THE CONCISE 21ST CENTURY CROSSWORD PUZZLE DICTIONARY

KEVIN McCANN & MARK DIEHL

PUZZLE
WRIGHT
PRESS

New York

An Imprint of Sterling Publishing
387 Park Avenue South
New York, NY 10016

PUZZLEWRIGHT PRESS and the distinctive Puzzlewright Press logo are
registered trademarks of Sterling Publishing Co., Inc.

This book is an abridged version of the 2009 book
The 21st Century Crossword Puzzle Dictionary.
This edition published in 2013.

© 2009 by Kevin McCann & Mark Diehl

ISBN 978-1-4549-0705-3

Distributed in Canada by Sterling Publishing
c/o Canadian Manda Group, 165 Dufferin Street
Toronto, Ontario, Canada M6K 3H6
Distributed in the United Kingdom by GMC Distribution Services
Castle Place, 166 High Street, Lewes, East Sussex, England BN7 1XU
Distributed in Australia by Capricorn Link (Australia) Pty. Ltd.
P.O. Box 704, Windsor, NSW 2756, Australia

For information about custom editions, special sales, and premium
and corporate purchases, please contact Sterling Special Sales at
800-805-5489 or specialsales@sterlingpublishing.com.

Manufactured in the United States of America

2 4 6 8 10 9 7 5 3 1

www.puzzlewright.com

Contents

Introduction

Crossword puzzles have been a part of American culture for nearly 100 years. The first crossword puzzle, then known as a "Word-Cross," was created by Arthur Wynne and appeared in the *New York World* on Dec. 21, 1913. In the 1920s, America experienced the "crossword craze," and since then crossword puzzles have been a regular feature in most daily newspapers. They can be found in magazine and book collections, topical publications, and now on the Internet.

But the puzzles we encounter today are not the same as those of the '20s, the '30s, or even the '80s. In days of yore, crossword puzzles were solely tests of vocabulary and facts, which did reward people who had broad knowledge of geography, mythology, history, and literature, but also tended to be dry and contained a great many entries that were highly obscure.

The 1990s brought in a new crossword era. Top puzzlemakers such as Merl Reagle and Stanley Newman sought to make the crossword puzzle less stodgy and more hip. And when Will Shortz took the helm as crossword editor of *The New York Times* in 1993, his goal was to make puzzles more appealing to a broader and younger audience by expanding the required knowledge, by including pop culture references, by using humorous wordplay, and by using unique and clever themes. In short, it was felt that crossword puzzles should be more fun. Nearly every syndicated publication has adopted this new style to some degree. Today's solver is the beneficiary of these changes.

Crossword puzzles are no longer just a test of one's vocabulary. They demand more from a solver and offer more in return. References to pop singers and television shows are commonplace. Tricky, punny, and sometimes diabolical clues are to be expected. But when solvers go to a typical crossword dictionary for assistance they find it to be of limited value. Most any dictionary will suffice if all the solver needs is a synonym for a straightforward clue. But most clues are not simple synonym clues. What about pop culture references, or clues that engage in wordplay? Today's crossword solver needs a better resource.

The Concise 21st Century Crossword Puzzle Dictionary

As creators of *The Concise 21st Century Crossword Puzzle Dic-*

tionary, we set out with one primary goal: to create a more useful resource for the modern crossword puzzle solver. We believe that goal has been reached.

How is *The Concise 21st Century Crossword Puzzle Dictionary* more useful?

- It has real answers to real clues, taken from a database of thousands of crossword puzzles.
- It does not aim to be a thesaurus with synonyms that never show up in puzzles.
- It highlights very common clue/answer pairs.
- It has up-to-date pop culture references.
- It uses entire clues, broken up into main entries and subentries.

Uses data from crossword database

The Concise 21st Century Crossword Puzzle Dictionary creators are also the maintainers of the cruciverb.com crossword database. This database includes, among other things, clues and answers extracted from thousands of puzzles offered by mainstream crossword publishers, and is used by most of today's professional crossword constructors and editors. This very same database was used to create *The Concise 21st Century Crossword Puzzle Dictionary*. What other dictionary can claim to derive its content from the same resource

used by nearly every crossword professional?

Not a thesaurus

Typical crossword dictionaries burden the solver with an abundance of synonyms, many of which have never appeared in crossword puzzles and likely never will. Such dictionaries are more like a thesaurus and tend to hide possible answers rather than highlight them. *The Concise 21st Century Crossword Puzzle Dictionary* only includes clue/answer pairs that have appeared at least twice in published puzzles in our database, which goes back 15 years. What this means is that you might see an entry like this:

Bashful
    companion: 3 DOC 5 DOPEY

Only Doc and Dopey are listed as answers because Bashful, Grumpy, Happy, Sleepy, and Sneezy don't show up often enough to merit inclusion.

Common clue/answer pairs are highlighted

If certain clue/answer pairs have appeared *many* times in previously published crosswords, *The Concise 21st Century Crossword Puzzle Dictionary* will highlight the answer in underlined boldface type. While there is no guarantee that a highlighted answer will be the one that a solver is looking for, the high occurrence rate indicates that it is a very strong possibility. No other crossword dictionary offers this highlighting feature.

Includes up-to-date pop culture references

Unlike crossword puzzles of yesteryear, today's puzzles contain a healthy amount of references to pop culture. *The Concise 21st Century Crossword Puzzle Dictionary* includes clues and answers that refer to recent songs, movies, television programs, authors, politicians, etc. It also includes common slang and other "in the language" words and phrases that have found their way into mainstream crossword puzzles. Some dictionaries have no pop culture references at all.

Uses the entire clue

The Concise 21st Century Crossword Puzzle Dictionary is made up of main entries, often with many subentries underneath. For example, the clues "Extinct bird" (answer: DODO or MOA) and "Flightless bird" (answer: EMU, KIWI, or RHEA) would share the same main entry of "Bird" and then have the rest of the clue in the subentries, like this:

Bird
Extinct: 3 MOA 4 DODO
Flightless: 3 EMU 4 KIWI RHEA

Other dictionaries may have one basic entry for "Bird," followed by the many possible answers:

Bird EMU MOA DODO KIWI
RHEA

The first method is more helpful, since the solver has more specific information and can narrow down the possibilities.

Dictionary Comparison

To further illustrate the difference between *The Concise 21st Century Crossword Puzzle Dictionary* and other dictionaries, see the table on page 9.

The differences are significant.

Many of the answers offered by other dictionaries have likely *never* appeared in a mainstream crossword puzzle. In fact, this is the case for the large majority of the answers provided for the "Agent" entry at right. Including these obscurities as if they were legitimately possible answers does nothing more than throw the solver off.

Other dictionaries lump all their answers together, separating them only by length. Our dictionary includes subentries such as "action" under "Affirmative," which help direct the solver to a smaller set of possible answers (in this case, one answer: NOD).

Also, since other crossword dictionaries largely contain nothing but synonyms, they're no help with more complex clues. Since we use whole clues, we can include very common answers such as ANT for "Aardvark morsel" and AGER for "Maturing agent." Other dictionaries do not offer this level of detail. Nor do they contain any references to pop culture (such as "American Idol").

For all these reasons, we think you'll find that *The Concise 21st Century Crossword Puzzle Dictionary* is clearly a more useful resource for today's crossword solver.

—Kevin McCann & Mark Diehl

The Concise 21st Century Crossword Puzzle Dictionary	Other Dictionary

Aardvark: 6 MAMMAL
   7 ANTBEAR 8 ANTEATER
   feature: 5 SNOUT
   land: 6 AFRICA
   meal: 4 ANTS
   morsel: 3 **ANT**

Affirmative: 3 YES
   action: 3 **NOD**
   Emphatic: 6 YESSIR
   French: 3 OUI
   NASA: 3 AOK
   Sailor: 3 AYE
   Shipboard: 6 AYEAYE
   Slangy: 4 YEAH
   Spanish: 4 SISI
   vote: 3 AYE **YEA** YES

Agent: 3 FED REP SPY
   7 VEHICLE
   amount: 3 CUT FEE
   Antiquing: 4 AGER
   Bleaching: 3 LYE
   Cleansing: 4 SOAP 5 BORAX
   DEA: 4 **NARC** 5 NARCO
   Diplomatic: 5 ENVOY
   Double: 4 **MOLE**
   Fed.: 4 GMAN TMAN
   Kind of: 3 IRS
   Leavening: 5 YEAST
   Maturing: 4 **AGER**
   of retribution: 7 NEMESIS
   Sales: 3 REP
   Secret: 3 SPY
   take: 5 TENTH
   Thickening: 4 AGAR
   Undercover: 3 SPY 4 NARC
   ~ 86: 5 SMART
   ~ Ness: 5 ELIOT
   ~ Scully: 4 DANA

"American Idol"
   winner Studdard: 5 RUBEN

Aardvark: ANTEATER
   EARTHHOG EDENTATE

Affirmative: AYE NOD YAH YEA
   YEP YES AMEN ATEN YEAH
   PONENT DOGMATIC
   POSITIVE

Agent: SPY AMIN DOER ETCH
   GENE ACTOR AMEEN BUYER
   CAUSE ENVOY MEANS
   ORGAN PROXY REEVE RIDER
   VAKIL WALLA ADUROL
   ASSIGN ATOPEN BROKER
   BURSAR COMMIS DEALER
   DEPUTY ENINE FACTOR
   FITTER KEYAHA LEDGER
   MEDIUM MINION MUKTAR
   PESKAR SELLER SYNDIC
   VAKEEL WALLAH BAILIFF
   BLISTER CHANNEL
   COUCHER DRASTIC FACIENT
   FEDERAL HUSBAND
   LEAGUER MOOKTAR
   MOUNTAR MUKTEAR
   MUTAGEN OFFICER
   PESHKAR PROCTOR
   SCALPER APPROVER
   ATTORNEY AUMILDAR
   CATALYST EMISSARY
   EXECUTOR GOMASHTA
   GOMASTAH IMPROVER
   INCITANT INSTITOR
   MINISTER MITICIDE
   MOOKHTAR OPERATOR
   PROMOTER QUAESTOR
   RESIDENT SALESMAN
   VIRUCIDE MIDDLEMAN
   OPERATIVE SATELLITE
   SENESCHAL MAINSPRING
   PROCURATOR
   PLENIPOTENTIARY

No entry for **"American Idol"**

How to Use This Book

Entry Parts

The user of this crossword dictionary needs to be familiar with the various entry parts. Here are some sample entries, followed by short descriptions of their different parts:

Affirmative: 3 YES
  action: 3 <u>NOD</u>
Tail
  Info: Suffix cue
Tribute
  Pay ~ to: 5 HONOR 6 SALUTE

Main entries: Affirmative, Tail, and Tribute
Subentries: "action" and "Pay ~ to"
Answers: YES, NOD, HONOR, and SALUTE (answers in underlined boldface type indicate very common clue/answer pairs)
Info indicator: provides further information
The swung dash (~): found in subentries and used to signify the part of the clue where the main entry would appear
Numbers: 3, 5, and 6 indicate the length of the answers

Main entries

Main entries often consist of a single word, which may be the only word in a clue, or the most prominent one. Other main entries consist of more than one word: Full names, places, titles, common phrases, and fill-in-the-blank clues account for many of these. When a clue ends with "e.g." or "for example" or "for one" or anything similar, the ending is dropped from the clue and the answer is listed under what remains. For example, the answer PET is listed under "Cat," even though the clue for PET would be "Cat, e.g." or "Cat, for example." Certain punctuation marks have also been removed, including question marks (which indicate punny clues) and some possessive indicators.

Subentries

Subentries are used in combination with main entries to provide a more detailed clue to an answer. Subentries that begin with a capital letter precede the main entry in their clues. Subentries that begin with a lowercase letter follow the main entry. A swung dash (~) is used as a placeholder when the main entry falls within the subentry, when it leads or follows a number, or when there is an exception to the capital letter rule.

  Observe the following examples:

Thick: 3 FAT 5 DENSE MIDST
  In the ~ of: 3 MID 4 **AMID**
    5 AMONG 6 AMIDST
  Lay on: 7 SLATHER
  slice: 4 **SLAB**
Woods
  Actor: 5 JAMES
  Golfer: 5 TIGER
  Neck of the: 4 **AREA**
  prop: 3 TEE

Joining the subentries with their main entries, the full clues are:

  Thick; In the thick of; Lay on thick; Thick slice
  Actor Woods; Golfer Woods; Neck of the woods; Woods's prop

Choose the Most Prominent Word(s)

When looking up a crossword entry, choose the most prominent word in the clue. If you have a clue such as "Aardvark feature" (answer: SNOUT), go to the "A" chapter and look up Aardvark, since "Aardvark" is more prominent than "feature."

Often two or more words in a clue will have equal prominence. In such cases, entries may be present for each word. For example, both "bleaching" and "agent" in the clue "Bleaching agent" are prominent. "Bleaching" may be somewhat stronger, but "agent" still has enough prominence to warrant inclusion.

For clues containing numbers, there will usually be an entry in the numbers chapter (the first chapter of the diction-

ary) in addition to any prominent word. For example, "36 inches" (answer: YARD) would have an entry under both "36" (in the numbers chapter) and "Inches" (in the I chapter).

Plurals, Tenses, and Other Inflections

Inflected forms of a word usually won't have their own entries and will instead be found under the root word. This is especially true where both the clue and answer end in -S, -ES, -ED, and -ING. For example, if a clue is "Extinct birds," the main entry would be "Bird." There would be no separate entry for "Birds."

Bird
  Extinct: 3 MOA 4 DODO

But since the real clue has "birds" and not "bird," the solver must append an S to the possible answer that will be placed in the grid. In the above example, the possible answers would be MOAS and DODOS.

There are exceptions. If either the answer or the clue is a less common inflection, such as a Latin or French plural, there will be a separate entry. If a plural word is part of a clue that has a non-plural answer, it, too, will have a separate entry. Plurals have their own entries when the answers are 3-letter plurals of 2-letter words. For example:

Addresses
  Change: 4 MOVE

Eggs: 3 <u>OVA</u> ROE
Vaccines: 4 <u>SERA</u>
VIPs
   Baseball: 3 GMS
   Courtroom: 3 DAS
   Hospital: 3 DRS MDS RNS
   Magazine: 3 EDS
   Radio: 3 DJS

People

These clues can include first names, middle names, last names, titles, and blanks. If a clue contains only a first name or last name, the main entry will be that single name. If a clue has both the first and last name, the main entry will be the last name followed by first name (e.g.: Nixon, Richard). Name titles such as Sir, Mr., and Mrs. will usually follow the last name (e.g.: O'Leary, Mrs.) unless the title and name is a film or book title (e.g., "Mrs. Miniver"). Name titles may also appear in the subentry instead of the main entry.

Places

Countries, cities, towns, rivers, buildings, monuments, and so forth are found under their *full name*. For example: South America, Niagara Falls, Lake Victoria, Eiffel Tower.

Titles of Works

Titles of books, film, plays, and the like are entered under the first letter of the first word unless the title begins with "The," "A," or "An." These entries will be found under the first letter of the next word. For example, if a clue contains "The Odd Couple," the solver should look for the entry "Odd Couple, The" in the O chapter.

Phrases With Quote Marks

Phrases with quote marks are found in their entirety under the first letter of the first word.

Phrases With Blanks

Phrases with blanks are found in their entirety under the first letter of the first word.

Alphabetization

Entries are alphabetized strictly on a letter-by-letter basis, ignoring all punctuation and spaces. The ampersand symbol (&) is counted as the letters "and." If two answers use the same letters, the simpler version comes first, with "simpler" meaning lowercase and no punctuation. So "Al" comes before "A.L." and they both come before "Al ___." Names listed under the last name are an exception to the strict alphabetization rule. They are alphabetized under the last name, following any listings that have the same letters.

Another exception to the alphabetization rule is when a parenthetical part follows a fill-in-the-blank clue; such clues are alphabetized immediately following the same clue without parentheses (or the place where such a clue would be). Note the order of these two, even though "Willa" follows "days" alphabetically:

"One of ___" (Willa Cather novel): 4 OURS	Al
"One of ___ days ...": 5 THESE	AL
	A.L.
	Al ___
	Al-___
	al-___, Bashar
	Ala.
	À la ___
	"Al Aaraaf"

Stone
___ Stone
Stone, Oliver
Stone Age
"Stoned Soul Picnic"
Stone-faced
Stonehenge
Stones

In subentries, the same alphabetization rules are followed. The only difference is the swung dash (~). If that's at the start of the subentry, it's listed at the end. If it's in the middle, then alphabetization stops at the swung dash.

If you can't find what you're looking for, look up and down a few inches and you might find it. Once you get used to the system, it will become easier.

Examples

Observing the above rules, some main entry examples can be found in the next column.

Other Information

In deciding which entries to include in this dictionary, the basic rule was that the clue/answer pairs had to have appeared in recent puzzles at least twice. Sometimes an answer that wouldn't have made the cut was added because we felt it was just a matter of time before that clue would appear in a crossword, but this was rare.

Main entry	Type	Chapter	Comment
1998	Number	#'s	Most numbers in a clue will have own entry
Aardvark	Single word	A	Normal lookup using first letter
West, Mae	Person	W	Last name, first name
Gellar, ___ Michelle	Person	G	Last name, other names
Atlas Mountains	Place	A	Full name
"Atlas Shrugged"	Title	A	First letter of title
"Simpsons, The"	Title	S	First letter of title, excluding "The," "An," or "A"
"Take it easy!"	Phrase	T	First letter of quote
"The doctor ___"	Phrase	T	First letter of quote, *including* "The," "An," or "A"
___ no good	Phrase	N	First letter of phrase

#'s

0: 3 NIL 8 GOOSEEGG
  Letter above: 4 OPER
  on a phone: 4 OPER
  Put back to: 5 RESET
0% ___: 3 APR
000
  Put back to: 5 RESET
007: 3 SPY 4 BOND 5 AGENT
  alma mater: 4 ETON
  creator Fleming: 3 IAN
  First ~ film: 4 DRNO
  foe: 3 KGB 4 DRNO
    6 SMERSH
  How ~ likes his martinis:
    6 SHAKEN
  portrayer Roger: 5 MOORE
  portrayer Timothy: 6 DALTON
1/640
  of a square mile: 4 ACRE
1/20
  of a ream: 5 QUIRE
1/8
  cup: 5 OUNCE
  ounce: 4 DRAM
1/6
  fl. oz.: 3 TSP
  inch: 4 PICA
1: 3 ODD RTE 4 CUBE 5 DIGIT
1-1
  score: 3 TIE
1/1
  song ender: 4 SYNE
  word: 4 AULD LANG SYNE
"1-2-3"
  singer Barry: 3 LEN
1.3
  cubic yards: 5 STERE
1.609
  kilometers: 4 MILE
1-800-COLLECT
  pitchman: 3 MRT
1-800-FLOWERS
  rival: 3 FTD

2
  on a phone : 3 ABC
2%
  The ~ in milk: 3 FAT
2.0
  average: 3 CEE
  average components:
    4 CEES
2:1: 5 RATIO
2.2
  pounds: 4 KILO
2.54
  centimeters: 4 INCH
2 to 1: 5 RATIO
3
  on a phone: 3 DEF
3.0
  ~, for example: 3 GPA
3:00: 4 EAST HOUR
3:1: 4 ODDS 5 RATIO
3.26
  light years: 6 PARSEC
3.5
  One of ~ billion: 5 ASIAN
  ~, for example: 3 GPA
3/17
  honoree: 5 STPAT
3-in-One
  product: 3 OIL
3-pointers
  in football: 3 FGS
  in Scrabble: 3 EMS
4
  He wore a: 3 ORR
  on a phone: 3 GHI
  ~ P.M.: 7 TEATIME
4.0
  ~, for example: 3 GPA
4-0
  The big ~, for one: 3 AGE
4:00
  social: 3 TEA
  ~ P.M.: 7 TEATIME

4×4: 3 **UTE**
4-F
  Like a: 5 UNFIT
4-sided
  fig.: 4 RECT
5
  on a phone: 3 JKL
5?-point
  type: 5 AGATE
5.5
  yards: 3 ROD
5.5-point
  type: 5 AGATE
5.88
  About ~ trillion mi.: 4 LTYR
5K: 4 RACE
5th: 3 AVE
6
  on a phone: 3 **MNO**
  They're worth ~ pts.: 3 TDS
  ___ 6: 5 MOTEL
6/6/44: 4 **DDAY**
6:50: 5 TENOF TENTO
6-pointers: 3 TDS
6-pt.
  plays: 3 TDS
6th
  sense: 3 ESP
7: 3 ODD 7 NATURAL
  on a phone: 3 PRS
7-10: 5 SPLIT
7/10/62
  launch: 7 TELSTAR
7/28/1914
  It started: 3 WWI
"7 Faces of Dr. ___": 3 LAO
7th-century
  date: 4 DCVI
  pope: 5 LEOII
  start: 3 DCI
7-Up
  rival: 6 FRESCA SPRITE
  ~, in old ads: 6 UNCOLA
8
  In base: 5 OCTAL
  on a phone: 3 TUV
  pts.: 3 GAL
8×10
  ~, often: 6 GLOSSY

"8 Mile"
  actress Basinger: 3 KIM
  star: 6 EMINEM
9
  on a phone: 3 WXY
  to 5: 5 RATIO SHIFT
9-3
  automaker: 4 SAAB
9-5
  automaker: 4 SAAB
9/8/66
  Noted debut of:
    8 STARTREK
9-iron
  Use a: 4 LOFT
9mm
  weapon: 3 UZI
10
  No.: 4 NEON
  out of 10: 5 IDEAL
"10"
  actress Bo: 5 DEREK
  director Edwards: 5 BLAKE
  music: 6 BOLERO
10%
  Give: 5 TITHE
  taker: 5 AGENT
10/7/82
  Notable debut of: 4 CATS
10/10/73
  resignee: 5 AGNEW
10/11/75
  Show that debuted: 3 SNL
10/30/74
  Champ of: 3 ALI
10K: 4 RACE
  Compete in a: 3 RUN
10-point
  type: 5 ELITE
10th anniversary
  gift: 3 TIN
10th-century
  emperor: 5 OTTOI
  pope: 4 LEOV 5 LEOVI
10th-grader: 4 SOPH
"10 Things ___ About You":
    5 IHATE
11: 3 ACE 5 PRIME
  Like: 3 ODD

11/11
  honorees: 4 VETS
12
  Name of ~ popes: 4 PIUS
12:00
  flasher: 3 VCR
  Revert to: 5 RESET
12/24: 3 EVE
12/31: 3 EVE
"12 Angry Men"
  role: 5 JUROR
12-point
  type: 4 PICA
12th-century
  poet: 4 OMAR
  year: 3 MCL 4 MCII
12-year-old: 5 TWEEN
  7 PRETEEN
13: 5 PRIME
  Group of: 5 COVEN
13th-century
  invader: 5 TATAR
  writings: 4 EDDA
14
  pounds, in Britain: 5 STONE
14-line
  poem: 6 RONDEL SONNET
14th-century
  ruler: 5 IVANI
15
  Score before: 4 LOVE
15.432
  grains: 4 GRAM
15th
  of a month: 4 IDES
15th-century
  vessel: 4 NINA 5 PINTA
16
  drams: 5 OUNCE
  Name of ~ popes:
    7 GREGORY
16.5
  feet: 3 ROD
16th
  president: 3 ABE
16th-century
  circumnavigator: 5 DRAKE
  fleet: 6 ARMADA
  start: 3 MDI

17
  Poem with ~ syllables: 5 HAIKU
"__ 17" (1953 film): 6 STALAG
17th-century
  diarist: 5 PEPYS
  poet laureate: 6 DRYDEN
  start: 4 MDCI
18
  holes: 5 ROUND
  Not yet: 8 UNDERAGE
  Play: 4 GOLF
"__ 18" (Uris novel): 4 MILA
18-wheeler: 3 RIG 4 SEMI
19th Amendment
  beneficiaries: 5 WOMEN
19th-century
  literary inits.: 3 RLS
20
  providers: 4 ATMS
  quires: 4 REAM
20%
  It might be: 3 TIP
  of cuarenta: 4 OCHO
20-20: 3 TIE
  It may be: 9 HINDSIGHT
"20/20"
  former cohost Downs: 4 HUGH
  former cohost Hugh: 5 DOWNS
  network: 3 ABC
20 Questions
  category: 6 ANIMAL
    7 MINERAL
20s
  dispenser: 3 ATM
20th-century
  art movement: 4 DADA
  Name of three ~ popes: 4 PIUS
20-vol.
  reference: 3 OED
21: 3 AGE 5 LEGAL OFAGE
  Cube with ~ dots: 3 DIE
  Exceeds: 5 BUSTS
21st-century
  start: 3 MMI
21-year-old: 5 ADULT
22
  One of ~ cards: 5 TAROT
22.5
  degrees: 3 NNE**

22-mile-high
  layer: 5 OZONE
23
  follower: 6 SKIDOO
23rd
  ~ Greek letter: 3 PSI
24
  cans: 4 CASE
  Every ~ hours: 4 ADAY
    5 DAILY
  horas: 3 DIA
  One of: 4 HOUR
  Poem of ~ books: 5 ILIAD
  sheets of paper: 5 QUIRE
24/7: 7 NONSTOP
  auction site: 4 EBAY
  bank device: 3 ATM
24-hr.
  bank feature: 3 ATM
  breakfast place: 4 IHOP
  convenience: 3 ATM
24-karat: 4 PURE
26
  fortnights: 4 YEAR
  Last of: 3 ZEE
27
  ~, to 3: 4 CUBE
"28 Days"
  subject: 5 REHAB
30
  ~, to a reporter: 3 END
30%
  of Africa: 6 SAHARA
  of the Earth's landmass: 4 ASIA
30-day
  mo.: 3 APR SEP
  month: 5 APRIL
30th
  Around the ~ (abbr.): 3 EOM
30-ton
  computer: 5 ENIAC
32
  Game sometimes using ~ cards:
      6 EUCHRE
  Game using ~ cards: 4 SKAT
32-card
  game: 4 SKAT
"32 Flavors"
  singer Davis: 5 ALANA

33rd
  pres.: 3 HST
34th
  pres.: 3 DDE IKE
34th Street
  happening: 7 MIRACLE
35.3
  cubic feet: 5 STERE
35mm
  camera type: 3 SLR
  Early ~ camera: 5 LEICA
  setting: 5 FSTOP
36
  inches: 4 YARD
36-24-36
  Part of: 4 HIPS 5 WAIST
38th
  parallel land: 5 KOREA
39
  About ~ inches: 5 METER
  ~, to Benny: 3 AGE
39.37
  inches: 5 METER 8 ONEMETER
39-line
  poem: 7 SESTINA
"39 Steps, The"
  actress Taina: 3 ELG
  star: 5 DONAT
40
  winks: 3 NAP 6 CATNAP
40-card
  Game with a ~ deck: 5 MONTE
40-day
  period: 4 LENT
41st
  president: 4 BUSH
42
  gal.: 3 BBL
"42nd Street"
  tune: 5 DAMES
43rd
  pres.: 4 BUSH 5 DUBYA
45: 4 DISC
  Half a: 5 BSIDE SIDEA
  inches: 3 ELL
  Old ~ player: 4 HIFI
  player: 5 PHONO
45th
  of 50: 4 UTAH

47-stringed
instrument: 4 HARP
"48 ___": 3 HRS
"48HRS"
actor Nick: 5 NOLTE
49%
About ~ of the world's population:
3 MEN
49th
state: 6 ALASKA
50%: 4 HALF
50–50: 3 TIE 4 EVEN
chance: 6 TOSSUP
proposition: 7 EVENBET
50-and-over
org.: 4 AARP
50 Cent: 7 RAPSTAR
50-oared
ship: 4 ARGO
52: 3 LII
54
Element: 5 XENON
55 minutes past the hour:
6 FIVETO
55th anniversary
stone: 7 EMERALD
56: 3 LVI
56-5
His won-lost record was: 3 ALI
60
Every ~ minutes: 5 HORAL
grains: 4 DRAM
secs.: 3 MIN
60%
Like ~ of the world's population:
5 ASIAN
60-homer
Three-time ~ man: 4 SOSA
"60 Minutes"
Alexander, formerly of:
5 SHANA
Andy of: 6 ROONEY
Lesley of: 5 STAHL
Morley of: 5 SAFER
network: 3 **CBS**
Original ~ correspondent:
8 REASONER
regular: 9 EDBRADLEY
Rooney of: 4 ANDY

60th
Capital near the ~ parallel:
4 OSLO
61
He hit ~ in '61: 5 MARIS
66: 3 **RTE** 5 ROUTE
67.5
deg.: 3 ENE
70
Did: 4 SPED
70%
of M: 3 DCC
70-millimeter
film format: 4 IMAX
72
~, often: 3 PAR
75%: 3 CEE
76ers
org.: 3 NBA
"77 Sunset Strip"
actor Byrnes: 3 EDD
character: 6 KOOKIE
costar of Edd: 5 EFREM
78: 4 DISC
79
for gold (abbr.): 4 ATNO
"80's Ladies"
singer: 5 OSLIN 7 KTOSLIN
86: 3 CAN NIX
Agent: 5 SMART
87
at the pump: 6 OCTANE
88
Piano's: 4 KEYS
~, briefly: 4 OLDS
90
degrees: 4 EAST
degrees from norte: 4 ESTE
Drove ~ mph: 4 SPED
Less than ~ degrees: 5 ACUTE
More than ~ degrees: 6 OBTUSE
90-degree
angle: 3 ELL
90s
It may be in the low: 6 OCTANE
90th
Hrs. on the ~ meridian: 3 CST
92
Pertaining to element: 6 URANIC

95: 3 RTE
98
~, briefly: 4 OLDS
98.6
Like a body temperature of:
  6 NORMAL
"99 Luftballons"
pop group: 4 NENA
100
clams: 5 CNOTE
cts.: 3 DOL
Got ~ on: 4 **ACED**
It seats: 6 SENATE
lbs.: 3 CWT
Less than ~ shares: 6 ODDLOT
One of ~ (abbr.): 3 SEN
percent: 3 ALL
yrs.: 3 **CEN**
100%: 3 ALL 4 PURE 6 PURELY
  8 ENTIRELY
100-eyed
giant: 5 ARGUS
100-meter
race: 4 DASH
100-yard
race: 4 DASH
"101 Dalmatians"
dog: 5 PONGO
106: 3 CVI
108
Game with ~ cards: 3 UNO
114
It has ~ suras: 5 KORAN
128
cubic feet: 4 CORD
150
One of ~ songs: 5 PSALM
151: 3 CLI
160
square rods: 4 ACRE
180: 3 UEY 5 UTURN
____ **180:** 3 DOA
180-degree
maneuver: 5 UTURN
180 degrees
from NNW: 3 SSE
from WNW: 3 ESE
from WSW: 3 ENE
turn: 3 UEY

200
fins: 3 GEE
milligrams: 5 CARAT
201: 3 CCI
202: 4 CCII
212: 8 AREACODE
Bring to ~ degrees: 4 BOIL
251: 4 CCLI
251.9
calories: 3 BTU
252
wine gallons: 3 TUN
300: 3 CCC
301: 4 CCCI
325i
maker: 3 BMW
347
Football coach with ~ victories:
  5 SHULA
365
days: 4 YEAR
dias: 3 ANO
389
Old car wih a ~ engine: 3 GTO
400
Society's: 5 ELITE
401: 3 CDI
401(k): 4 PLAN
alternative: 3 **IRA**
cousin: 3 **IRA**
404: 4 CDIV
435
One of: 3 REP
440: 4 RACE
440–461
pope: 4 LEOI
440-yard-long
path: 4 OVAL
450: 3 CDL
451: 4 CDLI
500
letters: 3 STP
sheets: 4 REAM
spot: 4 INDY
____ **500:** 4 INDY
500-mile
race: 4 INDY
501
brand: 5 LEVIS

502: 3 DII
503: 4 DIII
507: 4 DVII
511: 3 DXI
  Hitter of ~ homers: 3 OTT
516
  sheets: 4 REAM
525i
  maker: 3 BMW
551: 3 **DLI**
552: 4 DLII
601: 3 DCI
602: 4 DCII
640
  acres (abbr.): 4 SQMI
650: 3 DCL
660
  Hitter of ~ home runs: 4 MAYS
700: 3 DCC
705: 4 DCCV
747: 3 JET 5 PLANE
755
  Hitter with ~ homers:
    5 AARON
800
  preceder: 3 ONE
801
  Area code ~ locale: 4 UTAH
900
  automaker: 4 SAAB
901: 3 CMI
905: 3 CMV
911
  respondent: 3 **EMT**
  Subj. of a ~ call: 4 EMER
950: 3 CML
1,000
  G's: 3 MIL
  kilograms: 5 TONNE
  One in: 5 COMMA
"1000 Oceans"
  singer Tori: 4 AMOS
"1,001 ___": 4 USES
1002: 3 MII
1040: 4 FORM
  data: 6 INCOME
  info: 3 SSN
  issuer: 3 IRS
  reviewer: 3 CPA

1040EZ
  issuer: 3 IRS
1052: 4 MLII
1,093
  Holder of ~ patents: 6 EDISON
1102: 4 MCII
"___ 1138" (sci-fi film): 3 THX
1200
  hours: 4 NOON
1,281
  Scorer of ~ goals: 4 PELE
1300: 4 MCCC 5 ONEPM
  hours: 3 ONE
1302
  Exile of: 5 DANTE
1400: 5 TWOPM
1409
  Council site of: 4 PISA
1440
  School since: 4 **ETON**
1492
  discovery: 5 HAITI
  Ship of: 4 **NINA** 5 PINTA
1493
  landing site: 7 ANTIGUA
1500-meter
  gold medalist: 3 COE
1501: 3 MDI
1551: 4 MDLI
1600: 3 MDC
1605
  Pope of: 5 LEOXI
1614
  Groom of: 5 ROLFE
1692
  trial site: 5 SALEM
1701
  Institution since: 4 YALE
1711
  Race site since: 5 ASCOT
1719
  Classic of: 6 CRUSOE
1,760
  A mi. has: 3 YDS
  yards: 4 MILE
1773
  Jetsam of: 3 TEA
1776
  battleground: 7 TRENTON

pamphleteer: 5 PAINE
"1776"
  role: 5 ADAMS
1777
  battle site: 5 PAOLI 8 SARATOGA
1781
  discovery: 6 URANUS
1799
  discovery:
      15 THEROSETTASTONE
1801
  Company since: 6 DUPONT
  discovery: 5 CERES
1804
  dueler: 4 BURR
  symphony: 6 EROICA
1806
  It ended in ~ (abbr.): 3 HRE
1813
  battle site: 4 ERIE
1814
  exile site: 4 ELBA
  treaty site: 5 GHENT
1816
  notable novel: 4 EMMA
1825
  Canal completed in: 4 ERIE
  It opened in: 9 ERIECANAL
1829
  Mount first climbed in:
      6 ARARAT
1831
  Noted poem of: 6 LENORE
1836
  battle site: 5 **ALAMO**
1839–42
  war cause: 5 OPIUM
1846
  discovery: 7 NEPTUNE
1847
  noted novel: 4 OMOO
1850s
  war site: 6 CRIMEA
1852
  erupter: 4 ETNA
1,852
  meters: 7 SEAMILE
1,859
  Mel who scored ~ runs: 3 OTT

1860s
  govt.: 3 CSA
  insignia: 3 CSA
  nickname: 3 ABE
1862
  battle site: 6 SHILOH
      8 ANTIETAM
1864
  battle site: 9 MOBILEBAY
1867
  purchase: 6 ALASKA
1871
  opera debut: 4 AIDA
1876
  victor, by one vote: 5 HAYES
1880
  novel: 4 NANA
1883
  erupter: 8 KRAKATOA
1887
  novel: 3 SHE
  opera debut: 6 OTELLO
1890
  Org. since: 3 DAR
  State since: 5 IDAHO
1890s: 11 MAUVEDECADE
  ideal female: 10 GIBSONGIRL
1896
  State since: 4 UTAH
1898
  annexation: 6 HAWAII
  Famed hill of: 7 SANJUAN
  She sank in: 8 THEMAINE
      USSMAINE
  Soft drink since: 5 PEPSI
1899–1902
  war participant: 4 BOER
1900
  opera debut: 5 TOSCA
1903
  He debuted at the Met in:
      6 CARUSO
1909
  Pole seeker of: 5 PEARY
1912
  Cookie since: 4 OREO
  headline name: 7 TITANIC
1914
  battle site: 4 YSER 5 MARNE

"1914"
poet: 6 BROOKE
1915
Service club since: 7 KIWANIS
1917
newsmaker: 5 LENIN
Ruler until: 4 TSAR
1918
hit song: 7 KKKKATY
1919
musical: 5 IRENE
1920
novel: 5 CHERI
Rights org. since: 4 ACLU
1920s
auto: 3 REO
designer: 4 ERTE
style: 7 ARTDECO
1921
sci-fi play: 3 RUR
1922
discovery, familiarly: 3 TUT
documentary: 6 NANOOK
1923
Capital since: 6 ANKARA
1925
defendant: 6 SCOPES
Girl in a ~ musical:
    7 NANETTE
musical: 11 NONONANETTE
1926
Channel crosser of: 6 EDERLE
1927
Movie award since: 5 OSCAR
New auto of: 7 LASALLE
1928
musical, with "The":
    15 THREEPENNYOPERA
New auto of: 6 DESOTO
    MODELA
1930
discovery: 5 PLUTO
1930s
boxing champ: 4 BAER
From the: 6 PREWAR
migrant: 4 OKIE
movie dog: 4 ASTA
1931
convictee: 8 ALCAPONE

1933
film classic: 8 KINGKONG
Initials since: 3 TVA
1935
Country renamed in: 4 IRAN
musical: 7 ROBERTA
1936
best-selling novel:
    15 GONEWITHTHEWIND
First name in ~ politics: 3 ALF
1939
epic film:
    15 GONEWITHTHEWIND
film setting: 4 TARA
movie dog: 4 TOTO
1940s
agcy.: 3 OPA
computer: 5 ENIAC
first lady: 4 BESS
radio quiz show: 4 DRIQ
1941
attack site: 11 PEARLHARBOR
comics debut: 6 ARCHIE
musical: 13 MOONOVERMIAMI
1942
battle site: 8 CORALSEA
    9 ELALAMEIN
1944
battle site: 4 STLO 5 LEYTE
initials: 3 ETO
invasion city: 4 STLO
June 6: 4 **DDAY**
Paper launched in: 7 LEMONDE
Town in a ~ novel: 5 ADANO
turning point: 4 DDAY
1945
Aug. 15: 5 VJDAY
battle site: 7 OKINAWA
conference site: 5 YALTA
    7 POTSDAM
It started in: 9 ATOMICAGE
May 8: 5 VEDAY
summit site: 5 YALTA
1946
Airline founded in: 3 SAS
Computer unveiled in: 5 ENIAC
Govt. org. since: 3 SSA
1947
Mil. org. since: 4 USAF

1948
 Airline since: 4 ELAL
 Org. formed in: 3 OAS
 political quote:
  15 GIVEEMHELLHARRY
1949
 Defense org. since: 4 **NATO**
 Prize since: 4 EMMY
1950
 film noir classic: 3 **DOA**
1950s
 bomb: 5 EDSEL
 campaign name: 3 IKE
 experiment: 5 HTEST
 First name in ~ TV: 4 DESI
 political inits.: 3 AES
1952
 Magazine since: 3 MAD
 Weapon since: 5 HBOMB
1953
 classic film: 5 SHANE
 conquest: 7 EVEREST
 western: 5 SHANE
1954
 Alliance created in: 5 SEATO
1954–77
 alliance: 5 SEATO
1955
 animated film:
  15 LADYANDTHETRAMP
 hit song: 7 ONLYYOU
 merger gp.: 3 AFL CIO
 Name in ~ news: 9 ROSAPARKS
1956
 Awards since: 5 OBIES
 invasion site: 5 SINAI
 sci-fi classic:
  15 FORBIDDENPLANET
 trouble spot: 4 SUEZ
1957
 Car until: 4 NASH
 hit song: 5 DIANA
 River in a ~ film: 4 KWAI
1958
 chiller, with "The": 4 BLOB
 musical: 4 GIGI
 News org. since: 3 UPI
 Org. since: 4 NASA
 ~ #1 song: 6 VOLARE

1958–61
 political org.: 3 UAR
1959
 doo-wop classic:
  15 ATEENAGERINLOVE
1960
 Cartel since: 4 OPEC
 Fuel org. since: 4 OPEC
 hit song: 9 TEENANGEL
 inauguration speaker: 5 FROST
 U.N. member since: 4 TOGO
1960s
 atty. gen.: 3 RFK
 campus gp.: 3 SDS
 civil rights org.: 4 SNCC
 dance: 4 FRUG 5 TWIST
 do: 4 AFRO
 foursome: 7 BEATLES
 It was dropped in the: 3 LSD
 jacket style: 5 NEHRU
 protest: 5 SITIN
 radical gp.: 3 SDS
 Sign of the: 5 PEACE
 symbol: 5 PEACE
 war zone: 3 NAM
 ~ TV boy: 4 OPIE
1961
 space chimp: 4 ENOS
1962
 Launch of: 7 TELSTAR
 Retail chain since: 5 KMART
 spy film: 4 DRNO
1963–78
 pope: 6 PAULVI
1964
 Car of a ~ song: 3 GTO
 ~ #1 hit: 5 RINGO
1965
 march site: 5 SELMA
 unrest site: 5 WATTS
1966
 movie or song: 5 ALFIE
1967
 seceder: 6 BIAFRA
 war site: 5 SINAI
1968
 folk album: 4 ARLO
 groom, familiarly: 3 ARI
 New flier of: 3 SST

1969
bride: **3** ONO
Clothing retailer since:
  6 THEGAP
jazz album: **4** ELLA
landing site: **4** MOON
miracle team: **4** METS
Team created in: **5** EXPOS
1969–73
lottery org.: **3** SSS
1970
Govt. agency since: **3** EPA
hurricane: **5** CELIA
~ #1 hit: **7** LETITBE
1970s
bombing target: **5** HANOI
compact: **5** LECAR
hairdo: **4** AFRO
hit show: **5** RHODA
radical gp.: **3** SLA
sitcom: **5** ARNIE
space station: **6** SKYLAB
spin-off: **5** RHODA
1971
courtroom drama: **5** THEDA
Govt. agency since: **4** OSHA
1972
hit song: **5** LAYLA
hurricane: **5** AGNES
treaty subj.: **3** ABM
1973
court alias: **3** ROE
resignee: **5** AGNEW
space station: **6** SKYLAB
1974
abductee: **6** HEARST
biopic: **5** LENNY
dog film: **5** BENJI
Radical gp. in ~ news: **3** SLA
1975
blockbuster film: **4** JAWS
Comedy show since: **3** SNL
1976
bestseller: **5** ROOTS
raid site: **7** ENTEBBE
uprising site: **6** SOWETO
1977
Org. abolished in: **5** SEATO
TV event of: **5** ROOTS

1978
cult film: **10** ERASERHEAD
Science magazine since: **4** OMNI
thriller film: **4** COMA
1979
accident site: **3** TMI
disco hit: **4** YMCA
exile: **4** AMIN SHAH **7** IDIAMIN
It left orbit in: **6** SKYLAB
revolution locale: **4** IRAN
sci-fi classic: **5** ALIEN
1980
erupter: **8** STHELENS
    10 MTSTHELENS
~ TV debut: **3** CNN
1980s
Dolls of the: **3** ETS
Half of a ~ TV duo: **4** KATE
    5 ALLIE
1981
bride: **5** DIANA **6** LADYDI
1982
media debut: **8** USATODAY
recall subject: **7** TYLENOL
sci-fi film: **4** TRON
1983
invasion site: **7** GRENADA
1984: **4** YEAR **8** LEAPYEAR
Eclectic magazine started in:
    4 UTNE
film catchphrase: **9** ILLBEBACK
gas leak site: **6** BHOPAL
historical novel: **6** THEHAJ
sci-fi film: **7** STARMAN
"1984"
author: **6** ORWELL
setting: **7** OCEANIA
1986
It was launched in: **3** MIR
rock autobiography: **5** ITINA
sci-fi sequel: **6** ALIENS
self-titled album: **6** ARETHA
1988
country album: **4** REBA
1989
auto debut: **3** GEO
1990
Nation since: **7** NAMIBIA
~ #1 rap hit: **10** ICEICEBABY

1990s
music genre: 6 TECHNO
party: 4 RAVE
sitcom: 5 ELLEN

1991
Agcy. dismantled in: 3 KGB
Divorcée of: 5 IVANA
It dissolved in: 4 USSR
It regained independence in: 7 ESTONIA
They broke up in ~ (abbr.): 4 SSRS

1992
also-ran: 5 PEROT
erupter: 4 ETNA
presidential candidate: 5 PEROT 7 TSONGAS
TV host since: 4 LENO

1993
accord site: 4 OSLO
Nation since: 7 ERITREA
treaty: 5 NAFTA

1994
campus comedy: 3 PCU

1995
court VIP: 3 ITO
earthquake site: 4 KOBE
hurricane: 4 OPAL
Name in ~ news: 3 ITO
pig movie: 4 BABE

1996
also-ran: 4 DOLE
candidate: 4 DOLE
golf movie: 6 TINCUP
horror flick: 6 SCREAM
presidential hopeful: 5 LAMAR PEROT
running mate: 4 KEMP

1997
basketball film: 6 AIRBUD
biopic: 6 SELENA
blockbuster film: 7 TITANIC
Carrier until: 5 USAIR

1998
animated film: 4 ANTZ 5 MULAN
Car reintroduced in: 6 BEETLE
Computer since: 4 IMAC
report author: 5 STARR

1999
hurricane: 5 IRENE
name in the news: 5 ELIAN

2000: 4 YEAR 8 LEAPYEAR
also-ran: 4 GORE 5 NADER
Flier grounded in: 3 SST
Name in ~ news: 5 ELIAN
sci-fi film: 4 XMEN
World leader since: 5 PUTIN

2,000
pounds: 3 TON 6 ONETON

2001: 4 YEAR
biopic: 3 ALI
Carrier acquired in: 3 TWA
Co. in a ~ merger: 3 AOL
erupter: 4 ETNA
It came down in: 3 MIR

"2001: A Space Odyssey"
actor Dullea: 4 KEIR
computer: 3 HAL
extras: 4 APES

2002
erupter: 4 ETNA
scandal subject: 5 ENRON

2003
Its last trip was in: 3 SST
movie bomb: 5 GIGLI

2004
Auto discontinued in: 5 ALERO
biopic: 3 RAY
candidate: 5 NADER
hurricane: 4 IVAN

2005
hurricane: 4 RITA

2006: 4 YEAR

2,213
Ruth's: 4 RBIS

2,297
Aaron's: 4 RBIS

4,047
square meters: 4 ACRE

4,840
square yards: 4 ACRE 7 ONEACRE

5,000
Game played to ~ points: 7 CANASTA

"5,000 Fingers of ___, The":
3 DRT

5,280
feet: 4 MILE
5,714
He fanned: 4 RYAN
9000
automaker: 4 SAAB
11,000-foot
peak: 4 ETNA
24,902
Line that extends for ~ miles:
   7 EQUATOR

32,000
ounces: 3 TON
512,000
drams: 3 TON
6,272,640
square inches: 4 ACRE
1,000,000,000
years: 3 EON

Aa

A: 3 ONE 4 MARK SIDE TYPE
5 GRADE 7 ARTICLE
Get all ~ grades: 5 EXCEL
Got an ~ on: 4 ACED
in communications: 4 ALFA
major: 3 KEY
opposite, in England: 3 ZED
Took the ~ train: 4 RODE
Vitamin: 7 RETINOL
~, abroad: 3 EIN UNA UNE
A ___ (nonanalytic):
6 PRIORI
___ A: 4 QAND
A4
maker: 4 AUDI
A6
maker: 4 AUDI
A8
maker: 4 AUDI
AA: 7 BATTERY
concern: 3 DTS
offshoot: 6 ALANON
AAA
AA and: 4 ORGS
baseball team of Buffalo:
6 BISONS
offering: 3 MAP TOW
opposite: 3 EEE
Part of: 4 AMER ASSN
suggestion: 3 **RTE**
Aachen
article: 3 DER EIN
"Aah!"
accompanier: 3 **OOH**
A&E
Part of: 4 ARTS
A&M
Texas ~ player: 5 AGGIE
A&P
Part of: 3 ATL
A&W
rival: 4 DADS 5 HIRES
A ___ apple: 4 ASIN

Aar
Capital on the: 4 BERN
City on the: 5 BERNE
Aardvark: 6 MAMMAL
7 ANTBEAR 8 ANTEATER
feature: 5 SNOUT
land: 6 AFRICA
meal: 4 ANTS
morsel: 3 **ANT**
Aare
Capital on the: 4 BERN
City on the: 5 BERNE
Aaron
Brother of: 5 MOSES
Daughter of: 4 TORI
had 2,297: 4 RBIS
or Raymond: 4 BURR
Son of: 7 ELEAZAR
Aaron, Hank: 8 ALABAMAN
AARP
members: 3 SRS
membership determinant:
3 AGE
Part of: 3 RET 4 AMER ASSN
AAUW
Part of: 4 UNIV
Ab
neighbor: 3 PEC
Ab ___ (from the start): 3 **OVO**
6 INITIO
ABA
member: 3 **ATT** 4 ATTY
members: 3 DAS
superstar: 3 DRJ
___ Ababa: 5 **ADDIS**
Aback
Take: 4 STUN
Abacus
piece: 4 BEAD
Use an: 3 ADD
user: 5 ADDER
"Aba ___ Honeymoon, The":
4 DABA

Abalone
 eater: 5 OTTER
Abandon: 4 DROP SHED 5 DITCH
  LEAVE SCRAP 6 DESERT
  7 FORSAKE
 ~, as a lover: 4 JILT
Abase: 6 DEMEAN
Abate: 3 EBB 4 EASE WANE
  5 LETUP 6 EASEUP
  LESSEN
Abba
 1975 ~ hit: 3 SOS
 1976 ~ hit:
  15 IDOIDOIDOIDOIDO
 Music of: 7 EUROPOP
 of Israel: 4 **EBAN**
 roots: 6 SWEDEN
Abba, Mahmoud
 gp.: 3 PLO
Abbe
 or Nathan: 4 LANE
Abbé de l'___: 4 EPEE
Abbess
 Rank below: 8 PRIORESS
 underling: 3 NUN
Abbey: 4 ROAD
 and others: 3 RDS
 biggie: 5 PRIOR
Abbey Theatre
 name: 6 OCASEY
Abbott
 ~, to Costello: 6 COHORT
Abbott & Costello: 3 DUO
 1942 ~ movie: 7 RIORITA
Abbreviation
 An ~ of: 8 SHORTFOR
Abby
 Twin of: 3 **ANN**
 ~, to Ann: 6 SISTER
ABC: 7 NETWORK TRIGRAM
 Arledge of: 5 ROONE
 Early ~ show: 3 GMA
 Former ~ sitcom: 5 ELLEN
 Roberts of: 5 COKIE
 Sawyer of: 5 DIANE
ABC's: 6 BASICS
Abdicator
 of 1917: 4 TSAR
Abdomen: 3 GUT

Abduct: 6 KIDNAP
Abductee
 Paris: 5 HELEN
Abduction
 1974 ~ gp.: 3 SLA
Abductor
 craft: 3 UFO
 Elephant: 3 ROC
 Hearst: 3 SLA
 Helen: 5 PARIS
Abdul
 Singer: 5 PAULA
Abdul-___, Kareem: 6 JABBAR
"Abdul Abulbul ___": 4 AMIR
___ Abdul-Jabbar: 6 KAREEM
Abe
 Like: 6 HONEST
 Son of: 3 TAD
Abecedarian
 phrase: 4 ASIN
Abed
 Still: 5 NOTUP
Abel
 Brother of: 4 CAIN SETH
 Father of: 4 ADAM
 Mother of: 3 EVE
 Nephew of: 4 ENOS
 Newsman: 4 ELIE
Aberdeen
 denial: 3 NAE
 miss: 4 LASS
 native: 4 SCOT
 river: 3 DEE
Abet: 3 AID 4 HELP 5 COACT
Abeyance
 In: 5 ONICE
Abhor: 4 HATE 6 DETEST
  LOATHE
Abide
 Can't: 4 HATE 6 DETEST
  LOATHE
Abie
 Girl of: 4 ROSE
Ability: 5 SKILL 6 TALENT
 Creative: 3 ART
 Instinctive: 4 FEEL
 Musical: 3 **EAR**
 Paranormal: 3 ESP PSI
 to hit a target: 3 AIM

"A bit of talcum/Is always walcum"
poet: 4 NASH
Abject: 7 HANGDOG
Able
Art ~ to: 5 CANST
Is ~ to: 3 CAN
Isn't ~ to: 4 CANT
More than: 5 ADEPT
to feel: 7 SENSATE
to see through: 4 ONTO
"Able was ___ ...": 4 IERE
"Able was I ___ ...": 3 ERE
4 EREI
Ablutionary
vessel: 4 EWER
ABM
Part of: 4 ANTI
Abner
artist: 4 CAPP
last name: 5 YOKUM
love: 8 DAISYMAE
radio partner: 3 LUM
"___ Abner": 3 LIL
Abnormal
sac: 4 CYST
Suffix for the: 3 OSE
Abnormally: 3 TOO
Aboard: 4 ONTO
Put: 4 LADE STOW
Abode: 4 HOME 5 HOUSE
Alpine: 6 CHALET
Animal: 4 LAIR
Bird: 4 NEST
Conical: 5 TEPEE
Heavenly: 4 EDEN
Lofty: 5 AERIE
Abolish: 3 END 5 ANNUL
Abolished
Defense gp. ~ in 1977: 5 SEATO
Abolitionist
~ Harriet: 6 TUBMAN
Abominable: 6 HORRID
7 OBSCENE
Find: 4 HATE 6 DETEST
LOATHE
Abominable Snowman: 4 YETI
Abominate: 4 HATE 6 DETEST
LOATHE

___ a bone: 5 DRYAS
Aborigine
of Japan: 4 AINU
of New Zealand: 5 MAORI
Aborted
mission words: 4 NOGO
"Abou Ben ___": 5 ADHEM
Abound: 4 TEEM
Abounding: 4 RIFE
About: 4 ASTO INRE ORSO
5 ANENT CIRCA
Be up and: 4 STIR
Just: 4 NEAR ORSO 6 ALMOST
NEARLY
to happen: 8 IMMINENT
___ about: 4 NOSE ONOR
About-face: 5 UTURN
Above: 4 ATOP OVER UPON
5 SUPRA
As: 4 IDEM
From: 6 AERIAL
it all: 5 ALOOF
None of the: 5 OTHER
Word often seen from:
7 WELCOME
~, in German: 5 UBER
~, poetically: 3 OER
___ above: 4 ACUT
Aboveground
trains: 3 ELS
___ above the rest: 4 ACUT
Abracadabra
alternative: 6 PRESTO
Abrade: 3 RUB 4 RASP
Abraded: 4 WORE
Abraham
Grandson of: 4 ESAU 5 JACOB
Oscar role for: 7 SALIERI
Son of: 5 ISAAC
Wife of: 5 SARAH
Abrasion: 6 SCRAPE
Abrasive
cloth: 5 EMERY
particles: 4 GRIT
Use an: 5 SCOUR
**"Abra was ready ___ called her
name": Prior:** 4 EREI
Abreast
of: 4 UPON

Abridged
    Not: 5 UNCUT
Abroad
    Go: 4 TOUR 6 TRAVEL
Abrogate: 6 REPEAL
Abrupt: 4 CURT
    transition: 4 LEAP
Abruptly: 10 COLDTURKEY
    fired: 4 AXED
    Turn: 6 SWERVE
Abruzzi
    bell town: 4 ATRI
Abs
    exercise: 5 SITUP
    They're above the: 4 PECS
Abscam
    org.: 3 FBI
Absence: 4 LACK
    Feel the ~ of: 4 MISS
Absent: 4 AWAY
Absentee
    Roll call: 4 AWOL
Absinthe
    flavor: 5 ANISE
Absolut
    rival: 5 STOLI
Absolute: 5 FINAL SHEER TOTAL
        UTTER
    Not: 8 RELATIVE
    worst: 4 PITS
"Absolutely!": 3 **YES** 4 AMEN
        6 YOUBET
"Absolutely Fabulous"
    Patsy's pal on: 5 EDINA
Absorb: 3 EAT SOP 5 LEARN
        SOPUP
Absorbed: 4 **RAPT**
    as a cost: 3 ATE
    Be ~ slowly: 6 OSMOSE
    by: 4 **INTO**
    the loss: 5 ATEIT
Absorbent
    application: 4 TALC
    cloth: 5 TERRY
    Use ~ paper: 4 BLOT
Absorption
    Gradual: 7 OSMOSIS
Abstain
    from: 4 SHUN 5 AVOID

        6 ESCHEW RESIST
Abstract
    artist Mark: 6 ROTHKO
    composer Erik: 5 SATIE
    sculpture: 7 STABILE
    style: 5 OPART
    Swiss ~ artist: 4 KLEE
Abstraction: 4 IDEA
Abstractionist
    ~ Paul: 4 KLEE
Abstruse: 4 DEEP 6 ARCANE
        8 ESOTERIC
    stuff: 7 ESOTERY
Absurd: 4 ZANY 5 GOOFY INANE
Absurdist
    movement: 4 DADA
Abt.: 3 CIR
Abu ___ : 5 DHABI
Abu Dhabi: 7 EMIRATE
    denizen: 4 ARAB
    dignitary: 4 EMIR
    fed.: 3 UAE
Abuja
    Capital before: 5 LAGOS
    country: 7 NIGERIA
Abundance
    In: 6 GALORE
    Rapunzel: 4 HAIR
Abundant: 4 LUSH MUCH RIFE
        5 AMPLE
    Be: 4 TEEM
    Far from: 6 SPARSE
Abuse: 8 MALTREAT MISTREAT
Abut: 6 BORDER
    on: 6 ADJOIN
Abutting: 6 BESIDE NEXTTO
Abuzz
    It's ~ with activity: 4 HIVE
Abysmal: 4 DEEP
Abyss: 4 GULF 5 CHASM
Abyssinian: 3 CAT
Abzug
    Politico: 5 BELLA
AC: 4 ELEC
A/C
    measure: 3 BTU
    unit: 3 **BTU**
Acad.: 3 SCH 4 INST
    goal: 3 PHD

Academic
achievement: **6** TENURE
enclave: **10** IVORYTOWER
figure: **4** DEAN
Meas. of ~ excellence: **3** GPA
Purely: **4** MOOT
term: **8** SEMESTER
type: **7** SCHOLAR
Academy
founder: **5** PLATO
freshman: **5** PLEBE
graduate: **6** ENSIGN
Its ~ is in Colo. Spr.: **4** USAF
student: **5** CADET
Academy Award: 5 OSCAR
Acadia National Park
locale: **5** MAINE
Acapulco
Info: Spanish cue
appetizer: **5** NACHO
article: **3** LAS LOS UNA
assent: **4** SISI
aunt: **3** TIA
beach: **5** PLAYA
gold: **3 ORO**
Other, in: **4** OTRO
sun: **3** SOL
ACC
member: **3** UVA
Part of: **3** ATL
Accelerate: 3 REV **6** STEPUP
~, with "up": **3** REV
Accelerated: 6 SPEDUP
Acceleration
unit: **4** ONEG
Accelerator: 3 GAS **5** PEDAL
7 SMASHER
particle: **3** ION **4** ATOM
suffix: **4** TRON
Accent: 6 STRESS
Brand name with an: **4** RAGU
Irish: **6** BROGUE
Scottish: **4** BURR
Speak with a Jersey: **3** MOO
Accents
Like some: **5** ACUTE GRAVE
Accept: 3 BUY **5** ADOPT HONOR
7 AGREETO
eagerly: **5** LAPUP **6** LEAPAT

Acceptable: 4 OKAY
Acceptance
Gain ~ from: **7** GETINTO
on the street: **4** CRED
speech word: **5** THANK
Acceptances: 5 YESES **6** YESSES
Accepted: 3 OKD
customs: **5** MORES
eagerly: **7** LEAPTAT
practice: **5** USAGE
rule: **5** AXIOM
standard: **3** PAR **4** NORM
5 CANON
Accepter
Bet: **5** TAKER
Accepting
of: **6** OPENTO
Access: 5 ENTRY **6 ENTREE**
7 TAPINTO
ATM: **3** PIN
Freeway: **4** RAMP **6** ONRAMP
Gain computer: **5** LOGIN
Means of: **4** DOOR **6** AVENUE
Mine: **4** ADIT
suffix: **3** ORY
the Web: **5** LOGON
~, with "into": **3** TAP
"Access Hollywood"
host Nancy: **5** ODELL
Accessible
Most: **7** NEAREST
Accessory: 5 ADDON EXTRA
Accident: 3 HAP **6** MISHAP
1979 Pa. ~ site: **3** TMI
Comment after an: **4** IMOK
OHNO OOPS UHOH
monitoring agcy.: **4** OSHA
Multicar: **6** PILEUP
scene fig.: **3** EMT
U.S. ~ investigator: **4** NTSB
Accidental
Certain: **4** FLAT
Accidentally
Bump: **4** STUB
reveal: **7** LETSLIP
"Accidental Tourist, The"
Oscar winner for
10 GEENADAVIS
Acclaim: 4 LAUD **5** ECLAT KUDOS

Acclaimed
Not: 6 UNSUNG
Accolade: 4 RAVE 5 AWARD
Accolades: 5 KUDOS
Accommodate: 3 FIT 4 SEAT
    5 FITIN 6 OBLIGE
Accommodating: 4 EASY
    6 PLIANT
person: 5 SPORT
place: 3 INN
Accommodations
Cheap: 8 STEERAGE
Deluxe: 5 SUITE
Liner: 6 CABINS
Accompaniment
Improvised: 4 VAMP
Without: 4 SOLO
Accompany: 6 ESCORT
to the airport: 6 SEEOFF
Accompanying: 4 WITH
"___ accompli": 4 FAIT
Accomplice: 6 COHORT STOOGE
Con artist: 5 SHILL
Work without an: 8 ACTALONE
Accomplish: 6 ATTAIN
    7 ACHIEVE
perfectly: 4 NAIL
Accomplished: 3 **DID** 4 ABLE
    DONE FINE 7 PUTOVER
Accomplishes: 4 DOES
Accomplishment: 4 DEED **FEAT**
Cry of: 4 TADA 6 IDIDIT
Accord: 3 CAR 5 AMITY UNITY
    6 TREATY UNISON
    7 ENTENTE
1993 ~ site: 4 OSLO
Be in: 4 JIBE 5 ADDUP AGREE
Bring into: 6 ATTUNE
In: 5 ASONE
International: 4 PACT
    7 ENTENTE
maker: 5 HONDA
Perfect: 6 UNISON
Reach an: 5 AGREE
signed in 1992: 5 NAFTA
Were in: 5 JIBED
___ Accord: 3 WYE
Accordance
In ~ with: 3 PER 5 ASPER

According
to: 3 ALA **PER** 5 ASPER
Accordingly: 4 ERGO THEN
    THUS
According to ___: 5 HOYLE
"According to Jim"
actor: 7 BELUSHI
Accordion
feature: 5 PLEAT
Accost
for money: 5 HITUP
Account: 3 LOG 4 SAKE **TALE**
amt.: 3 BAL
book: 6 LEDGER
Contribute to an: 5 PAYIN
exec: 3 REP
Firsthand: 6 MEMOIR
Gave an: 4 TOLD
It may be called on ~ of rain:
    3 CAB
Kind of checking: 5 NOFEE
Long: 4 EPIC
Major: 4 SAGA
Rainy day: 7 NESTEGG
Settle an: 5 PAYUP
subtraction: 5 DEBIT
Third-party: 6 ESCROW
___ account (never): 4 ONNO
Accountant: 7 AUDITOR
    8 PREPARER
closing time: 7 YEAREND
job: 5 AUDIT
Accounting
plus: 5 ASSET
principle: 4 LIFO
Young's ~ partner: 5 ERNST
Accouter
anew: 5 REFIT
Accra
land: 5 GHANA
Accrual
IRA: 3 INT
Acct.
addition: 3 INT
datum: 3 SSN
entry: 3 BAL DEP
figures: 4 AMTS
Accumulate: 5 **AMASS** RUNUP
    STORE 6 ACCRUE PILEUP

SAVEUP 7 ACCRETE
STOREUP
Accumulated: 5 RANUP
Accumulation: 4 MASS **5** STACK
STORE
Chimney: **4** SOOT
Accuracy
Check for: **3** VET
Accurate: 4 TRUE **5** RIGHT
6 DEADON SPOTON
Accusation
Caesar's: **4** ETTU
Unjust: **6** BADRAP
Accuse: 5 BLAME **7** IMPEACH
Formally: **6** INDICT
Accused
cry: **5** WHOME
excuse: **5** ALIBI
Accustom: 5 ADAPT ENURE
INURE 6 ORIENT
AC/DC
record label: **3** EMI
Ace: 3 PRO **4** CARD WHIZ **5** FLIER
PILOT **6** TIPTOP TOPGUN
7 AVIATOR **9** HOLEINONE
Act like an: **6** AVIATE
place: **4** HOLE **6** SLEEVE
Acela: 5 TRAIN
operator: **6** AMTRAK
Acerbic: 4 TART **5** HARSH
Aces
Game with ~ and chips: **4** GOLF
Acetate
Any: **5** ESTER
Word before: **5** ETHYL
Acetyl
suffix: **3** ENE
Acetylacetone
form: **4** ENOL
Acetylene
prefix: **3** OXY
Ache: 4 HURT **5** YEARN
(for): **4** LONG PINE
Aches
and pains: **4** ILLS
Aches and ___: 5 PAINS
Acheson
Reader's Digest cofounder:
4 LILA

Achieve
success: **6** ARRIVE
Achievement: 4 DEED FEAT
Base runner: **5** STEAL
Grand: **4** COUP
Achille ___ : 5 LAURO
Achilles: 6 TENDON
He rescued the body of: **4** AJAX
Story of: **5** ILIAD
victim: **6** HECTOR
was dipped in it: **4** STYX
weak spot: **4** HEEL
"Achtung Baby"
producer Brian: **3** ENO
Achy: 4 SORE
Feels: **4** AILS
Acid: 3 LSD **4** TART
Antiseptic: **5** BORIC
Apple: **5** MALIC
Carbolic: **6** PHENOL
Draw with: **4 ETCH**
Essential: **5** AMINO
Fatty: **5** OLEIC
head: **5** AMINO
in tea: **6** TANNIC
Kind of: **5 AMINO** BORIC
MALIC OLEIC SALIC
6 ACETIC CITRIC NITRIC
TANNIC
letters: **3** LSD
neutralizer: **4** BASE
6 ALKALI
plus alcohol: **5** ESTER
Protein: **5** AMINO
Strong: **3** HCL **6** NITRIC
user: **6** ETCHER
Acid ___ : 4 RAIN TEST
___ acid: 5 AMINO BORIC FOLIC
OLEIC **6** ACETIC FORMIC
NITRIC
Acid-alcohol
compound: **5** ESTER
Acidic: 4 TART
Acidity
nos.: **3** PHS
Acknowledge: 3 OWN **4** AVOW
5 ADMIT NODTO THANK
applause: **3** BOW
frankly: **4** AVOW

Acknowledgment: 6 CREDIT
  Cockpit: **5** ROGER
  Debt: **3** IOU
  Frank: **6** AVOWAL
  Performer's: **11** CURTAINCALL
"A ___'clock scholar": 4 TENO
ACLU
  concerns: **3** RTS **6** RIGHTS
  Part of: **4** AMER
"A clue!": 3 AHA
Acme: 4 APEX PEAK
  At the ~ of: **4** ATOP
Acne
  sufferer: **4** TEEN
Aconcagua
  range: **5** ANDES
Acorn: 3 NUT **4** SEED
  source: **3** OAK **7** OAKTREE
A-courting
  Go: **3** SUE WOO
Acoustic
  unit: **4** SONE
"Acoustic Soul"
  singer: **9** INDIAARIE
Acquaintance
  Make the ~ of: **4** MEET
Acquainted
  Be ~ with: **4** KNOW
  Was ~ with: **4** KNEW
Acquiesce: 5 AGREE **6** ACCEDE
      ASSENT
Acquire: 3 <u>GET</u> NET WIN **4** GAIN
      REAP **5** GETIN INCUR
      6 OBTAIN SECURE
      8 COMEINTO
  molars: **6** TEETHE
Acquired: 6 CAMEBY
  deservedly: **6** EARNED
  It may be: **5** TASTE
  kin: **5** INLAW
Acquisition
  American: **3** TWA
  Aquarium: **5** TETRA
  Beach: **3** TAN
  Disney: **3** ABC
  Marriage: **5** INLAW
  Owner: **4** DEED
Acquitted
  Is: **11** BEATSTHERAP

Acre
  home: **6** ISRAEL
Acreage: 4 AREA LAND
Acred
  homes: **7** ESTATES
Acrimonious: 6 BITTER
Acrimony: 3 IRE **5** SPITE
Acrobat
  maker: **5** ADOBE
  security: **3** NET
Acrobatic: 5 AGILE
  performance: **5** STUNT
Acrobatics
  performed to music:
    10 BREAKDANCE
Acronym
  Alliance: **4** NATO **5** SEATO
  Anticrime: **4** RICO
  Breakfast: **4** IHOP
  Broadway: **4** ANTA
  Cartel: **4** OPEC
  Computer: **3** ROM **4** GIGO
    5 ASCII MSDOS
  Disney World: **5** EPCOT
  Diving: **5** SCUBA
  formed from Standard Oil:
    4 ESSO
  Great Lakes: **5** HOMES
  Military: **3** SAC **5** AWACS NORAD
  Navigation: **5** LORAN
  Oil: **4** OPEC
  part: **4** INIT
  Police jacket: **4** SWAT
  Record: **5** ASCAP
  Restaurant: **4** IHOP
  Sleep: **3** <u>REM</u>
  Sunscreen: **4** PABA
  Wall St.: **4** AMEX
Acrophobe
  dread: **6** HEIGHT
Acropolis
  figure: **6** ATHENA
  locale: **6** ATHENS
Across: 4 OVER
  Came: **3** MET
  Come: **4** FIND
  Come ~ as: **4** SEEM
  Directly ~ from (abbr.): **3** OPP
  Go: **4** SPAN

Reach: 4 **SPAN**
the ocean: 7 OVERSEA
~, in verse: 3 OER
Acrylic
fiber: 5 **ORLON**
Act: 4 DEED 6 BEHAVE
    7 STATUTE
as censor: 5 BLEEP
badly: 5 EMOTE
Catch in the: 3 NAB
Caught in the: 4 **SEEN**
Ceremonial: 4 RITE
crabby: 5 SIDLE
Failed to: 3 SAT
Formal: 7 STATUTE
human: 3 ERR
It's an: 4 SKIT
like: 3 APE 7 EMULATE
of faith: 4 LEAP
of war: 3 TUG
opener: 6 SCENEI 8 SCENEONE
Part of an: 5 **SCENE**
Prohibited: 4 NONO
properly: 6 BEHAVE
servile: 6 GROVEL
the ham: 5 RADIO
the snitch: 6 TATTLE
the snoop: 3 PRY
They: 5 DOERS
Time to: 4 DDAY
Trusting: 11 LEAPOFFAITH
Wrongful: 4 TORT
Act.
Not: 3 RET 4 RETD
Acting
ambassador: 5 AGENT
award: 4 OBIE
ensemble: 4 CAST
family: 5 ALDAS 6 FONDAS
like: 5 APING
Majors in: 3 LEE
part: 4 ROLE
Action: 4 DEED 5 STEPS
Affirmative: 3 **NOD**
Break in the: 4 **LULL**
centers: 6 ARENAS
figure: 5 GIJOE
film staple: 5 CHASE
First course of: 5 PLANA

Get ready for: 6 GEARUP
Inadvisable: 4 NONO
Incite to: 5 EGGON IMPEL
One who suspends an: 6 ABATOR
Out of: 5 IDLED ONICE
    6 LAIDUP
People of: 5 DOERS
Piece of the: 3 CUT 5 SHARE
Prepare for: 4 GIRD 6 GEARUP
Put into: 3 USE 5 EXERT
    6 DEPLOY
Rash: 5 HASTE
Refrain from taking: 6 SITPAT
spot: 5 ARENA
Stir to: 4 PROD URGE
    6 AROUSE
Take ~ against: 3 SUE
Where the ~ is: 5 **ARENA**
word: 4 VERB
Actionable
words: 5 LIBEL
Action-filled: 8 SLAMBANG
Actium
Victor at: 7 AGRIPPA
Activate: 3 USE 5 SPARK START
    6 ENABLE TURNON
Active: 4 SPRY 5 DOING
    7 ONTHEGO
by day: 7 DIURNAL
Not: 4 IDLE 5 INERT 6 ONHOLD
Not ~ (abbr.): 3 RET 4 RETD
one: 4 DOER
volcano: 4 ETNA
Activist: 4 DOER
An ~ has one: 5 CAUSE
Old ~ org.: 3 SDS
~ Chavez: 5 CESAR
~ Davis: 6 ANGELA
~ Parks: 4 **ROSA**
Activity
Busy: 3 ADO
Center of: 3 HUB
Centers of: 4 **LOCI**
Dirty: 4 POOL
Flurry of: 3 ADO 5 SPASM
Productive: 4 WORK
Spurts of: 6 SPASMS
"Act now!": 4 DOIT
Actor: 7 ARTISTE

accessory: 4 PROP
aid: 3 CUE
award: 5 OSCAR
Biggest fan of a child:
    8 STAGEMOM
Chain-wearing: 3 MRT
Crowd scene: 5 EXTRA
Lionized: 4 LAHR
milieu: 5 STAGE
minimum: 5 SCALE
Overacting: 3 HAM
part: 4 ROLE
Rapping: 4 ICET
rep: 5 AGENT
study: 5 LINES
Uncredited: 5 EXTRA
with no lines: 4 MIME
Actors
Change the: 6 RECAST
How ~ enter: 5 ONCUE
org.: 5 AFTRA
Actual: 4 REAL TRUE
    7 DEFACTO
being: 4 ESSE
Actually: 6 INESSE INFACT
    9 INREALITY
existing: 6 **INESSE**
"Act your ___!": 3 AGE
Acuff
Singer: 3 ROY
Acuity
Mental: 4 WITS
Musical: 3 EAR
Acupressure: 7 SHIATSU
Acupuncturist
life force: 3 CHI
Acura
model: 6 LEGEND 7 INTEGRA
___ a customer: 5 ONETO
Acute: 4 DIRE KEEN 5 SHARP
    6 SEVERE 7 INTENSE
Ad: 4 SPOT 5 PROMO
abbr.: 3 APR
Attack: 5 SMEAR
award: 4 CLIO
catchphrase: 6 SLOGAN
follower: 3 HOC LIB
A.D.
It began in 800: 3 HRE

Part of: 4 **ANNO** 6 DOMINI
Ad-___: 3 **HOC** LIB 4 LIBS
ADA
member: 3 DDS
Adage: 3 SAW 5 AXIOM MAXIM
Adagio: 4 SLOW
and allegro: 5 TEMPI
Slower than: 5 LENTO
Adah
Husband of: 4 ESAU
Adam
Actor: 5 ARKIN
and Eve locale: 4 EDEN
and Mae: 5 WESTS
First wife of ~, in Jewish lore:
    6 LILITH
Grandson of: 4 **ENOS** SETH
madam: 3 EVE
Son of: 4 ABEL CAIN SETH
"Adam ___": Eliot: 4 BEDE
"Adam Bede"
author: 5 ELIOT
Adams
Actor: 3 DON
Actress: 4 EDIE MAUD
Mrs. John Quincy: 6 LOUISA
Photographer: 5 **ANSEL**
Singer: 4 **EDIE** 5 BRYAN
Adams, John Quincy
Mrs.: 6 LOUISA
Adams, Scott
character: 7 DILBERT
Adam's ___ (water): 3 ALE
Adam's apple
locale: 4 EDEN 6 LARYNX
provider: 3 EVE
Adamson
lioness: 4 **ELSA**
Adaptable: 6 PLIANT
    7 ELASTIC
aircraft: 4 STOL
truck: 3 UTE
Adapter
letters: 4 ACDC
Adar
Month after: 5 NISAN
Month before: 6 SHEBAT
"Ad astra per ___": 6 ASPERA
Ad-___ committee: 3 HOC

ADCs: 5 ASSTS
Add: 5 MIXIN PUTIN TOTUP
  6 APPEND TACKON
  a lane to: 5 WIDEN
  as a bonus: 7 THROWIN
  booze to: 4 LACE
  color to: 4 TINT
  fizz to: 6 AERATE
  fringe to: 4 EDGE
  herbs to: 6 SEASON
  on: 5 ANNEX 6 APPEND
    ATTACH
  sugar: 7 SWEETEN
  to the payroll: 4 HIRE
  turf to: 5 RESOD
  up: 4 TOTE 5 TALLY TOTAL
    6 ACCRUE
  up (to): 6 AMOUNT
  value to: 6 ENRICH
  yeast to: 6 LEAVEN
Addams
  Cartoonist: 4 CHAS
  cousin: 3 ITT
  Mrs. ~, to Gomez: 4 TISH
Addams, Gomez
  portrayer: 5 ASTIN
"Addams Family, The"
  actor: 5 ASTIN
  actor Julia: 4 RAUL
  butler: 5 LURCH
  cousin: 3 ITT
Added
  details: 4 ANDS
  It's ~ to the bill: 5 RIDER
  stipulations: 4 **ANDS**
  topsoil to: 6 LOAMED
Addenda
  Ltr.: 3 **PSS**
Addendum
  Info: Suffix cue
Adder: 5 SNAKE
  kin: 3 ASP
Adderley
  instrument: 3 SAX
  Jazzman: 3 **NAT**
Adders: 5 ABACI
Addict: 4 USER 6 ABUSER
  helper: 7 ENABLER
  program: 5 DETOX REHAB

Adding
  Keep: 6 PILEON
Addis ___ : 5 **ABABA**
Addis Ababa
  land (abbr.): 3 ETH
Addison
  colleague: 6 **STEELE**
Addition: 3 ELL 4 GAIN WING
  Info: Suffix cue
  Acct.: 3 INT
  Building: 3 **ELL** 4 WING
    5 ANNEX
  column: 4 ONES TENS
  In: 3 AND TOO YET 4 ALSO
    ELSE PLUS 6 ATTHAT
    TOBOOT
  In ~ to: 8 ASWELLAS
  problems: 4 SUMS
  sign: 5 CARET
  Slight: 5 TINGE
Additional: 4 ELSE **MORE**
  5 EXTRA OTHER
  7 ANOTHER
  For an ~ cost: 5 EXTRA
  Make ~ changes to: 6 REEDIT
  ones: 6 OTHERS
  ~, in ads: 4 XTRA
Additionally: 3 AND TOO 4 **ALSO**
  ELSE PLUS
Additive
  Café: 4 LAIT
  Chinese food: 3 MSG
  Copier: 5 TONER
  Gas: 3 STP 5 ETHYL
  Lotion: 4 **ALOE**
  Tissue: 4 **ALOE**
Addle: 6 BEMUSE
  add-on: 5 PATED
Addlebrained: 4 DAFT 5 DITSY
Add-on: 3 ELL 5 EXTRA
  7 ADJUNCT
  Info: Suffix cue
Address: 4 TALK 6 SPEECH
  TALKTO 7 ORATION
  SPEAKTO
  abbr.: 3 RTE
  Abbr. under an: 4 ATTN
  a crowd: 5 ORATE
  book no.: 3 TEL

Family: 3 SIS
GI: 3 APO
Give an: 5 ORATE
Hood: 3 BRO
Indian: 5 SAHIB
Kingly: 4 SIRE
Mil.: 3 **APO**
Net: 3 URL
One sans permanent: 5 NOMAD
One with an: 8 KEYNOTER
Palindromic: 4 MAAM 5 MADAM
Polite: 3 SIR 4 **MAAM** 5 MADAM
Rev.: 3 SER
Royal: 4 SIRE 6 MYLORD
WWW: 3 **URL**
Addressee
  Apr.: 3 **IRS**
Addresses
  Change: 4 MOVE
Ade
  Astronaut's: 4 TANG
  cooler: 3 ICE
  flavor: 4 LIME
"A debt ... we ___ Adam": Twain:
    5 OWETO
Adele
  Dancer: 7 ASTAIRE
Aden
  land: 5 YEMEN
  native: 6 YEMENI
Adenauer
  epithet: 4 ALTE
  German chancellor: 6 KONRAD
  successor: 6 ERHARD
Adept: 3 ACE 4 DEFT
    7 SKILLED
  More: 5 ABLER
Adequacy
  Phrase of: 6 ITLLDO
Adequate: 4 OKAY SOSO
    6 DECENT ENOUGH
    8 PASSABLE
  Barely: 5 SCANT 6 SCANTY
    7 MINIMAL
  More than: 5 AMPLE EXTRA
  ~, old-style: 4 ENOW
  ~, slangily: 4 ENUF
Adhere: 3 HEW 4 BOND 5 CLING
    STICK

Adherent
  in Iran: 5 BAHAI
  suffix: 3 **IST** ITE
Adhesive: 3 GUM 4 GLUE
  Kindergarten: 5 PASTE
  Strong: 5 EPOXY
Adidas
  rival: 4 AVIA FILA KEDS NIKE
    PUMA
Adieu
  Bid the bed: 5 ARISE
Adipose: 5 FATTY
Adj.
  modifier: 3 ADV
Adjacent
  Be ~ to: 4 ABUT
Adjective
  suffix: 3 **ENT** IAL ILE INE
    4 IBLE ICAL
Adjoin: 4 ABUT
Adjudge: 3 TRY 4 DEEM
Adjunct: 4 AIDE
Adjust: 4 GEAR TUNE
    5 ALIGN ALTER
    RESET 6 ATTUNE
    ORIENT
  a brooch: 5 REPIN
  a clock: 5 RESET
  a hem: 5 RESEW
  for: 6 GEARTO
  one's sights: 5 REAIM
  shoelaces: 5 RETIE
  slightly: 5 TWEAK
  to fit: 5 ADAPT
Adjustable
  It has an ~ nose: 3 SST
  loop: 5 NOOSE
Adjuster
  concern: 5 CLAIM
  Piano: 5 TUNER
Adjustment
  Small: 5 TWEAK
  Steering: 5 TOEIN
  TV: 3 HOR
Adjutant: 4 AIDE
Adlai
  running mate: 5 **ESTES**
Adler
  of Holmes stories: 5 IRENE

Ad-lib: 4 SCAT 6 FAKEIT WINGIT
9 IMPROVISE
Adm.
org.: 3 USN
Adman: 9 SLOGANEER
award: 4 CLIO
~ Burnett: 3 LEO
Admin.
aide: 4 ASST
Administer: 4 DEAL
an oath to: 7 SWEARIN
EMTs ~ it: 3 CPR
medicine: 4 DOSE
the oath of office to:
7 INSTATE
They may ~ IVs: 3 RNS
Administration
Current: 3 INS
ER: 3 CPR
Hosp.: 3 TLC
Administrative
center: 4 SEAT
Administrator
CPR: 3 EMT
Online: 5 SYSOP
SAT: 3 ETS
Superfund ~ (abbr.): 3 EPA
Admiral
force: 4 NAVY 5 FLEET
German: 4 SPEE
Kind of: 4 REAR
org.: 3 USN
position: 4 REAR
WWII: 6 HALSEY
~ Zumwalt: 4 ELMO
Admiral Byrd
book: 5 ALONE
Admiration
Induce: 3 AWE
Sound of: 3 OOH
Admire
a lot: 7 ADULATE
amorously: 4 OGLE
Admired
one: 4 HERO **IDOL**
Admirer: 3 FAN 4 BEAU
Beauty: 5 BEAST
Male: 5 SWAIN
of Narcissus: 4 ECHO

Admiringly
fearful: 5 INAWE
Admission: 6 ACCESS AVOWAL
exams: 4 SATS
Fibber's: 5 ILIED
Frank: 6 AVOWAL
of 1890: 5 IDAHO
of defeat: 5 ILOSE ILOST
Admit: 3 OWN 4 AVOW 5 COPTO
LETIN LETON OWNUP
SEEIN 7 CONCEDE
OWNUPTO
a mistake: 7 EATCROW
openly: 4 AVOW
Refuse to: 4 DENY
to a poker game: 6 DEALIN
~, with "up": 3 OWN 4 FESS
Admittedly: 8 TOBESURE
Admitting
a draft: 4 AJAR
Admonish: 5 CHIDE 6 REBUKE
7 REPROVE
Admonishing
sounds: 4 TSKS
Admonition
Archie's ~ to Edith: 6 STIFLE
Librarian's: 3 SHH
to a child: 4 NONO 6 BENICE
to Fido: 4 STAY
Ado: 4 FLAP FUSS STIR
5 HOOHA 6 HOOPLA
Adobe
offering: 4 FONT
Adolescent: 4 TEEN 5 YOUTH
6 TEENER 7 TEENAGE
8 TEENAGER
Adolph
Brewer: 5 COORS
Publisher: 4 **OCHS**
"Adonais"
Shelley's: 5 ELEGY
Adonis: 4 HUNK STUD
killer: 4 BOAR
Adopt: 6 TAKEIN 7 EMBRACE
ESPOUSE
Adopt-a-Dog
month: 3 OCT
Adopted
name of Makonnen: 5 HAILE

son of Claudius: 4 NERO
Adoption
  agcy.: 4 SPCA 5 ASPCA
Adorable: 4 CUTE
  one: 4 IDOL 5 CUTIE
Adoration
  Object of: 4 IDOL
  Shout of: 7 HOSANNA
Adore: 4 LOVE 6 DOTEON
      REVERE
  ~, informally: 3 LUV
Adored
  one: 4 <u>IDOL</u>
Adorée
  Actress: 5 <u>RENEE</u>
Adoring
  trio: 4 MAGI
Adorn: 4 DECK 5 DRESS GRACE
      6 BEDECK
  Richly: 4 GILD
Adorned
  Elaborately: 6 ORNATE
  Less: 5 BARER
  ~, as an entrée: 5 GARNI
Adornment: 7 GARNISH
  Bejeweled: 5 TIARA
  Chin: 6 GOATEE
  Letter: 5 SERIF
  Model: 5 DECAL
  Uniform: 7 EPAULET
"Ad ___ per aspera": 5 ASTRA
Adrian
  Director: 4 LYNE
  portrayer: 5 TALIA
Adriatic
  Capital near the: 6 TIRANA
  country: 7 CROATIA
  feeder: 5 ADIGE
  peninsula: 6 ISTRIA
  port: 4 <u>BARI</u> 7 TRIESTE
  resort: 4 LIDO
  wind: 4 BORA
Adrien
  of cosmetics: 5 ARPEL
Adrienne
  Actress: 5 CORRI
Adroit: 4 ABLE DEFT 6 FACILE
      HABILE
  prefix: 3 MAL

Adroitness
  With: 4 ABLY
Ads
  Additional, in: 4 XTRA
  Dietary, in: 4 LITE
  Evening, in: 4 NITE
  Flat, in: 3 APT
  Shine, in: 3 GLO
  Skip the: 3 ZAP
  Times to call, in: 4 EVES
  Up to, in: 3 TIL
Adult: 5 GROWN OFAGE
      6 XRATED
  acorn: 3 OAK
  grig: 3 EEL
  insect: 5 IMAGO
  polliwog: 4 TOAD
Adulterate: 5 TAINT 6 DEBASE
Adulterated
  Less: 5 PURER
Adult-to-be: 4 TEEN
Advance: 4 GAIN LEND LOAN
      SPOT STEP 6 MOVEUP
      STEPUP STRIDE
  furtively: 5 SIDLE
  Have ready in: 6 PRESET
  in age: 5 GETON
  In ~ of: 3 ERE 5 AFORE
  Settled in: 7 PREPAID
  Take care of in: 6 PREPAY
  Take ~ orders for: 7 PRESELL
  warning: 5 ALERT
Advanced: 4 LENT
  deg.: 3 MBA PHD
  degree: 3 NTH
  degs.: 3 MAS
  More: 5 OLDER
  study group: 7 SEMINAR
  tests: 5 ORALS
Advantage: 3 PRO 4 <u>EDGE</u>
      5 ASSET AVAIL LEGUP
      STEAD
  Competitive: 4 <u>EDGE</u>
  Initial: 7 TOEHOLD
  Slight: 4 EDGE
  Take ~ of: 3 <u>USE</u>
  Used one's standing to:
      10 PULLEDRANK
  ___ **advantage: 4 ATAN**

Advantageous
  Be: 3 PAY
Advent
  song: 4 NOEL
Adventure: 4 GEST SAGA
  African: 6 SAFARI
  Carefree: 4 LARK
  Computer ~ game: 4 MYST
  hero Williams: 4 REMO
  Seeking: 6 ERRANT
  story: 4 GEST SAGA
"Adventures of Robin Hood, The"
  Little John portrayer in:
    8 ALANHALE
Adventurous
  rover: 6 ERRANT
  trip: 7 ODYSSEY
Adverb
  ending: 3 IAL
  Latin: 3 HIC HOC
  Legalese: 7 THERETO
  Nautical: 4 **ALEE**
  Poetic: 3 EEN **EER** OFT 4 ANON
    NEER
  Salty: 4 THAR
Adversary: 3 **FOE** 5 ENEMY
    RIVAL
Adverse
  fate: 4 DOOM
Adversely
  Affect: 8 WHIPLASH
Adversity
  Handle: 4 COPE
Advertise: 4 PLUG 5 PITCH
    6 MARKET
Advertiser: 7 SPONSOR
  award: 4 CLIO
  purchase: 7 AIRTIME
Advertising
  award: 4 **CLIO**
  photo label: 5 AFTER
  section: 6 INSERT
  sign: 4 NEON
  suffix: 5 ORAMA
Advice: 5 INPUT
  Ambulance chaser's: 3 SUE
  Bear: 4 SELL
  First name in: 3 ANN
  Follow, as: 5 **ACTON**

  Give meddlesome: 6 KIBITZ
  Kind of: 5 LEGAL 8 PATERNAL
  Medical: 4 REST
  One sought for: 5 ELDER
  Piece of: 3 TIP
  Takes, as: 6 ACTSON
Advil
  rival: 5 **ALEVE**
Advise: 4 WARN
  Strongly: 4 URGE
Adviser
  Apr. 15: 3 CPA
  Bush: 4 RICE ROVE
  Delphic: 6 ORACLE
  Reagan: 5 MEESE
  Spiritual: 4 GURU
  ~ Landers: 3 ANN
Advisory: 5 ALERT
  Defense ~ org.: 3 **NSC**
  group: 5 PANEL 7 CABINET
  P.D.: 3 APB
Advocacy
  Fem. ~ org.: 4 YWCA
  Rights ~ org.: 4 **ACLU**
  Sch. ~ org.: 3 PTA
Advocate: 7 ESPOUSE
    8 PROMOTER
  (abbr.): 4 ATTY
  Consumer: 5 NADER
Adz: 4 TOOL
Aeaea
  Sorceress of: 5 CIRCE
AEC
  logo: 4 ATOM
  successor: 3 NRC
Aegean: 3 SEA
  island: 5 SAMOS
  On the: 4 ASEA
  region: 5 IONIA
  vacation locale: 5 CRETE
Aeneas
  Lover of: 4 DIDO
"Aeneid": 4 EPIC
  First word of: 4 ARMA
  poet: 6 VIRGIL
Aerial: 7 ANTENNA
  defense acronym: 5 AWACS
  maneuver: 4 LOOP ROLL
    SPIN

Aerialist
getup: 7 LEOTARD
insurance: 3 NET
Aerie: 4 NEST
baby: 6 EAGLET
builder: 5 EAGLE
Aero
suffix: 3 SOL
Aerobatics
Do: 6 AVIATE
feat: 4 LOOP
Aerobics
action: 4 STEP
Kind of: 4 STEP
Rue the: 4 ACHE
Aerodynamic: 5 SLEEK
force: 4 DRAG
Aeronautics
feat: 4 SOLO
Aerosmith
1993 ~ hit: 5 CRYIN
vocalist: 5 TYLER
Aerosol
output: 4 MIST 5 SPRAY
Aerospatiale
Onetime ~ product: 3 SST
AES
defeater: 3 DDE
Aeschylus
trilogy: 8 ORESTEIA
Aesir
bigwig: 4 ODIN
Aesop
also-ran: 4 HARE
conclusion: 5 MORAL
Like ~ grapes: 4 SOUR
tale: 5 FABLE
Aesthetic
Affectedly: 4 ARTY
Aetna: 7 INSURER
offering: 3 HMO
Afar
Friend from: 6 PENPAL
Greet from: 6 WAVETO
Visitor from: 5 ALIEN
Visitors from: 3 ETS
AFC
1993 ~ Rookie of the Year:
5 MIRER

Affable
Least: 6 ICIEST
Affair: 5 EVENT FLING
7 LIAISON
Afternoon: 3 TEA
Court: 5 TRIAL
Debutante: 4 BALL
Evening: 6 SOIREE
Festive: 4 GALA
Genteel: 3 TEA
Hatfield-McCoy: 4 FEUD
Illicit: 5 AMOUR
Love: 5 **AMOUR**
Men-only: 4 STAG
of honor: 4 DUEL
Tortoise-hare: 4 RACE
Vanity: 7 EGOTRIP
___ Affair (1797–98): 3 XYZ
Affaire
de coeur: 5 AMOUR
d'honneur: 4 DUEL
Affairs: 3 DOS
Affect: 4 DOTO MOVE 5 ACTON
FEIGN GETTO 6 IMPACT
drastically: 5 UPEND
strongly: 4 STIR
~, as opinion: 4 SWAY
Affectation: 4 AIRS POSE
Affected: 4 ARTY 5 ARTSY GOTTO
STAGY 6 TOOTOO
Elegantly: 6 CHICHI
Excessively: 6 TOOTOO
look: 5 SMIRK
Tastelessly: 6 TOOTOO
Affection: 4 LOVE 8 FONDNESS
Lavish: 4 **DOTE**
Seek the ~ of: 3 WOO
Sign of: 4 KISS
Term of: 3 HON 5 CUTIE
6 DEARIE
Affectionate: 4 FOND 7 AMATIVE
10 LOVEYDOVEY
gesture: 3 PAT
touch: 6 CARESS
~, in slang: 5 KISSY
Affiliation: 3 TIE
Affirm: 4 AVER AVOW 5 STATE
SWEAR 7 PROFESS
SWEARTO

Affirmation
  Altar: 3 IDO
  Solemn: 4 OATH
Affirmative: 3 YES
  action: 3 **NOD**
  Emphatic: 6 YESSIR
  French: 3 OUI
  NASA: 3 AOK
  Sailor: 3 AYE
  Shipboard: 6 AYEAYE
  Slangy: 4 YEAH
  Spanish: 4 SISI
  vote: 3 AYE **YEA** YES
Affix: 3 SET 4 GLUE 5 PASTE
      7 STICKON
  a brand to: 4 SEAR
  a patch: 6 IRONON
Affleck
  Actor: 3 BEN 5 CASEY
  Oscar co-winner of: 5 DAMON
Afflict: 3 AIL 5 SMITE
Afflicted: 3 ILL 8 STRICKEN
  Be ~ with: 4 HAVE
  Is ~ with: 3 HAS
Affliction: 3 WOE 4 BANE
      6 MALADY
  Complexion: 4 ACNE
  FDR: 5 POLIO
  Skid row: 3 DTS
  Teen: 4 ACNE
"Affliction"
  actor Nick: 5 NOLTE
Affluence: 4 EASE 5 MEANS
Affront: 4 SLAP 6 OFFEND
      7 OUTRAGE
  Deliberate: 4 SNUB
Afghan: 5 ASIAN
  capital: 5 KABUL
  neighbor: 5 IRANI
Afghanistan
  capital: 5 KABUL
  city: 5 HERAT
  neighbor: 4 IRAN
  Pass to: 6 KHYBER
Aficionado: 3 FAN NUT 5 LOVER
  cheer: 3 OLE
"A fickle food upon a shifting
      plate": Dickinson: 4 FAME
___ a fiddle: 5 FITAS

Afield
  Go far: 4 TREK
Afire
  Set: 3 LIT 6 IGNITE
AFL
  partner: 3 **CIO**
AFL-___ : 3 CIO
Aflame
  Set: 6 IGNITE
AFL-CIO
  First president of the: 5 MEANY
  head John: 7 SWEENEY
  Part of: 4 AMER
Afloat: 6 NATANT
  Kept: 6 BUOYED
Afore: 3 ERE
Aforementioned: 4 SAID SAME
"A ___ formality": 4 MERE
___ a fox: 5 SLYAS
Afr.
  It's north of: 3 EUR
  nation: 3 ALG ETH
Afraid: 6 SCARED TREPID
  Be ~ to: 7 DARENOT
A-frame
  feature: 5 EAVES
Afresh: 5 NEWLY
  Lease: 5 RELET
Africa
  Film set in: 6 HATARI
  Fly from: 6 TSETSE
  Horn of ~ native: 6 SOMALI
  Lake of southeast: 5 NYASA
  Largest city in: 5 CAIRO
  Largest country in: 5 SUDAN
  Longest river of: 4 NILE
  Third-longest river of: 5 NIGER
African
  adventure: 6 SAFARI
  antelope: 3 GNU KOB 4 ORYX
      5 **ELAND** NYALA ORIBI
      6 IMPALA RHEBOK
  bloodsucker: 6 TSETSE
  capital: 5 ACCRA CAIRO RABAT
      TUNIS 7 ALGIERS NAIROBI
  cattle pen: 5 KRAAL
  charger: 5 RHINO
  cobra: 3 ASP
  danger: 9 TSETSEFLY

desert: 5 NAMIB 6 **SAHARA**
   8 KALAHARI
fly: 6 **TSETSE**
Former ~ capital: 5 LAGOS
fox: 4 ASSE
grassland: 5 VELDT
grazer: 3 GNU
language: 5 **BANTU** 6 RUANDA
lily: 4 ALOE
master: 5 BWANA
menace: 3 ASP 6 TSETSE
nation: 4 CHAD MALI TOGO
   5 BENIN GABON LIBYA
   SUDAN 6 ANGOLA UGANDA
   7 ERITREA LESOTHO
   SENEGAL
pullover: 7 DASHIKI
queen: 4 CLEO
river: 4 NILE 5 NIGER
   6 UBANGI
snake: 3 ASP 5 MAMBA
streambed: 4 WADI
tree: 4 KOLA
virus: 5 EBOLA
Westernmost ~ city: 5 DAKAR
African-American: 5 BLACK
"African Queen, The"
  author: 8 FORESTER
  screenwriter: 4 **AGEE**
Afrika Korps
  leader: 6 ROMMEL
Afrikaner: 4 **BOER**
Afros: 3 DOS
Aft: 5 ABACK 6 ASTERN
AFI
  rival: 3 NEA
After: 3 ALA 4 PAST 6 BEHIND
a long wait: 6 ATLAST
a while: 4 ANON
Come: 5 **ENSUE**
curfew: 4 LATE
expenses: 3 NET
Go: 3 SUE 4 SEEK SHAG
   5 CHASE SETAT 6 ASSAIL
   ATTACK PURSUE
hours: 4 LATE
Immediately: 4 UPON
Look: 3 RUN 4 TEND 5 SEETO
   6 TENDTO

Soon: 4 UPON
Take: 5 CHASE 7 EMULATE
Taking: 3 ALA
taxes: 3 NET
the bell: 4 LATE 5 TARDY
the hour: 4 PAST
Went: 8 ASSAILED
~, in French: 5 APRES
"___ After" (1998 film): 4 EVER
After-bath
  powder: 4 **TALC**
  wear: 4 ROBE
After-Christmas
  event: 4 SALE
After-class
  aide: 5 TUTOR
After-dinner
  candy: 4 MINT
  drink: 4 PORT 6 BRANDY
   8 ANISETTE
  offering: 3 TEA
  wine: 4 PORT
Aftereffect
  Lasting: 4 SCAR
  Workout: 4 ACHE
After-hours: 4 LATE
  depository: 3 ATM
After-lunch
  sandwich: 4 OREO
Aftermath: 4 WAKE
  Exercise: 4 ACHE
Afternoon
  affair: 3 TEA
  break: 3 NAP TEA
  delight: 6 SIESTA
  Early: 3 **ONE** TWO
  Early ~ time: 6 ONETEN
  fare: 4 SOAP
  gathering: 3 TEA
  Have an ~ break: 7 TAKETEA
  Rest of the: 6 SIESTA
  service: 6 TEASET
  show: 7 MATINEE
  social: 3 **TEA**
  ~, in Spanish: 5 TARDE
After-school
  drink: 5 COCOA
  gp.: 3 PTA
  treat: 4 OREO

Aftershock: 6 TREMOR
After-shower
   sprinkle: 4 TALC
Aftertaste
   Compound with a nutty:
      6 ACETAL
After-tax
   amount: 3 NET
"After the Bath"
   painter: 5 DEGAS
Afterthought
   Architectural: 5 ANNEX
   Legislative: 5 RIDER
   Second: 3 PPS
Afterward
   Come: 5 ENSUE
   Right: 4 THEN
A.G.
   Part of: 4 ATTY
Again: 4 ANEW OVER 6 AFRESH
   and again: 5 OFTEN 6 THRICE
      TRIPLY
   Back: 3 FRO
   Come up: 5 RECUR
   Employ: 5 REUSE
   Enlist: 4 REUP
   Go over: 6 REHASH 7 ITERATE
      RETRACE
   Happen: 5 RECUR
   Here: 4 BACK
   Over: 4 **ANEW**
   Say: 4 ECHO 6 REPEAT
      9 REITERATE
   Showed: 5 **RERAN**
Against: 3 CON 4 **ANTI** INTO
      6 VERSUS
   Dead: 4 ANTI
   Decide: 3 NIX
   Fit up: 6 BUTTTO
   Go up: 4 ABUT 6 OPPOSE
      TAKEON
   Lean: 6 RESTON
   Not: 3 FOR
   One: 4 ANTI
   Rest: 6 LEANON
   Stand: 6 OPPOSE
   Took action: 4 SUED
   Vote: 3 NAY
   Votes: 3 NOS 4 NOES

"... against ___ of troubles":
      4 ASEA
Aga Khan
   Son of: 3 ALY
Agamemnon
   Son of: 7 ORESTES
Agassi: 4 ACER
   It means nothing to: 4 LOVE
   of tennis: 5 **ANDRE**
Agate
   variety: 4 ONYX
Agatha
   contemporary: 4 **ERLE**
Agave
   fiber: 5 ISTLE SISAL
   root: 5 AMOLE
Agcy.: 3 ORG 4 DEPT
Age: 3 EON ERA 4 AEON
      5 EPOCH RIPEN
      7 SENESCE
   A dog's: 4 EONS 5 YEARS
   Advance in: 5 GETON
   Come of: 5 RIPEN
   Golden: 3 ERA 6 HEYDAY
   Of: 5 ADULT
   Of an: 4 ERAL
Aged: 3 OLD 6 GRAYED
   beer: 5 LAGER
Agee
   of baseball: 6 TOMMIE
Ageless: 7 ETERNAL
   ~, in poetry: 6 ETERNE
Agency
   By the ~ of: 3 VIA
   exec.: 3 DIR
   Govt.: 3 EPA GAO GSA IRS OMB
      SBA SSA
   Old news: 4 **TASS**
   Peace org.: 6 UNESCO
   U.N.: 3 **ILO**
   under FDR: 3 WPA
   WWII: 3 OPA
"Agency, The"
   actor Bellows: 3 GIL
Agenda: 4 LIST PLAN 5 SLATE
   entry: 4 **ITEM** 7 ITEMONE
   Hidden: 15 ULTERIORMOTIVES
   Opening words on an: 4 TODO
   ~, for short: 4 SKED

Agendum: 4 ITEM
Agent: 3 FED REP SPY
    7 VEHICLE
  amount: 3 CUT FEE
  Antiquing: 4 AGER
  Bleaching: 3 LYE
  Cleansing: 4 SOAP 5 BORAX
  DEA: **4 NARC** 5 NARCO
  Diplomatic: 5 ENVOY
  Double: 4 **MOLE**
  Fed.: 4 GMAN TMAN
  Kind of: 3 IRS
  Leavening: 5 YEAST
  Maturing: 4 **AGER**
  of retribution: 7 NEMESIS
  Sales: 3 REP
  Secret: 3 SPY
  take: 5 TENTH
  Thickening: 4 AGAR
  Undercover: 3 SPY 4 NARC
  ~ 86: 5 SMART
  ~ Ness: 5 ELIOT
  ~ Scully: 4 DANA
"Age of Anxiety, The"
  author: 5 AUDEN
    7 WHAUDEN
Age of Aquarius: 3 ERA
"Age of Bronze, The"
  artist: 5 RODIN
"Age of Reason, The"
  author: 5 PAINE
Ages: 3 EON
  badly: 5 RUSTS
  Wisdom of the: 4 LORE
Aggravate: 3 IRK 4 RILE ROIL
    5 EATAT
Aggravated: 5 WORSE
Aggregate: 3 SUM 4 PILE
    5 TOTAL 6 ENTIRE
    8 SUMTOTAL
Aggressive: 4 GOGO 5 PUSHY
    10 INYOURFACE
  dog: 5 BITER
  god: 4 ARES
  one: 5 TYPEA
  reformist: 9 YOUNGTURK
Aggressively
  Greet: 6 ACCOST
  Promote: 4 FLOG

  Went after: 5 HADAT
Agile: 4 SPRY 6 NIMBLE
    7 LISSOME
Agin
  Not: 3 **FER**
  One: 4 ANTI
Agitate: 4 RILE ROIL STIR
    5 CHURN SHAKE
Agitated: 5 ABOIL 7 INASTEW
    INASTIR 8 INASTATE
    9 INALATHER
  It may get: 4 WASH
  state: 4 FLAP **SNIT** STEW
    6 DITHER LATHER
  ~, with "up": 3 HET
Agitation: 6 UNREST
  State of: 4 FLAP **SNIT** STEW
    6 DITHER LATHER
Aglet
  site: 4 LACE
Agnes
  role: 6 ENDORA
  ~, to Cecil B.: 5 NIECE
"Agnes Grey"
  author: 6 BRONTE
Agnew
  Former veep: 5 SPIRO
  plea: 4 NOLO
"Agnus ___": 3 DEI
"___ agnus Dei": 4 ECCE
Ago: 4 PAST
  A while: 4 ONCE
  Long: 4 ONCE YORE 5 OFOLD
  Scottish: 4 SYNE
Agog: 7 BUGEYED
  All: 5 EAGER
  Stare: 4 GAPE
Agonize: 4 FRET STEW
Agony: 3 WOE 7 TORMENT
  Sound of: 4 MOAN
"A good walk spoiled": Twain:
    4 GOLF
Agorot
  100 ~: 6 SHEKEL
Agouti
  cousin: 4 PACA
Agra
  attire: 4 SARI
  locale: 5 INDIA

Agree: 4 JIBE 5 MATCH
6 ACCEDE ASSENT
CONCUR SAYYES
7 CONSENT
11 SEEEYETOEYE
with: 4 ECHO
without a word: 3 NOD
Agreeable: 4 NICE 6 GENIAL
answer: 3 YES
odor: 5 AROMA
"Agreed!": 3 YES 4 DEAL
Agreement: 4 DEAL **PACT**
5 TERMS UNITY 6 ACCORD
ASSENT
Altar: 3 IDO
at sea: 3 AYE
Emphatic: 4 AMEN 5 OHYES
6 YESYES 8 YESSIREE
Flat: 5 LEASE
Formal: 4 PACT
In: 3 ONE 5 ASONE ATONE
Indicate: 3 NOD
International: 6 ACCORD
7 DETENTE ENTENTE
Kind of: 4 ORAL 5 TOKEN
Nonverbal: 3 NOD
Nuptial: 3 IDO
Rental: 5 **LEASE**
Sign, as an: 9 ENTERINTO
Slangy: 3 YEP 4 YEAH
Word of: 3 AYE YES 4 **AMEN**
Words of: 4 ITOO 5 METOO
SOAMI SODOI 6 IDOTOO
Agricultural
business: 4 FARM
Agriculture
Goddess of: 5 CERES
7 DEMETER
Agrippina
Son of: 4 NERO
Agronomist
concern: 4 SOIL
Agt.: 3 REP
cut: 3 PCT
under Ness: 4 TMAN
Agua
~, in French: 3 EAU
Aguilera
Singer: 9 CHRISTINA

Ah
follower: 4 CHOO
"Ah!": 4 ISEE 6 IGETIT
"Aha!": 4 ISEE 5 GOTIT
6 EUREKA GOTCHA
IGETIT 7 THATSIT
Ahab
and crew: 7 WHALERS
Father of: 4 OMRI
obsession: 5 WHALE
~, in a song: 4 ARAB
A hard row ___: 5 TOHOE
Ahead: 5 ONTOP 6 ONWARD
TOCOME 7 EARLIER
LEADING 9 INTHELEAD
Look: 4 PLAN
Neither ~ nor behind: 4 TIED
of the game: 5 ONEUP
of the pack: 5 FIRST
of time: 5 EARLY
One looking: 4 SEER
Opposite of: 6 ASTERN
Slightly: 5 ONEUP
Spring: 5 RESET
Think: 4 PLAN
Time to look: 3 EVE
Was: 3 **LED**
"A ___ help you are!": 5 LOTTA
Ahem
Cousin of: 4 PSST
Ahmad
Sportscaster: 6 RASHAD
"Ah, me!": 3 WOE 4 **ALAS**
"Ah'm ___ it!": 4 AGIN
"A house ___ a home": 5 ISNOT
"Ah, Wilderness!"
character: 3 NAT
mother: 5 ESSIE
playwright: 6 ONEILL
Aid: 6 SUCCOR
Aiming: 5 SCOPE
Ask, as for: 6 TURNTO
Band: 3 AMP
Cleaning: 3 MOP
Driving: 3 **TEE**
Financial ~ criterion: 4 NEED
in crime: 4 **ABET**
Partner of: 4 ABET
Shopping: 4 CART LIST

Traction: 5 CLEAT
Aida: 5 SLAVE
  Love of: 7 RADAMES
"Aida": 5 OPERA
  backdrop: 4 NILE
  composer: 5 VERDI
  Where ~ premiered: 5 CAIRO
Aid and ___: 4 ABET
Aide: 6 HELPER
  (abbr.): 4 ASST
  Band: 6 ROADIE
  DA: 4 ASST
  Dictator: 5 STENO
  Legal ~, briefly: 4 PARA
  Mgr.: 4 ASST
  Reagan: 5 MEESE
Aide-___: 7 MEMOIRE
Aiea
  locale: 4 OAHU
___ Aigner: 7 ETIENNE
Aikman
  alma mater: 4 UCLA
  of football: 4 TROY
Ailey
  Choreographer: 5 ALVIN
Ailing: 3 ILL 4 SICK 6 LAIDUP
Ailment
  Common: 4 COLD
  Eye: 4 STYE
  Skid row: 3 DTS
  Stomach: 5 ULCER
  Throat: 5 STREP
  Winter: 3 FLU
Aim: 3 END TRY 4 GOAL MEAN
     5 POINT 6 ASPIRE
     INTEND INTENT
     TARGET
  Game: 3 WIN
  improver: 5 SCOPE
  Peddler: 4 SALE
  Perfectionist: 5 IDEAL
  Take careful ~ at:
    11 DRAWABEADON
Aimée
  Actress: 5 **ANOUK**
  title role: 4 LOLA
Aiming
  aid: 5 SCOPE
Aimless: 6 ADRIFT ERRANT

Aimlessly
  Move: 3 GAD 4 MILL
  Wander: 4 ROAM ROVE
Ain't
  right: 4 **ISNT** 5 ARENT
  Say it ~ so: 4 DENY
"___ ain't broke ...": 4 IFIT
"Ain't it the truth!": 4 AMEN
    6 ILLSAY
"Ain't She Sweet"
  composer: 4 AGER
"___ ain't so!": 5 SAYIT
"Ain't That a Shame"
  singer: 8 PATBOONE
Air: 4 AURA MIEN SHOW SONG
    TUNE 6 MANNER
    8 TELEVISE
  About one percent of: 5 ARGON
  agcy.: 3 FAA
  Alpine: 5 YODEL
  alternative: 4 RAIL
  apparent: 4 SMOG
  Attack from the: 6 STRAFE
  bag: 4 LUNG
  Bear in the: 4 URSA
  Chair in the: 5 SEDAN
  Christmas: 4 NOEL
  Dairy: 3 MOO
  December: 4 NOEL
  Distinctive: 4 AURA
  Drops in the: 4 MIST
  Eastern: 4 RAGA
  Get some: 6 INHALE 7 BREATHE
    RESPIRE
  gun ammo: 3 BBS
  hero: 3 ACE
  Hot: 3 GAS
  In the: 5 ALOFT
  Light: 4 LILT
  Like fall: 5 BRISK
  Like ocean: 5 SALTY
  Mountain: 5 YODEL
  Move on a puff of: 4 WAFT
  mover: 3 FAN
  Operated by: 9 PNEUMATIC
  out: 4 VENT 7 FRESHEN
  passage: 4 DUCT 7 NOSTRIL
  pollution: 4 SMOG 5 SMAZE
  prefix: 4 ATMO

quality org.: **3** EPA
safety org.: **3** FAA
Struggle for: **4** GASP
Take to the: **3** FLY **4** SOAR
    6 AVIATE
Took to the: **4** FLEW
Up in the: **4** IFFY **5** **ALOFT**
Walking on: **6** ELATED
Winter: **4** NOEL **5** CAROL

Airborne
honkers: **5** GEESE
targets: **5** SKEET

Airbrush: 7 RETOUCH

Air conditioner: 4 UNIT
measure (abbr.): **3** BTU

Aircraft: 4 BIRD
Arctic: **8** SKIPLANE

Aire
City of the: **5** LEEDS

Aired
again: **5** RERAN

Airedale: 7 TERRIER
Like an ~ coat: **4** WIRY

Airfone
corporation: **3** GTE

Air Force
1950s–60s ~ Chief of Staff:
    5 LEMAY
gp.: **3** SAC
hero: **3** ACE

Air Force One: 3 JET **5** PLANE
passenger (abbr.): **3** CIC **4** PRES

Air France
destination: **4** **ORLY**
plane: **3** SST

Air freshener
option: **4** PINE **5** LILAC
target: **4** ODOR

Airhead: 4 DITZ DOLT **5** SCHMO

Airing: 4 ONTV
Program: **8** TELECAST

Air Jordans
maker: **4** NIKE

Airline
Atlanta-based: **5** DELTA
Brazilian: **5** VARIG
Chilean: **3** LAN
Dutch: **3** KLM
European: **3** SAS

Israeli: **4** **ELAL**
Japanese: **3** ANA
patron: **5** FLIER
since 1948: **4** ELAL

Airliner
walkway: **5** AISLE

"Air Music"
composer: **5** ROREM

Airplane
boarding site: **4** GATE
Model ~ wood: **5** BALSA
roll control: **7** AILERON
seat feature: **7** ARMREST
seat option: **5** AISLE
server: **4** TRAY
shelter: **6** HANGAR
tracker: **5** RADAR
wing parts: **5** SLATS

"Airplane!"
actor Bridges: **5** LLOYD
actor Robert: **4** HAYS
heroine: **6** ELAINE

Airport
abbr.: **3** ARR ETA ETD
Accompany to the: **6** SEEOFF
area: **4** GATE
Bay area: **3** SFO
board word: **7** NONSTOP
Boston: **5** LOGAN
Calif.: **3** LAX
Chicago: **3** ORD **5** OHARE
conveyance: **4** TRAM
event: **7** ARRIVAL
French: **4** ORLY
info: **3** ARR ETA ETD
Israeli: **3** LOD
lineup: **4** CABS
Long Island: **5** ISLIP
Major: **3** HUB
National: **6** REAGAN
near Paris: **4** ORLY
near Tel Aviv: **3** LOD
NYC: **3** LGA
Paris: **4** **ORLY**
pickup: **4** LIMO **6** RENTAL
surface: **6** TARMAC
waiter: **3** CAB
Washington: **6** SEATAC
worry: **5** DELAY

Air-quality
  org.: 3 EPA
Air rifle: 5 BBGUN
  ammo: 3 **BBS** 6 BBSHOT
Air-safety
  org.: 3 FAA
Airtight
  It may be: 5 ALIBI
  Make: 4 SEAL 6 SEALUP
Air traffic
  control device: 5 RADAR
  screen sight: 4 BLIP
Airwaves: 5 ETHER
  Govt. ~ agency: 3 FCC
Airy
  Light and: 8 ETHEREAL
  melody: 4 LILT
Aisle
  Choose the window over the:
     5 ELOPE
  walker: 5 USHER
Aisles
  Have rolling in the: 4 SLAY
  Work the: 3 USH
AJ
  of Indy: 4 FOYT
Ajar: 8 HALFOPEN
  More than: 4 OPEN
  Not: 4 SHUT
  ~, poetically: 3 OPE
Ajax
  rival: 5 COMET
"A jealous mistress": Emerson:
     3 ART
"A jug of wine ..."
  poet: 4 OMAR
AKA
  Part of: 4 ALSO 5 KNOWN
Akaka
  of Hawaii (abbr.): 3 SEN
Akbar
  capital: 4 AGRA
Akela
  org.: 3 BSA
Aker
  Capital on the: 4 OSLO
Akhmatova
  Poet: 4 ANNA
Akihito: 7 EMPEROR

  (abbr.): 3 EMP
  ___ a kind: 5 ONEOF TWOOF
Akins
  Playwright: 3 ZOE
"Akira"
  genre: 5 ANIME
Akita
  home: 5 JAPAN
Akron
  baseball player: 4 AERO
  home: 4 OHIO
  product: 4 TIRE
  Rock group from: 4 DEVO
Al
  and Tipper: 5 GORES
  Discus champ: 6 OERTER
  of Indy: 5 UNSER
  Scarface: 6 CAPONE
  Trumpeter: 4 **HIRT**
  Veep before: 3 DAN
  Weatherman: 5 ROKER
  who drew Abner: 4 CAPP
AL
  and ME: 3 STS
A.L.
  1953 ~ MVP: 5 ROSEN
  1966 ~ Rookie of the Year:
     4 AGEE
  1993 ~ batting champ:
     6 OLERUD
  1996 ~ Rookie of the Year:
     5 JETER
  2002 ~ MVP: 4 AROD
  and N.L. city: 3 CHI
  Seven-time ~ batting champ:
     5 CAREW
  Some ~ batters: 3 DHS
  Three-time ~ batting champ:
     5 BRETT OLIVA
  Three-time ~ MVP: 5
     BERRA
Al ___: 5 **DENTE** FATAH
Al-___: 4 ANON
al-___, Bashar: 5 ASSAD
Ala.
  Neighbor of: 3 FLA
À la ___: 5 CARTE
"Al Aaraaf"
  author: 3 POE

Alabama
  city: **5 <u>SELMA</u>**
  footballers:
    11 CRIMSONTIDE
  native: **5 CREEK**
  One-named singer from:
    6 ODETTA
  port: **6 MOBILE**
Alack
  partner: **4 ALAS**
Aladdin: 4 ARAB
"Aladdin"
  baddie: **5 JAFAR**
  find: **4 LAMP**
  monkey: **3 <u>ABU</u>**
  parrot: **4 IAGO**
  prince: **3 ALI**
  vehicle: **6 CARPET**
  wish-granter: **5 GENIE**
al-Ahmed al-Sabah: 4 EMIR
___ alai: 3 <u>JAI</u>
Alain
  Actor: **5 DELON**
  Novelist: **6 LESAGE**
Alamance County
  college: **4 ELON**
___ Alamitos: 3 LOS
Alamo: 6 SHRINE
  defender: **5 BOWIE 6 TRAVIS**
  Mexican leader at the:
    9 SANTAANNA
  offering: **6 RENTAL**
  rival: **4 AVIS 5 HERTZ**
À la mode: 4 CHIC
Alamogordo
  county: **5 OTERO**
  event: **5 <u>ATEST</u>**
___ Alamos, New Mexico: 3 <u>LOS</u>
Alan
  Actor: **4 ALDA LADD 5 ARKIN**
    6 THICKE
  Conservative: **5 KEYES**
  South African author: **5 PATON**
Alarm: 4 FEAR 5 SCARE
    6 DISMAY
  Anticipate with: **5 DREAD**
  bell: **6 TOCSIN**
  Car: **4 HORN**
  Cause for: **4 FIRE**

  False: **5 SCARE**
  Gives a false: **9 CRIESWOLF**
  Heed the: **4 RISE**
  Ignore the: **7 SLEEPIN**
  Nature's ~ clock: **7 ROOSTER**
  Sound the: **4 WARN**
Alarmed
  Easily: **5 TIMID**
Alas
  Partner of: **5 ALACK**
  "Alas!": **4 AHME 5 SOSAD**
    6 DEARME 7 WOEISME
  ~, in German: **3 ACH**
Alaska: 5 STATE
  buyer: **6 SEWARD**
  city: **4 NOME**
  First capital of: **5 SITKA**
  First governor of: **4 <u>EGAN</u>**
  National park in: **6 DENALI**
  native: **5 ALEUT INUIT**
    6 ESKIMO
  radar site: **4 ATTU**
  river: **5 YUKON**
  Sen. Stevens of: **3 TED**
  ~, at one time (abbr.): **4 TERR**
___ Alaska: 5 BAKED
Alaskan
  bay: **7 PRUDHOE**
  Certain: **5 ALEUT INUIT**
    6 ESKIMO
  city: **4 NOME**
  island: **4 ATTU 6 KODIAK**
  islander: **5 ALEUT**
  native: **5 ALEUT INUIT**
    6 ESKIMO
  port: **4 NOME 5 SITKA**
  sled race: **8 IDITAROD**
  volcano: **6 KATMAI**
Alaskan Klee ___: 3 KAI
Al-Assad
  land: **5 SYRIA**
Alastair
  Actor: **3 SIM**
___ alba (gypsum): 5 TERRA
Albacore: 4 <u>TUNA</u>
Alban
  Composer: **4 BERG**
Albania
  Capital of: **6 TIRANA TIRANE**

Albanian
  coin: 3 **LEK**
Albany
  canal: 4 ERIE
  City near: 4 TROY
  College near: 5 SIENA
  leader: 6 PATAKI
Albatross: 4 ONUS 7 SEABIRD
  Black-footed: 6 GOONEY
Albee
  Alice from: 4 TINY
  Playwright: 6 EDWARD
Albéniz
  Composer: 5 ISAAC
  piano work: 6 IBERIA
Albers
  Artist: 5 JOSEF
Albert
  Actor: 5 EDDIE SALMI
  Author: 5 CAMUS
  of Minnesota: 3 LEA
  Sportscaster: 4 MARV
  ~, to Victoria: 7 CONSORT
Albert, Marv
  catchword: 3 YES
Alberta
  park: 5 BANFF 6 JASPER
Alberthal
  CEO: 3 LES
Albert the Alligator
  Friend of: 4 POGO
Albertville
  Skating medalist at: 3 ITO
Albion
  neighbor: 4 ERIN
Alborg
  native: 4 DANE
Albrecht
  Artist: 5 DURER
Albright
  headed it: 5 STATE
  or Falana: 4 LOLA
Album
  1968 folk ~: 4 ARLO
  1969 jazz ~: 4 ELLA
  1986 self-titled ~: 6 ARETHA
  1988 country ~: 4 REBA
  2001 self-titled ~: 3 JLO
  Country: 5 ATLAS

Albums
  Mini record: 3 EPS
  Old: 3 LPS
Alcatraz
  (abbr.): 3 ISL
  Birdman of: 5 LIFER 6 STROUD
  inmate: 7 BIRDMAN
Alchemist
  concoction: 6 ELIXIR
Alcindor
  of basketball: 3 LEW
Alcoa
  purchase: 3 ORE
Alcohol
  Allowing: 3 WET
  An end to: 3 ISM
  Grain: 7 ETHANOL
  Kind of: 4 AMYL 5 ETHYL
  Make ~ undrinkable:
      8 DENATURE
  plus acid: 5 ESTER
  Solid: 6 STEROL
  ___ alcohol: 5 BUTYL CETYL
      ETHYL
Alcohol-based
  solvent: 6 ACETAL
Alcoholic
  Excuse maker for an:
      7 ENABLER
  Hot ~ drink: 5 TODDY
Alcohol-laced
  dessert: 4 BABA
Alcott
  book: 11 LITTLEWOMEN
  Golfer: 3 AMY
Alcove: 3 BAY 4 NOOK 5 NICHE
      6 RECESS
  Church: 4 APSE
  Eating: 7 DINETTE
  Shady: 5 ARBOR
Alda
  Actor: 4 ALAN
  sitcom series: 4 MASH
Aldebaran: 4 STAR 5 KSTAR
Al dente: 4 FIRM
  It might be cooked: 5 PASTA
Alder: 4 TREE
Alderaan
  Princess from: 4 LEIA

Aldo
  Italian politician: 4 MORO
Aldrich
  Spy: 4 **AMES**
Aldrin, Buzz
  birth name: 5 EDWIN
  org.: 4 NASA
Ale: 4 BREW
  alternative: 5 LAGER
  cask: 3 TUN
  fellow: 6 BREWER
  Half ~, half stout:
      11 BLACKANDTAN
  holder: 3 MUG 5 STEIN
  order: 4 PINT
  quantity: 4 YARD
  seller: 3 PUB
Alec
  role: 6 OBIWAN
  ___ Alegre, Brazil: 5 PORTO
Alehouse: 3 PUB 6 TAVERN
Aleichem
  Writer: 6 SHOLOM
Alejandro
  Actor: 3 REY
  of baseball: 4 PENA
Alençon
  department: 4 ORNE
  product: 4 LACE
Aleppo
  land: 5 SYRIA
Alero
  maker: 4 OLDS
ALers
  Some: 3 DHS
Alert: 4 WARN 5 READY 6 TIPOFF
      10 ONONESTOES
  Coast Guard: 3 SOS
  color: 3 RED
  Golfer: 4 FORE
  Kind of: 4 SMOG
  Not: 7 NAPPING
  Not be: 4 DOZE
  P.D.: 3 **APB**
  Studio: 5 ONAIR
  Theater: 3 SRO
  ___ alert: 3 RED
Alerting
  light: 5 FLARE

Alessandro
  Physicist: 5 VOLTA
Aleutian
  island: 4 ADAK ATKA **ATTU**
Alewife
  relative: 4 SHAD
Alex
  Author: 5 HALEY
  Host: 6 TREBEK
Alexander: 4 TSAR
  1996 candidate ~: 5 LAMAR
  Aristotle, to: 5 TUTOR
  Artist: 6 CALDER
  Author: 5 SHANA
  Former Sec. of State: 4 HAIG
  Form of: 5 SASHA
  He slew: 5 AARON
Alexandra: 7 TSARINA
  husband: 4 TSAR
Alexandre
  Author: 5 DUMAS
Alexandria
  Capital near: 5 CAIRO
  river: 4 NILE
Alf
  and others: 3 ETS
  home planet: 6 MELMAC
Alfa ___: 5 ROMEO
Alfalfa: 6 RASCAL
  girlfriend: 5 DARLA
Alfa Romeo
  rival: 4 FIAT
Al Fatah
  Former ~ leader: 6 ARAFAT
  gp.: 3 PLO
"Alfie"
  lyricist David: 3 HAL
  star: 5 CAINE
      12 MICHAELCAINE
Alfonso
  queen: 3 ENA
Alfred
  GM president: 5 SLOAN
  IQ tester: 5 BINET
  of the theater: 4 LUNT
  Poet: 5 NOYES
  Psychologist: 5 ADLER
"Alfred"
  composer: 4 **ARNE**

Alfresco
eatery: 4 CAFE
meal: 6 PICNIC
Not: 6 INDOOR INSIDE
Alga
Microscopic: 6 DIATOM
Algae
product: 4 AGAR
Red: 7 SEAMOSS
Algebra: 4 MATH
Early writer on: 4 OMAR
equation: 9 QUADRATIC
Kind of: 6 LINEAR 7 BOOLEAN
topic: 6 MATRIX
Alger
beginning: 4 RAGS
Algeria
neighbor: 4 MALI
Algerian
pop music: 3 RAI
port: 4 **ORAN**
Algiers
area: 6 CASBAH KASBAH
governors: 4 DEYS
"Algiers"
actor Charles: 5 BOYER
actress Hedy: 6 LAMARR
Algonquian
language: 4 CREE 7 ARAPAHO
tribe: 6 MIAMIS 7 OTTAWAS
~ Indian: 8 KICKAPOO
Algonquin
home: 6 WIGWAM
Alhambra: 6 PALACE
builder: 4 MOOR
Site of the: 7 GRANADA
Ali
Boxer: 5 LAILA
Muhammad: 5 PASHA
Sharp left from: 3 JAB
trainer Dundee: 6 ANGELO
Where ~ KO'd Foreman: 5 ZAIRE
Ali ___: 4 BABA
"___ alia": 5 INTER
"Ali ___ and the 40 Thieves":
4 BABA
Alias: 3 **AKA**
Common: 5 SMITH
Dickens: 3 BOZ

Essayist: 4 **ELIA**
Lamb: 4 **ELIA**
Patty Hearst: 5 TANIA
Superman: 4 KENT
"Alias"
actress Lena: 4 OLIN
network: 3 ABC
Alibi: 5 STORY 6 EXCUSE
guy: 3 IKE
Perfect, as an: 8 AIRTIGHT
IRONCLAD
Alibi ___ (liars): 4 IKES
"___ Alibi": 3 HER
Alice
boss: 3 MEL
cat: 5 DINAH
chronicler: 4 ARLO
Event for: 8 TEAPARTY
He sang about: 4 **ARLO**
Musical star: 4 FAYE
She played ~ on TV: 5 LINDA
"Alice"
actress Martha: 4 RAYE
Alice, in: 8 WAITRESS
diner: 4 MELS
spin-off: 3 FLO
star: 5 LAVIN
"Alice in Wonderland"
cat: 5 DINAH
"Alice's Restaurant"
singer Guthrie: 4 ARLO
Alicia
Actress: 3 **ANA**
Ballerina: 6 ALONSO
Alien: 7 FOREIGN
Furry TV: 3 **ALF**
TV ~ home: 3 ORK
"Alien"
actor Holm: 3 IAN
Alienate: 8 ESTRANGE
"Alienist, The"
author: 4 CARR
author Carr: 5 CALEB
Aliens: 3 **ETS**
Course for U.S.: 3 ESL
Align: 4 TRUE
the cross hairs: 3 AIM
Alignment
Front wheel: 5 TOEIN

In: 4 TRUE
Alike
  Think: 5 AGREE
  ~, in French: 4 EGAL
"A likely story!": 3 HAH 4 IBET
Alimony
  receiver: 6 EXMATE EXWIFE
  receivers: 4 EXES
A-line
  line: 3 HEM 4 SEAM
Alison
  Author: 5 LURIE
A-list: 5 ELITE
Alistair
  Sam and: 6 COOKES
Alitalia
  stop: 4 ROMA
"Alive"
  setting: 5 ANDES
"___ alive!": 5 SAKES
"___ Alive!" (1974 film): 3 ITS
Al-Jazeera
  viewer: 4 ARAB
Alkali: 4 BASE
  neutralizer: 4 ACID
Alkaline
  solution: 3 LYE
Alka-Seltzer
  guy: 6 SPEEDY
  sound: 4 PLOP
All
  agog: 5 EAGER
  alternative: 3 ERA 4 NONE TIDE
    5 CHEER
  At: 3 ANY 4 EVER
  At ~ times: 4 EVER
  done: 4 OVER
  ears: 4 RAPT
  excited: 4 AGOG 7 ATINGLE
  fired up: 4 AVID 5 EAGER
  First of: 4 ADAM
  For ~ time: 4 EVER
    9 AGELESSLY
  For ~ to hear: 5 ALOUD
  For ~ to see: 5 OVERT 6 OPENLY
  hands on deck: 4 CREW
  Highest of: 7 TOPMOST
  in: 4 BEAT 5 SPENT TIRED
    WEARY

  Nearly: 4 MOST
  Not: 4 SOME
  Not at: 5 NOHOW 6 NOWISE
  Not ~ there: 5 DOTTY
  Opposite of: 4 NONE 6 NOTONE
  over: 4 ANEW 7 ATANEND
  over again: 4 **ANEW** 6 AFRESH
  possible: 5 EVERY
  prefix: 4 OMNI
  Second of: 3 EVE
  set: 5 READY
  smiles: 5 HAPPY
  spruced up: 4 NEAT
  Still and: 3 YET
  there: 4 **SANE** 6 INTACT
  the time: 4 ALOT 5 OFTEN
  They're ~ in the family: 4 SIBS
  tied up: 4 EVEN
  together: 5 ASONE 6 INTOTO
    7 **ENMASSE**
  tucked in: 4 ABED
  tuckered out: 5 SPENT
  With ~ one's might: 5 AMAIN
  worked up: 4 AGOG 5 IRATE
  you can carry: 7 ARMLOAD
  you can eat: 7 EDIBLES
  ~, in music: 5 TUTTI
All ___: 3 WET 4 EARS
"All ___!": 4 RISE 6 ABOARD
"All ___" (1967 hit): 5 INEED
"All ___" ('30s hit song): 4 OFME
"All ___" (Martin/Tomlin film):
  4 OFME
All-4-One
  ~ #1 hit: 6 ISWEAR
Alla ___ (2/2 time): 5 BREVE
"All About ___" (1950 film): 3 EVE
"All About Eve"
  actress Bette: 5 DAVIS
  actress Holm: 7 CELESTE
  role: 5 MARGO
Allah
  Religion of: 5 ISLAM
All-American
  name: 5 KNUTE
"All-American Girl"
  star Margaret: 3 CHO
"All ___ are off!": 4 BETS
Allay: 4 EASE

"All clear"
  signal: 5 SIREN
Allegation: 5 CLAIM
Allege: 4 **AVER**
Allegheny
  City on the: 5 OLEAN
  Company once called: 5 USAIR
  The ~ flows into it: 4 OHIO
Allegory: 7 PARABLE
Allegro: 4 FAST 5 TEMPO
  and others: 5 TEMPI
Allegro ___: 5 ASSAI
Allen
  Actor: 3 TIM
  Burns and ~ (abbr.): 4 SENS
  Burns, to: 7 PARTNER
  of the Green Mountain Boys:
    5 ETHAN
  or Martin: 5 STEVE
  Patriot: 5 **ETHAN**
  Sportscaster: 3 MEL
  successor: 4 PAAR
Allen, Ira
  Brother of: 5 ETHAN
Allen, Jay Presson
  play: 3 TRU
Allen, Woody
  1977 ~ film: 9 ANNIEHALL
  1978 ~ film: 9 INTERIORS
  1983 ~ film: 5 ZELIG
  1987 ~ film: 9 SEPTEMBER
  1998 film featuring the voice of:
    4 ANTZ
  Feeling for: 5 ANGST
All-encompassing: 5 BROAD
Allen County, Kansas
  Seat of: 4 IOLA
Allende
  Author: 6 ISABEL
  ___ aller (last resort): 3 PIS
Allergen
  Common: 4 DUST 6 DANDER
    POLLEN SPORES
    7 PETHAIR
Allergic
  reaction: 4 ITCH RASH 5 ACHOO
    6 ASTHMA SNEEZE
Allergy
  symptom: 4 RASH 5 HIVES

Alleviate: 4 **EASE** 6 SOOTHE
Alleviator: 5 EASER
Alley
  Bowling: 4 LANE
  button: 5 RESET
  cat: 5 STRAY
  Caveman: 3 OOP
  challenge: 5 SPLIT
  cry: 4 MEOW
  denizen: 3 RAT TOM
    5 STRAY
  follower: 3 OOP
  game: 7 TENPINS
  Kind of: 5 BLIND
  Like an ~ cat: 5 FERAL
  org.: 3 PBA
  pickup: 5 SPARE
  Play in the: 4 BOWL
  prowler: 3 TOM 6 TOMCAT
  target, at times: 7 NINEPIN
  targets: 4 PINS
"Alley ___": 3 **OOP**
Alley-___: 3 OOP
" ___ all, folks!": 5 THATS
All Fools' Day
  mo.: 3 APR
"All gone!": 4 PFFT
Allgood
  Actress: 4 SARA
Alliance: 4 BLOC PACT 6 LEAGUE
  7 ENTENTE
  acronym: 4 NATO 5 SEATO
  Defunct: 5 SEATO
  dissolved in 1977: 5 SEATO
  Onetime Egypt-Syr.: 3 UAR
  since 1948: 3 OAS
  since 1949: 4 NATO
"All I ___ Do" (Sheryl Crow hit):
  5 WANNA
Allie
  flat mate: 4 KATE
Allied: 5 SIDED
  1945 ~ conference site: 5 YALTA
    7 POTSDAM
  invasion site in WWII: 4 ORAN
  Menace to ~ ships: 5 UBOAT
  victory site: 4 STLO
Allies
  foe: 4 **AXIS**

Alligator
  kin: 6 CAIMAN
  pear: 7 AVOCADO
  Urban ~ home, they say:
    5 SEWER
Alligator ___: 4 PEAR
"All I gotta do ___ naturally":
    Beatles: 5 ISACT
All-inclusive: 4 ATOZ FULL
    6 ENTIRE
All-in-one
  meal: 4 STEW
"All in the Family"
  actress Stapleton: 4 JEAN
  daughter: 6 GLORIA
  producer Norman: 4 LEAR
  spin-off: 5 MAUDE
All in ___ work: 5 ADAYS
Allison
  Jazzman: 4 MOSE
"All I Wanna Do"
  singer: 10 SHERYLCROW
"All kidding ___ ...": 5 ASIDE
All-knowing: 4 WISE
" ___ All Laughed": 4 THEY
All-male: 4 STAG
Allman Brothers, The
  One of: 5 **DUANE** GREGG
"All My Children"
  actress Susan: 5 LUCCI
  character: 5 ERICA
"All My ___ Live in Texas": 3 EXS
All-natural
  food no-no: 3 BHT
All-night
  bash: 4 **RAVE**
All-nighter
  Pull an: 4 **CRAM**
Allocate: 4 METE 6 ASSIGN
    DEVOTE 7 DOLEOUT
"All of Me"
  director: 6 REINER
Allot: 4 METE
  ~, with "out": 4 **METE**
Alloted
  amount: 6 RATION
Allotment: 4 DOLE 5 PIECE
    QUOTA SHARE 6 RATION
  words: 4 APOP

All-out: 5 TOTAL 7 DOORDIE
Allow: 3 **LET** OWN 5 ADMIT
    OPINE 6 ENABLE PERMIT
  in: 5 ADMIT
  to pass: 5 LETBY
  to use: 4 LEND
Allowable: 5 LICIT
Allowance: 7 STIPEND
  Waste: 4 TRET
  Weight: 4 TARE TRET
Allowed: 5 LICIT
  number: 5 QUOTA
Allowing
  a draft: 4 AJAR
  alcohol: 3 WET
Alloy
  component: 5 METAL
  Electrician: 6 SOLDER
  Gold-imitating: 6 ORMOLU
  Iron: 5 STEEL
  Magnet: 6 ALNICO
  Tin: 6 PEWTER
All-points bulletin: 5 ALERT
All-purpose
  truck: 3 UTE
"All Quiet on the Western Front"
  star: 5 AYRES
"All right!": 3 YES
  ~, slangily: 3 OKE
All's
  opposite: 5 NOONE 6 NOTONE
    7 NOTABIT
  partner: 5 WARTS
All-star
  game side: 4 EAST WEST
  Player in 24 ~ games: 4 MAYS
Allstate
  rival: 5 AETNA
"All systems ___": 5 AREGO
"All systems go!": 3 AOK
"All That Jazz"
  actress Reinking: 3 ANN
  director: 5 FOSSE
All the ___: 4 RAGE SAME
"All the King's Men"
  actress Joanne: 3 DRU
"All the Things You ___": 3 ARE
"All the Way"
  lyricist: 4 CAHN

"All Things Considered"
　network: 3 **NPR**
　___ all-time high: 4 ATAN
All together: 5 ASONE INSUM
　　　6 INTOTO
Allude: 5 REFER
　to: 4 CITE 5 GETAT 6 HINTAT
All ___ up: 3 HET
Allure: 5 CHARM TEMPT
　Coffee: 5 AROMA
　competitor: 4 ELLE
Alluring: 4 FOXY **SEXY** 6 EROTIC
　skirt feature: 4 SLIT
Allusion
　Make: 5 REFER
Ally
　Actress: 6 SHEEDY
　Gulf war: 4 OMAN
　Missouri: 4 OTOE
　of Captain Hook: 4 SMEE
　WWII: 4 USSR
"___ All Ye Faithful": 5 OCOME
"Ally McBeal"
　actress Lucy: 3 LIU
　lawyer: 4 LING NELL
　　　7 GEORGIA
　secretary: 6 ELAINE
"All you had to do was ___":
　　　3 ASK
"All You Need Is ___" (Beatles
　song): 4 LOVE
Alma ___ : 5 MATER
Almanac
　datum: 4 STAT
　entry: 4 FACT
　tidbit: 5 ADAGE
　topic: 4 TIDE
Almighty: 3 GOD
　Muslim's: 5 ALLAH
　~, in French: 4 DIEU
Almodóvar
　Director: 5 PEDRO
Almond: 3 TAN 4 ECRU
　confection: 6 NOUGAT
　flavored liqueur: 8 AMARETTO
　paste: 8 MARZIPAN
Almost: 4 NIGH 6 NEARLY
　　　NIGHON
　boil: 5 SCALD 6 SIMMER

　closed: 4 AJAR
　forever: 3 EON 4 EONS
　here: 4 NEAR
　never: 4 ONCE
"Almost!":
　　　15 CLOSEBUTNOCIGAR
Alms
　Ask for: 3 BEG
Alnico: 5 ALLOY
"A loaf of bread ..."
　poet: 4 OMAR
Aloe ___ : 4 VERA
Aloft
　Glide: 4 SOAR
Aloha
　gift: 3 LEI
Aloha State
　bird: 4 NENE
　port: 4 HILO
Alone: 4 SOLO STAG
　Go it: 4 **SOLO**
　Leave: 5 LETBE
　Taken: 5 PERSE
___ alone (solo): 4 GOIT
Along
　Get: 4 FARE
　Go: 5 AGREE 6 SAYYES
　the way: 7 ENROUTE
Alongside
　Lie: 4 ABUT
Alonso
　Ballerina: 6 ALICIA
Aloof: 4 COOL
　Beyond: 3 ICY
Aloofness
　With: 5 ICILY
Alou
　of baseball: 5 JESUS 6 FELIPE
Aloud
　Marvel: 3 OOH
　Weep: 3 SOB
Alpaca
　kin: 5 CAMEL LLAMA
　tender: 5 INCAN
Alpes
　peak: 4 MONT
Alpha
　follower: 4 BETA
　opposite: 5 **OMEGA**

Alpha ___ : 4 MALE
Alphabet
  book phrase: **4** ASIN
  ender: **3** ZEE
  finaliser: **3** ZED
  quartet: **4** ABCD BCDE CDEF *etc.*
  quintet: **5** AEIOU **6** VOWELS
  soup letter: **6** NOODLE
  trio: **3** ABC BCD CDE *etc.*
Alphabetize: 4 SORT **5** ORDER
Alphonse
  partner: **6** GASTON
Alpine
  abode: **6** CHALET
  air: **5** YODEL
  assent: **3** OUI
  call: **5** YODEL
  capital: **4** BERN **5** BERNE
  heroine: **5** HEIDI
  region: **5** TIROL TYROL
  river: **3** AAR **4** AARE **5** ISERE
  sight: **4** MONT
  song: **5** YODEL
  tool: **5** ICEAX
  transport: **4** TBAR TRAM
Alpine Museum
  site: **4** BERN
Alps
  lake: **4** COMO
  peak: **5** EIGER
  river: **5** ISERE
  Sing in the: **5** YODEL
Already: 5 BYNOW
  in use: **5** TAKEN
"Already?": 6 SOSOON
Also: 3 AND **TOO 4** PLUS
      6 ASWELL
  known as: **5** ALIAS
Also-ran: 5 LOSER
  1992 ~: **5** PEROT
  1996 ~: **4** DOLE
  2000 ~: **4** GORE **5** NADER
      6 ALGORE
  Aesop: **4** HARE
  Fabled: **4** HARE
Alt: 3 KEY
  Opposite of: **3** NEU
Alt.: 4 ELEV
  spelling: **3** VAR

Altair: 5 ASTAR
  constellation: **6** AQUILA
Altar
  agreement: **3 IDO**
  area: **4** APSE
  boy: **7** ACOLYTE
  Bypass the: **5** ELOPE
  constellation: **3 ARA**
  ego: **3** MRS
  Leave at the: **4 JILT**
  words: **3** IDO **4** IDOS
Altared
  Get: **3** WED
Altdorf
  is its capital: **3** URI
"___ Alte" (Adenauer): 3 DER
Alter: 3 HEM **4** EDIT SPAY
      5 EMEND RESEW
      6 MUTATE
Alter ___ : 3 EGO **4** IDEM
Alterations
  Make ~ to: **5** REFIT
Altercation: 3 ROW **5** MELEE
      RUNIN SETTO **6** AFFRAY
      7 RHUBARB
  Minor: **4** SPAT
Alter ego
  Dracula: **3** BAT
  Famous: **4** HYDE **6** MRHYDE
  Jekyll: **4 HYDE**
  Superman: **4** KENT
Alterer: 6 TAILOR
Alternate: 5 OTHER **6** SEESAW
      7 STANDIN
      9 TAKETURNS
  handle: **5** ALIAS
  sp.: **3** VAR
Alternative: 5 OTHER **6** BACKUP
      CHOICE OPTION
  fuel: **7** ETHANOL GASOHOL
  magazine: **4** UTNE
  word: **4** ELSE **6** RATHER
Alternatively: 4 ELSE 5 IFNOT.
      7 INSTEAD
Altima
  maker: **6** NISSAN
Altitude
  Gain: **4** SOAR
___ Alto, California: 4 PALO

Altogether
In the: 4 BARE NUDE
Altoids
rival: 5 CERTS
___ **Altos, California:** 3 LOS
Altruist
opposite: 6 EGOIST
Alts.: 3 HTS
Alum: 4 GRAD
to be: 6 SENIOR
Aluminum
It may be: 6 SIDING
sheet: 4 FOIL
source: 3 ORE 7 BAUXITE
Alumna
word: 3 NEE
Alumni
Baseball: 9 OLDTIMERS
Alvar
Architect: 5 AALTO
Alvarado
Actress: 5 TRINI
Alveolus: 3 SAC
Alvin
Choreographer: 5 **AILEY**
Alway: 3 **EER**
Opposite of: 4 NEER
Always: 4 **EVER**
8 EVERMORE
~, in Italian: 6 SEMPRE
~, poetically: 3 **ERE**
"___ always say ...": 3 ASI
Alzheimer, Dr.: 5 ALOIS
A.M.
Part of: 4 ANTE
~ TV show: 3 GMA
AMA
members: 3 DRS GPS MDS
"Amadeus"
director Forman: 5 MILOS
star Tom: 5 HULCE
Amado
Novelist: 5 JORGE
Amahl
creator: 7 MENOTTI
Amalgamate: 3 WED 4 MELD
5 MERGE
Amanda
Actress: 4 PEET

"___ a man who wasn't ...":
4 IMET
Amaretto
flavor: 6 ALMOND
___, amas, amat: 3 AMO
"___, amas, I love ...": 3 AMO
Amass: 5 RUNUP 6 GARNER
PILEUP RACKUP RAKEIN
Amateur: 3 LAY 4 TYRO
6 NONPRO
Leave the ~ ranks: 5 GOPRO
No: 3 PRO
sports org.: 4 NCAA
Amateurish: 4 BUSH
10 BUSHLEAGUE
Amateurishly
Paint: 4 DAUB
Amati
Violinmaker: 6 NICOLO
Amatol
ingredient: 3 TNT
"___ Amatoria": 3 ARS
Amatory: 6 EROTIC
Amaze: 3 AWE WOW 4 STUN
13 SETONONESEARS
Amazed: 5 INAWE
Obviously: 5 AGAPE
outcries: 4 OOHS
Amazement: 3 AWE
Sound of: 4 GASP
Sounds of: 4 OOHS
"Amazin'"
team: 4 METS
Amazing
to behold: 10 EYEPOPPING
"Amazing"
magician: 5 RANDI
"Amazing!": 3 OOH
A-mazing
animal: 6 LABRAT
Amazing ___, The: 5 RANDI
"Amazing Grace"
ending: 4 ISEE
Amazon
burrower: 4 PACA
How the ~ flows: 4 EAST
River to the: 5 NEGRO
sales: 5 ETAIL
Source of the: 4 PERU 5 ANDES

squeezer: 3 BOA
zapper: 3 EEL
Ambassador
  forte: 4 TACT
  Israel's first U.N.: 4 EBAN
  Jack's U.N.: 5 ADLAI
  JFK's U.N.: 3 AES
     15 ADLAIESTEVENSON
  of old cars: 4 NASH
  Papal: 6 NUNCIO
"Am ___ believe ...?": 3 ITO
Amber: 5 RESIN
  brew: 3 ALE
  colored wine: 7 MADEIRA
Ambience: 4 AURA
Ambient
  music pioneer: 3 ENO
Ambiguous
  patterned style: 5 OPART
Ambition: 3 AIM
Ambitious
  Be: 6 ASPIRE
"Am ___ blame?": 3 ITO
Amble: 4 LOPE ROVE 5 MOSEY
     7 SAUNTER
  along: 6 STROLL
Ambler
  Author: 4 ERIC
Ambrose
  Writer: 6 BIERCE
Ambrosia
  accompaniment: 6 NECTAR
"Am ___ brother's keeper?":
     3 IMY
Ambulance
  attachment: 5 SIREN
  attendant (abbr.): 3 EMT
  chaser advice: 3 SUE
  destinations (abbr.): 3 ERS
  initials: 3 EMS
  ~ VIP: 3 EMT
Ambulatory
  Area next to an: 4 APSE
Ambush: 4 TRAP 6 WAYLAY
     7 SANDBAG
  One who waits in: 4 LIER
  Prepare for an: 4 LURK
AMC
  Old ~ model: 5 PACER

Amelia
  Women's rights advocate:
     7 BLOOMER
Ameliorate: 4 EASE
"Amen!": 3 YES 5 RIGHT
     6 IAGREE ILLSAY ITISSO
     SOBEIT 9 YOUSAIDIT
Amenable: 4 OPEN
Amend: 4 EDIT 5 ALTER
     6 REVISE
Amendment
  18th ~ state: 3 DRY
  19th ~ beneficiaries: 5 WOMEN
  First ~ defender: 4 ACLU
  Second ~ concern: 4 ARMS
  Second ~ supporter: 3 NRA
Amends
  Make: 5 ATONE
  One who makes: 6 ATONER
Amenhotep
  god: 4 ATEN ATON
Amenity
  Hotel: 3 ICE 4 POOL
  Suite: 6 WETBAR
Amer.
  counterpart: 4 NATL
Amerada ___: 4 HESS
America: 9 THESTATES
"America"
  Third word in: 3 TIS
  ___ America: 4 MISS
American
  Airline bought by: 3 TWA
  An ~ in Paris, maybe: 5 EXPAT
  Ancient: 4 INCA
  anthropologist: 4 MEAD
  buffalo: 5 BISON
  charge: 7 AIRFARE
  craft: 3 JET 5 PLANE
  dogwood: 5 OSIER
  First ~ in orbit: 5 GLENN
  First ~ saint: 5 SETON
  Native ~ group: 5 TRIBE
  naturalist: 4 MUIR
  of Japanese descent: 5 NISEI
  operative: 6 CIASPY
  plan offering: 4 MEAL
  rival: 5 DELTA 6 UNITED
  symbol: 5 EAGLE

Traditionally: **8** APPLEPIE
Typical ~, they say:
   7 PEORIAN
uncle: **3** SAM
~, to a Brit: **4** YANK
American ___: **3** ELM
"American ___"
  (Gere film): **6** GIGOLO
  (TV show): **4** IDOL
___ American: **6** NATIVE
___-American: **4** SINO
American Airlines Arena
  team: **9** MIAMIHEAT
"American Appetites"
  author: **5** OATES
American Beauty: **4** ROSE
  kin: **7** TEAROSE
"American Beauty"
  actor Bentley: **3** WES
  actress Suvari: **4** MENA
  director: **6** MENDES
American-born
  queen of Jordan: **4** NOOR
"American Buffalo"
  playwright: **5** MAMET
"___ American Cousin": **3** OUR
American Dance Theater
  founder: **5** AILEY
    10 ALVINAILEY
"American Dream, The"
  playwright: **5** ALBEE
American Express
  rival: **4** VISA
American Fur Company
  founder: **5** ASTOR
"American Gigolo"
  star: **4** GERE
"American Gothic"
  artist: **4** WOOD
"American Graffiti"
  actor Paul: **5** LEMAT
  director: **5** LUCAS
American Greetings
  logo: **4** ROSE
"American Idol"
  Compete on: **4** SING
  judge Abdul: **5** PAULA
  judge Cowell: **5** SIMON
  judge Paula: **5** ABDUL

  winner Studdard: **5** RUBEN
"American in Paris, An"
  actress: **8** NINAFOCH
  star: **5** CARON
Americanism
  Symbol of: **8** APPLEPIE
American League
  division: **4** EAST WEST
  team: **5** THEAS TWINS
    7 ORIOLES
American Legion
  member: **3** VET
"American Pie"
  actress Reid: **4** TARA
American Revolution
  general: **6** PUTNAM
Americans
  Faith of more than 5 million:
    5 ISLAM
  Like about 13% of: **6** LATINO
  Some: **6** LATINS
American Samoa
  capital: **8** PAGOPAGO
American Shakers
  founder: **6** ANNLEE
"American Tail, An"
  director: **5** BLUTH
American Theater Wing
  award: **4** TONY
"American Tragedy, An"
  writer: **7** DREISER
America's Cup
  activity: **8** YACHTING
  racer: **5** YACHT **7** YACHTER
  winner, perhaps:
    9 CATAMARAN
"___ America Singing": Whitman:
  5 IHEAR
"America's Most Wanted"
  host John: **5** WALSH
  letters: **3** AKA
"America, the Beautiful"
  closer: **3** SEA
  color: **5** AMBER
  pronoun: **4** THEE
"Amerika"
  author: **5** KAFKA
Amerind
  Western: **3** UTE

Amérique: 9 ETATSUNIS
"A merry heart ___ good like medicine": 5 DOETH
Ames
  and others: 3 EDS
AMEX
  counterpart: 4 NYSE
  listings: 3 COS
  unit: 3 SHR
AM/FM
  device: 5 RADIO
Amherst
  sch.: 5 UMASS
Amicus ___: 6 CURIAE
Amiens
  Info: French cue
  assent: 3 OUI
  is its capital: 5 SOMME
  Mine, in: 4 AMOI
Amigo: 3 PAL
"___ amigos!": 5 ADIOS
Amin
  Dictator: 3 IDI
  fate: 5 EXILE
  land: 6 UGANDA
  predecessor: 5 OBOTE
Amino ___: 4 ACID
Amino acid: 6 LYSINE
___ amis: 3 MES
Amish: 4 SECT
  feature: 5 BEARD
  pronoun: 4 THEE
Amiss: 3 OFF 5 WRONG
"Amistad"
  character: 5 SLAVE
"Amityville Horror, The"
  author Jay: 5 ANSON
"Am ___ late?": 4 ITOO
Amman
  land: 6 JORDAN
Ammo
  Air rifle: 3 BBS 6 BBSHOT
  Blowgun: 3 PEA 4 DART
  Put in more: 6 RELOAD
  Put ~ into: 4 LOAD
  Shooter: 3 PEA
  Slapstick: 3 PIE
  Sling: 5 STONE
  Toy pistol: 4 CAPS

Ammonia
  compound: 5 AMIDE AMINE
    IMIDE IMINE
  ___ ammoniac: 3 SAL
Ammunition
  Leading ~ maker: 4 OLIN
  unit: 5 ROUND
Amneris
  rival: 4 AIDA
Amnesiac
  question: 6 WHOAMI
Amniotic ___: 3 SAC
"Am not!"
  retort: 5 ARESO
Amo: 5 ILOVE
Amo, amas, ___: 4 AMAT
Amo, ___, amat: 4 AMAS
Amoeba: 4 BLOB
  An ~ has one: 4 CELL
  feature: 7 ONECELL
Amok
  Run: 4 RIOT
Among: 4 WITH
  others: 9 INTERALIA
"Am ___ only one?": 4 ITHE
Amontillado
  holder: 4 CASK
"___ Amore": 5 THATS
"Amores"
  poet: 4 OVID
Amorous
  complication: 8 TRIANGLE
Amorously
  Eye: 4 OGLE
  Talk: 3 COO
Amorphous
  critter: 5 AMEBA
  hunk: 4 GLOB
Amos
  and Spelling: 5 TORIS
  Book before: 4 JOEL
  Famous: 4 TORI
  partner: 4 ANDY
  Singer: 4 TORI
Amos Alonso ___: 5 STAGG
"Amos 'n' Andy"
  Amos last name on: 5 JONES
Amount: 3 SUM 4 DOSE
  A smaller: 4 LESS

Huge: 3 SEA TON 4 LOAD PILE
  RAFT SCAD SLEW 5 OCEAN
Minimal: 5 LEAST
Minimum: 4 WAGE
Minute: 4 IOTA 9 SCINTILLA
Paltry: 3 SOU
Small: 3 BIT DAB FIG JOT SOU
  TAD TOT 4 ATOM DRAM
  DRIB GRAM IOTA MITE
  WHIT 5 PINCH TRACE
  7 REDCENT
Vague: 4 SOME
"A mouse!": 3 EEK
Amp
  attachment: 4 MIKE
  toter: 6 ROADIE
Ampersand
  follower, sometimes: 3 SON
Amphibian
  Mil.: 3 LST
  Small: 3 EFT 4 NEWT
  Warty: 4 TOAD
Amphibious
  carriers: 4 LSTS
Amphilochus: 4 SEER
Amphitheater: 5 ARENA
  section: 4 TIER
  shape: 4 OVAL
Ample: 4 WIDE
Amplifier
  setting: 6 TREBLE
  Voice: 4 MIKE 9 MEGAPHONE
Ampule: 4 VIAL
"Amscray!": 3 GIT 4 SCAT SHOO
  5 SCOOT
Amsterdam
  Airline to: 3 KLM
  Comic: 5 MOREY
Amt.: 3 QTY
"Am ___ time?": 3 IIN
"Am too!"
  Reply to: 6 ARENOT
Amtrak
  express train: 5 **ACELA**
  stop (abbr.): 3 **STA**
  track: 4 RAIL
Amu Darya
  Sea the ~ flows into: 4 ARAL
Amulet: 5 CHARM 8 TALISMAN

Egyptian: 6 SCARAB
Polynesian: 4 TIKI
Voodoo: 4 MOJO
Amundsen
  Explorer: 5 ROALD
Amuse: 6 DIVERT TICKLE
  9 ENTERTAIN
  immensely: 4 SLAY
Amused
  Be ~ by: 6 GRINAT
Amusement: 5 MIRTH
  park lure: 4 RIDE
  Show: 4 GRIN 5 SMILE
Amusing
  Bitterly: 3 WRY
  Oddly: 5 DROLL
Amy
  Author: 3 TAN
  Sister of: 3 MEG 4 BETH
  ~, to Jo, Meg, or Beth: 3 SIS
"Am ___ your way?": 3 IIN
An: 7 ARTICLE
Anabaptists: 4 SECT
Anaconda: 3 BOA
Anaheim
  City north of: 4 BREA
  pro: 5 ANGEL
  team: 6 ANGELS
Anaïs
  Diarist: 3 **NIN**
Anakin
  Daughter of: 4 LEIA
  Son of: 4 LUKE
Analgesic
  target: 4 ACHE PAIN
Analogous: 4 **AKIN** LIKE 5 ALIKE
  7 SIMILAR
Analogy
  mark: 5 COLON
  words: 4 **ISTO**
Analysis: 5 ASSAY
Analyst: 7 ASSAYER
  concerns: 7 SYSTEMS
  need: 4 DATA
Analytical Psychology
  founder: 4 JUNG
Analytic Geometry
  giant: 5 EULER
Analyze: 4 TEST 5 ASSAY

Figures to: **7** RAWDATA
grammatically: **5** PARSE
verse: **4** SCAN

Analyzer
Echo: **5** SONAR

"Analyze This"
actor: **6** DENIRO

Ananias: 4 LIAR

"An apple ___ ...": 4 ADAY

Anarchist
1920s ~: **5** SACCO

Anastasia
dad: **4** TSAR

"Anastasia"
actor Brynner: **3** YUL
Oscar winner: **7** BERGMAN

Anat.: 3 SCI

Anatolia: 9 ASIAMINOR

Anatomical
canal: **4** ITER
cavity: **5** FOSSA
container: **3** SAC
duct: **3** VAS
foot: **3** PES
interstice: **6** AREOLE
knot: **4** NODE
network: **4** RETE
passage: **4** ITER
pouch: **3** **SAC**
ring: **6** AREOLA
sac: **5** BURSA

Anatomist
Second-century: **5** GALEN

Anatomy
class model: **8** SKELETON

Ancestral
group: **5** TRIBE

Ancestry: 4 LINE **5** ROOTS
6 ORIGIN **7** LINEAGE
One of mixed: **7** MULATTO
record: **4** TREE

Anchor: 4 MOOR
concern: **4** NEWS
Drop: **4** MOOR
Lift: **4** SAIL
NBC: **6** BROKAW
Pitch heavily at: **5** HAWSE
Plant: **4** ROOT
position: **4** DESK **5** APEAK

ATRIP
Raise an: **5** HEAVE WEIGH
Small: **5** KEDGE **7** GRAPNEL
Tooth: **4** ROOT
~ Paula: **4** ZAHN
~ Rather: **3** DAN

Anchorman
WJM: **3** TED
~ Rather: **3** DAN

"Anchors ___": 6 AWEIGH

"Anchors Aweigh"
gp.: **3** USN

Anchovies
How ~ are packed: **5** INOIL

Anchovy
container: **3** TIN

Ancient: 3 **OLD 4** AGED **5** HOARY
OLDEN **6** AGEOLD
article: **5** RELIC
ascetic: **6** **ESSENE**
beauty: **5** HELEN
character: **4** RUNE
colonnade: **4** STOA
consultant: **6** ORACLE
epoch: **6** ICEAGE
galley: **7** TRIREME
greeting: **3** AVE
kingdom: **4** MOAB
laborer: **4** ESNE
land: **5** IONIA **7** ALSATIA
lawgiver: **5** SOLON
letter: **4** **RUNE**
mariner: **4** NOAH
marketplace: **5** **AGORA**
medium: **6** ORACLE
meeting place: **4** STOA **5** AGORA
moralist: **5** AESOP
portico: **4** STOA
theaters: **4** ODEA
times, old-style: **3** ELD
~ Andean: **4** INCA
~ Briton: **4** CELT PICT
~ Celt: **5** DRUID
~ Iranian: **4** MEDE
~ Italian: **6** SABINE
8 ETRUSCAN
~ Mexican: **5** AZTEC OLMEC
6 TOLTEC
~ Palestinian: **6** **ESSENE**

~ Persian: 4 MEDE
~ Peruvian: 4 **INCA**
Ancient Greek
  city-state: 5 POLIS 6 SPARTA
  coin: 4 OBOL 6 STATER
  colony: 5 **IONIA**
  dialect (var.): 5 EOLIC
  garment: 5 TUNIC
  lyric poet: 6 SAPPHO
        8 ANACREON
  marketplace: 5 AGORA
  physician: 5 GALEN
  portico: 4 STOA
  region: 5 **IONIA**
  state: 6 ATTICA
  theater: 5 ODEON
Ancient Mariner
  poem: 4 RIME
Ancient Roman
  historian: 4 LIVY
  magistrate: 5 EDILE
  road: 4 ITER
And: 4 ALSO PLUS
  more: 3 ETC
  not: 3 **NOR**
  others: 3 ETC 4 **ETAL** 6 ETALIA
        ETALII
  so forth: 3 ETC 6 ETCETC
        8 ETCETERA
  the following: 5 ETSEQ
  ___ and aah: 3 OOH
"... and ___ a good-night!":
        5 TOALL
  ___ and all: 5 WARTS
Andalusia
  Info: Spanish cue
  Another, in: 4 OTRO
  home (abbr.): 3 ALA
Andalusian
  title: 5 SENOR 6 SENORA
  ___ and anon: 4 EVER
Andante
  or allegro: 5 TEMPO
  Slower than: 6 ADAGIO
"And a Voice to Sing With"
  writer: 4 BAEZ
"And away ___!": 4 WEGO
"___ and away!": 4 UPUP
"And ___ bed": Pepys: 4 SOTO

___ **and blood:** 5 FLESH
___ **and crafts:** 4 ARTS
___ **and dined:** 5 WINED
___ **and don'ts:** 3 DOS
Andean
  Ancient: 4 INCA
  animal: 5 LLAMA 6 ALPACA
        VICUNA
  capital: 4 LIMA
  nation: 4 PERU
  shrub: 4 COCA
  tuber: 3 OCA
Andersen
  birthplace: 6 ODENSE
  countrymen: 5 DANES
  portrayer: 4 KAYE
Anderson
  Actress: 4 **LONI** 6 PAMELA
  Comedian: 5 LOUIE
  Composer: 5 LEROY
  Director: 3 WES
  Jazz singer: 4 IVIE
  Like ~ in 1980 (abbr.): 3 IND
Anderson, Marian: 4 ALTO
Andes
  (abbr.): 3 MTS
  animal: 5 LLAMA
  capital: 4 LIMA
  High in the: 4 ALTO
  land: 4 PERU
  tuber: 3 OCA
___ **and far between:** 3 FEW
___ **and for all:** 4 ONCE
"___ and gimble ...": 4 GYRE
"And giving ___, up the
        chimney ...": 4 ANOD
"And ___ grow on": 5 ONETO
___ **and hearty:** 5 HALE
"And here it is!": 4 TADA
"___ and his money ...": 5 AFOOL
"And how!": 3 DOI
"... ___ and hungry look":
        Shakespeare: 5 ALEAN
"And I Love ___": 3 HER
Andiron: 7 FIREDOG
"And ___ I wrote ...": 4 THEN
___ **and kicking:** 5 ALIVE
___ **and kin:** 4 KITH
"___ and Lovers": 4 SONS

"And ___ off!": 6 THEYRE
___ and outs: 3 INS
Andover
  rival: 6 EXETER
"... and pretty maids all in ___":
      4 AROW
"___ and Punishment": 5 CRIME
Andre
  Ex of ~ and Frank: 3 MIA
  Literature Nobelist: 4 GIDE
  Pianist: 5 WATTS
Andrea ___: 5 **DORIA**
Andrea del ___: 5 SARTO
Andrea ___ Sarto: 3 DEL
___ **Andreas fault**: 3 SAN
Andrés
  Guitarist: 7 SEGOVIA
Andress
  Actress: 6 URSULA
  film: 3 SHE
Andretti
  Racer: 5 MARIO
Andrew
  Actor: 4 SHUE
  Brother of the Apostle:
      7 STPETER
  Painter: 5 WYETH
  Prince ~, to York: 4 DUKE
Andrews
  Actor: 4 DANA
  Cry at St.: 4 FORE
  or Vandenberg (abbr.): 3 AFB
Andrews Sisters, The: 4 TRIO
  One of: 6 MAXENE 7 LAVERNE
Andric
  Literature Nobelist: 3 IVO
Androcles
  extraction: 5 THORN
  Friend of: 4 LION
  Where ~ was spared: 5 ARENA
Android
  on the Enterprise: 4 DATA
"Andromeda Strain, The"
  actor James: 5 OLSON
"___ **Andronicus"**: 5 TITUS
Androphobe
  fear: 3 MEN
Andropov
  Former Soviet leader: 4 YURI

___ and sciences: 4 ARTS
"And so ___": Pepys: 5 TOBED
"And So It Goes"
  author: 8 ELLERBEE
"___ and sometimes ...": 5 AEIOU
___ and Span: 4 SPIC
"And Still I Rise"
  poet: 7 ANGELOU
"___ & Stitch": 4 LILO
___ and terminer: 4 OYER
"... and that ___ hay!": 4 AINT
"___ and the Art of Motorcycle
      Maintenance": 3 ZEN
"___ and the King": 4 ANNA
"And then again ...": 5 ORNOT
"___ and the Night Visitors":
      5 AMAHL
"And Then There Were ___":
      4 NONE
"___ and the Pussycats": 5 JOSIE
"And thereby hangs ___":
      Shakespeare: 5 ATALE
"And there you are!": 5 VOILA
"And there you have it!": 4 TADA
      5 VOILA
"___ and the Swan": Yeats:
      4 LEDA
"And this is the thanks ___?":
      4 IGET
___ and tuck: 3 NIP
___ and void: 4 NULL
"___ and weep!": 6 READEM
"And what ___ rare as ...": 4 ISSO
**"And what's he then that says
      I play the villain?" speaker:**
      4 IAGO
Andy
  Aunt of: 3 BEE
  of the comics: 4 CAPP
  or Ann: 7 RAGDOLL
  partner: 4 AMOS
  Son of: 4 OPIE
"Andy Capp"
  beverage: 3 ALE
  cartoonist Smythe: 3 REG
  hangout: 3 PUB
  wife: 3 **FLO**
"Andy Griffith Show, The"
  son: 4 OPIE

"___ Andy Warhol" (1996 film):
5 ISHOT
Anecdotal
collection: 3 ANA
knowledge: 4 LORE
Anemic
need: 4 IRON
Anent: 4 ASTO INRE
Anesthetic
gas: 6 ETHENE 8 ETHYLENE
Old: 5 **ETHER**
Anesthetics
Like some: 5 LOCAL
7 TOPICAL
Anesthetized: 4 NUMB 5 UNDER
7 SEDATED
Anew: 7 FRESHLY
Ang
Director: 3 LEE
Angel: 4 ALER 5 SAINT
6 SERAPH
Charlie's: 4 OONA
child: 6 CHERUB
dust: 3 PCP
Fallen: 5 SATAN
favorite letters: 3 SRO
hair: 5 PASTA
High-ranking: 6 SERAPH
instrument: 4 HARP
Jockey: 7 CORDERO
Kind of: 4 TEEN
No: 4 BRAT
topper: 4 HALO
TV ~ portrayer: 4 ROMA
5 REESE
"___ Angel" (Mae West film):
4 IMNO
"Angela's ___": 5 ASHES
"Angela's Ashes"
sequel: 3 TIS
___ Angeles: 3 LOS
Angelic
aura: 4 HALO
Angelica: 4 HERB
Angelico
Painter: 3 FRA
Angelina
Actress: 5 JOLIE
role: 4 LARA

Angelou
Poet: 4 **MAYA**
Angels
High-ranking: 8 SERAPHIM
home: 6 HEAVEN 7 ANAHEIM
in many images: 8 HARPISTS
"Angels in America"
figure: 4 COHN
Anger: 3 **IRE** 4 RAGE RILE
5 PIQUE STEAM UPSET
WRATH 6 ENRAGE
SPLEEN
Erupt in: 6 REARUP
Intense: 3 **IRE** 4 FURY RAGE
Internalize: 4 STEW
Shut in: 4 SLAM
With: 7 IRATELY
"Angie"
Stephen of: 3 REA
"Angie Baby"
singer: 5 REDDY
Angkor ___: 3 WAT
___ anglais (English horn): 3 COR
Angle: 4 FISH SKEW 5 SLANT
90-degree ~: 3 ELL
Cut at an: 5 BEVEL
iron: 4 LBAR
Leaf: 4 AXIL
prefix: 3 TRI
Right: 3 ELL
symbol: 5 THETA
Angler
aid: 4 LURE
basket: 5 CREEL
boot: 5 WADER
Certain: 5 EELER
gear: 6 TACKLE
hope: 4 BITE
need: 3 ROD 4 LURE REEL
spot: 4 PIER
Angles
At right ~ to the keel: 5 ABEAM
Like some: 5 ACUTE
They knew the: 6 SAXONS
Anglican
headgear: 5 MITRE
parish priest: 5 VICAR
Angling
area: 4 PIER

Go: 4 FISH
Anglo-___: 5 SAXON
Anglo-Saxon
  laborer: 4 ESNE
  lord: 5 THANE
Angola
  capital: 6 LUANDA
Angora
  fabric: 6 MOHAIR
  output: 4 WOOL
Angrily
  Speak: 5 SNARL
  Stare: 5 GLARE
Angry: 3 HOT MAD 4 IRED SORE
     5 CROSS IRATE IRKED
     RILED 6 IREFUL
  dispute: 7 QUARREL
  fits: 5 HUFFS
  Get: 6 SEERED
  Make: 3 IRE 4 RILE 6 ENRAGE
  Plenty: 4 SORE
  reaction: 4 RISE
  stare: 5 GLARE
  state: 4 SNIT
  Very: 5 IRATE LIVID
  with: 5 MADAT
  young man: 5 REBEL
  ~, with "off": 4 TEED
  ~, with "up": 3 HET
Angst
  Cause of Apr.: 3 IRS
Anguish: 3 WOE 4 PAIN 5 AGONY
  Cause ~ to: 6 TEARAT
  Extreme: 7 TORTURE
Angular
  prefix: 3 TRI 4 EQUI RECT
  shape: 3 ELL
Angus
  refusal: 3 NAE
Anima
  doctor: 4 JUNG
Animal: 5 BEAST
  catcher: 4 TRAP 5 SNARE
  den: 4 LAIR
  doc: 3 VET
  group suffix: 3 ZOA
  gullet: 3 MAW
  hide: 4 PELT
  home: 4 LAIR

  house: 3 ZOO 4 BARN CAGE
    LAIR
  in a roundup: 5 STEER
  life: 5 FAUNA
  park: 3 ZOO
  pouch: 3 SAC
  rights org.: 4 PETA SPCA
  shelter: 3 ARK 4 LAIR 5 POUND
  skin: 4 HIDE PELT
  stomach: 4 CRAW
  that bugles: 3 ELK
  that sleeps upside-down:
    5 SLOTH
  track: 5 SPOOR
  welfare org.: 4 SPCA
  with a snout: 5 TAPIR
  with striped legs: 5 OKAPI
"Animal Farm"
  author: 6 ORWELL
  form: 5 FABLE
"Animal House"
  brother: 5 OTTER
  group: 4 FRAT
  house: 5 DELTA
  party wear: 4 TOGA
Animals: 5 FAUNA
Animate: 5 ALIVE PEPUP
  7 ENLIVEN
Animated: 5 ALIVE
  1998 ~ film: 4 ANTZ 5 MULAN
  character: 4 TOON
  ~ Chihuahua: 3 REN
  ~ Olive: 3 OYL
Animation: 3 PEP VIM 4 LIFE
    ZING
  First name in: 4 WALT
  frame: 3 **CEL**
Animator
  unit: 3 CEL
  ~ Tex: 5 AVERY
Animosity: 6 HATRED
Anise-flavored
  liqueur: 4 **OUZO** 6 PERNOD
Aniston
  ex: 4 PITT
Anita
  Author: 4 LOOS
  Jazz singer: 4 **ODAY**
Anjou: 4 **PEAR**

agreement: **3** OUI
alternative: **4 BOSC**
Anka, Paul
1957 ~ hit: **5** DIANA
1962 ~ hit: **7** ESOBESO
Ankara
coin: **4** LIRA
resident: **4** TURK
title: **3** AGA
Ankh
feature: **4** LOOP
Ankle
bone: **5** TALUS
bones: **5** TARSI
Of the: **6** TARSAL
Anklebone: 5 TALUS
Anklebones: 4 TALI 5 TARSI
Ankle-knee
connector: **4** SHIN
Ankle-length
skirt: **4** MAXI
Ankles
Go in up to the: **4** WADE
Anklets: 5 SOCKS
Ann
and May: **5** CAPES
or Andy: **7** RAGDOLL
Shaker: **3** LEE
Sister of: **4** ABBY
Anna
Actress: **4** STEN
Author: **6** SEWELL
Diva: **5** MOFFO
Like students of: **7** SIAMESE
or Evangeline: **7** HEROINE
Where ~ taught: **4** SIAM
"Anna Christie"
playwright: **6** ONEILL
"Anna Karenina"
actress Garbo: **5** GRETA
author: **7** TOLSTOY
Annan
land: **5** GHANA
of the U.N.: **4** KOFI
Annan, Kofi ___: 4 ATTA
Annapolis
frosh: **5** PLEBE
grad.: **3** ENS
sch.: **4 USNA**

Anne
Actress: **5** HECHE
Author: **4** RICE
Funny: **5** MEARA
Pulitzer novelist: **5** TYLER
___ Anne de Beaupré: 3 STE
Annette
Actress: **6** OTOOLE
Annex: 3 ADD ELL **4** WING
5 ADDON
Info: **Suffix** cue
Annexation
1898 ~: **6** HAWAII
Annie: 6 ORPHAN **7** ADOPTEE
Actress: **5** POTTS
Deadeye: **6** OAKLEY
Dog of: **5** SANDY
of the comics: **6** ORPHAN
~, to Warbucks: **4** WARD
"Annie"
actress Quinn: **6** AILEEN
song: **8** TOMORROW
___ Annie ("Oklahoma!" role):
3 ADO
"Annie Get Your Gun"
1999 ~ star: **6** PETERS
subject: **6** OAKLEY
"Annie Hall"
actress Keaton: **5** DIANE
star: **6** KEATON
Woody role in: **4** ALVY
Anniversary: 4 DATE
4th ~ gift: **5** LINEN
10th ~ gift: **3** TIN
20th ~ gift: **5** CHINA
55th ~ gift: **7** EMERALD
Golden ~ number: **5** FIFTY
party: **7** JUBILEE
Ann-Margret
~, by birth: **5** SWEDE
Ann ___, Michigan: 5 ARBOR
Anno ___: 6 DOMINI
Annotation
Proof: **4** STET
Announce: 6 HERALD
Announcement
Circular: **4** SALE
"Coming soon": **5** PROMO
fanfare: **4** TADA

JFK: 3 ETA ETD
Marriage: 5 BANNS
Merger: 3 IDO
Proctor: 4 TIME

Announcements
It's used for: 8 PASYSTEM

Announcer
Baseball ~ phrase: 6 HESOUT
"Heeere's Johnny!":
    7 MCMAHON
Jay's former: 3 EDD
Old: 5 CRIER
Public: 5 CRIER
Soccer ~ cry: 4 GOAL
~ Don: 5 PARDO
~ Hall: 3 EDD
~ Johnny: 5 OLSON

Annoy: 3 EAT IRK VEX 4 MIFF
    RILE 5 BESET EATAT
    GETTO GRATE PEEVE
    TEASE 6 BOTHER HASSLE
    MOLEST NETTLE
    PESTER RANKLE
    7 AGITATE

Annoyance: 3 IRE 4 **PEST**
    5 PEEVE THORN
    6 HASSLE
Dorm: 5 SNORE 6 SNORER
Exclamation of: 4 DRAT
Eye: 4 STYE
Online: 4 SPAM 7 POPUPAD

Annoyed: 4 SORE
More than: 5 IRATE

Annoyer: 4 PEST PILL

Annoying: 5 PESKY 7 IRKSOME
child: 4 BRAT
insect: 4 GNAT
one: 4 PEST 5 VEXER
spots: 4 ACNE

Annuaire
listing: 3 NOM

Annual
award giver: 3 MTV
Bright: 6 ZINNIA
exhibition: 4 FAIR
foursome: 7 SEASONS
parade honoree: 5 STPAT
reference book: 7 ALMANAC
sled race: 8 IDITAROD

Annually: 7 PERYEAR
    9 ONCEAYEAR

Annul: 4 UNDO VOID 6 REPEAL
    REVOKE 7 RESCIND

Annum
Per: 5 AYEAR
___ annum: 3 PER

"Annus Mirabilis"
poet: 6 DRYDEN

Año
starter: 5 **ENERO**

Anomalous: 3 ODD

Anon: 4 SOON 5 LATER 6 INABIT
Partner of: 4 EVER

Anonymity
Woman of: 7 JANEDOE

Anonymous: 6 NONAME
    7 UNNAMED 8 NAMELESS
~ Jane: 3 DOE
~ John: 3 **DOE**
~ Richard: 3 ROE

Another: 7 ONEMORE
At ~ time: 4 ANON
Do ~ hitch: 4 REUP
One thing after: 6 SERIES
Put ~ way: 7 REWRITE
Take ~ shot: 5 RETRY
time: 4 ANEW 5 AGAIN
    7 LATERON
~, in Spanish: 4 OTRA OTRO

"Another Green World"
composer: 3 ENO

"Another interruption?":
    7 WHATNOW

"Another Pyramid"
musical: 4 AIDA

"Another Time"
poet: 5 AUDEN

"Another Woman"
actress Rowlands: 4 GENA

Anouk
Actress: 5 **AIMEE**

Ans.
Opposite of: 4 QUES

Answer: 4 RSVP 5 REACT REPLY
a charge: 5 PLEAD
Affirmative: 3 YES
Altar: 3 IDO
an invitation: 4 RSVP 5 REPLY

back: **4** SASS
(for): **5** ATONE
incorrectly: **3** ERR
man Trebek: **4** ALEX
Noncommittal: **5** MAYBE
Not ~ directly: **5** EVADE
Quiz: **4** TRUE **5** FALSE
to a charge: **4** PLEA

Answered
a charge: **4** PLED
a summons: **4** CAME

Answering
Avoid: **5** EVADE
machine button: **5** ERASE

Answers
Like some: **3** PAT
Man with all the: **6** TREBEK
Seek: **3** ASK

Ant: 5 EMMET **7** PISMIRE
group: **4** ARMY
magnet: **6** PICNIC
place: **6** COLONY
Pop singer: **4** ADAM

Ant.: 3 OPP
Opp. of: **3** SYN

Antacid
choice: **6** BICARB

Antagonist: 3 FOE **5** ENEMY
RIVAL

Antagonistic: 7 HOSTILE

Antal
Conductor: **6** DORATI

Antarctic
explorer Richard: **4** BYRD
explorer Shackleton: **6** ERNEST
explorer Sir James: **4** ROSS
flier: **4** SKUA
penguin: **4** ADELIE
sight: **6** ICECAP
volcano: **6** EREBUS
waters: **7** ROSSSEA

Antares: 4 STAR **7** REDSTAR

Ante
body: **3** POT
matter: **3** BET
Poker: **4** CHIP
Raised the: **5** UPPED
Up the: **5** RAISE

Ante-: 3 PRE

Anteater
feature: **5** SNOUT
Spiny: **7** ECHIDNA

Antebellum: 6 PREWAR

Antelope
African: **3** GNU KOB **4** ORYX
5 **ELAND** NYALA ORIBI
6 IMPALA **RHEBOK**
Bearded: **3** GNU
Female: **3** DOE
Small: **5** ORIBI
Where deer and ~ play:
5 RANGE
with twisty horns: **4** KUDU
5 ELAND

Antenna: 6 AERIAL
holder: **3** ANT
housing: **6** RADOME
Kind of: **4** DISH **6** DIPOLE
TV: **6** AERIAL
TV-top: **10** RABBITEARS

Antepenultimate
Greek letter: **3** CHI

Anthem
author: **3** KEY
contraction: **3** **OER**
opener: **4** **OSAY**
preposition: **3** **OER**
Show respect for the national:
4 RISE **5** STAND
up north: **7** OCANADA

Anther
It's got the: **6** STAMEN

Anthology: 3 ANA **6** READER
7 OMNIBUS

Anthony
Bowler: **4** EARL
British P.M.: **4** EDEN
Singer: **4** MARC **6** NEWLEY
~ Eden: **4** EARL

Anthony, ___ B.: 5 SUSAN

Anthony, St.
cross: **3** TAU

Anthropologist
~ Fossey: **4** DIAN
~ Margaret: **4** MEAD

Anti: 7 AGAINST
body: **3** CON
vote: **3** NAY

Antiaircraft
fire: 4 FLAK 6 ACKACK
Anti-art
art: 4 DADA
Antibiotic
target: 5 STREP
Antibody
sources: 4 SERA
Anti-Brady
org.: 3 NRA
Antic: 4 DIDO 5 CAPER
6 MADCAP
Anticipate: 5 AWAIT 6 PLANON
7 FORESEE
with alarm: 5 DREAD
Anticipated: 7 FORESAW
Anticipation
Time of: 3 EVE
Anticipatory
cry: 4 OHOH
times: 4 EVES
Anticrime
acronym: 4 RICO
Antidiscrimination
agcy.: 4 EEOC
Antidote: 4 CURE
Antidrug
cop: 4 NARC
honcho: 4 CZAR
mantra: 9 JUSTSAYNO
Anti-DWI
org.: 4 MADD
Antietam
fighter: 3 REB
general: 3 LEE
Antifreeze
additive: 8 METHANOL
Antifur
org.: 4 PETA
Antigen
attacker: 5 TCELL
Antigone
Father of: 7 OEDIPUS
Mother of: 7 JOCASTA
Uncle of: 5 CREON
Anti-gun-control
gp.: 3 NRA
Anti-ICBM
plan: 3 SDI

Antiknock
fluid: 5 ETHYL
Antilles
native: 5 CARIB
Antinuclear
treaty: 7 TESTBAN
Antiparticle
Certain: 8 POSITRON
Antipasto
ingredient: 5 **OLIVE** 6 SALAMI
Antipathetic: 6 AVERSE
Antipathy
Feel ~ toward: 4 HATE
Antipollution
org.: 3 EPA
Antiprohibitionist: 3 WET
___ **Antiqua:** 3 ARS
Antiquark
A quark and an: 5 MESON
Antiquated: 3 OLD 5 FUSTY
MOLDY MOSSY OLDEN
PASSE
interjection: 4 EGAD
Somewhat: 6 OLDISH
Antique: 3 OLD
auto: 3 **REO**
dealer's deal: 6 RESALE
gun: 4 STEN
shop item: 5 CURIO
~, once: 5 OLDE
"Antiques Roadshow"
network: 3 PBS
Antiquing
agent: 4 **AGER**
Antiquity: 3 **ELD**
Antony of: 4 MARC
Anti-Red
gp.: 4 HUAC
Antiroyalist: 4 WHIG
Antis: 3 NOS
Antiseptic
acid: 5 BORIC
element: 6 IODINE
Antislavery
leader Tuner: 3 NAT
Antismog
org.: 3 EPA
Antismoking
org.: 3 AMA

Antisocial
  sort: 5 LONER
Antisubversive
  Old ~ gp.: 4 HUAC
Antitank
  weapon: 7 BAZOOKA
Antithesis: 8 OPPOSITE
  Farm ~, in song: 5 PAREE
  Jock: 4 NERD
Antitoxin: 5 SERUM
Antitoxins: 4 **SERA**
Antitrust
  org.: 3 FTC
  suit defendant: 3 ITT
Antivenins: 4 SERA
Antiviral
  drug: 3 AZT
Antiwar
  gp.: 3 SDS
Antler
  point: 4 TINE 5 PRONG
Antlered
  animal: 3 **ELK** 4 DEER HART
    STAG 5 MOOSE 7 ROEDEER
Antoine
  ~ Domino: 4 FATS
Antoinette
  Tony award namesake: 5 PERRY
  ___ Antoinette: 5 MARIE
Antoinette, Marie: 5 REINE
Antonio
  Actor: 6 SABATO
  role: 3 CHE 5 ZORRO
  ___ Antonio: 3 SAN
Antony
  addressee: 5 ROMAN
  Love of: 4 AMOR CLEO
    9 CLEOPATRA
  of antiquity: 4 MARC
"Antony and Cleopatra"
  servant: 4 EROS
Antonym: 3 OPP
  opp.: 3 SYN
Ants
  flick: 4 THEM
Antsy: 6 ONEDGE 7 RESTIVE
Anvil: 7 EARBONE
  location: 3 EAR
  user: 5 SMITH

Anwar
  of Egypt: 5 **SADAT**
  successor: 5 HOSNI
Anxiety: 4 CARE 5 ANGST
    6 UNEASE 7 TENSION
  High: 6 STRESS
  Medication for: 6 VALIUM
Anxious: 4 EDGY 5 ANTSY EAGER
    ITCHY 6 ONEDGE RARING
    UNEASY 7 ALARMED
  Be: 4 STEW
Any: 4 SOME
  At ~ time: 3 EER 4 EVER
  boat: 3 SHE
  day now: 4 ANON SOON
  doctrine: 3 ISM
  Hardly: 3 FEW ONE 4 ATAD
    5 SCANT
  In ~ case: 7 ATLEAST
  In ~ way: 4 EVER 5 **ATALL**
    NOHOW
  Not: 4 NARY NONE ZERO
  Not in ~ way: 5 NOHOW
    6 NOWISE
  Not just: 3 THE
"Any ___?": 5 IDEAS 6 TAKERS
Anya
  Author: 5 SETON
Anybody: 7 SOMEONE
"... ___ any drop to drink": 3 NOR
"Any Given Sunday"
  star: 6 PACINO 8 ALPACINO
"Anyone home?": 6 YOOHOO
Anything
  He'll eat: 8 OMNIVORE
  Ready for: 5 ALERT 7 ONALERT
  Without doing: 4 IDLY
"Anything ___": 4 GOES
"Anything ___?": 4 ELSE
"___ Anything": 4 IDDO
"Anything for You"
  singer: 7 ESTEFAN
"Anything Goes"
  songwriter Porter: 4 COLE
"Anything you want!": 6 NAMEIT
Anytown, USA
  address: 6 MAINST
Anywhere
  Not going: 4 IDLE 7 STALLED

on earth: **11** UNDERTHESUN
Aoki
  Golfer: **4** ISAO
AOL: 3 ISP
  delivery: **5** EMAIL
  exchanges: **3** IMS
  Part of: **6** ONLINE
  rival: **3** MSN
A-one: 5 SUPER **8** TOPNOTCH
  ___ a one: **4** NARY
Aotearoa
  people: **5** MAORI
Août
  time: **3** ETE
AP
  Part of: **5** ASSOC
  rival: **3** UPI
Aparicio
  of baseball: **4** LUIS
Apart
  Come: **3** RIP **4** FRAY **7** UNRAVEL
  Fall: **3** ROT **7** GOTOPOT
  from this: **4** ELSE
  Kept: **6** SPACED
  Pull: **4** TEAR **8** SEPARATE
  Rip: **4** REND
  Set: **5** ALLOT **7** ISOLATE
  Split: **4** REND
  Spread: **5** SPLAY
  Take: **4** UNDO
  Tear: **3** RIP **4** REND RIVE
Apartment: 3 PAD **4** FLAT UNIT
  6 RENTAL
  Certain: **4** COOP LOFT
  6 SUBLET
  dweller: **6** TENANT
  Owned: **5** CONDO
  sharer: **6** ROOMIE
  sign: **5** TOLET
  Small: **6** STUDIO
  Super's ~, often: **4** ONEA
  Take an: **4** RENT
Apartments
  Like some: **5** RELET
Apathetic: 5 BLASE
  Isn't: **5** CARES
APB
  Part of: **3** ALL
  sources: **3** PDS

Ape: 4 COPY **5** MIMIC **6** SIMIAN
  7 IMITATE PRIMATE
  Big: **4** LOUT **5** ORANG
  7 GORILLA PALOOKA
  Go: **4** FLIP RANT **6** LOSEIT
  Movie: **4** KONG
Apennine
  Ancient ~ dweller: **6** SABINE
  volcano: **4** ETNA
Apéritif
  Cassis-flavored: **3** KIR
  Italian: **7** CAMPARI
  White wine: **3** KIR
Aperture: 4 HOLE
  Narrow: **4** SLIT SLOT
  Tiny: **7** PINHOLE
Apertures
  Leaf: **7** STOMATA
Apex: 3 TOP **4** ACME PEAK
  At the ~ of: **4** ATOP
Aphid: 4 PEST
  milker: **3** ANT
Aphorism: 3 SAW **5** GNOME
  MAXIM
  Hindu: **5** SUTRA
Aphrodite: 5 VENUS
  Beloved of: **6** ADONIS
  domain: **4** LOVE
  Lover of: **4** ARES
  Son of: **4** EROS
Apia
  is its capital: **5** SAMOA
Apiarist
  hazard: **8** BEESTING
Apiary: 4 HIVE
  resident: **3** BEE
Apiece: 3 PER **4** EACH
  ~, in scores: **3** ALL
A ___ pittance: 4 MERE
"A ___ plan, a canal ...": 4 MANA
Aplenty: 6 GALORE
  ~, old-style: **4** ENOW
Aplomb: 5 POISE
Apocalypse: 4 DOOM
"Apocalypse Now"
  setting: **3** NAM
Apocrypha
  archangel: **5** URIEL
  book: **5** TOBIT

character: 3 BEL
Apollo
  approval: 3 AOK
  astronaut Slayton: 4 DEKE
  birthplace: 5 DELOS
  destination: 4 MOON
  instrument: 4 LYRE
  launcher: 4 NASA
  Mother of: 4 LETO
  Nymph loved by: 6 DAPHNE
  or Ares: 3 GOD 5 DEITY
  path: 5 ORBIT
  Sister of: 7 ARTEMIS
  Son of: 3 ION
  twin: 7 ARTEMIS
  vehicle: 3 LEM
Apollo 11
  destination: 4 MOON
  lunar module: 5 EAGLE
  name: 4 NEIL
Apollo 13
  astronaut: 6 LOVELL
"Apollo 13"
  actor Gary: 6 SINISE
  actor Joe: 5 SPANO
  director Howard: 3 RON
Apollo 15
  astronaut James: 5 IRWIN
Apolo Anton ___
  Speed skater: 4 OHNO
Apology
  Brief: 5 SORRY
  Cause for an: 4 BUMP
  preceder: 4 OOPS
  Start of an: 3 MEA
Apostate: 8 RENEGADE
Apostle
  Brother of ~ Andrew:
    7 STPETER
  Epistle: 4 PAUL
Apostles
  One of the: 4 LUKE PAUL
    5 JUDAS PETER
"Apostles, The"
  composer: 5 ELGAR
Apostles' ___: 5 CREED
Apothecary
  weight: 4 DRAM
Apotheosis: 5 IDEAL 7 EPITOME

"... ___ a pound": 5 INFOR
"A pox upon thee!": 3 FIE
App.
  Job ~ no.: 3 SSN
Appalachian Trail
  Enjoy the: 4 HIKE
  terminus: 5 MAINE
Appalled: 6 AGHAST
Appaloosa
  Infant: 4 FOAL
Apparatus: 3 RIG 4 GEAR UNIT
    7 MACHINE
  Drilling: 6 OILRIG
  Gymnast's: 5 HORSE
  Lifting: 5 HOIST
  Playground: 5 SLIDE 6 SEESAW
  Weaving: 4 LOOM
Apparel: 4 GARB 5 DRESS
    7 RAIMENT
  Like some holiday: 3 GAY
  Mass: 3 ALB
Apparent: 5 OVERT
  Air: 4 SMOG
  Become ~ to: 6 DAWNON
  With no hair: 4 BALD
Apparently
  are: 4 SEEM
"Apparently": 6 SOISEE
Apparition: 5 GHOST 6 SPIRIT
    WRAITH 7 SPECTER
    8 PHANTASM
Appeal: 3 ASK 4 PLEA 5 CHARM
  Kind of: 3 SEX 4 SNOB
  Lose: 8 WEARTHIN
  Sex: 5 OOMPH
  strongly to: 5 TEMPT
  ___ appeal: 4 SNOB
Appealing: 4 CUTE SEXY
    5 SUING
Appear: 3 ACT 4 **SEEM**
    6 SHOWUP TURNUP
  dramatically: 4 LOOM
  gradually: 6 FADEIN
  suddenly: 5 ERUPT POPUP
Appearance: 3 AIR 4 LOOK **MIEN**
    5 GUISE 6 ASPECT VISAGE
  Brief: 5 CAMEO
  First: 5 DEBUT ONSET
  Make an: 4 COME SHOW

6 SHOWUP
Plate: 5 ATBAT
TV: 6 AIRING
Appeared: 4 CAME 5 AROSE
Appearing
live: 8 INPERSON
Appease: 4 CALM 7 PLACATE
fully: 4 SATE
Appellation: 4 NAME
Append: 3 ADD 5 ADDON AFFIX
  TAGON 6 TACKON
Appendage
Grain: 6 ARISTA
Grass: 3 AWN
Neural: 4 AXON
Appendages
Winglike: 4 ALAE
Appendectomy
evidence: 4 SCAR
Appendices: 7 ADDENDA
"___ appétit!": 3 BON
Appetite: 3 YEN
arouser: 5 AROMA
Stimulate an: 4 WHET
Appetizer
Chinese: 7 EGGROLL
French: 4 PATE
Italian ~ plates: 9 ANTIPASTI
Luau ~ array: 11 PUPUPLATTER
Mexican: 5 NACHO
Spanish: 4 TAPA
Appetizing: 5 TASTY 6 SAVORY
___ Appia: 3 VIA
Applaud: 4 CLAP 6 PRAISE
  7 CLAPFOR
(for): 4 ROOT
Applause: 4 HAND
Acknowledge: 3 BOW
  8 TAKEABOW
Round of: 4 HAND
Apple: 4 POME TREE
acid: 5 MALIC
alternative: 3 IBM
Apple's: 4 LOGO
application, once: 4 ALAR
Autumn: 6 RUSSET
Banned ~ spray: 4 **ALAR**
center: 4 CORE
coating: 7 CARAMEL

cofounder: 4 JOBS
Colorful: 4 IMAC
computer: 4 IMAC
drink: 5 CIDER
eater: 3 EVE
gadget: 5 CORER PARER
Go after an: 3 BOB
leftover: 4 CORE
Love: 6 TOMATO
MP3 player by: 4 IPOD
offering: 3 MAC 4 IMAC
pesticide: 4 ALAR
picker: 3 EVE
polisher: 5 TOADY
Prepare an: 4 CORE
product: 3 MAC 4 IMAC IPOD
  5 CIDER IBOOK
Singer: 5 FIONA
Skin an: 4 PARE
spray: 4 ALAR
Translucent: 4 IMAC
variety: 3 MAC 4 IMAC ROME
  6 RUSSET 7 WINESAP
Winter: 6 RUSSET
___ apple: 5 ADAMS
Appleby, Inspector
creator: 5 INNES
Applegate, Christina
sitcom: 5 JESSE
Apple of Discord
thrower: 4 ERIS
Apple pie
In ~ order: 4 **NEAT** TIDY
Like: 8 AMERICAN
order: 7 ALAMODE
pro: 3 MOM
Apples
Like some: 4 TART
Applesauce
maker: 5 MOTTS
Appleseed, Johnny
real surname: 7 CHAPMAN
Appliance
designation: 4 ACDC
Kitchen: 4 OVEN 5 RANGE
  STOVE 6 FRIDGE
Laundry: 5 DRYER
maker: 5 **AMANA**
on a board: 4 IRON

that sucks: **6** VACUUM
~, for short: **3** VAC
Applicable: 7 INFORCE
Applicant
  goal: **3** JOB
Applicants
  Coll.: **3** SRS
Application: 3 <u>USE</u> **5** USAGE
  Absorbent: **4** TALC
  After-bath: **4** TALC **6** TALCUM
  Apple: **4** ALAR
  Bow: **5** ROSIN
  College ~ part: **5** ESSAY
  Cut: **6** IODINE
  datum: **3** AGE SEX SSN **4** NAME
  Light: **3** DAB
  Lip: **4** BALM **5** GLOSS LINER
  Salon: **3** DYE GEL
  Soothing: **4** TALC
  Submit an: **6** SENDIN
Applier
  Pressure: **4** PEER
Appliqué: 5 SEWON
Apply: 3 USE **5** EXERT LAYON
    RUBON
  a basecoat to: **5** PRIME
  balm to: **6** SOOTHE
  crudely: **4** DAUB
  gently: **3** DAB
  haphazardly: **6** SLAPON
  macadam to: **4** PAVE
  oil to: **6** ANOINT
  spin to: **4** SKEW
  turf to: **3** SOD
Appoint: 4 NAME **6** ORDAIN
Appointee
  Pres.: **3** AMB **4** SECY
Appointment: 4 DATE POST
Appointments: 5 DECOR
Appomattox
  general: **3** LEE
Apportion: 4 METE **5** ALLOT
    7 PRORATE
  ~, with "out": **4** METE
Appraisal
  Nasal: **5** AROMA
Appraise: 4 RATE **6** ASSESS
    7 VALUATE
Appraiser: 6 VALUER

Appreciate: 3 GET **5** SAVOR
    VALUE
Appreciation
  Damsel's cry of: **6** MYHERO
  Express ~ to: **5** THANK
  Show: **4** CLAP
Apprehend: 3 BAG NAB **4** NAIL
    6 COLLAR
Apprehension: 4 FEAR **5** ALARM
    ANGST DREAD **6** UNEASE
Apprehensive: 5 ANTSY LEERY
    6 UNEASY
  feeling: **5** ANGST
Apprentice: 3 CUB **4** TYRO
    5 TUTEE **6** INTERN
    7 LEARNER TRAINEE
Apprised: 5 AWARE
  of: **4** INON
Approach: 4 COME NEAR PATH
    6 GOUPTO **7** CLOSEIN
  for a loan: **5** HITUP
  Means of: **6** ACCESS AVENUE
  midnight: **5** LATEN
  sneakily: **7** CREEPUP
  Special: **5** ANGLE
  the runway: **4** TAXI
  ~, with "for": **4** MAKE
Approaching: 4 NEAR NIGH
    6 ALMOST NEARTO
  the hour: **5** TENTO
Appropriate: 3 <u>APT</u> DUE FIT
    4 GRAB TAKE **5** ALLOT
    ANNEX COOPT RIGHT
    SEIZE STEAL SWIPE
    USURP **6** ASSUME SEEMLY
    SUITED
  Deem: **6** <u>**SEEFIT**</u>
  Most: **6** NICEST
  Not: **5** INAPT
  What a family film is ~ for:
    7 ALLAGES
Appropriating: 6 TAKING
Approval: 3 YES **5** SAYSO
    6 ASSENT **7** GOAHEAD
  Apollo: **3** AOK
  Express: **4** CLAP
  Final: **5** SAYSO
  Give: **4** OKAY
  Medicine ~ agcy.: **3** FDA

Quick ~ (abbr.): **4** INIT
Shout of: **3** OLE
Sign of: **3** **NOD**
Stamp of: **4** USDA
Approvals: 3 OKS **5** YESES
    6 YESSES
Approve: 4 OKAY **6** RATIFY
Approved: 3 OKD **4** OKED
  Generally: **8** ORTHODOX
Approves: 3 **OKS**
Approving
  cry: **3** OLE
Approx.: 3 EST
Approximately: 3 SAY **4** **ORSO**
    SOME **5** ABOUT CIRCA
Approximation
  Sched.: **3** ETA ETD
  suffix: **3** ISH
  Words of: **4** ORSO
Appt.
  book lines: **3** HRS
  calendar item: **3** MTG
APR
  Part of: **3** PCT **4** RATE
Apr.
  addressee: **3** **IRS**
  Busy one in: **3** **CPA**
Après-ski
  drink: **5** COCOA
April
  forecast: **4** RAIN
  honoree: **4** FOOL
  Many an ~ baby: **5** ARIES
  payment: **3** TAX
  ~, May, and June, to Daisy:
    6 NIECES
April 1
  victim: **4** FOOL
April 13: 4 IDES
April 15
  addressee: **3** IRS
April 22
  saint: **6** ANSELM
"April Love"
  composer Sammy: **4** FAIN
  singer: **5** BOONE
Apropos
  of: **4** ASTO INRE
  ___ apso (dog): **5** LHASA

Apt: 6 LIABLE LIKELY
  name for a cook: **3** STU
  to pry: **4** NOSY
Apt.
  coolers: **3** ACS
  divisions: **3** RMS
  feature: **3** EIK
  features: **3** BRS
  part: **4** BDRM
Apteryx australis: 4 KIWI
Aptitude: 4 BENT GIFT **5** KNACK
    SKILL **6** TALENT
  Musical: **3** EAR
Aptiva
  maker: **3** IBM
Aqua
  Color close to: **4** TEAL
  suffix: **4** NAUT
Aqua ___: 4 PURA **5** REGIA VITAE
Aqua-___: 4 LUNG
Aquamarine: 7 SEABLUE
Aquanaut
  base: **6** SEALAB
Aquarium: 4 TANK
  attraction: **8** PORPOISE
  bubbler: **7** AERATOR
  buildup: **5** ALGAE
  fish: **4** NEON **5** DANIO GUPPY
    TETRA **6** WRASSE
    9 NEONTETRA
  performer: **4** SEAL
  problem: **5** ALGAE
Aquarius
  Words with: **5** AGEOF
"Aquarius"
  musical: **4** HAIR
Aquatic
  bird: **4** COOT GULL TERN
  mammal: **4** SEAL **5** **OTTER**
  nymph: **5** NAIAD
  organisms: **5** ALGAE
  plant: **4** ALGA
Aquatint
  Make an: **4** ETCH
Aqua Velva
  rival: **4** AFTA
Aqueduct
  action: **3** BET
Aqueduct of Sylvius: 4 ITER

Aqueduct Racetrack
  nickname: 4 BIGA
Aquila
  Brightest star in: 6 ALTAIR
Aquiline
  weapon: 5 TALON
Aquitaine
  Home of ancient: 4 GAUL
  queen: 7 ELEANOR
Aquitania
  land: 4 GAUL
Arab: 5 HORSE 6 SEMITE
  Certain: 6 YEMENI
  ender: 5 ESQUE
  land: 7 EMIRATE
  leader: 4 EMIR 5 AMEER EMEER
    SHEIK
  lute: 3 OUD
  name part: 3 IBN
  Young: 4 FOAL
"Arabesque"
  actress: 5 LOREN
  ___ **Arabia:** 5 SAUDI
Arabian
  capital: 4 SANA
  Certain: 5 OMANI SAUDI
  cloak: 8 BURNOOSE
  gulf: 4 ADEN
  prince: 4 EMIR
  sailing vessel: 4 DHOW
  sultanate: 4 **OMAN**
"Arabian Nights"
  bird: 3 ROC
  group: 5 HAREM
  hero: 7 ALIBABA
Arabian Peninsula
  capital: 4 SANA
  land: 4 OMAN
Arabian Sea
  gulf: 4 ADEN
  nation: 4 OMAN
Arabic
  Gum: 6 ACACIA
  letter: 4 ALIF
  "reading": 5 KORAN
  "son of": 3 IBN
Arab League
  member: 3 PLO 4 IRAQ OMAN
    5 QATAR SYRIA YEMEN

Arachnid
  Tiny: 4 MITE
Arachnophobia: 4 FEAR
Arafat: 4 ARAB
  birthplace: 5 CAIRO
  gp.: 3 **PLO**
  of the PLO: 5 YASIR
    6 YASSER
Arafat, Yasir
  gp.: 3 PLO
Aragón
  Info: Spanish cue
  Are, in: 4 ESTA
  River of: 4 **EBRO**
Aral: 3 SEA
Aramis
  Athos, to: 3 AMI
  friend: 5 ATHOS
Arapaho: 5 TRIBE
  foe: 3 UTE
Ararat
  lander: 3 ARK 4 NOAH
"A rat!": 3 EEK
Arbiter: 3 REF UMP 6 UMPIRE
    7 REFEREE
Arbitrarily
  fine: 6 AMERCE
Arbitrary
  decree: 4 FIAT
Arbor
  abode: 4 NEST
Arbor Day
  honoree: 4 TREE
Arboreal
  abode: 4 NEST
  ape: 5 ORANG
  croaker: 8 TREETOAD
  lizard: 6 IGUANA
Arboretum
  item: 4 TREE
Arborist
  specimen: 4 TREE
  ___ **Arbor, Michigan:** 3 ANN
Arbuckle
  Like ~ films: 6 SILENT
Arbuckle, Jon
  dog: 4 **ODIE**
Arbus
  Photographer: 5 DIANE

Arc
  Hit in a high: 3 LOB
  lamp gas: 5 XENON
  on a score: 4 SLUR
Arcade
  attraction: 4 GAME 6 PACMAN
  coin: 5 TOKEN
  flub: 4 TILT
  name: 4 SEGA 5 ATARI
Arcade game: 6 TETRIS
  maker: 5 ATARI
  starter: 4 SKEE
Arcane: 8 ESOTERIC
Arcangelo
  Violinist: 7 CORELLI
  ___ Arc, Arkansas: 3 DES
Arcaro
  Jockey: 5 EDDIE
Arc de Triomphe
  site: 5 PARIS
Arch: 3 SLY 4 SPAN 6 IRONIC
  Kind of: 4 OGEE
  locale: 6 INSTEP
  Pointed: 4 OGEE 5 OGIVE
  type: 4 OGEE 6 GOTHIC
Arch.
  Kin of: 3 OBS
Archaeological
  find: 4 BONE TOMB 5 RELIC
      SHARD
  site: 3 DIG 4 RUIN
Archaeologist
  find: 4 BONE TOMB 5 RELIC
      SHARD
Archaeology
  site: 3 DIG
Archaic
  preposition: 3 ERE
  verb ending: 3 ETH
Archangel
  Apocryphal: 5 URIEL
Archbishop
  New York ~ before O'Connor:
      5 COOKE
  of New York: 4 EGAN
"Archduke ___": 4 TRIO
Archenemy: 7 NEMESIS
Archer: 5 AIMER
  Actress: 4 **ANNE**

  asset: 3 AIM
  bow wood: 3 YEW
  item: 3 BOW
  MacDonald's gumshoe: 3 LEW
  of myth: 4 AMOR EROS
  ~ William: 4 TELL
Arches National Park
  City near: 4 MOAB
  locale: 4 UTAH
Archibald
  of basketball: 4 **NATE**
  Watergate prosecutor: 3 COX
Archie: 4 TEEN
  admonition to Edith: 6 STIFLE
  Chum of: 5 MOOSE
  Mike, to: 5 INLAW
  Wife of: 5 EDITH
Archies, The
  1969 ~ hit: 10 SUGARSUGAR
Archilochus
  work: 5 EPODE
Archimedean
  tool: 5 LEVER
Archimedes
  cry: 6 EUREKA
Archipelago
  Pacific: 4 FIJI
  part: 4 ISLE 6 ISLAND
  unit (abbr.): 3 ISL
Architect
  addition: 3 ELL 5 ANNEX
  Kennedy Library: 5 **IMPEI**
  St. Louis bridge: 4 EADS
  St. Paul's: 4 **WREN**
  ~ Alvar: 5 AALTO
  ~ Christopher: 4 WREN
  ~ I.M.: 3 **PEI**
  ~ Jones: 5 INIGO
  ~ Lin: 4 MAYA
  ~ Maya: 3 LIN
  ~ Richard: 5 MEIER
  ~ Saarinen: 4 **EERO** 5 ELIEL
  ~ Sir Basil: 6 SPENCE
Architectural
  addition: 3 ELL 5 ANNEX
  curve: 4 OGEE
  detail: 4 SPEC
  drawing: 4 PLAN
  order: 5 DORIC IONIC

Ornamental ~ style: **6** ROCOCO
pier: **4** ANTA
sidepiece: **4** JAMB
style: **5** DORIC IONIC TUDOR
   6 GOTHIC
supporter: **6** LINTEL
wing: **3** ELL
Architecture
First name in: **4 EERO 5** ELIEL
Archives
Put in the: **4** FILE
Archrival: 7 NEMESIS
Arcing
shot: **3 LOB**
Arco ___ : 5 ARENA
Arctic: 5 GELID OCEAN POLAR
aircraft: **8** SKIPLANE
assistant: **3** ELF
barker: **4** SEAL
bird: **3** AUK **4** SKUA TERN
cover: **8** ICESHEET
dweller: **4** LAPP **5** INUIT
explorer John: **3** RAE
explorer Robert: **5** PERRY
floater: **4** BERG
ice: **4** FLOE
jacket: **5** PARKA **6** ANORAK
plain: **6** TUNDRA
sight: **4** FLOE
transport: **4** SLED **6** SLEDGE
Arctic Ocean
arm: **7** KARASEA
hazard: **4** BERG
sheet: **7** ICEFLOE
Arcturus: 4 STAR **5** KSTAR
Arden
Actress: **3 EVE**
Fictional: **5** ENOCH
"___ Arden": **5** ENOCH
Ardennes
river: **4** OISE
Ardent: 4 AVID **5** AFIRE EAGER
   7 AMATIVE DEVOTED
Ardor: 4 ELAN ZEAL
Arduous
journey: **4 TREK**
Are: 5 EXIST
Apparently: **4** SEEM
in the past: **4** WERE

~, in French: **4** ERES
~, in Spanish: **4 ESTA**
Area: 4 ZONE **6** SECTOR SPHERE
away from the battle: **4** REAR
Dark: **5** UMBRA
Depressed: **6** GHETTO
Developing: **4** WOMB
   8 DARKROOM
Grassy: **3** LEA
Low-lying: **4 VALE 5** SWALE
Marshy: **3** FEN
meas.: **4** SQIN
of land: **5** TRACT
of London: **7** EASTEND
of South Africa: **5** NATAL
Outlying: **5** EXURB
Recessed: **4** APSE **5** NICHE
Run-down: **4** SLUM
Swampy: **4** MIRE
Area ___ : 3 RUG **4** CODE
Area code
preceder: **3** ONE
Areas
Fertile: **5** OASES
Arena
Asian: **3** NAM
DDE: **3** ETO
Detroit: **4** COBO
Former Atlanta: **4 OMNI**
Jousting: **4** LIST
Kentucky: **4** RUPP
level: **4** TIER
NYC: **3** MSG
Sacramento: **4 ARCO**
San Antonio: **9** ALAMODOME
shout: **3** OLE RAH
WWII: **3 ETO**
Arenas: 6 STADIA
___ Arenas: 5 PUNTA
Arendt
Author: **6** HANNAH
"Are not!"
retort: **4** AMSO **5** AMTOO
Arens
of Israel: **5** MOSHE
"Aren't ___ lucky one!": 4 ITHE
"Aren't ___ pair?": 3 WEA
Ares: 3 GOD
area: **3** WAR

Mother of: **4 HERA**
Sister of: **4 ERIS**
Aretha
  genre: **4 SOUL**
"Are we there ___?": 3 YET
"Are you a man ___ mouse?":
    3 ORA
"Are you calling me ___?":
    5 ALIAR
"Are you coming ___ not?":
    4 INOR
"Are you looking ___?": 4 ATME
"Are you ___ out?": 4 INOR
"Are you some kind of ___?":
    4 ANUT
Arg.
  neighbor: **3 URU**
Argentina
  Info: Spanish cue
  Are, in: **4 ESTA**
  Big name in: **5 PERON**
  Eva of: **5 PERON**
  Hot time in: **5 ENERO**
  Musical set in: **5 EVITA**
  Perón of: **3 EVA**
Argentine
  Info: Spanish cue
  article: **3 LAS**
  aunt: **3 TIA**
  dance: **5 TANGO**
  plain: **5 PAMPA**
Argon: 3 GAS 7 RAREGAS
  Like: **5 INERT**
"Argonautica"
  character: **5 MEDEA**
Argonne Forest
  river: **5 AISNE**
Arguable: 4 MOOT
Argue: 5 PLEAD 6 DEBATE
  against: **7 CONTEST**
  Point to: **3 NIT**
Argued: 4 PLED
Argues: 7 HASAROW
    8 HASWORDS
Arguing: 4 ATIT
Argument: 3 ROW 4 FLAP
    5 RUNIN SETTO
    7 DISPUTE
  Brief: **5 SETTO**

Like a sound: **7 TENABLE**
Minor: **4 SPAT**
retort: **5 ISTOO**
Arguments
  Like some: **4 ORAL 6 HEATED**
  Some: **3 PRO**
Argus
  feature: **4 EYES**
Argus-eyed: 5 ALERT
Argyle: 4 SOCK
Argyles: 4 HOSE
Aria: 4 SOLO
  area: **5 OPERA**
  Perform an: **4 SING**
  singer: **4 DIVA**
  Verdi: **5 ERITU**
Arias: 4 SOLI 5 SOLOS
Arid: 3 DRY 4 SERE 7 STERILE
  expanse: **6 SAHARA**
  to the max: **7 SAHARAN**
Ariel
  of Israel: **6 SHARON**
  predecessor: **4 EHUD**
Aries: 3 CAR RAM 4 AUTO
    6 THERAM
Arise: 4 DAWN STEM 5 OCCUR
    6 COMEUP CROPUP
  (from): **4 STEM**
  without warning: **5 POPUP**
Arista
  or Epic: **5 LABEL**
Aristocracy: 5 ELITE 6 GENTRY
    7 PEERAGE
Aristocrat: 5 NOBLE
    9 BLUEBLOOD
  of old: **5 THANE**
Aristocratic: 5 ELITE NOBLE
Aristophanes
  comedy, with "The": **5 WASPS**
Aristotle
  subject: **5 LOGIC 6 ETHICS**
  Teacher of: **5 PLATO**
  walkway: **4 STOA**
  ~, to Alexander the Great:
    5 TUTOR
Arithmetic
  Do basic: **3 ADD**
  homework: **4 SUMS**
  Make, in: **3 ARE**

Ariz.
  clock setting: 3 MST
  neighbor: 3 NEV 4 NMEX
    5 CALIF
Arizona
  building block: 5 ADOBE
  city: 4 **MESA** YUMA 5 TEMPE
    7 NOGALES
  Former ~ congressman: 5 UDALL
  Morris of: 5 UDALL
  necktie: 4 BOLO
  neighbor: 6 SONORA
  river: 4 **GILA**
  sight: 4 MESA
  symbol: 7 SAGUARO
  tourist locale: 6 SEDONA
  ~ Indian: 4 **HOPI** PIMA
    6 NAVAHO NAVAJO
  ___ **Arizona:** 3 USS
Arizona State
  home: 5 TEMPE
Ark
  berth: 6 ARARAT
  builder: 4 **NOAH**
  contents: 5 TORAH 6 TORAHS
  Holy ~ home: 4 SHUL
  measure: 5 CUBIT
  units: 4 TWOS 5 PAIRS
Ark.
  neighbor: 4 OKLA
  ___ **Ark:** 5 NOAHS
Arkansas
  capital: 10 LITTLEROCK
  City on the: 5 TULSA
  footballer: 9 RAZORBACK
  Former ~ senator:
    11 DALEBUMPERS
  resort: 10 HOTSPRINGS
Arkin
  1969 ~ film: 4 POPI
  Actor: 4 ADAM **ALAN**
Arledge
  Late TV exec: 5 **ROONE**
Arlene
  Actress: 4 DAHL
Arles
  Info: French cue
  After, in: 5 APRES
  agreement: 3 OUI

A, in: 3 UNE
Are, in: 4 ETES
article: 3 LES UNE
river: 5 RHONE
Arlington
  landmark: 8 PENTAGON
  melody: 4 TAPS
Arlo
  Where ~ ate: 6 ALICES
Arm: 4 COVE LIMB 5 INLET
  6 WEAPON
  art: 6 TATTOO
  bone: 4 **ULNA**
  bones: 5 RADII ULNAE ULNAS
    6 HUMERI
  Broken ~ holder: 5 SLING
  Futuristic: 6 RAYGUN
  holder: 6 SLEEVE
  joint: 5 ELBOW
  Mediterranean: 6 AEGEAN
  muscle: 5 BICEP 6 BICEPS
  Of an ~ bone: 5 ULNAR
  of the sea: 5 INLET
  Shot in the: 4 HYPO 5 BOOST
  Tone ~ insert: 6 NEEDLE
  U.N.: 3 ILO
  ~, in French: 4 BRAS
Armada: 5 FLEET
Armageddon: 3 END 4 DOOM
  nation: 3 GOG 5 MAGOG
"Armageddon"
  actress Tyler: 3 LIV
  author: 4 URIS
Armand
  Actor: 7 ASSANTE
Armbone: 4 ULNA
Armchair
  quarterback channel: 4 ESPN
Armed
  conflict: 3 **WAR**
Armed Forces Day
  month: 3 MAY
Armenia
  capital: 7 YEREVAN
  capital, old-style: 6 ERIVAN
  neighbor: 4 IRAN
  peak: 6 ARARAT
  ~, formerly (abbr.): 3 SSR
Armistice: 5 TRUCE

Armistice Day
  mo.: 3 NOV
Armless
  couch: 5 DIVAN
Armor
  Fish: 5 SCALE
  Flexible: 9 CHAINMAIL
  plate: 6 TUILLE
  trouble: 5 CHINK
  Type of: 4 MAIL
Armor-busting
  weapon: 4 MACE
Armored
  goddess: 6 ATHENA
  vehicle: 4 TANK
Armory
  supply: 4 AMMO
Armour
  Parent company of: 4 DIAL
Armpit: 6 AXILLA
Armrest: 5 SLING
Arms
  Commando: 4 UZIS
  Comrade in: 4 ALLY
  Doll with: 5 GIJOE
  In the ~ of Morpheus: 6 ASLEEP
  Israeli: 4 UZIS
  Like some: 6 AKIMBO
  Org. with many: 3 NRA
  Supply of: 7 ARSENAL
  Up in: 5 IRATE
  ___ arms: 4 UPIN
Armstrong
  Actress: 4 BESS
  Astronaut: 4 **NEIL**
  Cyclist: 5 LANCE
  nickname: 7 SATCHMO
  of football: 4 OTIS
Arm-twisting: 6 DURESS
  Do some: 4 URGE 6 COERCE
Army
  address: 3 SIR
  attack helicopter: 5 COBRA
  base: 4 FORT
  bed: 3 COT
  brass: 5 BUGLE
  command: 6 ATEASE
  cops: 3 MPS
  corpsman: 5 MEDIC

Golfer with an: 5 **ARNIE**
group: 4 UNIT
Healthy, to the: 4 ONEA
helicopter: 4 HUEY 6 APACHE
Join the: 6 ENLIST
Kind of: 6 ONEMAN
leader: 5 ARNIE
meal: 4 MESS
member: 3 ANT
mule: 6 MASCOT
outfit: 4 UNIT
post: 4 BASE FORT
surgeon Walter: 4 REED
survey: 5 RECON
training center: 5 FTLEE
training loc.: 3 OCS
U.S. ~ medal: 3 DSC
vehicle: 4 JEEP TANK
~ E-3: 3 PFC
~ E-5: 3 NCO
~ NCO: 3 SGT 4 SSGT
~ VIP: 3 COL MAJ
___ Army: 6 ARNIES
Army of the Potomac
  leader: 5 MEADE
Army-style
  Polish: 9 SPITSHINE
Arnaz
  and Ball studio: 6 DESILU
  Entertainer: 4 DESI
Arnhem
  City near: 3 EDE
Arno
  Actor: 3 SIG
  Ancient land between ~ and
    Tiber: 7 ETRURIA
  Cartoonist: 5 PETER
  City on the: 4 PISA
Arnold
  Actor: 3 TOM
  co-conspirator: 5 ANDRE
  Comic: 5 STANG
  Country singer: 4 EDDY
  General: 3 HAP
  Wife of: 5 MARIA
"___ a Rock": 3 IAM
A-Rod
  first name: 4 ALEX
"___ a roll!": 4 IMON

Aroma: 4 NOSE **ODOR 5** SCENT
SMELL
Travel, like an: **4** WAFT
~, to a Brit: **5** ODOUR
Aromatic: 8 REDOLENT
compound: **5** **ESTER**
herb: **5** ANISE BASIL CUMIN
ointment: **4** BALM NARD
wood: **5** CEDAR
Arose: 5 GOTUP STOOD
6 CAMEUP
Around: 4 NEAR ORSO **5** ABOUT
CIRCA
Carry: **4** TOTE
Crowd: **3** MOB
Get: **4** ROVE **5** AVOID ELUDE
EVADE SKIRT
Go: **4** SPIN **5** AVOID ORBIT
SKIRT **6** BYPASS ROTATE
Going: **7** INORBIT
Hang: **4** LOLL **STAY** WAIT
6 LINGER LOITER
It goes: **7** ORBITER
Kid: **4** JEST JOSH
Knock: **4** ROAM
Nosed: **5** PRIED
Once: **3** LAP **5** ORBIT
Poke: **4** NOSE **5** SNOOP
Spread: **5** STREW
Stick: **4** STAY
Swing: **4** SLUE
the 30th (abbr.): **3** EOM
Way: **5** ORBIT
**"___ Around" (Beach Boys hit):
4** IGET
Arouse: 4 STIR **6** AWAKEN
EXCITE FIREUP FOMENT
interest: **5** PIQUE
Arousing: 4 SEXY **6** EROTIC
Arp: 7 DADAIST
art: **4** **DADA**
contemporary: **5** ERNST
Dadaist: **4** JEAN
Arpel
of cosmetics: **6** ADRIEN
Arraignment
offering: **4** PLEA
Arrange: 3 SET **4** SORT **5** ORDER
SETUP **6** LAYOUT

by class: **6** ASSORT
hair: **4** DOUP
in order: **7** SERIATE
strategically: **6** DEPLOY
Arrangement: 4 PLAN **5** SETUP
Driving: **7** CARPOOL
Floral: **3** LEI **4** POSY **5** SPRAY
Hair: **4** COIF
Kind of: **6** FLORAL
Orderly: **5** ARRAY
Arrangements
Make table: **7** PRESEAT
Array: 4 ROBE **5** ORDER
6 ATTIRE
Arrears: 4 DEBT
Be in: **3** OWE
In: **4** LATE
Arrest: 3 **NAB** **4** BUST STOP
5 RUNIN **6** COLLAR
HAULIN
Arrested: 5 **RANIN**
Arrid
rival: **3** BAN **4** SURE
target: **4** ODOR
Arrival: 6 ADVENT
Early: **6** REDEYE **7** PREEMIE
JFK: **3** SST
New: **6** EMIGRE
Recent: **6** NEWKID
8 NEWCOMER
Spring: **5** ARIES
Stable: **4** FOAL
Winter: **6** PISCES
Arrive: 4 COME LAND **5** GETIN
6 PULLIN SHOWUP
at: **5** GETTO REACH
6 ATTAIN
by air: **5** FLYIN
Expected to: **3** DUE
jauntily: **8** BREEZEIN
rapidly: **6** POURIN
Arrived: 4 **CAME 5** GOTIN
6 MADEIT
in time for: **4** MADE
"Arrivederci, ___": 4 ROMA
Arrogance: 6 HUBRIS
7 HAUTEUR
Arrogant
one: **4** SNOB

Arrow
competitor: 4 IZOD
poison: 4 INEE 6 CURARE
shooter: 3 BOW 4 EROS
stopper: 5 ARMOR
Words on an: 6 ONEWAY

Arrow-shaped
Plant with ~ leaves: 5 CALLA

Arrowsmith
Wife of: 5 LEORA

Arroz con ___ : 5 POLLO

Arroz ___ pollo: 3 CON

"Ars Amatoria"
About when ~ was written:
5 ONEBC
poet: 4 **OVID**

Arsenal
contents: 4 AMMO
Part of a nuclear: 4 ICBM
Update the: 5 REARM

Arsene
Gentleman burglar: 5 LUPIN

Arsenic: 6 POISON
user, perhaps: 8 POISONER

"Arsenic and Old Lace"
director: 5 CAPRA

"Ars longa, ___ brevis": 4 VITA

Arson: 6 FELONY
evidence: 5 ASHES

Arsonist: 5 FELON TORCH

"Ars Poetica"
poet: 6 HORACE

"Ars ___, vita brevis": 5 LONGA

Art
able to: 5 CANST
Body of: 5 TORSO
Cartoon: 5 ANIME
class: 5 GENRE
collectible: 3 CEL
colony of the Southwest:
4 **TAOS**
drawing: 5 SEPIA
follower: 4 DECO
gum: 6 ERASER
Italian ~ patron: 4 ESTE
Japanese: 7 ORIGAMI
Joan of: 4 MIRO
Kind of: 4 CAVE CLIP
Love of fine: 5 VIRTU

lover: 7 ESTHETE
major subj.: 4 ANAT
medium: 4 OILS 6 PASTEL
Modern: 3 ARE
Nihilistic: 4 DADA
of jazz: 5 TATUM
Paper: 7 ORIGAMI
photo: 5 SEPIA
print: 5 LITHO
songs: 6 LIEDER
stand: 5 EASEL
subject: 4 NUDE VASE 5 MODEL
TORSO
supporter: 5 EASEL
TV doc: 5 ULENE

Art ___ : 4 **DECO**

"Artaxerxes"
composer: 4 ARNE

Art Deco
designer: 4 **ERTE**

Artemis
Mother of: 4 LETO
slew him: 5 ORION
twin: 6 APOLLO
~, to the Romans: 5 DIANA

Arterial
trunk: 5 AORTA

Artery: 4 ROAD
Kind of: 5 ILIAC RENAL
Main: 5 **AORTA**
Of a main: 6 AORTIC

Artful: 3 SLY 4 WILY 6 CLEVER
dodge: 4 RUSE
dodger: 6 EVADER
tactic: 4 PLOY

Artful Dodger: 5 REESE

Art gallery: 5 SALON
London: 4 TATE
Manhattan ~ district: 4 SOHO

Artgum: 6 ERASER

Arthr-
suffix: 4 ITIC

Arthritis
prefix: 5 OSTEO

Arthroscopy
site: 4 KNEE

Arthur
Actress: 3 **BEA**
Author: 6 CLARKE

He beat ~ at the 1972 U.S. Open:
   4 ILIE
His real name was: 5 HARPO
of tennis: 4 **ASHE**
Arthur, Chester
   middle name: 4 ALAN
Arthur Conan ___ : 5 DOYLE
Arthur Gordon ___ : 3 PYM
Arthurian
   isle: 6 AVALON
   lady: 4 ENID
   locale: 7 ASTOLAT
   magician: 6 MERLIN
   paradise: 6 AVALON
   times: 4 YORE
Artichoke
   center: 5 HEART
   Jerusalem: 5 TUBER
Article: 4 ITEM
   addendum: 7 ENDNOTE
   Common: 3 **THE**
   French: 3 **LES** UNE
   German: 3 DAS **DER** EIN 4 EINE
   Italian: 3 GLI **UNA**
   lead-in: 8 DATELINE
   News: 4 ITEM
   of faith: 5 TENET
   Spanish: 3 LAS LOS **UNA** UNO
   supplement: 7 SIDEBAR
   Useful: 3 THE
Articulate: 3 SAY 5 UTTER
   6 FLUENT 7 ENOUNCE
Articulated: 4 SAID
Artie
   Clarinetist: 4 SHAW
   Ex of: 3 AVA 4 LANA
Artifact
   Ming: 4 VASE
   Religious: 4 ICON
Artifice: 4 RUSE WILE
Artificial: 4 FAUX 6 ERSATZ
   7 PLASTIC
   bait: 4 LURE
   leg: 5 STILT
   sweetener: 5 EQUAL
   tooth: 7 DENTURE
   waterway: 5 CANAL 6 SLUICE
Artillery
   burst: 5 SALVO

Artist
   apartment: 4 LOFT
   Art Deco: 4 **ERTE**
   cap: 5 BERET
   inspiration: 4 MUSE
   medium: 4 OILS
   One-named: 4 ERTE
   paint holder: 7 PALETTE
   pigment: 5 OCHER
   plaster: 5 GESSO
   prop: 5 EASEL
   stand: 5 EASEL
   studio: 7 ATELIER
   ~ Albrecht: 5 DURER
   ~ Guido: 4 RENI
   ~ Henri: 7 MATISSE
   ~ Jan: 5 STEEN
   ~ Joan: 4 MIRO
   ~ LeRoy: 6 NEIMAN
   ~ Mark: 6 ROTHKO
   ~ Max: 5 ERNST WEBER
   ~ Paul: 4 KLEE
   ~ Salvador: 4 DALI
Artistes
   wear them: 7 CRAVATS
Artistic
   category: 5 GENRE
   dynasty: 4 MING
   judgment: 5 TASTE
   Make an ~ impression: 4 ETCH
Artists
   Some: 7 ETCHERS
Artless
   one: 4 NAIF
Artlessness: 7 NAIVETE
"Art of Love, The"
   poet: 4 OVID
"Art of Loving, The"
   author: 5 FROMM
"Art of the Fugue"
   composer: 4 BACH
Artoo ___ : 5 DETOO
Art-rock
   British ~ combo: 3 XTC
Art Ross Trophy
   org.: 3 NHL
   Two-time ~ winner: 3 ORR
Arts
   partner: 8 SCIENCES

Artsy

90

Artsy
~ NYC area: 4 SOHO
Artsy-___: 7 CRAFTSY
Artwork
Religious: 5 PIETA
Arty
area: 7 BOHEMIA
~ NYC area: 4 SOHO
Aruba: 4 ISLE
Arugula
alternative: 8 ESCAROLE
Arum
family member: 4 TARO
lily: 5 CALLA
As: 3 QUA
a companion: 5 **ALONG**
a group: 7 ENMASSE
a joke: 5 INFUN
an alternative: 7 INSTEAD
a precaution: 6 INCASE
a result: 4 ERGO THUS
a rule: 9 INGENERAL
a substitute: 7 INSTEAD
a whole: 5 INALL 6 ENBLOC
expected: 4 DULY 5 ONCUE
far as: 4 **UPTO**
good as ever: 7 LIKENEW
it happens: 4 LIVE
located: 6 INSITU
many as: 4 UPTO
much: 6 NOLESS
much as you like: 5 AGOGO
of: 5 SINCE
of now: 6 TODATE
often as not: 9 ONAVERAGE
one: 6 UNITED
recently as: 4 ONLY
regards: 4 INRE
soon as: 4 ONCE
to: 4 INRE
well: 3 **TOO** 4 ALSO 6 TOBOOT
well as: 3 AND
we speak: 3 NOW
written: 3 SIC
yet: 5 SOFAR 6 ERENOW
you like it: 7 TOTASTE
A's
Former ~ player Sal: 5 BANDO
As ___: 5 ARULE

"As ___ and breathe!": 5 ILIVE
ASAP: 3 PDQ
in the ER: 4 STAT
Part of: 6 SOONAS
"As brisk as ___ in conversation":
4 ABEE
ASCAP
Part of: 3 SOC 4 AMER
rival: 3 **BMI**
Ascend: 4 RISE 5 ARISE CLIMB
Ascended: 4 ROSE 5 AROSE
RISEN 6 ARISEN
UPROSE
Ascent: 4 RISE
Ascetic
Ancient: 6 **ESSENE**
Hindu: 5 FAKIR
Ascot: 3 TIE
Ascribe: 6 IMPUTE
blame for: 5 PINON
to: 6 CREDIT
"... as devoid of rights as ___:
5 ABALE
"___ as directed": 3 USE
Asea
Assents: 4 AYES
Asgard
leader: 4 ODIN
prankster: 4 LOKI
"As Good As It Gets"
actor: 7 KINNEAR
11 GREGKINNEAR
studio: 7 TRISTAR
Ash: 4 TREE
Ashamed
Make: 5 ABASH
Ashcan School
painter: 6 SLOANE
Ashcroft
predecessor: 4 **RENO**
Ashe, Arthur
alma mater: 4 UCLA
Ashen: 3 WAN 4 GRAY PALE
5 PASTY
Turn: 4 PALE
Ashes
Don sackcloth and: 6 REPENT
holder: 3 URN
"___ Ashes": 7 ANGELAS

Ashe Stadium
  Ballpark near: 4 SHEA
  do-over: 3 LET
  event: 6 USOPEN
  org.: 4 USTA
"Ashes to Ashes"
  author Hoag: 4 TAMI
Ashley
  Actress: 4 JUDD 5 OLSEN
  Mom of: 5 NAOMI
  rival: 5 RHETT
  ~, to Mary-Kate: 4 TWIN
Ashore
  Go: 6 DEBARK
Ashram
  figure: 4 GURU
  visitor: 4 YOGI
Ashtabula
  lake: 4 **ERIE**
Ashtray
  item: 4 BUTT
Ashuelot
  City on the: 5 KEENE
Ash Wednesday
  start: 4 LENT
"Ash Wednesday"
  poet: 5 ELIOT
Ashworth
  Novelist: 5 ADELE
Asia
  About 25,000 square miles of:
      7 ARALSEA
  Inland sea of: 4 ARAL
  Turkey in: 8 ANATOLIA
  Western boundary of: 5 URALS
Asia Minor
  region: 5 **IONIA** 6 AEOLIA
Asian
  arena: 3 NAM
  border range: 4 URAL
  capital: 3 YEN 5 AMMAN DACCA
      HANOI KABUL LHASA
      SEOUL 6 TAIPEI TEHRAN
      7 JAKARTA
  carrier to Seoul: 3 KAL
  Central: 5 TATAR
  cuisine: 4 THAI
  desert: 4 GOBI
  destiny: 5 KARMA

festival: 3 TET
holiday: 3 **TET**
inland sea: 4 ARAL
language: 3 TAI 4 SHAN
nanny: 4 AMAH
nation: 4 LAOS 5 NEPAL
nursemaid: 4 **AMAH**
occasion: 3 TET
palm: 5 ARECA BETEL
peninsula: 5 KOREA MALAY
    6 ARABIA MALAYA
place-name suffix: 4 STAN
prefix: 3 EUR
republic: 4 IRAN LAOS
royal: 4 RANI
sash: 3 OBI
sea: 4 ARAL
secret society: 4 TONG
shrub: 5 HENNA
Southeast: 3 LAO 4 THAI VIET
tents: 5 YURTS
title: 3 AGA SRI
tongue: 4 THAI URDU
weight: 4 TAEL
Wild ~ dog: 5 DHOLE
~ New Year: 3 TET
Aside
  Brush: 5 SPURN
  Money set: 6 ESCROW
  Move: 5 SHUNT
  Put: 5 ALLOT 6 SHELVE
  Set: 4 SAVE 5 ALLOT
      8 RESERVED
  Sighed: 4 AHME
  Temporarily put: 5 ONICE
  Turn: 4 SNUB VEER 5 **AVERT**
      PARRY SHUNT 6 DIVERT
      7 DEFLECT
"As if!": 3 HAH NOT 4 IBET
      5 PSHAW
"As if ___!": 5 ICARE
"As if I care": 6 SOWHAT
"As I Lay Dying"
  father: 4 ANSE
Asimov
  Author: 5 ISAAC
  classic: 6 IROBOT
  genre: 5 SCIFI
Asinine: 4 DUMB 5 INANE

"As I ___ saying ...": 3 WAS
As it ___: 4 WERE
Ask: 4 POSE 5 QUERY 7 INQUIRE REQUEST
  for: 3 BEG 4 SEEK 7 SOLICIT
  for a hand: 7 PROPOSE
  for aid: 6 TURNTO
  for an opinion: 4 POLL
  for donations: 10 PASSTHEHAT
  for ID: 4 CARD
  for money: 5 HITUP
  More than just: 6 DEMAND
  ___ A Sketch: 4 ETCH
Asking
  For the: 4 FREE
ASL
  Use: 4 SIGN
Aslan: 4 LION
Asleep
  Be half: 6 DROWSE
  Fall: 5 CRASH
  Sound: 5 SNORE
Asmara
  is its capital: 7 ERITREA
Asner
  and others: 3 **EDS**
  array: 5 EMMYS
  title role: 8 LOUGRANT
"As ___ on TV!": 4 SEEN
  ___ a sour note: 5 ENDON
Asparagus
  unit: 5 **SPEAR**
ASPCA
  Part of: 3 SOC
Aspect: 4 AURA VIEW 5 ANGLE **FACET** PHASE 6 REGARD
  Harmful: 4 EVIL
  Negative: 3 CON
  Positive: 3 PRO 6 UPSIDE
Aspen: 4 TREE
  abode: 6 CHALET
  alternative: 4 VAIL 5 STOWE
  attire: 7 SKISUIT
  Do: 3 SKI
  feature: 6 SKITOW
  visitor: 5 SKIER
Asperity: 5 RIGOR
Aspersion: 4 SLUR
Asphalt: 4 PAVE

Aspin
  Former defense secretary: 3 LES
Aspiration: 3 AIM 4 HOPE 5 DREAM
  Common: 5 AITCH
Aspirin
  allotment: 4 DOSE
  maker: 5 BAYER
  Need an: 4 ACHE
  Open an ~ bottle: 5 UNCAP
  target: 4 ACHE 8 HEADACHE
  unit: 4 PILL
Aspiring
  atty. exam: 4 **LSAT**
  doc exam (abbr.): 4 MCAT
  musician handout: 4 DEMO
  one: 5 HOPER
As ___ resort: 5 ALAST
Ass: 4 DOPE
  Act like an: 4 BRAY
  Half: 4 MULE
  Wild Asian: 6 ONAGER
Assad: 6 SYRIAN
Assail: 5 BESET **SETAT** 6 ATTACK
Assailed: 5 BESET HADAT SETAT 6 CAMEAT 8 TOREINTO
Assassin: 6 SLAYER
  Stealthy: 5 NINJA
Assassinated: 5 SLAIN
Assassination
  Do some character: 5 ERASE
Assault: 5 ONSET 6 ATTACK ONRUSH
  Campaign: 5 SMEAR
  from Moe: 4 POKE SLAP
  or battery: 4 TORT
  Verbal: 4 SLAP
Assay: 3 TRY 4 TEST
  specimen: 3 ORE
Assayer
  concern: 3 ORE
"As ___ saying ...": 4 IWAS
Assemble: 3 SIT 5 ERECT RIGUP 6 GATHER
  Parts to: 3 KIT
Assembled: 3 MET 4 MADE
  again: 5 RESAT

Assemblies
General: 5 PLENA 6 ARMIES
Assembly: 4 DIET
Ancient ~ area: 5 AGORA
Church: 5 SYNOD
French: 5 SENAT
Full: 6 PLENUM
General: 4 ARMY 8 TOPBRASS
line worker: 5 ROBOT
Assent: 3 YEA YES 4 AMEN
6 SAYYES
French: 3 OUI
Indicate: 3 NOD
Informal: 3 YEH YEP 4 YEAH
Sailor's: 3 AYE 6 AYEAYE
Silent: 3 NOD
Slangy: 3 YEH YEP 4 YEAH
Spanish: 4 SISI
Sweetheart's: 7 YESDEAR
Assert: 4 AVER AVOW POSE
5 CLAIM POSIT STATE
6 ALLEGE
without proof: 6 ALLEGE
Assertion: 5 SAYSO
Assertions
Malicious: 3 MUD
Assertive
personality type: 5 ARIES
Assess: 4 RATE 5 GAUGE VALUE
6 SIZEUP
Assessment: 4 LEVY
Asset: 4 PLUS
Asseverate: 4 AVOW
"___ as she goes!": 6 STEADY
Assign: 3 PUT 5 ALLOT
8 DELEGATE
blame to: 5 PINON
new actors: 6 RECAST
stars to: 4 RATE
workers to: 3 MAN
Assignation: 5 TRYST
Assignment: 4 POST TASK
Detective: 4 CASE
English: 5 ESSAY THEME
P.O.: 3 RTE
RN: 3 ICU
School: 5 ESSAY 6 REPORT
Swimmer: 4 LANE
Teaching: 5 CLASS

Assignments
Between: 4 IDLE
Assimilate: 5 COOPT
Assimilation
process: 7 OSMOSIS
Assist: 3 AID 4 HELP 5 SERVE
in crime: 4 **ABET**
Assistance: 3 AID 4 HELP
6 RELIEF SUCCOR
Passing: 3 YEA
Road ~ org.: 3 AAA
Without: 5 ALONE 7 UNAIDED
Assistant: 4 **AIDE** 6 HELPER
Arctic: 3 ELF
Fictional: 4 IGOR
mil. branch: 3 ADC
with a hunch: 4 IGOR
Assn.: 3 **ORG** SOC
Hemispheric: 3 OAS
Associate: 4 ALLY PEER
6 COHORT HOBNOB
7 CONSORT
Close: 3 PAL
Staff: 3 ROD
with: 5 TIETO
Associated Press
rival: 7 REUTERS
Association: 3 TIE 4 CLUB
Assortment: 4 OLIO 5 ARRAY
8 MIXEDBAG
___ asst.: 5 ADMIN
Assuage: 4 EASE 5 ALLAY
Assume: 5 ADOPT POSIT USURP
6 TAKEON
blame: 10 TAKETHERAP
the role of: 5 ACTAS
Assumed: 5 GIVEN TACIT
It's: 5 ALIAS
truth: 5 AXIOM
Assuming
that: 4 IFSO
Assumption
Basic: 5 AXIOM
Assurance: 3 VOW 4 WORD
Say with: 4 AVER 5 CLAIM
Written: 9 GUARANTEE
Assure: 3 ICE
Assyrian
capital: 7 NINEVEH

king: 6 SARGON
Asta: 3 PET
owner: 4 **NORA**
Astaire
Dancer: 4 FRED 5 ADELE
headwear: 6 TOPHAT
partner: 6 ROGERS
    12 GINGERROGERS
sister: 5 **ADELE**
Astaire/Rogers
destination: 3 RIO
film: 6 TOPHAT
Asterisk: 4 STAR
Astern: 3 AFT
Asteroid
discovered in 1898: 4 EROS
First known: 5 CERES
Largest: 5 CERES
maker: 5 ATARI
path: 5 ORBIT
Third-largest: 5 VESTA
Underwater: 7 SEASTAR
As the ___ flies: 4 CROW
Asthmatic
need: 7 INHALER
"As Time Goes By"
pianist: 3 SAM
requester: 4 ILSA
Astin
Actor: 4 SEAN
Astolat
Maid of: 6 ELAINE
Astonish: 3 AWE 4 STUN 5 AMAZE
Astonished
Sound: 4 GASP
Visibly: 5 AGAPE
Astonishment: 3 AWE
Show: 4 GASP 6 GOGGLE
Astor
Actress: 4 MARY
line: 3 FUR
Astound: 4 DAZE STUN 5 AMAZE
    FLOOR
Astounded: 4 AGOG 5 AGAPE
Astral
hunter: 5 ORION
Astray: 5 AMISS 6 ERRING
Go: 3 **ERR** SIN 6 DERAIL
Astringent: 4 ALUM 6 TANNIC

Astro
or Asta: 3 PET
Astrodome
Former ~ player: 5 OILER
Astrologer
~ Sydney: 5 **OMARR**
Astrological
border: 4 CUSP
lion: 3 LEO
ram: 5 ARIES
scales: 5 LIBRA
Astronaut
apparel: 5 GSUIT
drink: 4 TANG
Elton John song about an:
    9 ROCKETMAN
excursion: 3 EVA
Friendship 7: 5 GLENN
milieu: 5 SPACE
org.: 4 NASA
"Thumbs up" to an: 3 AOK
~ Armstrong: 4 NEIL
~ Bean: 4 ALAN
~ Buzz: 6 ALDRIN
~ Collins: 6 EILEEN
~ Deke: 7 SLAYTON
~ Grissom: 3 **GUS**
~ James: 5 IRWIN
~ Jemison: 3 MAE
~ Judith: 6 RESNIK
~ Sally: 4 RIDE
~ Shepard: 4 **ALAN**
~ Slayton: 4 DEKE
~ Walter: 7 SCHIRRA
Astronomer
British: 6 HALLEY
favorite sky: 6 STARRY
Italian: 7 GALILEO
sighting: 4 NOVA STAR
    6 NEBULA
~ Carl: 5 SAGAN
~ Hubble: 5 EDWIN
~ Sagan: 4 CARL
~ Tycho: 5 BRAHE
Astronomical
altar: 3 ARA
bear: 4 URSA
distance: 6 PARSEC
event: 7 ECLIPSE MOONSET

object: **6** PULSAR QUASAR
phenomena: **5** NOVAE
Astronomy
  Major in: **4** URSA
  Muse of: **6** URANIA
  Star in: **5** SAGAN
AstroTurf
  alternative: **3** SOD **5** GRASS
  component: **5** VINYL
Asturias
  Capital of: **6** OVIEDO
Astute: **3** SLY **4** WILY **5** CANNY
    SHARP **6** SHREWD
Astuteness: **6** ACUMEN
Asunder: **5** RIVEN
  Tear: **4** REND
Aswan Dam
  builder: **6** NASSER
  river: **4** **NILE**
Asylum: **5** HAVEN
  Early: **3** ARK
  seeker: **6** **EMIGRE** **7** REFUGEE
"As you ___": **4** WERE
"As You Like It"
  forest: **5** **ARDEN**
  woman: **5** CELIA
**"As you sew, so shall you
    also ___":** **3** RIP
"As you wish": **6** SOBEIT
At
  a distance: **3** FAR **4** **AFAR**
  a good clip: **5** APACE
  all: **3** ANY **4** EVER
  all times: **4** EVER
  any time: **4** **EVER**
  a premium: **4** RARE
  attention: **5** ERECT
  birth: **3** NEE
  fault: **6** GUILTY
  first: **6** ONBASE
  first (abbr.): **4** ORIG
  full speed: **5** **AMAIN**
  hand: **4** **NEAR** NIGH **6** NEARBY
  large: **4** FREE **5** LOOSE
    10 ONTHELOOSE
  least one: **3** ANY
  liberty: **4** FREE
  lunch: **3** OUT
  no cost: **4** FREE

no time: **4** NEER **5** NEVER
once: **3** NOW **4** STAT
one's post: **6** ONDUTY
peace: **6** SERENE
rest: **4** IDLE
right angles to: **5** ABEAM
risk: **8** INDANGER
that time: **4** **THEN**
the center of: **4** AMID
the home of: **4** CHEZ
the movies: **7** ONADATE
the peak of: **4** **ATOP**
the right time: **5** ONCUE
the summit of: **4** **ATOP**
the time of: **4** UPON
this point: **4** HERE
what time: **4** WHEN
At ___
  (disagreeing): **4** ODDS
  (free): **5** LARGE
  (perplexed): **5** ALOSS
  (with consequences): **5** ACOST
Atahualpa
  land: **4** PERU
  subject: **4** INCA **5** INCAN
AT&SF
  and others: **3** RRS
  stop: **3** STA
AT&T
  acquisition: **3** NCR
  Cable co. that merged with:
    3 TCI
  computer system: **4** UNIX
  Former rival of: **3** GTE **MCI**
  Part of: **3** TEL
  wireless service: **5** MLIFE
Atari
  founder Bushnell: **5** NOLAN
Ataturk
  mausoleum city: **6** ANKARA
At-bat
  Successful: **3** HIT
Ate: **3** HAD **5** DINED
  into: **6** ERODED
  like a bird: **6** PECKED
"A-Team, The"
  member: **3** **MRT**
Atelier
  item: **5** EASEL **7** PALETTE

ATF
  agents: **4** FEDS
  employee: **3** AGT
At ___ for words: 5 ALOSS
Atheist
  ~ Madalyn: **5** OHAIR
Athena
  changed her into a spider:
     7 ARACHNE
  Epithet of: **4** ALEA
  Roman counterpart of:
     7 MINERVA
  shield: **5** AEGIS
  symbol: **3** OWL
Athenian
  emblem: **3** OWL
  lawgiver: **5** DRACO SOLON
  marketplace: **5** AGORA
  meeting place: **4** STOA
  or Corinthian: **7** HELLENE
  Shakespearean: **5** TIMON
  vowel: **3** ETA
  Wise: **5** PLATO
Athens
  attractions: **5** RUINS
  From: **5** GREEK
  Letter from: **3** ETA
  portico: **4** STOA
  Region around: **6** ATTICA
  rival: **6** SPARTA
  University in: **4** OHIO
Atherton, California
  college: **5** MENLO
"A thing of beauty is a joy
     forever"
  poet: **5** KEATS
Athirst: 5 EAGER
Athlete
  Career: **3** PRO
  Paid: **3** PRO
  prefix: **3 TRI**
  trouble spot: **4** KNEE
  ~ Jim: **6** THORPE
Athletic
  award: **5** MEDAL **6** LETTER
  Onetime ~ org.: **4** NASL
  shoe brand: **4** AVIA NIKE
  supporter: **3** TEE
  type: **5** ARIES

  wear company: **6** SPEEDO
Athos
  ~, to Porthos: **3** AMI
___ a time: 5 ONEAT
Atkins
  Actress: **6** EILEEN
  diet concern: **4** CARB
  Guitarist: **4 CHET**
  plan: **4** DIET
Atkinson, Rowan
  role: **4** BEAN
Atkov
  Salyut cosmonaut: **4** OLEG
Atl.
  based cable network: **3** TNT
  crosser: **3** SST
  It's across the: **3** EUR
Atlanta
  cable sta.: **3** TBS
  Former ~ arena: **4 OMNI**
  player: **5** BRAVE
  Turner of: **3** TED
  university: **5 EMORY**
Atlanta-based
  airline: **5** DELTA
  cable sta.: **3** TBS TNT
  health agcy.: **3** CDC
Atlantic: 5 OCEAN
  Arm of the: **8** IRISHSEA
  crosser: **3** SST
  food fish: **3** COD **4** SCUP
  island group: **6** AZORES
Atlantic City
  attraction: **4** KENO SLOT
  casino, with "The": **3** TAJ
  event: **7** PAGEANT
"Atlantic City"
  director: **5** MALLE
Atlantis
  docked with it: **3** MIR
Atlas: 4 ICBM **5** TITAN
  abbr.: **3** ISL MTN STR TPK
     4 ELEV USSR
  contents: **4** MAPS
  feature: **5** INSET
  It's right in the: **4** EAST
  Old ~ letters: **3** SSR **4** USSR
  page: **3** MAP
  rocket stage: **5** AGENA

section: 4 ASIA
stat: 4 AREA
Update an: 5 REMAP
Atlas, Charles: 5 HEMAN
Atlas Mountains
  site: 7 ALGERIA
"Atlas Shrugged"
  author Ayn: 4 RAND
  author Rand: 3 AYN
ATM
  input: 3 PIN
  maker: 3 NCR
  need: 3 PIN
  part: 6 KEYPAD
Atmosphere: 3 AIR 4 **AURA**
    8 AMBIENCE
  About 1% of the: 5 ARGON
  Bad: 6 MIASMA
  Distinctive: 4 **AURA**
  layer: 5 OZONE
  prefix: 3 AER
Atoll
  barrier: 4 REEF
  Bikini ~ event: 5 ATEST
  Bomb test: 8 ENIWETOK
  feature: 6 LAGOON
  material: 5 CORAL
Atom
  Charged: 3 **ION**
  Negatively charged: 5 ANION
Atomic: 3 WEE 4 TINY
    6 MINUTE
  cores: 6 NUCLEI
  energy org.: 3 NRC
  number 30: 4 ZINC
  particle: 5 MESON 6 PROTON
    7 NEUTRON
Atomizer
  output: 4 **MIST** 5 SPRAY
"At once!": 4 STAT
Atone: 6 REPENT 7 EXPIATE
  Reason to: 3 SIN
Atop: 4 ONTO OVER **UPON**
  Lie: 6 RESTON
  Place: 5 SETON
  Rest: 5 LIEON
"At Random"
  autobiographer: 4 CERF
At ___ rate: 3 ANY

Atrium
  locale: 5 HEART
Atropos: 4 FATE
  ~ , Clotho, and Lachesis: 5 FATES
"At Seventeen"
  singer: 3 IAN
Atsuta Shrine
  city: 6 NAGOYA
Attach: 5 ADDON AFFIX SCREW
    SEWON 6 APPEND
    GLUEON SNAPON
    7 PASTEON
  a brooch: 5 PINON
  a button: 5 SEWON
  a patch: 3 SEW 5 SEWON
  with a rope: 5 TIEON
Attached
  at the base: 7 SESSILE
  Be ~ (to): 6 ADHERE
  They come with strings: 5 KITES
    6 APRONS
Attachment: 3 TIE
  Info: Prefix or suffix cue
  adverb: 6 HERETO
Attack: 4 BOUT GOAT 5 BESET
    FLYAT ONSET RUNAT
    SETAT SETON SIEGE
    STORM 6 ASSAIL COMEAT
    HAVEAT JUMPON
    7 SETUPON 8 TEARINTO
  ad: 5 SMEAR
  a sub: 3 EAT
  by plane: 6 STRAFE
  Cause to: 5 SETAT SETON
  deterrent: 4 MACE MOAT
  Free to: 5 LETAT
  from above: 6 STRAFE
    7 AIRRAID
  from all sides: 5 **BESET**
  like an eagle: 5 SWOOP
  Main force of: 5 BRUNT
  Prolonged: 5 SIEGE
  Sneak: 4 RAID 6 AMBUSH
  Spirited: 5 SALVO
  Time to: 4 DDAY
  verbally: 8 TEARINTO
  vigorously: 6 ASSAIL
  word: 3 SIC
  ~, with "into": 3 LAY 4 LACE

___ attack: 4 SHAQ
Attacked: 5 HADAT RANAT
SETAT 6 CAMEAT FELLON
7 LITINTO 8 LAIDINTO
violently: 6 TOREAT
Attacker: 3 FOE 9 ASSAILANT
WWII: 5 UBOAT
"Attack, Fido!": 3 SIC
Attacking: 7 GOINGAT
Attacks: 5 **HASAT** 6 GOESAT
8 LAYSINTO
Attain
Endeavor to: 4 SEEK
status: 4 RISE
Attar
Major ~ source:
10 DAMASKROSE
"Atta Troll"
poet: 5 HEINE
Attempt: 3 TRY 4 SHOT **STAB**
5 ASSAY ESSAY GOFOR
6 EFFORT
Failed: 4 NOGO
Made an: 5 TRIED
Make a new: 5 RETRY
to get: 6 TRYFOR
Wild: 4 STAB
Attempts
~, with "at": 6 HASAGO
Attend: 4 GOTO
Fail to: 4 MISS SKIP
Attendance
bk. entry: 3 ABS
fig.: 3 **EST**
In: 6 ONHAND
taking: 8 ROLLCALL
Was in: 4 CAME
Attendance book
notation: 7 ABSENCE
Attendant: 5 VALET 6 ESCORT
Attendants: 7 RETINUE
Attended: 5 WASAT
Attendee: 4 GOER
Attends: 6 GOESTO
Attention: 3 **EAR** 4 CARE HEED
MIND
At: 5 ERECT
Centers of: 4 FOCI
getter: 3 HEY TAP 4 AHEM PSST

5 NUDGE
Give careful ~ to: 4 HEED
Hold, as: 5 RIVET
Lavish ~ (on): 4 DOTE
Media: 3 INK
Pay: 4 HARK 6 LISTEN
8 TAKENOTE 9 LENDANEAR
Paying: 5 ALERT AWARE
Pay no ~ to: 6 IGNORE
7 NEGLECT
Pay ~ to: 4 **HEED**
Sound for: 4 AHEM
Special: 3 TLC
Steal ~ from: 7 UPSTAGE
Sympathetic: 3 EAR
Attention ___: 4 SPAN
Attention-getter: 3 HEY 4 AHEM
PSST
First-grader's: 4 MEME
Half an: 3 YOO
Attentive: 7 ALLEARS
Fully: 4 RAPT
"At the ___" (1978 song phrase):
4 COPA
At the drop of ___: 4 AHAT
"___ at the office!": 5 IGAVE
Attic: 6 GARRET
In the: 6 STORED
Like an ~, perhaps: 5 DUSTY
sights: 4 WEBS
Attila: 3 HUN
group: 4 HUNS
Pope who persuaded ~ to spare
Rome: 4 LEOI
~, to God: 7 SCOURGE
Attila the ___: 3 HUN
Attire: 4 GARB TOGS 5 DRESS
HABIT 6 CLOTHE ENROBE
7 RAIMENT
Casual: 5 DENIM JEANS
Foreign: 4 SARI
Formal: 3 TUX
Senate: 4 TOGA
Summer: 6 SHORTS
Tattered: 4 RAGS
Attired: 4 CLAD
Attitude: 4 POSE 5 STAND
6 STANCE
Confident, as an: 5 CANDO

Pretentious: 4 AIRS
Attitudinize: 4 POSE
Attn.
Special: 3 TLC
Attorney
Abbr. after an ~ name: 3 ESQ
deg.: 3 LLB LLD
field: 3 LAW
follower: 5 ATLAW
Future ~ exam: 4 LSAT
org.: 3 **ABA**
Scopes: 6 DARROW
~ Melvin: 5 BELLI
Attorney-___: 5 ATLAW
Attorney General
1960s ~: 6 RAMSEY
1970s ~: 6 ELLIOT
1980s ~: 5 MEESE 7 EDMEESE
1990s ~: 4 RENO
Clinton's: 4 **RENO**
Reagan's: 5 **MEESE**
~ Janet: 4 RENO
Attract: 4 DRAW 6 DRAWIN
        ENTICE
Attracted: 4 DREW
Attraction: 4 DRAW LURE
        6 ALLURE
Fair: 4 RIDE
Main: 4 STAR
near Orlando: 5 EPCOT
Rush: 3 ORE
"___ Attraction": 5 FATAL
Attractive: 6 PRETTY
It's: 3 ION 6 MAGNET
legs: 4 GAMS
Make more: 7 SWEETEN
one: 5 CUTIE
quality: 6 APPEAL
        15 ANIMALMAGNETISM
Attribute: 3 OWE 5 REFER TRAIT
        6 IMPUTE 7 ASCRIBE
Golden: 7 SILENCE
Psychic: 3 ESP
Slot machine: 6 'ONEARM
Winemaking: 4 NOSE
Attu
resident: 5 ALEUT
Attucks
Patriot: 7 CRISPUS

Attuned: 5 KEYED
Atty.
degree: 3 LLD
Future ~ exam: 4 **LSAT**
Kind of: 4 DIST
org.: 3 ABA
title: 3 ESQ
Atty. Gen.
1960s ~: 3 RFK
ATV
Part of: 3 ALL
"At Wit's End"
author Bombeck: 4 ERMA
Au
79, for ~ (abbr.): 4 ATNO
courant: 5 AWARE
fait: 4 ABLE
naturel: 4 BARE NUDE
revoir: 5 ADIEU
Au ___: 3 JUS
Auberge: 3 INN
Auberjonois
Actor: 4 RENE
Auburn
hair dye: 5 HENNA
"Au contraire!": 5 NOTSO
Auction
action: 3 **BID** NOD 4 BIDS
amount: 3 LOT
caveat: 4 ASIS
cry: 4 SOLD
ending: 3 **EER**
Exceed at an: 6 OUTBID
Keep an ~ going: 5 REBID
off: 4 SELL
offering: 3 ART LOT
Online ~ site: 4 **EBAY**
Try for, at: 5 BIDON
vehicle, often: 4 REPO
Auctioneer
aid: 5 GAVEL
cry: 4 GONE SOLD
Audacity: 5 NERVE
        7 CHUTZPA
Auden, ___ Hugh: 6 WYSTAN
Audi
rival: 3 BMW
Audible
range: 7 EARSHOT

relief: 4 SIGH
warning: 3 GRR
Audibly: 5 ALOUD
  censor: 5 BLEEP
  Cry: 3 SOB
Audience: 3 EAR 9 LISTENERS
  Comment to the: 5 **ASIDE**
  member: 8 ATTENDEE
  shill: 5 PLANT
  Talk before an:
     15 PANELDISCUSSION
  USO: 3 GIS
Audiences
  For mature: 6 RATEDR
  Suitable for all: 6 RATEDG
Audio
  effect: 4 ECHO
  Match ~ and video: 4 SYNC
  system: 4 HIFI 6 STEREO
  systems, for short: 3 PAS
Audiophile
  collection: 3 CDS LPS
  purchase: 4 HIFI
  setup: 6 STEREO
Audit: 7 SITINON
  pro: 3 CPA
Audited: 7 SATINON
Auditing
  ace: 3 CPA
  Fed. ~ agency: 3 GAO
Audition: 4 TEST 6 TRYOUT
  (for): 4 READ
  Open: 10 CATTLECALL
  tape: 4 **DEMO**
Auditioner
  goal: 4 ROLE
Auditor
  Govt.: 3 GAO IRS
  initials: 3 CPA
Auditorium: 4 HALL
Auditory: 4 OTIC
  sensor: 3 EAR
Audrey
  1964 role for ~: 5 ELIZA
Audubon
  Of interest to: 5 AVIAN
Auel
  Author: 4 JEAN
  heroine: 4 AYLA

Auerbach
  Comic: 5 ARTIE
Aug.
  follower: 3 SEP 4 SEPT
  setting: 3 DST
Auger
  Use an: 4 BORE
Augment: 5 ADDTO
Augsburg
  Info: German cue
  Alas, in: 3 ACH
  article: 3 EIN
Augur: 4 OMEN SEER
     7 PORTEND
Augury: 4 OMEN 7 PORTENT
August: 5 NOBLE REGAL
     7 EMINENT
  birthstone: 7 PERIDOT
  hrs.: 3 DST
  Like Kansas in: 5 CORNY
  Most ~ babies: 4 LEOS
  person: 3 LEO
August 13: 4 IDES
Augusta
  11 through 13 at ~:
     10 AMENCORNER
  home: 5 MAINE
Auguste
  Painter: 6 RENOIR
  Sculpter: 5 RODIN
Auld
  lang syne: 4 YORE
"Auld Lang ___": 4 **SYNE**
Auld Sod, The: 4 EIRE ERIN
Aulin
  Actress: 3 EWA
Aunt
  Broadway: 4 MAME 5 ELLER
  Mayberry: 3 BEE
  ~, in French: 5 TANTE
  ~, in Spanish: 3 **TIA**
Aunt Bee
  charge: 4 **OPIE**
"Aunt ___ Cope Book": 5 ERMAS
"Auntie ___": 4 MAME
Aunt Jemima
  rival: 4 EGGO
Aunt Polly
  nephew: 3 TOM

"Au poivre"
  serving: 5 STEAK
Aura: 3 AIR 5 VIBES 6 NIMBUS
    8 MYSTIQUE
  Angelic: 4 HALO
Auréole
  wearer: 4 ANGE
"Au revoir!": 4 TATA 5 ADIEU
  ___ au rhum: 4 BABA
Auric
  creator: 3 IAN
Auricular: 4 OTIC
Auriga
  Star in: 7 CAPELLA
Aurora
  counterpart: 3 **EOS**
  or Alero: 4 OLDS
Aurora ___: 8 BOREALIS
Aus.
  neighbor: 3 GER
Auspices: 4 EGIS 5 AEGIS
Auspicious: 4 RIPE
Aussie
  Info: Australian cue
  bear: 5 KOALA
  bird: 3 EMU
  bounder: 3 ROO
  buddy: 4 MATE
  Colleges, to an: 4 UNIS
  gems: 5 OPALS
  greeting: 4 GDAY
  Grounded: 3 EMU
  hopper: 3 **ROO**
  lassie: 6 SHEILA
  marsupial: 5 KOALA 6 WOMBAT
  outlaw Kelly: 3 NED
  runner: 3 EMU
Austen
  Author: 4 JANE
  heroine: 4 **EMMA**
  novel: 4 **EMMA**
Austen, Jane
  novel: 4 **EMMA**
Austere: 5 HARSH STARK
    6 LENTEN 7 SPARTAN
Austerlitz
  Dancer born: 7 ASTAIRE
Austin
  Actress: 4 TERI

Australia
  Bird of: 3 EMU
  Gateway to: 6 SYDNEY
  Island off: 5 TIMOR
  Largest lake in: 4 EYRE
  Water off: 10 BASSSTRAIT
  Woman, in: 6 SHEILA
Australian
  bear: 5 KOALA
  bird: 3 EMU
  export: 4 OPAL
  Flightless: 3 EMU
  gem: 4 OPAL
  hard-rock band: 4 ACDC
  marsupial: 5 KOALA
  outlaw Kelly: 3 NED
Australian Open
  1970 ~ champ: 4 ASHE
  1998 ~ champ: 5 KORDA
  2000 ~ champ: 6 AGASSI
  Four-time ~ champ: 5 SELES
Austria
  A as in: 3 EIN
  Alpine region of: 5 TIROL TYROL
  article: 3 EIN
  Capital of: 6 VIENNA
  capital, to locals: 4 WIEN
Austrian
  composer: 5 ALBAN 6 MAHLER
  peak: 3 ALP
  psychologist: 5 ADLER
  region: 5 TIROL TYROL
  river: 4 ENNS
Auteur
  art: 6 CINEMA
Auth.
  unknown: 4 **ANON**
Authentic: 4 **REAL** TRUE 5 LEGIT
    VALID 7 GENUINE
Author: 3 PEN 6 PENNER
  of a 1998 report: 5 STARR
  offerings (abbr.): 3 MSS
  Rags-to-riches: 5 ALGER
  Uncredited: 5 GHOST
  unknown: 4 ANON
  Western: 4 GREY
  ~ Alexander: 5 SHANA
  ~ Ayn: 4 RAND
  ~ Bret: 5 HARTE

~ Eda: 6 LESHAN
~ Ennis: 4 REES
~ Frederik: 4 POHL
~ Hermann: 5 HESSE
~ James: 4 AGEE
~ John Dickson ___: 4 CARR
~ John Dos ___: 6 PASSOS
~ Josephine: 3 TEY
~ Joyce Carol: 5 OATES
~ Leonard: 6 ELMORE
~ Martin: 4 AMIS
~ Roald: 4 DAHL
~ Rona: 5 JAFFE
~ Scott: 5 ODELL
~ Umberto: 3 **ECO**

"Author! Author!"
actress: 10 DYANCANNON
star: 8 ALPACINO

Authoritative
decree: 4 FIAT
doctrine: 5 DOGMA
order: 7 MANDATE
source: 5 BIBLE

Authority: 5 POWER **SAYSO**
6 PUNDIT
Defy: 5 REBEL
Final: 5 **SAYSO**
Level of: 7 ECHELON
Mil.: 3 CMD
On the ~ of: 3 PER
Position of: 5 CHAIR
Quote an: 4 CITE
Symbol of: 4 MACE ROBE
5 BADGE 6 MANTLE
Wield, as: 5 EXERT

Authorize: 3 LET 4 OKAY
7 EMPOWER ENTITLE

Authorizes: 3 OKS

"Author unknown": 4 ANON

Auto: 3 CAR
1950s ~: 5 EDSEL
additive: 3 STP
Antique: 3 **REO**
Autobahn: 3 BMW 4 AUDI **OPEL**
buyer's bargain: 4 DEMO
Bygone ~ ornament: 3 FIN
Classic: 3 REO
club offering: 3 MAP TOW
damage: 5 DENTS

European: 4 OPEL YUGO
Family: 5 SEDAN
financing co.: 3 GMC
Former ~ mfr.: 3 AMC
frontpiece: 6 GRILLE
fuel: 3 GAS
German: 4 AUDI OPEL
graph: 3 MAP
Imported: 3 KIA 4 AUDI SAAB
inflatable: 6 AIRBAG
Italian: 4 ALFA FIAT
Like ~ shop floors: 4 OILY
loan letters: 3 APR
make: 4 MERC
making a comeback: 4 REPO
manufacturer woe: 6 RECALL
mechanic tool: 9 GREASEGUN
option: 3 AIR 5 ALARM
part: 3 CAM 4 CARB 6 GASCAP
parts brand: 4 NAPA
pioneer: 4 BENZ OLDS
race: 4 INDY 6 LEMANS
reversal: 3 UEY
Sad-sounding: 4 SAAB
safety device: 6 AIRBAG
7 ROLLBAR
selection: 5 SEDAN
steering system link: 6 TIEROD
style: 5 SEDAN
suffix: 4 CRAT
Swedish: 4 SAAB
trim: 6 CHROME
Vintage: 3 REO 5 ESSEX

Autobahn
auto: 3 BMW 4 AUDI **OPEL**

Autobio
Turner: 5 ITINA

Autobiographer
~ Bobby: 5 SEALE

Autobiography: 6 MEMOIR
7 MEMOIRS
Moss Hart: 6 ACTONE
Sammy Davis Jr.: 7 YESICAN

Auto-correcting
device: 5 SERVO

Autocrat: 4 CZAR **TSAR**
6 DESPOT

Auto financing
abbr.: 3 APR

Autograph: 4 SIGN
Auto grille
  covering: 3 BRA
Automaker
  9000 ~: 4 SAAB
  Early: 4 OLDS 6 DURYEA
  German: 4 AUDI OPEL
  Japanese: 5 ACURA
  ~ Citroën: 5 ANDRE
  ~ Ferrari: 4 ENZO
  ~ Maserati: 7 ERNESTO
Automat: 6 EATERY
Automatic: 4 ROTE
  pistol: 7 BURPGUN
  prefix: 4 SEMI
Automaton: 5 GOLEM ROBOT
      7 ANDROID
  play: 3 RUR
  ~, briefly: 3 BOT 5 DROID
Automne
  preceder: 3 ETE
Automobile
  pioneer: 4 OLDS
  sticker fig.: 3 MPG
Auto racer
  ~ Al: 5 UNSER
  ~ Bobby: 5 UNSER 7 ALLISON
  ~ Fabi: 3 TEO
  ~ Luyendyk: 4 ARIE
Autostrada
  auto: 4 ALFA FIAT
Autry
  pic: 5 OATER
Autumn: 4 FALL
  apple: 6 RUSSET 7 WINESAP
  birthstone: 4 OPAL
  bloomer: 5 **ASTER**
  color: 5 OCHER OCHRE
  drink: 5 CIDER
  mo.: 3 NOV OCT
  pear: 4 BOSC
  Sign of: 5 FROST
  toiler: 5 RAKER
"___ Autumn": 3 TIS
Autumnal equinox
  mo.: 3 SEP
"Autumn Sonata"
  actress Ullmann: 3 LIV
___ au vin: 3 COQ

Auxiliary: 3 AID 4 AIDE
  action: 7 SIDEBET
  proposition: 5 LEMMA
  track: 4 SPUR
  verb: 3 ARE
  WWII: 4 WACS
Av
  Month after: 4 ELUL
A/V
  Part of: 5 AUDIO
Ava
  Ex of: 5 ARTIE
"___ a vacation!": 5 INEED
Avail
  oneself of: 3 USE
  To no: 6 FUTILE INVAIN
      7 USELESS
___ avail: 4 TONO
Available: 3 OUT 4 OPEN
     5 <u>ONTAP</u> 6 ATHAND
     ONCALL ONHAND
     UNUSED 7 FORHIRE
  for rent: 5 TOLET 6 VACANT
  for work: 6 ONCALL
  from the publisher: 7 INPRINT
  Make: 6 FREEUP
  No longer: 4 SOLD 5 TAKEN
  Not: 5 INUSE 6 TIEDUP
  Readily: 5 ONTAP 6 ONCALL
     ONHAND
Avalanche: 5 SPATE
Avalon: 4 ISLE
Avalon, Frankie
  hit: 4 DEDE
Avant-___: 5 GARDE
Avant-garde
  artist: 3 ARP
Avarice: 5 GREED
"Avast!"
  responder: 4 SWAB
Avatar
  of Vishnu: 4 RAMA
Ave.
  crossers: 3 RDS <u>STS</u>
"Ave Maria"
  Opera with: 6 OTELLO
"Avengers, The"
  actor Patrick: 6 MACNEE
  actress Diana: 4 RIGG

actress Rigg: **5** DIANA
actress Thurman: **3** UMA
character Emma: **4** PEEL
Emma player in: **3** UMA
guy: **5** STEED
Mrs. Peel of: **4** EMMA

Avenging
spirits: **6** FURIES

Avenue
crosser: **6** STREET
liners: **4** ELMS
Monopoly: **8** ORIENTAL
that changes into Amsterdam
    Avenue: **5** TENTH

Average: 3 CEE PAR **4** MEAN
    NORM SOSO
Better than: **8** ABOVEPAR
grade: **3** __CEE__
guy: **3** JOE **4** NORM
Just above: **5** CPLUS
name: **3** DOE DOW
producer: **8** DOWJONES
They ~ 100: **3** IQS

Averred: 4 SAID **6** STATED

Averse: 5 LOATH
to exertion: **4** LAZY

Aversion: 5 ODIUM **8** DISTASTE
Cry of: **3** UGH

Avert
~, with "off": **4** WARD

Avery
Animator: **3** TEX

Aves.: 3 STS

Avg.: 3 PCT REG STD

Avian
chatterbox: **5** MYNAH
food holder: **4** CRAW
home: **4** NEST
mimic: **4** MYNA
wader: **5** STILT
~ Australians: **4** EMUS

Aviary: 4 CAGE
abode: **4** NEST
sound: **3** CAW **5** CHEEP TWEET

Aviate: 3 FLY

Aviation
First name in: **6** AMELIA
pioneer Clyde: **6** CESSNA
pioneer Post: **5** WILEY

pioneer Sikorsky: **4** IGOR
prefix: **3** AER **4** AERO

Aviator: 5 FLIER
Dance named for an: **5** LINDY
Famed: **8** REDBARON
~ Balbo: **5** ITALO
~ Earhart: **6** AMELIA
~ Post: **5** WILEY

Aviators
in tabloids: **3** ETS

Aviatrix
~ Earhart: **6** AMELIA

Avid: 4 KEEN **5** EAGER
    6 GUNGHO RAHRAH

Avignon
Info: French cue
aunt: **5** TANTE
River of: **5** RHONE

Avis
adjective: **4** RARA
Eventual: **4** OVUM
pair: **4** ALAE
Rara: **4** ONER
rival: **5** ALAMO HERTZ
___ avis: **4** __RARA__
___ Aviv: **3** TEL
___ Avivian: **3** TEL

Avocation: 3 BAG

Avoid: 4 SHUN **5** ELUDE SKIRT
    6 ESCHEW
a big wedding: **5** ELOPE
a trial: **6** SETTLE
Didn't: **5** FACED
doing: **5** EVADE
humiliation: **8** SAVEFACE
Publicly: **4** SHUN
responsibility: **11** PASSTHEBUCK
Something to: **4** NONO **5** TABOO
Try to ~ a tag: **5** SLIDE
Want to: **5** DREAD

Avoirdupois
alternative: **4** TROY

Avon
First Earl of: **4** EDEN

Avowal
Altar: **3** IDO

Avril
follower: **3** __MAI__

"Aw, ___!": 6 SHUCKS

Await
　jadgment: 4 **PEND**
Awaiting: 5 INFOR 7 INSTORE
　service: 6 INLINE
Awake
　Wide: 5 ALERT
"Awake and Sing!"
　playwright: 5 ODETS
Awaken: 4 STIR 5 GETUP ROUSE
　　6 AROUSE COMETO
　rudely: 5 ROUST
Awakening: 7 AROUSAL
　Cause of a rude: 5 SNORE
Awaker: 5 ALARM
"A waking dream": Aristotle:
　　4 HOPE
Award: 5 PRIZE
　Advertising: 4 **CLIO**
　Athletic: 5 MEDAL 6 LETTER
　bestowed by a queen: 3 OBE
　Broadway: 4 TONY
　Cable sports: 4 ESPY
　Drama: 4 OBIE
　Film: 5 OSCAR
　French film: 5 CESAR
　given by Chris Berman: 4 ESPY
　given by The Village Voice:
　　4 OBIE
　Mystery writer: 5 **EDGAR**
　Off-Broadway: 4 OBIE
　Olympic: 5 MEDAL
　recipient: 7 HONOREE
　Romance novelist: 4 RITA
　Science fiction: 4 HUGO
　since 1956: 4 OBIE
　Sports: 4 ESPY
　Television: 4 EMMY
　Theater: 4 **OBIE** TONY
　TV: 4 EMMY
　U.K.: 3 OBE
Aware
　Be ~ of: 4 KNOW
　Become ~ of: 5 LEARN SENSE
　Fully ~ of: 4 ONTO
　Make: 5 CUEIN 6 CLUEIN
　of: 4 INON **ONTO** UPON
　　5 HEPTO HIPTO 6 WISETO
　Was ~ of: 4 KNEW
　~, with "in": 5 CLUED

Away: 3 OFF OUT 5 ASIDE
　　NOTIN 6 ABSENT
　　7 NOTHOME ONLEAVE
　A ways: 4 AFAR
　Do ~ with: 3 OFF RID 4 OMIT
　　5 ERASE 7 ABOLISH
　from land: 4 ASEA
　from the bow: 3 AFT 6 ASTERN
　from the mouth: 6 ABORAL
　from the wind: 4 **ALEE**
　Get: 3 LAM 4 EXIT SLIP
　　6 ESCAPE
　Get ~ from: 5 **ELUDE** EVADE
　　6 ESCAPE
　Go: 5 LEAVE 6 DEPART
　　VACATE
　Not: 6 ATHOME
　Partner of: 3 FAR
　They got: 7 EVADERS
Awe: 3 WOW 5 AMAZE
　In: 4 AGOG 5 AGAPE
　Regard with: 8 VENERATE
　Sound of: 3 OOH
Aweather
　Opposite of: 4 **ALEE**
"Awesome!": 3 OOH **RAD**
Awestruck: 4 AGOG RAPT
　　5 AGAPE
　one: 5 GAPER
Awful: 3 BAD 4 DIRE 7 THEPITS
　Feel: 3 AIL
　smell: 5 FETOR
　tasting: 4 VILE
　Was: 5 STANK
"Aw, gee!": 4 DARN
Awkward: 5 GOONY 6 GANGLY
　It can put one in an ~ position:
　　4 YOGA
　situation: 12 STICKYWICKET
Awl: 4 TOOL
Awoke: 5 GOTUP 6 CAMETO
AWOL
　chasers: 3 **MPS**
　Part of: 5 LEAVE 6 ABSENT
　student: 6 TRUANT
"Awright!": 4 YEAH
Awry: 3 OFF 5 AMISS ASKEW
　Go: 3 ERR
　Seriously ~ scheme: 5 SNAFU

Ax: 3 CAN HEW 4 FIRE SACK
5 LETGO
Given the ~, with "off": 4 LAID
Give the: 3 CAN 4 FIRE SACK
5 LETGO
One with an ~ to grind:
5 HONER
relative: 3 ADZ
to grind: 6 AGENDA
wielder: 5 HEWER
Axed: 4 HEWN
Axel: 4 LEAP
Do an: 5 SKATE
Axes
Standard: 5 XANDY
Axis
foes: 6 ALLIES
leader: 4 TOJO
Turn on an: 4 SLUE
6 ROTATE
Axis of ___: 4 EVIL
Axle: 3 BAR
end: 3 HUB
holder: 5 UBOLT
Axlike
tool: 3 ADZ 4 ADZE
Axton
Country singer: 4 HOYT
Ayatollah: 4 IMAM
land: 4 IRAN
predecessor: 4 SHAH

Ayckbourn
Playwright: 4 ALAN
Aye
Apt anagram for: 3 YEA
opposite: 3 NAY
sayer: 3 PRO
Ayes
Spanish: 3 SIS 4 **SISI**
Aykroyd
Actor: 3 DAN
Ayn
Author: 4 RAND
Ayres
Actor: 3 **LEW**
Azalea: 5 HEATH
Azer.
~, once: 3 SSR
Azerbaijan
Capital of: 4 BAKU
~, once (abbr.): 3 SSR
Azerbaijani
neighbor: 5 IRANI
Azores
loc.: 3 ATL
Azov
On the: 4 ASEA
AZT
approver: 3 FDA
Azure: 4 BLUE 5 SKYEY
Azzo, Alberto
family name: 4 ESTE

Bb

B: 3 KEY 4 TYPE 6 LETTER
  followers: 3 CDE
  in chemistry: 5 BORON
B-2
  letters: 4 USAF
B-29
  Name on a famous: 5 ENOLA
B-52
  home: 3 AFB
B.A.
  Part of: 4 ARTS
Baa: 5 BLEAT
  maid: 3 EWE
Baal: 4 IDOL
Baba
  Fabled woodcutter: 3 ALI
  ingredient: 3 RUM
Baba ___ (Radner role): 4 WAWA
___ Baba: 3 <u>ALI</u>
Babar
  Wife of: 7 CELESTE
Babble: 5 PRATE RUNON
        7 PRATTLE
Babe
  Beasts like: 4 OXEN
  Family of: 5 RUTHS
  in the stable: 4 FOAL
  in the woods: 4 FAWN NAIF
"Babe"
  band: 4 STYX
  character Maa: 3 EWE
  Home for filmdom's: 3 STY
  in films: 3 PIG
Babel: 3 DIN
  building: 5 TOWER
Babilonia
  Skater: 3 <u>TAI</u>
Babka
  flavoring: 3 RUM
Babushka: 5 SCARF
Baby: 6 COSSET PAMPER
  bed: 4 CRIB
  bird: 5 OWLET STORK

        6 EAGLET
  bloomer: 3 BUD
  blues: 4 EYES 7 PEEPERS
  bouncer: 4 KNEE
  buggy: 4 PRAM
  carrier: 4 WOMB
  Cry like a: 4 MEWL
  food: 3 PAP
  goat: 3 KID
  grand: 5 PIANO
  in blue: 3 BOY
  powder: 4 <u>TALC</u>
  seal: 3 PUP
  seat: 3 LAP
  specialist: 7 DRSPOCK
  whale: 4 CALF
  word: 3 GOO 4 DADA MAMA
"Baby Baby"
  singer: 8 AMYGRANT
Baby-faced: 4 CUTE
Babylonian
  goddess: 6 ISHTAR
Babysit: 4 MIND TEND
Babysitter: 4 NANA
  bane: 3 IMP 4 BRAT
Bacall
  mate, familiarly: 5 BOGIE
Baccarat
  alternative: 4 FARO
  Best ~ hand: 4 NINE
  call: 5 BANCO
Bacchanal: 4 ORGY
Bacchanalian
  bash: 4 ORGY
Bacchus
  attendant: 5 SATYR
Bach
  contemporary: 6 HANDEL
  instrument: 5 ORGAN
  piece: 5 SUITE 7 CANTATA
        CHORALE TOCCATA
Bacharach
  Songwriter: 4 BURT

Bachelor
  home: 3 PAD
  Last words of a: 3 IDO
  pads, maybe: 5 STIES
  party: 4 STAG
  suffix: 4 ETTE
"Bachelor Father"
  actress Corcoran: 6 NOREEN
Bachman
  Singer: 3 TAL
Bacillus
  shape: 3 ROD
Back: 3 AGO FRO 4 HIND REAR
    5 STERN 7 ENDORSE
  Info: Suffix cue
  again: 3 FRO
  at sea: 3 AFT
  at the track: 5 BETON
  biter: 5 MOLAR
  bones: 5 SACRA
  Book: 5 SPINE
  Bounce: 4 ECHO
  Bring: 6 REVIVE 7 RESTORE
  Buy: 6 REDEEM
  Chair: 5 SPLAT
  Come: 4 ECHO 5 RECUR
  Come ~ again: 6 REECHO
  Cut: 4 PARE 5 PRUNE
  door: 7 POSTERN
  Draw: 6 RECEDE
  Drew: 5 SHIED
  Drive: 5 REPEL 7 REPULSE
  Drop: 3 LAG
  Fall: 3 EBB LAG 6 REVERT
    7 RELAPSE
  Far: 7 AGESAGO LONGAGO
  Flow: 3 **EBB**
  Force: 5 REPEL
  From way: 5 OFOLD
  Get: 6 RECOUP REGAIN
  Get ~ at: 5 SPITE
  Get ~ for: 6 AVENGE
  Give: 5 REPAY 7 RESTORE
  Go: 3 EBB 6 RETURN REVERT
    7 REGRESS
  Go ~ over: 7 RETRACE
  Hang: 3 LAG 5 TARRY
  Hold: 4 STEM 6 IMPEDE
    RETARD

  in: 5 RETRO
  in time: 3 AGO
  Kick: 4 LOAF REST
  Let ~ in: 7 READMIT
  Lying on one's: 6 SUPINE
  muscle: 3 **LAT**
  of a boat: 5 STERN
  of the neck: 4 **NAPE**
  out: 6 RENEGE
  Pay: 3 OLA 6 AVENGE
  Put: 4 STET 5 RESET
    7 RESTORE
  Quarter: 5 EAGLE
  Send: 4 ECHO 6 REMAND
  Set: 7 SCENERY
  Slip: 7 RELAPSE
  Spring: 6 RECOIL
  street: 5 ALLEY
  Strike: 5 REACT
  Take: 4 UNDO 6 RECANT
  talk: 3 **LIP** 4 ECHO GUFF **SASS**
    6 STATIC
  Talk ~ to: 4 **SASS**
  then: 4 ONCE
  tooth: 5 MOLAR
  Toward the: 5 AREAR
  Turn: 5 REPEL 6 REVERT
  Way ~ when: 4 ONCE
    7 AGESAGO LONGAGO
Backbone: 5 SPINE
  of a ship: 4 KEEL
Backbreaker
  Proverbial: 5 STRAW
"Backdraft"
  crime: 5 ARSON
Backdrop: 5 SCENE
  Theatrical: 5 SCRIM
Backfire: 9 BOOMERANG
  sound: 4 BANG
Backgammom
  impossibility: 3 TIE
  need: 4 DICE
  piece: 5 STONE
"Back in Black"
  band: 4 ACDC
"Back in the ___": 4 USSR
Backless
  couch: 5 DIVAN
  divan: 7 OTTOMAN

Backpacker: 5 HIKER
Backrub: 7 MASSAGE
  response: 3 AAH
Backs: 5 DORSA
Backside: 4 DUFF REAR
Backslide: 7 REGRESS RELAPSE
Backstabber: 3 RAT
  Comment to a: 4 ETTU
Backstreet Boys
  fan, usually: 4 TEEN
  rivals: 5 NSYNC
Backtalk: 3 LIP 4 ECHO SASS
Backup: 4 COPY
  procedure: 5 PLANB
Backward: 5 AREAR 6 ASTERN
Backwash
  creator: 3 OAR
Backwater
  Kind of: 5 BAYOU
Backyard
  building: 4 SHED 8 TOOLSHED
Baclanova
  Actress: 4 OLGA
Bacon: 6 AUTHOR
  Actor: 5 KEVIN
  bit: 5 ESSAY
  Bring home the: 4 EARN
  partner: 4 EGGS
  piece: 5 ESSAY
  portion: 4 SLAB 5 STRIP
  serving: 6 RASHER
Bacteria: 5 GERMS
  Dangerous: 5 ECOLI
  prefix: 6 ENTERO
  Spherical: 5 COCCI
Bacterium: 4 GERM
  Dangerous: 5 ECOLI
  Kind of: 6 AEROBE
Bad: 4 EVIL
  atmosphere: 6 MIASMA
  behavior: 3 SIN
  blood: 6 ANIMUS
  cut: 4 GASH
  dog: 5 BITER
  end: 4 DOOM
  Feel: 3 AIL
  Feel ~ about: 3 RUE
  Go: 3 **ROT** 4 TURN 5 SPOIL
  Gone: 6 SPOILT

  habit: 4 **VICE**
  impression: 4 DENT
  In a ~ way: 4 ILLY 6 EVILLY
  lighting: 5 ARSON
  look: 4 LEER 5 SNEER
  mark: 3 DEE ZIT 4 SCAR
    6 STIGMA 7 DEMERIT
  marks: 4 ACNE
  mood: 4 SNIT
  Not: 4 SOSO
  points: 4 CONS
  prefix: 3 DYS MAL 4 CACO
  reception: 4 HISS
  review: 3 PAN
  Smell: 4 REEK
  spell: 3 HEX
  start: 3 DYS MAL
  temper: 3 IRE
  throw: 5 ERROR
  Too: 4 ALAS
  to the bone: 4 **EVIL**
  treatment: 5 ABUSE
  Very: 5 AWFUL 7 ABYSMAL
"Bad, Bad Leroy Brown"
  singer: 5 CROCE
"Bad Behavior"
  actor: 3 REA
"Bad Boys"
  actor Morales: 4 ESAI
Baddie
  Barrie: 4 SMEE
  Bond: 4 DRNO
  Fairy tale: 4 OGRE
  Shakespeare: 4 IAGO
Bad Ems: 3 SPA
Baden-Baden: 3 SPA
Badge
  holder: 4 SASH
  Kind of: 5 MERIT
  material: 3 TIN
  Sheriff's: 4 STAR 7 TINSTAR
Badger: 3 NAG 6 HARASS
    PESTER
  group: 4 CETE
  Honey: 5 RATEL
Badges
  with names: 6 IDTAGS
Badlands
  sights: 5 MESAS

state (abbr.): **4** SDAK

Badminton
need: **3** NET **11** SHUTTLECOCK

Bad-mouth: 3 DIS 6 MALIGN
REVILE

Baer
Boxer: **3** MAX

Baez
Folk singer: **4** JOAN

Baffin Bay
sight: **4** BERG FLOE

Baffle: 5 STUMP

Baffled: 5 ATSEA **7** ATALOSS

Bag: 3 NAB SAC **5** SNARE
6 VALISE
Freezer: **6** ZIPLOC
It's in the: **3** TEA
Kind of: **4** GRAB TOTE
Mixed: **4** OLIO

Bagatelle: 6 TRIFLE
___ bagatelle: **5** AMERE

Bagel
alternative: **4** ROLL
flavoring: **6** SESAME
9 POPPYSEED
topper: **3** LOX **4** NOVA
variety: **5** PLAIN **6** SESAME

Baggage
handler: **6** PORTER REDCAP

Baggy: 5 LOOSE

Baghdad
country: **4** IRAQ
native: **5** IRAQI
river: **6** TIGRIS

Baglike
structure: **3** SAC

Bagnold
Author: **4 ENID**

Bagpipe
part: **5** DRONE
sound: **5** DRONE

Bagpiper
garment: **4** KILT
wear: **6** TARTAN

Baguette: 3 GEM **4** ROLL

Bah: 3 FIE
___ Bah: **4** POOH

Baha'i
birthplace: **4** IRAN

Bahamas
capital: **6** NASSAU

Bahrain
bigwig: **4** EMIR **5** AMEER
native: **4** ARAB

Baht
spender: **4** THAI

Bailey
bailiwick: **3** LAW
partner: **6** BARNUM
Singer: **5** PEARL

Bailey, F. ___
Attorney: **3** LEE

Bailiff
bellow: **4** OYEZ
command: **4** RISE **7** ALLRISE
execution: **4** WRIT
Reply to a: **3** IDO

Bailiwick: 4 AREA TURF
6 SPHERE
DDE: **3** ETO
Reporter's: **4** BEAT

Bailout
button: **5** EJECT
PC: **3** ESC

Baird
Attorney General nominee: **3** ZOE
Puppeteer: **3** BIL

Bairn
Like a: **3** SMA WEE

Bait: 4 LURE **5** TEASE TEMPT
Artificial: **4** LURE
buyer: **6** ANGLER
Drop ~ lightly: **3** DAP
Fish: **4** CHUM WORM
Take the: **4** BITE

Baiul
Ice skater: **6** OKSANA

Baja
Info: Spanish cue
bear: **3** OSO
buck: **4** PESO
capital: **8** MEXICALI
cheer: **3** OLE
Opposite of: **4** ALTA
port: **8** ENSENADA

Bake
eggs: **5 SHIRR**
sale org.: **3** PTA

Baked
  alternative: **6** MASHED
  dessert: **6** ALASKA
  ~, in Bologna: **5** COTTA
Baked in ___: 4 APIE
Bake-off
  appliance: **4** OVEN
Baker
  Brick: **4** KILN
  Corporate: **7** SARALEE
  dozen: **4** EGGS
  implement: **4** PEEL
  Jazz trumpeter: **4** CHET
  need: **4** OVEN **5** YEAST
  quantity: **5** BATCH
  Singer: **5** ANITA
___-Baker, Mark
  Actor: **4** LINN
Bakersfield
  neighbor: **6** DELANO
Bakery
  call: **4** NEXT
  emanation: **5** AROMA
  employee: **4** ICER
  enticement: **5** AROMA
  fixture: **4** OVEN
  need: **5** YEAST
  purchase: **4** LOAF
  treat: **4** TART **5** SCONE
       6 ECLAIR
  worker: **4** ICER
Baking
  chamber: **4** OVEN
  follower: **4** SODA
  ingredient: **5** YEAST
  Lee of: **4** SARA
  pan: **3** TIN
  soda target: **4** ODOR
Bakker, Jim
  former org.: **3** PTL
Balaam
  beast: **3** ASS
"Balalaika"
  actress Massey: **5** ILONA
Balance: 4 REST **6** SANITY
                    STASIS
  Card: **4** DEBT
  Fight for: **6** TEETER
  Hanging in the: **7** ATSTAKE

  Hang in the: **4** PEND
  Have a: **3** OWE
  Lose one's: **5** SPEND
  part: **3** PAN
  provider: **3** ATM
  sheet item: **5** ASSET
  sign: **5** LIBRA
Balanced: 4 EVEN SANE
Balancing
  pro: **3** CPA
Balbo
  Aviator: **5** ITALO
Balboa
  Explorer: **5** VASCO
  Mrs. Rocky: **6** ADRIAN
  Where to spend a: **6** PANAMA
Balbriggan
  Sight from: **8** IRISHSEA
Balcony
  barrier: **7** PARAPET
  Play to the: **5** EMOTE
       7 OVERACT
  section: **4** LOGE
"Balcony, The"
  playwright Jean: **5** GENET
Bald
  It's ~, possibly: **4** PATE
  Loss at a ~ spot: **5** TREAD
  spot cover: **3** SOD
Balder
  Father of: **4** ODIN
Balderdash: 3 <u>ROT</u> **4** HOKE
       5 HOKUM PSHAW
       7 EYEWASH **8** NONSENSE
Baldness: 8 ALOPECIA
Baldwin
  Actor: **4** ADAM <u>ALEC</u>
Bale
  binder: **4** WIRE **5** TWINE
  contents: **3** HAY
Balearic Islands
  One of the: **5** IBIZA **7** MAJORCA
       MINORCA
"Bali ___": 3 <u>HAI</u>
Balin
  Actress: **3** INA
Balkan
  capital: **5** SOFIA **6** TIRANA
  native: **4** SERB SLAV **5** CROAT

Ball: 3 ORB 4 GALA 6 SPHERE
  Bobble the: 3 ERR
  Cheese: 4 EDAM
  costar: 5 VANCE
  Drop the: 3 ERR
  game: 5 BOCCE LOTTO
  girl: 3 DEB 5 **BELLE**
  Great ~ of fire: 3 SUN 4 STAR
  Hand: 4 FIST
  High: 3 LOB
  holder: 3 TEE
  "i" ~: 3 DOT
  mate: 5 ARNAZ
  of yarn: 4 CLEW
  On the: 5 ALERT
  Soft ~ material: 4 NERF
  suffix: 3 OON
Ball, Lucille: 7 REDHEAD
Ballad: 3 LAY
  suffix: 3 EER
Ballade
  ending: 5 ENVOI
Balladeer
  aid: 4 LUTE
"Ballad of Jed Clampett, The"
  Oil, in: 8 TEXASTEA
"Ballad of John and __*, The":
  4 YOKO
"Ballad of Reading ___, The":
  4 GAOL
Ballantine
  brew: 3 ALE
  Publisher: 3 IAN
Ballerina
  exercise: 4 PLIE
  perch: 3 TOE
  Prima: 6 ETOILE
  skirt: 4 **TUTU**
  support: 5 BARRE
  Word before: 5 PRIMA
Ballesteros
  Golfer: 4 **SEVE**
Ballet: 5 DANCE
  bend: 4 **PLIE**
  Copland: 5 RODEO
  leap: 4 **JETE**
  rail: 5 BARRE
  Russian ~ company: 5 KIROV
  skirt: 4 TUTU

  slipper: 7 TOESHOE
  step: 3 PAS
  Stravinsky: 4 AGON
  Stravinsky ~ character: 4 SWAN
Ballet ___: 5 RUSSE
"Ballet Rehearsal"
  artist: 5 DEGAS
Ballfield
  cover: 4 TARP
Ballistic
  Go: 4 **RAGE** RAVE 6 LOSEIT
    SEERED
Ballmer, Steve: 3 CEO
Balloon: 5 BLOAT SWELL
    8 AEROSTAT
  Bust, like a: 3 POP
  filler: 3 AIR 5 WATER 6 HOTAIR
  Trial: 6 FEELER
  Water ~ sound: 5 SPLAT
Ballot: 4 VOTE
  Cast a: 4 VOTE
  Defeat by: 7 OUTVOTE
  Marked, as a: 3 XED
  marks: 3 XES 4 EXES
  Paper ~ part: 4 CHAD
Ballpark
  Big Apple: 4 SHEA
  Bite at the: 5 FRANK
  figure: 4 RBIS STAT
    8 ESTIMATE
  figure (abbr.): 3 **EST**
  figure follower: 4 ORSO
  instrument: 5 ORGAN
  level: 4 TIER
  official: 3 UMP
Ballpoint: 3 PEN
  brand: 3 BIC
Ballroom
  beat: 5 SAMBA
  Castle of the: 5 IRENE
  dance: 5 MAMBO TANGO
    6 CHACHA 7 ONESTEP
    TWOSTEP
  dance, when doubled: 3 CHA
  One of a ~ couple: 4 LEAD
Ball-shaped: 7 SPHERIC
  cheese: 4 EDAM
Ballyhoo: 4 HYPE 6 HOOPLA
    7 PROMOTE

Balm: 5 SALVE
Apply ~ to: 6 SOOTHE
Burn: 4 **ALOE**
ingredient: 4 **ALOE**
target: 3 LIP
Balmoral: 3 CAP
relative: 3 TAM
Balmoral Castle
river: 3 DEE
Balmy: 4 WARM
Baloney: 3 ROT 4 JIVE LIES
    5 TRIPE 7 EYEWASH
    HOGWASH 8 NONSENSE
Bit of: 3 FIB
Brit's: 4 TOSH
Balsa: 4 TREE
vessel: 4 RAFT
Balsam: 3 FIR 4 TREE
Baltic
capital: 4 RIGA
native: 4 LETT
One of the ~ States: 6 LATVIA
    7 ESTONIA
On the: 4 ASEA
republic: 7 ESTONIA
River to the: 4 **ODER**
Baltic Sea
feeder: 4 **ODER**
Baltimore
athlete: 5 RAVEN 6 ORIOLE
bird: 6 ORIOLE
paper: 3 SUN
"___ Baltimore, The": 4 HOTL
Balzac
character: 10 PEREGORIOT
character Père: 6 GORIOT
Bamako
is its capital: 4 MALI
Bambi: 4 DEER FAWN
aunt: 3 **ENA**
Father of: 4 STAG
kin: 4 DEER
Mother of: 3 DOE
Bambino: 3 TOT 4 TYKE
of baseball: 4 RUTH
watcher: 5 MAMMA
Bamboo
eater: 5 **PANDA**
swordplay: 5 KENDO

Bamboozle: 3 CON 4 FOOL SNOW
    6 TAKEIN
Ban: 6 OUTLAW
rival: 5 ARRID
site: 6 ARMPIT
target: 4 ODOR
Banana
oil, for one: 5 ESTER
relative: 8 PLANTAIN
skin: 4 PEEL
Top: 4 STAR
Bananas: 4 LOCO 5 CRAZY
Go: 4 RAVE
Go ~ over: 5 EATUP
"Bananas"
director: 5 ALLEN
star: 3 RAE
Bancroft
Actress: 4 ANNE
Band: 4 GANG 5 COMBO STRAP
    6 STRIPE 8 ENSEMBLE
aid: 3 AMP
aide: 6 ROADIE
Booking for a: 3 GIG
Bride's: 4 RING
command: 5 HITIT
Decorative: 6 ARMLET
Eight-man: 5 OCTET
follower: 3 AID
Heraldic: 4 ORLE
instrument: 3 SAX 4 FIFE OBOE
    TUBA
Kind of: 6 ONEMAN
Palindromic: 4 ABBA
Sheriff's: 5 POSSE
Small: 4 TRIO 5 COMBO
together: 5 UNITE
TV: 3 UHF VHF
Bandage: 6 SWATHE 7 SWADDLE
brand: 3 ACE
Band-aid
rival: 5 CURAD
site: 3 CUT 4 GASH
B&B: 3 INN 5 BETAS
Part of: 3 BED
Banded
quartz: 4 ONYX
rock: 6 GNEISS
stone: 5 AGATE

Banderas
  Actor: 7 ANTONIO
  role: 5 ZORRO
Banderillero
  Cheer for a: 3 OLE
  target: 6 ELTORO
Bandit
  Hun-armed: 6 ATTILA
  One-armed: 4 SLOT
  Title ~ of opera: 6 ERNANI
Bando
  of baseball: 3 SAL
B&O
  Part of: 4 OHIO
  stop: 3 STA
  ~, et al.: 3 RRS
"Band of Gold"
  singer Payne: 5 FREDA
Bandstand
  box: 3 AMP
Bandy: 4 SWAP
  words: 4 SPAR 5 ARGUE
Bang
  Big ~ producer: 3 TNT 5 NITRO
  shut: 4 SLAM
  up: 5 SMASH
Banger: 7 SAUSAGE
Bangkok
  bread: 4 BAHT
  money: 4 BAHT
  native: 4 THAI
Bangladesh
  capital: 5 DACCA
Bangor
  state: 5 MAINE
  Town near: 5 ORONO
Banish: 5 **EXILE**
Banished: 6 EXILED 7 INEXILE
  person: 5 EXILE 7 EVICTEE
Banister: 4 RAIL 7 RAILING
  post: 5 NEWEL
  Rode the: 4 SLID
Banjo
  perch: 4 KNEE
  Play a: 5 STRUM
  sound: 5 TWANG
Banjoist
  ~ Fleck: 4 BELA
  ~ Scruggs: 4 EARL

Bank: 4 RELY TIER 5 CAROM
    LEVEE 6 LIENOR
  acct. entry: 3 INT
  addition: 8 INTEREST
  claim: 4 **LIEN**
  customer: 5 SAVER
  deposit: 3 ORE 4 SILT SNOW
  device (abbr.): 3 ATM
  employee: 6 TELLER
  fixture: 4 SAFE
  holding: 4 LIEN
  holding (abbr.): 4 MTGE
  job: 5 HEIST
  offering: 3 IRA 4 LOAN
    7 CARLOAN
  of France: 4 RIVE
  (on): 4 **RELY**
  posting: 4 RATE
  Put in the: 4 SAVE 5 SAVED
  regulating gp.: 4 FDIC
  sign number: 6 CDRATE
  takeback: 4 **REPO**
Bankbook
  entry (abbr.): 3 DEP INT
Bankhead
  Actress: 8 TALLULAH
Banking
  British ~ name: 7 BARCLAY
  controller: 7 AILERON
  convenience: 3 ATM
  initials: 4 FDIC
Bankroll: 3 WAD 4 FUND
Bankrupt: 4 RUIN SUNK
Bankruptcy: 4 RUIN
  Be near: 3 AIL
  follow-up: 4 SALE
Banks
  It's found in: 3 ORE
  of baseball: 5 ERNIE
  Supermodel: 4 TYRA
  They may be found in: 4 OARS
  ___ Banks: 5 OUTER
Banner: 4 FLAG 6 ENSIGN
Banners
  Internet: 3 ADS
Bannister: 5 MILER
  Runner: 5 ROGER
Banquet: 3 SUP 4 DINE FETE
    MEAL 5 FEAST 6 DINNER

host: 5 EMCEE
hosts (abbr.): 3 MCS
platform: 4 DAIS
with barbs: 5 ROAST
Banquo: 5 THANE
Banshee
Act the: 4 KEEN
Cry like a: 4 WAIL
land: 4 EIRE
Like a: 6 GAELIC
Banter: 4 JEST 8 REPARTEE
Engage in: 4 JOSH
Online: 4 CHAT
Talent for: 3 WIT
Bantu
language: 4 ZULU 6 RUANDA
tribe: 6 RUANDA
tribesman: 4 ZULU
Banyan: 4 TREE
Bao ___: 3 DAI
Baptism: 4 RITE
One sponsored at a: 6 GODSON
Baptist
prefix: 3 ANA
Bar: 5 ESTOP INGOT 7 MEASURE
at the bar: 5 ESTOP
8 ESTOPPEL
Barbecue: 4 SPIT
Bathroom: 4 SOAP
bill: 3 **TAB**
Car: 4 **AXLE**
Car with a: 4 LIMO
chaser: 4 SHOT
employee: 7 BOUNCER
fare: 5 SALAD SUSHI
flier: 4 DART
Gold: 5 INGOT
High: 5 ROOST
ingredient: 7 GRANOLA
in the fridge: 4 OLEO
intro: 3 ISO
Kind of: 5 CANDY PIANO SPACE
Metal: 5 INGOT
One who can't pass the: 3 SOT
order: 3 ALE RUM RYE 4 BEER
NEAT 5 LAGER 6 CHASER
REFILL 7 MARTINI
order, with "the": 4 SAME
5 USUAL

Read a ~ code: 4 SCAN
regular: 6 PATRON
rocks: 3 ICE
Sand: 5 SHOAL
seat: 5 STOOL
Shot at the: 5 SNORT
sing-along: 7 KARAOKE
Snack: 7 GRANOLA
sound: 3 HIC
Straight, at the: 4 NEAT
Typing: 6 SPACER
Bar ___: 4 NONE
Bara
Actress: 5 THEDA
Baracus, B.A.
portrayer: 3 MRT
Barak: 7 ISRAELI
country: 6 ISRAEL
of Israel: 4 EHUD
Barb: 3 DIG
Barbara
Actress: 4 BAIN EDEN HALE
nickname: 4 BABS
"Barbara ___" (Beach Boys hit):
3 ANN
"Barbarella"
actor Milo: 5 OSHEA
Barbarian: 3 HUN 4 GOTH
OGRE
___ the: 5 CONAN
Barbaric: 5 CRUEL 6 SAVAGE
Barbarossa
realm (abbr.): 3 HRE
Barbary
beast: 3 **APE**
Barbary Coast
city: 5 TUNIS
Barbary State: 7 TRIPOLI
Former: 5 TUNIS 7 ALGIERS
Barbecue: 5 BROIL
bar: 4 SPIT
bit: 3 RIB
fare: 4 RIBS 9 SPARERIBS
fuel: 7 PROPANE
nugget: 4 COAL
offering: 5 KABOB KEBAB
receptacle: 6 ASHPIT
rod: 4 SPIT
site: 4 YARD 5 PATIO

Barbed
  barricade: 6 ABATIS
  comment: 3 JAB 4 GIBE
  It may be: 4 WIRE
Barbell
  abbr.: 3 LBS
  metal: 4 IRON
Barber
  call: 4 NEXT
  chair attachment: 5 STROP
  focus: 4 HAIR
  job: 4 TRIM 5 SHAVE
  motion: 4 SNIP
  obstacle: 3 EAR
  of music: 6 SAMUEL
  of Seville: 6 FIGARO
  powder: 4 TALC
  sharpener: 5 STROP
  shop sound: 4 SNIP
  Sports broadcaster: 3 RED
Barbera
  partner: 5 HANNA
"Barber of Seville, The": 5 OPERA
  composer: 7 ROSSINI
  role: 6 FIGARO
Barbershop
  band: 5 STROP
  call: 4 NEXT
  quartet member: 4 BASS
          5 TENOR
  request: 4 TRIM
  sound: 4 **SNIP**
  symbol: 4 POLE
Barbie: 4 DOLL
  beau: 3 **KEN**
  boyfriend: 3 KEN
  maker: 6 MATTEL
Barbieri
  Jazzman: 4 GATO
Barbizon School
  artist: 5 COROT DUPRE
Barbuda
  Island near: 7 ANTIGUA
Barcelona
  Info: Spanish cue
  beach: 5 PLAYA
  bear: 3 OSO
  boy: 4 NINO
  bravo: 3 OLE

  buck: 6 PESETA
  buddy: 5 AMIGO
  bull: 4 TORO
Bard: 4 POET
  Above, to a: 3 OER
  Before, to a: 3 **ERE**
  Below, to a: 5 NEATH
  Between, to a: 5 TWIXT
  Black, to a: 4 EBON
  Inspiration, to a: 5 ERATO
  Nightfall, to a: 3 EEN
  of boxing: 3 ALI
  River, to a: 4 **AVON**
  Soon, to a: 4 ANON
  Unclose, to a: 3 OPE
Bard of ___: 4 AVON
Bare: 4 MERE 6 DENUDE
  Lay: 6 DENUDE
  Not: 4 CLAD
Barefaced: 4 BOLD 6 BRAZEN
          7 BLATANT
Barefoot: 6 UNSHOD
  Not: 4 SHOD
"Barefoot Contessa, The"
  actor Brazzi: 7 ROSSANO
  actor O'Brien: 6 EDMOND
  actress Gardner: 3 AVA
Barents: 3 SEA
Barfly: 3 SOT
  perch: 5 STOOL
Bargain: 4 DEAL PACT PLEA
          5 STEAL 9 NEGOTIATE
  event: 4 SALE
  for leniency: 8 COPAPLEA
  Great: 5 **STEAL**
  hunter's stop: 7 TAGSALE
  site: 8 YARDSALE
Bargain-basement: 7 CUTRATE
Barge: 4 SCOW
Barge ___: 4 INON
Barilla
  rival: 4 RAGU
Baritone
  Voice above: 5 TENOR
Bark: 3 YAP 4 YELL
  beetle target: 3 ELM
  Comics: 3 **ARF**
  Little: 3 YIP
  Sharp: 3 YIP 4 YELP

Barker
and others: 3 MAS
Arctic: 4 SEAL
Baum: 4 TOTO
Circus: 4 SEAL
Novelist: 5 CLIVE
Barkin
Actress: 5 **ELLEN**
Barkless
dog: 7 BASENJI
Barkley
Boxer: 4 IRAN
title, slangily: 4 VEEP
Truman veep: 5 ALBEN
Barley
beard: 3 AWN
Germinated: 4 MALT
Bar mitzvah: 4 RITE
boy: 4 TEEN
dance: 4 **HORA**
official: 5 RABBI
reading: 5 TORAH
Barn
area: 4 LOFT
baby: 5 OWLET
bedding: 5 STRAW
bird: 3 OWL
dance: 4 REEL
7 HOEDOWN
neighbor: 4 SILO
Pile in a: 6 HAYMOW
topper: 4 VANE
"Barnaby Jones"
actor Buddy: 5 EBSEN
Barnard
graduate: 6 ALUMNA
Barnes
Critic: 5 CLIVE
of hockey: 3 STU
partner: 5 NOBLE
Barney
fan: 3 TOT
Neighbor of: 4 FRED
"Barney Miller"
actor Jack: 3 **SOO**
actor Linden: 3 HAL
actor Max: 4 GAIL
actor Vigoda: 3 ABE
Barnstorm: 6 AVIATE

Barnum, P.T.: 6 HOAXER
7 SHOWMAN
Exit, to: 6 EGRESS
Soprano who worked for:
4 LIND
Barnyard
baby: 3 KID
beast: 4 GOAT
bird: 4 FOWL
bleat: 3 MAA
cry: 5 BLEAT
enclosure: 3 STY
honker: 5 GOOSE
layer: 3 HEN
male: 3 TOM
mom: 3 EWE
perch: 5 ROOST
Barometer
type: 7 ANEROID
Baron
Scottish: 5 THANE
Baronet
title: 3 SIR
Baroque: 5 STYLE 6 ORNATE
composer: 4 BACH
style: 6 ROCOCO
Barr, William
successor: 4 RENO
Barracks
bed: 3 **COT**
boss: 5 SARGE
~ VIP: 3 NCO
Barracuda
Baby: 4 SPET
Barrage: 4 PELT 5 BLITZ SALVO
Barre
room bend: 4 PLIE
Barrel: 3 KEG 4 CASK
Beer: 3 **KEG**
Bottom of the: 4 LEES
Kind of: 4 PORK
Large: 4 DRUM
Lock, stock, and: 3 ALL
maker: 6 COOPER
material: 3 ELM
of laughs: 4 RIOT
part: 5 **STAVE**
Wine: 4 CASK
___ **barrel:** 5 OVERA

Barreled
along: 4 TORE
Barrelhead
bills: 4 CASH
Barrel race
participant: 7 COWGIRL
site: 5 RODEO
Barren: 4 ARID 6 DESERT
7 STERILE 8 DESOLATE
Barrett
Gossip columnist: 4 **RONA**
of Pink Floyd: 3 **SYD**
Barricade: 4 SHUT
Barbed-wire: 6 ABATIS
Barrie
baddie: 4 SMEE
boy: 3 PAN
dog: 4 NANA
Barrier: 4 WALL
Atoll: 4 REEF
Badminton: 3 NET
breaker: 3 SST
Cold War: 11 IRONCURTAIN
Corporate: 12 GLASSCEILING
Flood: 5 LEVEE
Subway: 5 STILE
Tennis: 3 NET
Water: 4 DIKE MOAT
Zoo: 4 MOAT
Barrio
Calif. ~ city: 6 EASTLA
grocery: 6 BODEGA
outsider: 5 ANGLO
resident: 6 LATINO
Barris, Chuck
game show prop: 4 GONG
Barrister
accessory: 3 WIG
Barroom
brawl: 5 MELEE
Barrow
native: 6 ESKIMO
Barry
Humorist: 4 DAVE
Singer: 3 LEN
Barrymore
Actress: 4 DREW 5 **ETHEL**
Bars
Behind: 5 CAGED

It's sold in: 4 OLEO SOAP
One behind: 3 CON
Opening: 5 INTRO
Bart
Father of: 5 HOMER
Football legend: 5 STARR
Grandpa of: 3 ABE
Homer, to: 3 DAD
Lisa, to: 3 SIS
Mother of: 5 MARGE
Sister of: 4 LISA
~, to Homer: 3 SON
Bartender
A ~ may run one: 3 TAB
need: 3 ICE
requests: 3 IDS
Rocks, to a: 3 ICE
Barter: 4 SWAP 5 TRADE
"Bartered Bride, The":
5 OPERA
composer: 7 SMETANA
mezzo: 5 AGNES
Barterer
Biblical: 4 ESAU
Bartlett: 4 PEAR
Abbr. from: 4 ANON
kin: 4 BOSC
piece: 5 QUOTE
Bartok
Actress: 3 EVA
Composer: 4 **BELA**
Bartoli
piece: 4 ARIA
Bartolomeu
Explorer: 4 DIAS
Barton
Red Cross nurse: 5 CLARA
___ **Barton (Triple Crown winner):**
3 SIR
Baryshnikov, Mikhail
birthplace: 4 RIGA 6 LATVIA
early influence: 7 ASTAIRE
leap: 4 JETE
nickname: 5 MISHA
~, by birth: 4 LETT
Basalt
source: 4 LAVA
Base: 4 EVIL VILE 6 ALKALI
SORDID TAWDRY

7 IGNOBLE IMMORAL
NONACID 8 SINISTER
address: 3 SIR
Be off: 3 ERR
eatery: 7 CANTEEN
8 MESSHALL
figure (abbr.): 3 NCO
greeting: 6 SALUTE
horn: 5 BUGLE
Illegally off: 4 AWOL
information: 4 DATA
.kid: 8 ARMYBRAT
Off: 4 AWOL 7 INERROR
Off ~ with permission:
7 ONLEAVE
runner's achievement: 5 STEAL
stealer Brock: 3 LOU
tune: 4 TAPS
~ 8: 5 OCTAL

Baseball
ancestor: 8 ROUNDERS
base: 3 BAG
bat wood: 3 **ASH**
blunder: 5 ERROR
club: 3 BAT
commissioner Bud: 5 SELIG
deal: 5 TRADE
diamond cover: 4 TARP
execs: 3 GMS
family name: 4 **ALOU**
feature: 4 SEAM
Former ~ commissioner Bowie:
4 KUHN
glove: 4 MITT
rarity: 3 TIE
stat: 3 **ERA RBI** 6 ATBATS
ERRORS STEALS
team: 4 NINE 6 ENNEAD

Baseballer
Certain ~ (abbr.): 4 ALER NLER
Detroit: 5 TIGER
Houston: 5 ASTRO
Montreal: 4 EXPO
San Diego: 5 PADRE

"Baseball Tonight"
network: 4 ESPN

Basecoat
Apply a: 5 PRIME
Paint: 6 SEALER

Baseless
rumor: 6 CANARD

Baseman
blunder: 5 ERROR
First ~ in a comedy routine:
3 WHO
Second ~ in a comedy routine:
4 WHAT

Basement
Bargain ~ sign: 4 SAVE
feature: 7 RECROOM
fixture: 7 FURNACE
Like a finished: 7 PANELED

Baserunner: 7 STEALER

Bash: 4 FETE
All-night: 4 RAVE
Bacchanalian: 4 ORGY
Big: 4 FETE **GALA** 7 SHINDIG
Evening: 6 SOIREE
Maui: 4 LUAU

Bashar
of Syria: 5 ASSAD

Bashful: 3 SHY 5 DWARF
6 DEMURE
companion: 3 DOC 5 DOPEY

Basic: 4 BARE MERE 6 ALKALI
8 NOFRILLS
9 ELEMENTAL
11 FUNDAMENTAL
bit: 4 ATOM
command: 4 GOTO
element: 4 UNIT
stuff: 4 ABCS

Basically: 9 INESSENCE

Basics: 4 **ABCS**

Basie, William "Count"
instrument: 5 PIANO

Basil: 4 HERB
sauce: 5 **PESTO**

Basil ___, Sir: 6 SPENCE

Basilica
area: 4 APSE NAVE
bench: 3 PEW
center: 4 NAVE
section: 4 APSE

Basin
accessory: 4 EWER
Boat: 6 MARINA
Essen: 4 RUHR

German: 4 SAAR
Holy-water: 5 STOUP
type: 5 TIDAL

Basinger
Actress: 3 KIM

Basis: 4 ROOT SEED 6 REASON

Bask: 3 TAN

Basket
Angler's: 5 CREEL
Easy: 5 LAYUP TAPIN TIPIN
fiber: 5 ISTLE
Jai alai: 5 **CESTA**
Long ~, in hoops lingo: 4 TREY
material: 5 OSIER 6 RAFFIA

Basketball
brand: 4 VOIT
College ~ tourney: 3 NIT
defense: 4 ZONE
hoop: 3 RIM
player: 5 CAGER
rim: 4 HOOP
shot: 5 LAYUP TIPIN
stadium: 5 ARENA
stat: 6 ASSIST 7 REBOUND
tactic: 5 PRESS
       9 FASTBREAK
target: 4 HOOP
Two-player ~ game:
       8 ONEONONE

Basketballer: 5 CAGER
Beehive State: 3 UTE
Boston: 6 CELTIC
Indiana: 5 PACER

Basketmaking
branch: 5 OSIER
need: 5 ISTLE
Palm used in: 4 NIPA

Baskin-Robbins
purchase: 4 CONE
serving: 5 SCOOP

Basque: 7 IBERIAN
ancestor: 7 IBERIAN
kingdom: 7 NAVARRE
org.: 3 ETA

Basra
land: 4 IRAQ
resident: 5 IRAQI

Bas-relief
medium: 5 GESSO

Bass: 3 ALE LOW 4 CLEF DEEP
       FISH 5 VOICE
line player: 4 TUBA
player: 6 ANGLER
product: 3 ALE
suffix: 3 OON

Bass ___ : 3 ALE

Basset hound
feature: 4 EARS
Like ~ ears: 6 DROOPY

Bassett
Actress: 6 ANGELA

Basso
~ Pinza: 4 **EZIO**

Bassoon: 4 **REED**
Like a: 5 REEDY
relative: 4 OBOE

Bassoonist
purchase: 4 REED

Baste: 3 SEW

Bastille Day
season: 3 ETE

Basutoland
~, today: 7 LESOTHO

Bat
again: 5 REHIT
home: 4 CAVE
navigation aid: 4 ECHO
Next to: 6 ONDECK
one's eyelashes: 5 FLIRT
Substance on a: 7 PINETAR
wood: 3 **ASH**

Batch
Auctioneer: 3 LOT
Dryer: 4 LOAD
Matched: 3 SET
of stew: 6 POTFUL

Bates
Actor: 4 ALAN
Actress: 5 KATHY
Author/poet: 4 ARLO
establishment: 5 MOTEL

Bath: 3 **SPA**
Info: British cue
county: 4 AVON
Enjoy a long: 4 SOAK
Finnish: 5 SAUNA
Need a ~ badly: 4 REEK
powder: 4 **TALC**

Relaxing: **4** SOAK
site (abbr.): **3** ENG
sponge: **6** LOOFAH
Steam: **5** SAUNA
suds: **3** ALE
Take a: **4** LAVE
water: **4** AVON
___ bath: **4** SITZ

Bathday
cake: **4** SOAP

Bathe: 4 LAVE **7** CLEANSE

"Bathers, The"
painter: **6** RENOIR **7** CEZANNE

Bathhouse: 6 CABANA

Bathing
suit top: **3** BRA
Type of ~ suit: **8** ONEPIECE
vessel: **3** TUB

Bathroom
bar: **4** SOAP
Bath: **3** LOO
flooring: **4** TILE
installation: **3** SPA
item: **3** MAT **5** SCALE
Like a ~ floor: **5** TILED
powder: **4** TALC

Bathsheba
husband: **5** URIAH
Son of: **7** SOLOMON

Baths of Caracalla
site: **4** ROME

Bathtub
booze: **3** GIN
Dirty ~ trait: **4** RING
feature: **5** DRAIN
murder victim: **5** MARAT

Bathwater
additive: **3** OIL
tester: **3** TOE

Bathysphere
designer: **5** BEEBE

Batik
artisan: **4** DYER
need: **3** DYE

Batista
successor: **6** CASTRO

Batman
and Robin: **3** DUO
and Robin, to villains:

7 NEMESES
butler: **6** ALFRED
costume part: **4** CAPE COWL
headquarters: **4** CAVE
Like: **5** CAPED
portrayer Adam: **4** WEST
portrayer Christian: **4** BALE
portrayer Kilmer: **3** VAL
sidekick: **5** ROBIN
~, to villains: **7** NEMESIS

"Batman"
actress Basinger: **3** KIM
sound effect: **3** BAM POW

Bat Masterson
trademark: **4** CANE **5** DERBY

Baton: 4 WAND **5** STICK
Handle a: **5** TWIRL
race: **5** RELAY
wielder: **7** MAESTRO

Baton Rouge
school (abbr.): **3** <u>LSU</u>
___ **Bator: 4** <u>ULAN</u>

Bats: 4 LOCO **5** DAFFY LOONY
NUTTY

Batten
down: **6** SECURE

Batter
Blend: **4** STIR
concern: **6** STANCE
position: **5** PLATE **6** STANCE
stat.: **3** RBI
success: **3** HIT **7** BASEHIT

Batteries
Small: **3** AAS **4** AAAS
Some: **3** AAS **4** AAAS
They may come in: **5** TESTS
Walkman: **3** AAS

Battering
device: **3** RAM
wind: **4** GALE

Battery
brand: **5** DELCO
component: **4** TEST
Electric ~ inventor: **5** VOLTA
fluid: **4** ACID
Of a ~ type: **6** ANODAL
part: **5** ANODE
size: **3** <u>AAA</u>
Small ~ size: **3** <u>AAA</u>

terminal: **5 ANODE**
terminal (abbr.): **3** NEG POS
type: **5** NICAD SOLAR
   7 DRYCELL
unit: **4** TEST VOLT
Batting
avg.: **3** PCT
stat.: **3** AVG RBI
Batting champ
1966 N.L. ~: **4** ALOU
Five-time: **5** BOGGS
Seven-time ~ Rod: **5** CAREW
Three-time ~ Tony: **5** OLIVA
Battle
Area away from the: **4** REAR
Court: **6** TENNIS
Engaged in: **5** ATWAR
Equip for: **3** ARM
field: **5** OPERA
memento: **4** SCAR
of behemoths: **4** SUMO
of wits: **5** CHESS
One-on-one: **4** DUEL
Ready for: **5** ARMED
song: **4** ARIA
Stage a ~, maybe: **7** REENACT
the clock: **4** RACE
"Battle Cry"
author Leon: **4** URIS
Battlefield: 5 ARENA
healer: **5** MEDIC
shout: **5** MEDIC
Battleground: 5 ARENA
Battle of Britain
gp.: **3** RAF
Battle of the ___ : 5 BANDS SEXES
Battle of the Bulge
locale: **8** ARDENNES
Battlers
Proverbial: **5** SEXES
Battleship
blast: **5** SALVO
color: **4** GRAY
letters: **3** USS
U.S. ~ destroyed in 1898:
   5 MAINE
Battle site
1836 ~: **5** ALAMO
1862 ~: **6** SHILOH **8** ANTIETAM

1914 ~: **4** YSER **5** MARNE
1944 ~: **4** STLO **5** BULGE
   LEYTE
490 B.C. ~: **8** MARATHON
Civil War: **6** SHILOH
Normandy: **4** STLO
Pacific: **7** OKINAWA
War of 1812: **4** ERIE
WWI: **4** YSER **5** MARNE SOMME
   YPRES
WWII: **4** STLO **6** BATAAN
WWII ~, for short: **3** IWO
"Battlestar Galactica"
commander: **5** ADAMA
Battling: 5 ATWAR
Batt. terminal: 3 POS
Batty: 4 LOCO **5** NUTSO
Bauble: 3 TOY **6** DOODAD
   GEEGAW GEWGAW
"Baudolino"
author Umberto: **3** ECO
Bauhaus
artist: **4** KLEE
Baum
canine: **4** TOTO
End of a ~ title: **4** OFOZ
princess: **4** OZMA
Bausch
partner: **4** LOMB
Bauxite: 3 ORE
component: **7** ALUMINA
Bavaria
river: **4** EGER ISAR
Bawdy: 4 LEWD
Bawdyhouse
manager: **5** MADAM
Bawl: 3 CRY SOB
Have a: **3** CRY SOB **4** WEEP
(out): **4** CHEW REAM
Baxter
Actress: **4** ANNE
Bandleader: **3** LES
Sitcom newsman: **3** TED
Bay: 4 COVE MARE **5** INLET
at the moon: **4** HOWL
Bring to: **4** TREE
Brought to: **5** TREED
city: **5** TAMPA
Maine: **5** CASCO

Scottish: 4 LOCH
Small: 5 INLET
Sound from a: 5 NEIGH
   window: 5 **ORIEL**
Bay ___: 4 AREA
Bayer
   alternative: 6 ANACIN
   brand: 5 ALEVE 7 ONEADAY
Bayes
   Vaudevillian: 4 NORA
Bayh
   Indiana senator: 4 **EVAN**
Baylor
   Basketball player: 5 ELGIN
Baylor University
   city: 4 WACO
Bay of Bengal
   city: 6 MADRAS
Bay of Biscay
   feeder: 5 LOIRE
Bay of Fundy
   feature: 4 TIDE
Bay of Naples
   isle: 5 CAPRI
Bay of Pigs
   locale: 4 CUBA
Bay of Whales
   sea: 4 ROSS
Bayonet: 4 STAB
Bay State
   cape: 3 ANN
   sch.: 5 UMASS
   symbol: 7 ELMTREE
"Baywatch"
   actress Anderson: 6 PAMELA
   actress Bingham: 5 TRACI
   actress Eleniak: 5 ERIKA
   actress ___ Lee Nolin: 4 GENA
   event: 6 RESCUE
Bazaar
   merchant: 4 ARAB
Bazin
   Author: 4 RENE
Bazooka: 4 TUBE
   product: 3 GUM
Bazooka Joe
   pal: 4 MORT
BB: 4 AMMO 6 PELLET
   gun: 8 AIRRIFLE

B-ball
   connection: 4 ASIN
   Place to play: 4 YMCA
BBC
   comedy: 5 ABFAB
   rival: 3 ITN
   Something to watch the ~ on:
     5 TELLY
"B ___ boy": 4 ASIN
BBS
   manager: 5 SYSOP
B.C.
   cartoonist: 4 HART
   neighbor: 4 ALTA
BCE
   Part of: 3 ERA
Be: 5 EXIST
   To ~, in French: 4 ETRE
   To ~, in Latin: 4 ESSE
   To ~, in Spanish: 3 SER
"Be ___!": 4 APAL
Bea
   Role for: 5 MAUDE
Beach: 5 SHORE 6 STRAND
   acquisition: 3 TAN
   Barcelona: 5 PLAYA
   bird: 4 TERN
   blanket: 4 SAND
   color: 3 TAN
   D-Day: 4 UTAH 5 **OMAHA**
   feature: 4 DUNE
   house: 6 CABANA
   Like a: 5 SANDY
   On the: 6 ASHORE
   Reach the: 4 LAND
   Rio: 7 IPANEMA
   scavenger: 4 GULL
   shade: 3 TAN
   sidler: 4 CRAB
   site: 4 ISLE
   souvenir: 5 SHELL
   They're caught at the: 4 RAYS
   toy: 4 PAIL
___ Beach: 4 VERO 5 PISMO
     6 LAGUNA MYRTLE
Beach Boys
   Car in a ~ tune: 5 TBIRD
   Girl in a ~ song: 6 RHONDA
   hit song: 6 KOKOMO

15 CALIFORNIAGIRLS
Beachgoer
goal: 3 TAN
worry: 4 BURN
Beachhead
D-Day: 4 UTAH 5 OMAHA
of 1/22/44: 5 ANZIO
Beachwear: 5 THONG 6 BIKINI
Beacon: 4 LAMP 5 LIGHT
Bead
counters: 5 ABACI
Draw a: 3 AIM
Draw a ~ on: 5 AIMAT
material: 5 NACRE
Rosary ~ representation:
    8 AVEMARIA
Beads
Item with: 6 ABACUS
on blades: 3 DEW
Prayer: 6 ROSARY
Produce: 8 PERSPIRE
Beagle
LBJ: 3 HER HIM
Writer aboard the: 6 DARWIN
Beak: 3 NEB NIB 4 NOSE
    5 SNOOT 6 SCHNOZ
Use the ~ on: 5 PREEN
"Be All That You Can Be"
group: 4 ARMY 6 USARMY
Beam: 3 RAY 4 GRIN 5 SMILE
Building: 4 **IBAR** 5 JOIST
Construction: 4 IBAR
of light: 3 RAY 6 SUNRAY
splitter: 5 PRISM
Support: 4 IBAR 5 JOIST TRUSS
Surgical: 5 LASER
Type of: 5 LASER
Use a surgical: 4 LASE
Beame
Mayor: 3 ABE
Beaming: 5 AGLOW 7 RADIANT
"Beam ___, Scotty!": 4 MEUP
Bean: 3 NOB 4 CONK HEAD
    6 NOGGIN NOODLE
Actor: 4 SEAN 5 ORSON
Astronaut: 4 ALAN
Broad: 4 FAVA
counter, for short: 3 CPA
cover: 3 HAT

curd: 4 **TOFU**
French: 4 TETE
holder: 3 POD
Judge: 3 ROY
Kind of: 4 FAVA NAVY SOYA
    5 CACAO CAROB PINTO
    6 KIDNEY
product: 4 IDEA
Protein: 4 SOYA
Succotash: 4 LIMA
town: 4 LIMA
Beanery
fare: 4 HASH
handout: 4 MENU
side: 4 SLAW
sign: 4 EATS
Beanie: 3 CAP HAT
Beanie Babies: 3 FAD 5 CRAZE
Beans: 8 SIDEDISH
Cook, as: 5 REFRY
It may be full of: 4 TACO
    7 BURRITO
partner: 4 RICE
Spill the: 3 RAT 4 **BLAB** SING
    TALK TELL 5 LETON
    6 TATTLE
Beantown
team: 3 SOX
Beany
friend: 5 CECIL
Bear: 5 ABIDE STAND 6 ENDURE
    MAMMAL 8 TOLERATE
Act like a: 4 SELL
advice: 4 SELL
Barcelona: 3 OSA OSO
Bring to: 5 EXERT
Cartoon: 4 YOGI
Celestial: 4 **URSA**
claw: 6 PASTRY
Cuddly: 5 TEDDY
feet: 4 PAWS
hands: 4 PAWS
Heavenly: 4 URSA
home: 3 DEN
in the air: 4 URSA
in the sky: 4 URSA
lair: 3 DEN 4 CAVE
Load to: 4 ONUS
Milne: 4 POOH

of literature: **4 MAMA PAPA**
of note: **6 SMOKEY**
Sky: **4 URSA**
suffix: **3 ISH**
witness: **6 ATTEST**
young, as sheep: **4 YEAN**
Bearable
Make: **4 EASE**
Beard
Barley: **3 AWN**
Pointed: **6 GOATEE**
Bearded
animal: **4 GOAT**
antelope: **3 GNU**
beast: **3 GNU**
bloom: **4 IRIS**
~, as barley: **5 AWNED**
Beardless: 6 SHAVEN
Bearer
Acorn: **3 OAK**
Biblical: **3 ASS**
Bindle: **4 HOBO**
Blame: **4 GOAT**
Cone: **3 FIR**
Flag: **4 MAST**
Needle: **4 PINE**
Ring: **4 WIFE 6 SATURN**
Sheepskin: **4 GRAD**
Bearing: 3 AIR 4 MIEN
    6 MANNER 8 CARRIAGE
    DEMEANOR PRESENCE
Bearings
Find one's: **6 ORIENT**
Bearish: 6 URSINE
Bearlike
beast: **5 KOALA PANDA**
Béarnaise: 5 SAUCE
ingredient: **8 TARRAGON**
Bears: 4 TEAM
coach: **5 DITKA HALAS**
What ~ do: **4 SELL**
Beast: 4 OGRE 5 BRUTE
    6 ANIMAL
African: **5 RHINO**
Andean: **5 LLAMA**
Antlered: **3 ELK**
Balaam: **3 ASS**
Barbary: **3 APE**
Bearded: **3 GNU**

Borneo: **5 ORANG**
Braying: **3 ASS**
Burrowing: **4 MOLE**
Caravan: **5 CAMEL**
Grimm: **4 OGRE**
Himalayan: **3 YAK**
Horned: **5 RHINO**
Long-snouted: **5 TAPIR**
of Borden: **5 ELSIE**
of burden: **3 ASS 5 LLAMA**
Stubborn: **4 MULE**
Tolkien: **3 ORC**
Zodiac: **3 RAM**
Beasts
Branded: **6 CATTLE**
Yoked: **4 OXEN**
Beat: 3 TOP 4 BEST 5 ALLIN
    OUTDO PULSE TEMPO
    THROB TIRED 6 BESTED
    PUMMEL 7 PULSATE
    8 DEFEATED
at the polls: **7 OUTVOTE**
back: **7 REPULSE**
badly: **4 ROUT 5 CREAM TROMP**
    7 SHELLAC
Barely: **3 NIP 4 EDGE 5 EDGED**
    7 EDGEOUT NOSEOUT
    8 EDGEDOUT
Brazilian: **5 SAMBA**
ending: **3 NIK**
it: **3 LAM 4 FLED FLEE**
    5 BONGO SCRAM
Mailman's: **5 ROUTE**
One with a: **3 COP**
the draft: **6 ENLIST**
the wheat: **6 THRESH**
to a pulp: **4 MASH**
to the tape: **6 OUTRAN OUTRUN**
Usher's: **5 AISLE**
Walk a: **6 PATROL**
walker: **3 COP**
with a stick: **4 FLOG**
Beaten
It may be: **3 EGG RAP 4 PATH**
It may be ~ at a party: **6 PINATA**
Was ~ by: **6 LOSTTO**
Beater
Birdie: **5 EAGLE**
Bogey: **3 PAR**

Breast: **5** HEART
Deuce: **4** TREY
Egg: **5** WHISK
King: **3** ACE
Proverbial sword: **3** PEN
Rock: **5** PAPER
Beating: 4 LOSS **6** ATHROB
   sound: **7** PITAPAT
Beatle
   bride: **3** ONO
   drummer: **5** RINGO STARR
   Early ~ Sutcliffe: **3** STU
Beatles
   adjective: **3** FAB
   album: **4** HELP **9** ABBEYROAD
   Best of the: **4** PETE
   Country in a ~ song: **4** USSR
   film: **4** HELP
   Girl in a ~ song: **4** ANNA RITA
      5 RIGBY SADIE
   hit song: **4** HELP **7** IMEMINE
      LETITBE **8** LOVEMEDO
      9 IFEELFINE
      15 HERECOMESTHESUN
      WHENIMSIXTYFOUR
      YELLOWSUBMARINE
   Instrument on some ~ songs:
      5 SITAR
   manager: **7** EPSTEIN
   meter maid: **4** RITA
   phenomenon: **5** MANIA
   refrain: **4** YEAH
   Start of a ~ title: **6** OBLADI
Beatnik
   abode: **3** PAD
   exclamation: **3** MAN **4** IDIG
      5 IMHIP
   instrument: **5** BONGO
Beatrice
   admirer: **5** DANTE
"Beats me!": 5 DUNNO **6** IDUNNO
      NOIDEA
Beattie
   Author: **3** **ANN**
Beat ___ to one's door: 5 APATH
Beatty
   Actor: **3** **NED** **6** WARREN
   bomb: **6** ISHTAR
   film: **4** REDS **5** BUGSY **6** ISHTAR

   flop: **6** ISHTAR
   role: **5** BUGSY
Beau: 5 ROMEO SWAIN WOOER
   Barbie's: **3** KEN
   Bordeaux: **3** AMI
   Doe's: **4** STAG
   Ewe's: **3** RAM
   Former: **8** OLDFLAME
   Rose's: **4** ABIE
Beau ___ (noble deed): 5 GESTE
"Beau ___": 5 GESTE
Beau Brummel: 3 FOP **5** DANDY
   concern: **6** ATTIRE
   school: **4** ETON
___ beaucoup: 5 MERCI
Beaufort: 5 SCALE
   scale category: **4** GALE **5** STORM
      11 FRESHBREEZE
Beaujolais: 4 WINE
Beauregard
   boss: **3** LEE
Beautician: 4 DYER **7** ADORNER
Beauties: 6 BELLES
   Group of: **4** BEVY
"Beautiful Mind, A": 6 BIOPIC
   actor: **5** CROWE **8** EDHARRIS
   subject: **4** NASH
Beauty: 3 GEM
   admirer: **5** BEAST
   Ancient: **5** HELEN
   Hardly a: **3** HAG **9** PLAINJANE
   Like a ~ queen: **7** TIARAED
   mark: **3** TEN
   pageant wear: **4** SASH
   parlor: **5** SALON
   preceder: **3** AGE
   queen's crown: **5** TIARA
___ Beauty (apple type): 4 ROME
"Beauty and the Beast"
   character: **5** BELLE
Beauvais
   department: **4** OISE
Beaux-Arts
   ___ des ~: 5 ECOLE
Beaver: 6 RODENT
   brother: **5** WALLY
   Chew as a: **4** **GNAW**
   creation: **3** DAM
   Like a: **5** EAGER

Beaver State: 6 OREGON
  (abbr.): 3 ORE 4 OREG
  capital: 5 SALEM
"Be-Bop-___": 5 ALULA
Because: 3 FOR 5 **SINCE**
  6 INTHAT
  of: 5 **DUETO**
  of this: 6 HEREAT
"Because ___!": 6 ISAYSO
Becker
  of tennis: 5 BORIS
"Becker"
  actor Danson: 3 TED
"Becket"
  actor Peter: 6 OTOOLE
Beckett
  award: 4 OBIE
  no-show: 5 GODOT
  title character: 5 GODOT
Beckon: 6 CALLTO INVITE
Becloud: 5 MUDDY 6 DARKEN
Become: 4 SUIT 8 TURNINTO
  ~, finally: 5 ENDUP
Bed
  Army: 3 COT
  Baby: 4 CRIB 6 CRADLE
  Barracks: 3 COT
  board: 4 SLAT
  ending: 5 STEAD
  Feather: 3 TAR
  Get out of: 4 RISE 5 ARISE
    ROUST
  Go to: 6 RETIRE
  Got out of: 5 AROSE
  Gotten out of: 6 ARISEN
  Kebab: 5 PILAF
  Make a: 3 HOE
  Out of: 5 ASTIR RISEN
    6 ARISEN
  Portable: 3 COT
  Push out of: 5 ROUST
  size: 4 TWIN
  Still in: 5 NOTUP
  support: 4 SLAT
Bed-and-breakfast: 3 **INN**
Bedaub: 5 SMEAR
Bedazzle: 3 AWE
Bedazzled: 5 INAWE
Bedding: 5 LINEN

  Barn: 5 STRAW
  item: 4 SHAM
  material: 5 LINEN SATIN
  Whack: 9 RAPSHEETS
Beddy-bye
  outfit: 7 JAMMIES
Bedeck: 4 DOUP 5 ADORN
Bedevil: 3 VEX 5 NAGAT TEASE
Bedim: 5 BLEAR
"Bed-in for Peace"
  participant: 3 ONO
Bedlam: 3 DIN 5 CHAOS
Bedmate
  Bother a: 5 SNORE
  Bothersome: 6 SNORER
Bedouin: 4 ARAB 5 NOMAD
  bigwig: 4 EMIR
  home: 4 TENT
  transport: 5 CAMEL
"Bed Riddance"
  poet: 4 NASH
Bedridden
  Be: 3 AIL
Bedrock
  pet: 4 DINO
Bedroom
  furniture: 6 BUREAU
    7 ARMOIRE DRESSER
Beds
  Like some: 4 MADE 6 UNMADE
Bedside
  awakener: 5 ALARM
  light: 4 LAMP
Bedtime
  Child's ~ request: 5 STORY
  Entertain at: 6 READTO
  Late: 5 ONEAM
  Nearing: 6 LATISH
  Put off: 6 STAYUP
  story: 5 DREAM
Bedwear
  ~, briefly: 3 PJS
Bee: 4 AUNT
  Be in a: 5 SPELL
  charge: 4 OPIE
  chaser: 3 CEE
  Competed in a: 5 SPELT
  flat: 4 HIVE
  formation: 5 SWARM

He stung like a: 3 ALI
house: 6 APIARY
Male: 5 DRONE
nephew: 4 ANDY OPIE
product: 5 QUILT
Bee ___: 4 GEES
Beech: 4 TREE
family member: 3 OAK
Beef: 4 CARP MEAT 5 GRIPE
     7 REDMEAT
Big piece of: 4 SIDE
Corned ~ concoction: 4 HASH
cut: 4 LOIN RUMP 5 TBONE
     9 CLUBSTEAK
dish: 4 STEW 10 SWISSSTEAK
How ~ may be served: 5 AUJUS
Improve, as: 3 AGE
Like some: 6 CORNED
One way to cook: 5 ROAST
on the hoof: 5 STEER
order: 4 RARE
rating org.: 4 USDA
Tenderized cut of: 9 CUBESTEAK
Beefcake: 4 HUNK
Beef-rating
agcy.: 4 USDA
Bee Gees, The: 4 TRIO 5 GIBBS
Beehive: 4 UPDO 5 STYLE
     6 HAIRDO
and others: 3 DOS
Build a: 5 TEASE
protector: 7 HAIRNET
Beehive State: 4 **UTAH**
athlete: 3 UTE
native: 3 UTE
Beekeeper: 8 APIARIST
in a 1997 film: 4 ULEE
Beelike: 5 APIAN
Beeline
Make a: 6 HASTEN
Beelzebub: 5 DEVIL SATAN
bailiwick: 4 EVIL
Been
Had: 3 WAS
"___ been fun!": 3 ITS
"___ been had!": 3 IVE
"Been there, done that":
     7 TRIEDIT
Beep: 4 PAGE

Beeper: 4 HORN 5 PAGER
Use a: 4 PAGE
Beer: 4 SUDS
Aged: 5 LAGER
barrel: 3 **KEG**
belly: 3 POT
Big name in: 5 PABST 6 AMSTEL
buy: 4 CASE
cheer: 5 SKOAL
Dark: 4 BOCK
holder: 5 STEIN
ingredient: 4 HOPS MALT
Japanese ~ brand: 5 ASAHI
keg outlet: 3 TAP
Like some: 5 ONTAP
Make: 4 BREW
mug: 5 STEIN
relative: 3 ALE
topper: 4 HEAD
variety: 4 LITE 5 LAGER
Word with: 4 NEAR
~, at times: 6 CHASER
"Beer Barrel ___": 5 POLKA
Beersheba
locale: 5 NEGEV
Beery
Actor: 4 NOAH
Beery, Wallace
film: 8 THECHAMP
Bees
Bunch of: 5 SWARM
home: 4 HIVE
Pertaining to: 5 **APIAN**
Beet
Comparable to a: 5 **ASRED**
extract: 5 SUGAR
variety: 5 CHARD
Beethoven
birthplace: 4 **BONN**
dedicatee: 5 **ELISE**
opera: 7 FIDELIO
Schiller work adapted by:
     8 ODETOJOY
symphony: 6 EROICA
wrote one: 5 OPERA
"Beethoven"
actor Charles: 6 GRODIN
Beetle: 3 CAR 4 AUTO
cousin: 5 JETTA

Egyptian: 6 SCARAB
juice: 3 GAS
Kind of: 3 ELM 4 STAG
larvae: 5 GRUBS
Spotted: 7 LADYBUG
"Beetle Bailey"
boss: 5 SARGE
creator Walker: 4 MORT
dog: 4 **OTTO**
Beeweed: 5 ASTER
Befit: 4 SUIT
Befitting: 3 APT
Before: 3 **ERE** 5 UNTIL
        7 AHEADOF PRIORTO
Come: 7 PRECEDE PREDATE
        8 ANTEDATE
long: 4 ANON SOON
Night: 3 EVE
now: 3 **AGO**
prefix: 3 PRE
surgery: 5 PREOP
the deadline: 5 EARLY
        6 INTIME
Time: 3 EVE
~, once: 3 **ERE**
~, poetically: 3 **ERE**
Befoul: 4 SOIL
Befuddled: 4 ASEA 5 **ATSEA**
Beg: 5 PLEAD 7 ENTREAT
One might ~ to do this: 6 DIFFER
Began: 5 AROSE 6 OPENED
Begat: 5 SIRED 7 SPAWNED
Begawan, Bandar __: 4 SERI
Beget: 4 **SIRE** 5 SPAWN
Beggar
request: 4 ALMS
Beggar's-___ (sticky seeds):
        4 LICE
Begged: 4 PLED 5 ASKED
        8 IMPLORED
Begin: 5 SETTO START 7 ISRAELI
        STARTON 8 STARTOFF
again: 4 REDO
a journey: 6 SETOUT
co-Nobelist: 5 SADAT
of Israel: 8 MENACHEM
Beginner: 4 TYRO 8 NEOPHYTE
Beginning: 3 TOP 4 ASOF SEED
        5 BIRTH **ONSET** START

        6 ORIGIN OUTSET
        7 INITIAL
From the: 4 ANEW 6 AFRESH
From the ~, in Latin: 5 ABOVO
The very: 6 DAYONE
        7 YEARONE
~, slangily: 5 GETGO
"Begin the Beguine"
bandleader Artie: 4 SHAW
Begley
and others: 3 EDS
"Begone!": 4 SCAT SHOO
        5 SCRAM 6 GETOUT
Begot: 5 SIRED
"Beg pardon ...": 4 AHEM
Begrudge: 4 ENVY 6 RESENT
Beguile: 5 AMUSE TEMPT
        6 SEDUCE 8 ENTRANCE
Beguiler: 5 SIREN
Beguiling
trick: 4 WILE
Behalf
On ~ of: 3 FOR
Behave: 3 ACT
badly: 3 ERR
rudely: 5 ACTUP
Behaving: 6 ACTING
Men ~ badly: 4 CADS
Behavior
Bad: 4 SINS
pattern: 5 HABIT
Behemoth: 5 TITAN
Highway: 4 SEMI
Sport for a: 4 SUMO
Behind: 3 AFT 4 LATE REAR
        9 INARREARS
bars: 5 CAGED
Be: 3 OWE 5 TRAIL
closed doors: 9 INPRIVATE
Come from: 5 RALLY
Fall: 3 **LAG** 8 LOSETIME
Following: 5 INTOW
Get: 7 ENDORSE 8 LOSETIME
Hit from: 7 REAREND
Is: 6 TRAILS
Not: 4 ANTI
One ~ bars: 3 CON
One ~ the other: 6 TANDEM
Pull from: 3 TOW

Running: **4** LATE
schedule: **4** LATE
Stay: **6** REMAIN
the eight ball: **7** INAHOLE
the scenes: **8** OFFSTAGE
Was ~ schedule: **7** RANLATE
Wet ~ the ears: **3** RAW **5** NAIVE
Behold: 3 SEE **8** LOOKUPON
Amazing to: **10** EYEPOPPING
"Behold!": **4** ECCE TADA
~, in Latin: **4** **ECCE**
"___ behold!": **5** LOAND
Beholden
Be ~ to: **3** OWE
Beholder: 4 EYER
Beiderbecke
Jazz musician: **3** BIX
Beige: 3 TAN **4** **ECRU**
Being: 4 ESSE **6** ENTITY
9 EXISTENCE
Came into: **5** AROSE
For the time: **6** PROTEM
Have: **5** EXIST
Supreme: **3** GOD
Time: **5** NONCE
~, in French: **4** ETRE
~, in Latin: **4** **ESSE**
Beirut
country (abbr.): **3** LEB
Bejewel: 5 ADORN
Bejeweled
headgear: **5** TIARA
Bel ___ : 5 PAESE
Bela
Actor: **6** LUGOSI
Colleague of: **3** LON
Composer: **6** BARTOK
Belafonte
Actress: **5** SHARI
Belafonte, Harry
Daughter of: **5** SHARI
song: **4** DAYO
Belarus
capital: **5** **MINSK**
~, once (abbr.): **3** SSR
Belbenoit
Devil's Island escapee: **4** RENE
Belch
forth: **4** SPEW

Shakespeare character: **4** TOBY
Belfast
gp.: **3** IRA
Town near: **6** ANTRIM
Belfry
locale: **7** STEEPLE
resident: **3** BAT
Belgian
city: **5** YPRES
composer Jacques: **4** BREL
Former ~ airline: **6** SABENA
resort: **3** SPA
river: **4** YSER
Belgium
City in: **5** YPRES
River in: **4** YSER
Belgrade
country: **6** SERBIA
Former ~ bigwig: **4** TITO
resident: **4** **SERB** SLAV
Belief: 3 **ISM** **5** CREDO **TENET**
Established: **5** DOGMA
in God: **5** DEISM **6** THEISM
Mideast: **5** ISLAM
Statement of: **5** CREDO CREED
system: **3** ISM
Beliefs
of a group: **5** ETHOS
Believable
Not: **4** LAME
Believe: 4 DEEM FEEL
Hard to: **4** TALL
Make: **7** PLAYACT PRETEND
without question: **5** EATUP
~, as a story: **3** BUY
"Believe"
singer: **4** CHER
Believed: 4 FELT HELD
without question: **5** ATEUP
"Believe it ___!": **5** ORNOT
"Believe ___ not!": **4** ITOR
Believer: 3 IST **5** DEIST
6 THEIST
Suffix for a: **3** IST
"___ Believer": **3** IMA
Belittle: 3 DIS **5** ABASE
9 DISPARAGE
Bell
After the: **4** LATE

Alarm: 6 TOCSIN
and others: 3 MAS
Evening: 6 VESPER
Noted ~ ringer: 8 AVONLADY
Ring a: 4 PEAL TOLL
ringer: 6 SEXTON
site: 7 STEEPLE
sound: 4 BONG DONG PEAL
    TING
the cat: 4 DARE
town: 4 ATRI 5 ADANO
Bell ___: 4 LABS
___ Bell: 4 TACO
Bella
Feminist politician: 5 ABZUG
Bell-bottoms
feature: 5 FLARE
Like: 5 RETRO
Belle
Bleating: 3 EWE
counterpart: 4 BETE
of the ball: 3 DEB
of the Old West: 5 STARR
"Bellefleur"
author: 5 OATES
"Bell for ___, A": 5 ADANO
Bellhop: 4 PAGE 5 TOTER
burden: 4 BAGS
employer: 5 HOTEL
Belli
Attorney: 6 MELVIN
Bellicose
god: 4 **ARES**
Belligerent
god: 4 ARES
"Belling the Cat"
author: 5 AESOP
Bellini: 7 ITALIAN
opera: 5 NORMA
"Bell Jar, The"
author: 5 PLATH
Belloc
Author: 7 HILAIRE
Bellow: 4 ROAR 5 SHOUT
Author: 4 SAUL
Bovine: 3 MOO
Bullring: 3 OLE
character March: 5 AUGIE
Bellowing: 5 AROAR

Bellows
Actor: 3 GIL
"Bells, The"
author: 3 POE
Bell-shaped
flower: 4 SEGO 5 TULIP
"Bells ___ Mary's, The": 4 OFST
"Bells of St. ___, The": 5 MARYS
Bellum
opposite: 3 PAX
Belly: 3 GUT 7 ABDOMEN
    STOMACH
Beer: 3 POT
Go ~ up: 4 FAIL FOLD
laugh: 4 ROAR
muscles: 3 ABS
On one's: 5 PRONE
pain: 4 ACHE
Bellyache: 4 BEEF CRAB MOAN
    5 GRIPE WHINE
Bellyacher: 4 CRAB 5 GRUMP
Bellybutton
type: 5 INNIE OUTIE
Bellyful
Give a: 4 SATE
Had a: 3 ATE
Belmont
bet: 6 EXACTA
event: 9 HORSERACE
Belmonts
lead singer: 4 DION
Belong: 3 FIT 5 FITIN 6 INHERE
Belonging
Cost of: 4 DUES
to moi: 3 MES
to us: 4 OURS
Belongings: 4 GEAR 6 ASSETS
    ESTATE
Beloved: 4 DEAR
animal: 3 PET
folk: 5 DEARS
Make: 6 ENDEAR
Name meaning: 5 AIMEE
"Beloved"
author Morrison: 4 TONI
director: 5 DEMME
Below: 5 UNDER
low: 5 EMPTY
~, in poetry: 5 NEATH

Belowdecks
  Put: 4 STOW
Belt: 4 AREA ZONE 5 PASTE
    STRAP 6 REGION WALLOP
  Bar: 4 SHOT
  clip-on: 5 PAGER
  Imaginary: 6 ZODIAC
  maker's tool: 3 AWL
  Ornamental: 4 SASH
  out: 4 SING
  site: 5 WAIST
  Tighten, as a: 4 GIRD
  ___ **Belt (constellation part):**
    6 ORIONS
Beluga
  delicacy: 3 ROE
Belushi
  venue, briefly: 3 SNL
Bemoan: 3 RUE 4 WAIL
    6 LAMENT REGRET
"Be My Baby"
  group: 8 RONETTES
Ben
  Golfer: 5 HOGAN
  Screenwriter: 5 HECHT
Ben-___: 3 HUR
Benaderet
  Actress: 3 BEA
"___ Ben Adhem": 4 **ABOU**
Ben and Jerry's
  alternative: 4 EDYS
Benatar
  Singer: 3 PAT
  ___ **Ben Canaan:** 3 ARI
Bench: 4 SEAT
  Church: 3 PEW
  Cry from the: 5 ORDER
  Lance of the: 3 ITO
  outfit: 4 ROBE
  site: 5 PIANO
  Warmed the: 3 SAT
Bench, Johnny
  team: 4 REDS
Bench-clearing
  incident: 5 MELEE SETTO
Benchley, Peter
  novel: 4 JAWS 7 THEDEEP
Benchmark: 4 NORM
  (abbr.): 3 STD

Bench-press
  unit: 3 REP
Benchwarmer: 3 SUB 5 SCRUB
    7 RESERVE
Bend: 3 ARC 4 FLEX 6 RELENT
  Ballet: 4 **PLIE**
  down: 5 STOOP
  out of shape: 4 WARP
  Pipe: 3 **ELL**
  Right-angle: 3 ELL
  Something to: 3 EAR
  Something to ~ or lend: 5 ANEAR
  under pressure: 3 SAG
Bended
  Asked on ~ knee: 4 PLED
Bender: 3 JAG 4 TEAR TOOT
    5 BINGE SPREE
  Eyeball: 5 OPART
  Fender: 4 DENT 6 MISHAP
  ___ **bender:** 6 FENDER
Bending
  muscle: 6 FLEXOR
  readily: 5 LITHE
Bendix
  role: 5 RILEY
  ___ **bene:** 4 NOTA
Beneath: 5 UNDER
Benedict
  suffix: 3 INE
  Traitor: 6 ARNOLD
  ___ **Benedict:** 4 EGGS
Benedictine
  title: 3 DOM
Benediction
  Give a ~ to: 5 BLESS
Benefactor: 5 ANGEL 6 PATRON
    7 DONATOR
  PBS: 3 NEA
Beneficial: 5 OFUSE UTILE
    6 USEFUL
Beneficiary: 4 HEIR 5 DONEE
    7 LEGATEE
  Primogeniture: 3 SON
Benefit: 3 AID 4 BOON PLUS
    SAKE 5 AVAIL
  Employee: 4 PERK
  event: 4 GALA
  Fed. ~ source: 3 SSA
  Fringe: 4 PERK

Benevolence: 5 MERCY
Benevolent: 4 KIND
  order member: 3 ELK
Bengali
  language group: 5 INDIC
Ben-Gay
  target: 4 ACHE
Ben-Gurion
  airline: 4 **ELAL**
Ben-Hur: 10 CHARIOTEER
"Ben-Hur": 4 EPIC
  author Wallace: 3 LEW
  studio: 3 MGM
Benigni
  Actor/director: 7 ROBERTO
Benin
  ~, once: 7 DAHOMEY
Bening
  Actress: 7 ANNETTE
Benjamin: 5 CNOTE
  British Prime Minister:
    8 DISRAELI
  Guitarist: 3 ORR
"___ Ben Jonson!": 5 ORARE
Bennett
  Publisher: 4 CERF
  Singer: 4 TONY
Bennett, Tony
  birthplace: 7 ASTORIA
  song title start: 5 ILEFT
Benny, Jack
  39, to ~: 3 AGE
  Like: 5 CHEAP
  sponsor: 5 JELLO
"Benny & Joon"
  actor Quinn: 5 AIDAN
"Benson"
  actress Swenson: 4 INGA
Bent: 7 STOOPED
  It may be ~ or lent: 3 EAR
  out of shape: 5 IRATE
    6 WARPED
  over: 6 ASTOOP
Bentley
  Actor: 3 WES
Bentley, E.C.
  detective: 5 TRENT
Bentsen
  Former senator: 5 LLOYD

Benz
  Auto pioneer: 4 KARL
  end: 3 ENE
Benzene
  prefix: 3 AZO
  source: 3 TAR
Benzi Box
  contents: 8 CARRADIO
Benzoyl peroxide
  target: 4 ACNE
Beowulf
  ~, to Grendel: 6 SLAYER
"Beowulf": 4 EPIC EPOS SAGA
  beast: 7 GRENDEL
  beverage: 4 MEAD
"Be patient": 6 NOTYET
    8 SITTIGHT
"Be Prepared"
  gp.: 3 BSA
Bequeath: 5 LEAVE
"Be quiet!": 4 HUSH
Berate: 5 SCOLD 6 RAILAT
    YELLAT
Bereavement: 5 GRIEF
Bereft: 4 LORN 6 DEVOID
Berenstain
  Writer: 4 STAN
Beret: 3 CAP HAT
  Leader in a: 3 CHE
  Place for a: 4 TETE
  Scottish: 3 TAM
Berg
  Composer: 5 ALBAN
  of baseball: 3 MOE
  opera: 4 LULU
Berganza
  Mezzo: 6 TERESA
Bergen
  dummy Mortimer: 5 **SNERD**
  Ventriloquist: 5 EDGAR
Berger
  Actress: 5 **SENTA**
Bergman: 5 SWEDE
  Actress: 6 INGRID
  Director: 6 INGMAR
  Last role for: 4 MEIR
  Oscar role for: 9 ANASTASIA
"Be right with you!": 6 INASEC
    ONESEC

Bering: 3 SEA 4 DANE 6 STRAIT
  (abbr.): 3 STR
Bering Sea
  bird: 3 AUK
  island: 4 ATTU
  native: 5 ALEUT
Berkeley
  School with a ~ campus (abbr.):
    4 UCAL
Berkow
  Sports columnist: 3 IRA
Berkshire
  school: 4 ETON
Berkshire Music Festival
  site: 5 LENOX
Berle, Milton
  sidekick Arnold: 5 STANG
  sponsor: 6 TEXACO
  theme: 7 NEARYOU
Berlin, Irving
  Original surname of: 6 BALINE
  output: 5 SONGS
  song: 6 ALWAYS
    15 PUTTINONTHERITZ
Berliner
  Inventor: 5 EMILE
Berman
  Sportscaster: 3 **LEN**
Berman, Chris
  award: 4 ESPY
Bermuda: 4 ISLE 5 ONION
  vehicle: 5 MOPED
  wear: 6 SHORTS
Bern
  river: 3 AAR 4 **AARE**
Bernadette
  (abbr.): 3 STE
  Performer: 6 PETERS
Bernard
  Author: 7 MALAMUD
  News anchor: 4 SHAW
  ___ Bernardino: 3 SAN
Berne
  river: 3 AAR 4 AARE
Bernese Alps
  Peak in the: 5 EIGER
  river: 3 AAR 4 AARE
Bernhardt
  Actress: 5 SARAH

Bernie
  Quarterback: 5 KOSAR
  Songwriting partner of: 5 ELTON
Bernini
  Sculptor: 4 GIAN
Bernstein
  Composer: 5 ELMER
  Journalist: 4 CARL
  musical: 7 CANDIDE
Berra
  of baseball: 4 YOGI
  teammate: 5 MARIS
Berry
  Actress: 5 **HALLE**
  Fuzzy: 4 KIWI
  Motown founder: 5 GORDY
  of baseball: 3 KEN
  prefix: 4 CRAN
  ___ Berry Farm: 6 KNOTTS
Berserk: 4 AMOK LOCO
  Go: 4 RAGE SNAP 7 RUNAMOK
Bert
  Actor: 4 **LAHR**
  Buddy of: 5 **ERNIE**
  Twin of: 3 NAN
Berth: 4 SLOT 5 SPACE
  Ark: 6 ARARAT
  Give a wide: 5 AVOID
  place: 4 DOCK PIER SLIP
    5 **UPPER** 6 MARINA
  Prebirth: 4 WOMB
Beryl
  variety: 7 EMERALD
Beseech: 3 BEG 4 PRAY 5 PLEAD
    7 ENTREAT IMPLORE
    8 APPEALTO
Beset: 6 ASSAIL
Beside: 5 ALONG
  oneself: 3 MAD 5 IRATE
Besides: 3 TOO 4 **ALSO ELSE**
    6 ATTHAT
Be silent
  ~, in music: 5 TACET
Besmirch: 3 **TAR** 4 SOIL 5 DIRTY
    SULLY 8 DISCOLOR
"___ Beso": 3 **ESO**
Bess
  follower: 5 MAMIE
  Harry and: 7 TRUMANS

partner: **5** PORGY
predecessor: **7** ELEANOR

Besson
Director: **3** LUC

Best: 3 TOP **4** AONE BEAT TOPS
5 ELITE IDEAL OUTDO
6 FINEST **7** OPTIMAL
OPTIMUM
Actress: **4** **EDNA**
conditions: **6** OPTIMA
In the ~ case: **7** IDEALLY
of the Beatles: **4** PETE
suited: **6** APTEST
The ~ of times: **9** GOLDENAGE

Best Actor
of 1958: **5** NIVEN
of 1961: **6** SCHELL
of 1967: **7** STEIGER
of 1971: **7** HACKMAN
of 1990: **5** IRONS
of 1995: **4** CAGE
of 1999: **6** SPACEY
of 2000: **5** CROWE

Best Actress
of 1936: **6** RAINER
of 1961: **5** LOREN
of 1963: **4** NEAL
of 1987: **4** CHER
of 1988: **6** FOSTER
of 1990: **5** BATES
of 1998: **4** HUNT
of 1999: **5** SWANK

Best Director
of the 1930s: **5** CAPRA
of 1997: **7** CAMERON
of 2005: **3** ANG **6** ANGLEE

Bested: 6 OUTDID **7** OUTDONE
8 OVERCAME
Be: **4** LOSE

Bestial
hideaway: **4** LAIR

"Best in Show"
org.: **3** AKC

Best Musical
of 1977: **5** ANNIE
of 1980: **5** EVITA
of 1996: **4** RENT
of 1999: **5** FOSSE

Best of the best: 8 CHOICEST

Bestow: 4 GIVE **5** AWARD ENDUE
GRANT **6** IMPART

Best Picture
of 1955: **5** MARTY
of 1958: **4** GIGI
of 1968: **6** OLIVER
of 1970: **6** PATTON
of 1976: **5** ROCKY
of 1977: **9** ANNIEHALL
of 1982: **6** GANDHI
of 1984: **7** AMADEUS
of 1986: **7** PLATOON
of 1997: **7** TITANIC
of 1998: **7** RAINMAN
of 2005: **5** CRASH

Best Play
of 1998: **3** ART

Best Supporting Actor
of 1958: **4** IVES
of 1985: **6** AMECHE
of 1986 and 1999: **5** CAINE
of 1988: **5** KLINE

Best Supporting Actress
of 1957: **5** UMEKI
of 1969: **4** HAWN
of 1973: **5** ONEAL
of 1992: **5** TOMEI

Best Western
competitor: **6** RAMADA

Bet: 4 LAID **5** WAGER
7 WAGERED
Match a: **3** SEE
preceder: **4** ANTE
Track: **6** EXACTA

Beta
follower: **3** RAY **5** GAMMA
___ Beta Kappa: **3** **PHI**

Betamax
creator: **4** SONY

Bête ___ : 5 **NOIRE**

Betel
palm: **5** ARECA

Betelgeuse: 4 STAR
constellation: **5** ORION

Beth
preceder: **5** ALEPH

Bethlehem
product: **5** STEEL
school: **6** LEHIGH

visitors: 4 MAGI
  Woman from: 5 NAOMI
Betray: 5 <u>RATON</u> 7 TWOTIME
  boredom: 4 YAWN
Betrothal
  symbol: 4 RING
Betrothed: 7 ENGAGED
Betsy
  Seamstress: 4 ROSS
"Betsy's Wedding"
  actor Alan: 4 ALDA
"Bette Davis Eyes"
  singer Carnes: 3 KIM
Bettelheim
  Psychologist: 5 BRUNO
Better: 5 AMEND EMEND
      6 ENRICH 7 ENHANCE
      IMPROVE 10 AMELIORATE
  copy: 4 EDIT
  equipped: 5 ABLER
  Get: 4 <u>HEAL</u>
  Get the ~ of: 5 <u>ONEUP</u> WORST
  Go one: 3 TOP 5 OUTDO
  half: 6 SPOUSE
  informed: 5 WISER
  Make: 4 CURE HEAL
      5 AMEND
  No ~ than: 4 MERE
  than average: 8 ABOVEPAR
"Better ___ than never": 4 LATE
Betting
  game: 5 BEANO
  group: 4 POOL
  info: 4 ODDS
  odds: 4 LINE
  setting: 4 <u>RENO</u> 5 VEGAS
      6 CASINO
Bettor
  aid: 6 SYSTEM
  figures: 4 ODDS
Betty
  of cartoons: 4 BOOP
  Pinup girl: 6 GRABLE
Between
  assignments: 4 IDLE
  Few and far: 4 RARE 6 SPARSE
  ports: 4 ASEA 5 ATSEA
  ~, in French: 5 ENTRE
  ~, poetically: 5 TWIXT

Beulah
  Actress: 5 BONDI
Bevan, Bev
  band: 3 ELO
Beveled
  edges: 5 CANTS
Beverage: 5 DRINK
  Ballpark: 4 BEER
  Brewed: 3 ALE
  Brown: 4 COLA
  Brunch: 6 MIMOSA
  Bubbly: 4 SODA
  French: 3 THE
  Honey: 4 MEAD
  Japanese: 4 SAKE
  Malt: 3 ALE
  nut: 4 KOLA
  Seasonal: 3 NOG
  Social: 3 TEA
  Wine and fruit: 7 SANGRIA
"Beverly Hillbillies, The"
  actor Buddy: 5 EBSEN
  actor Max: 4 BAER
  actress Ryan: 5 IRENE
  role: 3 JED 6 JETHRO
  role ___ May: 4 ELLY
"Beverly Hills Cop"
  character Foley: 4 AXEL
Beverly Hills Drive: 5 RODEO
Bewail: 5 MOURN 6 LAMENT
Beware
  Dog to: 5 BITER
  One who should: 5 BUYER
  Sign to: 4 OMEN
  Time to: 4 IDES
"Beware ... of jealousy"
  speaker: 4 IAGO
Bewhiskered: 5 HAIRY 7 HIRSUTE
  animal: 4 SEAL 5 OTTER
      6 WALRUS
Bewilder: 4 DAZE 5 ADDLE
      AMAZE 6 PUZZLE
Bewildered: 4 ASEA LOST
      5 <u>ATSEA</u> 7 ATALOSS
      INADAZE
Bewitch: 3 HEX 6 ENAMOR
      7 ENCHANT
"Bewitched"
  actress Moorehead: 5 AGNES

aunt: 5 CLARA
character: 6 ENDORA
   7 TABITHA
Beyond: 4 PAST
Go: 8 OVERSTEP
partner: 5 ABOVE
"Beyond Good and Evil"
author: 9 NIETZSCHE
"Beyond the Sea"
singer: 5 DARIN
B flat
equivalent: 6 ASHARP
Bhutan
locale: 4 ASIA
neighbor: 5 ASSAM
Bi
halved: 3 UNI
plus one: 3 TRI
Bias: 4 SKEW 5 SLANT
Biased: 7 COLORED SLANTED
   8 ONASLANT ONESIDED
   PARTISAN
person: 5 BIGOT
Biathlon
need: 4 SKIS 5 RIFLE
Bib
Need a: 5 DROOL
Bible
book: 4 ACTS AMOS 5 HOSEA
   MICAH 6 ESTHER
book (abbr.): 3 NEH 4 ESTH
division: 5 VERSE
Hotel ~ provider: 6 GIDEON
It has a part in the: 6 REDSEA
Last word of the: 4 AMEN
verb ending: 3 ETH
Biblical
beast: 3 ASS
Bit of ~ writing: 4 MENE
boat: 3 ARK
boat builder: 4 NOAH
brother: 4 ABEL **ESAU** 5 AARON
bushel: 4 EPHA
footwear: 6 SANDAL
garden: 4 EDEN
gift: 5 MYRRH
judge: 3 **ELI**
king: 5 HEROD
kingdom: 4 EDOM ELAM MOAB

measure: 5 CUBIT
miracle site: 4 CANA
no-no: 3 SIN
patriarch: 5 ISAAC
peak: 5 HOREB SINAI
   6 ARARAT
poem: 5 PSALM
possessive: 5 THINE
preposition: 4 **UNTO**
priest: 3 ELI
pronoun: 3 THY 4 THEE THOU
prophet: 4 AMOS 5 HOSEA
queendom: 5 SHEBA
query: 5 ISITI
shepherd: 4 ABEL
sin city: 5 SODOM
song: 5 PSALM
spy: 5 CALEB
strongman: 6 SAMSON
suffix: 3 ETH
twin: 4 **ESAU**
verb: 4 DOTH HAST HATH
   5 HADST
verb ending: 3 **ETH**
vessel: 3 ARK
villain: 5 HEROD
weed: 4 TARE
Bibliography
abbr.: 4 AUTH ETAL 5 OPCIT
info: 5 TITLE
phrase: 6 ETALII
word: 4 IDEM
Bibliophile
concern: 7 EDITION
purchase: 4 TOME
room: 3 DEN
Suffix for a: 3 ANA 4 IANA
Bic
buy: 3 PEN
filler: 3 INK
Biceps: 6 FLEXOR MUSCLE
builders: 7 CHINUPS
Show one's: 4 FLEX
Bicker: 5 ARGUE
Bickering: 4 ATIT TIFF
Bickle, Travis
drove one: 4 TAXI
Bicolor
bite: 4 OREO

Bicuspid: 5 TOOTH
 base: 4 ROOT
 neighbor: 5 MOLAR
Bicycle
 built for two: 6 TANDEM
 part: 4 DECK SEAT
  10 BANANASEAT
 wheel part: 5 SPOKE
 with an engine: 5 MOPED
"Bicycle Thief, The"
 director: 6 DESICA
Bid: 5 OFFER
 Bridge: 5 **ONENO**
 Final: 4 PASS
 first: 4 OPEN 6 OPENED
 It may be: 5 ADIEU
 No: 5 IPASS
 the bed adieu: 5 ARISE
Bidding: 6 BEHEST
 Begin: 4 OPEN
 Do the ~ of: 4 OBEY
 Place to do one's: 4 EBAY
 site: 4 EBAY
Biddy: 3 **HEN**
Bide
 one's time: 4 WAIT 5 AWAIT
Bide-___ : 4 AWEE
Bien
 opposite: 3 MAL
"___ bien!": 4 TRES
Biennial
 vegetable: 4 BEET
 ___ Bien Phu: 4 DIEN
Bierce
 Author: 7 AMBROSE
 In bad company, according to:
  5 ALONE
Big: 4 HUGE 5 LARGE OBESE
 do: 4 **AFRO** GALA
 game: 4 DEER ELKS
 Make it: 6 ARRIVE
 prefix: 4 MAXI MEGA
 shot: 3 VIP 4 CZAR 5 CELEB
  6 FATCAT
 show: 4 EXPO
 wheel: 5 CHIEF NABOB
  7 MAGNATE
Big ___ : 3 **BEN** MAC **SUR**
  6 BERTHA

"Big ___"
 of the comic pages: 4 NATE
Big Apple
 award: 4 OBIE
 ballpark: 4 ASHE SHEA
 cardinal: 4 EGAN
 inits.: 3 NYC 4 NYNY
 neighborhood: 4 SOHO
 stadium: 4 ASHE SHEA
 subway stop (abbr.): 3 LEX
"Big Bad John"
 actor Jack: 4 ELAM
Big Band: 3 ERA
 brother: 6 DORSEY
 follower: 3 ERA
 member: 3 SAX
 music: 5 SWING
Big bang
 producer: 3 TNT 5 NITRO
Big Bertha: 3 GUN
 birthplace: 5 ESSEN
Big-billed
 bird: 6 TOUCAN 7 PELICAN
"Big Blue": 3 IBM
Big Board
 letters: 4 NYSE
Big deal: 3 ADO
"Big deal!": 6 SOWHAT
Big East
 team: 4 PITT 5 HOYAS MIAMI
  6 SAINTS
Bigfoot
 cousin: 4 YETI
 Like: 5 HAIRY
Bigger
 Get: 4 GROW
 than med.: 3 LGE
Biggers
 detective: 4 CHAN
Biggers, Earl ___
 Author: 4 DERR
"___ bigger than a breadbox?":
  4 ISIT
Biggie
 Business: 3 CEO 4 EXEC 5 TITAN
 Media: 5 MOGUL
 Valhalla: 4 ODIN
Bight of Benin
 capital: 5 ACCRA

city: **5** LAGOS
Big Mama: **4** CASS
Bigmouth: **4** BASS
Big-mouthed
pitcher: **4** EWER
Bigot: **5** HATER **6** RACIST
on TV: **12** ARCHIEBUNKER
Big ___ outdoors: **5** ASALL
Big Red: **5** LENIN **6** STALIN
opponent: **3** ELI
"Big Red, The": **7** CORNELL
Big-screen
format: **4** IMAX
Big Ten
sch.: **3** OSU
school: **4** IOWA
team: **6** ILLINI
Big Twelve
athlete: **5** AGGIE
school: **6** KANSAS
Bigwig: **3** VIP **5** NABOB
Aesir: **4** ODIN
Business: **4** CZAR **5** MOGUL
Campus: **4** DEAN
Corp.: **3** CEO **4** EXEC
D.C.: **3** SEN
Kuwaiti: **4** EMIR
Mafia: **4** CAPO
Mideast: **4** EMIR **6** SULTAN
Mosque: **4** IMAM
Turkish: **3** AGA **5** PASHA
Valhalla: **4** ODIN
Venetian: **4** DOGE
Bijou: **3** GEM
Sign at the: **3** SRO
Bike: **5** CYCLE PEDAL
Go by: **5** PEDAL
type: **6** TANDEM **8** TENSPEED
with a small engine: **5** MOPED
Biker
A ~ might pop one: **7** WHEELIE
protection: **6** HELMET
wear: **7** LEATHER
Bikini: **5** ATOLL ISLET
alternative: **8** ONEPIECE
blast: **5** ATEST
experiment: **5** NTEST
part: **3** BRA
top: **3** BRA

~, once: **8** TESTSITE
Bil
Cartoonist: **5** KEANE
Puppeteer: **5** BAIRD
Bilbo: **5** SWORD
Bile: **3** IRE
Bilko: **5** ERNIE
actor: **7** SILVERS
nickname: **5** SARGE
rank (abbr.): **3** SGT **4** MSGT
Bilko, Sgt.: **5** ERNIE
Bill: **4** TAB **4** BEAK
(abbr.): **3** INV
add-on: **3** TAX **5** RIDER
8 SALESTAX
Bar: **3** TAB
Big: **5** CNOTE
Comedian ~, informally: **3** COS
Designer: **5** BLASS
Fill the: **3** EAT
Govt.: **5** TNOTE
Humorist: **3** NYE
in Washington: **5** GATES
killer: **4** VETO
Monthly: **5** CABLE
of fare: **4** MENU **5** CARTE
partner: **3** COO
Pass a: **5** ENACT
provider (abbr.): **3** ATM
Small: **3** ONE
Take care of, as a: **3** PAY **4** FOOT
They fill the: **5** CENTS
Till: **3** ONE
Utility ~ (abbr.): **4** ELEC
with a pyramid: **3** ONE
"Bill & ___ Excellent Adventure":
4 TEDS
Billboard: **4** SIGN
displays: **3** ADS
listings: **4** HITS
Billet-___: **4** DOUX
Billet-doux
beginner: **4** CHER DEAR
Billfold: **6** WALLET
contents: **4** ONES
Billiards
gadget: **4** RACK
need: **5** CHALK
shot: **5** CAROM MASSE

stick: 3 CUE
stroke: 5 MASSE 8 SIDESPIN

Billing
cycle: 5 MONTH
Get top: 4 STAR
One with equal: 6 COSTAR
unit: 4 HOUR

Billion
A ~ years: 3 EON 4 AEON
add-on: 4 AIRE
Faith of more than one: 5 ISLAM
Home to over one: 5 INDIA
Home to over three: 4 ASIA

Billionaire
Pockets of a: 4 DEEP
~ Bill: 5 GATES

Billions: 4 ALOT
Home to: 4 ASIA

Billionth
prefix: 4 NANO

Bill of Rights
defender (abbr.): 4 ACLU

Bills: 4 CASH 5 DEBTS
Big: 5 THOUS
Bologna: 4 LIRE
Bunch of: 3 WAD
Has: 4 OWES
Rare: 4 TWOS
Roll of: 3 WAD
Some: 4 TENS

Bill the Cat
statement: 3 ACK

"Bill ___, the Science Guy": 3 NYE

Billy
Actor: 4 ZANE
Evangelist: 6 GRAHAM
Melville's: 4 BUDD
Rocker: 4 IDOL
Singer: 4 JOEL 5 OCEAN
~, for one: 3 KID

"Billy Budd": 5 OPERA
captain: 4 VERE

"Billy, Don't Be ___": 5 AHERO

"Billy, Don't ___ Hero": 3 BEA

"___ Billy Joe": 5 ODETO

Biloxi-to-Mobile
dir.: 3 ENE

Binary: 4 DUAL
digit: 3 ONE

Binchy
Author: 5 MAEVE

Bind: 3 TIE 4 YOKE 5 UNITE
6 CEMENT ENLACE
OBLIGE
~, as fowl: 5 TRUSS

Binding
agreement: 3 IDO
material: 5 TWINE
Not: 4 VOID
order: 5 EDICT

Bindle
bearer: 4 HOBO
stiff: 4 HOBO

Binet, Alfred
creation: 6 IQTEST
data: 3 IQS

Bing
label: 5 DECCA
Milieu for ~ and Bob: 4 ROAD
Sing like: 5 CROON

Binge: 3 JAG 4 TOOT 5 SPREE
10 GOONASPREE

Bingham
Actress: 5 TRACI

Binghamton
City near: 5 OWEGO 6 ELMIRA
7 ONEONTA

"___ Bingle": 3 DER

Bingo
call: 4 BTEN
relative: 4 KENO 5 BEANO

"Bingo!": 3 AHA 5 RIGHT

Binoculars
Use: 3 SPY 4 SCAN

Bio: 4 LIFE 7 PROFILE
bit: 3 AGE
Broadway: 3 TRU
lab specimen: 6 AMOEBA
Postmortem: 4 OBIT
word: 3 NEE

Biochemical
catalyst: 6 ENZYME 7 OXIDASE

Bioelectric
swimmer: 3 EEL

Biography: 4 LIFE 9 LIFESTORY

"Biography"
network: 5 AANDE

Biol.: 3 SCI

branch: 4 ECOL
course: 4 ANAT
Biological
bristle: 4 SETA
classification: 7 SPECIES
classifications: 4 TAXA
    6 GENERA
container: 3 SAC
group: 5 GENUS
ring of color: 6 AREOLA
sci.: 4 ANAT
walls: 5 SEPTA
Biology
Attached, in: 6 ADNATE
prefix: 3 EXO 4 AERO AGRO
    5 ETHNO PALEO
subj.: 4 ANAT
topic: 3 DNA RNA
Bioluminescence
Marine: 7 SEAFIRE
Biondi
Swimmer: 4 MATT
"Bionic Woman, The"
role: 5 JAIME
Biopic
2001 ~: 3 ALI
Biotite: 4 MICA
Biplane
part: 5 STRUT
Birch: 4 TREE
craft: 5 CANOE
family member: 5 ALDER
of Indiana: 4 BAYH
Birchbark: 5 CANOE
Bird
abode: 4 NEST
beak: 3 NEB NIB
Big: 3 **EMU**
Diving: 3 AUK 4 LOON 5 GREBE
Extinct: 3 MOA 4 DODO
Fabulous: 3 ROC
Flightless: 3 EMU 4 KIWI RHEA
Flightless (var.): 4 EMEU
Hawaiian: 4 NENE
home: 4 NEST
instrument: 3 SAX 7 ALTOSAX
Marsh: 4 RAIL SORA 5 CRAKE
    EGRET HERON SNIPE
Mythical: 3 ROC

Night: 3 OWL
Nile: 4 IBIS
prefix: 3 AVI
raised on ranches: 3 EMU
Sea: 3 ERN 4 ERNE
Shore: 3 ERN 4 ERNE GULL
    TERN 5 HERON
Sinbad: 3 ROC
Small: 3 TIT 6 TOMTIT
sound: 5 TRILL
Talking: 4 MYNA
Three-toed: 4 RHEA
Wading: 4 **IBIS** 5 CRANE EGRET
    STILT STORK
Water: 4 COOT
White-tailed: 3 ERN 4 ERNE
Whooping: 5 CRANE
Word from a: 5 TWEET
~, in Latin: 4 AVIS
Birdbrain: 3 ASS 4 DODO DOLT
    5 IDIOT 6 NITWIT
Birdhouse
dweller: 4 WREN
Birdie: 8 UNDERPAR
beater: 5 EAGLE
Miss a: 7 MAKEPAR
plus one: 3 PAR
Birdlike: 5 **AVIAN**
Birdman of Alcatraz: 5 LIFER
    6 STROUD
"Bird on ___": 5 AWIRE
Bird-related: 5 AVIAN
Birds
For the: 5 **AVIAN**
It's for the: 6 **AVIARY**
"Birds, The"
actress Hedren: 5 TIPPI
heroine: 7 MELANIE
screenwriter Hunter: 4 EVAN
Birds-feather
connection: 3 OFA
Bird-to-be: 3 EGG
Birdy: 5 AVIAN
Bireme
feature: 3 OAR 4 TIER
Birkerts
Author: 4 SVEN
Birling
surface: 3 LOG

Birney, Alfred ___
 Poet: 5 EARLE
Birth: 5 ONSET
 Before: 7 INUTERO
 cert.: 5 IDENT
 control device (abbr.): 3 IUD
 Give ~ to: 4 HAVE 5 SPAWN
 Present from: 6 INNATE
 Regarding: 5 NATAL
Birthday
 attire: 4 SUIT
 dessert: 4 CAKE
 figure: 3 AGE
 In one's ~ suit: 4 BARE
  6 UNCLAD
 Like some ~ wishes: 7 BELATED
 suit: 4 SKIN
"Birth of a Nation, The"
 gp.: 3 KKK
 group: 4 KLAN
Birth-related: 5 **NATAL**
Birthright: 8 HERITAGE
 Biblical ~ seller: 4 **ESAU**
Birthstone
 Fall: 4 **OPAL** 5 TOPAZ
 February: 8 AMETHYST
 January: 6 GARNET
 July: 4 RUBY
 June: 5 PEARL
 May: 7 EMERALD
 November: 5 TOPAZ
 October: 4 **OPAL**
 September: 8 SAPPHIRE
Biscayne Bay
 city: 5 MIAMI
Biscotti
 flavoring: 5 ANISE
Biscuit
 English: 5 SCONE
 Teatime: 5 SCONE
Bisect: 5 HALVE
Bisected: 5 INTWO
Bisector
 Leaf: 6 MIDRIB
 Paris: 5 SEINE
Bishop: 7 PRELATE
 Comedian: 4 JOEY
 domain: 7 DIOCESE
 First ~ of Paris: 7 STDENIS

 First ~ of Rome: 7 STPETER
 headdress: 5 MITER
 headdress, in England: 5 MITRE
 jurisdiction: 3 SEE
 of early TV: 4 JOEY 5 SHEEN
 of Rome: 4 POPE
 South African: 4 TUTU
 subordinate: 6 PRIEST
Bishopric: 3 SEE
Bismarck
 state (abbr.): 4 NDAK
Bison
 Bunch of: 4 HERD
 feature: 4 MANE
Bisque: 4 SOUP
 morsel: 4 CLAM
Bissett
 Actress: 5 JOSIE
Bistro: 4 CAFE 6 EATERY
 menu: 5 CARTE
 sign word: 4 CHEZ
Bit: 3 DAB **TAD** 4 ATOM **IOTA**
   SOME 5 SHRED
  8 SOMEWHAT
 attachment: 4 REIN
 Basic: 4 ATOM
 Even a: 5 ATALL
 for a dog: 3 ORT
 for a horse: 3 OAT
 In a: 4 **ANON** SOON
 Least: 4 IOTA WHIT
 Little: 3 DAB JOT **TAD** 4 ATOM
   IOTA MITE
 modifier: 3 WEE
 Quite a: 4 LOTS 5 OFTEN
 Tiny: 3 DAB 4 ATOM **IOTA** MITE
   MOTE 5 TRACE
 Wee: 3 **TAD**
 ___ bit: 3 INA 4 AWEE NOTA
Bite: 3 NIP 4 NOSH TANG
   5 CHOMP NIPAT
 Grab a: 3 EAT
 Had a: 3 ATE
 Have a: 3 EAT SUP 4 NOSH
   5 TASTE
 Least likely to: 6 TAMEST
 like a beaver: 4 GNAW
 Prepare to: 6 TEETHE
 site: 4 CAFE

Small: **3** NIP
Sound: **5** QUOTE
Unlikely to: **4** TAME
Biter
Back: **5** MOLAR
Dog: **4** FLEA
Nile: **3** ASP
Small: **4** GNAT
Biting-: 4 TART **5** ACERB ACRID
TANGY **6** ACIDIC
7 ACERBIC
remark: **4** BARB
wit: **4** ACID
___ bitten: **4** ONCE
Biter: 5 ACERB ACRID
conflict: **6** STRIFE
drink: **3** ALE
end: **4** NESS
It may be: **3** ALE END
salad item: **9** DANDELION
Bitter-___ : 5 ENDER
Bittern: 5 HERON
relative: **5** EGRET
Bitterness: 8 ACRIDITY
ACRIMONY
Bivouac: 6 ENCAMP
bed: **3** COT
facility: **7** LATRINE
shelter: **4** TENT
Biz
biggie: **3** CEO **4** EXEC
Bizarre: 3 ODD **5** EERIE **OUTRE**
WEIRD
Bizet
opera: **6** CARMEN
priestess: **5** LEILA
work: **4** ARIA **5** OPERA
6 CARMEN
Bjorn
of tennis: **4** BORG
rival: **4** ILIE
Blab: 3 YAK **4** SING TELL
7 TELLALL
Blabbed: 4 SUNG TOLD
15 SPILLEDTHEBEANS
Blabbermouth: 5 YENTA
Hardly a: **4** CLAM
Black: 3 SEA **4** EBON **INKY**
5 EBONY SABLE

Actress: **5** KAREN
bird: **3** ANI DAW **5** RAVEN
cat: **4** OMEN
cuckoo: **3 ANI**
Deep: **3** JET **4** EBON INKY
5 RAVEN SABLE
eye: **6** SHINER
fly: **4** GNAT
gold: **3** OIL
gunk: **3** TAR
ink item: **5** ASSET
In the: **4** ASEA
Jet: **4** ONYX **5** SABLE
Justice: **4** HUGO
key: **5** AFLAT EFLAT **6** ASHARP
Lustrous: **5** RAVEN
mark: **6** STIGMA
One in a ~ suit: **5** SPADE
shade: **3** INK **4** COAL
Singer: **5** CLINT
tea: **5** PEKOE
Wear: **5** MOURN
wood: **5** EBONY
~, in French: **4** NOIR
~, to a bard: **4** EBON
~, to Blake: **4** EBON
"___ Black" (sci-fi film): 5 MENIN
Black and ___ (dog breed): 3 TAN
Black-and-orange
bird: **6** ORIOLE
Black-and-white
bamboo eater: **5** PANDA
cookie: **4** OREO
diver: **3** AUK
driver: **3** COP
killer: **4** ORCA
treat: **4** OREO
Blackball: 4 SHUN **9** OSTRACIZE
Black Bears
home: **5** ORONO
"Black Beauty"
actress Freeman: **4** MONA
author Anna: **6** SEWELL
Blackbird: 3 ANI **4** MERL
Where to find a baked: **6** INAPIE
Blackboard: 5 SLATE
Clear the: **5 ERASE**
"Blackboard Jungle, The"
author Hunter: **4** EVAN

Black-bordered
   bio: 4 OBIT
"Black Camel, The"
   detective: 4 CHAN
Black ___ cattle: 5 ANGUS
Blacken: 3 TAR 4 **CHAR** SEAR
Black-eyed
   legume: 3 PEA 6 COWPEA
Black-eyed ___ : 3 PEA 5 SUSAN
Black-footed
   animal: 6 FERRET
Blackguard: 3 CAD CUR RAT
         4 HEEL
Blackjack: 4 COSH
   card: 3 ACE TEN
   dealer's tip: 4 TOKE
   Good score in: 8 NINETEEN
   option: 4 STAY
   request: 5 HITME
Blackmore
   heroine: 5 DOONE
        10 LORNADOONE
   heroine Doone: 5 LORNA
"Black Narcissus"
   actress Deborah: 4 KERR
"Black Orpheus"
   setting: 3 RIO
Blackout: 3 BAN
Black Panthers
   founder Bobby: 5 SEALE
"Black Pearl, The": 4 PELE
Blacks
   out: 6 SWOONS
Black Sea
   country: 7 ROMANIA
   port: 6 **ODESSA**
Blacksmith: 5 SHOER
   attire: 5 APRON
   block: 5 ANVIL
   metal: 4 IRON
   tool: 4 RASP
"Black Stallion, The"
   boy: 4 ALEC
   horse: 7 ARABIAN
"Black Star, Bright Dawn"
   author Scott: 5 ODELL
Blackthorn: 4 SLOE
   fruit: 4 **SLOE**
Blade: 3 OAR

Blunted: 4 **EPEE**
brand: 4 ATRA
Bygone: 4 SNEE
Chopper: 5 ROTOR
Fencing: 4 **EPEE**
Fictional: 5 ATHOS
Gangster: 4 SHIV
handle: 4 HILT
metal: 5 STEEL
Precision: 5 XACTO
Shoulder: 7 SCAPULA
site: 5 SKATE
Sporting: 4 EPEE
Windmill: 4 VANE
Blades
   Singer: 5 RUBEN
   Use ~ on: 3 MOW
Blah: 5 HOHUM 7 PROSAIC
"Blah, blah, blah": 6 ETCETC
Blahs: 5 ENNUI
   Have the: 3 AIL
Blair
   Actress: 5 LINDA
   and others (abbr.): 3 PMS
   of Britain: 4 TONY
Blair, Tony
   Party of: 6 LABOUR
Blaise
   Mathematician: 6 PASCAL
Blake
   Actress: 6 AMANDA
   Jazz musician: 5 EUBIE
Blake, Robert
   series: 7 BARETTA
Blakey
   Jazz musician: 3 ART
Blakley
   Actress: 5 **RONEE**
Blame: 3 RAP 4 ONUS 5 FAULT
         6 ACCUSE
   Accept: 7 EATDIRT
   Assign, as: 5 PINON
   bearer: 4 GOAT
   Unfair: 6 BADRAP
   Who might be to: 5 NOONE
"Blame It on ___": 3 RIO
"Blame It on the ___ Nova":
         5 BOSSA
Blanc: 3 MEL

of Bugs Bunny: **3** MEL
___ **Blanc: 4** MONT **6** CHENIN
Blanche
　Carte: **8** FREEREIN
　Fictional: **6** DUBOIS
　Sister of: **6** STELLA
　___ **blanche: 5** CARTE
Blanched: 3 WAN **4** PALE
　　5 ASHEN
Blanchett
　Actress: **4** **CATE**
Blandness: 7 NOTASTE
Blank
　Draw a: **6** FORGET
　It may be: **5** STARE
　look: **5** STARE
　Make: **5** ERASE
　Word after: **5** VERSE
Blanket: 7 OVERLIE
　Beach: **4** SAND
　Boy with a: **5** LINUS
　Knitted: **6** AFGHAN
　Wet: **7** KILLJOY
　　11 PARTYPOOPER
　Winter: **4** SNOW
　___ **blanket: 3** WET
Blanks, Billy
　workout program: **5** TAEBO
Blare
　Trumpet: **7** TANTARA
Blaring: 4 LOUD **6** BRASSY
Blarney Stone
　home: **4** EIRE ERIN
"___ Blas" (LeSage novel): 3 GIL
Blasé: 5 BORED JADED
Blass
　competitor: **5** BEENE
Blast: 3 GAS **5** SALVO
　Clarion: **7** TANTARA
　from the past: **5** ATEST NTEST
　　OLDIE
　furnace input: **3** ORE
　　7 IRONORE
　It's a: **3** TNT
　maker: **3** TNT
　of wind: **4** GUST
　Short: **4** TOOT
　Trumpet: **7** TANTARA
"Blast!": 4 DANG DARN

Blaster
　need: **3** TNT
　Rock: **3** AMP
　___ **blaster: 6** GHETTO
Blastoff
　preceder: **3** ONE
Blatant: 5 OVERT
　deception: **7** CHARADE
Blather: 3 GAS **5** PRATE RUNON
　　6 HOTAIR
Blaze
　Big: **7** BONFIRE
　~, in French: **3** FEU
Blazer: 3 SUV
　cleaner: **7** CARWASH
　part: **5** LAPEL
　Slit in a: **4** VENT
Blazes
　It may go to: **4** HOSE
　Went like the: **4** TORE
Blazing: 3 LIT **5** **AFIRE**
　　6 AFLAME AFLARE
　　AGLARE
"Blazing Saddles"
　actress Madeline: **4** KAHN
　director Brooks: **3** MEL
Bldg.
　Municipal: **3** CTR
　unit: **3** APT
Bleach: 6 WHITEN **8** ETIOLATE
Bleacher
　creature: **3** FAN
　feature: **4** TIER
　suffix: **3** ITE
Bleachers
　Sell in the: **4** VEND
　sound: **3** BOO RAH
Bleaching
　agent: **3** LYE
Bleak: 4 GRIM **6** DISMAL
　~, in verse: **5** DREAR
Bleat: 3 BAA MAA
Bleater: 3 EWE **4** LAMB
　Baby: **3** KID
"Blecch!": 3 UGH
Bled: 3 RAN
Bleed: 3 RUN
Bleep: 7 EDITOUT
　out: **5** ERASE **6** CENSOR

Bleeped
It may be: 4 OATH
Blemish: 3 MAR 4 FLAW MOLE
SCAR SPOT 5 STAIN
Fender: 4 DENT
Shoe: 5 SCUFF
Skin: 4 MOLE WART
Blend: 3 MIX 4 MELD STIR
5 ADMIX IMMIX
with traffic: 5 MERGE
Blender
brand: 5 OSTER
setting: 3 MIX 5 **PUREE**
sound: 4 WHIR
Blessed
bread holder: 5 PATEN
event: 6 SNEEZE
It may be: 5 EVENT
Blessing: 4 BOON 7 GODSEND
Cause for a: 5 ACHOO 6 SNEEZE
preceder: 5 ACHOO 6 SNEEZE
" ___ bleu!": 5 **SACRE**
Blight: 7 EYESORE
Tomato: 5 EDEMA
Urban: 4 SLUM SMOG
victim: 3 ELM
Blimpie
rival: 7 QUIZNOS
Blind
It may be: 5 ALLEY
part: 4 **SLAT**
spot location: 6 RETINA
Blind as ___: 4 **ABAT**
Blindly
Search: 5 **GROPE**
Blini: 6 CREPES
Blink: 3 BAT
of an eye: 3 SEC
Blinker: 3 EYE 6 EYELID
10 TURNSIGNAL
Broadway: 4 NEON
Screen: 6 CURSOR
Blip
producer: 5 RADAR SONAR
Bliss: 6 HEAVEN 7 ECSTASY
8 EUPHORIA PARADISE
Place of: 4 EDEN
Blissful: 6 EDENIC ELATED
7 ELYSIAN

state: 4 EDEN
Blithe: 8 CAREFREE
spirit: 4 ELAN
Blithering
person: 5 IDIOT
"Blithe Spirit"
playwright: 10 NOELCOWARD
Blitz: 6 REDDOG
Kind of: 5 MEDIA
Blitzer
employer: 3 CNN
Journalist: 4 WOLF
Blixen
pseudonym: 7 DINESEN
Bloated: 5 GASSY
Blob
Move like the: 4 **OOZE**
Bloc: 5 UNION
Big voting: 5 LABOR
Doc: 3 **AMA**
Block: 3 BAN BAR 5 DAMUP
DETER 6 IMPEDE
Building: 4 UNIT 5 ADOBE
BRICK
Building ~ brand: 4 LEGO
buster: 6 ICEMAN
end: 3 ADE
house: 5 IGLOO
Illegal: 4 CLIP
legally: 5 ESTOP
Recent ~ arrival: 6 NEWKID
suffix: 3 ADE
Sun: 5 CLOUD 7 ECLIPSE
Tiny building: 4 ATOM
Toy ~ company: 4 LEGO
up: 3 DAM
Blockade: 5 SIEGE
Blockage: 4 CLOG CLOT
6 LOGJAM
Blood: 4 CLOT
Blockbuster
of 1975: 4 JAWS
rental: 3 DVD 5 VIDEO
transaction: 6 RENTAL
Blocker: 3 DAM
Actor: 3 DAN
Kind of: 4 BETA
Sun: 5 CLOUD
Ultraviolet: 5 OZONE

X-ray: **4** LEAD
___ blocker: **4** BETA
Blocker, Dan
  role: **4** HOSS
Blockhead: 3 ASS LUG OAF SAP
    4 CLOD DODO DOLT FOOL
Bloke: 3 EGG **4** **CHAP** GENT
    MATE
Blonde
  Go ~, maybe: **3** DYE
  Like some ~ hair: **4** DYED
  shade: **3** **ASH** **5** SANDY
Blondie: 7 CATERER
  Husband of: **7** DAGWOOD
"Blondie": 5 STRIP
  boy: **4** ELMO
  creator Young: **4** CHIC
  Mrs. Dithers of: **4** CORA
Blood: 3 KIN
  Bad: **6** ANIMUS ENMITY
    RANCOR
  bank supply: **6** PLASMA
  blockage: **4** CLOT
  carrier: **5** AORTA
  classification: **5** TYPEA TYPEB
  classification system: **3** ABO
  component: **5** SERUM **6** PLASMA
  components: **4** SERA
  Flesh and: **3** KIN
  giver: **5** DONOR
  Hot: **3** IRE **5** ARDOR
  line: **4** VEIN **5** AORTA **6** ARTERY
  measure: **4** UNIT
  Of the: **5** HEMAL
  of the gods: **5** ICHOR
  pigment: **4** HEME
  prefix: **4** HEMA HEMO
  Rare: **6** TYPEAB
  Related by: **4** AKIN
  type, briefly: **4** APOS ONEG
  vessel: **5** AORTA
Bloodhound: 7 TRACKER
  asset: **4** NOSE
  clue: **4** ODOR **5** SCENT
  trail: **5** SCENT
Bloodmobile
  Visit a: **6** DONATE
Bloodshot: 3 RED
Bloodsucker: 5 LEECH

African: **6** TSETSE
Blood-typing
  letters: **3** ABO
  system: **3** ABO
Bloom
  Actress: **6** CLAIRE
  Daisylike: **5** ASTER
  Purple: **5** LILAC
  September: **5** ASTER
  Spring: **4** IRIS **5** PEONY
  Thorny: **4** ROSE
"Bloom County"
  penguin: **4** OPUS
Bloomer
  Autumn: **5** ASTER
  Fall: **5** **ASTER**
  Late: **5** ASTER
  Spring: **5** LILAC **6** AZALEA
  Suffragist: **6** AMELIA
  Whitman: **5** LILAC
Blooming: 8 INFLOWER
  business: **3** FTD
  month: **5** APRIL
  neckwear: **3** LEI
Bloomingdale's
  competitor: **4** SAKS
Blooper: 4 SLIP **5** ERROR GAFFE
  Made a: **5** ERRED
Blossom: 5 BLOOM
  holder: **4** STEM
Blossom-to-be: 3 BUD
Blot: 6 STIGMA **7** EYESORE
  out: **5** ERASE
Blotch: 4 SPOT **5** STAIN
  Driveway: **3** OIL
Blotter
  info: **5** ALIAS
  letters: **3** AKA
Blotto: 3 LIT **5** FRIED OILED
    STIFF **6** LOOPED SOUSED
    STEWED STONED
    TANKED
Blount
  of football: **3** MEL
Blouse: 3 TOP **5** SHIRT
  Kind of: **7** PEASANT
Bloviate: 5 ORATE
Blow: 5 ERUPT
  a gasket: **5** GOAPE

away: 3 AWE 5 AMAZE
Big: 4 GALE
gently: 4 WAFT
it: 3 **ERR**
Karate: 4 CHOP
off steam: 4 HISS VENT
one's horn: 4 TOOT
one's top: 5 ERUPT
out: 6 EXHALE
Powerful: 4 SWAT
React to a: 8 SEESTARS
Severe: 4 GALE
Sharp: 4 SLAP
Sudden: 4 GUST
the whistle: 3 RAT
up: 4 RAGE 5 ERUPT
   6 GETMAD 7 ENLARGE
   GETSORE
up (abbr.): 3 ENL
~, as a game: 4 LOSE

Blower
  Sicilian: 4 ETNA
  Whistle: 3 **REF** 6 TOOTER

Blowfish: 6 PUFFER
  ___ & the: 6 HOOTIE

Blowgun
  ammo: 3 PEA 4 DART

Blowhard
  Act the: 4 BRAG
  offering: 5 BOAST
  trait: 3 EGO

Blowhole: 4 VENT

"Blowin' in the Wind"
  singer/composer: 5 DYLAN

Blown
  away: 4 AWED 5 INAWE
    6 AMAZED 7 STUNNED
  It may be: 4 FUSE 6 GASKET

Blowout: 4 **BASH** GALA

Blows
  Come to: 4 SPAR
  It ~ off steam: 6 GEYSER
  Where she: 4 THAR

Blowtorch
  Use a: 4 WELD

Blowup
  (abbr.): 3 ENL
  Atlas: 5 INSET
  Cause of a: 3 TNT

BLT
  part: 5 BACON 6 TOMATO
  spread: 4 MAYO

Blubber: 3 CRY FAT **SOB** 4 BAWL
   WEEP 6 BOOHOO
  Strip ~ from: 6 FLENSE

Bludgeon: 4 COSH

"___ Blu Dipinto di Blu": 3 **NEL**

Blue: 3 LOW **SAD** 6 EROTIC
  bird: 3 JAY
  blood, briefly: 6 ARISTO
  bloods: 5 ELITE
  Bluer than: 7 OBSCENE
  books: 4 PORN SMUT
    7 EROTICA
  cartoon character: 5 SMURF
  chip: 4 ANTE
  Dark: 4 NAVY
  Deep: 4 **ANIL**
  dye: 4 ANIL 6 INDIGO
  eyes: 5 TRAIT
  Feeling: 3 SAD
  flag: 4 IRIS
  follower: 4 NILE
  Get a ~ ribbon: 3 WIN
  Greenish: 4 **AQUA** CYAN **TEAL**
  Heraldic: 5 AZURE
  hue: 4 **AQUA** CYAN NAVY TEAL
    5 AZURE
  In a ~ funk: 3 SAD
  jeans: 5 LEVIS
  Like a ~ moon: 4 RARE
  of baseball: 4 VIDA
  ox: 4 BABE
  prints: 7 EROTICA
  shade: 3 SKY 4 ANIL AQUA
    NAVY NILE TEAL 5 ROYAL
    6 COBALT
  Sky: 5 AZURE
  Somewhat: 4 RACY
  Talk a ~ streak: 3 GAB YAK
    4 CUSS 5 RUNON SWEAR
  toon: 5 SMURF
  True: 5 LOYAL
  Turn: 3 DYE 6 SADDEN
  Wild ~ yonder: 3 SKY
    5 ETHER
"___ Blue": 4 NYPD
"___ Blue?": 3 AMI

Bluebeard
  Last wife of: 6 FATIMA
"Blueberry Hill"
  singer Domino: 4 FATS
Blue Bonnet
  product: 4 OLEO
Blue-book
  filler: 5 ESSAY
"Blue Chips"
  actor Nick: 5 NOLTE
BlueChoice: 3 HMO
Blue Cross
  alternative: 5 AETNA
"Blue Dahlia, The"
  actor: 4 LADD
  actress: 12 VERONICALAKE
Blue Devils
  home: 4 DUKE
Blue Eagle
  org.: 3 NRA
Bluefin: 4 TUNA
Bluegill
  relative: 5 BREAM
Bluegrass
  instrument: 5 BANJO
  musician Bill: 6 MONROE
  musician Lester: 5 FLATT
Blue-green: 4 AQUA CYAN TEAL
Blue Grotto
  locale: 5 CAPRI
"Blue Hawaii"
  star: 5 ELVIS
Bluejacket: 3 TAR
Blue Jays
  home: 7 TORONTO
  player: 4 ALER
  song: 7 OCANADA
Blue-law
  subject: 6 SUNDAY
"Blue Moon"
  of baseball: 4 ODOM
Blueness: 6 SORROW
Bluenose: 4 PRIG 5 PRISS PRUDE
    7 PURITAN 9 NICENELLY
Blue-pencil: 4 **EDIT** 5 EMEND
  user: 6 EDITOR
Bluepoint: 6 OYSTER
Blueprint: 4 **PLAN**
  detail: 4 **SPEC**

Blue-ribbon: 5 FIRST
Blue Ribbon
  maker: 5 PABST
Blues: 5 MUSIC
  Baby: 4 EYES
  singer Bonnie: 5 RAITT
  singer James: 4 ETTA
  singer Ma: 6 RAINEY
  singer Simone: 4 NINA
  singer Smith: 6 BESSIE
  singer Washington: 5 DINAH
  Singing the: 3 SAD
  Sing the: 4 WAIL
  street: 5 BEALE
"Blues Brothers, The"
  director: 6 LANDIS
  venue: 3 SNL
"Blue ___ Shoes": 5 SUEDE
"Blues in the Night"
  composer Harold: 5 ARLEN
"Blue Sky"
  actress Jessica: 5 LANGE
Bluesman
  ~ Mahal: 3 TAJ
  ~ Mo': 3 KEB
  ~ Spann: 4 OTIS
Blue ___ special: 5 PLATE
"Blue Suede Shoes"
  singer: 5 ELVIS
  songwriter Perkins: 4 CARL
Blue Triangle
  gp.: 4 YWCA
"Blue Velvet"
  actress Laura: 4 DERN
Bluffer
  game: 5 POKER
  ploy: 5 RAISE
Bluish
  duck: 4 TEAL
  gray: 5 SLATY
  green: 4 TEAL
  purple: 5 MAUVE
Blunder: 3 ERR 4 FLUB GOOF
    5 ERROR GAFFE
    7 MISSTEP
  Baseball: 5 ERROR
  Bridge: 6 RENEGE
  Make a: 3 ERR
  Social: 5 GAFFE

Blunderer: 7 SADSACK
Blunt: 6 OBTUSE
  blade: 4 EPEE
  sword: 4 EPEE
Blunted
  blade: 4 **EPEE**
  sword: 4 EPEE
Blurbs: 3 ADS 4 BIOS
Blurt
  Bleeped: 4 OATH
  Pert: 4 SASS
Blush: 5 ROUGE 6 REDDEN
Blushing: 3 **RED**
Bluster: 4 BRAG RANT
Blustery: 3 RAW
Bluto: 6 SAILOR
  dream girl: 5 OLIVE
  rival: 6 POPEYE
Blvd.: 3 AVE
  crossers: 3 RDS STS
Blyleven
  of baseball: 4 BERT
Blynken
  Partner of Wynken and: 3 NOD
Blyth
  Actress: 3 ANN
Blyton
  Author: 4 **ENID**
BMI
  rival: 5 ASCAP
B-movie
  bad guy: 4 YEGG
BMW: 6 IMPORT
  rival: 4 AUDI
Bo
  Actress: 5 DEREK
B.O.
  sign: 3 SRO
  ___ Bo: 3 TAE
Boa: 5 SCARF SNAKE 6 PYTHON
    7 FEATHER
Boar
  abode: 6 PIGSTY
  mate: 3 SOW
Board: 5 GETON HOPON MEALS
    7 CLIMBIN ENPLANE
  and lodging: 4 KEEP
  Back on: 3 AFT
  Bed: 4 SLAT

Bring on: 4 HIRE
Clear the: 5 **ERASE**
  game: 5 CHESS
  Manicurist's: 5 EMERY
  material: 5 EMERY
  member: 4 EXEC 7 TRUSTEE
  member (abbr.): 3 DIR
  Mystical: 5 OUIJA
  partner: 4 ROOM
  Put on: 4 LADE STOW
  Ship: 5 PLANK
  Thin: 4 SLAT
Boarded: 5 GOTON
Boarding
  area: 4 GATE
  place: 4 STOP
  place (abbr.): 3 STA
  sch.: 4 ACAD
Boardroom
  bigwig: 3 CEO
  visual aid: 5 GRAPH
Boards
  Clear the: 5 ERASE
  treader: 5 ACTOR
  Treading the: 7 ONSTAGE
  Tread the: 3 ACT
Boardwalk
  diversion: 6 STROLL
  refreshments: 4 ICES
Boars: 3 HES 5 MALES
  Place for: 3 STY
Boast: 4 BRAG CROW 7 POSSESS
  End of Jack's: 3 AMI
  Part of a famous: 4 ISAW VENI
    VICI VIDI 5 ICAME
Boaster: 6 GASBAG
Boastful: 5 GASSY
Boat: 3 HER SHE
  Back of a: 3 AFT 5 STERN
  basin: 6 MARINA
  Biblical: 3 ARK
  Biblical ~ builder: 4 NOAH
  bottom: 4 KEEL
  Coal: 4 SCOW
  contents: 5 GRAVY
  Dispatch: 5 **AVISO**
  Eskimo: 5 UMIAK
  Flat-bottomed: 4 DORY SCOW
  Garbage: 4 SCOW

Genesis: 3 ARK
Lake: 5 CANOE
Malayan: 4 PROA
Miss the: 7 LOSEOUT
Off the: 6 ASHORE
One-person: 5 SKIFF
Propel a: 3 ROW
propeller: 3 OAR
race: 7 REGATTA
Racing: 5 SCULL
trailer: 4 WAKE
Twin-hulled: 9 CATAMARAN
Boater: 3 HAT 8 STRAWHAT
Boathouse
inventory: 4 OARS
Bob: 6 HAIRDO
Choreographer: 5 FOSSE
Comedian: 5 SAGET
companion: 5 WEAVE
cousin: 4 LUGE
Former Ontario Premier: 3 RAE
Handyman: 4 VILA
of football: 6 GRIESE
of the Bob and Ray comedy team:
    6 ELLIOT
Rock singer: 5 SEGER
who lost to Bill: 4 DOLE
Bobbettes
hit song: 5 MRLEE
Bobbin: 5 SPOOL
Bobble: 3 ERR 4 MUFF 5 ERROR
Bobbsey
One of the ~ twins: 3 **NAN**
    4 BERT 7 FLOSSIE FREDDIE
Bobby
1960s radical ~: 5 SEALE
Auto racer: 5 RAHAL UNSER
Child star: 5 BREEN
of football: 5 LAYNE
of hockey: 3 **ORR**
of tennis: 5 RIGGS
of the Black Panthers: 5 SEALE
Singer: 3 VEE 5 DARIN
Bobby-___: 6 SOXERS
"___ Bobby McGee": 5 MEAND
Bobbysoxer: 4 GIRL
event: 3 HOP
Boca ___: 5 RATON
Bocelli, Andrea: 5 TENOR

performance: 4 ARIA
Bochco
Producer: 6 STEVEN
Bochco, Steven
series: 5 LALAW
Bock
holder: 5 STEIN
Bodega
owner: 6 GROCER
patron: 6 LATINO
setting: 6 BARRIO
Bodhidharma
philosophy: 3 ZEN
Bodine, Jethro
portrayer Max: 4 BAER
___ bodkins: 3 ODS
Body: 5 TORSO 6 CORPSE
    7 CADAVER
Ante: 3 POT
Anti: 3 CON
build: 5 FRAME
fluids: 4 SERA
French: 5 SENAT
Heavenly: 3 ORB 5 ANGEL
of art: 5 TORSO
of knowledge: 4 LORE
of speech: 4 TEXT
of values: 5 ETHIC
of water: 3 SEA 4 POND
    5 OCEAN
of work: 6 OEUVRE
passage: 4 ITER
Sci. of the: 4 ANAT
Study of the ~ (abbr.): 4 ANAT
Upper: 5 TORSO
Without: 4 LIMP
work: 6 TATTOO
wrap: 4 SKIN
Bodybuilder: 5 HEMAN
bane: 4 FLAB
pride: 3 ABS 4 LATS PECS
    6 BICEPS
unit: 3 REP
~ Charles: 5 ATLAS
~ Reeves: 5 STEVE
"Body Count"
rapper: 4 ICET
Bodyguards: 6 MUSCLE
Body shop: 3 SPA

challenge: 4 DENT
fig.: 3 EST
offering: 6 LOANER
Bodywork
In need of: 6 DENTED
Boeing: 3 JET 8 JETLINER
rival: 6 AIRBUS
Scrapped ~ project: 3 SST
Boer
migration: 4 TREK
Boesky
of Wall Street: 4 IVAN
Boff
suffix: 3 OLA
Boffo
letters: 3 SRO
review: 4 RAVE
show: 5 SMASH
Bog: 3 FEN 4 **MIRE**
down: 4 MIRE
fuel: 4 **PEAT**
Like a: 4 MIRY 5 PEATY
Bogarde
Actor: 4 DIRK
Bogart, Humphrey
costar: 6 BACALL 9 IDALUPINO
film: 6 SAHARA 8 KEYLARGO
role: 5 EARLE QUEEG SPADE
Spade, to: 4 ROLE
title role: 3 MRX
topper: 6 FEDORA
Bogey: 7 ONEOVER 8 ABOVEPAR
beater: 3 PAR
Bogeyman: 4 OGRE 6 SCARER
Bogged
down: 5 MIRED 6 INARUT
Boggs
of baseball: 4 WADE
Boggy: 4 MIRY
area: 3 FEN 4 MIRE 5 SWAMP
Bogosian
Actor: 4 ERIC
Bogotá
babies: 5 NENES
City southwest of: 4 CALI
Gp. founded in: 3 OAS
Bogus: 4 FAKE SHAM 5 FALSE
PHONY 6 ERSATZ
butter: 4 OLEO

Not: 4 REAL
Bohemian: 4 **ARTY** 5 ARTSY
CZECH
dance: 5 POLKA
More: 6 ARTIER
Bohr: 4 DANE
Physicist: 5 NIELS
study: 4 ATOM
Boiardo
patron: 4 ESTE
Boil: 6 SEETHE
Almost: 5 SCALD
Bring to a: 5 ANGER
6 ENRAGE
down: 6 DECOCT
in oil: 3 FRY
Boilermaker
Beer, in a: 6 CHASER
part: 4 BEER
"Boiler Room"
actress Long: 3 NIA
Boiling: 3 HOT MAD 5 IRATE
7 INARAGE
Extract by: 6 DECOCT
Heat without: 5 SCALD
___ **Boingo (rock band):** 5 OINGO
Boise
county: 3 ADA
state: 5 IDAHO
state (abbr.): 3 IDA
Boisterous: 4 LOUD 5 AROAR
Be: 7 ROLLICK
festivity: 5 REVEL
Boitano
Skater: 5 BRIAN
Bojangles
Emulate: 3 TAP 8 TAPDANCE
Bok ___: 4 CHOY
Bold: 5 BRAVE GUTSY
Be: 4 DARE
Not: 3 SHY 4 MEEK 5 TIMID
one: 5 DARER
Bolero
composer: 5 RAVEL
Boleyn: 4 ANNE
Bolger
costar: 4 LAHR
Bolívar, Simón
birthplace: 7 CARACAS

Bolivia
  Bear, in: 3 OSO
  capital: 5 LAPAZ SUCRE
  export: 3 TIN
  neighbor: 4 PERU
Bollix: 4 FLUB 5 SNAFU
Bollixed
  All ~ up: 7 INAMESS
Bolo: 3 TIE
Bologna: 8 DELIMEAT
  alternative: 6 SALAMI
  bills: 4 LIRE ·
  bread: 4 LIRA
  neighbor: 6 MODENA
  unit: 5 SLICE
Bolshevik: 3 RED
  leader: 5 LENIN
      7 TROTSKY
  target: 4 TSAR
Bolshevism
  founder: 5 LENIN
Bolshoi
  rival: 5 KIROV
Bolt: 3 LAM RUN 4 FLEE
  down: 3 EAT
  fastener: 3 NUT
  holder: 4 TNUT
  to bond: 5 ELOPE
Bomb: 4 FLOP 6 TURKEY
      7 FAILURE
      8 LAYANEGG
  Car: 5 EDSEL LEMON
  Kind of: 7 AEROSOL
  squad member: 5 ROBOT
  trial: 5 ATEST
Bombard: 4 PELT 5 SHELL
  suffix: 3 IER
Bombast: 3 GAS 8 RHETORIC
Bombastic: 5 GASSY TUMID
Bombay
  City ESE of: 5 POONA
  country: 5 INDIA
  garb: 4 SARI
  royal: 4 RANI
Bombeck
  Humorist: 4 **ERMA**
Bomber
  letters: 4 USAF
  Name on a: 5 ENOLA

  Noted: 8 ENOLAGAY
Bombs
  Like some: 5 SMART
"... bombs bursting ___ ...":
      5 INAIR
Bombshell: 6 SEXPOT
  actress Diana: 4 DORS
  actress Jean: 6 HARLOW
Bon ___: 3 **MOT** 4 SOIR
  of rock: 4 JOVI
"Bon ___!": 7 APPETIT
"___ bon!": 4 CEST
Bona ___: 4 FIDE 5 FIDES
Bona fide: 4 REAL 6 ACTUAL
Bon Ami
  competitor: 4 AJAX
Bonanza: 4 LODE
  find: 3 ORE
  Miner's: 4 LODE
"Bonanza"
  actor Blocker: 3 DAN
  actor Greene: 5 **LORNE**
  brother: 4 ADAM HOSS
Bonbon: 5 SWEET TREAT
Bond: 3 SPY 4 GLUE 5 AGENT
      UNITE 6 SURETY
  alma mater: 4 ETON
  creator Fleming: 3 IAN
  foe: 4 DRNO 6 SMERSH
  Govt.: 5 TNOTE
  on the run: 5 ELOPE
  order: 7 MARTINI
      10 DRYMARTINI
  portrayer: 5 MOORE 6 DALTON
  prefix: 4 EURO
  rating: 3 AAA BBB CCC
  recipient: 7 OBLIGEE
  Tax-free: 4 MUNI
  Type of: 5 EPOXY
Bond, James: 3 SPY
  (abbr.): 3 AGT
  alma mater: 4 ETON
  cocktail: 7 MARTINI
      10 DRYMARTINI
  creator Fleming: 3 IAN
  film: 4 **DRNO** 9 MOONRAKER
      10 GOLDFINGER
  foe: 4 DRNO 6 SMERSH
  portrayer: 5 MOORE 6 DALTON

Bonds
How some ~ are sold:
5 ATPAR
Like some: 5 RATED 6 RATEDA
7 TAXFREE
Bonds, Barry
stat: 3 HRS RBI
Bondsman: 4 SERF
payment: 4 BAIL
Bone: 5 FILET
Arm: 4 **ULNA**
Bad to the: 4 EVIL
connector: 5 SINEW
Dry as a: 4 ARID
Ear: 5 INCUS 6 STAPES
First ~ donor: 4 ADAM
Forearm: 4 **ULNA**
Largest human: 5 FEMUR
Leg: 4 SHIN 5 FEMUR TIBIA
Mouth: 3 JAW
Of an arm: 5 ULNAR
Pelvic: 5 ILIUM
prefix: 3 OST 4 OSSE **OSTE**
5 OSSEO OSTEO
Small: 7 OSSICLE
Smallest human: 6 STAPES
to pick: 4 BEEF 5 GRIPE
Work on a: 4 GNAW
~, in Latin: 4 OSSO
Bone-dry: 4 **ARID** SERE
Bonehead: 3 ASS OAF SAP
4 DOLT 5 IDIOT
Boneless
entrée: 5 FILET
Boner: 5 ERROR
Pull a: 3 ERR 4 GOOF
Bones: 4 DICE OSSA
Ankle: 5 TARSI
Arm: 5 RADII ULNAE ULNAS
6 HUMERI
Back: 5 SACRA
Foot: 5 TARSI
Forearm: 5 RADII ULNAE
ULNAS
Hip: 4 ILIA
Pelvic: 4 **ILIA** 5 SACRA
Wrist: 5 CARPI
___ **Bones (Ichabod's foe):**
4 BROM

"Bonesetter's Daughter, The"
author: 3 TAN 6 AMYTAN
Bonet
Actress: 4 **LISA**
Bonfire
remnant: 3 ASH
Bongo: 4 DRUM
Bonheur
Painter: 4 **ROSA**
Bon Jovi
Singer: 3 JON
Bonkers: 3 MAD 4 AMOK DAFT
GAGA LOCO NUTS
5 NUTSO 6 INSANE
Go: 4 RAVE SNAP
Not: 4 SANE
Bon mot: 4 QUIP 7 EPIGRAM
Bonn
Info: German cue
City near: 5 ESSEN
mister: 4 HERR
One in: 4 EINE
river: 5 RHINE
Bonner
Russian activist: 5 ELENA
Bonnet: 3 HAT
bug: 3 BEE
in Britain: 4 HOOD
Bonneville Flats
locale: 4 UTAH
Bonnie
Actress: 7 BEDELIA
partner: 5 CLYDE
portrayer: 4 FAYE
Singer: 5 **RAITT**
Bonnie Blue
Father of: 5 RHETT
Bonny
miss: 4 LASS
Bono
Pro: 6 UNPAID
Bonus: 3 TIP 5 EXTRA
Concert: 6 ENCORE
Bony: 6 OSTEAL 7 OSSEOUS
prefix: 5 OSTEO
Boo: 4 JEER
follower: 3 HOO
relative: 4 HISS
Boob: 3 ASS OAF

Boob ___: 4 TUBE
Boo-boo: 4 SLIP 5 BONER ERROR
  7 MISTAKE
  Book ~ *(plural):* 6 ERRATA
  remover: 6 ERASER
Boo Boo: 4 BEAR
  buddy: 4 YOGI
Boob tube: 5 TVSET
  (plural): 3 TVS
  ~, in Britain: 5 TELLY
Booby
  Get the ~ prize: 4 LOSE
  Taking the ~ prize: 4 LAST
  trap: 4 MINE 5 SNARE
Book
  after Daniel: 5 **HOSEA**
  after Ezra: 8 NEHEMIAH
  after Ezra (abbr.): 3 NEH
  after Galatians (abbr.): 3 EPH
  after II Chronicles: 4 EZRA
  after Joel: 4 AMOS
  after John: 4 ACTS
  after Jonah: 5 MICAH
  after Nehemiah: 6 ESTHER
  after Proverbs (abbr.): 4 ECCL
  back: 5 SPINE
  backbone: 5 SPINE
  before Amos: 4 JOEL
  before Daniel (abbr.): 4 EZEK
  before Deut.: 3 NUM
  before Esther (abbr.): 3 NEH
  before Jeremiah: 6 ISAIAH
  before Job (abbr.): 4 ESTH
  before Joel: 5 HOSEA
  before Micah: 5 JONAH
  before Nahum: 5 MICAH
  before Nehemiah: 4 EZRA
  before Obadiah: 4 AMOS
  before Romans: 4 ACTS
  Big: 4 **TOME** 5 FOLIO
  Cook: 4 COMA
  end: 5 INDEX
  Enjoy a: 4 READ
  Enjoy a ~ again: 6 REREAD
  Holy: 5 BIBLE KORAN
  jacket item: 3 BIO 5 BLURB
  leaf: 4 PAGE
  of Changes: 6 ICHING
  of hymns: 7 PSALTER

of legends: 5 ATLAS
of maps: 5 ATLAS
of memories: 5 ALBUM
of prophecies: 4 AMOS 5 HOSEA
OT: 3 LEV NEH 4 EZEK OBAD
page: 4 LEAF
Photo: 5 ALBUM
Prayer: 6 MISSAL
Ref.: 4 DICT
School: 4 TEXT 6 PRIMER
  7 SPELLER
size: 6 OCTAVO
supplements: 7 ADDENDA
World: 5 ATLAS
~ ID: 4 ISBN
~, in Spanish: 5 LIBRO
Bookbag
  item: 4 TEXT
Bookbinding
  leather: 4 ROAN
"Book 'em, ___!": 4 DANO
Booker T.
  backup band: 3 MGS
Bookie
  concern: 4 ODDS
  records: 4 BETS
Booking
  for a band: 3 GIG
  Take in for: 6 ARREST
Bookish: 8 STUDIOUS
  type: 4 NERD
Book jacket
  hype: 5 BLURB
Bookkeeper
  ~, at times: 5 ADDER
Bookkeeping
  entry: 5 DEBIT
Booklet
  Mass: 4 ORDO
Bookmark: 6 DOGEAR
  Browser: 3 URL
"Book of Days"
  singer: 4 ENYA
Books
  Blue: 4 PORN SMUT
  Check: 5 AUDIT
  Crack the: 4 READ
  He's found in: 5 WALDO
  Put on the: 5 **ENACT**

Reviewer of ~, for short: 3 CPA
Bookseller
  Online: 6 AMAZON
Bookstore
  Campus ~ purchase: 4 TEXT
  Enjoy a: 6 BROWSE
  feature: 4 CAFE
  section: 5 HOWTO HUMOR
    SCIFI
  section (abbr.): 4 BIOG
Bookworm: 4 NERD 6 READER
"Boola Boola"
  singer: 3 **ELI**
Boom: 4 SPAR 5 NOISE
  Kind of: 5 SONIC
  producer: 3 SST
  support: 4 MAST
  times: 3 UPS
___ boom: 5 **SONIC**
Boom-bah
  preceder: 3 SIS
Boom box: 5 RADIO
  button: 3 REC
  letters: 4 AMFM
  platters: 3 CDS
Boomer
  followers: 4 GENX
  of football: 7 ESIASON
Boomerang: 8 BACKFIRE
Booms: 9 GOODTIMES
  Like some: 5 SONIC
Boone
  of baseball: 4 BRET
  Singer: 3 PAT 5 DEBBY
  ~, to friends: 4 DANL
Boone, Daniel
  portrayer Parker: 4 FESS
Boop
  Miss: 5 BETTY
Boor: 3 CAD OAF 4 CLOD **LOUT**
    5 CHURL YAHOO
Boorish: 4 RUDE 5 CRASS
  sort: 3 CAD OAF 4 CLOD LOUT
    5 CHURL YAHOO
Boosler
  Comic: 6 **ELAYNE**
Boost: 3 AID 4 PUSH 5 LEGUP
    RAISE 7 ELEVATE
  It may need a: 3 EGO 6 MORALE

  Salary: 5 RAISE
Booster: 5 AGENA
  GI morale: 3 USO
  Paycheck: 8 OVERTIME
  Sound: 3 AMP
Boot: 4 OUST 6 UNSEAT
  attachment: 4 SPUR
  bottom: 4 SOLE
  Give the: 3 AXE CAN 4 OUST
  out: 5 EXPEL
  part: 3 TOE 6 TOECAP
  To: 3 TOO 4 **ALSO** 6 NOLESS
"___ Boot": 3 DAS
Bootblack
  offering: 5 SHINE
Boot camp
  boss: 5 SARGE
  reply: 6 YESSIR
Booted: 4 SHOD
Bootees
  Make: 4 **KNIT**
Booth
  Actor: 5 EDWIN
  Mall: 5 KIOSK
  Merchandise: 5 STALL
  Person in a: 5 VOTER
___ Boothe Luce: 5 CLARE
Bootlicker: 6 YESMAN
Bootlicking: 4 OILY
Boot-shaped
  country: 5 ITALY
Booty: 4 LOOT **SWAG**
    6 SPOILS
Booze: 5 HOOCH SAUCE
    6 HOOTCH
  Add ~ to: 4 LACE
  Avoid ~: 8 TEETOTAL
  Shot of: 5 SNORT
Boozehound: 3 SOT 4 LUSH
    WINO 5 DIPSO TOPER
Boozer: 3 SOT 4 LUSH WINO
    5 DIPSO TOPER
Bop: 4 CONK
"___ Bop" (Lauper hit): 3 SHE
Bo-Peep
  Call to: 3 BAA
  charges: 5 SHEEP
  Like ~ charges: 5 OVINE
___ Bora: 4 TORA

Bora Bora
  neighbor: 6 TAHITI
  ___ **Borch, Gerard**
  Painter: 3 TER
Bordeaux: 3 VIN 4 WINE
  Info: French cue
  bean: 4 TETE
  beau: 3 AMI
  Born, in: 3 NEE
  But, in: 4 MAIS
  To be, in: 4 ETRE
  wine: 5 MEDOC 6 CLARET
Bordelaise: 5 SAUCE
  ingredient: 7 SHALLOT
Borden
  Beast of: 5 ELSIE
  brand: 6 ELMERS
  cow: 5 ELSIE
  weapon: 3 AXE
Border: 4 ABUT EDGE SIDE
  marker: 5 FENCE
  on: 4 **ABUT**
  patrol concern: 6 ALIENS
  Put a ~ on: 5 EDGED
  Shield: 4 ORLE
  Stitched: 3 HEM
Bore: 4 DRAG DRIP TIRE
      6 NUDNIK
  Crashing: 4 DRIP
  It's a: 6 YAWNER
  Respond to a: 4 YAWN
  Utter: 4 DRAG
  Word before: 5 TIDAL
  ___ borealis: 6 AURORA
Bored
  Become: 4 TIRE
Boredom: 5 **ENNUI**
  Indicate: 4 SIGH YAWN
Borg: 5 SWEDE
  contemporary: 4 ASHE
  homeland: 6 SWEDEN
  of tennis: 5 BJORN
Borge, Victor: 4 DANE 7 PIANIST
  instrument: 5 PIANO
Borges, Jorge ___
  Author: 4 LUIS
Borgia
  Cardinal: 6 CESARE
  in-law: 4 ESTE

Borgnine
  Actor: 6 ERNEST
  Oscar-winning title role for:
      5 MARTY
Boric acid
  target: 4 ANTS
Boring: 4 BLAH DULL 5 HOHUM
  Become: 4 CLOY
  Do ~ work: 4 REAM
  Got: 4 WORE
  It may be: 3 BIT 5 DRILL
  person: 4 DRIP
  routine: 3 RUT
  tool: 5 **AUGER** 6 REAMER
      TREPAN
  voice: 8 MONOTONE
Boris
  contemporary: 3 LON 4 BELA
  partner: 7 NATASHA
  refusal: 4 NYET
  rival: 4 IVAN
Born: 3 **NEE**
  earlier: 5 ELDER OLDER
  First: 4 CAIN 6 ELDEST
      OLDEST
  in: 4 FROM
  yesterday: 5 NAIVE
  ~, in French: 3 **NEE**
Born and ___: 4 BRED
Borneo
  beast: 5 ORANG
  Island south of: 4 BALI
  ruler: 5 RAJAH
  Sultanate on: 6 BRUNEI
  ___ **Bornes (card game):** 5 MILLE
"Born Free"
  lioness: 4 **ELSA**
"Born in the ___": 3 USA
Borodin
  prince: 4 **IGOR**
Borodina
  Mezzo: 4 OLGA
Borrowed: 6 ONLOAN
Borscht: 4 SOUP
  belt bit: 3 GAG
  ingredient: 4 BEET 5 BEETS
"Borstal Boy"
  author Brendan: 5 BEHAN
Bosc: 4 PEAR

Bosley
  Actor: 3 TOM
Bosnia
  peacekeeping org.: 4 NATO
Bosnian: 4 SERB
Bosom
  buddy: 3 PAL 4 CHUM
"Bosom Buddies"
  musical: 4 MAME
Bosox
  outfielder: 3 YAZ
Bosporus: 6 STRAIT
  (abbr.): 3 STR
Boss: 4 HEAD 6 HONCHO
        8 OVERSEER
  (abbr.): 3 MGR
  Barracks: 5 SARGE
  Bus.: 3 CEO
  Mafia: 3 DON 4 CAPO
  Pfc.: 3 CPL
  Pvt.: 3 SGT
  request: 5 SEEME
  Safari: 5 BWANA
  Street: 5 MASON
Bossa nova
  relative: 5 SAMBA
Boss Tweed
  cartoonist: 4 NAST
Bossy: 3 COW
  baby: 4 CALF
  boss: 6 TYRANT
  chew: 3 CUD
  remark: 3 MOO
Boston
  airport: 5 LOGAN
  cager: 4 CELT
  newspaper: 5 GLOBE
  orchestra: 4 POPS
  suburb: 4 LYNN
  ~ NHLer: 5 BRUIN
Boston Bruins
  legend: 3 ORR
"Bostonians, The"
  actor: 5 REEVE
Boston Marathon
  month: 5 APRIL
"Boston Public"
  actor McBride: 3 CHI
  extra: 4 TEEN

Boston Red ___: 3 SOX
Boston Symphony
  Former ~ conductor: 5 OZAWA
Bot.: 3 SCI
Botanical
  beard: 3 AWN
  opening: 5 STOMA
  support: 4 STEM
Botanist
  expertise: 5 FLORA
  Flower named for a: 6 DAHLIA
  ~ Gray: 3 **ASA**
  ~ Mendel: 6 GREGOR
Botch: 3 ERR 4 BLOW FLUB
        MUFF RUIN 5 MISDO
        6 FOULUP MANGLE
"Botch-___" (Clooney tune):
        3 AME
Both
  prefix: 4 AMBI
Bother: 3 **ADO** AIL IRE IRK VEX
        4 FUSS PEST TODO
        5 ANNOY EATAT UPSET
        6 HARASS HASSLE
        PESTER
  Don't: 8 LETALONE
        10 LEAVEALONE
  persistently: 5 EATAT NAGAT
        6 HARASS
Botheration: 3 ADO
Bothered: 5 **ATEAT** GOTAT
Botswana
  blight: 6 TSETSE
Botticelli
  Painter: 6 SANDRO
Bottle
  Baby: 6 NURSER
  Dressing: 5 CRUET
  Hit the: 4 TOPE 5 BOOZE
  Large: 6 MAGNUM
  Medicine: 4 VIAL
  Message in a: 3 SOS
  Model in a: 4 SHIP
  Open, as a: 5 UNCAP
  part: 4 NECK
  Perfume: 4 VIAL
  size: 5 LITER
  size (British): 5 LITRE
  stopper: 4 CORK

Tiny: 4 VIAL
top: 3 CAP 6 NIPPLE
   8 SCREWCAP
Wicker-covered: 8 DEMIJOHN
Bottled
Not: 5 ONTAP
spirit: 4 DJIN 5 GENIE
(up): 4 PENT
water brand: 5 EVIAN
Bottleneck: 3 JAM 5 SNARL
Bottom: 4 FOOT 5 FANNY NADIR
Boat: 4 KEEL
Boot: 4 SOLE
Clear of the: 6 AWEIGH
Go to the: 4 SINK
Hit: 5 SPANK
It's on the: 6 DIAPER
line: 3 HEM **NET** SUM 5 TOTAL
   YIELD 6 AMOUNT
   10 NETRESULTS
of the barrel: 4 LEES 5 DREGS
   WORST
Rock: 5 NADIR
Shoe: 4 SOLE
Bottomless: 4 DEEP
It may be: 3 PIT
pit: 5 ABYSM **ABYSS**
Bottom-of-the-barrel: 5 WORST
stuff: 4 LEES 5 DREGS
"Bottoms up!": 5 SKOAL
Botulin: 5 TOXIN
Botvinnik
Defeater of ~ in chess: 3 TAL
Bough: 4 LIMB
Take a: 3 LOP
Bought: 7 PAIDFOR
and sold: 5 DEALT
back: 8 REDEEMED
It's ~ by the bar: 4 SOAP
Bouillabaisse: 4 STEW
Boulanger
Composer: 5 NADIA
Boulder: 3 DAM 4 ROCK 5 STONE
hrs.: 3 MST
Boulevard: 4 ROAD 6 AVENUE
Hollywood: 6 SUNSET
liners: 5 TREES
Boult
Conductor: 6 ADRIAN

Bounce: 3 BOB 4 BOOT ECHO
   LILT OUST 5 EJECT
   EVICT
back: 4 **ECHO**
Billiards: 5 CAROM
setting: 5 DRYER
Sonic: 4 ECHO
Bounced
check letters: 3 NSF
Bouncer: 4 BALL
Baby: 4 KNEE
requests: 3 IDS 7 IDCARDS
Bouncing
off the walls: 5 HYPER
Bouncy: 4 PERT 7 UPTEMPO
step: 4 LILT
Bound: 4 **LEAP** LOPE TIED
   6 LASHED
bundle: 5 SHEAF
Boundary: 3 END 4 EDGE
   5 AMBIT LIMIT
Plateau: 7 RIMROCK
Property: 5 FENCE
Racetrack: 4 RAIL
Sector: 3 ARC
Statistical: 8 QUARTILE
Strike zone: 5 KNEES
"Bound East for Cardiff"
Like O'Neill's: 6 ONEACT
Bounder: 3 **CAD** 4 ROUE
Aussie: 3 ROO
Bounding main: 3 SEA 5 OCEAN
On the: 4 ASEA 5 ATSEA
Boundless: 4 VAST
Bountiful
locale: 4 UTAH
Bounty: 5 PRICE 6 REWARD
competitor: 4 VIVA
destination: 6 TAHITI
Bouquet: 4 NOSE **ODOR** POSY
   5 **AROMA** SCENT
   7 NOSEGAY
Fall: 6 ASTERS
garni element: 5 THYME
holder: 4 VASE
item: 4 ROSE
Small: 4 POSY
Wine: 4 NOSE
Bouquet ___: 5 GARNI

Bouquets
Big name in: 3 FTD
Bourbon
and others (abbr.): 3 STS
Like good: 4 AGED
"Bourne Identity, The"
actor: 5 DAMON 9 MATTDAMON
Bourne, in: 5 JASON
8 AMNESIAC
Bourne's problem, in: 7 AMNESIA
Bout
ender: 3 **TKO**
Ends a ~ early: 3 KOS
locale: 5 ARENA
Prepare for a: 4 SPAR 5 TRAIN
Boutique: 4 SHOP 5 STORE
Boutonniere
site: 5 LAPEL
Boutros-___, Boutros
Diplomat: 5 GHALI
Boutros-Ghali, Boutros
successor: 4 KOFI 5 ANNAN
~, by birth: 7 CAIRENE
Bovary
Madame: 4 **EMMA**
Bovine
baby: 4 CALF
beasts: 4 OXEN
Borden: 5 ELSIE
bunch: 4 HERD
cry: 3 MOO
Hairy: 3 YAK 5 BISON
Humped: 4 ZEBU
Bow: 3 ARC
Actress: 5 CLARA
and scrape: 4 FAWN
application: 5 ROSIN
Away from the: 3 AFT 6 ASTERN
Boy with a: 4 AMOR EROS
God with a: 4 AMOR EROS
Low: 6 SALAAM
Make a: 3 TIE
Ma with a: 4 YOYO
of silents: 5 CLARA
Part of a: 4 LOOP 5 HAWSE
Polite: 6 CURTSY
Stern with a: 5 ISAAC
(to): 6 KOWTOW
With the ~, in music: 4 ARCO

wood: 3 YEW
Bowdlerize: 4 EDIT
Bower: 5 ARBOR
Bowery
bum: 4 WINO
___ Bowes (postage company):
6 PITNEY
Bowie: 3 JIM
Former baseball commissioner:
4 KUHN
last stand: 5 ALAMO
weapon: 5 KNIFE
Bowie, David
#1 hit of: 9 LETSDANCE
collaborator Brian: 3 ENO
Wife of: 4 IMAN
Bowl: 5 ARENA
org.: 4 NCAA
over: 3 AWE WOW 4 **STUN**
5 AMAZE
yell: 3 RAH
Bowler: 3 HAT 5 DERBY
button: 5 RESET
challenge: 5 SPLIT
edge: 4 BRIM
hangout: 5 ALLEY
pickup: 5 SPARE
target: 3 PIN 6 TENPIN
Bowlful
Bowser's: 4 ALPO
Breakfast: 6 CEREAL FARINA
Party: 8 ONIONDIP
Bowling
ball material: 7 EBONITE
British ~ pin: 7 SKITTLE
green: 4 LAWN
lane: 5 ALLEY
Lawn: 5 BOCCE BOCCI
pin wood: 5 MAPLE
site: 4 LANE LAWN
target: 3 PIN 6 TENPIN
unit: 5 FRAME
Bowling alley: 4 LANE
button: 5 RESET
letters: 3 AMF
"Bowling for Columbine"
Org. targeted in: 3 NRA
Bowser: 5 POOCH
alternative: 3 REX

bowlful: 4 ALPO
Brand for: 4 ALPO
Leftover for: 5 TBONE
Bowwow: 5 POOCH
Nickelodeon: 3 REN
Box: 4 LOGE SPAR 5 CRATE
   6 ENCASE
Balcony: 4 LOGE
Band: 3 AMP
Idiot: 5 TVSET 6 TEEVEE
In the: 5 ATBAT
Jewel: 6 CDCASE
Kind of: 5 IDIOT MITER PRESS
   6 LITTER
top: 3 LID
Boxcar
rider: 4 HOBO
Boxcars: 5 SIXES 6 TWELVE
Boxer: 3 DOG PUG
Baby: 3 PUP
bane: 5 FLEAS
blow: 3 JAB
Breathe like a: 4 PANT
Certain ~, informally: 6 WELTER
combination: 5 ONETWO
comment: 3 ARF GRR
doctor: 3 VET
fare: 4 ALPO
group: 6 SENATE
Instruction to a: 4 STAY
Rope-a-dope: 3 ALI
stat: 5 REACH
target: 3 JAW
vulnerability: 8 GLASSJAW
wear: 4 ROBE
Boxers
alternative: 6 BRIEFS
Boxing
Bard of: 3 ALI
boundary: 4 ROPE
decision: 3 TKO
great: 3 ALI
locale: 5 ARENA
match: 4 BOUT
official: 3 REF
Practice: 4 **SPAR**
prize: 4 BELT
punch: 3 JAB
signal: 4 BELL

stats: 3 KOS 4 TKOS
trainer Dundee: 6 ANGELO
venue: 5 ARENA
victory: 3 TKO 4 KAYO
Box office: 4 GATE
failure: 4 BOMB
sales, slangily: 3 TIX
sign: 3 SRO
Box score ˙
blemish: 5 ERROR
numbers: 5 STATS
stats: 3 RBI
Boy: 3 **LAD** TAD
king: 3 TUT
lead-in: 4 ATTA
Mama's: 3 SON
Mammy's: 5 ABNER
of TV: 4 BART OPIE
Poster: 4 IDOL 6 ADONIS
Sonny: 3 LAD
suffix: 3 ISH
toy: 3 KEN
Whipping: 4 GOAT
with a blanket: 5 LINUS
with a bow: 4 AMOR EROS
~, in Spanish: 4 NINO
___ boy: 5 MAMAS
"___ boy!": 4 **ATTA ITSA**
"Boy, am ___ trouble!": 3 IIN
Boyer
of baseball: 5 CLETE
Boyer, Charles
costar in "Algiers": 6 LAMARR
film: 7 ALGIERS
Boyfriend: 4 **BEAU**
Boyle
Cookbook author: 4 TISH
Boyle, ___ Flynn
Actress: 4 **LARA**
"Boy Named Sue, A"
singer: 4 CASH 10 JOHNNYCASH
Boys
Big: 3 MEN
club: 4 FRAT
in the hood: 4 BROS
Some ~ of summer: 4 LEOS
"___ Boys" (Alcott novel): 3 JOS
Boy Scout
action: 4 DEED

novice: **10** TENDERFOOT
outing: **4** HIKE
unit: **5** TROOP
"Boys Don't Cry"
 actor Brandon: **5** TEENA
 actress Swank: **6** HILARY
"Boys From Brazil, The"
 author Levin: **3** IRA
"Boys Town"
 neighbor: **5** OMAHA
Bozo: **3** ASS OAF **4** DOLT
  DOPE TWIT **5** CLOWN
  MORON
BP
 It merged with: **5** AMOCO
 purchase: **5** LITRE
BPOE
 Part of: **4** ELKS
Bra
 part: **5** STRAP
Brace: **3** DUO TWO **4** PAIR PROP
  5 STEEL **7** SHOREUP
 (oneself): **4** GIRD **5** STEEL
Bracelet
 attachment: **5** CHARM
 Rigid: **6** BANGLE
 site: **5** <u>ANKLE</u>
Bracer: **5** TONIC
Brachial: **7** ARMLIKE
Bracket
 Candle: **6** SCONCE
 Shelf: **3** ELL
Brackets
 Word in: **3** SIC
Brad: **4** NAIL
 Actor: **4** <u>PITT</u> **6** RENFRO
Bradbury
 Sci-fi writer: **3** RAY
Braddock
 Loser to: **4** BAER
Bradley
 and others: **3** EDS
 colleague: **5** STAHL
 General: **4** <u>OMAR</u>
Bradley University
 site: **6** PEORIA
Bradshaw
 of football: **5** TERRY
Bradstreet, Anne: **4** POET

Brady Bill
 opposers: **3** NRA
"Brady Bunch, The"
 actor Robert: **4** REED
 actress: **11** SHELLEYLONG
 actress Plumb: **3** EVE
 daughter: **3** JAN **5** CINDY
  6 MARCIA
 Greg, Peter, or Bobby, to Carol in:
  7 STEPSON
 housekeeper: **5** ALICE
 son: **4** GREG **5** BOBBY PETER
Brag: **4** CROW **5** BOAST GLOAT
  VAUNT
Braga
 Actress: **5** <u>SONIA</u>
Bragg: **4** FORT
Braggart: **6** CROWER
 A ~ has a big one: **3** EGO
 Fabled: **4** HARE
 Suffix for a: **3** EST
"___ bragh!": **6** ERINGO
Brahe: **4** DANE
Brahma
 sounds: **3** OMS
Brahman: **5** CASTE
Brahms
 Key of ~ Symphony No. 4:
  6 EMINOR
 Like ~ Symphony No. 3: **3** INF
Braid: **5** PLAIT TRESS **7** PIGTAIL
 Gold: **5** ORRIS
 Narrow hair: **7** CORNROW
Braille
 Bit of: **3** DOT
Brain
 area: **4** LOBE
 cell: **6** NEURON
 passage: **4** ITER
 PC's: **3** CPU
 protector: **5** SKULL
 Relating to the: **6** NEURAL
 scan (abbr.): **3** EEG
 Small ~ size: **3** PEA
 wave: **4** IDEA
Brainard
 Absent-minded professor: **3** NED
Braincases: **6** CRANIA
Brainchild: **4** <u>IDEA</u>

Brainiac: 4 WHIZ 6 GENIUS
    7 EGGHEAD 8 EINSTEIN
Brainpower: 3 WIT 5 SENSE
  measurer: 6 IQTEST
Brains: 5 SENSE
  Collection of: 5 MENSA
  Like: 5 LOBED
  They have: 6 CRANIA
Brainstorm: 4 **IDEA** 6 IDEATE
  announcement: 3 AHA
  product: 4 IDEA
Brainteaser: 5 POSER
    6 ENIGMA
Brainy: 5 SMART 6 BRIGHT
  bunch: 5 MENSA
  Not too: 3 DIM 5 DENSE
Brake: 5 PEDAL
  Do a ~ job: 6 RELINE
  Horse: 4 REIN
  part: 4 DISC SHOE
Brakes
  Apply quickly, as: 6 SLAMON
  Fix, as: 6 RELINE
  Hit the: 4 SLOW
  Type of: 4 DISC
Bran
  accompanier: 6 RAISIN
  source: 3 **OAT**
  substance: 5 FIBER
Branagh, Kenneth
  role of 1995: 4 IAGO
Branch: 3 ARM 4 LIMB
  headquarters: 4 NEST
  location: 4 TREE
  offshoot: 4 TWIG
  Peace: 5 OLIVE
  point: 4 NODE
  Religious: 4 SECT
  Small: 4 TWIG 5 SPRIG
  Union: 5 LOCAL
Branches: 4 RAMI
  Cut off, as: 3 LOP
  Remove: 5 PRUNE
  Tree with rooting: 6 BANYAN
  ~, in botany: 4 RAMI
Brand: 4 SEAR
  Name: 5 LABEL
Brandenburg
  river: 4 ODER

Brandenburg Concertos
  composer: 4 BACH
Branding
  Mark with a ~ iron: 4 SEAR
  tool: 4 IRON
Brandish: 5 WIELD
Brandless: 6 NONAME
Brand-new: 6 UNUSED
Brando, Marlon
  birthplace: 5 OMAHA
  by birth: 6 OMAHAN
  film: 8 SAYONARA
  role: 6 ZAPATA
Brandy: 6 COGNAC
  base: 4 PLUM
  cocktail: 7 SIDECAR STINGER
  flavor: 4 PEAR 7 APRICOT
  French: 6 COGNAC
    8 ARMAGNAC
  glass: 7 SNIFTER
  Grape: 4 MARC
  Italian: 6 GRAPPA
  letters: 3 VSO 4 VSOP
  Sitcom starring singer:
    6 MOESHA
Braque: 6 CUBIST
Brasi
  "The Godfather" villain: 4 LUCA
Brass: 4 GALL 5 ALLOY CHEEK
    NERVE 8 GENERALS
    OFFICERS
  Big: 4 TUBA 5 TUBAS
  component: 4 **ZINC**
  instrument: 4 TUBA
    10 FRENCHHORN
  Invigorate the: 7 REPLATE
  Military: 5 BUGLE
Brasserie
  order: 8 OMELETTE
Brat: 3 IMP 4 PEST 6 TERROR
  look: 5 SMIRK
  More than a: 5 DEMON
Brat Pack
  member: 4 LOWE 6 SHEEDY
Brauhaus
  brew: 4 BIER
Braun
  Hitler consort: 3 EVA
Braun, ___ Jackson: 6 LILIAN

___ **Braun, Wernher:** 3 VON
___ **Brava:** 5 COSTA
Brave: 4 DARE NLER 5 GUTSY
        6 HEROIC
  Home of the: 5 TEPEE
  legend: 5 AARON
"Braveheart"
  actor Gibson: 3 MEL
  group: 4 CLAN
"Brave New World"
  drug: 4 SOMA
Bravery: 5 VALOR
  Commend, as for: 4 CITE
Braves
  home: 7 ATLANTA
  home (abbr.): 3 ATL
  network (abbr.): 3 TBS
  player: 5 AARON
Braving
  the waves: 4 ASEA
Bravo: 3 RIO
  Bullring: 3 **OLE**
  competitor: 3 AMC
  preceder: 4 ALFA
"Bravo!": 3 OLE 8 WELLDONE
___ **Bravo:** 3 RIO
Bravura: 5 ECLAT
Brawl: 4 FRAY RIOT 5 MELEE
        SETTO 6 AFFRAY FRACAS
  Barroom: 5 MELEE
  Brief: 5 SETTO
  site: 6 SALOON
  souvenir: 6 SHINER
Brawny: 8 MUSCULAR
  guys: 5 HEMEN
Braxton
  Singer: 4 **TONI**
Bray: 6 HEEHAW
  beginning: 3 HEE
  ending: 3 HAW
  They: 5 ASSES
Brayer: 3 ASS 6 DONKEY
Braz.
  neighbor: 3 ARG BOL URU
Brazen: 5 SAUCY 9 SHAMELESS
  type: 5 HUSSY
Brazil
  neighbor: 4 PERU
  port: 5 BELEM NATAL

"Brazil"
  bandleader: 5 CUGAT
Brazilian
  airline: 5 VARIG
  dance: 5 **SAMBA**
  metropolis: 8 SAOPAULO
  port: 5 BELEM NATAL
  resort: 3 RIO
  soccer star: 4 PELE
  state: 5 BAHIA
Brazos River
  city: 4 **WACO**
Brazzi
  Actor: 7 ROSSANO
Breach: 3 GAP
  of security: 4 LEAK
Bread: 3 SOP 5 MOOLA 6 STAPLE
        11 STAFFOFLIFE
  Bit of: 5 CRUMB
  Break: 3 EAT 4 DINE
  Breakfast: 5 BAGEL TOAST
        13 ENGLISHMUFFIN
  Broke: 3 **ATE**
  Brown: 5 TOAST
  browner: 7 TOASTER
  chamber: 4 OVEN
  Corn: 4 PONE 10 JOHNNYCAKE
  Deli: 3 **RYE**
  Kind of: 3 RYE 6 RAISIN
  Like old: 5 STALE
  Like some: 5 OATEN 6 CRUSTY
  maker: 4 OVEN 5 BAKER
  of India: 3 NAN
  Pocket: 4 **PITA**
  Quick: 5 SCONE
  Ritual: 5 WAFER
  spread: 3 JAM 4 MAYO **OLEO**
  unit: 4 LOAF
  ___ bread: 4 PITA
Breadbasket: 5 BELLY TUMMY
  Square in a: 3 PAT
Breadth: 4 SPAN 5 RANGE SCOPE
Breadwinner: 6 EARNER
Break: 3 GAP NAP 4 REST RIFT
        TAME 6 HIATUS RECESS
        7 TAKETEN
        10 RESTPERIOD
  a fast: 3 EAT
  Afternoon: 3 NAP TEA

an oath: 3 LIE
away: 6 SECEDE
bread: 3 EAT
British: 7 TEATIME
Day: 3 NAP
down: 3 SOB 4 WEEP 5 PARSE
    7 ANALYZE
follower: 4 ALEG
ground: 3 HOE
in relations: 4 RIFT
in the action: 4 **LULL**
into bits: 5 SMASH 7 SHATTER
It's a good thing to: 5 HABIT
off: 3 END 4 WEAN 5 CEASE
    SEVER
out: 5 ERUPT 6 ESCAPE
point: 5 ADOUT
sharply: 4 SNAP
Something hard to: 5 HABIT
Take a: 4 **REST**
time: 5 TENAM
up: 5 ENDIT
Without a: 5 ONEND 6 ONEACT
"Break ___!": 4 ALEG
Breakaway
Glacier: 4 BERG
group: 4 SECT
Breakdown: 8 COLLAPSE
Diplomacy: 4 RIFT
It causes a: 6 ENZYME
Request after a: 3 TOW
Societal: 6 ANOMIE
Breaker
Barrier: 3 SST
Code: 3 KEY
Ground: 3 **HOE** 4 HOER
Ice: 4 PICK
Mach 1: 3 SST
on the road: 4 CBER
Tend to a: 5 RESET
Word before: 3 JAW
Breakfast: 4 MEAL
acronym: 4 IHOP
area: 4 NOOK
beverage: 5 JUICE
brand: 4 EGGO
bread: 5 BAGEL TOAST
    13 ENGLISHMUFFIN
chain: 4 IHOP

choice: 4 EGGS
companion: 3 BED
dish: 6 OMELET
drinks: 3 OJS
food: 7 GRANOLA
for Brutus: 3 OVA
fruit: 5 MELON
Had: 3 ATE
Hot: 7 OATMEAL
meat: 3 HAM 5 BACON
    13 CANADIANBACON
nook: 6 ALCOVE
pastry: 6 DANISH
sizzler: 5 BACON
staple: 4 EGGS
"Breakfast at Tiffany's"
author: 6 CAPOTE
Break-in
for snooping: 6 BAGJOB
Sound of a: 4 AHEM
"Breaking Away"
director Peter: 5 YATES
"Breaking Up Is Hard to Do"
singer Neil: 6 SEDAKA
Breakout: 6 ESCAPE
High school: 4 ACNE
Breakup
comment: 7 ITSOVER
"___ Breaky Heart": 4 ACHY
Breastbone: 7 STERNUM
Of the: 7 STERNAL
Breastbones: 6 **STERNA**
Breath
candy: 6 TICTAC
Catch one's: 4 REST
Dog: 4 PANT
Kind of: 5 BATED
mint: 5 CERTS 6 TICTAC
Struggle for: 4 GASP
Take a: 6 INHALE
Take a deep: 4 SIGH
Breathe: 7 RESPIRE
heavily: 4 PANT
life into: 7 ANIMATE
Live and: 3 **ARE** 5 EXIST
out: 6 EXHALE
Breather: 4 LUNG REST
Skin: 4 PORE
Take a: 4 **REST** 5 PAUSE

Breathing: 5 ALIVE
  fire: **5** IRATE
  organ: **4** GILL LUNG
  problem: **5** APNEA
  room: **5** SPACE
  sound: **4** RALE
  spell: **4** REST
Breathless: 5 EAGER
  condition: **5** APNEA
  Leave: **3** AWE
"Breathless"
  actress Jean: **6** SEBERG
Breathtaking
  beast: **3** BOA
Brecht
  collaborator: **5** WEILL
Breck
  competitor: **5** PRELL
  " ___ Breckinridge": **4** MYRA
Breed: 3 ILK **4** REAR SIRE SORT
    TYPE
  Mixed: **4** MUTT
Breeze: 4 EASY SNAP **5** CINCH
  Float on the: **4** WAFT
  Gentle: **6** ZEPHYR
  Like a certain: **7** ONSHORE
  producer: **3** FAN
  Shoot the: **3** FAN **GAB** JAW YAK
    4 CHAT
  through: **3** ACE
  (through): **4** SAIL
Breezy: 4 AIRY
  In a ~ way: **6** AIRILY
"Breezy"
  actress Kay: **4** LENZ
Brenda
  of the comics: **5** STARR
  Singer: **3** LEE
Brendan
  Playwright: **5** BEHAN
Brennan
  Actress: **6** EILEEN
  Justice who replaced: **6** SOUTER
Brenneman
  Actress: **3** AMY
Breslau
  river: **4** ODER
Brest
  Info: French cue

bridge: **4** PONT
friend: **3** AMI **4** AMIE
milk: **4** LAIT
To be, in: **4** ETRE
Bret
  Author: **5** HARTE
Bret Easton ___
  Author: **5** ELLIS
Breton: 4 CELT
___ breve: 4 **ALLA**
Brew: 3 ALE TEA **4** BEER
    5 STEEP
  Chinese: **3** CHA
  hue: **5** AMBER
  Japanese: **5** KIRIN
  Malt: **5** STOUT
  Pub: **3** ALE
  Weak: **8** NEARBEER
  Witch: **6** POTION
  ~, in German: **4** BIER
Brewed
  beverage: **3** ALE
  drink: **7** ICEDTEA
  Not: **7** INSTANT
Brewer
  Canadian: **6** LABATT
  Coffee: **3** URN
  need: **4** HOPS MALT **5** YEAST
  oven: **4** OAST
  Singer: **6** TERESA
Brewery
  container: **3** VAT
  fixture: **4** OAST
  need: **4** HOPS MALT **5** YEAST
Brewpub
  offering: **3** ALE
Brewski: 4 BEER SUDS
    7 COLDONE
  location: **6** COOLER
  topper: **4** HEAD
Breyers
  rival: **4** EDYS
Brezhnev
  Soviet leader: **6** LEONID
Brian
  Actor: **6** AHERNE
  Beatles manager: **7** EPSTEIN
  Figure skater: **5** ORSER
  of Roxy Music: **3** **ENO**

Rock producer: **3 ENO**
Bribe: 3 OIL SOP 6 GREASE
  Open to a: 5 VENAL
        9 ONTHETAKE
  to a DJ: 6 PAYOLA
Bric-a-___: 4 BRAC
Bric-a-brac
  event: 7 TAGSALE
  stand: 7 ETAGERE WHATNOT
Brice, Fanny
  theme song: 5 MYMAN
Brick
  bond: 6 MORTAR
  carrier: 3 HOD
  Hacienda: 5 ADOBE
  oven: 4 KILN
  Sun-dried: 5 **ADOBE**
  Toy ~ brand: 4 LEGO
  worker: 5 MASON
Brickell
  Singer: 4 **EDIE**
Bricklayer: 5 MASON
  burden: 3 HOD
Bricks
  measure: 3 TON
Bridal
  bio word: 3 NEE
  covering: 4 VEIL
  Part of a ~ dress: 5 TRAIN
  party: 4 WIFE
  path: 5 **AISLE**
  shower: 4 RICE
  wreath: 6 SPIREA
Bride
  band: 4 RING
  destination: 5 ALTAR
  headgear: 4 VEIL
  ride: 4 LIMO
  title: 3 MRS
  words: 3 IDO
"Bride of Frankenstein, The"
  actress Lanchester: 4 ELSA
Bridesmaid
  Many a: 6 SISTER
Bridge: 4 **SPAN**
  action: 3 BID 5 REBID
  ancestor: 5 WHIST
  beam: 4 IBAR
  bid, briefly: 5 **ONENO**

blunder: 6 RENEGE
call: 4 AHOY 5 IPASS
coup: 4 **SLAM**
declaration: 3 BID 5 IPASS
Defeats in: 4 SETS
Electrical: 3 ARC
expert Charles: 5 GOREN
expert Culbertson: 3 ELY
expert Sharif: 4 OMAR
feat: 4 SLAM
fee: 4 TOLL
First name in: 4 OMAR
guard of folklore: 5 TROLL
holding: 4 HAND 6 TENACE
ploy: 7 FINESSE
position: 4 **EAST** WEST
        5 NORTH SOUTH
section: 4 SPAN
site: 4 NOSE
support: 4 IBAR 5 TRUSS
        6 GIRDER 7 TRESTLE
tower: 5 PYLON
~, in French: 4 PONT
~, in Italian: 5 PONTE
"Bridge of San Luis ___, The":
        3 REY
"Bridge on the River ___, The":
        4 KWAI
Bridges
  Actor: 4 BEAU JEFF 5 LLOYD
  Like some rural: 7 ONELANE
Bridges, Jeff
  brother: 4 BEAU
  film: 4 TRON 7 STARMAN
Bridget
  She played ~ in 2001: 5 RENEE
  ~, to Jane: 5 NIECE
"Bridget Jones's Diary"
  actress Zellweger: 5 RENEE
"Bridge Too Far, A"
  author Cornelius: 4 RYAN
Bridle
  part: 3 BIT 4 REIN
  strap: 4 REIN
Brie
  carrier: 7 SALTINE
  covering: 4 RIND
  Mature, as: 3 AGE
  Mold, in: 7 RIPENER

Brief: 4 MINI 6 LITTLE
    7 CURSORY
  appearance: 5 CAMEO
  brawl: 5 SETTO
  message: 4 NOTE
  story: 3 BIO
  summary: 5 RECAP
  time: 6 MOMENT
  upturn: 4 BLIP
Briefly: 7 INAWORD INSHORT
  Visit: 6 STOPIN
Briefs
  alternative: 6 BOXERS
    11 BOXERSHORTS
  brand: 5 HANES
  ~, briefly: 4 BVDS
Brig
  British: 4 GAOL
  pair: 5 MASTS
Brigadier
  Like a ~ general: 7 ONESTAR
"Brigadoon"
  composer: 5 LOEWE
  lyricist: 6 LERNER
Brigantine
  gear: 4 SAIL
Brigham Young University
  city: 5 PROVO
Bright: 3 LIT 5 SMART SUNNY
    6 BRAINY
  annual: 6 ZINNIA
  bunch: 5 MENSA
  Extremely: 4 NEON
  It may be: 4 IDEA
  lights: 5 NEONS
  Not too: 4 PALE 5 DENSE
  star: 4 NOVA
  thought: 4 IDEA
Brighten: 6 PERKUP
Brightest
  star in a constellation:
    5 ALPHA
Brightly
  Burn: 5 BLAZE
  colored: 4 LOUD
  colored bird: 6 ORIOLE
  colored fish: 4 OPAH
  Shine: 7 RADIATE
  Shining: 6 AGLARE

Brightness
  Measurer of: 5 MENSA
  unit: 7 LAMBERT
Brighton
  Info: British cue
  buggy: 4 PRAM
  bye-bye: 4 TATA
Brigitte
  Actress: 6 BARDOT
Brilliance: 5 **ECLAT** 6 LUSTER
  Flash of: 4 IDEA
  Lose: 4 FADE
Brilliant: 6 SUPERB 7 STELLAR
  display: 4 RIOT
  stroke: 4 COUP
  success: 5 ECLAT
  suffix: 3 INE
"___ brillig ...": 4 TWAS
Brillo
  rival: 3 **SOS**
Brim: 4 EDGE TEEM
  Fill to the: 4 SATE
  Snap: 6 FEDORA
Brimless
  cap: 5 BERET
  hat: 3 FEZ 5 BERET TOQUE
  topper: 10 PILLBOXHAT
Brimstone: 6 SULFUR
  Spew fire and: 4 RANT
Brine-cured
  cheese: 4 FETA
  salmon: 3 LOX
Bring
  about: 5 BEGET CAUSE
    6 INDUCE 8 ENGENDER
  action: 3 SUE
  back: 6 REVIVE 7 RESTORE
  bad luck to: 4 JINX
  dishonor: 5 SHAME
  down: 4 RUIN UNDO 5 ABASE
  down the house: 4 RAZE
  forth: 6 ELICIT
  home: 3 NET 4 EARN
  home the bacon: 4 EARN
    11 MAKEALIVING
  in: 3 NET 4 **EARN REAP**
    6 IMPORT
  in the harvest: 4 REAP
  into accord: 6 ATTUNE

into being: 6 CREATE
into harmony: 6 ATTUNE
into play: 3 **USE** 6 ENTAIL
joy to: 5 ELATE
on: 4 HIRE
out: 5 **EDUCE** 6 ELICIT
(out): 4 TROT
the food: 5 CATER
to a boil: 6 ENRAGE
to a near boil: 5 SCALD
to bay: 4 TREE
to bear: 5 EXERT
together: 5 UNITE
to life: 7 ANIMATE
to light: 6 EXHUME EXPOSE
to mind: 5 EVOKE
to naught: 4 UNDO
to ruin: 4 UNDO
to the surface: 6 ELICIT
under control: 4 TAME
up: 4 REAR 5 **RAISE**
    7 MENTION
upon oneself: 5 INCUR
up the rear: 3 LAG 4 MOON
    5 TRAIL
"Bring ___!": 4 ITON
Brink: 3 EVE RIM 4 EDGE
    5 VERGE
Be on the: 6 TEETER
Brinker
Skater: 4 HANS
Briny: 3 SEA 5 OCEAN
Back on the: 3 AFT 5 STERN
On the: 4 **ASEA** 5 ATSEA
septet: 4 SEAS
Brio: 4 ELAN 6 SPIRIT
Brioche
ingredient: 3 EGG
Bris: 4 RITE
Brisk: 4 SPRY 5 NIPPY PERKY
    7 ALLEGRO
Bristle: 3 AWN 4 SETA
at: 6 RESENT
Barley: 3 AWN
Biological: 4 SETA
Grain: 6 ARISTA
Bristles: 5 SETAE 7 SEESRED
Grain: 7 ARISTAE ARISTAS
Bristly: 6 SETOSE

Bristol
baby carriage: 4 PRAM
cable channel: 4 ESPN
county: 4 AVON
Brit
Conservative: 4 TORY
Early: 4 PICT
Noble ~, briefly: 6 ARISTO
Brit.
fliers: 3 **RAF**
honor: 3 OBE
legislators: 3 MPS
lexicon: 3 OED
military decoration: 3 DSO
money: 4 STER
recording label: 3 EMI
sports cars: 3 MGS
Britannicus
Poisoner of: 4 NERO
___ **B'rith:** 4 **BNAI**
British
architect: 4 WREN 6 SPENCE
biscuit: 5 SCONE
blackbird: 4 MERL
bowling pin: 7 SKITTLE
break: 3 TEA
brew: 3 ALE
buddy: 5 MATEY
buggy: 4 PRAM
carbine: 4 STEN
coins: 5 PENCE
colony: 4 ADEN
composer: 4 ARNE
conservative: 4 TORY
ending: 3 ZED
exam: 6 ALEVEL OLEVEL
exclamation: 4 ISAY
flag: 9 UNIONJACK
flashlight: 5 TORCH
fliers (abbr.): 3 RAF
gun: 4 **STEN**
john: 3 LOO
music co.: 3 EMI
noble: 4 DAME DUKE EARL
    5 BARON
novelist: 5 READE
peer: 4 EARL 5 BARON
prep school: 4 **ETON**
prime minister: 4 EDEN 5 BLAIR

HEATH 6 ATTLEE
  8 DISRAELI
quart: 5 LITRE
racecourse: 5 ASCOT
raincoat: 3 MAC
record label: 3 **EMI**
ref. work: 3 OED
royal: 4 ANNE
rule in India: 3 **RAJ**
runner: 3 COE 5 OVETT
school: 4 ETON
servicewoman: 4 WREN
sports cars: 3 MGS
streetcar: 4 TRAM
submachine gun: 4 STEN
tar: 5 LIMEY
tax: 4 CESS
title: 4 DAME EARL
verb ending: 3 ISE
weapon: 4 STEN
weight: 5 STONE
British ___: 5 ISLES
British Honduras
  ~, today: 6 BELIZE
British Open
  winner: 3 ELS 4 DALY LEMA
    5 DUVAL FALDO 6 OMEARA
    WATSON
British Petroleum
  acquisition: 5 AMOCO
Briton
  Ancient: 4 CELT PICT
Brittany
  Info: French cue
  Being, in: 4 ETRE
  port: 5 BREST
Brittle: 5 CRISP
  cookie: 4 SNAP 10 GINGERSNAP
  pastry: 7 OATCAKE
Brno
  locale: 7 MORAVIA
Bro: 3 REL SIB 4 DUDE
  counterpart: 3 SIS
  of Dad or Mom: 3 UNC
  sib: 3 **SIS**
Broad: 4 DAME VAST WIDE
  bean: 4 FAVA
  necktie: 5 ASCOT
  sash: 3 OBI

shoe size: 3 EEE
tie: 5 ASCOT
valley: 4 **DALE**
Broadbent, Jim
  film: 4 IRIS
Broadcast: 3 **AIR** 4 EMIT ONTV
    SHOW 5 **AIRED** 6 STREWN
  Being: 4 ONTV 5 ONAIR
    6 AIRING
  component: 5 AUDIO
  inits.: 3 APB
  Not: 7 UNAIRED
  sign: 5 ONAIR
  slot: 7 AIRTIME
Broadcaster: 5 AIRER
  Cold war ~ (abbr.): 3 VOA
  Senate: 5 CSPAN
Broadcasting: 5 **ONAIR**
    8 ONTHEAIR
  watchdog (abbr.): 3 FCC
Broaden: 5 WIDEN 7 ENLARGE
Broadside
  Hit: 3 RAM
  Not: 5 ENDON
Broad-topped
  hill: 4 LOMA
Broadway
  1973 ~ revival: 5 IRENE
  1978 ~ musical: 5 EUBIE
  1990 one-man ~ show: 3 TRU
  1990s ~ smash: 4 RENT
  acronym: 4 ANTA
  aunt: 4 MAME 5 ELLER
  Auntie of: 4 MAME
  award: 4 TONY
  backer: 5 ANGEL
  Began on: 6 OPENED
  bio: 3 TRU
  brightener: 4 NEON
  hit: 4 CATS RENT
  hit letters: 3 SRO
  opening: 4 ACTI 6 ACTONE
  production: 4 PLAY SHOW
  role: 4 AIDA 5 ANNIE
Broadway Joe: 6 NAMATH
Brobdingnagian: 4 HUGE
    5 GIANT
Brocaded
  fabric: 4 LAME

Broccoli
  bit: 5 SPEAR 6 FLORET
Broccoli ___ : 4 RABE
___ broche: 3 ALA
Brock
  of baseball: 3 LOU
"___ Brockovich": 4 **ERIN**
Brogan: 4 SHOE
  bottom: 4 SOLE
Brogna
  of baseball: 4 RICO
Broil: 4 COOK
  Place to: 4 OVEN
Brokaw: 6 ANCHOR
  network: 3 NBC
  Newsman: 3 TOM
Broke: 8 STRAPPED
Broken: 4 TAME 5 KAPUT
  arm holder: 5 SLING
  It's ~ at parties: 6 PINATA
      THEICE
  Like a ~ horse: 4 TAME
  mirror: 4 OMEN
  piece: 5 SHARD
  They're ~ up: 4 EXES
  They run when: 4 EGGS
Broker: 5 AGENT
  charge: 3 FEE
  Information: 7 TIPSTER
  offering: 3 IRA TIP
  order: 4 SELL
  stat: 5 QUOTE
  suggestion: 3 BUY
Brokerage
  Online: 6 ETRADE
  phrase: 5 ATPAR
Brolly
  go-withs: 4 MACS
Bromide: 3 SAW 6 CLICHE
      OLDSAW
Bronco
  Break a: 4 TAME
  buster: 5 TAMER
  catcher: 5 LASSO
Broncos
  quarterback John: 5 ELWAY
Brontë
  Author: 4 ANNE 5 EMILY
  heroine Jane: 4 **EYRE**

  novel: 8 JANEEYRE
Bronx
  attraction: 3 ZOO
  cheer: 4 JEER RAZZ
  Give a ~ cheer: 4 JEER RAZZ
  Rhymer of ~ and thonx: 4 NASH
Bronx Bomber: 6 YANKEE
Bronx Zoo
  beasts: 4 APES
"Bronx Zoo, The"
  actor Ed: 5 ASNER
Bronze: 3 AGE 5 ALLOY
  coating: 6 PATINA
  component: 3 TIN
  Go for the: 3 TAN
Bronze ___ : 3 AGE
Brooch: 3 PIN 5 CLASP
  Adjust, as a: 5 REPIN
  Attach, as a: 5 PINON
  fastener: 5 CLASP
Brood: 3 SIT 4 CLAN MOPE POUT
      STEW SULK
  creator: 3 HEN
  Place to: 4 NEST
Brooder: 3 HEN
  place: 4 NEST
Brooding
  author: 3 POE
  place: 4 NEST
  type: 3 HEN
Brook: 4 RILL
  catch: 5 TROUT
  Small: 4 **RILL**
Brooke
  Ex-husband of: 5 ANDRE
Brooklet: 4 RILL
Brooklyn
  institute: 5 PRATT
  island: 5 CONEY
  pronoun: 3 DEM
  school (abbr.): 3 LIU
  suffix: 3 ESE ITE
  West of: 3 MAE
Brooklyn Dodgers
  Duke of the: 6 SNIDER
  great: 5 REESE
  ~, affectionately: 4 BUMS
Brookner
  Author: 5 ANITA

Brooks
 Actor: 5 AVERY 6 ALBERT
 Country singer: 5 GARTH
 Director: 3 MEL
Brooks, Foster
 persona: 3 SOT
Brooks, Garth
 birthplace: 5 TULSA
Brookville
 campus: 6 CWPOST
Broom
 Curling: 5 BESOM
 rider: 3 HAG
 Twig: 5 BESOM
 Use a: 5 SWEEP
 Used a: 5 SWEPT
"Broom ___": 5 HILDA
"Broom Hilda"
 cartoonist: 5 MYERS
Brosnan, Pierce
 role: 4 BOND 6 STEELE
Broten
 of hockey: 4 NEAL
Brother: 3 FRA SIB 4 MONK
 address: 3 FRA
 Biblical: 4 ABEL ESAU 5 AARON
 Daughter of a: 5 NIECE
 Kid ~, maybe: 4 PEST
 Lodge: 3 ELK
Brought
 about: 5 LEDTO
 forth: 5 BEGAT
 to life: 4 BORN
 up: 4 BRED
Brouhaha: 3 **ADO** 4 FLAP STIR
      TODO 5 SCENE 6 UPROAR
Browbeat: 7 HENPECK
Brown: 3 IVY 5 SAUTE
 and others: 5 IVIES
 bagger: 4 WINO
 Bandleader: 3 **LES**
 beverage: 3 ALE
 bread: 5 TOAST
 building: 4 DORM
 Dark: 5 SEPIA
 Editor: 4 TINA
 ermine: 5 **STOAT**
 Grayish: 3 DUN
 hue: 4 ECRU 5 SEPIA

 Light: 3 TAN 4 **ECRU** 5 BEIGE
 pigment: 5 SEPIA
 Question for a ~ cow:
      6 HOWNOW
 quickly: 4 SEAR
 rival: 4 PENN YALE
 seaweed: 4 KELP
 shade: 3 TAN 4 ECRU RUST
      5 BEIGE SEPIA TAUPE
      UMBER
Brown, Buster
 dog: 4 TIGE
Brown, Charlie
 exclamation: 4 RATS
Brown, ___ Mae
 Novelist: 4 RITA
Brown, Molly
 portrayer: 6 GRIMES
Brown, Murphy
 program: 3 FYI
 Son of: 5 AVERY
Brown, Rita ___
 Author: 3 MAE
Brown Bomber, The: 8 JOELOUIS
Browne
 Cartoonist: 3 DIK
Browner, Carol
 org.: 3 EPA
Brownie: 3 ELF 6 SPRITE
      9 GIRLSCOUT
 bunch: 5 TROOP
 org.: 3 GSA
 topper: 6 BEANIE
Brownie ___: 6 POINTS
Browning: 4 POET
 character: 5 PIPPA
 Director: 3 TOD
 output: 4 POEM
Brownish: 5 UMBER
 gray: 5 **TAUPE**
 purple: 4 PUCE
 yellow: 5 TAWNY
Brownstone
 feature: 5 STOOP
Brown-tinted
 photo: 5 SEPIA
Browse
 from outside: 10 WINDOWSHOP
 (through): 4 LEAF

~, in a way: **4** SURF
Browser
  bookmark: **3** URL
  target: **3** WEB
Broz, Josip: 4 TITO
"Brrr!": 6 IMCOLD
Brubeck
  Jazz pianist: **4** DAVE
  music: **4** JAZZ
Bruce
  Actor: **4** DERN **5** NIGEL
  Comedian: **5** LENNY
  Ex of: **4** DEMI
Bruckner
  Composer: **5** **ANTON**
  Like Symphony No. 7 by: **3** INE
Bruhn
  of ballet: **4** ERIK
Bruins: 4 TEAM
  home: **4** UCLA
  legend: **3** **ORR**
  player Phil, familiarly: **4** ESPO
  sch.: **4** UCLA
Bruised: 6 PURPLE
  It may be easily: **3** EGO
Bruiser: 5 HEMAN PASTE
  opposite: **5** SISSY
___ brûlée: 5 CREME
Brummell, Beau: 3 FOP
            5 DANDY
  school: **4** ETON
Brunch: 4 MEAL
  beverage: **6** **MIMOSA**
  entrée: **6** OMELET
  fish: **3** LOX
  Have: **3** EAT
  selection: **5** BAGEL CREPE
            6 OMELET QUICHE
            7 SAUSAGE
  time: **5** TENAM
Brundage
  Former Olympics head: **5** AVERY
Brunei: 9 SULTANATE
  locale: **4** ASIA **6** BORNEO
Brunette
  Become a: **3** DYE
  Go back to being a: **5** REDYE
Brunswick
  competitor: **3** AMF

Brunswick stew
  need: **5** ONION
Brush
  off: **4** SNUB **5** SPURN
  Ranch: **4** SAGE
  (up): **4** BONE
  up on: **7** RELEARN
Brusque: 4 CURT RUDE
          5 GRUFF SHORT TERSE
          6 ABRUPT
Brussels
  Alliance based in: **4** **NATO**
Brutal: 5 CRUEL **6** SAVAGE
Brute: 3 APE **4** LOUT **OGRE**
        5 BEAST **6** ANIMAL
        7 RUFFIAN
  leader: **4** ETTU
___ Brute: 4 **ETTU**
Brutus
  Info: Latin cue
  Bear, to: **4** URSA
  Behold, to: **4** ECCE
  Being, to: **4** ESSE
  Bird, to: **4** AVIS
  Breakfast for: **3** OVA
  Burdens, to: **5** ONERA
  But, to: **3** SED
  co-conspirator: **5** CASCA
  Rebuke to: **4** ETTU
Bryan: 6 ORATOR
  defeater, in 1908: **4** TAFT
Bryan, William Jennings
  birthplace: **5** SALEM
  Emulate: **5** ORATE
Bryant: 5 LAKER
  of basketball: **4** KOBE
  Singer: **5** ANITA
Bryant, Paul
  Movie about: **7** THEBEAR
  team, for short: **4** BAMA
Bryce Canyon
  locale: **4** **UTAH**
Brylcreem
  amount: **3** DAB
Bryn ___: 4 **MAWR**
Brynhild
  brother: **4** ATLI
Bryn Mawr
  grad: **6** ALUMNA

Brynner
  Actor: 3 <u>YUL</u>
Bryologist
  What a ~ studies: 4 MOSS
Bryson
  Singer: 5 PEABO
B's
  One of the three: 4 BACH
B.S.: 3 DEG
BSA
  part: 4 AMER
BTU
  Part of: 4 UNIT
  relative: 3 CAL
Bub: 3 <u>MAC</u>
Bubble: 4 BOIL 6 AERATE
  Enjoy ~ gum: 4 CHEW
  source: 3 GUM 4 SOAP
Bubble ___ : 4 WRAP
**"Bubble, bubble, ___ and
      trouble":** 4 TOIL
Bubblehead: 3 ASS 4 DOLT
Bubbler: 7 AERATOR
"Bubbles in the Wine"
  was his theme song: 4 WELK
Bubbletop: 4 DOME
Bubbling: 5 ABOIL
Bubbly
  beverage: 4 COLA SODA
      7 SELTZER
  Make: 6 AERATE
  name: 4 MOET
  prefix: 3 AER
  source: 4 ASTI
Bubkes: 3 NIL 4 NADA ZERO
Buccaneers
  home: 5 <u>TAMPA</u>
Buchanan
  Mystery writer: 4 EDNA
  Politico: 3 PAT
Buchholz
  Actor: 5 HORST
Buchwald
  Columnist: 3 ART
Buck: 4 CLAM DEER DEFY MALE
      STAG 6 DOLLAR RESIST
      7 ONESPOT 8 SIMOLEON
  add-on: 4 AROO
  Author: 5 PEARL

Bird on a: 5 EAGLE
Country singer: 5 OWENS
ender: 4 AROO
feature: 6 ANTLER
      7 ANTLERS
heroine: 4 OLAN
mate: 3 <u>DOE</u>
of baseball: 5 ONEIL
Buck, Pearl S.
  book: 12 THEGOODEARTH
  heroine: 4 OLAN
Bucked
  It may be: 6 SYSTEM
Bucker: 5 BRONC
Bucket: 4 PAIL SEAT
  Champagne: 4 ICER
  contents: 4 DROP
  Item in a: 3 MOP
  Like the ~ of song: 5 OAKEN
  locale: 4 WELL
  material: 3 OAK
  of bolts: 4 HEAP 5 CRATE
      LEMON 6 JALOPY
Buckets: 4 ALOT
  Come down in: 4 POUR
Buckeye: 6 OHIOAN
  sch.: 3 <u>OSU</u>
Buckeye State: 4 OHIO
Buckingham: 6 PALACE
Buckingham Palace
  letters: 3 HRH
Buckinghamshire
  school: 4 ETON
Buckle: 4 CAVE GIVE WARP
      6 FASTEN
  opener: 5 SWASH
  site: 4 BELT
  up: 7 STRAPIN
Buckley
  Actress: 5 BETTY
Bucko: 3 LAD
Bucks: 3 HES 4 CASH DEER KALE
      5 DOUGH MONEY MOOLA
  prefix: 4 MEGA
Buckwheat: 6 RASCAL
  dish: 5 KASHA
  pancakes: 5 BLINI
Bucky Beaver
  brand: 5 IPANA

Buco
Osso ~ meat: 4 VEAL
___ buco: 4 **OSSO**
Bucolic: 5 RURAL
byway: 4 LANE
Bucs
home: 5 TAMPA
Bud: 3 BRO MAC **PAL** 4 BEER
CHUM PARD 5 CRONY
6 FRIEND
Baseball commissioner: 5 SELIG
holder: 3 KEG 4 VASE
partner: 3 LOU
Pickled: 5 CAPER
~, to a botanist: 5 GEMMA
Budd
Olympic runner: 4 ZOLA
"Buddenbrooks"
novelist Thomas: 4 MANN
Buddha
birthplace: 5 NEPAL
sermon: 5 SUTRA
shade-giver: 6 BOTREE
Buddhist
discipline: 3 ZEN
Dome-shaped ~ shrine: 5 STUPA
language: 4 PALI
monk: 4 LAMA
sect: 3 **ZEN**
who has attained Nirvana:
5 ARHAT
Buddy: 3 BRO BUB **MAC PAL**
4 **CHUM** MATE PARD
5 AMIGO CRONY KIDDO
Actor: 5 EBSEN
British: 5 MATEY
Good: 3 PAL 4 CBER
Kind of: 5 BOSOM
of Bert: 5 **ERNIE**
of Bud: 3 LOU
of Ollie: 4 STAN
~, in French: 3 AMI
~, in Spanish: 5 AMIGO
Buddy-buddy: 5 CLOSE
"Buddy Holly Story, The"
actor Gary: 4 BUSEY
Budge: 4 MOVE STIR
Doesn't: 8 STAYSPUT
One who won't: 4 MULE

Budget
Monthly ~ item: 4 RENT
offering: 6 RENTAL
rival: 4 AVIS 5 ALAMO
Budgetary: 6 FISCAL
excess: 3 FAT
Budging
Not: 7 ADAMANT
Budweiser
rival: 5 COORS PABST
6 STROHS
___ Buena Island: 5 YERBA
Buenos ___ : 5 **AIRES**
"Buenos ___": 4 **DIAS**
Buenos Aires
musical: 5 EVITA
Buff: 3 FAN NUT RUB TAN
5 LOVER MAVEN SHINE
7 BURNISH
10 AFICIONADO
In the: 4 BARE NUDE 5 NAKED
Buffalo: 5 BISON STUMP
AAA baseball team: 6 BISONS
bunch: 4 HERD
canal: 4 ERIE
City near: 5 OLEAN
county: 4 ERIE
hockey player: 5 **SABRE**
hunter: 4 CREE
lake: 4 **ERIE**
Buffalo Bill: 4 CODY 5 IOWAN
colleague: 5 ANNIE
Buffalo Bob Smith
puppet: 10 HOWDYDOODY
Buffet: 4 MEAL PELT 6 REPAST
Enjoy a: 3 EAT 7 OVEREAT
patron: 5 EATER
table item: 3 URN
warmer: 6 STERNO
Buffoon: 3 ASS OAF 4 DOLT
Buffoonery: 5 ANTIC 6 ANTICS
8 ZANINESS
Buffy: 6 SLAYER
portrayer: 5 SARAH
weapon: 5 STAKE
"Buffy the Vampire Slayer"
actor Green: 4 SETH
actress ___ Michelle Gellar:
5 SARAH

Bug: 3 FLU IRK TAP VEX 4 GERM
RILE 5 ANNOY PEEVE
TEASE VIRUS 6 HASSLE
INSECT NEEDLE NETTLE
PESTER 7 WIRETAP
 Baby: 5 LARVA
 Busy: 3 BEE
 Computer: 6 GLITCH
 ending: 4 ABOO
 Fire: 3 ANT
 Have a: 3 **AIL**
 June ~, for one: 6 BEETLE
 killer: 3 DDT
 Like a ~ in a rug: 4 SNUG
 no end: 5 EATAT
 out: 5 LEAVE
 Pesky: 4 GNAT
 Tiny: 4 MITE
 with bounce: 4 FLEA
Bugaboo: 4 BANE FEAR
Bugbear: 4 OGRE 8 PETPEEVE
 9 BETENOIRE
Bug-eyed: 4 **AGOG GAGA**
 monsters: 3 ETS
Buggy
 Baby: 4 PRAM
 British: 4 PRAM
 Moon ~ (abbr.): 3 LEM
 Off-road ~ (abbr.): 3 ATV
 place: 4 DUNE
 power: 5 HORSE
Bugler
 call: 7 RETREAT
 evening call: 4 TAPS
 of the wild: 3 ELK
Bugling
 beast: 3 ELK
Bugs: 3 VWS 6 RABBIT
 chaser: 4 FUDD 5 ELMER
 9 ELMERFUDD
 co-creator Chuck: 5 JONES
 Columnist: 4 BAER
 Elmer, to: 3 DOC
 Gangster: 5 MORAN
 treat: 6 CARROT
 Voice of: 3 MEL 5 BLANC
"Bug's Life, A"
 character: 3 ANT
 princess: 4 ATTA

Build: 5 **ERECT**
 a fire under: 6 AROUSE
 on: 5 ADDTO
 (on): 3 ADD
 Place to: 4 SITE
 up: 5 AMASS 6 ACCRUE
Builder: 7 ERECTOR
 Ark: 4 **NOAH**
 Chair: 5 CANER
 Delta: 4 SILT
 Empire: 4 INCA
 guide: 5 SPECS
 Hill: 3 ANT
 Lodge: 6 BEAVER
 Molecule: 4 ATOM
 Navy: 6 SEABEE
 Nest: 3 ANT 4 BIRD
 Pot: 4 ANTE
Builders
 Pyramid: 5 MAYAS 6 MAYANS
Building
 addition: 3 **ELL** 4 WING
 5 ANNEX
 annex: 3 ELL 4 WING
 Babel: 5 TOWER
 Backyard: 4 SHED
 beam: 4 **IBAR** 5 JOIST
 block: 4 UNIT 5 ADOBE BRICK
 block brand: 4 LEGO
 brick: 5 ADOBE
 Brown: 4 DORM
 Campus: 4 DORM HALL
 courtyards: 5 ATRIA
 Diplomat's: 7 EMBASSY
 Domed: 7 ROTUNDA
 Farm: 4 BARN SILO
 front: 6 FACADE
 location: 4 SITE
 material: 5 ADOBE STONE
 near a silo: 4 BARN
 Quad: 4 DORM HALL
 site: 3 LOT
 support: 4 IBAR
 wing: 3 **ELL**
Buildup: 4 HYPE 6 HOOPLA
 Aquarium: 5 ALGAE
 Dryer: 4 LINT
 Flue: 4 SOOT
 Musical: 9 CRESCENDO

Navel: 4 LINT
Polar: 6 ICECAP
Pond: 5 ALGAE
Built: 4 MADE
for speed: 5 SLEEK
Built-up: 5 URBAN
Bulb: 5 CLOVE
Cartoon: 4 IDEA
Garden: 5 TULIP
holder: 6 SOCKET
Pungent: 5 ONION
unit: 4 WATT
___ **Bulba:** 5 TARAS
Bulfinch
subject: 4 MYTH
Bulgar: 4 SLAV
Bulgaria
capital: 5 **SOFIA**
money: 3 LEV
Bulgy
Battle of the: 4 SUMO
Bulk: 4 HEFT MASS
Bull: 4 MALE 5 EDICT NBAER
and others: 3 HES
artist: 4 LIAR
Barcelona: 4 TORO
Borden: 5 ELMER
Bullfight: 4 TORO
issuer: 4 POPE
It's no: 3 COW
markets: 3 UPS
prefix: 4 TAUR 5 TAURO
Rodeo: 6 BRAHMA
run: 3 LEA
sound: 5 SNORT
suffix: 3 ISH
target: 4 CAPE
Type of: 5 PAPAL
Bulldog: 3 ELI 5 YALIE 7 EDITION
of the comics: 4 OTTO
Bulldoze: 4 RAZE
Bullet: 4 SLUG
in a deck: 3 ACE
point: 4 ITEM
Bulletin: 5 ALERT
News: 6 UPDATE
Bulletin board
fastener: 4 TACK 7 PUSHPIN
notice: 4 MEMO 7 POSTING

overseer: 5 SYSOP
Put on a: 4 POST
Bullets: 4 **AMMO**
Fill with: 4 LOAD
Bullfight: 7 CORRIDA
bull: 4 TORO
cheer: 3 OLE
figure: 6 TORERO
Bullfighter: 6 TORERO
8 TOREADOR
cloak: 4 CAPA
Bullish: 7 TAURINE
"Bullitt"
director Peter: 5 YATES
Bullock
Actress: 6 SANDRA
film: 6 THENET
Bullpen
ace: 6 CLOSER
sound: 5 SNORT
stat: 3 ERA
Bullring
beast: 4 TORO
cheer: 3 **OLE**
Injured in the: 5 GORED
Bull Run
general: 5 MEADE 6 STUART
~, to the Rebs: 8 MANASSAS
Bulls: 4 TEAM
Like some: 5 PAPAL
org.: 3 NBA
Bull's-eye
(abbr.): 3 CTR
Eye the: 3 AIM
hitter: 4 DART
Like a: 8 ONTARGET
Bullwinkle: 5 MOOSE
foe: 5 BORIS 7 NATASHA
Bully: 3 COW 6 ABASER
ABUSER MEANIE
10 BROWBEATER
target: 4 NERD
Bullying: 6 DURESS
Engage in: 8 BROWBEAT
Bulova
rival: 5 ROLEX SEIKO TIMEX
Bulrush: 4 TULE 5 SEDGE
Bulwer-___
English author: 6 LYTTON

"Bulworth"
  actress Berry: 5 HALLE
Bum: 4 HOBO REAR
  Bowery: 4 WINO
  off of: 5 CADGE
  Word with: 3 SKI
Bum ___ : 3 RAP 5 STEER
Bumble Bee
  product: 4 TUNA
Bumbler: 3 OAF 7 SADSACK
  cry: 4 OOPS
Bumbling: 5 **INEPT**
Bummed: 3 SAD
  out: 3 SAD 4 BLUE 6 MOROSE
"Bummer!": 4 ALAS DRAG
Bump: 3 JAR 4 OUST STUB
     7 PREEMPT
  in the road: 4 SNAG
  into: 4 **MEET**
  Like a ~ on a log: 5 INERT
  off: 3 ICE 4 DOIN SLAY 5 ERASE
    WASTE
  on a log: 4 KNUR NODE
  Place for a: 3 LOG
Bumper
  bruise: 4 DENT
  coating: 6 CHROME
  sticker word: 4 HONK
Bumpkin: 4 HICK RUBE 5 YAHOO
    YOKEL
Bumpy: 6 UNEVEN
  Not: 4 EVEN
Bumstead
  boss: 7 DITHERS
  Dithers, to: 4 BOSS
Bun: 4 ROLL 6 HAIRDO
  Buttery: 7 BRIOCHE
  seed: 6 SESAME
Bunch: 4 HERD SLEW
    6 PASSEL
  A whole: 4 LOTS TONS
  Brainy: 5 MENSA
  Bright: 5 MENSA
  Crude: 4 OPEC
  Honey: 4 BEES
  of bees: 5 SWARM
  of bills: 3 WAD
  of brownies: 5 TROOP
"___ Bunch, The": 5 BRADY

Bunche
  Peace Nobelist: 5 RALPH
Bunco: 4 SCAM
Bundle: 5 **SHEAF** 6 PACKET
  Make a: 4 BALE
  of bills: 3 WAD
  of cotton: 4 BALE
  of energy: 6 DYNAMO
  of hay: 4 BALE
  of papers: 5 SHEAF
Bundy
  and others: 3 ALS
  Mrs.: 3 PEG
Bungle: 3 ERR 4 FLUB MUFF
     5 BOTCH GUMUP MISDO
     7 LOUSEUP SCREWUP
     8 BOLLIXUP
Bungling: 5 INEPT
Bunion
  locale: 3 TOE
Bunk: 3 COT ROT 4 GUFF
     5 HOKUM HOOEY
  Army: 3 COT
Bunker: 4 HILL
  Mr.: 6 ARCHIE
  Mrs.: 5 EDITH
  portrayer: 7 OCONNOR
Bunker, Archie: 5 BIGOT
  command: 6 STIFLE
  furniture: 8 ARMCHAIR
  humor: 6 ETHNIC
  portrayer: 7 OCONNOR
  Wife of: 5 EDITH
Bunny
  boss, briefly: 3 HEF
  bounce: 3 HOP
  Dumb: 5 STUPE
  makeup: 4 DUST
  Move like a: 3 HOP
  tail: 4 SCUT
Buns: 3 DOS
  Pat on the: 4 OLEO
Bunsen
  burner relative: 4 ETNA
  creation: 6 BURNER
Bunt
  situation: 5 ONEON
  ~, on a scorecard: 3 SAC
Bunting: 5 FINCH

place: **4** NEST
Buntline
Novelist: **3 NED**
Buñuel
collaborator: **4** DALI
Director: **4** LUIS
Bunyan, Paul
ox: **4** BABE
tool: **3 AXE**
"Buona ___": **4** SERA
Buoy: 5 ELATE
Red: **3** NUN
Where ~ meets gull: **3** SEA
5 OCEAN
Buoyancy: 10 RESILIENCE
Buoyant: 5 PERKY **6** FLOATY
7 SPRINGY
tune: **4** LILT
Burden: 3 TAX **4** LOAD **ONUS**
6 SADDLE
bearer: **5** BEAST
Beast of: **3** ASS YAK **5** CAMEL
LLAMA
Financial: **4** DEBT
of proof: **4 ONUS**
Burdened: 5 LADEN
No longer ~ by: **5** RIDOF
Burdensome: 7 ONEROUS
Burdette
of '50s–'60s baseball: **3** LEW
Burdon
Singer: **4** ERIC
Bureau: 5 CHEST **6** AGENCY
7 DRESSER
ender: **4** CRAT
Bureaucratic
bigwig: **6** POOBAH
tangle: **7** REDTAPE
Burg: 4 TOWN
Cheese: **4** EDAM
Icy: **4** NOME
Burger
bread: **3** BUN
side: **4** SLAW
topping: **5** ONION
Burglar: 4 YEGG **5** FELON THIEF
alarm feature: **6** SENSOR
deterrent: **4** BARK **5** ALARM
Kind of: **3** CAT

Like a cat: **8** STEALTHY
take: **4** LOOT
Burgle: 3 ROB **5** STEAL
Burgoo: 4 STEW
Burgundy: 3 VIN **4** WINE
being: **4** ETRE
buddy: **3** AMI
by another name: **5** ARLES
grape: **5** PINOT
Burial
vault: **4** TOMB **5** CRYPT
"Burial of the Count Orgaz"
painter: **7** ELGRECO
"Burke's Law"
Burke of: **4** AMOS
Burkina ___: 4 FASO
Burkina Faso
neighbor: **4** MALI
Burl
Folk singer: **4 IVES**
Burlap
bag: **4** SACK
material: **4** HEMP JUTE
Burlesque: 3 APE
bit: **4** SKIT
prop: **3** BOA
Burmese
prime minister: **3** UNU
Burn: 4 CHAR SEAR **5** SCALD
6 SCORCH
balm: **4 ALOE 8** ALOEVERA
brightly: **5** BLAZE
Do a slow: **4** STEW **6 SEETHE**
7 SMOLDER
Kind of: **4** SLOW
like a candle: **7** FLICKER
rubber: **5** SPEED
slightly: **5 SINGE**
soother: **4 ALOE 8** ALOEVERA
up: **3** IRE
without a flame: **7** SMOLDER
with water: **5** SCALD
Burner
Ceremonial: **6** CENSER
inventor: **6** BUNSEN
Lab: **4** ETNA
Oil: **4** LAMP
Burnett
Actress: **5** CAROL

Adman: 3 LEO
Burning: 3 LIT 5 **AFIRE** **AGLOW**
 6 AFLAME ONFIRE
desire: 5 ARSON
It's often: 6 DESIRE
Like ~ plastic: 5 ACRID
remnant: 3 ASH
the midnight oil: 6 UPLATE
with desire: 6 ARDENT
Burnish: 3 RUB
Burnoose
 wearer: 4 **ARAB**
Burnout
 cause: 6 STRESS
 treatment: 8 RESTCURE
Burns: 4 POET SCOT
 Info: Scottish cue
 and Allen (abbr.): 4 SENS
 Before, to: 3 ERE
 Bestow, to: 3 GIE
 birthplace: 3 AYR
 Documentarian: 3 KEN
 Hillside, to: 4 BRAE
 land: 6 SCOTIA
 Not large, to: 3 SMA WEE
 Not, to: 3 NAE
 partner: 5 ALLEN
 Possess, to: 3 HAE
 Pretty, to: 5 BONNY
 "sweet" stream: 5 AFTON
 title starter: 4 AULD
 ~, to Allen: 7 PARTNER
Burns, George
 film: 5 OHGOD
 partner ___ Allen: 6 GRACIE
 role: 3 GOD
 trademark: 5 CIGAR
Burnt
 color: 6 SIENNA
 residue: 3 ASH
Burnt ___ crisp: 3 TOA
Burpee
 unit: 4 SEED
Burr
 Duel participant: 5 AARON
 Event for ~ and Hamilton:
  4 DUEL
Burr, Raymond
 role: 5 MASON 8 IRONSIDE

Burrito
 alternative: 4 TACO
 filler: 4 BEEF
 kin: 6 TAMALE
 topping: 5 SALSA
 wrapper: 8 TORTILLA
Burro: 3 ASS 10 PACKANIMAL
 bellow: 4 BRAY
Burrow: 3 DEN 4 HOLE LAIR
Burrower
 Lawn: 4 MOLE
Burrowing
 animal: 4 MOLE 6 GERBIL
  WOMBAT
Burrows
 Playwright: 3 **ABE**
Bursa: 3 SAC
Burst: 3 POP 5 ERUPT
 Artillery: 5 SALVO
 of activity: 5 SPURT
 of energy: 5 SPASM
 of laughter: 4 PEAL
 of speed: 6 SPRINT
 of wind: 4 GUST
 Ready to: 5 SATED
 with pride: 5 KVELL
Bursting
 star: 4 NOVA
Burstyn
 Actress: 5 **ELLEN**
Burt
 and Loni: 4 EXES
 Ex of: 4 LONI
Burton
 Actor: 5 LEVAR
 Director: 3 TIM
 Miniseries role for: 5 KINTE
Burton, Richard
 film: 5 EQUUS 7 THEROBE
 Like: 5 WELSH
Burundi
 neighbor: 6 RWANDA
Bury: 5 **INTER** INURN
  6 ENTOMB INHUME
Bus
 alternative: 4 RAIL
 Board a: 5 GETON
 front: 4 OMNI
 Parks on a: 4 ROSA

passenger request: 8 TRANSFER
route: 4 LINE
starter: 4 MINI OMNI
station: 5 DEPOT
station info: 3 ETA
terminal (abbr.): 3 STN

Bus.
abbr.: 3 INC
bigwig: 3 CEO
card info: 3 TEL
heads: 4 MGMT
helper: 4 ASST
leader: 3 MGR
letter abbr.: 3 ENC 4 ATTN
school course: 4 ECON

Busboy
load: 4 TRAY

Busby: 3 HAT

Buscaglia
Author: 3 LEO

Busch Gardens
locale: 5 TAMPA

Busch Stadium: 5 ARENA
team (abbr.): 3 STL

Bush: 5 SHRUB
league: 3 GOP
outing: 6 SAFARI
Singer: 4 KATE

Bush, George H.W.: 3 ELI
    5 TEXAN YALIE
adviser Scowcroft: 5 BRENT
campaign adviser: 7 ATWATER
chief of staff: 6 SUNUNU
former org.: 3 CIA

Bush, George W.: 3 ELI 5 TEXAN
    YALIE
adviser Karl: 4 ROVE
alma mater: 4 YALE
degree (abbr.): 3 MBA
nickname: 5 DUBYA
opponent: 4 GORE
party: 3 GOP
spokesman Fleischer: 3 ARI
Wife of: 5 LAURA

Bush, Gov.
of Florida: 3 JEB
state (abbr.): 3 FLA

Bushed: 5 ALLIN TIRED WEARY
Become: 4 TIRE

Bushel
Biblical: 4 EPHA
fraction: 4 PECK

Bushel ___ peck: 4 ANDA

Bushels: 4 ALOT GOBS

Bushes
are in it: 3 GOP
One of the: 3 JEB

Bushmiller
Cartoonist: 5 ERNIE

Bushnell, Nolan
company: 5 ATARI

Bushwhacked: 7 WAYLAID

Bushy
hairdo: 4 **AFRO**

Bushy-tailed
beast: 7 RACCOON
rodent: 6 MARMOT

Busiest: 4 PEAK

Busily
Employ: 3 PLY
working: 4 ATIT

Business: 4 SHOP 5 TRADE
abbr.: 3 **INC** 4 CORP
attire: 4 SUIT 7 NECKTIE
banter: 8 SHOPTALK
bigwig: 4 CZAR EXEC 5 BARON
    MOGUL TITAN
Brand-new: 7 STARTUP
card abbr.: 3 **EXT** TEL
Do: 4 DEAL 8 TRANSACT
Do ~ with: 6 SELLTO
Doing: 4 OPEN
Funny: 5 ANTIC 6 ANTICS
Get down to: 10 TALKTURKEY
Go back into: 6 REOPEN
Head for: 4 BOSS
Its ~ is folding: 7 ORIGAMI
Its ~ was booming: 3 SST
letter abbr.: 3 **ENC** 4 ATTN
    ENCL
letters: 3 INC
lunch locale: 5 HOTEL
mag: 3 **INC**
marriage: 6 MERGER
Monkey: 5 APERY
news: 6 MERGER
Online: 5 ETAIL
Order of: 6 AGENDA

Out of: **4** SHUT **6** CLOSED
7 BELLYUP
partner, often: **3** SON
Place of: **4** SHOP
Port: **6** WINERY
prefix: **4** AGRI AGRO
Ready for: **4 OPEN**
school subj.: **4** ECON
sign abbr.: **4** ESTD **5** ESTAB
solicitor: **3** REP
transaction: **4** DEAL
You might give him the: **3** SON
~ VIP: **3** CEO
~, facetiously: **7** BEESWAX
Businessman
offering: **4** CARD
Businessmen: 5 SUITS
"Bus Stop"
playwright: **4 INGE**
Bust: 3 NAB **4** RAID **5** RUNIN
6 ARREST **10** POLICERAID
It may be a: **6** STATUE
Make a: **4** RAID **6** SCULPT
maker: **4** NARC
makers (abbr.): **3** DEA
opposite: **4** BOOM
Bust ___: 4 AGUT
Buster: 4 NARC
Drought: **4** RAIN
Drug: **4** NARC
of Flash Gordon fame: **6** CRABBE
of silent comedies: **6** KEATON
~, old-style: **6** SIRRAH
Bustle: 3 ADO HUM **4** STIR TODO
Busy: 4 ATIT **5** INUSE **6** ORNATE
TIEDUP **7** ONTHEGO
activity: **3** ADO
as a bee: **8** HARDATIT
bug: **3** BEE
Keep: **5** AMUSE
Not: **4** FREE IDLE SLOW
one: **3** BEE **4** DOER
one in Apr.: **3** CPA
place: **4** HIVE
time for the IRS: **3** APR
Busy as ___: 4 ABEE
Busybody: 5 SNOOP **YENTA**
7 MEDDLER
10 NOSYPARKER

Be a: **3** PRY **4** NOSE **5** SNOOP
Like a: **4** NOSY
But
end: **3** ANE
~, for short: **3** THO
~, in French: **4** MAIS
~, in German: **4** ABER
~, in Latin: **3** SED
"But ___ art?": 4 ISIT
Butcher
cut: **4** LOIN **5** TBONE
device: **5** SCALE
offering: **4** BEEF MEAT **5** STEAK
TBONE **10** SHELLSTEAK
Butches: 3 DOS
Butler: 4 HELP
Comic: **5** BRETT
Do the job of a: **5** ASKIN SEEIN
final word: **4** DAMN
love: **5** OHARA
of Batman: **6** ALFRED
of fiction: **5 RHETT**
portrayer: **5** GABLE
request: **5** ENTER
~, to Gable: **4** ROLE
Butler, Robert ___
Author: **4** OLEN
"But ___ me, give me liberty ...":
5 ASFOR
"But of course!": 3 AHA **5** OHYES
Butt: 3 END
Info: Suffix cue
bit: **3** ASH
Cigar: **4** ETTE
into: **3** RAM
place: **7** ASHTRAY
Butte
Big: **4** MESA
kin: **4** MESA
locale: **7** MONTANA
Butter: 3 RAM
alternative: **4 OLEO**
Bit of: **3** PAT
Clarified: **4** GHEE
holder: **3** TUB
Indian: **4** GHEE
knife: **8** SPREADER
Make: **5** CHURN
maker: **5** CHURN

serving: **3 <u>PAT</u>**
substitute: **4 OLEO**
up: **5 BASTE**
Buttercup
relative: **7 ANEMONE**
 8 LARKSPUR
"BUtterfield 8"
author John: **5 <u>OHARA</u>**
Butterfingers: 3 OAF 5 KLUTZ
cry: **4 OOPS**
Butterflies: 5 ANGST 6 NERVES
 7 ANXIETY
"Butterflies ___ Free": 3 ARE
Butterfly: 6 MADAME
Brightly colored: **7 MONARCH**
 10 REDADMIRAL
catcher: **3 NET**
Did the: **4 SWAM**
Float like a: **4 FLIT**
relative: **4 MOTH**
"Butterfly"
actress Zadora: **3 PIA**
"___ Butterfly": 6 MADAMA
"___ Buttermilk Sky": 3 OLE
Butterworth: 3 MRS
"___ but the Brave": 4 NONE
"___ but the wind": 4 TWAS
Butting
heads: **6 ATODDS**
Buttinsky: 4 PEST 5 PRIER YENTA
 YENTE
Barbecue: **3 ANT**
Like a: **4 NOSY**
Button
Alley: **5 RESET**
Attach, as a: **5 SEWON**
Blender: **5 PUREE**
Boom box: **3 REC**
Bowling alley: **5 <u>RESET</u>**
Calculator: **5 CLEAR**
Campaign ~ word: **5 ELECT**
Car radio: **6 PRESET**
Cash register: **6 NOSALE**
Cell phone: **4 SEND**
Clock radio: **6 SNOOZE**
Cockpit: **5 EJECT**
Cute as a: **8 ADORABLE**
Email: **4 SEND**
Fax: **4 SEND**

Furnace: **5 RESET**
Kind of: **5 PANIC**
Like a: **4 CUTE**
material: **5 NACRE**
On the: **5 EXACT**
PC panic: **3 ESC**
Phone: **4 OPER STAR 6 REDIAL**
Phone ~ trio: **3 ABC DEF GHI**
 JKL MNO PRS TUV WXY
Skater: **4 DICK**
up: **6 FASTEN**
~, to Frosty: **4 NOSE**
Buttoned: 4 SHUT
Not: **4 OPEN**
Buttonhole: 3 SEW 4 SLIT
 6 ACCOST
locale: **5 LAPEL**
Buttonless
shirt: **3 TEE**
Buttonlike: 4 CUTE
Buttons
Comedian: **3 RED**
Buttonwood: 8 SYCAMORE
Butyl
suffix: **3 ENE**
Buy
alternative: **5 LEASE**
and sell: **5 TRADE 6 DEALIN**
back: **6 REDEEM**
Great: **5 STEAL**
in a hurry: **6 SNAPUP**
One way to: **8 ONCREDIT**
stocks: **6 INVEST**
stuff: **4 SHOP**
Buyer: 6 VENDEE
Car ~ protection:
 8 LEMONLAW
caution: **4 ASIS**
concern: **4 COST**
incentive: **6 REBATE**
~, in Latin: **6 EMPTOR**
Buyoff: 5 BRIBE
Buzz: 3 HUM 4 NEWS 5 DRONE
 RUMOR
Astronaut: **6 ALDRIN**
Gave a: **4 RANG**
in space: **6 ALDRIN**
Moonmate of: **4 NEIL**
producer: **5 KAZOO**

Buzzard
  relative: 7 VULTURE
Buzzards Bay: 5 INLET
Buzzer: 3 BEE
  Bothersome: 4 GNAT
    8 HOUSEFLY
  Tiny: 4 GNAT
Buzzi
  Comedian: 4 RUTH
Buzzing: 4 AHUM 5 ASTIR
  about: 3 ADO
  cloud: 5 SWARM
  location: 6 APIARY
  pest: 4 GNAT
  with excitement: 5 ABOIL
"Buzz off!": 4 SHOO 5 SCRAM
B'way
  hit sign: 3 **SRO**
By: 3 VIA
  and by: 4 **ANON** SOON
    7 ERELONG
  and large: 7 ASARULE
    9 INTHEMAIN
  any chance: 4 EVER
  birth: 3 NEE
  far: 6 EASILY
  itself: 5 PERSE
  means of: 3 PER VIA
  way of: 3 **VIA**
  way of, briefly: 4 THRU
"By ___!": 3 GAR 4 JOVE 6 JIMINY
"Bye!": 4 CIAO TATA 5 ADIEU
    SEEYA 6 SEEYOU
"Bye-bye!": 4 CIAO TATA
    5 ADIEU SEEYA 6 SEEYOU
"Bye Bye Birdie"
  song: 4 KIDS 5 ROSIE
    15 PUTONAHAPPYFACE
  star: 10 JANETLEIGH
"Bye Bye Bye"
  pop group: 5 NSYNC

"By gar!": 4 EGAD
Bygone: 3 OLD 4 PAST 5 **OLDEN**
    7 OLDTIME
  days: 4 PAST YORE
"By Jove!": 4 EGAD ISAY 5 EGADS
"___ by land ...": 5 ONEIF
Bylaw
  ~, briefly: 3 REG
Byline
  Essay: 4 ELIA
"By me": 5 IPASS
BYOB
  Part of: 3 OWN 4 YOUR 5 BOOZE
    BRING
  provision: 5 SETUP
Bypass: 4 OMIT SKIP 5 SKIRT
  the altar: 5 ELOPE
Byrd, Admiral
  book: 5 ALONE
Byrnes
  Actor: 3 **EDD**
Byron: 4 POET
  daughter: 3 ADA
  piece written to Napoleon: 3 ODE
  poem: 4 LARA
"___ by Starlight": 6 STELLA
Byte
  parts: 4 BITS
  prefix: 4 GIGA KILO MEGA
    TERA
"___ by the bell!": 5 SAVED
"By the way ...": 3 SAY
Bytown
  was its first name: 6 OTTAWA
Byway: 4 LANE ROAD 6 AVENUE
    8 SIDEROAD
  Country: 4 LANE
Byways
  (abbr.): 3 RDS
Byword: 5 ADAGE MAXIM
"By yesterday!": 4 ASAP

Cc

C: 4 FAIR 5 GRADE 7 AVERAGE
  D and ~, in D.C.: 3 STS
  follower: 4 SPAN
  G in the key of: 3 SOL
  in a C scale: 5 TONIC
  in shop class: 5 CLAMP
  in UPC: 4 CODE
  Mark added to a: 7 CEDILLA
  minor: 3 KEY
  natural: 6 BSHARP
  Note above: 5 DFLAT
  sharp: 5 DFLAT
  The ~ of C.S. Lewis: 5 CLIVE
  to C: 6 OCTAVE
  Vehicle for the high: 4 ARIA
  What a ~ might be: 4 SOFT
  Work in: 4 CODE
  Worth a: 4 FAIR SOSO
C-___: 4 SPAN 5 CLAMP
C$_2$H$_6$: 6 ETHANE
C-3PO: 5 DROID ROBOT
C$_4$H$_8$: 6 BUTENE
C$_4$H$_8$O$_2$: 5 ESTER
C$_{14}$H$_9$Cl$_5$: 3 DDT
Ca^{++}: 3 ION
CAA
  employee: 3 AGT
Cab: 4 HACK TAXI
  caller: 6 HAILER
  counter: 5 METER
  Early: 6 HANSOM
  Flag a: 4 HAIL
  prefix: 4 PEDI
  Take a: 4 RIDE
Cabal: 4 PLOT RING 5 JUNTA
  member: 7 PLOTTER
"Cabaret"
  actor Grey: 4 JOEL
  actor Joel: 4 GREY
  actress Minnelli: 4 LIZA
  basis: 10 IAMACAMERA
  director Bob: 5 FOSSE
  lyricist: 3 EBB

  ~ Klub: 6 KITKAT
Cabbage: 4 GELT KALE LOOT
    5 MOOLA 6 DINERO
    MOOLAH
  Info: Money cue
  dish: 4 SLAW
  kin: 4 KALE
  Kobe: 3 YEN
  salad: 4 SLAW
  Spanish: 6 PESETA
Cabby: 4 HACK
  Call to a: 4 HAIL
  client: 4 FARE
  query: 7 WHERETO
Caber
  tosser: 4 SCOT
Cabernet: 3 RED 4 WINE
Cabeza
  across the Pyrenees: 4 TETE
Cabin
  bed: 3 COT
  component: 3 LOG
  Place for a: 4 LAKE
Cabinet
  Cleaning ~ supplies: 4 LYES
  department: 5 LABOR STATE
    7 DEFENSE 8 INTERIOR
  dept.: 3 **AGR** DOD HUD INT
    4 EDUC ENER USDA
  div.: 4 DEPT
  Kitchen: 8 CUPBOARD
  Medicine ~ item: 4 QTIP
    6 IODINE
  off.: 4 SECY
  TV: 7 CONSOLE
  wood: 5 ALDER CEDAR
Cabinet member
  Clinton: 4 PENA RENO
    5 COHEN 7 SHALALA
  Nixon: 6 ELLIOT
  Reagan: 4 HAIG 5 MEESE
Cable: 4 WIRE 5 PAYTV
  Atlanta-based ~ sta.: 3 TBS TNT

Basic ~ channel: **3** TNN
car: **4** TRAM
chan. for old films: **3** AMC TCM
channel: **3** AMC HBO SHO TBS
   TNN TNT USA
connection: **5** TVSET
co. that merged with AT&T: **3** TCI
kingpin Turner: **3** TED
modem alternative: **3** DSL
network: **3** AMC HBO SHO TBS
   TNN TNT USA
Provide with a new: **6** REWIRE
sports award: **4** ESPY
sports channel: **4** ESPN
superstation: **3** TBS
syst.: **4** CATV
worker: **5** WIRER

Caboodle
companion: **3** KIT
Kit and: **3** ALL LOT

Caboose: 4 <u>REAR</u>
place: **4** REAR

Cabral
Explorer: **5** PEDRO

Cabriolet
maker: **4** AUDI

Cache: 5 HOARD STORE TROVE
   7 SECRETE
Cash: **3** ATM **4** TILL

Cachet: 4 SEAL

Cackleberry: 3 EGG
producer: **3** HEN

Cackler: 3 HEN

Cacophony: 3 <u>DIN</u> 5 BLARE
   NOISE

Cacti
Flowering: **8** SAGUAROS

Cactus
Hallucinogenic: **6** MESCAL
   PEYOTE
Large: **7** SAGUARO
Like: **5** SPINY
ring: **6** AREOLE

Cad: 4 HEEL LOUT RAKE ROUE
   5 BEAST CREEP LOUSE
   6 ROTTER **7** BOUNDER
comeuppance: **4** SLAP

Cadbury
confection: **3** EGG

Caddie: 5 TOTER
suggestion: **4** IRON
supplies: **4** TEES

Caddies
Events with: **4** TEAS

Caddy
contents: **3** TEA
shack: **6** GARAGE
Word with: **3** TEA

Cadence
Rhythmic: **4** LILT
sound: **3** HUP

Cadenza
It might have a: **4** ARIA
Perform a: **4** SOLO
player: **7** SOLOIST

Cadet
First-year: **4** PLEB **5** PLEBE
org.: **4** ROTC
sch.: **4** USMA
Space ~ place: **8** LALALAND

Cadge: 3 BUM

Cadillac
model: **6** CATERA **7** SEVILLE
   8 ELDORADO

Cádiz
Info: Spanish cue
Cold, in: **4** FRIO
crafts: **5** ARTES

Cadmus
Daughter of: **3** INO

Caduceus
Org. with a ~ logo: **3** AMA

Caen
Info: French cue
In conclusion, in: **5** ENFIN
river: **4** ORNE
Town near: **5** STLO

Caesar: 3 SID **5** ROMAN SALAD
Info: Latin cue
accusation: **4** ETTU
cohort: **4** COCA
Comic: **3 <u>SID</u>**
Cry of: **4** ETTU
Dying words from: **4** ETTU
End of a ~ boast: **4** VICI
existence: **4** ESSE
farewell: **4** VALE
Fateful day for: **4** IDES

Hail, to: 3 AVE
hello: 3 AVE
Mo. named for a: 3 AUG
Opponent of: 4 CATO
Part of a ~ boast: 4 ISAW 5 ICAME
port: 5 OSTIA
Rebuke from: 4 ETTU
robe: 4 TOGA
salad ingredient: 3 OVA
server: 9 SALADBOWL
suffix: 3 EAN
That is, to: 5 IDEST
To be, to: 4 ESSE
tongue: 5 LATIN
topper: 7 CROUTON
Words from: 4 ETTU 5 ICAME
___ Caesar: 5 GAIUS
Caesarean
conquest: 4 GAUL
phrase: 4 ETTU
Caesura: 4 REST 5 PAUSE
Café: 6 BISTRO EATERY
additive: 4 LAIT
alternative: 3 THE
clientele: 6 EATERS
cup: 5 TASSE
feature: 6 AWNING
Café ___: 4 NOIR 6 AULAIT
Café au ___: 4 **LAIT**
Café con ___: 5 LECHE
Cafeteria
carrier: 4 **TRAY**
customer: 5 EATER
of yore: 7 AUTOMAT
Unappetizing ~ serving: 4 GLOP
wear: 7 HAIRNET
Caffè ___: 5 LATTE
Caffeinated
drink: 4 COLA
Caffeine
source: 3 TEA 4 COLA KOLA
Caftan: 4 ROBE
Cage
Actor ~, to friends: 3 NIC
part: 3 RIB
Talker in a: 4 MYNA
Worker in a: 6 TELLER
Cage, Nicolas
1997 ~ film: 6 CONAIR

Cager
Boston: 4 CELT
Cleveland: 3 CAV
Dallas: 3 MAV
favorite sound: 5 SWISH
Los Angeles: 5 LAKER
New Jersey: 3 NET
offense: 4 FOUL
org.: 3 NBA
San Antonio: 4 SPUR
target: 4 HOOP
~ Archibald: 4 NATE
~ Gilmore: 5 ARTIS
~ Mashburn: 5 JAMAL
~ O'Neal: 4 SHAQ
~ Shaq: 5 ONEAL
Cagers
Like most: 4 TALL
Cagey: 3 SLY
Cagney
1935 ~ film: 4 GMEN
1949 ~ film: 9 WHITEHEAT
portrayer: 5 GLESS
role: 5 COHAN
TV partner of: 5 LACEY
"Cagney & Lacey"
costar: 4 TYNE 5 GLESS
Cahoots
In: 6 ALLIED
Cain
Brother of: 4 **ABEL** SETH
Father of: 4 ADAM
Land where ~ dwelt: 3 NOD
Nephew of: 4 ENOS
Raise: 4 RAGE
raiser: 3 EVE 4 ADAM
Son of: 5 ENOCH
Caine
1966 ~ role: 5 **ALFIE**
title: 3 SIR
"Caine Mutiny, The"
author: 4 WOUK
captain: 5 QUEEG
Cairn
composition: 6 STONES
Cairngorms
River in the: 3 DEE
Cairo
debut of 1871: 4 AIDA

river: 4 **NILE** OHIO
suburb: 4 GIZA
Cajole: 4 COAX URGE
Cajun
  "Dirty" ~ dish: 4 RICE
  staple: 4 OKRA
  waterway: 5 BAYOU
Cake
  Bathday: 4 SOAP
  Corn: 4 PONE
  decoration: 5 ICING
  decorator: 4 **ICER**
  feature: 4 TIER 5 LAYER
  finisher: 4 **ICER**
  Finish the: 3 ICE
  ingredient: 5 SUGAR
  It's a piece of: 5 SLICE
  It takes the: 4 OVEN
  Kind of: 3 OAT 5 BUNDT LAYER
    6 SPONGE
  layer: 4 TIER
  Like a wedding: 6 TIERED
  Like fresh: 5 MOIST
  Make a: 4 BAKE
  Message on a: 5 EATME
  name: 7 SARALEE
  Nut: 5 TORTE
  Piece of: 4 EASY **SNAP** TIER
    5 CINCH LAYER WEDGE
    6 BREEZE PICNIC
  Popular snack: 5 SUZYQ
  Rich: 5 **TORTE** 6 GATEAU
  Rum: 4 **BABA**
  Small sponge:
    10 LADYFINGER
  Spongy: 5 BABKA
  Take the: 3 EAT WIN
  Tea: 5 SCONE
  topper: 4 ICER 5 ICING
  Wedding ~ feature: 4 **TIER**
Cake pan
  type: 5 BUNDT
Cakes
  partner: 3 ALE
  Rich: 7 GATEAUX
Cakewalk: 4 ROMP SNAP
    6 PICNIC
Cal
  Twin of: 4 ARON

Cal.
  Boxer from: 3 SEN
  column: 3 FRI MON SAT SUN
    THU TUE WED 4 THUR
    TUES
  entry: 4 APPT
  neighbor: 3 NEV ORE
  opener: 3 JAN
  page: 3 APR AUG FEB DEC JAN
    JUL JUN MAR NOV OCT
    SEP 4 SEPT
  pages: 3 MOS
  periods: 3 YRS
Cal ___ : 4 TECH
Calabash: 3 MRS
Calaboose: 4 STIR
Calais
  Info: French cue
  Cup, in: 5 TASSE
  ___ **Calais:** 5 PASDE
Calamari: 5 SQUID
Calamine
  ingredient: 4 ZINC
  target: 4 BITE ITCH
Calamitous: 4 **DIRE** 5 FATAL
    6 TRAGIC
Calamity: 3 ILL WOE 7 TROUBLE
Calc
  cousin: 4 TRIG
  prerequisite: 3 ALG
  readout: 3 LCD
Calcium-rich
  green: 4 KALE
Calculate
  astrologically: 4 CAST
Calculated
  It may be: 4 RISK
Calculating
  sort: 3 CPA
  subject: 4 MATH
Calculation
  Carpet: 4 **AREA**
  Cash register: 3 TAX
  Gambling: 4 ODDS
  Geometry: 4 **AREA**
  Graph: 5 SLOPE
  Physics: 4 MASS
  Statistics: 4 MEAN MODE
    5 RANGE

Trig: 5 SLOPE
Calculator: 5 ADDER
  Basic *(plural)*: 5 ABACI
  button: 5 CLEAR
  display: 3 LED
  Early: 6 ABACUS 9 SLIDERULE
  element: 5 DIODE
  figure: 6 ADDEND
  key: 3 COS 5 ENTER
  MPG: 3 EPA
  Use a: 3 ADD
Calculus: 6 TARTAR
  calculation: 4 AREA 5 LIMIT
    SLOPE
  pioneer: 5 EULER
  ___ calculus: 5 RENAL
Calcutta
  coin: 5 RUPEE
  costume: 4 **SARI**
  home: 5 INDIA
  Mother of: 6 TERESA
Calder, Alexander
  creation: 6 MOBILE 7 STABILE
Caldwell
  Actress: 3 **ZOE**
  Author: 7 ERSKINE
  Conductor: 5 SARAH
Caleb
  Author: 4 CARR
Caledonian: 4 SCOT
Calendar
  abbr.: 3 APR AUG DEC FEB FRI
    JAN JUL JUN MAR MON
    NOV OCT SAT SEP SUN
    THU TUE WED 4 SEPT
    THUR TUES
  Appt. ~ item: 3 MTG
  Church: 4 ORDO
  divs: 3 WKS
  End of the Jewish: 4 ELUL
  Kind of: 5 MAYAN PINUP
    6 JEWISH 7 ISLAMIC
  length: 4 YEAR
  Like the Muslim: 5 LUNAR
  line: 4 WEEK
  Lunar ~ event: 3 TET
  period: 4 WEEK YEAR
  pgs.: 3 MOS
  square: 3 DAY

"Calendar Girl"
  singer: 6 SEDAKA
Calendario
  opener: 5 **ENERO**
Calf
  catcher: 5 LASSO RIATA
  cry: 3 MAA 5 BLEAT
  Golden: 4 IDOL
  It covers half a: 4 MIDI
  meat: 4 VEAL
  Motherless: 5 DOGIE
  roping site: 5 RODEO
  Stray: 4 WAIF 5 DOGIE
Calf-length
  skirt: 4 MIDI
Calfless
  cow: 6 HEIFER
Calgary
  native: 8 ALBERTAN
  prov.: 4 ALTA
  province: 7 ALBERTA
Calgary Stampede: 5 RODEO
Calhoun
  Actor: 4 RORY
Calibrate: 3 SET
Calico
  comment: 4 MEOW
Calif.
  airport: 3 LAX
  barrio city: 6 EASTLA
  neighbor: 3 NEV 4 ARIZ OREG
  Old ~ fort: 3 ORD
  zone: 3 PST
California
  A ~ Santa: 3 ANA 5 CLARA
  Big in: 3 SUR
  border lake: 5 TAHOE
  city: 4 OJAI 6 ELTORO IRVINE
  college: 6 POMONA
  county: 4 NAPA 5 MARIN
    6 FRESNO ORANGE
    POMONA SHASTA
  first lady: 5 MARIA
  flag symbol: 4 BEAR
  Former ~ fort: 3 **ORD**
  giant: 7 REDWOOD
  gold rush name: 6 SUTTER
  golf locale: 11 PEBBLEBEACH
  hrs.: 3 PDT

Island off: 8 CATALINA
missionary: 5 SERRA
National forest in: 6 SHASTA
oak: 5 ROBLE
Onetime ~ capital: 8 MONTEREY
peak: 6 LASSEN SHASTA
peninsula: 4 BAJA
raisin center: 6 FRESNO
resort: 11 PALMSPRINGS
senator: 12 BARBARABOXER
Start of many ~ city names:
      3 SAN
valley: 4 NAPA SIMI
wind: 8 SANTAANA
wine region: 4 **NAPA** 6 SONOMA
___ California: 4 **BAJA**
Californie: 4 ETAT
Caligula
Nephew of: 4 NERO
"Caligula"
author: 5 CAMUS
Caliph
Early Muslim: 3 ALI 4 OMAR
faith: 5 ISLAM
Calista
role: 4 ALLY
Call: 3 REF SEE UMP 4 DIAL
      NAME TERM 5 PHONE
      RADIO VISIT
a game: 3 REF
a halt to: 3 END
at first: 4 SAFE
at home: 4 SAFE
before court: 7 ARRAIGN
Close: 5 SCARE 8 NEARMISS
counterpart: 3 PUT
for: 4 NEED PAGE 5 MERIT
      6 ENTAIL INVOKE
(for): 3 ASK
for attention: 4 PSST
for help: 3 **SOS** 6 MAYDAY
forth: 5 EVOKE
for the salt: 4 AHOY
into question: 6 OPPUGN
it a day: 4 QUIT STOP 6 RETIRE
Kind of: 4 MAIL TOLL 5 CLOSE
      6 MATING WAKEUP
      7 COLLECT
Like a 911: 4 EMER

Make a: 3 OPT 4 RULE 5 PHONE
off: 3 END 5 ABORT 6 CANCEL
of the wild: 4 ROAR
on: 3 SEE TAP USE 5 VISIT
out: 3 CRY
partner: 4 BECK
Part of an 800 collect ~ number:
      3 ATT
Place to ~ home: 5 ABODE
the shots: 4 LEAD 6 DIRECT
Times to ~, in ads: 4 EVES
to a mate: 4 AHOY
to attention: 4 PSST
to Bo Peep: 3 BAA
to court: 4 CITE
to Fido: 4 HERE
to mind: 5 EVOKE
to the USCG: 3 SOS
up: 4 DIAL RING 5 EVOKE
      PHONE
upon: 3 ASK 4 CITE 5 VISIT
      6 INVOKE
___ call: 4 TOLL
Calla lily
family: 4 ARUM
Callao
Capital near: 4 LIMA
country: 4 PERU
Callas: 4 DIVA
courter Onassis: 3 ARI
Soprano: 5 MARIA
"Call ___ cab!": 3 MEA
Call___ day: 3 **ITA**
Called
First to be: 4 ONEA
Formerly: 3 NEE
It may be ~ on account of rain:
      3 CAB
Once: 3 **NEE**
Originally: 3 NEE
Caller
Cab: 6 HAILER
Frequent: 4 AVON 8 AVONLADY
Strike: 3 UMP 5 UNION
      6 UMPIRE
Tech support: 4 USER
TKO: 3 REF
Calligrapher: 6 PENMAN
liquid: 3 INK

Calligraphy
need: 3 INK
stroke: 5 SERIF
Calling: 4 URGE 5 TRADE
6 CAREER
company: 4 **AVON**
Old ~ fee: 7 ONEDIME
"___ calling!": 4 AVON
Calliope: 4 MUSE
Sister of: 5 ERATO
Callisto
~, to Jupiter: 4 MOON
"Call Me ___": 5 MADAM
"Call Me Irresponsible"
songwriter Sammy: 4 CAHN
Callow
Less: 5 OLDER
Calloway, Cab
catchphrase: 6 HIDEHO
forte: 4 SCAT
"___ Calloways": 5 THOSE
"___ calls?": 3 ANY
"___ call us ...": 4 DONT
Calm: 4 COOL 5 ALLAY STILL
6 REPOSE SEDATE
SERENE 7 APPEASE
ATPEACE HALCYON
SILENCE 8 COMPOSED
Completely: 6 SERENE
down: 4 LULL 6 COOLIT PACIFY
SEDATE
On the ~ side: 4 ALEE
side: 3 LEE
"... calm, ___ bright": 5 ALLIS
"Calm down!": 4 EASY
6 NOWNOW
Calmer: 6 OPIATE
Calmness: 4 EASE 6 REPOSE
Caloric: 4 RICH
Calorie-laden: 4 RICH
Calories
Approx. 252: 3 BTU
Count: 4 DIET
Caltech
grad: 4 ENGR
Some ~ grads: 3 EES
Calumet: 9 PEACEPIPE
Calvary
letters: 4 **INRI**

Calverton
TV series set in: 6 LASSIE
Calvin
Columnist: 7 TRILLIN
Golfer: 5 PEETE
"Calvin and Hobbes"
bully: 3 MOE
girl: 5 SUSIE
Calvino
Author: 5 **ITALO**
Calypso
kin: 3 SKA
Calyx
component: 5 **SEPAL**
Cam
Bruin great: 5 NEELY
Camaro
model: 4 **IROC**
Onetime ~ rival: 3 GTO
Camay
alternative: 4 DOVE
Cambodia
continent: 4 ASIA
Lon of: 3 **NOL**
neighbor: 4 **LAOS**
Cambodian
currency: 4 **RIEL**
Former ~ leader: 3 NOL
6 LONNOL
neighbor: 3 LAO 4 THAI
Cambria: 5 WALES
Cambridge
bigwig: 3 DON
old coin: 5 PENCE
sch.: 3 **MIT**
Cambridgeshire
town: 3 ELY
Camcorder
abbr.: 3 REC
Camden Yards
player: 6 **ORIOLE**
Came
across: 3 MET SAW
after: 6 ENSUED
clean: 4 TOLD 8 FESSEDUP
down: 4 **ALIT** 6 RAINED
down to earth: 4 **ALIT**
down with: 3 GOT HAD
from behind: 7 RALLIED

home: 4 SLID
in: 7 ENTERED
in first: 3 WON
into being: 5 AROSE
on stage: 7 ENTERED
out: 7 EMERGED
out on top: 3 WON
out with: 4 SAID
to: 4 WOKE 5 AWOKE
    7 EQUALED
to a fast stop: 3 ATE
to a halt: 5 ENDED 6 CEASED
to a point: 7 TAPERED
to earth: 4 ALIT
together: 3 MET WED
    6 GELLED JELLED
    MASSED
to rest: 4 ALIT
to visit: 8 CALLEDON
up: 5 **AROSE**
upon: 3 MET
"___ Came Jones": 5 ALONG
Camel: 9 CIGARETTE
dropping: 3 ASH
feature: 4 HUMP
kin: 5 LLAMA 6 ALPACA
    7 GUANACO
lot: 5 OASIS
performer: 6 SKATER
pitstops: 5 OASES
resting place: 7 ASHTRAY
"Camel News Caravan"
anchor: 6 SWAYZE
Camelot
lady: 4 ENID
weapon: 5 LANCE
~, to Arthur: 5 REALM
    7 KINGDOM
"Camelot"
actor Franco: 4 NERO
composer: 5 LOEWE
Camembert
alternative: 4 BRIE
Cameo: 4 ROLE 7 BITPART
carving: 6 RELIEF
role of an actress, perhaps:
    7 HERSELF
shape: 4 OVAL
stone: 4 **ONYX**

Camera
attachment: 4 LENS
    8 ZOOMLENS
Canon: 3 **EOS**
Clown for the: 3 MUG
diaphragm: 4 IRIS
feature: 4 ZOOM
Follow with the: 3 PAN
inits.: 3 SLR
maker: 4 FUJI 5 CANON KODAK
    LEICA NIKON 7 MINOLTA
man: 4 FUNT
Mug for the: 4 POSE
part: 4 IRIS LENS 7 SHUTTER
Popular: 5 NIKON
Prepare a: 4 LOAD
protection: 7 LENSCAP
setting: 4 AUTO 5 FOCUS **FSTOP**
shop display: 4 SLRS
stand: 6 TRIPOD UNIPOD
type: 3 **SLR**
Words mouthed to a: 5 HIMOM
Word with: 4 DISC
Caméra ___ (Cannes prize): 3 DOR
"___ Camera": 4 **IAMA**
Cameraman
org.: 3 ASC
Cameron
Actor: 4 KIRK
Actress: 4 DIAZ
Cameron, James
1989 ~ film: 8 THEABYSS
Cameroon
neighbor: 4 CHAD 5 GABON
    7 NIGERIA
Camille
portrayer: 5 GRETA
Caminiti
of baseball: 3 KEN
Camouflage: 4 HIDE 5 BELIE
    7 BLENDIN
Camp
bed: 3 COT
Captives: 6 STALAG
craft: 5 CANOE
facility: 7 LATRINE
German prison: 6 STALAG
Military: 5 ETAPE
shelter: 4 TENT

Soviet labor: **5** GULAG
Word with: **3** DAY
WWII: **6** STALAG
Campaign: **3** RUN **4** RACE
    7 CRUSADE
1950s ~ nickname: **3** IKE
1996 ~ name: **4** DOLE
assault: **5** SMEAR
asset: **8** MOMENTUM
button word: **5** ELECT
concern: **5** IMAGE
contributor: **3** PAC
creator: **5** ADMAN
Dirty ~ stuff: **3** MUD
event: **6** DEBATE
(for): **3** RUN
funder: **3** PAC **6** FATCAT
Intense: **5** BLITZ
Long: **5** SIEGE
Perennial ~ issue: **4** JOBS
poster word: **7** REELECT
promise: **6** TAXCUT
strategy: **6** ATTACK
tactic: **5** SMEAR
Type of: **5** SMEAR
vet: **3** POL
worker: **4** AIDE
Campaigner: **3** POL
Dirty: **10** MUDSLINGER
Campanella
of baseball: **3** ROY
Campanile
Site of a famous: **4** PISA
sound: **4** PEAL
Campbell
Actress: **4** **NEVE** **5** TISHA
Country singer: **4** **GLEN**
creation: **4** SOUP
Supermodel: **5** **NAOMI**
Camp David Accords
participant: **5** BEGIN SADAT
Camped
out: **6** TENTED
Camper: **3** VAN **7** TRAILER
cover: **4** TENT
gear: **7** MESSKIT
Campers: **3** RVS
Campfire
remains: **3** ASH **5** ASHES EMBER

They're passed around a: **5** TALES
treat: **5** SMORE
Campground
letters: **3** KOA
Camphor: **6** KETONE
Camping
gear: **4** TENT
Campion
Director: **4** JANE
Camp Lejeune
letters: **4** USMC
Camp-out
treat: **5** SMORE
Camp Pendleton
City near: **9** OCEANSIDE
Campsite
Infantry: **5** ETAPE
sight: **4** TENT
Camp Swampy
dog: **4** OTTO
"Camptown Races"
syllable: **3** DAH
word: **6** DOODAH
Campus
1960s ~ gp.: **3** SDS
1994 ~ comedy: **3** PCU
Amherst: **5** UMASS
area: **4** **QUAD**
Baton Rouge: **3** LSU
Big man on: **4** DEAN
bigwig: **4** DEAN PROF
Brooklyn: **3** LIU
Bruin: **4** UCLA
building: **4** DORM HALL
buys: **5** TEXTS
Cambridge: **3** MIT
Cedar Rapids: **3** COE
climber: **3** IVY
Connecticut: **4** YALE
digs: **4** DORM
E. Lansing: **3** MSU
figure: **4** COED
gp.: **4** ROTC
hangout: **4** QUAD
Jewish ~ organization: **6** HILLEL
L.A.: **3** USC
letter: **3** ETA RHO **4** BETA
    5 SIGMA THETA
Lewiston: **5** BATES

Maine ~ site: **5** ORONO
marchers: **4** ROTC
Militant ~ org.: **3** SDS
military org.: **4 <u>ROTC</u>**
New Haven: **4** YALE
official: **4** DEAN
quarters: **4** DORM **5** DORMS
Sch. with a Berkeley: **4** UCAL
Sch. with a Providence: **3** URI
sports org.: **4** NCAA
tie-ups: **6** SITINS
West Coast: **4** UCLA

Camry
maker: **6** TOYOTA

Camus
birthplace: **7** ALGERIA
Plague, to: **5** PESTE

Can: 3 AXE MAY TIN **4** FIRE JAIL
    JOHN SACK **5** LETGO
    6 LAYOFF
Kind of: **7** AEROSOL
material: **3** TIN
Meat in a: **4** SPAM
opener: **3** CEE TAB **7** PULLTAB
    9 CHURCHKEY
Spray: **7** AEROSOL
Word on a drink: **4** LITE

Can.
heads: **3** PMS
neighbor: **3** USA
province: **3** ONT PEI QUE
    4 ALTA NFLD SASK

"Can ___?": 4 ITBE

**"___ Can" (Sammy Davis Jr.
    book): 4** YESI

Canaan
spy: **5** CALEB
suffix: **3** ITE

Canaanite
deity: **4** BAAL

Canada
capital: **6** OTTAWA
Exxon, in: **4** ESSO
lake: **4** ERIE
province: **7** ONTARIO

Canada Day
month: **4** JULY

Canadian
Abbr. in many ~ city names:

    3 STE
capital: **3** CEE **6** OTTAWA
coin: **4** CENT
coin bird: **4** LOON
comedian Mort: **4** SAHL
cop: **7** MOUNTIE
distance measures (abbr.): **3** KMS
Eastern ~ Indian: **6** MICMAC
flag symbol: **4** LEAF
gas name: **4** ESSO
mayor: **5** REEVE
Native: **4** CREE
peninsula: **5** GASPE
prov.: **3** ONT PEI QUE **4** ALTA
    NFLD SASK
province: **7** ONTARIO
territory: **5** YUKON
tribe: **4** CREE
verb ending: **3** ISE
~ Arctic explorer: **3** RAE
~ Conservative: **4** TORY
~ Indian: **4 <u>CREE</u>**

"Canadian Bacon"
president portrayer: **4** ALDA

Canadiens: 4 TEAM
org.: **3** NHL

Canal: 4 DUCT **7** SHIPWAY
Albany: **4** ERIE
Anatomical: **4** ITER
buildup: **6** EARWAX
completed in 1825: **4** ERIE
craft: **5** BARGE
Egyptian: **4** SUEZ
examiner aid: **8** OTOSCOPE
feature: **4** LOCK
of Sal: **4** ERIE
of song: **4 <u>ERIE</u>**
opened in 1869: **4** SUEZ
problem: **7** EARACHE
River connected by ~ to the Tiber:
    4 ARNO
site: **3 <u>EAR</u> 6** PANAMA
to Buffalo: **4** ERIE
to the Baltic: **4** KIEL
to the Hudson: **4** ERIE
to the Mediterranean: **4** SUEZ
Word before: **4** ROOT
zone: **3** EAR
___ Canals: 3 <u>SOO</u>

Canapé
  and so on: **10** FINGERFOOD
  topper: **4** PATE
Canary: 3 PET **6** YELLOW
  kin: **5** SERIN
  Largest: **8** TENERIFE
  nose: **4** CERE
  sound: **5** TWEET
Canary Islands
  One of the: **7** LAPALMA
Canasta
  combo: **4** MELD
Canaveral
  org.: **4** NASA
  stop: **5** ABORT
Canberra
  comrade: **4** MATE
Cancel: 3 AXE NIX **4** NULL UNDO
     XOUT **5** ABORT ANNUL
     ERASE SCRAP SCRUB
     6 NEGATE REPEAL
     REVOKE **7** CALLOFF
     REDLINE VOIDOUT
  a dele: **4** STET
  out: **6** NEGATE
Canceled: 4 NOGO VOID
     6 XEDOUT
Canceler
  Nay: **3** YEA
Cancer
  follower: **3** LEO
" ___ Can Cook": 3 YAN
Cancún
  Info: Spanish cue
  coin: **4 PESO**
  kin: **3** TIO
Candelabrum
  Religious: **7** MENORAH
Candice
  Father of: **5** EDGAR
Candid: 4 OPEN **5** FRANK
     6 HONEST
  Be: **5** LEVEL
"Candida"
  playwright: **4** SHAW
Candidate
  1936 ~ Landon: **3** ALF
  1950s ~ Stevenson: **5** ADLAI
  1992 ~: **5** PEROT

  1996 ~: **4** DOLE **5** LAMAR
     NADER PEROT
  2000 ~: **5** NADER **6** ALGORE
  2004 ~: **4** DEAN **5** NADER
  concern: **4** POLL **5** IMAGE
  Day care: **3** TOT
  Florida governor: **4** RENO
  goal: **4** SEAT
  Green Party: **5** NADER
  list: **5 SLATE**
  Losing: **7** ALSORAN
  Perennial ~ of old: **7** STASSEN
  Reform Party: **5** PEROT
  Tony: **4** PLAY
  Unlikely ~ for prom king:
    4 NERD
Candidates
  discussion: **6** DEBATE
  Like some ~ (abbr.): **3** IND
"Candid Camera"
  cohost Durward: **5** KIRBY
  host Allen: **4** FUNT
"Candide"
  author: **8** VOLTAIRE
Candied: 5 GLACE SWEET
  dish: **4** YAMS
Candies
  Cinnamon: **7** REDHOTS
  Spicy: **7** REDHOTS
Candle
  Add a ~ to the cake: **3** AGE
  bracket: **6** SCONCE
  Burn like a: **7** FLICKER
  center: **4** WICK
  count: **3** AGE
  dripping: **3** WAX
  holder: **4** CAKE **6** SCONCE
  Kind of: **5** ROMAN
  Like a: **5** WAXEN
  material: **3** WAX **4** SUET
    6 TALLOW
  Slender: **5** TAPER
Candlelight
  Song sung by: **4** NOEL
Candler
  Coca-Cola founder: **3** ASA
Candles
  Like prank: **5** RELIT
  Like some: **7** SCENTED

What ~ may reveal: 3 AGE
C&O
and others: 3 RRS
C&W
Chet of: 6 ATKINS
Former ~ channel: 3 TNN
K.T. of: 5 OSLIN
Leann of: 5 RIMES
McEntire of: 4 REBA
Tritt of: 6 TRAVIS
Candy: 6 SWEETS
After-dinner: 4 MINT
Big name in: 4 MARS
brand: 3 PEZ 4 ROLO 6 KITKAT
    REESES RIESEN
Caramel: 4 ROLO
Chewy: 5 TAFFY 6 NOUGAT
    TOFFEE 7 CARAMEL
Coated: 5 MANDM
Craving for: 10 SWEETTOOTH
Dispenser: 3 **PEZ**
Hard: 10 JAWBREAKER
Hard ~, in Britain: 5 LOLLY
Hershey: 4 HUGS ROLO
    6 KITKAT
in a dispenser: 3 PEZ
Ingredient in some ~ bars:
    6 ALMOND
Lemon: 4 DROP
Like cotton: 4 SPUN
Like taking ~ from a baby:
    4 EASY
shape: 3 BAR 4 CANE
striper: 4 AIDE
Candy, John
Old show featuring: 4 SCTV
Cane: 4 FLOG 5 STICK 6 RATTAN
cutter: 7 MACHETE
extract: 5 SUGAR
Sugar ~ menace: 6 AGOUTI
~, to Charlie Chaplin: 4 PROP
Canea
Where ~ is capital: 5 CRETE
Canetti
Literature Nobelist: 5 ELIAS
Canful
Cook's: 4 LARD
Canin
Novelist: 5 ETHAN

Canine: 5 TOOTH 8 EYETOOTH
Camp Swampy: 4 OTTO
Cartoon: 3 **REN** 4 ODIE
checker (abbr.): 3 DDS
coat: 6 ENAMEL
Comics: 4 ODIE OTTO 5 SNERT
command: 3 BEG SIT 4 HEEL
    STAY
comment: 3 **ARF** 4 WOOF
cry: 3 ARF 4 HOWL YELP
from Kansas: 4 TOTO
Hollywood: 4 ASTA
Kiddie lit: 4 SPOT
neighbor: 8 PREMOLAR
Oz: 4 TOTO
warning: 3 GRR
Welsh: 5 CORGI
Canines: 5 TEETH 8 EYETEETH
Cut: 6 TEETHE
Raise: 6 TEETHE
Caning
material: 6 RATTAN
Canis Major
Constellation south of: 4 ARGO
Canned
heat: 6 STERNO
meat: 4 SPAM
Canner
job: 5 AXING
supply: 4 LIDS
Cannery
row: 4 JARS TINS
Cannes
Info: French cue
cap: 5 BERET
cash: 5 FRANC
co.: 3 CIE
concept: 4 IDEE
confidant: 3 AMI
cup: 5 TASSE
showing: 4 CINE
Water in: 3 EAU
Cannibal
Tolkien: 3 ORC
Cannon
Actress: 4 **DYAN**
Kind of: 5 LOOSE
Loose: 6 MENACE
suffix: 3 ADE EER

Water ~ target: 6 RIOTER
"___ Cannonball": 6 WABASH
Cannonballs: 4 AMMO
Cannoneer
command: 4 FIRE
"Can ___ now?": 3 IGO
Canny: 3 SLY 5 SMART
6 SHREWD
Canoe
challenge: 6 RAPIDS
Enclosed: 5 KAYAK
paddle: 3 OAR
___ can of worms: 5 OPENA
Canon
camera: 3 **EOS**
competitor: 4 MITA 5 KODAK
LEICA NIKON RICOH
6 KONICA 7 MINOLTA
Canonical
hour: 4 NONE 5 MATIN NONES
Canonized
mlle.: 3 STE
pope known as "the Great":
5 STLEO
Canopy: 6 TESTER
support: 7 BEDPOST
Cans
24 ~: 4 CASE
Canseco
of baseball: 4 JOSE
Cant: 4 LEAN 5 ARGOT
6 JARGON
Can't
abide: 6 DETEST
bear: 4 HATE
do without: 4 NEED 5 NEEDS
help but: 4 MUST 5 HASTO
stand: 4 HATE 5 ABHOR HATES
6 DETEST LOATHE
7 DETESTS
stomach: 4 HATE 5 ABHOR
wait for: 8 NEEDASAP
Cantab
rival: 3 ELI
Cantabrian Mountains
river: 4 EBRO
Cantaloupe: 5 MELON
cover: 4 RIND
kin: 6 CASABA 8 HONEYDEW

Cantankerous: 5 TESTY
6 ORNERY
~ Ryan: 5 IRENE
Cantata
composer: 4 BACH
melody: 4 ARIA
singers: 5 CHOIR
"... can't believe ___ the whole
thing": 4 IATE
Canter: 4 **GAIT** LOPE
Canterbury
can: 3 LOO TIN 4 GAOL
county: 4 KENT
John of: 3 LOO
saint: 6 ANSELM
"Canterbury"
episode: 4 TALE
"Canterbury Tales, The"
author: 7 CHAUCER
pilgrim: 5 REEVE
"Can't Fight the Moonlight"
singer: 5 RIMES
"Can't Get It Out of My Head"
rock gp.: 3 ELO
"Can't Get Used to Losing You"
singer Williams: 4 ANDY
"Can't Help Lovin' ___ Man":
3 DAT
Canticle: 3 ODE
Perform a: 6 INTONE
Cantilevered
window: 5 ORIEL
Cantina
cooker: 4 OLLA
offering: 4 TACO 6 TAMALE
tidbit: 4 TAPA
___ canto: 3 **BEL**
Canton
designer: 3 PEI
locale: 4 OHIO
neighbor: 5 AKRON
suffix: 3 ESE
Swiss: 3 URI 6 GENEVA
William Tell: 3 **URI**
Cantor
Mrs.: 3 IDA
"Cantos de ___": 6 ESPANA
Cantrell
Singer: 4 LANA

"Can ___ true?": 4 ITBE
"Can't Take My Eyes Off You"
singer Frankie: 5 VALLI
Canucks: 4 TEAM
Canute
foe: 4 OLAF
Canvas
bag: 4 TOTE
cover: 4 TARP 8 OILPAINT
holder: 5 EASEL
Knock to the: 4 DECK
Practice on: 4 SPAR
Send to the: 4 KAYO
shelter: 4 TENT
sunscreen: 6 AWNING
support: 5 EASEL
Waterproof: 4 TARP
Canvasback
cousin: 4 TEAL
"Can we talk?"
comic: 6 RIVERS 10 JOANRIVERS
Canyon: 5 GORGE
comeback: 4 ECHO
edge: 3 RIM
of comics: 5 STEVE
phenomenon: 4 ECHO
sound: 4 ECHO
Utah: 4 SEGO 5 BRYCE
Canyonlands
locale: 4 UTAH
___ Canyon National Park:
5 BRYCE
Cap: 3 LID TAM 4 ACME COIF
5 LIMIT
Artist: 5 BERET
attachment: 5 PLUME 6 EARLAP
Bird on a: 6 ORIOLE
Brimless: 5 BERET 6 BEANIE
Capitol: 4 DOME
Cardinal ~ letters: 3 STL
Clergy: 7 BIRETTA
Dunce: 4 CONE
feature: 5 VISOR
flap: 6 EARLAP
Foreign Legion: 4 KEPI
Freshman's: 6 BEANIE
Joint with a: 4 KNEE
Like a dunce: 5 CONIC
locale: 4 KNEE
material: 3 ICE
Military force: 4 KEPI
Mushroom ~ part: 4 GILL
Nut with a: 5 ACORN
on a leg: 7 PATELLA
Put a ~ on: 5 LIMIT
Put on one's thinking: 6 IDEATE
Red: 3 FEZ
Scottish: 3 TAM
setting: 4 KNEE
Shriner's: 3 FEZ
Skye: 3 TAM
source: 4 COON
Special Forces: 5 BERET
Tasseled: 3 FEZ
Tip a: 4 DOFF
Visored: 4 KEPI
Cap.
Abu Dhabi is its: 3 UAE
Dover is its: 3 DEL
Vilnius is its: 4 LITH
Cap-___ (head-to-toe): 4 APIE
Capability
Military: 9 FIREPOWER
Capable
More than: 5 ADEPT
of: 4 UPTO
Capacious: 5 AMPLE ROOMY
Capacitance
Unit of: 5 FARAD
Capacitor
Primitive: 9 LEYDENJAR
Capacity: 4 ROLE ROOM
AC ~ measure: 3 BTU
Calendar: 4 YEAR
Computer ~ unit: 4 BYTE
descriptor: 3 SRO
Diary: 4 YEAR
Garage: 6 ONECAR
Hospital: 4 BEDS
In the ~ of: 3 QUA
Serve in the ~ of: 5 ACTAS
Cape: 4 NESS 5 CLOAK
Bay State: 3 ANN
Massachusetts: 3 ANN COD
North Carolina: 4 FEAR
8 HATTERAS
of Portugal: 4 ROCA
Pope: 5 ORALE

Cape ___: 3 ANN COD 4 ROCA
5 VERDE
"Cape ___" (De Niro film): 4 FEAR
Cape Canaveral
org.: 4 NASA
Cape Cod
catch: 4 TUNA
town: 5 **TRURO**
"Cape Fear"
actor: 5 NOLTE
Capek
play: 3 **RUR**
Playwright: 5 KAREL
Cape of Good Hope
country (abbr.): 3 RSA
discoverer: 4 DIAS
Caper: 4 DIDO LARK 5 **ANTIC**
PRANK
Bank: 5 HEIST
Cape Town
cash: 4 RAND
Diplomat born in: 4 EBAN
home (abbr.): 3 RSA
Cape Tres Puntas
locale (abbr.): 3 ARG
Capework
reaction: 3 OLE
Capita
Per: 4 EACH
___ capita: 3 **PER**
Capital: 4 AONE
Info: Money cue
Info: See specific country, state,
etc.
African: 5 ACCRA CAIRO RABAT
TUNIS
Alpine: 4 BERN
Andean: 4 LIMA
Arabian: 4 SANA
Asian: 5 AMMAN DACCA HANOI
KABUL LHASA SEOUL
6 TAIPEI TEHRAN
7 JAKARTA
Assyrian: 7 NINEVEH
at the center of Czechoslovakia:
4 OSLO
Balkan: 5 SOFIA 6 TIRANA
Baltic: 4 RIGA
before Brasilia: 3 RIO

Chinese: 6 TAIPEI
Cold: 4 OSLO 8 HELSINKI
Continental: 4 EURO
European: 4 BERN KIEV OSLO
RIGA 6 TIRANA ZAGREB
First U.S.: 3 NYC
Former European: 4 BONN
Former Japanese: 4 NARA
5 KYOTO
Former Polish: 6 KRAKOW
Former Serbian: 3 NIS
Mediterranean: 5 TUNIS
7 NICOSIA
Mideast: 4 SANA 5 AMMAN
6 TEHRAN 7 TEHERAN
Mogul: 4 AGRA
near the 60th parallel: 4 OSLO
North African: 5 RABAT TUNIS
Northern: 4 OSLO
of Österreich: 4 WIEN
on a fjord: 4 **OSLO**
Pacific: 4 APIA
South American: 4 LIMA 5 LAPAZ
QUITO SUCRE
transit: 5 METRO
Western: 5 BOISE SALEM
6 HELENA
Westernmost African: 5 DAKAR
Working: 3 PAY
Capitale
European: 4 ROMA
Capitalist
Fur: 5 ASTOR
Capitalize
on: 3 USE
Capitol: 10 STATEHOUSE
feature: 4 **DOME** 7 ROTUNDA
fig.: 3 POL SEN
Like the: 5 DOMED
Record label with: 3 EMI
topper: 4 DOME
worker: 4 AIDE
~ VIPs: 4 SENS
Capitol ___, The: 5 STEPS
Capitol Hill
fig.: 3 SEN
figure: 3 POL
first name: 4 NEWT
prize: 4 SEAT

~ VIP: 3 SEN
Capitulate: 6 CAVEIN
Caplet
count: 4 DOSE
Cap'n
mate: 4 BOSN
Say "~": 5 ELIDE
Capo
crew: 5 MAFIA
Capone
and others: 3 **ALS**
associate: 5 NITTI
captor: 4 NESS
facial feature: 4 SCAR
nemeses: 4 TMEN
nemesis: 4 **NESS**
rival: 5 MORAN
Capote
nickname: 3 **TRU**
Play about: 3 **TRU**
Capp
and others: 3 **ALS**
contraction: 3 LIL
creation: 5 ABNER
hyena: 4 LENA
of comics: 4 ANDY
Capp, Andy
hangout: 3 PUB
quaff: 3 ALE
Wife of: 3 **FLO**
wife, often: 3 NAG
Capped
joint: 4 KNEE
They're: 5 KNEES
Capping: 4 ATOP
Cappuccino
cousin: 5 LATTE
Prepare milk for: 5 STEAM
topper: 4 FOAM 5 FROTH
Capri: 4 **ISLE** 5 ISOLA
attraction: 6 GROTTO
cash: 4 LIRA
suffix: 3 **OTE**
Caprice: 4 WHIM
Capricious: 9 WHIMSICAL
notion: 4 WHIM
Capriciously: 7 ONAWHIM
Capricorn: 4 GOAT
Capris: 5 PANTS

Caps
Like some: 6 WOOLEN
Capsize: 5 UPEND UPSET
Caps Lock
neighbor: 3 TAB
Capstone: 4 ACME
Capsule
contents: 4 DOSE
Cotton: 4 BOLL
Time ~ event: 6 BURIAL
Capsule-mate
of Buzz: 4 NEIL
Capt.
aide: 3 ENS
heading: 3 ESE SSE
prediction: 3 ETA
Rank below: 5 LIEUT
saluters: 3 LTS
superior: 3 MAJ
Captain: 4 RANK
command: 5 AVAST TOSEA
diary: 3 LOG
Enterprise: 4 KIRK
Fictional: 4 AHAB NEMO
Golden Hind: 5 DRAKE
Melville: 4 AHAB
offering: 4 MENU
of Ishmael: 4 AHAB
of Queequeg: 4 AHAB
of Starbuck: 4 AHAB
One-handed: 4 HOOK
position: 4 HELM
Reply to the: 3 AYE 6 AYEAYE
staff: 4 CREW
superior: 5 MAJOR
Verne: 4 **NEMO**
Wouk: 5 QUEEG
"Captain Blood"
actor Flynn: 5 ERROL
costar of Basil: 5 ERROL
Captain Davies
portrayer: 7 EDASNER
Captain Hook
sidekick: 4 SMEE
Captain Kangaroo
portrayer: 7 KEESHAN
Captain Kirk
helmsman: 4 SULU
Captain Lou Albano: 7 RASSLER

Captain Marvel
  magic word: 6 SHAZAM
Captain Nemo
  creator: 5 VERNE
Captain Picard
  counselor: 4 TROI
Capt. Davies
  portrayer: 5 ASNER
Capt. Hook
  biter: 4 CROC
Caption
  Diet-ad photo: 5 AFTER
      6 BEFORE
Captivate: 6 ENAMOR ENGAGE
      RAVISH 8 ENTHRALL
  a crowd, perhaps: 5 ORATE
Captivated
  by: 4 INTO
Captive
  MP's: 4 AWOL
  of Hercules: 5 IOLE
  of Paris: 5 HELEN
Captor
  Capone: 4 NESS
Captors
  Patty Hearst: 3 SLA
Capture: 3 BAG GET NAB NET
      WIN 4 CAGE GRAB LAND
      TAKE 5 LASSO SEIZE
      SNARE 6 CORRAL
      7 ENSNARE
  electronically: 4 SCAN
  the bronze: 3 TAN
Captured: 3 WON 4 TOOK
  again: 5 REWON
Car: 4 AUTO
  1960s muscle ~: 3 GTO
  accessory: 3 MAG
  ad abbr.: 3 APR MPG
  alarm: 4 HORN
  Antique: 3 REO
  Balloon: 7 NACELLE
  bar: 4 **AXLE** 5 STRUT
  bomb: 5 **EDSEL** LEMON
  buyer protection: 8 LEMONLAW
  Cable: 4 TRAM
  Classic: 3 GTO **REO** 5 TBIRD
      6 MODELA 7 BEARCAT
  club: 3 AAA

co. bought by Chrysler: 3 AMC
Collectible: 5 EDSEL
Company: 4 PERK
  contract: 5 LEASE
  dealer offering: 5 LEASE
Drive the getaway: 4 ABET
Early touring: 3 REO
Enter a: 5 GETIN
European: 4 OPEL
Family: 5 SEDAN
Fancy: 5 ROLLS
for hire: 3 CAB
Four-door: 5 SEDAN
"Fun, Fun, Fun": 5 TBIRD
German: 4 AUDI OPEL
Gun in a: 3 REV
Italian: 4 FIAT
Italian ~, for short: 4 ALFA
Junky: 4 HEAP
Kind of: 4 SLOT TOWN USED
    5 SQUAD 6 KIDDIE MUSCLE
    PATROL
Korean: 3 KIA
Last: 6 HEARSE 7 CABOOSE
lifter: 4 JACK
Light: 4 NEON
"Little" ~ of song: 3 GTO
loan fig.: 3 APR
Long: 4 LIMO
Lousy: 5 LEMON
Mine: 4 TRAM
Monogrammatic: 3 REO
nut: 3 LUG
Olds: 3 REO
owner proof: 5 TITLE
parker: 5 VALET
part: 4 AXLE FUSE TIRE
payment: 4 TOLL
Police ~ device: 5 SIREN
prefix: 4 SIDE
protector: 3 BRA 5 ALARM
Race ~ sponsor: 3 STP
rack item: 3 SKI
radio button: 6 PRESET
Railroad: 5 DINER
Retro: 6 BEETLE
roof feature: 4 TTOP
safety feature: 6 AIRBAG
    7 ROLLBAR

scar: **4** DENT DING
Seized: **4** REPO
shopper option: **5** LEASE
show car: **9** STREETROD
Showroom: **4** DEMO
since 1949: **4** SAAB
Sleek, in ~ lingo: **4** AERO
sound: **7** SCREECH
Souped-up: **6** HOTROD
Sports ~, for short: **3** JAG
   4 ALFA
Squad: **7** CRUISER
starter: **5** CRANK
starter (abbr.): **3** IGN
Subway ~ part: **5** STRAP
Swedish: **4** SAAB
Taken-back: **4** REPO
Test-driven: **4** DEMO
top: **4** ROOF
Touring: **5** SEDAN
Two-door: **5** COUPE
until 1957: **4** NASH
Used ~ deal: **6** RESALE
Vintage: **3** REO
Wait in the: **4** IDLE
wash option: **3** WAX
window sticker: **5** DECAL
with a bar: **4** LIMO
with four linked rings: **4** AUDI

Cara
Singer/actress: **5** IRENE

Caracas
lass (abbr.): **4** SRTA

Carafe
kin: **4** EWER
size: **5** LITER

Caramel
candy brand: **4** ROLO
Crème: **4** FLAN
Like: **5** CHEWY
topped dessert: **4** FLAN

Carangi
Supermodel: **3** GIA

Carapace: **5** SHELL

Caravan
beast: **5** CAMEL
maker: **5** DODGE
stop: **5** OASIS
stops: **5** OASES

Caravel
Historic: **4** **NINA** **5** PINTA

Caraway: **4** HERB SEED

Carbine
British: **4** STEN

Carbohydrate
ending: **3** OSE

Carbolic
acid: **6** PHENOL

Carbo-loader
fare: **5** PASTA

Carbon
compound: **4** **ENOL** **5** ESTER
   6 KETONE
compound suffix: **3** ENE
monoxide lack: **4** ODOR
Test for ~ **14**: **4** DATE
~ **13**: **7** ISOTOPE

Carbon ___: **7** DIOXIDE

Carbonated
drink: **4** COLA **SODA**

Carbon dioxide
Treat with: **6** AERATE

Carbonium: **3** ION

Carbs
Cut: **4** DIET

Carburetor
regulator: **5** CHOKE

Card: **3** WIT **4** NLER RIOT
   5 CUTUP
balance: **4** DEBT
Birthday ~ subject: **3** AGE
Blackjack: **3** ACE TEN
Bus. ~ info: **3** TEL
combination: **4** MELD
Conceal a: **4** PALM
Diner's: **4** MENU
Drawing: **4** LURE
Green ~ holder: **5** ALIEN
Greeting ~ item: **4** POEM
He's a real: **4** JACK
High: **3** ACE
"in the hole": **3** ACE
Kind of: **3** ATM **5** HONOR INDEX
   6 CREDIT
Low: **3** TWO **4** TREY **5** DEUCE
Low ~ in a royal flush: **3** TEN
Low ~ in euchre: **5** SEVEN
Low ~ in pinochle: **4** NINE

Monopoly: 4 **DEED**
Picture: 5 TAROT
Plays the wrong: 7 RENEGES
Poker: 3 ACE 4 TREY 5 DEUCE
Punch ~ remnant: 4 CHAD
Read a credit: 5 SWIPE
Restaurant: 4 MENU
Sci-fi writer: 5 ORSON
Seer's: 5 TAROT
spot: 3 PIP
Take a: 4 DRAW
Tarot ~ user: 4 SEER
Took a: 4 DREW
Top: 3 ACE
Used a credit: 4 OWED
Wild: 5 JOKER
with one pip: 3 ACE
X, on a greeting: 4 KISS
Card-carrying: 4 REAL
Card catalogue
abbr.: 4 ETAL
entry: 5 TITLE
Carder
requests: 3 IDS
Card game: 3 GIN **LOO** UNO
    WAR 4 SKAT STUD
    6 ECARTE GOFISH
    7 CANASTA
also called sevens: 6 FANTAN
authority Edmond: 5 HOYLE
Children's: 3 UNO **WAR**
    6 GOFISH 7 OLDMAID
    11 CRAZYEIGHTS
cry: 3 GIN 6 GOFISH
Easy: 3 WAR
Family: 3 UNO
Fast-paced: 4 SPIT
for three: 4 **SKAT** 5 OMBRE
Fortuneteller: 5 TAROT
for two: 3 WAR 6 ECARTE
Lively: 3 UNO
Old: 3 LOO 4 SKAT 5 OMBER
    OMBRE
Popular: 3 **UNO**
stake: 4 ANTE
start: 4 DEAL
Trick-taking: 6 EUCHRE
with a "good ten": 6 CASINO
with forfeits: 3 LOO

Cardiff
country: 5 WALES
natives: 5 WELSH
Cardigan: 4 KNIT
Make a: 4 KNIT
Cardin
rival: 6 ARMANI
Cardinal: 4 MAIN 7 DEEPRED
    REDBIRD
Big Apple: 4 EGAN
insignia: 3 STL
letters: 3 STL
point: 4 NEST
The first: 3 ONE
topper: 6 REDHAT
~ O'Connor successor: 4 EGAN
~ Slaughter: 4 ENOS
Cardinale
Actress: 7 CLAUDIA
Cardinals
great Brock: 3 LOU
great Musial: 4 STAN
home (abbr.): 3 STL
manager: 4 POPE
Marrero of the: 3 ELI
Cardiologist
concern: 5 AORTA
Cards
Big name in sports: 5 FLEER
    TOPPS
Cost of: 4 ANTE
Distributed the: 5 DEALT
Extra hand of: 5 WIDOW
Hard-to-find: 5 RARES
In the: 5 FATED
Like some: 5 SMART
Place for: 5 TABLE
Care
Day ~ attendee: 3 TOT
Dress with: 5 PREEN PRIMP
Enter with: 6 EASEIN
for: 4 LIKE MIND REAR TEND
    5 NURSE SEETO VALUE
    6 TENDTO
Great: 5 PAINS
Handle without: 3 PAW
Managed ~ gp.: 3 HMO
Med. ~ option: 3 HMO
packages: 3 AID

prefix: **4** MEDI
Taken ~ of: **6** SEENTO
Take ~ of: **4** TEND **5** **SEETO**
 TREAT **6** HANDLE TENDTO
 8 SEEAFTER
Take ~ of business: **7** SEETOIT
Taking ~ of business: **4** ONIT
Took ~ of: **3** DID **4** KEPT
 5 SAWTO
Tooth ~ org.: **3** ADA
Word with: **3** DAY
"___ care!": **5** IDONT
Career: 4 TEAR
 athlete: **3** PRO
 Calls it a: **7** RETIRES
 Certain ~ path:
  10 MOMMYTRACK
 soldier: **5** LIFER
Carefree: 3 GAY **4** EASY **6** BLITHE
 7 CONTENT
 adventure: **4** LARK
Careful
 about spending: **6** FRUGAL
 Give ~ attention to: **4** HEED
 "___ careful!": **4** DOBE
Carefully
 Enter: **6** EASEIN EDGEIN
 Examine: **4** SIFT
 Move: **4** EASE
 Not ~ considered: **4** RASH
 Read: **6** PERUSE
 Study ~, with "over":
  4 PORE
 Watch: **3** EYE
Caregivers
 Hosp.: **3** RNS
 ___ **care in the world: 4** NOTA
Careless: 3 LAX **6** REMISS
 8 SLAPDASH SLIPSHOD
"Careless Hands"
 singer: **5** TORME
Carelessly
 Let fall: **5** DRAPE
Caress: 3 PET **5** TOUCH
Caretaker: 6 SITTER
 Baby: **4** NANA
Carey
 Comic: **4** DREW
 Singer: **6** MARIAH

Carey, Mariah
 Former label of: **3** EMI
Cargo: 4 LOAD
 carrier: **4** SEMI
 Clipper ship: **3** TEA
 Fill with: **4** **LADE**
 hauler: **3** VAN
 Load: **4** STOW
 measure: **3** TON
 Put on: **4** LADE
 Schooner: **3** ALE
 Stow: **4** LADE
 Tram: **3** ORE
Carhop
 load: **4** TRAY
Caribbean: 3 SEA
 and others: **4** SEAS
 getaway: **5** ARUBA
 group: **7** CAYMANS
  8 ANTILLES
 music: **3** SKA
 republic: **5** HAITI
 resort island: **5** ARUBA
Caribou
 kin: **3** ELK **4** DEER
Caricaturist
 Tweed: **4** NAST
 ~ Daumier: **6** HONORE
 ~ Thomas: **4** NAST
Caring: 6 HUMANE
Carioca
 city: **3** RIO
 country: **6** BRASIL
Cariou
 Actor: **3** **LEN**
Carl
 Astronomer: **5** SAGAN
 Composer: **4** ORFF
 Corporate raider: **5** ICAHN
 Ex-Viking: **5** ELLER
 or Rob: **6** REINER
 Rob, to: **3** SON
Carle
 Author: **4** ERIC
Carle, Frankie
 theme song:
  15 SUNRISESERENADE
Carlisle, Belinda
 was one: **4** GOGO

Carlo
  Author: 4 LEVI
  Sophia's: 5 PONTI
  ___ Carlo: 5 **MONTE**
Carlos
  Spanish king before Juan:
     7 ALFONSO
Carlos, Juan: 3 REY
  Daughter of: 5 ELENA
Carlos III
  Museum founded by: 5 PRADO
Carlsbad
  river: 5 PECOS
Carlson
  Former governor: 4 ARNE
Carly
  Singer: 5 SIMON
Carmaker
  9-5 ~: 4 SAAB
  French: 7 PEUGEOT
  Korean: 3 KIA
  woe: 6 RECALL
  ~ Maserati: 7 ERNESTO
  ~ Ransom Eli: 4 OLDS
Carmela
  player: 4 **EDIE**
Carmen
  Jazz singer: 5 MCRAE
  Pop singer: 4 ERIC
  Spanish actress: 5 MAURA
"Carmen": 5 OPERA
  composer: 5 BIZET
  highlight: 4 ARIA 8 HABANERA
Carmichael
  Composer: 5 HOAGY
Carmichael, Hoagy
  classic: 8 STARDUST
"Carmina Burana"
  composer: 4 ORFF
Carmine: 3 RED
Carnaby Street
  setting: 4 SOHO
Carnac: 4 SEER
Carnation: 4 PINK
  container: 4 VASE
  emanation: 5 AROMA
  site: 5 LAPEL
Carnegie: 4 SCOT
  Author: 4 DALE

  foundation: 5 STEEL
  or Mellon: 6 ANDREW
Carnegie ___: 4 DELI HALL
Carnegie Hall
  event: 7 RECITAL
Carnera
  Champ after: 4 BAER
Carnes
  Singer: 3 KIM
Carney
  Actor: 3 ART
  role: 6 NORTON
Carney, Art
  role: 8 EDNORTON
Carnival
  area: 6 MIDWAY
  attraction: 4 RIDE
  city: 3 **RIO**
  doll: 6 KEWPIE
  follower: 4 LENT
  locale: 3 RIO
  oddball: 4 GEEK
  prize: 5 PANDA
  show: 5 RAREE
  sight: 4 TENT
  stock-in-trade: 3 FUN
  treat: 7 SNOCONE
"Carnivàle"
  network: 3 HBO
Carnivore: 9 MEATEATER
  Catlike: 5 CIVET
  diet: 4 MEAT
  Doglike: 5 HYENA
  Jurassic: 8 ALLOSAUR
  Mountain: 4 PUMA
Carol: 4 NOEL SING SONG
  contraction: 3 TIS
  Cover girl: 3 ALT
  Greg Brady, to: 7 STEPSON
  Model: 3 **ALT**
  starter: 5 OCOME 6 **ADESTE**
  syllables: 3 LAS
  time: 4 YULE
Carole Bayer ___
  Songwriter: 5 SAGER
Caroled: 4 SANG
Caroler
  song: 4 NOEL
  syllable: 3 TRA

Carolina
  college: 4 ELON
  First name in ~ politics:
    5 STROM
  rail: 4 SORA
  river: 6 PEEDEE
Caroline
  group: 5 PALAU
  of TV: 4 RHEA
  Uncle of: 3 TED
"Caroline in the City"
  Thompson of: 3 LEA
Carolyn
  Nancy Drew creator: 5 KEENE
Caron
  1953 ~ film: 4 **LILI**
  Actress: 6 LESLIE
  role: 4 GIGI LILI
"Caro nome": 4 ARIA
___ carotene: 4 BETA
Carouse: 5 REVEL
"Carousel"
  choreographer: 7 DEMILLE
"___ Carousel" (Hollies hit): 3 ONA
Carousing: 7 ONATEAR
    8 ONASPREE
Carp: 5 CAVIL
  at: 3 NAG
  Japanese: 3 KOI
  Tiny: 3 NIT
Carpe ___: 4 DIEM
"Carpe diem!": 11 SEIZETHEDAY
Carpenter: 5 KAREN
  clamp: 4 VISE
  cutter: 3 SAW
  fastener: 4 TNUT
  groove: 4 **DADO**
  machine: 5 LATHE 6 PLANER
    SANDER
  mouthful: 5 NAILS
  Singer: 5 KAREN
  tool: 3 ADZ AWL SAW 4 ADZE
    RASP VISE 5 DRILL LATHE
    LEVEL PLANE 6 NAILER
    RIPSAW ROUTER SANDER
  wear: 5 APRON
  ~, at times: 6 NAILER PLANER
    SANDER 7 STAINER
    TENONER

Carpenter, John
  movie: 6 THEFOG
Carpenters
  Some: 4 ANTS
Carpentry: 5 TRADE
  fastener: 4 NAIL 5 SCREW
  groove: 4 DADO
  joint: 5 MITER
  tool: 3 ADZ AWL SAW 4 ADZE
    RASP VISE 5 DRILL LATHE
    LEVEL PLANE 6 NAILER
    RIPSAW ROUTER SANDER
Carper: 3 NAG
Carpet: 3 RUG
  calculation: 4 AREA
  cleaner: 3 VAC
  color: 3 RED
  fastener: 4 TACK
  feature: 3 NAP 4 PILE
  fiber: 5 ISTLE
  Install: 3 LAY
  Kind of: 4 SHAG
  leftover: 7 REMNANT
  Like a: 5 PILED
  meas.: 4 SQYD
  measure: 4 AREA
  quality: 4 PILE
  store purchase: 7 AREARUG
  Thick: 4 SHAG
  Wear out the: 4 PACE
Carpooling
  Lane for ~ (abbr.): 3 HOV
  path: 7 HOVLANE
Carr
  Author: 5 CALEB
  Singer: 5 VIKKI
Carreras: 5 TENOR
  piece: 4 ARIA
  Tenor: 4 JOSE
Carreras, Jose: 5 TENOR
Carrere
  Actress: 3 **TIA**
Carrey
  Comical: 3 JIM
  role: 7 VENTURA
Carrey, Jim
  1994 ~ movie: 7 THEMASK
  1997 ~ movie: 8 LIARLIAR
  role: 6 GRINCH 10 ACEVENTURA

Carriage: 4 MIEN 5 COACH
  Brit's baby: 4 PRAM
  Four-wheel: 6 LANDAU
  Fringed: 6 SURREY
  Light: 8 STANHOPE
  One-horse: 3 GIG 4 SHAY
  Open: 4 SHAY
  Russian: 6 TROIKA
  Three-horse: 6 TROIKA
  Traveling: 4 SHAY
Carrie
  Actress: 3 NYE
  Role for: 4 LEIA
  Suffragist: 4 **CATT**
"Carrie"
  star: 6 SPACEK
Carried: 5 **BORNE**
  chair: 5 SEDAN
  Get ~ away: 4 RIDE
  on: 5 PLIED **WAGED**
  out: 3 DID
Carrier: 4 CASE 5 TOTER
  Common: 3 BUS
  European: 3 SAS 8 ALITALIA
  Former U.K.: 4 BOAC
  name until 1997: 5 USAIR
  since 1948: 4 ELAL
  to Ben-Gurion: 4 ELAL
  to Copenhagen: 3 **SAS**
  to Karachi: 3 PIA
  to Kyoto: 3 JAL
  to Stockholm: 3 SAS
  to Tel Aviv: 4 ELAL
Carrion
  feeder: 5 HYENA
Carroll
  Actor: 4 LEOG
  cake phrase: 5 EATME
  creature: 5 SNARK
  heroine: 5 ALICE
  slithy thing: 4 TOVE
Carroll, Lewis: 7 PENNAME
  critter: 5 SNARK
  heroine: 5 ALICE
Carrot: 4 ROOT 6 VEGGIE
    7 TAPROOT
  cutter: 5 DICER
  Dangle a: 5 TEMPT 6 ENTICE
  on a snowman: 4 NOSE

Carrot-top: 7 REDHEAD
Carry: 4 BEAR HAUL **TOTE**
    6 SCHLEP
  All you can: 7 ARMLOAD
  along: 4 TOTE
  A movie star may ~ one: 4 AURA
  away: 5 ELATE
  It's hard for some to: 4 TUNE
  off: 6 ABDUCT
  on: 3 PLY 4 RAGE **RANT** RAVE
    WAGE 8 TRANSACT
  out: 4 OBEY 5 ACTON STAGE
    7 ENFORCE EXECUTE
  Partner of: 4 CASH
  Runners ~ it: 4 SLED
  the day: 3 WIN
  They ~ a charge: 4 IONS
  They ~ on: 7 RANTERS
  to excess: 6 OVERDO
  with effort: 3 LUG
Carry-___: 3 ONS
Carryall: 4 CASE TOTE
  Western: 9 SADDLEBAG
Carrying
  a grudge: 4 SORE
  current: 4 LIVE
  no guarantees: 4 ASIS
Carry-on: 4 TOTE 7 TOTEBAG
Cars
  British sports: 3 MGS
  Some sports: 3 GTS
  Used: 4 RODE
Cars, The
  Ocasek of: 3 RIC
Carson
  Author: 6 RACHEL
  character: 6 CARNAC
  Frontiersman: 3 KIT
  predecessor: 4 PAAR
  successor: 4 LENO
  target: 3 DDT
Carson, Johnny: 5 IOWAN
  announcer: 7 MCMAHON
Carson, Kit
  home: 4 TAOS
Carson City
  City north of: 4 RENO
  Lake near: 5 TAHOE
  state: 6 NEVADA

state (abbr.): **3** NEV
Cart: 4 HAUL
  before the ores: **4** TRAM
  Bring by ~, maybe: **7** WHEELIN
  Farm: **4** WAIN
  Kind of: **4** GOLF
  Shopping ~ path: **5** AISLE
  Sturdy: **4 DRAY**
  ___ Carta: **5** MAGNA
"Car Talk"
  network: **3** NPR
Carte
  du jour: **4** MENU
  start: **3 ALA**
  ___ carte: **3 ALA**
Carte blanche: 8 FREEREIN
  offer: **6** NAMEIT
Cartel: 4 BLOC
  acronym: **4** OPEC
  city: **4** CALI
  Oil: **4 OPEC**
Carter
  Actress: **4** NELL **5** LYNDA
  and Grant: **4** AMYS
  and Gwyn: **5** NELLS
  Country singer: **5** DEANA
  First daughter: **3** AMY
  had one: **4** TERM
  sch.: **4** USNA
  Secretary of State under:
     5 VANCE
  Singer: **4** NELL
  successor: **6** REAGAN
Carter, Howard
  discovery: **3** TUT
Carter, James ___ : 4 EARL
Carter, Jimmy
  coll.: **4** USNA
  Daughter of: **3** AMY
  Where ~ taught: **5** EMORY
Carter Center
  university: **5** EMORY
Cartesian
  conclusion: **3 IAM**
  conjunction: **4** ERGO
  line: **4** AXIS
Carthage
  founder: **4** DIDO
  hater: **4** CATO

language: **5** PUNIC
  neighbor: **5** TUNIS UTICA
"Carthage must be destroyed"
  speaker: **4** CATO
Carthaginian: 5 PUNIC
Cartier-Bresson
  Photographer: **5** HENRI
Cartland
  title: **4** DAME
Cartographer
  creation: **3** MAP
  do over: **5** REMAP
Cartographic
  collection: **5** ATLAS
  extra: **5** INSET
Carton
  contents: **4** EGGS
  count: **5** DOZEN
  Egg ~ abbr.: **3** DOZ **4** USDA
  sealer: **4** TAPE
Cartoon
  art: **3** CEL **5** ANIME
  bear: **4** YOGI
  Bilingual ~ character: **4** DORA
  bird: **10** ROADRUNNER
  Blue ~ character: **5** SMURF
  canine: **3 REN 4** ODIE **5** ASTRO
    GOOFY PLUTO SNERT
    9 SCOOBYDOO
  cat: **3** TOM **6** STIMPY
  catalog company: **4** ACME
  caveman: **3** OOP
  chihuahua: **3 REN**
  chipmunk: **4** DALE **5** ALVIN
    SIMON
  clown: **4** KOKO
  collectible: **3 CEL**
  cry: **3** EEK
  First Mickey Mouse:
    15 STEAMBOATWILLIE
  flapper: **4** BOOP
  frame: **3** CEL
  George Herriman: **8** KRAZYKAT
  Half a ~ duo: **3** REN **4** LOIS
  Japanese ~ art: **5** ANIME
  light bulb: **4** IDEA
  mirage: **5** OASIS
  Nearsighted ~ character:
    5 MAGOO

part: 5 PANEL
partner of Barbera: 5 HANNA
shriek: 4 YEOW
sidekick: 5 BORIS
skunk: 4 PEPE 5 LEPEW
squeal: 3 EEK
therapist Dr. ___: 4 KATZ
voiceman Mel: 5 BLANC

Cartoonist
Cat: 6 KLIBAN
Dogpatch: 4 CAPP
Harper's Weekly: 4 NAST
~ Addams: 4 **CHAS**
~ Browne: 3 DIK
~ Chast: 3 ROZ
~ Drake: 4 STAN
~ Drucker: 4 MORT
~ Edward: 5 SOREL
~ Gardner: 3 REA
~ Goldberg: 4 RUBE
~ Groening: 4 MATT
~ Guisewite: 5 CATHY
~ Hoff: 3 SYD
~ Johnny: 4 HART
~ Keane: 3 **BIL**
~ Kelly: 4 WALT
~ Key: 3 TED
~ Larson: 4 GARY
~ Lazarus: 4 MELL
~ Peter: 4 ARNO
~ Rall: 3 TED
~ Silverstein: 4 SHEL
~ Soglow: 4 OTTO
~ Tex: 5 AVERY
~ Thomas: 4 NAST
~ Trudeau: 5 GARRY
~ Walker: 4 MORT
~ Wilson: 5 GAHAN

Cartridge
contents: 3 INK 4 AMMO
　　5 TONER
holder: 3 PEN
Cartridges: 4 AMMO
Cartwheel
spinner: 4 AXLE
Cartwright, Ben
~, for one: 7 NEVADAN
Cartwright, Hoss
real name: 4 ERIC

Cartwright, Nancy
supplies his voice: 4 BART
Cartwrights
One of the: 3 BEN 4 ADAM HOSS
Caruso: 5 TENOR
portrayer: 5 LANZA
Singer: 6 ENRICO
Carve: 6 INCISE
with acid: 4 ETCH
Carved
gem: 4 JADE 5 CAMEO
Island with ~ heads: 6 EASTER
Letters ~ in stone: 3 RIP
out: 4 HEWN
pillar: 5 STELA
pole: 5 TOTEM
Carver
Kachina: 4 HOPI
Carver, G.W.
concern: 6 PEANUT
Carvey
Comedian: 4 **DANA**
Carving
Cameo: 6 RELIEF
Green: 4 JADE
Polynesian: 4 TIKI
Cary
Actor: 5 ELWES
Ex of: 4 DYAN
Casa
cookware: 4 OLLA
division: 4 SALA
Lady of la: 6 SENORA
material: 5 ADOBE
title: 5 SENOR
Casa ___: 4 LOMA
Casaba: 5 MELON
Casablanca
Capital near: 5 RABAT
City near: 3 FEZ
"Casablanca"
actor: 5 LORRE RAINS
actor Wilson: 6 DOOLEY
Bergman role in: 4 LUND
café: 5 RICKS
café owner: 4 RICK
heroine: 4 ILSA
Ingrid role in: 4 **ILSA**
Lorre role in: 6 UGARTE

pianist: **3** SAM
producer Hal: **6** WALLIS
Rick's love in: **4 ILSA**
Casals: 5 PABLO
instrument: **5** CELLO
Casanova: 4 RAKE ROUE
9 LADIESMAN
Casbah
headgear: **3** FEZ
Cascade Range
peak: **6** SHASTA
Cascades
mount: **4** HOOD
peak: **6** MTHOOD SHASTA
7 RAINIER
Case: 6 SHEATH **8** INSTANCE
Dairy ~ item: **4** OLEO
Decorative: **4 ETUI**
for a lawyer: **7** ATTACHE
Hopeless: **5 GONER**
In: **4** LEST
In any: **4** EVER **7** ATLEAST
In that: **4** IFSO THEN
Just in: **4** LEST
Kind of: **4** TEST **6** CLOSET
DATIVE **7** ATTACHE
Knickknack: **7** ETAGERE
Latin: **6** DATIVE
Make a: **5** ARGUE PLEAD
maker: **4** SUER
Name in a famous: **3** ROE **4** DRED
Needle: **4 ETUI**
Nut: **3** BUR **5** CRANK
Seed: **4** ARIL
Sewing: **4 ETUI**
Should that be the: **4** IFSO
Small: **4** ETUI
Stated one's: **4** PLED
State one's: **5** OPINE
Try a: **4** HEAR
Vanity: **7** EGOTRIP
worker: **5** JUROR **6** LAWYER
worker org.: **3** ABA
workers (abbr.): **3** DAS **5** ATTYS
___ case-by-case basis: **3** ONA
Casement: 4 SASH
Cases
Head: **6** CRANIA
Some ER: **3 ODS**

Spore: **4** ASCI
Vanity: **4** EGOS
Casey
Deejay: **5** KASEM
Storied: **5** JONES
Cash: 5 ASSET MOOLA
24-hr. ~ source: **3** ATM
Boy in a ~ tune: **3** SUE
cache: **3** ATM **4** TILL
closing: **3** IER
dispenser, for short: **3** ATM
drawer: **4** TILL
in: **6** REDEEM
Large amount of: **3** WAD **4** PILE
of the courts: **3** PAT
on hand: **4** ANTE
Prison in a ~ tune: **6** FOLSOM
source: **3** ATM
Strapped for: **5** SHORT
substitute: **3** IOU
suffix: **3 IER**
Casher
Check: **5** PAYEE
Cashew: 3 NUT **4** TREE
kin: **5** SUMAC
Cashier: 4 FIRE
stack: **4** ONES
Cashless
deal: **4** SWAP **5** TRADE
trade: **6** BARTER
Cash lost in 'em:
12 SLOTMACHINES
Cashmere: 4 WOOL
brand: **3** TSE
Cash register: 4 TILL
calculation: **3** TAX
key: **6** NOSALE
output: **4** TAPE
stack: **4** ONES TENS
Casing: 4 SKIN
Prickly: **3** BUR
Casino
action: **4** BETS
area: **3** PIT
Atlantic City ~, with "The": **3** TAJ
city: **4 RENO**
cube: **3** DIE
cubes: **4** DICE
Does ~ work: **5** DEALS

employee: 6 DEALER
figures: 4 ODDS
game: 4 **FARO** KENO 5 CRAPS
   POKER
gear: 5 RAKES
gratuity: 4 TOKE
lure: 5 SLOTS
machine: 4 SLOT
opening: 4 SLOT
request: 5 HITME
supervisor: 7 PITBOSS
three: 4 TREY
Throw in a: 4 ROLL
Vegas ~, with "The": 5 DUNES
"Casino"
costar: 5 PESCI
Cask
contents: 3 ALE
dregs: 4 LEES
Large: 3 TUN VAT
Put another hole in a: 5 RETAP
Unfilled part of a: 6 ULLAGE
Wine: 3 TUN
wood: 3 OAK
"Cask of Amontillado, The"
author: 3 POE
Casks
Like some: 5 OAKEN
Caspary
Author: 4 VERA
novel: 5 LAURA
Casper: 5 GHOST
Caspian: 3 SEA
Capital on the: 4 BAKU
Country on the: 4 IRAN
feeder: 4 **URAL**
neighbor: 4 ARAL
River to the: 4 **URAL**
Sea east of the: 4 **ARAL**
Cass: 4 MAMA
Mama: 6 ELLIOT
Cassandra: 4 SEER 6 ORACLE
alter ego: 5 ELVIRA
Brother of: 7 TROILUS
Father of: 5 PRIAM
Cassatt
Painter: 4 MARY
Cassava
product: 7 TAPIOCA

Casserole
Kind of: 5 DIVAN
staple: 4 TUNA
Cassette: 4 TAPE
contents: 5 VIDEO
half: 5 SIDEA SIDEB
Make a new: 6 RETAPE
Cassidy, Hopalong
portrayer: 4 **BOYD**
Cassin
Peace Nobelist: 4 RENE
Cassini
Designer: 4 **OLEG**
Cassino
cash: 4 LIRA LIRE
Cassio
rival: 4 IAGO
Cassis
aperitif: 3 KIR
Cassiterite: 6 TINORE
Cassius
Loser to: 5 SONNY
Cassowary
kin: 3 **EMU** 4 RHEA
Cast: 3 HUE 4 HURL MIEN SENT
   SHED TOSS 5 FLING
   FLUNG HEAVE SLING
   SLUNG THREW TINGE
   6 ACTORS HURLED
   THROWN
a ballot: 4 VOTE
aspersions on: 4 SLUR
Be a ~ member of: 5 ACTIN
Be in a: 3 ACT
forth: 4 EMIT 6 SPEWED
Head the ~ of: 6 STARIN
iron: 5 ALLOY
It may be: 3 DIE 4 IRON ROLE
   5 SPELL
Join the ~ of: 5 ACTIN
leader: 4 TELE
member: 5 **ACTOR** 6 PLAYER
off: 4 SHED
off from the body: 5 EGEST
of mind: 4 BENT
One in a: 5 ACTOR
out: 4 SPEW 5 EGEST EXILE
   6 BANISH 7 EGESTED
Something to: 6 BALLOT

supporter: **5** SLING
They're: **6** ACTORS
wearer problem: **4** ITCH

Castaway
call: **3** SOS
creation: **4** RAFT
home: **4** ISLE **5** ISLET
Literary: **6** CRUSOE

"Cast Away"
setting: **4** ISLE

Caste
member: **3** ANT **5** HINDU

Castel Gandolfo
resident: **4** POPE

Castel Nuovo
site: **6** NAPLES

Caster
Ballot: **5** VOTER

Castile
Hero of: **5** ELCID

Castilian
hero: **5** ELCID
kinsmen: **4** TIOS

Casting
assignment: **4** ROLE
Do some: **4** FISH
requirement: **3** ROD **4** REEL

Castle: **4** ROOK
Cuban: **5** MORRO
defense: **4** __MOAT__
feature: **4** KEEP **5** TOWER
    6 TURRET
material: **4** SAND
mistress: **10** CHATELAINE
Movable: **4** ROOK
of dance: **5** __IRENE__
or Cara: **5** IRENE
protector: **4** MOAT
Queenside ~, in notation: **3** OOO
with lots of steps: **5** IRENE
___ Castle: **5** MORRO

"Castle, The"
author: **5** KAFKA

Cast-of-thousands
film: **4** EPIC

Castor
Mother of: **4** __LEDA__
or Olive: **3** OYL
or Pollux: **4** STAR TWIN

Castro
country: **4** CUBA
Cuba, to: **4** ISLA
of Cuba: **5** FIDEL
predecessor: **7** BATISTA

Casual
attire: **5** DENIM JEANS
day (abbr.): **3** FRI
eatery: **6** BISTRO
fabric: **5** DENIM
pants: **5** JEANS
shirt: **3** TEE **4** POLO
talk: **4** CHAT
top: **3** TEE **6** TSHIRT
wear: **5** JEANS LEVIS **6** CHINOS
    DENIMS

Casually
Turns ~, with "through":
    5 LEAFS

Casualty
Euro: **5** FRANC
Hamelin: **3** RAT
Titanic: **5** ASTOR

Cat: **3** __PET__
Alice's: **5** DINAH
Alley ~, perhaps: **5** STRAY
Bell the: **4** DARE
Big: **4** LION LYNX PUMA
Black: **7** PANTHER
Black ~, maybe: **4** OMEN
breed: **7** SIAMESE
call: **3** MEW **4** __MEOW__
Cartoon: **3** TOM
cartoonist: **6** KLIBAN
catcher: **4** CLAW
Colorful: **6** CALICO
Cool: **6** DADDYO
Curly-haired: **3** REX
Dogs on a: **4** PAWS
Drink like a: **3** LAP **5** LAPUP
Endangered: **4** PUMA **6** OCELOT
Fast: **7** CHEETAH
Fat: **5** MOGUL NABOB
    9 MONEYBAGS
feet: **4** PAWS
food flavoring: **4** TUNA
hangout: **5** ALLEY
Kind of: **3** HEP **4** MANX **5** ALLEY
    7 SIAMESE

Leopardlike: **6** OCELOT
Let the ~ out of the bag: **4** BLAB TOLD
Like a ~ burglar: **8** STEALTHY
Like an alley: **5** FERAL
Long-haired: **6** ANGORA
Made ~ calls: **5** MEWED
Male: **3** GIB TOM
Mountain ~ perch: **5** ARETE
of ads: **6** MORRIS
pajamas: **3** FUR
preceder: **3** SNO **4** ONEO
prey: **3** RAT
scanner: **3** VET
Spotted: **5** CIVET **6** CALICO OCELOT
Tailless: **4** **MANX**
that earns its keep: **6** MOUSER
weapon: **4** CLAW
Wild: **4** PUMA
with ear tufts: **4** LYNX
~, in Spanish: **4** GATO
CAT
scan kin: **3** MRI
CAT ___: **4** SCAN
Catalan
artist: **4** MIRO
Catalina: **4** ISLE **6** ISLAND
(abbr.): **3** ISL
Catalog: **4** LIST **6** ASSORT
abbr.: **4** ETAL
Card ~ entry: **5** TITLE
Kind of: **9** MAILORDER
Old ~ maker: **5** SEARS
Catalogs
Big name in: **5** JCREW **6** LLBEAN **7** SPIEGEL
Catalonia
cat: **4** GATO
Catalyst
Biochemical: **6** ENZYME
Catamaran
mover: **4** SAIL
Catamount: **4** PUMA
"Cat and the Curmudgeon, The"
author: **5** AMORY
Catania
View from: **4** **ETNA**
Catapult: **4** HURL

Medieval: **6** ONAGER
Catastrophe
prefix: **3** ECO
Word before: **4** NEAR
"Cat Ballou"
actor Marvin: **3** LEE
Catbird
seat: **4** NEST TREE **5** PERCH ROOST
Catboat
has one: **4** MAST
Catcall: **3** BOO **4** HISS HOOT JEER
Catch: **3** BAG GET NAB NET RUB SEE **4** HEAR HOOK LAND NAIL ROPE SNAG **5** CLASP LASSO SNARE **6** ENMESH REELIN **7** **ENSNARE**
a break: **5** SLEEP
a glimpse of: **4** ESPY SPOT
Atlantic: **3** COD
Brook: **5** TROUT
but good: **4** NAIL
Cape Cod: **4** TUNA
Coastal: **4** SOLE
Cop's: **4** PERP
forty winks: **3** NAP
Hard to: **4** EELY
in a net: **6** ENMESH
in a sting: **6** ENTRAP
in the act: **3** NAB
Marine: **7** SEABASS
New England: **3** COD **5** SCROD
on: **3** SEE **5** LEARN SEEIT
one's breath: **4** REST
on to: **3** GET **5** GRASP
phrase: **6** IGOTIT SLOGAN
red-handed: **3** NAB **4** NAIL
sight of: **4** **ESPY** SPOT **6** DESCRY
some extra Z's: **7** SLEEPIN
some rays: **3** SUN TAN **4** BASK **6** SUNTAN
some z's: **3** NAP **4** DOZE **5** SLEEP **6** SNOOZE
up with: **8** OVERTAKE
What nodders: **4** ZEES
"Catch!": **4** HERE
Catch ___: **4** ONTO
Catch-22: **4** SNAG **7** DILEMMA

"Catch-22"
  actor: 5 ARKIN
  Minderbinder of: 4 MILO
  pilot: 3 ORR
"Catch a Falling Star"
  singer: 4 COMO
Catchall
  abbr.: 3 **ETC** 4 ETAL MISC
  category: 5 OTHER 6 OTHERS
    7 POTLUCK
Catcher: 3 NET 5 SNARE
  Animal: 4 TRAP
  Catcher's: 4 MITT
  Circus: 3 NET
  communication: 4 SIGN
  Cow: 5 LASSO REATA RIATA
    6 LARIAT
  Drip: 3 BIB
  Fly: 3 WEB 4 MITT
  in the Rhine: 5 SEINE
  in the wry: 5 BERRA
  locale: 3 RYE
  Mouse: 3 OWL 4 TRAP
  Pass: 3 END
  position: 5 SQUAT 6 CROUCH
  Quotable: 5 BERRA
  Read the sign of a: 6 PEERIN
  Splash: 5 APRON
  Wave: 7 ANTENNA
  ~ Berra: 4 YOGI
  ~ Tony: 4 PENA
"Catcher in the ___, The": 3 RYE
"Catcher in the Rye, The"
  author: 8 SALINGER
Catching
  It may be: 4 TRAP
Catchphrase: 6 SLOGAN
  Austin Powers: 8 OHBEHAVE
  Chef: 3 ALA
  Skelton: 7 IDOODIT
Catchword: 6 SLOGAN
  1960s ~: 5 PEACE
  Belafonte: 4 DAYO
  Dieter's: 4 LITE 5 LOFAT
    6 LOWFAT NONFAT
  Emeril: 3 BAM
  Jack Benny: 4 WELL
  Marv Albert: 3 YES
  Procrastinator's: 6 MANANA

"Catch you later!": 3 BYE
"Categorical imperative"
  philosopher: 4 KANT
Categorically
  State: 4 AVER 6 ASSERT
Categorize: 4 SORT 5 LABEL
  6 ASSORT
Category: 4 TYPE 5 CLASS
  GENRE
  Artistic: 5 GENRE
  Blood: 4 TYPE
  Book: 5 HOWTO
  Catchall: 5 OTHER 6 OTHERS
    7 POTLUCK
  Clothing: 4 MENS
  Fencing: 4 EPEE
  Figure skating: 5 PAIRS
  Grammy: 3 POP **RAP** 4 FOLK
    ROCK 5 LATIN RANDB
    6 GOSPEL
  Literary: 5 GENRE
  Music: 4 SOUL
  Nobel: 4 ECON 5 PEACE
  Poll: 9 UNDECIDED
  Pulitzer: 5 **DRAMA**
  Skating: 5 PAIRS
  Skiing: 6 ALPINE
  SSS: 4 ONEA
  Ticket: 5 ADULT
  Trivia: 5 SPORTS
  Twenty Questions: 6 ANIMAL
    7 MINERAL
Cater
  basely: 6 PANDER
Catered
  event: 6 AFFAIR
Caterer
  carrier: 4 TRAY
  coffeepot: 3 URN
  heater: 6 STERNO
  job: 5 EVENT
Caterpillar: 5 LARVA
  case: 6 COCOON
  construction: 4 TENT
  hairs: 5 SETAE
  product: 7 TRACTOR
  rival: 5 DEERE
  Tent: 5 EGGER
  Vehicle with ~ treads: 6 SNOCAT

Caterwaul: 4 HOOT HOWL YOWL
Cathartic
herb: **5** SENNA
Cathay
visitor: **4** POLO
Cathedral
area: **4 APSE**
center: **4** NAVE
English ~ city: **3** ELY **6** EXETER
French ~ city: **5** REIMS
6 AMIENS
topper: **5** SPIRE
Tuscany ~ city: **5** SIENA
Cather
Author: **5** WILLA
title heroine: **7** ANTONIA
Catherine
Henry VIII's: **4** PARR
Home of: **6** ARAGON
Husband of: **5** HENRY
Catherine of ___: 6 ARAGON
Catherine the Great: 7 EMPRESS
TSARINA
Cathode
counterpoint: **5** ANODE
Catholic
devotion: **6** NOVENA
Eastern: **5** UNIAT
prayer: **8** AVEMARIA
~ Bible version: **5** DOUAY
"Cat ___ Hot Tin Roof": 3 ONA
Catkin
producer: **5 ALDER**
Catlike: 6 AGILE **6** FELINE
carnivore: **5** CIVET
Cat-mouse
connector: **3** AND
Catnap: 4 DOZE
Cat Nation
members: **5** ERIES
Cato: 5 ROMAN
Info: Latin cue
To be, to: **4** ESSE
"Cat on a Hot Tin Roof"
actor Burl: **4** IVES
Cat-o'-nine-tails
blow: **4** LASH
Use a: **4** FLOG
"Cat on ___ Tin Roof": 4 AHOT

Cats
Copy: **3** MEW **4** MEOW PURR
Like some: **3** HEP
Rain ~ and dogs: **4** POUR
Striped: **7** TABBIES
"Cats"
director Trevor: **4** NUNN
monogram: **3** TSE
poet: **5** ELIOT
Cat's ___: 7 PAJAMAS
Catskills
resort area: **11** BORSCHTBELT
Cat's-paw: 3 SAP **4** DUPE TOOL
6 STOOGE
Catsup
catcher: **3** TIE
Cattail: 4 REED
setting: **5** MARSH
Cattails
Full of: **5** REEDY
Cat-tails
connector: **5** ONINE
Cattle: 4 KINE **5** STEER
African ~ pen: **5** KRAAL
Black ~ breed: **5 ANGUS**
call: **3** LOW **MOO**
catcher: **5** LASSO REATA RIATA
catching weapon: **4** BOLA
encourager: **4** PROD
English ~ breed: **5** DEVON
genus: **3** BOS
group: **4** HERD
identifier: **5** BRAND
Raised: **4** BRED
Scottish ~ breed: **5** ANGUS
Steal: **6** RUSTLE
unit: **4** HEAD
Work with: **6** DEHORN
Cattleman
concern: **4** BEEF
Catty
remark: **3** MEW **4 MEOW**
Catullus
composition: **3** ODE
Catwoman
portrayer Kitt: **6** EARTHA
~, to Batman: **3** FOE
Caucasus
native: **5** OSSET

Caucus
  selection: 8 DELEGATE
  state: 4 IOWA
Caught: 3 GOT 4 SEEN 5 ROPED
      6 NAILED NETTED
      SNARED 7 INATRAP
      SNAGGED 8 ENSNARED
  a calf: 5 ROPED
  a few winks: 5 SLEPT
  Fish ~ in a pot: 3 EEL
  Fish ~ in winter: 4 SHAD
  He ~ a perfect game:
    9 YOGIBERRA
  He ~ his adversary's ear:
    5 TYSON
  in a trap: 6 SNARED
  in the act: 4 **SEEN**
  One ~ off base: 4 AWOL
  on video: 5 TAPED
  on, with "up": 5 WISED
  sight of: 5 SPIED 6 ESPIED
  some rays: 6 SUNNED TANNED
  some Z's: 5 **SLEPT**
  They're ~ at the beach: 4 RAYS
  up in a cliffhanger: 6 ONEDGE
  Where some fish are: 6 EELERY
Caught in ___: 4 ALIE
"Caught you!": 3 AHA
Cauldron
  1996 Olympic ~ lighter: 3 ALI
  stirrer: 3 HAG
Caulfield
  creator: 8 SALINGER
Cauliflower
  cousin: 8 BROCCOLI
Caulk: 4 SEAL 7 SEALANT
Caulking
  material: 5 OAKUM PUTTY
Cause: 4 SAKE 7 CRUSADE
  '70s–'80s ~: 3 ERA
  a major disturbance in:
    7 UPHEAVE
  anguish to: 6 TEARAT
  Bygone polit.: 3 ERA
  damage to: 3 MAR
  for a blessing: 5 ACHOO
    6 SNEEZE
  for alarm: 4 FIRE
  for an apology: 4 BUMP

  for a pause: 5 COMMA
  for cramming: 4 EXAM
  for overtime: 3 TIE
  Interruption: 5 PAGER
  It can ~ a blowup: 3 TNT
  Losing: 4 DIET
  Lost: 5 GONER
  NOW: 3 ERA
  of burnout: 6 STRESS
  of inflation: 3 AIR
  of ruin: 4 BANE
  Overtime: 3 TIE
  They ~ breakdowns: 7 ENZYMES
  to attack: 5 SETAT SETON
  to err: 6 TRIPUP
  to expand: 6 DILATE
  to laugh: 5 AMUSE
  to see red: 6 ENRAGE
  to swell: 5 BLOAT
  to vanish: 6 DISPEL
  to yawn: 4 BORE
  trouble: 15 CREATEANUISANCE
  Underlying: 4 ROOT
Cause ___: 7 CELEBRE
Caused: 5 LEDTO 7 LEDUPTO
  by: 5 DUETO
  to go: 6 BETOOK
Causing
  goose bumps: 5 EERIE 6 CREEPY
  laughter: 7 COMICAL
Caustic: 4 TART 5 ACRID
    7 EROSIVE
  chemical: 3 **LYE**
  Comparatively: 6 TARTER
  stuff: 3 **LYE**
  wit: 7 SARCASM
Cauterize: 4 SEAR
Cauthen
  Jockey: 5 STEVE
Caution: 4 WARN
  Road: 3 **SLO** 4 SLOW
  Sale: 4 ASIS
Cautionary
  word: 4 DONT
Cautious: 4 WARY
Cautiously
  Enter: 6 EASEIN EDGEIN
  Move: 6 TIPTOE
  ___ cava: 4 **VENA**

Cavaliers
NCAA: 3 UVA
Cavalry
British ~ sword: 5 SABRE
command: 6 CHARGE
member: 6 LANCER
unit: 5 TROOP
weapon: 5 LANCE **SABER**
Cavalryman
European ~ sight: 6 HUSSAR
in an oater: 5 EXTRA
Cavaradossi
Lover of: 5 TOSCA
Cave: 3 DEN 4 LAIR 5 ANTRE
6 GROTTO RELENT
Alley in a: 3 OOP
art: 5 MURAL
dweller: 3 BAT 5 TROLL
effect: 4 ECHO
Explore a: 7 SPELUNK
Small: 6 GROTTO
Caveat
Issue a ~ to: 4 WARN
Sale: 4 **ASIS**
Caveat ___: 6 EMPTOR
Caveman: 9 SPELUNKER
Comics: 3 OOP 8 ALLEYOOP
discovery: 4 FIRE
weapon: 4 CLUB
~ Alley: 3 OOP
Cavern: 6 GROTTO
comeback: 4 ECHO
~, in poetry: 4 GROT 5 ANTRE
Caviar: 3 **ROE** 4 EGGS
Roman: 3 OVA
source: 6 BELUGA 8 STURGEON
They may be served with: 5 BLINI
variety: 7 SHADROE
Caving
Go: 7 SPELUNK
Cavities: 6 FOSSAE
Bone: 5 ANTRA
Cavity: 4 HOLE
Deep: 5 ABYSM
filler: 5 GROUT
filler (abbr.): 3 DDS
Kind of: 5 NASAL
Skull: 5 SINUS
Cavort: 4 ROMP 6 PRANCE

Cavs
org.: 3 NBA
Cavy
Spotted: 4 PACA
Cay: 4 ISLE 5 ISLET
___ Cayes, Haiti: 3 LES
Cayuga
relative: 6 SENECA
Cayuga Lake
City on: 6 ITHACA
Cayuse
controller: 4 REIN
CB: 5 RADIO
Emergency ~ channel: 4 NINE
CBC
Onetime ~ newsman:
6 TREBEK
CBer
relative: 3 HAM
sign-off: 4 OVER
CBS
anchor Dan: 6 RATHER
eye: 4 LOGO
forensic drama: 3 CSI
Former ~ anchor: 4 MUDD
6 RATHER
Former ~ chairman Laurence:
5 TISCH
founder: 5 PALEY
hit series: 3 CSI
logo: 3 **EYE**
Part of: 3 **SYS** 4 SYST
Rather of: 3 DAN
CD: 4 ACCT
acronym: 5 ASCAP
earnings: 3 INT
follower: 3 ROM
Make a: 4 BURN
Part of: 4 DISC
Pitch a: 4 TOUR
player part: 5 LASER
players: 3 DJS
predecessors: 3 **LPS**
Promo: 4 DEMO
selection: 4 SONG 5 TRACK
source: 5 SANDL
CD-___: 3 **ROM**
Cease: 3 END 4 HALT STOP
6 DESIST

"Cease!"
at sea: 5 AVAST
Cease-fire: 5 TRUCE
Ceaselessly: 5 NOEND ONEND
7 ONANDON
Cecil
Cartoon pal of: 5 BEANY
Cecil B.
Agnes, to: 5 NIECE
Cedar Rapids
college: 3 COE
Ceded: 6 GAVEUP
Ceiling: 3 CAP LID 5 LIMIT
fixture: 3 FAN
Sistine ~ figure: 4 ADAM
support: 5 JOIST
Cel
character: 4 TOON
mates: 5 TOONS
Celeb: 4 NAME STAR
life story: 3 BIO
Soccer: 4 PELE
Celebrant
June: 4 GRAD
Celebrate: 5 REVEL
15 PAINTTHETOWNRED
Time to: 3 EVE
Celebrated: 4 STAR 5 FAMED
FETED 7 EMINENT
STORIED
Celebration: 4 FEST FETE GALA
5 PARTY REVEL 6 FIESTA
Asian: 3 TET
Day of: 4 FETE
Environmentalist: 8 EARTHDAY
Passover: 5 SEDER
Sunday: 4 MASS
Thanksgiving: 5 FEAST
times: 4 EVES
Celebratory
dance: 4 HORA
poem: 3 ODE
___ célèbre: 5 CAUSE
Celebrex
maker: 6 SEARLE
Celebrity: 4 FAME LION NAME
5 ECLAT 6 RENOWN
7 STARDOM 9 SUPERSTAR
A ~ may have one: 4 AURA

concern: 5 IMAGE
Treat as a: 7 LIONIZE
Celerity: 5 HASTE SPEED
With: 5 APACE
Celery
piece: 5 STALK
Celeste
Husband of: 5 BABAR
Oscar winner: 4 HOLM
Celestial
altar: 3 ARA
array: 4 ORBS
bear: 4 URSA
being: 6 SERAPH
hunter: 5 ORION
ice ball: 5 COMET
It lies on the ~ equator: 5 ORION
messenger: 5 ANGEL
radio source: 6 PULSAR
ram: 5 ARIES
sphere: 3 ORB
Celestial Seasonings
product: 3 TEA
Celine
Singer: 4 DION
Cell
Brain: 6 NEURON
centers: 6 NUCLEI
component: 3 DNA RNA
division: 7 MITOSIS
Egg: 4 OVUM
Germ: 5 SPORE
Immature egg: 6 OOCYTE
Kind of: 4 GERM STEM
5 SOLAR
messenger: 3 RNA
Nerve: 6 NEURON
Nerve ~ part: 4 AXON
Reproductive: 5 OVULE
6 GAMETE
Retina: 3 ROD
Sea: 4 BRIG
Stuff in a: 3 RNA
terminal: 5 ANODE
Cellar
door device: 4 HASP
dweller's place: 4 LAST
It's in the: 9 TABLESALT
Like many a: 4 DAMP DANK

Sit in the: **3** AGE
stock: **4** WINE
Word before: **5** STORM
Cellist
direction: **4** ARCO
French-born: **6** YOYOMA
purchase: **5** ROSIN
~ Casals: **5** PABLO
~ Ma: **4** YOYO
~ Starker: **5** JANOS
Cello
feature: **5** FHOLE
kin: **4** VIOL **5** VIOLA
Ma with a: **4** YOYO
Cellophane: 4 WRAP
Cell phone
button: **4** SEND
kin: **5** PAGER
lack: **4** CORD
maker: **5** NOKIA
Pioneer ~ co.: **3** GTE
Cells
Dissolve: **4** LYSE
Egg: **3** OVA
Element in photoelectric:
    6 CESIUM
Reproductive: **3** OVA
Cellular
prefix: **3** UNI **5** MULTI
stuff: **3** RNA
Cellular ___: 3 ONE **5** PHONE
Celluloid
canine: **4** ASTA
Cellulose
fiber brand: **5** ARNEL
Celsius: 5 SWEDE
freezing point: **4** ZERO
Thermometer developer:
    6 ANDERS
Celt: 4 GAEL
Ancient: **5** DRUID
Celtic
group: **4** CLAN
language: **4** **_ERSE_** **5** IRISH
    6 GAELIC
priest of old: **5** DRUID
sea god: **3** LER
tongue: **4** ERSE
~ Bird: **5** LARRY

Celtics
coach, 1995–97: **6** MLCARR
Hall of Famer: **7** KCJONES
M.L. of the: **4** CARR
star White: **4** JOJO
"Celts, The"
singer: **4** ENYA
Cement: 4 GLUE **5** PASTE
Like the "c" in: **4** SOFT
Like wet: **5** UNSET
Cemetery
sights: **4** URNS
Cen.
parts: **3** YRS
Cenozoic: 3 **_ERA_**
Censor: 5 BLEEP
concern: **4** OATH SMUT
Roman: **4** CATO
"Censor, The": 4 CATO
Censoring
device: **5** VCHIP
Censorship
fighting gp.: **4** ACLU
Censure: 4 DAMN **7** DEPLORE
    REPROVE
Census
data: **4** AGES
info: **3** AGE SEX **4** RACE
Cent: 5 PENNY
Word on a: **4** UNUM
Cent.
parts: **3** YRS
Centaur
~, in part: **5** HORSE
Centaurs
Home of the: **6** PELION
Centavos
100 ~: **4** PESO
Centennial
prefix: **3** TER
Center: 3 HUB **4** CORE SNAP
    5 FOCUS HEART **_MIDST_**
At the ~ of: **4** AMID
Bagel: **4** HOLE
Basilica: **4** NAVE
Church: **4** NAVE
Combat: **5** ARENA
County: **4** SEAT
Cyclone: **3** EYE

Dead: 4 TOMB
Diamond: 5 MOUND
Fitness: 3 **SPA**
Florida citrus: 5 OCALA
Football: 3 AIR
front: 3 EPI
Fruit: 3 PIT 4 CORE
Game: 3 TAC
Health: 3 SPA
Heat ~, once: 5 ONEAL
Hurricane: 3 EYE
In the ~ of: 4 **AMID**
It may be left of: 3 EPI
Kind of: 3 REC 4 ARTS 5 REHAB
    6 CRISIS TRAUMA
Lincoln: 3 CEE
Lines from the: 5 RADII
Military: 4 BASE
Nearest the: 7 MIDMOST
Near the: 3 MID
Nut: 4 MEAT
of a ball: 3 DEB 5 BELLE
of activity: 3 HUB 4 HIVE
    5 LOCUS
of a roast: 7 HONOREE
of Florida: 5 EPCOT
of government: 4 SEAT
of Miami, once: 4 SHAQ 5 ONEAL
of power: 5 LOCUS
of rotation: 4 AXIS
opening: 3 EPI
or end: 7 ATHLETE
prefix: 3 **EPI**
Raisin: 6 FRESNO
Remove the ~ of: 4 CORE
Self: 3 EGO
Shopping: 4 MALL MART
    5 PLAZA
Simile: 3 **ASA** 4 ASAN
Sports: 5 ARENA
starter: 3 EPI
Storm: 3 EYE
Taste: 6 PALATE
Third from: 3 END
Trade: 4 MART
Wheel: 3 HUB
X or O: 3 TAC
___ center: 3 REC
___ Center: 5 EPCOT

Centerpiece
    Still-life: 4 VASE
    Wedding reception: 4 CAKE
Centers
    Cell: 6 NUCLEI
    of activity: 4 **LOCI**
    of attention: 4 FOCI
    of power: 4 LOCI
    Trauma: 3 ERS
Centesimi
    100 ~: 4 LIRA 7 ONELIRA
Centesimos
    100 ~: 4 PESO
Centimes
    Five or ten ~, once: 3 SOU
Centimeter-gram-second
    unit: 3 ERG 4 DYNE
Centimeters
    2.54 ~: 4 INCH
Centimos
    100 ~: 6 PESETA
Centipede
    maker: 5 ATARI
Central: 3 MID 4 MAIN 5 FOCAL
    INNER NODAL
    church area: 4 NAVE
    computer: 4 HOST 6 SERVER
    courtyards: 5 ATRIA
    feature: 4 CRUX
    leaf vein: 6 MIDRIB
    line: 4 AXIS
    part: 4 CORE PITH YOLK
        5 MIDST
    parts: 6 NUCLEI
    point: 4 CRUX GIST NODE
        5 HEART MIDST NAVEL
        NEXUS 6 THESIS
    points: 4 FOCI
    spots: 4 LOCI
    street: 4 MAIN
    truth: 3 TAO
Central American
    ~ Indian: 4 MAYA
Central Florida
    city: 5 OCALA
Central New York
    city: 5 UTICA
Central Pennsylvania
    city: 7 ALTOONA

___ **Centre:** 5 EATON
Centric
  prefix: 4 AFRO ENDO EURO
    5 ETHNO HELIO
Centrifuge
  stresses: 7 GFORCES
Centripetally: 7 INWARDS
Centrum
  rival: 7 ONEADAY
Cents
  100 ~: 4 EURO RAND 5 RUPEE
  Make: 4 MINT
  Put in one's two: 4 ANTE
    5 OPINE
Centuries
  and centuries: 3 EON
Century
  1st ~ emperor: 4 NERO
  4th ~ invader: 4 GOTH
  5th ~ pope: 5 STLEO
  10th ~ emperor: 5 OTTOI
  11th ~ hero: 5 ELCID
  13th ~ invader: 5 TATAR
  16th ~ council site: 5 TRENT
  16th ~ painter: 5 PAOLO
  16th ~ poet: 5 TASSO
  divs.: 3 YRS
  Like some 20th ~ music:
    6 ATONAL
  One of a 15th ~ trio: 4 NINA
  plant: 4 ALOE 5 AGAVE
Century 21
  rival: 3 ERA
CEO: 3 VIP 4 PRES
  aide: 4 ASST
  degree: 3 MBA
  Former Disney: 6 EISNER
  Part of: 4 EXEC
  perk: 3 JET
  "stat!": 4 ASAP
Ceramic
  square: 4 TILE
Ceramics: 5 CRAFT
  oven: 4 KILN
Cereal: 5 GRAIN
  brand: 3 KIX 4 CHEX 5 TOTAL
    10 FROOTLOOPS
  choice: 4 BRAN 6 FLAKES
  Cooked: 6 FARINA

  fruit: 6 BANANA RAISIN
  fungus: 5 ERGOT
  grain: 3 **OAT** RYE 4 RICE
    6 BARLEY
  grass: 3 RYE
  ingredient: 4 BRAN
  Kids': 4 TRIX 10 CAPNCRUNCH
  killer: 5 ERGOT
  Like some: 4 OATY 5 OATEN
  Quaker: 3 OHS
  serving: 4 BOWL
  sound: 4 SNAP
  utensil: 5 SPOON
Cereal box
  stat.: 3 RDA 5 NETWT
  tiger: 4 TONY
Cerebellum
  section: 4 LOBE
Cerebral
  output: 4 IDEA
Cerebral ___ : 6 CORTEX
Ceremonial
  act: 4 RITE
  dinner: 5 SEDER
  gown: 4 TOGA
  procession: 6 PARADE
  splendor: 4 POMP
  staff: 4 MACE
Ceremony: 4 POMP **RITE**
    6 RITUAL
  Skip the: 5 ELOPE
  Solemn: 4 RITE
___ **ceremony:** 7 STOODON
Ceres: 8 ASTEROID
    9 PLANETOID
  birthplace: 4 ENNA
Cereus
  and others: 5 CACTI
Cerf
  Publisher: 7 BENNETT
  specialty: 3 PUN
Cerium: 9 RAREEARTH
Cert.
  Birth: 5 IDENT
Certain: 4 SURE
  Far from: 4 IFFY
  Made: 7 SAWTOIT
  Make: 6 ASSURE ENSURE
    INSURE

That ~ something: 4 AURA
    6 ALLURE
To a ~ extent: 6 INPART
Was ~ of: 4 KNEW
"Certainly!": 3 YES 4 SURE
    5 NATCH
Certainty: 5 CINCH
    State with: 4 AVER
Certifiable: 3 MAD 6 INSANE
Certificate: 5 SCRIP
    Ownership: 4 DEED 5 TITLE
    Village Voice: 4 OBIE
Certified
    It may be: 4 MAIL
Certify: 6 **ATTEST** 8 ACCREDIT
    ATTESTTO
    ~, in a way: 8 NOTARIZE
Certs
    rival: 6 TICTAC 7 TICTACS
Cerulean: 5 AZURE
Cervantes
    title: 5 SENOR
Cerveza
    Snack with: 4 TAPA
Cesar
    Actor: 6 ROMERO
Cessation: 3 END 4 HALT REST
Cesspool: 3 STY 4 SUMP
"C'est ___": 5 LAVIE
"C'est magnifique!": 6 OOLALA
    7 OOHLALA
"___ c'est moi": 5 LETAT
Cetus
    Star in: 4 MIRA
C. Everett ___: 4 KOOP
Ceylon
    ~, today: 8 SRILANKA
Cézanne
    Artist: 4 PAUL
    summer: 3 ETE
CFO: 4 EXEC
CGS
    unit: 3 ERG
Chablis: 4 WINE
Cha-cha
    cousin: 5 MAMBO
Cha cha cha: 5 STEPS
Chachi
    portrayer: 4 BAIO

Chacon
    of baseball: 4 ELIO
"Chacun ___ goût": 4 ASON
Chad
    Cont. of: 3 AFR
    neighbor: 5 LIBYA NIGER
        8 CAMEROON
Chadwick, Sir James
    discovery: 7 NEUTRON
Chafe: 3 IRK RUB 6 ABRADE
Chaff
    Free grain from: 6 WINNOW
Chaffee
    Skier: 4 SUZY
Chagall
    Artist: 4 **MARC**
Chai: 9 SPICEDTEA
Chain
    Breakfast restaurant: 4 IHOP
    Cinema: 5 LOEWS
    component: 4 LINK 5 DAISY
    concern: 8 WEAKLINK
    Early discount gas: 4 HESS
    European: 4 ALPS
    Fast-food: 3 KFC 4 ROYS
        5 ARBYS 7 HARDEES
    Flowery: 3 LEI
    found in cells: 3 RNA
    Home furnishings: 4 IKEA
    hotel, for short: 4 HOJO
    Island: 3 LEI
    letters: 3 DNA RNA
    Mountain: 5 RANGE RIDGE
        6 SIERRA 7 SIERRAS
    of hills: 5 RIDGE 6 SIERRA
    Sawlike: 6 SIERRA
    Supermarket: 5 AANDP
    Swedish: 4 IKEA
    units (abbr.): 3 MTS
    Watch: 3 FOB
    wearer: 3 MRT
    with links: 4 IHOP
"Chain Gang"
    singer: 5 COOKE
"Chain Reaction"
    actor Reeves: 5 KEANU
Chains
    Actor in: 3 MRT
Chair: 4 SEAT

back: **5** SPLAT
Barber ~ attachment: **5** STROP
builder: **5** CANER
Carried: **5** SEDAN
designer: **5** EAMES
Easy ~ site: **3** DEN
Fall into a: **4** PLOP
Kind of: **5** EAMES
Left the: **5** AROSE
man: **5** EAMES
part: **3** ARM LEG **4** SLAT
person: **5** TAMER
piece: **4** SLAT
Pull up a: **3** SIT
raising experience: **4** HORA
supporter: **3** LEG
Take a: **3** SIT
Took a: **3** SAT
Use an easy: **7** RECLINE
Working on a ~, perhaps:
   6 CANING
Chaired: 3 LED
Chairlift
  alternative: **4** TBAR
Chairmaker: 5 CANER
Chairman
  Chinese: **3** MAO
  Former CBS: **5** TISCH
  need: **3** GAVEL **6** AGENDA
  Nixon impeachment: **6** RODINO
  of note: **3** MAO
  ~ Arafat: **5** YASIR
  ~ Greenspan: **4** ALAN
Chairperson: 5 CANER
  list: **6** AGENDA
Chairs
  Like some: **5** CANED
Chairwoman: 5 MADAM
Chaka
  Singer: **4** KHAN
Chakra
  releasing discipline: **4** YOGA
Chalcedony: 4 SARD **5** AGATE
Chalet
  backdrop: **3** ALP
  environs: **7** SKIAREA
  Like a: **5** EAVED
  shape: **6** AFRAME
  Strand at the: **5** ICEIN

Chaliapin: 5 BASSO
  and others: **5** BASSI
Chalice: 5 GRAIL
  partner: **5** PATEN
Chalk
  French: **4** TALC
  remover: **6** ERASER
  user: **6** TAILOR
Chalkboard
  Clear the: **5** ERASE
Chalky-cheeked: 5 ASHEN
Challenge: 4 <u>**DARE**</u> DEFY
  Alley: **5** SPLIT
  Barber's: **3** MOP
  Climber's: **3** ALP **4** CRAG
  for a nonnative speaker: **5** IDIOM
  Golfer's: **6** DOGLEG
  Lab rat: **4** MAZE
  Laundry: **5** STAIN **6** GREASE
  Mover's: **5** PIANO
  Oater's: **4** DRAW
  Parenting: **4** TEEN
  Poker: **5** ICALL
  Presents a:
    15 TESTSONESMETTLE
  Ready for any: **5** CANDO
  Schoolyard: **4** DARE **6** MAKEME
  ~, metaphorically: **4** HILL
Challenged
  Socially ~ person: **4** NERD
  When: **7** ONADARE
Challenger: 5 RIVAL
  astronaut Judith: **6** RESNIK
  Clinton's: **4** DOLE
  Dwight's: **5** ADLAI
  letters: **4** NASA
  quest: **5** TITLE
  Stalin's: **4** TITO
Chalmers
  business partner: **5** ALLIS
Châlons
  Loser at: **6** ATTILA
Chalupa
  kin: **4** TACO
Chamber: 4 ROOM
  Baking: **4** OVEN
  Casa: **4** SALA
  Cloud ~ particle: **3** ION
  composition: **5** NONET

Firing: 4 KILN
group: 4 TRIO 5 NONET OCTET
    6 SEPTET
Harem: 3 ODA
Kind of: 3 ION 4 ECHO
opening: 4 ANTE
piece: 7 ARMOIRE
Schubert ~ work:
    12 TROUTQUINTET
Underground: 4 CAVE 5 CRYPT
worker (abbr.): 3 SEN

Chambered
mollusks: 7 NAUTILI

Chamberlain
of basketball: 4 WILT
TV role for: 7 KILDARE

Chamberlain, Neville
reputation: 8 APPEASER

Chambers
Heart: 5 ATRIA

Chamomile: 3 TEA

Chamonix
nix: 3 NON
View from: 3 ALP 4 ALPE ALPS
    5 ALPES

Champ
Batting: 4 ALOU 5 BRETT
    CAREW OLIVA
Boxing: 3 ALI 4 BAER ZALE
Chess: 3 TAL
Golf: 3 ELS 4 LEMA 5 SNEAD
    15 SEVEBALLESTEROS
holding: 5 TITLE
Home run: 3 OTT 5 KINER
    MARIS
Indy: 4 ARIE
Ski: 5 MAHRE
Tennis: 4 ASHE BORG GRAF
    5 EVERT LAVER LENDL
    SELES 6 AGASSI

Champagne
bucket: 4 **ICER**
city: 5 REIMS
cocktail: 6 MIMOSA
designation: 3 SEC 4 BRUT
does this: 7 SPARKLE
Dry: 4 BRUT
glass: 5 FLUTE
glass part: 4 STEM

name: 4 **MOET** MUMM

"Champagne music"
player: 4 WELK

Champagne Tony
of golf: 4 LEMA

Champaign
st.: 3 ILL

Champigny-___-Marne: 3 SUR

Champing
at the bit: 5 ANTSY EAGER
    READY

Champion: 3 ACE
boast: 4 IWON
claim: 5 TITLE
Its ~ is called "yokozuna":
    4 SUMO
rider: 5 AUTRY

Championship: 5 TITLE

Champs ___: 6 ELYSEE

Champs Élysées
feature: 4 CAFE

Chan
phrase: 4 AHSO
player of TV: 5 NAISH
portrayer: 5 **OLAND** TOLER

Chan, Charlie
creator Earl ___ Biggers: 4 DERR

Chance: 3 BET HAP LOT 4 RISK
    5 BETON
50–50 ~: 6 TOSSUP
By any: 4 EVER
Discover by: 5 HITON
Discovered by: 5 LITON
Even: 6 TOSSUP
for a hit: 5 ATBAT
Game of: 4 KENO 5 BEANO
    LOTTO
Meet by: 8 BUMPINTO
Second: 15 ANEWLEASEONLIFE
Student's second: 6 RETEST
Take a: 3 BET 4 DARE 5 WAGER
    6 GAMBLE
Take a ~ on: 4 RISK
Take the: 6 RISKIT
to play: 4 TURN
to speak: 3 SAY
upon: 4 MEET
With zero: 5 NOHOW

"___ chance!": 3 FAT 4 NOTA

Chanced
  upon: 3 MET
Chancel
  cross: 4 ROOD
Chancellor
  First ~ of reunified Germany:
      4 KOHL
  ~ Adenauer: 6 KONRAD
  ~ Bismarck: 4 OTTO
  ~ Willy: 6 BRANDT
Chancellorsville
  fighter: 3 REB
Chances: 4 ODDS
  Like some: 4 SLIM
  ~, briefly: 3 OPS
"Chances ___": 3 ARE
"Chances Are"
  singer: 6 MATHIS
Chandler
  Actress: 5 ESTEE
  Buddy of: 4 ROSS
  Publisher: 4 OTIS
  ___ & Chandon: 4 MOET
Chanel
  Designer: 4 COCO
Chaney
  Actor: 3 LON
Chang: 4 TWIN
  homeland: 4 SIAM
  Twin of: 3 ENG
Change: 4 REDO VARY 5 ALTER
      AMEND EMEND 6 AFFECT
      MUTATE REVISE SWITCH
  a bill: 5 AMEND
  addresses: 4 MOVE
  Bit of: 4 CENT DIME
  chemically: 5 REACT
  color: 3 DYE
  color again: 5 REDYE
  Continuous: 4 FLUX
  course: 3 ZIG 4 TURN VEER
  Editor's ~ of heart: 4 STET
  Element of: 4 CENT COIN DIME
  for a five: 4 ONES
  for a twenty: 4 TENS
  form: 5 MORPH
  for the better: 4 EDIT 5 AMEND
  in Chile: 4 PESO
  Kind of: 5 LOOSE

machine input: 4 ONES
  Minimal: 4 CENT
  on the beach: 3 TAN
  over time: 6 EVOLVE
  places: 4 MOVE 7 MIGRATE
  Resist: 8 STANDPAT
  Resistance to: 7 INERTIA
  Seek: 3 BEG
  Sharp ~ in direction: 3 ZIG
  Short: 3 CTS
  Small: 5 CENTS DIMES PENNY
  Spare: 4 TIRE
  states: 4 MELT
  the borders of: 5 REMAP
      6 REZONE
  the décor: 4 REDO
  the focus of: 8 REDIRECT
  the look of: 7 RESTYLE
  the price on: 5 RETAG
  to suit: 5 ADAPT
  Without: 4 ASIS
"___ changed man!": 3 IMA
Changer
  Lane ~ concern: 9 BLINDSPOT
  Money: 6 EDITOR
Changes
  Book of: 6 ICHING
  If nothing: 6 ASITIS
  Scene of many: 6 CABANA
Changing
  place: 6 CABANA
  Without money ~ hands:
      7 INTRADE
Channel: 3 RUT WAY 4 DUCT
      LANE 5 STEER 6 GROOVE
      STRAIT STREAM TRENCH
  Artificial water: 6 SLUICE
  Cable: 3 AMC HBO TNT USA
      4 ESPN 5 AANDE
  Chimney: 4 FLUE
  choker: 4 SILT
  Emergency CB: 4 NINE
  English: 3 BBC
  Former cable: 3 TNN
  marker: 4 BUOY
  Political: 5 CSPAN
  Premium: 3 HBO
  Shopping: 3 QVC
  surfer locale: 8 RECLINER

swimmer Gertrude: 6 EDERLE
Water: 6 SLUICE
___ Channel: 5 SCIFI
Channeling
state: 6 TRANCE
Channel Islands
One of the: 4 SARK 6 JERSEY
Channels
Turner of: 3 TED
TV ~ 2–13: 3 VHF
TV ~ 14 and up: 3 UHF
Went through: 6 SURFED
Channing
of Broadway: 5 CAROL
Chanson de ___: 5 GESTE
Chant: 6 INTONE
Olympics: 3 USA 6 USAUSA
Start of a pirate: 4 YOHO
with the cheerleaders: 4 ROOT
Chanted
word: 6 MANTRA
Chanteuse
~ Adams: 4 EDIE
~ Edith: 4 PIAF
~ Horne: 4 LENA
Chantey
locale: 3 SEA
singer: 6 SAILOR
Chantilly: 4 LACE
department: 4 OISE
product: 4 LACE
river: 4 OISE
Chaos: 4 MESS RIOT 6 MAYHEM
7 ANARCHY
Daughter of: 4 GAEA GAIA
It's: 3 ZOO
Son of: 4 EROS
Tendency toward: 7 ENTROPY
Utter: 6 BEDLAM
Chaotic: 5 MESSY SNAFU
6 HECTIC
Cause of ~ weather: 6 ELNINO
scene: 3 ZOO
situation: 5 SNAFU
Chap: 3 GUY JOE LAD MAN
4 DUDE GENT 5 BLOKE
BUCKO FELLA
Chelsea: 4 BRIT
Words to an old: 4 ISAY

Chapeau: 3 HAT 5 BERET
holder: 4 TETE
Chapel
fixture: 3 PEW
part: 4 APSE
Run off to the: 5 ELOPE
Sound from a ~ tower: 4 PEAL
top: 5 SPIRE
vow: 3 IDO
___ **Chapel: 7 SISTINE**
Chapel Hill
sch.: 3 UNC
student: 7 TARHEEL
Chaperone: 6 ESCORT
Chaplain
Military: 5 PADRE
Chaplin
brother: 3 SYD
employer: 7 SENNETT
Mrs.: 4 OONA
persona: 5 TRAMP
prop: 4 CANE
title: 3 SIR
"Chaplin"
actress Kelly: 5 MOIRA
Chaplin, Geraldine
Mother of: 4 OONA
Chapped: 3 RED
Chaps: 3 MEN
Chapter: 4 PART
Chaucer: 4 TALE
in history: 3 ERA
partner: 5 VERSE
Serial: 7 EPISODE
Textbook: 4 UNIT
Chapter 11
cause: 4 DEBT
Chapter and ___: 5 VERSE
"Chapter on Ears, A"
writer: 4 ELIA
Chapters
They have: 6 UNIONS
Char: 4 SEAR 5 SINGE
Character: 4 ROLE TONE
5 AROMA ETHOS TENOR
6 ASPECT NATURE
Ancient: 4 RUNE
Animated: 4 TOON
Blue: 5 SMURF

builder: 4 GENE
Community: 5 ETHOS
Crowd-scene: 5 EXTRA
Do some ~ assassination:
    5 ERASE
Homeric: 3 ETA
Mysterious: 4 RUNE
Opposite in: 5 POLAR
part: 4 GENE 5 TRAIT
PC ~ set: 5 ASCII
Step into: 3 ACT
Uncool: 4 NERD
Characteristic: 5 TRAIT
carrier: 4 **GENE**
Characterize: 6 DEPICT
Charade: 3 ACT 4 MIME
Charades: 4 GAME
Play: 4 MIME 6 ACTOUT
~, basically: 6 MIMING
    8 GESTURES
Charcoal
wood: 5 ALDER
Chardonnay: 4 WINE
Charen
Author: 4 MONA
Charge: 3 FEE 4 BILL CARE
    COST FARE GOAT TASK
    WARD 5 DEBIT PRICE
    RUNAT STORM 6 ACCUSE
    ALLEGE INDICT IONIZE
    ONRUSH RUSHAT TILTAT
Answer a: 5 PLEAD
Answered a: 4 PLED
Answer to a: 4 PLEA
At no: 4 FREE
Atom with a: 3 ION
Bee's: 4 OPIE
Be in: 4 RULE 5 REIGN
Be in ~ of: 4 HEAD
carrier: 3 ION
Club: 4 FEES
Criminal: 3 RAP
Daily: 4 RATE
Depth: 6 ASHCAN
Eunuch's: 3 ODA 5 HAREM
Extra: 5 ADDON
Fixed: 6 SETFEE
In: 15 WEARINGTHEPANTS
In ~ of: 4 OVER

It has a negative: 5 ANION
It's not free of: 3 ION
Membership: 3 FEE
per unit: 4 RATE
Professional: 3 FEE
Service: 3 **FEE** 4 TOLL
Sitter: 3 TOT
the passer: 5 BLITZ
Took: 3 LED
Took ~ of: 3 RAN
Unfair: 6 BADRAP BUMRAP
Charged: 5 HADAT IONIC
    RANAT 6 WENTAT
Create ~ particles: 6 IONIZE
Negatively: 7 ANIONIC
particle: 3 **ION** 5 ANION
Weight not ~ for: 4 **TARE**
Charger: 5 STEED 8 WARHORSE
African: 5 RHINO
array: 5 DEBTS
Corrida: 4 TORO 6 ELTORO
Chargers: 4 TEAM
home: 8 SANDIEGO
Charges
Facing: 7 ONTRIAL
Teacher's: 5 CLASS
Charging
need: 6 CREDIT
Chariot
rider of myth: 3 EOS 4 THOR
suffix: 3 EER
"Chariots of Fire"
actor Charleson: 3 IAN
Charismatic
trait: 4 AURA
Charisse
Dancer: 3 **CYD**
Charitable
Be: 6 DONATE
donation: 4 ALMS
offering: 4 ALMS
Charitably
hand out: 4 DOLE
Charity: 4 ALMS DOLE 5 DONEE
event: 6 BAZAAR
Give to: 6 DONATE
Hope and ~ partner: 5 FAITH
Popular: 9 UNITEDWAY
recipient: 5 DONEE

Charlatan: 5 FAKER FRAUD
Charlemagne
  capital: 6 AACHEN
  domain:
    15 HOLYROMANEMPIRE
  domain (abbr.): 3 **HRE**
Charles: 3 ROI 4 HEIR
  and others: 4 RAYS 5 NORAS
  Author: 5 READE
  barker: 4 ASTA
  Bodybuilder: 5 ATLAS
  Bridge expert: 5 **GOREN**
  Chair designer: 5 EAMES
  Composer: 4 IVES
  Former senator: 4 ROBB
  Mrs.: 4 **NORA**
  Newsman: 6 OSGOOD
  Newsreel pioneer: 5 PATHE
  or Louis: 3 ROI
  pastime: 4 POLO
  Poet: 5 OLSON
  Sch. on the: 3 MIT
  Singer: 3 RAY
Charles, Ray
  hit: 5 NOONE
    15 GEORGIAONMYMIND
Charles ___, Sir
  Geologist: 5 LYELL
Charles II
  mistress: 4 NELL
  painter: 4 LELY
"Charles in Charge"
  actor Willie: 5 AAMES
  star: 4 BAIO
Charleston
  fort: 6 SUMTER
  st.: 3 WVA
Charley
  horse: 4 ACHE 5 CRAMP
    SPASM
Charlie: 4 TUNA
  Actor: 5 SHEEN
  Detective: 4 CHAN
  of PBS: 4 ROSE
  of the Honolulu P.D.: 4 CHAN
  Wife of: 4 OONA
"Charlie and the Chocolate
    Factory"
  author: 4 DAHL

"Charlie Hustle": 4 ROSE
  8 PETEROSE
"Charlie's Angels"
  actress Lucy: 3 LIU
  actress Roberts: 5 TANYA
  actress Smith: 6 JACLYN
  angel: 4 KRIS
Charlize
  Actress: 6 THERON
Charlotte
  Actress: 3 **RAE**
  Comic: 3 **RAE**
  creation: 3 WEB
Charlotte ___: 5 **RUSSE** 6 AMALIE
Charlottesville
  sch.: 3 UVA
"Charlotte's Web"
  author: 7 EBWHITE
  boy: 5 AVERY
  monogram: 3 EBW
Charlottetown
  prov.: 3 PEI
Charlton
  Actor: 6 HESTON
  role: 5 MOSES
"Charly"
  actress Bloom: 6 CLAIRE
Charm: 3 HEX 4 MOJO 5 AMUSE
  6 ALLURE AMULET
  DISARM ENAMOR
  ENDEAR FETISH
  7 ENCHANT 8 TALISMAN
  Magic: 4 MOJO 6 AMULET
  Radiate: 4 OOZE 5 EXUDE
  Voodoo: 4 MOJO 5 OBEAH
Charmed
  one: 5 COBRA
  particle: 5 QUARK
Charmee
  Snake: 3 EVE
Charmer
  Snake for a: 5 COBRA
Charming: 6 QUAINT
  8 ENGAGING
Charon
  is its moon: 5 PLUTO
  river: 4 **STYX**
Charred: 5 BURNT
Chart: 3 MAP 5 GRAPH TABLE

anew: 5 REMAP
Genealogy: 4 TREE
Heart: 3 EKG
holder: 5 EASEL
Kind of: 3 PIE 4 FLIP 5 NATAL
shape: 3 PIE
topper: 3 HIT
Charter: 3 LET 4 HIRE RENT
    5 LEASE
again: 5 RELET
Chas.
Mother of: 4 ELIZ
Chase: 4 SHAG SHOO
    7 GOAFTER
Actress: 4 **ILKA**
off: 4 SHOO
Chaser
Info: Suffix cue
Bar: 4 SHOT
Bugs: 5 ELMER
Magnum: 4 OPUS
Mob: 4 STER
Narc: 4 OTIC
Nymph: 5 SATYR
Pusher: 4 NARC
Status: 3 QUO
Whiskey: 5 AGOGO
Chasers: 5 POSSE
AWOL: 3 MPS
Chasing: 5 AFTER
Chasm: 4 GULF 5 ABYSS GORGE
Deep: 5 ABYSS 6 CANYON
Chast
Cartoonist: 3 ROZ
Chaste: 4 PURE
Chastity
Mom of: 4 CHER
Sonny or: 4 BONO
Chat: 3 JAW 4 TALK
    9 TETEATETE
    14 SHOOTTHEBREEZE
Cat: 4 MEOW
Have a ~ with: 6 TALKTO
Informal: 10 RAPSESSION
Private: 9 TETEATETE
sites: 9 FIRESIDES
You may ~ on it: 3 AOL
___ chat: 5 PASDE
Chateaubriand: 5 STEAK

Chateau-Thierry
river: 5 MARNE
Chatelaine
rival: 4 ELLE
Chat room
chuckle: 3 **LOL**
initials: 4 IMHO
nonparticipant: 6 LURKER
provider: 3 AOL
Chats
online: 3 IMS
Chatter: 3 GAB JAW YAK YAP
    4 BLAB 5 PRATE RUNON
Idle: 10 YACKETYYAK
Like some: 4 IDLE
on the road: 4 CBER
Chatterbox: 6 MAGPIE TALKER
    YABBER
Chatty
bird: 4 MYNA 5 MYNAH
Chaucer
offering: 4 **TALE**
pilgrim: 5 REEVE
Wife's place in a ~ tale: 4 BATH
Chaud
time: 3 ETE
Chauffeur: 6 DRIVER
Order to a: 4 HOME
vehicle: 4 LIMO
Word to the: 5 DRIVE
Chauncey
Orator: 5 DEPEW
Chauvinistic
type: 6 SEXIST
Chavez
Labor leader: 5 **CESAR**
Che
compadre: 5 FIDEL
Revolutionary: 7 GUEVARA
~, formally: 7 ERNESTO
Cheap: 5 TATTY 6 TRASHY
    7 CHINTZY
accommodations: 8 STEERAGE
bar: 7 GINMILL
cigar: 6 STOGIE
jewelry: 5 PASTE
Like ~ pianos: 5 TINNY
liquor: 6 ROTGUT
mags: 5 PULPS

Not: 4 DEAR
so-and-so: 5 PIKER
tire: 7 RETREAD
way to live: 8 RENTFREE
"Cheap Detective, The"
   star: 4 FALK
Cheapen: 6 DEBASE 7 DEVALUE
Cheaper: 6 ONSALE
Cheaply: 8 FORASONG
Cheapskate: 5 MISER PIKER
      7 SCROOGE STINTER
Cheat: 3 GYP 4 BILK GULL HOSE
      REAM ROOK SCAM
      5 COZEN 6 CHISEL
      CONMAN
   on: 7 TWOTIME
   sheet: 4 TROT
   ~, in a way: 4 COPY PEEK
Cheater
   aid: 4 CRIB
Check: 3 TAB 4 BILL CURB HALT
      REIN STEM STOP TEST
      5 BLOCK DETER 6 ARREST
      REININ REREAD STANCH
   Alimony ~ cashers: 4 EXES
   Bad ~ letters: 3 NSF
   books: 5 AUDIT
   Bouncers ~ them: 3 IDS
   casher: 5 PAYEE
   copy: 4 EDIT
   endorser: 5 PAYEE
   entry: 4 DATE 6 AMOUNT
   falsifier: 5 KITER
   fig.: 3 AMT
   for accuracy: 3 VET
   for Checkers: 5 LEASH
   for fit: 5 TRYON
   for prints: 4 DUST
   Grab the: 5 TREAT
   In: 5 ATBAY
   letters: 3 NSF
   Make a ~ for later: 8 POSTDATE
   mark: 4 TICK
   mate: 4 STUB
   out: 3 EYE VET 4 OGLE SCAN
      TEST 5 AUDIT TALLY
      7 EXAMINE 8 LOOKINTO
   (out): 5 SCOPE
   out before a heist: 4 CASE

out the sites: 4 SURF
payee: 6 BEARER
Pick up the: 5 TREAT
point: 4 BANK
Rain ~, often: 4 STUB
recipient: 5 PAYEE
Sign the back of a: 7 ENDORSE
Something to: 3 BAG HAT IDS
   4 COAT
the check: 3 ADD 5 READD
Traveler's: 3 MAP
Word on a sample: 4 VOID
words: 5 PAYTO
writer: 5 PAYER
Checkbook
   item: 4 STUB
Check-cashing
   needs: 3 IDS
Checked
   for fit: 7 TRIEDON
Checker: 4 DISC TAXI
   Double: 4 KING
   Spot: 3 VET 4 SPCA 5 LEASH
Checker, Chubby
   dance: 5 TWIST
Checkerboard
   rows, e.g.: 6 OCTETS
Checkered: 5 PLAID
   It has a ~ past: 4 TAXI
   It may be: 4 PAST
Checkers: 3 MEN 4 GAME
   Check for: 5 LEASH
   color: 3 RED
   Half the: 4 REDS
Checking
   Kind of ~ account: 5 NOFEE
   out: 5 EYING 6 EYEING
"check is in the mail, The": 3 LIE
"Check it out!": 4 LOOK 5 GOSEE
Checklist
   part: 4 **ITEM**
Checkout
   bars (abbr.): 3 UPC
   count: 5 ITEMS
   item: 7 SCANNER
   task: 4 SCAN
   Work at a ~ counter: 3 BAG
Checkpoint
   requests: 3 IDS

Checkroom
  item: 3 HAT 4 COAT
Checks
  Like some ~ (abbr.): 4 CERT
"Check this out!": 4 PSST
Checkup: 4 EXAM TEST
  request: 5 SAYAH
  sounds: 3 AHS
Cheddar
  Like some: 4 AGED MILD
      5 SHARP
Cheech
  Actor: 5 MARIN
  Ex-partner of: 5 CHONG
Cheek: 4 JOWL SASS 5 NERVE
  coloring: 5 ROUGE
  dampener: 4 TEAR
  Of the: 5 MALAR
Cheekiness: 4 SASS
Cheeks
  Like some: 4 ROSY
"Cheek to Cheek"
  musical: 6 TOPHAT
Cheeky: 4 PERT WISE 5 SASSY
Cheep
  place: 4 NEST
Cheer: 3 RAH 4 ROOT YELL
      5 ELATE 7 GLADDEN
      HEARTEN
  Beer: 5 SKOAL
  Bronx: 4 GIBE HOOT JEER
      RAZZ
  Bullring: 3 **OLE**
  competitor: 3 ERA
  (for): 4 **ROOT**
  Full of: 5 MERRY
  Half a: 5 BOOLA
  Object of an old French: 5 LEROI
  Olympics: 3 USA
  Palindromic: 3 YAY
  School: 4 YELL 6 GOTEAM
  Spanish: 3 OLE
  Stadium: 3 RAH
  starter: 3 HIP SIS 4 VIVA
  Word of: 3 RAH YEA
  Yale: 5 BOOLA
Cheerful: 3 GAY 4 GLAD ROSY
      5 RIANT SUNNY 6 BLITHE
      UPBEAT 8 SANGUINE

  tune: 4 LILT
Cheering: 5 AROAR
  sound: 3 RAH
"Cheerio!": 4 **TATA** 5 SEEYA
Cheerios
  grain: 3 OAT
  Like: 4 **OATY** 5 OATEN
Cheerleader
  cheer: 4 YELL
  cry: 3 RAH 6 GOTEAM
  feat: 6 SPLITS
  skirt: 4 MINI
Cheerleaders
  Chant with the: 4 ROOT
  Group of: 5 SQUAD
  Most: 4 SHES
Cheerless: 4 DRAB GRIM 5 BLEAK
      DREAR STARK 6 DISMAL
"Cheers"
  actor Danson: 3 TED
  actor George: 5 WENDT
  actor Roger: 4 REES
  actress Neuwirth: 4 BEBE
  actress Perlman: 4 **RHEA**
  barfly: 4 NORM
  barmaid: 5 CARLA
  bartender: 3 SAM 6 MALONE
  Bebe on: 6 LILITH
  Carla on: 4 RHEA
  Diane's successor on: 7 REBECCA
  fixture: 8 BARSTOOL
  Norm's wife on: 4 VERA
  perch: 5 STOOL
  regular: 4 NORM
  Rhea on: 5 CARLA
  role: 3 SAM 5 CARLA DIANE
  setting: 3 BAR
  star: 6 DANSON
  waitress: 5 CARLA DIANE
"Cheers!": 5 SKOAL
      9 BOTTOMSUP
Cheery: 3 GAY 4 GLAD ROSY
      5 RIANT SUNNY 6 BLITHE
      UPBEAT 8 SANGUINE
  tune: 4 LILT
Cheese
  Ball-shaped: 4 EDAM
  Big: 4 BOSS EXEC 5 NABOB
      6 TOPDOG

Big name in: 5 KRAFT
Brine-cured: 4 FETA
burg: 4 EDAM
choice: 4 BRIE 5 SWISS
coating: 4 RIND
Creamy: 4 BRIE
Crumbly: 4 FETA
dish: 7 RAREBIT
Dutch: 4 **EDAM** 5 GOUDA
etc.: 5 DAIRY
for crackers: 4 BRIE
French: 4 **BRIE**
Goat: 4 FETA
Greek: 4 **FETA**
Hunk of: 4 SLAB
Italian: 6 ROMANO
    8 PARMESAN
Kind of: 5 NACHO 7 PIMENTO
Like some: 4 AGED 5 SHARP
Like Swiss: 5 HOLEY
made from ewe's milk:
    6 ROMANO
Mild: 4 EDAM 5 GOUDA
Mold-ripened: 4 BRIE
nibblers: 4 MICE
Party: 4 BRIE EDAM
Pickled: 4 FETA
Red-wrapped: 4 EDAM 5 GOUDA
region: 4 BRIE
Romano ~ source: 3 EWE
Round: 4 EDAM
Salad: 4 FETA
Sharp: 6 ROMANO
Soft: 4 **BRIE**
Spreadable: 4 BRIE
Wax-coated: 4 **EDAM**
White: 4 BRIE
with holes: 7 HAVARTI
"Cheese"
action: 5 SMILE
___ cheese: 4 BLEU
Cheeseboard
ball: 4 EDAM
Cheesecake
Bit of: 3 GAM
Cheesehead
st.: 4 WISC
Cheesemaking
leftover: 4 WHEY

Cheesy
dish: 7 RAREBIT
morsel: 5 NACHO
sandwich: 4 MELT
Cheetah
Like a: 4 FAST
Chef
catchphrase: 3 ALA
collection: 7 RECIPES
d'état: 3 ROI
direction: 5 STIR
flavoring: 4 HERB
French ~ cry: 7 ETVOILA
gadget: 5 DICER RICER
Good name for a: 3 STU
herb: 4 SAGE
mixture: 4 ROUX
phrase: 3 ALA
protector: 5 APRON
protectors: 5 MITTS
seasoning: 4 HERB
~, at times: 4 ICER 5 DICER
    6 SPICER
~ Graham: 4 KERR
~ Julia: 5 CHILD
~ Lagasse: 6 EMERIL
~ Martin: 3 YAN
"Che gelida manina": 4 ARIA
Chekhov
First play of: 6 IVANOV
Playwright: 5 **ANTON**
Sister in a ~ play: 4 OLGA
    5 IRINA MASHA
Uncle in a ~ play: 5 VANYA
Chekov
neighbor: 4 SULU
Chelsea
Info: British cue
chap: 4 BRIT
Chem.: 3 **SCI**
class: 3 **LAB**
class data: 5 ATNOS
lab array: 5 ACIDS
neurotransmitter: 3 ATP
pollutant: 3 PCB
unit: 3 MOL
Chemical
analysis: 5 ASSAY
Aromatic: 5 ESTER

Caustic: **3** LYE
compound: **4** ENOL **5** ESTER
   6 ISOMER
Copier: **5** TONER
Corrosive: **4** ACID
ending: **3** ANE **ENE** IDE INE ITE
extract: **5** EDUCT
Fertilizer: **4** UREA
prefix: **5** PETRO
salt: **6** IODIDE
suffix: **3** ANE **ENE** IDE INE ITE
Type of ~ bond: **5** IONIC
Chemical-free: 7 NATURAL
Chemically
Change: **5** REACT
nonreactive: **5** INERT
Chemicals
Big name in: **3** DOW **4** OLIN
   6 DUPONT
Chemin de ___ : 3 FER
Chemist
condiment: **4** NACL
workplace: **3** LAB
Chemistry
B in: **5** BORON
class cost: **6** LABFEE
Kind of: **7** ORGANIC
Nobelist in: **4** HAHN UREY
   5 CURIE
Twin, in: **6** ISOMER
Cheney: 4 VEEP
predecessor: **4** GORE
   6 ALGORE
Cheng-chou
province: **5** HONAN
Chenin ___ : 5 BLANC
Cher
Ex of: **4** BONO **5** SONNY
film: **4** MASK
Cherbourg
Info: French cue
"Cherchez la ___": 5 FEMME
Cheri
Actress: **5 OTERI**
Cherish: 4 LOVE **5 ADORE** PRIZE
   6 ESTEEM
Cherished
relation: **8** LOVEDONE
Chero-Cola

Company formerly known as:
   4 NEHI
Cherokee: 4 JEEP
Cherokee Strip
city: **4** ENID
Cheroot: 5 CIGAR **6** STOGIE
Cherry: 3 RED **4** TREE
and others: **4** REDS
brandy: **6** KIRSCH
holder: **4** STEM
picker: **5** CRANE
Pie: **7** MORELLO
pit: **5** STONE
red: **6** CERISE
Singer: **5** NENEH
stone: **3** PIT
Sweet: **4** BING
variety: **4 BING**
Cherry ___ : 4 COLA
Cherub: 5 ANGEL
archer: **4** AMOR
superior: **6** SERAPH
Chervil: 4 HERB
Cheryl
Actress: **4** LADD
and Alan: **5** LADDS
Supermodel: **5** TIEGS
Chesapeake
catch: **4** CRAB
Cheshire Cat
look: **4** GRIN
Chess: 4 GAME
1960 ~ champ: **3 TAL**
action: **4** MOVE
castle: **4** ROOK
champion Mikhail: **3** TAL
Computer ~ machine:
   8 DEEPBLUE
ending: **4** MATE
Japanese: **5** SHOGI
Least valuable ~ piece: **4** PAWN
opening: **3** CEE **6** GAMBIT
piece: **3** MAN **4** KING PAWN
   ROOK
pieces (abbr.): **3** KTS
Queenside castle, in ~ notation:
   3 OOO
rival of Bobby: **5** BORIS
sequence: **7** ENDGAME

Won at: 5 MATED
World ~ org.: 4 FIDE

Chessboard
row: 4 RANK

Chest: 5 TORSO 6 THORAX
beater: 3 APE 5 HEART
display: 5 MEDAL
filler: 4 LUNG
Kind of: 3 ICE TOY WAR
5 CEDAR
material: 5 CEDAR
Medieval: 4 ARCA
muscle: 3 **PEC**
of drawers: 6 BUREAU
7 DRESSER
part: 6 DRAWER
protector: 3 BIB RIB 4 VEST
Sacred: 3 ARC
Trunk with a: 5 TORSO
wood: 5 CEDAR

Chesterfield: 4 COAT SOFA
8 OVERCOAT

Chester White
home: 3 STY

Chestnut: 4 TREE 5 HORSE
coating: 3 BUR
horse: 4 ROAN

Chestnut-colored: 4 ROAN
ruminant: 7 REDDEER

Chestnuts
Cook: 5 ROAST

Chest-thumping: 5 MACHO

Chet
Guitarist: 6 ATKINS

Chevalier
film: 4 GIGI
song: 4 MIMI
trademark: 8 STRAWHAT

Chevrolet
introduced in 1966: 6 CAMARO

Chevron
Chevron's: 4 LOGO
rival: 4 ARCO ESSO
wearer (abbr.): 3 NCO

Chevy
Classic: 6 IMPALA
cohort: 5 GILDA
minivan: 5 ASTRO
model: 4 AVEO 6 CAMARO

LUMINA MALIBU
7 CORSICA
Old: 4 NOVA VEGA 6 IMPALA
Sporty: 5 VETTE 6 CAMARO
truck: 5 TAHOE
vehicle of the 1970s: 3 SNL
~ SUV: 5 TAHOE 6 BLAZER

Chew: 4 GNAW
Cow: 3 CUD
(on): 4 **GNAW** 5 MUNCH
out: 5 SCOLD 7 TELLOFF
Something to: 3 CUD GUM
6 THEFAT
the fat: 3 GAB JAW YAK 4 CHAT
8 SCHMOOZE
the rag: 3 YAK
the scenery: 5 **EMOTE**
7 HAMITUP OVERACT

Chewable
nut: 5 BETEL

Chewer
Bamboo: 5 PANDA
Scenery: 3 HAM 6 EMOTER

Chewing gum: 6 CHICLE

Chewy
candy: 5 TAFFY 6 NOUGAT
TOFFEE 7 CARAMEL

Cheyenne
ally: 7 ARAPAHO
county: 7 LARAMIE
shelter: 5 TEPEE

Chg.
Type of: 3 NEG

Chi
follower: 3 PSI 4 MINH
hrs.: 3 CDT CST
paper: 4 TRIB
preceder: 3 TAI

Chi.
setting: 3 CDT CST
___ chi: 3 **TAI**

Chiang
opponent: 3 MAO

Chiang Kai-shek
capital: 6 TAIPEI

Chiang ___ -shek: 3 KAI

Chianti: 4 VINO WINE
color: 3 RED
Like: 3 DRY SEC

Chic: 5 STYLE **6** CLASSY SWANKY
TRENDY **7** ALAMODE
ELEGANT INSTYLE
STYLISH
getaways: **4** SPAS
More: **6** TONIER
Revivalist: **5** RETRO
___ chic: **4** TRES
Chicago
1974 ~ hit: **8** CALLONME
airport: **5** **OHARE**
airport code: **3** ORD
area: **4** LOOP
Banks of: **5** ERNIE
Big name in: **5** DALEY
Boston or: **4** BAND
critic: **5** EBERT
Downtown: **7** THELOOP
exchange: **4** MERC
footballer: **4** BEAR
hrs.: **3** CST
hub: **5** OHARE
Like: **5** WINDY
maestro: **5** SOLTI
mayor: **5** DALEY
Mrs. of: **6** OLEARY
paper, briefly: **4** **TRIB**
state (abbr.): **3** ILL
suburb: **5** ELGIN NILES
6 CICERO SKOKIE
7 OAKLAWN
team: **3** SOX **4** CUBS
terminal: **5** OHARE
trains: **3** **ELS**
university: **6** DEPAUL LOYOLA
"Chicago"
actor: **4** GERE
actress Lucy: **3** LIU
actress Neuwirth: **4** BEBE
actress Zellweger: **5** RENEE
lyricist: **3** EBB
role: **5** VELMA
Chicagoan
Legendary: **9** MRSOLEARY
Chicago Cubs
Sammy of the: **4** SOSA
spring training site: **4** MESA
"Chicago Hope"
actor Adam: **5** ARKIN

actor Arkin: **4** ADAM
actress: **5** LAHTI
Chichén ___: 4 ITZA
Chichén Itzá
attraction: **5** RUINS
resident: **4** MAYA
Chichester
chap: **3** SOD **5** BLOKE
Chichi: 4 ARTY TONY
5 ARTSY SWANK
7 ALAMODE
___ **chi ch'uan: 3** TAI
Chick
Jazz pianist: **5** **COREA**
mate: **4** DUDE
sound: **4** PEEP
suffix: **4** ADEE
Chick-___-A: 3 FIL
Chickadee: 8 TITMOUSE
Chickadees: 7 TITMICE
Chickasaw: 5 TRIBE
Chicken: 4 WIMP **5** SISSY
6 COWARD SCARED
TREPID
Big name in: **5** TYSON
7 SANDERS
choice: **3** LEG **4** WING **5** FRYER
THIGH **6** BREAST
7 ROASTER
dinner: **4** FEED
dish: **8** YAKITORI
Fixed: **5** CAPON
General ___ ~: **4** TSOS
house: **4** COOP **5** ROOST
in some dish names: **3** COQ
Little: **6** BANTAM
organ: **6** GIBLET
part: **4** NECK
preceder: **3** EGG
style: **4** KIEV **7** ALAKING
~, in Spanish: **5** POLLO
Chicken ___: 3 POX **4** KIEV
6 LITTLE
Chicken cordon ___: 4 BLEU
Chicken-king
link: **3** ALA
Chicken ___ king: 3 **ALA**
Chicken Little: 8 ALARMIST
9 PESSIMIST

"Chicken Run"
  characters: 4 HENS
Chickens
  and others: 4 FOWL
Chico: 4 MARX
Chide: 3 NAG 5 SCOLD
Chiding
  sound: 3 TSK
Chief: 3 KEY TOP 4 ARCH BOSS
      HEAD MAIN 5 MAJOR
      6 LEADER 7 HEADMAN
  Arab: 4 EMIR 5 EMEER
  Clan: 5 THANE
  Corp.: 4 EXEC
  exec: 4 PRES PREZ
  Former ~ Palestinian: 6 ARAFAT
  Indian: 5 RAJAH
  Magazine: 6 EDITOR
  Muslim: 4 IMAM
  point: 9 ESSENTIAL
  steward: 9 MAJORDOMO
  Tribal: 4 KHAN 6 SACHEM
  Turkish: 3 AGA
  ~ Big Bear: 4 CREE
  ~ Greek god: 4 ZEUS
  ~ Norse god: 4 ODIN
  ~ Pontiac: 6 OTTAWA
  ~ Whitehorse: 4 OTOE
Chief Justice
  1836–64 ~: 5 TANEY
  1920s ~: 4 TAFT
  1953–69 ~: 10 EARLWARREN
  Dred Scott: 5 TANEY
  First: 7 JOHNJAY
  ~ Warren: 4 EARL
Chief of Staff
  Bush: 6 SUNUNU
  Nixon: 4 HAIG
  Reagan: 5 REGAN
Chieftain
  Arab: 4 EMIR 5 EMEER
  Mafia: 4 CAPO
  Norse: 5 ROLLO
Chiffon
  Like: 5 SHEER
  Sturdy: 5 NINON
Chiffons
  hit: 10 ONEFINEDAY
Chigger: 5 LARVA

Chignon
  setting: 4 NAPE
Chihuahua: 5 STATE
  Info: Spanish cue
  Bark like a: 4 YELP
  Cartoon: 3 **REN**
  cash: 4 PESO
  celebration: 6 FIESTA
  cheer: 3 **OLE**
  chicken: 5 POLLO
  child: 4 NINO
  home: 4 CASA
  neighbor (abbr.): 4 NMEX
  TV: 3 REN
  wrap: 6 SERAPE
Child: 3 KID SON 4 BABE TYKE
  Admonition to a: 4 NONO
      6 BENICE
  Annoying: 4 BRAT
  appliance: 4 OVEN
  Chihuahua: 4 NINO
  direction: 4 STIR
  Flower: 4 SEED 6 HIPPIE
  god: 4 AMOR
  Homeless: 4 WAIF
  hood: 3 IMP
  Kind of: 4 ONLY 5 INNER
  Love: 4 EROS
  Mexican: 4 NINA
  of fortune: 4 HEIR
  play: 3 TAG
  seat: 3 LAP
  Small: 3 TAD TOT
  Spoiled: 4 BRAT
  support: 4 KNEE
  Wee: 5 BAIRN
  welfare gps.: 4 PTAS
  ~, for one: 4 CHEF
  ~, in Spanish: 4 NINO
Child-care
  writer LeShan: 3 EDA
Childhood
  They're often removed in:
    8 ADENOIDS
Childish: 7 PUERILE
Children
  Bring up: 4 REAR
  Card game for: 3 WAR
    7 OLDMAID

doctor: **5** SEUSS
Game for: **3** TAG
Like proper: **4** SEEN
Nursery rhyme home of many:
    4 SHOE
rhyme start: **4** EENY
song refrain: **5** EIEIO
"Children of a ___ God":
    6 LESSER
"Children of a Lesser God"
    director Haines: **5** RANDA
"Children of the Albatross"
    author: **3** NIN
"Children of the Poor"
    author: **4** RIIS
Children's author
    ~ Blyton: **4** ENID
    ~ Eleanor: **5** ESTES
    ~ Ennis: **4** REES
    ~ Scott: **5** ODELL
Chile
    Much of: **5** ANDES
    neighbor: **4** PERU
    Range in: **5** ANDES
    When it's warm in: **5** ENERO
Chilean
    1970s ~ leader: **7** ALLENDE
    airline: **3** LAN
    change: **4** PESO
    pianist: **5** ARRAU
    poet Pablo: **6** NERUDA
    range: **5** ANDES
Chili
    companion: **5** CARNE
    hotness unit: **5** ALARM
    ingredient: **10** PINTOBEANS
    powder ingredient: **5** CUMIN
    verde: **4** STEW
Chiliads
    Many: **3** EON
Chili ___ carne: 3 CON
Chili con ___: 5 CARNE
Chill: 3 NIP **4** REST **5** RELAX
    Causing ~ bumps: **5** EERIE
    Feverish: **4** AGUE
    out: **5** RELAX
    Take a ~ pill: **6** COOLIT
"Chill!": 5 RELAX
Chilled: 4 COLD ICED **5** ONICE

garnish: **5** ASPIC
soup: **5** SCHAV
Chiller: 3 ICE
    1958 ~, with "The": **4** BLOB
Chill-inducing: 5 EERIE
Chilling: 3 ICY **5** **EERIE** ONICE
    out: **6** ATEASE ATREST
    ~ Chaney: **3** LON
Chills: 4 AGUE
    and fever: **4** **AGUE**
Chilly
    and damp: **3** RAW
    and wet: **4** DANK
    powder: **4** SNOW
    Really: **6** ARCTIC
Chime: 4 RING
    ominously: **5** KNELL
    time: **4** NOON
Chimed: 4 RANG
Chimers: 5 BELLS
Chimney
    channel: **4** FLUE
    Like a: **5** SOOTY
    nester: **5** STORK
    residue: **4** **SOOT**
    Vulcan's: **4** ETNA
Chimp: 3 APE
    in space: **4** **ENOS**
    relative: **5** ORANG
Chimpanzee: 3 APE **5** JOCKO
Chin
    adornment: **6** GOATEE
    end: **3** ESE
    indentation: **5** CLEFT
    stroker's words: **4** ISEE
    Take it on the: **4** LOSE
Ch'in
    Dynasty after: **3** HAN
China
    and others: **7** FAREAST
    border river: **4** YALU
    city: **8** SHANGHAI
    Fine: **5** SPODE
    Former leader of: **3** MAO
    group: **6** TEASET
    name: **5** SPODE
    neighbor: **4** LAOS
    piece: **4** DISH **5** PLATE
        6 TEACUP

prefix: 4 **INDO**
problem: 4 CHIP
province: 5 HONAN HUNAN
purchase: 6 TEASET
river: 7 YANGTZE
setting: 4 **ASIA** 7 FAREAST
shop problem: 4 BULL
prefix: 4 SINO
Use: 5 EATON
Used: 5 ATEIN
Zhou of: 5 ENLAI
China ___ : 5 ASTER
"China Beach"
setting: 3 NAM
star Dana: 6 DELANY
Chinatown
Street in New York's: 4 MOTT
"Chinatown"
screenwriter Robert: 5 TOWNE
Chinchilla: 3 FUR 6 RODENT
Chinese: 5 ASIAN
4th to 6th century ~ dynasty:
    3 WEI
1960s ~ leader: 3 MAO
appetizer: 7 EGGROLL
Artistic ~ dynasty: 4 MING
association: 4 TONG
Big name in ~ history: 5 ENLAI
boat: 4 JUNK
brew: 3 CHA
calendar animal: 3 RAT
capital: 6 TAIPEI
coin: 4 YUAN
cuisine: 5 HUNAN
Dark ~ principle: 3 YIN
discipline: 3 ZEN 6 TAICHI
dollar: 4 YUAN
drink: 3 TEA 8 GREENTEA
dumpling: 6 WONTON
dynasty: 3 HAN 4 CHOU HSIA
    MING TONG 5 LIANG
    SHANG
dynasty overthrown by the
    Mongols: 4 SUNG
food additive: 3 MSG
Former ~ leader: 3 MAO 4 DENG
gang: 4 TONG
gelatin: 4 AGAR
general: 3 TSO

gooseberry: 4 KIWI
ideal: 3 TAO
idol: 4 JOSS
island: 6 TAIWAN
leader: 4 INDO SINO
Like some ~ dishes:
    9 STIRFRIED
martial art: 6 KUNGFU
menu general: 3 **TSO**
menu phrase: 5 NOMSG
money: 4 YUAN
nurse: 4 AMAH
nut: 6 LITCHI
Old ~ money: 4 TAEL
opening: 4 SINO
percussion: 4 GONG
philosopher: 6 LAOTSE
philosophy: 3 TAO
poet: 4 LIPO
port: 4 AMOY
potable: 8 GREENTEA
prefix: 4 INDO SINO
principle: 3 TAO
secret society: 4 **TONG**
Start of a ~ game: 3 MAH
takeout freebie: 4 RICE
tea: 3 **CHA**
temple: 6 PAGODA
toy: 4 PEKE
way: 3 TAO
~ Chairman: 3 MAO
"Chinese Parrot, The"
hero: 4 CHAN
Chinese restaurant
drink: 6 HOTTEA
flower: 7 TEAROSE
freebie: 3 TEA
offering: 8 GREENTEA
Chinese restaurant syndrome
cause: 3 MSG
___ Chinmoy: 3 SRI
Chinny
chatter: 4 LENO
Chinook: 6 SALMON
Chinua
Novelist: 6 ACHEBE
Chinwag: 3 GAB
Chip
accompanier: 8 ONIONDIP

away at: 5 **ERODE**
Blue or white: 4 ANTE
Cheesy ~ flavor: 5 NACHO
dip: 5 SALSA
feature: 5 RIDGE
flavoring: 4 SALT
giant: 5 INTEL
in: 4 **ANTE**
Initial: 4 ANTE
Kick in a: 4 ANTE
Kind of: 5 NACHO
Main ~, for short: 3 CPU
maker: 3 AXE 4 WISE 5 INTEL
    7 ICEPICK
making supply: 4 LARD
off the old block: 3 LAD SON
    5 IMAGE 6 SLIVER
on the table: 4 ANTE
or drive: 6 STROKE
Partner of: 4 **DALE**
Popular: 5 FRITO
Snack: 5 NACHO
Snack for ~ or Dale: 5 ACORN
topper: 3 DIP
tossing comment: 4 IMIN
~, to a Brit: 5 CRISP
Chipmunk: 6 RODENT
  Cartoon: 4 DALE 5 ALVIN
Chippendale
  feature: 4 OGEE
  Like ~ furniture: 6 ROCOCO
Chipper: 3 GAY 4 PERT 5 PERKY
  Nipper and ~ co.: 3 RCA
Chips
  and such: 4 NOSH 8 JUNKFOOD
    9 SNACKFOOD
  Apples with: 4 MACS
  Bag of: 4 NOSH
  Big name in: 4 LAYS WISE
    5 INTEL 6 FRITOS
  Element in: 7 SILICON
  Game with aces and: 4 GOLF
  Have some: 4 NOSH
  In the: 4 RICH
  Like some: 5 SALTY 6 RIDGED
"CHiPs"
  actor Erik: 7 ESTRADA
  actor Estrada: 4 ERIK
  actress Oakes: 5 RANDI

Chips, Mr.
  portrayer: 5 DONAT 6 OTOOLE
  subject: 5 LATIN
"Chiquitita"
  quartet: 4 ABBA
Chirac
  palace: 6 ELYSEE
  state: 4 ETAT
Chiromancer
  study: 5 PALMS
Chiropractor
  concern: 5 SPINE
Chirp: 4 PEEP 5 TWEET
Chirper
  Little: 4 WREN
  Tiny: 7 KATYDID
Chisel: 4 TOOL 5 GOUGE
  feature: 4 EDGE
  relative: 3 ADZ
Chisholm Trail
  city: 4 ENID WACO
  group: 4 HERD
  terminus: 7 ABILENE
Chit: 3 **IOU**
  Has a ~ out: 4 OWES
Chitchat: 3 GAB YAK 4 TALK
    7 PALAVER
Chi-town
  paper: 4 TRIB
"Chitty Chitty Bang Bang"
  actor Frobe: 4 GERT
  screenwriter: 4 DAHL
  ~, literarily: 12 ONOMATOPOEIA
Chivalrous: 5 NOBLE 7 GALLANT
  Hardly: 4 RUDE
Chive: 4 HERB
Chloe
  Love of: 7 DAPHNIS
Chlor-
  suffix: 3 IDE
Chloride
  prefix: 3 TRI
  Sodium: 4 SALT
Chlorine
  compound: 6 HALIDE
Chloroform
  kin: 5 ETHER
Chlorophyll
  maker: 4 ALGA 5 PLANT

Chmn.
cousin: 4 PRES
Choate
Attend: 4 PREP
Chocoholic
bane: 5 CAROB
"Chocolat"
actress Lena: 4 OLIN
Chocolate
bar nut: 6 ALMOND
bean: 5 CACAO
Big name in: 6 NESTLE
candy brand: 6 RIESEN
dessert: 6 MOUSSE MUDPIE
Ersatz: 5 CAROB
flavoring: 5 MOCHA
Half a ~ drink: 3 YOO
marshmallow snack: 5 SMORE
sauce: 4 MOLE
shape: 3 BAR 4 KISS
snacks: 5 ROLOS
source: 5 **CACAO**
substitute: 5 **CAROB**
syrup brand: 5 BOSCO
treat: 3 BAR 4 KISS OREO
    5 FUDGE 6 MOUSSE
    7 MARSBAR
Chocolate Creme
cookie: 4 OREO
Chocolatier
Fictional: 5 WONKA
Choctaw: 5 TRIBE
Choice: 4 PICK PLUM RARE
    5 ELECT ELITE PRIME
    6 OPTION
cut: 4 LOIN 5 FILET
location: 4 FORK MENU
marble: 3 TAW
morsel: 6 TIDBIT
word: 3 ANY 4 EENY **ELSE**
    5 OTHER 6 EITHER
words: 3 ORS 4 IFSO 5 ANDOR
    6 ORELSE
"___ Choice": 7 SOPHIES
Choir
attire: 4 ROBE
member: 4 **ALTO** 5 TENOR
neighbor: 4 APSE
section: 5 ALTOS

Some ~ members: 4 ALTI
    5 ALTOS 6 BASSES
stands: 6 RISERS
voice: 4 **ALTO**
Choke: 3 GAG JAM 8 OVERGROW
Choker: 5 NOOSE
Channel: 4 SILT
site: 4 NECK
Choler: 3 **IRE** 5 ANGER WRATH
Cholesterol
Bad ~ letters: 3 LDL
Good ~ letters: 3 HDL
Chollas: 5 CACTI
Chomolungma
alias: 7 EVEREST
Chomsky
Linguist: 4 **NOAM**
Chong, ___ Dawn: 3 **RAE**
Choo-choo
part: 6 ENGINE
sound: 4 TOOT
Choose: 3 **OPT** TAP 4 PICK
    5 ELECT 6 DECIDE
    OPTFOR SELECT
not to choose: 7 ABSTAIN
the window instead of the aisle:
    5 ELOPE
Chooser
word: 4 EENY
Choosing
Having a hard time: 4 TORN
Chop: 3 HEW 5 MINCE
down: 3 AXE HEW 4 FELL
finely: 4 HASH 5 MINCE
In a ~ shop: 6 STOLEN
into cubes: 4 DICE
Kind of: 4 JUDO LOIN PORK
    6 KARATE
off: 3 LOP
up: 4 HASH 5 MINCE
Chop ___: 4 **SUEY**
Chop-chop: 4 ASAP 5 APACE
    6 PRESTO
Go: 3 HEW
Chophouse
choice: 5 STEAK TBONE
request: 4 RARE
Chopin
piece: 5 **ETUDE** WALTZ

7 MAZURKA 9 POLONAISE
Sand, to: 4 AMIE
work: 8 NOCTURNE
Chopped
side dish: 4 SLAW
Chopper: 3 **AXE**
blade: 5 ROTOR
Clod: 3 HOE
Choppers: 5 TEETH
Grow: 6 TEETHE
Chopping
tool: 3 AXE 4 ADZE
Chops: 4 MEAT
Chop suey
additive: 3 MSG
Choral
part: 4 ALTO
piece: 5 MOTET 7 CANTATA
section: 5 ALTOS
syllable: 3 TRA
"Choral"
Beethoven's ~ Symphony:
5 NINTH
Chord
Common: 5 **TRIAD**
Chore: 4 TASK 6 ERRAND
list header: 4 TODO
shortcut: 9 TIMESAVER
Choreographer
~ Agnes de ___: 5 MILLE
~ Ailey: 5 ALVIN
~ Alvin: 5 AILEY
~ Bob: 5 FOSSE
~ Cunningham: 5 MERCE
~ de Mille: 5 AGNES
~ Lubovitch: 3 LAR
~ Sir Frederick: 6 ASHTON
~ Tharp: 5 TWYLA
~ Twyla: 5 THARP
Choreography
bit: 4 STEP
Choristers
Some: 4 ALTI 5 ALTOS
Chorus: 7 REFRAIN
A ~ line: 4 ALTO 5 TRALA
Church: 5 AMENS
girl: 4 ALTO
member: 4 **ALTO** BASS 5 TENOR
syllable: 3 TRA

voice: 4 ALTO
"Chorus Line, A"
producer: 4 PAPP
song: 3 ONE
Chose: 5 **OPTED**
Chosen: 5 ALIST ELECT
few: 5 ELITE
number: 3 FEW
one: 8 SELECTEE
ones: 5 ELECT
Chou ___: 5 ENLAI
Chou En-___: 3 **LAI**
Chow: 4 **EATS** FEED FOOD
GRUB 5 SPITZ
chow: 4 ALPO
down: 3 **EAT**
holder: 5 LEASH
Luau: 3 POI
mein additive: 3 MSG
Sow: 4 SLOP
Chow ___: 4 MEIN
Chowder
ingredient: 4 CLAM
Manhattan clam ~ seasoning:
5 THYME
Chowderhead: 3 ASS LUG SAP
4 DOLT DOPE SIMP
5 IDIOT STUPE
___ choy: 3 BOK
Chris
NHL goalie: 6 OSGOOD
of tennis: 5 EVERT
Singer: 3 REA 5 ISAAK
Christ
Follower of: 3 IAN
Sect member during time of:
6 ESSENE
Vicar of: 4 POPE
Christen: 4 NAME
Christian: 3 ERA
Egyptian: 4 COPT
of fashion: 4 DIOR
symbol: 5 CROSS
Christian ___: 3 ERA
Christiania
Capital formerly called: 4 OSLO
Christianity
(abbr.): 3 REL
Creed of: 6 NICENE

Early center of: 6 EDESSA
Christians
Like some: 6 REBORN
9 BORNAGAIN
Christian Science
founder: 4 EDDY
"___ Christian Soldiers":
6 ONWARD
Christie
and Karenina: 5 ANNAS
contemporary: 3 TEY
detective: 6 MARPLE POIROT
of mystery: 6 AGATHA
Singer: 3 LOU
"___ Christie": 4 ANNA
Christie, Agatha
River in an ~ title: 4 NILE
title: 4 DAME
Christie's
Compete at: 3 BID
Christina
Actress: 5 RICCI
Father of: 3 ARI
Singer: 8 AGUILERA
"Christina's World"
painter: 5 WYETH
Christine
Actress: 5 **LAHTI**
TV actress: 5 ELISE
Christmas: 4 NOEL YULE
(abbr.): 3 ISL
air: 4 NOEL
buy: 3 FIR TOY 4 TREE
carol: 4 **NOEL**
Classic ~ present: 4 SLED
decoration: 4 TREE 5 HOLLY
SANTA 6 WREATH
display: 6 CRECHE
eave decoration: 6 ICICLE
poem opener: 4 TWAS
quaff: 3 NOG 6 EGGNOG
season: 4 NOEL YULE
song: 4 NOEL 5 CAROL
sounds: 3 HOS
stamp subject: 7 MADONNA
Start of a ~ carol: 5 OCOME
6 ADESTE
Start of a ~ poem: 4 TWAS
time (abbr.): 3 DEC

~, in Italian: 6 NATALE
Christmas ___: 3 EVE 4 SEAL
5 CAROL SEALS
"Christmas Carol, A"
character: 3 TIM
exclamation: 3 BAH
"Christmas Song, The"
co-composer: 5 TORME
Christmas tree: 3 FIR
glitter: 6 TINSEL
topper: 4 STAR 5 ANGEL
"Christ of St. John of the Cross"
artist: 4 DALI
Christogram
letter: 3 RHO
Christopher
Actor: 5 LLOYD **REEVE**
Architect: 4 WREN
Connecticut senator: 4 DODD
"Christ's Entry Into Brussels"
painter James: 5 ENSOR
"Christ Stopped at ___": 5 EBOLI
"Christ Stopped at Eboli"
author: 4 LEVI
Chromosome
component: 3 DNA 4 GENE
map: 6 GENOME
molecule: 3 RNA
Y ~ carrier: 4 MALE
Chronic
critic: 3 NAG
nag: 5 SHREW
Not: 5 ACUTE
Chronicler
1666 London fire ~: 5 PEPYS
Alice's: 4 ARLO 5 LEWIS
Narnia: 7 CSLEWIS
Poker Flat: 5 HARTE
Chronicles: 6 ANNALS
"Chronicles of ___": 6 NARNIA
Chronological
brinks: 4 EVES
Chronology
component: 3 ERA
Chrysalis: 4 PUPA
Chrysler: 4 AUTO
1980s ~ model: 4 KCAR
Car co. bought by: 3 AMC
Former head of: 7 IACOCCA

Old ~ model: **6** DESOTO
Chrysler Building
  architect William Van ___:
    4 ALEN
  style: **4** DECO
"Chuang Tzu"
  principle: **3** TAO
Chubby: 3 FAT **5** PLUMP
Chuck: 3 PEG **4** HURL TOSS
    5 FLING **7** DEEPSIX
  A ~ holds it: **3** BIT
  alternative: **4 CHAS**
  Former Steelers coach: **4** NOLL
  of Watergate: **6** COLSON
  Test pilot: **6** YEAGER
  wagon honcho: **4** COOK
Chuckle
  Bit of a: **3** HEH
  Cause to: **5** AMUSE
  Chat room: **3 LOL**
  More than: **4** ROAR
Chucklehead: 3 ASS SAP **4** BOOB
    DOPE **5** DUNCE SCHMO
Chug-___: 4 ALUG
Chukkers
  Game of: **4 POLO**
Chum: 3 BRO BUB BUD **PAL**
    5 AMIGO CRONY
  Longtime: **6** OLDPAL
  ~, to a Brit: **4** MATE
Chump: 3 SAP **5** SCHMO
Chung, Connie
  employer: **3** CNN
Chunk: 3 GOB **4** SLAB
  Big ~ of earth: **4** ASIA
  in the Arctic Ocean: **4** BERG
  of fairway: **5** DIVOT
  of history: **3** ERA
Chunky
  More than: **5** OBESE
Church
  agreement: **4** AMEN
  area: **4 APSE** NAVE **5** ALTAR
    6 VESTRY
  assembly: **5** SYNOD
  bench: **3** PEW
  calendar: **4** ORDO
  center: **4** NAVE
  chorus: **5** AMENS

  council: **5 SYNOD**
  dignitary: **7** PRELATE
  donation: **5** TITHE
  ending: **4** GOER
  feature: **5** SPIRE
  gallery: **4** LOFT
  holding: **5** DOGMA TENET
  instrument: **5** ORGAN
  key: **6** OPENER
  lady: **3** NUN
  law: **5** CANON
  leader: **5** ELDER
  Letters in some ~ names: **3** AME
  Like a ~ mouse: **4** POOR
  Like some ~ matters: **4** LAIC
  Millennial ~ member: **6** SHAKER
  music: **5** MOTET
  niche: **4** APSE
  offering: **5** TITHE
  official: **5** ABBOT **ELDER** VICAR
    6 DEACON PASTOR SEXTON
    7 PRELATE
  recess: **4 APSE**
  seating: **3** PEW
  service: **4** MASS
  singers: **5** CHOIR
  song: **4** HYMN **5** MOTET
  Split for: **5** TITHE
  support: **5** TITHE
  Title acquired in: **3** MRS
  topper: **5** SPIRE **7** STEEPLE
  Unification ~ member:
    6 MOONIE
  Vaulted ~ area: **4** APSE
  vestment: **3** ALB
Churchgoers
  Many ~ (abbr.): **5** CATHS
Churchill: 4 TORY
  Barrier named by:
    11 IRONCURTAIN
  gesture: **3** VEE **5** VSIGN
  "So few," to: **3** RAF
  successor: **4 EDEN 6** ATTLEE
  The RAF, to: **5** SOFEW
Churchill Downs
  drink: **5** JULEP
  event: **5** DERBY
Church Lady
  sound: **3** TSK

Churchyard
tree: 3 YEW
Churl: 3 CAD OAF 4 BOOR LOUT
Like a: 4 RUDE
Churn
up: 4 RILE ROIL
Chute
Deliver by: 4 DROP
fabric: 5 NYLON
opener: 4 PARA
Chutist
~, briefly: 4 PARA
Chutney
fruit: 5 MANGO
ingredient: 8 TAMARIND
Chutzpah: 4 GALL 5 BRASS
  CRUST MOXIE **NERVE**
  6 HUBRIS
Full of: 5 BRASH NERVY
CIA
1980s ~ director: 5 CASEY
agent: 3 SPY
director under Bush and Clinton:
  5 TENET
film spoof: 4 SPYS
Former ~ opponent: 3 KGB
operative: 3 AGT
Part of: 6 AGENCY
predecessor: 3 **OSS**
problem: 4 MOLE
relative: 3 NSA
"Ciao!": 3 BYE 4 TATA 5 LATER
  SEEYA
~, in Spanish: 5 ADIOS
Cicatrix: 4 SCAR
Cicely
Emmy winner: 5 TYSON
Cicero
Emulate: 5 ORATE
Cider
girl: 3 IDA
Like some: 4 HARD
"Cider House Rules, The"
Oscar winner: 5 CAINE
  12 MICHAELCAINE
Cigar
butt: 4 ETTE
Cheap: 6 STOGIE
Cherished: 6 HAVANA

choice: 6 CORONA
holder: 7 HUMIDOR
Kind of: 5 CUBAN
Long: 9 PANATELLA
Mild: 5 **CLARO**
residue: 3 ASH
suffix: 4 ETTE
tip: 3 ASH 4 ETTE
Cigarette: 4 WEED
Illicit: 6 REEFER
ingredient: 3 TAR
pkg.: 3 CTN
residue: 3 ASH
stuff: 3 TAR
Cigs: 5 WEEDS
Cilium: 4 LASH
"Cimarron"
actress Dunne: 5 IRENE
C in C: 4 PRES 5 POTUS
Part of: 3 CDR
Cinch: 3 ICE 4 SNAP 6 ENSURE
in Japan: 3 OBI
Cincinnati
state: 4 OHIO
team: 4 REDS 7 BENGALS
Cinco
follower: 4 SEIS
y dos: 5 SIETE
y tres: 4 OCHO
Cinco de Mayo: 3 DIA
event: 6 FIESTA
Cincy
player: 3 RED
Cinderella
event: 4 BALL
horses: 4 MICE
Like stepsisters of: 4 UGLY
loss: 7 SLIPPER
"Cinderella Liberty"
Wallach of: 3 ELI
Cinders
of comics: 4 **ELLA**
Turn to: 4 CHAR
"___ Cinders" (old comic): 4 ELLA
Cine
suffix: 4 RAMA
Cinema
canine: 4 ASTA
chain: 5 LOEWS

Delon of: 5 ALAIN
Hall of: 5 ANNIE
name: 5 ODEON
snippet: 4 CLIP
Sommer of: 4 ELKE
statuette: 5 OSCAR
supplies: 5 REELS
trigram: 3 MGM
West of: 3 MAE
Cinemas
Local: 5 NABES
Cinematographer
org.: 3 ASC
~ Nykvist: 4 SVEN
Cinemax
sister: 3 HBO
Cineplex ___ : 5 ODEON
Cinerary
vessel: 3 URN
Cinergy Field
team: 4 REDS
Cinnabar: 3 ORE
Cinnamon: 5 SPICE
candy: 6 REDHOT
Chinese: 6 CASSIA
Cinque
follower: 3 SEI
minus due: 3 TRE
CIO
partner: 3 AFL
Cio-Cio-___ : 3 SAN
Cipher: 4 CODE NULL ZERO
Put in: 6 ENCODE
Circa: 4 NEAR 5 **ABOUT**
6 AROUND
Circle: 3 SET 4 AREA LOOP RING
5 ORBIT 7 COTERIE
bit: 3 ARC
Colorful: 6 AREOLA
constants: 3 PIS
dance: 4 **HORA**
Flattened: 4 OVAL
Floral: 3 LEI
Form a: 4 LOOP
Full: 3 LAP
Inner: 4 LOOP 5 CADRE
line: 6 RADIUS
Line connecting points on a:

5 CHORD
lines: 5 RADII
Line through a: 6 SECANT
meas.: 4 DIAM
of light: 4 HALO
overhead: 4 HALO
preceder: 5 INNER
section: 3 **ARC**
stat: 8 DIAMETER
Tiny: 3 DOT
Traffic: 6 ROTARY
Word with: 5 INNER
"Circle of Friends"
author Binchy: 5 MAEVE
Circles
Colorful: 7 AREOLAE
Go around in: 4 EDDY ROLL
SPIN 5 ORBIT
Going in: 4 LOST
Circlet
Angelic: 4 HALO
Circling: 7 INORBIT
Circuit: 4 LOOP
breaker word: 3 AMP
Full: 3 LAP
part: 4 FUSE
Racing: 3 LAP
Circuitous
path: 3 ARC
Circular: 5 FLIER 6 MAILER
announcement: 4 SALE
course: 4 GYRE
current: 4 EDDY
file: 7 ROLODEX
gasket: 5 ORING
waffle: 4 EGGO
"Circular file": 8 TRASHCAN
Circulation
Took out of: 8 CALLEDIN
~, in a way: 7 READERS
Circulatory
blockage: 4 CLOT
Circumference: 5 AMBIT GIRTH
part: 3 ARC
Circumflex
lookalike: 5 CARET
Circumnavigator
16th-century ~: 5 DRAKE
Fictional: 4 FOGG

Circumspect: 5 CHARY
Circumstance
  Partner of: 4 POMP
Circumstances
  Under any: 5 ATALL
  Under the most favorable:
    6 ATBEST
Circumvent: 5 AVOID ELUDE
    EVADE 6 BYPASS OUTWIT
Circus
  act: 4 FEAT
  barker: 4 SEAL
  catcher: 3 NET
  clapper: 4 SEAL
  clown Kelly: 6 EMMETT
  cries: 3 OHS 4 OOHS
  employee: 5 TAMER
  housing: 4 TENT
  Kind of: 4 FLEA 5 MEDIA
  Like ~ lions: 5 TAMED
  lineup: 4 ACTS
  performer: 4 FLEA SEAL
    5 CLOWN TAMER
    7 ACROBAT 9 AERIALIST
    LIONTAMER
  prop: 5 STILT
  safeguard: 3 NET
  setups: 5 TENTS
  sight: 4 TENT 5 STILT
  site: 5 ARENA
  Work with ~ cats: 4 TAME
  ___ Circus: 5 NEROS
Circus Hall of Fame
  site: 8 SARASOTA
Cirque du ___: 6 SOLEIL
Cirrus: 5 CLOUD
  cloud formation: 4 WISP
CIS
  members, once: 4 SSRS
  predecessor: 4 USSR
Cisco Kid
  horse: 6 DIABLO
  player: 6 ROMERO
  ~, to Pancho: 5 AMIGO
Cistern: 3 VAT
  ___ cit.: 3 LOC
Citadel
  Like The ~, now: 4 COED
  student: 5 CADET

  The ~ rival, briefly: 3 VMI
Citation
  and Corsair: 6 EDSELS
  Court ~ abbr.: 5 ETSEQ
  Earned a: 4 SPED
  jockey: 6 ARCARO
  Reason for a ~ (abbr.): 3 DWI
  ___ citato: 5 OPERE
Cite: 5 QUOTE 6 ADDUCE
    7 REFERTO
"Cities of the Interior"
  author: 3 NIN 8 ANAISNIN
Cities Service
  competitor: 4 ESSO
Citified: 5 URBAN
Citium
  Stoic from: 4 ZENO
Citizen: 7 FREEMAN
  Muscat: 5 OMANI
  New: 6 EMIGRE
  Noted: 4 KANE
  rights org.: 4 ACLU
  Riyadh: 4 ARAB
  Saudi: 4 ARAB
  Seoul: 6 KOREAN
  Sultanate: 5 OMANI
  U.S. ~ to be: 9 DECLARANT
"Citizen ___": 4 KANE
"Citizen Kane"
  actor Everett: 6 SLOANE
  actor Joseph: 6 COTTEN
  Last word of: 7 ROSEBUD
  portrayer: 6 WELLES
  prop: 4 SLED
  sled: 7 ROSEBUD
  studio: 3 **RKO**
Citizenship
  Good ~ org.: 3 GSA
"Citizen X"
  actor: 3 REA
Citric ___: 4 ACID
Citrine
  cooler: 3 ADE
Citroën
  Automaker: 5 ANDRE
Citron
  suffix: 4 ELLA
Citrus
  Big ~ fruit: 6 POMELO

city: **5** OCALA
cooler: **3** ADE
drink: **3 ADE 7** LIMEADE
fruit: **4** LIME UGLI **5** LEMON
    6 ORANGE
hybrid: **4** UGLI **5** LIMON
    7 TANGELO
Jamaican: **4** UGLI
juice cocktail: **7** SIDECAR
peel: **4** ZEST **5** TWIST
source: **8** LIMETREE
Wrinkly: **4** UGLI

Città
capitale: **4** ROMA

Città ___ Vaticano: 3 DEL

City: 4 BURG **5** URBAN
Ancient: **5** TANIS UTICA
    6 EDESSA SPARTA
    7 BABYLON
area: **3** URB
Bay: **5** TAMPA
Biblical: **5** SODOM
Big ~ woe: **4** SMOG
bond, for short: **4** MUNI
"by the sea, oh": **3** RIO
council rep.: **3** ALD
"Gay": **5** PAREE
Half a: **4** PAGO **5** WALLA
Holy: **5** MECCA **6** TOLEDO
Inner ~ area: **6** BARRIO
    GHETTO
It's far from the big city: **5** EXURB
leader: **5** MAYOR
map: **4** PLAT
NFL: **5** TAMPA
NHL: **6** OTTAWA
N.L.: **3** ATL STL
Sin: **5** SODOM
Southernmost U.S.: **4** HILO
Strange-sounding: **4** ERIE
Word with: **5** INNER

___ City
(easy street): **3** FAT
(PC game): **3** SIM

City-state
Greek: **5** POLIS **6** SPARTA
    7 CORINTH

"City Without Clocks, The":
    5 VEGAS

"City Without Walls"
poet: **5** AUDEN

Ciudad Juárez
neighbor: **6** ELPASO

Civic: 5 HONDA
group: **4** ELKS **5** LIONS

Civil: 6 POLITE
action cause: **4** TORT
disorder: **4** RIOT
It may be: **3** WAR
punishment: **4** FINE
suffix: **3** ITY
They may be ~ (abbr.): **3** RTS
wrong: **4 TORT**

"Civil Disobedience"
author: **7** THOREAU

Civilian
clothes: **5** MUFTI

Civil rights
1960s ~ gp.: **4** SNCC
city: **5** SELMA
figure Parks: **4** ROSA
lawyer Morris: **4** DEES
leader Medgar: **5** EVERS
org.: **5** NAACP

Civil Rights Memorial
designer: **3** LIN

Civil War
authority Shelby: **5** FOOTE
battle site: **6** SHILOH
biography: **5** RELEE
fort: **6** SUMTER
general: **3** LEE **4** RENO
    5 GRANT MEADE
    7 SHERMAN
gp.: **3** CSA
guerrilla: **6** REDLEG
nickname: **3** ABE
photographer: **5** BRADY
side: **4** REBS **5** NORTH SOUTH
    UNION
soldier: **3** REB **4** GRAY
song: **15** TRAMPTRAMPTRAMP
veterans gp.: **3** GAR

Civvies: 5 MUFTI

Cl⁻: 3 ION **5** ANION

Clack: 5 NOISE

Clad: 7 ATTIRED
Was ~ in: **4** WORE

Claiborne
 Designer: 3 **LIZ**
 Food writer: 5 CRAIG
Claim: 4 AVER AVOW DIBS
    6 **ALLEGE** ASSERT
    7 PROFESS PURPORT
 Champion's: 5 TITLE
 Clairvoyant's: 3 ESP
 Ex: 7 ALIMONY
 First: 4 DIBS
 Legal: 4 LIEN
 Property: 4 **LIEN**
 Psychic's: 3 ESP
 Vain: 5 BOAST
Claimant: 6 LIENOR
 cry: 4 DIBS
Claimed
 the title: 3 WON
Claiming
 Quit: 5 CEDED
Clair
 Director: 4 **RENE**
"Clair de ___": 4 LUNE
Claire
 Actress: 3 INA
 ___ **Claire**
 (Quebec): 6 POINTE
 (Wisconsin): 3 EAU
Clairol
 choice: 4 TINT 8 BRUNETTE
 user: 4 DYER
Clairvoyance: 3 ESP PSI
Clairvoyant: 4 **SEER** 5 SIBYL
 cards: 5 TAROT
 claim: 3 ESP
 gift: 3 ESP
 opener: 4 ISEE
Clam
 digs: 5 SHORE
 Edible: 6 QUAHOG
 home: 5 SHELL
 Soft-shell: 7 STEAMER
Clambake
 item: 7 STEAMER
Clammy: 4 DAMP DANK
    5 MOIST
Clamor: 3 ADO CRY **DIN** HUE
    5 HOOHA NOISE
    6 RACKET

Clamorous: 4 LOUD 5 AROAR
    NOISY VOCAL
 criticism: 4 FLAK
Clamp: 4 VISE
 shape: 3 CEE
Clampett
 patriarch: 3 JED
Clampett, Jed: 9 HILLBILLY
 portrayer: 5 EBSEN
Clampett, ___ May: 4 ELLY
Clams
 100 ~: 5 CNOTE CSPOT
 Cook: 5 STEAM
 or lettuce: 5 BREAD
Clan
 chief: 5 THANE
 clash: 4 FEUD
 emblem: 5 **TOTEM**
 pattern: 6 TARTAN
 unit: 4 SEPT
Clancy
 Author: 3 TOM
Clancy, Tom
 hero: 4 RYAN
 org.: 3 CIA
 subj.: 3 CIA
Clandestine: 3 SLY 6 SECRET
 maritime org.: 3 ONI
 meeting: 5 TRYST
Clangor: 3 DIN 5 NOISE
"Clan of the Cave Bear, The"
 author: 4 AUEL
 heroine: 4 AYLA
Clansman
 cap: 3 TAM
Clanton
 foe: 4 EARP
 gang leader: 3 IKE
Clap: 4 PEAL
Clapper
 Circus: 4 SEAL
Clapton
 Guitarist: 4 **ERIC**
 tune: 5 LAYLA
 ___ **Clara, California:** 5 SANTA
Clare
 and Henry: 5 LUCES
Clarence
 accuser: 5 ANITA

Saxophonist: **7** CLEMONS
Claret: 4 WINE
and chianti: **4** REDS
color: **3** RED
relative, for short: **3** ZIN
Clarification
preceder: **5** IDEST
starter: **5** IMEAN
Words of: **4** ASIN **5** IDEST
TOWIT
Clarified
butter: **4** GHEE
Clarifier
Latin: **5** IDEST
words: **5** IMEAN
Clarinet: 4 REED
cousin: **4** __OBOE__
part: **4** REED
Clarinetist
Dixieland: **12** PETEFOUNTAIN
need: **4** REED
~ Artie: **4** SHAW
~ Shaw: **5** __ARTIE__
Clarion
blast: **7** TANTARA
Clark
Country singer: **3** ROY
5 TERRI
of The Daily Planet: **4** KENT
partner: **4** LOIS **5** LEWIS
Role for: **5** RHETT
Singer: **6** PETULA
Clark, Gen. Wesley
Like: **3** RET
Clarke
Actress: **3** MAE
computer: **3** HAL
Claro: 5 CIGAR
Clash
of clans: **4** FEUD
of heavyweights: **4** SUMO
Petty: **4** SPAT
They may: **4** EGOS
"Clash by Night"
playwright: **5** ODETS
Clasp
Men's: **6** TIEBAR
Resting spot for a: **4** NAPE
Tie with a: **4** BOLO

Class: 3 ILK **4** SORT TIER
5 CASTE GENRE GRADE
STYLE
action gp.: **3** PTA
Airline: **7** ECONOMY
Anatomy ~ model: **8** SKELETON
Arrange by: **6** ASSORT
Art: **5** GENRE
Audited a: **5** SATIN
Beginning drawing: **4** ARTI
Biology ~ subject: **6** AMOEBA
Chem: **3** LAB
Cushy: **5** EASYA
cutter: **6** TRUANT
ender: **4** BELL
for new arrivals (abbr.): **3** ESL
Grad.: **3** SRS
High school: **3** GYM **4** MATH
SHOP
H.S.: **3** ALG ENG SCI **4** ECON
GEOG GEOM TRIG **5** SEXED
Law school: **5** TORTS
leader: **4** PROF
Math ~ abbr.: **3** QED **4** CALC
Med. school: **4** ANAT
of racing car: **6** MIDGET
of submarines: **4** ALFA
Physics ~ topic: **3** ERG
pres.: **4** BMOC
Privileged: **5** ELITE
reunion attendee: **4** ALUM
Science: **3** LAB
Ship: **8** STEERAGE
Social: **5** CASTE
struggle: **4** EXAM TEST
Unlikely ~ president: **4** NERD
With: **6** FINELY
work: **6** LESSON
Yoga ~ need: **3** MAT
Class-conscious
gp.: **3** PTA
Classic
art subject: **4** NUDE
beginning: **3** NEO
board game: **4** LIFE RISK
5 SORRY
car: **3** GTO __REO__ **5** TBIRD
VETTE **6** MODELA
card game: **3** UNO

clown: 4 BOZO
computer game: 4 MYST
film noir: 3 DOA
gas brand: 4 ESSO
opener: 3 NEO
sneakers: 4 KEDS
soft drink: 4 **NEHI**
sports cars: 3 MGS
theater: 4 ROXY 5 ODEON
western: 5 SHANE

Classical
beginning: 3 NEO
finale: 5 OMEGA
Light ~ music orchestra: 4 POPS
lyric poet: 6 SAPPHO
meeting place: 4 STOA
prefix: 3 NEO
style: 5 DORIC IONIC

Classification: 4 TYPE 5 GENRE
Biological: 6 FAMILY
Blood ~ system: 3 ABO
Draft: 4 ONEA
Kennel club: 5 BREED
Racehorse: 3 AGE

Classifications
Biological: 6 GENERA

Classified: 6 SECRET SORTED
WANTAD
ad abbr.: 3 EEO EOE
ad no.: 3 TEL
Highly: 9 TOPSECRET
info: 3 ADS
It's: 6 WANTAD
offers: 4 JOBS

Classifieds: 3 ADS
Times in: 4 EVES

Classifier: 8 ASSORTER

Classify: 3 PEG 4 SORT 5 LABEL
6 **ASSORT**

Classmates
See old: 5 REUNE

"Class Reunion"
author Jaffe: 4 RONA

Classroom
aid: 5 GLOBE
book: 4 TEXT
drudgery: 4 ROTE
favorite: 3 PET
furniture: 5 DESKS

helper: 4 AIDE
need: 7 ERASERS
supply: 5 CHALK

Classy: 4 POSH 7 ELEGANT
entrance: 4 ARCH

Clatter: 3 DIN 5 NOISE

Clattery
trains: 3 ELS

Claude
Actor: 5 AKINS RAINS
Author: 5 MCKAY

Claudio
Pianist: 5 **ARRAU**

Claudius
Info: Latin cue
I, to: 3 EGO
Successor to: 4 NERO
To be, to: 4 ESSE

Claus
Subordinate: 3 ELF

Clause
connector: 3 AND
Contract ~ (abbr.): 4 COLA
Escape: 3 OUT
negator: 3 NOR

Claustrophobic
patient's dread: 3 MRI

Clavell, James
novel: 6 SHOGUN TAIPAN
7 KINGRAT

"C'___ la vie!": 3 EST

Claw: 5 **TALON** 6 TEARAT
Bear: 6 PASTRY
Lobster: 6 PINCER

Clay
brick: 5 ADOBE
clump: 4 CLOD
Desert: 5 ADOBE
Lump of: 4 GLOB
Made of: 7 EARTHEN
Nee: 3 ALI
Remodeled: 3 ALI
today: 3 **ALI**
Work: 5 KNEAD

Clay, Henry: 6 ORATOR

Clayey
deposit: 4 MARL

Clay pigeon: 5 SKEET 6 TARGET
tosser: 4 TRAP

Clean: 5 MOPUP
 air org.: **3 EPA**
 Came: 4 TOLD
 Come: 4 ADMIT BATHE
   6 FESSUP
 Hard to: 5 GRIMY
 It's not: 4 SMUT
 kind of energy: 5 SOLAR
 Make: 5 REHAB
 off: 5 ERASE
 Squeaky: 6 CHASTE
 tables: 3 BUS
 the deck: 4 SWAB
 the furniture: 4 DUST
 the slate: 5 ERASE
 They ~ locks: 8 SHAMPOOS
 up: 4 LAVE WASH 5 BATHE
 up copy: 4 EDIT
 Wipe: **5 ERASE**
 with effort: 5 SCOUR SCRUB
Clean Air Act
 concern: 4 SMOG
 org.: 3 EPA
Cleaned
 one's plate: 3 ATE
Cleaner
 Blazer: 7 CARWASH
 Caustic: 3 LYE
 Clorox: 7 PINESOL
 Cotton-tipped: 4 SWAB
 Dry ~ challenge: 4 SPOT
 Ear: 4 QTIP SWAB
 Flat: 4 CHAR
 Pipe: 5 DRANO 6 REAMER
 Plate: 3 UMP 7 DISHRAG
 Rug: 3 VAC
 Strong: 3 LYE
Cleaners
 One may be taken to the: 5 STAIN
 Take to the: 4 BILK SOAK
   6 FLEECE 7 SWINDLE
Cleaning
 agent: 3 LYE
 aid: 3 MOP 5 BROOM 6 SPONGE
   7 DUSTMOP
 cloth: 3 RAG 4 WIPE
 Do a ~ chore: 4 DUST
 Spring ~ event: 7 TAGSALE
Cleanliness: 7 HYGIENE

Cleanse: 3 RID 4 LAVE 5 BATHE
   PURGE 7 DETERGE
Cleanser
 brand: 4 AJAX 5 COMET LYSOL
   6 BONAMI
 scent: 4 PINE
 Strong: 3 LYE
Cleansing
 agent: 4 SOAP 5 BORAX
Cleanup
 Fall ~ aid: 4 RAKE
 org.: 3 EPA
Clear: 3 NET RID 4 EARN
   5 DEFOG **ERASE** LUCID
   PLAIN 6 DELETE LIMPID
   PATENT UNCLOG
   UNSTOP 7 EVIDENT
   9 EXONERATE
 a hurdle: 4 LEAP
 Became: 6 SANKIN
 for takeoff: 5 DEICE
 Just ~ of the bottom: 5 ATRIP
 (of): 3 RID
 off: 4 WIPE 5 ERASE
 of the bottom: 6 AWEIGH
 of vermin: 5 DERAT
 Partner of: 4 LOUD
 Perfectly: 5 LUCID
 sky: 5 ETHER
 sky color: 5 AZURE
 soup: 8 CONSOMME
 Steer ~ of: 4 DUCK SHUN
   5 **AVOID** ELUDE EVADE
 tables: 3 BUS
 the board: 5 **ERASE**
 the leaves: 4 RAKE
 the tape: 5 ERASE
 the windshield: 5 DEFOG
 up: 5 SOLVE
 Words before: 5 INTHE
Clearance
 condition: 4 ASIS
 event: 4 SALE
 sign: 6 ONSALE
Clear as ___: 5 ABELL
Clearasil
 target: 3 ZIT 4 **ACNE**
Clear-cut
 They're often: 5 TREES

"___ Clear Day ...": 3 ONA
Clearheaded: 4 SANE 5 LUCID
   SOBER
Clearing
  Forest: 5 **GLADE**
  Throat: 4 AHEM
Clearly
  Hears: 4 GETS
  Outline: 4 ETCH
  Show: 6 EVINCE
Cleary, Beverly
  character: 6 RAMONA
Cleats
  What ~ increase: 4 GRIP
Cleave: 4 REND TEAR 5 SEVER
   6 ADHERE
Cleaver
  Mrs.: 4 JUNE
Cleaver, Theodore
  ~, to Wally: 4 BEAV
Cleaver, Wally
  pal: 5 EDDIE
  portrayer: 3 DOW 7 TONYDOW
Cleaving
  tool: 3 AXE 4 FROE
Cleek: 7 ONEIRON
Cleese
  cohort: 4 IDLE 5 PALIN
  Fish in a ~ film: 5 WANDA
Clef
  Kind of: 4 ALTO BASS 6 TREBLE
  Violinist: 4 **ALTO**
Clematis: 4 VINE
Clemens
  pen name: 5 TWAIN
  Pitcher: 5 ROGER
  stat: 3 ERA
  ~, as of 2004: 5 ASTRO
Clement
  Director: 4 RENE
  Poet: 5 MOORE
  ___ **Clemente:** 3 SAN
Clementine
  Father of: 5 MINER
Clemson
  athlete: 5 TIGER
Cleo
  of jazz: 5 LAINE
  river: 4 NILE

  undoing: 3 **ASP**
  wooer: 4 MARC
Cleopatra
  charm: 6 SCARAB
  He defeated Antony and:
    7 AGRIPPA
  killer: 3 ASP
  love: 4 MARC 6 ANTONY
  portrayer in 1917: 4 BARA
  river: 4 NILE
"Cleopatra"
  backdrop: 4 NILE 5 EGYPT
  portrayer:
    15 ELIZABETHTAYLOR
Cleopatra's Needle: 7 OBELISK
Clergy
  Not of the: 4 LAIC
  Some French: 5 ABBES
Clergyman: 5 VICAR 7 PRELATE
  cap: 7 BIRETTA
  Catholic: 6 PRIEST
  French: 4 ABBE
  Noted: 5 PEALE
  quarters: 5 MANSE
Cleric: 5 VICAR 6 DEACON
    PRIEST
  council: 5 SYNOD
  famous for bloopers: 7 SPOONER
  French: 4 **ABBE**
Clerical
  abode: 5 MANSE
  garb: 3 ALB
  Not: 4 LAIC
  One doing ~ work: 6 PRIEST
  vestment: 4 ROBE 5 AMICE
Clerk: 6 SELLER
  Dickens: 4 HEEP 5 URIAH
    8 CRATCHIT
  Do a ~ job: 4 SELL
  File: 12 PENCILPUSHER
  Kwik-E-Mart: 3 APU
  "M*A*S*H": 5 RADAR
Clermont
  designer: 6 FULTON
  power: 5 STEAM
Cleveland: 4 CITY 6 GROVER
  Abbr. after: 3 HTS
  Author: 5 AMORY
  cager: 3 **CAV**

City near: 5 AKRON 6 ELYRIA
lake: 4 **ERIE**
~ Indian: 4 ERIE
Cleveland Indians
mascot: 5 WAHOO
Clever: 3 APT 4 CAGY DEFT WILY
       5 CANNY QUICK SHARP
       SLICK SMART
comment: 3 MOT 4 QUIP
maneuver: 4 PLOY
one: 3 WIT
opening: 3 CEE
ploy: 4 RUSE
Cleverly
effective: 4 NEAT
skillful: 6 ADROIT
Cliburn: 7 PIANIST
Clichéd: 5 BANAL TRITE
movie ending: 6 SUNSET
Click: 8 HITITOFF
beetle: 6 ELATER
It's sent with a: 5 EMAIL
Morse: 3 DIT
Request before a: 5 SMILE
site: 4 ICON
They: 8 TAPSHOES
Clickable
image: 4 ICON
Clicked
image: 4 ICON
"send": 7 EMAILED
Clicker: 6 REMOTE 8 CASTANET
Clickers: 4 MICE
Client: 4 USER
of Darrow: 4 LOEB
"Client, The"
actor Brad: 6 RENFRO
Clientele
Café: 6 EATERS
Cliff: 5 SCARP 6 ESCARP
dwelling: 5 AERIE
hanger: 5 AERIE
line: 5 SCARP
Rocky: 4 SCAR
Rough: 4 CRAG
Clifford
Playwright: 5 **ODETS**
Cliffside
dwelling: 5 AERIE

Climactic
opening: 4 ANTI
time in a Cooper film: 4 NOON
Climatologist
concern: 6 ELNINO
Climax: 3 CAP 4 ACME PEAK
Musical: 4 CODA
Oater: 8 SHOOTOUT
Race: 7 LASTLAP
Climb: 4 GOUP RISE SHIN
       5 SCALE 6 ASCEND
       ASCENT SHINNY
They ~ walls: 5 IVIES VINES
Tough to: 5 STEEP
up: 5 MOUNT 6 ASCEND
Climber: 4 SNOB VINE
Campus: 3 IVY
challenge: 3 ALP 4 CRAG
descent: 6 RAPPEL
Hill: 3 ANT
Mountain: 4 TBAR
need: 7 TOEHOLD
Showy: 8 CLEMATIS
Social ~ goal: 6 STATUS
spike: 5 PITON
stop: 5 LEDGE
tool: 5 ICEAX
Climbing
plant: 3 IVY 4 VINE 5 LIANA
       8 SWEETPEA
spike: 5 PITON
vine: 5 LIANA
Clinch: 3 **ICE** 4 NAIL SEAL
       5 SEWUP
Cline
Country singer: 5 PATSY
record label: 5 DECCA
Cling: 6 **ADHERE** COHERE
Word before: 6 STATIC
Clinger
Sock: 3 BUR
Clinic
name: 4 MAYO
Recovery: 5 REHAB
___ Clinic: 4 MAYO
Clink: 3 CAN 4 JAIL STIR
glasses: 5 TOAST
Klink: 6 STALAG
Ship: 4 BRIG

Clinker: 3 DUD 4 GOOF 5 ERROR
  Drink: 3 ICE
Clinky: 8 METALLIC
Clint
  "costar": 5 ORANG
Clinton: 8 ARKANSAN
  (abbr.): 3 DEM SEN
  aide Leon: 7 PANETTA
  aide Myers: 6 DEEDEE
  alma mater: 4 YALE
  and Bush: 4 ELIS
  attorney general: 4 RENO
  birthplace: 4 HOPE
  blew it: 3 SAX
  cabinet member: 4 PENA RENO
    7 SHALALA
  canal: 4 ERIE
  cat: 5 SOCKS
  CIA director under: 5 TENET
  defense secretary: 5 COHEN
  inaugural poet: 7 ANGELOU
  investigator: 5 STARR
  opponent: 4 DOLE
  or Kennedy: 7 SENATOR
  treaty: 5 NAFTA
  veep: 4 GORE 6 ALGORE
  was one: 5 YALIE
  Where Bill and Hillary ~ met:
    4 YALE
  ~ FBI director: 5 FREEH
  ~, to Yale: 4 ALUM
"Clinton's Ditch": 9 ERIECANAL
Clio: 4 MUSE 5 AWARD
  Sister of: 5 ERATO 6 THALIA
    URANIA
  winner: 5 ADMAN
  winners: 3 ADS 5 ADMEN
Clip: 4 CHOP GAIT PACE RATE
    5 SHEAR 6 ATTACH
    7 SCISSOR
  alternative: 6 STAPLE
  At a good: 5 APACE
  News: 5 VIDEO 7 FOOTAGE
  out: 7 SCISSOR
  wool: 5 SHEAR
Clip-fed
  machine gun: 4 BREN
Clip-on
  Belt: 5 PAGER

Clipped: 5 SHORN **TERSE**
  Musically: 8 STACCATO
Clipper: 4 SHIP
  feature: 4 MAST SAIL
  name: 5 PANAM
  target: 4 NAIL 7 TOENAIL
Clippers: 6 SHEARS
  org.: 3 NBA
  Using: 4 ASEA
Clipper-ship
  cargo: 3 TEA
Clipping: 4 ITEM
  holder: 9 SCRAPBOOK
  Item for: 7 TOENAIL
  Shopper's: 6 COUPON
Clique: 3 SET 4 GANG 7 COTERIE
    FACTION INCROWD
    INGROUP
  member: 7 INSIDER
Cloak: 4 CAPE 6 MANTLE
  Arabian: 8 BURNOOSE
  Bullfighter: 4 CAPA
  partner: 6 DAGGER
  Roman: 4 TOGA
  Sleeveless: 6 MANTLE
Cloak-and-dagger
  org.: 3 CIA
  type: 3 SPY
Clobber: 3 BOP LAM 4 BASH
    DECK DRUB ROUT
    5 PASTE SMITE TROMP
    6 THRASH 7 SHELLAC
  with snowballs: 4 PELT
Clobbered
  Is: 9 SEESSTARS
Clock
  Adjust a: 3 SET 5 RESET
  face: 4 DIAL
  function: 5 ALARM
  Kind of: 4 SHOT 6 ANALOG
    ATOMIC 7 DIGITAL
  Midnight on a grandfather: 3 XII
  numeral: 3 III VII XII 4 IIII VIII
  part: 4 DIAL FACE GEAR
  radio button: 6 SNOOZE
  sound: 4 TICK TOCK
  std.: 3 GMT GST
"Clockers"
  director Spike: 3 LEE

Clockmaker
~ Terry: 3 **ELI**
~ Thomas: 4 **SETH**
Clock setting
Ala.: 3 CST
Ariz.: 3 MST
at LAX: 3 PST
Cal.: 3 PST
Chi.: 3 CDT CST
Colo.: 3 **MST**
D.C.: 3 EDT EST
Halifax ~ (abbr.): 3 AST
L.A.: 3 PST
N.S.: 3 AST
NYC: 3 EDT EST
Okla.: 3 CST
Penna.: 3 EST
Phila.: 3 EST
Seattle ~ (abbr.): 3 PST
S.F.: 3 PST
Summer ~ (abbr.): 3 DST EDT
"Clockwork Orange, A"
hooligan: 4 ALEX
Clod: 3 ASS OAF 4 BOOR
Big: 3 APE
chopper: 3 HOE
Clodhopper: 3 OAF 4 BOOR
LOUT
Clog: 4 SHOE 5 DAMUP JAMUP
6 STOPUP
bottom: 4 SOLE
clearer: 5 DRANO
kin: 5 SABOT
Cloisonné: 6 ENAMEL
"Cloister and the Hearth, The"
author: 5 **READE**
Cloistresse: 3 NUN
Clone: 4 COPY 7 REPLICA
Famous: 5 DOLLY
Cloned
They may be: 3 PCS
Cloning
basic: 3 DNA
Clop
Foot that goes: 4 HOOF
Clorox
cleaner: 7 LESTOIL PINESOL
Close: 3 END 4 NEAR **SHUT**
5 LATCH TIGHT ZIPUP

6 ENDING NEARBY
NEARTO
Actress: 5 GLENN
again: 6 RESEAL
associate: 3 PAL
at hand: 4 NEAR NIGH
6 NEARBY
Brings to a: 4 ENDS
by: 4 **NEAR** NIGH 6 ATHAND
NEARTO
by, once: 5 ANEAR
call: 5 SCARE 8 NEARMISS
Came to a: 5 ENDED
companion: 8 SOULMATE
Cut: 4 CROP MOWN 5 SHAVE
Doesn't just: 5 SLAMS
down: 3 END
Draw to a: 3 END 4 WANE
enough: 7 INRANGE
friend: 3 PAL 8 SIDEKICK
Get: 6 NESTLE
Get ~ to: 4 NEAR
Getting: 4 WARM
Hardly a ~ win: 4 ROMP
(in): 3 HEM
in films: 5 GLENN
in on: 4 NEAR
It may be: 5 SHAVE
Like a ~ neighbor: 8 NEXTDOOR
loudly: 4 SLAM
Not: 4 AFAR 5 APART
Not even: 3 FAR
one: 3 PAL
Reason to ~ up shop: 6 SIESTA
shave: 5 SCARE
tightly: 4 SEAL 6 SEALUP
to: 4 NEAR WARM 5 ABOUT
to closed: 4 **AJAR**
up: 4 SEAL
Closed
Almost: 4 AJAR
Behind ~ doors: 9 INPRIVATE
Not quite: 4 **AJAR**
Sing with a ~ mouth: 3 HUM
Close-fitting: 4 SNUG
hat: 5 TOQUE
Closely
confined, with "up": 4 PENT
connected: 7 SIAMESE

Examine: 4 SIFT
Follow: 3 APE DOG 4 HEEL TAIL
    5 STALK 6 SHADOW
Following: 6 ATHEEL
Look: 4 PEER 5 DELVE
Read: 6 PERUSE
resemble: 5 MIMIC
Watch: 3 EYE
    15 KEEPASHARPEYEON
Closemouthed: 3 MUM
Closeout
  caveat: 4 ASIS
Closer
  Clothes: 4 SNAP
  Fairy tale: 5 AFTER
  Gate: 5 LATCH
  Get ~ to: 6 GAINON
  Kimono: 3 OBI 4 SASH
  Letter: 5 YOURS
  Newscast: 5 RECAP
  Prayer: 4 AMEN
  stat: 3 ERA
Closest: 8 NEARMOST
Closet
  contents: 5 LINEN
  Forced from the: 5 OUTED
  invader: 4 MOTH
  item: 5 BROOM 6 HANGER
  items: 6 SHEETS
  Kind of: 5 CEDAR LINEN
  pest: 4 MOTH
  ___ close to schedule: 4 ONOR
Close-up
  map: 5 INSET
Closing
  Info: Suffix cue
  Auctioneer's ~ word: 4 SOLD
  document: 4 DEED
  notes: 4 CODA
  passage: 4 CODA
  remarks: 4 OBIT
  Road: 4 STER
Cloth
  Abrasive: 5 EMERY
  Absorbent: 5 TERRY
  Cleaning: 3 RAG
  Coarse: 5 TWEED
  Cover with: 5 DRAPE
  Cut from the same: 4 AKIN

finish: 3 IER
joint: 4 SEAM
Kind of: 3 LAY 4 LAIC
Not of the: 3 LAY 4 LAIC
sample: 6 SWATCH
Scrap of: 3 RAG
suffix: 3 IER
unit: 4 BOLT
Woolen: 7 WORSTED
Worsted: 6 TRICOT
Clothed: 6 DECENT
Clothes: 4 DUDS GARB TOGS
    6 ATTIRE 7 THREADS
  alterer: 6 TAILOR
  Civilian: 5 MUFTI
  closer: 4 SNAP
  Iron: 5 ARMOR PRESS
  Knight: 4 MAIL 5 ARMOR
  line: 3 **HEM** 4 SEAM 6 CREASE
    INSEAM
  Nice, as: 6 DRESSY
  presser: 4 IRON
  Put some ~ on: 6 ENROBE
  with slogans: 7 TSHIRTS
Clothes-drying
  frame: 5 AIRER
Clothesline
  alternative: 5 DRYER
Clothespin: 3 PEG
  Reason for a comic strip: 4 ODOR
Clothier
  concern: 3 FIT
  ~ Strauss: 4 LEVI
Clothing: 3 TOG 4 DUDS GARB
    GEAR TOGS 5 DRESS
    6 ATTIRE 7 RAIMENT
  Calcutta: 4 SARI
  category: 4 MENS SIZE 6 MISSES
  chain, with "The": 3 GAP
  Food, ~, or shelter: 4 NEED
  Knight: 5 ARMOR
  label word: 4 MADE
  line: 3 HEM 4 SEAM 6 CREASE
    INSEAM
  size: 6 PETITE
  Without: 5 NAKED
Clothing store: 6 THEGAP
  department: 4 MENS
  designations: 9 MENSSIZES

Clotho: 4 FATE
Cloud: 4 BLUR
  Bit of a: 4 WISP
  chamber particle: 3 ION
  Interstellar: 6 NEBULA
  layers: 6 STRATA
  locale: 3 SKY
  Low-altitude: 7 STRATUS
  Mushroom ~ maker: 5 ABOMB
    HBOMB
  number: 4 NINE
  On ~ nine: 6 ELATED
  Put on ~ nine: 5 **ELATE**
  Space: 6 NEBULA
  Start of some ~ names: 4 ALTO
  ___ cloud: 4 OORT
Cloudiness: 5 BLEAR
Cloudless: 5 CLEAR
  sky hue: 5 AZURE
Cloud-nine
  feeling: 7 ELATION
Clouds
  Dark: 4 OMEN
  Dense: 6 CUMULI
  in space: 7 NEBULAE
  Move quickly, as: 4 SCUD
  Rain: 5 **NIMBI**
  Wispy: 5 CIRRI
Clouseau
  portrayer: 7 SELLERS
  valet: 4 KATO
  ~, briefly: 4 INSP
Clove hitch: 4 KNOT
Clover
  Kind of: 8 FOURLEAF
Cloverleaf
  feature: 4 LOOP RAMP
    6 ONRAMP
  parts: 5 EXITS LOOPS ROADS
Clown: 4 BOZO
  Cartoon: 4 KOKO
  Court: 6 JESTER
  first name: 6 RONALD
  of renown: 4 BOZO KOKO
  "Pagliacci": 5 TONIO
  pole: 5 STILT
  prop: 5 PIE WIG 5 STILT
  Sidewalk: 4 MIME
  suffix: 3 ISH

  TV: 4 BOZO
  ~ Kelly: 6 EMMETT
"___ Clown": 3 BEA
Clownish: 4 ZANY
Cloying
  stuff: 7 TREACLE
Club: 6 CUDGEL
  alternative: 3 BLT
  at a club: 4 IRON 5 WEDGE
  Baseball: 3 BAT
  Big: 3 ACE
  Car: 3 AAA
  charge: 4 DUES
  Cricket: 3 BAT
  Cub with a: 4 SOSA
  date: 3 GIG
  Diamond: 3 BAT
  dressing: 4 MAYO
  for swingers: 3 BAT
  Golf: 4 IRON WOOD 5 WEDGE
    6 PUTTER
  Health: 3 SPA
  High-IQ: 5 MENSA
  Join, as a: 5 ENTER
  Kind of: 3 FAN 4 GLEE GOLF
    6 KENNEL
  Knight: 4 MACE
  of song: 4 COPA
  Private: 3 USO
  soda: 7 SELTZER
  Some ~ members: 4 ELKS
  Spiked: 4 MACE
  steak: 9 DELMONICO
  U.S. motor: 3 AAA
  Word after: 4 SODA
Club ___ : 3 **MED** 4 SODA
___ Club: 4 SAMS 6 SIERRA
"___ Club, The": 3 PTL
Club Med
  locale: 4 ISLE
Clubroot
  cause: 9 SLIMEMOLD
Clubs
  Big name in book: 5 OPRAH
  or spades: 4 SUIT
  Woods with: 5 TIGER
Cluck: 3 OAF
  Condescending: 3 **TSK**
  Dumb: 4 DODO 5 IDIOT

Clucker: 3 HEN
Clucking
  sounds: 4 TSKS
Clue: 4 HINT IDEA
  Bloodhound: 4 ODOR 5 SCENT
  character: 11 MISSSCARLET
  Give a: 4 HINT
  hunter: 3 TEC
  Misleading: 10 REDHERRING
  room: 4 HALL 5 STUDY
  Small: 4 HINT
  weapon: 4 ROPE 8 LEADPIPE
Clued
  in: 5 AWARE
  in about: 4 ONTO
Clueless: 4 LOST 5 ATSEA
    BLANK INEPT NAIVE
    7 ATALOSS
"Clueless"
  actress Dash: 6 STACEY
  catchphrase: 4 ASIF
  Cher in: 6 ALICIA
  Inspiration for: 4 EMMA
  lead role: 4 CHER
Clues
  Some crossword: 4 PUNS
  ~, to a cop: 5 LEADS
Clump: 4 GLOB
  Clay: 4 CLOD
  of grass: 4 TUFT
  of hair: 4 TUFT
  Small: 4 TUFT
Clumsily
  Handle: 3 PAW 5 PAWAT
  Move: 6 LUMBER
  Spill: 5 SLOSH
Clumsy: 5 INEPT 6 OAFISH
    9 ALLTHUMBS
  craft: 3 ARK
  dancer's problems: 4 TOES
  one: 3 OAF 4 LOUT 5 KLUTZ
  one's cry: 4 OOPS
  ship: 3 TUB
Clunker: 3 DUD 4 BOMB HEAP
    5 LEMON 6 JALOPY
Clunky
  shoe: 5 SABOT
Cluster: 4 CLOT KNOT TUFT
    5 BUNCH GROUP

Clutch: 4 GRAB GRIP 5 CLASP
    GRASP PEDAL
  neighbor: 5 BRAKE
  producer: 3 HEN
Clutched: 4 HELD
Clutcher: 4 CLAW 5 TALON
Clutches
  Escape the ~ of: 5 ELUDE
Clutter: 4 MESS
  E-mail: 4 SPAM
  Sink: 6 DISHES
  Web site: 3 ADS
Cluttered: 5 MESSY
  Less: 5 BARER 6 NEATER
Clutter-free: 4 NEAT
Clyde
  Aviation pioneer: 6 CESSNA
  Cap on the: 3 TAM
  City on the: 7 GLASGOW
  Partner of: 6 BONNIE
Clytemnestra
  Mother of: 4 LEDA
  Slayer of: 7 ORESTES
"C'mon in!": 5 ENTER
CNBC
  analyst Ron: 6 INSANA
CNN
  anchor Paula: 4 ZAHN
  founder: 6 TURNER
  home (abbr.): 3 ATL
  interviewer: 9 LARRYKING
  offering (abbr.): 4 REPT
  Part of: 4 NEWS 5 CABLE
  reporter David: 5 ENSOR
C-note
  Change for a: 4 TENS
C-notes
  Ten: 3 GEE 4 ONEG THOU
CN Tower
  city: 7 TORONTO
CO
  setting: 3 MST
Co.
  auditors: 4 CPAS
  bigwig: 3 CEO 4 PRES
  designation: 3 INC
  Electric: 4 UTIL
  French: 3 CIE
  unit: 4 DEPT

Coach: 3 BUS 5 CLASS TRAIN
    TUTOR 6 ADVISE MENTOR
    7 TRAINER
 ~ Chuck: 4 NOLL
 ~ Dan: 5 ISSEL
 ~ Don: 5 SHULA
 ~ Ewbank: 4 WEEB
 ~ George: 5 HALAS
 ~ Greasy: 5 NEALE
 ~ Hank: 5 STRAM
 ~ Jackson: 4 PHIL
 ~ Joe: 7 PATERNO
 ~ Karolyi: 4 **BELA**
 ~ Mike: 5 DITKA
 ~ Parseghian: 3 **ARA**
 ~ Pat: 5 RILEY
 ~ Rockne: 5 KNUTE
"Coach"
 actress Georgia: 5 ENGEL
Coagulate: 3 SET 4 CLOT
Coal
 boat: 4 SCOW
 carrier: 3 **HOD** 4 TRAM
 container: 3 **BIN**
 Covers with ~ dust: 5 SOOTS
 deposit: 4 SEAM
 German ~ region: 4 RUHR **SAAR**
 hole: 4 MINE
 Hot: 5 EMBER
 layer: 4 VEIN
 product: 4 COKE
 scuttle: 3 HOD
 stratum: 4 SEAM
 unit: 3 TON 4 LUMP
Coalfield
 city: 5 ESSEN
Coalition: 4 BLOC 5 UNION
 Form a: 5 UNITE
"Coal Miner's Daughter"
 subject: 5 LYNN
Coals
 Rake over the: 5 CHIDE ROAST
    SCOLD
Coarse: 4 LEWD 5 BAWDY
    ROUGH 6 EARTHY
 fabric: 5 TWEED
 file: 4 **RASP**
 flour: 4 MEAL
 Opposite of: 4 FINE

person: 5 BEAST
Coarsely
 irreverent: 6 RIBALD
Coast: 5 GLIDE SHORE
    7 SEASIDE
 On the: 6 INLAND
 ___ Coast, Antarctica: 6 ADELIE
Coastal
 catch: 4 SOLE
 city: 4 PORT
 feature: 5 INLET
 flier: 3 ERN 4 ERNE
 prefix: 5 INTRA
 region: 8 SEABOARD
 resorts: 8 RIVIERAS
Coasted: 4 SLID
Coaster: 4 LUGE SLED
 cry: 4 WHEE
 Roller: 4 RIDE
Coast Guard
 alert: 3 SOS
 rank (abbr.): 3 ADM CPO ENS
 ___ Coast, Hawaii: 4 KONA
Coastline
 feature: 3 RIA 5 INLET
Coat: 5 LAYER
 Apply a new: 7 REPAINT
 Canine: 6 ENAMEL
 Expensive: 3 FUR
 feature: 5 LAPEL
 Fir: 4 BARK
 First: 6 PRIMER
 Fix a: 6 RELINE
 Grass: 3 DEW
 Heavy: 6 ULSTER
 holder: 3 PEG
 House: 5 PAINT
 It has a red: 4 EDAM
 Kind of: 3 LAB PEA 4 BASE
 Like an Airedale: 4 WIRY
 Mink: 3 FUR
 of paint: 5 LAYER
 on Santa's coat: 4 SOOT
 Orange: 4 RIND SKIN
 part: 3 ARM 4 HOOD
 Put a ~ on: 4 GILD 5 PAINT
 Red: 4 RUST
 Seaman's: 9 PEAJACKET
 Seed: 4 ARIL 5 TESTA

Short: 5 TUNIC 6 REEFER
   TABARD
Sugar: 5 ICING
Take a ~ off: 4 PARE
White: 4 RIME
Winter: 3 ICE 4 RIME SNOW
   6 ANORAK ULSTER
with a coat of arms: 6 TABARD
with gold: 4 GILD 5 PLATE
Coated
candy: 5 MANDM
Coating: 4 FILM RIND 5 LAYER
Bronze: 6 PATINA
Bumper: 6 CHROME
Canine: 6 ENAMEL
Ember: 3 ASH
Floss: 3 WAX
Icy: 4 HOAR RIME
Nonstick: 6 TEFLON
Sandpaper: 4 GRIT
Coat-of-arms
border: 4 ORLE
Coatrack
item: 3 PEG
Coax: 4 URGE
Cob: 3 PEN
Cobalt
~ 60: 7 ISOTOPE
Cobb
Actor: 4 **LEEJ**
and others: 3 **TYS**
salad ingredient: 5 BACON
"Cobb"
Ty Cobb portrayer, in:
   13 TOMMYLEEJONES
Cobbled
together: 4 MADE
~, in a way: 5 SOLED
Cobbler: 3 PIE
container: 6 PIEPAN PIETIN
Do a ~ job: 6 REHEEL RESOLE
form: 4 LAST
output: 5 SHOES
stock: 5 HEELS SOLES
tool: 3 AWL
~, at times: 5 SOLER
Cobblestone
sound: 4 CLOP
___ Cob, Connecticut: 3 COS

Cobra: 5 SNAKE
Egyptian: 3 ASP
killer: 8 MONGOOSE
kin: 3 ASP 5 MAMBA
Coburn, D.L.
~ Pulitzer play, with "The":
   7 GINGAME
Cobweb
Filmy: 8 GOSSAMER
site: 5 ATTIC
Coca
Comic: 7 IMOGENE
Coca-Cola
brand: 3 TAB 6 FRESCA MRPIBB
Cochise: 6 APACHE
player Michael: 6 ANSARA
Cochran
Mississippi senator: 4 THAD
Cock
and bull: 3 HES 5 MALES
Cock-a-doodle-doo: 4 CROW
Cockamamie: 5 **INANE** 7 ASININE
Cockatoo
kin: 5 MACAW
Cocked: 5 ATILT
It may be: 3 HAT
Cockeyed: 4 ALOP LOCO 5 AMISS
   ASKEW INANE 6 ABSURD
   ALLWET ASLANT
Cockney: 4 BRIT
Info: British cue
coins: 5 PENCE
greeting: 4 ELLO
residence: 3 OME
Cockpit
abbr.: 3 **ALT**
acknowledgment: 5 ROGER
button: 5 EJECT
calculation: 3 ETA
figure: 5 PILOT 7 COPILOT
Cockroach
Fictional keyboarding: 5 ARCHY
Cocktail
Brandy: 7 SIDECAR STINGER
Brunch: 6 MIMOSA
Champagne: 6 MIMOSA
Fruit ~ fruit: 4 PEAR
Fruity: 6 MAITAI
Gin and lime: 6 GIMLET

Half a: **3** MAI TAI
made with grenadine: **7** BACARDI
Molotov ~ fuse: **3** RAG
nibble: **6** CANAPE
party spread: **4** PATE
Popular: **7** MARTINI
Rum: **6** MAITAI
Vodka: **12** WHITERUSSIAN

Coco
of fashion: **6** CHANEL

Coconut
cookie: **8** MACAROON
Dried: **5** COPRA
fiber: **4** COIR
Oranges and shredded:
    8 AMBROSIA
source: **4** PALM

Cocoon
dwellers: **5** PUPAE
Exit one's: **6** EMERGE
fiber: **4** SILK
resident: **4** PUPA

"Cocoon"
actor: **6** AMECHE
actor Cronyn: **4** HUME
director Howard: **3** RON

Cod: **4** CAPE
kin: **4** HAKE
piece: **3** FIN
___ **Cod:** **4** CAPE LING

Coda
kin: **6** EPILOG **8** EPILOGUE
place: **3** END

Coddle: **4** BABY **6** PAMPER

Cuddled
It may be: **3** EGG

Code
ATM: **3** PIN
Bar: **3** LAW
Bar ~ reader: **7** SCANNER
breaker: **3** KEY
carrier: **3** DNA **4** GENE
component: **3** LAW
Computer: **5** ASCII
cracker comment: **3** AHA
creator: **5** MORSE
Gangster: **6** OMERTA
Genetic: **3** DNA
Govt. ~ breakers: **3** NSA

It has a: **4** AREA GENE
Kind of: **3** ZIP **4** AREA **5** DRESS
    MORSE PENAL
Long, in: **3** DAH **4** DASH
Moral: **5** ETHIC
name: **5** **MORSE**
of conduct: **5** ETHIC
of silence: **6** OMERTA
Org. with a: **3** IRS
subject: **4** AREA **5** DRESS
syllable: **3** DAH **4** DASH
Web prog.: **4** HTML
word: **3** DAH DIT **4** **ALFA**
    6 SIERRA
___ **code:** **3** ZIP **4** AREA **5** MORSE
    PENAL

Code-cracking
org.: **3** **NSA**

Coded
message: **6** CIPHER

Codeine: **6** OPIATE
source: **5** OPIUM

Codfish
Young: **5** SCROD

Codger: **4** COOT CUSS **6** GEEZER
replies: **3** EHS

Coed
It may be: **4** DORM

Coeducation
pioneering college: **7** OBERLIN

Coen
brothers film: **5** FARGO
Filmmaker: **4** JOEL **5** **ETHAN**

Coerce: **5** FORCE

Coercion: **6** DURESS

___ **Coeur:** **5** SACRE

Coeur d'___, Idaho: **5** **ALENE**

Coffee: **3** JOE **4** JAVA
add-in: **5** CREAM
allure: **5** AROMA
alternative: **3** TEA
brewer: **3** URN
choice: **7** INSTANT
container: **3** URN
flavor: **5** MOCHA
gathering: **6** KLATCH
    7 KLATSCH
harvest: **5** BEANS
Hawaiian: **4** KONA

holder: 3 CUP MUG POT **URN**
Hot ~ hazard: 5 SCALD
How ~ may be served: 6 AULAIT
Just sit, like: 7 GETCOLD
Kind of: 4 DRIP ICED 5 DECAF
   IRISH
lightener: 5 CREAM
Like some: 4 ICED
liqueur: 6 KAHLUA 8 TIAMARIA
Made: 6 PERKED
maker: 3 **URN**
order: 5 BLACK DECAF LATTE
   LIGHT MOCHA SANKA
   6 GRANDE 7 REGULAR
order (abbr.): 3 REG
Place for: 5 TABLE
Quick: 7 INSTANT
server: 3 **URN**
size: 4 TALL
source: 4 BEAN
Strong black ~ after dinner:
   9 DEMITASSE
table item: 7 ARTBOOK
variety: 5 MOCHA
~, in slang: 3 JOE MUD 4 **JAVA**
Coffee ___ : 3 URN
"Coffee ___?": 5 ORTEA
___ coffee: 5 IRISH
"___ coffee?": 5 TEAOR
Coffee break
hr.: 5 TENAM
snack: 5 DONUT
time: 3 TEN
When some take a: 5 ATTEN
Coffeehouse
choice: 5 MOCHA
container: 3 URN
draw: 5 AROMA
order: 5 LATTE 8 ESPRESSO
"Coffee, ___ Me?": 5 TEAOR
Coffeepot: 3 URN
"Coffee, Tea ___?": 4 ORME
Coffee-to-go
need: 3 LID
Coffin
stand: 4 BIER
Cog
Slip a: 3 ERR
Coghlan, Eamonn: 5 MILER

Cogitate: 5 THINK
Cogitating
Result of: 4 IDEA
"Cogito ___ sum": 4 ERGO
Cognac
Big name in: 4 REMY
Cognate: 4 AKIN
Cognizant: 5 AWARE
of: 4 INON ONTO 5 HIPTO
Cohabitant: 6 POSSLQ ROOMIE
Cohen
Skater: 5 SASHA
Coherent
Emit ~ light: 4 **LASE**
Cohesive
group: 4 UNIT
Cohn
Grammy winner: 4 MARC
Coho: 6 SALMON
Cohort: 3 PAL 4 ALLY CHUM
   5 CRONY
Coif
Frizzy: 4 AFRO
High: 4 UPDO
Coiffure: 6 HAIRDO
Coiffures: 3 DOS
Coil: 5 HELIX SKEIN TWINE
   6 SPIRAL
Inventor of a: 5 TESLA
of hair: 4 HANK
___ coil: 5 TESLA
Coiled: 5 WOUND
Coin: 4 MINT 6 INVENT SPECIE
$10 ~: 5 EAGLE
collection: 4 ROLL
collector: 4 SOFA
factory: 4 MINT
Fake: 4 SLUG
flip: 4 TOSS
flipper phrase: 6 CALLIT
hole: 4 SLOT
New: 4 EURO
Old gold: 5 DUCAT
reverse: 5 TAILS
side: 7 OBVERSE
Small: 3 SOU 4 CENT
Thin: 4 DIME
toss call: 5 HEADS TAILS
word: 3 GOD 4 UNUM 5 TRUST

Worthless: **3** SOU
Coincide: 5 AGREE
  with: **7** OVERLAP
Coined
  money: **6** SPECIE
  word: **4** UNUM
Coin-edge
  ridge: **5** KNURL
Coins: 6 SPECIE
  and bills: **4** CASH
  Roll of: **7** ROULEAU
  Some: **6** TOKENS
Coke: 4 COLA
  alternative: **5** PEPSI
  and Pepsi: **5** COLAS
  partner: **3** RUM
  vs. Pepsi event: **9** TASTETEST
Col.
  boss: **3** GEN
Cola
  choice: **5** PEPSI
  container: **3** CAN
  cooler: **3** ICE
  Part of: **4** COST
Colada
  liquor: **3** RUM
  ___ colada: **4** **PINA**
Colander: 8 STRAINER
  kin: **5** SIEVE
Colbert
  role: **9** CLEOPATRA
Colchester
  county: **5** ESSEX
Colchis
  Ship to: **4** ARGO
Cold: 4 ICED **5** ALGID HARSH
        RHEUM **6** WINTRY
        8 UNHEATED
  and clammy: **4** DANK
  and damp: **6** CLAMMY
  and wet: **3** RAW
  Bitterly: **3** RAW **7** GLACIAL
  call: **3** BRR
  capital: **4** BERN OSLO
        8 HELSINKI
  Crack from the: **4** CHAP
  cube: **3** ICE
  cuts: **4** MEAT
  desserts: **4** ICES

development: **7** REDNOSE
draft: **4** BEER
drops: **5** SLEET
era: **6** ICEAGE
feet: **4** FEAR
front: **3** CEE
Give the ~ shoulder: **4** SHUN
        SNUB **5** SPURN
Go ~ turkey: **4** QUIT
Had down: **4** KNEW
Like a ~ shower: **6** SLEETY
Like many ~ meds: **3** OTC
mold: **5** ASPIC
one: **4** BEER BREW
or hot drink: **5** CIDER
reaction: **3** BRR
Really: **3** ICY **6** FROSTY
response: **5** ACHOO
shoulder: **4** SNUB
shower: **4** HAIL **5** SLEET
Soup served: **5** SCHAV
spell: **6** ICEAGE
symptom: **7** SNIFFLE
temperatures: **5** TEENS
Very: **3** ICY **5** GELID **6** ARCTIC
weather protector: **5** PARKA
        7 EARFLAP
~, in Spanish: **4** FRIA FRIO
Cold-blooded
  killer: **3** ASP **4** TREX
Cold-caller
  goal: **4** SALE
"Cold Case Files"
  carrier: **5** AANDE
Cold-cock: 4 STUN
"Cold Mountain"
  role for Nicole: **3** ADA
"Cold one": 4 BEER
Cold-shoulder: 4 SHUN SNUB
        5 SPURN
Cold War
  abbr.: **3** SSR
  capital: **4** BONN
  concern: **5** HBOMB
  country: **4** USSR
  defense gp.: **4** NATO
  foe: **4** REDS USSR
  initials: **3** SDI **4** USSR
  news name: **4** TASS

org.: 3 KGB
power: 4 USSR
threat: 5 HBOMB
winner: 4 NATO
Cold-weather
cap part: 6 EARLAP
coat: 5 PARKA
Cole
of song: 3 NAT 7 NATALIE
or Abdul: 5 PAULA
Cole ___: 4 SLAW
Coleman
Songwriter ~ et al.: 3 CYS
Coleridge
character: 7 MARINER
sacred river: 4 ALPH
work: 3 ODE 4 RIME
Coles
Dancer: 4 HONI
Colette
1920 ~ novel: 5 CHERI
pal: 4 AMIE
work: 4 GIGI
Colgate
rival: 3 AIM 5 CREST GLEEM
Coliseum: 5 ARENA
Coll.: 3 SCH
admissions concerns: 4 SATS
aides: 3 TAS
course: 3 SOC 4 ECON
degrees: 3 BAS
dorm figures: 3 RAS
figure: 4 PROF
hoops competition: 3 NIT
hopefuls: 3 SRS
hotshot: 4 BMOC
major: 3 BIO ENG SOC 4 ECON
marchers: 4 ROTC
record no.: 3 GPA
senior's test: 3 GRE
Some ~ exams: 5 LSATS
Some ~ students: 3 SRS
sports group: 4 NCAA
Collaborative
number: 4 DUET
"Collages"
author: 3 NIN
Collagist
French: 3 ARP

need: 4 GLUE
Collapse: 4 GIVE 6 CAVEIN
FALLIN
Collapsed: 4 FELL GAVE WENT
Collapsible
bed: 3 COT
lid: 8 OPERAHAT
Collar: 3 **NAB** 4 NAIL 5 PINCH
RUNIN SEIZE 6 ARREST
attachment: 5 IDTAG LEASH
extension: 5 LAPEL
Hot under the: 4 SORE 5 ANGRY
IRATE RILED
Inquisition: 7 GAROTTE
insert: 4 STAY
Kind of: 4 ETON FLEA
Make a: 3 NAB 4 BUST 6 ARREST
on a pipe: 6 FLANGE
Put the ~ on: 3 NAB 5 RANIN
6 ARREST
Ring around the: 3 LEI TIE
stiffener: 4 STAY
victim: 4 PERP
White ~ worker: 6 CLERIC
Collared: 5 RANIN
Collate: 4 SORT
Colleague: 4 PEER
Collect: 4 REAP SAVE 5 AMASS
RAISE 6 GATHER
Part of a ~ call number: 3 ATT
slowly: 5 GLEAN
Collected: 3 MET 4 CALM COOL
6 SEDATE SERENE
dust: 3 SAT
sayings: 3 ANA
Collectible: 5 CURIO
candy dispenser: 3 PEZ
cap: 3 POG
car: 5 EDSEL
Cartoon: 3 **CEL**
illustrator: 4 ERTE
~ Ming: 4 VASE
Collectibles
Music: 3 LPS
Collecting
a pension (abbr.): 3 RET
Collection: 3 ANA SET 5 ARRAY
BATCH TROVE
8 ENSEMBLE

agcy.: 3 IRS
Complete: 3 SET
Literary: 3 **ANA**
Map: 4 ATLAS
Monopoly: 4 RENT
of anecdotes: 3 ANA
of brains: 5 MENSA
of Hindu truths: 5 SUTRA
of online discussion groups:
   6 USENET
of poetry: 4 EDDA EPOS
Record: 7 DATASET
   8 DATABASE
Smithsonian: 9 AMERICANA
Stock: 4 HERD
Valuable: 5 TROVE
Vinyl: 3 LPS
Collectively: 5 ASONE INALL
Collector
  Coin: 4 SOFA
  Garbage: 6 ASHMAN
  goal: 3 SET
  Lint: 4 TRAP 5 INNIE
  Nectar: 3 BEE
  quests: 4 SETS
  Specimen: 4 SWAP
  Trash: 3 BIN
"Collector, The"
  actress Samantha: 5 EGGAR
Colleen: 4 LASS
  country: 4 EIRE
College
  administrator: 4 DEAN
  application part: 5 ESSAY
  area: 4 QUAD
  bigwig: 4 **DEAN** 7 PROVOST
  book: 4 TEXT
  bulldogs: 4 ELIS
  California: 6 POMONA
  Carolina: 4 ELON
  Cedar Rapids: 3 COE
  Certify, as a: 8 ACCREDIT
  cheer: 3 RAH
  course, briefly: 3 LIT 5 PSYCH
  entrance exam: 3 SAT
  exam: 4 ORAL
  First coed ~ in U.S.: 7 OBERLIN
  grad: 4 ALUM
  head: 5 PREXY

Hold aside as a ~ athlete:
   8 REDSHIRT
housing: 4 DORM
Iowa: 3 COE
Kentucky: 5 BEREA
lecturer: 4 PROF
life: 7 ACADEME
Like some ~ curricula: 4 CORE
Like some ~ walls: 5 IVIED
maj.: 5 PSYCH
major: 3 **ART** 4 MATH 5 DRAMA
member: 7 ELECTOR
Michigan: 5 **ALMA**
military gp.: 4 ROTC
New Rochelle: 4 **IONA**
North Carolina: 4 **ELON**
NY: 3 RPI
official: 4 DEAN 6 BURSAR
   7 PROVOST
Ohio: 4 KENT 5 HIRAM
   7 OBERLIN
Portland: 4 REED
Poughkeepsie: 6 MARIST
   VASSAR
quarters: 5 DORMS
Some ~ students: 5 COEDS
sports org.: 4 NCAA
sr.'s exam: 4 GMAT LSAT
sr.'s test: 3 GRE
unit: 6 CREDIT
web address suffix: 3 **EDU**
Wisconsin: 5 RIPON 6 BELOIT
Word in many ~ names: 4 TECH
~ QB, often: 4 BMOC
~, to Aussies: 3 UNI
~ VIP: 4 BMOC DEAN
College Park
  athlete: 4 TERP
College World Series
  site: 5 OMAHA
Collegian
  Connecticut: 3 **ELI**
  declaration: 5 MAJOR
  Florida: 5 GATOR
  Maryland: 4 TERP
  New Haven: 3 ELI 5 YALIE
  quest: 6 DEGREE
Collette
  Actress: 4 TONI

Collide
  with: 7 REAREND
Collie
  of film: 6 LASSIE
Colliery
  carrier: 4 TRAM
Collin
  Country singer: 4 RAYE
Collins
  Astronaut: 6 EILEEN
  Pop singer: 4 PHIL
Collins, Michael
  land: 4 EIRE
  Org. founded by: 3 IRA
Collision: 5 CRASH 6 IMPACT
  Kind of: 6 MIDAIR
  result: 4 DENT
  Serious: 7 SMASHUP
  sound: 3 BAM 4 BANG
Colloquialism: 5 IDIOM SLANG
Collusion: 7 CAHOOTS
Colmes
  of Hannity & Colmes: 4 ALAN
Colo.
  clock setting: 3 MST
  neighbor: 3 KAN NEB WYO
    4 NEBR
Cologne
  Info: German cue
  Article of: 3 EIN
  City near: 5 ESSEN
  conjunction: 3 UND
  cooler: 3 EIS
  cry: 3 ACH
  German name for: 4 KOLN
  "Oh!" de: 3 ACH
  Popular: 4 TABU
  river: 5 RHINE
  scent: 4 MUSK
  trio: 4 DREI
  water: 3 EAU
___ **Cologne:** 5 EAUDE
Colombian
  border river: 7 ORINOCO
  capital: 6 BOGOTA
  city: 4 **CALI**
  coin: 4 PESO
  kin: 4 TIOS
  Onetime ~ drug kingpin:

  7 ESCOBAR
Colon
  Abbr. that may precede a: 4 ATTN
  translation: 4 ISTO
Colonel: 4 RANK
  Comics: 5 BLIMP
  insignia: 5 EAGLE
  TV: 5 HOGAN
Colonel Klink
  Foil for: 5 HOGAN
Colonel Mustard
  game: 4 CLUE
Colonel Sanders
  feature: 6 GOATEE
Colonel Tibbets
  Mother of: 5 ENOLA
Colonial
  descendants gp.: 3 DAR
  diplomat Silas: 5 DEANE
  estate owner: 5 SAHIB
  insect: 3 ANT
  leader: 3 NEO
  newsman: 5 CRIER
  or Cape Cod: 5 HOUSE
  prefix: 3 NEO
  ~ British rule in India: 3 RAJ
  ~ Virginia: 4 DARE
Colonies
  Like some: 5 APIAN
  One of the 13 orig.: 3 DEL
    4 CONN PENN
Colonist
  Molokai: 5 LEPER
  Small: 3 ANT
  Virginia: 5 ROLFE
Colonizer
  of Greenland: 4 ERIC
Colonnade
  Ancient: 4 STOA
  tree: 3 ELM
Colony
  Ancient Greek: 5 **IONIA**
  Art ~ of New Mexico: 4 TAOS
  Former British: 4 ADEN
  Former Portuguese: 3 GOA
    5 MACAO
  Insect: 4 HIVE
  Kind of: 5 PENAL 6 NUDIST
  member: 3 **ANT** BEE 4 WASP

5 LEPER
Southwestern art: 4 TAOS
Color: 3 DYE HUE 5 TINCT
Add ~ to: 4 TINT
anew: 5 REDYE
Burnt: 6 SIENNA
Change: 3 DYE
changer: 4 DYER
Drained of: 3 WAN 4 PALE
    5 ASHEN
fabric: 6 TIEDYE
Get some: 3 TAN
Intense, as: 5 VIVID
Lacking: 4 PALE
Lack of: 6 PALLOR
lightly: 4 TINT
Lose: 4 FADE PALE
Lost: 5 FADED PALED
Neutral: 3 TAN 4 ECRU 5 FLESH
of honey: 4 GOLD 5 AMBER
of money: 5 GREEN
of raw silk: 4 ECRU
of sand: 3 TAN
of water: 4 AQUA
on the Irish flag: 6 ORANGE
prefix: 3 TRI UNI
Primary: 3 RED
quality: 4 TONE
Ring of: 6 AREOLA
separator: 5 PRISM
Subdued: 6 PASTEL
Touch of: 5 TINCT TINGE
Turn: 5 RIPEN
variation: 5 SHADE
wheel display: 5 TONES
Coloradan
Early: 3 UTE
Colorado
city: 5 ASPEN 7 DURANGO
creek: 3 RIA
Former ~ governor Roy:
    5 ROMER
hrs.: 3 MST
native: 3 **UTE**
neighbor: 4 UTAH
resort: 4 VAIL 5 ASPEN
Western ~ sight: 4 MESA
~ NHL team: 3 AVS
~ Park: 5 ESTES

Colorado River
city: 4 YUMA
feeder: 4 GILA
"Colorado Serenade": 5 OATER
Colorado Springs
initials: 4 USAF
Colorado State
player: 3 RAM
Colorant: 3 DYE
Coloration: 5 TINCT
Slight: 4 TINT 5 TINGE
Coloratura
piece: 4 ARIA
Colored
Brightly: 4 LOUD NEON
Brightly ~ bird: 6 ORIOLE
Brightly ~ fish: 4 OPAH
eye part: 4 IRIS
glasses color: 4 ROSE
Colorfast
Wasn't: 3 RAN 4 BLED
Colorful
amphibian: 4 NEWT
arc: 7 RAINBOW
bands: 7 SPECTRA
card game: 3 UNO
cat: 6 CALICO
circle: 6 AREOLA
computer: 4 IMAC
diaphragm: 4 IRIS
fish: 4 **OPAH** 5 TETRA
    6 TETRAS
Hardly: 4 DRAB 5 ASHEN
horse: 4 ROAN
insects: 7 REDANTS
Least: 6 PALEST
parrot: 5 **MACAW**
seashell: 6 TRITON
songbird: 6 ORIOLE
talk: 5 SLANG
Used ~ language: 5 SWORE
wrap: 6 SERAPE
writing: 7 IMAGERY
~ Apple: 4 IMAC
Coloring: 4 TINT 5 TINCT
Cheek: 5 ROUGE
expert: 4 DYER
Hair: 3 DYE
Horse: 4 ROAN

Salon: 5 HENNA
Colorist: 4 DYER
Colorless: 3 WAN 4 DRAB PALE
  ketone: 6 ACETOL
  liqueur: 4 OUZO
  liquor: 7 TEQUILA
  solvent: 7 ACETONE
"Color Purple, The"
  author Walker: 5 ALICE
  role: 5 CELIE
  Sofia in: 5 OPRAH
  Whoopi in: 5 CELIE
Colors
  Having a range of: 7 OPALINE
  Like some: 4 NEON
  Pass with flying: 3 ACE
"Colors"
  actor Sean: 4 PENN
  actress Maria Conchita:
    6 ALONSO
Color TV
  knob: 4 TINT
  pioneer: 3 **RCA**
Colo. Spr.
  Initials at: 4 USAF
Colossal: 4 EPIC HUGE 7 TITANIC
Colosseum
  sights: 5 LIONS
  wear: 4 TOGA
Colossus: 5 TITAN
  locale: 6 RHODES
"Colossus, The"
  poet: 5 PLATH
Colour
  Autumn: 5 OCHRE
Colt
  coddler: 4 MARE
  mother: 4 MARE
  of fame: 6 UNITAS
Colt 45
  maker: 5 PABST
Colt .45s
  ~, today: 6 ASTROS
Columba
  island: 4 IONA
Columbia
  athlete: 4 LION
  City on the: 7 ASTORIA
  launcher: 4 NASA

Columbian
  prefix: 3 PRE
  vessel: 5 PINTA
Columbia Pictures
  cofounder: 4 COHN
Columbo: 3 TEC
  and others (abbr.): 3 LTS
  Bandleader: 4 RUSS
  employer: 4 LAPD
  portrayer: 4 FALK
Columbus
  birthplace: 5 GENOA
  death year: 4 MDVI
  discovery: 5 HAITI 7 ANTIGUA
    JAMAICA
  Home to: 4 OHIO
  in NYC: 3 AVE
  Native encountered by: 5 CARIB
  port: 5 PALOS
  sch.: 3 **OSU**
  Second voyage start for: 5 CADIZ
  ship: 4 NINA 5 PINTA
Columbus Day
  event: 4 SALE 6 PARADE
  mo.: 3 OCT
Column: 6 PILLAR
  Addition: 4 ONES TENS
  Cal.: 3 FRI MON SAT SUN THU
    TUE WED 4 THUR TUES
  crossers: 4 ROWS
  Grooved, as a: 6 FLUTED
  Kind of: 4 LOSS ONES OPED
    5 IONIC 6 SPINAL
  Ledger: 4 ASSETS
  Memorial: 4 OBIT
  P&L ~ heading: 3 YTD
  piece: 4 ITEM
  Rightmost: 4 ONES
  Society ~ word: 3 NEE
  Sports: 4 WINS 6 LOSSES
  style: 5 DORIC IONIC
  worker: 5 ADDER
  ~ A or B selection: 6 ENTREE
Columnist
  Advice: 3 ANN 4 ABBY
  page: 4 OPED
  ~ Barrett: 4 **RONA**
  ~ Bombeck: 4 ERMA
  ~ Buchwald: 3 ART

~ Coulter: 3 ANN
~ Goodman: 5 ELLEN
~ Herb: 4 CAEN
~ Hopper: 5 HEDDA
~ Joseph: 5 ALSOP
~ Landers: 3 ANN
~ LeShan: 3 EDA
~ Marilyn ___ Savant: 3 VOS
~ Maureen: 4 DOWD
~ Mike: 5 ROYKO
~ Rowland: 5 EVANS
~ Smith: 3 LIZ

Com
preceder: 3 DOT
prefix: 4 TELE
relative: 3 EDU GOV ORG

Comanche
enemy: 3 UTE

Comaneci
Gymnast: 5 **NADIA**

Comb
again and again: 5 PREEN
backwards: 5 TEASE
Divide with a: 4 PART
Kind of: 7 RATTAIL
maker: 3 BEE
Place for a: 4 HIVE MANE
    5 TRESS
projections: 5 TEETH
Combat: 3 WAR 4 DUEL
    6 OPPOSE
area: 7 WARZONE
gear: 5 ARMOR
zone: 5 ARENA 6 SECTOR
Combatant: 3 FOE 4 VIER
    5 ENEMY
1999 ~: 4 SERB
Civil War: 3 REB
Corrida: 6 TORERO
Combative
Small ~ ones: 7 BANTAMS
Combination: 7 AMALGAM
Boxing: 6 ONETWO
Card: 4 MELD
Combinations
Info: Prefix cue
Combine: 3 ADD MIX WED
    4 MELD POOL 5 UNITE
with: 5 ADDTO

~, as resources: 4 POOL
Combined: 5 INONE 8 ALLINONE
Combing
attractions: 6 SHELLS
Combo: 4 BAND
Card: 4 MELD
Largish: 5 NONET OCTET
Musical: 5 CHORD
offering: 3 SET
Ring: 6 ONETWO
Small: 4 **TRIO**
Combs
of baseball: 5 EARLE
Ones with: 4 BEES
Rapper: 4 SEAN
Combs, ___ "Puffy": 4 SEAN
Combust: 4 BURN
Combustible
heap: 4 **PYRE**
Come: 6 ARRIVE
about: 4 TURN 5 ARISE OCCUR
    PIVOT
across: 4 FIND
across as: 4 SEEM
after: 5 **ENSUE**
again: 5 RECUR
and go: 5 RECUR
apart: 3 RIP 7 UNRAVEL
apart at the seams: 4 FRAY
back: 4 ECHO 5 RECUR
    6 ANSWER
back again: 6 REECHO
before: 6 LEADTO 7 PRECEDE
    PREDATE 8 ANTECEDE
    ANTEDATE
by: 3 GET 5 VISIT 6 ATTAIN
clean: 4 TELL 5 ADMIT BATHE
    LEVEL 6 FESSUP
clean, with "up": 4 FESS
closer to: 4 NEAR
down: 3 SET 4 LAND RAIN
    TEEM
down hard: 4 POUR TEEM
down to earth: 4 LAND
down with: 3 GET 5 CATCH
forth: 6 **EMERGE**
from behind: 5 RALLY
Hard to ~ by: 4 RARE
in: 5 ENTER 6 ARRIVE

in second: **4** LOSE **5** PLACE
in third: **4** SHOW
into one's own: **7** BLOSSOM
into view: **4** LOOM **6** APPEAR
   EMERGE
It may ~ after you: **3** ARE
It may ~ before long: **3** ERE
next: **5** ENSUE **6** FOLLOW
out: **5** DEBUT **6** **EMERGE**
   7 EMANATE
out on top: **3** WIN
Really ~ down: **4** POUR
Sign of things to: **4** **OMEN**
to: **5** REACH TOTAL WAKEN
   6 ATTEND **AWAKEN**
   8 ARRIVEAT
to a halt: **3** END **4** STOP **5** CEASE
to a point: **5** TAPER
together: **3** **GEL** **4** JELL KNIT
   MASS MESH **5** AMASS
   MERGE REUNE UNITE
   8 COALESCE
to light: **5** ARISE **6** EMERGE
to mind: **5** ARISE OCCUR
too: **8** TAGALONG
to pass: **5** ENSUE **OCCUR**
   6 BETIDE HAPPEN
to terms: **5** AGREE
to the plate: **3** BAT
to the rescue of: **3** AID
up: **5** **ARISE**
up again: **5** RECUR
up against: **4** ABUT
up short: **3** OWE **4** FAIL FALL
   LOSE
up with: **6** CREATE
Come-___: 3 ONS **6** HITHER
"Come again?": 3 HUH **4** WHAT
Comeback: 4 ECHO **5** REPLY
   6 ANSWER RETORT
   7 RIPOSTE **8** RESPONSE
   Playground: **5** AMNOT ARESO
   ISNOT ISTOO **6** CANTOO
   Snappy: **6** RETORT
"Come Back, Little ___": 5 SHEBA
"Come Back, Little Sheba"
   playwright: **4** **INGE**
   wife: **4** LOLA
Comedian: 6 AMUSER

stock: **4** GAGS
Violin-playing: **5** BENNY
~ Bill, briefly: **3** COS
~ Bruce: **5** LENNY
~ Charlotte: **3** RAE
~ George: **5** GOBEL
~ Louis: **3** NYE
~ Margaret: **3** CHO
~ Martha: **4** RAYE
~ Richard: **5** PRYOR
Comedians
~ Bob and Chris: **8** ELLIOTTS
Comedy
Anne of: **5** MEARA
Caesar of: **3** SID
club sound: **4** HAHA ROAR
Costello of: **3** LOU
Fields of: **5** TOTIE
First name in: **3** EMO
Half a ~ duo: **5** MEARA OLLIE
Idle in: **4** ERIC
Inits. in: **3** SNL
King of: **4** **ALAN**
Muse of: **6** THALIA
props: **4** PIES
Rivers of: **4** JOAN
Rock of: **5** CHRIS
Comedy Central
game show host: **5** STEIN
Come from ___ : 4 AFAR
"Come here ___?": 5 OFTEN
"Come in!": 5 ENTER
Come-on: 4 LINE LURE **5** OFFER
   6 TEASER
   Commercial: **6** TRYONE
   Credit card: **5** NOFEE
Comet: 8 REINDEER
competitor: **4** **AJAX** **6** BONAMI
head: **4** COMA
leader: **5** SANTA
Moves like a: **4** ARCS
Cometh
He: **6** ICEMAN
"___ Cometh, The": 6 ICEMAN
Comets
Leader of the: **5** HALEY
Comeuppance
Cad's: **4** SLAP
Defaulter's: **4** REPO

Mugger's: **4** MACE
Comfort: 4 EASE 5 SALVE
    6 RELIEF SOLACE
    SOOTHE **7** CONSOLE
Give ~ to: **6** SOOTHE
    8 REASSURE
Words of: **5** ITSOK
Comfortable: 5 HOMEY **6** ATEASE
    ATHOME
room: **3** DEN
with: **6** USEDTO
Comfortable ___ old shoe: 4 ASAN
Comforter: 5 DUVET
filling: **5** EIDER
Comforting
words: **5** ICARE
Comforts
Forgo: **7** ROUGHIT
Comfy: 4 SNUG **5** HOMEY
    6 ATEASE
Get: **6** NESTLE
room: **3** DEN
shirt: **3** TEE
shoe: **3** MOC
spot: **4** SOFA
Warm and: **6** TOASTY
Comic: 3 WIT
actor Jack: **5** OAKIE
actress Tessie: **5** OSHEA
bit: **3** GAG
intro: **5** SERIO
pianist Victor: **5** BORGE
prefix: **5** SERIO
reward: **4** HAHA
~ Charlotte: **3** RAE
~ Cheech: **5** MARIN
~ Howie: **6** MANDEL
~ Judy: **6** TENUTA
~ Lillie: **3** BEA
~ Louie: **3** NYE
~ Margaret: **3** CHO
~ Martha: **4** RAYE
~ Mort: **4** SAHL
~ Soupy: **5** SALES
Comic book
cry: **3** EEK
punch sound: **3** POW
Comics
Andy of: **4** CAPP

bark: **3** ARF
Brenda of: **5** STARR
canine: **4 ODIE** OTTO **5** SNERT
Canyon of: **5** STEVE
Capp of: **4** ANDY
caveman: **3** OOP **8** ALLEYOOP
Cinders of: **4** ELLA
colonel: **5** BLIMP
cry: **3** EEK
diminutive: **3** LIL
Etta of: **4 KETT**
exclamation: **3** ACK
ghost: **6** CASPER
heroes: **4** XMEN
Kett of: **4 ETTA**
Krazy ___ of: **3** KAT
Light bulb, in: **4** IDEA
Magician of: **8** MANDRAKE
Miss in the: **5** PEACH
Morgan of: **3** REX
Mrs. Dithers of: **4** CORA
Olive in: **3** OYL
orphan: **5** ANNIE
possum: **4** POGO
Rich kid in: **5** ROLLO
Snores, in: **4** ZEES
sound: **5** SPLAT
Spitting sound, in: **4** PTUI
Trueheart of: **4** TESS
Wavy lines, in: **4** ODOR
Comic strip
canine: **4** ODIE **5** SNERT
Greg Evans: **5** LUANN
Jeff MacNelly: **4** SHOE
Jerry Marcus: **5** TRUDY
Mell Lazarus: **5** MOMMA
pair: **11** MUTTANDJEFF
segment: **5** PANEL
viking: **5** HAGAR
"Comin' ___!": 4 ATYA
Coming: 3 DUE **6** ADVENT
    7 ENROUTE ONORDER
before (abbr.): **4** PREC
Have: **4** EARN **5** MERIT
    7 DESERVE
into existence: **7** NASCENT
Keep it: **5** RENEW
One who has it: **4** HEIR
or going: **7** ENROUTE

out even: **5** TYING
Second: **6** ENCORE
Short: **3** ARR
up: **5** AHEAD ONTAP
   7 INSTORE
Young lady ~ out: **3** DEB
"___ Coming": 4 ELIS
"Coming Home"
actor: **4** DERN **6** VOIGHT
subject: **3** NAM
Coming-out: 5 DEBUT
party: **3** DEB
Comings
Word used for ~ and goings:
   5 ALOHA
"Comin' ___ the Rye": 4 THRO
Comma
Abbr. after a: **3** ETC
connotation: **5** PAUSE
Command: 4 FIAT LEAD
   5 ORDER PILOT **6** BEHEST
   ORDAIN
for DDE: **3** ETO
for Queeg: **5** CAINE
level (abbr.): **3** ECH
posts (abbr.): **3** HQS
to a dog: **3** BEG SIT **4** HEEL
   STAY **5** FETCH SICEM
   SPEAK
to a horse: **3** GEE **4** WHOA
to a sailor: **5** AVAST
to Macduff: **5** LAYON
to the band: **5** HITIT
Took: **3** LED
Commanded: 3 LED RAN **4** BADE
Commander
Arabic: **4** EMIR
British: **4** HOWE
ETO: **3** DDE
Revolutionary War: **4** ASHE
Waterloo: **3** NEY
Commanding
phrase: **4** DOIT
Commandment: 7 PRECEPT
Break a: **3** SIN **5** COVET
count: **3** TEN
Final: **5** TENTH
pronoun: **3** THY
verb: **5** SHALT

word: **3** NOT THY **5** COVET
   SHALT
Commando: 6 RAIDER
action: **4** RAID
Navy: **4** SEAL
weapon: **3** UZI
"Comme ci, comme ça": 4 SOSO
   8 NOTSOHOT
Commedia dell'___ : 4 ARTE
Commemoration
Exodus: **5 SEDER**
Commemorative
marker: **5** STELE
writing: **3** ODE
Commence: 5 ARISE ENTER
   START **7** STARTIN
Commenced: 5 BEGAN BEGUN
Commencement: 5 ONSET
   START
composer: **5** ELGAR
Commencement Bay
city: **6** TACOMA
Commencing: 4 ASOF
Commend: 4 CITE **6** SALUTE
Commendation: 4 STAR **6** PRAISE
School: **8** GOLDSTAR
Comment
after an accident: **4** IMOK
after the fog clears: **4** ISEE
Barbed: **3** JAB
Clever: **3** MOT **4** QUIP
Cutting: **4** BARB
Disparaging: **4** SLUR
Klutz's: **4** OOPS
Quitter: **5** ICANT
Skeptic's: **4** IBET
suffix: **4** ATOR
to the audience: **5** ASIDE
Winter: **3** BRR **4** BRRR
Commentator
page: **4** OPED
~ Rooney: **4** ANDY
Comments
Make nasty: **5** SNIPE
Puzzled: **3** EHS
Commerce
agcy.: **3** FTC
Online: **5** ETAIL **6** ETRADE
org.: **4** GATT

pact: 5 NAFTA
restriction: 7 EMBARGO
Commerce Secretary
~ Maurice: 5 STANS
Commercial
bovine: 5 ELSIE
Designate as: 6 REZONE
designer: 5 ADMAN
makers: 5 ADMEN
prefix for winter items: 3 SNO
prefix with foam: 5 STYRO
producer: 7 SPONSOR
shine: 3 GLO
silencer: 4 MUTE
suffix with Motor: 3 OLA
TV: 4 SPOT
Commercially
Become ~ successful:
6 GETHOT
Commercials: 3 ADS
Cow of: 5 ELSIE
Skip the: 3 ZAP
Commies: 4 REDS
Commiserate
with: 4 PITY
Commiserative
comment: 4 ALAS
"Commish, The"
actress McGraw: 7 MELINDA
Commission
Out of: 5 KAPUT 6 LAIDUP
Put out of: 7 DISABLE
Commissioned
Lowest ~ USN officer: 3 ENS
Commit
a court infraction: 6 TRAVEL
a deadly sin: 4 LUST
a faux pas: 3 ERR
perjury: 3 LIE
to memory: 5 LEARN
unalterably: 6 LOCKIN
Commitment
Avoid: 5 HEDGE
Words of: 3 IDO
Committee: 5 PANEL
head: 5 CHAIR
Judiciary ~ head: 5 BIDEN
Kind of: 5 **ADHOC**
sess.: 3 MTG

Committer
Crime: 4 PERP
Commodious: 5 ROOMY
Commodity
OPEC: 3 OIL
Commodore
Old ~ computer: 5 AMIGA
Commodore Perry
headquarters: 4 ERIE
Common: 4 MERE 6 COARSE
NORMAL VULGAR
It may be: 5 SENSE
Least: 6 ODDEST RAREST
Not so: 7 SCARCER
sense: 5 SIGHT SMELL TASTE
6 SMARTS
Commoner: 4 **PLEB**
Common-interest
group: 4 BLOC
Commonly: 4 ALOT 5 OFTEN
Common Market
initials: 3 EEC
money: 3 ECU 4 EURO
Common Mkt.: 3 **EEC**
Commonplace: 5 BANAL TRITE
USUAL 6 OLDHAT
"Common Sense": 5 TRACT
author: 5 PAINE
Commonsensical: 4 SANE
Commotion: 3 **ADO** 4 FUSS STIR
TODO 5 HOOHA 6 CLAMOR
HOOPLA TUMULT
UPROAR 7 TEMPEST
Public: 5 SCENE
Commune
Dutch: 3 EDE
Iowa: 5 AMANA
Italian: 4 ESTE
Communicate
manually: 4 SIGN
online: 5 EMAIL
Communication
Catcher's: 4 SIGN
Mass: 5 LATIN
Office: 3 FAX
Old style of: 5 TELEX
syst.: 3 ASL
Communications
A, in: 4 ALFA

co.: 3 GTE ITT
satellite: 5 RELAY 7 TELSTAR
Communion: 4 RITE
cup: 7 CHALICE
plates: 7 PLATENS
site: 5 ALTAR
Communiqué
Interoffice: 4 MEMO
segue: 4 ASTO
Communism
First name in: 4 KARL
Communist
Old ~ letters: 3 SSR
Communist-hunting
gp.: 4 HUAC
"Communist Manifesto"
coauthor: 6 ENGELS
Communities
Like some: 5 GATED
Community
bldg.: 3 CTR
characteristic: 5 ETHOS
Complex: 5 BIOME
contest: 3 BEE
Jewish: 6 SHTETL
org.: 4 YMCA
outside the city: 5 EXURB
program: 8 OUTREACH
spirit: 5 **ETHOS**
Commute: 4 RIDE
prefix: 4 TELE
Commuter
cost: 4 TOLL
hassle: 5 TIEUP
home: 5 BURBS EXURB
6 SUBURB
line: 4 RAIL
NYC ~ line: 4 LIRR
obstacle: 5 SNARL
prefix: 4 TELE
Some ~ trains: 3 ELS
"Cómo ___?": 4 ESTA
Como, Perry
1956 ~ hit: 4 MORE
"Cómo ___ usted?": 4 **ESTA**
"___ Como Va": 3 OYE
Comp.
course: 3 ENG
key: 3 ESC

Compact: 5 DENSE TERSE
6 TREATY 7 ENTENTE
Dodge: 4 NEON
item: 4 DISC 5 ROUGE
name: 5 ESTEE
Saturn: 3 ION
weapon: 3 UZI
Compact ___: 4 DISC
Compacted
coal: 6 CANNEL
Compadre: 3 PAL 5 AMIGO
of Che: 5 FIDEL
of Fidel: 3 CHE
Companies
Combine: 5 MERGE
Companion: 3 PAL 6 COHORT
As a: 5 ALONG
Close: 8 SOULMATE
Companionless: 5 ALONE
Company: 4 FIRM 5 TROOP
avoider: 5 LONER
Calling: 4 **AVON**
car: 4 PERK
dishes: 5 CHINA
emblem: 4 LOGO
In need of: 8 LONESOME
in the news: 5 ENRON
In the ~ of: 4 WITH 5 AMONG
Keep ~ with: 3 SEE
lover: 6 MISERY
name tag: 3 INC
that has its ups and downs:
4 OTIS
Theater: 3 REP
Without: 4 LONE 8 ALLALONE
LONESOME
Word after some ~ names:
3 SON
~, in French: 3 CIE
~, proverbially: 3 TWO
~ VIP: 3 CEO 4 EXEC PRES
"___ company, ...": 4 TWOS
"Company, The": 3 **CIA**
"company for women, The":
4 AVON
Compaq
acquisition: 3 DEC
competitor: 3 IBM 4 DELL
products: 3 PCS

Comparable: 4 **AKIN** 5 ALIKE
    EQUAL
  to a beet: 5 ASRED
  to a pancake: 6 ASFLAT
  to a pig: 5 ASFAT
  to a pin: 6 ASNEAT
Comparably: 5 ALIKE
Comparative
  phrase: 4 ASAN ISTO
  suffix: 3 IER
  word: 4 THAN
Compare: 5 LIKEN
Compared
  to: 4 **THAN** 7 AGAINST
Comparison: 6 SIMILE
  center: 3 ASA
  figure: 4 NORM
  Numeric: 5 RATIO
  word: 4 THAN
  words: 3 ASA
Compartment: 5 STALL
  Elevator: 3 CAB CAR
  Glove ~ item: 3 MAP
  Protective: 3 POD
  Put in the overhead: 4 STOW
  Till: 4 ONES TENS
  Truck: 3 CAB
Compass: 4 AREA 6 EXTENT
  Any point of the: 5 RHUMB
  creation: 3 ARC
  dir.: 3 ENE ESE NNE NNW **SSE**
    SSW WNW WSW
  line: 3 ARC
  Spanish ~ point: 4 ESTE
  Use a: 6 ORIENT
Compassion: 4 PITY 5 HEART
    MERCY 6 PATHOS
  Feel: 4 ACHE
  Lacking: 8 INHUMANE
  Letters of: 3 TLC
Compassionate: 4 KIND
    6 CARING HUMANE
  letters: 3 TLC
Compel: 4 HALE 5 EXACT FORCE
    6 COERCE
Compelled
  Was: 5 HADTO
Compensate: 3 PAY 5 ATONE
    REPAY

  for: 6 OFFSET
Compensation: 3 PAY 4 WAGE
    6 OFFSET SALARY
    7 PAYMENT
"___ Compères": 3 LES
Compete: 3 **VIE** 4 RACE
  6 STRIVE
  in logrolling: 4 BIRL
  with: 5 RIVAL
Competence
  With: 4 ABLY
Competent: 4 **ABLE**
  ~, slangily: 3 EPT
Competing
  team: 4 SIDE
Competition: 3 BEE 4 MEET
  Crush, in: 4 ROUT
  In: 5 VYING
  Lumberjack: 5 ROLEO
  Pub: 5 DARTS
  site: 5 ARENA
  Spelling: 3 BEE
  Trucker: 6 ROADEO
Competitive: 9 RIVALROUS
  advantage: 4 **EDGE**
  personality: 5 TYPEA
  Ruthlessly: 9 DOGEATDOG
Competitor: 3 FOE 5 RIVAL
    7 ENTRANT
Complacent: 4 SMUG
Complain: 4 CARP CRAB FUSS
    MOAN 5 GRIPE GROAN
    6 GROUSE REPINE
    YAMMER
  bitterly: 4 RAIL
  in a murmur: 6 MUTTER
  loudly: 12 RAISETHEROOF
  too often: 3 NAG
Complainer: 4 CRAB 5 GRUMP
    6 MOANER WHINER
Complaining: 5 GRIPY WHINY
Complaint: 4 **BEEF** MOAN
    5 GRIPE PEEVE WHINE
    6 MALADY 7 AILMENT
  Grounds for: 5 ACHES
    9 GRIEVANCE
  Long: 4 RANT
"Compleat Angler, The"
  author Walton: 5 IZAAK

Complement
 Baseball: 4 NINE
 Football: 6 ELEVEN
 Lacrosse: 3 TEN
Complete: 4 ATOZ OVER REAL
     5 TOTAL UTTER WHOLE
     6 **ENTIRE**
 a sentence: 6 DOTIME
     9 SERVETIME
 a street: 3 TAR
 collection: 3 **SET**
 failure: 6 FIASCO
 prefix: 3 HOL
 range: 4 ATOZ
 reversal: 5 UTURN
 ~, informally: 5 THORO
Completed: 4 DID 4 DONE OVER
Completely: 3 ALL 4 ATOZ
     5 FULLY INALL QUITE
     6 INFULL **INTOTO**
     8 FROMATOZ
     9 EVERYINCH
 botch: 4 RUIN
 confused: 7 CHAOTIC
 consumed: 5 ATEUP 7 ALLGONE
 convinced: 4 SOLD SURE
 cooked: 4 DONE
 demolish: 4 RAZE
 full: 5 SATED
 infatuated: 4 GAGA
 mistaken: 6 ALLWET
 new: 6 REMADE
 surrounding: 7 AMBIENT
Completeness
 Sense of: 7 CLOSURE
Complex
 division: 4 UNIT
 Like a certain: 7 OEDIPAL
 Sports: 5 ARENA
Complexion
 affliction: 4 ACNE
 tone: 5 OLIVE
Compliant
 Be: 4 OBEY
 one: 6 OBEYER
Complicated
 Less: 6 EASIER
Complication: 3 ADO RUB 4 SNAG
     5 SNARL

Compliment
 Give, as a: 3 PAY
 Response to a: 4 ITRY
 to the cook: 3 YUM
Complimentary: 4 FREE
Compliments: 5 KUDOS
Comply: 4 OBEY
 with: 4 MEET OBEY
     8 ADHERETO
Component: 6 FACTOR MODULE
     7 ELEMENT
Comportment: 4 MIEN
Compose: 3 PEN 4 CALM
     7 TYPESET
 prose: 5 WRITE
Composed: 4 EVEN 5 STAID
     WROTE 6 SEDATE SERENE
Composer
 base: 5 THEME
 British: 4 ARNE
 French: 5 SATIE
 Hungarian: 5 LISZT 6 BARTOK
 Knighted: 5 ELGAR
 New Age: 4 TESH
 Norwegian: 5 GRIEG
 org.: 5 ASCAP
 Rock: 3 ENO
 work: 4 OPUS
 ~ Alban: 4 BERG
 ~ ___ Carlo Menotti: 4 GIAN
 ~ Charles: 4 IVES
 ~ Erik: 5 **SATIE**
 ~ Gustav: 6 MAHLER
 ~ Harold: 5 ARLEN
 ~ Jacques: 4 BREL 5 IBERT
 ~ Jerome: 4 KERN
 ~ Ned: 5 ROREM
 ~ Thomas: 4 ARNE
Composite
 Bilingual: 6 PIDGIN
 kin: 5 DORIC
Composition: 4 OPUS 5 ESSAY
 Musical: 4 **OPUS** 5 ETUDE
     6 ARIOSO SONATA
 Short: 8 SONATINA
Compos mentis: 4 SANE
 ___ compos mentis: 3 NON
Compost
 Become: 3 ROT

Composure: 4 COOL WITS
  5 POISE 6 APLOMB
Compote
  fruit: 4 PEAR 5 PEARS
Compound
  Aromatic: 5 ESTER
  Carbon: 4 ENOL
  Chemical: 4 ENOL 5 ESTER
    6 ISOMER
  Fatty: 5 LIPID
  Fragrant: 5 **ESTER**
  Hydroxyl: 4 **ENOL**
  Nitrogen: 5 AMIDE AMINE
    AZIDE
  Organic: 4 **ENOL** 5 AMIDE
    ESTER
  with two double bonds: 5 DIENE
Comprehend: 3 GET SEE 4 KNOW
    5 GRASP 6 FATHOM
  Hard to: 4 DEEP
Comprehension: 3 KEN 5 GRASP
    6 UPTAKE
  Words of: 4 ISEE
Comprehensive: 5 BROAD
    6 GLOBAL 7 OVERALL
Compress
  a file: 3 ZIP
  ~, informally: 5 SMUSH
Compression
  It operates by: 6 AIRGUN
Compromise: 5 BUDGE
    8 TRADEOFF
Compromised
  Financially: 7 INAHOLE
"Compromising Positions"
  author Susan: 6 ISAACS
Compulsion: 4 NEED URGE
Compulsive
  thief: 6 KLEPTO
Compunction: 7 REMORSE
Computation
  Carpet: 4 AREA
Computer
  1940s ~: 5 ENIAC
  accessory: 5 MODEM MOUSE
    7 PRINTER
  acronym: 4 GIGO 5 ASCII
  add-on: 3 ESE
  Apple: 4 IMAC

bug: 6 GLITCH
bulletin board manager: 5 SYSOP
capacity: 5 BYTES 6 MEMORY
Central: 6 SERVER
chip maker: 5 INTEL
choice: 3 MAC
clickers: 4 MICE
Colorful: 4 IMAC
command: 4 GOTO OPEN SAVE
  UNDO 5 ENTER ERASE
  PRINT 7 RESTART
core (abbr.): 3 CPU
data unit: 4 BYTE
device: 5 MODEM MOUSE
document: 4 FILE
Dot on a: 5 PIXEL
Early: 5 **ENIAC** 6 UNIVAC
expert: 6 TECHIE
fodder: 4 DATA 5 INPUT
game: 4 MYST 6 TETRIS
game maker: 5 ATARI
geek: 4 NERD
giant: 3 NEC 4 DELL 5 APPLE
graphic: 4 ICON
image: 4 ICON
image file format: 4 JPEG
input: 4 DATA 7 DATASET
introduced in 1985: 5 AMIGA
Japanese ~ giant: 3 NEC
Jobs in the ~ biz: 5 STEVE
key: 3 ALT ESC TAB 5 ARROW
  ENTER 6 DELETE
Kind of ~ drive: 5 CDROM
language: 4 JAVA 5 ALGOL
  BASIC COBOL 6 PASCAL
  7 FORTRAN
letters: 5 EMAIL
Like a certain ~ system: 5 OCTAL
list: 4 MENU
memory unit: 3 MEG 4 BYTE
message: 5 EMAIL
monitor, for short: 3 CRT
Most ~ buyers: 8 ENDUSERS
network: 6 SYSTEM
networking device: 6 ROUTER
Old: 5 AMIGA
Old ~ tube: 6 TRIODE
operating system: 4 UNIX
  5 MSDOS

operator: 4 **USER**
owner: 4 **USER**
peripheral: 7 SCANNER
picture: 4 SCAN
Pioneer: 5 ENIAC
Portable: 6 LAPTOP
printer maker: 5 EPSON
problem: 5 CRASH VIRUS
program feature: 4 LOOP
program, for short: 3 APP
record: 7 DATASET
reseller (abbr.): 3 OEM
screen, for short: 3 CRT
Shared ~ sys.: 3 LAN
shortcut: 5 MACRO
Start up a: 4 BOOT
suffix: 3 ESE IZE
symbol: 4 **ICON**
text: 5 ASCII
TRS-80 ~ maker: 5 TANDY
unit: 3 MEG 4 BYTE
whiz: 6 TECHIE
Computerphile: 4 USER
Computes
net weight: 5 TARES
Comrade: 3 PAL 4 ALLY
British: 4 MATE
French: 3 AMI
Russian: 8 TOVARICH
Comstock
load: 3 ORE
Comtes
etc.: 8 NOBLESSE
"Comus"
composer: 4 ARNE
Con: 4 **ANTI** DUPE RUSE SCAM
      SNOW 6 INMATE
counter: 3 PRO
cover: 5 ALIAS
decoy: 5 SHILL
game: 4 **SCAM** 5 BUNCO
   BUNKO STING
Help with a: 4 ABET
man: 4 ANTI
men: 5 ANTIS
Pro or: 4 SIDE
Three-card: 5 MONTE
vote: 3 NAY
Con ___: 4 BRIO 5 AMORE

ConAgra
Home of: 5 OMAHA
"Con Air"
actor Nicolas: 4 CAGE
Conan
former sidekick: 4 ANDY
Host: 6 OBRIEN
Con artist: 5 DUPER 7 FLEECER
aide: 5 SHILL
art: 4 SCAM
Concave
lint trap: 5 INNIE
Conceal: 4 BURY HIDE MASK
      PALM VEIL 6 HUSHUP
      SCREEN SHIELD
      7 SECRETE
Concealed: 3 HID 5 PERDU
      6 HIDDEN UNSEEN
Not: 5 OVERT
Concealer
Floorboard: 7 AREARUG
Concealment
Hunter: 5 BLIND
Concede: 4 GIVE 5 ADMIT
      ALLOW YIELD
Conceit: 3 **EGO** 4 IDEA
      7 EGOTISM
Conceited: 4 VAIN
Conceive: 6 IDEATE
Concentrate: 5 FOCUS
      7 DISTILL
Concentration
Points of: 4 FOCI
"Concentration"
puzzle: 5 REBUS
Concept: 4 **IDEA**
Cannes: 4 IDEE
Confucian: 3 TAO
Flawless: 5 IDEAL
Freudian: 3 EGO 6 LIBIDO
Newtonian: 7 INERTIA
Physics: 4 MASS
Conception: 4 IDEA 5 IMAGE
Conceptualize: 6 IDEATE
Concern: 4 CARE FIRM NEED
      5 ALARM WORRY
      6 MATTER 8 INTEREST
Concerned
with: 4 INTO

**Concerning: 4 <u>ASTO</u> INRE
5 ABOUT ANENT ASFOR**
this: 6 HEREOF
~, in legalese: 4 INRE
Concert: 5 EVENT
bonus: 6 ENCORE
ending: 3 INA
equipment: 4 AMPS
hall: 5 ODEUM
halls: 4 <u>ODEA</u>
In: 5 ASONE
pianist Claudio: 5 ARRAU
setting: 5 ARENA
souvenir: 3 TEE 6 TSHIRT
take: 4 GATE
venue: 5 ARENA
Concertina: 10 SQUEEZEBOX
Concerto
climax: 7 CADENZA
finale: 4 CODA
highlight: 4 SOLO
instrument: 4 OBOE 5 PIANO
movement: 5 RONDO
Concession
Concise: 5 ILOSE
Make a: 4 BEND
suffix: 4 AIRE
Conch
cousin: 6 LIMPET
Conciliatory: 6 IRENIC
gift: 3 SOP
**Concise: 4 CURT 5 PITHY SHORT
TERSE**
summary: 5 RECAP 6 PRECIS
Concisely
Describe: 5 SUMUP
**Conclude: 3 END 4 WRAP
5 ENDUP INFER**
by: 5 ENDAT
**Concluded: 4 DONE OVER
6 SEWNUP**
Concluding
passage: 4 CODA
**Conclusion: 3 <u>END</u> 4 CODA
5 FINIS 6 ENDING EPILOG
FINALE**
Info: Suffix cue
Cartesian: 3 <u>IAM</u>
Congregational: 4 AMEN

Draw a: 5 INFER
Horner: 3 AMI
In: 6 LASTLY
In ~, in French: 5 ENFIN
lead-in: 4 ERGO IFSO 5 HENCE
Legal: 3 ESE
Major: 4 ETTE
Musical: 4 CODA
Start of a legal: 5 IREST
Conclusive: 4 LAST
trial: 8 ACIDTEST
**Concoct: 4 BREW 5 HATCH
6 DEVISE 7 DREAMUP**
Concoction
Bean: 4 IDEA
Café: 5 MOCHA
Corn: 4 PONE
Corned beef: 4 HASH
Crockpot: 4 STEW
Custard: 4 FLAN
Noodle: 4 IDEA
Scotch: 6 ROBROY
Witches': 4 BREW
**Concord: 5 AMITY PEACE UNITY
6 UNISON**
Concorde: 3 <u>SST</u>
maker: 8 CHRYSLER
Take a: 3 JET
"Concord Sonata"
composer: 4 IVES
Concrete: 4 <u>REAL</u> 6 ACTUAL
Cover with: 4 PAVE
kin: 6 CEMENT
Like fresh: 5 UNSET
reinforcer: 5 REBAR
section: 4 SLAB
Concubine
room: 3 ODA
**Concur: 5 <u>AGREE</u> 6 ACCEDE
ASSENT 7 GOALONG
11 SEEEYETOEYE**
Condé ___: 4 NAST
Condemn: 4 DOOM
openly: 5 DECRY
Condé Nast
magazine: 4 SELF
Condensation
Morning: 3 DEW
Condense: 7 ABRIDGE

on a surface: 6 ADSORB
Condensed
 In ~ form: 8 CAPSULAR
Condescend: 5 **DEIGN** STOOP
Condescending
 cluck: 3 **TSK**
 one: 4 SNOB 5 SNOOT
Condiment
 Breakfast: 5 SYRUP
 Cannes: 3 SEL
 Chemist: 4 NACL
 Chili: 8 HOTSAUCE
 Japanese: 8 SOYSAUCE
  9 SOYASAUCE
 Ocean: 7 SEASALT
 source: 8 SALTMINE
 Sushi: 6 WASABI
 TexMex: 5 SALSA
Condition: 4 MODE 5 INURE
  SHAPE **STATE** 6 FETTLE
  7 PROVISO
 In perfect: 4 MINT
 Muscle: 4 TONE
 Physical: 5 SHAPE
 Pique: 3 IRE
 Sale: 4 **ASIS**
 Undesirable: 6 MALADY
 Untidy: 4 MESS
Conditional
 release: 6 PAROLE
Conditionally
 out: 8 ONPAROLE
Conditioned
 reflex researcher: 6 PAVLOV
Conditioner
 Kind of: 3 AIR
Conditions: 3 IFS
 Best: 6 OPTIMA
 Contract: 5 TERMS
 Harsh: 6 RIGORS
 Prevailing: 7 CLIMATE
Condo: 4 **UNIT**
 alternative: 4 COOP
 division: 4 **UNIT**
Condor
 claw: 5 TALON
 condo: 4 NEST 5 AERIE
 Kind of: 6 ANDEAN
 Like a ~ in the wild: 4 RARE

Conduct: 3 RUN 4 LEAD
 Code of: 5 **ETHIC**
 (oneself): 6 DEPORT
Conductance
 unit: 3 **MHO**
Conducted: 3 **LED**
Conducting
 First name in: 6 ARTURO
 rod: 5 BATON
Conductor: 7 MAESTRO
 Bombay-born: 5 MEHTA
 concern: 5 TEMPO
 Former Boston Symphony:
  5 OZAWA
 Hungarian-born: 5 SOLTI
 intro: 4 SEMI
 Longtime NBC Symphony:
  9 TOSCANINI
 platforms: 5 PODIA
 reference: 5 SCORE
 Semi: 4 CBER
 Slowly, to a: 6 ADAGIO
 stick: 5 BATON
 ~ Antal: 6 DORATI
 ~ Georg: 5 SOLTI
 ~ Kurt: 5 MASUR
 ~ Lucas: 4 FOSS
 ~ Riccardo: 4 MUTI
 ~ Seiji: 5 OZAWA
 ~ Sir Georg: 5 SOLTI
 ~ Walter: 5 BRUNO
 ~ Zubin: 5 **MEHTA**
Conduit: 4 DUCT 8 PIPELINE
 bend: 3 ELL
 Engine: 4 HOSE
 in an ICU: 6 IVTUBE
 Poison: 4 FANG
 Underground: 5 SEWER
 Vital engine: 7 OILLINE
 Water: 4 MAIN
Cone
 bearer: 3 FIR 4 PINE
 It may be found in a: 4 LAVA
 prefix: 3 SNO
 Traffic: 5 PYLON
Cone-bearing
 tree: 3 FIR 7 CYPRESS
Cones
 It contains rods and: 6 RETINA

Partners of: **4** RODS

Cone-shaped
  heater: **4** ETNA

Conestoga: 5 WAGON

Confection
  Cadbury: **3** EGG
  Cold: **3** ICE **5** BOMBE
  French: **7** PRALINE
  Frozen: **4** ICEE
  Nutty: **6** NOUGAT **7** PRALINE

Confectionary
  worker: **4** ICER

Confederacy
  foe: **5** UNION

"Confederacy of Dunces, A"
  author: **5** TOOLE

Confederate: 4 ALLY
  general: **3** LEE **6** STUART
  Quebec: **3** AMI
  soldier: **3** REB

Confer: 6 BESTOW

Conference: 6 POWWOW
       7 PALAVER SEMINAR
  1945 ~ site: **5** **YALTA**
  Court: **7** SIDEBAR
  Football: **6** HUDDLE
  prefix: **4** TELE
  Press ~ activity: **5** QANDA
  WWII ~ site: **5** CAIRO YALTA

Conferral
  A-student: **5** HONOR
  College: **6** DEGREE

Confess: 3 OWN **4** **AVOW** TALK
      TELL **5** ADMIT OWNTO
      OWNUP
  ~, with "up": **3** OWN

Confession
  collection: **4** SINS
  starter: **3** MEA

Confessions
  Like some: **4** ORAL

"Confessions of ___ Turner, The":
  3 NAT

Confetti: 6 SHREDS
  Make: **5** SHRED
  Turn into: **5** RIPUP

Confidante: 4 AMIE

Confidence: 5 FAITH TRUST
      6 SECRET SURETY

Declare with: **4** AVER **6** ASSERT
game: **4** SCAM **5** BUNKO STING
Give ~ to: **6** ASSURE
Have: **4** RELY
Have ~ in: **5** TRUST
Restore ~ to: **8** REASSURE
Vote of: **3** AYE
Words of: **4** ICAN

Confident: 4 SURE
  solver's tool: **3** PEN
  way to solve: **5** ININK

Confidential
  matter: **6** SECRET

Confidently
  State: **4** **AVER** **6** ASSERT
      ASSURE

Confine: 4 SHUT **5** BOXIN
      HEMIN LIMIT PENIN
      6 COOPUP ENCAGE
      INTERN
  ~, with "in": **3** HEM

Confined: 4 **PENT**

Confines: 3 RIM **4** AREA
      7 PURLIEU SHUTSIN
  Swine: **5** STIES

Confirmation: 4 RITE
  Used as: **5** CITED

Confiscate: 5 SEIZE
  ~, in law: **7** ESCHEAT

Conflagration: 5 BLAZE

Conflict: 3 WAR **4** SPAT **5** CLASH
      6 STRIFE **7** COLLIDE
  1960s ~ site: **3** NAM
  Armed: **3** **WAR**
  Confused: **5** MELEE
  Field of: **5** ARENA
  In: **4** TORN **5** ATWAR **6** ATODDS
  In ~ with, with "of": **5** AFOUL
  Literary: **4** AGON

Conflicted: 4 TORN

Conform: 4 JIBE **5** ADAPT FITIN
      6 ADHERE
  (to): **3** HEW

Conforming: 6 INSTEP

Confound: 5 ADDLE **6** BEMUSE

Confounded: 5 ATSEA

"Confound it!": 4 DANG DRAT

Confront: 4 **FACE** MEET
      6 ACCOST

Confrontation: 5 RUNIN
    8 ONEONONE
    SHOWDOWN
  In direct: 8 TOETOTOE
  Rink: 7 FACEOFF
Confronted
  with: 9 UPAGAINST
Confucian
  path: 3 TAO
Confucius
  Dynasty of: 4 CHOU
Confuse: 3 VEX 5 **ADDLE** BEFOG
    MUDDY RAVEL 6 BAFFLE
    TANGLE
Confused: 4 LOST 5 **ATSEA**
    MUDDY 6 INAFOG
    7 OUTOFIT
  Completely: 7 CHAOTIC
  fight: 5 MELEE
  Make: 5 ADDLE
  state: 3 FOG 4 HAZE
Confusing
  pathway: 4 MAZE
Confusion: 4 HAZE MESS MOIL
    8 DISARRAY
  Total: 5 CHAOS
Cong.
  meeting: 4 SESS
  member: 3 SEN
  ___ Cong: 4 **VIET**
Conga: 4 DRUM
"Conga"
  singer: 7 ESTEFAN
Congeal: 3 GEL SET 4 CLOT
    CURD JELL
Congenial: 4 NICE
  Less: 5 ICIER
  Like Miss: 6 NICEST
Congenital: 6 INNATE
Conger: 3 **EEL** 6 SEAEEL
  catcher: 5 **EELER**
  Caught a: 5 EELED
Congested
  area: 5 SINUS
Conglomerate: 5 AMASS
    UNITE
  Corp.: 3 ITT
Conglomeration: 4 OLIO
    6 RAGBAG

Congo
  animal: 5 HIPPO OKAPI RHINO
  First ~ P.M. Lumumba:
    7 PATRICE
  neighbor: 6 ANGOLA RWANDA
  river: 4 UELE 5 EBOLA
    6 UBANGI
  suffix: 4 LESE
  ~, formerly: 5 ZAIRE
"Congratulations!": 5 KUDOS
    8 MAZELTOV
  in action: 3 PAT
Congregate: 4 MEET
Congregation
  area: 4 NAVE
  divider: 5 AISLE
  leader: 5 RABBI 6 PASTOR
  members: 5 LAITY
  shout: 4 AMEN
Congress
  creation: 3 ACT
  Mem. of: 3 REP
  Part of: 6 SENATE
  Send to: 5 ELECT
  Vote in: 3 YEA
  Where to see: 5 CSPAN
Congressional
  approval: 3 YEA
  committee: 6 ETHICS
  gofer: 4 PAGE
  mtg.: 4 SESS
  output: 3 ACT 4 ACTS BILL
    LAWS
  period: 7 SESSION
  ~ VIP: 4 WHIP
Conical
  dryer: 4 OAST
  home: 5 TEPEE
Coniferous
  tree: 3 YEW 4 PINE 5 CEDAR
    LARCH
Conjecture: 5 GUESS 7 GUESSAT
    SURMISE
Conjugation
  Latin I: 3 AMO 4 AMAS **AMAT**
Conjunction
  Cartesian: 4 ERGO
  Common: 3 AND NOR
  couplet: 5 ANDOR

German: 3 UND
Latin: 4 ERGO
Negative: 3 NOR
Poetic: 3 ERE
Conjure
up: 5 EVOKE
Conjurer
prop: 4 WAND
Conk: 3 BOP 4 BEAN 5 BRAIN
    CROWN
out: 3 **DIE** 4 FAIL QUIT 5 STALL
Conker
Curly: 3 MOE
Conn
Actress: 4 DIDI
Take the: 5 STEER
Conn.
school: 5 YALEU
Connect: 3 TIE 4 JOIN LINK
    5 TIEIN UNITE 6 FASTEN
    PLUGIN
to an outlet: 6 PLUGIN
via phone: 6 DIALIN
with: 5 **TIETO** 7 TIEINTO
Connected
Closely: 7 SIAMESE
Is: 6 TIESIN
to the Internet: 6 ONLINE
Connecticut
campus: 4 YALE
city: 7 BRISTOL
collegian: 3 ELI 5 YALIE
Former ~ governor: 6 GRASSO
motto word: 3 QUI
senator: 4 DODD
Connecting
flight: 9 STAIRCASE
point: 4 NODE
strips of land: 6 ISTHMI
wd.: 4 CONJ
word: 3 AND
Connection: 3 TIE 4 BOND LINK
    5 NEXUS TIEIN 6 HOOKUP
    7 LIAISON
Have a: 6 RELATE
Inner: 5 SINEW
Connections: 3 **INS**
French: 3 **ETS**
Connective tissue: 6 TENDON

Connect the ___: 4 DOTS
Conned: 3 GOT HAD 5 TAKEN
Connell
Author: 4 EVAN
Connelly
Playwright: 4 **MARC**
Connery
Actor: 4 **SEAN**
role: 4 BOND
successor: 5 MOORE
~, by birth: 4 SCOT
Connick Jr., Harry
1994 ~ album: 3 SHE
Sing like: 5 CROON
Connie
Newswoman: 5 CHUNG
of baseball: 4 MACK
portrayer: 5 TALIA
Conniption: 6 CATFIT
Connivance: 6 SCHEME
Connive: 4 PLAN 6 SCHEME
with: 4 ABET
Conniving: 3 SLY
sort: 7 SCHEMER
Connoisseur: 5 MAVEN
Food: 7 EPICURE GOURMET
Wine ~ concern: 4 YEAR
Connors
adversary: 4 ASHE BORG
Conoco
rival: 4 ESSO
___ con pollo: 5 ARROZ
Conquer: 4 BEAT BEST TAME
Conqueror
11th century ~: 6 NORMAN
of Mexico: 6 CORTEZ
of Valencia: 5 ELCID
Sword: 3 PEN
Conquest
for Caesar: 4 GAUL
Hillary: 7 EVEREST
of 1953: 7 EVEREST
Salk's: 5 POLIO
Conquistador
fighter: 4 INCA
quest: 3 ORO
Conrad
Actor: 4 BAIN
novel: 7 LORDJIM

of old films: **5** NAGEL
Conrad, Robert
  series: **5** THEDA
Conried
  Actor: **4** HANS
Cons
  Discuss pros and: **6** DEBATE
  do it: **4** TIME
Conscience: 8 SUPEREGO
  burden: **5** GUILT
Conscious: 5 ALERT AWARE
        8 SENTIENT
  prefix: **3** ECO
Consciousness
  Lose: **5** SWOON
  Regained: **6** CAMETO
Conscriptable: 4 ONEA
Conscription
  org.: **3** SSS
Conseco Fieldhouse
  player: **5** PACER
Consecrate: 5 BLESS **6** ANOINT
        HALLOW ORDAIN
Consecrated: 4 HOLY **5** BLEST
        6 SACRED
Consecutively: 6 INAROW
Consensus
  Come to a: **5** AGREE
Consent: 9 ACQUIESCE
  Give: **5** AGREE **6** ACCEDE
Consequence: 6 IMPORT
        RESULT
  Workout: **4** ACHE
  ___ consequence: **4** OFNO
Consequently: 4 ERGO THEN
        THUS **5** HENCE
Conservationist
  ~ John: **4** MUIR
Conservative: 4 TORY **5** STAID
  prefix: **3** NEO **5** ULTRA
  ~ Alan: **5** KEYES
Conservatives: 5 RIGHT
Conservatory
  Ohio: **7** OBERLIN
  subj.: **3** MUS
Consider: 4 **DEEM** HEED
        5 WEIGH **6** DEBATE
        HEAROF LOOKAT
  again: **6** REHEAR

officially: **4** HEAR
  ~, with "over": **4** CHEW MULL
Considerable: 4 TIDY **5** AMPLE
        BROAD LARGE
  amount: **3** TON
  sum: **11** PRETTYPENNY
Considerably: 3 FAR **4** ALOT
        MUCH **5** QUITE
Considerate: 4 KIND NICE
Consideration: 4 HEED SAKE
Considered
  Everything: **8** ALLINALL
  Not carefully: **4** RASH
"Consider it done": 6 IMONIT
Consign: 6 DEVOTE **8** RELEGATE
  to oblivion: **4** DOOM
Consist
  suffix: **3** ENT **4** ENCY
Consistency
  It's used for the sake of:
        7 THINNER
Consolidate: 4 MELD POOL
        5 MERGE UNITE
Consonant: 6 INSYNC
  Greek: **3** CHI PSI RHO TAU
        4 BETA ZETA **5** SIGMA
Consonants
  Greek: **3** MUS NUS **6** THETAS
  Some: **6** NASALS
Consort
  of Aphrodite: **4** ARES
  of Zeus: **4** HERA
Conspicuous: 5 OVERT
        7 EMINENT SALIENT
  success: **5** ECLAT
Conspiracy: 4 PLOT **5** CABAL
**"Conspiracy Against Childhood,
        The"**
  author LeShan: **3** EDA
"Conspiracy Zone, The"
  network: **3** TNN
Conspirator
  Shakespearean: **4** IAGO
  ~ Guy: **6** FAWKES
Conspiratorial
  group: **5** CABAL
Conspire: 4 PLOT **6** SCHEME
        7 COLLUDE
  with: **4** ABET

Constable
  Where to see a: 4 TATE
"Constant Craving"
  singer: 4 LANG 6 KDLANG
Constantine
  Mother of: 6 HELENA
Constantly: 4 EVER 5 NOEND
  find fault with: 3 NAG
  ~, to Keats: 3 EER
Constants
  Circle: 3 PIS
Constellation
  Altar: 3 **ARA**
  animal: 4 URSA
  Belted: 5 ORION
  brightest star: 5 ALPHA
  component: 4 STAR
  Northern: 5 DRACO
  Peacock: 4 PAVO
  Southern: 3 ARA 4 ARGO
  Vega: 4 **LYRA**
Consternate: 6 APPALL
Consternation: 5 ALARM
        6 DISMAY
Constituent: 4 PART 6 MEMBER
        7 ELEMENT
  Cell: 3 RNA
  Convoy: 4 SEMI
Constitution
  Change the: 5 AMEND
  clause: 7 ARTICLE
  drafter: 6 FRAMER
  lead-in: 3 USS
  States' rights amendment to the:
        5 TENTII
  ___ Constitution: 3 USS
Constitutional: 4 WALK 6 STROLL
  Failed ~ amendment: 3 ERA
Constriction
  of the pupils: 6 MIOSIS
Constrictor: 3 BOA
  ___ constrictor: 3 BOA
Construct: 4 MAKE 5 BUILD
        ERECT
Constructed: 4 MADE
Construction
  beam: 4 **IBAR**
  Big name in: 4 LEGO
  Caterpillar: 4 TENT

co. project: 4 BLDG
  Coral: 4 REEF
  crew: 8 HARDHATS
  Fed. ~ overseer: 3 GSA
  girder: 5 IBEAM
  Naval ~ crew: 7 SEABEES
  piece: 4 **IBAR** ZBAR 5 IBEAM
  setting: 4 SITE
  site sight: 4 CONE 5 CRANE
        7 HARDHAT
  Stage: 3 SET
  support: 4 IBAR
  worker: 7 ERECTER HARDHAT
Constructive
  Be: 6 CREATE
Constructor
  Crossword ~, seemingly: 6 SADIST
Consult: 3 SEE 6 LOOKTO
Consultant
  Ancient: 6 ORACLE
  Manual: 4 USER
Consultation
  Send for: 5 REFER
Consume: 3 **EAT** USE 5 EATUP
  Safe to: 6 EDIBLE
Consumed: 3 **ATE** HAD 4 GONE
        5 EATEN 6 USEDUP
  Completely: 7 ALLGONE
  quickly: 5 ATEUP
Consumer: 4 USER 5 BUYER
        EATER 7 ENDUSER
  advocate Ralph: 5 NADER
  concern: 4 COST
  protection org.: 3 BBB
  reading: 5 LABEL
Consumerist
  ~ Ralph: 5 NADER
Consumer Reports
  employee: 5 RATER 6 TESTER
"___ consummation devoutly ...":
        Hamlet: 4 TISA
Consumption: 3 USE
  Fit for: 6 EDIBLE
Cont.
  Second-largest: 3 AFR
Contact: 4 LENS 5 EMAIL RADIO
  contact: 6 CORNEA
  Don't make ~ with: 4 MISS
  Make: 6 LIAISE

Reporter: **6** SOURCE
site: **3** EYE
"Contact"
author: **5** SAGAN
They make contact in: **3** ETS
Contact ___: 4 LENS
Container: 3 BIN CAN JAR TUB
Big: **3** VAT
cover: **3** LID
Small: **4** VIAL
weight: **4 TARE**
Containing
nothing: **5** EMPTY
Contains: 3 HAS
Contaminant
Chem.: **3** PCB
free: **4** PURE
Water: **5** ECOLI
Contaminate: 5 TAINT **6** DEFILE
INFECT POISON
7 POLLUTE
Contemplate: 4 MUSE **6** PONDER
Subject to: **5** NAVEL
Contemporary: 6 COEVAL
MODERN
Contempt: 5 ODIUM SCORN
Beneath: **4** VILE
Cry of: **3** BAH **4** PISH POOH
TUSH
Show: **4** JEER **5** SCOFF SNEER
Treat with: **4** SNUB **5** SCORN
SPURN **6** DERIDE
Uttered with: **4** SPAT
Contemptible: 4 BASE MEAN
VILE **5** MANGY
one: **3** CAD CUR **4** CRUD HEEL
TOAD WORM **5** LOUSE
SWINE TWERP **7** DASTARD
Contemptuous
look: **5** SNEER
noise: **5** SNORT
Contend: 3 VIE 6 STRIVE
colloquially: **6** RASSLE
Contender: 4 VIER
___ contendere: 4 NOLO
Content: 7 ATPEACE
prefix: **3** MAL
Contented
sound: **3** AAH **4** PURR

Contention
Drop out of: **4** FADE
Matter of: **4** BONE
Still in: **5** ALIVE
Contentment: 4 EASE
Sound of: **3** AAH **4** PURR
Sounds of: **3** AHS
Contest: 3 BEE VIE **4** BOUT
MEET **5** ARGUE
Cowboy: **5** RODEO
form: **5** ENTRY
for two: **4** DUEL
Greek: **4** AGON
hopeful: **7** ENTRANT
Kind of: **3** BEE
Logger: **5** ROLEO
Medieval: **4** TILT
No: **4** ROMP
Oldest hoops: **3** NIT
Ring: **4** SUMO
Speed: **4** RACE
Spelling: **3** BEE
submission: **5** ENTRY
venue: **5** ARENA
Contestant: 4 VIER **5** ENTRY
Become a: **5** ENTER
rank: **4** SEED
Regatta: **3** OAR
Slalom: **5** SKIER
Continent
Currency on the: **4** EURO
Largest: **4 ASIA**
Second-largest: **6** AFRICA
separator: **5** OCEAN
south of Eur.: **3** AFR
The: **6** EUROPE
"Continent, The": 6 EUROPE
Continental
border: **5** URALS
competitor: **5** DELTA
currency: **4 EURO 5** EUROS
divide: **5** OCEAN
prefix: **4** AFRO EURO
trade gp.: **3** EEC
Continental Airlines Arena
team: **4** NETS
Continental Congress
Silas of the: **5** DEANE
Contingencies: 3 IFS ·

Contingency
  Event: 8 RAINDATE
Continually: 4 EVER
  Bother: 5 EATAT NAGAT
    6 HARASS
Continue: 3 ADD 4 GOON MOVE
    6 KEEPON MOVEON
    ROLLON
  a subscription: 5 RENEW
Continued: 6 KEPTON WENTON
  drama: 6 SERIAL
  ~, with "on": 4 KEPT
Continuing
  story: 6 SERIAL
Continuous
  change: 4 FLUX
Continuously: 4 EVER 5 ONEND
Contort: 4 BEND CURL WARP
    5 GNARL 6 DEFORM
Contoured
  Finely: 5 SLEEK
Contra-
  relative: 4 ANTI
Contract: 3 GET 4 HIRE PACT
    WANE
  add-on: 5 RIDER
  Certain: 5 LEASE
  conditions: 5 TERMS
  Defeat a ~ in bridge: 3 SET
  escalator: 4 COLA
  Extend a: 5 RENEW
  Kind of: 10 SWEETHEART
  Lucrative, as a: 3 FAT
  negotiator: 5 AGENT
  negotiator (abbr.): 3 AGT
  provision: 6 CLAUSE
  Rental: 5 LEASE
  seeker: 9 FREEAGENT
  Sign a: 3 INK
  Unbreakable, as a: 8 IRONCLAD
  Without a: 6 ONSPEC
  worker: 6 HITMAN
"Contract Bridge Complete"
  author: 5 GOREN
Contracted: 3 GOT 8 SHRUNKEN
  cost: 7 SETRATE
Contraction: 5 SPASM
  Anthem: 3 **OER**
  Carol: 3 **TIS**

  Muscle: 5 SPASM
  Poetic: 3 EEN EER OER TIS
    4 NEER
  Quaint: 5 SHANT TWERE
Contractor
  detail: 4 SPEC
  fig.: 3 EST
  Sub: 4 DELI
  Top: 6 ROOFER
Contracts
  Like some: 4 ORAL
Contradict: 4 DENY 5 **BELIE**
    REBUT
Contradicted
  Apt to be: 8 DENIABLE
Contrapuntal
  composition: 5 CANON
Contrary
  girl: 4 MARY
  to expectation: 5 ODDLY
  votes: 4 NAYS
Contrasts
  Like some: 5 STARK
  Opposite of: 6 LIKENS
Contretemps: 6 MISHAP
Contribute: 3 ADD 5 ADDIN
    PAYIN PUTIN 6 CHIPIN
    DONATE IMPART KICKIN
Contributing
  element: 6 FACTOR
Contribution
  Church: 5 TITHE
  Insured's: 5 COPAY
  Kind of: 3 IRA
  of ideas: 5 INPUT
  Pot: 4 ANTE
Contributor
  Campaign: 3 PAC
  Wealthy: 6 FATCAT
Contrite: 5 SORRY
  Feel: 6 REPENT
  one: 4 RUER
Contrition: 6 REGRET 7 REMORSE
  Show: 3 RUE
Contrive: 4 BREW MAKE PLAN
    5 HATCH STAGE 6 DEVISE
Contrived: 5 HOKEY 7 TREACLE
Control: 3 OWN 4 REIN 5 REINS
    7 HARNESS

Bring under: 4 TAME 6 REININ
Crew's: 3 OAR
Dashboard: 5 DEFOG
Electronic ~ system: 5 SERVO
Emissions ~ gp.: 3 EPA
Flood ~ device: 4 DIKE
Have ~ of: 3 OWN
Lose: 4 FLIP RAGE SKID SNAP
Means of: 4 REIN
Mission ~, for short: 3 OPS
Organ: 4 STOP
Out of: 4 **AMOK** WILD 5 ARIOT
   7 ONATEAR
Pest ~ brand: 4 DCON
Pollution ~ org.: 3 EPA
post: 4 HELM
Steer out of: 8 STAMPEDE
tower image: 4 BLIP
TV: 3 VOL 4 DIAL TINT
   5 TUNER
Under: 4 TAME 5 TAMED
   6 INHAND INLINE

Controller
Horse: 4 REIN
Pupil: 4 IRIS
Traffic: 5 LIGHT

Controls
Like some: 4 DUAL

Controversial: 7 ERISTIC
1990s ~ sitcom: 5 ELLEN
blowup: 5 ATEST
chemical: 3 PCB
spray: 4 **ALAR**
talk: 7 EBONICS
Very: 6 REDHOT
war zone: 3 NAM

Controvert: 4 DENY 5 BELIE
   REBUT
Contumely: 5 SCORN
Conundrum: 5 POSER 6 ENIGMA
   RIDDLE
Convection: 4 OVEN
Convene: 3 SIT 4 MEET
Convened: 3 MET SAT
again: 5 REMET
Convenience: 4 EASE
24-hr. ~: 3 ATM
Airline: 7 ETICKET
Bank: 3 ATM

Hotel: 4 SAFE
Shopping: 4 TOTE
store convenience: 3 ATM
Convenient: 5 HANDY
enc.: 3 SAE

Convent
dweller: 3 NUN
leader: 6 ABBESS
Convention: 4 MORE NORM
   5 USAGE
address: 7 KEYNOTE
center event: 4 EXPO
group: 4 BLOC
handout: 5 IDTAG
   7 NAMETAG
site: 4 HALL
~ VIP: 7 NOMINEE
   8 KEYNOTER
Conventional
Make: 7 STYLIZE
Convergence
points: 4 FOCI
Conversant
with: 4 UPON
Conversation: 6 DIALOG
filler: 4 ISEE
Friendly: 4 CHAT
Have a: 4 TALK
piece: 5 PHONE
starter: 5 HELLO 6 LISTEN
Conversational
filler: 5 IMEAN
fillers: 3 ERS
Conversationalist: 6 TALKER
Converse: 3 RAP 4 CHAT TALK
   5 SPEAK
competitor: 4 AVIA KEDS
To's: 3 FRO
Convert: 5 ADAPT
~, with "over": 3 WIN
Converted: 6 REBORN
Convertible: 6 RAGTOP
   7 SOFABED
alternative: 5 SEDAN
couch: 6 DAYBED 7 SOFABED
cover: 7 SOFTTOP
It may be: 4 SOFA
Mazda: 5 MIATA
Convertiplane: 4 STOL

Convex
molding: 5 OVOLO
Conveyance
Airport: 4 TRAM
Skier's: 4 TBAR
Whitewater: 4 RAFT
Winter: 4 SLED
Conveyed: 6 DEEDED
Conveyor
Tear: 4 DUCT
Conviction: 5 FAITH TENET
6 BELIEF
One with a: 5 FELON
State with: 4 AVER 6 ASSERT
Unfair: 3 RAP
Convince: 4 SELL SWAY
Convinced: 4 SOLD SURE
Convincing
one: 6 SWAYER
Convocation
Quilting: 3 BEE
Convoy
component: 3 RIG 4 SEMI
Convulsive
sound: 3 SOB
Convy: 4 BERT
Conway
Comic: 3 TIM
Cooer: 4 DOVE
Cook: 4 CHEF 7 PREPARE
abbr.: 3 TSP
Apt name for a: 3 STU
book: 4 COMA
canful: 4 LARD
clams: 5 STEAM
cookies: 4 BAKE
cover-up: 5 APRON
exhortation: 5 DIGIN
Gourmet: 4 CHEF
in a microwave: 3 ZAP 4 NUKE
in a wok: 5 SAUTE
in the oven: 5 ROAST
meas.: 3 TSP
one's goose: 5 ROAST
One way to: 3 FRY 4 BOIL STEW
5 BROIL ROAST 6 BRAISE
too long: 6 OVERDO
up: 4 BREW 5 HATCH 6 INVENT
wear: 5 APRON

Cook, Robin
book: 4 **COMA**
Cookbook
abbr.: 3 TBS TSP 4 TBSP TSPS
author Boyle: 4 TISH
author Rombauer: 4 IRMA
direction: 4 SIFT STIR 5 PUREE
phrase: 3 ALA 5 ADDIN
Cooke
Singer: 3 SAM
TV host: 8 ALISTAIR
Cooked: 4 DONE MADE 5 READY
6 STEWED
cereal: 6 FARINA
It's ~ up: 3 LIE
Less: 5 RARER RAWER
Not: 3 RAW
~ Indian-style: 8 TANDOORI
Cooker: 4 OVEN 5 STOVE
7 ROASTER
Asian: 3 WOK
Cantina: 4 OLLA
Old-fashioned: 8 OILSTOVE
Stew: 3 POT
Cookie
Black-and-white: 4 **OREO**
Brittle: 4 SNAP 10 GINGERSNAP
Computer: 4 DATA
cooker: 4 OVEN
Creme-filled: 4 **OREO**
"Famous" ~ maker: 4 **AMOS**
filling: 5 CREME
flavorer: 5 ANISE
Ginger: 4 SNAP
holder: 3 **JAR** TIN
Keebler ~ maker: 3 ELF
Kind of: 5 SMART 7 OATMEAL
litter: 6 CRUMBS
maker Wally: 4 AMOS
Nabisco: 4 **OREO**
Pepperidge Farm: 6 MILANO
sandwich: 4 OREO
since 1912: 4 OREO
Cookies
Cook: 4 BAKE
quantity: 5 BATCH
"Cookie's Fortune"
actress Patricia: 4 NEAL
director: 6 ALTMAN

Cooking
   direction: 4 HEAT
   Enjoyed home: 5 ATEIN
   fat: 4 **LARD** SUET
   First name in: 6 EMERIL
   Leaves for: 4 SAGE
   meas.: 3 TSP
   output: 5 AROMA
   pot: 4 OLLA
   Prepares for: 7 DRESSES
   spray brand: 3 **PAM**
   style: 4 THAI 6 CREOLE
   Sunken ~ site: 7 FIREPIT
   up: 6 MAKING
Cook Inlet
   city: 9 ANCHORAGE
Cook-off
   dish: 5 CHILI
Cookout: 3 BBQ
   fare: 4 RIBS 5 STEAK
   Hawaiian: 4 LUAU
   intruder: 3 ANT
   leftover: 3 ASH 5 EMBER
   locale: 5 PATIO
   throwaway: 3 COB
Cookware
   Big name in nonstick: 4 TFAL
   Glass: 5 PYREX
   item: 3 POT WOK
Cool: 3 FAN HEP HIP RAD
         4 CALM NEAT 5 ALOOF
         NEATO NIFTY POISE
         6 APLOMB SEDATE
         SERENE 10 NONCHALANT
   drink: 3 ADE
   dude: 3 CAT 6 HEPCAT
   Heat and then: 6 ANNEAL
   in manner: 5 ALOOF
   it: 4 STOP 5 CEASE 6 DESIST
       8 CHILLOUT
   Lose one's: 4 SNAP 5 PANIC
   Not: 5 UNHIP
   rap artist: 4 ICET
   red giants: 6 SSTARS
   treat: 6 SUNDAE 7 SHERBET
        SNOCONE
   Way: 3 RAD 5 GELID
   ~, updated: 3 DEF 4 PHAT
"Cool!": 3 RAD 4 NEAT 5 **NEATO**

"___ cool!": 3 WAY
Cool, Joe
   Hardly: 4 NERD
Coolant
   Nature's: 5 SWEAT
Cool ___ Bell (of baseball): 4 PAPA
Cool cat: 6 DADDYO
   Like a: 3 HEP
   quality: 7 HIPNESS
Cool ___ cucumber: 3 ASA
"Cool, dude!": 3 RAD
Cooled: 4 ICED
Cooler: 3 FAN PEN 4 JAIL STIR
        6 ICEBOX
   Citrus: 3 **ADE**
   Drink: 3 ICE
   in a cooler: 3 ADE
   In the: 5 ONICE
   Sailor's: 4 BRIG
   Stay in the: 6 DOTIME
   Summer: 3 **ADE** FAN 4 POOL
        6 ICETEA
   than cool: 3 RAD
   Water: 3 ICE
Coolers
   Apt.: 3 ACS
Coolidge: 3 DAM
   President: 3 CAL
   Singer: 4 **RITA**
   veep: 5 **DAWES**
Coolidge Dam
   river: 4 GILA
Cooling-off
   period: 6 ICEAGE
   place: 4 SILL
Coolio
   genre: 3 RAP
"Cool it!": 4 STOP 5 CHILL
Coolpix
   maker: 5 NIKON
Coon
   kin: 5 COATI
Coop: 3 PEN 5 HUTCH
   clutch: 4 EGGS
   flier: 7 ESCAPEE
   group: 4 HENS
   Pigeon: 4 COTE
Co-op
   Soviet: 5 ARTEL

unit (abbr.): **3** APT
Cooped
  (up): **4** PENT
Cooper
  1936 ~ role: **5** DEEDS
      7 MRDEEDS
  Actress: **6** GLADYS
  classic: **9** BEAUGESTE
  hero: **5** UNCAS
  piece: **5** STAVE
  Time in a ~ film: **4** NOON
  tool: **4** ADZE
Cooperate
  Won't: **7** RESISTS
Cooperative
  action: **7** SYNERGY
      8 TEAMWORK
  Iowa: **5** AMANA
  Russian: **5** **ARTEL**
Cooperstown
  Info: Baseball cue
  Banks in: **5** ERNIE
  bldg.: **3** HOF
  first elected member: **6** TYCOBB
  Mel in: **3** OTT
  Monte of: **5** IRVIN
  nickname: **4** TRIS YOGI
  Slaughter in: **4** ENOS
  Speaker in: **4** TRIS
  Warren of: **5** SPAHN
Coordinate: 4 MESH
  system base: **5** XAXIS
Coordinated: 5 AGILE
Coordination: 4 SYNC
  Loss of. **6** ATAXIA
Coordinators
  Flight ~ (abbr.): **3** ATC
Coors
  brand: **4** ZIMA
  Brewer: **6** ADOLPH
  rival: **5** PABST **6** STROHS
Coos Bay
  state: **6** OREGON
Coot: 6 GEEZER
Cooties: 4 LICE
Cop
  Antidrug: **4** NARC
  calls (abbr.): **4** APBS
  catch: **4** PERP

French: **8** GENDARME
  milieu: **4** BEAT
  Offender, to a: **4** PERP
  out: **6** RENEGE
  Traffic ~, at times: **5** CITER
  Unarmed, to a: **5** CLEAN
  ~ ID: **5** BADGE
Cop ___ : 5 APLEA
Cop a ___ : 4 PLEA
Copacabana
  site: **3** **RIO**
"Copacabana"
  showgirl: **4** LOLA
Copacetic: 3 AOK **4** JAKE OKAY
Copal: 5 RESIN
Copays
  Gp. requiring: **3** HMO
Cope: 4 DEAL **6** HACKIT
      MAKEDO MANAGE
  with: **5** STAND **6** HANDLE
"Cope Book"
  aunt: **4** ERMA
Coped: 5 DEALT **6** MADEDO
Copenhagen
  carrier: **3** **SAS**
  currency: **5** KRONE
  park: **6** TIVOLI
  resident: **4** DANE
Copernicus: 6 CRATER
  sci.: **4** ASTR
Copied: 4 APED **7** XEROXED
  Something ~ (abbr.): **4** ORIG
Copier: 3 APE **4** APER **5** MIMIC
      6 SCRIBE
  additive: **5** TONER
  company: **4** MITA **5** CANON
      RICOH
  function: **4** SORT
  Large: **3** APE
  Old-style: **5** MIMEO
  setting: **5** LEGAL
Copilot
  Fly without a: **4** SOLO
Copious: 5 AMPLE
"Cop Killer"
  rapper: **4** ICET
Copland
  ballet: **5** RODEO
  composer: **5** **AARON**

Copley
 Actress: 4 TERI
Copped
 Something: 4 PLEA
"Coppélia"
 costume: 4 TUTU
Copper: 4 **CENT** 5 PENNY
 Big ~ exporter: 4 PERU
 coverings: 7 PATINAE
 head: 3 ABE
Copperfield
 field: 5 MAGIC
 Mrs.: 4 **DORA**
 villain: 4 HEEP
Copperhead: 5 SNAKE
Coppers
 English: 5 PENCE
Coppertone
 no.: 3 SPF
Coppola
 Director: 5 SOFIA
Coppola, Francis
 Sister of: 5 TALIA
Cops: 6 POLICE
 Army: 3 MPS
 Like some undercover: 5 WIRED
 Pressure from the: 4 HEAT
 Watch for the: 4 ABET
Copter
 Early: 4 GIRO
 part: 5 ROTOR
Coptic
 title: 4 ABBA
Copy: 3 **APE** 4 DUPE TEXT
     5 CLONE MIMEO MIMIC
     REPRO XEROX 6 PARROT
     7 EMULATE IMITATE
     REPLICA
 Better: 4 EDIT
 cats: 3 MEW 4 MEOW PURR
 Check: 4 EDIT
 Exact: 4 TWIN 5 CLONE
 Hard: 8 PRINTOUT
 machine need: 5 TONER
 Magazine: 5 ISSUE
 Not a ~ (abbr.): 4 ORIG
 Old: 5 MIMEO
 Remove from: 4 DELE
 to a floppy: 4 SAVE

Copycat: 3 APE 4 **APER** 5 MIMIC
     7 METOOER
 cry: 5 METOO
Copying: 3 ALA
 Worth: 8 IMITABLE
Copyist: 4 APER 6 SCRIBE
     9 SCRIVENER
Copyright
 letter: 3 CEE
 page abbr.: 4 ISBN
 "Copy that": 5 ROGER
Coq au ___: 3 VIN
Coquette: 4 MINX VAMP 5 FLIRT
     TEASE
 Like a: 3 COY
Coquettish: 3 COY
Coral: 3 SEA 4 PINK
 formation: 4 **REEF** 5 ATOLL
 island: 3 CAY
 producer: 5 POLYP
Coral ___: 3 SEA
Corbeled-out
 window: 5 ORIEL
Corby
 Actress: 5 ELLEN
Corcoran
 Actress: 6 NOREEN
Cord: 5 TWINE
 About ?: 5 STERE
 components: 4 LOGS
 Jumper's: 6 BUNGEE
 Kind of: 3 RIP 6 SPINAL
 Sailor: 7 LANYARD
 Strong: 4 ROPE
 Tie with a: 4 BOLO
 ___ corda: 3 UNA
Cordage
 fiber: 5 ISTLE SISAL
Corday
 victim: 5 **MARAT**
Cordelia
 Father of: 4 **LEAR**
 Sister of: 5 **REGAN**
Cordial: 4 WARM 8 ANISETTE
 flavoring: 5 ANISE
 French ~ flavoring: 4 ANIS
 Less: 5 ICIER
Cordiant
 ad agency: 5 BATES

Cordillera Real
home: **5** ANDES
Córdoba
Info: Spanish cue
cheer: **3** OLE
kinswoman: **3** TIA
Cordon ___: 4 BLEU
Cords: 5 PANTS
Cut: **3** HEW
Corduroy
feature: **3** RIB **4** WALE **5** RIDGE
Like: **5** WALED **6** RIBBED
RIDGED
Cordwood
measure: **5** **STERE**
Core: 3 HUB NUB NUT **4** GIST
PITH **5** HEART MIDST
7 ESSENCE
Corn: **3** COB
group: **5** CADRE
PC: **3** CPU
Peach: **3** PIT
CORE
Roy of: **5** INNIS
Cores: 6 NUCLEI
Corey
Actor: **4** HAIM
Professor: **5** IRWIN
Corfu
Letter from: **3** ETA
Corgi
or collie: **5** BREED
Coriander
cousin: **5** ANISE
or basil: **4** HERB
Corinth
Play set in: **5** MEDEA
Corinthian: 7 HELLENE
alternative: **5** DORIC
"Coriolanus"
setting: **4** ROME
Cork: 7 STOPPER
dance: **3** JIG
locale: **4** EIRE **7** IRELAND
shooter: **6** POPGUN
source: **3** OAK **4** BARK
Corker: 3 PIP **4** **LULU**
Corkers: 5 IRISH
Corkscrew: 4 COIL **6** SPIRAL

pasta: **6** ROTINI
Corkwood: 5 BALSA
Corleone: 5 FREDO SONNY
creator: **4** PUZO
Head: **4** VITO
title: **3** DON
Corleone, Sonny
portrayer: **4** CAAN
Corn: 4 CROP **5** MAIZE
Bit of: **6** KERNEL
bread: **4** PONE
10 JOHNNYCAKE
concoction: **4** PONE
core: **3** COB
country: **4** IOWA
covering: **4** HUSK
flower: **6** TASSEL
Golden-___: **5** EARED
grower: **3** TOE
holder: **3** CAN COB **4** CRIB
How ~ is planted: **6** INROWS
Indian: **5** **MAIZE**
Order of: **3** EAR
prefix: **3** TRI UNI
product: **4** OLEO
serving: **3** **EAR**
site: **3** TOE
spikes: **4** EARS
Store, as: **6** ENSILE
syrup brand: **4** **KARO**
unit: **3** COB **EAR**
Corn ___: 4 BELT CHEX PONE
5 SYRUP
Cornball: 5 HOKEY TRITE
Corn Belt
state: **4** IOWA
Cornbread
cake: **4** PONE
Cornea
companion: **6** SCLERA
repository: **7** EYEBANK
Corned beef
concoction: **4** **HASH** **6** REUBEN
sandwich bread: **3** RYE
Corneille
play: **5** ELCID
Cornell
city: **6** ITHACA
rival: **4** PENN YALE

Cornell University
  founder: 4 **EZRA**
Corner: 4 NOOK TREE 5 ANGLE
      HEMIN NICHE
  Cozy: 4 NOOK
  Diamond: 3 BAG 4 BASE
      6 SECOND
  From ~ to ~ (abbr.): 4 DIAG
  In a: 5 TREED
  Just around the: 4 SOON
  key: 3 ESC
  map: 5 INSET
  Monopoly: 4 JAIL
  One in your: 4 ALLY
  piece: 3 ELL 4 **ROOK**
  Secluded: 4 NOOK
Cornerback
  ~ Sanders: 5 DEION
Cornered: 5 **ATBAY** TREED
      7 UPATREE
Cornerstone
  abbr.: 3 EST 4 **ESTD** 5 ESTAB
  features: 5 DATES
  word: 4 ANNO
Cornetist
  ~ Adderley: 3 NAT
  ~ Beiderbecke: 3 BIX
Cornfield
  bird: 4 CROW
  cry: 3 **CAW**
  measure: 4 ACRE
"Cornflake Girl"
  singer Tori: 4 AMOS
"... corn ___ high ...": 4 ISAS
Cornhusker
  city: 5 OMAHA
  rival: 6 SOONER
  st.: 3 NEB 4 NEBR
  ___ Corning: 5 OWENS
Cornishman: 4 CELT
Cornmeal
  bread: 4 PONE
  mush: 7 POLENTA
  treat: 7 HOECAKE
Corn-oil
  spread: 4 OLEO
Cornrow: 5 PLAIT
Cornrows
  Like: 7 PLAITED

Cornstalks
  Like: 5 EARED
Cornstarch
  brand: 4 ARGO
Cornwall: 5 SHIRE
Cornwallis
  surrender site: 8 YORKTOWN
Corny
  bit: 6 KERNEL
  item: 3 EAR 4 PONE
"___ corny as Kansas ...": 4 IMAS
Corolla
  part: 5 PETAL
Corona: 5 CIGAR 7 AUREOLE
Coronado
  quest: 3 ORO
Coronet: 5 TIARA
Corot
  Painter: 4 JEAN
Corp.
  bigwig: 3 **CEO** 4 EXEC PRES
  exec degree: 3 MBA
  money handler: 3 CFO
  takeover: 3 LBO
Corporal
  punishment unit: 4 LASH
Corporally
  punish: 5 SPANK
Corporate
  alias (abbr.): 3 DBA
  baker: 7 SARALEE
  budget part: 5 RANDD
  cow: 5 ELSIE
  department: 5 LEGAL SALES
  exec.: 3 CEO CFO
  flunky: 5 DRONE
  image: 4 LOGO
  mouthpiece: 9 SPOKESMAN
  raider Carl: 5 ICAHN
  rule: 5 BYLAW
  symbol: 4 LOGO
  ~ VIP: 3 **CEO** 4 EXEC
Corporation
  called "Big Blue": 3 IBM
  Giant chemicals: 4 OLIN
  that gave a bad account of itself:
      5 ENRON
Corporeal
  quintet: 6 SENSES

Corps
member: 6 MARINE
Corpsman: 5 MEDIC
Corpulent: 3 FAT 5 OBESE STOUT
Corpus
follower: 7 DELICTI
Habeas: 4 WRIT
___ corpus: 6 HABEAS
Corral: 3 PEN 5 PENIN 6 ROPEIN
       7 ENCLOSE
Correct: 4 MEND TRUE
       5 AMEND EMEND RIGHT
       6 PROPER REMEDY
       7 REDRESS
Ain't: 4 ISNT 5 ARENT
copy: 4 EDIT 5 EMEND
Correction: 7 ERASURE
list: 6 ERRATA
Make a ~ to: 5 EMEND
Need: 3 ERR
Correctly: 6 ARIGHT
Correlative
Common: 3 NOR
Correo ___ (airmail): 5 AEREO
Correspond: 5 AGREE TALLY
Corresponded: 5 WROTE
Correspondence: 4 MAIL
       6 PARITY 7 LETTERS
High-tech: 5 EMAIL
Kind of: 8 ONETOONE
Office: 4 MEMO
Correspondent
Foreign: 6 PENPAL
WWII ~ Pyle: 5 ERNIE
Corresponding: 4 SAME
Corrida
beast: 4 TORO 6 ELTORO
cheer: 3 **OLE**
combatant: 6 TORERO
Enthusiastic ~ cry: 6 OLEOLE
Hurt in the: 5 GORED
Corridor: 4 HALL 5 AISLE
bullet train: 5 ACELA
Corrode: 3 EAT 4 RUST
       7 EATINTO
Corroded: 3 ATE 5 ATEAT EATEN
       7 ATEINTO
Corrosive
chemical: 4 ACID

Corrupt: 3 BAD ROT 4 HOSE
       5 TAINT VENAL 6 DEBASE
       POISON 7 DEPRAVE
       SUBVERT
Corruptible: 5 VENAL
Corsage
Attach, as a: 5 PINON
flower: 6 ORCHID
Corsair: 5 EDSEL
Corset
part: 4 STAY
tightener: 5 LACER
Corsica: 3 CAR
Isle near: 4 ELBA
Corsican
hero: 5 PAOLI
Cortés
quest: 3 ORO
victim: 5 AZTEC
Cortex
prefix: 3 NEO
product: 4 IDEA
Cortisone: 7 STEROID
Corundum: 4 RUBY
Corvair
critic: 5 NADER
Corvine
cry: 3 CAW
Cosa ___: 6 NOSTRA
___ cosa: 4 OTRA
Cosby
1960s ~ show: 4 ISPY
costar: 4 CULP 6 RASHAD
heavy creation: 6 ALBERT
specialty: 8 ANECDOTE
"Cosby Show, The"
actress Lisa: 5 BONET
actress Phylicia: 6 RASHAD
kid: 4 THEO
Cosecant
reciprocal: 4 SINE
Cosell
Longtime ~ foil: 3 ALI
Cosgrave
Former Irish P.M.: 4 LIAM
Cosine: 5 RATIO
Cosmetic
additive: 4 ALOE
Cheek: 5 ROUGE

goo: 5 GELEE
Lash: 7 MASCARA
Liquid: 6 LOTION
Cosmetician
~ Lauder: 5 ESTEE
Cosmetics
Adrien of: 5 ARPEL
Arpel of: 6 ADRIEN
company: 4 AVON
Curtis of: 6 HELENE
dye: 5 EOSIN
First name in: 5 **ESTEE** MERLE
Mary ___ of: 3 KAY
name: 4 COTY 5 ESTEE
overseeing agcy.: 3 FDA
"Cosmicomics"
author Calvino: 5 ITALO
Cosmo: 3 MAG
feature: 7 SEXQUIZ
rival: 4 ELLE
Cosmonaut: 7 RUSSIAN
home: 3 MIR
insignia, once: 4 CCCP
~ Atkov: 4 OLEG
~ Gagarin: 4 **YURI**
Cosmopolitan
rival: 4 ELLE
Cosmos
star: 4 PELE
"Cosmos"
creator: 5 SAGAN
Cost: 5 PRICE RANTO RUNTO
6 OUTLAY 7 EXPENSE
Absorb, as: 3 EAT
At no: 4 FREE
Contracted: 7 SETRATE
Determine: 5 PRICE
For an additional: 5 EXTRA
Housing: 4 RENT
Maintenance: 6 UPKEEP
of belonging: 4 DUES
of leaving: 4 BAIL
of living: 4 RENT
Pump: 6 GASTAX
to cross: 4 TOLL
~, in slang: 6 DAMAGE
___ cost: 4 ATNO
Costa ___ : 4 MESA **RICA**
Costa del ___ : 3 **SOL**

Costa del Sol
feature: 5 PLAYA
Costanza
Mother of George: 7 ESTELLE
Costa ___ Sol: 3 DEL
Costello
Abbott and: 3 DUO
Abbott, to: 6 COHORT
Comedian: 3 **LOU**
Partner of: 6 ABBOTT
Costly: 4 DEAR
Costner
1987 ~ role: 4 **NESS**
1988 ~ film: 10 BULLDURHAM
1994 ~ role: 4 EARP
1996 ~ film: 6 TINCUP
Actor: 5 KEVIN
Cost-of-living
stat: 3 CPI
Costs
(abbr.): 3 EXP
Cover: 9 BREAKEVEN
~, with "to": 5 COMES
"___ cost to you!": 4 ATNO
Costume: 6 GETUP GUISE
6 ATTIRE
Ballet: 4 TUTU
Calcutta: 4 SARI
Halloween: 5 GHOST SHEET
part: 4 CAPE MASK
"___ cost you!": 4 ITLL
Cote
call: 3 BAA COO
girls: 4 EWES
It's off la: 3 MER
Côte ___ : 3 DOR
Côte d'___ : 4 **AZUR**
Cotillion: 4 BALL
honoree: 3 DEB
___ cotta: 5 TERRA
Cottage
and condo: 6 REALTY
site: 4 LAKE
Ski: 5 LODGE 6 CHALET
Summer: 5 DACHA LODGE
Summer ~, often: 6 RENTAL
Cotton: 7 TEXTILE
bundle: 4 BALE
bundler: 5 BALER

candy: **5** SUGAR
fabric: **4** PIMA **5** CHINO RAMIE
    6 DAMASK SATEEN
    7 GINGHAM
Fine: **4** PIMA **5** LISLE
fuzz: **4** LINT
gin inventor Whitney: **3** ELI
Lightweight: **7** ETAMINE
Like ~ candy: **4** SPUN
pest: **6** WEEVIL
pod: **4** BOLL
Process: **3** GIN
Sheer: **5** TOILE
Strong: **4** PIMA
stuffing: **4** BATT
thread: **5** LISLE
unit: **4** BALE
Cotton Bowl
city: **6** DALLAS
Three-time ~ champs: **3** SMU
"Cotton Candy"
trumpeter: **4** HIRT **6** ALHIRT
Cotton Club
site: **6** HARLEM
"Cotton Club, The"
setting: **6** HARLEM
star: **4** GERE
Cotton State (abbr.): **3** ALA
Cottontail: 6 RABBIT
tail: **4** SCUT
Cotton-tipped
cleaner: **4** SWAB
Cottonwood: 5 ALAMO **6** POPLAR
    10 POPLARTREE
Coty
of France: **4** RENE
Couch: 4 SOFA **6** PHRASE
    SETTEE
Backless: **5** DIVAN
Convertible: **6** DAYBED
Couch potato: 5 IDLER
Be a: **4** LAZE LOLL
device: **6** REMOTE
    13 REMOTECONTROL
Like a: **4** IDLE **5** INERT
No: **4** DOER
perch: **4** SOFA
Cougar: 3 CAR CAT **4** AUTO
    PUMA

maker: **4** MERC
quarters: **4** LAIR
Cough
drop flavor: **5** ANISE
    7 MENTHOL
Polite: **4** AHEM
quieter: **7** CODEINE
syrup amt.: **3** TSP
up: **4** ANTE
Could
It ~ be a lot: **4** ACRE
tell: **6** SENSED
"... could ___ fat": 5 EATNO
Couldn't
abide: **5** HATED
help but: **5** HADTO
remember: **6** FORGOT
stand: **5** HATED **8** DETESTED
"Couldn't help it!": 5 HADTO
Coulomb
per sec: **3** AMP **6** AMPERE
Coulter
Author: **3** ANN
Council
1409 ~ site: **4** PISA
1545 ~ site: **5** TRENT
Church: **5** **SYNOD**
City ~ rep.: **3** ALD
member: **5** ELDER
___ Council: **6** NICENE
Council Bluffs
neighbor: **5** OMAHA
Counsel: 4 WARN **6** ADVISE
Hire, as ~: **6** RETAIN
Counseling: 4 HELP
Counselor
at Troy: **6** NESTOR
org.: **3** ABA
Personal: **6** MENTOR
Count: 3 ADD **4** RELY **6** MATTER
Attendance: **5** NOSES
calories: **4** DIET
Candle: **3** AGE
Checkout: **5** ITEMS
Commandments: **3** TEN
Down for the: **3** KOD
Drop for the: **4** KAYO
ending: **3** ESS
equivalent: **4** EARL

Hospital: 4 BEDS
It may: 8 NEATNESS
of jazz: 5 BASIE
(on): 4 **RELY**
player: 6 LUGOSI
Ring: 3 **TEN**
Start for a Spanish: 3 UNO
Start of a: 4 EENY 5 BALLS
suffix: 3 ESS
Supreme Court: 4 NINE
Swimmer's: 4 LAPS
Workout: 3 REP
You can ~ on it: 6 ABACUS
"Count ___": 4 MEIN
Countdown
deejay Casey: 5 KASEM
start: 3 TEN
Counted
Fully: 5 INALL
They're: 5 NOSES
Countenance: 4 MIEN 6 VISAGE
Counter: 5 REBUT 6 OPPOSE
7 RESPOND
Cab: 5 METER
call: 4 NEXT
Kind of: 5 LUNCH 6 GEIGER
7 CALORIE
Kitchen: 5 TIMER
KO: 3 REF
man: 6 GEIGER
Mileage: 8 ODOMETER
offer: 3 BLT 4 SODA
opener: 4 EENY
Counteract: 6 NEGATE OFFSET
Counterargue: 5 REBUT
Counterbalance: 6 OFFSET
SETOFF
Counterculture
guru: 5 LEARY
Countercurrent: 4 **EDDY**
Counterfeit: 3 BAD 4 FAKE SHAM
5 BOGUS
catcher: 4 TMAN
coin: 4 SLUG
Countermand: 3 NIX 6 CANCEL
NEGATE
Countermeasures
Take: 5 REACT
Counterpart: 4 MATE 8 OPPOSITE

Counters: 5 ABACI
11 to 20, for some ~: 4 TOES
What ~ count: 5 NOSES
Counterstroke: 6 RIPOST
Countertenor: 4 ALTO
Countess
spouse: 4 **EARL**
Counting
everything: 5 **INALL** 6 INTOTO
method: 4 TENS
(on): 7 RELIANT
rhyme start: 4 EENY
Stop ~ sheep: 5 SLEEP
Counting-out
word: 4 **EENY**
Countless: 4 MANY 6 UNTOLD
years: 3 EON 4 AGES
"Count me in!": 6 IMGAME
7 IMFORIT
"Count of ___ Cristo, The":
5 MONTE
"Count of Monte ___, The":
6 CRISTO
"Count of Monte Cristo, The"
setting: 7 DUNGEON
Countrified: 5 RURAL
Country: 4 LAND 5 RURAL
6 NATION
1988 ~ album: 4 REBA
African: 4 MALI 5 SUDAN
album: 5 ATLAS
Andean: 4 PERU
Arabian: 4 OMAN
Biblical: 4 EDOM
Black of: 5 CLINT
Boot-shaped: 5 ITALY
bumpkin: 4 CLOD JAKE RUBE
5 YAHOO YOKEL
Bush: 5 USOFA
byway: 4 LANE
cousin: 4 RUBE
crossing: 5 STILE
Divided: 5 KOREA
estate: 5 MANOR VILLA
First name in: 4 **REBA**
founded by freed slaves:
7 LIBERIA
Hill of: 5 FAITH
in a Beatles song: 4 USSR

It's a free: 3 USA
Leave the: 6 SECEDE
lodging: 3 INN
mail rte.: 3 RFD
Medit.: 3 ISR
Mideast: 5 YEMEN
name: 4 REBA
Of ~ life: 5 RURAL
on the Caspian: 4 IRAN
Out of the: 6 ABROAD
quartet: 7 ALABAMA
rtes.: 3 RDS
SA: 3 ARG
Scand.: 4 NORW
Split: 5 KOREA
U.K.: 3 ENG
with a blue, black, and white flag:
    7 ESTONIA
"___ Country": 4 AFAR
Country club
(abbr.): 5 THEUN
figure: 3 PRO
rental: 4 CART
Country dance: 4 REEL
spot: 4 BARN
"Country Doctor, A"
author Sarah ___ Jewett:
    4 ORNE
"Country Gentleman"
Atkins: 4 CHET
"Country Girl, The"
playwright: 5 ODETS
Tony winner: 8 UTAHAGEN
Countryman
Neither a friend nor a: 5 ROMAN
Country music: 6 ANTHEM
network, once: 3 TNN
Country road: 4 LANE
feature: 3 ESS RUT
Unlike a: 5 PAVED
Country singer
~ Black: 5 CLINT
~ Bonnie: 5 RAITT
~ Brenda: 3 LEE
~ Brooks: 5 GARTH
~ Carter: 5 DEANA
~ Clark: 3 ROY 5 TERRI
~ Collin: 4 RAYE
~ Crystal: 5 GAYLE

~ David Allan ___: 3 COE
~ Davis: 3 MAC 7 SKEETER
~ Evans: 4 SARA
~ George: 6 STRAIT
~ Gibbs: 5 TERRI
~ Haggard: 5 MERLE
~ Jackson: 4 ALAN
~ Kathy: 6 MATTEA
~ Ketchum: 3 HAL
~ K.T.: 5 OSLIN
~ LeAnn: 5 RIMES
~ Lynn: 7 LORETTA
~ McCann: 4 LILA
~ McCoy: 4 NEAL
~ McDaniel: 3 MEL
~ McEntire: 4 **REBA**
~ McGraw: 3 TIM
~ Morgan: 6 LORRIE
~ Murray: 4 ANNE
~ Randy: 6 TRAVIS
~ Reeves: 3 DEL
~ Rimes: 5 LEANN
~ Tillis: 3 MEL PAM
~ Travis: 5 TRITT
~ Tubb: 6 ERNEST
~ Tucker: 5 TANYA
~ Yearwood: 6 TRISHA
County
center: 4 SEAT
English: 4 AVON KENT 5 ESSEX
    SHIRE 6 DORSET
festival: 4 FAIR
Scottish: 5 CLARE KERRY SLIGO
    6 ARGYLL
County Clare
capital: 5 ENNIS
County Kerry
seat: 6 **TRALEE**
Coup
Bridge: 4 **SLAM**
Court: 3 ACE
follower: 5 DETAT
Golf: 3 ACE 5 EAGLE
group: 5 CABAL JUNTA
Narc's: 4 BUST
Coup ___ : 5 DETAT
Coup d'___ : 4 ETAT
Coupe: 3 CAR 4 AUTO
alternative: 5 SEDAN

Couple: 3 DUO TWO WED
    4 DUAD DYAD ITEM PAIR
    5 UNITE 7 TWOSOME
  Divorced: 4 EXES
  in the news: 4 ITEM
  Odd: 4 DEES
  of cups: 3 BRA
  pronoun: 3 OUR 4 OURS
Coupler: 4 YOKE
Couples
  carrier: 3 ARK
  Golfer: 4 FRED
  may swing here: 3 TEE
Coupling
  device: 4 YOKE
Coupon
  clipper: 8 REDEEMER
  for the needy: 9 FOODSTAMP
  Removes, as a: 5 CLIPS
    8 TEARSOUT
Courage: 4 GUTS 5 HEART
    NERVE PLUCK SPINE
  Deprive of: 5 UNMAN
  Have the: 4 DARE
Courageous: 5 BRAVE 6 GRITTY
  Be: 4 DARE
Couric
  Former ~ cohost: 5 LAUER
  Former ~ show: 5 TODAY
  Newscaster: 5 **KATIE**
Courier: 4 FONT
Course: 4 DISH FLOW PATH
    ROAD 5 ROUTE TREND
    6 STREAM
  Change: 3 ZIG 4 TURN VEER
  Circular: 4 GYRE
  climax: 4 TEST
  Coll.: 3 SOC 4 ECON
  Cushy: 5 EASYA
  deviation: 3 YAW
  Dinner: 4 SOUP 5 SALAD
    6 ENTREE 7 DESSERT
  dir.: 3 ENE ESE NNE SSE
  Downhill: 6 SKIRUN
  Early: 5 SALAD
  First: 4 SOUP 5 PLANA
  for U.S. aliens: 3 ESL
  Freshman language: 6 LATINI
  Go off: 3 ERR YAW 4 VEER

  guide: 3 PAR
  Gut: 5 EASYA
  hazard: 4 TRAP
  Horse: 4 OATS OVAL
  H.S.: 3 ENG 4 TRIG
  list abbr.: 3 TBA
  listing: 4 MENU
  Main: 6 **ENTREE**
  Math: 4 CALC TRIG
  Med.: 4 **ANAT**
  of events: 4 TIDE
  Off: 4 AWRY 6 ASTRAY ERRANT
  requirement: 3 TEE
  Second: 5 PLANB
  section: 4 UNIT
  start: 3 TEE
  Took a: 3 ATE
  with greens: 5 SALAD
  Zigzag: 6 SLALOM
Courses
  Like some golf: 8 NINEHOLE
  Slalom: 5 ESSES
  Takes: 4 SUPS
Court: 3 **WOO**
  1973 ~ name: 3 ROE
  1995 ~ VIP: 3 ITO
  action: 4 PLEA
  activity: 5 TRIAL
  arbiter: 3 REF
  Argued in: 4 PLED
  battle: 6 TENNIS
  Bring to: 3 SUE
  calendar: 6 DOCKET
  call: 3 **LET** 4 ADIN 5 ORDER
  Call before a: 7 ARRAIGN
  Call to: 4 CITE
  clown: 6 JESTER
  conference: 7 SIDEBAR
  coup: 3 ACE
  covering: 4 ROBE
  cry: 4 OYEZ 6 HEARYE
  decision: 3 LET
  defense: 4 ZONE
  divider: 3 **NET**
  Dressed for: 5 ROBED
  event: 5 TRIAL
  fig.: 3 ATT 4 ATTY
  figs.: 3 DAS
  figure: 4 EARL SUER 5 JUROR

NOBLE STENO
game: 8 ONEONONE
Gentleman of the: 4 ASHE
hearing: 4 OYER
Hoop at a: 3 RIM
huddle: 7 SIDEBAR
legend: 3 DRJ 4 ASHE
Like ~ testimony: 5 SWORN
matter: 3 RES
Open: 6 ATRIUM
order: 4 RISE WRIT 7 ALLRISE
org.: 3 ABA 4 USTA
Papal: 5 CURIA
plea, briefly: 4 NOLO
procedure: 4 OATH
records: 4 ACTA
reporter: 5 STENO
response: 4 PLEA
ruling: 3 LET
score: 4 ADIN
Send back to a lower: 6 REMAND
site, with "The": 5 HAGUE
statistic: 4 PLEA
story: 5 ALIBI
summons: 8 SUBPOENA
Take to: 3 **SUE**
They come to: 5 BEAUS
They're taken in: 5 OATHS
Zero, on a: 4 LOVE
~ VIPs: 3 DAS

Courteney
Actress: 3 COX
Courteous: 4 NICE 5 CIVIL
          6 POLITE 7 GENTEEL
Courtesan
Zola: 4 NANA
Courtesy
Reply ~, briefly: 4 SASE
"Court Jester, The"
star: 9 DANNYKAYE
Courtroom
1970s ~ drama: 5 THEDA
attire: 4 ROBE
entry: 4 PLEA
fig.: 3 ATT
First name in ~ fiction: 4 ERLE
pledge: 4 OATH
statement: 4 PLEA
~ VIPs: 3 DAS

Courts: 5 **ATRIA**
Court TV
fare: 5 TRIAL
topic: 3 LAW
Courtyard: 6 **ATRIUM**
Courtyards: 5 **ATRIA**
Cous.: 3 REL
Cousins: 3 **KIN**
mothers: 5 AUNTS
Cousteau
milieu: 3 MER 5 OCEAN
Cousy, Bob
team: 7 CELTICS
Couth
Lacking: 4 RUDE 5 CRASS
____ couture: 5 HAUTE
Couturier
initials: 3 YSL
~ Cassini: 4 OLEG
~ Christian: 4 DIOR
Cove: 3 BAY RIA 5 **INLET**
____ Cove: 5 CABOT
Covenant: 4 PACT
holder: 3 ARK
Covent Garden
architect Jones: 5 INIGO
landmark: 10 OPERAHOUSE
offering: 5 OPERA
solo: 4 ARIA
Coventry
Info: British cue
cleaner: 4 CHAR
coins: 5 PENCE
Cover: 3 **LID** 4 COAT VEIL
          5 ALIAS ALIBI 6 CLOTHE
          ENCASE INSURE
          7 OVERLAY OVERLIE
After-bath: 4 ROBE
anew: 5 RESOD
Arctic: 8 ICESHEET
Camper: 4 TENT
Canvas: 4 TARP
Catch-basin: 5 GRATE
Crown: 6 ENAMEL
Diamond: 4 TARP
Engine: 4 HOOD
Front end: 3 BRA
Ground: 3 SOD 7 MACADAM
Head: 3 HAT

Infield: 4 **TARP**
Lamp: 5 SHADE
Lens: 6 EYELID
letter letters: 3 SAE
Orange: 4 PEEL RIND
over: 6 REWRAP 7 REPAPER
Pillow: 4 CASE SHAM
Pot: 3 LID
Road: 3 TAR
Seed: 4 **ARIL**
Slip: 5 DRESS
Stadium: 4 DOME
story: 5 **ALIBI**
Take: 4 HIDE
Teapot: 4 COZY
Took: 3 HID
Under: 4 ABED 5 INBED
up: 4 HIDE VEIL 6 ENROBE
Waterproof: 4 TARP
Wheel: 6 HUBCAP
Window: 5 BLIND DRAPE
with crumbs: 5 BREAD
with dirt: 4 BURY
with goo: 5 SLIME
with graffiti: 6 DEFACE
with turf: 3 SOD
Wound: 4 SCAB
Coverage
letters: 3 HMO
Press: 3 INK
Rug: 4 AREA
Covered: 4 CLAD
(in): 5 AWASH
It's got you: 4 SKIN
passageway: 6 ARCADE
with dirt: 5 GRIMY
with vines: 5 IVIED
Cover girl
~ Banks: 4 TYRA
~ Carol: 3 ALT
Covering: 4 ATOP
Head: 3 CAP 4 HAIR
Outer: 4 PEEL RIND SKIN
Polar: 6 ICECAP
Pond: 5 ALGAE
Protective: 4 TARP
Seed: 4 **ARIL** HULL 5 TESTA
up: 6 HIDING
Coverlet: 5 QUILT 6 AFGHAN

Covert
org.: 3 CIA
~ WWII org.: 3 OSS
Cover-up: 4 ROBE TARP TOGA
5 APRON 6 CAFTAN
Calcutta: 4 SARI
Covet: 4 ENVY WANT 6 DESIRE
Coveted
statue: 5 OSCAR
Covetous
feeling: 4 ENVY
Covetousness: 4 ENVY 5 GREED
Cow: 3 AWE 5 BULLY DAUNT
catcher: 5 LASSO REATA RIATA
6 LARIAT
chew: 3 CUD
comment: 3 MOO
Corporate: 5 ELSIE
Dairy: 8 HOLSTEIN
hand: 4 HOOF
Have a: 5 CALVE
Having a: 5 UPSET
Her symbol was a: 4 ISIS
hurdle, in rhyme: 4 MOON
kid: 4 CALF
name: 5 BOSSY
or sow: 3 **SHE** 6 FEMALE
owner: 6 OLEARY
Query to a: 6 HOWNOW
Sea: 7 MANATEE
Coward: 10 WEAKSISTER
11 YELLOWBELLY
lack: 5 HEART SPINE
Playwright: 4 **NOEL**
Cowardly Lion
alter ego: 4 ZEKE
portrayer: 4 **LAHR**
"Coward of the County"
actress Alicia: 3 ANA
Cowboy: 5 ROPER 6 HERDER
boot attachment: 4 SPUR
contest: 5 RODEO
date: 3 GAL
gear: 5 RIATA 6 LARIAT
Legendary: 9 PECOSBILL
Mexican: 6 CHARRO
nickname: 4 SLIM
pal: 4 PARD
rope: 5 LASSO REATA RIATA

Singing: 5 AUTRY
stray: 5 DOGIE
~ Ritter: 3 TEX
~ Rogers: 3 ROY
Cowboys
gp.: 3 NFL
home: 6 DALLAS
or Indians: 4 TEAM
"Cowboys"
Like Shepard's: 6 ONEACT
Cowcatcher: 6 GRILLE
"Cow Cow Boogie"
singer Morse: 7 ELLAMAE
Cower: 5 QUAIL
Cowgirl
~ Dale: 5 EVANS
Cowhand
moniker: 3 TEX
Cow-horned
goddess: 4 ISIS
Cowley
composition: 3 ODE
Cowpoke
contest: 5 RODEO
pal: 4 PARD
Pampas: 6 GAUCHO
rope: 5 RIATA 6 LARIAT
Cows: 4 KINE
Like some: 6 SACRED
Cox
TV role for: 7 PEEPERS
Coxcomb: 3 FOP
Coxswain
charges: 4 OARS
Obey the: 3 ROW
Coyote
Cartoon: 5 WILEE
clamor: 4 HOWL
supplier: 4 ACME
___ Coyote: 5 WILEE
Coyote, ___ E.: 4 WILE
Cozumel
Info: Spanish cue
cash: 4 PESO
Cozy: 4 SNUG 5 COMFY HOMEY
contents: 6 TEAPOT
corner: 4 NOOK
Get: 6 NESTLE
Kind of: 3 TEA

retreat: 3 DEN 4 NEST
up: 6 NESTLE
CPA
busy mo.: 3 APR
concern: 6 TAXLAW
employer: 3 IRS
expertise: 3 NOS
Part of: 3 ACC 4 ACCT CERT
suggestion: 3 IRA
Cpl.: 3 **NCO**
NCO two levels above: 4 SSGT
Rank above: 3 **SGT**
Rank below: 3 PFC PVT
CPO
org.: 3 USN
CPR
expert: 3 EMT
CPU
attachment: 3 CRT
Part of: 4 UNIT
CQD
successor: 3 SOS
Crab: 3 NAG 5 GRIPE
Move like a: 5 **SIDLE**
weapon: 4 CLAW
Crab ___: 6 NEBULA
Crabby
Act: 5 SIDLE
Crab Key
resident: 4 DRNO
Crack: 3 ACE TRY 4 CHAP JOKE
OPEN QUIP SLIT STAB
5 ADEPT SOLVE
7 ATTEMPT FISSURE
8 APERTURE
a book: 4 READ
and redden: 4 CHAP
At the ~ of dawn: 5 EARLY
cop: 4 NARC
Creep through the: 4 SEEP
Enter via a: 6 SEEPIN
fighter pilot: 3 ACE
in the cold: 4 CHAP
Likely to: 7 BRITTLE
Open a: 4 **AJAR**
Org. with a ~ staff: 3 DEA
result: 4 HAHA
Something to: 4 CODE
squad: 5 ATEAM

Take a ~ at: **3** TRY
Tough nut to: **5** POSER
6 ENIGMA
Cracked: 3 MAD **4 AJAR** BATS
DAFT LOCO NUTS **5** BATTY
LOONY NUTTY **6** INSANE
It might be: **4** SAFE
open: **4** AJAR
Cracker
box: **4** SAFE
brand: **4** HIHO RITZ
flavoring: **6** SESAME
Kind of: **6** GRAHAM
Seder: **5** MATZO
shape: **6** ANIMAL
Soup: **7** SALTINE
spread: **3** ROE **4** PATE
topper: **4** BRIE
Vault: **4** YEGG
Crackerjack: 3 ACE PRO **5** ADEPT
Cracker Jack
surprise: **3** TOY
Crackers: 3 MAD **4** BATS DAFT
LOCO NUTS **5** BATTY
LOONY NUTTY **6** INSANE
Cracking
Get: **5** START
Crackle
colleague: **4** SNAP
Crackler
Year-end: **7** YULELOG
Crackpot: 3 NUT **6** MANIAC
Cradle
Odd place for a: **7** TREETOP
part: **6** ROCKER
"Cradle of Love"
singer Billy: **4** IDOL
Craft: 3 ART **4** BOAT MAKE SHIP
5 GUILE SKILL **6** VESSEL
Camp: **5** CANOE
Canal: **5** BARGE
Clumsy: **3** ARK
Eskimo: **5** KAYAK UMIAK
E.T.: **3** UFO
Harbor: **3** TUG
Indian: **5** CANOE
Lunar: **3** LEM **6** LANDER
Paper: **7** ORIGAMI
Simple: **4** DORY

Small-runway: **4** STOL
WWII: **3 LST 5** EBOAT
Crafted: 4 MADE
on a loom: **5** WOVEN
Craftiness: 5 GUILE
Crafts
Cádiz: **5** ARTES
partner: **4 ARTS**
Craftsperson: 7 ARTISAN
Crafty: 3 SLY **4** ARCH WILY
5 SLICK **6** ASTUTE
More: **5** SLIER SLYER
move: **4** RUSE
one: **5** SNEAK **7** ARTISAN
Crag: 3 TOR
Craggy
hill: **3 TOR**
ridge: **5** ARETE
Craig, Jenny
client: **6** DIETER
Cram: 4 SATE **5** STUFF
6 BONEUP PACKIN
Reason to: **4** EXAM TEST
Crammed: 5 DENSE
Cramp: 5 SPASM
Cranberry: 3 RED
locale: **3** BOG
product: **5** SAUCE
Crane: 5 DAVIT HOIST WADER
cousin: **5** HERON
Irving's: **7** ICHABOD
Poet: **4** HART
Crane, Frasier
Brother of: **5** NILES
Crane, Martin
dog: **5** EDDIE
Crane, Niles
Wife of: **6** DAPHNE
Crank
up: **3** REV
Crankcase
base: **6** OILPAN
fluid: **3** OIL
Crankshaft
attachment: **7** FANBELT
Cranky
one: **5** GRUMP
Cranny
partner: **4 NOOK**

Cranston
of old radio: 6 LAMONT
Craps
action: 3 BET
Losing come-out roll in: 3 TWO
5 THREE
natural: 5 SEVEN 6 ELEVEN
need: 4 DICE
turn: 4 ROLL
Crapshoot: 4 RISK
Crash: 4 REST
cause: 5 PANIC
course: 4 ECON
into: 3 RAM
Prepares for a: 6 BRACES
Roswell ~ victim, supposedly:
5 ALIEN
site: 3 PAD 4 SOFA 5 PARTY
Crashed
It ~ in 2001: 3 MIR
Crasher
Garden: 4 WEED
Picnic: 3 ANT
Crashing
bore: 4 DRIP
Bring ~ down: 4 RUIN
sound: 3 BAM
Crass
one: 3 OAF
Cratchit: 5 CLERK
Cry to: 3 BAH
Son of: 7 TINYTIM
Tiny Tim, to: 3 SON
Crate: 3 BOX 4 HEAP
6 ENCASE
component: 4 SLAT
marking: 7 STENCIL
Upturned, as a: 5 ONEND
Crater: 4 LAKE
feature: 3 RIM
Volcanic: 7 CALDERA
Crater Lake
Like: 4 DEEP
state: 6 OREGON
___ **Crater, Maui:** 3 EKE
Craters of the Moon
locale: 5 IDAHO
Cravat: 3 TIE
cousin: 5 ASCOT

Crave: 4 WANT 6 BEGFOR
DESIRE
Craved: 8 THIRSTED
Craven
Director: 3 **WES**
Craving: 3 **YEN** 4 ITCH LUST
NEED URGE 6 DESIRE
THIRST
Crawford
Model: 5 CINDY
Crawford, Christina
book: 13 MOMMIEDEAREST
Crawford, Cindy
Ex of: 4 GERE
Crawl: 4 WORM 6 GROVEL
10 SNAILSPACE
Did the: 4 SWAM
Do the: 4 SWIM
(with): 4 TEEM
Crawler: 3 TOT
Dangerous: 3 ASP
Hairy: 9 TARANTULA
Night ~, perhaps: 4 BAIT
stop: 3 PUB
Tiny: 3 ANT
Crawling: 6 ASWARM
Cray
ending: 3 OLA
Crayola
choice: 5 COLOR
color until 1990: 9 ORANGERED
shade: 6 SIENNA
Crayon
Burnt ~ color: 6 SIENNA
Like a: 4 WAXY
Use a: 5 COLOR
Craze: 3 FAD 5 FEVER **MANIA**
TREND
Latest: 4 RAGE
Crazed: 5 MANIC
Crazily: 4 AMOK
busy: 6 HECTIC
Craziness
Symbol of: 4 LOON
Crazy: 4 BATS GAGA LOCO NUTS
5 GONZO LOONY NUTSO
WACKO 6 ABSURD INSANE
Be ~ about: 5 ADORE
Like: 4 ALOT

Not: 4 SANE
quilt: 4 OLIO
Talk like: 4 RANT
"Crazy"
singer: 5 CLINE
Crazy ___: 6 EIGHTS
Crazy as ___: 5 ALOON
Crazy as a ___: 4 LOON
Crazy Eights
Game similar to: 3 UNO
"Crazy for You"
singer: 7 MADONNA
Crazy Horse: 5 CHIEF 6 LAKOTA
OGLALA
Crazy Horse Memorial
loc.: 4 SDAK
Cream: 4 TRIO 5 ELITE
Bit of: 3 DAB
cooler: 4 SODA
Depilatory: 4 NAIR
ingredient: 4 **ALOE**
of the crop: 4 BEST 5 ATEAM
ELITE
puff: 4 WIMP 6 ECLAIR
quantity: 4 PINT
Whipped ~ amount: 4 GLOB
6 DOLLOP
Cream ___: 3 ALE 4 SODA
Creamer
etc.: 6 TEASET
Cream-filled
cookie: 4 OREO
pastry: 6 ECLAIR
Cream-of-the-crop: 4 AONE
Creamy
cheese: 4 BRIE
dessert: 6 MOUSSE
white: 5 IVORY
Crease
It has a ~ on top: 6 FEDORA
player: 6 GOALIE
Creasing
Skill in: 7 ORIGAMI
Create: 4 FORM MAKE 5 CRAFT
batik: 3 DYE
friction: 5 CLASH
~, as a word: 4 COIN
Created: 4 MADE
a basket: 4 WOVE

a web site: 4 SPUN
Creation
at the Creation: 3 MAN
"Creation, The"
composer: 5 HAYDN
Creative: 4 ARTY
ability: 3 ART
person: 7 IDEAMAN
spark: 4 **IDEA**
story: 3 LIE
types: 7 IDEAMEN
work: 4 OPUS
Creator: 3 GOD 5 MAKER
Creature: 5 BEING 6 ANIMAL
Bearded: 3 GNU
Carroll: 5 SNARK
Elusive: 4 YETI
Folklore: 3 ROC 5 GNOME
home, in film: 6 LAGOON
Microscopic: 5 AMEBA
6 AMOEBA
of habit: 3 NUN
Sea: 7 ANEMONE
Seuss: 5 LORAX
Shy: 4 DEER
Thick-skinned: 5 RHINO
Tolkien: 3 **ENT** ORC 6 HOBBIT
Two-footed: 5 BIPED
Zodiac: 3 RAM
Crèche
trio: 4 MAGI
Credibility
problem: 3 GAP
Credit: 7 ASCRIBE
12 BROWNIEPOINT
agcy.: 3 TRW
counterpart: 5 DEBIT
Extend: 4 LEND
Letters of: 3 IOU
Take: 3 OWE
union offering: 4 LOAN
Used: 4 OWED
Write without: 5 GHOST
Credit card
ad abbr.: 3 APR
alternative: 4 CASH
Bank name on a: 6 ISSUER
come-on: 5 NOFEE
feature: 6 STRIPE

kind: 4 VISA
Read, as a: 5 SWIPE
Credit-checking
corp.: 3 TRW
Creditor
claim: 4 LIEN
Credits
listing: 4 ROLE
Part of the: 4 CAST
Credo: 3 ISM 5 ETHIC TENET
Creed
Kind of: 6 NICENE
Postal ~ word: 3 **NOR**
___ **Creed:** 6 NICENE
Creedence Clearwater Revival
1968 ~ hit: 6 SUZIEQ
Creek: 3 RIA 6 STREAM
barrier: 4 WEIR
Up the: 6 INAJAM 7 INASPOT
9 INTROUBLE
___ **creek:** 5 UPTHE
Creep: 4 BOZO DRIP INCH POKE
5 STEAL 6 GOSLOW
Look like a: 4 LEER
through the cracks: 4 SEEP
Creeper: 3 IVY TOT 4 VINE
5 SNAIL
keeper: 7 TRELLIS
"Creepshow"
director: 6 ROMERO
Creepy: 5 **EERIE** SCARY WEIRD
feeling: 6 UNEASE
one: 5 SNAIL
thing: 4 VINE
Creepy-crawlies: 6 LARVAE
Creepy-crawly: 6 SPIDER
Creighton
Vietnam War general: 6 ABRAMS
Creighton University
site: 5 OMAHA
Crème
caramel: 4 FLAN
cookie: 4 OREO
flavorer: 6 MENTHE
Crème ___ crème: 4 DELA
Crème de ___: 5 CACAO
6 MENTHE
Crème de la crème: 4 BEST
5 ELITE

Creme-filled
cookie: 4 **OREO**
Cremona
artisan: 5 **AMATI**
crowd: 3 TRE
Former coin of: 4 LIRA
product: 5 STRAD
Crenshaw: 5 MELON
Golfer: 3 BEN
Relative of: 6 CASABA
Creole
veggie: 4 OKRA
Creosote
source: 3 TAR
Crepe
de Chine: 4 SILK
Crêpe ___: 7 SUZETTE
Crescent: 4 LUNE
Its emblem is the: 5 ISLAM
point: 4 CUSP
shape: 3 ARC
Crescent-shaped: 6 LUNATE
Cressida
Love of: 7 TROILUS
Crest: 4 ACME APEX 5 RIDGE
6 SUMMIT
competitor: 3 AIM
Mountain: 5 ARETE
On the ~ of: 4 ATOP
Crested
bird: 3 JAY 7 BLUEJAY
8 COCKATOO
Crestfallen: 3 SAD
Cretan
king: 5 MINOS
peak: 3 IDA
Crete
Capital of: 5 CANEA
Highest peak in: 5 MTIDA
Crew: 4 GANG 5 HANDS
Ahab and: 7 WHALERS
Construction: 8 HARDHATS
equipment: 4 OARS
Film ~ member: 4 GRIP
Hotel: 5 MAIDS
leader: 3 COX
member: 3 OAR 5 ROWER
7 OARSMAN
Naval construction: 7 SEABEES

need: 3 OAR
Participate in: 3 ROW
Road ~ supply: 3 TAR
UFO: 3 ETS 6 ALIENS
Crewman: 4 HAND
Dhow: 4 ARAB
under Kirk: 4 SULU
Crib: 3 BIN PEN 4 TAKE 5 FILCH
    STEAL
cry: 4 MAMA
kid: 3 TOT
part: 4 SLAT
toy: 6 RATTLE
Use ~ notes: 5 CHEAT
Cribbage
knave: 3 NOB
piece: 3 **PEG**
Crichton
critter: 8 DINOSAUR
Crick
site: 4 NECK
spirals: 3 DNA
Cricket: 4 FAIR
club: 3 BAT
player: 7 BATSMAN
position: 4 SLIP
sides: 3 ONS
sound: 5 CHIRP
team: 6 ELEVEN
wicket: 3 END
Crickets, The
1957 hit for ~: 5 OHBOY
Cried: 4 WEPT 6 SOBBED
"___ Cried" (1962 hit): 3 SHE
Crier
Kind of: 4 TOWN
"Crikey!": 4 EGAD
Crime
Aid in: 4 **ABET**
boss: 4 CAPO
committer: 4 PERP
fiction name: 4 ERLE
Fiery: 5 **ARSON**
job: 5 CAPER
Lure into: 6 ENTRAP
scene find: 5 PRINT
Torch: 5 ARSON
White collar: 5 FRAUD
"___ crime?": 5 ISITA

Crimean
conference site: 5 YALTA
native: 5 TATAR
resort: 5 YALTA
"Crime and Punishment"
heroine: 5 SONYA
Crime-fighter
~ Eliot: 4 NESS
Crime lab
job: 7 DNATEST
study: 3 DNA
"Crimes & Misdemeanors"
actor: 4 ALDA
"Crimes of Love, The"
author: 6 DESADE
Crime-solving
game: 4 CLUE
Criminal: 4 PERP THUG 5 FELON
    7 ILLEGAL
A ~ may have one: 5 ALIAS
charge: 3 RAP
haul: 4 LOOT
patterns: 3 MOS
Serious: 5 FELON
They are broken by a: 4 LAWS
Criminalize: 3 BAN
Crimp: 4 KINK
Crimson: 3 RED 7 DARKRED
    8 BLOODRED
    9 CHERRYRED
rival: 3 **ELI**
Crimson Glory: 4 ROSE
Crimson Tide: 4 BAMA
Cringe: 5 COWER
Crinkled
fabric: 5 CREPE
Cripple: 4 MAIM
Crisis
period: 8 REDALERT
point: 4 HEAD
Crisp
biscuit: 4 RUSK
Burn to a: 4 CHAR
cookie: 4 SNAP
fabric: 7 TAFFETA
veggie: 8 SNAPBEAN
Crisper: 3 BIN
Crispy
sandwich: 3 BLT

Crisscross
pattern: 4 GRID 7 LATTICE
___ Cristo: 5 MONTE
Criteria
(abbr.): 4 STDS
Coll. entrance: 4 SATS
Criterion
(abbr.): 3 STD
Scholarship: 4 NEED
Critic: 5 RATER
1987 Pulitzer ~: 4 EDER
Be a: 4 RATE
Canadian literary: 4 FRYE
Chicago film: 5 EBERT
Film: 7 REXREED
pick: 3 NIT
Thumb-turning: 5 EBERT
~ Barnes: 5 CLIVE
~ James: 4 AGEE
~ Janet: 6 MASLIN
~ Pauline: 4 KAEL
~ Rex: 4 REED
~ Roger: 5 EBERT
~ Sheraton: 4 MIMI
~ Walter: 4 KERR
Critical: 3 KEY 5 ACUTE GRAVE
    VITAL
care ctrs.: 3 ERS
evaluation: 4 TEST 8 ACIDTEST
inning: 5 NINTH
It may be: 4 MASS
point: 4 CRUX 5 BRINK
Criticism: 3 DIG 4 **FLAK** GAFF
    6 STATIC
Defend against: 6 UPHOLD
Harsh: 5 LUMPS
Random: 7 POTSHOT
Strong: 4 FLAK
Tiny: 3 NIT
Criticize: 3 DIS PAN RAP RIP
    4 CARP FLAY REAM SLAM
    5 CAVIL FAULT KNOCK
    SNIPE TRASH 6 ATTACK
    IMPUGN LEANON RAILAT
    RAILON SCATHE YELLAT
"Critique of Pure Reason"
writer: 4 KANT
Croak: 4 RASP
Croaker: 4 FROG TOAD

Croat: 4 **SLAV**
Croatian
born inventor: 5 TESLA
capital: 6 ZAGREB
prefix: 5 SERBO
Croc
cousin: 5 **GATOR**
Crock: 3 JAR POT 4 OLLA
suffix: 3 ERY
Crockett
cohort: 5 BOWIE
Frontiersman: 4 DAVY
hat critter: 4 COON
last stand: 5 **ALAMO**
portrayer Parker: 4 FESS
rifle: 5 BETSY
Crockpot
concoction: 4 STEW
Crocodile
shirt maker: 4 IZOD
Crocodile Dundee
greeting: 4 GDAY
"Crocodile Rock"
rocker John: 5 ELTON
Crocus: 4 IRID
bulb: 4 CORM
cousin: 4 IRIS
Croesus
Conquest of: 5 IONIA
kingdom: 5 LYDIA
"___ Croft: Tomb Raider": 4 LARA
Croissant: 4 ROLL
Crone: 3 HAG
Like a: 5 ANILE
Cronus: 5 TITAN
Daughter of: 4 HERA
Son of: 4 ZEUS
Crony: 3 PAL
Cronyn
Actor: 4 **HUME**
Crook: 4 BEND CANE 5 THIEF
    8 CHISELER 9 CHISELLER
Help a: 4 ABET
Crooked: 4 ALOP AWRY BENT
    5 ASKEW 6 ASLANT
lass of rhyme: 6 BOPEEP
"Crooklyn"
director: 3 LEE
Crooned: 4 SANG

Crooner
  Hawaiian: 5 DONHO
  ~ Cole: 3 NAT
  ~ Columbo: 4 RUSS
  ~ Jerry: 4 VALE
  ~ Paul: 4 ANKA
  ~ Perry: 4 COMO
Crooning
  First name in: 4 BING
Crop: 3 MAW 4 CRAW TRIM
  Bring in the: 4 REAP
  Cream of the: 4 BEST 5 ATEAM
    ELITE
  Many a ~ duster: 7 BIPLANE
  pest: 5 APHID
  Raise a: 4 FARM
  up: 5 **ARISE** 6 EMERGE
Cropped
  up: 5 **AROSE**
Cropper
  Come a: 4 FAIL
  ___ cropper: 5 CAMEA COMEA
Croquet
  area: 4 LAWN
  need: 6 MALLET
Crosby
  Bandmate of ~ and Stills: 4 NASH
  Love interest of ~ and Hope:
    6 LAMOUR
  partner: 4 HOPE
  Sing like: 5 CROON
  ~, Stills, and Nash: 4 TRIO
Crosby, Bing
  1944 ~ hit: 4 AMOR
  Emulate: 5 CROON
  record label: 5 DECCA
Cross: 4 FORD ROOD SPAN
    5 MEDAL TESTY
    6 GOOVER 8 TRAVERSE
  Align the ~ hairs: 3 AIM
  Ancient: 3 TAU
  a shallow creek: 4 WADE
  Cost to: 4 TOLL
  Egyptian: 4 **ANKH**
  Greek: 3 **TAU**
  It may have a ~ to bear: 5 ALTAR
  Kind of: 3 TAU 5 PAPAL
  Large: 4 ROOD
  letters: 4 INRI

  over: 4 SPAN
  product: 3 PEN
  shape: 3 TAU
  Sportscaster: 3 IRV
  St. Anthony's: 3 TAU
  the goal line: 5 SCORE
  the threshold: 4 GOIN 5 ENTER
    6 STEPIN
  to bear: 4 ONUS
  word: 3 BAH
  words: 4 SPAT
  ___ cross: 3 TAU
Crossbones
  partner: 5 SKULL
  Word seen on a skull and:
    6 POISON
Crossbow
  Medieval: 8 ARBALEST
Crossbreed: 3 MIX
Cross-country
  gear: 4 SKIS
  Go: 3 SKI
Crosscut: 3 SAW
Crossed: 3 MET
  one's fingers: 5 HOPED
  out: 3 XED 4 EXED
  They can be: 4 EYES
  They're ~ in competition:
    5 EPEES
Crosser
  Atl.: 3 **SST**
  Avenue: 6 STREET
  Column: 3 ROW
  Gorge: 7 TRESTLE
  Hollywood: 4 VINE
  Line: 4 SCAB
  Long.: 3 **LAT**
  Ocean: 5 LINER
  Rubicon: 6 CAESAR
  St.: 3 **AVE**
  Street: 6 AVENUE
Crossing
  cost: 4 TOLL
  Country: 5 STILE
  Exodus: 6 REDSEA
  Kind of: 5 ZEBRA
  Making a: 4 ASEA
  sign silhouette: 4 DEER
  swords: 5 ATWAR

Crosspiece: 4 RUNG
  ___ **crossroads:** 3 ATA
Crosswise: 5 **ABEAM** 7 ATHWART
Crossword
  Complete a: 5 SOLVE
  hint: 4 CLUE
  maker, at times: 5 CLUER
  pattern: 4 GRID
  Potential ~ clue: 7 SYNONYM
  solving tool: 3 PEN
  Some ~ clues: 4 PUNS
  wipeout: 7 ERASURE
  worker: 4 ESNE
Crotchety
  sort: 4 COOT
Crothers
  Actor: 7 SCATMAN
Crouch
  down: 5 SQUAT
"Crouching Tiger, Hidden
    Dragon"
  director: 3 LEE 6 ANGLEE
Croupier: 5 RAKER
  accessory: 8 EYESHADE
  tool: 4 RAKE
Croutons
  Place for: 5 SALAD
Crow: 4 BRAG 5 BOAST EXULT
    7 AMERIND
  cousin: 3 DAW
  cry: 3 **CAW**
  home: 4 NEST 5 TEPEE
    6 TEEPEE
  Time to: 4 DAWN 5 SUNUP
Crowbar: 3 PRY 5 LEVER
  Use a ~ on: 5 FORCE
    7 PRYOPEN
Crowd: 3 MOB 4 CRAM HERD
    HOST SLEW 5 HORDE
    THREE 6 THRONG
  Address a: 5 ORATE
  Cremona: 3 TRE
  Feed a: 5 CATER
  German: 4 DREI
  In: 5 ELITE
  Like a loud: 5 AROAR
  noise: 3 BOO RAH 4 ROAR
    8 APPLAUSE
  One in a: 5 EXTRA

  scene actor: 5 EXTRA
  Sign near a: 3 SRO
  Spanish: 4 TRES
  to capacity: 7 JAMPACK
Crowd-___: 7 PLEASER
Crowded: 5 DENSE
Crowd-pleasing
  hit: 7 HOMERUN
Crowds
  Like some: 4 UGLY 5 AROAR
Crowe
  2001 ~ role: 4 NASH
Crower: 7 ROOSTER
  ___ **crow flies:** 5 ASTHE
Crown: 3 TOP 4 APEX **PATE**
    5 TIARA 6 DIADEM
    7 CORONET
  and scepter: 7 REGALIA
  covering: 6 **ENAMEL**
  Jeweled: 5 TIARA
  sparkler: 5 JEWEL
Crowned
  It may be: 5 MOLAR
Crowning: 4 ATOP
  event: 8 CAPSTONE
  glory: 4 MANE
  point: 4 ACME APEX
Crown jewels
  quality: 6 LUSTRE
Crows
  Collection of: 6 MURDER
Crow's-feet: 5 LINES
Crow's-nest
  cry: 4 AHOY LAND 5 AVAST
    6 LANDHO
  locale: 4 MAST
CRT
  Part of: 3 RAY
Cru
  product: 3 VIN
  ___ **Cruces, New Mexico:** 3 **LAS**
Crucial: 3 KEY
"Crucible, The"
  actress: 5 RYDER
  setting: 5 **SALEM**
Crucifix: 4 **ROOD**
  inscription: 4 **INRI**
Crucifixion
  site: 8 GOLGOTHA

Crude: 3 RAW
  bunch: 4 OPEC
  carrier: 5 OILER
  dude: 3 CAD 4 BOOR
  dwelling: 3 HUT 5 SHACK
  gp.: 4 OPEC
  metal: 3 ORE
  stuff: 3 OIL
Crudely
  Apply: 4 DAUB
Cruel: 6 UNKIND 8 INHUMANE
  fellow: 4 OGRE
  one: 6 SADIST
"Cruel Intentions"
  costar Phillippe: 4 RYAN
Cruellest
  month: 5 APRIL
Cruelty: 6 SADISM
Cruet
  contents: 3 OIL
Cruise
  destination: 3 RIO 6 NASSAU
  in style: 5 YACHT
  On a: 4 <u>ASEA</u>
  or Mix: 3 TOM
  quarters: 5 CABIN
      9 STATEROOM
  ship: 5 LINER
  ship deck: 4 LIDO
  stop: 4 ISLE PORT 5 ISLET
Cruiser
  Highway: 7 TROOPER
  Retired: 3 SST
Cruising: 4 <u>ASEA</u> 5 ATSEA
Cruller
  cousin: 5 DONUT
Crumb: 3 ORT 6 MORSEL
  Tiniest: 4 IOTA
Crumble: 3 ROT 5 ERODE
      6 MOLDER 7 GOTOPOT
Crumbly: 7 FRIABLE
  and dry: 5 MEALY
  cheese: 4 FETA
Crumbs
  Cover with: 5 BREAD
Crumhorn
  cousin: 4 OBOE
Crummy
  Feel: 3 AIL

Crumpets
  partner: 3 TEA
Crumple
  into a ball: 5 WADUP
Crumpled: 4 GAVE
Crunch
  creator: 6 NESTLE
  Lunch with a: 4 TACO
  Numbers to: 4 DATA
  targets: 3 ABS
  ___ Crunch: 4 CAPN
Cruncher
  No.: 3 CPA
Crunchy: 5 CRISP
  Like ~ vegetables: 3 RAW
  munchie: 4 TACO
  salad toppers: 5 BACOS
  sandwich: 3 BLT 4 TACO
  vegetable: 6 CELERY
Crusade: 5 JIHAD 7 HOLYWAR
"Crusade in Europe"
  auth.: 3 DDE
Crusader
  foes: 8 SARACENS
  ~ Ralph: 5 NADER
Crusader Rabbit
  weapon: 5 LANCE
Crush: 4 MASH RUIN 7 SODAPOP
      TRAMPLE
  Have a ~ on: 5 ADORE
  in a Cuisinart: 5 PUREE
  with one's foot: 6 STEPON
      7 STAMPON
Crushed: 4 TROD
Crusher: 6 PESTLE
Crusoe
  creator: 5 DEFOE
  Strand like: 6 ENISLE
Crust
  Dessert with a: 3 PIE
  Form a: 4 CAKE
  layer of Earth: 4 SIMA
  Like a pie: 5 FLAKY
  Pie ~ ingredient: 4 LARD
  Upper: 5 ELITE
  Word before: 5 UPPER
Crustacean: 4 CRAB
      6 ISOPOD
Crusted: 5 CAKED

Cruster
Upper: 7 ELITIST
Crusty
Get: 4 CAKE
one: 3 PIE
Crux: 4 ESSE GIST MEAT
7 ESSENCE
Cruz
Salsa singer: 5 CELIA
Cry: 3 SOB 4 WEEP YELL YELP
6 HOLLER
a river: 4 BAWL
at home: 4 SAFE
before a fall: 6 TIMBER
before disaster: 4 OHNO
companion: 3 HUE
for help: 3 SOS
from above: 6 UPHERE
from the bench: 5 ORDER
like a baby: 4 BAWL MEWL PULE
loudly: 3 SOB 4 BAWL
out: 4 WAIL YELL YELP
out for: 4 NEED
over: 6 BEMOAN
___ cry: 4 AFAR
Crybaby: 6 WEEPER
Be a: 4 PULE
Crying: 7 INTEARS
shame: 4 PITY
"Crying"
singer Orbison: 3 ROY
"Crying Game, The"
star: 3 REA
Cryogenic
refrigerant: 4 NEON
Cryptic
character: 4 RUNE
Make: 6 ENCODE
Cryptogram: 4 CODE
Solve a: 6 DECODE
Cryptographer
aid: 3 KEY
Cryptologic
gp.: 3 NSA
Cryptozoology
subject: 6 NESSIE
"Cry ___ River": 3 MEA
Crystal
Country singer: 5 GAYLE

Crystal ball: 3 ORB 5 GEODE
gazer: 4 SEER
Look into a: 4 GAZE
Crystalline
rock: 6 SCHIST
Crystal-lined
rock: 5 GEODE
Crystallize: 3 GEL
Crystals
1960s ~ hit: 9 HESAREBEL
11 DADOORONRON
Icy: 4 HOAR RIME
"Cry, the Beloved Country"
author: 5 PATON
CSA
general: 5 RELEE
monogram: 3 REL
Part of a ~ signature: 4 ELEE
soldier: 3 REB
state: 3 ALA
"CSI": 5 DRAMA
actress Helgenberger: 4 MARG
evidence: 3 DNA
network: 3 CBS
"CSI: Miami"
network: 3 CBS
CST
Part of: 3 STD
Ctrl
cousin: 3 ALT
Cuatro
halved: 3 DOS
Twice: 4 OCHO
Cub: 4 NLER
Former ~ Sandberg: 4 RYNE
house: 3 DEN 4 LAIR
Joy's: 4 ELSA
slugger: 4 SOSA
Cuba: 4 ISLA ISLE
(abbr.): 3 ISL
Coin of: 4 PESO
Dance from: 5 MAMBO RUMBA
6 RHUMBA
Gp. of which ~ is a member:
3 OAS
is in it: 8 ANTILLES
leader: 5 FIDEL 6 CASTRO
U.S. base in: 5 GITMO
Cuba ___ : 5 LIBRE

Cuban
boy: 4 NINO 5 ELIAN
currency: 4 PESO 5 PESOS
dance: 5 MAMBO RUMBA
    6 RHUMBA
drum: 5 CONGA
leader: 5 FIDEL 6 CASTRO
line dance: 5 CONGA
patriot: 5 MARTI
Cuban Revolution
figure: 3 CHE 7 GUEVARA
Cubby
hole: 3 DEN
Cubbyhole: 4 CELL NOOK
    5 NICHE
Cube: 4 DICE
A ~ has twelve: 5 EDGES
Casino: 3 DIE
Gaming: 3 DIE
grippers: 5 TONGS
inventor Rubik: 4 **ERNO**
Like a: 5 SOLID
Sugar: 4 LUMP
with 21 dots: 3 DIE
Cubed
Dos: 4 OCHO
Zwei: 4 ACHT
Cubemaker
~ Rubik: 4 ERNO
Cubes: 4 DICE 5 DICES
Cut into: 5 DICED
Grab, as ice: 4 TONG
Some: 5 SUGAR
Cubic
128 ~ feet: 4 CORD
decimeter: 5 LITER
meter: 5 **STERE**
~ Rubik: 4 ERNO
Cubicle
fixture: 4 DESK
Cubist
~ Fernand: 5 LEGER
~ Juan: 4 GRIS
~ Rubik: 4 ERNO
Cubits
Vessel measured in: 3 ARK
Cubs: 4 TEAM
Banks of the: 5 ERNIE
Home of the: 3 DEN

Org. with ~ and Eagles: 3 BSA
Sammy of the: 4 SOSA
~, on scoreboards: 3 CHI
Cub Scout: 3 LAD
group: 3 **DEN**
leader: 5 AKELA
Cuckoo: 3 ANI MAD 4 NUTS
    5 CRAZY INANE NUTSY
    NUTTY 6 INSANE
Black: 3 **ANI**
Cucumber
Like a: 4 COOL
Cuddle: 5 SPOON 6 NESTLE
Cuddly
carnival prize: 5 PANDA
pet: 6 LAPDOG
Cuddly-looking
critter: 5 KOALA
Cue: 6 PROMPT
application: 5 CHALK
Fix a: 5 RETIP
Jazzman's: 5 HITIT
Queue: 4 NEXT
Cuff
Speak off the: 5 ADLIB
Cuffs
Put on ~, perhaps: 5 ALTER
Slap ~ on: 3 NAB 6 ARREST
Cugat, Xavier
Half a ~ hit: 4 TICO
Lane who sang with: 4 ABBE
Cuisinart
Crush in a: 5 PUREE
Cuisine
Asian: 4 THAI
Chinese: 5 HUNAN
Curried: 6 INDIAN
Hardly haute: 4 GLOP SLOP
Kind of: 5 HAUTE 6 ETHNIC
    8 NOUVELLE
Lover of lean: 5 SPRAT
New Orleans: 5 CAJUN
Spicy: 4 **THAI** 6 CREOLE
    TEXMEX
___ cuisine: 5 HAUTE
Cul-___: 5 **DESAC**
Culbertson
Bridge expert: 3 **ELY**
Cul-de-___: 3 **SAC**

Culinary
artiste: 4 CHEF
cover-up: 5 APRON
directive: 4 STIR
herb: 5 THYME
Culkin
Actor: 4 RORY
Cull: 6 SCREEN SELECT
7 WEEDOUT
Culmination: 4 ACME 6 APOGEE
Culp
and Cosby TV series: 4 ISPY
___ culpa: 3 **MEA**
Culpable: 7 ATFAULT
___ Culp Hobby: 5 OVETA
Cultist
Jamaican: 5 RASTA
Cultivate: 3 HOE 4 FARM GROW
PLOW TEND TILL WEED
5 BREED
Cultivation
Fit for: 6 ARABLE
Cultivator: 3 HOE
Cultural: 6 ETHNIC
character: 5 ETHOS
funding org.: 3 NEA
Govt. ~ org.: 4 USIA
interests: 4 ARTS
Intl. ~ org.: 6 UNESCO
NYC ~ center: 4 MOMA
prefix: 4 AGRI 5 MULTI
values: 5 ETHOS
Culturally
showy: 4 ARTY
Cultural Revolution
figure: 3 MAO
Culture
base: 4 AGAR
character: 5 ETHOS
dish: 5 PETRI
Kind of: 3 POP
medium: 4 **AGAR**
prefix: 3 AVI 4 AGRI
Cultured
gem: 5 PEARL
With ~ airs: 4 ARTY
Cum ___: 5 LAUDE
Cumberland ___: 3 GAP
Cumberland Gap

explorer: 5 BOONE
___ cum laude: 5 **MAGNA**
SUMMA
Cummerbund: 4 SASH
feature: 5 PLEAT
kin: 3 OBI
Cumming
Tony winner: 4 ALAN
Cumulus
prefix: 4 ALTO
Cuneiform
discovery site: 6 AMARNA
Cunning: 3 ART **SLY** 4 ARCH
CAGY FOXY WILE WILY
5 GUILE 7 SLYNESS
More: 5 CUTER SLIER SLYER
6 WILIER
With: 5 SLYLY
Cunningham
Choreographer: 5 MERCE
Cuomo
Former governor: 5 MARIO
successor: 6 PATAKI
Cup: 5 CALIX 6 TROPHY
1/16 of a ~ (abbr.): 4 TBSP
Café: 5 TASSE
Court: 5 DAVIS
Golf: 5 RYDER
handle: 3 EAR
holder: 6 SAUCER
part: 3 RIM 4 BRIM 5 OUNCE
Place to buy a: 4 CAFE
Put in the: 5 HOLED
___ Cup: 5 DAVIS 8 AMERICAS
Cup-and-saucer
heaters: 5 ETNAS
Cupboard
Like Hubbard's: 4 BARE
Tall: 7 ARMOIRE
Cupcake
topper: 4 ICER 5 ICING
Cupful
Diner: 3 JOE 4 JAVA
Cupid: 4 **AMOR** EROS
8 AMORETTO REINDEER
projectile: 5 ARROW
Struck by: 6 INLOVE 7 SMITTEN
~, to Greeks: 4 EROS
Cupidity: 5 GREED 7 AVARICE

Cupids
　Little: 8 AMORETTI
"Cup of Tea, The"
　painter: 7 CASSATT
Cupola: 4 DOME
Cuppa
　contents: 3 TEA
Cuprite: 3 ORE
Cups
　A couple of: 3 BRA
　deck: 5 TAROT
　etc.: 6 TEASET
Cur
　curb: 5 LEASH
Curaçao
　has one: 7 CEDILLA
　neighbor: 5 **ARUBA**
Curative
　locale: 3 SPA
Curator
　deg.: 3 MFA
Curb: 4 REIN 6 REININ STIFLE
　Get to the other: 5 CROSS
　Run at the: 4 IDLE
Curbside
　call: 4 **TAXI**
　fixture: 5 METER
Curd
　Bean: 4 TOFU
Curdle: 5 GOBAD
Curdler
　Milk: 6 RENNET
Cure: 4 HEAL 6 REMEDY
　hides: 3 TAN
　Place to take a: 3 SPA
　prefix: 3 EPI 4 PEDI
Cure-all: 6 ELIXIR 7 PANACEA
Cured
　cheese: 4 FETA
　Something to be: 3 HAM
Curfew
　After: 4 LATE
　___ curiae: 5 AMICI
Curie
　Daughter of: 5 IRENE
　Madame: 5 MARIE
　title: 6 MADAME
　title (abbr.): 3 MME
Curio: 9 OBJETDART

　shelf: 7 WHATNOT
Curiosity
　Raise: 5 PIQUE
　Show: 3 ASK
Curious: 3 ODD 4 NOSY 5 NOSEY
　　7 STRANGE
"Curious George"
　author: 3 REY
Curl: 7 RINGLET
　Kind of: 4 SPIT
　One ~, say: 3 REP
　one's lip: 5 SNEER
　Place to ~ up and dye:
　　5 SALON
Curled
　Dog with a ~ tail: 3 PUG
　lip look: 5 SNEER
　Tightly: 5 KINKY
Curler: 7 ATHLETE
　place: 4 RINK
Curlew
　cousin: 5 SNIPE
Curlicue: 4 COIL LOOP
Curling
　lines: 4 ARCS
　Mark aimed at in: 3 TEE
　place: 4 RINK
　surface: 3 ICE
Curly: 6 STOOGE
　associate: 3 MOE
　bopper: 3 MOE
　cabbage: 4 KALE
　coif: 4 AFRO
　diacritic: 5 TILDE
　do: 4 AFRO
　lock: 5 TRESS
　of the Globetrotters: 4 NEAL
　replacement: 5 SHEMP
　strand: 7 TENDRIL
　syllable: 3 WOO
Curly-haired
　cat: 3 REX
Curly-leafed
　cabbage: 4 KALE
Curly-tailed
　dog: 5 AKITA
Curmudgeon: 4 COOT CRAB
　　6 GROUCH
　TV: 6 ROONEY

Currant
Black ~ liqueur: 6 CASSIS
Current: 3 HIP NEW 4 FLOW
TIDE 5 TREND 6 LATEST
7 PRESENT 8 UPTODATE
10 PRESENTDAY
administration: 3 INS
amount: 6 AMPERE
Carrying: 4 LIVE
choice: 4 **ACDC**
Circular: 4 EDDY
Dangerous: 3 RIP 7 RIPTIDE
entry points: 6 ANODES
event: 4 TIDE 6 ELNINO
fashion: 4 MODE RAGE 5 TREND
gadget: 7 AMMETER
letters: 4 ACDC
location: 5 OCEAN
measure: 4 VOLT WATT
6 AMPERE
strength: 8 AMPERAGE
unit: 3 AMP 6 **AMPERE**
Weather-affecting: 6 ELNINO
with the wind: 7 LEETIDE
Currently
employed: 5 INUSE
popular: 3 HOT
serving status: 4 ONEC
Curricula vitae: 4 BIOS
Curriculum
division: 4 UNIT 6 MODULE
Gp. concerned with: 3 PTA
range, briefly: 4 ELHI
Curriculum ___: 5 VITAE
Curried
cuisine: 6 INDIAN
Currier
Lithographer: 3 NAT
9 NATHANIEL
Partner of: 4 **IVES**
Curry
herb: 5 CUMIN
or Rice: 3 TIM
powder ingredient: 8 TURMERIC
Curse: 3 HEX POX 4 BANE DAMN
DOOM OATH 5 SWEAR
6 REVILE
"___ Curse, The": 4 DAIN
Cursed: 5 SWORE 7 SWOREAT

team, some say: 3 SOX
"Curse of the Starving Class"
Award for: 4 OBIE
"Curses!": 3 BAH 4 DRAT OHNO
Cursive
opposite: 5 PRINT
Cursor
mover: 5 MOUSE
target: 4 ICON
Curt: 5 SHORT TERSE 6 ABRUPT
SNIPPY
Sportscaster: 5 GOWDY
Curtail: 4 CLIP PARE TRIM
5 ELIDE 8 CUTSHORT
Curtain: 5 DRAPE
call: 6 ENCORE
call call: 5 BRAVO
Drop the ~ on: 3 END
fabric: 4 LACE 5 NINON **SCRIM**
VOILE
folds: 6 PLEATS
holder: 3 **ROD**
raiser: 4 ACTI
shade: 4 ECRU
___ Curtain: 4 IRON
Curtin
Comical: 4 JANE
Curtin, Jane
role: 5 ALLIE
Curtis
Actor: 4 TONY
of cosmetics: 6 HELENE
Curtsy
Ballet: 4 PLIE
Curvaceous
character: 3 ESS
Curve: 3 ARC 4 ARCH BEND
Architectural: 4 OGEE
Double: 3 **ESS** 4 OGEE
Geometric: 3 ARC 7 ELLIPSE
8 PARABOLA
Kind of: 4 BELL SINE
shape: 3 ESS
Slalom: 3 **ESS**
Curved: 4 BENT
arch: 4 OGEE
basket: 5 CESTA
entranceway: 4 ARCH
letter: 3 ESS

molding: 4 **OGEE**
shape: 3 ESS
sword: 5 SABER 8 SCIMITAR
Curvy
letter: 3 **ESS**
Cushiness: 4 EASE
Cushion: 3 PAD
Billiard: 4 BANK RAIL
Hit the: 5 CAROM
It gives players a:
      9 POOLTABLE
Pin: 3 MAT
Cushy: 4 EASY SOFT 5 DOWNY
course: 5 EASYA
Cusp: 4 EDGE
Holiday: 3 EVE
Cuspid: 5 TOOTH
Cuspidor
Used the: 4 SPAT
Cuss: 5 SWEAR
Cussed: 5 SWORE
Cussler
Author: 5 CLIVE
Custard
apple relative: 5 PAPAW
base: 3 EGG
dessert: 4 **FLAN**
Like: 4 EGGY
Custer
colleague: 4 RENO
Custodian: 5 SUPER
collection: 4 KEYS
Custody: 7 KEEPING
Hold in: 6 DETAIN
In: 4 HELD 8 ARRESTED
Take into: 3 NAB 6 ARREST
Custom: 3 TAX 4 WONT 5 HABIT
      USAGE 6 MANNER
Customarily: 7 ASARULE
Customary: 5 USUAL
practice: 4 RITE 5 USAGE
Customer: 4 USER 6 CLIENT
      PATRON
Cafeteria: 5 EATER
file entry: 8 AREACODE
Hack: 4 FARE
Have as a: 6 SELLTO
S&L: 4 ACCT
Utility: 4 USER

Customers
Ready for: 4 OPEN
Customs: 5 MORES
duty: 6 IMPOST
Cut: 3 AXE HEW LOP MOW SAW
      4·AXED DELE ETCH HEWN
      MOWN OMIT SAWN SLIT
      SNIP 5 HEWED SAWED
      SEVER SHARE SHEAR
      SHORN 6 DELETE
      DILUTE FELLED
      7 ABRIDGE SHEARED
      8 DECREASE
abruptly: 3 AXE
and paste: 4 **EDIT**
application: 6 IODINE
a rug: 5 DANCE
at an angle: 5 BEVEL
back: 4 PARE 5 PARED PRUNE
Bad: 4 GASH
Beef: 4 LOIN RUMP 5 TBONE
      9 CLUBSTEAK
Boneless: 5 FILET
canines: 6 TEETHE
close: 4 CROP MOWN 5 SHAVE
corners: 5 SKIMP 6 SCRIMP
Deep: 4 GASH
down: 3 HEW 4 AXED FELL
      5 HEWED
down on: 6 LESSEN
drastically: 5 SLASH
Dress: 4 BIAS 5 ALINE
flower: 4 STEM
from the same cloth: 4 AKIN
glass: 4 ETCH
into: 5 ERODE 6 INCISE
into cubes: 4 DICE 5 DICED
into pieces: 4 CHOP
It may be ~ and dried: 3 HAY
line: 4 SCAR
Narrow: 4 SLIT
Neckline: 3 VEE
off: 3 END LOP 4 CROP STEM
      5 ALONE APART SEVER
      7 ABSCISE ISOLATE
of marble: 4 SLAB
One getting a: 5 AGENT
out: 3 END 4 BAIL CLIP OMIT
      STOP 5 CEASE

partner: 5 DRIED PASTE
Quick: 4 SNIP
short: 3 END 4 CLIP CROP SNIP
   5 ABORT ELIDE 7 CURTAIL
taker: 5 AGENT
the grass: 3 MOW
through: 9 PENETRATE
time: 9 ALLABREVE
Took a: 5 SWUNG
up: 4 DICE 5 SHRED
V-shaped: 5 NOTCH
with a knife, old-style: 4 SNEE
with small strokes: 4 SNIP
wood: 5 SAWED
~, old-style: 4 SNEE

Cut ___ : 4 ARUG 5 INTWO

Cute
as a button: 8 ADORABLE

Cutesy-___ : 3 POO

Cutie: 4 DOLL

Cutie ___ : 3 PIE

"Cut it out!": 4 DONT STOP
   5 CEASE 6 DESIST

Cutlass
Former ~ model: 5 CIERA
maker: 4 OLDS

Cutlery: 6 KNIVES

Cutlet: 4 NICK SNIP
meat: 4 VEAL

Cutoff
point: 3 END

Cutter: 3 AXE SAW 4 EDGE SHIP
   5 PARER
Cane: 7 MACHETE
Carrot: 5 DICER
Class: 6 TRUANT
kin: 5 SLOOP
part: 4 MAST
Portable: 8 SABERSAW
Record: 6 STYLUS
Wood: 3 AXE SAW 4 ADZE

"Cut that out!": 4 STOP 6 STOPIT

Cutting: 4 KEEN TART 5 SNIDE
edge: 5 BLADE
It lacks a ~ edge: 4 EPEE
It may be: 4 EDGE
Make ~ remarks: 5 SNIPE
remark: 3 DIG 4 **BARB**
the mustard: 4 ABLE

tool: 3 ADZ AXE BUR 4 ADZE
   5 KNIFE
Work in the ~ room: 4 EDIT

Cuttlefish
ejection: 3 INK
ink: 5 SEPIA

"Cutty ___": 4 SARK

Cutup: 4 CARD
Act the: 7 OPERATE

Cuyahoga
outlet: 4 ERIE

Cuzco
From: 5 INCAN
land: 4 PERU
native: 4 **INCA**

C-worthy: 4 FAIR SOSO

Cyber
chuckle: 3 LOL
junk: 4 SPAM

Cyberauction
site: 4 EBAY

Cybercafe
patron: 4 USER

Cyberflick
1982 ~: 4 TRON

Cyberheads
Where ~ surf: 3 NET

Cybermessage: 5 EMAIL

Cybername: 6 USERID

Cyberspace
bidding site: 4 EBAY
initials: 3 AOL
letters: 5 EMAIL
nuisance: 6 HACKER
traveler: 4 USER

"Cybill"
actress Witt: 6 ALICIA

Cyborg
enforcer: 7 ROBOCOP
movie prefix: 4 ROBO

Cyclades
island: 3 IOS
sea: 6 AEGEAN

Cycle
Economic: 11 BOOMANDBUST
Gentle ~ items: 5 KNITS
Kind of: 5 LUNAR SLEEP
   SOLAR
part: 5 PHASE

Cyclist
prefix: 3 EPI TRI **UNI**
Wash: 4 SPIN 5 RINSE
Cyclist
choice: 4 GEAR
protection: 6 HELMET
stunt: 7 WHEELIE
~ Armstrong: 5 LANCE
~ LeMond: 4 GREG
Cyclo-
suffix: 4 TRON
Cyclone
center: 3 EYE
Cyclones
Home of the: 4 AMES
9 IOWASTATE
Cyclopes
workplace: 4 ETNA
Cyclops
and others: 4 XMEN
Site of the smithy of: 4 ETNA
Cyclotron
bit: 3 ION 4 ATOM
Cygnet
Former: 4 SWAN
mother: 3 PEN
Cygnus
Bright star in: **5 DENEB**
Cylinder
filler: 6 PISTON
Storage: 4 SILO
Cylindrical: 6 TERETE
structure: 4 SILO
Cymbal
relative: 4 GONG
sound: 5 CLASH
"Cymbeline"
heroine: 6 IMOGEN
Cyndi
Singer: 6 LAUPER
Cynic
look: 5 SNEER
retort: 4 IBET

Cynical
Cause to be: 4 JADE
Cynthia
Author: 5 OZICK
___ Cynwyd, Pennsylvania:
4 BALA
Cypress
feature: 4 KNEE
Cyprus
capital: 7 NICOSIA
Opera set in: 6 OTELLO
Cyrano
Love of: 6 ROXANE
portrayer: 6 GERARD
Cyrus
Book that tells of: 4 EZRA
realm: 6 PERSIA
Cyst: 3 WEN
Cytoplasm
material: 3 RNA
Cy Young Award
winner: 4 LYLE 5 SPAHN
6 GOODEN
Czar: 5 RULER
edict: 5 UKASE
Terrible: 4 IVAN
The Great: 6 PETERI
Czarist
edict: 5 UKASE
parliament: 4 DUMA
Czech: 4 SLAV
chief Vaclav: 5 HAVEL
composer Janacek: 4 LEOS
dialect: 8 MORAVIAN
mark: 5 HACEK
river: 4 ODER OHRE
runner Zatopek: 4 EMIL
tennis star Ivan: 5 LENDL
Czechoslovakia
Capital in the middle of: 4 OSLO
Czechs
neighbors: 7 SLOVAKS

Dd

D: 4 POOR
  Half of: 3 CCL
  neighbor: 5 EFLAT
  Worth a: 4 POOR
  ___ d': 6 MAITRE

Da
  opposite: 4 NYET

Da ___ (from the beginning):
  4 CAPO

D.A.
  Kind of: 4 ASST
  Part of: 3 ATT

da ___, Leonardo: 5 VINCI

da ___, Vasco
  Explorer: 4 GAMA

"___ Daba Honeymoon, The":
  3, ABA

Dabble
  in: 6 PLAYAT 7 SMATTER

Dabbler: 4 TEAL

Dabbling
  duck: 4 TEAL

Dachshund
  doc: 3 VET
  features: 4 EARS

Dacia
  Year ~ was captured by Trajan:
    3 CVI

Dacron: 8 MATERIAL

Dactyl: 3 TOE
  opening: 5 PTERO

Dad: 3 POP 4 PAPA 6 OLDMAN
  Bro of: 3 UNC
  Mate of: 3 MOM
  Mom and: 7 PARENTS
  Sister of: 4 AUNT
  ~, to Grandpa: 3 SON

Dada
  artist: 3 ARP
  daddy: 3 ARP
  pioneer: 3 ARP

Dadaism
  founder: 3 ARP

Dadaist
  Early: 7 JEANARP
  German: 5 ERNST
  ~ Jean: 3 **ARP**
  ~ Max: 5 **ERNST**

Dad-blasted: 8 DOGGONED

Daddy: 4 **PAPA** 5 POPPA

Daddy-longlegs: 8 ARACHNID

Daddy-o: 4 POPS

Daddy Warbucks
  kid: 5 ANNIE

Daedalus
  creation: 4 MAZE
  Son of: 6 ICARUS

Daffy Duck: 4 TOON
  impediment: 4 LISP
  Speak like: 4 LISP
  Voice of: 3 MEL

da Gama
  destination: 5 INDIA
  Explorer: 5 VASCO

Dagger
  handle: 4 HAFT HILT
  Highlands: 4 DIRK
  of yore: 4 SNEE
  Old: 4 SNEE
  partner: 5 CLOAK
  Slender: 6 STYLET 8 STILETTO
  Small: 7 PONIARD 8 STILETTO

Daggers
  Look: 5 GLARE 6 GLOWER

"Dagnabbit!": 5 NERTS

Dagwood: 8 BUMSTEAD
  Herb, to: 8 NEIGHBOR
  Neighbor of: 4 HERB
  Wife of: 7 BLONDIE
  Young neighbor of: 4 ELMO

Dah
  partner: 3 DIT

Dahl
  Actress: 6 **ARLENE**
  Author: 5 ROALD
  ex: 5 LAMAS

Dahl, Roald
　book: 7 MATILDA
Dahomey
　~, today: 5 BENIN
Dail
　land: 4 EIRE
Daily
　delivery: 4 MAIL 6 USMAIL
　drama: 4 SOAP
　event: 7 SUNRISE
　grind: 3 RUT 7 RATRACE
　One of a ~ trio: 4 MEAL
　record: 3 LOG
Daily Bruin
　sch.: 4 UCLA
Daily Planet
　Clark of the: 4 KENT
　Lois of the: 4 LANE
　name: 4 LOIS
　reporter: 5 OLSEN 8 LOISLANE
Daintily
　Drink: 3 SIP
　Walk: 5 MINCE
Dainty: 4 TWEE 8 DELICATE
Daiquiri
　ingredient: 3 RUM
Dairy
　animal: 3 COW
　case purchase: 4 OLEO
　cow: 8 HOLSTEIN
　Cultured ~ product: 6 YOGURT
　dozen: 4 EGGS
　herd: 4 COWS
　implement: 5 CHURN
　purchase: 5 CREAM
　section selection: 5 OLEOS
　staple: 4 MILK
Dairy Queen
　order: 4 CONE 6 SUNDAE
Daisy
　Michaelmas: 5 ASTER
　relative: 5 ASTER
　variety: 5 **OXEYE** 6 SHASTA
　White: 5 OXEYE
Daisy ___: 3 **MAE**
Daisylike
　flower: 5 ASTER
Daisy Mae
　creator: 4 CAPP

　Husband of: 5 ABNER
Daisy ___ Yokum: 3 MAE
Dakar
　land: 7 SENEGAL
Dakota
　home: 5 TEPEE
　~ Indian: 3 REE 6 OGLALA
　~, once (abbr.): 4 TERR
Dalai ___: 4 LAMA
Dalai Lama
　land: 5 TIBET
Dale
　Cowgirl: 5 EVANS
　Husband of: 3 ROY
　Snack for: 5 ACORN
Dalgliesh, Adam
　creator: 7 PDJAMES
Dali
　contemporary: 4 MIRO
　Like a ~ watch: 4 LIMP
Dallas
　cager: 3 MAV
　campus (abbr.): 3 SMU
　City north of: 5 PLANO
　City SSW of: 4 WACO
　hoopster: 3 MAV
　sch.: 3 **SMU**
　suburb: 5 PLANO
"Dallas"
　actor Larry: 6 HAGMAN
　family name: 5 EWING
　Jock's wife, in: 5 ELLIE
　matriarch: 5 **ELLIE**
　Miss on: 5 ELLIE
　One of the Ewings on: 3 PAM
　setting: 5 RANCH
Dallas Cowboys
　emblem: 4 STAR
Dallas-to-Houston
　dir.: 3 SSE
"___ Dalloway": 3 MRS
Dalmatia
　native: 5 CROAT
Dalmatian: 5 CROAT
　detail: 4 SPOT
　Good name for a: 4 SPOT
　marking: 4 SPOT
Daly
　Actress: 4 **TYNE**

costar: **5** GLESS
Daly, Tyne
  role: **5** LACEY
Dam: 3 SHE **4** WEIR
  Egyptian: **5** ASWAN
  mate: **4** SIRE
  on the Nile: **5** ASWAN
  org.: **3** TVA
  Ram's: **3** EWE
  River: **4** WEIR
  Small: **4** WEIR
Damage: 3 <u>**MAR**</u> **4** COST HARM
      6 IMPAIR
  Auto: **5** DENTS
  Cause ~ to: **3** MAR
  Do ~ to: **4** HARM
  done: **4** TOLL
  Sign of: **4** SCAR
  Widespread: **5** HAVOC
"Damage"
  director: **5** MALLE
Damages
  Seek: **3** SUE
Damascus
  land: **5** SYRIA
  native: **6** SYRIAN
D'Amato
  and others: **3** ALS
Dam-building
  org.: **3** TVA
Dame: 5 TITLE
  intro: **5** NOTRE
  of the piano: **4** HESS
___ Dame: 5 <u>**NOTRE**</u>
Daminozide
  brand: **4** ALAR
"Damn Yankees"
  composer Richard: **5** ADLER
  Lola portrayer in: **4** GWEN
  role: **4** LOLA
  vamp: **4** <u>**LOLA**</u>
Damocles
  Sword of: **5** PERIL
Damon
  Actor: **4** MATT
  Writer: **6** RUNYON
Damone
  Singer: **3** VIC
___ d'amore: 4 OBOE

Damp: 4 DANK DEWY **5** MOIST
      SOGGY
  More than: **3** WET
Dampen: 3 WET
Damper
  Put a ~ on: **5** DETER
Damsel: 4 GIRL LASS MAID
  cry: **4** HELP **6** MYHERO
  deliverer: **4** HERO
  Yonder: **3** HER
___ Dan (rock group):
      6 STEELY
Dana
  Actor: **5** ELCAR
  Actress: **6** DELANY
  perfume brand: **4** TABU
Dance: 3 ART HOP
  1860s ~ tune:
      15 BLUEDANUBEWALTZ
  1930s ~: **5** LINDY
  1940s ~:
      15 BEERBARRELPOLKA
  1960s ~: **4** FRUG **6** WATUSI
  1960s ~ tune:
      15 PEPPERMINTTWIST
  1970s ~ music: **5** DISCO
  1990s ~ craze: **8** MACARENA
  All-night ~ party: **4** RAVE
  Ballroom: **5** TANGO **7** ONESTEP
      TWOSTEP
  Barn: **4** REEL **7** HOEDOWN
  bit: **4** STEP
  Brazilian: **5** <u>**SAMBA**</u>
  Circle: **4** <u>**HORA**</u>
  Cork: **3** JIG
  Country: **4** REEL
  Cuban: **5** CONGA MAMBO
      RUMBA **6** RHUMBA
  Dramatic: **5** TANGO
  energetically: **6** BOOGIE
  First name in: **5** TWYLA
      7 ISADORA
  Formal: **4** BALL
  for two: **5** TANGO
  Gliding ~ step: **6** CHASSE
  Half a: **3** CAN <u>**CHA**</u>
  Hawaiian: **4** HULA
  Hip: **4** HULA
  in duple (2/4) time: **5** POLKA

in quadruple (4/4) time:
  7 GAVOTTE
instruction: 4 STEP
Interrupt on the ~ floor: 5 CUTIN
Island: 4 HULA
Israeli: 4 HORA
Jazz: 5 STOMP
Jewish: 4 HORA
Latin: 5 MAMBO SAMBA
  TANGO
Latin ~ music: 5 SALSA
lesson: 4 STEP
Line: 5 CONGA
Lively: 4 HORA **REEL** 5 GALOP
  GIGUE
Maui: 4 HULA
move: 3 DIP 4 STEP
Old French: 7 GAVOTTE
partner: 4 **SONG**
pattern: 4 STEP
Ragtime: 7 ONESTEP
Ring: 4 HORA
Round: 4 HORA
Sailor's: 8 HORNPIPE
School: 3 HOP
Sensuous: 5 TANGO
Song and: 4 ARTS
Spring: 7 MAYPOLE
Stately: 6 MINUET PAVANE
step: 3 CHA PAS
under the bar: 5 LIMBO
unit: 4 STEP
U.S. ~ gp.: 3 ABT
Vigorous: 8 FLAMENCO
Virginia: 4 REEL
Wedding: 4 HORA
When repeated, a: 3 **CHA**
with a kick: 5 CONGA
~, in French: 3 BAL
"Dance On Little Girl"
  singer: 4 ANKA
Dancer
  1968 ~ biopic: 7 ISADORA
  garment: 4 TUTU 7 LEOTARD
  handrail: 5 BARRE
  Kind of: 4 GOGO
Dancers
  Like some: 6 EXOTIC
  Snake: 4 HOPI

"___ Dances" (Dvořák work):
  8 SLAVONIC
"Dancing Queen"
  group: 4 **ABBA**
Dandelion: 4 WEED
Dander: 3 **IRE** 5 IRISH
  Get one's ~ up: 3 IRE 4 RILE
Dandling
  spot: 4 KNEE
Dandy: 3 **FOP** 4 FINE
  beginning: 3 JIM
  dresser: 3 FOP
  Fine and: 3 AOK
  neckwear: 5 ASCOT
Danes
  Actress: 6 CLAIRE
Danger: 4 RISK 5 **PERIL**
  In: 6 ATRISK
  Inviting: 15 PLAYINGWITHFIRE
  Out of: 4 SAFE
  sign: 7 REDFLAG
  signal: 5 ALERT 7 REDFLAG
Dangerfield
  Comedian: 6 RODNEY
Dangerous: 5 RISKY 6 UNSAFE
  Least: 6 SAFEST
  partner: 5 ARMED
"Dangerous When Wet"
  star: 5 LAMAS
Dangle: 4 HANG
  a carrot in front of: 5 TEMPT
  Decorative: 6 TASSEL
Dangler: 6 TASSEL
  Deli: 6 SALAMI
  Palate: 5 UVULA
  Throat: 5 UVULA
Daniel
  Book after: 5 **HOSEA**
  Follower of: 5 HOSEA
  Hawaiian senator: 6 INOUYE
  of Nicaragua: 6 ORTEGA
  Trailblazer: 5 BOONE
"Daniel Boone"
  actor: 4 AMES 6 EDAMES
  actor Parker: 4 FESS
"Daniel Deronda"
  author: 5 ELIOT
Danielle
  Novelist: 5 STEEL

Danilova
dip: 4 PLIE
Danish
city: 6 ODENSE
coin: 5 KRONE
filler: 5 PRUNE
Kind of: 5 PRUNE
money: 5 KRONE
seaport: 6 ODENSE
show brand: 4 ECCO
toy company: 4 LEGO
Danish-born
journalist: 4 RIIS
reformer: 4 RIIS
Danny
Actor: 6 AIELLO DEVITO
Comedic actor: 4 KAYE
Daughter of: 5 MARLO
of basketball: 5 AINGE
"Danny Boy"
actor: 3 REA
Danson
Actor: 3 **TED**
Dante
locale: 7 INFERNO
translator John: 6 CIARDI
Dantès
Dumas character: 6 EDMOND
Danube
City on the: 3 ULM 4 LINZ
Danza
Actor: 4 TONY
Daphnis
God offended by: 4 EROS
Lover of: 5 **CHLOE**
"Daphnis et ___" (Ravel work):
5 CHLOE
Dapper: 5 NATTY SMART
6 SPORTY
fellow: 3 DAN
Dapper ___ : 3 DAN
Dappled: 4 PIED
horse: 4 ROAN
d'Arc, Jeanne: 6 SAINTE
(abbr.): 3 STE
Dare
alternative: 5 TRUTH
Defiant: 6 MAKEME
Daredevil: 6 RISKER

name: 4 EVEL
Robbie's ~ dad: 4 EVEL
Daredeviltry
First name in: 4 **EVEL**
Daring: 4 BOLD
deed: 4 GEST
exploit: 4 GEST
feat: 5 STUNT
Hardly a ~ do: 3 BUN
Darius I
land: 6 PERSIA
Darjeeling: 3 TEA
duds: 4 SARI
Dark: 5 **UNLIT** 6 GLOOMY
and dreary: 5 DINGY
area: 5 UMBRA
Grow: 5 **LATEN**
In the: 7 UNAWARE
Not in the ~ about: 5 HEPTO
suit: 6 SPADES
The ~ force: 4 EVIL
The ~ side: 3 YIN
times, in verse: 4 EENS
Very: 4 INKY
~, in poetry: 4 EBON
"Dark Angel"
actress Jessica: 4 ALBA
**"Dark at the Top of the Stairs,
    The"**
playwright: 4 INGE
Dark-complexioned: 7 SWARTHY
Darken: 3 DIM TAN 5 BEDIM
Darkening: 7 ECLIPSE
"Dark Lady"
singer: 4 CHER
Darkness: 4 MURK
Force of: 4 EVIL
personified: 6 EREBUS
Darkroom
abbr.: 3 ENL NEG
Darlin': 3 HON
"___ Darlin": 3 LIL
Darling: 3 PET 4 DEAR IDOL
7 SWEETIE
dog: 4 NANA
of baseball: 3 RON
~, in French: 5 CHERI 6 CHERIE
Darn: 3 SEW 4 MEND
Give a: 3 SEW 4 CARE MIND

"Darn!": 4 DRAT NUTS RATS
5 SHOOT
"Darn ___!": 5 ITALL
Darned: 4 SEWN VERY
spot: 3 TOE 4 TEAR
"Darn it!": 4 DRAT HECK NUTS
RATS
"Da ___ Ron Ron": 3 DOO
Darrow
Actress: 3 ANN
client: 4 LOEB 6 SCOPES
Dart: 3 ZIP 4 **FLIT** 5 SCOOT
about: 4 FLIT
Make a: 3 SEW
___ d'art: 5 OBJET
D'Artagnan
creator: 5 DUMAS
Friend of: 5 ATHOS 6 ARAMIS
Dartboard: 6 TARGET
Drink by a: 3 ALE
Darth Vader
Daughter of: 4 LEIA
Like: 4 EVIL
Son of: 4 LUKE
Dartmoor
crag: 3 TOR
Darts
quaff: 3 ALE
venue: 3 PUB
"Das Boot"
setting: 5 UBOAT
Dash: 3 PEP RUN VIM 4 **ELAN**
RACE 5 VERVE 6 SPRINT
7 PANACHE
counter: 8 ODOMETER
gauge: 4 TACH
lengths: 3 EMS ENS
off: 5 WRITE
Dashboard
abbr.: 3 MPH RPM
control: 5 DEFOG
device: 4 DIAL
dial: 4 TACH
gauge: 4 TACH 8 ODOMETER
Dashed: 3 RAN 4 TORE
Dashes: 3 EMS ENS
Dashiell
contemporary: 4 ERLE
detective: 4 NORA

dog: 4 ASTA
Dashing: 5 SHARP
sort: 5 RACER
style: 4 ELAN
___ dash of ...: 4 ADDA
"Das Kapital"
author: 4 MARX
"Das Lied von der Erde"
composer: 6 MAHLER
"Das Rheingold"
goddess: 4 ERDA
Dastardly: 4 EVIL
Data: 4 INFO 5 STATS
holder: 4 DISK
Like some: 3 RAW
storage medium: 5 CDROM
to enter: 5 INPUT
transfer rate unit: 4 BAUD
transmission path:
6 UPLINK
Database
operation: 4 SORT
Data-sharing
system (abbr.): 3 LAN
Date: 3 **SEE**
Get ready for a: 5 PRIMP
Guy's: 3 GAL
Have a: 3 EAT
Invite on a: 6 ASKOUT
Kind of: 3 DUE
On a: 3 OUT
producer: 4 PALM
Prom: 6 ESCORT
To: 3 **YET** 5 **ASYET** SOFAR
Where to get a: 5 OASIS
with a Dr.: 4 APPT
Without a: 4 STAG
___ date (makes wedding plans):
5 SETSA
"___ date!": 4 ITSA
Datebook
abbr.: 3 APR AUG DEC FEB FRI
JAN JUL JUN MAR MON
NOV OCT SAT SEP SUN
THU TUE WED 4 APPT
THUR TUES
Dated: 3 OLD SAW 4 SEEN
5 PASSE 6 OLDHAT
Dateless: 4 **STAG** 5 ALONE

Dates
  Like some: 6 PITTED
  Where to find: 5 OASES OASIS
Dating
  couple: 4 ITEM
  from: 4 ASOF
  letters: 3 BCE
  Word used in: 4 ANNO
Datum: 4 FACT STAT
Daughter
  Brother's: 5 NIECE
  Mom's: 3 SIS
  Sister's: 5 NIECE
  ~, for example: 3 SHE
Daumier
  Artist: 6 HONORE
Daunt: 4 FAZE 5 SCARE
     6 DISMAY
Dauntless: 5 STOUT 6 HEROIC
Dave
  Computer nemesis of: 3 HAL
  Humorist: 5 BARRY
  of baseball: 5 STIEB
  of the PGA: 4 MARR
"Dave"
  star: 5 KLINE
Davenport: 4 SOFA
  resident: 5 IOWAN
  site: 4 IOWA
David: 4 CAMP 6 STATUE
  Actor: 5 NIVEN 6 CARUSO
  Coanchor of: 4 CHET
  Golfer: 5 DUVAL
  Impressionist: 4 FRYE
  Journalist: 5 ENSOR
  Lyricist: 3 HAL
  Philosopher: 4 HUME
  Playwright: 5 MAMET
  Song of: 5 PSALM
  Weapon used by: 5 SLING
  ___ David (Jewish star): 5 MOGEN
Davidic
  song: 5 PSALM
Davies
  Golfer: 5 LAURA
Davies, Capt.
  portrayer: 7 EDASNER
  ___-Davies, John: 4 RHYS
Da ___, Vietnam: 4 NANG

Davis
  Activist: 6 ANGELA
  Actor: 5 **OSSIE**
  Actress: 5 BETTE **GEENA**
  Nutritionist: 6 ADELLE
  Singer: 3 MAC 7 SKEETER
Davis, Jefferson
  org.: 3 CSA
  supporter: 3 REB
Davis, Jim
  dog: 4 **ODIE**
Davis Cup
  Former ~ captain: 4 ASHE
Davis Jr., Sammy
  book: 7 YESICAN
Davit: 5 CRANE HOIST
Daw, Marjorie
  vehicle: 6 SEESAW
Dawber
  Actress: 3 **PAM**
Dawdle: 3 LAG 5 TARRY
     6 LOITER 8 LOSETIME
Dawdling: 4 POKY
Dawn: 4 MORN 5 ARISE ONSET
     SUNUP 6 AURORA
  deity: 3 **EOS**
  droplets: 3 DEW
  goddess: 3 **EOS** 6 AURORA
  Greet the: 5 ARISE
  riser: 3 SUN
  to dusk: 3 DAY
  Toward the: 4 EAST
Dawnlike: 7 AURORAL
Dawson
  of football: 3 **LEN**
"Dawson's Creek"
  actress Holmes: 5 KATIE
  extra: 4 TEEN
Day
  Actress: 5 DORIS
  Any ~ now: 4 SOON
  at the movies: 5 DORIS
  break: 3 NAP 6 RECESS SIESTA
  Break of: 4 DAWN MORN
     5 SUNUP 6 SIESTA
  Call it a: 4 QUIT
  care attendee: 3 TOT
  divs.: 3 HRS
  Face the: 5 ARISE

Fateful: 4 IDES
fraction: 4 HOUR
Greet the: 4 RISE 5 **ARISE**
Hebrew: 3 YOM
It's another: 8 TOMORROW
laborer: 4 PEON
march: 5 ETAPE
of celebration: 4 FETE
of rest: 7 SABBATH
of the wk.: 3 FRI MON SAT SUN
    THU TUE WED
Plain as: 8 CLEARCUT
preceding: 3 EVE
prefix: 3 MID 6 YESTER
saver: 4 HERO
To this: 3 YET
~, in Spanish: 3 DIA
Day-___ : 3 **GLO**
___ **day (dosage):** 4 ONEA
___ **Day (November 2):**
    8 ALLSOULS
Day, Doris
film: 10 PILLOWTALK
Word repeated in a ~ song:
    4 SERA
Dayan
contemporary: 4 MEIR
of Israel: 5 **MOSHE**
Daybed: 6 CHAISE
Daybreak: 4 DAWN 5 SUNUP
Daydream: 4 MOON 7 REVERIE
    10 WOOLGATHER
"___ **day now ...":** 3 ANY
Days
Bygone: 4 PAST YORE
In the old: 4 **ONCE**
In those: 4 THEN
In ~ past: 3 AGO
Like ~ of yore: 5 OLDEN
of old: 4 YORE
of yore: 3 ELD 4 PAST
Days ___ : 3 INN 5 OFOLD
"___ **Days" (Woody Allen film):**
    5 RADIO
"___ **Day's Night":** 5 AHARD
Days of ___ : 4 YORE
"**Days of ___ Lives":** 3 OUR
Daytime
drama: 4 SOAP 6 SERIAL

First name in ~ TV: 5 OPRAH
show: 7 MATINEE
Dayton
City near: 5 XENIA
Daytona 500: 4 RACE
entrant: 7 RACECAR
org.: 6 NASCAR
Daytona Beach
City west of: 5 OCALA
"___ **Day Will Come":** 3 OUR
"**Day Without Rain, A"**
singer: 4 ENYA
Daze: 3 FOG 4 STUN 6 STUPOR
Dazed: 4 ASEA 6 INAFOG
and confused: 5 ATSEA
    6 INAFOG 7 OUTOFIT
condition: 6 STUPOR
___ **d'Azur:** 4 COTE
Dazzle: 3 AWE 4 STUN 5 AMAZE
    ECLAT
Dazzled: 5 INAWE
Dazzling
display: 5 ECLAT
effect: 5 ECLAT
light: 5 GLARE
performance:
    11 SHOWSTOPPER
success: 5 ECLAT
D'back: 4 NLER
D.C.
bigwig: 3 SEN
donor: 3 PAC
figure: 3 POL SEN
fund-raiser: 3 PAC
insider: 3 POL
lobby: 3 NRA 4 AARP
lobbying gp.: 3 PAC
One of a ~ 100: 3 SEN
pol: 3 SEN
setting: 3 EDT EST
stadium: 3 RFK
TV from: 5 CSPAN
type: 3 POL
~ VIP: 3 **SEN**
D-Day
beach: 4 UTAH 5 **OMAHA**
craft: 3 LST 4 LSTS
invasion town: 4 STLO
link: 4 ASIN

transport: 3 LST
vessel: 3 LST
DDE
command: 3 **ETO**
foe: 3 AES
follower: 3 JFK
Loser to: 3 AES
nickname: 3 IKE
party: 3 GOP
predecessor: 3 HST
DDT
Org. that banned: 3 EPA
De ___
(actual): 5 FACTO
(again): 4 NOVO
(excessive): 4 TROP
De ___, Brian
Director: 5 PALMA
de ___, Cabeza
Explorer: 4 VACA
de ___, Charles: 6 GAULLE
de ___, Cyrano: 8 BERGERAC
de ___, Hernando
Explorer: 4 SOTO
de ___, Honoré
Novelist: 6 BALZAC
De ___, Robert
Actor: 4 NIRO
De ___, Vittorio
Director: 4 SICA
DEA
agent: 4 NARC
Dead: 3 SEA
against: 4 ANTI
center: 4 TOMB
duck: 5 GONER
end: 3 DEE 10 BLINDALLEY
follower: 3 END
giveaway: 6 ESTATE
heat: 3 **TIE**
In a ~ heat: 4 EVEN
It may be: 3 END
letters: 3 RIP
to the world: 5 INERT 6 ASLEEP
~, as an engine: 5 KAPUT
"Dead ___"
Francis book: 4 CERT
Deaden: 4 DAMP MUTE NUMB
6 BENUMB

Dead-end
job: 3 RUT
street: 8 CULDESAC
Deadeye
of legend: 6 OAKLEY
Deadline
Add just before the: 6 EDGEIN
After the: 4 LATE
Before the: 5 EARLY 6 INTIME
Past the: 4 LAST
Deadlock: 3 TIE 4 DRAW
7 IMPASSE
Deadlocked: 4 EVEN TIED
Deadly: 5 FATAL 6 LETHAL
defoliant: 11 AGENTORANGE
poison: 4 BANE
sin: 4 ENVY LUST 5 ANGER
GREED PRIDE SLOTH
8 GLUTTONY
sin count: 5 SEVEN
snake: 3 ASP 5 KRAIT MAMBA
virus: 5 EBOLA
Dead Sea
document: 6 SCROLL
kingdom: 4 MOAB
region: 4 EDOM
scribe: 6 ESSENE
Dead Sea Scrolls
language: 7 ARAMAIC
Presumed authors of: 7 ESSENES
"Dead Souls"
novelist: 5 GOGOL
Deaf
Communication for the ~ (abbr.):
3 ASL
Falling on ~ ears: 7 UNHEARD
Deaf as ___: 5 APOST
___ deaf ear to: 5 TURNA
Deafening: 4 LOUD 5 AROAR
Deal: 4 PACT
Bank: 4 LOAN
Big: 3 ADO
Cashless: 4 SWAP 5 TRADE
Conclude, as a: 5 CLOSE
Get in on a: 4 ANTE
Good: 3 BUY LOT 4 LOTS
Great: 3 LOT TON 4 SLEW
5 NOEND
in: 4 SELL

Kind of: **10** SWEETHEART
maker: **5** AGENT
preceder: **4** ANTE
Secondhand: **6** RESALE
Secure, as a: **3** ICE
Sports: **4** SWAP **5** TRADE
with: **5** TREAT **7** ADDRESS
(with): **4** COPE
"___ deal!": **4** ITSA
Dealer
buster: **4** NARC
in cloth: **6** DRAPER
in stolen goods: **5** FENCE
Kind of: **4** ARMS
nemesis: **4** NARC
Order to a: **5** HITME
request: **4** ANTE
Tip for a: **4** TOKE
Dealt
(with): **5** COPED
Dean
concern: **8** ACADEMIA
list fig.: **3** GPA
of diplomacy: **7** ACHESON
of Jan & Dean: **8** TORRENCE
Partner of: **3** JAN
Dean, James: 4 ICON
film: **5** GIANT
persona: **5** REBEL
Deane
Diplomat: **5** SILAS
Deanna
Enterprise counselor: **4** TROI
Dear: 6 VALUED **7** BELOVED
companion: **4** NEAR
Hold: **4** LOVE **5** ADORE
    7 CHERISH
~, in French: **5** CHERE
    CHERI
~, in Italian: **4** CARA CARO
~, in Spanish: **4** CARA CARO
"Dear"
advice-giver: **4** ABBY
one: **3** SIR **4** ABBY
Dear Abby
Sister of: **3** ANN
"___ Dearest": 6 MOMMIE
Dearie: 3 HON PET
"Dear me!": **4** ALAS

"Dear old"
family member: **3** DAD
Dearth: 4 LACK
Death
Done to: **3** OLD
Love to: **5** ADORE
Thrill to: **5** ELATE
"___ Death" (Grieg work): **4** ASES
"Death Be Not Proud"
author: **5** DONNE
"Death in the Family, A"
author: **4** **AGEE**
"Death in Venice"
author: **4** MANN
"Death of a Naturalist"
poet: **6** HEANEY
"Death of a Salesman"
name: **5** LOMAN
"Death on the ___": **4** NILE
Death Valley
Like: **4** ARID
Debacle: 6 FIASCO
___ de Balzac
Novelist: **6** HONORE
Debatable: 4 **MOOT**
Debate: 5 **ARGUE**
focus: **5** TOPIC
side: **3** CON **PRO** **4** ANTI
subject: **5** ISSUE TOPIC
topic: **5** ISSUE
Under: **7** ATISSUE
Debating
Not worth: **4** MOOT
Debauchee: 4 ROUE **5** SATYR
Debbie
Actress: **8** REYNOLDS
Swimmer: **5** MEYER
Debby
Singer: **5** BOONE
de Beauvoir
Writer: **6** SIMONE
Debilitated: 6 FEEBLE
Debonair: 5 SUAVE **6** URBANE
Deborah
Actress: **4** KERR **5** ADAIR
___ de Boulogne (Paris park):
    4 BOIS
Debra
Actress: **5** PAGET

Debra Jo
  Actress: 4 RUPP
Debris
  Ocean: 6 JETSAM 7 FLOTSAM
  Rocky: 5 SCREE
Debt
  acknowledgment: 3 IOU
  Be in: 3 OWE
  Clear a: 5 REPAY
  Govt.: 5 TNOTE
  Letters of: 3 IOU
  memo: 3 IOU
  National ~ word: 8 TRILLION
  Satisfy, as a: 5 REPAY
  security: 4 LIEN
  Settle a: 5 REPAY 6 PONYUP
  Unpaid: 6 ARREAR
Debtor
  claim: 4 LIEN
  letters: 3 IOU
  note: 3 IOU
  woe: 4 REPO
Debt-ridden: 8 INTHERED
Debts: 6 REDINK
  Acquire, as: 5 INCUR RUNUP
  Have: 3 OWE
Debussy
  Composer: 6 CLAUDE
  contemporary: 5 SATIE
  subject: 3 MER
  work: 5 LAMER
Debut: 5 ENTRY 7 PREMIER
      ROLLOUT
  NASDAQ: 3 IPO
  NYSE: 3 IPO
  of Oct. 7, 1982: 4 CATS
  of Oct. 11, 1975: 3 SNL
  Wall St.: 3 IPO
Débutante
  affair: 3 BAL 4 BALL
Dec.
  holiday: 4 XMAS
Decade
  divs.: 3 YRS
Decadent: 6 EFFETE
Decaf
  brand: 5 SANKA
Decalogue
  deliverer: 5 MOSES

  word: 5 SHALT
Decant: 4 POUR
Decapitate: 6 BEHEAD
DeCarlo
  Actress: 6 YVONNE
Decathlon
  component: 5 EVENT
  event: 7 JAVELIN SHOTPUT
Decay: 3 ROT
  Sign of: 4 RUST
Deceit: 4 RUSE 5 GUILE
Deceitful
  Be: 3 LIE 8 TELLALIE
  one: 4 LIAR
Deceive: 4 DUPE SNOW 5 COZEN
      LIETO 6 LEADON
Deceived: 5 LEDON 6 LIEDTO
      MISLED
  Not ~ by: 4 ONTO
Deceiving: 7 LYINGTO
Decelerate: 4 SLOW
December
  24th or 31st: 3 EVE
  air: 4 NOEL
  decoration: 8 ORNAMENT
  song: 4 NOEL 5 CAROL
  temp: 5 SANTA
  The first of: 3 DEE
Decennial
  event: 6 CENSUS
Decent: 4 CLAD
  chap: 4 GENT
  Not: 4 LEWD
  sort: 6 MENSCH
Deception: 3 LIE 4 HOAX RUSE
      SHAM
  Blatant: 7 CHARADE
  on the ice: 4 DEKE
Deceptive: 6 TRICKY
  move: 5 FEINT
  plan: 4 RUSE
Decide: 3 OPT
  against: 3 NIX
  on: 5 ELECT
  to withdraw: 6 OPTOUT
  Unable to: 4 TORN
Decide at the flip of ___: 5 ACOIN
Deciding
  Have trouble: 6 SEESAW

Decimal
base: 3 TEN
follower: 5 CENTS
fraction: 5 TENTH
No. after the: 3 CTS
point: 3 DOT
unit: 3 TEN
___ decimal system: 5 DEWEY
Decimeter
Cubic: 5 LITER
Decision: 4 CALL
Await a: 4 PEND
Bout: 3 TKO
Court: 3 LET
Judicial: 5 AWARD
Make a: 3 OPT 4 RULE 5 ELECT
point: 4 FORK
Ref's: 3 **TKO**
Right of: 5 SAYSO
Ring: 3 TKO
Split: 7 DIVORCE
Time of: 4 DDAY
Decisive
Be: 3 OPT
defeat: 8 WATERLOO
time: 4 DDAY
Deck: 4 KAYO
22-card ~: 5 TAROT
assent: 6 AYEAYE
Clean the: 4 SWAB
Diviner's: 5 **TAROT**
expert: 9 CARDSHARK
Fortuneteller's: 5 TAROT
Gave from a: 5 DEALT
hands: 4 CREW
Lowest: 5 **ORLOP**
Mystical: 5 TAROT
No longer on: 5 ATBAT
Not on: 5 BELOW
On: 4 NEXT 7 TOPSIDE
On a ~, perhaps: 4 ASEA
out: 5 ADORN ARRAY 6 CLOTHE
    7 FESTOON
Playing with a full: 4 SANE
    8 ALLTHERE
salt: 3 TAR
Seer's: 5 TAROT
Ship: 5 ORLOP
wood: 4 TEAK

Decked: 3 KOD 4 CLAD
Get ~ out: 5 DRESS
out: 4 **CLAD** 7 ADORNED
    ARRAYED
Decks: 3 KOS
"Deck the Halls": 5 CAROL
contraction: 3 TIS
sequence: 6 LALALA
syllables: 3 LAS
Declaim: 5 ORATE SPOUT
Declaration
Altar: 3 IDO
Bridge: 5 IPASS
Formal: 6 DICTUM
Make a: 4 AVER
Pinochle: 4 MELD
Poker: 4 **IMIN** 5 ICALL 6 IRAISE
Senate: 3 YEA
Solemn: 4 OATH
Wedding: 3 IDO
Declare: 3 SAY 4 **AVER AVOW**
    5 STATE 6 ASSERT
false: 4 DENY
openly: 4 **AVOW**
positively: 4 **AVER**
untrue: 4 **DENY**
Decline: 3 EBB SAG 4 DROP FALL
    PASS WANE 5 SAYNO
    SLIDE 6 REFUSE WORSEN
in value: 3 SAG
On the: 6 ASLOPE WANING
Period of: 3 EBB 7 EBBTIDE
to bid: 4 PASS
to vote: 7 ABSTAIN
___ Deco: 3 ART
___ de coeur: 3 CRI
___ de Cologne: 3 **EAU**
___ de combat: 4 HORS
Decompose: 3 ROT
Décor
Change the: 4 **REDO**
Wall: 5 MURAL
Decorate: 5 **ADORN** 7 GARNISH
anew: 4 **REDO**
Decorated
Richly: 6 ORNATE
Decoration: 5 AWARD
    9 ADORNMENT
Cake: 5 ICING

Christmas: 4 TREE 5 HOLLY
   6 TINSEL
Garden: 3 URN 5 GNOME
Gift: 3 BOW
Hat: 5 PLUME
Mil.: 3 DSC DSM
Object of: 4 HERO
Party: 8 STREAMER
Shoe: 6 TASSEL
Uniform: 7 EPAULET
Decorative
  band: 6 ARMLET FRIEZE
  case: 4 **ETUI**
  jug: 4 EWER
  metalwork: 6 NIELLO
  noose: 3 TIE
  Not just: 5 UTILE
  pitcher: 4 **EWER**
  trim: 4 LACE
  vase: 3 URN
Decorator
  Cake: 4 ICER
  Hire a: 4 REDO
  shade: 4 ECRU
  suggestion: 3 HUE
Decorous: 4 PRIM 6 SEEMLY
___ de corps: 6 ESPRIT
Decoy: 4 LURE
  Con's: 5 SHILL
Decrease: 3 EBB 4 WANE
   5 ABATE LOWER
De-crease: 4 IRON 5 PRESS
Decree: 4 FIAT RULE 5 **EDICT**
   UKASE 6 ORDAIN
  Imperial: 5 UKASE
  Islamic: 5 FATWA
  Not final, as a: 4 NISI
  Official: 5 EDICT
Decrepit: 6 CREAKY
  horse: 3 NAG
___ de deux: 3 PAS
Dedicated: 4 AVID 5 LOYAL
   6 ARDENT
  poem: 3 ODE
Dedicatory
  verse: 3 ODE
  words: 3 TOA
Deduce: 5 GLEAN **INFER**
   6 GATHER

Deduction
  Scale: 4 TARE
Deductions
  After: 3 NET
Deductive: 7 APRIORI
Dee
  Actress: 6 SANDRA
  predecessor: 3 CEE
  Singer: 4 KIKI
Dee, Ruby
  Husband of: 5 OSSIE
Deed: 3 ACT
  Daring: 4 GEST
  Have the ~ to: 3 OWN
  Heroic: 4 FEAT 7 EXPLOIT
  holder: 5 OWNER
  No good: 3 SIN
"Deed I Do"
  singer: 5 HORNE
Deejay: 7 SPINNER
  worry: 4 SKIP
Deem
  appropriate: 6 **SEEFIT**
Deep: 4 RICH 7 INTENSE
  black: 3 JET 4 EBON INKY
  blue: 4 **ANIL**
  cavity: 5 ABYSM
  chasm: 5 ABYSS 6 CANYON
  cut: 4 **GASH**
  dish: 6 TUREEN
  down: 7 ATHEART 8 INWARDLY
  draft: 4 SWIG
  Go off the ~ end: 4 DIVE SNAP
  green: 7 EMERALD
  pink: 4 ROSE 5 MELON
  pit: 5 ABYSS
  red: 4 RUBY 6 CERISE
  secrets: 6 ARCANA
  sleep: 4 **COMA** 5 SOPOR
  voice: 4 BASS
Deep Blue
  game: 5 CHESS
  maker: 3 IBM
Deep-dish
  meal: 6 POTPIE
Deepen
  ~, as a canal: 6 DREDGE
Deep-frying
  need: 3 OIL 6 HOTOIL

"Deep Impact"
   star: 5 LEONI
Deep-seated: 6 INBRED
   INNATE
Deep-six: 3 CAN 4 TOSS 5 DITCH
   SCRAP **TRASH**
Deep-space
   energy source: 6 QUASAR
   mission: 5 PROBE
"Deep Space Nine"
   character: 3 ODO
Deep Throat: 6 SOURCE
Deep-voiced
   singer: 5 BASSO
Deer: 3 DOE ROE
   Baby: 4 FAWN
   cousin: 3 ELK
   dad: 4 STAG
   Female: 3 DOE 4 HIND
   herder: 4 LAPP
   Male: 4 HART **STAG**
   mom: 3 DOE
   sir: 4 STAG
   Young: 4 FAWN
Deere
   headquarters: 6 MOLINE
   product: 4 PLOW
___ Dee River: 3 PEE
Deerstalker: 3 HAT
Deface: 3 **MAR**
De facto: 6 ACTUAL
Defamation
   Written: 5 LIBEL
Defame: 5 ABASE LIBEL
   in print: 5 LIBEL
Defat
   ~, as a whale: 6 FLENSE
Defaulter
   loss: 4 REPO
Defeat: 3 TOP 4 BEST LICK LOSS
     5 WORST
   Admission of: 5 ILOSE ILOST
   Barely: 4 EDGE
   Cry of: 5 UNCLE
   decisively: 4 DRUB ROUT
     5 STOMP 6 THRASH
     15 MOPTHEFLOORWITH
   Narrowly: 3 NIP 4 EDGE
   Overwhelmingly: 4 ROUT

Defeated: 5 DIDIN 6 BEATEN
Defeatist
   word: 4 CANT 6 CANNOT
Defect: 4 FLAW 5 FAULT
Defective: 3 BAD
   Slightly ~ (abbr.): 3 IRR
Defector: 6 EMIGRE
Defendant
   answer: 4 PLEA
   excuse: 5 ALIBI
   of 1925: 6 SCOPES
Defendants
   ~, in old law: 3 REI
Defender
   Bridge: 4 EAST
   Perennial: 4 EAST
Defense
   acronym: 4 NATO
   advisory org.: 3 NSC
   Castle: 4 MOAT
   Court: 4 ZONE
   Former ~ gp.: 5 SEATO
   gp.: 4 NATO
   Medieval: 4 MOAT
   org.: 4 NATO
   Polecat's: 4 ODOR
   Skunk's: 4 ODOR
   type: 4 ZONE
   Weaponless ~ system: 4 JUDO
Defenseless: 5 NAKED
   Render: 5 UNARM
Defenseman
   Legendary: 3 ORR
Defensive
   ditch: 4 MOAT
   effort: 5 STAND
   spray: 4 MACE
   wall: 7 PARAPET
Defer
   Suffix with: 4 ENCE
   (to): 6 KOWTOW
___ deferens: 3 VAS
Defiant
   act: 4 DARE
   remark: 7 SOTHERE
   reply: 5 NEVER
   words: 6 MAKEME
Defibrillator
   yell: 5 CLEAR

Deficiency: 3 GAP 5 MINUS
   8 SHORTAGE
  Result of iron: 6 ANEMIA
  Result of thiamine: 8 BERIBERI
Deficient
  Be ~ in: 4 LACK
Deficit
  indicator: 6 REDINK
Definitive
  statement: 8 LASTWORD
Deflated
  It can be: 3 EGO
Deflation
  victim: 3 EGO
Deflect: 5 AVERT
Defoe
  Author: 6 DANIEL
  character: 6 CRUSOE
   12 MOLLFLANDERS
  character Flanders: 4 MOLL
Defoliant
  Deadly: 11 AGENTORANGE
  ___ de France: 3 **ILE**
Defraud: 4 BILK SCAM 5 CHEAT
   COZEN 6 FLEECE
Defrost: 4 MELT THAW
Deft: 5 AGILE HANDY SLICK
   6 ADROIT
Deftness: 4 EASE 5 SKILL
Defunct
  alliance: 5 SEATO
  humor magazine: 3 SPY
  sports org.: 3 ABA
Defy: 4 DARE
Degas
  Artist: 5 EDGAR
  Item in a ~ painting: 4 TUTU
  Many a: 6 PASTEL
  subject: 7 DANCERS
De Gaulle
  alternative: 4 ORLY 5 LILLE
  birthplace: 5 LILLE
Degauss: 5 ERASE
DeGeneres
  Comic: 5 **ELLEN**
Degrade: 5 **ABASE**
Degree: 4 STEP 6 EXTENT
  Advanced: 3 NTH PHD
  Atty.'s: 3 LLD

CEO's: 3 MBA
div.: 3 MIN
High: 3 **NTH** PHD 7 MASTERS
Highest: 3 NTH
In the slightest: 5 ATALL
Math: 3 NTH
Nth: 3 MAX
Prof.'s: 3 PHD
Second: 3 MBA
Third: 3 PHD
To a: 4 SOME 5 QUITE
To any: 5 ATALL
Ultimate: 3 **NTH**
Utmost: 3 NTH
___ degree: 3 NTH TOA
Degrees
  22.5 ~: 3 NNE
  90 ~: 4 EAST
  ___ de guerre: 3 NOM
Dehydrated: 4 SERE
Dehydration
  remedy: 7 LIQUIDS
  "___ Dei": 5 AGNUS
Deicer
  Road: 4 SALT
Deighton
  Author: 3 **LEN**
Deimos: 4 MOON
  Father of: 4 ARES
Deity
  Bellicose: 4 **ARES**
  Dawn: 3 **EOS**
  Discord: 4 ERIS
  dismisser: 7 ATHEIST
  doubter: 8 AGNOSTIC
  Hindu: 4 RAMA 5 SHIVA
   6 VISHNU
  Islamic: 5 ALLAH
  Lascivious: 5 SATYR
  Lustful: 5 SATYR
  Semitic: 4 BAAL
  Shi'ite: 5 ALLAH
  Subordinate: 6 DAEMON
  Supreme Greek: 4 ZEUS
  Supreme Norse: 4 ODIN
  Supreme Theban: 6 AMENRA
  Viking: 4 ODIN
  War: 4 ARES
  Woodland: 4 FAUN 5 **SATYR**

___ **de Janeiro:** 3 RIO
Déjà vu
  Have: 6 RELIVE
Dejected: 3 SAD 4 BLUE DOWN
    GLUM 5 MOPEY
Deke: 5 FEINT
  Astronaut: 7 SLAYTON
de la ___, Oscar
  Boxer: 4 HOYA
  Designer: 5 **RENTA**
  ___ **de la Cité:** 3 ILE
Delaney
  Actress: 3 KIM
Delany
  Actress: 4 DANA
de la Renta
  Designer: 5 OSCAR
De Laurentiis
  Producer: 4 DINO
Delaware
  Capital on the: 7 TRENTON
  City on the: 6 CAMDEN
  senator: 4 ROTH 5 BIDEN
  ~ Indian: 6 LENAPE
"Delaware Water Gap"
  painter George: 6 INNESS
Delay: 5 SITON TARRY 6 PUTOFF
    7 TIMELAG
  After much: 6 ATLAST
  progress: 6 RETARD
  Time: 3 LAG
  Without: 3 NOW 5 APACE
    6 ATONCE
    15 ATTHEDROPOFAHAT
  Without ~, in a memo: 4 ASAP
Delayed: 4 LATE 6 HELDUP
Dele
  Cancel a: 4 STET
  undoer: 4 STET
Delectable: 5 TASTY YUMMY
Delegate: 5 ENVOY 8 EMISSARY
  U.N.: 3 AMB
___ **de Leon**
  Explorer: 5 PONCE
Delete: 3 ZAP 4 XOUT 5 ERASE
Deleted: 3 XED 6 XEDOUT
___ **del Fuego:** 6 TIERRA
Delhi
  Info: Indian cue

  address: 3 SRI
  bread: 5 RUPEE
  dough: 5 RUPEE
  dress: 4 **SARI**
  dweller: 5 HINDU
  language: 5 HINDI
  princess: 4 RANI
  wrap: 4 **SARI**
Deli
  bread: 3 **RYE**
  dangler: 6 SALAMI
  display: 5 MEATS
  donut: 5 BAGEL
  fixture: 6 SLICER
  jarful: 4 MAYO
  loaf: 3 RYE
  loaves: 4 **RYES**
  meat: 3 HAM 6 SALAMI
    7 BOLOGNA
  need: 6 SLICER
  order: 3 BLT 5 SWISS 6 REUBEN
    8 HAMONRYE PASTRAMI
  request: 3 BLT 5 ONRYE
    6 NOMAYO
  sandwich: 3 BLT 4 HERO
    6 REUBEN
  sausage: 6 SALAMI
  side: 4 **SLAW**
  spread: 4 MAYO
  Word on a ~ scale: 4 TARE
Deliberate: 4 MUSE SLOW
  loss: 4 DIVE
Delibes
  Composer: 3 LEO
Delicacy: 4 TACT 7 FINESSE
  Fish: 3 EEL 7 SHADROE
  Jellied: 3 EEL
  Pickled: 3 EEL
  Seafood: 3 ROE
  Shad: 3 ROE
  Stuffed: 5 DERMA
  Sturgeon: 3 ROE
Delicate: 4 FINE LACY SOFT
    5 FRAIL 6 TENDER
    8 ETHEREAL
  fabric: 4 LACE
"Delicate Balance, A"
  playwright: 5 ALBEE
Delicious: 5 TASTY

discard: **4** CORE
leftover: **4** CORE
thing: **5** APPLE
"Delicious!": **3** MMM YUM
    4 MMMM **5** TASTY
Delight: **3** JOY **4** GLEE **5** ELATE
    6 PLEASE REGALE
    TICKLE
in: **5** ENJOY
Insurer's: **7** LOWRISK
Sound of: **3** AAH OOH
Sounds of: **3** AHS
___ delight: **6** IDIOTS
Delighted: **4** GLAD SENT
    6 ENRAPT
exclamation: **3** AAH OOH
"___ delighted!": **4** IDBE
Delightful: **4** NICE **8** PLEASING
place: **4** EDEN
Delilah
portrayer: **6** LAMARR
wooer: **6** SAMSON
DeLillo
Writer: **3** DON
Delineate: **4** ETCH LIMN
Delirious: **4** AGOG **5** GIDDY
    6 RAVING
person: **5** RAVER
Deliver: **6** RESCUE
a diatribe: **4** RANT
an address: **5** ORATE
a speech: **5** ORATE
a tirade: **4** RANT
by parachute: **4** DROP
    7 AIRDROP
It may ~ the goods: **4** SEMI
Suffix with: **4** ANCE
Deliverance: **6** RESCUE
    7 RELEASE
"Deliverance"
actor Beatty: **3** NED
Delivered: **4** BORN **5** DEALT
    6 SENTIN
Had food: **5** ATEIN
Have food: **5** EATIN **7** ORDERIN
Deliverer
Baby: **5** STORK
Damsel's: **4** HERO
of old: **6** ICEMAN

Pkg.: **3** UPS
Serum: **7** SYRINGE
Delivery
AOL: **5** EMAIL
co.: **3** UPS
Daily: **4** MAIL **6** USMAIL
Diva's: **4** ARIA
docs: **3** OBS
Early: **7** PREEMIE
entrance: **8** SIDEDOOR
Fast: **5** SPIEL
Male: **3** SON
Postal: **4** MAIL
Sun.: **3** SER
Sunday: **6** SERMON
truck: **3** VAN
UPS: **3** PKG
USPS: **3** LTR
Dell: **4** VALE
competitor: **3** IBM **4** ACER
products: **3** PCS
Della
Actress: **5** REESE
creator: **4** **ERLE**
of mystery: **6** STREET
Singer: **5** REESE
Delmonico
alternative: **5** TBONE
order: **4** RARE
Delon
Actor: **5** **ALAIN**
"___ De-Lovely": **3** ITS
Delphi
figure: **6** ORACLE
prophet: **6** ORACLE
temple god: **6** APOLLO
Delphic: **8** ORACULAR
medium: **6** ORACLE
shrine: **6** ORACLE
Del Rio
Actress: **7** DOLORES
___ del Sol: **5** COSTA
Delt
neighbor: **3** LAT PEC
Delta: **7** AIRLINE
Actress: **5** BURKE
builder: **4** SILT
deposit: **4** SILT
Former ~ competitor: **3** TWA

"Delta Dawn"
  singer Tucker: 5 TANYA
"Delta of Venus"
  author Anais: 3 **NIN**
Delude: 6 LEADON
Deluge: 6 ENGULF 7 TORRENT
DeLuise
  Comic: 3 **DOM**
DeLuise, Dom
  film: 5 FATSO
"___ de Lune": 5 CLAIR
Deluxe: 4 POSH
  accommodations: 5 SUITE
  seat: 3 BOX
  sheet fabric: 5 SATIN
Dem.
  foe: 3 REP
  Neither ~ nor Rep.: 3 **IND**
Demagnetize: 5 ERASE
Demand: 5 EXACT
  Court: 5 ORDER
  In: 3 HOT 7 DESIRED
  Kidnapper's: 6 RANSOM
  payment: 3 DUN
  Striker's: 5 RAISE
  Union: 5 RAISE
Demanding: 5 STERN
      7 EXIGENT
  Less: 6 EASIER
  star: 4 DIVA
Demarcate: 6 DEFINE
Demarcation
  Mountain: 8 TREELINE
  Pool: 4 LANE
___ de Mayo: 5 CINCO
Demean: 5 ABASE
Demeanor: 3 AIR 4 **MIEN** MOOD
de' Medici, Catherine: 5 REINE
___ de menthe: 5 CREME
Dementieva
  of tennis: 5 ELENA
"___ de mer": 3 MAL
Demeter
  counterpart: 5 CERES
Demi
  Actress: 5 MOORE
  and Bruce: 4 EXES
"Demian"
  author: 5 HESSE

de Mille
  Choreographer: 5 **AGNES**
  Dancer: 5 AGNES
DeMille
  Director: 5 CECIL
  film: 4 EPIC
  specialty: 4 EPIC
Demise: 3 END
Demme
  Director: 3 TED
Demo
  ender: 4 CRAT
Democratic
  donkey creator: 4 NAST
Democratic Party
  symbol: 6 DONKEY
Demoiselle: 3 GAL 4 GIRL
Demolish: 4 **RAZE** RUIN 5 LEVEL
      TOTAL WRECK
Demolition
  compound: 3 TNT
  letters: 3 TNT
Demolitionist
  supply: 3 TNT
Demon: 3 IMP
  Female: 5 LAMIA
  Little: 3 IMP
  Speed: 5 RACER
Demon ___: 3 RUM
Demond
  TV costar: 4 REDD
Demonic: 4 EVIL
Demonstrate: 4 SHOW 5 PROVE
Demonstration
  End of a: 3 QED
  Nonviolent: 5 SITIN
Demosthenes: 6 ORATOR
  Emulate: 5 **ORATE**
Demure: 3 COY
Den: 4 **LAIR** NEST
  denizen: 4 BEAR 7 BEARCUB
  din: 4 ROAR
  Kind of: 5 OPIUM
  Lion's: 4 LAIR
  mother: 7 LIONESS
  outburst: 4 ROAR
  sets: 3 TVS
  system: 6 STEREO
Den ___ (Dutch city): 4 HAAG

Dench
Actress: 4 JUDI
film: 4 IRIS
title: 4 DAME
Dendrologist
study: 5 TREES
Deng
land: 5 CHINA
Denial: 4 VETO 7 REFUSAL
Dundee: 3 **NAE**
Military: 5 NOSIR
Slangy: 3 NAH 4 NOPE
Spouse's: 6 NODEAR
Terse: 5 NOTME
Words of: 4 NOTI 5 NOTME
6 IDONOT
Denials: 3 NOS 4 NOES
Denier
words: 4 NOTI 5 NOTME
Denim: 8 MATERIAL
fabric: 8 DUNGAREE
First name in: 4 LEVI
De Niro, Robert
film: 5 RONIN 6 CASINO
8 CAPEFEAR
10 GOODFELLAS
role: 6 CAPONE
Denison
denizen: 5 TEXAN
Denizen
Alley: 3 TOM
Coop: 3 HEN
Den: 4 BEAR 7 BEARCUB
Desert: 5 CAMEL
Dorm: 4 COED
Down under: 3 EMU 6 AUSSIE
Forest: 4 DEER
Hill: 3 ANT
Marsh: 4 RAIL 5 HERON
Pen: 3 CON
Pond: 4 NEWT TOAD
Dennis: 6 MENACE
Actor: 3 DAY
of basketball: 6 RODMAN
Dennis the Menace: 4 BRAT
dog: 4 RUFF
girl: 4 GINA
Like: 5 PESKY
Mother of: 5 ALICE

Denomination: 4 SECT 5 ORDER
Denouement: 3 END 6 ENDING
FINALE
Denounce: 4 DAMN 6 RAILAT
7 CONDEMN
De novo: 4 **ANEW**
Dense: 6 OBTUSE
fog: 7 PEASOUP
Not: 4 RARE 6 SPARSE
Density
symbol: 3 RHO
Dent: 3 MAR 4 DING
prefix: 3 TRI
Dental
cleaner: 5 FLOSS
exam: 4 ORAL
filling: 5 INLAY
records: 5 XRAYS
Dentist
deg.: 3 DDS
directive: 4 BITE OPEN 5 **RINSE**
WIDER 8 OPENWIDE
handiwork: 5 INLAY
org.: 3 ADA
request: 4 BITE OPEN 5 **RINSE**
WIDER 8 OPENWIDE
tool: 5 DRILL
Denver
dish: 6 OMELET
elevation: 4 MILE
hrs.: 3 MST
summer hrs.: 3 MDT
university: 5 REGIS
Denver-to-Chicago
dir.: 3 ENE
Deny: 6 NAYSAY NEGATE
Deodorant
type: 5 SPRAY 6 ROLLON
7 AEROSOL
"De oratore"
author: 6 CICERO
Dep.
opposite: 3 ARR
De Palma
Director: 5 BRIAN
Depardieu
Actor: 6 GERARD
Depart: 5 LEAVE 6 SETOFF
9 TAKELEAVE

Departed: 4 GONE LEFT WENT
Department: 4 AREA
  Cabinet: **5** LABOR STATE
     7 DEFENSE **8** INTERIOR
  Corporate: **5** LEGAL SALES
  French: **3** AIN **4** OISE ORNE
     5 AISNE
Department of Labor
  agcy.: **4** OSHA
Department store
  section: **4** MENS **6** LINENS
     MISSES **8** MENSWEAR
  ~ Santa: **4** TEMP
Departs: 4 GOES
Departure: 4 EXIT **5** DEATH
  Mass: **6** EXODUS
  notice: **4** OBIT
Depend: 4 **RELY** **5** HINGE
  (on): **4** **RELY** **5** HINGE
  suffix: **4** ENCE
Dependable: 4 SAFE **5** SOLID
     6 TRUSTY
Dependent
  Be: **4** RELY
Depict: 4 LIMN
  unfairly: **4** SKEW
Depilatory
  brand: **4** NAIR NEET
Deplaned: 4 ALIT
Deplete: 3 SAP **5** DRAIN EATUP
     USEUP **7** EATINTO
Depleting: 7 USINGUP
___ de plume: 3 **NOM**
Deportment: 4 MIEN
Depose: 4 OUST
Deposed
  leader: **4** SHAH **5** EXILE
Deposit: 3 BED LAY PUT
     5 PLACE
  Bank: **3** ORE **4** **SILT** SNOW
  Big: **4** LODE
  Clayey: **4** MARL
  Coal: **4** SEAM
  Delta: **4** SILT **8** SEDIMENT
  Earthy: **4** MARL
  Glacial: **7** MORAINE
  Gold: **4** LODE
  in a tray: **3** ASH
  Loamy: **5** **LOESS**

  Metal: **4** LODE
  Mineral: **4** VEIN
  Rich: **4** LODE
  River: **4** SILT
  Silt: **5** LOESS
Depot: 4 STOP **7** STATION
  (abbr.): **3** **STA**
  letters (abbr.): **3** ARR
  posting, for short: **4** SKED
  RR: **3** STA STN
Depp, Johnny
  role: **6** BRASCO EDWOOD
Depraved: 4 EVIL
Depreciation
  cause: **11** WEARANDTEAR
Depressed: 3 LOW SAD **4** BLUE
     DOWN **7** INAFUNK
  area: **6** GHETTO
Depressing: 3 SAD **6** DREARY
     GLOOMY
  situation: **6** DOWNER
Depression: 3 ERA **4** DALE DENT
     FUNK HOLE
  agcy.: **3** NRA TVA
  Big: **6** CRATER
  Geological: **5** BASIN
  Great: **5** ABYSS
  migrant: **4** OKIE
Deprive
  of courage: **5** UNMAN
  of food: **6** STARVE
  of heat: **5** UNARM **6** DISARM
  of weapons: **5** UNARM
Deprived: 6 BEREFT
Dept.
  head: **3** MGR
  store stock: **4** MDSE
Depth: 5 ABYSS NADIR
  checker: **5** PLUMB
  Lacking: **4** TWOD
  Lacking ~ and width: **4** ONED
  Like a ~ finder: **5** SONIC
Depth charge: 6 ASHCAN
  target: **5** UBOAT
Dept. of Justice
  employee: **4** ATTY
Dept. of Labor
  agency: **4** **OSHA**
  division: **4** OSHA

Deputized
group: 5 POSSE
Deputy: 4 AIDE
(abbr.): 4 ASST
Deputy ___ (cartoon character):
4 DAWG
Der ___ (Adenauer): 4 **ALTE**
Deranged: 3 MAD 6 INSANE
Derby: 3 HAT 4 RACE
distance: 4 MILE 5 METRE
feature: 4 BRIM
material: 4 FELT
prize: 5 PURSE ROSES
prospect: 4 COLT
site: 5 EPSOM
town: 5 EPSOM
Derek
and others: 3 BOS
of baseball: 5 JETER
Derek, Bo
film: 3 TEN 4 ORCA
Derek and the Dominos
hit song: 5 LAYLA
Derelict: 3 BUM 4 HOBO
6 REMISS TRUANT
Deride: 4 GIBE JEER 7 SCOFFAT
SNEERAT
Derision: 5 SCORN
Express: 4 JEER 5 SNEER
Sound of: 5 SNORT
Derisive: 5 SNIDE
cry: 3 YAH
laugh: 3 HAH 4 HAHA
look: 5 SNEER
sound: 5 SNORT
Derive: 5 INFER
Derm
prefix: 4 ECTO ENDO ENTO
Dermal
dilemma: 4 ACNE
opening: 3 EPI 4 PORE
prefix: 3 EPI 4 ENTO
Dermatologist
concern: 4 ACNE CYST ITCH
MOLE
Dermis
prefix: 3 EPI
Dern
Actor: 5 BRUCE

Actress: 5 LAURA
Dernier ___ : 3 **CRI**
Derogatory: 5 SNIDE
Derrière: 4 **REAR** TUSH
Derring-do
Bit of: 4 FEAT
First name in: 4 EVEL
Tale of: 5 GESTE
Derringer: 3 GUN 8 SMALLARM
"___ Derringer" (TV oldie):
5 YANCY
"Der Ring ___ Nibelungen": 3 DES
Dershowitz
field: 3 LAW
Lawyer: 4 ALAN
Der Spiegel
Article in: 3 EIN 4 EINE
Dervish: 5 FAKIR
faith: 5 ISLAM
Des ___ : 6 MOINES
___ de sac: 3 CUL
Desai
Author: 5 ANITA
___ des Beaux-Arts: 5 ECOLE
Descartes
concept: 4 IDEE
conclusion: 3 IAM
Philosopher: 4 **RENE**
quote word: 4 ERGO
Therefore, to: 4 ERGO
Descend: 4 SINK
Descendant: 5 **SCION**
Descent: 4 DROP
Climber's: 6 RAPPEL
Hawk's: 5 SWOOP
Describe: 4 LIMN 6 RELATE
Descriptive
wd.: 3 ADJ
Desdemona
Husband of: 7 OTHELLO
opera: 6 OTELLO
Desecrate: 6 DEFILE
Desert
African: 6 SAHARA 8 KALAHARI
Asian: 4 GOBI
bloomers: 5 CACTI
clay: 5 ADOBE
denizen: 5 CAMEL
Dry as a: 4 ARID 7 SAHARAN

flora: 5 CACTI
group: 7 CARAVAN
havens: 5 OASES
home: 5 ADOBE
Israeli: 5 **NEGEV**
Like ~ vegetation: 6 SPARSE
Mideast: 5 NEGEV
Mongolian: 4 **GOBI**
near Sinai: 5 NEGEV
plant: 5 AGAVE
plants: 5 CACTI
rest stop: 5 OASIS
rest stops: 5 OASES
sight: 4 DUNE 6 MIRAGE
stopover: 5 OASIS
stream: 4 WADI
wanderer: 5 NOMAD
Western: 6 MOHAVE MOJAVE
World's largest: 6 SAHARA
Deserted: 5 ALONE 6 LONELY
Deserter: 3 RAT 7 RUNAWAY
    8 RENEGADE
Desert Fox, The: 6 ROMMEL
Desertlike: 4 **ARID** SERE
    7 SAHARAN
___ Desert of the Southwest:
    7 SONORAN
Desert Storm
missile: 4 SCUD
reporter Peter: 6 ARNETT
site: 4 IRAQ
Deserve: 4 **EARN** RATE 5 **MERIT**
a hand: 4 ANTE
Deserved: 3 DUE
Desi
Bandleader: 5 ARNAZ
Daughter of: 5 **LUCIE**
Wife of: 4 LUCY
Desideratum: 4 NEED
Design: 3 AIM 4 PLAN
detail: 4 SPEC
Inlaid: 6 MOSAIC
Interior: 5 DECOR
Stick-on: 5 DECAL
with acid: 4 ETCH
Designate: 3 TAP 4 NAME TERM
    5 ALLOT ELECT 6 ANOINT
    DENOTE
a new use for: 6 REZONE

Designation: 4 NAME 5 TITLE
Designer
concern: 5 DECOR
One-named: 4 ERTE
studio: 7 ATELIER
tool: 7 STENCIL
"Designing Women"
actress: 10 DELTABURKE
actress Annie: 5 POTTS
actress Delta: 5 BURKE
Desilu
partner: 5 ARNAZ
Desirable
guests: 5 ALIST
Most: 7 OPTIMAL
position: 4 PLUM
quality: 5 ASSET
Desire: 3 YEN 4 EROS ITCH
    URGE **WANT** 5 COVET
    CRAVE 6 THIRST
    7 HOPEFOR 9 STREETCAR
Burning: 5 ARSON
Passionate: 4 LUST
Persistent: 7 CRAVING
Restless: 4 ITCH
Strong: 3 YEN 4 URGE 6 THIRST
Desist: 4 STOP 5 CEASE
partner: 5 CEASE
Desk
item: 6 ERASER 7 STAPLER
type: 7 ROLLTOP
wood: 3 OAK
words: 5 INOUT
Desktop
item: 4 ICON
products: 3 PCS
symbol: 4 ICON
Des Moines
hrs.: 3 CST
resident: 5 IOWAN
state: 4 IOWA
university: 5 DRAKE
Desmond
of South Africa: 4 TUTU
___ de soie: 4 PEAU
Desolate: 4 LORN 5 STARK
region: 5 WILDS
Despair
Cry of: 4 OHNO

Desperate: 4 DIRE **7** DOORDIE
  measure: **10** LASTRESORT
"Desperate Housewives"
  actress Hatcher: **4** TERI
  Longoria of: **3 EVA**
  network: **3** ABC
  role: **4** EDIE BREE
Desperation
  Act of: **15** LASTDITCHEFFORT
  tactic: **8** LASTGASP
Despicable: 3 LOW **4** VILE
  More: **5** BASER
  sort: **3** CUR **4** TOAD WORM
Despise: 4 HATE 5 ABHOR
    6 LOATHE
Despoil: 3 ROB **5** TAINT
Despondent: 3 SAD
  cry: **4** OHME
Despot: 4 TSAR 6 TYRANT
  1970s ~: **7** IDIAMIN
  Bygone: **4** TSAR
  Persian: **6** SATRAP
  Roman: **4** NERO
  Ugandan: **4** AMIN **7** IDIAMIN
Despotism: 7 TYRANNY
  First name in: **3** IDI
Dessert
  choice: **3** PIE **4** CAKE
  Cold: **3** ICE **6** GELATO SORBET
    7 SHERBET
  Creamy: **6** MOUSSE
  Crusty: **3** PIE
  Custard: **4** FLAN
  Dense: **6** GELATO
  Dixie: **8** PECANPIE
  Double: **10** PIEALAMODE
  Eggy: **4** FLAN
  Frozen: **6** SORBET **7** SHERBET
  Fruity: **3** PIE **4** TART
  Green: **7** LIMEPIE
  Rich: **4** CAKE **5** TORTE
    8 TIRAMISU **9** CREAMCAKE
    10 CHEESECAKE
  sandwich: **4** OREO
  Southern: **8** PECANPIE
    10 SHOOFLYPIE
  Spanish: **4** FLAN
  style: **7** ALAMODE
  vehicle: **4** CART

  Wedding: **4** CAKE
  wine: **4** PORT **6** MALAGA
    8 SAUTERNE
Dessert ___ : 4 MENU
Dest.
  Mail: **5** POBOX
Destiny: 3 LOT **4** FATE **5 KARMA**
    6 KISMET
  Asian: **5** KARMA
  Dire: **4** DOOM
Destiny's Child: 4 TRIO
Destitute: 4 POOR **5 NEEDY**
Destroy: 4 RUIN UNDO **5** ERASE
    TOTAL TRASH
  by degrees: **5** ERODE
  gradually: **5** ERODE
  ~, as documents: **5** SHRED
Destroyed: 7 INRUINS
    8 TOREDOWN
  Not: **6** EXTANT
Destroyer
  detector: **5** SONAR
  Hindu: **4** SIVA **5** SHIVA
  letters: **3** USS
  ~, slangily: **6** TINCAN
Destroyer, The: 4 SIVA **5** SHIVA
Destruction: 4 BANE LOSS RUIN
    5 HAVOC
Destructive
  compound: **3** TNT
  episode: **7** RAMPAGE
  insect: **5** BORER
Detach: 5 UNFIX UNPIN
    6 UNCLIP UNHOOK
    7 TEAROFF
  gradually: **4** WEAN
Detached: 5 ALOOF APART
    8 STACCATO
  ~, in mus.: **4** STAC
Detail: 4 ITEM **7** ITEMIZE
  Job: **4 SPEC**
  Map: **5** INSET
  Small: **4** SPEC
  Type: **5** SERIF
Details
  Contract: **10** SMALLPRINT
  Like some: **4** GORY
  Missing: **7** SKETCHY
Detained: 4 HELD

Detainee: 6 INTERN
  privilege: 7 ONECALL
Detect: 4 SPOT 5 SENSE
Detected: 4 SEEN
Detection
  device: 5 RADAR SONAR
  Escape: 5 ELUDE
  Means of: 5 SCENT
Detective: 4 TAIL 6 SLEUTH
      TRACER 7 GUMSHOE
  1950s ~: 4 GUNN
  1970s TV ~: 4 TOMA
  1990s TV ~ drama:
      15 DIAGNOSISMURDER
  assignment: 4 CASE
  dilemmas: 8 DEADENDS
  discovery: 4 CLUE
  dog: 4 ASTA
  Fictional ~ name: 4 CHAN ERLE
      NERO
  need: 4 LEAD
Detectives: 3 PIS
Detective story: 7 MYSTERY
  discovery: 4 BODY
  pioneer: 3 POE
  writer ___ Stanley Gardner:
      4 ERLE
Detector
  Destroyer: 5 SONAR
  Motion: 6 SENSOR
  Smoke: 4 NOSE
  Sub: 5 SONAR
  Submarine: 5 SONAR
  Type of: 3 LIE 5 METAL
Détente: 4 THAW
  Abandon: 5 REARM
Detergent: 4 SOAP
  brand: 3 ERA 4 TIDE 5 CHEER
      PUREX
  ingredient: 5 BORAX
  Old ~ brand: 3 DUZ
  target: 4 DIRT
Deteriorate: 3 ROT 4 RUST
      6 WORSEN 7 GOTOPOT
      8 GOTOSEED
  Gradually: 5 ERODE
Deterioration: 4 WEAR
Determinant
  Gender: 11 XCHROMOSOME

  Trait: 4 GENE
Determination: 7 RESOLVE
      8 SELFWILL
Determined: 3 SET 8 RESOLUTE
  to follow: 5 SETON
Deterrent
  Attack: 4 MACE MOAT
  Burglar: 4 BARK 5 ALARM
  Teamwork: 3 EGO
Detest: 4 HATE 5 ABHOR
      6 LOATHE
Detestation: 5 ODIUM
Dethrone: 4 OUST
de Tirtoff, Romain
  pseudonym: 4 ERTE
  ___ de toilette: 3 EAU
Detonate: 6 SETOFF 7 EXPLODE
  It doesn't: 3 DUD
Detonating
  device: 3 CAP 6 PETARD
  ___ Detoo: 5 **ARTOO**
de Torquemada, ___: 5 TOMAS
Detour: 5 AVERT 6 BYPASS
      DIVERT
  Send on a: 7 REROUTE
Detox
  center: 5 REHAB
Detractor: 4 ANTI
Detrained: 4 ALIT
  ___ d'etre: 6 RAISON
Detriment: 4 HARM
  ___ de Triomphe: 3 ARC
Detritus: 7 REMAINS
  Cigarette: 3 ASH
  Dryer: 4 LINT
  Volcano: 3 ASH
  ___ de trois: 3 PAS
Detroit
  baseballer: 5 TIGER
  brewery name: 5 STROH
  dud: 5 **EDSEL**
  footballer: 4 LION
  founder: 8 CADILLAC
  labor gp.: 3 UAW
  org.: 3 UAW
  product: 3 CAR 4 AUTO
Deuce: 3 TWO 4 CARD
  beater: 4 **TREY**
  follower: 4 **ADIN**

pair: 4 PIPS
Score after: 4 **ADIN** 5 ADOUT
topper: 4 **TREY**
~, in tennis: 3 TIE
Deucey
lead-in: 4 ACEY
Deut.
Book before: 3 NUM
Deuterium
discoverer: 4 UREY
Deutsch: 6 GERMAN
"Deutschland ___ Alles": 4 UBER
"Deutschland uber ___": 5 ALLES
Deux
follower: 5 TROIS
Pas de ~ section: 6 ADAGIO
plus trois: 4 CINQ
preceder: 3 UNE
___ deux: 5 PASDE
De Valera
land: 4 EIRE
of Ireland: 5 EAMON
Devalue: 7 CHEAPEN
Devastate: 4 RUIN 6 RAVAGE
Devastation: 4 RUIN 5 HAVOC
Develop: 4 GROW 5 ARISE
6 EMERGE EVOLVE
UNFOLD
Begin to: 4 DAWN
into: 6 BECOME
slowly: 6 EVOLVE 7 GESTATE
Starting to: 7 NASCENT
Developed: 6 MATURE
Fully: 4 RIPE
Developer
map: 4 PLAT
site: 3 LOT
Developing: 7 NASCENT
9 INCIPIENT
area: 4 WOMB 8 DARKROOM
Development
Land: 6 CAMERA
phase: 5 STAGE
Place for: 7 SEEDBED
site: 8 PHOTOLAB
Stage of: 5 PHASE
unit: 4 ACRE HOME
Devereux, Robert
earldom: 5 ESSEX

Devers
Runner: 4 GAIL
Deviate: 3 YAW 4 SKEW VARY
VEER
Deviation: 3 YAW 7 ANOMALY
9 ABERRANCE
Course: 3 YAW
Standard ~ symbol: 5 SIGMA
Device: 4 RUSE 6 GADGET
"___ de vie" (brandy): 3 EAU
Devil: 5 DEMON SATAN
dog: 6 MARINE
doing: 4 EVIL
Little: 3 IMP
"Devil and Daniel Webster, The"
author: 5 BENET
Deviled
item: 3 EGG
Devilfish: 5 MANTA
Devilish: 7 SATANIC
look: 4 GRIN
sort: 3 IMP
Devilkin: 3 IMP
DeVille: 3 CAR 4 AUTO
Devil-may-care: 4 RASH
Devil Rays
home: 5 TAMPA
Devil's Island
escapee Belbenoit: 4 RENE
Devious: 3 SLY
More: 5 SLYER
move: 4 PLOY
plan: 5 ANGLE 6 SCHEME
Devise: 6 CREATE
~, as a plot: 5 HATCH
Devitalize: 3 SAP
DeVito
Actor: 5 DANNY
sitcom: 4 TAXI
___ de vivre: 4 JOIE
Devoid: 6 BEREFT
Devon
capital: 6 EXETER
river: 3 EXE
Devonshire
city: 6 EXETER
dad: 5 PATER
river: 3 EXE
seat: 6 EXETER

Devoted: 5 LOYAL 6 ARDENT
Devotee: 3 FAN NUT 7 ACOLYTE
    8 IDOLATER
Devotion: 6 NOVENA
  Blind: 8 IDOLATRY
  Intense: 5 ARDOR
  Object of: 4 IDOL
Devour: 3 EAT 5 EATUP
Devoured: 3 ATE 5 EATEN
Devout: 5 GODLY PIOUS
  petition: 6 ORISON
Devoutness: 5 PIETY
Dew
  Bit of: 4 DROP
  Frozen: 4 HOAR
de Waart
  Conductor: 3 EDO
Dewey
  Donald, to: 4 UNCA
  ~, for one (abbr.): 3 ADM
  ~, to Donald Duck: 6 NEPHEW
Dewey, Thomas
  hometown: 6 OWOSSO
Dewlap: 4 JOWL
de Wolfe
  Decorator: 5 ELSIE
De-wrinkle: 4 IRON
Dewy: 3 WET 4 DAMP
Dewy-eyed: 5 NAIVE
  Get: 4 TEAR
Dexterity: 3 ART 4 EASE 5 CRAFT
    SKILL
  prefix: 4 AMBI
Dexterous: 4 DEFT 5 AGILE
    6 ADROIT
Dextrous
  prefix: 4 AMBI
Dey, Susan
  TV series: 5 LALAW
D flat
  equivalent: 6 CSHARP
DH: 4 ALER
  stat: 3 RBI
  ___ Dhabi: 3 **ABU**
Dharma
  Husband of: 4 GREG
  She played: 5 JENNA
"Dharma & Greg"
  actress Elfman: 5 JENNA

  actress Jenna: 6 ELFMAN
d'honneur
  Affaire: 4 DUEL
  ___ d'hôtel: 6 MAITRE
Dhow: 4 BOAT
  crewman: 4 ARAB
Di-
  doubled: 5 TETRA
Diablo
  He rode: 5 CISCO
Diabolical: 4 EVIL 5 CRUEL
Diacritical
  mark: 5 HACEK TILDE
    6 UMLAUT
Diagnostic
  scanner (abbr.): 3 MRI
  test: 4 SCAN
  tool: 6 CTSCAN 7 TESTKIT
  tool (abbr.): 3 EEG MRI
Diagonal: 4 BIAS
Diagonally: 6 ASLOPE
    11 KITTYCORNER
Diagram: 4 GRID 6 SCHEMA
  Family: 4 TREE
  Genealogy: 4 TREE
  grammatically: 5 PARSE
  Guitar: 5 CHORD
Dial: 4 KNOB
  0 on a ~: 4 OPER
  2 on a ~: 3 ABC
  3 on a ~: 3 DEF
  4 on a ~: 3 GHI
  5 on a ~: 3 JKL
  6 on a ~: 3 MNO
  7 on a ~: 3 PRS
  8 on a ~: 3 TUV
  9 on a ~: 3 WXY
  Dashboard: 4 TACH
  Find on the: 6 TUNETO
  on a dash: 4 TACH
  Radio: 4 KNOB
  sound: 4 TONE
  Top of a: 3 XII
Dialect: 5 ARGOT IDIOM LINGO
    6 PATOIS
Dialogue
  writer: 5 PLATO
Dial-up
  device: 5 MODEM

Diameter
  halves: 5 RADII
  Inside: 4 BORE
  Wire ~ measure: 3 MIL
  ~, in ballistics: 7 CALIBER
Diametrically
  opposed: 5 POLAR
Diamond: 4 CARD 5 SHAPE
  Info: Baseball cue
  arbiter: 3 UMP
  authority: 3 UMP
  bag: 4 BASE
  call: 3 OUT 4 SAFE
  center: 5 MOUND
  club: 3 BAT
  corner: 3 BAG 4 **BASE**
  cover: 4 **TARP**
  data: 4 OUTS 5 STATS
  datum: 5 STEAL
  execs: 3 GMS
  family name: 4 ALOU
  flaw: 5 ERROR
  girl: 3 LIL
  group: 4 NINE
  makeup: 6 CARBON
  number: 4 NINE
  of note: 4 NEIL
  pattern: 6 ARGYLE
  plate: 4 HOME
  protection: 4 TARP
  side: 5 FACET
  Singer: 4 NEIL
  situation: 5 ONEON
  stat: 3 ERA RBI 5 ATBAT
  sultanate: 4 SWAT
  surface: 5 FACET
  Up on the: 5 ATBAT
  weight: 5 CARAT
Diamond ___: 3 LIL
Diamondback: 8 TERRAPIN
Diamondbacks, The
  ~, on scoreboards: 3 ARI
Diamond Head
  locale: 4 **OAHU**
Diamonds: 3 ICE 4 SUIT
  Big name in: 7 DEBEERS
"Diamonds and Rust"
  singer Joan: 4 BAEZ
"Diamonds ___ Forever": 3 ARE

Diamond-shaped
  pattern: 6 ARGYLE
Diana
  Actress: 4 DORS RIGG
  Singer: 4 ROSS
  Swimmer: 4 NYAD
"Diana"
  singer: 4 **ANKA**
Diane
  Actress: 4 LADD 6 KEATON
"Dianetics"
  author Hubbard: 4 LRON
Dianne
  Actress: 5 WIEST
Diaper
  ~, in Britain: 5 NAPPY
Diaphanous: 4 THIN 5 SHEER
Diaphragm
  Camera: 4 IRIS
  Colorful: 4 IRIS
  spasm noise: 3 HIC
Diarist
  French: 3 NIN
  of note: 3 NIN 5 PEPYS
  Palindromic: 3 NIN
Diary: 3 LOG 6 MEMOIR
        7 JOURNAL
  capacity: 4 YEAR
  item: 5 ENTRY
  name: 4 ANNE
  opener: 4 DEAR
  passage: 5 ENTRY
"Diary of ___ Housewife": 4 **AMAD**
Dias
  365 ~: 3 ANO
Diatribe: 4 RANT 6 SCREED
        TIRADE
Diaz de Vivar, Rodrigo: 5 ELCID
DiCaprio
  role: 5 ROMEO
  ~, to friends: 3 LEO
Dice: 5 BONES CUBES
  Loser at the ~ table:
        9 SNAKEEYES
  roll: 5 THROW
  Throw, as: 4 CAST TOSS
  Throw the ~ again: 6 REROLL
Diciembre
  follower: 5 **ENERO**

Dick
  1956 counterpart of ~: 5 ESTES
  Detective: 5 TRACY
  Ex of: 3 LIZ
  Sportscaster: 6 ENBERG
  Tom, ~, or Harry: 4 MALE NAME
  "___ Dick": 4 MOBY
Dick and Jane
  dog: 4 SPOT
Dickens
  alias: 3 BOZ
  boy: 3 TIM 7 TINYTIM
  character: 5 DROOD RUDGE
      URIAH 7 TINYTIM
  character Drood: 5 EDWIN
  character Heep: 5 URIAH
  character Pecksniff: 4 SETH
  character Uriah: 4 HEEP
  clerk: 4 HEEP
  girl: 4 NELL
  pen name: 3 BOZ
  title starter: 5 **ATALE**
  villain: 5 FAGIN
  Went like the: 4 FLEW SPED
      TORE
Dickensian
  clerk: 5 URIAH
  cry: 3 BAH
  lad: 3 TIM
  outburst: 3 BAH
Dicker: 6 HAGGLE
Dickerson
  of football: 4 ERIC
Dickinson: 4 POET
  Actress: 5 **ANGIE**
  Poet: 5 EMILY
Dickinson, Emily: 4 POET
      7 POETESS
  home: 7 AMHERST
Dict.
  entries: 3 WDS
  entry: 3 DEF SYN
  label: 3 ADJ OBS
  listing: 3 SYN
  offering: 3 DEF SYN 4 ETYM
Dictation
  taker: 5 **STENO**
Dictator: 8 AUTOCRAT
  aide: 5 STENO

  problem: 8 EGOMANIA
Dictatorship: 10 ONEMANRULE
Dictionary
  abbr.: 3 OBS VAR
  entry: 4 WORD
  Hi-tech ~ medium: 5 CDROM
  info: 5 USAGE
  listing: 5 ENTRY
  word: 5 ENTRY
  ___ dictum: 6 OBITER
Did
  in: 4 SLEW
  nothing: 3 SAT 5 SATBY
Diddley
  and others: 3 BOS
Diddley, Bo
  hit song: 6 IMAMAN
Diddly: 3 NIL
Diddly-squat: 3 NIL
Diddy, P.
  First name of: 4 SEAN
Didion
  Novelist: 4 JOAN
"Didn't I tell you?": 3 SEE
Dido
  Lover of: 6 AENEAS
  Work in which ~ died: 6 AENEID
Didrikson
  Sportswoman: 4 BABE
"Did you ___?": 4 EVER
"Did You Ever ___ Lassie?": 4 SEEA
"Did you forget about me?":
      4 AHEM
Die: 4 CUBE 6 EXPIRE
  down: 3 EBB 4 WANE 5 **ABATE**
  (out): 5 PETER
Dieciseis
  Half of: 4 OCHO
"Die Fledermaus": 5 OPERA
  composer: 7 STRAUSS
  maid: 5 ADELE
  ___ Diego: 3 SAN
Diehard
  Like ~ fans: 4 AVID
"Die Lorelei"
  poet: 5 HEINE
  ___ diem: 3 PER 5 **CARPE**
"Die Meistersinger"
  soprano: 3 EVA

"___ Dien" (Prince of Wales
     motto): 3 ICH
"Dies ___": 4 **IRAE**
Diesel
 Actor: 3 VIN
Diet: 4 FARE 5 LOFAT NOCAL
     6 LOWCAL
 doctor: 6 ATKINS
 Kind of: 6 NOSALT
     9 SCARSDALE
 Like many ~ foods: 6 NONFAT
 Overdo a: 6 STARVE
 Soft: 3 PAP
 Stable: 4 OATS
 successfully: 4 LOSE
 Word on a ~ product: 4 LITE
 ___ diet: 3 ONA
Dietary
 abbr.: 3 RDA
 concern: 3 FAT
 label: 5 LOFAT
 need: 4 IRON
 ~, in ads: 4 LITE
Diet Coke
 forerunner: 3 TAB
Dieter
 concern: 3 FAT 9 WAISTLINE
 dish: 5 SALAD
 dread: 4 GAIN
 no-no: 3 FAT 6 SWEETS
 of rhyme: 5 SPRAT
 temptation: 5 AROMA
 unit: 7 CALORIE
 word: 4 LITE
Dietetic: 5 LOFAT NOFAT
"___ dieu!": 3 MON
Differ
 suffix: 3 ENT 4 ENCE
Difference
 Make a: 5 ALTER 6 MATTER
     14 CHANGETHEWORLD
 Subtle: 6 NUANCE
 Time: 3 LAG
"___ difference!": 4 SAME
Different: 4 **ELSE** 5 **OTHER**
 In a ~ form: 4 ANEW
 In a ~ manner: 4 ELSE
Differently: 4 ELSE
"Different Read on Life, A"

 magazine: 4 UTNE
Difficult: 4 HARD 6 ORNERY
     TAXING TRYING
     7 LABORED
 duty: 4 ONUS
 journey: 4 TREK
 Make less: 4 EASE
 Not: 4 EASY
 spot: 7 HOTSEAT
 test: 6 ORDEAL
Difficulty: 3 ADO RUB 4 SNAG
 Get with: 3 EKE
 Manage with: 4 COPE
Diffident: 3 SHY
"Diff'rent Strokes"
 actress Charlotte: 3 RAE
 actress Plato: 4 DANA
Diffuse: 6 OSMOSE
DiFranco
 Singer: 3 **ANI**
Dig: 5 DELVE 6 TUNNEL
 a lot: 5 ADORE
 deeply: 5 ADORE
 find: 5 RELIC
 for: 4 SEEK
 fragment: 5 SHARD
 in: 3 **EAT**
 into: 3 EAT
 (into): 5 DELVE
 it: 3 ORE 4 HOLE
 like a pig: 4 ROOT
 this: 3 ORE
 (up): 6 DREDGE
 You can ~ it: 3 **ORE** 4 HOLE
     6 TRENCH
"Dig?": 5 GETIT
Digestive: 6 PEPTIC
 aid: 4 BILE 6 SALIVA
Digger: 5 SPADE 6 TROWEL
 Gold: 5 MINER
Digging: 4 INTO
 tool: 5 SPADE 6 SHOVEL
Diggs
 Actor: 4 TAYE
"Dig in!": 3 **EAT** 7 LETSEAT
Digit
 Binary: 3 ONE
 Hitchhiker's: 5 THUMB
 Largest: 4 NINE

Low: 3 **TOE**
Pedal: 3 TOE
Digital
communication (abbr.): 3 ASL
First ~ computer: 5 ENIAC
Not: 6 ANALOG
readout: 3 LCD
Digitize: 4 SCAN
Digits
ID: 3 SSN
Number with 101: 6 GOOGOL
Dignified: 5 STAID
Stiffly: 7 STILTED
woman: 6 MATRON
Dignify: 7 ENNOBLE
Dignitary: 3 VIP
Church: 7 PRELATE
Foreign: 4 EMIR
Indian: 5 RANEE
Dignity
Amount of: 5 SHRED
Retain some: 8 SAVEFACE
With: 5 NOBLY
Digress: 5 STRAY
15 GOOFFONATANGENT
Digression: 5 ASIDE 7 TANGENT
Digs: 5 ABODE
Campus: 4 DORM
Dirty: 3 STY
Dog's: 6 KENNEL
of twigs: 4 NEST
Pig's: 3 PEN **STY**
Squalid: 4 SLUM
DIII
doubled: 3 MVI
Dik-dik: 8 ANTELOPE
Dike: 5 LEVEE
problem: 4 LEAK
~, Eunomia, and Irene: 5 HORAE
Dilapidated: 5 RATTY 6 SHABBY
8 DECREPIT
dwelling: 5 SHACK 7 RATTRAP
Dilbert
creator: 5 ADAMS
Like: 5 NERDY
Note for: 4 MEMO
"Dilbert"
cartoonist: 5 ADAMS
10 SCOTTADAMS

intern: 4 ASOK
Dilemma: 4 BIND
Dermal: 4 ACNE
Dilettante: 7 AMATEUR
Be a: 6 DABBLE
dabblings: 4 ARTS
Dilettantish: 4 ARTY 5 ARTSY
Diligent
worker: 5 PLIER
Diligently
Work: 3 PLY
Dillinger
Org. that stopped: 3 FBI
Dillon
Actor: 4 MATT
Actress: 7 MELINDA
Dillon, Marshal
portrayer: 6 ARNESS
Dilly: 4 LULU ONER 5 BEAUT
PEACH
Dillydally: 3 LAG 4 IDLE
6 DAWDLE LOITER
Dilute: 4 THIN
Diluted: 4 WEAK 6 WATERY
Not: 4 PURE
Dim: 4 FADE 5 BLEAR UNLIT
6 DARKEN
Become: 4 FADE
DiMaggio
nickname: 13 YANKEECLIPPER
of baseball: 3 DOM JOE
Dime: 4 COIN
A ~ a dozen: 4 RATE
Item shown on a: 5 TORCH
Like a: 4 THIN
Word on a: 3 ONE 7 LIBERTY
Words before: 3 ONA
Dimension: 5 DEPTH WIDTH
The fourth: 4 TIME
Dimensions: 4 SIZE
Dimethyl
sulfate: 5 ESTER
Dimin.
Opposite of: 5 CRESC
Diminish: 3 EBB 4 BATE FADE
WANE 5 ABATE 6 LESSEN
RECEDE
Diminished
by: 4 LESS 5 MINUS

Diminutive: 3 WEE **5** SMALL
TEENY **6** PETITE TEENSY
Comics: **3** LIL
Dogpatch: **3** LIL
suffix: **3** CLE INO ULA **ULE**
4 ETTA **ETTE** LING
Dimmer: 8 RHEOSTAT
Dimwit: 4 BOZO DOLT SIMP
5 IDIOT STUPE **6** STOOGE
Din: 4 ROAR **5 NOISE 7** CLATTER
Den: **4** ROAR
"___ **Din": 5** GUNGA
Dinah
Singer: **5** SHORE
"___ **Dinah" (Frankie Avalon hit):**
4 DEDE
Dinars
100 ~: **4** RIAL
spender: **5** IRANI IRAQI
Dine: 3 EAT **SUP**
at home: **5 EATIN**
Wine and: **3** WOO **4** FETE
6 REGALE
Dined: 3 ATE **5** ATEIN
Diner: 3 CAR **5** EATER **6** EATERY
card: **4** MENU
cupful: **3** JOE
dish: **4** HASH
display: **4** PIES
Down, at a: **7** ONTOAST
employee: **7** FRYCOOK
handout: **4** MENU
hodgepodge: **4** HASH
On toast, at a: **4** DOWN
order: **3 BLT 6** OMELET
sandwich: **3** BLT
side dish: **4** SLAW
sign: **4 EATS 7** EATHERE
Sitcom: **4** MELS
Sitcom ~ owner: **3** MEL
TV: **4** MELS
TV ~ owner: **3** MEL
Dinero: 4 GELT **5** MOOLA PESOS
6 MOOLAH
Bit of: **4** PESO
Dines
at home: **6** EATSIN
Dinesen
Author: **4 ISAK**

Real name of: **6** BLIXEN
Dinette
spot: **4** NOOK
Ding: 4 DENT
Ding-a-___ : 4 LING
Dingbat: 5 IDIOT NINNY
Dinghy: 4 BOAT
need: **3** OAR
propeller: **3** OAR
___ Dinh Diem: 3 NGO
Dining
Like patio: **8** ALFRESCO
option: **8** ALACARTE
"___ **Dinka Doo": 4** INKA
Dinner: 4 MEAL
and a movie: **4** DATE
Ceremonial: **5** SEDER
course: **4** SOUP **5** SALAD
6 ENTREE **7** DESSERT
Had: **3** ATE
Had ~ at home: **5** ATEIN
Have: **3** EAT SUP
Have ~ at home: **5** EATIN
jacket: **6** TUXEDO
Offers for: **8** SERVESUP
Pay for: **5** TREAT
Point at the ~ table: **4** TINE
Private: **4** MESS
Rude ~ guest: **7** REACHER
Served ~ to: **3** FED
Dinnerware: 5 CHINA **6** PLATES
Piece of: **5** PLATE
Dinning, Mark
hit song: **9** TEENANGEL
Dino
Master of: **4** FRED
tail: **4** SAUR
~, to Fred: **3** PET
Dinosaur: 5 RELIC **7** HASBEEN
Frightening: **4** TREX
Tall: **4** TREX
Dinsdale, Shirley
award: **4** EMMY
Dinsmore
of children's literature: **5** ELSIE
Dinty Moore
product: **4** STEW
Diocese
head: **6** BISHOP

Diogenes: 5 CYNIC 6 SEEKER
Dion
  Singer: 6 CELINE
Dion and the Belmonts
  hit song: 10 NOONEKNOWS
    15 ATEENAGERINLOVE
Dionne
  kid: 5 QUINT
  Where the ~ quints were born:
    7 ONTARIO
Dionysus
  attendant: 5 SATYR
  Bride of: 7 ARIADNE
  Mother of: 6 SEMELE
  Priestess of: 6 MAENAD
Dior
  creation: 5 ALINE
Dip: 3 SAG
  Chip: 5 SALSA
  Go for a: 4 SWIM
  into coffee: 4 DUNK
  Zesty: 5 SALSA
Diphthong: 7 PHONEME
Diploma
  (abbr.): 4 CERT
  holder: 4 GRAD
  word: 3 CUM 5 LAUDE MAGNA
    SUMMA
Diplomacy: 4 TACT
  breakdown: 4 RIFT
  Root of: 5 ELIHU
Diplomatic
  agent: 5 ENVOY
  etiquette: 8 PROTOCOL
  goal: 7 ENTENTE
  representative: 5 ENVOY
  trait: 4 TACT
  woe: 4 RIFT
Dipper
  Big: 5 LADLE
  Skinny: 3 EEL
  unit: 4 STAR
Dipsomaniac: 3 SOT
Dipstick: 3 ROD
  word: 3 ADD
Dir.: 3 ENE ESE NNE NNW SSE
    SSW WNW WSW
Dire
  fate: 4 DOOM

In ~ straits: 5 NEEDY
___ dire: 4 VOIR
Direct: 5 ORDER REFER **STEER**
  6 HEADON 7 OVERSEE
  15 STRAIGHTFORWARD
  elsewhere: 5 REFER
  ending: 3 IVE
  route: 7 BEELINE
Directed: 3 LED RAN 4 BADE
  against a thing: 5 INREM
  at: 6 SENTTO
  Do as: 4 OBEY
  skyward: 6 UPCAST
"___ directed": 5 USEAS
Direction: 4 PATH 5 ROUTE
  (abbr.): 3 ENE ESE NNE NNW
    SSE SSW WNW WSW
  Change: 4 VEER
  Chef's: 4 STIR
  Cookbook: 4 HEAT STIR
    5 PUREE
  Dawn's: 4 EAST
  General: 5 TREND
  German: 3 OST
  In the ~ of: 6 TOWARD
  Nautical: 3 AFT 4 ALEE
    5 ABEAM APORT
  Paint can: 4 STIR
  Point in the right: 6 ORIENT
  Recipe: 4 **STIR** 6 STIRIN
  Sailor's: 4 ALEE
  Script: 5 ENTER
  Stage: 4 EXIT 5 **ENTER**
  Sunrise: 4 **EAST**
  Sunset: 4 WEST
  Sunup: 4 EAST
  Whaler's: 4 THAR
Directional
  prefix: 3 UNI
  suffix: 3 **ERN**
Directions
  In need of: 4 LOST
  It follows: 3 ERN
Directive: 5 ORDER 6 BEHEST
  7 PRECEPT
  Culinary: 4 STIR
  Drill: 6 ATEASE
  Memo: 4 ASAP
  Recipe: 4 STIR

Directly: 3 DUE 4 ANON
    8 ONEONONE
  Go: 7 BEELINE
  opposed: 8 TOETOTOE
Direct-mail
  sticker: 3 YES
Director: 4 BOSS
  bane: 3 HAM
  cry: 3 **CUT** 6 ACTION
  Personnel: 5 HIRER
  prerogative: 5 RECUT 6 RETAKE
  Traffic: 4 CONE 5 ARROW
Directory: 4 LIST
  contents: 5 NAMES
Dirigible: 5 BLIMP 8 AEROSTAT
  Like a: 5 RIGID
  parts: 5 KEELS
Dirk: 6 DAGGER
  Use a: 4 STAB
Dirksen
  Senator: 7 EVERETT
Dirndl: 5 SKIRT
Dirt: 4 INFO SMUT 5 FILTH
    GRIME PORNO
  bike cousin: 3 ATV
  Dish the: 6 GOSSIP
  Flue: 4 SOOT
  Lump of: 4 CLOD
  Pay: 3 **ORE**
  road feature: 3 RUT
  Stubborn: 5 GRIME
  Treat like: 5 ABUSE
Dirtbag: 3 CAD
Dirty: 4 LEWD SOIL 6 SOILED
    7 POLLUTE UNCLEAN
  air: 4 SMOG
  dealing: 8 FOULPLAY
  digs: 3 STY
  dog: 3 CAD CUR RAT
  Get: 4 SOIL
  look: 4 LEER 5 GLARE
  Make: 4 SOIL
  money: 4 PELF
  rat: 5 LOUSE 7 SOANDSO
"Dirty"
  activity: 4 POOL
  dish: 4 RICE
"Dirty Dancing"
  star: 6 SWAYZE

Dirty Harry
  employer (abbr.): 4 SFPD
  portrayer: 5 CLINT
Dis: 4 SASS SLAM 6 INSULT
  Not: 3 DAT
Disable: 4 MAIM
Disabled
  On the ~ list: 4 HURT
  ___ disadvantage: 3 ATA
Disadvantaged: 5 NEEDY
Disagree: 5 CLASH 6 DIFFER
Disagreeable: 4 SOUR UGLY
    5 TESTY
  burden: 4 ONUS
  people: 5 PILLS
Disagreeing: 6 ATODDS
Disagreement: 3 ROW 4 SPAT
  In: 6 ATODDS
Disallow: 3 BAN 4 DENY
Disappear: 6 PERISH VANISH
  gradually: 4 FADE
  into thin air: 9 EVAPORATE
  Some things ~ into it:
    7 THINAIR
Disappearance
  Sound of: 4 POOF
Disappearing
  sea: 4 ARAL
  transports: 3 ELS
Disappoint: 7 LETDOWN
Disappointment: 7 LETDOWN
  Sound of: 3 TSK
  Sounds of: 3 AWS
Disapproval
  Look of: 5 FROWN
  One showing: 6 CHIDER
  Shout of: 3 BOO
  Sound of: 3 **TSK** TUT 6 TUTTUT
    9 RASPBERRY
  Voice ~ of: 6 HISSAT
Disapproving
  sound: 3 TSK TUT
Disarrange: 4 MUSS 7 UNSTACK
Disarray: 4 MESS
  In: 5 MESSY 7 CHAOTIC
Disassemble: 5 UNRIG
Disaster: 6 FIASCO 7 DEBACLE
    8 CALAMITY
  Environmental: 7 ECOCIDE

relief org.: 4 FEMA
Small: 6 MISHAP
Disastrous: 4 DIRE 5 FATAL
Disavow: 4 DENY
Disburden: 4 EASE
Disburse: 5 SPEND
Discard: 5 SCRAP
Corn eater's: 3 COB
Delicious: 4 CORE
Discarded: 7 OFFCAST
    9 TOSSEDOUT
Discern: 3 SEE 4 ESPY TELL
Discerning: 4 SAGE 7 SAPIENT
Discernment: 3 EYE 5 TASTE
Musical: 3 EAR
Discharge: 4 **EMIT** FIRE SPEW
    5 **EGEST** LETGO
    7 RELEASE 8 EMISSION
Brit's: 5 DEMOB
letters: 3 TNT
Disciple: 7 APOSTLE
query: 5 ISITI
Disciplinarian
Like a: 5 STERN
reading: 7 RIOTACT
Discipline: 5 RIGOR
Dojo: 6 KARATE
Eastern: 3 ZEN 4 YOGA
Exercise: 4 YOGA
Hindu: 4 YOGA
Meditative: 3 ZEN
Tranquil: 4 YOGA
Disclaimer: 8 NEGATION
Tag: 4 ASIS
Disclose: 6 IMPART REVEAL
    7 CONFIDE
Disco
dancer type: 4 GOGO
fixture: 6 STROBE
hit song: 4 YMCA
light: 6 STROBE
musical style: 6 TECHNO
Phrase in ~ names: 5 AGOGO
Rick of: 4 DEES
**Disco ___ (character on "The
    Simpsons"):** 3 STU
Discolor: 5 STAIN
Discombobulate: 5 ADDLE UPSET
Discombobulated: 5 ATSEA

Discomfit: 4 FAZE 5 ABASH
    UPSET
Discomfort: 4 ACHE 6 UNEASE
    7 MALAISE
Discompose: 5 ABASH
    7 PERTURB
Disconcert: 4 **FAZE** 5 **ABASH**
Disconnect: 6 UNPLUG
Discontinue: 4 DROP QUIT STOP
    5 **CEASE** SEVER
    8 SURCEASE
Discord: 6 STRIFE
Goddess of: 4 **ERIS**
Norse god of: 4 LOKI
Discordant: 4 AJAR
Discordia
counterpart: 4 ERIS
Discotheque
effect: 6 STROBE
phrase: 5 AGOGO
Discount: 6 IGNORE REBATE
label abbr.: 3 IRR
rack abbr.: 3 IRR 5 IRREG
With a ~ of: 4 LESS
Words before: 3 ATA
Discounted: 4 LESS 6 ONSALE
by: 4 LESS
Some ~ items: 5 DEMOS
Discourage: 5 DETER
Discouraging
word: 3 BAH TUT
words: 3 NOS 4 NOES
Discourse
Lengthy: 6 SCREED
Discourteous: 4 RUDE
Discover: 5 LEARN 6 DETECT
    7 FINDOUT UNEARTH
by chance: 5 HITON
~, as an idea: 5 HITON
Discovered: 5 FOUND 6 LEARNT
Discoverer
cry: 3 AHA OHO
Discovery: 4 FIND
Cry of: 3 AHA OHO 6 EUREKA
Dawn: 3 DEW
Detective's: 4 CLUE
Dig: 5 RELIC
gp.: 4 NASA
Pollster's: 5 TREND

Valuable: **5** TROVE
Discovery Channel
  subj.: **3** SCI
Discredit: 5 DECRY TAINT
    6 DEFAME **8** TEARDOWN
Discreet: 7 POLITIC
Discrete: 5 APART
  part: **4** UNIT
  unit: **6** ENTITY
Discretion: 4 TACT **5** SAYSO
Discriminating
  person: **6** AGEIST
Discrimination: 5 TASTE
  basis: **4** RACE
  Type of: **6** AGEISM SEXISM
  watchdog (abbr.): **4** EEOC
Discriminator: 6 AGEIST SEXIST
Discs: 3 LPS
Discus
  champ Al: **6** OERTER
Discuss: 6 GOINTO **7** GETINTO
  again: **6** REHASH
  in detail: **7** HASHOUT
  pros and cons: **6** DEBATE
  ~, with "out": **4** HASH
Discussion: 7 PALAVER
  group: **5** **PANEL**
  Informal: **10** RAPSESSION
        11 BULLSESSION
  Online: **4** CHAT
  panel: **5** FORUM
  Under: **7** ATISSUE
  venue: **5** FORUM
Disdain: 5 SCORN **8** CONTEMPT
  Feigned: **10** SOURGRAPES
  Look of: **5** SNEER
  Reject with: **5** SPURN
  Show: **5** SCORN SNEER
  Word of: **4** POOH
Disease
  Grass: **5** ERGOT
  Teen: **4** MONO
Disenchanted
  Become: **4** SOUR
Disencumber: 3 **RID**
Disentangle: 5 RAVEL **6** UNKNOT
        7 UNSNARL
Disfigure: 3 MAR **4** MAIM
Disgorge: 4 SPEW

Disgrace: 5 ODIUM SHAME
Disgruntled: 4 SORE
  sound: **3** UGH
Disguise: 4 MASK **5** CLOAK
Disguised: 9 INCOGNITO
  ~, for short: **5** INCOG
Disgust: 6 NAUSEA OFFEND
        SICKEN
  Cry of: **3** BAH FIE PAH UGH
  Sound of: **3** UGH
Disgusted: 5 FEDUP
Disgusting: 4 ICKY **5** GROSS
Dish: 5 CUTEY CUTIE PLATE
  alternative: **5** CABLE
        7 ANTENNA
  Beef: **4** STEW
  Brunch: **6** OMELET
  Cabbage: **4** SLAW
  Cheese: **7** RAREBIT
  Deep: **6** TUREEN
  Diner: **4** HASH
  Dixie: **5** GRITS
  Dover: **4** SOLE
  Egg: **6** OMELET
  Fish: **3** COD **4** HAKE SOLE
        5 SCROD
  Folded: **6** OMELET
  for culture: **5** PETRI
  Garlicky: **6** SCAMPI
  Hawaiian: **3** POI
  Islands: **3** POI
  Japanese: **5** SUSHI
  Jellied: **5** ASPIC
  Kind of: **5** PETRI
  Leftovers: **4** HASH
  Luau: **3** **POI**
  Main: **6** ENTREE
  manufacturer: **3** RCA
  Meat: **4** STEW **7** ROULADE
  name: **5** PETRI
  Picnic: **4** SLAW
  Rice: **5** **PILAF** **6** PAELLA
  Russian: **5** BLINI
  Scottish: **6** HAGGIS
  Shrimp: **6** SCAMPI
  Side: **4** DISH
  Slung: **4** HASH
  Southern: **5** GRITS
  Spanish: **6** PAELLA

Taro: **3** POI
Tasty: **5** VIAND
___ **dish: 5** PETRI
Dishearten: 5 DAUNT **6** DEJECT
    7 DEPRESS
Dishes
  Company: **5** CHINA
  Help with the: **3** DRY **4** WIPE
  List of: **4** MENU
Dishevel: 6 TOUSLE
Disheveled: 5 MESSY **6** RAGTAG
    7 UNKEMPT
Dishonest
  Be ~ with: **5** LIETO
  sort: **5** SNEAK
  Was ~ with: **6** LIEDTO
Dishonesty
  Suspect: **9** SMELLARAT
Dishonor: 5 ABASE SHAME
    STAIN TAINT
  Trace of: **5** TAINT
Dishwasher
  cycle: **5** RINSE
Dishwater
  Dull as: **4** BLAH DRAB
  Like: **4** DULL **5** SUDSY
Disinclined: 5 LOATH **6** __AVERSE__
Disinfectant: 5 LYSOL
Disinfest: 5 DERAT
Disk
  Clear, as a: **5** ERASE
  contents: **4** DATA
  function: **7** STORAGE
  On: **6** STORED
  Prepare a ~ for writing:
    6 FORMAT
  suffix: **4** ETTE
  Thrown: **7** FRISBEE
Dislike
  Intense: **5** ODIUM **6** HATRED
  More than: **4** HATE **5** ABHOR
    6 DETEST LOATHE
Disloyal: 5 FALSE **6** UNTRUE
Dismal: 4 GRIM **5** AWFUL SORRY
    6 DREARY
Dismay: 4 FAZE **5** ALARM APPAL
    6 APPALL
  Cries of: **3** OYS
  Cry of: **4** ALAS OHNO

Words of: **4** OHNO **5** OYVEY
Dismiss: 3 AXE **4** SACK **5** LETGO
  derisively: **7** SNEERAT
  lightly: **8** POOHPOOH
  unceremoniously: **4** BOOT
Dismounted: 4 __ALIT__
Disney
  1940 ~ film: **8** FANTASIA
  1955 ~ film:
    15 LADYANDTHETRAMP
  1957 ~ film: **9** OLDYELLER
  1982 ~ film: **4** TRON
  1998 ~ film: **5** MULAN
  acquisition: **3** ABC
  Animator: **4** WALT
  collectible: **3** CEL
  deer: **3** ENA **5** BAMBI
  dog: **4** __LADY__ **5** PLUTO SCAMP
  duck: **6** __DONALD__
  dwarf: **3** DOC
  dwarfs: **6** SEPTET
  fish: **5** NEMO
  Former ~ head: **6** EISNER
  frame: **3** CEL
  leader: **4** EURO
  lioness: **4** NALA
  mermaid: **5** ARIEL
  middle name: **5** ELIAS
  musical: **4** AIDA
  parrot: **4** IAGO
  prefix: **4** EURO
  sci-fi film: **4** TRON
Disney, Walt
  Middle name of: **5** ELIAS
Disneyland
  attraction: **4** RIDE
  locale: **7** ANAHEIM
  transport: **8** MONORAIL
Disney World
  anagram: **5** EPCOT
  attraction: **4** RIDE **5** EPCOT
  city: **7** ORLANDO
  transport: **4** TRAM
Disobedience:
    15 INSUBORDINATION
Disorder: 4 MESS **5** CHAOS
    HAVOC **6** MAYHEM
  Civil: **4** RIOT
  Sleep: **5** APNEA

Utter: 5 CHAOS
Disordered: 5 MESSY 6 UNTIDY
Disorderly: 6 UNRULY UNTIDY
      7 INAMESS
  crowd: 3 MOB
  disturbance: 6 FRACAS
  do: 3 MOP
  group: 3 MOB
Disoriented: 4 LOST
Disown: 8 RENOUNCE
Disparage: 4 SLUR 5 DECRY
      8 BADMOUTH
Disparaging: 5 SNIDE
  comment: 4 SLUR
Disparity: 3 GAP
Dispatch: 4 **SEND** SHIP 5 HASTE
  boat: 5 **AVISO**
  identifier: 8 DATELINE
  ~, as a dragon: 4 SLAY
Dispatched: 4 **SENT** 7 SENTOUT
Dispensable
  candy: 3 PEZ
Dispense: 5 ALLOT 7 DOLEOUT
      METEOUT
  ~, with "out": 4 METE
Dispenser
  candy: 3 **PEZ**
  Cash: 3 ATM
  Coffee: 3 URN
  Dough: 3 ATM
Disperse: 5 STREW 6 FANOUT
      7 SCATTER
Disperser
  Light: 5 PRISM
Dispirit: 5 UNMAN
Displace: 4 BUMP 6 UPROOT
Displaced
  person: 5 EXILE 6 EMIGRE
Display: 3 AIR 4 SHOW 5 SPORT
      6 EVINCE
  Calc.: 3 LCD
  case: 7 ETAGERE
  Dazzling: 5 ECLAT
  Deli: 5 MEATS
  Dizzying: 5 OPART
  Elaborate: 5 ECLAT
  Embarrassing: 5 SCENE
  Gallery: 3 ART
  Historical: 7 DIORAMA

  Met: 3 ART
  Museum: 3 ART
  Ostentatious: 4 POMP RITZ
  Showy: 5 **ECLAT**
  Wide-ranging: 7 PANOPLY
  Wild: 4 RIOT
Displeased
  look: 5 FROWN
  with: 5 MADAT
Displeasure: 7 UMBRAGE
  Look of: 5 SCOWL
  Show: 3 BOO 4 HISS SULK
Disposable
  Some are: 7 INCOMES
Disposal
  button: 5 RESET
  item: 3 ORT
Disposed: 3 APT 5 GIVEN PRONE
Disposition: 4 BENT MOOD
      6 NATURE 8 ATTITUDE
Dispossess: 4 OUST 5 EVICT
Disprove: 5 REBUT
Dispute: 3 ROW 4 DENY SPAR
      SPAT 5 ARGUE 7 QUARREL
  handler: 8 MEDIATOR
  Matter of: 5 ISSUE
Disqualify: 6 RECUSE
Disquiet: 4 ROIL 6 UNEASE
      UNREST
Disraeli: 4 EARL TORY
"Disraeli"
  actor George: 6 ARLISS
Disregard: 4 OMIT SKIP
      6 IGNORE 8 SHRUGOFF
Disreputable: 5 SEAMY SEEDY
      SHADY SLIMY
  group: 8 RIFFRAFF
  newspaper: 3 RAG
Disrepute: 5 ODIUM
Disrespect: 4 SASS 7 IMPIETY
      9 INSOLENCE
  Show ~ to: 4 SASS
Disrobe: 4 PEEL 7 UNDRESS
Dissect: 5 PARSE
Disseminate: 3 SOW 5 STREW
      6 EFFUSE
Dissent
  Vote of: 3 NAY
  Without: 5 ASONE

Dissenter: 4 ANTI
  Religious: 7 HERETIC
  word: 3 NAY
Dissenting
  vote: 3 NAY
  votes: 3 NOS
Dissertation: 6 THESIS
      8 TREATISE
Dissertations: 6 THESES
Disservice: 4 HARM
Dissimilar: 6 UNLIKE
Dissolute
  man: 4 ROUE
Dissolve: 4 MELT 5 SEVER
  ~, as cells: 4 LYSE
Dissonant
  Not: 5 TONAL
Dissuade: 5 DETER
Distance
  Astronomical: 6 PARSEC
  At a: 3 FAR 4 **AFAR**
  Derby: 5 METRE
  Dueler's: 4 PACE
  From a: 4 AFAR
  Go the: 4 LAST
  In the: 3 YON 4 AFAR
  Long ~ letters: 3 ATT MCI
  Off in the: 4 AFAR
  Pool: 3 LAP
  Race: 4 MILE
  runner: 5 MILER
  Short: 4 STEP
    11 STONESTHROW
Distant: 3 **FAR** ICY 4 AFAR
    5 ALOOF 6 REMOTE
  beginning: 4 EQUI
  friends: 7 PENPALS
  prefix: 4 TELE
  Prefix with: 4 EQUI
Distaste: 8 AVERSION
  Cry of: 3 FIE UGH
Distasteful: 4 ICKY 8 UNSAVORY
Distillery
  ingredient: 4 MALT
  tank: 3 VAT
Distinct: 8 SEPARATE
  period: 3 ERA
  style: 5 IDIOM
Distinction: 4 NOTE

  Subtle: 6 NUANCE
  Woman of: 4 DAME
Distinctive
  air: 4 AURA
  atmosphere: 4 AURA
  doctrine: 3 ISM
  flavor: 4 TANG
  manner: 5 STYLE
  period: 3 ERA 5 EPOCH
  quality: 4 AURA
  style: 4 ELAN
  time: 3 ERA
Distinguish: 8 SETAPART
Distinguished: 5 GREAT
    6 OFNOTE 7 EMINENT
    NOTABLE 8 SETAPART
Distort: 4 BEND **SKEW** WARP
    5 COLOR GNARL
Distress: 3 AIL WOE 4 PAIN
    5 ANGST 6 UNEASE
  call: 3 SOS
  Cry of: 4 YOWL
  In: 6 PAINED
  Muscular: 4 ACHE
  Sighs of: 3 OHS
  signal: 3 **SOS** 4 ACHE 5 FLARE
  Sound of: 5 GRUNT
  Woman in: 6 DAMSEL
Distribute: 4 DOLE METE
    5 ALLOT 7 DOLEOUT
    HANDOUT
  anew: 6 REDEAL
  cards: 4 DEAL
  ~, with "out": 4 METE
Distributed: 5 DEALT
District: 4 AREA ZONE
  Theater: 6 **RIALTO**
  Voting: 5 WARDS
Distrustful: 5 LEERY
Disturb: 4 RILE ROIL
  Do not: 5 LETBE
Disturbance: 5 MELEE SCENE
    6 POTHER
  Civil: 4 RIOT
  Disorderly: 6 FRACAS
Disturbed: 5 UPSET 6 AWOKEN
  state: 4 SNIT
Disuse
  Fall into: 5 LAPSE

Sign of: 4 RUST
Dit
partner: 3 DAH
Ditch: 4 LOSE 6 TRENCH
digger: 5 SPADE
that divides: 9 SUNKFENCE
Watery: 4 MOAT
Dither: 4 STEW
Dithers
Mrs.: 4 **CORA**
~, to Bumstead: 4 BOSS
"Ditto": 4 SAME 5 METOO SODOI
8 SAMEHERE
Ditty: 4 LILT TUNE
December: 4 NOEL 5 CAROL
Ditz: 7 AIRHEAD
Diurnal: 5 DAILY
Diva
delivery: 4 ARIA
problem: 3 EGO
solo: 4 **ARIA**
song: 4 ARIA
Divan: 4 SOFA
Backless: 7 OTTOMAN
Dive: 6 PLUNGE
Hollywood: 5 STUNT
Splashy: 9 BELLYFLOP
Takes a: 5 SCUBA
Type of: 4 SWAN
Diver
acronym: 5 SCUBA
Black-and-white: 3 AUK
concern: 5 BENDS
device: 5 SCUBA
Flying: 3 AUK
Kind of: 7 DEEPSEA
Navy: 4 SEAL
Ocean: 3 ERN
Skilled: 4 LOON
wear: 7 WETSUIT
Divergence: 3 GAP
Diverse: 6 MOTLEY VARIED
Diversify: 4 VARY 9 VARIEGATE
Diversion: 3 TOY 4 RUSE 5 SPORT
7 PASTIME 9 AMUSEMENT
Divert: 5 AMUSE SHUNT
Divest: 3 RID
Divide: 4 REND
equally: 5 HALVE

in threes: 7 TRISECT
up: 5 ALLOT
Divided: 4 TORN 5 CLEFT INTWO
country: 5 KOREA
~, as a highway: 5 LANED
Dividend: 6 PAYOUT
Divider
Continent: 5 OCEAN
Court: 3 **NET**
Highway: 6 MEDIAN
Notebook: 3 TAB
Room: 4 WALL
Tennis: 3 NET
Theater: 5 AISLE
word: 4 INTO
Dividers
Nasal: 5 SEPTA
Dividing
It multiplies by: 6 AMOEBA
membranes: 5 SEPTA
walls: 5 SEPTA
word: 4 INTO
Divination: 4 OMEN 6 AUGURY
Book of: 6 ICHING
deck: 5 TAROT
practitioner: 4 SEER
Divine
entertainer: 5 MISSM
food: 5 MANNA
hunter: 5 DIANA
revelation: 6 ORACLE
"Divine Comedy, The"
opening: 7 INFERNO
poet: 5 DANTE
"Divine Miss M, The": 5 BETTE
Diviner
deck: 5 TAROT
Diving
acronym: 5 SCUBA
bird: 3 **AUK** 4 **LOON** 5 **GREBE**
duck: 4 SMEW 6 SCOTER
position: 4 PIKE TUCK
seabird: 3 AUK 6 PETREL
Divining
one: 6 DOWSER
tool: 3 ROD
Use a ~ rod: 5 **DOWSE**
Divisible
by two: 4 EVEN

Division: 6 SCHISM SECTOR
      7 SEGMENT
  Cell: 7 MITOSIS
  Condo: 4 **UNIT**
  Corporate: 5 SALES
  Farm: 4 ACRE
  Game: 4 HALF
  Hair: 4 PART
  Like some: 4 LONG
  Match: 3 SET
  Opera: 3 ACT
  Play: 3 ACT
  Poem: 5 CANTO
  Pool: 4 LANE
  preposition: 4 INTO
  result: 8 QUOTIENT
  School: 5 GRADE
  Social: 5 CASTE
  Timeline: 3 ERA
  word: 4 **INTO**
Divorce
  mecca: 4 RENO
Divorced
  couple: 4 EXES
"___ Divorcee, The": 3 GAY
Divorcees: 4 EXES
Divorces
  Like some: 5 MESSY 7 NOFAULT
Divulge: 4 TELL 5 LETON SPILL
      6 EXPOSE LETOUT
      REVEAL
Divulged: 4 TOLD
Divvy
  up: 5 ALLOT SHARE 6 RATION
Dix
  follower: 4 ONZE
  Painter: 4 OTTO
Dixie: 9 DEEPSOUTH
  bread: 4 PONE
  dessert: 8 PECANPIE
  dish: 5 GRITS
  drink: 5 JULEP
  letters: 3 CSA
  pronoun: 4 YALL
  soldier: 3 REB
  suffix: 4 CRAT
  talk: 5 DRAWL
"Dixie"
  composer: 6 EMMETT

Dixie Chicks, The: 4 TRIO
Dixieland
  clarinetist: 12 PETEFOUNTAIN
  favorite: 8 TIGERRAG
  trumpeter Al: 4 HIRT
  ___ dixit: 4 **IPSE**
Dixon, Jeane
  supposed gift: 3 ESP
Dizzy: 5 AREEL
  Feel: 8 SEESTARS
  of baseball: 4 DEAN
Dizzying
  designs: 5 **OPART**
  display: 5 OPART
  pictures: 5 OPART
DJ
  assortment: 3 CDS LPS
  gear: 3 AMP
DJIA
  Part of: 3 DOW
Djibouti
  language: 6 SOMALI
  neighbor: 7 ERITREA
DKNY
  Part of: 5 DONNA
Dmitri
  denial: 4 NYET
DMV
  datum: 3 DOB
  document: 3 LIC
  offering: 7 EYETEST
DMZ
  Part of: 4 ZONE
DNA
  component: 7 ADENINE
  holder: 4 GENE
  source: 8 GENEPOOL
  structure: 4 GENE 5 HELIX
Dnieper
  Capital on the: 4 KIEV
Do: 4 COIF NOTE PERM 5 PARTY
      6 SOIREE 7 HAIRCUT
  1960s ~: 4 AFRO
  as told: 4 OBEY
  away with: 5 ERASE 7 ABOLISH
  Big: 4 **AFRO** BASH FETE GALA
  Bushy: 4 **AFRO**
  Can't ~ without: 4 NEED
      5 NEEDS

doer: 7 STYLIST
followers: 4 REMI
in: 4 KILL **SLAY**
nothing: 4 IDLE LAZE LOAF
over: 7 ITERATE
poorly: 3 AIL
well: 7 PROSPER
without: 5 FORGO
"Do ___!": 4 TELL
Do-___: 4 REMI 5 ORDIE
Dobbin
  command: 4 WHOA
  home: 6 STABLE
  morsel: 3 OAT
  pulls one: 4 SHAY
  tow: 4 SHAY
Dobbs
  of CNN: 3 LOU
Doberman
  boss: 5 BILKO
  doc: 3 VET
  ___ doble: 4 PASO
Doc: 5 MEDIC 6 MEDICO
  bloc: 3 **AMA**
  Dog: 3 VET
  Friend of: 5 WYATT
  Future ~ exam: 4 MCAT
Docile: 4 MEEK TAME
Dock: 4 PIER QUAY 5 WHARF
  Tie up at the: 4 MOOR
  Work on the: 4 LADE
Docked
  Not: 4 ASEA
Dockers
  org.: 3 ILA
Dockworkers
  org.: 3 **ILA**
Docs: 3 GPS MDS
  Delivery: 3 OBS
  org.: 3 AMA
Doctor: 5 ALTER CURER MEDIC
      TREAT 6 HEALER
  aid: 5 PAGER
  Available, as a: 6 ONCALL
  charge: 3 FEE
  directive: 5 SAYAH
  interruption: 4 PAGE
  Kind of: 4 SPIN
  New: 6 INTERN

Nonresident: 6 EXTERN
order: 4 REST TEST 5 REHAB
      SAYAH
prescription: 4 DOSE
Sci-fi: 3 WHO
Spin: 5 PRMAN
TV: 4 PHIL
Word to a: 3 AAH
Doctorate
  dissertations: 6 THESES
  hurdle: 5 ORALS 8 ORALEXAM
Doctorow
  novel: 7 RAGTIME
Doctors
  make them: 6 ROUNDS
  org.: 3 **AMA**
  Spin: 5 PRMEN
"Doctor Zhivago"
  heroine: 4 LARA
Doctrine: 3 **ISM** 5 CREDO CREED
      DOGMA **TENET**
  doubter: 7 HERETIC
  Prescribed: 5 DOGMA
  Religious: 5 TENET
  Secret: 6 CABALA
Document
  Computer: 4 FILE
  end: 3 ARY
  Legal: 4 DEED WRIT
  Owner's: 4 DEED 5 TITLE
  subsection: 7 ARTICLE
  Title: 4 DEED
Documentation: 6 PAPERS
Doddering: 5 ANILE 6 SENILE
Dodecanese Islands
  Largest of the: 6 RHODES
Dodge: 4 RUSE 5 AVOID ELUDE
      EVADE SHIRK
  compact: 4 NEON
  model: 4 DART OMNI 5 ARIES
  Old: 4 DART **OMNI** 5 ARIES
  truck: 3 RAM
Dodge City
  lawman: 4 EARP
Dodger
  Artful: 5 REESE 6 EVADER
  Like a certain: 6 ARTFUL
"Do ___ Diddy Diddy": 3 WAH
Dodo: 4 BIRD

Like the: 7 EXTINCT
Doe: 3 SHE 4 DEER
  beau: 4 STAG
  follower in song: 5 ADEER
  mate: 4 STAG
"Doe, ___ ...": 5 ADEER
Doer
  of dos: 7 STYLIST
  suffix: 3 IST
  ~, in crime-speak: 4 PERP
Does: 4 DEER
  ___ d'oeuvres: 4 HORS
Dog: 3 PET 5 POOCH 6 HARASS
    PURSUE
  Bad: 5 BITER
  bane: 4 FLEA LICE 5 FLEAS
  bark: 3 YIP
  biter: 4 FLEA
  Cartoon: 3 **REN** 4 ODIE
  collar attachment: 5 IDTAG
  Comics: 4 ODIE 5 SNERT
  command: 3 SIC SIT 4 COME
    STAY 5 SICEM
  days mo.: 3 AUG
  Devil: 6 MARINE
  Dirty: 3 CUR
  doc: 3 **VET**
  Drink like a: 3 LAP 5 LAPUP
  English: 6 SETTER
  Film: 4 ASTA TOTO
  food brand: 4 ALPO
  hand: 3 PAW
  Have ~ breath: 4 PANT
  Herding: 6 COLLIE
  holder: 3 BUN
  Hot: 6 WEENIE WIENER
  Hunting: 6 SETTER
  in Oz: 4 **TOTO**
  Irish: 6 SETTER
  Is a good: 5 OBEYS
  Japanese: 5 **AKITA**
  Junkyard: 3 CUR
  Kind of: 4 SLED
  Lap ~, for short: 3 POM 4 PEKE
  Latin: 5 CANIS
  Movie: 4 ASTA TOTO
  Outback: 5 DINGO
  pest: 4 FLEA
  Put on the: 3 SIC

Sea: 3 GOB **TAR** 4 SALT
Snarly: 3 CUR
Snub-nosed: 3 PUG
star: 4 ASTA 5 BENJI 6 LASSIE
Start of a ~ name: 3 RIN
tag datum: 5 OWNER
Top: 5 CHAMP 9 NUMEROUNO
treat: 4 BONE
TV: 3 REN 5 ASTRO
warning: 3 GRR
Welsh: 5 CORGI
Wild: 5 DINGO
Wiry-coated: 8 AIREDALE
with a blue-black tongue:
    4 CHOW
with a curled tail: 3 PUG 5 AKITA
Word before: 3 RED SEA
Work like a: 4 TOIL 5 SLAVE
    SWEAT
Wrinkled: 3 PUG
Dog-___: 5 EARED
Dogbane
  shrub: 8 OLEANDER
Dogcatcher
  quarry: 5 STRAY
Dog-eared: 4 WORN
Dogfaces: 3 GIS
Dogfight
  participant: 3 ACE
Doggie bag
  morsel: 3 ORT
Doggone: 7 DRATTED
"Doggone it!": 4 DRAT RATS
Doggy: 5 POOCH
Dogie: 4 CALF 6 ORPHAN
  catcher: 5 LASSO RIATA
Doglike
  scavenger: 5 HYENA
Dogma: 5 TENET 6 BELIEF
  disputer: 7 HERETIC
"Dog of Flanders, A"
  author: 5 OUIDA
Dog-paddle: 4 SWIM
Dog-paddled: 4 SWAM SWUM
Dogpatch
  adjective: 3 LIL
  cartoonist: 4 CAPP
  creator: 4 CAPP 6 ALCAPP
  denizen: 5 ABNER SADIE

8 LILABNER
10 MAMMYYOKUM
diminutive: 3 LIL
Hawkins of: 5 SADIE
Opposed to, in: 4 AGIN
possessive: 4 HISN
resident: 5 ABNER
Dog-tired: 5 ALLIN 6 POOPED
Dogwood
variety: 5 OSIER
Doha
land: 5 QATAR
Doherty
Actress: 7 SHANNEN
of the Mamas & the Papas:
5 DENNY
Dohnányi
Composer: 4 ERNO
"Do I dare to ___ peach?":
4 EATA
Doilies
Make: 3 TAT
Doily
Like a: 4 LACY
Make a: 3 TAT
material: 4 LACE
Doing: 4 DEED UPTO
Not ~ much: 4 IDLE
nothing: 4 **IDLE**
Without ~ much: 4 IDLY
Do-it-yourselfer
purchase: 3 KIT
words: 5 HOWTO
Dojo
teaching: 6 KARATE
Dol.
parts: 3 CTS
Doldrums: 5 BLAHS
In the: 3 SAD
Dole: 4 METE
out: 5 **ALLOT**
(out): 4 **METE**
running mate: 4 KEMP
Dolin
Dancer: 5 ANTON
Doll: 3 HON TOY 5 CUTIE SUGAR
Carnival: 6 KEWPIE
cry: 4 DADA **MAMA**
Fad: 5 TROLL

for boys: 5 GIJOE
He's a: 3 KEN 4 ELMO
Kachina ~ maker: 4 **HOPI**
Kind of: 6 VOODOO
Living: 5 CUTIE
Mattel: 3 KEN
Raggedy: 3 **ANN** 4 ANDY
She's a: 3 ANN
Ticklish: 4 **ELMO**
Dollar
bill: 3 ONE
competitor: 4 AVIS 5 ALAMO
divs.: 3 CTS
Kind of: 4 SAND
Latin word on a: 4 ORDO
Like a new ~ bill: 5 CRISP
Parts of a: 5 CENTS
prefix: 4 EURO
rival: 4 AVIS EURO 5 ALAMO
Dollop: 3 DAB GOB 4 GLOB
Dolls
companions: 4 GUYS
Like some Russian: 6 NESTED
of the 1980s: 3 ETS
"Doll's House, A"
author: 5 IBSEN
heroine: 4 NORA
Dolly: 3 EWE 5 CLONE SHEEP
Singer: 6 PARTON
the clone: 3 EWE
Dolores
Actress: 6 DELRIO
Dolphin
habitat: 5 MIAMI OCEAN
Largest: 4 ORCA
relative: 4 ORCA
Dolphins
coach: 5 SHULA
Dan of the: 6 MARINO
home: 5 MIAMI
Dolt: 3 ASS OAF 4 BOOB CLOD
LOUT 5 IDIOT MORON
SCHMO 6 NITWIT
11 KNUCKLEHEAD
Domain: 4 **AREA** LAND
5 **REALM**
Royal: 5 REALM
"Domani"
singer: 6 LAROSA

Dome: 6 CUPOLA
  home: 5 IGLOO
  openings: 5 OCULI
  player: 5 ASTRO
Domed
  building: 7 ROTUNDA
  home: 5 IGLOO
  recess: 4 APSE
Domenica
  Day before: 6 SABATO
Domenici
  Senator: 4 PETE
Dome-shaped
  building: 7 ROTUNDA
  home: 5 IGLOO
  ~ Buddhist memorial: 5 STUPA
Domestic: 4 MAID 6 AUPAIR
    8 HOMEMADE
  Some are: 4 ARTS
Domesticate: 4 TAME
Domesticated: 4 **TAME**
  insect: 3 BEE
  Not: 4 WILD 5 FERAL
Domicile: 5 ABODE
Dominant: 5 ONTOP
  It may be: 4 GENE
  Socially: 5 ALPHA
Domineering: 5 BOSSY
Domingo: 3 DIA 5 TENOR
  domain: 5 OPERA
  solo: 4 ARIA
  ___ **Domingo:** 5 **SANTO**
  ___ **Domini:** 4 **ANNO**
Dominican
  dollar: 4 PESO
  slugger: 4 SOSA
Dominican Republic
  neighbor: 5 HAITI
Dominik
  NHL goalie: 5 HASEK
Dominion: 5 REALM
Domino: 4 MASK
  dot: 3 PIP
  Middle: 4 TREY
  Singer: 4 FATS
Don: 4 WEAR 8 SLIPINTO
  Announcer: 5 PARDO
  Deejay: 4 IMUS
  of football: 5 SHULA

  of game shows: 5 PARDO
  of talk radio: 4 IMUS
Doña ___ (Las Cruces's county):
  3 ANA
Donahue
  Actor: 4 TROY
  Actress: 6 ELINOR
  TV host: 4 PHIL
Donald
  and Ivana: 4 EXES
  Ex of: 5 IVANA MARLA
  First ex of: 5 IVANA
Donald Duck: 4 TOON
  nephew: 4 HUEY 5 DEWEY
    LOUIE
  ~, to his nephews: 4 UNCA
Donaldson
  TV newsman: 3 SAM
Donate: 4 GIVE
Donation
  Charitable: 4 ALMS
  Church: 5 TITHE
  Eye bank: 6 CORNEA
  Generous: 5 ORGAN
  Parish: 5 TITHE
Donations: 4 ALMS
  Ask for: 10 PASSTHEHAT
Don ___ de la Vega: 5 DIEGO
Done: 4 OVER 5 ENDED
    7 THROUGH
  for: 4 DEAD SUNK 5 KAPUT
    SPENT
  in: 5 **SLAIN**
  It's: 4 DEED
  Just not: 5 TABOO
  Less: 5 RARER
  to death: 3 OLD
  with: 4 OVER
  with a wink: 3 SLY
  ~, in French: 4 FINI
  ~, to Donne: 3 OER
"___ done!": 6 NICELY
Donegal
  From: 5 IRISH
  Island of: 4 ARAN
Donegal Bay
  River to: 4 **ERNE**
"___ Done Him Wrong": 3 SHE
Done to ___: 5 ATURN

Done ___ turn: 3 TOA
"Don Giovanni": 5 OPERA
  composer: 6 MOZART
"Don Juan"
  poet: 5 BYRON
"Don Juan DeMarco"
  actor: 4 DEPP
Donkey: 3 **ASS**
  remark: 6 HEEHAW
  sound: 4 BRAY
  uncle: 3 ASS
  ~, in German: 4 ESEL
Donna
  Designer: 5 KARAN
  ___ donna: 5 PRIMA
Donne: 4 POET
  Info: Poetic cue
  Dawn, to: 4 MORN
  Done, to: 3 OER
  Dusk, to: 3 EEN
Donner Pass
  City near: 4 RENO
Donny
  Marie, to: 3 SIS
  Singer: 6 OSMOND
  Sister of: 5 **MARIE**
Donnybrook: 3 ROW 4 FRAY RIOT
  5 **MELEE** SETTO
  6 FRACAS
Donohoe
  Actress: 6 AMANDA
Donor
  Become a: 4 GIVE
  Big: 3 PAC
  D.C.: 3 PAC
  Noted bone: 4 ADAM
  Universal: 5 TYPEO
"Do not give up !": 3 TRY
Do-nothing: 5 IDLER
Donovan
  crew: 3 OSS
  Daughter of: 4 IONE
"Don't ___!": 3 ASK
"Don't bet ___!": 4 ONIT
"Don't bother": 6 NONEED
"Don't Bring Me Down"
  gp.: 3 ELO
"Don't count ___!": 4 ONIT
"Don't Cry for Me, Argentina"

  musical: 5 EVITA
"Don't dawdle!": 4 ASAP
"Don't ___, don't tell": 3 ASK
"Don't Drop Bombs"
  singer Minnelli: 4 LIZA
"Don't evade the question!":
  7 YESORNO
"Don't even bother": 5 NOUSE
"Don't even go ___!": 5 THERE
"Don't get any funny ___!":
  5 IDEAS
"Don't give up!": 3 TRY
"Don't go": 4 STAY
"Don't have ___, man!": 4 ACOW
"Don't look ___!": 4 ATME
"Don't look at me!": 4 NOTI
"Don't make ___!": 5 AMESS
  AMOVE
"Don't mind ___!": 5 IFIDO
"Don't mind ___ do": 3 IFI
"Don't move!": 4 STAY
  7 STAYPUT
"Don't ___ surprised": 5 ACTSO
"Don't tell ___!": 5 ASOUL
"Don't tell me!": 4 OHNO
"Don't throw bouquets ___":
  4 ATME
"Don't You Know"
  singer: 5 REESE
Donut
  Dip, as a: 3 SOP
  feature: 4 HOLE
  quantity: 5 DOZEN
  shape: 5 TORUS 6 TOROID
Donut-and-dance
  org.: 3 USO
Doo-___ : 3 WOP
Doodlebug
  Adult: 7 ANTLION
  prey: 3 ANT
Doodler
  aid: 10 SCRATCHPAD
Doofus: 3 ASS OAF 4 BOOB BOZO
  CLOD DODO DOLT TWIT
  5 IDIOT SCHMO 6 NITWIT
  10 STUMBLEBUM
Doohickey: 5 GIZMO 6 GADGET
Doolittle
  Ms.: 5 ELIZA

Poet: 5 HILDA
Doolittle, Eliza
Inspiration for: 7 GALATEA
Doom: 3 END 4 FATE
partner: 5 GLOOM
Doomsayer: 9 PESSIMIST
sign: 6 REPENT
Doone
of fiction: 5 **LORNA**
"___ Doone": 5 **LORNA**
"Doonesbury"
cartoonist: 7 TRUDEAU
character: 4 DUKE
Door: 5 ENTRY 8 ENTRANCE
fastener: 4 HASP
feature: 4 KNOB
frame: 4 JAMB
frame part: 6 LINTEL
handle: 4 KNOB
opener: 3 KEY 4 KNOB
Open the ~ to: 5 LETIN
part: 4 JAMB 5 HINGE
sign: 3 MEN 4 EXIT PULL PUSH
   5 ENTER
sound: 4 SLAM
Sound at the: 3 RAP
word: 3 MEN 4 PULL PUSH
Doorbell
Eschew the: 5 KNOCK
Used a: 4 RANG
Doorframe
part: 4 JAMB
Doorkeeper
Masonic: 5 TILER
Doors
Like French: 5 PANED
Like many: 4 AJAR
Opener of many: 7 PASSKEY
Doorway: 5 ENTRY 6 PORTAL
   8 ENTRANCE
part: 4 JAMB
"Do ___ others ...": 4 UNTO
Do-over
Tennis: 3 **LET**
Doo-wop
instrument: 3 SAX
member: 4 ALTO
song: 5 OLDIE
syllable: 3 **SHA**

Doozy: 3 PIP 4 **LULU** ONER
Dope: 3 SAP 4 **INFO** POOP
   7 SCHNOOK
Dopey: 5 DWARF INANE
picture: 3 CEL
Doppelgänger: 4 TWIN 5 CLONE
___ d'Or (award at Cannes):
   5 PALME
Dorati
Conductor: 5 ANTAL
Do-re-mi: 4 GELT KALE LOOT
   5 MOOLA 6 DINERO
"___ Doria": 6 ANDREA
Do-Right, Dudley
beloved: 4 NELL
org.: 4 RCMP
Doris
Actress and singer: 3 DAY
Dork: 4 NERD 5 DWEEB SCHMO
   6 DOOFUS
___ d'Orléans: 3 ILE
Dorm
alternative: 4 FRAT
annoyance: 5 SNORE
dweller: 4 COED
sharer: 6 ROOMIE
unit: 4 ROOM
~ VIPs: 3 RAS
Dormant: 6 ASLEEP LATENT
   7 RESTING
Dormitory: 4 HALL
annoyance: 6 SNORER
Dorothea
Reformer: 3 DIX
Dorothy
dog: 4 TOTO
Em, to: 4 AUNT
home: 6 KANSAS
Mystery writer: 6 SAYERS
Skater: 6 HAMILL
~, to Em: 5 NIECE
Dors
Actress: 5 DIANA
___ d'Orsay: 4 QUAI
Dorsey, Jimmy
hit: 6 SORARE
Dorsey, Tommy
hit: 7 OPUSONE
Dortmund-___ Canal: 3 EMS

Dory: 4 BOAT
  propeller: 3 OAR
Dos: 6 NUMERO
  cubed: 4 OCHO
  follower: 4 TRES
  halved: 3 UNO
  Notes after: 3 RES
  preceder: 3 UNO
  Uno plus: 4 TRES
  Where ~ are done: 5 SALON
Dos ___, John
  Author: 6 PASSOS
Dosage
  amt.: 3 TSP
  Radiation: 3 REM
  unit: 3 RAD 4 PILL
  units: 3 CCS
Do-say
  link: 3 ASI
"Do ___ say": 3 ASI
Dose
  amt.: 3 TSP
  Medicinal: 4 PILL
  prefix: 4 MEGA
  Prevention: 5 OUNCE
Do-___ situation: 5 ORDIE
Dos Passos, John
  trilogy: 3 USA
Dossier: 4 FILE
  letters: 3 AKA
Dostoevsky
  Author: 6 FYODOR
  novel: 8 THEIDIOT
  title character: 5 IDIOT
Dot
  follower: 3 COM ORG
  Map: 4 ISLE TOWN 5 ISLET
  of land: 5 ISLET
  on a domino: 3 PIP
  on a monitor: 5 PIXEL
  On the: 5 SHARP
  Small: 6 TITTLE
  Video: 5 PIXEL
Dot-___: 3 COM
Dotage
  In one's: 6 SENILE
Dot-com: 7 STARTUP
  address: 3 URL
  giant: 6 AMAZON

Dote
  on: 5 ADORE
Doth
  speak: 5 SAITH
"Do the ___!": 4 MATH
"Do the Right Thing"
  pizzeria: 4 SALS
  star: 6 AIELLO
Doting: 4 FOND
Dotty: 4 DAFT GAGA 6 SENILE
  Not as: 5 SANER
Douay
  prophet: 4 OSEE
Double: 3 HIT 4 TWIN 7 STANDIN
    TWOFOLD
  agent: 4 **MOLE**
  curve: 3 **ESS** 4 **OGEE**
  dessert: 10 PIEALAMODE
  duty: 5 STUNT
  Exact: 5 CLONE
  fold: 5 PLEAT
  header: 3 DUO
  job: 5 STUNT
  negative: 4 NONO
  On the: 4 ASAP 5 APACE
    6 ATONCE PRONTO
  reed: 4 OBOE
  standard: 3 TWO
  Stunt: 7 STANDIN
  twist: 3 ESS
  whole note: 5 BREVE
Double ___: 4 DARE
    8 ENTENDRE
Double-___: 5 EDGED 6 TALKER
    7 CROSSER
Double-check: 6 REREAD
    RETEST
  a sum: 5 READD
Double-clicked
  item: 4 ICON
Double-crosser: 5 SNAKE
    8 TWOTIMER
Doubleday
  of baseball: 5 ABNER
Double-decker: 3 BUS
  part: 4 TIER
Double Delight
  snack: 4 OREO
Double-edged: 6 IRONIC

"Double Fantasy"
  singer: 3 ONO 7 YOKOONO
Doubleheader
  First game of a: 6 OPENER
Double-helix
  stuff: 3 DNA
"Double Indemnity"
  novelist: 4 CAIN
Doublemint: 3 GUM
  figures: 5 TWINS
Double-reed
  instrument: 4 **OBOE**
  player: 6 OBOIST
Double Stuf
  cookie: 4 OREO
  ___ double take: 3 DOA
Doubly: 5 TWICE
Doubt: 8 MISTRUST QUESTION
  Free from: 6 ASSURE
  Free of: 4 SURE
  Had no: 4 KNEW
  Sounds of: 3 EHS
  Without a: 4 SURE
Doubter: 7 SKEPTIC
  Deity: 8 AGNOSTIC
  Response to a: 6 ICANSO
  words: 4 IBET
"___ Doubtfire": 3 MRS
Doubtful: 4 IFFY
Doubting Thomas: 5 CYNIC
Doubtless: 4 SURE
Dough: 4 KALE 5 BREAD MONEY
     MOOLA 6 MOOLAH
  Delhi: 5 RUPEE
  dispenser: 3 ATM
  Like: 6 YEASTY
  Like some: 4 SOUR
  Pisa: 4 LIRA
  raiser: 5 YEAST
  Rolling in: 4 RICH
  Turkish: 4 LIRA
  Work: 5 KNEAD
Doughnut
  center: 4 HOLE
  Dip, as a: 4 DUNK
  Finish a: 5 GLAZE
  shape: 5 TORUS
  shapes: 4 TORI
Doughnut-shaped: 5 TORIC

Douglas: 3 FIR 7 DEBATER
Douglas ___: 3 FIR
Douglas, Michael
  film: 4 COMA
  ~, to Kirk: 3 SON
Douglas-Home
  British P.M.: 4 ALEC
Dour: 4 GLUM 5 MOODY
    6 SULLEN
Dove: 4 SOAP 5 COOER
    8 PACIFIST
  call: 3 COO
  goal: 5 PEACE
  into second: 4 SLID
  Like a: 7 ANTIWAR
  Poet: 4 RITA
  shelter: 4 COTE
  sound: 3 COO
Dover
  dish: 4 SOLE
  state (abbr.): 3 DEL
Dovetail: 4 MESH
  part: 5 TENON
Dow: 5 INDEX
  figures: 5 HIGHS
  rise: 4 GAIN
Do-well
  starter: 4 NEER
Down: 3 EAT **SAD** 4 BLUE GLUM
    6 MOROSE
  at the heels: 5 SEEDY
  at the pond: 5 EIDER
  for the count: 3 KOD
  Go: 3 SET 4 DROP LOSE SINK
    WANE 5 ABATE 6 SHRINK
  Got: 3 ATE 4 **ALIT**
  Had ~ pat: 4 KNEW
  in the dumps: 3 **SAD** 4 BLUE
    GLUM 6 MOROSE
  in the mouth: 3 SAD 4 BLUE
    GLUM 6 MOROSE
  Is ~ with: 3 HAS
  It may be laid: 6 THELAW
  Marked: 6 **ONSALE**
  opposite: 6 ACROSS
  Put: 3 DIS LAY SET 4 LAID
    5 ABASE QUELL 6 BERATE
    DEMEAN DERIDE DISSED
    STIFLE

Set: 3 LAY PUT 4 ALIT LAID
   5 WROTE
source: 5 EIDER
the road: 5 AHEAD 6 INTIME
too much: 7 OVEREAT
Went: 4 FELL SANK SLID
Where to get: 5 EIDER
with, in French: 4 ABAS
with the flu: 3 ILL
~, at a diner: 7 ONTOAST
Down ___ (Maine): 4 EAST
Down-and-out: 5 NEEDY
Downcast: 3 SAD 4 BLUE GLUM
   6 MOROSE
Down East: 5 <u>MAINE</u>
Downed: 3 <u>ATE</u> 5 EATEN
Downer: 4 DRAG
It's a real: 6 OPIATE
Scud: 3 ABM
Downey
Actress: 4 ROMA
costar: 5 REESE
TV angel: 4 ROMA
Downfall: 4 BANE RUIN
   6 DEMISE
Downhearted: 3 SAD 4 BLUE
   GLUM 6 MOROSE
Downhill
course: 6 SKIRUN SLALOM
Go: 4 SLED 6 WORSEN
   8 GETWORSE
Go ~ fast: 3 SKI 4 LUGE SLED
   6 SCHUSS
racer: 4 LUGE SLED
runner: 3 SKI
Downpour: 4 RAIN
Downright: 5 PLUMB SHEER
   6 ARRANT 7 UTTERLY
Downs
It has its ups and: 4 YOYO
   6 SEESAW
town: 5 EPSOM
TV host: 4 HUGH
___ Downs: 5 EPSOM
Downsize: 4 PARE 7 RESCALE
Downspout
site: 4 EAVE
Downstairs
~, at sea: 5 BELOW

Downtime: 4 LULL REST
   5 RANDR
Toddler's: 3 NAP
Down-to-earth: 4 REAL
folks: 3 ETS
"Downtown"
singer Clark: 6 PETULA
Downturn: 3 DIP
Down Under
Info: Australian cue
bird: 3 EMU
critter: 5 KOALA
denizen: 6 AUSSIE
dog: 5 DINGO
girl: 6 SHEILA
hopper: 3 ROO
soldier: 5 ANZAC
Downward
bend: 3 SAG
Downwind: 4 <u>ALEE</u>
Downy: 4 SOFT
duck: 5 EIDER
surface: 3 NAP
Dowsing
tool: 3 ROD
Dowson
English poet: 6 ERNEST
"Do Ya"
rock gp.: 3 ELO
Doyle, Popeye
prototype Eddie: 4 EGAN
Doyle, Sir Arthur ___: 5 CONAN
"Do you come here often?":
   4 LINE
"Do you get it?": 3 SEE
Doz.
Twelve: 3 GRO
Doze: 3 NAP NOD 6 NODOFF
(off): 3 NOD
Dozed: 5 SLEPT
Dozen
A dime a: 4 RATE
Baker's: 4 EGGS 8 THIRTEEN
Dairy: 4 EGGS
Half a: 3 SIX
Item sold by the: 5 DONUT
Price of a: 4 DIME
DPL
One with ~ plates: 3 AMB EMB

Dr.
  group: **3** AMA HMO
  magazine: **4** JAMA
  of literature: **5** SEUSS
  of rap: **3** <u>DRE</u>
  order: **3** MRI
  orders: **3** RXS
  org.: **3** AMA
  TV: **4** PHIL
Dr. ___
  Rapper: **3** <u>DRE</u>
Drab: 4 BLAH PALE
  color: **5** OLIVE
Drachma
  replacer: **4** EURO
Draconian: 5 HARSH **6** SEVERE
Dracula: 5 COUNT **7** VAMPIRE
  creator: **6** STOKER
  Inspiration for: **4** VLAD
  Mother-in-law of: **6** OLDBAT
  portrayer: **6** LUGOSI
  portrayer Lugosi: **4** BELA
  ~, at times: **3** BAT
"Dracula"
  author: **6** STOKER
  author Stoker: **4** BRAM
  director Browning: **3** TOD
Draft: 4 BEER
  Admitting a: **4** AJAR
  animals: **4** OXEN
  Beat the: **6** ENLIST
  Bit of a: **3** SIP
  choice: **3** <u>ALE</u>
  classification: **4** ONEA
  device: **3** TAP **4** YOKE
  drink: **3** ALE
  Hearty: **5** QUAFF
  holder: **8** SCHOONER
  letters: **3** SSS
  org.: **3** NBA NFL <u>SSS</u>
  pick: **3** <u>ALE</u>
  rating: **4** ONEA
  source: **7** BEERKEG
  status: **4** <u>ONEA</u> **5** ONTAP
Draftable: 4 <u>ONEA</u> **5** ONTAP
"Draft Dodger Rag"
  singer Phil: **4** OCHS
Drafting
  Fit for: **4** ONEA

Drag: 4 BORE HAUL TOKE
  It's a: **3** TOW
  It's off the main: **10** SIDESTREET
  Kind of a: **4** MAIN
  one's feet: **5** STALL
  Prepare to: **3** REV
  race participant: **6** HOTROD
  through the mud: **5** SMEAR
Dragnet: 5 TRAWL
"Dragnet"
  background for credits:
    5 BADGE
  org.: **4** LAPD
  role: **9** JOEFRIDAY
  star: **4** WEBB
Dragon: 6 TATTOO
  Did in, as a: **4** SLEW
  Do in, as a: **4** <u>SLAY</u>
  land: **7** HONALEE
  puppet: **5** OLLIE
  ___ dragon: **6** KOMODO
"Dragons of ___, The" (Carl
    Sagan novel): 4 EDEN
"Dragons of Eden, The"
  author: **5** SAGAN
"Dragonwyck"
  author Anya: **5** SETON
  author Seton: **4** ANYA
Drag queen
  topper: **3** WIG
  wrap: **3** BOA
Drain: 3 SAP **4** TIRE **5** EMPTY
    SEWER
  bane: **4** CLOG
  cleaner: **3** LYE
  of color: **8** ETIOLATE
  problem: **4** CLOG
  sight: **4** EDDY
Drained: 5 SPENT
  of color: **5** ASHEN
Drainer
  Pasta: **5** SIEVE
Drainpipe
  section: **4** TRAP
Drake: 4 MALE
  Cartoonist: **4** STAN
  Fake: **5** DECOY
"Drake"
  poet: **5** NOYES

Drake, Francis
  title: 3 SIR
Dram: 3 TOT
Drama
  award: 4 OBIE
  Daytime: 4 SOAP 6 SERIAL
  Forensic: 3 CSI
  Japanese: 3 NOH 6 KABUKI
  Musical: 5 OPERA
  opening: 4 ACTI
  prefix: 4 MELO
  Robot: 3 RUR
  Short: 7 PLAYLET
  TV ~ settings: 3 ERS
Dramatic
  beginning: 4 ACTI
  dance: 5 TANGO
  opening: 4 ACTI MELO
  Overly: 5 HAMMY
  segment: 3 ACT 5 SCENE
  wail: 4 ALAS
Dramatist
  French: 6 SARTRE
  Irish: 5 SYNGE
Drambuie
  Scotch and ~ drink:
    9 RUSTYNAIL
Drams
  16 ~: 5 OUNCE
  512,000 ~: 3 TON
Drang
  partner: 5 STURM
Drano
  ingredient: 3 LYE
  target: 4 CLOG
Drape
  edge: 3 HEM
Draped
  garment: 4 SARI TOGA
Draperies
  Decorative: 5 SWAGS
"Drat!": 4 DANG OATH 5 NERTS
Draught: 3 ALE 4 SWIG
Dravidian
  language: 5 TAMIL
Draw: 3 TIE 4 PULL 6 ALLURE
    7 ATTRACT TIEGAME
  a bead: 3 AIM
  a bead on: 5 **AIMAT**

a blank: 6 FORGET
a conclusion: 5 INFER
forth: 5 EDUCE EVOKE
  · 6 ELICIT
in: 6 ENTICE
on a board: 9 STALEMATE
on glass: 4 ETCH
out: 5 **EDUCE** 6 **ELICIT**
Ready to: 5 ONTAP
Something to: 4 BATH
to a close: 3 END 4 WANE
upon: 3 USE 7 TAPINTO
with acid: 4 **ETCH**
Drawbridge
  Water under the: 4 MOAT
Drawer
  Big: 5 MECCA
  Cash: 4 TILL
  part: 4 KNOB
  Produce: 7 CRISPER
  Top: 4 AONE
Drawers
  Chest of: 6 BUREAU 7 DRESSER
Drawing: 6 SKETCH
  card: 4 LURE
  place: 4 WELL
  Ready for: 5 ONTAP
  Represent in: 4 LIMN
  room: 5 SALON
  support: 5 EASEL
Drawing board
  staple: 7 TSQUARE
Drawings
  Like some: 6 RANDOM
Drawn
  Ready to be: 5 ONTAP
  They're: 4 LOTS
Dre, Dr.
  genre: 3 RAP
Dread: 4 FEAR 5 ANGST
  Cry of: 4 OHNO
  Feeling of: 5 ANGST
Dreadful: 3 BAD 4 DIRE
    6 HORRID 9 ATROCIOUS
Dreadlocks
  wearer: 5 RASTA
Dream: 6 ASPIRE
  Kind of: 4 PIPE
  location: 3 BED

state: 3 REM
up: 6 DEVISE 7 CONCOCT
~, in French: 4 REVE
"Dream a Little Dream of Me"
singer: 8 MAMACASS
    14 MAMACASSELLIOT
Dreamcast
maker: 4 SEGA
Dreamer: 8 IDEALIST
    10 LOTUSEATER
Fictional: 5 ALICE
opposite: 7 REALIST
Dreaming
phenomenon: 3 REM
"___ dreaming?": 3 **AMI**
Dreamland: 5 SLEEP 6 UTOPIA
Out of: 5 AWAKE
"Dreamlover"
singer Carey: 6 MARIAH
Dreamscape
artist: 4 DALI
Dreary: 4 DRAB GREY 5 BLEAK
    7 HUMDRUM
Dregs: 4 LEES
Drench: 3 **SOP** 4 **SOAK** 5 DOUSE
Drenched: 3 WET 5 SOGGY
Drescher
Actress: 4 FRAN
Drescher, Fran
Like the voice of: 5 **NASAL**
role: 5 NANNY
Dresden
Info: German cue
denial: 4 NEIN
native: 5 SAXON
river: 4 ELBE
Dress: 4 GARB 6 ATTIRE
Ballet: 4 TUTU
cut: 5 ALINE
Delhi: 4 **SARI**
down: 5 BASTE 6 BERATE
Elegant: 5 SATIN
Formal: 4 GOWN
Indian: 4 SARI
line: 4 SEAM
Longish: 4 MIDI
Loose-fitting: 4 TENT
Mend a: 5 REHEM
Peasant: 6 DIRNDL

Prom: 4 GOWN
Prom ~ material: 5 TULLE
Roomy: 5 ALINE
size: 6 PETITE
smartly: 5 PREEN
style: 4 MAXI 5 **ALINE**
up: 5 ADORN PREEN 6 TOGOUT
(up): 3 **TOG**
up, with "out": 3 TOG
with a flare: 5 ALINE
Dressed: 4 **CLAD** 6 GARBED
Get: 5 TOGUP
It's often: 5 SALAD
like a judge: 5 ROBED
Sharply: 5 NATTY
to the nines: 7 DUDEDUP
Dressed to the ___ : 5 **NINES**
Dresser
Dandy: 3 FOP
Messy: 4 SLOB
Smart: 3 FOP
Dressing
bottle: 5 CRUET
choice: 5 RANCH 7 ITALIAN
    RUSSIAN
Course with: 5 SALAD
holder: 5 CRUET
ingredient: 3 OIL 7 VINEGAR
Surgical: 5 GAUZE
tool: 3 ADZ
Window: 5 DRAPE 6 FACADE
Dressmaker
cut: 4 BIAS
dummy: 4 FORM
Dress to the ___ : 5 NINES
Dressy
accessory: 3 TIE
event: 4 GALA
Drew
a blank: 6 FORGOT
Actor: 5 CAREY
back: 5 SHIED
in: 5 LURED
in novels: 5 NANCY
on: 4 USED
Drew, Nancy
beau: 3 **NED**
boyfriend: 3 **NED**
creator Carolyn: 5 KEENE

"Drew Carey Show, The"
  character: 4 MIMI
  setting: 4 OHIO
Drexler
  of basketball: 5 CLYDE
Dreyer
  partner in ice cream: 3 EDY
Dreyfus
  Defender of: 4 ZOLA
    9 EMILEZOLA
  trial city: 6 RENNES
Dribble: 4 SEEP
Dried
  fruit: 5 PRUNE
  It may be cut and: 3 HAY
  out: 4 **SERE** 5 SOBER
  up: 4 **SERE**
Drier: 5 TOWEL
  Hops: 4 OAST
Drift: 4 ROAM ROVE 5 STRAY
    TENOR
  Get the: 3 SEE
  off: 4 DOZE
Drifter: 4 HOBO
Drifters
  hit song: 11 UPONTHEROOF
    15 THISMAGICMOMENT
  Plains: 5 BISON
Driftwood
  Groucho's: 4 OTIS
  Where ~ drifts: 6 ASHORE
Drill: 4 BORE 5 BORER
  command: 6 ATEASE
  License to: 3 DDS
  through: 6 PIERCE
Driller: 3 SGT
  deg.: 3 DDS
  org.: 3 ADA
Drilling
  gp.: 4 ROTC
  machine: 6 OILRIG
  Ready for: 4 NUMB
  tool: 8 BRACEBIT
Drill sergeant
  call: 3 HEP HUP
  command: 6 ATEASE FALLIN
  Obey the:
    15 SNAPTOATTENTION
Drink: 3 SEA 5 OCEAN 6 IMBIBE

After-dinner: 4 PORT
    8 ANISETTE
a little: 3 SIP
Apple: 5 CIDER
Autumn: 5 CIDER
Big: 4 SWIG
Brewed: 7 ICEDTEA
Brunch: 6 MIMOSA
Carbonated: 4 SODA
Chinese: 6 HOTTEA
    8 GREENTEA
Citrus: 3 **ADE** 7 LIMEADE
cooler: 3 ICE
Dad's: 8 ROOTBEER
daintily: 3 SIP
Dixie: 5 JULEP
Draft: 3 ALE
Eggy: 3 NOG
Fizzy: 4 COLA SODA
from a bag: 3 TEA
from a dish: 3 LAP
Fruit: 3 ADE
Fruity: 3 **ADE** 7 SANGRIA
garnish: 4 LIME PEEL 5 TWIST
Green: 3 TEA
Half a: 3 MAI TAI
Herbal: 3 TEA
Holiday: 3 NOG
Honey: 4 MEAD
Hot: 3 TEA 5 COCOA TODDY
impolitely: 5 SLURP
in a can: 4 COLA
in a mug: 3 ALE
Japanese: 4 SAKE
Juice: 3 ADE
like a cat: 3 LAP 5 LAPUP
like a dog: 3 LAP 5 LAPUP
like a fish: 4 TOPE
Lime: 3 ADE
Malt: 3 ALE
mixer: 4 SODA
No-cal: 5 WATER
noisily: 5 SLURP
of the gods: 6 NECTAR
on board: 4 GROG
on draft: 3 ALE
Orange: 3 ADE
Pirate's: 3 RUM
Pub: 3 ALE

Quick: 3 NIP 5 SNORT
Rum: 4 GROG 6 COLADA
   MAITAI
Sailor's: 4 GROG
slowly: 3 SIP
Small: 3 NIP SIP
Soft: 4 **COLA** SODA 7 SODAPOP
Stiff: 6 BRACER
suffix: 3 ADE
Summer: 3 **ADE**
too much: 4 TOPE
with a straw: 4 SODA 5 FLOAT
Yule: 3 NOG

Drinker
debt: 6 BARTAB
Heavy: 3 SOT

Drinking
Marked by: 3 WET
party: 7 WASSAIL
spree: 6 BENDER

Drinks
Like some: 4 NEAT
   10 ONTHEHOUSE

"Drinks are ___!": 4 ONME

Drip: 4 BORE
catcher: 3 BIB
drops: 4 OOZE
site: 4 EAVE

Dripping: 3 WET
Candle: 3 WAX
Plant: 5 RESIN
sound: 4 PLOP

Drive: 4 URGE 5 IMPEL MOTOR
   6 COMPEL STROKE
away: 4 SHOO 5 REPEL
   6 BANISH 8 ALIENATE
back: 5 REPEL 7 REPULSE
bananas: 5 ANNOY
   7 DERANGE
Finish a: 4 PAVE
forward: 5 **IMPEL** 6 PROPEL
Get ready to: 5 TEEUP
Got ready to: 4 TEED
Inner: 4 URGE
Kind of: 5 CDROM
off: 4 SHOO 5 REPEL
Prepare to: 3 **TEE** 5 TEEUP
Quick: 4 SPIN
the getaway car: 4 ABET

Drive-___ : 4 THRU

Drive-in
employee: 6 CARHOP

Drivel: 3 PAP ROT 5 BILGE
   DROOL TRIPE 6 SALIVA
   SLAVER

Driven
group: 4 HERD
Like the ~ snow: 4 PURE
They're: 4 CARS

Driver: 4 WOOD
aid: 3 TEE
Back seat: 3 NAG
caution: 3 SLO
choice: 4 GEAR 5 SEDAN
device: 3 TEE
Dory: 3 OAR
Elephant: 6 MAHOUT
Gondola: 5 POLER
invitation: 5 HOPIN
lic. *(plural)*: 3 IDS
license datum: 3 AGE DOB SEX
licenses: 3 IDS
lic. info: 3 DOB HGT 5 IDENT
need: 3 GAS
need (abbr.): 3 LIC
New: 4 TEEN
one-eighty: 5 UTURN
org.: 3 AAA PGA
shield: 5 VISOR
Stake: 4 MAUL
warning: 4 FORE

Drive-thru
dispenser: 3 ATM
request: 5 ORDER

Driveway
blotch: 3 OIL
surface: 3 TAR 6 GRAVEL

Driving
aid: 3 **TEE**
choice: 7 ONEIRON
danger: 3 FOG ICE 4 SNOW
   5 GLARE SLEET
hazard: 3 FOG ICE 4 SNOW
   5 GLARE SLEET
need: 3 GAS TEE 7 EYETEST
place: 3 TEE 4 LANE
Rare ~ result: 3 ACE

Drizzle: 4 MIST RAIN

"Dr. Kildare"
  actor Raymond: 6 MASSEY
"Dr. No"
  actor Connery: 4 SEAN
  Sean's costar in: 6 URSULA
Droid
  of movies: 5 ARTOO
Droll: 3 WRY 7 AMUSING
  folks: 4 WAGS
Drome
  prefix: 4 AERO
Drone: 3 BEE 4 MALE
  home: 4 HIVE
Drones: 4 HUMS
  Like some: 5 APIAN
Droning
  reed: 7 BAGPIPE
  sound: 3 HUM
Drood
  Dickens character: 5 EDWIN
Drool: 6 SLAVER 7 SLOBBER
Drooling
  dog of comics: 4 ODIE
Droop: 3 LOP **SAG** 4 WILT
Drooping: 5 SAGGY
Droopy-eared
  dog: 7 SPANIEL
  hound: 6 BASSET
Drop: 3 EBB 4 LOSE **OMIT**
    6 PLUNGE 7 DESCEND
  a line: 4 FISH
  back: 3 LAG
  by: 5 POPIN 6 STOPIN
  down: 4 MOLT
  Eye: 4 **TEAR**
  for the count: 4 KAYO
  from the eye: 4 TEAR
  Get the ~ on: 3 NAB
  in: 5 VISIT
  in on: 3 SEE
  in the ocean: 3 EBB
  off: 3 NAP NOD 4 DOZE WANE
    5 ABATE SLEEP
  one's jaw: 4 GAPE
  out: 6 SECEDE
  Ready to: 5 ALLIN SPENT
  Salty: 4 TEAR
  shot: 4 DINK
  Sweat: 4 BEAD

  Theater: 5 SCRIM
  the ball: 3 ERR
Drop ___ (write): 5 ALINE
Drop-down
  list: 4 MENU
Droplets
  Adorn with: 5 BEDEW
  Form: 4 BEAD
  Morning: 3 DEW
___ drop of a hat: 5 ATTHE
Drop-off
  point: 4 EDGE
Dropout
  doc.: 3 GED
Dropped
  a line: 5 WROTE
  It was ~ in the 1960s: 3 LSD
    4 ACID
  off: 8 TOOKANAP
    10 FELLASLEEP
Dropper
  Acorn: 3 OAK
  Eaves: 6 ICICLE
  Needle: 4 PINE
Drought
  buster: 4 RAIN
  ender: 4 RAIN
Drought-damaged: 4 SERE
Drove: 4 HERD
  (around): 6 TOOLED
  too fast: 4 SPED
Drowned
  valley: 3 RIA
"Drowning ___" (2000 film):
    4 MONA
Drowse
  Begin to: 3 NOD
Droxie
  rival: 4 OREO
"Dr. Strangelove"
  actor Wynn: 6 KEENAN
Drub: 4 LICK 5 PASTE
Drubbing: 4 ROUT
Drucker
  Mad cartoonist: 4 MORT
Drudge: 4 MOIL **PEON** SERF
    5 SLAVE
  Feudal: 4 SERF
  Internet columnist: 4 MATT

work: 4 TOIL
Drudgery: 4 TOIL 5 LABOR
  Classroom: 4 ROTE
  Do: 4 MOIL
Drug: 6 OPIATE SEDATE
  agent: 4 NARC 5 NARCO
  buster: 4 NARC 5 NARCO
  cop: 4 NARC 5 NARCO
  Hallucinogenic: 3 LSD
  Psychedelic: 3 LSD
  source: 6 IPECAC
  unit: 4 KILO
Druggie: 4 USER
Druggist
  Thrice, to a: 3 TER
  ~, to a Brit: 7 CHEMIST
Druid: 4 CELT 6 PRIEST
Drum
  accompanier: 4 FIFE
  attachment: 5 SNARE
  Beatnik's: 5 BONGO
  Fifer's: 5 TABOR
  Hand: 6 TOMTOM
  Indian: 5 TABLA
  major's hat: 5 SHAKO
  material: 5 STEEL
  out: 4 OUST
  part: 5 SNARE
  played with the hands: 5 BONGO
  site: 3 EAR
  Small: 5 TABLA TABOR
  sound: 4 ROLL
  string: 5 SNARE
Drummer: 8 SALESMAN
"Drums Along the Mohawk"
  hero: 3 GIL
Drumstick: 3 LEG
  source: 4 FOWL
Drunk: 3 SOT 5 SOUSE 7 PIEEYED
  Get: 5 BESOT
  suffix: 3 ARD
Drunkard: 3 SOT 4 LUSH 5 SOUSE
Drunken: 5 BEERY 6 SOTTED
  daze: 6 STUPOR
Drury
  Novelist: 5 ALLEN

Drury Lane
  composer: 4 ARNE
Dry: 3 SEC 4 **ARID SERE** 7 SAHARAN
  and crumbly: 5 MEALY
  as a bone: 4 ARID
  as a desert: 7 SAHARAN
  as dust: 4 ARID SERE
  Extra: 4 ARID
  In a ~ manner: 6 ARIDLY
  Make: 5 PARCH
  Not quite: 4 DAMP
  (off): 5 TOWEL
  On ~ land: 6 ASHORE
  out: 5 DETOX PARCH
  Place to ~ out: 5 REHAB
  run: 4 **TEST**
  Stay: 8 TEETOTAL
  Very: 4 ARID BRUT SERE
  ~, as Champagne: 4 BRUT
  ~, as wine: 3 SEC
  ~, in a way: 5 WRING
Dry ___: 3 MOP ROT
Dry as ___: 5 ABONE
Dryden, John
  year of death: 4 MDCC
Dryer
  batch: 4 LOAD
  buildup: 4 LINT
  Hops: 4 OAST
  Like a ~ trap: 5 LINTY
  outlet: 4 VENT
  residue: 4 LINT
Drying
  cloth: 5 TOWEL
  Keep from ~ out: 5 REWET
  oven: 4 OAST
Drying-out
  facility: 5 REHAB
  stint: 5 REHAB
Drysdale
  of baseball: 3 DON
"Dr. Zhivago"
  actor Rod: 7 STEIGER
  heroine: 4 LARA
D sharp
  equivalent: 5 EFLAT
DST
  When ~ begins: 3 APR

When ~ ends: **3** OCT
Duane
  Guitarist: **4** EDDY
Duarte, Maria Eva
  after marriage:
      10 EVITAPERON
  He married: **5** PERON
Dub: 4 NAME
Dubai: 7 EMIRATE
  dignitary: **4** EMIR
Dubbed: 5 NAMED **6** TITLED
  one: **3** SIR
  Prepared to be: **5** KNELT
Dubious: 4 IFFY
  gift: **3** ESP
Dublin
  dance: **3** JIG
  denizens: **5** IRISH
  land: **4** EIRE ERIN
  theater: **5** ABBEY
Dublin-born: 5 IRISH
  poet: **5** YEATS
Dubuque
  native: **5** IOWAN
  state: **4** IOWA
Dubya
  and classmates: **4** ELIS
  deg.: **3** MBA
  Wife of: **5** LAURA
  ~, as a collegian: **3** ELI
Ducat
  word: **5** ADMIT
Duchamp
  art movement: **4** DADA
  contemporary: **3** ARP
Duchess: 5 TITLE
  Goya's: **4** ALBA
Duchess of ___: 4 YORK
"Duchess of ___" (Goya work):
    4 ALBA
"Duchess of Alba"
  painter: **4** GOYA
Duchess of York: 5 SARAH
Duchin
  Bandleader: **5** PETER
Duchovny, David
  Wife of: **3** TEA **8** TEALEONI
Duchy
  Old German: **4** SAXE

Duck: 5 AVERT AVOID DODGE
      ELUDE **EVADE**
      8 SIDESTEP
  Dabbling: **4** TEAL
  Dead: **5** GONER
  Diving: **4** SMEW **6** SCOTER
  down: **4** HIDE **5** EIDER
  Downy: **5** EIDER
  Eurasian: **4** SMEW
  Freshwater: **4** **TEAL**
  home: **4** POND
  Male: **5** DRAKE
  Pintail: **4** SMEE
  Pond: **4** TEAL
  Sea: **5** EIDER
  Small: **4** TEAL
  suffix: **4** LING
  Walk like a: **6** WADDLE
"Duck ___": 4 SOUP
Duck, Daffy: 4 TOON
"___ Duckling, The": 4 UGLY
"Duck soup!": 4 EASY
"Duck Soup"
  name: **4** MARX
Ducky
  color: **4** TEAL
  Just: **3** AOK
Ducommun
  Nobelist: **4** ELIE
Duct: 4 MAIN **5** CANAL
  Anatomical: **3** VAS
  Chimney: **4** FLUE
  follower: **4** TAPE
  prefix: **3** OVI
  suffix: **3** ILE
Ductile
  element: **3** TIN
Dud: 4 FLOP **5** LEMON
  Detroit: **5** EDSEL
  Social: **6** MISFIT
Dude: 3 BRO BUB CAT **5** FELLA
  Cool: **3** CAT
  Crude: **3** CAD **4** BOOR
  Macho: **5** HEMAN
  Mean: **4** OGRE
  Rich: **6** FATCAT
  Rude: **3** CAD **4** BOOR
  Stewed: **3** SOT
Dudgeon: 3 IRE **5** ANGER

High: 3 **IRE**
___ du Diable: 3 **ILE**
Dudley
  Actor: 5 MOORE
  Beloved of: 4 NELL
Duds: 4 GARB 5 GETUP 6 ATTIRE
    7 THREADS
Due: 4 OWED
  Amount past: 3 TRE
  Before the ~ date: 5 EARLY
  follower: 3 TRE
  In ~ time: 4 ANON
  It may be: 4 EAST RENT WEST
    5 NORTH SOUTH
  It's past: 3 TRE
  Landlord's: 4 RENT
  Past: 4 LATE
  Uno plus: 3 TRE
Duel
  invitation: 4 SLAP
  personality: 4 BURR 6 SECOND
  prelude: 4 SLAP
  souvenir: 4 SCAR
  tool: 4 EPEE 5 SABER
Dueler
  distance: 4 PACE
Dueling
  souvenir: 4 SCAR
  sword: 4 EPEE
  weapon: 4 EPEE
Dues
  payer: 6 MEMBER
  payer (abbr.): 3 MEM
  receiver: 4 CLUB
Duet: 4 PAIR
  plus one: 4 TRIO
Duff: 4 REAR RUMP
Duffel: 4 GEAR
  filler: 4 GEAR
Duffer
  cry: 4 FORE
  dream: 3 ACE 5 EAGLE
  goal: 3 PAR
  headache: 4 TRAP
  problem: 5 SLICE
Dufy
  Artist: 5 RAOUL
Dug: 3 GOT
  in: 3 **ATE** 10 ENTRENCHED

  Really: 5 ATEUP
  up: 5 MINED
  ~, in a way: 6 SPADED
Dugong: 6 SEACOW
Dugout: 4 BOAT 5 CANOE
  fig.: 3 MGR
  gear: 5 MITTS
  shelter: 4 ABRI
  vessel: 5 CANOE
  ~ VIP: 3 MGR
Duisburg
  river: 4 RUHR
___ du jour: 4 PLAT
Duke: 4 FIST PEER 5 NOBLE
    TITLE
  (abbr.): 4 UNIV
  His wife was a: 5 ASTIN
  home: 4 DORM
  of baseball: 6 SNIDER
  She performed with: 4 ELLA
  st.: 4 NCAR
Duke, The: 5 WAYNE
"Duke Bluebeard's Castle"
  composer: 6 BARTOK
Dukedom
  Notable: 4 YORK
"Duke of ___" (1962 hit): 4 EARL
Duke of York: 6 ANDREW
**"___ Dukes, The" (Ted Nugent's
    old band):** 5 AMBOY
"Dukes of Hazzard, The"
  Boss of: 4 HOGG
  deputy: 4 ENOS
  spin-off: 4 ENOS
Duke University
  locale: 6 DURHAM
"___ du lieber!": 3 ACH
Dull: 4 BLAH DRAB 5 HOHUM
    6 BORING
  finish: 3 ARD 5 **MATTE**
  pain: 4 ACHE
  routine: 3 RUT 4 ROTE
  sound: 4 THUD
  suffix: 3 ARD
  ~, as text: 5 PROSY
Dullard: 4 BORE CLOD SIMP
Dull-colored: 4 DRAB
Dullea
  Actor: 4 KEIR

Dulles, Allen
  org.: 3 CIA
Dulles Airport
  designer: 12 EEROSAARINEN
Dullsville: 4 BLAH 5 NOFUN
Dull-witted
  person: 4 DODO
Duma
  denial: 4 NYET
Dumas
  character: 5 ATHOS 6 ARAMIS
      7 PORTHOS 9 MUSKETEER
  motto word: 3 ALL
Dumb: 5 INANE 7 ASININE
  bunny: 5 STUPE
  cluck: 4 DODO 5 IDIOT
"Dumb"
  girl of comics: 4 DORA
"Dumb & Dumber"
  actress: 4 GARR
Dumbarton
  denial: 3 NAE
  denizen: 4 SCOT
Dumbarton ___ : 4 OAKS
Dumbbell: 4 DODO DOLT 5 IDIOT
      SCHMO STUPE
  material: 4 IRON
Dumbfound: 3 AWE WOW 4 DAZE
      5 AMAZE 7 STUPEFY
Dumbo
  wing: 3 EAR
Dumbstruck: 4 AWED 5 AGAPE
      INAWE
  Leave: 3 AWE
Dumfries
  denial: 3 NAE
  denizen: 4 SCOT
Dummkopf: 3 ASS 4 CLOD DODO
      5 IDIOT
Dummy: 3 ASS 4 BOZO DODO
      DOLT 6 NITWIT STOOGE
  name: 5 SNERD
  perch: 4 KNEE
  ~, at times: 4 EAST WEST
      5 NORTH SOUTH
Dump: 3 CAN STY 4 JILT 5 SCRAP
      6 UNLOAD 7 EYESORE
  emanation: 4 ODOR
  output: 4 ODOR

Dumpling
  Chinese: 6 WONTON
  Potato: 7 GNOCCHI
Dumps: 5 STIES
  Down in the: 3 **SAD** 4 BLUE
      GLUM 6 MOROSE
Dumpster
  contents: 5 TRASH
  emanation: 4 ODOR
Dunaway
  Actress: 4 FAYE
Dunaway, Faye
  film: 13 MOMMIEDEAREST
      15 EYESOFLAURAMARS
Duncan
  Dancer: 7 ISADORA
  of basketball: 3 TIM
  product: 4 YOYO
  When Macbeth slays:
      5 ACTII
Dunce: 3 OAF 4 SIMP 7 AIRHEAD
      PINHEAD
Dunce cap: 4 CONE
  shape: 5 CONIC
  wearer: 4 DOLT DOPE
"Dunciad, The"
  poet: 4 ROPE
Dundee
  Info: Scottish cue
  Boxing trainer: 6 ANGELO
  denial: 3 **NAE**
  denizen: 4 **SCOT**
  portrayer: 5 HOGAN
  Wee, in: 3 SMA
Dunderhead: 3 **ASS** OAF SAP
      4 BOZO DOLT DOPE
      5 IDIOT MORON
"Dune"
  composer Brian: 3 ENO
Dungeon
  Like a: 4 DANK
  restraints: 5 IRONS
Dungeons & Dragons
  co.: 3 TSR
  fan: 5 GAMER
  monster: 3 ORC
  spellcaster: 4 MAGE
Dunk: 7 IMMERSE
___ dunk: 4 SLAM

Dunkable
cookie: 4 OREO
treat: 4 OREO 5 DONUT

Dunked
It may be: 4 OREO 5 DONUT

Dunkers: 4 SECT

Dunn
Comic: 4 NORA

Dunne
Actress: 5 **IRENE**

Dunne, Irene
film: 13 IREMEMBERMAMA

Duo: 3 TWO
times four: 5 OCTET

Dup.
Not a: 4 ORIG
___ du pays: 3 MAL

Dupe: 3 SAP 5 REPRO 6 DELUDE
7 CATSPAW

Duped: 3 HAD 7 TAKENIN
Easily: 5 NAIVE
Not ~ by: 4 **ONTO**

Dupin
creator: 3 POE

Duple
Dance in ~ time: 5 POLKA

Duplicate: 4 TWIN 5 CLONE
DITTO REPRO
Sent a: 4 CCED

Duplicitous: 6 SNEAKY
7 CROOKED

Duplicity: 5 GUILE 6 DECEIT

DuPont
introduced it: 5 ORLON
invention: 6 LUCITE

Durability: 4 WEAR

Durable
fabric: 5 CHINO SERGE
wood: 3 OAK 4 TEAK
5 LARCH

Duracell
competitor: 7 RAYOVAC

Durango
Info: Mexican cue
day: 3 DIA
dough: 5 PESOS
dwelling: 4 CASA

Durant
Historian: 5 ARIEL

Durante
Prominent ~ feature: 4 NOSE
song starter: 4 INKA

Duration: 4 TERM 6 LENGTH
7 STRETCH

D'Urbervilles
lass: 4 TESS

Durbeyfield
girl: 4 TESS

Durbin
Actress: 6 DEANNA

Dürer
Emulate: 4 ETCH

Durham
sch.: 3 UNH

During: 4 **AMID** 6 AMIDST
the time that: 5 WHILE

Durkheim
Sociologist: 5 EMILE

"___ durn tootin'!": 3 YER
___ Duro Canyon: 4 PALO

Durocher
Baseball manager: 3 LEO
shortstop: 5 REESE

Dusk
Like: 6 TWILIT
Poet's: 3 EEN
~, to Donne: 3 **EEN**

Düsseldorf
Info: German cue
denial: 4 NEIN
direction: 3 OST
donkey: 4 ESEL

Dust
Bit of: 4 MOTE
Chimney: 4 SOOT
Collected: 3 SAT
Dry as: 4 ARID SERE
jacket feature: 3 BIO
Kind of: 6 COSMIC
Leave in the: 4 LOSE
Like a ~ bowl: 4 ARID
speck: 4 MOTE
Volcanic: 3 ASH
Word after: 3 BIN 5 CLOTH
___ dust: 5 DRYAS

Dust Bowl
migrant: 4 OKIE
refugee: 4 OKIE

Dustcloth: 3 RAG
Duster: 3 RAG 4 MAID
Dustin
  Role for: 5 RATSO
Dusting: 5 CHORE
  cloth: 3 RAG
  target: 4 CROP
"Dust in the Wind"
  group: 6 KANSAS
Dustup: 3 ROW 4 SPAT STIR
        5 SETTO
Dutch
  airline: 3 KLM
  bloom: 5 TULIP
  carrier: 3 KLM
  cheese: 4 **EDAM** 5 GOUDA
  city: 3 EDE
  commune: 3 EDE
  explorer: 6 TASMAN
  export: 4 **EDAM** 5 TULIP
  humanist: 7 ERASMUS
  It may be ~: 4 DOOR OVEN
  It may be ~ or French: 4 DOOR
  master: 5 STEEN
  painter: 4 HALS 5 STEEN
  sights: 5 DIKES
  town: 4 EDAM
  treat: 4 EDAM 5 GOUDA
Dutch ___: 4 OVEN
Dutch Guiana
  ~, today: 7 SURINAM
        8 SURINAME
Dutch South African: 4 BOER
Dutra
  Golfer: 4 OLIN
Duty: 3 TAX 4 ONUS TASK
        6 IMPOST TARIFF
  Customs: 6 IMPOST
  Import: 6 TARIFF
  Kind of: 5 CIVIC
  Period of: 4 TOUR
  Tour of: 5 **STINT**
Duun
  Novelist: 4 OLAV
Duvalier, Papa Doc:
        6 DESPOT
  domain, once: 5 HAITI
Duvall, Robert
  title role: 7 SANTINI

Duvall, Shelley
  role: 8 OLIVEOYL
___ du Vent: 4 ILES
DVD
  maker: 3 RCA
  part: 5 VIDEO
DVD player
  alternative: 3 VCR
  maker: 3 RCA
  necessities: 3 TVS
Dvorak: 5 CZECH
Dwarf: 4 STAR
  Bespectacled: 3 DOC
  complement: 5 SEVEN
  Folklore: 5 GNOME
  Silent: 5 DOPEY
  Subterranean: 5 GNOME
  tree: 6 BONSAI
Dwarfs
  Disney's: 6 SEPTET
Dweeb: 4 GEEK **NERD** TWIT
        5 LOSER
Dweebish: 5 NERDY
Dweezil
  Musician: 5 ZAPPA
Dwell: 4 BIDE 5 ABIDE
        6 RESIDE
  on: 6 PONDER
        7 BELABOR
  (on): 4 HARP
  permanently: 6 RESIDE
Dweller
  Apartment: 6 TENANT
  Arctic: 4 LAPP 5 INUIT
  Attu: 5 ALEUT
  Brook: 5 TROUT
  Cave: 3 BAT
  Convent: 3 NUN
  Coop: 3 HEN
  Cuzco: 4 INCA
  Delhi: 5 HINDU
  Dorm: 4 COED
  Flat: 6 LESSEE
  Forest: 3 DOE
  Hill: 3 **ANT**
  Igloo: 6 ESKIMO
  Lamp: 5 GENIE
  Mesa: 4 HOPI
  Palace: 5 ROYAL

Pueblo: 4 HOPI
Reef: 3 EEL
Sty: 3 HOG SOW
Dwelling: 5 __ABODE__
Cliffside: 5 AERIE
Conical: 5 TEPEE
Crude: 3 HUT 5 SHACK
Durango: 4 CASA
Indian: 5 TEPEE
Lofty: 5 AERIE
Makeshift: 3 HUT
Miserable: 5 HOVEL
Navajo: 5 HOGAN
Dwelt: 5 LIVED 7 RESIDED
Dwight
General under: 4 OMAR
Loser to: 5 ADLAI
Opponent of: 5 ADLAI
Dwindle: 3 EBB 4 WANE
~, with "out": 5 PETER
Dye: 5 TINCT
at the salon: 5 HENNA
Blue: 4 ANIL 6 INDIGO
Hair: 5 HENNA
Indigo: 4 ANIL
Nitrogen-based: 3 AZO
Place to curl up and: 5 SALON
plant: 4 ANIL
Red: 5 EOSIN HENNA
worker: 7 STAINER
Dyeing
art: 5 BATIK
Dyemaking
chemical: 7 ANILINE
Dyer
container: 3 VAT

Dye-yielding
plant: 4 ANIL
Dying
words: 4 ETTU
Dykstra
of baseball: 3 LEN
Dylan
Singer: 3 BOB
Dynamic
Leader: 4 AERO
opening: 4 __AERO__
Prefix for: 4 __AERO__
start: 4 __AERO__
Dynamite: 3 FAB 4 AONE
Form of: 7 GELATIN
ingredient, for short: 5 NITRO
inventor: 5 NOBEL
Dynamo: 8 FIREBALL LIVEWIRE
part: 6 STATOR
Dynasty
after the Ch'in: 3 HAN
Chinese: 3 HAN WEI 4 CHOU
    MING
Early Chinese: 4 HSIA
of Confucius: 4 CHOU
"Dynasty"
actress Emma: 5 SAMMS
actress Linda: 5 EVANS
conniver: 6 ALEXIS
role for Joan: 6 ALEXIS
Dyne
Prefix with: 4 AERO
Dyne-centimeter: 3 ERG
Dzhugashvili
Leader originally surnamed:
    6 STALIN

Ee

E: 3 DIR KEY 4 NOTE
  Morse: 3 DIT DOT
  Three before: 3 BCD
E-3: 3 PFC
E-4
  to E-7: 3 NCO
Each: 3 PER 4 **APOP** 5 AHEAD
      EVERY 6 APIECE ATHROW
  and every: 3 ALL
  For: 3 **PER** 6 APIECE
  in scores: 3 ALL
  Partner of: 5 EVERY
"Each Dawn ___": 4 IDIE
"___ each life ...": 4 INTO
Eager: 4 AGOG AVID KEEN
      5 DYING 6 ARDENT
      7 ATHIRST
  eater: 9 CHOWHOUND
  Far from: 5 LOATH
  Like an ~ guest: 5 EARLY
  to try: 6 KEENON
Eagerly
  Accept: 5 LAPUP 6 LEAPAT
  excited: 4 AGOG
  expectant: 4 ATIP
Eagerness: 4 ZEAL 5 ARDOR
Eagle: 6 SOARER
  Attack like an: 5 SWOOP
  claw: 5 TALON
  Fish-eating: 4 ERNE
  Fly like an: 4 SOAR
  Like an: 7 TALONED
  Muppet: 3 SAM
  nest: 5 AERIE
  org.: 3 BSA
  Sea: 3 ERN 4 **ERNE**
  Silver ~ wearer: 7 COLONEL
  The ~ that landed: 3 LEM
Eagles: 4 TEAM
Eagles, The
  Glenn of: 4 FREY
Eaglet
  nursery: 5 AERIE

Ear: 5 ORGAN
  bone: 5 INCUS 6 STAPES
  cleaner: 4 QTIP SWAB
  coverings: 5 MUFFS
  Inner: 3 COB
  Lend an: 4 HEED 6 LISTEN
  Like a turned: 4 DEAF
  Of the: 4 **OTIC** 5 AURAL
  part: 4 DRUM **LOBE** 5 CANAL
  prefix: 3 **OTO**
  problem: 6 OTITIS
  Stick it in your: 4 QTIP
  Word before: 3 TIN 5 INNER
Earache: 7 OTALGIA
"___ ear and out ...": 5 INONE
Eared
  pitcher: 4 EWER
  seal: 5 OTARY
Earhart: 8 AVIATRIX
  Aviator: 6 AMELIA
  Emulate: 6 AVIATE
  plane: 7 ELECTRA
Earl: 4 PEER 5 NOBLE TITLE
  Banjo player: 7 SCRUGGS
  French: 5 COMTE
  Jockey: 5 SANDE
  of Avon: 4 EDEN
  of jazz: 5 HINES
  Tea: 4 GREY
Earldom
  Anthony Eden: 4 AVON
  Devereux: 5 **ESSEX**
Earl Grey: 3 TEA
Earlier: 3 AGO ERE 5 OLDER
      PRIOR 6 BEFORE
  At an ~ time: 4 ONCE
  Born: 5 OLDER
  Of an ~ style: 5 RETRO
  Throwback to an ~ time:
      7 ATAVIST
Early: 3 WEE
  afternoon: 3 **ONE** TWO
      5 ONEPM

afternoon time: 6 ONETEN
arrival: 6 PREMIE
bird: 3 EGG
cab: 6 HANSOM
car: 3 REO
course: 4 SOUP 5 SALAD
End: 5 ABORT
evening: 5 SEVEN
evictee: 3 EVE
game score: 6 ONEONE
hour: 5 ONEAM
hrs.: 3 AMS
in the morning: 6 ATDAWN
man prefix: 3 CRO
pulpit: 4 AMBO
Put an ~ end to:
    11 NIPINTHEBUD
release: 6 PAROLE
round: 6 PRELIM
stage: 5 ONSET
times: 3 AMS 5 MORNS
Very: 3 WEE
word: 4 MAMA
years: 5 YOUTH
~ P.M.: 3 AFT
"Early Edition"
network: 3 CNN
Earmark: 5 ALLOT 7 DESTINE
    8 SETAPART
Earn: 4 MAKE 5 CLEAR GROSS
    MERIT 6 PULLIN
    TAKEIN 7 BRINGIN
    REALIZE
after taxes: 3 NET
and then some: 6 RAKEIN
Earned: 3 WON 4 MADE
a citation: 4 SPED
Earnest: 7 INTENSE SINCERE
request: 4 PLEA
Earnestly
hope: 4 PRAY
Earnhardt
Racer: 4 DALE
Earnings: 5 WAGES 6 SALARY
Acct.: 3 INT
Earp
Lawman: 5 WYATT
Ear-piercing
It can be: 4 STUD

Earring
site: 4 **LOBE**
Small: 4 STUD
style: 4 HOOP
Ears
All: 4 RAPT
Falling on deaf: 7 UNHEARD
It's all: 4 CORN 5 MAIZE
Like basset: 6 DROOPY
Like some: 3 TIN
Rabbit: 6 DIPOLE 7 ANTENNA
Up to one's: 5 AWASH
Wet behind the: 3 **RAW** 5 NAIVE
Earshot
Within: 4 NEAR
Earsplitting: 4 LOUD
Earth: 3 SOD 4 DIRT LOAM SOIL
    5 TERRA 6 SPHERE
Anywhere on:
    11 UNDERTHESUN
Came down to: 4 **ALIT**
Clump of: 4 CLOD
Come down to: 4 LAND
crust layer: 4 SIMA
Ends of the: 5 POLES
force: 4 ONEG
goddess: 4 GAEA GAIA
Good: 4 LOAM
Heaven on: 4 EDEN 6 UTOPIA
hue: 5 OCHER OCHRE
inheritors: 4 MEEK
Most of ~ surface: 5 OCEAN
Not from: 5 ALIEN
On: 4 HERE
Orbital point farthest from:
    6 APOGEE
orbiter: 3 MIR
pigment: 5 OCHER OCHRE
    6 SIENNA
remover: 6 DREDGE
sci.: 4 ECOL GEOG
tone: 4 ECRU 5 BEIGE OCHER
    OCHRE UMBER
Wet: 3 MUD 4 CLAY MIRE
Word after: 4 TONE
~, in German: 4 **ERDE**
~, in sci-fi: 5 TERRA
Eartha
Singer: 4 KITT

Earthbound
bird: 3 EMU
Earth Day
mo.: 3 APR
month: 5 APRIL
subj.: 4 ECOL
Earthen
pot: 4 **OLLA**
Earthenware
pot: 4 **OLLA** 5 CROCK
source: 4 CLAY
Earth First
prefix: 3 ECO
Earth-friendly
prefix: 3 **ECO**
sci.: 4 ECOL
"Earth in the Balance"
author: 4 GORE 6 ALGORE
Earthling: 5 HUMAN
~, in sci-fi: 6 TERRAN
Earthlings
Most: 6 ASIANS
EarthLink: 3 ISP
competitor: 3 AOL
Earthmover: 5 DOZER
maker, for short: 3 CAT
Earthquake: 5 SEISM 7 TEMBLOR
1995 ~ site: 4 KOBE
origins: 4 FOCI
Earthquake-related: 7 SEISMAL
SEISMIC
Earthshaking: 7 SEISMIC
It's: 6 TREMOR
Earth-sky
boundary (abbr.): 3 HOR
Earth Summit
site: 3 RIO
Earthy
deposit: 4 MARL
desire: 4 LUST
pigment: 5 OCHER **OCHRE**
UMBER
Ear-to-ear
smile: 4 GRIN
Ease: 5 ABATE LETUP 6 LESSEN
Less at: 6 EDGIER
up: 5 ABATE 6 LOOSEN
___ ease: 5 ILLAT
Easel: 5 STAND

"Ease on Down the Road"
musical: 6 THEWIZ
Easier
Make ~ to take: 9 SUGARCOAT
version, in music: 5 OSSIA
"Easier said ___ done": 4 THAN
Easiness
Epitome of: 3 ABC PIE
Easing
of tension: 4 THAW
East: 6 ORIENT
end: 3 ERN
ender: 3 **ERN**
From the: 5 ASIAN
of the Urals: 4 ASIA
Priest of the: 4 LAMA
suffix: 3 ERN
The: 4 ASIA 6 ORIENT
Way of the: 3 TAO
wind: 5 EURUS
~, in German: 3 OST
~, in Spanish: 7 ORIENTE
East China Sea
island: 5 MATSU
East Coast
rte.: 5 USONE
Easter
egg coloring: 3 DYE
entrée: 3 HAM 4 LAMB
event: 6 PARADE
flower: 4 **LILY**
follower: 4 SEAL
headgear: 6 BONNET
lead-in: 3 NOR
Like ~ eggs: 4 **DYED**
or Christmas (abbr.): 3 ISL
preceder: 3 NOR 4 LENT
10 PALMSUNDAY
Easter Island
owner: 5 CHILE
statues: 7 COLOSSI
Eastern: 5 ASIAN
air: 4 RAGA
cuisine: 4 THAI
discipline: 3 ZEN 4 YOGA
holiday: 3 TET
ideal: 3 TAO
leader: 3 AGA
music: 4 RAGA

nanny: 4 **AMAH**
nursemaid: 4 AMAH
philosophy: 3 TAO
royal: 4 RANI
sash: 3 OBI
tie: 3 OBI
title: 3 AGA SRI
way: 3 **TAO**
wrap: 4 SARI
~ Canadian indian: 6 MICMAC
~ Christian: 6 UNIATE
~ European: 4 **SERB** SLAV
~ Indian: 4 ERIE

East German
secret police: 5 STASI

East Indian
sailor: 6 LASCAR

East Lansing
sch.: 3 MSU

"East of ___": 4 EDEN

"East of Eden"
brother: 3 CAL 4 ARON
character Cathy: 4 AMES
director Kazan: 4 ELIA
family name: 5 TRASK
girl: 4 ABRA

Easton
Singer: 6 SHEENA

Easton ___, Bret
Author: 5 ELLIS

Eastwood
1980 ~ film: 11 BRONCOBILLY
Actor: 5 CLINT
series: 7 RAWHIDE
TV role for: 5 YATES

Easy: 7 LENIENT
basket: 5 LAYUP
dupe: 3 SAP
gait: 4 LOPE TROT 5 AMBLE
gallop: 6 CANTER
job: 4 SNAP
mark: 3 **SAP** 4 DUPE PREY
SIMP 5 CHUMP PATSY
6 PIGEON 7 LIVEONE
Not ~ to find: 4 RARE
on the eyes: 6 PRETTY
out: 5 POPUP
pace: 4 LOPE TROT 5 AMBLE
Proverbial ~ life leader: 5 RILEY

Take it: 4 LAZE LOAF LOLL
REST 5 COAST RELAX
target: 3 SAP 11 SITTINGDUCK
task: 4 SNAP
The ~ life: 10 BEDOFROSES
threesome: 3 ABC
throw: 3 LOB 4 TOSS
to fool: 5 NAIVE
to manage: 4 TAME
to understand: 5 CLEAR
two-pointer: 4 DUNK
victory: 4 ROMP ROUT
7 RUNAWAY
way out: 4 DOOR
"Easy!": 5 ASNAP
Easy ___: 5 ASABC **ASPIE**
6 STREET
"___ Easy" (1977 hit): 5 ITSSO
Easy as ___: 3 ABC
Easy as falling off ___: 4 ALOG
Easy chair
site: 3 DEN
Use an: 7 RECLINE
Easygoing
Not: 5 TESTY
Easy-listening: 4 LITE
Easy Street
On: 4 RICH
Was on: 9 HADITMADE
Where ~ is: 7 FATCITY
"Easy to Be Hard"
musical: 4 HAIR
Easy-to-prepare: 6 NOBAKE
Eat: 3 SUP 4 DINE HAVE
6 FEEDON INGEST
All you can: 7 EDIBLES
away: 4 GNAW 5 ERODE
7 CORRODE
away at: 5 **ERODE**
between meals: 4 NOSH 5 SNACK
He'll ~ anything: 8 OMNIVORE
in style: 4 DINE
into: 5 **ERODE**
like a bird: 4 PECK
Ready to: 4 DONE RIPE
sumptuously: 5 FEAST
Unable to ~ another bite:
7 STUFFED
voraciously: 5 SCARF

well: 4 DINE
What you: 4 DIET
"Eat Drink Man Woman"
director Lee: 3 ANG
"Eat ___ eaten!": 4 ORBE
Eaten
up: 4 GONE
Eater
Abalone: 5 OTTER
Apple: 3 EVE
Bamboo: 5 PANDA
Eucalyptus: 5 KOALA
Lean: 5 SPRAT
Pumpkin: 5 PETER
Seaweed: 7 ABALONE
Slop: 5 SWINE
Sweater: 4 MOTH
Eatery: 4 **CAFE** 5 DINER
Casual: 6 BISTRO
Famed New York: 7 ELAINES
Outmoded: 7 AUTOMAT
Puck's: 5 SPAGO
Small: 7 TEAROOM
"Eat hearty!": 5 DIGIN
Eating
alcove: 7 DINETTE
plan: 4 DIET
Start: 5 DIGIN
"Eating ___" (1982 film):
5 RAOUL
Eat like ___ : 4 APIG 5 ABIRD
6 AHORSE
Eats: 3 HAS 4 CHOW GRUB
Eau ___, Wisconsin: 6 CLAIRE
Eaves
dropper: 6 ICICLE
Eavesdrop: 3 TAP 4 HEAR
Eavesdropper: 5 SNOOP
Eban
of Israel: 4 **ABBA**
eBay
action: 3 BID
Beat on: 6 OUTBID
user: 6 SELLER
Ebb: 4 WANE WILT 6 RECEDE
and neap: 5 TIDES
Of ~ and neap: 5 TIDAL
Ebbets Field
great: 5 **REESE**

Ebenezer
exclamation: 3 **BAH**
Partner of: 5 JACOB
Eberhard ___ : 5 FABER
Ebert
Emulate: 4 RATE
Former partner of: 6 SISKEL
Ebony
counterpart of song: 5 IVORY
Ebro: 3 RIO
City on the: 9 SARAGOSSA
Ebullience: 3 VIM
Ecbatana
resident: 4 MEDE
Eccentric: 3 NUT ODD 4 KOOK
5 BATTY DOTTY KOOKY
LOOPY NUTTY OUTRE
WACKO 6 SCREWY
7 ODDBALL
people: 9 HEADCASES
type: 5 FLAKE
wheel: 3 CAM
Eccentricity: 3 TIC 7 ODDNESS
Ecclesiastes
Phrase repeated in: 5 ATIME
Ecclesiastical
council: 5 SYNOD
office: 3 SEE
Echelon: 4 RANK TIER
Top: 5 ELITE
Echidna
morsel: 3 ANT
Echo: 4 RING 5 NYMPH OREAD
6 ANSWER REPEAT
7 ITERATE RESOUND
8 RESONATE
effect: 6 REVERB
Emulate: 4 PINE
finder: 5 SONAR
spot: 6 CANYON
Echolocation
device: 5 SONAR
"Echo Park"
actress: 3 DEY
Eclectic
magazine: 4 UTNE
mix: 4 OLIO
Eclipse: 4 OMEN
Kind of: 5 LUNAR SOLAR

shadow: 5 UMBRA
sight: 4 RING 6 CORONA
Eco-friendly
org.: 3 EPA
Ecol.
watchdog: 3 **EPA**
Ecological
adjective: 5 SERAL
community: 5 BIOME
Econ.
measure: 3 **GNP**
Economic
cycle: 11 BOOMANDBUST
extremes: 10 BOOMORBUST
fig.: 3 GNP
prefix: 5 SOCIO
stat.: 3 CPI
warfare tactic: 7 EMBARGO
What ~ sanctions can lead to:
    8 TRADEWAR
Economical: 4 LEAN
Economics
prefix: 5 MACRO MICRO
Economize: 4 SAVE 6 SCRIMP
    10 CUTCORNERS
Economy: 4 SIZE 6 THRIFT
Failed ~ car: 4 YUGO
Lack of: 5 WASTE
Economy-size: 5 GIANT JUMBO
Ecru: 5 BEIGE
Ecstasy: 5 BLISS
Go into: 5 SWOON
In: 4 SENT
"Ecstasy"
actress Hedy: 6 LAMARR
Ecstatic
Make: 5 ELATE
Ecto-
Opposite of: 4 **ENDO** ENTO
Ecuador
Capital of: 5 QUITO
East, in: 7 ORIENTE
Ending for: 3 EAN
Ecuadoran
cash: 6 SUCRES
Ed
Actor: 5 ASNER
and Mel of baseball: 4 OTTS
Comedian: 4 WYNN

Former NYC mayor: 4 KOCH
Former SAG president: 5 ASNER
Mingo portrayer: 4 AMES
of the Reagan cabinet: 5 MEESE
Singer: 4 AMES
Wife of: 6 TRIXIE
"Ed"
network: 3 NBC
Ed.
Enclosure to an: 4 SASE
First: 4 ORIG
Fixed by an: 4 CORR
group: 3 PTA
provider: 3 SCH
Submissions to an: 3 MSS
___ **Ed.:** 4 PHYS
Eda
Author: 6 LESHAN
Edam: 6 CHEESE
relative: 5 GOUDA
Edberg
of tennis: 6 STEFAN
or Borg: 5 SWEDE
Eddas
Language of the: 8 OLDNORSE
Eddie
and Edward: 7 ALBERTS
Ex of: 3 LIZ
Famous cop: 4 EGAN
of baseball: 4 YOST 5 LOPAT
Rocker: 8 VANHALEN
Vaudevillian: 3 FOY
Eddy: 5 SWIRL
Guitarist: 5 DUANE
Eddying: 6 ASWIRL
Edelweiss
source: 4 ALPS
Eden
event: 4 FALL
evictee: 3 EVE 4 ADAM
Like Nod, to: 4 EAST
Eden, Anthony: 4 EARL
earldom: 4 AVON
Eden, Barbara
role: 5 GENIE
"___ ed Euridice": 5 ORFEO
Edgar: 5 AWARD
Painter: 5 DEGAS
Psychic: 5 CAYCE

Edgar Allan ___ : 3 POE
Edgard
  Composer: **6** VARESE
Edge: 3 HEM LIP **RIM 4** TRIM
      6 BORDER
  along: **5** SIDLE
  Beveled: **4** CANT
  Bowler: **4** BRIM
  Canyon: **3 RIM**
  Cutting: **3** LIP **5** BLADE
  Drape: **3** HEM
  Extreme: **5** BRINK
  Give an ~ to: **4** HONE WHET
  Golf-hole: **3** LIP
  Had an: **3** LED
  Hat: **4** BRIM
  Have an ~ against: **4** ABUT
  It lacks a cutting: **4** EPEE
  On: **5** JUMPY TENSE TESTY
      6 UNEASY
  Outer: **3** RIM **6** FRINGE
  Put an ~ on: **4 HONE** WHET
  Racer's: **9** HEADSTART
  Rock on the: **6** TEETER
  Roof: **4 EAVE**
  Server: **4** ADIN
  Skirt: **3** HEM
  Tennis: **4** ADIN
  The ~ of night: **4** DUSK
  Water's: **5** SHORE
  Wear at the: **4** FRAY
Edger
  Lid: **8** EYELINER
Edgy: 5 TENSE WIRED
Edible
  Become: **5** RIPEN
  clam: **6** QUAHOG
  mollusk: **6** OYSTER **7** ABALONE
  mushroom: **5** MOREL
  No longer: **3** BAD
  pocket: **4** PITA
  pod: **4** OKRA **5** CAROB
  root: **3** YAM **4** TARO
  snail: **8** ESCARGOT
  spikes: **4** EARS
  tuber: **3** OCA YAM **4** TARO
      6 POTATO
Edict: 4 FIAT **6** DECREE
      7 MANDATE

1598 ~ site: **6** NANTES
Czar: **5** UKASE
Edinburgh
  native: **4** SCOT
Edison
  contemporary: **5 TESLA**
  grant: **6** PATENT
  middle name: **4 ALVA**
  product: **4** IDEA
Edison, Thomas ___ : 4 ALVA
Edit: 5 AMEND **EMEND**
      6 REDACT REVISE
  anew: **5** RECUT
  film: **6** SPLICE
  menu choice: **4** UNDO
  out: **4** DELE **5** BLEEP **6** DELETE
Edited
  Not: **5** UNCUT
Edith
  Archie's admonition to: **6** STIFLE
  Chanteuse: **4** PIAF
  Mike, to: **5** INLAW
  portrayer: **4** JEAN
  ~, to Archie: **7** DINGBAT
Edith ___
  Tomlin character: **3** ANN
Editing
  Do some film: **6** SPLICE
  Do some tape: **3** DUB
  Film ~ technique: **4** WIPE
  Work at film: **5** RECUT
Edition
  Later: **7** REPRINT
  Mag.: **3** ISS
  Magazine: **5** ISSUE
  Most-used ~ (abbr.): **3** STD
  Special: **5** EXTRA
Editor
  Encl. to an: **3** SAE **4** SASE
  Film: **7** SPLICER
  find: **4** TYPO
  Leave in, to an: **4** STET
  mark: **4** DELE **STET**
  Material for an: **4** COPY
  of the New Yorker: **4** ROSS
  Remove, to an: **4** DELE
  ~ Brown: **4** TINA
Editorial
  submissions (abbr.): **3** MSS

Editorialize: 5 OPINE
"Editorially speaking"
~, in chat rooms: **3** IMO
Edmond
Card game authority: **5** HOYLE
Edmonton
hockey player: **5** **OILER**
province: **7** ALBERTA
Edmund
Actor: **5** GWENN
Shakespearean actor: **4** KEAN
"Ed, ___ n' Eddy": 3 EDD
Edom
Ancient kingdom near: **4** MOAB
Edomite
city: **5** PETRA
Edouard
Composer: **4** LALO
Eds.
Submissions to: **3** **MSS**
Edson
Athlete born: **4** PELE
"EDtv"
director Howard: **3** RON
Edu
alternative: **3** ORG
Educ.
group: **3** PTA
institution: **3** SCH
Educate: 5 TEACH **6** SCHOOL
Educated
It may be: **5** GUESS
Education
Basics of: **3** RRR
Early: **4** ABCS
gp.: **3** PTA
grant name: **4** PELL
K-12, in: **4** ELHI
station: **4** DESK
Uncreative: **4** ROTE
Educational
items used to illustrate everyday
life: **6** REALIA
Educator
org.: **3** NEA
Royal: **4** ETON
Edward
and Eddie: **7** ALBERTS
Archbishop: **4** EGAN

New Yorker cartoonist: **5** SOREL
Playwright: **5** **ALBEE**
Poet: **4** LEAR
Edward G.
role: **4** RICO
Edward James ___
Actor: **5** OLMOS
Edwards
(abbr.): **3** AFB
Director: **5** BLAKE
Edwin
Former Attorney General:
5 MEESE
"Ed Wood"
director Burton: **3** TIM
star: **4** DEPP
~ Oscar winner: **6** LANDAU
EEC
Part of: **3** EUR
Eel: 6 CONGER
Feared: **5** MORAY
Glass: **5** ELVER
lookalike: **7** LAMPREY
Where to find: **8** SUSHIBAR
Young: **5** ELVER
E'en
if: **3** THO
Not ~ once: **4** **NEER**
Eerie: 6 SPOOKY **7** STRANGE
feeling: **6** DEJAVU
sighting: **3** UFO
E'erlasting: 6 ETERNE
Eero
Dad of: **5** ELIEL
Eeyore
Creator of: **5** MILNE **7** AAMILNE
Effect
Audio: **4** ECHO
Canyon: **4** ECHO
Dazzling: **5** ECLAT
Discotheque: **6** STROBE
Echo: **6** REVERB
Guitar: **4** WAWA
Have an: **4** TELL WORK
Having: **7** INURING
Ice cream: **5** SWIRL
Jacuzzi: **4** EDDY
Lasting: **4** SCAR
Lunar: **4** TIDE

Magic sound: 4 POOF
Meteorological: 4 HALO
Muted: 4 WAWA
Organ: 7 TREMOLO
Partner of: 5 CAUSE
Put into: 5 ENACT
Replay: 5 SLOMO
Singing: 7 TREMOLO
Sound: 4 ECHO
Take: 5 INURE SETIN
Vibrating: 7 TREMOLO
Effective: 7 INFORCE OPERANT
Cleverly: 4 NEAT
power: 5 TEETH
Effectively
Use: 5 WIELD
Effectiveness
Range of: 5 SCOPE
Effects
Reverse the ~ of: 4 UNDO
Effervescent
Make: 6 AERATE
Efficiency
experts: 15 SYSTEMSANALYSTS
Fuel ~ abbr.: 3 MPG
symbol: 3 ETA
Efficient: 4 ABLE
Effigy: 5 IMAGE
Effluvia
Noxious: 6 MIASMA
Effluvium
Emit: 4 REEK
Effort: 4 DINT STAB
Carry with: 3 LUG 4 HAUL
Clean with: 5 SCRUB
Contest: 5 ENTRY
Exert no: 5 COAST
Gather with: 7 SCAREUP
High mark with low: 5 EASYA
Kind of: 9 LASTDITCH
Last-ditch: 5 STAND
Lift with: 4 HEFT 5 HEAVE
Make an: 3 TRY 6 STRIVE
Put forth: 5 EXERT
Throw with: 5 HEAVE
Vigorous: 11 ELBOWGREASE
Walk with: 4 PLOD SLOG
    6 TRUDGE
Waste: 14 SPINONESWHEELS

With little: 6 EASILY
___ effort: 4 AFOR EFOR
Effortless: 4 EASY
pace: 4 ROMP
Effortlessly
Move: 5 GLIDE
Effortlessness: 4 EASE
Effrontery: 4 GALL 5 BRASS
    CHEEK
Effusive
Be: 4 GUSH
E-file
org.: 3 IRS
E flat
equivalent: 6 DSHARP
Eft: 4 NEWT
Eg.
and Syr., once: 3 UAR
E.g.
relative: 3 VIZ
"Egad!": 4 OATH OHMY YIPE
Egg: 4 OVUM URGE 6 GAMETE
beater: 5 WHISK
carton abbr.: 3 DOZ 4 USDA
cell: 4 OVUM
cells: 3 OVA
container: 4 NEST 6 OVISAC
cream ingredient: 4 SODA
    5 SYRUP
dish: 6 OMELET
drink: 3 NOG
Goose: 3 NIL ZIP 4 NADA **ZERO**
    6 NAUGHT
holder: 3 SAC 4 NEST
Immature ~ cell: 6 OOCYTE
Kind of nest: 7 ROTHIRA
Lay an: 4 BOMB FLOP
layers: 4 HENS
Like a good: 6 GRADEA
Louse: 3 NIT
Nest: 3 IRA 7 ROTHIRA
on: 4 COAX DARE GOAD PROD
    SPUR **URGE** 6 INCITE
One with a nest: 3 HEN
order: 4 OVER
    11 SUNNYSIDEUP
Paint with ~ in it: 7 TEMPERA
part: 5 YOLK
prefix: 3 OVI OVO

Prepare an: 5 POACH
producer: 3 HEN
purchase: 5 DOZEN
qty.: 3 DOZ
shape: 4 OVAL
size: 5 JUMBO LARGE
Small: 5 OVULE
warmer: 3 HEN
white: 7 ALBUMIN
Word following: 4 ROLL
"Egg ___, The": 4 ANDI
Egg foo ___: 4 YUNG
Egghead: 4 NERD 5 BRAIN
6 SAVANT
Egg-laying
animal: 7 ECHIDNA
Egglike: 6 OVULAR
Eggnog
spice: 6 NUTMEG
Time for: 4 NOEL YULE
Eggplant
dish: 8 MOUSSAKA
Egg roll
place: 4 LAWN
time: 6 EASTER
Eggs: 3 **OVA** ROE
Bake: 5 **SHIRR**
partner: 3 HAM
Egg-shaped: 4 OVAL 5 **OVATE**
OVOID
instrument: 7 OCARINA
Eggshell: 4 ECRU
Eggy
cake: 5 TORTE
dessert: 4 FLAN
drink: 3 NOG
entrée: 6 OMELET
Egg ___ yung: 3 FOO
Ego: 4 SELF
Altar: 3 MRS 5 GROOM
of Freud: 3 ICH
Egotist
interest: 4 SELF
Egoyan
Director: 4 ATOM
Egret: 5 WADER
relative: 4 IBIS 5 HERON
Egypt
Anwar of: 5 SADAT

Capital of: 5 **CAIRO**
Gulf between Saudi Arabia and:
5 AQABA
Lake of: 6 NASSER
Mubarak of: 5 **HOSNI**
Nasser of: 5 GAMAL
neighbor (abbr.): 3 ISR
Opera set in: 4 **AIDA**
Port of: 4 SAID
President of: 7 MUBARAK
River of: 4 NILE
Sacred bird of: 4 IBIS
Sadat of: 5 ANWAR
Symbol of ancient: 3 ASP
~, in the 1960s: 3 UAR
Egyptian
beetle: 6 SCARAB
bird: 4 IBIS
boy king: 3 TUT
canal: 4 SUEZ
cobra: 3 **ASP**
cross: 4 **ANKH**
dam: 5 ASWAN
deity: 6 AMENRA
Former ~ leader: 5 SADAT
god: 4 PTAH
goddess of fertility: 4 **ISIS**
god of the underworld: 6 OSIRIS
money: 7 PIASTER
peninsula: 5 SINAI
pharoah: 7 RAMESES
port: 4 SUEZ
pyramid: 4 TOMB
queen: 4 CLEO
snake: 3 ASP
sun deity: 4 ATEN
symbol of life: 4 ANKH
symbol of resurrection: 6 SCARAB
viper: 3 ASP
~ Christian: 4 COPT
"Eh": 4 SOSO
Ehud
of Israel: 5 BARAK
successor: 5 ARIEL
E-I
connection: 3 FGH
Eiffel ___: 5 TOWER
Eiffel Tower
home: 5 PARIS

Eiger: 3 ALP
Eight
  Based on: 5 OCTAL
  Behind the ~ ball: 6 INAJAM
    7 INAHOLE
  bits: 4 BYTE
  furlongs: 4 MILE
  Group of: 5 OCTAD OCTET
  Half a figure: 3 ESS
  Name of ~ popes: 5 URBAN
  One of ~ Eng. kings: 3 EDW
  prefix: 4 OCTA OCTO
  pts.: 3 GAL
  quarts: 4 PECK
  Word in ~ Commandments:
    3 NOT
  ~, in German: 4 ACHT
  ~, in Spanish: 4 OCHO
Eight-armed
  creature: 7 OCTOPUS
  creatures: 6 OCTOPI
Eightball
  choice: 6 SOLIDS
  shot: 5 MASSE
Eight-based: 5 OCTAL
Eight-day
  observance: 8 CHANUKAH
"Eight Days ___": 5 AWEEK
Eighteenth Amendment
  state: 3 DRY
Eighteen-wheeler: 3 RIG 4 SEMI
Eighth
  Greek letter: 5 THETA
"Eight Is Enough"
  actor Willie: 5 AAMES
Eight-legged
  Deity with an ~ horse: 4 ODIN
Eight-line
  verse: 7 TRIOLET
Eight-member
  ensemble: 5 OCTET
Eightsome: 5 OCTAD OCTET
Eighty Eight: 4 OLDS
Eighty-eight: 5 PIANO
Eighty-six: 3 NIX 4 TOSS
  5 DITCH
EIK
  Part of: 5 EATIN
  site: 3 APT

Eins
  und zwei: 4 **DREI**
Einstein: 5 BRAIN
  birthplace: 3 **ULM**
  Everything, to: 5 ALLES
  factor: 4 MASS
  ~, for one: 6 EMIGRE
Eisaku
  1974 Peace Nobelist: 4 SATO
Eisenhower
  and others: 4 IKES
  Mrs.: 5 MAMIE
  nickname: 3 IKE
  Secretary of State under:
    6 DULLES
  WWII command: 3 ETO
Eisenhower Center
  city: 7 ABILENE
Eisenstein
  Director: 6 SERGEI
"Either he goes, ___ do!": 3 ORI
Eithne Ní Bhraonáin
  Singer born: 4 ENYA
Eject: 4 BOOT OUST SPEW
  6 CASTUP
  lava: 5 ERUPT
E-junk: 4 SPAM
Ekberg
  Actress: 5 **ANITA**
Eke
  out a living: 6 MAKEDO
EKG
  Part of: 4 GRAM
Ekland
  Actress: 5 BRITT
El ___
  (Spanish hero): 3 **CID**
  (Spanish painter): 5 GRECO
  (Texas city): 4 PASO
  (treasure city): 6 DORADO
  (weather phenomenon): 4 **NINO**
  (western peak): 7 CAPITAN
  (WWII battle site): 7 ALAMEIN
"El ___" (Marty Robbins hit):
  4 PASO
Elaborate: 6 ORNATE
  display: 5 ECLAT
  party: 4 FETE GALA
  tapestry: 5 ARRAS

Elaine
Friend of Jerry and: 5 COSMO
Home of: 7 ASTOLAT
El Al
destination: 3 LOD 7 TELAVIV
___ el Amarna, Egypt: 3 TEL
Elan: 4 DASH
Elapse: 4 GOBY
Elastic: 7 RUBBERY
wood: 3 ASH YEW
Elasticity: 4 GIVE
Elate: 4 SEND 7 OVERJOY
Elated: 4 GLAD SENT 5 HAPPY
11 ONCLOUDNINE
Be visibly: 4 GLOW
Where the ~ walk: 5 ONAIR
Elath
neighbor: 5 AQABA
Elation: 3 JOY 4 GLEE
Elba
Send to: 5 EXILE
Elbe
tributary: 4 EGER
Elbow: 3 JAB 4 POKE PROD
5 JOINT NUDGE SHOVE
6 JOSTLE
Bend one's: 4 TOPE 6 IMBIBE
Bone below the: 4 ULNA
Gently: 5 NUDGE
site: 3 ARM
Use ~ grease: 4 TOIL 5 SCOUR
SCRUB
Elbow-bender: 3 SOT 4 LUSH
5 SOUSE
Elbow room: 5 SPACE
Elbows: 5 PASTA
on the table: 5 PASTA
8 MACARONI
Pipe: 4 ELLS
Elbow-wrist
connection: 4 ULNA
El Capitan
Like the face of: 5 STEEP
El Cid: 4 HERO
foe: 4 MOOR
Elder: 4 TREE
elver: 3 EEL
of Isaac: 4 ESAU
~ Judd: 5 NAOMI

~ Saarinen: 5 ELIEL
"Elder"
Roman: 4 CATO
Elderly: 3 OLD 4 AGED
Eldest
of Cain: 5 ENOCH
of Eve: 4 CAIN
of Isaac: 4 ESAU
of Noah: 4 SHEM
El Dorado
treasure: 3 ORO
"Eldorado"
rock gp.: 3 ELO
" ___ e Leandro": 3 ERO
Eleanor
Children's author: 5 ESTES
Feminist: 5 SMEAL
First Lady before: 3 LOU
in a Beatles hit: 5 RIGBY
successor: 4 BESS
~, to Teddy: 5 NIECE
Eleanora
Actress: 4 DUSE
Eleazar: 8 AARONITE
Elec.
company: 4 UTIL
designation: 4 ACDC
system component: 3 IGN
Elect: 3 OPT 6 CHOOSE CHOSEN
VOTEIN
Elected
officials: 3 **INS**
Try to get: 3 RUN
Electees: 3 INS
Election
data: 7 RETURNS
day (abbr.): 4 TUES
Fix an: 3 RIG
hanger-on: 4 CHAD
loser: 3 OUT 7 ALSORAN
mo.: 3 NOV
news: 5 UPSET
winners: 3 INS
Elective
High school: 3 ART
Electoral
Winner by one ~ vote:
5 HAYES
Electorate: 6 VOTERS

Electra
Brother of: 4 ORIN
  7 ORESTES
Electric
co.: 4 UTIL
coil inventor: 5 TESLA
current blocker: 8 RESISTOR
eye: 6 SENSOR
fish: 3 EEL
flux symbol: 3 PSI
measure: 3 AMP
One with ~ organs: 3 EEL
partner: 3 GAS
swimmer: 3 EEL
unit: 4 VOLT
Electric ___: 3 ARC EEL EYE
Electrical
bridge: 3 ARC
device: 7 ADAPTER ADAPTOR
Do ~ work: 4 WIRE
gauge: 7 AMMETER
inventor Nikola: 5 TESLA
letters: 4 ACDC
Make ~ improvements:
  6 REWIRE
network: 4 GRID
pioneer: 5 TESLA
problem: 9 SHORTFUSE
resistance: 6 OHMAGE
resistance unit: 3 OHM
safeguard: 4 FUSE
unit: 3 AMP MHO OHM REL
  4 **VOLT** WATT 5 FARAD
  6 AMPERE
Electrically
flexible: 4 ACDC
Electric guitar
effect: 4 WAWA
hookup: 3 AMP
Electrician: 5 WIRER
alloy: 6 SOLDER
need: 6 PLIERS
Electricity: 5 JUICE POWER
Jolt with: 3 ZAP
Kind of: 6 STATIC
pioneer: 5 TESLA VOLTA
Electrified
fish: 3 EEL
particle: 3 ION

Electrify: 3 AWE WOW 4 WIRE
  6 AROUSE THRILL
Electrode
Certain: 7 EMITTER
flow: 3 ARC
Electrolux: 3 VAC
Electrolysis
particle: 3 ION 5 ANION
Electrolytic
cell part: 5 ANODE
Electromagnetic
wave amplifier: 5 MASER
Electron
home: 4 ATOM
loser or gainer: 3 ION
stream: 7 BETARAY
tube: 5 DIODE
Electronic
control system: 5 SERVO
drug in Shatner novels: 3 TEK
First ~ computer: 5 ENIAC
game pioneer: 5 ATARI
info source: 5 CDROM
music pioneer: 4 MOOG
  6 VARESE
Electronically
Capture: 4 SCAN
Electronic Data Systems
founder: 5 PEROT
Electronics
Big name in: 3 IBM RCA 4 SONY
  5 CASIO SANYO 7 TOSHIBA
  8 MOTOROLA
co.: 3 ITT RCA
device: 5 DIODE
expert: 4 TECH 6 TECHIE
Electrophorus
member: 3 EEL
Elegance: 4 LUXE TONE
  5 CLASS GRACE STYLE
  6 POLISH
Elegant: 4 FINE POSH 5 SLEEK
  SWANK 6 CLASSY SWANKY
  7 REFINED
Has an ~ supper: 5 DINES
Elegantly
lean: 6 SVELTE
stylish: 6 CLASSY
"___ eleison": 5 KYRIE

"Elektra"
composer: 7 STRAUSS
Elem.
school aux.: 3 PTA
Element: 4 UNIT
Antiseptic: 6 IODINE
Blind: 4 SLAT
Brake: 4 SHOE
Brass: 4 ZINC
Containing ~ 76: 5 OSMIC
Contributing: 6 FACTOR
element: 4 ATOM
Forest: 4 TREE
Graphite: 6 CARBON
Jigsaw: 5 PIECE
Moral: 5 ETHOS
of change: 4 CENT COIN
    DIME
Ointment: 4 ZINC
Photoelectric cell: 6 CESIUM
Psyche: 3 EGO
Revue: 4 SKIT
Solder: 3 TIN
The fifth: 5 BORON
~ 5: 5 BORON
~ 5 compound: 6 BORATE
~ 10: 4 NEON
~ 34: 8 SELENIUM
~ 39: 7 YTTRIUM
~ 50: 3 TIN
~ 53 salt: 6 IODATE
~ 54: 5 XENON
~ 76: 6 OSMIUM
~ 77: 7 IRIDIUM
~ 86: 5 RADON
Elemental
ending: 3 IUM
unit: 4 ATOM
variant: 7 ISOTOPE
Elementary: 4 EASY 5 BASIC
education: 4 ABCS
particle: 3 ION 4 ATOM MUON
    5 MESON QUARK
    8 NEUTRINO
school trio: 3 RRR
Elements
One of the four: 3 AIR
Protected from the: 6 INDOOR
    INSIDE

"Elements"
author: 6 EUCLID
___ elements: 9 RAREEARTH
"Elements of Style, The"
coauthor: 6 STRUNK
"Eleni"
author Nicholas: 4 GAGE
director Peter: 5 YATES
star: 8 NELLIGAN
Eleniak
Actress: 5 **ERIKA**
Elephant
abductor: 3 ROC
ancestor: 8 MASTODON
Big ~ features: 4 EARS
driver: 6 MAHOUT
group: 3 GOP
Kid-lit: 5 BABAR
Republican ~ creator: 4 NAST
seat: 6 HOWDAH
suffix: 3 INE
tooth: 4 TUSK
Vicious: 5 ROGUE
White: 6 ALBINO
"Elephant Boy"
boy: 4 SABU
Elephantine: 4 HUGE 5 GIANT
Elephants
Opera with: 4 AIDA
Some: 4 COWS
Elev.: 3 ALT HGT
Elevate: 4 LIFT REAR 5 EXALT
    RAISE 6 UPLIFT
    7 ENHANCE RAISEUP
Lines that: 3 ODE
Elevated
dwelling: 5 AERIE
Elevation: 4 HILL
Western: 4 MESA
Elevator
alternative: 6 STAIRS
    8 STAIRWAY*
compartment: 3 CAR
inventor: 4 OTIS
Links: 3 TEE
man: 4 **OTIS**
part: 3 CAR
pioneer Otis: 6 ELISHA
Some ~ buttons: 3 UPS

Élève
place: 5 ECOLE
Eleven
through thirteen at Augusta:
   10 AMENCORNER
Two of these make: 4 ONES
~, in French: 4 ONZE
Eleventh ___: 4 HOUR
Eleventh-hour: 4 LATE
Elevs.: 3 HTS
Elf: 3 HOB 6 SPRITE
"Elf"
Ed who played Santa in: 5 ASNER
Elfin: 3 WEE 6 LITTLE
Elfman
Actress: 5 JENNA
Elfman, Danny
band: 11 OINGOBOINGO
Elfman, Jenna
role: 6 DHARMA
Elgar
King in an ~ work: 4 OLAF
Elgart
Bandleader: 3 LES
El Greco: 6 CRETAN
homeland: 5 CRETE
subject: 6 TOLEDO
Elhi
org.: 3 PTA
Eli
school: 4 YALE
word: 5 BOOLA
Eli, Ransom
Carmaker: 4 OLDS
Elia: 7 PENNAME
output: 5 ESSAY
Elias
Inventor: 4 HOWE
Elicit: 5 EDUCE EVOKE
Elicitor
Groan: 3 PUN
Elide: 4 OMIT
Eliel
Son of: 4 EERO
Eligibility
Org. with ~ rules: 4 NCAA
Eligible
for Mensa: 5 SMART
for service: 4 ONEA

Most: 4 ONEA
Elijah
role: 5 FRODO
Elimelech
Wife of: 5 NAOMI
Eliminate: 3 BAR END RID
   5 ERASE 6 REMOVE
Elimination
game: 9 ODDMANOUT
Elinor
Poet: 5 WYLIE
Writer: 4 GLYN
Eliot: 4 POET
character: 4 ADAM BEDE
   5 SILAS 6 MARNER
Untouchable: 4 NESS
Eliot, George
Real last name of: 5 EVANS
Eliphaz
Father of: 4 ESAU
Elisabeth
Actress: 4 SHUE
Elisha
Inventor: 4 OTIS
Elite: 3 TOP 5 ALIST CREAM
   6 CHOSEN 7 ALLSTAR
alternative: 4 PICA
athlete: 11 ALLAMERICAN
group: 5 ALIST ATEAM
Navy: 4 SEAL 5 SEALS
seats: 4 LOGE
Sports: 6 ALLPRO
Elitist: 4 SNOB 5 SNOOT
Elixir: 5 TONIC
Eliz., Queen
Honor from: 3 OBE
Eliza
Inspiration for: 7 GALATEA
Mentor of: 4 ENRY
Elizabeth
Actress: 4 PENA
Bob or: 4 DOLE
Initials for: 3 HRH
Makeup mogul: 5 ARDEN
player: 4 CATE
TV newswoman: 6 VARGAS
"Elizabeth"
actress Blanchett: 4 CATE
Elizabethan ___: 3 ERA

Elizabeth I
  Elizabeth II, to: 8 NAMESAKE
  favorite: 5 ESSEX
  Mother of: 4 ANNE
  Sister of: 4 MARY
Elk: 7 WAPITIS
  feature: 6 ANTLER
Elke
  Actress: 6 SOMMER
Elks
  Group of: 5 LODGE
Ella
  Actress: 6 RAINES
  Emulate: 4 **SCAT**
  Former Conn. governor:
    6 GRASSO
Elle
  rival: 5 VOGUE
"Ellen": 6 SITCOM
Ellerbee
  Newscaster: 5 **LINDA**
Ellington
  Bandleader: 4 DUKE
  classic: 9 SATINDOLL
    13 TAKETHEATRAIN
  colleague: 5 BASIE
  inits.: 3 EKE
  mood: 6 INDIGO
  vehicle: 6 ATRAIN
Elliot, ___ Cass: 4 MAMA
Elliot, Mama ___: 4 CASS
Ellipse: 4 OVAL
  points: 4 LOCI
Ellipsis: 4 DOTS
  part: 3 DOT
Ellipsoid: 4 OVAL
Elliptical: 4 OVAL 5 OVATE OVOID
    TERSE
Ellis
  (abbr.): 3 ISL
  Novelist: 4 BRET
Ellison
  Sci-fi writer: 6 HARLAN
Ellison, Larry
  company: 6 ORACLE
Elly May
  Pa of: 3 JED
Elm: 4 TREE 9 SHADETREE
  and others (abbr.): 3 STS

offering: 5 SHADE
Elm City
  student: 3 ELI
Elmer
  Partner of: 5 ELSIE
  Voice of: 3 MEL
  who bugs Bugs: 4 FUDD
  ~, to Bugs: 3 DOC
Elmer's: 4 GLUE
El Misti
  locale: 4 PERU
  range: 5 ANDES
Elmore
  of basketball: 3 LEN
Elm Street
  terrorizer: 6 FREDDY
Elocution
  Practice: 5 ORATE
Eloise
  creator Thompson: 3 KAY
  The likes of: 4 IMPS
Elongated
  fish: 3 EEL
  pastry: 6 ECLAIR
Eloquent: 10 ORATORICAL
  equine: 4 MRED
  speaker: 6 ORATOR
  Wax: 5 ORATE
El Prado
  city: 6 MADRID
Elroy
  Dog belonging to: 5 **ASTRO**
Els
  followers: 3 EMS
  Golfer: 5 **ERNIE**
  org.: 3 PGA
Elsa: 7 LIONESS
  chronicler: 7 ADAMSON
Else
  Everything: 4 REST
Elsewhere: 4 AWAY 7 NOTHERE
  Direct: 5 REFER
  Here: 3 ICI
  Usher: 6 RESEAT
Elsie
  chew: 3 CUD
  Emulate: 3 MOO
Elton
  john: 3 LOO

Partner of: **6** BERNIE
Title for: **3** SIR
Elude: 4 LOSE **5** AVOID DODGE
the seeker: **4** HIDE
Elusive: 4 EELY **6** SCARCE
creature: **4** YETI
one: **3** EEL
Elver: 3 EEL
Elvin
of basketball: **5** HAYES
Elvis: 4 IDOL
1956 ~ song: **6** LOVEME
       15 HEARTBREAKHOTEL
1958 ~ song: **4** DONT
       15 HARDHEADEDWOMAN
1961 ~ song: **10** BLUEHAWAII
1964 ~ song: **5** ASKME
1969 ~ movie: **6** CHARRO
birthplace: **6** TUPELO
Emulate: **6** GYRATE
first label: **3** SUN
hit: **13** JAILHOUSEROCK
middle name: **4 ARON**
record label: **3** RCA
Rocker: **8** COSTELLO
swiveled his: **4** HIPS
Elwes
Actor: **4** CARY
Elwood P. ___ : 4 DOWD
Ely
Actor: **3 RON**
Elysium: 4 EDEN
Elzie
Popeye creator: **5** SEGAR
Em: 6 AUNTIE
and Bee: **5** AUNTS
Dorothy, to: **5** NIECE
~, to Dorothy: **4** AUNT
E-mail: 4 MEMO SEND
       7 MESSAGE WRITETO
       8 MESSAGES
(abbr.): **3** MSG
address ending: **3** COM **EDU** GOV
       ORG
address part: **3** AOL **DOT**
again: **6** REPOST RESEND
alternative: **3** FAX **6** LETTER
button: **4** SEND
command: **4 SEND**

forerunner: **5** TELEX
guffaw: **3** LOL
header: **4** FROM
Junk: **4 SPAM**
nuisance: **4** SPAM
option: **5** REPLY
symbol: **8** EMOTICON
Unwanted: **4** SPAM
E-mailed: 4 SENT **5** WROTE
Emanate: 4 EMIT **5** ARISE
Emanation: 4 AURA
Bakery: **5** AROMA
Kitchen: **4** ODOR **5** AROMA
Radiator: **4** HEAT
Sachet: **5** AROMA SCENT
Sun: **3** RAY
Emancipate: 4 FREE **7** MANUMIT
       SETFREE
Emasculate: 4 GELD **5** UNMAN
Embankment: 5 LEVEE
Build an: **5** REVET
Protective: **6** ESCARP
Soil: **4** BERM
Embargo: 3 BAN
Embargoed
land: **4** CUBA
Embarrass: 5 ABASH SHAME
Embarrassed: 3 RED
Visibly: **7** BEETRED
       10 REDASABEET
Embarrassing
display: **5** SCENE
situation: **7** HOTSEAT
Embarrassment: 5 SHAME
Show: **5** BLUSH
Embassy
fig.: **3** AMB
Embattle: 5 BESET
Embellish: 5 ADORN **6** BEDECK
       7 DRESSUP
richly: **4** GILD
Embellished: 6 ORNATE
Embellishment
Entrée: **5** GARNI
Letter: **5** SERIF
Musical: **5** TRILL **7** ROULADE
       9 GRACENOTE
Ember
coating: **3** ASH

Embezzler
fear: **5** AUDIT
Emblem: 4 ICON
Clan: **5** TOTEM
Company: **4** LOGO
Its ~ is the crescent: **5** ISLAM
Official: **4** SEAL
of power: **3** ORB
of victory: **6** LAUREL
Embodiment: 6 AVATAR
7 EPITOME
Embrace: 3 HUG **5** ADOPT
7 ESPOUSE
Strong: **7** BEARHUG
Embroider: 3 SEW
Embroidered
mat: **5** DOILY
Embroidery
aid: **4** HOOP
Bit of ~ (abbr.): **4** INIT
loop: **5** PICOT
style: **11** CROSSSTITCH
Towel: **3** HIS
yarn: **6** CREWEL
Embroiled
Seriously: **8** KNEEDEEP
Embryo
Of the ~ sac: **8** AMNIOTIC
Embryonic
Beyond: **5** FETAL
plant: **5** OVULE
sac: **6** AMNION
Emcee: 4 HOST
need: **4** MIKE
task: **5 INTRO**
Emerald: 3 GEM **5** BERYL
Emerald ___ : 4 ISLE
Emerald City
creator: **4** BAUM
princess: **4** OZMA
Emerald Isle: 4 EIRE ERIN
From the: **5** IRISH
Emerge: 4 DAWN **5** ARISE
6 APPEAR
from being out: **6** COMETO
Emerged: 5 AROSE **7** CAMEOUT
Emergencies: 6 CRISES
Emergency: 4 NEED **6** CRISIS
exit: **10** FIREESCAPE

fund: **8** MADMONEY
job: **3** TOW
light: **5** FLARE
link: **7** HOTLINE
safeguard: **8** FIREDOOR
signal: **5** FLARE SIREN
supply: **5** SERUM **6** PLASMA
treatment: **8** FIRSTAID
~ CB channel: **4** NINE
~ PC key: **3** ESC
Emerging: 7 NASCENT
Emeril: 4 CHEF
exclamation: **3** BAM
need: **4** OVEN
Emeritus
(abbr.): **3 RET 4** RETD
Emerson
contemporary: **4** ASHE
middle name: **5** WALDO
of tennis: **3** ROY
piece: **5** ESSAY
Emerson, Ralph ___ : 5 WALDO
Emery
Use ~ on: **6** ABRADE
Emetic
plant: **6** IPECAC
Emigration
Loss through: **10** BRAINDRAIN
Mass: **6** EXODUS
Emil
Expressionist: **5** NOLDE
of track: **7** ZATOPEK
Emile
Author: **4** ZOLA
portrayer: **4** EZIO
Emilia
Husband of: **4** IAGO
Emiliano
Mexican revolutionary:
6 ZAPATA
Emilio
Actor: **7** ESTEVEZ
Designer: **5** PUCCI
~, to Martin: **3** SON
Emily
Sister of: **4** ANNE
Eminem: 7 RAPSTAR
genre: **3** RAP
Mentor of: **3** DRE **5** DRDRE

Eminent: 4 HIGH 5 NOTED
   6 OFNOTE
Emirate
  Mideast: 4 OMAN 5 DUBAI
   QATAR 8 ABUDHABI
Emissary: 6 LEGATE
Emission
  control gp.: 3 EPA
  Volcanic: 3 ASH 4 LAVA
Emit: 4 SHED 7 GIVEOFF
   SENDOUT
  coherent light: 4 **LASE**
EMK: 3 SEN
Emma
  Actress: 5 SAMMS
  Avenger: 4 PEEL
"Emma"
  author Austen: 4 JANE
Emmenthaler: 5 SWISS
   6 CHEESE
Emmet
  Muppet: 5 OTTER
Emmy: 5 AWARD
  1977 ~ winner: 5 ROOTS
  1986–87 ~ winner: 5 GLESS
  Daytime ~ candidate: 4 SOAP
  Four-time ~ winner: 5 LALAW
  Sally Field ~ role: 5 SYBIL
  Seven-time ~ winner: 5 ASNER
   7 EDASNER
  Susan Lucci ~ role: 5 ERICA
  winner Arthur: 3 BEA
  winner Christine: 5 LAHTI
  winner Cicely: 5 TYSON
  winner Falco: 4 **EDIE**
  winner Lewis: 5 SHARI
  winner Loretta: 4 SWIT
  winner Lucci: 5 SUSAN
  winner Susan: 5 LUCCI
  winner Thompson: 4 SADA
  winner Ward: 4 SELA
Emollient: 4 BALM 6 LOTION
  Natural: 4 **ALOE**
Emolument: 3 FEE
Emote
  Hardly: 8 UNDERACT
Emotion
  A verse to: 3 ODE
  Overwhelming: 3 AWE

Emotional: 5 TEARY 6 MOVING
   8 CHOKEDUP
  feeling: 4 VIBE
  flower: 4 TEAR
  Less: 5 ICIER
  Not: 5 STOIC
  pang: 6 TWINGE
  poem: 3 ODE
  situation: 5 DRAMA
Emotionally
  Affect: 4 MOVE STIR 5 GETTO
   TOUCH
Emotions
  Has: 5 FEELS
  Like some: 6 PENTUP
Empathetic
  words: 5 ICARE
Empathize: 6 RELATE
Empathy
  One showing: 7 SOLACER
  Words of: 10 ICANRELATE
"Empedocles on ___": 4 ETNA
Emperor
  10th-century ~: 5 OTTOI
  after Galba: 4 OTHO
  after Nero: 5 GALBA
  Cruel: 4 NERO
  Fiddling: 4 NERO
  Holy Roman: 4 OTTO 6 TRAJAN
   7 LOTHAIR
  Japanese: 7 AKIHITO
  Mo. named for an: 3 AUG
"Emperor Jones, The"
  playwright: 6 ONEILL
  star: 7 ROBESON
Emphasis: 6 STRESS
  Phrase tacked on for: 6 NOLESS
Emphasize: 6 ACCENT STRESS
Emphatic
  agreement: 4 AMEN 6 IDOIDO
   YESYES 8 YESSIREE
  Be: 6 INSIST
  denial: 5 NOSIR 6 NONONO
   7 NOSIREE
  ending: 5 SIREE
  refusal: 5 NEVER NOHOW
   6 NOMAAM
  type (abbr.): 4 **ITAL**
Empire: 5 REALM

Bygone: 4 INCA
Former: 4 USSR
Like a bygone: 5 INCAN
Empire State
canal: 4 ERIE
leader: 6 PATAKI
Empire State Building
climber: 4 KONG
site: 3 NYC
style: 7 ARTDECO
Employ: 3 **USE** 4 HIRE 5 APPLY
6 HIREON
again: 5 REUSE
They: 5 USERS
vigorously: 5 EXERT
Employed
as: 7 USEDFOR
Currently: 5 INUSE
Employee: 6 EARNER
benefit: 4 PERK 7 DAYCARE
request: 5 RAISE
reward: 5 BONUS
Transferred ~ concern: 4 RELO
~ ID: 3 SSN
Employees: 4 HELP 5 STAFF
Employer: 4 **USER** 5 HIRER
Employment: 3 USE
agency listing: 3 JOB
extra: 4 PERK
Emporium: 4 MART
event: 4 SALE
Empower: 3 LET 6 ENABLE
Empowered: 4 ABLE
Empress
Former Iranian: 5 FARAH
Russian: 7 TSARINA
Emptiness: 4 VOID
Empty: 4 BARE IDLE NULL VOID
5 DRAIN INANE 6 HOLLOW
VACANT VACATE
7 DEPLETE
hand, literally: 6 KARATE
house feature: 4 ECHO
(of): 3 RID
out: 6 UNPACK
space: 4 VOID
stomach sound: 5 GROWL
talk: 3 GAS 4 CANT WIND
5 HOKUM 6 HOTAIR

~, as an apartment: 5 UNLET
Empty ___ : 4 NEST 6 NESTER
Empty-headed: 5 INANE
___ empty stomach: 4 ONAN
Empty-vehicle
weight: 4 TARE
Ems: 3 SPA
followers: 3 ENS
EMT
destinations: 3 ERS
Part of: 4 EMER
skill: 3 CPR
Emu
kin: 4 RHEA
or ostrich: 6 RATITE
Emulate: 3 APE
Emulsion
Photo lab ~ compound:
6 HALIDE
En ___ : 5 MASSE
"En ___ !": 5 GARDE
Enact
anew: 8 REORDAIN
Enameled
metalware: 4 TOLE
Enamored
of: 4 INTO 6 KEENON
Enc.
to an editor: 3 SAE 4 SASE
Encase: 7 SHEATHE
Enceladus
burial place: 4 ETNA
Enchanted: 3 FEY 4 RAPT
"___ Enchanted": 4 ELLA
"Enchanted April"
setting: 5 ITALY
Enchanting: 7 MAGICAL
Enchantress: 5 SIREN
Mythical: 5 CIRCE
Enchilada
alternative: 6 TAMALE
The whole: 3 **ALL** 4 ATOZ
5 TOTAL
Encircle: 4 **GIRD** RING 5 HEMIN
7 CLOSEIN
Encircled: 4 GIRT
Encirclements: 5 SIEGE
Encl.
to an editor: 3 SAE 4 **SASE**

Enclave
Academic: **10** IVORYTOWER
Enclose: 7 ROPEOFF
Enclosed
canoe: **5** KAYAK
car: **5** SEDAN
Enclosure
Baby: **7** PLAYPEN
Farm: **3** PEN STY
Jamboree: **4** TENT
Ms.: **3** SAE **4** SASE
Ranch: **6** CORRAL
Software: **5** CDROM
Yard: **5** HEDGE
Zoo: **4** CAGE
"Encomium Moriae"
author: **7** ERASMUS
Encompassing: 7 AMBIENT
Encore
performance: **5** RERUN
"Encore!": 4 MORE **5** AGAIN
Encounter: 4 MEET **5** RUNIN
7 MEETING RUNINTO
8 MEETWITH
Encountered: 3 MET
7 RANINTO
Encourage: 4 COAX URGE
5 EGGON **6** EXHORT
FOSTER SPURON
URGEON **7** HEARTEN
NURTURE
a crook: **4** ABET
Encouragement
at the bullring: **3** OLE
Shout of: **5** CHEER
Word of: **3** OLE RAH TRY YES
4 AMEN CMON
Encourager
Cattle: **4** PROD
Encouraging
sound: **3** RAH
touch: **3** PAT
word: **3 OLE** RAH TRY YES
4 AMEN CMON
Encroach: 7 IMPINGE
on: **6** INVADE
Encroachment: 6 INROAD
Encrusted: 4 CAKY **5** CAKED
Encrypted: 5 CODED

Encumbered
Be: **3** OWE
Encumbrance: 4 LIEN ONUS
Encyclopedia
medium: **5** CDROM
unit (abbr.): **3** VOL
volume: **5** ATLAS INDEX
Walking: **7** EGGHEAD
End: 3 TIP **4** GOAL HALT REAR
STOP **5** CEASE DEATH
FINIS OMEGA **6** RESULT
WRAPUP
Info: Suffix cue
a fast: **3** EAT
Ages on: **4** EONS
at: **4** ABUT
Bad: **4** DOOM
Book: **5** INDEX
Dead: **3** DEE **10** BLINDALLEY
early: **5** ABORT
Go off the deep: **4** DIVE SNAP
Hammer: **4** CLAW **PEEN**
Land's: **5** SCAPE
Match: **3** TKO
notes: **4** CODA
of a #2: **6** ERASER
of a 1/1 song: **4** SYNE
of a bridal path: **5** ALTAR
of a demonstration: **3** QED
of a list abbr.: **4** ETAL
of a race: **8** ELECTION
of a series: **3** ZEE **5** OMEGA
of a shooting: **4** WRAP
of a threat: **4** ELSE **6** ORELSE
of grace: **4** AMEN
piece: **4** CODA
product: **6** RESULT
Put an early ~ to:
11 NIPINTHEBUD
Put an ~ to: **3** CAN **4** DOIN
STOP **5** CEASE
result: **6** UPSHOT
River: **7** ESTUARY
Shoelace: **5** AGLET
Short: **4** STUB
Short ~ of the stick: **7** BUMDEAL
RAWDEAL
Striking: **4** PEEN
Tail: **4** REAR

The: **3** ZEE **5** FINIS OMEGA
Time on: **3** EON
to sex: **3** ISM
Untimely: **6** DEMISE
up with: **3** NET
What some games ~ in: **4** ATIE
Where breeches: **4** KNEE
End ___: 4 USER
___ end: 4 ATAN
Endangered: 4 RARE
  antelope: **4** ORYX
  cat: **4** PUMA **6** OCELOT
  goose: **4** NENE
  layer: **5** OZONE
  sea cow: **7** MANATEE
  state bird: **4** NENE
Endearment
  Italian term of: **7** CARAMIA
  Term of: **3** HON PET **4** BABE
    5 HONEY TOOTS **7** TOOTSIE
    10 HONEYBUNCH
Endeavor: 3 AIM TRY **7** VENTURE
  to attain: **4** SEEK
Endeavored: 6 STROVE
Endeavour
  org.: **4** NASA
  Travel like: **5** ORBIT
Ended: 4 OVER
  ~, as a subscription: **6** LAPSED
Ender
  Info: Suffix cue
Endgame
  ender: **4** MATE
End in ___: 4 ATIE
Ending
  Info: Suffix cue
Endless
  ~, in poetry: **6** ETERNE
Endnote
  abbr.: **4** ETAL IBID
Endo-
  Opposite of: **3** EXO **4** ECTO
End of ___: 5 ANERA
End-of-class
  signal: **4** BELL
End-of-proof
  letters: **3** QED
End-of-week
  cry: **4** **TGIF**

Endora
  portrayer: **5** AGNES
Endorse: 4 OKAY SIGN
Endorsed: 3 OKD **4** OKED
Endorsement
  Passport: **4** VISA
Endorser: 6 SIGNEE
  Check: **5** PAYEE
  Toothpaste ~ (abbr.): **3** ADA
Endorses: 3 OKS
Endow: 4 FUND VEST **5** BLESS
    GRANT **6** PAYFOR
Endower
  College: **4** ALUM
  Cornell: **4** EZRA
Endowment: 4 GIFT **5** GRANT
Ends
  Book: **7** ADDENDA
  It ~ in a point: **5** FABLE
  It ~ in Oct.: **3** DST
  Leave no loose: **3** TIE
  of letters: **3** PSS
  of the earth: **5** POLES
Endurance: 4 LEGS **7** STAMINA
Endure: 4 BEAR COPE **LAST**
    5 ABIDE **7** PERSIST
    WEATHER
  successfully: **7** RIDEOUT
Endured: 5 STOOD **7** RODEOUT
Enduring: 7 ETERNAL
"Endymion"
  poet: **5** KEATS
ENE
  Opposite of: **3** WSW
Enemy: 3 FOE
  Allies: **4** AXIS
  C.O.N.T.R.O.L.: **4** KAOS
  Iroquois: **4** ERIE
  Kind of: **6** MORTAL
  leader: **4** ARCH
  Minuteman: **7** REDCOAT
  Superman: **6** LUTHOR
  The: **4** THEM
Energetic: 4 GOGO SPRY **5** BRISK
Energetically
  Begin: **6** WADEIN **8** WADEINTO
  Dance: **6** BOOGIE
Energize: 4 STIR **5** LIVEN REVUP
    7 ANIMATE

Energy: 3 GAS PEP VIM ZIP
4 ZEST 5 DRIVE POWER
STEAM
bit: 3 ERG
Bundle of: 6 DYNAMO
Burst of: 5 SPASM
choice: 5 SOLAR
Clean kind of: 5 SOLAR
Former ~ giant: 5 ENRON
Full of: **4 GOGO** 5 ALIVE PEPPY
VITAL ZIPPY 6 BOUNCY
Full of nervous: 5 ANTSY
Kind of: 5 SOLAR
Lack of: 6 ANEMIA
Lose: 3 SAG 4 TIRE 5 DROOP
source: 3 SUN 4 ATOM COAL
FUEL
unit: 3 **ERG** 5 JOULE
Enero: 3 MES
to enero: 3 ANO
Enervate: 3 SAP 4 TIRE
6 WEAKEN
Enfants
Place for les: 5 ECOLE
Song pour les: 8 ALOUETTE
Enfield: 5 RIFLE
Enforcement
Big Apple ~ gp.: 4 NYPD
orgs.: 3 PDS
Ottawa-based ~ gp.: 4 RCMP
power: 5 TEETH
Enforcer: 7 EXACTER
Law ~ since 1873: 7 MOUNTIE
Yukon law: 4 RCMP
"Enforcer, The"
Frank: 5 NITTI
Eng
homeland: 4 SIAM
Twin of: 5 CHANG
Eng.
award: 3 OBE
channel: 3 BBC
course: 3 LIT
Engage: 4 HIRE MESH
in logrolling: 4 BIRL
Engaged: 4 ATIT
in: 4 UPTO
in battle: 5 ATWAR
Not: 4 IDLE 5 ALOOF

Engagement: 6 BATTLE
Arranged: 9 BLINDDATE
Evening: 6 SOIREE
gift: 4 RING
Ring: 4 BOUT
Engagements
Series of: 4 TOUR
Engager
Ratchet: 4 PAWL
Engaging: 7 WINSOME
one: 5 HIRER
Engels
collaborator: 4 MARX
Engender: 4 SIRE 5 BEGET
10 GIVERISETO
Engendered: 4 BRED 5 BEGOT
Engine: 5 MOTOR
additive: 3 OIL STP
Aircraft: 6 RAMJET
Air to a jet: 6 INTAKE
attachment: 4 HOSE
Bike with an: 5 MOPED
booster: 5 TURBO
cover: 4 HOOD
Gun the: 3 **REV**
housing: 9 CRANKCASE
knock: 4 PING
need: 3 OIL
part: 3 **CAM** ROD 4 GEAR
5 ROTOR 7 STARTER
part, briefly: 4 CARB
Powerful: 4 VTEN 5 TURBO
Rev an: 3 GUN
Rotating ~ part: 3 CAM
sound: 4 PING PURR ROAR
WHIR 5 COUGH KNOCK
8 PUTTPUTT
stat: 3 RPM
type: 4 HEMI VSIX 5 TURBO
6 DIESEL
Vital ~ conduit: 7 OILLINE
Engineer
French: 6 EIFFEL
Kind of: 5 CIVIL
place: 3 CAB
Engineering
NY ~ sch.: 3 RPI
project: 4 DIKE 7 TRESTLE
sch.: 4 TECH

England
County of: 5 ESSEX
French port nearest: 6 CALAIS
Head of: 3 LOO
John of: 3 LOO 5 ELTON
River in: 4 OUSE
English: 4 SPIN 7 BRITONS
Any of three ~ rivers: 4 OUSE
article: 3 THE
assignment: 5 ESSAY THEME
cathedral city: 3 ELY 6 EXETER
cattle breed: 5 DEVON
channel: 3 BBC
channel, with "the": 4 BEEB
china: 5 SPODE
composer: 4 ARNE
coppers: 5 PENCE
county: 4 AVON KENT 5 ESSEX
  SHIRE
earldom: 5 ESSEX
earth tone: 5 OCHRE
equivalent of a count: 4 EARL
governor: 4 EARL
homework: 5 ESSAY
paper: 5 ESSAY
Pigeon: 3 COO
poet: 5 KEATS
prep school: 4 ETON
race place: 5 ASCOT EPSOM
river: 3 EXE 4 AVON OUSE
  TYNE 5 TRENT
royal house: 4 YORK 5 TUDOR
spa: 4 BATH
sports car: 3 JAG
university city: 5 LEEDS
variety: 5 SCOTS
English ___: 3 LIT
English Channel
1926 ~ swimmer: 6 EDERLE
county: 6 DORSET
feeder: 3 EXE 4 AVON ORNE
  5 SEINE SOMME
isle: 5 WIGHT
seaport: 7 LEHAVRE
English horn
cousin: 4 OBOE
need: 4 REED
"English Patient, The"
setting: 6 SAHARA

Engorge
oneself: 6 PIGOUT
Engr.
Kind of: 4 ELEC MECH
Engrave: 4 ETCH 6 INCISE
with acid: 4 ETCH
Engraver: 6 ETCHER
Engraving: 7 LINECUT
tools: 5 STYLI
Engrossed: 4 **RAPT**
by: 4 INTO
Engulf: 5 DROWN WHELM
Enhance: 5 ADDTO
Enhancer
Café: 4 LAIT
Flavor: 3 MSG 4 SALT 5 SPICE
Grade: 4 PLUS
Enid
Knight who wed: 7 GERAINT
Enigma: 5 POSER 6 RIDDLE
Extraterrestrial: 3 UFO
"Enigma Variations"
composer: 5 ELGAR
Enjoined: 4 BADE
Enjoy: 4 LIKE 5 EATUP SAVOR
  6 RELISH
a favorite book: 6 REREAD
a long bath: 4 SOAK
a novel: 4 READ
a snowy slope: 3 SKI 4 SLED
bubble gum: 4 CHEW
fine whiskey: 3 SIP
the sun: 4 BASK
Enjoyed
home cooking: 5 ATEIN
immensely: 5 ATEUP
oneself: 7 ATEITUP
  9 HADABLAST
Enjoying: 4 INTO
Enjoyment: 3 FUN 5 KICKS
  8 PLEASURE
___ En-lai: 4 **CHOU**
Enlarge: 4 GROW 6 DILATE
a hole: 4 REAM
a house: 7 ADDONTO
a photo: 6 BLOWUP
Enlargement
Atlas: 5 INSET
Enlighten: 5 **EDIFY** TEACH

Enlightenment
  Cry of: 3 AHA
  Means of: 3 ZEN
  Mock words of: 4 AHSO
  Zen: 6 SATORI
Enlist
  again: 4 REUP
  in: 4 JOIN
Enlisted
  men: 3 GIS
  ~ VIPs: 4 NCOS
Enlistee
  WWII: 3 WAC 5 GIJOE
Enlistees
  Some: 4 PFCS
Enliven: 5 PEPUP
  ~, with "up": 3 PEP 4 PERK
      5 SPICE
En masse
  Enter: 6 PILEIN
  Exist: 3 ARE
Enmity: 4 HATE 6 ANIMUS
Ennead: 5 NONET
  Feline: 5 LIVES
Ennis
  Author: 4 REES
Ennoble: 5 EXALT 7 ELEVATE
Ennui: 5 BLAHS 6 TEDIUM
      7 BOREDOM 8 THEBLAHS
  Exhibit: 4 YAWN
Enoch
  Tennyson's: 5 ARDEN
Enola Gay
  payload: 5 ABOMB
Enormous: 4 HUGE VAST
      6 COSMIC
  bird of myth: 3 ROC
Enormously: 4 ALOT
Enos
  Father of: 4 SETH
Enough: 5 AMPLE
  Close: 7 INRANGE
  Hardly: 5 SCANT 5 SCANTY
  It may be: 4 ONCE
  Just firm: 7 ALDENTE
  Just ~ to wet the lips: 3 SIP
  More than: 4 MANY 5 AMPLE
      6 OODLES PLENTY
  Not good ~ for: 7 BENEATH

  Old: 5 **OFAGE**
  Old ~ to know better: 5 ADULT
  Quite: 5 AMPLE
  Seen: 5 HADIT
  ~, for some: 4 ONCE
  ~, in Italian: 5 BASTA
"Enough!": 4 STOP 5 CANIT
      IGIVE UNCLE 6 DROPIT
      NOMORE QUITIT STOPIT
      7 SPAREME
"Enough already!": 5 CANIT
      UNCLE 6 QUITIT STOPIT
      8 IVEHADIT
En passant
  capture: 4 PAWN
"___ en paz, fierro en guerra":
      3 ORO
Enrage: 3 IRE 4 GALL
Enrapture: 4 SEND 5 RIVET
Enraptured: 4 GAGA SENT
Enrich: 4 LARD
Enrico
  Physicist: 5 FERMI
  Tenor: 6 CARUSO
Enríquez
  Actor: 4 RENE
En route: 4 SENT
  by ship: 4 ASEA
Ens.
  producer: 4 USNA
"___ en scene": 4 MISE
Ensemble: 4 CAST 6 OUTFIT
  Acting: 4 CAST
  Certain string: 5 NONET
  Furniture: 5 SUITE
  Jazz: 4 TRIO 5 COMBO
  Midsized: 5 OCTET
Ensign
  Shakespearean: 4 IAGO
Ensler
  Playwright: 3 EVE
Ensnare: 4 TRAP
Ensuing: 4 NEXT
Ensure
  failure: 4 DOOM
  ~, with "up": 3 SEW
Entail: 7 INVOLVE
Entangle: 4 MIRE 5 SNARE
      SNARL

Entangled: 5 AFOUL
Entanglement: 3 WEB 4 KNOT
     MESH SNAG 5 SKEIN
     SNARL TIEUP
Enter: 3 LOG 4 **GOIN** 5 INPUT
     KEYIN 6 GOINTO READIN
     STEPIN TYPEIN
     7 GETINTO
 again: 5 REKEY
 cautiously: 6 EASEIN EDGEIN
 forcefully: 6 BUSTIN INVADE
 gradually: 6 EASEIN
 Invite to: 5 ASKIN
 One way to: 5 ONCUE
 secretly: 7 SNEAKIN
 Signal to: 3 CUE
 the picture: 6 APPEAR
 uninvited: 7 BARGEIN
 via cracks: 6 SEEPIN
 with care: 6 EASEIN
Entered: 6 CAMEIN GONEIN
     WENTIN 7 KEYEDIN
 en masse: 9 PILEDINTO
 in the record: 6 LOGGED
 the race: 3 RAN
Enterprise: 8 STARSHIP
 captain: 4 KIRK
 communications officer: 5 UHURA
 counselor: 4 TROI
 helmsman: 4 SULU
 initials: 3 USS
 Klingon on the: 4 WORF
 Letters on the: 3 NCC
 navigator: 4 SULU
 off.: 3 ENS
 rival: 4 AVIS 5 ALAMO
 voyage: 4 TREK
"___ Enterprise": 3 USS
Enterprising
 one: 8 GOGETTER
Entertain: 4 DINE FETE HOST
     WINE 5 **AMUSE** 6 DIVERT
     REGALE
 at bedtime: 6 READTO
 lavishly: 6 REGALE
Entertainer: 4 HOST 7 ARTISTE
 Island: 5 DONHO
 Japanese: 6 GEISHA
 Late, great: 7 BOBHOPE

 trademark: 7 TAGLINE
Entertainers
 GI: 3 USO
"Entertaining Mr. ___": 6 SLOANE
Entertainment
 Cowboy: 5 RODEO
 GI: 7 USOSHOW
 gp.: 3 USO
 Home ~ option: 5 WEBTV
 Luau: 4 HULA
"___ Entertainment!": 5 THATS
"Entertainment Tonight"
 Former host of: 4 TESH
 Gibbons of: 5 LEEZA
 topic: 4 ITEM
"___ Entertain You": 5 LETME
Enthrall: 4 SEND 6 RAVISH
Enthralled: 4 AGOG RAPT
Enthuse: 4 RAVE
Enthusiasm: 4 ELAN FIRE **ZEAL**
     ZEST 5 ARDOR DRIVE
     GUSTO 6 SPIRIT
 Excessive: 5 MANIA
 Infuse with: 6 PUMPUP
 With: 6 AVIDLY
Enthusiast: 3 NUT 4 BUFF
     5 LOVER
 Extreme: 4 NERD
Enthusiastic: 4 **AVID** GOGO KEEN
     WILD 5 CANDO EAGER
     HETUP 6 ONFIRE
     RAHRAH STOKED
 about: 4 INTO 5 UPFOR
     6 HIGHON KEENON
 approval: 6 YESYES
 Became ~ about: 7 GOTINTO
 Extremely: 5 RABID
 Hardly: 5 TEPID
 Like ~ fans: 5 AROAR
 overseas assent: 4 SISI
 verse: 3 ODE
 Wildly: 4 GAGA
 words: 5 YESES
 ~, with "up": 3 HET
Enthusiastically
 Receive: 5 LAPUP
Entice: 4 BAIT COAX LURE
     5 TEMPT 6 BECKON
     LEADON LUREIN ROPEIN

Enticement: 4 BAIT HOOK WILE
    6 ALLURE COMEON
  Bakery: 4 ODOR 5 AROMA
  Fish: 4 LURE
Entire
  range: 5 GAMUT
Entirely: 3 ALL 5 FULLY INALL
    6 INTOTO
  sensible: 4 SANE
Entity: 4 UNIT
  Single: 5 MONAD
Entomb: 5 INTER
Entomologist
  subject: 6 INSECT 7 INSECTS
Entourage: 7 RETINUE
Entr'___: 4 **ACTE**
Entrance: 4 ADIT DOOR 5 INLET
    WAYIN 6 PORTAL
    7 BEWITCH GATEWAY
  Classy: 4 ARCH
  College ~ exam: 3 SAT
  Curved: 4 ARCH
  Delivery: 8 SIDEDOOR
  Freeway: 4 RAMP 6 ONRAMP
  Metro: 5 STILE
  Mine: 4 **ADIT**
Entranced: 4 RAPT
Entrant
  Derby: 5 HORSE
  Iditarod: 4 SLED 5 RACER
  Indy: 5 RACER
  Regatta: 5 YACHT
Entrap: 5 **SNARE**
  ~, with "up": 3 SET
Entre ___ : 4 **NOUS**
Entreat: 3 ASK BEG 4 PRAY URGE
Entreated: 4 PLED
Entreaty: 4 **PLEA**
Entrée: 5 WAYIN 6 ACCESS
    8 MAINDISH
  Barbecue: 4 RIBS
  Brunch: 6 OMELET
  Crusty: 6 POTPIE
  Easter: 3 HAM 4 LAMB
  Eggy: 6 OMELET
  fowl: 5 CAPON
  Greek: 4 GYRO
  Hearty: 5 STEAK TBONE
  item: 4 MEAT

  Layered: 7 LASAGNA
  Mexican: 4 TACO 7 TOSTADA
  Pounded: 10 SWISSSTEAK
  preceder: 5 SALAD
  Salsa-topped: 4 TACO
  School-lunch: 11 MYSTERYMEAT
  Seafood: 4 SOLE 5 FILET SCROD
    11 FILETOFSOLE
  Shrimp: 6 SCAMPI
  Sunday: 5 ROAST 8 POTROAST
Entrench: 5 DIGIN
Entrepreneur
  deg.: 3 MBA
  mag: 3 INC
Entrepreneur-aiding
  org.: 3 SBA
Entry: 4 DOOR 6 ACCESS
    7 LISTING
  Agenda: 4 ITEM 7 ITEMONE
  Almanac: 4 FACT
  Bank acct.: 3 DEP INT
  Black ink: 5 **ASSET**
  Bookkeeping: 5 DEBIT
  Cal.: 4 APPT
  Card catalogue: 5 TITLE
  Check: 4 DATE 6 AMOUNT
  Courtroom: 4 PLEA
  Customer file: 8 AREACODE
  Dict.: 3 DEF SYN
  Dictionary: 4 WORD
  Gain: 5 GETIN
  Glossary: 4 TERM
  Grant ~ to: 5 ADMIT LETIN
  Illegal: 6 BAGJOB
  Indy: 7 RACECAR
  Ledger: 4 ITEM 5 ASSET DEBIT
    6 CREDIT
  List: 4 ITEM
  PDA: 4 APPT
  permit: 4 VISA
  Poker ~ fee: 4 ANTE
  Rap sheet: 5 PRIOR
  Red ink: 4 DEBT 5 DEBIT
  requirement: 5 IDTAG
  Savings acct.: 3 INT
  Sched.: 3 ETD 4 APPT
  Thesaurus ~ (abbr.): 3 SYN
  To-do list: 4 TASK
  Web browser: 3 URL

"Entry of Christ Into Brussels"
artist: 5 ENSOR
Entryway: 4 DOOR 6 PORTAL
Enumerate: 4 LIST 6 DETAIL
RECITE 7 ITEMIZE
Enumeration
abbr.: 3 ETC
Env.
contents: 3 LTR 4 ENCS
extra: 3 ENC
info: 4 ADDR
In this: 4 ENCL
notation: 4 ATTN
stuffer: 3 ENC
Envelope
abbr.: 4 **ATTN**
closer: 4 FLAP SEAL 5 CLASP
encl.: 4 SASE
feature: 5 CLASP
Kind of: 6 MANILA
Letters on a love letter:
4 SWAK
Open an: 4 SLIT 6 UNSEAL
part: 4 FLAP GLUE
sticker: 5 STAMP
Enveloping
glow: 4 AURA
Environment: 6 MILIEU
Stable: 5 STALL
Environmental
disaster: 7 ECOCIDE
prefix: 3 ECO
sci.: 4 **ECOL**
subgroup: 7 ECOTYPE
subj.: 4 ECOL
toxin: 3 PCB
Environmentalist
celebration: 8 EARTHDAY
concern: 4 SMOG
Dr. Seuss's: 5 LORAX
magazine: 6 SIERRA
maj.: 4 ECOL
Environs: 4 AREA 6 CLIMES
MILIEU
Chalet: 7 SKIAREA
Envision: 3 **SEE**
Envy: 3 SIN
Enya
Musical style of: 6 NEWAGE

Enzyme
ending: 3 **ASE**
Kidney: 5 RENIN
suffix: 3 **ASE**
Eocene: 5 EPOCH
Eon: 3 AGE
subdivision: 3 ERA
Eos
Lover of: 5 ORION
EPA
banned it: 3 DDT
concern: 4 ECOL SMOG
determination: 3 MPG
Epcot
home: 3 FLA
Épée
Wield an: 5 FENCE
Ephesus
Home of: 5 IONIA
Ephron
Author: 4 **NORA** 5 DELIA
Director: 4 **NORA**
Screenwriter: 4 **NORA**
5 DELIA
Epic
Homeric: 5 **ILIAD**
Icelandic: 4 EDDA
poem: 5 ILIAD
tale: 4 **SAGA**
Trojan War: 5 **ILIAD**
Virgil: 6 AENEID
___ epic scale: 4 ONAN
Epicure
asset: 6 PALATE
Epidermal
eruption: 4 RASH
Epilogue: 3 END
Musical: 4 CODA
Epinephrine
prefix: 3 NOR
producer: 7 ADRENAL
Epinicion: 3 ODE
Epiphany
figures: 4 MAGI
sound: 3 AHA
Episcopal
cleric: 6 RECTOR
Episode: 5 EVENT 8 INCIDENT
Old TV show: 5 RERUN

Epistle
apostle: 4 PAUL
writer: 4 PAUL

Epistolary
friend: 6 PENPAL

Epitaph
opener: 4 **HERE**

Epithet: 4 NAME SLUR 5 LABEL
Dickensian: 3 BAH
Homer: 3 DOH
Mild: 4 EGAD
of Athena: 4 ALEA

Epitome: 5 IDEAL 8 PARADIGM
of easiness: 3 ABC PIE
of hardness: 5 NAILS
of neatness: 3 PIN
of redness: 4 BEET
of simplicity: 3 ABC
of slowness: 5 SNAIL
   8 MOLASSES
of thinness: 4 RAIL REED
   5 RAZOR

"E pluribus ___": 4 UNUM

"E pluribus unum": 5 MOTTO

Epoch: 3 AGE **ERA**
Ancient: 6 ICEAGE
from 10 to 2 million years ago:
   8 PLIOCENE
Glacial: 6 ICEAGE
Pleistocene: 6 ICEAGE
when mammals arose:
   6 EOCENE

Eponym
for failure: 5 EDSEL
of a lemon: 9 EDSELFORD

Eponymous
general: 3 TSO

Epoxy: 4 GLUE 5 RESIN

Epps
Actor: 4 **OMAR**

Epsilon
follower: 4 **ZETA**

Epsilon ___: 3 ERI

Equal: 3 ARE 4 **PEER** SAME
Miss: 4 MILE
prefix: 3 ISO 4 PARI
Sharing ~ value: 6 ONAPAR
Social: 4 **PEER**
to the task: 4 ABLE

Try to: 7 EMULATE
Without: 5 ALONE

Equally: 5 ALIKE
Divide: 5 HALVE
divided: 4 EVEN
matched: 4 EVEN

Equanimity: 6 APLOMB

Equation
Kind of: 6 LINEAR

Equator
Constellation above the:
   5 ORION
Fly over the: 6 TSETSE
Island crossed by the:
   7 SUMATRA

Equatorial
Opposite of: 5 AXIAL

Equestrian: 5 RIDER
attire: 5 HABIT
brake: 4 REIN
equipment: 10 RIDINGCROP
event: 8 DRESSAGE

Equi-: 3 **ISO**

Equiangular: 8 ISOGONAL
figure: 6 ISOGON

Equilibrium: 6 STASIS

Equine: 5 HORSY
Eloquent: 4 MRED
Energetic: 5 STEED
Striped: 5 ZEBRA
Stubborn: 3 ASS 4 MULE

Equinox
mo.: 3 SEP 4 SEPT

Equip: 3 RIG 6 TOOLUP
anew: 5 REFIT RERIG
for battle: 3 ARM

Equipment: 4 **GEAR**
Backgammon: 4 DICE
Bowling ~ mfr.: 3 AMF
Brewery: 4 OAST
Coffeehouse: 3 URN
Concert: 3 AMP
Crew: 4 OARS
ER: 3 IVS
Farm ~ name: 5 DEERE
Fire truck: 6 LADDER
Fronton: 5 CESTA
Lab: 4 ETNA
Olympics: 4 EPEE

Playground: 5 SWING
  6 SEESAW SLIDES
    SWINGS
Trawling: 3 NET
Equipped: 4 ABLE
Equitable: 4 EVEN FAIR JUST
  5 RIGHT
Equitably
  Assessed: 7 PRORATA
Equivalent
  Aurora: 3 EOS
  C: 6 BSHARP
  Count: 4 EARL
  C sharp: 5 DFLAT
  D flat: 6 CSHARP
  D sharp: 5 EFLAT
  E flat: 6 DSHARP
  F: 6 ESHARP
  French ~ of the Oscar:
    5 CESAR
  F sharp: 5 GFLAT
  G sharp: 5 AFLAT
  Helios: 3 SOL
Equivocator
  spot: 5 FENCE
Equivoque: 3 PUN
ER
  cry: 4 STAT
  equipment: 3 IVS
  figure: 3 DOC
  hookups: 3 IVS
  locale: 4 HOSP
  Part of: 4 EMER
  pronouncement: 3 DOA
  readout: 3 EEG
  skill: 3 CPR
  Some ~ cases: 3 ODS
  units: 3 CCS
  workers: 3 DRS MDS RNS
"ER"
  actor Epps: 4 OMAR
  actor La Salle: 4 ERIQ
  actor Noah: 4 WYLE
  actress Laura: 5 INNES
  and others: 6 DRAMAS
  doctor: 4 ROSS
  extra: 5 NURSE
  extras: 3 RNS
  network: 3 NBC

  order: 4 STAT
  roles: 3 MDS
  setting: 3 ICU
"Er ...": 5 IMEAN
Era: 3 AGE 4 TIME 5 EPOCH
    TIMES
  From a prior: 3 OLD
  Suffix on ~ names: 4 ZOIC
ERA: 4 STAT
  Part of: 5 EQUAL 6 EARNED
Eras
  Two or more: 3 EON
    4 AEON
Erase: 4 UNDO WIPE
    6 DELETE
  a magnetic tape: 7 DEGAUSS
Eraser
  Kind of: 6 ARTGUM
  leaving: 6 SMUDGE
"Eraser"
  star: 4 CAAN
"Eraserhead"
  actor Jack: 5 NANCE
Erasers
  Clean: 4 CLAP
Erato: 4 MUSE
  instrument: 4 LYRE
  is their Muse: 5 POETS
Ere: 5 AFORE
Erect
  Not quite: 5 ATILT
  Wasn't: 5 LEANT
  ___ erectus: 4 HOMO
Erelong: 4 ANON SOON
Eremite: 5 LONER
  Like an: 4 LONE 5 ALONE
Erenow: 3 AGO
Ergo: 4 THEN THUS 5 HENCE
Ergs
  100 ~ per gram: 3 RAD
  Ten million: 5 JOULE
Erhard, Werner
  system: 3 EST
Eric
  Actor: 4 IDLE 5 BLORE
    6 STOLTZ
  Author: 6 AMBLER
  Magazine founder: 4 UTNE
  Son of: 4 LEIF

Erica
Author: 4 JONG
Erich
Author: 5 SEGAL
Ericson
Mariner: 4 LEIF
tongue: 5 NORSE
Eric the Red: 5 NORSE
Son of: 4 LEIF
Erie: 4 LAKE 5 CANAL
hockey player: 5 OTTER
Erie Canal
city: 5 UTICA
mule: 3 **SAL**
Erik
Actor: 7 ESTRADA
Composer: 5 **SATIE**
Erin
Actress: 5 MORAN
"Erin go ___!": 5 BRAGH
Eritrea
border: 6 REDSEA
Capital of: 6 **ASMARA**
"Eri tu": 4 ARIA
Erle
Contemporary of: 6 AGATHA
Ermine: 6 WEASEL
Brown: 5 STOAT
Summer: 5 STOAT
Erne: 7 SEABIRD 8 SEAEAGLE
Ernest
Offscreen pal of: 4 VERN
of honky-tonk: 4 TUBB
Winemaker: 5 GALLO
Ernestine
~, for one: 8 OPERATOR
Ernesto
nickname: 3 CHE
Ernie
Golfer: 3 ELS
Home of: 12 SESAMESTREET
Journalist: 4 PYLE
Keebler's: 3 ELF
Pal of: 4 BERT
Ernst
colleague: 3 ARP
style: 4 DADA
Ernst & Young
staff: 4 CPAS

Erode: 3 EAT 4 GNAW WEAR
5 DECAY EATAT
7 EATAWAY EATINTO
Eroded: 3 ATE 4 WORE WORN
5 ATEAT EATEN
7 ATEINTO 8 WOREDOWN
valley: 6 RAVINE
"Eroica"
Key of: 5 EFLAT
Eros
Love of: 6 PSYCHE
Roman: 4 AMOR
Erosion
cause: 4 TIDE
loss: 4 SOIL
Product of: 6 RAVINE
Erotic: 4 SEXY 6 STEAMY
Erotica
First name in: 5 ANAIS
Err: 4 GOOF SLIP
Cause to: 4 TRIP
Errand: 3 JOB 4 TASK
runner: 4 PAGE 5 **GOFER**
Erratic
move: 3 ZAG ZIG 4 FLIT
Erratum: 4 SLIP
Errol
Emulate: 11 SWASHBUCKLE
Erroneous
conviction: 6 BUMRAP
Error: 6 MISCUE 7 MISSTEP
indicator: 3 SIC
Key: 4 TYPO
message: 4 OOPS
Minor: 5 LAPSE
Partner of: 5 TRIAL
Pitching: 4 BALK
Remove an: 5 DEBUG
Sign of an: 7 ERASURE
Errors: 4 STAT
Ersatz: 4 FAKE SHAM
(abbr.): 4 IMIT
butter: 4 OLEO
chocolate: 5 CAROB
fat: 5 OLEAN
gold: 6 ORMOLU
Erstwhile: 3 OLD 4 ONCE
Erté
forte: 4 DECO 7 ARTDECO

Erudite: 4 WISE 7 LEARNED
Erudition: 4 LORE
Erupt: 4 SPEW 7 FLAREUP
  suddenly: 5 FLARE
Erupter
  1786 ~: 8 MTSHASTA
  European: 4 ETNA
  Sicilian: 4 ETNA
Eruption
  Epidermal: 4 RASH
Erving
  nickname: 3 DRJ
Erwin
  Actor: 3 **STU**
Erykah
  Singer: 4 BADU
Esai
  Actor: 7 MORALES
Esau
  Descendant of: 7 EDOMITE
  Father of: 5 ISAAC
  home: 4 EDOM
  Jacob, to: 4 TWIN
  Twin of: 5 JACOB
  Wife of: 4 ADAH
ESC: 3 KEY
Escalator
  clause: 4 COLA
  feature: 5 TREAD
  part: 4 STEP
"Escales"
  composer: 5 IBERT
Escamillo
  Cheer for: 3 OLE
Escapade: 4 **LARK** 5 CAPER
Escape: 3 FLY LAM 4 BOLT FLEE
      5 ELUDE 6 GETOUT
      7 RUNAWAY
      10 FLYTHECOOP
  artist: 6 ELUDER
  clause: 3 OUT
  Close, as an: 6 NARROW
  from: 5 EVADE
  Hasty: 3 **LAM**
  mechanism: 4 VENT
  slowly: 4 SEEP
  Unable to: 5 TREED
  vehicle: 3 POD
Escapee: 6 ELUDER

  Pandora: 4 EVIL
  Political: 6 EMIGRE
  Sodom: 3 LOT
Escaping
  Keep from: 6 SEALIN
Escargot: 5 SNAIL
Escher
  genre: 5 OPART
Eschew: 4 SHUN 5 AVOID
  the doorbell: 5 KNOCK
  the leftovers: 6 EATOUT
Eschewed
  fast food: 5 ATEIN
Escort: 3 SEE 6 GIGOLO SQUIRE
      7 TAKEOUT
  Lady's: 4 GENT
  offering: 3 **ARM**
  to the door: 6 SEEOUT
Escorted: 3 LED 5 LEDIN
  by: 4 WITH
Escorts
  to the penthouse: 6 SEESUP
ESE
  Opposite of: 3 WNW
  ___ e sempre: 3 ORA
Eshkol
  of Israel: 4 LEVI
  successor: 4 MEIR
Eskimo: 5 INUIT
  craft: 5 KAYAK UMIAK
  home: 5 IGLOO 6 ALASKA
  knife: 3 ULU
  relative: 5 ALEUT
  transport: 4 SLED
ESL
  student challenge: 5 IDIOM
Esne: 4 SERF
Eso
  Not esto or: 4 OTRO
"Eso ___" (Anka hit): 4 BESO
Esophagus: 6 GULLET
Esoteric: 4 DEEP 6 ARCANE
      OCCULT
ESP: 4 GIFT
  and such: 3 PSI
España
  Info: Spanish cue
"___ espanol?": 5 HABLA
Espied: 3 SAW 4 SEEN

Espionage
  1960 ~ show: 4 ISPY
  First name in: 4 MATA
  insider: 4 MOLE
  org.: 3 CIA
ESPN
  figure: 4 STAT
  subject: 4 NCAA
"Espolio"
  artist: 7 ELGRECO
Esposito
  of hockey: 4 PHIL
  teammate: 3 ORR
Espouse: 5 ADOPT
Espresso
  drink: 5 LATTE
  Spot for: 4 CAFE
Esprit de corps: 6 MORALE
Espy: 3 SEE 4 SPOT 6 DETECT
        NOTICE
Esq.
  user: 4 ATTY
Esquivel
  1980 Peace Nobelist: 6 ADOLFO
  ___ es Salaam: 3 **DAR**
Essay: 3 TRY 5 PROSE
        7 ATTEMPT
  An ~ may be part of it: 4 EXAM
  byline: 4 ELIA
  page: 4 OPED
"Essay ___, An": 5 ONMAN
Essayist
  alias: 4 ELIA
  Newspaper ~ page: 4 OPED
"Essay on Criticism, An"
  writer: 4 POPE
"Essay on Man"
  author: 4 POPE
"Essays of ___": 4 LAMB
Essen
  Info: German cue
  exclamation: 3 ACH
  river: 4 RUHR
Essence: 3 NUB 4 CORE CRUX
        GIST MEAT ODOR PITH
        SOUL 6 FLAVOR KERNEL
        THRUST 8 SUMTOTAL
  Rose: 5 ATTAR
  Spiritual: 4 SOUL

Essential: 3 KEY 4 NEED 5 VITAL
        6 NEEDED
  acid: 5 AMINO
  Be an ~ part of: 6 INHERE
  It may be: 3 OIL
  part: 4 GIST PITH ROOT
Essentially: 7 ATHEART
Essentials: 4 ABCS
        10 BRASSTACKS
Esses
  Have trouble with: 4 LISP
Essex: 3 CAR
  contemporary: 3 REO
Est
  founder: 6 ERHARD
EST
  Part of: 3 STD
Est.: 3 SSR
Esta
  Not ~ or esa: 4 OTRA
Establish: 3 SET 5 ERECT SETUP
  as fact: 5 PROVE
  as law: 5 ENACT
Established
  Become: 5 SETIN
  fact: 5 GIVEN
  Long: 7 OLDTIME
  rule: 5 AXIOM
Establishment
  Quaint: 6 SHOPPE
Estate: 5 MANOR
  Country: 5 MANOR VILLA
  division: 4 ACRE
  Feudal: 4 FIEF
  Fourth: 5 PRESS
  home: 5 MANOR
  Kane: 6 XANADU
  Lord's: 7 DEMESNE
  Luxurious: 5 VILLA
  Rancher's: 8 HACIENDA
  recipient: 4 HEIR
  Scarlett's: 4 TARA
Estates
  Like some: 5 GATED
"¿___ está usted?": 4 COMO
Estee
  Cosmetician: 6 LAUDER
Esteem: 5 VALUE 6 ADMIRE
        REGARD REPUTE

Lower in: 5 ABASE
Object of: 4 ICON
to the extreme: 5 ADORE
Esteemed
one: 3 GEM
title: 3 SIR
Estefan
Singer: 6 GLORIA
Estelle
Actress: 5 GETTY
Costar of: 3 BEA
Ester
Soap: 6 OLEATE
Estevez
Actor: 6 EMILIO
Dad of: 5 SHEEN
Esth.
Book before: 3 **NEH**
Esther
Actress: 5 **ROLLE**
festival: 5 PURIM
Estimate: 4 STAB 5 ASSAY GAUGE
follower: 4 ORSO
formally: 6 ASSESS
Estimator
words: 4 ORSO
Esto
Not ~ or eso: 4 OTRO
Estonia
~, once (abbr.): 3 SSR
" ___ est percipi": 4 ESSE
Estrada
Actor: 4 **ERIK**
Estragon
expected him: 5 GODOT
Estrange: 8 ALIENATE
Estrangement: 4 RIFT
Estuary: 3 **RIA** 5 DELTA INLET
ET
craft: 3 UFO
on TV: 3 ALF
"E.T."
Wallace of: 3 DEE
Et ___: 3 SEQ 4 ALIA **ALII**
6 CETERA
Eta
Letter after: 5 THETA
ETA
Part of: 3 ARR

Et al.
and others: 5 ABBRS
Etats-___: 4 UNIS
Etc.
kin: 4 ETAL
Etch: 4 DRAW LIMN
___ et Chandon: 4 MOET
Etch-a-Sketch
feature: 4 KNOB
Shake an: 5 ERASE
Etcher
need: 4 **ACID**
Etching
fluid: 4 ACID
Etchings: 3 ART
Eternal: 7 AGELESS
AGELONG UNAGING
UNDYING
It springs: 4 HOPE
Eternal City: 4 ROME
Eternally: 4 EVER
~, in poetry: 3 EER
Eternity: 3 EON 4 AEON
Ethan
Actor: 5 HAWKE
Filmmaker: 4 **COEN**
"Ethan ___": 5 FROME
Ethel
or Fred: 5 MERTZ
Ethelbert
Composer: 5 NEVIN
Ethelred
Descriptor for: 7 UNREADY
Ethereal: 4 AERY AIRY
prefix: 4 AERI
Etheridge
Singer: 7 MELISSA
Ethical: 5 MORAL
standards: 5 MORES
Ethically
neutral: 6 **AMORAL**
Ethiopian
emperor Selassie: 5 HAILE
map word: 5 ABABA
neighbor: 6 SOMALI
of opera: 4 AIDA
title: 3 RAS
Ethnic: 6 RACIAL
cuisine: 4 THAI

suffix: 3 ESE
Ethyl
  acetate: 5 ESTER
  ending: 3 **ENE**
Ethylene: 4 AGER 7 RIPENER
Etiquette
  Diplomatic: 8 PROTOCOL
  expert: 4 POST
    11 MISSMANNERS
  Post of: 5 EMILY
  subjects: 5 NONOS
"___ et labora": 3 ORA
"___ et mon droit": 4 DIEU
Etna
  Emulate: 5 ERUPT
  Gush like: 4 SPEW
  output: 3 ASH 4 LAVA
ETO
  commander: 3 DDE
  name: 3 IKE
Etonian
  dad: 5 PATER
ETS
  exam: 3 SAT
  offering: 4 PSAT
Etta
  Jazz singer: 5 JAMES
  of old comics: 4 **KETT**
"**Et voilà!**": 4 TADA
EU
  language: 3 ENG GER
  member: 3 GER
  Part of: 3 EUR
Eubanks
  is on his show: 4 LENO
Eucalyptivore: 5 KOALA
Eucalyptus
  eater: 5 **KOALA**
Eucharist
  bread: 5 WAFER
  plate: 5 PATEN
  vessel: 3 PYX
Euchre
  kin: 6 ECARTE
  low card: 5 SEVEN
Euclid
  lake: 4 ERIE
  subj.: 4 GEOM
  suffix: 3 EAN

Eugene
  Belgian composer: 5 YSAYE
  Daughter of: 4 OONA
  home: 6 OREGON
  Playwright: 6 **ONEILL**
    7 IONESCO
  Socialist: 4 DEBS
"**Eugene Onegin**"
  mezzo: 4 OLGA
Eulogist
  B.C.: 6 ANTONY
Eulogize: 4 LAUD 5 EXTOL
Eunomia
  ~, Dike, and Irene: 5 HORAE
Eunuch
  Area guarded by a: 5 HAREM
Euphoric: 5 GIDDY
  states: 5 HIGHS
  Where the ~ walk: 5 ONAIR
Euphrates
  land: 4 IRAQ 5 SYRIA
Eur.
  Bygone ~ realm: 3 HRE
  carrier: 3 SAS
  Former ~ carrier: 4 BOAC
  It's south of: 3 AFR
  nation: 3 GER IRE
Eurasian
  divide: 5 URALS
  duck: 4 SMEW
  wild goat: 4 IBEX
Eure-et-Loir
  neighbor: 4 ORNE
"**Eureka!**": 3 **AHA** OHO 5 MOTTO
    7 THATSIT
  cause: 8 SOLUTION
Euripides
  play: 3 ION 5 HELEN MEDEA
    7 ELECTRA ORESTES
Euro
  exchange (abbr.): 3 DOL
  fraction: 4 CENT
  predecessor: 3 **ECU** 4 LIRA
    5 FRANC 6 PESETA
Europe
  "boot": 5 ITALY
  East end of: 5 URALS
  highest volcano: 4 ETNA
  In: 6 ABROAD

Longest river of: **5** VOLGA
~, to the U.S.: **8** OLDWORLD
European
airline: **3** SAS
auto: **4** AUDI OPEL SAAB
    YUGO
blackbird: **4** MERL
capital: **4** BERN KIEV OSLO
    RIGA **5** BERNE MINSK
    6 TIRANA VIENNA ZAGREB
    7 TALLINN
chain: **4** ALPS
Eastern: **4** **SERB** SLAV
erupter: **4** **ETNA**
fashion center: **5** MILAN
finch: **5** SERIN **6** LINNET
Former ~ capital: **4** BONN
high points: **4** ALPS
hot spot: **4** ETNA
language: **4** ERSE
peak: **3** ALP
peninsula: **6** IBERIA
prefix: **4** INDO
river: **4** ARNO ELBE
rocket: **6** ARIANE
stock exchange: **6** BOURSE
tree: **4** SORB
viper: **3** ASP **5** ADDER
European-made
jet: **6** AIRBUS
Europe-Asia
divider: **5** URALS
Eurydice
Lover of: **7** ORPHEUS
Euterpe: **4** MUSE
Sister of: **4** CLIO **5** ERATO
Eva
half-sister: **3** ZSA
of Argentina: **5** PERON
or Zsa Zsa: **5** GABOR
Sister of: **5** MAGDA **6** ZSAZSA
Evade: **5** DODGE SHIRK SKIRT
~, with "out of": **6** WEASEL
Evader
Famed tax: **6** CAPONE
Tax ~ nightmare: **5** AUDIT
Evaluate: **4** RATE **5** ASSAY WEIGH
    6 **ASSESS** SIZEUP
    8 APPRAISE

Evaluation: **4** TEST
Critical: **8** ACIDTEST
Evan
Senator: **4** BAYH
suffix: **4** ESCE
Evanesce: **4** FADE WANE
    8 FADEAWAY
Evangeline: **7** ACADIAN
"Evangeline"
setting: **6** ACADIA
Evangelist
cry: **6** REPENT
Early: **11** BILLYSUNDAY
Eminent: **11** BILLYGRAHAM
prefix: **3** TEL
Evans
Actress: **5** LINDA
Country singer: **4** SARA
Cowgirl: **4** DALE
Jazz arranger: **3** GIL
partner in journalism:
    5 NOVAK
Evans, Greg
comic strip: **5** LUANN
Evans, Janet
Emulated: **4** SWAM
Evaporation
product: **7** SEASALT
Evasive: **3** COY **4** EELY **5** CAGEY
maneuver: **5** SLASH STALL
    6 ENDRUN
Eve
Actress: **5** ARDEN
counterpart: **4** MORN
Early: **3** RIB
Eldest of: **4** CAIN
Grandson of: **4** ENOS
Home of: **4** EDEN
Mate of: **4** ADAM
Second son of: **4** ABEL
Son of: **4** ABEL CAIN SETH
Tempter of: **7** SERPENT
Youngest of: **4** SETH
Yves's: **4** SOIR
Evel
deed: **5** STUNT
Evelyn
Actress: **5** KEYES
Writing brother of: **4** ALEC

Even: 3 TIE YET 4 **TIED** 5 ALIGN
     FLUSH 6 INATIE ONAPAR
     SEDATE TIEDUP
   a little: 3 ANY 5 ATALL
   chance: 6 TOSSUP
   Get ~ for: 6 AVENGE
   if: 3 **THO** 5 ALTHO 6 ALBEIT
   Make: 4 TRUE
   Not: 3 ODD 5 ASKEW 6 ASLOPE
     UNTRUE
   one: 3 ANY
   prime: 3 TWO
   score: 3 TIE
   so: 3 YET 5 STILL
   start: 4 EQUI
   though: 6 ALBEIT
   ~, once: 4 EVER
   ~, with "in": 4 ATIE
Evenhanded: 4 FAIR
Evening
   affair: 6 SOIREE
   bell: 6 VESPER
   do: 6 SOIREE
   Early: 5 SEVEN
   Eat in the: 3 SUP 4 DINE
   event: 6 SOIREE SUNSET
   hour: 3 TEN 4 NINE
   Informal: 4 NITE
   Like a romantic: 7 MOONLIT
   Like some ~ gowns:
     9 STRAPLESS
   party: 6 SOIREE
   Suitable for ~ wear: 6 DRESSY
   ~, in French: 4 SOIR
   ~, in Italian: 4 SERA
   ___ even keel: 4 **ONAN**
Evenly
   matched: 8 ONETOONE
   Split: 6 BISECT
"Even ___ speak ...": 4 ASWE
Even-steven: 4 TIED
Event
   1944 ~: 4 DDAY
   1977 ~: 5 ROOTS
   1998 ~: 5 NTEST
   After-Christmas: 4 SALE
   Airport: 7 ARRIVAL
   Annual sports: 6 USOPEN
   Annual TV: 6 OSCARS

Bargain: 4 SALE
Blessed: 6 SNEEZE
Campaign: 6 DEBATE
Catered: 6 AFFAIR
Community: 4 SING
Court: 5 TRIAL
Current: 4 EDDY TIDE
   6 ELNINO
Dressy: 4 GALA
Easter: 6 PARADE
Eden: 4 FALL
Emotional: 5 DRAMA
Equestrian: 8 DRESSAGE
Festive: 4 GALA
Field: 7 SHOTPUT
for Alice: 8 TEAPARTY
Friars: 5 ROAST
Fundraising: 8 BAKESALE
Gallery: 7 ARTSALE
Garage: 4 SALE
Hoops: 3 NIT
Ice skating: 5 PAIRS
Inauguration: 4 OATH
Lunar: 7 ECLIPSE
Mall: 4 SALE
May: 4 INDY
Meet: 4 DASH RACE
Musical: 7 RECITAL
Olympic: 4 EPEE LUGE
Pentathlon: 4 EPEE
Pointless: 4 EPEE
Prefight: 7 WEIGHIN
Quadrennial:
   11 SUMMERGAMES
Quantum: 4 LEAP
Red-tag: 4 SALE
Significant: 9 MILESTONE
Speakeasy: 4 RAID
Sports: 4 MEET
Spring: 4 THAW
Stock mkt.: 3 IPO
Tent: 4 SALE
Thanksgiving Day: 6 PARADE
Track: 3 BET 4 DASH **MEET**
   RACE TROT 5 RELAY
   6 SPRINT 7 JAVELIN
with caddies: 3 TEA
WWII: 4 DDAY
Yachting: 7 SEARACE

Yard: 4 SALE
Events: 6 DOINGS
Course of: 4 TIDE
Eventual
avis: 4 OVUM
Eventually: 3 YET 6 INTIME
ONEDAY 7 SOMEDAY
13 SOONERORLATER
become: 5 ENDUP
Ever
As good as: 7 LIKENEW
Hardly: 5 RARELY
Partner of: 4 **ANON**
so slight: 3 WEE
Everage
Dame: 4 EDNA
Title: 4 DAME
Ever and ___: 4 ANON
Everest: 5 MOUNT
and others: 3 MTS
guide: 6 SHERPA
locale: 5 NEPAL
Everett
Actor: 4 CHAD 6 SLOANE
Everglades
bird: 5 EGRET
deposit: 4 PEAT
terrain: 5 SWAMP
wader: 4 IBIS 5 EGRET HERON
Everglades Parkway
City west of: 6 NAPLES
Evergreen: 3 FIR YEW 4 PINE
6 SPRUCE 7 CONIFER
hedge: 6 PRIVET
Northern ~ forest: 5 TAIGA
Poisonous: 8 OLEANDER
scented: 4 PINY
Tropical: 5 CACAO
West Coast: 6 TANOAK
Everhart
Model: 5 ANGIE
Everlasting: 7 AGELESS
ETERNAL 8 CONSTANT
~, old-style: 6 ETERNE
Everly Brothers: 3 DUO 4 DUET
1957 ~ hit: 10 BYEBYELOVE
1960 ~ hit: 5 SOSAD
9 LETITBEME
One of the: 4 PHIL

Sleeping girl in an ~ hit: 5 SUSIE
"___ Ever Need Is You": 4 ALLI
"___ ever so humble ...": 4 BEIT
Evert
of tennis: 5 CHRIS
Every: 3 ALL 4 EACH
bit: 3 ALL
Each and: 3 ALL
For: 3 PER
last one: 3 ALL
~ 24 hours: 4 ADAY 5 DAILY
~, on an Rx: 3 OMN
Everybody: 3 ALL
Opposite of: 5 NOONE
"Everybody Loves Raymond":
6 SITCOM
actor Peter: 5 BOYLE
actor Ray: 6 ROMANO
network: 3 CBS
"Everybody's Talkin'"
singer: 7 NILSSON
Everyday: 5 PLAIN USUAL
6 NORMAL 7 PROSAIC
ROUTINE
vocabulary: 10 VERNACULAR
Everydog: 4 FIDO
Everyone: 3 ALL
Buy ~ beers: 9 GETAROUND
For: 4 COED 6 RATEDG
For ~ to hear: 5 ALOUD
~, on boxes: 7 ALLAGES
Everything: 3 ALL 6 THELOT
considered: 8 ALLINALL
Counting: 5 **INALL** 6 INTOTO
7 ALLTOLD INTOTAL
OVERALL
else: 4 REST
It means: 4 OMNI
Lose: 6 GOBUST
They fix: 8 PANACEAS
~, in German: 5 ALLES
Everytown, USA: 6 PEORIA
Everywhere: 7 ALLOVER
10 HIGHANDLOW
"Every ___ winner!": 4 ONEA
Evian
and others: 4 SPAS
output: 3 EAU
Evict: 4 OUST SHOO

Evictee
Early: 3 EVE 4 ADAM
Eviction: 6 OUSTER
site: 4 EDEN
Evidence
Appendectomy: 4 SCAR
Burning: 5 SMOKE
Carpet: 6 FIBERS
Conclude from the: 5 INFER
Examine: 4 SIFT
Hide: 15 COVERONESTRACKS
in court: 7 EXHIBIT
Indisputable: 5 PROOF
Minimal: 5 SHRED
Modern-day: 3 DNA
of change: 7 ERASURE
of rot: 4 ODOR
of sloppiness: 5 TYPOS
Paternity suit: 3 DNA
Piece of: 4 TAPE
Stop introducing: 4 REST
Type of: 3 DNA
Watergate: 4 TAPE
Evil: 3 BAD ILL 4 BASE 6 UNHOLY
  7 SATANIC
Believer in good and: 7 DUALIST
deed: 3 SIN
emperor: 4 NERO
It may be: 3 EYE
Like a certain: 6 LESSER
look: 4 LEER
one: 3 ORC 4 OGRE 5 DEMON
  FIEND SATAN
repeller: 6 AMULET
spell: 3 HEX
spirit: 5 DEMON
spirits: 6 INCUBI
~, in French: 3 MAL
~ Norse god: 4 LOKI
"___ evil ...": 5 SEENO
"Evil That ___, The": 5 MENDO
"Evil Ways"
band: 7 SANTANA
"Evil Woman"
band: 3 **ELO**
Evinced: 5 SHOWN
Eviscerate: 3 GUT
"Evita"
Antonio in: 3 CHE

Madonna costar in: 7 ANTONIO
role: 3 **CHE** 5 PERON
Evoke: 6 ELICIT
love: 6 ENDEAR
Evoker
Blessing: 5 ACHOO 6 AHCHOO
Evoking
the past: 5 RETRO
Evolution
Steps in human: 4 APES
Evolutionary
link: 6 APEMAN
Evolutionist
interest: 7 ORIGINS
"___ Ev'ry Mountain": 5 CLIMB
Ewbank
Coach: 4 WEEB
Ewe
Cheese from ~ milk: 6 ROMANO
He loves: 3 RAM
It comes from: 4 WOOL
kids: 5 LAMBS
Like a: 5 OVINE
milieu: 3 LEA
said it: 3 **BAA** MAA
Ewing
A ~ on TV: 3 PAM
mother: 5 ELLIE
Ewing, J.R.: 6 OILMAN
Mother of: 5 **ELLIE**
show: 6 DALLAS
Ewing, Patrick: 6 CENTER
Ewok
home: 5 ENDOR
"Ew-w-w!": 3 ICK 5 GROSS
Ex
claim: 7 ALIMONY
of André: 3 MIA
of Artie: 3 AVA 4 LANA
of Barbie: 3 KEN
of Brooke: 5 ANDRE
of Bruce: 4 **DEMI**
of Burt: 4 **LONI**
of Cher: 4 BONO 5 SONNY
of Crawford: 4 GERE
of Dahl: 5 LAMAS
of Dick: 3 LIZ
of Donald: 5 IVANA 6 MAPLES
of Duke: 5 ASTIN

of Frank: 3 AVA MIA
of Frasier: 6 LILITH
of George Hamilton: 5 ALANA
of Ike: 4 **TINA**
of Julia: 4 LYLE
of Loni: 4 BURT
of Madonna: 4 SEAN
of Mick: 6 BIANCA
of Mickey: 3 AVA
of Puffy: 3 JLO
of Richard Gere: 5 CINDY
of Rita: 3 ALY
of Rod Stewart: 5 ALANA
of Sonny: 4 CHER
of Tina: 3 IKE
of Turner: 5 FONDA
of Woody: 3 MIA
of Xavier: 4 ABBE 5 CHARO
~ GI: 3 VET
Exact: 4 EVEN VERY 6 STRICT
7 LITERAL PRECISE
copy: 4 TWIN 5 CLONE
7 REPLICA
Not an ~ fig.: 3 EST
satisfaction for: 6 AVENGE
Exacta: 3 BET
"Exactamundo!": 5 RIGHT
Exacting: 5 HARSH RIGID STERN
6 SEVERE STRICT
Exactitude: 5 RIGOR
Exactly: 3 PAT 4 TOAT 6 NOLESS
TOATEE 8 ONTHEDOT
SMACKDAB VERBATIM
9 ONTHENOSE
like this: 6 JUSTSO
right: 6 DEADON SPOTON
"Exactly!": 5 RIGHT
Exaggerate: 6 OVERDO
7 INFLATE
Exaggerated: 4 TALL
melodrama:
15 BLOODANDTHUNDER
publicity: 4 HYPE
sense of power: 8 MACHISMO
Exaggerator
ending: 3 EST
Exalt: 4 LAUD 6 LIFTUP
7 ENNOBLE LIONIZE
Exam: 4 TEST

3-D ~: 3 MRI
Atty.-to-be: 4 **LSAT**
Breeze through an: 3 ACE
British: 6 ALEVEL OLEVEL
College: 4 ORAL
Coll. senior's: 3 GRE 4 GMAT
Cram for an: 6 BONEUP
Dental: 4 ORAL XRAY
Doc-to-be: 4 MCAT
English: 5 ESSAY
Face-to-face: 4 ORAL
for jrs.: 4 PSAT
H.S.: 3 SAT 4 PSAT
Jr.: 4 **PSAT**
Kind of: 4 **ORAL** 5 FINAL
8 OPENBOOK
Makeup: 6 RETEST
no-no: 4 CRIB
part: 5 ESSAY
Sr.: 3 SAT
taker: 6 TESTEE
Tough: 4 BEAR ORAL
Examination: 4 TEST 5 ASSAY
Stiff: 7 AUTOPSY
Examine: 3 EYE 4 QUIZ TEST
5 ASSAY STUDY 6 GOINTO
GOOVER LOOKAT PERUSE
again: 5 RESEE
closely: 4 SIFT
hastily: 4 SCAN
in detail: 4 SCAN 5 PROBE
~, with "out": 5 SCOPE
Examiner: 6 TESTER
Ear: 8 OTOSCOPE
Future: 4 SEER
Ticket: 5 VOTER
X-file: 4 GMAN
Example: 4 TYPE 5 MODEL
6 LESSON 8 SPECIMEN
Fine: 5 PEARL
One with an: 5 CITER
___ example: 4 ASAN
Exasperate: 3 IRE IRK VEX
4 GALL RILE
Exasperation: 3 IRE
Excalibur: 5 SWORD
Excavate: 3 DIG 6 DEEPEN
Excavated
again: 5 REDUG

Excavation
  find: 3 ORE 5 RELIC
Excedrin
  rival: 5 ALEVE BAYER
     6 ANACIN
Exceed: 3 TOP 5 OUTDO
     6 GOOVER 7 OUTSTEP
     RUNOVER 8 OVERSTEP
  the limit: 5 SPEED
Exceeding: 4 OVER 5 ABOVE
Exceedingly: 4 VERY 5 NOEND
     6 EVERSO
Excel: 4 STAR 5 SHINE
     7 ACHIEVE
Excelled: 5 SHONE
Excellence: 5 MERIT
  Mark of: 3 TEN 5 APLUS
  Meas. of academic: 3 GPA
  Model of: 7 PARAGON
  Standard of: 5 IDEAL
Excellent: 4 **AONE** 5 AOKAY
     SUPER 6 BANGUP SUPERB
     TIPTOP 8 SPLENDID
  mark: 5 APLUS
  rating: 4 AONE
  service: 3 ACE
  Unusually: 4 RARE
  ~, slangily: 3 DEF RAD 4 PHAT
     5 PRIMO
"Excellent!": 5 GREAT SWELL
Except: 3 BAR BUT 4 OMIT SAVE
     5 DEBAR 6 ALLBUT
     7 BESIDES
  if: 6 UNLESS
Exception: 7 ANOMALY
  Take: 5 **DEMUR** 6 OBJECT
     RESENT
  Without: 3 ALL 6 ALWAYS
     TOAMAN 7 BARNONE
Exceptional: 4 RARE 8 ABERRANT
Excerpt: 5 QUOTE
  Film: 4 CLIP
  Opera: 4 ARIA
Excess: 3 FAT
  Carry to: 6 OVERDO
  Drink to: 4 TOPE
  Fill to: 4 SATE 7 SATIATE
  In ~ of: 4 OVER 8 MORETHAN
  Love to: 4 DOTE

  Spell of: 5 SPREE
  Use to: 6 OVERDO
  Weary by: 4 CLOY
Excessive: 5 ULTRA **UNDUE**
     6 DETROP 8 ALLFIRED
     10 INORDINATE
  excitement: 5 MANIA
  fondness: 6 DOTAGE
  interest: 5 USURY
  pride: 6 HUBRIS
  sentimentality: 8 SCHMALTZ
  sweetness: 7 TREACLE
Excessively: 3 TOO 4 OHSO
  affected: 6 TOOTOO
  excited: 5 MANIC
  glib: 3 PAT
  Talk: 5 PRATE
Exchange: 4 MART SWAP
     5 BANDY TRADE 6 SWITCH
     7 TRADEIN
  allowance: 4 AGIO
  Chicago: 4 MERC
  Church: 4 IDOS
  Currency ~ board (abbr.): 3 USD
  European stock: 6 BOURSE
  Foreign: 4 EURO
  membership: 4 SEAT
  premium: 4 AGIO
  Tech-heavy: 6 NASDAQ
  verbal blows: 4 SPAR
  vows: 3 WED
  Wedding: 4 IDOS
Exchanged
  items: 4 IONS
  Where vows are: 5 ALTAR
  words: 3 IDO 4 IDOS
Exchanges
  AOL: 3 IMS
Excise: 3 TAX 4 DELE
Excite: 3 WOW 4 SEND 5 KEYUP
     REVUP 6 AROUSE THRILL
     TICKLE TURNON
     7 ENTHUSE
  ~, as interest: 5 PIQUE
Excited: 4 AGOG SENT 5 HETUP
     6 INHEAT ONFIRE
     PUMPED 7 ATINGLE
     KEYEDUP
  about: 4 INTO 5 UPFOR

Got: 5 RAVED
sensation: 6 TINGLE
"___ Excited": 4 IMSO
Excitedly: 4 AGOG
Excitement: 3 ADO 5 DRAMA
    6 HOOPLA 7 AROUSAL
Buzzing with: 5 ABOIL
Cry of: 4 OHOH
Excessive: 5 MANIA
Full of: 4 AGOG
Exciting
Far from: 4 BLAH TAME
Exclaim
over: 3 OOH
Exclamation
Beatnik: 3 MAN
Brit: 4 **ISAY**
Comics: 3 ACK
Ebenezer: 3 BAH
Emeril: 3 BAM
French: 5 VOILA 7 OOHLALA
German: 3 ACH
Magician: 6 PRESTO
of annoyance: 4 DRAT
of discovery: 3 AHA
of disdain: 4 POOH
of disgust: 3 UGH
of relief: 4 PHEW
of surprise: 3 OHO 4 LORD YIPE
    5 WOWIE
Old-time: 3 FIE 4 EGAD
Part of a WWII: 4 TORA
Taunting: 3 OHO
Triumphant: 3 AHA
Weary worker: 4 TGIF
Exclamations
Surprised: 3 OHS
Exclude: 3 BAN BAR 4 OMIT
    5 DEBAR
Excluding: 3 NOT 7 SHORTOF
Exclusive: 4 **SOLE** 5 ELITE
    SCOOP 6 SNOOTY
group: 4 CULT 5 CASTE ELITE
    6 CHOSEN 7 COTERIE
    INCROWD
Exclusively: 3 ALL 4 ONLY
    5 ALONE
Excommunication
Reason for: 6 HERESY

Excoriate: 4 FLAY PARE SKIN
    6 REVILE SAVAGE SCATHE
    7 CHEWOUT
Excursion: 4 RAID TRIP 5 FORAY
    JAUNT
NASA: 3 EVA
Excursions
Like some: 5 LUNAR
Excuse: 3 OUT 5 **ALIBI** 6 LETOFF
    PARDON 7 CONDONE
    FORGIVE
Kind of: 4 LAME
Lame: 6 COPOUT 7 IFORGET
Legal: 5 ALIBI
Like a poor: 4 LAME
Many an: 3 LIE
"Excuse me ...": 4 **AHEM**
Exec: 4 SUIT
Agency: 3 DIR
Chief: 4 PRES PREZ
College: 5 PREXY
Corp.: 4 PRES 5 TREAS
degree: 3 MBA
Ex-Disney: 6 EISNER
extra: 4 PERK
Fiscal: 3 CFO
note: 4 MEMO
request: 4 ASAP
Right away, to an: 4 ASAP
TV ~ work: 4 SKED
Execrate: 5 ABHOR 6 DETEST
    LOATHE
Execs
Account: 4 REPS
Baseball: 3 GMS
Magazine: 3 EDS
Mag for: 3 INC
Some: 3 VPS
Execute
perfectly: 4 NAIL
Executed: 3 DID
Executes: 4 DOES
Executive: 4 SUIT 7 MANAGER
(abbr.): 4 PRES
extra: 4 PERK 11 STOCKOPTION
staff: 5 AIDES
~ Roone: 7 ARLEDGE
Executor
concern: 6 ESTATE

Exemplar: 5 IDEAL
of easiness: **3** PIE
of grace: **4** SWAN
of greed: **5** MIDAS
of might: **3** OAK
of twinship: **4** PEAS
Exempt: 4 FREE **6** IMMUNE
Exemption
Tournament: **3** BYE
Exercise: 3 PLY USE **5** EXERT
WIELD
aftermath: **4** ACHE
Ballerina: **4** PLIE
Bar: **6** CHINUP
based on karate: **5** TAEBO
discipline: **4** YOGA
Dumbbell: **4** CURL
for the abs: **5** SITUP
Kind of: **7** AEROBIC
Swimming: **4** LAPS
target: **3** ABS **4** DELT FLAB
unit: **3** SET **5** SITUP **6** PULLUP
Weightlifting: **4** CURL
Exerciser
target: **3** ABS **4** FLAB
wear: **7** SPANDEX
Exert
One may ~ pressure: **4** PEER
Exertion: 4 DINT TOIL **5** SWEAT
6 EFFORT STRAIN
Averse to: **4** LAZY
Aversion to: **5** SLOTH
Exhalation
Wistful: **4** SIGH
Exhaust: 3 SAP **4** POOP TIRE
5 DRAIN SPEND **USEUP**
7 DEPLETE TIREOUT
WEAROUT
tube: **8** TAILPIPE
Exhausted: 4 BEAT DEAD SHOT
5 ALLIN **SPENT** WEARY
6 DONEIN USEDUP
9 WASHEDOUT
~, slangily: **5** FRIED
Exhausts
Like some: **4** DUAL
Exhibit: 4 SHOW
scorn: **5** SNEER
subject: **3** ART

Exhibition: 4 FAIR SHOW
Exhibitionist: 8 SHOWBOAT
Exhibits: 8 EVIDENCE
Exhilarate: 5 ELATE
Exhort: 4 URGE
Exhortation
Cook's: **5** DIGIN
Demonstration: **5** UNITE
November: **4** VOTE
Exigency: 4 <u>NEED</u>
Exile
1979 ~: **4** AMIN SHAH
7 IDIAMIN
Early: **3** EVE **4** ADAM
isle: **4** <u>ELBA</u> **8** STHELENA
of 1302: **5** DANTE
Political: **5** EXPAT
Renowned: **9** DALAILAMA
Exiled
Leader ~ to Hawaii: **4** RHEE
Where Napoleon was: **4** ELBA
~ Amin: **3** IDI
~ Cambodian leader: **6** LONNOL
~ Irani: **4** SHAH
~ Roman poet: **4** OVID
~ Ugandan: **4** AMIN
Exist: 3 <u>ARE</u> **4** LIVE
Did not: **6** WERENT
Does not: **4** ISNT
Do not: **5** ARENT
suffix: **3** ENT **4** ENCE
Existed: 3 <u>WAS</u> **4** BEEN WERE
Never: **5** WASNT
Existence: 4 LIFE **5** BEING
Coming into: **7** NASCENT
Have: **3** ARE
Hectic: **7** RATRACE
Latin: **4** ESSE
Existential
woe: **5** ANGST
Existing: 5 ALIVE
Exit: 4 DOOR **5** LEAVE **6** BOWOUT
DEPART EGRESS WAYOUT
7 STEPOUT
Discreet: **8** SIDEDOOR
Emergency: **10** FIREESCAPE
Freeway: **4** RAMP
Head for the: **5** LEAVE
location: **4** REAR

one's cocoon: **6** EMERGE
Secret: **8** TRAPDOOR
___ ex machina: **4** DEUS

Exmoor
Doone of: **5** LORNA

Exo-
Opposite of: **4** ENDO ENTO

Exodus
Bk. after: **3** LEV
commemoration: **5 SEDER**
crossing: **6** REDSEA
figure: **5** MOSES **7** PHARAOH
food: **5** MANNA
High priest in: **5** AARON
miracle: **5** MANNA
mount: **5** SINAI
pharoah: **6** RAMSES
vllain: **7** PHARAOH

"Exodus"
actor: **5** MINEO
actor John: **5** DEREK
actor Mineo: **3** SAL
author: **4 URIS**
author Uris: **4** LEON
director Preminger: **4** OTTO
hero: **3 ARI**
role for Paul Newman: **3** ARI

Exonerate: 5 CLEAR
Exorbitant: 4 HIGH **5** STEEP
interest: **5** USURY

"Exorcist, The"
actress Blair: **5** LINDA
Board used in: **5** OUIJA
quarry: **5** DEMON

Exotic: 5 ALIEN **7** STRANGE
fruit: **5** MANGO
meat: **3** EMU
stamp receiver: **6** PENPAL

Expand: 4 GROW **5** ADDON
SPLAY WIDEN **6** DILATE
7 ADDONTO BROADEN
ENLARGE
Cause to: **6** DILATE
Expanded: 4 GREW
Expanding
gp.: **4** NATO
Expanse: 3 SEA **4** AREA
6 SPREAD
African: **6** SAHARA

Argentine: **5** PAMPA
Arid: **6** SAHARA
Green: **3** LEA **4** ACRE LAWN
Iranian: **15** GREATSALTDESERT
Mongolian: **4** GOBI
of land: **5** TRACT
Pastoral: **3** LEA
Sandy: **6** DESERT
Treeless: **5** PAMPA
Vast: **3** SEA **5** OCEAN

Expansion
Room for: **5** ANNEX
team of 1962: **4** METS

Expansive: 4 VAST **5** BROAD
7 OCEANIC
Expatriate: 8 EMIGRANT
Expect: 4 HOPE **5 AWAIT**
6 PLANON **7** WAITFOR

Expectant
Act the ~ father: **4** PACE
Eagerly: **4** ATIP
father: **5** PACER
parent: **5** NAMER

Expectations
Grate: **3** ASH **5** ASHES
Like some: **5** UNMET
Meet, as: **6** RISETO
Met: **5** ARIAS **6** OPERAS
Expected: 3 DUE 5 USUAL
6 NORMAL
As: **4** DULY **5** ONCUE
7 UPTOPAR
Exactly what's:
15 PARFORTHECOURSE
Is ~ (to): **5** OUGHT
It's: **3** PAR
result: **3** PAR **4** NORM
soon: **4** NIGH
to arrive: **3** DUE
What's: **4** NORM
When: **5** ONCUE

Expecting: 8 PREGNANT
Eagerly: **4** ATIP
the worse: **7** BEARISH
Expectorate: 4 SPIT
Expedition: 4 TREK **5** HASTE
SPEED
African: **6** SAFARI
Expeditious: 6 PROMPT SPEEDY

Expel: 4 OUST SPEW 5 EJECT
    EVICT 6 DEPORT
  from law practice: 6 DISBAR
Expend: 3 USE 5 USEUP
Expenditure: 4 COST 5 OUTGO
    6 OUTLAY
Expense: 4 COST 6 OUTLAY
  Monthly: 4 RENT
  Nightclub: 11 COVERCHARGE
  Trucker: 4 TOLL
Expenses
  After: 3 NET
  Reduce: 4 PARE
Expensive: 4 DEAR HIGH
    5 STEEP 6 COSTLY
Experience: 4 FEEL HAVE
    7 UNDERGO
  again: 6 RELIVE
  Bound to: 5 INFOR
  Chair-raising: 4 HORA
  Exciting: 4 TRIP
  Pique: 3 IRE 4 SNIT
  Trying: 6 ORDEAL
Experienced: 3 PRO 4 FELT
    KNEW 7 VETERAN
  Least: 6 RAWEST
  ~, old-style: 5 VERST
Experiences: 3 HAS
Experiment: 4 TEST 5 TRIAL
  Alamogordo: 5 ATEST
  Bikini: 5 NTEST
  site: 3 LAB
  subject: 6 LABRAT
  Subject of a psych.: 3 ESP
  Underwater ~ site: 6 SEALAB
Expert: 3 **ACE** PRO WIZ 4 GURU
    WHIZ 5 ADEPT MAVEN
    SHARP 7 MAESTRO
    OLDHAND
  Bridge: 5 GOREN
  Card game: 5 HOYLE
  Coloring: 4 DYER
  CPR: 3 **EMT**
  ending: 3 ISE
  Gregg: 5 STENO
  group: 5 PANEL
  in futures: 4 SEER
  Law: 6 JURIST
  Martial arts: 5 NINJA

  Mideast: 7 ARABIST
  PC: 4 TECH
  Policy: 4 WONK
  Service: 4 ACER
  suffix: 3 **ISE**
  Talmud: 5 RABBI
  Tax prep.: 3 CPA
  with a deck: 9 CARDSHARK
"___ expert, but ...": 4 IMNO
Expertise: 3 ART 5 SKILL
    7 KNOWHOW
  Field of: 4 **AREA**
  Level of karate: 3 DAN
  PT: 5 REHAB
  Sailor: 5 KNOTS
Expiate: 5 **ATONE**
Expire: 3 DIE END 5 LAPSE
    6 RUNOUT
Explain
  away, with "over": 5 GLOSS
  Hard to: 5 EERIE
"___ Explains It All": 8 CLARISSA
Explanation: 3 WHY
  Phrase of: 5 IDEST
  Propose as an: 5 POSIT
Expletive
  Charlie Brown: 4 **RATS**
  Dated: 4 EGAD
  Ebenezer: 3 BAH
  Fields: 4 DRAT
  Mild: 4 EGAD
Explicable
  Least: 6 ODDEST
Explicit
  Not: 5 VAGUE
Explode: 5 BURST ERUPT
    6 BLOWUP GOBOOM
  Ready to: 5 IRATE
Exploded: 4 BLEW 7 WENTOFF
Exploding
  gag item: 5 CIGAR
  star: 4 NOVA
  stars: 5 NOVAE
  Still capable of: 4 LIVE
Exploit: 3 ACT **USE** 4 DEED FEAT
    GEST MILK 5 GESTE
    7 TRADEON UTILIZE
Exploitive
  boss: 7 PADRONE

one: **4** USER
Exploration
   org.: **4** NASA
Exploratory
   expedition: **5** PROBE
Explore: 5 DELVE PROBE
      6 GOINTO
   caves: **7** SPELUNK
Explorer
   Antarctic: **4** BYRD ROSS
      6 ERNEST
   Arctic: **3** RAE **5** PEARY
   called "the Red": **4** ERIC
   Cumberland Gap: **5** BOONE
   Down Under: **6** TASMAN
   Early: **4** ERIC
   Ford: **3** SUV
   Internet: **4** USER
   maker: **4** FORD
   Mississippi River: **6** DESOTO
      7 LASALLE
   NASA: **5** ROBOT
   need: **3** MAP
   Norse: **4** ERIC
   of Florida: **6** DESOTO
   org.: **3** BSA
   Scottish: **3** RAE
   Space: **5** PROBE
   Victoria Island: **3** RAE
   who named Louisiana:
      7 LASALLE
   ~ La ___: **5** SALLE
   ~ Polo: **5** MARCO
Explosion: 5 BLAST
Explosive: 3 TNT **5** NITRO
   compound: **6** AMATOL
   letters: **3** **TNT**
   liquid: **5** NITRO
   sound: **4** BANG BLAM WHAM
      6 KABOOM
   trial: **5** NTEST
Expo
   1970 ~ site: **5** OSAKA
Exponential
   inverse: **7** ANTILOG
Export
   Australian: **4** OPAL
   Bolivian: **3** TIN
   Dutch: **4** EDAM **5** TULIP

   Holland: **5** TULIP
   Jamaican: **3** RUM
   Malaysian: **3** TIN
   Mideast: **3** OIL
   North Pole: **3** TOY
   Sri Lanka: **3** TEA **5** PEKOE
      8 PEKOETEA
   Swedish: **4** SAAB
   Venezuelan: **3** OIL
Expos
   Former ~ manager: **4** ALOU
Expose: 4 BARE **6** DEBUNK
      UNMASK **7** LAYBARE
      LAYOPEN
   ~, in verse: **3** OPE
Exposed: 4 OPEN SEEN **5** NAKED
      8 LAIDBARE
Exposition: 4 FAIR
Exposure: 4 RISK
Express: 3 AIR SAY **4** AVER VENT
      5 OPINE STATE UTTER
      VOICE **6** PHRASE
   alternative: **5** LOCAL
   appreciation to: **5** THANK
   approval: **4** CLAP
   checkout word: **4** ITEM
      5 ITEMS
   disapproval: **4** HISS
   discontent: **6** REPINE
   disdain: **3** TUT
   gratitude to: **5** THANK
   grief: **5** MOURN
   letters: **4** ASAP
   Not: **5** LOCAL TACIT
   regret: **4** MOAN SIGH
   shock: **4** GASP
Expressed: 3 PUT **4** SAID
   delight: **5** AAHED OOHED
   disapproval: **5** TSKED
   joy: **4** WEPT
   Vocally: **4** ORAL
   ~, as a farewell: **4** BADE
Expression: 4 LOOK TERM
      5 IDIOM VOICE
   All-inclusive: **4** ATOZ
   following an accident: **4** UHOH
   of contempt: **5** SNEER
   of discovery: **3** AHA
   of pride: **4** ROAR

of sorrow: 4 ALAS 6 LAMENT
of surprise: 3 OHO
Unhappy: 5 SCOWL
Without: 5 STONY 7 STONILY
Expressionist
~ Nolde: 4 EMIL
~ Schiele: 4 EGON
Expressionless: 5 BLANK STONY
    6 GLASSY
Expressions
of surprise: 3 OHS
Pained: 3 OWS
Expressway
access: 4 RAMP
___ **Expressway:** 5 EDENS
Expunge: 4 DELE 5 ERASE
    6 EFFACE
Exquisite: 6 DAINTY
trinket: 5 BIJOU
Extend: 3 ADD JUT RUN 5 RANGE
    RENEW SPLAY 6 OUTLIE
    7 ADDONTO
across: 4 SPAN
a subscription: 5 RENEW
credit: 4 LEND
Extended: 4 LONG
family: 4 CLAN 5 TRIBE
period: 3 EON ERA 4 AEON
Extender
Info: Suffix cue
List: 4 ETAL
Pay: 3 OLA
Sail: 5 SPRIT
Extension: 3 ARM 4 LIMB
    5 ADDON
Info: Suffix cue
Building: 3 **ELL** 4 WING
    5 ANNEX
Computer filename: 3 EXE
East: 3 ERN
Florida: 4 KEYS
Home: 5 STEAD
Keel: 4 SKEG
Kitchen: 4 ETTE
Manila folder: 3 TAB
Program file: 3 EXE
Right-angled: 3 ELL
Shoulder: 6 SLEEVE
Stage: 5 APRON

Switch: 4 EROO
Table: 4 LEAF
Extensive: 4 VAST WIDE 5 MAJOR
Extensively: 4 ALOT 8 ATLENGTH
Extent: 4 AREA SIZE SPAN
    5 GAMUT REACH SCOPE
    6 DEGREE
Full: 4 SPAN
Fullest: 4 HILT
To a certain: 6 INPART
To a greater: 6 MORESO
To any: 5 ATALL
To a smaller: 4 LESS
To some: 3 ANY 4 ATAD
To such an: 7 INSOFAR
To the ~ that: 7 ASFARAS
Two-dimensional: 4 AREA
Utmost: 9 NTHDEGREE
Extents
Vast: 5 DEEPS
Exterior: 5 OUTER
finish: 6 STUCCO
Tough: 4 HIDE
Exterminator
target: 4 PEST
External: 5 OUTER
Not: 5 INNER
Extinct
Become: 3 DIE 6 DIEOUT
bird: 3 **MOA** 4 DODO
Extinction
Facing: 4 RARE
Extinguish: 4 DAMP KILL
    5 DOUSE SNUFF
    6 PUTOUT
Extol: 4 LAUD TOUT 6 PRAISE
Extort: 5 BLEED WREST WRING
Extorted: 4 BLED
Extra: 4 MORE 5 ADDED ADDON
    SPARE 7 ADDEDON
    SURPLUS TOSPARE
(abbr.): 4 ADDL
Bus. letter: 3 ENC
charge: 5 ADDON
dry: 4 ARID
Env.: 3 ENC
Exec: 4 PERK
inning: 5 TENTH
innings cause: 3 TIE

It's a lot of ~ work:
   11 ELBOWGREASE
Ltr.: 3 ENC
Movie ~, for short: 4 SUPE
number: 6 ENCORE
periods: 3 OTS
perk: 5 FRILL
Something: 3 TIP 4 PLUS
   5 BONUS
stipulations: 4 ANDS
tire: 5 SPARE
wager: 7 SIDEBET
___ **extra cost:** 4 ATNO
Extract: 5 WREST 6 ELICIT
Beet: 5 SUGAR 7 SUCROSE
Rose: 5 ATTAR
Seaweed: 4 AGAR 6 POTASH
Shale: 3 OIL
Soybean: 4 TOFU
Extraction: 7 LINEAGE
Androcles: 5 THORN
Mine: 3 ORE
Extracts
Make: 6 DECOCT
Extra-large: 4 SIZE
Extra-long: 4 MAXI
Extraordinary: 4 EPIC
Be: 11 TAKETHECAKE
Most: 6 RAREST
server: 4 ACER
talent: 6 PHENOM
Extras
These have many: 5 EPICS
Extraterrestrial: 5 ALIEN
TV: 3 ALF
Extravagant: 6 LAVISH
party: 4 GALA
Extravagantly
theatrical: 4 CAMP
Extra-wide: 3 EEE 4 EEEE
Extreme: 3 END FAR NTH
   5 ACUTE OUTER **ULTRA**
   UNDUE 6 ARRANT
   SEVERE 7 INTENSE
   RADICAL
anguish: 7 TORTURE
cruelty: 6 SADISM
degree: 3 NTH
dislike: 6 HATRED

edge: 5 BRINK
fear: 5 DREAD 6 TERROR
Global: 4 POLE
Orbital: 6 APOGEE
suffix: 3 EST
~, as a fan: 5 RABID
Extremely: 3 TOO 4 VERY
   5 AWFUL NOEND QUITE
   SUPER 6 DAMNED
   EVERSO SORELY
Extremes
Go to: 6 OVERDO
Extremist: 5 **ULTRA** 6 ZEALOT
   7 RADICAL
group: 4 CULT
Extremity: 3 END TOE
Extrinsic: 5 ALIEN
Exuberance: 3 PEP VIM 4 ELAN
   GLEE
Exuberant: 6 ELATED HEARTY
   YEASTY 7 RIOTOUS
   ZESTFUL
cry: 5 WAHOO
Exudate
Tree: 3 SAP
Exudation
Pine: 5 RESIN
Exude: 4 EMIT OOZE SEEP
   6 REEKOF 7 SECRETE
Exult: 4 CROW 7 REJOICE
Exultant
joy: 4 GLEE
Exultation: 4 GLEE
Exxon
It merged with: 5 MOBIL
rival: 4 ARCO HESS 5 AMOCO
   SHELL
tiger: 4 TONY
~, formerly: 4 **ESSO**
Exxon Valdez: 5 OILER
mishap: 5 SPILL 8 OILSPILL
Eye: 3 TEC 4 HOLE LENS OGLE
   5 ORGAN 6 PEEPER
   7 STAREAT
amorously: 4 **OGLE**
annoyance: 4 STYE
bank donation: 6 CORNEA
Black: 5 MOUSE 6 SHINER
   STIGMA

Blink of an: **3** SEC
Camera: **4** LENS
closer: **3** LID
color: **5** HAZEL
Colored ~ part: **4** IRIS
covering: **3** LID **6** SCLERA
drop: **4 TEAR**
Electric: **6** SENSOR
Flower of one's: **4** IRIS
Give the: **4** OGLE **6** LEERAT
irritation: **4** STYE
It brings a tear to the: **4** DUCT
It keeps an ~ on TV: **3** CBS
It may have a black: **3** PEA
Keep an ~ on: **4** TEND
lasciviously: **6** LEERAT
layer: **4 UVEA 6** RETINA
liner: **3** LID
Of the: **5** OPTIC
opener: **5** ALARM
opening: **4** SLIT
part: **4 IRIS** UVEA
parts (var.): **6** IRIDES
Perform ~ surgery: **4** LASE
piece: **4** LENS
Poetic: **3** ORB
prefix: **5** OCULO
Private: **3** TEC **5** SNOOP
6 SHAMUS
problem: **4 STYE 6** IRITIS
protector: **4** LASH
rakishly: **4** OGLE
shade: **5** HAZEL
shape: **6** ALMOND
signal: **4** WINK
site: **5** STORM **6** POTATO
slyly: **4** OGLE
Snake: **7** ONESPOT
sore: **4 STYE**
surgery procedure: **5** LASIK
the bull's-eye: **3** AIM
up and down: **4** OGLE
Use the mind's: **7** IMAGINE
White of the: **6** SCLERA
woe: **4** STYE **6** IRITIS
~, in Spanish: **3** OJO
Eyeball: 3 ORB **4** LEER OGLE
6 GAPEAT SIZEUP
benders: **5** OPART

part: **6** RETINA
Eyebrow
Pluck ~ hairs: **6** TWEEZE
shape: **4** ARCH
Eyeful
Get an: **4** GAPE GAWK LEER
OGLE
Eyeglass
frames: **4** RIMS
part: **4** LENS
parts: **7** TEMPLES
Eyeglasses: 5 SPECS
Eyelash
cosmetic: **7** MASCARA
Eyelashes: 5 CILIA
Bat one's: **5** FLIRT
Eyelet
maker: **8** STILETTO
Eyelid
attachment: **4** LASH
problem: **4** STYE
Eye of ___: 4 NEWT
Eye-opener: 5 LATTE
Eyepiece: 6 OCULAR
Eye-related: 5 OPTIC
Eyes: 5 OCULI
Blue ~, for one: **5** TRAIT
Cry one's ~ out: **4** BAWL
Easy on the: **6** PRETTY
Frosty's: **4** COAL
Hard on the: **4** UGLY
It brings tears to one's: **4** DUCT
Kind of: **6** GOOGOO
Lay ~ on: **3** SEE **4** ESPY SPOT
Like some: **5** BEADY
7 DEEPSET
Make ~ at: **4 OGLE**
Open your: **5** AWAKE
Snake: **3** TWO **4** ACES ONES
Some have black: **4** PEAS
The ~ have them: **4** LIDS
They may make your ~ roll:
4 PUNS
Turn away, as one's: **5** AVERT
What some ~ do: **4** DART
"___ Eyes" (Eagles hit): 4 LYIN
Eyesore: 3 STY **4** DUMP
Garden: **4** WEED
Urban: **4** SLUM

"Eyes Wide ___" (Cruise film):
    4 SHUT
Eye to eye
  Not seeing: 6 ATODDS
     10 ATVARIANCE
  See: 4 JIBE 5 **AGREE**
    6 CONCUR
Eyetooth: 6 CANINE
Eyewear: 5 SPECS 6 SHADES
Eyewitness
  phrase: 4 ISAW

Eyre, Jane: 7 HEROINE
  pupil: 5 ADELE
Ezekiel
  Book after: 6 DANIEL
  Prince in: 3 GOG
Ezio: 4 BASS 5 BASSO
  and others: 5 BASSI
  Basso: 5 PINZA
Ezra
  Bk. after: 3 NEH
  Book after: 8 NEHEMIAH

Ff

F
Avoid an: 4 PASS
equivalent: 6 ESHARP
Letters before: 3 CDE TGI
major or minor: 3 KEY
M or: 3 SEX
on a test: 5 FALSE
sharp equivalent: 5 GFLAT
T or: 3 ANS

F-14
fighter: 6 TOMCAT
home: 3 AFB

Fa
follower: 3 **SOL**
followers: 4 LALA
lead-in: 4 REMI

Fab: 5 BOFFO SUPER
intro: 3 PRE
rival: 3 ERA

Fabergé
creation: 3 **EGG**

Fab Four: 7 BEATLES
film: 4 HELP
member: 4 PAUL 5 RINGO
    STARR 6 GEORGE LENNON

Fabi
Auto racer: 3 **TEO**

Fabian
, once. 4 IDOL

Fable
creator: 4 LIAR 5 AESOP

Fabled
also-ran: 4 HARE
bird: 3 ROC
cow owner: 6 OLEARY
ending: 5 MORAL
Like the ~ piper: 4 PIED
monster: 4 OGRE
racer: 4 HARE 8 TORTOISE
warrior: 6 AMAZON

"___ Fables": 6 AESOPS
"Fables in Slang"
author: 3 ADE

Fabray
Emmy winner: 7 NANETTE
Fabric: 4 WEFT 5 CLOTH
Angora: 6 MOHAIR
Brocaded: 4 LAME
Casual: 5 DENIM
Colorful: 6 TIEDYE
Cotton: 6 SATEEN
Crinkled: 5 CREPE
Crisp: 7 TAFFETA
Curtain: 4 LACE 5 NINON
    SCRIM
Decorative strip of: 6 RIBAND
Delicate: 4 LACE
Durable: 5 SERGE
Fancy: 6 SATEEN
Feltlike: 5 BAIZE
Filmy: 5 GAUZE
Fine: 5 SATIN
Flaxen: 5 LINEN
fold: 5 PLEAT
fuzz: 4 LINT
Glazed: 6 CHINTZ
Glossy: 5 SATIN 6 SATEEN
Gown: 5 TULLE
Hat: 4 FELT
Jeans: 5 DENIM
Lightweight: 5 VOILE
Linen: 5 TOILE
Lustrous: 5 SATIN 6 SATEEN
    7 TAFFETA
meas.: 3 YDS
Metallic: 4 LAME
Open: 4 MESH
Pants: 5 CHINO
Patterned: 5 TOILE 6 DAMASK
    MADRAS
Puckered: 6 PLISSE
Reversible: 6 DAMASK
rib: 4 WANE
Ribbed: 5 TWILL 6 FAILLE
Robe: 5 TERRY
Roll of: 4 BOLT

Sheer: **5** NINON
Sheet: **7** PERCALE
Shiny: **4** LAME
Soft: **5** TERRY
suffix: **3** EEN **4** ATOR
Suit: **4** WOOL **5** SERGE TWEED
Synthetic: **5** ORLON
Tie: **3** REP
Twilled: **5** **SERGE**
Upholstery: **5** TOILE **6** VELOUR
Veil: **5** TULLE
with metallic threads: **4** LAME
Wrinkle-resistant: **5** ORLON
Fabricate: 4 FAKE MAKE SPIN
   6 MAKEUP
Fabrication: 3 LIE **4** TALE YARN
   5 STORY
Fabricator: 4 LIAR
Fabrics
for sale: **8** DRYGOODS
Fabulist
Greek: **5** AESOP
Fabulous: 5 SUPER
bird: **3** ROC
fellow: **5** AESOP
"Fabulous Baker Boys, The"
star: **7** BRIDGES
Façade: 4 POSE **5** FRONT
   6 VENEER
part: **7** CEDILLA
Face: 4 MEET PUSS **6** VISAGE
Certain watch: **3** LCD
Clock: **4** DIAL
cover: **4** VEIL
defacer: **4** ACNE
down: **5** BEARD PRONE
Fly in the ~ of: **4** DEFY
Happy: **4** BEAM GRIN **5** SMILE
Have a long: **4** MOPE
In the ~ of: **7** DESPITE
It makes your ~ red: **5** ROUGE
Make a: **4** GRIN **5** SCOWL
   SNEER
Make a funny: **3** MUG
mask wearer: **6** GOALIE
New: **8** STRANGER
on a five: **3** ABE
Pouty: **4** MOUE
prefix: **5** INTER

shape: **4** OVAL
Smack in the: **4** KISS
Stuff one's: **6** PIGOUT
that launched a thousand ships:
   5 HELEN
the day: **5** ARISE
the pitcher: **3** BAT
Watch: **4** DIAL
Wear a long: **4** MOPE POUT
Without ~ value: **5** NOPAR
~, in French: **3** VIS
Face-off: 4 DUEL
preceder, often: **7** OCANADA
"Face/Off"
director John: **3** WOO
Facet: 6 ASPECT
"Face the Nation"
network: **3** CBS
Facetious: 5 DROLL **7** JOCULAR
five: **5** AEIOU
Face-to-face
exam: **4** **ORAL**
Face-up: 6 SUPINE
Face-valued: 5 ATPAR
Facial
feature: **4** JOWL MOLE NOSE
firmer-upper: **5** TONER
hair: **4** LASH **7** EYELASH
movement: **3** TIC
spot: **3** SPA
tissue additive: **4** ALOE
Facil.
Research: **4** INST
Facile
Unconvincingly: **3** PAT
Facilitate: 4 **EASE** **6** ENABLE
a felony: **4** ABET
Facilitator
Breakfast-in-bed: **4** TRAY
Rush-hour traffic: **7** HOVLANE
Facilities: 4 JOHN **7** LATRINE
Sports: **6** STADIA
Facility: 4 **EASE**
Health: **3** SPA **6** CLINIC
London: **3** LOO
Medical: **6** CLINIC
Mil. ed.: **3** OCS
Research ~ (abbr.): **4** INST
Sports: **5** ARENA

Underground: 4 SILO
Facing: 6 TOWARD
  charges: 7 ONTRIAL
  extinction: 4 RARE
  Not ~ the truth: 8 INDENIAL
  the pitcher: 5 **ATBAT**
Facsimile: 4 COPY
Fact: 5 GIVEN
  Allege as: 4 **AVER**
  Assume as: 5 POSIT
  Declare as: 5 STATE
  Despite the ~ that, for short:
    3 THO
  Establish as: 5 PROVE
  filled volume: 7 ALMANAC
  fudger: 4 LIAR
  It's a: 5 DATUM
  Perceive as: 4 KNOW
  State as: 5 SAYSO
  suffix: 3 OID
Faction: 4 BLOC CAMP **SECT**
    SIDE
  Political: 4 BLOC
  Religious: 4 SECT
  ___ facto: 5 **IPSO**
Factoid: 4 STAT 5 DATUM
Factor: 5 PIECE
  in: 8 ALLOWFOR
  Inheritance: 4 GENE
  Weigh station: 4 TARE
Factory: 4 SHOP 5 PLANT
  Flour: 4 MILL
  Honey: 4 HIVE
  item: 4 TOOL
  Modern ~ worker: 5 ROBOT
  Right from the: 3 NEW
  second (abbr.): 3 IRR
  Update a: 6 RETOOL
Factotum: 5 DOALL
  Frankenstein: 4 IGOR
Facts: 4 DATA INFO 6 SKINNY
  Had the: 4 KNEW
  The ~ of life: 3 BIO
"Facts of Life, The"
  actress Charlotte: 3 RAE
  actress Mindy: 4 COHN
  Mrs. Garrett of: 4 EDNA
Factual: 4 TRUE
Faculties: 6 SENSES

They keep control of their:
  5 DEANS
Faculty: 5 KNACK SKILL STAFF
  head: 4 DEAN
Fad: 4 RAGE 5 CRAZE MANIA
    TREND
  1950s ~: 8 HULAHOOP
  1961 ~: 4 YOYO
  1970s ~: 7 PETROCK
  1970s ~ participant:
    8 STREAKER
  1990s ~: 7 CHIAPET
  doll: 5 TROLL
  Therapy: 3 EST
Faddish
  pet: 4 CHIA
Fade
  away: 3 DIE EBB 6 DIEOUT
    8 EVANESCE
  out: 3 DIE DIM
Faded
  star: 7 HASBEEN
"Faerie Queene, The"
  division: 5 CANTO
  victim: 5 IRENA
Fahd: 4 ARAB 5 SAUDI
  subject: 4 ARAB 5 SAUDI
Fail: 4 BOMB TANK 5 FLUNK
    7 LOSEOUT
  Does not: 6 PASSES
  suffix: 3 URE
  to attend: 4 MISS SKIP
  to impress: 8 CUTNOICE
  to include: 4 OMIT
  to make: 4 MISS
  to medal: 4 LOSE
  to mention: 4 **OMIT**
  to pronounce: 5 ELIDE
  to see: 4 MISS
  ___ Fail (Irish coronation stone):
    3 LIA
Failed
  amendment: 3 ERA
  attempt: 4 NOGO
  to: 5 DIDNT
  to act: 3 SAT
Fails
  If all else: 7 ATWORST
  to: 6 DOESNT

Failure: 3 DUD **4** FLOP MISS
    5 LAPSE
  Ensure the ~ of: **4** DOOM
  Memory: **5** LAPSE
  Power: **6** OUTAGE
  Show-biz: **4** BOMB
  Total: **6** FIASCO
Faint: 3 WAN **4** PALE **5 SWOON**
    WISPY **7** PASSOUT
  from excitement: **5** PLOTZ
  Grow: **3** DIM **4** WANE
  ~, with "over": **4** KEEL
"Faint heart ___ won ...": 4 NEER
Fainthearted: 5 TIMID
Fair: 4 EVEN EXPO JUST **SOSO**
    5 BLOND CLEAR
    6 HONEST **7** AVERAGE
    CRICKET **8** UNBIASED
  attraction: **4 RIDE**
  Big: **4** EXPO
  features: **5** TENTS
  grade: **3** CEE
  hiring abbr.: **3** EOE
  It may be: **4** DEAL
  Kind of ~ (abbr.): **3** SCI
  Like a ~ playing field: **5** LEVEL
  mark: **3** CEE
  Not: **5** RAINY
  share: **4** HALF
  sight: **4** TENT
  to middling: **4** SOSO
"___ Fair" (Cornell song):
    6 ITISNT
Fair, A.A.
  monogram: **3** ESG
  real first name: **4** ERLE
Fairbanks
  Highway to: **5** ALCAN
Fair Deal
  pres.: **3** HST
  president: **6** TRUMAN
Fairground
  attraction: **4** RIDE
Fair-haired: 5 BLOND
Fair-hiring
  letters: **3 EEO 4** EEOC
Fairies
  King of the: **6** OBERON
  Queen of the: **3** MAB

"___ fair in love ...": 4 ALLS
Fairly
  modern: **6** NEWISH
Fair-minded: 4 JUST
Fairness: 6 EQUITY
  in hiring (abbr.): **3** EEO
Fair-sized
  musical group: **5** NONET
Fairway
  border: **5** ROUGH
  choice: **4** IRON
  chunk: **5** DIVOT
  Fix the: **5** RESOD
  position: **3** LIE
  vehicle: **4** CART
  warning: **4** FORE
Fairy
  Kind of: **5** TOOTH
  king: **6** OBERON
  Persian: **4** PERI
  queen: **3 MAB**
  story: **4** TALE
Fairy tale
  baddie: **4** OGRE
  beginning: **4** ONCE
  closer: **5** AFTER
  figure: **3** HAG **5** GNOME
  heroine: **6** GRETEL
  last word: **5** AFTER
  meanie: **4** OGRE **10** STEPSISTER
  opener: **4** ONCE
  penultimate word: **4** EVER
  second word: **4** UPON
  start: **4 ONCE**
Faisal II: 5 IRAQI
Faith: 5 CREED TRUST
  Act of: **4** LEAP
  Article of: **5** TENET
  Fight to keep the: **7** HOLYWAR
  Forsaker of the: **8** APOSTATE
  Have: **4** RELY **5** TRUST
  healer command: **4** RISE
  of over one billion: **5** ISLAM
  prefix: **5** INTER
  that arose in Persia: **5** BAHAI
Faith-based
  system (abbr.): **3** REL
Faithful: 4 TRUE **5** LOYAL
  Is: **7** ADHERES

Fajita
  cuisine: 6 TEXMEX
  flavorer: 5 SALSA
Fake: 4 COPY MOCK SHAM
     5 BOGUS FEIGN PHONY
     6 ERSATZ RINGER
     7 NOTREAL 8 IMPOSTER
  coin: 4 SLUG
  drake: 5 DECOY
  fanfare: 4 TADA
  fat: 5 OLEAN
  handle: 5 ALIAS
  it: 3 ACT 7 PRETEND
  jewelry: 5 PASTE
  Not: 4 REAL
  on the ice: 4 DEKE
  Teens may have ~ ones: 3 IDS
Fala: 7 SCOTTIE
Falafel
  holder: 4 PITA
  sauce: 6 TAHINI
Falana
  Entertainer: 4 **LOLA**
Falco
  Emmy winner: 4 **EDIE**
Falcon
  Fictional ~ home: 5 MALTA
  Small: 7 KESTREL
"___ Falcon, The": 7 MALTESE
"Falcon Crest"
  actress Alicia: 3 ANA
Falcon-headed
  god: 5 HORUS
Falcons: 4 TEAM
  home (abbr.). 3 ATL
Faline
  Mother of: 3 ENA
Falkland Islands
  city: 7 STANLEY
Falklands War
  participant: 4 BRIT
Fall: 3 ERR 4 DROP 6 AUTUMN
    7 DESCEND
  apart: 3 ROT 7 GOTOPOT
  away: 3 EBB
  back: 3 EBB LAG 4 REEL
    5 RESET 6 REVERT
    7 RELAPSE
  behind: 3 **LAG** OWE 5 TRAIL

    8 LOSETIME
  birthstone: 4 **OPAL** 5 TOPAZ
  bloomer: 5 **ASTER**
  color: 4 RUST 5 OCHRE
    6 ORANGE
  Cry before a: 6 TIMBER
  Do a ~ chore: 4 RAKE
  drink: 5 CIDER
  faller: 4 LEAF
  flower: 5 **ASTER**
  for: 4 BITE
  from grace: 3 ERR **SIN**
  guy: 3 SAP 4 ADAM GOAT
    5 CHUMP **PATSY** RAKER
    6 STOOGE 9 SCAPEGOAT
  heavily: 4 PLOP THUD
  Kind of: 4 PRAT
  lead-in: 4 PRAT
  Let: 4 DROP
  Like ~ weather: 5 BRISK
  locale: 4 EDEN
  mo.: 3 NOV **OCT** SEP 4 SEPT
  off: 3 DIP EBB 4 WANE 5 ABATE
    ERODE
  Opposite of: 4 RISE
  (over): 4 KEEL
  over in a faint: 5 PLOTZ
  place: 4 EDEN
  planting: 4 BULB
  preceder: 4 PRAT TRIP 5 PRIDE
    6 TIMBER
  setting: 4 EDEN
  shade: 4 RUST
  short: 4 FAIL
  sign: 5 LIBRA 7 SCORPIO
  site: 4 EDEN
  sound: 4 PLOP THUD
  Start to: 3 TIP
  Threaten to: 6 TEETER
  times (abbr.): 4 OCTS
  tool: 4 RAKE
  Winter: 4 SNOW 5 SLEET
  worker: 5 RAKER
Fallaci
  Auhor: 6 ORIANA
Fallback
  option: 5 PLANB
Fallen
  angel: 5 SATAN

space station: 3 MIR
"___ fallen ...": 3 IVE
Fallibility
  Show: 5 ERASE
Falling
  flakes: 4 SNOW
  Like ~ off a log: 4 EASY
  out: 4 RIFT
  pellets: 4 HAIL
  star: 6 METEOR
Falling-out: 4 SPAT TIFF
"Fall of the House of Usher, The"
  author: 3 POE
Fallopian tube
  travelers: 3 OVA
Fallout
  Volcanic: 3 ASH
Fall River
  tool: 3 AXE
Falls
  for lovers: 7 NIAGARA
  on the border: 7 NIAGARA
  on, as responsibility: 8 LIESWITH
  ___ Falls (Venezuela): 5 ANGEL
"Fall, The"
  author: 5 CAMUS
False: 5 NOTSO 6 PSEUDO
        UNTRUE
  alarm: 5 SCARE
  coin: 4 SLUG
  Declare: 4 DENY
  Expose as: 6 DEBUNK
  friend: 4 IAGO
  front: 3 ACT 4 POSE 5 GUISE
        PSEUD 6 FACADE
  Gives a ~ alarm: 9 CRIESWOLF
  god: 4 **BAAL** IDOL
  It may be: 5 ALARM
  locks: 4 WIGS
  move: 5 FEINT
  Not: 4 TRUE
  prefix: 5 PSEUDO
  Prove: 5 BELIE
  Reject as: 4 DENY
  rumor: 6 CANARD
  Some are: 5 HOPES
  start: 6 PSEUDO
  Was: 4 LIED
  witness: 4 LIAR

"False!": 5 NOTSO
Falsehood: 3 FIB LIE
Falsetto
  1960s ~ singer: 7 TINYTIM
Falsified: 6 COOKED
Falsifier
  Check: 5 KITER
Falstaff
  Like: 3 FAT
"Falstaff": 5 OPERA
  composer: 5 VERDI
  prince: 3 HAL
Fam.
  doctors: 3 GPS
  member: 3 BRO **REL** SIS
  tree member: 4 DESC
Fame: 5 ECLAT 6 RENOWN
        REPUTE
"Fame"
  actress Irene: 4 **CARA**
  actress Peeples: 3 NIA
  singer: 9 IRENECARA
  singer Irene: 4 CARA
Familia
  member: 3 TIA TIO
  New ~ member: 4 BEBE
Familial
  address: 3 SIS
Familiar
  Become ~ with: 8 EASEINTO
        9 GETTOKNOW
  Comfortably: 5 HOMEY
  saying: 6 OLDSAW
  Sound: 9 RINGABELL
  Was ~ with: 4 KNEW
  with: 4 INTO UPON 6 USEDTO
  ~, as friends: 3 OLD
Familiarize: 6 **ORIENT**
        8 ACQUAINT
Famille
  member: 4 MERE PERE
        5 FRERE
Family: 3 ILK **KIN** 4 CLAN
        5 GROUP
  1950s TV ~: 7 NELSONS
  Acting: 6 FONDAS
  auto: 5 SEDAN
  Big: 5 TRIBE
  Blended ~ member: 7 STEPSON

card game: 3 UNO
diagram: 4 TREE
docs: 3 GPS
dog: 3 LAB
emblem: 5 TOTEM
Extended: 4 CLAN 5 TRIBE
follower: 4 TREE
girl: 3 SIS 5 NIECE
group: 4 CLAN
guy: 3 BRO DAD
head: 3 DON 4 CAPO
life, figuratively: 6 HEARTH
Like ~ films: 6 RATEDG
man: 3 DAD
map: 4 TREE
mem.: 3 REL
member: 3 DAD SIB SIS SON
    4 AUNT 5 NIECE UNCLE
    6 SISTER
men: 3 PAS
nickname: 3 **SIS** UNC 4 NANA
    6 GRAMPA
problem: 4 FEUD
subdivision: 5 GENUS
subdivisions: 6 GENERA
They're all in the: 4 SIBS
They're new to the:
    9 SONSINLAW
tree word: 3 NEE
Word after: 4 TREE
    8 ORIENTED
"Family Circus, The"
  cartoonist Bil: 5 KEANE
  cartoonist Keane: 3 BIL
Family-friendly
  ~, in films: 6 RATEDG
"Family Matters"
  nerd: 5 URKEL
"Family Plot"
  actor Bruce: 4 DERN
Family reunion
  attendee: 5 NIECE
Family room: 3 **DEN**
  piece: 6 SETTEE
"Family Ties"
  mother: 5 ELYSE
  son: 4 ALEX
Famished
  Far from: 5 SATED

Famous: 3 BIG 5 KNOWN NOTED
    7 EMINENT NOTABLE
cow owner: 6 OLEARY
fed: 4 NESS
fiddle: 5 STRAD
fiddler: 4 NERO
flop: 5 EDSEL
fountain piazza: 5 TREVI
jour.: 3 AMA
last word: 4 AMEN
last words: 3 IDO 4 ETTU
    5 ELEGY 6 THEEND
lioness: 4 ELSA
loch: 4 NESS
palindrome middle: 5 IEREI
redhead: 4 ERIC
Site of some ~ hangings:
    5 PRADO
twin: 3 ENG
~ B-29: 5 ENOLA
"Famous"
  cookie maker: 4 **AMOS**
Famous ___: 4 AMOS
"Famous Potatoes"
  Its license plates say: 5 IDAHO
Fan: 3 BUG 4 COOL 5 LOVER
    6 ADORER ROOTER
    7 DEVOTEE 8 ADULATOR
A ~ of: 4 **INTO**
club focus: 4 IDOL
Extreme, as a: 5 RABID
fave: 4 IDOL
Jazz: 3 CAT 6 UTAHAN
mag: 4 ZINE
noise: 3 RAH
setting: 3 LOW 5 ARENA
sound: 3 RAH 4 CLAP WHIR
Unhappy: 5 BOOER
Unhappy ~ noise: 4 HISS
Fanatic: 3 NUT 5 ULTRA
    6 MANIAC ZEALOT
Fanatical: 5 RABID 7 EXTREME
    8 OBSESSED
devotion: 8 ZEALOTRY
Fanciful: 4 TALL
  story: 8 TALLTALE
Fancily
  Dress ~, with "out": 3 TOG
  Walk: 6 SASHAY

Fancy: 4 IDEA WHIM 5 ADORE COVET DREAM HAUTE 6 DESIRE ORNATE PREFER 7 IMAGINE
case: 4 ETUI
cover: 4 SHAM
desk: 7 ROLLTOP
dinnerware: 5 CHINA
fabric: 4 LAME
Made: 5 DIDUP
Not ~ at all: 6 LOATHE
Passing: 3 FAD
Really: 5 ADORE
Sudden: 4 WHIM
Tickle the: 5 AMUSE
"Fancy"
singer McEntire: 4 REBA
Fancy-schmancy: 4 POSH 5 RITZY 7 ELEGANT
"Fancy that!": 3 GEE 4 GOSH MYMY
Fanfare: 5 ECLAT 6 HOOPLA 7 TANTARA
Mock: 4 **TADA**
Fangs: 7 CANINES
Fannie
Author: 5 FLAGG HURST
Funny: 5 FLAGG
Fannie ___: 3 **MAE**
Fanny: 4 DUFF REAR TUSH
"Fanny"
author Jong: 5 ERICA
Fans
Like: 4 AVID 7 ADORING
Like enthusiastic: 5 AROAR
Where ~ may be found: 6 STANDS
Fantail: 4 DEER
Fan-tan: 6 SEVENS
Fantasia
alternative: 7 TOCCATA
"Fantasia"
dancer: 5 HIPPO
frame: 3 CEL
Fantasize: 5 DREAM
Fantastic: 5 GREAT SUPER 6 UNREAL 7 SURREAL
"Fantastic Mr. Fox"
author Roald: 4 DAHL

"Fantasy Island"
prop: 3 LEI
"___ fan tutte": 4 **COSI**
Fanzine: 3 MAG
focus: 4 IDOL 5 CELEB
Streisand, in a: 4 BABS
FAO Schwarz
offering: 3 TOY
Far
As ~ as: 4 **UPTO**
back: 7 AGESAGO
By: 6 EASILY
Few and ~ between: 4 RARE 6 SPARSE
Not: 4 NEAR
So: 3 YET 5 **ASYET** 6 TODATE 7 UPTONOW
Take too: 6 OVERDO
Thus: 3 YET 5 ASYET 6 TODATE
Far ___: 4 EAST
Faraway
place: 8 TIMBUKTU
Fare: 4 DIET FOOD 5 GETON
Had: 3 ATE
question: 7 WHERETO
reduction: 4 DIET
Trendy: 5 SUSHI
Unappetizing: 4 GLOP MUSH SLOP
War: 4 SPAM
Far East
cuisine: 4 THAI
From the: 5 ASIAN
nurse: 4 AMAH
Farewell: 5 ADIEU
Expressed a: 4 BADE
Forum: 3 AVE 4 VALE
French: 5 ADIEU
Informal: 5 LATER
Italian: 4 CIAO
party: 7 SENDOFF
Spanish: 5 ADIOS
"Farewell!": 4 TATA 5 ADIEU ADIOS
Farewells
Like some: 4 FOND
"Farewell to ___, A": 4 ARMS
"Farewell to Thee"
translated: 7 ALOHAOE

"___ far, far better thing ...":
5 ITISA
Farfetched: 4 TALL
Far-flung: 4 VAST
Far-flying
seabird: 6 PETREL
Fargo
Partner of: 5 WELLS
state (abbr.): 4 NDAK
"Fargo"
director: 4 COEN
Faris
Actress: 4 ANNA
Farlow
Jazz guitarist: 3 TAL
Farm
animal: 3 ANT ASS EWE 4 GOAT
antithesis, in song: 5 PAREE
building: 4 BARN
bundle: 4 BALE
butter: 3 RAM
call: 3 BAA 5 SOOEY
cart: 4 WAIN
crawler: 3 ANT
cry: 4 OINK
division: 4 ACRE
dweller: 3 ANT
enclosure: 3 PEN STY
equipment name: 5 DEERE
fare: 4 SLOP
Fat: 3 SPA
father: 4 SIRE
feature: 4 SILO
female: 3 DAM **EWE** HEN SOW
4 MARE
gathering: 3 HAY
hauler: 4 DRAY
Health: 3 SPA
It's left on the: 3 HAW
It's pulled on a: 5 UDDER
It's raised on a: 4 SILO
layer: 3 HEN
letters: 5 EIEIO
machine: 5 BALER 6 REAPER
SEEDER TILLER 7 COMBINE
measure: 4 ACRE
Milk: 5 DAIRY
prefix: 4 AGRI AGRO
soil: 4 LOAM

sound: 3 BAA CAW MOO 4 BRAY
OINK 5 BLEAT
Store on a: 6 ENSILE
structure: 4 BARN SILO
team: 4 **OXEN** SPAN
team unifier: 4 YOKE
tool: 6 SCYTHE
tower: 4 SILO
unit: 4 **ACRE**
vehicle: 7 TRACTOR
worker: 3 ANT 9 PLOWHORSE
yield: 4 CROP
Farmed
Fit to be: 6 ARABLE
Farmer: 4 HOER 6 PLOWER
SEEDER TILLER
Feudal: 4 SERF
field: 3 LEA
field (abbr.): 3 AGR
in the spring: 5 SOWER
place: 4 DELL 7 THEDELL
purchase: 4 SEED
Transvaal: 4 BOER
victims of the ~'s wife: 4 MICE
"Farmer in the Dell, The"
syllables: 4 HIHO
"Farmer's Daughter, The"
actress Stevens: 5 INGER
Farming
abbr.: 3 AGR
Fit for: 6 ARABLE
Kind of: 7 ONECROP
prefix: 4 AGRI AGRO
Refrain from: 5 EIEIO
Farmland: 5 ACRES
unit: 4 **ACRE**
Far-out: 5 OUTRE WACKO
Org. with ~ goals: 4 NASA
"Far out!": 3 **RAD** 5 NEATO
6 UNREAL 7 AWESOME
Farr
Actor: 5 JAMIE
Farragut
word: 4 DAMN
Far-reaching
view: 5 VISTA
Farrell
costar: 4 ALDA
Soprano: 6 EILEEN

Farrier
  tool: 4 RASP
Farrow
  Actress: 3 **MIA**
Farsi
  speaker: 5 **IRANI**
        7 IRANIAN
  Where ~ is spoken: 4 **IRAN**
"Far Side, The"
  cartoonist Gary: 6 LARSON
Farsighted
  one: 4 SEER
Farther
  Extend ~ down: 6 DEEPEN
Farthest: 6 UTMOST
        7 ENDMOST
  from the hole: 4 AWAY
  orbital point: 6 APOGEE
Fascinated
  by: 4 **INTO**
Fascination: 6 ALLURE
Fashion: 3 TON WAY 4 FORM
        MAKE **MODE** 5 CRAFT
        SHAPE STYLE TREND
        VOGUE 6 CREATE
  1970s ~ fad: 8 HOTPANTS
  Big name in: 4 DIOR IZOD
        5 BLASS KLEIN PRADA
        6 ARMANI
  center: 5 MILAN
  Current: 4 MODE RAGE
        5 TREND
  First name in: 3 LIZ 4 COCO
        OLEG YVES
  Fleeting: 3 FAD
  High: 3 TON
  illustrator: 4 ERTE
  In: 3 HIP HOT 4 CHIC
  industry: 8 RAGTRADE
  initials: 3 YSL 4 DKNY
  issue: 4 ELLE
  It's long in: 4 MAXI
  letters: 3 YSL
  line: 3 HEM
  magazine: 4 **ELLE**
  model: 4 IMAN
  monogram: 3 **YSL**
  Nostalgic: 5 RETRO
  Out of: 5 PASSE

Fashionable: 3 MOD 4 CHIC LATE
        6 MODISH TRENDY
        7 INSTYLE
  cashmere company: 3 TSE
  monogram: 3 YSL
  necktie: 5 ASCOT
  resort: 3 SPA
  ~ Christian: 4 DIOR
  ~ Geoffrey: 5 BEENE
  ~ Simpson: 5 ADELE
Fashion designer
  monogram: 3 YSL
  ~ Geoffrey: 5 BEENE
  ~ Giorgio: 6 ARMANI
  ~ Ralph: 6 LAUREN
  ~ Vera: 4 WANG
Fashioned: 4 MADE
"Fashion Emergency"
  host: 4 EMME
Fast: 5 APACE BRISK QUICK
        RAPID
  Break a: 3 EAT
  Came to a ~ stop: 3 ATE
  feline: 4 PUMA
  finish: 4 MEAL
  flier: 3 JET **SST**
  food order: 6 BURGER
  gait: 6 GALLOP
  Hold: 6 ADHERE COHERE
  horse: 4 ARAB
  Make: 3 TIE
  movement: 7 ALLEGRO
  Not very: 7 ANDANTE
  pace: 4 CLIP
  Pull a ~ one: 4 YANK
  Ran ~, to a Brit: 5 HARED
  runner: 4 HARE
  start: 5 STEAD
  time: 4 **LENT** 7 RAMADAN
  Went: 4 SPED TORE
"___ fast!": 5 NOTSO
Fastball: 4 HEAT 6 HEATER
  Famous ~ thrower: 4 RYAN
        5 NOLAN
Fasten: 3 TIE 4 BIND DOUP
        SHUT 5 LATCH SCREW
        6 ATTACH
  again: 5 RETIE
  anew: 5 REPIN

at sea: **5** BELAY
with a pop: **6** SNAPON
with rope: **4** LASH
Fastened: 5 DIDUP **6** HASPED
Fastener: 4 BOND SNAP STUD
    5 CLASP LATCH
Bolt: **3** NUT **4** TNUT
Door: **4** HASP
for Rosie: **5** RIVET
Gate: **4** HASP **5** LATCH
Letter-shaped: **4** TNUT **5** UBOLT
Metal: **4** BOLT HASP NAIL
    5 RIVET SCREW
Necklace: **5** CLASP
Office: **9** PAPERCLIP
Paper: **6** STAPLE
Small: **4** BRAD TACK
Threaded: **4** TNUT **5** SCREW
Fastening
device: **4** HASP TNUT
pin: **5** RIVET
Faster
No: **5** EATER
Fastest
runner: **7** CHEETAH
Fast-food
chain: **4** ROYS **5** ARBYS
    7 HARDEES
drink: **4** COLA SODA
inits.: **3** KFC
option: **4** TOGO
Fast ___ get-out: 5 ASALL
Fastidious: 4 NEAT TIDY **5** FUSSY
Fast-moving
object: **4** BLUR
Fast-shrinking
sea: **4** ARAL
Fast-talking: 4 GLIB
Fat: 4 LARD **5** LIPID **6** TALLOW
Big ~ mouth: **3** YAP
Big ~ zero: **3** NIL
cat: **5** NABOB **9** MONEYBAGS
Chew the: **3** GAB JAW YAK
    4 CHAT **8** SCHMOOZE
Cooking: **4** LARD SUET
Cut the: **4** TRIM
Fake: **5** OLEAN **7** OLESTRA
farm: **3** SPA
foot spec: **3** EEE

in a can: **4** LARD
letters: **3** EMS
Liquid: **5** OLEIN
Low in: **4** **LEAN**
More than: **5** OBESE
Pat of: **4** OLEO
substitute: **5** OLEAN **7** OLESTRA
unit: **4** GRAM
Wool: **7** LANOLIN
~, in French: **4** GRAS
"Fatal Attraction"
director Adrian: **4** LYNE
___ fatale: **5** FEMME
Fatality
Genesis: **4** ABEL
Fata morgana: 6 MIRAGE
"Fat chance!": 3 HAH **4** NOPE
    5 NEVER **6** NOSOAP
Fate: 3 LOT **4** DOOM **5** KARMA
    6 KISMET
Adverse: **4** DOOM
of Wednesday's child: **3** WOE
Tempt: **4** DARE
Fateful
date: **4** IDES
Fates, The: 4 TRIO
One of: **6** CLOTHO **7** ATROPOS
Fat-free: 4 SLIM
"Fatha"
Jazzman: **5** HINES
~ Hines: **4** EARL
Father: 3 DAD **4** PAPA **SIRE**
    5 BEGET
Act the expectant: **4** PACE
Become a: **4** SIRE
Expectant: **5** PACER
First: **4** ADAM
in the army: **5** PADRE
in the Bible: **4** ABBA
Make a: **6** ORDAIN
Related on the ~ side: **5** AGATE
talk (abbr.): **3** SER
wear: **3** ALB
word form: **5** PATRI
~, in French: **4** **PERE**
Father ___ : 6 DAMIEN
Father-and-son
actors: **5** ALDAS
physicists: **5** BOHRS

Fathered: 5 BEGAT BEGOT
Father-in-law
  of Jacob: 5 LABAN
  of Meathead: 6 ARCHIE
"Father Knows Best"
  family name: 8 ANDERSON
"Father Murphy"
  actor Merlin: 5 OLSEN
  extra: 6 ORPHAN
"Father of the Bride"
  actor Martin: 5 SHORT STEVE
Fathers
  and sons: 3 HES MEN
  Unwed: 7 PRIESTS
"Fathers and Sons"
  novelist Turgenev: 4 IVAN
Father's Day
  gift: 3 TIE 4 BELT 5 RAZOR
    6 TIEPIN TIETAC WALLET
  month: 4 JUNE
Fathom: 3 GET 5 GRASP
  Hard to: 4 DEEP 6 ARCANE
Fatigue: 4 TIRE
  Showing: 3 WAN
Fatima
  faith: 5 ISLAM
  Husband of: 3 ALI
Fat lady
  What the ~ sings: 4 ARIA
  Where the ~ sings: 5 OPERA
Fatman, The
  Partner of: 4 JAKE
Fat-removing
  surgery: 4 LIPO
Fat Tuesday
  Fat, in: 4 GRAS
Fatty: 7 ADIPOSE
  acid: 5 OLEIC
  compound: 5 LIPID
  It may be: 4 ACID
  Not: 4 LEAN
  oil: 6 CANOLA
  tissue: 4 SUET
Fatuous: 5 INANE SILLY
    7 ASININE
___ **fatuus (delusion):** 5 IGNIS
Faucet: 3 TAP 6 SPIGOT
  attachment: 7 AERATOR
  brand: 4 MOEN

  fault: 4 **DRIP** LEAK
  problem: 4 **DRIP** LEAK
Faulkner
  character Varner: 4 EULA
  title start: 3 ASI
Fault: 3 SIN 4 FLAW 5 ERROR
  At: 6 GUILTY
  Find: 4 CARP CRAB 5 BLAME
    CAVIL
  Find ~ with: 5 NAGAT
Faults
  It has its: 6 TENNIS
Faulty: 5 AMISS
  Most: 5 WORST
Faun
  half: 4 GOAT
Fauna
  collection: 3 ZOO
  Flora and: 4 LIFE 5 BIOTA
  Partner of: 5 FLORA
  prefix: 3 AVI
Fauntleroy
  title: 4 LORD
"Faust": 5 OPERA
  author: 6 GOETHE
Fauvism
  founder: 7 MATISSE
Faux: 4 FAKE MOCK SHAM
  (abbr.): 4 IMIT
Faux ___ (social misstep): 3 PAS
Faux pas: 4 NONO SLIP 5 ERROR
    GAFFE 6 BOOBOO
    7 MISSTEP
  Commit a: 3 ERR
Fava: 4 BEAN
Fave
  Teacher: 3 PET
  Teen: 4 IDOL
Favor: 4 BOON 5 BLESS
    6 ESTEEM PREFER
  Do a ~ for: 6 OBLIGE
  In ~ of: 3 FOR **PRO**
  Not in ~ of: 4 ANTI
  one side: 4 LIMP
  Out of: 5 INBAD
  Return the: 5 REPAY
  Seek ~ with: 3 WOO
  Votes in: 4 YEAS 5 YESES
___ **favor:** 3 POR

Favorable: 6 BENIGN
  factor: 4 PLUS
  Less: 5 WORSE
  opinion: 6 ESTEEM
  Under the most ~ conditions:
    6 ATBEST
Favored
  few: 5 ELITE
  Highly: 6 ODDSON
Favoring: 3 PRO
Favorite: 3 **PET** 4 IDOL SEED
    5 TOAST 7 TOPSEED
  Crowd: 7 PLEASER
  Enjoy a ~ book: 6 REREAD
  hangout: 5 HAUNT
  Hardly a: 8 LONGSHOT
  one: 3 SON
  son, maybe: 6 ELDEST
  Tournament: 4 SEED
Favoritism: 4 BIAS
Favre
  Quarterback: 5 **BRETT**
  target: 3 END
___ Fawkes Day: 3 GUY
"Fawlty Towers"
  airer: 3 BBC
  star John: 6 CLEESE
Fawn: 5 TOADY
  Mature: 4 DEER
  mom: 3 DOE
  (on): 4 DOTE
  over: 7 ADULATE
Fawning: 7 SERVILE
  one: 3 DOE
Fax: 4 SEND
  button: 4 SEND
  cover-page word: 4 FROM
  forerunner: 5 TELEX
  user: 6 SENDER
Faxed: 4 SENT
Fayed
  "Hook" producer: 4 DODI
Faze: 5 DAUNT 6 RATTLE
FBI
  agent: 4 GMAN
  datum: 5 CRIME
  director after Sessions: 5 FREEH
  employee: 3 AGT 4 GMAN
    5 AGENT

  info: 4 FILE
  Part of: 7 FEDERAL
  sting of the late 1970s: 6 ABSCAM
FCC
  concerns (abbr.): 4 STDS
FDR: 3 DEM 4 PRES
  coin: 4 DIME
  Mother of: 4 **SARA**
  opponent Landon: 3 ALF
  Part of: 4 INIT 6 DELANO
  program: 3 CCC **NRA** TVA WPA
  project: 3 TVA
  quote word: 6 INFAMY
  successor: 3 **HST**
  ~ Interior Secretary: 5 ICKES
  ~ Scottie: 4 FALA
  ~ Secretary of State: 4 HULL
Fe: 4 IRON
Fear: 4 CAPE 6 PHOBIA
  and wonder: 3 AWE
  For ~ that: 4 **LEST**
  Great: 5 DREAD
  Instill ~ in: 5 SCARE
  Intense: 5 PANIC 6 TERROR
  Reduce a: 5 ALLAY
  Show: 4 PALE 5 COWER QUAKE
    7 TREMBLE
  Shrink in: 6 CRINGE
Feared
  fly: 6 TSETSE
  mosquito: 5 AEDES
Fearful: 5 MOUSY 6 AFRAID
    TREPID
  Be ~ of: 5 DREAD
  fate: 4 DOOM
Fearless: 4 BOLD
  flyer: 3 ACE
Fearless Fosdick
  creator: 6 ALCAPP
"Fear of Fifty"
  author: 9 ERICAJONG
  author Erica: 4 JONG
  author Jong: 5 ERICA
Fearsome
  dinosaur: 4 TREX
  fellow: 4 OGRE
  fly: 6 TSETSE
Fearsome Foursome
  member: 5 GRIER

Feast: 4 DINE **6** REPAST
  finale: **7** DESSERT
  Island: **4** LUAU
  Passover: **5 SEDER**
  Put on a: **6** REGALE
  Spring: **5** SEDER
Feast of Lots
  book: **6** ESTHER
Feat: 3 ACT **4** DEED
  Brilliant: **4** COUP
  Daring: **5** STUNT
  on ice: **4** AXEL
Feather: 5 PENNA PINNA PLUME
  bed: **3** TAR
  Light as a: **4** AIRY
  partner: **3** TAR
  scarf: **3** BOA
Feathered
  bigfoot: **3** EMU
  fisher: **6** OSPREY
  stole: **3** BOA
Feathers
  Duck: **5** EIDER
  Fix: **5** PREEN
  Fuss and: **3** ADO
  Lose: **4** MOLT
  Ruffle: **3** IRE IRK VEX **4** RILE
Feathery: 4 SOFT
  wrap: **3 BOA**
Feature: 5 MOVIE TRAIT
        6 ASPECT
Feb.
  Month after: **3** MAR
Febrero
  preceder: **5** ENERO
Febreze
  target: **4** ODOR
February
  birthstone: **8** AMETHYST
  forecast: **5** SLEET
February 14
  figure: **4** EROS
  word: **4** LOVE
February 29: 7 LEAPDAY
Fed: 4 GMAN TMAN
  after a dealer: **4** NARC
  Famous: **4** NESS
  first name: **4** ALAN
  Got ~ up: **3** ATE

  on: **3** ATE
  the kitty: **5** ANTED
  They're ~ at curbside: **6** METERS
Fed.
  Abu Dhabi: **3** UAE
  agent: **4** GMAN TMAN
  auditors: **3** GAO
  benefit source: **3** SSA
  emissions watchdog: **3** EPA
  fiscal agency: **3** OMB
  funder: **3** NEA
  hush-hush group: **3** NSA
  loan agency: **3** SBA
  med. research agency: **3** NIH
  monetary-aid program: **3** SSI
  money overseer: **3** OMB
  pollution monitor: **3** EPA
  property overseer: **3 GSA**
  retirement org.: **3** SSA
  support benefit: **3** SSI
  watchdog: **3** EPA
  workplace watchdog: **4** OSHA
Federal
  agcy.: **3** AEC
  agt.: **4** GMAN TMAN
  Like ~ tax laws: **6** ARCANE
  purchasing org.: **3** GSA
"Federalist, The"
  pieces: **6** ESSAYS
Federation
  Mideast ~ (abbr.): **3** UAE
Federico
  Clinton Cabinet member: **4** PENA
Federico Garcia ___
  Poet: **5** LORCA
FedEx: 4 SEND SHIP
  arrival: **6** PARCEL
  rival: **3 UPS**
Fedora: 3 HAT
  feature: **4** BRIM **6** CREASE
Feds: 4 GMEN **TMEN**
Fee: 6 CHARGE
  Bridge: **4** TOLL
  Currency exchange: **4** AGIO
  Docking: **7** MOORAGE
  Flat: **4** RENT
  Hourly: **4** RATE
  Import: **6** TARIFF
  Lawyer: **8** RETAINER

Mutual fund: 4 LOAD
Old calling: 7 ONEDIME
Poker: 4 ANTE
Stud: 4 ANTE
Feeble: 6 ANEMIC
Feeble-minded: 4 DOTY
Feebly
Walk: 6 TOTTER
Feed: 4 SLOP 6 REPAST
      7 NOURISH
a crowd: 5 CATER
Don't: 6 FAMISH
fuel to: 5 STOKE
Livestock: 4 MASH SLOP
      7 SOILAGE
Off one's: 3 ILL
Part of a TV: 5 AUDIO
seed: 3 OAT
the kitty: 4 ANTE
the pigs: 4 SLOP
Feedback: 5 INPUT
Positive: 5 YESES
Feed bag
Attach, as a: 5 TIEON
Don the: 3 EAT
feed: 4 **OATS**
item: 3 **OAT**
Feeder
filler: 4 SEED SUET
Horse: 7 NOSEBAG
Line: 4 CUER
Pig: 6 TROUGH
"Fee, fi, fo, fum"
caller: 4 OGRE 5 GIANT
Feel: 4 AURA 5 GROPE SENSE
      7 BELIEVE
Able to: 7 SENSATE
bad: 3 AIL
bad about: 3 **RUE**
contrite: 6 REPENT
excitement: 6 TINGLE
indignant toward: 6 RESENT
in one's bones: 4 KNOW 5 SENSE
longing for: 4 MISS
Nice way to: 6 NEEDED
off: 3 AIL
one's way: 5 GROPE
poorly: 3 **AIL**
remorse: 3 RUE

sore: 4 **ACHE**
sorry about: 3 RUE 6 LAMENT
sorry for: 4 PITY
the same: 5 AGREE
Feeler: 4 PALP TEST 7 ANTENNA
Feelers: 8 ANTENNAE
Feeling: 4 AURA VIBE 5 CHORD
      SENSE 7 SENSATE
      TACTILE
Apprehensive: 5 ANGST
blue: 3 SAD 4 DOUR GLUM
Cloud-nine: 7 ELATION
Covetous: 4 ENVY
Creepy: 6 UNEASE
Distressed: 4 PANG
Emotional: 4 VIBE
faint: 5 WOOZY
Fluish: 4 AGUE
Full of: 5 LYRIC
Gung-ho: 4 ZEAL
Have a: 5 **SENSE**
Kind of: 3 GUT
no pain: 4 NUMB
off: 3 ILL
of hunger: 4 PANG
of pity: 6 PATHOS
Parched: 6 THIRST
poorly: 3 ILL
Queasy: 6 NAUSEA
sore: 4 ACHY
Tickled-pink: 4 GLEE
Uneasy: 5 ANGST QUALM
Vengeful: 5 SPITE
Feelings: 3 EGO
Feign: 5 EMOTE
Have good ~ about: 4 LIKE
Ill: 10 NOLOVELOST
Feet: 4 DOGS
128 cubic ~: 4 CORD
43,560 square ~: 4 ACRE
5,280 ~: 4 MILE
Cold: 4 FEAR
Drag one's: 5 STALL
Feline: 4 PAWS
Get one's ~ wet: 4 WADE
Got to one's: 5 STOOD
Hard on the: 6 PEBBLY
Having ~ pointing inward:
      10 PIGEONTOED

in meter: 5 IAMBS
Light on one's: 4 SPRY 5 AGILE
One who works with: 4 POET
Poetic: 5 IAMBS
Work with: 4 POEM
Feign: 3 ACT 6 AFFECT
      7 PRETEND 8 SIMULATE
  feelings: 5 EMOTE
  ___ **Fein:** 4 **SINN**
Feinstein
  (abbr.): 3 DEM SEN
  Senator: 6 DIANNE
Feint: 4 PLOY RUSE
  Fencing: 5 APPEL
  Football: 4 JUKE
  Hockey: 4 DEKE
Feldman
  Actor: 5 COREY
  Comical: 5 MARTY
Feldman, Marty
  role: 4 IGOR
Felicia
  Actress: 4 FARR
Feliciano
  Singer: 4 JOSE
"Felicity"
  star Russell: 4 KERI
Feline: 5 CATTY
  defense: 5 CLAWS
  ennead: 5 LIVES
  fancy: 6 CATNIP
  Fast: 4 PUMA 7 CHEETAH
  feet: 4 PAWS
  female: 7 TIGRESS
  Film: 4 ELSA
  film heroine: 4 ELSA
  hybrid: 5 LIGER
  line: 4 MEOW
  Male: 6 TOMCAT
  sign: 3 LEO
  Spotted: 6 OCELOT
  ~, in Spanish: 4 GATO
  ~, to Tweety: 3 TAT
Felipe
  farewell: 5 ADIOS
  of baseball: 4 **ALOU**
Felis
  member: 4 PUMA
Felix: 3 CAT

Like: 4 NEAT TIDY
  roommate: 5 OSCAR
"Feliz ___ Nuevo!": 3 ANO
Fell: 3 HEW 4 SLAY
  It ~ in 1836: 5 ALAMO
  It ~ in 2001: 3 MIR
  off: 5 EBBED WANED
  with a blade: 3 MOW
Fell, Gideon
  creator: 4 CARR
Fella: 3 BUD GUY MAC 4 CHAP
      GENT 5 KIDDO
Feller: 3 **AXE** MAN
  targets: 5 TREES
  What a ~ needs: 3 AXE SAW
      8 CHAINSAW
Fellini: 7 ITALIAN
  film: 8 LASTRADA
  Musical based on a ~ film:
      4 NINE
Fellow: 3 BUB GUY LAD MAN
      4 **CHAP** GENT
  Ale: 6 BREWER
  Clumsy: 3 OAF
  Contemptible: 3 CAD
  Cruel: 4 OGRE
  Dapper: 3 DAN
  Deer: 4 STAG
  Fabulous: 5 AESOP
  Fiery: 7 HOTHEAD
  Foolish: 4 TWIT
  Fraternal: 3 ELK
  Fun-loving:
      15 GOODTIMECHARLIE
  Furtive: 5 SNEAK
  Hilarious: 3 WAG 4 RIOT
  Ode: 4 POET
  Philandering: 4 ROUE
  Singular: 4 ONER
  Smart: 5 ALECK
  Young: 3 **LAD** SON
Fellows: 3 HES MEN
  For ~ only: 4 STAG
Fellowship
  Fund a: 5 ENDOW
Felon
  Aid a: 4 ABET
Felony
  Fiery: 5 ARSON

Felt: 6 SENSED
  hat: **6** FEDORA
Feltlike
  fabric: **5** BAIZE
Fem.
  leadership gp.: **4** YWCA
  Neither ~ nor masc.: **4 NEUT**
  Not: **4 MASC**
Female: 3 SEX
  antelope: **3** DOE
  cells: **3** OVA
  Common ~ middle name: **3** MAE
  deer: **3** DOE **4** HIND
  demon: **5** LAMIA
  domestic: **4** MAID
  donkey: **5** JENNY
  Farm: **3** DAM **EWE** HEN SOW
    4 MARE
  Feline ~ of film: **4** ELSA
  Fleecy: **3** EWE
  Forest: **3 DOE**
  fowl: **3** HEN **6** PEAHEN
  fox: **5** VIXEN
  friend, in French: **4** AMIE
  gamete: **4** OVUM
  hare: **3** DOE
  horse: **4** MARE
  kangaroo: **3** DOE
  lobster: **3 HEN**
  Low ~ voice: **4** ALTO
  Male and: **5** SEXES
  octopus: **3** HEN
  pheasant: **6** PEAHEN
  pig: **3** SOW
  principle: **3** YIN
  pronoun: **3** SHE
  prophet: **5** SIBYL
  rabbit: **3** DOE
  red deer: **4** HIND
  sheep: **3** EWE
  suffix: **3** INE **4** ENNE
  swan: **3** PEN
  swimmer: **5** NAIAD
  vampire: **5** LAMIA
  whale: **3** COW
  WWII gp.: **4** WAAC WACS
  ~ bear, in Spanish: **3** OSA
"Female Eunuch, The"
  author: **5** GREER

Feminine: 7 WOMANLY
  Hardly: **7** MANNISH
  principle: **3** YIN
  suffix: **3** ESS INA **4 ENNE** ETTA
    ETTE TRIX
Feminist
  ~ Abzug: **5** BELLA
  ~ Bella: **5** ABZUG
  ~ Eleanor: **5** SMEAL
  ~ Germaine: **5** GREER
  ~ Lucretia: **4** MOTT
Femme
  Canonized ~ (abbr.): **3** STE
  fatale: **5** SIREN **7** MANTRAP
    8 MANEATER
  That: **4** ELLE
Femme ___ : 6 FATALE
**Fen-___ (diet drug combo):
    4** PHEN
Fence
  alternative: **5** HEDGE
  Be a ~ for: **4** ABET
  feature: **4** GATE POST RAIL
    5 STILE
  Get off the: **3** ACT OPT
    6 CHOOSE DECIDE
  Like ~ wares: **6** STOLEN
  On the: **4** TORN
  opening: **4** GATE **5** STILE
  Racetrack: **4** RAIL
  stake: **4** PALE
  Steps over a: **5** STILE
  supplier: **5** THIEF
Fencer
  blade: **4** EPEE
  cry: **7** ENGARDE
  defense: **5** PARRY
  feint: **5** APPEL
  move: **5** LUNGE
Fence-sitter
  sounds: **3** ERS
Fencing
  blade: **4** EPEE
  event: **4** EPEE **5** SABER
  Japanese: **5** KENDO
  move: **5 LUNGE** PARRY
    6 THRUST
  piece: **4** RAIL
  sword: **4 EPEE 5** SABER

Fender
bender: 4 **DENT** 6 MISHAP
flaw: 4 **DENT** DING
Fenway
Imposing ~ sight:
   15 THEGREENMONSTER
team: 5 BOSOX
Feodor: 4 TSAR
Fer
Not: 4 **AGIN**
Feral: 6 UNTAME
Least: 6 TAMEST
Ferber
Author: 4 **EDNA**
novel: 5 GIANT **SOBIG**
   8 CIMARRON 9 ICEPALACE
Ferde
Composer: 5 GROFE
Ferdinand
First lady of: 6 IMELDA
kingdom: 6 ARAGON
of WWI: 4 FOCH
queen: 8 ISABELLA
Ferdinand III
Daughter of: 7 ELEANOR
Fergie
~, formally: 5 **SARAH**
Ferment: 6 SIMMER
Fermentation
ingredient: 5 YEAST
Fermented: 7 YEASTED
drink: 3 ALE
honey drink: 4 MEAD
milk drink: 5 KEFIR
rice drink: 4 SAKE SAKI
Fermenter: 5 YEAST
Fermi
Physicist: 6 **ENRICO**
study: 4 ATOM
Fern
Future: 5 SPORE
leaf: 5 FROND
seed: 5 SPORE
Fernand
Cubist: 5 LEGER
Fernandez
Pitcher: 3 SID
Fernando
Info: Spanish cue

Actor: 3 **REY** 5 LAMAS
"Fernando"
group: 4 **ABBA**
Ferocious: 6 SAVAGE
fish: 7 PIRANHA
Ferrara
Director: 4 ABEL
family name: 4 **ESTE**
Ferrari
Automaker: 4 ENZO
Ferraro
Ms. ~, to friends: 4 GERI
Ferrell
film: 3 ELF
Ferrer
Actor: 3 MEL 4 JOSE
Ferret
foot: 3 PAW
kin: 5 OTTER
out: 4 FIND SEEK 5 DIGUP
Ferrigno
Actor: 3 LOU
Ferris wheel: 4 RIDE
Ferry
destination: 4 ISLE
How a ~ goes: 8 TOANDFRO
river of myth: 4 STYX
Ferryman
Styx: 6 CHARON
Fertile
area: 5 OASIS
areas: 5 OASES
soil: 4 LOAM 5 LOESS
Fertile Crescent
land: 4 ASIA 5 SYRIA
river: 6 TIGRIS
Fertility
god: 6 OSIRIS
goddess: 4 **ISIS** 7 ASTARTE
Fertilization
Kind of: 7 INVITRO
site: 5 OVULE
targets: 3 OVA
Fertilizer
brand: 5 ORTHO
chemical: 4 UREA 7 NITRATE
ingredient: 4 PEAT 5 NITER
   6 MANURE POTASH
Loamy: 4 MARL

Organic: 5 GUANO
source: 7 PEATBOG
Fervency: 4 ZEAL
Fervent: 4 AVID 5 EAGER RAPID
Fervid: 6 ARDENT
Fervor: 4 ZEAL 5 ARDOR
Full of: 6 ONFIRE
With: 5 HOTLY
Fess
up: 4 AVOW 5 **ADMIT**
(up): 3 OWN
Fest
month: 7 OKTOBER
Fester
Morticia, to: 5 NIECE
Festival
Asian: 3 TET
Colorado ~ site: 5 ASPEN
County: 4 FAIR
Jewish: 5 PURIM
opener: 3 EVE
Redford: 8 SUNDANCE
Spring: 6 EASTER
Vietnamese: 3 TET
Festival d' ___: 3 ETE
Festive: 3 GAY 4 **GALA**
event: 4 FETE GALA
night: 3 EVE
time: 4 YULE
Festoon: 4 SWAG 5 ADORN
DRAPE
Fetch: 3 GET 4 SHAG 5 BRING
GOFOR GOGET
Thing to: 5 STICK
with force: 3 LUG
Fetching: 4 CUTE
ones: 6 GOFERS
Fete: 4 GALA 5 HONOR
6 REGALE
Friars: 5 ROAST
Feted
with alcohol: 5 WINED
Fetes
Fancy: 3 DOS
Fettle
In fine: 3 AOK FIT 4 HALE
WELL
Fettuccine: 5 PASTA
Fettuccine ___: 7 ALFREDO

Feud
Bitter: 8 VENDETTA
family: 6 MCCOYS
Feudal
estate: 4 FIEF
Like ~ times: 8 MEDIEVAL
lord: 5 **LIEGE**
worker: 4 ESNE **SERF** 6 VASSAL
Feudin'
with: 4 AGIN
Feuding: 4 ATIT 5 ATWAR
Fever
cause: 3 FLU
Chills and: 4 **AGUE**
Have, as a: 3 RUN
Malarial: 4 AGUE
symptom: 5 CHILL
"Fever"
singer Peggy: 3 LEE
___ fever: 4 RANA
Feverish: 3 ILL 4 WARM 6 HECTIC
chill: 4 AGUE
Feel: 3 AIL
Few
A: 4 **SOME**
A ~ bucks: 4 DEER
A ~ chips: 4 ANTE
A ~ last words: 4 OBIT
A ~ laughs: 4 HAHA
and far between: 4 RARE
6 SPARSE
Favored: 5 ELITE
Known by: 6 ARCANE
Like very ~ games: 5 NOHIT
Of ~ words: 5 TERSE
Select: 5 ELITE
Understood by: 8 ESOTERIC
Fewer: 4 LESS
No ~ than: 7 ATLEAST
"Few Good ___, A": 3 MEN
"Few Good Men, A"
actress: 5 MOORE
director: 6 REINER
9 ROBREINER
___ few rounds: 3 GOA
Fey
Comedienne: 4 TINA
Fez: 3 HAT
feature: 6 TASSEL

F.G.s

452

F.G.s
They're worth two: 3 TDS

Fi
lead-in: 3 SCI

Fiasco: 4 BOMB 7 DEBACLE
    8 DISASTER
Ford: 5 EDSEL

Fiat: 5 EDICT
homeland: 5 ITALY

Fib: 3 LIE 8 TELLALIE

Fibber: 4 LIAR
admission: 5 ILIED
and Molly: 6 MCGEES
of old radio: 5 MCGEE

Fiber
Acrylic: 5 **ORLON**
Agave: 5 SISAL
Basket: 5 ISTLE
Burlap: 4 JUTE
Carpet: 5 ISTLE
Caulking: 5 OAKUM
Cellulose: 5 ARNEL RAYON
Cereal: 4 BRAN
Coconut: 4 COIR
Cocoon: 4 SILK
Cordage: 5 SISAL
Dupont: 5 ORLON
Flaxlike: 5 RAMIE
Hemp: 5 SISAL
Rope: 4 BAST COIR HEMP JUTE
    5 **SISAL** 6 STRAND
source: 4 BEAN BRAN HEMP
    5 AGAVE
Strong: 5 RAMIE
Synthetic: 5 ARNEL NYLON
    ORLON RAYON
    7 ACETATE
Twine: 5 SISAL

Fiber-yielding
plant: 4 ALOE

Fibster: 4 LIAR

Fibula: 4 BONE
neighbor: 5 TIBIA

FICA
funds it: 3 SSA

Fiction: 5 GENRE 6 NOVELS
expert: 4 LIAR
Opposite of: 4 FACT
Work of: 5 NOVEL

Fictional
alter ego: 4 HYDE
bell town: 5 ADANO
blade: 5 ATHOS
captain: 4 AHAB NEMO
circumnavigator: 4 FOGG
dreamer: 5 ALICE
elephant: 5 BABAR
governess: 4 ANNA EYRE
hunchback: 4 IGOR
lab assistant: 4 IGOR
pirate: 4 SMEE
planet: 3 ORK
plantation: 4 TARA
salesman: 5 LOMAN
surname of 1847: 4 EYRE
terrier: 4 ASTA
weaver: 6 MARNER
wirehair: 4 ASTA
~ Butler: 5 RHETT
~ Doone: 5 LORNA
~ Frome: 5 ETHAN
~ Gantry: 5 ELMER
~ Georgia home: 4 TARA
~ Heep: 5 URIAH
~ Helm: 4 MATT
~ Honolulu detective: 4 CHAN
~ Italian town: 5 ADANO
~ Jane: 4 EYRE
~ Lorna: 5 DOONE
~ Marner: 5 SILAS
~ Plaza Hotel brat: 6 ELOISE
~ Swiss miss: 5 HEIDI
~ Uncle: 5 REMUS
~ Uriah: 4 HEEP
~ Wolfe: 4 NERO

Fictitious
~ Richard: 3 ROE

Fiddle
Early: 4 VIOL
Emperor with a: 4 NERO
finale: 5 DEDEE 6 DEEDEE
Fine: 5 AMATI STRAD
Fit as a: 4 HALE
Kind of: 4 BASS
Like a: 3 FIT
Renaissance: 5 REBEC
stick: 3 BOW
(with): 6 TAMPER

with a fiddle: 4 TUNE
Fiddled: 5 TOYED
Fiddle-de-___ : 3 DEE
Fiddlehead: 4 FERN
Fiddlemaker
  Famed: 5 AMATI
Fiddler
  Famous: 4 NERO
  of kids' rhyme: 3 CAT
  on the reef: 4 CRAB
"Fiddler on the Roof"
  concern: 6 POGROM
  matchmaker: 5 YENTE
  role: 5 TEVYE
  setting: 6 SHTETL
  star: 5 TOPOL
"Fiddlesticks!": 4 BOSH DRAT
      POSH RATS 5 PSHAW
      SHOOT
___ fide: 4 **BONA**
Fidel
  Friend of: 3 CHE
  Philippine president: 5 RAMOS
"___ Fideles": 6 **ADESTE**
"Fidelio": 5 OPERA
  jailer: 5 ROCCO
Fidelity: 5 TROTH
  High: 5 TROTH
Fidget
  Inclined to: 5 ANTSY
Fidgety: 5 ANTSY 8 RESTLESS
Fido
  Bit for: 3 ORT 5 SCRAP
  Call to: 4 HERE
  Command to: 3 BEG SIT 4 HEEL
      STAY 5 FETCH SICEM
      SPEAK 6 DROPIT
  doc: 3 VET
  Food for: 4 ALPO
  foot: 3 PAW
  Friend of: 3 REX 5 ROVER
  warning: 5 SNARL
Fiduciary
  entity: 5 TRUST
Field: 4 **AREA** 5 ARENA
      6 DOMAIN MEADOW
      METIER SPHERE
  Attorney: 3 LAW
  Battle: 5 OPERA

call: 3 CAW
Clear the: 4 REAP
cover: 4 TARP
event: 7 SHOTPUT
Farmer ~ (abbr.): 3 AGR
furrower: 4 PLOW
Grassy: 3 LEA
house: 5 TEPEE
Level the playing: 3 MOW
Like a fair playing: 5 LEVEL
marshal: 3 REF
measure: 4 ACRE
mouse: 4 VOLE
of expertise: 4 AREA
official: 3 REF UMP
of honor event: 4 DUEL
of play: 5 ARENA
of study: 4 AREA
of work: 4 LINE
Partner of: 5 TRACK
Plow the ~: 4 TILL
prefix: 4 AGRO
protector: 4 TARP
Rice: 5 PADDY
Rock ~ (abbr.): 4 GEOL
Small: 4 ACRE
trip: 5 ERROR
unit: 4 **ACRE**
Word before: 3 AIR
yield: 4 CROP
Field ___ : 4 GOAL
Field, Sally
  Emmy-winning role: 5 SYBIL
  Oscar film: 8 NORMARAE
  TV role: 3 NUN
Fielding
  goof: 5 ERROR
  novel: 6 AMELIA
"Field of Dreams"
  setting: 4 IOWA
Fields
  Bandleader: 4 SHEP
  Comedienne: 5 TOTIE
  oath: 4 DRAT
  persona: 3 SOT
  School with historic playing:
      4 ETON
___ Fields (mythical paradise):
      7 ELYSIAN

Fields, W.C.
  expletive: 4 DRAT
  persona: 3 SOT 4 LUSH 5 SOUSE
Fiend: 3 NUT 4 **OGRE** 5 DEMON
Fiendish: 4 EVIL VILE 7 SATANIC
Fiennes
  1998 ~ role: 5 STEED
Fierce
  fighter: 7 BEARCAT
  one: 5 TIGER
  Smell something: 4 REEK
"Fierce Creatures"
  star John: 6 CLEESE
Fierceness: 4 FURY
Fierstein, Harvey
  Talk like: 4 RASP
Fiery
  crime: 5 **ARSON**
  fellow: 7 HOTHEAD
  gemstone: 4 OPAL
  heap: 4 PYRE
  saint: 4 ELMO
"Fiesque"
  composer: 4 LALO
Fiesta: 4 GALA
  fare: 5 TACOS
  prop: 6 PINATA
Fiesta Bowl
  site: 5 TEMPE
Fife
  accompaniment: 5 TABOR
  companion: 4 DRUM
  player: 6 KNOTTS
Fifth
  element: 5 BORON
  note: 3 SOL
  of NYC: 3 AVE
  qtrs.: 3 OTS
  wheel: 5 SPARE
  zodiac sign: 3 LEO
Fifth Avenue
  store: 4 **SAKS**
"Fifth Beatle"
  ~ Sutcliffe: 3 STU
Fifth-century
  pope: 4 LEOI 5 STLEO
  scourge: 6 ATTILA
  start: 3 CDI
  warrior: 3 HUN

Fifty
  Change for a: 4 TENS
  minutes past: 5 TENTO
  One of: 5 STATE
  percent: 4 HALF
  Two of: 4 EFFS
Fifty-fifty: 4 **EVEN**
"Fifty-four-forty or Fight"
  territory: 6 OREGON
Fig
  Give a: 4 CARE
  pollinator: 4 WASP
Fig.
  Attendance: 3 EST
  Ballpark: 3 AVG EST
  Capitol: 3 SEN
  Check: 3 AMT
  Court: 3 **ATT** 4 ATTY
  Dugout: 3 MGR
  Financial: 3 APR
  Geometric: 3 CIR 4 RECT
  Global positioning: 3 LAT
  Invoice: 3 AMT
  Nutritional: 3 CAL **RDA**
  Pilot: 3 ALT
  Transcript: 3 GPA
  Yield: 3 ROI
Fight: 3 ROW 4 BOUT 5 MELEE
        SETTO 6 OPPOSE SCRAPE
        TUSSLE
  back: 6 RESIST
  Brief: 5 SETTO
  Confused: 5 MELEE
  down and dirty: 6 RASSLE
  ender: 3 TKO
  enders: 3 KOS
  Fix a: 3 RIG
  for balance: 6 TEETER
  Give up the: 4 CAVE
  grime: 5 CLEAN
  like a knight: 4 TILT
  Noisy: 5 BRAWL
  off: 5 REPEL
  Prepare to: 4 SPAR
        9 SQUAREOFF
  Put up a: 6 RESIST
  Rural: 6 RASSLE
  site: 4 RING 5 ARENA
  Slight: 4 SPAT

to keep the faith: 7 HOLYWAR
Two-person: 4 DUEL
Valiant: 5 STAND
with fists: 3 BOX
Fighter
Crack ~ pilot: 3 ACE
Fierce: 7 BEARCAT
Fire: 4 HOSE
Flu: 5 SERUM
Good: 4 EVIL
Infection: 5 SULFA
Inflation:
    15 PRICEREGULATION
in grey: 3 REB
Korean War: 3 MIG
Polio: 5 SABIN
Russian: 3 **MIG**
Fighters
Flu: 4 SERA
___ Fighters: 3 FOO
Fighting: 4 ATIT 5 **ATWAR**
    7 HOSTILE WARFARE
fleet: 6 ARMADA
In ~ shape: 4 TRIM
Scene of WWI: 4 YSER
Them's ~ words: 7 ENGARDE
"Fighting"
~ Big Ten team: 6 ILLINI
Fighting ___: 5 IRISH
Fighting Irish
Rockne of the: 5 KNUTE
Fighting Tigers
sch.: 3 LSU
"___ fightin' words!": 5 THEMS
Figs.: 3 **NOS**
Court: 3 DAS
Figure: 3 BOD 4 STAT 5 ADDUP
    TOTUP 6 DECIDE PERSON
    RECKON 7 NUMERAL
Adored: 4 IDOL
Do ~ eights: 5 SKATE
Go: 3 ADD
Half a ~ eight: 3 ESS
in geometry: 4 AREA
of speech: 5 IDIOM **TROPE**
    6 LECTOR ORATOR SIMILE
on a fin: 3 ABE
out: 3 GET SEE 5 INFER SOLVE
    6 DECODE DEDUCE

    REASON 7 REALIZE
(out): 4 DOPE SUSS
Figured
out: 3 GOT
Figurehead
place: 4 PROW
Figures: 4 DATA
to analyze: 7 RAWDATA
Watch the: 4 OGLE
Figure skater
category: 5 PAIRS
figure: 5 EIGHT
jump: 4 AXEL
~ Babilonia: 3 TAI
~ Baiul: 6 OKSANA
~ Cohen: 5 SASHA
~ Katarina: 4 WITT
~ Lipinski: 4 TARA
~ Paulsen: 4 AXEL
~ Rodnina: 5 IRINA
~ Sasha: 5 COHEN
~ Sonja: 5 HENIE
~ Thomas: 4 DEBI
Figurine
mineral: 4 ONYX
Polynesian: 4 TIKI
Fiji
Neighbor of: 5 SAMOA **TONGA**
One of three in: 3 DOT
Filament: 6 THREAD
element: 8 TUNGSTEN
Filbert: 3 NUT
Filch: 3 COP ROB 5 STEAL SWIPE
    6 THIEVE
File: 4 RASP SORT 5 EMERY
    QUEUE
box filler: 6 RECIPE
Brokerage ~ (abbr.): 4 ACCT
Change a ~ listing: 6 RENAME
Circular: 7 ROLODEX
    8 TRASHCAN
Coarse: 4 **RASP**
Common text ~ name:
    6 README
Compress a data: 3 ZIP
Computer ~ format: 4 JPEG
Customer ~ entry: 8 AREACODE
Delete a: 5 ERASE
Expand a: 5 UNZIP

folder feature: 3 TAB
holder: 4 DISC 6 FOLDER
material: 5 EMERY
Program ~ extension: 3 EXE
"___ File, The": 6 ODESSA
Filed
item: 4 NAIL
Filer: 4 RASP 5 EMERY
Form: 3 CPA
worry: 5 AUDIT
Filet
fish: 4 SOLE
Filet ___: 6 MIGNON
Filet mignon
source: 4 LOIN
Filigreed: 4 LACY
Filing
aid: 3 TAB 5 EMERY
Court: 10 LEGALBRIEF
Miner: 5 CLAIM
mo.: 3 APR
Filippo Lippi: 3 FRA
Fill: 4 SATE 7 SATIATE
a hold: 4 LADE
Get one's: 6 LOADUP
in: 4 TELL TEMP 5 BRIEF
Something to ~ out: 4 FORM
space: 3 ARE
the bill: 3 EAT
the lungs: 6 INHALE
the tank: 5 GASUP
They ~ the bill: 5 CENTS
Till: 4 CASH ONES
up: 4 SATE 7 SATIATE
with cargo: 4 **LADE**
with fizz: 6 AERATE
with joy: 5 **ELATE**
with love: 6 ENAMOR
with resolution: 5 STEEL
with wonder: 3 AWE
Filled
pastry: 6 ECLAIR
They may be ~ with jets: 4 SPAS
to overflowing: 5 ABRIM
tortilla: 4 TACO
up: 3 ATE
with wonder: 5 INAWE
Filler
Balloon: 3 **AIR**

Boat: 5 GRAVY
Conversation: 4 ISEE 5 IMEAN
Duffel: 4 GEAR
Feeder: 4 SEED SUET
Flagon: 3 ALE
Flask: 5 BOOZE
Floppy: 4 DATA
Football: 3 AIR
Hourglass: 4 SAND
Pen: 3 INK
Pillow: 4 FOAM 5 EIDER
Reservoir: 4 RAIN
Sandwich: 4 TUNA 8 TUNAFISH
Scuttle: 4 COAL
Sleeve: 3 ARM
Slot: 3 TAB
Tank: 3 GAS
Tankard: 3 ALE
Tire: 3 AIR
Tram: 3 ORE
Fillet: 4 BONE 6 DEBONE
Like a: 8 BONELESS
Filleted
fish: 3 COD 4 SHAD SOLE
Fill-in: 3 SUB 4 TEMP
Filling
Bagel: 3 LOX
Burrito: 4 BEEF
Cookie: 5 CREME
Dental: 5 INLAY
It's removed before ~ up:
  6 GASCAP
material: 7 AMALGAM
Pie: 3 MUD
Pillow: 5 EIDER
station letters: 3 DDS
Fillmore: 4 WHIG
Filly: 4 LASS
brother: 4 COLT
father: 4 SIRE
filler: 4 OATS
footfall: 4 CLOP
Former: 4 MARE
Film: 4 CINE 5 MOVIE 6 PATINA
1944 ~: 5 LAURA
1950 ~: 3 **DOA**
1953 ~: 4 LILI
1958 ~: 4 GIGI
1962 ~: 4 DRNO

1965 ~: 4 HELP
1971 ~: 5 KLUTE
1974 ~: 5 BENJI
1975 ~:
    15 DOGDAYAFTERNOON
1977 ~: 4 ORCA
1978 ~: 4 COMA
    10 ERASERHEAD
1979 ~: 5 ALIEN
1982 ~: 4 TRON
1985 ~: 5 ELENI
1996 ~: 5 FARGO
1997 ~: 7 TITANIC
1998 ~: 4 ANTZ
1999 ~: 4 EDTV
    13 THESIXTHSENSE
2001 ~: 3 ALI 6 AMELIE
Action ~ highlight: 5 CHASE
award: 5 OSCAR
Big name in: 5 KODAK
box letters: 3 ASA
buff network: 3 AMC
Cast-of-thousands: 4 EPIC
changes: 5 EDITS
composer Morricone: 5 ENNIO
composer Nino: 4 ROTA
composer Rota: 4 NINO
composer Schifrin: 4 LALO
crew member: 4 GRIP
critic James: 4 AGEE
critic Pauline: 4 KAEL
critic Reed: 3 REX
critic Rex: 4 REED
critic Roger: 5 EBERT
Do ~ work: 3 ACT
dog: 4 ASTA
Do some ~ editing: 6 SPLICE
editing effect: 4 WIPE
editor: 7 SPLICER
ending: 4 GOER
excerpt: 4 CLIP
feline: 4 ELSA
festival site: 6 CANNES
fish: 4 NEMO 5 WANDA
format: 4 IMAX
fragment: 4 CLIP
frame: 3 CEL
French ~ award: 5 CESAR
genre: 4 **NOIR** 6 ACTION

    HORROR 7 ROMANCE
holder: 4 **REEL**
Home ~ player: 3 VCR
Kind of: 4 CULT
material: 7 ACETATE
Non-studio: 5 INDIE
ogre: 5 SHREK
part: 4 ROLE
plantation: 4 TARA
Pond: 4 SCUM
princess: 4 LEIA
Private ~ producer: 5 INDIE
Put in more: 6 RELOAD
Put ~ into: 4 LOAD
rat: 3 BEN
rating org.: 4 MPAA
river: 4 KWAI
Sci-fi ~ extra: 5 ALIEN
segment: 4 CLIP
Some ~ ratings: 3 PGS
spool: 4 REEL
studio: 3 LOT
technique: 5 SLOMO
terrier: 4 ASTA
unit: 4 **REEL**
Western: 5 OATER
What a family ~ is appropriate
    for: 7 ALLAGES
winds up on it: 4 REEL
Word with: 3 ART
~, in French: 4 CINE
Film ___ : 4 NOIR
Film director
cry: 3 CUT
unit: 4 TAKE
~ Kazan: 4 ELIA
~ Lee: 3 ANG
~ Nicolas: 4 ROEG
~ Petri: 4 ELIO
~ Resnais: 5 ALAIN
Filmed: 4 SHOT
again: 6 RESHOT
Filming
Bit of: 4 TAKE
locale: 3 SET
Filmmaker
with creative control: 6 AUTEUR
~ Craven: 3 WES
~ Lee: 3 ANG

~ Riefenstahl: **4** LENI
~ Spike: **3** LEE
~ Wertmuller: **4** LINA
Film noir: **5** GENRE
classic: **3** <u>DOA</u>
Films
Its ~ begin with a roar: **3** MGM
Like horror: **6** RATEDR RRATED
Like many independent: **4** ARTY
Like some R-rated: **4** GORY
6 EROTIC
Filmy: **8** GOSSAMER
fabric: **5** GAUZE
Fils
father: **4** PERE
Filter: **4** SEEP **6** SCREEN
Flounder: **4** GILL
Filthy
lucre: **4** PELF
money: **5** LUCRE
place: **3** STY
Fin: **5** FIVER
Change for a: **4** ONES
Figure on a: **3** ABE
Finagle: **3** RIG **6** WANGLE
Final: **3** NET **4** EXAM LAST TEST
Info: Suffix cue
(abbr.): **3** <u>ULT</u>
authority: **5** <u>SAYSO</u>
bio: **4** OBIT
exams: **5** ORALS
inning, usually: **5** NINTH
Let have the ~ word:
7 DEFERTO
notice: **4** <u>OBIT</u>
Not yet: **4** NISI
preceder: **4** SEMI
Prepare for a: **4** CRAM
stage: **7** ENDGAME
stanza: **5** ENVOI
story: **4** OBIT
taker: **6** TESTEE
transport: **6** HEARSE
word: **4** AMEN **5** ADIEU SAYSO
~ Commandment: **5** TENTH
"Final answer?"
asker: **5** REGIS
"Final Days, The"
author: **5** OLSON

Finale: **3** <u>END</u> **4** CODA **5** OMEGA
6 ENDING
Info: Suffix cue
Brit: **3** ZED
Classical: **5** OMEGA
English-exam: **5** ESSAY
Fable: **5** MORAL
Feast: **7** DESSERT
Gerund: **3** ING
Grand: **3** DEE **4** PRIX
Major: **4** ETTE
Musical: **4** CODA
Proof: **3** QED
Series: **3** ETC **4** ETAL
Social: **3** ITE
Threat: **6** ORELSE
Waltz: **3** ZEE
Final Four
1998 ~ team: **4** UTES
game: **4** SEMI
org.: **4** <u>NCAA</u>
"Final frontier": **5** SPACE
Finalize: **8** NAILDOWN
~, as a deal: **3** INK
~, with "up": **3** SEW
Finally: **6** ATLAST
Become,: **5** ENDUP
~, in French: **5** ENFIN
"Finally!": **3** AHA **6** ATLAST
Finance
co. takeback: **4** REPO
deg.: **3** MBA
Fannie of: **3** MAE
Financial: **6** FISCAL **8** ECONOMIC
aid criterion: **4** NEED
backer: **5** ANGEL
Bit of ~ planning: **3** IRA
burden: **4** DEBT
claim: **4** LIEN
Federal ~ planning gp.: **3** OMB
fig.: **3** APR
independence: **10** EASYSTREET
It may be: **3** AID
obligation: **4** DEBT
page letters: **4** NYSE
Party to a ~ exchange: **6** DRAWEE
standing: **5** WORTH
transaction: **4** LOAN
wherewithal: **5** MEANS

windfall: **5** MELON
Financial ___ : **3** AID
Financially
  compromised: **7** INAHOLE
  Set up: **5** ENDOW
  solvent: **6** AFLOAT
Financier
  Fugitive ~ Robert: **5** VESCO
  Powerful: **5** BARON
  with his own law: **7** GRESHAM
  ~ Cornell: **4** EZRA
Financing
  abbr.: **3** APR
  Auto ~ co.: **4** GMAC
  ___ financing: **3** APR
Finch
  European: **6** LINNET
  home: **4** NEST
  Long-tailed: **6** TOWHEE
  Small: **5** SERIN
Finch, Atticus
  creator: **3** LEE
Find: **4** SPOT **5** DIGUP **6** DETECT
     LOCATE **7** UNEARTH
  Hard to: **4** **RARE** **5** SCANT
     6 SCARCE
  Hard to ~, in Latin: **4** RARA
  Manage to: **7** SCAREUP
  out: **3** SEE **4** HEAR **5** LEARN
     7 UNCOVER
  out about: **6** HEAROF
  the origin of: **5** TRACE
  Try to: **4** SEEK
  Try to ~ out: **3** ASK
Fin de ___ : **6** SIECLE
Finder
  cry: **3** AHA
  Fish: **5** SONAR
  Like a depth: **5** SONIC
  Scent: **4** NOSE
  Stash: **4** NARC
  View: **3** EYE
Finder's ___ : **3** FEE
Find ___ for: **5** AMATE
"Finding ___": **4** NEMO
Findlay, Mrs. Walter: **5** MAUDE
Fine: **3** AOK **4** GOOD NICE OKAY
     6 AMERCE CHOICE
     7 PENALTY

and dandy: **3** AOK
china: **5** SPODE
cotton: **4** PIMA
cotton thread: **5** LISLE
dinnerware: **5** CHINA
Enjoy ~ food: **4** DINE
fabric: **5** SATIN
fur: **5** SABLE **6** ERMINE
Impose a: **6** AMERCE
In ~ fettle: **3** AOK FIT **4** HALE
     WELL
Just: **3** AOK
Like ~ wine: **4** **AGED**
Love of ~ art: **5** VIRTU
netting: **5** TULLE
or Howard: **6** STOOGE
point: **6** DETAIL NICETY
Punish by: **6** AMERCE
rain: **4** MIST
Risk a: **5** SPEED
silver: **8** STERLING
Some are: **4** ARTS
spray: **4** MIST
suit material: **5** TWILL
They may be: **4** ARTS
things: **4** ARTS
wool: **6** MERINO
work: **3** ART
"Fine!: **3** AOK
" ___ Fine": **5** HESSO
" ___ Fine Day": **3** ONE
Fine-grained
  wood: **3** YEW
Finely
  Chop: **4** DICE HASH
     5 MINCE
  contoured: **5** SLEEK
  sharpened: **4** KEEN
Fineness
  unit: **5** KARAT
Finer
  Made: **6** SIFTED
Finesse: **4** TACT
  With: **4** ABLY
Finest: **4** BEST
  One of the: **3** COP
" ___ Finest Hour": **5** THEIR
Fine-tune: **4** **HONE** **5** TWEAK
     6 ADJUST

Fine-tuned
  engine sound: 4 PURR
Finger: 4 FEEL NAME 5 DIGIT
      RATON
  Do ~ painting: 5 SMEAR
  feature: 4 NAIL
  Jab with a: 4 POKE
  Largest ~ Lake: 6 SENECA
  Little: 5 PINKY
  Luau ~ food: 3 POI
  Point a ~ at: 5 BLAME RATON
      6 ACCUSE
  pointer: 6 BLAMER 7 ACCUSER
  Put one's ~ on: 7 PINDOWN
  Use the ~ bowl: 5 RINSE
Fingerboard
  ridge: 4 FRET
Finger-choosing
  call: 5 EVENS
Fingered: 4 IDED
Finger-paint: 4 DAUB 5 SMEAR
Fingerprint: 4 CLUE
  feature: 5 WHORL
  Kind of: 3 DNA
Fingerprints
  Check for: 4 DUST
  Like some: 6 LATENT
Fingers: 3 IDS
  count: 3 TEN
  Cross one's: 4 HOPE
  Work your ~ to the bone: 5 SLAVE
Fingertip: 4 NAIL
Finger-wagging: 5 STERN
Finis: 3 END 4 OVER 5 DEATH
Finish: 3 **END** 5 ENDUP MOPUP
      SEWUP USEUP 6 VENEER
      WRAPUP 9 POLISHOFF
  Info: Suffix cue
  a basement: 5 PANEL
  a drive: 4 PAVE
  a highway: 3 TAR
  Big: 6 FINALE
  by: 5 ENDAT
  Dull: 3 ARD 5 **MATTE**
  Exterior: 6 STUCCO
  first: 3 WIN
  line: 4 TAPE WIRE
  Lineup: 4 ETAL
  Lusterless: 5 MATTE

  off: 3 EAT 4 DOIN 5 USEUP
      6 DEVOUR
  option: 5 GLOSS MATTE
  Photo: 5 GENIC **MATTE**
  Pottery: 5 GLAZE
  protector: 7 COASTER
  second: 5 PLACE
  Stay to the: 4 LAST
  the cake: 3 ICE
  third: 4 SHOW
  (up): 3 MOP SEW 4 WRAP
  with: 5 ENDAT ENDON
  Wood: 5 STAIN
Finished: 3 DID 4 DONE **OVER**
      THRU 5 ENDED KAPUT
      6 CAMEIN 7 ALLDONE
      ALLOVER ATANEND
      ENDEDUP
  Expensively: 4 GILT
  first: 3 WON
  with: 5 RIDOF
"Finished!": 5 THERE
Finisher
  Cake: 4 **ICER**
  Furniture: 7 STAINER
  Late: 7 ALSORAN
Finito: 4 DONE OVER 5 ENDED
      KAPUT
Fink: 3 RAT 4 SCAB SING TELL
      6 TELLON 7 STOOLIE
      TATTLER
Finless
  fish: 3 EEL
Finn
  carrier: 4 RAFT
  chronicler: 5 TWAIN
  Fictional: 4 HUCK
"Finnegans Wake"
  author James: 5 JOYCE
  wife: 4 ANNA
Finnish
  architect Alvar: 5 AALTO
  bath: 5 SAUNA
Fins
  200 ~: 3 GEE
  Twenty: 5 CNOTE
  Two: 6 TENNER 7 TENSPOT
Fiord
  city: 4 OSLO

Fir
coat: 4 BARK
fluid: 3 SAP
Kind of: 6 BALSAM
Fire: 3 **AXE** CAN 4 SACK ZEAL
      5 ARDOR BLAZE LETGO
      6 EXCITE
Antiaircraft: 4 FLAK
Baptism of: 6 ORDEAL
Breathing: 5 IRATE
bug: 3 ANT
Build a ~ under: 6 AROUSE
Dying ~ feature: 5 EMBER
engine warning: 5 SIREN
Feed a: 5 STOKE
fiddler: 4 NERO
fighters: 5 HOSES
from a plane: 6 STRAFE
Great ball of: 3 SUN 4 STAR
Hang: 4 PEND
Kind of: 5 ENEMY
man: 4 ELMO
On: 3 LIT 6 ABLAZE AFLAME
On ~, in a restaurant: 6 FLAMBE
opal: 7 GIRASOL
Partner of: 6 BRIMSTONE
preceder: 3 AIM
Prepare to: 3 **AIM**
proof: 3 **ASH**
Ready to: 5 ARMED 6 COCKED
remnant: 3 ASH 5 EMBER
saint: 4 ELMO
Set on: 3 LIT 6 IGNITE
Set ~ to: 5 TORCH
sign: 3 LEO 5 EMBER SMOKE
Spew ~ and brimstone: 4 RANT
Started a ~ again: 5 RELIT
starter: 5 SPARK 6 TINDER
Trial by: 6 ORDEAL
truck item: 3 AXE 4 HOSE
      6 LADDER
up: 6 AROUSE ENRAGE
      FOMENT 7 INSPIRE
Went out, as a: 4 DIED
work: 5 ARSON
~, in French: 3 FEU
~, in Spanish: 5 FUEGO
"Fire!"
preceder: 3 AIM

Fire ___: 3 ANT 4 OPAL
"___ Fire" (Springsteen hit):
      4 IMON
Firearm: 6 WEAPON
filler: 4 AMMO
Fireballer
~ Nolan: 4 RYAN
~ Ryan: 5 NOLAN
Firebird: 6 ORIOLE
Firebox
feature: 5 ALARM
Fire-breathing
beast: 6 DRAGON 7 CHIMERA
Firebug
crime: 5 ARSON
Firecracker
Fizzled: 3 DUD
Kind of: 6 PETARD
      10 CHERRYBOMB
Fired
on: 6 SHOTAT
Singer ~ on live TV: 6 LAROSA
up: 4 AVID 5 EAGER 6 AFLAME
"___ fired!": 5 YOURE
Firedog: 7 ANDIRON
Firedome: 6 DESOTO
Firefighter: 5 HOSER 7 RESCUER
fixture: 7 HYDRANT
need: 4 HOSE
protection: 7 GASMASK
tool: 3 AXE 7 BROADAX
~ Red: 5 **ADAIR**
Firehouse
Used a ~ pole: 4 SLID
Firenze
Info: Italian cue
farewell: 4 CIAO
friends: 5 AMICI
land: 6 ITALIA
Fireplace: 5 INGLE
accessory: 7 ANDIRON
adjunct: 6 MANTEL
fill: 4 LOGS
floor: 6 HEARTH
frame: 5 GRATE 6 MANTEL
glower: 5 EMBER
Like a: 4 ASHY
projection: 3 HOB
receptacle: 6 ASHPIT

residue: 3 ASH 5 ASHES
shelf: 3 HOB 6 MANTEL
tool: 5 POKER
Firepower
Exceed in: 6 OUTGUN
Fireproof
material: 8 ASBESTOS
Fireside: 6 HEARTH
chat medium: 5 RADIO
Firewood
measure: 4 CORD 5 STERE
Firework
Revolving: 8 PINWHEEL
Fireworks
Big name in: 6 GRUCCI
cries: 3 AHS 4 OOHS
Firing
It does a lot of: 6 NEURON
place: 4 KILN 5 RANGE
squad (abbr.): 3 NRA
Unlawful: 5 ARSON
Firm: 3 SET 5 SOLID 7 ALDENTE
        STAUNCH
and fresh: 5 CRISP
Be: 6 INSIST
head: 4 EXEC PRES
Just ~ enough: 7 ALDENTE
Law ~ employee: 4 PARA
Stand: 6 INSIST RESIST
Stood: 4 HELD
up: 3 GEL
___ firma: 5 **TERRA**
Firmament: 3 SKY
Firmer-upper
Facial: 5 TONER
Firm-fleshed
pear: 5 ANJOU
Firmly
Declare: 4 AVER
Fix: 4 MOOR 5 EMBED
        IMBED RIVET
        8 ENSCONCE
Hold: 4 GRIP
Imprint: 4 ETCH
Plant: 5 EMBED
State: 4 **AVER**
Stick: 6 ADHERE
Firms
(abbr.): 3 COS

First: 4 BASE GEAR 6 PRIMAL
        7 INITIAL ORDINAL
and second: 8 ORDINALS
appearance: 5 DEBUT ONSET
At: 6 ONBASE
At ~ (abbr.): 4 ORIG
born: 4 CAIN 6 ELDEST OLDEST
cardinal: 3 ONE
claim: 4 DIBS
coat: 6 PRIMER
Come in: 3 WIN
course: 4 SOUP 5 PLANA SALAD
Finish: 3 WIN
follower: 3 AID
game: 6 OPENER
garden: 4 EDEN
Go: 5 START
home: 4 EDEN
in a series: 5 ALPHA
In ~ place: 5 AHEAD ONTOP
It's a: 8 PREMIERE
light: 4 DAWN
Make the ~ bid: 4 OPEN
man: 4 ADAM
man, to Polynesians: 4 TIKI
mate: 3 **EVE** 4 ADAM
miracle site: 4 CANA
of all: 4 ADAM
of December: 3 DEE
of September: 3 ESS
person, in German: 3 ICH
place: 4 **EDEN**
Play: 4 LEAD
Played: 3 LED
Ran: 3 LED
Show for the ~ time: 6 UNVEIL
sign: 5 ARIES
state (abbr.): 3 DEL
strategy: 5 PLANA
to be called: 4 ONEA
to be counted: 4 EENY
Took: 3 WON
to putt: 4 AWAY
victim: 4 ABEL
video game: 4 PONG
Went: 3 LED 6 LEDOFF
X: 3 TIC
~, in German: 4 ERST
First ___: 3 AID 4 BASE GEAR

"First ___, The": 4 NOEL
First-aid
  item: 6 IODINE
  provider: 5 MEDIC
First Amendment
  defenders: 4 ACLU
"First Blood"
  director Kotcheff: 3 TED
  hero: 5 RAMBO
Firstborn: 6 ELDEST OLDEST
  Genesis: 4 CAIN
  Ingrid's: 3 PIA
  Isaac's: 4 ESAU
First-century
  emperor: 4 NERO
First-class: 3 ACE 4 AONE 5 ELITE
        PRIMO 6 GRADEA
  Not: 5 COACH
First Daughter
  1970s ~: 3 AMY
  1990s ~: 7 CHELSEA
First Dog
  ~, once: 4 FALA
First-draft: 8 UNEDITED
First-grade
  attention-getter: 4 MEME
First Lady: 3 **EVE**
  1940s ~: 4 BESS 7 ELEANOR
  1950s ~: 5 MAMIE
  after Hillary: 5 LAURA
  before Eleanor: 3 LOU
  before Mamie: 4 BESS
  First: 6 MARTHA
  in 1900: 3 IDA
  of Harry: 4 BESS
  of jazz: 4 ELLA
  Second: 7 ABIGAIL
"First Lady of Song": 4 ELLA
First name
  at Gettysburg: 3 ABE
  at the Fed: 4 ALAN
  at Woodstock: 4 ARLO JIMI
  Dickensian: 5 URIAH
  Dog star's: 3 RIN
  in 1950s TV: 4 DESI
  in 1970s tennis: 4 ILIE
  in 1970s TV comedy: 4 REDD
  in 2000 news: 5 ELIAN
  in advice: 3 ANN
  in animation: 4 WALT
  in architecture: 4 **EERO** 5 ELIEL
  in aviation: 6 AMELIA
  in bridge: 4 OMAR
  in clowns: 6 RONALD
  in coaching: 3 ARA
  in comedy: 3 EMO
  in Communism: 4 KARL
  in conducting: 6 ARTURO
  in cooking: 6 EMERIL
  in cosmetics: 5 **ESTEE** MERLE
  in country: 4 **REBA**
  in courtroom fiction: 4 ERLE
  in crooning: 4 BING
  in dance: 7 ISADORA
  in daredeviltry: 4 **EVEL**
  in daytime TV: 5 OPRAH
  in despotism: 3 IDI
  in diaries: 5 ANAIS
  in espionage: 4 MATA
  in exiles: 3 IDI
  in exploration: 7 AMERIGO
  in fashion: 3 LIZ 4 COCO **OLEG**
        YVES
  in game shows: 4 ALEX MERV
        5 REGIS
  in gins: 3 ELI
  in gospel: 7 MAHALIA
  in gossip: 4 RONA
  in gymnastics: 4 OLGA 5 NADIA
  in horror: 3 **LON** WES 4 BELA
        BRAM 6 FREDDY
  in humor: 4 **ERMA**
  in jazz: 4 **ELLA**
  in jeans: 4 LEVI
  in late-night TV: 5 CONAN
  in lexicography: 4 NOAH
  in linguistics: 4 NOAM
  in modern dance: 5 TWYLA
  in mysteries: 4 **ERLE** 6 AGATHA
  in one-liners: 5 HENNY
  in photography: 5 ANSEL
  in puppetry: 5 SHARI
  in rock: 5 ELTON
  in scat: 4 **ELLA**
  in shoes: 6 IMELDA
  in Solidarity: 4 LECH
  in soul: 6 ARETHA
  in spydom: 4 MATA

in stunts: 4 **EVEL**
in swashbuckling: 5 ERROL
in swing: 5 ARTIE
in talk: 5 CONAN ELLEN
   OPRAH REGIS ROSIE
   6 MONTEL
in tyranny: 3 IDI
in westerns: 5 CLINT
in whodunits: 4 ERLE
of Fergie: 5 SARAH
Whale: 4 MOBY
___ first-name basis: 3 ONA
First-place: 4 BEST GOLD
First-rate: 3 ACE DEF TIP TOP
    4 ACES **AONE** BEST NEAT
    TOPS 5 PRIME PRIMO
    6 CHOICE CLASSA TIPTOP
    7 STELLAR
First-stringer: 7 STARTER
First-stringers: 5 **ATEAM**
"First Time Ever ___ Your Face,
   The": 4 ISAW
"First Wives' Club, The"
  actress: 4 HAWN
  members: 4 EXES
First word
  Baby's: 4 DADA
  Giant's: 3 FEE
  in a fairy tale: 4 ONCE
  in Massachusetts' motto: 4 ENSE
First-year
  cadet: 5 PLEBE
  law student: 4 ONEL
  student: 5 FROSH
"___ first you don't ...": 4 **IFAT**
Firth of Clyde
  island: 5 ARRAN
  port: 3 AYR
Firth of Tay
  port: 6 DUNDEE
Fiscal
  exec: 3 CFO
  Fed. ~ agency: 3 OMB
  period: 4 YEAR
Fischer
  forte: 5 CHESS
  opponent: 7 SPASSKY
Fish: 5 ANGLE GROPE
  Aquarium: 5 DANIO GUPPY

NEONS **TETRA** 6 TETRAS
   9 NEONTETRA
Atlantic: 3 COD 4 SCUP
   6 TARPON
bait: 4 WORM
basket: 5 CREEL
Bony: 6 TARPON
Brunch: 3 LOX
catcher: 3 NET
caught in a pot: 3 EEL
Caviar: 6 BELUGA
Colorful: 4 NEON **OPAH**
   5 TETRA
Curtainlike ~ catcher:
   7 GILLNET
delicacy: 3 EEL
dish: 3 COD 4 SOLE 5 SCROD
Disney: 4 NEMO
Dover: 4 SOLE
Drink like a: 4 TOPE
eggs: 3 **ROE**
Electrified: 3 **EEL**
Fast: 6 DARTER
feature: 4 GILL
Filleted: 4 SHAD SOLE
Film: 4 NEMO 5 WANDA
fin: 6 DORSAL
finder: 5 SONAR
Finless: 3 EEL
Flat: 3 RAY 4 SOLE
Flexible: 3 EEL
Food: 3 COD 4 BASS CARP LING
   PIKE SHAD SOLE 5 SMELT
   7 HALIBUT SEABASS
fooler: 4 BAIT
for: 4 SEEK
Future: 3 **ROE**
Game: 4 BASS CERO TUNA
   5 TROUT 6 MARLIN
   TARPON
Go: 5 ANGLE
Go ~ request: 5 NINES
Great Lakes: 4 CHUB
Group of: 6 SCHOOL
hawk: 6 **OSPREY**
Herringlike: 4 SHAD
holder: 4 TANK 5 CREEL
   6 KETTLE
hook: 4 GAFF

in a tin: **7** SARDINE
ladder setting: **3** DAM
Land a: **6** REELIN
Like sushi: **3** RAW
Like ~ sticks: **7** BREADED
Long: **3** EEL
Long-snouted: **3** **GAR**
market feature: **4** ODOR
Melt: **4** TUNA
Migratory: **3** EEL **4** SHAD
Needle-nosed: **3** GAR
order: **5** FILET
Place to: **6** STREAM
Pond: **4** CARP
propeller: **3** FIN
Puffer: **4** FUGU
Rainbow: **5** TROUT
Red: **3** TAI **7** SNAPPER
Salad: **4** TUNA
Sandwich: **4** TUNA
Scaleless: **3** EEL
Side dish with: **4** SLAW
Silvery: **5** **SMELT**
Slippery: **3** **EEL**
Small: **3** FRY **4** DACE
Snakelike: **3** **EEL**
Sound at a ~ fry: **3** SSS
spawn: **3** ROE
Spawning: **3** EEL **4** SHAD
story: **3** LIE **4** TALE YARN
story suffix: **3** EST
Striped: **4** BASS
Sucker: **6** REMORA
Sushi: **3** **EEL**
that's big enough: **6** KEEPER
Toothy: **3** GAR
Tropical: **4** SCAD **5** TETRA
Winter: **4** SHAD
with a net: **5** SEINE TRAWL
Wriggly: **3** EEL
"Fish Called Wanda, A"
actor John: **6** CLEESE
actor Kevin: **5** KLINE
actor Michael: **5** PALIN
Oscar winner: **5** KLINE
Fish-eating
bird: **3** ERN **4** ERNE
duck: **4** SMEW
hawk: **6** OSPREY

Fisher
Feathered: **6** OSPREY
Flying: **3** ERN **4** ERNE
known as "The Long Island
    Lolita": **3** AMY
Long-legged: **5** HERON
Singer: **5** EDDIE
Fisher, Avery
field: **4** HIFI
___ **Fisher Hall: 5** AVERY
Fisherman: 6 ANGLER BAITER
    REELER
A ~ may spin one: **4** TALE
Certain: **5** EELER
hook: **4** GAFF
lure: **4** BAIT
signal: **4** BITE
wear: **6** WADERS
Fish-foul
connector: **3** NOR
Fishhook
attachment: **5** **SNELL**
feature: **4** BARB
Iron: **4** GAFF
Fishing
boots: **6** WADERS
gear: **3** NET **4** LURE NETS
    REEL RODS **5** LURES
    6 TACKLE
Go: **5** ANGLE
hole: **4** POND
hook: **4** GAFF
Kind of: **7** DEEPSEA
Let out a ~ line: **6** UNREEL
line: **5** SNELL
locale: **4** LAKE PIER **5** CREEK
    WHARF **6** STREAM
need: **3** ROD **4** POLE
net: **5** SEINE TRAWL
Out: **4** ASEA
pole: **3** ROD
Primitive ~ tool: **5** SPEAR
reel winder: **5** SPOOL
Revolving ~ lure: **7** SPINNER
rod attachment: **4** REEL
Start: **4** CAST
Fishline
adjunct: **4** LURE
hangup: **4** SNAG

"Fish Magic"
  painter: 4 KLEE
Fishnet: 4 MESH
Fishtail: 3 YAW 4 SKID
Fishy
  It may be: 4 ODOR
  sign: 6 PISCES
  yarn: 4 TALE
Fisk, Carlton
  nickname: 5 PUDGE
Fissile
  rock: 5 SHALE
Fission
  Nuclear ~ discoverer Otto:
      4 HAHN
  subject: 4 ATOM
Fissure: 4 GASH RENT RIFT
      5 CLEFT CRACK
  Deep: 5 CHASM
Fist: 4 DUKE
  Hit with a: 4 SLUG
  part: 7 KNUCKLE
  Tighten, as a: 6 CLENCH
  Word with: 4 IRON
Fistfight: 5 SETTO
  result: 6 SHINER
"Fistful of Dollars, A"
  director: 5 LEONE
Fists
  Fight with: 3 BOX
Fit: 4 **ABLE** HALE TRIM 5 ADAPT
      SPASM 6 PROPER SUITED
      7 INSHAPE
  Adjust to: 5 ADAPT
  Angry: 4 HUFF
  as a fiddle: 4 HALE
  Check for: 5 **TRYON**
  for a king: 4 POSH 5 NOBLE
      REGAL ROYAL
  for consumption: 6 EDIBLE
  for cultivation: 6 ARABLE
  for drafting: 4 ONEA
  for farming: 6 ARABLE
  for sainthood: 4 HOLY
  for service: 4 ONEA
  Fully: 4 ABLE
  Get to: 5 ADAPT
  Hissy: 4 SNIT
  in: 6 BELONG

  It's ~ for a queen: 5 TIARA
  It's ~ to be tied: 8 SNEAKERS
  Kind of: 5 HISSY
  Make: 5 ADAPT ALTER
      6 TAILOR
  Not: 5 UNAPT
  of agitation: 4 SNIT
  of fever: 4 AGUE
  of pique: 4 SNIT
  of wrath: 4 RAGE
  one inside another: 4 NEST
  out: 3 RIG 5 EQUIP
  Shivering: 4 AGUE
  Snit: 5 ANGER
  Test for: 5 TRYON
  Think: 5 DEIGN
  Throw a: 4 RAGE
  to be tied: 3 MAD 5 **IRATE** LIVID
      RILED 7 INARAGE
      STEAMED
  to be tried: 4 SANE
  together: 4 MESH NEST
  Trim to: 4 EDIT
  up against: 6 BUTTTO
  well: 4 MESH
  within: 6 NESTED
  ___ fit: 4 HADA
Fit ___ fiddle: 3 ASA
Fitness: 6 HEALTH
  center: 3 **SPA**
  Muscular: 4 TONE
Fitting: 3 **APT** DUE 4 MEET
      5 RIGHT TRYON
      7 APROPOS
  As is: 4 DULY
  End of a ~ phrase: 4 ATEE
  In a ~ manner: 5 APTLY
  Not: 5 INAPT UNAPT
Fit to ___: 4 ATEE
Fitzgerald
  Singer: 4 **ELLA**
  specialty: 4 SCAT
Fitzgerald, F. Scott
  Wife of: 5 ZELDA
Five
  centimes: 3 SOU
  cents a minute, say: 4 RATE
  Change for a: 4 ONES
  Cleveland: 4 CAVS

Group of: **6** PENTAD
Having ~ sharps: **3** INB
High: **4** SLAP
hundred sheets: **4** REAM
in front: **5** PENTA
iron: **6** MASHIE
It follows four but not: **4** TEEN
New Jersey: **4** NETS
One of: **5** QUINT SENSE
prefix: **5** PENTA
Take: **4 REST 5** RELAX
word form: **5** PENTA
~, in French: **4** CINQ
Five-alarm
  item: **5** CHILI
Five-alarmer: 5 BLAZE
Five-dollar
  bill: **3** FIN
"Five Guys Named ___": 3 MOE
Five-line
  verse: **8** LIMERICK
Five Nations
  tribe: **6** ONEIDA SENECA
Five o'clock shadow: 7 STUBBLE
  remover: **5** RAZOR
Fiver: 3 FIN
  Face on a: **3** ABE
Fivescore
  yrs.: **3** CEN
Five-spot: 3 FIN
Five-star
  name: **4** OMAR
Five-time
  Derby winner: **6** ARCARO
    7 HARTACK
  Wimbledon champ: **4 BORG**
Five W's
  One of the: **3** WHO WHY **4** WHAT
    WHEN **5** WHERE
Fix: 3 JAM PUT RIG SET **4** CURE
    DARN MEND MESS REDO
    SPAY **5** ALTER AMEND
    DEBUG EMBED EMEND
    6 DEFINE REMEDY
    REPAIR SCRAPE
  a loose lace: **5** RETIE
  a road: **5** RETAR
  a seam: **3** SEW
  a squeak: **3** OIL

deeply: **5** EMBED **7** INGRAIN
feathers: **5** PREEN
firmly: **4** MOOR **5** EMBED RIVET
  8 ENSCONCE
illegally: **3** RIG
program problems: **5** DEBUG
Start to: **3** PRE
Temporary: **7** STOPGAP
text: **4** EDIT
the fairway: **5** RESOD
the soundtrack: **5** REDUB
They ~ locks: **6** SALONS
up: **4** MEND **REDO 5** REHAB
~, as a fight: **3** RIG
Fixate: 6 OBSESS
___ fixe: 4 IDEE PRIX
Fixed: 3 SET **5** RIGID **6** INTENT
    REDONE
  by an ed.: **4** CORR
  charge: **3** FEE **4** RATE
  chicken: **5** CAPON
  look: **4** GAZE **5** STARE
  Not: **7** MOVABLE **8** MOVEABLE
  quantity: **4** UNIT
  They may be: **6** ASSETS
  up: **6** REDONE
Fixer
  Boxer: **3** VET
  Flat: **5** SUPER
  Piano: **5** TUNER
Fixer-upper: 8 REPAIRER
Fizz
  Add ~ to: **6** AERATE
  ingredient: **7** SLOEGIN
  producer: **4** SODA
Fizzle
  out: **3** DIE
  sound: **3** SSS
Fizzler: 3 DUD
Fizzless: 4 FLAT
Fizzling-out
  sound: **4** PFFT
Fizzy
  drink: **4** COLA SODA
  Make: **6** AERATE
  No longer: **4** FLAT
  prefix: **3** AER
Fjord: 5 INLET
  Capital on a: **4 OSLO**

kin: **3** RIA
land (abbr.): **4** ICEL

Fla.
It borders: **3** ALA ATL
Living in ~, maybe: **4** RETD

Flabbergast: 3 AWE **4** DAZE **STUN**
5 AMAZE FLOOR SHOCK
7 ASTOUND

Flabby
Not: **5** TONED

Flaccid: 4 LIMP
flesh: **4** FLAB

Flack
forte: **4** SPIN

Flag: 3 SAG **4** FADE IRIS TIRE
WANE **6** COLORS
British: **9** UNIONJACK
Common ~ feature: **4** STAR
Country with a blue, black, and
white: **7** ESTONIA
down: **4** HAIL
holder: **4** POLE
Open a: **6** UNFURL
Red: **5** ALERT
Roll up a: **4** FURL
tosser: **3** REF
Verbal white: **5** UNCLE
waver: **4** WIND
White ~ message: **5** TRUCE

Flagmaker
Betsy: **4** ROSS

Flagon
filler: **3** ALE

Flagrant: 5 GROSS

Flagstaff
sch.: **3** NAU
setting: **7** ARIZONA

Flagston, Mrs.
of the comics: **4** LOIS

Flaherty
man: **4** ARAN

Flair: 4 BENT **ELAN 5** ECLAT
KNACK STYLE **6** PIZAZZ
TALENT
Musical: **3** EAR
of wrestling: **3** RIC

Flake: 4 CHIP KOOK PEEL
5 WACKO **6** WEIRDO
10 SPACECADET

Feedbag: **3** OAT
material: **4** BRAN

Flakes
Falling: **4** SNOW
Fireplace: **5** ASHES

Flaky
dessert: **3** PIE
mineral: **4 MICA**
pastry: **4** FILO

Flamboyance: 4 ELAN
7 PANACHE

Flamboyant
pianist: **8** LIBERACE
~ Flynn: **5** ERROL

Flame
Burn without: **7** SMOLDER
follower: **4** MOTH
Rick's: **4** ILSA

Flamenco
cheer: **3** OLE
clicker: **8** CASTANET

Flames
In: **5 AFIRE 6** ABLAZE
Old: **4** EXES
Stand in the: **4** PYRE

Flamethrower
fuel: **6** NAPALM

Flaming: 5 AFIRE
felony: **5** ARSON

Flamingo
color: **4** PINK

Flammable
garment: **3** BRA
gas: **6** ETHANE ETHENE
jelly: **6** STERNO

Flanders
fields flower: **5** POPPY
of fiction: **4** MOLL
river: **4** YSER

"___ Flanders": 4 MOLL

Flanders, Rod
Dad of: **3** NED

Flange: 3 RIM

Flanged
girder: **5** IBEAM

Flank
alternative: **5** TBONE

Flannel
makeup: **4** WOOL

Flap: 3 **ADO** TAB 4 BEAT SNIT
SPAT STIR TODO
Cap: 6 EARLAP
Home with a ~ door: 5 TEPEE
Jacket: 5 LAPEL
Public: 5 SCENE
Flapjack: 7 PANCAKE
Fancy: 5 CREPE
flipper: 7 SPATULA
franchise: 4 IHOP
Flapper
Cartoon: 4 BOOP
hairdo: 3 BOB
wrapper: 3 BOA
Flare: 5 FUSEE
Dress with a: 5 ALINE
Kind of: 5 SOLAR
Flareup
of crime: 5 ARSON
Flash: 3 SEC 4 IDEA JIFF
7 INSTANT
in the can: 6 GORDON
light: 6 STROBE
Mental: 4 IDEA
of brilliance: 4 IDEA
of light: 5 GLEAM GLINT
point: 6 CAMERA
Radar screen: 4 BLIP
___ flash: 3 INA
Flashback
causer: 3 LSD
"Flashdance"
singer Irene: 4 CARA
song: 6 MANIAC
star Jennifer: 5 BEALS
Flashed
sign: 3 VEE
Flasher
Disco: 6 STROBE
on the Strip: 4 NEON
Flashing
lights: 6 ALERTS 7 STROBES
Flashlight
British: 5 TORCH
carrier: 5 USHER
Flashy: 5 GAUDY 6 SPORTY
car accessories: 4 MAGS
display: 10 RAZZMATAZZ
flower: 5 PEONY

outfit: 8 ZOOTSUIT
Flask
Drink from a: 4 SWIG
filler: 5 BOOZE
Vacuum ~ inventor: 5 DEWAR
___ flask: 5 DEWAR
Flat: 4 EVEN TWOD 5 LEVEL
PRONE 6 PLANAR
7 INSIPID
agreement: 5 LEASE
B ~: 6 ASHARP
Bee: 4 HIVE
cleaner: 4 CHAR
D ~: 6 CSHARP
dweller: 6 LESSEE
fee: 4 RENT
fish: 3 RAY 4 SOLE
fixer: 5 PATCH SUPER
floater: 4 RAFT
Go: 3 LIE
hat: 3 TAM 5 BERET
Having one: 3 INF
High ~ area: 4 MESA
in ads: 3 APT
key material: 5 EBONY
Knock: 4 DECK
land: 7 PRAIRIE
Leave: 6 DESERT
Lying: 5 PRONE
Neither sharp nor: 5 ONKEY
on one's back: 6 SUPINE
payment: 4 RENT
rate: 4 RENT
replacement: 5 SPARE
sharer: 6 ROOMIE
sign: 5 TOLET
sound: 3 SSS 4 SSSS
spot: 4 MESA
surface: 5 PLANE
They pay a ~ rate: 6 RENTER
Where the world is: 3 MAP
Word after: 4 RATE
Flatboat: 4 SCOW
Old: 3 ARK
Flat-bottomed
boat: 4 DORY **SCOW** 5 BARGE
Flatbush
Duke of: 6 SNIDER
Flatfish: 4 SOLE 6 PLAICE

Flat-fixing
  tool: 8 TIREIRON
Flatfoot: 3 COP
  lack: 4 ARCH
Flatow
  Host: 3 IRA
Flat ___ pancake: 3 ASA
Flats
  Key with no ~ or sharps:
      6 AMINOR
  Level: 4 RASE
Flatt
  Bluegrass musician: 6 LESTER
Flat-tasting: 5 BLAND
Flatten: 4 DECK IRON KAYO
      MASH RAZE 5 PRESS
      6 LAYLOW
  ~, in Britain: 4 RASE
Flattened: 6 OBLATE
  circle: 4 OVAL
Flattener
  Fly: 7 SWATTER
Flattens: 3 KOS
Flatter: 7 IMITATE
  servilely: 7 ADULATE
Flattering: 6 SMARMY
  deception: 7 SNOWJOB
Flattery
  False: 5 SMARM
Flattop: 7 CARRIER
  letters: 3 USS
Flat-topped
  hill: 4 **MESA** 5 BUTTE
Flaubert
  birthplace: 5 ROUEN
  character: 6 BOVARY
  heroine: 4 EMMA
Flaunt: 6 PARADE
Flavius
  Foot, to: 3 PES
Flavor: 5 SAPOR TASTE
  Absinthe: 5 ANISE
  Amaretto: 6 ALMOND
  Brandy: 4 PEAR 7 APRICOT
  Coffee: 5 MOCHA
  Distinctive: 4 TANG
  Dressing: 5 RANCH
  enhancer: 3 MSG 4 SALT
  Fudge: 5 MAPLE

  Gin: 4 SLOE
  Half a: 5 TUTTI
  Ice cream: 4 OREO 5 PECAN
  Jelly: 5 GUAVA
  Jelly bean: 8 LICORICE
  Nectar: 4 PEAR
  Nehi: 5 GRAPE
  Pernod: 5 ANISE
  Pop: 4 COLA
  Popsicle: 6 ORANGE
  Potato chip: 3 BBQ
  Sharp: 3 NIP 4 TANG
  Soda: 4 COLA 5 GRAPE
  Syrup: 5 MAPLE
  Tangy pie: 5 LEMON
  Tropical: 5 MANGO
Flavorer
  Amaretto: 6 ALMOND
  Crème: 6 MENTHE
  Liqueur: 5 ANISE 7 ANISEED
Flavorful: 5 SAPID TANGY TASTY
Flavoring
  Bagel: 6 SESAME
  Biscotto: 5 ANISE
  Brandy: 7 APRICOT
  Cat food: 4 TUNA
  Chef's: 4 HERB
  Coffee: 5 MOCHA
  Cordial: 5 **ANISE**
  Cream soda: 7 VANILLA
  French cordial: 4 ANIS
  Gimlet: 4 LIME
  Gin: 4 **SLOE**
  Julep: 4 MINT
  Licorice: 5 **ANISE**
  Ouzo: 5 **ANISE** 7 ANISEED
  Soup: 4 DILL MISO
Flaw: 4 WART 6 DEFECT
  Diamond: 5 ERROR
  Face: 3 ZIT
  Fairway: 5 DIVOT
  Faucet: 4 DRIP LEAK
  Fender: 4 DENT
  Fruit: 6 BRUISE
  Logical: 4 HOLE
  LP: 4 SKIP
  Surfboard: 4 DING
  Upholstery: 3 RIP
  Without a: 5 IDEAL

Flawed
~, as mdse.: **3** IRR
Flaws
Like some: **6** TRAGIC
Flax
fabric: **5** LINEN
Soak: **3** RET
Flaxlike
fiber: **5** RAMIE
Flea: **4** PEST
Fleabag
Like a: **5** SEEDY
Flea market
find: **5** CURIO
warning: **4** ASIS
Fleck: **4** SPOT
Banjoist: **4** BELA
Fled: **3** RAN
Fledgling: **4** TYRO
Barn: **5** OWLET
pigeon: **5** SQUAB
Flee: **3** LAM
to wed: **5** ELOPE
Unable to: **5** ATBAY
Fleece: **3** CON ROB **4** BILK CLIP
MILK ROOK SCAM SKIN
5 SHEAR
Fine: **5** LLAMA
Made from: **6** WOOLEN
ship: **4** ARGO
Fleeced: **5** SHORN
They get: **4** EWES
Fleecy
babe: **4** LAMB
female: **3** EWE
Fleeing: **8** ONTHELAM
Fleet: **4** FAST NAVY **5** RAPID
6 ARMADA SPEEDY
Far from: **4** POKY
fleet: **4** SSTS
letters: **3** USS
member: **4** TAXI
One of a 15th-century:
4 NINA
Street: **4** CABS
WWII: **3** RAF
~ VIP: **3** ADM
FleetCenter
player: **4** CELT

Fleeting
fashion: **3** FAD
trace: **4** WISP
Fleetwood ___ : **3** MAC
Fleetwoods, The: **4** TRIO
1959 #1 hit for ~: **6** MRBLUE
Flegenheimer, Arthur
Gangster: **12** DUTCHSCHULTZ
Fleischer
Boxing historian: **3** NAT
Bush spokesman: **3** **ARI**
Fleming
Actress: **6** RHONDA
Author: **3** **IAN**
Soprano: **5** RENEE
villain: **4** DRNO
Flesh
and blood: **3** KIN
Flaccid: **4** FLAB
In the: **4** LIVE
Pound of: **4** DEBT
Fleshy
fruit: **4** PEAR POME **5** PAPAW
mushroom: **3** CEP
part: **4** JOWL
Fleshy-leafed
plant: **4** ALOE
Fleshy-snouted
beast: **5** TAPIR
Fletcher
product: **5** ARROW
Fleur-___ : **5** DELYS
Fleur-de-___ : **3** **LIS** LYS
Flew: **4** SPED TORE **7** AVIATED
alone: **6** SOLOED
Flex: **4** BEND
suffix: **4** IBLE
Flexed
It may be: **6** BICEPS
Flexibility: **4** GIVE PLAY
Show: **4** BEND **5** ADAPT
Flexible: **5** AGILE LITHE
6 LIMBER PLIANT
7 ELASTIC
armor: **9** CHAINMAIL
Electrically: **4** ACDC
fish: **3** EEL
mineral: **4** MICA
Most: **7** LOOSEST

response: **6** EITHER
schedule part: **8** OPENDATE
wood: **3** YEW
Flexible Flyer: 4 SLED
Flick: 3 PIC **5** MOVIE
Hot: **3** ASH
Local ~ shower: **4** NABE
Mix: **5** OATER
Flicks: 3 PIX
Like horror: **4** GORY
"___ fliegende Holländer": 3 DER
Flier
Andean: **6** CONDOR
Bar: **4** DART
Coastal: **3** ERN **4** ERNE
Coop: **7** ESCAPEE
Fabled: **3** ROC
Fast: **3** JET **SST**
Fork-tailed: **4** TERN
Frequent: **4** BIRD
Grounded: **3** SST
Hawaiian: **4** NENE
Ill-fated: **6** ICARUS
Israeli: **4** ELAL
Mythical: **3** ROC
Night: **3** OWL **4** MOTH
Pesky: **4 GNAT**
seat choice: **5** AISLE
Swedish: **3** SAS
Tabloid: **3** UFO
Tailed: **4** KITE
Fliers
Brit.: **3** RAF
Formation: **5** GEESE
Mil.: **4** USAF
WWII: **3** RAF
Flies: 5 PESTS
Chase: **4** SHAG
Dangerous: **7** TSETSES
in the face of: **6** DEFIES
Small: **5** GNATS
without a motor: **6** GLIDES
"Flies, The"
playwright: **6** SARTRE
Flight: 3 LAM 4 WING
board abbr.: **3** ARR ETA
component: **5** STAIR
Connecting: **9** STAIRCASE
coordinators (abbr.): **3** ATC

data: **4** ETAS
Designed for: **4** AERO
Expensive: **3** SST
formation: **3** VEE
from justice: **3** LAM
Hasty: **3** LAM
Incoming ~ info: **3** ETA
Night: **6** REDEYE
part: **4** STEP **5** RISER STAIR
Post in a: **5** NEWEL
Short: **3** HOP
stat.: **3** ALT
student's test: **4** SOLO
Take: **4** SOAR
Take ~ to unite: **5** ELOPE
Flight-board
abbr.: **3** ARR
Flightless
bird: **3 EMU 4** KIWI RHEA
bird (var.): **4** EMEU
Extinct ~ bird: **3** MOA
Flights
First name in: **6** AMELIA
Like many JFK: **4** INTL
Like some: **6** SPIRAL
7 NONSTOP
Flighty
Far from: **5** STAID
Flimflam: 3 CON GYP **4** FOOL
SCAM **5** BUNCO **6** CONJOB
EUCHRE FAKERY
"Flim ___ Man, The": 4 FLAM
Flimsy
~, as an excuse: **4** LAME
Flinch: 5 REACT START WINCE
Fling: 4 CAST HURL TOSS
5 SPREE
with effort: **5** HEAVE
Flintstone
Mr.: **4** FRED
Mrs.: **5** WILMA
yell part: **5** DABBA YABBA
"Flintstones, The"
boss: **5** SLATE
pet: **4** DINO
setting: **8** STONEAGE
wife: **5** WILMA
Flip: 4 PERT TOSS **5** EVERT
GOAPE SASSY UPEND

6 INVERT LOSEIT RESELL
  7 REVERSE
and bob: **3** DOS
Coin: **4** TOSS
out: **4** SNAP **5** GOAPE **6** LOSEIT
  8 HAVEACOW
over: **5** ADORE UPEND
  6 INVERT
response: **5** HEADS TAILS
  7 SOSUEME
Something to: **3** LID
through: **4** SCAN
Flip ___: 5 ACOIN
Flip-chart
  stand: **5** EASEL
Flip-flop: 5 THONG UTURN
  6 SANDAL
  Wearing a: **4** SHOD
Flippant: 4 PERT **5** SASSY SAUCY
Flipped: 7 WENTAPE
  Heads: **5** TAILS
  It may be: **3** LID
Flipper: 3 FIN **7** ACROBAT
  SPATULA **8** FORELIMB
Flippered
  animal: **4** SEAL **7** SEALION
Flirt: 5 TEASE
  badly: **4** OGLE
  signal: **4** WINK
Flirtatious
  overture: **4** PASS
  signal: **4** WINK
  sort: **4** MINX
  stare: **4** OGLE
Flit: 3 GAD
___ Flite (bicycle brand): 4 AERO
Flo
  TV boss of: **3** MEL
Float: 3 BOB **4** BUOY RAFT WAFT
  base: **4** COLA
  ingredient: **8** ICECREAM
    ROOTBEER
  material: **5** BALSA
Float ___ (finance): 5 ALOAN
Floater
  Arctic: **4** BERG
  Flat: **4** RAFT
  Genesis: **3** ARK
  Pond: **4** ALGA

Floating: 4 ASEA **6** NATANT
  Go for ~ apples: **3** BOB
  zoo: **3** ARK
"Float like a butterfly"
  boxer: **3** ALI
Flock: 4 BEVY **5** COVEY DROVE
  female: **3** EWE
  Flightless: **4** EMUS
  head (abbr.): **3** REV
  holder: **3** PEW
  leader: **3** RAM **6** PASTOR PRIEST
  Leave the: **5** STRAY
  member: **3** EWE RAM
  Of the: **4** LAIC
  place: **3** LEA
  Sea: **5** ERNES
  sound: **3** BAA
Flockhart
  Actress: **7** CALISTA
  role: **6** MCBEAL
Flog: 4 CANE LASH WHIP
  6 THRASH
Flo-Jo
  alma mater: **4** UCLA
Flood: 5 SPATE **6** DELUGE
  7 TORRENT **8** ACTOFGOD
    INUNDATE
  barrier: **5** LEVEE
  prevention: **3** DAM **4** DIKE
  refuge: **3** ARK
  survivor: **4** NOAH
Flooded: 5 AWASH
Floodgate: 3 DAM **6** SLUICE
Flooding
  factor: **4** TIDE
Flooey
  lead-in: **3** KER
Floor: 4 STUN **5** AMAZE NADIR
  STORY **7** ASTOUND
  8 ASTONISH
  Clean a tile: **7** DAMPMOP
  cleaner: **7** DUSTMOP
  covering: **3** MAT RUG **4** LINO
  7 AREARUG
  10 SHAGCARPET
  Fireplace: **6** HEARTH
  Food on the: **4** ALPO
  Hold the: **5** ORATE
  Interrupt on the dance: **5** CUTIN

it: **4** TEAR **5** SPEED
Japanese ~ covering: **6** TATAMI
layer: **5** TILER
model: **4** **DEMO**
Ocean: **6** SEABED
piece: **4** TILE
Some ~ votes: **4** NAYS
square: **4** TILE
Top: **5** ATTIC
worker: **5** TILER WAXER
 6 TRADER
Work on the: **6** RETILE
~, in French: **5** ETAGE

Floorboard
concealer: **7** AREARUG
sound: **5** CREAK

Floored: 5 INAWE
it: **4** SPED TORE

Flooring
calculation: **4** AREA
material: **3** OAK **4** TEAK **5** VINYL
Short: **4** LINO
square: **4** TILE

Floors: 3 KOS
Like some: **4** WAXY **5** TILED

Floozy: 4 TART

Flop: 3 DUD **4** BOMB BUST
Famed film: **6** ISHTAR
Ford: **5** EDSEL
Opposite of: **5** SMASH
prefix: **3** KER

Floppy: 4 DISK
Copy to a: **4** SAVE
filler: **4** DATA

Flora
and fauna: **4** LIFE **5** BIOTA
Desert: **5** CACTI
partner: **5** FAUNA
Unwanted: **5** WEEDS
Wrigley Field: **3** IVY

Floral
arrangement: **4** POSY **5** SPRAY
 7 COROLLA
fragrance: **5** ATTAR
leaf: **5** SEPAL
loop: **3** LEI

Florence
City near: **5** SIENA
flooder: **4** ARNO

river: **4** **ARNO**
ruling family: **6** MEDICI

Florentine
artist: **6** GIOTTO
attraction: **5** DAVID
family: **6** MEDICI
flower: **4** ARNO
poet: **5** DANTE
river: **4** ARNO

Florid: 3 RED **6** ORNATE
 ROCOCO
Far from: **5** ASHEN

Florida: 9 PENINSULA
Bush of: **3** JEB
Center of: **5** EPCOT
city: **5** **OCALA** TAMPA
city, for short: **4** BOCA
collegian: **5** GATOR
county: **4** DADE
explorer: **6** DESOTO
extension: **5** KEYS
footballer: **5** GATOR
football stadium:
 10 ORANGEBOWL
fruit: **6** ORANGE
island: **7** SANIBEL
islands: **4** KEYS
keys: **5** ISLES
port: **5** TAMPA
port, for short: **3** JAX
sea creature: **7** MANATEE
swinger: **4** CHAD
vacation area: **4** KEYS
~ ZIP code starter: **5** THREE

Florida State
player: **8** SEMINOLE
rival: **5** MIAMI

Florist
piece: **4** VASE
unit: **4** STEM

Floss
coating: **3** WAX
Kind of: **6** DENTAL

Flossing
advocacy gp.: **3** ADA

Flotilla: 6 ARMADA

Flounder
Future: **3** ROE
through water: **5** SLOSH

Flour
  factory: 4 MILL
  Future: 5 GRIST
  Kind of: 3 RYE SOY 6 FARINA
    or sugar: 6 STAPLE
  Prepare: 4 SIFT
Flourish: 5 BLOOM 6 THRIVE
    7 BLOSSOM
  Letter: 5 SERIF
  Signer: 8 CURLICUE
Flourless
  cake: 5 TORTE
Flout: 4 DEFY 6 DERIDE
Flouter
  Union: 4 SCAB
Flow: 6 STREAM
  back: 3 EBB
  Forceful: 5 SPATE
  Go with the: 5 ADAPT
  It goes with the: 4 LAVA
  out: 6 EFFUSE 7 EMANATE
  Outward: 3 EBB
  Partner of: 3 EBB
  Rhythmic: 7 CADENCE
  slowly: 4 OOZE **SEEP**
    7 TRICKLE
  Steady: 6 STREAM
  stoppage: 4 CLOT 6 STASIS
  stopper: 4 CLOG
  Volcanic: 4 LAVA
Flower: 4 POSY 5 BLOOM RIPEN
    6 MATURE 7 BLOSSOM
  base: 5 BRACT
  Bell-shaped: 4 SEGO 5 TULIP
  child: 4 SEED 6 HIPPIE
  Corsage: 6 ORCHID
  Daisylike: 5 ASTER
  Dutch: 5 TULIP
  Easter: 4 LILY
  Fall: 5 **ASTER**
  feature: 5 PETAL
  Flashy: 5 PEONY
  Fragrant: 7 TEAROSE
    8 GARDENIA
  Fresh: 5 DAISY
  Friend of: 5 BAMBI
  Funnel-shaped: 7 PETUNIA
  Garden: 4 IRIS 5 PANSY TULIP
    10 SNAPDRAGON

girl, perhaps: 5 NIECE
holder: 3 POT URN 4 STEM
  VASE 5 LAPEL
Imaginary eternal:
  8 AMARANTH
In full: 4 OPEN 6 ABLOOM
of one's eye: 4 IRIS
Ornamental: 6 DAHLIA
part: 4 STEM 5 CALYX OVARY
  PETAL **SEPAL** 6 ANTHER
  PISTIL RACEME STAMEN
  7 COROLLA
Purple: 5 LILAC
Red: 4 ROSE
shop letters: 3 FTD
Showy: 4 IRIS LILY ROSE
  5 ASTER CALLA CANNA
  PEONY PHLOX POPPY
  6 AZALEA DAHLIA
  7 ANEMONE 8 HIBISCUS
Showy ~, for short: 4 GLAD
site: 3 BED
Spring: 4 IRIS
stalk: 4 STEM
visitor: 3 BEE
"Flower Drum Song"
  actor: 3 SOO
Flowering: 6 ABLOOM
  7 INBLOOM
  shrub: 6 AZALEA SPIREA
"Flowering Peach, The"
  playwright: 5 ODETS
Flowerless
  plant: 4 FERN
Flowerlike
  polyp: 7 ANEMONE
"Flower of my heart": 7 ADELINE
Flowerpot
  spot: 4 SILL 5 LEDGE
Flowers
  Like: 7 PETALED
  Oil from: 5 ATTAR
**"... flowers that bloom in the
    spring, ___":** 5 TRALA
Flowery: 6 ORNATE
  greeting: 3 LEI
  verse: 3 ODE
"Flow gently, sweet ___": Burns:
  5 AFTON

Flowing
  Musically: 6 LEGATO
  tresses: 5 MANES
  ___ Flow, Scotland: 5 SCAPA
Fl. oz.
  ⅙ ~: 3 TSP
  Half a: 4 TBSP
Flu
  Down with the: 3 ILL
  fighter: 4 SHOT 5 SERUM
    6 HOTTEA
  fighters: 4 SERA
  Kind of: 5 ASIAN
  Like the: 5 VIRAL
  symptom: 4 ACHE **AGUE**
    5 FEVER
  ___ flu: 5 ASIAN
Flub: 3 ERR 5 ERROR MISDO
  Arcade: 4 TILT
Fluctuate: 4 VARY YOYO
Flue
  residue: 4 SOOT
Fluent: 4 GLIB
Fluff: 4 LINT
  up: 5 TEASE WHISK
Fluffy
  scarf: 3 BOA
  trio: 4 EFFS
Fluid
  ⅛ of a ~ ounce: 4 DRAM
  Antiknock: 5 ETHYL
  Battery: 4 ACID
  Blood: 5 SERUM
  container: 3 SAC
  rock: 4 LAVA
  Tree: 3 SAP
Fluidity
  unit: 3 RHE
Fluids: 4 **SERA**
Fluke: 8 ACCIDENT
Flummox: 4 FOOL 5 ADDLE
Flummoxed: 5 ATSEA 7 ATALOSS
Flung: 5 THREW
Flunk: 4 FAIL
Flunking
  letters: 3 EFS
Flunky: 4 AIDE 6 STOOGE
    YESMAN
  Corporate: 5 DRONE

  Frankenstein: 4 IGOR
  reply: 3 YES
Fluor-
  suffix: 3 IDE 4 ESCE
Fluorescent
  lamp filler: 5 ARGON
  paint: 6 DAYGLO
Fluoride
  prefix: 5 TETRA
Flurry: 3 **ADO**
Flush: 4 **EVEN** 5 COLOR LEVEL
    6 LOADED 7 REDNESS
    TURNRED 8 ROSINESS
Flushed: 3 **RED** 4 ROSY
  Hardly: 4 PALE
Flushes
  Like some: 5 ROYAL 7 ACEHIGH
Flushing
  stadium: 4 **ASHE**
Fluster: 4 FAZE
Flute
  innovator Theobald: 5 BOEHM
  Kind of: 4 ALTO
  Small: 4 FIFE
  sound: 6 TOOTLE
Flutie
  Quarterback: 4 DOUG
Flutist
  ~ Herbie: 4 MANN
Fluttering
  tree: 5 ASPEN
Flux
  Symbol of electric: 3 PSI
  Unit of magnetic: 5 WEBER
  Unit of magnetic ~ density:
    5 TESLA
Fly: 4 LURE PEST SOAR TEAR
    6 **AVIATE**
  African: 6 **TSETSE**
  alone: 4 SOLO
  Attack a: 4 SWAT
  ball path: 3 ARC
  Biting: 4 GNAT
  catcher: 3 WEB 4 MITT
  Dangerous: 6 **TSETSE**
  flattener: 7 SWATTER
  Flew like a: 5 ARCED
  Half a: 3 TSE
  Harvest: 6 CICADA

high: 4 **SOAR**
in the face of: 4 DEFY
in the ointment: 3 RUB 4 SNAG
It'll never: 3 EMU
like a butterfly: 4 FLIT
like an eagle: 4 **SOAR** 5 SWOOP
off the handle: 4 RAGE RANT
   RAVE
Prepare to: 4 TAXI
Run after a: 5 TAGUP
Sacrifice ~ stat: 3 RBI
Small: 4 GNAT
They ~ by night: 4 OWLS
trap: 3 WEB
Try for a: 4 SWAT 6 SWATAT
Word to a: 4 SHOO
___ fly: 3 SAC 6 TSETSE
"Fly away home"
nursery rhyme critter:
   7 LADYBUG
Flybelt
pest: 6 TSETSE
Flyboy
place: 7 AIRBASE
Fly-by-night: 6 REDEYE
sort: 3 OWL
Flycatcher: 4 MITT 5 PEWEE
Flyer
Coastal: 4 ERNE
Fast: 3 SST
Fearless: 3 ACE
Flexible: 4 SLED
Night: 3 OWL
Transatlantic: 3 SST
Flyers
org.: 3 NHL
WWII Brit.: 3 RAF
Flying: 5 ALOFT
fish eater: 3 ERN 4 ERNE
formation: 3 VEE
Go like a ~ squirrel: 5 GLIDE
honkers: 5 GEESE
jib: 4 SAIL
mammal: 3 BAT
monster: 5 RODAN
Pass with ~ colors: 3 ACE
pest: 4 GNAT
prefix: 4 AERO
solo: 5 ALONE

start: 4 AERO
stinger: 4 WASP
watchdog (abbr.): 3 FAA
~ Pan: 5 PETER
Flying "A"
rival: 4 ESSO
Flying Cloud
automaker: 3 REO
"Flying Down to ___": 3 RIO
"Flying Dutchman, The"
heroine: 5 SENTA
huntsman: 4 ERIK
Flying Dutchman's
choice: 3 KLM
Flying Finn: 5 PAAVO
Flying saucer: 3 UFO
pilots: 3 ETS
Flynn
Actor: 5 **ERROL**
"___ Fly Now": 5 GONNA
Flyspeck: 3 DOT 4 MOTE SPOT
Flytrap, Venus
radio station: 4 WKRP
Fo
Playwright: 5 DARIO
Foal
father: 4 SIRE
mother: 4 MARE
Foam: 4 SUDS 5 FROTH SPUME
at the mouth: 4 RAGE 6 SEETHE
ingredient: 8 URETHANE
prefix: 5 STYRO
Foaming
at the mouth: 5 IRATE RABID
"Foaming cleanser": 4 AJAX
Foamy
brew: 3 ALE
Fob: 10 WATCHCHAIN
locale: 4 VEST
Focal
point: 3 HUB 4 NODE
   9 EPICENTER
points: 4 LOCI
prefix: 3 TRI
Foch
Actress: 4 NINA
Focus: 3 AIM HUB 5 RIVET
   6 ZEROIN
again: 5 REAIM

Debate: 5 TOPIC
I ~: 3 EGO
Lose: 4 BLUR
Focused: 6 INTENT
Focusing
agent: 4 LENS
Fodder: 3 HAY 6 SILAGE
grain: 3 OAT
holder: 4 **SILO**
Store: 6 **ENSILE**
Foe: 4 ANTI 5 ENEMY RIVAL
Fog: 4 HAZE 7 STEAMUP
Comment after the ~ clears:
    4 ISEE
Dense: 7 PEASOUP
    9 PEASOUPER
In a: 5 ATSEA DAZED
Light: 4 MIST
Mental: 4 DAZE
Not in a: 5 AWARE
Fogelberg
Singer: 3 DAN
Fogg, Phileas
creator: 5 VERNE
portrayer: 5 NIVEN
"Fog of War, The"
director Morris: 5 ERROL
Fogy: 4 DODO
Foible: 3 TIC
Foie ___: 4 GRAS
Foie gras
source: 5 GOOSE
Foil: 4 EPEE 6 STOOGE STYMIE
    THWART TRIPUP
alternative: 4 EPEE 5 SABER
    SARAN
Big name in: 5 ALCOA
for Bugs: 5 ELMER
for Colonel Klink: 5 HOGAN
for Garfield: 4 ODIE
kin: 4 EPEE
material: 3 TIN
prefix: 4 AERO
Tin: 4 WRAP
Foist: 6 IMPOSE
Fold: 3 PEN 4 BEND TUCK
    5 PLAIT PLEAT 6 CREASE
Don't: 4 STAY 6 STAYIN
female: 3 EWE

Press, ~, and stretch: 5 KNEAD
sound: 3 BAA
~, spindle, or mutilate: 3 MAR
Folded
food: 4 TACO 5 CREPE TACOS
    6 OMELET 7 OMELETS
    8 OMELETTE
Folder
feature: 3 **TAB**
What a ~ wouldn't say: 4 IMIN
Words from a: 5 IMOUT
work: 7 ORIGAMI
Fold-in
Magazine with a ~ cover: 3 MAD
Folding
Its business is: 7 ORIGAMI
Folds
Arrange in: 5 DRAPE
Fold-up
bed: 3 COT
mattress: 5 FUTON
Folgers
rival: 5 SANKA 7 NESCAFE
Foliage
Bit of: 4 LEAF
Folies-Bergère
designer: 4 **ERTE**
Foliovore: 5 KOALA
Folk
1968 ~ album: 4 ARLO
Beloved: 5 DEARS
First name in: 4 ARLO JONI
history: 4 LORE
music instrument: 5 BANJO
Simple: 5 AMISH
story: 4 TALE
wisdom: 4 LORE
Folklore
being: 3 ORC 4 OGRE 5 GNOME
    TROLL
Bridge protector of: 5 TROLL
Door opener of: 7 ALIBABA
Dream producer of: 3 MAB
fiend: 4 **OGRE**
Wailer of: 7 BANSHEE
Folks: 3 KIN 7 PARENTS
Droll: 4 WAGS
Food for regular: 4 BRAN
Funny: 5 RIOTS

Folk singer
 Irish: 4 ENYA
 One-named: 6 ODETTA
 ~ Burl: 4 IVES
 ~ DiFranco: 3 ANI
 ~ Guthrie: 4 ARLO
 ~ Joan: 4 BAEZ
 ~ Mitchell: 4 JONI
 ~ Pete: 6 SEEGER
 ~ Phil: 4 OCHS
 ~ Seeger: 4 PETE
Folk-song
 mule: 3 SAL
Folktales: 4 LORE
Folkways: 5 MORES
Follett
 Author: 3 KEN
Follow: 3 DOG GET 4 HEED
        OBEY TAIL 5 ACTON
        ENSUE TRACE TRAIL
        6 GONEXT 7 ABIDEBY
        ACTUPON EMULATE
        IMITATE SUCCEED
        8 ADHERETO
        9 COMELATER
 a pattern: 3 SEW
 a trail: 4 HIKE
 closely: 3 APE DOG 4 HEEL TAIL
        5 STALK 6 SHADOW
 Fail to ~ suit: 6 RENEGE
        REVOKE
 It may ~ a dot: 3 COM
 It may ~ directions: 3 ERN
 It may ~ something: 4 ELSE
 It may ~ you: 3 ARE
 orders: 4 **OBEY**
 Something to: 4 SUIT 5 ARROW
 the rainbow: 3 ARC
 too closely: 8 TAILGATE
Follow ___: 5 ALEAD
Follower: 3 FAN IST 4 TAIL
        8 ADHERENT
 Info: Suffix cue
 follower: 3 IST
 suffix: 3 IST ITE
Followers: 5 SHEEP
Following: 3 ALA 4 NEXT SECT
        THEN 5 **AFTER** INTOW
        7 RETINUE

 And the ~ (abbr.): 5 ETSEQ
 behind: 5 INTOW
 closely: 6 ATHEEL
 Loyally: 6 TRUETO
 orders: 8 OBEDIENT
"Follow me!": 4 CMON COME
Follows
 He ~ Jay: 5 CONAN
 He ~ the news: 4 LENO
 It often ~ you: 3 ARE
 It ~ that: 4 ERGO
Follow-up
 (abbr.): 3 SEQ
Folly: 7 MADNESS
 Ford: 5 EDSEL
"___ Folly" (Alaska): 7 SEWARDS
"___ folly to be wise": Gray:
        3 TIS
Foment: 3 SOW
Fond
 Become ~ of: 6 TAKETO
 Be too: 4 DOTE
 of: 4 INTO 5 BIGON 6 KEENON
Fonda
 1940 ~ role: 4 JOAD
 1981 ~ film:
        12 ONGOLDENPOND
 1997 ~ role: 4 **ULEE**
 Actor: 5 PETER
 Actress: 4 JANE 7 BRIDGET
Fonda, Jane
 role: 9 CATBALLOU
 ~ Oscar movie: 5 KLUTE
Fonda, Peter
 title role: 4 **ULEE**
Fond du ___: 3 **LAC**
Fondle: 3 PET
Fondness: 8 APPETITE
 Excessive: 6 DOTAGE
 Show much: 4 DOTE
Fondue: 3 DIP
Fong
 Senator: 5 HIRAM
Font
 flourish: 5 SERIF
Fontana di ___: 5 TREVI
Fontanne
 of Broadway: 4 LYNN
 Partner of: 4 **LUNT**

Fonteyn
  garb: 4 TUTU
  title: 4 DAME
Fonz
  Richie's father, to the: 3 MRC
  Richie's mother, to the: 4 MRSC
  sitcom: 9 HAPPYDAYS
Food: 4 CHOW EATS FARE
     7 ALIMENT EDIBLES
     VICTUAL
  additive: 3 DYE MSG
  All-natural ~ no-no: 3 BHT
  and drink: 6 REPAST
  and shelter: 5 NEEDS
  Baby: 3 PAP 5 PUREE
  bar: 4 OLEO 5 SALAD
  Bird: 4 SEED SUET
  Breakfast: 6 CEREAL
  Bring the: 5 CATER
  Deprive of: 6 STARVE
  Divine: 5 MANNA
  Dog: 4 ALPO
  fish: 3 COD 4 BASS CARP LING
     PIKE SHAD SOLE 5 SMELT
     7 HALIBUT SEABASS
     SNAPPER
  Folded: 4 TACO 5 CREPE TACOS
     6 OMELET 7 OMELETS
     8 OMELETTE
  from heaven: 5 MANNA
  Frozen ~ brand: 6 OREIDA
     8 BIRDSEYE
  Furnish: 5 CATER
  Half a ~ fish: 4 MAHI
  Health ~ flavor: 5 CAROB
  High-fiber: 4 BRAN
  Hog: 4 SLOP
  holder: 3 TIN
  in a red coat: 4 EDAM
  in a shell: 4 TACO
  Infant: 3 PAP
  Italian: 5 PIZZA
  label abbr.: 3 RDA 4 NTWT
  Luau: 3 POI
  Mexican: 4 TACO
  morsel: 3 ORT
  Mushy: 3 PAP
  of the gods: 8 AMBROSIA
  on the floor, maybe: 4 ALPO

  Orange: 3 YAM
  order: 4 TOGO
  Pig: 4 SLOP
  plan: 4 DIET
  poisoning: 8 PTOMAINE
  preparer: 4 COOK
  Provide: 5 CATER
  Put through a ~ press: 4 RICE
  pyramid org.: 4 USDA
  scrap: 3 ORT
  Search for: 6 FORAGE
  seeker: 7 FORAGER
  Shell: 4 TACO
  shop: 4 **DELI**
  Soft: 3 PAP
  Squirrel: 3 NUT 5 ACORN
  stabilizer: 4 AGAR
  stamp: 4 USDA
  stat.: 3 RDA
  sticker: 4 TINE
  storage material: 5 SARAN
  supply: 6 LARDER
  Supply the: 5 CATER
  thickener: 4 **AGAR**
  Twice-chewed: 3 CUD
  Word with: 6 ETHNIC
"Food Glorious Food"
  musical: 6 OLIVER
Foodie: 5 EATER
Food Network
  chef: 6 EMERIL
Foofaraw: 3 ADO 4 TODO
     5 HOOHA
Fool: 3 **ASS** CON KID SAP
     4 BOOB BOZO DOPE DUPE
     SIMP 5 BOOBY CLOWN
     GOOSE IDIOT MORON
     NINNY 6 DELUDE
  (around): 5 HORSE
  follower: 3 ISH
  Old: 4 COOT
  Pompous: 3 ASS
"___ Fool Believes" (1979 hit):
     5 WHATA
Fooled: 3 GOT HAD
  Not ~ by: 4 **ONTO** 6 WISETO
  on the ice: 5 DEKED
Fooler
  Fish: 4 BAIT

Foolhardy: 4 **RASH** 5 BRASH
 HASTY 6 UNWISE
Foolish: 4 DAFT GAGA 5 GOOSY
 INANE LOONY SAPPY
 6 UNWISE 7 WITLESS
 behavior: 6 IDIOCY
 fellow: 4 COOT SIMP TWIT
 It might be: 4 GRIN
 month: 5 APRIL
"___ Foolish Things": 5 THESE
"Fool Such ___, A": 3 ASI
"___ Fool to Care": 5 IWASA
"___ Fool to Want You": 3 IMA
Foot: 4 IAMB
 Anatomical: 3 PES
 Big: 3 EEE
 bones: 5 TARSI
 Crush with the: 7 STAMPON
 fault: 4 CORN
 Feline: 3 PAW
 fraction: 4 INCH
 Furry: 3 PAW
 Hand or: 4 **UNIT**
 It's about a: 4 SHOE
 It's just over a: 5 ANKLE
 It's under: 4 SOLE
 Latin: 3 PES
 Left ~ of Orion: 5 RIGEL
 Measured on: 5 PACED
 Metric: 4 IAMB
 Move a: 4 STEP
 part: 3 TOE 4 ARCH BALL HEEL
  INCH SOLE 6 INSTEP
 Poetic: 4 IAMB
 prefix: 4 PEDI
 Put one's ~ down: 4 **STEP** TROD
  5 STOMP TREAD
 Wait on hand and: 7 CATERTO
 Wide ~ spec: 3 EEE
 word form: 4 PEDE PEDI PEDO
Footage
 Square: 4 **AREA**
Football
 blitz: 6 REDDOG
 center: 3 AIR
 conference: 6 HUDDLE·
 feint: 4 JUKE
 filler: 3 AIR
 formation: 7 SHOTGUN

 gains: 5 YARDS
 gains (abbr.): 3 YDS
 gear: 4 PADS
 holder: 3 TEE
 Kind of: 5 ARENA
 Kind of ~ kick: 6 ONSIDE
 lineman: 3 END
 official: 3 REF
 part: 4 LACE
 play: 4 PASS TRAP 7 LATERAL
  REVERSE
 position: 3 END 7 LINEMAN
 positions (abbr.): 3 RTS
 scores (abbr.): 3 TDS
 shorthand: 7 XSANDOS
 shutout line score: 4 OOOO
 squad: 6 ELEVEN
 stat.: 3 INT YDS
 supporter: 3 TEE
 team: 6 ELEVEN
 ___ football: 5 ARENA
Football-shaped: 4 OVAL 5 OVATE
 OVOID
Footboard-headboard
 connector: 7 BEDRAIL
Footed
 vase: 3 URN
Footfall: 4 STEP
 Horse: 4 CLOP
Footing
 Lose one's: 4 SLIP
Footless
 animal: 4 APOD
Footlike
 part: 3 PES
"Footloose"
 singer: 7 LOGGINS
 Singer of: 4 LORI
Footnote
 abbr.: 3 VID 4 ETAL **IBID** IDEM
  5 ETSEQ OPCIT
 datum: 4 PAGE
 word: 4 IDEM 6 IBIDEM
Footprint: 4 CLUE STEP 5 TRACK
 maker: 4 SOLE
Footrest: 7 OTTOMAN
 Pole with: 5 STILT
Footstool: 7 OTTOMAN
Footwear: 5 PUMPS

Quaint: 5 SPATS
Summer: 7 SANDALS
Winter: 5 BOOTS
Wooden: 5 SABOT
Fop: 5 DANDY
prop: 4 CANE
For: 3 PRO
each: 3 **PER** 6 APIECE
every: 3 PER
everyone: 6 RATEDG
example: 3 **SAY** 6 SUCHAS
fear that: 4 **LEST**
fun: 7 ONALARK
instance: 3 SAY
now: 6 PROTEM
one: 3 PER 4 APOP EACH
    6 APIECE
real: 5 LEGIT
rent: 5 TOLET
the most part: 6 MAINLY
Those: 4 AYES YEAS
For ___
(cheap): 5 ASONG
(suitable for everyone):
    7 ALLAGES
Forage
holder: 4 SILO
Forager
Forest: 4 DEER
Tiny: 3 ANT
"For ___ a jolly ...": 3 HES
"___ for All Seasons": 4 AMAN
Foray: 4 RAID 6 SORTIE
Forbear: 7 ABSTAIN
"For better or for ___": 5 WORSE
Forbid: 3 BAN
Forbidden: 5 TABOO
fruit site: 4 EDEN
They're: 5 NONOS
thing: 4 NONO
(var.): 4 TABU
"Forbidden City, The": 5 LHASA
Forbidding: 3 ICY 4 DOUR GRIM
    5 STERN 6 SEVERE
Force: 4 **DINT** 5 IMPEL MIGHT
    6 COERCE COMPEL
    OBLIGE
along: 4 URGE
(apart): 3 PRY

back: 5 REPEL
Bit of: 4 DYNE
Cold war: 4 NATO
Dark: 4 EVIL
down: 4 TAMP
Driving: 5 MOTOR
Earth: 4 ONEG
Fetch with: 3 LUG
Fighting: 6 ARMADA
Fling with: 4 HURL
French: 5 ARMEE
Full: 5 BRUNT
Gaza: 3 PLO
Having no: 4 NULL
In: 5 VALID
Kind of: 4 GALE 5 BRUTE
Life: 3 CHI
Main: 5 BRUNT
Naval: 5 FLEET
One on a: 3 REP 8 SALESREP
One with the: 4 JEDI
open: 5 JIMMY
Opposing: 5 ENEMY
out: 4 OUST 5 EVICT EXILE
    ROUST 6 DEPOSE
Rotational: 6 TORQUE
Sales: 4 REPS
Take by: 4 REFT 5 SEIZE USURP
    WREST
Throw with: 5 HEAVE
to leave: 5 EXILE 6 UPROOT
unit: 4 **DYNE**
Wield: 5 EXERT
With full: 5 AMAIN
~, in Latin: 3 VIS
Forced
Was: 5 HADTO
Forceful: 6 COGENT 7 DYNAMIC
flow: 5 SPATE
Forcefully
Eject: 4 SPEW
Fling: 4 HURL
Say: 4 AVER
Take: 5 WREST
Forces
Join: 4 ALLY 5 MERGE **UNITE**
    6 TEAMUP
Forcibly
Put down: 5 QUELL

Take: 5 USURP WREST
Ford
1950s ~: 5 **EDSEL**
Actor: 5 GLENN
A Tennessee: 5 ERNIE
Classic: 3 LTD 5 TBIRD WOODY
    6 MODELA MODELT
    7 MUSTANG
contemporary: 4 OLDS
flop: 5 **EDSEL**
model: 5 PINTO 6 ESCORT
    FIESTA TAURUS
of fashion: 6 EILEEN
of football: 3 LEN
Old: 3 **LTD** 5 EDSEL PINTO
or Lincoln: 3 CAR 4 AUTO
predecessor: 5 AGNEW
press secretary: 6 NESSEN
product, briefly: 4 MERC
role: 4 SOLO
son: 5 EDSEL
~ Explorer: 3 SUV
Ford, President: 6 GERALD
Fore
for four: 5 TETRA
Opposite of: 3 AFT
site: 3 TEE
Fore-and-after: 4 YAWL 5 SLOOP
Forearm
bone: 4 **ULNA**
bones: 5 ULNAE
Forebear: 8 ANCESTOR
Foreboding: 4 OMEN
Feeling of: 5 DREAD
Forecast
April: 4 RAIN
Icy: 5 SLEET
Part of a summer: 4 HAZE
Welcome: 5 CLEAR
Wet: 4 RAIN
Winter: 4 SNOW 5 SLEET
    TEENS
Forecaster
~ Al: 5 ROKER
Forecasting
aid: 5 RADAR
Forehead: 4 BROW
cover: 5 BANGS
Foreign: 5 ALIEN

assembly: 5 SENAT
correspondent: 6 PENPAL
dignitary: 3 AGA 4 EMIR
follower: 3 AID
Like some ~ films: 7 UNRATED
money: 4 LIRE
prefix: 4 XENO
settler: 6 EMIGRE
"Foreign Affairs"
author Alison: 5 LURIE
~ Pulitzer-winner Lurie:
    6 ALISON
Foreigner: 5 ALIEN
prefix: 4 XENO
Forelimb
bone: 4 ULNA
Foreman
Deck: 4 BOSN
KO'er of: 3 ALI
place: 4 RING
Where Ali kayoed: 5 ZAIRE
Foremast
attachment: 8 HEADSAIL
Forensic
CBS ~ show: 3 CSI
tool: 3 DNA
workplace: 8 CRIMELAB
Forensics
expert: 7 DEBATER
Foresail: 3 JIB
Foreshadow: 4 BODE OMEN
    5 AUGUR
Forest
clearing: 5 **GLADE**
denizen: 3 ELK 4 DEER
element: 4 TREE
feller: 3 AXE
female: 3 **DOE**
growth: 4 MOSS
Like a rain: 4 LUSH 5 DENSE
plant: 4 FERN
quaker: 5 ASPEN
ranger: 3 ELK
runner: 3 SAP
Shakespearean: 5 **ARDEN**
Subarctic: 5 TAIGA
unit: 4 TREE
vine: 5 LIANA
Forestall: 5 AVERT

Forest floor
  sight: 8 PINECONE
Forest Service
  dept.: 4 USDA
Foretopman
  Melville: 4 BUDD
Forever: 4 AGES 6 ALWAYS
    9 INDELIBLY
  Almost: 3 EON 4 EONS
  Lasting: 7 ETERNAL
  Partner of: 4 ADAY
  Seemingly: 3 EON 4 AEON AGES
    EONS
  young: 7 AGELESS
  ~, poetically: 6 ETERNE
"Forever, ___" (1996 humor
    book): 4 ERMA
Forever and ___ : 4 ADAY
Forever ___ day: 4 ANDA
"Forever Your Girl"
  singer: 5 ABDUL
"___ for Evidence" (Grafton
    novel): 3 EIS
Forewarned: 8 ONNOTICE
Foreword: 5 INTRO
  (abbr.): 4 INTR
Forfeit: 4 CEDE LOSE 5 WAIVE
Forfeits
  Card game with: 3 LOO
Forge
  worker: 5 SMITH
Forgery: 4 FAKE
Forget: 4 OMIT
Forget-___ : 5 MENOT
"___ Forget": 5 TRYTO
Forgetfulness
  Drink of: 8 NEPENTHE
  River of: 5 LETHE
"Forget it!": 3 NAH NOT 4 NOPE
    UHUH 5 IWONT IXNAY
    NOHOW NOWAY 6 ISAYNO
    NODEAL NODICE NOSOAP
Forging
  When ~ began: 7 IRONAGE
"___ forgiven": 5 ALLIS
Forgiveness
  Start of a saying on: 5 TOERR
"... ___ forgive those ...":
    4 ASWE

Forgiving: 8 PLACABLE
  Less: 7 STERNER
Forgo
  Cannot: 5 NEEDS
"For goodness ___!": 4 SAKE
    5 SAKES
"Forgot About ___" (rap song):
    3 DRE
"___ for Innocent" (Grafton
    novel): 3 IIS
"For ___ jolly ...": 4 HESA
Fork: 7 DIVERGE UTENSIL
  feature: 4 TINE 5 PRONG
  in the road: 3 WYE
  Kind of: 5 SALAD 6 OYSTER
  Like a: 5 TINED
  One with a: 5 TUNER
  over: 3 PAY 5 REMIT SPEND
  over, with "up": 4 ANTE
  part: 4 **TINE**
  site: 4 ROAD
  Stick a ~ in: 4 STAB
Forked
  Not yet ~ over: 4 OWED
  Speak with ~ tongue: 3 LIE
"For ___ know ...": 4 ALLI
Fork-tailed
  flier: 4 TERN 6 MARTIN
Form: 4 MODE 7 FASHION
  a coalition: 5 UNITE
  a jury: 7 EMPANEL
  an opinion: 4 DEEM
  follower: 3 ULA
  Foundary: 4 MOLD
  Good: 7 DECORUM
  heading: 3 UNI
  In a different: 4 ANEW
  letters: 3 IRS
  of ID: 3 LIC
  Poetic: 3 ODE
  prefix: 3 UNI
  Relating to: 5 MODAL
  Sculpted: 5 TORSO
  Shoemaking: 4 LAST
  Short: 4 ABBR
  suffix: 3 ULA
  Tax: 6 RETURN
  Tiny life: 5 AMEBA
  Vb.: 3 INF

Form 1040
completer: 3 CPA
deduction: 3 IRA
issuer: 3 IRS
~ ID: 3 SSN
Formal: 4 PRIM 6 DRESSY
accessory: 4 STUD
act: 7 STATUTE
agreement: 4 PACT
attire: 3 TUX
avenue: 5 ALLEE
ceremony: 4 RITE
dance: 4 BALL
declaration: 6 DICTUM
decree: 5 EDICT
dress: 4 GOWN
Go: 5 DRESS 7 DRESSUP
headgear: 6 TOPHAT
introduction: 4 SEMI
need: 3 TIE
order: 4 WRIT 6 DECREE
pronoun: 7 ROYALWE
rulings: 5 DICTA
speech: 7 ORATION
Spring: 4 PROM
Stiffly: 7 STILTED
wear: 3 TUX 5 TAILS
"___ for Malice" (Grafton novel):
    3 MIS
Forman
Director: 5 MILOS
Format
Big-screen: 4 **IMAX**
Computer data: 5 ASCII
Early VCR: 4 BETA
Home movie: 3 DVD
Image file: 4 JPEG
Interview: 5 QANDA
Radio: 4 TALK 6 OLDIES
Videotape: 3 VHS 4 BETA
Formation
Coral: 4 **REEF** 5 ATOLL
fliers: 5 GEESE
Flight: 3 VEE
Glacial: 5 ARETE
In: 7 ARRAYED
Orderly: 5 ARRAY
River mouth: 5 DELTA
Sand: 4 DUNE

Southwestern land: 4 MESA
Triangular: 5 DELTA
Formative: 7 SEMINAL
Formatting
key: 6 TABSET
"For Me and My ___": 3 GAL
Former: 3 OLD 4 ONCE PAST
    5 PRIOR 6 BYGONE
    7 CREATOR **ONETIME**
Formerly: 3 AGO NEE 4 ERST
    ONCE 9 ATONETIME
Formic acid
source: 3 ANT
Formicary: 4 NEST
resident: 3 ANT
Formula: 6 RECIPE
of belief: 5 CREDO
Part of a circle: 3 PIR
Salt: 4 NACL
Formula ___: 3 ONE
Formulary
entry: 4 DRUG
Formulate: 4 DRAW 5 FRAME
    SHAPE
"___ for Murder": 5 DIALM
"___ for Noose" (Grafton novel):
    3 NIS
___ for oneself: 4 FEND
"Forrest Gump"
actor Gary: 6 SINISE
Oscar actor for: 8 TOMHANKS
Forsake: 6 DESERT
"For ___ sake!": 5 PETES
Forsaken: 4 LORN 5 ALONE
child: 4 WAIF
Forsaker
of the faith: 8 APOSTATE
"For shame!": 3 FIE TSK TUT
    6 TSKTSK TUTTUT
Forster
novel: 15 APASSAGETOINDIA
novel setting: 5 INDIA
title with a view: 5 AROOM
Forsyth
title city: 6 ODESSA
Fort: 7 BASTION 8 GARRISON

attacked by Goldfinger: 4 KNOX
California: 3 **ORD**
Civil War: 6 SUMTER
Kentucky: 4 KNOX
near McGuire Air Force Base:
    3 DIX
North Carolina: 5 BRAGG
Fort ___
(California): 3 ORD
(Florida): 5 MYERS
(gold site): 4 KNOX
(North Carolina): 5 BRAGG
(New Jersey): 3 DIX
(Ontario): 4 ERIE
(South Carolina): 6 SUMTER
Fortas
Justice: 3 **ABE**
___ for tat: 3 TIT
Fort Baxter
sergeant: 5 BILKO
Fort Bliss
city: 6 ELPASO
Fort Courage
company: 6 FTROOP
group: 6 FTROOP
Forte: 4 LOUD 5 SKILL 6 METIER
Fort Erie
home (abbr.): 3 ONT
Forth
And so: 3 ETC 8 ETCETERA
Belch: 4 SPEW
Bring: 5 EDUCE SPAWN
    6 ELICIT
Call: 5 EVOKE
Cast: 4 EMIT 6 SPEWED
Come: 6 **EMERGE**
Draw: 5 EDUCE EVOKE
    6 ELICIT
Flow: 7 EMANATE
Give: 4 EMIT 5 EXUDE
Gush: 4 **SPEW**
Hold: 5 OPINE **ORATE**
Issue: 4 EMIT
Put: 3 ASK 5 EXERT POSIT
Send: 4 EMIT
Spew: 5 ERUPT
They go back and: 4 SAWS
Walk back and: 4 PACE
Words before: 5 ANDSO

Forthcoming
Not: 3 SHY 5 CAGEY
"For ___ the Bell Tolls": 4 WHOM
"For the Boys"
gp.: 3 USO
"For the life ___, ...": 4 OFME
"___ for the Misbegotten":
    5 AMOON
___ for the money: 4 INIT
"___ for the poor!": 4 ALMS
Forthright: 4 BOLD OPEN
    6 CANDID 7 SINCERE
Fortification: 7 RAMPART
V-shaped: 5 REDAN
Fortify: 3 ARM MAN 4 GIRD
    5 STEEL 7 BOLSTER
Fortitude: 4 GRIT GUTS
    6 METTLE
Fort Knox
bar: 5 INGOT
Fort Lauderdale
City near: 5 MIAMI
Fortnight
fourteen: 4 DAYS
Half a: 4 WEEK
Fortnights
26 ~: 4 YEAR
Fort Peck: 3 DAM
Fortress: 7 CITADEL
Dead Sea: 6 MASADA
Medieval Italian: 4 ESTE
Mountaintop: 5 AERIE
Fortunate: 5 LUCKY 6 INLUCK
Fortune: 3 HAP LOT 4 FATE PILE
    6 KISMET RICHES
    WEALTH
Good ~ source: 6 AMULET
partner: 4 FAME
Soldier of: 4 MERC
Wheels of: 4 LIMO
Fortune 500
abbr.: 3 INC 4 CORP
inits.: 3 ITT
listings (abbr.): 3 COS
Fortuneteller: 4 SEER
    6 ORACLE
deck: 5 TAROT
phrase: 4 ISEE
sign: 4 OMEN

Fort Wayne
  river: 7 STMARYS
  state (abbr.): 3 IND
Fort Worth
  sch.: 3 TCU
Forty
  One of the back: 4 ACRE
  winks: 3 **NAP** 4 DOZE
      6 CATNAP SNOOZE
      7 SHUTEYE
Forty-___ : 5 NINER
Forty-niner: 5 MINER
  filing: 5 CLAIM
  find: 3 ORE
Forum
  Info: Latin cue
  farewell: 3 AVE
  garb: 4 TOGA
  greeting: 3 **AVE**
  language: 5 LATIN
  matter: 3 RES
  player: 5 LAKER
  site: 4 ROME
  wear: 4 TOGA 5 TOGAE TOGAS
"For ___ us a child ...": 4 UNTO
"For want of ___ ...": 5 ANAIL
Forward: 4 BOLD PERT 5 AHEAD
      BRASH FRESH REMIT
      6 BRASSY RESEND
      SENDON
  Come: 6 EMERGE
  Drive: 5 **IMPEL** 6 PROPEL
  Look ~ to: 5 AWAIT
  Move: 6 PROPEL
  Nudge: 4 PROD
  pass: 6 AERIAL
  Put: 4 POSE 5 OFFER POSED
      POSIT 6 ASSERT
  sail: 3 JIB
  Urge: 5 IMPEL
Forwarded: 4 SENT 6 SENTON
Forward-looking
  group: 5 SEERS
"For Your Eyes Only"
  singer Sheena: 6 EASTON
Fosse
  film: 11 ALLTHATJAZZ
  musical: 6 DANCIN 7 CABARET
      CHICAGO

Fossey
  Anthropologist: 4 DIAN
  subject: 3 APE 6 SIMIAN
Fossil
  Famed ~ site: 4 JAVA
  fuel blocks: 5 PEATS
  holder: 5 SHALE
  preserver: 6 TARPIT
  resin: 5 AMBER
Fossil fuel: 3 GAS OIL 4 COAL
Foster: 4 ABET REAR 5 BREED
      RAISE 7 NURTURE
  Actress: 5 JODIE
  home crowd: 5 FOLKS
  uncle: 3 NED
Foster, Jodie
  1999 ~ role: 4 ANNA
  alma mater: 4 YALE
  movie: 4 **NELL**
  role: 4 ANNA NELL
  title role: 4 NELL
"Foucault's Pendulum"
  author: 3 **ECO**
Foul: 4 VILE 5 NASTY 6 PUTRID
      SORDID 7 NOTFAIR
  caller: 3 REF UMP
  mood: 4 SNIT
  odor: 6 STENCH
  Pinball: 4 TILT
  up: 3 ERR 5 BOTCH MISDO
  (up): 6 BOLLIX
Foul-mouth: 6 CURSER
Foul-smelling: 4 OLID RIPE
      5 FETID FUNKY 6 PUTRID
      RANCID
Foul-tempered
  fellow: 4 OGRE
Foul-up: 4 GOOF 5 BONER
      ERROR SNAFU 6 BOOBOO
Found: 5 BEGIN 6 CREATE
      7 LOCATED
  As originally: 6 INSITU
  out: 6 LEARNT 7 LEARNED
  Partner of: 4 LOST
Foundation: 3 BED 4 BASE
      5 **BASIS** 7 ENDOWER
  Carnegie: 5 STEEL
  figure: 7 TRUSTEE
  garment: 6 CORSET

Oxford: 4 SOLE
plant: 5 SHRUB
Plaster: 4 LATH
Stone: 6 RIPRAP
"Foundation"
author: 6 ASIMOV
Founded: 5 BASED
(abbr.): 3 EST 4 ESTD 5 ESTAB
"Found it!": 3 AHA
Foundry
form: 4 MOLD
need: 3 ORE
refuse: 4 SLAG
Fountain
drink: 4 COKE COLA MALT
SODA 5 SHAKE 6 MALTED
Famous: 5 TREVI
freebie: 5 STRAW
of jazz: 4 PETE
Roman: 5 TREVI
treat: 4 MALT 6 MALTED
11 BANANASPLIT
Fountain, Pete
collaborator: 6 ALHIRT
"Fountainhead, The"
author Rand: 3 AYN
character: 5 ROARK
Four
A quarter of: 3 ONE
duos: 5 OCTET
gills: 4 PINT
Give ~ stars: 4 RATE
Having ~ sharps: 3 INE
inferior: 4 TREY
It follows ~ but not five: 4 TEEN
Key with ~ sharps: 6 EMAJOR
Lake in ~ states: 4 ERIE
of a kind: 6 TETRAD
One of the ~ elements: 3 AIR
prefix: 5 TETRA
quarters: 3 ONE 4 YEAR
Round of: 5 SEMIS
seasons in Spain: 3 ANO
Three or: 4 AFEW
times a day, on an Rx: 3 QID
Top: 4 ACES
Four-___: 7 ALARMER
___ four: 5 PETIT
___ Four, The: 3 FAB

Fourbagger: 5 HOMER
Fourbaggers
in MLB: 3 HRS
Four Corners
state: 4 **UTAH**
Four-door: 5 SEDAN
"Four Essays on Liberty"
author Berlin: 6 ISAIAH
Four-footed
friend: 3 PET
Four Forest Cantons
lake: 7 LUCERNE
Four Freedoms
subject: 4 FEAR
Four-hand
piano piece: 4 DUET
Four Horsemen
One of the: 3 WAR
Four-in-hand: 3 TIE
Four-letter
Use a ~ word: 4 CUSS
word: 4 OATH 5 SWEAR
Four o'clock
fare: 8 TEACAKES
Leaves at: 3 TEA
service: 6 TEASET
Four-page
sheet: 5 FOLIO
Four-person
event: 5 RELAY
Fourposter: 3 BED
"Four Quartets"
poet: 5 ELIOT 7 TSELIOT
Fours: 5 CAKES
___ fours (crawling): 5 ONALL
Fourscore: 6 EIGHTY
Four Seasons, The
Frankie of: 5 VALLI
song: 6 SHERRY
"Four Seasons, The"
director: 4 **ALDA**
Four-sided
fig.: 4 RECT
Foursome: 6 TETRAD
Annual: 7 SEASONS
Grand slam: 4 RBIS
Half a 1960s: 5 MAMAS PAPAS
Monopoly ~ (abbr.): 3 RRS
Four-star: 4 AONE RAVE 5 GREAT

Hardly ~ fare: **4** SLOP
review: **4 RAVE**

Four-stringed
instrument: **3** UKE

Four-term
pres.: **3** FDR

Fourth
anniversary gift: **5** LINEN
dimension: **4** TIME
in a series: **3** DEE
little piggy's share: **4** NONE
man: **4** SETH
person: **4** ABEL
planet: **4** MARS

Fourth-down
option: **4** PUNT

Fourth Estate: 5 PRESS

Fourth-largest
lake: **7** ARALSEA

Fourths
of gals.: **3** QTS

Four-time
~ Australian Open champ:
5 SELES
~ Emmy-winning drama:
5 LALAW
~ Indy 500 winner: **4** FOYT
5 UNSER **7** ALUNSER
~ Japanese P.M.: **3** ITO
~ Super Bowl champs:
8 STEELERS
~ Wimbledon champ: **5** LAVER

Four-to-midnight
group: **10** SWINGSHIFT

Four-wheeler: 5 WAGON
6 LANDAU
Recreational: **3** ATV

Four-year
degs.: **3** BAS BSS

Fowl
Entrée: **5** CAPON
Female: **3** HEN **6** PEAHEN
Flightless: **3** EMU
pole: **5** ROOST
product: **3** EGG
territory: **4** COOP
Young: **5** POULT

Fox: 7 REYNARD
African: **4** ASSE

comedy series: **5** MADTV
Female: **5** VIXEN
follower: **4** TROT
Former ~ sitcom: **3** ROC
6 MARTIN
Fox Mulder program on:
9 THEXFILES
honorific: **4** BRER
hunt cry: **5** HALLO **6** YOICKS
7 TALLYHO
kin: **3** SAC
Like a: **3** SLY
Partner of: **4** DANA
prey: **4** HARE
relative: **7** ARAPAHO
show: **4** COPS
Young: **3** KIT
~, in Spanish: **5** ZORRO
___ Fox: **4** BRER

"Fox and the Grapes, The"
storyteller: **5** AESOP

Foxhole
Fix a: **5** REDIG

Foxlike: 3 SLY

Foxx
Actor: **5** JAMIE
Comedian: **4 REDD**
Singer: **4** INEZ

Foxy: 3 SLY
lady: **5** VIXEN

Foy
Vaudevillian: **5** EDDIE

Foyer: 4 HALL

Foyt
et al.: **3** AJS

Fr.
company: **3** CIE
father: **4** PERE
holy woman: **3 STE**
holy women: **4 STES**
miss: **4** MLLE
title: **3** MME **4** MLLE

Fra
Painting: **5** LIPPI

Fracas: 4 TODO **5** MELEE SCRAP
SETTO

Fraction
Bushel: **4** PECK
Day: **4** HOUR

Farm: 4 ACRE
Foot: 4 INCH
Inch: 3 MIL
Joule: 3 ERG
Min.: 4 NSEC
Newton: 4 DYNE
Ounce: 4 DRAM
Peso: 7 CENTAVO
Sawbuck: 3 ONE
Sen: 3 RIN
Square-mile: 4 ACRE
Fractional
prefix: 4 DEMI HEMI NANO
Fractions
Make: 6 DIVIDE
Ton ~ (abbr.): 3 LBS
Fragile
It may be: 3 EGO
layer: 5 OZONE
Fragment: 5 PIECE SCRAP
SHARD 7 ATOMIZE
SNIPPET
Pottery: 5 SHARD
Fragrance: 4 **ODOR** 5 AROMA
SCENT
Floral: 5 ATTAR
Gucci: 4 ENVY
Popular: 4 COCO TABU
6 ARAMIS
YSL: 5 OPIUM
Fragrant: 8 REDOLENT
compound: 5 **ESTER**
fir: 6 BALSAM
flower: 5 LILAC 7 TEAROSE
8 GARDENIA
oil: 5 **ATTAR**
resin: 5 ELEMI
ring: 3 LEI
root: 5 ORRIS
shrub: 5 LILAC 6 AZALEA
tree: 3 FIR 4 PINE
wood: 5 CEDAR 8 REDCEDAR
___ fraîche: 5 CREME
Fraidy-cat: 5 SISSY
Frame: 5 SETUP
Animation: 3 **CEL**
a photo again: 5 REMAT
Clothes-drying: 5 AIRER
Door ~ part: 4 JAMB 6 LINTEL

Fireplace: 5 GRATE
insert: 4 LENS
of mind: 4 MOOD 5 HUMOR
6 MORALE
Pane: 4 SASH
shape: 4 OVAL
Ship: 4 HULL
Time: 3 ERA
Window: 4 SASH
Framed: 5 SETUP
It may be: 3 ART CEL
Framer
need: 3 MAT
Framework: 7 LATTICE
Bridge: 7 TRESTLE
Rigid: 5 TRUSS
Window: 4 SASH
Fran
Friend of: 5 KUKLA OLLIE
Franc
Former ~ fraction: 3 SOU
successor: 4 EURO
Française
feature: 7 CEDILLA
___ française: 3 ALA
France
Ancient region of: 7 ALSATIA
Author: 7 ANATOLE
Bank of: 4 RIVE
Born in: 3 NEE
City of: 4 CAEN 5 LILLE
Department of: 3 AIN
France of: 7 ANATOLE
Friend in: 3 AMI 4 AMIE
Head of: 4 TETE
King of: 3 **ROI**
Longest river in: 5 LOIRE
Neighbor of: 7 ANDORRA
One in: 3 UNE
Patron saint of: 5 DENIS
President of: 4 COTY
Queen of: 5 REINE
Region of: 4 BRIE
River of: 4 OISE YSER 5 ISERE
RHONE
Saint of: 6 TROPEZ
State of: 4 ETAT
Story of: 5 ETAGE
Summer in: 3 ETE

The king of: **5** LEROI
The south of: **4** MIDI
~, formerly: **4** GAUL
___ **France: 5** ILEDE
Franchise: 4 VOTE
Flapjack: **4** IHOP
Francis: 5 SAINT
Actress: **6** ARLENE
of 1950s films: **4** MULE
or Frank: **4** ANNE
Francis ___, Sir
Explorer: **5** DRAKE
Francis, St.
birthplace: **6** ASSISI
Franciscan: 5 FRIAR
___ **Francisco: 3** SAN
Franck
Composer: **5** CESAR
Franco
Actor: **4** NERO
friend: **5** AMIGO
François
Info: French cue
Farewell from: **5** ADIEU
Friend of: **3** AMI **4** AMIE
Frank: 3 DOG **4** OPEN
6 CANDID DIRECT
HONEST REDHOT
WIENER
admission: **6** AVOWAL
comic colleague: **6** ERNEST
Diarist: **4 ANNE**
Director: **5** CAPRA
Ex of: **3** AVA MIA
Gangster: **5** NITTI
of rock: **5** ZAPPA
Songwriter: **7** LOESSER
topper: **5** KRAUT **6** RELISH
work: **5** DIARY
Frank, Anne
account: **5** DIARY
Franken
and others: **3** ALS
Frankenstein
assistant: **4 IGOR**
feature: **4** SCAR
workplace: **3** LAB
"Frankenstein"
Like: **6** GOTHIC

Frankfurt
Info: German cue
First in: **4** ERST
river: **4 ODER**
Frankfurter
Justice: **5** FELIX
link: **3** UND
Frankie
Singer: **5 LAINE** VALLI
Franklin
flier: **4** KITE
forte: **4** SOUL
invention: **5** STOVE
invention (abbr.): **3** DST
is on it: **5** CNOTE
Loser to ~ in 1936: **3** ALF
Mother of: **4 SARA**
of soul: **6** ARETHA
or Jefferson: **5** DEIST
successor: **5** HARRY
Wife of: **7** ELEANOR
Franks
Of: **5** SALIC
Franny
Father of: **3** LES
Frans
Painter: **4 HALS**
Frantic
Get: **13** CLIMBTHEWALLS
Franz
Author: **5** KAFKA
Composer: **5** LEHAR LISZT
Hypnotist: **6** MESMER
Fraser
of tennis: **5 NEALE**
"Frasier"
actress Gilpin: **4** PERI
actress Peri: **6** GILPIN
brother: **5 NILES**
character: **3 ROZ 5** NILES
6 DAPHNE
dog: **5 EDDIE**
Ex-wife on: **5** MARIS
Peri on: **3** ROZ
portrayer: **6** KELSEY
Surname on: **5** CRANE
Frat
house wear: **4** TOGA
letter: **3** CHI **ETA** PHI PSI RHO

TAU 4 BETA ZETA 5 KAPPA
SIGMA THETA
party staple: 3 KEG
recruits: 5 FROSH
Fraternal
group: 4 BPOE ELKS 6 MASONS
member: 3 ELK
twin, in chemistry: 6 ISOMER
Fraternity
hopeful: 6 RUSHEE
letter: 3 CHI **ETA** PHI PSI RHO
TAU 4 BETA ZETA 5 KAPPA
SIGMA THETA
letters: 3 NUS XIS
member: 5 GREEK
members: 3 MEN
party wear: 4 TOGA
travail: 8 HELLWEEK
Fratricide
victim: 4 ABEL
Frau
abode: 4 HAUS
mate: 4 HERR
Fraud: 4 HOAX SCAM SHAM
6 POSEUR
finder (abbr.): 3 BBB
monitoring agcy.: 3 FTC
Fray: 4 WEAR 5 RAVEL SETTO
Frayed: 4 WORN
Frazier
foe: 3 ALI
Freak
out: 5 GOAPE 6 LOSEIT
Freaked
out: 6 LOSTIT 7 GONEAPE
HADACOW
"Freaks"
director Browning: 3 TOD
Hyams of: 5 LEILA
Freberg
Satirist: 4 STAN
Fred
1966 U.S. Open champ ~:
6 STOLLE
Dancer: 7 ASTAIRE
Lyricist: 3 EBB
Partner of: 5 ADELE
Ricky vis-à-vis: 6 TENANT
Sister of: 5 **ADELE**

Wife of: 5 WILMA
~, to Pebbles: 3 DAD
Freda
Singer: 5 PAYNE
"Fred Basset"
cartoonist Graham: 4 ALEX
Freddie
Comic: 6 PRINZE
Freddie the Freeloader: 4 HOBO
5 TRAMP
portrayer: 10 REDSKELTON
Freddy
street: 3 ELM
Frederic
Photoengraving innovator: 4 IVES
Frederick
Composer: 5 LOEWE
Frederick ___, Sir
Choreographer: 6 ASHTON
Fredericksburg
Victor at: 3 LEE
Frederik
Sci-fi author: 4 POHL
Free: 3 RID 4 ONME 5 LETGO
LOOSE **UNTIE** 6 GRATIS
LETOUT 7 ATLARGE
MANUMIT PROBONO
RELEASE UNLOOSE
8 ATNOCOST LIBERATE
SETLOOSE
Add for: 7 THROWIN
from: 5 RIDOF
from contaminants: 4 PURE
from strife: 7 ATPEACE
gift, sometimes: 7 TOTEBAG
It may be: 4 RIDE 5 TRIAL
VERSE
It's a ~ country: 3 USA
It's not ~ of charge: 3 ION
Let: 5 UNTIE
Not: 5 CAGED INUSE 6 EARNED
(of): 3 **RID**
of charge: 6 GRATIS
of frost: 5 DEICE
Set: 5 UNTIE 6 UNCAGE
7 UNLOOSE
speech obstacle: 3 GAG
suffix: 3 DOM
throw score: 3 ONE

ticket: **4 COMP PASS**
tix: **5 COMPS**
to attack: **5 LETAT**
~, in French: **5 LIBRE**
~ TV ad: **3 PSA**
Free as ___: 5 ABIRD
Freebie: 4 COMP PASS
  Chinese restaurant: **3 TEA**
  Chinese takeout: **4 RICE**
  Diner: **5 MINTS**
  Gas station: **3 AIR**
  Hotel: **3 ICE 4 SOAP**
  Motel: **3 ICE 4 SOAP**
  Restaurant: **4 ROLL 5 WATER
    8 ICEWATER**
  Soda shop: **5 STRAW**
Freebooter: 6 PIRATE
Freed
  Rock pioneer: **4 ALAN**
Freedom
  from worry: **4 EASE**
  Put a price on: **7 SETBAIL**
  Swahili for: **5 UHURU**
  ~, briefly: **3 LIB**
**Free-for-all: 4 RIOT 5 BRAWL
    MELEE 6 FRACAS**
Freeh
  org.: **3 FBI**
Freelancer
  encl.: **4 SASE**
Freeload: 5 MOOCH
**Freeloader: 5 LEECH 6 SPONGE
    7 SPONGER**
Freely: 6 ATWILL
Freeman
  Actress: **4 MONA**
Freemen
  Anglo-Saxon: **6 CEORLS**
Freesia
  family: **4 IRIS**
Freestone
  fruit: **5 PEACH**
Freethinker: 7 HERETIC
Free-throw
  area: **4 LANE**
Freetown
  currency: **5 LEONE**
Freeway
  access: **4 RAMP**

  caution: **7 NOUTURN**
  Enter the: **5 MERGE**
  feature: **6 ONRAMP**
Freeze: 5 ICEUP
  over: **5 ICEUP**
  prefix: **4 ANTI**
  Word with: **4 DEEP**
Freezer
  bag name: **6 ZIPLOC**
  brand: **5 AMANA**
  stuff: **3 ICE**
  Take out of the: **4 THAW**
Freezing: 4 COLD 7 ICECOLD
  point: **4 ZERO**
  temperatures: **5 TEENS**
Freight: 5 CARGO
  carrier: **6 BOXCAR 7 FLATCAR**
  Filled with: **5 LADEN**
  hauler: **4 SEMI**
  unit: **6 ONETON**
  weight: **3 TON**
Freighter
  filler: **5 CARGO**
**"___ Freischütz" (Weber opera):
    3 DER**
Freleng
  Animator: **7 ISADORE**
Fremont
  guide: **9 KITCARSON**
**French: 6 GALLIC
    15 ROMANCELANGUAGE**
  1950s ~ president: **4 COTY**
  2001 ~ film: **6 AMELIE**
  actor Delon: **5 ALAIN**
  actress Anouk: **5 AIMEE**
  affirmative: **3 OUI**
  airport: **4 ORLY**
  article: **3 LES UNE**
  assembly: **5 SENAT**
  avant-garde artist: **3 ARP**
  bank: **4 RIVE**
  bean: **4 TETE**
  bench: **4 BANC**
  beverage: **3 THE**
  brandy: **6 COGNAC
    8 ARMAGNAC**
  bread: **5 FRANC**
  brother: **5 FRERE**
  cathedral city: **5 REIMS**

chalk: 4 TALC
cheer ending: 5 LEROI
cheese: 4 **BRIE** 7 FROMAGE
city: 4 CAEN LYON METZ NICE
   5 ARLES 6 CALAIS
cleric: 4 **ABBE**
collagist: 3 ARP
composer Edouard: 4 LALO
composer Erik: 5 SATIE
connections: 3 **ETS**
cop: 8 GENDARME
cordial flavoring: 4 ANIS
corp.: 3 CIE
cubist Fernand: 5 LEGER
cup: 5 TASSE
curve creation: 3 ARC
dear: 5 CHERI
department: 4 OISE ORNE
   5 AISNE
diarist: 3 NIN
director Clair: 4 RENE
door part: 4 PANE
evening: 4 SOIR
existentialist: 6 SARTRE
explorer: 7 LASALLE
farewell: 5 ADIEU
fashion designer: 6 CHANEL
   10 COCOCHANEL
fashion magazine: 4 ELLE
father: 4 **PERE**
females: 5 ELLES
film: 4 CINE
film award: 5 CESAR
force: 5 ARMEE
Former ~ coin: 3 SOU
friar: 4 ABBE
friend: 3 **AMI** 4 AMIE
friends: 4 AMIS
funnyman Jacques: 4 TATI
girlfriend: 4 AMIE
handle: 3 NOM
hat: 5 BERET
head: 4 TETE
holy woman (abbr.): 3 STE
honey: 5 CHERI
illustrator Gustave: 4 DORE
impressionist: 5 DEGAS MANET
   MONET
income: 5 RENTE

infinitive: 4 ETRE
inn: 7 AUBERGE
islands: 4 ILES
jeweler Lalique: 4 RENE
key: 3 CLE
king: 3 ROI
king Hugh: 5 CAPET
landscapist: 5 COROT
leave: 5 ADIEU
legislature: 5 SENAT
Like some ~ accents: 5 ACUTE
Like some ~ sounds: 5 NASAL
Like ~ doors: 5 PANED
Like ~ toast: 4 EGGY
love: 5 AMOUR
map word: 3 ILE
mark below C: 7 CEDILLA
mathematician: 6 PASCAL
military cap: 4 KEPI
mother: 4 MERE
movie: 4 CINE
mushroom: 4 CEPE
naval base: 5 BREST
negative: 3 NON
nobleman: 3 DUC 5 COMTE
noodle: 4 TETE
novelist: 4 GIDE LOTI ZOLA
   6 BALZAC
Old ~ coin: 3 **ECU** SOU
Old ~ dance: 7 GAVOTTE
one: 3 UNE
painter: 5 COROT LEGER
   MANET MONET 6 RENOIR
   7 UTRILLO
peak: 4 ALPE
physicist: 6 AMPERE
pianist: 5 SATIE
play part: 4 ACTE
pointillist: 6 SEURAT
port: 5 BREST ROUEN 6 CALAIS
   7 LEHAVRE
possessive: 3 MES SES TES
   4 AMOI ATOI
preposition: 3 DES 4 AVEC SANS
   5 APRES ENTRE
president Jacques: 6 CHIRAC
president residence: 6 ELYSEE
pronoun: 3 CES ILS LUI MOI
   MON SES TES TOI UNE

4 AMOI ELLE
protest phrase: 4 ABAS
pupil: 5 ELEVE
queen: 5 REINE
restaurant name part: 4 CHEZ
revolutionary: 5 MARAT
river: 4 EURE OISE ORNE
   5 ISERE LOIRE MARNE
   RHONE SAONE SARRE
   SELLE SOMME
roast: 4 ROTI
rocket: 6 ARIANE
romance: 5 AMOUR
room: 5 SALLE
satellite launcher: 6 ARIANE
school: 5 **ECOLE** LYCEE
sculptor: 5 RODIN
sea: 3 **MER**
seaport: 5 BREST
season: 3 ETE
seasoning: 3 SEL
silk: 4 SOIE
silk center: 4 LYON
soldier: 5 POILU
Some ~ sounds: 6 NASALS
soul: 3 AME
spa: 5 EVIAN
spot of land: 3 ILE
star: 6 ETOILE
states: 5 ETATS
story: 5 ETAGE
street: 3 RUE
student: 5 ELEVE
summer: 3 **ETE**
surname start: 3 DES
teacher: 6 MAITRE
textile city: 5 LILLE
tire: 4 PNEU
toast: 5 SALUT
toast portion: 5 SANTE
verb: 4 **ETRE**
vineyard: 3 CRU
water: 3 EAU 5 EVIAN
wave: 4 ONDE
way: 3 RUE
weapon: 4 ARME
When the ~ fry: 3 **ETE**
wine: 3 VIN 5 MEDOC
wine region: 6 ALSACE

wine valley: 5 LOIRE
~ Mrs.: 3 MME
~ Nobelist André: 4 GIDE
~ Oscar: 5 CESAR
French Chantilly: 4 LACE
"French Connection, The"
  Hackman role in ~: 5 DOYLE
French Foreign ___: 6 LEGION
"French Kiss"
  actress Meg: 4 RYAN
  costar: 5 KLINE
Frenchman: 4 GAUL
French Open
  1973 ~ champ Nastase: 4 ILIE
  1983 ~ champ: 4 NOAH
  1989 ~ champ: 5 CHANG
  1990–92 ~ champ: 5 SELES
  1999 ~ champ: 6 AGASSI
  Three-time ~ champ: 5 SELES
French Polynesia
  capital: 7 PAPEETE
French Riviera
  city: 4 NICE
French Sudan
  ~, today: 4 **MALI**
Frenzied: 4 AGOG AMOK WILD
   5 MANIC 6 HECTIC
   RAVING 7 BERSERK
  In a ~ way: 4 AMOK
  routine: 7 RATRACE
  (var.): 5 AMUCK
Frenzy: 4 RAGE 5 FUROR MANIA
  In a: 4 **AMOK**
Freon: 3 GAS
Frequency
  unit: 5 HERTZ
Frequent: 5 HAUNT
  author: 4 ANON
  caller: 4 AVON
  Far from: 4 RARE
  flier: 4 BIRD 5 PILOT
  fliers: 6 JETSET
  hangout: 5 HAUNT
  song subject: 4 LOVE
  ~ 007 foe: 3 KGB
Frequently: 3 OFT 4 ALOT
   5 **OFTEN** 8 OFTTIMES
  It's ~ 72: 3 PAR
  ~, in poetry: 3 **OFT**

Frère
  sibling: 5 SOEUR
Fresh: 3 NEW 4 AIRY ANEW PERT
      5 NOVEL **SASSY**
      6 RECENT RESTED
      UNUSED
  and firm: 5 CRISP
  Far from: 5 BANAL TRITE
  from the laundry: 5 CLEAN
  Get ~ with: 4 SASS
  information: 4 NEWS
  kid: 4 BRAT
  Least: 7 STALEST TRITEST
  Like ~ cake: 5 MOIST
  More: 5 NEWER
  No longer: 5 STALE
  Not: 5 STALE TRITE
  start: 3 NEO 7 RENEWAL
  Stay: 4 KEEP
  Still: 7 UNJADED
  talk: 4 SASS
"Fresh Air"
  airer: 3 NPR
Fresh as a ___: 5 DAISY
Freshen: 5 RENEW 6 AERATE
    AIROUT
Freshener: 6 SACHET
  Breath: 6 TICTAC
  scent: 4 PINE
  target: 4 ODOR
Freshly: 4 **ANEW**
  made: 3 NEW
  painted: 3 WET
"Freshmaker, The": 6 MENTOS
Freshman: 4 TEEN
  Academy: 5 PLEBE
  cap: 6 BEANIE
  language course: 6 LATINI
Fresh-mouthed: 4 PERT 5 SASSY
Freshness: 3 LIP 4 SASS
  Lose: 4 WILT 5 STALE
  Protect: 6 SEALIN
  Sign of: 4 SLAP
  Symbol of: 5 DAISY
"Fresh Prince of Bel Air"
  actress Tatyana: 3 ALI
Freshwater
  crustacean: 6 ISOPOD
  duck: 4 **TEAL**

  fish: 4 CHUB DACE PIKE RUDD
    5 BREAM 6 DARTER
  minnow: 6 REDFIN
Fresno
  paper: 3 BEE
Fret: 4 **STEW** 5 WORRY
Fretful: 7 INASTEW
Freud
  Article written by: 3 DER
  contemporary: 4 JUNG 5 **ADLER**
  ego: 3 ICH
  First stage of: 4 ORAL
  focus: 3 EGO
  focus (abbr.): 4 ANAL
  Psychoanalyst: 4 ANNA
  Surrealist influenced by: 4 DALI
Freudian
  concept: 3 **EGO** 6 LIBIDO
  error: 4 SLIP
  subject: 5 DREAM
  subjects: 3 IDS
Fri.
  Gal: 4 ASST
  preceder: 3 THU
___ Fria National Monument:
    4 AGUA
Friar: 5 ABBOT
  French: 4 ABBE
  Sherwood: 4 TUCK
Friars Club
  event: 5 **ROAST**
  official: 5 ABBOT
Frick
  collection: 3 ART
Friction: 6 STRIFE
  easer: 3 OIL
"Frida"
  actress Hayek: 5 SALMA
Friday: 3 COP
  Abbr. before: 3 SGT
  and Bilko: 4 SGTS
  Casual ~ castoff: 3 TIE
  catchphrase ender: 4 MAAM
  creator: 5 DEFOE
  Friend of: 6 CRUSOE
  Man: 4 AIDE
  org.: 4 LAPD
  player: 4 WEBB
  preceder: 3 GAL

program: 7 DRAGNET
rank (abbr.): 3 SGT
Sergeant: 3 JOE
What ~ wanted: 5 FACTS
___ **Friday:** 3 GAL SGT
Friday, Joe: 3 COP
Friday, Sgt.
  employer: 4 **LAPD**
  ___ **Friday's (restaurant):** 3 TGI
Fridge
  accessory: 6 MAGNET
  foray: 4 **RAID**
  name: 5 AMANA
  Old: 6 ICEBOX
  Raid the: 4 NOSH
  Stick in the: 4 **OLEO**
Fried
  lightly: 7 SAUTEED
  Pan for ~ rice: 3 WOK
"Fried Green Tomatoes"
  actress Cicely: 5 TYSON
  author Fannie: 5 FLAGG
Friedman
  subj.: 4 ECON
Friedrich
  German mineralogist: 4 MOHS
Friend: 3 PAL 4 ALLY 5 AMIGO
  address: 4 THEE
  As a ~, in French: 5 ENAMI
  Close: 3 PAL
  False: 4 IAGO USER 5 JUDAS
  Formal: 4 ALLY
  Four-footed: 3 PET
  French: 3 AMI 4 AMIE
  from afar: 6 PENPAL
  Good: 6 BONAMI
  in the 'hood: 3 BRO
  in war: 4 ALLY
  Like a best: 6 TRUEST
  opposite: 3 FOE
  Spanish: 5 AMIGO
  Western: 4 PARD
"Friend ___?": 5 ORFOE
Friendlier
  Become: 4 THAW
Friendliness: 5 AMITY
      8 BONHOMIE
Friendly: 4 WARM 6 GENIAL
      7 AMIABLE CORDIAL

Become: 4 WARM
Break in ~ relations: 4 RIFT
conversation: 4 CHAT
dog offering: 3 PAW
femme: 4 AMIE
intro: 3 ECO 4 USER
Kind of: 4 USER
Less: 5 ICIER
nation: 4 ALLY
prefix: 3 **ECO**
term of address: 5 KIDDO
Very: 5 CLOSE 10 BUDDYBUDDY
Friendly Islands: 5 TONGA
Friends
  and family: 4 KITH
  Familiar, as: 3 OLD
  in France: 5 AMIES
  in Italy: 5 AMICI
  pronoun: 4 THEE THOU
"Friends": 6 SITCOM
  actor Matt: 7 LEBLANC
  actor Matthew: 5 PERRY
  baby: 4 EMMA
  costar: 3 COX 6 KUDROW
      7 ANISTON
  friend: 4 JOEY ROSS 6 MONICA
      PHOEBE
  network: 3 NBC
  Phoebe's sister on: 6 URSULA
  ___ **friends:** 5 AMONG
Friendship: 5 **AMITY**
Friendship 7
  astronaut: 5 GLENN
Fries: 6 TATERS
  condiment: 4 SALT
  Future: 4 SPUD
  go-with: 6 CATSUP
  Kind of: 4 HOME
  order: 5 LARGE
  or slaw: 4 SIDE 8 SIDEDISH
Frigate
  front: 4 PROW
Frigg
  Husband of: 4 ODIN
Fright: 5 SCARE 6 TERROR
  Pale with: 5 ASHEN
  site: 5 STAGE
  Sound of: 3 EEK 4 GASP
  Sudden: 5 PANIC START

Frighten: 5 ALARM DAUNT
  SCARE UNMAN 7 STARTLE
  off: 5 DETER
Frightened
  horse: 6 REARER
  Visibly: 5 ASHEN
Frightening: 5 EERIE
  8 FEARSOME
  shout: 3 BOO
Frigid: 3 ICY 4 ICED 5 POLAR
  6 ARCTIC
  finish: 4 **AIRE**
  time: 6 ICEAGE
Frigidaire
  rival: 5 AMANA
Frilly: 4 LACY
Fringe: 4 EDGE
  benefit: 4 PERK
  Beyond the: 5 OUTRE
  material: 7 TASSELS
Frisbee: 4 **DISC** DISK
  inspiration: 6 PIETIN
  maker: 5 WHAMO
Frisco
  footballer: 5 NINER
Frisk
  ~, with "down": 3 PAT
Friskies
  Ask for: 3 MEW
  eater: 3 CAT
Frisky
  mammal: 5 OTTER
  pet: 6 KITTEN
Frist
  predecessor: 4 LOTT
Frito-Lay
  product: 9 CORNCHIPS
Frittata: 6 OMELET
  needs: 4 EGGS
Fritter
  away: 5 WASTE
Fritz
  Director: 4 LANG
  Go on the: 4 FAIL 5 ACTUP
  On the: 5 KAPUT
Frivolous
  gal of song: 3 SAL
Frizzy
  coif: 4 AFRO

Fro
  Flowed to and: 5 TIDED
  Go to and: 4 SWAY
  ___ fro: 5 TOAND
Frobe
  Actor: 4 GERT
Frock: 5 DRESS
  Forum: 4 TOGA
  German: 6 DIRNDL
  wearer: 5 FRIAR
Frodo
  Friend of: 3 ENT SAM
  portrayer: 10 ELIJAHWOOD
Frog: 6 LEAPER 7 CROAKER
  Future: 7 TADPOLE
  genus: 4 RANA
  kin: 4 **TOAD**
  Made like a: 5 LEAPT
  seat: 7 LILYPAD
  sound: 5 CROAK
  spit: 4 ALGA
  Twain's: 4 DANL
Froggy
  Talk like: 4 RASP
Frogman
  gear: 5 SCUBA
Frogner Park
  city: 4 OSLO
Frolic: 4 LARK PLAY ROMP
  5 SPORT 6 CAVORT
  PRANCE
Frolicking
  animal: 5 OTTER
From: 4 ASOF 5 SINCE
  above: 6 AERIAL
  birth: 6 INNATE
  l. to r.: 3 ACR
  now: 5 HENCE
  scratch: 4 **ANEW** 6 AFRESH
  square one: 4 **ANEW** 5 AGAIN
    6 AFRESH
  that place: 6 THENCE
  the beginning: 4 ANEW 5 ABOVO
    6 AFRESH DENOVO
  the beginning, in music:
    6 DACAPO
  the heart: 6 AORTAL 7 EARNEST
  then on: 5 SINCE
  the top: 4 **ANEW** 5 AGAIN

the U.S.: **4** AMER
the year one: **3** OLD
way back: **5** OFOLD
what source: **6** WHENCE
From ___
  (completely): **4** ATOZ
  (opening bit): **4** ATOB
From A ___ : 3 TOZ
Frome
  Fictional: **5** **ETHAN**
  "___ Frome": **5** ETHAN
From head ___ : 5 TOTOE
"From Here to Eternity"
  actor Montgomery: **5** CLIFT
  actress: **4** KERR
  wife: **5** KAREN
Fromm
  Psychoanalyst: **5** **ERICH**
  "___ From Muskogee": **4** OKIE
From the ___ : 5 GETGO
"From the Earth to the Moon"
  writer: **5** VERNE
"From the Terrace"
  author: **5** OHARA
"From ___ to Eternity": 4 HERE
"From ___ to Mozart": 3 MAO
"From where ___ ...": 4 ISIT
"From ___ With Love": 6 RUSSIA
From ___ Z: 3 **ATO**
Fronds
  Plant with: **4** FERN
  With ~ aplenty: **5** FERNY
Front: 3 ACT **4** FORE **6** VENEER
  Info: Prefix cue
  At the ~ of the line: **4** NEXT
  Back at the: **5** RETRO
  end: **3** IER
  False: **3** ACT **4** POSE **5** GUISE
      PSEUD **6** FACADE
  In: **5** AHEAD
  line: **6** ISOBAR
  money: **4** ANTE
  Out in: **5** AHEAD
  part: **11** BUSINESSEND
  porch: **5** STOOP
  Ship: **4** **PROW**
  Sock: **3** TOE
  Stage: **5** APRON
  Was in: **3** LED

wheel alignment: **5** TOEIN
Fronted: 3 LED
Frontier
  Final: **5** SPACE
  nickname: **4** DANL
  settlement: **7** OUTPOST
  trophy: **5** SCALP
Frontiersman
  ~ Carson: **3** KIT
  ~ Crockett: **4** DAVY
Frontman
  U2: **4** BONO
Fronton
  gear: **6** CESTAS
Front-page
  stuff: **4** NEWS
"Front Page, The"
  coauthor: **5** HECHT
Front-runner: 6 LEADER
Frosh
  Academy: **5** PLEBE
  Former: **4** **SOPH**
  topper: **6** BEANIE
Frost: 3 ICE **4** **HOAR** POET RIME
  bite: **3** NIP
  Bit of: **4** POEM
  lines: **4** POEM **5** VERSE
  Melt the ~ from: **5** DEICE
  over: **5** ICEUP
  prefix: **5** PERMA
  remover: **6** DEICER
  Touch of: **3** NIP
Frost, Jack
  touch: **3** NIP
Frost, Robert
  farm site: **5** DERRY
  piece: **4** POEM
Frost-covered: 4 RIMY **5** RIMED
Frosted: 4 **ICED** RIMY
  Get: **5** ICEUP
Frostflower: 5 ASTER
Frostiness: 3 NIP
Frosting
  pro: **4** ICER
  Put ~ on: **3** ICE
Frosty: 3 ICY **5** CRISP
      7 SNOWMAN
  Button, to: **4** NOSE
  covering: **4** HOAR RIME

eyes: 4 COAL
Froth: 4 FOAM
Frothy: 5 BARMY FOAMY LIGHT
Get: 4 FOAM
quaff: 3 ALE
Frowned-on
thing: 4 NONO
thing (var.): 4 TABU
Frowning: 3 SAD
Frozen
confection brand: 4 ICEE
dessert: 3 ICE 6 GELATO
    SORBET 7 SHERBET
dessert chain: 4 TCBY
dew: 4 HOAR
food brand: 4 EGGO 6 OREIDA
    8 BIRDSEYE
quarters: 6 IGLOOS
rain: 4 HAIL 5 SLEET
They can be: 6 ASSETS
treats: 4 ICES
waffle brand: 4 EGGO
~ Wasser: 3 **EIS**
Frug
Dance like the: 10 HULLYGULLY
Frugal
Be: 5 STINT 6 SCRIMP
fellow: 5 SAVER
Fruit
Aptly named: 4 UGLI
Big citrus: 6 POMELO
Big name in: 4 DOLE
Big name in ~ drinks: 5 MOTTS
Blackthorn: 4 **SLOE**
Breakfast: 5 MELON
center: 3 PIT 4 CORE
Cereal: 6 RAISIN
Chinese: 6 LITCHI
Chutney: 5 MANGO
Citrus: 4 LIME UGLI 5 LEMON
    6 ORANGE
cocktail fruit: 4 PEAR
Compote: 4 PEAR
covering: 4 RIND
Dried: 5 PRUNE
Early winter: 9 SNOWAPPLE
flaw: 6 BRUISE
Fleshy: 4 PEAR POME 5 PAPAW
for a twist: 4 LIME

Forbidden ~ site: 4 EDEN
Fuzzy: 4 **KIWI** 5 PEACH
Green: 4 KIWI LIME 5 OLIVE
Hybrid: 4 UGLI 7 TANGELO
Jamaican: 4 UGLI
Jelly: 5 GRAPE GUAVA
Juicy: 4 PEAR 5 MELON PEACH
    6 ORANGE
Margarita: 4 LIME
Mediterranean: 3 FIG 4 DATE
Melonlike: 5 PAPAW 6 PAPAYA
Newton: 3 FIG
Not a pretty: 4 UGLI
Oak: 5 ACORN
Oblong: 5 PAPAW
Orchard: 4 PEAR
Palm: 4 DATE
pastry: 7 STRUDEL
peel: 4 RIND SKIN
Pie: 5 APPLE
Plumlike: 4 SLOE
Purple: 4 SLOE
Sour: 4 SLOE 5 LEMON
spray: 4 ALAR
Tart: 4 SLOE
Trademarked: 4 UGLI
tree: 4 PEAR
Trifling: 3 FIG
Tropical: 4 DATE 5 DATES
    GUAVA MANGO 6 PAPAYA
Turkish: 3 FIG
Wintergreen: 8 TEABERRY
Wrinkly: 4 **UGLI** 5 PRUNE
Fruitcake: 3 NUT 4 LOON
Nutty as a: 5 LOOPY
Fruit drink: 3 **ADE** 5 CIDER
brand: 3 HIC
suffix: 3 ADE
Fruit-filled
dessert: 3 PIE
pastry: 7 STRUDEL
Fruitless: 4 ARID VAIN
Fruit of the Loom
rival: 5 HANES
Fruits de ___: 3 MER
Fruity
cocktail: 6 MAITAI
cooler: 3 ADE
dessert: 3 PIE 4 TART

drink: 3 **ADE** 7 SANGRIA
liqueur: 7 SLOEGIN
pastry: 4 TART
quaff: 3 ADE
spread: 3 JAM
Fruity-smelling
  compound: 5 ESTER
Frustrate: 4 FOIL 6 STYMIE
    THWART
Frustration
  Cry of: 5 AARGH
  ___-frutti: 5 TUTTI
Fry: 5 SAUTE
  Fish ~ sound: 3 SSS
  Small: 3 TOT 4 TOTS TYKE
    6 NIPPER
  When the French: 3 ETE
  Word before: 4 DEEP STIR
    5 SMALL
Frying
  medium: 4 LARD 7 DEEPFAT
  pan: 7 SKILLET
  Prepare for: 5 FLOUR
  Source of rings for: 5 ONION
Frypan
  Chinese: 3 WOK
"F Troop"
  corporal: 5 AGARN
  sergeant: 7 OROURKE
Ft. Worth
  school: 3 TCU
"___ Fu" (1970s western): 4 KUNG
Fudd
  Elmer: 4 TOON
  of cartoons: 5 **ELMER**
Fuddy-duddy: 4 DODO FOGY
    6 GEEZER STODGY
    13 STICKINTHEMUD
Fudge: 5 CHEAT
  flavor: 5 MAPLE MOCHA
  ~, to a dieter: 4 NONO
"Fudge!": 4 DARN RATS
Fudger
  Fact: 4 LIAR
Fuel
  Add ~ to: 5 STOKE
  additive: 3 STP
  Alternative: 7 GASOHOL
  Auto: 3 GAS

Barbecue: 7 PROPANE
Blast-furnace: 4 COKE
Bog: 4 PEAT
carrier: 5 OILER 6 TANKER
cartel: 4 OPEC
Chafing dish: 6 STERNO
Commercial: 7 COALGAS
efficiency abbr.: 3 MPG
Flamethrower: 6 NAPALM
Fossil: 3 GAS OIL 4 COAL
Funny-car: 5 NITRO
Furnace: 4 COKE
gas: 6 ETHANE
Hybrid: 7 GASOHOL
Lighter: 6 BUTANE
org.: 4 OPEC
Organic: 4 PEAT
prefix: 3 SYN
Vegetable: 4 PEAT
Fugard
  Playwright: 5 **ATHOL**
  title word: 5 ALOES
Fugitive: 7 ESCAPEE
  financier: 5 VESCO
  Help a: 4 ABET
"Fugitive, The"
  actor Barry: 5 MORSE
  actress Ward: 4 **SELA**
  pursuer: 6 GERARD
Fugue
  master: 4 BACH
Fuji
  competitor: 4 AGFA 5 KODAK
  outflow: 4 LAVA
Fujimori
  land: 4 PERU
  of Peru: 7 ALBERTO
Fulcrum
  locale: 6 SEESAW
  Oar: 5 THOLE
Fulda
  feeder: 4 **EDER**
Fulfill
  Fully: 4 SATE
Fulfilled: 3 MET
  Not: 5 UNMET
Full: 5 LADEN SATED 6 ENTIRE
  assemblies: 5 PLENA
  At ~ gallop: 5 APACE

At ~ speed: **5 AMAIN**
circle: **3 LAP**
Completely: **5 SATED**
Do a ~. monty: **5 STRIP**
extent: **4 SPAN**
Fill beyond: **4 SATE 7 SATIATE**
force: **5 BRUNT**
For the ~ orchestra: **5 TUTTI**
Going ~ tilt: **4 ATIT**
Hardly the ~ gamut: **4 ATOB**
house: **4 HAND**
house sign: **3 SRO**
In ~ flower: **4 OPEN 6 ABLOOM**
moon: **5 PHASE**
name part: **3 III**
Not at ~ power: **5 ONLOW**
of (suffix): **3 OSE**
of back talk: **5 SASSY**
of chutzpah: **5 NERVY**
of energy: **4 GOGO 5 ALIVE**
    PEPPY VITAL ZIPPY
of excitement: **4 AGOG**
of feeling: **5 LYRIC**
of fervor: **6 ONFIRE**
of good cheer: **5 MERRY**
of gossip: **5 DISHY**
of guile: **3 SLY 4 WILY**
of meaning: **4 DEEP**
of merriment: **6 JOCOSE**
of nervous energy: **5 ANTSY**
of oneself: **4 SMUG VAIN**
of pep: **4 PERT SPRY 5 ALIVE**
of school spirit: **6 RAHRAH**
of streaks: **5 LINY**
of substance: **5 MEATY**
of vice: **4 EVIL**
of vinegar: **5 PEPPY 6 ACETIC**
of wonder: **5 INAWE**
of zip: **4 PERT**
Playing with a ~ deck: **4 SANE**
    8 ALLTHERE
range: **5 GAMUT**
skirt: **6 DIRNDL**
With ~ force: **5 AMAIN**
Full-bodied: 4 RICH 6 ROBUST
Fuller
  figure: **4 DOME**
Fullest
  Enjoy to the: **5 SAVOR**

  extent: **4 HILT**
Full-house
  notice: **3 SRO**
"Full House"
  actor Bob: **5 SAGET**
Full-length: 5 UNCUT
"Full Metal Jacket"
  setting: **3 NAM**
Fullness: 7 SATIETY
Full-price
  payer: **5 ADULT**
Full-scale: 6 ALLOUT
Fully: 3 ALL 5 INALL
  fulfill: **4 SATE**
  grown: **5 ADULT**
  Not ~ closed: **4 AJAR**
Fulminate: 4 RAGE RAIL
Fulton
  power: **5 STEAM**
Fumble: 3 ERR
  for words: **3 HAW**
Fume: 4 BOIL STEW 5 STEAM
    6 SEERED SEETHE
  More than: **4 RAGE**
Fuming: 5 IRATE 7 ENRAGED
Fun: 4 JEST
  For: **7 ONALARK**
  Have: **4 PLAY 5 ENJOY**
  Make ~ of: **3 RAG RIB 4 JAPE**
    MOCK RAZZ 5 RAGON
    TEASE 6 DERIDE HOOTAT
    JEERAT PARODY
    7 SNEERAT
  Partner of: **5 GAMES**
  Poke ~ at: **3 KID RIB 4 MOCK**
    TWIT 5 TEASE 6 NEEDLE
  time: **3 GAS**
  ~, for short: **3 REC**
Function: 3 ACT JOB USE 4 ROLE
    TASK WORK
  Kind of: **4 TRIG**
  prefix: **3 DYS MAL**
  suffix: **3 ARY**
  Trig: **4 SINE 5 COSEC COTAN**
    6 COSINE SECANT
    7 ARCSINE
Functional: 5 UTILE 6 USABLE
  prefix: **3 DYS**
Fund: 5 ENDOW

for the future: **7** NESTEGG
Kind of: **5** SLUSH TRUST
   6 NOLOAD
org.: **3** SSA
Svgs.: **3** IRA
Fundamental: 3 KEY **4** CORE
   5 BASAL **BASIC**
position: **5** TENET
Fundamentals: 4 ABCS
Funder
   Campaign: **3** PAC
   PBS: **3** NEA
Fund-raiser: 7 BENEFIT
   8 TELETHON
   D.C.: **3** PAC
   Government: **5** LOTTO
   Popular: **6** RAFFLE **8** BAKESALE
Fund-raisers
   pass it: **3** HAT
   Some: **7** DINNERS
Fund-raising
   gp.: **3** PAC PTA
   letter: **6** APPEAL
   suffix: **4** THON
Funeral
   bell: **5** KNELL
   fire: **4** PYRE
   march symphony: **6** EROICA
   stand: **4** BIER
"Funeral in Berlin"
   author Deighton: **3** LEN
Funereal
   fires: **5** PYRES
Funfair
   feature: **4** RIDE
"Fun, Fun, Fun"
   car: **5** TBIRD
Fungi
   Fermenting: **6** YEASTS
   partner to form lichens: **5** ALGAE
   Tasty: **6** MORELS
Fungus
   Cereal: **5** ERGOT
   Grain: **4** SMUT
   growth: **4** MOLD **6** MILDEW
Funhouse
   sounds: **4** EEKS
Funk
   In a: **3** SAD

of Funk & Wagnalls: **5** ISAAC
Puts in a: **7** BUMSOUT
"Funky Cold Medina"
   rapper: **7** TONELOC
Fun-loving
   fellow: **15** GOODTIMECHARLIE
Funnel
   shape: **4** CONE
Funnel-shaped: 5 CONED CONIC
   flower: **7** PETUNIA
Funnies: 6 COMICS
Funny: 3 ODD **4** JOKE **5** ANTIC
   COMIC **7** COMEDIC
   RISIBLE STRANGE
   brothers: **6** MARXES
   business: **5** ANTIC **6** ANTICS
   guy: **3** WAG
   Have a ~ feeling: **5** SENSE
   Ironically: **3** WRY
   joke: **6** GASSER
   one: **4** RIOT **5** COMIC
   person: **4** CARD **5** CUTUP
   sketch: **4** SKIT
"Funny!": 4 HAHA
Funny-car
   fuel: **5** NITRO
"Funny Girl"
   actor Omar: **6** SHARIF
   composer Jule: **5** STYNE
Funnyman: 3 WIT
   ~ Jacques: **4** TATI
   ~ Jay: **4** LENO
   ~ Mort: **4** SAHL
Funt
   gear: **6** CAMERA
   TV host: **5** ALLEN
   Word from: **5** SMILE
Fur: 4 COAT HIDE **6** PELAGE
   Brown: **5** OTTER STOAT
   6 NUTRIA
   Expensive: **4** MINK **5** SABLE
   6 ERMINE
   Like the ~ seal: **5** EARED
   Lose: **4** SHED
   Make the ~ fly: **4** SHED
   piece: **4** WRAP **5** STOLE
   Rabbit: **4** CONY **5** CONEY LAPIN
   Royal: **6** ERMINE
   tycoon: **5** **ASTOR**

"Für ___": 5 ELISE
Furbys
    and others: 4 FADS
Furies
    Avenging: 9 EUMENIDES
    One of the: 6 ALECTO
Furious: 5 ANGRY **IRATE**
    with: 5 MADAT
"Fur Is Dead"
    org.: 4 PETA
Furlongs
    Eight: 4 MILE
Furlough: 5 LEAVE
Furloughed: 7 ONLEAVE
Furnace: 4 KILN
    Blast ~ input: 3 ORE 7 IRONORE
    button: 5 RESET
    fodder: 4 COAL
    fuel: 3 OIL 4 COKE
    output: 4 HEAT
    Put through a: 5 SMELT
    tender: 6 STOKER
Furnish: 4 LEND 5 ENDOW
        EQUIP YIELD 6 RENDER
        7 ENTITLE
    food: 5 CATER
    with gear: 5 EQUIP
Furnished
    Less: 5 BARER
Furnishing
    Cubicle: 4 DESK
    style: 5 DECOR
Furnishings: 5 DECOR
    Big name in: 4 IKEA
Furniture
    Bar: 5 STOOL 6 STOOLS
    Classroom: 5 DESKS
    Clean the: 4 DUST
    designer Charles: 5 EAMES
    ensemble: 5 SUITE
    finisher: 7 STAINER
    Fix some: 6 RECANE
    giant: 4 IKEA
    Hawaiian ~ wood: 3 KOA
    Like Chippendale: 6 ROCOCO
    Like some: 5 OAKEN 6 INLAID
    Living room: 4 SOFA 5 DIVAN
        8 ARMCHAIR
    mover: 3 VAN

Nursery: 4 CRIB
Office: 4 DESK 5 DESKS
Parlor: 10 POOLTABLES
polish scent: 5 LEMON
store section: 5 SOFAS
Versatile: 6 DAYBED 7 SOFABED
wheel: 6 CASTER
wood: 3 ASH OAK 4 TEAK
    5 CEDAR
worker: 7 STAINER
Furor: 3 ADO 4 RAGE 5 MANIA
Furrier
    Famed: 5 **ASTOR**
    offering: 4 PELT 6 ERMINE
Furrow: 3 **RUT** 4 KNIT LINE
        SEAM
    fillers: 5 SEEDS
    former: 3 HOE 4 PLOW
    Narrow: 5 STRIA
Furrowed: 4 KNIT 7 STRIATE
    It may be: 4 BROW
Furry: 6 PILOSE
    feet: 4 PAWS
    frolicker: 5 OTTER
    neckwear: 3 BOA
    sci-fi critter: 4 **EWOK**
    sitcom E.T.: 3 ALF
    swimmer: 5 **OTTER**
    ~ Australian: 5 KOALA
Furry-tailed
    rodent: 8 DORMOUSE
Furtado
    Singer: 5 NELLY
Further: 3 AND TOO 4 ALSO ELSE
        MORE
    Go no: 3 END 4 STOP
    Refrain from taking ~ action:
        6 SITPAT
    Say: 3 **ADD**
    shorten: 5 RESAW
    Without ~ delay: 3 NOW
Furthermore: 3 **AND** TOO 4 ALSO
        PLUS
Furtive: 3 SLY 6 SNEAKY
    In a ~ manner: 5 SLYLY
    look: 4 PEEK
    one: 5 SNEAK
    whisper: 4 PSST
Furtively: 8 ONTHESLY

Follow: **4** TAIL
Move: **5** SIDLE SLINK SNEAK
    6 TIPTOE
Fury: 3 IRE **4** RAGE **5** ANGER
    WRATH
Fusco, Paul
  TV puppet voiced by: **3** ALF
Fuse: 3 WED **4** MELD WELD
    5 SMELT UNITE
    6 CEMENT SOLDER
  metal: **4** WELD
  Molotov cocktail: **3** RAG
  unit: **3** AMP **6** AMPERE
  Word on a: **4** AMPS
Fuselage
  fastener: **5** RIVET
Fusilli: 5 PASTA
Fusion: 5 ALLOY
Fuss: 3 ADO **4** FRET STEW STIR
    TODO **5** HOOHA STINK
    6 HASSLE HOOPLA
  over oneself: **5** PREEN
  over, with "on": **4** DOTE
  Put up a: **4** BALK **6** BEEFED
    7 PROTEST
Fussbudget: 4 PRIG **5** BIDDY
Futhark
  symbol: **4** RUNE
Futile: 4 VAIN **5** NOUSE **6** OTIOSE
    7 USELESS
Future
  atty.'s exam: **4** LSAT
  DA's course: **6** PRELAW
  Deck of the: **5** TAROT
  doc's exam: **4** MCAT
  examiner: **4** SEER **6** ORACLE
    7 SEERESS
  fern: **5** SPORE
  fish: **3** ROE
  flour: **5** GRIST
  flower: **4** SEED

frog: **7** TADPOLE
fry: **3** ROE
Funds for the: **8** NESTEGGS
indicator: **4** OMEN
In the: **5** AHEAD HENCE LATER
In the near: **4** ANON SOON
Know the: **7** SEEINTO
Near: **6** OFFING
Now or in the: **4** EVER
oak: **5** ACORN
One with a promising:
    7 STARLET
Past, present, or: **5** TENSE
plant: **4** SEED
queen: **4** PAWN
school: **3** ROE
Sign of the: **4** OMEN
tulip: **4** BULB
"Future Shock"
  writer Toffler: **5** ALVIN
Futurist: 4 SEER
Futuristic
  play: **3** RUR
  servant: **5** ROBOT
Fuzz: 3 NAP **4** COPS HEAT LINT
Fuzzbuster
  finding: **5** RADAR
Fuzzy: 5 VAGUE **7** UNCLEAR
  Become: **4** BLUR
  fruit: **4** KIWI **5** PEACH
  hang-ups: **4** DICE
  image: **4** BLUR
Fuzzy Wuzzy
  lack: **4** HAIR
"Fuzzy Wuzzy ___ fuzzy":
    5 WASNT
FX
  subjects: **3** ETS
FYI
  Part of: **3** FOR
___ Fyne, Scotland: 4 LOCH

Gg

G: 3 KEY 4 CLEF NOTE THOU
  Black key above: 5 AFLAT
  follower: 4 SUIT
  neighbor: 5 AFLAT
  The ~ in GTO: 4 GRAN
G, Kenny
  buy: 4 REED
  instrument: 3 SAX
  record label: 6 ARISTA
G4
  computer: 3 MAC
G-8
  member: 3 USA
Ga.
  city: 3 ATL
  neighbor: 3 ALA FLA 4 TENN
  setting: 3 EST
Gab: 3 JAW YAK 4 CHAT CHIN
    TALK 6 NATTER
    7 PRATTLE
  suffix: 4 FEST
Gab and gab: 5 RUNON
    8 NATTERON
Gable
  Butler, for: 4 ROLE
  part: 4 EAVE
  place: 4 ROOF
Gabler
  creator: 5 IBSEN
  Ibsen's: 5 HEDDA
  "___ Gabler": 5 HEDDA
  ___ Gables, Florida: 5 CORAL
Gabor
  and Perón: 4 **EVAS**
  sister: 3 **EVA** 5 MAGDA 6 ZSAZSA
Gabor, Zsa Zsa
  1966 ~ comedy:
    15 ARRIVEDERCIBABY
Gabriel: 3 SAN
  companion: 5 URIEL
  ___ Gabriel: 3 SAN
Gabrielle
  Model: 5 REECE

Gad
  about: 4 ROAM **ROVE**
    6 RAMBLE 7 TRAIPSE
Gadabout: 4 GOER 5 ROVER
    6 ROAMER
Gadget: 5 GIZMO 6 DOODAD
  Kitchen: 5 CORER DICER
    PARER **RICER** TIMER
    6 BASTER BEATER
    GRATER OPENER PEELER
    REAMER
  Sharp: 3 AWL
Gadsden Purchase
  city: 6 TUCSON
"Gadzooks!": 4 EGAD OATH
Gaea
  Child of: 5 TITAN
Gael: 4 CELT SCOT
  college: 4 IONA
  tongue: 4 ERSE
Gaelic: 4 **ERSE**
  name for Ireland: 4 EIRE
  poet: 6 OSSIAN
  pop star: 4 ENYA
  Scots: 4 **ERSE**
  tongue: 4 **ERSE**
Gaetano
  Librettist: 5 ROSSI
Gaff: 4 SPAR
Gaffe: 5 ERROR
  Half a: 3 BOO
Gaffer
  aide: 7 BESTBOY
Gag: 4 JAPE JEST JOKE
  reflex: 4 HAHA
  response, informally: 4 LAFF
Gaga
  Be ~ over: 4 RAVE 5 ADORE
  Went ~ over: 5 LOVED
Gagarin
  Cosmonaut: 4 **YURI**
Gage, Nicholas
  book: 5 **ELENI**

Gaggle
  formation: 3 VEE
  greeting: 4 HONK
  member: 5 GOOSE
  members: 5 GEESE
Gagné
  of baseball: 4 ERIC
Gailey
  Actor: 4 FRED
Gain
  access: 5 ENTER LOGIN
  altitude: 4 SOAR
  entry: 5 GETIN
  Grid: 5 YARDS
  in the polls: 5 SURGE
  Monetary: 5 LUCRE
  Small football: 4 YARD
  Unrealized: 11 PAPERPROFIT
Gained
  a lap: 3 **SAT**
Gainesville
  athlete: 5 GATOR
  City near: 5 **OCALA**
Gains
  Ill-gotten: 4 LOOT PELF SWAG
      5 BOOTY LUCRE
      11 FILTHYLUCRE
  NFL: 3 **YDS**
Gainsay: 4 DENY 5 BELIE
Gait: 4 PACE STEP
  Easy: 4 LOPE TROT 5 AMBLE
  Fast: 6 GALLOP
  Hobbling: 4 GIMP
Gaius
  garb: 4 TOGA
  greeting: 3 AVE
Gal
  counterpart: 3 GUY
  of song: 3 **SAL**
  Society: 3 DEB
  ~ Fri.: 4 ASST
Gal.
  Book before: 3 EPH
  parts: 3 QTS
Gala: 4 BASH FETE 5 EVENT
      6 SOIREE
Galahad
  Like: 4 PURE
  Mother of: 6 ELAINE

  title: 3 SIR
Galápagos
  creature: 6 IGUANA
  owner: 7 ECUADOR
Galatea
  Love of: 4 ACIS
Galatians
  Book before ~ (abbr.): 3 EPH
Galba
  Emperor after: 4 OTHO
  greeting: 3 AVE
  predecessor: 4 NERO
Gale: 5 STORM
  family pet: 4 TOTO
  Novelist: 4 ZONA
  Sail in a: 4 SCUD
Galena: 3 ORE 7 LEADORE
Galería de ___: 4 ARTE
Galilee: 3 SEA
  town: 4 CANA
Galileo: 5 **PISAN**
  birthplace: 4 PISA
Gall: 5 CRUST NERVE
Gallagher
  Actress: 5 MEGAN
  of Oasis: 4 NOEL
Gallantry
  RAF award for: 3 DSO
Gallery
  Art: 5 SALON
  display: 3 **ART**
  district of NYC: 4 SOHO
  Do a ~ job: 4 HANG 6 REHANG
  Flashy ~ display: 5 OPART
  Fruit in a: 9 STILLLIFE
  London: 4 **TATE**
  NYC: 4 MOMA
  Washington: 5 FREER
Galley
  Ancient: 7 TRIREME
  Do ~ work: 4 EDIT 7 TYPESET
  gear: 4 OARS
  goofs: 5 TYPOS 6 ERRATA
  Like a: 5 OARED
  marking: 4 STET 5 CARET
  need: 3 OAR
  Remove from the: 4 DELE
  tool: 3 OAR
  Two-tiered: 6 BIREME

Gallic
girlfriend: 4 **AMIE**
goodbye: 5 ADIEU
Gallico, Paul
title character: 5 ARRIS
Gallic Wars
hero: 6 CAESAR
Gallimaufry: 4 OLIO 7 MELANGE
Gallivant: 3 GAD 4 ROAM ROVE
       7 TRAIPSE
Gallo
brother: 5 JULIO 6 ERNEST
Gallon
fraction: 4 PINT 5 QUART
Gallons
252 wine ~: 3 TUN
Gallop: 3 HIE 4 GAIT LOPE RACE
At full: 5 APACE
Easy: 6 CANTER
Galloper
Graceful: 4 ARAB
Galloping: 5 RAPID SWIFT
"Galloping Ghost"
of football: 9 REDGRANGE
"Galloping Gourmet, The"
Graham: 4 KERR
Galloway
gal: 4 LASS
Gallows
loop: 5 NOOSE
reprieve: 4 STAY
Gallup
concern: 5 TREND
work: 4 POLL
Galoot: 3 **APE** LUG MUG OAF
       6 BIGAPE
Galore: 7 APLENTY
Gals.
Fourths of: 3 QTS
Galvanization
metal: 4 ZINC
Galway, James
hometown: 7 BELFAST
instrument: 5 FLUTE
Galway Bay
island group: 4 ARAN
Gambia
neighbor: 7 SENEGAL
Gambit: 4 RUSE 6 TACTIC

Gamble: 3 BET 4 DARE RISK
Gambler
asset: 4 LUCK
loss: 5 SHIRT
marker: 3 IOU 4 CHIT
mecca: 4 RENO 6 CASINO
method: 6 SYSTEM
money: 5 STAKE
woe: 4 LOSS
Gambling: 4 VICE
city: 4 RENO
game: 3 LOO 4 FARO KENO
       5 BEANO LOTTO MONTE
mecca: 4 RENO
site (abbr.): 3 OTB
Gambol: 4 PLAY ROMP SKIP
Place to: 3 LEA
Game
32-card ~: 4 **SKAT**
48-card ~: 8 PINOCHLE
accessory: 8 EGGTIMER
Ahead of the: 5 ONEUP
aim: 3 WIN
Alley: 7 TENPINS
Ball: 5 BOCCE
Be in the: 4 PLAY
Big: 3 ELK 4 DEER
Big ~ venue: 5 ARENA
bird: 8 PHEASANT
Board: 5 CHESS PENTE SORRY
Call a: 3 REF UMP
Card: 3 GIN **LOO** UNO WAR
       4 SKAT STUD 6 CASINO
       ECARTE FANTAN GOFISH
       7 OLDMAID
Casino: 4 **FARO** KENO 5 CRAPS
catcher: 5 SNARE
center: 3 TAC
Close, in a: 4 WARM
Computer: 4 DOOM MYST
Con: 4 **SCAM** 5 BUNKO STING
       8 FLIMFLAM
division: 4 HALF
ender: 4 HORN MATE
ending: 4 ALAI
Final Four: 4 SEMI
First: 6 OPENER
fish: 4 BASS TUNA 5 TROUT
       6 MARLIN TARPON

Gets: **6** SNARES
Go for: **4** HUNT
Half court: **4** ALAI
High-risk:
   15 RUSSIANROULETTE
"It": **3** TAG
keeper: **5** SNARE **6** ARCADE
Kids': **3** TAG **8** PATACAKE
   REDROVER **9** HOPSCOTCH
   SIMONSAYS
   11 HIDEANDSEEK
Lawn: **5** BOCCI
Like a perfect: **5** NOHIT
maker: **5** ATARI
Match: **3** NIM **7** OLDMAID
Mating: **5** CHESS
Middle of a: **3** TAC
named for a king: **4** FARO
needs: **5** RULES
Numbers: **4** KENO **5** BEANO
   BINGO LOTTO
of chance: **4** KENO **5** BEANO
   LOTTO
of chukkers: **4** POLO
one: **6** OPENER
on horseback: **4** POLO
opener: **3** TIC
piece: **3** DIE MAN PEG **4** TILE
plan: **4** IDEA **8** SCENARIO
   STRATEGY
played with dollar bills:
   10 LIARSPOKER
point: **4** ADIN
Pub: **5** DARTS **7** SNOOKER
ragout: **5** SALMI
room: **3** DEN **6** ARCADE
Running: **3** TAG
segment: **4** HALF
Shell: **4** SCAM
Simple: **4** PONG
Small: **4** PREY **5** HARES
Spelling: **5** GHOST
stick: **6** CROSSE
stickers: **6** SPEARS
Still in the: **5** **ALIVE**
Three-card: **5** MONTE
Three-player: **4** **SKAT**
winner: **3** OOO
with aces and chips: **4** GOLF

with car tokens: **4** LIFE
with mallets: **4** POLO
with matchsticks: **3** NIM
with pitching: **4** GOLF
with Skip cards: **3** UNO
with trump cards: **4** SKAT
with two bases: **7** ONEACAT
Won every: **5** SWEPT
Word: **5** GHOST
"___ Game, The": **6** PAJAMA
"Game, ___, and match": **3** SET
Game-ending
   cry: **3** GIN **4** IWIN MATE
Games
   Big name in: **4** SEGA **5** ATARI
      HOYLE
   Fun and: **3** REC
   gp.: **3** IOC
   Like some: **5** NOHIT
   Site of ancient: **5** NEMEA
   Some big: **5** BOWLS
   What some ~ end in: **4** ATIE
Game show
   announcer Don: **5** PARDO
   announcer Johnny: **5** OLSON
   Comedy Central ~ host: **5** STEIN
   first name: **4** ALEX MERV
      5 REGIS
   host: **5** EMCEE
   host Pat: **5** SAJAK
   host Trebek: **4** ALEX
   offer: **5** PRIZE
   panelist Peggy: **4** CASS
   prize: **3** CAR **4** TRIP **6** NEWCAR
   request: **3** ANA ANE ANI ANO
Gamesmanship
   Turn on the: **5** PSYCH
"Games People Play"
   author: **5** BERNE
Gamete
   Female: **4** OVUM
Gametes: 3 OVA
Gaming
   cube: **3** DIE
   device: **10** PUNCHBOARD
Gamma
   preceder: **4** BETA
Gamma ___: 8 GLOBULIN
Gamut: 4 **ATOZ** **5** RANGE

Hardly the full: 4 ATOB
Gamy: 3 OFF
Gance
  Director: 4 ABEL
Gandalf
  Letter for: 4 RUNE
  portrayer McKellen: 3 IAN
Gander: 4 MALE 5 GOOSE
  Take a ~ at: 3 EYE SEE
Ganders: 5 GEESE
Gandhi: 5 HINDU RAJIV
    6 INDIRA
  associate: 5 NEHRU
  Father of: 5 NEHRU
  land: 5 INDIA
  Mrs. ~: 6 INDIRA
  Rule opposed by: 3 RAJ
  Title for: 7 MAHATMA
Gandolfini
  costar: 5 FALCO
  role: 7 SOPRANO
G&S
  title character: 3 IDA
Gang: 3 MOB 5 POSSE 6 CIRCLE
  addition: 4 STER
  Chinese: 4 TONG
  L.A. ~ member: 4 CRIP
  land: 4 TURF
  leader: 4 KOOL
  Like the ~, in song: 7 ALLHERE
  See the old: 5 REUNE
  Some ~ members: 6 BIKERS
  suffix: 4 STER
  territory: 4 TURF
  weapon: 4 SHIV
"___ Gang": 3 OUR
Gangbuster
  ~ Ness: 5 ELIOT
Ganges
  city: 5 PATNA
  garb: 4 SARI 5 SARIS
  Where the ~ flows: 5 INDIA
Gangling: 5 LANKY
Gangplank: 4 RAMP
  Down the: 6 ASHORE
Gangsta
  recitals: 4 RAPS
"Gangsta's Paradise"
  rapper: 6 COOLIO

Gangster: 4 HOOD THUG
  blade: 4 SHIV
  chaser: 4 GMAN
  gal: 4 **MOLL**
  gun: 3 **GAT** 6 ROSCOE
  known as Scarface: 6 CAPONE
  nickname: 5 BUGSY
  toppers: 7 FEDORAS
  ~ Frank: 5 NITTI
  ~ Lansky: 5 MEYER
Gangway: 5 AISLE
Gannet: 5 SOLAN
Gannon University
  locale: 4 ERIE
"___ Gantry": 5 ELMER
Ganymede: 4 MOON
Gap: 4 VOID 5 CHASM SPACE
    6 HIATUS LACUNA
  Neuron: 7 SYNAPSE
Gape: 4 GAWK OGLE YAWN
Gaping
  hole: 3 MAW 5 CHASM
  pit: 5 ABYSS
Garage
  band tape: 4 DEMO
  capacity: 6 ONECAR
  contents: 3 CAR 4 AUTO
  event: 4 SALE
  figs.: 4 ESTS
  Gun in the: 3 REV
  job: 4 LUBE
  Kind of: 6 ONECAR TWOCAR
  Large: 4 BARN
  Like most ~ sale goods: 4 USED
  occupant: 4 AUTO
  sale caveat: 4 ASIS
  Sitcom in a: 4 TAXI
  stain: 3 OIL
Garam ___ (spice mix): 6 MASALA
Garb: 4 TOGS 5 DRESS 6 ATTIRE
    ENROBE
Garbage: 5 TRASH
  barge: 4 SCOW
  can, on a PC: 4 ICON
  collector: 6 ASHMAN
  hauler: 4 SCOW
  receptacle: 3 BIN 6 ASHCAN
  Taking out the: 5 CHORE
Garbed: 4 CLAD 5 ROBED

Garbo: 5 SWEDE 7 SWEDISH
  1932 ~ role: 8 MATAHARI
  1936 ~ role: 7 CAMILLE
  Actress: 5 **GRETA**
  homeland: 6 SWEDEN
  line ender: 5 ALONE
Garcia
  Actor: 4 ANDY
Garcia ___, Frederico
  Poet: 5 LORCA
Garciaparra
  of baseball: 5 NOMAR
Garçon: 6 WAITER
  has one: 7 CEDILLA
  list: 5 CARTE
Garden
  area: 3 BED 4 PLOT
  Biblical: 4 EDEN
  bulb: 5 TULIP
  decoration: 3 URN 5 GNOME
  Do ~ work: 3 HOE 4 WEED
  entrance: 4 GATE
  fertilizer: 4 PEAT
  fertilizer brand: 5 ORTHO
  figure: 4 ADAM 5 GNOME
  First: 4 EDEN
  flower: 4 IRIS 5 PANSY
    7 BEGONIA TEAROSE
    10 SNAPDRAGON
  Genesis: 4 **EDEN**
  Hose not for the: 6 NYLONS
  hose problem: 4 KINK
  intruder: 4 WEED
  Kind of: 4 BEER
  Make a row in the: 3 HOE
  party: 3 EVE 4 ADAM
  pest: 4 SLUG 5 APHID
  products name: 5 ORTHO
  product word: 3 GRO
  Rock ~ herb: 5 SEDUM
  shelter: 5 ARBOR 6 GAZEBO
  shrub: 6 AZALEA
  spot: 4 **EDEN**
  spot of London: 3 KEW
  star: 5 ASTER
  starter: 4 SEED
  statue: 5 GNOME
  tool: 3 HOE 4 RAKE 5 EDGER
    SPADE

  variety: 4 SOSO
  worker: 4 HOER
Garden City
  ~ University: 7 ADELPHI
Gardener
  bane: 5 WEEDS
  in action: 4 HOER
  need: 4 HOSE
  of rhyme: 4 MARY
  Original: 4 ADAM
  purchase: 4 BULB LIME SEED
  soil: 4 LOAM 5 LOESS
  tool: 3 HOE 4 RAKE 5 EDGER
    SPADE 6 TROWEL
  ~, at times: 4 HOER 5 HOSER
    RAKER 6 PRUNER SPADER
    WEEDER
Gardening
  Do some: 4 WEED
  tool: 3 HOE 5 EDGER SPADE
    6 WEEDER
"Garden of ___, The" (Wilde):
  4 EROS
"Garden of Earthly Delights"
  author: 5 OATES
  painter: 5 BOSCH
___ Gardens: 3 KEW 5 BUSCH
Garden-variety: 5 PLAIN
  USUAL 6 NORMAL
  7 AVERAGE
Gardner
  1948 ~ film:
    15 ONETOUCHOFVENUS
  Actress: 3 **AVA**
  Author: 4 **ERLE**
  creation: 5 MASON
  pen name: 6 AAFAIR
Garfield: 3 CAT 6 PETCAT
  TOMCAT
  middle name: 5 **ABRAM**
  predecessor: 5 HAYES
  successor: 6 ARTHUR
"Garfield"
  dog: 4 **ODIE**
  foil: 4 **ODIE**
  girlfriend: 6 ARLENE
  guy: 3 JON
  waitress: 4 IRMA
Garfield, James ___: 5 **ABRAM**

Garfield County, Oklahoma
Seat of: 4 ENID
Garfunkel
Ex-partner of: 5 SIMON
Singer: 3 ART
"Gargantua and Pantagruel"
author: 8 RABELAIS
Gargantuan: 4 HUGE
Gargle: 5 RINSE
Gargoyle
Like a: 4 UGLY
Garibaldi
Gen.: 8 GIUSEPPE
Garish: 4 LOUD 5 GAUDY
6 ROCOCO
light: 4 NEON
Garland
Hawaiian: 3 **LEI**
~, originally: 4 GUMM
Garlic
Dish made with ~ and butter:
6 SCAMPI
mayonnaise: 5 AIOLI
portion: 5 CLOVE
trait: 4 ODOR
Garment
border: 3 HEM
Draped: 4 SARI TOGA
Foundation: 6 CORSET
Hooded: 4 COWL 5 PARKA
Loose: 4 ROBE SARI TOGA
5 TUNIC
Protective: 5 SMOCK
Sleeveless: 4 CAPE VEST
Garner: 3 NET 4 EARN 5 AMASS
6 TAKEIN
of jazz: 6 ERROLL
Garner, Jennifer
series: 5 ALIAS
Garner, John ___ : 5 NANCE
Garnet: 3 RED 7 DEEPRED
Garnish
Bar: 5 OLIVE
Burger: 5 ONION
Drink: 4 LIME RIND 5 OLIVE
Gelatin: 5 ASPIC
Gibson: 5 ONION
Gimlet: 4 LIME
Green: 5 CRESS

Martini: 5 **OLIVE**
Meat: 5 ASPIC
Salad: 5 CRESS
Garr
Actress: 4 **TERI**
role: 4 INGA
Garret: 4 LOFT
Garrick
Newsman: 5 **UTLEY**
Garrison: 8 PRESIDIO
pl. (abbr.): 3 FTS
Garroway
TV host: 4 DAVE
Garson
Actress: 5 GREER
Garson, Greer
role: 5 CURIE 7 MINIVER
Gary
Actor: 5 BUSEY 6 OLDMAN
SINISE
Cartoonist: 6 LARSON
Former senator: 4 HART
Golfer: 6 PLAYER
Pundit: 5 BAUER
state (abbr.): 3 IND
Gas: 4 FUEL
additive: 3 STP 5 ETHYL
Anesthetic: 6 ETHENE
Bottled: 7 PROPANE
brand in Canada: 4 ESSO
choice: 8 UNLEADED
co.: 4 UTIL
Dangerous: 5 RADON
Early discount ~ chain: 4 HESS
E, on a ~ gauge: 5 EMPTY
Flammable: 6 ETHANE
from the past: 4 ESSO
Fuel: 6 ETHANE
gauge reading: 4 FULL
gauge warning: 5 EMPTY
Give the: 3 REV
guzzler: 6 ENGINE
Inert: 4 NEON 5 ARGON XENON
in glass: 4 NEON
It's a: 4 **NEON**
Laughing: 5 OXIDE
Light: 4 **NEON**
Like some: 6 LEADED
Marsh: 7 METHANE

Natural ~ component:
  6 ETHANE
Nerve: 5 SARIN
Noble: 4 NEON 5 XENON
Odorless: 5 ARGON 6 ETHANE
Old ~ brand: 4 **ESSO**
or clutch: 5 PEDAL
Out of: 5 TIRED
Past: 4 ESSO
prefix: 3 AER
provider: 4 PUMP
pump choice (abbr.): 3 REG
Radioactive: 5 RADON
rating: 6 OCTANE
Refrigerant: 5 FREON
Run out of: 4 TIRE
Sign: 4 NEON
thief device: 6 SIPHON
Treat with: 6 AERATE
~, to a Brit: 6 PETROL
Gasconade: 4 BRAG
Gases
  Heaviest of the noble: 5 RADON
  Like some: 5 INERT
Gasket: 5 **ORING**
  Blow a: 4 RAGE 5 GOAPE
Gaslight ___: 3 ERA
Gasohol: 4 FUEL
Gasoline: 4 FUEL
  rating: 6 OCTANE
  type: 6 HITEST
Gasp: 4 PANT
  Famous last ~ start: 4 ETTU
  in delight: 3 OOH
"Gaspard de la ___": 4 NUIT
Gasser: 4 RIOT
Gasset, ___ y
  Philosopher: 6 ORTEGA
Gas station
  freebie: 3 AIR
  store: 8 MINIMART
Gasteyer
  Comic: 3 **ANA**
Gaston
  of baseball: 4 CITO
Gastric
  Like ~ juice: 4 ACID
Gastroenteritis
  cause: 5 ECOLI

Gastronome: 7 EPICURE
Gat: 3 ROD 6 HEATER
Gate: 4 TAKE
  fastener: 4 HASP 5 LATCH
  Get out of the: 5 START
  Give the: 4 OUST
  Open, as a: 5 UNBAR
  part: 5 HINGE
  Starting: 4 POST
  Water: 3 DAM
Gate-crash: 6 IMPOSE
  7 INTRUDE
Gatekeeper: 5 GUARD
  7 STPETER
Gates
  and others: 4 CEOS
  Like heaven's: 6 PEARLY
  Race with: 6 SLALOM
Gateway
  Like a: 6 ARCHED
  products: 3 PCS
  rival: 4 DELL
  Shinto temple: 5 TORII
  to Australia: 6 SYDNEY
Gateway Arch
  designer Saarinen: 4 EERO
Gather: 4 CULL REAP 5 **AMASS**
  GLEAN INFER 6 RAKEIN
  gradually: 5 GLEAN
  grain: 4 **REAP**
  in bundles: 6 SHEAVE
  intelligence: 3 SPY
  leaves: 4 RAKE
  on a surface: 4 SORB 6 ADSORB
  one's strength: 6 RESTUP
  together: 5 **AMASS**
  with difficulty: 8 SCRAPEUP
  with effort: 7 SCAREUP
Gatherer
  Clue ~ (abbr.): 3 DET
  Pollen: 3 BEE
Gathering: 3 BEE 4 BEVY
  5 GROUP
  Afternoon: 3 TEA
  Ancient ~ place: 4 STOA
  5 AGORA
  clouds: 4 OMEN
  Farm: 3 HAY
  Hippie: 4 BEIN

Social: 3 BEE 5 EVENT 6 AFFAIR
tool: 4 RAKE
Gator: 7 REPTILE
kin: 4 **CROC**
tail: 3 ADE
___ Gatos, California: 3 LOS
Gatsby
portrayer of 1949: 4 LADD
"Gattaca"
actor Hawke: 5 ETHAN
actress Thurman: 3 UMA
Gauche: 6 COARSE
"___ gauche": 4 RIVE
Gaucho
area: 6 PAMPAS
gear: 5 REATA RIATA
gold: 3 ORO
plain: 5 LLANO
rope: 5 **REATA** RIATA
weapon: 4 **BOLA**
Gaudy: 4 LOUD 6 ORNATE
sign: 4 NEON
Gauge: 4 DIAL 5 METER
        6 ASSESS
Dash: 4 TACH
Electrical: 7 AMMETER
Gauguin
Artist: 4 PAUL
island home: 6 TAHITI
Gaul
girlfriend: 4 AMIE
invader: 6 ATTILA
Gaunt: 4 BONY LANK
        8 RAWBONED
Gauntlet: 5 GLOVE
Throw down the: 4 DARE
Gauze
fabric: 5 LISSE
Gave
in: 5 CAVED
it a go: 5 TRIED
off: 7 EMITTED
out: 8 ASSIGNED
up: 5 CEDED 6 WAIVED
what for: 7 TOLDOFF
Gavel
pounder's word: 4 SOLD
        5 ORDER
word: 4 GONE

Gawk: 4 GAPE 5 STARE
at: 3 EYE 4 **OGLE**
Gawking
sort: 6 STARER
Gay
Author: 6 TALESE
leader: 5 ENOLA
"Gay ___": 5 PAREE
___ Gay: 5 ENOLA
Gaye, Marvin
genre: 4 SOUL
Gay Nineties: 3 ERA 6 DECADE
Gaynor
Actress: 5 **MITZI**
Gaza
gp.: 3 PLO
Gaze: 5 STARE
at: 3 EYE 6 BEHOLD
Gazelle
hound: 6 SALUKI
~, at times: 5 LOPER
Gazer
Crystal: 4 SEER
Gazetteer
datum: 4 **AREA**
Gazillions: 4 ALOT ATON
        5 SCADS
Gazpacho
ingredient: 5 ONION 6 TOMATO
Like: 4 COLD
Gazzara
Actor: 3 BEN
Gdansk
resident: 4 POLE
"G'day"
recipient: 4 MATE
Gds.: 4 MDSE
GE
competitor: 5 AMANA
Part of: 4 ELEC
product: 5 TVSET
purchase of 1986: 3 RCA
subsidiary: 3 NBC
Gear: 9 EQUIPMENT
Run out of: 4 IDLE
tooth: 3 **COG**
Gearshift
sequence: 5 PRNDL
Gecko: 6 LIZARD

___ Geddes, Barbara
  Actress: 3 BEL
Gee: 4 THOU
  follower: 5 AITCH
  preceder: 3 EFF
  preceders: 3 EFS
"Gee!": 4 GOSH
  Scottish: 3 OCH
Geek: 4 **NERD**
Geeky: 5 UNHIP
  sort: 4 NERD
Geena
  Actress: 5 DAVIS
  Role for: 6 THELMA
Geese
  formation: 3 VEE
  Why ~ migrate: 8 INSTINCT
"Gee whillikers!": 4 GOSH
"Gee whiz!": 3 BOY MAN 4 GOSH
Geezer: 4 COOT
  queries: 3 EHS
Gefilte-fish
  fish: 4 CARP
Gehrig
  of baseball: 3 **LOU**
  on the diamond: 4 FOUR
"___ geht's?": 3 WIE
Geiger
  Element in a ~ counter: 4 NEON
  Mr.: 4 HANS
Geisel
  pen name: 5 SEUSS
Geisha
  garb: 6 KIMONO
  sash: 3 **OBI**
Gel: 3 SET
  additive: 4 ALOE
  amount: 3 DAB
  effect: 7 WETLOOK
  Lab: 4 **AGAR**
Gelatin
  Culture: 4 AGAR
  garnish: 5 ASPIC
  shaper: 4 MOLD
Gelcap
  alternative: 6 TABLET
Gellar
  role: 5 BUFFY
Gellar, ___ Michelle: 5 SARAH

Geller
  Mentalist: 3 **URI**
Gem
  Australian: 4 OPAL
  Cameo: 4 ONYX
  Carvable: 4 JADE
  Fiery: 4 OPAL
  Green: 4 JADE 5 BERYL
    7 EMERALD PERIDOT
  Iridescent: 4 **OPAL** 5 PEARL
  Milky: 4 **OPAL**
  mineral: 5 BERYL
  Necklace: 5 PEARL
  Pendant ~ shape: 8 TEARDROP
  Red: 4 RUBY 6 SPINEL
  Reddish-brown: 4 SARD
  shape: 6 SCARAB
  Silicon: 4 OPAL
  surface: 5 FACET
  Verbal: 3 MOT
  weight: 5 CARAT
Gemini: 15 CASTORANDPOLLUX
  figure: 6 CASTOR
  month: 4 JUNE
  rocket: 5 AGENA
Gemologist
  concern: 6 CARATS
Gems
  Like some: 7 OPALINE
Gemsbok: 4 ORYX
Gem State: 5 IDAHO
  capital: 5 BOISE
  product: 5 TATER
Gemstone: 4 JADE OPAL 5 LAPIS
    7 CATSEYE
Gen.
  CSA: 5 RELEE
  follower: 4 EXOD
  WWII: 3 DDE
Gen-___ : 3 **XER**
Gender: 3 SEX
  (abbr.): 3 FEM 4 MASC
Gender-neutral
  Make: 5 DESEX
Gene
  Actress: 7 TIERNEY
  Critic: 6 SHALIT
  Drummer: 5 KRUPA
  Film cowboy: 5 AUTRY

form: 6 ALLELE
Golfer: 7 SARAZEN
material: 3 DNA RNA
Genealogical
record: 4 TREE
Genealogy: 5 ROOTS 7 LINEAGE
chart: 4 TREE 10 FAMILYTREE
gp.: 3 DAR
word: 3 NEE
General
address: 3 SIR
assemblies: 5 PLENA 6 ARMIES
assembly: 4 ARMY 8 TOPBRASS
command: 6 ATEASE
direction: 5 TREND
drift: 5 TENOR
Gettysburg: 5 MEADE
Greet a: 6 SALUTE
helper: 4 AIDE
In: 7 ASARULE OVERALL
in gray: 3 LEE
insignia: 4 STAR
Japanese: 4 TOJO
Kind of: 7 ONESTAR
meaning: 4 GIST
on Chinese menus: 3 **TSO**
pardon: 7 AMNESTY
plan: 7 ROADMAP
Revolutionary War: 4 GAGE
Turkish: 3 AGA 4 AGHA
under Dwight: 4 OMAR
vicinity: 4 AREA
General ___ chicken: 4 **TSOS**
"General Hospital": 4 SOAP
extra: 5 NURSE
Generally: 7 ASARULE
8 ALLINALL
approved: 8 ORTHODOX
General Mills
brand: 3 KIX 4 CHEX TRIX
5 TOTAL
General Motors
division: 3 GEO 4 SAAB
6 SATURN
Generals: 5 BRASS
Like some: 7 TWOSTAR
Generate: 5 SPAWN
It can ~ some interest: 4 LOAN
Generation: 3 AGE ERA

Generation ___: 3 XER
Generational
misunderstanding: 3 GAP
Generations
Story of: 4 SAGA
**"Generations of healthy, happy
pets"**
brand: 4 ALPO
Generator
part: 5 ROTOR
Random number: 3 DIE
Rumor: 4 MILL
Generic: 6 **NONAME**
dog: 4 FIDO
___ generis: 3 **SUI**
Generous: 5 AMPLE 6 GIVING
Be: 4 GIVE 5 TREAT 6 DONATE
donation: 5 ORGAN
gifts: 8 LARGESSE
sort: 5 DONOR 6 SHARER
7 DONATOR
Generously
Gave: 8 LAVISHED
Genesis: 4 SEED 5 ONSET START
6 ORIGIN SOURCE
boat: 3 ARK
brother: 4 ABEL CAIN ESAU
SETH
builder: 4 NOAH
City destroyed in: 5 SODOM
figure: 3 EVE 4 ADAM
garden: 4 **EDEN**
grandchild: 4 ENOS
setting: 4 EDEN
son: 4 ABEL CAIN ENOS SETH
twin: 4 **ESAU**
victim: 4 **ABEL**
Genetic
attribute: 5 TRAIT
carrier: 3 DNA RNA
double: 5 CLONE
letters: 3 DNA **RNA**
material: 3 DNA **RNA**
Genetically
Copy: 5 CLONE
related organisms: 7 BIOTYPE
Geneticist
creation: 5 CLONE
Pioneering: 6 MENDEL

study: **3** RNA
Geneva
  native: **5** SWISS
Genève
  nation: **6** SUISSE
Genevieve: 3 STE
Genghis ___: 4 KHAN
Genghis Khan: 6 MONGOL
  follower: **5** TATAR
Genie
  home: **4** LAMP
  offering: **4** WISH
  on TV: **4** EDEN
  summoner: **7** ALADDIN
Genius: 5 BRAIN **8** EINSTEIN
  Not exactly a: **5** DENSE
Genoa
  Region NW of: **4** ASTI
Genome
  stuff: **3** DNA
Genre
  1960s ~: **5** OPART
  1970s ~: **5** DISCO
  Comedy: **7** STANDUP
  Film: **4 NOIR 5** ANIME SCIFI
      6 ACTION HORROR
      8 WHODUNIT
  Jazz: **3** BOP **4** JIVE **5** BEBOP
  Music: **3** POP RAP **4** FOLK ROCK
      5 METAL RANDB
  Novel: **7** ROMANCE
  Practical literary: **5** HOWTO
Gent: 4 CHAP
  German: **4** HERR
  Spanish: **5** SENOR
Genteel: 4 NICE
  affair: **3** TEA
  Hardly: **4** RUDE **5** CRASS
Gentile: 6 NONJEW
Gentle: 4 KIND MILD SOFT
      TAME
  breeze: **6** ZEPHYR
  cycle items: **5** KNITS
  handling: **3** TLC
  In a ~ way: **6** TAMELY
  Isn't ~ with: **4** PAWS
  one: **4** LAMB
  pace: **7** DOGTROT
  prod: **5** NUDGE

  rhythm: **4** LILT
  slope: **4** RISE **6** GLACIS
  touch: **3** PAT **6** CARESS
  TV bear: **3** BEN
Gentle as ___: 5 ALAMB
Gentleman
  Gentleman's: **5** VALET
  Hindu: **4** BABU
  No: **3** CAD **4** BOOR **5** BRUTE
  of the court: **4** ASHE
"Gentleman Jim"
  Jim in: **5** ERROL
"Gentleman's Agreement"
  director Kazan: **4** ELIA
  ~ Oscar winner Celeste: **4** HOLM
Gentlemen: 4 SIRS
"Gentlemen Prefer Blondes"
  author: **4** LOOS **9** ANITALOOS
Gentlewoman: 4 DAME **5** MADAM
Gently
  Apply: **3** DAB
  Blow: **4** WAFT
  Hold: **6** CRADLE
  Pat: **3** DAB **5** DABAT
  persuade: **4** COAX
  Prod: **5** NUDGE
  Stroke: **3** PAT PET
Gentry: 5 ELITE
Genuflected: 5 KNELT
Genuflection
  point: **4** KNEE
Genuine: 4 REAL TRUE
      6 KOSHER **8** BONAFIDE
  article: **3** THE
  Not ~ (abbr.): **4** IMIT
Genuine Risk: 4 MARE
Genus
  Cattle: **3** BOS
  Dog: **5** CANIS
  Goose: **5** ANSER
  Holly: **4** ILEX
  Maple: **4** ACER
  of garden pests: **5** APHIS
  Olive: **4** OLEA
  Our: **4** HOMO
Gen Xer
  predecessor: **6** BOOMER
Geo: 3 CAR
  model: **5** METRO PRIZM STORM

Geodesic
  item: 4 DOME
Geoffrey
  Designer: 5 **BEENE**
Geog.
  Old ~ initials: 3 SSR
Geographic
  area: 7 TERRAIN
Géographie
  feature: 3 ILE
Geol.: 3 SCI
Geological
  layers: 6 STRATA
  period: 3 AGE EON ERA
    5 EPOCH
  ridge: 5 ARETE ESKER
Geom.
  figure: 3 CIR 4 RECT
  Kin of: 3 ALG
  point: 3 CTR
  solid: 3 SPH
Geometer
  product: 4 AREA
Geometric
  calculation: 4 AREA
  curve: 3 ARC
  fig.: 3 CIR 4 RECT
  figure: 5 PRISM
  locus: 7 EVOLUTE
  reference line: 4 AXIS
  solid: 5 TORUS
  solids: 4 TORI
  suffix: 3 GON
  Works with ~ patterns:
    5 OPART
Geometry
  adjective: 7 SCALENE
  Big name in: 5 EULER
  calculation: 4 **AREA**
  curve: 8 PARABOLA
  Kind of: 5 PLANE SOLID
  line: 4 AXIS
  ratios: 3 PIS
Geopolitical
  Former ~ initials: 3 SSR 4 USSR
Georg
  Physicist: 3 OHM
Georg ___, Sir
  Conductor: 5 **SOLTI**

George
  Actor: 5 SEGAL TAKEI WENDT
    6 ARLISS 7 PEPPARD
  and George W.: 4 ELIS
  Author: 5 ELIOT
  bill: 3 ONE
  Brother of: 3 **IRA** JEB
  Colleague of ~, Hap, and Ike:
    4 OMAR
  Comedian: 5 GOBEL 6 CARLIN
  Country singer: 6 STRAIT
  Director: 5 LUCAS
  English dramatist: 5 PEELE
  He ran against ~ and Bill:
    4 ROSS
  Humorist: 3 ADE
  John, Paul, and ~ (abbr.): 3 STS
  Logician: 5 BOOLE
  NFL pioneer: 5 HALAS
  of baseball: 5 BRETT
  of jazz: 6 BENSON
  or Victoria: 4 LAKE
  Partner of: 6 GRACIE
  Partner of John, Paul, and:
    5 RINGO
  spokesman: 3 ARI
  TV friend of Jerry and: 6 ELAINE
  Veep after: 3 DAN
  Wife of: 6 MARTHA
George ___: 3 III
George M. ___: 5 COHAN
"George of the Jungle"
  elephant: 4 SHEP
  obstacle: 4 TREE
Georges
  Composer: 6 ENESCO
  French writer: 5 PEREC
  Pointillism founder: 6 SEURAT
Georgetown
  athlete: 4 **HOYA**
Georgia: 3 SSR 5 STATE
  Actress: 5 ENGEL
  capital: 7 ATLANTA
  city: 5 MACON 6 ATHENS
    8 MARIETTA SAVANNAH
  Ex-Senator from: 4 **NUNN**
  Fictional ~ home: 4 TARA
  It's south of: 4 IRAN
  Leader born in: 6 STALIN

neighbor: **7** ARMENIA
product: **7** PEACHES
Rock group from: **3** REM
state tree: **7** LIVEOAK
Where ~ is: **4** ASIA
~, et al.: **4** SSRS
Georgia ___: **4** TECH
Georgian
neighbor: **8** ARMENIAN
"Georgia Peach": **4** COBB
Georgia Tech
grad: **4** ENGR
Géorgie
~, for one: **4** ETAT
"Georgy Girl"
star: **8** REDGRAVE
Geppetto
goldfish: **4** CLEO
Geraint
Love of: **4** **ENID**
Geraint, Sir
Wife of: **4** ENID
Gerald
Veep before: **5** SPIRO
Geraldo
News reporter: **6** RIVERA
Gerard
Actor: **3** GIL
Gerbil: **3** PET
Gere
title role: **3** DRT
Geriatrics
subject: **6** OLDAGE
Geritol
ingredient: **4** IRON
Germ: **4** SEED **5** SPORE
It has a: **4** IDEA
Rod-shaped: **5** ECOLI
Some ~ cells: **3** OVA
Germaine
Feminist: **5** GREER
German: **6** TEUTON **8** TEUTONIC
admiral: **4** SPEE
article: **3** DAS **DER** EIN **4** EINE
art songs: **6** LIEDER
auto: **4** AUDI OPEL
auto pioneer: **4** BENZ
border river: **4** ODER
capital: **4** BONN

city: **5** BADEN ESSEN STADT
  6 BREMEN
city with a canal: **4** KIEL
coal region: **4** RUHR **SAAR**
crowd: **4** DREI
cry: **3** ACH
dadaist: **5** ERNST
direction: **3** OST
donkey: **4** ESEL
Early: **6** TEUTON
First president of the ~ republic:
  5 EBERT
Former ~ chancellor: **4** KOHL
  6 BRANDT
Former ~ state: **5** BADEN LIPPE
gent: **4** HERR
gun: **5** LUGER **6** MAUSER
historian: **5** WEBER
industrial city: **5** **ESSEN**
industrial family: **6** KRUPPS
industrial region: **4** **RUHR**
king: **4** OTTO
mark: **6** UMLAUT
mister: **4** HERR
name part: **3** VON
one: **3** EIN **4** EINS
philosopher: **4** **KANT**
physicist: **3** OHM
port: **4** KIEL **5** EMDEN ESSEN
  6 BREMEN
Pre-euro ~ money: **5** MARKS
prison camp: **6** STALAG
pronoun: **3** ICH SIE **4** EINE
resort: **3** EMS
river: **3** EMS **4** **EDER** ELBE
  ODER RUHR SAAR **5** FULDA
  RHINE WESER
ruler: **6** KAISER
series start: **4** EINS
spa: **3** EMS **5** BADEN
  10 BADENBADEN
steel city: **5** ESSEN
sub: **5** **UBOAT**
surrealist: **5** ERNST
thoroughfare: **7** STRASSE
title: **4** HERR
town: **5** STADT
valley: **4** RUHR SAAR
wine valley: **5** MOSEL RHINE

~ 101 word: **3** ICH
Germane: 3 APT **8** RELEVANT
Germanic
   invader: **4** GOTH
   tribesman: **6** TEUTON
Germ-free: 7 ASEPTIC STERILE
"Germinal"
   author Émile: **4** ZOLA
Germinated
   barley: **4** MALT
Germs
   may grow in it: **4** AGAR
Gernreich
   Designer: **4** <u>RUDI</u>
Geronimo: 6 APACHE
"Gerontion"
   monogram: **3** TSE
   poet: **5** ELIOT
Gerontologist
   study: **6** OLDAGE
Gershon
   Actress: **4** <u>**GINA**</u>
Gershwin
   biographer David: **4** EWEN
   first hit: **6** SWANEE
   hero: **5** PORGY
   heroine: **4** BESS
   Lyricist: **3** <u>**IRA**</u>
   tune: **4** LIZA
Gershwin, Ira
   creation: **5** LYRIC
Gerstner
   of IBM: **3** LOU
Gertrude
   and Hamlet: **5** DANES
   Channel swimmer: **6** <u>**EDERLE**</u>
   Writer: **5** STEIN
Gerund: 4 NOUN
   maker: **3** ING
   ___ gestae: **3** RES
Gesturer: 4 MIME
"Gesundheit!"
   preceder: **5** ACHOO **6** AHCHOO
   Reason to say: **6** SNEEZE
Get: 3 NAB **4** EARN REAP
   5 GRASP **6** ATTAIN OBTAIN
   7 RECEIVE
   by: **4** COPE PASS **5** ELUDE
   EXIST **6** MAKEDO MANAGE

in: **6** ARRIVE
it: **3** SEE
off: **6** DEBARK
on: **3** AGE **4** RIDE **5** BOARD
   TEASE
to: **3** IRK **4** RILE **5** ANNOY
   REACH **6** ATTAIN RANKLE
up: **4** RISE **5** <u>**ARISE**</u> AWAKE
   ROUST STAND
~, as a job: **4** LAND
"Get ___ !": 4 REAL **5** AGRIP
   ALIFE AROOM
   (hit song): **4** AJOB
Get ___ a good thing: 4 INON
Get an ___ effort: 4 <u>**AFOR**</u> EFOR
Getaway
   Chic: **3** SPA
   Drive a ~ car: **4** ABET
   Healthful: **3** SPA
   spot: **4** ISLE **6** RESORT
   Summer: **4** CAMP
   time: **7** WEEKEND
   Weekend: **3** INN **5** BANDB
"Get away!": 4 SCAT SHOO
"Get clean"
   program: **5** REHAB
Get ___ for effort: 3 ANA ANE
Get ___ for one's money: 4 ARUN
Get-go: 5 <u>**ONSET**</u>
Get ___ goat: 4 ONES
"Get going!": 3 NOW **4** MOVE
   6 MOVEIT
"Get it?": 3 <u>SEE</u>
"___ get it": 5 IDONT
"Get lost!": 4 SCAT SHOO
   5 SCRAM **6** BEATIT
   BEGONE GOHOME
"Get my drift?": 3 SEE
Get ___ of: 3 RID **5** AHOLD
"Get ___ of yourself!": 5 AHOLD
Get ___ on the back: 4 APAT
Get ___ on the wrist: 5 ASLAP
"Get out!": 4 SCAT **5** LEAVE
   SCRAM
Get-out-of-jail
   money: **4** BAIL
"Get outta here!": 4 SCAT SHOO
   5 SCRAM
"Get real!": 4 ASIF **6** COMEON

Get-rich-quick
scheme: 5 HEIST
Get ___ shape: 4 INTO
"Get Shorty"
author: 6 ELMORE
"Get Smart"
evil gp.: 4 KAOS
Getter
Attention: 3 HEY TAP 4 AHEM
PSST 5 NUDGE
Get ___ the ground floor: 4 INON
"Get the picture?": 3 SEE
Getting
on: 3 OLD 5 AGING 6 AGEING
Getting ___ years: 4 __ONIN__
Get-together
Coffee: 6 KLATCH
Evening: 6 SOIREE
Gala: 4 FETE
Island: 4 LUAU
Rural: 3 BEE
Getty
Actress: 7 ESTELLE
Getty Center
architect: 5 MEIER
Gettysburg
First name at: 3 ABE
general: 5 MEADE
loser: 3 LEE
victor: 5 MEADE
Gettysburg Address
adjective: 3 AGO
Getup: 4 TOGS 5 DRESS
6 ATTIRE
Get-up-and-go: 3 __PEP__ VIM ZIP
4 BRIO PUSH ZEAL ZEST
5 DRIVE MOXIE OOMPH
6 ENERGY
Get-well
program: 5 REHAB
Get ___ writing: 4 ITIN
Getz
instrument: 3 SAX 8 TENORSAX
of jazz: 4 __STAN__
Geyser
output: 5 STEAM
Ghana
capital: 5 __ACCRA__
neighbor: 4 TOGO

people: 7 ASHANTI
river: 5 VOLTA
___ ghanouj: 4 BABA
Ghastly: 7 MACABRE
Ghent
river: 3 LYS
Ghost
Comics: 6 CASPER
cry: 3 BOO
Give up the: 3 DIE
Like ~ stories: 5 EERIE
Pale as a: 4 ASHY
When Hamlet sees the: 4 ACTI
White as a: 3 WAN 4 ASHY PALE
5 ASHEN
Word following: 4 TOWN
"Ghost"
costar: 4 DEMI
role: 3 ODA
"... ___ ghost!": 5 SEENA
"Ghost and Mrs. ___, The":
4 MUIR
"Ghost and ___ Muir, The":
3 MRS
"Ghostbusters"
actor Harold: 5 RAMIS
character: 4 EGON
goo: 5 __SLIME__
Ghostlike: 5 ASHEN
Ghostly: 4 PALE 5 ASHEN EERIE
greeting: 3 BOO
"Ghosts"
playwright: 5 __IBSEN__
GI
address: 3 APO
ally of the 1950s: 3 ROK
chow: 3 MRE
duties: 3 KPS
entertainers: 3 USO
entertainment: 7 USOSHOW
gear: 7 MESSKIT
Like a ~ series: 5 BARIC
mail drop: 3 APO
meal: 7 CRATION
Missing: 4 AWOL
neckwear: 5 IDTAG
offense: 4 AWOL
squads: 3 KPS
uniforms: 3 ODS

Gia
Actress: 5 SCALA
Giant: 4 NLER 5 LARGE
TITAN
100-eyed ~: 5 ARGUS
Global: 4 ASIA
Himalayan: 4 YETI
Rabelaisian: 9 GARGANTUA
Red: 4 MIRA 5 SSTAR
7 ANTARES
screen format: 4 IMAX
syllable: 3 FEE FIE FUM
Tolkien: 3 ENT
Took ~ steps: 6 STRODE
Wrestling: 5 ANDRE
"Giant"
author Ferber: 4 EDNA
ranch: 5 REATA
Giants
Former ~ manager Felipe:
4 ALOU
Hollywood: 4 EGOS
Mel of the: 3 OTT
Some: 5 OGRES
Gibb
Singer: 4 ANDY
Gibbon: 3 APE
Gibbons
Oscar designer: 6 CEDRIC
TV host: 5 **LEEZA**
Gibbs
Actress: 5 MARLA
Country singer: 5 TERRI
Giblets
part: 5 LIVER
Gibraltar
City near: 5 CADIZ
Port near: 7 TANGIER
~, for one (abbr.): 3 STR
Gibran
birthplace: 7 LEBANON
Gibson
1981 ~ film, with "The":
11 ROADWARRIOR
1996 ~ film: 6 RANSOM
Actor: 3 MEL
garnish: 5 ONION
of tennis: 6 ALTHEA
role: 5 RIGGS 6 MADMAX

Giddy
Make: 5 ELATE
Gide
Author: 5 ANDRE
God, to: 4 DIEU
"Gidget"
actress Sandra: 3 DEE
Gift: 7 PRESENT
10th anniversary ~: 3 TIN
20th anniversary ~: 5 CHINA
55th anniversary ~:
7 EMERALD
bearers: 4 MAGI
Biblical: 5 MYRRH
Clairvoyant: 3 ESP
Conciliatory: 3 SOP
decoration: 3 BOW
Diplomat: 4 TACT
Dubious: 3 ESP GAB
Engagement: 4 RING
for Dad: 3 TIE 5 RAZOR
6 TIEPIN
for an exec: 7 DESKSET
Fourth anniversary: 5 LINEN
Give as a: 6 BESTOW
Hanukkah: 4 GELT
Hawaiian: 3 LEI
Heavenly: 5 MANNA
holder: 3 BOX
It's a: 3 GAB
Musical: 3 EAR
Pledge drive: 4 TOTE
recipient: 5 **DONEE**
tag word: 4 FROM
Temporary: 4 LOAN
Gift ___: 5 OFGAB
Gifted
person: 5 DONEE
Gift-giver
urging: 6 OPENIT
"Gift of the ___, The": 4 MAGI
"Gift of the Magi, The"
author: 6 OHENRY
gift: 3 FOB 5 COMBS
Like: 6 IRONIC
Gifts: 7 TALENTS
Generous: 8 LARGESSE
Gift-wrapping
time: 3 EVE

Gig
  Acting: 4 ROLE
  after gig: 4 TOUR
  gear: 3 AMP
  Part of a: 3 SET
Gigantic: 4 HUGE
Giggle: 5 LAUGH TEHEE
      6 TEEHEE TITTER
  Part of a: 3 HEE
  Start of a: 3 TEE
Giggling
  muppet: 4 ELMO
  sound: 5 TEHEE 6 TEEHEE
"Gigi"
  actress Leslie: 5 CARON
  ___ Gigio (TV mouse): 4 TOPO
  "___ Gigolo" (Cole Porter): 3 IMA
Gigs
  Between: 4 IDLE
"G.I. Jane"
  actress Demi: 5 MOORE
  actress Moore: 4 **DEMI**
"Gil ___": 4 BLAS
Gila monster
  home: 6 DESERT
Gilbert
  Actress: 4 **SARA** 7 MELISSA
Gilbert & Sullivan
  fairy queen: 8 IOLANTHE
  princess: 3 IDA
  production: 8 OPERETTA
  work, with "The": 6 MIKADO
Gilberto
  Singer: 6 ASTRUD
"Gil Blas"
  novelist Alain: 6 LESAGE
  novelist Lesage: 5 ALAIN
Gilda
  character Baba: 4 WAWA
  Comic: 6 RADNER
"Gilda"
  star Hayworth: 4 RITA
Gilded: 7 AUREATE
Gilels
  Pianist: 4 **EMIL**
"Gilgamesh": 4 EPIC
Gill
  of country music: 5 VINCE
  opening: 4 SLIT

Gillespie
  genre: 3 BOP 5 BEBOP
  ~, to fans: 3 DIZ
Gillette
  brand: 4 **ATRA**
  product: 5 FOAMY RAZOR
  razor brand: 4 **ATRA**
      6 SENSOR
Gilliam
  Comic: 3 STU
Gillian
  role: 4 DANA
Gilligan
  boat: 6 MINNOW
  was stranded on one: 4 ISLE
"Gilligan's Island"
  actor Hale: 4 ALAN
  actress Louise: 4 TINA
  Ginger portrayer on: 4 TINA
  Skipper portrayer on:
      8 ALANHALE
Gillis
  buddy: 5 KREBS
  of TV: 5 DOBIE
Gills
  Fill to the: 4 **SATE**
  Four: 4 PINT
  Green around the: 3 ILL
      4 SICK
Gilmore
  of basketball: 5 **ARTIS**
Gilpin
  Actress: 4 **PERI**
Gimel
  Letter before: 4 BETH
Gimlet: 4 TOOL
  garnish: 4 **LIME**
  ingredient: 9 LIMEJUICE
  liquor: 3 GIN
Gimme
  Like a: 4 EASY
  on the green: 5 TAPIN
"Gimme ___!": 3 ANA ANE
"Gimme a Break"
  star Carter: 4 NELL
"Gimme a break!": 4 CMON
"Gimme a ...!" etc.: 4 YELL
Gimmick: 4 PLOY 6 SHTICK
  Marketing: 5 TIEIN

Gin
    accompanier: 5 TONIC
    drink: 4 FIZZ
    flavoring: 4 **SLOE**
    game: 5 RUMMY
    Kind of: 4 SLOE
    ___ gin fizz: 4 **SLOE**
Ginger: 3 PEP
    cookie: 4 **SNAP**
Ginger ale
    Like: 7 PALEDRY
Gingerbread
    house visitor: 6 HANSEL
Gingerly
    Drink: 3 SIP
    Go: 4 EASE
Gingersnap: 6 COOKIE
Gingivitis
    What ~ affects: 4 GUMS
Gingrich
    Former Speaker: 4 NEWT
    Speaker before: 5 FOLEY
Ginnie ___ : 3 **MAE**
Ginsberg, Allen: 8 BEATPOET
    and others: 5 BEATS
    poem: 4 HOWL
Ginsburg
    Garbed like: 5 ROBED
Ginsburg, Ruth ___
    Justice: 5 BADER
Ginza
    cash: 3 YEN
    girdle: 3 OBI
    light: 4 NEON
    locale: 5 TOKYO
Giorgio
    Fashion designer: 6 ARMANI
    "___ giorno!": 4 BUON
Giotto
    fresco town: 6 ASSISI
    work: 5 MURAL
"Giovanna d'___": 4 ARCO
Gipper
    grippers: 6 CLEATS
Gipper, The: 6 REAGAN
Giraffe
    feature: 4 NECK
    kin: 5 **OKAPI**
Girasol: 4 OPAL

Gird: 5 STEEL
Girded
    They may be: 5 LOINS
Girder: 4 IBAR 5 IBEAM
    Letter-shaped: 5 HBEAM
        IBEAM
    material: 5 STEEL
Girdle: 6 CORSET
Girl: 4 LASS 5 MISSY 6 LASSIE
    Ball: 3 DEB 5 **BELLE**
    Chorus: 4 ALTO
    Diamond: 3 LIL
    Dickens: 4 NELL
    Down Under: 6 SHEILA
    Family: 3 SIS 5 NIECE
    Graceful: 5 SYLPH
    Hardy: 4 TESS
    Impudent: 5 HUSSY
    Mischievous: 6 GAMINE
    Nice: 5 NELLY
    or boy of song: 3 SUE
    preceder: 4 **ATTA**
    Salinger: 4 **ESME**
    Slave ~ of opera: 4 AIDA
    Society: 3 DEB
    Stowe: 3 EVA
    That: 3 HER **SHE**
    Valley: 4 LILY
    Young: 5 MISSY
    "___ girl!": 4 **ATTA**
    "___ Girl Friday": 3 HIS
Girlfriend
    French: 4 **AMIE**
    of Peter Gunn: 4 EDIE
    of Sundance: 4 **ETTA**
    of Superboy: 4 LANA LANG
"Girl Like I, A"
    author: 4 LOOS 9 ANITALOOS
**"___ Girl Like You Loved a Boy
        Like Me":** 3 IFA
"___ Girls": 3 LES
Girl Scout
    emblem: 7 TREFOIL
    group: 5 TROOP
    "___ Girls Go": 5 ASTHE
Girl-watch: 4 OGLE
Girth
    They practice ~ control:
        7 DIETERS

Gish, Lillian
  film, with "The":
    14 BIRTHOFANATION
Gist: 3 **NUB** 4 CRUX IDEA MEAT
  5 HEART POINT 6 UPSHOT
  7 ESSENCE 8 MAINIDEA
"Git!": 4 SCAT SHOO 5 SCRAM
"Git ___ Little Dogies": 5 ALONG
Giuliani
  Former mayor: 4 RUDY
Give: 4 PLAY 5 ENDOW GRANT
  6 DONATE
  away: 4 CEDE 6 REVEAL
  in: 4 CAVE 5 YIELD 6 ACCEDE
    RELENT
  off: 4 **EMIT** OMIT 5 EGEST
    EXUDE 7 RADIATE
  or take: 5 ABOUT
  out: 3 DIE 4 CEDE **EMIT** FAIL
    5 ALLOT ISSUE 6 ASSIGN
  (out): 4 METE
  up: 3 DIE 4 **CEDE** EMIT QUIT
    5 FORGO WAIVE YIELD
    6 VACATE
Giveaway
  Gambler: 4 TELL
"Give ___ break!": 3 MEA
Give ___ for one's money:
  4 ARUN
Give-go
  link: 3 ITA
Give ___ go: 3 ITA
Give-hand
  connection: 3 MEA
"Give it ___!": 3 AGO 4 ATRY
  5 **AREST**
Given
  away: 6 UNKEPT
Give ___ of one's own medicine:
  5 ADOSE
Give ___ on the back: 4 APAT
Giver
  Blood: 5 DONOR
  CPR: 3 EMT
  Party: 4 HOST
  Shade: 3 ELM 4 TREE
"Give ___ rest!": 3 **ITA**
Giverny
  Artist at: 5 MONET

Givers
  Hug: 4 ARMS
  TLC: 3 RNS
Give ___ to Cerberus: 4 ASOP
"Give ___ whirl!": 3 ITA
Giza
  neighbor: 5 CAIRO
Gizmo: 6 DOODAD GADGET
  Kitchen: 5 CORER DICER
    PARER
  Office: 7 LABELER
  Post office: 5 DATER
  Tackle box: 6 SCALER
Glace
  Melted: 3 EAU
Glacial
  deposit: 7 MORAINE
  epoch: 6 ICEAGE
  matter: 7 ICEFALL
  pinnacle: 5 SERAC
  ridge: 5 ARETE ESKER
Gladden: 4 BUOY 5 **ELATE**
Glade
  rival: 5 LYSOL
  target: 4 ODOR
Gladiator
  domain: 5 **ARENA**
  weapon: 7 TRIDENT
"Gladiator"
  actor Russell: 5 CROWE
  garment: 4 TOGA
  setting: 4 ROME 5 ARENA
Gladly: 4 FAIN LIEF
Gladstone
  P.M. before: 8 DISRAELI
"Glad that's over!": 4 WHEW
Gladys
  guys: 4 PIPS
Glamour
  rival: 4 ELLE
Glance: 5 CAROM
    8 ONCEOVER
  at: 3 EYE
  Impolite: 4 **LEER**
  over: 4 READ SCAN SKIM
  Quick: 4 PEEK
  ___ glance: 3 **ATA**
Glances
  Like some: 8 SIDELONG

Gland
Kind of: 6 PINEAL 7 ADRENAL
prefix: 5 ADENO
Reproductive: 5 OVARY
Glare
Villainous: 5 SNEER
Glaringly
vivid: 5 LURID
Glasgow
gal: 4 LASS
negative: 3 NAE
Novelist: 5 ELLEN
resident: 4 SCOT
river: 5 CLYDE
Glass
Actor: 3 RON
Brandy: 7 SNIFTER
component: 6 SILICA
Cut: 4 ETCH
eels: 6 ELVERS
finish: 3 INE
Gas in: 4 NEON
Heat-resistant: 5 PYREX SILEX
Jeweler: 5 LOUPE
Like some: 6 LEADED
 7 STAINED
Makeshift drinking: 8 JELLYJAR
marble: 5 AGATE
of public radio: 3 IRA
part: 4 STEM
Raise a ~ to: 5 TOAST
sheet: 4 PANE
Small liqueur: 4 PONY
Small ~ container: 4 VIAL
 5 PHIAL
suffix: 3 INE
Toughen, as: 6 ANNEAL
Type of: 4 SHOT
Window: 4 PANE
Word with: 3 ART
Glass-enclosed
porches: 7 SOLARIA
Glasses: 5 SPECS
Champagne: 6 FLUTES
Clink: 5 TOAST
Colored ~ color: 4 ROSE
Kind of: 5 OPERA
Like some: 6 TINTED
Opera: 9 LORGNETTE

option: 4 TINT
parts: 4 RIMS
piece: 4 LENS
Glassful
Toddler's: 4 WAWA
Glassmaker
~ Lalique: 4 RENE
Glass-polishing
compound: 5 CERIA
Glassware
material: 5 PYREX
oven: 4 LEHR
Glassworker: 8 ANNEALER
Glassy
look: 5 STARE
Glaswegian: 4 SCOT
negative: 3 NAE
Glaze
Pottery: 6 ENAMEL
Glazed
fabric: 6 CHINTZ TAMMIE
square: 4 TILE
Glazier
need: 5 PUTTY
unit: 4 PANE
Gleam: 5 SHINE
Gleamed: 5 SHONE
Gleason
Early ~ role: 5 RILEY
Glee: 5 MIRTH
club member: 4 ALTO
"Glengarry Glen Ross"
actor Baldwin: 4 ALEC
playwright: 5 MAMET
Glenn
Actress: 5 CLOSE
of the Eagles: 4 FREY
represented it: 4 OHIO
Rocker: 4 FREY
Glenn, John
portrayer: 8 EDHARRIS
state: 4 OHIO
Glib
Excessively: 3 PAT
Gift of the: 3 GAB
quality: 7 PATNESS
responses: 10 PATANSWERS
Glide: 5 COAST SKATE 6 SASHAY
 8 ICESKATE

high: 4 SOAR
on snow: 3 SKI
Glided: 4 SLID
Glider: 5 SKATE
On a: 5 ALOFT
Snow: 4 SLED
wood: 5 BALSA
Gliding
Go: 4 SOAR
step: 6 CHASSE 8 GLISSADE
Glimmering: 4 IDEA
Glimpse: 3 SEE 4 **ESPY** LOOK
    PEEK 5 SIGHT
    6 PEEKAT
Glimpsed: 4 SEEN
Glisten: 5 SHINE
Glistened: 5 SHONE
Glistener
Cheek: 4 TEAR
Morning: 3 DEW
Glistens
It: 3 DEW 5 ASPIC
Glitch: 3 BUG 4 **SNAG**
Glitter: 6 TINSEL
Bit of: 7 SPANGLE
Glitterati: 5 ELITE 6 JETSET
    8 SMARTSET
Glittery
material: 4 LAME
stone: 5 GEODE
topper: 5 TIARA
Gloaming: 3 EVE 4 DUSK
Gloater
cry: 3 HAH SEE
Glob
suffix: 3 **ULE**
Global
currency org.: 3 IMF
extreme: 4 POLE
giant: 4 ASIA
positioning fig.: 3 LAT
septet: 4 SEAS
warming treaty city: 5 KYOTO
Globe: 3 **ORB** 6 SPHERE
    7 THEATRE
Company with a blue ~ logo:
    5 PANAM
It circles the: 6 TROPIC
plotter: 4 IAGO

Globin
prefix: 4 HEMO
Globular: 5 ORBED
Globule: 4 BEAD DROP
Gloom: 4 MURK 7 SADNESS
Mood of: 4 PALL
Partner of: 4 DOOM
"___ gloom of night ...":
    3 NOR
Gloomy: 3 DUN 4 DARK **DOUR**
    DRAB GRAY GRIM
    6 MOROSE SOLEMN
Act: 4 MOPE
guy: 3 **GUS**
More: 5 BLUER
~, in poetry: 5 DREAR
Gloomy Gus: 4 MOPE
Glop: 3 GOO
Gloria
Pop singer: 7 ESTEFAN
Writer: 7 STEINEM
"Gloria"
actress Rowlands: 4 GENA
Gloria ___ : 5 PATRI
"Gloria in excelsis ___": 3 DEO
Glorified
gofer: 4 AIDE
Glorify: 4 LAUD 5 ADORE BLESS
    EXALT EXTOL
Glory: 4 KUDO 5 ECLAT EXALT
Crowning: 4 MANE
Vein: 3 ORE 4 LODE
Gloss: 5 SHEEN
target: 3 LIP 4 LIPS
Glossary
entry: 4 TERM
Glossed
It might be ~ over: 3 LIP
Glossina
Fly of the genus: 6 TSETSE
Glossiness: 5 SHEEN
Glossy: 5 SLEEK
brown fur: 5 OTTER
coating: 6 ENAMEL
fabric: 5 SATIN 6 SATEEN
Not: 5 MATTE
paint: 6 ENAMEL
Glottis
prefix: 3 EPI

Gloucester
  cape: 3 ANN
Glove
  Baseball: 4 **MITT**
  compartment item: 3 MAP
  material: 5 LATEX LISLE SUEDE
  Oven: 4 MITT
Gloves
  Place to wear: 4 OVEN
  Train with: 4 SPAR
Glow: 4 **AURA** 5 ARDOR SHINE
      8 RADIANCE
  Saintly: 4 AURA HALO
  Vegas: 4 NEON
Glower: 4 NEON
  Fireplace: 5 EMBER
Glowing: 3 LIT 6 ASHINE
      7 RADIANT
  personality: 4 AURA
  remnant: 5 EMBER
  review: 4 RAVE
Gluck
  hero: 5 ORFEO
  Soprano: 4 **ALMA**
Glue: 4 BIND TACK 5 EPOXY
      PASTE 6 CEMENT
  Bull on ~ bottles: 5 ELMER
  name: 5 ELMER
  Stick like: 6 ADHERE
  Strong: 5 EPOXY
Glued
  Stay ~ to: 7 STAREAT
Glum: 3 SAD 4 DOUR 6 MOROSE
  drop: 4 TEAR
Glut: 4 SATE 7 ENGORGE
      SATIATE
Glutton: 3 HOG PIG
Gluttony: 3 SIN
Glyceride: 5 ESTER
Glycerin
  opener: 5 NITRO
Glyn
  Author: 6 ELINOR
Glyph
  prefix: 3 TRI 5 HIERO
GM
  line: 4 OLDS
  Negotiator with: 3 UAW
  subsidiary: 4 OPEL

G-man: 3 FED 4 NARC
      8 FBIAGENT
  (abbr.): 3 AGT
  org.: 3 FBI
GMC
  truck: 6 SIERRA
GMT
  Part of: 4 MEAN
Gnat: 4 PEST
  Go after a: 4 SWAT
  Like a: 5 PESKY
Gnatlike
  insect: 5 MIDGE
Gnaw
  on: 5 EATAT
Gnawed
  away: 5 EROSE
Gnocchi
  ingredient: 6 POTATO
Gnome
  kin: 5 TROLL
GNP: 4 STAT
Gnu
  kin: 5 ELAND
Go: 3 TRY 4 EXIT PART 5 LEAVE
      6 ELAPSE
  across: 4 SPAN
  after: 3 SUE 4 SEEK SHAG
      5 CHASE SETAT 6 ASSAIL
      ATTACK PURSUE
  along: 5 AGREE 6 SAYYES
  along (with): 5 AGREE
  along with: 6 ESCORT
      7 AGREETO
  around: 4 SPIN 5 AVOID ORBIT
      SKIRT 6 BYPASS
  at it: 5 ARGUE 6 TUSSLE
  away: 5 LEAVE
  by: 4 PASS 6 **ELAPSE**
  Caused to: 6 BETOOK
  Cause to: 4 SEND
  Come and: 5 RECUR
  Doesn't: 5 STAYS
  for: 4 COST LIKE
  (for): 3 **OPT** TRY VIE
  Get up and: 4 MOVE
  Give it a: 3 TRY
  Have a ~ at: 3 **TRY**
  in: 5 ENTER

It must ~ on: 7 THESHOW
Let: 3 AXE CAN CUT 4 AXED
　　CEDE DROP FIRE FREE
　　SACK 5 FIRED FREED
　　RELAX WAIVE 6 LAYOFF
　　UNHAND 7 RELEASE
　　UNLOOSE
　　15 RELEASEONESHOLD
off: 3 ERR 5 ERUPT LEAVE
on: 4 LAST RANT 6 NATTER
One way to: 3 APE
On the: 6 ACTIVE
out: 3 DIE EBB 4 EXIT 5 LEAVE
　　SLEEP 6 EGRESS
over: 3 TOP 4 READ SPAN
　　5 CROSS ELIDE RECAP
　　7 RUNLATE
(over): 4 PORE
Partner of: 5 GETUP
through: 5 SPEND
(through): 4 SIFT
to: 3 SEE 4 ATTEND
to the dogs: 4 MUSH
under: 4 FAIL FOLD SINK
　　5 DROWN
up: 4 RISE SOAR 5 CLIMB
　　SCALE 6 ASCEND
Way to ~ (abbr.): 3 **RTE**
with: 3 SEE 4 DATE 6 ESCORT
without: 4 FAST
Go ___: 3 APE 4 ATIT 5 ALONG
　　6 TOSEED
Go-___: 4 KART 6 GETTER
"___ go!": 4 LETS 5 GOTTA
Goad: 4 PROD SPUR URGE
　　5 EGGON
Go-ahead: 3 NOD 4 OKAY
　　5 SAYSO 6 ASSENT
Gave the: 3 OKD 4 OKED
　　6 OKAYED
Gives the: 3 OKS 5 OKAYS
"Go ahead!": 4 DOIT 5 SHOOT
Goal: 3 **AIM** END
Set a high: 6 ASPIRE
Goalie
area: 6 CREASE
Beat the: 5 SCORE
feat: 4 SAVE
protection: 4 MASK PADS

Goalpost
part: 8 CROSSBAR
Goals
(abbr.): 3 PTS
or assists: 4 STAT
Goat
Baby: 3 KID
cheese: 4 FETA
coat: 6 MOHAIR
Get one's: 3 IRK 4 RILE
Half: 5 SATYR
Mountain: 4 IBEX
Navy ~, e.g.: 6 MASCOT
or rabbit: 6 ANGORA
sound: 3 MAA
Wild: 4 **IBEX**
~, ox, or sheep: 5 BOVID
"Goat, The"
playwright: 5 ALBEE
"___ Goat-Boy": 5 GILES
Goat-drawn
chariot rider: 4 THOR
Goatee: 5 BEARD
site: 4 CHIN
Goat-footed
one: 5 SATYR
Goatish
glance: 4 LEER
Goat-man: 4 FAUN 5 SATYR
"Go away!": 4 SCAT
Gob: 3 TAR WAD 4 SALT
　　6 SEAMAN
greeting: 4 AHOY
"Go back!"
in word processing: 4 UNDO
on a PC: 3 ESC
Gobble: 3 EAT
up: 3 EAT 5 SCARF 6 DEVOUR
Gobbled
up: 3 ATE 5 EATEN
Gobbler: 3 TOM
Go-between: 5 AGENT 7 LIAISON
　　8 EMISSARY MEDIATOR
Man-mouse: 3 ORA
Pi-sigma: 3 RHO
Gobi: 6 DESERT
continent: 4 ASIA
Like the: 4 ARID SERE
refuge: 5 OASIS

Goblet: 7 CHALICE
  part: 4 **STEM**
Goblin
  prefix: 3 HOB
  word: 3 BOO
"___ go bragh!": 4 **ERIN**
Gobs: 4 **ALOT** ATON 5 SLEWS
  6 SEAMEN
Go-cart: 5 RACER
God: 4 LORD 5 DEITY
  Aggressive: 4 ARES
  attended by Valkyries: 4 ODIN
  Belief in: 6 THEISM
  Celtic sea: 3 LER
  Chariot-riding: 4 THOR
  Chief Greek: 4 ZEUS
  Chief Norse: 4 ODIN
  Child: 4 AMOR
  Egyptian: 4 ATEN PTAH
    6 AMENRA OSIRIS
  Falcon-headed: 5 HORUS
  False: 4 **BAAL** IDOL
  Greek love: 4 EROS
  Greek war: 4 **ARES**
  Greek wind: 6 AEOLUS
  Handsome: 6 APOLLO
  He played: 5 BURNS
  Hebrew title for: 6 ADONAI
  Hindu: 4 DEVA SIVA 5 SHIVA
  Love: 4 AMOR **EROS**
  Mischievous: 4 LOKI
  Norse: 4 **ODIN**
  Norse peace: 4 FREY
  Norse war: 3 TYR 4 ODIN
  Norse ~ of discord: 4 LOKI
  of Islam: 5 ALLAH
  of love: 4 AMOR EROS
  of the Koran: 5 ALLAH
  of thunder: 4 THOR
  of war: 4 ARES MARS ODIN
  One-handed: 3 TYR
  prefix: 4 DEMI
  Red-bearded: 4 THOR
  Roman household: 3 LAR
  Roman love: 4 AMOR
  Roman sun: 3 SOL
  Scandinavian: 4 ODIN
  Sea: 7 NEPTUNE
  Theban: 4 AMON

The Lion of: 3 ALI
Thunder: 4 THOR
War: 4 **ARES** MARS
Winged: 4 **EROS**
with a bow: 4 AMOR EROS
  5 CUPID
with a hammer: 4 THOR
with an eight-legged horse:
  4 ODIN
You may thank ~ for it (abbr.):
  3 FRI
~, in French: 4 DIEU
~, in Italian: 3 DIO
~, in Spanish: 4 DIOS
~, with "the": 7 CREATOR
  ETERNAL
Godard
  Actress: 8 PAULETTE
  style: 7 NEWWAVE
Godard, Jean-___: 3 LUC
God-awful: 5 LOUSY
Goddess
  Agriculture: 5 CERES
  Armored: 6 ATHENA
  Babylonian: 6 ISHTAR
  Cow-horned: 4 ISIS
  Dawn: 3 **EOS** 6 AURORA
  Earth: 4 GAEA GAIA
  Egyptian: 4 **ISIS**
  Fertility: 4 ISIS 7 ASTARTE
  Greek war: 4 ENYO
  Harvest: 3 OPS
  Hearth: 5 VESTA 6 HESTIA
  Moon: 4 **LUNA** 6 SELENA
    SELENE
  Nature: 4 ISIS
  Norse: 3 HEL 4 NORN 5 FREYA
  of discord: 4 ERIS
  of plenty: 3 OPS
  of recklessness: 3 ATE
  of sorcery: 6 HECATE
  of the hunt: 5 DIANA 7 ARTEMIS
  of wisdom: 6 ATHENA
  Parthenon: 6 ATHENA
  Peace: 5 IRENE
  Rainbow: 4 **IRIS**
  Victory: 4 NIKE
  Vindictive: 4 HERA
  Winged: 4 NIKE

Goddesses
  of the seasons: 5 HORAE
  Trio of: 5 FATES
"Godfather, The"
  actor: 4 CAAN
  actress Shire: 5 TALIA
  author: 4 PUZO
  character: 5 SONNY
  composer Nino: 4 ROTA
  Henchman Luca of: 5 BRASI
  John Cazale in: 5 FREDO
  Marlon's role in: 4 VITO
  Portrayer of Connie in: 5 TALIA
  star: 6 BRANDO
  Word not used in: 5 MAFIA
Godfrey
  instrument: 3 UKE
  Singer fired by: 6 LAROSA
Godhead
  Like the: 6 TRIUNE
"God in Ruins, A"
  author: 4 URIS
Godiva: 4 LADY
  Emulate: 4 RIDE
  Unlike: 4 CLAD
Godlike: 6 DIVINE
Godliness: 5 PIETY
Gods
  Blood of the: 5 ICHOR
  Drink of the: 6 NECTAR
  Food of the: 5 MANNA
      8 AMBROSIA
  Home of the Norse: 6 ASGARD
  Household: 5 LARES
  Queen of the: 4 HERA
  Race of Norse: 5 AESIR
  Way of the: 6 SHINTO
Godsend: 4 BOON
"God's Little ___": 4 ACRE
Godunov, Boris: 4 TSAR
  singer: 5 BASSO
"God willing!": 7 IHOPESO
Godzilla
  creator: 6 TANAKA
  target: 5 TOKYO
"Go Eat Worms!"
  author: 7 RLSTINE
"___ goes": 4 SOIT
"___ goes nothing!": 4 HERE

Goethe
  classic: 5 FAUST
  Playwright: 6 JOHANN
Gofer: 4 AIDE
  (abbr.): 4 ASST
  job: 6 ERRAND
  Senate: 4 PAGE
"Go fly ___!": 5 AKITE
Go ___ for: 5 TOBAT
Go-getter: 4 DOER 5 TIGER
      6 DYNAMO
Goggle: 4 GAPE GAWK GAZE
      5 STARE
  at: 4 LEER OGLE
Go-go
  Like ~ boots, nowadays: 5 RETRO
Going
  Coming or: 7 ENROUTE
  Get: 4 MOVE ROLL 5 HOPTO
      START 6 BOOGIE
      8 COMMENCE
  It'll keep you: 7 INERTIA
  Keep: 4 LAST 5 RUNON
      7 PERSIST
  on and on: 7 ETERNAL
  out: 6 DATING
Going ___: 4 ATIT
Goings-on: 3 ADO 6 EVENTS
Goiter
  treatment: 6 IODINE
Gold: 5 METAL 7 ELEMENT
  $10 ~ piece: 5 EAGLE
  79, for ~ (abbr.): 4 ATNO
  Band of: 3 ORE
  bar: 5 INGOT
  Black: 3 OIL 8 TEXASTEA
  braid: 5 ORRIS
  brick: 5 INGOT
  Coat with: 4 GILD
  compound: 6 AURATE
  Containing: 5 AURIC
  deposit: 4 LODE
  digger: 5 MINER
  Ersatz: 6 ORMOLU
  fabric: 4 LAME
  Fort of: 4 KNOX
  Go for the: 3 DIG PAN VIE
      4 MINE 7 COMPETE
  Got the: 3 WON

Legendary city of: **8** ELDORADO
Look for: **3** PAN
measure: **5** KARAT
measures (abbr.): **3** KTS
mine: **9** MONEYTREE
mold: **5** INGOT
Old ~ coin: **5** DUCAT
prefix: **3** AUR
standard: **5** KARAT
statuette: **5** OSCAR
Take the: **3** WIN
They go for the: **6** MINERS
unit: **3** BAR **5** KARAT OUNCE
watch recipient: **7** RETIREE
~, in Spanish: **3** **ORO**
Gold ___ : 4 LAME
" ___ Gold" (1997 film): 5 ULEES
Golda
of Israel: **4** **MEIR**
Goldberg
Cartoonist: **4** **RUBE**
Oscar emcee: **6** WHOOPI
"Goldberg Variations"
composer: **4** BACH
Goldbrick: 4 LOAF **5** DOGIT
    IDLER SHIRK **7** SHIRKER
    SLACKER
"Gold Bug, The"
author: **3** POE
author monogram: **3** EAP
Gold Coast
locale: **5** GHANA
Golden: 5 AURIC **7** AUREATE
age: **6** HEYDAY
ager: **7** OLDSTER
anniversary number: **5** FIFTY
attribute: **7** SILENCE
boy of film: **5** OSCAR
finish: **4** AGER
It may be: **5** OLDIE
King with a ~ touch: **5** **MIDAS**
rule word: **4** **UNTO**
song: **5** OLDIE
years: **6** OLDAGE
~, in French: **3** DOR
Golden ___ : 4 AGER GATE RULE
    5 OLDIE
Golden- ___ : 4 AGER
corn: **5** EARED

Golden ___, The: 4 HIND
Golden Arches
offering: **6** BIGMAC
Golden Bears
(abbr.): **4** UCAL
"Golden Boy"
playwright: **5** **ODETS**
Golden-brown
quartz: **8** TIGEREYE
Golden Calf: 4 **IDOL**
builder: **5** AARON
Golden-coated
horse: **8** PALOMINO
Golden-egg
layer: **5** GOOSE
Golden Fleece
hunter: **5** JASON
princess: **5** MEDEA
ship: **4** **ARGO**
"Goldengirl"
actress Susan: **5** ANTON
"Golden Girls, The"
actress Arthur: **3** BEA
actress Getty: **7** ESTELLE
actress McClanahan: **3** RUE
Blanche portrayer on: **3** RUE
character: **4** ROSE
Golden Hind
skipper: **5** DRAKE
Golden Horde
member: **5** TATAR
    6 MONGOL
Golden Pong
bird: **4** LOON
"Golden rule"
last word: **3** YOU
preposition: **4** UNTO
Golden Spike
locale: **4** UTAH
Golden State
sch.: **3** USC **4** UCLA
Golden Triangle
country: **4** LAOS
native: **4** THAI
Goldfinger
assistant: **6** ODDJOB
first name: **5** AURIC
Fort attacked by: **4** KNOX
portrayer Frobe: **4** GERT

Goldie
  Actress: 4 HAWN
  Costar of ~ and Ruth: 4 ARTE
Goldilocks
  adversary: 8 PAPABEAR
  Like some porridge, to:
    6 TOOHOT
Goldin
  Photographer: 3 NAN
Goldman
  Anarchist: 4 EMMA
  broker partner: 5 SACHS
Gold Rush
  mecca: 4 NOME
  name: 6 SUTTER
  territory: 5 YUKON
Goldsmith: 7 ARTISAN
Goldwyn: 6 SAMUEL
  star Anna: 4 STEN
Golf
  1996 ~ movie: 6 TINCUP
  bag item: 3 TEE 4 IRON
  Best, in a ~ score: 6 FEWEST
  California ~ locale:
    11 PEBBLEBEACH
  coup: 3 ACE 5 EAGLE
  Easy ~ shot: 5 TAPIN
  Farthest from the hole, in:
    4 AWAY
  gadget: 3 **TEE**
  goal: 3 PAR
  goof: 4 HOOK
  great: 5 **SNEAD**
  Half a ~ course: 4 NINE
  hazard: 4 **TRAP**
  instructor: 3 PRO
  lesson topic: 6 STANCE
  Like some ~ balls: 4 TEED
  Like some ~ courses:
    8 NINEHOLE
  Like some ~ tourneys: 5 PROAM
  Major ~ event: 6 USOPEN
  Miami ~ resort: 5 DORAL
  peg: 3 TEE
  position: 3 LIE
  Rare ~ shot: 3 ACE
  shoe feature: 5 CLEAT
  stroke: 4 CHIP PUTT SHOT
  Word after: 5 WIDOW

Golf ball
  material: 6 BALATA
  position: 3 LIE
  support: 3 TEE
"Golf Begins at Forty"
  author: 5 SNEAD
Golf club: 4 IRON WOOD
    6 DRIVER
  part: 3 TOE 4 GRIP 5 SHAFT
  socket: 5 HOSEL
Golf course
  area: 3 TEE
  feature: 6 DOGLEG
Golfer
  accessory: 5 VISOR
  aide: 5 CADDY
  bagful: 4 TEES
  challenge: 6 DOGLEG
  choice: 4 IRON NINE
    5 WEDGE
  concern: 3 LIE 4 GRIP 5 SWING
    6 STANCE
  coup: 3 ACE
  cry: 4 FORE
  gadget: 3 TEE
  goal: 3 **PAR** 4 HOLE
  headache: 6 BADLIE
  purchase: 5 BALLS IRONS
  target: 4 HOLE
  transport: 4 CART
  with an army: 5 ARNIE
  ~ Aoki: 4 ISAO
  ~, at times: 4 TEER
  ~ Ballesteros: 4 SEVE
  ~ Calvin: 5 PEETE
  ~ Dutra: 4 OLIN
  ~ Hale: 5 IRWIN
  ~ Isao: 4 AOKI
  ~ Mattiace: 3 LEN
  ~ Mediate: 5 ROCCO
  ~ Norman: 4 GREG
  ~ Palmer: 5 ARNIE
  ~ Trevino: 3 LEE
  ~ Wadkins: 5 LANNY
Golf hole
  edge: 3 LIP
  start: 3 TEE
Golfing
  group: 8 FOURSOME

Golgi
Physician: 7 CAMILLO
Goliath: 5 GIANT
Golightly
creator: 6 CAPOTE
"Golly!": 3 GEE
Gomer
and Goober: 5 PYLES
"Gomer ___, U.S.M.C.": 4 PYLE
Gomez
Cousin of: 3 ITT
Mrs. Addams, to: 4 TISH
Gomorrah
Sister city of: 5 SODOM
Gompers, Samuel
org.: 3 AFL
org., informally: 5 AFOFL
Gondola
driver: 5 POLER
locale: 5 CANAL
propeller: 4 POLE
Some ~ users: 6 SKIERS
Gondolier: 5 POLER
need: 4 POLE
"Gondoliers, The"
girl: 5 TESSA
Gone: 4 AWAY DEAD 5 EATEN
6 USEDUP 7 EXTINCT
bad: 6 SPOILT
by: 3 AGO 4 PAST 5 OFOLD
out with: 4 SEEN
wrong: 4 AWOL
"___ Gone": 4 SHES
Goner: 5 TOAST 8 DEADDUCK
Goneril
Father of: 4 LEAR
Sister of: 5 REGAN
"Gone ___ the Wind": 4 WITH
"Gone With the Wind"
actor Howard: 6 LESLIE
actress Barbara: 5 ONEIL
actress McDaniel: 6 HATTIE
actress Vivien: 5 LEIGH
plantation: 4 TARA
star: 5 GABLE
Gong: 6 TAMTAM
"___ Gonna Take It": 7 WERENOT
Gonzales
of tennis: 6 PANCHO

González
in 2000 news: 5 ELIAN
Goo: 4 GLOP MIRE 5 SLIME
7 TREACLE
Cosmetic: 5 GELEE
Do: 3 GEL
Greasy: 4 GUNK
Hair: 3 **GEL**
La Brea: 3 TAR
Lip: 4 BALM
Road: 3 TAR
Styling: 3 GEL
Goober
of Mayberry: 4 PYLE
Good
A ~ deal: 4 TONS
As ~ as ever: 7 LIKENEW
Believer in ~ and evil:
7 DUELIST
Body of ~ conduct: 5 ETHIC
buddy: 3 BRO PAL 4 CBER
CHUM 6 FRIEND
buy: 4 DEAL
cheer: 3 OLE
deal: 3 BUY LOT TON
earth: 4 LOAM
feller: 3 AXE
form: 7 DECORUM
Full of ~ cheer: 5 MERRY
grade: 5 BPLUS
guy: 6 MENSCH
In ~ health: 4 HALE WELL
In ~ order: 4 NEAT TIDY
In ~ shape: 3 FIT 4 HALE TRIM
It doesn't look: 7 EYESORE
It's not: 4 EVIL
judgment: 5 SENSE
10 HORSESENSE
looker: 3 EYE
Make: 5 ATONE REPAY
7 RESTORE
name: 3 REP 6 REPUTE
Not as: 5 WORSE
Not ~ enough for: 7 BENEATH
ol' boy: 5 BUBBA
Partner of: 4 EVIL
point: 5 ASSET
relations: 5 AMITY
run: 6 STREAK

shot: 4 GOAL 6 RINGER
Show a really ~ time: 6 REGALE
sign: 4 HALO
Tell a ~ one: 3 LIE
The ~ life: 4 EASE
thing: 4 PLUS 5 **ASSET**
times: 3 **UPS**
witch: 6 GLINDA
~, in French: 4 BIEN
~, in slang: 3 BAD DEF
~, in Spanish: 5 BUENO
Good ___: 5 ASNEW
"Good ___!": 5 GRIEF
Good Book: 5 BIBLE
"Good buddy": 4 CBER
Goodbye: 4 CIAO TATA 5 ADIEU
   Hello or: 5 ALOHA 6 SHALOM
"Goodbye Columbus"
   author: 4 ROTH
"Goodbye Girl, The"
   Mason of: 6 MARSHA
"___ good cheer!": 4 BEOF
___ good deed: 3 DOA
"Good Earth, The"
   author: 9 PEARLBUCK
   heroine: 4 **OLAN**
___ good example: 4 SETA
___ Good Feeling: 5 ERAOF
"GoodFellas"
   costar: 6 LIOTTA 9 RAYLIOTTA
   Oscar winner: 5 PESCI
   star: 6 DENIRO
Goodfellow
   (abbr.): 3 AFB
Goodfellow, Robin: 3 IMP
   6 SPRITE
Good-for-nothing: 3 BUM
   5 IDLER ROGUE 6 BADEGG
   7 NOCOUNT USELESS
Good-gets
   connector: 4 ASIT
"Good going!": 4 NICE
"Good grief!": 4 EGAD 5 EGADS
Good Housekeeping
   award: 4 SEAL
Good-humored: 7 AMIABLE
Goodie: 5 TREAT
   Bakery: 5 SCONE
   from Linz: 5 TORTE

Fruity: 4 TART
Gumbo: 4 OKRA
Gooding Jr., ___
   Actor: 4 CUBA
Good-looking
   guy: 10 STUDMUFFIN
"Good Luck, Miss Wyckoff"
   novelist: 4 INGE
Goodly
   A ~ number: 4 MANY
Goodman
   Columnist: 5 ELLEN
   drummer: 5 KRUPA
Goodman, Benny
   genre: 5 SWING
"___ Good Men": 4 AFEW
Good-natured: 4 NICE
   banter: 4 JOSH
Goodness: 5 WORTH 6 VIRTUE
   Symbol of: 4 HALO
"Goodness!": 4 MYMY OHMY
   6 DEARME
"Goodness gracious!": 4 EGAD
   MYMY OHMY 6 DEARME
Goodnight
   girl: 5 **IRENE**
"Goodnight ___": 5 IRENE
"Good one!": 4 NICE
___ good race: 4 RANA
"Good riddance": 6 NOLOSS
Goods: 5 WARES
   It may deliver the: 4 SEMI
   Piece: 5 CLOTH
   Stolen: 4 LOOT
   Store ~ (abbr.): 4 MDSE
Good Samaritan: 5 AIDER
"Good shot!": 4 NICE
   7 NICEONE
Good-sized
   combo: 5 NONET OCTET
Goodson
   TV partner of: 6 TODMAN
"Good Times"
   actress Esther: 5 ROLLE
___ good turn: 3 DOA
Goodwill: 5 ASSET
"... good will ___": 5 TOMEN
Goodwill Ambassadors
   org.: 6 UNESCO

"Good Will Hunting"
actor: 5 DAMON
actress: 12 MINNIEDRIVER
campus: 3 MIT
"Good work!": 4 NICE
"Goody!": 5 OHBOY
Goody, Sam
purchases: 3 CDS
Goodyear
home: 5 AKRON
product: 4 TIRE
Goody-goody: 5 PRUDE
"Goody Two Shoes"
singer Adam: 3 ANT
Gooey
dessert: 5 SMORE
stuff: 3 GEL 4 GLOP MIRE OOZE
5 SLIME
Goof: 3 **ERR** 4 SLIP 5 ERROR
6 BOOBOO MISCUE
off: 4 LAZE LOAF
Printing: 4 TYPO
up: 3 **ERR** 4 FLUB
Goofball: 4 BOZO NERD YOYO
5 FLAKE
Goof-off: 5 IDLER
Goofs: 6 ERRATA
Goofy: 3 ODD 4 DAFT LOCO
TOON 5 INANE SAPPY
Google
rival: 5 YAHOO
Goo-goo
Make ~ eyes at: 4 OGLE
Goo Goo Dolls
1998 ~ hit: 4 IRIS
Goolagong
of tennis: 6 EVONNE
rival: 5 EVERT
Goombah: 3 PAL
Goon: 3 **APE** 4 HOOD THUG
6 GALOOT
"Go on!": 6 DOTELL
"Go on ...": 3 AND
"___ go on?": 6 SHALLI
Goop
Hair: 3 GEL
Goose
Black-necked: 5 BRANT
Causing ~ bumps: 5 EERIE

Cook one's: 5 ROAST
egg: 3 NIL ZIP 4 NADA **ZERO**
6 NAUGHT
genus: 5 ANSER
Hawaiian: 4 **NENE**
Like a: 8 ANSERINE
Silly: 3 ASS 5 NINNY
sound: 4 HONK
Gooseberry
Chinese: 4 KIWI
Goosebumps
Causing: 5 EERIE 6 CREEPY
"Goosebumps"
author: 5 STINE 7 RLSTINE
Goosefoot
plant: 4 BEET
Gooselike: 8 ANSERINE
Gooseneck: 4 LAMP
Goosey: 5 INANE
GOP
elephant drawer: 4 NAST
foe: 3 DEM
hq.: 3 RNC
member: 3 REP
Part of: 3 OLD
Gopher wood
vessel: 3 ARK
Gorbachev
Its last pres. was: 4 USSR
Mrs.: 5 **RAISA**
policy: 8 GLASNOST
Gorcey
Actor: 3 LEO
Gordie
of hockey: 4 **HOWE**
Gordimer
Novelist: 6 NADINE
Gordius
tied one: 4 KNOT
Gordon
Auto racer: 4 JEFF
Gordon, Flash
foe: 4 MING
portrayer Buster: 6 CRABBE
Gordon, Jeff
org.: 6 NASCAR
Gore
and others: 3 ALS
gp.: 4 DEMS

home st.: 4 TENN
~, formerly: 4 VEEP
Gorge: 4 SATE 5 CHASM FEAST
    6 RAVINE 7 SATIATE
crosser: 7 TRESTLE
Gorged: 7 ATEALOT
Gorgon: 3 HAG 6 MEDUSA
Like a: 4 UGLY
Gorilla: 3 APE 4 HOOD THUG
leader: 10 SILVERBACK
researcher Fossey: 4 DIAN
Sign language: 4 KOKO
Toon: 7 MAGILLA
"Gorillas in the Mist"
author Dian: 6 FOSSEY
author Fossey: 4 DIAN
Gorky Park
setting: 6 MOSCOW
Gormé
Singer: 5 EYDIE
Gorton
Senator: 5 SLADE
"Gosh!": 3 GEE OOH 4 ISAY
Gospel
First name in: 7 MAHALIA
singer Winans: 4 CECE
writer: 4 JOHN LUKE MARK
Gospels
follower: 4 ACTS
One of the: 4 JOHN LUKE MARK
Gossamer: 4 AIRY LACY 5 LIGHT
    WISPY 7 SPIDERY
    8 ETHEREAL
Gossip: 3 GAB JAW YAK 4 BLAB
    CHIN DIRT DISH POOP
    TALK 5 YENTA 6 TATTLE
Bit of: 4 ITEM 5 ONDIT
columnist Barrett: 4 RONA
columnist Smith: 3 LIZ
Full of: 5 DISHY
Juicy: 4 DIRT 6 EARFUL
Piece of: 4 ITEM 5 ONDIT
tidbit, with "the": 6 LATEST
Gossipy: 5 NEWSY
Got
along: 5 FARED 6 MADEDO
by: 6 MADEDO
down: 3 ATE 4 **ALIT**
off: 4 **ALIT**

on: 5 FARED
up: 4 ROSE WOKE 5 **AROSE**
    AWOKE STOOD
"Got ___?": 4 MILK
"___ Got a Crush on You": 3 IVE
"___ Got a Secret": 3 IVE
"Gotcha!": 3 **AHA** OHO 4 IDIG
    ISEE
"Go team!": 3 RAH
Gotham City
protector: 6 BATMAN
Gothic
adornment: 5 GABLE
governess: 4 EYRE
"Got it!": 3 AHA 4 IDIG ISEE
"___ got it!": 3 IVE
"Got me!": 5 DUNNO
"Got milk?"
cry: 4 MEOW
"___ Got Sixpence": 3 IVE
"___ gotta be kidding!": 3 YOU
"___ Gotta Be Me": 3 IVE
"___ Gotta Crow": 3 IVE
"Gotta have it"
sloganeer: 5 PEPSI
"___ Gotta Have It": 4 SHES
"Gotti"
actor Armand: 7 ASSANTE
"___ Got You Under My Skin":
    3 IVE
Gouda
alternative: 4 EDAM
Gouge: 4 TOOL
Goulash: 4 STEW
seasoning: 7 PAPRIKA
Gould
Novelist: 4 LOIS
railroad: 4 ERIE
Gould, Jay
railroad: 4 ERIE
Gould/Sutherland
film: 4 SPYS
Gounod
composition: 8 AVEMARIA
opera: 5 FAUST
Gourd
fruit: 4 PEPO
instrument: 6 MARACA
Out of one's: 4 LOCO

Gourde
 Its currency is the: 5 HAITI
Gourmand: 5 EATER 6 GORGER
Gourmet
 cook: 4 CHEF
 mushroom: 5 MOREL
 sense: 6 PALATE
Govern: 4 RULE
Governess
 Fictional: 4 ANNA EYRE
Governessy: 4 PRIM
Governing
 body: 6 SENATE
Government
 agent: 3 FED 4 TMAN
 Center of: 4 SEAT
 in power: 6 REGIME
 issue: 5 TNOTE
 security: 5 TNOTE
 worker: 10 BUREAUCRAT
Governor
 domain: 5 STATE
 First ~ of Alaska: 4 **EGAN**
 Former Connecticut: 6 GRASSO
 Former NJ: 6 FLORIO
 Former NY: 5 CUOMO 6 PATAKI
 option: 4 VETO
Govt.
 1860s ~: 3 CSA
 agent: 4 TMAN
 airwaves board: 3 FCC
 auditor: 3 IRS
 banking org.: 4 FDIC
 certified: 4 REGD
 code breakers: 3 NSA
 home loan gp.: 3 FHA
 hush-hush gp.: 3 NSA
 investigation: 3 INQ
 lawyers: 3 DAS
 lender: 3 SBA
 medical agcy.: 3 NIH
 mortgage gp.: 3 FHA
 narcotics watchdog: 3 DEA
 obligation: 5 TBILL TNOTE
 old-age insurer: 3 SSA
 product-testing org.: 3 FDA
 property overseer: 3 GSA
 security: 5 TNOTE
 watchdog: 3 EPA 4 OSHA

Go-with
 Brolly: 3 MAC
 Early PC: 5 MSDOS
 Gin: 5 TONIC
 Muumuu: 3 LEI
 Oil change: 4 LUBE
 Soup: 7 SALTINE
 Tonic: 3 GIN
Gown: 5 DRESS
 accessory: 5 STOLE
 fabric: 5 SATIN TULLE
 Kind of: 6 BRIDAL
 Priest: 3 ALB
 renters (abbr.): 3 SRS
Gowns
 Like some: 9 STRAPLESS
 partners: 4 CAPS
 Pricey: 5 DIORS
Goya
 homeland: 5 SPAIN
 museum: 5 PRADO 7 ELPRADO
 patron: 4 ALBA
 subject: 4 **MAJA**
Gp.: 3 ORG 4 ASSN
G.P.
 gp.: 3 AMA
G.P.'s: 3 MDS
GQ: 3 MAG
Grab: 5 SEIZE 6 SNAPUP
  SNATCH
 a bite: 3 EAT
 bag: 4 OLIO
 by the collar: 6 ACCOST
 (onto): 4 GLOM
 some z's: 5 SLEEP
 the check: 5 TREAT
 tightly: 6 CLENCH
 ~, in a way: 4 TONG
Grab ___ : 5 ABITE
"Grab ___!": 5 AHOLD
Grabber: 4 CLAW 5 TALON
 Tab ~ words: 4 ONME
Grabbers: 5 TONGS
Grable, Betty
 asset: 4 LEGS
Grabs
 Up for: 4 FREE OPEN
 ___ grabs: 5 UPFOR
Grace: 6 PRAYER

End of: 4 AMEN
Fall from: 3 **SIN**
land: 6 MONACO
period: 4 AMEN
Say: 4 PRAY
Symbol of: 4 SWAN
under pressure: 5 POISE
word: 5 BLESS
Grace, Bud
strip: 5 ERNIE
Graceful
bend: 4 PLIE
bird: 4 SWAN
girl: 5 SYLPH
horse: 4 ARAB
plunge: 8 SWANDIVE
runner: 7 ARABIAN
seabird: 4 TERN
Trim and: 5 SLEEK
Graceland: 6 ESTATE
home (abbr.): 4 TENN
icon: 5 ELVIS
"... grace of God ___": 3 GOI
"Gracias"
reply: 6 DENADA
Gracile: 4 SLIM
Grad: 4 **ALUM**
class: 3 SRS
Gregg: 5 STENO
MIT: 4 ENGR
USNA: 3 **ENS**
Yale: 3 ELI
Grade: 4 HILL RATE 5 SLOPE
        7 INCLINE
Average: 3 **CEE**
Barely passing: 3 DEE
        5 DPLUS
enhancer: 4 PLUS
Good: 5 BPLUS
Great: 5 APLUS
of tea: 5 PEKOE
point avg.: 4 CUME
Poor: 3 **DEE**
prefix: 5 CENTI
school class (abbr.): 3 SCI
They make the: 5 TESTS
Grader
Govt. beef: 4 USDA
Seventh: 7 PRETEEN

Grades
~ 1–12: 4 ELHI
~ K–6 (abbr.): 4 ELEM
Grads
Many college: 3 BAS
Many MIT: 3 EES
OCS: 3 LTS
Grads-to-be
(abbr.): 3 **SRS**
Grad student
hurdle: 4 ORAL
work: 6 THESIS
Grad-to-be: 6 SENIOR
Gradually: 8 BITBYBIT
        OVERTIME
        10 STEPBYSTEP
Graduate: 6 ALUMNA
Academy: 6 ENSIGN
deg.: 3 PHD
garb: 4 GOWN
Seminary: 5 RABBI
USNA: 3 ENS
"Graduate, The"
actress Katharine: 4 ROSS
hero: 3 BEN
heroine: 6 ELAINE
Graduated: 6 SCALAR
Graduates: 6 ALUMNI
        7 ALUMNAE
Graduating
class (abbr.): 3 SRS
Graduation
composer: 5 ELGAR
dangler: 6 TASSEL
month: 4 JUNE
Graf
Husband of: 6 AGASSI
of tennis: 6 STEFFI
rival: 5 **SELES**
Graf ___: 4 **SPEE**
Graff
Actress: 5 **ILENE**
Graffiti
artist: 6 VANDAL
Biblical ~ start: 4 MENE
Cover with: 6 DEFACE
Like most ~ (abbr.): 4 ANON
~, to some: 3 ART
Graft: 6 BOODLE

Grafting
shoot: 5 SCION
Grafton
Author: 3 SUE
Graham
Author: 6 GREENE
Cartoonist: 4 ALEX
of football: 4 OTTO
of rock: 4 NASH
Grain
alcohol: 7 ETHANOL
beard: 3 AWN
Brewer: 4 MALT
bristle: 6 ARISTA
bristles: 7 ARISTAE
Cereal: 3 **OAT** RYE
for grinding: 5 GRIST
Free ~ from chaff: 6 WINNOW
fungus: 4 SMUT
Gather: 4 REAP
Granola: 3 OAT
grinder: 4 MILL
Ground: 4 MEAL 5 GRIST
holder: 3 BIN 4 SILO
husk: 4 BRAN
Made of a certain: 5 OATEN
Saw with the: 3 RIP
Skeptic's: 4 SALT
Store: 6 ENSILE
thresher: 5 FLAIL
Grains
60 ~: 4 DRAM
About 3 ~: 5 CARAT
About 15 ~: 4 GRAM
Buckwheat: 6 KASHAS
Gritty: 4 SAND
Grain-sized
Made: 5 RICED
Grainy: 5 OATEN
Gram: 4 NANA
prefix: 3 ANA EPI 4 IDEO
Gramercy Five
leader Shaw: 5 ARTIE
Gramm: 7 SENATOR
Senator: 4 PHIL
Grammar
Analyze: 5 PARSE
class subject: 5 NOUNS TENSE
no-no: 4 AINT

school trio: 3 RRR
Subj. including: 3 ENG
Grammarian
concern: 5 USAGE
Grammy
1988 ~ winner: 5 OSLIN
1989 ~ winner: 5 RAITT
1991 ~ winner: 6 ARETHA
1992 ~ winner: 4 ENYA
6 KDLANG
2003 ~ winner Jones: 5 NORAH
category: 3 RAP 4 FOLK JAZZ
5 RANDB 6 GOSPEL
winner Bonnie: 5 RAITT
winner Cohn: 4 MARC
Gramps
Wife of: 4 NANA
Grams
1000 ~: 4 KILO
Like: 6 METRIC
Granada
Info: Spanish cue
God, in: 4 DIOS
gold: 3 ORO
Good, in: 5 BUENO
greeting: 4 HOLA
Gran Canaria: 4 ISLA
Grand: 3 GEE 4 EPIC POSH **THOU**
6 SUPERB 8 THOUSAND
Baby: 5 PIANO
duke's father: 4 CZAR
finale: 4 PRIX
It may be: 4 TOUR 7 LARCENY
It's less than: 6 SPINET
On a ~ scale: 4 EPIC
slam foursome: 4 RBIS
theft: 6 FELONY
Word after: 5 OPERA
"Grand"
hotel: 5 HYATT
ice cream: 4 EDYS
island: 6 BAHAMA
thing: 5 PIANO
Grand ___ : 3 CRU PRE 4 PRIX
Grand Canal
bridge: 6 RIALTO
Grand Canyon
beast: 5 BURRO
feature: 3 RIM

sight: 4 MESA
st.: 4 ARIZ
transport: 5 BURRO
view: 8 PANORAMA
"Grand Canyon Suite"
composer Ferde: 5 GROFE
composer Grofé: 5 FERDE
Grand Central
(abbr.): 3 STA
Grandchild
Genesis: 4 ENOS
Grandchildren
Watch the: 3 SIT
Grand Coulee: 3 DAM
Granddaddy
of computers: 5 ENIAC
Grand ___ Dam: 6 COULEE
Grande: 3 RIO
___ Grande: 3 RIO 4 CASA
Grandee
inferior: 7 HIDALGO
Grandfather
Hour not on a ~ clock: 4 XIII
of Bart: 3 ABE
"Grand Illusion"
director: 6 RENOIR
Grandiloquize: 5 ORATE
Grand ___ island: 6 BAHAMA
Grandma: 4 NANA
impersonator: 4 WOLF
in galleries: 5 MOSES
Grand Marquis
~, for short: 4 MERC
Grandmother: 4 NANA
Grand ___ National Park:
5 **TETON**
Grand Ole ___: 4 **OPRY**
"Grand Ole Opry"
network: 3 TNN
Grand ___ Opry: 3 **OLE**
Grandparent
~, often: 5 DOTER
Grand Prix
feature: 3 ESS
site: 6 LEMANS
Grand Slam
winner: 4 GRAF 5 LAVER
Grandson
add-on: 3 III

of Abraham: 4 ESAU
of Adam: 4 **ENOS**
Grandstand
shout: 3 RAH
Grand Teton
grazer: 3 ELK
Granny: 4 KNOT NANA
portrayer: 5 IRENE
Granola
grain: 3 **OAT**
ingredient: 6 RAISIN
Like: 5 OATEN
___ grano salis: 3 CUM
Grant: 4 CEDE GIVE 5 AWARD
ENDOW 6 BESTOW
7 STIPEND
(abbr.): 3 GEN
Actor: 4 CARY HUGH
basis: 4 NEED
bill: 5 FIFTY
entry to: 5 LETIN
foe: 3 LEE
General: 7 ULYSSES
Genie: 4 WISH
money: 5 ENDOW
portrayer: 5 **ASNER**
7 EDASNER
Singer: 3 AMY 4 GOGI
source (abbr.): 3 NEA
successor: 5 HAYES
Tey investigator: 4 ALAN
Grant-___: 5 INAID
Grant, Inspector
creator: 3 TEY
Grant, Lou
paper: 4 TRIB
portrayer: 5 ASNER
7 EDASNER
Grant, U.S.
birthplace: 4 OHIO
Granted: 4 GAVE
Be: 7 RECEIVE
Take for: 6 ASSUME
Granter
Wish: 5 **GENIE**
Granters
Wish: 5 GENII
Granting
gp.: 3 NEA

that, briefly: 3 THO
Grantorto
  victim: 5 IRENA
Granular
  coating: 4 RIME
Grape
  Burgundy: 5 **PINOT**
  Dried: 6 RAISIN
  holder: 4 VINE
  Red wine: 6 MERLOT
  soda: 4 NEHI
  suffix: 3 ADE
  Wine: 5 PINOT
Grapefruit
  kin: 6 POMELO
Grapefruit League
  state (abbr.): 3 FLA
Grapes
  Like some: 4 SOUR 8 SEEDLESS
  Like sour: 4 TART 6 ACIDIC
"Grapes of Wrath"
  character: 4 **OKIE**
  family name: 4 JOAD
  star: 5 FONDA
Grapevine
  Get from the: 4 HEAR
  item: 5 RUMOR
Graph: 5 CHART
  (0,0) on a: 6 ORIGIN
  3-D ~ line: 5 ZAXIS
  calculation: 5 SLOPE
  horizontal line: 5 XAXIS
  line: 4 AXIS
  lines: 4 AXES
  Make a: 4 PLOT
  pattern: 4 GRID
  point: 4 PEAK
  points: 4 LOCI
  prefix: 3 EPI 4 IDEO PARA TELE
  vertical line: 5 YAXIS
  X or Y, on a: 4 AXIS
Graphic
  Computer: 4 ICON
  descriptions: 6 IMAGES
  prefix: 3 GEO 4 IDEO
  symbol: 4 ICON
Graphic ___ : 4 ARTS
Graphics
  machine: 6 IMAGER

Graphite
  element: 6 CARBON
  remover: 6 ERASER
Grapple: 6 RASSLE
Grappler
  surface: 3 MAT
___ Gras: 5 **MARDI**
Grasp: 3 GET KEN SEE 4 HOLD
      KNOW 5 SEIZE 6 ATTAIN
      FATHOM
  Hard to: 4 DEEP EELY
  Mental: 6 UPTAKE
Grasped: 4 HELD
Graspers: 5 TONGS
Grass: 4 LAWN
  appendage: 3 AWN
  Cereal: 3 OAT
  Clump of: 4 TUFT
  coat: 3 DEW
  Cut the: 3 MOW
  Drops on the: 3 DEW
  Kind of: 3 OAT
  Like early morning: 4 DEWY
  Marsh: 4 REED 5 SEDGE
  Put in new: 5 RESOD
  Rye ~ disease: 5 ERGOT
  section: 3 SOD
  unit: 5 BLADE
  Word with: 5 WIDOW
___ grass: 3 OAT
Grasshopper
  associate: 3 ANT
  kin: 7 KATYDID
  sound: 5 CHIRR
Grassland: 3 **LEA**
  African: 5 VELDT
  Russian: 6 STEPPE
Grasso
  Former governor: 4 **ELLA**
Grassy
  area: 3 LEA
  expanse: 5 LLANO
  field: 3 LEA
  plain: 5 LLANO 7 SAVANNA
  surface: 5 SWARD
Grate: 4 RASP
  expectations: 3 ASH 5 ASHES
  on: 3 IRK
  stuff: 3 ASH 5 ASHES

G-rated: 5 CLEAN
  What ~ is for: 7 ALLAGES
Grateful: 5 ASHES
Grater
  input: 6 ROMANO
___ gratia: 3 DEI
"___ gratia artis": 3 **ARS**
___ gratias: 3 **DEO**
Gratify: 4 FEED SATE 6 PLEASE
Grating: 4 GRID 5 HARSH RASPY
     6 HOARSE 8 STRIDENT
  sound: 4 RASP
  Window: 6 GRILLE
Gratis: 4 COMP FREE
     7 FORFREE
Gratitude
  Express ~ to: 5 THANK
Gratuity: 3 TIP
  Casino: 4 TOKE
Grave: 4 TOMB 5 ACUTE SOBER
     STAID STERN 6 SEVERE
     SOLEMN SOMBER
     7 SERIOUS
  marker: 5 STELA STONE
  risk: 5 PERIL
  robber: 5 GHOUL
Gravel ___ (Dick Tracy character):
     6 GERTIE
Gravelly
  ridge: 5 ESKER
  utterance: 5 RASP
Graven
  image: 4 IDOL
Graves
  Actress: 6 TERESA
Gravitate: 4 TEND
  (toward): 4 LEAN
Gravity
  Give in to: 3 SAG 5 DROOP
Gravity-powered
  vehicle: 4 SLED
Gravy
  Absorb, as: 5 SOPUP
  absorber: 3 SOP
  flaw: 4 LUMP
  holder: 4 **BOAT**
  Like bad: 5 LUMPY
  morsel: 6 GIBLET
  Red-eye ~ base: 3 HAM

Gravy Train
  rival: 4 ALPO
Gray: 3 AGE CSA REB 4 ASHY
     DRAB REBS 5 ASHEN
     7 ELEGIST
  Actress: 4 ERIN
  area (abbr.): 4 ANAT
  Botanist: 3 **ASA**
  Brownish: 5 **TAUPE**
  Fighter in: 3 REB
  General in: 3 LEE
  Go: 3 AGE
  Like the ~ mare: 3 OLD
  matter output: 4 IDEA
  piece: 3 ODE 5 ELEGY
  remover: 4 DYER
  shade: 5 TAUPE
  Silvery: 3 ASH
  Soldier in: 3 REB 5 REBEL
  subj.: 4 ANAT
  wolf: 4 **LOBO**
Gray ___: 4 AREA
Gray, Dorian
  creator: 5 WILDE
  What ~ didn't do: 3 AGE
Gray, Thomas
  ode subject: 4 ETON
  work: 3 ODE 5 ELEGY
Grayback: 3 REB
Graycoat: 3 REB
Grayish: 4 ASHY DRAB
     5 ASHEN
  brown: 3 DUN
  yellow: 4 ECRU
Gray Panthers
  (abbr.): 3 SRS
Graze: 3 EAT 4 FEED
  Place to: 3 LEA
Grazed: 3 ATE
Grazer
  African: 3 GNU
  Bearded: 3 GNU
  Female: 3 EWE
  Grand Teton: 3 ELK
  Roadside: 4 DEER
  Serengeti: 3 GNU 5 ELAND
     6 IMPALA
Grazie
  Response to: 5 PREGO

Grazing
  ground: 3 **LEA** 6 MEADOW
    7 PASTURE
GRE
  takers: 3 SRS
Grease: 4 LARD LUBE
  Clean with elbow: 5 SCOUR
    SCRUB
  job: 4 LUBE
  target: 4 AXLE
"Grease"
  actress: 8 EVEARDEN
  actress Conn: 4 DIDI
  actress Eve: 5 ARDEN
  Costar of John in: 6 OLIVIA
  girl: 5 SANDY
  group: 7 SHANANA
  singer: 5 VALLI
Greasy: 4 OILY
  goo: 4 GUNK
  of football: 5 NEALE
Greasy spoon: 5 DINER
  sign: 4 EATS
Great: 3 RAD 4 AONE EPIC
    5 NOTED SWELL
  ball of fire: 4 STAR
  bargain: 5 STEAL
  care: 5 PAINS
  deal: 3 LOT TON 4 HEAP SCAD
    SLEW
  In ~ shape: 3 FIT
  move: 4 COUP
  Neither ~ nor terrible: 4 SOSO
  No ~ shakes: 4 SOSO
  number: 3 TON 4 HEAP RAFT
    SCAD
  review: 4 **RAVE**
  score: 3 TEN
  service: 3 ACE
  time: 3 ERA GAS 4 BALL
    5 BLAST
  unwashed: 5 PLEBS
  work: 4 OPUS
"Great"
  czar: 6 PETERI
  detective of kid lit: 4 NATE
  pope: 5 STLEO
"Great!": 5 NEATO SUPER
    SWELL

Great ___ : 4 DANE 6 DIVIDE
"Great, The"
  Pope known as: 4 LEOI
"Great ___, The": 7 SANTINI
Great Britain
  emblem: 4 LION
"Great Dictator, The"
  costar Jack: 5 OAKIE
Greater: 4 MORE
  To a ~ extent: 6 MORESO
Greatest: 6 UTMOST
  degree: 3 MAX
  part: 4 MOST
"Greatest, The": 3 **ALI**
"Great Expectations"
  girl: 7 ESTELLA
  hero: 3 PIP
  Magwitch of: 4 ABEL
"Great Forest, The"
  painter: 6 ERNEST
Great Lake: 4 ERIE
  Second largest: 5 HURON
  Shallowest: 4 ERIE
  Smallest: 7 ONTARIO
  Southernmost: 4 ERIE
Great Lakes
  acronym: 5 HOMES
  fish: 4 CHUB 5 CISCO SMELT
  port: 4 ERIE
  salmon: 4 COHO
  whitefish: 5 CISCO
  ~ Indians: 5 ERIES
Great Leap Forward
  leader: 3 MAO
Great Mosque
  site: 6 ALEPPO
Great ___ Mountains: 5 SMOKY
"Great ___ Pepper, The": 5 WALDO
Great Salt Lake
  site: 4 UTAH
Great Society
  pres.: 3 LBJ
Great Trek
  participant: 4 BOER
Great white ___ : 5 HERON
Great White North, The:
    6 CANADA
Grecian
  urn work: 3 ODE

Grecian Formula
target: 8 GRAYHAIR
Greece
Dawn of: 3 EOS
Divine agency of: 6 ORACLE
Letter from: 3 ETA RHO TAU
Peak in NE: 6 MTOSSA
Region of ancient: 5 IONIA
~, to the Greeks: 5 ELLAS
Greed: 3 SIN 7 AVARICE
Exemplar of: 5 MIDAS
Greedy
Be: 3 HOG
cry: 4 MINE 5 METOO
one: 3 HOG PIG 5 TAKER
Greek: 7 HELLENE
1st ~ letter: 5 ALPHA
3rd ~ letter: 5 GAMMA
6th ~ letter: 4 ZETA
7th ~ letter: 3 ETA
8th ~ letter: 5 THETA
19th ~ letter: 3 TAU
Ancient ~ coin: 4 OBOL
    6 STATER
Ancient ~ colony: 5 **IONIA**
Ancient ~ dialect: 5 EOLIC
Ancient ~ lyric poet: 6 SAPPHO
    8 ANACREON
Ancient ~ physician: 5 GALEN
Ancient ~ region: 5 IONIA
Ancient ~ state: 6 ATTICA
bread: 4 PITA
cheese: 4 FETA
Chief ~ god: 4 ZEUS
city-state: 5 POLIS 6 SPARTA
    7 CORINTH
colonnade: 4 STOA
column style: 5 IONIC
consonant: 3 CHI RHO TAU
    4 BETA ZETA 5 SIGMA
consonants: 3 MUS NUS
cross: 3 **TAU**
ending: 5 OMEGA
epic: 5 ILIAD
fabulist: 5 AESOP
for "many": 6 POLLOI
garment: 5 TUNIC
god of love: 4 **EROS**
god of war: 4 **ARES**

group: 4 FRAT
harp: 4 LYRE
island: 5 CRETE SAMOS
legislature: 5 BOULE
letter: 3 CHI **ETA** PHI PSI RHO
    TAU 4 BETA IOTA ZETA
    5 ALPHA GAMMA KAPPA
    OMEGA SIGMA THETA
letters: 3 MUS NUS PIS XIS
liqueur: 4 **OUZO**
marketplace: 5 **AGORA**
mountain: 4 OSSA
Paradoxical: 4 ZENO
peak: 4 **OSSA**
philosopher: 4 ZENO 5 PLATO
portico: 4 **STOA**
sandwich: 4 GYRO
sea: 6 AEGEAN
temple: 4 NAOS
theater: 5 ODEON
theaters: 4 ODEA
Triangular ~ letter: 5 DELTA
underworld: 5 HADES
vowel: 3 **ETA** 4 IOTA
    7 OMICRON UPSILON
wine: 7 RETSINA
~ H: 3 ETA
~ I: 4 IOTA
~ P: 3 RHO
~ T: 3 TAU
~ X: 3 CHI
Greek salad
cheese: 4 FETA
Greeley
direction: 4 WEST
Newsman: 6 HORACE
Green: 3 ECO NEW RAW 4 CASH
    5 MOOLA NAIVE
    6 MOOLAH UNRIPE
    8 IMMATURE
Actor: 4 SETH
and others: 3 ALS
around the gills: 3 ILL 4 SICK
beans: 5 LIMAS
beginner: 4 EVER
Bluish: 4 AQUA TEAL
Bowling: 4 LAWN
carvings: 4 JADE
course: 5 SALAD

Deep: **7** EMERALD
dessert: **7** LIMEPIE
drink: **3** TEA **7** LIMEADE
eggs and ham promoter:
   6 SAMIAM
feeling: **4** ENVY
film: **6** PATINA
fruit: **4** KIWI LIME **5** OLIVE
garnish: **5** CRESS
gem: **4** **JADE** **5** BERYL
   7 EMERALD PERIDOT
Gimme on the: **5** TAPIN
Gives the ~ light: **3** OKS
growth: **4** ALGA MOSS
guarder: **4** TRAP
hole: **3** CUP
hue: **4** JADE
land: **4** **EIRE** ERIN
light: **4** OKAY **6** ASSENT
lights: **3** OKS **5** YESES
liqueur: **8** ABSINTHE
Little ~ man: **5** **ALIEN**
Little ~ men: **3** ETS
Long: **4** CASH KALE **5** BREAD
   DOUGH MONEY MOOLA
   6 MOOLAH
moth: **4** LUNA
perimeters: **6** APRONS
pet: **4** CHIA
prefix: **3** ECO
Pungent: **5** CRESS
Salad: **3** COS **5** **CRESS**
   6 CELERY ENDIVE
   8 ESCAROLE
sauce: **5** PESTO
sci.: **4** ECOL
shade: **3** PEA SEA **4** JADE LEEK
   LIME MOSS NILE **5** BERYL
   KELLY OLIVE **7** AVOCADO
shot: **4** PUTT
spot: **5** OASIS
stuff: **4** CASH **5** MOOLA
   6 DOREMI
suffix: **3** ERY
target: **3** CUP PIN **4** HOLE
Turn: **3** DYE **4** ENVY
Word seen in: **4** WALK
"Green ___": **5** ACRES
"Green ___, The": **4** MILE

"Green Acres"
  costar: **5** GABOR **6** ALBERT
  Gabor of: **3** EVA
  pig: **6** ARNOLD
Green Bay
  gridder: **6** PACKER
"Green Berets, The"
  actor Ray: **4** ALDO
Green card
  holder: **5** ALIEN
  org.: **3** INS
  ~, informally: **4** AMEX
Greene
  Actor: **5** **LORNE**
  Critic: **4** GAEL
Greene, Mean Joe: 7 STEELER
Greene County, Ohio
  seat: **5** XENIA
Greenery
  Pond: **5** ALGAE
  Yuletide: **5** HOLLY
Green-eyed
  monster: **4** ENVY
Greenfield
  Columnist: **3** MEG
Green Gables
  girl: **4** **ANNE**
Greenhorn: 4 COLT NAIF TIRO
    TYRO **6** ROOKIE
  Like a: **3** NEW
Green Hornet
  real first name: **5** BRITT
  real last name: **4** REID
  sidekick: **4** **KATO**
Greenhouse
  area: **6** HOTBED
  Do a ~ job: **5** REPOT
  gadget: **6** MISTER
Greenish: 5 OLIVE
  blue: **4** AQUA CYAN NILE **TEAL**
  yellow pear: **4** BOSC
Greenland
  air base site: **5** THULE
  explorer: **4** ERIC
  feature: **6** ICECAP
Green Mountain Boys
  leader Allen: **5** ETHAN
Green Party
  candidate: **5** NADER

Greens: 5 SALAD
    ___ greens: 4 BEET
Greenside
    hazard: 4 TRAP
Greenskeeper
    supply: 3 SOD
Greenspan
    Economist: 4 **ALAN**
    group: 3 FED 6 THEFED
    subj.: 4 ECON
Green Wave
    school: 6 TULANE
Greenwich
    Songwriter: 5 ELLIE
Greenwich Village
    Area below: 4 SOHO
    Like: 4 ARTY
Greet: 4 HAIL 7 SAYHITO
    and seat: 5 SEEIN
    from afar: 6 WAVETO
    the day: 4 RISE 5 **ARISE**
    the judge: 4 RISE
    the villain: 3 BOO 4 **HISS**
    with laughter: 6 ROARAT
Greeting: 5 HELLO
    at sea: 4 AHOY
    Aussie: 4 GDAY
    Bygone: 3 AVE
    Cockney: 4 ELLO
    Cowboy: 5 HOWDY
    Flowery: 3 LEI
    Forum: 3 AVE
    Informal: 3 HEY 4 HIHO HIYA
       5 HOWDY HULLO
       6 YOOHOO 7 HITHERE
    Island: 5 **ALOHA**
    On-field: 5 HIMOM
    Ritual: 6 SALAAM
    Silent: 4 WAVE
    Spanish: 4 HOLA
    Tail: 3 WAG
"Greetings": 5 HELLO
    org.: 3 SSS
Greg
    Actor: 6 EVIGAN 7 KINNEAR
    TV wife of: 6 DHARMA
Gregarious: 6 SOCIAL
    Not: 7 ASOCIAL
    Not the ~ type: 5 LONER

Gregg
    expert: 5 STENO
    Rocker: 6 ALLMAN
Gregor
    Kafka hero: 5 SAMSA
Gregory
    Dancer: 5 HINES
    of reggae: 6 ISAACS
Gregory I
    papacy year: 3 DCI
Gremlin
    maker: 3 AMC
Gremlins: 4 AMCS
Grenada: 4 ISLE
    Info: Spanish cue
    gold: 3 ORO
Grenade
    throw: 3 LOB
Grenadine
    Cocktail made with: 7 BACARDI
Grenoble
    Info: French cue
    girlfriend: 4 AMIE
    Goodbye, in: 5 ADIEU
    Good, in: 4 BIEN
    river: 5 ISERE
Greta
    Actress: 5 GARBO
    role: 4 MATA
Gretel
    Brother of: 6 HANSEL
Gretna Green
    Visit: 5 ELOPE
Gretzky
    of hockey: 5 WAYNE
    score: 4 GOAL
    was one: 5 OILER
Grew
    fond of: 6 TOOKTO
    like ivy: 5 VINED
Grey
    Actor: 4 JOEL
    Actress: 3 NAN
    Author: 4 **ZANE**
    ___ Grey: 4 EARL
Grey Cup
    org.: 3 CFL
Greyhound: 3 BUS
    stop (abbr.): 3 STN

Grid
 figure, slangily: **5** ZEBRA
 infraction: **4** CLIP
 stat: **4** GAIN
 TV screen: **6** RASTER
Gridder
 Frisco: **5** NINER
 Green Bay: **6** PACKER
 St. Louis: **3** RAM
 Tennessee: **5** TITAN
Griddle
 sound: **3** SSS
Gridiron
 complement: **6** ELEVEN
 divs.: **3** YDS
 figure: **3** REF
 gains: **5** YARDS
 kick: **4** PUNT
 official: **3** REF
 org.: **3** NFL
 pass: **7** LATERAL
 play: **5** SNEAK **6** ENDRUN
 prop: **3** TEE
 stat: **3** YDS **5** SACKS
 team: **6** ELEVEN
 unit: **4** YARD
 "zebra": **3** REF
Gridlock: 3 JAM
 component: **3** CAR **4** AUTO
Grief: 3 WOE **4** PAIN **5** DOLOR
  6 SORROW
 Express: **5** MOURN
Grief-stricken
 cry: **4** ALAS
Grieg
 Composer: **6** EDVARD
 dancer: **6** ANITRA
 homeland: **6** NORWAY
 Peer of: **4** GYNT
 ~ Piano Concerto key: **6** AMINOR
Grier
 Actress: **3** PAM
 of football: **5** ROSEY
Grievance: 4 BEEF
Grieve: 5 MOURN
 (for): **4** WEEP
Griever
 word: **4** ALAS
Grievously: 6 SORELY

 Injure: **4** MAIM
Griffey
 of baseball: **3** __KEN__
 stat: **3** RBI
Griffin
 Game show creator: **4** MERV
 Half of a: **4** LION **5** EAGLE
Griffith
 Actor: **4** ANDY
 Actress: **7** MELANIE
 Boxer: **5** EMILE
 Folk singer: **5** NANCI
 role: **7** MATLOCK
Grifter
 speciality: **4** SCAM
Grig
 Adult: **3** EEL
Grill: 3 ASK **5** BROIL
 Blacken on a: **4** SEAR
 partner: **3** BAR
 Patio: **7** HIBACHI
Grille
 cover: **3** BRA
 Horse-collar ~ car: **5** EDSEL
Grilled
 sandwich: **4** MELT **6** PANINI
Grim
 figure: **6** REAPER
Grimace: 4 MOUE **5** WINCE
 Uttered: **3** UGH
Grimaldis
 ruling site: **6** MONACO
Grime: 4 DIRT SOIL
 Fight: **5** CLEAN
Grimm
 beast: **4** __OGRE__
 Elder ~ brother: **5** JACOB
 girl: **6** GRETEL
 lad: **6** HANSEL
 offering: **4** TALE
Grim Reaper
 prop: **6** SCYTHE
Grin: 5 SMILE
 Begin to: **11** CRACKASMILE
 Big ~ terminus: **3** EAR
 from ear to ear: **4** BEAM
 Twisted, as a: **3** WRY
Grinch
 creator: **5** SEUSS

dog: **3** MAX
smile: **5** SNEER
victim: **3** WHO
Grind: 3 RUT **5** GNASH
　　6 ABRADE CRUNCH
　　7 RATRACE
Axe to: **6** AGENDA
Daily: **3** RUT **7** RATRACE
One with an axe to: **5** HONER
Grinder: 3 SUB **4** HERO MILL
　　5 HOAGY MOLAR
　　6 HOAGIE
Grain: **4** MILL
Pepper: **4** MILL
Grinding
Grain for: **5** GRIST
material: **5** EMERY
tool: **6** PESTLE
tooth: **5** MOLAR
Grinned: 5 LITUP
Grins
Like some: **3** SLY **6** TOOTHY
　　8 SHEEPISH
Grip: 5 CLASP
Get a ~ on: **4** HOLD **5** GRASP
It helps you get a: **4** VISE
　　7 PINETAR
workplace: **3** SET
Gripe: 4 BEEF MOAN **5** PEEVE
　　6 KVETCH PLAINT
Grippe: 3 FLU
Gripper: 5 TALON
for the Gipper: **5** CLEAT
Workbench: **4** VISE **5** CLAMP
　　6 CCLAMP
Gris-gris: 6 AMULET
Grisham
title bird: **7** PELICAN
Grissom
Astronaut: **3** **GUS**
TV show featuring: **3** CSI
Grist
for processors: **4** DATA
place: **4** MILL
Grit: 4 GUTS SAND **5** GNASH
　　SPUNK **6** METTLE
Gritty
intro: **5** NITTY
Grizabella: 3 CAT

Grizzlies
org.: **3** NBA
Grizzly: 3 OLD **4** BEAR
home: **4** LAIR
Young: **3** CUB
Groan
causer: **3** PUN **4** CORN
Groaner: 3 PUN
Groats
Buckwheat: **5** KASHA
Groceries
holder: **3** BAG
Pack the ~ again: **5** REBAG
Grocery
carrier: **4** CART
containers: **5** SACKS
holder: **3** BAG
part: **5** AISLE
Spanish: **6** BODEGA
stick: **4** OLEO
Groening
Cartoonist: **4** MATT
Grofé
Composer: **5** FERDE
Grog
house: **3** INN
ingredient: **3** RUM
Groggery: 3 BAR
Grok: 3 GET
Grommet: 6 EYELET
Gromyko
Diplomat: **6** ANDREI
Groom: 5 PRIMP
attendant: **5** USHER
carefully: **5** PREEN
garb: **3** TUX
Greek ~ of 1968: **3** ARI
of 1614: **5** ROLFE
vow: **3** IDO
Groomer
Jungle: **3** APE
Grooming
process: **6** TOILET
Groove: 3 RUT **4** SLOT
Carpentry: **4** **DADO** **6** RABBET
It's in the: **6** NEEDLE
Narrow: **5** STRIA
Groove-billed
bird: **3** ANI

Grooved
Toy on a ~ track: **7** SLOTCAR
~, as a column: **6** FLUTED

Grooving
on: **4** INTO

Groovy
music: **3** LPS
track: **3** RUT

"Groovy!": **3** FAB RAD **4** COOL
NEAT **5** NEATO

Grope: **3** PAW
for words: **3** HEM

Grosbard
Director: **3** ULU

Gross: **4** ICKY
minus net: **4** TARE
minus taxes: **3** NET
out: **5** REPEL

"Gross!": **3** ICK UGH **4** YUCK
5 YECCH

Grosse ___, Michigan: **6** POINTE

Grotesque
figure: **8** GARGOYLE
imitation: **8** TRAVESTY

Grotto: **4** CAVE **6** CAVERN

Grouch: **4** CRAB **5** CRANK
8 SOURPUSS

Groucho
Glance from: **4** __LEER__
of comedy: **4** MARX
prop: **5** CIGAR
remark: **4** QUIP
role: **4** OTIS **5** RUFUS
Tattooed lady of: **5** LYDIA

Grouchy: **4** SOUR
person: **4** CRAB **5** CRANK
~ Muppet: **5** OSCAR

Ground: **4** SOIL **5** EARTH
Break: **3** HOE
breaker: **3** __HOE__ **4** HOER
cover: **3** SOD **4** TARP **5** GRASS
MULCH **7** MACADAM
Drops on the: **3** DEW
Gooey: **4** MIRE
grain: **4** MEAL **5** GRIST
Grazing: **3** __LEA__
High: **6** UPLAND
Hit the: **4** ALIT
Hold one's: **8** STANDPAT

It's found in the: **3** ORE
Lose: **5** __ERODE__
Marshy: **6** MORASS
On solid: **6** ASHORE
Play: **5** ARENA
Soggy: **4** MIRE
Solid: **10** TERRAFIRMA
Swampy: **3** BOG **4** MIRE
They never get off the: **4** EMUS
Touched: **4** ALIT

Groundbreaker: **3** HOE

Groundbreaking
discovery: **3** ORE

Grounded
bird: **3** __EMU__
flier: **3** SST

Grounder
Kicks a: **4** ERRS
Like an easy: **6** ONEHOP

Ground-floor
apartment, perhaps: **4** ONEB

Groundhog
Noted: **4** PHIL

"Groundhog Day"
actress MacDowell: **5** ANDIE

Groundless: **4** IDLE

Grounds: **5** BASIS DREGS
for complaint: **9** GRIEVANCE
for excommunication: **6** HERESY
Grand: **6** ESTATE

Groundskeeper
purchase: **3** SOD
~, at times: **5** RAKER

Ground-up
bait: **4** CHUM

Groundwork: **5** BASIS

Group: **3** LOT SET **4** BLOC
6 ASSORT
belief: **5** TENET
character: **5** ETHOS
"In": **5** ELITE
In a ~ of: **4** AMID
Kind of: **3** AGE **4** PEER
Large: **4** BEVY **5** ARRAY
of 13: **5** COVEN
of associates: **6** COHORT
of beauties: **4** BEVY
of bees: **5** SWARM
of cattle: **4** HERD

of eight: **5** OCTAD OCTET
of experts: **5** PANEL
of fish: **6** SCHOOL
of five: **6** PENTAD
of horses: **4** TEAM
of lions: **5** PRIDE
of nine: **5** NONET **6** ENNEAD
of officers: **5** CADRE
of periods: **3** ERA
of planes: **5** FLEET
of seven: **6** HEPTAD
of ships: **5** FLEET
of students: **5** CLASS
of three: **5** TRIAD TRINE
   6 TROIKA
of two: **4** DUAD DYAD
of whales: **3** POD
of witches: **5** COVEN
principle: **5** TENET
spirit: **6** MORALE
values: **5** ETHOS
voters: **4** BLOC

Grouper
group: **6** SCHOOL
Groupie: 3 FAN
Grouping: 5 ARRAY
Group Theatre
playwright: **5** ODETS
Grouse: 4 BEEF CRAB KICK RAIL
Grove
fruit: **6** ORANGE
growth: **10** ORANGETREE
Grovel: 7 EATDIRT
Grover
Second veep of: **5** ADLAI
___ **Grove Village, Illinois: 3** ELK
Grow
dark: **5** LATEN
dim: **4** FADE
faint: **4** WANE
It'll ~ on you: **4** HAIR
old: **3** AGE **7** SENESCE
One to ~ on: **4** ACRE
together: **7** ACCRETE
up: **3** AGE
wearisome: **4** PALL
weary: **4** TIRE
Grower: 6 FARMER
concern: **6** WEEVIL

Vegetable: **11** TRUCKFARMER
Growing
area: **4** FARM
   10 GREENHOUSE
Good for: **6** ARABLE
out: **5** ENATE
room: **4** ACRE
"Growing Pains"
actor Alan: **6** THICKE
"Growing Up in ___":
   9 NEWGUINEA
"Growing Up in New Guinea"
author: **4** MEAD
Growl: 4 GNAR
Grown: 5 ADULT
Grownup: 5 ADULT
Grown-up: 5 ADULT
acorn: **3** OAK
kid: **4** GOAT
"___ Grows in Brooklyn":
   5 ATREE
Growth
Forest: **4** MOSS
Marsh: **4** REED
Pond: **4** ALGA
Rock: **4** MOSS
Sea: **5** ALGAE
~, briefly: **4** INCR
Groza
of football: **3** LOU
Grp.: 3 ORG **4** ASSN
Grub: 4 CHOW **EATS** FOOD
   5 LARVA
Give ~ to: **4** FEED
Grubstake: 4 LOAN
Grudge
Carrying a: **4** SORE
Grueling
test: **4** ORAL
Gruesome: 5 LURID **6** MORBID
Gruff: 6 HOARSE
Grumble: 4 CARP CRAB **5** GRIPE
   6 GROUSE MUTTER
Grump: 4 CRAB
"Grumpier Old Men"
actress Sophia: **5** LOREN
Grumpy: 4 SOUR
companion: **3** DOC
glare: **5** SCOWL

mood: 4 SNIT
"Grumpy ___" (1993 film):
    6 OLDMEN
"Grumpy Old Men"
actor Davis: 5 OSSIE
Grunt
Disgusted: 3 UGH
of surprise: 3 HUH
Grunts: 3 GIS
GTO
The "G" in: 4 GRAN
Guacamole: 3 DIP
ingredient: 7 AVOCADO
Guadalajara
Info: Spanish cue
gold: 3 ORO
goodbye: 5 ADIOS
Good, in: 5 BUENO
guy: 5 SENOR
Guadalquivir
and others: 4 RIOS
Guadeloupe
and others: 4 ILES
Guam
(abbr.): 3 TER 4 TERR
capital: 5 **AGANA**
Point between ~ and Hawaii:
    10 WAKEISLAND
Guanabara Bay
city: 3 RIO
Guanaco
kin: 5 LLAMA
Guantánamo
locale: 4 CUBA
Guarantee: 4 AVOW SEAL
    6 ASSURE AVOUCH
    ENSURE INSURE
Guaranteed: 4 ICED MADE
    6 NOLOSE 8 FAILSAFE
(abbr.): 4 CERT
to work: 8 SUREFIRE
Guarantees
Carrying no: 4 ASIS
Guarantor
Acct.: 4 FDIC
Guard: 4 TEND 6 PATROL
    SENTRY SHIELD
    7 GATEMAN PROTECT
    8 SENTINEL

dog warning: 5 SNARL
Harem: 6 EUNUCH
Like a good: 5 ALERT
On: 4 WARY 5 ALERT
Place for a: 4 SHIN
Prison: 5 SCREW
shout: 4 HALT
Some ~ dogs: 5 SHEPS
Guarded: 4 SAFE 5 LEERY
Sword with a ~ tip: 4 EPEE
Guarder
Green: 4 TRAP
Guardian
charge: 4 WARD
spirits: 5 GENII LARES
Treasures: 5 GNOME
Guardian Angels
wear: 5 BERET
"Guarding ___" (1994 film):
    4 TESS
Guards: 7 LINEMEN
Guatemala
Info: Spanish cue
gold: 3 ORO
native: 4 MAYA
Guayaquil
locale: 7 ECUADOR
Gucci
Designer: 4 **ALDO**
fragrance: 4 ENVY
rival: 5 FENDI
Guernsey: 3 COW 4 ISLE
greeting: 3 MOO
___ guerre: 5 NOMDE
Guerrero
of baseball: 5 PEDRO
Guerrilla
1970s ~ org.: 3 SLA
action: 4 RAID
Guess: 4 IDEA STAB 5 OPINE
    6 RECKON
(abbr.): 3 EST
Didn't: 4 KNEW
Hazard a: 5 OPINE
Sked: 3 ETA ETD
Wild: 4 **STAB**
Winetaster: 4 YEAR
Guessing
Close to: 4 WARM

Guesstimate
  phrase: 4 ORSO
Guest
  Homecoming: 4 ALUM
  Honored ~ spot: 4 DAIS
  Like an eager: 5 EARLY
  of note: 5 EDGAR
  Uninvited:
    11 GATECRASHER
  Unwelcome: 4 BOOR PEST
  work: 5 VERSE
Guesthouse: 3 INN
Guests
  Desirable: 5 ALIST
Guevara
  Revolutionary: 3 **CHE**
Guevara, Che
  real first name: 7 ERNESTO
Guff: 3 GAS LIP 4 SASS
Guffaw: 3 YUK 4 ROAR
  E-mail: 3 LOL
  Hardly a: 5 TEHEE
  React to with a: 6 ROARAT
  syllable: 3 HAR
  ~, à la Variety: 4 LAFF
Guggenheim
  (abbr.): 3 MUS
  display: 3 ART
"Guh-ross!": 5 YECCH
Guidance
  Seek divine: 4 PRAY
Guide: 4 LEAD 5 PILOT STEER
    8 LODESTAR
  Himalayan: 6 SHERPA
  Magi: 4 STAR
  Museum: 6 DOCENT
  posts: 5 TOURS
  Road: 3 MAP
  Saw: 3 JIG
  Spiritual: 4 GURU
  Theater: 5 USHER
  the ride: 5 STEER
  Tour: 3 MAP
  Travel ~ name: 5 FODOR
Guidebook
  for travelers: 8 BAEDEKER
Guided: 3 LED
  It might be: 7 MISSILE
  trip: 4 TOUR

Guideline
  FDA: 3 RDA
Guiding
  beliefs: 5 ETHOS
  light: 6 BEACON 7 POLARIS
    8 LODESTAR POLESTAR
  principle: 5 CREDO CREED
    ETHIC TENET
  tower: 5 PYLON
Guido
  high note: 3 ELA
  Italian artist: 4 RENI
Guidry
  Pitcher: 3 RON
Guild
  Medieval: 5 HANSA HANSE
Guildenstern
  or Rosencrantz: 4 DANE
    8 COURTIER
Guile
  Full of: 3 SLY 4 WILY
Guileful: 3 SLY 4 WILY
Guilt: 7 REMORSE
  Sign of: 3 TIC
Guilty: 4 PLEA
  Find not: 6 ACQUIT
Guinea
  pig: 3 PET 4 CAVY
"Guinevere"
  actor Stephen: 3 REA
Guinier
  Legal scholar: 4 LANI
Guinness
  Actor: 4 **ALEC**
  adjective: 5 FIRST
  category: 7 LARGEST
  order: 4 PINT
  suffix: 3 **EST**
Guinness, Alec
  film, with "The":
    15 LAVENDERHILLMOB
Guisado
  cooker: 4 OLLA
Guisewite
  Cartoonist: 5 CATHY
Guitar
  Adjust a: 4 TUNE
  attachment: 5 STRAP
  bar: 4 FRET

book diagrams: **6** CHORDS
Country music: **5** DOBRO
cousin: **3** UKE **4** LUTE **5** BANJO
    SITAR
device: **4 CAPO**
Electric ~ effect: **4** WAWA
forerunner: **4** LUTE
innovator Paul: **3** LES
One of two on a: **7** ESTRING
part: **4** FRET NECK
picker Chet: **6** ATKINS
Play the: **5** STRUM THRUM
sound: **5** TWANG
suffix: **3** IST
Twang, as a: **5** PLUNK
~, slangily: **3** AXE
Guitarist
Classical: **7** SEGOVIA
"Guitar Town"
singer Steve: **5** EARLE
Gulager
Actor: **3 CLU**
Gulch: 6 ARROYO RAVINE
biter: **4** TOTO
Gules
~, in heraldry: **3** RED
Gulf: 3 GAP **5** ABYSS BIGHT
    CHASM
Arabian: **4 ADEN**
Bottomless: **5** ABYSS
competitor: **4** ESSO **5** AMOCO
    SHELL
emirate: **5** QATAR **8** ABUDHABI
leader: **4** EMIR
Libyan: **5** SIDRA
Mideast: **4** ADEN OMAN
    5 AQABA
north of Somalia: **4** ADEN
port: **4** ADEN
Red Sea: **5** AQABA
relatives: **4** BAYS
ship: **5** OILER
st.: **3** ALA
sultanate: **4** OMAN
Gulf of ___
(Algeria): **4** ORAN
(Arabia): **4** ADEN
(Baltic): **4** RIGA
(Caribbean): **7** SANBLAS

(China): **6** TONKIN
(Mideast): **4 ADEN** OMAN
    5 AQABA
(New Guinea): **5** PAPUA
(Spain): **5** CADIZ
(Yemen): **4** ADEN
Gulf of Aden
country: **5** YEMEN
Gulf of Aqaba
city: **5** EILAT
Gulf of Bothnia
country: **6** SWEDEN
Gulf of California
peninsula: **4** BAJA
Gulf of Finland
capital: **8** HELSINKI
feeder: **4** NEVA
Land on the: **7** ESTONIA
Gulf of Guinea
capital: **5** ACCRA
river: **5** NIGER
Gulf of Mexico
sight: **6** OILRIG
Gulf State: 4 OMAN **7** ALABAMA
Gulf War
ally: **4** OMAN
foe: **4** IRAQ
gulf: **4** ADEN
missile: **4 SCUD**
planes: **5** AWACS
Gulfweed: 8 SARGASSO
Gull: 4 DUPE **6** VICTIM
relative: **4** SKUA **TERN**
Where buoy meets: **5** OCEAN
Gullet: 3 MAW **4** CRAW
Gullible: 5 NAIVE
one: **3** SAP **4** DUPE FOOL
    5 PATSY
"Gulliver's Travels"
author: **13** JONATHANSWIFT
brute: **5** YAHOO
Like: **7** SATIRIC
Gully: 6 RAVINE
Gulp
Big: **4** SWIG
down: **4** CHUG
Gulped
down: **3** ATE
Gum: 4 TREE **5** RESIN

arabic tree: 6 ACACIA
Art: 6 ERASER
Chewing ~ base: 6 CHICLE
Enjoy some: 4 CHEW
gob: 3 WAD
source: 6 CHICLE
tree dweller: 5 KOALA
Use art: 5 ERASE
___ gum: 4 GUAR

Gumball
machine feature: 4 SLOT

Gumbo
ingredient: 4 **OKRA**

Gummo
Last name of: 4 MARX

Gump
of the comics: 4 ANDY

Gumption: 4 GRIT GUTS 5 MOXIE
NERVE SPINE SPUNK
6 METTLE
Have the: 4 DARE

Gums
Beat one's: 3 YAP

Gumshoe: 3 **TEC** 4 DICK
6 SHAMUS SLEUTH
job: 4 CASE

Gun: 3 **REV** 6 HEATER
Air ~ ammo: 3 BBS
Big: 6 BERTHA CANNON
MORTAR
British: 4 **STEN**
cleaner: 4 SWAB
Clip-fed machine: 4 BREN
Gangster: 3 **GAT**
German: 5 LUGER
gp.: 3 **NRA**
Hit with a ray: 3 ZAP
Hood: 3 GAT
Israeli: 3 **UZI**
Kind of: 3 CAP RAY 5 RADAR
SPRAY
Machine ~ sound: 7 RATATAT
Machine ~ syllable: 3 TAT
maker: 7 ARMORER
offspring: 3 SON
Radar ~ wielder: 3 COP
recoil: 4 KICK
stat: 4 BORE
Stun: 5 TASER

Submachine: 3 UZI 4 BREN
STEN
the engine: 3 REV
Top: 3 ACE
Toy ~ ammo: 3 CAP
WWII: 4 **STEN**
"___ Gun, The": 5 NAKED

Gund Arena
player: 3 CAV

Gunfight
command: 4 DRAW

"Gunfight at the O.K. Corral"
role: 4 EARP

Gunfighter
cry: 4 DRAW

"___ Gun for Hire": 4 THIS

"Gunga Din"
setting: 5 INDIA

Gung-ho: 4 **AVID** 5 CANDO
EAGER 6 ARDENT
RAHRAH
about: 4 INTO
feeling: 4 ZEAL
sort: 6 ZEALOT

Gunk: 4 CRUD GLOP GOOP
MUCK OOZE 5 SLIME
6 SLUDGE
Roofer: 3 TAR

Gunn, Peter
girlfriend: 4 **EDIE**

Gunners
org.: 3 NRA

Gunning
for: 5 AFTER

Gunpowder: 3 TEA
ingredient: 5 **NITER**

Guns
Filler for some: 4 GLUE
Give ~ to: 3 ARM

Gunslinger
cry: 4 DRAW

"Gunsmoke"
actor James: 6 **ARNESS**
actress Blake: 6 AMANDA
bartender: 3 SAM
deputy: 7 CHESTER
role: 3 DOC

Guns N' Roses
singer Rose: 3 AXL

Gunther, John
  book: 10 INSIDEASIA
Gunwale
  pin: 5 THOLE
Gurkha: 6 NEPALI
  home: 5 NEPAL
Gurley
  mag: 5 COSMO
Gurney
  Poet: 4 IVOR
Guru: 4 SAGE 5 TUTOR
      6 MASTER
  1960s ~: 5 LEARY
  Counterculture: 5 LEARY
  Home repair: 4 VILA
  Policy: 4 WONK
Gus
  Gloomy: 4 MOPE
  Lyricist: 4 KAHN
Gush: 4 RAVE **SPEW** 5 EMOTE
      SPOUT SPURT
Gussy
  up: 5 ADORN PREEN PRIMP
Gustatory
  organ: 8 TASTEBUD
Gustav
  Composer: 5 HOLST 6 MAHLER
Gustave
  Artist: 4 DORE
Gustavus
  subject: 5 SWEDE
Gusto: 3 PEP 4 BRIO ELAN ZEAL
      ZEST
Gut
  course: 5 EASYA
  feeling: 4 PANG
  Get a ~ feeling: 5 SENSE
  Listen to one's: 3 EAT
  reaction: 3 OOF
"___ gut!": 4 SEHR
Guthrie
  Folk singer: 4 **ARLO**
  restaurant owner: 5 ALICE
Guts: 4 GRIT 5 MOXIE VALOR
      7 INSIDES
  Have the: 4 DARE
  Scarecrow: 5 STRAW
Guttenberg
  Actor: 5 STEVE

Gutter
  site: 4 **EAVE**
Guy: 3 MAC MAN 4 CHAP DUDE
      GENT MALE 5 FELLA
  Average: 3 JOE 4 NORM
  Belonging to that: 3 HIS
  Big ~ nickname: 4 TINY
  Fall: 3 SAP 4 ADAM GOAT
      5 CHUMP **PATSY** 6 STOOGE
      9 SCAPEGOAT
  Funny: 3 WAG
  Gloomy: 3 GUS
  Good: 6 MENSCH
  Great: 5 SCOTT
  Grim: 6 REAPER
  Handsome: 6 ADONIS
  Little: 3 LAD
  Macho: 5 HEMAN
  Partner of: 3 GAL
  Regular: 4 BEAU
  Sly: 5 RAMBO
  Smart: 4 ALEC 5 **ALECK** BRAIN
  Sneaky: 4 PETE
  Stand-up kind of: 5 COMIC
  Sty: 4 BOAR
  That: 3 HIM
  Tough: 7 IRONMAN
      8 HARDNOSE
  Wise: 3 OWL 4 GURU **SAGE**
      5 SWAMI 6 SAVANT SMARTY
      11 SMARTYPANTS
Guy Fawkes Day
  mo.: 3 NOV
  sight: 7 BONFIRE
Guys
  only: 4 STAG
  partners: 4 GALS 5 DOLLS
  The bad: 4 THEM
  Wise: 4 MAGI
"Guys and Dolls"
  actor Robert: 4 ALDA
  composer: 7 LOESSER
  guy: 7 DETROIT
      13 NATHANDETROIT
  song: 5 SUEME
      15 ADELAIDESLAMENT
  writer: 6 RUNYON
Guzzle: 4 CHUG
  Not: 3 SIP

What cars: **3** GAS
Guzzled: 5 DRANK
Guzzler: 3 SOT
  Gas: **6** ENGINE
Gwen
  Role for: **4** LOLA
Gwyn
  Actress: **4** NELL
Gwyneth
  1996 role for: **4** EMMA
Gym
  accessory: **3** MAT
  ball: **4** PROM
  exercise: **4** CHIN
  garb: **6** SWEATS
  It's pumped at a: **4** IRON
  pad: **3** MAT
  set: **4** REPS
  site: **4** YMCA
  stretcher: **7** SPANDEX
Gym-goer
  concern: **3** BOD
Gymnast
  assistant: **7** SPOTTER
  dream: **3** TEN
  goal: **3** TEN
  Like a: **5** AGILE LITHE
  Olympic ~, often: **4** TEEN
  perch: **4** BEAM
Gymnastic
  event: **5** HORSE RINGS

feat: **6** SPLITS
  finale: **8** DISMOUNT
Gymnastics
  coach Karolyi: **4 BELA**
  competition: **4** MEET
  device: **3** BAR
  First name in: **4** OLGA
    5 NADIA
  move: **4** FLIP
  Rare ~ score: **3** TEN
"Gymnopédies"
  composer Erik: **5** SATIE
Gynt, Peer
  composer: **5** GRIEG
  creator: **5** IBSEN
  Mother of: **3 ASE**
Gypsum
  painting surface: **5** GESSO
  variety: **8** SELENITE
Gypsy: 6 ROMANY
  deck: **5** TAROT
"Gypsy"
  composer Jule: **5** STYNE
Gyrate: 4 SPIN **5** WHIRL
Gyrene
  org.: **4** USMC
Gyro
  bread: **4 PITA**
  meat: **4** LAMB
Gyrocompass
  part: **5** ROTOR

Hh

H
  Greek: 3 ETA
  Hellenic: 3 **ETA**
  lookalike: 3 ETA
Häagen-___: 4 DAZS
Häagen-Dazs
  alternative: 4 EDYS
Haakon
  successor: 4 OLAV
Habaneros
  Like: 3 HOT
Habeas corpus: 4 WRIT
Haberdashery
  item: 3 TIE 6 TIEBAR TIEPIN
    7 TIETACK
Habiliments: 4 GARB 6 ATTIRE
Habit: 4 GARB WONT 5 USAGE
    6 ATTIRE
  Bad: 4 VICE
  Creature of: 3 NUN
  In the ~ of: 6 USEDTO
  Woman of: 3 NUN
Habitation: 5 ABODE
Habitually: 5 OFTEN
  Take: 3 USE
Habituate: 5 **ENURE INURE**
Habitué: 7 REGULAR
Hacienda: 5 RANCH
  brick: 5 ADOBE
  hand: 4 PEON
  room: 4 SALA
Hack: 3 **CAB** HEW 4 CHOP TAXI
    6 CABBIE 7 TAXICAB
  auto: 3 CAB
  charge: 7 CABFARE
  customer: 4 FARE
  it: 4 COPE
  off: 3 LOP
  question: 7 WHERETO
Hackberry
  cousin: 3 ELM
Hackensack
  City near: 4 LODI

Hacker: 3 AXE
  Cry from a: 4 IMIN
Hacking
  fee: 4 FARE
  knife: 4 BOLO
Hackles
  Raise one's: 3 IRK 4 RILE
Hackman
  Actor: 4 GENE
  role: 5 DOYLE
Hackneyed: 5 **BANAL** STALE
    TIRED TRITE
Had: 3 ATE 5 OWNED
  been: 3 WAS
  on: 4 **WORE**
"___ Had a Hammer": 3 IFI
Haddock
  Young: 5 SCROD
"Had enough?": 4 GIVE
Hades
  entryway: 6 EREBUS
  Mother of: 4 RHEA
  river: 4 STYX 5 LETHE
  Traveler to: 7 ORPHEUS
"___ had it!": 3 IVE
Hadn't
  Wish one: 3 RUE
Hadrian: 7 EMPEROR
  Info: Latin cue
Hafez al-___: 5 ASSAD
Hafiz
  object of study: 5 KORAN
Hag: 5 **CRONE**
Hägar the Horrible
  creator Browne: 3 DIK
  Daughter of: 4 HONI
  dog: 5 SNERT
  Wife of: 5 HELGA
Hagen
  Actress: 3 **UTA**
  Tony winner: 3 **UTA**
Hagfish
  relative: 3 EEL

Haggadah
  Meal at which the ~ is read:
    5 SEDER
Haggard: 4 WORN **5** DRAWN
    GAUNT
  Country singer: **5** MERLE
  heroine: **3** SHE
Haggard, H. Rider
  book: **3** SHE
Haggis
  ingredient: **4** SUET
Hagia ___: 6 SOPHIA
Hagiologist
  subject: **5** SAINT
Hagman
  costar: **4** EDEN
  role: **5** EWING
"Ha-ha"
  Mini: **5** TEHEE
  Online: **3** LOL
Hahn
  Nobelist: **4** OTTO
" ___ Ha'i": 4 BALI
Haifa
  airline: **4** ELAL
  country: **6** ISRAEL
  country (abbr.): **3** ISR
  greeting: **6** SHALOM
Haig
  and others: **3** ALS
Haiku: 4 POEM **5** VERSE
Hail: 5 EXTOL GREET
  Sailor's: **4** AHOY
  sound: **7** PITAPAT
  ~, in Latin: **3** AVE
Hail ___: 4 ACAB
Haile ___: 8 SELASSIE
Hailed
  vehicle: **3** CAB **4** TAXI
Hailey, Arthur
  novel: **5** HOTEL
Hailing
  Sailing: **4** AHOY
Hail Mary: 4 PASS
"Hail the Conquering Hero"
  actress Raines: **4** ELLA
Haiphong
  Capital west of: **5** HANOI
  holiday: **3** TET

Hair
  Angel: **5** PASTA
  application: **3** GEL
  Bit of: **4** HANK
  braid: **5** PLAIT
  cluster: **4** TUFT
  color: **3** ASH
  colorer: **3** DYE
  conditioner: **5** RINSE
  dressing: **6** POMADE
  dryer brand: **6** CONAIR
  feature: **5** BRAID
  goo: **3** __GEL__
  goop: **3** GEL
  He had a bad ~ day: **6** SAMSON
  High ~ style: **4** UPDO
  highlights: **7** STREAKS
  holder: **3** GEL
  Horse: **4** MANE
  Lid: **4** LASH
  Like permed: **4** WAVY
  line: **4** __PART__
  Lock of: **5** __TRESS__
  Long: **4** MANE
  Lose: **4** SHED
  Make big, as: **5** TEASE
  Mass of: **4** SHAG
  Muss one's: **6** TOUSLE
  net: **5** __SNOOD__
  ointment: **6** POMADE
  piece: **4** CURL **5** TRESS
    6 STRAND
  removal brand: **4** NAIR NEET
  rinse: **5** HENNA
  Stiff: **4** SETA
  style: **3** BUN **4** AFRO COIF
  Thick: **3** MOP **4** MANE
  treatment: **6** POMADE
  Unruly head of: **3** MOP
  untangler: **4** COMB
"Hair"
  cowriter James: **4** RADO
  producer: **4** PAPP
Haircut
  Layered: **4** SHAG
  Quick: **4** TRIM
  Short: **3** BOB
  Very short: **4** BURR
Hairdo: 4 COIF

Bushy: 4 **AFRO**
Short: 3 BOB
Spheroid: 4 AFRO
Uneven: 4 SHAG
Hairless: 4 BALD
Hairnet: 5 SNOOD
Hairpiece: 3 RUG WIG
Hair-raiser: 7 ROGAINE
Hair-raising: 5 EERIE SCARY
place: 5 SALON
Hairs
Split: 7 NITPICK
Stiff: 5 SETAE
Hairsplitter: 6 PEDANT
"Hairspray"
actress Zadora: 3 PIA
award: 4 TONY
Hairstyle: 4 COIF
Bushy: 4 AFRO
High: 4 UPDO
Hairstyles: 3 DOS
Hairstyling
goo: 3 GEL
Hairy: 6 PILOSE 7 HIRSUTE
bovine: 3 YAK
crawler: 9 TARANTULA
~ Himalayan: 4 YETI
~ TV cousin: 3 ITT
Hairy-chested: 5 MANLY 6 VIRILE
Haiti
Info: French cue
Head of: 4 TETE
Here in: 3 ICI
season: 3 ETE
Haitian
dictator: 7 PAPADOC
leader: 8 ARISTIDE
monetary unit: 6 GOURDE
season: 3 ETE
"Haj, The"
author Leon: 4 **URIS**
Hajj
destination: 5 MECCA
Hajji
belief: 5 ISLAM
destination: 5 MECCA
Hal
Actor: 6 LINDEN
Hale: 3 FIT 5 SOUND

Actor: 4 ALAN
alma mater: 4 YALE
Golfer: 5 IRWIN
Not: 3 ILL
Patriot: 6 NATHAN
Hale-___ (comet): 4 BOPP
Hale, Edward Everett
character: 5 NOLAN
Haleakala National Park
locale: 4 MAUI
Hale-Bopp: 5 COMET
Haley
Author: 4 **ALEX**
costar: 4 LAHR
Haley, Alex
saga: 5 **ROOTS**
Haley, Bill
group: 6 COMETS
Half: 6 MOIETY
Better: 6 SPOUSE
More than: 4 MOST
prefix: 4 DEMI HEMI SEMI
Half-___
(flag position): 4 MAST
(ill-considered): 5 BAKED
Half and half: 3 ONE
Half-and-half
half: 3 ALE 5 CREAM
Half-asleep: 4 DOZY 6 DROWSY
Half-baked: 4 DONE
Not even: 3 RAW
Half-brother
of Ishmael: 5 ISAAC
of Tom Sawyer: 3 SID
Half-dozen
~, in Spanish: 4 SEIS
Halfhearted: 5 **TEPID**
Half-inch
stripe wearer (abbr.): 3 ENS
"Half ___ is better than none":
5 ALOAF
Half-moon
shape: 4 LUNE
tide: 4 NEAP
Half-pint: 6 PEEWEE
Half-sister
Eva's: 3 ZSA
Halftime
lead: 4 EDGE

marchers: 4 BAND
Halfway
house: 3 INN
Half-witted: 4 DUMB
Halifax
clock setting (abbr.): 3 AST
Hall
Comedian: 7 ARSENIO
Concert: 5 ODEUM
Former late show announcer:
    3 EDD
Kind of: 4 BEER
Large: 4 SALA
Music: 5 ODEUM
partner: 5 OATES
watcher: 7 MONITOR
Word with: 4 CITY
___ hall: 3 REC
___ Hall: 5 SETON
Hall & Oates: 3 DUO
Halle
Actress: 5 BERRY
"Hallelujah, ___ Bum": 3 IMA
Halley
observation: 5 COMET
Halliday, Brett
detective: 6 SHAYNE
Halliwell
Former Spice Girl: 4 **GERI**
Hallmark
card feature: 4 POEM
product: 4 CARD
Hall of Famer: 5 GREAT
    6 LEGEND
Giant: 3 OTT 6 MELOTT
pitcher Warren: 5 SPAHN
Polo Grounds: 3 OTT
with exactly 3,000 hits:
    8 CLEMENTE
~ Aparicio: 4 LUIS
~ Bobby: 3 ORR
~ Combs: 5 EARLE
~ Hank: 5 AARON
~ Hubbard: 3 CAL
~ Koufax: 5 SANDY
~ Mel: 3 OTT
~ QB Bob: 6 GRIESE
~ QB Johnny: 6 UNITAS
~ QB Y.A.: 6 TITTLE

~ Ralph: 5 KINER
~ Ryan: 5 NOLAN
~ Slaughter: 4 ENOS
~ Tony: 5 PEREZ
~ Williams: 3 TED
~ Yogi: 5 BERRA
Hall of Famer, Aviation
member: 6 CESSNA
Hall of Famer, Baseball
First: 4 COBB
~ Al: 6 KALINE
~ Combs: 5 EARLE
~ Duke: 6 SNIDER
~ Mel: 3 OTT
~ Rod: 5 CAREW
~ Roush: 3 EDD
~ Slaughter: 4 ENOS
~ Speaker: 4 TRIS
~ Waite: 4 HOYT
~ Warren: 5 SPAHN
Hall of Famer, Basketball
nickname: 3 DRJ
~ Archibald: 4 NATE
~ Dan: 5 ISSEL 6 LANIER
~ Harshman: 4 MARV
~ Holman: 3 NAT
~ Monroe: 4 EARL
~ Thurmond: 4 NATE
~ Unseld: 3 WES
Hall of Famer, Football
coach Greasy: 5 NEALE
~ Blount: 3 MEL
~ Dawson: 3 LEN
~ Ewbank: 4 WEEB
~ Ford: 3 LEN
~ George: 5 HALAS
~ Graham: 4 OTTO
~ Hirsch: 5 ELROY
~ Luckman: 3 SID
~ Lynn: 5 SWANN
~ Marchetti: 4 GINO
~ Merlin: 5 OLSEN
~ Ronnie: 4 LOTT
~ Sayers: 4 GALE
~ Wellington: 4 MARA
Hall of Famer, Golf
~ Sam: 5 SNEAD
Hall of Famer, Hockey
~ Bobby: 3 ORR

~ Phil, familiarly: **4** ESPO
Hall of Famer, Horse racing
  ~ Earl: **5** SANDE
Hall of Famer, Rock and Roll
  ~ James: **4** ETTA
  ~ Shannon: **3** DEL
Hallow: 5 BLESS
  ending: **3** EEN
Hallowed: 6 SACRED
  site: **6** SHRINE
  ~, old-style: **5** BLEST
Halloween
  Basic ~ costume: **5** GHOST
    SHEET
  choice: **5** TREAT
  color: **6** ORANGE
  costume part: **4** MASK
  decoration: **3** BAT **8** SKELETON
  greeting: **3** BOO
  hue: **6** ORANGE
  mo.: **3** OCT
  option: **5** TREAT
Halls
  Concert: **4** ODEA
  Music: **4** ODEA
Hallucinogen: 3 LSD
Hallucinogenic
  cactus: **6** MESCAL PEYOTE
  drug: **3** LSD
Halo: 4 AURA **6** NIMBUS
  7 AUREOLE
  wearer: **5** ANGEL
Halogen
  salt: **6** IODATE
  suffix: **3** INE
Halsey, William: 3 ADM
Halt: 3 END **4** STEM STOP
  5 ABORT CEASE
  Call a ~ to: **3** END
  Come to a: **5** CEASE
"Halt!"
  ~, to a salt: **5** AVAST
Halter: 3 TOP **6** SENTRY
  Horse: **4** REIN WHOA
  Traffic: **8** STOPSIGN
"Halt, salt!": 5 AVAST
Halvah
  ingredient: **6** SESAME
Halved: 5 INTWO

Bi-: **3** UNI
Dos: **3** UNO
Sei: **3** TRE
Halves: 8 MOIETIES
  Course: **5** NINES
  Diameter: **5** RADII
  Sawbuck: **4** FINS
  Sextet: **5** TRIOS
Ham: 4 MEAT **6** **EMOTER**
  8 BADACTOR
  Brother of: **4** SHEM
  Father of: **4** NOAH
  holder: **3** RYE
  How ~ may be ordered: **5** ONRYE
  it up: **5** **EMOTE**
  need: **5** RADIO **7** ANTENNA
  Place for a: **4** DELI
  raiser: **4** NOAH
  spice: **5** CLOVE
  ~, to Noah: **3** SON
Ham ___ (overact): 4 ITUP
Hambletonian
  Compete in the: **4** TROT
  pace: **4** TROT
Hamburg
  river: **4** **ELBE**
Hamburger: 5 PATTY
  grade: **4** LEAN
  holder: **3** BUN
  topping: **5** ONION
  unit: **5** PATTY
Hamelin
  casualty: **3** RAT
  hero: **5** PIPER
  Like the ~ piper: **4** PIED
Ham-handed: 5 INEPT
Hamill
  Actor: **4** MARK
  Journalist: **4** PETE
Hamilton: 10 FEDERALIST
  Actress: **5** LINDA
  bill: **3** TEN
  dueling opponent: **4** BURR
  place: **3** TEN
  prov.: **3** ONT
  Skater: **5** SCOTT
  undoing: **4** DUEL
Hamilton, George
  Ex of: **5** ALANA

Hamilton, Scott: 6 SKATER
  gear: 9 ICESKATES
Hamilton-Burr
  event: 4 DUEL
Hamlet: 4 BURG DANE ROLE
  choice: 4 TOBE
  cousin: 4 TOWN
  expression: 4 ALAS
  Father of ~, for one: 5 GHOST
  friend: 6 YORICK 7 HORATIO
  home: 8 ELSINORE
  Mother of: 8 GERTRUDE
  realm: 7 DENMARK
  slayer: 7 LAERTES
  What ~ smelled: 4 ARAT
  When ~ dies: 4 ACTV
  When ~ goes mad: 5 ACTII
  When ~ see his father's ghost:
      4 ACTI
"Hamlet": 5 DRAMA
  actor Hawke: 5 ETHAN
  courtier: 5 **OSRIC**
  has five: 4 ACTS
  hiding place: 5 ARRAS
  maiden: 7 OPHELIA
  setting: 8 ELSINORE
  soliloquy starter: 4 TOBE
Hamlin, Harry
  onetime costar: 3 DEY
  series: 5 LALAW
Hamm
  of soccer: 3 **MIA**
  score: 4 GOAL
Hammarskjöld
  Nobelist: 3 DAG
  successor: 6 UTHANT
  U.N. Secretary: 3 DAG
Hammer: 4 TOOL
  Businessman: 6 ARMAND
  end: 4 **PEEN**
  God with a: 4 THOR
  Heavy: 4 MAUL 6 SLEDGE
  in oil: 6 ARMAND
  on a slant: 3 TOE
  part: 4 CLAW **PEEN**
  Shape with a: 4 PEEN
  site: 3 EAR
  sound: 3 BAM
  target: 4 NAIL

  Tool used with a: 7 NAILSET
  user: 6 NAILER
  wielder: 4 THOR
Hammer, Mike
  actor Keach: 5 STACY
  creator Mickey: 8 SPILLANE
Hammering
  block: 5 ANVIL
Hammerin' Hank: 5 **AARON**
Hammers
  Instrument with: 5 PIANO
Hammerstein
  creation: 5 LYRIC
Hammer-wielding
  god: 4 THOR
Hammett
  detective: 5 SPADE
  heroine: 4 NORA
  hound: 4 **ASTA**
  sleuth: 5 SPADE
Hammock
  holder: 4 TREE
  Use a: 4 LAZE LOLL REST
Hammond
  product: 5 ATLAS ORGAN
Hamper: 5 CRIMP
  filler: 4 WASH 7 LAUNDRY
Hamperer
  Picnic: 4 ANTS RAIN
  Tamperer: 4 SEAL
Hampton
  instrument: 5 VIBES
  of jazz: 6 LIONEL
Hampton Court
  feature: 4 MAZE
Hamster: 3 PET
  home: 4 CAGE
Hamsun
  Author: 4 KNUT
Han
  beloved: 4 LEIA
  Furry ally of: 4 EWOK
  of sci-fi: 4 SOLO
Hancock, John: 6 SIGNEE
      SIGNER
  (abbr.): 3 SIG
  Add your: 3 INK
  Put your ~ on: 4 SIGN
  site: **10** DOTTEDLINE

Hand: 4 UNIT
Ask for a: **7** PROPOSE
At: **4 NEAR** NIGH **6** NEARBY
At ~, old style: **5** ANEAR
ball: **4** FIST
Band: **6** ROADIE
Bridge: **4** EAST
Cash on: **4** ANTE
Close at: **4** NEAR NIGH
   6 NEARBY
Cow: **4** HOOF
cream ingredient: **4** ALOE
Gave a: **5** DEALT
Give a: **3** AID **4** CLAP DEAL
Helping: **3** AID
holder: **3 ARM 4** MITT **5** GLOVE
Hook: **4** SMEE
Lend a: **3 AID 4** ABET HELP
   6 ASSIST
lotion ingredient: **4** ALOE
Old: **3 PRO**
One in a: **3** ACE
On the other: **3** BUT YET
   5 AGAIN
out: **3** PAY **4** DEAL **5** ALLOT
(out): **4** METE
over: **4 CEDE 5** REFER
Part of a: **4** CARD
Pay for a: **4** ANTE
Ranch: **7** COWPOKE
Right: **4** AIDE
Seek the ~ of: **3** WOO
Start a: **4** ANTE DEAL
suffix: **3** FUL
Turn one's ~ down: **4** FOLD
Upper: **4 EDGE**
Wait on ~ and foot: **7** CATERTO
warmer: **4** MITT **5** GLOVE
   6 MITTEN
Word before: **3** OLD **5** UPPER
You may have a ~ in it: **5** GLOVE
   6 MITTEN
~ down, as a verdict: **6** RENDER
~, in Spanish: **4** MANO
~, slangily: **3** PAW
"___ hand?": **5** NEEDA
___ hand (help): **5** LENDA
Handbag: 5 PURSE
handle: **5** STRAP

   Large: **4** TOTE
   material: **5** SUEDE
   Open: **4** TOTE
Handball
   relative: **7** JAIALAI
Handbill: 5 FLIER FLYER
Handbook: 5 GUIDE
Hand-color: 6 TIEDYE
Handcuff: 7 MANACLE
Hand-dyed
   fabric: **5** BATIK
   technique: **5** BATIK
Handed
   down: **6** RETOLD
   out: **5** DEALT
Handed-down
   history: **4** LORE
Handel
   bars: **6** SONATA **8** ORATORIO
   contemporary: **4** ARNE
   oratorio: **4** SAUL
Handford, Martin
   character: **5** WALDO
Handful: 3 FEW
   A ~ of: **4** SOME
Handheld
   computer (abbr.): **3** PDA
   harp: **4** LYRE
   lunch: **4** WRAP
Handhold
   Subway: **5** STRAP
Handicapper
   hangout, for short: **3** OTB
"Hand it over!": 4 GIVE
Handle: 3 USE **4** NAME **5 SEETO**
   WIELD
   adversity: **4** COPE
   Alternate: **5** ALIAS
   clumsily: **3** PAW **5** PAWAT
   Cup: **3** EAR
   Dagger: **4** HAFT
   Door: **4** KNOB
   Fake: **5** ALIAS
   Fly off the: **4** RAGE RANT RAVE
   holder: **4** CBER
   Hook on a: **4** GAFF
   Jug: **3** EAR
   Knife: **4** HAFT HILT
   Looped: **4** ANSA

One with a: **4** CBER
Razor: **4** ATRA
roughly: **4** MAUL
Scythe: **5** SNATH
Sword: **4** HAFT **HILT**
Teacup: **3** EAR
the helm: **5** STEER
Tractor: **5** DEERE
Vase: **4** ANSA
Word above a: **4** PULL
Handled: 3 RAN **5** SAWTO
     6 SEENTO
Easily ~, as a ship: **4** YARE
Handler
  Baggage: **6** REDCAP
  Honey: **3** BEE
  Horse: **5** GROOM
  Money: **6** TELLER
  Pan: **4** CHEF
Handling
  Gentle ~, initially: **3** TLC
Handout: 4 ALMS DOLE
  Beanery: **4** MENU
  Diner: **4** MENU
  New father's: **5** CIGAR
  Party: **5** FAVOR
  Revival: **5** TRACT
  Spa: **5** TOWEL
  Waiter's: **4** MENU
Handrail
  Ballet: **5** BARRE
H&R Block
  employee: **3** CPA
Hands
  Deck: **4** CREW
  Gave new: **7** REDEALT
  Join: **4** CLAP
  One's ~ and knees: **8** ALLFOURS
  Put your ~ together: **4** CLAP
  Shake ~ with: **4** MEET **5** GREET
  Show of: **4** VOTE
  Sitting on one's: **4** IDLE
  Talk with one's: **4** SIGN
  Time when both ~ are up:
     4 NOON
  With ~ on hips: **6** AKIMBO
  Work with the: **5** KNEAD
Handshake
  Reason for a: **4** DEAL

Result of a: **4** PACT
  words: **8** ITSADEAL
Handsome
  god: **6** APOLLO
  guy: **6** ADONIS
  Hardly: **4** UGLY
"Handsome ___ handsome does":
     4 ISAS
Hands-up
  time: **4** NOON
Handwriting
  feature: **5** SLANT
  on the wall: **4** OMEN
Handy: 4 DEFT **5** OFUSE UTILE
     6 NEARBY
  bag: **4** TOTE
  reference: **7** ALMANAC
"Handy"
  man: **4** ANDY
Handyman: 5 DOALL FIXER
  need: **4** TOOL
  TV ~ Bob: **4** VILA
Hanes
  competitor: **3** BVD **5** LEGGS
Hanff
  Author: **6** HELENE
Hang: 4 PEND **5** DRAPE HOVER
     7 SUSPEND
  around: **4** LOLL STAY WAIT
     6 LINGER LOITER
  around for: **5** AWAIT
  back: **3** LAG **5** TARRY
  Hard to ~ on to: **4** EELY
  in the air: **5** HOVER
  in the balance: **4** PEND
  in there: **4** LAST **6** ENDURE
  It may ~ by the neck: **4** JOWL
  loose: **4** LOLL **5** CHILL RELAX
  loosely: **3** LOP **5** DRAPE
     6 DANGLE
  One to ~ with: **3** PAL
  on the line: **6** AIRDRY
  on to: **4** KEEP **6** RETAIN
  out: **4** LOLL **6** AIRDRY LOITER
  out (with): **6** HOBNOB
  over one's head: **4** LOOM
  ten: **4** SURF
Hangar
  Cliff: **5** AERIE

Hanged Man, The: 5 TAROT
Hanger
  Cliff: 5 AERIE
  Deli: 6 SALAMI
  Frozen: 6 ICICLE
  Hat: 3 PEG
  Throat: 5 UVULA
Hanger-on: 5 LEECH
  Boat: 8 BARNACLE
  Election: 4 CHAD
Hang-glide: 4 SOAR
Hang ___ Index: 4 SENG
Hanging
  around: 4 IDLE
  Deli: 6 SALAMI
  Elegant: 5 ARRAS
  in the balance: 7 ATSTAKE
  It's often left: 3 ART
  Kind of: 3 OIL
  Locker: 5 PINUP
  loose: 6 ATEASE
  need: 5 NOOSE
  Public: 3 ART
  tapestry: 5 ARRAS
  Wall: 5 ARRAS
Hangings
  Public: 7 ARTSHOW
  Site of some: 5 PRADO
"Hanging Up"
  novelist Ephron: 5 DELIA
Hangman
  knot: 5 NOOSE
  line: 3 ARM
  request: 3 ANI
Hangout: 3 DEN 4 LAIR 5 HAUNT
       7 PURLIEU
  Bowler's: 5 ALLEY
  Campus: 4 QUAD
  Cat's: 5 ALLEY
  GI: 3 USO
  Handicapper: 3 OTB
  Herd: 3 LEA
  High king: 4 TARA
  Hippie: 3 PAD
  Jersey: 3 LEA
  Oater's: 6 SALOON
  Owl's: 4 BARN
  Regular: 5 HAUNT 7 PURLIEU
  Sloth's: 4 TREE

  Teal: 4 POND
  Teen: 4 MALL
  Thieves': 3 DEN
  Tout: 3 OTB
Hangover: 4 EAVE
Hang-up: 4 SNAG
Hang-ups
  Serious: 3 ART
Hank
  Football coach: 5 STRAM
  of baseball: 5 AARON BAUER
  Slugger: 5 AARON
Hanker: 5 YEARN
  (for): 5 YEARN
Hankering: 3 YEN 4 ITCH URGE
  Have a: 5 YEARN
Hanks
  Actor: 3 TOM
Hanks, Tom
  awards: 6 OSCARS
  film: 3 BIG 11 THEMONEYPIT
  film, with "The": 5 BURBS
  Wife of: 4 RITA
Hanky
  Use a: 4 WIPE
Hanna
  animation partner: 7 BARBERA
Hannah
  Actress: 5 DARYL
Hannah, Daryl
  film: 6 SPLASH
"Hannah and Her Sisters"
  actress Farrow: 3 MIA
Hannibal
  hurdle: 4 ALPS
  Mountains crossed by: 4 ALPS
  opponent: 6 SCIPIO
Hannity
  Talk show host: 4 SEAN
Hanoi
  holiday: 3 TET
Hans
  Dadaist: 3 ARP
  ~, in Ireland: 4 SEAN
"Hansel and Gretel"
  prop: 4 OVEN
Hansen
  NPR host: 5 LIANE
Hanson: 4 TRIO

hit song: **6** MMMBOP
Hanukkah
  centerpiece: **7** MENORAH
  gift: **4** GELT
  treat: **5** LATKE
Haole
  gift: **3** LEI
Haphazard: 6 RANDOM
      8 SLAPDASH
Haphazardly: 6 ANYHOW
      8 ATRANDOM
  Apply: **6** SLAPON
Happen: 4 PASS **5** ARISE OCCUR
  About to: **8** IMMINENT
  again: **5** RECUR
  Be about to: **6** IMPEND
  They may not: **3** IFS
  to: **6** BEFALL BETIDE
Happening: 5 AFOOT **EVENT**
      7 EPISODE
  Hippie: **4** BEIN **6** LOVEIN
  Keep: **5** RECUR
  Keep from: **5** AVERT
  place: **5** ARENA SCENE
  Spring: **4** THAW
  Track: **4** MEET
  What's: **4** NEWS **5** EVENT
      TREND **6** DOINGS
Happens
  As it: **4** LIVE
  It: **5** EVENT
"___ happens ...": 4 ASIT
"... happily ___ after": 4 EVER
Happiness: 4 GLEE
  Bird symbolizing: **4** LARK
  Symbol of: **4** CLAM LARK
Happy: 4 GLAD **6** ELATED
      7 CONTENT
  colleague: **6** SLEEPY SNEEZY
  ending: **4** HOUR
  follower: **4** MEAL
  loser: **6** DIETER
  Make: **5** **ELATE**
  Not: **5** UPSET
  Not a ~ fate: **4** DOOM
  Put on a ~ face: **4** BEAM
      5 SMILE
  song: **4** LILT
  sounds: **3** AHS

  Very: **6** ELATED
  Visibly: **5** AGLOW
Happy ___ : 4 HOUR
"Happy Anniversary"
  writer: **4** ICER
Happy as ___ : 5 ACLAM
"Happy Birthday"
  writer: **4** ICER
"Happy Birthday ___": 5 TOYOU
"Happy Days"
  actor Howard: **3** RON
  actor Scott: **4** BAIO
  actor Williams: **5** ANSON
  actress: **9** ERINMORAN
  actress Erin: **5** MORAN
  actress Moran: **4** ERIN
  character: **4** FONZ **6** CHACHI
  malt shop owner: **6** ARNOLD
  role: **6** RICHIE
  surname: **5** MALPH
"Happy Days Are Here Again"
  composer Milton: **4** AGER
Happy-go-lucky: 8 CAREFREE
  syllables: **7** TRALALA
"Happy Motoring"
  company: **4** **ESSO**
Harald
  Capital city founded by: **4** OSLO
  Father of: **4** OLAV
Harangue: 4 RANT **5** ORATE
      6 BERATE TIRADE
Harass: 4 RIDE **5** ANNOY **BESET**
      NAGAT TEASE **6** BADGER
      MOLEST
  ~, in a way: **4** HAZE
Harassed: 4 RODE
Harbach
  Lyricist: **4** OTTO
Harbinger: 4 **OMEN** **6** HERALD
  Spring: **5** ROBIN
Harbor: 4 HIDE PORT
  alert: **4** TOOT
  craft: **3** TUG
  hauler: **4** SCOW
  Leave the: **4** SAIL
  marker: **4** BUOY
  protection: **5** JETTY
  pronoun: **3** SHE
  pusher: **3** TUG

Safe: 4 COVE
sight: 3 TUG 4 SHIP
structure: 5 WHARF
Tie up in the: 4 MOOR
workhorse: 3 TUG
___ Harbour, Florida: 3 BAL

Harburg
Lyricist: 3 YIP

Hard: 6 STEELY
candy: 10 JAWBREAKER
Come down: 4 POUR TEEM
copy: 8 PRINTOUT
ending: 4 WARE
finish: 6 ENAMEL
Get: 3 SET
Give a ~ time to: 6 HARASS
    HASSLE
Hit: 3 RAM 5 SMITE WHACK
It's ~ to believe: 4 TALE
It's ~ to tell: 4 SAGA
knocks: 4 BOPS
Not as: 6 EASIER
on the eyes: 4 UGLY
on the feet: 6 PEBBLY
Playing ~ to get: 3 COY
rain: 4 HAIL
rubber: 7 EBONITE
shot: 5 SMASH
stuff: 5 BOOZE SAUCE
suffix: 4 WARE
throw: 3 PEG
to believe: 4 TALL
to catch: 4 EELY
to clean: 5 GRIMY
to come by: 4 RARE
to comprehend: 4 DEEP
to fathom: 4 DEEP
to find: 4 **RARE** 6 SCARCE
to get: 4 RARE 7 ELUSIVE
to grasp: 4 EELY
to hold: 4 **EELY**
to lift: 6 LEADEN
to make out: 5 FAINT
to penetrate: 5 DENSE
to please: 5 PICKY
to resolve: 5 MESSY
to understand: 6 OPAQUE
Tried: 6 STROVE
Try: 6 STRIVE

up: 4 POOR 5 NEEDY
water: 3 ICE 4 HAIL
wear: 5 ARMOR
wood: 3 ASH OAK
work: 4 TOIL 5 SWEAT
worker: 6 TOILER

Hard ___ (slaving away): 4 ATIT
"Hard ___!" (ship command):
    4 ALEE
"Hardball"
broadcaster: 5 MSNBC
"Hard Cash"
author Charles: 5 READE
"Hard Day's Night, A"
director Richard: 6 LESTER
Harden: 3 SET 5 **ENURE**
    INURE
in the heat: 4 BAKE
Hardhearted: 5 STONY
"Hard Hearted Hannah"
composer: 4 AGER
Hardin
Actor ~ and others: 3 TYS
Harding
Actress: 3 ANN
opponent: 3 COX
Skater: 5 **TONYA**
successor: 8 COOLIDGE
Hardliner: 4 HAWK
Hardly
any: 3 FEW 4 ATAD 5 SCANT
enough: 5 SCANT
ever: 6 RARELY SELDOM
seen: 4 RARE
"Hardly!": 3 NOT
"___ hardly wait!": 4 ICAN
Hardness
Epitome of: 5 NAILS
Hard-nosed: 5 STERN
Hardly: 3 LAX
"Hard Road to Glory, A"
author: 4 ASHE
Hard-rock
connection: 3 ASA
Hardship: 5 RIGOR
Accustom to: 5 INURE
Hardware
item: 4 BOLT BRAD TNUT
    5 UBOLT

Hardwood
  Made of a: **5** OAKEN
  source: **6** REDOAK **7** OAKTREE
  tree: **3** ASH OAK **5** MAPLE
Hardy: 4 HALE
  follower: **3** HAR
  heroine: **4 TESS**
  lass: **4** TESS
  partner: **6** LAUREL
  soul: **4** TESS
  ~, to Laurel: **5** OLLIE
  ~, vis-à-vis Laurel: **6** LARGER
Hardy, Joe
  tempter: **4** LOLA
Hare: 6 MAMMAL
  constellation: **5** LEPUS
  Female: **3** DOE
  opponent: **8** TORTOISE
  tail: **4** SCUT
  Young: **7** LEVERET
Harebrained: 5 INANE **6** ABSURD
Harem: 8 SERAGLIO
  chamber: **3** ODA
  guard: **6** EUNUCH
  room: **3 ODA**
  ___ **Hari: 4 MATA**
Hari, Mata: 3 SPY
Haricot: 4 STEW
Harkin, Tom
  state: **4** IOWA
Harlem
  suffix: **3** ITE
  theater: **6** APOLLO
Harlem Globetrotters
  promoter Saperstein: **3** ABE
  star: **15** MEADOWLARKLEMON
Harley: 3 HOG
Harlin
  Director: **5** RENNY
Harlow: 14 PLATINUMBLONDE
  Actress: **4** JEAN
Harm: 3 ILL **4** MAIM **6** DAMAGE
    INJURE
Harmless: 6 BENIGN
  Render: **5** UNARM **6** DEFANG
    DEFUSE DISARM
Harmon
  Actor: **4** MARK
  Actress: **5** ANGIE

Harmonia
  Father of: **4** ARES
Harmonica
  part: **4** REED
Harmonious
  Make: **6** ATTUNE
Harmonize: 5 AGREE **6** ATTUNE
    7 BLENDIN
Harmony: 4 SYNC 5 AMITY
    ORDER **6** ACCORD
  Be in: **4** JIBE **5** AGREE
  Bring into: **4** SYNC **6** ATTUNE
  Having: **5** TONAL
  In: **5** ASONE
Harness
  Oxen: **4** YOKE
  part: **4** HAME REIN
  race: **4** TROT
  race pace: **4** TROT
  racer: **5** PACER
  ring: **6** TERRET
  strap: **4** REIN
Harold
  Chemistry Nobelist: **4** UREY
  Composer: **5 ARLEN**
  Editor: **5** EVANS
  Presidential candidate:
    7 STASSEN
Haroseth
  When ~ is eaten: **5** SEDER
Harp
  cousin: **4** LYRE
  ending: **3** IST
  on: **7** BELABOR
  output: **3** ALE
Harped: 5 DWELT
Harper
  Actress: **4 TESS**
  Author: **3** LEE
Harper, Valerie
  role: **5 RHODA**
Harper's Bazaar
  illustrator: **4 ERTE**
Harper's Weekly
  artist: **4** NAST
  Piece in: **5** ESSAY
Harper Valley
  gp.: **3** PTA
"Harper Valley ___": 3 PTA

Harpist
  Heavenly: 5 ANGEL
Harpo
  of comedy: 4 MARX
Harpoon: 5 SPEAR
Harpoonist
  Nemo's: 3 NED
Harpo Productions
  Head of: 5 OPRAH
Harp seal
  lack: 4 EARS
Harpsichord: 7 CLAVIER
  Small: 6 SPINET
Harrah's
  locale: 4 RENO
Harridan: 3 NAG
Harriet
  hubby: 5 OZZIE
Harriman
  Diplomat: 6 PAMELA
Harris
  Actress: 3 MEL
  and others: 3 EDS
  Country singer: 7 EMMYLOU
Harris, Joel Chandler
  creation: 10 UNCLEREMUS
  title: 4 BRER
  Uncle: 5 REMUS
Harrisburg
  suburb: 5 ENOLA
Harrison
  Actor: 3 REX
  associate: 5 STARR
  role: 3 HAN
Harrison, George: 6 BEATLE
  Instrument played by: 5 SITAR
Harrow
  blade: 4 DISK
  rival: 4 **ETON**
"Harrumph": 3 BAH
Harry: 4 MALE NAME 6 MOLEST
  Candy maker: 5 REESE
  Mother of: 5 DIANA
  successor: 3 IKE
  U.S. President: 6 TRUMAN
  veep: 5 ALBEN
  Wife of: 4 BESS 5 LEONA
Harsh: 5 STERN 6 COARSE
       SEVERE

  conditions: 6 RIGORS
  cry: 3 CAW
  light: 5 GLARE
  Not: 3 LAX
  review: 3 PAN
  sound: 4 RASP
  treatment: 4 GAFF
Harshman
  of basketball: 4 MARV
Hart, Moss
  autobiography: 6 ACTONE
  memoir: 6 ACTONE
Harte
  Author: 4 **BRET**
Harte, Bret
  play: 5 AHSIN
Hartebeest
  cousin: 3 GNU
Hartford
  home (abbr.): 4 CONN
  symbol: 3 ELK
Hartman
  Comedian: 4 PHIL
  portrayer: 6 LASSER
Hart Trophy
  winner: 3 ORR
Harvard
  and others: 5 IVIES
  First-year ~ law student: 4 ONEL
  hater: 3 ELI
  Like ~ walls: 5 IVIED
  rival: 4 **YALE**
  Sch. near: 3 MIT
  Some ~ grads: 3 DRS
  student: 6 CANTAB
Harvest: 4 **REAP**
  Bring in the: 4 REAP
  fly: 6 CICADA
  goddess: 3 OPS
  Ready for: 4 RIPE
  wool: 5 SHEAR
Harvester: 3 ANT
  Anglo-Saxon: 4 ESNE
  haul: 4 CROP
Harvey
  Actor: 6 KEITEL
"Harvey"
  hero: 4 DOWD
Harvey ___ College: 4 MUDD

Has: 4 <u>OWNS</u>
  been: 3 WAS
  on: 5 WEARS
  to: 4 MUST
  to have: 5 NEEDS
  too much: 3 ODS
Has ___ (is connected): 4 ANIN
Has-been
  Track: 3 NAG
Hasbro
  division: 9 PLAYSKOOL
  line of trucks: 5 TONKA
Hasbrouck ___, N.J.: 3 HTS
Hasenpfeffer: 4 STEW
Has ___ for (is skilled at):
    5 ABENT
___ Hashanah: 4 <u>ROSH</u>
___ ha-Shanah: 4 ROSH
Hash house: 5 DINER 7 BEANERY
  handout: 4 MENU
Hasidic
  leaders: 6 REBBES
Hasidism: 4 SECT
Hassle: 4 FUSS 5 ANNOY
    6 PESTER
Hasso
  Actress: 5 SIGNE
Hassock
  Use a: 5 KNEEL
"Hasta ___!": 5 LUEGO
"Hasta la ___!": 5 VISTA
Haste: 5 SPEED
  Go in: 3 HIE
  Make: 3 HIE
  Marry in: 5 ELOPE
"Haste makes waste": 5 ADAGE
Hasten: 3 <u>HIE</u>
Hasty: 4 RASH
  ___ hasty retreat: 5 BEATA
Hat: 3 LID
  Brimless: 3 FEZ 5 BERET
    TOQUE
  Canterbury: 5 MITRE
  Close-fitting: 5 TOQUE
  edge: 4 BRIM
  fabric: 4 FELT
  Felt: 6 FEDORA
  Flat: 3 TAM 5 BERET
  French: 5 BERET

  High: 5 MITER 9 STOVEPIPE
  Highland: 3 TAM
  Jipijapa: 6 PANAMA
  material: 4 FELT 5 STRAW
  Military: 5 SHAKO
  Old: 5 DATED **PASSE** STALE
    TRITE
  Part of a ~ trick: 4 GOAL
  Place to hang your: 3 PEG
  Remove, as a: 4 DOFF
  Shriner's: 3 FEZ
  stand: 4 HEAD
  Straw: 6 BOATER
  Summer: 6 PANAMA
  Tasseled: 3 FEZ
  Tip, as a: 4 DOFF
  White ~ wearer: 4 CHEF
  with a pompon: 3 TAM
  Word before: 3 OLD
Hatch: 6 DEVISE
  Senator: 5 <u>ORRIN</u>
  state: 4 UTAH
Hatcher
  Actress: 4 <u>TERI</u>
Hatcher, Teri
  role: 8 LOISLANE
Hatchery
  sound: 4 PEEP
  supply: 3 ROE
Hatchet: 3 AXE
  handle: 4 HAFT
  Native: 8 TOMAHAWK
  Shaped with a: 4 HEWN
Hatching
  place: 4 NEST
Hatchling
  Aerie: 6 EAGLET
  group: 5 BROOD
  home: 4 NEST
  Nocturnal: 5 OWLET
  noise: 4 PEEP
Hate: 5 ABHOR VENOM
    6 DETEST LOATHE
  group: 4 KLAN
  State of: 5 ODIUM
  the thought of: 5 DREAD
Hatfield
  foe: 5 MCCOY
  ~, to a McCoy: 3 FOE 5 ENEMY

Hatfield-McCoy
affair: 4 FEUD
Hatfields: 4 CLAN
Hathaway
Shakespeare's: 4 ANNE
"Hath ___ sister?": Shakespeare:
3 HEA
Hatred: 5 **ODIUM** 6 ANIMUS
ENMITY
Hatter
Like the: 3 MAD
Hat-tipper
word: 4 MAAM
Haughtiness: 4 AIRS
Haughty: 5 PROUD
one: 4 SNOB
response: 5 SNIFF
Haul: 3 LUG TOW 4 DRAG TOTE
5 CARRY 6 SCHLEP
Heist: 4 LOOT
into court: 3 SUE
Long: 4 TREK
to jail: 5 RUNIN
Hauled
Being: 5 INTOW
Hauler
Cargo: 3 VAN
Farm: 4 DRAY
Freight: 4 SEMI
Garbage: 4 SCOW
Highway: 3 RIG 4 **SEMI**
Long: 4 SEMI
Haunt: 6 OBSESS
Haunted house
Like a: 5 EERIE
reaction: 6 SCREAM
sound: 4 **MOAN** 5 CREAK
Haunting: 5 EERIE
Haus
Man of the: 4 HERR
wife: 4 FRAU
Woman of the: 4 FRAU
Hautboy: 4 OBOE
Haute
Hardly ~ cuisine: 4 GLOP SLOP
___ **Haute, Indiana:** 5 **TERRE**
Hauteur: 4 AIRS
Havana
castle: 5 MORRO

country: 4 CUBA
home: 4 CASA
honcho: 6 CASTRO
residue: 3 ASH
"Havana"
actress Lena: 4 OLIN
actress Olin: 4 LENA
Have: 3 **OWN** 7 POSSESS
a go at: 3 **TRY**
Had to: 6 NEEDED
Has to: 5 NEEDS
Long to: 5 COVET
Must: 4 NEED
no use for: 4 HATE 6 DETEST
on: 4 **WEAR**
one's say: 5 OPINE
something: 3 AIL EAT
What we: 4 OURS
What we ~ here: 4 THIS
Have ___
(be connected): 4 ANIN
(freak out): 4 ACOW
"Have a bite": 5 TRYIT
"Have a good time!": 5 ENJOY
"Have a piece!": 6 TRYONE
Have ___ at: 3 AGO
"Have ___ day": 5 ANICE
Have ___ for: 4 ITIN 5 ANEED
Have ___ for news: 5 ANOSE
Have ___ good authority: 4 ITON
Have ___ in one's bonnet: 4 ABEE
Havelock
Author: 5 ELLIS
Haven: 5 OASIS
Gambling: 4 RENO
Health: 3 SPA
Hog: 3 STY
Safe: 4 NEST
Havens: 5 ASYLA OASES
"Haven't a clue": 6 NOIDEA
**"Haven't ___ you somewhere
before?":** 4 IMET
"Have one": 5 TRYIT
Have ___ on one's shoulder:
5 ACHIP
Haves
One of the: 5 NABOB
The ~ have it: 6 WEALTH
"Have some": 3 EAT

Have ___ to grind: 4 ANAX
    5 ANAXE
Have to have: 4 NEED
Have ___ to pick: 4 ANIT 5 ABONE
Have ___ to play: 5 AROLE
Have ___ with
  (know well): 4 ANIN
  (speak to): 5 ACHAT
"Have you ___ wool?": 3 ANY
Having "it": 4 SEXY
Havoc: 4 RUIN
  Cause: 5 WREAK
Havoline
  competitor: 3 STP
Haw
  Hem and: 7 STAMMER
  partner: 3 HEM
  preceder: 3 HEE
"___ Haw": 3 HEE
Hawaii: 5 STATE
    10 ALOHASTATE
  coastal region: 4 KONA
  hi: 5 ALOHA
  Ho of: 3 DON
  It gets picked in: 3 UKE
  Outsider, in: 5 HAOLE
  porch: 5 LANAI
  senator Hiram: 4 FONG
  state bird: 4 NENE
Hawaiian
  bird: 4 NENE
  carving: 4 TIKI
  city: 4 HILO
  coffee: 4 KONA
  crooner: 5 DONHO
  dance: 4 HULA
  dish: 3 POI
  feast: 4 LUAU
  garland: 3 LEI
  goose: 4 NENE
  hello: 5 ALOHA
  honker: 4 NENE
  instrument: 3 UKE
  island: 4 MAUI OAHU 5 LANAI
    7 MOLOKAI
  Like ~ shirts: 4 LOUD
  music maker: 3 UKE
  necklace: 3 LEI
  porch: 5 LANAI

port: 4 HILO
souvenir: 3 LEI
state bird: 4 NENE
tree: 3 KOA
tuber: 4 TARO
tuna: 3 AHI
veranda: 5 LANAI
wind: 4 KONA
Hawaii County
  seat: 4 HILO
"Hawaii Five-O"
  locale: 4 OAHU
  network: 3 CBS
  nickname: 4 DANO 5 DANNO
  star: 4 LORD
Hawk: 4 SELL VEND 5 NBAER
    6 PEDDLE
  descent: 5 SWOOP
  Fish: 6 OSPREY
  gripper: 5 TALON
  home: 4 NEST 5 AERIE
  Like a: 7 TALONED
  Mythical: 4 ARES
  opposite: 4 DOVE
  weapon: 5 TALON
Hawke
  Actor: 5 ETHAN
Hawkeye: 5 IOWAN
  home: 4 IOWA
  portrayer: 4 ALDA
  show: 4 MASH
  Where ~ served: 5 KOREA
Hawkeye State: 4 IOWA
Hawkins
  creator: 4 CAPP
  of Dogpatch: 5 SADIE
  ___ Hawkins Day: 5 SADIE
Hawkish: 6 PROWAR
  deity: 4 ARES
Hawks
  former home: 4 OMNI
Hawley
  cosponsor: 5 SMOOT
Hawley-___ Tariff Act: 5 SMOOT
Haws
  Hems and: 3 ERS
Hawthorne
  birthplace: 5 SALEM
  English actor: 5 NIGEL

Hay
bundle: 4 BALE
Hit the: 5 CRASH SLEEP
home: 4 BARN
Ready to hit the: 4 BEAT
Spread, as: 3 TED
storage area: 4 LOFT
Store, as: 6 ENSILE
unit: 4 BALE
Haydn: 4 PAPA
piece: 6 SONATA 8 ORATORIO
sobriquet: 4 PAPA
Hayek
Actress: 5 SALMA
Hayes
Actress: 5 HELEN
of basketball: 5 ELVIN
Singer: 5 ISAAC
Hayloft
bundle: 4 BALE
site: 4 BARN
Haymaker
Nails with a: 3 KOS
React to a: 4 REEL 8 SEESTARS
Haymarket Square
event: 4 RIOT
Hayseed: 4 HICK RUBE 5 YOKEL
Haystack
hider: 6 NEEDLE
"Haystacks"
painter: 5 MONET
Hayworth
Actress: 4 **RITA**
husband Khan: 3 ALY
Hazard: 4 RISK PERIL
a guess: 5 OPINE
Arctic: 4 BERG
Boating: 4 EDDY
Course: 4 TRAP
Driving: 3 FOG ICE 4 SNOW
    5 GLARE SLEET
Golf: 4 **TRAP** 8 SANDTRAP
Home: 5 RADON
Links: 4 TRAP
Navigational: 4 BERG REEF
prefix: 3 BIO ECO HAP
River: 5 SHOAL
Road: 3 ICE
Sailing: 5 SHOAL

Shipping: 4 FLOE 7 ICEBERG
Underwater: 4 REEF
Urban: 4 SMOG
Water: 4 REEF
Winter: 3 ICE 5 SLEET
Hazardous: 5 RISKY
for driving: 6 SLEETY
gas: 5 RADON
Less: 5 SAFER
Haze
London: 3 FOG
Morning: 4 MIST
Urban: 4 SMOG
Hazel
cousin: 5 BIRCH
occupation: 4 MAID
"Hazel"
cartoonist Key: 3 TED
Hazy: 6 UNSURE
Become: 4 BLUR
Hazzard County
boss: 4 HOGG
deputy: 4 ENOS
HBO
alternative: 3 AMC SHO TMC
    TNT
Part of: 4 HOME
sports agent: 6 ARLISS
HCl: 4 ACID
Head: 3 NOB 4 BEAN BOSS
    DOME FOAM PATE
    5 FROTH 6 NOODLE
A: 4 EACH
Big: 3 EGO
cases: 6 CRANIA
Cone: 3 SNO
Corp.: 3 CEO
cover: 3 HAT 5 SCALP
covering: 3 CAP 4 HAIR 5 SCALP
Dept.: 3 MGR
Egg: 3 OVI OVO
follower: 4 ACHE
for: 4 GOTO
for the hills: 4 BOLT FLEE
Hit on the: 3 BOP 4 CONK
Hole in the: 4 PORE 5 SINUS
honcho: 4 BOSS 5 MRBIG
    6 TOPDOG
hunters: 4 LICE

It comes to a: 4 BEER
It gets hit on the: 4 NAIL
It has a ~ and hops: 4 BEER
It may have a big: 4 BEER
It's over your: 3 SKY 4 ROOF
light: 4 HALO IDEA
lines: 3 EEG
lock: 4 HAIR 5 **TRESS**
of the class: 4 PROF
off: 5 AVERT
out: 5 LEAVE
over heels: 4 GAGA
Red: 5 LENIN
set: 4 EARS EYES
start: 4 EDGE
Swelled: 3 **EGO**
Top of the: 4 PATE
toward: 7 MAKEFOR
up: 5 CLIMB
wreath: 6 ANADEM
~, in French: 4 TETE
Head-___ (thorough): 5 TOTOE
Headache: 6 HASSLE
augmenter: 5 NOISE
helper: 7 ASPIRIN
Highway: 5 TIEUP
Headband: 4 HALO
Jeweled: 5 TIARA
Royal: 6 DIADEM
Sidekick with a: 5 TONTO
Headdress
Bishop's: 5 MITER
British bishop's: 5 MITRE
Egyptian ~ symbol: 3 ASP
Jeweled: 5 TIARA
Wound: 6 TURBAN
Headed: 3 LED RAN
(for): 5 BOUND
Header
Double: 3 DUO
Take a: 4 FALL TRIP
Headey
Actress: 4 LENA
Headgear
Angel's: 4 HALO
Bride's: 4 VEIL
Formal: 6 TOPHAT
Hardy: 5 DERBY
Highland: 3 TAM

Pageant: 5 TIARA
Royal: 5 CROWN TIARA
Soldier's: 6 TINHAT
Heading: 3 ENE ESE NNE NNW
  SSE SSW WNW WSW
  6 COURSE
Invitation: 5 WHERE
List: 4 TODO
Memo: 4 INRE
Menu: 7 ENTREES
Pioneer: 4 WEST
Poster: 6 WANTED
Headland: 3 RAS 4 CAPE NESS
Headley, Heather
role: 4 AIDA
Headlight: 4 HALO
component: 4 LENS
lamp type: 7 HALOGEN
setting: 3 DIM
Headline: 4 STAR 6 BANNER
Sensational: 8 SCREAMER
Headliner: 4 **STAR**
"Headlines"
host: 4 LENO
Headlong: 4 RASH
Rush: 4 TEAR 8 STAMPEDE
Rushed: 4 TORE
Send: 4 TRIP
Headly
Actress: 6 GLENNE
Head-on
Hit: 3 RAM
Meet: 4 FACE
Head-over-heels: 4 GAGA
Headphones: 4 EARS
Headpiece: 5 TIARA
Headquartered: 5 BASED
Headquarters: 4 BASE HOME
  SEAT
Branch: 4 NEST TREE
"___ Headroom": 3 MAX
"Heads ___ ...": 4 IWIN
Headstone
letters: 3 RIP
Heads-up: 5 ALERT
"Heads up!": 4 FORE 5 ALERT
Headwaiter: 7 MAITRED
Headware
Angel's: 4 HALO

Heavenly: 4 HALO
Regal: 5 TIARA
Headway: 4 DENT
Heady
posture: 3 EGO
stuff: 3 ALE 4 BEER
Heal: 4 KNIT MEND
~, as bones: 4 KNIT
Healer
Animal: 3 VET
Battlefield: 5 MEDIC
Tribal: 6 SHAMAN
Ward: 5 NURSE
Healing
attn.: 3 TLC
ointment: 4 BALM
plant: 4 ALOE
sign: 4 SCAB
Health
Atlanta-based ~ agcy.: 3 CDC
club: 3 SPA
Drink to one's: 7 WASSAIL
facility: 3 SPA
food flavor: 5 CAROB
Home ~ hazard: 5 RADON
In good: 4 HALE WELL
org.: 3 AMA
Picture of: 4 XRAY
resort: 3 **SPA** 6 CLINIC
Restore to: 4 CURE
Run for: 3 JOG
Urban ~ hazard: 4 SMOG
~, in French: 5 SANTE
Health and Human Services
division (abbr.): 3 FDA
Healthful: 8 SALUTARY
getaway: 3 SPA
resort: 3 SPA
routine: 7 REGIMEN
Healthy: 4 **HALE** WELL 5 SOUND
look: 4 GLOW
Not: 3 ILL
Perfectly ~, to the Army: 4 ONEA
Heaney
Poet: 6 SEAMUS
Heap: 3 TON 4 **PILE**
A: 5 LOADS SCADS
Combustible: 4 PYRE
Fiery: 4 PYRE

Hearth: 5 ASHES
Top of the: 4 ACME
Whole: 4 SLEW
Heaps: 4 **ALOT** ATON 5 APILE
Hear: 3 TRY
For all to: 5 **ALOUD**
So all can: 5 **ALOUD**
"___ Hear a Waltz?": 3 DOI
Heard: 5 AURAL
Hearing: 5 SENSE
aid: 3 AMP EAR 5 STENO
Court: 4 OYER
Of: 5 AURAL
Open: 4 OYER
things: 4 EARS
Hearing-related: 4 OTIC 5 **AURAL**
    8 AUDITORY
Hearst
book division: 4 AVON
Hearst, Patty: 7 HEIRESS
alias: 5 TANIA
kidnap gp.: 3 SLA
Heart: 3 NUB 4 CORE CRUX ESSE
    GIST PITH 5 ORGAN
    6 TICKER 7 ESSENCE
Big: 3 ACE
chambers: 5 ATRIA
chart (abbr.): 3 ECG EKG
Eat one's ~ out: 5 YEARN
From the: 6 AORTAL 7 EARNEST
It comes from the: 5 AORTA
    PULSE
It gets to your: 8 VENACAVA
It's from the: 5 AORTA
line: 5 AORTA
of a PC: 3 CPU
Of a ~ part: 6 ATRIAL
of the matter: 3 NUB 4 CRUX
    MEAT PITH
outlet: 5 AORTA
Say by: 6 RECITE
starter: 3 CPR
Take to: 4 HEED
Take to one's: 6 ENDEAR
test (abbr.): 3 EKG
The way to a man's: 4 VEIN
ward (abbr.): 3 CCU
Where the ~ is: 4 HOME
    5 CHEST

Win the ~ of: 6 ENAMOR
Word after: 4 ACHE
~, in French: 5 COEUR
Heartache: 3 WOE 5 GRIEF
"___ Heartache" (Bonnie Tyler hit):
    4 ITSA
Heartbeat: 5 PULSE
___ heartbeat: 3 INA
"___ Heartbeat" (Amy Grant hit):
    5 EVERY
Heartbreaker: 3 CAD
    type: 8 CASANOVA
"Heartbreak House"
    author: 4 SHAW
Heartburn: 5 AGITA
    remedy: 7 ANTACID
Heartfelt: 4 DEEP REAL
    7 EARNEST SINCERE
Hearth: 5 INGLE 8 FIRESIDE
    goddess: 6 HESTIA
    heap: 5 ASHES
    residue: 3 ASH 5 ASHES
    Roman ~ goddess: 5 VESTA
Heartless: 4 COLD 5 CRUEL
    fellow: 6 TINMAN
Heart of Dixie (abbr.): 3 ALA
Hearts
    How two ~ may beat: 5 ASONE
    Parts of: 5 ATRIA
    Two: 3 BID
    What lurks in the ~ of men:
        4 EVIL
Heart-shaped
    Tree with ~ leaves: 6 LINDEN
Heartthrob: 4 IDOL
    Small-screen: 6 TVIDOL
Hearty
    brew: 3 ALE
    cheer: 3 OLE
    companion: 4 HALE
    draft: 5 QUAFF
    entrée: 5 STEAK TBONE
    hello: 4 HAIL
    partner: 4 **HALE**
    Party: 5 REVEL 8 LIVEITUP
    pint: 5 STOUT
Heat: 4 COPS TEAM
    and then cool: 6 ANNEAL
    Beat the: 7 AIRCOOL

Canned: 6 STERNO
center, once: 5 ONEAL
Cook with high: 4 SEAR
Dead: 3 TIE
Deprive of: 6 DISARM
Feel the: 4 BAKE
home: 5 MIAMI
In a dead: 4 EVEN
meas.: 3 **BTU**
Packing: 5 ARMED
shield location: 8 NOSECONE
source: 3 GAS SUN 5 STEAM
    6 BOILER
Source of: 3 IRE
unit: 5 THERM
up: 4 WARM
without boiling: 5 SCALD
"Heat"
    actor: 8 ALPACINO
"Heat ___, The": 4 ISON
Heated: 4 WARM 5 ANGRY
    argument: 5 SETTO
Heater: 3 **GAT** ROD
    Caterer's: 6 STERNO
    feature: 4 COIL
    Lab: 4 **ETNA**
    Space: 3 SOL
Heath
    family shrub: 5 ERICA 6 AZALEA
    ___ Heath ("The Return of the
        Native" setting): 5 EGDON
Heathcliff: 3 CAT
Heathen: 5 PAGAN
Heather: 5 ERICA
    lands. 5 MOORS
Heathrow
    Former ~ arrival: 3 SST
Heating
    device: 4 ETNA
    fuel: 3 GAS OIL 7 COALGAS
    Strengthen by: 6 ANNEAL
Heat-resistant
    glass: 5 PYREX
Heaved
    It may be: 4 SIGH
Heave-ho: 4 BOOT 6 OUSTER
    Give the: 3 CAN 4 OUST TOSS
        5 EJECT
Heaven: 3 SKY 5 BLISS

Food from: 5 MANNA
Hog: 3 STY
In: 5 ABOVE 6 ONHIGH
In seventh: 6 ELATED
on earth: 4 EDEN 6 UTOPIA
Queen of: 4 HERA
Seventh: 5 BLISS 7 ECSTASY
    8 EUPHORIA 9 CLOUDNINE
Smell to high: 4 REEK
"Heaven forbid!": 4 OHNO
Heavenly: 6 DIVINE 9 CELESTIAL
altar: 3 ARA
bear: 4 URSA
body: 3 **ORB** 5 ANGEL
circle: 4 HALO
food: 5 MANNA
gift: 5 MANNA
glow: 4 AURA
headwear: 4 HALO
hunter: 5 **ORION**
instrument: 4 HARP
opener: 5 URANO
ring: 4 HALO
streaker: 6 METEOR
Heavenly ___ (ice cream flavor):
    4 HASH
Heavens: 3 SKY 5 ETHER
Head for the: 4 SOAR
Hunter in the: 5 ORION
In the: 6 ONHIGH
prefix: 5 URANO
"Heavens!": 4 EGAD 6 DEARME
Heaven-sent
food: 5 MANNA
"Heavens to Betsy!": 4 EGAD
Heavenward: 5 ABOVE
Heavily
Breathe: 4 PANT
Drop: 4 PLOP THUD
favored: 6 ODDSON
Sit: 4 PLOP
Stepped: 4 TROD
Walk: 4 PLOD SLOG 5 STOMP
    TROMP
Walked: 4 TROD
Weigh: 8 MILITATE
Heavy: 6 LEADEN 7 VILLAIN
book: 4 TOME
burden: 4 LOAD

cart: 4 DRAY
Fairy-tale: 4 OGRE
hammer: 4 MAUL 6 SLEDGE
knock: 5 THUMP
metal: 4 **LEAD**
More than: 5 OBESE
overcoat: 6 ULSTER
reading: 4 **TOME**
weight: 3 **TON**
wts.: 3 TNS
Heavy ___ music: 5 METAL
Heavyweight
Japanese: 4 SUMO
Light: 6 EDISON
Zoo: 5 HIPPO RHINO
Heavyweight champ
1930s ~: 4 BAER
1940s ~: 8 JOELOUIS
Three-time: 3 ALI
~ Holyfield: 7 EVANDER
~ Johansson: 7 INGEMAR
~ Max: 4 BAER
~ Willard: 4 JESS
Heb.
judge: 4 SAML
Hebrew: 6 SEMITE
beginning: 4 ROSH
day: 3 YOM
First ~ letter: 4 ALEF 5 **ALEPH**
judge: 3 ELI
letter: 3 MEM TAV YOD 4 ALEF
    TETH YODH 5 ALEPH
month: 4 ADAR ELUL
opener: 5 ALEPH
prophet: 4 AMOS 5 HOSEA
    6 ELIJAH ISAIAH
Sons of, in: 4 BNAI
title of respect for God:
    6 ADONAI
Hebrews
Bk. after: 3 JAS
Hebrides
hill: 4 BRAE
island: 4 **IONA SKYE**
language: 4 ERSE
Heche
Actress: 4 **ANNE**
Heckart
Actress: 6 EILEEN

Heckelphone
  cousin: 4 OBOE
Heckerling
  Director: 3 AMY
Heckle: 3 BOO 4 BAIT HISS
      RAZZ RIDE 6 HARASS
      NEEDLE
Heckler
  holler: 3 BOO
  missile: 3 EGG
Hector: 6 TROJAN
  died in it: 5 ILIAD
  Father of: 5 PRIAM
"Hedda Gabler"
  playwright Henrik: 5 IBSEN
Hedgehog
  of video games: 5 SONIC
Hedin
  Explorer: 4 SVEN
Hedonistic:
      15 PLEASURESEEKING
Hedren
  Actress: 5 TIPPI
"___ he drove out of sight ...":
      3 ERE
Hedwig
  Harry Potter's: 3 OWL
Hedy
  Actress: 6 LAMARR
Hee
  follower: 3 HAW
"Hee ___": 3 HAW
Heed: 4 OBEY 8 LISTENTO
  Give: 6 HARKEN
  Pay: 4 OBEY
  Pay no ~ to: 6 IGNORE
  Sign to: 4 OMEN
  the alarm: 4 RISE
Heedless: 4 DEAF
"Hee Haw"
  character: 4 RUBE
  cohost: 5 OWENS
  performer Pickens: 4 SLIM
Heel: 3 CAD CUR 5 LOUSE
  Kind of: 8 STILETTO
Heeler
  Ward: 3 POL
Heelless
  shoe: 4 FLAT

Heels
  Bite, as the: 5 NIPAT
  Cool one's: 4 WAIT
  Down at the: 5 SEEDY
  Head over: 4 GAGA
  Kick up one's: 6 GAMBOL
  Took to one's: 3 RAN
Heep: 5 CLERK
  Dickens's: 5 URIAH
  of fiction: 5 URIAH
Hefty
  competitor: 4 GLAD
  sandwich: 4 HERO
  volume: 4 TOME
Hegelian
  article: 3 EIN
"___ he grown!": 5 HASNT
Heidelberg
  trio: 4 DREI
Heiden
  Skater: 4 ERIC
Heidi: 5 SWISS
  height: 3 ALP
  Hollywood madam: 6 FLEISS
  home: 4 ALPS 6 CHALET
"Heidi"
  author: 5 SPYRI
Heifer: 3 SHE
  housing: 4 BARN
Heifetz
  teacher: 4 AUER
  Violinist: 6 JASCHA
Height: 4 ACME APEX
      7 STATURE
  (abbr.): 3 ALT 4 ELEV
  Having ~, width, and depth:
      6 THREED
  Lacking ~ or depth: 4 ONED
  prefix: 3 ACR 4 ACRO ALTI
Heighten: 5 RAISE 7 ENHANCE
Heights
  Mideast: 5 GOLAN
  ___ Heights: 5 GOLAN
Hein
  Mathematician: 4 PIET
Heineken
  brand: 6 AMSTEL
  symbol: 4 STAR
Heinie: 4 TUSH

Heinous: 4 EVIL
Heinrich
  Poet: 5 HEINE
Heinz, H.J.
  Company owned by: 6 OREIDA
"Heinz 57"
  dog: 4 MUTT
Heinz Field
  player: 7 STEELER
Heir: 7 LEGATEE
  concern: 6 ESTATE
  lines: 4 WILL
  ~, in law: 7 ALIENEE
  ~, often: 3 SON 6 ELDEST
Heiress
  ~, perhaps: 5 NIECE
Heirloom
  locale: 5 ATTIC
Heirs
  Biblical: 4 MEEK
Heisman Trophy
  winner Doug: 6 FLUTIE
Heist: 5 CAPER
  haul: 4 LOOT
  Help in a: 4 **ABET**
Held: 3 HAD 4 KEPT 6 DEEMED
  off: 5 ATBAY
  on to: 4 KEPT
  up: 4 LATE 5 BORNE
"___ Heldenleben" (Strauss opus):
  3 EIN
Helen
  Actress: 5 HAYES
  of radio soaps: 5 TRENT
  Paris dumped her for:
    6 OENONE
  Singer: 5 REDDY
  Where Paris took: 4 TROY
Helena
  rival: 5 **ESTEE**
Helen of ___: 4 TROY
Helen of Troy
  abductor: 5 PARIS
  Mother of: 4 **LEDA**
Helga
  Husband of: 5 HAGAR
Helgenberger
  Actress: 4 MARG
  hit on CBS: 3 CSI

Helicopter
  Army: 5 COBRA 6 APACHE
  blade: 5 ROTOR
  inventor Igor: 8 SIKORSKY
  part: 5 ROTOR
  pioneer Sikorsky: 4 IGOR
Helios: 6 SUNGOD
  Mother of: 4 THEA
  Roman counterpart of: 3 SOL
Helium: 3 GAS 8 INERTGAS
  Like: 5 INERT
  One of a ~ pair: 6 PROTON
Helix: 4 COIL 6 SPIRAL
  Heredity: 3 DNA
Hell
  He went to ~, so to speak:
    5 DANTE
  Like: 6 ABLAZE
  of a place: 5 HADES
Hellenic
  hangouts: 6 AGORAE
  ~ H: 3 **ETA**
Hellish: 7 AVERNAL 8 INFERNAL
"Hell ___ no fury ...": 4 HATH
Hello
  Caesar's: 3 AVE
  Hawaiian: 5 ALOHA
  Hilo: 5 **ALOHA**
  Sailor's: 4 AHOY
"Hello": 7 HITHERE
  follower, often: 9 HOWAREYOU
  It may say: 7 NAMETAG
"Hello, Dolly!"
  character Dolly: 4 LEVI
Hells Canyon
  state: 5 IDAHO
"Hellzapoppin"
  actress Martha: 4 RAYE
  star Ole: 5 OLSEN
Helm
  Fictional spy: 4 MATT
  Handle the: 5 STEER
  Have the: 5 STEER
  heading: 3 ENE ESE NNE NNW
    SSE SSW WNW WSW
  position: 4 ALEE
  Quick to the: 3 YAR 4 YARE
  Take the: 5 **STEER**
Helmet: 7 HARDHAT

accessory: 5 PLUME
feature: 5 STRAP
Pith: 5 TOPEE
plume: 5 CREST
Soldier's: 6 TINHAT
Visored: 5 ARMET
___ helmet (safari wear): 4 PITH
Helmets: 8 HEADGEAR
Helmsley
Hotelier: 5 **LEONA**
Helmsman: 7 STEERER
Enterprise: 4 SULU
Helmut
German statesman: 4 KOHL
Heloise
Info: French cue
love: 7 ABELARD
offering: 4 HINT
Help: 3 **AID** 4 ABET 5 AVAIL
a hood: 4 ABET
a hooligan: 4 ABET
Bit of: 4 HINT
Call for: 3 **SOS** 6 MAYDAY
Can't ~ but: 5 HASTO
Couldn't ~ but: 5 HADTO
for the stumped: 4 HINT
Holiday: 3 ELF
in a heist: 4 **ABET**
It'll ~ you up: 4 TBAR
on the way up: 4 STEP
out: 6 ASSIST
Requiring: 6 INNEED
Seek ~ from: 6 PRAYTO
   TURNTO
settle: 7 MEDIATE
with homework: 5 TUTOR
Without: 4 SOLO 5 ALONE
   7 UNAIDED
with the dishes: 3 DRY 4 WIPE
"Help!": 3 SOS 6 SAVEME
Helper: 4 **AIDE**
(abbr.): 4 ASST
Dictator's: 5 STENO
Driver's: 3 TEE
Holiday: 3 ELF
Hook's: 4 SMEE
Little: 3 ELF 4 ASST
Mgr.'s: 4 **ASST**
Mother's: 9 NURSEMAID

Off.: 4 ASST
Reception: 6 AERIAL
   7 ANTENNA
Santa's: 3 ELF
Wedding: 5 USHER
Helpers
Hwy.: 3 AAA
Prof's: 3 TAS
Helpful: 5 OFUSE UTILE
contacts: 3 INS
hint: 3 TIP
sort: 5 AIDER
Helpless: 4 SOLO 5 ALONE
   6 UNABLE
Helpmate: 6 SPOUSE
"Help ___ the way!": 4 ISON
Help wanted
abbr.: 3 EEO EOE
"___ help you?": 4 CANI MAYI
Helsinki
native: 4 FINN
Year ~ was founded: 3 MDL
Helter-skelter: 8 PELLMELL
Helvetica: 4 FONT
Hem
again: 5 RESEW
and haw: 7 STAMMER
Fix, as a: 5 RESEW
in: 5 BESET
line: 4 KNEE
partner: 3 **HAW**
Prepare to: 5 PINUP
Raise the: 5 ALTER
He-man
Hardly a. 5 SISSY
Like a: 5 MACHO
Hematite: 3 ORE 7 IRONORE
Hemingway
Actress: 6 MARIEL
Author: 6 ERNEST
End of a ~ title: 6 THESEA
nickname: 4 PAPA
novel: 15 AFAREWELLTOARMS
Pronoun in a ~ title: 4 WHOM
sobriquet: 4 PAPA
title character: 6 OLDMAN
Writer: 6 ERNEST
Hemispherical
home: 5 IGLOO

roof: 4 DOME
Hemmed: 4 SEWN
Hemming
  and hawing: 3 ERS
Hemoglobin
  component: 4 IRON
Hemp: 5 BHANG
  fiber: 5 SISAL
Hems
  and haws: 3 ERS
Hen: 5 LAYER 6 FEMALE
  home: 4 COOP
  pen: 4 COOP
  Type of: 7 CORNISH
Hence: 4 **ERGO** THUS
Henchman
  Hook's: 4 SMEE
Henderson, Rickey
  Emulate: 5 STEAL
Hendricks
  of football: 3 TED
Hendrix
  genre: 8 ACIDROCK
  Guitarist: 4 **JIMI**
  hairdo: 4 AFRO
Hendryx
  Singer: 4 NONA
Henhouse: 4 COOP 5 ROOST
  unit: 3 EGG
Henie
  Skater: 5 SONJA
Henie, Sonja
  birthplace: 4 OSLO
Henley
  crew: 4 OARS
  event: 7 REGATTA
  Playwright: 4 BETH
  propeller: 3 OAR
Henley-on-Thames
  Annual ~ event: 7 REGATTA
Henley Regatta
  site: 6 THAMES
Henna: 3 DYE
  user: 4 DYER
Henner
  Actress: 6 MARILU
Henning
  Magician: 4 DOUG
Henpeck: 3 **NAG**

Henri: 3 NOM
  Info: French clue
  Painter: 7 MATISSE
Henrik
  Playwright: 5 IBSEN
Henry
  Actor: 5 FONDA
  Publisher: 4 LUCE
  Sculptor: 5 MOORE
  Son of: 5 EDSEL
  tutee: 5 ELIZA
Henry ___: 4 VIII
Henry, O.
  device: 5 IRONY
  Like a story by: 6 IRONIC
Henry ___, Sir
  gallery: 4 TATE
"Henry & June"
  character: 3 NIN 5 ANAIS
  She was June in: 3 UMA
Henry II
  He played ~ twice: 6 OTOOLE
  Queen of: 7 ELEANOR
Henry VI
  School founded by: 4 ETON
Henry VIII
  family: 5 TUDOR
  house: 5 TUDOR
  Last wife of: 4 PARR
  Like: 5 OBESE
  Second wife of: 4 ANNE
  sextet: 5 WIVES
  Sixth wife of: 4 **PARR**
  wife Boleyn: 4 ANNE
  wife Catherine: 4 PARR
Henson
  of Muppets fame: 3 JIM
Hentoff
  Writer: 3 **NAT**
Heparin
  target: 4 CLOT
Hepburn
  film: 8 ADAMSRIB
      12 MORNINGGLORY
      15 THELIONINWINTER
  quartet: 6 OSCARS
  role: 7 SABRINA
Hepcat
  jargon: 4 JIVE

Hephaestus
  workshop: 4 ETNA 6 MTETNA
Hepta-
  plus one: 4 OCTA
Her
  His and: 5 THEIR
  partner: 3 HIS
  ~, in French: 3 SES
"Her ___" ("Miss Saigon" song):
    4 ORME
Hera
  counterpart: 4 JUNO
  Husband of: 4 ZEUS
  Mother of: 4 RHEA
  Son of: 4 ARES
Herald: 7 USHERIN
  Home of the: 5 MIAMI
Heraldic
  band: 4 ORLE
  blue: 5 AZURE
  border: 4 ORLE
Herb
  Aromatic: 5 ANISE
  Cathartic: 5 SENNA
  Chef's: 4 SAGE
  Columnist: 4 CAEN
  Culinary: 5 THYME
    8 MARJORAM
  Curry: 5 CUMIN
  Medicinal: 5 SENNA
  of regret: 3 RUE
  of the parsley family:
    8 ANGELICA
  Pesto: 5 BASIL
  Pickling: 4 DILL
  Pizza: 7 OREGANO
  Stuffing: 4 SAGE
  "Sweet": 5 BASIL
  Trumpeter: 6 ALPERT
Herbal
  drink: 3 TEA
  quaff: 3 TEA
Herber
  of football: 5 ARNIE
Herbert
  Actor: 3 LOM
  Pulitzer winner: 4 AGAR
Herbert, Frank
  classic novel: 4 DUNE

Herbicide
  target: 4 WEED
Herbie
  Jazz flutist: 4 MANN
  ~, in Disney films: 5 VWBUG
Herbivore
  Horned: 5 RHINO
  Hulking: 5 HIPPO
Hercule
  creator: 6 AGATHA
Herculean
  dozen: 5 TASKS
  Hardly: 4 PUNY
  labor site: 5 NEMEA
Hercules: 5 HEMAN
  captive: 4 IOLE
  challenges: 6 LABORS
  victim: 5 HYDRA
  Where ~ slew a lion: 5 NEMEA
"Hercules"
  spin-off: 4 XENA
Herd: 5 DROVE
  bird: 3 EMU
  Dairy: 4 COWS
  hangout: 3 LEA
  in Africa: 5 ELAND
  It's heard in a: 3 BAA MOO
  Name for a ~ dog: 4 SHEP
  noise: 3 MOO
  of seals: 3 POD
  orphan: 5 DOGIE
  word: 3 MOO
Herder
  Reindeer: 4 **LAPP**
Herding
  dog: 6 COLLIE
  dog name: 4 SHEP
Here
  again: 4 BACK
  Almost: 4 NEAR
  and there: 5 ABOUT APART
    6 PASSIM
  Go ~ and there: 4 ROAM ROVE
  It's neither ~ nor there: 5 LIMBO
  No longer: 4 GONE
  Not for: 4 TOGO
  The one: 4 THIS
  The ones: 5 THESE
  What's: 5 THESE

You are: 5 EARTH
~, in French: 3 ICI
~, in Spanish: 3 ACA 4 AQUI
"Here ___ Again": 3 IGO
"Here comes trouble!": 4 OHOH
    UHOH
Hereditary: 6 INBORN INBRED
    INNATE LINEAL
    8 FAMILIAL
helix: 3 DNA
ruler: 6 DYNAST
unit: 4 GENE
Heredity: 5 GENES
carrier: 4 GENE
helix: 3 DNA
"Here Is Your War"
author Ernie: 4 PYLE
"Here it is!": 4 TADA
"Here's to you!": 5 SKOAL TOAST
The "you" of: 7 TOASTEE
Here today, gone tomorrow:
    9 EPHEMERAL
Heretofore: 5 ASYET SOFAR
    6 ERENOW
"Here we ___!": 3 ARE
"___ Her Go" (Frankie Laine
    song): 4 ILET
Herman, Jerry
musical: 4 MAME
Hermann
Author: 5 HESSE
Gold medalist skier: 5 MAIER
Herman's Hermits
singer Peter: 5 NOONE
Hermes
Half brother of: 4 ARES
Mother of: 4 MAIA
Hermit: 5 LONER 7 RECLUSE
It may be a ~ or fiddler: 4 CRAB
Like a: 5 ALONE
Hermitic: 4 LONE
Hernando
Info: Spanish cue
Hernando de ___
Explorer: 4 SOTO
"Hernando's Hideaway":
    5 TANGO
Hero: 3 SUB 4 **IDOL**
Air: 3 ACE

ending: 3 INE
love: 7 LEANDER
maker: 4 DELI
Place for a: 4 DELI
reward: 5 MEDAL
suffix: 3 INE ISM
worshiper: 7 LEANDER
"Hero"
singer Mariah: 5 CAREY
Heroes
Like some: 6 UNSUNG
Where ~ are made: 4 DELI
Heroic: 5 BRAVE
act: 6 RESCUE
action: 9 DERRINGDO
deed: 4 FEAT
narrative: 4 SAGA
story: 4 EPIC
tale: 4 EPIC **SAGA**
Heroics: 9 DERRINGDO
Heron: 5 WADER
home: 4 NEST
Plumed: 5 EGRET
relative: 4 IBIS
Small: 7 BITTERN
White: 5 EGRET
Herr
home: 4 HAUS
mate: 4 FRAU
Herriman, George
cartoon: 8 KRAZYKAT
"Krazy" creation of: 3 KAT
Herring
cousin: 4 SHAD
Red: 4 PLOY
Type of: 4 SHAD 5 SPRAT
Herringlike
fish: 4 SHAD
Hersey
bell town: 5 **ADANO**
Hershey
brand: 4 ROLO 6 REESES
candy bar: 6 KITKAT
product: 4 KISS
Hershiser
of baseball: 4 OREL
Hertz
prefix: 4 TERA
rival: 4 **AVIS**

Herzegovina
  partner: 6 BOSNIA
Herzigova
  Model: 3 EVA
**"He's Got the Whole World ___
    Hands": 5 INHIS**
Hesitant: 6 UNSURE
    9 TENTATIVE
  sounds: 3 ERS UHS UMS
Hesitate: 3 HAW HEM 5 HEDGE
    WAVER
  It may make you: 5 COMMA
Hesitation: 3 HAW HEM
  Show: 6 FALTER
  Sounds of: 3 **ERS** UHS UMS
  Without: 6 FLATLY
**"He's ___ nowhere man" (Beatles
    lyric):** 5 AREAL
Hess
  Pianist: 4 MYRA
Hesse
  Novelist: 7 HERMANN
  River of: 4 **EDER**
  Sculptor: 3 EVA
Hessian
  pronoun: 3 ICH
  river: 4 EDER
Hester
  portrayer: 4 DEMI
Heston, Charlton
  film: 5 ELCID 6 BENHUR
  org.: 3 **NRA**
  role: 5 **ELCID** MOSES
    6 BENIIUR
Het
  up: 5 IRATE
Hew: 3 AXE LOP 4 CHOP
Hewing
  tool: 3 AXE
Hex: 4 JINX 5 SPELL
  ending: 3 ANE
  halved: 3 TRI
  sign site: 4 BARN
"Hey!": 4 **PSST**
Heyerdahl
  Author: 4 THOR
  craft: 3 RAI
  Explorer: 4 THOR
  raft: 7 KONTIKI

"Hey, over here!": 4 **PSST**
"Hey, sailor!": 4 AHOY
"Hey there!": 4 PSST
"Hey, wait ___!": 4 ASEC
"Hey, what's the big ___?":
    4 IDEA
"Hey you!": 4 PSST
Hgt.: 3 ALT 4 ELEV
HHH: 4 ETAS
HHS
  division: 3 SSA
Hi
  from Ho: 5 ALOHA
  HI: 5 ALOHA
  Wife of: 4 LOIS
"Hi"
  Hawaiian: 5 ALOHA
  Ho: 5 ALOHA
Hi-___: 3 FIS RES
  graphics: 3 RES
  monitor: 3 RES
"Hi and Lois"
  pet: 4 DAWG
Hiatus: 3 GAP 5 LAPSE PAUSE
Hiawatha
  craft: 5 CANOE
Hibachi
  residue: 5 ASHES
  site: 5 PATIO
Hibernate
  Place to: 4 LAIR
Hibernation: 5 SLEEP
  location: 3 DEN 4 LAIR
Hibernia: 4 EIRE ERIN
Hibiscus: 6 MALLOW
Hiccup
  cause: 5 SPASM
  cure: 5 SCARE
Hic, ___, hoc: 4 HAEC
Hick: 4 RUBE 5 YAHOO YOKEL
Hickey
  beginning: 3 DOO
Hickory: 3 NUT
Hid: 7 HOLEDUP STASHED
Hidalgo
  Info: Spanish cue
  Here, in: 3 ACA
  home: 4 CASA
  hooray: 3 OLE

Hidden: 5 INNER PERDU
    6 CACHED COVERT
    LATENT UNSEEN VEILED
  advantage: **12** ACEINTHEHOLE
  agenda: **15** ULTERIORMOTIVES
  Hardly: **5** OVERT
  It may be: **6** AGENDA
  loot: **5** STASH
  Not: **5** OVERT
  obstacle: **4** SNAG
  problem: **5** CATCH
  supply: **5** CACHE STASH
  treasure: **5** TROVE
  valley: **4** GLEN
Hide: 4 MASK **PELT** SKIN VEIL
    5 CLOAK STASH **6** SCREEN
    7 SECRETE
  away: **5** STASH
  from view: **6** SHROUD
  out: **6** LIELOW
  partner: **4** **SEEK**
  Prepare: **3** TAN
  Untanned: **4** PELT
  well: **4** BURY
  worker: **6** TANNER
Hide-and-seek
  Cheat at: **4** PEEK
Hideaway: 3 DEN **4** CAVE **LAIR**
  High: **5** AERIE
"Hideaway"
  actress Christine: **5** LAHTI
Hide-hair
  connector: **3** NOR
Hideki
  Pitcher: **5** IRABU
Hideo
  Pitcher: **4** NOMO
Hideous: 4 UGLY
  fellow: **4** OGRE
Hideout: 3 DEN **4** **LAIR**
Hider
  Haystack: **6** NEEDLE
Hiding
  out: **8** ONTHELAM
  place: **3** DEN **4** LAIR NOOK
    5 CACHE
Hierarchy: 6 LADDER
    9 TOTEMPOLE
  level: **4** RUNG

Top, in a: **5** ALPHA
Hieroglyphics
  bird: **4** IBIS
  snake: **3** ASP
  stone: **7** ROSETTA
Hieronymus
  Painter: **5** BOSCH
Hi-fi: 6 STEREO
  component: **3** AMP
  discs: **3** LPS
  pioneer Fisher: **5** AVERY
Higgins, Henry
  creator: **4** SHAW
High: 4 TALL **5** LOFTY TIPSY
    6 STONED WASTED
  ball: **3** LOB
  bar: **5** ROOST
  card: **3** **ACE**
  degree: **3** **NTH PHD**
  dudgeon: **3** **IRE**
  fashion: **3** TON
  flier: **4** KITE
  Fly: **4** **SOAR**
  Get really: **4** SOAR
  grade: **5** APLUS
  ground: **6** UPLAND
  guy: **4** ALTO
  hat: **5** MITER **9** STOVEPIPE
  Hold: **6** ESTEEM
  home: **5** **AERIE**
  Home on: **4** NEST **5** AERIE
  It may be: **4** NOON
  It may get ~ marks: **5** LEVEE
  jinks: **6** ANTICS
  land: **5** NEPAL
  Leave ~ and dry: **6** STRAND
  light: **4** HALO
  lines: **3** ELS
  mark with low effort: **5** EASYA
  mountain: **3** ALP
  note of old: **3** ELA
  On: **5** ALOFT
  On a: **6** ELATED
  opening: **4** ALTI
  peak: **3** ALP TOR
  pitch: **3** LOB
  point: **4** **ACME APEX** PEAK
    6 APOGEE **7** EVEREST
    8 PINNACLE

prefix: 4 ALTI
pt.: 3 MTN
regard: 6 ESTEEM
return: 3 LOB
rollers: 3 ELS
roller's roll: 3 WAD
schooler: 4 **TEEN** 6 TEENER
society: 5 ELITE
spirits: 4 **GLEE** 7 ELATION
spot: 3 ALP 4 APEX
standard: 5 IDEAL
station: 3 MIR
style: 4 UPDO
time: 4 BOOM **NOON**
times: 3 UPS
wind: 4 GALE OBOE 5 FLUTE
~, in music: 3 ALT
High ___: 3 TEA
"High ___"
  (Anderson play): 3 TOR
  (Bogart film): 6 SIERRA
High-___: 3 RES 4 TECH
Highball
  ingredient: 3 RYE
Highborn: 5 NOBLE
Highbrow: 4 SNOB 5 SNOOT
Highbrows: 8 LITERATI
Highchair
  feature: 4 TRAY
  Like a baby in a: 6 BIBBED
  wear: 3 BIB
High-class: 5 ELITE
  tie: 5 ASCOT
  ___ High Dam: 5 ASWAN
High-energy
  snack: 4 GORP
Higher
  ground: 6 UPLAND
  than: 4 OVER 5 ABOVE
"Higher Learning"
  actor Epps: 4 OMAR
Higher-ranking: 6 SENIOR
Higher-ups: 8 TOPBRASS
Highest: 3 NTH
  degree: 3 NTH PHD
  honor: 3 ACE
  of all: 7 TOPMOST
  Of the ~ quality: 4 BEST
  point: 4 ACME APEX 5 CREST

  6 APOGEE ZENITH
  power: 3 NTH
Highfalutin: 5 ARTSY LOFTY
  6 SNOOTY
High-fashion
  mag: 4 ELLE
High-fiber
  food: 4 BRAN
High-five: 4 **SLAP**
  sound: 4 SLAP
Highflier
  home: 5 AERIE
High-flying
  clique: 6 JETSET
  toy: 4 KITE
High-grade: 6 RATEDA
High-hat: 4 SNOB 5 SNOOT
  6 SNOOTY
High-hatter: 4 **SNOB** 5 SNOOT
"High Hopes"
  insect: 3 ANT
  lyricist Sammy: 4 CAHN
High-IQ
  group: 5 MENSA
High-jump
  hurdle: 3 BAR
Highland
  girl: 4 LASS
  hat: 3 TAM
  headgear: 3 TAM
  hillside: 4 BRAE
  horde: 4 CLAN
  pattern: 6 TARTAN
  refusal: 3 NAE
  tongue. 4 **ERSE**
  topper: 3 TAM
  valley: 4 CLAN
  wear: 6 TARTAN
Highlander: 4 **GAEL SCOT**
  8 CLANSMAN
  hat: 3 TAM
Highlight
  Opera: 4 ARIA
Highlights
  ESPN: 3 TDS
  Hair: 7 STREAKS
  Musical: 4 SOLI
Highminded: 5 NOBLE
High-minded: 5 MORAL NOBLE

High-muck-a-muck: 5 MOGUL
   NABOB
"High Noon"
  heroine: 3 AMY
  lawman: 4 KANE
High-pH
  substance: 3 LYE 6 ALKALI
High-pitched: 5 SHARP 6 TREBLE
  cry: 4 YELP
High-priced
  spread: 6 ESTATE
  ticket area: 4 LOGE
High-profile
  hairdo: 4 AFRO
High-protein
  food: 4 TOFU
High-ranking
  angel: 6 SERAPH
  clergyman: 7 PRELATE
  NCO: 4 MSGT
High-rise
  feature: 7 TERRACE
  locales: 4 URBS
  support: 4 IBAR
High school
  book: 4 TEXT
  breakout: 4 ACNE
  class: 3 ART GYM 4 SHOP
  dance: 4 PROM
  exam: 4 PSAT
  misfit: 4 NERD
  subj.: 3 ALG **ENG** SCI 4 BIOL
    HIST
"High Sierra"
  actress: 9 IDALUPINO
  actress Lupino: 3 IDA
  director: 5 WALSH
  role: 5 EARLE
High-spirited: 6 ELATED
  horse: 5 STEED 7 ARABIAN
High-strung: 4 EDGY TAUT
    5 HYPER TENSE
Hightail
  it: 3 LAM 4 FLEE SCAT TEAR
Hightailed
  it: 3 RAN 4 SPED
High-tech
  identifier: 3 DNA
  memo: 5 EMAIL

  recordings: 3 CDS
  Suffix used in: 4 TRON
Highway: 4 **ROAD** 6 ARTERY
  (abbr.): 3 RTE
  access: 4 **RAMP**
  behemoth: 4 SEMI
  curve: 3 ESS
  divider: 6 MEDIAN
  division: 4 LANE
  entrance: 4 RAMP
  exit: 4 RAMP
  fee: 4 TOLL
  hauler: 3 RIG 4 **SEMI**
  hazard: 5 SLEET
  headache: 5 TIEUP
  Like a main: 8 ARTERIAL
  Main: 6 ARTERY
  no-no: 5 UTURN
  Northern: 5 ALCAN
  Old ~ name: 5 ALCAN
  owner: 7 ROADHOG
  patroller: 7 TROOPER
  rig: 4 SEMI
  sign: 5 MERGE
  warning: 3 SLO 5 FLARE
Highwayman: 6 BANDIT
"Highwayman, The"
  poet Alfred: 5 NOYES
"Hi-___, Hi-Lo": 4 LILI
Hike: 4 SNAP TREK 5 BOOST
    RAISE TROOP
  Long: 4 TREK
  Take a: 4 WALK
  Words before a: 6 HUTONE
Hiked: 5 UPPED
Hiker
  burden: 8 KNAPSACK
  path: 5 TRAIL
  route: 4 PATH 5 TRAIL
  snack: 4 GORP
  woe: 4 CORN
Hikes: 3 UPS 7 JACKSUP
Hiking
  path: 5 TRAIL
  trail: 4 PATH
Hilarious
  joke: 11 KNEESLAPPER
  person: 4 RIOT
Hilarity: 4 GLEE 5 MIRTH

Hildegarde
  Actress: 4 NEFF
Hill
  builder: 3 **ANT** 4 MOLE
  climber: 3 **ANT**
  companion: 4 DALE
  Craggy: 3 TOR
  dweller: 3 **ANT**
  Flat-topped: 4 MESA 5 BUTTE
  Highland: 4 BRAE
  in 1991 news: 5 ANITA
  Isolated: 5 BUTTE
  resident: 3 ANT
  Rocky: 3 TOR
  Sand: 4 DUNE
  Send to the: 5 ELECT
  Small: 5 KNOLL
  Way up a: 4 TBAR
  worker: 3 ANT
___ Hill
  of San Francisco: 3 NOB
  R&B band: 3 DRU
Hill, Faith
  hit song: 8 THISKISS
Hillary
  challenge: 7 EVEREST
  conquest: 7 EVEREST
  successor: 5 LAURA
  supporters: 7 SHERPAS
  Where Bill met: 4 YALE
  ~, at birth: 6 RODHAM
Hillenbrand
  of baseball: 4 SHEA
Hillock: 4 RISE 5 KNOLL
       MOUND
Hills
  Chain of: 5 RANGE
  City of seven: 4 ROME
  Head for the: 4 BOLT **FLEE**
  Home in the: 3 DEN
  Like the: 3 OLD
Hillside: 5 SLOPE
  Highland: 4 BRAE
  Scottish: 4 **BRAE**
  shelter: 4 ABRI
"Hill Street Blues"
  actor Joe: 5 SPANO
  actress Veronica: 5 HAMEL
Hilltop: 3 TOR 4 RISE

Hilo
  feast: 4 LUAU
  garland: 3 LEI
  hello: 5 ALOHA
  strings: 4 UKES
Hilton
  rival: 5 HYATT
"___ Hilton, The": 5 HANOI
Him
  ~, in French: 3 LUI
Himalayan
  beast: 3 YAK
  continent: 4 ASIA
  country: 5 NEPAL
  danger: 9 AVALANCHE
  guide: 6 SHERPA
  Hairy: 4 YETI
  humanoid: 4 YETI
  kingdom: 5 NEPAL 6 BHUTAN
  legend: 4 **YETI**
  sighting: 4 YETI
  summit: 7 EVEREST
Himalayas
  Area south of the: 5 ASSAM
  continent: 4 ASIA
"___ Him on a Sunday": 4 IMET
Hind: 3 DOE 4 DEER
  mate: 4 STAG
Hindenburg
  predecessor: 5 EBERT
Hinder: 5 DETER EMBAR
       6 IMPEDE
  legally: 5 ESTOP
  Opposite of: 4 ABET
Hindi
  language group: 5 INDIC
  master: 5 SAHIB
Hindquarters: 4 RUMP
Hindrance: 5 CRIMP
Hindu
  aphorism: 5 SUTRA
  ascetic: 5 FAKIR
  deity: 4 RAMA 5 SHIVA
       6 VISHNU
  destroyer: 4 SIVA
  discipline: 4 YOGA
  doctrine: 6 TANTRA
  garment: 4 SARI
  gentleman: 4 BABU

god: 4 DEVA SIVA
hero: 4 RAMA
honorific: 3 **SRI** 5 RAJAH SWAMI
incarnation: 6 **AVATAR**
loincloth: 5 DHOTI
master: 5 SWAMI
melody: 4 RAGA
Member of a ~ trio: 5 SHIVA
monk: 5 SADHU
music: 4 RAGA
Of ~ scriptures: 5 VEDIC
prince: 5 RAJAH
princess: 4 **RANI** 5 RANEE
queen: 4 RANI 5 RANEE
religious teacher: 5 SWAMI
retreat: 6 ASHRAM
sacred writing: 4 VEDA
sage: 5 RISHI SWAMI
self: 5 ATMAN
social division: 5 CASTE
teacher: 4 GURU 5 SWAMI
title: 3 **SRI**
wrap: 4 SARI 5 SAREE

Hinduism
The Creator, in: 6 BRAHMA
The Destroyer, in: 4 SIVA
The Preserver, in: 6 VISHNU

Hines
Dance like: 3 TAP
Jazzman "Fatha": 4 EARL

Hines, Earl
nickname: 5 FATHA

Hines, Gregory
forte: 3 TAP

Hinge
Silence a: 3 OIL

Hinged
cover: 3 LID
fastener: 4 HASP

Hingis
of tennis: 7 MARTINA
rival: 4 GRAF 5 SELES

Hinkle
Golfer: 3 LON

"Hinky Dinky Parlay ___": 3 VOO

Hinny
kin: 4 MULE

Hint: 3 TIP 4 CLUE 5 TINGE
TRACE

at: 7 SUGGEST
at, with "to": 6 ALLUDE
of color: 5 TINGE
of light: 5 GLEAM
Words before: 5 DROPA

Hints
Needing many: 4 SLOW
Woman with: 7 HELOISE

Hip: 3 MOD 4 COOL 5 AWARE
6 TRENDY WITHIT
bones: 4 ILIA
dance: 4 HULA
ending: 4 STER
Got: 5 WISED
joint: 4 COXA
Part of the: 6 HAUNCH
suffix: 4 **STER**

Hipbone: 5 ILIUM
Of the: 5 ILIAC
Of the ~ (prefix): 4 ILIO

Hipbones: 4 **ILIA**

"Hip hip ___!": 6 HOORAH

Hip-hop: 3 RAP
Dr. of: 3 DRE
fan: 4 BBOY

Hippie: 11 FLOWERCHILD
attire: 5 BEADS
Color, as ~ clothing: 6 TIEDYE
greeting: 5 PEACE
happening: 4 BEIN 6 LOVEIN
home: 3 PAD
purchase: 4 WEED
Understand, like a: 3 DIG

Hippo
add-on: 5 DROME
relative: 5 TAPIR
tail: 5 DROME

Hippodrome: 5 ARENA
shape: 4 OVAL

Hippomenes
Loser to ~ in a footrace:
8 ATALANTA

Hippy
dance: 4 HULA

Hips
With hands on: 6 AKIMBO

Hipster: 3 CAT 7 COOLCAT
exclamation: 3 MAN
Not a: 4 NERD

Hiram
 of Hawaii: 4 FONG
Hire: 6 ENGAGE TAKEON
 Car for: 3 CAB
 New: 7 TRAINEE
 new staff: 5 REMAN
 Summer: 4 TEMP
 ~, as a lawyer: 6 RETAIN
Hired
 Just: 3 NEW
Hiree
 Annual: 3 CPA
 Holiday: 5 SANTA
 Vacationer's: 6 SITTER
Hires: 7 TAKESON 8 ROOTBEER
 competition: 4 DADS
 New corp.: 4 MBAS
Hirohito: 7 EMPEROR
"Hiroshima"
 writer: 6 HERSEY
Hirsch
 of football: 5 ELROY
Hirsch, Judd
 sitcom: 4 TAXI
Hirschfeld
 and others: 3 ALS
 daughter: 4 NINA
Hirt
 and others: 3 **ALS**
His
 and her: 5 THEIR
 partner: 4 HERS
 ~, in French: 3 SES
His ___ (big shot): 4 NIBS
"His Master's Voice"
 org.: 3 RCA
Hispanic: 6 LATINO
Hispaniola: 4 ISLA 5 HAITI
Hiss: 8 SIBILATE
 Gp. that accused: 4 HUAC
 of history: 5 ALGER
 relative: 3 BOO
Hisser
 Household: 9 STEAMIRON
Hissy fit: 4 SNIT
Historian
 German: 5 WEBER
 interest: 4 PAST
 Roman: 4 LIVY

 subject: 3 ERA
 unit: 3 ERA
 Venerable: 4 BEDE
 ~ Muse: 4 CLIO
Historic
 age: 3 ERA
 beginning: 3 PRE
 leader: 3 PRE
 period: 3 **ERA**
 start: 3 PRE
 time: 3 **ERA**
Historical
 display: 7 DIORAMA
 memento: 5 RELIC
 period: 3 AGE **ERA** 5 EPOCH
 records: 6 ANNALS
History: 4 PAST
 Chapter in: 3 ERA
 Folk: 4 LORE
 Handed-down: 4 LORE
 homework: 5 ESSAY
 Hunk of: 3 ERA
 Kind of: 4 **ORAL**
 Muse of: 4 **CLIO**
 Piece of: 3 ERA 5 RELIC
 Time in: 3 **ERA**
 ___ history: 4 ORAL
Hit: 3 BOP RAM 4 BEAT BELT
      SLAP SWAT 5 SMACK
 alternative: 4 MISS
 Big: 5 HOMER SMASH 6 TRIPLE
      7 HOMERUN
 bottom: 5 SPANK
 broadside: 3 RAM
 hard: 3 RAM 4 BELT SLAM
      5 SMACK SMITE SMOTE
 letters: 3 SRO
 lightly: 3 TAP
 maker: 3 BAT
 man: 4 ICER 8 ASSASSIN
 music: 3 RAP
 one's toe: 4 STUB
 on the green: 4 PUTT
 on the head: 3 BOP 4 CONK
 openhanded: 4 SLAP
 show sign: 3 SRO
 sign: 3 **SRO**
 Surprise: 7 SLEEPER
 the beach: 4 LAND

the big time: **6** ARRIVE MAKEIT
the books: **5** STUDY
the bottle: **4** TOPE **5** BOOZE
the deck: **5** ARISE
the ground: **4** ALIT
the hay: **5** CRASH SLEEP
the jackpot: **12** STRIKEITRICH
the mall: **4** SHOP
the road: **4** LEFT TOUR WENT
    5 LEAVE SCRAM
the roof: **6** SEERED
the slopes: **3** **SKI**
the spot: **7** SATISFY
the tarmac: **4** LAND
Try to ~, as a fly: **6** SWATAT
with a laser: **3** ZAP
~, old-style: **5** SMITE SMOTE
Hitch: 4 KNOT **SNAG** YOKE
Clove: **4** KNOT
Do another: **4** REUP
Half: **4** KNOT
on the run: **5** ELOPE
Start another: **4** REUP
Hitchcock, Alfred
film: **4** ROPE **5** TOPAZ **6** FRENZY
    MARNIE PSYCHO
    7 REBECCA VERTIGO
film appearance: **5** CAMEO
film title start: **5** DIALM
genre: **8** SUSPENSE
menaces: **5** BIRDS
Wife of: **4** ALMA
Hitchcockian: 5 EERIE
Hitched: 3 WED
Get: **3** WED
Get ~ quick: **5** ELOPE
It may be: **4** RIDE
Not: **5** UNWED
Hitchhike: 4 RIDE
Hitchhiker: 5 RIDER
digit: **5** THUMB
quest: **4** LIFT RIDE
Words to a: **5** GETIN HOPIN
"Hitchin' ___" (1970 hit): 5 ARIDE
Hitching
place: **4** POST RENO
post: **5** **ALTAR**
Hite
Author: **5** SHERE

Sex researcher: **5** SHERE
Hi-tech
address: **3** URL
dictionary medium: **5** CDROM
message: **5** EMAIL
Hither
partner: **3** **YON**
Hither and ___ : 3 YON
Hitherto: 5 ASYET SOFAR
Hit-or-miss: 6 RANDOM
    8 SLAPDASH
Hits
Big ~ (abbr.): **3** HRS
the roof: **7** SEESRED
They're rarely: **6** BSIDES
"Hits the spot"
sloganeer: **5** PEPSI
Hitter
Heavy: **6** SLEDGE
of 660 home runs: **4** MAYS
of 755 home runs: **5** AARON
ploy: **4** BUNT
stat: **3** RBI
Hitting: 5 ATBAT
opportunity: **5** ATBAT
Hittites
home: **9** ASIAMINOR
Hive
dweller: **3** BEE **5** DRONE
house: **6** APIARY
Hiver
opposite: **3** ETE
Hives
Like: **5** APIAN
Person with: **8** APIARIST
problem: **4** ITCH
Hizzoner: 5 MAYOR
H-L
connectors: **3** IJK
"Hmmm ...": 4 ISEE **7** LETSSEE
    8 LETMESEE
HMO
listing: **3** GPS
members: **3** MDS **4** DOCS
Part of: **6** HEALTH
HMS
Part of: **3** HER HIS
Ho
Hello from: **5** ALOHA

of Hawaii: **3** DON
"___ ho!": **5** HEAVE
Ho, Don
  hit: **11** TINYBUBBLES
  neckwear: **3** LEI
Hoad
  of tennis: **3** LEW
Hoag
  Author: **4** TAMI
Hoagie
  Had a: **3** ATE
Hoard: 5 CACHE STASH TROVE
Hoarfrost: 4 RIME
Hoarse: 5 RASPY
  sound: **4** RASP
Hoarsely
  Speak: **4** RASP
Hoary: 3 OLD **4** AGED
Hoax: 4 SHAM **6** CANARD
"Hobbit, The"
  character: **5** BILBO FRODO
  home: **5** SHIRE
Hobble: 4 LIMP
Hobbling: 4 GIMP LAME
Hobby: 7 PASTIME
  Making a ~ of: **4** INTO
  shop purchase: **3** KIT
  suffix: **3** IST
Hobbyist
  purchase: **3** KIT
  Radio: **3** HAM
Hobnob: 9 ASSOCIATE
Hobo: 5 TRAMP **7** VAGRANT
       8 VAGABOND
  fare: **4** STEW
Ho Chi ___ : 4 MINH
Ho Chi Minh City
  former name: **6** SAIGON
Hock: 4 PAWN
  Be in: **3** OWE
  In: **6** PAWNED
Hockey
  fake out: **4** DEKE
  great Bobby: **3** **ORR**
  great Gordie: **4** HOWE
  infraction: **5** ICING
  legend: **3** ORR
  objective: **4** GOAL
  official: **3** REF

position: **4** WING
score: **4** GOAL
shot: **4** SLAP
Song played at some ~ games:
  7 OCANADA
stat: **7** ASSISTS
stick wood: **3** ASH
surface: **3** ICE
team: **6** SEXTET
venue: **4** RINK
"Hocus Pocus"
  actor Katz: **4** OMRI
Hod
  worker: **5** MASON
Hodgepodge: 4 HASH MESS **OLIO**
       STEW **5** SALAD **7** FARRAGO
       MELANGE **8** PASTICHE
       10 CRAZYQUILT
Hodges
  of baseball: **3** GIL
  teammate: **5** REESE
Hoe: 4 TILL
  home: **4** SHED
  target: **4** WEED
Hoedown
  move: **6** DOSIDO
  participant: **3** GAL
  seat: **4** BALE
  setting: **4** BARN
Hoff
  Cartoonist: **3** SYD
"Hoffa"
  screenwriter: **5** MAMET
Hoffer
  Author: **4** ERIC
Hoffman
  Actor: **6** DUSTIN
  Author: **5** ABBIE
  offerings: **5** TALES
  Radical: **5** ABBIE
Hoffman, Dustin
  film: **5** LENNY **7** RAINMAN
       TOOTSIE
  role: **5** LENNY RATSO
Hog
  cheek: **4** JOWL
  fat: **4** LARD
  food: **4** SLOP
  heaven: **3** STY

home: **3** STY
opposite: **6** SHARER
sound: **5** GRUNT
Stage: **3** HAM
Wild: **4** BOAR

Hogan
contemporary: **5** SNEAD
dweller: **6** NAVAHO NAVAJO
Golfer: **3** BEN
in a sitcom: **7** COLONEL
Wrestler: **4** HULK

Hogan, Paul
film: **15** CROCODILEDUNDEE

"Hogan's Heroes"
keeper: **12** COLONELKLINK
sergeant: **7** SCHULTZ
setting: **6** **STALAG**

Hoggett, Farmer
prize pig: **4** BABE
Wife of: **4** ESME

Hoglike
beast: **5** TAPIR

Hogs
Feed the: **4** SLOP

Hogwarts
accessory: **4** WAND
attendee: **11** HARRYPOTTER
mail carrier: **3** OWL
Malfoy at: **5** DRACO

Hogwash: **3** PAP ROT **4** BOSH
BULL BUNK LIES SLOP
5 BILGE HOOEY PSHAW
TRIPE **6** HOTAIR
7 BALONEY

"Ho, ho, ho!"
speaker: **15** JOLLYGREENGIANT

Ho-hum: **4** **BLAH** DRAB DULL
SOSO **5** BLASE
feeling: **5** ENNUI
grade: **3** CEE
~ TV fare: **5** RERUN

"Ho-hum": **7** IMBORED

Hoi ___: **6** POLLOI

Hoi polloi: **6** MASSES RABBLE
character: **7** OMICRON
disdainer: **4** SNOB **7** ELITIST

Hoist: **5** CRANE RAISE
7 ELEVATE UPRAISE
Lifeboat: **5** DAVIT

Hoisted
~, nautically: **4** HOVE

Hoister: **6** PETARD

Hoity-___: **5** TOITY

Hoity-toity
type: **4** SNOB

Hokey: **5** CORNY

Hokkaido
city: **5** OTARU
native: **4** AINU
people: **4** AINU
port: **5** OTARU

Hokum: **3** ROT

Holbein
Painter: **4** HANS

"Holberg Suite"
composer: **5** GRIEG

Holbrook
Actor: **3** **HAL**

Hold: **3** OWN **4** DEEM GRIP
5 GRASP **6** ASSERT
DETAIN RETAIN
7 POSSESS **8** MAINTAIN
back: **4** REIN STEM **6** IMPEDE
dear: **5** ADORE **7** CHERISH
Didn't: **3** RAN
Doesn't ~ up well: **4** SAGS
Don't ~ back: **4** TELL
fast: **6** ADHERE COHERE
Fill the: **4** LADE
firmly: **4** GRIP
forth: **5** **ORATE**
gently: **6** CRADLE
Hard to: **4** **EELY**
in high regard: **6** ADMIRE
In the: **4** ALOW **5** BELOW
off: **4** WAIT **5** DEFER
on: **4** WAIT
one's ground: **8** STANDPAT
one's horses: **4** WAIT
Put in the: **4** LADE STOW
Put on: **6** SHELVE
responsible: **5** BLAME
stuff: **5** CARGO
sway: **4** **RULE** **5** REIGN
Take: **5** SETIN
the deed to: **3** OWN
the floor: **5** ORATE
Tight: **4** GRIP

title to: **3** OWN
together: **6** COHERE
up: **3 ROB 4** LAST
Wrestling: **6** NELSON
~, as attention: **5** RIVET
"__ Holden" (Bacheller novel):
      4 EBEN
Holding: 5 ASSET TENET
gadget: **4** VISE
Third-party: **6** ESCROW
Holdings: 6 ESTATE
"Hold it!": 4 WHOA
"Hold it right there!": 6 FREEZE
"Hold Me"
Grammy winner for: **5** OSLIN
"Hold on!": 4 WAIT **6** NOTYET
      ONESEC **8** WAITASEC
"Hold on __!": 4 ASEC
"Hold on a __!": 3 SEC
"Hold on there!": 4 WHOA
"Hold On Tight"
band: **3 ELO**
Holdover: 5 RELIC
Holds: 3 HAS
Holdup: 4 SNAG **5** DELAY HEIST
      7 BANKJOB
Help in a: **4** ABET
"Hold your horses!": 4 WAIT
      WHOA **6** NOTYET
Hole
Be in the: **3** OWE
enlarger: **6** REAMER
fixer: **6** DARNER
for a lace: **6** EYELET
Gaping: **5** CHASM
Get a ~ in one: **3** ACE
goal: **3** PAR
Green: **3** CUP
in one: **3** ACE
in the head: **5** SINUS
in the wall: **4** VENT
Is in the: **4** OWES
Make a new: **5** REDIG
maker: **3 AWL**
Needle: **3** EYE
number: **3 PAR**
Place to start a: **3** TEE
puncher: **3 AWL**
Roll with a: **5** BAGEL

Shoe: **6** EYELET
Start a: **5** TEEUP
starter: **3** AWL TEE
Start of a: **3** TEE
up: **4** HIDE
Widen a: **4** REAM
Words after: **5** INONE
Hole __ : 5 INONE
Holed
up: **3** HID
Hole-in-one: 3 ACE
Hole-making
pest: **5** BORER
tool: **3** AWL **5** BORER
Hole-punching
tool: **3** AWL
Holes
18 ~: **5** ROUND
Maker of: **4** MOTH
Poke ~ in: **4** STAB **6** AERATE
Holey
roll: **5** BAGEL
utensil: **5** SIEVE
Holiday
Asian: **3 TET**
cusp: **3** EVE
Dec.: **3** XMAS
drink: **3** NOG
Hanoi: **3 TET**
helper: **3** ELF
Hué: **3** TET
Italian: **5** FESTA
lead-in: **3** EVE
mo.: **3** DEC
Mo. without a: **3** AUG
music: **5** BLUES
number: **4** NOEL
poem opener: **4** TWAS
preceder: **3 EVE**
quaff: **3** NOG **7** WASSAIL
Roman: **5** FESTA
season: **4** NOEL
song: **4** NOEL
team leader: **7** RUDOLPH
time: **4** YULE
tree: **3** FIR
tune: **4** NOEL **5** CAROL
Vietnamese: **3** TET
visitor: **5** INLAW SANTA

warmer: **7** YULELOG
Holiday ___: **3** INN
Holiday Inn
competitor: **6** RAMADA
Holier-than-___: **4** THOU
Holier-than-thou
type: **10** GOODYGOODY
Holier-___-thou: **4** THAN
Holiness: **8** SANCTITY
Symbol of: **4** HALO
Holland
cheese: **4** EDAM
export: **4** EDAM **5** TULIP
flower: **5** TULIP
humanist: **7** ERASMUS
Hollandaise: **5** SAUCE
Holler: **3** CRY **4** HOWL YELL
YOWL **5** SHOUT **6** SCREAM
Heckler's: **3** BOO
partner: **4** HOOT
"**___** hollers ...": **4** IFHE
Holliday
and others: **4** DOCS
associate: **4** EARP
Holliday, Polly
role: **3** FLO
Holliman
Actor: **4** EARL
Hollow: **3** PIT **4** DELL GLEN
VALE **6** CAVITY
grass: **4** REED
Not: **5** SOLID
pastry: **7** POPOVER
reply: **4** ECHO
rock: **5** GEODE
stone: **5** GEODE
Hollowed: **5** CORED
Hollowing
tool: **6** ROUTER
"**Hollow Man**"
actress Elisabeth: **4** SHUE
"**Hollow Men, The**"
poet: **5** ELIOT
Holly: **4** ILEX
genus: **4** ILEX
piece: **5** SPRIG
Holly, Buddy
portrayer Gary: **5** BUSEY
song: **5** OHBOY

Hollywood: **7** FILMDOM
Info: Film capital; often a
reference to actors, actresses,
and directors
award: **5** OSCAR
boulevard: **6** SUNSET
Bridges in: **4** BEAU JEFF
canine: **4** ASTA
crosser: **4** VINE
crowd: **6** EXTRAS
Day in: **5** DORIS **7** LARAINE
deal maker: **5** AGENT
dive: **5** STUNT
favorite: **4** IDOL
First name in ~ dirt: **4** RONA
giants: **4** EGOS
headliner: **4** STAR
Head of: **5** EDITH
hopeful: **7** STARLET
Hunt in: **5** HELEN LINDA
Miles from: **4** VERA
Power in: **6** TYRONE
pursuit: **7** STARDOM
treasure: **5** OSCAR
West of: **3** **MAE**
Hollywood Boulevard
sight: **4** STAR
"**Hollywood Ending**"
actress Téa: **5** LEONI
"**Hollywood Squares**"
option: **5** AGREE
regular: **5** LYNDE
win: **3** OOO
Hollywood Walk of Fame
feature: **4** STAR
Holm
Actor: **3** **IAN**
Actress: **7** **CELESTE**
oak: **4** ILEX
Holman
of basketball: **3** NAT
Holmes
Actress: **5** KATIE
creator: **5** DOYLE
hint: **4** CLUE
Task for: **4** CASE
Holmes, Sherlock: **6** SLEUTH
Brother of: **7** MYCROFT
Bruce of ~ films: **5** NIGEL

friend Adler: **5** IRENE
portrayer: **13** BASILRATHBONE
portrayer Rathbone: **5** BASIL
prop: **4** PIPE
Holmesian
exclamation: **4** ISAY
Hologram
creator: **5** LASER
Holography
need: **5** LASER
Holstein: 3 COW
hello: **3** MOO
home: **5** DAIRY
Holster
item: **3** GUN **6** PISTOL
Holt
of westerns: **3** TIM
Holy: 6 SACRED **7** BLESSED
    SAINTED
Apply ~ oil to: **6** ANOINT
book: **5** BIBLE KORAN
city: **5** MECCA **6** TOLEDO
Fr. ~ woman: **3** **STE**
Fr. ~ women: **4** **STES**
Make: **5** BLESS
men (abbr.): **3** STS
one: **5** SAINT **6** TERROR
place: **6** SHRINE **7** SANCTUM
places: **6** SANCTA
Russian name meaning: **4** OLGA
scroll: **5** TORAH
war: **5** JIHAD **7** CRUSADE
water receptacle: **4** FONT
    5 STOUP
"Holy ___!": 4 MOLY
Holy Ark
locale: **4** SHUL
"Holy cow!": 3 GEE **4** EGAD JEEZ
    YIPE **5** EGADS GOLLY
    YIKES
Holyfield
Boxer: **7** EVANDER
defeater: **4** BOWE
Hit like: **3** BOX
Loser to: **5** TYSON
punch: **3** JAB
"Holy moly!": 3 GEE **4** EGAD
    JEEZ YIPE **5** EGADS
    GOLLY YIKES

Holy Roman
emperor: **4** OTTO **5** OTTOI
    7 LOTHAIR
"Holy smokes!": 3 GEE **4** EGAD
    JEEZ YIPE **5** EGADS
    GOLLY YIKES
"Holy Sonnets"
poet: **5** DONNE
"Holy Toledo!": 3 GEE **4** EGAD
    JEEZ YIPE **5** EGADS
    GOLLY YIKES
Homage: 6 SALUTE
Poetic: **3** ODE
"Homage to Clio"
poet: **5** AUDEN
Hombre
home: **4** CASA
title: **5** SENOR
Home: 4 BASE DIGS NEST
    5 ABODE **6** HEARTH
    7 HABITAT **9** RESIDENCE
Almost make it: **6** TRIPLE
At the ~ of: **4** CHEZ
Bring: **3** NET **4** **EARN** **5** CLEAR
Call at: **4** SAFE
Clay: **5** ADOBE
Conical: **5** TEPEE
Desert: **5** ADOBE
Dome: **5** **IGLOO**
ending: **5** STEAD
Estate: **5** MANOR
extension: **3** ELL **5** STEAD
Farm: **3** STY
First: **4** EDEN
fries: **6** TATERS
Get ~ safely: **5** SCORE
High: **5** **AERIE**
in a 1936 novel: **4** TARA
in a tree: **4** NEST
Leaves: **4** TREE
Log: **5** CABIN
Make a: **4** NEST
maker: **6** NESTER
Mobile: **4** TENT **5** TEPEE
    7 ALABAMA
Not: **3** OUT **4** AWAY
Not at: **3** OUT **4** AWAY
of the brave: **5** TEPEE
One who works at: **3** UMP

on high: **5** AERIE
on the range: **5 TEPEE**
 6 TEEPEE
planet: **5** EARTH
products seller: **5** AMWAY
Remain at: **6** STAYIN
Returns: **3** IRS
room: **3** DEN
Rose: **3** BED
Royal: **6** CASTLE
site: **3** LOT
Stately: **5** MANOR
Stuck at ~, in a way:
 9 SNOWBOUND
Take: **3** NET **4 EARN**
territory: **4** TURF
to billions: **4** ASIA
to most: **4** ASIA
with a flap door: **5** TEPEE
with a view: **5** AERIE
wrecker: **7** TERMITE
Home ___: 4 INON **5** PLATE
"Home ___": 5 ALONE
___ home (out): 5 NOTAT
"Home Alone"
 actor: **5** PESCI
Homeboy: 3 PAL
 turf: **4** HOOD
Homebuilders
 Storied: **15** THREELITTLEPIGS
Homebuyer
 need: **4** LOAN
Homecoming
 guest: **4** ALUM
 guests: **6** ALUMNI
 queen headwear: **5** TIARA
"Homecoming, The"
 playwright: **6** PINTER
Home-cooked
 Have a ~ meal: **5** EATIN
Home Depot
 competitor: **5** LOWES
Home ec
 alternative: **4** SHOP
Homegrown: 5 LOCAL
"Home Improvement"
 actor Allen: **3** TIM
 prop: **4** TOOL
 star: **5** ALLEN

Homeless
 animal: **5** STRAY
 child: **4** WAIF
Homemade
 hooch: **10** BATHTUBGIN
 SNEAKYPETE
Homeowner
 paper: **4** DEED
 pride: **4** LAWN
 pymt.: **4** MTGE
Homer: 3 HIT **4** POET
 8 EPICPOET
 Bart, to: **3** SON
 Cry from: **3** DOH
 Daughter of: **4** LISA
 epic: **5** ILIAD
 Father of: **3** ABE
 leader: **5** AARON
 neighbor: **3** NED
 outburst: **3** DOH
 Son of: **4** BART
 Two-run ~ prerequisite:
 5 ONEON
 work: **4** EPIC EPOS
 ~, to Bart: **3** DAD
Homeric: 4 EPIC
 epic: **5 ILIAD 7** ODYSSEY
 work: **5** ILIAD
Home run
 great: **5** MARIS
 king: **5** AARON
 pace: **4** TROT
 ~, slangily: **5** TATER
HOMES
 member: **4** ERIE
 Part of: **4 ERIE**
Homesite: 3 LOT
"Home to Harlem"
 novelist: **5** MCKAY
Homework
 Arithmetic: **4** SUMS
 English: **5** ESSAY
 Give, as: **6** ASSIGN
 Help with: **5** TUTOR
 History: **5** ESSAY
Homey: 4 COZY
 in the 'hood: **3** BRO
Homicide
 First ~ victim: **4** ABEL

Homily: 6 SERMON
Ho ___ Minh: 3 CHI
Hominoid
  family member: 3 APE
Hominy
  kin: 4 SAMP
Homme ___ (statesman): 5 DETAT
Homme d'___ (statesman): 4 ETAT
"___ homo!": 4 ECCE
Homo sapiens: 7 SPECIES
  Like: 5 ERECT
  The "Homo" in: 5 GENUS
Hon: 3 PET 4 BABY DEAR DOLL
    LOVE 5 DEARY SUGAR
    TOOTS 6 DEARIE
    7 DEAREST SWEETIE
    10 SWEETIEPIE
Honcho: 4 BOSS 5 MRBIG NABOB
    8 BIGWHEEL
  Corp.: 3 CEO 4 EXEC
  Head: 4 BOSS 5 MRBIG
    6 TOPDOG
  Monastery: 5 ABBOT
Honda: 3 CAR 4 AUTO
  competitor: 6 YAMAHA
  division: 5 ACURA
  model: 5 CIVIC 6 ACCORD
Hone: 7 SHARPEN
Honed: 4 KEEN
Honest: 4 REAL
  Be ~ (with): 5 LEVEL
"Honest"
  one: 3 ABE
  president: 3 ABE
"Honest!": 5 NOLIE 6 ISWEAR
    7 FORREAL TRUSTME
Honest ___: 3 ABE
Honest-to-goodness: 4 REAL
    TRUE 6 ACTUAL
Honey: 3 PET 4 BABY DEAR
    DOLL LOVE 5 DEARY
    SUGAR TOOTS 6 DEARIE
    7 DEAREST SWEETIE
    10 SWEETIEPIE
  badger: 5 RATEL
  bunch: 4 BEES
  drink: 4 MEAD
  factory: 4 HIVE
  Fermented: 4 MEAD

  French: 5 CHERI
  handler: 3 BEE
  holder: 3 JAR
  maker: 3 BEE
  Take the ~ and run: 5 ELOPE
  The color of: 4 GOLD 5 AMBER
  Word after: 3 PIE
"Honey, ___!": 6 IMHOME
Honeybun: 3 PET 4 BABY DEAR
    DOLL LOVE 5 DEARY
    SUGAR TOOTS 6 DEARIE
    7 DEAREST SWEETIE
    10 SWEETIEPIE
Honeybunch: 3 PET 4 BABY DEAR
    DOLL LOVE 5 DEARY
    SUGAR TOOTS 6 DEARIE
    7 DEAREST SWEETIE
Honeycomb
  maker: 3 BEE
  shape: 7 HEXAGON
  unit: 4 CELL
Honeycreeper
  cousin: 7 TANAGER
Honeydew: 5 MELON
  eater: 3 ANT
  relative: 6 CASABA
Honeyed
  beverage: 4 MEAD
Honeymoon
  choice: 5 SUITE
  haven: 7 NIAGARA
"Honeymooners, The"
  actor Carney: 3 ART
  actress Jane: 4 KEAN
  role: 5 ALICE 6 NORTON TRIXIE
Hong Kong
  harbor craft: 6 SAMPAN
  neighbor: 5 MACAO
Honk: 4 BEEP TOOT
  provoker: 7 ROADHOG
Honker: 4 BEAK HORN NOSE
    5 GOOSE
  Barnyard: 5 GOOSE
  Hawaiian: 4 NENE
Honkers: 5 GEESE
Honking
  birds: 5 GEESE
Honky-___: 4 TONK

Honky-tonk: 6 SALOON
7 RAGTIME
musician Ernest: **4** TUBB
player: **5** PIANO
Honolulu
fictional detective: **4** CHAN
hello: **5** ALOHA
home: **4** OAHU
island: **4** **OAHU**
Honor: 4 LAUD **5** ADORE AWARD
6 ESTEEM
Brit.: **3** DSO
Highest: **3** ACE
In ~ of: **3** FOR
It's an: **3** TEN
Pay ~ to: **4** FETE
Place of: **4** DAIS
society letter: **3** PHI
Title of: **3** SIR
with a party: **4** FETE
with humor: **5** ROAST
Word of: **4** OATH
Honoraria: 4 FEES
Honorarium: 3 FEE
Honorary
Brit. ~ title: **3** OBE
deg.: **3** LLD
title: **7** EMERITA
Honored
lady: **4** DAME
Honoré de ___ (French novelist):
6 BALZAC
Honoree
April: **4** FOOL
Cotillion: **3** DEB
Jan.: **3** MLK
June: **3** **DAD**
Mar.: **5** **STPAT**
March: **9** STPATRICK
March ~, for short: **5** **STPAT**
May: **3** **MOM** **6** MOTHER
Nov.: **3** VET
Parade: **4** HERO
Parade ~, for short: **5** STPAT
place: **4** DAIS
Purim: **6** ESTHER
Wartime: **4** HERO
Honorific: 5 TITLE
Asian: **3** SRI

Hindu: **3** **SRI** **5** SWAMI
Honshu: **3** SAN
Indian: **3** SRI **5** SAHIB
Japanese: **3** **SAN**
Royal: **4** SIRE
Turkish: **3** AGA **4** **AGHA**
Honor ___ thieves: 5 AMONG
"Honor Thy Father"
author: **6** **TALESE**
"Honour is ___ scutcheon":
Shakespeare: 5 AMERE
Honshu
city: **5** OSAKA
honorific: **3** SAN
peak: **4** FUJI
port: **4** KOBE **5** **OSAKA**
Hoo
preceder: **3** YOO
Hooch: 5 BOOZE
holder: **5** FLASK
Homemade: **10** BATHTUBGIN
SNEAKYPETE
Hood: 4 COWL THUG
Child actress: **5** DARLA
gun: **3** GAT
Help a: **4** ABET
Job for a: **5** HEIST
knife: **4** SHIV
Monk's: **4** COWL
weapon: **3** GAT
Young: **4** PUNK
~, to a Brit: **6** BONNET
Hood, Robin: 6 ARCHER
OUTLAW
gang: **8** MERRYMEN
portrayer Flynn: **5** ERROL
weapon: **5** ARROW **7** LONGBOW
Hooded
garment: **4** COWL **5** PARKA
jacket: **6** ANORAK
snake: **3** ASP **5** COBRA
Hoodlum: 4 GOON THUG
Help a: **4** ABET
Hoodwink: 3 **CON** GYP **4** DUPE
FOOL SCAM **5** LIETO
9 BAMBOOZLE
Hooey: 3 ROT **4** BOSH **5** PSHAW
Hoof
Beef on the: **5** **STEER**

it: 4 WALK
protector: 4 SHOE
sound: 4 CLOP
Hoofbeat: 4 CLOP
sound: 4 CLOP
Hoo-ha: 3 **ADO** 4 FLAP STIR
TODO
Hook: 6 PIRATE
Fishing: 4 GAFF
hand: 4 SMEE
Hawk's: 5 TALON
henchman: 4 SMEE
It's on the: 4 BAIT
Let off the: 6 EXEMPT
mate: 4 SMEE
nemesis: 4 CROC
Off the: 4 FREE
Prepare a: 4 BAIT
projection: 4 BARB
shape: 3 CEE **ESS**
target: 3 JAW
"Hook"
producer Fayed: 4 DODI
role: 4 SMEE
Hook, Captain
cohort: 4 **SMEE**
nemesis: 4 CROC
Hookah
part: 3 URN
Hooked
It often gets: 4 BAIT
on: 4 INTO
"___ hooks": 5 USENO
Hook-shaped
peninsula: 7 CAPECOD
Hookup: 4 LINK
Hydrant: 4 HOSE
PC: 3 CRT LAN
R-V: 3 STU
TV: 3 VCR
Hookups
ER: 3 IVS
ICU: 3 IVS
Hooky
Playing: 4 AWOL 6 ABSENT
Hooligan: 4 GOON THUG
5 ROWDY
British: 3 YOB
Help a: 4 ABET

Hoop
edge: 3 RIM
gp.: 3 NBA
hanger: 3 NET
Hula: 3 **LEI**
Kind of: 4 HULA
site: 3 EAR
Hoopla: 3 ADO 4 HYPE TODO
Hoople, Major
outburst: 4 EGAD
Hoops: 5 **BBALL**
Info: Basketball cue
Coll. ~ competition: 3 **NIT**
gp.: 3 NBA
nickname: 4 SHAQ
org.: 3 NBA
pos.: 3 CTR
target: 3 RIM
tournament org.: 4 NCAA
Hoopster: 5 CAGER
Info: Basketball player cue
Boston ~, briefly: 4 CELT
Cleveland ~, briefly: 3 CAV
Dallas ~, briefly: 3 MAV
gp.: 3 NBA
Hoosier: 5 PACER
L.A.: 5 LAKER
New Jersey: 3 NET
New York: 5 KNICK
org.: 3 NBA
Salt Lake City: 3 UTE
Seattle: 5 SONIC
target: 3 RIM
"Hooray!": 3 OLE
~, to José: 3 OLE
"Hooray for me!": 4 TADA
Hoosegow: 3 CAN 4 **STIR**
5 POKEY
Naval: 4 BRIG
Hoosier
hoopster: 5 PACER
hub: 4 GARY
humorist: 3 ADE
state: 7 INDIANA
"Hoosier Poet, The": 5 RILEY
Hoot
Give a: 4 **CARE** HONK JEER
YELL
It gives a: 3 OWL

Hootenanny: 4 SING
Hooter: 3 OWL
  Baby: 5 OWLET
  Little: 5 OWLET
Hoover: 3 DAM
  birthplace: 4 IOWA
  org.: 3 FBI
  rival: 5 ORECK 6 EUREKA
  vice president: 6 CURTIS
  ~, briefly: 3 VAC
Hoover ___: 3 DAM
Hoover, Herbert: 5 IOWAN
  It was named for ~ in 1947:
    10 BOULDERDAM
Hoover, J. ___: 5 EDGAR
Hoover, J. Edgar
  gp.: 3 FBI
Hoover Dam
  lake: 4 MEAD
Hooves
  Split like: 6 CLOVEN
Hop
  Giant: 4 LEAP
  Sock: 5 DANCE
  ~, skip, or jump: 4 VERB
"Hop ___!": 4 TOIT
Hopalong Cassidy
  portrayer William: 4 **BOYD**
Hope: 6 ASPIRE
  Actress: 5 LANGE
  and charity partner:
    5 FAITH
  Bit of: 3 RAY
  Comic: 3 BOB
  Give up: 7 DESPAIR
  Gp. that brought ~ to the troops:
    3 USO
  Lose: 7 DESPAIR
  Losing: 4 DIET
  Not much: 3 RAY
  One beyond: 5 GONER
  sponsor: 3 USO
"___ Hope" (former soap):
    5 RYANS
Hope/Crosby
  costar Dorothy: 6 LAMOUR
  destination: 3 RIO 4 BALI
Hoped-for
  reply: 3 YES

"Hope Floats"
  actress Rowlands: 4 GENA
Hopeful
  Contest: 7 ENTRANT
  Fraternity: 6 RUSHEE
  Hollywood: 7 STARLET
  Military: 5 CADET
Hopeless: 5 NOWIN 6 ABJECT
  case: 5 **GONER**
  situation: 9 LOSTCAUSE
Hopes
  Have high: 6 ASPIRE
Hopi
  doll: 7 KACHINA
  reservation site: 4 MESA
  ritual: 9 RAINDANCE
Hopkins, Anthony: 5 WELSH
  role: 5 NIXON 6 LECTER
  title: 3 SIR
___ Hopkins University: 5 JOHNS
Hopper: 3 BIN ROO 4 FLEA HARE
    TOAD
  Aussie: 3 **ROO**
  Columnist: 5 HEDDA
  Gossipy: 5 HEDDA
  load: 3 ORE
  Long-eared: 4 HARE
  Outback: 3 ROO
  Warty: 4 TOAD
Hopping
  Be ~ mad: 4 BOIL
  mad: 5 **IRATE** LIVID
Hoppy
  brew: 3 ALE
  quaff: 3 ALE
Hops
  dryer: 4 KILN OAST
  It has a head and: 3 ALE
    4 BEER
  kiln: 4 OAST
  product: 4 BEER
"Hop to it!": 4 MOVE
Hor.
  Opposite of: 4 VERT
Hora: 5 DANCE
Horace: 5 ODIST
  collection: 4 ODES
  Educator: 4 MANN
  work: 3 ODE

Horae
One of the: 5 IRENE
Horas
24 ~: 3 DIA
Horatian
creation: 3 ODE 5 EPODE
Horatio
Author: 5 ALGER
Horde: 4 SLEW 5 DROVE
6 THRONG
Highland: 4 CLAN
Member of a: 3 HUN
Horizon
Go below the: 3 SET
On the: 4 NIGH 5 AHEAD
Rise on the: 4 LOOM
Horizontal
handrail: 5 BARRE
line on a graph: 5 XAXIS
Make: 5 LEVEL
Hormel
product: 4 SPAM
Hormone
drug: 7 STEROID
Female: 8 ESTROGEN
Pituitary: 4 ACTH
Horn: 6 ANTLER
Big: 4 TUBA
blower: 6 TOOTER
Blow one's: 4 CROW TOOT
Get on the: 5 PHONE
Hit the: 4 HONK
Honk the: 4 TOOT
sound: 4 BEEP TOOT
Toot one's own: 4 BRAG 5 BOAST
Horne: 4 DIVA
Singer: 4 **LENA**
solo: 4 ARIA
Horned
beast: 5 RHINO
flyer: 3 OWL
goddess: 4 ISIS
lizard: 6 IGUANA
viper: 3 **ASP**
Horned Frogs
sch.: 3 TCU
Horner, Little Jack
dessert: 3 PIE
find: 4 PLUM

last words: 3 AMI
Hornet
home: 4 NEST
nest: 3 ADO
relative: 4 WASP
Horn of Africa
native: 6 SOMALI
Horns
Animal with curved: 4 IBEX
Animal with twisted: 5 ELAND
It may have: 7 DILEMMA
Hornswoggle: 3 CON 4 DUPE
HOAX HOSE ROOK
5 CHEAT
Hornswoggled: 3 HAD
Horny
bill: 4 BEAK
Horoscope
columnist Sydney: 5 OMARR
datum: 4 SIGN
Horrible: 5 AWFUL 8 GRUESOME
"Horrible"
comics character: 5 HAGAR
Horrified: 6 AGHAST
sound: 4 GASP
Horrify: 5 APPAL 6 APPALL
Horripilation: 10 GOOSEFLESH
Causing: 5 EERIE
Horror
Cry of: 4 OHNO
Cry of mock: 4 EGAD
First name in: 3 LON WES
4 BELA 5 BORIS 6 FREDDY
Horror film
actor Chaney: 3 LON
director Craven: 3 WES
Like a: 4 GORY 5 EERIE
11 HAIRRAISING
of 1954: 4 THEM
of 1996: 6 SCREAM
reaction: 4 GASP
sound: 6 SHRIEK
staple: 4 GORE
street: 3 ELM
Word in a ~ title: 8 CREATURE
"Horrors!": 3 EEK 4 EGAD OHMY
OHNO
Hors d'oeuvre: 6 CANAPE
Fancy: 6 CAVIAR

Spanish: 4 TAPA
spread: 4 PATE
Horse: 5 STEED 6 EQUINE
bit: 3 OAT
Came down off a: 4 ALIT
Charley: 4 ACHE
color: 4 **ROAN**
Colorful: 4 ROAN
controller: 4 REIN
course: 4 OATS OVAL
Dark: 4 ROAN
Fast: 4 ARAB
father: 4 SIRE
Female: 4 MARE
Fine: 4 ARAB 5 STEED
gait: 4 TROT
Graceful: 4 ARAB 7 ARABIAN
hair: 4 MANE
halter: 4 REIN WHOA
handler: 5 GROOM
High-spirited: 5 STEED
hoof sound: 4 CLOP
house: 4 BARN 6 STABLE
hue: 4 ROAN
Jousting: 5 STEED
lead: 6 HALTER
Like a: 5 MANED
Like a broken: 4 TAME
mackerel: 4 TUNA
morsel: 3 OAT
Mottled: 4 ROAN
of a different color: 4 ROAN
Old: 3 NAG
opera: 5 **OATER**
pace: 4 GAIT
play: 4 POLO 5 EQUUS
Reddish: 4 ROAN
Reddish-brown: 3 BAY 6 SORREL
River: 5 HIPPO
Show: 4 ARAB MRED
Small: 4 PONY
Spirited: 4 ARAB 5 STEED
Spot on a: 6 DAPPLE
Stereotypical: 6 DOBBIN
Swift: 4 ARAB
Talking ~ of TV: 4 MRED
TV: 4 MRED
Unbroken: 5 BRONC
War: 5 STEED

Winged ~ of myth: 7 PEGASUS
Word after: 5 SENSE
Young: 4 COLT
"___ horse!": 4 GETA
Horse-and-buggy: 3 ERA
travelers: 5 AMISH
Horseback
Game on: 4 POLO
Go on: 4 RIDE
Horse-drawn
vehicle: 6 HANSOM
"Horsefeathers!": 3 BAH ROT
5 PSHAW
Horsehide: 4 BALL
Pitch a: 4 HURL
"Horsepower"
coiner James: 4 WATT
Horses
Hold one's: 4 WAIT
Like show: 4 SHOD
Horseshoe
site: 4 HOOF
Horseshoe Curve
City near: 7 ALTOONA
Horseshoes
player: 6 TOSSER
scorer: 6 LEANER
Horseshoe-shaped
fastener: 5 UBOLT
symbol: 5 OMEGA
"___ horse to water ...": 5 LEADA
Horticulturist
of note: 13 LUTHERBURBANK
topic: 6 BOTANY
Horton
creator: 5 SEUSS
heard one: 3 WHO
Seuss's: 8 ELEPHANT
"Horton Hears ___": 4 AWHO
"Horton Hears a ___": 3 WHO
Horus
Father of: 6 OSIRIS
Mother of: 4 **ISIS**
Hose: 3 WET 5 SPRAY 6 NYLONS
color: 4 ECRU NUDE
Garden ~ problem: 4 KINK
hue: 4 ECRU 5 BEIGE TAUPE
ladder: 3 RUN
material: 5 NYLON

part: 3 TOE 6 NOZZLE
problem: 4 SNAG
shade: 4 ECRU 5 BEIGE TAUPE
woe: 3 RUN 4 SNAG
Word before: 5 PANTY

Hosea
Book after: 4 JOEL

Hosiery: 6 NYLONS
choice: 5 LEGGS
hue: 4 ECRU 5 BEIGE TAUPE
item: 6 ANKLET
material: 5 LISLE NYLON
problem: 4 SNAG
shade: 4 **ECRU** NUDE 5 TAUPE
thread: 5 LISLE
woe: 4 SNAG

Hoskins, Bob
role: 4 SMEE

Hosni
predecessor: 5 ANWAR

Hosp.
aide: 3 LPN
area: 3 **ICU**
areas: 3 **ERS ORS**
diagnostic: 3 MRI
employees: 3 DRS RNS
hookups: 3 IVS
machine: 3 MRI
picture: 3 MRI
readout: 3 EEG EKG
section: 3 ICU
sections: 3 ERS
Some ~ cases: 3 ODS
specialty: 3 TLC
staffer: 3 LPN
staffers: 3 RNS
test: 3 EKG
units: 3 ERS
ward: 3 ICU
worker: 3 LPN
workers: 3 MDS RNS

Hospice
Eastern: 6 IMARET
Hospitable: 8 PLEASANT
Less: 5 ICIER

Hospital
area: 5 PREOP
capacity: 4 BEDS
depts.: 3 ERS

figure: 5 NURSE
fluids: 4 SERA
helper: 4 AIDE
item: 6 BEDPAN
Like some ~ care: 8 NEONATAL
solution: 6 SALINE
staffer: 4 AIDE 6 INTERN
supplies: 4 **SERA**
unit: 3 BED
worker: 6 INTERN
    7 ORDERLY

Hospitality
area: 5 SUITE

Hoss
brother: 4 ADAM
dad: 3 BEN

Host: 4 ARMY SLEW 5 **EMCEE**
Answer to the: 4 RSVP
handout: 4 MENU
Late-night: 4 LENO
Roast: 5 **EMCEE**
Show: 5 EMCEE

Hostage
1979–81 ~ site: 4 IRAN
crisis group: 4 SWAT
Former ~ Terry: 5 WAITE

Hostel: 3 INN
Ute: 5 TEPEE

Hostelry: 3 **INN**

Hostess
Famous: 5 MESTA
snack cakes: 5 HOHOS

Hostile: 4 UGLY 5 ENEMY
    6 BITTER 7 ADVERSE
party: 5 ENEMY
reaction: 4 FLAK
to: 4 ANTI

Hostilities
Break in: 5 TRUCE
ender: 4 PACT 6 TREATY
Ongoing: 4 FEUD

Hosts: 3 MCS
MTV: 3 VJS
Roast: 3 MCS

Hot: 4 FOXY IRED RACY SEXY
    5 AFIRE IRATE RILED
    SPICY 6 EROTIC **STOLEN**
    TRENDY 7 ONAROLL
    PICANTE STEAMED

9 ONASTREAK
        10 ALLTHERAGE
air: 3 GAS
and dry: 7 SAHARAN
blood: 3 IRE 5 ARDOR
coal: 5 EMBER
drink: 3 TEA 4 GROG 5 TODDY
flick: 3 ASH
Get ~ and bothered: 7 STEAMUP
Get really: 6 SEERED
issue: 4 LAVA
It gets in ~ water: 6 TEABAG
It makes one: 3 IRE
Leaves in ~ water: 3 TEA
No longer: 3 OUT
Not: 4 COLD MILD
Not so: 4 WARM 5 **TEPID**
Not too: 4 SOSO
Not very: 5 TEPID
off the press: 3 NEW
pepper: 7 CAYENNE
pot: 4 STEW
rock: 4 LAVA
sandwich: 4 MELT
sauce: 5 SALSA 7 TABASCO
shot: 3 ACE
Some like it: 3 TEA 5 TODDY
        6 CEREAL TAMALE
spot: 3 SPA 4 HELL **OVEN**
        5 HADES SAUNA STOVE
        7 INFERNO
spring: 3 SPA
stuff: 4 LAVA LOOT 5 ANGER
        CHILI SALSA 7 CAYENNE
        TABASCO
temper: 3 IRE 5 ANGER
time: 4 JULY
time (abbr.): 3 AUG
time, in French: 3 ETE 4 AOUT
to trot: 4 AGOG AVID KEEN
        5 EAGER
tub: 3 **SPA**
tub part: 3 JET
under the collar: 4 SORE
        5 ANGRY IRATE RILED
Hot ___ (rock band): 4 TUNA
Hotbed: 4 NEST
Hotcakes
  Go like: 4 SELL

"Hot Diggity"
  singer: 4 COMO
Hot dog: 6 WEENIE WIENER
        WIENIE
  picker-upper: 5 TONGS
  topping: 5 CHILI 6 RELISH
  ~, once: 6 LASSIE
Hotel
  convenience: 4 SAFE
  employee: 4 MAID 5 VALET
        11 BELLCAPTAIN
  freebie: 3 ICE 4 SOAP
  Luxury ~, familiarly: 7 THERITZ
  name: 4 RITZ 5 HYATT LEONA
        6 HILTON
  offering: 5 SUITE
  posting: 5 RATES
  Resort: 3 SPA
  Rural: 3 INN
  sign: 3 ICE
  suffix: 3 IER
  upgrade: 5 SUITE
  ~ Bible name: 6 GIDEON
Hotfoot: 5 PRANK
  it: 3 HIE 5 SCOOT SPEED
Hothead
  Italian: 4 ETNA
Hotpoint
  competitor: 5 AMANA
Hot rod
  propellant: 5 NITRO
  rod: 4 AXLE
  sound: 5 VROOM
Hots: 4 LUST
Hotshot: 3 ACE
  Coll.: 4 BMOC
  Company: 4 EXEC
  pilot: 3 ACE
  Univ.: 4 BMOC
Hotsy-___: 5 TOTSY
"Hot Zone, The"
  topic: 5 EBOLA
Houdini: 8 ESCAPIST MAGICIAN
  feat: 6 ESCAPE
Houlihan
  portrayer: 4 SWIT
  rank: 5 MAJOR
Hound: 3 DOG NAG PET
        6 BASSET HARASS

Gazelle: **6** SALUKI
hint: **5** SCENT
holder: **5** LEASH
hounder: **4** FLEA
Long-eared: **6** BASSET
Low-slung: **6** BASSET
prey: **4** HARE

Hour
After the: **4** PAST
Evening: **4** NINE **5** SEVEN
Lunch: **3** ONE
Man of the: **4** HERO
Nearing the: **5** TENOF TENTO
   6 FIVETO
News: **6** ELEVEN
Prime-time: **3** TEN **4** NINE
Wee: **3** ONE TWO **5** ONEAM
   THREE TWOAM **6** FOURAM
Whistle: **4** NOON

Hourglass: 5 TIMER
filler: **4** <u>**SAND**</u>

Hourly
charge: **4** RATE
pay: **4** WAGE
wage: **4** RATE

Hours
1200 ~: **4** NOON
1300 ~: **3** ONE
After: **4** LATE
Every 24: **4** ADAY **5** DAILY
Keep late: **6** STAYUP
L.A.: **3** PST
Like early: **3** WEE
Many: **4** DAYS
Mass. summer: **3** EDT
NYC: **3** EST
Tenn.: **3** CST

House: 4 STOW **6** ENCASE
addition: **3** ELL
adjunct: **4** YARD
and grounds: **6** ESTATE
Animal: **3** ZOO **4** BARN CAGE
   LAIR
Bee: **6** APIARY
Big: **5** MANOR **7** MANSION
Bird: **4** CAGE NEST
Bring down the: **4** <u>**RAZE**</u>
call: **3** NAY YEA **4** VOTE
coat: **5** PAINT

Country: **5** DACHA
cover: **4** ROOF
extension: **3** ELL
Feature of an empty: **4** ECHO
Field: **5** TEPEE
Full: **4** HAND
Hash: **5** DINER
Horse: **4** BARN **6** STABLE
Ice: **5** IGLOO
It may be on the: **4** LIEN
Lady of the: **5** MADAM
Lord's: **5** MANOR
mem.: **3** REP
member: **4** LORD
of the lord: **5** MANOR
of worship: **6** TEMPLE
On the: **4** FREE
pet: **3** CAT
Place for a small: **4** TREE
Public: **3** INN
Religious: **6** PRIORY
Rough: **6** LEANTO
School: **4** FRAT
shower: **5** CSPAN
Sign of a full: **3** SRO
style: **5** TUDOR **7** CAPECOD
   8 COLONIAL
The big: **4** STIR
top: **5** ATTIC
Tree: **4** <u>**NEST**</u>
Upper: **6** SENATE
vote: **3** NAY YEA
wing: **3** ELL
work: **3** ACT
wrecker: **7** TERMITE
~, in Spanish: **4** CASA

"House"
actor Epps: **4** OMAR

Housecat: 3 PET
perch: **4** SILL

Housecleaning
Do some: **4** DUST

Housecoat: 6 DUSTER

Household: 6 MENAGE
animal: **3** PET
helper: **7** HELOISE
pest: **3** ANT **5** ROACH **6** REDANT
spirit: **3** LAR
spray target: **4** ODOR

task: 5 CHORE
"House Is Not ___, A": 5 AHOME
Housekeeping
Do some light: 4 DUST
"House of Blue Leaves, The"
playwright: 5 GUARE
House of Lords
member: 4 PEER
"House of the Seven Gables, The"
locale: 5 SALEM
House of York
symbol: 4 ROSE
Houseplant
Popular: 4 ALOE 8 ALOEVERA
9 AMARYLLIS
Spiny: 4 **ALOE**
Housework
Do some: 4 DUST
Housing
College: 4 DORM
cost: 4 RENT
Engine: 9 CRANKCASE
Fodder: 4 SILO
Hen: 4 COOP
Missile: 4 SILO
unit: 5 CONDO
Houston
baseballer: 5 ASTRO
footballer: 5 OILER
hockey player: 4 AERO
of Texas: 3 SAM
player: 5 ASTRO
Private eye: 4 MATT
pro: 5 ASTRO
team: 6 ASTROS
university: 4 RICE
Houston, Whitney
recording label: 6 ARISTA
Houstonian: 5 TEXAN
HOV
lane users: 8 CARPOOLS
Hovel: 5 SHACK 6 SHANTY
Hover: 4 HANG
Hoverer
Sci-fi: 3 UFO
Stadium: 5 BLIMP
How
Show: 5 TEACH
"How ___!": 4 RUDE TRUE

How-___ (instruction books):
3 TOS
"How about that!": 3 GEE
Howard
Actor: 4 DUFF
and others: 4 RONS
Director: 3 **RON**
of baseball: 6 ELSTON
Shock jock: 5 STERN
Sportscaster: 6 COSELL
Howard, Ron
film: 4 **EDTV** 6 RANSOM
role: 4 OPIE
"How awful!": 3 ICK 4 OHNO
"How can ___?": 5 ILOSE
"How Can ___ Sure" (1967 hit):
3 IBE
"How Can We Be Lovers"
singer Michael: 6 BOLTON
"How cute!"
exclamations: 3 AWS
"How disgusting!": 3 ICK UGH
"How Do I Live"
singer LeAnn: 5 RIMES
How-do-you-dos: 3 HIS
"How do you like ___ apples?":
4 THEM
"How dry ___": 3 IAM
Howdy
Hawaiian: 5 ALOHA
"Howdy": 4 HIYA
Howdy Doody
network: 3 NBC
original name: 5 ELMER
spot: 7 FRECKLE
"___ Howdy Doody time!": 3 ITS
Howe
Inventor: 5 **ELIAS**
of hockey: 6 GORDIE
Playwright: 4 TINA
Howe'er: 3 **THO**
However: 3 BUT YET
~, briefly: 3 **THO**
Howie
Comic: 6 MANDEL
Howl: 3 BAY 7 ULULATE
Howland Island
She never made it to: 7 EARHART
Howler: 4 RIOT WOLF 6 COYOTE

"How nice!": 3 AAH
"How obvious!": 3 DUH
"How revolting!": 3 UGH
"How sexy!": 7 OOHLALA
"How stupid of me!": 3 DOH
"How sweet ___!": 4 **ITIS**
"How the Grinch Stole Christmas"
  director Howard: 3 RON
"How the Other Half Lives"
  author Jacob: 4 RIIS
How-to
  help: 8 TUTORIAL
  listing: 4 STEP
"How to Handle a Woman"
  lyricist: 6 LERNER
**"How to Make an American
    Quilt"**
  author Whitney: 4 OTTO
"How to Murder Your Wife"
  actress Virna: 4 LISI
"How've you ___?": 4 BEEN
"How was ___ know?": 3 ITO
___ Hoya, Oscar
  Boxer: 4 DELA
Hoyle
  topic: 5 RULES
Hr.
  Lunch: 5 ONEPM
  part: 3 MIN
  Wee: 5 ONEAM
HRH
  Part of: 3 HER HIS
Hrs.
  Early: 3 AMS
H.S.
  class: 3 ALG ENG SCI 4 GEOG
    HIST TRIG
  exam: 3 SAT 4 PSAT
  math: 3 ALG 4 TRIG
  proficiency test: 3 GED
  promoter: 3 PTA
  requirement: 3 ENG
  subject: 3 ALG ENG SCI 4 GEOG
    HIST TRIG
Hsing-Hsing: 5 PANDA
___ Hsin-liang
  Taiwanese dissident: 3 HSU
HST
  predecessor: 3 FDR

  successor: 3 **DDE**
Ht.: 3 ALT 4 ELEV
http
  Address that begins with: 3 URL
HUAC
  Part of: 4 COMM
Huáscar
  subject: 4 INCA
Hub: 5 MECCA
  In the ~ of: 4 AMID
  Wheel: 4 NAVE
"Hubba hubba!": 6 OOLALA
       7 OOHLALA
  Person who might say: 5 OGLER
Hubbard
  Author: 4 LRON
  Hall of Famer: 3 CAL
  Scientology founder: 4 LRON
Hubbell
  of baseball: 4 CARL
  teammate: 3 OTT
Hubble
  Astronomer: 5 EDWIN
Hubbub: 3 **ADO** 4 STIR TODO
     5 NOISE 6 CLAMOR
     8 BROUHAHA
Huber
  of tennis: 4 ANKE
Hubert
  successor: 5 SPIRO
  Veep after: 5 SPIRO
Hubris
  source: 3 EGO
Huck
  conveyance: 4 RAFT
  follower: 4 STER
  of fiction: 4 FINN
  transport: 4 RAFT
"Huckleberry Finn"
  character: 3 JIM
HUD
  Former ~ head Jack: 4 KEMP
  Part of: 5 URBAN
  ~, for one: 4 DEPT
"Hud"
  actress Patricia: 4 **NEAL**
  director Martin: 4 RITT
  Oscar winner: 4 NEAL
Huddle: 6 POWWOW

Court: **7** SIDEBAR
Hudson: 3 CAR
Actress: **4** KATE
Canal to the: **4** ERIE
City on the: **4** TROY **6** ALBANY
N.J. city on the: **5** FTLEE
Hudson, Henry
ship: **8** HALFMOON
Hudson Bay
prov.: **3** ONT
tribe: **4** CREE
Hudson/Day
film: **10** PILLOWTALK
Hue: 4 TINT TONE **5** COLOR
SHADE
and cry: **5** FUROR **6** CLAMOR
Blue: **4 AQUA** NAVY TEAL
5 AZURE
Earth: **5** OCHER OCHRE
Green: **4** JADE
Horse: **4** ROAN
Hose: **4** ECRU **5** BEIGE TAUPE
Linen: **4** ECRU
Neutral: **4** ECRU
partner: **3** CRY
Pastel: **4** AQUA
Purple: **5** LILAC MAUVE
Shoe: **3** TAN
Huey
of politics: **4** LONG
~, Dewey, and Louie: **4** TRIO
~, Dewey, or Louie: **6** NEPHEW
Huff: 4 SNIT
and puff: **4** BLOW GASP **PANT**
Be in a: **4** STEW
Horsy: **5** SNORT
In a: **5** IRATE **7** STEAMED
Leave in a: **5** STORM
Huffington
Columnist: **7** ARIANNA
Huffy: 4 SORE
state: **4** SNIT
Hug: 5 CLASP **7** ENCLASP
givers: **4** ARMS
Huge: 4 EPIC VAST **5** GIANT
7 IMMENSE MASSIVE
amount: **3** SEA TON **5** OCEAN
~, in French: **6** ENORME
~, poetically: **5** ENORM

Hugh
French king: **5** CAPET
Magazine publisher: **6** HEFNER
nickname: **3** HEF
TV host: **5** DOWNS
Hughes
Poet: **3 TED**
Skater: **5** SARAH
Hughes, Howard
aircraft: **11** SPRUCEGOOSE
Company once owned by: **3** TWA
Studio once owned by: **3** RKO
Hughes, Langston
poem: **4 ITOO**
Hughes, Sarah
Emulate: **5** SKATE
leap: **4** AXEL LUTZ
Hugo: 5 AWARD
fugitive: **7** VALJEAN
Hugs
~, in letters: **3** OOO
~, symbolically: **3** OOO
"Huh?": 3 WHA **10** IDONTGETIT
Huitzilopochtli: 6 WARGOD
worshiper: **5** AZTEC
Hula: 5 DANCE
follower: **5** SKIRT
hoop: **3** FAD LEI
skirt material: **5** GRASS
Hulk
of wrestling: **5** HOGAN
"Hulk, The"
actor Bana: **4** ERIC
director Lee: **3** ANG
Hull
Captain: **5** ISAAC
marking: **8** LOADLINE
packing: **5** OAKUM
part: **4** KEEL **5** BILGE
Hullabaloo: 3 ADO DIN **4** STIR
5 HOOHA **6** RUMPUS
Hull House
founder: **6** ADDAMS
Hum: 4 WHIR **5** DRONE
Human: 5 BIPED **6** MORTAL
PERSON **7** ADAMITE
Act: **3** ERR
Be: **3** ERR
being: **5** BIPED **6** MORTAL

PERSON 7 ADAMITE
It's: 5 **TOERR**
Largest ~ organ: 4 SKIN
Period in ~ development:
   7 IRONAGE
rights gp.: 3 ILO 4 ACLU
suffix: 3 OID
The ~ senses: 6 PENTAD
trunk: 5 TORSO
Was: 5 ERRED

"Human Concretion"
sculptor: 3 ARP

"Human Condition, The"
author Arendt: 6 HANNAH

Humane
org.: 4 SPCA 5 ASPCA

Human Genome Project
topic: 3 DNA

Humanist
Dutch: 7 ERASMUS

Humanities: 4 ARTS
degs.: 3 BAS MAS
subj.: 3 ENG

Humanoid
Hairy: 4 YETI 7 BIGFOOT
Himalayan: 4 YETI

Humans: 4 RACE 6 PEOPLE

Humbert, Humbert
obsession: 6 LOLITA

Humble: 5 **ABASE** LOWLY
   6 DEMEAN
home: 3 HUT 5 ABODE
oneself: 7 EATDIRT
reply: 4 ITRY
Word after: 3 PIE

Humbled
Was: 7 ATECROW ATEDIRT

Humble Oil
Company that bought: 4 ESSO

Humboldt
City on the: 4 ELKO

Humbug
preceder: 3 BAH

Humdinger: 4 LULU ONER
   5 BEAUT DILLY DOOZY

Humdrum: 4 BLAH 8 TIRESOME

Humerus
locale: 3 ARM
neighbor: 4 **ULNA**

Humid: 3 WET 4 DAMP 5 MOIST

Humidifier
output: 5 VAPOR

Humidity
React to: 4 WILT

Humidor
item: 5 CIGAR CLARO
   6 HAVANA

Humiliate: 5 **ABASE** SHAME
   6 DEMEAN 7 DEGRADE

Humiliated
person: 7 DOORMAT
Was: 7 ATECROW ATEDIRT

Humiliation: 5 SHAME
Avoid: 8 SAVEFACE
Suffer: 7 EATCROW EATDIRT

Hummable: 6 CATCHY

Humming: 5 ABUZZ

Hummingbird
Hang like a: 5 HOVER

Hummus
holder: 4 **PITA**
ingredient: 6 SESAME TAHINI

Humongous: 5 GIANT LARGE

Humor: 7 CATERTO
First name in: 4 **ERMA**
Good ~ man: 3 WIT
Ill: 4 BILE 6 SPLEEN
Like some: 3 DRY WRY
   6 ETHNIC
magazine: 3 MAD
Often-missed: 5 IRONY
Old-fashioned: 4 CORN
Overwhelm with: 4 SLAY
Sense of: 3 WIT
with a twist: 5 IRONY

Humorous
Dryly: 3 WRY
fellow: 3 WAG
Whimsically: 5 DROLL

Humpback: 5 WHALE
herd: 3 POD

Humpbacked
helper: 4 IGOR

Humped
bovine: 4 ZEBU

Humperdinck
hero: 6 HANSEL
heroine: 6 GRETEL

Humperdinck, Engelbert
  hit song: 9 RELEASEME
Humphrey
  1960s veep ~: 6 HUBERT
  costar: 3 IDA
  nickname: 5 BOGIE
  role: 3 SAM
  successor: 5 AGNEW
Humphries, Barry
  character: 8 DAMEEDNA
Hump-shouldered
  animal: 3 GNU
Humpty Dumpty: 3 EGG
  Like: 5 OBESE OVATE
    OVOID
Humvee
  forerunner: 4 JEEP
Hun
  Head: 6 ATTILA
  king: 4 ATLI 6 ATTILA
Hunch
  Assistant with a: 4 IGOR
  Have a: 4 FEEL 5 **SENSE**
Hunchback
  Fictional: 4 IGOR
"Hunchback of Notre Dame, The"
  woman: 9 ESMERALDA
Hundred
  A ~ sawbucks: 4 ONEG
  dollar bill: 5 CSPOT
  Five ~ sheets: 4 REAM
  One of a D.C.: 3 SEN
  smackers: 5 CSPOT
Hundred Acre Wood
  denizen: 3 ROO 4 POOH
Hundredweight
  20 ~: 3 TON
Hung.
  neighbor: 3 AUS
Hungarian: 6 MAGYAR
  composer: 5 LISZT 6 BARTOK
  conductor: 5 SOLTI
  leader Kádár: 5 JANOS
  premier Imre: 4 NAGY
  premier Nagy: 4 IMRE
  sheepdog: 4 PULI
  spa town: 4 EGER
  stew: 7 GOULASH
  wine: 5 TOKAY

"Hungarian Dances"
  composer: 6 BRAHMS
"Hungarian Rhapsodies"
  composer: 5 LISZT
Hungary
  Nagy of: 4 **IMRE**
Hunger: 3 YEN
  Feeling of: 4 PANG
  for: 5 CRAVE
  (for): 4 LUST 5 YEARN
  Halt a ~ strike: 3 EAT
  It's from: 4 PANG
Hung-jury
  result: 7 RETRIAL
Hungry: 5 UNFED
  feeling: 4 PANG
  Still: 7 UNSATED
Hunk: 3 GOB 4 SLAB 6 ADONIS
    APOLLO
  of cheese: 4 SLAB
  of history: 3 ERA
  of meat: 4 SLAB
  pride: 3 BOD
Hunker
  down: 5 SQUAT
Hunky-dory: 3 AOK 4 FINE JAKE
    OKAY 5 DANDY SWELL
"Hunny"
  bear: 4 POOH
Huns
  King of the: 4 ATLI 6 ATTILA
Hunt: 8 SCAVENGE
  Actress: 5 HELEN LINDA
  for: 4 SEEK
  illegally: 5 POACH
  partner: 4 PECK
Hunted: 4 PREY
  animal: 4 PREY
  spheroid: 3 EGG
Hunter
  Actor: 3 IAN
  Actress: 3 KIM
  Author: 4 **EVAN**
  Bugs: 4 FUDD 5 ELMER
  Celestial: 5 ORION
  dog: 6 SETTER
  Heavenly: 5 **ORION**
  in the night sky: 5 ORION
  Moray: 5 EELER

Nocturnal: 3 OWL
Novelist: 4 **EVAN**
quarry: 3 ELK 4 PREY
target: 4 PREY
trail: 5 SPOOR
Writer: 4 **EVAN**
Hunter, Kim
role: 6 STELLA
"___ Hunter, The": 4 DEER
Hunting
dog: 5 HOUND 6 SETTER
expedition: 6 SAFARI
Legal ~ period: 10 OPENSEASON
Huntley
Newsman: 4 CHET
Huntress
Mythical: 5 DIANA 8 ATALANTA
Hupmobile
contemporary: 3 REO
Hurdle
Aspiring atty.'s: 4 LSAT
Classroom: 4 EXAM TEST
Clear a: 4 LEAP
Cow's ~, in rhyme: 4 MOON
Doctorate: 5 ORALS
Hannibal: 4 ALPS
Legal: 3 BAR
Hurdy-gurdy: 5 ORGAN
Hurl: 4 SPEW 5 THROW
Hurler
asset: 3 ARM
stat: 3 **ERA**
Hurley
Actress: 3 LIZ
Hurling: 5 SPORT
stat: 3 ERA
"Hurlyburly"
actor Sean: 4 PENN
playwright: 4 RABE
~ Tony winner Judith: 4 IVEY
Hurly-burly: 3 ADO
Hurok
Impresario: 3 **SOL**
Huron: 4 LAKE
neighbor: 4 ERIE
"Hurrah!": 3 YAY
for José: 3 OLE
"Hurray for me!": 6 IDIDIT
Hurricane: 5 STORM

center: 3 EYE
heading (abbr.): 3 ENE ESE
   NNE NNW SSE SSW WNW
   WSW
home: 5 MIAMI
of 1964: 4 DORA
of 1970: 5 CELIA
of 1972: 5 AGNES
of 1975: 6 ELOISE
of 1995: 4 OPAL
of 1999: 5 IRENE
of 2004: 4 IVAN
Hurriedly: 5 APACE 7 INHASTE
Hurry: 3 **HIE** 4 RUSH 5 SPEED
up: 4 RUSH
"Hurry!": 4 ASAP
Hurry-scurry: 3 ADO
"Hurry up!": 4 CMON 6 COMEON
   7 HOPTOIT 8 STEPONIT
Hurston, ___ Neale
Writer: 4 ZORA
Hurston, Zora ___
Author: 5 **NEALE**
Hurt: 3 AIL MAR 4 ACHE HARM
   PAIN 5 ACHED AILED
   SMART 6 HARMED
   OFFEND 7 SMARTED
badly: 4 MAIM
Hurting: 4 ACHY SORE
Husband: 4 MATE 5 STORE
   6 OLDMAN SAVEUP
   SPOUSE
~, in French: 4 MARI
Hush-hush: 6 SECRET
   9 TOPSECRET
Govt. ~ group: 3 CIA NSA
org.: 3 CIA **NSA**
WWII ~ group: 3 OSS
Hush puppy
material: 8 CORNMEAL
Husk: 8 SEEDCASE
Prickly: 3 BUR
site: 3 OAT
Wheat: 4 BRAN
Huskies
of the NCAA: 5 UCONN
Husk-wrapped
dish: 6 TAMALE
Husky: 6 HOARSE

burden: 4 SLED
cry: 3 ARF
trailer: 4 SLED
Husky-voiced: 6 HOARSE
Hussein, King
Widow of: 4 NOOR
Hussy: 4 MINX 7 JEZEBEL
Hustle: 3 HIE 4 RACE 5 DANCE
    SCOOT SPEED
and bustle: 3 ADO
music: 5 DISCO
"Hustler, The"
actress Piper: 6 LAURIE
game: 4 POOL
locale: 8 POOLHALL
    POOLROOM
prop: 3 CUE
role: 5 EDDIE
Hut: 5 HOVEL
material: 5 ADOBE
Hutchinson
Congressman: 3 ASA
Hutchison
Senator: 3 KAY
Hutu
country: 6 RWANDA
Huxley
Author: 6 ALDOUS
work: 13 BRAVENEWWORLD
Huxtable
mom: 5 CLAIR
son: 4 THEO
Huxtable, ___ Louise
Critic: 3 ADA
"Huzzah!": 3 YAY
~, in Spanish: 3 OLE
HVAC
measure: 3 BTU
Hwy.: 3 **RTE**
Coast: 4 RTEI
helpers: 3 AAA
Numbered: 3 **RTE**
with tolls: 3 TPK
Hwys.: 3 **RDS**
Hyacinth
holder: 4 VASE
Hyalite: 4 OPAL
Hyams
Actress: 5 LEILA

Hyannis
entrée: 5 SCROD
Hybrid
animal yielding low-fat meat:
    7 BEEFALO
cat: 5 LIGER TIGON
fruit: 4 UGLI 7 TANGELO
fuel: 7 GASOHOL
Hyde: 5 FIEND
alterego: 6 JEKYLL
~, to Jekyll: 8 ALTEREGO
Hyde Park
buggy: 4 PRAM
Hydra: 5 POLYP
Hydrant
hookup: 4 HOSE
___ hydrate (sedative):
    7 CHLORAL
Hydrocarbon
ending: 3 ANE ENE
Simple: 6 ETHANE
suffix: 3 **ANE ENE**
Type of: 6 OLEFIN
used as a solvent: 6 HEXANE
with a double bond: 6 ALKENE
Hydroelectric
agcy.: 3 TVA
project: 3 DAM
Hydrogen: 3 GAS
atomic number: 3 ONE
Heavy: 7 ISOTOPE
Hydrolysis
atom: 3 ION
product: 5 ANION
Hydromassage
facility: 3 SPA
Hydrophane: 4 OPAL
Hydrotherapy
place: 3 SPA
Hydrox
rival: 4 **OREO**
Hydroxide
Potassium: 3 LYE 6 ALKALI
Sodium: 3 LYE
Sodium ~, to a chemist: 4 NAOH
Hydroxyl
compound: 4 **ENOL**
Hygiene
Kind of: 4 ORAL

Hygienist
Dental ~ request: **5** RINSE
Hymn: 5 PSALM **8** DOXOLOGY
book: **7** PSALTER
Joyous: **5** PAEAN
Kind of: **7** CHORALE
of praise: **5** PAEAN
opener: **6** ADESTE
part: **4** ALTO
Sacred: **5** PSALM
Start of a: **4** OGOD
word: **4** AMEN
Hymnal
holder: **3** PEW
Hype: 4 PLUG **6** HOOPLA
7 PROMOTE **8** BALLYHOO
Hyperion: 5 TITAN
Daughter of: **3** EON
"Hyperion"
poet: **5** KEATS
Hyphen: 4 DASH
Hyphenated
~ ID: **3** SSN
Hypnotic
name: **6** MESMER

state: **6** TRANCE
Hypnotist
command: **5** SLEEP
Evil ~ of fiction: **8** SVENGALI
Pioneering ~ Franz: **6** MESMER
Hypnotized: 5 UNDER
Hypo
units: **3** CCS
Hypothesis
Start of a: **4** IFSO
___ hypothesis: **4** GAIA
Hypothesize: 5 POSIT
Hypothetical: 4 MOOT **6** WHATIF
particle: **5** AXION
primate: **6** APEMAN
question: **6** WHATIF
Hypotheticals: 3 IFS
Hyson: 3 TEA
Hysteria: 5 PANIC
area: **7** DEEPEND
Hysterical: 5 MANIC
person: **4** RIOT
Hyundai: 3 CAR **4** AUTO
competitor: **3** KIA
model: **6** SONATA **7** ELANTRA

Ii

I: 3 EGO ONE 4 ELEM 5 VOWEL
focus: 3 EGO
It may start with: 3 RTE
Latin: 3 EGO
problem: 3 EGO 7 EGOTISM
   8 EGOMANIA
The ~ of I.M. Pei: 4 IEOH
The ~ of IV: 5 INTRA
The ~ of TGIF: 3 ITS
topper: 3 DOT
~, in German: 3 ICH
~, in Greek: 4 IOTA
"¡"
ball: 3 DOT
I-5: 3 RTE
I-79
terminus: 4 ERIE
I-80: 3 RTE
Nevada city on: 4 ELKO
I-95: 3 <u>RTE</u>
Iacocca
Businessman: 3 LEE
IAD
posting: 3 ARR ETA ETD
Iago: 4 LIAR
Superior of: 7 OTHELLO
Wife of: 6 EMILIA
"I agree!": 4 AMEN
"I Ain't Marching Anymore"
singer: 4 <u>OCHS</u>
Iambs: 4 FEET
"I am ___ crook!": Nixon: 4 NOTA
Iams
competitor: 4 ALPO
"I Am Woman"
singer: 5 REDDY
Ian
Actor: 4 HOLM
"___ I a stinker?": 4 AINT
" ___ I a woman?": Sojourner
Truth: 5 ARENT
"I before E except after C":
   4 RULE

"I Believe"
singer Frankie: 5 LAINE
Iberia
Part of: 5 SPAIN
River that gives ~ its name:
   4 EBRO
Ibid.
relative: 5 OPCIT
IBM: 4 CORP
compatibles: 3 PCS
competitor: 3 NEC
Gerstner of: 3 LOU
Part of: 4 INTL
products: 3 PCS
Ibn ___: 4 SAUD
iBook: 3 MAC
Ibsen
character: 3 ASE 4 GYNT
   6 GABLER
city: 4 OSLO
dancer: 6 ANITRA
heroine: 4 NORA 5 HEDDA
play: 6 GHOSTS 8 PEERGYNT
Playwright: 6 HENRIK
Ibuprofen
brand: 5 ADVIL
target: 4 ACHE
"I burn"
Mount whose name means:
   4 ETNA
"I called it!": 4 DIBS
"I ___ Camera": 3 AMA
"___ I can help it!": 5 NOTIF
"I cannot ___ lie": 5 TELLA
"I cannot tell ___": 4 <u>ALIE</u>
"I can take ___!": 5 AHINT
"I can't believe ___ ...": 4 IATE
"I can't ___ satisfaction":
   5 GETNO
"I can't ___ thing!": 4 EATA
"___ I care!": 4 ASIF
Icarus
Father of: 8 DAEDALUS

"Icarus Agenda, The"
author: 6 LUDLUM
ICBM
First U.S.: 5 ATLAS
Part of: 5 INTER
Ice: 3 OFF 6 ENSURE
alternative: 7 SNOCONE
Arctic: 4 FLOE
Bobby on the: 3 ORR
breaker: 4 PICK
Celestial ~ ball: 5 COMET
device: 5 TONGS
Fake on the: 4 DEKE
Glide on: 5 SKATE
hockey team: 6 SEXTET
house: 4 IGLU 5 IGLOO
Jump on the: 4 **AXEL**
legend: 3 ORR
Lose control on: 5 SLIDE
mass: 4 BERG
melter: 3 SUN 4 SALT
pick: 3 AWL
pinnacle: 5 SERAC
Put on: 4 COOL 5 CHILL TABLE
Sans: 4 NEAT
sheet: 4 FLOE
They're kept on: 5 PUCKS
unit: 4 CUBE
Without: 4 **NEAT**
~, in German: 3 EIS
Ice ___ : 3 AGE 4 FLOE
Ice Age
elephant: 8 MASTODON
Iceberg
alternative: 7 ROMAINE
Ice cream
brand: 4 **EDYS**
drink: 4 MALT SODA 5 FLOAT
effect: 5 SWIRL
flavor: 4 **OREO** 5 MOCHA
    PECAN 6 COFFEE
    7 VANILLA 9 ROCKYROAD
    11 COOKIEDOUGH
Half an ~ flavor: 5 TUTTI
holder: 4 CONE
ingredient: 4 AGAR
maker Joseph: 3 EDY
One of an ~ duo: 3 BEN
parlor order: 6 FRAPPE SUNDAE

pattern: 5 SWIRL
purchase: 4 PINT
serving: 3 DIP 5 SCOOP
thickener: 4 AGAR
With: 7 ALAMODE
Ice Cube: 6 RAPPER
Real first name of: 5 OSHEA
Iced: 5 DIDIN
tea garnish: 5 LEMON
~, with "in": 3 DID
~, with "up": 4 SEWN
Iceland
feature: 5 FJORD
money: 5 KRONA
ocean (abbr.): 3 ATL
"Iceland"
star: 5 HENIE
"Iceland Fisherman, An"
author Pierre: 4 LOTI
Icelandic
epic: 4 **EDDA**
singer: 5 BJORK
Iceless: 4 NEAT
Iceman
Legendary: 3 ORR
"Iceman ___ , The": 6 COMETH
"Iceman Cometh, The"
playwright: 6 ONEILL
Ice skater
event: 5 PAIRS
figures: 6 EIGHTS
leap: 4 AXEL
"Ice Storm, The"
director Lee: 3 ANG
Ice-T
genre: 3 RAP
"Ich bin ___ Berliner": 3 EIN
"Ich ___ dich": 5 LIEBE
"I Ching"
reader: 6 TAOIST
Icicle
former: 4 DRIP
site: 4 **EAVE**
"Ici on ___ français": 5 PARLE
"Ick!": 5 GROSS
Icky
stuff: 3 GOO 4 CRUD GLOP
    GOOK GUNK OOZE 5 SLIME
    6 SLUDGE

"I, Claudius"

"I, Claudius"
role: 4 NERO
star: 6 JACOBI
Icon: 5 IMAGE
Place for an: 4 APSE
unit: 5 PIXEL
"I could ___ horse!": 4 **EATA**
"I couldn't care less"
attitude: 6 APATHY
"I could write ___": 5 ABOOK
ICU
conduit: 6 IVTUBE
hookups: 3 IVS
Quickly, in the: 4 STAT
staff: 3 RNS
The U in: 4 UNIT
Icy: 4 COLD 5 ALOOF GELID
burg: 4 NOME
coating: 4 HOAR RIME
forecast: 5 SLEET
It can be: 5 STARE
mass: 4 BERG
rain: 4 HAIL 5 SLEET
remark: 4 BRR
Tended to ~ roads: 6 SANDED
threat: 4 BERG
treat: 7 SNOCONE
ID
Ask for: 4 CARD
Book: 4 ISBN
Common: 3 SSN
Cop: 5 BADGE
Driver's: 3 LIC
High-tech: 3 DNA
IRS: 3 SSN
Library: 4 ISBN
Merchandise: 3 UPC
Nine-digit: 3 SSN
"Id ___": 3 EST
Ida.
neighbor: 3 NEV ORE WYO
4 MONT
Idaho: 4 SPUD 5 TATER
capital: 5 BOISE
motto word: 4 ESTO
nickname: 8 GEMSTATE
product: 4 SPUD 6 POTATO
"I dare you!": 4 DOIT
5 TRYME

Idea: 4 CLUE 6 NOTION
7 CONCEPT
Central ~, in music: 4 TEMA
Discover, as an: 5 HITON
7 HITUPON
Main: 4 GIST 5 THEME
Novel: 4 PLOT 5 STORY
Start of an: 4 GERM SEED
Took hold, as an: 6 SANKIN
Unifying: 5 THEME
Ideal: 5 DREAM 6 EDENIC
7 PARAGON
Eastern: 3 **TAO**
place: 4 EDEN 6 UTOPIA
___ ideal: 3 EGO
Idealist: 7 UTOPIAN
Idealistic
one: 7 QUIXOTE
Ideally: 6 ATBEST
15 INAPERFECTWORLD
"___ Ideas" (1951 song): 4 IGET
Idée ___: 4 FIXE
Identical: 4 **SAME** TWIN 5 ALIKE
EQUAL 6 CLONED
8 SELFSAME
Regard as: 6 EQUATE
to: 6 SAMEAS
Identification
Formal phrase of: 5 ITISI
Miss: 3 SHE
Old station: 4 ESSO
Identifier
Corporate: 4 LOGO
High-tech: 3 DNA
Wildlife: 6 EARTAG
Identify: 3 PEG 4 **NAME**
5 LABEL
Identifying
mark: 4 SCAR
Identity: 3 EGO 7 ONENESS
Assumed: 5 ALIAS
Give new ~ to: 6 RENAME
Question of: 3 WHO
Secret ~ preserver: 4 MASK
"___ Identity, The": 6 BOURNE
Ideology: 3 ISM
Ides
Ninth day before the: 5 NONES
rebuke: 4 **ETTU**

618

"I'd hate to break up ___":
4 ASET

Idi
Notorious: 4 AMIN

"I did it!": 4 **TADA**

"I didn't know that!": 3 GEE

Idiom
Specialized: 5 ARGOT

Idiosyncrasy: 3 TIC 5 QUIRK

Idiosyncratic: 3 ODD

Idiot: 4 BOZO DODO DOLT
5 MORON
box: 5 TVSET 6 TEEVEE
boxes: 3 TVS
light word: 3 OIL

Idiotic: 4 DUMB 5 INANE
7 ASININE

Iditarod
command: 4 MUSH
destination: 4 NOME
racer: 4 SLED
setting: 6 ALASKA
terminus: 4 NOME
vehicle: 4 SLED

Idle: 4 LOAF 5 NOTON 6 OTIOSE
Comic: 4 **ERIC**
Stays: 4 SITS
Was: 3 SAT

Idler: 9 DONOTHING
opposite: 4 DOER

"I'd like to buy ___": 3 ANA ANE
ANI ANO

Idly
Chatter: 5 PRATE
Pass time: 4 LAZE
Scribble: 6 DOODLE

"I do": 3 VOW

"I do!": 3 YES

"I Do I Do I Do I Do I Do"
group: 4 ABBA

Idol
Biblical: 4 BAAL
Chinese: 4 JOSS
Kind of: 4 TEEN 7 MATINEE
Like an: 6 ADORED
Polynesian: 4 TIKI
worshipper: 3 FAN

Idolize: 5 **ADORE** 6 DOTEON

Idolizer: 6 ADORER

"I don't buy it!": 5 PSHAW

"I Don't Buy Kisses Anymore"
costar Peeples: 3 NIA

"I don't give ___!": 4 ARAP
5 AHOOT

"I don't think so!": 3 NAH 4 NOPE
UHUH

"I don't want to hear it!":
5 SHUSH 7 SPAREME

"I'd rather not": 3 NAH

"I Dream of Jeannie"
star Barbara: 4 EDEN

"I dropped it!": 4 OOPS

IDs
Corp.: 3 TMS

"I'd walk ___ for ...": 5 AMILE

Idyllic
place: 4 **EDEN**
setting: 3 LEA

Idylls: 5 POEMS

"Idylls of the King"
lady: 4 ENID

i.e.: 5 IDEST 6 THATIS
Part of: 3 EST
Relative of: 3 VIZ

If: 6 INCASE
all else fails: 7 ATWORST
all goes well: 6 ATBEST
E'en: 3 THO
Even: 3 THO 5 ALTHO 6 ALBEIT
Except: 6 UNLESS
need be: 8 INAPINCH
not: 4 **ELSE**
nothing changes: 6 ASITIS

"If all ___ fails ...": 4 **ELSE**

"I Fall to Pieces"
singer Patsy: 5 CLINE

"If ___ a nickel ...": 4 IHAD

"If ___ Answers": 4 AMAN

"If ___ be so bold ...": 4 IMAY

"If He Walked Into My Life"
musical: 4 MAME

"If I Could Turn Back Time"
singer: 4 CHER

"If I Had a Hammer"
singer: 10 PETESEEGER

"If I ___ Hammer": 4 HADA

Ifill
Newswoman: 4 GWEN

"If I Only Had the Nerve"
  singer: 4 LAHR
"If I ___ Rich Man": 5 WEREA
"If I Ruled the World"
  rapper: 3 NAS
"If it ___ broke ...": 4 AINT
"If I Were a Rich Man"
  singer: 5 TEVYE
"If I Were King of the Forest"
  singer: 4 LAHR
"If I Were ___ Man": 5 ARICH
"If ___ nickel ...": 5 IHADA
"If only!": 5 IWISH
"If only that were true!": 5 IWISH
"I forbid": 4 VETO
"I forgot the words"
  syllables: 4 LALA
"I found it!": 3 AHA
"If they could ___ now ...":
  5 SEEME
"If ___ Would Leave You":
  5 EVERI
"If ___ you ...": 5 IWERE
"If You Knew ___": 5 SUSIE
"I get it!": 3 AHA
"I give!": 5 UNCLE
"I give up!": 5 UNCLE
  8 ITSNOUSE
Iglesias
  tune: 4 AMOR
Igloo
  dweller: 5 INUIT 6 ESKIMO
  dwellers (abbr.): 4 ESKS
Ignatius
  of Loyola: 6 JESUIT
Igneous
  rock: 6 BASALT 7 DIORITE
    8 FELDSPAR
  rock source: 5 MAGMA
Ignite: 5 LIGHT 6 KINDLE
Ignited: 3 **LIT**
  again: 5 RELIT
Igniter
  Lighter: 5 FLINT
Ignominy: 5 ODIUM SHAME
Ignorance
  ~, in an adage: 5 BLISS
"Ignorance ___ excuse!": 4 ISNO
Ignorant: 7 UNAWARE

of right and wrong: 6 AMORAL
Ignore: 4 OMIT SKIP 5 ELIDE
  7 TUNEOUT
  15 CLOSEONESEYESTO
  Doesn't: 5 HEEDS OBEYS
  intentionally: 4 SNUB
  the alarm clock: 7 SLEEPIN
  the limit: 5 SPEED
  the script: 5 ADLIB
  ~, with "out": 4 TUNE
"I Got ___" (1973 song): 5 ANAME
"I ___ Grow Up": 4 WONT
Iguana
  relative: 5 ANOLE
"I had no ___!": 4 IDEA
"I Hated, Hated, Hated This
  Movie"
  author: 5 EBERT
"I hate to break up ___": 4 ASET
"I have found it!": 6 EUREKA
"I have ___ good authority":
  4 ITON
IHOP
  order: 5 STACK 7 LARGEOJ
    SMALLOJ
  Part of: 4 INTL
___ II (Gillette razor brand):
  4 TRAC
II Chronicles
  Book after: 4 EZRA
___ II Men: 4 BOYZ
"I ___ it!": Red Skelton: 4 DOOD
Ijsselmeer
  City on the: 4 EDAM
"I Just Wanna Stop"
  singer Vannelli: 4 GINO
Ike
  Colleague of: 4 OMAR
  command in WWII: 3 ETO
  Ex-wife of: 4 **TINA**
  hometown: 7 ABILENE
  initials: 3 DDE
  Opponent of: 5 ADLAI
  She didn't like: 4 TINA
  Wife of: 5 MAMIE
"___ Ike" ('50s slogan): 5 ILIKE
Ikhnaton
  successor: 3 TUT
"I ___ kick ...": 5 GETNO

"I Kid You Not"
autobiographer: 4 PAAR
"I kiss'd thee ___ I kill'd thee":
Othello: 3 ERE
"___ I Kissed You" (Everly Brothers
hit): 3 TIL
"I knew it!": 3 AHA
"I know what you're up to!":
3 OHO
Il ___ (Mussolini): 4 DUCE
Ile ___-Hélène: 3 STE
Iliac
prefix: 5 SACRO
"Iliad": 4 EPIC EPOS
bickerer: 4 HERA
king: 5 PRIAM
Like the: 4 EPIC
sage: 6 NESTOR
setting: 4 TROY
warrior: 4 AJAX ARES
Ilie
of tennis: 7 NASTASE
Iliescu
Former Romanian president:
3 ION
"I Like ___" ('50s slogan): 3 IKE
Ilium: 4 TROY 7 HIPBONE
Ilk: 4 KIND SORT TYPE
Ill
Be: 3 AIL
feelings: 10 NOLOVELOST
humor: 4 BILE 6 SPLEEN
It may be: 6 REPUTE
temper: 3 IRE 4 BILE
treatment: 5 ABUSE
Was ~ with: 3 HAD
will: 3 IRE 4 HATE 5 SPITE
6 ANIMUS ENMITY MALICE
RANCOR
Ill.
neighbor: 3 IND WIS
Ill at ___: 4 EASE
Ill-behaved: 3 BAD
"I'll be ___ of a gun!": 4 ASON
"I'll be right there!": 6 ONESEC
Ill-considered: 4 RASH 5 HASTY
6 UNWISE 7 ASININE
"I'll do it!": 5 LETME
"I'll drink to that!": 4 AMEN

Illegal
block: 4 CLIP
entry: 6 BAGJOB
firing: 5 ARSON
interest: 5 USURY
liquor: 9 MOONSHINE
Make: 3 BAN
parker's foe: 5 TOWER
Illegally
Fix: 3 RIG
Hunt: 5 POACH
off base: 4 AWOL
resell: 5 SCALP
seize: 5 USURP
Take: 3 ROB 4 SKIM
Illegible
signature: 6 SCRAWL
Ill-fated: 5 HEXED 6 DAMNED
DOOMED TRAGIC
auto: 5 EDSEL
flier: 6 ICARUS
mission of 1967: 7 APOLLOI
sub of 2000: 5 KURSK
"I'll get right ___!": 4 ONIT
"I'll go along with that": 4 OKAY
Ill-gotten
gains: 4 LOOT PELF SWAG
5 BOOTY GRIFT
11 FILTHYLUCRE
Ill-humored: 4 DOUR 5 CROSS
SURLY
Illicit
cigarette: 6 REEFER
drug inits.: 3 PCP
Illinois
city: 5 ALTON CAIRO ELGIN
SALEM 6 MOLINE PEORIA
URBANA
City on the: 6 PEORIA
neighbor: 4 IOWA
port: 5 CAIRO 6 PEORIA
Illiterate
Signed like an: 3 XED
Ill-mannered: 4 RUDE
sort: 4 BOOR LOUT
"Illmatic"
rapper: 3 NAS
Illness
End of an: 4 ITIS

Infant: **5** COLIC
Severe: **7** BADCASE
"I'll say!": **4** AMEN
"I'll speak a prophecy ___ go":
Shakespeare: 4 EREI
Ill-suited: 5 INAPT UNFIT
"I'll take that as ___": 3 ANO
Ill-tempered: 4 MEAN **5** NASTY
SURLY TESTY **6** ORNERY
Illuminated: 5 LITUP
sign: **4** EXIT
Illuminating
gas: **4** NEON
Illumination
Evening: **10** NIGHTLIGHT
Vegas: **4** NEON
Illusion: 6 MIRAGE
Illusionist
feat: **15** DISAPPEARINGACT
Illusory
paintings: **5** OPART
promise: **11** PIEINTHESKY
Illustrator
One-named: **4** ERTE
Illustrious: 5 FAMED NOBLE
NOTED **6** FAMOUS
7 EMINENT
"Ill wind that no one blows
good": 4 OBOE
"Il mio tesoro": 4 ARIA
"Il Nome Della Rosa"
author: **3** ECO
"I Lost It at the Movies"
author: **4** KAEL
I love
~, in French: **5** JAIME
~, in Latin: **3** _AMO_
"I Love a Parade"
composer: **5** ARLEN
"I Love Lucy"
network: **3** CBS
"I Love Rock 'n Roll"
singer Joan: **4** JETT
"I Loves You, Porgy"
singer: **4** BESS
singer Nina: **6** SIMONE
Ilsa
Love of: **4** RICK
maiden name: **4** LUND

Where ~ met Rick: **5** PARIS
~, to Rick: **3** KID
"Il Trovatore": 5 OPERA
soprano: **4** INEZ
___ Ilyich
Tolstoy's: **4** IVAN
IM
carrier: **3** AOL
I.M.
Architect: **3** PEI
"I'm ___!": 4 ONIT
iMac
maker: **5** APPLE
rivals: **3** PCS
"___, I'm Adam": 5 MADAM
Image: 4 ICON **7** PERSONA
8 LIKENESS
Computer: **4** ICON
Computer ~ format: **3** GIF
4 JPEG
Corporate: **4** LOGO
Graven: **4** IDOL
maker: **5** PRMAN
Medical: **4** SCAN
Photog: **3** NEG
Public: **3** REP **7** PERSONA
Radar: **4** BLIP
receiver: **6** RETINA
Imaginary: 6 UNREAL
belt: **6** ZODIAC
eternal flower: **8** AMARANTH
line: **4** AXIS
Not: **4** REAL
Imaginative: 5 NOVEL
Was: **8** HADIDEAS
Imagine: 5 OPINE **6** IDEATE
7 PICTURE
"Imagine ___!": 4 THAT
Imagined: 6 DREAMT
Not: **4** REAL
Imago
Future: **4** PUPA
"I'm all ___": 4 EARS
"I'm all ears!": 5 TRYME
6 DOTELL
Imam
book: **5** KORAN
Iman
Model ~, for one: **6** SOMALI

Imbalance
Economic: 8 TRADEGAP
Imbibe: 5 DRINK
to excess: 4 TOPE
Imbibed
some: 7 HADANIP
Imbroglio: 4 MESS SPAT
Imbue: 5 STEEP 6 INFUSE
"I mean ...": 6 THATIS
Imelda
collection: 5 SHOES
"___, I'm Falling in Love Again":
4 OHOH
"I'm freezing!": 3 BRR
"I'm game!": 4 LETS
"I'm ___ here!": 4 OUTA
5 OUTTA
"I'm impressed!": 3 GEE OOH
WOW 4 NICE 5 NEATO
I-minded
individual: 6 EGOIST
"I'm innocent!": 5 NOTME
Imitate: 3 APE 4 COPY 5 MIMIC
6 MIRROR PARROT
7 ACTLIKE
Imitating: 5 APING
Imitation: 4 FAUX MOCK SHAM
5 APERY 6 ERSATZ
Grotesque: 8 TRAVESTY
In ~ of: 5 AFTER
Prone to: 5 APISH
Imitative: 5 APISH 6 ECHOIC
7 COPYCAT
sort: 4 APER
Imitator: 4 APER
Life: 3 ART
"I'm kidding!": 3 NOT
"I'm listening": 4 GOON
Immaculate: 4 PURE 5 CLEAN
Immanuel
Philosopher: 4 KANT
Immature: 5 YOUNG 6 UNRIPE
7 PUERILE
egg cell: 5 OVULE 6 OOCYTE
newt: 3 EFT
Immeasurable
chasm: 5 ABYSS
time: 3 EON 4 AEON
Immediate: 4 NEAR

Immediately: 3 NOW 4 STAT
6 ATONCE PRESTO
after: 4 UPON
if not sooner: 3 PDQ
~, in the ER: 4 STAT
"Immediately!": 4 ASAP STAT
Immense: 3 BIG 4 HUGE VAST
Immensely: 4 ALOT ATON
5 NOEND
Enjoyed: 5 ATEUP
Immerse: 3 DIP 4 SOAK 5 BATHE
SOUSE STEEP 6 PLUNGE
Immigrant
course (abbr.): 3 ESL
island: 5 ELLIS
Japanese: 5 ISSEI
Japanese ~ descendant:
6 SANSEI
subj.: 3 ESL
Immigration
island: 5 ELLIS
Imminent: 4 NEAR
Be: 4 LOOM
Imminently: 4 SOON
Immobilize: 6 HOGTIE SPLINT
Immobilized: 7 INACAST
Immoderate
revelry: 4 ORGY
"Immoralist, The"
author: 4 GIDE
Immortal
coaching name: 5 KNUTE
Soccer: 4 PELE
~ Giant: 3 OTT
Immovable
blockage: 6 LOGJAM
Immune
response stimulus: 7 ANTIGEN
system agent: 5 TCELL
Immunity
One with: 8 DIPLOMAT
Immunization: 4 SHOT
letters: 3 DPT
Immunologist
study: 7 ANTIGEN
"I'm not ___ complain ...":
5 ONETO
Imogene
Comedienne: 4 COCA

Partner of: 3 SID
"I'm OK, You're OK"
  author: 6 HARRIS
"I'm outta here!": 4 CIAO 5 ADIOS
      LATER SEEYA
Imp: 4 BRAT PEST 5 DEMON
      DEVIL 6 RASCAL URCHIN
      8 DEVILKIN
Impact
  Main: 5 BRUNT
  sound: 3 BAM 4 BANG THUD
      WHAM 5 SPLAT
Impair: 3 MAR 4 HARM HURT
      MAIM
Impala
  kin: 5 ELAND
Impale: 5 SPEAR
Impaler, The
  Ruler known as: 4 VLAD
Impart: 4 LEND LOAN 7 INSTILL
Impartial: 4 FAIR JUST
___ impasse (stuck): 4 **ATAN**
Impassioned: 6 ARDENT
Impassive: 5 **STOIC** STONY
      6 STOLID WOODEN
      7 STOICAL
Impatience:
      15 ANTSINONESPANTS
  Sign of: 4 HONK
Impatient: 5 ANTSY HASTY
  acknowledgment: 6 YESYES
  cry: 3 NOW YAH
Impeach: 6 ACCUSE
Impeachment
  juror: 7 SENATOR
  Nixon ~ chairman: 6 RODINO
Impecunious: 4 POOR 5 NEEDY
Impedance
  unit: 3 OHM
Impede: 5 DETER 6 HINDER
      HOBBLE RETARD
  legally: 5 ESTOP
Impeder
  Progress: 4 SNAG
Impediment: 4 SNAG
  Speech: 4 LISP
Impel: 4 GOAD URGE 5 DRIVE
Impend: 4 LOOM
Impending: 4 NEAR

Impenetrable: 5 DENSE
Imperative: 4 MOOD 5 AMUST
  Sentry: 4 HALT
Imperfect: 6 MARRED
  Be: 3 ERR
  Make: 3 MAR
Imperfection: 4 **FLAW** WART
      5 STAIN 6 DEFECT
  Hose: 4 SNAG
  Mug: 3 ZIT
  Road: 4 BUMP
  Sign of: 7 ERASURE
Imperial
  autocrat: 4 TSAR
  decree: 5 UKASE
  product: 4 OLEO
Imperil: 8 ENDANGER
Impersonate: 3 APE 6 POSEAS
Impersonator: 4 APER
Impertinence: 3 LIP 4 SASS
      5 CHEEK
Impertinent: 4 FLIP RUDE
      5 SASSY SAUCY
  one: 4 SNIP
  stare: 4 OGLE
Imperturbable: 5 STOIC
      6 SERENE
Impetuous: 4 **RASH** 5 BRASH
      6 MADCAP
  ardor: 4 ELAN
  motion: 6 PLUNGE
Impetuously: 7 ONADARE
  Begin: 8 PLUNGEIN
Impetus: 4 FUEL 5 DRIVE FORCE
Impiety: 3 SIN
Impish: 6 ELFISH
  smile: 4 GRIN
  sort: 5 PIXIE
Implant: 3 SOW 5 EMBED
      6 ENROOT
"I'm pleased!": 4 GOOD
Implement: 4 TOOL
Implied: 5 GOTAT MEANT **TACIT**
Implore: 3 BEG 4 PRAY URGE
      5 PLEAD 7 ENTREAT
Imply: 4 MEAN 5 AIMAT GETAT
      6 HINTAT 7 CONNOTE
Impolite: 4 RUDE
  look: 4 **LEER** OGLE 5 STARE

sound: 5 SLURP
Import: 5 SENSE TENOR
　　6 WEIGHT
　duty: 6 TARIFF
Importance
　Of no: 5 PETTY
　___ importance: 4 OFNO
Important: 3 BIG KEY 6 OFNOTE
　　9 REDLETTER
　exam: 5 FINAL
　grain: 4 OATS
　Is: 7 MATTERS
　Most: 4 MAIN
　Not as: 6 LESSER
　numero: 3 UNO
　period: 3 ERA
　sort: 7 SOMEONE
　time: 3 **ERA**
Imported
　auto: 4 AUDI
　cheese: 4 EDAM
Imports
　Pricey: 4 BMWS
Importune: 3 BEG 4 URGE
　　7 ENTREAT
Impose: 3 PUT 4 LEVY 5 FOIST
　a fine: 6 AMERCE
　a second levy on: 5 RETAX
Impose ___ on: 4 ABAN
Imposing
　entrance: 6 PORTAL
　structure: 7 EDIFICE
"Impossible!": 6 CANTBE
　　7 NOCANDO
"___ impossible!": 3 ITS
Impostor: 4 FAKE SHAM
Impoverished: 4 POOR 5 NEEDY
　　6 INNEED
Impractical: 8 QUIXOTIC
　idealist: 9 STARGAZER
　one: 7 DREAMER
Imprecise
　ordinal: 3 NTH
Impresario
　production: 5 OPERA
Impress: 3 WOW 4 DENT 5 PRINT
　deeply: 3 AWE 4 ETCH
　It may be added to: 3 IVE
　More than: 3 AWE

Impressed
　Not: 6 UNAWED
Impression: 4 DENT IDEA
　　5 SENSE
　Do an ~ of: 3 APE
　Lasting: 4 **SCAR**
　Make an: 4 DENT ETCH
Impressionist: 4 APER
Impressive
　grouping: 5 ARRAY
　Long and: 4 EPIC
Imprint: 5 STAMP
　firmly: 4 ETCH
Imprison: 5 EMBAR
Impromptu
　bookmark: 6 DOGEAR
　percussion: 6 SPOONS
　playing: 10 JAMSESSION
Improper: 5 AMISS UNDUE
Improprieties: 5 NONOS
Improv
　style: 4 SCAT
Improve: 4 HONE MEND
　　5 AMEND 6 ENRICH
　　7 ENHANCE
　~, as beef: 3 AGE
　~, as text: 5 EMEND
Improvement: 7 UPGRADE
Improvisational
　composition: 7 TOCCATA
　style: 4 SCAT
Improvise: 4 VAMP 5 ADLIB
　　6 FAKEIT NOODLE
　　WINGIT
　vocally: 4 SCAT
Improvised: 5 ADHOC ADLIB
　　7 STOPGAP
　accompaniment: 4 VAMP
Impudence: 3 LIP 4 GALL SASS
　　5 BRASS CHEEK SAUCE
Impudent: 4 PERT 5 BRASH
　　SASSY
　girl: 4 MINX 5 HUSSY
　talk: 3 LIP
　youth: 5 WHELP
Impulse: 4 **URGE** WHIM
　carrier: 4 AXON
　conductor: 4 AXON 6 NEURON
　Nerve ~ region: 7 SYNAPSE

transmitter: 4 AXON
Impulsive: 4 RASH
Impurities
Free from: 6 REFINE
Impute: 7 ASCRIBE
Imre
Former Hungarian premier:
4 NAGY
"I'm Real"
singer, familiarly: 3 JLO
"I'm ___ Sexy": 3 TOO
"I'm so glad!": 3 YAY
"I'm Sorry"
singer Brenda: 3 LEE
"I'm thinking ...": 3 HMM
"___ I'm told": 4 ORSO
"I'm too ___ for my shirt": 4 SEXY
"I'm ___ you!": 4 ONTO
"I ___ my wit's end": 4 AMAT
In: 3 HOT MOD 4 AMID CHIC
6 AMIDST **ATHOME**
TRENDY 7 ELECTED
ELECTEE
Not: 4 AWAY 5 PASSE UNHIP
on: 5 HEPTO 6 WISETO
7 PRIVYTO
In ___
(actually): 4 **ESSE**
(as found): 4 SITU
(bored): 4 ARUT
(calmly): 6 STRIDE
(entirely): 4 TOTO
(even): 4 ATIE
(existing): 4 ESSE
(harmonious): 4 SYNC
(intrinsically): 6 ITSELF
(lined up): 4 AROW
(not yet born): 5 UTERO
(soon): 4 ABIT
(stuck): 4 AJAM ARUT 5 ABIND
(together): 4 SYNC 6 UNISON
(unborn): 5 UTERO
(undisturbed): 4 SITU
(untidy): 5 AMESS
___ in (cozy in bed): 6 TUCKED
"___ In" (1976 Wings hit):
5 LETEM
Ina
Actress: 5 BALIN

Inability
Musical: 6 TINEAR
___ in a blue moon: 4 ONCE
Inaccurate: 3 OFF 5 NOTSO
6 UNTRUE
Be: 3 ERR
Inactive: 4 IDLE 6 ATREST
7 DORMANT
Inactivity: 6 STASIS 7 INERTIA
Inadequate: 3 BAD LOW 4 LAME
POOR 5 SCANT 6 SCARCE
Inadvertently
Say: 7 LETSLIP
Inadvisable
action: 4 NONO
"I ___ Name": 4 GOTA
___ in a million: 3 ONE
Inamorata
of Valentino: 5 NEGRI
Inamorato: 4 BEAU 5 LOVER
Inane: 5 DOPEY LOONY
9 SENSELESS
___ in apple: 3 AAS
"In apprehension how like ___":
Hamlet: 4 AGOD
Inasmuch
as: 5 SINCE
(as): 6 SEEING
Inaugural
ball: 4 GALA
Inauguration
1960 ~ speaker: 5 FROST
highlight: 4 **OATH**
In-basket
item: 4 MEMO
stamp (abbr.): 4 RECD
"___ in Boots": 4 PUSS
In-box
clutter: 4 SPAM
Ed.'s ~ filler: 3 MSS
filler: 5 MEMOS
input: 5 EMAIL
Inc.
alternative: 3 LTD
workers: 3 EDS
~, abroad: 3 CIE **LTD**
Inca
land: 4 PERU
Incalculable: 6 UNTOLD

"___ in Calico": 4 AGAL
Incan
  capital: 5 CUZCO
Incandescence: 4 GLOW
Incandescent: 5 AGLOW
  lamp gas: 5 ARGON
Incantation: 5 SPELL
  opener: 4 **ABRA**
Incarcerate: 4 JAIL
Incarnation
  Hindu: 6 AVATAR
  of Vishnu: 4 RAMA
Incendiary: 8 ARSONIST
  stuff: 6 NAPALM
Incense: 3 IRE 5 ANGER
      6 ENRAGE 7 MAKEMAD
  resin: 5 MYRRH
  stick: 4 JOSS
Incensed: 5 ANGRY IRATE
Incentive
  Sales: 6 **REBATE**
  Worker's: 5 BONUS
Inception: 4 DAWN 5 ONSET
      6 ORIGIN
Incessantly: 4 EVER 5 NOEND
      7 NONSTOP ONANDON
  Bother: 5 EATAT
Inch: 4 UNIT 5 SIDLE
  .001 ~: 3 MIL
  Part of an: 4 PICA
  ___ in Charlie: 3 CAS
Inched: 5 CREPT
Inches
  36 ~: 4 YARD
  45 ~: 3 ELL
  6,272,640 square ~: 4 ACRE
  About 39 ~: 5 METER METRE
  Nine: 4 SPAN
Inchon
  City near: 5 SEOUL
Incident: 5 EVENT 7 EPISODE
  Bench-clearing: 5 SETTO
"___ Incident, The": 5 OXBOW
Incidentally
  ~, in e-mail shorthand: 3 BTW
Incidentals
  cash: 8 PINMONEY
Incision: 4 SLIT 5 NOTCH
Incisor: 5 TOOTH

  neighbor: 6 CANINE
Incite: 4 GOAD PROD URGE
      5 EGGON ROUSE
      6 SPURON 7 PROVOKE
  to action: 5 EGGON IMPEL
Inclement: 5 NASTY RAINY
Inclination: 4 BENT BIAS 5 BEVEL
      SLANT SLOPE 7 MINDSET
      8 TENDENCY
Incline: 3 TIP 4 LEAN RAMP
      TEND TILT 5 GRADE
      SLANT SLOPE 7 DISPOSE
Inclined: 3 **APT** 5 ATILT LEANT
      PRONE 6 ASLOPE
      7 OFAMIND
  Be: 4 TEND
  Not: 6 AVERSE
  Very: 5 STEEP
Include: 3 ADD 4 HAVE 5 ADDIN
  Fail to: 4 **OMIT**
Includes: 3 HAS
Including: 4 WITH 6 SUCHAS
      8 ASWELLAS
Inclusion
  MS.: 4 SASE
  Phrase of: 6 ETALII
Inclusive
  abbr.: 3 ETC 4 ETAL
  ___ incognita: 5 TERRA
Income: 4 FEES 7 REVENUE
  component: 8 NETSALES
  French: 5 RENTE
  Landlord: 4 RENT
  Like some: 8 UNEARNED
  Madison Ave.: 6 ADFEES
  Magazine: 3 ADS
  Some ~ (abbr.): 3 INT
Incoming
  flight (abbr.): 3 ARR
  flight info: 3 ETA
Incomparable: 6 UNIQUE
  ending: 3 EST
Incompatible
  Be: 5 CLASH
Incompetent: 6 UNABLE
  sort: 3 OAF
Incomplete: 7 PARTIAL
"Incompleteness theorem"
  formulator: 5 GODEL

Incongruity
  Literary: **5** IRONY
Inconsiderate: 4 RUDE
Inconsistent: 6 SPOTTY UNEVEN
       7 ERRATIC
  Be: **4** VARY
Inconvenience: 6 HASSLE
Incorporate
  new territory: **5** ANNEX
Increase: 4 BUMP GOUP GROW
       HIKE RISE **5** ADDTO
       BOOST REVUP RUNUP
       6 STEPUP **7** ENHANCE
  by 200%: **6** TREBLE
  gradually: **6** ACCRUE
  Sudden: **5** SURGE
  ~, with "up": **3** REV
Increaser
  IRA: **3** INT
  Price: **3** TAX
  Signal: **3** AMP
Incredible
  bargain: **5** STEAL
  story: **4** YARN
Incredulous
  Visibly: **5** AGAPE
Incriminate: 5 RATON
Incriminating
  info: **4** DIRT
Incubation
  station: **4** NEST
Incubator
  occupant: **7** NEONATE
  spot (abbr.): **3** ICU
Incur: 5 RUNUP
Incurred: 5 **RANUP**
Incursion: 4 RAID **5** FORAY
Ind.
  neighbor: **3** ILL
Indebted: 7 OBLIGED
  Be ~ to: **3** **OWE**
Indecisive
  Be: **3** HEM **5** WAVER **6** WAFFLE
Indeed: 3 YEA **6** REALLY
"Indeed!": 3 YES **5** OHYES
Indelicate: 4 RACY
Indemnify: 5 REPAY
Indentation: 5 CLEFT NOTCH
       6 RECESS

Independence
  Financial: **10** EASYSTREET
  It gained ~ in 1991: **7** ESTONIA
"Independence Day"
  actor: **5** QUAID
  invaders: **3** ETS
Independent
  emirate since 1971: **5** QATAR
  land since 1991: **8** SLOVENIA
  Like many ~ films: **4** ARTY
  Make: **4** WEAN
Independently: 5 APART
Index
  Market: **3** DOW
  UV ~ monitor: **3** EPA
  Wall St.: **4** NYSE
India
  1998 headline event in ~:
       5 NTEST
  Ancient invader of: **5** ARYAN
  British rule in: **3** **RAJ**
  City of: **4** AGRA **5** DELHI
       6 MADRAS MYSORE
  Coin of: **5** RUPEE
  Conductor born in: **5** MEHTA
  First P.M. of: **5** **NEHRU**
  Language of: **5** HINDI TAMIL
  Like ~ paper: **4** THIN
  neighbor: **5** NEPAL
  Nursemaid of: **4** AMAH
  Prince of: **4** RAJA
  Princess of: **4** RANI **5** RANEE
  Sir, in: **5** SAHIB
  Song of: **4** RAGA
  State of: **5** **ASSAM**
  tourist mecca: **4** AGRA
  Where ~ is: **4** ASIA
  ~ Inc.: **3** LTD
India.___
  Singer: **4** ARIE
Indian: 5 ASIAN OCEAN
  address: **5** SAHIB
  Alabama: **4** CREE
  Andean: **4** INCA
  Arizona: **4** HOPI PIMA
       6 NAVAHO NAVAJO
  attire: **4** SARI
  Big: **4** RAJA
  bread: **3** NAN

butter: 4 GHEE
Canadian: 4 CREE
chief: 4 RAJA 5 RAJAH
city: 5 DELHI
coin: 5 RUPEE
Colorado: 3 UTE
corn: 5 MAIZE
craft: 5 CANOE
Dakota: 3 REE
Delaware: 6 LENAPE
dress: 4 SARI
drum: 5 TABLA 6 TOMTOM
dwelling: 5 HOGAN TEPEE
elephant driver: 6 MAHOUT
garment: 4 SARI
head: 4 CENT
home: 4 ASIA
honorific: 3 SRI 5 SAHIB
instrument: 5 SITAR
king: 4 RAJA
Lake: 4 ERIE
language: 5 HINDI
lentil dish: 3 DAL
Longfellow: 8 HIAWATHA
Manitoba: 4 CREE
Midwest: 3 SAC 4 OTOE
movie area: 9 BOLLYWOOD
music: 4 RAGA
music first name: 4 RAVI
Nebraska: 3 OTO 4 OTOE
    5 OMAHA 6 PAWNEE
New Mexico: 4 ZUNI
nursemaid: 4 AMAH
Oklahoma: 3 OTO SAC 4 **OTOE**
    5 OSAGE 6 PAWNEE
Peruvian: 4 INCA
Plains: 3 OTO 4 CREE OTOE
    5 KIOWA OSAGE 6 PAWNEE
    7 ARAPAHO
poet: 6 TAGORE
pole: 5 TOTEM
Pre-Aztec: 6 TOLTEC
prince: 4 RAJA 5 **RAJAH**
princess: 4 RANI 5 RANEE
Pueblo: 4 **HOPI** TIWA ZUNI
silk center: 5 ASSAM
Southwestern: 3 UTE 4 HOPI
state: 5 **ASSAM**
title: 3 SRI 5 SAHIB

tourist city: 4 **AGRA**
Western: 3 OTO **UTE** 4 HOPI
    OTOE
Indian ___ : 5 OCEAN
Indiana
basketballer: 5 PACER
city: 4 GARY PERU 7 ELKHART
county: 7 LAPORTE
Former ~ governor Bayh: 4 EVAN
Former ~ senator Birch: 4 BAYH
river: 6 WABASH
senator: 5 LUGAR
state flower: 5 **PEONY**
Indiana Jones: 4 HERO
quest: 3 ARK
trademark: 6 FEDORA
Indianapolis
team: 5 COLTS
university: 6 PURDUE
Indiana University
locale: 6 KOKOMO
Indian Ocean
vessel: 4 DHOW
Indians: 4 TEAM 6 ASIANS
on scoreboards: 3 CLE
Indic
language: 4 URDU
Indicate: 6 DENOTE SIGNAL
    7 BESPEAK POINTAT
    POINTTO
assent: 3 NOD
Indicated: 7 BESPOKE
Indication: 4 HINT OMEN SIGN
Little-hand: 4 HOUR
Tree-ring: 3 AGE
Indicator
Econ.: 3 GNP
Future: 4 OMEN
Insertion: 5 CARET
Maiden-name: 3 **NEE**
Market: 3 DOW
Pause: 5 COMMA
Pitch: 4 CLEF NOTE
Price: 3 TAG
RPM: 4 TACH
Sale: 6 REDTAG
Second-sequel: 3 III
Sellout: 3 SRO
Tie: 3 ALL

Wind: **4** SOCK VANE
Indifference: 6 APATHY
Indifferent: 4 SOSO **5** ALOOF
JADED
Ethically: **6** AMORAL
Indigence: 4 NEED
Indigenous: 6 ETHNIC NATIVE
Indigent: 5 NEEDY
Indigestion
cause: **4** ACID
Indignant: 5 HETUP
Feel ~ about: **6** RESENT
reaction: **4** SLAP
~, with "up": **3** HET
Indignation: 3 <u>IRE</u> **7** OUTRAGE
Indigo: 3 DYE **4** ANIL
source: **4** <u>ANIL</u>
Indira
Father of: **5** NEHRU
Son of: **5** RAJIV
Indirect: 3 WRY
10 ROUNDABOUT
Make ~ reference: **6** ALLUDE
Indiscretion: 4 SLIP
Indispensable: 5 VITAL
Indisposed: 3 ILL **6** AVERSE
UNWELL
15 UNDERTHEWEATHER
Indistinct: 3 DIM **4** HAZY **5** BLEAR
FAINT MISTY
Become: **4** BLUR FADE
Indistinctly
Speak: **4** SLUR **6** MUTTER
Indistinguishable: 4 SAME
Individual: 3 ONE **4** LONE SELF
6 ENTITY PERSON
effort: **4** SOLO
performances: **4** SOLI
share: **4** ANTE
Individualist: 5 LONER
Individuality: 4 SELF **5** STYLE
Individually: 4 APOP EACH
6 APIECE
Indivisible: 3 <u>ONE</u>
Indochinese
language: **3** LAO
Indo-European: 5 <u>ARYAN</u>
Indolence: 5 SLOTH
Indolent: 4 LAZY **6** OTIOSE

Indomitable
spirit: **4** GRIT
Indonesia
is in it: **4** OPEC
Part of: **4** BALI
Indonesian
ape: **5** ORANG
Certain: **8** SUMATRAN
island: **4** <u>BALI</u> JAVA **5** CERAM
TIMOR **6** BORNEO
7 SUMATRA
islands: **3** ARU
ox: **4** ANOA
Indoor
ball: **4** NERF
"In Dreams"
actor: **3** REA
"Indubitably": 3 YES
Induce
to a crime: **6** SUBORN
Inducement
Illegal: **5** BRIBE
Inducer
Admiration: **3** AWE
Sleep: **6** OPIATE **7** SANDMAN
Yawn: **4** BORE
Induction
motor inventor: **5** TESLA
unit: **5** GAUSS TESLA
Indulge: 5 HUMOR **7** CATERTO
in daydreaming:
10 WOOLGATHER
oneself: **7** SPLURGE
to excess: **6** OVERDO
Indulged
in vanity: **6** PRIDED
Indulgence
Bout of: **5** SPREE
Period of: **4** ORGY
Indus
Where the ~ flows: **4** ASIA
Industrial
container: **3** VAT
German ~ city: **5** <u>ESSEN</u>
German ~ region: **4** <u>RUHR</u>
giant: **4** CZAR
Japanese ~ center: **5** OSAKA
Industrious
group: **5** DOERS

insect: 3 **ANT**
Industriousness
  Symbol of: 3 ANT
Industry
  big shot: 4 CZAR 5 BARON
  Captain of: 7 MAGNATE
  Cloning: 7 BIOTECH
  Fashion: 8 RAGTRADE
  prefix: 4 AGRO
  Symbol of: 3 ANT 4 LOGO
"Industry"
  Its motto is: 4 UTAH
Indy
  Al of: 5 UNSER
  Big initials at: 3 STP
  Compete at: 4 RACE
  entrant: 5 RACER 7 RACECAR
  Family name at: 5 UNSER
  leader: 7 PACECAR
  letters: 3 STP
  mishap: 7 SPINOUT
  path: 4 OVAL
  service area: 3 PIT
  sponsor: 3 STP
  stop: 3 PIT
  The Unsers of: 3 ALS
Indy 500
  1983 ~ winner: 5 SNEVA
  1986 ~ winner: 5 **RAHAL**
  and others: 5 RACES
  area: 3 PIT
  entrant: 3 CAR 5 RACER
  Four-time ~ winner: 4 FOYT
      5 UNSER
  letters: 3 STP
  sponsor: 3 STP
  winner Luyendyk: 4 ARIE
Inebriate: 3 SOT
Inebriated: 3 LIT
Inedible
  Become: 3 ROT
  mushroom: 9 TOADSTOOL
  orange: 5 **OSAGE**
"I Need to Know"
  singer Anthony: 4 MARC
Ineffective: 4 VOID WEAK
      6 OTIOSE
  Make: 6 NEGATE
Ineffectual: 6 NOHELP

Inefficiency
  Eliminate: 10 CLEANHOUSE
Inept: 4 POOR 6 GAUCHE
  Less: 5 ABLER
  Socially: 5 NERDY
  soldier: 7 SADSACK
Ineptitude
  Musical: 6 TINEAR
Inert
  gas: 4 NEON 5 ARGON RADON
      XENON
  Some are: 5 GASES
Ines, ___ Juana (Mexican poet):
  3 SOR
"I never ___ man ...": 4 META
Inevitable: 4 SURE 5 FATED
      8 FOREGONE
Inexact
  words: 4 ORSO
Inexperienced: 3 NEW RAW
      5 GREEN 6 CALLOW
Infamy
  Symbol of: 6 STIGMA
Infant: 4 BABY
  Appaloosa: 4 FOAL
  food: 3 PAP
  illness: 5 COLIC
  word: 4 DADA
Infantile
  outburst: 3 WAH
Infantry
  campsite: 5 ETAPE
  group: 11 SHOCKTROOPS
Infatuate: 5 BESOT
Infatuated: 4 GAGA 7 SMITTEN
  with: 6 SOFTON
Infatuation: 5 CRUSH
Infected: 5 GERMY 6 SEPTIC
Infection
  fighter: 5 SULFA
  Kind of: 5 STAPH VIRAL
  site: 4 STYE
  suppressants: 4 SERA
Infer: 5 EDUCE 6 DERIVE
      GATHER
Inferior: 4 POOR 5 WORSE
      6 CHEAPO CHEESY
      LESSER SHABBY
  in quality: 6 TRASHY

liquor: 6 ROTGUT
"Inferiority complex"
coiner Alfred: 5 ADLER
Infernal: 6 NETHER
"Inferno, The"
author: 5 **DANTE**
First word of: 3 NEL
Infest: 7 OVERRUN
Infidel
in Islam: 5 KAFIR
Infield
cover: 4 **TARP**
Hit beyond the: 5 BLOOP
Infielder
stat.: 3 DPS
Infiltrator: 4 MOLE 5 PLANT
In fine ___ : 6 FETTLE
Infinitesimal: 4 TINY
amount: 4 IOTA
Infinitive
French 101: 4 ETRE
Latin I: 4 ESSE
Inflame: 5 ANGER
Inflamed: 3 LIT RED 5 ANGRY
suffix: 4 ITIC
Inflammation
Eyelid: 4 STYE
Joint: 4 GOUT
Inflammatory
suffix: 4 ITIS
Inflatable
item: 3 EGO 4 RAFT
Inflate: 3 PAD
Inflated
It may be: 3 EGO
Sell at an ~ price: 5 SCALP
Inflation
Cause of: 3 AIR
fighter: 15 PRICEREGULATION
fighting WWII org.: 3 OPA
meas.: 3 CPI PSI
victim: 3 EGO
Inflationary
path: 6 SPIRAL
Inflection: 4 TONE
Inflexibility: 5 RIGOR
Inflexible: 4 IRON 5 RIGID
7 ADAMANT 8 CASTIRON
OBDURATE

Inflict: 5 WREAK
upon: 4 DOTO
In-flight
info: 3 ETA 4 ETAS
Influence: 4 BIAS HEFT PULL
SWAY 5 CLOUT COLOR
JUICE 6 AFFECT
Area of: 6 SPHERE
Sphere of: 5 ORBIT REALM
6 DOMAIN
Wield: 5 EXERT
Influential
group: 5 ELITE
Highly ~ and original:
7 SEMINAL
individual: 5 NABOB
member: 5 ELDER
Org. with an ~ journal: 3 AMA
Info: 4 DATA DOPE NEWS POOP
STAT
gathering: 5 RECON
Inside: 3 TIP 4 DOPE POOP
Infomercial
directive: 5 TRYIT 6 ACTNOW
muscles: 3 ABS
Infomercials: 3 ADS
Big name in: 5 RONCO
Popeil of: 3 RON
Inform: 7 APPRISE
(on): 3 RAT
Informal
affirmative: 3 YEP YUP 4 YEAH
bid: 5 ONENO
chat: 10 RAPSESSION
evening: 4 NITE
goodbyes: 5 CIAOS
greeting: 3 HEY 4 HIHO HIYA
5 HOWDY HULLO
refusal: 4 NOPE
shirt: 3 TEE
sign-off: 3 LUV 5 LATER
speech: 5 SLANG
talk: 4 CHAT
Information: 4 DATA DOPE
bank: 8 DATABASE
Bit of: 4 FACT 5 DATUM
broker: 7 TIPSTER
Fresh: 4 NEWS
Kind of: 6 INSIDE

medium: **5** CDROM
One way to get: **5** DIALO
Seek: **3** ASK
unit: **4** BYTE
Informative: 5 NEWSY
Informed: 5 AWARE CLUED
about: **4** UPON
Better: **5** WISER
of: **4** ONTO
Informer: 3 RAT **6** CANARY
     7 STOOLIE
     11 STOOLPIGEON
Infraction
Grid: **4** CLIP
Hockey: **5** ICING
Pinball: **4** TILT
Infrequent: 4 RARE
Infrequently: 6 SELDOM
Infuriate: 3 IRE **4** RILE **5** ANGER
     6 ENRAGE MADDEN
Infuse: 5 STEEP
with oxygen: **6** AERATE
Inge
dog: **5** SHEBA
Ingenious: 6 CLEVER
Ingenuous: 5 NAIVE
Least: **6** SLYEST
Ingest: 3 EAT
Ingle
glowers: **5** COALS
Ingot: 3 BAR
Ingrain: 4 ETCH
Ingratiate: 6 ENDEAR
Ingredient: 6 FACTOR
Ingrid
Daughter of: **3** PIA
role: **4** ILSA
Inhabitant
suffix: **3** ITE
Inhalation
Noisy: **5** SNORT
of fright: **4** GASP
Inhaler
target: **6** ASTHMA
Inherent
quality: **6** NATURE
Inherently: 5 PERSE
Inheritance
factor: **4** GENE

Genetic: **5** TRAIT
Inherited: 3 GOT **8** CAMEINTO
They're: **5** GENES
wealth: **8** OLDMONEY
Inheritors
Earth: **4** MEEK
"Inherit the Wind"
star: **5** TRACY
Inhibit: 5 CRIMP DETER
Inhibited
Less: **5** FREER
Iniquity: 3 SIN **4** EVIL VICE
site: **3** DEN
Initial: 4 OKAY
advantage: **7** TOEHOLD
chip: **4** ANTE
instruction: **7** STEPONE
stake: **4** ANTE
Initialed: 3 OKD
Initiated: 5 BEGAN
Initiation: 5 ONSET
practice: **4** RITE
Initiative
Took the: **3** LED
Injecting
device: **4** HYPO
Injection: 4 SHOT
fluids: **4** SERA
selection: **7** SYRINGE
Injure: 3 MAR **4** HARM HURT
     MAIM 5 WOUND
a knee: **4** SKIN
Injured: 4 HURT
sneakily: **5** KNEED
Support for an ~ arm: **5** SLING
~, literally: **4** LESE
Injuries
Like some: **6** SPINAL
Injury: 4 HARM
Muscle: **6** STRAIN
Psychological: **6** TRAUMA
sign: **4** SCAR
Injustice: 5 WRONG
Ink: 4 SIGN
Black ~ entry: **5** ASSET
Cuttlefish: **5** SEPIA
Kind of: **3** SOY **5** INDIA
Like a debtor's: **3** RED
Like some: **8** ERASABLE

Like wet: 6 SMEARY
Red: 4 DEBT
Red ~ amount: 4 LOSS
smear: 4 BLOT
sources: 6 OCTOPI
stain: 4 BLOT
~, in French: 5 ENCRE
Ink-jet
alternative: 5 LASER
Inkless
pen: 3 STY
Inkling: 4 CLUE HINT **IDEA**
    5 GLINT
Have an: 5 SENSE
Inks
Chemical salt in some:
    7 TANNATE
Inky
mess: 4 BLOT
Inlaid
design: 6 MOSAIC
Inland
sea: 4 **ARAL**
In ___ land: 4 **LALA**
In-law: 6 AFFINE
Borgia: 4 ESTE
LBJ: 4 ROBB
Lennon: 3 ONO
Lincoln: 4 TODD
Inlay
material: 5 NACRE 6 NIELLO
Inlet: 3 ARM **RIA** 4 COVE
    7 ESTUARY
Marshy: 5 BAYOU
Narrow: 3 **RIA** 5 FJORD
River: 3 **RIA**
Scottish: 5 FIRTH
Sheltered: 4 COVE
In-line
item: 5 SKATE
Inmate: 3 CON
hope: 6 PAROLE
Long-term: 5 LIFER
In medias ___: 3 **RES**
"In memoriam"
item: 4 OBIT
Inn: 5 HOTEL 8 HOSTELRY
Arabian: 5 SERAI
French: 7 AUBERGE

Inexpensive: 6 HOSTEL
inventory: 4 ALES BEDS
Kind of: 5 BANDB
name: 6 RAMADA
Spanish: 6 POSADA
Turkish: 5 SERAI 6 IMARET
Innards
Virus: 3 RNA
Watch: 5 WORKS
Inner
circle: 4 LOOP 5 CADRE
city area: 6 BARRIO GHETTO
connection: 5 SINEW
drive: 4 URGE
ear: 3 COB
prefix: 3 ESO 4 ENDO ENTO
self: 5 ANIMA
tubes: 4 TORI
tube surrounder: 4 TIRE
turmoil: 5 ANGST
vision: 4 XRAY
Inner Hebrides
island: 4 IONA SKYE
Innermost: 4 CORE
Innie: 5 NAVEL
Inning
enders: 4 OUTS
Extra: 5 TENTH
half: 6 BOTTOM
Last ~, usually: 5 NINTH
Like a good ~ for a pitcher:
    5 NOHIT
trio: 3 ENS
Innings
Cause for extra: 3 TIE
Pitches between: 3 ADS
Innisfree
He celebrated: 5 YEATS
Innkeeper: 8 HOSTELER
Italian: 4 OSTE 7 PADRONE
Innocence
Affected: 7 COYNESS
Epitome of: 4 LAMB
Innocent: 4 BABE LAMB NAIF
    5 NAIVE 6 CHASTE
    CHERUB
and others: 5 POPES
one: 4 BABE LAMB
Plead: 4 DENY

remark: 5 NOTME
Innovative: 3 NEW
Innsbruck
is its capital: 5 TYROL
province: 5 TIROL
Innuendo: 4 SLUR
Inoculation
fluids: 4 SERA
In ___ of: 5 LIEU
___ in on (near): 4 HOME
Inoperative: 4 NOGO
Inopportune: 8 ILLTIMED
"In other words ...": 5 IMEAN
In ___ parentis (legal doctrine):
4 LOCO
"In principio ___ verbum": 4 ERAT
Input: 5 ENTER
anew: 6 RETYPE 7 REENTER
Inquest: 6 ASSIZE
Inquire: 3 **ASK**
Inquiries
Make: 9 ASKAROUND
Inquiry: 5 PROBE
Judicial: 6 ASSIZE
Shipping: 6 TRACER
Inquisition
choker: 7 GARROTE
Inquisitive: 4 NOSY
Be: 3 PRY
Ins.
choice: 3 HMO
Insane: 3 MAD 8 DERANGED
Inscribe: 4 ETCH
Inscribed
pillar: 5 STELA **STELE**
Inscription
Ancient: 4 RUNE
Calvary: 4 INRI
Crucifix: 4 **INRI**
Part of a cornerstone: 4 ANNO
Statue: 8 EPIGRAPH
Tombstone: 3 RIP
Towel: 3 HIS 4 HERS
Insect
Adult: 5 IMAGO
Annoying: 4 GNAT
Colorful hill: 6 REDANT
Destructive: 5 BORER 6 LOCUST
Domesticated: 3 BEE

egg: 3 NIT
feelers: 5 PALPS
Flying: 4 MOTH
form: 4 PUPA
Gnatlike: 5 MIDGE
Industrious: 3 **ANT**
midsection: 6 THORAX
nest: 4 NIDI
Nocturnal: 6 EARWIG
Noisy: 6 CICADA
Pesky: 4 **GNAT**
Praying: 6 MANTIS
repellent: 4 DEET
Sap-sucking: 5 APHID
Showy: 6 IOMOTH
Shrill: 6 CICADA
Slender-waisted: 4 WASP
Social: 3 ANT
stage: 4 **PUPA** 5 IMAGO LARVA
Stinging: 4 WASP 6 HORNET
Strong: 3 ANT
study (abbr.): 5 ENTOM
wings: 4 ALAE
with pincers: 6 EARWIG
Insecticide
Banned: 3 **DDT**
ingredient: 7 ARSENIC
Insectivorous
insect: 6 MANTIS
Insensitive
Isn't: 5 FEELS
sort: 4 BOOR
Inseparable: 3 ONE
He and his brother were: 3 ENG
Insert: 3 ADD 5 PANEL
mark: 5 CARET
Insertion
mark: 5 **CARET**
Inset: 3 MAP
site: 5 ATLAS
Inside
diameter: 4 BORE
Fit one ~ another: 4 NEST
Go: 5 ENTER
info: 3 TIP 4 DOPE POOP
look: 4 XRAY 7 CATSCAN
prefix: 4 ENDO
scoop: 4 DIRT
shot: 4 XRAY

Turn ~ out: 5 **EVERT**
"Inside Politics"
    broadcaster: 3 CNN
Insider
    D.C.: 3 POL
    Espionage: 4 MOLE
    vocabulary: 5 ARGOT
"Inside the Actors Studio"
    network: 5 BRAVO
"Inside the NFL"
    network: 3 HBO
"Inside the Third Reich"
    author: 5 SPEER
Insidious: 3 SLY 4 EVIL
    sort: 5 SNAKE
Insight: 5 SENSE 6 ACUMEN
    Cry of: 3 AHA
    Mock phrase of: 4 AHSO
Insightful: 4 DEEP KEEN
        6 ASTUTE
Insignia: 6 EMBLEM
    1860 ~: 3 CSA
    Cardinal: 3 STL
    Colonel: 5 EAGLE
    Old cosmonaut: 4 CCCP
    site: 3 CAP
    Superman: 3 ESS
Insignificant: 4 **MERE** PUNY
        SLIM 5 DINKY MINOR
        SMALL 6 MEASLY TWOBIT
        8 ONEHORSE
        13 SMALLPOTATOES
    amount: 3 SOU TAD 4 IOTA
        5 MINIM
    one: 4 SNIP TWIT 5 TWERP
Insincere: 4 OILY 5 PHONY
    talk: 4 CANT 10 LIPSERVICE
    Verbally: 4 GLIB
Insinuate: 5 GETAT
Insinuating: 5 SNIDE
Insinuation: 8 OVERTONE
Insinuative
    remark: 5 SNEER
Insipid: 4 BLAH 5 BLAND
        6 JEJUNE
Insist
    on: 6 DEMAND
    suffix: 3 ENT
Insolence: 3 LIP

Insolent: 5 SASSY SAUCY
Insomnia
    Evidence of: 7 REDEYES
    Royal ~ cause: 3 PEA
"Insomnia"
    star: 6 PACINO
Insomniac
    lack: 5 SLEEP
Inspect
    the figures: 4 OGLE
Inspection: 7 LOOKSEE
    Food ~ inits.: 4 USDA
    Kind of: 6 ONSITE
Inspector: 4 EYER
    employer (abbr.): 4 USDA
    Nectar: 3 BEE
Inspiration: 4 IDEA
    Have a sudden: 4 GASP
    Poet: 5 ERATO
    Source of: 4 MUSE
Inspirational
    phrase: 5 MOTTO
    talk (abbr.): 3 SER
Inspire: 4 FIRE 5 ELATE IMBUE
        6 AROUSE PROMPT
    reverence: 3 AWE
Inspired
    It's: 3 AIR AWE
    poem: 3 ODE
    with love, old-style: 4 SMIT
Inst.: 4 ACAD
Instability
    Show: 4 YOYO
    Social: 6 ANOMIE
Install
    a door: 4 HANG
    a sidewalk: 4 PAVE
    carpeting: 3 LAY
    to new specs: 5 REFIT
    turf: 3 SOD
Installation
    Bath: 3 SPA
    Glazier: 4 PANE
Installed: 4 LAID
Installer
    Floor: 5 TILER
Installment: 7 EPISODE
Instamatic
    maker: 5 KODAK

Instance: 4 CASE
  For: 3 SAY
Instant: 3 SEC 5 FLASH JIFFY
     TRICE 6 MOMENT
  brand: 7 NESCAFE
  lawn: 3 SOD
  message sender: 5 AOLER
  replay format: 5 SLOMO
  This: 3 NOW
  ___ instant (quickly): 4 **INAN**
Instant Message
  sender: 5 AOLER
Instead: 15 ASANALTERNATIVE
  of: 3 FOR 4 THAN
Instinctive: 3 GUT
  ability: 4 FEEL
Instinctual
  energy: 6 LIBIDO
Institute
  Brooklyn: 5 PRATT
  Educ.: 3 SCH
  MD: 4 USNA
Institutes
  Prestigious: 5 IVIES
In ___ straits: 4 DIRE
Instruct: 5 EDIFY TEACH
Instruction
  Cookbook: 4 STIR
  Dance: 4 STEP
  Dotted-line: 4 TEAR
  Initial: 7 STEPONE
  Rx: 3 TID
  to a boxer: 4 STAY
  Yoga: 6 EXHALE
Instructions
  Set of: 6 RECIPE
Instructor
  Dance ~ call: 4 STEP
  Drill ~ directive: 6 ATEASE
  Golf: 3 PRO
  Private: 5 TUTOR
Instrument: 5 AGENT
     7 UTENSIL
  Kind of: 4 REED
  Long-necked: 4 LUTE 5 SITAR
Insulated
  Poorly: 6 DRAFTY
Insulating
  tubing: 9 SPAGHETTI

Insulation
  material: 4 MICA
Insulin: 7 HORMONE
Insult: 4 BARB SLAM SLAP SLUR
  response: 6 INEVER
  Response to an: 4 SLAP
  ~, slangily: 3 DIS RIP 4 ZING
Insulting: 5 SNIDE
  look: 5 SNEER
  remark: 4 SLUR
Insurable
  item: 4 AUTO
  It's: 4 LIFE
Insurance
  Aerialist's: 3 NET
  Big name in: 5 AETNA GEICO
     6 LLOYDS
  Case for an ~ detective: 5 ARSON
  city: 8 HARTFORD
  company with a duck: 5 AFLAC
  concern: 7 METLIFE
  Flood: 3 ARK
  Kind of: 4 TERM 7 NOFAULT
  Med. ~ group: 3 HMO
  seller: 5 AGENT
  spokeslizard: 5 GECKO
  subject: 4 LOSS
  worker: 5 AGENT
Insured
  contribution: 5 COPAY
  report: 4 LOSS
Insurer
  calculation: 4 RISK
  delight: 7 LOWRISK
  Mortgage: 3 FHA
Insurgent: 5 REBEL
Insurrectionist: 5 REBEL
Int.
  disclosure: 3 APR
  They earn: 3 CDS
Intaglio
  opposite: 5 CAMEO
  stone: 4 ONYX
Intake
  Limited food: 4 DIET
  Quick: 4 GASP
  Small: 3 SIP
Intangible
  quality: 4 AURA

Integer
  Smallest positive: 3 ONE
Integers
  Half of the: 4 ODDS 5 EVENS
Integra
  maker: 5 **ACURA**
Integrated
  circuit: 9 MICROCHIP
  It may be: 7 CIRCUIT
Intel
  Grove of: 4 ANDY
Intellect: 4 MIND
Intellectuals: 8 LITERATI
Intelligence: 4 NEWS 5 SENSE
  Former ~ org.: 3 OSS
  Gather: 3 SPY
  Lively: 6 ESPRIT
  org.: 3 NSA
  test developer: 5 BINET
Intelligent: 5 SMART
  Unusually: 3 APT
Intelligently
  planned progress: 7 TELESIS
Intelligentsia: 8 LITERATI
Intend: 3 AIM 4 MEAN
Intended: 5 MEANT 6 FIANCE
    TARGET 7 FIANCEE
Intense: 4 AVID DEEP EDGY
    5 ACUTE 6 FIERCE
    RAGING
  Become more: 6 DEEPEN
  desire: 4 ITCH
  devotion: 5 ARDOR
  dislike: 5 ODIUM
  fear: 6 TERROR
  Make less: 4 BATE
  More: 7 FIERCER
  pain: 5 AGONY
  ~, as color: 5 VIVID
Intensifier
  Slangy: 3 OLA
Intensify: 6 DEEPEN HEATUP
    STEPUP 7 ENHANCE
Intensity: 4 ZEAL ZEST 5 ARDOR
    6 FERVOR
  Diminish in: 5 ABATE
  With: 5 HOTLY
Intent: 3 AIM 4 RAPT
  look: 4 GAZE 5 STARE

Intention: 3 AIM END 4 IDEA
    PLAN 6 DESIGN
Intentional
  grounding: 3 SOD
Intentionally
  lose: 5 THROW
Intentions
  Have good: 8 MEANWELL
Intently
  Look: 4 GAZE PEER
  Staring: 5 AGAZE
Inter ___ (among others): 4 **ALIA**
Intercom
  speaker: 9 SQUAWKBOX
Interdiction: 3 BAN
Interest: 4 GRAB 5 STAKE
    8 APPEALTO
  Accumulate: 6 ACCRUE
  Arouse: 5 PIQUE
  Excessive: 5 USURY
  Field of: 4 AREA
  figure: 4 RATE
  Garner: 4 EARN
  group: 4 BLOC
  Item of: 4 LOAN
  Lose: 4 TIRE
  Lose ~ in: 6 TIREOF
  One of great: 6 USURER
    9 LOANSHARK
  Place of: 4 BANK
  Show ~ in: 8 ASKABOUT
  Showed: 5 SATUP
Interested
  Overly: 4 NOSY
Interfere: 6 MEDDLE TAMPER
  (with): 4 MESS
Interference: 6 STATIC
  TV: 4 SNOW
Interim
  ruling group: 5 JUNTA
Interior
  design: 5 DECOR
Interior Secretary
  1960s ~: 5 UDALL
  FDR: 5 ICKES
  Reagan: 4 WATT
Interject: 3 ADD
Interjection
  Brit: 4 ISAY

German: 3 ACH
Klutz: 4 OOPS
of disapproval: 3 TUT
Old-style: 3 FIE
Psalms: 5 SELAH
Triumphant: 4 TADA
Interjections
Pirate: 3 ARS
Questioning: 3 EHS
Interlace: 4 KNIT
Interlaced: 5 WOVEN 6 TWINED
Interlaken
river: 4 AARE
Interlock: 4 **MESH**
Interlude
Romantic: 4 IDYL 5 IDYLL
Intermediary: 9 GOBETWEEN
Interminable: 7 ENDLESS
time: 3 EON
Interminably: 5 NOEND ONEND
Intermission: 4 LULL
8 ENTRACTE
follower: 5 ACTII 6 ACTTWO
preceder: 4 ACTI
Intermissionless: 6 ONEACT
Intermittently: 8 ONANDOFF
Intern: 4 AIDE
Internalize
anger: 4 STEW
International
accord: 7 ENTENTE
agcy.: 6 UNESCO
agreement: 6 ACCORD
7 ENTENTE
court site, with "The": 5 HAGUE
money: 4 EURO
thaw: 7 DETENTE
trade spot: 8 OPENPORT
waters: 7 OPENSEA
Internet
abbr.: 3 WWW
auction site: 4 EBAY
Big name on the: 3 AOL
Browse the: 4 SURF
Connected to the: 6 ONLINE
connection need: 5 MODEM
Drudge of the: 4 MATT
explorer: 4 USER
High-speed ~ inits.: 3 DSL

initials: 4 HTTP
letters: 3 AOL WWW
marketing: 5 ETAIL
messages: 5 EMAIL
novice: 6 NEWBIE
Popular ~ company: 5 YAHOO
popups: 3 ADS
Profitable ~ business: 4 PORN
program language: 4 JAVA
Short ~ message: 5 ENOTE
Internet address: 3 URL
component: 3 DOT
ending: 3 COM EDU ORG
starter: 4 HTTP
Internist
org.: 3 AMA
Interoffice
note: 4 MEMO
Interpret: 4 READ 8 CONSTRUE
incorrectly: 7 MISREAD
Interpretation: 4 SPIN
Kind of: 5 LOOSE
Interpreter
Omen: 4 SEER
Interrogate: 3 ASK 4 PUMP QUIZ
5 GRILL
after a mission: 7 DEBRIEF
Interrogation
Intense: 11 THIRDDEGREE
room excuse: 5 ALIBI
Interrogative
interjections: 3 EHS
Interrupt: 5 CUTIN
Interrupter
word: 4 AHEM
Interruption: 3 GAP 4 AHEM
5 BREAK LAPSE
6 HIATUS
cause: 5 PAGER
Doctor's: 4 PAGE
Follow without: 5 SEGUE
TV show: 9 NEWSFLASH
Without: 5 ONEND
Interruptions
TV show: 3 ADS
Intersect: 4 MEET 5 CROSS
Intersection: 4 NODE
sign: 4 STOP
Three-way: 3 TEE

Interstate
  entrance: 4 RAMP
  sight: 4 SEMI
  sign: 3 GAS 4 EXIT
  stop: 8 RESTAREA
Interstate H1
  Where ~ is: 4 OAHU
Interstellar
  cloud: 6 NEBULA
  dist.: 4 LTYR
Interstice: 3 GAP 6 AREOLA
  Anatomical: 6 AREOLE
Intertwine: 4 LACE MESH
      5 WEAVE 6 ENLACE
Interval: 3 GAP LAG 4 SPAN
  between cause and effect:
      7 TIMELAG
  Musical: 4 REST 5 NINTH
      6 OCTAVE 7 TRITONE
Intervene: 6 STEPIN
Intervening
  stretch: 8 MEANTIME
Interview: 3 ASK
  format: 5 QANDA
  wear: 4 SUIT
Interviewer
  CNN: 9 LARRYKING
  Emmy-winning: 5 FROST
"Interview With the Vampire"
  author Rice: 4 ANNE
  vampire: 6 LESTAT
Interweave: 4 KNIT MESH
      5 BRAID 7 ENTWINE
Intestinal
  bacteria: 5 ECOLI
  parts: 4 ILEA
  prefix: 6 ENTERO
Intestine
  Of the small: 5 ILEAC
"In that case ...": 4 IFSO
      THEN
"___ in the bag": 3 ITS
"In the Bedroom"
  actress: 5 TOMEI
In the blink ___ eye: 4 OFAN
In the blink of ___: 5 ANEYE
___ in the bucket: 5 ADROP
"___ in the Dark": 5 ASHOT
"___ in the Family": 3 ALL

"In the Good Old Summertime"
  lyricist Shields: 3 REN
"In the headlights"
  animal: 4 DEER
"In the Heat of the Night"
  setting: 6 SPARTA
"In the Land of Israel"
  author: 6 AMOSOZ
"___! In the Name of Love":
      4 STOP
Intimate: 3 PAL 4 CHUM HINT
      NEAR 5 BOSOM CLOSE
      CRONY GETAT 6 HINTAT
"Intimate ___, The": 4 ELLA
"Intimations of Immortality":
      3 ODE
Intimidate: 3 COW 5 **DAUNT**
      DETER PSYCH
      7 OVERAWE
Intimidating: 6 FEARED
Into
  Is: 4 DIGS
  ___ into (attack): 3 LAY
Intolerance
  Source of: 7 LACTOSE
Intolerant
  one: 5 BIGOT
Intone: 5 CHANT
Intoxicate: 5 BESOT ELATE
Intoxicating: 5 HEADY
  drink: 4 KAVA
"___ in Toyland": 5 BABES
Intraoffice
  linkup (abbr.): 3 LAN
Intrepid: 4 BOLD 5 BRAVE
      8 FEARLESS
Intricate
  Cleverly: 6 DAEDAL
  pattern: 3 WEB
Intrigue: 4 PLOT 5 CABAL
  League of: 5 CABAL
Intrigued
  by: 4 INTO
Intrinsically: 5 **PERSE**
Intro: 5 PROEM 6 LEADIN
      OPENER PROLOG
  Info: Prefix cue
  maker: 5 EMCEE
  NYSE: 3 IPO

Introduce
  slowly: 7 PHASEIN
  to the mix: 5 ADDIN
Introduction: 5 DEBUT PROEM
      6 LEADIN
  Info: Prefix cue
Introductory
  material: 4 ABCS
Introvert: 5 LONER
Intrude: 6 HORNIN
  upon: 6 INVADE
  ~, with "in": 4 BUTT 5 BARGE
Intruder
  Garden: 4 WEED
  Kitchen: 3 ANT
Intrusive: 4 NOSY
Intrusively
  Greet: 6 ACCOST
Intuit: 5 SENSE
Intuition: 5 HUNCH SENSE
  More than: 3 ESP
Intuitive
  ability: 4 FEEL
Intuitively
  Feel: 5 SENSE
Inuit: 6 ESKIMO
  craft: 5 KAYAK UMIAK
  kin: 5 ALEUT
  transport: 4 SLED
Inundate: 5 DROWN SWAMP
      6 DELUGE ENGULF
Inundated: 5 AWASH
Inundation: 5 SPATE
Invader
  5th-century : 6 ATTILA
  13th-century ~: 5 TATAR
  Ancient: 4 GOTH
  Mongol: 5 TATAR
  of Gaul: 6 ATTILA
  of Rome: 4 GOTH
  Picnic: 3 ANT
  Sci-fi: 7 MARTIAN
Invalid: 4 NULL
  Make: 4 VOID 6 NEGATE
Invalidate: 5 ANNUL
Invasion
  Roman ~ resister: 5 DRUID
  site of 1944: 4 STLO
  site of 1956: 5 SINAI

  site of 1983: 7 GRENADA
"Invasion of the Body Snatchers"
  prop: 3 POD
Inveigh
  against: 6 RAILAT
Inveigle: 4 COAX LURE 6 ENTICE
Inveigled: 5 LEDON
Invent: 4 COIN 6 CREATE DEVISE
      7 DREAMUP
Invented
  word: 7 COINAGE
Invention
  beginning: 4 IDEA
  Bell: 5 PHONE
  Franklin: 5 STOVE
  Whitney: 9 COTTONGIN
Inventions: 4 FIBS LIES
  Second name in: 4 ALVA
Inventor
  cry: 3 AHA
  document: 6 PATENT
  goal: 15 BETTERMOUSETRAP
  monogram: 3 TAE
  start: 4 IDEA
Inventory: 5 STOCK 6 STORES
  (abbr.): 4 MDSE
  Bit of: 4 ITEM
  syst.: 4 FIFO LIFO
"In ___ veritas": 4 VINO
Inverness
  inhabitant: 4 SCOT
  instrument: 7 BAGPIPE
  Lake near: 4 NESS
Invert: 5 UPEND
  a pencil: 5 ERASE
Inverted
  e: 5 SCHWA
Invest: 5 ENDUE
Investigate: 5 DELVE PLUMB
      PROBE 7 DIGINTO
      8 LOOKINTO
  again: 6 REOPEN
Investigation: 5 PROBE
  Govt.: 3 INQ
Investigative
  gp.: 4 HUAC
  tool: 13 FINETOOTHCOMB
Investigator: 6 PROBER
  Crack: 4 NARC

P.D.: 3 DET
question: 3 WHY
U.S. accident: 4 NTSB
~, briefly: 3 TEC
Investing
Online ~ service: 6 ETRADE
options: 3 CDS
Investment: 5 STAKE
Certain: 4 BOND 5 TNOTE
Govt.: 5 TBILL
option: 3 IRA
options: 3 CDS
Sound: 3 AMP 6 STEREO
Investor
goal: 6 RETURN
hope: 4 GAIN
mail-in: 5 PROXY
Online ~ company: 6 ETRADE
Org. that protects an: 3 SEC
Invigorate
the brass: 7 REPLATE
Invigorating: 5 BRISK CRISP
drink: 5 TONIC
place: 3 SPA
Invincible
Not: 8 BEATABLE
Inviolate: 6 SACRED
Invisible: 6 UNSEEN
emanation: 4 AURA
follower: 3 INK
It may be: 3 INK
troublemaker: 7 GREMLIN
"Invisible Man"
author: 7 ELLISON
"Invisible Man, The"
author: 5 WELLS
Invitation
Answer an: 4 RSVP 5 REPLY
Driver's: 5 HOPIN
Duel: 4 SLAP
heading: 5 WHERE
letters: 4 BYOB **RSVP**
Positive reply to an: 4 LETS
turndown: 7 REGRETS
Invite: 3 ASK
on a date: 6 ASKOUT
to a penthouse: 5 ASKUP
to enter: 5 ASKIN
to one's house: 7 ASKOVER

Invited
Not: 7 UNASKED
Invitee: 5 GUEST
Invitees
Most-wanted: 5 **ALIST**
Inviting
smell: 5 AROMA
Invoice
abbr.: 3 AMT
amount: 3 FEE
fig.: 3 AMT
phrase: 6 SHIPTO
stamp: 4 PAID
word: 3 DUE NET 5 REMIT
Invoke
Bad thing to: 3 IRE
Involuntary
contraction: 5 SPASM
muscle movement: 3 TIC
Involve: 6 **ENTAIL** 7 EMBROIL
Involved: 9 ELABORATE
Get: 6 STEPIN
with: 4 INON INTO 6 SEEING
In ___ way: 4 ABAD 5 HARMS
"In what way?": 5 HOWSO
"In your dreams!": 4 ASIF
5 NOWAY 10 NOTACHANCE
Io: 4 MOTH
Protector of: 5 ARGUS
Iodine
creator: 5 HATLO
source: 4 KELP 7 SEAWEED
Iolani Palace
locale: 4 OAHU
Ion
suffix: 3 IZE
Iona College
athlete: 4 GAEL
Ione
Actress: 4 SKYE
Ionian Sea
island: 5 CORFU
Sight from the: 4 ETNA
Ionic
alternative: 5 DORIC
Ionized
gas: 6 PLASMA
Iota: 3 TAD 4 WHIT 5 SPECK
TRACE

follower: 5 KAPPA
preceder: 5 THETA
IOU: 4 CHIT DEBT NOTE
      6 MARKER
Part of: 3 OWE
Iowa
city: 4 **AMES**
college: 3 COE
college town: 4 **AMES**
commune: 5 AMANA
state tree: 3 OAK
Iowa State
location: 4 **AMES**
Ipanema
locale: 3 RIO
"I pass": 5 NOBET
"Ipcress File, The"
author Deighton: 3 LEN
Ipecac: 6 EMETIC
iPod
maker: 5 APPLE
Ipse ___: 5 DIXIT
Ipso
Meaning of: 6 ITSELF
Ipso ___: 5 FACTO
IQ
test name: 5 BINET
Ira
Author: 5 LEVIN
IRA: 7 NESTEGG
holder: 5 SAVER
increaser: 3 INT
legislation: 5 ERISA
Part of: 3 RET 4 ACCT 5 IRISH
renewal: 8 ROLLOVER
Tapping an: 3 RET
type: 3 SEP 4 ROTH
Iran
Adherent in: 5 BAHAI
capital: 6 TEHRAN
Coin of: 4 RIAL
Former name of: 6 PERSIA
Former ruler of: 4 SHAH
Iran-Contra
name: 5 NORTH
North of: 5 OLLIE
org.: 3 CIA NSC
Iranian: 5 ASIAN
Ancient: 4 MEDE

city: 3 QOM
coin: 4 **RIAL**
expanse: 15 GREATSALTDESERT
Former ~ leader: 4 **SHAH**
island: 6 ABADAN
language: 5 FARSI
money: 4 **RIAL**
mountain dweller: 4 KURD
Iraq
money: 5 DINAR
neighbor: 4 IRAN
port: 5 BASRA
resource: 3 OIL
Iraqi: 4 ARAB
Northern: 4 KURD
Irascible: 4 EDGY 5 TESTY
      7 BRISTLY
Irate: 3 MAD 4 SORE 5 ABOIL
      6 FUMING 7 TEEDOFF
Ire: 5 ANGER 6 SPLEEN
Ireland: 4 EIRE ERIN
      11 EMERALDISLE
County of: 4 CORK 5 CLARE
      DERRY
De Valera of: 5 EAMON
Island off: 4 ARAN
John, in: 4 SEAN
poetic name: 5 IRENA
Singer from: 4 ENYA
"I Remember Mama"
son: 4 NELS
Irene
Actress: 4 RYAN 5 DUNNE
      PAPAS
Dike, Eunomia, and: 5 HORAE
She played: 5 RENEE
Singer: 4 CARA
"I ___ return": 5 SHALL
Iridescent: 7 OPALINE
gem: 4 **OPAL**
Iris
center: 5 PUPIL
covering: 6 CORNEA
locale: 3 EYE 4 UVEA
Part of the: 6 AREOLA
Irises: 8 GLADIOLI
Irish
accent: 6 BROGUE
Ancient ~ capital: 4 TARA

county: 5 CLARE KERRY SLIGO
   6 GALWAY 7 DONEGAL
dance: 3 JIG
dramatist: 5 SYNGE
flag color: 6 ORANGE
folk singer: 4 ENYA
Former ~ P.M. Cosgrove: 4 LIAM
hero: 5 STPAT
homeland: 4 EIRE
instrument: 4 HARP
Ireland, to the: 4 EIRE
islands: 4 ARAN
lass: 7 COLLEEN
lass name: 4 ERIN
lullaby start: 5 TOORA
moonshine: 6 POTEEN
nationalist Robert: 5 EMMET
native: 4 CELT
offshoot: 4 ERSE
Old ~ alphabet: 5 OGHAM
poet: 5 YEATS
port: 4 COBH CORK 5 DERRY
   SLIGO 6 GALWAY TRALEE
republic: 4 EIRE
singer: 4 **ENYA**
tongue: 4 ERSE
wailing spirit: 7 BANSHEE
word on coins: 4 EIRE
~ Gaelic: 4 ERSE
Irish ___ : 6 SETTER
Irishman: 4 CELT
Irish Rose
  lover: 4 **ABIE**
  " ___ Irish Rose": 5 ABIES
Irk: 3 VEX 4 RILE 5 ANNOY
      GETAT GETTO PEEVE
      6 NEEDLE NETTLE
      PESTER
  More than: 4 GALL
Irked: 4 SORE
"I, Robot"
  author: 6 ASIMOV
  author Asimov: 5 ISAAC
"I ___ Rock" (Simon and
    Garfunkel song): 3 AMA
Iron: 5 PRESS
  alloy: 5 STEEL
  and Ice: 4 AGES
  Angle: 4 LBAR

clothes: 5 ARMOR
fishhook: 4 GAFF
Five: 6 MASHIE
In need of: 6 ANEMIC
Kind of: 3 PIG 4 NINE
Mark with a branding: 4 SEAR
One with ~ hands: 6 DESPOT
output: 5 STEAM
pigment: 5 OCHER
prefix: 5 FERRI FERRO
product: 6 WAFFLE
Refined: 5 STEEL
setting: 5 STEAM
Shooting: 6 SIXGUN
source: 3 ORE 5 LIVER
target: 6 ANEMIA CREASE
Use an: 5 PRESS
Ironed: 9 DECREASED
Ironfisted: 5 STERN
Ironic: 3 WRY
"Ironic"
  singer Morissette: 6 ALANIS
"Iron Mike": 5 DITKA TYSON
Iron-on: 5 DECAL
Iron-pumper
  muscles: 4 LATS PECS
    5 DELTS
  unit: 3 REP
Irons: 5 ACTOR
  Actor: 6 JEREMY
Irony: 5 TROPE
Iroquoian
  Indian: 4 ERIE 6 SENECA
  language: 4 ERIE 6 ONEIDA
    8 CHEROKEE
  tribe: 6 ONEIDA
Iroquois
  foe: 4 **ERIE**
  tribe: 5 HURON 6 ONEIDA
    SENECA
Irrational: 3 MAD 6 INSANE
  fear: 6 PHOBIA
  numbers: 5 SURDS
Irreconcilables: 8 DIEHARDS
Irrefutable: 4 SURE TRUE
Irregular: 5 EROSE
Irregularly
  notched: 5 **EROSE**
Irrelevant: 4 MOOT

Irreligious
  one: 5 PAGAN
Irresistible
  It may be: 4 URGE
Irreverence: 7 IMPIETY
Irreverent: 4 FLIP
  Coarsely: 6 RIBALD
Irrigation
  aid: 5 CANAL
  Needing: 4 ARID
Irritable: 4 EDGY 5 TESTY
    6 TETCHY 7 PECKISH
Irritably
  Speak ~ to: 6 SNAPAT
Irritant
  Dog's: 4 FLEA
  Major: 5 THORN
  Royal: 3 PEA
Irritate: 3 IRK NAG VEX 4 GALL
    MIFF RASP **RILE** ROIL
    5 CHAFE EATAT GRATE
    PIQUE 6 BOTHER NETTLE
    PESTER RANKLE TEEOFF
Irritated
  state: 4 SNIT
Irritation: 5 PEEVE
  Eye: 4 STYE
  State of: 4 SNIT
IRS
  check: 5 AUDIT
  employee: 3 AGT CPA 4 TMAN
  mo.: 3 APR
  Percentage for the: 7 TAXRATE
  review (abbr.): 3 AUD
  ~ ID: 3 <u>SSN</u>
IRT
  and BMT partner: 3 IND
Irvin
  Illustrator: 3 REA
Irving
  Actress: 3 AMY
  hero: 3 RIP 4 GARP 6 TSGARP
  Talent agent: 5 LAZAR
Irving, John
  character: 4 GARP 6 TSGARP
Irwin
  Actor: 3 STU
  Golfer: 4 HALE
Is: 6 EXISTS

  for two: 3 ARE
  in the past: 3 WAS
  no longer: 3 WAS
  without: 6 HASNOT
  ~, in Spanish: 4 ESTA
"Is ___?": Matt. 26:22: 3 ITI
Isaac
  Eldest son of: 4 ESAU
  Mother of: 5 SARAH
  Sci-fi writer: 6 ASIMOV
  Singer/actor: 5 HAYES
  Violinist: 5 STERN
Isabel II: 5 REINA
Isabella: 5 REINA
Isabella d'___: 4 ESTE
Isaiah: 7 PROPHET
Isak
  Real first name of: 5 KAREN
I Samuel
  priest: 3 ELI
"___ is an island": 5 NOMAN
Isao
  Golfer: 4 AOKI
"___ is as good as a wink":
    4 ANOD
"___ is a terrible thing ...":
    5 AMIND
"... ___ I saw Elba": 3 ERE
"I saw ___ sawing wood ...":
    4 ESAU
"I say!"
  sayer: 4 BRIT CHAP
"___ I say!": 4 DOAS
"___ I say more?": 4 NEED
ISBN
  Part of: 4 INTL
"___ Is Born": 5 ASTAR
"I see!": 3 AHA OHO
  ~, facetiously: 4 AHSO
"I see it now!": 3 AHA
"... is fear ___": FDR: 6 ITSELF
Isherwood
  collaborator: 5 AUDEN
    7 WHAUDEN
Ishmael
  Captain of: 4 AHAB
  One of ~'s people: 4 ARAB
"I Shot Andy Warhol"
  star Taylor: 4 LILI

"Ishtar"
  director: 9 ELAINEMAY
  extras: 6 CAMELS
"___ is human ...": 5 TOERR
Isidor
  Physics Nobelist: 4 RABI
Isinglass: 4 MICA
Isis
  Brother of: 6 OSIRIS
"Is it soup ___?": 3 YET
Islam
  (abbr.): 3 REL
  follower: 3 ITE 5 SUNNI
  God of: 5 ALLAH
  holy city: 5 MECCA
  One of the Pillars of: 4 HADJ
Islamabad
  country: 8 PAKISTAN
Islamic
  chief: 4 EMIR
  crusade: 5 JIHAD
  decree: 5 FATWA
  deity: 5 ALLAH
  holy war: 5 JIHAD
  leader: 4 EMIR IMAM 5 AMEER
  republic: 4 IRAN
  spirit: 5 DJINN
  text: 5 KORAN
  title: 4 EMIR
Island
  accompaniment: 3 UKE
  Adriatic: 4 LIDO
  Aegean: 5 SAMOS
  Alaskan: 4 ATTU 6 KODIAK
  Aleutian: 4 ADAK ATKA **ATTU**
  Atlantic ~ group: 6 AZORES
  attire: 6 SARONG
  Bering Sea: 4 ATTU
  Big ~ port: 4 HILO
  Caribbean: 5 ARUBA
  chain: 3 LEI
  Chinese: 6 TAIWAN
  Coral: 5 **ATOLL**
  dance: 4 HULA
  dish: 3 POI
  East China Sea: 5 MATSU
  east of Java: 4 BALI
  Exile: 4 ELBA
  feast: 4 LUAU

Firth of Clyde: 5 ARRAN
Florida: 7 SANIBEL
Greek: 5 CRETE SAMOS
  6 LESBOS
greeting: 5 **ALOHA**
group near Fiji: 5 SAMOA
Hawaiian: 4 **MAUI** OAHU
  5 LANAI 7 MOLOKAI
Hebrides: 4 **IONA** SKYE
Immigration: 5 ELLIS
in a computer game: 4 MYST
Indonesian: 4 **BALI** JAVA
  5 CERAM TIMOR 6 BORNEO
Italian: 4 LIDO
Japanese: 6 HONSHU
  7 OKINAWA
Largest Mediterranean: 6 SICILY
Low: 3 CAY
Mediterranean: 5 MALTA
More: 6 UTOPIA
New York: 5 CONEY **ELLIS**
  6 STATEN
of Brooklyn: 5 **CONEY**
Philippine: 4 CEBU 5 LEYTE
  LUZON PANAY SAMAR
ring: 3 LEI
River: 3 AIT
South Pacific: 5 SAMOA
  6 EASTER TAHITI
  8 BORABORA
strings: 3 UKE
U.S. Pacific: 4 GUAM
welcome: 3 LEI
West Indies: 5 ARUBA
WWII: 5 LEYTE
~, in French: 3 ILE
___ Island: 5 ELLIS RHODE
  6 STATEN
~, Florida: 5 MARCO
Islander
  Alaskan: 5 ALEUT
  Pacific: 6 SAMOAN
Islanders
  org.: 3 NHL
"Island of the Blue Dolphins"
  author: 5 ODELL
"Island of the Day Before, The"
  author Umberto: 3 ECO
___ **Island Red: 5 RHODE**

___ **Islands:** 6 BAHAMA BIMINI
"___ Island With You": 4 ONAN
Isle of ___: 5 WIGHT
Isle of Man
 man: 4 GAEL
Islet: 3 AIT CAY
Ism: 5 DOGMA TENET
"___ is me!": 3 WOE
"I smell ___!": 4 **ARAT**
"Isn't ___ bit like you and me?":
  3 HEA
Iso-
 Relative of: 4 EQUI
Isolate: 5 ICEIN 6 ENISLE
  8 SETAPART
Isolated: 4 LONE 5 ALONE APART
  STRAY 8 ALLALONE
 district: 7 ENCLAVE
 hill: 5 BUTTE
Isolde
 Love of: 7 TRISTAN
"I ___ Song Go Out of My Heart":
  4 LETA
Isotope
 Radioactive: 6 IONIUM
ISP
 Popular: 3 **AOL**
"I Spy"
 costar Bill: 5 COSBY
 costar Robert: 4 CULP
Isr.
 neighbor: 3 LEB **SYR**
Israel
 Abba of: 4 **EBAN**
 Airline to: 4 ELAL
 American Revolutionary general:
  6 PUTNAM
 Ariel of: 6 SHARON
 Bank ___ of: 5 LEUMI
 Barak of: 4 EHUD
 carrier to Seoul: 4 ELAL
 Dayan of: 5 MOSHE
 Eban of: 4 ABBA
 First king of: 4 **SAUL**
 Follower of: 3 ITE
 Golda of: 4 MEIR
 Gun designed in: 3 UZI
 legislature: 7 KNESSET
 Meir of: 5 GOLDA

 Moshe of: 5 ARENS
 neighbor: 5 SYRIA
 Port of: 4 ACRE ELAT 5 EILAT
  HAIFA
 Sharon of: 5 **ARIEL**
 Shimon of: 5 PERES
 suffix: 3 ITE
 Tribe of: 3 DAN 5 ASHER
 Weizman of: 4 EZER
Israeli: 5 SABRA 6 SEMITE
 airline: 4 **ELAL**
 airport: 3 LOD
 author Oz: 4 AMOS
 carrier: 4 ELAL
 city: 5 HAIFA
 dance: 4 **HORA**
 desert: 5 **NEGEV**
 Former ~ P.M.: 4 MEIR 5 PERES
  RABIN
 gun: 3 **UZI**
 money: 6 SHEKEL
 native: 5 **SABRA**
 political party: 5 LIKUD
 port: 4 ACRE ELAT 5 EILAT
  HAIFA
 resort: 4 ELAT 5 EILAT
 statesman Abba: 4 **EBAN**
 statesman Dayan: 5 MOSHE
 statesman Weizman: 4 EZER
 weapon: 3 **UZI**
"Is so!"
 rebuttal: 4 AINT
Issue: 4 **EMIT** 5 SCION TOPIC
  6 EMERGE 7 EMANATE
  RELEASE
 a summons to: 4 CITE
 Became an: 5 AROSE
 Burning: 3 ASH
 Business: 3 INC
 Campaign: 4 JOBS
 Fashion: 4 ELLE
 forth: 4 EMIT
 For the ~ price: 5 ATPAR
 Government: 5 TNOTE
 Hot: 4 LAVA
 Labor: 5 CHILD
 New: 3 IPO
 Newspaper: 7 EDITION
 One side of an: 3 CON

Royal: **6** PRINCE
Issues
  Agree to more: **5** RENEW
  How some ~ are debated:
    5 HOTLY
Istanbul
  inn: **6** IMARET
  native: **4** **TURK**
  region: **6** THRACE
  title: **3** AGA
"Is that ___?": **3** ANO **5** AFACT
"Is that a fact!": **6** DOTELL
"Is That All There Is"
  singer: **8** PEGGYLEE
"Is that so?": **3** GEE **6** DOTELL
  REALLY
"Is this a dagger which ___ ...":
  Macbeth: **4** ISEE
Isthmus
  Malay: **3** KRA
  splitter: **5** CANAL
"I Still See ___" ("Paint Your
  Wagon" tune): **5** ELISA
Isuzu
  model: **5** RODEO
"I swear!": **5** NOLIE **6** HONEST
"Is Your Mama a ___?" (kids'
  book): **5** LLAMA
It
  game: **3** TAG
  Like: **6** NEUTER
  They may have: **4** AYES
  ~, in Italian: **4** ESSA ESSO
It.
  is there: **3** EUR
  It borders: **3** AUS
  peak: **6** MTETNA
"It ___": **3** ISI
"___ it!" ("Amen!"): **4** SOBE
"It ain't over till it's over"
  speaker: **5** BERRA
Italia
  Capital of: **4** **ROMA**
  city: **6** TORINO
  seaport: **6** NAPOLI
Italian: **6** ETHNIC
  alternative: **5** RANCH
  Ancient: **6** SABINE **8** ETRUSCAN
  aperitif: **7** CAMPARI

article: **3** UNA
artist: **4** RENI
art patron: **4** ESTE
author: **3** ECO
auto: **4** ALFA FIAT
beach resort: **4** LIDO
brandy: **6** GRAPPA
bread: **4** LIRA LIRE
bridge: **5** PONTE
bubbly source: **4** ASTI
cheese: **6** ROMANO **7** RICOTTA
  8 PARMESAN
city: **4** ESTE PISA **5** CUNEO
  MILAN TURIN UDINE
  7 TARANTO
dessert: **3** ICE
dish: **5** PASTA
Fictional ~ town: **5** ADANO
Former ~ money: **4** LIRA LIRE
Former ~ P.M.: **4** MORO
holiday: **5** FESTA
hot spot: **4** ETNA
ice alternative: **7** SNOCONE
ice cream: **6** GELATI GELATO
innkeeper: **4** OSTE **7** PADRONE
island resort: **4** LIDO
isle: **5** CAPRI
lady: **5** DONNA
lawn game: **5** BOCCI
love: **5** AMORE
loved one: **4** CARA
money: **4** **LIRA** LIRE
monk: **3** FRA
noble family: **4** **ESTE**
number: **3** TRE UNO
peak: **4** ETNA
poet: **5** TASSO
port: **4** BARI **5** GENOA
  6 NAPLES **7** SALERNO
  TRIESTE
possessive: **3** MIO
prime minister Aldo: **4** MORO
pronoun: **3** MIA
province: **4** ASTI **5** SIENA UDINE
  7 SALERNO
resort: **4** LIDO
resort lake: **4** COMO
rice dish: **7** RISOTTO
river: **4** ARNO

sauce: 5 PESTO
sculptor: 6 PISANO
smoker: 4 ETNA
sonnet end: 6 SESTET
soup ingredient: 4 ORZO
staple: 5 PASTA
Stuffed ~ pockets: 7 RAVIOLI
term of endearment: 7 CARAMIA
town: 6 ASSISI
treat: 3 ICE
trio: 3 TRE
volcano: 4 ETNA
white: 5 SOAVE
wine: 4 VINO 5 SOAVE
        7 MARSALA
wine region: 4 **ASTI**
Italics
  Like: 6 ASLANT
  What ~ do: 5 SLANT
"It ___ All Velvet": 5 WASNT
Italy
  Alpine region of: 5 TIROL
  Former denomination in:
        7 ONELIRA
  Largest lake of: 5 GARDA
  Moro of: 4 ALDO
  Part of: 3 TOE
  shape: 4 BOOT
  Wine region of: 4 ASTI
"___ It a Pity?": 4 ISNT
Itar-___: 4 **TASS**
"___ it a shame!": 4 ISNT
"I tawt I taw a puddy ___!": 3 TAT
"It ___ Be You": 5 HADTO
"It can't be!": 4 OHNO
Itch: 3 YEN 4 URGE
Itchy: 5 EAGER 8 PRURIENT
Item: 7 ARTICLE
  of interest: 4 LOAN
  of value: 5 ASSET
  The ~ here: 4 THIS
Itemize: 4 LIST
Iterate: 5 RESAY 6 RETELL
"___ It Goes": 5 ANDSO
"It Had to ___": 5 BEYOU
"It Had to Be ___": 3 YOU
"It Had to Be You"
  composer Jones: 5 ISHAM
  lyricist Gus: 4 KAHN

"It Happened One Night"
  director: 5 CAPRA
  producer: 4 COHN
"I thought we ___ deal!": 4 HADA
"I thought we had ___!": 5 ADEAL
Itinerant: 5 NOMAD
  Be: 4 ROVE
Itinerary: 5 ROUTE
  abbr.: 3 ARR RTE
  Concert: 4 TOUR
  info: 4 ETAS
  word: 3 **VIA**
"It is rumored ...": 7 SOMESAY
"It is ___ told by an idiot ...":
        5 ATALE
"It Must Be ___": 3 HIM
"It must be him, ___ shall die":
        3 ORI
"It Must Be Him" singer: 4 CARR
"It must have been
        something ___!": 4 IATE
"It must have been
        something I ___!": 3 ATE
"___ it my best": 5 IGAVE
"It ___ Necessarily So": 4 AINT
"I told you so!": 3 HAH **SEE**
        5 THERE
  Word before: 3 SEE
"___ it or lose it": 3 USE
___ it over (dominated):
        6 LORDED
"___ It Romantic?": 4 ISNT
Its
  ~, in French: 3 SES
"It's ___!": 4 ABOY 5 ADATE
        ADEAL AGIRL ASNAP
"It's ___ ...": 4 AGAS
"It's about time!": 6 ATLAST
"It's a deal!": 4 DONE OKAY
"It's all ___": 5 ANACT
"It's all clear now": 4 ISEE
"It's Alright" singer: 3 ONO
"It's a ___ situation!": 5 NOWIN
"It's ___ a while": 4 BEEN
"It's a Wonderful Life"
  angel: 8 CLARENCE
  cabdriver: 5 ERNIE
  director Frank: 5 CAPRA
"It's been ___ pleasure": 5 AREAL

"It's ___ big mistake!": 4 ALLA
"It's c-c-c-cold!": 3 BRR
"It's ___ country!": 5 AFREE
Itself
  By: 5 PERSE
  In: 5 PERSE 6 ASSUCH
  ~, in Latin: 4 IPSA
"It's ___ ever wanted": 4 ALLI
"It's ___ in the right direction":
  5 ASTEP
"It slices, it ___ ...": 5 DICES
"It's ___ Love": 4 YOUI
"It's My Party"
  singer: 4 GORE
"It's no ___!": 3 USE
"It's not gonna happen": 4 NOPE
"It's only ___!": 5 AGAME
"It's on me!": 7 MYTREAT
"It's ___ real!": 4 BEEN
"It's rumored ...": 7 SOMESAY
"It's the end of ___": 5 ANERA
"It's the truth!": 5 NOLIE
"It's Too Late Now"
  autobiographer: 7 AAMILNE
"It's ___ to tell ...": 4 ASIN
"It's true!": 5 NOLIE
"It's ___ vu all over again!":
  4 DEJA
"It's ___-win situation": 3 ANO
"It's ___ world": 5 AMANS
"It's worth ___": 4 ATRY 5 ASHOT
Itsy-___: 5 BITSY
Itsy-bitsy: 3 WEE 4 TINY 5 TEENY
  6 TEENSY
  biter: 4 GNAT MITE
  bits: 5 ATOMS
ITT
  Part of: 3 TEL
"It takes two"
  dance: 5 TANGO
"___ it the truth!": 4 AINT
Itty-___: 5 BITTY
Itty-bitty: 3 WEE 4 TINY 5 TEENY
  6 TEENSY
  bit: 4 IOTA
  bug: 4 MITE
"It Walks by Night" author:
  4 CARR
"It was ___ and ...": 5 ADARK

"It was ___ mistake!": 4 ALLA
"It was the ___ I could do":
  5 LEAST
"I understand": 4 AHSO 5 GOTIT
  ROGER
IV
  givers: 3 RNS
  measurements: 3 CCS
  part: 5 INTRA
  place: 3 ICU
  sites: 3 ORS
"I ___ vacation!": 5 NEEDA
Ivan: 4 TSAR
  of tennis: 5 LENDL
Ivana
  and Donald: 4 EXES
"Ivanhoe"
  author: 5 SCOTT
  love: 6 **ROWENA**
  weapon: 5 LANCE
Ivan the Terrible: 4 TSAR
"I vant to be alone"
  actress: 5 GARBO
"I've been ___!": 3 HAD
"I've been framed!": 7 ITSALIE
"I've Got ___ in Kalamazoo":
  4 AGAL
"I've got it!": 3 AHA
"I've got my ___ you!": 5 EYEON
"I've Gotta ___": 4 BEME
"I've ___ had!": 4 BEEN
Ives
  Oscar-winner: 4 BURL
  Singer: 4 BURL
"I've ___ up to here!": 5 HADIT
Ivey, Artis
  Rapper born: 6 COOLIO
Ivied
  alcove: 5 ARBOR
  Student inside ~ walls: 3 ELI
Ivies
  One of the: 4 PENN YALE
Ivins, Molly
  Presidential bio by: 5 SHRUB
Ivories: 4 KEYS
  place: 5 PIANO
  Tickle the: 4 PLAY
Ivory
  product: 4 SOAP

rival: 4 DIAL 5 CAMAY
source: 4 TUSK
tower setting: 8 ACADEMIA
Ivory Coast
neighbor: 4 MALI
Ivy
feature: 4 VINE 7 TENDRIL
Ivy League
city: 6 ITHACA
school: 4 PENN YALE
5 BROWN
team: 4 ELIS PENN
Ivy Leaguer: 3 <u>ELI</u> 5 YALIE
I.W.
Labor leader: 4 ABEL
"I ___ Walrus": 5 AMTHE

"I wanna!": 5 LEMME
"I want it!": 5 GIMME
"I was elsewhere"
excuse: 5 ALIBI
"___ I Went Mad": 3 ERE
"I will sing ___ the Lord ...":
Exodus: 4 UNTO
"I Will Survive"
singer Gloria: 6 GAYNOR
Iwo ___: 4 JIMA
"I wouldn't send ___ out ...":
4 ADOG
"I would rather not": 3 NAH
"Ixnay!": 6 NODICE
Izmir
native: 4 TURK

Jj

J
  topper: 3 DOT
Ja
J
  Opposite of: 4 NEIN
  ~, across the Rhine: 3 OUI
Jab: 4 POKE PROD
  Many a: 4 LEFT
Jabba
  prisoner: 4 LEIA
  ___-Jabbar, Kareem: 5 ABDUL
Jabba the ___: 4 HUTT
Jabber: 3 GAS JAW YAK YAP
    5 PRATE
"Jabberwocky"
  opener: 4 **TWAS**
  Slithy ~ thing: 4 TOVE
Jabs
  Trade: 4 SPAR
"J'accuse"
  author: 4 ZOLA
  author Zola: 5 EMILE
  ___ Jacinto: 3 SAN
Jack: 4 CARD 5 KNAVE
    6 MOOLAH SEAMAN
  Actor: 3 **SOO** 4 ELAM WEBB
    5 BENNY OAKIE 6 LEMMON
    7 PALANCE 9 ALBERTSON
    NICHOLSON
  and the missus: 6 SPRATS
  Author: 7 KEROUAC
  Boxer: 7 DEMPSEY
  Clancy hero: 4 RYAN
  Golfer: 8 NICKLAUS
  inferior: 3 TEN
  Like: 6 NIMBLE
  of nursery rhyme: 5 SPRAT
  of politics and football: 4 KEMP
  partner: 4 JILL
  predecessor: 3 IKE
  TV host: 4 PAAR
  ___ Jack: 5 UNION
Jackal: 5 CANID

Jack and Jill
  vessel: 4 PAIL
Jacket: 4 COAT 5 PARKA
    6 BLAZER
  1960s-style ~: 5 NEHRU
  Arctic: 6 ANORAK
  buildup: 4 LINT
  fabric: 5 SUEDE TWEED
  feature: 3 ARM 4 SNAP VENT
    5 LAPEL 6 SLEEVE
    8 COATTAIL
  Kind of: 3 MAO 4 ETON FLAK
    5 NEHRU
  partner: 3 TIE
  Police ~ letters: 4 SWAT
  Short: 6 BOLERO
Jackie
  Actor: 4 CHAN 7 GLEASON
  Designer for: 4 **OLEG**
  predecessor: 5 MAMIE
  Sister of: 3 LEE
"Jackie Brown"
  star: 5 GRIER
"Jackie Gleason Show, The"
  network: 3 CBS
Jackie O
  Husband of: 3 **ARI**
"Jackie Robinson Story, The"
  actress: 7 RUBYDEE
Jack-in-the-pulpit: 4 ARUM
Jackknife: 4 DIVE
  It may: 4 SEMI
Jack-o'-lantern
  feature: 4 GRIN
Jackpot
  game: 5 LOTTO
  Hit the: 12 STRIKEITRICH
Jacks: 7 OPENERS
Jackson
  Actress: 4 KATE 6 GLENDA
  Country singer: 4 ALAN
  Gospel singer: 7 MAHALIA
  Jazzman: 4 MILT

NBA coach: 4 PHIL
Reverend: 5 JESSE
Singer: 5 JANET 6 BROWNE
    LATOYA 7 MICHAEL
Jackson, Jesse
intro: 3 REV
Jackson 5
hairdo: 4 AFRO
hit song: 3 ABC
member: 4 TITO
Jackson County, Texas
seat: 4 EDNA
Jackson Hole
backdrop: 6 TETONS
beast: 3 ELK
Jack-tar: 3 GOB 6 SAILOR
    SEAMAN
Jaclyn
TV angel: 5 SMITH
Jacob
Author: 4 **RIIS**
Father of: 5 ISAAC
Furrier: 5 ASTOR
Magnate: 5 ASTOR
Reformer: 4 **RIIS**
Son of: 4 **LEVI** 5 ASHER
Twin brother of: 4 **ESAU**
Wife of: 4 **LEAH** 6 RACHEL
~, to Esau: 4 TWIN
Jacobi
Actor: 5 DEREK
Jacobin
leader: 5 MARAT
Jacob ___ Park: 4 RIIS
Jacqueline
Actress: 6 BISSET
Author: 6 SUSANN
Jacques: 3 NOM
Actor: 4 **TATI**
Composer: 4 **BREL** 5 IBERT
Director: 4 TATI
French president: 6 CHIRAC
___ Jacques: 5 FRERE
Jacuzzi: 3 SPA
effect: 4 EDDY
feature: 3 JET
product: 6 HOTTUB
Jaffe
Author: 4 **RONA**

Jag: 5 SPREE
Classic: 3 XKE
rival: 3 BMW
"JAG"
network: 3 CBS
Jagged: 5 **EROSE** 6 UNEVEN
Jagger
and mates: 6 STONES
Ex of: 6 BIANCA
Rock star: 4 MICK
Jaguar: 3 CAR 4 AUTO 6 FELINE
Classic: 3 **XKE**
Jahan: 4 SHAH
city: 5 DELHI
tomb site: 4 AGRA
Jai ___: 4 **ALAI**
Jai alai
ball: 6 PELOTA
basket: 5 **CESTA**
locale: 7 FRONTON
Jail: 3 CAN 6 PRISON
feature: 7 IRONBAR
key: 9 CANOPENER
Navy: 4 BRIG
Out of: 4 FREE
Take to: 5 RUNIN
___ jail: 4 GOTO
Jailbird: 3 CON 6 INMATE
Jailbreak: 6 ESCAPE
participant: 7 ESCAPEE
Jaipur
City east of: 4 AGRA
Jakarta
island: 4 JAVA
Jake: 3 AOK
TV partner of: 6 FATMAN
"Jake's Thing"
author: 4 AMIS
Jalapeno: 6 PEPPER
Like a: 3 HOT
Jalopy: 4 HEAP 5 CRATE WRECK
Jalousie
part: 4 SLAT
Jam: 3 FIX 4 CRAM MESS
    5 SNARL TIEUP 6 SCRAPE
ingredient: 3 CAR 4 AUTO
Popular ~ band: 5 PHISH
up: 4 CLOG
Word with: 3 LOG

Jamaica
  gent: 3 MON
"Jamaica ___": 3 INN
Jamaican
  Certain: 5 **RASTA**
  export: 3 RUM
  fruit: 4 UGLI
  music: 3 **SKA** 6 REGGAE
Jamb
  insert: 4 DOOR
Jambalaya
  ingredient: 4 RICE
  Like: 6 CREOLE
Jamboree
  gp.: 3 BSA
  sight: 4 **TENT**
James
  Actor: 4 **CAAN** COCO
    5 WOODS 6 ARNESS
    SPADER
  Astronaut: 5 IRWIN
  Author: 4 **AGEE** 5 JOYCE
  Bk. before: 3 HEB
  Lyricist: 4 RADO
  Magician: 5 RANDI
  of the Met: 6 LEVINE
  Outlaw: 5 JESSE
  Revolutionary orator: 4 OTIS
  Singer: 4 **ETTA**
  Spy: 4 BOND
"James and the Giant Peach"
  author: 4 DAHL
James II
  Daughter of: 4 ANNE
"James Joyce"
  Author Leon: 4 EDEL
Jamestown
  John of: 5 ROLFE
James Whitcomb ___
  Poet: 5 RILEY
Jamie
  Actor: 4 FARR
Jammies: 3 PJS
Jam-pack: 4 CRAM
Jan
  Painter: 5 **STEEN**
Jan.
  honoree: 3 MLK
  preceder: 3 DEC

Jan. 1
  to now: 3 YTD
Jan. 1, 1994
  Act of: 5 NAFTA
Janacek
  Composer: 4 **LEOS**
Jane
  Actress: 5 FONDA
  Brother of: 5 PETER
  Dog of: 4 SPOT
  Fictional: 4 **EYRE**
  Lady: 4 GREY
Jane ___: 3 DOE
"Jane ___": 4 EYRE
"Jane Eyre": 7 HEROINE
  pupil: 5 ADELE
Janeiro
  starts it: 3 ANO
___ Janeiro: 5 RIODE
Janet
  Actress: 5 LEIGH
  Attorney General: 4 RENO
  Film critic: 6 MASLIN
  Olympic swimmer: 5 EVANS
  ~, to Michael: 3 SIB SIS
Janeway
  Economist: 5 ELIOT
Jangler: 5 ALARM
Janis
  Actress: 5 PAIGE
  Comic strip mate of: 4 **ARLO**
  Old comic actress: 5 ELSIE
  Singer: 3 IAN
Janitor
  tool: 3 MOP
Jann
  Rolling Stone founder:
    6 WENNER
Jannings
  Actor: 4 **EMIL**
Janowitz
  Author: 4 **TAMA**
January
  Big game in: 8 ROSEBOWL
  birthstone: 6 GARNET
  popper: 4 CORK
  song word: 4 AULD SYNE
  warm spell: 4 THAW
  ~, in Spanish: 5 **ENERO**

January 13th: 4 IDES
Japan: 7 FAREAST
  capital: 5 TOKYO
  city: 5 OSAKA OTARU
  ending: 3 ESE
  Former capital of: 3 EDO 4 **NARA**
    5 KYOTO
  Highest peak of: 4 FUJI
  island: 6 HONSHU 7 OKINAWA
  legislature: 4 DIET
Japanese: 5 ASIAN 9 EASTASIAN
  airline: 3 ANA
  art form: 7 ORIGAMI
  assassin: 5 **NINJA**
  band: 3 **OBI**
  Beatle: 3 ONO
  beer: 5 ASAHI KIRIN
    7 SAPPORO
  capital: 3 YEN
  car: 5 MIATA
  carp: 3 KOI
  cartoon art: 5 ANIME
  Certain: 6 OSAKAN
  chess: 5 SHOGI
  computer giant: 3 NEC
  dish: 5 SUSHI 7 TEMPURA
    8 SUKIYAKI
  dog: 5 **AKITA**
  drama: 3 **NOH** 6 KABUKI
  entertainer: 6 GEISHA
  fencing: 5 KENDO
  gateway: 5 TORII
  honorific: 3 **SAN**
  immigrant: 5 **ISSEI**
  leader of old: 6 SHOGUN
  martial art: 6 AIKIDO
  mat: 6 **TATAMI**
  miniature tree: 6 BONSAI
  money: 3 **YEN**
  noodles: 5 RAMEN
  novelist Kobo: 3 ABE
  parliament: 4 DIET
  porcelain: 5 IMARI
  port: 4 KOBE 5 OSAKA OTARU
    6 SASEBO 9 HIROSHIMA
  prime minister: 4 SATO
  rice drink: 4 SAKE
  sandal: 4 ZORI
  sash: 3 **OBI**

  soup: 4 **MISO**
  statesman: 3 ITO
  stringed instrument: 4 KOTO
  temple: 6 PAGODA
  vegetable: 3 UDO
  verse: 5 HAIKU
  warrior: 7 SAMURAI
Japanese-American: 5 ISSEI
    NISEI 6 SANSEI
Japheth
  Brother of: 4 SHEM
  Father of: 4 NOAH
Jar: 4 STUN
  Kind of: 5 MASON 6 LEYDEN
  part: 3 LID
Jardin zoologique
  inhabitant: 4 BETE
Jared
  Actor: 4 LETO
Jargon: 4 CANT JIVE 5 ARGOT
    LINGO
  suffix: 3 **ESE**
Jarreau
  and others: 3 ALS
Jarrett
  Jazzman: 5 KEITH
  NASCAR racer: 3 NED
Jasmine: 4 VINE
Jason
  Field goal kicker: 4 ELAM
  Ship of: 4 **ARGO**
  Wife of: 5 **MEDEA**
Jasper
  Painter: 5 JOHNS
Jaundiced: 6 SALLOW
Jaunt: 4 RIDE TRIP 8 SIDETRIP
Jauntily
  Wear: 5 SPORT
Jaunty: 4 AIRY PERT 6 RAKISH
  greeting: 4 HIHO
  hat: 5 BERET
  rhythm: 4 LILT
Java: 3 JOE
  holder: 3 CUP MUG URN
  Island near: 4 **BALI**
  selection: 5 DECAF
"Java"
  trumpeter: 4 HIRT 6 ALHIRT
Javelin: 5 SPEAR

Javits Center
  architect: 3 PEI
Jaw: 3 GAB YAP
  Drop your: 4 GAPE
  Make the ~ drop: 3 AWE
  With dropped: 5 AGAPE
Jawaharlal
  Daughter of: 6 INDIRA
Jawbone: 8 MANDIBLE
  Biblical ~ source: 3 ASS
Jaworski
  of Watergate: 4 LEON
"Jaws"
  boat: 4 **ORCA**
  omen: 3 **FIN**
Jay
  Actor: 4 MOHR
  Author: 5 ANSON
  follower: 3 KAY
  Former announcer for: 3 EDD
  home: 4 NEST
  Host: 4 **LENO**
  Host after: 5 CONAN
  preceder: 3 DEE
  Rival of: 4 DAVE
Jayvee
  athlete, perhaps: 4 SOPH
Jaywalking: 4 NONO
"Jaywalking"
  comedian: 4 LENO
Jay-Z: 7 RAPSTAR
  genre: 3 RAP
Jazz: 4 TEAM
  accompaniment: 4 VAMP
  album: 4 ELLA
  bandleader: 5 SUNRA
  band member: 7 SIDEMAN
  bit: 4 RIFF
  club unit: 3 SET
  combo: 4 TRIO 5 OCTET
  dance: 5 STOMP
  drummer: 8 MAXROACH
  fan: 3 CAT 6 HEPCAT
  form: 5 BLUES
  genre: 4 JIVE
  gp.: 3 NBA
  group: 5 COMBO
  instrument: 3 SAX 7 ALTOSAX
    8 TENORSAX

  job: 3 GIG
  lick: 4 RIFF
  Like some: 4 COOL
  nickname: 5 SATCH 7 SATCHMO
  performance: 3 JAM
    10 JAMSESSION
  phrase: 4 LICK RIFF
  pianist: 5 TATUM 8 ARTTATUM
    10 COUNTBASIE
    15 JELLYROLLMORTON
  saxophonist: 8 COLTRANE
    STANGETZ
  score: 4 HOOP
  setting: 4 UTAH
  singing: 4 SCAT
  style: 3 BOP 5 BEBOP
  trumpeter: 6 ALHIRT
  Type of: 4 ACID
  up: 7 ENLIVEN
  (up): 4 HOKE 5 SPICE
Jazzman: 3 CAT
  cue: 5 HITIT
  instrument: 3 AXE
"Jazz Singer, The": 6 TALKIE
J. Carroll ___: 5 NAISH
JCPenney
  rival: 5 SEARS
Jct.
  component: 3 HWY RTE
J.D.
  holder: 3 ATT
  hurdle: 4 LSAT
Jean: 3 NOM
  Actress: 6 HARLOW SEBERG
  Author: 4 AUEL
  Dadaist: 3 **ARP**
  Playwright: 5 GENET
  Psychologist: 6 PIAGET
Jeanmaire
  Dancer: 5 RENEE
Jeanne: 3 STE
Jeanne ___ : 4 DARC
Jeannette
  First Congresswoman: 6 RANKIN
Jean-Paul
  French revolutionary: 5 MARAT
Jeans: 5 LEVIS PANTS
  brand: 3 LEE
  fabric: 5 DENIM

feature: **5** RIVET
Like old: **5** FADED
Jeb
of Bull Run: **6** STUART
J.E.B. ___ : **6** STUART
Jedi
master: **4** YODA
Jeep
maker, once: **3** AMC
"Jeepers!": **4** EGAD GOSH
Jeer: **4** GIBE HOOT **5** SCOFF
TAUNT **7** CATCALL
Jeff
Pal of: **4** MUTT
Racer: **6** GORDON
Jefferson: **5** DEIST
bill: **3** TWO
portrayer: **5** NOLTE
Pres.: **4** THOS
Sch. founded by: **3** <u>UVA</u>
veep: **4** BURR
"Jefferson in Paris"
actor: **5** NOLTE **9** NICKNOLTE
"Jeffersons, The"
Sanford of: **6** ISABEL
star: **7** HEMSLEY
Jehoshaphat
Father of: **3** ASA
Jehovah's Witnesses: **4** SECT
Jejune: **4** ARID **5** STALE
Jekyll, Dr.
Alter ego of: **4** <u>**HYDE**</u>
6 MRHYDE
creator's initials: **3** RLS
~, to Mr. Hyde: **8** ALTEREGO
"Jekyll & Hyde"
Linda of: **4** EDER
Jellied
delicacy: **3** EEL
garnish: **5** <u>**ASPIC**</u>
Jelling
agent: **4** AGAR
Jell-O
Like ~, often: **6** MOLDED
Move like: **6** WIGGLE
Jelly: **6** SPREAD
bean flavor: **8** LICORICE
container: **3** <u>**JAR**</u>
Flammable: **6** STERNO

flavor: **4** MINT **5** GRAPE <u>**GUAVA**</u>
Inedible: **8** VASELINE
ingredient: **6** PECTIN
Royal ~ maker: **3** BEE
Savory: **5** <u>**ASPIC**</u>
Word following: **4** ROLL
Jellyfish: **6** MEDUSA
appendage: **8** TENTACLE
Jelly Roll
of jazz: **6** MORTON
"Jelly's Last Jam"
dancer: **5** HINES
Jellystone Park
bear: **4** YOGI **6** BOOBOO
Jemima: **4** AUNT
Jemison
Astronaut: **3** MAE
Je ne ___ quoi: **4** SAIS
Jenna
Actress: **6** ELFMAN
Jennifer
Actress: **5** BEALS LOPEZ
Former husband of: **4** BRAD
"Jennifer 8"
actress Thurman: **3** UMA
Jennings: **6** ANCHOR
Newscaster: **5** PETER
Jenny: **3** ASS
Diet guru: **5** CRAIG
Little ~, in nursery rhyme:
4 WREN
Soprano: **4** LIND
Jeopardy: **4** RISK **5** PERIL
In: **6** ATRISK
Out of: **8** HOMEFREE
"Jeopardy!"
ans.: **4** QUES
clue: **6** ANSWER
column: **8** CATEGORY
contestant: **5** ASKER
host Alex: **6** TREBEK
host Trebek: **4** ALEX
millionaire Jennings: **3** KEN
Respond on: **3** ASK
staple: **6** TRIVIA
Jer.
Book before: **3** ISA
Jeremiah
Book before: **6** ISAIAH

"Jeremiah Johnson"
  actor Will: 4 GEER
Jeremy
  Actor: 5 IRONS
  Singing partner of: 4 CHAD
Jerk: 3 ASS BOB TIC TUG 4 BOZO
    TWIT YANK 5 IDIOT
    MORON REACT **SCHMO**
    SPASM
  Kind of: 4 KNEE SODA
Jerky
  Made: 5 DRIED
  Make: 4 CURE
Jermaine
  Brother of: 4 TITO
Jerome
  Composer: 4 KERN
  novel: 15 THREEMENINABOAT
Jerry
  Cartoonist: 6 SIEGEL
  Comedian: 5 LEWIS
  of basketball: 4 WEST
  of the Grateful Dead: 6 GARCIA
  Partner of: 3 **BEN** 4 DEAN
  Singer: 4 VALE
Jerry-built: 6 SHODDY
Jerry Lee ___: 5 LEWIS
"Jerry Maguire"
  actress Zellweger: 5 RENEE
  Oscar winner:
    13 CUBAGOODINGJR
Jersey: 3 COW 4 KNIT
  chew: 3 CUD
  hangout: 3 LEA
  remark: 3 MOO
"Jersey Lily, The": 7 LANGTRY
Jerusalem
  airline: 4 ELAL
  Capital east of: 5 AMMAN
  country: 6 ISRAEL
  day: 3 YOM
  temple hill: 4 ZION
Jesse
  Olympian: 5 OWENS
  Outlaw: 5 JAMES
Jessica
  Actress: 4 ALBA 5 **LANGE**
    TANDY
  portrayer on TV: 6 ANGELA

Jest: 4 JAPE 5 PUTON
Jester: 4 FOOL
Jesus
  Language of: 7 ARAMAIC
  letters: 4 INRI
  miracle site: 4 CANA
  of baseball: 4 ALOU
  story: 7 PARABLE
"Jesus ___" (shortest Bible verse):
    4 WEPT
Jet: 4 EBON
  Air, to a ~ engine: 6 INTAKE
  black: 4 INKY ONYX 5 EBONY
    SABLE
  follower: 3 LAG
  giant: 4 LEAR
  Mil. ~ letters: 4 USAF
  Mil. ~ locale: 3 AFB
  prefix: 5 TURBO
  Russian: 3 MIG
  speed unit: 4 MACH
  stream heading: 4 EAST
Jeté: 4 LEAP
Jeter
  of baseball: 5 **DEREK**
Jethro
  Agriculturalist: 4 TULL
Jethro ___ (rock band): 4 TULL
Jet Propulsion Lab
  org.: 4 NASA
  site: 7 CALTECH
Jets: 4 GANG TEAM
  Joe of the: 6 NAMATH
  Like the: 5 ANGLO
  one-time org.: 3 AFL
Jetsam
  of 1773: 3 TEA
Jet-set
  destination: 7 RIVIERA
Jetson
  dog: 5 **ASTRO**
  maid: 5 ROSIE
  mom: 4 JANE
  son: 5 **ELROY**
Jetson, Judy
  Brother of: 5 ELROY
Jettison: 4 DUMP TOSS 5 SCRAP
Jetty: 4 PIER QUAY
___ Jeunesse: 3 UNE

Jewel: 3 GEM 5 BIJOU STONE
  box: 6 CDCASE
Jeweled
  crown: 5 **TIARA**
Jeweler
  item: 3 GEM
  magnifier: 5 LOUPE
  unit: 5 **CARAT** KARAT
Jewelry
  Big name in: 5 ZALES
  Carved: 5 CAMEO
  Fake: 5 **PASTE**
  item: 3 PIN 4 RING 6 BROOCH
    CHOKER 7 PENDANT
    8 BRACELET
  Showy ~, in slang:
    10 BLINGBLING
"Jewel Song": 4 ARIA
Jewett, Sarah ___ : 4 ORNE
Jewish
  campus organization: 6 HILLEL
  community: 6 SHTETL
  dance: 4 HORA
  feast: 5 SEDER
  festival: 5 PURIM
  Like much ~ food: 6 KOSHER
  month: 4 ADAR ELUL 6 TISHRI
  mystical doctrine: 6 CABALA
  Old ~ scholar: 4 ABBA
  robot: 5 GOLEM
  scripture: 5 TORAH
  teacher: 5 RABBI REBBE
Jew's-harp
  sound: 5 TWANG
Jezebel: 5 HUSSY
  Husband of: 4 **AHAB**
  idol: 4 BAAL
  portrayer: 5 BETTE
JFK: 3 DEM 4 PRES 7 AIRPORT
  arrival: 3 SST
  carrier: 3 KLM 4 ELAL
  info: 3 ARR **ETA** ETD
  Like: 4 INTL
  opponent: 3 RMN
  part: 4 INIT
  predecessor: 3 **DDE**
  quote start: 3 ASK 6 ASKNOT
  regulator: 3 FAA
  successor: 3 LBJ

  terminal: 3 TWA
  was in it: 3 USN
  ~ U.N. ambassador: 3 AES
    15 ADLAIESTEVENSON
"JFK"
  actor Joe: 5 PESCI
  director Oliver: 5 STONE
JFK Library
  designer: 3 PEI 5 IMPEI
J. Geils Band
  song: 10 LOVESTINKS
Jib: 4 SAIL
  Racing: 5 GENOA
Jibe: 4 MESH 5 AGREE
Jidda
  locale: 6 REDSEA
Jiff: 3 **SEC**
Jiffy: 3 **SEC** 5 TRICE 6 MOMENT
Jiggermast
  Like a: 3 AFT
Jigsaw
  part: 5 PIECE
Jillian
  Actress: 3 ANN
Jillions: 4 ALOT LOTS 6 OODLES
Jim
  Athlete: 6 THORPE
  Newsman: 6 LEHRER
  Olympics sportscaster: 5 MCKAY
  Singer: 5 CROCE
___ Jima: 3 **IWO**
Jim and Tammy
  org.: 3 PTL
Jim-dandy: 4 AONE NEAT NICE
    5 SWELL
Jimenez, Jose
  portrayer: 4 DANA
    8 BILLDANA
Jimjams: 3 DTS
Jimmie
  Mouseketeer: 4 DODD
Jimmy: 3 PRY 5 LEVER
  Actor: 5 SMITS
  Labor leader: 5 HOFFA
  Predecessor of: 6 GERALD
  Rival of: 4 ILIE
  Successor of: 6 RONALD
Jingle
  writer: 5 ADMAN

"Jingle Bells"
  contraction: 3 OER
Jinx: 3 HEX
Jipijapa
  hat: 6 PANAMA
Jitterbug
  relative: 5 LINDY
Jitteriness: 6 NERVES
Jitters: 6 UNEASE
  Worse than: 5 ANGST
Jittery: 4 EDGY 5 ANTSY TENSE
    6 ONEDGE
Jo
  Sister of: 4 BETH
Joad, Tom: 4 **OKIE**
Joan: 3 STE
  Folk singer: 4 BAEZ
  Rock singer: 4 **JETT**
  Surrealist painter: 4 **MIRO**
"Joanie Loves Chachi"
  costar Moran: 4 ERIN
Joanna
  Actress: 5 KERNS
Joanne
  Actress: 3 **DRU**
Joan of ___: 3 ARC
Joan of Arc: 6 MARTYR
  City saved by: 7 ORLEANS
  death site: 5 ROUEN
"Joan of Arc"
  actress Sobieski: 6 LEELEE
___ João: 3 SAO
Job: 3 GIG 4 POST TASK
    5 CHORE HEIST
  ad letters: 3 EOE
  Barber: 4 TRIM
  Bk. before: 4 ESTH
  Con: 4 SCAM
  Crime: 5 CAPER
  Dead-end: 3 RUT
  detail, briefly: 4 SPEC
  Detective: 4 CASE
  Did a smithy: 4 SHOD 5 SHOED
  Double: 5 STUNT
  Emcee: 5 INTRO
  extra: 4 PERK
  follower: 6 PSALMS
  Friend of: 5 ELIHU
  Grease: 4 LUBE

  Kind of: 4 RUSH SNOW
  Off the: 4 IDLE
  On the: 4 ATIT 6 ATWORK
  opening: 4 SLOT
  preceder: 6 ESTHER
  safety org.: 4 OSHA
  Salon: 3 SET 4 PERM TINT
    5 RINSE
  Scout: 5 RECON
  security: 6 TENURE
  Time on the: 5 STINT
  Torch: 5 ARSON
  Tow: 4 REPO
  Up to the: 4 ABLE
  Wrecker: 3 TOW
"___ Job": 4 GETA
Jobs
  Like some: 3 ODD 5 CUSHY
    6 INSIDE
  of computers: 5 STEVE
  offering: 4 IMAC
  ~, so to speak: 4 HATS
Jock: 7 ATHLETE
  antithesis: 4 NERD
  Wife of: 5 ELLIE
Jockey: 5 RIDER
  1930 Triple-Crown ~: 5 SANDE
  attire: 5 SILKS
  Kind of: 4 DISC
  need: 4 CROP
  strap: 4 REIN
  Two-time Triple-Crown:
    6 ARCARO
  ~ Angel: 7 CORDERO
  ~ Arcaro: 5 EDDIE
Jocular
  nickname: 5 KIDDO
Joe: 4 JAVA 6 COFFEE
  Actor: 5 PESCI SPANO
  and Jane: 3 GIS
  Baseball manager: 5 **TORRE**
  holder: 3 CUP URN
  Joltless: 5 DECAF SANKA
  Playwright: 5 ORTON
  ~, in French: 4 CAFE
___ Joe: 5 INJUN
Joel
  Actor: 4 GREY 6 MCCREA
  Book after: 4 AMOS

Book before: **5** HOSEA
Director: **4** **COEN**
Joel, Billy
   instrument: **5** PIANO
Joey
   mom: **8** KANGAROO
   of twister fame: **3** DEE
   Punk rocker: **6** RAMONE
Joffrey
   of ballet: **6** ROBERT
Jog: 3 RUN **4** TROT
Jogger
   purchase: **5** NIKES
Johann
   Author: **4** WYSS
Johannes
   Astronomer: **6** KEPLER
Johann Sebastian ___: 4 BACH
Johansson
   Boxer: **7** INGEMAR
John: 3 LAV **4** POPE **6** TOILET
   Actor: **5** ASTIN **6** CLEESE
   AFL-CIO: **7** SWEENEY
   Anonymous: **3** DOE
   Arctic explorer: **3** RAE
   Author: **5** OHARA **6** UPDIKE
      7 GRISHAM
   Batting champ: **6** OLERUD
   Book after: **4** ACTS
   Book before: **4** LUKE
   Brewer: **6** LABATT
   British: **3** **LOO**
   Broncos QB: **5** ELWAY
   Cards expert: **6** SCARNE
   Comedian: **5** BYNER
   Dante translater: **6** CIARDI
   Director: **3** WOO
   Explorer: **5** CABOT
   Farm equipment maker: **5** DEERE
   Former TV host: **4** TESH
   Furrier ~ Jacob: **5** **ASTOR**
   Justice: **3** JAY
   Naturalist: **4** **MUIR**
   New Age musician: **4** **TESH**
   or Jane: **3** DOE
   or Paul: **6** BEATLE
   Painter: **4** OPIE
   Philosopher: **5** LOCKE
   Pilgrim: **5** **ALDEN**

Playwright: **7** OSBORNE
Poet: **5** DONNE KEATS
Politician: **6** SUNUNU
Russian: **4** IVAN
Scottish: **3** IAN
Singer: **5** **ELTON** RAITT
TV pioneer: **5** BAIRD
Welsh: **4** EVAN
Widow of: **4** YOKO
Wife of: **4** YOKO
with a wild wardrobe: **5** ELTON
~, Paul, and George (abbr.): **3** STS
John ___: 3 DOE
___ John: 4 DEAR
John, Elton
   title: **3** SIR
John Boy
   Sister of: **4** ERIN
John Boyd ___: 3 ORR
"John Brown's Body"
   poet: **5** BENET
John Dickson ___: 4 CARR
"___ John, M.D.": 7 TRAPPER
Johnny
   Actor: **4** DEPP
   Announcer: **5** **OLSON**
   of baseball: **4** MIZE
   Quarterback: **6** UNITAS
   Singer: **6** MATHIS
Johnny ___: 3 REB
"___ Johnny!": 5 HERES
Johnny Appleseed
   last name: **7** CHAPMAN
"Johnny B. ___": 5 GOODE
Johnnycake: 4 PONE
"Johnny Mnemonic"
   actor/rapper: **4** ICET
Johnny Reb
   gp.: **3** CSA
John Paul II: 4 POLE POPE
   Given name of: **5** KAROL
   Like: **5** PAPAL
John Philip ___: 5 SOUSA
John/Rice
   musical: **4** AIDA
Johns, Jasper
   genre: **6** POPART
Johnson
   Comic: **4** **ARTE**

Decathlete: 5 RAFER
dog: 3 HER HIM
in-law: 4 ROBB
Johnson, Claudia ___ Taylor:
    4 ALTA
Johnson, Dame ___: 5 CELIA
Johnson & Johnson
  item: 4 QTIP
Johnstown
  disaster: 5 FLOOD
John Wooden Center
  site: 4 UCLA
Joie de vivre: 4 **ELAN**
Join: 3 WED 4 BAND KNIT
        LINK WELD 5 ENROL
        ENTER UNITE
        6 ENLIST
  forces: 4 ALLY 5 MERGE UNITE
        6 TEAMUP
  metal items: 6 SOLDER
  securely: 5 TENON
        .7 MORTISE
  temporarily: 5 SITIN
  the team: 4 YOKE
  together: 4 TEAM 6 SPLICE
  up: 6 SIGNON
Joiner
  Common: 3 AND
  Woodworking: 5 DOWEL
Joining
  words: 3 IDO
Joint: 6 MUTUAL REEFER
  ailment: 4 GOUT
  Arm: 5 ELBOW
  Fix, as a pipe: 6 REWELD
  Jacuzzi: 3 SPA
  Kind of: 5 HINGE MITER
  Leg: 4 KNEE 5 ANKLE
  Oink: 3 STY
  part: 5 TENON 7 MORTISE
  Pipe: 3 ELL TEE
  point: 4 NODE
  problem: 4 ACHE
  protection: 7 KNEEPAD
  Quirky: 9 TRICKKNEE
  Seedy: 4 DIVE
  Swivel: 3 HIP
  Tailor: 4 SEAM
  tenant: 3 CON 5 FELON

Three-way: 3 TEE
Jointly
  Held: 6 POOLED
Joke: 3 GAG KID 4 JAPE JEST
  around with: 3 KID
  As a: 5 INFUN
  Butt of a: 4 GOAT 6 STOOGE
  Cohort of priest and minister in a:
      5 RABBI
  Funny: 4 RIOT 6 GASSER
  Get the: 5 LAUGH
  Kind of: 10 KNOCKKNOCK
  Knock-knock: 3 PUN
  Like an old: 5 CORNY STALE
  Old: 6 WHEEZE
  Online ~ response: 3 LOL
  Practical: 3 GAG 4 JAPE
      5 PRANK 7 LEGPULL
  React to a bad: 5 WINCE
  response: 4 HAHA 6 IGETIT
  setting: 3 BAR
  Short: 8 ONELINER
  target: 4 BUTT
  Way to pass on a: 5 EMAIL
Joker: 3 WAG 4 CARD 5 CUTUP
  portrayer Cesar: 6 **ROMERO**
  Practical: 9 LEGPULLER
Jokers
  Game with four: 7 CANASTA
Jokester: 3 WAG
Jokingly: 5 INFUN 6 INJEST
Jolie
  Actress: 8 ANGELINA
Jollies: 3 FUN
Jolliet
  1669 ~ discovery: 4 ERIE
Jollity: 3 FUN 4 GLEE 5 MIRTH
Jolly
  Season to be: 4 NOEL YULE
Jolly ___: 5 ROGER
Jolly Roger
  feature: 4 BONE 5 BONES
        SKULL
  mate: 4 SMEE
"___ jolly swagman": 5 ONCEA
Jolson
  and others: 3 ALS
  portrayer Parks: 5 LARRY
  real first name: 3 **ASA**

song: 6 SWANEE
       15 TOOTTOOTTOOTSIE
Jolt: 3 JAR ZAP 4 BUMP 5 SHOCK
"Joltin' Joe": 5 DIMAG 6 YANKEE
Joltless
  joe: 5 DECAF SANKA
Jon
  Director: 5 AMIEL
  Dog of: 4 ODIE
  Illustrator: 4 AGEE
  Rock singer: 7 BONJOVI
Jonah
  Book after: 5 MICAH
  swallower: 5 WHALE
Jonas
  Vaccine developer: 4 SALK
Jonathan: 5 APPLE
  Director: 5 DEMME
Jones: 7 SURNAME
  Architect: 5 **INIGO**
  Bandleader: 5 SPIKE
  Casey: 8 ENGINEER TRAINMAN
  Composer: 5 ISHAM
  Grammy winner: 5 NORAH
  Jazz singer: 4 **ETTA**
  Jazz trumpeter: 4 THAD
  of the Miracle Mets: 5 CLEON
  Playwright: 5 LEROI
  Poet: 5 LEROI
  ___ Jones: 3 DOW
Jones, Davy
  domain: 3 SEA
Jones, Dr.
  nickname: 4 INDY
Jones, Indiana
  quest: 3 ARK
  trademark: 6 FEDORA
Jones, Marion
  Where ~ won: 6 SYDNEY
Jones, Tommy Lee
  movie: 4 COBB
  ___ Jones's locker: 4 DAVY
Jong
  Author: 5 **ERICA**
Jonson: 4 POET
  work: 3 ODE
Joplin
  genre: 7 RAGTIME
  Singer: 5 JANIS

Joplin, Scott
  piece: 3 **RAG**
Jordan
  capital: 5 AMMAN
  Director: 4 NEIL
  Former queen of: 4 NOOR
  neighbor: 5 SYRIA
  neighbor (abbr.): 3 SYR
  Seaport city of: 5 AQABA
Jordan, Michael
  alma mater (abbr.): 3 UNC
  epithet: 3 AIR
  former team: 5 BULLS
  org.: 3 NBA
  underwear: 5 HANES
Jordanian: 4 ARAB
Jorge
  Author: 5 AMADO
  Pianist: 5 BOLET
"Jo's Boys"
  author: 6 ALCOTT
José
  Flamenco dancer: 5 GRECO
  Pet name for: 4 PEPE
  Pianist: 6 ITURBI
  preceder: 3 SAN
  Uncle: 3 TIO
  World Series MVP: 4 RIJO
  ___ Jose: 3 SAN
José Marie ___
  Muralist: 4 SERT
Joseph
  Columnist: 5 ALSOP
  Journalist: 5 ALSOP
  Theater producer: 4 PAPP
Josephine
  Mystery author: 3 **TEY**
Josh: 3 **KID** RIB 5 TEASE
Joss: 4 IDOL
Jostle: 3 JAR 5 ELBOW SHOVE
Jot: 3 TAD 4 ATOM IOTA WHIT
     5 SPECK 6 TITTLE
  down: 4 NOTE
Jottings: 5 NOTES
Joule
  fraction: 3 **ERG**
  per second: 4 WATT
"Jour de Fete"
  star: 4 TATI

Journal: 3 LOG
  British medical: 6 LANCET
  ending: 3 ESE
  Nautical: 3 LOG
  Org. with a: 3 **AMA**
Journalist: 6 SCRIBE
  idea: 5 ANGLE
  WWII: 4 PYLE
Journey: 4 **TREK** TRIP
  7 ODYSSEY
  Begin a: 6 SETOUT
  Muslim: 4 HADJ HAJJ
  part: 3 LEG
  Self-directed: 7 EGOTRIP
  Tough: 4 TREK
"Journey Into Fear"
  author Ambler: 4 ERIC
  author Eric: 6 AMBLER
"Journey of Natty ___, The":
  4 GANN
Joust: 4 TILT
  verbally: 4 SPAR
Jousting: 5 ATILT
  arena: 5 LISTS
  Defeat at: 7 UNHORSE
  weapon: 5 LANCE
Jovi, Jon ___: 3 BON
Joy: 4 GLEE 7 ELATION
  Author: 7 ADAMSON
  Bring ~ to: 5 ELATE
  Express: 3 OOH 4 WEEP
  Exude: 4 BEAM
  Jump for: 5 EXULT
  Partner of: 5 PRIDE
  With: 5 GAILY
"___ Joy": 5 ODETO
Joyce
  epic: 7 ULYSSES
  Nation of: 4 EIRE
Joyce Carol ___
  Author: 5 **OATES**
Joyful
  dance: 4 HORA
  Make: 5 ELATE
"___ joy keep you": Sandberg:
  4 LETA
"Joy Luck Club, The"
  author: 3 TAN 6 AMYTAN
  game: 8 MAHJONGG

"Joy of Cooking, The"
  author: 8 ROMBAUER
  author Rombauer: 4 IRMA
"___, Joy of Man's Desiring":
  4 JESU
"Joy of Sex, The"
  Author Comfort: 4 ALEX
Joyous: 3 GAY 5 MERRY
  affair: 4 GALA
  hymn: 5 PAEAN
Joyride: 4 SPIN
Joystick: 5 LEVER
  Use a: 6 AVIATE
J.P.
  Flee to a: 5 ELOPE
  visitor: 6 ELOPER
J. Paul
  Oil magnate: 5 GETTY
Jr.
  exam: 4 PSAT
  Son of ~, maybe: 3 III
  Yr. before: 4 SOPH
Jr. high
  Sch. before: 4 ELEM
Jrs.
  Former: 3 SRS
Juan
  Cubist: 4 GRIS
  or Eva: 5 PERON
  preceder: 3 SAN
  Wife of: 3 EVA
Juan, Don: 4 ROUE
  9 LADIESMAN
  Mother of: 4 INEZ
___ Juana Ines: 3 SOR
Juan Carlos: 3 REY
  Daughter of: 5 ELENA
Juárez
  of Mexico: 6 BENITO
Jubilance: 7 ELATION
Jubilant: 6 ELATED
  Be: 5 EXULT
Judah
  Mother of: 4 LEAH
  Son of: 4 **ONAN**
Judd
  Actor: 6 HIRSCH
  Mother: 5 NAOMI
  Singer: 5 **NAOMI**

Jude
Actor: 3 LAW
Judean
king: 5 **HEROD**
Judge: 4 **DEEM** RATE 5 TRIER
      6 ASSESS CRITIC
      7 ARBITER
Biblical: 3 ELI
Consider, as a: 4 HEAR
cry: 5 ORDER
demand: 5 ORDER
Dressed like a: 5 ROBED
Former TV: 4 KOCH 6 EDKOCH
    WAPNER
garb: 4 ROBE
in Judges: 6 GIDEON
Like a: 5 SOBER
need: 5 GAVEL
O.J. Simpson: 3 ITO
    8 LANCEITO
seat in court: 4 BANC
TV: 4 JUDY
~ Fortas: 3 ABE
Judges: 4 REFS
Book after: 4 RUTH
Group of: 5 PANEL
Judge in: 6 GIDEON
"Judging Amy"
actress Daly: 4 **TYNE**
actress Tyne: 4 DALY
Judgment
Artistic: 5 TASTE
Await: 4 PEND
Good: 5 SENSE
    10 HORSESENSE
Kind of: 4 SNAP
Unjust: 6 BADRAP
"Judgment at Nuremberg"
director: 6 KRAMER
___ judicata: 3 RES
Judicial
comments: 5 DICTA
delay: 4 STAY
inquiry: 6 ASSIZE
order: 4 WRIT
Judicious: 4 SAGE WISE 5 SOBER
Judith
Actress: 4 **IVEY**
Astronaut: 6 RESNIK

"Judith"
composer: 4 **ARNE**
Judo
level: 3 DAN
master: 6 SENSEI
Judy
Comic: 5 CARNE 6 TENUTA
Daughter of: 4 LIZA
Jug: 4 **EWER**
band instrument: 5 KAZOO
beverage: 5 CIDER
handle: 3 EAR
Wide-mouthed: 4 EWER OLLA
Juggler
fruits: 7 ORANGES
Jughead: 4 TEEN 8 TEENAGER
Friend of: 6 ARCHIE
Juice
Beetle: 3 GAS
Bug: 3 GAS
drink: 3 **ADE**
Extract ~ from: 4 REAM
Kind of: 3 MOO
Medicinal: 4 ALOE
Pickle: 5 BRINE
Pour ~ over: 5 BASTE
Provide ~ for: 6 PLUGIN
source: 6 OUTLET
Tree: 3 SAP
with punch: 9 HARDCIDER
Juicer: 3 SOT
refuse: 4 PULP
Juices: 6 SALIVA
Big name in: 5 MOTTS
Juicy: 5 MOIST
fruit: 4 PEAR
gossip: 4 DIRT
morsel: 6 TIDBIT
Juillet
season: 3 ETE
Juilliard
deg.: 3 MFA
subj.: 3 MUS
Juin
preceder: 3 MAI
season: 3 ETE
Juju: 6 AMULET
Jukebox
part: 4 SLOT

verb: 6 SELECT
Jule
 Composer: 5 **STYNE**
Julep
 enhancer: 4 MINT
Jules
 Author: 5 VERNE
 Composer: 8 MASSENET
 Painter: 5 DUPRE
 school: 5 ECOLE
Juli
 Golfer: 7 INKSTER
Julia
 2000 role for ~: 4 **ERIN**
 Actor: 4 **RAUL**
 Ex of: 4 LYLE
 TV chef: 5 CHILD
Julian
 of rock music: 6 LENNON
Julia Ward ___
 Reformer: 4 HOWE
Juliet
 Beloved of: 5 ROMEO
 Dancer: 6 PROWSE
 Emulate: 5 ELOPE
 Home of: 6 VERONA
 Last name of: 7 CAPULET
 Romeo, to: 5 LOVER
 ~, to Romeo: 3 SUN
Julio: 3 MES
 Vintner: 5 GALLO
Julius
 avenger: 4 MARC
 Crooner: 6 LAROSA
 Villain named: 4 DRNO
"Julius Caesar"
 costume: 4 TOGA
 role: 5 CASCA
 setting: 4 ROME 6 SENATE
Julius III
 Start of ~ papacy: 3 MDL
July
 birthstone: 4 RUBY
 Late ~ birth: 3 LEO
 noisemaker:
  11 FIRECRACKER
July 4, 1776
 ~, for one: 4 DATE
July 15: 4 IDES

Jumble: 4 HASH MESS OLIO
  5 CHAOS MIXUP
  8 MISHMASH
Jumbo: 5 LARGE
Jumna
 City on the: 4 AGRA
Jump: 3 HOP 4 LEAP VERB
 Ballet: 4 JETE
  9 PASDECHAT
 electrodes: 3 ARC
 for joy: 5 EXULT
 Make: 5 SCARE
 of surprise: 5 START
 on the ice: 4 **AXEL** LUTZ
  7 SALCHOW
 over: 4 LEAP OMIT
 Triple ~ feature: 3 HOP
 What to ~ for: 3 JOY
Jumped: 5 LEAPT 6 SPRANG
 It may be: 4 BAIL
 to one's feet: 5 AROSE
Jumper
 Aussie: 3 ROO
 cable connection: 5 ANODE
 Cord for a: 6 BUNGEE
 High: 4 FLEA
Jumping
 Big name in: 4 EVEL
 Twain's ~ frog: 4 DANL
Jumping-off
 point: 4 EDGE
"Jumpin' Jack Flash, it's ___ ...":
  4 AGAS
Jump-starting
 org.: 3 AAA
Jumpy: 5 TENSE 6 ONEDGE
Junction
 Petticoat: 4 SEAM
 point: 4 **NODE**
"___ Junction": 9 PETTICOAT
June: 4 NAME
 Actress: 5 HAVER HAVOC
 bug: 6 BEETLE
 celebrant: 4 GRAD
 honoree: 3 **DAD** 4 GRAD
  8 OLDGLORY
 Early ~ birth: 6 GEMINI
June 6, 1944: 4 DDAY
June 14: 7 FLAGDAY

Jung
　Inner soul, to: 5 ANIMA
　Psychiatrist: 4 CARL
Jungfrau: 3 ALP
Jungian
　principle: 5 ANIMA
　topic: 3 EGO
Jungle
　crusher: 3 BOA 8 ANACONDA
　groomer: 3 APE
　growth: 4 VINE
　King of the: 4 LION
　sound: 4 ROAR
　swinger: 3 **APE**
　vine: 5 LIANA
　woman: 4 JANE
"Jungle, The"
　novelist: 8 SINCLAIR
　novelist Sinclair: 5 UPTON
"Jungle Book, The"
　bear: 5 BALOO
　boy: 6 MOWGLI
　setting: 5 INDIA
　snake: 3 KAA
　star: 4 SABU
　tiger: 9 SHEREKHAN
Junho to Junho: 3 ANO
Junior: 3 SON 4 YEAR
　Dolphins linebacker: 4 SEAU
　Future: 4 SOPH
　H.S. ~ test: 4 **PSAT**
　of a junior: 3 III
　Watch: 3 SIT
　watcher: 6 SITTER
　Whopper: 3 FIB
　~, to Senior: 8 NAMESAKE
Juniper
　drink: 3 GIN
Junipero
　Missionary: 5 SERRA
Junk: 4 SHIP 5 SCRAP TRASH
　e-mail: 4 **SPAM**
　Some of it is: 4 MAIL
Junket: 4 TRIP 5 SPREE
Junkie: 4 USER
Junk mail: 3 ADS
　Like much: 6 UNREAD
Junky
　car: 4 HEAP

Junkyard
　dog: 3 CUR
Juno
　Greek counterpart of: 4 HERA
"Juno and the Paycock"
　playwright: 6 OCASEY
Junta: 5 CABAL
Jupiter: 3 GOD 4 DEUS JOVE
　　　　　5 DEITY
　Greek counterpart of: 4 ZEUS
　Moon of: 3 OPS 4 LEDA
　　　　　6 EUROPA
　probe: 7 GALILEO
　Wife of: 4 JUNO
Jurado
　Actress: 4 KATY
Jurassic
　carnivore: 8 ALLOSAUR
"Jurassic Park"
　actor Sam: 5 NEILL
　actress Laura: 4 **DERN**
　actress Richards: 6 ARIANA
　mathematician ___ Malcolm:
　　　3 IAN
　menace: 4 **TREX** 6 RAPTOR
　role for Laura: 5 ELLIE
　sequel: 12 THELOSTWORLD
"Jurassic Park III"
　star Téa: 5 LEONI
　___ jure: 4 IPSO
Jurgensen
　Sportscaster: 5 SONNY
Juries
　Like some: 4 HUNG
　___ juris: 3 SUI
Jurisdiction
　of a bishop: 7 DIOCESE
Jurisprudence: 3 LAW
Juror: 4 PEER
Jury: 5 PANEL
　member: 4 **PEER**
　Seat a: 7 EMPANEL IMPANEL
　Serve on a: 3 SIT
　size: 6 TWELVE
Jury-___: 3 RIG
　___ jury: 5 PETIT
"___ Jury": 4 ITHE
Just: 4 FAIR MERE **ONLY**
　　　　　6 BARELY MERELY

a bit: 3 TAD
about: 6 ALMOST NEARLY
above average: 5 CPLUS
beat: 4 EDGE
fine: 3 **AOK**
for fun: 7 ONALARK
for kicks: 5 INFUN
get by: 6 EDGEIN
hired: 3 NEW
in case: 4 LEST
know: 5 SENSE 6 INTUIT
make, with "out": 3 EKE
not done: 5 TABOO
Not ~ any: 3 THE
Not ~ one: 4 BOTH
okay: 4 SOSO
one of those things: 4 THAT
open: 4 AJAR
out: 6 NEWEST 8 BRANDNEW
peachy: 3 AOK 5 SWELL
right: 4 TOAT 5 IDEAL
   6 TOATEE
slightly: 4 ATAD
They may be: 7 DESERTS
Just ___: 4 ABIT ATAD
"Just ___": 4 ASEC DOIT
   6 INCASE
"Just a ___!": 3 SEC
"Just as I thought!": 3 AHA OHO
Just for Men
  product: 3 DYE
"Just for the heck ___": 4 OFIT
Justice
  attire: 4 ROBE
  Flight from: 3 LAM
  Janet of: 4 RENO
  Kind of: 6 POETIC

  Wild West: 5 NOOSE
Justice Dept.
  division: 3 ATF DEA FBI
  employee: 3 ATT
Justification: 6 REASON
Justifiers
  Means: 4 **ENDS**
"Justine"
  author: 4 SADE 6 DESADE
  star: 5 AIMEE
Just ___ in the bucket: 5 ADROP
"Just kidding!": 3 NOT
"___ just kidding!": 4 IWAS
Just-passing
  grade: 3 DEE
"Just say ___ drugs": 4 NOTO
"Just Shoot Me"
  actor George: 5 SEGAL
  actress Malick: 6 WENDIE
Just the ___: 4 SAME
"Just the facts, ___": 4 MAAM
"Just this ___": 4 ONCE
"Just ___ thought!": 3 ASI
"Just you wait, ___ 'iggins!":
   4 ENRY
Jute
  Language that gives us:
   7 BENGALI
Jutland
  native: 4 DANE
  Old ~ resident: 6 TEUTON
Jutlander: 4 DANE
___ Juvante (motto of Monaco):
   3 DEO
Juxtapose: 4 ABUT
JVC
  competitor: 3 RCA

Kk

K
  follower: 4 MART
  followers: 3 LMN 4 LMNO
  through 12: 4 **ELHI**
K-___: 3 TEL
K2
  continent: 4 ASIA
K-5: 4 **ELEM**
Kabibble
  Comic: 3 **ISH**
Kabob
  holder: 6 SKEWER
  skewer: 4 SPIT
Kabuki
  kin: 3 NOH
  sash: 3 OBI
Kachina: 4 DOLL
  carver: 4 **HOPI**
Kadar
  Hungarian leader: 5 JANOS
Kadett
  maker: 4 OPEL
Kadiddlehopper
  Skelton character: 4 **CLEM**
Kael
  Critic: 7 PAULINE
Kaelin
  Simpson trial figure: 4 KATO
Kaffiyeh
  wearer: 4 ARAB
Kafka
  hero: 5 SAMSA
  novel: 7 AMERIKA
  Writer: 5 FRANZ
Kaftan
  Kyoto: 6 KIMONO
Kahanamoku, Duke
  Emulate: 4 SURF
Kahlil
  Author: 6 GIBRAN
Kahn
  Art patron: 4 OTTO
  Banker: 4 OTTO

Composer: 3 GUS
Kai-___, Chiang: 4 SHEK
Kaiser: 4 ROLL 5 RULER
Kai-shek, Chiang
  capital: 6 TAIPEI
Ka Ka ___ : 3 LAE
Kal-___ : 3 KAN
Kalahari: 6 DESERT
  layover: 5 OASIS
  layovers: 5 OASES
  Like the: 4 ARID
Kalamazoo
  lass: 3 GAL
Kale
  Variety of: 7 COLLARD
Kal-Kan
  rival: 4 **ALPO**
Kama ___ : 5 **SUTRA**
Kamali
  Designer: 5 NORMA
Kamehameha
  Island conquered by: 4 OAHU
Kaminska
  Actress: 3 IDA
Kamoze
  Singer: 3 INI
Kampala
  country: 6 UGANDA
  native: 7 UGANDAN
"___ Kampf": 4 MEIN
Kan.
  neighbor: 3 NEB 4 OKLA
Kander
  Broadway partner of: 3 EBB
Kandinsky
  contemporary: 3 ARP 4 KLEE
Kane
  of "All My Children": 5 ERICA
  portrayer on TV: 5 LUCCI
  Rosebud, to: 4 SLED
Kane, Marshall
  deadline: 4 NOON
  Wife of: 3 AMY

Kanga
  creator: **5** MILNE
  Kid of: **3** ROO
Kangaroo: 6 HOPPER
  Female: **3** DOE
  Young: **4** JOEY
  ___ **Kangaroo: 4** CAPT
"___ Kangaroo Down, Sport":
      5 TIEME
Kans.
  neighbor: **4** OKLA
Kansai International Airport
  site: **5** OSAKA
Kansas
  canine: **4** TOTO
  capital: **6** TOPEKA
  city: **4** IOLA
  Dorothy of: **4** GALE
  end of the Chisholm Trail:
      7 ABILENE
  Landon from: **3** ALF
  Like ~ in August:
      5 CORNY
  motto word: **5** ASTRA
  playwright: **4** INGE
  She never left: **6** AUNTEM
      8 AUNTIEEM
Kansas City
  athlete: **5** CHIEF ROYAL
  team: **6** CHIEFS ROYALS
"___ Kapital": 3 <u>**DAS**</u>
Kaplan
  Comic: **4** <u>**GABE**</u>
Kappa
  follower: **6** LAMBDA
  preceder: **4** IOTA
Kaput: 4 DONE GONE OVER
      SHOT **5** RUINED
  Go: **3** DIE **4** FAIL
Karachi
  airline: **3** PIA
Karamazov
  brother: **4** IVAN **6** DMITRI
Karan
  Designer: **5** DONNA
Karaoke
  need: **4** MIKE
Kara Sea
  border: **4** ASIA

Karate
  award: **4** BELT
  blow: **4** CHOP
  Exercise based on: **5** TAEBO
  instructor: **6** SENSEI
  kin: **4** JUDO
  level: **3** DAN
  school: **4** DOJO
"Karate Kid, The"
  costar Pat: **6** MORITA
  hero: **6** DANIEL
Kareem
  Alma mater of: **4** UCLA
  ~, as a kid: **3** LEW
Karel
  Playwright: **5** CAPEK
Karen
  Actress: **7** GRASSLE
Karen ___ (Isak Dinesen):
      6 BLIXEN
Karenina
  portrayer: **5** GARBO
"___ Karenina": 4 <u>**ANNA**</u>
Karl
  Actor: **6** MALDEN
  Auto pioneer: **4** BENZ
  Bush adviser: **4** ROVE
  of the NBA: **6** MALONE
Karloff
  Actor: **5** BORIS
  film: **6** THEAPE
  Real last name of: **5** PRATT
  role: **5** MUMMY
Karma: 5 VIBES
Karmann ___: 4 GHIA
Karnak
  ruler: **6** RAMSES
Karolyi
  Coach: **4** <u>**BELA**</u>
Karras
  of football: **4** ALEX
Karrie
  Golfer: **4** WEBB
Karsavina
  Ballerina: **6** TAMARA
Kasbah
  native: **4** ARAB
Kasparov
  game: **5** CHESS

Queens, to: 3 MEN
sixteen: 3 MEN
win: 4 MATE
Youngest chess champion before:
   3 TAL
Kassel
river: 4 EDER
Katarina
Skater: 4 WITT
Kate
Model: 4 MOSS
TV mate of: 5 ALLIE
Katey
Actress: 5 SAGAL
Katharina: 5 SHREW
Kathie Lee
Former cohost of: 5 REGIS
~, formerly: 6 COHOST
Kathmandu
land: 5 NEPAL
native: 6 NEPALI
Kathryn
Actress: 4 ERBE
Kathy
Country singer:
   6 MATTEA
Katmandu
land: 5 NEPAL
native: 6 NEPALI
Katz
Actor: 4 OMRI
Katzenjammer
kid: 4 HANS
Kauai
flier: 4 NENE
Island near: 4 OAHU
keepsake: 3 LEI
Kaufman
Comedian: 4 ANDY
role: 5 LATKA
TV show: 4 TAXI
Kay
Actress: 4 LENZ
Bandleader: 5 KYSER
follower: 3 ELL
Singer: 5 STARR
Kayak
kin: 5 CANOE UMIAK
propeller: 3 OAR

Kaye
Actor: 5 DANNY
Bandleader: 5 SAMMY
Kayo
count: 3 TEN
Kayoed: 3 OUT
Kazakh
river: 4 URAL
Kazakhstan
capital: 6 ASTANA
former capital: 6 ALMATY
   7 ALMAATA
lake: 7 ARALSEA
river: 4 URAL
sea: 4 ARAL
~, formerly (abbr.): 3 SSR
Kazakh-Uzbek
sea: 4 ARAL
Kazan
Actress: 6 LAINIE
Director: 4 **ELIA**
native: 5 TATAR
Kazoo
Play a: 3 HUM
k.d.
Singer: 4 **LANG**
___ **Kea:** 5 MAUNA
Keach
Actor: 5 STACY
Keane
Cartoonist: 3 BIL
Keanu
Actor: 6 REEVES
Keaton
Actress: 5 DIANE
Keaton, Buster
Like: 7 DEADPAN
Keaton, Michael
film: 5 MRMOM 6 BATMAN
title role: 5 MRMOM 6 BATMAN
Keats: 4 POET 5 ODIST
Always, to: 3 EER
creation: 3 **ODE**
Frequently, to: 3 OFT
Shelley elegy to: 7 ADONAIS
subject: 3 URN
title starter: 5 ODEON
Kebab
bed: 5 PILAF

holder: 4 SPIT
Like: 8 SKEWERED
___ kebab: 5 SHISH
Kedrova
  Actress: 4 **LILA**
Keds
  competitor: 4 AVIA
Keebler
  baker: 3 ELF
  cracker: 4 HIHO
  crew: 5 ELVES
  spokes-elf: 5 ERNIE
Keebler, Ernie
  Like: 5 ELFIN
Keel
  Across the: 5 ABEAM
  connector: 4 SKEG
Keen: 4 AVID NEAT WAIL
    5 ACUTE NEATO 6 ASTUTE
  about: 4 INTO
  of sight: 9 EAGLEEYED
Keenan
  Actor: 4 WYNN
Keep: 4 HAVE HOLD LAST SAVE
    STOW 6 RETAIN
    7 LEAVEIN 8 HANGONTO
  adding: 6 PILEON
  afloat: 4 BUOY
  an eye on: 4 TEND
  apart: 5 SPACE
  at it: 4 GOON 8 PLUGAWAY
  away: 5 REPEL
  away from: 4 SHUN 5 AVOID
    EVADE
  company with: 3 SEE
  Fail to: 3 ROT
  Fail to ~ up: 3 LAG
  for later: 5 STORE
  from: 5 DETER
  from happening: 5 AVERT
  from leaving: 6 DETAIN
  getting: 5 RENEW
  going: 4 LAST 5 RUNON
    7 PERSIST
  happening: 5 RECUR
  in: 4 STET
  in a barrel: 3 AGE
  in mind: 8 REMEMBER
  It'll ~ you going: 7 INERTIA

It won't ~ you up: 5 DECAF
    SANKA
  out: 3 BAN BAR 5 DEBAR
  possession of: 6 RETAIN
  secret: 4 HIDE
  time: 3 TAP
  to oneself: 3 HOG
  up: 7 SUSTAIN 8 MAINTAIN
Keep ___: 4 ATIT
Keep an ___: 5 EYEON
Keep an ___ the ground: 5 EARTO
Keeper: 6 WARDEN
  A ~ may keep it: 3 INN
  Creeper: 7 TRELLIS
  Game: 5 SNARE 6 ARCADE
  Key: 4 RING
  Rhythm: 3 TOE
  Sheep: 8 HERDSMAN
  ~, so it's said: 6 FINDER
Keeping: 7 CUSTODY
Keep ___ on: 5 ANEYE
Keep ___ profile: 4 ALOW
Keepsake: 5 RELIC TOKEN
    7 MEMENTO
  Concert: 4 STUB
  holder: 6 LOCKET
  Kauai: 3 LEI
  Personal: 5 TRESS
  Wedding: 5 ALBUM
Kefauver
  Politician: 5 **ESTES**
Keg
  contents: 4 BEER
  From the: 5 ONTAP
  outlet: 3 TAP
  stopper: 4 BUNG
Kegger: 5 PARTY
Kegler
  org.: 3 PBA
  place: 5 ALLEY
  target: 3 PIN 4 PINS
Keillor, Garrison
  Where ~ began (abbr.): 3 NPR
Keir
  Actor: 6 DULLEA
Keister: 4 REAR RUMP
Keller, Helen
  birthplace: 7 ALABAMA
  Org. cofounded by: 4 ACLU

Kellogg
  brand: 4 EGGO
  selection: 4 POPS
Kelly
  Actor: 4 GENE
  Actress: 5 GRACE MOIRA
  Cartoonist: 4 WALT
  Clown: 6 EMMETT
  Cohost: 4 RIPA
  Cohost of: 5 REGIS
  Outlaw: 3 NED
Kelly, Gene
  classic: 15 SINGININTHERAIN
Kelly, Walt
  comic strip: 4 POGO
Kelp: 4 ALGA 5 ALGAE
        7 SEAWEED
Kelsey
  Costar of: 4 PERI RHEA
  She played the ex of: 4 BEBE
Kemal
  Turkish leader: 7 ATATURK
Kemelman
  character: 5 RABBI
Kemo ___ : 4 **SABE**
Kemo Sabe
  sidekick: 5 TONTO
Ken: 4 DOLL
  Actor: 4 **OLIN**
  Author: 5 KESEY
  Boxer: 6 NORTON
  Friend of: 6 BARBIE
  Golfer: 7 VENTURI
Kenan
  Partner of: 3 KEL
Ken-L Ration
  competitor: 4 ALPO
Kenmore
  competitor: 5 AMANA
  seller: 5 SEARS
Kennedy: 3 TED 4 ROSE 5 ETHEL
        JOHNF 6 EUNICE
        7 SENATOR 8 CAROLINE
  (abbr.): 3 SEN
  coin: 4 HALF
  colleague: 6 SCALIA
  matriarch: 4 ROSE
  Mrs.: 5 ETHEL
  Start of a ~ quote: 6 ASKNOT

Kennedy Center
  architect: 3 PEI 5 IMPEI
Kennedy Library
  architect: 3 PEI 5 IMPEI
Kennel
  club info: 5 BREED
  command: 3 SIT
  cry: 3 ARF YAP YIP 4 WOOF
        YELP YOWL 6 ARFARF
Kenneth
  Critic: 5 TYNAN
  Judge: 5 STARR
  Prosecutor: 5 STARR
Kenny
  Rocker: 7 LOGGINS
Kenny G
  accessory: 4 REED
  instrument: 3 SAX
  label: 6 ARISTA
Keno
  kin: 5 LOTTO
Kenobi
  trainee: 5 VADER
Kenobi, ___-Wan: 3 **OBI**
Kent
  associate: 4 LANE 5 OLSEN
Kenton
  Director: 4 ERLE
  Jazzman: 4 **STAN**
Kent State
  state: 4 OHIO
Kentucky
  college: 5 BEREA
  fort: 4 KNOX
  landmark: 11 MAMMOTHCAVE
Kentucky Derby
  1955 ~ winner: 5 SWAPS
  1984 ~ winner: 5 SWALE
  drink: 5 JULEP
  Five-time ~ winner: 6 ARCARO
        7 HARTACK
  prize: 5 ROSES
  time: 3 MAY
Kenya
  capital: 7 NAIROBI
  caravan: 6 SAFARI
  neighbor: 6 SOMALI
  president: 3 MOI
  revolutionary: 6 MAUMAU

tribesman: 5 MASAI
Kenyatta University
  city: 7 NAIROBI
Keogh
  relative: 3 IRA
Keokuk
  state: 4 IOWA
Kepler
  Teacher of: 5 BRAHE
Kerensky
  successor: 5 LENIN
Kerfuffle: 3 ADO 4 TODO
Kern
  Composer: 6 JEROME
  creation: 4 SONG
Kernel: 3 NUB 4 GIST
  site: 3 COB EAR
Kerns
  Actress: 6 JOANNA
Kerouac: 4 BEAT 7 BEATNIK
Kerr
  Actress: 7 DEBORAH
Kerri
  Gymnast: 5 STRUG
Kerrigan
  Skater: 5 NANCY
Kertesz
  Nobelist: 4 IMRE
Kesey
  Author: 3 KEN
Kesselring
  Killer in a ~ play: 7 ARSENIC
Ketch: 4 BOAT 5 YACHT
  cousin: 4 YAWL
  pair: 5 MASTS
Ketcham
  Country singer: 3 HAL
  menace: 6 DENNIS
Ketone
  Colorless: 6 ACETOL
Kett
  of comics: 4 **ETTA**
Kettle
  and others: 3 MAS
  Large: 8 CAULDRON
  of fish: 4 MESS
Kettles: 7 MAANDPA 8 IRONWARE
Kevin
  Actor: 5 KLINE 6 SPACEY

"SNL" alum: 6 NEALON
Kewpie: 4 DOLL
Key: 4 ISLE 5 ISLET 6 OPENER
  7 CENTRAL
  (abbr.): 3 ALT ESC MAJ MIN
  Black: 5 AFLAT BFLAT DFLAT
    EFLAT GFLAT 6 ASHARP
  Calculator: 5 ENTER
  Cartoonist: 3 TED
  Cash register: 6 NOSALE
  Church: 6 OPENER
  color: 5 EBONY
  Computer: 3 ALT DEL ESC TAB
    5 ENTER 6 DELETE SPACER
  contraction: 3 OER
  food: 4 LIME
  French: 3 CLE
  Having a: 5 TONAL
  Hit the plus: 3 ADD
  Important piano: 7 MIDDLEC
  in: 4 TYPE 5 ENTER
  in again: 6 RETYPE 7 REENTER
  Indent: 3 TAB
  Jail: 9 CANOPENER
  Lacking a: 6 ATONAL
  letter: 3 **PHI** 4 BETA 5 KAPPA
  locale: 5 PIANO
  material: 5 CORAL EBONY
    IVORY
  Musical: 5 AFLAT BFLAT CFLAT
    DFLAT EFLAT FFLAT
    GFLAT 6 EMAJOR
  PC: 3 ALT END **ESC** 5 ENTER
    6 DELETE
  player: 7 PIANIST
  preposition: 3 OER
  state (abbr.): 3 FLA
  Type of: 5 MINOR
  Wide: 5 ENTER
  with four sharps: 6 EMAJOR
  with no black keys: 6 CMAJOR
  with no sharps or flats: 6 AMINOR
  with three sharps (abbr.): 4 AMAJ
Key ___: 4 LIME 5 LARGO
Key Arena
  team: 6 SONICS
    11 SUPERSONICS
Keyboard
  bar: 6 SPACER

Count with a: 5 BASIE
expert: 6 TYPIST
instrument: 5 PIANO 6 SPINET
    7 CELESTA
key: 3 ALT DEL ESC TAB
    5 ENTER 6 DELETE
    SPACER
Largest ~ key: 8 SPACEBAR
symbol: 8 ASTERISK
Use a: 4 **TYPE**
Keyed up: 5 HYPER TENSE
Keyes
Commentator: 4 ALAN
Keyhole
Look through a: 3 SPY 4 PEEK
    6 PEERIN
Keyless: 6 ATONAL
Keynes
alma mater: 4 ETON
subj.: 4 ECON
Keynote
Giva a: 5 ORATE
Keypad
key: 5 ENTER
Keystone
officer: 3 KOP
place: 4 ARCH
Keystone Kops: 7 CHASERS
creator Mack: 7 SENNETT
Like the: 4 ZANY
Keystone State
city: 7 ALTOONA
founder: 4 PENN
port: 4 ERIE
KFC
piece: 3 LEG 4 WING 6 BREAST
side order: 4 SLAW
KGB
employee: 3 AGT
rival: 3 CIA
Kgs.: 3 WTS
Khachaturian
Composer: 4 **ARAM**
composition: 10 SABERDANCE
Khakis: 4 TANS
Like: 4 DRAB
Khan
foe: 4 KIRK
title: 3 **AGA**

___ **Khan:** 3 **AGA** ALY 4 AGHA
    BATU 5 SHERE 7 GENGHIS
Khan, Genghis
follower: 5 TATAR 6 MONGOL
    TARTAR
___ **Khan, Yasmin:** 3 AGA
Khartoum
country: 5 SUDAN
river: 4 NILE
Khayyam
Poet: 4 **OMAR**
Khomeini: 5 IRANI 6 SHIITE
country: 4 IRAN
title: 4 IMAM
Khrushchev
country (abbr.): 4 USSR
Premier: 6 NIKITA
Khyber Pass
city: 5 KABUL
Ki ___ (founder of Korea): 3 TSE
Kibbutz
dance: 4 HORA
Kibosh
Put the ~ on: 3 END **NIX** 4 KILL
    STOP VETO 5 CEASE
    ENDED NIXED
Kick: 3 VIM 4 BOOT PUNT ZEST
    5 GRIPE 6 GROUSE RECOIL
Add a ~ to: 4 LACE
a grounder: 3 ERR
back: 4 LOAF REST 5 RELAX
Cake with a: 4 BABA
Dance with a: 5 CONGA
in: 4 ANTE
Kind of: 6 ONSIDE 7 SCISSOR
Little: 4 TANG
off: 4 OPEN 5 BEGIN START
    8 INITIATE
out: 3 BAN 4 OUST 5 EJECT
    EVICT EXILE EXPEL
    6 BANISH DEPORT
    10 DISPOSSESS
Place to ~ something: 5 REHAB
Stick with a: 3 TNT
target: 4 SHIN
Thing to: 5 HABIT
Top: 6 NONCOM
up your heels: 6 GAMBOL
Kickback: 6 RECOIL

Kicker
  aid: 3 TEE
  Famous: 4 PELE
  target: 4 SHIN 8 CROSSBAR
    GOALPOST
Kicking: 5 ALIVE
  partner: 5 **ALIVE**
Kickoff: 5 ONSET START
    6 OPENER OUTSET
  aid: 3 TEE
  NFL: 4 NATL
"___ Kick Out of You": 5 **IGETA**
Kicks
  They get their: 5 TIRES
Kid: 3 RIB TOT 4 JEST JIVE
    JOKE JOSH TYKE 5 TEASE
  Annoying: 4 BRAT
  Base: 8 ARMYBRAT
  Composer: 3 ORY
  Cow: 4 CALF
  cry: 3 BAA MAA 5 MOMMY
  Ewe: 4 LAMB
  Grownup: 4 GOAT
  Jazzman: 3 ORY
  king: 3 TUT
  name: 5 CISCO
  plea: 4 CANI
  retort: 5 CANSO DIDSO
  Well-behaved: 4 DOLL
  wheels: 4 BIKE 5 WAGON
    7 SCOOTER 10 SKATEBOARD
Kid-___: 3 VID
"___ Kid, The": 5 CISCO
Kidd
  Captain: 6 PIRATE
  stuff: 5 BOOTY 6 PIRACY
Kidd, Jason
  team: 4 NETS
Kidder
  Actress: 6 MARGOT
Kiddie
  Play in a ~ pool: 4 WADE
  racer: 6 GOCART GOKART
  transport: 7 SCOOTER
Kiddie ___: 3 LIT
Kiddie lit
  brat: 6 ELOISE
  dog: 4 SPOT
  elephant: 5 BABAR

  giant: 5 SEUSS
  trio: 5 BEARS
Kidding
  Just: 3 NOT
  No: 3 GEE 4 GOSH 5 TRULY
    6 DOTELL HONEST
    7 IMEANIT ITSTRUE
    8 ITSAFACT
Kiddy
  litter: 4 TOYS
Kidman
  Actress: 6 NICOLE
Kidnap: 6 SNATCH
  Hearst ~ gp.: 3 **SLA**
Kidnapper
  demand: 6 RANSOM
Kidney
  enzyme: 5 RENIN
  related: 5 RENAL
Kids
  card game: 3 UNO WAR
    6 GOFISH
  cereal: 4 TRIX 10 CAPNCRUNCH
  game: 3 TAG 7 STATUES
    8 PATACAKE REDROVER
    9 HOPSCOTCH SIMONSAYS
    11 HIDEANDSEEK
  Not for: 5 ADULT
  question: 3 WHY
  Raise: 4 REAR
  Watch the: 3 SIT
  wheels: 6 TRIKES
Kierkegaard: 4 DANE
  Philosopher: 5 **SOREN**
Kiev
  land: 7 UKRAINE
Kigali
  land: 6 RWANDA
  resident: 7 RWANDAN
Kiki
  Singer: 3 DEE
Kilauea
  flow: 4 LAVA
Kilborn
  TV host: 5 CRAIG
Kildare
  and others: 3 DRS
Kilimanjaro
  covering: 4 SNOW

Kill: 3 NIX OFF 4 SLAY VETO
      7 BUMPOFF
      10 STRIKEDOWN
  time: 4 IDLE LAZE LOAF
  with a click: 3 ZAP
Killarney
  From: 5 IRISH
  Land of: 4 ERIN
Killebrew
  of baseball: 6 HARMON
Killed: 4 SLEW 5 SLAIN
Killer
  Banned: 3 DDT
  Bill: 4 VETO
  Bug: 3 DDT 4 DCON
  Cereal: 5 ERGOT
  Cobra: 8 MONGOOSE
  Cold-blooded: 3 ASP 4 TREX
  of Scarpia: 5 TOSCA
  Sci-fi: 3 RAY
  Weed: 3 HOE
  whale: 3 ORC 4 **ORCA**
Killer ___: 3 APP
"Killers, The"
  Gardner of: 3 AVA
Killjoy: 11 PARTYPOOPER
Kill ___ killed: 4 ORBE
Kilmer
  Actor: 3 **VAL**
  concern: 4 TREE
  creation: 4 POEM
  poem: 5 **TREES**
  Poet: 5 JOYCE
Kiln: 4 **OAST** OVEN
  Put in a: 3 DRY 4 FIRE
Kilograms
  1,000 ~: 5 TONNE
Kilometers
  1.6 ~: 4 MILE
Kilowatt-hour
  fraction: 3 ERG
Kilt
  accessory: 3 TAM
  feature: 5 PLEAT
  pattern: 5 PLAID 6 TARTAN
  Pouch worn with a: 7 SPORRAN
  wearer: 4 SCOT
Kilter
  Out of: 4 AWRY 5 AMISS ASKEW

Kiltie
  dance: 5 FLING
  Young: 3 LAD
Kim
  Actress: 5 NOVAK
  Ex-husband of: 4 ALEC
  Singer: 6 CARNES
  ___ Kim of hip-hop: 3 LIL
Kimberly
  Actress: 5 ELISE
Kimono
  accessory: 3 **OBI** 4 SASH
  kin: 4 ROBE 6 CAFTAN
Kin: 9 RELATIONS
  (abbr.): 3 FAM REL
  Acquired: 5 INLAW
  Certain: 3 MAS
  group: 4 CLAN
  Kissin': 6 COUSIN
  of a spouse: 5 INLAW
  Partner of: 4 KITH
Kind: 3 **ILK** 4 NICE SORT TYPE
      5 BREED 6 HUMANE
  of: 5 QUASI SORTA 8 INASENSE
  Of that: 4 SUCH
  One of a: 4 UNIT
  words: 6 PRAISE
Kindergarten
  basics: 4 **ABCS**
  break: 3 **NAP**
  disrupter: 4 BRAT
  period: 8 PLAYTIME
  song start: 3 ABC 4 ABCD
      5 ABCDE
Kindergartner: 3 TOT 4 TYKE
Kindled: 3 LIT
  again: 5 RELIT
Kindling
  Bit of: 4 TWIG
**"... kindness begets kindness
    ___":** 8 EVERMORE
Kine: 6 CATTLE
Kinetoscope
  inventor: 6 EDISON
Kinfolk: 4 CLAN
  (abbr.): 4 RELS
King: 4 CARD SIRE 5 PIECE
      RULER TITLE 7 CHECKER
      ROYALTY 8 FACECARD

1965 ~ arrest site: 5 SELMA
Actor: 4 ALAN
address: 4 SIRE
À la: 5 EERIE REGAL SCARY
beater: 3 ACE
Biblical: 4 JEHU OMRI SAUL
   5 HEROD 7 SOLOMON
Boy: 3 TUT
Comic: 4 ALAN
Cretan: 5 MINOS
domain: 3 CNN 5 REALM
Egyptian: 3 TUT 6 RAMSES
   7 RAMESES
Elgar: 4 OLAF
Eng.: 3 EDW
English: 5 HENRY 6 GEORGE
   7 RICHARD
Fairy: 6 OBERON
First ~ of Israel: 4 SAUL
Fit for a: 5 NOBLE REGAL
   ROYAL
Golden touch: 5 MIDAS
High ~ hangout: 4 TARA
Home run: 5 AARON
Indian: 4 RAJA 5 RAJAH
lead-in: 3 ALA
Merry old: 4 COLE
Norwegian: 4 OLAF **OLAV**
of beasts: 4 LION
of Judea: 5 HEROD
of Phrygia: 5 MIDAS
of Siam phrase: 8 ETCETERA
of the Huns: 4 ATLI 6 ATTILA
of the jungle: 4 LION
of the road: 4 HOBO
of tragedy: 4 LEAR
of Troy: 5 PRIAM
of TV talk: 5 LARRY
Persian: 4 SHAH
Place for a: 4 DECK PROM
Pop songwriter: 6 **CAROLE**
Portuguese: 3 REI
proclamation: 5 EDICT
protector: 4 PAWN ROOK
Ring: 3 ALI
ring thing: 4 SEAL
Saudi: 4 FAHD
seat: 6 THRONE
Shakespearean: 4 LEAR

   6 OBERON
Strikeout: 4 RYAN
title (abbr.): 3 REV
topper: 3 ACE
~, in French: 3 ROI 5 LEROI
~, in Latin: 3 REX
~, in Spanish: 3 REY
King ___ : 4 KONG 5 COBRA
___ king: 3 **ALA**
King, Larry
  employer: 3 CNN
  has a few: 4 EXES
King, Stephen
  format: 5 EBOOK
  home: 5 MAINE
  novel: 4 CUJO 6 CARRIE MISERY
    8 THESTAND 9 SALEMSLOT
    10 ROSEMADDER
    11 FIRESTARTER
  novel setting: 5 SALEM
    9 SHAWSHANK
    10 CASTLEROCK
    11 BANGORMAINE
  short story collection:
    12 SKELETONCREW
King, The: 5 ELVIS
  Middle name of: 4 ARON
"King ___, The": 4 **ANDI**
"___ King, The": 4 LION 6 FISHER
"___-King, The": 3 ERL
"King and I, The"
  actor Brynner: 3 YUL
  actress: 4 KERR
  character: 4 **ANNA**
  country: 4 SIAM
  role: 4 ANNA
King Arthur
  Father of: 5 UTHER
  Foster brother of: 3 KAY 6 SIRKAY
  home: 7 CAMELOT
  Nephew of: 6 GARETH
  paradise: 6 AVALON
  Sister of: 4 ANNE
  slayer: 7 MORDRED
King Atahualpa: 4 INCA 5 INCAN
King Cole
  fiddlers: 4 TRIO 5 THREE
  request: 4 PIPE
  ___ King Cole: 3 **NAT**

King David: 8 PSALMIST
  creation: 5 PSALM
  Father of: 5 JESSE
  instrument: 4 HARP
  predecessor: 4 SAUL
  Son of: 7 ABSALOM
Kingdom: 5 **REALM**
  Ancient: 4 MOAB 5 NUBIA
    SHEBA
  Biblical: 4 EDOM ELAM MOAB
  Himalayan: 5 NEPAL 6 BHUTAN
  of Croesus: 5 LYDIA
  of Henry IV: 7 NAVARRE
  Old Spanish: 4 LEON
  South Pacific: 5 TONGA
King Faud: 5 SAUDI
King Features
  competitor: 3 NEA
King Harald
  Father of: 4 OLAV
King Hussein: 4 ARAB
  Queen of: 4 NOOR
  Widow of: 4 NOOR
King-jack
  card combination: 6 TENACE
King James
  (abbr.): 3 VER
"King Kong": 3 APE
  costar: 4 WRAY
  studio: 3 **RKO**
King Lear
  Daughter of: 5 REGAN
Kingly: 5 REGAL ROYAL
      6 REGNAL
  address: 4 SIRE
King Mark
  Nephew of: 7 TRISTAN
  Wife of: 7 ISOLDE
King Minos
  Daughter of: 7 ARIADNE
  Mother of: 6 EUROPA
  realm: 5 CRETE
King Mongkut
  realm: 4 SIAM
  visitor: 4 ANNA
"King of Comedy, The"
  star: 6 DENIRO
King of Torts, The: 5 BELLI
Kingpin: 4 CZAR EXEC

Kuwaiti: 4 EMIR
King ___ Saud: 3 IBN
King Sisters, The
  One of: 5 ALYCE
Kingsley
  Actor: 3 BEN
  Author: 4 **AMIS**
Kings Peak
  range: 5 UINTA
  state: 4 UTAH
Kingston
  group: 4 TRIO
  sch.: 3 URI
Kingston Trio, The
  hit song: 3 **MTA** 9 TOMDOOLEY
Kinison
  Comic: 3 SAM
Kinks, The
  hit song: 4 **LOLA**
  Ray of: 6 DAVIES
Kinky
  do: 4 AFRO
Kinnear
  Actor: 4 GREG
Kinshasa
  country, once: 5 ZAIRE
  river: 5 CONGO
Kinship: 3 TIE
  emblem: 5 TOTEM
Kinski
  role: 4 TESS
Kinsman: 3 SIB
  (abbr.): 3 REL
  ~, in Spanish: 3 TIO
  _ Kinte: 5 KUNTA
Kip
  spender: 7 LAOTIAN
  Where ~ are spent: 4 LAOS
Kipling
  lad: 3 KIM
  novel: 3 KIM
  poem: 8 GUNGADIN
    10 FUZZYWUZZY
  python: 3 KAA
  story setting: 5 INDIA
  wolf: 5 AKELA
___ Kippur: 3 **YOM**
Kirby
  Actor: 5 BRUNO

Kirghizia
  city: 3 OSH
Kirk
  (abbr.): 4 CAPT
  diary: 3 LOG
  Journey for: 4 TREK
  Officer under: 4 SULU 5 UHURA
  portrayer: 7 SHATNER
Kirkland
  Labor-leader: 4 LANE
Kirkuk
  country: 4 IRAQ
  native: 4 KURD
Kirlian
  photography image: 4 AURA
Kirsten
  Actress: 5 DUNST
Kishke: 5 DERMA
Kismet: 4 FATE 5 KARMA
    7 DESTINY
Kiss: 4 BUSS 5 SMACK 6 SMOOCH
    8 OSCULATE
  partner: 4 TELL
  Prelude to a: 3 IDO
  Prepare to: 6 PUCKER
  Quick: 4 PECK
  sound: 5 SMACK
  ~, in Spanish: 4 BESO
"Kiss, The"
  sculptor: 5 RODIN
Kisser: 3 LIP MUG YAP 4 PUSS
    TRAP
  Baby: 3 POL
  Nickname for a good: 7 HOTLIPS
Kisses
  Like some: 6 STOLEN
  partner: 4 HUGS
Kit
  and caboodle: 3 ALL 4 ALOT
  call: 4 MEOW
  First aid ~ item: 4 TAPE
    6 IPECAC
  item: 4 TOOL
  Like ~ pieces: 6 PRECUT
  Makeup ~ item: 5 LINER
    7 MASCARA
  partner: 8 CABOODLE
  Scout: 6 CARSON
  Sewing ~ item: 5 SPOOL

    6 NEEDLE
Kitchen: 4 ROOM
  add-on: 4 **ETTE**
  appliance: 4 OVEN 5 RANGE
    STOVE 6 FRIDGE 7 TOASTER
    8 DISPOSAL 9 CANOPENER
  appliance brand: 5 AMANA
  bar: 4 OLEO SOAP
  basin: 4 SINK
  cleaner: 3 MOP 5 COMET
  cloth: 7 DISHRAG
  counter: 5 TIMER
  coverup: 5 APRON
  filter: 5 SIEVE
  fixture: 4 SINK 5 RANGE
    7 CABINET
  foil: 5 ALCOA
  gadget: 5 CORER DICER LADLE
    PARER **RICER** SIEVE TIMER
    TONGS 6 BASTER BEATER
    GRATER OPENER PEELER
    SLICER 7 SPATULA UTENSIL
    8 STRAINER 9 CANOPENER
  gadget maker: 3 OXO
  glove: 4 MITT
  hanger: 7 POTHOOK
  intruder: 3 ANT
  item: 6 SPONGE 7 UTENSIL
  It runs in the: 3 TAP
  Kind of: 5 **EATIN**
  light: 5 PILOT
  pest: 3 ANT
  spray: 3 PAM
  spread: 4 OLEO
  tear-jerker: 5 ONION
  utensil maker: 3 OXO
  vessel: 3 PAN POT
  whistler: 6 TEAPOT
  worker: 4 CHEF COOK
  wrap: 5 SARAN
"Kitchen God's Wife, The"
  Author: 3 TAN
Kite: 4 BIRD
  Golfer: 3 TOM
  home: 4 NEST
  Kind of: 3 BOX
  part: 4 BEAK TAIL
Kith
  partner: 3 KIN

Kitsch
opposite: 5 TASTE
Kitschy: 9 TASTELESS
film monster: 5 RODAN
lawn figure: 8 FLAMINGO
Kitt
Singer/actress: 6 EARTHA
Kitt, Eartha
hit: 9 CESTSIBON
Kitten
cry: 3 MEW
plaything: 4 YARN
quality: 8 CUTENESS
Kitty: 3 POT 4 PUSS
Comment to: 4 SCAT
Contented ~ sound: 4 PURR
cry: 3 MEW 4 MEOW
Feed the: 4 **ANTE**
Kitty ___ : 5 OSHEA 6 LITTER
Kiva
builder: 4 HOPI
Kiwi: 6 RATITE
Native: 5 MAORI
relative: 3 EMU **MOA**
Klaxon: 5 ALARM
cause: 5 ALERT
Klee: 5 SWISS
Artist: 4 PAUL
contemporary: 3 ARP
Klein
Designer: 4 ANNE
" ___ kleine Nachtmusik": 4 **EINE**
Klemperer
Actor: 6 WERNER
Conductor: 4 **OTTO**
Klensch
CNN style maven: 4 ELSA
Klimt
birthplace: 6 VIENNA
Painter: 6 GUSTAV
Kline
Actor: 5 KEVIN
movie: 4 DAVE
Kline, Kevin
Wife of: 5 CATES
Klinger
hometown: 6 TOLEDO
portrayer: 4 **FARR**
rank (abbr.): 3 CPL

Klingon: 5 ALIEN
and others: 3 ETS
Enterprise: 4 WORF
Klink
clink: 6 STALAG
Prisoner of: 5 HOGAN
Secretary to: 5 HELGA
Klink, Colonel
portrayer:
15 WERNERKLEMPERER
KLM
rival: 3 **SAS**
Klondike
find: 3 ORE 4 GOLD
territory: 5 YUKON
Kluszewski
of baseball: 3 TED
Klutz: 3 **OAF** 4 CLOD 6 GALOOT
cry: 4 OHNO OOPS
Klutzy: 5 INEPT
one: 3 OAF
Knack: 3 ART WAY 5 FLAIR
6 TALENT
Lacking the: 5 INEPT
Knapsack: 6 KITBAG
Knave: 3 CAD 5 ROGUE 6 RASCAL
loot: 4 TART
Knead: 7 MASSAGE
Kneading
Needing: 4 ACHY SORE 5 TENSE
Kneads
Person who: 5 BAKER
7 MASSEUR 8 MASSEUSE
Knee: 5 HINGE JOINT
Ask on bended: 5 PLEAD
bend: 4 PLIE
Injure a: 4 SKIN 6 SCRAPE
It goes below the: 4 MIDI
Jerk your: 5 REACT
neighbor: 4 SHIN
protector: 3 PAD
Knee-ankle
connection: 5 TIBIA 6 FIBULA
Kneecap: 7 PATELLA
Knee-high
to a grasshopper: 4 TINY
Knee-slapper: 4 HOOT JOKE
RIOT 6 GASSER HOTONE
Knell: 4 PEAL

Knickers: 5 PANTS
Knickknack: 4 ITEM 5 CURIO
　　6 DOODAD NOTION
　　7 MEMENTO TRINKET
　holder: 5 SHELF 7 ETAGERE
Knicks
　coach: 5 RILEY
　coach Riley: 3 PAT
　org.: 3 NBA
　venue: 3 MSG
Knievel
　Daredevil: 4 **EVEL**
　specialty: 5 STUNT 6 STUNTS
Knife: 4 SHIV STAB 6 WEAPON
　Butter: 8 SPREADER
　Eskimo: 3 ULU
　Hacking: 4 BOLO 7 MACHETE
　handle: 4 HAFT HILT
　holder: 6 SHEATH
　Kind of: 5 BOWIE XACTO
　Large ~ of yore: 4 **SNEE**
　Like a good: 5 SHARP
　maker: 6 CUTLER
　on TV: 5 GINSU
　sharp part: 4 EDGE
　Use a: 4 PARE SLIT STAB
Knight: 3 SIR 5 TITLE
　Actor: 3 TED
　address: 3 SIR
　aide: 4 PAGE
　apprentice: 6 SQUIRE
　award (abbr.): 3 OBE
　cap: 6 HELMET
　clothes: 4 MAIL 5 ARMOR
　　9 CHAINMAIL
　club: 4 MACE
　duel: 5 JOUST
　fight: 4 TILT
　game: 5 JOUST
　job: 5 QUEST
　lady: 4 DAME
　Like a: 6 TITLED
　Make a: 3 DUB
　mare: 5 STEED
　mount: 5 STEED
　neighbor: 4 ROOK 6 BISHOP
　noise: 5 CLANK
　of note: 6 GLADYS
　of the Round Table: 3 KAY

　　4 BORS 6 GARETH GAWAIN
　　7 GALAHAD MORDRED
　　TRISTAN 8 LANCELOT
　Roving, as a: 6 ERRANT
　spot: 5 MALTA
　Star Wars: 4 JEDI
　superior: 7 BARONET
　time: 4 YORE
　title: 3 SIR
　tunic: 6 TABARD
　weapon: 5 LANCE
　work: 5 QUEST
Knight ___: 7 TEMPLAR
Knighted
　actor Guinness: 4 ALEC
　actor McKellen: 3 IAN
　architect: 4 WREN
　composer: 5 ELGAR
　conductor: 5 SOLTI 6 PREVIN
　Prepare to be: 5 KNEEL
Knightwear: 5 ARMOR
Knish
　ingredient: 6 POTATO
　noshery: 4 DELI
Knit: 4 HEAL MEND
　alternative: 4 PURL
　shirt: 4 POLO
Knitted
　blanket: 6 AFGHAN
　shoe: 6 BOOTEE
　wrap: 5 SHAWL
Knitting
　item: 5 SKEIN
　need: 4 YARN
　project: 6 AFGHAN
　stitch: 4 PURL
　tool: 6 NEEDLE
Knob: 4 NODE
　Control: 4 DIAL
　Organ: 4 STOP
　Radio: 5 TUNER
　TV: 4 TINT VERT
Knobby: 5 NODAL
Knock: 3 DIS RAP
　about: 4 ROAM
　down: 4 DECK FELL RAZE
　　TAMP 5 UPSET 6 DEBASE
　　DEFAME DEMOTE
　　LAYLOW

down a peg: 5 ABASE
Engine: 4 PING
follower: 5 KNEED
for a loop: 4 DAZE STUN
Hard: 3 BOP RAP 5 THUMP
It'll ~ you out: 5 ETHER
off: 4 DOIN SLAY STOP 5 CEASE
on the noggin: 4 CONK
out: 3 AWE 6 SEDATE
   7 FLATTEN
over: 3 AWE ROB 6 TOPPLE
prefix: 4 ANTI
response: 5 ENTER 6 COMEIN
senseless: 4 DAZE STUN
the socks off: 3 WOW 5 AMAZE
   6 DAZZLE
Knock-___: 5 KNEED
Knocked
for a loop: 5 AREEL
over: 5 SPILT
Knocker: 6 CRITIC
place: 4 DOOR
reply: 5 ITSME
Knock for ___: 5 **ALOOP**
Knocking
sound: 4 PING 7 RATATAT
   10 RATATATTAT
Source of: 3 GIN
Knock-knock
joke: 3 PUN
Knockoff: 5 CLONE
Knockout: 4 LULU
It's a: 5 ETHER
Knoll: 5 MOUND
Knossos
King of: 5 MINOS
locale: 5 CRETE
Knot: 3 TIE 4 NODE 5 SKEIN
   TIEUP UNITE
again: 5 RETIE
In a: 5 TENSE
Loosen a: 4 UNDO 5 UNTIE
Tie the: 3 **WED**
type: 7 BOWLINE
Wild West: 5 NOOSE
work: 7 MACRAME
Knotted
neckwear: 3 TIE 5 ASCOT
up: 5 TENSE

Knotty
craft: 7 MACRAME
wood: 4 PINE
Knot-tying
phrase: 3 IDO
place: 5 ALTAR 6 CHAPEL
Know
A way to: 3 ESP
Before you ~ it: 4 SOON
In the: 3 HEP HIP 5 **AWARE**
In the ~ about: 4 ONTO
   5 HEPTO
Just: 5 SENSE 6 INTUIT
Old enough to ~ better: 5 ADULT
Wanted to: 5 ASKED
___ Know: 4 ALLI
Know-how: 3 ART
Knowing
about: 4 ONTO
Know-it-all: 8 WISEACRE
Knowledge: 3 KEN 4 LORE
   7 SCIENCE
Body of: 4 LORE
Field of: 6 SPHERE
Gain: 5 LEARN
Impart: 5 TEACH
Range of: 3 KEN
Traditional: 4 **LORE**
" ___ Knowledge": 6 CARNAL
Knowledgeable: 4 WISE
   5 AWARE
about: 4 INON
Known
Least: 6 RAREST
Make: 3 AIR 4 TELL
Once ~ as: 3 **NEE**
Well: 8 ONTHEMAP
___ known: 4 HADI
Knows
about: 6 ISONTO
What the nose: 4 ODOR
   5 AROMA SMELL
" ___ Knows" (Dion & the Belmonts
   hit): 5 NOONE
" ___ know you?": 3 DOI
Knox: 4 FORT
and others (abbr.): 3 FTS
Knoxville
athlete: 3 VOL

org.: 3 TVA
sch.: 5 UTENN
Knuckle: 5 JOINT
dragger: 3 APE
Knucklehead: 4 BOZO DODO
DOPE TWIT 5 IDIOT
MORON
KO
counter: 3 REF
K-O
filler: 3 LMN
Koala
home: 4 TREE
Koan
teaching: 3 ZEN
Kobe: 5 LAKER
City near: 5 OSAKA
cummerbund: 3 OBI
currency: 3 YEN
Koblenz
cry: 3 ACH
Koch
and others: 3 EDS
Mayor before: 5 BEAME
memoir: 5 MAYOR
Kodak
competitor: 4 FUJI 8 FUJIFILM
film brand: 4 TMAX
moments: 3 ADS
Kodaly
Composer: 6 ZOLTAN
Kofi
country: 5 GHANA
of the U.N.: 5 ANNAN
predecessor: 3 DAG
Koh-i-___: 4 NOOR
Kohoutek: 5 COMET
Kojak
Detective: 4 **THEO**
Lt.: 4 THEO
portrayer: 7 SAVALAS
Kol ___ (Hebrew prayer): 5 NIDRE
Köln: 5 STADT
crowd: 4 DREI
Kong: 3 APE
costar: 4 WRAY
___ **Kong:** 4 HONG
Konica
competitor: 4 AGFA 5 CANON

Königsberg
philosopher: 4 KANT
Kon-Tiki: 4 RAFT
wood: 5 BALSA
Kon-Tiki Museum
site: 4 OSLO
Kook: 3 NUT
Kooky: 3 ODD 4 LOCO NUTS
ZANY
Koontz
Author: 4 DEAN
Koop
and others: 3 SGS
Kopecks
100 ~: 5 RUBLE
Koppel
News host: 3 **TED**
Koran
deity: 5 ALLAH
language: 6 ARABIC
Like the: 7 ISLAMIC
religion: 5 ISLAM
Korbut
Gymnast: 4 **OLGA**
Korda
of tennis: 4 PETR
Korea
and others: 7 FAREAST
8 EASTASIA
continent: 4 ASIA
Sitcom set in: 4 MASH
Syngman of: 4 RHEE
Korea Bay
feeder: 4 YALU
Korean: 5 ASIAN 9 EASTASIAN
carmaker: 3 KIA
money: 3 WON
river: 4 YALU
soldier: 3 ROK
statesman: 4 RHEE
Korean War
fighter: 3 MIG
Korngold
Composer: 5 ERICH
Kosher: 5 **LEGIT** LICIT
Airline that serves only ~ food:
4 ELAL
It may be: 4 DELI
Not: 4 TREF

685

One who keeps things:
5 RABBI
Kosovo
ally: 7 ALBANIA
citizen: 4 SERB
defense gp.: 4 NATO
Koss, Johann ___
Speed skater: 4 OLAV
Kostelanetz
Conductor: 5 ANDRE
Kosygin
Soviet leader: 6 ALEXEI
Kotcheff
Director: 3 TED
Kotter
portrayer: 6 KAPLAN
portrayer Kaplan: 4 GABE
student: 8 SWEATHOG
Kotter, Mrs.
portrayer: 9 STRASSMAN
Koufax
Pitcher: 5 SANDY
stat.: 3 ERA
Kournikova
of tennis: 4 **ANNA**
Koussevitzky
Conductor: 5 SERGE
Kovacs
Comic: 5 **ERNIE**
Kovacs, Mrs.: 4 **EDIE**
Kovic
War memoirist: 3 RON
Kowalski
portrayer: 6 BRANDO
shout: 6 STELLA
K.P.
Do ~ work: 4 PEEL
tool: 5 PARER 6 PEELER
K-P
filler: 4 LMNO
Kraft Foods
brand: 4 OREO 5 SANKA
Krait
kin: 3 ASP
Kramden
laugh: 3 HAR
Mr.: 5 RALPH
Mrs.: 5 ALICE
Norton, to: 3 PAL

Pal of: 6 NORTON 8 EDNORTON
portrayer: 7 GLEASON
vehicle: 3 BUS
Kramer
Quarterback: 4 ERIK
"Kramer vs. Kramer"
director: 6 BENTON
Krantz, Judith
novel: 8 SCRUPLES
Krasner
Artist: 3 LEE
Krauss
Pop singer: 6 ALISON
Kravitz
Pop singer: 5 LENNY
Krazy
of comics: 3 KAT
Krazy ___: 3 **KAT**
Kresge, S.S.
~, now: 5 KMART
Kreskin
forte: 3 ESP
Kringle
Mr.: 4 KRIS 5 KRISS
Krishna
chant: 6 MANTRA
preceder: 4 HARE
Krispy ___: 5 KREME
Kristin
Swimmer: 4 OTTO
Kristofferson
Actor/singer: 4 **KRIS**
Kroc
of McDonald's: 3 RAY
"___ Kröger" (Thomas Mann novella): 5 TONIO
Krona
part: 3 ORE
Krone
part: 3 ORE
Kroon
country: 7 ESTONIA
___ Kross (rap duo): 4 KRIS
Krueger
of Elm Street: 6 FREDDY
street: 3 ELM
Kruger
Actor: 4 OTTO
NBA coach: 3 LON

Kruger, ___ Paul: 3 OOM
Krupa
  Drummer: 4 GENE
  instrument: 4 DRUM
  portrayer: 8 SALMINEO
Krupp
  of hockey: 3 UWE
  works city: 5 **ESSEN**
Krusty: 5 CLOWN
Krypton: 3 **GAS** 6 PLANET
  7 RAREGAS
  Like: 5 **INERT**
K.T.
  Singer: 5 **OSLIN**
Kuala Lumpur
  country: 8 MALAYSIA
  language: 5 MALAY
  native: 5 MALAY
Kublai ___: 4 KHAN
Kubrick
  computer: 3 HAL
  Director: 7 STANLEY
Kudos: 5 HONOR 6 PRAISE
Kudrow
  Actress: 4 **LISA**
Kudu: 8 ANTELOPE
Kudzu: 4 VINE
Kukla
  friend: 4 FRAN 5 **OLLIE**
Kukoc
  of basketball: 4 TONI
Kulik
  Figure skater: 4 ILIA
Kumquat
  shape: 4 OVAL
Kung ___: 3 PAO
Kunta ___: 5 KINTE
Kunta Kinte
  slave name: 4 TOBY
Kupcinet
  Journalist: 3 IRV
Kurdistan
  Bit of: 4 IRAN
  peak: 6 ARARAT
Kurds
  Home to some: 4 IRAN IRAQ
Kurosawa
  Director: 5 **AKIRA**
  film: 3 RAN 8 RASHOMON

Kurt
  Conductor: 5 ADLER MASUR
  denial: 4 NEIN
  Quarterback: 6 WARNER
  Wife of: 5 LOTTE
Kurtz
  Actress: 7 SWOOSIE
  Conductor: 5 EFREM
Kuwait: 7 EMIRATE
  peninsula: 6 ARABIA
Kuwaiti: 4 ARAB
  money: 5 DINAR
  ruler: 4 **EMIR** 5 EMEER
Kvass
  ingredient: 3 RYE
Kvetch: 4 CARP CRAB MOAN
  5 GRIPE WHINE 6 GROUSE
  MOANER
  cry: 5 OYVEY
Kwai
  River ~ locale: 4 SIAM
Kwan: 6 SKATER
  Actress: 5 NANCY
  move: 4 AXEL
Kwanzaa
  principle: 5 FAITH UNITY
KwaZulu-___: 5 NATAL
Kwik-E-Mart
  clerk: 3 APU
___ kwon do: 3 **TAE**
Ky,
  neighbor: 4 TENN
Kyle
  Brother of: 3 IKE
  of football: 4 ROTE
Kyoto
  carrier: 3 JAL
  cash: 3 YEN
  cummerbund: 3 OBI
  garment: 6 KIMONO
  killer: 5 NINJA
Kyrgyz
  city: 3 OSH
  range: 4 ALAI
Kyrgyzstan
  city: 3 OSH
  range: 4 ALAI
Kyser
  Bandleader: 3 KAY

L1

L: 5 FIFTY LARGE

La
 lead-in: 3 SOL TRA

La ___
 (Milan opera house): 5 SCALA
 (San Diego resort): 5 JOLLA

"La ___"
 (Debussy work): 3 MER
 (Fellini film): 6 STRADA
 (Puccini work): 6 BOHEME
 (Ravel work): 5 VALSE
 (Ritchie Valens hit): 5 BAMBA

Lab
 animal: 3 RAT
 burner: 4 **ETNA**
 container: 4 VIAL
 cry: 3 AHA
 dish: 5 PETRI
 eggs: 3 OVA
 employee: 6 TESTER
 Fictional ~ assistant: 4 IGOR
 fluids: 4 SERA
 gel: 4 **AGAR**
 heater: 4 **ETNA**
 procedure: 4 TEST
 rat's course: 4 MAZE
 runner: 3 RAT
 slide objects: 6 AMEBAE
 subj.: 3 SCI
 swimmer: 5 AMEBA
 Take back to the: 6 RETEST
 tube: 7 BURETTE PIPETTE
 unit: 4 GRAM
 work: 5 TESTS

"La Bamba"
 actor Morales: 4 **ESAI**
 actress Elizabeth: 4 PENA

Label: 3 TAG 4 NAME 5 IDTAG
  7 NAMETAG
 anew: 5 RETAG
 info: 4 SIZE
 Lapel: 5 IDTAG
 Loo: 5 GENTS

Put a new ~ on: 5 RETAG
  6 RENAME
 Record: 3 EMI MCA RCA SUN
  4 KTEL 5 ASCAP DECCA
  6 ARISTA

LaBelle
 Singer: 5 **PATTI**
 song: 13 LADYMARMALADE

"La Belle et la ___": 4 BETE

Labine
 Pitcher: 4 CLEM

"La Bohème": 5 OPERA
 heroine: 4 MIMI
 highlight: 4 ARIA
 Updated version of: 4 RENT

La ___, Bolivia: 3 PAZ

"La ___ Bonita": 4 ISLA

Labor: 4 TOIL WORK 6 STRIVE
 camp: 5 GULAG
 group: 5 UNION
 issue: 5 CHILD
 output: 4 BABY
 partner: 5 PARTS

Labor Day
 mo.: 3 SEP 4 **SEPT**

Laborer
 Anglo-Saxon: 4 ESNE
 Lowly: 4 **PEON**
 Medieval: 4 ESNE SERF
 Menial: 4 PEON
 Migrant: 7 BRACERO

Laborious: 6 UPHILL
  8 TOILSOME
 routine: 5 GRIND

Labrador: 3 DOG
 retriever: 4 SPCA

La Brea
 attraction: 6 TARPIT
 goo: 3 TAR

Labyrinth: 4 **MAZE**
 King who had the ~ built:
  5 MINOS
 suffix: 3 INE

Lac
  contents: 3 EAU
"La Campanella": 5 ETUDE
Lace: 3 TIE 7 TATTING
  again: 5 RETIE
  color: 4 ECRU
  Hole for a: 6 EYELET
  Loosen a: 5 UNTIE
  Made: 6 TATTED
  Make: 3 **TAT**
  place: 4 SHOE 6 EYELET
  tip: 5 AGLET
Lacework
  Do: 3 TAT
Lachesis
  Clotho, ~, and Atropos: 5 FATES
Lachrymal
  secretion: 4 TEAR
Lachrymose: 5 TEARY
Lack: 4 NEED 6 DEARTH
      7 ABSENCE
Lackadaisical: 4 SLOW
  response: 6 MANANA
Lackawanna
  lake: 4 ERIE
  ___ Lackawanna Railroad: 4 ERIE
Lacking: 3 SHY 4 LESS SANS
      5 NEEDY OUTOF SHORT
  a key: 6 ATONAL
  color: 4 PALE
  compassion: 8 INHUMANE
  couth: 4 RUDE
  in variety: 7 ONENOTE
  locks: 4 BALD
  moisture: 3 DRY 4 ARID
  muscle: 4 WEAK
  play: 4 TAUT
  principles: 6 AMORAL
  siblings: 4 ONLY
  skill: 5 INEPT
  slack: 4 **TAUT**
  substance: 4 AIRY 5 INANE
  value: 3 NIL
  vitality: 6 ANEMIC
Lackluster: 4 DRAB DULL
Lacks: 5 **HASNT**
"L.A. Confidential"
  actress Basinger: 3 KIM
Laconic: 5 TERSE

Lacoste
  of fashion: 4 IZOD
  of tennis: 4 **RENE**
Lacquer: 5 JAPAN
  ingredient: 5 ELEMI RESIN
Lacquered
  metalware: 4 TOLE
Lacrosse
  team: 3 TEN
Lact-
  suffix: 3 OSE
Lacto-___ vegetarian: 3 OVO
Lacuna: 3 GAP
Lacy
  item: 5 DOILY
  loop: 5 PICOT
Lad: 3 BOY
  love: 4 LASS
Ladd
  Actor: 4 **ALAN**
  Actress: 5 DIANE 6 CHERYL
Ladd, Alan
  film: 3 OSS 5 SHANE
  role: 5 SHANE
Ladder
  Climb the: 4 RISE
  He dreamt about a: 5 JACOB
  Hose: 3 RUN
  Item with a: 5 SLIDE
  Lover with a: 6 ELOPER
  part: 4 RUNG STEP
  step: 4 **RUNG**
  Top of the corporate: 3 CEO
  ~, in Italian: 5 SCALA
"Ladders to Fire"
  novelist: 3 NIN
Laddie: 4 BOYO
  love: 4 LASS
La-di-da: 6 TOOTOO
Ladies
  man: 4 GENT 5 ROMEO
      8 CASANOVA
  room: 5 HAREM
Ladle: 5 SPOON 6 DIPPER
"La Dolce ___": 4 VITA
"La Dolce Vita"
  director: 7 FELLINI
  setting: 4 ROME
  star Anouk: 5 AIMEE

"___ la Douce": 4 **IRMA**
Lady: 7 PEERESS
  Church: 3 NUN
  escort: 4 GENT
  First: 3 **EVE**
  Foxy: 5 VIXEN
  Lea: 3 EWE
  Little: 4 GIRL
  Loved: 4 LUCY
  of the house: 5 MADAM
  of the knight: 4 DAME
  Scat: 4 ELLA
  That: 3 HER SHE
  title: 3 MRS 5 MADAM
  What the fat ~ sings: 4 ARIA
    5 OPERA
  Young: 4 GIRL LASS MISS
  ~, in Italian: 5 DONNA
  ~, in Spanish: 3 SRA 4 DONA
    6 SENORA
"___ Lady": 5 SHESA
"Lady ___, The": 3 EVE
    5 INRED
"Lady and the Tramp"
  breed: 7 SIAMESE
Ladybug
  feature: 5 SPOTS
  prey: 5 APHID
"Lady Jane Grey"
  dramatist: 4 ROWE
Lady-killer: 5 ROMEO
  8 LOTHARIO
"Lady Lindy": 7 EARHART
"Lady Love"
  singer: 5 RAWLS
Lady Macbeth: 4 ROLE
___ Lady of Fatima: 3 OUR
"Lady of the Lake, The"
  author: 5 SCOTT
"Lady Sings the Blues"
  star: 4 ROSS
Lady's man: 3 SIR 4 BEAU EARL
  GENT LORD 5 ROMEO
Lady's-slipper: 6 ORCHID
"Lady ___ Tramp, The": 3 ISA
Laertes
  sister: 7 OPHELIA
Lafayette
  recruiter Silas: 5 DEANE

Lafayette College
  home: 6 EASTON
Lag: 5 TRAIL
Lagasse
  Chef: 6 EMERIL
L'Age ___ : 3 DOR
Lager
  holder: 5 STEIN
  kin: 3 ALE
  Light: 7 PILSNER
Lagerlöf
  Novelist: 5 SELMA
Laggard: 4 POKE 6 SLOUCH
Lago
  contents: 4 AGUA
Lagomorphic
  leaper: 4 HARE
Lagoon
  surrounder: 5 **ATOLL**
LaGuardia Airport
  Stadium near: 4 ASHE SHEA
"___ la guerre!": 4 CEST
"Lah-di-___!": 3 DAH
Lahore
  garb: 4 SARI
  language: 4 URDU
Lahr
  Actor: 4 BERT
  role: 4 LION
"La ___ Humaine" (Jean Renoir
  film): 4 BETE
Laid
  Be ~ up: 3 AIL
  It's often ~ down: 6 THELAW
  low: 3 HID
  off: 5 IDLED
  up: 3 **ILL** 4 ABED 5 INBED
Laid-back: 5 STAID TYPEB
  6 ATEASE
  Hardly: 5 TYPEA
  In a ~ fashion: 4 IDLY
  quality: 4 EASE
  sort: 5 TYPEB
Laila
  Boxer: 3 **ALI**
Laine
  Jazz singer: 4 **CLEO**
Laine, Frankie
  hit song: 8 IBELIEVE

Lair: 3 **DEN** 7 HIDEOUT
  Bear: 3 **DEN**
  Lofty: 5 AERIE
Laissez-___: 5 FAIRE
Lake
  boat: 5 CANOE
  craft: 5 CANOE
  dweller: 5 TROUT
  Fictional: 7 WOBEGON
  lander: 8 SEAPLANE
  Land in a: 5 ISLET
  maker: 3 DAM
  rental: 5 CANOE
  Resort: 5 TAHOE
  tribe: 4 ERIE
  Western: 5 TAHOE
Lake ___
  (Blue Nile source):
    4 TANA
  (Mississippi river source):
    6 ITASCA
Lake Assad
  setting: 5 SYRIA
Lake Geneva
  spa: 5 EVIAN
Lake Mead
  Like: 7 MANMADE
Lake Michigan
  city: 4 GARY 6 RACINE
Lake Nasser
  City near: 5 ASWAN
"Lake ___ of Innisfree, The":
  4 ISLE
Lake Okeechobee
  state: 3 FLA
Lake Ontario
  River to: 7 GENESEE
Laker
  Great: 4 SHAQ 5 ONEAL
  org.: 3 NBA
Lake Tahoe
  City near: 4 RENO
Lake Titicaca
  is partly here: 4 PERU
  locale: 5 ANDES
Lake Volta
  locale: 5 GHANA
"Lakmé"
  soprano: 5 ELLEN

La-la
  lead-in: 3 OOH **TRA**
___ la la: 3 TRA
"___ La La" (Manfred Mann hit):
  3 SHA
"L.A. Law"
  actor Richard: 6 DYSART
  actress Susan: 3 **DEY**
  lawyer: 5 ARNIE
Lalique
  Glassmaker and jeweler: 4 RENE
Lallygag: 4 LOAF
"La Loge"
  painter: 6 RENOIR
Lam
  Go on the: 4 FLEE
  One on the: 5 FLEER
    7 ESCAPEE
  On the: 5 LOOSE
  Went on the: 6 LITOUT
Lama
  land: 5 TIBET
  Like Nash's: 4 **ONEL**
___ Lama: 5 **DALAI**
"___ Lama Ding Dong": 4 **RAMA**
La Mancha
  Lady of: 6 SENORA
  Man of: 5 SENOR
Lamarr
  Actress: 4 **HEDY**
"La Marseillaise": 6 ANTHEM
Lamb: 4 MEAT 8 ESSAYIST
  alias: 4 **ELIA**
  A little: 4 CHOP
  Had a little: 3 ATE
  Like a: 4 MEEK
  mother: 3 EWE
  noise: 3 BAA
  of literature: 4 ELIA
  pen name: 4 **ELIA**
  product: 5 ESSAY
  sandwich: 4 GYRO
  serving: 4 CHOP RACK
  sound: 5 BLEAT
  Tender: 3 EWE
Lamb, Charles: 8 ESSAYIST
  pen name: 4 ELIA
Lambaste: 4 SLAM 5 CREAM
    SCOLD 6 RAILAT

Lamb Chop
  puppeteer Lewis: 5 SHARI
Lambert Airport
  code: 3 STL
Lamborghini
  owner: 4 AUDI
Lambs
  Like: 5 OVINE
  ~, in Latin: 4 AGNI
Lame: 6 FEEBLE FLIMSY
  excuse: 7 IFORGOT
Lament: 3 RUE 4 MOAN 5 MOURN
        6 BEMOAN GRIEVE
        7 DEPLORE
  loudly: 4 KEEN WAIL
  Poem of: 5 ELEGY
Lamentation: 4 MOAN 6 PLAINT
  in verse: 5 ELEGY
Laminated
  rock: 5 SHALE
Lammermoor
  bride: 5 LUCIA
Lamont ___ ("The Shadow"):
        8 CRANSTON
LaMotta
  Boxer: 4 JAKE
Lamour
  garment: 6 SARONG
L'Amour, Louis
  novel: 5 HONDO
Lamp
  cover: 5 SHADE
  dweller: 5 GENIE
  dwellers: 5 GENII
  filler: 4 NEON 5 ARGON XENON
  fuel: 8 KEROSENE
  insert: 4 BULB
  Kind of: 4 LAVA 7 HALOGEN
        8 INFRARED
  locale: 8 ENDTABLE
  On, as a: 3 LIT
  part: 4 HARP
  ___ lamp: 3 ARC
Lampblack: 4 SOOT
Lamplighter: 8 KEROSENE
Lampoon: 5 SPOOF 6 SATIRE
        SENDUP
Lamprey: 3 EEL
  hunter: 5 EELER

Lamprey-like: 4 EELY
LAN
  Part of: 4 AREA
Lana
  Ex of: 5 ARTIE
Lanai
  event: 4 LUAU
  neighbor: 4 MAUI OAHU
Lancaster
  group: 5 AMISH
  symbol: 4 ROSE 7 REDROSE
Lancaster, Burt
  role: 4 EARP
  thriller: 14 SEVENDAYSINMAY
Lancastrian
  symbol: 4 ROSE 7 REDROSE
Lance: 4 STAB 5 SPEAR
  cpl. inferior: 3 PFC
  Judge: 3 ITO
  of the bench: 3 ITO
  With ~ in hand: 5 ATILT
Lancelot
  lover: 6 ELAINE
  portrayer: 4 GERE
  Son of: 7 GALAHAD
  title: 3 SIR
Lanchester
  Actress: 4 **ELSA**
Land: 5 TERRA 6 ALIGHT
        ARRIVE NATION REALTY
        7 ACREAGE
  Area of: 5 TRACT
  development: 6 CAMERA
  Divided: 5 KOREA
  Dot of: 4 ISLE
  down under: 5 HADES
  Expanse of: 5 TRACT
  Far from: 4 ASEA
  Feudal: 4 FIEF
  Flat: 4 MESA 7 PRAIRIE
  French spot of: 3 ILE
  Gang: 4 TURF
  Grazing: 3 LEA
  Green: 4 **EIRE** ERIN
  Having: 5 ACRED
  High: 5 NEPAL
  hopper: 4 TOAD
  in la mer: 3 ILE
  in the lake: 5 ISLET

in the ocean: 5 ISLET
in the sea: 4 ISLE 5 ISLET
in the water: 4 ISLE 5 ISLET
Kind of: 4 LALA
Large ~ mass: 4 ASIA
    7 EURASIA
Lots of: 5 ACRES
Low bit of: 5 SWALE
map: 4 **PLAT**
measure: 4 **ACRE**
Narrow strip of: 7 ISTHMUS
Not on: 4 ASEA
of a billion: 5 INDIA
of literature: 4 ERIN
of poetry: 4 ERIN
On: 6 ASHORE
On dry: 6 ASHORE
Our ~, informally: 5 USOFA
parcel: 3 LOT 4 ACRE
Plot of: 4 ACRE 5 TRACT
Promised: 6 CANAAN UTOPIA
Speck of: 5 ISLET
Spot of: 4 ISLE
Stretch of: 5 TRACT
suffix: 5 SCAPE
unit: 4 **ACRE**
Work the: 4 FARM TILL
~, as a fish: 6 REELIN
~, in French: 5 TERRE
~, in Latin: 5 TERRA
"Land ___!": 5 SAKES
___ land: 4 LALA
Landed: 4 **ALIT** 5 ACRED
    estate: 5 MANOR
    property: 5 MANOR
Landers
    Advice columnist: 3 ANN
Landfall
    Biblical: 6 ARARAT
Landfill: 4 DUMP
    emanation: 4 ODOR
Landing: 4 QUAY
    area: 5 STRIP WHARF
    field: 9 AERODROME
    info: 3 ETA
    pier: 4 DOCK
    place: 4 PIER 8 AIRSTRIP
Landlady
    Lucy's: 5 ETHEL

Landlocked
    land: 4 MALI 6 UGANDA
        7 BOLIVIA
    sea: 4 ARAL
Landlord: 5 OWNER 6 LESSOR
    due: 4 RENT
    income: 4 RENT
    need: 6 TENANT
    sign: 5 TOLET 10 ROOMSTOLET
    Sitcom: 5 MERTZ
"Land of Smiles, The"
    composer Franz: 5 LEHAR
Land of the Rising Sun: 5 JAPAN
Landon
    1936 candidate ~: 3 ALF
Landon, Michael
    role: 15 TEENAGEWEREWOLF
Landowner
    Like a: 5 ACRED
    Scottish: 5 **LAIRD**
Landscaper
    need: 3 SOD
    tool: 5 EDGER
Landscaping
    tool: 5 EDGER
Landscapist
    French: 5 COROT
Landvetter
    airline: 3 SAS
Lane
    Add a ~ to: 5 WIDEN
    Bowling: 5 ALLEY
    changer's concern:
        9 BLINDSPOT
    colleague: 4 KENT
    for carpoolers: 3 HOV
    Lovers': 5 AISLE
    Singer: 4 **ABBE**
    with lines: 6 NATHAN
Lane, Rocky
    spoke for him: 4 MRED
Lanes
    Join: 5 MERGE
    org.: 3 PBA
Lang
    of Smallville: 4 LANA
    Superboy's girlfriend: 4 LANA
Langdon, Sue ___
    Actress: 3 **ANE**

Langer
 Philosopher: 7 SUSANNE
Langerhans
 ___ of ~ (pancreatic parts):
  6 ISLETS
Langley
 org.: 3 CIA
" ___ Lang Syne": 4 AULD
Langtry
 Actress: 6 LILLIE
Language
 columnist William: 6 SAFIRE
 Computer: 4 JAVA 5 ALGOL
  BASIC COBOL 7 FORTRAN
 ending: 3 **ESE**
 Forum: 5 LATIN
 Highland: 4 ERSE
 Kids': 8 PIGLATIN
 Limerick: 4 ERSE
 Mass: 5 LATIN
 peculiarity: 5 IDIOM
 Secret: 4 CODE
 Sine: 4 TRIG
 suffix: 3 **ESE** ISH
Languish: 3 ROT SAG 4 PINE
  5 DROOP
Languor: 5 ENNUI
Lanin
 Bandleader: 6 LESTER
Lanka
 lead-in: 3 SRI
 ___ Lanka: 3 **SRI**
Lanky: 4 LEAN SLIM THIN
  6 GANGLY
L'année
 Part of: 3 ETE
Lansbury
 Actress: 6 ANGELA
 role: 4 MAME
Lansing
 E. ~ school: 3 MSU
Lansky
 Mobster: 5 MEYER
Lantern-jawed
 celebrity: 4 LENO
L.A.-N.Y.
 flight path: 3 ENE
Lanza
 role: 6 CARUSO

 Singer: 5 MARIO
Lanzoni
 Male model: 5 FABIO
Lao
 follower: 3 TSE
Lao- ___ : 3 **TSE** TZU
La ___ of Milan: 5 **SCALA**
Laos
 locale: 4 ASIA
Laotian: 5 ASIAN
 money: 3 KIP
 neighbor: 4 THAI
Lao-tzu
 follower: 6 TAOIST
 system: 6 TAOISM
 way: 3 TAO
Lap
 Create a: 3 SIT
 dog, for short: 3 POM 4 PEKE
 Gained a: 3 **SAT**
 Lose a: 5 STAND
 Made a: 3 **SAT**
" ___ Lap" (1983 film): 4 PHAR
La Paz
 country (abbr.): 3 BOL
LAPD
 alert: 3 **APB**
 rank: 3 DET
Lapel
 device: 4 MIKE
 jewelry: 3 PIN
 label: 5 IDTAG
Lapidarist
 item: 3 GEM
 unit: 5 CARAT
Lapin
 Lady: 3 DOE
Laps
 Did: 4 SWAM
 Do: 4 SWIM
 Done: 4 SWUM
Lapse: 3 SIN 4 SLIP 5 ERROR
Lapsed: 6 RANOUT
Lapses: 6 ERRATA
Laptev Sea
 River to the: 4 LENA
Laptop
 Apple: 5 IBOOK
 IBM: 8 THINKPAD

Lara
694

item: 6 NAPKIN
Lara
Tomb raider: 5 CROFT
Laraine
cohort: 5 GILDA
Larcenous: 7 PIRATIC
Larceny: 5 THEFT
Type of: 5 PETIT
Larch: 4 TREE 8 TAMARACK
___ **Laredo, Mexico:** 5 NUEVO
Large: 3 BIG 4 SIZE
amount: 3 SEA TON 4 SCAD
5 OCEAN
At: 4 FREE 5 LOOSE
10 ONTHELOOSE
group: 4 BEVY 5 ARRAY
More than: 4 HUGE 5 OBESE
number: 4 HERD HOST
SLEW
quantity: 4 SCAD SLEW
6 OODLES
Too: 5 OBESE
Large-eyed
lemur: 5 LORIS
primate: 5 LEMUR
Larger ___ life: 4 THAN
Larger-than-life: 4 EPIC
Large-scale: 4 EPIC MASS
Large-screen
film format: 4 IMAX
Largo: 5 TEMPO
and others: 5 TEMPI
Faster than: 6 ADAGIO
Lariat: 4 ROPE 5 LASSO REATA
RIATA
loop: 5 NOOSE
Lark: 5 ANTIC SPREE
8 ESCAPADE
Words before: 3 ONA
___ **lark:** 3 ONA
"L'Arlésienne"
composer: 5 BIZET
Larrup: 3 TAN
Larry: 6 STOOGE
Cohort of: 3 MOE
"Larry King Live"
broadcaster: 3 CNN
Larsen
of baseball: 3 DON

Larson
Cartoonist: 4 GARY
Larson, Jonathan
musical: 4 RENT
Larvae
Beetle: 5 GRUBS
Fly: 7 MAGGOTS
Laryngology
prefix: 3 OTO
Lasagna
ingredient: 7 RICOTTA
La Salle
Actor: 4 ERIQ
La Scala
1887 ~ debut: 6 OTELLO
highlight: 4 **ARIA**
home: 5 MILAN
offering: 5 **OPERA**
solo: 4 **ARIA**
star: 4 DIVA
"La Scala di ___" (Rossini opera):
4 SETA
Las ___, Canary Islands:
6 PALMAS
Lascivious: 4 LEWD
deity: 5 SATYR
look: 4 **LEER**
Lasciviously
Look: 4 LEER OGLE 6 LEERAT
Laser
Hit with a: 3 ZAP
light: 4 BEAM
output: 3 RAY 4 BEAM
Lash: 3 TAN TIE 4 CANE WHIP
cosmetic: 7 MASCARA
Cowboy star: 5 LARUE
of westerns: 5 LARUE
out at: 6 ASSAIL
Lash ___: 5 OUTAT
"Lasher"
novelist Anne: 4 RICE
Lashes: 5 CILIA
Site for: 6 EYELID
Lashing
reminder: 4 WELT
Lass: 3 GAL 4 GIRL 5 BELLE
6 DAMSEL
partner: 3 LAD
Lassie: 6 COLLIE

Aussie: 6 SHEILA
mate: 3 LAD
Lassitude: 5 ENNUI
Lasso: 4 ROPE 5 REATA **RIATA**
6 LARIAT
loop: 5 NOOSE
wielder: 5 ROPER
Last: 5 FINAL 6 ENDURE
(abbr.): 3 ULT
call: 4 TAPS
Come in: 4 LOSE
in a series: 3 NTH ZEE 5 OMEGA
mo.: 3 DEC
part: 3 END
place: 6 CELLAR
shot: 4 PUTT
word: 3 END
"Last Days of Pompeii, The"
heroine: 4 IONE
Last-ditch
effort: 5 STAND
"Last Don, The"
author: 4 PUZO
"Last Emperor, The"
star: 4 LONE
"Last Essays of ___," 1833: 4 ELIA
Lasting: 7 DURABLE
do: 4 PERM
forever: 7 ETERNAL
impression: 4 **SCAR**
start: 4 EVER
"Last of the Mohicans, The"
heroine: 4 CORA
"Last one ___ a rotten egg!":
4 INIS
Last Supper
cup: 5 GRAIL
guest: 7 APOSTLE
query: 5 ISITI
"Last Supper, The": 5 MURAL
city: 5 MILAN
painter: 7 DAVINCI
"Last Temptation of Christ, The"
actor: 5 DAFOE
Last word: 3 END 4 AMEN
in a threat: 4 ELSE
in prayer: 4 AMEN
Last words: 4 OBIT 7 EPITAPH
Famous: 3 IDO 4 ETTU 5 AMENS

6 THEEND
Las Vegas
area: 5 STRIP
gas: 4 NEON
illumination: 4 NEON
TV drama set in: 3 CSI
"Las Vegas"
actor James: 4 CAAN
Laszlo
of cosmetics: 4 ERNO
Laszlo, Victor
Wife of: 4 ILSA
La ___ Tar Pits: 4 **BREA**
Latch: 4 GLOM GRAB
Door: 4 HASP
Word after: 4 ONTO
Latch ___: 4 ONTO
Latched
Not: 4 AJAR
Late: 5 TARDY 6 RECENT
7 OVERDUE 8 DECEASED
news: 4 OBIT
Not: 5 ONCUE 6 ONTIME
Of: 5 NEWLY
Running: 5 TARDY
Lateef
Composer: 5 YUSEF
Lateen-rigged
vessel: 4 DHOW
Late-night
flight: 6 REDEYE
host: 4 **LENO** PAAR 5 CONAN
Later: 4 ANON 5 NEWER
6 NOTNOW NOTYET
No ~ than: 3 TIL 5 UNTIL
"Later!": 3 BYE 4 TATA 5 ADIOS
SEEYA 6 MANANA
NOTNOW
Lateral
prefix: 3 TRI UNI 4 **EQUI**
remark: 5 ASIDE
Laterally
Move: 5 SIDLE
Late-show
watcher: 8 NIGHTOWL
Latest
info: 4 DOPE
The: 4 NEWS
thing: 4 RAGE

word: 4 NEWS 6 UPDATE
Lather: 4 FOAM SNIT STEW
In a: 3 MAD 4 AGOG 5 HETUP
  SOAPY
Producing: 5 SUDSY
Lathered: 6 SOAPED
Latin
abbr.: 3 ETC 4 ETAL
adverb: 3 HIC HOC
bear: 4 URSA
being: 4 ESSE
carol word: 6 ADESTE
case: 6 DATIVE
clarifier: 5 IDEST
dance: 5 SAMBA TANGO
dance music: 5 SALSA
dog: 5 CANIS
egg: 4 OVUM
eggs: 3 OVA
existence: 4 ESSE
First of a ~ trio: 3 AMO
foot: 3 PES
king: 3 REX
land: 5 TERRA
law: 3 LEX
Like ~, today: 4 DEAD
list ender: 6 ETALII
love: 4 **AMOR**
lover's word: 3 **AMO** 4 AMAT
music: 5 SALSA
others: 4 ALII
passage: 4 ITER
Pertinent, in: 5 ADREM
poet: 4 OVID
preposition: 4 ANTE
pronoun: 3 MEA 4 ILLE
salutation: 3 AVE
That is, in: 5 IDEST
thing: 3 RES
trio member: 3 AMO 4 AMAS
  AMAT
word on a coin: 4 UNUM
word on a dollar bill: 4 ORDO
year: 4 ANNO
Latin 101
word: 3 **AMO** EGO 4 **AMAS**
  AMAT ERAT ESSE
Latino
cry: 7 CARAMBA

Latish
bedtime: 5 ONEAM
lunch hr.: 5 ONEPM
lunchtime: 3 ONE
Latitude: 4 PLAY ROOM
  6 LEEWAY
Pole: 6 NINETY
Latke
ingredient: 6 POTATO
"La Traviata"
composer: 5 VERDI
mezzo: 5 FLORA
Lats
neighbors: 3 ABS
___ latte: 5 CAFFE
Latter-day Saint: 6 MORMON
Lattice
for plant growers: 7 TRELLIS
Latticework
strip: 4 LATH
Lattisaw
Singer: 5 STACY
Latvia
capital: 4 **RIGA**
Like: 6 BALTIC
~, once (abbr.): 3 SSR
Latvian: 4 BALT LETT
capital: 4 RIGA
Laud: 5 EXTOL 6 PRAISE
Laudatory
lines: 3 ODE
Lauder
of cosmetics: 5 **ESTEE**
Lauderdale
neighbor: 4 BOCA
Lauer
Host: 4 MATT
show: 5 TODAY
Laugh
Belly: 4 ROAR
Big: 6 HAHAHA
Cause to: 5 AMUSE
Derisive: 3 HAH 6 HAWHAW
Half a: 3 HEE HEH
Have a good: 4 HOOT ROAR
Little: 5 **TEHEE** 6 GIGGLE
  TEEHEE
Loud: 3 YUK 4 ROAR
loudly: 4 ROAR

Make: 5 AMUSE
riot: 6 SCREAM
syllable: 3 HAR HEE
unit: 4 PEAL
Witch's: 6 CACKLE
~, in French: 4 RIRE
Laughable: 5 COMIC INANE
    7 ASININE
"Laughable Lyrics"
  writer: 4 LEAR
Laugh-a-minute: 4 HOOT RIOT
  type: 4 RIOT
Laughfest: 4 HOOT RIOT
"Laugh-In"
  actress Goldie: 4 HAWN
  actress Judy: 5 CARNE
  cohost Dan: 5 ROWAN
  comedian Johnson: 4 ARTE
  comedienne Lily: 6 TOMLIN
  comedienne Ruth: 5 BUZZI
  line: 10 SOCKITTOME
  segment: 4 SKIT
Laughing: 5 RIANT
  animal: 5 HYENA
  gas: 5 OXIDE
  It may be: 3 GAS
  matter: 3 GAS
  scavenger: 5 HYENA
"Laughing Cavalier, The"
  painter: 4 HALS
Laughs: 4 HAHA
  Barrel of: 4 RIOT
Laughter
  Burst of: 4 GALE PEAL
  Cause of: 7 COMICAL
  Loud: 4 ROAR
  Sound of: 4 HAHA PEAL
    6 TEEHEE
"Laughter in the Rain"
  singer/songwriter: 6 SEDAKA
Launch: 4 BOAT 6 PROPEL
    8 INITIATE
  agcy.: 4 NASA
  Cancel a: 5 ABORT
  cancellation: 4 NOGO
  of 1962: 7 TELSTAR
  of 1986: 3 MIR
  Scrub, as a: 5 ABORT
  site: 3 PAD

Launcher
  French satellite: 6 ARIANE
  org.: 4 NASA
  Rocket: 4 NASA
Launder: 4 WASH 5 CLEAN
Laundering
  In need of: 6 SOILED
Laundromat
  appliance: 5 DRYER
  Like a ~ machine: 6 COINOP
Laundry: 4 WASH
  Do a ~ task: 4 SORT
  Early ~ brand: 5 RINSO
  load: 4 WASH
  mysteries: 8 ODDSOCKS
  Prepare: 4 SORT
  supply: 6 STARCH
  unit: 4 LOAD
  woe: 5 STAIN
  worker: 6 IRONER
Lauper
  Singer: 5 CYNDI
Laura
  Actress: 4 DERN 5 INNES
  Fashion designer: 6 ASHLEY
  Songwriter: 4 NYRO
"Laura"
  actress Gene: 7 TIERNEY
  author Caspary: 4 VERA
  director Preminger: 4 OTTO
Laurel
  Comedian: 4 **STAN**
  Hardy, to: 5 OLLIE
  Hardy, vis-à-vis: 6 LARGER
  topper: 5 DERBY
Lauren
  Actress: 5 TEWES
  Designer: 5 RALPH
Lauren, Ralph
  brand: 4 POLO
  line: 5 CHAPS
Laurence
  Former CBS chairman: 5 TISCH
Laurentiis, De
  Film producer: 4 DINO
Lav
  of London: 3 LOO
Lava
  Eject: 4 SPEW 5 ERUPT

Like: 6 MOLTEN
rock: 6 BASALT
Spew: 5 ERUPT
Lavatory
London: 3 LOO
sign: 5 INUSE
Laver
of tennis: 3 ROD
"___ la vie": 4 CEST
"La Vie en Rose"
singer Edith: 4 PIAF
Lavigne
Singer: 5 AVRIL
Lavin
Actress: 5 LINDA
Lavish: 7 OPULENT
affection: 4 **DOTE**
party: 4 FETE GALA
"___ la vista": 5 HASTA
"La ___ Vita": 5 DOLCE
"La vita nuova"
poet: 5 DANTE
Law: 7 STATUTE 9 ORDINANCE
It's the: 5 EDICT
Lay down the: 4 RULE
Make into: 5 **ENACT**
Man with a: 3 OHM
partner: 5 ORDER
Pass into: 5 ENACT
Religious: 5 CANON
school class: 5 TORTS
suffix: 3 YER
Thing, in: 3 RES
~, in French: 3 LOI
~, in Latin: 3 LEX
___ law
(old German code): 5 SALIC
(physics topic): 4 OHMS
"Law & ___": 5 ORDER
"Law & Order: SVU"
actor: 4 ICET
Lawful: 5 LEGIT LICIT
Lawgiver
Ancient: 5 SOLON
Athenian: 5 DRACO SOLON
Harsh: 5 DRACO
Wise: 5 SOLON
La ___, Wisconsin: 6 CROSSE
Lawless: 8 ANARCHIC

character: 4 **XENA**
Lawman
Comical: 3 KOP
Legendary: 4 EARP
Tombstone: 4 EARP
Lawn: 5 GRASS
additive: 4 LIME
bowling: 5 BOCCE BOCCI
burrower: 4 MOLE
decoration: 5 GNOME
    8 FLAMINGO
Do ~ work: 3 SOD 5 RESOD
    6 RESEED
Instant: 3 SOD
Lay down the: 3 SOD
layer: 3 SOD
Name in ~ care: 4 TORO
    5 ORTHO 6 SCOTTS
Neaten the: 4 EDGE
pest: 4 MOLE
Start a: 4 SEED
tool: 5 EDGER MOWER
    6 SEEDER
Lawn mower
brand: 4 TORO 5 DEERE
path: 5 SWATH
site: 4 SHED
"Lawnmower Man"
actor Jeff: 5 FAHEY
Lawrence
land: 6 ARABIA
portrayer: 6 OTOOLE
Lawrence, D.H.
ranch site: 4 TAOS
"Lawrence of Arabia"
actor: 6 OTOOLE
Lawsuit
cause: 4 TORT
issue: 7 DAMAGES
Lawyer: 8 ATTORNEY
(abbr.): 3 ATT ESQ 4 ATTY
assistant, briefly: 4 PARA
Case for a: 7 ATTACHE
charge: 3 FEE
Good name for a: 3 SUE
org.: 3 ABA
take: 3 FEE
thing: 3 RES
undertaking: 4 CASE

Lawyers
  gp.: 3 **ABA**
  org.: 3 **ABA**
  ~, collectively: 6 THEBAR
LAX
  posting: 3 **ARR ETA ETD**
Lay: 3 SET 4 POEM SONG
  an egg: 4 BOMB
  concrete: 4 PAVE
  down the law: 4 RULE
  down the lawn: 3 SOD
  eyes on: 4 ESPY
  into: 5 SETAT
  low: 3 HID 4 HIDE 7 HIDEOUT
  One way to ~ it on: 5 THICK
  on thick: 7 SLATHER
  out: 5 SPEND
  person: 8 MINSTREL
  to rest: 5 INTER 6 ENTOMB
  turf: 3 SOD
  up: 5 STORE
  waste to: 4 RUIN
Lay ___ : 5 ANEGG
Layabout: 5 IDLER
  Not a: 4 DOER
"___ Lay Dying": 3 ASI
Layer: 3 HEN PLY 4 COAT TIER
    7 STRATUM
  Atmospheric: 5 OZONE
  Barnyard: 3 HEN
  Cake: 4 TIER
  Coal: 4 SEAM VEIN
  Damaged: 5 OZONE
  Eye: 4 **UVEA**
  Farm: 3 HEN
  Floor: 5 TILER
  Golden egg: 5 GOOSE
  Green egg: 3 EMU
  Lawn: 3 SOD
  on a wall: 4 COAT
  Paint: 4 **COAT**
  Plywood: 6 VENEER
  Skin: 5 **DERMA**
  Thin: 6 LAMINA
  Tissue: 3 PLY
  with a hole: 5 OZONE
Layered
  cookie: 4 OREO
  entrée: 7 LASAGNA

  haircut: 4 SHAG
  lunch: 3 BLT
  rock: 5 SHALE
  skirt: 4 TUTU
Layers: 6 **STRATA**
  Thin: 7 LAMINAE
"Lay it ___!": 4 ONME
"Layla"
  singer Clapton: 4 ERIC
"Lay Lady Lay"
  singer: 5 DYLAN
"___ Lay Me Down": 3 ASI
"___ lay me down ...": 4 NOWI
Layout: 5 SETUP 6 FORMAT
  Printer's: 7 PASTEUP
Layover: 4 STOP
Layperson: 6 OBLATE
Lay ___ the line: 4 ITON
Lay ___ thick: 4 ITON
Lazarus
  Cartoonist: 4 MELL
  Poet: 4 **EMMA**
Lazarus, Mell
  comic strip: 5 MOMMA
Laze: 4 LOLL
  about: 4 LOLL
Lazily
  Recline: 4 LOLL
Laziness: 5 SLOTH
  ___ lazuli: 5 LAPIS
Lazy: 6 OTIOSE
  one: 5 IDLER SLOTH
Lazybones: 5 IDLER
"___ Lazy River": 3 UPA
Lazy Susan: 4 TRAY
Lb.
  and others: 3 WTS
LBJ: 4 PRES 5 TEXAN
  beagle: 3 HER HIM
  in-law: 4 ROBB
  successor: 3 RMN
  veep: 3 HHH
Lbs.
  100 ~: 3 CWT
  and others: 3 WTS
  Parts of: 3 OZS
LCD
  Part of: 5 LEAST
"L'___ c'est moi": 4 ETAT

"L'chaim!": 6 TOLIFE
"L'___ des Femmes" (Moliere work): 5 ECOLE
"L'___ de siège" (Camus work): 4 ETAT
Le ___ (Paris paper): 5 MONDE
Le ___, John
  Author: 5 CARRE
Lea
  lady: 3 EWE
  Low in a: 3 MOO
Leaching
  product: 3 LYE
Lead: 4 CLUE ROLE STAR 5 GUIDE STEER 9 SPEARHEAD TITLEROLE
  Get the ~ out: 4 MINE 5 ERASE SMELT
  Have the: 4 STAR
  In the: 5 AHEAD ONTOP 8 OUTFRONT
  ore: 6 GALENA
  player: 4 STAR
  sharer: 6 COSTAR
  Silver: 4 REIN
  Take the: 4 STAR
  to: 5 CAUSE
Lead ___: 6 ASTRAY
Leadbelly
  Real first name of: 6 HUDDIE
Leaden: 4 GREY
Leader: 4 HEAD 6 TOPDOG
  Info: Prefix cue
  Arab: 4 EMIR 5 AMEER EMEER
  Bearded: 6 CASTRO
  Brute: 4 ETTU
  Bus.: 3 MGR
  Bygone: 4 TSAR
  Cast: 4 TELE
  Church: 5 ELDER
  City: 5 MAYOR
  Corp.: 3 CEO
  Crew: 3 COX
  Deposed: 4 SHAH 5 EXILE
  Dynamic: 4 AERO
  Enemy: 4 ARCH
  Flock: 3 RAM 6 PASTOR PRIEST
  Functional: 3 DYS
  Gay: 5 ENOLA

Historic: 3 PRE
in a beret: 3 CHE
League: 3 IVY
Liberal: 3 NEO
Likeable: 3 IKE
Loss: 3 ATA
Mosque: 4 IMAM
of the pack: 5 AKELA PACER
Party: 4 HOST
Potent: 4 OMNI
Prayer: 4 IMAM
preceder: 4 BORN
Ring: 5 CHAMP 6 TORERO
Sect: 3 TRI
Space: 4 AERO
Staff: 4 CLEF
Supreme: 4 ROSS
Team: 7 CAPTAIN
Temple: 5 RABBI
Tour: 5 GUIDE
World: 6 NETHER
Leadership: 8 GUIDANCE
  position: 4 HELM
Leadfoot: 7 SPEEDER
  detector: 5 RADAR
Lead-in
  Info: Prefix cue
Leading: 3 TOP 5 **AHEAD** FIRST ONTOP 7 AHEADOF INFRONT
"Leading With My Chin"
  author: 4 LENO 7 JAYLENO
Leadoff
  Result of a ~ walk: 5 ONEON
Leaf: 4 PAGE 5 FOLIO
  bisector: 6 MIDRIB
  Book: 4 PAGE
  Fern: 5 FROND
  Floral: 5 SEPAL
  gatherer: 4 RAKE
  Half a: 4 PAGE
  holder: 4 STEM
  line: 4 VEIN
  opening: 4 PORE 5 STOMA
  Palm: 5 FROND
  part: 6 MIDRIB
  pore: 5 STOMA
  Salad: 6 ENDIVE
  Uneven like a: 5 EROSE

unit: 4 PAGE
vein: 3 RIB
Leafed: 5 PAGED
  through: 4 READ
Leaflike
  appendage: 5 BRACT
Leaf-loving
  ~ Aussie: 5 KOALA
Leafstalk: 7 PETIOLE
Leafy
  climber: 3 IVY
  recess: 5 ARBOR BOWER
  shelter: 5 BOWER
  vegetable: 4 KALE
League
  Certain ~ (abbr.): 4 AMER NATL
  leader: 3 IVY
  member: 4 ARAB TEAM
  of intrigue: 5 CABAL
  ___ League: 3 IVY 4 ARAB
        6 LITTLE
League of Nations
  home: 6 GENEVA
"League of ___ Own, A":
        5 THEIR
"League of Their ___, A": 3 OWN
League of Women Voters
  founder: 4 CATT
Leah
  Son of: 4 LEVI
Leak: 4 SEEP 6 GETOUT
  slowly: 4 OOZE SEEP
  sound: 3 SSS 4 SSSS
Leakey, Richard: 6 KENYAN
  home: 5 KENYA
Leaking: 4 OOZY 5 ADRIP
Lean: 4 LANK LIST THIN TILT
        TRIM WIRY 5 SPARE
        6 MEAGER
  against: 6 RESTON
  and lovely: 6 SVELTE
  and muscular: 4 WIRY
  eater of rhyme: 5 SPRAT
  Long and: 4 LANK
  Make: 5 DEFAT
  (on): 4 RELY
  to one side: 4 LIST
  toward: 5 FAVOR 6 PREFER
Lean-___ (sheds): 3 TOS

Leander
  love: 4 HERO
Leaning: 4 BENT BIAS 5 ATILT
        6 ASLANT
  against: 4 ANTI
  to the right: 6 ITALIC
Leaning Tower
  town: 4 PISA
LeAnn
  Country singer: 5 RIMES
Lean-to: 4 SHED
Leap
  at the rink: 4 AXEL
  Ballet: 4 JETE
  Skater's: 4 AXEL LUTZ
"___ Leap": 7 QUANTUM
Leaper
  Aussie: 3 ROO
  Long-eared: 4 HARE
  Savanna: 6 IMPALA
Leapfrog: 3 HOP
Leaping: 7 SALTANT
  game fish: 5 WAHOO
"Leap of Faith"
  Queen who wrote: 4 NOOR
Leapt: 6 SPRANG
Lear: 4 KING
  Daughter of: 5 REGAN
Learn: 4 HEAR
  about: 6 HEAROF
  gradually: 5 GLEAN
  One way to: 4 ROTE 6 BYROTE
  Quick to: 3 APT
Learned: 4 SAGE 5 HEARD
        7 ERUDITE 8 LITERATE
  Not: 6 INNATE
  one: 4 SAGE 6 SAVANT
Learning: 4 LORE
  inst.: 4 ACAD
  Mechanical: 4 ROTE
  method: 4 ROTE
  One ~ on the job: 7 TRAINEE
Leary, Denis
  1994 ~ film: 6 THEREF
Leary, Timothy
  drug: 3 LSD
Lease: 3 LET 4 RENT
  anew: 5 RELET
  length: 4 YEAR

Leash: 5 CHAIN 6 TETHER
  Off the: 5 LOOSE
Least: 6 FEWEST MEREST
    7 MINIMUM
  At ~ one: 3 ANY
  bit: 3 FIG 4 IOTA WHIT
  In the: 3 ANY 5 ATALL AWHIT
    6 ONEBIT
  The ~ bit: 5 ATALL 7 ONEIOTA
Leather
  Bookbinding: 4 ROAN
  ending: 4 ETTE
  Napped: 5 SUEDE
  piercer: 3 AWL
  Pliable: 3 ELK
  Prepare: 3 TAN
  Soft: 3 ELK 5 SUEDE
  sticker: 3 AWL
  strap: 4 REIN
  tool: 3 AWL
  Unpolished: 6 RUSSET
  worker: 6 TANNER
Leatherneck: 6 MARINE
  lunch: 4 MESS
  org.: 4 USMC
Leatherworker
  tool: 3 **AWL**
L'eau
  land: 3 ILE
Leave: 4 EXIT QUIT 5 SPLIT
    6 DEPART SECEDE
    7 HEADOUT PULLOUT
    TAKEOFF
  alone: 5 LETBE
  at the altar: 4 JILT
  be: 4 STET
  Force to: 5 EXILE 6 UPROOT
  in: 4 STET
  in a hurry: 4 BOLT
  in the dust: 4 LOSE
  Not: 4 STAY
  off: 4 **OMIT** 5 CEASE
  one's mark: 4 ETCH 7 IMPRESS
  out: 4 **OMIT** SKIP 5 ELIDE
  port: 4 SAIL 7 SETSAIL
  the country: 6 SECEDE
  the flock: 5 STRAY
  the stage: 4 EXIT
  the union: 6 SECEDE

  unsaid: 4 OMIT
Leave ___: 4 ATIP
"Leave ___ Beaver": 4 ITTO
"Leave it": 4 STET
"Leave It to Beaver"
  role: 5 EDDIE
Leaven: 5 YEAST
Leavening
  agent: 5 YEAST
Leavenworth: 6 PRISON
Leaves: 4 GOES 7 FOLIAGE
  Clear the: 4 RAKE
  for lunch: 5 SALAD
  Gather: 4 RAKE
  home: 4 NEST **TREE** 6 TEABAG
  in a bag: 3 TEA
  in hot water: 3 TEA
  Like some: 5 EROSE OVATE
    6 LOBATE 7 TERNATE
  Uneven, as: 5 EROSE
Leaving: 3 ORT
  Cost of: 4 BAIL 7 ALIMONY
  Keep from: 6 DETAIN
"___ Leaving Home" (Beatles
    tune): 4 SHES
"Leaving Las Vegas"
  actress Elisabeth: 4 SHUE
"Leaving on ___ Plane": 4 AJET
Leb.
  neighbor: 3 **ISR** SYR
Lebanese: 4 ARAB
Lebanon
  capital: 6 BEIRUT
  tree: 5 CEDAR
Leblanc
  detective Lupin: 6 ARSENE
LeBlanc
  Actor: 4 MATT
Lebowitz
  Humorist: 4 FRAN
Le Carré
  character: 3 SPY 6 SMILEY
Lech
  of Poland: 6 WALESA
Lecher: 4 ROUE 5 SATYR
  look: 4 LEER OGLE
Lecherous: 5 RANDY 7 GOATISH
  look: 4 LEER
  sort: 4 ROUE 5 SATYR

"Le Coq ___": 3 **DOR**
Lectern
  locale: 4 DAIS
Lecterns: 5 PODIA 6 ROSTRA
Lecture
  Give a: 5 ORATE
  hall: 6 LYCEUM
  jottings: 5 NOTES
  locale: 4 HALL
Lecturer: 4 PROF
  platform: 4 DAIS
  spots: 5 PODIA
Led: 3 RAN 5 PACED RULED
      7 USHERED
  on: 7 ENTICED
  to a seat: 7 USHERED
LED
  Part of: 5 DIODE
"Le ___ d'Arthur": 5 MORTE
Lederer
  known as Ann Landers:
      5 EPPIE
Ledge: 5 SHELF
  Window: 4 **SILL**
Ledger
  column: 6 ASSETS
  entry: 5 DEBIT
  item: 5 ENTRY
"Le ___ d'Or" (Rimsky-Korsakov
    title): 3 COQ
Le Duc Tho
  capital: 5 HANOI
"Le ___ du printemps": 5 SACRE
Lee
  Actress: 4 RUTA
  Cake lady: 4 SARA
  Director: 3 ANG
  foe: 5 MEADE
  gp.: 3 CSA
  of comics: 4 STAN
  side: 3 CSA 4 GRAY
  soldier: 3 REB
  ___ Lee: 4 SARA 6 KATHIE
"___ Lee"
  (folk song): 4 AURA
  Poe work: 7 ANNABEL
Lee, Ann: 6 SHAKER
Lee, Brenda
  hit song: 7 IMSORRY

Lee, Peggy
  song: 5 FEVER
Lee, Robert E.: 3 GEN 4 GENL
  org.: 3 CSA
  soldier: 3 REB
  waiting area: 5 LEVEE
Lee, Spike
  film: 15 DOTHERIGHTTHING
Lee, Tsung-___
  Nobelist: 3 DAO
Leeds
  lockup: 4 GAOL
  river: 4 AIRE
Leek
  relative: 5 CHIVE ONION
Leer
  at: 4 OGLE
Lees: 5 DREGS
Leeward Island: 7 STKITTS
Leeway: 4 ROOM 7 LICENSE
      8 LATITUDE
"___ le feste": 5 TUTTE
Le ___, France: 5 **HAVRE**
Left: 4 GONE WENT 7 VACATED
      8 DEPARTED
  Are: 6 REMAIN
  at sea: 5 APORT
  end: 3 IST
  Go: 3 HAW 4 TURN
  in a hurry: 4 HIED
  in the dust: 6 OUTRAN
  Not ~ over: 5 EATEN
  on a map: 4 WEST
  one's seat: 5 AROSE
  out: 7 OMITTED
  over: 7 UNEATEN
  They're ~ behind: 7 ESTATES
  To the ~, at sea: 5 APORT
  What's: 3 NET 4 REST 6 ESTATE
Left Bank
  city: 5 PARIS
  river: 5 SEINE
Left Coast
  airport, for short: 3 LAX
Left-hand
  entry: 5 DEBIT
  page: 5 **VERSO**
Left-handed
  Game that can't be played: 4 POLO

Leftover: 3 ORT 5 CRUMB SCRAP 6 EXCESS
  Apple: 4 CORE
  morsel: 3 ORT
Leftovers: 4 REST
  dish: 4 HASH
  Have: 5 EATIN
  Like: 7 UNEATEN
  Prepare: 6 REHEAT
Left-winger: 5 PINKO 7 LIBERAL
Lefty: 8 SOUTHPAW
  of baseball: 5 ODOUL
Leg: 3 GAM 4 **LIMB**
  bone: 4 SHIN 5 FEMUR TIBIA
  Give a ~ up: 5 BOOST
  joint: 4 **KNEE** 5 ANKLE
  muscle: 4 QUAD
  part: 4 CALF SHIN 5 SHANK
  Shake a: 3 HIE 6 HASTEN
  up: 4 **EDGE** 5 BOOST
Legacy: 8 HERITAGE
  recipient: 4 HEIR
Legal: 5 LICIT OFAGE
  action: 4 SUIT 6 APPEAL
  add-on: 3 ESE
  aide: 4 PARA 5 CLERK
  claim: 4 **LIEN**
  conclusion: 3 **ESE**
  cover-up: 4 ROBE
  deg.: 3 LLB
  document: 4 DEED WRIT
  excuse: 5 ALIBI
  gp.: 3 ABA
  It may be: 6 TENDER
  Like some ~ proceedings: 5 INREM
  matter: 3 **RES**
  memo opener: 4 INRE
  order: 4 WRIT
  org.: 3 **ABA**
  plea: 4 NOLO
  postponement: 4 STAY
  rep.: 4 ATTY
  rights org.: 4 ACLU
  scholar: 6 JURIST
  Some ~ tender: 6 TNOTES
  Start of a ~ conclusion: 5 IREST
  suffix: 3 ESE
  thing: 3 **RES**

  wrong: 4 TORT
Legalese
  adverb: 6 HEREBY HEREIN HERETO 7 THEREIN THERETO
  Bit of: 4 INRE
Legalistic
  phrase: 4 INRE
Legally
  bar: 5 **ESTOP**
  prevent: 5 **ESTOP**
  responsible: 6 LIABLE
"Legally Blonde"
  actress Witherspoon: 5 REESE
  role: 4 ELLE
Legate: 8 EMISSARY
Legatee: 4 HEIR
Legend: 4 MYTH
  maker: 5 ACURA
Legends
  Book with: 5 ATLAS
  The stuff of: 4 LORE
"Leggo my ___!": 4 EGGO
L'eggs
  rival: 5 HANES
Leghorn
  locale: 5 ITALY
Legion: 4 ARMY
Legislate: 5 ENACT
Legislation: 3 LAW 4 ACTS
  Pass: 5 ENACT
  Pension ~ letters: 5 ERISA
Legislative
  add-on: 5 RIDER
  assemblies: 5 PLENA
  house: 6 SENATE
Legislator: 3 SEN 7 ENACTOR
  Municipal ~ (abbr.): 3 ALD
  Wise: 5 SOLON
Legislature
  French: 5 SENAT
  Greek: 5 BOULE
  Japanese: 4 DIET
  Russian: 4 DUMA
Legit: 5 LICIT VALID 6 KOSHER
Legitimate: 5 LICIT VALID 6 KOSHER
Legman
  list: 7 ERRANDS

Leg-puller: 5 JOKER 6 KIDDER
Legrand
  Composer: 6 MICHEL
Legree, Simon: 6 TYRANT
        8 OVERSEER
  creator: 5 STOWE
  look: 5 SNEER
Legume: 3 PEA
  Black-eyed: 6 COWPEA
  Medicinal: 5 SENNA
  Soup: 3 PEA 6 LENTIL
  Southern: 6 COWPEA
  Tiny: 3 PEA
Le Havre
  Info: French cue
  City near: 4 CAEN
Lehman
  Conductor: 5 ENGEL
Lehmann
  Soprano: 5 **LOTTE**
Leia
  cohort: 3 HAN
  Furry friend of: 4 EWOK
  portrayer: 6 CARRIE
  Princess ~ ___: 6 ORGANA
Leibovitz
  Photographer: 5 ANNIE
Leif
  Father of: 4 **ERIC**
  language: 5 NORSE
Leigh
  Actress: 5 JANET 6 VIVIEN
  role: 5 OHARA
Leinsdorf
  Conductor: 5 ERICH
Leisure: 4 EASE 8 FREETIME
  Like a ~ suit: 5 RETRO
Leisurely: 4 SLOW
  stroll: 5 PASEO
  Walk: 5 AMBLE 6 STROLL
LEM
  Part of: 5 LUNAR
  ___ Leman: 3 LAC
LeMans: 3 GTO
Le Mans
  event: 4 RACE
Lemieux
  milieu: 3 ICE 4 RINK
"Lemme ___!": 4 ATEM

Lemmon, Jack
  comedy: 6 AVANTI
"___ Le Moko": 4 PEPE
Lemon: 3 DUD
  candy: 4 DROP
  drink: 3 ADE
  Like a: 4 SOUR
  Noted: 5 EDSEL
  peel: 4 RIND ZEST
  rind: 4 PEEL ZEST
  suffix: 3 ADE
  zest: 4 PEEL RIND
LeMond
  Cyclist: 4 GREG
Le Monde
  article: 3 UNE
Lemons
  locale: 5 GROVE
  Where to find: 6 CARLOT
"Lemon Tree"
  singer Lopez: 5 TRINI
Lemony: 4 SOUR TART
Lemur
  Large-eyed: 5 LORIS
Len
  of football: 6 DAWSON
Lena
  Actress: 4 **OLIN**
  Singer: 5 **HORNE**
Lend: 6 IMPART
  a hand: 3 **AID** 4 HELP 6 ASSIST
  an ear: 6 LISTEN
  Something to: 3 EAR 5 ANEAR
Lend ___: 5 **ANEAR**
Lender
  claim: 4 LIEN
  Govt.: 3 SBA
  offering: 5 BAGEL
Lending
  figures: 5 RATES
Lendl
  of tennis: 4 **IVAN**
Length
  Biblical: 5 CUBIT
  Lease: 4 YEAR
  of time: 5 SPELL
  of yarn: 4 HANK 5 SKEIN
  Ruler: 4 FOOT
  Skirt: 4 MAXI MIDI MINI

times width: 4 AREA
Lengthen: 3 EKE 6 EXTEND
Lengths
Dash: 3 EMS ENS
Lenient: 3 LAX 4 EASY SOFT
Less: 7 STERNER
with: 6 SOFTON
Lenin
foe: 7 TSARIST
Leader before: 4 TSAR
middle name: 5 ILICH
Lennon
lady: 3 **ONO**
love: 3 **ONO**
Singer: 4 SEAN
widow: 3 ONO
Lennon, John
hit: 5 WOMAN 7 IMAGINE
middle name: 3 ONO
Wife of: 7 YOKOONO
Lennon, Sean
Mother of: 3 ONO 7 YOKOONO
Lennox
Singer: 5 ANNIE
Lenny
Comic: 5 BRUCE
Leno
Former ~ announcer Hall: 3 EDD
Host: 3 JAY
Notable ~ feature: 4 CHIN
predecessor: 6 CARSON
welcome: 5 INTRO
"Lenore"
poet: 3 POE
Lens
cover: 6 EYELID
holders: 4 RIMS
Instrument: 5 OPTIC
Powerful: 5 MACRO
setting: 5 FSTOP
type: 4 ZOOM 7 BIFOCAL
    CONCAVE
Lenska
Actress: 4 RULA
Lent: 4 GAVE
a hand: 5 AIDED
ender: 6 EASTER
First day of: 12 ASHWEDNESDAY
It may be: 3 EAR

Lenten
symbol: 3 ASH
treat: 11 HOTCROSSBUN
Lentil: 6 LEGUME
Indian ~ dish: 3 DAL
Lento: 4 SLOW 5 TEMPO
Lenya
Actress: 5 **LOTTE**
Leo: 4 SIGN
follower: 5 VIRGO
home: 3 DEN 4 LAIR
Singer: 5 SAYER
sound: 4 ROAR
Leon
Actor: 4 AMES
Author: 4 **URIS**
Biographer: 4 EDEL
Clinton aide: 7 PANETTA
Singer: 7 REDBONE
Leonard
Author: 6 **ELMORE**
foe: 5 DURAN
Songwriter: 5 COHEN
Leonard ___ (Roy Rogers): 4 SLYE
Leonardo da ___: 5 VINCI
Leoncavallo
opera: 9 PAGLIACCI
Leone
Director: 6 SERGIO
___ **Leone:** 6 SIERRA
Leonhard
Mathematician: 5 EULER
Leoni
Actress: 3 TEA
Leonine
locks: 4 MANE
sound: 4 ROAR
Leontyne
piece: 4 ARIA
Leopard
Leap like a: 6 POUNCE
markings: 5 SPOTS
relative: 6 OCELOT
spot: 7 ROSETTE
Leopardlike
cat: 6 OCELOT
Leopold
partner in crime: 4 LOEB
Violinist: 4 **AUER**

Le Pew
Cartoon skunk: 4 PEPE
Lepidopterist
gear: 3 NET
Leporine
creature: 4 HARE
___ **Leppard**: 3 DEF
Leprechaun: 3 ELF
land: 4 **EIRE ERIN**
Like a: 5 ELFIN
Lepton
Kind of: 3 TAU
locale: 4 ATOM
Unstable: 4 MUON
Lepus: 4 HARE
Lerner
partner: 5 LOEWE
Lerner, ___ Jay: 4 ALAN
"___ le roi!": 4 ABAS VIVE
"Le roi d'Ys"
composer: 4 **LALO**
LeRoy
Sports artist: 6 NEIMAN
Les
WKRP news director: 7 NESSMAN
"Les ___" (Broadway show, for
short): 3 MIZ
Lesage
Author: 5 ALAIN
hero: 4 BLAS
Lesbos
poet: 6 SAPPHO
Les États-___: 4 **UNIS**
"Les Girls"
actress Taina: 3 ELG
LeShan
Author: 3 **EDA**
Lesley
Newscaster: 5 STAHL
Leslie
Actress: 5 CARON
"Les Misérables"
author: 4 HUGO
Lesotho
capital: 6 MASERU
Less: 5 MINUS NOTAS
Get for: 6 SAVEON
More or: 5 **ABOUT**
Much: 8 LETALONE

No ~ than: 7 ATLEAST
than: 5 UNDER
Lessee: 6 TENANT
Lessen: 4 BATE EASE 5 **ABATE**
8 DECREASE DIMINISH
Lesser of two ___: 5 EVILS
Lesser Sunda
island: 4 BALI 5 TIMOR
Lessing
Author: 5 DORIS
Lesson
Dance: 4 STEP
Early: 4 ABCS
Kindergarten: 4 ABCS
Piano: 5 ETUDE
"Lesson From ___, A" (Fugard
play): 5 **ALOES**
"Less Than Zero"
author Bret Easton ___: 5 ELLIS
Lest: 6 INCASE
Lestat
creator Anne: 4 RICE
Lester
Bluegrass guitarist: 5 FLATT
Sci-fi writer: 6 DELREY
"Lest we lose our ___": 5 EDENS
Les ___-Unis: 5 **ETATS**
Let: 4 RENT 5 ALLOW LEASE
6 RENTED
back in: 7 READMIT
down: 5 ALTER
fall: 4 DROP
free: 5 UNTIE
go: 3 AXE CAN 4 AXED FIRE
FREE 5 FIRED FREED
7 RELEASE UNLEASH
UNLOOSE
15 RELEASEONESHOLD
go of: 4 DROP
in: 5 ADMIT 8 ADMITTED
loose: 5 FREED UNPEN UNTIE
off: 4 VENT 6 ACQUIT
out: 4 EMIT RENT 5 ALTER
UNPEN WIDEN 6 LOOSEN
PAROLE
slip: 4 TELL TOLD
stand: 4 STET
up: 4 EASE 5 **ABATE EASED**
6 ABATED LESSEN RELENT

~, in tennis: 6 DOOVER
"Let ___" (Beatles song): 4 ITBE
Let ___ a secret: 4 INON
"Let ___ cake": 5 EMEAT
Letch: 5 SATYR
"Let 'er ___!": 3 RIP
"Lethal Weapon"
  costar of Danny: 3 MEL
  director Richard: 6 DONNER
  role: 5 RIGGS
"Let ___ hang out": 5 ITALL
Lethargic: 4 LOGY 5 INERT
      6 DROWSY SUPINE
Lethargy: 5 SOPOR 6 STUPOR
      TORPOR 7 MALAISE
"Let It ___" (Everly Brothers hit):
      4 BEME
"Let it stand": 4 STET
"Let me repeat ...": 5 ISAID
      7 ASISAID
"Let's ___": 4 ROLL
"Let's Dance"
  singer David: 5 BOWIE
"Let's Eat Right to Keep Fit"
  author Davis: 6 ADELLE
"Let's Fall in Love"
  composer: 5 ARLEN
"Let's get going!": 4 CMON
"Let's Get It On"
  singer: 4 GAYE
"Let's go!": 4 CMON
"Let's just leave ___ that": 4 ITAT
"Let's Make ___": 5 ADEAL
"Let's Make a Deal"
  option: 4 DOOR
Letter: 7 EPISTLE
  abbr.: 3 ENC PPS 4 ATTN ENCL
  additions (abbr.): 3 PSS
  adornment: 5 SERIF
  after chi: 3 PSI
  after epsilon: 4 ZETA
  after eta: 5 THETA
  after pi: 3 RHO
  after theta: 4 IOTA
  after zeta: 3 ETA
  Ancient: 4 RUNE
  ⁓before beth: 5 ALEPH
  before gimel: 4 BETH
  before iota: 5 THETA

before omega: 3 PSI
before sigma: 3 RHO
before upsilon: 3 TAU
Campus: 3 ETA RHO 5 THETA
Curvy: 3 ESS
embellishment: 5 SERIF
enc.: 3 SAE 4 SASE
flourish: 5 SERIF
Frat: 3 CHI ETA PHI PSI RHO
      TAU 5 SIGMA THETA
Greek: 3 CHI ETA PHI PSI RHO
      TAU 4 IOTA ZETA 5 ALPHA
      KAPPA OMEGA SIGMA
      THETA
Hebrew: 3 MEM TAV YOD 4 ALEF
      KOPH TETH 5 ALEPH
Key: 3 PHI 4 BETA 5 KAPPA
Kind of: 4 FORM 5 CHAIN
Last: 3 ZEE
Last ⁓ in London: 3 ZED
Old English: 3 EDH
Online: 5 EMAIL
opener: 3 SIR 4 DEAR SIRS
      5 STEAM 7 DEARSIR
Penultimate: 3 WYE
Pluralizing: 3 ESS
Scarlet: 6 STIGMA
signoff: 6 ASEVER
Sorority: 3 CHI ETA RHO
starter: 4 DEAR
Sweater: 3 RHO VEE 4 ZETA
      5 THETA
to Santa: 8 WISHLIST
Triangular: 5 DELTA
Trident-shaped: 3 PSI
Undeliverable: 5 NIXIE
Use a ⁓ opener: 4 SLIT
Letterhead
  abbr.: 3 INC TEL
  symbol: 4 LOGO
Lettering
  device: 7 STENCIL
Letterless
  phone button: 3 ONE
Letterman
  rival: 4 LENO
  ⁓, to pals: 4 DAVE
Letterman, David
  dental feature: 3 GAP

list: 6 TOPTEN
network: 3 CBS
rival: 7 JAYLENO
Lettermen, The: 4 TRIO
Letters: 4 MAIL
Alias: 3 AKA
at sea: 3 HMS USS
Chain: 3 DNA
Cross: 4 **INRI**
Dead: 3 RIP
Draft: 3 SSS
Explosive: 3 **TNT**
Fashion: 3 YSL
Fleet: 3 USS
Form: 3 IRS
Full house: 3 SRO
Genetic: 3 **DNA RNA**
Greek: 3 MUS NUS PIS XIS
Hit: 3 **SRO**
Invitation: 4 RSVP
Key: 3 ESC
Links: 3 PGA
Lodge: 4 BPOE
Lotion: 3 SPF
Love: 4 SWAK
Marker: 3 IOU
Memo: 3 FYI
News: 3 UPI
of concern: 3 TLC
of credit: 3 IOU
of success: 3 SRO
of urgency: 4 ASAP
Online: 5 EMAIL
Package: 3 COD
partner: 4 ARTS
Proof: 3 QED
Red: 4 USSR
Regal: 3 HRH
Rush: 4 ASAP
Shingle: 3 DDS
Tach: 3 RPM
Tanning: 3 SPF
Trading: 4 NYSE
Urgent: 4 ASAP
Wanted: 3 AKA
with no stamps: 5 EMAIL
Woman of: 5 VANNA
Letter-shaped
beam: 4 IBAR

fastener: 4 TNUT 5 UBOLT
girder: 5 HBEAM
opening: 5 TSLOT
support: 5 IBEAM
Letter-writing
device: 7 STENCIL
Letts
live here: 4 RIGA
Lettuce: 5 BREAD MOOLA
6 DOREMI
Big piece of: 5 CNOTE
Like: 5 LEAFY
unit: 4 HEAD
variety: 3 COS 4 BIBB
Letup
Without: 5 NOEND ONEND
"Let Us Now Praise Famous Men"
writer James: 4 AGEE
Levant
Pianist: 5 OSCAR
Levee: 4 DIKE
Level: 4 **EVEN RAZE TIER** TOOL
TRUE 5 PLANE
7 ECHELON STRATUM
Ballpark: 4 TIER
connector: 4 RAMP
Hierarchy: 4 RUNG
Highest: 4 ACME
Not: 5 ATILT 6 ASLOPE
Not on the: 6 ASLANT
SLOPED
of authority: 7 ECHELON
Stadium: 4 TIER
Theater: 4 LOGE
~, in London: 4 RASE
Levelheaded: 4 SANE
Leveling
device: 4 SHIM
Levels: 6 STRATA
of society: 6 STRATA
Lever: 3 PRY
Foot: 5 PEDAL
Kind of: 7 CROWBAR
Leveret: 4 HARE
Levertov
Poet: 6 DENISE
Lévesque
Former Quebec premier:
4 RENE

Levi
Former Israeli prime minister:
6 ESHKOL
Mother of: 4 LEAH
Levi, Carlo
novel town: 5 EBOLI
Leviathan: 4 HULK 8 BEHEMOTH
Levin
Author: 3 **IRA**
Levinson, Barry
film: 5 DINER 6 TINMEN
Levi's
line: 4 SEAM
material: 5 DENIM
rival: 3 LEE
Levitate: 4 RISE 5 FLOAT
Levy: 3 TAX 6 IMPOSE
collector: 3 IRS
Lew
Actor: 5 AYRES
Wimbledon champion: 4 HOAD
Lewd: 6 SMUTTY 7 OBSCENE
look: 4 LEER
Lewis
Bandleader: 3 TED
Jazz pianist: 6 RAMSEY
puppet: 8 LAMBCHOP
Puppeteer: 5 **SHARI**
Ventriloquist: 5 SHARI
with Lamb Chop: 5 SHARI
Lewis, C.S.
fictional land: 6 NARNIA
The "C" of: 5 CLIVE
Lewis, Huey (and the News)
hit song: 13 HIPTOBESQUARE
Lewis, John L.
org.: 3 UMW
Lewiston, Maine
campus: 5 BATES
Lex
Superman foe: 6 LUTHOR
Lexicographer
concern: 5 USAGE
Lexicography
First name in: 4 NOAH
Lexicon
Brit.: 3 OED
U.K.: 3 OED
Lexington: 3 AVE

sch.: 3 VMI
Lhasa
land: 5 TIBET
priest: 4 LAMA
Lhasa ___: 4 **APSO**
Liability: 4 DEBT
Musical: 6 TINEAR
opposite: 5 ASSET
Liable: 3 APT
Become: 5 INCUR
Liam
Actor: 6 NEESON
Liar
Biblical: 7 ANANIAS
"Liar Liar"
actress Cheri: 5 OTERI
star: 9 JIMCARREY
Libation: 8 BEVERAGE
Postprandial: 4 PORT
Yuletide: 3 NOG
Libel: 4 TORT
Liberace: 7 PIANIST
Like a ~ outfit: 6 ORNATE
Liberal
follower: 4 ARTS
Former: 6 NEOCON
leader: 3 NEO
pursuits: 4 ARTS
Liberal ___: 4 ARTS
Liberate: 4 FREE
~, so to speak: 5 SWIPE
Liberator
Simón: 7 BOLIVAR
Liberia
capital: 8 MONROVIA
Libertine: 4 RAKE **ROUE**
6 LECHER
opposite: 4 PRIG
Liberty: 4 EASE 5 LEAVE
6 STATUE 7 FREEDOM
At: 4 FREE
On: 6 ASHORE
Taking: 6 ASHORE
Libido: 4 **EROS**
Libra: 4 SIGN
Gem for a ~, maybe: 4 OPAL
Librarian
admonition: 3 SHH
gadget: 5 DATER

motto: 15 SILENCEISGOLDEN

Library
Bellow in the: 4 SAUL
command: 3 SHH
device: 5 DATER
innovator: 5 DEWEY
item: 4 BOOK
microfilm: 5 FICHE
no-no: 5 NOISE
patron: 4 USER
ref.: 3 OED
study area: 6 CARREL
unit: 5 SHELF
Use a: 4 READ
~ ID: 4 ISBN

Libreville
country: 5 GABON

Libya
capital: 7 TRIPOLI
Much of: 6 SAHARA
Neighbor of: 4 CHAD

Lice: 4 NITS 6 VERMIN

License: 6 PERMIT 7 ENTITLE
Driver's ~ datum: 3 DOB SEX
    4 NAME
issuer (abbr.): 3 FCC
Kind of: 6 POETIC
plate: 3 TAG
to drill: 3 DDS

Licenses: 3 IDS

Licentious: 7 IMMORAL
man: 4 ROUE

Lichen
component: 4 ALGA 5 ALGAE
Velvety: 4 MOSS

Lichtenstein
Artist: 3 ROY
output: 6 POPART

Lick
Musical: 4 RIFF
Not a: 4 NONE

Lickable
cookie: 4 OREO

Licked: 6 BEATEN
Get: 4 LOSE

Lickety-split: 3 PDQ 5 APACE
    8 INNOTIME
Go: 4 TEAR
Went: 4 SPED TORE

Licking
It may get a ~ after dinner:
    4 OREO

Lick ___ promise: 4 ANDA

Licorice
flavoring: 5 **ANISE**
liqueur: 5 ANISE 8 ANISETTE
plant: 5 ANISE

Lid: 3 CAP
attachment: 4 LASH
edger: 8 EYELINER
problem: 4 STYE
Take the ~ off: 5 UNCAP

Liddy
of politics: 4 DOLE

Lie: 4 REST 7 UNTRUTH
at rest: 6 REPOSE
in store for: 5 AWAIT
in the sun: 4 BASK
in wait: 4 LURK
Little: 3 FIB
low: 4 HIDE
next to: 4 ABUT
One way to: 5 PRONE
on the beach: 4 BAKE
White: 3 FIB

Liechtenstein
capital: 5 VADUZ

Lied
article: 4 EINE
"___ lied!": 3 SOI

Lieder: 5 SONGS
Follow the: 4 SING

Life: 3 PEP 6 CEREAL
    8 SENTENCE
Animal: 5 FAUNA
Bring to: 7 ANIMATE
Brought to: 4 BORN
College: 7 ACADEME
Come back to: 7 REAWAKE
follower: 4 SPAN
form: 5 BEING
Had a: 3 WAS
Have a: 3 ARE 5 EXIST
jacket: 4 VEST 7 MAEWEST
lines: 3 BIO 4 OBIT
Local: 5 BIOTA
Lot in: 4 FATE
Low: 5 AMEBA

Mark for: 4 SCAR
Nice: 3 VIE
partner: 4 LIMB MATE
Pertaining to: 6 BIOTIC
Plant: 5 FLORA
Pool: 4 ALGA
prefix: 3 MID
preserver: 4 OBIT
Regional: 5 BIOTA
saver: 4 HERO
Short: 3 BIO
Show signs of: 4 STIR
Sign of: 5 PULSE
sources: 3 OVA
story: 3 **BIO**
Succeed in: 5 GOFAR
support: 3 AIR
Symbol of: 4 ANKH
The easy: 10 BEDOFROSES
The facts of: 3 BIO
The good: 4 EASE
This is your: 3 BIO
time: 3 AGE
Time of one's: 3 AGE
Tiny ~ form: 5 AMEBA
work: 6 CAREER
"___ life!": 4 GETA
"Life ___ a dream": 5 ISBUT
Lifeboat
  item: 3 OAR
  lowerer: 5 DAVIT
"Lifeboat"
  actress Bankhead: 8 TALLULAH
"Life ___ cabaret": 3 ISA
"Life in London"
  author Pierce: 4 EGAN
Lifeless: 4 ARID DEAD 5 INERT
  ~, old-style: 5 AMORT
Lifelike: 4 REAL
Lifeline
  site: 4 PALM
Lifelines
  OR: 3 IVS
Life of ___ (ease): 5 RILEY
"Life of Brian"
  star: 8 ERICIDLE
Life of Riley: 4 <u>EASE</u>
"Life of Riley, The"
  character Digger: 5 ODELL

Lifesaver: 3 EMT NET 4 HERO
      6 AIRBAG
  Biblical: 3 ARK
Lifesaving
  skill: 3 CPR
"Life ___ short ...": 5 ISTOO
"Lifestyles of the Rich and
    Famous"
  host Robin: 5 LEACH
Lifetime: 3 AGE 4 DAYS
Lifework: 5 TRADE 6 CAREER
Liffey
  locale: 4 EIRE
LIFO
  Part of: 6 LASTIN
Lift: 3 COP 4 HIKE RIDE 5 HOIST
     RAISE STEAL 6 REPEAL
     THIEVE 7 ELEVATE
     RESCIND UPRAISE
     8 ELEVATOR
  anchor: 4 SAIL
  Hard to: 6 LEADEN
  He gave us a: 4 OTIS
  It might give you a: 4 TBAR
  Need a: 3 SAG
  Shoe: 7 HEELTAP
  Ski: 4 **TBAR**
  the spirits of: 5 ELATE
  They may need a: 6 SKIERS
  up: 5 ELATE EXALT HOIST
     RAISE 7 ELEVATE
  up a mountain: 4 TBAR
  with effort: 5 HEAVE
  "___ lift?": 5 NEEDA
Lifted: 5 STOLE
  with effort: 4 HOVE
Lifter
  Car: 4 JACK
  Mythical: 5 ATLAS
  Weight: 5 CRANE
Lifting
  apparatus: 5 HOIST
  Job involving: 5 HEIST
  unit: 3 REP
Light: 4 AIRY LAMP PALE
     6 IGNITE
  air: 4 LILT
  Alerting: 5 FLARE
  and airy: 8 ETHEREAL

as a feather: 4 AIRY
Beam of: 3 RAY
Blinding: 5 GLARE
Bring to: 6 EXHUME EXPOSE
Circle of: 4 HALO
Come to: 5 ARISE 6 EMERGE
Disco: 6 STROBE
Emit coherent: 4 **LASE**
Emitted: 5 SHONE
First: 4 DAWN
Flash of: 5 GLEAM GLINT
Gas: 4 NEON
Green: 4 OKAY 6 ASSENT
Guiding: 6 BEACON 7 POLARIS
    8 POLESTAR
Head: 4 HALO IDEA
High: 4 HALO
Hint of: 5 GLEAM
into: 3 RIP 6 ASSAIL
Kitchen: 5 PILOT
Laser: 4 BEAM
Make ~ of: 8 POOHPOOH
Night: 4 NEON STAR
on one's feet: 4 SPRY 5 **AGILE**
opening: 3 TWI
prefix: 3 TWI 4 PHOS
Ray of: 4 BEAM
Science of: 6 OPTICS
show: 6 AURORA
Sky: 3 UFO 4 STAR
source: 3 SUN 4 LAMP
splitter: 5 PRISM
starter: 3 TWI
Stove: 5 PILOT
stuff: 4 NEON
Theater: 4 SPOT
unit: 5 LUMEN
Light ___: 5 ASAIR
Lighten: 4 EASE
up: 4 EASE PALE
"Lighten up!": 10 TONEITDOWN
Lighter: 5 BARGE
feature: 4 WICK
fuel: 6 BUTANE
Get: 4 FADE
igniter: 5 FLINT
Made: 5 EASED
maker: 3 BIC
Light-footed: 5 AGILE 6 NIMBLE

Lightheaded: 5 GIDDY WOOZY
Light-Horse Harry: 3 LEE
Lighthouse
locale: 4 ISLE
of note: 6 PHAROS
Lighting
Bad: 5 ARSON
Overhead: 4 HALO
"Light My Fire"
band: 8 THEDOORS
Lightning: 4 TEAM
drawer: 3 ROD
home: 5 TAMPA
sound: 3 ZAP
"___ Light Up My Life": 3 YOU
Lightyear, Buzz
movie: 8 TOYSTORY
Light-years
3.26 ~: 6 PARSEC
Lignite: 4 COAL
Ligurian Sea
feeder: 4 ARNO
Likable: 4 NICE
Like: 3 **ALA** DIG 4 ASIF 5 GOFOR
    6 AKINTO SUCHAS
    7 SIMILAR
so: 4 THUS
suffix: 3 ISH OID
Like ___ (quickly): 5 ASHOT
Likeable
leader: 3 IKE
Like a ___ bricks: 5 TONOF
"Like a Rock"
singer Bob: 5 SEGER
"Like a Rolling Stone"
singer Bob: 5 DYLAN
Liked: 3 DUG
Like ___ from the blue: 5 ABOLT
"___ Like It Hot": 4 SOME
Likelihood: 4 ODDS
Likely: 3 **APT** 6 LIABLE
Not: 5 UNAPT
(to): 5 PRONE
Like-minded: 9 SIMPATICO
voters: 4 BLOC
Likeness: 5 IMAGE
prefix: 5 ICONO
"Like ___ not": 4 ITOR
"Like, no way!": 4 ASIF

Like ___ of bricks: 4 ATON
Like ___ of sunshine: 4 ARAY
Like ___ out of hell: 4 ABAT
"... like ___ planted by the rivers":
　　5 ATREE
Likewise: 3 TOO 4 **ALSO** SAME
　not: 3 NOR
"Likewise": 5 DITTO
Likhovtseva
　of tennis: 5 ELENA
Liking: 3 YEN 4 INTO 5 FANCY
　　TOOTH 7 SWEETON
　Start: 6 TAKETO
Likud
　leader: 6 SHAMIR
"Li'l Abner"
　cartoonist: 4 CAPP 6 ALCAPP
　Mother of: 10 PANSYYOKUM
　Opposed to, in: 4 AGIN
　Say: 5 ELIDE
Lilac: 4 ODOR 5 SHRUB
"Lilies of the Field"
　role: 3 NUN
Lille
　Info: French cue
　Laugh, in: 4 RIRE
　Lily, in: 3 LIS LYS
　Little, in: 3 PEU
　Love, in: 5 AMOUR
Lillehammer
　City near: 4 OSLO
　country: 6 NORWAY
Lillian
　Actress: 4 GISH
Lillie
　Comic: 3 BEA
Lilliputian: 3 WEE 4 TINY
Lilly
　of pharmaceuticals: 3 **ELI**
　___ Lilly & Co.: 3 **ELI**
Lilongwe
　country: 6 MALAWI
Lilting
　refrain: 3 TRA 5 TRALA
Lily
　African: 4 ALOE
　Arum: 5 CALLA
　Medicinal: 4 ALOE
　plant: 4 ALOE

　Plantain: 5 HOSTA
　Showy: 4 SEGO
　Soprano: 4 PONS
　Type of: 5 CALLA
　Utah: 4 SEGO
　Western: 4 SEGO
Lily-livered: 6 CRAVEN
Lily-white: 4 PURE
Lima: 4 BEAN
　land: 4 **PERU**
　state: 4 OHIO
Limb: 3 ARM
　grabber: 5 TALON
　holder: 5 TORSO
　It may be out on a: 4 NEST
　Out on a: 5 TREED
Limber: 5 AGILE LITHE
Limbo
　requirement: 3 BAR
　resident: 4 SOUL
　USPS: 3 DLO
Limburger
　feature: 4 ODOR
　relative: 6 TILSIT
Lime: 5 **OXIDE**
　drink: 3 **ADE**
Limelites
　leader: 4 SHEP
Limerick: 4 POEM
　County north of: 5 CLARE
　land: 4 EIRE ERIN
　language: 4 ERSE
　maker: 4 LEAR
　Second word of a ~, often:
　　4 ONCE
　Third word of a ~, often: 3 WAS
Limit: 3 CAP
　Go over the: 5 SPEED
　Kind of: 3 AGE
　Outer: 3 RIM 4 EDGE
　Salary: 3 CAP
　Speed ~ letters: 3 MPH
　Spending: 3 CAP
　Upper: 3 CAP MAX
　Went over the: 4 SPED
Limited: 5 SCANT 6 FINITE
　　NARROW
　It may be: 7 EDITION
　number: 3 FEW

support: 5 RAILS
Limitless: 4 VAST
  quantity: 3 SEA 5 OCEAN
Limo
  destination: 4 PROM
  passenger: 3 VIP
Limp
  Go: 4 WILT
  watch painter: 4 **DALI**
Limp as ___: 4 ARAG
Limping: 4 LAME 5 LAMED
Lin
  Architect: 4 MAYA
Linchpin: 8 KEYSTONE
  site: 4 AXLE
Lincoln: 3 CAR 4 AUTO 7 CAPITAL
  Actor: 4 ELMO
  birthplace: 8 LOGCABIN
  center: 3 CEE
  feature: 5 BEARD
  First VP of: 6 HAMLIN
  in-law: 4 TODD
  nickname: 3 **ABE**
  portrait site: 4 CENT
  President: 3 ABE
  Son of: 3 TAD
Lind, Jenny: 5 SWEDE
Linda
  Actress: 4 DANO HUNT 5 EVANS
    LAVIN
  of the soaps: 4 DANO
  Singer: 4 EDER
  ___ Linda, California: 4 **LOMA**
Lindbergh
  feat: 10 SOLOFLIGHT
  Like the ~ flight: 4 SOLO
  Writer: 4 ANNE
Lindbergh, Anne ___: 6 MORROW
Lindbergh, ___ Morrow: 4 ANNE
Linden: 4 TREE
  Actor: 3 **HAL**
Lindgren
  character Longstocking: 5 PIPPI
  Novelist: 6 ASTRID
Lindley
  Actress: 5 AUDRA
  of golf: 4 LETA
Lindros
  of hockey: 4 ERIC

Lindsay
  Poet: 6 VACHEL
Lindstrom
  Newswoman: 3 PIA
Lindy
  Fly like: 4 SOLO
Line: 5 QUEUE
  Bottom: 3 HEM **NET** SUM
    5 TOTAL 10 NETRESULTS
  Central: 4 AXIS
  crosser: 4 SCAB
  Curved: 3 ARC
  Cut: 4 SCAR
  dance: 5 CONGA
  Drop a: 4 FISH 5 WRITE
  feeder: 6 STOOGE
  Hang on the: 6 AIRDRY
  It holds the: 4 REEL
  Kind of: 3 AIR DEW 5 CONGA
    WAIST
  Like a ~, briefly: 4 ONED
  Main: 5 AORTA 6 ARTERY
  On the: 6 ATRISK 7 **ATSTAKE**
  Out of: 5 ASKEW
  Put on the: 4 RISK
  Stand in: 4 WAIT
  Stop on a: 5 DEPOT
  Toe the: 4 **OBEY**
Lineage: 5 BREED 7 DESCENT
  8 ANCESTRY
Linear: 4 ONED
  prefix: 5 RECTI
Lined
  up: 4 AROW 6 INAROW
Lineman: 3 END
Linemen: 3 LGS LTS RGS RTS
  TES 4 ENDS
Linen: 5 CLOTH
  color: 4 ECRU
  fabric: 5 TOILE 6 DAMASK
  items: 6 SHEETS
  Sheer: 5 TOILE
  source: 4 FLAX
  Table: 6 NAPERY
  tape: 5 INKLE
  Transparent: 5 TOILE
  vestment: 3 ALB
Liner: 4 SHIP
  Eye: 3 LID

Kind of: 5 OCEAN
letters: 3 USS
On a: 4 ASEA
Place for a: 5 OCEAN
Shoe: 6 INSOLE

Lines
Circle: 5 RADII
Dedicated: 3 ODE
Graph: 4 AXES
Head: 3 EEG
Heir: 4 WILL
High: 3 ELS
Like some: 6 DOTTED
Lyrical: 3 ODE
Map ~ (abbr.): 3 RDS STS
of music: 5 STAFF
on a musical staff: 5 EGBDF

Lineup: 5 ARRAY
Circus: 4 ACTS
finish: 4 ETAL
Kind of: 7 ALLSTAR
Picked out of a: 4 IDED
Picks out of a: 3 IDS
Rest stop: 5 SEMIS
Wasn't in the: 6 SATOUT

"Lineup, The"
enforcement gp.: 4 SFPD

___ Ling (Chinese mountain range): 3 NAN

Linger: 4 STAY WAIT 5 TARRY

Lingerie
item: 3 **BRA** 5 TEDDY
7 NIGHTIE

Lingering
effect: 4 ECHO
sensation: 10 AFTERTASTE
sign: 4 SCAR

Ling-Ling: 5 PANDA
Lingo: 5 ARGOT SLANG 6 PATOIS
Lingua ___: 6 FRANCA
Lingual
prefix: 3 TRI
Linguine: 5 **PASTA**
topper: 5 PESTO
Linguistics
First name in: 4 NOAM
gp.: 3 MLA
Suffix used in: 3 **ESE**
___ Lingus: 3 **AER**

Liniment
Need: 4 ACHE
Needing: 4 ACHY SORE
target: 4 ACHE

Lining
Hat: 4 CAUL
Warm: 3 FUR

Link: 3 TIE 4 BOND 5 NEXUS
TIEIN UNITE
with: 5 TIETO

Linking
toy: 4 LEGO
verb: 6 COPULA

Linkletter
Emcee: 3 ART

Links
Info: Golf cue
carrier: 4 CART
cry: 4 FORE
figure: 3 PRO
gadget: 3 TEE
gp.: 3 PGA
hazard: 4 TRAP
letters: 3 **PGA**
Missing: 6 APEMEN
nickname: 5 ARNIE
norm: 3 PAR
org.: 3 **PGA**
peg: 3 TEE
position: 3 LIE
rarity: 3 ACE 5 EAGLE
rental: 4 CART
Take to the: 4 GOLF
target: 4 HOLE

Linkup
PC: 3 **LAN**

Linoleum
alternative: 4 TILE
protector: 3 WAX

Linseed oil
source: 4 FLAX

Lint: 5 FLUFF
collector: 4 TRAP
trap: 5 INNIE

Lintel
locale: 9 DOORFRAME

Linz
Goodie from: 5 TORTE
locale (abbr.): 3 AUS

Linzer
follower: 5 TORTE
Lion: 3 CAT
den: 4 LAIR
home: 3 DEN
Like a: 5 MANED
Like a sea: 5 EARED
Mountain: 4 PUMA
of Narnia: 5 ASLAN
portrayer: 5 LAHR
pride: 4 MANE
share: 4 MOST
sound: 4 ROAR
suffix: 3 ESS IZE
Young: 5 WHELP
Zodiac: 3 LEO
Lion-colored: 5 TAWNY
Lionel
product: 8 TRAINSET
Sister of: 5 ETHEL
Lioness
lack: 4 MANE
Lionized: 4 ELSA
Literary: 4 **ELSA**
Movie: 4 ELSA
"Lion in Winter, The"
queen: 7 ELEANOR
star: 6 OTOOLE
Lionized
actor: 4 LAHR
lioness: 4 ELSA
"Lion King, The"
hero: 5 SIMBA
lion: 4 NALA 5 **SIMBA**
villain: 4 **SCAR**
Lions: 4 TEAM
Group of: 5 PRIDE
Like circus: 5 TAMED
org.: 3 NFC
Lip: 3 RIM 4 BRIM EDGE **SASS**
application: 5 GLOSS LINER
attachment: 4 SYNC
Curl one's: 5 SNEER
Give ~ to: 4 SASS
goo: 4 BALM
service: 4 KISS
Lip-___: 4 SYNC
Lipinski
leap: 4 **AXEL**

milieu: 3 ICE
Skater: 4 **TARA**
Lippi, Filippo: 3 FRA
Lipstick
container: 5 PURSE
Like: 4 WAXY
mishap: 5 SMEAR
Lipton
offering: 3 TEA
rival: 6 NESTEA SALADA
TETLEY
Liq.
measures: 3 PTS QTS
Liquefy: 4 MELT THAW 5 PUREE
Liqueur
Almond-flavored: 8 AMARETTO
Anise-flavored: 4 OUZO
6 PERNOD
Black currant: 6 CASSIS
Coffee-flavored: 8 TIAMARIA
flavoring: 5 ANISE 7 ANISEED
APRICOT
Greek: 4 OUZO
Green: 8 ABSINTHE
Small ~ glass: 4 PONY
Spanish: 4 ANIS
Sweet: 8 ANISETTE
Thick: 5 CREME
Liquid: 5 FLUID
asset: 4 CASH
Burn with hot: 5 SCALD
Corrosive: 4 ACID
cosmetic: 6 LOTION
Explosive: 5 NITRO
fat: 5 OLEIN
Make: 4 CASH
Pickling: 5 BRINE
suffix: 4 ATOR
Volatile: 5 NITRO
Liquidate: 4 SELL 7 SELLOUT
Liquid-Plumr
alternative: 5 DRANO
Liquor
Colada: 3 RUM
Gimlet: 3 GIN
Jamaican: 3 RUM
Kind of: 4 MALT
lover: 3 SOT
Martini: 3 GIN

Selling: 3 WET
Small drink of: 3 NIP

Lira
replacement: 4 EURO

Lire
Where ~ are spent: 5 ITALY

Lisa
Actress: 5 BONET
of basketball: 6 LESLIE
Singer: 4 LOEB
~, to Bart: 3 SIS

"___ Lisa": 4 MONA

Lisbon
Info: Portuguese cue
City north of: 6 OPORTO
Lady, in: 4 DONA 7 SENHORA
Man, in: 6 SENHOR
native: 7 IBERIAN

Lisi
Actress: 5 VIRNA

Lisper
Problematic letter for a: 3 ESS

Lissome: 5 AGILE

List: 4 MENU 6 ROSTER
abbr.: 3 ETC 4 ETAL
component: 4 ITEM
divider: 5 COMMA
ender: 3 **ETC** 4 **ETAL** 6 ETALIA
  8 ETCETERA
entry: 4 ITEM
Get on the: 5 ENROL
heading: 4 TODO
of candidates: 5 SLATE
of choices: 4 MENU
of dishes: 4 MENU
Official with a: 4 DEAN
of lapses: 6 ERRATA
of options: 4 MENU
of priors: 8 RAPSHEET
of topics: 6 AGENDA
One with a: 4 DEAN
On the A: 5 ELITE
On the disabled: 4 HURT
Part of a: 4 ITEM
preceder: 5 COLON
price: 6 RETAIL
recipient: 5 SANTA
shortener: 3 ETC 4 **ETAL**
Type of: 4 TODO

___ list: 4 TODO 5 DEANS

Listed: 5 LEANT
Not ~ above: 5 OTHER

Listen: 4 HARK 6 ATTEND
here: 3 EAR
in on: 7 WIRETAP
Refusing to: 4 DEAF
to: 4 HEAR HEED OBEY

"Listen!": 4 HARK

List-ending
abbr.: 3 **ETC** 4 **ETAL**

Listener: 3 EAR

Listening: 7 ALLEARS TUNEDIN
device: 3 **EAR**
to music, maybe: 6 ONHOLD

"Listen up!": 3 HEY
  8 TAKEHEED

Listerine
target: 4 GERM

Listlessness: 5 ENNUI 6 TORPOR
  7 MALAISE 8 LETHARGY

Liston
Boxer: 5 SONNY
defeater: 3 ALI

List-shortening
abbr.: 3 ETC 4 ETAL

Liszt
Composer: 5 FRANZ
Lively, to: 7 ANIMATO
piece: 5 ETUDE
symphonic poem: 5 TASSO

Lit: 4 HIGH 5 AFIRE AGLOW
  OILED 6 LOOPED STONED
  7 IGNITED SMASHED
Barely: 3 DIM
into: 5 HADAT
No longer: 5 SOBER
Poorly: 3 DIM
up: 5 AGLOW

Lit ___ (college course): 4 CRIT

Lite: 5 LOFAT NOCAL

Literacy
Prove one's: 4 READ

Literary
adverb: 3 OFT 4 NEER
alias: 4 ELIA
assortment: 3 ANA
captain: 4 AHAB NEMO
category: 5 GENRE

collection: 3 **ANA**
conflict: 4 AGON
device: 5 IRONY 6 SIMILE
figure: 4 LION
inits.: 3 EAP GBS RLS RWE **TSE**
lioness: 4 ELSA
monogram: 3 EAP GBS RLS RWE
   TSE
olio: 3 ANA
pen name: 4 ELIA
postscript: 6 EPILOG
pseudonym: 4 ELIA
Literature: 7 LETTERS
Lewd: 4 PORN
Liters
  Like: 6 METRIC
Lith.
  ~, once: 3 SSR
Lithe: 4 SLIM 6 SUPPLE SVELTE
Lithographer
  Highly collectible: 4 ERTE
  Noted: 4 IVES
Litigant: 4 SUER
  Unnamed: 3 ROE
Litigate: 3 SUE
Litigator
  org.: 3 ABA
Litigious
  Be: 3 SUE
  type: 4 SUER
Litmus: 3 DYE
  It turns ~ blue: 6 ALKALI
  It turns ~ red: 4 ACID
  reddener: 4 **ACID**
Litter: 5 BROOD
  critter: 3 PUP
  cry: 3 MEW
  Littlest of a: 4 RUNT
  member: 3 PUP 4 RUNT
  Theater: 5 STUBS
Literae: 3 ARS
Litterbug: 4 SLOB
Little: 3 WEE 5 SMALL
  A: 4 SOME
  bit: 3 DAB **TAD** 4 ATOM DRIB
    IOTA 5 SKOSH
  Even a: 3 ANY 5 ATALL
  Give a: 4 BEND
  more than: 4 MERE

  one: 3 ELF TAD **TOT** 4 RUNT
    TYKE
  'un: 3 TAD TOT
"Little"
  car of song: 3 GTO
  comics fellow: 4 NEMO
Little ___
  (nickname of a state): 5 RHODY
  (tots): 3 UNS
"Little ___": 4 NEMO 5 WOMEN
Little ___ (60's singer): 3 EVA
Little, Rich: 4 APER
"Little ___ Annie": 6 ORPHAN
Little Anthony and the Imperials
  hit song:
    15 TEARSONMYPILLOW
"Little Bitty Tear, A"
  singer: 4 IVES
"Little Caesar"
  role: 4 RICO
"Little Darlings"
  actress: 5 ONEAL
"Little Flower of Jesus":
    7 THERESA
"Little Girls"
  musical: 5 ANNIE
Little-hand
  indication: 4 HOUR
"Little House on the Prairie"
  actor Nels: 6 OLESON
"___ Little Indians" (Christie
    mystery): 3 TEN
Little Joe
  Brother of: 4 ADAM
Little League
  coach, often: 3 DAD
  membership restriction:
    8 AGELIMIT
  precursor: 5 TBALL
Little Leaguer: 7 PRETEEN
"Little Mermaid, The"
  mermaid: 5 ARIEL
  prince: 4 ERIC
Little Oil Drop
  was its mascot: 4 ESSO
Little pig
  count: 5 THREE
Little piggy: 3 TOE
  cry: 3 WEE

What the fourth ~ had: 4 NONE

"Little Plastic Castle"
singer DiFranco: 3 ANI

"___ Little Prayer": 5 ISAYA

"Little Red Book"
adherents: 7 MAOISTS
author: 3 MAO

"Little Red Hen, The"
reply: 4 NOTI

"Little Shop of Horrors"
demand: 6 FEEDME

Littlest
of a litter: 4 RUNT

"___ little teapot ...": 3 IMA

"___ Little Tenderness": 4 **TRYA**

"Little Women"
author: 6 ALCOTT
costar: 5 RYDER
woman: 3 AMY 4 BETH

Liturgy: 4 RITE

Litvak
Director: 7 ANATOLE

Liu
Actress: 4 LUCY

Live: 3 **ARE** 5 EXIST 6 RESIDE
7 UNTAPED
and breathe: 3 **ARE** 5 EXIST
Appearing: 8 INPERSON
Can't ~ without: 5 NEEDS
in fear of: 5 DREAD
it up: 5 REVEL
Not: 5 **TAPED** 6 ONTAPE
partner: 5 LEARN
Place to: 5 ABODE
(up): 3 PEP
Where you: 5 ABODE
wire: 4 DOER

Live Aid: 7 BENEFIT
founder Bob: 6 GELDOF

"___ live and breathe!": 3 ASI

Lived: 3 WAS 4 WERE 5 DWELT
7 RESIDED
it up: 9 HADABLAST

"Live Free or Die"
~, to New Hampshire:
5 MOTTO

Liveliness: 4 BRIO ELAN
5 VERVE 6 ENERGY
ESPRIT

Lively: 4 PERT SPRY 5 AGILE
BRISK 6 ACTIVE
7 ANIMATO
dance: 3 JIG 4 HORA REEL
5 GALOP GIGUE
Less: 8 SLEEPIER
one: 4 GRIG
outing: 5 SPREE
party: 4 BASH
wit: 6 ESPRIT
~, in music: 7 ANIMATO
~, in music (abbr.): 4 ANIM

Liven: 4 ZEST

Liver: 5 GLAND
accompaniment: 6 ONIONS
Chopped: 4 PATE
product: 4 BILE
~, in French: 4 FOIE

Liverpool
river: 6 MERSEY

Liverpudlian: 4 BRIT

Livery
Did ~ work: 5 SHOED

Livestock
farm: 5 RANCH
feed: 4 MASH 7 SOILAGE

Livid: 5 ANGRY ASHEN IRATE

Living: 5 TRADE
Barely make, as a: 6 EKEOUT
Cost of: 4 RENT
doll: 5 CUTIE
Eke out a: 6 MAKEDO
end, once: 9 BEESKNEES
follower: 3 END
quarters: 5 ABODE
thing: 5 BEING

Living room
furniture: 4 SOFA 5 COUCH
6 SETTEE

**"Livin' La Vida ___" (Ricky Martin
hit):** 4 LOCA

Livorno
Info: Italian cue
Love, in: 5 AMORE

Livy
Info: Latin cue
Land, to: 5 TERRA
language: 5 LATIN
Like: 5 ROMAN

Love, to: 4 AMOR
Lixivium: 3 LYE
Liz
  Role for: 4 **CLEO**
Liza
  sister Lorna: 4 LUFT
Lizard
  Brightly-colored: 5 AGAMA
  Large: 6 IGUANA
  Like a: 5 SCALY 6 SCALED
  Small: 5 GECKO SKINK
  Tropical: 5 GECKO 6 IGUANA
  Type of: 6 LOUNGE
  ~, old-style: 3 EFT
Lizardlike: 5 SCALY 7 SAURIAN
Lizzie
  Tin: 6 MODELT
  ___ Lizzie: 3 TIN
Llama
  country: 4 PERU
  cousin: 6 ALPACA VICUNA
      7 GUANACO
  feature: 7 SILENTL
  habitat: 5 ANDES
  land: 4 PERU
  Like the: 6 ANDEAN
Llano
  rarity: 4 TREE
LLD
  holder: 3 ATT 4 ATTY
Lloyd
  Actor: 5 NOLAN
Lloyd Webber, Andrew:
      6 KNIGHT
  musical: 4 CATS 5 EVITA
  title: 3 SIR
"Lo!"
  ~, in Latin: 4 ECCE
Lo ___ (noodle dish): 4 MEIN
Lo-___: 3 CAL RES
  ___ Loa: 5 MAUNA
Load: 4 ONUS SLEW STOW
      6 BURDEN
  Got a ~ of: 3 SAW 4 EYED
  hauler: 4 DRAY
  Heavy: 4 ONUS
  in a basket: 4 WASH
  Lode: 3 **ORE**
  on a ship: 5 CARGO

Take a ~ off: 3 **SIT** 4 REST
      5 RELAX
  Tram: 3 ORE
Loaded: 4 RICH RIFE 6 STINKO
      7 WEALTHY
  It may be: 3 DIE
  They may be: 4 DICE 5 BASES
  They're: 7 FATCATS
Loader
  Musket: 6 RAMROD
  Muzzle: 6 RAMROD
Loading
  area: 4 DOCK
  site: 4 PIER
Loads: 4 **ALOT** **ATON** GOBS
      LOTS MANY TONS
      5 HEAPS SCADS 6 OCEANS
      OODLES SCORES
Loaf: 4 LAZE
  about: 4 LOLL
  Deli: 3 RYE
  end: 4 HEEL
  on the job: 5 DOGIT
  part: 3 END
Loafer: 4 SHOE 5 IDLER
      6 SLIPON
  attachment: 6 TASSEL
  lack: 5 LACES
  sin: 5 SLOTH
Loafers
  Wearing: 4 SHOD
  Where to find: 8 SHOETREE
Loafing: 4 IDLE
"___ loaf is better ...": 5 HALFA
Loam: 4 SOIL
  component: 4 SILT
  Rich: 5 LOESS
Loamy
  deposit: 5 LOESS
  soil: 5 LOESS
Loan
  Ask for a: 5 HITUP
  figure (abbr.): 3 APR PCT
  Have a ~ from: 5 OWETO
  payment (abbr.): 3 INT
  Settle a: 5 REPAY
  source: 8 PAWNSHOP
"Lo and behold!": 3 OHO
Loaned: 4 LENT

Loaner
Like a: 4 USED
Loan shark: 6 USURER
offense: 5 USURY
Loath: 6 AVERSE
Loathe: 4 HATE 5 ABHOR
6 DETEST 7 DESPISE
Loathing: 4 HATE 5 ODIUM
6 HATRED
Object of: 8 ANATHEMA
Loathsome: 4 VILE
person: 4 TOAD
Lob: 4 TOSS
path: 3 ARC
Lobbed: 5 THREW
Lobby: 4 URGE
Big D.C.: 3 NRA
Gun ~ org.: 3 NRA
suffix: 3 IST
Lobbying
org.: 3 **PAC**
Lobe
locale: 3 EAR
Loblolly: 4 PINE
"___ Lobo" (John Wayne film):
3 RIO
___ Lobos: 3 LOS
Lobster
catcher: 4 TRAP
eater's need: 3 BIB
eggs: 3 **ROE**
Female: 3 HEN
Like a boiled: 3 RED
locale: 5 MAINE
pincer: 4 CLAW
relative: 7 CRAWDAD
serving: 4 TAIL
Lobster ___ Diavolo: 3 FRA
"L'Oca ___ Cairo" (Mozart opera):
3 DEL
Local: 4 NEAR 6 NATIVE
cinema: 4 NABE
group: 5 UNION
life: 5 BIOTA
self-government: 8 HOMERULE
theater: 4 NABE
Lo-cal: 4 **LITE**
Locale: 4 AREA SITE ZONE
5 PLACE SCENE

Locality: 4 AREA SITE
Locate: 4 FIND SITE
Located: 5 SITED
As: 6 INSITU
Location: 4 AREA **SITE** SPOT
5 PLACE
Loch
Legendary: 4 NESS
Monster's: 4 NESS
monster's nickname: 6 NESSIE
Scottish: 4 NESS
Loch ___: 4 NESS
Lock: 5 **TRESS** 6 SHOOIN
fastener: 4 HASP
Head: 5 **TRESS**
It fits in a: 3 OAR
Long: 5 TRESS
maker: 4 YALE
of hair: 5 **TRESS**
opener: 3 KEY
prefix: 4 ANTI 5 INTER
site: 5 CANAL
Thin: 4 WISP
(up): 3 SEW
~, stock, and barrel: 3 ALL
Locked
in: 8 ICEBOUND
They may be: 5 HORNS
up: 5 CAGED 6 INJAIL
JAILED
(up): 4 PENT
Locker
hanging: 5 PINUP
photo: 5 PINUP
Locker room
emanation: 4 ODOR
item: 5 TOWEL
powder: 4 TALC
shower: 4 ESPN
Locket
shape: 4 OVAL
"Lockhorns, The"
husband: 5 LEROY
Locks: 4 HAIR
Change: 3 DYE
False: 3 WIG 6 TOUPEE
Head: 4 HAIR
in a barn: 4 MANE
Lacking: 4 BALD

Leonine: 4 MANE
They can fix: 6 SALONS
Unruly: 3 MOP
Lockup: 4 CELL JAIL
London: 4 GAOL
Navy: 4 BRIG
Loco: 4 BATS
Less: 5 SANER
"Loco-Motion, The"
singer: 9 LITTLEEVA
Locomotive: 6 ENGINE
9 IRONHORSE
fuel: 4 COAL
power: 5 STEAM
sound: 4 CHUG
Locum ___ (temporary substitute):
6 TENENS
Locus
Geometrical: 7 EVOLUTE
Locust: 3 BUG 4 TREE
tree: 6 ACACIA
Lod
land (abbr.): 3 ISR
lander: 4 ELAL
Lod Airport
carrier: 4 ELAL
Lode
Get a ~ of this: 3 ORE
load: 3 **ORE**
locale: 4 VEIN
Lodge: 3 INN 4 ROOM STOW
6 HOSTEL RESIDE
brother: 3 ELK
builder: 6 BEAVER
letters: 4 BPOE
member: 3 **ELK** 5 MOOSE
Motor: 3 INN
opening: 5 ECONO
resident: 5 SKIER
___ Lodge (motel chain):
5 ECONO
Lodging
Country: 3 INN
Inexpensive: 6 HOSTEL
Military: 6 BILLET
Quaint: 3 INN
Roadside: 5 MOTEL
Loeb
Singer: 4 LISA

___ l'oeil: 6 TROMPE
Loewe
Partner of: 6 LERNER
Loewenstein, Laszlo
Actor born: 5 LORRE
Lo-fat: 4 LITE
Lofgren
Guitarist: 4 **NILS**
Loft: 5 ATTIC
contents: 3 HAY
group: 5 CHOIR
locale: 4 BARN
Voice in a: 4 ALTO BASS
Lofts
Author: 5 NORAH
Lofty: 4 HIGH TALL 5 NOBLE
6 AERIAL 8 RAREFIED
abode: 5 AERIE
lyric: 3 ODE
nest: 5 AERIE
poem: 3 ODE
Set a ~ goal: 6 ASPIRE
Log: 5 ENTER
Bump on a: 4 KNAR NODE
cutter: 6 PITSAW
home: 5 CABIN
item: 5 ENTRY
Kind of: 4 YULE
prefix: 3 ANA EPI
Logan
and others (abbr.): 3 MTS
home: 4 UTAH
Logarithms
inventor: 6 NAPIER
Logged
One ~ on: 4 USER
Loggers
contest: 5 ROLEO
Loggins
partner: 7 MESSINA
Singer: 5 KENNY
Logic: 5 SENSE 6 REASON
Hence, in: 4 ERGO
negation mark: 5 TILDE
Use: 6 REASON
Logical
Be: 6 REASON
conclusion: 3 QED
flaw: 4 HOLE

prefix: 3 ECO GEO 4 **IDEO**
   THEO 5 PATHO 6 CHRONO
Logically
   Think: 6 REASON
Logician: 8 REASONER
   letters: 3 QED
   phrase: 7 APRIORI
   word: 4 ERGO
Logo: 6 EMBLEM
Log-on
   need: 6 USERID
Logos
   (abbr.): 3 TMS
Logrolling
   Compete in: 4 BIRL
Logs
   Cut, as: 4 SAWN
   Like: 4 SAWN
   One who ~ on: 4 USER
   Saw: 5 SNORE
   Sawing: 6 ASLEEP
Lohengrin
   love: 4 **ELSA**
"Lohengrin": 5 OPERA
   role: 4 ELSA
Loin
   steak: 5 TBONE
Loincloth
   Hindu: 5 DHOTI
Loire
   City on the: 5 TOURS 6 NANTES
Lois
   love: 5 CLARK
   portrayer: 4 TERI
"Lois & Clark"
   actor Dean: 4 CAIN
   actress Hatcher: 4 **TERI**
Loiter: 5 DALLY TARRY
Loki
   Daughter of: 3 HEL
"LOL"
   vocalized: 4 HAHA
"Lola"
   actress Anouk: 5 AIMEE
   band: 8 THEKINKS
"Lolita"
   actress Lyon: 3 SUE
   actress Sue: 4 LYON
Loll: 4 LAZE

Lollapalooza: 3 PIP 4 LULU ONER
   5 BEAUT
Lolling: 6 ATEASE
Lollobrigida
   Actress: 4 **GINA**
Lollygag: 4 IDLE LAZE LOAF
___ Loma, California: 4 ALTA
Loman, Willy: 8 SALESMAN
   field: 5 SALES
   Son of: 4 BIFF
Lombard
   Actress: 6 CAROLE
Lombardi
   Coach: 5 VINCE
Lombardy
   Info: Italian cue
   attraction: 8 LAKECOMO
   city: 5 MILAN
   lake: 4 COMO
   Love, in: 5 AMORE
Lo mein
   morsel: 6 NOODLE
Lomond: 4 LOCH
Lon
   contemporary: 4 BELA
   of Cambodia: 3 NOL
London
   airport: 8 HEATHROW
   area: 4 SOHO 7 EASTEND
   district: 4 **SOHO**
   facility: 3 LOO
   gallery: 4 TATE
   Garden spot of: 3 KEW
   Inc., in: 3 LTD
   land (abbr.): 3 ENG
   landmark: 6 BIGBEN
        15 ROYALALBERTHALL
   Last letter in: 3 ZED
   lavatory: 3 LOO
   length: 5 METRE
   Level, in: 4 RASE
   locale: 7 ONTARIO
   lockup: 4 GAOL
   neighborhood: 4 SOHO
   Notorious ~ prison:
        7 NEWGATE
   park name: 4 HYDE
   Place to go in: 3 LOO
   river: 6 THAMES

section: 7 EASTEND
stroller: 4 PRAM
subway: 4 TUBE
theater: 6 OLDVIC
~ TV inits.: 3 BBC
London ___ : 5 BROIL
Londoner: 4 BRIT 6 BRITON
  Wealthy: 3 NOB
London Magazine
  essayist: 4 ELIA
Lone: 4 SOLE
"Lonely Boy"
  singer Paul: 4 **ANKA**
"Lonely Rage, A"
  author Bobby: 5 SEALE
Loner: 6 HERMIT MISFIT
Lone Ranger
  sidekick: 5 TONTO
"Lonesome Dove"
  author: 13 LARRYMCMURTRY
Lonesome George
  of early TV: 5 GOBEL
Lone Star State: 5 TEXAS
  sch.: 4 **UTEP**
Long: 4 ACHE PINE 5 YEARN
            6 HANKER
  A ~ way off: 3 FAR 4 AFAR
  Actress: 3 **NIA**
  After a ~ wait: 6 ATLAST
  ago: 4 ONCE YORE
  and lean: 4 LANK
  Before: 4 ANON SOON
  Certain ~ shot: 8 ONEINTEN
  Football commentator: 5 HOWIE
  for: 5 CRAVE 6 DESIRE
  Go: 5 RUNON
  intro: 3 ERE
  It comes before: 3 ERE
  It may be: 3 TON
  Politician: 4 HUEY
  Went: 7 RANOVER
Long.
  crosser: 3 LAT
Long ___ : 3 AGO TON 5 JOHNS
"Long ___ and Far Away": 3 AGO
Long-armed
  ape: 5 ORANG
  entity: 3 LAW
"___ longa, vita brevis": 3 **ARS**

Long-billed
  bird: 4 IBIS 5 HERON SNIPE
  wader: 4 IBIS 5 HERON
Longbow
  wood: 3 YEW
Long-distance
  letters: 3 ATT MCI
  Start of a ~ call: 3 ONE
Long-eared
  animal: 3 ASS 4 HARE
  hound: 6 BASSET
Longer: 4 MORE
  Is no: 3 WAS
  No: 4 ONCE
  No ~ here: 4 GONE
  No ~ hot: 3 OUT
  No ~ in: 5 DATED PASSE
  No ~ in bed: 5 ASTIR
  No ~ in use: 7 DEFUNCT
  No ~ lit: 5 SOBER
  No ~ mint: 4 USED
  No ~ on deck: 5 ATBAT
"Longest Day, The"
  city: 4 CAEN
Longevity: 4 LEGS
Long-faced: 3 SAD 6 SULLEN
Longfellow
  bell town: 4 ATRI
  ~ Indian: 8 HIAWATHA
Long-gone
  bird: 4 DODO
Longhair: 6 HIPPIE
Long-haired
  cat: 6 ANGORA
Longhorn: 5 STEER
  rival: 5 AGGIE
Longing: 3 **YEN** 4 ACHE ITCH
            6 DESIRE
  Feel ~ for: 4 MISS
Longish
  skirt: 4 MIDI
Long Island
  airport: 5 ISLIP
  town: 5 ISLIP
  university: 7 ADELPHI
Long-jawed
  fish: 3 **GAR**
Long John Silver
  feature: 6 PEGLEG

Long-lasting
  wave: 4 PERM
Long-legged
  bird: 4 IBIS 5 HERON STILT
    STORK 6 AVOCET
Longley
  of basketball: 3 LUC
Long-limbed: 5 LEGGY RANGY
"Long Long Time"
  singer Linda: 8 RONSTADT
Long March
  leader: 3 MAO
Long-necked
  bird: 4 SWAN 5 HERON
  instrument: 4 LUTE 5 SITAR
  lute: 5 SITAR
Long-nosed
  fish: 3 GAR 4 PIKE
Long-plumed
  bird: 5 EGRET
Long-range
  weapon: 4 ICBM
Longship
  mover: 3 OAR
Longshoreman: 5 LADER
    9 STEVEDORE
Long-snouted
  beast: 5 TAPIR
  fish: 3 **GAR**
Longstocking
  creator Lindgren: 6 ASTRID
  of children's books: 5 PIPPI
Long-tailed
  finch: 6 TOWHEE
  parrot: 5 MACAW
"Long time ___": 5 NOSEE
"Long Time No See"
  novelist Susan: 6 ISAACS
  ___ longue: 6 CHAISE
  ___ long way (last): 3 GOA
Long-winded: 5 GASSY
    6 PROLIX
  Less: 6 TERSER
  type: 6 GASBAG
Loni
  and Burt: 4 EXES
  Ex of: 4 BURT
Loo
  sign: 5 GENTS INUSE

Looie
  subordinate: 5 SARGE
Look: 4 PEER **SEEM** 6 APPEAR
  Affected: 5 SMIRK
  after: 4 TEND 5 SEETO
    6 TENDTO
  at: 3 EYE SEE 4 VIEW 6 REGARD
  at the stars: 4 GAZE
  Blank: 5 STARE
  closely: 4 PEER 5 DELVE
  Contemptuous: 5 SNEER
  daggers: 5 GLARE
  Derisive: 5 SNEER
  Dirty: 4 LEER 5 GLARE
  Displeased: 5 FROWN
  Evil: 4 LEER
  Fixed: 4 GAZE 5 STARE
  for: 4 **SEEK** 5 AWAIT
  forward to: 5 AWAIT
  Give a new ~ to: 4 REDO
  good on: 6 BECOME
  Have a: 3 SEE
  Healthy: 4 GLOW
  Impolite: 4 **LEER** 5 STARE
  Intent: 4 GAZE
  It doesn't ~ good: 7 EYESORE
  Lascivious: 4 **LEER**
  Lecherous: 4 LEER
  Lecher's: 4 LEER OGLE
  like: 8 RESEMBLE
  like a wolf: 4 LEER OGLE
  Long: 4 GAZE 5 STARE
  Lustful: 4 LEER
  lustfully: 4 OGLE
  of contempt: 5 SNEER
  of disdain: 5 SNEER
  over: 3 EYE 4 SCAN
  Pouty: 4 MOUE
  Quick: 4 PEER 6 GLANCE
    7 GLIMPSE
  Salacious: 4 LEER
  Scornful: 5 SNEER
  Sheepish: 4 GRIN
  Sinister: 4 LEER
  Sly: 4 **LEER**
  Sneak a: 4 PEEK
  Suggestive: 4 LEER
  sullen: 4 POUT
  through a keyhole: 6 PEERIN

to be: 4 SEEM
up and down: 4 OGLE
upon: 6 REGARD
up to: 6 ADMIRE ESTEEM
   REVERE
Villainous: 4 LEER 5 SNEER
Wanton: 4 LEER
Wolfish: 4 LEER
~, slangily: 6 GANDER
Look ___
(explore): 4 INTO
(visit): 4 INON
"Look ___ ..." ("Misty" starter):
   4 ATME
Lookalike: 4 TWIN 6 RINGER
   10 CARBONCOPY
   DEADRINGER
   13 SPITTINGIMAGE
H ~: 3 ETA
Hydrox: 4 OREO
"Look at Me, I'm Sandra ___":
   3 DEE
"Look Back in Anger"
playwright John: 7 OSBORNE
Looker: 3 EYE
Good: 3 EYE 4 EYER
Lewd: 5 OGLER
"Look ___ hands!": 4 MANO
"Look here!": 3 OHO
Looking
down from: 4 ATOP
One ~ ahead: 4 SEER
over: 6 EYEING
up: 4 ROSY
Lookout: 8 SENTINEL
Act as: 4 ABET
Be a ~ for: 4 ABET
On the: 5 ALERT
point: 5 AERIE
"Look out!": 7 HEADSUP
Look-see: 4 PEEK PEEP
"Looks ___ everything": 5 ARENT
"Looks like trouble!": 4 UHOH
"Look what I did!": 4 TADA
"Looky here!": 3 OHO
Loom
Crafted on a: 5 WOVEN
Use a: 5 WEAVE
Used a: 4 WOVE

Loon: 8 CRACKPOT
   9 SCREWBALL
relative: 5 GREBE
Looney Tunes
devil, for short: 3 TAZ
prey: 6 TWEETY
Loony: 4 BATS DAFT NUTS
   5 NUTSO 6 INSANE
Less: 5 SANER
Loop: 4 COIL RING
Embroidery: 5 PICOT
Floral: 3 LEI
Gallows: 5 NOOSE
Knock for a: 4 DAZE JOLT STUN
Lariat: 5 NOOSE
Lasso: 5 NOOSE
loopers: 3 **ELS**
Throw for a: 4 FAZE STUN
Looped
fabric: 5 FRISE
handle: 4 ANSA
rope: 5 NOOSE
Loophole: 3 OUT
Use a: 5 EVADE
Loopy: 4 DAFT 6 SPACED
Loos: 3 WCS
Author: 5 **ANITA**
woman: 7 LORELEI
Loose: 3 LAX 4 FREE 5 FREED
   6 ATEASE 7 ATLARGE
   SETFREE
cannon: 6 MENACE
garment: 4 TOGA
Hang: 3 SAG 4 LOLL 5 CHILL
   RELAX
Hanging: 6 ATEASE
Let: 4 **FREE** 5 FREED UNPEN
   UNTIE 7 UNLEASH
Not: 6 CHASTE
On the: 7 ATLARGE
overcoat: 6 RAGLAN ULSTER
Set: 5 UNTIE
snow: 6 POWDER
Some are: 4 ENDS
talk: 5 SLANG
Turn: 7 UNLEASH
~, as shoelaces: 6 UNTIED
Loose-fitting: 5 BAGGY
dress: 4 TENT

Loose-limbed: 5 AGILE LITHE
Loosen: 4 THAW UNDO 5 **UNTIE**
    6 UNKNOT UNLACE
Looseness: 4 GIVE 5 SLACK
Loosestrife
  dye: 5 HENNA
Loot: 3 ROB 4 SWAG 7 RANSACK
  Hidden: 5 STASH
  Lot of: 4 PILE
  Stolen: 4 HAUL
"Loot"
  playwright Joe: 5 ORTON
Lop
  off: 5 SEVER
  the crop: 4 REAP
Lopez
  Singer: 5 **TRINI**
  ___ Lopez (chess opening): 3 RUY
Lopez, Jennifer
  film: 6 SELENA 7 THECELL
  role: 6 SELENA
Lopez, Vincent
  theme song: 4 **NOLA**
Lopsided: 5 ASKEW ATILT
  win: 4 ROUT
Loquacious: 5 TALKY
  horse: 4 MRED
"Lorax, The"
  author: 5 SEUSS
Lord: 4 PEER 5 LIEGE NOBLE
    TITLE
  Feudal: 5 **LIEGE**
  home: 5 MANOR
  House of the: 5 MANOR
  laborer: 4 SERF
  land: 4 FIEF
  mate: 4 LADY
  of La Mancha: 5 SENOR
  of poetry: 5 BYRON
  Turkish: 3 AGA
  worker: 4 SERF 5 THANE
"Lord ___" (Conrad work): 3 JIM
"Lord, ___?": 5 ISITI
"Lord, is ___?": 3 **ITI**
"Lord Jim"
  actor: 6 OTOOLE
"Lord of the Rings, The"
  actor McKellen: 3 IAN
  actor Sean: 5 ASTIN

  actress Tyler: 3 LIV
  beast: 3 ORC 4 OGRE
  hero: 5 FRODO
  tree creature: 3 ENT
Lords
  Actress: 5 TRACI
Lord's Prayer: 5 PATER
  pronoun: 3 THY
  start: 3 **OUR**
Lorelei: 5 SIREN
  river: 5 RHINE
Loren
  Actress: 6 SOPHIA
  Husband of: 5 PONTI
Lorenz
  Lyricist: 4 **HART**
Lorenzo
  Actor: 5 LAMAS
"Lorenzo's Oil"
  actor Nick: 5 NOLTE
Loretta
  Actress: 4 SWIT
  portrayer: 5 SISSY
  Singer: 4 LYNN
Lorgnette
  part: 4 LENS
Lorillard
  brand: 4 KENT
Lorna
  Actress: 4 LUFT
  of literature: 5 DOONE
"Lorna ___": 5 DOONE
Lorne
  Actor: 6 GREENE
Lorraine
  neighbor: 6 ALSACE
Lorre, Peter
  role: 4 MOTO 6 MRMOTO
    UGARTE
Los Alamos
  scientist: 4 BOHR
Los Angeles
  Beach near: 6 MALIBU
  cager: 5 LAKER
  Center of ~, once: 5 ONEAL
  City near: 6 POMONA
  suburb: 6 ENCINO RESEDA
Los ___, California: 5 ALTOS
    GATOS

Lose: 4 SHED 6 MISLAY
  a lap: 5 STAND
  color: 4 FADE
  control: 4 SKID
  energy: 4 TIRE
  everything: 6 GOBUST
  ground: 5 **ERODE**
  hair: 4 SHED
  Having a lot to: 5 OBESE
  Intentionally: 5 THROW
  it: 4 **SNAP** 5 **GOAPE** GOMAD
  one's cool: 5 PANIC
  one's footing: 4 SLIP
  one's mind: 5 GOMAD
  one's nerve: 10 CHICKENOUT
  steam: 4 TIRE
  strength: 4 FADE FLAG TIRE
  traction: 4 SKID SLIP
  Try to: 4 DIET
  weight: 4 SLIM
  You stand to ~ it: 3 LAP
Loser: 5 DWEEB 7 ALSORAN
  Election: 7 ALSORAN
  Fabled: 4 HARE
  Happy: 6 DIETER
  of 1588: 6 ARMADA
  of 1996: 4 DOLE
  to DDE: 3 AES
Losers
  Election: 4 OUTS
  Like some: 4 SORE
  Place for: 3 SPA
Losing: 7 ONADIET
  cause: 4 DIET
  money: 8 INTHERED
  proposition: 4 DIET
"Losing My Religion"
  band: 3 **REM**
Los ___, New Mexico: 6 ALAMOS
Loss
  Deliberate: 4 DIVE
  leader: 3 ATA
  of coordination: 6 ATAXIA
  of courage: 8 COLDFEET
  of memory: 7 AMNESIA
  Suffer a: 5 EATIT
  ___ loss: 3 ATA
Losses
  How ~ are shown: 5 INRED

  ~, in accounting: 6 REDINK
  ___ loss for words: 3 ATA
"Loss of Roses, A"
  playwright: 4 INGE
Lost: 4 ASEA 5 ATSEA
  a lap: 5 AROSE STOOD
  in thought: 7 PENSIVE
  on purpose: 5 THREW
  traction: 4 **SLID**
"Lost Boys, The"
  actor: 4 HAIM
"Lost Horizon"
  director: 5 CAPRA
"Lost in Space"
  character: 5 ROBOT
"Lost World, The"
  menace: 4 TREX
Lot: 3 TON 4 FATE GOBS HEAP
    MUCH SCAD SLEW TONS
    5 BATCH LOADS **OFTEN**
    RAFTS 8 GOODDEAL
  A whole: 4 TONS 6 OCEANS
  Bit of a: 4 ACRE
  choice: 5 SEDAN
  in life: 4 FATE
  It could be a: 4 ACRE
  Not a: 3 FEW
  They make a: 5 ACRES
  Use a: 4 PARK
  Whole: 3 TON 4 SLEW
Lothario: 4 RAKE
  look: 4 OGLE
Lotion
  additive: 4 **ALOE**
  Apply, as: 5 RUBON
  ingredient: 4 **ALOE** 8 ALOEVERA
  letters: 3 SPF
Lots: 4 AGOB ATON GOBS MUCH
    MANY TONS 5 AHEAP
    LOADS OFTEN RAFTS
    REAMS SCADS 6 OCEANS
    OODLES PLENTY
Lott
  of football: 6 RONNIE
  Senator: 5 **TRENT**
Lotte
  Actress: 5 **LENYA**
Lottery
  cry: 4 IWON

Onetime ~ org.: **3** SSS
Lotto
  cousin: **4 KENO 5** BEANO
  variant: **4** KENO
Lotto-like
  game: **4** KENO
Lotus
  owner: **3** IBM
  position activity: **4** YOGA
Lotus-___: 5 EATER
Lou
  Singer: **5** RAWLS
Loud: 5 AROAR GAUDY NOISY
      6 BRASSY GARISH
  and clear: **7** CLARION
  laugh: **3** YUK **4** ROAR
  speaker: **7** STENTOR
  thud: **3** BAM
  Very ~, in music: **3** FFF
  ~, as a crowd: **5 AROAR**
Loudness
  increaser: **3** AMP
  unit: **3** BEL **4** PHON **SONE**
"Lou Dobbs Moneyline"
  carrier: **3** CNN
Louganis
  Diver: **4** GREG
Louganis, Greg: 5 DIVER
Loughlin
  Actress: **4 LORI**
"Lou Grant"
  reporter: **5** ROSSI
  star: **5** ASNER **7** EDASNER
Louie
  ~, to Donald Duck: **6** NEPHEW
Louis
  Comedian: **3 NYE**
  FBI director: **5** FREEH
Louise
  Actress: **4** TINA **6** LASSER
  cohort, in film: **6** THELMA
"Louise"
  soprano: **4** IRMA
Louisiana
  Capital of: **3** ELL
  county: **6** PARISH
  feature: **5** BAYOU
  lingo: **6** CREOLE
  marsh: **5** BAYOU

  namer: **7** LASALLE
  symbol: **7** PELICAN
  ~, in Orléans: **4** ETAT
Louisville
  river: **4** OHIO
  slugger: **3** ALI
"Louisville Lip, The": 3 ALI
Louisville Slugger: 3 BAT
  wood: **3** ASH
Louis XIV: 3 ROI
  ~, to himself: **5** LETAT
Lounge: 3 LIE **4** IDLE LAZE LOAF
      LOLL SOFA **6** REPOSE
  group: **4** TRIO
Lounging: 6 ATEASE
  robe: **6** CAFTAN
  slipper: **4** MULE
Louse: 3 CAD
  egg: **3** NIT
  Plant: **5** APHID
  up: **4** RUIN
  Wood: **6** ISOPOD
Lousy: 3 BAD
  car: **5** LEMON
  egg: **3** NIT
  Feel: **3** AIL
  pick: **3** NIT
Lout: 3 APE OAF **4** BOOR CLOD
      5 YAHOO
Louver: 4 SLAT
  part: **4** SLAT
Louvre: 5 MUSEE
  collection: **6** MANETS
      7 RENOIRS
  display: **3** ART
  highlight: **8** MONALISA
  sculpture: **11** VENUSDEMILO
  Works at the: **4** OILS
Louvre Pyramid
  architect: **3** PEI **5** IMPEI
Lovable
  Make: **6** ENDEAR
Love: 5 ADORE
  affair: **5 AMOUR**
  apple: **6** TOMATO
  god: **4 AMOR EROS**
  Greek god of: **4 EROS**
  In: **7** SMITTEN
  In ~ with oneself: **4** VAIN

Inspire ~ in: 6 ENAMOR
Latin: 4 AMOR
letters: 4 SWAK 6 XOXOXO
lots: 5 ADORE
Madly in: 4 GAGA
of fine art: 5 VIRTU
opposite: 4 HATE
personified: 4 **AMOR** EROS
Roman god of: 4 AMOR
song: 6 BALLAD
symbol: 4 EROS 7 REDROSE
To ~, in Italian: 5 AMARE
to death: 5 ADORE
to pieces: 5 **ADORE**
You ~, in Latin: 4 AMAS
~, in Italian: 5 AMORE
~, in Spanish: 4 AMOR
Love ___ : 4 NEST
"Love ___" (Beatles hit): 4 MEDO
"___ Love" (Pat Boone hit):
        5 APRIL
"___ Love, The"
    (Gershwin tune): 4 MANI
    (R.E.M. tune): 4 ONEI
Love, Courtney
    band: 4 HOLE
"___ Love Again" (Porter song):
        4 IMIN
"Love and Basketball"
    actor Omar: 4 EPPS
"Love Boat, The"
    actress Lauren: 5 TEWES
Lovecraft, H.P
    Like ~ stories: 5 EERIE
Loved
    by: 6 DEARTO
    Just: 5 ATEUP
    one: 4 DEAR IDOL
"Love Hangover"
    singer Ross: 5 DIANA
"___ Love Her" (Beatles hit):
        4 ANDI
"Love Is a Hurtin' Thing"
    singer: 5 RAWLS
Lovelace
    Mathematician: 3 ADA
"Love Letters in the Sand"
    singer: 8 PATBOONE
"Lovely ___" (Beatles tune): 4 RITA

"Love ___ Madly" (Doors hit):
        3 HER
"Love Me, I'm a Liberal"
    singer Phil: 4 OCHS
"Love Me Tender"
    ~, originally: 7 AURALEE
"Love ___ neighbor ...": 3 THY
Lover: 5 ROMEO
    boy: 4 EROS
Loverboy: 4 BEAU 5 ROMEO
        8 LOTHARIO
"Lovergirl"
    singer Marie: 5 TEENA
    singer Teena: 5 MARIE
Lovers
    meeting: 5 TRYST
    place: 4 LANE
Loves
    He ~, in Latin: 4 AMAT
    too much: 7 DOTESON
"Love ___ Simple Thing": 3 ISA
"Love Sneakin' Up on You"
    singer: 5 RAITT
"Love Story"
    author Erich: 5 SEGAL
    author Segal: 5 ERICH
    composer Francis: 3 LAI
"Love the skin you're in"
    company: 4 OLAY
Lovett
    label: 3 MCA
    Singer: 4 **LYLE**
Lovey: 3 PET 4 DEAR
Lovey-dovey: 7 AMOROUS
    Act: 3 COO
"___ Love You" (Beatles hit): 3 PSI
"Love ___ you need" (Beatles
        lyric): 5 ISALL
Loving
    Act: 4 DOTE
    murmur: 3 COO
    touch: 6 CARESS
    Word before: 4 EVER
Lovingly
    Talk: 3 COO
    Touch: 6 FONDLE
Low: 3 MOO SAD 4 BASE
    As ~ as it gets:
        10 ROCKBOTTOM

Below: 5 EMPTY
bow: 6 SALAAM
card: 4 **TREY**
digit: 3 **TOE**
grade: 3 DEE
in fat: 4 LEAN
joint: 5 ANKLE
Laid: 3 HID
Lay: 3 HID 4 HIDE 7 HIDEOUT
Lie: 4 HIDE
life: 5 AMEBA
man: 5 BASSO
mark: 3 DEE
men: 5 BASSI 6 BASSOS
point: 5 NADIR
sock: 6 ANKLET
spot: 4 DELL
They get: 5 BASSI
tract: 4 VALE
voice: 4 BASS
woman: 4 ALTO
Low-___: 3 CAL
Low-budget
prefix: 5 ECONO
Low-cal: 4 DIET **LITE**
Low-cholesterol
spread: 4 OLEO
Low-class
~, in London: 4 NONU
Low-___ diet: 4 CARB
Lowdown: 4 DIRT DOPE INFO
         POOP 5 SCOOP
Low-down
joint: 5 ANKLE
Lowe
Actor: 3 ROB 4 CHAD
Lowell
Poet: 3 AMY
Lower: 3 DIM 4 BATE LESS
         5 ABASE SCOWL
         6 NETHER 7 DEPRESS
oneself: 5 DEIGN STOOP
~, as lights: 3 DIM
~, south of the border: 4 BAJA
Lowest
deck: 5 ORLOP
lake: 7 DEADSEA
point: 5 **NADIR**
tide: 4 NEAP

Lowey
Congresswoman: 4 NITA
Low-fat: 4 LEAN
meat: 3 EMU 7 BEEFALO
Low-grade
wool: 5 MUNGO
Low-heeled
shoe: 6 BROGUE
Lowland: 4 DALE VALE
Boggy: 3 FEN
Wet: 5 SWALE
Lowlife: 3 CAD 4 SCUM 5 SLIME
         SNAKE SWINE 6 SLEAZE
Lowly: 4 BASE 6 MENIAL
worker: 3 ANT 4 **PEON** SERF
Low-lying
area: 4 **VALE** 5 SWALE
Low-paying
position: 5 MCJOB
Low-pH
substance: 4 ACID
Low-pressure
pitch: 8 SOFTSELL
Low-quality: 4 POOR 7 ONESTAR
Lowry
Newbery-winning author: 4 LOIS
Low-slung
hound: 6 BASSET
Low-tech
calculators: 5 ABACI
missile: 3 PEA
propeller: 3 OAR
Low-voiced
lady: 4 ALTO
man: 5 BASSO
Lox
Kind of: 4 NOVA
partner: 5 BAGEL
Loy
Actress: 5 **MYRNA**
Loyal: 4 TRUE 8 TRUEBLUE
lodger: 5 MOOSE
subject: 5 LIEGE
Loyalist: 4 TORY
Loyally
following: 6 TRUETO
Lozenge: 4 DROP PILL 6 TROCHE
LP
contents: 3 MNO

cover: 6 SLEEVE
flaw: 4 SKIP
measure: 3 RPM
player: 4 HIFI 5 PHONO
successors: 3 CDS
Word on an: 6 STEREO

L-P
filler: 3 MNO

L-Q
filler: 4 MNOP

LSAT: 4 EXAM

LSD: 4 ACID

Lt.
Rank below: 3 ENS
saluter: 3 NCO
superior: 4 CAPT
trainer: 3 OCS

Ltd.
~, in France: 3 CIE
~, in the U.S.: 3 INC

Ltr.
addenda: 3 **PSS**
addendum: 3 PPS
enclosure: 4 SASE
extra: 3 ENC
holder: 3 ENV
opener: 4 INIT

Luanda
land: 6 ANGOLA

Luau
chow: 3 POI
dance: 4 **HULA**
dish: 3 **POI**
fare: 3 POI
greeting: 5 ALOHA
instrument: 3 UKE 7 UKELELE
    UKULELE
memento: 3 LEI
souvenir: 3 LEI
staple: 3 POI
strings: 3 UKE

Lubber: 3 OAF

Lubbock
home: 5 TEXAS

Lubitsch
Director: 5 ERNST

Lubovitch
Choreographer: 3 LAR

Lubricate: 3 **OIL** 6 GREASE

Lubrication
opening: 7 OILHOLE

Lucas, George
critter: 4 EWOK
letters: 3 THX

Lucci
Actress: 5 SUSAN

Lucci, Susan
Award that ~ finally won:
    4 EMMY
role: 5 ERICA

Luce
Playwright: 6 CLAIRE

Lucerne
view: 4 ALPS

Lucid: 4 **SANE** 5 CLEAR

Lucie
Brother of: 4 DESI
Father of: 4 **DESI**

Lucifer: 5 SATAN
Like: 4 EVIL

Luck
Bad: 6 HOODOO
Bring bad ~ to: 4 JINX
Down on one's: 5 NEEDY
personification: 4 LADY
Stroke of: 5 BREAK FLUKE
"___ luck!": 5 **LOTSA**
"___ luck?": 3 **ANY**

Luckman
of football: 3 SID

Lucky
charm: 6 AMULET
number: 5 SEVEN
strike: 3 OIL ORE 5 TROVE
tip: 3 ASH

"Lucky Jim"
author: 4 AMIS

Lucrative: 3 FAT

Lucre
Filthy: 4 PELF

Lucretia
Feminist: 4 MOTT

Lucy
Actress: 3 **LIU** 7 LAWLESS
He loved: 4 **DESI**
landlady: 5 ETHEL
neighbor: 5 ETHEL
partner: 4 DESI

Where ~ was found: 8 ETHIOPIA
Ludicrous: 5 ANTIC INANE
Ludwig
  Biographer: 4 EMIL
  dedicatee: 5 ELISE
  lament: 3 ACH
  "___ luego!": 5 HASTA
Luening
  Composer: 4 OTTO
Luft
  Actress: 5 LORNA
Luftwaffe
  battler: 3 RAF
Lug: 3 APE 4 LOUT **TOTE**
      5 SHLEP 6 SCHLEP
      7 SCHLEPP
  Big: 3 OAF
  nut cover: 6 HUBCAP
Luge: 4 SLED
Luggage: 4 BAGS
  attachment: 3 TAG 5 IDTAG
      7 NAMETAG
Lugosi
  Actor: 4 **BELA**
Luigi
  Info: Italian cue
  ___ Luis, Brazil: 3 SAO
Luise
  Actress: 6 RAINER
  ___ Luis Obispo: 3 SAN
"Luka"
  singer Suzanne: 4 VEGA
Lukas
  Actor: 4 HAAS
  Conductor: 4 FOSS
Luke
  Mentor of: 6 OBIWAN
  Sister of: 4 LEIA
  Teacher to: 4 YODA
Lukewarm: 5 **TEPID**
Lull: 4 REST 5 LETUP
Lullaby
  Irish ~ start: 5 TOORA
  Soldier's: 4 TAPS
Lulu: 3 PIP 4 **ONER** 5 BEAUT
      DOOZY 6 CORKER
"Lulu": 5 OPERA
  Composer Alban: 4 BERG
  Composer Berg: 5 ALBAN

Lum
  partner: 5 ABNER
Lumbago: 4 ACHE
Lumber: 4 WOOD
  mill fixture: 3 SAW
  processor: 7 SAWMILL
Lumberjack: 5 AXMAN HEWER
      6 AXEMAN LOGGER
  competition: 5 ROLEO
  shout: 6 TIMBER
  tool: 3 AXE
Luminary: 4 STAR
Luminous: 5 AGLOW
  radiation: 4 AURA
  ring: 4 HALO
  sign: 4 NEON
Lummox: 3 APE OAF 4 CLOD
      LOUT
Lump: 3 NUB 4 GLOB
  Large: 3 GOB
  of clay: 4 GLOB
  of dirt: 4 CLOD
  ___ Lumpur: 5 KUALA
Lumumba
  Congo P.M.: 7 PATRICE
Luna: 4 MOTH
Lunar
  calendar holiday: 3 TET
  craft: 6 LANDER
  descent: 7 MOONSET
  feature: 5 RILLE 6 CRATER
  new year: 3 TET
  plain: 4 MARE
  trench: 5 RILLE
  valley: 5 **RILLE**
  ___ Lunas, New Mexico: 3 LOS
Lunatic: 5 RAVER 6 MADMAN
Lunch: 4 MEAL
  At: 3 OUT
  Brief: 3 BLT
  Did: 3 ATE
  Dieter's: 5 SALAD
  Do: 5 CATER
  Had: 3 ATE
  Have: 3 EAT
  holder: 3 BAG
  hour: 3 ONE
  Light: 5 SALAD
  Long: 4 **HERO**

meat: 3 HAM
order: 3 BLT
Out to: 6 EATING
time: 3 ONE 4 NOON 5 ONEPM
Words before: 5 OUTTO
___ lunch: 5 OUTTO

Lunchbox
fruit: 5 APPLE
treat: 4 **OREO**

Luncheon
ending: 4 **ETTE**

Luncheonette
list: 4 MENU

"Luncheon on the Grass"
painter: 5 MANET

Lunchtime: 3 ONE 4 NOON
7 NOONDAY
Latish: 3 ONE
___ Lund (of "Casablanca"): 4 ILSA

Lundgren
Actor: 5 DOLPH

Lundi
Day after: 5 MARDI

Lunes: 3 DIA

Lung
Of ~ membranes: 7 PLEURAL
section: 4 LOBE
starter: 4 AQUA

Lung, Wang
Wife of: 4 OLAN

Lungful: 3 AIR
Get a: 6 INHALE

Lungs
Fill the: 6 INHALE
Pertaining to the: 5 LOBAR

Lunkhead: 3 ASS SAP 4 CLOD
DOLT

Lupin
Fictional detective: 6 ARSENE
Leblanc's: 6 ARSENE

Lupino
Actress: 3 **IDA**

LuPone
Actress: 5 PATTI
role: 5 EVITA PERON

Lurch: 4 REEL 6 CAREEN

Lure: 4 BAIT 5 DECOY TEMPT
6 COMEON ENTICE
ENTRAP ROPEIN

into crime: 6 ENTRAP
with music: 7 TWEEDLE

Lurie
Novelist: 6 ALISON

Lush: 3 **SOT** 4 WINO 5 SOUSE
TOPER 7 TIPPLER
locale: 3 BAR
sound: 3 HIC
with vegetation: 7 VERDANT

Lusitania: 5 LINER
sinker: 5 **UBOAT**

Lust: 3 SIN
Look of: 4 LEER

Luster: 5 **SHEEN**
Lacking: 5 MATTE
Legendary: 5 SATYR
Lose: 4 FADE

Lusterless: 4 DRAB
finish: 5 MATTE

Lustful: 5 RANDY
deity: 5 SATYR
god: 4 EROS
look: 4 LEER OGLE

Lustrous: 5 SILKY SLEEK
6 GLOSSY PEARLY
SHEENY
black: 5 RAVEN
fabric: 5 SATIN 6 **SATEEN**
gem: 4 OPAL

Lusty
deity: 5 SATYR

Lute
Arab: 3 OUD
Long-necked: 5 SITAR
part: 4 FRET
shape: 4 PEAR

Lutefisk
fish: 3 COD

Lutetia
Modern: 5 PARIS

Luth.: 3 REL

Luther, Martin
article: 3 DER
had 95: 6 THESES
lang.: 3 GER
opposer: 3 ECK

Luthor
Superman foe: 3 LEX

Lutz: 4 LEAP

Lux.
  locale: 3 EUR
  neighbor: 3 GER 4 BELG
Luxemburg
  Revolutionary: 4 ROSA
Luxor
  river: 4 NILE
Luxuriant: 4 LUSH
Luxuriate: 4 BASK 5 REVEL
    6 WALLOW
Luxurious: 4 LUSH POSH TONY
    5 PLUSH 7 OPULENT
    UPSCALE
  fur: 5 SABLE
  life: 4 EASE
  material: 5 SATIN
  place: 3 LAP
  resort: 3 SPA
  retreat: 5 VILLA
Luxury: 4 EASE
  Big name in: 4 RITZ
  resort: 3 SPA
  resort feature: 5 SAUNA
  Seat of: 3 LAP
  ___ luxury: 5 LAPOF
Luyendyk
  Racer: 4 **ARIE**
Luzinski
  of baseball: 4 GREG
Lycée: 5 ECOLE
Lydia
  Foe of ancient: 5 IONIA
Lying: 4 ABED
  around: 4 IDLE
  facedown: 5 PRONE
  flat: 5 PRONE
  on: 4 ATOP
  on one's back: 6 SUPINE

  Stopped: 5 AROSE
Lymph ___ : 4 NODE
Lymphatic
  mass: 4 NODE
Lymphocyte
  Immune system: 5 TCELL
Lynch, David
  film: 10 ERASERHEAD
Lyne
  Director: 6 ADRIAN
Lynn
  of country: 7 LORETTA
  of football: 5 SWANN
  sister: 7 VANESSA
Lynne, Jeff
  rock gp.: 3 ELO
Lyon
  Info: Also spelled Lyons
  Actress: 3 SUE
  Organization based in:
    8 INTERPOL
  river: 5 RHONE SAONE
Lyonnaise
  Ingredient in ~ cuisine: 5 ONION
Lyra
  Star in: 4 **VEGA**
Lyre
  cousin: 4 HARP
  Muse with a: 5 ERATO
Lyric
  Lofty: 3 ODE
  poem: 3 **ODE** 5 **EPODE**
  poet: 4 BARD 5 ODIST
Lyrical: 4 ODIC 6 POETIC
  lines: 3 ODE
  work: 5 EPODE
Lysol
  target: 4 GERM ODOR

Mm

M: 4 SIZE
Quarter of: 3 CCL
Two signal an: 4 DAHS
What an ~ may indicate: 3 SEX
"M"
director Fritz: 4 LANG
star: 5 LORRE
M.
mate: 3 MME
M-1: 5 RIFLE
inventor: 6 GARAND
M-16: 5 RIFLE
Equip with an: 3 ARM
Ma
Cellist: 4 YOYO
instrument: 5 CELLO
or Pa: 6 KETTLE
Sister of: 4 AUNT
MA
and PA: 3 STS
M.A.
entry test: 3 GRE
Ma, Yo-Yo
instrument: 5 CELLO
___ Maar (Picasso subject): 4 DORA
___ Mable (WWI humor book):
4 DERE
Mabley
Comic: 4 MOMS
Mac: 3 BUB 5 KIDDO
alternatives: 3 **PCS**
insert: 5 CDROM
maker: 5 APPLE
Macabre: 5 EERIE
In a ~ way: 6 EERILY
___ Macabre: 5 DANSE
Macadam
Apply ~ to: 4 PAVE
Macao
money: 3 AVO
Macarena: 3 FAD 5 DANCE
Macaroni: 5 PASTA
shape: 5 **ELBOW**

MacArthur
dismisser: 3 HST
quote ender: 6 RETURN
victory site: 5 LEYTE
MacArthur Airport
site: 5 ISLIP
Macaw: 6 PARROT
Macbeth
burial place: 4 IONA
title: 5 THANE
weapon: 6 DAGGER
When ~ dies: 4 ACTV
When ~ slays Duncan: 5 ACTII
"Macbeth": 5 DRAMA
opener: 4 ACTI
quintet: 4 ACTS
trio: 4 HAGS
witch: 6 HECATE
MacDonald
Like: 3 OLD
Partner of: 4 EDDY
sleuth: 6 ARCHER
spread: 4 FARM
MacDowell
Actress: 5 **ANDIE**
MacDuff: 5 THANE
Command to: 5 LAYON
Mace
source: 6 NUTMEG
Macedonia
Early capital of: 6 EDESSA
Macedonian
neighbor: 4 SERB
MacGraw
Actress: 3 **ALI**
Mach
Physicist: 5 ERNST
Mach 1
breaker: 3 **SST**
Mach 2
plane: 3 SST
Mach 3
alternative: 4 ATRA

Machete: 4 BOLO
Machiavellian: 3 SLY
Machinating: 4 UPTO
Machine
  Assembly line: 5 ROBOT
  Bread: 3 ATM
  Deli: 6 SLICER
  Farm: 5 BALER 6 REAPER
    SEEDER 7 COMBINE
  Graphics: 6 IMAGER
  Office: 5 ADDER 8 SHREDDER
  part: 3 **CAM** COG 4 GEAR
    5 ROTOR
  Sowing: 6 SEEDER
  tooth: 3 COG
  Vegas: 4 SLOT
  Voting ~ part: 5 LEVER
  Weaving: 4 LOOM
  Woodworking: 5 LATHE
  Word with: 4 SLOT
  ___ machine: 4 SLOT
Machine gun
  sound: 7 RATATAT
  syllable: 3 TAT
Machinery
  Big name in farm: 5 DEERE
  Run, as: 7 OPERATE
  Update the: 6 RETOOL
Macho: 5 MANLY
  Hardly: 3 FEY 5 MOUSY SISSY
    6 GIRLIE
  type: 4 STUD 5 HEMAN RAMBO
  types: 5 HEMEN
Machu Picchu
  resident: 4 **INCA** 5 INCAN
  site: 4 PERU
Macintosh
  maker: 5 APPLE
Mack
  of early TV: 3 TED
  predecessor: 5 BOWES
  Producer: 7 SENNETT
MacKenzie
  Actor: 5 ASTIN
  Singer: 6 GISELE
Mackerel
  Horse: 4 TUNA
  kin: 6 BONITO
  Large: 5 WAHOO

  shark: 4 MAKO
Mackinac Island
  lake: 5 HURON
"Mack the Knife"
  singer: 5 DARIN
MacLachlan
  Actor: 4 KYLE
MacLaine, Shirley
  1963 ~ role: 4 IRMA
  1969 ~ musical:
    12 SWEETCHARITY
  1994 ~ role: 4 TESS
MacLeod
  Actor: 5 GAVIN
Macmillan
  predecessor: 4 EDEN
MacMurray, Fred
  sitcom: 11 MYTHREESONS
MacNeil
  Partner of: 6 LEHRER
MacNelly, Jeff
  comic strip: 4 SHOE
Macon
  breakfast: 5 GRITS
Macpherson
  Model: 4 **ELLE**
Macramé: 5 CRAFT
  unit: 4 KNOT
Macro
  suffix: 4 COSM
Macroeconomic
  stat: 3 GNP
Macy's: 5 STORE
  alternative: 5 SEARS
  event: 4 SALE
  section: 4 MENS
Mad: 4 LOCO 5 ANGRY FEDUP
    IRATE LIVID 7 STEAMED
  (at): 4 SORE
  Be ~ about: 5 ADORE
  Be hopping: 4 BOIL 6 SEETHE
  Get: 5 STEAM 6 SEERED
  one of fiction: 6 HATTER
  Plenty: 4 IRED
Mad. ___: 3 AVE
"Mad About You"
  actress Helen: 4 HUNT
  cousin: 3 IRA
Madagascar: 6 ISLAND

primate: **5** LEMUR
Madalyn
  Atheist: **5** OHAIR
Madam: **4** BAWD **5** TITLE
  Mate of: **3** SIR
"Madama Butterfly"
  Pinkerton, in: **5** TENOR
Madame
  Reply to a: **6** OUIOUI
Madame Bovary: 4 EMMA
Madame Butterfly
  Sash for: **3** OBI
Madame de ___: 5 STAEL
Madame Karenina: 4 ANNA
Madame Tussaud
  medium: **3** WAX
"Madame X"
  painter: **7** SARGENT
"Madamina": 4 ARIA
Madcap: 4 ZANY **5** ANTIC
  comedy: **4** ROMP
MADD
  concern: **3** DUI
  Part of: **7** AGAINST
Madden: 3 IRE **4** RILE **6** ENRAGE
    7 DERANGE
Maddox
  Former Georgia governor:
    6 LESTER
Maddux
  of baseball: **4** GREG
Made: 6 EARNED
  Barely ~ it: **4** EKED
  certain: **7** SAWTOIT
  Freshly: **3** NEW
  like: **4** APED
  out: **5** FARED **6** NECKED
  over: **5** REDID **6** REDONE
  possible: **7** ENABLED
  up (for): **6** ATONED
  use of: **6** DREWON
Made in the ___: 3 USA
Madeleine
  Actress: **5** STOWE
Madeline
  Actress: **4** __KAHN__
"___ Made to Love Her": 4 IWAS
Mad Hatter
  drink: **3** TEA

Madhouse: 3 ZOO
Madigan
  Actress: **3** AMY
"___ Madigan": 6 ELVIRA
Madison: 6 AVENUE
  (abbr.): **3** AVE JAS
  Friend of: **5** UNGER
  Mrs.: **6** DOLLEY
  Sch. in ~, N.J.: **5** DREWU
  state (abbr.): **3** WIS
  successor: **6** MONROE
  veep: **5** GERRY
Madison, Oscar: 4 SLOB
  Like: **5** MESSY
  secretary: **5** MYRNA
Madison Ave.
  address: **4** NYNY
  guys: **5** ADMEN
  income: **6** ADFEES
  output: **3** ADS
Madison Avenue
  award: **4** CLIO
  reading: **6** ADWEEK
  type: **5** ADMAN
  types: **5** ADMEN **7** IDEAMEN
Madison Square Garden:
    5 ARENA
Madlyn
  Actress: **4** RHUE
Mad magazine
  cartoonist Drucker: **4** MORT
  Get ~ again: **5** RENEW
  piece: **6** SATIRE
  publisher: **6** GAINES
Mad Max
  portrayer: **3** MEL
"Mad Max"
  Max in: **3** MEL
  villain: **5** BIKER
"___ Madness": 6 REEFER
Madonna
  1996 ~ film: **5** EVITA
  Ex of: **4** SEAN
  portrayal: **5** PIETA
  role: **5** __EVITA__ PERON
    8 EVAPERON
  stagewear: **3** BRA
"___ Madonna"
  (Beatles tune): **4** LADY

(Raphael): 7 SISTINE
Madras
Info: India cue
dress: 4 SARI
master: 5 SAHIB
money: 5 RUPEE
music: 4 RAGA
~ Mr.: 3 SRI
Madre
Brother of: 3 TIO
Child of: 4 NENE NINO
title (abbr.): 3 SRA
___ Madres: 6 SIERRA
Madrid
Info: Spanish cue
airline: 6 IBERIA
City NW of: 4 LEON
mister: 5 SENOR
money: 6 PESETA
month: 5 ENERO
museum: 5 **PRADO**
Walled city near: 5 **AVILA**
~ Mrs.: 3 **SRA** 6 SENORA
~ Ms.: 4 SRTA
Madrileña
Married: 6 SENORA
Madrileño: 5 SENOR
"Mad TV"
rival: 3 SNL
Mae
Actress: 4 WEST
role: 3 LIL
___ Mae (Oscar role for Whoopi):
3 ODA
Maelstrom: 4 EDDY
Maestro
Bombay-born: 5 MEHTA
wand: 5 BATON
~ Georg: 5 SOLTI
Mafia
boss: 3 **DON** 4 CAPO
Chinese: 4 TONG
code of silence: 6 OMERTA
Mag
edition: 3 ISS
Fan: 4 ZINE
Fan ~ subject: 4 IDOL
features: 3 ADS
for execs: 3 INC

magnate: 3 HEF
Web: 5 EZINE
workers: 3 EDS
Magazine: 7 ARSENAL
about celebs: 6 PEOPLE
Arm with a: 3 UZI
Business: 3 INC
contents: 4 AMMO
copy: 5 **ISSUE**
Do ~ work: 4 EDIT
Dr.'s: 4 JAMA
Eclectic: 4 **UTNE**
execs.: 3 **EDS**
extra: 6 INSERT
Fashion: 4 **ELLE**
fillers: 3 ADS
for men: 7 DETAILS
Former humor: 3 SPY
Former science: 4 OMNI
Former women's: 5 ROSIE
for women: 4 SELF
genre: 4 MENS
magnate, for short: 3 HEF
Noted online: 5 SLATE
Satire: 3 MAD
Women's ~, for short: 5 COSMO
Word in some ~ titles: 6 DIGEST
~ VIPs: 3 **EDS**
Magaziner: 3 IRA
Magazines
and papers: 10 PRINTMEDIA
Magda
Sister of: 3 EVA 6 ZSAZSA
Magellan: 6 STRAIT
org.: 4 NASA
Maggie
Husband of: 5 JIGGS
Maggot: 5 LARVA
Magi: 4 TRIO
Any of the: 6 ADORER
gift: 5 MYRRH
guide: 4 STAR
Home of the: 6 ORIENT
Like the: 4 WISE
One of the: 6 CASPAR
origin: 4 EAST
Magic
charm: 4 MOJO 6 AMULET
org.: 3 NBA

stick: **4** WAND
The ~ word: **6** PLEASE
town: **7** ORLANDO
West Indies: **5** OBEAH
word: **6** PRESTO
words: **10** HOCUSPOCUS
~, formerly: **5** LAKER
    7 LALAKER
"___ magic!": **3** ITS
___ magica: 3 ARS
Magical
character: **4** RUNE
Cult using ~ rites: **6** VOODOO
drink: **6** POTION
object: **6** FETISH
opening: **4** ABRA **5** HOCUS
sound: **4** POOF
wish granter: **5** GENIE
"Magic Flute, The": 5 OPERA
Magician
Amazing: **5** RANDI
cry: **5** VOILA **6** PRESTO
Famous: **7** HOUDINI
hiding place: **6** SLEEVE
hiding spot: **4** PALM
name suffix: **3** INI
prop: **3** HAT **4** WAND
secret exit: **8** TRAPDOOR
source: **7** THINAIR
Tribal: **6** SHAMAN
Magistrate
Muslim: **4** CADI
Roman: **5** EDILE
Venetian: **4** DOGE
Maglie
of baseball: **3** SAL
Magma
on the go: **4** LAVA
Magna ___ : 5 CARTA
Magna cum ___ : 5 LAUDE
Magna ___ laude: 3 CUM
Magnani
Actress: **4 ANNA**
Magnate: 4 CZAR **5** BARON
    TITAN
Fur: **5** ASTOR
nickname: **3** ARI HEF
Magnavox
rival: **3** RCA **4** SONY

Magnet
alloy: **6** ALNICO
end: **4** POLE
holder: **6** FRIDGE
Kitchen: **5** AROMA
metal: **4** IRON
Tourist: **5** MECCA
"Magnet and Steel"
singer Walter: **4** EGAN
Magnetic
flux unit: **5** WEBER
induction unit: **5** GAUSS **TESLA**
prefix: **4** AERO
ribbon: **4** TAPE
Magnetism: 6 ALLURE
    8 CHARISMA
Magnetite: 3 ORE **7** IRONORE
Magnificence: 4 POMP
    8 SPLENDOR
Magnificent: 5 REGAL
"Magnificent Seven, The"
Chris in: **3** YUL
"___ magnifique!": 4 CEST
Magnify: 7 ENHANCE
Magnifying
device: **5** LOUPE
Magniloquize: 5 ORATE
Magnitude: 4 SIZE **6** EXTENT
Having ~, but no direction:
    6 SCALAR
___ Magnon: 3 CRO
Magnum
and others (abbr.): **3** PIS
follower: **4** OPUS
Magnus
Newswoman: **4** EDIE
Magoo: 5 MYOPE
Nephew of: **5** WALDO
vision: **4** BLUR
voice: **6** BACKUS
Magritte
Painter: **4 RENE**
___ Mahal: 3 TAJ
Mahalia
music: **6** GOSPEL
Maharani
garb: **4** SARI
Mahayana
master: **4** LAMA

movement: 3 ZEN
"Ma, He's Making Eyes ___":
    4 ATME
Mah-jongg
    piece: 4 **TILE**
Mahler
    Composer: 6 GUSTAV
    Earth, to: 4 ERDE
Mahler, Gustav
    Wife of: 4 ALMA
Mahogany: 4 TREE
Mahre
    Emulate: 3 SKI
Mai ___ (cocktail): 3 **TAI**
___ mai (dim sum dish): 3 SHU
Maid
    Baa: 3 EWE
    cloth: 3 RAG
    Comics: 5 HAZEL
    need: 7 PASSKEY
    of Astolat: 6 ELAINE
Maiden: 4 LASS
    name preceder: 3 **NEE**
    Poe: 6 LENORE
    voyage preceder:
        15 SHAKEDOWNCRUISE
Maidenform
    product: 3 BRA
Maidenhair: 4 FERN
"Maid of Athens, ___ part": Byron:
    5 EREWE
"Maids, The"
    playwright: 5 GENET
"... maids all in ___": 4 AROW
Maidstone
    county: 4 KENT
Mail: 4 POST SEND 7 SENDOUT
    again: 6 RESEND
    carrier beat: 5 ROUTE
    carrier beat (abbr.): 3 RTE
    Country ~ rte.: 3 RFD
    French: 5 POSTE
    GI ~ drop: 3 **APO**
    In the: 4 SENT
    Junk ~, often: 3 ADS 6 UNREAD
    Kind of: 4 BULK HATE 5 SNAIL
        7 METERED
    Main ~ ctr.: 3 GPO
    motto word: 3 NOR

opening: 4 SLOT
org.: 4 USPS
Piece of ~ (abbr.): 3 LTR
Put in the: 4 SEND SENT
Snail ~ attachment: 5 STAMP
The check is in the ~, often: 3 LIE
Unwelcome: 4 BILL
You've got ~ co.: 3 **AOL**
Mailbox
    attachment: 4 FLAG
Mail Boxes ___: 3 ETC
Mailed: 6 SENTIN
Mailer, Norman: 6 AUTHOR
    novel: 12 HARLOTSGHOST
Mailing
    courtesy (abbr.): 4 SASE
    list items: 5 NAMES
    Ready for: 7 STAMPED
    Software: 5 CDROM
    supply: 6 LABELS
Mailman
    beat: 5 ROUTE
    "Cheers": 5 CLIFF
Mail order
    giant: 6 LLBEAN
    record co.: 4 KTEL
Main: 3 SEA 5 CHIEF OCEAN
    and others (abbr.): 3 STS
    artery: 5 **AORTA**
    attraction: 4 STAR
    course: 6 **ENTREE**
    idea: 4 CRUX **GIST**
    impact: 5 BRUNT
    In the: 7 ASARULE
    Like a ~ highway: 8 ARTERIAL
    line: 5 **AORTA** 6 ARTERY
    men: 4 TARS
    Of a ~ line: 6 AORTIC
    On the: 4 **ASEA** 5 ATSEA
    pronoun: 3 HER
    role: 4 LEAD
    route: 7 SEALANE
    squeeze: 6 STEADY
    theme: 5 MOTIF
Maine: 5 STATE
    Bay in: 5 CASCO
    college town: 5 **ORONO**
    national park: 6 ACADIA
    resort: 9 BARHARBOR

symbol: 8 PINETREE
tree: 4 PINE
Maine ___ cat: 4 COON
Mainframe
2001 ~: 3 HAL
Send to a: 6 UPLOAD
Maintain: 4 **AVER** HOLD 5 CLAIM
    6 ALLEGE ASSERT
    HOLDTO
Maintenance: 6 UPKEEP
Like some computer: 6 ONSITE
worker: 7 JANITOR
Mainz
mister: 4 HERR
"Mais ___!": 3 OUI
Mai tai
ingredient: 3 RUM
Maj.
College: 3 BIO ENG SOC 4 ECOL
    ECON 5 PSYCH
Rank above: 3 COL 5 LTCOL
Maja
painter: 4 GOYA
"Maja Nude"
painter: 4 GOYA
___ majesté: 4 **LESE**
Majestic: 4 EPIC 5 GRAND REGAL
    7 STATELY
poem: 4 EPIC
"___ Majesty's Secret Service":
    5 ONHER
Major
Λ: 3 KEY
account: 4 SAGA
addition: 4 ETTE
airport: 3 HUB
animal: 4 URSA
artery: 5 **AORTA**
Coll.: 3 BIO ENG SOC 4 ECOL
    ECON 5 PSYCH
College: 3 ART 4 MATH 5 DRAMA
conflict: 3 WAR
in the sky: 4 URSA
leaguer: 3 PRO
meal: 5 FEAST
mix-up: 5 SNAFU
successor: 5 BLAIR
Uncommon: 5 CFLAT
util.: 4 ELEC

work: 4 OPUS
Major ___: 4 DOMO
___ Major: 4 **URSA** 5 CANIS
"Major Barbara"
playwright: 4 SHAW
Majorca: 4 ISLA
capital: 5 PALMA
Majorette
motion: 5 TWIRL
need: 5 BATON
Major Hoople
holler: 4 EGAD
Majority: 4 MOST
Major leagues
One of the ~ (abbr.): 4 NATL
~, in slang: 4 BIGS
Major Major
portrayer: 7 NEWHART
Majors
Actor: 3 LEE
Makarova
Ballerina: 7 NATALIA
of tennis: 5 ELENA
Make: 4 **EARN**
amends: 5 **ATONE**
Barely: 6 EKEOUT
Barely ~ it: 5 GETBY
    8 SQUEAKBY
better: 4 HEAL 5 AMEND
certain: 6 ASSURE ENSURE
    INSURE
do: 4 COPE
Hard to ~ out: 5 FAINT
it: 3 TAG 4 COME 5 GOFAR
    6 ARRIVE
like: 3 APE
one: 3 WED 5 UNITE
one's own: 5 ADOPT
(one's way): 4 WEND
out: 3 SEE 4 ESPY FARE NECK
    READ 6 DETECT 7 DISCERN
(out): 3 EKE
over: 5 ALTER 7 RESTYLE
    8 RECREATE
up: 5 ATONE ELATE
up for: 5 **ATONE** 6 RECOUP
use of: 3 TAP
"Make ___!" (captain's order):
    4 ITSO

Make ___ (get rich): 5 AMINT
Make ___ at: 5 APASS
Makeba
  Singer: 6 MIRIAM
Make-believe: 4 SHAM
        8 PRETENSE
Make ___ buck: 5 AFAST
Make ___ dash for: 4 **AMAD**
"Make ___ double": 3 ITA
Make ___ for: 5 ACASE
Make ___ for it: 4 ARUN
Make ___ for oneself: 5 ANAME
"Make it snappy!": 4 ASAP
"Make love, not war": 6 SLOGAN
Make ___ meet: 4 ENDS
Make ___ of: 5 ANOTE
Make ___ of things: 5 AMESS
Makeover: 4 REDO
Makes
  What one: 6 INCOME
Makeshift: 7 STOPGAP
  drinking glass: 8 JELLYJAR
  dwelling: 3 HUT
  money: 5 SCRIP
  swing: 4 TIRE
Make the ___: 6 MOSTOF
Makeup: 4 EXAM TEST 6 RETEST
  artist: 4 LIAR
  Cube: 3 ICE
  Do a ~ job: 5 ATONE
  Jury: 5 PEERS
  Model: 5 BALSA
  name: 5 ESTEE
  Rio: 4 AGUA
Make ___ with: 4 AHIT
Making
  a crossing: 4 ASEA
  all stops: 5 LOCAL
  no progress: 6 INARUT
  no sense: 5 INANE
"Makin' Whoopee"
  lyricist Gus: 4 KAHN
Mal-
  relative: 3 MIS
Mal ___: 5 DEMER
Malady: 7 AILMENT DISEASE
Malaga
  mister: 5 SENOR
  Mmes. in: 4 SRAS

Mrs. in: 3 SRA
Malaise: 8 THEBLAHS
  ~, with "the": 5 BLAHS
Malamud, Bernard
  novel: 10 THENATURAL
Malamute
  tow: 4 SLED
Malaprop: 3 MRS
Malaria
  symptom: 4 **AGUE**
Malarkey: 3 ROT
Malay
  boat: 4 PROA
  Export of: 3 TIN
  isthmus: 3 KRA
  monarch: 5 RAJAH
Malay Archipelago
  island: 6 BORNEO
Malcolm
  role: 4 THEO
  TV dad of: 3 HAL
Malcolm-___ Warner: 5 JAMAL
Malcolm X
  biographer: 9 ALEXHALEY
"Malcolm X"
  director: 3 LEE 8 SPIKELEE
Malcontent: 5 REBEL
Mal de ___: 3 **MER**
Malden
  Actor: 4 **KARL**
Male
  admirer: 5 SWAIN
  bee: 5 DRONE
  cat: 3 TOM
  deer: 4 HART **STAG**
  duck: 5 DRAKE
  heirs: 4 SONS
  Kind of: 5 ALPHA
  pig: 4 BOAR
  sheep: 3 RAM
  sibs: 4 BROS
  swan: 3 COB
  turkey: 3 **TOM**
___ male: 5 ALPHA
Maleficent: 4 EVIL
Males: 3 HES
Malevolence: 4 EVIL HATE
        5 SPITE
Malevolent: 4 EVIL

Malfoy
  of Hogwarts: 5 DRACO
Malfunction: 5 ACTUP
Mali
  neighbor: 5 NIGER
  river: 5 NIGER
Malibu: 4 AUTO 5 SEDAN
Malice: 5 **SPITE**
"Malice"
  Baldwin of: 4 ALEC
Malicious: 4 EVIL MEAN 5 CATTY
      NASTY SNIDE
  gossip: 4 DIRT
  look: 4 LEER
  ones: 7 MEANIES
Maliciously
  Treat: 5 SPITE
Malick
  Actress: 6 WENDIE
Malign: 5 ABUSE 7 ASPERSE
      TRADUCE
  in print: 5 LIBEL
Malihini
  Gift for a: 3 LEI
Malkovich, John
  1985 ~ film: 5 ELENI
Mall
  Ancient: 5 AGORA
  areas: 5 ATRIA
  bag: 4 TOTE
  binge: 5 SPREE
  chain, with "The": 3 GAP
  event: 4 SALE
  feature: 6 ARCADE CINEMA
  Greek: 5 AGORA
  Kind of: 5 STRIP
  rat: 4 TEEN
  Shopping: 8 GALLERIA
  stand: 5 KIOSK
  tenant: 10 CHAINSTORE
  unit: 4 SHOP 5 **STORE**
Mallard
  Male: 5 DRAKE
  relative: 4 TEAL
Mallet: 5 GAVEL
  game: 4 POLO
Mallorca: 4 **ISLA**
  Info: Spanish cue
  Mlle. in: 4 SRTA

  Mrs. in: 3 SRA
Mallow
  shrub: 4 OKRA
Malmo
  citizen: 5 SWEDE
  setting: 6 SWEDEN
Malodorous: 5 FETID
      7 REEKING
  animal: 7 POLECAT
Malone
  Actress: 4 JENA
  of basketball: 4 KARL
Malraux
  Novelist: 5 ANDRE
Malt
  alternative: 4 SODA
  beverage: 3 ALE 4 BEER
      5 STOUT
  dryer: 4 OAST
  kiln: 4 OAST
  liquor yeast: 4 BARM
Malta
  capital: 8 VALLETTA
  money: 4 LIRA
Maltese
  cry: 4 MEOW
"Maltese Falcon, The"
  actor Peter: 5 LORRE
  actress Mary: 5 ASTOR
  role: 3 SAM 5 SPADE
Maltreat: 5 ABUSE 6 ILLUSE
___ Malvinas (the Falklands):
      5 ISLAS
Mama
  Big: 4 CASS
  boy: 3 **SON**
  Lamb: 3 EWE
  of papa: 4 NANA
  Partner of: 4 PAPA
  ~ bear, in Spanish: 3 OSA
Mama Cass ___: 6 ELLIOT
"Mamas & the Papas, The"
  singer Doherty: 5 DENNY
  singer Elliot: 4 CASS
Mambo
  king Puente: 4 TITO
"Mambo Kings, The"
  star: 7 ASSANTE 8 BANDERAS
Mame: 6 AUNTIE

Mamet, David
1992 ~ play: 7 OLEANNA
award: 4 OBIE
Mamie
Husband of: 3 IKE
predecessor: 4 **BESS**
"Mamma ___!": 3 MIA
Mammal
Aquatic: 4 SEAL 5 **OTTER**
Burrowing: 4 MOLE
Flying: 3 BAT
Long-eared: 4 HARE
Mammoth: 5 WHALE
Marine: 6 WALRUS 7 SEALION
of Madagascar: 5 LEMUR
Piglike: 5 TAPIR
Slow-moving: 5 SLOTH
Thick-skinned: 5 HIPPO RHINO
Tropical: 5 TAPIR
"Mamma Mia!"
group: 4 **ABBA**
Mammoth
era: 6 ICEAGE
part: 4 TUSK
Mammy Yokum
creator: 6 ALCAPP
Son of: 5 ABNER
Man: 3 BRO 4 GENT ISLE
5 VALET 7 PRIMATE
(abbr.): 3 ISL
at the wheel: 5 SAJAK
Chair: 5 EAMES
Con: 4 ANTI
Dadaist: 3 RAY
Dirty old: 6 LECHER
Elevator: 4 **OTIS**
Family: 3 DAD
First: 4 ADAM
Fourth: 4 SETH
High: 4 ALTO
Hit: 4 ICER
in a suit: 5 SANTA
Iron: 5 ROBOT
Jazz: 3 CAT
Little green: 5 ALIEN
Low: 5 BASSO
Macho: 4 STUD
March: 5 SOUSA
of La Mancha: 5 **SENOR**

of many words: 5 ROGET
of morals: 5 **AESOP**
of mystery: 3 MRX
of parts: 5 ACTOR
of photos: 3 RAY
of Principle: 5 PETER
of the haus: 4 HERR
of the hour: 4 HERO
Old: 3 DAD POP 5 POPPA
Right-hand: 4 AIDE
Straight: 4 FOIL 6 STOOGE
Third: 4 ABEL
Third ~ in the ring: 3 REF
Top: 5 MRBIG
Tractor: 5 DEERE
Unmannered: 3 CAD
who would be queen: 4 PAWN
with a law: 3 OHM
with a mission: 5 PADRE
SERRA
Young: 3 LAD
~ Fri.: 4 ASST
~ Friday: 4 AIDE
~, in Italian: 4 UOMO
~, in Latin: 3 VIR
"Man!": 5 OHWOW
Man ___ (racehorse): 4 OWAR
___ man: 3 TOA
" ___ Man"
(1984 film): 4 REPO
(1992 film): 6 ENCINO
(Village People hit): 5 MACHO
" ___ Man, The" (Heston film):
5 OMEGA
Manacle: 8 HANDCUFF
Manage: 4 COPE FEND 5 GETBY
SEETO 6 EKEOUT
MAKEDO 7 OPERATE
OVERSEE SWINGIT
Barely ~, with "out": 3 EKE
Easy to: 4 TAME
moguls: 3 SKI
to find: 7 SCAREUP
Managed: 3 **RAN** 5 SAWTO
care org.: 3 HMO
Management
Fed. ~ gp.: 3 GSA
Middle: 4 DIET
prefix: 5 MICRO

Manager
  Cardinal: 4 POPE
  Corp. money: 3 CFO
  deg.: 3 MBA
  Fed. property: 3 GSA
  Money: 6 EDITOR
Manager of the Year
  1994 N.L.: 4 ALOU
  1998 A.L.: 5 TORRE
Mañana
  Opposite of: 4 AYER
  ___ mañana!: 5 HASTA
"Man and a Woman, A"
  actress: 5 AIMEE
"Man and Superman"
  playwright: 4 SHAW
"___ Man Answers" (1962 film):
    3 IFA
Manatee: 6 SEACOW
  home: 3 SEA
Manche
  capital: 4 **STLO**
Manchester
  man: 5 BLOKE
  Singer: 7 MELISSA
Manchurian
  border river: 4 YALU
Manco Capac: 4 INCA
Mandamus: 4 WRIT
Mandarin: 6 ORANGE
Mandate: 5 ORDER
Mandel
  Comic: 5 **HOWIE**
Mandela: 6 NELSON
  org.: 3 **ANC**
Mandible
  part: 4 JOWL
Mandlikova
  of tennis: 4 **HANA**
Mandolin
  feature: 4 FRET
  kin: 4 LUTE
Mandrake
  assistant: 6 LOTHAR
  field: 5 MAGIC
"Mandy"
  singer: 7 MANILOW
Mane
  Antelope with a: 3 GNU

  area: 4 NAPE
  Thick: 3 MOP
  thing: 4 HAIR
Man-eating
  monster: 4 OGRE
Manet: 6 ARTIST
Maneuver
  180-degree ~: 5 UTURN
  carefully: 4 EASE
  Clever: 4 PLOY
  Dance: 3 DIP
  Evasive: 6 ENDRUN
  Sailing: 4 TACK
  Skating: 4 AXEL LOOP
  Skiing: 8 SIDESLIP
  Wall St.: 3 LBO
Maneuverable: 4 YARE
Manfred
  Detective story writer: 3 LEE
  Pop singer: 4 MANN
Mangel-wurzel: 4 BEET
Manger
  bedding: 3 HAY
  visitors: 4 MAGI
"Mangia!": 3 EAT
Mangle: 4 MAIM
  Use a: 4 IRON
Man-goat: 5 SATYR
Manhandle: 3 PAW 4 MAUL
    5 PAWAT
Manhattan: 5 DRINK 6 ISLAND
  (abbr.): 3 ISL
  Arty ~ district: 4 SOHO
  eatery: 7 ELAINES
  ingredient: 3 RYE
  Island near: 5 ELLIS
  landmark:
    11 CENTRALPARK
  letters: 4 NYNY
  locale (abbr.): 4 KANS
  neighborhood: 4 SOHO
    7 TRIBECA
  sch.: 3 NYU 4 CCNY
  section: 8 EASTSIDE
  site: 3 BAR
  Suffix with: 3 ITE
  ~, for short: 4 BORO
"Manhattan Murder Mystery"
  star: 4 ALDA

Manhattan Project
 Agcy. created after the: 3 AEC
 It followed the: 9 ATOMICAGE
 result: 5 ABOMB
 scientist: 5 FERMI
Manhunt
 letters: 3 APB
 target: 7 ESCAPEE
Mania: 3 FAD 4 RAGE
     5 CRAZE
 source of the 1630s: 5 TULIP
Maniac: 5 FIEND 6 MADMAN
 Kind of: 3 EGO
Manicured
 expanse: 4 LAWN
Manicurist
 board: 5 **EMERY**
 concern: 4 NAIL 7 CUTICLE
 tool: 4 FILE
Manifest: 5 OVERT 6 EVINCE
 7 EVIDENT
Manifesto
 writer: 4 MARX 6 ENGELS
Manila
 envelope fastener: 5 CLASP
 folder extension: 3 TAB
 island: 5 LUZON
 Territory east of: 4 GUAM
Manilow, Barry
 1975 ~ hit: 5 MANDY
 song setting: 4 **COPA**
"Man in Full, A"
 author: 5 WOLFE
Manipulate: 3 USE 5 WIELD
 dishonestly: 4 COOK
Manipulative
 one: 4 **USER**
Manipulator: 4 USER
Manitoba
 native: 4 **CREE**
Manjula
 Husband of: 3 APU
Manliness: 8 MACHISMO
Manly: 5 MACHO 6 VIRILE
Man-made
 Not: 7 NATURAL
"Man ___ Mancha": 4 OFLA
Man-mission
 link: 3 ONA

Man-mouse
 link: 3 **ORA**
"... man ___ mouse?": 3 ORA
Mann
 of education: 6 HORACE
 Singer: 5 **AIMEE**
Mann, Manfred
 1964 ~ hit: 7 SHALALA
Manner: 4 MIEN
 Cool in: 5 ALOOF
 Distinctive: 5 STYLE
 In the ~ of: 3 **ALA**
 In this: 6 LIKESO
 Kind of: 7 BEDSIDE
 of action: 4 MODE
 of speaking: 5 IDIOM
 suffix: 3 ISM
Mannerism: 5 TRAIT
 Odd: 3 TIC
Mannerly
 guy: 4 GENT
 ___ manner of speaking: 3 INA
Manners: 5 MODES
     7 PSANDQS
 of moving: 5 GAITS
 Post of: 5 EMILY
Mannheim
 Mr.: 4 HERR
Manning
 of football: 3 ELI
Manny
 of baseball: 4 MOTA
Mano a mano: 4 DUEL
     8 ONEONONE
"Man of ___": 4 ARAN
"Man of a Thousand Faces"
 actor Chaney: 3 LON
Man of Steel
 portrayer: 5 REEVE
Man of the Year
 1971 ~: 5 NIXON
 1977 ~: 5 SADAT
 1981 ~: 6 WALESA
Manolete
 Cheer for: 3 OLE
 nemesis: 6 ELTORO
Manor: 6 ESTATE
 master: 4 LORD
 Mitchell: 4 TARA

... ___ man put asunder: 5 LETNO

Mansard: 4 ROOF
  overhang: 4 EAVE

Manse
  dweller: 6 PARSON

Man-shaped
  mug: 4 TOBY

Mansion
  and grounds: 6 ESTATE
  Man with a: 6 HEFNER
  Mitchell: 4 TARA

Mantel
  piece: 3 URN 4 VASE

Mantilla: 5 SCARF

Mantle
  number: 5 SEVEN
  teammate: 5 MARIS

Mantra
  Antidrug: 9 JUSTSAYNO
  sounds: 3 **OMS**

Manual
  Kind of: 5 USERS
  Not: 5 STICK
  reader: 4 USER
  transmission: 5 STICK

Manufacture: 4 MAKE

Manufacturer: 5 MAKER
  bane: 6 RECALL
  Dish: 3 RCA
  Egg: 3 HEN
  offer: 6 REBATE

Manuscript
  book: 5 CODEX
  copyist: 6 SCRIBE
  Correct a: 4 EDIT
  encl.: 4 SASE
  Fix, as a: 6 RETYPE
  marking: 4 **STET**
  Pertaining to a: 7 TEXTUAL
  Remove from a: 4 DELE
  sheet: 5 FOLIO

Manuscripts
  Unsolicited: 5 SLUSH

Manute
  of basketball: 3 BOL

"Man Who Fell to Earth, The"
  director: 4 ROEG

"Man Who Knew Too Much, The"
  actress: 8 EDNABEST

... ___ man who wasn't there:
      5 IMETA

"Man Wasn't There, The"
  director: 4 COEN

"Man Without ___, The" (1993
      film): 5 AFACE

"Man Without a Country, The":
      5 NOLAN

... ___ man with seven wives:
      5 IMETA

Manx: 3 CAT
  feature: 6 NOTAIL
  lack: 4 TAIL
  of the house: 3 PET
  relative: 4 ERSE
  thanks: 4 PURR

Many: 4 ALOT 6 ALOTOF
      LOTSOF
  As ~ as: 4 UPTO
  (Greek): 6 POLLOI
  Is for: 3 ARE
  Not: 3 FEW 4 AFEW
  Not as: 5 FEWER

Many-___: 4 HUED

"___ many and many a year ...":
      Poe: 5 ITWAS

___ many cooks ...: 3 TOO

Many-headed
  monster: 5 HYDRA

Many moons ___: 3 AGO

___ many words: 4 **INSO**

Mao
  colleague: 4 CHOU
  follower: 3 TSE
  Like the Book of: 3 RED
  opponent: 6 CHIANG
  successor: 4 DENG

Map
  abbr.: 3 AVE ISL LAT **RTE**
  abbrs.: 3 STS
  collection: 5 ATLAS
  Corner: 5 INSET
  dot: 4 ISLE TOWN 5 ISLET
  Family: 4 TREE
  feature: 5 INSET SCALE
  Former ~ abbr: 4 USSR
  In need of a: 4 LOST
  It's right on the: 4 EAST
  Land: 4 PLAT

line: 4 ROAD
lines (abbr.): 3 RDS STS
Modern ~ subject: 6 GENOME
out: 4 PLAN
overlay: 4 GRID
Surveyor: 4 PLAT
Treasure ~ distance: 4 PACE
Up, on a: 5 NORTH
Weather ~ line: 6 **ISOBAR**
within a map: 5 **INSET**
WWII ~ (abbr.): 3 ETO

Maple
fluid: 3 SAP
genus: 4 **ACER**
Like a ~ leaf: 5 EROSE
product: 5 SYRUP

Maple Leaf
org.: 3 NHL

"Maple Leaf ___": 3 RAG

Maples
Actress: 5 MARLA

MapQuest
request (abbr.): 3 RTE

Maps
Big name in: 4 RAND
Book of: 5 ATLAS
Org. with: 3 AAA

Mar: 4 DENT
Site in el: 4 ISLA

Mar.
follower: 3 APR
honoree: 5 STPAT

Maracaibo: 4 LAGO

Maradona
of soccer: 5 DIEGO

Marais ___ Cygnes: 3 DES

Marañón
Where the ~ flows: 4 PERU

Marathon: 4 RACE 5 EVENT
data: 5 TIMES
Do a: 3 RUN
mementos: 7 TSHIRTS
Prep for a ~, with "up":
    4 CARB
unit: 4 MILE

Marathoner
gorge: 5 CARBS
need: 7 STAMINA
woe: 4 ACHE

"Marat/Sade"
Patrick of: 5 MAGEE
playwright Peter: 5 WEISS

Maravich
nickname: 10 PISTOLPETE

Marble
Cut of: 4 SLAB
Glass: 5 AGATE
Italian ~ city: 5 MASSA
Like: 6 VEINED
Metal: 7 STEELIE
Noted Italian: 5 PIETA
Playing: 3 TAW 5 **AGATE**
    AGGIE IMMIE 7 CATSEYE
    STEELIE
Shooting: 3 **TAW** 5 AGATE

Marbled
bread: 3 RYE
Fully: 4 SANE
stone: 5 AGATE

Marbles
game: 4 MIBS
Having all one's: 4 SANE
~, so to speak: 6 SANITY

___ Marbles: 5 ELGIN

Marc
Love of: 4 CLEO
of distinction: 6 ANTONY
Painter: 7 CHAGALL

Marc Antony
love: 4 AMOR
request: 4 EARS
Wife of: 7 OCTAVIA
    9 CLEOPATRA

Marceau
character: 3 BIP
Emulate: 4 MIME
Mime: 6 MARCEL

Marcel
Mime: 7 MARCEAU
Mother, to: 4 MERE
Novelist: 6 PROUST

Marcellus II
Pope after: 6 PAULIV

March: 5 TROOP
1965 ~ city: 5 SELMA
event: 6 EASTER PARADE
follower: 4 HARE 5 APRIL
gp., once: 3 SDS

honoree: 5 **STPAT** 9 STPATRICK
Host: 3 HAL
It came down in ~ 2001: 3 MIR
lead-in (abbr.): 3 FEB
marchers: 5 IRISH
Military day's: 5 ETAPE
name: 5 SOUSA
sound: 3 HUP
March 15: 4 IDES
March 17
 dance: 3 JIG
 honoree, briefly: 5 STPAT
 slogan word: 4 ERIN
March 21
 occurrence: 7 EQUINOX
"March comes in like ___ ...":
  5 ALION
Marchers
 Coll.: 4 **ROTC**
 March: 5 IRISH
 November: 4 VETS
 Sugar bowl: 4 ANTS
Marchetti
 of football: 4 **GINO**
Marching
 band instrument: 4 FIFE TUBA
  5 FLUTE
 order: 4 HALT
 practice: 5 DRILL
 together: 6 INSTEP
 words: 4 HEPS
"Marching Along"
 autobiographer: 5 SOUSA
"March King, The": 5 SOUSA
"March Madness"
 org.: 4 NCAA
March of ___: 5 DIMES
Marciano
 birth name: 5 ROCCO
Marcie
 Peppermint Patty, to: 3 SIR
Marco
 Traveler: 4 POLO
Marcos
 Mrs.: 6 **IMELDA**
 successor: 6 AQUINO
Marcus
 MGM founder: 4 **LOEW**
 Partner of: 6 NEIMAN

Marcus, Jerry
 comic strip: 5 TRUDY
"Marcus Welby, M.D."
 actress Verdugo: 5 ELENA
 network: 3 ABC
Mardi ___: 4 **GRAS**
Mardi Gras
 accessory: 4 MASK
 follower: 4 LENT
 ~ VIP: 3 REX
Mare
 Knight: 5 STEED
 Like the gray: 3 OLD
 meal: 4 OATS
 Mottled: 5 PINTO
 offspring: 4 FOAL
 on the moon: 3 SEA
Mare, Walter ___
 Poet: 4 DELA
Mare's-nest: 4 MESS
Margaret
 Anthropologist: 4 MEAD
 Comic: 3 **CHO**
 Comics tormentor of: 6 DENNIS
 hero: 5 RHETT
 nickname: 3 PEG
Margaret Higgins ___: 6 SANGER
Margarine: 4 **OLEO**
Margarita: 4 ISLA
 fruit: 4 LIME
 need: 4 SALT
Margery
 of rhyme: 3 DAW
Margin: 3 RIM 4 EDGE
 Large: 4 MILE
 mark: 4 STET
 Narrow: 4 HAIR INCH NOSE
  7 EYELASH WHISKER
 Suffix with: 4 ALIA
 Victory: 6 LENGTH
Marginal: 10 BORDERLINE
 jotting: 8 NOTATION
 mark: 4 STET
Marginalia
 Bit of: 4 STET
Margins
 Like some: 4 SLIM
Margot
 role: 4 LOIS

Margrethe
Queen ~ subjects: 5 DANES
Maria
Soprano: 6 CALLAS
"Maria ___" (old song): 5 **ELENA**
___ Maria (liqueur): 3 TIA
"___ Maria": 3 **AVE**
Mariachi
wrap: 6 SERAPE
Mariah
Former label of: 3 EMI
Singer: 5 CAREY
Marian: 4 MAID
Marianas
Largest of the: 4 GUAM
One of the: 6 SAIPAN
Marianne
Poet: 5 MOORE
Marie
(abbr.): 3 STE
Donny or: 6 OSMOND
~, to Donny: 3 SIS
___ Marie
Singer: 5 **TEENA**
Marie Claire
rival: 4 ELLE
Marienbad: 3 SPA
Marigold: 6 ANNUAL
Marijuana
source: 4 HEMP
Marilu
Actress: 6 HENNER
role: 6 ELAINE
Marilyn
birth name: 5 NORMA
Like: 4 SEXY
Mezzo-soprano: 5 HORNE
Marin
Comic: 6 CHEECH
Marin, Cheech
film setting: 6 EASTLA
Marina
feature: 4 PIER
sight: 5 BOATS YACHT
Marina del ___ : 3 REY
Marinara: 5 SAUCE
alternative: 5 PESTO
ingredient: 6 TOMATO
Marinate: 4 SOAK

Marine: 3 SEA 8 DEVILDOG
bioluminescence: 7 SEAFIRE
eagle: 3 ERN 4 ERNE
food fish: 7 SEABASS
mammal: 7 SEALION
meal: 4 MESS
menace: 4 ORCA
plant: 4 ALGA
rock-clinger: 7 ABALONE
shade: 4 AQUA
snail: 5 WHELK
TV ~ Gomer: 4 PYLE
Marine ___ : 5 CORPS
Mariner: 3 TAR 6 SEAMAN
Ancient: 4 NOAH
call: 4 AHOY
Genesis: 4 NOAH
"Mayday!": 3 SOS
measure: 7 SEAMILE
menace: 3 FOG
patron: 6 STELMO
~ Ericson: 4 LEIF
~ Melville: 4 AHAB
"Marines' Hymn, The"
port: 7 TRIPOLI
Marino
Quarterback: 3 DAN
___ Marino: 3 SAN
Mario
Author: 4 PUZO
Former NY governor: 5 CUOMO
Linguist: 3 PEI
of basketball: 4 ELIE
Tenor: 5 LANZA
Mario Brothers
One of the: 5 LUIGI
Marion County, Florida
Seat of: 5 OCALA
Marionette
maker Tony: 4 SARG
surname: 5 DOODY
Mariposa
relative: 4 SEGO
Maris
~, to pals: 3 ROG
Marisa
Actress: 5 **TOMEI**
Marital
skirmish: 4 SPAT

Maritime
  Clandestine ~ org.: **3** ONI
  One of the ~ Provinces (abbr.):
    3 PEI
  trio member: **4** NINA
Marjoram: 4 HERB
  Wild: **7** OREGANO
Marjorie
  of rhyme: **3** DAW
Mark: 5 GRADE **6** DENOTE
    7 APOSTLE
  alternative: **4** EURO
  Bad: **7** DEMERIT
  Beauty: **3** TEN
  below C in French: **7** CEDILLA
  Black: **6** STIGMA
  Check: **4** TICK
  Czech: **5** HACEK
  down, perhaps: **5** RETAG
  Easy: **3 SAP 5** CHUMP PATSY
    6 PIGEON **7** LIVEONE
  Editor: **4** DELE **STET**
  Excellent: **5** APLUS
  for life: **4** SCAR
  German: **6** UMLAUT
  Golfer: **6** OMEARA
  High ~ with low effort: **5** EASYA
  Insertion: **5 CARET**
  Kind of: **4** SKID
  King ~ queen: **6** ISOLDE
  Leave a ~ on: **4** SCAR
  Leave one's: **7** IMPRESS
  Low: **3** DEE
  Made one's: **3** XED
  Make one's: **4** SIGN
  Mediocre: **3 CEE**
  Miss the: **3 ERR**
  Musical: **4** REST
  Official: **5** STAMP
  Off the: **4** WIDE **6** AFIELD
    ERRANT
  On the: **3** APT **4** TRUE
  or Dorothy: **6** HAMILL
  permanently: **4** ETCH
  Proofreader: **4** DELE **STET**
  Punctuation: **5** COMMA
  Spanish: **5** TILDE
  Squiggly: **5** TILDE
  Swimmer: **5** SPITZ

  Tally: **5** NOTCH
  the beginning of: **7** USHERIN
  the boundaries of: **7** DELIMIT
  Wide of the: **3** OFF **6** ERRANT
  with blotches: **6** MOTTLE
Markdown: 4 SALE
Marked
  a ballot: **3** XED
  down: **6 ONSALE**
  Not ~ up: **6** ATCOST
Marker: 3 IOU 4 CHIT DEBT
    5 STELE
  Air-race: **5** PYLON
  Channel: **4** BUOY
  Commemorative: **5** STELE
  Cribbage: **3** PEG
  Desktop: **4** ICON
  Gambling: **4** CHIT
  Grave: **5** STONE
  Highway: **8** MILEPOST
  Traffic: **4** CONE
Markers
  Has ~ out: **4** OWES
  Spot: **4** EXES
Market: 4 SELL
  activity: **7** TRADING
  aid: **4** CART
  Ancient Greek: **5** AGORA
  Ending for: **3** EER
  figure: **6** SELLER
  Fish ~ feature: **4** ODOR
  Flea ~ find: **5** CURIO
  indicator: **3** DOW
  Kind of: **4** BULL FLEA
    7 OPENAIR
  opportunist, briefly: **3** ARB
  oversupply: **4** GLUT
  price: **5** VALUE
  Put on the: **4** SELL
  section: **4** DELI
  town: **5** BOURG
  unit: **5** SHARE
Marketing
  Internet: **5** ETAIL
  Intro to: **4** TELE
  lures: **7** REBATES
  ploy: **4** TEST **5** TIEIN
Marketplace: 6 BAZAAR RIALTO
  Ancient Greek: **5 AGORA**

Online: 4 EBAY
Markets
Bull: 3 UPS
Markey
Silents actress: 4 ENID
Marking
Crate ~, often: 7 STENCIL
Manuscript: 4 STET
Martian: 5 CANAL
Maze: 5 ENTER
Meat: 4 USDA
Music: 4 SLUR
Shoebox: 3 EEE
Markova
Ballerina: 6 ALICIA
Marks
Bad: 4 ACNE
They take ~ off: 7 ERASERS
Marksman: 5 AIMER 7 DEADEYE
org.: 3 NRA
weapon: 5 RIFLE
Marla
predecessor: 5 IVANA
Marlee
Actress: 6 MATLIN
"___ Marlene": 4 LILI
Marley, Bob: 5 RASTA
genre: 6 REGGAE
Marlin: 4 NLER
Marlon
costar: 3 EVA
He directed: 4 ELIA
role: 4 VITO
Marmalade
ingredient: 4 RIND
Marner: 5 MISER
Fictional: 5 **SILAS**
"___ Marner": 5 **SILAS**
Maroon: 6 ENISLE STRAND
home: 4 ISLE
"Mârouf"
baritone: 3 ALI
Marquand
sleuth: 4 MOTO 6 MRMOTO
Marquee
filler: 4 NEON
name: 4 STAR
time: 4 NITE
word: 4 NITE 6 TONITE

Marquette
Title for: 4 PERE
Marquis
Rank above: 4 DUKE
Rank below: 4 EARL
Marquis ___: 6 DESADE
Marquis de ___: 4 **SADE**
Marrero
of baseball: 3 ELI
Marriage: 4 RITE 5 UNION
acquisition: 5 INLAW
Invalidate, as a: 5 ANNUL
Ready for: 6 NUBILE
requirement: 3 TWO
Unite in: 3 WED
vows: 4 IDOS
Marriageable: 6 NUBILE
"Marriage of ___, The": 6 FIGARO
Married: 3 ONE
mujer: 6 SENORA
"___ Married an Axe Murderer":
3 SOI
"Married ... With Children"
actor Ed: 6 ONEILL
actress Katey: 5 SAGAL
Marriott
rival: 5 HYATT 6 RAMADA
Marrow, Tracy
Rapper: 4 ICET
Marry: 3 WED
in haste: 5 ELOPE
Marryin' Sam
creator: 4 CAPP 6 ALCAPP
Mars: 3 GOD ORB 4 DEUS 5 DEITY
6 WARGOD 9 REDPLANET
Counterpart of: 4 ARES
Man from: 5 ALIEN
Moon of: 6 DEIMOS
Phobos, to: 4 MOON
prefix: 4 AREO
Marsalis
Jazz pianist: 5 ELLIS
Marseille
Info: French cue
Mail, in: 5 POSTE
Mine, in: 4 AMOI
Mrs., in: 3 MME
They, in: 3 ILS
View from: 3 MER

Marsh: 3 FEN
  Author: **5** NGAIO
  bird: **4** RAIL SORA **5** CRAKE
    EGRET HERON SNIPE
  critter: **4** CROC
  duck: **4** TEAL
  gas: **7** METHANE
  Like ~ plants: **5** REEDY
  Louisiana: **5** BAYOU
  material: **4** PEAT
  plant: **4** REED **5 SEDGE**
    7 CATTAIL
  wader: **5** EGRET HERON
Marshal: 5 ARRAY
  at Waterloo: **3 NEY**
  Field: **3** REF
  of Yugoslavia: **4** TITO
Marshaled: 3 LED
Marshall
  Director: **5** PENNY
Marshall ___: 4 PLAN
Marshall Islands: 6 ATOLLS
Marshland: 3 FEN
Marshmallow
  Chocolate ~ snack: **5** SMORE
  Drink with a: **5** COCOA
  sandwich: **7** MOONPIE
Marshy
  area: **3** FEN
  ground: **6** MORASS
  inlet: **5** BAYOU
Marsupial
  American: **7** OPOSSUM
  Australian: **5** KOALA **6** WOMBAT
  Comics: **4** POGO
  Milne: **3 ROO**
Mart
  start: **4** EURO
Martes: 3 DIA
Martha
  Comedienne: **4 RAYE**
  successor: **7** ABIGAIL
Martial ___: 4 ARTS
Martial art: 4 JUDO **6** KARATE
  TAICHI
  Japanese: **6** AIKIDO
Martial arts
  degree: **3** DAN
  expert: **5** NINJA

  master: **6** SENSEI
  school: **4** DOJO
"Martial Law"
  actor Hall: **7** ARSENIO
Martian: 5 ALIEN
  feature: **6** ICECAP
  marking: **5** CANAL
  rover: **3** UFO
Martians: 3 ETS
Martin
  Author: **4** AMIS
  Comic: **5** STEVE
  Director: **4** RITT
  of Broadway: **4** MARY
  Partner of: **5** ROWAN
  TV chef: **3** YAN
"Martin"
  actress Campbell: **5** TISHA
"Martin ___": 4 EDEN
___ Martin
  (auto): **5** ASTON
  (cognac): **4** REMY
Martin, Dean
  Home of: **4** OHIO
  subject: **5** AMORE
Martin, Mary
  1966 ~ musical: **6** IDOIDO
Martin, Ricky: 4 IDOL
  Like ~ "vida": **4** LOCA
Martin, Steve
  movie: **7** ALLOFME
  song: **7** KINGTUT
  ~, at the 2001 Oscars: **5** EMCEE
Martin, ___ Sue
  Actress: **6** PAMELA
Martina
  of tennis: **6** HINGIS
  rival: **4** HANA **6** STEFFI
Martinelli
  Actress: **4** ELSA
Martinez
  of baseball: **4 TINO**
  Pitcher: **5 PEDRO**
Martinez, Pedro: 3 MET
  stat: **3** ERA
Martini
  garnish: **5 OLIVE**
  ingredient: **3** GIN
  Like a James Bond: **6** SHAKEN

Partner of: 5 **ROSSI**
Ruin a James Bond: 4 STIR
Martinique: 3 **ILE**
  mountain: 5 PELEE
Martinis
  Like some: 3 DRY
Marty
  role: 4 IGOR
"Marty"
  Marty's friend in: 5 ANGIE
Marvel Comics
  founder Lee: 4 STAN
  superhero: 4 THOR
  superheroes: 4 **XMEN**
Marveled
  aloud: 5 OOHED
Marvin
  Actor: 3 LEE
  Journalist: 4 KALB
  Singer: 4 **GAYE**
Marvy: 3 FAB
Marx
  A ~ brother: 5 CHICO GUMMO
    HARPO ZEPPO 7 GROUCHO
  article: 3 DAS 4 EINE
  collaborator: 6 ENGELS
  forte: 3 WIT 8 ONELINER
  Silent: 5 HARPO
  Socialist: 4 KARL
  with a horn: 5 HARPO
Marx, Groucho
  Prop for: 5 CIGAR
Marx Brothers
  Like the: 4 ZANY 5 ANTIC
    6 MADCAP
  mom: 6 MINNIE
Mary
  Actress: 3 URE 5 ASTOR
  and John Jacob: 6 ASTORS
  Fashion designer: 5 QUANT
  Follower of: 4 LAMB
  had a little one: 4 LAMB
  of Peter, Paul, and Mary:
    7 TRAVERS
  Painter: 7 CASSATT
  TV boss of: 3 LOU
Mary ___ (cosmetics): 3 KAY
Mary-Kate: 4 TWIN
  Actress: 5 OLSEN

Mary Kay
  rival: 4 **AVON** 5 ESTEE
Maryland
  athlete: 4 **TERP** 8 TERRAPIN
  battle site: 8 ANTIETAM
  pro: 6 ORIOLE
  state bird: 6 ORIOLE
"Mary ___ Little Lamb": 4 HADA
Mary Lou
  Gymnast: 6 RETTON
"Mary, Mary, Quite Contrary"
  prop: 11 SILVERBELLS
Mary McLeod ___
  Educator: 7 BETHUNE
"Mary Poppins"
  chimney sweep: 4 BERT
Mary Tyler ___ : 5 MOORE
"Mary Tyler Moore Show, The"
  costar: 7 EDASNER
  spin-off: 5 RHODA
  unseen character: 4 LARS
Mas
  mates: 3 PAS
Masc.
  Neither ~ nor fem.: 4 **NEUT**
  Not: 3 FEM
Mascara
  First name in: 5 **ESTEE**
  target: 4 **LASH** 7 EYELASH
Mascot
  MGM: 4 LION
  Navy: 4 GOAT
  Qantas: 5 KOALA
Masculine
  side: 4 YANG
Maserati
  Carmaker: 7 **ERNESTO**
"M*A*S*H"
  actor Jamie: 4 FARR
  actress Loretta: 4 SWIT
  cops: 3 MPS
  extra: 5 MEDIC NURSE
  Pierce portrayer on: 4 ALDA
  procedure: 6 TRIAGE
  role: 5 RADAR
    13 HAWKEYEPIERCE
    15 CORPORALKLINGER
  setting: 5 KOREA
  soda: 4 NEHI

staffers: 3 DRS 4 DOCS
Star of: 8 ASTERISK
vehicle: 4 JEEP
Winchester rank on: 3 MAJ
Mashburn
of basketball: 5 JAMAL
Mashed
dish: 4 YAMS
Masher
Response to a: 4 SLAP
Mashie: 4 IRON
Mask
feature: 7 EYEHOLE
Kind of: 3 SKI
wearer: 3 UMP 6 GOALIE
"Mask"
actor Eric: 6 STOLTZ
actor Stoltz: 4 ERIC
star: 4 CHER
Masked
critter: 4 **COON**
swordsman: 5 **ZORRO**
Masks
Play with: 3 NOH
Sport with: 4 EPEE
Masochistic
beginning: 4 SADO
Mason
(abbr.): 4 ATTY
Actress: 6 MARSHA
assistant: 6 STREET
burden: 3 HOD
field: 3 LAW
job: 4 CASE
portrayer: 4 BURR
tool: 6 TROWEL
wedge: 4 SHIM
Mason, James
1954 ~ role: 4 NEMO
Masonic
doorkeeper: 5 TILER
Masqat
land: 4 OMAN
___ masque: 3 BAL
Masquerade: 3 ACT
item: 6 DOMINO
Mass: 3 GOB 4 RITE 5 HORDE
        7 REQUIEM
apparel: 4 ALBS

booklet: 4 ORDO
confusion: 5 CHAOS
declaration: 4 AMEN
departure: 6 EXODUS
figure: 6 PRIEST
Icy: 4 **BERG**
Knotlike tissue: 4 NODE
language: 5 LATIN
Large land: 4 ASIA 7 EURASIA
music: 4 HYMN
name: 4 JESU
of hair: 3 MOP 4 SHAG
seating: 4 PEWS
segment: 5 CREDO
transit carrier: 3 BUS
unit: 4 GRAM KILO
Mass.
neighbor: 4 CONN
Sen. from: 3 EMK
setting: 3 EST
summer hours: 3 EDT
Massachusetts
cape: 3 **ANN** COD
motto opener: 4 ENSE
nickname: 8 BAYSTATE
senator John: 5 KERRY
state tree: 3 ELM
Tip of: 6 ONEILL
university: 5 TUFTS
Massage: 3 RUB 5 KNEAD
deeply: 4 ROLF
locale: 3 SPA
Need a: 4 ACHE
Needing a: 4 ACHY 5 TENSE
reaction: 3 AAH
reactions: 3 AHS
target: 5 SCALP 7 TENSION
Massaged
It may be: 3 EGO
Massenet
Composer: 5 JULES
opera: 5 LECID THAIS
Masseur/Masseuse
application: 6 HOTOIL
concern: 9 TENSENESS
employer: 3 SPA
In need of a: 4 SORE
supply: 3 OIL 4 OILS
target: 4 ACHE KNOT

Massey
 Actress: 5 **ILONA**
"Mass in B Minor"
 composer: 4 BACH
Massive: 4 HUGE 5 GREAT
"Mass ___ Minor": 3 INB
Mast: 4 SPAR
 pole: 5 SPRIT
 support: 4 STAY
 Turn, as a: 4 SLUE
Master: 3 ACE PRO 4 GURU
  5 SAHIB
 anew: 7 RELEARN
 Fugue: 4 BACH
 Hindu: 5 SWAMI
 Judo: 6 SENSEI
 Kind of: 3 ZEN
 Madras: 5 SAHIB
 Mahayana: 4 LAMA
 Ring: 3 ALI 7 JEWELER
 Scout: 5 TONTO
 Web: 6 SPIDER
 ~, in Hindi: 5 SAHIB
 ~, in Swahili: 5 BWANA
"Master Builder, The"
 playwright: 5 IBSEN
MasterCard
 alternative: 4 VISA
Masterful: 5 ADEPT
"Master Melvin"
 of baseball: 3 OTT
Masterpiece: 3 GEM
"Masterpiece Theatre"
 airer: 3 PBS
Masters
 1996 ~ winner: 5 FALDO
 1997 ~ winner: 5 WOODS
  10 TIGERWOODS
 1998 ~ winner: 6 OMEARA
 and Jonson: 5 POETS
 city: 7 AUGUSTA
 holder (abbr.): 3 PGA
 Old: 4 OILS
 Three-time ~ winner: 5 FALDO
  SNEAD
 Two-time ~ winner: 4 SEVE
  15 SEVEBALLESTEROS
Master's
 follower: 3 PHD

 ordeal: 5 ORALS
 requirement: 6 THESIS
Masterson
 Friend of: 4 EARP
 weapon: 4 CANE
Masterstroke: 4 COUP
"___ Master's Voice": 3 HIS
Masterwork: 4 OPUS
Masthead
 title: 6 EDITOR
 ~ VIPs: 3 EDS
Mastic: 5 RESIN
Masticate: 4 CHEW
Mat
 Embroidered: 5 DOILY
 Go to the ~, slangily: 6 RASSLE
 Japanese: 6 **TATAMI**
 Lace: 5 DOILY
 material: 5 SISAL
 Sent to the: 3 KOD
Mata ___ : 4 **HARI**
Matador: 6 TORERO
 Cheer for a: 3 **OLE**
 foe: 4 TORO 6 ELTORO
 move: 4 PASE
 trophy: 3 EAR
Mata Hari: 3 SPY
Matalin
 Martin and: 5 MARYS
Matamoros
 mister: 5 SENOR
 Mrs., in: 3 SRA
Match: 3 SEE 4 BOUT PAIR SYNC
  TWIN 5 AGREE EQUAL
 Don't: 5 CLASH
 ender: 3 TKO
 game: 7 OLDMAID
 Missing a: 3 ODD
 part: 3 SET
 play: 5 ARSON
 Put a ~ to: 3 LIT 6 IGNITE
 Shoving: 4 SUMO
 site: 5 ARENA
 Start a tennis: 5 SERVE
 Tournament: 4 SEMI
Matchbox
 item: 6 TOYCAR
Matched
 Equally: 4 EVEN

Evenly: 8 ONETOONE
Half a ~ set: 4 HERS
Matches
Play with: 6 TENNIS
Matching: 4 SAME TWIN
Matchless: 3 ODD
Matchmaker: 5 CUPID
Musical: 5 YENTE
of myth: 4 EROS
Play ~ for: 5 FIXUP
Play ~ to: 5 SETUP
Matchstick
game: 3 **NIM**
Match-up: 7 PAIRING
Mate: 3 PAL
assent: 6 AYESIR
First: 3 EVE 4 ADAM
greeting: 4 AHOY GDAY
Madam: 3 SIR
preceder: 4 SOUL
Quest for a: 5 CHESS
Soul: 4 BODY
___ maté (tealike drink): 5 YERBA
___ Mateo, California: 3 SAN
___ mater: 3 PIA 4 **ALMA** DURA
"___ Mater": 6 STABAT
Material
Genetic: 3 DNA **RNA**
Net: 4 MESH
Pat: 4 OLEO
Raw: 3 ORE
Soft ball: 4 NERF
Star: 3 TIN
Sturdy: 5 DENIM
Materialize: 6 APPEAR
Materiel
Brief: 4 AMMO
Maternally
related: 5 **ENATE**
Math
abbr.: 3 QED
amts.: 4 LCMS
calculation: 4 AREA 5 SLOPE
degree: 3 NTH
Do the: 3 ADD
Empty, in: 4 NULL
groups: 4 SETS
makes up half of it (abbr.): 4 PSAT
Old ~ tool: 9 SLIDERULE

Ordered group in: 6 NTUPLE
ratio: 4 SINE
rings: 4 TORI
Squiggly ~ symbol: 5 TILDE
subj.: 3 **ALG** 4 CALC GEOM TRIG
Mathematical
grouping: 5 COSET
points: 4 LOCI
proof letters: 3 QED
proportion: 5 RATIO
symbol: 7 NUMERAL
Mathematician
Blind: 5 EULER
~ Blaise: 6 PASCAL
~ Charles: 7 BABBAGE
~ George: 5 BOOLE
~ Leonhard: 5 **EULER**
~ Lovelace: 3 ADA
~ Paul: 5 ERDOS
Mathers, Jerry
role: 6 BEAVER
Mathew
Photographer: 5 BRADY
Mathis, Johnny
1959 ~ hit: 5 MISTY
1962 ~ hit: 4 GINA
"Matilda"
Wilson of: 4 MARA
Matinee
hero: 4 IDOL
Matinee ___: 4 IDOL
Mating
game: 5 CHESS
Matisse
Painter: 5 **HENRI**
pieces: 3 ART
Matriculate: 5 ENROL 6 ENROLL
Matrimony
Enter into: 3 WED
"Matrix, The"
Keanu in: 3 **NEO**
Neo in: 5 KEANU
Matson
of football: 5 OLLIE
Matt
Actor: 7 LEBLANC
Former cohost with: 5 KATIE
Internet reporter: 6 DRUDGE
Olympic swimmer: 6 BIONDI

TV host: **5** LAUER
Mattel
  doll: **3** KEN
  game: **3** UNO
Matter: 4 CASE **5** COUNT
  Bit of: **4** ATOM
  Confidential: **6** SECRET
  Court: **3** RES
  Heart of the: **3** NUB **4** CRUX
    MEAT PITH
  In the ~ of: **4** ASTO
  Legal: **3** RES
  Mined-over: **3** ORE
  No ~ what:
    15 COMERAINORSHINE
  of contention: **4** BONE
  Subject: **5** TOPIC
  Will: **6** ESTATE
Matterhorn: 3 ALP
  (abbr.): **3** MTN
"Matter of Fact"
  columnist: **5** ALSOP
Matters: 6 COUNTS
  in dispute: **6** ISSUES
  Mysterious: **6** ARCANA
  PBS: **4** ARTS
Matthau
  Actor: **6** WALTER
Matthew: 7 APOSTLE
  Actor: **5** PERRY **6** MODINE
  Question in: **5** ISITI
  Trio in: **4** MAGI
Mattiace
  Golfer: **3** LEN
Mattingly
  of baseball: **3** DON
Mattress
  Fold-up: **5** FUTON
  maker: **5** SEALY SERTA
  part: **4** COIL
  problem: **3 SAG 4** LUMP
  support: **4** SLAT
  Thin: **5** FUTON
  type: **4** TWIN
Matty
  of baseball: **4 ALOU**
Mature: 3 AGE 4 RIPE **5** ADULT
    RIPEN **7** GROWNUP
    9 COMEOFAGE

For ~ audiences: **6** RATEDR
Matured: 4 GREW **6** GREWUP
Maturing
  agent: **4** AGER
Maturity
  Attain: **5** RIPEN
Matzo
  lack: **5** YEAST
  meal: **5** SEDER
Maude
  portrayer Arthur: **3** BEA
"Maude"
  Maude on: **3** BEA
Maudlin: 5 SAPPY
Maugham, Somerset
  heroine: **5** SADIE
  novel: **13** THERAZORSEDGE
  satire: **11** CAKESANDALE
Maugham, W. ___: 8 SOMERSET
Maui
  dance: **4** HULA
  dish: **3** POI
  flier: **4** NENE
  greeting: **5** ALOHA
  music-maker: **3** UKE
  necklace: **3** LEI
  neighbor: **5** LANAI
Mauna ___: 3 KEA **LOA**
Mauna Loa
  City near: **4** HILO
  flow: **4** LAVA
Maupin
  effort: **4** TALE
Maureen
  Actress: **5** OHARA
  Columnist: **4** DOWD
Maurice
  Actor: **5** EVANS
  Author: **6** SENDAK
  Barry, Robin, and: **5** GIBBS
  Composer: **5** JARRE
  Illustrator: **6** SENDAK
  Nixon Commerce Secretary:
    5 STANS
  Painter: **7** UTRILLO
Mauritania
  Most of: **6** SAHARA
  Neighbor of: **4** MALI
    7 SENEGAL

Mauritius
Extinct bird of: **4** DODO
Mausoleum: 4 TOMB
Ataturk ~ city: **6** ANKARA
Maven: 3 PRO **4** GURU
Media:
15 MARSHALLMCLUHAN
Maverick
One of the ~ brothers: **4** BART
BRET
type: **5** LONER
"Maverick"
Maverick of: **4** BRET
Mavs
The ~ play in it: **3** NBA
Mawkish: 5 SAPPY SOPPY
material: **4** CORN
___ Mawr: **4** BRYN
Max
Artist: **5** WEBER
Author: **5** WEBER
Boxer: **4** BAER
Buddy, Bugs, or: **4** BAER
Dadaist: **5** **ERNST**
Movie scorer: **7** STEINER
Surrealist: **5** ERNST
Max.
Opposite of: **3** MIN
Maxi
Opposite of: **4** MINI
Maxim: 3 SAW **5** ADAGE MOTTO
TENET
Russian writer: **5** GORKI
Maxima
maker: **6** NISSAN
Maximally: 6 ATMOST
Maximilian
Actor: **6** SCHELL
Maximilian I
Realm of ~ (abbr.): **3** HRE
Maxims
Religious: **5** LOGIA
Maximum: 3 NTH **6** UTMOST
Reach a: **4** PEAK
"Maximus Poems, The"
author: **5** OLSON
Maxwell
Hostess: **4** ELSA
Socialite: **4** ELSA

Maxwell House
brand: **5** SANKA
May
April, ~, and June, to Daisy Duck:
6 NIECES
Be that as it: **6** EVENSO
9 ATANYRATE
birthstone: **7** EMERALD
Director: **6** ELAINE
event, for short: **4** INDY
honoree: **3** **MOM** **6** MOTHER
in New Jersey: **4** CAPE
Psychologist: **5** ROLLO
May 8, 1945: 5 VEDAY
May 15: 4 IDES
Maya
Architect: **3** LIN
"Maybe": 6 ILLSEE
"Maybellene"
singer: **5** BERRY
10 CHUCKBERRY
Mayberry
aunt: **3** BEE
Goober or Gomer of: **4** PYLE
kid: **4** **OPIE**
Like: **5** RURAL
Pyle of: **5** GOMER
sheriff: **4** ANDY
tippler: **4** **OTIS**
"Mayberry ___": 3 RFD
Mayday: 3 SOS
"Mayday!": 3 SOS
Mayer, Louis B.
birthplace: **5** MINSK
Mayfair
It borders: **4** SOHO
moms: **6** MATERS
Mayflower
employee: **5** MOVER
pilgrim John: **5** ALDEN
Mayhem: 5 HAVOC
"May I have your attention?":
4 AHEM
"May I help you?": 3 YES
"May I speak?": 4 AHEM
Maynard G. ___: 5 KREBS
"May ___ now?": 3 IGO
Mayo: 3 MES
Garlicky: **5** AIOLI

holder: **3** JAR
Sandwich with: **3** BLT
serving: **4** GLOB
"May ___ of service?": 3 IBE
Mayonnaise
Garlic: **5** **AIOLI**
Mayor
Canadian: **5** REEVE
Chicago: **5** DALEY
Former Cincinnati:
   13 JERRYSPRINGER
Former L.A. ~ Sam: **5** YORTY
Former N.Y.: **6** EDKOCH
   8 ABEBEAME
Former N.Y. ~ Abe: **5** BEAME
Former N.Y. ~ Beame: **3** ABE
Former N.Y. ~ Ed: **4** KOCH
Former N.Y. ~ Giuliani:
   4 RUDY
Former Philly ~ Wilson:
   5 GOODE
L.A. ~ Jim: **4** HAHN
"Mayor"
author: **6** EDKOCH
author Ed: **4** KOCH
Mayo to Mayo: 3 ANO
Maytag
rival: **5** AMANA
Mazar
Actress: **4** DEBI
Mazda
model: **5** **MIATA**
Maze
runner: **3** RAT **6** LABRAT
solution: **4** PATH
word: **5** **ENTER**
"Mazel ___!": 3 TOV
"Mazes and Monsters"
author Jaffe: **4** RONA
Mazuma
Monterrey: **4** PESO
MB
It is measured in: **3** RAM ROM
MBA: 3 DEG
subj.: **4** ECON
McAn
Shoemaker: **4** THOM
McAn, Thom
spec.: **3** EEE

McArdle
of Broadway: **6** ANDREA
role: **5** ANNIE
McBain, Ed
Author Hunter who used the pen
   name: **4** EVAN
McBeal: 6 LAWYER
on TV: **4** ALLY
McCaffrey
Sci-fi author: **4** ANNE
McCain
State of ~ (abbr.): **4** ARIZ
~, once: **3** POW
McCann
Country singer: **4** LILA
McCarey
Director: **3** LEO
McCarthy
aide Roy: **4** COHN
quarry: **3** RED **4** REDS
trunkmate: **5** SNERD
McCarthy, Charlie
Like: **6** WOODEN
McCarthy, Joe
attorney Roy: **4** COHN
McCarthy-era
hearings gp.: **4** HUAC
McCartney, Paul: 4 BRIT
1982 ~ hit with Stevie Wonder:
   13 EBONYANDIVORY
1984 ~ hit: **5** SOBAD
instrument: **4** BASS
title: **3** SIR
McCarver
Sportscaster: **3** TIM
McClanahan
Actress: **3** RUE
McClellan
victory site: **8** ANTIETAM
McClure
Actor: **4** DOUG
McClurg
Actress: **4** **EDIE**
McConaughey, Matthew
1999 ~ film: **4** EDTV
McCormack
Actor: **4** ERIC
McCormick
Inventor: **5** CYRUS

McCorvey, Norma
alias in a famous court case:
3 ROE
McCourt, Frank
book: 3 __TIS__
Mother of: 6 ANGELA
McCowen
Actor: 4 ALEC
McCoy
Country singer: 4 NEAL
Hatfield, to a: 3 FOE 5 ENEMY
Jazz pianist: 5 TYNER
McCoy, Dr.
nickname: 5 BONES
spray: 4 HYPO
___ McCoy, The: 4 REAL
McCoys: 4 CLAN
McCrea
Actor: 4 JOEL
McCullough
Novelist: 7 COLLEEN
McDaniel
Actress: 6 HATTIE
Country singer: 3 MEL
McDonald's
arches: 4 LOGO
clown: 6 RONALD
equipment: 6 FRYERS
founder: 7 RAYKROC
founder Kroc: 3 RAY
founder Ray: 4 KROC
freebie: 6 CATSUP
order: 4 TOGO
symbol: 6 ARCHES
McDonough
Actor: 4 NEAL
McDowall
Actor: 5 RODDY
McEnroe
foe: 4 BORG 5 LENDL
McEntire
Country singer: 4 __REBA__
McEwan
Author: 3 IAN
McFuzz, Gertrude
creator: 5 SEUSS
McGee
Principal ~ portrayer:
8 EVEARDEN

McGraw
Actress: 7 MELINDA
Country singer: 3 TIM
of baseball: 3 TUG
McGregor
Actor: 4 __EWAN__
McGrew
Service's: 3 DAN
McGuire Air Force Base
Fort near: 3 DIX
McGwire, Mark
cap monogram: 3 STL
home run rival: 4 SOSA
speciality: 5 HOMER
stat (abbr.): 3 HRS
stats: 4 RBIS
McHenry: 4 FORT
and others (abbr.): 3 FTS
McIntosh: 5 APPLE
alternative: 7 WINESAP
McKellen
Actor: 3 __IAN__
McKenna
Folk singer: 4 LORI
McKenzie
Series set at ~, Brackman, et al.:
5 LALAW
McKinley
and others (abbr.): 3 MTS
Mount: 6 DENALI
Mrs.: 3 __IDA__
Ohio birthplace of:
5 NILES
McKinney
Olympic skier: 6 TAMARA
McKuen
Poet: 3 ROD
McLachlan
Pop singer: 5 SARAH
McLachlan, Sarah
hit: 4 __ADIA__
McLain
of baseball: 5 DENNY
McLean
Singer: 3 DON
"___ McLean" (Owen Wister
novel): 3 LIN
McLean, Don
song: 11 AMERICANPIE

McLean, VA
Group based in: 3 CIA
McLuhan
study: 5 MEDIA
McMahon
and others: 3 EDS
McMillan
of basketball: 4 NATE
Writer: 5 TERRY
McMuffin
ingredient: 3 EGG
McMurtry
Film based on a ~ novel: 3 HUD
McNally
Partner of: 4 **RAND**
McPherson
Evangelist: 5 **AIMEE**
"McQ"
first name: 3 LON
McQueen
Actor: 4 CHAD 5 STEVE
McQueen, Steve
First movie starring: 7 THEBLOB
McShane
Actor: 3 IAN
"McSorley's Bar"
painter: 5 SLOAN
M.D.: 4 PHYS
ASAP, to an: 4 STAT
Date with an: 4 APPT
Family ~ (plural): 3 GPS
measures: 3 CCS
order: 3 MRI 6 CTSCAN
org.: 3 AMA
speciality: 3 ENT
wall hanging: 3 DEG
workplaces: 3 ERS ORS
Md.
neighbor: 3 DEL
Mdse.: 3 **GDS**
Flawed, as: 3 IRR
Me
It's all about: 6 EGOISM
    7 EGOTISM
To ~, in French: 4 AMOI
~, in French: 3 MOI
~, myself, and I: 3 EGO
"___ me!": 5 WOEIS
"___ me?": 4 ISIT

Mea ___ : 5 CULPA
Mead
base: 5 HONEY
research site: 5 SAMOA
subject: 5 SAMOA
Mead, Margaret
Island studied by: 5 SAMOA
subject: 6 SAMOAN
Meadow: 3 **LEA**
Like a: 6 GRASSY
mother: 3 EWE
mouse: 4 VOLE
sound: 3 BAA MAA
Meadowlands
pace: 4 TROT
team: 4 NETS
Meadowlark
kin: 6 ORIOLE
Meadowsweet: 6 SPIREA
Meager: 4 SLIM 5 **SCANT**
    6 SCANTY SPARSE
Not: 5 AMPLE
Meagerly
maintain, with "out": 3 EKE
Meal: 6 **REPAST**
Army: 4 MESS
Carbo-loading: 5 PASTA
Crusty: 6 POTPIE
Exodus: 5 SEDER
Gave a ~ to: 3 FED
GI: 7 CRATION
Had a home-cooked: 5 ATEIN
Have a: 3 EAT SUP 4 DINE
in a pot: 4 STEW
in a shell: 4 TACO
Kind of: 3 OAT
Light: 5 SALAD
Major: 5 FEAST
Military: 4 MESS
on a stick: 5 KABOB
One-dish: 4 STEW
Passover: 5 **SEDER**
starter: 3 OAT 5 SALAD
When repeated, a kid's: 3 DIN
Meals
Eat between: 4 NOSH 5 SNACK
Mean: 3 LOW 5 CRUEL NASTY
    6 DENOTE INTEND
    ORNERY STINGY

Didn't ~ to tell: 7 LETSLIP
dude: 4 OGRE
It makes men: 3 ANA
mien: 5 SNEER
mood: 4 SNIT
mutt: 3 CUR
What little things: 4 ALOT
"Me and Bobby ___": 5 MCGEE
Meander: 3 GAD 4 ROAM ROVE
    WIND 5 AMBLE STRAY
    6 RAMBLE
Meandering
  curve: 3 ESS
Meanie: 4 **OGRE**
  face: 5 SCOWL
  Fairy tale: 4 OGRE
    10 STEPSISTER
Meaning: 5 SENSE 6 INTENT
  Full of: 4 DEEP
  General: 4 GIST
  Give the ~ of: 6 DEFINE
  Shade of: 6 NUANCE
Meaningless
  talk: 4 JIVE
Meanness
  Symbol of: 11 JUNKYARDDOG
Means: 4 MODE 6 AVENUE
  By ~ of: 3 PER VIA
  justifiers: 4 **ENDS**
  of access: 6 AVENUE
  of approach: 6 ACCESS
  of control: 4 REIN
  of enlightenment: 3 ZEN
  of support: 3 BRA
  Partner of: 4 WAYS
  Without ~ of support: 7 BRALESS
Mean-spirited: 5 NASTY SNIDE
  6 ORNERY
Meantime: 7 INTERIM
Meany
  Fairy tale: 4 OGRE
  Irving's: 4 OWEN
Meara
  Comic: 4 ANNE
  Partner of: 7 STILLER
Measles
  Like: 5 VIRAL
Measly: 4 MERE
  amount: 3 SOU

Measure: 3 ACT 4 METE STEP
  5 GAUGE 6 AMOUNT
  AC: 3 BTU
  Biblical: 5 CUBIT
  Blood: 4 UNIT
  Cordwood: 5 **STERE**
  Current: 6 AMPERE
  Econ.: 3 GNP
  Electrical: 3 AMP OHM 4 VOLT
  Energy: 3 ERG
  Gold: 5 KARAT
  Heavy: 3 TON
  Jeweler: 5 KARAT
  Land: 4 ACRE
  LP: 3 RPM
  Mariner's: 7 SEAMILE
  Memory: 4 BYTE
  metal: 5 ASSAY
  Metric: 3 ARE 4 KILO 5 LITER
  Musical: 3 BAR
  of conductance: 3 MHO
  of purity: 5 KARAT
  on foot: 4 PACE
  (out): 4 METE
  Paper: 4 REAM
  Petrol: 5 LITRE
  Prevention: 5 OUNCE
  Wire: 3 **MIL**
"Measure for Measure"
  heroine: 8 ISABELLA
  villain: 6 ANGELO
Measurement
  Middle: 5 WAIST
  of work: 3 ERG
  Pants: 6 INSEAM
  Wing: 4 SPAN
Measurements
  IV: 3 CCS
  Recipe ~ (abbr.): 4 TSPS
Measurer
  Brainpower: 6 IQTEST
  Current: 7 AMMETER
  RPM: 4 TACH
  Thickness: 7 CALIPER
Measures
  Liq.: 3 PTS QTS
  Mensa: 3 IQS
  Printer's: 3 **EMS** ENS
  Take: 3 ACT

"Measure twice, cut ___":
4 ONCE
Measuring
device: 4 TAPE 5 GAUGE SIZER
instrument: 5 METER
Meat: 4 GIST
and potatoes: 4 FOOD
avoider: 5 VEGAN
Breakfast: 3 HAM 5 BACON
Calf: 4 VEAL
Canned: 4 SPAM
Cutlet: 4 VEAL
Cut of: 4 LOIN 5 ROAST SHANK
Deli: 3 HAM 6 SALAMI
dish: 7 ROULADE
filled treat: 4 TACO
garnish: 5 ASPIC
Gyro: 4 LAMB
Hunk of: 4 SLAB
inspection inits.: 4 USDA
It does ~ to a turn:
    10 ROTISSERIE
Like some: 4 LEAN
locker, for example: 4 AGER
Low-fat: 3 EMU 7 BEEFALO
Lunch: 3 HAM
marking: 4 USDA
pie: 5 PASTY
substitute: 4 TOFU
The other white: 4 PORK
Treat: 4 CORN CURE
Meat-and-potatoes: 5 BASIC
Meathead: 3 OAF
Father-in-law of: 6 ARCHIE
Mother-in-law of: 5 EDITH
player: 6 REINER
Meat-rating
org.: 4 USDA
Mecca
Gambler's: 4 **RENO** 6 CASINO
Indian: 4 AGRA
Journey to: 4 **HADJ** HAJJ
native: 4 ARAB 5 SAUDI
Pilgrimage to: 4 HADJ HAJJ
Pilgrim to: 5 HAJJI 6 MOSLEM
    MUSLIM
Shopping: 4 MALL
Ski: 4 ALPS 5 ASPEN
Surfing: 4 OAHU 7 WAIKIKI

Mechanic
Part of a ~ bill: 5 LABOR
prefix: 4 AERO
service: 4 LUBE
tool: 9 GREASEGUN
Mechanical
learning: 4 ROTE
man: 5 ROBOT
method: 4 ROTE
Slangy prefix meaning: 4 ROBO
Mechanism
Control: 5 SERVO
Defense: 6 DENIAL
Watch: 6 DETENT
Med
school subj.: 4 ANAT
Med.
Bigger than: 3 LRG
care option: 3 **HMO**
country: 3 ISR LEB SYR
course: 4 ANAT
diagnostic tool: 3 EEG
drama sets: 3 ERS
people: 3 DRS RNS
plan: 3 **HMO**
readout: 3 EKG
research funder: 3 NIH
specialty: 3 **ENT** GYN
test: 3 MRI
Medal: 5 HONOR
Fail to: 4 LOSE
giver: 7 HONORER
Mil.: 3 DSC DSO
recipient: 4 HERO
U.K.: 3 OBE
U.S. Army: 3 DSC
Winning: 4 GOLD
worthy behavior: 5 VALOR
Medalist
1984 and 1988 skating ~: 4 WITT
1984 skiing ~: 5 MAHRE
1988 swimming ~ Kristin:
    4 OTTO
Four-time Olympic discus:
    6 OERTER
Gold ~ Lipinski: 4 TARA
Gold ~ skater Michelle: 4 KWAN
Gold ~ skier Hermann: 5 MAIER
Gold ~ skier Phil: 5 MAHRE

Gold ~ skier Tommy: **3** MOE
Three-time skating: **5** HENIE
Two-time 1500-meter gold: **3** COE

Medallion
site: **3** CAB **4** TAXI

"Medallion, The"
star: **4** CHAN

Meddle: 3 PRY **5** SNOOP
(with): **4** MESS

Meddler: 5 SNOOP YENTA

Meddlesome: 4 NOSY **5** NOSEY
sort: **5** YENTA

Medea
rode on it: **4** ARGO

Medevac
destinations: **3** ERS

Medgar
Civil rights leader: **5** EVERS

Media
Alternative ~ magazine: **4** UTNE
attention: **3** INK
exec Roger: **5** AILES
gadfly Huffington: **7** ARIANNA
Govt. ~ watchdog: **3** FCC
law topic: **5** LIBEL
maven:
　　　　15 MARSHALLMCLUHAN
Modern music: **3** CDS
mogul Turner: **3** TED
Noted ~ merger:
　　　　10 TIMEWARNER
Print: **5** PRESS
Toronto ~ inits.: **3** CBS
workers' union: **5** AFTRA

Media ___ : 5 EVENT

Mediate
Golfer: **5** ROCCO

Mediator
Freudian: **3** EGO
skill: **4** TACT

Medic: 3 DOC
prefix: **4** PARA
treatment: **8** FIRSTAID

Medical
advice, often: **4** REST
amount: **4** DOSE
beam: **5** LASER
breakthrough: **4** CURE
British ~ journal: **6** LANCET

care gp.: **3** HMO
disappointment: **7** RELAPSE
facility: **6** CLINIC
Govt. ~ agency: **3** NIH
image: **4** SCAN
picture: **4** XRAY
plan, briefly: **3** HMO
prefix: **5** OSTEO
procedure: **4** TEST
research agcy.: **3** NIH
resident: **6** INTERN
staffer: **6** INTERN
suffix: **3** ESE OMA **4** ITIS OSIS
supply: **5** SERUM
test: **4** SCAN
wiper: **4** SWAB

"Medical Center"
star: **7** EVERETT
　　　　11 CHADEVERETT

Medicare
org.: **3** SSA

Medicate: 4 DOSE

Medication
for anxiety: **6** VALIUM
How most ~ is taken:
　　　　6 ORALLY
Sleep: **6** OPIATE

Medicinal
amount: **4** DOSE **6** DOSAGE
amt.: **3** TSP
fluids: **4** SERA
form: **4** PILL
herb: **5** SENNA
juice: **4** ALOE
plant: **4** ALOE HERB **5** **SENNA**
shrub: **5** SENNA **6** CASSIA
syrup: **6** IPECAC

Medicine
Amount of: **4** DOSE
bottle: **4** VIAL
cabinet item: **4** QTIP
holder: **7** CAPSULE
Like some: **4** ORAL
man: **6** HEALER SHAMAN
show product: **6** ELIXIR
Soothing: **7** NERVINE
yielding legume: **5** SENNA
~ Metchnikoff: **4** ELIE

Medico: 3 DOC

Medieval
catapult: 6 ONAGER
chest: 4 ARCA
contest: 4 TILT
defense: 4 MOAT
guild: 5 HANSA HANSE
helmet: 5 ARMET
Hero of ~ romances: 6 ROLAND
laborer: 4 ESNE SERF
weapon: 6 POLEAX 7 POLEAXE
8 CROSSBOW
Medina
resident: 4 ARAB
Mediocre: 4 BLAH **SOSO**
mark: 3 **CEE**
writer: 4 HACK
Medit.
country: 3 **ISR**
Meditate: 4 MUSE
Meditation
sounds: 3 OMS
system: 3 ZEN 4 YOGA
Meditative
discipline: 3 ZEN
sect: 3 ZEN
sounds: 3 OMS
Meditator: 4 YOGI
Mediterranean
Arm of the: 6 AEGEAN
8 ADRIATIC
Canal to the: 4 SUEZ
capital: 5 TUNIS 7 NICOSIA
feeder: 4 NILE 5 RHONE
fruit: 3 FIG
island: 5 MALTA 7 MINORCA
Largest ~ island: 6 SICILY
port: 4 GAZA ORAN
resort: 4 RIVIERA
Spanish river to the: 4 EBRO
tourist destination: 5 IBIZA
Méditerranée: 3 MER
Medium: 4 SEER SIZE SOSO
7 PSYCHIC
board: 5 OUIJA
distance run: 4 TENK
grade: 3 CEE
meeting: 6 SEANCE
range missile: 4 THOR
setting: 6 ORACLE

sized sofa: 6 SETTEE
skill: 3 ESP
Medley: 4 OLIO
Médoc: 3 RED 4 WINE
**"___ me down to rest me" (old
        prayer start):** 4 ILAY
Medulla
place: 9 BRAINSTEM
Medusa
Snake, to: 5 TRESS
transformer: 6 ATHENA
Meek
Comics partner of: 3 EEK
one: 4 LAMB
Meeny
preceder: 4 EENY
Meerschaum: 4 PIPE
part: 4 STEM
Meese
and others: 3 EDS
Meet: 3 APT FIT SIT 6 RISETO
component: 4 RACE 5 EVENT
head-on: 4 FACE
in Las Vegas: 3 SEE
in poker: 3 SEE
Kind of: 4 SWAP
One you might not want to:
        5 MAKER
people: 6 RACERS
They ~ at a center: 5 RADII
Tries not to: 6 AVOIDS
Where roads ~ (abbr.): 3 JCT
with: 3 SEE
~, as expectations: 6 RISETO
Meeting: 7 SESSION
1945 ~ site: 5 YALTA
Ancient ~ place: 4 STOA
        5 AGORA
Big ~ (abbr.): 4 CONF
Cong.: 4 SESS
Hold a: 3 SIT
Kind of: 3 PTA 6 SUMMIT
leader: 5 CHAIR
Lovers': 5 TRYST
Medium: 6 SEANCE
minimum: 6 QUORUM
of the minds: 3 ESP
outline: 6 AGENDA
plan: 6 AGENDA

Propose at a: 4 MOVE
Public: 5 FORUM
Secret: 5 TRYST
Short: 4 SESS
Speak at a: 12 TAKETHEFLOOR
Meetings
Formal: 8 SYMPOSIA
Pregame: 10 PEPRALLIES
Town: 4 FORA
"Meet Joe Black"
actor: 4 PITT
"Meet John Doe"
director: 5 CAPRA
"Meet Me ___ Louis": 4 INST
"Meet the Parents"
actress Polo: 4 TERI
"Meet the Press"
host Russert: 3 TIM
"Mefistofele": 5 BASSO
composer: 5 BOITO
role: 5 ELENA
Meg
Actress: 4 RYAN 5 TILLY
Sibling of: 3 AMY 4 BETH
Mega
follower: 4 BYTE
Megacorporation: 5 GIANT
Megalomaniac: 6 MADMAN
Megaphone
Crooner with a: 6 VALLEE
Shaped like a: 5 CONIC
Mehitabel
Pal of: 5 ARCHY
Mehta
Conductor: 5 ZUBIN
Meir: 7 ISRAELI
Foreign minister under: 4 EBAN
of Israel: 5 GOLDA
successor: 5 RABIN
Mei Xiang: 5 PANDA
Mekong
nation: 4 LAOS
native: 3 LAO 7 LAOTIAN
Mel
Giant: 3 OTT
of baseball: 3 OTT
of many voices: 5 BLANC
Singer: 5 TORME
Melancholy: 3 SAD 6 SOMBER

poem: 5 ELEGY
"___ Melancholy" (Keats work):
5 ODEON
Mélange: 4 **OLIO** 8 MIXEDBAG
Melba
of peaches and toast: 6 NELLIE
___ Melba: 5 PEACH
Melba, Nellie
title: 4 DAME
Meld
40-point ~: 8 PINOCHLE
Melee
memento: 4 SCAR
Mello ___ (Coca-Cola brand):
5 YELLO
Mellon: 6 ANDREW
Mellow: 3 AGE
More: 5 RIPER
Mellower
Got: 4 AGED
Melmac
alien: 3 ALF
Melodic: 5 TONAL 6 ARIOSE
ARIOSO
passage: 6 ARIOSO
pieces: 6 ARIOSI
syllable: 3 TRA
~ Mel: 5 TORME
___ Melodies (old cartoons):
6 MERRIE
Melodious: 6 ARIOSE ARIOSO
singer: 4 WREN
~ Horne: 4 LENA
Melodrama
Exaggerated:
15 BLOODANDTHUNDER
Musical: 5 OPERA
Melodramatic: 5 SOAPY SUDSY
cry: 4 ALAS
Get: 5 EMOTE
Melody: 3 AIR 4 TUNE
Airy: 4 LILT
Diva's: 4 ARIA
Hindu: 4 RAGA
Light: 4 LILT 6 ARIOSO
Little: 7 ARIETTA
Recurring: 5 MOTIF THEMA
Melon
Kind of: 6 CASABA

8 HONEYDEW
Winter: 6 CASABA
Melonlike
fruit: 5 PAPAW 6 PAPAYA
Melpomene
Sister of: 5 ERATO
"Melrose Place"
actor Andrew: 4 SHUE
actor Rob: 5 ESTES
role: 6 AMANDA
Mel's: 5 DINER
Mel's Diner
Waitress at: 3 FLO 4 VERA
5 ALICE
Melt: 4 THAW 5 DEICE
down: 6 RENDER
ingredient: 4 TUNA
It can ~ in your mouth: 4 OLEO
together: 4 FUSE
Meltdown
site: 4 CORE
victim of myth: 6 ICARUS
Melted
glace: 3 EAU
Melter
Ice: 4 SALT
Mel-Tones
leader: 5 TORME
Melville
Author: 6 HERMAN
captain: 4 AHAB
hero: 4 BUDD 9 BILLYBUDD
novel: 4 **OMOO** 5 TYPEE
Melvin
Attorney: 5 BELLI
Mem.
Bar: 3 ATT
Family: 3 REL
House: 3 REP
Member
Become a: 4 JOIN 5 ENROL
Influential: 5 ELDER
Membership
charge: 3 FEE
Exchange: 4 SEAT
fees: 4 DUES
Take out: 5 ENROL
Membrane
Eye: 6 SCLERA

Pass through a: 6 OSMOSE
Membranes
Of lung: 7 PLEURAL
Memento: 5 RELIC TOKEN
8 KEEPSAKE
Battle: 4 SCAR
Historical: 5 RELIC
Scuffle: 6 FATLIP
Memnon
Mother of: 3 EOS
Memo: 4 **NOTE**
abbr.: 4 **ATTN**
Debt: 3 IOU
directive: 4 ASAP
heading: 4 ATTN
opener: 4 **INRE** 5 ASPER
phrase: 4 ASTO **INRE**
Memorable: 6 OFNOTE
9 REDLETTER
time: 3 **ERA** 5 EPOCH
Memorial
column: 4 OBIT
marker: 5 STELE
Stone: 5 CAIRN
Memorial Day
event: 4 INDY
setting: 3 MAY
solo: 4 TAPS
Memories
Place for: 4 LANE
"Memories Are Made of ___":
4 THIS
Memorization: 4 ROTE
Memorize: 5 LEARN
Memorized
Have: 4 KNOW
Memory: 6 RECALL
failure: 5 LAPSE
Having a good: 9 RETENTIVE
Loss of: 7 AMNESIA
Nudge the: 3 JOG
Remove from: 5 ERASE
Speak from: 6 RECITE
trace: 6 ENGRAM
unit: 3 MEG 4 BYTE
"Memory"
musical: 4 CATS
Memphis
home (abbr.): 4 TENN

locale: 5 EGYPT
middle name: 4 ARON
Opera that opens in: 4 AIDA
Sight in: 4 NILE
street: 5 BEALE

Memsahib
nurse: 4 AMAH

"Me, myself ___": 4 ANDI

"Me, Myself & ___" (Jim Carrey flick): 5 IRENE

Men: 3 HES 4 SIRS 5 MALES
behaving badly: 4 CADS
Con: 5 ANTIS
Family: 3 PAS 4 DADS
For ~ only: 4 **STAG**
Holy ~ (abbr.): 3 STS
It makes ~ mean: 3 ANA
Little green: 3 ETS 6 ALIENS
Main: 4 TARS
of La Mancha: 6 SENORS
Org. for young: 3 BSA
or women: 6 PLURAL
She turned ~ into swine: 5 CIRCE
Wise: 4 MAGI 5 SAGES
Young: 4 LADS

___ Men ("Who Let the Dogs Out" band): 4 BAHA

"___ Men" ("Kiss Me, Kate" tune): 5 IHATE

Menace: 6 THREAT
African: 3 ASP 6 TSETSE
Marine: 4 ORCA
Mariner: 3 FOG
Meteorological: 6 ELNINO
Toothy: 4 CROC
WWII: 5 UBOAT

Menachem
co-Nobelist of: 5 **ANWAR**

Menacing: 7 OMINOUS
look: 5 GLARE

Menagerie: 3 ZOO

Mend: 3 FIX 4 DARN HEAL TAPE
a dress: 5 REHEM
again: 5 RESEW 6 REHEAL
Be on the: 4 HEAL

Mendel
Botanist: 6 GREGOR
subject: 3 PEA

Mendelssohn
Key of ~ Symphony No. 3: 6 AMINOR
oratorio: 6 ELIJAH

Mendes
Actress: 3 EVA
of the bossa nova: 6 SERGIO

Mendicant
Money for: 4 ALMS
moniker: 3 FRA

"Me neither": 4 NORI

Menelaus
Realm of: 6 SPARTA
Wife of: 5 HELEN

"Mene, mene, ___, upharsin": 5 TEKEL

"Men ___ From Mars, ...": 3 ARE

Menial: 4 PEON 6 FLUNKY

"... men in ___": 4 ATUB

Menjou
Actor: 7 ADOLPHE

Menken
1860s actress ~: 4 ADAH

Menlo Park
middle name: 4 ALVA
monogram: 3 **TAE**
name: 6 EDISON

Mennonite
group: 5 **AMISH**

Meno ___ (less rapid): 5 MOSSO

Men-only: 4 STAG

Menotti
Composer: 4 GIAN
title character: 5 AMAHL

Mens ___ (criminal intent): 3 REA

Mensa
data: 3 IQS
Eligible for: 5 SMART
Hardly ~ material: 5 DENSE
hurdle: 6 IQTEST

Menswear
brand: 4 IZOD

Mental
acuity: 4 WITS
flash: 4 IDEA
fog: 4 DAZE
grasp: 6 UPTAKE
picture: 4 IDEA 5 IMAGE
pictures: 7 IMAGERY

quickness: 3 WIT
Mentalist
  claim: 3 **ESP**
  ~ Geller: 3 **URI**
Mentality
  Kind of: 5 SIEGE
Mentally
  quick: 5 AGILE
  twisted: 4 SICK
Menth-
  suffix: 3 ENE
Mention: 4 CITE 7 REFERTO
  Fail to: 4 **OMIT**
  Make ~ of: 4 NOTE
  Not to: 3 AND 4 ALSO PLUS
    8 LETALONE
  Passing: 4 OBIT
Mentioned: 4 SAID
  prefix: 5 AFORE
Mentioning
  Worth: 6 OFNOTE
Mentor: 4 **GURU**
  One under a: 7 PROTEGE
Menu: 5 CARTE
  Bistro: 5 CARTE
  Chinese ~ general: 3 TSO
  Chinese ~ letters: 3 MSG
  Chinese ~ phrase: 5 NOMSG
  heading: 7 ENTREES
    8 ALACARTE
  Japanese ~ item: 7 SASHIMI
    8 TERIYAKI
  option: 4 SAVE UNDO
  Phone ~ imperative: 5 PRESS
  phrase: 3 **ALA** 8 ALACARTE
  pick: 6 ENTREE
  Pick from the: 5 ORDER
Menuhin
  Violinist: 6 YEHUDI
Méphistophélès
  player: 5 BASSO
Mer
  contents: 3 EAU
  sight: 3 ILE
Mercator
  creation: 3 MAP
Mercedes
  rival: 3 BMW 4 AUDI
Mercedes-___ : 4 BENZ

Mercenary: 5 VENAL
  Japanese: 5 NINJA
  Revolutionary: 7 HESSIAN
Mercer
  Singer: 5 MABEL
Merchandise: 5 GOODS WARES
  booth: 5 STALL
  Stocking: 4 TOYS
  ~ ID: 3 UPC
Merchant: 6 SELLER 8 RETAILER
  Food: 6 GROCER
  Large ~ ship: 6 ARGOSY
  Mail order: 6 LLBEAN
  NYC ~ Horace: 4 SAKS
  of music: 7 NATALIE
  Online: 7 ETAILER
  vessel officer: 5 BOSUN
  vessel officer, briefly: 4 BOSN
"Merchant of Venice, The"
  heroine: 6 PORTIA
  title character: 7 ANTONIO
Merci
  relative: 5 DANKE
Merciless: 5 CRUEL
  one: 4 MING
Mercilessly
  Tease: 4 RIDE
Mercredi
  Day after: 5 JEUDI
"Mercure"
  composer: 5 SATIE
Mercury: 5 METAL
  model: 5 SABLE
  org.: 4 NASA
  or Saturn: 3 CAR GOD 4 AUTO
    5 DEITY
Mercutio
  Friend of: 5 ROMEO
  Queen described by: 3 MAB
Mercy
  Have ~ on: 5 SPARE
  Mother of: 6 TERESA
  Show: 5 SPARE
Mercyhurst College
  site: 4 ERIE
"... mercy on such ___": Kipling:
    4 ASWE
Mere: 4 POND 5 SCANT
  No ~ spectator: 4 DOER

taste: 3 SIP
Mère
  sibling: 5 ONCLE
Merely: 4 ONLY
Merganser: 4 SMEW
Merge: 5 UNITE
Merged
  It ~ into Verizon: 3 GTE
  It ~ with BP: 5 AMOCO
  It ~ with Exxon: 5 MOBIL
  It ~ with GE: 3 RCA
  It ~ with Mobil: 5 EXXON
  It ~ with Time Warner: 3 AOL
  news agency: 4 TASS
Merger: 5 UNION
  1955 ~: 3 AFL CIO
  1998 ~: 5 AMOCO
  2001 ~: 3 AOL
  agreement: 3 IDO
  Form a secret: 5 ELOPE
  Have a: 3 WED
  Media: 10 TIMEWARNER
Mérida
  Mrs., in: 3 SRA
Meridian: 4 ACME
  Hrs. on the 90th: 3 CST
  ___ meridiem: 4 ANTE
Meringue
  ingredient: 8 EGGWHITE
Merino
  coat: 4 WOOL
  mama: 3 **EWE**
Morit: 4 **EARN** RATE 7 DESERVE
Merit badge
  holder: 4 SASH
  org.: 3 BSA
Merkel
  Actress: 3 **UNA**
Merle
  Actress: 6 OBERON
Merlin: 4 MAGE SEER
  Actor: 5 OLSEN
  of football: 5 OLSEN
  Sportscaster: 5 OLSEN
Merlot: 3 RED 7 REDWINE
Mermaid
  Disney: 5 **ARIEL**
  feature: 4 TAIL
  habitat: 3 **SEA**

  movie: 6 SPLASH
Merman
  Singer: 5 ETHEL
Merrick
  Half a ~ musical: 3 IDO
Merrie
  follower: 4 OLDE
Merrill
  Actress: 4 **DINA**
Merrily
  Play: 6 CAVORT
"Merrily, we roll ___": 5 ALONG
Merrimack
  City on the: 6 NASHUA
Merriment: 4 **GLEE**
  Full of: 6 JOCOSE
Merry: 3 GAY 4 GLAD
  Make: 5 ELATE REVEL
  month: 3 MAY
  prank: 4 JEST
  ~, in Basque: 4 ALAI
"Merry Company"
  artist: 5 STEEN
"Merry Drinker, The"
  painter: 4 HALS
Merry-go-round
  figure, to a kid: 5 HORSY
  music: 4 LILT
"Merry Widow, The"
  composer: 5 **LEHAR**
  role: 5 SONIA
Mertz
  Ethel: 8 LANDLADY
  Mrs.: 5 ETHEL
  Ricardo, to: 6 TENANT
Meryl
  1982 ~ role: 6 SOPHIE
  Actress: 6 STREEP
Mes
  Primero: 5 ENERO
Mesa
  dweller: 4 HOPI
  Small: 5 BUTTE
Mesa ___: 5 VERDE
Mesabi Range
  find: 3 ORE 7 IRONORE
___ Mesa, California: 5 COSTA
Mescal
  source: 5 AGAVE

Mescaline
  source: 6 PEYOTE
Meses
  12 ~: 3 ANO
Mesh: 5 AGREE FITIN
  It's a: 3 NET WEB
  Like: 5 NETTY
  Resembling: 7 NETLIKE
  ~, as gears: 6 ENGAGE
Meshed
  land: 4 IRAN
  resident: 5 IRANI
Meshuga: 6 INSANE
Mesmerized: 4 RAPT 6 ENRAPT
    9 INATRANCE
Mesopotamia
  today: 4 IRAQ
Mesopotamian
  city: 6 EDESSA
  ruler: 6 SARGON
Mesozoic: 3 **ERA**
Mess
  Big: 5 SNAFU
  hall mess: 4 SLOP
  It's a: 3 STY
  Make a ~ of: 4 RUIN 6 FOULUP
  maker: 4 SLOB
  One in a: 5 EATER
  place: 4 HALL
  Stuck in a: 4 ONKP
  up: 3 **ERR** 4 FLUB 5 BOTCH
      MISDO SPOIL 6 BLOWIT
  Went to: 3 ATE
Mess ___: 3 KIT
Message
  board: 5 OUIJA
  Brief: 4 NOTE
  Coded: 6 CIPHER
  Computer: 5 EMAIL
  Error: 4 OOPS
  Get the: 3 SEE
  Got the: 5 HEARD
  in a bottle: 3 SOS
  Kind of: 5 ERROR
  Newsgroup: 4 POST
  Office: 4 MEMO
  Short Internet: 5 ENOTE
  starter: 4 INRE
  White flag: 5 TRUCE

___ message: 5 SENDA
Messages
  Pitched: 3 ADS
Messenger
  Genetic: 3 **RNA**
  Official: 6 HERALD
Messenger ___: 3 **RNA**
Messiah
  Muslim: 5 MAHDI
"Messiah": 8 ORATORIO
  composer: 6 HANDEL
Messina
  Sight from: 4 ETNA
Messing
  Actress: 5 DEBRA
Messy
  dresser: 4 SLOB
  Less: 6 NEATER
  mass: 4 GLOB
  place: 3 STY
  situation: 5 SNAFU
Mesta
  Hostess: 5 PERLE
  Perle: 7 HOSTESS
Met: 3 SAT 4 NLER 7 RANINTO
    8 CONVENED
  display: 3 ART
  expectations: 5 ARIAS 6 OPERAS
  He debuted at the ~ in 1903:
      6 CARUSO
  James of the: 6 LEVINE
  offering: 4 ARIA 5 OPERA
  solo: 4 ARIA
  Some ~ stars: 6 TENORS
  squarely: 5 FACED
  star: 4 DIVA
Metabolism
  Kind of: 5 BASAL
Metal
  bar: 5 INGOT
  Can: 3 TIN
  container: 3 ORE
  Crude: 3 ORE
  Cut into: 4 ETCH
  deposit: 4 LODE
  Enameled: 4 TOLE
  fastener: 4 BOLT HASP 5 RIVET
      SCREW UBOLT
  Fuse: 4 WELD

Galvanizing: 4 ZINC
Heavy: 4 **LEAD**
in brass: 4 ZINC
in steel: 4 IRON
Join: 4 WELD 6 SOLDER
marble: 7 STEELIE
Measure: 5 ASSAY
mix: 5 ALLOY
mold: 3 PIG
Pewter: 3 TIN
Precious: 4 GOLD
Put the pedal to the: 4 SPED
Refine: 5 SMELT
refuse: 4 SLAG
rim: 6 FLANGE
shaping aid: 5 ANVIL
Soft: 3 TIN
source: 3 ORE
strand: 4 WIRE
Temper: 6 ANNEAL
Threaded ~ fastener: 4 TNUT
Unrefined: 3 ORE
waste: 5 DROSS

Metal-bearing
mineral: 3 ORE

Metallic
fabric: 4 LAME
marble: 7 STEELIE
mixture: 5 ALLOY
rock: 3 **ORE**
sound: 5 CLANG
waste: 4 SLAG

Metallica
drummer Ulrich: 4 LARS

Metallurgist
sample: 3 ORE

Metals
Big name in: 5 ALCOA

Metalworker: 5 SMITH

Metamorphic
rock: 5 SLATE

"Metamorphoses"
poet: 4 OVID

Metamorphosis
stage: 4 PUPA 5 LARVA

"Metamorphosis, The"
author: 5 KAFKA
Hero of: 5 SAMSA

___ me tangere: 4 **NOLI**

Metaphor: 5 TROPE
Economic: 3 PIE
Fog: 7 PEASOUP
Scolding: 7 RIOTACT

Metaphorically
Challenge, ~: 4 HILL
Punishment, ~: 3 ROD

Metaphysical
poet: 5 DONNE

Metaphysics
Giant of: 4 KANT

Metcalf
Actress: 6 LAURIE

Metchnikoff
Nobelist: 4 ELIE

Mete
out: 4 DOLE 5 ALLOT

Meteor
path: 3 ARC
tail: 3 ITE

"Meteorologica"
writer: 9 ARISTOTLE

Meteorological
concern: 7 AIRMASS
effect: 4 HALO 6 AURORA
line: 6 ISOBAR
menace: 6 ELNINO

Meteorologist
comfort meas.: 3 THI
device: 9 BAROMETER
study: 5 SKIES

Meter
Cubic: 5 **STERE**
feed: 5 DIMES
Feet in: 5 IAMBS
maid of song: 4 **RITA**
man: 4 POET
Millionth of a: 6 MICRON
Millionths of a: 5 MICRA
opening: 4 ALTI
prefix: 3 ODO 4 PERI 5 ANEMO
reader: 6 GASMAN
reading: 4 FARE 5 USAGE
site: 4 TAXI

Metered
vehicle: 3 CAB 4 TAXI

Meters
100 square ~: 3 ARE
1,852 ~: 7 SEAMILE

4,047 square ~: 4 ACRE
Meth
  suffix: 3 **ANE**
Meth.: 3 REL SYS 4 PROT
Methane
  lack: 4 ODOR
Method: 3 WAY 4 MODE 5 STYLE
        6 SYSTEM TACTIC
  (abbr.): 3 SYS 4 SYST
  A question of: 3 HOW
  Counting: 4 TENS
  Gambler's: 6 SYSTEM
  Learning: 4 ROTE 7 OSMOSIS
  of meditation: 3 ZEN 4 YOGA
  of reasoning: 5 LOGIC
Methuselah: 7 OLDSTER
  claim to fame: 6 OLDAGE
  Father of: 5 ENOCH
  Like: 3 OLD
Methyl
  ending: 3 ENE
Methyl acetate: 5 ESTER
Meticulousness: 4 CARE
Metier: 5 TRADE
MetLife: 7 INSURER
  competitor: 5 AETNA
"Me too": 5 ASAMI SODOI
Metric
  distances (abbr.): 3 KMS
  foot: 4 IAMB
  heavyweight: 5 TONNE
  mass unit: 4 GRAM
  measure: 3 ARE 4 KILO 5 LITER
        STERE
  prefix: 3 **ISO** 4 DECA DECI
        5 CENTI MILLI
  quart: 5 LITER
  weight: 4 GRAM KILO
Metro
  area: 3 URB
  entrance: 5 STILE
  maker: 3 GEO
Metrodome
  lack: 4 TARP
  player: 4 TWIN
Metroliner
  company: 6 AMTRAK
Metronome
  setting: 5 TEMPO

  settings: 5 TEMPI
Metropolis: 4 CITY
  Indian: 5 DELHI
  Japanese: 5 OSAKA
  Norwegian: 4 OSLO
  Pakistani: 6 LAHORE
Metropolitan: 5 URBAN
Mets: 4 TEAM
  1969 ~ victims: 7 ORIOLES
  div.: 6 NLEAST
  First ~ manager: 7 STENGEL
  Former ~ outfielder: 4 AGEE
  Jones of the: 5 CLEON
  stadium: 4 **SHEA**
  Tommie in ~ history: 4 AGEE
Mettle: 4 GUTS 5 SPUNK VALOR
Metz
  Mine, in: 4 AMOI
  ~ Mrs.: 3 MME
Mex.: 4 ABBR
  miss: 4 SRTA
  Neighbor of: 3 **USA** 4 ARIZ
  ~ Mrs.: 3 SRA
Mexicali
  mister: 5 SENOR
  peninsula: 4 BAJA
        15 LOWERCALIFORNIA
Mexican
  Ancient: 5 AZTEC OLMEC
  beans: 5 PESOS
  blanket: 6 SERAPE
  bread: 4 PESO
  cactus: 6 PEYOTE
  child: 4 NINA
  coin: 4 PESO
  cowboy: 6 CHARRO
  food: 4 TACO 6 TAMALE
        7 TOSTADA
  general: 9 SANTAANNA
  mister: 5 **SENOR**
  money: 4 **PESO**
  month: 3 MES
  munchie: 4 TACO
  muralist: 6 RIVERA
  peninsula: 4 BAJA
  Prepare ~ beans: 5 REFRY
  revolutionary: 5 VILLA 6 ZAPATA
  saloon: 7 CANTINA
  sandal: 8 HUARACHE

sandwich: **4** TACO
shawl: **6** SERAPE
silverwork center: **5** TAXCO
snack: **4** TACO **5** NACHO
state: **7** TABASCO
The U.S., to a: **7** ELNORTE
treat holder: **6** PINATA
water: **4** AGUA
wrap: **6** SERAPE
~ Mrs.: **3** SRA

Mexican War
president: **4** POLK

Mexico
Conqueror of: **6** CORTES
It is in: **4** ESTA
Mme., in: **3** SRA
More, in: **3** MAS
State of: **6** OAXACA
This, in: **4** ESTO
Up from: **5** NORTE

Meyer
Crime boss: **6** LANSKY
Director: **4** RUSS

Meyers
Actress: **3** ARI
of basketball: **3** ANN

Mezzo
offering: **4** ARIA
~ Berganza: **6** TERESA
~ Borodina: **4** OLGA

Mezzo-soprano
~ Marilyn: **5** HORNE

MFA
Part of: **4** ARTS

"___ M for Murder": **4** DIAL

Mfr.
detail: **4** SPEC

Mfume, Kweisi
org.: **5** NAACP

Mg.
and others: **3** WTS

MGM: 6 STUDIO
Cofounder of: **4** LOEW
Former ~ rival: **3** RKO
lion: **3** LEO
motto word: **3** ARS **5** ARTIS
movie sound: **4** ROAR
Part of: **5** MAYER METRO

Mgmt.: 5 ADMIN

Mgr.
degree: **3** MBA
helper: **4** ASST

Mgrs.
Online: **6** SYSOPS

MHz
Part of: **4** MEGA

Mi
followers: **3** FAS

Mi.
A ~ has 1,760: **3** YDS
About ⅝: **3** KIL
About 5.88 trillion: **4** LTYR

Mia
An ex of: **5** ANDRE
of soccer: **4** HAMM
Role for: **6** HANNAH
"___ mia!": **5** MAMMA
"___ Mia" (1965 hit): **4** CARA

Miami
basketball team: **4** HEAT
City near: **11** CORALGABLES
county: **4** DADE
golf resort: **5** DORAL
newspaper: **6** HERALD
Tree in: **4** PALM
Where ~ is: **4** OHIO

Miamian
Certain: **5** ANGLO

Miami Sound Machine
singer: **7** ESTEFAN

"Miami Vice"
actor Edward James: **5** OLMOS
star: **10** DONJOHNSON

Miata
maker: **5** MAZDA

Mica: 8 SILICATE

Micah
Book before: **5** JONAH

Mice
catchers: **4** OWLS
Field: **4** VOLE
Reactions to: **4** EEKS
Sites for: **4** PADS
~, to cats: **4** PREY

Mich.
neighbor: **3** IND ONT **4** WISC

Michael
Actor: **5** NOURI

and others: 5 TSARS
Batman after: 3 VAL
Brother of: 4 TITO
Cochise portrayer: 6 ANSARA
Former Disney exec: 6 EISNER
Janet, to: 3 SIS
of tennis: 5 CHANG STICH
Sister of: 5 JANET 6 LATOYA
Sleuth: 6 SHAYNE
~, to Kirk: 3 SON

"Michael"
actress Garr: 4 TERI
actress MacDowell: 5 ANDIE

"Michael Collins"
star: 3 REA

Michaelmas
daisy: 5 **ASTER**

Michaels
TV producer: 5 LORNE

Michel
Napoleonic marshal: 3 NEY

Michelangelo
masterpiece: 5 DAVID **PIETA**
works: 4 ARTE 7 FRESCOS

Michelin
product: 4 TIRE 6 RADIAL
rival: 6 DUNLOP

Michelle
and Cass: 5 MAMAS
of soccer: 5 AKERS
Rival of: 4 TARA
Skater: 4 KWAN

Michener
epic: 5 SPACE TEXAS 6 ALASKA
    HAWAII IBERIA
work: 4 EPIC SAGA

"Mi chiamano Mimi": 4 ARIA

Michigan: 4 LAKE 6 AVENUE
city: 4 OWOSSO 7 PONTIAC
    SAGINAW
college: 4 ALMA

Mick
Bandmates of: 6 STONES
Ex of: 6 BIANCA

Mickey
Actor: 6 ROONEY
and Minnie: 4 MICE
Ex of: 3 AVA
of baseball: 6 MANTLE

Mickey ___ (loaded drink): 4 FINN

Mickey Mouse
courses: 6 EASYAS
creator: 4 WALT 6 DISNEY
dog: 5 PLUTO
First ~ cartoon:
    15 STEAMBOATWILLIE
Girlfriend of: 6 MINNIE
Like: 8 ANIMATED

Microbe: 4 **GERM**

Microbiologist
gel: 4 AGAR

Microbrewery
offering: 3 ALE 4 BEER

Microfilm
sheet: 5 FICHE

Micromanager
concern: 6 DETAIL

Micronesia
Group that includes: 7 OCEANIA

Microphone
He patented the: 6 EDISON
inventor Berliner: 5 EMILE

Microscope
item: 5 SLIDE
Kind of: 8 ELECTRON
part: 4 LENS 5 OPTIC
sample: 5 SMEAR

Microscopic: 3 WEE 4 TINY
critter: 5 AMEBA 6 AMOEBA
critters: 6 AMEBAE
sea life: 4 ALGA

Microscopy
supply: 5 STAIN

Microsoft
boss: 5 GATES
employee: 5 CODER
game system: 4 XBOX
product: 4 WORD
reference: 7 ENCARTA

Microwave: 3 ZAP 4 NUKE OVEN
brand: 5 AMANA
option: 4 THAW

Midafternoon: 5 THREE
on a sundial: 3 III

Mid-American Conference
team: 6 TOLEDO

Midas
undoing: 5 GREED

Midday: 4 NOON
  errand: 6 NOONER
  nap: 6 SIESTA
Middies
  sch.: 4 USNA
Middle
  (abbr.): 3 CTR
  ear bone: 5 INCUS 6 STAPES
  Give in the: 3 SAG
  grade: 3 CEE
  In the ~ of: 5 AMONG
    7 AMONGST
  management: 4 DIET
  measurement: 5 WAIST
  middle: 4 DEES
  Minuet: 4 TRIO
  Most red in the: 6 RAREST
  of a game: 3 TAC
  of an insect: 6 THORAX
  of March: 4 IDES
  of some plays: 5 ACTII
  of summer: 3 EMS
  prefix: 4 MESO
  QED: 4 ERAT
  Simile: 3 ASA
  Split down the: 6 BISECT
  weight: 9 SPARETIRE
  ~ X or O: 3 TAC
Middlecoff
  Golfer: 4 CARY
Middle East
  bread: 4 PITA
  denizen: 4 ARAB
  faith: 5 ISLAM
  gp.: 3 PLO
  leader: 4 EMIR 5 EMEER
  port: 4 ADEN
  strip: 4 GAZA
  sultanate: 4 OMAN
Middle Easterner: 4 ARAB
    5 SAUDI 7 IRANIAN
"Middlemarch"
  author: 5 **ELIOT**
Middle name
  Common girl's: 3 ANN MAE
  Disney's: 5 ELIAS
  Edison's: 4 **ALVA**
  Elvis's: 4 ARON
  Emerson's: 5 WALDO

  Garfield's: 5 ABRAM
  Lenin's: 5 ILICH
  Lennon's: 3 ONO
  Mystery: 5 CONAN
  Poe's: 5 ALLAN
  Polk's: 4 KNOX
  Presidential: 4 ALAN 5 ABRAM
    6 DELANO
Middlesex
  Middle of: 6 CENTRE
Middleweight
  1940s ~ champ Tony: 4 ZALE
Middling: 4 FAIR **SOSO**
    7 AVERAGE
  grade: 3 **CEE**
Mideast
  airline: 4 ELAL
  belief: 5 ISLAM
  canal: 4 SUEZ
  capital: 4 SANA 5 AMMAN
    7 TEHERAN
  carrier: 4 **ELAL**
  chief: 4 EMIR
  chief (var.): 4 AMIR
  desert: 5 NEGEV
  emirate: 4 OMAN 5 DUBAI
  expert: 7 ARABIST
  export: 3 OIL
  federation (abbr.): 3 UAE
  Former ~ first name: 5 YASIR
  Former ~ gp.: 3 **UAR**
  Former ~ leader: 4 SHAH
  gp.: 3 **PLO** 5 HAMAS
  gulf: 4 ADEN
  heights: 5 GOLAN
  land: 4 OMAN
  land (abbr.): 3 ISR
  leader: 5 ASSAD
  Like some ~ politics: 7 PANARAB
  missile: 4 SCUD
  money: 4 RIAL 5 DINAR
  nation: 5 QATAR
  peninsula: 5 SINAI 6 ARABIA
  port: 4 ADEN
  prince: 4 EMIR
  region: 4 GAZA
  royal name: 4 SAUD
  ruler: 4 AMIR EMIR SHAH
    5 AMEER EMEER

sultanate: **4** OMAN
Midge: 4 GNAT
Singer: **3** URE
Midland
City near: **6** ODESSA
Midleg: 4 KNEE
Midler: 4 DIVA
1979 ~ film: **7** THEROSE
Singer: **5** **BETTE**
Mid-level
army rank: **10** FIELDGRADE
Mid-month
day: **4** IDES
Midmorning: 3 TEN **5** TENAM
Midnight: 3 XII
Approach: **5** LATEN
Burning the ~ oil: **6** UPLATE
Burn the ~ oil: **6** STAYUP
fridge visit: **4** RAID
Hour after: **5** ONEAM
Hour before: **6** ELEVEN
rider: **6** REVERE
Word heard around: **4** AULD
"Midnight Cowboy"
role: **5** **RATSO**
Midori
Skater: **3** **ITO**
Midpoint
(abbr.): **3** CTR
Midriff
revealing top: **6** HALTER
Midsection: 3 GUT **5** BELLY
TORSO WAIST
Midshipman
rival: **5** CADET
sch.: **4** USNA
Midshipmen, The: 4 NAVY
Mid-sized
ensemble: **5** OCTET
Midst
In the ~ of: **5** AMONG
Midsummer
sign: **3** LEO
"Midsummer Night's Dream, A"
King of: **6** OBERON
Queen of: **7** TITANIA
trickster: **4** PUCK
Midterm: 4 EXAM TEST
Midvoyage: 4 ASEA

Midway
alternative: **5** **OHARE**
attraction: **4** RIDE
Midwest
Big ~ sch.: **3** OSU
city: **5** OMAHA
city, familiarly: **3** CHI
hub: **5** **OHARE**
Indian: **3** SAC **4** OTOE **5** OMAHA
university town: **4** AMES
Midwife
instruction: **4** PUSH
Midwives
Some ~ (abbr.): **3** RNS
Mien: 3 AIR
Mean: **5** SNEER
"Mi ___ es su ...": 4 CASA
Mies van der ___
Architect Ludwig: **4** ROHE
Mies van der Rohe
More, to: **4** LESS
motto: **10** LESSISMORE
Miff: 3 IRE **4** RILE SNIT **5** STEAM
Miffed: 4 SORE
More than: **5** IRATE
state: **4** SNIT
~, with "off": **4** TEED
Might: 3 MAY **4** DINT **5** FORCE
POWER
Symbol of: **3** **OAK**
Mighty
long time: **3** EON
tree: **3** OAK
"Mighty Aphrodite"
Sorvino of: **4** MIRA
"Mighty ___ a Rose": 3 LAK
Mighty Ducks
Home of the: **7** ANAHEIM
org.: **3** NHL
"Mighty Ducks, The"
star: **7** ESTEVEZ
Mighty Joe Young: 3 APE
"Mighty Lak' a Rose"
composer: **5** NEVIN
___ mignon: **5** FILET
Migraine
omen: **4** AURA
omens: **5** AURAE
Migrant: 5 NOMAD

Depression era: 4 OKIE
Migrate
  Why geese: 8 INSTINCT
Migration: 4 TREK
Migratory
  fish: 3 EEL 4 SHAD
  goose: 5 BRANT
  ___ **Miguel:** 3 SAO
"Mikado, The": 8 OPERETTA
  attire: 3 OBI
  role: 4 KOKO
  weapon: 4 SNEE
Mike
  Archie or Edith, to: 5 INLAW
  Boxer: 5 TYSON
  Columnist: 5 ROYKO
  Hidden: 4 WIRE
  holder: 4 BOOM 5 EMCEE
    LAPEL STAND
  Iron: 5 TYSON
  of football: 5 DITKA
  Producer ~ and others: 5 TODDS
Mikhail
  of chess: 3 **TAL**
  Wife of: 5 RAISA
Mikita
  of hockey: 4 **STAN**
"Mikrokosmos"
  composer: 6 BARTOK
Mil.
  address: 3 **APO**
  advisory gp.: 3 NSC
  alliance: 4 NATO
  assistant: 3 ADC
  authority: 3 CMD
  award: 3 DSC DSM DSO
  bigwig: 3 GEN
  branch: 4 USAF USAR USMC
  drop site: 3 APO
  entertainers: 3 USO
  group on campus: 4 ROTC
  jet locale: 3 AFB
  mail drop: 3 APO
  No longer in the: 3 RET
  officers: 3 LTS
  rank: 3 COL GEN MAJ PFC PVT
    SGT 5 LTCOL
  registration group: 3 SSS
  school: 4 ACAD

stores: 3 PXS
student body: 4 ROTC
training academy: 3 **OCS**
transport: 3 LST
truant: 4 AWOL
unit: 4 REGT
"Mila 18"
  author: 4 URIS
Milan
  attraction: 7 LASCALA
  money: 4 LIRA
  Seaport south of: 5 GENOA
Milano
  Actress: 6 ALYSSA
  moola: 4 LIRA LIRE
Mild: 4 TAME 5 TEPID
  cheese: 4 EDAM 5 GOUDA
  cigar: 5 **CLARO**
  oath: 4 DRAT **EGAD** GOSH
    HECK 5 EGADS NERTS
  ~, as weather: 5 BALMY
Mildew
  and mold: 5 FUNGI
Mildly
  Scold: 5 CHIDE
Mile
  1/640 of a square ~: 4 ACRE
  A ~ a minute: 5 SIXTY
  fraction: 4 YARD
Mileage
  counter: 8 ODOMETER
  Get more ~ out of: 5 REUSE
  rating gp.: 3 EPA
  Square: 4 AREA
Mile High Center
  architect: 3 PEI
Miler
  ~ Sebastian: 3 COE
Miles
  About 25,000 square ~ of Asia:
    7 ARALSEA
  Actress: 4 VERA 5 SARAH
  and miles: 3 FAR
  Many ~ off: 4 **AFAR**
  of jazz: 5 DAVIS
  per hour: 4 RATE
Milestone
  Baby: 9 FIRSTSTEP
Milieu: 4 AREA 7 ELEMENT

Militant
  campus gp.: **3** SDS
  ~ Muslim group: **5** HAMAS
Military
  1980s ~ inits.: **3** SDI
  academy frosh: **4** PLEB
  address: **3** SIR
  address (abbr.): **3** APO
  adversary: **5** ENEMY
  Arm of the British: **4** STEN
  assault: **5** SIEGE
  award: **5** MEDAL
  band: **6** ARMLET
  band instrument: **7** HELICON
  bigwigs: **5** BRASS
  Brit. ~ decoration: **3** DSO
  camp: **5** ETAPE
  Campus ~ org.: **4** <u>ROTC</u>
  cap: **4** KEPI **5** SHAKO
  capability: **9** FIREPOWER
  chaplain: **5** PADRE
  classification: **4** ONEA
  command: **6** ATEASE
  "Currently serving" ~ status:
    4 ONEC
  day's march: **5** ETAPE
  defense parts: **5** SAMS
  denial: **5** NOSIR
  Discharge from the ~, informally:
    3 RIF
  Elite ~ unit: **5** ATEAM
  French ~ cap: **4** KEPI
  group: **4** ARMY UNIT
  helicopter: **4** HUEY **6** APACHE
  hopeful: **5** CADET
  inits.: **3** SDI
  Join the: **6** ENLIST
  meal: **4** **MESS**
  mess: **5** SNAFU
  mission: **5** RECON
  pilots: **6** AIRMEN
  Pres., to the: **3** CIC **4** CINC
  response: **5** NOSIR **6** YESSIR
  sch.: **4** ACAD
  school: **7** ACADEMY
  squad: **4** UNIT
  station: **4** POST
  stronghold: **4** FORT
  student: **5** CADET

  subdivision: **4** UNIT
  tactic: **4** RAID
  tenure: **4** TOUR
  trainee: **5** CADET
  training group: **5** CADRE
  training site: **8** BOOTCAMP
  U.K. ~ fliers: **3** RAF
  unit: **5** SQUAD TROOP
  vehicle: **4** JEEP
Milk
  amts.: **3** QTS
  Brest: **4** LAIT
  choice: **4** SKIM
  component: **4** WHEY
  container: **6** CARTON
  Cry over spilled: **3** RUE **4** OOPS
    5 WHINE
  curdler: **6** RENNET
  delivery cry: **3** MOO
  Drink with: **5** LATTE
  etc.: **5** DAIRY
  farm: **5** DAIRY
  Like skim: **6** NONFAT
  Nonfat: **4** SKIM
  pitcher: **5** ELSIE
  prefix: **4** LACT **5** LACTI **LACTO**
  Prepare cappuccino: **5** STEAM
  Produce skim: **5** DEFAT
  purchase: **5** QUART
  related: **6** LACTIC
  Remove from a mother's:
    4 WEAN
  Request for: **3** MEW
  snake: **5** ADDER
  source: **3** COW EWE **4** GOAT
    5 UDDER
  sugar: **7** LACTOSE
  train: **5** LOCAL
  Treat with: **4** OREO
  Turn bad, as: **4** SOUR
  Word before: **4** SOYA
  ~, in a way: **3** USE
  ~, in French: **4** LAIT
  ~, in prescriptions: **3** LAC
  ~, in Spanish: **5** LECHE
Milk-Bone: **5** TREAT
Milker
  Aphid: **3** ANT
  need: **4** PAIL **5** STOOL

Milking
  machine attachment: 5 UDDER
  the cows: 5 CHORE
Milk of ___: 8 MAGNESIA
Milkshake
  in New England: 6 FRAPPE
  insert: 5 STRAW
Milksop: 4 WIMP
  lack: 5 SPINE
Milky
  gemstone: 4 **OPAL**
Milky Way: 3 BAR
  component: 6 NOUGAT
  maker: 5 MARS
  part: 4 STAR
Mill: 5 GRIND
  fodder: 5 GRIST
  input: 3 ORE 5 GRIST
  Kind of: 3 GIN 5 GRIST STEEL
  material: 4 IRON
  output: 5 PAPER STEEL
  site: 6 STREAM
  Steel ~ refuse: 4 SLAG
Millais
  Site of some ~ works: 4 TATE
Millay
  muse: 5 ERATO
  Poet: 4 **EDNA**
Milldam: 4 WEIR
Millennia
  Many: 3 EON 4 AEON EONS
    5 AEONS
Millennial Church
  member: 6 SHAKER
Millennium
  start: 3 MMI
  unit: 4 YEAR
Millennium Falcon
  pilot: 7 HANSOLO
  pilot Solo: 3 HAN
Miller: 4 BEER
  Bandleader: 5 GLENN MITCH
  beer: 4 LITE
  character: 5 LOMAN
  Comic ranter: 6 DENNIS
  Dancer: 3 ANN
  Designer: 6 NICOLE
  mistress: 3 NIN
  need: 5 GRIST

  offering: 4 BEER LITE
  salesman: 5 LOMAN
Miller ___: 4 LITE
"___ Miller": 5 LUISA
Miller, Arthur
  character: 5 LOMAN
Miller, Dennis
  monologue: 4 RANT
Miller, Glenn
  protégé Ray: 6 EBERLE
Miller, Henry
  Friend of: 8 ANAISNIN
  genre: 7 EROTICA
  title start: 6 TROPIC
Miller, Mitch: 6 OBOIST
  instrument: 4 **OBOE**
Miller, Roger
  hit: 6 DANGME
    13 KINGOFTHEROAD
Miller, William E.
  was his running mate:
    14 BARRYGOLDWATER
Miller Lite
  alternative: 6 AMSTEL
Milli ___: 7 VANILLI
Milligrams
  200 ~: 5 CARAT
  It may be measured in: 4 DOSE
Milliner: 6 HATTER
  stock: 4 HATS
Millinery
  accessory: 6 HATPIN
Million
  Capital of 2.6: 6 TAIPEI
  Ending for: 4 AIRE
  Most of a: 5 ZEROS
  One in a: 4 RARE
  suffix: 4 **AIRE**
Millionaire
  maker: 5 LOTTO 7 LOTTERY
  on the Titanic: 5 ASTOR
  prefix: 5 MULTI
  transport: 5 YACHT
"Millionairess, The"
  star: 5 LOREN
Million Moms March
  target: 3 NRA
Millions
  of years: 4 EONS

"___ Millions" (O'Neill play):
    5 MARCO
Millionth
    of a meter: 6 MICRON
Millionths
    of a meter: 5 MICRA
"Mill on the Floss, The"
    author: 5 ELIOT
Mills
    or Sills: 4 DIVA
Millstone: 4 ONUS
Milne
    baby: 3 ROO
    bear: 4 POOH
    marsupial: 3 **ROO** 5 KANGA
Milo
    Actor: 5 **OSHEA**
    Partner of ~ in film: 4 OTIS
Milosevic: 4 SERB
Milquetoast: 4 WIMP
    Like a: 4 MEEK
Milsap
    Singer: 6 RONNIE
Miltie
    Memorable: 5 BERLE
Milton: 5 ODIST
    Funnyman: 5 BERLE
    muse: 5 ERATO
    overthrower: 3 IDI
    pearl: 3 ODE 5 ELEGY
Mime: 4 APER
    Muse of: 5 ERATO
    ~ Marceau: 6 MARCEL
Mimeo: 4 COPY
Mimic: 3 APE 4 **APER** COPY
    ECHO MYNA 6 PARROT
    7 COPYCAT
    ability: 5 APING
    skill: 5 APERY
Mimieux
    Actress: 6 YVETTE
Miming
    dance: 4 HULA
Mimosa
    family tree: 6 ACACIA
Min.
    15 ~ of football: 3 QTR
    Fraction of a: 4 NSEC
    part: 3 SEC

Three ~ in the ring: 3 RND
"Min and Bill"
    Oscar winner: 8 DRESSLER
Mince: 4 HASH
Minced
    It may be: 4 OATH
Mincemeat
    dessert: 3 PIE
    ingredient: 4 SUET
Mind: 4 HEED **OBEY** TEND
    5 SEETO 6 LISTEN
    RESENT
    Be of one: 5 AGREE
    Bring to: 5 **EVOKE**
    Call to: 5 EVOKE
    Cast of: 4 BENT
    Come to: 5 **ARISE** OCCUR
    Frame of: 4 MOOD
    Had in: 5 MEANT
    Have in: 4 **MEAN** PLAN
        6 INTEND
    It comes to: 4 IDEA
    Keep in: 8 REMEMBER
    Kind of: 8 ONETRACK
    Lose one's: 5 GOMAD
    Of sound: 4 SANE
    Peace of: 4 EASE REST
        6 REPOSE
    Prey on the: 5 EATAT
    set: 5 IDEAS 6 IMAGES
    Soundness of: 6 SANITY
    Speak one's: 5 OPINE
    State of: 4 MOOD
    the kids: 3 SIT
    Things to: 7 PSANDQS
    What comes to: 4 IDEA
    Words before: 5 OUTOF
"___ mind?": 5 DOYOU
Mind-boggler: 6 ENIGMA
Mind-boggling
    span: 3 EON
Minded
    junior: 3 SAT
Minderbinder
    of fiction: 4 MILO
Mindful: 5 AWARE
Mindless: 5 INANE
    card game: 3 WAR
    process: 4 ROTE

Mind reader
(abbr.): 3 EEG
knack: 3 ESP
Mind-reading: 3 ESP
Minds
Meeting of the: 3 ESP
Mind's
eye view: 5 IMAGE
Use the ~ eye: 7 IMAGINE
Mindspring
(abbr.): 3 ISP
Mindy
portrayer: 3 PAM
Where ~ honeymooned: 3 ORK
Mine
access: 4 ADIT
A load off one's: 3 ORE
and yours: 4 OURS
A relative of: 4 OURS
car: 4 TRAM
entrance: 4 **ADIT**
find: 3 **ORE**
line: 4 SEAM
passage: 5 SHAFT
prefix: 5 UNDER
Stuff of: 3 ORE
yield: 3 ORE
~, in French: 4 **AMOI**
"___ Mine"
(Beatles song): 3 IME
(Platters song): 3 HES
Mined
find: 3 ORE 7 IRONORE
over matter: 3 ORE
"Mine eyes have seen the ___ ...":
5 GLORY
Mineo
Actor: 3 **SAL**
Miner
bonanza: 4 LODE
concern: 3 ORE
hat feature: 8 HEADLAMP
Mineral
Bone: 7 APATITE
Chalky: 4 TALC
deposit: 4 LODE VEIN
Figurine: 4 ONYX
Flaky: 4 **MICA**
Gem: 5 BERYL

Green: 4 JADE
hardness scale: 4 MOHS
in pesticide: 4 TALC
Iridescent: 4 OPAL
Layered: 4 MICA
Metal-bearing: 3 ORE
Monterrey: 3 ORO
Nail file: 5 EMERY
Nutritive: 4 IRON
Outback: 4 OPAL
Shiny: 4 MICA
Silica: 4 OPAL
Soft: 4 TALC
spring: 3 **SPA**
suffix: 3 ITE
Supplement: 4 ZINC
Translucent: 4 MICA
___ minérale: 3 EAU
Minero
find: 3 ORO
Miners
sch.: 4 UTEP
Minerva
Greek: 6 ATHENA
Symbol of: 3 OWL
Minesweeper
Fictional: 5 CAINE
Miney
follower: 3 MOE
Ming: 7 DYNASTY
artifact: 4 VASE
of basketball: 3 YAO
thing: 4 VASE
Mingle
at a banquet: 8 TABLEHOP
Mingled
with: 5 AMONG
Mingo
portrayer: 4 AMES 6 EDAMES
___ Minh: 4 VIET
___ Minh City, Vietnam: 5 HOCHI
Mini
albums, for short: 3 EPS
Change a: 5 REHEM
feature: 3 HEM
ha-ha: 5 TEHEE
map: 5 INSET
pictures: 5 ICONS
whirlpool: 4 EDDY

Miniature: 3 TOY 5 PYGMY
  golf club: 6 PUTTER
  map: 5 INSET
  racer: 4 KART 6 GOCART
    7 SLOTCAR
  sci-fi vehicles: 4 PODS
Minibar
  site: 4 LIMO
Minibike
  kin: 5 MOPED
Minicam
  abbr.: 3 REC
Minima: 6 LEASTS
Minimal: 5 **LEAST** 6 BAREST
  amount: 4 IOTA 5 LEAST
  change: 4 CENT 5 PENNY
  evidence: 5 SHRED
  money: 4 CENT
  moola: 7 REDCENT
  Most: 6 BAREST
  swimwear: 5 THONG
Minimalist
  More to a: 4 LESS
Minimally: 4 ATAD 7 ATLEAST
Minimize
  Designed to ~ drag: 4 AERO
Minimovies: 6 SHORTS
Minimum: 5 LEAST 6 BAREST
  amount: 4 WAGE
  Meeting: 6 QUORUM
  Morse: 3 DIT
  Sales: 5 QUOTA
  wage: 5 SCALE
Minimum ___: 4 WAGE
Mining
  Montana ~ town: 5 BUTTE
  nail: 4 SPAD
Minirecord
  albums: 3 EPS
Miniseries
  1981 ~: 6 MASADA
  Haley: 5 ROOTS
  role of 1977: 5 KINTE
Minister: 6 PARSON
  (abbr.): 3 REV
  assistant: 6 DEACON
  cohort: 5 RABBI
  home: 5 MANSE
  nickname: 3 REV

  request: 8 BESEATED
  school: 8 SEMINARY
  to: 4 TEND 5 CATER
Ministry
  TV: 3 PTL
Minivan
  alternative: 3 SUV
  Chevy: 5 ASTRO
  model: 8 AEROSTAR
Miniver
  Mr.: 4 CLEM
"___ Miniver": 3 MRS
Mink: 3 FUR
  kin: 5 OTTER STOAT
  wrap: 5 STOLE
Minn.
  neighbor: 3 ONT WIS 4 NDAK
    SDAK WISC
Minneapolis
  Magazine based in: 4 UTNE
  suburb: 5 **EDINA**
Minnelli
  Singer: 4 LIZA
Minnelli, Liza
  1977 ~ musical: 6 THEACT
Minnesota
  10,000 of ~: 5 LAKES
  ballplayer: 4 TWIN
  Former ~ governor Ventura:
    5 JESSE
  governor Carlson: 4 ARNE
  lake: 6 ITASCA
  range: 6 MESABI
  state bird: 4 LOON
  twin: 6 STPAUL
  twins: 3 ENS
Minnesota ___: 4 FATS
Minnesota Fats
  rival, in film: 9 FASTEDDIE
  stick: 3 CUE
Minnesotan: 6 GOPHER
Minnie
  Memorable: 5 PEARL
  Mickey and: 4 MICE
"Minnie the Moocher"
  singer: 11 CABCALLOWAY
Minnow
  Freshwater: 6 REDFIN
  variety: 4 DACE

Minnows: 4 BAIT
Minoan
  domain: 5 CRETE
Minolta
  rival: 5 RICOH
Minolta Maxxum: 3 SLR
Minor: 4 TEEN 5 PETTY 6 LESSER
  A: 3 KEY
  argument: 4 SPAT
  dent: 4 DING
  falling-out: 4 TIFF
  First ~ prophet: 5 HOSEA
  No longer a: 5 OFAGE
  obsession:
      15 BEEINONESBONNET
  player: 3 COG
  prophet: 5 JONAH
  quarrel: 4 SPAT
  setback: 4 SNAG 6 HICCUP
  ~, in law: 5 PETIT
  ___ Minor: 4 ASIA **URSA**
Minorca
  Capital of: 5 MAHON
Minority
  Mideastern: 4 KURD
  Writer in the: 5 LEFTY
Minors
  Not for: 5 ADULT
Minos: 6 CRETAN
  Daughter of: 7 ARIADNE
  King ~ capital: 7 KNOSSOS
  Kingdom of: 5 CRETE
  Mother of: 6 EUROPA
Minotaur
  Half sister of: 7 ARIADNE
  home: 5 CRETE
Mins.
  Extra game: 3 OTS
  Many: 3 HRS
  Parts of: 4 SECS
Minsk
  money: 5 RUBLE
Minstrel
  instrument: 4 **LUTE** LYRE
  song: 3 LAY
Minstrel show
  figure: 6 ENDMAN
Mint: 3 NEW 4 COIN HERB
      7 POTHERB

family member: 4 CHIA SAGE
    5 BASIL THYME 7 OREGANO
No longer: 4 USED
output: 4 CENT COIN
Popular breath: 6 TICTAC
They make a: 5 CERTS
Weed of the ~ family: 6 HENBIT
Mint-condition: 3 NEW
Minted
  Coin no longer: 4 LIRA
      7 ONELIRA
Mints
  Brand of: 5 CERTS
Minty
  drink: 5 JULEP
Minuet
  middle: 4 TRIO
"Minuet ___": 3 ING
Minus: 4 **LESS** SANS
Minuscule: 3 WEE 4 ITSY TINY
      5 TEENY
  amount: 3 TAD 4 IOTA
  margin: 4 HAIR
  part of a min.: 4 NSEC
Minuses
  It has pluses and: 4 MATH
  They have their pluses and:
      4 IONS
Minute: 3 WEE 4 TINY 5 MICRO
      TEENY 6 ATOMIC TEENSY
  A mile a: 5 SIXTY
  amount: 4 IOTA 9 SCINTILLA
  Any: 4 ANON **SOON**
  bit: 4 ATOM
  In a: 4 SOON
  In a New York: 6 ATONCE
  More: 7 TEENIER
  opening: 4 PORE
  piece: 6 SECOND
  Right this: 3 NOW
  Study at the last: 4 CRAM
  This: 3 NOW 6 ATONCE
Minute ___: 5 STEAK
Minute Maid
  product: 3 HIC
Minute Maid Park
  player: 5 ASTRO
Minuteman
  enemy: 7 REDCOAT

home: 4 SILO
Minutemen
of college sports: 5 UMASS
Minutes
30 ~ in football: 4 HALF
50 ~ spent with a shrink:
    7 SESSION
55 ~ past the hour: 6 FIVETO
Fifty ~ past: 5 TENTO
Of sixty: 5 HORAL
taker: 5 STENO
Minuti
60 ~: 3 ORA
Minx: 4 VAMP 5 HUSSY
Like a: 4 PERT
"___ Mio": 5 **OSOLE**
Miquelon: 3 ILE
Mir
Travel à la: 5 ORBIT
Mira
Paul Sorvino, to: 3 DAD
Miracle
Biblical ~ site: 4 CANA
drink: 6 ELIXIR
Exodus: 5 MANNA
response: 3 AWE
team of 1969: 4 METS
Miracle-___: 3 **GRO**
"Miracle Mets"
manager: 6 HODGES
pitcher: 6 SEAVER
"Miracle on 34th Street"
actor Gailey: 4 FRED
actor John: 5 PAYNE
Oscar winner: 5 GWENN
store: 5 MACYS
"Miracle Worker, The"
actress Swenson: 4 INGA
Mirage
sight: 5 OASIS
"___ Mir Bist Du Schön": 3 BEI
Mire
Move in: 4 SLOG
Mired: 8 KNEEDEEP
"Miró, Miró on the wall"
Like: 5 PUNNY
Mirror: 3 APE 5 IMAGE
Broken ~, say: 4 OMEN
Fuss at the: 5 PREEN

marrer: 5 SMEAR
material: 5 GLASS
reflection: 5 IMAGE
Mirrors
Like some: 4 OVAL
    10 FULLLENGTH
Partner of: 5 SMOKE
Mirth: 4 GLEE
Mirthful: 5 RIANT
sounds: 4 HAHA
Mis
followers: 3 FAS
preceders: 3 RES
Misanthrope: 5 **HATER**
Misbehave: 5 **ACTUP**
    7 CARRYON
Misbehaving: 3 BAD
Miscalculate: 3 **ERR**
Miscellaneous
collection: 3 ANA
mixture: 4 OLIO
Miscellany: 3 ANA 4 **OLIO**
    8 CATCHALL
Mischa
Actor: 4 AUER
Violinist: 5 **ELMAN**
Mischief: 4 HARM
night activity: 5 PRANK
Mischief-maker: 3 IMP 5 PIXIE
    6 RASCAL
Norse: 4 LOKI
Mischievous: 3 BAD 4 ARCH
    5 ELFIN 6 ELFISH IMPISH
bird: 6 MAGPIE
one: 3 ELF IMP 5 DEVIL PIXIE
    ROGUE 6 RASCAL
Small and: 5 ELFIN
sprite: 5 PIXIE
Misconduct
Mark for: 7 DEMERIT
Miscue: 4 SLIP 5 ERROR
Misdeed: 3 SIN
Miser
Fictional ~ Marner: 5 SILAS
fixation: 5 MONEY
word: 4 MINE
Miserable
dwelling: 5 HOVEL
"___ Misérables": 3 **LES**

Miserably
Fail: 4 BOMB
Miserere: 5 PSALM
Misery: 3 WOE
"Misery"
costar: 4 CAAN
director: 6 REINER
star: 5 BATES
~ Oscar winner Bates: 5 KATHY
Misfire
QB: 3 INT
Misfit
Social: 4 DORK GEEK **NERD**
5 DWEEB
Misfortune: 3 WOE
Misfortunes: 4 **ILLS**
Misgivings: 6 QUALMS
Have ~ about: 3 RUE
Mishandle: 4 MUFF 5 ABUSE
Mishap
One-in-a-million:
13 FREAKACCIDENT
Shaving: 4 NICK
Mishmash: 4 **OLIO**
Misinform: 5 LIETO
Misjudge: 3 ERR
Mislay: 4 LOSE
Mislead: 5 LIETO
Misleading: 8 ILLUSIVE
clue: 10 REDHERRING
Misogynist: 5 HATER
Mispickel: 3 ORE
Misplace: 4 LOSE
Misplay: 5 ERROR
Misprints: 6 ERRATA
"Misreadings"
author: 3 ECO
Misrepresent: 4 SKEW 5 BELIE
7 DISTORT
Miss: 3 GAL SHE 4 GIRL LASS
OMIT
a cue: 3 ERR
after marriage: 3 MRS
a step: 6 FALTER
Bonny: 4 LASS
counterpart: 3 HIT
equal: 4 MILE
Fictional Swiss: 5 HEIDI
identification: 3 SHE

in a 1934 song: 4 OTIS
Kind of: 4 NEAR
Mex.: 4 **SRTA**
Mexican: 8 SENORITA
of comics: 5 PEACH
out: 3 DEB
Oxford: 3 OLE
Porter's: 4 OTIS
the mark: 3 ERR
TV psychic: 4 CLEO
~, in French: 4 MLLE
~, in Spanish: 4 SRTA
Miss.
neighbor: 3 **ALA** 4 TENN
___ miss: 5 HITOR
___ Miss: 3 **OLE**
Miss America
Accessory for: 4 SASH 5 TIARA
Former ~ host Parks: 4 BERT
Former ~ host Ron: 3 ELY
to some: 5 IDEAL
Miss Brooks
Eve who played: 5 ARDEN
"___ Miss Brooks": 3 OUR
Miss by ___ : 5 AMILE
Miss Cinders
of old comics: 4 ELLA
Miss Clairol
user: 4 DYER
Miss Congeniality
Like: 6 NICEST
Miss Daisy
Driver of: 4 HOKE
Missed: 5 UNHIT
It may be: 3 CUE
List of what was: 6 ERRATA
Missile
American: 5 TITAN
Blowgun: 4 DART
Deadly: 4 NUKE
Gulf War: 4 **SCUD**
Heckler: 3 EGG
housing: 4 SILO
Kind of: 6 CRUISE 8 AIRTOAIR
Low-tech: 3 PEA
Medium-range: 4 THOR
Mideast: 4 SCUD
path: 3 ARC
Pub: 4 **DART**

Slapstick: 3 PIE
Two-stage: 5 TITAN
Underwater: 7 POLARIS
"Missile Crisis, The"
author Abel: 4 ELIE
Missing: 4 GONE LOST 5 OUTOF
    6 ABSENT
a deadline: 4 LATE
a match: 3 ODD
details: 7 SKETCHY
links: 6 APEMEN
nothing: 6 ENTIRE
~ GI: 4 AWOL
Mission: 4 TASK 5 QUEST
Aborted ~ words: 4 NOGO
Bomber: 6 SORTIE
control, for short: 3 OPS
Historic: 5 ALAMO
Ill-fated ~ of 1967: 7 APOLLOI
Info-gathering: 5 RECON
Interrogate after a: 7 DEBRIEF
Man with a: 5 PADRE SERRA
Memorable: 5 ALAMO
Person on a: 6 LEGATE
Scout: 5 RECON
Scrubbed: 4 NOGO
___ mission: 3 ONA
Missionary
Molokai: 6 DAMIEN
target: 5 PAGAN
~ Junipero: 5 SERRA
Mission ___, California: 5 VIEJO
Mission Control
gp.: 4 NASA
order: 5 ABORT
"Mission: Impossible"
actor Greg: 6 MORRIS
actress Barbara: 4 BAIN
Mr. on: 6 PHELPS
theme composer Schifrin:
    4 LALO
"Mission: Impossible II"
director: 3 WOO
Mississippi
city: 6 BILOXI TUPELO
City on the: 7 MEMPHIS
explorer: 6 DESOTO
feeder: 3 RED 4 OHIO 5 YAZOO
inlet: 5 BAYOU

Lake source of the: 6 ITASCA
Lott of: 5 TRENT
Mouth of the: 5 DELTA
Much of: 5 ESSES
senator: 9 TRENTLOTT
senator Cochran: 4 THAD
senator Trent: 4 LOTT
state tree: 8 MAGNOLIA
Ward of: 4 SELA
"Mississippi ___": 6 MASALA
Mississippi River
explorer: 6 DESOTO
source: 6 ITASCA
transport: 5 BARGE
Missive: 6 LETTER
(abbr.): 3 LTR
Modern: 5 EMAIL
Unsigned:
    15 ANONYMOUSLETTER
Miss Manners
Like: 6 POLITE
Unlike: 4 RUDE
Miss Marple
discovery: 4 CLEW
of mystery: 4 JANE
Miss Muffet
bugaboo: 6 SPIDER
fare: 4 WHEY
Like: 9 SCAREDOFF
morsel: 4 CURD
Miss-named: 3 NEE
Missouri: 5 RIVER
Capital on the: 6 PIERRE
City on the: 5 OMAHA
feeder: 5 OSAGE 6 PLATTE
motto end: 4 ESTO
mountains: 5 OZARK
river: 5 OSAGE
town where Truman was born:
    5 LAMAR
tribe: 4 OTOE
___ Missouri: 3 USS
"Miss Peaches"
James nicknamed: 4 ETTA
Miss Piggy: 3 SOW
query: 3 **MOI**
"Miss Pym Disposes"
author Josephine: 3 TEY
"Miss ___ Regrets": 4 OTIS

"Miss Saigon"
homeland: **7** VIETNAM
Salonga of: **3** LEA
setting: **3** NAM
Misstep: 4 TRIP **5** ERROR GAFFE
Make a: **3** ERR
Missus
Jack and the: **6** SPRATS
Miss Woodhouse
of fiction: **4** EMMA
Mist: 4 HAZE **5** VAPOR
Get the ~ off: **5** DEFOG
Mistake: 5 ERROR LAPSE
7 ERRATUM
Big: **5** BONER
By: **7** INERROR
Like many a: **4** RUED
Make a: **3 ERR**
Minor: **4** SLIP
Printed: **4** TYPO
QB: **3** INT
remover: **6** ERASER
Sign of a: **7** ERASURE
Mistaken: 7 INERROR
Be: **3** ERR
Mistakenly: 7 INERROR
Mistakes: 6 ERRATA
Mister: 3 SIR
Madras: **3** SRI
~, in German: **4** HERR
~, in Spanish: **5 SENOR**
"Mister Ed"
actor Leon: **4** AMES
morsel: **3** OAT
Mister Roberts
portrayer: **5** FONDA
Mister Rogers: 4 FRED
Mistletoe
mo.: **3** DEC
Mistreat: 5 ABUSE **6** ILLUSE
Mistreatment: 5 ABUSE
Mistress
Like ~ Mary's maids: **6** INAROW
"Mistress of the Dark": 6 ELVIRA
"Misty"
composer Garner: **6** ERROLL
Where to look, in: **4** ATME
Misunderstanding: 4 TIFF
Generational: **3** GAP

MIT: 3 SCH
grad: **4** ENGR
Many ~ grads: **3 EES**
Part of: **4** INST TECH
Mitchell
Actor: **5** SASHA
Dennis: **4** BRAT
Diva: **5** LEONA
heroine: **5** OHARA
mansion: **4** TARA
Singer: **4 JONI**
Songwriter: **4** JONI
Mite: 4 ATOM **6** ACARID
Mitigate: 4 EASE
"Mitla Pass"
author: **4** URIS
Mitochondrion
material: **3** RNA
Mitt: 5 GLOVE
Kind of: **4** OVEN
Kit: **3** PAW
Mittens
Make: **4 KNIT**
Mitterrand
successor: **6** CHIRAC
Mittimus
or mandamus: **4** WRIT
Mitty
portrayer: **4** KAYE
Mitzi
Actress: **6** GAYNOR
Mix: 4 STIR **5** BLEND
Actor: **3** TOM
anew: **6** RETOSS
Contribute to the: **5** ADDIN
flick: **5** OATER
it up: **6** RASSLE
Metal: **5** ALLOY
Moonshine: **4** MASH
more thoroughly: **6** RESTIR
movie: **5** OATER
of football: **3** RON
Snack: **4** GORP
together: **4** STIR **5** BLEND
Trail: **4** GORP
Trail ~ fruit: **6** RAISIN
up: **4** STIR **5** ADDLE
Mix-a-Lot
title: **3** SIR

Mixed
bag: 4 **OLIO**
One of ~ ancestry: 7 MULATTO
Mixer: 5 TONIC 6 SOCIAL
Bar: 4 SODA 5 TONIC
    8 CLUBSODA
Rum: 4 COLA
Sans: 4 NEAT
Mixologist
measure: 4 SHOT
spot: 6 WETBAR
workplace: 3 BAR
Mixture: 4 MELD OLIO
    7 AMALGAM
Chef's: 4 ROUX
Metal: 5 ALLOY
Mix-up: 5 SNAFU
Miyoshi
Oscar winner: 5 UMEKI
"___ Miz": 3 **LES**
Mizrahi
Designer: 5 ISAAC
Mizzen: 4 SAIL
Mjolnir
His hammer was named:
    4 THOR
Mkt.
Common: 3 **EEC**
Like a school supplies: 4 ELHI
Stock ~ event: 3 IPO
ml.
About five: 3 TSP
MLB
stat: 3 ERA HRS
MLK
Part of: 6 MARTIN
title: 3 REV
Mlle.
Canonized: 3 STE
cousin: 4 **SRTA**
Mme.
of Madrid: 3 **SRA**
"Mm-hmm!": 4 ISEE
"MMMBop"
Group with 1997 hit: 6 HANSON
"Mmm, mmm!": 5 TASTY
M ___ mnemonic: 4 ASIN
Mnemonic
Lakes: 5 HOMES

Mnemosyne
Daughter of: 5 ERATO
Mo
preceder: 3 SLO
MO
city: 3 STL
Mo.
Autumn: 3 NOV OCT
Back-to-school: 4 SEPT
Dog days: 3 AUG
Equinox: 3 SEP 4 SEPT
Fall: 3 NOV **OCT** SEP 4 SEPT
Last: 3 DEC
named for a Caesar: 3 AUG
Presents: 3 DEC
Schoolmaster: 3 OCT
Showery: 3 APR
Spring: 3 **APR**
Summer: 3 **AUG**
town: 3 STL
Winter: 3 DEC FEB JAN
without a holiday: 3 AUG
Moab
Ancient region near: 4 EDOM
Moat
critter: 4 CROC
Mob: 4 BAND 5 HORDE
    6 RABBLE THRONG
action: 4 RIOT
boss: 4 CAPO
follower: 4 STER
hitman weapon: 7 GARROTE
scene: 4 RIOT
thug: 4 GOON
tough: 8 ENFORCER
"Mo' Better Blues"
director Spike: 3 LEE
Mobil
Company that merged with:
    5 EXXON
logo: 7 PEGASUS
rival: 5 AMOCO
Mobile
home: 4 TENT 5 TEPEE
    6 TEEPEE 7 ALABAMA
home (abbr.): 3 ALA
person: 8 ALABAMAN
Mobiles: 3 ART
Big name in: 6 CALDER

Mobuto
land: 5 ZAIRE
Mobuto Sese ___: 4 SEKO
Moby Dick: 5 WHALE
"Moby Dick"
captain: 4 **AHAB** 5 PELEG
Moccasin: 4 SHOE
Move like a: 7 SLITHER
Water: 11 COTTONMOUTH
Mocedades
1974 ~ hit: 6 ERESTU
Mocha
setting: 5 YEMEN
Mock: 4 GIBE JAPE JEER
      5 SCOFF SCORN TAUNT
      TEASE 6 DERIDE JEERAT
fanfare: 4 TADA
laugh syllable: 3 HAR
suffix: 3 ERY
words of understanding: 4 **AHSO**
~, in a way: 3 APE
"Mocker Mocked, The"
artist: 4 KLEE
Mockery: 5 FARCE
Make a ~ of: 7 SNEERAT
"Mockingbird"
singer Foxx: 4 INEZ
Mockingly
Laugh: 5 FLEER
"Mod ___, The": 5 SQUAD
Mode: 5 STYLE
lead-in: 3 ALA
___ mode: 3 **ALA**
Model: 4 POSE 5 IDEAL
adornment: 5 DECAL
airplane wood: 5 BALSA
asset: 4 FACE 5 POISE
Big name in ~ trains: 4 TYCO
Floor: 4 DEMO
from Somalia: 4 IMAN
in a bottle: 4 SHIP
Kind of: 4 ROLE 5 SCALE
maker's purchase: 3 KIT
material: 5 BALSA
of excellence: 7 PARAGON
of perfection: 5 IDEAL
One-named: 4 EMME IMAN
      5 FABIO
partner: 4 MAKE

Perfect game: 5 IDEAL
Plus-size: 4 EMME
Role: 4 HERO IDOL 5 IDEAL
Rolled: 5 PINUP
Runway: 5 PLANE
session: 5 SHOOT
Showroom: 4 DEMO
stance: 4 POSE
train layout: 4 OVAL
wood: 5 BALSA
~ Carol: 3 **ALT**
~ Gabrielle: 5 REECE
~ Macpherson: 4 **ELLE**
Modeler
purchase: 3 KIT
wood: 5 BALSA
Modeling
material: 4 CLAY
wood: 5 BALSA
Models
Like many: 6 SVELTE
Like Playboy: 4 SEXY
Very thin: 5 WAIFS
Model T: 4 AUTO
contemporary: 3 REO
Modem
Cable ~ alternative (abbr.): 3 DSL
Kind of: 5 CABLE
message: 3 FAX
Message via: 5 EMAIL
speed unit: 4 BAUD
termini: 3 EMS
Moderate: 4 EASE 5 ABATE
      TEPID 8 CENTRIST
Politically:
      15 MIDDLEOFTHEROAD
Moderately
slow: 7 ANDANTE
Moderator: 4 HOST
~ Jim: 6 LEHRER
Modern: 3 NEW 8 UPTODATE
address: 3 URL
art: 3 ARE
evidence: 3 DNA
Fairly: 6 NEWISH
First name in ~ dance: 5 TWYLA
letters: 5 EMAIL
Like some ~ music: 6 ATONAL
map subject: 6 GENOME

music media: 3 CDS
music style: 3 RAP
office staples: 3 PCS
pentathlon weapon: 4 EPEE
phone feature: 6 REDIAL
prefix: 3 NEO
recorder: 4 TIVO
rock genre: 3 EMO
sci. course: 4 ECOL
surgical tool: 5 LASER
viewer's choice: 4 HDTV
workout system: 5 TAEBO
~, in German: 3 NEU
Modernist: 3 NEO
"Modern Maturity"
  org.: 4 AARP
Modest: 6 DEMURE
  response to praise: 4 ITRY
  Skirt for the: 4 MAXI
Modesto
  winery name: 5 GALLO
"Modest Proposal, A"
  author: 5 SWIFT
Modicum: 3 TAD
Modifier
  abbr.: 3 ADJ
Modify: 4 EDIT 5 ADAPT ALTER
    AMEND 6 RECAST
  text: 4 EDIT
Modifying
  wd.: 3 ADJ
Modigliani
  Painter: 6 AMEDEO
Modish: 4 CHIC
"Mod Squad, The"
  actor Andrews: 4 TIGE
  actor Epps: 4 OMAR
  costar: 4 EPPS
  role: 4 LINC PETE
Modular
  home: 6 PREFAB
Module: 4 UNIT
  Apollo 11: 5 EAGLE
Modus ___: 8 OPERANDI
Modus operandi: 3 HOW WAY
    6 METHOD SYSTEM
Moe: 6 STOOGE
  Assault from: 4 POKE SLAP
  Missile for: 3 PIE

Moe, Tommy
  Emulate: 3 SKI
Moffo
  Diva: 4 **ANNA**
  Soprano: 4 **ANNA**
Mogadishu
  country: 7 SOMALIA
  resident: 6 SOMALI
"Mogambo"
  costar: 3 **AVA**
Mogul: 5 NABOB 6 TYCOON
  Early movie: 4 LOEW
  Industry: 4 CZAR
  Movie ~ Laemmle: 4 LOEW
Mogul Empire
  capital: 4 AGRA 5 DELHI
Moguls
  One among the: 5 SKIER
  Tackle: 3 SKI
Mohair
  source: 6 ANGORA
Mohammed
  Descendant of: 7 AGAKHAN
Mohawk
  Actor with a: 3 MRT
  City on the: 5 UTICA
  Literary: 5 UNCAS
Mohs scale
  1 on the ~: 4 TALC
  8 on the ~: 5 TOPAZ
  Higher on the: 6 HARDER
  top: 3 TEN
Moi
  Belonging to: 3 MES
  ___ Moines: 3 **DES**
Moises
  of baseball: 4 **ALOU**
Moist: 3 WET 4 DAMP DEWY
  and musty: 4 DANK
  application: 3 DAB
  In a ~ way: 5 WETLY
  Keep: 5 BASTE
  Less: 5 DRIER
  suffix: 3 URE
Moisten: 5 BEDEW
  the turkey: 5 BASTE
Moistener
  Muffin: 4 OLEO
Moisture: 7 WETNESS

Lacking: 3 DRY 4 ARID
Morning: 3 DEW
remover: 5 DRIER
Moistureless: 4 ARID
Moisturizer
ingredient: 4 ALOE
Mojave: 6 DESERT
Like the: 4 ARID
plant: 5 AGAVE
state (abbr.): 5 CALIF
Mojo: 6 AMULET
Molar: 5 TOOTH
Acquire a: 6 TEETHE
Molars: 5 TEETH
Molasses
Dessert made from:
10 SHOOFLYPIE
Like: 4 SLOW
Move like: 4 OOZE
Slow as: 4 POKY
Molasses-based
liquor: 3 RUM
Mold: 5 SHAPE
anew: 7 RESHAPE
Cold: 5 ASPIC
Gold: 5 INGOT
Metal: 3 PIG
React to: 5 RIPEN
ripened cheese: 4 BRIE
source: 5 SPORE
Moldavia
~, once (abbr.): 3 SSR
Molded
dessert: 5 BOMBE
dish: 5 ASPIC
Easily: 4 SOFT
Molder: 3 ROT
Molding
Convex: 5 OVOLO
Curved: 4 **OGEE**
Horizontal: 7 CORNICE
S-shaped: 4 **OGEE**
Window: 5 LEDGE
Moldings
Semicircular: 4 TORI
Molds: 5 FUNGI
Mole: 3 SPY 5 AGENT
kin: 5 SHREW
passageway: 6 TUNNEL

Molecular
biology topic: 3 RNA
bit: 4 ATOM
Molecule
Genetic: 3 RNA
part: 4 **ATOM**
Part of a complex: 6 LIGAND
Single-strand: 3 RNA
Molehill
It can make a ~ out of a
mountain: 3 TNT
Molière
metier: 6 SATIRE
play part: 4 ACTE
Moline
Company based in: 5 DEERE
"Moll Flanders"
author: 5 DEFOE
Mollify: 4 CALM 5 ALLAY
6 SOFTEN SOOTHE
7 ASSUAGE PLACATE
Mollusk
Bivalve: 4 CLAM
Edible: 6 OYSTER 7 ABALONE
Spiral-shelled: 5 SNAIL WHELK
Tentacled: 5 SQUID
7 OCTOPOD
Mollusks
Tentacled: 6 OCTOPI
Molly
Fibber and: 6 MCGEES
Mollycoddle: 4 BABY 6 PAMPER
Molokai
meal: 4 LUAU
neighbor: 4 MAUI OAHU
Molotov cocktail
fuse: 3 RAG
Molson
product: 4 BEER
Molson Centre
music: 7 OCANADA
Molt: 4 SHED
Molten
rock: 4 LAVA 5 **MAGMA**
Mom: 6 PARENT
1950s sitcom ~: 4 REED
Bro of: 3 UNC
Coop: 3 HEN
Cousin's: 4 AUNT

Mate of: 3 DAD
Meadow: 3 EWE
Mom's: 4 GRAN NANA
Question to ~ or dad: 4 CANI
Related to: 5 ENATE
Sister of: 4 AUNT
specialty: 3 TLC
Stable: 4 MARE
MoMA
artist: 4 DALI KLEE MIRO
Part of: 3 ART 6 MODERN
Part of ~ address: 4 NYNY
Mom-and-pop
lender (abbr.): 3 SBA
org.: 3 PTA
Mombasa
home: 5 KENYA
Moment
Brief: 3 SEC
Met: 4 ARIA
Quiet: 4 LULL
Senior: 4 PROM
___ moment: 3 INA
Momentarily: 4 SOON 6 INASEC
Momentary
flash: 5 GLINT
"___ momento!": 3 UNO
Momentous: 8 EVENTFUL
       15 EARTHSHATTERING
"___ Mommy Kissing Santa
       Claus": 4 ISAW
"Momo"
author Michael: 4 ENDE
Mon.
follower: 3 TUE 4 TUES
"Mon ___!": 4 DIEU
"Mona ___": 4 LISA
Monaco
resort: 10 MONTECARLO
Monarch: 5 RULER
Be a: 4 RULE
Bygone: 4 TSAR
catcher: 3 NET
domain: 5 REALM
Future: 4 HEIR
Old: 4 SHAH
Monarchy
Himalayan: 5 NEPAL
near Fiji: 5 TONGA

Monastery: 5 ABBEY
address: 3 DOM
head: 5 ABBOT
music: 5 CHANT
resident: 4 MONK 6 OBLATE
Monastic
jurisdiction: 6 ABBACY
title: 3 FRA
Mondale
running mate: 7 FERRARO
Mondavi
rival: 5 GALLO
"Monday, Monday"
Half the ~ group: 5 MAMAS
       PAPAS
"Monday Night Football"
Former ~ commentator:
       7 ESIASON
network: 3 ABC
___ monde (high society): 4 **HAUT**
Mondesi
of baseball: 4 RAUL
Mondrian
Painter: 4 **PIET**
Monet: 6 ARTIST
medium: 4 OILS
Monetary
gain: 5 LUCRE
Money: 4 CASH KALE 5 MOOLA
       6 TENDER
Advance: 4 LEND
back: 6 REBATE REFUND
Big: 9 MEGABUCKS
Box office: 4 GATE
Bribe: 4 SOAP
Bygone: 6 PESETA
changer: 6 EDITOR
Coined: 6 SPECIE
Color of: 5 GREEN
Continental: 4 EURO
Corp. ~ man: 3 CFO
Dirty: 4 PELF
dispenser: 3 ATM
drawer: 4 TILL
Extort ~ from: 5 BLEED
Fed. ~ overseer: 3 OMB
for old age (abbr.): 3 IRA
for the poor: 4 ALMS
Front: 4 ANTE

Get-out-of-jail: 4 BAIL
Grant: 5 ENDOW
guarantor, for short: 4 FDIC
handler: 6 TELLER
International: 4 EURO
In the: 4 RICH
in the bank: 5 ASSET
Kind of: 3 MAD 4 HUSH SEED
Lay ~ on: 3 BET
Losing: 8 INTHERED
machine: 3 ATM
Make: 4 COIN EARN MINT
maker: 4 MINT
Makeshift: 5 SCRIP
manager: 6 EDITOR
Minimal: 4 CENT
New: 4 **EURO** 5 EUROS
Old: 4 LIRE 5 SCRIP
overseas: 5 EUROS
owed: 4 DEBT
Paper: 5 NOTES
player: 3 PRO
Prize: 5 PURSE
Provide ~ for: 5 ENDOW
Put ~ in the bank: 4 SAVE
Put up, as: 4 LEND
roll: 3 WAD
Run for the: 4 RACE
Send: 5 REMIT
set aside: 6 ESCROW
Slangy: 4 KALE
Slightest bit of: 3 SOU
Solicit ~ from: 5 HITUP
spent: 5 OUTGO
substitute: 5 SCRIP
Take the ~ and run: 3 ROB
    7 ABSCOND
The color of no: 3 RED
Upfront: 4 ANTE
Use: 5 SPEND
Without ~ changing hands:
    7 INTRADE
Words before: 7 ALACKOF
"Money"
novelist Martin: 4 AMIS
Moneybags: 5 NABOB 6 FATCAT
Moneyed
one: 4 HAVE
"Money ___ everything!": 4 ISNT

Money-losing
proposition: 4 SCAM
Moneymaker: 4 MINT
Sure: 7 CASHCOW
Moneymakers
Magazine: 3 ADS
Money-making: 3 PRO
device: 3 DIE
Money-managing
exec.: 3 CFO
"Money ___ object!": 4 ISNO
Money-related
(abbr.): 4 FISC
Money-saving
~, in product names: 5 ECONO
Mongibello
Mount known locally as:
    4 ETNA
Mongkut, King
realm: 4 SIAM
visitor: 4 ANNA
Mongol
invader: 5 TATAR
ruler: 4 KHAN
tent: 4 YURT
Mongolia
Like: 4 ARID
Much of: 4 GOBI
___ Mongolia: 5 OUTER
Mongolian: 5 ASIAN
desert: 4 **GOBI**
expanse: 10 GOBIDESERT
It means "ocean" in: 5 DALAI
It means "red" in: 4 ULAN
monk: 4 LAMA
mountain range: 5 ALTAI
tent: 4 YURT
Mongoose
prey: 5 COBRA
Mongrel: 3 **CUR** 4 MUTT
Monica
of tennis: 5 **SELES**
___ Monica, California:
    5 SANTA
Monicagate
prosecutor: 5 STARR
Moniker: 3 TAG 4 NAME
    6 HANDLE
Cowboy: 3 **TEX**

Monk: 3 FRA
Monster: 6 NESSIE
Satanic: 7 EVILONE

Monitor
Airport ~ (abbr.): 3 ARR ETA
beat: 4 HALL
Dot on a: 5 PIXEL
image: 4 ICON
Kind of PC: 3 LCD
PC: 3 **CRT**
Place for a ~ (abbr.): 3 ICU
TV: 3 FCC 5 VCHIP

Monk
Buddhist: 4 LAMA
home: 5 ABBEY 6 PRIORY
hood: 4 COWL
Like a: 6 HOODED
Main: 5 ABBOT
music: 3 BOP
quarters: 4 CELL
title: 3 DOM **FRA**

"Monkees"
1967 ~ song: 3 SHE
Peter of the: 4 TORK

Monkey
African: 6 BABOON
Aladdin: 3 **ABU**
business: 5 APERY
Grease ~ job: 4 LUBE
Kind of: 6 RHESUS
Mini: 4 TITI
South American: 4 TITI
suit: 3 TUX
wrench: 4 SNAG

Monkey's
uncle: 3 APE

Monkeyshine: 5 ANTIC

Monkey Trial
defendant: 6 SCOPES
lawyer: 6 DARROW

Mono
Not: 6 STEREO
relative: 3 **UNI**

Monocle
part: 4 LENS

Monogram
1950s ~: 3 AES DDE
CSA: 3 REL
Fashion: 3 **YSL**

Inventor: 3 TAE
Jan.: 3 MLK
letter: 7 INITIAL
Literary: 3 EAP GBS RLS RWE
    TSE
ltr.: 4 INIT
N.L.: 3 STL
Poet: 3 TSE
Presidential: 3 DDE FDR HST
pt.: 4 INIT

Monogrammatic
car: 3 REO

Monokini
lack: 3 BRA

Monologist
Late-night: 4 LENO
need: 5 STOOL
~ Mort: 4 SAHL

Monologue
Miller: 4 RANT

"Mon Oncle"
actor: 4 TATI
Tati's ~ Monsieur: 5 HULOT

Monopolize: 3 HOG
~, with "up": 3 SEW

Monopoly: 4 GAME
asset: 5 HOTEL
avenue: 8 ORIENTAL
card: 4 DEED
Cheap ~ purchase: 6 BALTIC
Corner square in: 4 JAIL
fee: 4 RENT
maker: 6 HASBRO
need: 4 DICE
payment: 4 RENT
props.: 3 RRS 4 AVES
purchase: 5 HOTEL HOUSE
purchase (abbr.): 4 UTIL
token: 3 HAT 4 IRON SHOE
    7 SCOTTIE
White ~ bill: 3 ONE

Monorail
unit: 4 TRAM

Monotone
Speak in a: 5 DRONE

Monotonous: 7 ONENOTE
    8 SINGSONG

Monotonously
Talked: 8 DRONEDON

Monotony: 6 TEDIUM
    8 SAMENESS
Monounsaturated
  Oil high in ~ fatty acids:
    6 CANOLA
Monroe: 6 BLONDE
  movie: 7 BUSSTOP
  or Madison (abbr.): 3 JAS
  policy: 8 DOCTRINE
  successor: 5 ADAMS
Monroe, Marilyn: 4 ICON
    6 BLONDE
  birth name: 5 NORMA
  feature: 4 MOLE
Monsoon
  Like ~ season: 5 RAINY
Monster: 4 HUGE **OGRE**
  Fairy tale: 4 OGRE
  Flying ~ of sci-fi: 5 RODAN
  Green-eyed: 4 ENVY
  Kind of: 4 GILA
  lizard: 4 GILA
  loch: 4 NESS
  Many-headed: 5 HYDRA
  Mythical: 3 **ORC** 5 HARPY
    7 GRIFFIN
  nickname: 6 NESSIE
  Sea: 3 ORC 6 SCYLLA
  Southwestern: 4 GILA
___ monster: 4 **GILA**
"Monsters, ___": 3 INC
"Monster's Ball"
  actress Berry: 5 HALLE
Mont.
  neighbor: 3 IDA 4 ALTA NDAK
    SASK SDAK
Montague
  foe: 7 CAPULET
  Young: 5 ROMEO
Montaigne
  output: 5 ESSAI ESSAY
Montana: 3 JOE 5 STATE
  capital: 6 HELENA
  city: 5 BUTTE
  motto starter: 3 ORO
  native: 4 CREE
  neighbor: 7 ALBERTA
  tribe: 4 CROW
  ~, once: 5 NINER

Montand
  Actor: 4 **YVES**
Mont Blanc: 3 **ALP** PEN
  range: 4 ALPS
  ~, in French: 4 ALPE
Monte
  Three-card: 4 SCAM
Monte ___: 5 CARLO 6 CRISTO
  (peak): 4 ROSA
___ Monte: 3 DEL
Monte Carlo: 4 AUTO
Montecristo
  Island north of: 4 ELBA
Montel
  rival, once: 5 OPRAH
Montenegro
  native: 4 SLAV
Monterey
  Fort near: 3 ORD
Monte Rosa: 3 ALP
Monterrey
  jack: 4 PESO
  mineral: 3 ORO
  ~ Mrs.: 3 SRA
Monteverdi
  opera: 5 ORFEO 7 ARIANNA
Montevideo
  land (abbr.): 3 URU
Montez
  Dancer: 4 LOLA
Montezuma: 5 AZTEC
Montgomery
  Actor: 5 CLIFT
  City SSE of: 5 OZARK
  City west of: 5 SELMA
  Jazz guitarist: 3 **WES**
Month
  A ~ of Sundays: 4 AGES
  Day of the: 4 IDES
  First Spanish: 5 ENERO
  Hebrew: 4 ADAR ELUL 5 NISAN
  In the previous: 6 ULTIMO
  "Merry": 3 MAY
  ~, in Spanish: 3 MES
Monthly: 6 MENSAL
  bill: 4 RENT 5 CABLE
  bill (abbr.): 3 TEL 4 ELEC
Months
  Like non-oyster: 5 RLESS

Monticello: 6 ESTATE
Montmartre
menu: 5 CARTE
Montreal: 6 ISLAND
1967 ~ event: 4 EXPO
player: 4 **EXPO**
prov.: 3 QUE
season: 3 ETE
~ Mrs.: 3 MME
Monty
Do a full: 5 STRIP
"Monty Python"
actor Idle: 4 ERIC
actor John: 6 CLEESE
actor Michael: 5 PALIN
airer: 3 BBC
offering: 4 SKIT
Monument: 5 STELE
designer Maya: 3 LIN
rock: 7 GRANITE
Stone: 5 CAIRN STELE
Year, on a: 4 ANNO
Monumental: 4 **EPIC**
year: 4 ANNO
Monument Valley
feature: 4 MESA
state: 4 UTAH
Moo: 3 LOW
Alley from: 3 OOP
Mooch: 3 BUM 5 CADGE
6 SPONGE
Mood: 4 TONE
Foul: 4 SNIT
In a peeved: 5 TESTY
In the: 7 AMOROUS
ring, once: 3 FAD
"Mood ___": 6 INDIGO
Moody: 4 DOUR 6 MOROSE
Actor: 3 RON
Moody Blues
hit: 5 GONOW
"Moody River"
singer: 8 PATBOONE
Moo ___ gai pan: 3 GOO
Moo goo gai pan
pan: 3 WOK
Moo goo ___ pan: 3 **GAI**
Mooing
Still ~, so to speak: 4 RARE

Moolah: 4 CASH GELT JACK
KALE 5 BREAD DOUGH
LUCRE 6 DINERO DOREMI
Moon: 3 ORB
Bay at the: 4 HOWL
Blue: 6 RARITY
craft: 3 LEM
First name on the: 4 NEIL
Full: 5 PHASE
goddess: 4 **LUNA** 6 SELENE
Howl at the: 3 BAY
lander: 3 **LEM**
Like a blue: 4 RARE
Many a: 4 AGES
material: 11 GREENCHEESE
mission name: 6 APOLLO
New: 5 PHASE
of Jupiter: 4 LEDA 6 EUROPA
of Mars: 6 DEIMOS PHOBOS
of Neptune: 6 NEREID TRITON
of Saturn: 4 RHEA 5 DIONE
TITAN 6 TETHYS
Of the: 5 LUNAR
of Uranus: 5 ARIEL 6 OBERON
7 MIRANDA TITANIA
Once in a blue: 6 RARELY
ring: 4 HALO
Second man on the: 6 ALDRIN
shape: 8 CRESCENT
Shoot for the: 6 ASPIRE
stage: 5 PHASE
suffix: 5 SCAPE
Unseen part of the: 7 FARSIDE
valley: 4 RILL 5 **RILLE**
vehicle: 3 LEM
Moonfish: 4 OPAH
"Moonlight ___": 6 SONATA
8 SERENADE
Moon of Endor
critter: 4 EWOK
"Moon Over Parador"
actress: 5 BRAGA
"Moonraker"
actor Richard: 4 KIEL
"Moon River"
composer: 7 MANCINI
lyricist: 6 MERCER
Moonroof
alternative: 4 TTOP

Moons
Many: 3 EON 4 AGES
Moonscape
Like a: 5 STARK
Moonshine: 5 HOOCH
11 MOUNTAINDEW
Irish: 6 POTEEN
maker: 5 STILL
mix: 4 MASH
Mouthful of: 4 SWIG
Moonstone: 4 OPAL
Moonstruck: 4 DAFT GAGA
6 INLOVE
"Moonstruck"
Oscar winner: 4 CHER
Moo ___ pork: 3 SHU
Moor: 5 HEATH TIEUP
betrayer: 4 IAGO
Place to: 4 COVE 5 INLET
Shakespearean: 7 OTHELLO
Moore
Actress: 4 DEMI
costar: 5 ASNER
Filmmaker: 7 MICHAEL
poem opener: 4 TWAS
Singer: 5 MELBA
___ Moore (stew): 5 DINTY
Moore, Demi
1990 ~ film: 5 GHOST
1997 ~ film: 6 GIJANE
Moore, Dudley
film: 6 ARTHUR
Moore, Mary ___: 5 TYLER
Moore, Thomas
land: 4 ERIN
Moorehead
Actress: 5 **AGNES**
Mooring
rope: 6 HAWSER
Moorish
palace: 7 ALCAZAR
Moose
kin: 3 ELK 4 DEER
Mop
mate: 4 PAIL
up: 4 **SWAB**
Mop & ___: 3 GLO
Mope: 4 POUT SULK
5 BROOD

Mopped
It may be: 4 BROW
Moppet: 3 TOT 4 TYKE
Mayberry: 4 OPIE
Moral
author: 5 AESOP
element: 5 ETHOS
principle: 5 **ETHIC**
Story with a: 5 FABLE
7 PARABLE
values: 6 ETHICS
Morale: 6 ESPRIT
GI ~ booster: 3 USO
Morales
Actor: 4 **ESAI**
Moralist
Noted: 5 AESOP
Roman: 6 SENECA
Morality: 5 ETHIC
Morally
reprehensible: 6 SORDID
strict: 7 PURITAN
Morals
Man of: 5 **AESOP**
Moran
Actress: 4 **ERIN**
rival: 6 CAPONE
Moranis
Actor: 4 RICK
Morante
Novelist: 4 ELSA
Moravia
Capital of: 4 BRNO
Moravian: 4 SLAV
Moray: 3 **EEL**
home: 6 EELERY
hunter: 5 EELER
Mordant: 5 ACERB
~ Mort: 4 SAHL
More: 4 ELSE 5 EXTRA
And: 3 ETC 4 ETAL
Does ~ than see: 6 RAISES
Get ~ out of: 5 REUSE
Is for ~ than one: 3 ARE
Little ~ than: 4 MERE
No ~ than: 4 MERE ONLY UPTO
6 ATMOST
of the same: 7 WHATNOT
Once: 4 ANEW 5 **AGAIN**

6 AFRESH
One: 7 ANOTHER
One or: 3 **ANY** 4 SOME
or less: 5 **ABOUT** SORTA
6 KINDOF
Say: 3 ADD
What's: 3 AND 4 **ALSO**
work: 6 UTOPIA
~, in Spanish: 3 MAS
~, musically: 3 PIU
~, proverbially: 4 LESS
"More!": 6 ENCORE
Morel
morsel: 4 STEM
Morelos, José
Place to see: 4 PESO
Moreno
Actress: 4 **RITA**
More or ___ : 4 LESS
Moreover: 3 AND TOO 4 ALSO
"More's the pity": 4 ALAS
Morgan
Country singer: 6 LORRIE
of the comics: 3 REX
Senior golfer: 3 GIL
Morgan, J.P.: 6 BANKER
___ morgana (mirage): 4 FATA
Morgenstern
of TV: 5 RHODA
Morgiana
Master of: 7 ALIBABA
Morgue: 3 RUE
"Moriae encomium"
author: 7 ERASMUS
Morissette
hit: 6 IRONIC
singer: 6 **ALANIS**
Morita
Sony cofounder: 4 AKIO
Mork: 5 ALIEN
and others: 3 ETS
home planet: 3 ORK
Like: 5 ORKAN
sign-off: 8 NANUNANU
spaceship: 3 EGG
supervisor: 5 ORSON
word: 4 NANU
"Mork & Mindy"
actress Dawber: 3 PAM

leader: 5 ORSON
planet: 3 ORK
Morley
Reporter: 5 SAFER
Morlocks
victims: 4 ELOI
Mormon
gp.: 3 LDS
Many a: 6 UTAHAN
stronghold: 4 UTAH
Mormon Church
founder: 5 SMITH
Morn
Moist in the: 4 DEWY
opposite: 3 EVE
Mornay: 5 SAUCE
Morning
bowlful: 6 CEREAL
condensation: 3 DEW
Early ~ arrivals: 7 REDEYES
Early in the: 6 ATDAWN
eyeopener: 4 JAVA 5 LATTE
6 COFFEE
haze: 4 MIST
hrs.: 3 AMS
It breaks every: 3 DAY
Like ~ grass: 4 DEWY
NBC ~ show: 5 TODAY
noisemaker: 5 ALARM
radio host: 4 IMUS
Red sky at: 4 OMEN
talk show cohost: 4 RIPA
~, in French: 5 MATIN
Morning ___ : 5 GLORY
"Morning ___ Broken": 3 HAS
"Morning Edition"
network: 3 NPR
Mornings
~, for short: 3 **AMS**
"Morning Watch, The"
writer: 4 AGEE
Morns: 3 AMS
opposites: 4 EENS
Moro
of Italy: 4 ALDO
Moroccan
city: 3 FES FEZ
Morocco
Capital of: 5 RABAT

Former Spanish enclave in: 4 IFNI
Morocco-like
  leather: 4 ROAN
Moron: 3 ASS
Moronic: 3 DIM 5 INANE
  intro: 3 OXY
Morose: 6 SULLEN
Morph
  prefix: 4 ECTO ENDO
  suffix: 3 EME
Morpheus
  In the arms of: 6 ASLEEP
  Realm of: 6 DREAMS
Morphine: 6 OPIATE
Morricone
  Composer: 5 **ENNIO**
Morris
  Civil rights lawyer: 4 DEES
  Director: 5 ERROL
  Politico: 5 UDALL
Morrison
  Author: 4 **TONI**
  Singer: 3 VAN
Morrison, Jim
  group, with "The": 5 DOORS
  portrayer Kilmer: 3 VAL
Morrison, Toni
  novel: 4 SULA 7 BELOVED
    TARBABY
Morrow
  Actor: 3 VIC
Morrow, Tracy
  Rapper born: 4 ICET
Morse: 4 CODE
  bit: 3 DAH DIT DOT 4 DASH
  "E": 3 DIT DOT
  message: 3 SOS
  Singer: 7 ELLAMAE
  "T": 3 DAH
  Three dots, in: 3 ESS
Morse, Robert
  Tony role for: 3 TRU
Morsel: 3 ORT 4 BITE 6 TIDBIT
Mort
  Comedian: 4 **SAHL**
  Satirist: 4 **SAHL**
  ___ mort (melancholy): 3 ALA
Mortal
  wrong: 3 SIN

___ **mortals:** 4 MERE
Mortar
  partner: 6 PESTLE
  tool: 6 TROWEL
  tray: 3 HOD
Mortarboard: 3 CAP
  attachment: 6 TASSEL
  Like a: 8 TASSELED
  wearer: 4 GRAD
Mortgage: 4 DEBT LIEN
  figure: 4 RATE
  Govt. ~ org.: 3 FHA
  Have a: 3 OWE
  Satisfy a: 5 REPAY
  Take out a: 6 BORROW
Morticia: 6 ADDAMS
  Cousin of: 3 ITT
  creator, briefly: 4 CHAS
  Husband of: 5 GOMEZ
Mortification: 5 SHAME
    7 CHAGRIN
Mortify: 5 ABASE ABASH APPAL
    6 DEMEAN
Mortimer
  Dummy: 5 **SNERD**
  Philosopher: 5 ADLER
Mortise
  mate: 5 **TENON**
Morton
  product: 4 SALT
Morton, ___ P.: 4 LEVI
Mos.
  Fall: 4 OCTS
  Many: 3 **YRS**
  School: 5 SEPTS
Mosaic: 5 INLAY
  Like ~ stones: 6 INLAID
  piece: 4 TILE
    7 TESSERA
  pieces: 8 TESSERAE
  technique: 5 INLAY
Mosconi
  game: 4 POOL
  maneuver: 5 MASSE
Moscow
  City near: 4 OREL
  money: 5 RUBLE
Mose
  Jazzman: 7 ALLISON

Moselle
  City on the: 4 METZ
  tributary: 4 SAAR
Moses
  Brother of: 5 AARON
  Grandma: 4 ANNA
  mount: 4 NEBO
  Mount climbed by: 5 SINAI
  Obstacle for: 6 REDSEA
  of basketball: 6 MALONE
  of track: 5 EDWIN
  portrayer: 6 HESTON
  Successor of: 6 JOSHUA
  Where ~ was buried: 4 MOAB
"Moses"
  novelist: 4 ASCH
Moses, Grandma
  first name: 4 ANNA
"Moses und ___": 4 ARON
Mosey: 5 AMBLE
Mosh: 9 SLAMDANCE
Moshe
  Israeli general: 5 DAYAN
  of Israel: 5 ARENS
Moslem
  leader: 4 EMIR IMAM
Mosque
  Great ~ site: 6 ALEPPO
  leader: 4 **IMAM**
  tower: 7 **MINARET**
Mosque of ___: 4 OMAR
Mosquito: 4 PEST 5 BITER
  Dangerous: 5 **AEDES**
  lookalike: 5 MIDGE
  protection: 3 NET
  ~, to a dragonfly: 4 PREY
Moss
  Kind of: 4 PEAT
  maker: 5 SPORE
  Model: 4 KATE
  Sea: 4 ALGA
  Sphagnum: 4 PEAT
  ___ moss: 4 PEAT
Mossback: 4 FOGY
Most
  At: 4 TOPS
  For the ~ part: 6 MAINLY
    7 ASARULE
  Home to: 4 **ASIA**

  Like ~ of us: 5 ASIAN
  likely: 6 APTEST
  More than: 3 ALL
Mostel
  Actor: 4 ZERO
  role: 5 TEVYE
"Most likely ...": 7 ODDSARE
"___ Most Unusual Day": 4 ITSA
Most-wanted
  group: 5 ALIST
Mosul
  native: 5 IRAQI
Mot
  Bon: 4 JEST QUIP 7 EPIGRAM
Mote: 5 SPECK
Motel: 3 INN
  employee: 4 MAID
  freebie: 3 ICE 4 SOAP
  Kind of: 5 ROACH
  meeting: 5 TRYST
  posting: 5 RATES
  rater: 3 AAA
  They're non grata at a: 4 PETS
  unit: 4 ROOM
___ motel (tryst site): 6 NOTELL
Motet
  group: 5 CHOIR
Moth
  Draw for a: 5 FLAME
  Kind of: 4 LUNA
  meal: 4 WOOL
  repellent: 5 CEDAR
Moth-___: 5 EATEN
Moth-eaten: 3 OLD 5 RATTY
    STALE TATTY
  More: 6 HOLIER
Mother
  Act the ~ hen: 4 FUSS
  Brooding: 3 HEN
  Farm: 3 EWE HEN SOW
  group: 3 DEN
  helper: 9 NURSEMAID
  of renown: 6 TERESA
  relative: 5 ENATE
  superior: 6 ABBESS
  ~, in Spanish: 5 MADRE
Mother ___: 4 LODE 6 TERESA
"Mother Goose Suite"
  composer: 5 RAVEL

Mother Hubbard
  Like: 3 OLD
Mothering
  sort: 5 DOTER
  type: 3 HEN
Mother-in-law
  of Dracula: 6 OLDBAT
  of Meathead: 5 EDITH
  of Ruth: 5 NAOMI
Motherless
  calf: 5 DOGIE
"Mother Night"
  star: 5 NOLTE
Mother-of-pearl: 5 NACRE
  source: 7 **ABALONE**
Mother's Day
  baby: 6 TAURUS
  Busy co. on: 3 FTD
Mothers of Invention
  rocker Frank: 5 ZAPPA
Mother Teresa: 3 NUN
Moths
  Showy: 3 IOS
Motif: 5 THEME
  Jazz: 4 RIFF
Motion
  detector: 6 SENSOR
  First law of ~ subject: 7 INERTIA
  Manner of: 4 GAIT
  Ocean: 4 **TIDE**
  Pertaining to: 7 KINETIC
  picture: 4 CINE
  Put into: 7 ACTUATE
  Put off, as a: 5 TABLE
  Support a: 6 SECOND
Motionless: 5 INERT STILL
  6 ATREST
Motion picture
  spool: 4 REEL
Motivate: 4 STIR 5 IMPEL
  7 INSPIRE
Motivator
  Certain: 7 PEPTALK
Motive: 6 REASON
  A question of: 3 WHY
  Crime: 7 REVENGE
  Secret: 5 ANGLE
Motley: 4 PIED 6 RAGTAG
Mötley ___ : 4 CRUE

Motor
  Adjust a: 4 TUNE
  attachment: 4 CADE
  club: 3 AAA
  Fly without a: 5 GLIDE
  Gun the: 3 REV
  Induction ~ inventor: 5 TESLA
  lodge: 3 INN
  oil additive: 3 STP
  oil amount: 5 QUART
  suffix: 3 OLA 4 CADE
  trailer: 4 CADE
  vehicle: 3 CAR
Motorboat
  tow: 9 AQUAPLANE
Motor City
  gp.: 3 UAW
Motorcycle
  attachment: 7 SIDECAR
  Big: 3 HOG
  daredevil: 7 KNIEVEL
  First name in ~ stunts: 4 EVEL
  maker: 6 YAMAHA
Motorcyclist
  ~ Knievel: 4 EVEL
Motorist
  choices: 4 RTES
  offense: 3 DWI
  org.: 3 AAA
  Red, to a: 4 STOP
  Stranded ~ need: 3 TOW
  Stranded ~ signal: 5 FLARE
Motown: 5 LABEL 7 DETROIT
  Franklin of: 6 ARETHA
  genre: 4 SOUL
  Marvin of: 4 GAYE
Motown Records
  founder Berry: 5 GORDY
Motrin
  rival: 5 ADVIL ALEVE 6 ANACIN
Mott
  Reformer: 8 LUCRETIA
Mottled: 4 PIED 5 PINTO
  horse: 4 ROAN 5 PINTO
  6 DAPPLE
Motto
  U.S. ~ word: 4 UNUM
"Moulin Rouge"
  actor McGregor: 4 EWAN

dance: 6 CANCAN
Mound: 4 DUNE HEAP HILL
     PILE 5 KNOLL
  builder: 3 ANT
  Insect: 7 ANTHILL
  stat: 3 ERA
  Stone: 5 CAIRN
  Take the: 4 HURL
Mount: 5 GETON HORSE **STEED**
  climbed by Moses: 5 SINAI
  Colorful: 4 ROAN
  for Noah: 6 ARARAT
  in Crete: 3 IDA
  near Catania: 4 ETNA
  They may: 8 TENSIONS
  whose name means "I burn":
     4 ETNA
Mount ___: 5 SINAI 6 VERNON
Mountain
  air: 5 YODEL
  ashes: 6 ROWANS
  Biblical: 5 HOREB
  cat: 4 PUMA
  chain: 5 RANGE 7 SIERRAS
  climber equipment: 5 ICEAX
     PITON
  crest: 5 ARETE RIDGE
  curve: 3 ESS
  debris: 5 SCREE
  demarcation: 8 TREELINE
  Genesis: 6 ARARAT
  goat: 4 IBEX
  Greek: 4 OSSA
  High: 3 ALP
  home: 5 AERIE 6 CHALET
  lake: 4 **TARN**
  Lift up a: 4 TBAR
  lion: 4 **PUMA**
  man pursuit: 4 PELT
  man trap: 5 SNARE
  Martinique: 5 PELEE
  Mongolian ~ range: 5 ALTAI
  nymph: 5 **OREAD**
  pass: 3 COL GAP
  pool: 4 TARN
  ridge: 5 **ARETE**
  road feature: 3 ESS
  road sign: 10 STEEPGRADE
  sighting: 4 YETI

  sign (abbr.): 4 ELEV
  suffix: 3 EER
  top: 4 PEAK
  topper: 4 SNOW
  tree: 3 ASH
  Trip up a: 6 ASCENT
  Way up a: 4 TBAR
  World's highest: 7 EVEREST
  ~, to some: 8 MOLEHILL
Mountain ___: 3 DEW
Mountaineer: 6 SCALER
     7 CLIMBER
  challenge: 4 CRAG
  descent: 6 RAPPEL
  rest stop: 5 LEDGE
  tool: 5 ICEAX
"Mountain Music"
  group: 7 ALABAMA
___ Mountains: 4 URAL 5 OZARK
     UINTA
Mountaintop: 4 APEX PEAK
  home: 5 AERIE
Mountbatten
  Lady: 6 EDWINA
Mount Carmel
  locale: 6 ISRAEL
Mount Desert Island
  park: 6 ACADIA
Mountebank: 4 FAKE 5 ROGUE
Mounted: 4 ROSE
  on: 4 ATOP
Mount Fuji
  setting: 6 HONSHU
Mount Hood
  locale: 6 OREGON
Mount Katahdin
  locale: 5 MAINE
Mount McKinley: 6 DENALI
Mount Olympus
  chief: 4 ZEUS
  dwellers: 4 GODS
  queen: 4 HERA
Mount Rainier
  range: 8 CASCADES
  View from: 6 TACOMA
Mount Rushmore
  pres.: 3 ABE
  state (abbr.): 4 SDAK
Mount Saint ___: 6 HELENS

Mount Saint Helens
 fallout: 3 ASH
Mount Vernon: 6 ESTATE
Mourn: 6 BEWAIL GRIEVE
Mournful: 7 ELEGIAC
 cry: 4 YOWL
 melody: 5 DIRGE
 peal: 5 KNELL
 poem: 5 ELEGY
Mourning
 of basketball: 6 ALONZO
"Mourning Becomes Electra"
 brother: 4 ORIN
 playwright: 6 ONEILL
Mouse: 6 RODENT
 catcher: 3 CAT OWL 4 TRAP
 Eat like a: 4 GNAW
 hater cry: 3 EEK
 home: 3 PAD
 Like a: 3 WEE
 Like a church: 4 POOR
 manipulator: **4 USER**
 Move like a: 4 DRAG
 pad: 3 MAT
 Reaction to a: 3 EEK
 sound: 5 CLICK
 target: 4 ICON
 Word with: 3 PAD
 ~, to some: 4 PREY
Mouseketeer
 An original: 6 DOREEN
   7 ANNETTE
 ~ Jimmy: 4 DODD
Mouselike
 animal: 4 VOLE
Mousquetaires
 Number of: 5 TROIS
Moussaka
 meat: 4 LAMB
Mousse
 alternative: 3 GEL
Mousy: 3 SHY 4 MEEK 5 TIMID
Mouth
 area: 5 DELTA
 Away from the: 6 ABORAL
 Big: 3 MAW YAP 4 TRAP
 bone: 3 JAW
 By: 6 ORALLY
 Down in the: 3 SAD

 Foam at the: 4 RAGE
 Foaming at the: 5 RABID
 It has a big: 4 EWER
 off: 4 RANT SASS
 off to: 6 SNAPAT
 Of the: 4 ORAL
 part: 4 ROOF
 piece: 3 LIP
 prefix: 3 ORI
 River: 5 DELTA
 Roof of the: 6 PALATE
 Run at the: 5 DROOL
 Sing with closed: 3 HUM
 Taken by: 4 ORAL
 They exist from hand to: 5 REINS
 Toward the: 4 ORAD
 Word of: 5 PAROL
 ~, in slang: 3 YAP 4 **TRAP**
Mouthed
 Words ~ to a camera: 5 HIMOM
Mouthful: 3 WAD 4 CHAW
 Carpenter: 5 NAILS
 Cows': 3 CUD
 of a sort: 4 SWIG
Mouthing
 off: 8 INSOLENT
Mouthless
 comic strip character: 7 DILBERT
Mouthpiece
 piece: 4 REED
Mouths: 3 ORA
Mouth-shaped
 flower: 10 SNAPDRAGON
Mouthwash
 Like a: 5 MINTY
 Use: 6 GARGLE
Mouth-watering: 5 TASTY
Mouthy: 4 ORAL
Movable
 castle: 4 ROOK
Movado
 rival: 5 ROLEX
Move: 4 STIR 8 RELOCATE
   RESETTLE
 a bit: 5 BUDGE
 aimlessly: 3 GAD 4 MILL ROVE
 a muscle: 4 STIR
 a picture: 6 REHANG
 a plant: 5 REPOT

aside: 5 SHUNT
away: 6 RECEDE
Ballet: 4 PLIE
carefully: 4 EASE
cautiously: 6 TIPTOE
Crafty: 4 RUSE
Dance: 3 DIP 4 STEP
Don't: 4 STAY STOP
effortlessly: 6 GLIDE
Erratic: 3 ZAG ZIG
False: 5 FEINT
Fencing: 5 LUNGE PARRY
forward: 5 IMPEL 6 PROPEL
furtively: 5 SIDLE SLINK SNEAK
Get a ~ on: 3 HIE
gradually: 4 OOZE
Gymnastics: 4 FLIP
Hard to: 6 LEADEN
How groups: 7 ENMASSE
it: 3 HIE
It can ~ a star: 4 LIMO
It may ~ you: 3 VAN
Karate: 4 CHOP
laterally: 5 SIDLE
like a bunny: 3 HOP
like a butterfly: 4 FLIT
like a cat: 5 PROWL
like a crab: **5 SIDLE**
like a snake: 7 SLITHER
like Jell-o: 6 WIGGLE
like molasses: **4 OOZE**
Make a: 3 ACT 4 STEP 5 REACT
obliquely: 5 SIDLE
on all fours: 5 CRAWL
on a puff of air: 4 WAFT
One on the: 4 GOER
one's tail: 3 WAG
On the: 5 ASTIR GOING
    6 ACTIVE
out: 6 VACATE
Powerless to: 5 INERT
Priced to: 6 ONSALE
quickly: 3 HIE ZIP 4 DART RUSH
    SCUD
Really: 4 ZOOM
sideways: 4 CRAB
Skittish: 5 START
slowly: 4 INCH OOZE PLOD
    SLOG 5 MOSEY

stealthily: 5 SKULK SLINK
    SNEAK
to the side: 5 SHUNT
unsteadily: 6 TEETER
upward: 5 ARISE
with a hum: 4 WHIR
Wrong: 5 ERROR
~, in Realtor-speak: 4 **RELO**
" ___ move": 4 YOUR
Moved
  Barely: 5 CREPT
  furtively: 5 SLUNK
"Move it, already!": 6 LETSGO
Movement
  Art: 4 DADA
  Ballet: 4 PLIE
  Concerto: 5 RONDO
  Dance: 4 STEP
  Fast: 7 ALLEGRO
  Hippy: 4 HULA
  Muscle: 3 TIC
  Slow: 4 OOZE 5 LARGO
    6 ADAGIO 7 ANDANTE
  Sonata: 5 RONDO
  Start of many ~ names: 3 NEO
  Upward: 6 ASCENT
  word: 3 LIB
"Move on": 7 LETITGO
Mover: 3 VAN
  Air: 3 FAN
  and shaker: 4 DOER 5 NABOB
  Boat: 3 OAR
  challenge: 5 PIANO
  Cursor: 5 MOUSE
  How a ~ moves a sofa:
    7 ENDWISE
  need: 3 VAN
  rental: 5 UHAUL
  Slow: 5 SNAIL
Movie: 4 CINE FILM SHOW
    5 FLICK
  1958 ~, with "The": 4 BLOB
  1966 ~: 5 ALFIE
  1969 ~: 3 CHE
  1977 ~: 4 ORCA
  1982 ~: 4 TRON
  1987 ~: 6 ISHTAR
  1997 ~: 7 AMISTAD
  1998 ~: 4 ANTZ

2003 ~: 5 GIGLI
award: 5 OSCAR
backdrop: 3 SET
Beatles: 4 HELP
buy: 3 DVD
channel letters: 3 HBO
Chase: 10 CADDYSHACK
color: 4 BLUE
critic Roger: 5 EBERT
Dinner and a: 4 DATE
dog: 4 ASTA TOTO
Early ~ mogul: 4 LOEW
ending: 4 GOER
ending cliché: 6 SUNSET
extra, for short: 4 SUPE
French: 4 CINE
genre: 6 HORROR 8 WHODUNIT
Hot: 14 CHARIOTSOFFIRE
     ISPARISBURNING
     15 TOWERINGINFERNO
house: 6 CINEMA
Jungle ~ omen: 5 DRUMS
lioness: 4 ELSA
location: 3 LOT SET
maven: 5 EBERT
monster: 4 BLOB
Part of a ~ collection: 7 VCRTAPE
pooch: 4 ASTA
Poor ~ rating: 7 ONESTAR
preview: 7 TRAILER
previewer: 5 RATER
princess: 4 LEIA
promo: 7 TRAILER
ratings: 3 PGS
shot: 4 TAKE 5 STILL
spool: 4 REEL
that rates 0 stars: 4 BOMB
     7 STINKER
theater: 4 CINE 6 CINEMA
trailer: 4 GOER
Western: 5 OATER
Whale of a: 4 ORCA
Movies: 3 PIX 4 FLIX
At the ~, maybe: 7 ONADATE
Day at the: 5 DORIS
In the: 8 ONSCREEN
Like many ~ nowadays:
     5 ONDVD
Like most: 5 RATED

Power of the: 6 TYRONE
The last word in: 3 END
Moving: 5 ASTIR
aid: 3 VAN 6 CASTER
Not: 5 INERT 6 ATREST
part: 5 ROTOR
Run without: 4 IDLE
vehicle: 3 **VAN**
Moviola
Work at the: 4 EDIT
Mowed
row: 5 SWATH
Mower
maker: 4 TORO 5 DEERE
path: 5 SWATH
storage: 4 SHED
Mowgli
portrayer: 4 SABU
Mowing: 5 CHORE
Moxie: 3 PEP 4 GRIT 5 NERVE
Alternative to: 4 NEHI
Have the: 4 DARE
Mozambique
neighbor: 6 MALAWI
Mozart
article: 4 EINE
birthplace: 7 AUSTRIA
movement: 5 RONDO
opera title starter: 4 COSI
portrayer Tom: 5 HULCE
rival: 7 SALIERI
MP
quarry: 4 **AWOL**
MP3
player: 4 IPOD
mpg
Part of: 3 PER
rater: 3 **EPA**
mph
Part of: 3 PER
Mr.
and Mr.: 6 MESSRS
Cartoon: 5 MAGOO
German: 4 HERR
Hindu: 4 BABU
Myopic: 5 MAGOO
~, abroad: 3 SRI
Mr. ___
(baseball mascot): 3 MET

(old whodunit game): 3 REE
(soft drink): 4 PIBB
"Mr. Apollinax"
 poet: 5 ELIOT
"Mr. Belvedere"
 actress Graff: 5 ILENE
Mr. Big: 5 NABOB
Mr. Bill
 shriek: 4 OHNO
Mr. Boddy
 game: 4 CLUE
Mr. Chips
 class: 5 LATIN
 portrayer: 5 DONAT 6 OTOOLE
Mr. Cool
 Hardly: 4 NERD
"Mr. Deeds Goes to Town"
 director: 5 CAPRA
Mr. Green
 game: 4 CLUE
Mr. Heep: 5 URIAH
"Mr. Holland's ___": 4 OPUS
"Mr. Hulot's Holiday"
 star/director: 4 TATI
Mr. Hyde: 5 FIEND
 8 ALTEREGO
MRI: 4 SCAN
Mr. 'iggins: 4 ENRY
Mr. Kramden: 5 RALPH
Mr. Kringle: 4 KRIS 5 KRISS
Mr. Magoo: 5 MYOPE
 malady: 6 MYOPIA
 nephew: 5 WALDO
 portrayer: 7 NIELSEN
"Mr. Mom"
 actress: 8 TERIGARR
 actress Garr: 4 **TERI**
 Costar of Keaton in: 4 GARR
 Costar of Michael in: 4 TERI
Mr. Moneybags: 5 NABOB
Mr. Moto: 6 SLEUTH
 portrayer: 5 LORRE
 remark: 4 AHSO
Mr. Nahasapeemapetilon: 3 APU
"___ Mr. Nice Guy!": 6 NOMORE
"Mr. ___ Passes By": 3 PIM
Mr. Peanut
 attire: 5 SPATS
Mr. Pecksniff: 4 SETH

"Mr. Peepers"
 actor Wally: 3 COX
Mr. Potato Head: 3 TOY
 part: 3 EAR EYE 4 NOSE
Mr. Pulver
 rank: 3 ENS
Mr. Right
 Hardly: 5 CREEP
Mrs.
 and Mrs.: 4 MMES
 Chicago: 6 OLEARY
 German: 4 FRAU
 Spanish: 6 SENORA
 ~, in French: 3 **MME**
 ~, in Spanish: 3 **SRA**
Mrs. Addams
 ~, to Gomez: 4 TISH
Mrs. Andy Capp: 3 FLO
"Mrs. Bridge"
 author Connell: 4 EVAN
Mrs. Cleaver: 4 JUNE
Mrs. Copperfield: 4 **DORA**
Mrs. Dithers: 4 **CORA**
Mrs. Kramden: 5 ALICE
"Mrs. Miniver"
 Mr. Miniver in: 4 CLEM
 ~ Oscar winner: 6 GARSON
Mrs. Munster: 4 LILY
Mrs. Peel: 4 EMMA
 partner: 5 STEED
 portrayer: 4 RIGG
Mr. Spock
 forte: 5 LOGIC
 Like: 7 LOGICAL
 Mother of: 6 AMANDA
 portrayer: 5 NIMOY
Mrs. Smith
 product: 3 PIE
Mrs. Sprat
 no-no: 4 LEAN
Mrs. Zeus: 4 HERA
Mr. T
 group: 5 **ATEAM**
 movie: 5 DCCAB
"Mr. Tambourine Man"
 group, with "The": 5 BYRDS
Mr. Television: 5 BERLE
Mr. Turkey: 3 TOM
Mr. Unexciting: 4 DRIP

Mr. Universe
pride: 3 ABS
"Mr. Wrong"
actress: 9 DEGENERES
MS.
enclosure: 4 **SASE**
founder: 7 STEINEM
markers: 3 EDS
~, in Spanish: 4 SRTA
MS-___: 3 DOS
"MS. Found in a Bottle"
author: 3 POE
MSG
decisions: 4 TKOS
Part of: 4 MONO
tourney: 3 NIT
Msg.
Sabbath: 3 SER
MSgt: 3 NCO
MSN: 3 ISP
rival: 3 AOL
MSNBC
entertainer: 4 IMUS 7 DONIMUS
rival: 3 CNN
Ms. Pac-Man
ghost: 3 SUE
Mtg.: 4 SESS
Mtge.
units: 3 PTS
MTM
Part of: 5 TYLER
Mtn.
stat: 3 ALT 4 ELEV
MTV
cartoon girl: 5 DARIA
fans: 5 TEENS
fare: 6 VIDEOS
figure: 6 VEEJAY
hosts: 3 VJS
prize: 3 AVA
Mubarak
of Egypt: 5 **HOSNI**
predecessor: 5 SADAT
Much: 3 FAR 4 ALOT 6 ALOTOF
As: 6 NOLESS
As ~ as you like: 5 AGOGO
Be too: 4 CLOY
Had too: 4 ODED
Has too: 3 ODS

It doesn't take: 4 TREY
less: 8 LETALONE
Not: 4 ABIT **ATAD**
Not as: 4 **LESS**
Not so: 4 **LESS**
Not up to: 4 IDLE
So ~, musically: 5 TANTO
the same: 5 ALIKE
Too ~, musically: 6 TROPPO
Took too ~ of: 6 ODEDON
Very: 4 **ALOT** ATON TONS
     5 BYFAR NOEND 6 SORELY
~, musically: 5 MOLTO
"___ Much" (Presley hit): 3 TOO
"Much ___ About Nothing":
     3 **ADO**
"Much Ado About Nothing"
friar: 7 FRANCIS
Mucho: 4 ALOT LOTS 5 LOTSA
"Much obliged!": 6 THANKS
Much-quoted
Org. with a ~ journal: 3 AMA
Much-used
key: 5 ENTER
Mucilage: 4 GLUE 5 PASTE
Muck: 3 GOO 4 CRUD MIRE OOZE
Muck-a-muck
High: 3 VIP 4 EXEC 7 BIGSHOT
Mideast: 4 AMIR
Muckraker
~ Sinclair: 5 UPTON
~ Tarbell: 3 IDA
Mud: 3 JOE 4 GOOP JAVA
bath place: 3 SPA
Drag through the: 5 SMEAR
hole: 3 STY
Like: 4 OOZY
Like thick, dry: 5 CAKED
Move through: 4 SLOG 5 SLOSH
Sling ~ at: 4 SLUR 5 SMEAR
     7 ASPERSE
Stick in the: 4 MIRE 5 EMBED
"Mud": 3 JOE
Mud ___: 3 EEL PIE
Mudder
fodder: 3 HAY 4 OATS
Muddle: 4 HASH MESS 5 BEDIM
     BEFOG SNAFU
In a: 4 ASEA

Muddleheaded: 6 ADDLED
Muddy: 4 ROIL 6 OPAQUE
  up: 4 **ROIL**
Mudhole: 3 STY
"___ mud in your eye!": 5 HERES
Mud-sliding
  mammal: 5 OTTER
Mudville
  complement: 4 NINE
  slugger: 5 CASEY
Mueller, Robert
  org.: 3 FBI
Muesli
  morsel: 3 **OAT**
Muezzin
  call to prayer: 4 AZAN
  perch: 7 MINARET
Muff: 3 ERR
  site: 3 EAR
Muffet
  bugaboo: 6 SPIDER
  fare: 4 CURD WHEY 5 CURDS
Muffet-to-tuffet
  words: 6 SATONA
Muffin
  choice: 3 OAT 4 BRAN CORN
  ingredient: 3 OAT 4 **BRAN**
  Make a: 4 BAKE
  topper: 4 **OLEO**
Muffin Man
  lane: 5 DRURY
Muffle: 6 DEADEN
Muffler: 5 SCARF
  Trumpet: 4 MUTE
Mug: 3 ROB 4 FACE PUSS
    6 KISSER
  Big: 5 STEIN
  Drink in a: 3 ALE
  filler: 3 ALE 4 BEER
  for the camera: 4 POSE
  imperfections: 4 ZITS
  Man-shaped: 4 TOBY
Mugger: 3 HAM
  repellent: 4 MACE
Muggy: 5 HUMID
Muhammad
  birthplace: 5 MECCA
  Boxer: 3 ALI
  Descendant of: 4 EMIR

  faith: 5 ISLAM
Muhammad ___: 3 ALI
Muhammad Ali
  was one: 5 PASHA
Muir
  milieu: 7 SIERRAS
  Poet: 5 EDWIN
Mujer
  Married: 6 SENORA
  Married ~ (abbr.): 3 SRA
___ Mujeres, Mexico: 4 ISLA
Mukluk
  material: 8 SEALSKIN
  wearer: 5 INUIT
Mulberry
  fruit: 3 FIG
  relative: 5 OSAGE
Mulder
  and Scully org.: 3 FBI
  folder: 5 XFILE
  or Scully: 5 AGENT
  or Scully (abbr.): 3 AGT
**"Mulder, ___" (Gillian Anderson
    biography):** 5 ITSME
Mule: 4 SHOE
  Army: 6 MASCOT
  Canal with a: 4 ERIE
  Erie Canal: 3 **SAL**
  father: 3 ASS
  Like a: 7 STERILE
  mother: 4 MARE
  of song: 3 **SAL**
  team: 4 ARMY
"Mule Train"
  singer: 5 LAINE
Mulgrew
  Actress: 4 KATE
Mull
  Island near: 4 IONA
  over: 6 PONDER
Mullah
  home: 4 IRAN
  Taliban: 4 OMAR
Mullally
  Actress: 5 MEGAN
Mullens, Miss
  Caller on: 5 ALDEN
Mulligan: 4 STEW
Mulligatawny: 4 SOUP

Multi
  suffix: 4 PLEX
Multichannel: 6 STEREO
Multicolored: 4 PIED
Multi-day
  prayer: 6 NOVENA
Multilingual: 8 POLYGLOT
Multinational
  currency: 4 EURO
Multiple
  Abbr. before ~ surnames:
    6 MESSRS
Multiple-choice
  choice: 5 OTHER
"Multiplicity"
  director: 5 RAMIS
Multiplies
  It ~ by dividing: 6 AMOEBA
Multipurpose
  truck: 3 UTE
Multiroofed
  structure: 6 PAGODA
Multitude: 3 SEA 4 ARMY BEVY
    HEAP HOST SLEW
    5 HORDE 6 LEGION
Multivitamin
  brand: 7 GERITOL
  supplement: 4 IRON
Multivolume
  ref.: 3 OED
Mum: 5 MATER 6 SILENT
Mummy
  Celebrated: 3 TUT
  God in ~ wrappings: 6 OSIRIS
  home: 4 TOMB
  Make a: 6 EMBALM
Mun.
  official: 3 ALD
Munch: 3 EAT 5 CHOMP
Munch, Edvard
  subject: 6 SCREAM
Munched
  on: 3 ATE
München
  mister: 4 HERR
Munches
  on: 5 CHEWS
Münchhausen
  Baron: 4 KARL

Munchie
  Crunchy: 4 TACO
  Mexican: 4 TACO 7 TOSTADA
Munchies: 4 URGE
  Party: 7 CANAPES
  Satisfy the: 4 NOSH
Munchkin: 3 ELF
Munch Museum
  site: 4 OSLO
___ **mundi:** 4 ANNO
Mungojerrie
  musical: 4 CATS
Muni
  role: 4 ZOLA
Munic.
  legislator: 3 ALD
Munich
  Info: German cue
  river: 4 ISAR
Munich ___ of 1938: 4 PACT
Municipal: 5 CIVIC
  offering: 4 BOND
Municipality: 4 TOWN
  Suffix in some ~ names:
    4 BORO
Munro, H.H.
  pen name: 4 **SAKI**
Munson
  Actress: 3 ONA
Munster
  Mr.: 6 HERMAN
  Mrs.: 4 LILY
  pet bat: 4 IGOR
  pet dinosaur: 4 SPOT
  son: 5 EDDIE
Münster
  mister: 4 HERR
"Munsters, The"
  DeCarlo of: 6 YVONNE
Muppet: 4 ELMO 5 ERNIE
  eagle: 3 SAM
  Ernie's ~ pal: 4 BERT
  Giggly: 4 ELMO
  Grouchy: 5 OSCAR
  Red: 4 ELMO
  Spanish-speaking: 6 ROSITA
  Ticklish: 4 ELMO
  with a unibrow: 4 BERT
  ~ Emmet: 5 OTTER

Muppets
  creator: 6 HENSON
  creator Henson: 3 JIM
Mural
  prefix: 5 INTRA
  site: 4 WALL
Muralist
  Mexican: 6 RIVERA
  Spanish: 4 SERT
  ~ José María: 4 SERT
  ~ Rivera: 5 DIEGO
Murals
  and such: 3 ART
Murder
  Christie ~ setting: 4 NILE
  First ~ victim: 4 ABEL
  mystery plot device: 5 TWIST
  Some ~ mystery suspects:
    5 HEIRS
  ~, in slang: 3 OFF
"Murder, ___": 3 INC
"Murder in the Cathedral"
  playwright: 5 ELIOT
"Murder in the First"
  Christian of: 6 SLATER
"Murder Must Advertise"
  writer: 6 SAYERS
"Murder on the ___ Express":
  6 ORIENT
"Murders in the ___ Morgue,
  The": 3 RUE
"Murders in the Rue Morgue, The"
  beast: 3 APE
"Murder, ___ Wrote": 3 SHE
Murdoch
  Author: 4 IRIS
Murmur: 3 COO
Murphy: 3 BED
  Actor: 5 EDDIE
  Actress: 4 ERIN
  bed place: 6 CLOSET
  Decorated: 5 AUDIE
  War hero: 5 **AUDIE**
Murphy, Eddie
  1996 ~ film: 5 METRO
  2002 ~ film: 4 ISPY
  old show, for short: 3 SNL
"Murphy Brown"
  bar owner: 4 PHIL

  show: 3 FYI
  son: 5 AVERY
  star: 6 BERGEN
Murphy's ___: 3 LAW
Murray
  Actor: 4 BILL
  Actress: 3 MAE
  ref. work: 3 OED
  Singer: 4 ANNE
Murray, Arthur
  lessons: 5 STEPS
Murrow
  and others: 3 EDS
  network: 3 CBS
Mus.
  Get slower, in: 3 RIT
  Lively, in: 4 ANIM
  major degrees: 3 BAS
  version: 3 ARR
Musante, Tony
  series: 4 TOMA
Musberger
  Sportscaster: 5 **BRENT**
Muscat
  land: 4 **OMAN**
  money: 5 RIALS
  resident: 5 **OMANI**
Muscateer: 5 OMANI
Muscatel: 4 WINE
Muscle: 5 SINEW
  Arm: 5 BICEP 6 BICEPS
  Back: 3 **LAT**
  Bending: 6 FLEXOR
  car: 3 **GTO**
  Certain: 6 TENSOR
  Chest: 3 **PEC**
  condition: 4 TONE
  connector: 6 TENDON
  contraction: 5 SPASM
  fiber ridge: 5 STRIA
  injury: 4 TEAR
  Involuntary ~ movement: 3 TIC
    5 SPASM
  Lacking: 4 WEAK
  Leg: 4 QUAD
  Move a: 4 STIR
  pain: 4 ACHE
  power: 5 SINEW
  problem: 3 TIC 5 CRAMP SPASM

6 STRAIN
protein: 5 ACTIN
Shoulder: 4 DELT 7 DELTOID
    ROTATOR
Show: 4 FLEX
spasm: 4 KINK
Stretching: 6 TENSOR
Thoracic: 3 PEC

Muscle Beach
sight: 3 BOD

Musclebound
guy: 5 HEMAN

Muscleman
Mohawked: 3 MRT
~ Reeves: 5 STEVE
~ Steve: 6 REEVES

Muscles: 5 BRAWN
Belly: 3 ABS
Like overused: 4 ACHY
Mold: 6 TONEUP
Sitting: 6 GLUTEI GLUTES
Tummy: 3 **ABS**

Muscular: 4 ROPY 5 BEEFY BUILT
    6 SINEWY
condition: 4 TONE
dog: 5 AKITA
Lean and: 4 WIRY
power: 5 SINEW

Muse
Astronomy: 6 URANIA
Comedy: 6 THALIA
count: 4 NINE
History: 4 **CLIO**
Instrument: 4 LYRE
Music: 7 EUTERPE
Poetry: 5 **ERATO**
Tenth: 6 SAPPHO

Museo
in Madrid: 5 PRADO
works: 4 ARTE

Muses, The: 4 NINE 5 NONET
    6 ENNEAD

Museum
area: 8 GIFTSHOP
artifact: 5 RELIC
display: 3 **ART**
Do ~ work: 7 RESTORE
guide: 6 DOCENT
Like some ~ exhibits: 6 ONLOAN

Natural history ~ display:
    4 TREX
piece: 5 RELIC TORSO
worker deg.: 3 MFA
Museum ___ : 5 OFART

Museum Folkwang
setting: 5 ESSEN

Mush
Cornmeal: 7 POLENTA
Reduce to: 5 PUREE

Musher
vehicle: 4 **SLED**

Mushroom
cap part: 4 GILL
cloud maker: 5 ABOMB
Edible: 5 MOREL
Fleshy: 3 CEP
French chef's: 4 CEPE
Gourmet: 5 MOREL
Inedible: 9 TOADSTOOL
Japanese: 5 ENOKI
part: 3 CAP 4 STEM
seed: 5 SPORE
stem: 5 STIPE

Mushy
food: 3 PAP
Get all: 4 MELT

Musial
of baseball: 4 **STAN**

Musial, Stan
nickname: 6 THEMAN

Music
"10" ~: 6 BOLERO
1950s ~ store purchase: 4 HIFI
African ~ genre: 3 BIS
A little night: 4 TAPS 5 SNORE
Ambient ~ composer: 3 **ENO**
Be silent, in: 5 TACET
Big Band: 5 SWING
box: 6 CDCASE
British ~ co.: 3 EMI
Caribbean: 3 SKA
carrier: 4 IPOD
category: 4 SOUL
Church: 5 MOTET
collectibles: 3 LPS
compilation name: 4 KTEL
Count in: 5 BASIE
Country: 6 ANTHEM

creators' org.: **5** ASCAP
Easier version, in: **5** OSSIA
Eastern: **4** RAGA
for two: **4** DUET
genre: **3** POP RAP **4** FOLK ROCK
   SOUL **5** BLUES
group: **4** BAND
hall: **5** ODEON ODEUM
halls: **4** **ODEA**
Hit: **3** RAP
Holiday: **5** BLUES
Home ~ system: **6** STEREO
Kind of: **5** SHEET
Knack for: **3** EAR
Latin: **5** SALSA
Like some: **6** ATONAL
Lines of: **5** STAFF
Lure with: **7** TWEEDLE
marking: **4** SLUR
Merchant of: **7** NATALIE
Mexican: **8** MARIACHI
Modern ~ media: **3** CDS
Modern ~ style: **3** RAP
Muse of: **7** EUTERPE
Music box: **4** LILT
Night: **4** TAPS
Page of: **5** PATTI
Piece of: **5** SHEET
player: **4** JUKE **6** STEREO
preceder: **4** SOUL
rights org.: **5** ASCAP
sampler: **4** DEMO
sheet abbr.: **3** ARR
Sound of: **4** TONE
Summer: **5** DISCO
Summer ~ festival site: **5** ASPEN
Swing: **4** JIVE
TV ~ vendor: **4** KTEL
With the bow, in: **4** **ARCO**
~, to a matador: **3** OLE
~, to a musician: **5** FORTE
Musical
1925 ~: **11** NONONANETTE
1943 ~:
   15 ONETOUCHOFVENUS
1948 ~: **6** CASBAH
1953 ~: **4** LILI
1958 ~: **4** GIGI
1960s rock ~: **4** HAIR

1966 ~: **6** **IDOIDO**
1969 ~: **12** SWEETCHARITY
1973 ~: **6** PIPPIN
1978 ~: **5** EUBIE
1996 ~: **4** RENT **5** EVITA
ability: **3** **EAR**
based on a Fellini film: **4** NINE
based on a strip: **5** ANNIE
beat: **5** TEMPO
break: **4** REST
buildup: **9** CRESCENDO
chairs goal: **4** SEAT
chord: **5** TRIAD
climax: **4** CODA
combo: **5** CHORD
composition: **4** OPUS **5** ETUDE
conclusion: **4** CODA
dir.: **3** RIT
direction: **5** LENTO
discernment: **3** EAR
drama: **5** OPERA
embellishment: **7** ROULADE
   9 GRACENOTE
ending: **4** CODA
event: **7** RECITAL
exercise: **5** ETUDE
Fair-sized ~ group: **5** NONET
gift: **3** EAR
gourd: **6** MARACA
ineptitude: **6** TINEAR
interval: **5** NINTH **6** OCTAVE
   7 TRITONE
key: **5** AFLAT BFLAT CFLAT
   DFLAT EFLAT FFLAT
   GFLAT **6** AMINOR BMINOR
   CMINOR DMINOR EMINOR
   FMINOR GMINOR
leads: **5** SOLOS
Light ~ work: **8** OPERETTA
mark: **4** NOTE REST SLUR
measure: **3** BAR
melodrama: **5** OPERA
miscellany: **4** OLIO
motif: **5** THEME
notes: **3** FAS LAS MIS RES TIS
number: **5** PIECE
Of ~ quality: **5** TONAL
Part of a ~ gig: **3** SET
pause: **4** REST

phrase: 5 TRALA
pitch: 4 TONE
postscript: 4 CODA
potpourri: 6 MEDLEY
quality: 4 TONE
refrain: 5 TRALA
sense: 3 EAR
Short ~ composition:
    8 SONATINA
sign: 4 CLEF
silence: 4 REST
speed: 5 TEMPO
staff lines: 5 EGBDF
study: 5 ETUDE
syllable: 3 TRA
symbol: 4 CLEF NOTE REST
talent: 3 EAR
theme: 5 MOTIF
toy: 5 KAZOO
vamp: 5 INTRO
work: 4 OPUS

Musically
A little, ~: 4 POCO
flowing: 6 LEGATO
From the top, ~: 6 DACAPO
keyless: 6 ATONAL
More, ~: 3 PIU
Slow, ~: 5 LARGO
Smooth, ~: 6 LEGATO
So much, ~: 5 TANTO
Together, ~: 4 **ADUE**
Twice, ~: 3 BIS
Very, ~: 5 ASSAI
Wing it, ~: 3 JAM

"Music for Airports"
composer: 3 ENO

Musician
asset: 3 EAR
booking: 3 GIG
gift: 3 EAR
inspiration: 5 ERATO
job: 3 GIG
of old: 6 LUTIST
One-named: 4 MOBY 5 YANNI
org.: 5 ASCAP
Rolling: 5 STONE
~ Brian: 3 **ENO**
~ John: 4 **TESH**
~ Yoko: 3 ONO

Music-licensing
org.: 5 ASCAP

"Music Man, The"
setting: 4 IOWA

Music store
frequenters: 5 TEENS

Musing
Meadow: 3 MOO

Musk: 4 ODOR 5 SCENT
secreter: 5 OTTER

Musket
ammo: 4 BALL
attachment: 3 EER 7 BAYONET
loader: 6 RAMROD
suffix: 3 EER

Musketeers: 4 TRIO
One of the: 5 **ATHOS** 6 ARAMIS
Three: 3 BAR

Muskie
successor: 4 HAIG

Muskogee
native: 4 OKIE

Muslim: 7 ISLAMIC
Certain: 5 SUNNI 6 SHIITE
chief: 4 IMAM
crusade: 5 JIHAD
destination: 5 MECCA
general: 4 AGHA
judge: 5 HAKIM
leader: 4 EMIR IMAM
Like the ~ calendar: 5 LUNAR
magistrate: 4 CADI
messiah: 5 MAHDI
palace area: 5 HAREM
Philippine: 4 MORO
pilgrim: 4 HAJI
pilgrimage: 3 HAJ 4 HADJ HAJJ
sect: 5 SUNNI
title: 3 AGA 5 HAFIZ
~ Almighty: 5 ALLAH

Muss: 6 RUMPLE TOUSLE

Mussel
home: 6 SEABED

Mussolini
moniker: 4 DUCE 6 ILDUCE

Mussorgsky
bass: 5 BORIS

Must: 5 HASTO 6 HAVETO
    NEEDTO 7 NEEDSTO

have: 4 NEED
It ~ go on: 7 THESHOW
pay: 3 OWE
You ~ remember this: 5 ALAMO
~, informally: 5 GOTTA
"Musta been something ___":
      4 IATE
Mustache
  style: 9 HANDLEBAR
Mustachioed
  artist: 4 DALI
  Last ~ president: 4 TAFT
  ~ Surrealist: 4 DALI
Mustang: 3 CAR 4 AUTO
  home: 6 GARAGE
Mustangs
  Home of the: 3 **SMU**
Mustard: 7 COLONEL
  Cut the: 4 REAP
  Cutting the: 4 ABLE
  family member: 4 KALE
      6 RADISH WASABI
  rank (abbr.): 3 COL
  town: 5 DIJON
Mustard, Colonel
  game: 4 CLUE
"Must be something ___": 4 IATE
Must-have: 4 NEED
"Must've been something ___":
      4 IATE
Musty: 4 **DANK**
Mutated
  gene: 6 ALLELE
Mute
  Some are: 5 SWANS
  ~ Marx: 5 HARPO
Muted
  effect: 4 WAWA
  ~, with "down": 5 TONED
Mutilate: 3 MAR 4 MAIM
Mutineer: 5 REBEL
Mutinied
  ship: 7 AMISTAD
Mutiny
  Potemkin ~ city: 6 ODESSA
  site: 5 CAINE
"___ Mutiny, The": 5 CAINE
Mutt: 3 **CUR** 7 MONGREL
  Pal of: 4 JEFF

Mutton
  fat: 4 SUET
  serving: 3 LEG
"___ Mutual Friend": 3 OUR
Mutual fund
  fee: 4 LOAD
  holdings: 7 NESTEGG
  Kind of: 4 REIT 6 NOLOAD
  Some ~ accts.: 4 IRAS
Mutuel
  lead-in: 4 PARI
Muumuu
  accessory: 3 LEI
  Where to wear a: 4 LUAU
Muzak
  locale: 8 ELEVATOR
Muzzle: 5 SNOUT
  Gun with a flared:
      11 BLUNDERBUSS
  loader: 6 RAMROD
MVP
  1953 A.L. ~: 5 ROSEN
  1998 N.L. ~: 4 SOSA
  2000 World Series ~: 5 JETER
      10 DEREKJETER
  First Super Bowl: 5 STARR
  Super Bowl III: 6 NAMATH
  Super Bowl XXXIII: 5 ELWAY
  Three-time NHL: 3 ORR
  Three-time Super Bowl:
      10 JOEMONTANA
My
  Your and: 3 OUR
  ~, in French: 3 MES
"My ___!": 4 HERO
Myanmar
  locale: 4 ASIA
  neighbor: 4 LAOS
  ~, formerly: 5 BURMA
"My bad!": 4 OOPS
"My Big Fat Greek Wedding"
  Vardalos of: 3 NIA
"My boy": 3 SON
"___ my brother's keeper?":
      3 AMI
"___ my case": 5 IREST
"My Cherie ___": 5 AMOUR
"My Children! My ___!":
      6 AFRICA

"My Country"
　author: 4 **EBAN**

"My country, ___ of thee ...":
　3 TIS

"My country, 'tis of thee"
　song: 7 AMERICA

"My Cousin Vinny"
　actress Marisa: 5 TOMEI
　Oscar winner: 5 TOMEI
　star: 5 PESCI 8 JOEPESCI

"My Cup Runneth Over"
　musical: 6 IDOIDO
　singer: 6 EDAMES

"My Darling Clementine"
　role: 4 EARP

"My dear man": 3 SIR

"My Dinner With Andre"
　actor: 5 SHAWN
　director: 5 MALLE

"My dog ___ fleas": 3 HAS

Myers
　Former press secretary:
　　6 DEEDEE
　Political analyst: 6 DEEDEE

"___ Myers": 3 NED

Myerson
　Miss America: 4 BESS

"My Fair Lady"
　composer: 5 LOEWE
　director: 5 CUKOR
　lady: 5 ELIZA
　race place: 5 ASCOT

"My fault!": 5 SORRY

"My Favorite Martian"
　headgear: 8 ANTENNAS

"My Favorite Year"
　star: 6 OTOOLE

"My Friend ___": 4 IRMA

"My Friend Flicka"
　author: 5 OHARA

"My gal": 3 SAL

"___ my God, thou art very
　great": 5 OLORD

"___, My God, to Thee":
　6 NEARER

"My goodness!": 5 EGADS

"___ My Heart": 4 PEGO

"___ My Heart in San Francisco":
　5 ILEFT

"My Heart Will Go On"
　singer: 4 DION

"My karma ran over my ___":
　5 DOGMA

"My kingdom for ___": 6 AHORSE

"My Life as ___": 4 ADOG

"My life ___ open book": 4 ISAN

"___ my lips!": 4 READ

"My Little Chickadee"
　actress West: 3 MAE
　costar: 7 MAEWEST

"My mama done ___ me ...":
　3 TOL

"My man!": 3 BRO

"My Michael"
　author Oz: 4 AMOS

"My mistake!": 4 OOPS

"My Name Is ___": 4 ARAM

"My Name Is Asher ___": 3 LEV

"My Name Is ___ Lev": 5 ASHER

MYOB
　Part of: 3 OWN 4 YOUR

Myopic
　Mr.: 5 MAGOO

"___ My Party": 3 ITS

"My People"
　author: 4 EBAN

Myra
　Dame: 4 **HESS**
　Pianist: 4 **HESS**

"Myra Breckinridge"
　author: 5 VIDAL

"___ my reasons ...": 5 IHAVE

Myriad: 4 MANY

Myrmecologist
　study: 4 **ANTS**

Myrna
　Actress: 3 **LOY**
　Role for: 4 NORA

Myron
　Humorist: 5 COHEN

Myrrh: 5 RESIN

Myshkin: 5 IDIOT

"My So-Called Life"
　actor Jared: 4 LETO
　actress Danes: 6 CLAIRE

Mysore
　master: 5 SAHIB
　mister: 3 SRI

Myst: 4 GAME
"My stars!": 4 EGAD 5 EGADS
Mysteries: 6 ARCANA
Mysterious: 5 EERIE QUEER 6 ARCANE
  character: 4 RUNE
  matters: 6 ARCANA
  (var.): 4 EERY
Mystery: 5 GENRE 6 ENIGMA
  First name in: 4 ERLE 5 EDGAR 6 AGATHA
  Man of: 3 MRX
  middle name: 5 CONAN
  Street of: 5 DELLA
"Mystery!"
  host Diana: 4 RIGG
  station: 3 **PBS**
"Mystery of ___ Vep, The": 4 IRMA
Mystery writer
  award: 5 EDGAR RAVEN
  ~ Josephine: 3 **TEY**
Mystic: 4 YOGI 5 SWAMI
  letter: 4 RUNE
Mystical: 5 RUNIC
  character: 4 RUNE
  deck: 5 TAROT
  emanation: 4 AURA
  poem: 4 RUNE
"Mystic Pizza"
  actress Taylor: 4 LILI
Mystique: 4 AURA
"___: My Story": 3 AVA 4 REBA
Myth: 4 TALE
  Peak of: 4 OSSA
  River of: 4 STYX

Ship of: 4 ARGO
Twin of: 5 REMUS
Mythical
  archer: 4 EROS
  beast: 3 ORC
  bird: 3 **ROC**
  goat-man: 4 FAUN
  hammer wielder: 4 THOR
  hunter: 5 ORION
  huntress: 5 DIANA
  man-goat: 3 PAN 5 SATYR
  meanie: 4 OGRE
  monster: 3 **ORC** 7 GRIFFIN
  river: 4 STYX
  sorceress: 5 CIRCE MEDEA
  strongman: 5 ATLAS
  trio: 5 FATES
  weaver: 7 ARACHNE
  weeper: 5 NIOBE
Mythology
  anthology: 4 EDDA
Mythomaniac: 4 LIAR
"My Three ___": 4 SONS
"My Three Sons"
  son: 5 ERNIE
"My treat": 4 ONME
My ___, Vietnam: 3 LAI
"My Way"
  songwriter: 4 **ANKA**
"___ my way": 4 IMON
"My Wicked, Wicked Ways"
  author: 5 ERROL
"___ my wit's end!": 4 IMAT
"My word!": 4 EGAD ISAY
"___ my word!": 4 UPON

Nn

N: 3 DIR
followers: 4 OPQR
N/A
Part of: 4 APPL
NAACP
Part of: 4 ASSN NATL 5 ASSOC
Nab: 3 BAG 4 NAIL 5 CATCH
6 ARREST COLLAR
Nabber
Cry of a: 6 GOTCHA
Nabisco
cookie: 4 **OREO**
cracker: 4 RITZ
steak sauce: 4 AONE
wafer: 5 NILLA
Nabokov, Vladimir
novel: 3 **ADA** 4 **PNIN** 6 **LOLITA**
Nabors, Jim
role: 4 PYLE
Nachos
topping: 5 SALSA
"___ Nacht" (German carol):
6 STILLE
NaCl: 4 SALT
Containing: 6 SALINE
Nada: 3 **NIL ZIP** 4 NONE ZERO
5 ZILCH ZIPPO
~, in French: 4 RIEN
Nadelman
Sculptor: 4 **ELIE**
Nader: 7 ALSORAN
Activist: 5 RALPH
Nadir: 6 BOTTOM
opposite: 6 ZENITH
Nae
sayer: 4 SCOT
NAFTA
Part of: 5 TRADE
predecessor: 4 GATT
signer: 3 USA
Nag: 4 CARP 5 SHREW 6 BADGER
7 HENPECK
nibble: 3 OAT

pad: 6 STABLE
Nagana
carrier: 6 TSETSE
Nagano
noodles: 5 RAMEN
Nagger: 5 SHREW
"___ Nagila": 4 HAVA
Nagy
Hungarian leader: 4 **IMRE**
"Nah!": 4 UHUH
Nahuatl: 5 AZTEC
Nahum
Book before: 5 MICAH
British poet laureate: 4 TATE
Naif: 4 BABE
Nail
cousin: 5 SCREW
file: 5 EMERY
holder: 3 TOE
Mining: 4 SPAD
polish: 6 ENAMEL
puller: 4 CLAW
site: 3 TOE
Small: 4 BRAD
Thin: 4 BRAD
Nail-biters
(abbr.): 3 OTS
Nails
100 pounds of ~: 3 KEG
Target for: 4 ITCH
Work on: 4 FILE
Nair
rival: 4 NEET
Nairn
negative: 3 NAE
Nairobi
nation: 5 KENYA
native: 6 KENYAN
Naish, J. ___: 7 CARROLL
Naive: 7 ARTLESS
crusader: 8 DOGOODER
Not so: 5 SLYER
Naked: 4 BARE 6 UNCLAD

Make: 6 DENUDE
Not: 4 CLAD
"Naked ___" (Goya work): 4 MAJA
___ naked: 5 STARK
"Naked Jungle, The"
menace: 4 ANTS
"Naked Maja"
painter: 4 GOYA
Nala: 4 LION
Naldi
Actress: 4 **NITA**
Namath, Joe: 3 JET
Last team of: 4 RAMS
Super Bowl with: 3 III
Name: 3 DUB 4 CITE 5 TITLE
7 APPOINT
Assumed: 5 **ALIAS**
Average: 3 DOW
Big: 4 STAR
Fail to: 4 OMIT
Give a ~ to: 3 DUB 7 ENTITLE
Give a new ~ to: 7 RETITLE
Given a: 6 TERMED
Good: 6 REPUTE
Good ~, briefly: 3 REP
part (abbr.): 4 INIT
Named: 4 IDED
names: 4 SANG
Once: 3 NEE
Originally: 3 **NEE**
Name-dropper: 4 SNOB
word: 3 NEE
"___ Named Sue": 4 ABOY
Namely: 5 IDEST **TOWIT**
(abbr.): 3 VIZ
"Name of the Rose, The"
author: 3 **ECO**
Namesake
of Jr.: 3 III
(plural): 3 JRS SRS
Nametag
Like many a: 7 STICKON
word: 5 HELLO
"Name That Tune"
clue: 4 NOTE
Namibia
neighbor: 6 ANGOLA
8 BOTSWANA
~, until 1990 (abbr.): 3 SWA

"Nana"
actress Anna: 4 **STEN**
author Émile: 4 ZOLA
author Zola: 5 EMILE
___ Na Na: 3 **SHA**
Nanakuli
necklace: 3 LEI
Nancy
Actress: 5 OLSON
City near: 4 METZ
Friend of: 6 SLUGGO
Golfer: 5 LOPEZ
Rival of: 5 TONYA
When ~ bakes: 3 ETE
"Nancy"
rich kid: 5 ROLLO
Nanette
Words to: 4 NONO
"___ Nanette": 4 NONO
Nanjing
nanny: 4 AMAH
Nanki-___ : 3 POO
Nanking
nanny: 4 AMAH
Nanny: 4 GOAT 9 NURSEMAID
Eastern: 4 AMAH
trio: 3 ENS
"Nanny, The"
actress Taylor: 5 **RENEE**
butler: 5 NILES
portrayer Drescher: 4 **FRAN**
Nanook
nook: 5 IGLOO
Nantes
Info: French cue
noggin: 4 TETE
Nothing, in: 4 RIEN
notion: 4 IDEE
river: 5 LOIRE
Nantucket: 6 ISLAND
Nap: 4 DOZE 5 SLEEP
6 SIESTA SNOOZE
10 FORTYWINKS
It has a: 5 SUEDE
Long: 4 SHAG
Noontime: 6 SIESTA
Place for a: 3 COT
sack: 3 BED
Take a: 4 REST

Napa
  business: 6 WINERY
  County east of: 6 SOLANO
  growth: 4 VINE
  nabob: 5 GALLO
  Prefix used in: 4 OENO

Naphthalene
  target: 4 MOTH

Napkin
  for a slob: 6 SLEEVE
  holder: 3 LAP
  material: 5 LINEN

Naples
  City near: 7 SALERNO

Napoleon: 5 EXILE 7 DESSERT
  (abbr.): 3 EMP
  birthplace: 7 CORSICA
  Exile site for: 4 ELBA
  Fate of: 5 EXILE
  Marshal under: 3 NEY

Napoleon III
  Wife of: 7 EUGENIE

Napoli
  City NW of: 4 ROMA
  locale: 6 ITALIA
  Nothing, in: 6 NIENTE
  Three, in: 3 **TRE**

Napping: 5 ADOZE 6 ASLEEP
        ATREST
  ~, so to speak: 7 UNAWARE

Narc
  activity: 4 BUST RAID
  chaser: 4 OSIS OTIC
  find: 3 PCP 4 KILO 5 STASH
  org.: 3 **DEA**

Narcissist
  love: 4 SELF
  problem: 3 EGO
  vacation: 7 EGOTRIP

Narcissus
  Like: 4 VAIN
  Lover of: 4 ECHO

Narcotic: 4 DRUG 6 OPIATE
  Govt. ~ watchdog: 3 DEA
  Poppy: 5 OPIUM

Narnia
  chronicler: 7 CSLEWIS
  lion: 5 ASLAN

Narrate: 4 TELL

  anew: 6 RETELL
Narration: 4 TALE
Narrative: 4 **TALE** 5 STORY
  Heroic: 4 SAGA
  Lengthy: 4 EPIC

Narrator
  Literary: 7 PERSONA
  Notable: 7 ISHMAEL

Narrow: 5 TAPER
  access: 5 ALLEY
  Become: 5 TAPER
  cut: 4 SLIT
  groove: 5 STRIA
  inlet: 3 **RIA**
  margin: 4 HAIR NOSE
      7 EYELASH
  opening: 4 SLIT
  passage: 4 LANE 5 INLET
  peninsula: 4 SPIT
  piece: 5 STRIP
  ridge: 5 STRIA
  street: 4 LANE
  strip: 4 SLAT
  valley: 4 GLEN
  waterway (abbr.): 3 STR
  zone: 4 BELT
  ~, as a bridge or road:
      7 ONELANE

Narrow-bodied
  fish: 3 GAR

Narrowly: 7 BYAHAIR
  defeat: 3 NIP 4 EDGE

Narrow-waisted
  insect: 4 WASP

Narthex
  neighbor: 4 NAVE

Nary
  a soul: 5 **NOONE** 6 NOTONE

NASA
  affirmative: 3 AOK
  cancellation: 4 NOGO
  Cancel, to: 5 ABORT
  chimp: 4 ENOS
  concern: 3 UFO
  Creator of: 3 DDE
  gasket: 5 ORING
  moon craft: 3 LEM
  outfit: 5 GSUIT
  Part of: 4 NATL 5 SPACE

Perfect, at: 3 AOK
rocket stage: 5 AGENA
spacewalk: 3 EVA

Nasal
appraisal: 4 ODOR 5 AROMA
cavity: 5 SINUS
partitions: 5 SEPTA
passage: 4 NARE
tone: 5 TWANG

NASCAR
qualifier: 9 TIMETRIAL
sponsor: 3 STP

NASDAQ
cousin: 3 ASE
debut: 3 IPO
Like ~ trades: 3 OTC
listings (abbr.): 3 COS
New ~ listing: 3 IPO
offering: 5 STOCK
Part of ~ (abbr.): 4 ASSN
    5 ASSOC
rival: 4 NYSE

Nash
Crosby, Stills, and: 4 TRIO
Like a ~ lama has: 4 **ONEL**
Poet: 5 OGDEN
portrayer: 5 CROWE
priest: 4 LAMA 8 ONELLAMA
specialty: 3 PUN

Nashville
attraction: 4 OPRY
school (abbr.): 3 TSU
venue: 4 OPRY

"Nashville"
actress: 10 KARENBLACK
actress Blakley: 5 RONEE
song: 6 IMEASY

Nassau
country: 7 BAHAMAS

Nasser
Egyptian leader: 5 GAMAL
org.: 3 UAR
successor: 5 SADAT

Nast
of publishing: 5 CONDE
target: 9 BOSSTWEED
___ Nast: 5 CONDE

Nastase
Netman: 4 **ILIE**

of tennis: 4 **ILIE**

Nastassja
Actress: 6 KINSKI
Father of: 5 KLAUS
Role for: 4 TESS

Nasty: 4 ACID BASE MEAN UGLY
    VILE 5 SNIDE
Not so: 5 NICER
sort: 4 OGRE 6 MEANIE

Nasty-smelling: 5 FETID

Nat
Singer: 4 COLE

Natal
native: 4 ZULU
starter: 3 **NEO** PRE

Natalie
Singer: 4 COLE

Natasha
No, to: 4 NYET
Partner of: 5 BORIS

Nathan
Actor: 4 LANE
Patriot: 4 **HALE**

Nathanael
Author: 4 WEST

National
competitor: 4 AVIS 5 ALAMO
prefix: 5 INTER
service: 8 RENTACAR
song: 6 ANTHEM
symbol: 5 EAGLE
___ National Forest, Florida:
    5 OCALA

National Gallery
architect: 3 PEI
center: 6 ARMORY

National Institutes of Health
city: 8 BETHESDA

Nationalists
city: 6 TAIPEI

Nationality
suffix: 3 ESE

National League
division: 4 EAST
stadium: 4 SHEA
team: 4 METS REDS 6 ASTROS

National Park
of Alaska: 6 DENALI
of California: 7 REDWOOD

of Canada: 5 BANFF
of Maine: 6 ACADIA
of Utah: 4 ZION
"National Velvet"
author Bagnold: 4 **ENID**
National Zoo
animal: 5 PANDA
Native: 6 INBRED 7 ENDEMIC
        8 INHERENT
        10 ABORIGINAL
suffix: 3 ITE OTE
Nativity
scene: 6 CRECHE
Natl. Courtesy Mo.: 4 SEPT
NATO
founder: 3 HST
member: 3 GER USA
member since '99: 3 POL
Part of ~ (abbr.): 3 ATL ORG
Natter: 3 GAB 4 CHAT
Natterjack: 4 TOAD
Natty: 4 NEAT
Natural: 4 BORN 6 INBORN
        INNATE UNDYED
do: 4 AFRO
emollient: 4 **ALOE**
habitat: 7 ELEMENT
Isn't a: 4 DYES
It may be: 3 GAS
necklace: 3 LEI
Not: 4 DYED 7 MANMADE
resource: 3 ORE
talent: 4 GIFT 5 FLAIR
~, in craps: 5 SEVEN
"Natural, The"
role: 5 HOBBS
Natural gas: 4 FUEL
component: 6 ETHANE
"Natural History"
author: 5 PLINY
Naturalist
Roman: 5 PLINY
"Natural Man, A"
singer: 5 RAWLS
Naturalness: 4 EASE
Nature: 3 ILK 4 SORT
        7 ASPECTS
By its very: 9 IPSOFACTO
goddess: 4 ISIS

prefix: 3 ECO
Similar in: 4 **AKIN**
"Nature"
author: 7 EMERSON
Naught: 3 NIL
Bring to: 4 UNDO
Naughty: 3 BAD
Not: 4 NICE
"Naughty, naughty!": 3 TSK
"Naughty you!": 5 SHAME
"Nausea"
novelist: 6 SARTRE
Nautical
adverb: 4 **ALEE**
assent: 3 AYE
cry: 4 AHOY 5 AVAST
danger: 4 REEF
direction: 4 ALEE 5 APORT
journal: 3 LOG
pole: 4 SPAR 5 SPRIT
prefix: 4 AERO
speed unit: 4 KNOT
Nautilus: 3 SUB
attacker: 5 SQUID
captain: 4 **NEMO**
Nav.
officer: 3 ADM ENS
rank: 3 CPO **ENS**
school: 4 ACAD
Navajo: 5 TRIBE
dwelling: 5 HOGAN
foes: 4 UTES
neighbor: 4 HOPI
Naval
agreement: 3 AYE
base: 4 KEEL
builder: 6 SEABEE
force: 5 FLEET 8 SEAPOWER
hoosegow: 4 BRIG
initials: 3 HMS USS
noncom: 3 CPO
officer (abbr.): 3 ADM ENS
petty officer: 6 YEOMAN
pronoun: 3 SHE
rank (abbr.): 3 CDR CPO **ENS**
standard: 6 ENSIGN
~ VIP: 3 ADM
Naval Academy
freshman: 4 PLEB 5 PLEBE

Nave
  bench: 3 PEW
  neighbor: 4 **APSE**
Navel: 6 ORANGE
  buildup: 4 LINT
  Type of: 5 INNIE OUTIE
Navigate: 5 PILOT STEER
Navigation
  acronym: 5 LORAN
  aid: 5 SONAR
  Bat's ~ aid: 4 ECHO
  need: 3 MAP
  Old ~ instrument:
      9 ASTROLABE
  route: 7 SEALANE
  tool: 7 SEXTANT
  unit: 7 SEAMILE
Navigator
  heading (abbr.): 3 ENE ESE NNE
      NNW SSE SSW WNW WSW
  instrument: 6 OCTANT
  need: 3 MAP
Navigator Islands
  ~, today: 5 SAMOA
Navratilova
  It means nothing to: 4 LOVE
  rival: 5 **EVERT**
Navy: 4 BEAN
  builder: 6 SEABEE
  commando: 4 SEAL
  Elite ~ group: 5 SEALS
  mascot: 4 GOAT
  noncom: 3 CPO
  officer: 6 ENSIGN
  sport rival: 4 ARMY
Nay
  canceler: 3 YEA
  opposite: 3 YEA
  sayer: 4 **ANTI**
Naysay: 4 DENY
Naysayer: 4 ANTI
"Nazarene, The"
  novelist: 4 **ASCH**
Nazarenes: 4 SECT
Nazareth
  native: 7 ISRAELI
N.B.
  Part of: 4 BENE NOTA
  Prov. east of: 3 PEI

NBA
  Like many ~ players: 4 TALL
  nickname: 4 SHAQ
  Part of: 4 ASSN
  stats: 3 PTS
  team: 4 HEAT NETS 5 SPURS
      6 LAKERS PACERS
  ~ MVP of 1981: 3 DRJ
NBC
  comedy show since '75: 3 SNL
  founder: 3 RCA
  host: 4 LENO
  morning show: 5 TODAY
  news show: 8 DATELINE
  Part of: 4 NATL
  Peacock, to: 4 LOGO
N.C.
  city: 3 RAL
NC-17: 5 ADULT
  assigning gp.: 4 MPAA
  Reason for an ~ rating: 4 GORE
NCAA
  1995 ~ champs: 4 UCLA
  Part of: 3 ATH 4 ASSN
      8 ATHLETIC
  rival: 3 NIT
NCO: 3 CPL SGT 4 MSGT SSGT
  Certain ~, familiarly: 5 SARGE
  Navy: 3 CPO
  Part of: 3 NON
  USAF: 4 TSGT
NEA
  member: 4 TCHR
  Part of: 4 ARTS ASSN EDUC
Neal, Patricia
  film: 3 HUD
Neanderthal: 7 CAVEMAN
  wear: 4 PELT
Neap: 4 TIDE
  Pertaining to: 5 TIDAL
Near: 4 NIGH 5 ABOUT
      6 ATHAND BESIDE
      7 CLOSEBY CLOSETO
  Draw: 7 CLOSEIN
  future: 6 OFFING
  Not: 3 FAR
Near ___ : 4 EAST
Nearby: 5 CLOSE LOCAL
      6 AROUND ATHAND

Not: 4 AFAR
things: 5 THESE
Near East
inn: 5 SERAI
Near Eastern
honorific: 3 AGA
hotel: 5 SERAI
Neared: 10 CLOSEDINON
Nearest: 8 PROXIMAL
the center: 7 MIDMOST
Near-eternity: 3 EON 4 AEON
Nearing
bedtime: 6 LATISH
the hour: 5 TENTO
Nearly: 4 NIGH 5 ABOUT
6 ALMOST 7 CLOSETO
all: 4 MOST
Very: 6 ALLBUT
Near-perfect
grade: 6 AMINUS
rating: 4 NINE
Neat: 4 TIDY 5 KEMPT NIFTY
7 INORDER
Make: 5 GROOM
Not: 5 MESSY ONICE
7 OVERICE
Stiffly: 4 PRIM
suffix: 3 NIK
Neat as ___: 4 APIN
Neaten: 4 TIDY 6 TIDYUP
8 SPRUCEUP
~, as a lawn: 4 EDGE
Neath
Not: 3 OER
Neatnik
opposite: 4 **SLOB**
"Neato!": 4 COOL KEEN 5 SWELL
Neb.
neighbor: 3 KAN WYO 4 SDAK
Nebraska
city: 5 **OMAHA**
county: 4 OTOE
First capital of: 5 OMAHA
native: 3 OTO 4 OTOE
6 PAWNEE
neighbor: 4 IOWA
river: 6 **PLATTE**
Nebuchadnezzar
realm: 7 BABYLON

Nebula
composition:
10 COSMICDUST
Necessary
(abbr.): 4 REQD
Deem: 6 SEEFIT
Necessitate: 6 **ENTAIL**
Necessity: 4 MUST NEED
Neck
and neck: 4 **EVEN** TIED
6 INATIE
Back of the: 4 **NAPE**
It may hang by the: 4 JOWL
of the woods: 4 **AREA**
Pain in the: 4 KINK **PEST**
5 CRICK 6 HASSLE
part: 4 NAPE
region: 6 SCRUFF
shape: 3 VEE
wrap: 3 BOA 5 ASCOT SCARF
~, slangily: 5 SCRAG
Necklace
component: 4 BEAD
fastener: 5 CLASP
Floral: 3 LEI
gem: 5 PEARL
item: 6 AMULET
Kind of: 6 CHOKER
Natural: 3 LEI
Neckline
shape: 3 **VEE**
type: 3 VEE
Neckpiece
Feathered: 3 BOA
Necktie: 6 CRAVAT
Arizona: 4 BOLO
Broad: 5 ASCOT
Fancy: 5 ASCOT
Western: 4 BOLO 5 NOOSE
Neckwear: 3 TIE
Floral: 3 LEI
Furry: 3 BOA
Knotted: 5 ASCOT
Oxen: 4 YOKE
Winter: 5 SCARF
Nectar
collector: 3 BEE
inspector: 3 BEE
source: 4 PEAR

Ned
  Composer: 5 **ROREM**
Need
  Has ~ of: 5 LACKS
  If ~ be: 8 INAPINCH
  It's all you: 4 LOVE
Needle: 4 RIDE TWIT 5 NAGAT
      TAUNT **TEASE**
  bearer: 4 PINE
  case: 4 **ETUI**
  holder: 3 FIR 4 ETUI
      7 TONEARM
  hole: 3 **EYE**
  part: 3 EYE
  Ply a: 3 SEW
  point: 3 ENE ESE NNE NNW
      SSE SSW WNW WSW 4 EAST
      WEST 5 NORTH SOUTH
  source: 3 FIR
  Use a: 3 SEW
  With a ~ (prefix): 3 ACU
Needlefish: 3 **GAR** 4 GARS
Needle-nosed
  fish: 3 GAR
Needles
  On pins and: 4 **EDGY** 5 ANTSY
      TENSE
  Phonograph: 5 STYLI
  Work with: 4 KNIT
Needle-shaped: 7 ACEROSE
Needlework
  Do: 3 SEW
Needs: 5 HASNT
Needy: 4 POOR
  Is: 5 WANTS
Ne'er-do-well: 3 BUM 5 IDLER
      ROGUE 7 LOWLIFE
Neeson
  Actor: 4 **LIAM**
Neet
  rival: 4 **NAIR**
Nefarious: 4 **EVIL**
  plan: 6 SCHEME
Neg.
  blowup: 3 ENL
  opposite: 3 **POS**
Negate: 4 UNDO
Negation
  symbol, in logic: 5 TILDE

Negative
  conjunction: 3 NOR
  Double: 4 NONO
  link: 3 NOR
  particle: 5 ANION
  Poetic: 4 NEER
  Russian: 4 NYET
  Scottish: 3 NAE
  Slangy: 3 NAH
  vote: 3 NAY
  votes: 3 NOS 4 **NOES**
  ~, in German: 4 NEIN
Negev
  Like the: 4 ARID
Neglect: 4 OMIT 6 DISUSE
  May ~ to: 6 NEEDNT
  Sign of: 4 RUST
Neglected
  area: 4 SLUM
  ~, as a lawn: 5 WEEDY
Neglectful: 6 REMISS
Negligent: 3 LAX 6 REMISS
Negligible: 4 SLIM
Negotiating
  goal: 4 DEAL
Negotiation
  result: 4 DEAL
Negotiations: 5 TALKS
  hang-up: 4 SNAG
Negotiator: 5 AGENT
  asset: 4 TACT
Negri
  Silent film actress: 4 **POLA**
Neh.
  Book after: 4 ESTH
  Book before: 3 EZR
Nehemiah
  Book after: 6 ESTHER
  Book before: 4 EZRA
Nehi
  drinker on TV: 5 RADAR
  flavor: 5 GRAPE
Nehru
  Daughter of: 6 INDIRA
Neigh
  sayer: 5 HORSE
Neighbor: 4 **ABUT**
  A: 5 BFLAT
  on: 4 ABUT

Neighborhood: 4 <u>AREA</u> 5 LOCAL
  event: **10** GARAGESALE
  In the: **4** NEAR **5** ABOUT LOCAL
    6 NEARBY
  Needy: **6** GHETTO
  store: **4** DELI
Neigh-sayer: 5 HORSE
  on TV: **4** MRED
Neil
  Playwright: **5** SIMON
  Singer: **6** SEDAKA
Neill
  Actor: **3** SAM
Neiman
  Artist: **5** LEROY
Neisse
  partner: **4** ODER
Neither
  partner: **3 <u>NOR</u>**
Neither fish ___ fowl: 3 NOR
Neither here nor there:
    7 ENROUTE INLIMBO
Neither here ___ there: 3 NOR
"Nel ___, dipinto ...": 3 BLU
Nell
  British actress: **4** GWYN
"Nell"
  actor Neeson: **4** LIAM
  actress Foster: **5** JODIE
Nellie
  Journalist: **3** BLY
  Soprano: **5** MELBA
Nelligan, Kate
  film: **5 <u>ELENI</u>**
Nelly
  Poet: **5** SACHS
Nels
  Actor: **6** OLESON
Nelson
  Nobelist: **7** MANDELA
  Singer: **4** EDDY
Nelson, Willie
  Like the voice of: **5** NASAL
  movie: **15** HONEYSUCKLEROSE
Nemesis: 3 FOE **4** BANE
    5 ENEMY
Nemo
  creator: **5** VERNE
  harpoonist: **3** NED

Nen
  of baseball: **4** ROBB
Neo
  portrayer: **5** KEANU
Neo-
  opposite: **5** PALEO
Neolith: 4 TOOL
Neologism: 7 COINAGE
  Create, as a: **4** COIN
Neon: 3 GAS **7** RAREGAS
    8 INERTGAS
  Like: **5** INERT
Neon ___: 5 TETRA
Neophyte: 4 TYRO
    10 FIRSTTIMER
Nepal
  capital: **8** KATMANDU
  legend: **4** YETI
  locale: **4** ASIA
Nephrite: 4 JADE
Nephritic: 5 RENAL
Ne plus ultra: 4 <u>ACME</u>
Nepotism
  beneficiary (abbr.): **3** REL
Neptune: 3 GOD **6** SEAGOD
  Celtic: **3** LER
  moon: **6** NEREID TRITON
  neighbor: **6** URANUS
  realm: **3** SEA **5** OCEAN
  spear: **7** TRIDENT
Nerd: 4 GEEK **5 <u>DWEEB</u>** TWERP
Nerdy: 5 UNHIP **6** UNCOOL
  Not: **3** HEP **4** COOL
Nero
  (abbr.): **3** EMP
  instrument: **5** PIANO
  successor: **5** GALBA
  Tutor of: **6** SENECA
  Wife of: **7** OCTAVIA
  Year during reign of: **3** LIV LIX
    LVI LXI
"Nerts!": 4 DRAT
Neruda
  Nobelist poet: **5** PABLO
  specialty: **4** ODES
Nerve: 5 CRUST MOXIE
  cell: **6** NEURON
  cell part: **4** AXON
  Deadly ~ gas: **5** SARIN

Have the: 4 **DARE**
impulse region: 7 SYNAPSE
Kind of: 5 **OPTIC**
Lose one's: 10 CHICKENOUT
network: 4 RETE
opening: 4 NEUR
Some: 5 OPTIC
___ nerve: 5 OPTIC
"___ nerve!": 4 SOME

Nerves
More than just: 4 FEAR
Sign of: 3 TIC

Nervous: 4 **EDGY** 5 ANTSY
TENSE 6 ONEDGE
UNEASY 9 ILLATEASE
girl: 6 NELLIE
laugh: 6 TITTER
spasm: 3 TIC
twitch: 3 **TIC**
~, with "up": 5 KEYED

Nervous ___: 6 NELLIE
Nervousness: 6 UNEASE
Nervy: 4 BOLD 5 BRASH
Ness: 3 FED 4 LOCH TMAN
Agent: 5 ELIOT
nemesis: 5 NITTI
Untouchable: 5 ELIOT

Nessen
Press secretary: 3 RON

Nessie
Home of: 4 LOCH

Nessman
WKRP newsman: 3 LES
___ **Ness monster:** 4 LOCH

Nest: 5 NIDUS
builder: 3 ANT 4 BIRD
Eagle's: 5 **AERIE**
Lofty: 5 AERIE
Lofty ~ (var.): 5 EYRIE
material: 5 TWIGS
noise: 4 PEEP 5 CHEEP CHIRP
TWEET
part: 4 TWIG

Nest egg: 3 **IRA**
choice: 7 ROTHIRA

Nester: 3 HEN
Chimney: 5 STORK

Nesting
spot: 4 EAVE

Nestlé
pet food brand: 4 ALPO

Nestling
noise: 4 PEEP 5 CHEEP

Nestor: 4 SAGE

Nests
Insect: 4 NIDI
Like some: 5 EMPTY

Net: 5 SNARE 7 REALIZE
8 AFTERTAX TAKEHOME
address: 3 URL
Catch in a: 6 ENMESH
domain part: 3 COM EDU ORG
Fishing: 5 SEINE TRAWL
giant: 3 AOL
Hair: 5 SNOOD
letters: 3 WWW
material: 4 MESH
Surfing the: 6 ONLINE
Where the ~ hangs: 3 RIM

Netanyahu
predecessor: 5 PERES
~, familiarly: 4 BIBI

Neth.
neighbor: 3 GER

Netherlands
cheese: 4 EDAM
city: 3 EDE

Netherlands Antilles
island: 5 ARUBA

Netherworld: 5 HADES
river: 4 STYX

Netizen: 4 USER

Netscape
purchaser: 3 AOL

Netting: 4 MESH

Nettle: 3 IRK 4 RILE ROIL

Network: 3 WEB 4 GRID 5 AIRER
6 SYSTEM
(abbr.): 4 SYST
Cable: 3 AMC HBO TNT USA
Kind of: 6 NEURAL
logo: 3 EYE
Major TV: 3 ABC CBS NBC
Nerve: 4 RETE
Overseas: 3 BBC
(plural): 5 RETIA
point: 4 NODE
signal: 4 FEED

Telly: 3 BBC
terminal: 4 NODE
U.K.: 3 BBC
"Network"
actor: 10 PETERFINCH
director: 5 LUMET
"___ Network 90" (1980s
        comedy): 4 SCTV
Neuman, Alfred E.
feature: 4 GRIN
magazine: 3 MAD
Neur-
Suffix: 4 OTIC
Neural
transmitter: 4 AXON
Neurologist
request: 3 EEG
Neuron
gap: 7 SYNAPSE
Part of a: 4 AXON
Neurotransmission
site: 4 AXON
Neuss
Never, in: 3 NIE
Neut.
Not ~ or fem.: 4 MASC
Neuter: 4 GELD SPAY 5 DESEX
    7 SEXLESS
Neutral: 4 GEAR
color: 3 TAN 4 ECRU 5 BEIGE
Ethically: 6 AMORAL
Run in: 4 IDLE
Neutrality
Eschew: 9 TAKESIDES
Neutralize: 5 ANNUL
Neutralizer
Acid: 4 BASE 6 ALKALI
Alkali: 4 ACID
Neutrinos
Symbols for: 3 NUS
Neuwirth
Actress: 4 BEBE
Nev.
neighbor: 3 IDA ORE 4 ARIZ
    5 CALIF
Nevada
city: 4 ELKO RENO
lake: 5 TAHOE
Novelist: 4 BARR

senator Harry: 4 REID
town: 3 ELY 4 ELKO
___ Nevada: 6 SIERRA
Never: 4 NARY 5 NOHOW
    7 NOTONCE 8 ATNOTIME
Almost: 4 ONCE
Better than: 4 LATE
say this: 3 DIE
~, in German: 3 NIE
Never-ending: 7 ETERNAL
story: 9 SOAPOPERA
~, in poetry: 6 ETERNE
"Neverending Story, The"
author: 4 ENDE
"___ never fly!": 4 ITLL
"___ never happen!": 4 ITLL
"Never mind!": 6 SKIPIT
    8 NOMATTER
~, to an editor: 4 STET
"Nevermore!"
speaker: 5 RAVEN
Nevertheless: 3 BUT THO YET
    6 EVENSO 8 AFTERALL
"___ never too late!": 3 ITS
"Never Wave at a ___" (1952
    film): 3 WAC
"___ never work!": 4 ITLL
Nevil
Novelist: 5 SHUTE
Neville
Singer: 5 AARON
Nevins
Biographer: 5 ALLAN
Nevis
partner: 7 STKITTS
New
follower: 4 AGER
moon: 5 PHASE
Not: 4 USED
Not as: 5 OLDER
prefix: 3 NEO
~, in Spanish: 5 NUEVA NUEVO
New-___: 4 AGER
New Age
musician: 5 YANNI
musician John: 4 TESH
singer: 4 ENYA
Newark
County of: 5 ESSEX

neighbor: **10** EASTORANGE
New Balance
  competitor: **4** AVIA NIKE
Newbery Medal
  winner Lowry: **4** LOIS
  winner Scott: **5** ODELL
Newbie: 4 TYRO
  Military: **5** PLEBE
  Society: **3** DEB
Newborn: 4 BABE BABY
      7 NEONATE
  outfit: **7** LAYETTE
  place: **4** CRIB
  Stable: **4** FOAL
Newcastle
  product: **4** COAL
  river: **4 TYNE**
Newcomer: 3 NEO **6** ROOKIE
  Academy: **4** PLEB **5** PLEBE
  Law school: **4** ONEL
  Society: **3 DEB**
  Stable: **4** FOAL
New Deal
  agcy.: **3** CCC NRA **REA** TVA WPA
  monogram: **3** FDR
  org.: **3** CCC NRA REA TVA **WPA**
  pres.: **3** FDR
  prog.: **3** CCC NRA REA TVA WPA
New Delhi
  garment: **4** SARI
New England
  cape: **3** ANN
  catch: **3** COD **5** SCROD
  college town: **7** AMHERST
  collegian: **3** ELI
  player: **7** PATRIOT
  sch.: **3** UNH URI
  soda fountain: **3** SPA
New Englander: 6 YANKEE
Newer: 8 UPGRADED
  version: **6** REMAKE
New Guinea
  port: **3** LAE
  ___ **New Guinea: 5 PAPUA**
New Hampshire
  city: **5** KEENE **6** NASHUA
  college town: **5** KEENE
  prep school: **6** EXETER
  state flower: **5** LILAC

Newhart
  Comedian: **3** BOB
"Newhart"
  actor Tom: **6** POSTON
  setting: **3** INN
New Haven
  campus: **4** YALE
  collegian: **3** ELI
  founder Theophilus: **5** EATON
  nickname: **7** ELMCITY
  school: **4 YALE**
  student: **3 ELI 5** YALIE
Newhouser
  of baseball: **3** HAL
New ___, India: 5 DELHI
"New Jack City"
  costar: **4** ICET
New Jersey
  county: **5** ESSEX
  five: **4 NETS**
  hoopsters: **4 NETS**
  resort: **7** CAPEMAY
  seaport: **10** PERTHAMBOY
  skater: **5** DEVIL
  state tree: **6** REDOAK
  team: **4** NETS
  town: **4** LODI **6** LEONIA
"New Life, A"
  actor and director: **4** ALDA
New Look
  designer: **4 DIOR**
Newly
  formed: **8** EMERGENT
  made: **5** FRESH
Newlyweds
  trip: **9** HONEYMOON
Newman
  Newsman: **5 EDWIN**
Newman, Paul
  film: **3 HUD 10** THEHUSTLER
      12 COOLHANDLUKE
      15 THECOLOROFMONEY
  role: **3** ARI HUD
      12 BUTCHCASSIDY
Newman, Randy
  song: **7** ILOVELA
New Mexico
  art colony: **4 TAOS**
  mountains: **6** SANDIA

native: 4 ZUNI
resort: 4 TAOS
state flower: 5 YUCCA
town: 4 TAOS
New Orleans
cuisine: 6 CREOLE
sandwich: 5 POBOY
   7 POORBOY
university: 6 TULANE
Newport Folk Festival
performer: 4 BAEZ
New Rochelle
college: 4 **IONA**
News
agcy.: 3 UPI
bit: 4 **ITEM**
bulletin: 6 UPDATE
Business: 6 MERGER
clip: 5 VIDEO
Election: 5 UPSET
feature: 5 STORY
hour: 6 ELEVEN
Late: 4 OBIT
Latest: 6 UPDATE
letters: 3 UPI
Like old: 5 PASSE
Old ~ source: 5 CRIER
org.: 3 **UPI**
Reaction to bad: 5 GROAN
segment: 5 RECAP
Short ~ bit: 5 SQUIB
source: 4 LEAK
Sports: 5 TRADE
subject: 5 EVENT
summary: 5 RECAP
TV ~ source: 3 CNN
When some ~ airs: 5 ATSIX
   ATTEN
Newsboy
cry: 5 EXTRA
Newscast
ender: 5 RECAP
feature: 6 SPORTS
Newsgroup
message: 4 POST
system: 6 **USENET**
Newshawk
asset: 4 NOSE
query: 3 HOW WHO WHY

   4 WHAT WHEN 4 WHERE
source: 4 LEAK
"NewsHour"
airer: 3 PBS
Newsletter
Corporate: 5 ORGAN
   10 HOUSEORGAN
Newsman
of yore: 5 CRIER
New South Wales
capital: 6 SYDNEY
Newspaper
advertising piece: 6 INSERT
Do ~ work: 4 EDIT
employee: 8 PRESSMAN
executive: 6 EDITOR
inserts: 3 ADS
issue: 7 EDITION
notice: 4 **OBIT**
Old ~ section: 4 ROTO
opinion piece: 9 EDITORIAL
page: 4 **OPED**
piece: 4 ITEM
section: 6 COMICS SPORTS
Newspapers: 5 PRESS
Like most: 5 DAILY
~, television, etc.: 5 MEDIA
Newsreel
inventor: 5 PATHE
segment: 5 EVENT
Newsroom
fixture: 4 DESK
Old ~ machine (abbr.): 3 TTY
unit: 4 PICA
Newsstand: 5 KIOSK
purchase: 5 DAILY
Newsweek
rival: 4 TIME
Newswire
initials: 3 UPI
Newt: 3 EFT
Young: 3 **EFT**
___ newt: 5 EYEOF
New Testament
book: 4 **ACTS** LUKE
king: 5 HEROD
letter: 7 EPISTLE
Newton: 4 UNIT
fraction: 4 DYNE

fruit: **3** FIG
Scientist: **5** ISAAC
Newtonian
concept: **7** INERTIA
Newton-John
Singer: **6** OLIVIA
New World
(abbr.): **4** AMER
gp.: **3** OAS
New Year
Vietnamese: **3** **TET**
New Year's ___: **3** EVE
New Year's Day
event: **4** BOWL
New Year's Eve
word: **4** AULD LANG SYNE
New York: **5** STATE **6** COLONY
7 SEAPORT
archbishop: **4** EGAN
bridge, formerly: **7** TRIBORO
canal: **4** ERIE
city: **5** **OLEAN** **UTICA**
6 ELMIRA
college: **4** **IONA**
county: **4** ERIE
gallery district: **4** SOHO
island: **5** CONEY ELLIS
6 STATEN
lake: **6** ONEIDA
mayor Giuliani: **4** RUDY
mountains: **6** RAMAPO
Place name in: **5** ASTOR
port: **6** OSWEGO
restaurateur: **5** SARDI
river: **4** EAST **7** AUSABLE
GENESEE
stadium: **4** ASHE
team: **4** METS
tribe: **7** ONEIDAS
university: **7** CORNELL
New York City
archbishop: **4** EGAN
former mayor: **8** ABEBEAME
New Yorker, The
cartoonist Edward: **5** SOREL
cartoonist Peter: **4** ARNO
___ New York minute: **3** INA
New York Times
publisher Adolph: **4** OCHS

New York World
journalist: **3** BLY
New Zealand
bird: **4** KIWI
native: **5** **MAORI**
parrot: **3** KEA
tongue: **5** MAORI
New Zealander: **4** KIWI
5 MAORI
Next: **4** THEN **6** ONDECK
Be ~ to: **4** ABUT **6** ADJOIN
Come: **5** **ENSUE**
in line: **4** HEIR
Lie ~ to: **4** ABUT
Put ~ to: **6** APPOSE
to: **6** BESIDE
to bat: **6** ONDECK
Up: **6** ONDECK
"___ next?": **4** WHOS
Next-to-last
syllable: **6** PENULT
Nez ___: **5** PERCE
Nez Perce
leader: **6** JOSEPH
mount: **9** APPALOOSA
NFL
city: **5** TAMPA
coach Dan: **5** SHULA
gains: **3** **YDS**
linemen: **3** RTS TES
official: **3** REF
scores: **3** **TDS**
stat: **3** YDS
tiebreakers: **3** OTS
~ 3-pointers: **3** FGS
~ 6-pointers: **3** TDS
NFLer: **3** BUC PRO **7** STEELER
Former: **5** LARAM
Top: **6** ALLPRO
Ngaio
Contemporary of: **4** ERLE
Ngo Dinh ___ (Vietnamese
dictator): **4** DIEM
NHL
city: **6** OTTAWA
Extra ~ periods: **3** OTS
legend: **3** ORR **4** HOWE
player: **5** BRUIN OILER SABRE
Play in the: **5** SKATE

Niagara Falls
  feeder: 4 ERIE
  Like: 5 MISTY
  prov.: 3 ONT
  sound: 4 ROAR
  veil: 4 MIST
Niamey
  Its capital is: 5 NIGER
Nibble: 4 GNAW NOSH
  Nag: 3 OAT
  on: 3 EAT 5 TASTE
  Take a: 5 TASTE
Nibblers
  Cheese: 4 MICE
Niblick: 4 IRON
Nicaragua
  city: 4 LEON
  Daniel of: 6 ORTEGA
  Nothing, in: 4 NADA
Nice: 4 KIND
  girl: 5 NELLY
  life: 3 VIE
  notion: 4 IDEE
  Not so: 7 NASTIER
  response: 3 OUI
  summer: 3 ETE
  touch: 6 CARESS
  view: 3 MER
  water: 3 EAU
"Nice!": 3 AAH OOH 7 GOODONE
Nice ___: 5 NELLY
"___ nice day!": 5 HAVEA
Niche: 4 NOOK 6 RECESS
  Church: 4 APSE
Nichelle
  role: 5 UHURA
Nicholas: 4 TSAR 5 SAINT
  Poet: 4 ROWE
"Nicholas Nickleby"
  actor Roger: 4 REES
Nichols
  partner: 3 MAY
Nichols, Anne
  hero: 4 ABIE
Nicholson, Jack
  film: 14 FIVEEASYPIECES
  role: 5 HOFFA
Nick: 4 DENT DING 5 GRAZE
  Actor: 5 NOLTE

  Golfer: 5 FALDO
  name: 5 SANTA
  Old: 5 SATAN 9 BEELZEBUB
  Wife of: 4 **NORA**
Nick and Nora
  dog: 4 **ASTA**
Nick at ___: 4 **NITE**
Nickel: 4 COIN 7 ELEMENT
  animal: 5 BISON
  Word on a: 5 CENTS
Nickel-and-___: 4 DIME
Nickelodeon: 7 JUKEBOX
  Kenan's pal on: 3 KEL
  pooch: 3 REN
Nickels: 6 CHANGE
Nicklaus, Jack
  Norm for: 3 PAR
  org.: 3 PGA
Nickname: 3 DUB TAG
        7 AGNOMEN EPITHET
"Nick of Time"
  singer: 5 RAITT
Nicks
  Singer: 6 STEVIE
Nicolas
  Actor: 4 CAGE
  Film director: 4 ROEG
Nicolò
  Violin maker: 5 AMATI
Nicotine
  partner: 3 TAR
  source: 5 PATCH
___ Nidre (Hebrew prayer): 3 KOL
Niels
  Physicist: 4 **BOHR**
Nielsen
  Actor: 6 LESLIE
  Actress: 8 BRIGITTE
  output: 7 RATINGS
Nieuwpoort
  river: 4 YSER
Nifty: 4 NEAT 5 NEATO
Niger
  Much of: 6 SAHARA
  neighbor: 4 CHAD **MALI**
        5 BENIN
Nigeria
  city: 5 LAGOS
  Gp. that includes: 4 OPEC

language: 3 EDO
neighbor: 4 CHAD 5 BENIN
    8 CAMEROON
Pop singer from: 4 SADE
tribesman: 3 IBO

Nigh: 6 NEARBY
Draw: 4 NEAR
Draw ~ to: 5 ANEAR
Not: 4 AFAR

Night
before: 3 **EVE**
bird: 3 OWL
flier: 3 OWL 4 MOTH
flight: 6 REDEYE
In for the: 4 ABED
light: 4 NEON STAR
    8 MOONBEAM
Like a clear: 6 STARRY
    7 STARLIT
noise: 4 HOOT 5 SNORE
Out for the: 4 ABED 6 ASLEEP
Poetic: 3 EEN
prefix: 3 MID **TWI** 5 NOCTI
school subj.: 3 ESL
sight: 4 STAR
sound: 5 SNORE
Spend the: 4 STAY
spot: 3 BED
star: 4 LENO
stick: 5 ROOST
The ~ before: 3 EVE
vision: 5 DREAM
watch: 5 VIGIL

"Night"
author Wiesel: 4 ELIE

"Night at the Opera, A"
song: 5 ALONE

Nightclub: 5 BOITE DISCO
    6 BISTRO 7 CABARET
    HOTSPOT
employee: 5 BGIRL
expense: 11 COVERCHARGE
offering: 9 FLOORSHOW
of song: 4 COPA
performer: 5 COMIC

Nightfall
Bard's: 3 **EEN**

Nightgown
wearer of rhyme:
    15 WEEWILLIEWINKIE

Nightingale: 5 NURSE

"Nightingale, The"
author: 8 ANDERSEN

"Nightline"
host Koppel: 3 TED
host Ted: 6 KOPPEL
network: 3 ABC

Nightly
comic: 4 LENO

Nightmare: 5 DREAM
cause: 7 BUGABOO
street: 3 ELM

"Nightmare on ___ Street, A":
    3 ELM

Nightmarish
street: 3 ELM

"Night Music"
playwright: 5 ODETS

"Night of the Hunter, The"
screenwriter: 4 AGEE

Nightshade
Plant of the ~ family:
    7 HENBANE

"Nights in White ___": 5 SATIN

Nightspot: 4 CAFE 7 CABARET

Nightstand: 8 BEDTABLE
item: 4 EWER LAMP

**"Night They Invented
    Champagne, The"**
musical: 4 GIGI

Nighttime
disorder: 5 APNEA
noise: 5 SNORE
Poetic: 3 EEN

"Night Watch, The"
painter: 9 REMBRANDT

Nightwear: 3 PJS

Nihilistic
art: 4 DADA

Nike: 5 DEITY
home: 6 OREGON
logo: 6 SWOOSH
rival: 4 AVIA 6 ADIDAS
    REEBOK
swoosh: 4 LOGO

Nikita
"No," to: 4 NYET
successor: 6 ALEXEI

Nikkei
  unit: 3 YEN
Nikola
  Inventor: 5 **TESLA**
Nikolai
  Author: 5 GOGOL
Nikon
  rival: 5 LEICA
Nil: 4 NADA ZERO
Nile
  bird: 4 IBIS
  biter: 3 **ASP**
  city: 5 ASWAN CAIRO
  delta town: 7 ROSETTA
  Opera set on the: 4 AIDA
  queen: 4 CLEO
  reptile: 3 **ASP**
  slitherer: 3 **ASP**
  wader: 4 **IBIS**
Nimbi: 5 AURAS
Nimble: 4 DEFT SPRY 5 **AGILE**
    LITHE 6 ADROIT
Nimbus: 4 AURA HALO
NIMBY
  Part of: 3 NOT
Nimitz
  title (abbr.): 3 ADM
Nin
  Diarist: 5 **ANAIS**
Nin, Anais
  output: 7 EROTICA
Nina
  Actress: 4 FOCH
  Designer: 5 RICCI
Nincompoop: 3 **ASS** SAP
    4 BOZO SIMP TWIT
    5 IDIOT
Nine
  Group of: 6 ENNEAD
  Half of: 3 ENS
  inches: 4 SPAN
  On cloud: 6 ELATED
  One of: 6 INNING
  Piece for: 5 NONET
  Put on cloud: 5 ELATE
  The whole ~ yards: 3 ALL
    4 ATOZ
  Third of ~, once: 5 EARTH
  Two of: 3 ENS

Nine-___ (short golf course):
    5 HOLER
Nine-day
  ritual: 6 NOVENA
Nine-digit
  no. issuer: 3 SSA
  sequence: 3 ZIP
  ~ ID: 3 **SSN**
Nine-headed
  serpent: 5 HYDRA
Nine-millimetre
  gun: 4 STEN
Nines
  Dressed to the: 7 DUDEDUP
    9 GUSSIEDUP
  Pair of: 3 ENS
Nine-sided
  shape: 7 NONAGON
Ninesome: 6 ENNEAD
Nine-to-fiver
  cry: 4 TGIF
Nineveh
  Book about: 5 NAHUM
  locale: 7 ASSYRIA
  locale (abbr.): 5 ASSYR
  Modern site of: 4 IRAQ
  river: 6 TIGRIS
Ninny: 3 **ASS** SAP 4 BOOB DODO
    DOLT DOPE SIMP TWIT
    5 GOOSE
Nino
  Film composer: 4 ROTA
"Ninotchka"
  actress: 9 INACLAIRE
  director Lubitsch: 5 ERNST
  portrayer: 5 GRETA
Nino Tempo
  Singer with: 12 APRILSTEVENS
Nintendo
  character: 5 MARIO
  forerunner: 5 ATARI
  rival: 4 **SEGA**
Ninth
  day before the ides: 5 NONES
  month (abbr.): 4 SEPT
Niobe: 6 WEEPER
Nip: 4 BITE
  partner: 4 TUCK
Nipper: 3 DOG

co.: 3 RCA
company: 9 RCAVICTOR
Nile: 3 ASP
Nose: 9 JACKFROST

Nirvana
attainer: 5 ARHAT
seeker: 5 HINDU

Nisan
Month after: 4 IYAR
Month before: 4 ADAR

Nissan
model: 6 ALTIMA MAXIMA
    SENTRA
~, once: 6 DATSUN

Nita
of silents: 5 NALDI

Nitpick: 5 CAVIL 10 SPLITHAIRS
Nitpicker: 6 PEDANT
___ nitrate: 4 AMYL
___ nitrite: 4 AMYL
Nitrogen: 3 GAS
compound: 5 AMIDE AMINE
    AZINE
lack: 4 ODOR

Nitrogen-based
dye: 3 AZO

Nitrous ___ (laughing gas):
    5 OXIDE

Nits
Adult: 4 LICE

Nittany Lions
school (abbr.): 3 PSU

Nitti
nemesis: 4 NESS

Nitty-gritty: 3 NUB 4 MEAT PITH
    6 BASICS
Nitwit: 3 ASS 4 BOOB DODO
    DOLT FOOL

Niven
role: 4 FOGG

Nix: 4 VETO 6 SCOTCH
Nixon
aide: 5 STANS
chief of staff: 4 HAIG
Commerce Secretary of: 5 STANS
Defense Secretary of: 5 LAIRD
impeachment chairman:
    6 RODINO
nemesis Sam: 5 ERVIN

policy: 7 DETENTE
target: 4 HISS
undoing: 5 TAPES
Vice President of: 5 AGNEW

"Nixon in China": 5 OPERA
role: 3 MAO

"Nixon's the One": 6 SLOGAN
N.J.
and others: 3 STS
base: 5 FTDIX
city: 5 FTLEE
neighbor: 3 DEL
summer hrs.: 3 EDT

N.L.
city: 3 ATL CHI STL

N.L. Central
team: 3 CHI MIL STL

NNE
opposite: 3 SSW
U-turn from: 3 SSW

NNW
opposite: 3 SSE
U-turn from: 3 SSE

No
and others: 3 DRS
follower: 3 SIR 5 SIREE
Russian: 4 NYET
vote: 3 NAY
voter: 4 ANTI
~, in German: 4 NEIN

No.
after a no.: 3 EXT

No-
follower: 3 CAL

"No ___!": 4 PROB
No-___ (gnat): 5 SEEUM
"No ___" (menu phrase): 3 MSG
No. 2: 4 ASST
No. 5
maker: 6 CHANEL

No. 10: 4 NEON
"No. 10"
painter: 6 ROTHKO

Noah
Actor: 4 WYLE 5 BEERY
boat: 3 ARK
challenge: 5 FLOOD
landfall: 6 ARARAT
mount: 6 ARARAT

number: 3 TWO
Son of: 3 HAM 4 SHEM
"___ No Angels": 4 WERE
Nob: 4 HILL
Nobel: 5 SWEDE
category: 5 PEACE
category (abbr.): 4 CHEM ECON
Inventor: 6 ALFRED
suffix: 3 IST
Nobel Institute
city: 4 OSLO
Nobelist: 8 LAUREATE
Nobelist, Chemistry
1911 ~ Marie: 5 CURIE
1913 ~ Alfred: 6 WERNER
1918 ~ Fritz: 5 HABER
1928 ~ Windhaus: 5 ADOLF
1934 ~ Harold: 4 UREY
1936 ~ Peter: 5 DEBYE
1937 ~ Norman: 7 HAWORTH
1944 ~ Hahn: 4 OTTO
1944 ~ Otto: 4 HAHN
1967 ~ Manfred: 5 EIGEN
1968 ~ Onsager: 4 LARS
Nobelist, Economics
1974 ~ Myrdal: 6 GUNNAR
1980 ~ Lawrence: 5 KLEIN
1990 ~ William: 6 SHARPE
1997 ~ Scholes: 5 MYRON
2001 ~ Michael: 6 SPENCE
Nobelist, Literature
1909 ~ Lagerlöf: 5 SELMA
1913 ~ Rabindranath: 6 TAGORE
1921 ~ France: 7 ANATOLE
1923 ~ William Butler: 5 YEATS
1927 ~ Henri: 7 BERGSON
1929 ~ Thomas: 4 MANN
1930 ~ Sinclair: 5 LEWIS
1933 ~ Ivan: 5 BUNIN
1936 ~ Eugene: 6 ONEILL
1946 ~ Hermann: 5 HESSE
1947 ~ André: 4 GIDE
1948 ~: 5 ELIOT 7 TSELIOT
1954 ~:
   15 ERNESTHEMINGWAY
1957 ~ Albert: 5 CAMUS
1961 ~ Andric: 3 IVO
1966 ~ Nelly: 5 SACHS
1966 ~ Sachs: 5 NELLY

1971 ~ Neruda: 5 PABLO
1971 ~ Pablo: 6 NERUDA
1976 ~ Bellow: 4 SAUL
1981 ~ Canetti: 5 ELIAS
1984 ~ Simon: 6 CLAUDE
1989 ~ Camilo José: 4 CELA
1990 ~ Octavio: 3 PAZ
1990 ~ Paz: 7 OCTAVIO
1991 ~ Gordimer: 6 NADINE
1992 ~ Walcott: 5 DEREK
1993 ~: 4 TONI
   12 TONIMORRISON
1995 ~ Seamus: 6 HEANEY
1997 ~ Fo: 5 DARIO
2002 ~ Kertesz: 4 IMRE
Nobelist, Medicine
1904 ~ Pavlov: 4 IVAN
1908 ~ Metchnikoff: 4 ELIE
1919 ~ Jules: 6 BORDET
1936 ~ Otto: 5 LOEWI
1949 ~ Walter: 4 HESS
1950 ~ Philip: 5 HENCH
1970 ~ Bernard: 4 KATZ
1970 ~ von Euler: 3 ULF
1974 ~ George: 6 PALADE
1975 ~ Dulbecco: 6 RENATO
1977 ~ Rosalyn: 5 YALOW
1977 ~ Yalow: 7 ROSALYN
Nobelist, Peace
1907 ~ Ernesto: 6 MONETA
1912 ~ Root: 5 ELIHU
1925 ~ Charles: 5 DAWES
1927 ~ Ludwig: 6 QUIDDE
1946 ~ John: 4 MOTT
1949 ~ John Boyd ___: 3 ORR
1949 ~ John ___ Orr: 4 BOYD
1950 ~: 6 BUNCHE
   11 RALPHBUNCHE
1958 ~ Georges: 4 PIRE
1961 ~ Hammarskjöld: 3 DAG
1963 ~: 7 PAULING
   12 LINUSPAULING
1968 ~ Cassin: 4 RENE
1969 ~: 3 ILO
1971 ~ Willy: 6 BRANDT
1974 ~ Eisaku: 4 SATO
1975 ~ Sakharov: 6 ANDREI
1978 ~ Anwar: 5 SADAT
1978 ~ Sadat: 5 ANWAR

1980 ~ ___ Pérez Esquivel:
 6 ADOLFO
1983 ~ Lech: 6 WALESA
1983 ~ Walesa: 4 LECH
1984 ~ Desmond: 4 TUTU
1986 ~ Elie: 6 WIESEL
1986 ~ Wiesel: 4 ELIE
1987 ~ Oscar ___ Sánchez:
 5 ARIAS
1989 ~: 9 DALAILAMA
1989 ~ the ___ Lama: 5 DALAI
1993 ~ Nelson: 7 MANDELA
1994 ~ Shimon: 5 PERES
1994 ~ Yasser: 6 ARAFAT
1994 ~ Yitzhak: 5 RABIN
2001 ~ Kofi: 5 ANNAN
Nobelist, Physics
1902 ~ Pieter: 6 ZEEMAN
1903 ~ Pierre and Marie:
 5 CURIE
1909 ~ Guglielmo: 7 MARCONI
1918 ~ Max: 6 PLANCK
1918 ~ Planck: 3 MAX
1922 ~ Bohr: 5 NIELS
1922 ~ Niels: 4 BOHR
1930 ~ Venkata: 5 RAMAN
1933 ~ Paul: 5 DIRAC
1938 ~ Enrico: 5 FERMI
1938 ~ Fermi: 6 ENRICO
1944 ~ Isidor: 4 RABI
1944 ~ Rabi: 6 ISIDOR
1945 ~ Wolfgang: 5 PAULI
1955 ~ Polykarp: 5 KUSCH
1957 ~ Tsung-___ Lee: 3 DAO
1958 ~ Tamm: 4 IGOR
1959 ~ Segrè: 6 EMILIO
1962 ~ Landau: 3 LEV
1967 ~ Hans: 5 BETHE
1973 ~ Giaever: 4 IVAR
1978 ~ Penzias: 4 ARNO
Nobel Prize
 decliner: 6 SARTRE
 subj.: 4 ECON
"No bid": 5 IPASS
Nobility: 5 PEERS
 Indian: 5 RAJAS RANIS
 Some: 4 SIRS
Noble
 British: 4 EARL 5 BARON

 7 BARONET
British ~ (briefly): 6 ARISTO
French: 5 COMTE
gas: 4 NEON 5 XENON
Heaviest ~ gas: 5 RADON
Hindu: 4 RANI
Italian ~ family: 4 ESTE
It may be: 3 GAS
mount: 5 STEED
objective: 5 IDEAL
Of a certain: 5 DUCAL
partner: 6 BARNES
state: 7 EARLDOM
Nobleman: 4 EARL LORD
 5 BARON
 French: 3 DUC 5 COMTE
 Spanish: 7 GRANDEE HIDALGO
Noblewoman: 7 PEERESS
 8 BARONESS
"No ___, Bob!": 6 SIRREE
Nobody
 in particular: 6 ANYONE
"Nobody doesn't like ___ Lee":
 4 SARA
No-brainer: 5 MORON
 7 EASYONE
 15 OPENANDSHUTCASE
 Like a: 4 EASY
No-cal
 drink: 5 WATER
Noche
 opposite: 3 DIA
___ noche (tonight, in Spanish):
 4 ESTA
No-cholesterol
 spread: 4 OLEO
Nocturnal
 bird: 3 OWL
 flier: 4 MOTH
 hunter: 5 ORION
 insect: 6 EARWIG
 lizard: 5 GECKO
 primate: 5 LEMUR
Nod: 3 CUE 4 DOZE 5 SLEEP
 6 ASSENT SIGNAL
 ending: 3 ULE
 Gives the: 3 OKS
 Give the: 4 OKAY 5 AGREE
 6 ASSENT

Land west of: 4 **EDEN**
off: 3 NAP 4 DOZE 6 DROWSE
to: 5 GREET
Visit the land of: 5 SLEEP
Words with a: 4 ISEE
Nodding: 6 ASLEEP SLEEPY
"No dice": 3 NAH 4 UHUH
Nods: 3 OKS 5 YESES
Nodule: 5 POLYP
Crystal-lined: 5 GEODE
Noel: 4 YULE 5 CAROL
___ Noël: 4 PERE
"No Exit"
playwright: 6 SARTRE
No-frills: 5 BASIC PLAIN
        7 GENERIC SPARTAN
bed: 3 COT
Nofziger
Reagan aide: 3 LYN
Nog
ingredient: 3 EGG
Nogales
Info: Spanish cue
Nap, in: 6 SIESTA
Nothing, in: 4 NADA
Now, in: 5 AHORA
Noggin: 4 **BEAN** DOME HEAD
        PATE 5 GOURD
        6 NOODLE
Knock on the: 4 BONK CONK
~, in French: 4 TETE
No-good: 6 ROTTEN
___ no good: 4 UPTO
No-goodnik: 3 CAD RAT 4 HEEL
        5 LOUSE 6 BADDIE
        BADEGG MEANIE
        7 SOANDSO STINKER
No-holds-barred: 6 ALLOUT
        7 EXTREME
___ No Hooks: 3 USE
"___ no idea!": 4 IHAD
"No ifs, ands, or ___": 4 BUTS
"No ifs, ___, or buts!": 4 ANDS
___ noir: 4 CAFE 5 PINOT
___ noire: 4 **BETE**
Noise
Crowd: 3 RAH 8 APPLAUSE
Fan: 3 RAH 4 WHIR
Herd: 3 MOO

Lot of: 3 DIN
Nest: 4 PEEP 5 CHEEP
Night: 5 SNORE
of the lambs: 3 BAA
Radio: 6 STATIC
Trumpet: 5 BLARE
Noisemaker
Celebration: 11 FIRECRACKER
Flying: 6 CICADA
Nighttime: 6 SNORER
Nursery: 6 RATTLE
Noisily
Drink: 5 SLURP
Proclaim: 5 BLARE
Revel: 7 ROISTER
Walk: 5 CLOMP
Noisy: 4 LOUD 5 AROAR
bird: 3 JAY
fight: 5 BRAWL
flier: 3 SST
insect: 6 CICADA
napper: 6 SNORER
quarrel: 3 ROW
sleeper: 6 SNORER
toy: 6 POPGUN
trains: 3 ELS
"No kidding!": 3 GEE 4 GOSH
        6 DOTELL 7 IMEANIT
        ITSTRUE 8 ITSAFACT
Nol
of Cambodia: 3 LON
Nolan
of baseball: 4 RYAN
Nolan, Philip: 5 EXILE
No later than: 3 TIL 5 UNTIL
Nolde
Expressionist painter: 4 EMIL
No less than: 7 ATLEAST
Nolin, ___ Lee
Actress: 4 GENA
Nolo: 4 PLEA
contendere: 4 PLEA
No longer: 3 NOT
here: 4 GONE
hot: 3 OUT
in: 5 DATED PASSE
Nolte
Actor: 4 NICK
Cape in a ~ film: 4 FEAR

Nomad: 5 ROVER 6 ROAMER
    8 WANDERER
Nomadic
  Be: 4 ROAM ROVE
  tribe: 5 HORDE
"No man is an island"
  author: 5 DONNE
"No man ___ island": 4 ISAN
No matter what:
    15 COMERAINORSHINE
Nom de plume: 5 ALIAS
  Lamb's: 4 **ELIA**
Nome
  dome home: 5 IGLOO
  home: 6 ALASKA
  knife: 3 ULU
"___ nome" ("Rigoletto"
    highlight): 4 CARO
Nominate: 4 NAME
Nomination
  Kind of: 4 EMMY
Nominee
  Clio: 5 ADMAN
  list: 5 SLATE
Nomo
  birthplace: 5 OSAKA
  Number for: 3 ERA
  of baseball: 5 HIDEO
"No more!": 5 UNCLE
Non
  opposite: 3 OUI
Non ___ (unwelcome): 5 GRATA
Nonaffiliated
  (abbr.): 3 IND
No-name: 7 GENERIC
Nonbeliever: 5 PAGAN 7 ATHEIST
Nonchalance: 4 EASE
    8 EASINESS
Nonchalant: 4 COOL
Nonchalantly
  Walk: 6 SASHAY
Nonchooser: 6 BEGGAR
Non-clashing
  color: 4 ECRU
Nonclerical: 3 LAY 4 LAIC
  group: 5 LAITY
Noncom
  (abbr.): 3 SGT 4 MSGT
  Navy: 3 CPO

  nickname: 5 SARGE
Noncombat
  gp.: 4 WAAC
Noncommercial
  ~ TV network: 3 PBS
Noncommittal
  answer: 5 MAYBE
  words: 4 IMAY
Noncompromiser: 6 PURIST
Nonconformist: 5 FLAKE
    6 MISFIT 7 HERETIC
Nondairy
  spread: 4 OLEO
None
  of the above: 5 **OTHER**
Non-earthling: 5 ALIEN
"No need to explain": 6 IGETIT
Nonetheless: 3 YET 6 ANYWAY
    EVENSO
  ~, for short: 3 THO
Nonexistent: 3 **NIL** 4 NULL
Nonfat
  milk: 4 SKIM
Nonflowering
  plant: 4 FERN
  ___ non grata: 7 PERSONA
Non-Jew: 7 GENTILE
Nonkosher
  sandwich: 3 BLT
Nonnational: 5 ALIEN
Nonnative: 5 ALIEN
  Subj. for a: 3 ESL
  ~ Hawaiian: 5 HAOLE
No-no: 4 DONT 5 **TABOO**
  (var.): 4 TABU
"No ___, no gain": 4 PAIN
"No, No, Nanette"
  lyricist Harbach: 4 OTTO
  tune: 9 TEAFORTWO
"No No Song, The"
  singer: 5 STARR
Non-oyster
  Like ~ months: 5 RLESS
Nonpastoral: 4 LAIC
Nonpayment
  result: 4 REPO
Non-P.C.
  suffix: 3 ESS 4 ENNE ETTE
Nonplussed: 5 ATSEA

Non-Polynesian: 5 HAOLE
Nonpro
 sports gp.: **3** AAU
Non-pro: 4 ANTI
Nonprofessional: 3 LAY
Nonprofit
 website suffix: **3** ORG
Nonreactive: 5 INERT
Nonrecurring: 7 ONESHOT
Nonresident
 doctor: **6** EXTERN
 Place for ~ patients: **6** CLINIC
Nonreturnable
 It's: **3** ACE
Non-Rx: 3 OTC
Nonsense: 3 PAP **ROT** **4** BOSH
      HOKE TOSH **5** BILGE
      HOOEY TRIPE **6** BUSHWA
      DRIVEL **7** HOGWASH
      TWADDLE
      10 BALDERDASH
 Kind of: **5** UTTER
 singing: **4** SCAT
 Talk: **4** JIVE
 ~, to a Brit: **4** TOSH
"Nonsense!": 3 BAH **4** BUNK
      PISH TOSH **5** NERTS
      PSHAW
Nonsensical: 5 **INANE** SILLY
      7 ASININE IDIOTIC
Non-sharer: 3 HOG
Nonsmoking ___ : 4 AREA
Nonstick
 spray: **3** PAM
 surface: **6** TEFLON
Nonstop: 5 NOEND **7** ENDLESS
      ETERNAL **9** CEASELESS
 Talk: **5** RUNON
Non-studio: 5 INDIE
Nonsurfer: 5 HODAD
Nonverbal
 agreement: **3** NOD
Nonviolent
 demonstration: **5** SITIN
Nonwinner: 7 ALSORAN
Nonwoody
 plant: **4** HERB
Nonwritten
 test: **4** ORAL

Noodge: 3 NAG **4** PEST
 Be a: **6** PESTER
Noodle: 4 BEAN
 concoction: **4** IDEA
 dish: **5** RAMEN
 French: **4** TETE
 Like a wet: **4** LIMP
 Use one's: **5** THINK **6** REASON
Noodlehead: 3 OAF SAP
      5 SCHMO **9** BIRDBRAIN
Noodles: 5 PASTA
 Japanese: **5** RAMEN
Nook: 6 ALCOVE
 Church: **4** **APSE**
 Kitchen: **7** DINETTE
 Shady: **5** ARBOR
 Sheltered: **4** COVE
Noon: 6 MIDDAY
 Nap after: **6** SIESTA
 ~, in France: **4** MIDI
 ~, to Nero: **3** XII
"No Ordinary Love"
 singer: **4** SADE
Noose
 Decorative: **3** TIE
 material: **4** ROPE
"Nope": 3 NAH **4** **UHUH**
 rebuttal: **3** YUP
"No problem!": 4 EASY SURE
      5 CANDO
"___ no questions ...": 5 ASKME
Nor
 partner: **7** NEITHER
Nor.
 neighbor: **3** SWE
Nora
 Director: **6** EPHRON
 portrayer: **5** MYRNA
Norah
 Father of: **4** RAVI
Nord
 opposite: **3** SUD
Nordic
 alternative: **6** ALPINE
 carrier: **3** SAS
Nordland
 native: **4** LAPP
Nordstrom
 rival: **4** SAKS

Nor'easter: 5 STORM
"No returns": 4 ASIS
Norgay, Tenzing: 6 SHERPA
Norm: 3 PAR
  (abbr.): 3 **STD**
  Wife of: 4 VERA
  ~, in golf: 3 PAR
Norma
  Constellation near: 3 ARA
"Norma": 5 OPERA
  composer: 7 BELLINI
  highlight: 4 ARIA
"Norma ___": 3 **RAE**
Normal: 3 PAR 4 SANE 5 USUAL
  (abbr.): 3 STD
  Not: 3 ODD
  prefix: 4 PARA
  They're not: 8 DEVIANTS
Normally: 7 ASARULE
Norman
  Author: 6 MAILER
  Golfer: 4 GREG
  home (abbr.): 4 OKLA
  of cosmetics: 5 MERLE
  Playwright: 6 MARSHA
  Producer: 4 LEAR
  Soprano: 6 JESSYE
Normand
  of silent films: 5 **MABEL**
Normandy
  battle site: 4 **STLO**
  city: 4 CAEN
  event: 4 DDAY
  town: 4 **STLO**
Norman Vincent ___: 5 PEALE
"Norma Rae"
  director: 4 PITT
No ___ roses: 5 BEDOF
Norris Dam
  project (abbr.): 3 TVA
Norris Trophy
  winner: 3 ORR
Norse
  capital: 4 OSLO
  chieftain: 5 ROLLO
  epic: 4 EDDA
  Evil ~ god: 4 LOKI
  explorer: 4 ERIC
  god: 4 **ODIN**

  goddess: 3 HEL
  goddess of love: 5 FREYA
  god of discord: 4 LOKI
  god of strife: 3 TYR
  god of thunder: 4 THOR
  god of war: 3 TYR 4 ODIN
  Home of the ~ gods:
    6 ASGARD
  name: 4 OLAF
  pantheon: 5 AESIR
  Race of ~ gods: 5 AESIR
  saint: 4 OLAV
Norte
  90 degrees from ~: 4 ESTE
  opposite: 3 SUR
North: 3 SEA
  Actress: 6 SHEREE
  end: 3 ERN
  of Irangate: 5 OLLIE
  of Virginia: 5 OLLIE
  suffix: 3 ERN
North Africa
  Much of: 6 SAHARA
North African
  capital: 5 RABAT TUNIS
  desert: 6 SAHARA
  tribesman: 6 BERBER
  viper: 3 ASP
"North and South"
  novelist: 5 JAKES
North Atlantic
  fish: 3 COD
  menace: 4 BERG
"North by Northwest"
  costar: 3 EVA
North Carolina
  cape: 4 FEAR 8 HATTERAS
  capital: 7 RALEIGH
  college: 4 ELON
  county: 4 **ASHE**
  fort: 5 BRAGG
  motto beginning: 4 ESSE
  resident: 7 TARHEEL
  senator: 5 HELMS
  university: 4 **ELON**
North Dakota
  city: 5 FARGO MINOT
Northeast
  college town: 5 ORONO

Northeast Corridor
train: 5 ACELA
Northeast India
State in: 5 ASSAM
Northern: 6 BOREAL
Bright ~ star: 6 ALTAIR
capital: 4 OSLO
constellation: 5 DRACO
diving bird: 3 AUK
forest: 5 TAIGA
highway: 5 ALCAN
Northern ___ (apple): 3 SPY
"Northern Exposure"
setting: 6 ALASKA
Northern Manhattan
dweller: 8 UPTOWNER
Northern Spy: 5 APPLE
North Pole
explorer: 5 PEARY
exports: 4 TOYS
resident: 5 SANTA
worker: 3 ELF
Northrop
Literary critic: 4 FRYE
North Sea
diver: 3 AUK
feeder: 3 DEE EMS 4 **ELBE**
TYNE **YSER** 5 MEUSE
port: 8 ABERDEEN
structure: 6 OILRIG
tributary: 5 MEUSE
Northumberland
river: 4 TYNE
Northwest
(abbr.): 4 TERR
Sound of the: 5 PUGET
Northwest Rebellion
tribe: 4 CREE
Northwest Territories
capital: 11 YELLOWKNIFE
North Yorkshire
river: 3 URE
Norton
and others: 3 EDS
Boxer: 3 KEN
Norton, Ed
wear: 4 VEST
workplace: 5 SEWER
~, to Ralph Kramden: 3 PAL

Norton Sound
city: 4 NOME
Norway
capital: 4 OSLO
patron saint: 4 **OLAF OLAV**
Norwegian
capital: 4 OSLO
coin: 3 ORE
composer: 5 GRIEG
inlet: 5 FJORD
king: 4 **OLAF OLAV**
Northern: 4 LAPP
playwright: 5 IBSEN
saint: 4 OLAF OLAV
"Norwegian Wood"
instrument: 5 SITAR
Nor'wester: 5 STORM
Nose
around: 3 PRY 5 SNOOP
Beat by a: 3 NIP 4 EDGE
Canary's: 4 CERE
Kind of: 5 ROMAN
nipper: 9 JACKFROST
notifier: 5 AROMA
Offend the: 4 REEK
On the: 5 EXACT
(out): 4 **EDGE**
prefix: 4 NASI RHIN
Turn up one's ~ at: 4 SNUB
What the ~ knows: 4 ODOR
5 AROMA
Words before: 3 BYA
wrinkler: 4 ODOR
~, slangily: 5 SNOOT
"No seats left": 3 SRO
Nosebag
filler: 4 OATS
Nosebleed
seats: 6 TOPROW
Nosedive: 4 FALL 6 TUMBLE
No-see-um: 4 **GNAT**
Nosegay: 4 POSY
Nose-in-the-air
type: 4 SNOB
Nosh: 3 EAT 4 BITE 5 SNACK
Nag's: 3 OAT
on: 3 EAT
No-show: 4 AWOL
8 ABSENTEE

Literary: 5 GODOT
Military: 4 AWOL
Score for a: 4 ZERO
Nostalgia
Bit of: 5 OLDIE
Nostalgic
Be ~ for: 4 MISS
fashion: 5 RETRO
location: 10 MEMORYLANE
pop: 4 NEHI
song: 5 OLDIE
style: 5 RETRO
times: 5 OLDDAYS
tune: 5 OLDIE
___ Nostra: 4 **COSA**
Nostradamus: 4 SEER
Sign for: 4 OMEN
Nostrils: 5 **NARES**
"No Strings Attached"
pop group: 5 NSYNC
Nostromo
Film set on the spaceship:
5 ALIEN
Nostrum: 6 REMEDY
"___ No Sunshine": 4 AINT
"No sweat!": 4 EASY
Nosy
Be: 3 PRY
Get: 3 PRY 5 SNOOP
sort: 5 SNOOP
Nosy Parker: 5 PRIER SNOOP
  YENTA 7 SNOOPER
Be a: 3 PRY
Not: 4 NARY
And: 3 NOR
any: 4 NARY NONE
~, to a Scot: 3 NAE
Not ___ (mediocre): 5 SOHOT
"Not ___!": 4 THAT 5 AGAIN
Nota ___: 4 BENE
Notable
period: 3 ERA 5 EPOCH
time: 3 ERA 5 EPOCH
"Not a chance!": 5 MYEYE
  NOWAY
"Not again!": 4 OHNO
"No talking!": 3 SHH
Notary
need: 4 SEAL

Not at all: 5 NOHOW 6 HARDLY
  NOWISE 7 INNOWAY
Notation
Editor's: 4 STET
Env.: 4 ATTN
ER: 3 DOA
Invitation: 4 RSVP
Margin: 4 STET
Memo: 4 ASAP INRE
Proofreader's: 4 STET
Quotation: 4 ANON
Sale: 4 ASIS
Staff: 4 CLEF
"Not ___ bet!": 3 ONA
Notch: 3 VEE 4 NICK
___ notch: 3 UPA
Notched: 5 JAGGY 7 CRENATE
  SERRATE
Irregularly: 5 EROSE
Note: 3 IOU SOL 4 MEMO
  7 JOTDOWN
above C: 5 DFLAT
above G: 5 AFLAT
after fa: 3 SOL
High ~ of old: 3 ELA
in the A-major scale: 6 GSHARP
Office: 4 MEMO
Promissory: 3 IOU
Sour: 7 CLINKER
Staff: 3 SOL 4 MEMO
Sticky: 6 POSTIT
Take ~ of: 4 HEED
taker: 5 STENO
Notebook: 6 LAPTOP
divider: 3 TAB
Like ~ paper: 5 LINED RULED
maker: 3 IBM
Noted: 6 FAMOUS 7 EMINENT
Notes
after do: 3 RES 4 REMI
Closing: 4 CODA
End: 4 CODA
Musical: 3 FAS LAS MIS RES TIS
Pound: 6 ARFARF
Scale: 3 **FAS** LAS MIS **RES** TIS
"___ note to follow ...": 3 LAA
Noteworthy
period: 3 ERA 5 EPOCH
time: 3 ERA 5 EPOCH

Not ___ eye in the house: 4 ADRY
"Not from where ___": 4 ISIT
"Not guilty": 4 PLEA
Nothin': 4 NADA
"Nothin' ___!": 4 DOIN
"Nothin' doin'!": 4 UHUH
Nothing: 3 **NIL** ZIP 4 NADA ZERO
  at all: 3 NIL
  but: 3 ALL 4 MERE ONLY
  Did: 3 SAT 5 SATBY
  Do: 4 IDLE LAZE LOAF
  Doing: 4 **IDLE**
  Have ~ to do with: 4 SHUN
  If ~ changes: 6 ASITIS
  It beats: 4 PAIR
  It means: 3 NIL
  It means ~ in tennis: 4 LOVE
  It's ~ new: 5 RERUN
      7 ROUTINE
  It's next to: 3 ONE
  more than: 4 **MERE** ONLY
  One with ~ to do: 5 IDLER
  special: 4 SOSO
  Sweet: 10 ENDEARMENT
  Take ~ in: 4 FAST
  to write home about: 4 SOSO
  ~, in French: 4 RIEN
  ~, in Italian: 6 NIENTE
  ~, in Spanish: 4 NADA
  ~, to Nero: 5 NIHIL
Nothing ___: 4 LESS
"Nothing ___!": 5 DOING
___ nothing: 5 ALLOR
"Nothing new": 7 SAMEOLD
"Nothing runs like a ___":
      5 DEERE
Notice: 3 **SEE** 4 ESPY SPOT
      6 DETECT
  Final: 4 **OBIT**
  Give: 4 QUIT
  Give ~ to: 5 ALERT
  Passing: 4 **OBIT**
  Put on: 4 WARN
  Take: 5 SITUP
Noticed: 3 SAW 4 SEEN 6 ESPIED
Notify: 5 ALERT 6 ADVISE
      INFORM
Not in: 4 AWAY 5 PASSE
Not ___ in the world: 5 ACARE

Not in use: 4 IDLE
Not in yet: 7 ONORDER
Notion: 4 **IDEA**
  Capricious: 4 WHIM
  Nice: 4 IDEE
  ~, in French: 4 IDEE
Notions
  case: 4 ETUI
Not know from ___: 4 ADAM
"Not likely!": 4 IBET
Not ___ many words: 4 **INSO**
Not miss ___: 5 ABEAT
Not much: 4 ABIT **ATAD**
Not now: 4 THEN 5 LATER
      7 LATERON
"Not on ___!": 4 ABET
Notoriety: 4 FAME 6 REPUTE
      7 RECLAME
"Notorious"
  actor Grant: 4 CARY
Not quite: 6 ALMOST
"No ___ traffic": 4 THRU
Notre ___: 4 DAME
Notre Dame
  area: 4 APSE
  bench: 3 PEW
  city: 5 PARIS
  coach Parseghian: 3 ARA
  coach Rockne: 5 KNUTE
  river: 5 SEINE
  team: 5 IRISH
"Not so fast!": 6 HOLDIT
Not so many: 5 FEWER
Not so much: 4 **LESS**
Nottingham
  John of: 3 LOO
  river: 5 TRENT
"Not to worry!": 5 ITSOK
"Not true!": 7 ITSALIE
      9 THATSALIE
"___ Not Unusual": 3 ITS
Not up to much: 4 IDLE
Notwithstanding: 7 DESPITE
  ~, briefly: 3 THO 5 ALTHO
Not worth ___: 4 AFIG ASOU
Not worth a ___: 3 FIG SOU
"Not you ___!": 5 AGAIN
Noun
  gender (abbr.): 3 FEM 4 MASC

NEUT
suffix: 4 NESS SION TION
Noun-forming
suffix: 3 ION 4 ENCE
Nourish: 4 FEED
Nourished: 3 **FED**
Nourishing
~, in Latin: 4 ALMA
Nourishment: 4 FOOD
___ nous: 5 **ENTRE**
Nouveau ___ : 5 **RICHE**
Nouvelle-Calédonie: 3 ILE
Nova: 3 LOX 4 STAR
follower: 6 SCOTIA
"Nova"
network: 3 **PBS**
subj.: 3 SCI
Nova ___ : 6 SCOTIA
___ nova: 3 ARS 5 **BOSSA**
Novak
Actress: 3 KIM
Onetime partner of: 5 EVANS
Novarro
Actor: 5 **RAMON**
Novel: 3 NEW 5 FRESH
ending: 3 IST 4 **ETTE**
6 EPILOG
idea: 4 PLOT
~ ID: 4 ISBN
Novell
city: 4 OREM
state: 4 UTAH
Novello
Actor: 4 **IVOR**
November
birthstone: 5 TOPAZ
choice: 4 VOTE
honoree: 3 VET
veggie: 3 YAM
winner: 7 ELECTEE
winners: 3 INS
Novgorod
No, in: 4 NYET
Novice: 4 TIRO TYRO 6 ROOKIE
10 TENDERFOOT
Internet: 6 NEWBIE
Novi Sad
native: 4 SERB
___ Novo: 5 PORTO

Novocain
Shoot up with: 4 NUMB
6 DEADEN
target: 5 NERVE
Novotna
of tennis: 4 JANA
Novus ___ seclorum: 4 ORDO
Now: 5 TODAY 6 ATONCE
and again: 5 TWICE 7 ATTIMES
10 ONOCCASION
and then: 7 ATTIMES
10 ONOCCASION
From ~ on: 5 HENCE
Not: 4 ANON THEN 5 LATER
7 LATERON
or in the future: 4 EVER
partner: 4 THEN
Until: 3 YET 5 ASYET SOFAR
6 TODATE
Up to: 3 YET 5 ASYET SOFAR
6 TODATE
~, in Spanish: 5 AHORA
"Now!": 4 ASAP STAT 6 ATONCE
PRONTO
Nowadays: 7 ANYMORE
"No way!": 3 NAH 4 ASIF UHUH
5 ICANT MYEYE PSHAW
6 CANTBE
10 NOTACHANCE
"No way, ___!": 4 JOSE
"Now hear ___!": 4 THIS
Nowhere
Going: 6 INARUT
Went: 5 IDLED
Nowheresville: 6 PODUNK
"Now I get it!": 3 AHA
"Now I ___ me down to ...": 3 LAY
No-win
situation: 3 **TIE** 4 DRAW
"Now I see!": 3 AHA 4 AHSO
"Now ___ it!": 4 IGET
"Now it makes sense": 4 ISEE
"Now it's clear": 4 ISEE
"Now I've ___ everything!":
4 SEEN
"Now ___ me down ...": 4 ILAY
"___ now or never": 3 ITS
"Now ___ seen everything!":
3 IVE

"Now ___ theater near you!":
   3 ATA
"Now, Voyager"
  actress Chase: 4 ILKA
"Now We Are Six"
  author: 5 MILNE
"Now, where ___?": 4 WASI
"Now, where ___ I?": 3 WAS
"Now you ___ ...": 5 SEEIT
"Now ___ you ...": 4 IASK
Noxious
  emanation: 6 MIASMA
Noyes
  Poet: 6 ALFRED
Nozzle: 3 JET 6 GASJET
NPR
  host Glass: 3 IRA
  host Hansen: 5 LIANE
  puzzlemaster: 6 SHORTZ
  reporter Totenberg: 4 NINA
NRA: 4 ASSN
  supporter: 3 FDR
NRC
  predecessor: 3 **AEC**
NT
  book: 3 EPH
Nth
  (abbr.): 3 ULT
  degree: 3 MAX
Nuance: 4 TONE 7 SHADING
Nuanced: 6 SUBTLE
Nubian Desert
  site: 5 SUDAN
Nuclear
  accident site (abbr.): 3 TMI
  experiment: 5 ATEST
  fission discoverer: 4 HAHN
  Former ~ agcy.: 3 AEC
  missile acronym: 4 MIRV
  physicist Niels: 4 BOHR
  physics suffix: 4 TRON
  trial: 5 ATEST
  weapon: 5 ABOMB HBOMB
Nuclei: 5 CORES
Nucleotide
  prefix: 3 TRI
Nucleus: 4 CORE 5 CADRE
  Part of a cell: 3 RNA
Nude: 4 BARE 5 MODEL

Not: 4 CLAD
Nudge: 3 JOG 4 POKE PROD
    5 ELBOW
  forward: 4 PROD
  rudely: 5 ELBOW
  ~, as memory: 3 JOG
Nudist: 7 ADAMITE
Nudnik: 4 PAIN **PEST**
  Be a: 6 PESTER
"___ nuff!": 3 SHO
Nugent
  Guitarist: 3 **TED**
Nugget
  Barbecue: 4 COAL
___ Nui (Easter Island): 4 RAPA
Nuisance: 4 PAIN **PEST**
  E-mail: 4 SPAM
  Garden: 4 WEED
"___ nuit!": 5 BONNE
Nuke: 3 **ZAP** 6 REHEAT REWARM
  prefix: 4 ANTI
Nullify: 4 UNDO VOID 6 NEGATE
Num.
  follower: 4 DEUT
Numb: 6 DEADEN
  ~, as a foot: 6 ASLEEP
Number: 3 ACT 4 SONG TUNE
  Allowed: 5 QUOTA
  Best-selling: 3 ONE
  Chosen: 3 FEW
  Clock: 3 III VII XII 4 IIII VIII
  Cloud: 4 NINE
  Did a: 4 SANG
  Diva's: 4 ARIA
  Do a: 4 SING
  for Nomo: 3 ERA
  for one: 4 ARIA
  for two: 4 DUET
  Gas pump: 6 OCTANE
  Great: 4 RAFT
  Hole: 3 **PAR**
  Holiday: 4 NOEL
  in black: 5 ASSET
  Kind of: 6 ATOMIC 7 ORDINAL
  Large: 4 HERD HOST SLEW
  Like a certain ~ system: 5 OCTAL
  Limited: 3 FEW
  Lonely: 3 ONE
  Met: 4 ARIA

next to a plus sign: 6 ADDEND
Old: 5 ETHER
Opera: 4 ARIA
Page: 5 FOLIO
Perfect: 3 TEN
Pump: 6 OCTANE
Round: 4 ZERO
Small: 3 FEW
Sundial: 3 III VII XII 4 IIII VIII
Tango: 3 TWO
Three-digit: 8 AREACODE
two: 4 VICE
Unspecified: 3 ANY
Whole: 7 INTEGER
Work with a: 4 OPUS

Number-calling
game: 5 BEANO

Number cruncher: 3 CPA

Numbered
club: 4 IRON
composition: 4 OPUS
hwy.: 3 **RTE**
rd.: 3 **RTE**
work: 4 **OPUS**
___ number on: 3 DOA

"Number One Son"
Father of: 4 CHAN

Numbers
after "1": 8 AREACODE
Bookie's: 4 ODDS
Box score: 5 STATS
game: 4 KENO 5 BEANO BINGO
    LOTTO
holder: 5 TORAH
on horses: 4 ODDS
person: 8 OPERATOR
Recital: 4 SOLI
Set of: 6 MEDLEY
to crunch: 4 DATA
Track: 4 ODDS

Numbskull: 3 ASS OAF 4 BOZO
    DODO DOPE 5 IDIOT

Numeral: 5 DIGIT
Clock: 3 III VII XII 4 IIII VIII

Numerals
Like our: 6 ARABIC
Like some: 5 ROMAN

"Numerals, The"
painter: 4 ERTE

Numerical
ending: 3 ETH 4 TEEN
prefix: 3 **TRI** 4 DECA HEPT
    HEXA MONO OCTA OCTO
    5 PENTA TETRA
suffix: 3 ETH 4 TEEN

Numero
Important: 3 UNO
uno: 4 BEST

Numero ___ : 3 **UNO**

Numerous: 4 MANY 6 LEGION
    UNTOLD
Less: 5 FEWER
Most ~ people: 6 ASIANS
~, slangily: 5 LOTSA

Numismatist
item: 4 COIN

Numskull: 3 ASS OAF 4 BOZO
    DODO DOPE 5 IDIOT

Nun: 6 SISTER
attire: 5 HABIT
headcloth: 6 WIMPLE

Nuncupative: 4 ORAL

Nunn
Georgia senator: 3 SAM

Nuptial
agreement: 3 IDO
lane: 5 AISLE
pronoun: 4 OURS
starter: 3 PRE
Take a ~ flight: 5 ELOPE

Nuremberg
Info: German cue
Never, in: 3 NIE
No, in: 4 NEIN
trial figure: 5 SPEER

Nureyev: 7 DANSEUR
Ballet dancer: 6 RUDOLF

Nurmi
Olympic medalist: 5 PAAVO

Nürnberg
Info: German cue
Never, in: 3 NIE
No, in: 4 NEIN

Nurse: 3 SIP 4 FEED 6 SUCKLE
Asian: 4 AMAH
Eastern: 4 AMAH

Nursemaid: 5 NANNY
Asian: 4 AMAH

Hindu: 4 AYAH
Indian: 4 AMAH
Nursery
color: 4 PINK
cry: 4 MAMA
denizen: 7 NEONATE
furniture: 4 CRIB
product: 3 SOD
purchase: 4 CRIB 5 PLANT
supply: 4 LOAM
Nursery rhyme
boy: 5 PETER
girl: 6 BOPEEP
name: 5 SPRAT
residence: 4 SHOE
start: 5 PEASE 6 BAABAA
10 RUBADUBDUB
trio: 4 MICE
Nursing
Need: 3 AIL
Nurture: 4 GROW REAR TEND
Nus
followers: 3 XIS
~, to us: 3 ENS
Nut: 4 KOOK LOON 6 MANIAC
WEIRDO
cake: 3 BUR 5 TORTE
Car: 3 LUG
center: 4 MEAT
Kind of: 3 LUG 4 KOLA 5 BEECH
BETEL 6 LITCHI 7 LUNATIC
9 MACADAMIA
Oak: 5 ACORN
partner: 4 BOLT
Pie: 5 PECAN
Praline: 5 PECAN
Soft drink: 4 KOLA
source: 4 TREE
Tough: 5 POSER
tree: 5 BEECH
Tropical: 4 KOLA 5 BETEL
with a cap: 5 ACORN
Nutcase: 4 KOOK LOON 5 WACKO
Nutcracker
suite: 4 NEST
"Nutcracker, The"
girl: 5 CLARA
Nuthatch
home: 4 NEST

"Nuthin' but a 'G' Thang"
rapper: 5 DRDRE
Nutmeg: 4 SEED
covering: 4 ARIL
spice: 4 MACE
NutRageous
maker: 6 REESES
Nutrient
Important: 4 IRON
stat.: 3 RDA
Nutrition
inits.: 3 **RDA**
units: 5 GRAMS
Nutritional
fig.: 3 CAL **RDA**
std.: 3 **RDA**
Nutritive
mineral: 4 IRON
Nuts: 4 BATS GAGA LOCO
5 CRAZY KOOKY
LOONY
and bolts: 4 ABCS
Be ~ over: 5 ADORE
Go: 4 RAGE RAVE
Like many: 6 SALTED
"Nuts!": 3 BAH 4 DARN DRAT
RATS
___ nutshell: 3 INA
Nutso: 4 LOCO 5 LOOPY
Nutty: 4 DAFT 5 LOOPY
cake: 5 TORTE
confection: 6 NOUGAT
7 PRALINE
Not as: 5 SANER
"Nutty Professor, The"
actor Murphy: 5 EDDIE
N.Y.
college: 3 RPI
hrs.: 3 EST
neighbor: 3 ONT QUE
summer hrs.: 3 EDT
team: 4 METS
winter·hrs.: 3 EST
Nyasaland
~, today: 6 MALAWI
NYC
airport: 3 LGA
arena: 3 MSG
art center: 4 MOMA

Artsy ~ area: 4 SOHO
clock setting: 3 EDT EST
commuter line: 4 LIRR
gallery: 4 MOMA
hours: 3 EST
Part of: 4 CITY
radio station: 4 WABC
subway: 3 IND IRT
subway line: 3 IRT
subway org.: 3 MTA
subway overseer: 3 MTA
summer hours: 3 EDT
They're numbered in: 3 STS
Train line to: 4 LIRR
Uptown, in: 3 NNE

Nyctophobic:
       15 AFRAIDOFTHEDARK

Nye, Bill
subj.: 3 SCI

Nykvist
Cinematographer: 4 **SVEN**

Nylon: 7 POLYMER

NY Mets: 5 NLERS
division: 6 NLEAST

Nymph
Aquatic: 5 NAIAD
chaser: 5 SATYR

Mountain: 5 **OREAD**
River: 5 NAIAD
Sea: 6 NEREID 7 OCEANID
who fled Apollo: 6 DAPHNE
Wood: 5 DRYAD

"Nymphéas"
painter: 5 MONET

Nymphet: 6 LOLITA

NYPD
alert: 3 APB
figure: 3 DET
rank: 3 DET SGT
title: 3 DET

"NYPD Blue"
actor Jimmy: 5 SMITS
actor Morales: 4 ESAI
network: 3 ABC

Nyro
Singer: 5 LAURA

NYSE: 3 MKT
competitor: 4 AMEX
cousin: 6 NASDAQ
debut: 3 IPO
listings: 3 COS
regulator: 3 SEC
rival: 4 AMEX
unit: 3 SHR

Oo

O: 3 MAG 4 ELEM RING TYPE
    8 for ~: 4 ATNO
    Center X or: 3 TAC
    Greek: 7 OMICRON
    in old radio lingo: 4 OBOE
    in REO: 4 OLDS
    in SRO: 4 ONLY
    of O magazine: 5 OPRAH
    preceders: 3 LMN
Oaf: 3 APE LUG 4 BOZO CLOD
       DOLT LOUT 6 GALOOT
       7 PALOOKA
Oafish: 5 INEPT
Oahu
    dance: 4 HULA
    goose: 4 NENE
    greeting: 5 ALOHA
    landmark: 11 DIAMONDHEAD
    neighbor: 5 KAUAI
    souvenir: 3 **LEI**
    wear: 6 MUUMUU
    wingding: 4 LUAU
Oak: 4 TREE
    California: 5 ROBLE
    fruit: 5 ACORN
    Future: 5 ACORN
    Holm: 4 ILEX
    Like ~ leaves: 5 EROSE
       LOBED
    Live: 6 ENCINA
    nut: 5 ACORN
    Silver ~ leaf wearer (abbr.):
       5 LTCOL
    White: 5 ROBLE
Oakes
    Actress: 5 RANDI
Oakland
    county: 7 ALAMEDA
    neighbor: 7 ALAMEDA
    player: 6 RAIDER 8 ATHLETIC
    transit sys.: 4 BART
Oakley
    Sharpshooter: 5 ANNIE

Oakley, Annie: 4 PASS
    7 DEADEYE
    Like the aim of: 4 TRUE
Oak Ridge Boys
    hit: 6 ELVIRA
Oar: 6 PADDLE
    pin: 5 THOLE
Oarlock: 5 THOLE
Oar-powered
    ship: 7 TRIREME
OAS
    member: 4 PERU 5 CHILE
    Part of: 3 ORG 4 AMER
Oasis
    animal: 5 CAMEL
    Roadside: 3 INN
    8 RESTSTOP
Oast: 4 OVEN
Oater: 10 HORSEOPERA
    actor Jack: 4 ELAM
    actor Lash: 5 LARUE
    affirmative: 3 YEP YUP
    challenge: 4 DRAW
    Classic: 5 SHANE
    climax: 8 SHOOTOUT
    Entered, in an: 8 RODEINTO
    group: 5 POSSE
    locale: 6 SALOON
    omen: 5 NOOSE 6 TOMTOM
    prop: 5 LASSO RIATA
    Scram, in an: 3 GIT
    sound effect: 7 GUNFIRE
    sound effects: 5 CLOPS
    transport: 5 STAGE
    wear: 7 BANDANA
Oates, Joyce Carol
    novel: 4 THEM
Oath: 3 VOW
    Administer the ~ to: 7 INSTATE
       SWEARIN
    Affirm under: 7 SWEARTO
    Break an: 3 LIE
    Kind of: 6 SOLEMN

Mild: 4 DRAT EGAD GOSH
HECK
Name in an old: 4 JOVE
Name on which an ancient ~ was
taken: 4 STYX
Old: 4 **EGAD** 5 NERTS
Start of an: 5 SACRE
Take an: 5 SWEAR
Testify under: 6 DEPONE
DEPOSE
Oatmeal: 6 CEREAL
alternative: 6 FARINA
Oats: 4 FEED 5 GRAIN
holder: 7 FEEDBAG
Like some: 6 ROLLED
Oaxaca
Other, in: 4 **OTRA**
water: 4 AGUA
OB-___: 3 GYN
**"O ___ babbino caro" (Puccini
aria):** 3 MIO
Obadiah
Book before: 4 AMOS
Obdurate: 4 HARD 5 STONY
Obedience school
command: 3 SIT 4 HEEL STAY
Obedient: 8 AMENABLE
dogs: 7 STAYERS
Obeisance: 6 SALAAM
Show: 5 KNEEL
Obelisk: 8 MONUMENT
Oberon
Actress: 5 **MERLE**
Wife of: 7 TITANIA
"O, beware, my lord, of jealousy!"
speaker: 4 IAGO
Obey: 4 HEED
10 TOETHELINE
the coxswain: 3 ROW
the drill sergeant:
15 SNAPTOATTENTION
the photographer: 5 SMILE
the sentry: 4 HALT
Obfuscate: 5 BEFOG
OB-GYN
job: 5 AMNIO
Obi: 4 SASH
Obie: 5 AWARD
cousin: 4 TONY

Obit
word: 3 NEE
Obi-Wan: 4 JEDI
portrayer: 4 **ALEC** EWAN
Obi-Wan ___: 6 KENOBI
Object: 3 AIM 4 MIND 5 ARGUE
DEMUR THING
of devotion: 4 **IDOL**
of esteem: 4 ICON
of gossip: 4 ITEM
of loathing: 8 ANATHEMA
of worship: 4 IDOL
Three-dimensional: 5 SOLID
Ultimate: 6 ENDALL
Objection
Trivial: 5 CAVIL
Vocal: 3 NAY
Objective: 3 **AIM** END 4 GOAL
5 POINT 6 TARGET
Heist: 4 LOOT
Noble: 5 IDEAL
Objectivism
advocate Rand: 3 AYN
"Object of My Affection, The"
actor: 4 ALDA
Objet
d'art: 5 CURIO
Objeto
That: 3 ESO
"Ob-La-Di, Ob-La-Da"
Last name in: 5 JONES
Oblast
on the Oka: 4 OREL
Obligated: 6 LIABLE
Be ~ to: 3 OWE
Obligation: 4 DEBT DUTY MUST
ONUS
Govt.: 5 TNOTE
Word of: 5 OUGHT
Obligatory: 6 MUSTDO
___ oblige: 8 NOBLESSE
Obliged
Be ~ to: 3 OWE
Obliging
spirit: 5 GENIE
Oblique: 5 BEVEL
Obliquely: 6 ASKANT ASLANT
Move: 5 SIDLE
Obliterate: 5 **ERASE**

Oblivion: 5 LETHE
  Consign to: **4** DOOM
Oblivious: 7 UNAWARE
  Hardly: **5** AWARE
Oblong
  yellow fruit: **5** PAPAW
Obloquy: 5 ABUSE
Oboe: 4 REED
  Sounding like an: **5** REEDY
Oboist
  need: **4** REED
Obote
  Deposer of: **4** AMIN
O'Brian, Hugh
  TV role: **4** EARP
O'Brien
  Actor: **6** EDMOND
  Author: **4** EDNA
  Talk show host: **5** CONAN
  thriller: **3** DOA
Obringa
  River known anciently as:
    4 AARE
OBs: 3 MDS
Obscene: 4 LEWD
  material: **4** SMUT
Obscenity: 4 SMUT
Obscure: 3 DIM **4** BLUR VEIL
    5 BEDIM BEFOG
    6 DARKEN
  stuff: **7** ESOTERY
Obsequious
  Be ~ (to): **6** KOWTOW
  ono: **6** FAWNER
Observance: 4 RITE
  Hanoi: **3** TET
  Ramadan: **4** FAST
Observant: 5 AWARE
  one: **5** NOTER
  Very: **9** EAGLEEYED
Observation: 6 ESPIAL
Observatory
  find: **4** NOVA
Observe: 3 EYE SEE **4** HEED
    NOTE OBEY SPOT VIEW
    5 WATCH **6** BEHOLD
    LOOKAT
Observer: 4 EYER **5** NOTER
  U.N.: **3** PLO

Obsessed
  by: **4** INTO
  captain: **4** AHAB
  with: **4** INTO
Obsession: 5 MANIA **8** IDEEFIXE
Obsidian
  source: **4** LAVA
Obstacle: 3 RUB **4** SNAG
  Limbo: **3** BAR
  Slalom: **4** GATE
  Underwater: **4** REEF
  ___ obstat: **5** NIHIL
Obstetrician
  Of interest to an: **8** PRENATAL
Obstinate: 5 BALKY **6** ORNERY
  one: **3** ASS **4** MULE
Obstruct: 3 DAM **5** DAMUP
    JAMUP **6** IMPEDE
Obstruction: 3 DAM
  Blood vessel: **4** CLOT
Obtain: 3 GET **4** REAP
  by force: **6** EXTORT
Obtuse: 3 DIM **4** DULL **5** DENSE
    THICK
  It may be ~ (abbr.): **3** ANG
  one: **6** CRETIN
Obvious: 5 OVERT **6** PATENT
    7 EVIDENT
  flirt: **5** OGLER
  It is: **6** TRUISM
"O Canada": 6 ANTHEM
Ocasek
  Rocker: **3** **RIC**
O'Casey
  Playwright: **4** SEAN
Occasion
  Asian: **3** TET
  Festive: **4** GALA **5** PARTY
  March: **6** PARADE
  On a single: **4** ONCE
  Present: **4** XMAS **5** NONCE
  Quilting: **3** BEE
  Suitable for the: **3** APT
Occasionally: 7 ATTIMES
    11 EVERANDANON
    15 EVERYNOWANDTHEN
Occident
  It is no: **6** ORIENT
Occult: 6 MYSTIC

doctrine: 6 CABALA
Occupant: 6 TENANT
Occupation: 3 JOB 4 LINE
    5 TRADE 6 METIER
  Start an: 6 MOVEIN
Occupational
  suffix: 3 EER IER IST 4 STER
Occupied: 4 BUSY 5 **INUSE**
  TAKEN
Occupy: 3 USE 4 FILL 5 TIEUP
  6 LIVEAT TAKEUP
  ~, as a table: 5 SITAT
Occur: 5 EXIST
  to: 6 DAWNON
Occurrence: 3 HAP 5 EVENT
  March 21: 7 EQUINOX
  Spring: 4 THAW
Ocean: 3 SEA TON 4 DEEP SLEW
  5 BRINE
  (abbr.): 3 ATL
  bottom: 6 DEPTHS
  crosser: 5 LINER
  debris: 7 FLOTSAM
  Dot in the: 5 ISLET
  Drop in the: 3 EBB
  flier: 3 ERN 4 ERNE
  Land in the: 4 ISLE
  liner: 4 SAND
  motion: 4 **TIDE**
  Mongolian: 5 DALAI
  On the: 4 **ASEA** 5 ATSEA
  predator: 4 ORCA
  Spot in the: 5 ISLET
  vessel: 4 SHIP
Oceania
  Much of: 6 ATOLLS
Oceanic
  ice: 4 FLOE
Océano
  contents: 4 AGUA
  feeder: 3 RIO
Oceans: 4 ALOT 5 DEEPS
"Ocean's Eleven"
  star: 7 SINATRA
Ocean State
  coll.: 3 URI
Oceanus: 5 TITAN
  Wife of: 6 TETHYS
Ochlocracy: 7 MOBRULE

Ocho ___, Jamaica: 4 RIOS
Ochs
  of folk: 4 PHIL
O'clock
  Five ~ shadow: 7 STUBBLE
  Four ~ drink: 3 TEA
  Four ~ fare: 8 TEACAKES
  Six ~ fare: 4 NEWS
"___ o'clock scholar": 4 **ATEN**
"O Come, ___ Faithful": 5 ALLYE
"O Come, O Come Emmanuel":
  5 CAROL
O'Connor
  Actress: 3 UNA
  Singer: 6 SINEAD
O'Connor, Cardinal
  successor: 4 EGAN
O'Connor, ___ Day
  Justice: 6 SANDRA
OCS
  driller: 3 SGT
  grads: 3 LTS
  relative: 4 ROTC
Oct.
  It used to end in: 3 DST
Octagon
  Roadside: 8 STOPSIGN
  Word in an: 4 STOP
Octave
  follower: 6 SESTET
Octavio
  Author: 3 PAZ
Octet
  plus one: 5 NONET
October
  birthstone: 4 **OPAL**
  Many ~ babies: 6 LIBRAS
October 31
  option: 5 TREAT
Octopus
  arm: 8 TENTACLE
  defense: 3 INK
  eater: 3 EEL
  Female: 3 HEN
  octet: 4 ARMS
Ocular
  output: 5 TEARS
  woe: 4 STYE
"Ocupado": 5 INUSE

Odalisque
quarters: 6 HAREMS
O'Day
Singer: 5 ANITA
Odd: 4 RARE 7 STRANGE
8 ABNORMAL
couple: 4 DEES
It may be: 3 JOB LOT
Not: 4 EVEN
Oddball: 4 KOOK NERD 5 WACKO
6 WEIRDO
Carnival: 4 GEEK
"Odd Couple, The"
cop: 6 MURRAY
director: 4 SAKS 8 GENESAKS
Half of: 5 OSCAR UNGER
playwright: 5 SIMON
Oddity: 5 FREAK
Oddly
amusing: 5 DROLL
Odd-numbered
page: 5 RECTO
Odds
Betting: 4 LINE
Long: 8 ONEINTEN
Partner of: 4 ENDS
Take: 3 BET
"Odds ___ ...": 3 ARE
Odd-toed
ungulate: 5 TAPIR
Ode: 4 POEM
fellow: 4 POET
preposition: 3 ERE
subject: 3 URN
title starter: 3 TOA
Odense
citizen: 4 DANE
"Odense" Symphony
Key of Mozart's: 6 AMINOR
Oder
region: 7 SILESIA
Odessa
native: 5 TEXAN
"Ode to Psyche"
poet: 5 KEATS
"O Deus Ego ___ Te" (hymn):
3 AMO
Odin
hall: 8 VALHALLA

Home of: 6 ASGARD
Like: 5 NORSE
race: 5 AESIR
Son of: 3 TYR 4 THOR
Wife of: 5 FRIGG
Odist: 4 POET
Odometer
reading: 7 MILEAGE
unit: 4 MILE
O'Donnell
Actor: 5 CHRIS
Quarterback: 4 NEIL
TV host: 5 **ROSIE**
O'Donnell, Chris
role: 5 ROBIN
Odor: 5 SMELL 6 REPUTE
Agreeable: 5 AROMA
Foul: 6 STENCH
Oxygen with an: 5 OZONE
Slight: 5 WHIFF
Odorizer: 6 SACHET
Odorless
gas: 5 ARGON 6 ETHANE
Odysseus
Father of: 7 LAERTES
Guardian for: 6 ATHENA
Home of: 6 ITHACA
Wife of: 8 PENELOPE
~, to Polyphemus: 5 NOMAN
Odyssey
maker: 5 HONDA
"Odyssey": 4 EPIC
enchantress: 5 CIRCE
OED
offering: 3 DEF SYN
Part of: 4 DICT
"Oedipe"
composer Georges: 6 ENESCO
Oedipus
follower: 3 REX
"Oedipus ___": 3 REX
Oenologist
Dry, to an: 3 SEC
interest: 4 WINE YEAR
O'er
Not: 5 **NEATH**
O'er and o'er: 3 OFT
Oerter
and others: 3 ALS

sport: **6** DISCUS
"Of ___ and Men": 4 MICE
O'Faolain
  Writer: **4** SEAN
___ of Avon, The: 4 BARD
___ of Capricorn: 6 TROPIC
"Of course!": 3 YES **4** ISEE
  5 NATCH
"___ of Eden": 4 EAST
Off: 3 ICE **4** AWAY AWRY DOIN
  IDLE LESS SENT **5** AMISS
  ASKEW ERASE NOTON
  and on: **7** ATTIMES
  base: **4** AWOL **7** ONLEAVE
  course: **4** AWRY **6** AFIELD
    ASTRAY ERRANT
  in the distance: **4** AFAR
  one's feed: **3** ILL
  one's rocker: **4** LOCO
  the boat: **6** ASHORE
  the hook: **4** FREE
  the job: **4** IDLE
  the leash: **5** LOOSE
  the mark: **4** WIDE **6** ERRANT
  the track: **6** ASTRAY
  yonder: **4** AFAR
Off.
  helper: **4** ASST
  Naval: **3** ADM CDR ENS
  Not: **3** RES
  Three-star: **5** LTGEN
  ___ off: 4 **TEED**
Off-Broadway
  award: **4** OBIE
Off-center: 5 ASKEW
Off-color: 3 RAW **4** BLUE LEWD
  RACY **5** SALTY
Off-duty: 4 IDLE **7** ONLEAVE
Offed: 4 SLEW **5** DIDIN
Offend: 4 MIFF **6** INSULT
  the nose: **4** REEK
Offended: 4 **HURT** **5** HUFFY
Offender: 7 CULPRIT
  ~, to a cop: **4** PERP
Offense: 3 SIN **7** UMBRAGE
  Bum's: **8** VAGRANCY
  Cager's: **4** FOUL
  GI's: **4** AWOL
  Loan shark's: **5** USURY

  Meas. of passing: **3** YDS
  Motorist ~, briefly: **3** DWI
  On ~, on a diamond: **5** ATBAT
  Take ~ at: **6** RESENT
Offensive: 4 VILE **5** GROSS
  NASTY
  Some are: **4** ENDS
  time: **3** TET **4** DDAY
  Was: **5** STANK
  ___ Offensive: 3 TET
Offer: 3 BID **6** HITMAN TENDER
  8 ASSASSIN
  AAA: **3** RTE
  Escort: **3** ARM
  for dinner: **7** SERVEUP
  Manufacturer's: **6** REBATE
  One with lots to: **7** REALTOR
  Shark's: **4** LOAN
  Treater's: **4** ONME
Offering: 4 ALMS **5** TITHE
  to voters: **5** SLATE
Offhand: 5 ADLIB **6** CASUAL
Office
  aide (abbr.): **4** ASST SECY
  assistant: **4** AIDE
  communication: **3** FAX
  crew: **5** STAFF
  D.C. ~ shape: **4** OVAL
  diversion: **4** POOL
  fastener: **9** PAPERCLIP
  fill-in: **4** TEMP
  Force from: **6** DEPOSE
  furniture: **4** DESK **5** DESKS
  Kind of: **4** HOME
  Like some ~ jobs: **8** CLERICAL
  machine: **5** ADDER **6** COPIER
    8 SHREDDER
  Many an ~ has one: **4** OATH
  Modern ~ staple: **3** PCS
  note: **4** **MEMO**
  novice: **7** TRAINEE
  Period of: **4** TERM
  phone nos.: **4** EXTS
  Put back in: **7** REELECT
  Put in: **5** **ELECT**
  Remove from: **4** OUST **6** UNSEAT
  Seek: **3** RUN
  seeker: **3** POL
  skills meas.: **3** WPM

solution: 5 TONER
Sought: 3 **RAN**
stamp: 4 PAID RECD 5 DATER
supply: 5 TONER 6 ERASER
Those holding: 3 INS
worker: 5 CLERK STENO
Officeholders: 3 INS
Officer
. Antidrug: 4 NARC
Church: 5 ELDER 6 DEACON
Merchant vessel: 5 BOSUN
Nav.: 3 ADM ENS
Navy: 6 ENSIGN
order: 6 ATEASE
ornament: 7 EPAULET
Ottoman: 3 AGA
Patrol ~ rounds: 4 BEAT
University: 6 REGENT
Officers
Group of: 5 CADRE
Mil.: 3 LTS
Petty: 6 YEOMEN
Official: 3 REF
Ballpark: 3 UMP
College: 4 DEAN
decree: 5 EDICT
emblem: 4 SEAL
mark: 5 STAMP
Muslim: 3 AGA 4 EMIR IMAM
proceedings: 4 ACTA
record: 4 ACTA
Roman: 5 EDILE 7 SENATOR
seal: 6 SIGNET
Turkish: 3 AGA 5 PASHA
Officiate: 3 REF UMP
Offing
Be in the: 4 PEND
In the: 4 NEAR 5 AHEAD
Off-limits: 5 TABOO
item: 4 NONO
(var.): 4 TABU
Off-peak
call: 5 YODEL
Off-ramp: 4 EXIT
Off-road
goer, for short: 3 ATV
vehicle: 8 DIRTBIKE
Off-season
in the Alps: 3 ETE

Offshoot: 3 ARM 4 SPUR
5 SCION
Religious: 4 SECT
Offshore: 4 ASEA 5 ATSEA
sight: 6 OILRIG
Offspring: 3 SON 4 KIDS SONS
5 BROOD ISSUE SCION
YOUNG
(abbr.): 4 DESC
Off-target: 5 AMISS 6 ERRANT
"Off the Court"
autobiographer: 4 ASHE
Off-the-cuff: 5 ADLIB
Off-the-wall: 3 ODD 4 LOCO
ZANY 5 MANIC WACKO
WEIRD
play: 5 CAROM
reply: 4 ECHO
Off-white: 4 BONE ECRU 5 BEIGE
IVORY
"___ of God": 5 AGNES
"___ of Honey": 6 ATASTE
"Of ___ I Sing": 4 THEE
"___ of Iwo Jima": 5 SANDS
O'Flaherty
Novelist: 4 LIAM
___ of Man: 4 ISLE
"Of Mice and Men"
actor Bob: 6 STEELE
___ of office: 4 OATH
"___ of One's Own": 5 AROOM
"___ of Pooh, The": 3 TAO
"___ of robins ...": 5 ANEST
"Of ___ Sing": 5 THEEI
Oft-broken
promise: 3 IDO
Often: 4 ALOT
Often-repeated
abbr.: 3 ETC
___ of the Apostles, The: 4 ACTS
"Of Thee ___" (Gershwin musical):
5 ISING
"___ of the Flies": 4 LORD
"___ of the Mind" (Shepard play):
4 ALIE
Oft-mispunctuated
pronoun: 3 ITS
Oft-stubbed
digit: 3 TOE

Oft-told
tales: 4 LORE
"___ of Two Cities": 5 **ATALE**
___ of vantage: 5 COIGN
Ogden
Humorist/poet: 4 **NASH**
Ogle: 3 EYE 4 LEER 5 STARE
        6 LEERAT 7 STAREAT
        10 MAKEEYESAT
O'Grady
of song: 5 ROSIE
Ogre: 3 ORC 5 BEAST FIEND
        6 MEANIE
Oh
Word before and after: 3 MAN
"Oh!": 4 ISEE
~, in German: 3 ACH
"Oh, ___!": 4 MAMA
O'Hara
home: 4 **TARA**
O'Hara, Mary
Horse in a ~ book: 6 FLICKA
O'Hara, Scarlett: 5 BELLE
O'Hare
abbr.: 3 ARR ETA
airport designation: 3 ORD
Strand at ~, perhaps: 5 ICEIN
"Oh, bother!": 4 DRAT
"Oh boy!": 5 GOODY
"Oh, brother!": 3 MAN
"Oh dear!": 4 ALAS
O. Henry
group: 4 MAGI
Like an ~ story: 6 IRONIC
specialty: 5 IRONY
"Oh, fudge!": 4 DRAT
"Ohh, that's why!":
        8 NOWONDER
Ohio
city: 5 AKRON XENIA
        6 DAYTON TOLEDO
college: 7 OBERLIN
political name: 4 TAFT
River to the: 5 MIAMI
~ Indians: 5 ERIES
Ohm
Physicist: 5 GEORG
symbol: 5 OMEGA
"Oh my!": 4 EGAD GOSH

"Oh my goodness!": 5 EGADS
"Oh no!": 4 YIPE
"Oh, nonsense!": 4 PISH
"Oh, sure!": 4 **IBET**
"Oh, that's silly!": 4 POOH
"Oh, what's the ___?": 3 USE
"Oh, woe!": 4 ALAS
"Oh yeah?": 3 GEE 7 SAYSWHO
"Oh yeah? ___ who?": 3 SEZ
Oil: 4 FUEL 8 TEXASTEA
        9 BLACKGOLD
additive: 3 STP
Apply ~ to: 6 ANOINT
Big ~ company, informally: 3 OXY
Big name in: 4 ARCO HESS
        5 AMOCO GETTY MOBIL
        6 CRISCO WESSON
Burning the midnight: 6 UPLATE
Canadian ~ company: 4 ESSO
cartel: 4 **OPEC**
Cook in hot: 3 FRY
Fragrant: 5 **ATTAR**
gp.: 4 OPEC
Hammer in: 6 ARMAND
holder: 3 CAN 4 DRUM TANK
        5 CRUET EASEL
Like some: 7 IRANIAN
Linseed ~ source: 4 FLAX
Motor ~ abbr.: 3 SAE
Orange blossom: 6 NEROLI
Paint: 7 LINSEED
Perfume: 5 ATTAR 6 NEROLI
Rose: 5 ATTAR
source: 3 SOY 4 PALM WELL
        5 OLIVE SHALE 6 CANOLA
        OLIVES PEANUT SESAME
        7 COCONUT LINSEED
        SOYBEAN
Oil-bearing
rock: 5 SHALE
Oilcan
size: 5 QUART
Oil-measuring
device: 8 DIPSTICK
Oil of ___: 4 **OLAY**
Oil-rich
land: 5 QATAR
peninsula: 6 ARABIA 7 ARABIAN
Oils: 3 ART

Oil well
firefighter: 5 ADAIR
Oily: 5 SLICK
Oink
joint: 3 STY
Ointment
Apply: 5 RUBON
Fly in the: 4 SNAG
Hair: 6 POMADE
ingredient: 7 LANOLIN
Pharmaceutical; 6 OLEATE
Soothing: 4 BALM 5 SALVE
**"O! it is my love; O! that she
    knew she were"**
speaker: 5 ROMEO
O.J.
trial judge: 3 ITO 8 LANCEITO
OK: 3 NOD 4 FAIR JAKE
    5 ALLOW 6 ASSENT
    10 ACCEPTABLE
in any outlet: 4 ACDC
Radio: 5 ROGER
sign: 3 NOD
Oka
City on the: 4 **OREL**
Okay: 4 SOSO 5 LEGIT LICIT
"Okay": 4 SURE
à la Opie: 4 YESM
O.K. Corral
brothers: 5 EARPS
gunfighter: 4 **EARP**
occurrence: 8 SHOOTOUT
Okeechobee
loc.: 3 FLA
O'Keeffe, Georgia
locale: 4 TAOS
Okefenokee
possum: 4 POGO
Okinawa
city: 4 **NAHA**
port: 4 NAHA
Okla.
neighbor: 3 KAN TEX 4 KANS
~, before 1907: 4 TERR
Oklahoma
athlete: 6 SOONER
city: 3 ADA 4 **ENID** 5 TULSA
native: 3 OTO 4 **OTOE** 5 OSAGE
    6 PAWNEE

"Oklahoma!"
actor Gordon: 6 MACRAE
aunt: 5 ELLER
girl: 8 ADOANNIE
Okra
stew: 5 GUMBO
unit: 3 POD
Oksana
successor: 4 TARA
Oktoberfest
dance: 5 POLKA
order: 4 BEER
souvenir: 5 STEIN
vessel: 5 STEIN
Olajuwon
of basketball: 5 AKEEM
Oland
role: 4 CHAN
"Ol' Blue Eyes": 7 SINATRA
Old: 4 AGED 5 DATED PASSE
enough: 5 **OFAGE**
hand: 3 **PRO**
hat: 5 DATED **PASSE** STALE
    TRITE
salt: 3 **TAR**
saw: 5 **ADAGE**
Suffix with: 4 STER
The ~ man: 3 DAD POP
    5 POPPA
The ~ Sod: 4 EIRE ERIN
Very ~ (abbr.): 3 ANC
Old ___: 3 VIC
"Old ___" (1957 Disney film):
    6 YELLER
"Old ___ Bucket, The": 5 OAKEN
"___, old chap!": 4 ISAY
Old ___, Connecticut: 4 LYME
"___ old cowhand ...": 4 **IMAN**
"Old Curiosity Shop, The"
girl: 4 NELL
"Olde"
establishment: 6 SHOPPE
Olden
In ~ days: 4 ONCE
Old English
letter: 3 **EDH** ETH
Older
Grow: 3 AGE
Old Faithful: 6 GEYSER

Old-fashioned: 5 DATED
      6 STODGY
  Fashionably: 5 RETRO
Old Glory: 4 FLAG 6 USFLAG
    15 STARSANDSTRIPES
"Old Guitarist, The"
  painter: 7 PICASSO
"Old MacDonald"
  refrain: 5 EIEIO
  sound: 4 OINK
"Old Man and the Sea, The"
  Old man in: 8 SANTIAGO
Old Nick: 5 SATAN
      9 BEELZEBUB
Olds
  Middle name of: 3 ELI
  model: 5 **ALERO**
  Old: 3 REO 5 CIERA
Olds, Ransom ___: 3 ELI
Old Scratch: 5 SATAN 7 EVILONE
Oldsmobile
  model: 5 **ALERO**
Old Sod, The: 4 EIRE ERIN
Old Testament
  boat: 3 ARK
  book: 3 JOB 4 AMOS EZRA
    RUTH 5 HOSEA JONAH
    MICAH 6 ESTHER ISAIAH
    PSALMS 8 JEREMIAH
  priest: 3 ELI
  prophet: 4 AMOS 5 HOSEA
    6 ISAIAH
  scroll: 5 TORAH
  verse: 5 PSALM
Old-timer: 3 VET 5 ELDER
"Old Uncle"
  in a Stephen Foster song: 3 NED
Old West
  outlaw family: 7 DALTONS
"Old Wives' Tale, The"
  dramatist: 5 PEELE
Old World
  deer: 3 ROE 4 ROES
  language: 4 ERSE
"Olé ___" (1976 hit album): 3 ELO
"Oleanna"
  playwright: 5 MAMET .
Oleo
  holder: 3 TUB

  square: 3 PAT
Olfactory
  stimulus: 4 ODOR 5 AROMA
    SMELL
Olin
  Actor: 3 KEN
  Actress: 4 **LENA**
Olio: 6 MEDLEY
  Literary: 3 ANA
Olive
  Animated: 3 OYL
  genus: 4 OLEA
  kin: 3 ASH
  lover: 6 POPEYE
  product: 3 OIL
Olive ___: 3 OYL 4 DRAB
Oliver
  Actor: 5 PLATT
  Actress: 4 EDNA
  Director: 5 STONE
"Oliver!"
  choreographer White: 4 ONNA
  composer Lionel: 4 BART
  Oliver of: 4 REED
"Oliver Twist"
  dish: 5 GRUEL
  request: 4 MORE
  villain: 5 FAGIN SIKES
Olives
  Like some: 7 SPEARED
Olivier
  role: 4 LEAR 6 HAMLET
Olla: 3 POT 7 STEWPOT
Ollie
  Friend of: 4 FRAN 5 KUKLA
  Partner of: 4 **STAN**
"Olly, Olly, ___ Free": 4 OXEN
"Ol' Man River"
  composer: 4 KERN
Ologies
  (abbr.): 4 SCIS
Olsen
  Comic: 3 OLE
"Olympia"
  painter Édouard: 5 MANET
Olympian: 7 ATHLETE
  1936 ~: 5 OWENS
  hawk: 4 ARES
  queen: 4 HERA

quest: **4** GOLD **5** MEDAL
ruler: **4** ZEUS
sword: **4** EPEE
Olympic
award: **5** MEDAL
contest: **5** EVENT
judge: **5** RATER
sled: **4** LUGE
weapon: **4** EPEE
Olympics
1936 ~ star: **5** OWENS
1952 ~ site: **4** **OSLO**
1960 ~ site: **4** ROME
1964 ~ site: **5** TOKYO
1972 ~ site: **7** SAPPORO
1984 ~ site: **8** SARAJEVO
1988 ~ site: **5** KOREA SEOUL
1996 ~ host: **3** USA
1998 ~ site: **6** NAGANO
2000 ~ host: **6** AUSSIE
2000 ~ site: **6** SYDNEY
2002 ~ host: **3** USA
2002 ~ site: **4** UTAH
2004 ~ host: **6** ATHENS
Ancient ~ site: **4** ELIS
broadcaster Jim: **5** MCKAY
chant: **3** USA
event: **4** EPEE
jump: **4** AXEL
no-no: **7** STEROID
prize: **5** MEDAL
Olympic Stadium
team: **5** EXPOS
Olympus
neighbor: **4** OSSA
Queen of: **4** HERA
resident: **3** GOD
"Om": **6** MANTRA
Omaha
beach craft (abbr.): **3** LST
river: **6** PLATTE
state (abbr.): **3** NEB
Oman
neighbor: **5** YEMEN
Omani: **4** ARAB
money: **4** RIAL
title: **4** EMIR
Omar
Actor: **4** **EPPS**

O'Meara, Mark
org.: **3** PGA
Omega: **3** END
Its symbol is an: **3** OHM
opposite: **3** ALPHA
preceder: **3** PSI
rival: **5** ROLEX SEIKO
Omelet
base: **4** EGGS
Western ~ ingredient: **3** HAM
Omen: **4** SIGN **7** PORTENT
Be an ~ of: **4** BODE
interpreter: **4** SEER
Shark: **3** FIN
"Omen, The"
boy: **6** DAMIEN
"O, ___ me the lass that ...":
Burns: **3** GIE
"Omigosh!": **4** EGAD **5** YIKES
Ominous: **4** DIRE
"O mio babbino ___" (Puccini
aria): **4** CARO
Omission: **3** SIN
indication: **8** ELLIPSIS
Omit: **4** SKIP
in pronunciation: **5** ELIDE
~, in diners: **4** HOLD
"Omnia vincit ___": Virgil:
4 AMOR
Omnibus
alternative: **4** TRAM
"Omnibus"
host: **5** COOKE
Omnium-gatherum: **4** OLIO
On: **3** LIT **4** **ATOP** **6** ABOARD
AIRING **7** ASTRIDE
again: **5** RELIT
Off and: **7** ATTIMES
On ___: **4** SPEC **5** AROLL ATEAR
ATOOT THEGO **6** THEDOT
"___ on $45 a Day": **6** EUROPE
Onager: **3** ASS
"On Aggression"
author: **6** LORENZ
On and on: **5** NOEND
8 ATLENGTH
On a scale of one ___: **5** TOTEN
Onassis
nickname: **3** **ARI**

On bended ___: 4 KNEE
Once: 8 ASSOONAS
  again: 4 ANEW
  around: 3 LAP 5 ORBIT
  a year: 6 ANNUAL
  called: 3 **NEE**
  in a while: 7 ATTIMES
  more: 4 ANEW 5 **AGAIN**
  Not: 4 NEER
  ~, formerly: 4 **ERST**
___ once: 5 ALLAT
"Once and Again"
  actress Ward: 4 SELA
Once ___ blue moon: 3 INA
**"Once ___ Honeymoon" (1942
    film)**: 5 UPONA
"Once in Love With ___": 3 AMY
"Once Is Not Enough"
  author Jacqueline: 6 SUSANN
**"Once ___ Mattress" (1959
    Broadway show)**: 5 UPONA
Once-over
  Give the: 3 **EYE** 4 OGLE SCAN
"Once upon ___ ...": 5 ATIME
Once ___ while: 3 INA
Oncle
  Wife of: 5 TANTE
One: 6 UNITED
  against: 4 ANTI
  and one: 4 PAIR
  and only: 4 LONE SOLE
  and the other: 4 BOTH
  As: 6 UNITED
  by one: 6 ELEVEN
  Even: 3 ANY
  Every: 3 ALL
  For: 3 PER 4 APOP 6 APIECE
  more: 7 ANOTHER
  More than: 6 PLURAL
  more time: 4 ANEW 5 AGAIN
  Not: 4 NARY
  Not ~ or the other: 7 NEITHER
  Not just: 4 BOTH
  of a kind: 4 UNIT
  of fifty: 5 STATE
  of five: 5 QUINT
  of those: 4 THAT
  of two: 4 HALF 6 EITHER
  or more: 3 ANY

  or the other: 6 EITHER
  out: 7 PAROLEE
  over par: 5 BOGEY
  over there: 4 THAT
  Partner of: 4 ONLY
  prefix: 3 UNI
  The ~ that got away: 4 YARN
  ~, in French: 3 UNE
  ~, in German: 3 EIN 4 EINE
    EINS
  ~, in Spanish: 3 UNO
"One"
  has one (abbr.): 3 SYL
  in a one-two: 3 JAB
  on a one: 4 UNUM
One-___: 4 OCAT 6 REELER
O'Neal
  Actor: 4 RYAN
  Actress: 5 TATUM
  nickname: 4 SHAQ
One-armed
  bandit: 4 SLOT
One-billionth
  prefix: 4 NANO
One-celled
  animal: 5 AMEBA 6 AMOEBA
One ___ customer: 3 TOA
"One Day at ___": 5 ATIME
"One Day ___ Time": 3 ATA
One-dimensional: 6 **LINEAR**
  SCALAR
One-eighty: 3 UEY 5 UTURN
  9 ABOUTFACE
**"One Flew Over the Cuckoo's
    Nest"**
  author: 5 KESEY
    8 KENKESEY
"One for My Baby"
  composer: 5 ARLEN
O'Neill
  daughter: 4 OONA
  offering: 5 DRAMA
  play: 3 ILE
  title character: 4 ANNA
    6 ICEMAN
  title ender: 4 ELMS 6 COMETH
"One I Love, The"
  group: 3 REM
One ___ kind: 3 OFA

"One Life to Live"
  Kristen of: 5 ILENE
  Slezak of: 5 ERICA
One-liner: 3 GAG 4 JOKE QUIP
"One Mic"
  rapper: 3 NAS
One-million
  link: 3 INA
One ___ million: 3 INA
"One More Night"
  singer Collins: 4 PHIL
One-name
  actress: 4 CHER
  designer: 4 ERTE
  folk singer: 6 **ODETTA**
  Irish singer: 4 **ENYA**
  musician: 5 YANNI
  Nigerian singer: 4 SADE
  singer: 4 CHER 5 CHARO
  sports star: 4 PELE
  supermodel: 4 EMME IMAN
Oneness: 5 UNITY
"One O'Clock Jump"
  composer: 5 BASIE
"One of ___" (Willa Cather novel):
  4 OURS
"One of ___ days ...": 5 THESE
One-on-one: 4 DUEL
  sport: 4 EPEE
One-piece
  undergarment: 9 UNIONSUIT
Oner: 4 LULU
"One ringy-dingy"
  lady: 9 ERNESTINE
One-seater
  Speedy: 6 GOKART
One-sided: 6 UNEVEN
  win: 4 ROUT
One-spot: 3 ACE
___ one's time: 4 BIDE
One-striper: 3 PFC
One-time
  link: 3 **ATA**
One ___ time: 3 **ATA**
"One Touch of Venus"
  composer: 5 WEILL
One-two
  connector: 4 ANDA
  Start of a: 3 JAB

One-up: 4 BEST 8 OUTSMART
One-way
  sign: 5 ARROW
On-field
  greeting: 5 HIMOM
"___ on first?": 4 WHOS
Ongoing
  saga: 9 SOAPOPERA
  story: 6 SERIAL
"On Golden ___": 4 POND
"On Golden Pond"
  bird: 4 LOON
Onion: 4 BULB
  Cocktail with an: 6 GIBSON
  Kind of: 7 BERMUDA
  relative: 4 **LEEK** 5 CHIVE
Onions
  partner: 5 LIVER
"___ on it!": 4 STEP
"On Language"
  columnist: 6 SAFIRE
Online
  activity: 4 CHAT
  auction site: 4 EBAY
  bookseller: 6 AMAZON
  brokerage: 6 ETRADE
  group: 5 USERS
  help: 3 FAQ
  message: 5 EMAIL
  newsgroup: 6 USENET
  novice: 6 NEWBIE
  publication: 4 EMAG 5 EZINE
  response to a joke: 3 LOL
  VIP: 5 SYSOP
Only: 3 ONE 4 LONE MERE SOLE
  fair: 4 SOSO
"___ Only Just Begun": 4 WEVE
"Only the Lonely"
  Milo of: 5 OSHEA
"Only Time"
  singer: 4 **ENYA**
"Only When I ___" (1968 British
  comedy): 4 LARF
"On ___ Majesty's Secret Service":
  3 HER
Ono
  Singer: 4 YOKO
On ___ of: 6 BEHALF
On one's ___: 3 OWN 4 TOES

"___ on parle français": 3 ICI
On-ramp
  sign: 5 MERGE
Onsager
  Nobel chemist: 4 LARS
Onstage
  Go: 5 ENTER
  Overplay: 5 EMOTE
Ont.
  neighbor: 3 QUE
Ontario
  capital: 7 TORONTO
  native: 4 CREE 6 OTTAWA
  neighbor: 4 ERIE
On the ___: 3 LAM SLY 4 OUTS 5 FRITZ
"On the Beach"
  actress Gardner: 3 AVA
  author: 5 SHUTE
  costar of Gregory: 3 AVA
"On the double!": 3 NOW 4 ASAP
"On the ___ hand ...": 5 OTHER
On the qui ___: 4 VIVE
On the qui vive: 5 ALERT
"___ on the Range": 4 HOME
"On the Road Again"
  singer: 6 NELSON
"On the Street Where You Live"
  composer: 5 LOEWE
"On the Town"
  actor: 7 SINATRA
On the ___ vive: 3 QUI
"On the Waterfront"
  director: 9 ELIAKAZAN
  director Kazan: 4 ELIA
  ___ onto: 4 GLOM
Ontologist
  concern: 5 BEING
On ___ with: 4 APAR
"___ on your life!": 3 NOT
Onyx: 3 GEM
Oocytes
  ~, eventually: 3 OVA
Oodles: 4 ALOT GOBS LOTS TONS 5 SCADS 6 OCEANS
Ooh and ___: 3 AAH
"Ooky"
  ~ Addams Family cousin: 3 ITT

Oologist
  studies: 3 OVA
Oolong: 3 TEA
Oompah
  instrument: 4 TUBA
Oomph: 3 PEP 4 ELAN
  Lose: 3 SAG
"Oops!": 4 OHNO UHOH
Ooze: 4 SEEP 5 EXUDE
Oozing: 5 SEEPY
Op ___: 3 ART
Op. ___: 3 CIT
Opal: 3 GEM 6 SILICA
  Fire: 7 GIRASOL
  suffix: 4 ESCE
"O patria mia"
  singer: 4 AIDA
OPEC: 6 CARTEL
  concern: 3 OIL
  figure: 4 EMIR
  Many ~ delegates: 5 ARABS
  member: 4 IRAN
  unit: 3 BBL 6 BARREL
Open: 4 AIRY 5 OVERT UNBAR UNCAP 6 UNBOLT UNSEAL 7 SINCERE 8 UNFASTEN
  a bottle: 5 UNCAP
  a gate: 5 UNBAR
  a jacket: 5 UNZIP
  house org.: 3 PTA
  Out in the: 5 OVERT 6 PUBLIC
  Slightly: 4 AJAR
  wide: 4 GAPE YAWN
"Open ___": 6 SESAME
"Open ___ 9": 3 TIL
Opener: 3 KEY 5 INTRO 7 PASSKEY
  for two tins: 3 RIN
Open-eyed: 5 ALERT AWAKE
Open-handed
  blow: 4 SLAP
Opening: 3 GAP 4 SLOT 5 INTRO 7 ORIFICE
  at an opening: 6 ACTONE
  bars: 5 INTRO
  day: 4 XMAS
  remarks: 5 INTRO
  run: 4 ABCD

stake: 4 ANTE
time: 4 NINE
word: 6 **SESAME**
Openings: 3 ORA
Open-mouthed: 5 AGAPE
  Leave: 5 AMAZE
  stare: 4 GAPE
Openness: 6 CANDOR
Open ___ of worms: 4 ACAN
"Open Sesame"
  sayer: 7 ALIBABA
Open-textured
  weave: 4 MESH
Open-wide
  word: 3 AAH
Opera
  1887 ~ debut: 6 OTELLO
  about an opera singer: 5 TOSCA
  and others: 4 ARTS
  cast member: 8 BARITONE
  hero, often: 5 TENOR
  NYC ~ house: 3 MET
  opener: 4 ACTI
  Prince of: 4 IGOR
  prop: 5 SPEAR
  set in Egypt: 4 **AIDA**
  Slave girl of: 4 AIDA
  solo: 4 **ARIA**
  star: 4 DIVA
  villain, often: 5 BASSO
  villains, often: 5 BASSI
  ___ operandi: 4 MODI 5 MODUS
Operate: 3 RUN
  Prepare to: 5 SCRUB
  properly: 4 WORK
Operated
  by air: 9 PNEUMATIC
Operatic
  Brief ~ solo: 7 ARIETTA
  Extended ~ solo: 5 SCENA
  passage: 6 ARIOSO
  prince: 4 **IGOR**
  slave: 4 AIDA
  solo: 4 ARIA
Operating: 5 INUSE
  at a loss: 8 INTHERED
  room pro: 10 SCRUBNURSE
  Start: 9 SETUPSHOP
  system: 4 UNIX

Operation
  Kind of: 5 STING
  Sting: 4 TRAP
Operation Allied Force
  gp.: 4 NATO
Operation Overlord
  time: 4 DDAY
Operative: 3 SPY 5 AGENT
  American: 6 CIASPY
  DEA: 4 NARC
  Undercover: 4 MOLE
Operator
  Computer: 4 USER
  need: 7 SCALPEL
  Radio: 3 HAM
  wear: 7 HEADSET
Operetta
  title character: 6 MIKADO
Ophelia: 4 DANE
  Brother of: 7 LAERTES
Ophthalmologist
  case: 4 STYE
  study: 3 EYE
Opie
  Bee, to ~: 4 AUNT
  Father of: 4 ANDY
  portrayer: 3 RON
Opinion: 3 SAY 4 IDEA VIEW
  Ask for an: 4 POLL
  Favorable: 6 ESTEEM
  Form an: 4 DEEM
  Hold the same: 5 AGREE
  Not shy with an: 5 VOCAL
  opener: 8 ASISEEIT
  page, briefly: 4 OPED
  piece: 5 ESSAY
Opossum
  gripper: 4 TAIL
Opp.: 3 ANT
Opponent: 3 FOE 4 ANTI
     5 ENEMY RIVAL
Opportune: 4 RIPE 6 TIMELY
Opportunity: 4 SHOT
  Equitable: 9 FAIRSHAKE
  Hitting: 5 ATBAT
  Seize an: 7 MAKEHAY
  ~, so to speak: 4 DOOR
Oppose: 6 RESIST
  boldly: 5 BEARD

Opposed: 4 <u>**ANTI**</u> 6 AVERSE
  Diametrically: 5 POLAR
  Those: 4 NAYS 5 ANTIS
  to, in the sticks: 4 <u>**AGIN**</u>
Opposing: 4 ANTI
  force: 5 ENEMY
Opposite: 5 POLAR
Opposition
  member: 4 ANTI
  vote: 3 NAY
Oppositionist: 4 ANTI
"Oppression and Liberty"
  author Simone: 4 WEIL
Oppressor: 6 DESPOT
Oprah
  rival, once: 5 ROSIE
Ops
  Husband of: 6 SATURN
Opt: 5 ELECT 6 CHOOSE
Optic
  screens: 7 RETINAE
  ___ optics: 5 FIBER
Optima
  automaker: 3 KIA
Optimally: 6 <u>**ATBEST**</u>
Optimist
  focus: 6 UPSIDE
  words: 4 ICAN
Optimistic: 4 <u>**ROSY**</u> 6 UPBEAT
  Be: 4 HOPE
  Be unrealistically:
    15 HOPEAGAINSTHOPE
"Optimist's Daughter, The"
  author: 5 WELTY
    11 EUDORAWELTY
Option
  No longer an: 3 OUT
Optional
  Not: 6 NEEDED
  Not ~ (abbr.): 3 REQ
Options
  list: 4 MENU
Optometrist
  interest: 3 EYE
Opulence: 4 LUXE
Opulent: 4 LUSH
Opus ___: 3 DEI
OR
  On the double, in the: 4 STAT

  workers: 3 DRS RNS
"Or ___!": 4 ELSE
Oracle: 4 SEER
  sire: 6 DELPHI
Oral: 4 EXAM
  history: 4 LORE
  poetry: 4 EPOS
  surgeon deg.: 3 DDS
Orally: 5 ALOUD
Orang: 3 APE
Orange: 4 BOWL
  container: 5 CRATE
  cover: 4 PEEL RIND SKIN
  drink: 3 ADE
  feature: 5 NAVEL
  food: 3 YAM
  Inedible: 5 OSAGE
  Kind of: 5 NAVEL OSAGE
    8 MANDARIN
  seed: 3 PIP
Orange ___: 5 PEKOE
___ orange: 5 OSAGE
Orange Bowl
  city: 5 MIAMI
  org.: 4 NCAA
Orange County
  seat: 7 ORLANDO
"Orange Crush"
  band: 3 REM
Orangeish: 5 OCHRE
___ Orange, New Jersey: 4 EAST
Orange-red
  rock: 4 SARD
Oranges
  and shredded coconut:
    8 AMBROSIA
Orangutan: 3 APE
Oranjestad
  island: 5 ARUBA
Oration: 6 SPEECH
  station: 4 DAIS
Oratorio
  piece: 4 ARIA
  that debuted in 1742:
    7 MESSIAH
Orb: 6 SPHERE
Orbison
  hit song: 4 LEAH
  Singer: 3 ROY

Orbit
bit: 3 ARC
First American in: 5 GLENN
Kind of: 5 LUNAR
Leave: 7 REENTER
period: 4 YEAR
Where electrons: 4 ATOM
Orbital
high point: 6 APOGEE
point: 4 NODE 5 APSIS
   7 PERIGEE
Orbs: 4 EYES
Orch.
section: 3 **STR**
Orchard
Banned ~ spray: 4 **ALAR**
fruit: 4 PEAR
pest: 5 APHID
unit: 4 TREE
Orchard Field
~, now: 5 OHARE
Orchestra
alternative: 4 LOGE
area: 3 PIT
member: 4 OBOE 5 CELLO
   6 OBOIST
output: 5 MUSIC
sec.: 3 STR
section: 5 BRASS REEDS
Orchestrate: 4 PLAN
Orchid
products: 4 LEIS
starch: 5 SALEP
Order: 4 FIAT TELL 5 EDICT
(around): 4 BOSS
In: 4 NEAT 6 ARIGHT
In ~ that: 6 SOASTO
In ~ (to): 4 SOAS
Kind of: 3 GAG
member: 3 NUN
One way to: 4 TOGO
   8 ALACARTE
Out of: 5 AMISS
Partner of: 3 LAW
request: 4 ASAP
room service: 5 EATIN
Ordered: 4 BADE NEAT
Orderly: 4 NEAT TIDY
grouping: 5 **ARRAY**

Orders: 5 DICTA
One who takes: 4 CHEF
Short: 4 BLTS
Take ~ from: 4 OBEY
Take ~, in a way: 4 WAIT
Ordinal
ending: 3 **ETH**
Imprecise: 3 NTH
Ordinance: 3 LAW
Ordinarily: 7 ASARULE
Ordinary: 5 USUAL 7 MUNDANE
Hardly: 3 ODD
language: 5 PROSE
Out of the: 3 ODD 7 STRANGE
"___ Ordinary Man": 4 IMAN
Ordnance
supplier: 5 ARMER
Ore
analysis: 5 ASSAY
carrier: 4 TRAM
deposit: 4 LODE VEIN
ending: 3 ITE
Process: 5 SMELT
Ore.
neighbor: 3 CAL IDA NEV
   5 CALIF
setting: 3 PST
summer setting: 3 PDT
Oreck
product: 3 VAC
Oregano: 4 HERB
Oregon
capital: 5 SALEM
city: 6 EUGENE 7 ASTORIA
college: 4 REED
motto's first word: 4 ALIS
volcanic peak: 6 MTHOOD
Oregon Trail
fort: 5 BOISE
Ore-Ida
product: 9 TATERTOTS
O'Reilly, Radar
drink: 4 NEHI
rank: 3 CPL
Orenburg
river: 4 URAL
Oreo
center: 5 CREME
makers: 7 NABISCO

Org.: 4 <u>ASSN</u> 5 ASSOC
  founded in 1970: 3 EPA
  that sticks to its guns: 3 NRA
  with a journal: 3 AMA
Organ
  effect: 7 TREMOLO
  Kind of: 4 PIPE REED
  knob: 4 STOP
  Largest human: 4 SKIN
  part: 5 PEDAL
  transplant need: 5 DONOR
Organic
  compound: 4 <u>ENOL</u> 5 AMIDE
    ESTER
  ending: 3 ENE
  fertilizer: 5 GUANO
  fuel: 4 PEAT
Organism
  Plantlike: 4 ALGA
  Single-cell: 5 MONAD
    6 AMOEBA
Organisms
  Genetically related: 7 BIOTYPE
Organization
  (abbr.): 4 ASSN
  Worker in a big: 3 COG
Organized
  crime: 6 THEMOB
  It may be: 5 CRIME
Organizer
  Cry of an: 5 UNITE
Organs
  Like some: 5 VITAL
Orient: 4 EAST
  From the: 7 EASTERN
Oriental: 7 EASTERN
Orienteering
  need: 3 MAP
Orig.
  Not: 4 IMIT
  Photo: 3 NEG
Origami
  bird: 5 CRANE
  Do: 4 FOLD
  need: 5 PAPER
Origin: 4 ROOT SEED 6 SOURCE
    7 GENESIS
  Find the ~ of: 5 TRACE
  suffix: 4 ATOR

Original: 5 NOVEL
  gardener: 4 ADAM
  Highly ~ and influential:
    7 SEMINAL
  In its ~ form: 5 UNCUT
  It may be: 3 SIN
  Not the ~ color: 4 DYED
  sinner: 3 EVE
"Original Gangster"
  rapper: 4 ICET
Originally: 3 <u>NEE</u>
  As ~ placed: 6 INSITU
Originate: 4 STEM 5 ARISE
O-ring: 6 GASKET
Orinoco: 3 RIO
"Orinoco Flow"
  singer: 4 <u>ENYA</u>
Oriole: 4 ALER
  home: 3 ELM
Orion
  has one: 4 BELT
  Part of: 4 STAR
  Star in: 5 RIGEL
Ork: 6 PLANET
Orlando
  attraction: 5 EPCOT
  City NW of: 5 OCALA
"Orlando"
  author: 5 WOOLF
  princess: 5 SASHA
Orlando-Miami
  dir.: 3 SSE
Orléans
  Louisiana, in: 4 ETAT
  river: 5 LOIRE
"___ or lose it!": 5 USEIT
Orly
  arrival: 5 AVION
  plane, once: 3 SST
Ornament: 5 ADORN
Ornamental
  band: 6 ARMLET
  case: 4 ETUI
  container: 8 CACHEPOT
  fabric: 4 LAME
  flower: 6 DAHLIA
  loop: 5 PICOT
  shell: 7 ABALONE
  shrub: 6 SPIREA 8 OLEANDER

stone: **9** TIGERSEYE
style: **6** ROCOCO
trinket: **10** KNICKKNACK
vase: **3** URN
Ornamentation: 5 DECOR
Ornate
  Overly: **6** ROCOCO
Orne
  City on the: **4** CAEN
"Oro y ___" (Montana motto):
    5 PLATA
Orphan
  Fictional: **4** EYRE
  of comics: **5** ANNIE DONDI
  Range: **5** DOGIE
"Orphée"
  painter: **5** COROT
Orpheus
  instrument: **4** <u>**LYRE**</u>
  poet: **5** RILKE
Orr
  org.: **3** NHL
  teammate, familiarly: **4** ESPO
Orr, Bobby
  team: **6** BRUINS
Orsk
  river: **4** <u>**URAL**</u>
Orson
  Planet of: **3** ORK
Orthodontist
  concern: **4** BITE
  deg.: **3** DDS
  device: **8** RETAINER
  org.: **3** ADA
Orthodox
  prefix: **3** NEO
Orthopedist
  tool: **4** XRAY
ORU
  Part of: **4** ORAL
Orwell, George
  alma mater: **4** ETON
Orzo: 5 PASTA
___ O's (Post cereal): 4 OREO
Osage oranges
  Like: **8** INEDIBLE
Osaka
  City near: **4** KOBE
  sash: **3** OBI

Osbourne
  music: **5** METAL
  of rock: **4** OZZY
Oscar: 5 AWARD
  1953 ~ winner: **7** SINATRA
  1992 ~ winner: **5** TOMEI
  Actor/pianist: **6** LEVANT
  An ~ is mostly this: **3** TIN
  French: **5** CESAR
  org.: **5** AMPAS
  Three-time ~ winner for
    directing: **5** CAPRA
Oscar the Grouch
  passion: **5** TRASH
Oscillated: 5 SWUNG
O'Shea
  Actor: **4** <u>**MILO**</u>
  Actress: **6** TESSIE
"O Ship of State!"
  Words before: **6** SAILON
Osiris
  Sister/wife of: **4** <u>**ISIS**</u>
Oskar
  portrayer: **4** LIAM
Oslo
  airline: **3** SAS
  Word on ~ coins: **5** NORGE
Osmonds
  birthplace: **5** OGDEN
  One of the: **5** DONNY **MARIE**
  ~, by birth: **7** UTAHANS
"O Sole ___": 3 MIO
Osprey
  asset: **5** TALON
OSS
  successor: **3** CIA
Osso ___: 4 BUCO
Ostentatious: 5 SHOWY
    7 SPLASHY
  display: **4** POMP RITZ
Ostracize: 4 SHUN
Ostracized
  one: **5** LEPER
Ostrich: 6 RATITE
  kin: **3** <u>**EMU**</u> MOA **4** RHEA
O.T.
  book: **3** EZR GEN ISA LEV NEH
    4 ECCL ESTH EZEK OBAD
Otalgia: 7 EARACHE

"Otello"
  composer: 5 VERDI
  offering: 4 ARIA
"O tempora! O mores!"
  speaker: 6 CICERO
Oteri
  "SNL" alum: 5 CHERI
Othello: 4 MOOR
  foe: 4 IAGO
  Like: 7 MOORISH
  piece: 4 DISC
"Othello"
  fellow: 4 IAGO
  villain: 4 **IAGO**
Other: 4 ELSE
  Go to the ~ side: 6 DEFECT
  In ~ words: 5 IDEST
  Look the ~ way: 6 IGNORE
  Not one or the: 7 NEITHER
  One and the: 4 BOTH
  One behind the: 6 TANDEM
  One or the: 6 EITHER
  On the ~ hand: 3 BUT YET
  side: 3 FOE 5 ENEMY
  than that: 4 ELSE
  ~, in French: 5 AUTRE
  ~, in Spanish: 4 OTRA OTRO
Others: 5 THOSE
  And: 6 ETALII
  And ~ (abbr.): 4 ETAL
  ~, in Latin: 4 ALII
Otherwise: 4 ELSE 5 IFNOT
Otherworldly: 5 EERIE
Otis
  Inventor: 6 ELISHA
Otitis: 7 EARACHE
Otologist
  study: 3 EAR
Ott
  of baseball: 3 MEL
Ottawa
  chief: 7 PONTIAC
  prov.: 3 ONT
Otter
  Friend of: 4 TOAD
Otto
  1936 Medicine Nobelist ~:
    5 LOEWI
  1944 Chemistry Nobelist ~:

    4 HAHN
  preceder: 5 SETTE
Otto I
  Realm of ~ (abbr.): 3 HRE
Ottoman
  bigwig: 6 SULTAN
  governor: 3 BEY
  official: 3 AGA 4 AGHA
  sultan name: 5 AHMED
  title: 5 PASHA
"Ouch!": 4 YEOW 5 YOWIE
Ought
  to have, informally: 7 SHOULDA
Oui: 3 YES
  Opposite of: 3 NON
" ___ oui!": 4 MAIS
Ouija board
  word: 3 YES
Ounce
  .035 ~: 4 GRAM
  ⅛ ~: 4 DRAM
Ounces
  32,000 ~: 3 TON
  Four fluid: 4 GILL
Our
  genus: 4 HOMO
  lang.: 3 ENG
  Not: 5 THEIR
  ~, in French: 5 NOTRE
Ouray, Chief
  Tribe of: 3 UTE
"Our Gang"
  actress Hood: 5 DARLA
  assent: 4 OTAY
  dog: 4 PETE 5 PETEY
  girl: 5 DARLA
  kid with a cowlick: 7 ALFALFA
" ___, Our Help in Ages Past":
    4 OGOD
"Our Miss Brooks"
  star: 5 ARDEN 8 EVEARDEN
"Our Town": 5 DRAMA
  character Emily: 4 WEBB
  family: 5 WEBBS
  heroine: 5 EMILY
Oust: 4 BOOT 5 EVICT 6 DEPOSE
    UNSEAT
Out: 4 AWAY 5 ALIBI NOTIN
    PASSE 6 ASLEEP ONLOAN

7 ONADATE
9 NOTATHOME
for the night: 4 ABED
   6 ASLEEP
in front: 5 AHEAD
in the open: 5 OVERT
Not: 4 SAFE 5 AWAKE
   6 ATHOME
of: 4 FROM
of it: 6 INAFOG
One: 7 PAROLEE
Partner of: 4 OVER
there: 4 AFAR 6 YONDER
"Out!": 4 CALL SCAT
Opposite of: 4 SAFE
___ out
(cancels): 3 XES
(decline): 3 OPT
(relax): 3 VEG
(scrape by): 3 EKE
"___ out!": 3 **YER**
"___ out?": 4 INOR
___ out a living: 3 **EKE** 4 EKED
   EKES 5 EKING
Out-and-out: 5 **UTTER**
Outback
bird: 3 **EMU**
canine: 5 DINGO
hopper: 3 **ROO**
mineral: 4 OPAL
runner: 3 EMU
Outbreak: 4 RIOT 5 ONSET
Unwanted: 4 ACNE
"Outbreak"
actress Rene: 5 RUSSO
actress Russo: 4 RENE
Outbuilding: 4 SHED
Outburst: 3 CRY 5 SPASM
   6 TIRADE
of laughter: 4 GALE
Outcast: 5 LEPER 6 MISFIT
   PARIAH
Social: 4 NERD
"Outcasts of Poker Flat, The"
author: 5 HARTE
Outcome: 3 END 6 RESULT
   UPSHOT
Outcropping: 4 CRAG
Outcry: 3 HUE 4 ROAR

Outdo: 3 TOP 4 BEST 5 ONEUP
   6 SHOWUP
Outdoor: 7 OPENAIR
   8 ALFRESCO
party: 4 LUAU
Outer
limit: 3 RIM 4 EDGE
prefix: 3 ECT EXO 4 ECTO
Outerwear
Arctic: 6 ANORAK
Outfield
surface: 3 SOD
Outfielder
cry: 4 MINE 6 IGOTIT
Outfit: 4 UNIT 5 EQUIP GETUP
   6 ATTIRE
Outflow
Opposite of: 6 INTAKE
Outing
African: 6 SAFARI
Rural: 7 HAYRIDE
Scout: 4 HIKE
Outlaw: 3 **BAN**
chaser: 5 POSSE
Outlay: 4 COST
Outlet: 4 VENT 5 STORE
insert: 4 PLUG
option: 4 ACDC
Outline: 4 LIMN 6 AGENDA
   SKETCH
Make an ~ of: 5 TRACE
Outlook: 4 VIEW 5 VISTA
Outlying: 3 FAR
area: 4 BURB 5 EXURB
Outmoded: 5 PASSE 6 OLDHAT
"Out of Africa"
author Dinesen: 4 ISAK
author Isak: 7 DINESEN
director: 7 POLLACK
star: 6 STREEP
Out-of-date: 5 PASSE
(abbr.): 3 OBS
Out-of-doors: 4 OPEN
"Out of Sight"
costar of Clooney: 5 LOPEZ
"Out of sight!": 3 RAD
"Out of Time"
Group with the #1 album: 3 REM
Out on ___: 5 **ALIMB**

Outpost: 4 CAMP FORT
Outpouring: 5 **SPATE**
Outrage: 3 IRE 5 ANGER
Outrageousness: 8 ENORMITY
Outs
  partner: 3 INS
Outscore: 4 BEAT
Outshine: 7 ECLIPSE
Outside: 8 EXTERNAL
  prefix: 3 EXO
Outsider: 5 ALIEN
  in Hawaii: 5 HAOLE
Outstanding: 4 **OWED** 6 UNPAID
    7 STELLAR
"Outta sight!": 5 NEATO
Outward
  Growing: 5 ENATE
  Turn: 5 EVERT SPLAY
"Out with it!": 4 GIVE
Ouzo
  flavoring: 5 **ANISE** 7 ANISEED
Oval: 7 ELLIPSE
Oven: 4 KILN OAST 7 ROASTER
  glove: 4 MITT
  output: 4 HEAT
  Ready to come out of the: 4 DONE
  setting: 5 BROIL
  Use the: 4 BAKE 5 ROAST
Over: 4 **ANEW** ATOP DONE PAST
    UPON 5 ABOVE AGAIN
    ENDED 6 ACROSS AFRESH
    7 ONTOPOF
  again: 4 **ANEW** 8 ONCEMORE
  Do: 7 ITERATE
  One: 5 BOGEY
  prefix: 3 EPI
  there: 3 **YON** 6 YONDER
  there, poetically: 4 YOND
  yonder: 5 THERE
  ~, in French: 3 SUR
  ~, in German: 4 UBER
  ~, slangily: 6 FINITO
"Over ___": 5 THERE
___ over: 4 KEEL TIDE 5 PORED
Over-50
  gp.: 4 AARP
Overabundance: 4 GLUT
Overact: 3 HAM 5 **EMOTE**
    7 HAMITUP

Overactor: 3 HAM
Overall
  material: 5 DENIM
  part: 3 BIB
Over and over:
    10 REPEATEDLY
Overblown: 5 HYPED
Overcast: 4 GRAY
Overcharge: 4 SOAK 5 GOUGE
    SCALP STING
Overcoat: 6 RAGLAN ULSTER
Overcome: 6 DEFEAT
  Most: 8 TEARIEST
  utterly: 5 WHELM
Overcook: 4 CHAR
Overdone: 5 BANAL STALE
    TRITE
Overdue: 4 LATE
  debt: 6 ARREAR
Overeater: 3 PIG
Overfill: 4 SATE
Overflow: 4 **TEEM**
  point: 3 RIM
Overflowing: 5 AWASH
  Filled to: 5 ABRIM
Overfond
  Was: 5 DOTED
Overgrown
  ~, in a way: 5 IVIED
Overhang: 4 **EAVE**
Overhaul: 4 **REDO** 5 REFIT
    REHAB 6 REVAMP
Overhead: 5 ABOVE ALOFT
  Circle: 4 HALO
  Pack: 4 STOW
  trains: 3 **ELS**
"Over here!": 4 PSST
Overindulge: 4 GLUT 5 SPOIL
Overindulgent: 4 FOND
  one: 5 DOTER
Overjoy: 5 **ELATE**
Overlay
  Map: 4 GRID
  material: 7 ACETATE
Overload: 4 CRAM 5 SWAMP
  protection: 4 FUSE
Overlook: 4 MISS OMIT
    6 IGNORE 7 NEGLECT
Overly: 3 **TOO** 6 TOOTOO

Overpermisisve: 3 LAX
Overplay: 5 EMOTE HAMUP
Overrun: 6 INFEST
Overseas: 6 ABROAD
 carrier: 4 ELAL
Oversell: 4 HYPE
Overshadow: 7 ECLIPSE
        UPSTAGE
Overshoe: 6 GALOSH
 liner: 3 PAC
Oversight: 5 LAPSE
Oversized: 3 BIG
Overstuff: 4 CRAM SATE
Oversupply: 4 GLUT 5 SPATE
"Over the Rainbow"
 composer Harold: 5 **ARLEN**
"Over There"
 composer: 5 COHAN
"Over there!": 4 LOOK
Overthrow: 5 ERROR UPEND
Overthrown
 leader: 4 SHAH
Overtime
 cause: 3 TIE
Overture
 follower: 4 ACTI 6 ACTONE
Overturn: 3 TIP 5 **UPEND** UPSET
        7 CAPSIZE
Overused: 5 STALE TRITE
Overweight: 5 OBESE
Overwhelm: 3 AWE 4 DAZE ROUT
        STUN 5 SWAMP
        8 INUNDATE
Ovid
 opus: 6 AMORES
Ovine
 utterance: 3 BAA
 whine: 5 BLEAT
Ovum: 6 GAMETE
Owl: 6 HOOTER
 hangout: 4 BARN
 Like an: 7 TALONED
 question: 3 WHO
 sound: 4 HOOT
Own: 4 HAVE
 Come into one's: 7 BLOSSOM
 On one's: 4 SOLO 5 ALONE
 (Scottish): 3 HAE
 Take as one's: 5 **ADOPT**

 up to: 4 AVOW 5 ADMIT
 (up to): 4 FESS
Owner: 6 HOLDER
 certificate: 4 DEED 5 TITLE
"Owner of a Lonely Heart"
 band: 3 YES
Ownership: 5 TITLE
 Proof of: 4 DEED 5 TITLE
Owns: 3 **HAS**
Ox: 5 BOVID
 Indian: 4 ZEBU
 Tibetan: 3 YAK
Oxen
 holder: 4 YOKE
 Pair of: 4 SPAN TEAM
Oxeye
 Like an ~ window: 4 OVAL
Oxford: 4 SHOE
 bigwig: 3 DON
 choice: 3 EEE
 Miss in: 3 OLE
 tie: 4 LACE
 university: 7 OLEMISS
 ___ oxide: 7 NITROUS
Oxidize: 4 RUST
Oxlike
 antelope: 3 GNU 5 ELAND
Oxy
 target: 3 ZIT
Oxygen
 container: 4 TENT
 Creature dependent on:
        6 AEROBE
 Fill with: 6 AERATE
 Form of: 5 OZONE
"Oy ___!": 3 VEY
"Oye Como Va"
 band: 7 SANTANA
 composer Puente: 4 TITO
Oyster
 home: 3 BED
 prize: 5 PEARL
"Oysters ___ season": 3 RIN
Oz
 Author: 4 AMOS
 creator: 4 BAUM
 denizen: 4 LION
 Dog in: 4 **TOTO**
 Transport to: 7 TORNADO

"Oz"
  network: 3 HBO
Oz.
  ⅛ fl. ~: 3 TSP
  ½ fl. ~: 4 TBSP
  and others: 3 WTS

Many: 3 LBS
Sixteen: 5 ONELB
Ozone
  alert prompter: 4 HAZE
Ozzy
  Wife of: 6 SHARON

Pp

P: 3 **RHO** 5 PENCE
  followers: 3 QRS
  Greek: 3 RHO
  of mpg: 3 PER
  of rpm: 3 PER
PA
  and others: 3 STS
  announcement: 3 ETA
  neighbor: 3 DEL
  nuclear accident site: 3 TMI
  summer hrs.: 3 EDT
PABA
  Part of: 5 AMINO
Pablo
  Former drug kingpin: 7 ESCOBAR
  Poet: 6 NERUDA
PAC
  man, often: 6 FATCAT
  Powerful: 3 NRA
Pac.
  borderer: 3 CAL
  counterpart: 3 ATL
Pac-10
  sch.: 3 ASU ORE USC 4 UCLA
  team: 4 **UCLA**
Pace: 4 CLIP STEP 5 TEMPO
      6 STRIDE
  Easy: 4 LOPE TROT 5 AMBLE
  Fast: 4 CLIP
  Gentle: 7 DOGTROT
  Horse: 4 GAIT TROT
Pacer: 5 EDSEL
  maker: 3 AMC
  place: 6 STABLE
Paces
  Musical: 5 TEMPI
Pacesetter: 6 LEADER
Pachyderm
  of fiction: 5 BABAR
  with a horn: 5 RHINO
Pacific: 5 OCEAN 6 SERENE
  battle site: 7 OKINAWA
  capital: 4 APIA

coast land: 4 PERU
goose: 4 NENE
greeting: 5 ALOHA
Half a ~ island city: 4 PAGO
Half a ~ isle: 4 BORA
island: 4 OAHU
islander: 6 SAMOAN
island nation: 4 FIJI 5 NAURU
kingdom: 5 TONGA
party: 4 LUAU
paste: 3 POI
phenomenon: 6 ELNINO
ring: 3 LEI
sighter: 6 BALBOA
tuber: 4 TARO
U.S. ~ island: 4 GUAM
Pacific ___: 3 RIM
Pacific Fur Company
  founder: 5 ASTOR
Pacifier: 3 SOP
Pacifist: 4 DOVE
Pacify: 5 QUIET 7 APPEASE
      PLACATE
Pacino
  and others: 3 **ALS**
  film: 15 DOGDAYAFTERNOON
  role: 7 SERPICO
___ Pacis (Rome): 3 ARA
Pack: 4 LADE STOW
  again: 5 REBAG
  Ahead of the: 5 FIRST
  animal: 3 ASS RAT 4 MULE
     5 BURRO LLAMA
  away: 3 EAT 4 **STOW**
  down: 4 **TAMP**
  in tightly: 4 CRAM
  it in: 4 QUIT
  Kind of: 3 ICE
  Leader of the: 5 AKELA PACER
  member: 4 BRAT
  of pennies: 4 ROLL
  rat: 5 SAVER
  Trail the: 3 LAG

up: 6 ENCASE
Word before or after: 3 RAT
Pack ___: 4 **ITIN**
Package: 6 ENCASE PARCEL
Benefit ~ gp.: 3 HMO
info: 4 NTWT
Kind of: 4 CARE
letters: 3 COD
string: 5 TWINE
Wired: 4 BALE
Packages: 4 MAIL
Care: 3 AID
Packaging
abbr.: 5 NETWT
amt.: 3 GRO
material: 5 SARAN
need: 4 TAPE
Packard: 4 AUTO
Packed: 5 DENSE
away: 3 ATE
How tuna is: 5 INOIL
in: 3 ATE
Tightly: 5 DENSE
Packers
org.: 3 NFL
Packing: 5 ARMED
a punch: 6 POTENT
cord: 5 TWINE
heat: 5 ARMED
Send: 3 AXE CAN 4 OUST
Packinghouse
stamp: 4 USDA
Pact: 6 TREATY
1990s U.S./Can./Mex.: 5 NAFTA
city: 6 WARSAW
Defunct def.: 5 SEATO
Western: 4 NATO
Pad: 4 DIGS 6 TABLET
Brake: 4 SHOE
Gym: 3 MAT
Kind of: 4 KNEE LILY 5 STENO
7 HEATING
Mouse: 3 MAT
Paper for a: 5 LEASE
Parson: 5 MANSE
Pig: 3 STY
Place for a: 4 KNEE
prefix: 4 HELI
Rice: 4 DORM

user: 5 STENO
Pad ___: 4 THAI
Padded
covering: 4 COZY
Paddle: 3 OAR TAN 5 SPANK
boat: 5 CANOE
Do the dog: 4 SWIM
Paddock
female: 4 MARE
newcomer: 4 FOAL
parent: 4 SIRE
Paddy
product: 4 RICE
Padlock
piece: 4 HASP
Padre: 4 NLER
brother: 3 TIO
Padres
Former owner of the: 4 KROC
Pads
Lizard with clingy toe: 5 GECKO
Things on: 4 MICE
Padua
City near: 4 ESTE
Paean
Poetic: 3 ODE
Paella
accompaniment: 7 SANGRIA
base: 4 RICE
pot: 4 OLLA
Paesano
land: 6 ITALIA
___ Paese cheese: 3 BEL
Paganini
birthplace: 5 GENOA
Page: 4 BEEP LEAF
Atlas: 3 MAP
Book: 4 LEAF
Essay: 4 OPED
Kind of: 4 OPED
Left-hand: 5 VERSO
Newspaper: 4 **OPED**
number: 5 FOLIO
Odd-numbered: 5 RECTO
of columns: 4 OPED
of music: 5 **PATTI**
On this: 4 HERE
Right-hand: 5 **RECTO**
Singer: 5 PATTI

Society ~ word: 3 **NEE**
Stock ~ abbr.: 3 OTC 4 AMEX
Title: 4 DEED
Pageant
 accessory: 4 SASH
 crown: 5 TIARA
 Like a ~ winner: 7 TIARAED
 Parks at a: 4 BERT
 prize: 5 TIARA
 rating subject: 5 POISE
 venue: 12 ATLANTICCITY
Page-bottom
 abbr.: 4 IBID
Pageboy: 6 HAIRDO
Pager
 letters: 3 MCI
 sound: 4 BEEP
"Pagliacci": 5 OPERA
 clown: 5 TONIO
 soprano: 5 NEDDA
"___, Pagliacci" (aria): 4 RIDI
Pagoda
 roofing: 5 TILES
 sight: 5 IDOL
 sound: 4 GONG
Pago Pago
 native: 6 SAMOAN
 site: 5 **SAMOA**
Pah
 lead-in: 3 OOM
Pahlavi: 4 SHAH
 Shah: 4 REZA
Pahoehoe: 4 LAVA
Paid
 admission: 4 GATE
 Debt to be: 3 IOU
 holiday: 13 FRINGEBENEFIT
 out: 5 SPENT
 player: 3 **PRO**
 Price: 4 COST
 spots: 3 ADS
 (up): 5 ANTED 6 PONIED
Paige
 of baseball: 7 SATCHEL
Pail
 Be clumsy with a: 5 SLOSH
Pain: 4 ACHE HURT 6 HASSLE
 Be a: 5 ANNOY 6 PESTER
 Cries of: 3 OWS

Cry of: 4 OUCH YELP YIPE
    YOWL
Dull: 4 ACHE
Feeling no: 4 NUMB
In: 4 HURT 6 ACHING
Intense: 5 AGONY
in the neck: 4 ACHE KINK **PEST**
    5 CRICK 6 HASSLE
Lessen a: 4 EASE
Little: 3 IMP
React to: 5 WINCE
Royal: 4 PEST
soother: 4 BALM 6 BENGAY
Spasm of: 5 THROE
Sudden: 6 TWINGE
Pained
 expression: 4 MOUE
Painful: 4 SORE
 state: 5 THROE
Painkiller: 5 OPIUM 7 ANODYNE
 Popular: 5 ALEVE
Pain reliever: 6 OPIATE
    7 ANODYNE
 brand: 5 ALEVE BAYER
Pains: 4 CARE ILLS
 Partner of: 5 **ACHES**
Paint: 4 LIMN
 Apply more ~ to: 6 RECOAT
 base: 5 LATEX
 basecoat: 6 PRIMER SEALER
 can direction: 4 STIR
 crudely: 4 DAUB
 Eggy: 7 TEMPERA
 Glossy: 6 ENAMEL
 ingredient: 5 LATEX 7 ACETONE
 Kind of: 5 LATEX 6 ENAMEL
    7 ACRYLIC
 layer: 4 **COAT**
 like Pollock: 7 SPATTER
 oil: 7 LINSEED
 pigment: 5 OCHRE
 Place to: 7 ATELIER
 Poster: 7 TEMPERA
 Prepare: 4 STIR
 Prepare to: 6 SCRAPE
 Remove: 5 STRIP
 Smear: 4 DAUB
 the town red: 7 CAROUSE
 Uneven, as a ~ job: 7 STREAKY

Painted
Freshly: 3 WET
horse: 5 PINTO
It may be: 3 TOE 4 NAIL
tinware: 4 TOLE
vessel: 4 EWER
Painted Desert
feature: 4 MESA
site (abbr.): 4 ARIZ
Painter
Belgian ~ James: 5 ENSOR
calculation: 4 AREA
choice: 3 HUE
cover-up: 5 SMOCK
Dutch: 4 HALS 5 STEEN
English ~ John: 4 OPIE
French: 5 COROT LEGER
    MANET MONET 7 MATISSE
    UTRILLO
Like a: 4 ARTY
Limp watch: 4 DALI
Maja: 4 GOYA
of ballerinas: 5 DEGAS
pigment: 8 OILCOLOR
plaster: 5 GESSO
Pointillist: 6 SEURAT
Spanish: 4 GOYA MIRO SERT
stand: 5 EASEL
Surrealist: 4 DALI 5 ERNST
Swiss: 4 KLEE
~ Ashan: 5 SLOAN
~ Fernand: 5 LEGER
~ Frans: 4 HALS
~ Henri: 7 MATISSE
~ Hieronymus: 5 BOSCH
~ Jan: 5 STEEN
~ Jan Van ___: 4 EYCK
~ Joan: 4 MIRO
~ Mary: 7 CASSATT
~ Maurice: 7 UTRILLO
~ Max: 5 ERNST WEBER
~ Rembrandt: 5 PEALE
~ Richard: 5 ESTES
~ Salvador: 4 DALI
Painting
Do finger: 5 SMEAR
genre: 9 LANDSCAPE
guide: 7 STENCIL
(Italian): 4 ARTE

Kind of: 3 OIL
on plaster: 6 FRESCO
Prepare for: 5 PRIME
Put up a: 4 HANG
School of: 6 ASHCAN
surface: 5 **GESSO**
Wall: 5 MURAL
Paintings: 3 ART
Illusory: 5 OPART
Some: 4 OILS
Pair: 3 DUO TWO 4 DUAD DYAD
    ITEM 5 BRACE 6 COUPLE
    7 TWOSOME
of nines: 3 ENS
of socks: 6 ONETWO
One of a matched: 3 HIS 4 HERS
picker: 4 NOAH
The: 4 BOTH
The best: 4 ACES
up: 4 MATE
with drums: 4 EARS
Wrestling: 7 TAGTEAM
Yoked: 4 OXEN
Pairing: 5 UNION
Paisley
Irish leader: 3 IAN
"Pajama Party"
actress: 8 DORISDAY
Pajamas
Cat's: 3 FUR
Exec in: 3 HEF
Pak
LPGA star: 4 SERI
Pak, Se Ri
org.: 4 LPGA
Pakistan
city: 6 LAHORE
language: 4 **URDU**
money: 5 RUPEE
neighbor: 4 IRAN 5 INDIA
river: 5 INDUS
Pakistani: 5 ASIAN
president of the 80s: 3 ZIA
Pal: 3 BRO BUD 4 CHUM 5 AMIGO
    BUDDY
French: 3 **AMI** 4 AMIE
Spanish: 5 AMIGO
Western: 4 PARD
___ pal (girlfriend): 3 GAL

Palace
dweller: 5 ROYAL
Like many a: 6 ORNATE
Moorish: 7 ALCAZAR
　　8 ALHAMBRA
Muslim ~ area: 5 HAREM
Paris: 6 ELYSEE
Pinball: 6 ARCADE
protector: 4 MOAT
resident: 4 EMIR TSAR
Sports: 5 ARENA
Palais
resident: 3 ROI
Palatable: 5 TASTY
Make: 9 SUGARCOAT
Palate
dangler: 5 UVULA
pleasing: 5 TASTY
Palatine Hill
site: 4 ROME
Pale: 3 WAN 4 ASHY 5 ASHEN
as a ghost: 4 ASHY
color: 4 TINT
drink: 3 ALE
More: 6 ASHIER
Paler than: 4 ASHY
purple: 5 **LILAC** MAUVE
Turn: 6 BLANCH
Very: 4 ASHY
yellow: 5 MAIZE
Pale ___: 3 ALE
Paleo-
Opposite of: 3 **NEO**
Paleontological
estimate: 3 AGE
find: 6 FOSSIL
period: 3 ERA
Paleozoic: 3 ERA
Palermo
Prior ~ pelf: 4 LIRE
Palestine
Ancient city of: 6 BETHEL
Ancient neighbor of: 4 EDOM
Northernmost city of ancient:
　　3 DAN
~, long ago: 6 CANAAN
Palestinian: 4 ARAB
Ancient: 6 ESSENE
ascetic: 6 ESSENE

Former ~ leader: 6 ARAFAT
Palestrina
piece: 5 MOTET
Palillo
Actor: 3 RON
Palindrome
center: 3 ERE
Island in a: 4 ELBA
part: 4 EREI
Poetic: 3 ERE
start: 4 AMAN
Palindromic
address: 4 MAAM 5 MADAM
animal: 3 EWE
cheer: 3 YAY
comics dog: 4 OTTO
cry: 3 AHA OHO
diarist: 3 NIN
exiled dictator: 6 LONNOL
magazine: 4 ELLE
name: 3 ASA EVE 4 OTTO
nickname: 3 NAN
parent: 3 DAD MOM
plea: 3 SOS
pop group: 4 **ABBA**
preposition: 3 **ERE**
principle: 5 TENET
songbird: 3 TIT
spinner: 5 ROTOR
suffix: 4 ETTE
tennis pro: 5 SELES
time: 4 NOON
title: 4 MAAM 5 MADAM
Palladium: 5 METAL
Palliate: 4 EASE
Pallid: 3 WAN 4 ASHY 5 ASHEN
　　WAXEN
Palm: 4 TREE
Asian: 5 ARECA BETEL
Basketry: 4 NIPA
Betel: 5 ARECA
fruit: 4 DATE
Kind of: 4 SAGO 5 BETEL
leaf: 5 FROND
reader: 4 SEER
spring: 5 OASIS
starch: 4 SAGO
Wicker: 6 RATTAN
___ Palmas: 3 LAS

Palme
  of Sweden: 4 OLOF
Palme ___ (Cannes award): 3 DOR
Palmer
  Actress: 5 LILLI
  Golfer: 5 **ARNIE**
  peg: 3 TEE
  with an "army": 5 ARNIE
Palmer, Jim: 6 ORIOLE
Palminteri
  Actor: 5 CHAZZ
Palmist: 4 SEER
  concern: 4 LINE
Palm Pilot: 3 PDA
Palo Alto
  City near: 8 SANMATEO
Palo ___, California: 4 ALTO
Paloma
  Pop of: 5 PABLO
Palomino
  TV: 4 MRED
Palooka: 3 APE OAF 4 LOUT
Palpable: 7 EVIDENT
Paltrow, Gwyneth
  title role: 4 EMMA
Paltry: 4 MERE 6 MEASLY
  amount: 3 SOU
Pam
  Actress: 5 GRIER
Pampas
  bird: 4 RHEA
  cowpoke: 6 GAUCHO
Pamper: 4 BABY 5 SPOIL
     6 CODDLE COSSET
     11 MOLLYCODDLE
  One to: 3 TOT
  Place to ~ oneself: 3 SPA
Pampering: 3 TLC
  place: 3 SPA
Pamphlet: 5 TRACT
  suffix: 3 EER
Pamphleteer
  of 1776: 5 PAINE
Pamplona
  Info: Spanish cue
  pal: 5 AMIGO
  runner: 4 TORO
  shout: 3 OLE
  Stick at: 4 GORE

Pan: 4 SLAM
  Baking: 3 TIN
  creator: 6 BARRIE
  Flying: 5 PETER
  Frying: 7 SKILLET
  handler: 4 CHEF
  Opposite of: 4 RAVE
  Oven: 7 ROASTER
  Played like: 5 PIPED
  Stir-fry: 3 **WOK**
Panacea: 7 CUREALL
Panache: 4 **ELAN** 5 STYLE
Pan Am
  Old ~ rival: 3 TWA 5 USAIR
Panama: 3 HAT 7 ISTHMUS
  currency: 6 BALBOA
Panasonic
  rival: 3 RCA 4 AIWA 5 SANYO
Panatella: 5 CIGAR
Pancake
  Fancy: 5 CREPE
  French: 5 CREPE
  Light: 4 BLIN
  Like a: 4 FLAT
  palace: 4 IHOP
  Russian: 4 BLIN
  Russian *(plural):* 5 BLINI
  serving: 5 STACK
  Thin: 5 CREPE
  topper: 4 OLEO 5 SYRUP
  Turn over a: 4 FLIP
Panchen ___: 4 LAMA
Pancho
  Mexican revolutionary: 5 VILLA
  pal: 5 AMIGO CISCO
  poncho: 6 SERAPE
Pancreas: 5 GLAND
Panda
  Toon: 4 ANDY
Pandemonium: 5 CHAOS HAVOC
P&L
  column heading: 3 YTD
  preparer: 3 CPA
Pandora
  released them: 4 **ILLS** 5 EVILS
Pandora's box:
     10 CANOFWORMS
  remnant: 4 HOPE
Pandowdy: 3 PIE

Pane
frame: 4 SASH
Panel
Court: 4 JURY
Dress: 5 INSET
Kind of: 5 **SOLAR**
suffix: 3 IST
Paneling
material: 8 MASONITE
Panelist: 5 JUROR
Panels
Car with removable roof: 4 TTOP
Panetta
Political: 4 LEON
Pan-fry: 5 SAUTE
Pang: 4 ACHE 5 **THROE**
6 TWINGE
Emotional: 6 TWINGE
Panhandle: 3 **BEG**
loc.: 4 OKLA
site: 6 ALASKA
State with a: 5 IDAHO
Panic
In a: 6 SCARED
PC ~ button: 3 ESC
Study in a: 4 CRAM
___ Panisse (restaurant): 4 CHEZ
Panorama: 4 VIEW 5 VISTA
Pans
Partners of: 4 POTS
Some: 7 TINWARE
Pant: 4 GASP
Pantheon
member: 3 GOD
Norse: 5 AESIR
Panther: 5 NHLER
Cartoon ~ color: 4 PINK
Panthers
of the Big East: 4 PITT
Panties
Short: 7 STEPINS
Pantomime: 6 ACTOUT
character: 7 PIERROT
Song title spelled in: 4 YMCA
Pantomimist
Jacques: 4 TATI
Pantry: 6 LARDER 9 STOREROOM
items: 4 TINS
pest: 3 ANT

Pants: 5 GASPS 6 SLACKS
alternative: 5 SKIRT
Alternative to hot: 4 MINI
Casual: 5 JEANS
feature: 6 CREASE
holder: 6 HANGER
maker Strauss: 4 LEVI
material: 5 CHINO
measure: 6 INSEAM LENGTH
One with ~ on fire: 4 LIAR
part: 3 LEG 4 KNEE **SEAT**
problem: 3 RIP
Short: 4 TROU
style: 5 CAPRI
___ pants: 5 CAPRI
Pantyhose
Brand of: 5 LEGGS
shade: 4 ECRU
woe: 4 SNAG
Pantywaist: 5 SISSY
Panza, ___: 6 SANCHO
Panza, Sancho
mount: 3 ASS
Papa: 3 DAD
Mama of: 4 NANA
Partner of: 4 MAMA
Stable: 4 SIRE
"Papa Bear"
of football: 5 HALAS
"Papa, Can You Hear Me?"
Film with the song: 5 YENTL
Papa Doc
ruled it: 5 HAITI
Papa Hemingway: 6 ERNEST
Papal
ambassador: 6 NUNCIO
bull: 5 EDICT
cape: 5 FANON
court: 5 CURIA
headgear: 5 TIARA
name: 4 PIUS
representative: 6 LEGATE
vestment: 5 **ORALE**
Papandreou
Former Greek P.M.: 7 ANDREAS
Paparazzi
target: 4 STAR 5 CELEB
Paparazzo
need: 6 CAMERA

prize: 3 PIC
target: 4 STAR 5 CELEB

Papas
Actress: 5 IRENE
Singing partner of: 5 MAMAS

Papeete
island: 6 TAHITI

Paper
24 sheets of: 5 QUIRE
art: 7 ORIGAMI
Baltimore: 3 SUN
Chi-town: 4 TRIB
container: 3 BAG
craft: 7 ORIGAMI
Do ~ work: 4 EDIT
Enjoy the: 4 READ
fastener: 6 STAPLE
Flat: 5 LEASE
flier: 4 KITE
holder: 3 PAD
Holds the ~ to: 4 OWNS
Homeowner: 4 DEED
Kind of: 3 FAX 4 RICE TERM
    5 CREPE GRAPH TRADE
Like India: 4 THIN
Like notebook: 5 LINED RULED
money: 4 NOTE
name, briefly: 4 TRIB
Not on: 4 ORAL
Old ~ money: 5 SCRIP
Old ~ part: 4 ROTO
Party: 5 CREPE
Piece of: 4 SLIP 5 SCRAP SHEET
Pitch on: 7 PRINTAD
Pulitzer: 5 WORLD
pusher: 7 NEWSBOY
Put on: 5 WRITE
quantity: 4 REAM 5 QUIRE
Renter: 5 LEASE
Scrap: 5 SHRED
section: 6 SPORTS
size: 5 LEGAL
Sleazy: 3 RAG
Term ~ abbr.: 4 IBID
Term ~ citation: 6 IBIDEM
towel: 4 WIPE
Translucent: 9 ONIONSKIN
Travel: 4 VISA
unit: 5 SHEET

Washington: 4 POST
worker: 6 EDITOR
Yellow: 6 MANILA

Paperback: 4 BOOK
Big inits. in: 3 NAL
publisher: 4 AVON DELL
    6 SIGNET

Paperboy
path: 5 ROUTE

"Paper Chase, The"
topic: 3 LAW

Paper Mate: 3 PEN
rival: 3 BIC

"Paper Moon"
actor or actress: 5 ONEAL

"Paper Roses"
singer Marie: 6 OSMOND

Papers: 5 MEDIA
(abbr.): 3 MSS
Bundle of: 5 SHEAF
Give walking ~ to: 3 AXE
Research: 6 THESES
Walking: 5 THEAX

Paperwork: 5 FORMS 7 REDTAPE

Papier-___: 5 MACHE

Paprika
Stew with: 7 GOULASH

Papua
city: 3 LAE

Papyrus: 5 SEDGE

Paquin
Oscar winner: 4 **ANNA**

Par: 4 NORM
On a: 4 EVEN
On a ~, in French: 4 EGAL
On a ~ with: 7 EQUALTO
One over: 5 BOGEY
One under: 6 BIRDIE
Two under: 5 EAGLE

Par ___ (airmail label): 5 AVION

Parable
message: 5 MORAL

Parabola
part: 3 ARC

Parabolic
path: 3 ARC

Parachute
Deliver by: 7 AIRDROP
Kind of: 6 GOLDEN

material: 5 NYLON
part: 4 CORD 6 CANOPY
Small: 6 DROGUE
"Parachutes and Kisses"
author Erica: 4 JONG
Parade: 5 STRUT
group: 4 VETS
honoree: 4 HERO 5 STPAT
NY ~ sponsor: 5 MACYS
sight: 5 FLOAT
spinner: 5 BATON
spoiler: 4 RAIN
time: 6 EASTER
Word before: 3 HIT
"Parade"
actor: 4 TATI
Paradigm: 5 IDEAL
Paradise: 4 EDEN
evictee: 4 ADAM
Like: 6 EDENIC
lost: 4 EDEN
of Gauguin: 6 TAHITI
of King Arthur: 6 AVALON
"Paradise Lost": 4 EPIC
character: 4 ADAM
figure: 5 SATAN
poet: 6 MILTON
setting: 4 EDEN
Paradisiacal: 6 EDENIC
"Paradiso"
writer: 5 DANTE
Paradoxical
question, in Zen: 4 KOAN
~ Greek: 4 ZENO
Paraffin
Like: 4 WAXY
Paragon: 5 IDEAL
8 NONESUCH
Paragraph
Playbill: 3 BIO
Start a: 6 INDENT
Parakeet: 3 PET
home: 4 CAGE
Parallel: 4 AKIN 6 ANALOG
7 ALIGNED
Capital on the 60th: 4 OSLO
It's ~ to the radius: 4 ULNA
Parallelograms
Some: 6 RHOMBI

Paramecium
propellers: 5 CILIA
Paramedic
(abbr.): 3 EMT
Paramount: 4 MAIN
Paramour
French: 4 AMIE
Paranoiac
worry: 4 PLOT
Paranormal
power: 3 **ESP**
Paranormalist
~ Geller: 3 URI
Paraphernalia: 4 GEAR
Paraphrase: 7 RESTATE
Parapsychology
subj.: 3 ESP
Parasailing
Go: 4 SOAR
Parasite: 5 LEECH
home: 4 HOST
Plant: 5 APHID
prefix: 4 ECTO
Tiny: 4 MITE
Young: 3 NIT
Parasites
Some: 4 LICE
Their parents are: 4 NITS
Parasol: 8 SUNSHADE
offering: 5 SHADE
Paratrooper
cry: 8 GERONIMO
need: 5 CHUTE
Parboil: 5 SCALD
Parcel: 4 DOLE METE
Land: 4 ACRE 5 TRACT
out: 5 ALLOT
Partner of: 4 PART
Realty: 3 LOT
Parched: 4 **ARID** SERE
feeling: 6 THIRST
Pardon
General: 7 AMNESTY
~, with "off": 3 LET
Pardoned
president: 5 NIXON
"Pardon me": 4 AHEM 5 SORRY
7 SOSORRY
abroad: 5 SCUSI

Pare: 4 PEEL
  pounds: **4** SLIM
Parent: 4 REAR **6** RAISER
    REARER
  New: **5** NAMER
  order: **3** NOW
  Palindromic: **3** DAD MOM POP
  Parisian: **4** MERE PERE
  Piglet: **3** SOW
  Reason from a: **6** ISAYSO
  Show biz: **8** STAGEMOM
  Stable: **4** **SIRE**
  warning: **4** DONT
Parenthesis: 3 ARC
Parenthetical
  amount: **4** LOSS
  remark: **5** ASIDE
Parenthood
  Plant ~ setting:
    10 GREENHOUSE
"Parenthood"
  actress Dianne: **5** WIEST
Parenting
  challenges: **5** TEENS
  Do: **4** REAR
Paretsky
  Mystery writer: **4** **SARA**
Pariah: 5 LEPER
  Union: **4** SCAB
Parimutuel: 4 TOTE
  Use a: **3** BET
Paris
  Info: French cue
  abductee: **5** HELEN
  airport: **4** **ORLY**
  American in: **5** ANGLO
  bank: **4** RIVE
  based org.: **6** UNESCO
  City of: **4** TROY
  divider: **5** SEINE
  evening: **4** SOIR
  Father of: **5** PRIAM
  First bishop of: **7** STDENIS
  foe: **5** ROMEO
  girl: **4** ELLE
  Hot time in: **3** ETE
  museum: **6** LOUVRE
  newspaper, with "Le": **5** MONDE
  pal: **3** AMI

  palace: **6** ELYSEE
  papa: **4** PERE
  path: **5** ALLEE
  Plaster of: **5** GESSO
  playground: **4** PARC
  possessive: **3** MON SES **4** AMOI
  pronoun: **3** TOI
  river: **5** SEINE
  River near: **4** OISE
  school: **5** ECOLE LYCEE
  springtime: **3** MAI
  star: **6** ETOILE
  Suburb of: **4** ORLY
  subway: **5** METRO
  summer: **3** ETE
  Washington in: **4** ETAT
  Wife of: **6** OENONE
  yes: **3** OUI
  ~ Ltd.: **3** CIE
"___ Paris" (Cole Porter): 5 ILOVE
Parish
  leader: **6** RECTOR
  priest: **5** VICAR **6** CURATE
Parishes
  Long in the: **4** HUEY
Parishioners: 5 LAITY
  donation: **5** TITHE
Parisian
  Info: French cue
  article: **3** UNE
  coin: **5** FRANC
  diner: **4** CAFE
  goodbye: **5** ADIEU
  pal: **3** AMI
  palace: **6** ELYSEE
  parent: **4** MERE PERE
  passion: **5** AMOUR
  possessive: **3** SES **4** AMOI
  preposition: **4** AVEC
  pronoun: **3** ILS
  pupil: **5** ELEVE
  season: **3** ETE
  street: **3** RUE
Park: 6 AVENUE
  Alberta: **5** BANFF
  Animal: **3** ZOO
  Big Apple: **4** SHEA
  concern (abbr.): **4** ECOL
  Copenhagen: **6** TIVOLI

in NYC: 3 AVE
it: 3 SIT
Kind of: 5 THEME 7 TRAILER
London: 4 HYDE
Out of the: 4 GONE
person: 6 RANGER
place: 3 LOT 4 CURB 6 GARAGE
shelter: 6 GAZEBO

___ Park
(California): 5 BUENA MENLO
(Colorado): 5 **ESTES**
(Illinois): 3 OAK
(New Jersey): 5 MENLO
(New York): 4 REGO
(Pirates' field): 3 PNC

Parka: 6 ANORAK
part: 4 HOOD

Park Avenue: 3 CAR

Parkay
product: 4 OLEO

Parked
it: 3 SAT

Parker: 3 PEN
Actor: 4 FESS
Actress: 5 POSEY
Car: 5 VALET
Illegal ~ worry: 5 TOWER
Nosy: 5 SNOOP YENTA

Parker, Charlie
genre: 5 BEBOP
instrument: 7 ALTOSAX
nickname: 4 BIRD

Parker, Dorothy
quality: 3 WIT

Parker, ___ Jessica: 5 SARAH

Parker House: 4 ROLL

Parking
Airport ~ area: 5 APRON
attendant: 5 VALET
lot device: 5 METER
meter opening: 4 SLOT
place: 3 LOT 4 CURB SPOT
    6 GARAGE

Parkinsonism
treatment: 5 LDOPA

Parks
at a pageant: 4 BERT
Civil rights activist: 4 **ROSA**
on a bus: 4 ROSA

Parks, Rosa: 8 ALABAMAN

Parliament
First woman in: 5 ASTOR
Head of: 3 LOO
Israeli: 7 KNESSET
Japanese: 4 DIET
John in: 3 LOO
member: 4 LORD
Russian: 4 DUMA

Parliamentary
govt. leaders: 3 PMS
proposal: 6 MOTION
response: 3 AYE

Parlor
Beauty: 5 SALON
game: 4 POOL
Ice cream ~ order: 6 FRAPPE
    SUNDAE
letters: 3 OTB
piece: 4 SOFA 5 DIVAN
    6 SETTEE
Spider's ~ invitee: 3 FLY
Stick in a: 3 CUE
~, in Spanish: 4 SALA

Parmenides
home: 4 ELEA

Parmesan
Prepare: 5 GRATE

Parody: 3 APE 5 SPOOF
    6 SENDUP 7 LAMPOON
Yankovic: 5 EATIT

Paroxysm: 5 THROE

Parquet
Like a ~ floor: 6 INLAID

Parrot: 3 APE 4 APER **ECHO**
    6 REPEAT 7 IMITATE
Colorful: 5 **MACAW**
cry: 3 AWK
Disney: 4 IAGO
Large: 3 KEA 5 MACAW
Showy: 8 COCKATOO

Parry: 5 AVERT
follower: 7 RIPOSTE
Item to ~ with: 4 EPEE

Parseghian
Coach: 3 **ARA**
of football: 3 **ARA**

Parsifal
quest: 5 GRAIL

Parsing
choice: 4 NOUN
Parsley: 4 HERB
piece: 5 SPRIG
relative: 4 DILL 5 ANISE
6 FENNEL 8 ANGELICA
With: 5 GARNI
Parson
place: 5 MANSE
Parsonage: 5 MANSE 7 RECTORY
Parsons
Actress: 7 ESTELLE
Musician: 4 ALAN
Part: 4 AREA **ROLE** 6 DIVIDE
7 ELEMENT 8 SEPARATE
Bit: 5 CAMEO
Discrete: 4 UNIT
Do one's: 3 ACT
Essential: 4 PITH
Film: 4 ROLE
of: 4 INON
Worst: 5 DREGS
Partake
of: 3 EAT USE 4 **HAVE**
Parted
It ~ in Exodus: 6 REDSEA
Parthenon
goddess: 6 ATHENA
Partial: 6 BIASED 8 ONESIDED
Partiality: 4 BIAS
Partially: 4 SOME
Participate: 5 ENTER OPTIN
SHARE SITIN
Decide to: 5 OPTIN
Hope to: 6 WANTIN
Not ~ in: 6 SITOUT
Particle: 4 ATOM
Charged: 3 **ION** 5 ANION
Cyclotron: 3 ION
Dust: 4 MOTE
Electrolysis: 5 ANION
Elementary: 4 ATOM 5 MESON
8 NEUTRINO
Hypothetical: 5 AXION QUARK
Kind of: 3 PSI 5 ALPHA
6 LAMBDA
Negative: 5 ANION
Positive: 6 PROTON
prefix: 4 ANTI

Quantum physics: 5 MESON
Small: 4 MOTE
Soot: 4 SMUT
Stable: 3 OAT
Subatomic: 4 MUON PION
5 MESON 6 PROTON
Tiny: 4 ATOM
Unstable: 4 MUON
___ particle: 3 PSI TAU
Particle accelerator
particle: 3 ION 4 ATOM
Particles
Abrasive: 4 GRIT
Create charged: 6 IONIZE
Remove ~ from: 4 SIFT
Sandy: 4 GRIT
Particular: 4 **ITEM** 5 FUSSY
6 DETAIL
Agenda: 4 ITEM
Drive nowhere in: 4 SPIN
In ~ (abbr.): 3 ESP
Nobody in: 6 ANYONE
period: 3 ERA
Parties: 3 DOS
Like some: 4 STAG
War: 6 ARMIES
Parting
Pacific: 5 ALOHA
word: 4 CIAO 5 **ADIEU** ADIOS
ALOHA LATER 7 GOODBYE
8 SAYONARA
words: 4 BYES OBIT TATA
5 IQUIT OBITS 6 ADIEUS
8 AUREVOIR
"Parting is ___ sweet sorrow":
4 SUCH
Partisan
prefix: 3 NON
Partisanship: 4 SIDE
Partition: 5 SEVER 6 DIVIDE
Ping-Pong: 3 NET
Safety: 8 FIREWALL
~, with "off": 4 ROPE
Partitions
Nasal: 5 SEPTA
Partly
coincide: 7 OVERLAP
open: 4 AJAR
Partner: 4 ALLY MATE 5 UNITE

Talk show: **6** COHOST
Partnership: 7 CAHOOTS
Partnership for Peace
  gp.: **4** NATO
Partook
  of: **3** ATE
Partridge
  boy: **5** DANNY
  Eldest: **5** KEITH
  perch in song: **8** PEARTREE
  Slang expert: **4** ERIC
Partridge, Laurie
  portrayer: **3** DEY
"Partridge Family, The"
  actor Bonaduce: **5** DANNY
  actress Susan: **3** DEY
"___ partridge in ...": 4 ANDA
"... partridge in ___ tree":
      5 APEAR
Parts
  of qts.: **3** PTS
Part-time
  player: **7** SEMIPRO
  worker: **4** TEMP
Party: 4 FETE **5** REVEL
  1990s ~: **4** RAVE
  A ~ to: **4 INON**
  activist: **3** POL
  Afternoon: **3** TEA
  All-night: **4** RAVE
  animal: **4** STAG **6** DONKEY
  attendee: **5** GUEST
  big shot: **4** WHIP
  Block party. **9** HOMEOWNER
  bowlful: **3** DIP
  brewer: **3** URN
  Bridal: **4** WIFE
  cheese: **4** BRIE EDAM
  Coming-out: **3** DEB
  decoration: **8** STREAMER
  Fancy: **4** GALA
  follower: **4** GOER
  Frat ~ staple: **3** KEG
  Frat ~ wear: **4** TOGA
  Furnish ~ food: **5** CATER
  game pin-on: **4** TAIL
  Garden: **3** EVE **4** ADAM
  gift: **5** FAVOR
  Give a ~ for: **4** FETE

giver: **4** HOST **7** HOSTESS
handout: **5** FAVOR
hearty: **5** REVEL **8** LIVEITUP
Held by a third: **8** INESCROW
Hostile: **5** ENEMY
invitee: **5** GUEST
Israeli political: **5** LIKUD
Kind of: **3** HEN TEA **4** POOL
      STAG TOGA **6** PAJAMA
Lavish: **4** FETE
Lawn ~ site: **4** YARD
leader: **4** HOST **5** EMCEE
      7 HOSTESS
Life of the:
      15 GOODTIMECHARLIE
Like a dull: **4** DEAD
line: **5** CONGA **8** WHATSNEW
Lively: **4** BASH
member: **3** HEN
member, briefly: **3** DEM
munchies: **7** CANAPES
Not the ~ sort (abbr.): **3** IND
offering: **5** SLATE
paper: **5** CREPE
Pool: **5** STENO
pooper: **4** BORE DRAG DRIP
      10 WETBLANKET
popper: **4** CORK
purchase: **3** ICE
Quilting: **3** BEE
Quite a: **4** BASH
Search: **5** POSSE
snacks: **4** NUTS
spread: **4** PATE
Stag: **4** DEER
Tea ~ crasher: **5** ALICE
Tea ~ member: **8** DORMOUSE
thrower: **4** HOST
time: **3** EVE
to: **4** INON
Uncrashable: **9** OPENHOUSE
Wild: **4** ORGY
Work: **4** CREW
Party-giver: 4 HOST
  ~ Mesta: **5** PERLE
  ~ Perle: **5** MESTA
Parvenu: 7 UPSTART
Pas
  Partners of: **3** MAS

Pas ___: 4 ALLE SEUL
"___ pasa?": 3 QUE
Pasadena
parade flowers: 5 ROSES
Pascal
Philosopher: 6 BLAISE
thought: 6 PENSEE
___ Pascal (computer language):
5 TURBO
Pas de ___: 4 DEUX
Pas de deux
part: 6 ADAGIO
Pass: 4 GOBY 5 BADGE **ENACT**
6 ELAPSE 8 OVERTAKE
again: 5 RELAP
Allow to: 5 LETBY
along: 5 RELAY 6 RELATE
and then some: 3 ACE
by: 6 ELAPSE
catcher: 3 **END**
Come to: 5 ENSUE **OCCUR**
6 BETIDE HAPPEN
Didn't ~ the bar: 5 DRANK
Didn't just: 4 ACED
Don't: 3 BID
Forward: 6 AERIAL
Give a free: 4 COMP
into law: 5 ENACT
Kind of: 7 LATERAL
Long: 4 BOMB
Make a ~ at: 5 HITON
8 COMEONTO
Mountain: 3 COL GAP
on: 4 SKIP 5 REFER RELAY
out: 4 ZONK 5 ALLOT SWOON
out cards: 4 DEAL
over: 4 **OMIT** SKIP 5 ELIDE
prefix: 3 SUR
Press: 5 IDTAG
quickly: 4 FLIT
slowly: 4 DRAG 6 WEARON
the time: 4 LAZE
They're hard to: 8 ROADHOGS
through a wall: 4 GATE
Tourney: 3 BYE
~, as time: 5 SPEND 6 ELAPSE
"Pass ___!": 4 ITON
Passable: 4 SOSO
Passage: 4 PATH

Anatomical: 4 ITER
Brain: 4 ITER
Chimney: 4 FLUE
Closing: 4 CODA
Diary: 5 ENTRY
Melodic: 6 ARIOSO
Mine: 4 ADIT 5 SHAFT
Narrow: 4 LANE 5 ALLEY INLET
Narrow water ~ (abbr.): 3 STR
Operatic: 6 ARIOSO
Right of: 8 EASEMENT
Sermon: 4 TEXT
Symbol of safe: 3 ARK
~, in Latin: 4 ITER
Passages
Nasal: 5 NARES
"Passage to India, A"
author: 9 EMFORSTER
doctor: 4 AZIZ
heroine: 5 ADELA
Passageway
Body: 4 ITER
Covered: 6 ARCADE
Vine-covered: 7 PERGOLA
Passbook
abbr.: 3 DEP INT
amt.: 3 DEP
Passé: 3 OLD OUT 5 DATED
STALE 6 DEMODE
OLDHAT
preposition: 4 UNTO
Passed: 3 OKD 6 GONEBY
It may be: 3 ACT HAT
out cards: 5 DEALT
the puck to: 3 FED
Passel: 4 SLEW
Passenger: 5 RIDER
Ark: 3 HAM
Cheap ~ place: 8 STEERAGE
info: 3 ETA
Limo: 3 VIP
Paying: 4 FARE
Was a: 4 RODE
Passport
info: 3 NOM
Passer
Buck: 3 ATM
Charge the: 5 BLITZ
Leading NFL ~ of 1980: 4 SIPE

"___ Passes" (Rumer Godden novel): 5 PIPPA
"___ Pass Go ...": 5 DONOT
Passing
assistance: 3 YEA
Barely ~ grade: 3 DEE
fancy: 3 FAD 4 WHIM
grade: 3 CEE
mention: 4 OBIT
notice: 4 OBIT
Sounds of time: 5 TICKS
stats (abbr.): 3 YDS
Passing ___: 4 LANE
Passion: 4 FIRE HEAT LOVE ZEAL 5 ARDOR 6 FERVOR
Hate with a: 6 DETEST
Parisian: 5 AMOUR
personified: 4 EROS
Uncontrolled: 4 LUST
Passionate: 4 AVID 5 AFIRE 6 ARDENT TORRID 7 INTENSE
about: 4 INTO
desire: 4 LUST
"Passions": 4 SOAP
Passive
Be: 5 SITBY
protest: 5 SITIN
Passive-aggressive
response: 15 SILENTTREATMENT
___ Passos, John: 3 DOS
Passover
meal: 5 **SEDER**
month: 5 NISAN
staple: 5 MATZO
Passport
maker: 5 HONDA
stamp: 4 VISA
Passports: 3 IDS
___ passu (equably): 4 PARI
Password
Fictional ~ user: 7 ALIBABA
Person with a: 4 USER
preceder: 6 USERID
requester: 4 USER
Type a: 5 LOGIN
Verify a: 7 REENTER
What a ~ allows: 5 ENTRY

Past: 3 **AGO** 7 ONETIME
Are in the: 4 WERE
Blast from the: 5 ATEST NTEST OLDIE
due: 4 LATE
Ending for: 3 URE
Evoking the: 5 RETRO
Fifty minutes: 5 TENTO
Get: 5 ELUDE
Go: 4 OMIT SKIP
In days: 3 AGO
In the: 3 **AGO** 4 ONCE
In the ~, in the past: 4 ERST
In the recent: 6 LATELY OFLATE
Is in the: 3 WAS
Long: 6 OFYORE
Not long: 6 RECENT
Of time: 5 OLDEN
one's prime: 4 AGED
or present: 5 TENSE
Piece of the: 3 ERA 5 RELIC
Put one: 3 ACE
Slip: 5 ELUDE
Song from the: 5 OLDIE
The ~, in the past: 3 ELD
the deadline: 4 LATE
Thing of the: 5 RELIC
Time: 4 THEN **YORE**
Times: 4 ERAS YORE
Went: 8 OVERSHOT
Pasta
choice: 4 ZITI 5 PENNE
Corkscrew: 6 ROTINI
dish: 7 LASAGNA
Firm: 7 ALDENTE
Green ~ sauce: 5 PESTO
ingredient: 8 SEMOLINA
in product names: 4 RONI
order: 7 ALDENTE
Popular ~, for short: 3 MAC
Ricelike: 4 ORZO
sauce maker: 4 RAGU
shape: 5 ELBOW SHELL 6 BOWTIE
Soup: 4 ORZO
suffix: 3 INI
topper: 5 PESTO SAUCE
Tubular: 4 ZITI 5 PENNE 8 RIGATONI

With ~, in product names:
5 ARONI
with pockets: 7 RAVIOLI
~, to an athlete: 4 CARB
Paste: 4 SOCK 6 WALLOP
Cut and: 4 EDIT
ingredient: 6 TOMATO
Polynesian: 3 POI
Sesame: 6 TAHINI
Soybean: 4 MISO
Pasted
in the ring: 3 KOD
Pastel
Hardly: 4 NEON
shade: 4 AQUA 5 LILAC
Pastels: 3 ART
Pasternak
heroine: 4 LARA
Pasteur
Chemist: 5 LOUIS
portrayer: 4 MUNI
Pastiche: 4 OLIO
Pastime
for Prince Charles: 4 POLO
Pub: 5 DARTS
Pastis
flavor: 5 ANISE
Pastoral: 5 IDYLL RURAL
6 SERENE
deity: 4 FAUN
pipe: 4 REED
place: 3 **LEA**
poem: 4 **IDYL** 5 IDYLL
7 ECLOGUE
sound: 3 BAA
"Pastoral" Symphony
Like Beethoven's: 3 INF
Pastrami
Like good: 4 LEAN
purveyor: 4 DELI
Pastry
Breakfast: 6 DANISH
Cream-filled: 6 ECLAIR
finisher: 4 ICER
Flaky: 4 FILO
French: 7 RISSOLE
Fruit: 4 TART 7 STRUDEL
Indian: 6 SAMOSA
Rich: 5 TORTE

shell: 4 PUFF
thickener: 4 AGAR
Pasture: 3 **LEA** 5 FIELD
mom: 3 EWE
sound: 3 BAA MAA MOO
Pastureland: 3 LEA
Pasty: 3 WAN 5 ASHEN
Pat: 3 DAB
Actor: 6 MORITA
Alternative nickname for: 5 TRISH
Didn't stand: 4 DREW
down: 4 TAMP
Former Knicks coach: 5 RILEY
gently: 3 DAB 5 DABAT
Had down: 4 KNEW
Host: 5 SAJAK
of fat: 4 OLEO
on the back: 4 BURP 6 PRAISE
on the buns: 4 OLEO
Vanna, to: 6 COHOST
Pataki
Gov. ~ place: 3 NYS
predecessor: 5 CUOMO
Patch: 6 REPAIR
Attach a: 5 SEWON 6 IRONON
Kind of: 3 PEA 6 IRONON
More than ~ up: 4 REDO
Needing a: 4 WORN
place: 3 EYE 4 KNEE
Place for a: 3 RIP 4 TEAR
up: 3 SEW 4 DARN HEAL MEND
6 REPAIR
Patchwork
Make a: 3 SEW
Some: 6 QUILTS
Patchy: 4 PIED
Pat-down: 5 FRISK
Paté
meat: 5 LIVER
Paté de foie ___: 4 GRAS
Paté de ___ gras: 4 FOIE
Patella: 7 KNEECAP
place: 4 **KNEE**
Patented
product names (abbr.): 3 TMS
Patents
Holder of 1,093: 6 EDISON
Pater ___ (Lord's Prayer):
6 NOSTER

Paternal
relative: 6 AGNATE
Paternity test
material: 3 DNA
site: 6 DNALAB
Path: 4 LANE 5 AISLE ROUTE
TRAIL
Bridal: 5 **AISLE**
Curved: 3 ESS
Data: 6 UPLINK
finder: 5 HIKER
Kind of: 4 BASE
Like a planetary: 7 ORBITAL
Mowing: 5 SWATH
Off the: 6 ASTRAY
Orbital: 7 ELLIPSE
Paperboy: 5 ROUTE
Pendulum: 3 **ARC**
Planetary: 5 ORBIT
Racer's: 4 OVAL
Runner's: 8 BASELINE
Slalom ~ part: 3 ESS
Spiritual: 3 TAO ZEN
Sprinter: 4 LANE
Wagon-wheel: 3 RUT
Winding: 3 ESS
Pathet ___ (Asian Party): 3 LAO
Pathetic: 3 SAD 4 LAME
person: 7 SADSACK
"Pathétique": 6 SONATA
Pathfinder
challenge: 4 MAZE
launcher: 4 NASA
target: 4 MARS
Pathogen
Rod-shaped: 5 ECOLI
Pathological
One might be: 4 LIAR
Paths
Puzzle with: 4 MAZE
Patience: 6 VIRTUE
Her ~ is legendary: 4 ENID
Paragon of: 3 JOB
Tax one's: 3 TRY
Patient
Be: 4 WAIT
gp.: 3 HMO
people: 7 ABIDERS
remark: 3 AHH

responses: 3 AHS
state: 4 COMA
wear: 4 GOWN
Patient-care
gp.: 3 HMO
Patients
A number of dental: 3 GAS
Place for nonresident:
6 CLINIC
Patina; 4 COAT 5 SHEEN
Patio
grill: 7 HIBACHI
Patisserie
product: 6 ECLAIR
worker: 4 ICER
Patois: 5 ARGOT
Paton
Author: 4 ALAN
___ patriae (patriotism): 4 AMOR
Patriarch: 5 ELDER 6 NESTOR
Biblical: 4 ENOS 5 ABRAM
ISAAC
Genesis: 4 ADAM
~ Clampett: 3 JED
Patricia
Actress: 4 **NEAL**
Patrick: 5 SAINT
Mame, to: 6 AUNTIE
of basketball: 5 EWING
Tony-winner: 5 MAGEE
Patriot: 3 SAM
Cuban: 5 MARTI
Hungarian ~ Nagy: 4 IMRE
Irish: 5 EMMET
Yugoslav: 4 TITO
~ Nathan: 4 **HALE**
~ Silas: 5 DEANE
"Patriot Games"
gp.: 3 IRA
Patriotic
chant: 3 USA 6 USAUSA
org.: 3 **DAR** SAR
symbol: 4 FLAG
women's org.: 3 DAR
Patriots
gp.: 3 AFC
org.: 3 NFL
Patriots' Day
month: 5 APRIL

Patrol
  Border ~ concern: 6 ALIENS
  car alert (abbr.): 3 APB
  Cop: 4 BEAT
  Vietnam ~ boat: 8 RIVERRAT
Patroller
  Highway: 7 TROOPER
Patron: 4 USER 6 CLIENT
  Airlines: 5 FLIER
  Bank: 5 SAVER
  Goya: 4 ALBA
  Library: 4 USER
  Pol: 6 FATCAT
  Renaissance: 4 ESTE
  Restaurant: 5 EATER
  Sailor: 6 STELMO
Patronage: 5 AEGIS
Patronize: 5 BUYAT 6 SHOPAT
  a motel: 6 STAYAT
  a restaurant: 5 EATAT 6 DINEAT
Patronizing
  person: 4 SNOB
Patrons
  Starts to receive: 5 OPENS
Patron saint
  of France: 5 DENIS
  of Norway: 4 OLAF OLAV
  of sailors: 4 ELMO
Patsy: 3 **SAP** 4 DUPE FOIL
      5 CHUMP 8 EASYMARK
  Make a ~ of: 3 USE
  Pal of: 5 EDINA
  Singer: 5 **CLINE**
Patter
  Pigeon: 3 COO
Pattern
  Behavior: 5 HABIT
  Dance: 4 STEP
  Follow a: 3 SEW
  Graph: 4 GRID
  Ice cream: 5 SWIRL
  Intricate: 3 WEB
  Kilt: 6 TARTAN
  of diamonds: 6 ARGYLE
  Predictable: 8 SYNDROME
  Quatrain: 4 ABBA
  Radial: 5 TREAD
  Ripply: 5 MOIRE
  Sock: 6 ARGYLE

  Tartan: 5 PLAID 6 ARGYLE
  Tire: 5 TREAD
  Wavy: 5 MOIRE
  Wood: 5 GRAIN
Patterned
  Delicately: 4 LACY
  fabric: 5 TOILE 6 DAMASK
Patterns
  Criminal: 3 MOS
  Paintings with geometric:
      5 OPART
Patti
  Singer: 4 PAGE 6 LUPONE
      7 ADELINA LABELLE
Patton
  protrayer: 5 SCOTT
Patty
  place: 3 BUN
  Rock singer: 5 SMYTH
Paucity
  of pep: 6 ANEMIA
Paul: 3 MRS 4 POPE TSAR
      5 SAINT 6 BEATLE
      7 APOSTLE
  1933 Nobelist ~: 5 DIRAC
  1943 Oscar winner ~:
      5 LUKAS
  1992 presidential hopeful ~:
      7 TSONGAS
  Acting daughter of: 4 MIRA
  Comedian: 5 LYNDE
  Director: 9 VERHOEVEN
  Guitarist: 3 **LES**
  Longest letter of: 6 ROMANS
  of Peter, Paul, and Mary:
      7 STOOKEY
  or Carly: 5 SIMON
  Peter and ~ (abbr.): 3 STS
  role: 3 **ARI**
  Singer: 4 **ANKA**
  status: 8 SAINTDOM
  suffix: 3 INE
  Swiss painter: 4 KLEE
Paula
  Actress: 8 PRENTISS
  Newscaster: 4 ZAHN
  Singer: 5 ABDUL
Pauley Pavilion
  team: 4 UCLA

Pauline
Film critic: 4 **KAEL**
problem: 5 **PERIL**
___ Paulo: 3 **SAO**
Paulsen
Skater: 4 AXEL
Paul V
predecessor: 5 LEOXI
Paunch: 3 POT
Pause: 4 REST 5 LETUP
Cause for: 5 COMMA
9 SEMICOLON
in the action: 4 LULL
Poet: 7 CAESURA
sign: 5 COMMA
Pauses
Speaker: 3 ERS
Pavarotti: 5 **TENOR**
birthplace: 6 MODENA
piece: 4 ARIA
Tenor: 7 LUCIANO
Pave
over: 5 RETAR
Pavement: 7 MACADAM
caution: 3 **SLO**
material: 3 TAR
Paves
It ~ the way: 3 TAR 7 ASPHALT
Pavilion: 6 GAZEBO
Pavin
Golfer: 5 COREY
Paving
In need of: 5 RUTTY
material: 3 TAR 7 MACADAM
pieces: 6 STONES
stone: 4 SETT
Pavlov
dog output: 6 SALIVA
Nobelist: 4 IVAN
Physiologist: 4 IVAN
Pavlova
attire: 4 TUTU
Ballerina: 4 **ANNA**
portrayal: 4 SWAN
Paw: 4 MITT
Cat's: 3 TOM
Pal with a: 3 PET
part: 3 PAD
Partner of: 3 MAW

Pawn: 4 DUPE HOCK 5 AGENT
"Pawnbroker, The"
actor Rod: 7 STEIGER
Pawned: 6 INHOCK
Pawns: 5 OCTET
Pawnshop
Leave at a: 4 HOCK
Pax ___: 6 ROMANA
Pay: 5 REMIT WAGES 6 ANTEUP
PONYUP SALARY
attention: 6 LISTEN
9 LENDANEAR
attention to: 4 HEED OBEY
back: 3 OLA 6 AVENGE
Bills to: 5 DEBTS
dirt: 3 **ORE**
ending: 3 OLA
for: 4 FOOT
for a hand: 4 ANTE
for dinner: 5 TREAT
Have to ~ back: 3 OWE
heed: 4 OBEY
Hourly: 4 WAGE
Kind of: 4 BASE
Need to: 3 OWE
no attention to: 6 IGNORE
7 NEGLECT
One way to: 4 CASH 6 CHARGE
INCASH
out: 5 SPEND
period: 4 WEEK
phone feature: 4 SLOT
Promise to: 3 IOU
Small price to: 4 CENT
stub: 3 **OLA**
stub abbr.: 3 YTD
stub fig.: 4 FICA
suffix: 3 **OLA**
Take-home: 3 NET
They play for: 4 PROS
to play: 4 **ANTE**
tribute to: 5 HONOR 6 SALUTE
up: 5 REMIT SPEND
6 SETTLE
(up): 4 PONY
What you: 4 COST
with plastic: 6 CHARGE
Payable: 3 DUE
Become: 7 FALLDUE

It may be ~ (abbr.): **4** ACCT

Payback
Get ~ for: **6** AVENGE
Manufacturer: **6** REBATE

"Payback"
actor Kristofferson: **4** KRIS

Paycheck
abbr.: **4** FICA
booster: **8** OVERTIME
deduction: **8** STATETAX

Pay dirt: 3 ORE

Payee: 6 BEARER
Apr.: **3** IRS

Payer
Dues ~ (abbr.): **3** MEM
Full-price: **5** ADULT
Rent: **6** LESSEE TENANT

Paying
attention: **5** ALERT
passenger: **4** FARE

Payment: 8 REMITTAL
Car: **4** TOLL
Demand: **3** DUN
Lawyer: **3** FEE
Monthly: **4** RENT
option: **4** CASH
Pester for: **3** DUN
Poker: **4 ANTE**
Press for: **3 DUN**
Send: **5 REMIT**
Simple ~ form: **4** CASH
Tenant: **4** RENT
Tiny: **4** CENT
Under-the-table: **5** BRIBE
Upfront: **4** ANTE

"Pay ___ mind": 4 ITNO

Payne
Golfer: **7** STEWART
Singer: **5** FREDA

Payoff: 3 SOP **6** REWARD
Ransom: **4** DROP

Payola: 5 GRAFT

Payout
Commuter: **4** TOLL

Payroll
Add to the: **4** HIRE
category: **4** RATE
On the: **8** SALARIED
Put on the: **4 HIRE**

Put on the ~ again: **6** REHIRE
~ ID: **3** SSN

Pay-___-view: 3 PER

Pb: 4 LEAD

PBS
Charlie of: **4** ROSE
funder: **3 NEA**
newsman: **6** LEHRER
NYC ~ flagship: **4** WNET
"science guy": **3** NYE
science show: **4 NOVA**
supporter: **3** NEA

PC
alternative: **3** MAC **4 IMAC**
bailout: **3** ESC
brain: **3** CPU
component: **3** CPU CRT
core: **3** CPU
environment: **5** MSDOS
expert: **4** TECH
format: **5** MSDOS
hookup: **3** CRT LAN
insert: **5** CDROM
key: **3** ALT **ESC 5** ENTER
   6 DELETE
Kind of ~ monitor: **3** LCD
letters: **5** EMAIL
linkup: **3 LAN**
listing: **4** MENU
maker: **3** IBM
monitor: **3 CRT**
owner: **4** USER
panic button: **3** ESC
part: **3** CRT
perch: **3** LAP
person: **4** USER
pic: **4** ICON
platform: **3** DOS
Popular ~ game: **4** DOOM
Portable: **6** LAPTOP
program: **3** APP
screen: **3** CRT
shortcut: **5** MACRO
software: **5** MSDOS
storage medium: **5** CDROM
support staff: **5** TECHS
troubleshooter: **4** TECH

PCBs
Org. concerned about: **3** EPA

P.D.
 alert: 3 APB
 employee: 4 INSP
 rank: 3 DET 4 INSP
PDA
 entry: 4 APPT
 no.: 4 NSEC
P. Diddy
 First name of: 4 SEAN
PDQ: 4 **ASAP**
 in the ER: 4 STAT
P/E: 5 RATIO
Pea: 6 LEGUME
 holder: 3 CAN POD
 jacket: 3 POD
Pea-___ (dense fog): 6 SOUPER
___' Pea: 4 **SWEE**
Peace
 agreement: 4 PACT
 and quiet: 4 CALM
 At: 6 SERENE
 bird: 4 DOVE
 goddess: 5 IRENE
 Gp. in ~ accords: 3 IRA
 In: 8 SERENELY
 Kind of: 5 INNER
 maker: 7 ENTENTE
 Norse god of: 4 FREY
 offering: 6 AMENDS
 of mind: 4 EASE REST
   6 REPOSE
 personified: 5 IRENE
 Promoting: 6 IRENIC
 Russian: 3 MIR
 suffix: 3 NIK
 symbol: 3 VEE 4 DOVE
 treaty: 4 PACT
Peace Corps
 cousin: 5 VISTA
Peaceful: 6 IRENIC SERENE
 greeting: 6 SALAAM
 place: 7 ARCADIA
 protest: 5 SITIN
Peace Garden State
 (abbr.): 4 NDAK
Peacekeeping
 gp.: 4 NATO
 skill: 4 TACT
Peacenik: 4 DOVE

 slogan: 7 NONUKES
Peace Nobelist
 1912 ~: 4 ROOT
 1962 ~: 12 LINUSPAULING
 1969 ~ gp.: 3 ILO
 1971 ~: 6 BRANDT
 1974 ~: 4 SATO
 1978 ~: 5 SADAT
 1983 ~: 6 WALESA
 1984 ~: 4 **TUTU**
 1987 ~: 5 ARIAS
 1989 ~: 9 DALAILAMA
 1993 ~: 7 MANDELA
 1994 ~: 5 PERES RABIN
   6 ARAFAT
 South African: 4 TUTU
 ~ Cassin: 4 RENE
 ~ Ducommun: 4 ELIE
 ~ Eisaku: 4 SATO
 ~ John Boyd ___: 3 ORR
 ~ Ralph: 6 BUNCHE
 ~ Root: 5 ELIHU
 ~ Sakharov: 6 ANDREI
 ~ Wiesel: 4 ELIE
Peace Prize
 city: 4 OSLO
Peach: 3 HUE 4 TREE 5 COLOR
 pulpy portion: 5 FLESH
 seed: 3 PIT
Peach ___: 5 **MELBA**
Peachy
 follower: 4 KEEN
 Just: 3 AOK 5 SWELL
 "Peachy!": 4 NEAT 5 NEATO
   NIFTY SWELL
Peachy-keen: 4 NEAT 5 NEATO
   NIFTY SWELL
Peacock
 Act like a: 5 PREEN
 constellation: 4 PAVO
 feather: 5 PLUME
 feather feature: 6 OCELLI
   7 EYESPOT
 Like a: 5 PROUD
 NBC: 4 LOGO
 network: 3 NBC
 pride: 4 TAIL 7 PLUMAGE
 Strut like a: 6 PARADE
 Walk like a: 5 STRUT

Peacock Throne
occupant: 4 SHAH
Peak: 4 ACME APEX 5 CREST
    MOUNT 6 APOGEE
    8 PINNACLE
At the: 5 ONTOP
Biblical: 5 HOREB
California: 6 **SHASTA**
Craggy: 3 TOR
Cretan: 3 IDA
French: 4 ALPE
Greek: 4 **OSSA**
High: 3 ALP
in myth: 4 OSSA
in W. Turkey: 5 MTIDA
Japanese: 4 FUJI
no.: 4 ELEV
On the ~ of: 4 ATOP
Ore.: 6 MTHOOD
peak: 9 MTEVEREST
performance: 5 YODEL
Reach a: 5 CREST
Rocky: 3 TOR
Sicilian: 4 ETNA
Swiss: 3 **ALP**
Thessaly: 4 OSSA
Turkish: 6 ARARAT
Peaked
A bit: 6 PALISH
Peaks
(abbr.): 3 MTS 4 MTNS
Austrian: 4 ALPS
Peruvian: 5 ANDES
Peal: 4 TOLL
Mournful: 5 KNELL
Pealed: 4 RANG
Peanut: 6 GOOBER LEGUME
product: 3 **OIL**
Peanut butter: 6 SPREAD
brand: 3 JIF
choice: 6 SMOOTH
container: 3 JAR
cup maker: 6 REESES
___ **Peanut Butter Cups:** 6 REESES
Peanut Butter Lovers Mo.: 3 NOV
Peanuts
Like many: 6 SALTED
"Peanuts"
boy: 5 LINUS

Dirty ~ character: 6 PIGPEN
expletive: 4 RATS
girl: 4 LUCY
One never seen in: 5 ADULT
Pear: 4 POME TREE
Alligator: 7 AVOCADO
Prickly: 6 CACTUS
Type of: 6 SECKEL
variety: 4 **BOSC** 5 ANJOU
Pearl: 5 ONION
Fake: 6 OLIVET
Milton: 3 ODE
Perlman who played: 4 RHEA
producer: 6 OYSTER
Pearl City
locale: 4 OAHU
Pearl Harbor
attack plane: 4 ZERO
island: 4 OAHU
ship: 4 UTAH 6 NEVADA
    7 ARIZONA
"Pearl Harbor"
Baldwin of: 4 ALEC
Pearl Mosque
city: 4 **AGRA**
Pearly
Show one's ~ whites: 5 SMILE
whites: 5 TEETH
Pearly Gates
keeper: 7 STPETER
Pear-shaped
fruit: 3 FIG
instrument: 4 LUTE 5 SITAR
Pearson
Canadian statesman:
    6 LESTER
Peary
Of interest to: 5 POLAR
Peas
Resembling two ~ in a pod:
    5 ALIKE
~, to a prankster: 4 AMMO
Peasant: 4 SERF
costume part: 6 BODICE
dress: 6 DIRNDL
skirt: 6 DIRNDL
Peat: 4 MOSS
source: 3 BOG
Peau de ___ (silk cloth): 4 SOIE

Pebble Beach
  hazard: 4 TRAP
  pastime: 4 GOLF
  peg: 3 TEE
Pebbles
  Fred, to: 3 DAD
  hair accessory: 4 BONE
  Mother of: 5 WILMA
  pet: 4 DINO
Pec
  neighbor: 3 LAT
Pecan: 3 NUT PIE 4 TREE
  confection: 7 PRALINE
Peccadillo: 3 SIN
Peck: 4 TYPE
  and Remick film: 7 THEOMEN
  Partner of: 4 HUNT
  pic topic: 4 OMEN
  role: 4 AHAB
Pecker
  Woodpecker: 4 BEAK
Peckinpah
  Director: 3 SAM
Pecksniff
  Dickens's: 4 SETH
Pecs
  display case: 3 BOD
  kin: 3 ABS
Pectin
  React to: 3 GEL
Peculiar: 3 ODD 5 WEIRD
  expression: 5 IDIOM
  It's: 7 ANOMALY
  prefix: 4 IDIO
Peculiarity: 5 TRAIT
  Language: 5 IDIOM
PED ___: 4 XING
Pedagogic
  org.: 3 NEA
Pedal: 4 BIKE
  digit: 3 TOE
  pusher: 4 FOOT 5 BIKER
  pushers: 4 FEET
  Put the ~ to the metal: 4 SPED
Peddle: 4 HAWK SELL VEND
  Peddlers ~ them: 5 WARES
Peddler
  aim: 4 SALE
Pedestal: 4 BASE

figure: 4 IDOL
part: 4 BASE **DADO**
Piece on a: 3 URN
Put on a: 5 **ADORE** DEIFY
    EXULT 6 ADORED ESTEEM
    7 ADULATE ELEVATE
    8 IDEALIZE VENERATE
topper: 4 IDOL
Pedestrian
  Law-breaking: 9 JAYWALKER
  Like an unlucky winter:
    7 SLUSHED
  path: 4 WALK
Pediatrician
  Noted: 7 DRSPOCK
Pedicurist
  target: 7 TOENAIL
  workplace: 4 TOES 5 SALON
Pedigree
  org.: 3 AKC
  part: 4 SIRE
  rival: 4 ALPO
Pedometer
  New ~ reading: 3 OOO
Pedro
  Info: Spanish cue
  Intro to: 3 SAN SAO
  pal: 5 AMIGO
  parlor: 4 SALA
Pedro, Dom
  Wife of: 4 INES
Peek: 4 LOOK 6 GLANCE
  follower: 4 **ABOO**
  in (on): 3 SPY
  Sneak ~ (var.): 6 PREVUE
Peek-___: 4 **ABOO**
Peekaboo
  follower: 7 ISEEYOU
  words: 4 ISEE
Peel: 4 **PARE** RIND SKIN 5 STRIP
  Fruit: 4 RIND
  Fruit with a: 6 BANANA
  in a drink: 5 TWIST
  Lemon: 4 RIND ZEST
Peel, Mrs.: 7 AVENGER
  Partner of: 5 STEED
  portrayer: 4 RIGG
Peeler: 5 PARER
"Peel ___ grape": 3 MEA

Peeling
  potatoes, perhaps: 4 ONKP
Peep
  Sheep: 3 BAA
"Peep at Polynesian Life, A"
  Novel subtitled: 5 TYPEE
Peeper: 3 EYE 5 CHICK SNOOP
  place: 7 KEYHOLE
  problem: 4 STYE
  protector: 4 EYELID
Peepers: 4 ORBS
  Use one's: 3 SEE
Peeping Tom: 4 EYER 5 SPIER
  Play the: 6 PEERIN
Peeples
  Actress: 3 **NIA**
Peer: 5 EQUAL
  at a page: 4 READ
  British: 4 EARL LORD
    5 BARON
  group: 4 EYES JURY
  Without: 5 ALONE
"Peer ___": 4 GYNT
Peerage
  member: 4 EARL
"Peer Gynt"
  character: 3 ASE
  composer: 5 GRIEG
  dancer: 6 ANITRA
  playwright: 5 IBSEN
Peerless: 4 AONE 5 ALONE
Peeve: 3 IRK 4 RILE
  Pet: 4 FLEA
  PETA: 3 FUR
Peeved: 4 SORE 5 ANGRY CROSS
    6 INAPET 7 INASNIT
  In a ~ mood: 5 TESTY
  mood: 4 SNIT
  More: 5 IRATE
Peevish: 4 SOUR 5 TESTY
  complaint: 4 CARP
  state: 4 SNIT
  temper: 4 BILE
Peevishness: 4 BILE
Peewee: 4 MINI RUNT TINY
    6 TEENSY
Pee Wee
  of baseball: 5 **REESE**
  Teammate of: 3 GIL

Peg
  Golf: 3 TEE
  Small: 3 TEE
  Square ~ in a round hole:
    6 MISFIT
  Take down a: 5 ABASE
  Wooden: 5 DOWEL
Peggy
  Panelist: 4 CASS
  Singer: 3 LEE
  Speechwriter: 6 NOONAN
"Peg Woffington"
  author: 5 READE
PEI
  setting: 3 AST
Pei, Ieoh ___: 4 MING
Pei, I.M.
  alma mater: 3 MIT
  The "I" of: 4 IEOH
Pei, ___ Ming: 4 IEOH
Peke
  perch: 3 LAP
  squeak: 3 YIP
Peking
  suffix: 3 ESE
Pekoe: 3 **TEA**
  holder: 6 TEABAG
  server: 6 TEAPOT
  unit: 7 TEALEAF
Pelé
  given name: 5 EDSON
  org.: 4 NASL
Pelée
  spew: 4 LAVA
Pelion
  neighbor: 4 OSSA
Pell-___: 4 MELL
Pellagra
  preventer: 6 NIACIN
Pellet: 7 GRANULE
  propeller: 8 AIRRIFLE
  shooter: 3 PEA
Pellets
  Air-gun: 3 BBS
  Falling: 4 HAIL
Peloponnesian
  P: 3 RHO
Peloponnesian War
  victor: 6 SPARTA

Pelota
catcher: 5 CESTA
Pelt: 3 FUR 4 HIDE SKIN
    5 STONE 6 PEPPER
Pelvic: 5 ILIAC
bone: 5 ILIUM
bones: 4 ILIA 5 SACRA
parts: 4 ILIA
Pelvis
part: 6 SACRUM 7 HIPBONE
Pelvis-knee
connector: 5 FEMUR
Pemmican
Language that gives us: 4 CREE
Pen: 3 STY 4 SWAN 5 WRITE
    6 CORRAL FEMALE
    7 ENCLOSE
African cattle: 5 KRAAL
British: 4 GAOL
Bull ~ sound: 5 SNORT
Bull ~ stat: 3 ERA
fare: 4 SLOP
Farm: 3 STY
feature: 7 FELTTIP
filler: 3 INK
Hen's: 4 COOP
holder: 4 CELL
Kind of: 5 STATE
mother: 3 SOW
pal: 3 CON PIG SOW 5 SWINE
    6 INMATE OINKER
part: 4 CELL
partner: 3 PAD
point: 3 **NIB**
resident: 3 CON
sound: 4 OINK
stroke: 5 SERIF
Penalized: 5 FINED
Penalty: 4 FINE
caller: 3 REF
for not paying on time:
    7 LATEFEE
Paid the: 6 ATONED
Subject to a: 7 PASTDUE
Penance
Do: 5 **ATONE**
Penchant: 4 BIAS
Pencil
end: 6 ERASER

game entries: 7 XSANDOS
holder: 3 EAR
Much-used: 3 NUB 4 STUB
pusher: 5 CLERK 6 WRITER
puzzle: 4 MAZE
Styptic ~ stuff: 4 ALUM
topper: 6 ERASER
Use a ~ end: 5 ERASE
Use a blue: 4 EDIT
Pencil-and-paper
game: 4 DOTS MAZE
Pencil box
item: 5 RULER
Penciled
It may be ~ in: 7 EYEBROW
"Pencils down": 7 TIMESUP
Pendant
Fashionable: 7 EARDROP
gem shape: 8 TEARDROP
Polynesian: 4 TIKI
Pending
item: 6 PATENT
Pendleton
Actor: 3 NAT
Pendulum
direction: 3 FRO
Like a ~ motion: 8 TOANDFRO
partner: 3 PIT
path: 3 **ARC**
Penetrate: 5 ENTER
Hard to: 5 DENSE
slowly: 4 SEEP
Penetrating: 4 KEEN 5 ACUTE
    6 ASTUTE COGENT
quality: 4 EDGE
reed: 4 OBOE
Penguin
Antarctic: 6 **ADELIE**
Comics page: 4 OPUS
Penguins
1955 ~ hit: 10 EARTHANGEL
org.: 3 NHL
___ **Penh, Cambodia:** 4 PNOM
    5 PHNOM
Penicillin: 4 DRUG
source: 4 MOLD
target: 5 STREP
Peninsula
Adriatic: 6 ISTRIA

Asian: **5** KOREA MALAY
   6 ARABIA MALAYA
Black Sea: **6** CRIMEA
European: **6** IBERIA
It is mostly a ~ (abbr.): **3** FLA
Mexican: **4** BAJA
Mideast: **5** SINAI **6** ARABIA
Portugal: **6** IBERIA
Québec: **5** GASPE
Red Sea: **5** SINAI
World's largest: **6** ARABIA
___ Peninsula: 6 ARABIA BALKAN
   7 IBERIAN
Penitence
Period of: **4** LENT
Show: **5** ATONE
Penitent: 6 ATONER
person: **4** RUER **6** ATONER
Penlight
battery: **3** AAA
Penman: 6 SCRIBE
Penn: 4 SEAN **5** ACTOR
(abbr.): **3** STA
Actor: **4** <u>SEAN</u>
Like: **3** IVY
name: **4** <u>SEAN</u>
pal: **6** TELLER
specialty: **5** MAGIC
Penna
neighbor: **3** DEL
Pen name: 3 BIC **5** ALIAS FLAIR
Literary: **3** BOZ **4** ELIA SAKI
   5 TWAIN
Pennant: 4 FLAG
Took the: **3** WON
Penne: 5 PASTA
kin: **4** ZITI
Penned: 5 WROTE
Pennies: 5 ANTES
(abbr.): **3** CTS
Pack of: **4** ROLL
Pinch: **5** SKIMP STINT
Penniless: 5 BROKE
person: **4** HOBO
Penn Sta.
traffic: **3** RRS
Penn State
city: **4** ERIE
coach: **7** PATERNO

Penn Station
inits.: **4** LIRR
Pennsylvania: 6 AVENUE
(abbr.): **3** AVE
city: **4** ERIE **6** EASTON
   7 ALTOONA
county: **4** ERIE
port: **4** <u>ERIE</u>
resort area: **7** POCONOS
sect: **5** AMISH
university: **6** LEHIGH
Pennsylvania Dutch
Some: **5** AMISH
Penny: 4 <u>CENT</u>
component: **4** ZINC
pincher: **5** MISER PIKER
   6 CHEAPO
portrayal: **7** LAVERNE
Prez on a: **3** ABE
Word on a: **3** GOD ONE **4** UNUM
Penny ___: 4 ANTE
"... ___ penny earned": 3 ISA
Penny-pinching: 4 MEAN
Penobscot
City on the: **6** BANGOR
   11 BANGORMAINE
Penobscot River
city: **5** ORONO
Penpoint: 3 <u>NIB</u>
"Penrod"
pal: **3** SAM
Pens: 5 STYLI
Pension
agcy.: **3** SSA
alternative: **3** IRA
Become owned, as a: **4** VEST
On a ~ (abbr.): **3** RET **4** RETD
plan law: **5** ERISA
supplement: **3** IRA
Pensioner: 7 RETIREE
Pensive
sounds: **3** HMS
Pent
ending: **3** ANE
up: **5** CAGED
Penta
minus one: **5** TETRA
Pentacles
Deck with: **5** TAROT

Pentad
 Common: **6** SENSES
Pentagon
 bigwigs: **5** BRASS
Pentagram: 4 STAR
Pentameter
 parts: **5** IAMBS
Pentateuch: 5 TORAH
Pentathlete
 weapon: **4** EPEE
Pentathlon
 event: **4 EPEE**
Penthouse
 Escorts to a: **6** SEESUP
 Invite to a: **5** ASKUP
 plus: **4** VIEW
Pentium
 maker: **5** INTEL
Penultimate
 fairy tale word: **4** EVER
 Greek letter: **3** PSI
 letter: **3** WYE
Penury: 4 NEED
Penzance
 prison: **4** GAOL
Peony
 part: **5** PETAL **6** PISTIL
People
 Dear: **4** SIRS
 Home to most: **4** ASIA
 Laid-back ~ category: **5** TYPEB
 Med.: **3** DRS
 Meet: **6** RACERS
 of action: **5** DOERS
 Party: **5** HOSTS
 people (abbr.): **3** EDS
 person: **5** CELEB
 PR: **4** AGTS
 prefix: **5** ETHNO
 Prized: **5** DEARS
 Self-employed: **3** EDS
 Short ~ write them: **4** IOUS
 Some ~ can't take one: **4** HINT
 Spirit of a: **5** ETHOS
 Those: **4** THEY
 to hang with: **4** PALS
 Where ~ rush: **4** FRAT
 who knead people: **8** MASSEURS
 with pistols: **8** STARTERS

 Work with: **4** EDIT
"People's Court, The"
 former judge: **4** KOCH
Pep: 3 VIM **4** BRIO ELAN ZEST
    5 VIGOR **6** ENERGY
 Full of: **4** PERT SPRY **5** ALIVE
 Give a ~ talk to: **6** EXHORT
 rally cry: **3** RAH
 up: **7** ANIMATE
Pepe
 Cartoon skunk: **5** LEPEW
Pepe Le ___ (Boyer role): 4 MOKO
Pepe Le Pew
 defense: **4** ODOR
Peppard, George
 1980s ~ costar: **3** MRT
 TV series, with "The": **5** ATEAM
Pepper
 (abbr.): **3** SGT
 and others: **3** DRS **4** SGTS
 from above: **6** STRAFE
 Hot: **7** CAYENNE **8** JALAPENO
 Kind of: **4** BELL **5** BETEL
    7 CAYENNE **8** JALAPENO
 Partner of: **4** SALT
 Pickled ~ measure: **4** PECK
 plant: **5** BETEL
 reaction: **6** SNEEZE
___ Pepper: 3 SGT
Pepperidge Farm
 cookie brand: **6** MILANO
Peppermint
 candy: **6** PATTIE
Peppermint Patty
 ~, to Marcie: **3** SIR
"Peppermint Twist"
 singer: **7** JOEYDEE
 singer Joey: **3** DEE
Peppery: 3 HOT **7** PUNGENT
Peppy: 4 SPRY **8** SPIRITED
Pepsi: 4 COLA SODA
 bottle size: **5** LITER
 Coke vs. ~ event: **9** TASTETEST
 rival: **4** COKE **6** RCCOLA
Pepsin: 6 ENZYME
Pepsi-owned
 juice drink: **4** SOBE
Peptic
 problem: **5** ULCER

Pepys: 7 DIARIST
  kept one: 5 DIARY
Pequod
  captain: 4 **AHAB**
  hand: 7 ISHMAEL
Per: 4 **APOP** EACH 6 APIECE
Per ___ : 4 **DIEM** 5 ANNUM
    6 CAPITA
Pera
  Author: 3 PIA
Perambulate: 4 WALK
___ Percé: 3 NEZ
Perceive: 4 ESPY FEEL 5 SENSE
    6 DESCRY 7 DISCERN
Perceived: 4 KNEW SEEN
  to be: 6 SEENAS
Percent
  100 ~: 3 ALL 4 PURE
  Fifty: 4 HALF
  Increase by 200: 6 TREBLE
  suffix: 3 **ILE**
Percentage: 4 PART 5 SHARE
  for the IRS: 7 TAXRATE
Percenter
  Ten ~ (abbr.): 3 AGT
Perception: 3 EYE 7 INSIGHT
  General: 5 IMAGE
  Of: 7 SENSATE
  Sound: 3 EAR
Perceptive: 4 KEEN 5 ACUTE
    SHARP 6 ASTUTE
Perch: 3 SIT 5 **ROOST**
  Bird: 4 WIRE 5 LEDGE ROOST
    7 TREETOP
  Came to: 4 ALIT
  Church: 3 PEW
  Couch potato: 4 SOFA
  Dummy's: 4 KNEE
  Lofty: 7 TREETOP
  Mountain cat: 5 ARETE
  Mountain goat: 4 CRAG
  Muezzin: 7 MINARET
  Pet: 3 LAP
  Pie: 4 SILL
  Pigskin: 3 TEE
  Pub: 5 STOOL
  Toddler: 4 KNEE
  Yodeler: 3 ALP
Perched: 3 SAT

  on: 4 **ATOP**
Percolate: 4 OOZE **SEEP** 5 LEACH
Percussion
  cap: 9 DETONATOR
  Chinese: 4 GONG
  Impromptu: 6 SPOONS
  instrument: 4 DRUM GONG
    5 GOURD 6 BONGOS
    TOMTOM 7 MARIMBA
    9 SNAREDRUM
    10 KETTLEDRUM
  set: 7 TYMPANI
Percussionist
  ~ Puente: 4 TITO
Père
  sibling: 5 ONCLE
Père ___ : 6 GORIOT
"Perelandra"
  author: 7 CSLEWIS
Perennial
  campaign issue: 4 JOBS
  defender: 4 EAST
  Garden: 7 BEGONIA
  Showy: 6 DAHLIA
Perennials
  Showy: 5 CROCI
Peres
  of Israel: 6 SHIMON
  predecessor: 5 RABIN
___ Peres, Missouri: 3 DES
Peretti
  Designer: 4 ELSA
Perez
  Actress: 5 ROSIE
Pérez de Cuéllar
  home: 4 PERU
Pérez Esquivel, ___
  1980 Peace Nobelist ~:
    6 ADOLFO
Perfboard
  insert: 3 PEG
  Repair a: 5 REPEG
Perfect: 3 AOK 4 HONE MINT
    5 **IDEAL** 9 ERRORLESS
  accord: 6 UNISON
  for NASA: 3 AOK
  game catcher: 9 YOGIBERRA
  In ~ condition: 4 MINT
  It may be: 5 TENSE

Like a ~ game: 5 NOHIT
Like a ~ plan: 9 FOOLPROOF
model: 5 IDEAL
Not: 6 FLAWED
number: 3 TEN
or present: 5 TENSE
place: 4 **EDEN** 6 UTOPIA
prose: 4 EDIT
rating: 3 TEN
score: 3 **TEN**
serve: 3 ACE
world: 6 UTOPIA
"Perfect!": 3 AOK
"Perfect Fool, The": 6 EDWYNN
Perfection
First name in Olympic: 5 NADIA
Gymnastic: 3 TEN
Standard of: 5 IDEAL
Perfectionist: 8 STICKLER
aim: 5 IDEAL
Perfectly: 3 PAT 4 TOAT
6 **TOATEE**
clear: 5 LUCID
Do: 4 NAIL
draftable: 4 ONEA
Execute: 4 NAIL
matched: 8 ONETOONE
Not ~ round: 5 OVOID
Served: 4 ACED
timed: 5 ONCUE
vertical: 5 PLUMB
Perfecto: 5 CIGAR
"Perfect Peace, A"
author: 6 AMOSOZ
Perfect Sleeper
maker: 5 SERTA
"Perfect Spy, A"
author: 7 LECARRE
"... ___ perfect union ...":
5 AMORE
Perform: 3 ACT 6 RENDER
a canticle: 6 INTONE
again: 4 REDO
better than: 5 OUTDO
penance: 5 ATONE
Performance: 3 GIG
Diva: 4 ARIA
hall: 5 ODEUM
Individual: 4 SOLO

Jazz: 3 JAM
Kind of: 4 GALA
Like a super: 5 BOFFO
Met: 5 OPERA
Peak: 5 YODEL
Price: 5 OPERA
Repeat: 4 ECHO 6 ENCORE
Performed: 3 **DID**
in Shakespeare: 5 DIDST
Poorly: 4 LAME
satisfactorily: 5 DIDOK
Performer: 4 DOER 7 ARTISTE
Aquarium: 4 SEAL
Camel: 6 SKATER
Circus: 4 FLEA SEAL
9 LIONTAMER
15 HUMANCANNONBALL
CPR: 3 EMT
Nightclub: 5 COMIC
Public: 7 ARTISTE
Rodeo: 5 ROPER
Street: 4 MIME
thrill: 15 STANDINGOVATION
"Wave": 3 FAN
with lions: 5 TAMER
Performing: 7 ONSTAGE
Performing ___ : 4 ARTS
Performs: 4 DOES
Perfume: 5 AROMA ATTAR
CENSE SCENT 7 ESSENCE
Apply: 5 SPRAY
bottle name: 5 ESTEE
brand: 4 TABU
compound: 5 ESTER
holder: 4 VIAL
ingredient: 4 MUSK 5 ATTAR
6 ACETAL
oil: 5 ATTAR 6 NEROLI
Petal: 5 ATTAR
resin: 5 ELEMI
root: 5 ORRIS
Pergola: 5 ARBOR
Perhaps: 5 MAYBE
Peri
Actress: 6 GILPIN
role: 3 ROZ
Pericles
Opponent of: 5 CLEON
___ **Perignon:** 3 DOM

Peril: 6 DANGER HAZARD
   MENACE
   Sailor: 4 REEF
Perimeter: 3 RIM 4 EDGE
   contents: 4 AREA
   Green: 5 APRON
Per ___ income: 6 CAPITA
Period: 3 AGE DOT END **ERA**
   4 TERM 5 EPOCH STAGE
   6 TENURE
   Calendar: 4 WEEK YEAR
   Cong.: 4 SESS
   Crisis: 8 REDALERT
   Geologic: 3 EON 5 EPOCH
   Grace: 4 AMEN
   Historical: 3 AGE **ERA** 5 EPOCH
   Interim: 8 MEANTIME
   Legal hunting: 10 OPENSEASON
   Long: 3 EON 5 EPOCH
   Notable: 3 ERA 5 EPOCH
   of decline: 7 EBBTIDE
   of devotions: 6 NOVENA
   of duty: 4 TOUR
   of greatest success: 6 HEYDAY
   of note: 3 ERA
   of office: 4 TERM
   of penitence: 4 LENT
   of power: 5 REIGN
   of time: 4 SPAN 5 SPELL STINT
   on the throne: 5 REIGN
   Pay: 4 WEEK
   piece: 3 ERA 5 EPOCH
   Pique: 4 SNIT
   place: 3 END
   Postwar: 9 PEACETIME
   Preceding: 3 EVE
   Prosperous: 4 BOOM
   Quiet: 4 LULL
   School: 4 TERM
   Significant: 3 ERA
   "Spring fwd.": 3 DST
   Subscription: 4 YEAR
   Telegram: 4 STOP
   Time: 3 ERA 4 SPAN 5 SPELL
   Tiny time ~ (abbr.): 4 NSEC
Periodical
   Fan ~, for short: 4 ZINE
   for short: 3 MAG
   Online: 4 EMAG 5 EZINE

   piece: 7 ARTICLE
Periodically: 7 ATTIMES
Periodic Table
   abbr.: 4 ATNO ATWT
   entry: 7 ELEMENT
   stat.: 4 ATNO
"Periodic Table, The"
   author: 4 LEVI 9 PRIMOLEVI
Periodontist
   deg.: 3 DDS
   gp.: 3 ADA
Periods
   Good: 3 UPS
   Group of: 3 ERA
   Morning: 3 AMS
   Tie-breaking ~ (abbr.): 3 OTS
Peripheral: 5 ADDON
Periphery: 3 RIM 4 EDGE
   6 FRINGE
Periscope
   part: 4 LENS 5 PRISM
   6 MIRROR
Perjure
   oneself: 3 LIE
Perjurer: 4 LIAR
Perjury
   Commit: 3 LIE
Perk: 6 REWARD
   Executive: 11 STOCKOPTION
   up: 4 WHET 5 LIVEN
   7 ANIMATE
Perking
   place: 3 URN
Perkins
   role: 5 BATES
   Songwriter: 4 CARL
Perky: 4 SPRY
Perle
   Hostess: 5 **MESTA**
Perlman
   Actress: 4 **RHEA**
   instrument: 6 VIOLIN
   Violinist: 6 ITZHAK
Permafrost
   region: 6 TUNDRA
Permanent
   feature: 4 WAVE
   location: 5 SALON
   Make: 4 ETCH

mark: 4 SCAR
One sans ~ address: 5 NOMAD
pen pal: 5 LIFER
Permanently: 5 ININK
    7 FORGOOD
Dwell: 6 RESIDE
Mark: 4 ETCH
~, in poetry: 3 EER
Permeate: 4 SEEP 5 IMBUE
Permed
Like ~ hair: 4 WAVY
Permissible: 5 LICIT
Permission: 5 LEAVE
Give ~ to: 3 LET 5 ALLOW
Legal: 7 RELEASE
Refuse to give: 5 SAYNO
to go: 5 LEAVE
Permissive: 3 LAX 7 LENIENT
Permit: 3 **LET** 5 ALLOW
    6 ENABLE 7 LICENSE
Passport: 4 VISA
"Permit Me Voyage"
author: 4 AGEE
Permitted: 5 LEGAL LICIT
Pernod
flavoring: 5 **ANISE**
Peron
Ms.: 3 EVA
Musical about: 5 EVITA
Perot: 7 ALSORAN
Businessman/candidate: 4 ROSS
    5 HROSS
Co. founded by: 3 EDS
party (abbr.): 3 IND
Treaty opposed by: 5 NAFTA
Perp
alert: 3 APB
Help a: 4 ABET
Pinch a: 3 NAB
prosecutors: 3 DAS
story: 5 ALIBI
Perpendicular
to long.: 3 LAT
to radial: 5 AXIAL
to the keel: 5 ABEAM
Perpetrator: 4 DOER 5 FELON
    7 CULPRIT
Genesis: 4 CAIN
Rue Morgue: 3 APE

"___ perpetua" (Idaho's motto):
    4 **ESTO**
Perpetual: 7 AGELESS ENDLESS
    ETERNAL
~, in poetry: 6 ETERNE
Perplex: 5 STUMP 6 BEMUSE
Perplexed: 4 ASEA LOST 5 **ATSEA**
    7 ATALOSS
~, after "at": 5 ALOSS
Perplexing
path: 4 MAZE
Perrier
rival: 5 **EVIAN**
Perrins
Partner of: 3 LEA
Perry
creator: 4 ERLE
Designer: 5 **ELLIS**
secretary: 5 **DELLA**
Singer: 4 COMO
victory site: 4 ERIE
Persecute: 6 HARASS
Persephone
Husband of: 5 HADES
Mother of: 7 DEMETER
Persepolis
Home of ancient: 4 IRAN
Perseus
Monster slain by: 6 MEDUSA
Mother of: 5 DANAE
Person ~ petrified: 5 ATLAS
star: 5 **ALGOL**
Persevere: 4 COPE 6 HANGIN
    KEEPAT 7 PRESSON
Pershing
nickname: 9 BLACKJACK
~ WWI gp.: 3 AEF
Persia
Faith that arose in: 5 BAHAI
Queen of ~, in the Bible:
    6 ESTHER
today: 4 **IRAN**
Persian: 3 CAT RUG 5 FARSI
Ancient: 4 MEDE
despot: 6 SATRAP
emperor: 5 CYRUS
fairy: 4 PERI
for "king": 4 SHAH
Former ~ ruler: 4 SHAH

for "rose water": 5 JULEP
Modern: 5 FARSI IRANI
Person in ~ folklore: 7 ALIBABA
plaint: 3 MEW
pleasure: 6 CATNIP
poet: 4 OMAR
religion: 5 BAHAI
royal name: 6 DARIUS XERXES
ruler: 4 SHAH
Speak: 4 MEOW
Persian Gulf
capital: 6 TEHRAN 8 ABUDHABI
emirate: 5 DUBAI QATAR
    8 ABUDHABI
fed.: 3 UAE
nation: 4 IRAN 5 QATAR
port: 5 BASRA DUBAI
ruler: 4 EMIR
ship: 5 OILER
Persiflage: 6 BANTER
Persist: 4 LAST 5 RECUR
    6 KEEPAT LINGER
suffix: 3 ENT 4 ENCE
Persisted: 6 HUNGON KEPTAT
"Persistence of Memory, The"
painter: 4 DALI
Persistent
desire: 7 CRAVING
Persistently
Bother: 3 NAG 5 EATAT **NAGAT**
    6 HARASS PESTER
Follow: 3 DOG
Person: 3 ONE 4 NOUN
Accommodating: 5 SPORT
Active: 4 DOER
Adored: 4 IDOL
Any: 3 ONE
August: 3 LEO
Chair: 5 TAMER
Cruel: 4 OGRE
Delivery ~ path: 5 ROUTE
Displaced: 6 EMIGRE
First: 4 ADAM
First ~ in Berlin: 3 ICH
Fourth: 4 ABEL
Funny: 5 CUTUP
Gifted: 5 DONEE
Hilarious: 4 RIOT
Hill ~ (abbr.): 3 SEN

Holy: 6 TERROR
Impertinent: 4 SNIP
In: 4 LIVE
in a mask: 3 UMP
in a pool: 5 STENO
in the left lane: 6 PASSER
of action: 4 DOER
of great interest: 6 USURER
on a soapbox: 6 ORATOR
Patronizing: 4 SNOB
PC: 4 USER
People: 5 CELEB
Per: 4 APOP EACH
Personnel: 5 HIRER
Pompous: 3 ASS
Powerful: 5 NABOB
PR: 5 AGENT
Promising: 5 COMER
Remarkable: 4 LULU
Right-hand: 4 AIDE
Second: 3 EVE YOU
Singular: 4 ONER
Support: 5 AIDER
Twisted: 5 SICKO
Unique: 4 ONER
Which: 3 WHO
Wise: 4 SAGE
with a mike: 5 EMCEE
with hives: 8 APIARIST
~, informally: 3 EGG
Persona: 4 ROLE 5 IMAGE
Chaplin: 5 TRAMP
Fields: 3 SOT
non grata: 5 LEPER
Public: 5 IMAGE
Skelton: 4 HOBO
Persona ___ grata: 3 NON
Personal: 3 OWN
account: 6 MEMOIR
ad abbr.: 3 SWF SWM
appearance: 4 MIEN
bugbear: 8 PETPEEVE
creed: 5 ETHIC
history: 4 PAST
instructor: 5 TUTOR
magnetism: 8 CHARISMA
prefix: 4 IDIO
quirk: 3 TIC
Some are: 3 ADS

taste: 8 CUPOFTEA
Personalities: 4 EGOS
  Split: 4 EXES
Personality
  aspect: 5 TRAIT
  Assertive: 5 ARIES TYPEA
  Duel: 4 BURR 6 SECOND
  Kind of: 5 ONAIR TYPEA
  part: 3 EGO 5 ANIMA
Personalize: 7 ENGRAVE
Personals: 3 ADS
Persona non ___: 5 GRATA
Personification: 6 AVATAR
  Luck: 4 LADY
  Moon: 4 LUNA
  of wind: 4 AURA
Personified: 9 INCARNATE
  Darkness: 6 EREBUS
  Love: 4 **AMOR** EROS 5 VENUS
  Moon: 4 LUNA
  Passion: 4 EROS
  Peace: 5 IRENE
  Sun: 3 SOL
Personify: 6 EMBODY
Personnel: 5 STAFF
  Ambulance: 4 EMTS
  director: 5 HIRER
  ER: 3 DRS RNS
  group: 5 CADRE
  listing: 6 ROSTER
  Mil.: 4 NCOS
  OR: 3 RNS
  person: 5 HIRER
Person of the Year
  of 2005: 4 BONO
Person-to-person: 8 ONEONONE
"Person to Person"
  host: 6 MURROW
Perspective: 4 VIEW 5 ANGLE
      SLANT
Perspicacity: 6 ACUMEN
Perspiration: 5 SWEAT
  point: 4 PORE
Persson
  Actress: 4 ESSY
Persuade: 4 COAX SELL SWAY
      6 CAJOLE ENTICE INDUCE
      7 WINOVER
  Try to: 4 COAX URGE

Persuaded: 4 SOLD 7 WONOVER
Pert: 5 SASSY
  blurt: 4 SASS
Pertain: 6 RELATE
Pertaining
  to a manuscript: 7 TEXTUAL
  to bees: 5 APIAN
  to birds: 5 AVIAN
  to life: 6 BIOTIC
  to most students: 4 ELHI
  to planes: 4 AERO
  to plants: 7 BOTANIC
  to punishment: 5 PENAL
  to spring: 6 VERNAL
Perth
  pal: 4 MATE
  river: 3 TAY
Perth ___, New Jersey: 5 AMBOY
Pertinent: 3 APT 7 APROPOS
  ~, in Latin: 5 ADREM
Perturb: 4 FAZE 7 AGITATE
Perturbed: 8 INASTATE
  state: 4 SNIT
Peru
  Capital of: 4 **LIMA**
  From early: 5 INCAN
  native: 4 INCA
  Neighbor of: 7 ECUADOR
  range: 5 ANDES
  Sumac of: 3 YMA
Perugia
  Town near: 6 ASSISI
Peruse: 4 READ
  again: 6 REREAD
Peruvian
  Ancient: 4 **INCA** 5 INCAN
  beast: 5 LLAMA 6 ALPACA
  capital: 4 LIMA
  coin: 3 SOL
  singer: 8 YMASUMAC
  singer Sumac: 3 **YMA**
  ~ Peter: 5 PEDRO
Pervasive
  quality: 4 **AURA**
Pervert: 5 SICKO
Pesci, Joe
  title role: 5 VINNY
Peseta
  replacer: 4 EURO

Pesky
e-mail: 4 SPAM
flier: 4 **GNAT**
insect: 4 **GNAT** 5 MIDGE
6 TSETSE 7 SKEETER
kid: 4 BRAT PAIN
Peso
fraction: 7 CENTAVO
Spanish: 4 DURO
Pessimist: 4 BEAR 8 NAYSAYER
reply: 5 ICANT
word: 4 CANT
Pessimistic: 4 DOUR
pal of Pooh: 6 EEYORE
sort: 4 BEAR
Pest: 4 GNAT TWIT 5 TWERP
6 NOODGE NUDNIK
African: 6 TSETSE
Closet: 4 MOTH
control brand: 4 DCON
control device: 10 FLYSWATTER
Cornfield: 4 CROW
Dog: 4 FLEA
Garden: 4 SLUG 5 APHID
Household: 5 ROACH 6 REDANT
Little: 3 IMP
Pantry: 3 ANT
Picnic: 3 **ANT** 4 GNAT
Plant: 5 APHID BORER
Subterranean: 4 MOLE
Summer: 4 GNAT
Summer ~, informally:
7 SKEETER
Tiny: 4 GNAT MITE
Wharf: 3 RAT
Pester: 3 BUG NAG 5 ANNOY
NAGAT TEASE 6 HARASS
HASSLE NEEDLE
NOODGE
for payment: 3 DUN
like a pup: 5 NIPAT
Pesticide
Apple: 4 ALAR
Banned: 3 **DDT**
mineral: 4 TALC
Pestle
Partner of: 6 MORTAR
Pesto: 5 SAUCE
herb: 5 BASIL

ingredient: 7 PINENUT
Pet: 4 SNIT 6 CARESS
adoption org.: 4 SPCA
Caged: 8 PARAKEET
carrier feature: 7 AIRHOLE
checker: 5 LEASH
Cuddly: 6 LAPDOG
Flintstone: 4 DINO
Green: 4 CHIA
House: 3 CAT
Is in a: 5 SULKS
Kind of: 4 CHIA
lovers' org.: 4 SPCA
master: 5 OWNER
name: 3 HON 4 DEAR FIDO
Nestlé ~ food brand: 4 ALPO
peeve: 4 FLEA
Popular: 3 CAT DOG
Potted: 4 CHIA
Primer: 4 SPOT
protection org.: 4 SPCA 5 ASPCA
restraint: 6 TETHER
rocks, once: 3 FAD
Screen: 4 ASTA
store purchase: 4 CAGE 5 LEASH
Treat as a: 6 COSSET
Pet __: 5 PEEVE
__ Pet: 4 CHIA
PETA
Kin of: 4 SPCA
peeve: 3 FUR
Petal
perfume: 5 ATTAR
plucker word: 3 NOT SHE
pusher: 3 BEE
Pete
Folk singer: 6 SEEGER
Peter: 4 TSAR
Actor: 5 **LORRE** 6 OTOOLE
and Annette: 7 OTOOLES
and Franco: 5 NEROS
and Paul (abbr.): 3 STS
Author: 4 MAAS
Cartoonist: 4 **ARNO**
Director: 4 WEIR 5 YATES
Newsman: 6 ARNETT
of Herman's Hermits: 5 **NOONE**
of Peter and Gorden: 5 ASHER
of Peter, Paul, and Mary:

6 YARROW
or Paul: 4 TSAR 5 SAINT
    7 APOSTLE
out: 3 DIE EBB 4 WANE
Pianist: 4 **NERO**
Playwright: 5 WEISS
Reggae singer: 4 TOSH
Synonymist: 5 ROGET
the Great: 4 CZAR TSAR
~, Paul, and Mary: 3 **STS**
    4 TRIO
~, Paul, or Mary: 5 SAINT
"Peter ___": 4 GUNN
"Peter and the Wolf"
    bird: 5 FLUTE SASHA
    duck: 4 OBOE 5 SONIA
"Peter Grimes": 5 OPERA
Peter Pan
    foe: 4 HOOK 11 CAPTAINHOOK
    rival: 3 JIF
"Peter Pan"
    critter: 4 CROC
    pirate: 4 HOOK **SMEE**
    playwright: 6 BARRIE
    pooch: 4 **NANA**
"Peter, Peter, Pumpkin ___":
    5 EATER
Peters
    Soprano: 7 ROBERTA
Petersburg, Virginia
    Base near: 5 FTLEE
Peterson, Cassandra
    alter ego: 6 ELVIRA
Petite: 4 SIZE
    dessert: 4 TART
    pasta: 4 ORZO
Petit four: 4 CAKE
    finisher: 4 ICER
Petition: 3 BEG SUE 4 PLEA PRAY
    5 PLEAD 7 ENTREAT
    8 ENTREATY
    Devout: 6 ORISON
Petrarch
    Beloved of: 5 LAURA
    work: 6 SONNET
Petri
    Director: 4 ELIO
Petri dish
    gelatin: 4 **AGAR**

Petrie, Laura
    plaint: 5 OHROB
"Petrified Forest, The"
    Bogart role in: 6 MANTEE
Petrifying
    Her looks were: 6 MEDUSA
Petrocelli
    of baseball: 4 RICO
Petrol
    brand: 4 ESSO
    measure: 5 **LITRE**
    unit: 5 **LITRE**
Petroleum
    distillate: 7 NAPHTHA
    gp.: 4 OPEC
    jelly: 8 VASELINE
    name: 4 ARCO 5 AMOCO
    product: 8 KEROSENE
Petruchio
    activity: 6 TAMING
Pet Shop Boys
    record label: 3 EMI
Petticoat: 4 SLIP
    junction: 4 SEAM
Petting
    place: 3 ZOO
    zoo animal: 5 LLAMA
Petty: 5 SMALL
    Actress: 4 **LORI**
    clash: 4 SPAT
    officer: 4 BOSN 5 BOSUN
        6 YEOMAN
    or Singer: 4 LORI
    quarrel: 4 **SPAT** TIFF
    tyrant: 6 SATRAP
Petty, Richard
    Son of: 4 KYLE
    sponsor: 3 STP
Petula
    Singer: 5 CLARK
Petunia
    Boyfriend of: 5 PORKY
    part: 5 PETAL SEPAL
Peut-___ (maybe, in French):
    4 ETRE
Pew
    adjunct: 7 KNEELER
    area: 4 NAVE
    divider: 5 AISLE

Pewter: 5 ALLOY
  component: 3 TIN 4 LEAD
  Kind of: 3 LEY
Peyote
  cactus: 6 MESCAL
  Sacramental user of: 3 UTE
"Peyton Place"
  actor: 5 ONEAL
  actress Hope: 5 LANGE
  actress Turner: 4 LANA
PFC
  superior: 3 CPL
PG
  Gave a: 5 RATED
Pg.
  Turn to the next: 4 CONT
PG-13: 6 RATING
PGA
  1965 ~ champ Dave: 4 MARR
  1998 ~ champ: 5 SINGH
  Annual ~ event: 6 USOPEN
  nickname: 4 SEVE 5 ARNIE
  Part of: 4 ASSN
  player: 3 PRO
  Three-time ~ champ: 5 SNEAD
  Winner of 81 ~ tournaments:
    5 SNEAD
pH
  It has a low: 4 ACID
Phair
  Singer: 3 LIZ
Phantom: 8 SPECTRAL
  portrayer Chaney: 3 LON
"Phantom Lady"
  1944 ~ star: 6 RAINES
"Phantom Menace, The"
  actor McGregor: 4 EWAN
  boy: 3 ANI
"Phantom of the Opera, The"
  1962 ~ star: 3 LOM
  name: 4 ERIK
Pharaoh
  cross: 4 ANKH
  land: 5 EGYPT
  of Genesis: 7 RAMESES
  river: 4 NILE
  symbol: 3 ASP
Pharm.
  watchdog: 3 FDA

Pharmaceutical
  giant: 5 MERCK ROCHE
    8 ELILILLY
  Lilly of ~ fame: 3 **ELI**
  ointment: 6 OLEATE
  watchdog gp.: 3 FDA
Pharmacist
  compound: 3 SAL
  concern: 4 DOSE
  item: 4 DRUG
  thrice: 3 TER
Phase: 4 STEP 5 STAGE 6 ASPECT
  out: 3 END
  Sea: 4 TIDE
  Sleep: 3 REM
  Washer: 5 CYCLE
Phased-out
  flier: 3 SST
  toxin: 3 PCB
Phaser
  Hit with a: 3 ZAP
  setting: 4 **STUN**
Phat: 3 RAD
Ph.D.: 3 DEG
  hurdle: 5 ORALS
Pheasant
  female: 3 HEN 6 PEAHEN
  stew: 5 SALMI
"Phèdre"
  playwright: 6 RACINE
Phenom: 3 ACE
  Golf ~ Michelle: 3 WIE
Phenomena
  Astronomical: 5 NOVAE
  Kind of: 3 PSI
Phenomenon
  Cave: 4 ECHO
  Eclipse: 6 CORONA
  Foreboding: 4 OMEN
  Ocean: 4 TIDE 8 NEAPTIDE
  Pacific weather: 6 ELNINO
  Sleep: 3 REM 5 APNEA
  Solar: 5 FLARE
  Spring: 4 THAW
  Winter: 8 COLDSNAP
"Phew!"
  inducer: 4 ODOR
Phi
  follower: 3 CHI

Phi Beta Kappa
concern (abbr.): 3 GPA
Phidias
subject: 6 ATHENA
Phi ___ Kappa: 4 BETA
Phil
Don or ~ of pop: 6 EVERLY
Folk singer: 4 OCHS
of hockey, familiarly: 4 ESPO
Quarterback: 5 SIMMS
Skier: 5 MAHRE
Texas senator: 5 GRAMM
Wife of: 5 MARLO
Phil.
Book before: 3 EPH
Phila.
clock setting: 3 EST
transit: 5 SEPTA
Philadelphia
former mayor: 5 GOODE
founder: 4 PENN
suburb: 5 ASTON PAOLI
university: 6 TEMPLE
7 LASALLE
"Philadelphia"
director: 5 DEMME
Philanderer: 3 CAD 4 ROUE
of filmdom: 5 ALFIE
Philanthropic
Was: 4 GAVE
Philanthropist: 5 DONOR
No: 5 MISER
~ Barton: 5 CLARA
~ Cornell: 4 EZRA
~ Yale: 5 ELIHU
Philatelist
book: 5 ALBUM
purchase: 4 PANE 5 STAMP
Philbin
cohort: 4 RIPA
TV host: 5 REGIS
Phileas
Verne hero: 4 FOGG
Philemon: 7 EPISTLE
Book before: 5 TITUS
Philharmonic
gp.: 4 ORCH
Philip
Author: 4 **ROTH** 5 WYLIE

Philip II
fleet: 6 ARMADA
Philippe: 3 ROI
Philippic: 4 RANT 6 TIRADE
Philippine
capital: 6 MANILA
city: 6 ILOILO
Former ~ leader: 5 RAMOS
6 MARCOS
island: 4 CEBU 5 LEYTE LUZON
SAMAR
peak: 3 APO
sea: 4 SULU
~ Muslim: 4 MORO
Philippines
1990s ~ president: 5 RAMOS
Capital of the: 6 MANILA
island: 5 LEYTE
Marcos of the: 6 IMELDA
Philips
Comic: 3 **EMO**
product: 5 TVSET
Philistines
Where Samson slew the: 4 LEHI
Phillies
star Del: 5 ENNIS
Phillippe
Actor: 4 RYAN
Phillips
and Elliot: 5 MAMAS
head: 5 SCREW
Newsman: 5 STONE
Phillips Academy
city: 7 ANDOVER
Phillips ___ Academy: 6 EXETER
Phillips University
city: 4 ENID
Phillpotts
Author: 4 EDEN
Philly
player: 5 EAGLE SIXER
Philo
S.S. Van Dine sleuth: 5 VANCE
Philosopher: 4 SAGE
Chinese: 6 LAOTSE
English: 5 LOCKE
French: 6 PASCAL
German: 4 KANT
Greek: 5 PLATO

Roman: 4 CATO 6 SENECA
Philosophical: 4 DEEP
  ending: 3 ISM
  ideal: 3 TAO
Philosophy: 5 CREDO
  Chinese: 3 TAO
  giant: 4 KANT 5 PLATO
"Philosophy of Right, The"
  author: 5 HEGEL
Phinehas
  Father of: 3 ELI
Phlebotomy
  target: 4 VEIN
Phnom ___: 4 **PENH**
Phobia: 4 FEAR
  prefix: 4 **ACRO** XENO 5 AGORA
Phobos: 4 MOON
  Father of: 4 ARES
  orbits it: 4 MARS
Phoebe
  Actress: 5 CATES
  portrayer: 4 LISA
  Sister of: 6 URSULA
Phoenician: 6 SEMITE
  deity: 4 BAAL
  love goddess: 7 ASTARTE
  port: 4 TYRE 5 SIDON
Phoenix
  cager: 3 SUN
  City near: 4 MESA 5 TEMPE
  setting (abbr.): 3 MST
  source: 5 ASHES
  team: 4 SUNS
Phone: 4 CALL HORN
  abbr.: 4 OPER
  answerer word: 5 HELLO
  attachment: 3 EAR 5 SOUSA
  bk. listings: 3 NOS
  Bug a: 7 WIRETAP
  Bulk-rate ~ line (abbr.): 4 WATS
  Business ~ button: 4 HOLD
  button: 4 OPER STAR 6 REDIAL
  Bygone pay ~ amount: 4 DIME
  Cell ~ button: 4 SEND
  Cell ~ kin: 5 PAGER
  Cell ~ maker: 5 NOKIA
  cord shape: 4 COIL
  crew: 7 LINEMEN
  Emergency: 7 HOTLINE

  enclosure: 5 BOOTH
  In ~ limbo: 6 ONHOLD
  Kind of: 4 CELL
  Letterless ~ button: 3 ONE
  Like most ~ numbers:
    6 LISTED
  Like some ~ nos.: 3 RES
  Long-distance ~ number part:
    8 AREACODE
  menu imperative: 5 PRESS
  Modern ~ feature: 6 REDIAL
  no. add-on: 3 EXT
  Office ~ nos.: 4 EXTS
  Old ~ company nickname:
    6 MABELL
  Old ~ lack: 4 STAR
  Old ~ user: 6 DIALER
  part: 7 HANDSET
  Pay ~ feature: 4 SLOT
  Pioneer cell ~ co.: 3 GTE
  prefix: 4 MEGA TELE
  Report by: 6 CALLIN
  Retro ~ feature: 4 DIAL
  Run up a ~ bill: 3 GAB
  Send via: 3 FAX
  six: 3 MNO
  Tie up the: 3 YAK
  trio: 3 ABC DEF GHI JKL MNO
    PRS TUV WXY
  ~ 0: 4 OPER
  ~ 2: 3 ABC
  ~ 3: 3 DEF
  ~ 4: 3 GHI
  ~ 5: 3 JKL
  ~ 6: 3 MNO
  ~ 7: 3 PRS
  ~ 8: 3 TUV
  ~ 9: 3 WXY
  ~, slangily: 4 HORN
Phone ___: 3 TAG
Phoned: 4 RANG
Phones
  Like some: 6 ROTARY
Phonograph
  needles: 5 STYLI
  part: 3 ARM
  record: 4 DISC
Phony: 4 SHAM 5 BOGUS FAKER
    POSER 6 POSEUR

"Phooey!": 3 BAH FIE PAH
    4 CRUD DANG DARN
    DRAT NUTS RATS
    5 NERTS 6 DANGIT
    DARNIT
Phosphate: 5 ESTER
Photo: 3 PIC 4 SNAP
  Advertising ~ label: 5 AFTER
  book: 5 ALBUM
  Brown-tinted: 5 SEPIA
  Enlarge a: 6 BLOWUP
  finish: 4 STAT 5 GENIC **MATTE**
  Frame a ~ again: 5 REMAT
  holder: 5 ALBUM
  lab svc.: 3 ENL
  Locker: 5 PINUP
  Magazine: 4 STAT
  Old: 5 SEPIA 7 TINTYPE
  prefix: 4 TELE
  session: 5 SHOOT
  Sit for a: 4 POSE
  Take a: 4 SNAP 5 SHOOT
  tint: 5 SEPIA
  Took a: 4 SHOT
Photo ___ : 3 **OPS**
Photocopier
  part: 6 SORTER
  problem: 3 JAM
Photocopy: 4 STAT 5 REPRO
  precursor: 5 DITTO
Photoelectric cell
  element: 6 CESIUM
Photoengraving
  innovator Frederic: 4 IVES
Photog
  choice: 3 SLR
  image: 3 NEG
  request: 5 SMILE
Photog.
  service: 3 ENL
Photograph: 5 SHOOT
  Trim a: 4 CROP
Photographed: 4 SHOT
Photographer
  Civil War: 5 BRADY
  request: 5 SMILE
  setting: 5 FSTOP
  Word to the: 6 CHEESE
  Yosemite: 10 ANSELADAMS

  ~ Adams: 5 **ANSEL**
  ~ Arbus: 5 DIANE
  ~ Cartier-Bresson: 5 HENRI
  ~ Goldin: 3 NAN
  ~ Leibovitz: 5 ANNIE
  ~ Richard: 6 AVEDON
Photography
  brand: 5 KODAK
  First name in: 5 ANSEL
  lens: 5 MACRO
  light: 6 STROBE
Photomuralist
  ~ Adams: 5 ANSEL
Photos: 3 PIX
  Some have: 3 IDS
Phrase
  after break or shake: 4 ALEG
  before phrase: 5 COINA
  in disco names: 5 AGOGO
  Musical: 5 TRALA
  of inclusion: 6 ETALII
  of understanding: 4 ISEE
  Ratio: 4 ISTO
  Speller: 4 ASIN
  tacked on for emphasis:
      6 NOLESS
  Twist of: 7 ANAGRAM
Phrygia
  King of: 5 MIDAS
Phx.
  Sch. near: 3 ASU
Phylicia
  Cosby costar: 6 RASHAD
Phyllis
  Comic: 6 DILLER
  TV husband of: 4 LARS
Phylum
  subdivision: 5 CLASS
Phys.: 3 SCI
Physical: 4 EXAM
  condition: 5 SHAPE
  Having ~ presence:
      15 BRICKSANDMORTAR
  likeness: 5 IMAGE
  prefix: 4 META
  sounds: 3 AHS
Physician: 6 HEALER
  Ancient: 5 GALEN
  Canadian: 5 OSLER

English ~ and scholar: 5 ROGET
Greek: 5 GALEN
Hypnotism: 6 MESMER
org.: 3 AMA
~, briefly: 3 DOC
Physicist
Austrian: 4 MACH 5 PAULI
Danish: 4 BOHR
French: 6 AMPERE
German: 3 OHM
particle: 3 ION
study: 4 ATOM 6 ENERGY
unit: 3 RAD
~ Alessandro: 5 VOLTA
~ Enrico: 5 FERMI
~ Fermi: 6 ENRICO
~ Georg: 3 OHM
~ Mach: 5 ERNST
~ Niels: 4 BOHR
~ Nikola: 5 TESLA
~ Ohm: 5 GEORG
~ Sakharov: 6 ANDREI
Physics
Branch of: 6 OPTICS
    7 STATICS
calculation: 4 MASS
concept: 4 MASS
particle: 5 BOSON MESON
prefix: 4 META 5 ASTRO
Suffix in nuclear: 4 TRON
unit: 3 ERG RAD 4 DYNE
Physics Nobelist
1918 ~: 6 PLANCK
1922 ~: 4 BOHR
1933 ~: 5 DIRAC
1938 ~: 5 FERMI
. 1957 ~ Tsung-___ Lee: 3 DAO
Physique: 3 BOD 4 BODY
    5 FRAME SHAPE
Having a good: 5 BUILT
Pi: 5 RATIO
follower: 3 **RHO**
PI: 3 TEC
Pia
Actress: 6 ZADORA
Piaf
Singer: 5 EDITH
Pianist
Chilean: 5 ARRAU

Comic: 5 BORGE
Flamboyant: 8 LIBERACE
Jazz: 10 COUNTBASIE
Jazz ~ Allison: 4 MOSE
Jazz ~ Art: 5 TATUM
Jazz ~ with eight Grammys:
    5 COREA
New Age: 5 YANNI
purchase: 10 SHEETMUSIC
span: 6 OCTAVE
~ André: 5 WATTS
~ Chick: 5 COREA
~ Claudio: 5 ARRAU
~ John: 4 TESH
~ Myra: 4 **HESS**
~ Peter: 4 **NERO**
~ Rudolf: 6 SERKIN
Piano: 4 SOFT
Dame of the: 4 HESS
dedicatee: 5 ELISE
exercise: 5 ETUDE
Fix a: 4 TUNE 6 RETUNE
fixer: 5 TUNER
Four-hand ~ piece: 4 DUET
key material: 5 EBONY IVORY
keys: 7 IVORIES
Kind of: 6 SPINET
    9 BABYGRAND
lesson: 5 ETUDE
Like some ~ keys: 4 EBON
part: 5 PEDAL
piece: 3 LEG RAG 5 **ETUDE**
    6 DAMPER
pieces: 4 KEYS
reference point: 7 MIDDLEC
Sharp and flat ~ keys:
    7 EBONIES
Small: 6 SPINET
technician: 5 TUNER
~ 88: 4 KEYS
"Piano, The"
actor Harvey: 6 KEITEL
actor Sam: 5 NEILL
extra: 5 MAORI
Heroine in: 3 ADA
Oscar winner:
    11 HOLLYHUNTER
"Piano Lesson, The"
painter: 7 MATISSE

"Piano Man"
  songwriter: **4** JOEL
Piao
  of China: **3** LIN
Piaster
  place: **5** SYRIA
Piazza
  with a fountain: **5** TREVI
Piazza, Mike: 3 MET
Piazza del Campo
  site: **5** SIENA
Pic: 4 FOTO SNAP
  PC: **4** ICON
  Quick: **4** SNAP
  source: **3** NEG
Pica
  alternative: **5** ELITE
Picador
  cheer: **3** OLE
  target: **4** TORO
Picante: 5 ZESTY
Picard
  Counselor to: **4 TROI**
Picard, Jean-___
  Captain: **3** LUC
Picasso: 6 CUBIST
  contemporary: **4** DALI MIRO
  Designer: **6** PALOMA
  home: **5** SPAIN
  Painter: **5** PABLO
  phase: **10** BLUEPERIOD
  style: **6** CUBISM
Picasso, Pablo ___ y: 4 RUIZ
Picayune: 5 PETTY
Piccadilly Circus
  Area north of: **4** SOHO
  statue: **4 EROS**
Piccata
  meat: **4** VEAL
  ___ Picchu: 5 MACHU
Piccolo
  player: **4** CAAN
  relative: **4** FIFE **5** FLUTE
Pick: 3 OPT TAP **4** CULL **5** ELECT
      6 CHOICE SELECT
  a target: **3** AIM
  Bone to: **4** BEEF **5** GRIPE
  Critic: **3** NIT
  Do with a: **4** AFRO

Draft: **3** ALE
from the menu: **5** ORDER
Ice ~, essentially: **3** AWL
Lousy: **3** NIT
Menu: **6** ENTREE
on: **3** NAG **5** TEASE
out: **4** SPOT **5** ELECT **6** CHOOSE
Place for a: **4** AFRO
preceder: **3** ICE
prefix: **3** NIT
Ready to: **4** RIPE
Something to: **3** NIT **4** BONE
Take your: **3** OPT **6** CHOOSE
Top: **4** FAVE
Try to ~ up: **5** HITON
up: **3** GET NAB **4** GAIN HEAR
      LIFT TAKE **5** LEARN SENSE
      6 ARREST
up, as cubes: **4** TONG
up on: **5** SENSE
up the tab: **5 TREAT**
Worker with a: **5** MINER
~, with "for": **3** OPT
Pickable: 4 RIPE
Picked: 5 CHOSE **6** CHOSEN
  from a lineup: **4** IDED
  It can be ~ out: **3** ORE
  It gets ~ in Hawaii: **3** UKE
  It may be: **4** LOCK
  It's ~ up at a pizza place:
      5 AROMA
  Something that's: **3** NIT
  up: **3** GOT **4** ROSE TOOK
  up item: **3** TAB
Pickens
  Actor: **4** SLIM
Picker
  A ~ may pick one: **5** BANJO
  Apple: **3** EVE
  prefix: **3** NIT
Picker-upper: 4 MAID TAXI
      5 TALON
  Ice: **5** TONGS
  Quicker: **3** CAB
Picket
  line: **5** FENCE
  line crosser: **4 SCAB**
Picketer
  foe: **4** SCAB

Pickle: 3 FIX JAM **4** BIND CURE
    MESS SPOT **5** SOUSE
  brand: **6** VLASIC
  flavoring: **4** DILL
  holder: **3** JAR
  juice: **5** BRINE
  pick: **4** DILL
  producer: **5** HEINZ
  purveyor: **4** DELI
  ___ pickle: **3** INA **4** DILL
Pickled: 6 STINKO
  bud: **5** CAPER
  cheese: **4** FETA
  delicacy: **3** EEL
  Somewhat: **5** TIPSY
  veggie: **4** BEET
Pickler: 5 BRINE
Pick-me-up: 4 LIFT **5** TONIC
    6 BRACER ELIXIR
  Morning: **5** LATTE
Pickup
  Airport: **4** LIMO **6** RENTAL
  Bowling: **5** SPARE
  capacity: **3** TON **6** ONETON
  Curbside: **5** TRASH
  line: **5** HELLO HOPIN
    13 WHATSYOURSIGN
    15 HAVEWEMETBEFORE
  shtick: **4** LINE
  Tow truck: **4** REPO
  Yardage: **4** GAIN
Pick-up-sticks
  game: **3** NIM
Picky
  Be: **4** CARP
  It is picked by the: **3** NIT
Picnic
  beverage: **4** COLA
  carry-all: **6** BASKET
  container: **6** COOLER
  event: **8** SACKRACE
  hamperer: **3** ANT **4** RAIN
  lunch: **10** SANDWICHES
  Paris ~ place: **4** PARC
  pest: **3** ANT **4** GNAT
  side dish: **4** SLAW **8** COLESLAW
    10 PASTASALAD
  Spoil, as a: **6** RAINON
  spoiler: **4** ANTS RAIN

  take-along: **8** ICECHEST
"Picnic"
  playwright: **4 INGE**
Picone
  of fashion: **4** EVAN
Pictograph: 4 ICON
Picture: 3 SEE **4** CINE **5** IMAGE
    7 IMAGINE
  Big: **4** EPIC **5** MURAL
  Big ~ (abbr.): **3** ENL
  book: **5** ALBUM
  card: **5** TAROT
  Computer: **4** ICON
  Enter the: **6** APPEAR
  frame shape: **4** OVAL
  Get the: **3 SEE**
  Got the: **3** SAW
  holder: **5** ALBUM
  Hosp.: **3** MRI
  in a picture: **5** INSET
  Iron-on: **5** DECAL
  Match sound to: **5** SYNCH
  Medical: **4** XRAY
  Motion: **4** CINE
  Move a: **6** REHANG
  of health: **4** XRAY
  prize: **5** OSCAR
  Put up a: **4** HANG
  puzzle: **5** REBUS
  receivers: **7** RETINAE
  Revealing: **4** XRAY
  Sacred: **4** ICON
  Take a: **5** SHOOT
  taker, briefly: **3** CAM
  Transfer: **5** DECAL
  ~, informally: **4** FOTO
"Picture of Dorian Gray, The"
  writer: **5** WILDE
"Picture of ___ Gray, The":
    6 DORIAN
Pictures
  Dizzying: **5** OPART
  Mental: **7** IMAGERY
  Pair of: **7** DIPTYCH
"___ Pictures" (Wyeth): 5 HELGA
Picturesque: 6 SCENIC
Piddling: 6 MEAGER
Pie: 4 TART
  chart lines: **5** RADII

choice: 5 PECAN
cooling place: 4 SILL
crust ingredient: 4 LARD
cuts, essentially: 5 RADII
fight sound: 5 SPLAT
filling: 3 MUD
French: 5 TARTE
fruit: 5 APPLE
ingredient: 3 MUD 5 MINCE
   PECAN
in the sky: 3 UFO
Italian: 5 PIZZA
Kind of: 3 MUD 5 MINCE
   6 ESKIMO
   11 BANANACREAM
   BOSTONCREAM
Like: 4 EASY
Like many a: 8 HOMEMADE
maker: 3 MOM
Meat: 5 PASTY
nut: 5 PECAN
part: 5 CRUST
perch: 5 SILL
Piece of the: 5 SHARE
portion: 5 SLICE
preference: 7 ALAMODE
   8 DEEPDISH
slice: 5 WEDGE
Small: 4 TART
Tangy ~ flavor: 5 LEMON
___ Pie: 5 CUTIE 6 ESKIMO
   TWEETY
Piece: 3 BIT 4 ITEM
activists: 3 NRA
Big: 5 CHUNK
Broken: 5 SHARD
End: 4 CODA
goods: 5 CLOTH
In one: 5 WHOLE 6 ENTIRE
It's a ~ of cake: 5 SLICE
maker: 5 REESE
Numbered: 4 OPUS
of advice: 3 TIP
of cake: 4 SNAP TIER 5 CINCH
   WEDGE 6 BREEZE PICNIC
of china: 5 PLATE
of cookware: 7 STEWPAN
of dinnerware: 5 PLATE
of eight piece: 4 REAL

of farmland: 4 ACRE
of history: 3 ERA 5 RELIC
of land: 5 TRACT
of mail (abbr.): 3 LTR
of music: 5 SHEET
of news: 4 ITEM
of paper: 4 SLIP 5 SHEET
of the action: 3 CUT
of the past: 3 ERA 5 RELIC
of the pie: 5 SHARE
of turf: 3 SOD
of work: 3 ERG JOB 4 TASK
on a pedestal: 3 URN
Packing a: 5 ARMED
Parlor: 4 SOFA 5 DIVAN
   6 **SETTEE**
Period: 5 EPOCH
Practice: 5 ETUDE
Recital: 4 SOLO
Rotating: 3 CAM
Set: 4 PROP
Short opera: 7 ARIETTA
Show: 3 ACT 7 EPISODE
Signature: 3 PEN
Single: 4 UNIT
Thick: 4 SLAB
Top: 3 BRA
Wooden: 4 SLAT
___ piece (alike): 3 OFA
Pieced
together: 4 SEWN
Piecemeal: 8 ALACARTE
"Piece of cake!": 4 EASY 5 CANDO
   6 NOPROB 7 NOSWEAT
Pieces: 3 MEN
Go to: 5 PANIC 7 SHATTER
In: 5 APART
Love to: 5 **ADORE**
Small: 4 NUBS
Tear to: 4 REND 5 RIPUP
   SHRED
Thrill to: 5 ELATE
To: 5 APART
___ Pieces: 6 REESES
Pied-___: 6 ATERRE
Pied-à-___: 5 TERRE
Piedmont
capital: 5 TURIN
Carrier that bought: 5 USAIR

province: 4 **ASTI**
wine center: 4 **ASTI**
Pied Piper
Emulate the: 5 DERAT
follower: 3 RAT
understatement: 10 ISMELLARAT
Pie-eyed: 5 OILED 6 STEWED
STINKO
Makes: 6 BESOTS
Pielet: 4 TART
Pie ___ mode: 3 ALA
Pie-mode
connection: 3 ALA
Pier: 5 WHARF
Architectural: 4 ANTA
gp.: 3 ILA
Landing: 4 DOCK
Pierce: 4 STAB 5 LANCE
Author: 4 EGAN
portrayer: 4 **ALDA**
Pierce, Hawkeye
portrayer: 8 ALANALDA
Pierce Arrow
rival: 3 REO
Pierced
item: 3 EAR
places: 5 LOBES 8 EARLOBES
Pierced-lip
people: 6 UBANGI
Piercer: 3 AWL
Piercing: 4 KEEN
site: 3 EAR 4 LOBE
tool: 3 ADZ AWL 4 ADZE
Pierre
Impressionist: 6 RENOIR
Novelist: 4 LOTI
pal: 3 AMI
South Dakota, to: 4 ETAT
state (abbr.): 4 SDAK
Pietà
figure: 4 MARY
Pietermaritzburg
province: 5 NATAL
Pig: 4 SLOB
Big: 3 HOG 4 BOAR
Comparable to a: 5 ASFAT
Dig like a: 4 ROOT
digs: 3 **STY**
feed: 4 SLOP

feeder: 6 TROUGH
Kind of: 6 GUINEA
Male: 4 BOAR
nose: 5 SNOUT
of film: 4 BABE
out: 3 EAT 5 BINGE GORGE
7 OVEREAT
place: 3 PEN STY 4 POKE
tail: 3 LET
Wild: 4 BOAR
Word after: 4 IRON
Pig ___: 5 LATIN
Pigeon: 3 SAP 4 DUPE
Clay: 6 TARGET
Clay ~ sport: 5 SKEET
coop: 4 COTE
follower: 4 TOED
perch: 5 LEDGE
shelter: 4 COTE
sound: 3 COO
Stool: 3 RAT
variety: 7 FANTAIL
Young: 5 SQUAB
Pigeon-___: 4 TOED
Pigeon English: 3 COO
Pigeonhole: 4 SLOT SORT
5 LABEL 6 ASSORT
place: 4 DESK
Pigged
out: 3 ATE 7 OVERATE
Piggery: 3 STY
Piggies
Little: 4 **TOES**
protector: 6 BOOTEE
Piggy: 3 TOE
bank opening: 4 SLOT
Little: 3 **TOE**
Little ~ cry: 3 WEE
What the fourth little ~ had:
4 NONE
Piggy bank
opening: 4 SLOT
Pig in ___: 5 APOKE
Piglet: 5 SHOAT
Creator of: 5 MILNE
Mom of: 3 SOW
Pal of: 3 ROO 4 POOH
parent: 3 SOW
Piglike: 5 MESSY

animal: 5 TAPIR

Pigment
Blood: 4 HEME
Brown: 5 SEPIA
deficient: 6 ALBINO
Earthy: 5 OCHER OCHRE
    UMBER 6 SIENNA
Paint: 5 OCHER
Red: 4 LAKE
Skin: 7 MELANIN
Yellowish: 5 OCHER

Pigmented
eye part: 4 UVEA

Pigpen: 3 STY

Pig-poke
connector: 3 INA

Pig ___ poke: 3 INA

Pigs: 5 SWINE

"___ pig's eye!": 3 **INA**

Pigskin
Give up the: 4 PUNT
prop: 3 TEE

Pigsty: 3 PEN 4 MESS SLUM

Pigtail: 5 BRAID PLAIT TRESS

Pigtails
Like: 6 TWINED

Pigweed: 7 REDROOT

Pika
kin: 4 HARE

Pikake
Wreath of ~ flowers: 3 LEI

Pike: 4 ROAD

Pikes Peak
locale (abbr.): 4 COLO

Pilaf
staple: 4 RICE

Pilaster: 4 ANTA

Pilate
Behold, to: 4 ECCE
Word from: 4 ECCE

Pilates
alternative: 4 YOGA

Pile: 4 HEAP 5 STACK
Atomic: 7 REACTOR
by a pitchfork: 3 HAY
Combustible: 4 PYRE
Ed.'s: 3 MSS
Make a: 5 AMASS STACK
maker: 4 RAKE

Rite: 4 PYRE
up: 5 **AMASS** 6 RAKEIN

Piled
deeply: 5 PLUSH
up: 7 INAHEAP

Piles: 4 ALOT
Place on: 4 PIER
Put into: 4 SORT

Pileup
Messy: 6 LOGJAM

Pilfer: 3 NIP 4 GLOM 5 FILCH
    STEAL SWIPE

Pilfered: 5 STOLE

Pilgrim
Chaucer: 5 REEVE
destination: 5 MECCA
    6 SHRINE
Plymouth: 5 ALDEN
to Mecca: 5 HADJI HAJJI
    6 MOSLEM
~ John: 5 ALDEN

Pilgrimage
destination: 5 MECCA
Muslim: 4 HADJ HAJJ
to Mecca: 4 **HADJ** HAJJ

Pill: 6 TABLET
form: 6 CAPLET
Kind of: 3 PEP
Open a ~ bottle: 5 UNCAP
Sugar: 7 PLACEBO
Take a chill: 6 COOLIT

Pillage: 4 LOOT 6 MARAUD

Pillager: 3 HUN

Pillar
His wife was a: 3 LOT
Inscribed: 5 STELA STELE
Of a stone: 6 STELAR
Stair: 5 NEWEL
Stone: 5 STELA

Pillars
It has five: 5 ISLAM
One of the ~ of Islam: 4 HADJ
    HAJJ

Pillbox: 3 HAT

Pill-gobbling
video icon: 6 PACMAN

Pillow
cover: 4 CASE **SHAM**
filler: 4 FOAM 5 EIDER

Pillowcase
  and others: 5 LINEN
      8 BEDLINEN
"Pillow Talk"
  actress: 3 DAY
  actress Day: 5 DORIS
Pillowy: 4 SOFT
Pills
  ~, briefly: 4 MEDS
  ___ Pills: 5 DOANS
Pillsbury
  competitor: 7 SARALEE
Pillsbury Bake-Off
  fixture: 4 OVEN
Pilot: 5 STEER 6 AVIATE
  Did a ~ job: 5 RELIT
  fig.: 3 ALT
  guidepost: 5 PYLON
  heading (abbr.): 3 ENE NNE SSE
  Hotshot: 3 ACE
  Kind of: 4 TEST
  Legendary test: 6 YEAGER
  Military ~ post: 7 AIRBASE
  place: 5 STOVE 8 GASRANGE
  prediction (abbr.): 3 ETA
  prefix: 4 AUTO
  problem: 3 YAW
  Sky: 5 PADRE
  UFO: 5 ALIEN
  wind problem: 5 SHEAR
  worry: 4 FLAK
  ~, slangily: 6 FLYBOY
Pilothouse
  abbr.: 3 ENE
Pilotless
  plane: 5 DRONE
Pilots
  Signal to: 8 AIRALERT
  UFO: 3 ETS
Pilsener: 5 LAGER
  holder: 5 STEIN
  kin: 3 ALE
Piltdown Man: 4 HOAX
Pimiento
  holder: 5 OLIVE
Pimples: 4 ACNE
Pin: 5 RIVET 6 BROOCH
  Accessory: 6 TIETAC
  Bowling ~ wood: 5 MAPLE

British bowling: 7 SKITTLE
Carpentry: 5 DOWEL
Comparable to a: 6 ASNEAT
cushion: 3 MAT
Fastening: 5 RIVET
Gunwale: 5 THOLE
Hard to ~ down: 4 EELY
    5 DODGY VAGUE
Holding: 6 COTTER
Oar: 5 THOLE
Place for a: 3 MAT TIE
    5 LAPEL
Poke with a: 5 PRICK
Stick with a: 5 BURST
up: 6 SECURE
Wooden: 5 DOWEL
PIN
  requester: 3 **ATM**
Pin ___ : 3 OAK
Piña colada
  ingredient: 3 RUM
"___ Pinafore": 3 **HMS**
Pinatubo
  product: 3 ASH
Pinball
  infraction: 4 TILT
  palace: 6 ARCADE
  path: 3 ARC
  problem: 4 TILT
Pince-___ : 3 **NEZ**
Pincer: 4 CLAW
Pincers
  Insect with: 6 EARWIG
Pinch: 3 NAB NIP 5 CRIMP STEAL
    SWIPE 6 ARREST
  One to watch in a: 6 KLEPTO
  pennies: 5 STINT 6 SCRIMP
  Playful: 5 TWEAK
  ___ pinch: 3 INA
Pincher
  Penny: 5 MISER PIKER
Pinch-hit: 7 STANDIN
"___ pinch of salt ...": 4 ADDA
Pincushion
  alternative: 4 ETUI
Pindar: 5 ODIST
  work: 3 **ODE**
Pindaric
  poem: 3 ODE

Pine: 4 ACHE LONG **5** SCENT
        YEARN
   aloud: **4** SIGH
   cone, essentially: **4** SEED
   exudate: **5** RESIN
   family tree: **3** FIR
   (for): **4** ACHE
   leaf: **6** NEEDLE
   Like ~ scent: **6** WOODSY
   product: **3** TAR **5** RESIN
   Sauce with ~ nuts: **5** PESTO
Pine-___ (cleaning brand):
        3 SOL
Pineapple: 7 GRENADE
   Big name in: **4** DOLE
   island: **5** LANAI
Pine Tree
   state: **5** MAINE
Pine Valley
   resident: **5** ERICA
Ping: 5 NOISE
Ping-___: 4 PONG
Ping-Pong
   partition: **3** NET
Pinhead: 3 ASS **4** BOOB DODO
        TWIT **5** IDIOT
Piniella
   of baseball: **3** LOU
Pink: 4 RARE ROSE ROSY
   Deep: **4** ROSE **5** MELON
   Give a ~ slip to: **3** AXE CAN
        9 TERMINATE
   In the: **4** HALE RARE ROSY
        WELL
   lady ingredient: **3** GIN
   Not in the: **3** ILL
   Reddish: **4** RARE
   slip: **13** WALKINGPAPERS
   Tickle: **5** AMUSE **ELATE**
        6 PLEASE
   Tickled: **4** **GLAD**
   wine: **4** ROSE
   Yellowish: **7** TEAROSE
Pinker
   inside: **5** RARER
Pinkerton
   Detective: **5** **ALLAN**
Pinkett Smith
   Actress: **4** JADA

Pink Floyd
   album, with "The": **4** WALL
   guitarist Barrett: **3** **SYD**
Pinkish: 4 RARE
   yellow: **5** CORAL
Pink-legged
   bird: **5** STILT
"Pink Panther, The"
   actor David: **5** NIVEN
   actor Herbert: **3** LOM
Pink-slip: 3 **AXE** CAN **4** BOOT
        FIRE SACK
Pinky
   Key hit with a: **5** ENTER
   or Peggy: **3** LEE
Pinnacle: 3 TOP TOR **4** ACME
        APEX PEAK **5** SPIRE
   Rocky: **3** **TOR**
Pinocchio: 4 LIAR
   Emulate: **3** LIE
   goldfish: **4** CLEO
   lie detector: **4** NOSE
Pinochle
   combo: **4** MELD
   king beater: **3** TEN
   low card: **4** NINE
   play: **4** **MELD**
Pin-on
   Conference: **5** IDTAG
   Party: **4** TAIL
Pinot ___ (wine): 4 NOIR
"___ pin, pick ...": 4 SEEA
Pinpoint: 6 LOCATE
Pins
   On ~ and needles: **4** **EDGY**
        5 ANTSY TENSE
Pinsk
   Peace, in: **3** MIR
Pinstripes
   Manager in ~, once: **5** TORRE
   wearer: **4** YANK **6** YANKEE
Pint
   fraction: **4** GILL
   Half: **3** CUP
   Hearty: **5** STOUT
   Place for a: **3** PUB
   Pub: **3** **ALE**
Pinta
   partner: **4** NINA

Pintail
  duck: **4** SMEE
Pinter
  Playwright: **6** HAROLD
Pinto: 4 BEAN
Pint-size: 4 MINI
Pint-sized: 4 PUNY TINY **5** SHORT
    TEENY
Pinup
  '40s ~ Betty: **6** GRABLE
  feature: **3** GAM
  legs: **4** GAMS
  Like a: **4** SEXY
Pinza
  and others: **5** BASSI
  Basso: **4** EZIO
  Singer: **4** EZIO
Pinzón
  Ship commanded by: **5** PINTA
Pion
  Home to a: **4** ATOM
Pioneer: 7 SETTLER
    11 TRAILBLAZER
  automaker: **4** OLDS
  cell phone co.: **3** GTE
  computer: **5** ENIAC
  heading: **4** WEST
  in Surrealism: **5** ERNST
  product: **6** STEREO
  vehicle: **5** WAGON
Pioneer Day
  Where ~ is celebrated: **4** UTAH
Pioneering
  video game: **4** PONG
  video game system: **5** ATARI
Pious: 5 GODLY **6** DEVOUT
    8 REVERENT
Pip: 4 LULU ONER SEED
    5 BEAUT PEACH
  Beloved of: **7** ESTELLA
  Card with a single: **3** ACE
Pipe
  bend: **3** ELL **5** ELBOW
  cleaner: **5** DRANO **6** REAMER
  Collar on a: **6** FLANGE
  elbows: **4** ELLS
  joint: **3** ELL TEE
  Kind of: **5** BRIAR
  Large: **4** MAIN

  material: **3** COB **5** BRIAR
    BRIER
  part: **3** ELL **4** BOWL STEM
  Pastoral: **4** REED
  problem: **4** CLOG DRIP LEAK
    RUST
  residue: **6** DOTTLE
  section: **4** TRAP
  type: **3** ELL **5** BRIAR BRIER
    7 CORNCOB
  up: **5** SPEAK **7** CHIMEIN
  Vertical: **5** RISER
  Water: **4** MAIN **6** HOOKAH
"Pipe down!": 3 SHH **4** HUSH
    5 SHUSH
Pipeline
  Fuel: **7** GASMAIN
Piper
  Actress: **6** LAURIE
  Greek: **3** PAN
  Legendary: **3** PAN
  Like the: **4** PIED
  Son of the: **3** TOM
  wear: **4** KILT
  ___ Piper: **4** PIED
Pipes
  Some bagpipe: **6** DRONES
Pipeye
  Popeye, to: **5** UNCLE
Piping: 5 REEDY
Pippig
  Marathoner: **3** UTA
"Pippi Longstocking"
  author Lindgren: **6** ASTRID
"Pippin"
  actress Ryan: **5** IRENE
  director: **5** FOSSE
Pipsqueak: 4 RUNT **5** TWERP
    6 SHRIMP
Piquancy: 3 NIP **4** TANG ZEST
    5 SPICE
Piquant: 4 RACY TART **5** SALTY
    TANGY ZESTY
Pique: 3 IRE IRK PET **4** RILE
    SNIT **6** AROUSE
  condition: **3** IRE
  experience: **3** IRE **4** SNIT
  Fit of: **4** HUFF SNIT
  period: **4** SNIT

Piqued
state: 4 HUFF SNIT
Pirandello
Author: 5 LUIGI
Pirate: 6 SEADOG 7 CORSAIR
    8 SEAROVER
captain: 4 KIDD
feature: 6 PEGLEG
Fictional: 4 SMEE
interjections: 3 ARS
knife: 4 SNEE
of note: 15 ROBERTOCLEMENTE
place: 7 OPENSEA
plunder: 4 LOOT 5 BOOTY
potable: 3 RUM 4 GROG
punishment: 4 LASH
rival: 5 ASTRO
ship: 7 CORSAIR 8 SEAROVER
Start of a ~ chant: 4 YOHO
"Pirates of the Caribbean"
star: 4 DEPP
Pirelli
product: 4 TIRE
Pirouette: 5 TWIRL
follower: 4 PLIE
Pisa
dough, formerly: 4 LIRA
Emulate the ~ tower: 4 LEAN
Like the ~ tower: 5 ATILT
place: 5 ITALY
river: 4 **ARNO**
Pisan
payments, formerly: 4 LIRE
Pisces
Sign after: 5 ARIES
Pistachio: 3 NUT
Piste
Sport played on a: 4 EPEE
Pistil
partner: 6 STAMEN
Pistol: 3 GUN ROD 7 FIREARM
    SIDEARM
Fully automatic: 7 BURPGUN
German: 5 LUGER
kickback: 6 RECOIL
Kind of: 3 CAP
Point a: 3 AIM
pointer: 5 AIMER
Toy: 6 CAPGUN POPGUN

Toy ~ ammo: 4 CAPS
~, slangily: 3 GAT ROD 4 IRON
Pistol-packing: 5 ARMED
Piston
chamber: 8 CYLINDER
Press: 3 RAM
Pit: 4 SEED
Bottomless: 5 ABYSM **ABYSS**
bull sound: 3 GRR
Caravan ~ stop: 5 OASIS
contents: 3 TAR
Deep: 5 ABYSS CHASM
Do a ~ job: 6 REFUEL
Fruit: 5 STONE
Gaping: 5 ABYSS
Reed in a: 4 OBOE
stuff: 3 TAR
Water: 4 SUMP
Wind in a: 4 OBOE
Pit-___ (heart sound): 3 PAT
Pita
sandwich: 4 GYRO
"Pit and the Pendulum, The"
author: 3 POE
Pitapat
Go: 5 THROB
Pitch: 3 TAR 4 HURL SELL TONE
    TOSS 5 ERECT RESIN
    SLANT SLOPE SPIEL
    THROW
Black as: 4 INKY
catcher: 4 MITT
Certain: 8 HARDSELL
Dangerous: 8 BEANBALL
High: 3 LOB 4 BALL
Hit with a: 4 BEAN
in: 3 AID 4 HELP
In: 5 TUNED
indicator: 4 CLEF NOTE
It may follow a: 4 SALE
Low: 4 BASS
Lowest: 8 SOFTSELL
Musical: 4 TONE
Of: 5 TONAL
One way to: 7 OVERARM
on paper: 7 PRINTAD
Pitcher's: 6 SLIDER
preceder: 3 SLO
Sales: 3 PIE 5 SPIEL

Slow: 3 LOB
Softball: 3 ARC
Successful: 4 SALE
symbol: 4 CLEF
tents: 6 ENCAMP
Tricky: 8 CHANGEUP
Vocal: 4 TONE
Pitch-black: 4 INKY
Pitchblende: 3 ORE
Pitched: 5 THREW
It might be: 3 WOO 4 ROOF
    TENT 7 ROOFTOP
Perfectly: 5 NOHIT
Properly: 5 ONKEY
roof: 4 TENT
too low: 4 FLAT
**Pitcher: 4 EWER 5 ADMAN
    8 SALESMAN**
1950s ~: 5 LOPAT 6 MAGLIE
asset: 3 ARM
Decorative: 4 EWER
dream: 8 NOHITTER
Face the: 3 BAT
Facing the: 5 ATBAT
handle: 3 EAR
nicknamed "Tornado": 4 NOMO
of milk: 5 ELSIE
part: 3 EAR LIP
Perfect game: 6 LARSEN
place: 5 MOUND
plant catch: 6 INSECT
Porcelain: 4 EWER
pride: 3 ARM
prize: 4 CLIO
Relief: 5 SAVER 7 FIREMAN
Relief ~ goal: 4 SAVE
Star: 3 ACE
stat: 3 ERA
target: 4 MITT
Top: 3 ACE
Water: 4 EWER
with a big mouth: 4 EWER
with a record 5,714 strikeouts:
    4 RYAN
~ Early: 4 WYNN
~ Hideki: 5 IRABU
~ Hideo: 4 NOMO
~ Nolan: 4 RYAN
~ Robb: 3 NEN

~ Ryan: 5 NOLAN
~ Satchel: 5 PAIGE
~ Shawn: 5 ESTES
~ Warren: 5 SPAHN
Pitcherful
~, maybe: 3 ALE
Pitches
between innings: 3 ADS
Like some: 7 OUTSIDE SIDEARM
Pitchfork
part: 4 TINE 5 PRONG
Pile by a: 3 HAY
wielder: 5 DEVIL
Pitchfork-shaped
letter: 3 PSI
Pitch ___-hitter: 3 ANO
Pitching
choice: 3 TAR
Game with: 4 GOLF
star: 3 ACE
stat: 3 ERA 4 WINS 5 SAVES
style: 7 SIDEARM
Pitchman: 6 BARKER
___-pitch softball: 3 SLO
Pitfall: 4 TRAP 5 SNARE
Pith: 4 MEAT 7 ESSENCE
helmet: 4 TOPI 5 TOPEE
Pithy: 5 TERSE
Pitiful: 5 SORRY
Pits: 5 NADIR
Took ~ from: 6 STONED
Pit stop
can: 3 STP
maker: 7 RACECAR
Pitt
1995 ~ flick: 5 SEVEN
Actor: 4 BRAD
Penn or: 5 ACTOR
Pittance: 3 SOU 4 MITE
preceder: 4 MERE
~, slangily: 3 HAY
Pitter-patter
maker: 4 RAIN
Pitts
Actress: 4 ZASU
Pittsburgh
co.: 7 USSTEEL
German: 5 ESSEN
pro: 7 STEELER

river: 4 OHIO
team: 7 PIRATES 8 STEELERS
Pituitary: 5 GLAND
hormone: 4 ACTH
Pity
Feeling of: 6 PATHOS
"Pity!": 4 ALAS
Pius
and others: 5 POPES
Pivot: 4 SLUE 6 ROTATE SWIVEL
around: 4 SLUE
Pivotal: 3 KEY
point: 4 CRUX 5 HINGE
Pix
Pose for: 3 SIT
Pixar
character: 4 NEMO
Pixel: 3 DOT
Alter ~ by pixel: 5 MORPH
Pixie: 3 ELF IMP 6 SPRITE
Pizarro
City founded by: 4 LIMA
conquest: 4 PERU
gold: 3 ORO
victim: 4 INCA
Pizazz: 3 ZIP 4 BRIO **ELAN** ZEST
ZING 5 FLAIR OOMPH
SPICE STYLE VERVE
Lacking: 8 LIFELESS
Without: 5 DRYLY
Piz Bernina: 3 ALP
Pizza: 3 PIE
brand: 7 CELESTE
feature: 5 CRUST
Had a ~ delivered: 5 ATEIN
herb: 7 OREGANO
It's picked up at a ~ parlor:
5 AROMA
order: 3 PIE 4 TOGO
perimeter: 5 CRUST
piece: 5 SLICE
place: 4 OVEN
portion: 8 ONESLICE
slice, often: 6 EIGHTH
topping: 5 BACON ONION
6 OLIVES SALAMI
7 OREGANO SAUSAGE
Pizza Quick
sauce maker: 4 RAGU

Pizzeria
fixture: 4 **OVEN**
lure: 5 AROMA
order: 3 PIE 5 SLICE
patron: 5 EATER
Pizzeria ___ (fast food chain):
3 UNO
Pizzicato
Not: 4 ARCO
Play: 5 PLUCK
Pkg.
Cigarette: 3 CTN
deliverer: 3 UPS
How a ~ may arrive: 3 COD
Placard: 6 POSTER
Placate: 7 APPEASE
Place: 3 LAY PUT SET 4 **LIEU**
SITE SPOT 5 LOCUS
STEAD WHERE 6 LOCALE
7 SITUATE
All over the: 4 RIFE
At the original: 6 INSITU
At this: 4 HERE
First: 4 **EDEN**
for an X: 3 MAP
for losers: 3 SPA
for memories: 4 LANE
for portraits: 4 HALL
for sweaters: 3 SPA
for the night: 3 INN
From that: 6 THENCE
From what: 6 WHENCE
In: 3 SET 4 NEAT
In ~ of: 3 FOR
In first: 5 ONTOP
In that: 5 THERE
In the first: 5 AHEAD
in the Old West: 4 ETTA
In this: 4 HERE
of bliss: 4 EDEN
of honor: 4 DAIS
of refuge: 3 ARK 5 HAVEN
on piles: 4 PIER
on the schedule: 4 SLOT
Person, ~, or thing: 4 NOUN
place: 6 SECOND
Put in: 5 SITED
Run in: 4 IDLE
Show: 5 STAGE THIRD

side by side: 6 APPOSE
Take: 5 OCCUR 6 HAPPEN
Taking-off: 3 SPA
Taking the ~ (of): 6 INLIEU
Third: 4 SHOW
to be taken: 9 CLIPJOINT
to build: 4 SITE
to crash: 3 PAD
to do one's bidding: 4 EBAY
to fish: 6 STREAM
to gambol: 3 LEA
to graze: 3 LEA
to kick something: 5 REHAB
to lay over: 3 INN
to live: 5 ABODE
to moor: 5 INLET
Took: 3 WAS
to park: 3 LOT
to play: 5 ARENA 7 RECROOM
to play b-ball: 4 YMCA
to relax: 3 DEN SPA
to roll: 5 AISLE
to sign: 10 DOTTEDLINE
to sit: 5 CHAIR
to stand a round: 3 BAR
to start a hole: 3 TEE
to stay: 3 INN
to step: 5 ASIDE
to surf: 3 NET
to trade: 4 MART
to unwind: 3 SPA
to work: 4 DESK
" ___ Place": 7 MELROSE
Placed: 4 LAID
Placekicker: 3 TOE
prop: 3 TEE
Place-name
Asian ~ ender: 4 STAN
Places: 4 LOCI
To distant: 4 AFAR
Placid: 4 LAKE 6 SERENE
Plácido
Tenor: 7 DOMINGO
Plagiarize: 4 COPY CRIB LIFT
5 STEAL
Plague: 3 AIL POX VEX 4 PEST
5 BESET 6 HARASS
7 BEDEVIL
Avoid like the: 4 SHUN

Biblical: 7 LOCUSTS
~, to Camus: 5 PESTE
"Plague, The"
setting: 4 ORAN 7 ALGERIA
Plaid: 6 TARTAN
Kind of: 4 GLEN
Plain: 3 DRY 4 BARE 7 GENERIC
Arctic: 6 TUNDRA
Argentine: 5 PAMPA
as day: 8 CLEARCUT
Author: 5 BELVA
Grassy: 5 LLANO 7 SAVANNA
homes: 6 TEPEES
Just ~ bad: 5 AWFUL
Lunar: 4 MARE
Russian: 6 STEPPE
Southwestern: 5 LLANO
to see: 5 OVERT
Treeless: 5 LLANO 6 STEPPE
Tropical: 7 SAVANNA
writing: 5 PROSE
~ Jane: 4 EYRE
Plain ___ : 5 TOSEE
___ Plaines, Illinois: 3 **DES**
Plain-living
sect: 5 AMISH
Plains
drifters: 5 BISON
shelter: 5 TEPEE
tribe: 3 OTO 4 OTOE OTOS
5 KIOWA OSAGE 6 PAWNEE
7 ARAPAHO
Plains Indian: 3 OTO 4 OTOE
5 KIOWA OSAGE
6 PAWNEE 7 ARAPAHO
"Plains of Passage, The"
author: 4 AUEL
Plaint
Kennel: 4 YELP
Persian: 3 MEW
Pooped person's: 6 IMBEAT
Porker: 4 OINK
Plaintext
Translate from: 6 ENCODE
Plaintiff: 4 **SUER** 7 ACCUSER
Certain ~, at law: 4 USEE
Plaintive
cry: 3 MEW 4 MEOW
poem: 5 ELEGY

"__ plaisir!": 4 **AVEC**
Plait: 5 BRAID
Plan: 4 IDEA 6 AGENDA DESIGN
    INTEND SCHEMA
    SCHEME
    Anti-ICBM: 3 SDI
    Food: 4 DIET
    for later yrs.: 3 IRA
    Game: 8 SCENARIO STRATEGY
    General: 7 ROADMAP
    Like a perfect: 9 FOOLPROOF
    Med.: 3 **HMO**
    Meeting: 6 AGENDA
    Nefarious: 6 SCHEME
    on it: 8 INTENDTO
    part: 4 **STEP**
    Part of a: 4 STEP
    Retirement ~ name: 5 KEOGH
    Roth: 3 IRA
    Spending: 6 BUDGET
    to lose: 4 DIET
    Vacation: 4 TRIP
    Word with: 4 GAME
Planchette
    Board with a: 5 OUIJA
Plane: 4 TOOL 6 EVENER
    Attack by: 6 STRAFE
    detector: 5 RADAR
    Famous ~ name part: 5 ENOLA
    Fast: 3 JET
    Fast ~, for short: 3 SST
    flier: 5 PILOT
    Kind of: 6 ASTRAL
    measure: 4 **AREA**
    Old ~ handle: 5 USAIR
    part: 4 NOSE 7 AILERON
    Pilotless: 5 DRONE
    place: 3 SKY
    prefix: 4 AERO AQUA
    reservation: 4 SEAT
    seating choice: 5 AISLE
    Shuttle: 6 AIRBUS
    site: 6 HANGAR
    Small: 9 ONESEATER
    surface: 6 TARMAC
    WWI: 4 SPAD
    WWII: 4 ZERO
Plane-regulating
    gp.: 3 FAA

Plane-related: 4 AERO
Planes
    Big name in small: 6 CESSNA
    Group of: 5 FLEET
    Large fleet of: 6 ARMADA
    Unidentified: 6 BOGIES
Planet: 3 ORB 5 GLOBE 6 SPHERE
    Fourth: 4 MARS
    of Mork: 3 **ORK**
    Outer: 6 URANUS
    Poet's: 3 ORB
    Red: 4 MARS
    Ringed: 6 SATURN
    Seventh: 6 URANUS
    Sitcom: 3 **ORK**
    suffix: 3 OID
    Third: 5 EARTH
    TV: 3 ORK
Planetarium
    display: 5 STARS
Planetary
    path: 5 ORBIT
    revolution: 4 YEAR
    shadow: 5 UMBRA
"**Planet of the __**": 4 APES
"**Planet of the Apes**"
    planet: 5 EARTH
"**Planets, The**"
    composer: 5 HOLST
Plank
    Playground: 6 SEESAW
Plankton
    component: 5 ALGAE
Planned
    Intelligently ~ progress:
        7 TELESIS
Planning
    Bit of financial: 3 IRA
    Federal financial ~ gp.: 3 OMB
    time: 3 EVE
Plans: 8 SCHEMATA
Plant: 3 SOW SPY 5 EMBED
    again: 5 RESOW
    anchor: 4 ROOT
    anew: 5 RESOW
    Aquatic: 4 ALGA
    bristle: 3 AWN
    Climbing: 3 IVY 4 VINE
    Dye: 4 ANIL

firmly: 5 EMBED
fungus: 5 ERGOT
life: 5 FLORA
louse: 5 APHID
malady: 5 EDEMA
more seed: 5 RESOW
Move, as a: 5 REPOT
Nonflowering: 4 FERN
Nonwoody: 4 HERB
of the future: 4 SEED
one on: 4 KIDD
parasite: 5 APHID
parenthood setting:
   10 GREENHOUSE
part: 4 ROOT STEM
pest: 4 MITE 5 APHID BORER
Pet: 4 CHIA
place: 7 NURSERY
Pond: 4 ALGA
pores: 7 STOMATA
pouch: 3 SAC
Prepare to: 3 HOE
Prickly: 5 BRIER 6 TEASEL
Prickly-leafed: 6 TEASEL
Related to ~ life: 7 BOTANIC
reproductive part: 5 SPORE
root: 5 RADIX
Seedless: 4 FERN
stem: 5 STALK
Succulent: 4 **ALOE**
suffix: 4 WORT
swelling: 5 EDEMA
Terrarium: 4 FERN
tissue: 5 XYLEM
with a bitter root: 7 DOGBANE
with arrow-shaped leaves:
   5 CALLA
~, so to speak: 5 INTER
Plantain
lily: 5 HOSTA
Plantation
of fiction: 4 **TARA**
Planted: 4 **SOWN**
How corn is: 6 INROWS
Planter
Large: 3 URN
purchase: 4 SEED
Planting
Fall: 4 BULB

Fit for: 6 ARABLE
Prepare for: 4 PLOW
Plants: 5 FLORA
Desert: 5 CACTI
Plant-to-be: 4 SEED
Plaque
place: 4 WALL
Plasm
prefix: 4 **ECTO** ENDO
Plaster: 5 BESOT
Apply, as: 4 DAUB
backing: 4 LATH
Harden, as: 3 SET
Painter's: 5 GESSO
Painting on: 6 FRESCO
support: 4 LATH
Wall: 6 STUCCO
Plastered: 3 LIT
Plaster of ___: 5 PARIS
Plasterwork
Some: 6 STUCCO
Plastic: 6 CREDIT
alternative: 4 CASH 5 PAPER
item: 3 BAG
Name in: 4 VISA
Pay with: 6 CHARGE
prefix: 5 OSTEO
Switch from ~ to paper: 5 REBAG
Transparent: 6 LUCITE
wrap: 5 **SARAN**
Plastic ___ Band: 3 **ONO**
Plata
Partner of: 3 ORO
Plate
appearance: 5 ATBAT
cleaner: 3 UMP 7 DISHRAG
Diamond: 4 HOME
Do better at the: 6 OUTHIT
Eucharist: 6 PLATEN
License: 3 TAG
No longer on the: 5 EATEN
scrap: 3 ORT
Step to the: 3 BAT
Still on the: 7 UNEATEN
Plateau
boundary: 7 RIMROCK
Western: 4 MESA
___ Plateau (Missouri region):
   5 OZARK

Platform
Choir: 5 RISER
Golf ball: 3 TEE
Old PC: 3 DOS
over the water: 4 PIER
part: 5 PLANK
Place for a ~ (abbr.): 3 STA
Portable: 4 SKID
Speaker: 4 **DAIS**
Platforms: 5 PODIA 6 ROSTRA
Plath, Sylvia
book: 5 ARIEL
novel, with "The": 7 BELLJAR
Plating
material: 3 TIN 4 ZINC
Platinum: 5 METAL
Went: 4 DYED
Platitude: 6 CLICHE TRUISM
Plato
Home of: 6 ATHENS
school: 7 ACADEMY
Teacher of: 8 SOCRATES
Platoon: 4 UNIT
"Platoon"
actor: 5 DEFOE SHEEN
setting: 3 **NAM**
Platte
People of the: 3 OTO 4 OTOS
Platter: 4 DISC
1950s ~: 5 OLDIE
Kind of: 4 PUPU
part: 5 SIDEB
player: 4 HIFI 5 PHONO
Top of a: 5 SIDEA
___ platter: 4 PUPU
Platters
Groovy: 3 LPS
Plaudits: 4 OLES
Plausible
Less: 5 LAMER
Play: 8 RECREATE
again: 7 REPRISE
an ace: 6 AVIATE
area: 4 YARD 5 ARENA
    7 RECROOM
a role: 3 ACT
(around): 5 HORSE
a round: 4 GOLF
backer: 5 ANGEL

ball: 9 COOPERATE
break: 8 ENTRACTE
Bring into: 3 **USE** 6 ENTAIL
by oneself: 4 SOLO
Chance to: 4 TURN
Child's: 3 TAG
Did not: 3 SAT
Does not: 5 RESTS
first: 4 STAR
footsie: 5 FLIRT
for a sap: 3 USE
for reading only:
    11 CLOSETDRAMA
for time: 5 **STALL**
French ~ part: 4 ACTE
ground: 5 ARENA
group: 4 CAST
hard to get: 5 EVADE
How some: 8 FORKEEPS
In: 4 LIVE
in a puddle: 5 SLOSH
in the pool: 6 SPLASH
Lacking: 4 TAUT
lightly: 5 STRUM
Like a short: 6 ONEACT
matchmaker for: 5 FIXUP
mates: 4 CAST
merrily: 6 CAVORT
Off-the-wall: 5 CAROM
One way to: 5 BYEAR
on words: 3 PUN
opener: 4 **ACTI**
part: 3 **ACT** 4 ROLE 5 ACTII
    SCENE
Part to: 4 **ROLE**
Pay to: 4 **ANTE**
place: 5 ARENA
Put on a: 5 STAGE
Roulette: 3 RED
Serious: 5 DRAMA
start: 4 ACTI
Start of a: 4 ACTI 6 ACTONE
Still in: 4 LIVE 5 ALIVE
Students ~ it: 5 HOOKY
the flute: 6 TOOTLE
the lead: 4 STAR
the part: 3 ACT
the part of: 5 ENACT
the role of: 5 ACTAS

They ~ for pay: 3 PRO
thing: 4 PROP ROLE
time: 6 RECESS
to the balcony: 5 EMOTE
tricks: 4 JAPE
Unable to: 4 HURT
unit: 5 SCENE
up: 6 STRESS
Urban ~ area: 7 SANDLOT
What some ~ for: 5 KEEPS
(with): 3 TOY
with masks: 3 NOH
with matches: 6 TENNIS
with robots: 3 RUR
Play-___: 3 DOH
Playback
magazine org.: 5 ASCAP
Playbill
feature: 3 BIO
listing: 4 CAST ROLE
paragraph: 3 BIO
Playboy: 4 ROUE
bunny: 4 LOGO
Featured in: 4 BARE
founder, familiarly: 3 **HEF**
Like ~ cartoons: 6 RIBALD
Like ~ models: 4 SEXY
publisher: 6 HEFNER
**"Playboy of the Western World,
The"**
author: 5 SYNGE
Played
again: 5 RERAN
first: 3 LED
out: 5 STALE
over: 5 RERAN
Player: 5 GAMER
Bit: 5 EXTRA
Bygone: 4 HIFI
Card ~ cry: 3 GIN
Contest: 7 ENTRANT
Golfer: 4 GARY
in a dome: 5 ASTRO
J.V.: 4 SOPH
Key: 7 PIANIST
Lead: 4 STAR
Minor: 3 COG
Money: 3 PRO
Music: 4 JUKE

Paid: 3 **PRO**
Part: 5 ACTOR
Part-time: 7 SEMIPRO
Poker: 6 RAISER 8 GAMESTER
Top: 4 STAR
turn: 4 MOVE
Players: 4 CAST
CD: 3 DJS
Top: 5 ATEAM
Playful
animal: 5 OTTER
mammal: 5 OTTER
one: 3 IMP
pinch: 5 TWEAK
prank: 5 ANTIC
sort: 5 PIXIE
swimmer: 5 **OTTER**
Playfully: 5 INFUN
roguish: 4 ARCH
Run: 4 ROMP
Playground
comeback: 6 CANTOO
cry: 4 WHEE
equipment: 5 SWING 6 SEESAW
   SLIDES
game: 3 TAG
item: 5 SLIDE
marble: 5 AGATE
plank: 6 SEESAW
retort: 4 AMSO 5 AMNOT ARESO
   CANSO ISNOT ISTOO
sight: 5 SLIDE
Playhouse
Parma: 6 TEATRO
Play ___ in (influence): 5 AROLE
Playing
field: 5 ARENA
hard to get: 3 COY
hooky: 4 AWOL 6 ABSENT
marble: 3 TAW 5 **AGATE** AGGIE
   7 STEELIE
Not: 4 IDLE 11 OUTOFACTION
solitaire: 5 ALONE
with a full deck: 4 SANE
Playing card: 4 TREY
spot: 3 PIP
Playing field
Level the: 3 MOW
Like a fair: 5 LEVEL

"___ Playing Our Song":
6 THEYRE
"Play it, Sam"
speaker: 4 ILSA
"Play It ___, Sam": 5 AGAIN
Playlet: 4 SKIT
Playoff
game: 4 SEMI
Playpen
item: 3 TOY
Plays
6-pt. ~: 3 TDS
Tic-tac-toe: 7 XSANDOS
Playskool
parent company: 6 HASBRO
PlayStation
maker: 4 SONY
Playtex
parent company: 7 SARALEE
product: 3 BRA
Plaything: 3 TOY
Beach: 4 PAIL
Kitten: 4 YARN
Playthings
Construction: 10 TINKERTOYS
Play to ___ (draw): 4 ATIE
Play ___ with (damage): 3 HOB
Playwright
1953 Pulitzer: 4 INGE
dream: 4 OBIE
Kansas: 4 INGE
turned president: 5 HAVEL
~ Clifford: 5 ODETS
~ David: 5 MAMET
~ Henrik: 5 IBSEN
~ Jean: 5 GENET
~ Zoe: 5 AKINS
Plaza: 4 MALL 6 SQUARE
of Plato: 5 AGORA
___ Plaza: 4 ESSO
Plaza Hotel
imp: 6 **ELOISE**
Plea
Court ~, for short: 4 **NOLO**
Kid's: 4 ICAN
Sea: 3 **SOS**
Plead: 3 ASK BEG 7 ENTREAT
a case: 5 ARGUE
innocent to: 4 DENY

Pleasant: 4 **NICE** 6 POLITE
and mild: 5 BALMY
smell: 5 AROMA
to look at: 6 SCENIC
way to walk: 5 ONAIR
Please
Hard to: 5 FUSSY PICKY
6 CHOOSY
More than: 5 ELATE
~, in German: 5 **BITTE**
~, in Siamese: 4 MEOW
___ please (do one's best):
5 AIMTO
Pleased: 4 **GLAD** 5 HAPPY
"Please stay!": 6 DONTGO
"___ please the court ...": 4 IFIT
Pleasing: 4 NICE
scent: 5 AROMA
Pleasure
boat: 5 SLOOP YACHT
dome site: 6 XANADU
Expressed: 5 AAHED OOHED
Great: 4 GLEE
seeker: 8 HEDONIST
Sounds of: 4 AAHS
Take ~ in: 5 EATUP REVEL
6 RELISH
trip: 5 JAUNT
Unexpected: 5 TREAT
Pleasure ___ (hedonists):
7 SEEKERS
Pleasure-seeking: 7 HEDONIC
Pleat: 4 FOLD
Plebe
place: 7 ACADEMY
West Point: 5 CADET
Pledge: 3 VOW 4 OATH 6 COMMIT
SURETY
Courtroom: 4 OATH
drive reward: 4 TOTE
7 TOTEBAG
of fidelity: 5 TROTH
Pledged: 5 SWORE
Pledge of Allegiance
ender: 3 ALL
Pledges
Harass the: 4 HAZE
Pleiades
Father of the: 5 ATLAS

number: 5 SEVEN
One of the: 4 MAIA
pursuer: 5 ORION
Pleistocene: 5 EPOCH
beast: 7 MAMMOTH
epoch: 6 ICEAGE
Plentiful: 4 RIFE 5 AMPLE
Be: 6 ABOUND
Plenty: 4 **ALOT** ATON GOBS
LOTS TONS 6 OODLES
8 OPULENCE
angry: 4 SORE
Biblical place of: 6 GOSHEN
Goddess of: 3 OPS
loud: 5 AROAR
mad: 4 IRED
of: 5 AMPLE
of yore: 4 ENOW
~, slangily: 4 ENUF
"___ Plenty o' Nuttin'" (Gershwin
song): 4 IGOT
Plexiglas: 7 POLYMER
Plexus
Word before: 5 SOLAR
Pliable: 5 WAXEN
leather: 3 ELK
Plied
with port: 5 WINED
Pliers
Kind of: 10 NEEDLENOSE
Plies
a needle: 4 SEWS
Plight: 4 MESS
Plimpton, George
1982 ~ bestseller: 4 EDIE
Pliny the ___: 5 ELDER
PLO
Arafat of the: 5 YASIR 6 YASSER
Former ~ leader: 6 ARAFAT
Plod
along: 4 SLOG 6 TRUDGE
Plop
down: 3 SIT
prefix: 3 **KER**
Plot: 4 PLAN 5 CABAL TRACT
6 SCHEME
Devise, as a: 5 HATCH
in the suburbs: 4 LAWN
of land: 4 ACRE 5 TRACT

outline: 8 SCENARIO
over: 5 REMAP
part: 4 ACRE 5 TWIST
Perfect: 4 EDEN
Shady: 5 ARBOR
unit: 4 ACRE
Plotter
Globe: 4 IAGO
Plotters: 5 CABAL
Plotting: 4 UPTO
group: 5 CABAL
"Plough and the Stars, The"
playwright: 6 OCASEY
Plow: 4 TILL
Hitch to a: 4 YOKE
into: 3 RAM
maker: 5 DEERE
pioneer: 5 **DEERE**
Pull a: 4 TILL
pullers: 4 OXEN TEAM
Reason to: 4 SNOW
Plowshares
Beat swords into: 5 UNARM
Ploy: 4 RUSE TRAP 6 GAMBIT
TACTIC
Marketing: 4 TEST 5 TIEIN
Poker: 5 BLUFF RAISE
Pluck: 4 GRIT 5 MOXIE SPUNK
6 METTLE SPIRIT
out: 6 TWEEZE
Ready to: 4 RIPE
Plucked
instrument: 3 UKE 4 HARP LYRE
Plucky: 4 GAME 5 BRAVE
Plug: 4 TOUT 5 DAMUP PROMO
away: 5 SLOG TOIL
of tobacco: 4 CHAW
part: 5 PRONG
Pull the ~ on: 3 **END** 4 STOP
suffix: 3 OLA
up: 4 FILL
Plugging
away: 4 **ATIT**
Plugs: 3 ADS
Plum: 3 HUE 4 TREE 5 COLOR
center: 3 PIT
Dried: 5 PRUNE
Exec: 4 PERK
finder of rhyme: 6 HORNER

pudding ingredient: 4 SUET
relative: 7 MAGENTA
Tart: 4 SLOE
variety: 4 GAGE SLOE
   6 DAMSON
wild: 4 SLOE

Plumb
Actress: 3 EVE
crazy: 4 **LOCO**

Plumb ___: 4 LOCO

Plumber
Good name for a: 3 FLO
Job for a: 4 DRIP LEAK
joint: 3 ELL TEE
tool: 5 SNAKE

Plumbing
convenience: 12 RUNNINGWATER
joint: 3 ELL
Kind of: 6 INDOOR
problem: 4 CLOG DRIP LEAK

Plume
owner: 5 TANTE
source: 5 EGRET
___ plume: 5 NOMDE

Plumed
hat: 5 SHAKO
heron: 5 EGRET
wader: 5 EGRET

Plumlike
fruit: 4 **SLOE**

Plummer
Actress: 6 **AMANDA**

Plummet: 4 DIVE DROP FALL
   8 NOSEDIVE

Plump
and then some: 5 **OBESE**

Plunder: 3 ROB 4 LOOT SACK
   SWAG 5 BOOTY RIFLE
   6 MARAUD RAVAGE
~, old-style: 5 REAVE

Plundered
~, old-style: 4 REFT

Plunderer
take: 4 SWAG

Plunge: 4 DIVE DROP
Take the: 3 WED
Took the: 4 DOVE 5 LEAPT

Plunk
(down): 3 PUT

preceder: 3 **KER**

Pluperfect: 5 TENSE

Plural
suffix: 3 IES 4 EERS

Pluralized
~ Y: 3 IES

Pluralizing
letter: 3 ESS

Plus: 3 **AND** 4 ALSO 5 ASSET
item: 5 ASSET
others (abbr.): 4 ETAL

Pluses and minuses
It has: 4 MATH
They have their: 4 IONS

Plus-size
model: 4 **EMME**

Plutarch
subject: 4 CATO

Pluto
and others: 4 GODS
ender: 4 CRAT
realm: 5 HADES

Plutocrat
backer: 6 FATCAT

Pluvial: 3 WET 5 RAINY

Ply: 3 USE 5 LAYER
the seas: 4 SAIL
with a feast: 6 REGALE

Plymouth
1970s ~: 6 DUSTER
pilgrim: 5 ALDEN 8 STANDISH
Standish of: 5 MILES MYLES

Plymouth Reliant: 4 KCAR

Plywood
feature: 6 VENEER
section: 5 PANEL

P.M.
4 ~: 7 TEATIME
11 ~, to some: 7 BEDTIME
British ~ Douglas-Home: 4 ALEC
British ~ educator: 4 ETON
British ~ Tony: 5 BLAIR
Early: 3 AFT
First Burmese: 3 UNU
First Indian: 5 NEHRU
Former British: 4 EDEN PITT
   8 DISRAELI
Former Greek ~ Papandreou:
   7 ANDREAS

Former Irish ~ Cosgrave:
  4 LIAM
Former Israeli: 4 MEIR
Former Italian: 4 MORO
Former Japanese: 4 SATO
Former Swedish ~ Palme:
  4 OLOF
times: 4 AFTS

Pmt.
Bank: 3 INT
Homeowner: 4 MTGE
Loan: 3 INT
Proof of: 4 RCPT
Security: 3 DEP

Pneumo
What ~ means: 4 LUNG

Po
City on the: 5 TURIN
land: 5 ITALY

P.O.
assignment: 3 RTE
piece: 3 LTR

Poached
edibles: 4 EGGS

Poacher
meal: 4 EGGS
nemesis: 10 GAMEWARDEN

Pocahontas
Husband of: 5 **ROLFE**

Pocatello
state: 5 IDAHO

Pocket: 5 STEAL
bread: 4 PITA
change sound: 6 JINGLE
Edible: 4 PITA
money: 4 CASH
problem: 4 HOLE
residue: 4 LINT
Watch: 3 FOB

Pocket Books
logo: 8 KANGAROO

Pocketful
Golfer: 4 TEES
Nursery rhyme: 3 RYE

"Pocketful of Miracles"
director: 5 CAPRA

Pocket protector
item: 3 PEN
wearer: 4 NERD

Pockets
Like rich: 4 DEEP
Pasta with: 7 RAVIOLI
They're found in: 4 ORES

Pod
Cotton: 4 BOLL
Edible: 5 CAROB
member: 5 WHALE
prefix: 3 TRI
veggie: 3 PEA 4 **OKRA**
  8 SNAPBEAN

Podiatrist
case: 5 CORNS

Podium
Take the: 5 ORATE
___ podrida: 4 **OLLA**

Poe
family: 5 USHER
Like ~ works: 5 EERIE
maiden: 6 LENORE 7 ANNABEL
middle name: 5 ALLAN
poem: 6 LENORE 7 ULALUME
  8 THEBELLS THERAVEN
  9 TAMERLANE
story setting: 3 PIT
visitor: 5 RAVEN

Poe, ___ Allan: 5 EDGAR
Poe, Edgar ___ : 5 ALLAN

Poem: 5 VERSE
14-line ~: 6 RONDEL SONNET
Classic: 5 EPODE
final stanza: 5 ENVOI
Holiday ~ opener: 4 TWAS
Inspired: 3 ODE
Kind of: 3 ODE
Long: 4 EPIC
Love ~ of 1849:
  10 ANNABELLEE
Lyric: 3 ODE 5 EPODE
Mournful: 5 ELEGY
Mystical: 4 RUNE
of 24 books: 5 ILIAD
of homage: 3 ODE
of lament: 5 ELEGY
Old Testament: 5 PSALM
part: 5 CANTO VERSE 6 STANZA
Pastoral: 4 **IDYL** 5 IDYLL
Plaintive: 5 ELEGY
Praiseful: 3 **ODE**

Sacred: 5 PSALM
Short: 6 RONDEL
Six-line: 6 SESTET
Symphonic ~ creator: 5 LISZT
with 17 syllables: 5 HAIKU
with a punch line: 8 LIMERICK
"... poem lovely as ___": 5 ATREE
Poet: 4 BARD
  1948 Pulitzer Prize: 5 AUDEN
  Chilean: 6 NERUDA
  Chinese: 4 LIPO
  Classical lyric: 6 SAPPHO
        8 ANACREON
  concern: 5 METER
  contraction: 3 EEN TIL TIS
  English: 4 TATE 5 KEATS
  eye: 3 ORB
  foot: 4 IAMB
  Indian: 6 TAGORE
  Irish: 5 YEATS
  Italian: 5 TASSO
  laureate Nicholas: 4 ROWE
  laureate of 1692: 4 TATE
  Lyric: 4 BARD 5 ODIST
  Metaphysical: 5 DONEN
  monogram: 3 TSE
  muse: 5 **ERATO**
  pause: 7 CAESURA
  Persian: 4 OMAR
  preposition: 3 **ERE** OER
        5 ANEAR
  Roman: 4 **OVID**
  suffix: 4 ICAL
  ~ Crane: 4 HART
  ~ Federico García: 5 LORCA
  ~ Heinrich: 5 HEINE
  ~ Mark Van: 5 DOREN
  ~ Nahum: 4 TATE
  ~ Ogden: 4 NASH
  ~ Stephen Vincent: 5 BENET
  ~ T.S.: 5 ELIOT
  ~ W.H.: 5 AUDEN
Poetic
  adverb: 3 EEN **EER** OFT
        4 ANON NEER
  conjunction: 3 ERE
  contraction: 3 EEN EER OER TIS
        4 NEER
  Exaltedly: 4 ODIC

foot: 4 IAMB
form: 3 ODE
It may be: 7 LICENSE
preposition: 3 **ERE** OER
pugilist: 3 ALI
time: 3 EEN 4 MORN
tribute: 3 **ODE**
verb: 3 OPE
~ Muse: 5 **ERATO**
"___ Poetica" (Horace poem):
    3 ARS
Poet laureate
  17th-century: 6 DRYDEN
  ~ Hughes: 3 TED
  ~ Nahum: 4 TATE
  ~ Nicholas: 4 ROWE
Poetry: 5 VERSE
  fight: 4 SLAM
  Icelandic: 4 EDDA
  Land of: 4 ERIN
  Muse of: 5 **ERATO**
  Norse ~ collection: 4 EDDA
  Oral: 4 EPOS
"___ Poets Society": 4 DEAD
Pogo: 6 POSSUM 7 OPOSSUM
  cartoonist Kelly: 4 WALT
Pogs: 3 FAD
Poi
  party: 4 LUAU
  source: 4 **TARO**
Point: 3 AIM DOT NIB USE
        4 CRUX GIST ITEM NODE
        TINE
  a finger at: 5 BLAME 6 ACCUSE
  after deuce: 4 ADIN
  At any: 4 EVER
  At that: 4 THEN
  at the dinner table: 4 TINE
  At this: 4 HERE
  Ball: 3 TEE
  Break: 5 ADOUT
  Central: 4 CRUX GIST NODE
        5 MIDST NAVEL
  Come to a: 5 TAPER
  Connecting: 4 NODE
  Crisis: 4 HEAD
  Decimal: 3 DOT
  Drop-off: 4 EDGE
  Fine: 6 DETAIL NICETY

Focal: 3 HUB 4 NODE
9 EPICENTER
Get the: 3 SEE
Get to the: 5 TAPER
Good: 5 ASSET
Highest: 3 TOP 4 **ACME** APEX
5 CREST 6 APOGEE ZENITH
7 EVEREST
in the right direction: 6 ORIENT
It ends in a: 5 FABLE
Junction: 4 NODE
Kind of: 5 FOCAL
Lookout: 5 AERIE
Lowest: 5 **NADIR**
Made a: 6 SCORED
Main: 4 CRUX GIST
Make a: 5 TAPER
More to the: 6 TERSER
Needle: 3 ENE ESE 4 EAST
5 NORTH
of decline: 3 EBB
of no return: 3 ACE
of view: 5 ANGLE SLANT STAND
Orbital: 4 NODE 5 APSIS
6 APOGEE 7 PERIGEE
Orbital high: 6 APOGEE
out: 7 MENTION
15 CALLATTENTIONTO
Overflow: 3 RIM
Perspiration: 4 PORE
Pivotal: 4 CRUX
Regarding this: 6 HERETO
Selling: 5 ASSET KIOSK STORE
Starting: 4 GERM 6 ORIGIN
Sticking: 4 CRAW TINE
Strong: 5 ASSET FORTE
Talking: 3 JAW 5 TOPIC
To the: 3 APT 5 PITHY **TERSE**
To this: 3 YET 5 ASYET SOFAR
Turning: 4 AXIS AXLE EDDY
5 HINGE PIVOT 6 CRISIS
Up to this: 3 YET 5 ASYET
___ point
(never): 4 ATNO
(somewhat): 5 UPTOA
(stitch): 4 GROS
"___ Pointe Blank" (John Cusack
film): 6 GROSSE
Pointed: 5 SHARP 6 ACUATE

arch: 4 OGEE 5 OGIVE
beard: 6 GOATEE
end: 3 NIB
remark: 4 BARB
tool: 3 AWL
Pointer: 3 TIP 5 ARROW
11 INDEXFINGER
Finger: 7 ACCUSER
West: 5 CADET
word: 4 THAT
Pointer Sisters
hit: 6 DAREME 8 HESSOSHY
One of the: 5 ANITA
Pointillist
painter Georges: 6 SEURAT
point: 3 DOT
Pointless: 5 **INANE** NOUSE
6 FUTILE OTIOSE
event: 4 EPEE
Point ___ return: 4 OFNO
Points: 4 FOCI
High: 6 APICES
Pointy
beard: 6 GOATEE
shoe wearer: 3 ELF
Poirot
Hercule: 6 SLEUTH
job: 4 CASE
portrayer: 7 USTINOV
Poise: 6 APLOMB
Poison: 4 BANE 5 TOXIN
Arrow: 4 INEE 6 CURARE
checker: 6 TASTER
conduit: 4 FANG
Snake: 5 VENOM
Poison ___ : 3 OAK 5 SUMAC
Poisoner
of Britannicus: 4 NERO
Poison ivy
relative: 5 SUMAC
symptom: 4 ITCH RASH
Poison Ivy
portrayer: 3 UMA
Poisonous: 5 TOXIC
plant: 5 SUMAC 7 HENBANE
8 OLEANDER
snake: 3 **ASP** 5 VIPER
Poitier
Actor: 6 SIDNEY

film: 15 ARAISININTHESUN
role: 3 SIR 5 TIBBS
Poitiers
pal: 3 AMI
Poivre
Partner of: 3 SEL
Poke: 3 JAB 4 GOAD PROD
      5 NUDGE
around: 5 SNOOP
fun at: 3 KID RIB 4 MOCK TWIT
      5 **TEASE** 6 NEEDLE
holes in: 4 STAB
Sharp: 3 JAB
with a pin: 5 PRICK
Pokémon: 3 FAD
Poker
action: 3 BET 4 CALL
buy-in: 4 ANTE
card: 3 ACE 4 TREY 5 DEUCE
declaration: 4 **IMIN** 5 ICALL
      IFOLD 6 IRAISE
dream: 10 ROYALFLUSH
fee: 4 ANTE
holding: 4 PAIR
Match in: 3 SEE
Maximum ~ bet: 5 ALLIN
payment: 4 **ANTE**
phrase: 4 IMIN 5 ICALL 6 IRAISE
player: 6 RAISER 8 GAMESTER
prize: 3 POT
stake: 4 **ANTE**
starter: 4 ANTE
strategy: 5 BLUFF RAISE
Stud. 4 SPUR
token: 4 CHIP
variety: 4 DRAW STUD
winnings: 4 POTS
Poker Flat
creator: 5 HARTE
Poky: 3 CAN JUG 4 SLOW STIR
Pol
backer: 6 FATCAT
Certain: 3 DEM
concern: 5 IMAGE
D.C.: 3 SEN
Minor: 6 HEELER
Pol.
neighbor: 3 GER 4 LITH
Old ~ division: 3 SSR

Pola
of the silents: 5 NEGRI
Poland
capital: 6 WARSAW
Gp. joined by: 4 NATO
Lech of: 6 WALESA
river: 4 ODER
Walesa of: 4 **LECH**
Poland Spring
rival: 5 EVIAN
Polanski
Director: 5 ROMAN
film: 4 TESS
Polar: 6 ARCTIC
buildup: 6 ICECAP
crew: 5 ELVES
explorer: 4 BYRD
feature: 6 ICECAP
formation: 6 ICECAP
      8 ICESHEET
jacket: 6 ANORAK
worker: 3 ELF
Polaris: 4 STAR
place: 9 URSAMINOR
Polaroid: 4 SNAP
Pole: 4 **SLAV** 8 EUROPEAN
Carved: 5 TOTEM
Climb a: 4 SHIN
Fishing: 3 ROD
Fowl: 5 ROOST
image: 5 TOTEM
Indian: 5 TOTEM
Kind of: 5 TOTEM
length: 7 TENFEET
Nautical: 4 MAST SPAR
      5 SPRIT
Positive: 5 ANODE
seeker of 1909: 5 PEARY
star: 5 CLAUS SANTA
tossed by Scots: 5 CABER
Toward Santa's: 5 NORTH
Used a firehouse: 4 SLID
vault: 5 EVENT
vault unit: 5 ZLOTY
worker: 3 ELF
___ Pole: 5 TOTEM
Polecat
defense: 4 ODOR
kin: 6 FERRET

Pole Position
  company: 5 ATARI
Poles
  Chair on: 5 SEDAN
  Flattened at the: 6 OBLATE
  with footrests: 6 STILTS
Pole-to-pole
  line: 4 AXIS
Poli ___ : 3 SCI
Police: 4 COPS
  1980s TV ~ comedy: 4 ENOS
  action: 4 RAID 6 ARREST
      8 STAKEOUT
  alert (abbr.): 3 **APB**
  area: 8 PRECINCT
  blotter entry: 3 AKA 5 ALIAS
  car warning: 5 SIREN
  cry: 4 RAID 6 OPENUP
  dept. employee: 3 DET
  Former East German secret:
      5 STASI
  Half a TV ~ duo: 5 LACEY
  informer: 7 STOOLIE
      11 STOOLPIGEON
  line: 6 CORDON
  round: 6 PATROL
  search: 7 DRAGNET
  team: 4 SWAT
  The ~, e.g.: 4 TRIO
  WWII USSR secret: 4 NKGB
  ~, with "the": 3 LAW
Policeman: 3 COP
  British: 5 BOBBY
  insignia: 5 BADGE
  patrol: 4 BEAT
"Police Woman"
  Dickinson of: 5 ANGIE
Policy
  1970s Nixon ~: 7 DETENTE
  Get a: 6 INSURE
  gurus: 5 WONKS
  opposer: 4 ANTI
  position: 5 STAND
  reversal: 5 UTURN 8 FLIPFLOP
  Words before: 3 ASA
Polio
  vaccine developer: 4 **SALK**
      5 SABIN
Polish: 4 BUFF EDIT 5 SHINE

Former ~ capital: 6 KRAKOW
Furniture ~ scent: 5 LEMON
language: 4 EDIT
locale: 4 NAIL
Nail: 6 ENAMEL
Nail ~ brand: 5 CUTEX
off: 3 **EAT**
Partner of: 4 **SPIT**
prose: 4 EDIT
remover: 7 ACETONE
river: 4 ODER
sausage: 8 KIELBASA
seaport: 6 GDANSK
Shoe ~ brand: 4 KIWI
      7 SHINOLA
Polished: 5 ADEPT SLEEK SUAVE
      6 SMOOTH URBANE
      7 ELEGANT
  It may be: 4 RICE
  off: 3 **ATE** 5 EATEN
Polishing
  agent: 5 EMERY
"Polish Wedding"
  star: 5 OLIN
Polit.
  label: 3 IND
  Old ~ cause: 3 ERA
Polite: 5 CIVIL
  address: 3 SIR 4 **MAAM**
      5 MADAM
  Far from: 4 RUDE
  interruption: 4 AHEM
  refusal: 5 **NOSIR** 6 NOMAAM
  response: 7 YESMAAM
  Start of a ~ offer: 9 IFYOUWISH
Politely
  Ax: 7 EASEOUT
  Tip: 4 DOFF
Political
  1958–71 ~ inits.: 3 UAR
  buff channel: 5 CSPAN
  cartoonist Thomas: 4 NAST
  faction: 4 BLOC
  Former ~ divs.: 4 SSRS
  funny business: 5 GRAFT
  group: 4 CAMP 5 BLOCK PARTY
  housecleaning: 5 PURGE
  influence: 5 CLOUT
  intrigue: 5 CABAL

Israeli ~ party: 5 LIKUD
mascot creator: 4 NAST
Occasional suffix on ~ titles:
    5 ELECT
Ohio ~ name: 4 TAFT
pamphlet: 5 TRACT
power structure: 7 APPARAT
prefix: 3 GEO
refugee: 6 EMIGRE
satirist Mort: 4 SAHL
scandal: 6 ABSCAM
slant: 4 SPIN
suffix: 3 IST 4 CRAT
ticket: 5 SLATE
Type of ~ campaign: 5 SMEAR
Wealthy ~ patron: 6 FATCAT
~ VIP: 4 BOSS

Politically
incorrect suffix: 4 ETTE
moderate:
        15 MIDDLEOFTHEROAD
neutral sort: 7 MUGWUMP

"Politically Incorrect"
host Bill: 5 **MAHER**

Politician
concern: 5 IMAGE
~ Alexander: 5 LAMAR
~ Bob: 4 DOLE

Politico
Elected (plural): 3 INS
Nasty: 7 SMEARER
~ Alexander: 5 LAMAR
~ Morris or Stewart: 5 UDALL

Politics
Big name in Chicago: 5 DALEY
First name in Mideast: 5 YASIR
Long in: 4 HUEY
prefix: 3 GEO
Root of: 5 ELIHU

Politique
Division: 4 ETAT

Polk
1844 loser to: 4 CLAY
middle name: 4 KNOX
President after: 6 TAYLOR
President before: 5 TYLER

Poll
amt.: 3 PCT
category: 5 OTHER

9 UNDECIDED
finding: 5 TREND
Kind of: 4 EXIT 5 STRAW
suffix: 4 STER

Pollack
Director: 3 SYD
kin: 3 COD

Pollen
gatherer: 3 BEE
producer: 6 **STAMEN**
React to: 6 SNEEZE

Pollen-bearing
part: 6 ANTHER STAMEN

Pollinator
Fig: 4 WASP

Polliwog
Adult: 4 TOAD
place: 4 POND

Pollock
cousin: 3 COD
Paint like: 7 SPATTER

"Pollock"
actress Amy: 7 MADIGAN

Pollock, Jackson
player: 8 EDHARRIS
___ polloi: 3 **HOI**

Polls
Big name in: 5 ROPER
Gain in the: 5 SURGE

Pollster
discovery: 5 TREND
~ Roper: 4 ELMO

Pollutant: 3 ASH
Banned: 3 PCB
Chem.: 3 PCB

Pollute: 5 TAINT 6 DEFILE

Pollution
Air: 4 **SMOG** 5 SMAZE
Kind of: 5 NOISE
monitoring org.: 3 **EPA**
problem: 4 SMOG

Pollux
Mother of: 4 **LEDA**
Twin of: 6 CASTOR

Polly: 4 AUNT
Nephew of Aunt ~: 3 TOM
~, to Tom Sawyer: 4 **AUNT**

"Pollyanna"
author Porter: 7 ELEANOR

Polo: 5 SHIRT
  Actress: 4 TERI
  animal: 4 PONY
  competitor: 4 IZOD
  Explorer: 5 MARCO
  grounds: 4 ASIA
  homeland: 5 ITALY
  in China: 5 MARCO
  period: 7 CHUKKER
Polo, Marco
  crossed it: 4 ASIA
Polo Grounds
  legend: 3 **OTT**
  team: 6 GIANTS
  team, once: 4 METS
Polonaise
  composer: 6 CHOPIN
Polonius
  Daughter of: 7 OPHELIA
  Hiding place for: 5 ARRAS
  Son of: 7 LAERTES
Poltergeist: 6 SPIRIT
Poly
  finish: 5 ESTER
  kin: 5 MULTI
Poly ___ (college major): 3 SCI
___ Poly (West Coast school):
  3 CAL
Polyester
  brand: 6 DACRON
  film brand: 5 MYLAR
Polygon
  measurement: 4 AREA
Polygonal
  recess: 4 APSE
Polygraph
  test failer: 4 LIAR
  wave, maybe: 3 LIE
Polyhymnia: 4 MUSE
  Sister of: 5 ERATO
Polynesian
  drink: 4 KAVA
  First man, in ~ myth: 4 TIKI
  food: 4 TARO
  idol: 4 TIKI
  kingdom: 5 TONGA
  language: 5 MAORI
  paste: 3 POI
  pendant: 4 TIKI

  porch: 5 LANAI
  treat: 11 PUPUPLATTER
Polyp
  Flowerlike: 7 ANEMONE
    10 SEAANEMONE
Polyphemus
  Odysseus, to: 5 NOMAN
Polyphonic
  piece: 5 MOTET
___ Polytechnique: 5 ECOLE
Polytheist: 5 PAGAN
Pom
  alternative: 4 PEKE
Pomade
  relative: 3 GEL
Pomegranate
  Like a: 5 SEEDY
Pomeranian: 6 LAPDOG
  variety: 5 SPITZ
Pomme de ___ (potato):
  5 TERRE
Pomp: 5 ECLAT
  Proclaim with: 5 ORATE
"Pomp and Circumstance"
  composer: 5 ELGAR
Pompano
  relative: 4 SCAD
Pompeii
  attraction: 5 RUINS
  burier: 3 ASH 4 LAVA
  City near: 6 NAPLES
  heroine: 4 IONE
Pompey the Great
  Supporter of: 6 CICERO
Pompom
  Hat with a: 3 TAM
Pompous
  people: 5 ASSES
  sort: 3 **ASS**
  walk: 5 STRUT
Pompously
  Speak: 5 ORATE
Ponce ___: 6 DELEON
Ponce de ___: 4 LEON
Ponch
  Erik who played ~ on TV:
    7 ESTRADA
Poncho
  relative: 6 SERAPE

Pond
 denizen: 3 EFT 4 NEWT TOAD
 Down at the: 5 EIDER
 duck: 4 TEAL
 film: 4 SCUM
 fish: 4 CARP
 floater: 4 ALGA
 greenery: 5 ALGAE
 High: 4 TARN
 Like some ~ life: 5 ALGAL
 plant: 4 ALGA
 Poetic: 4 MERE
 scum: 5 ALGAE
 sound: 5 CROAK
 swimmer: 4 TEAL
 youngster: 3 EFT
Ponder: 4 MULL MUSE 5 BROOD
     WEIGH 8 COGITATE
Ponderosa: 6 SPREAD
 son: 4 HOSS
Pong
 maker: 5 **ATARI**
Pongid
 Certain: 5 ORANG
Ponied
 up: 6 AHORSE
Ponies
 Place to play the ~ (abbr.): 3 OTB
 Play the: 3 BET
Pons
 delivery: 4 ARIA
Ponselle
 Soprano: 4 ROSA
Ponta Delgada
 locale: 6 AZORES
Pont ___ Arts: 3 DES
Ponte Vecchio
 river: 4 **ARNO**
 Water under the: 4 **ARNO**
Ponti
 Director: 5 CARLO
 Wife of: 5 LOREN
Pontiac
 model: 3 GTO 5 FIERO
     7 GRANDAM
 Old ~ model: 3 **GTO**
 place (abbr.): 4 MICH
 tribe: 6 OTTAWA
Pontifical: 5 PAPAL

Pontificate: 5 ORATE
Ponty, Jean-___
 Violinist: 3 LUC
Pony
 American Indian: 6 CAYUSE
 pace: 4 GAIT TROT
 player's loc.: 3 OTB
 prodder: 4 SPUR
 up: 3 PAY
Pony Express
 employee: 5 RIDER
 stop: 4 ELKO
Ponzi
 scheme: 4 SCAM
Pooch: 3 DOG 6 DOGGIE
 Big: 3 LAB
 Comics: 4 ODIE
 Generic: 4 FIDO
 Inge: 5 SHEBA
 Movie: 4 ASTA
 Nickelodeon: 3 REN
 Oz: 4 TOTO
 Primer: 4 SPOT
 Silky-coated: 7 SPANIEL
 Snorkel: 4 OTTO
 Toon: 3 REN
 White House: 4 FALA
Poodle: 3 DOG PET
 Kind of: 3 TOY
 name: 4 FIFI
Pooh: 3 BAH 4 BEAR
 creator: 5 MILNE 7 AAMILNE
 Greeting from: 5 HALLO
 pal: 3 **ROO** 5 KANGA 6 EEYORE
     PIGLET TIGGER
Pooh-bah
 Mideast: 4 AGHA EMIR
 Persian: 4 SHAH
Pooh-pooh: 5 DECRY SCOFF
     6 DERIDE 7 SCOFFAT
     SNEERAT
Pool
 accessory: 3 CUE 4 RACK
     5 CHALK
 color: 4 AQUA
 contents: 5 GENES
 distance: 3 LAP
 division: 4 LANE
 Fix a ~ cue: 5 RETIP

Get in a: 3 BET
Gone across a: 4 SWUM
Kind of: 4 GENE 5 STENO
life: 4 ALGA
Like one end of the: 4 DEEP
member: 5 STENO
Mountain: 4 TARN
Part of a: 4 GENE
party: 5 STENO
Play in the: 6 SPLASH
problem: 5 ALGAE
shot: 5 CAROM MASSE
site: 4 YMCA
stick: 3 CUE
stroke: 5 MASSE
tester: 3 TOE
Toddler in a: 5 WADER
tool: 3 CUE
Type of: 7 SNOOKER
worker: 5 STENO

Poolroom
cube: 5 CHALK
ploy: 5 MASSE
stick: 3 CUE
triangle: 4 RACK

Pools
Like some: 6 HEATED INDOOR
They're in: 5 GENES

Poolside
enclosure: 6 CABANA

Pool table
feature: 8 SLATEBED
material: 4 FELT
rim: 4 RAIL

Poona
place: 5 INDIA

Poop: 4 INFO
out: 4 TIRE

Pooped: 4 BEAT 5 ALLIN WEARY
person's cry: 6 IMBEAT
___ pooped to pop: 3 TOO

Poor: 5 NEEDY 6 INNEED
blokes: 4 SODS
dog's portion: 4 NONE
grade: 3 **DEE**
Like ~ losers: 4 SORE
Like a ~ excuse: 4 LAME
mark: 3 DEE
Money for the: 4 ALMS

movie rating: 7 ONESTAR
woodcutter of folklore:
    7 ALIBABA

Poor box
filler: 4 ALMS
___ poor example: 4 SETA

Poorhouse
In the: 5 NEEDY

"Poor Little Fool"
singer: 11 RICKYNELSON

Poorly: 3 ILL
behaved: 3 BAD
Do: 3 AIL
Feel: 3 **AIL**
Feeling: 3 ILL
kept: 5 SEEDY
lit: 3 DIM
performed: 4 LAME
Treat: 5 ABUSE

"Poor me!": 4 ALAS

"Poor Poor Pitiful Me"
singer Clark: 5 TERRI

Poor Richard: 3 BEN
book: 7 ALMANAC

"Poor Richard's Almanack"
tidbit: 5 ADAGE

"___, poor Yorick!": 4 ALAS

Pop: 3 **DAD** 4 SODA 5 DADDY
    6 PARENT
A: 3 **PER** 4 EACH
Bro of: 3 UNC
Classic: 4 NEHI
Fasten with a: 6 SNAPON
flavor: 4 COLA
follower: 3 ART
hero: 4 IDOL
Jamaican: 3 SKA
John of: 5 ELTON
King of: 6 CAROLE
maker: 6 WEASEL
Mama of: 4 CASS
measure: 5 LITER
Open with a: 6 UNSNAP
Partner of: 3 MOM
Popular: 4 COLA
quiz: 4 TEST
Radar's: 4 NEHI
Singer: 4 IGGY
Sir of: 5 ELTON

star: 4 **IDOL**
stars, often: 9 TEENIDOLS
the question: 3 ASK
They may ~ up: 3 ADS
up: 5 ARISE 6 APPEAR
Word with: 3 ART

Popcorn
additive: 4 SALT
How some ~ is popped: 5 INAIR

Pope
5th-century: 4 LEOI 5 STLEO
7th-century ~: 5 LEOII
10th-century ~: 5 LEOVI
after Marcellus II: 6 PAULIV
cape: 5 ORALE
from 440 to 461: 4 LEOI
nicknamed "the Great": 4 LEOI
of 1605: 5 LEOXI
output: 4 POEM 5 ESSAY
who persuaded Attila not to attack
    Rome: 4 LEOI 5 STLEO

Pope, Alexander
piece: 5 ESSAY

Popeil
of infomercials: 3 RON

Pope John Paul II
first name: 5 KAROL

Pope John XXIII
first name: 6 ANGELO

Popes
First of 13: 4 LEOI
Name of 6: 6 ADRIAN
Name of 8: 5 URBAN
Name of 12: 4 PIUS
Name of 13: 3 LEO

Popeye: 6 SAILOR
creator Elzie: 5 SEGAR
Olive of: 3 **OYL**
phrase: 4 IYAM
power source: 7 SPINACH
rival: 5 BLUTO
Son of: 7 SWEEPEA
sweetie: 5 OLIVE 8 OLIVEOYL
tattoo: 6 ANCHOR
tooter: 4 PIPE
verb: 3 YAM
~, to Pipeye: 5 UNCLE

Popeyed: 4 AGOG
Popinjay: 3 FOP

Poplar: 5 ASPEN
Southwestern: 5 ALAMO
White: 5 **ABELE**

Poppaea
Husband of: 4 NERO

Popped: 5 BURST
up: 5 AROSE 6 ARISEN

Popper
of song: 6 WEASEL
Party: 4 CORK

Poppy
derivative: 6 OPIATE
product: 5 OPIUM

Poppycock: 3 **ROT** 5 BILGE
    HOOEY
"Poppycock!": 3 BAH 4 BOSH
Poppycockish: 5 INANE
Pops: 3 PAS
(abbr.): 3 SRS

Popsicle
flavor: 6 ORANGE

Pop singer
~ Leo: 5 SAYER
~ Taylor: 5 DAYNE
~ Tori: 4 AMOS

Popular: 3 BIG HOT 5 LOVED
Extremely: 3 HOT 4 HUGE
    6 REDHOT
No longer: 3 OUT
Not a ~ type: 4 NERD
resort: 3 RIO
sauce: 4 RAGU
side: 4 SLAW
toast: 3 RYE
___ populi: 3 VOX

Populous
area: 3 URB

Pop-up
breakfast brand: 4 EGGO
nuisances: 3 ADS
Word after: 4 MENU
Pop-ups: 3 ADS

Porcelain
Fine: 9 BONECHINA
Japanese: 5 **IMARI**
making dynasty: 4 MING
pitcher: 4 EWER
Some English: 5 SPODE

Porch: 7 VERANDA

Ancient: 4 STOA
Polynesian: 5 LANAI
Porches
Glassed-in: 7 SOLARIA
Porcine
pad: 3 STY
reply: 4 OINK
title role: 4 BABE
Porcupine: 6 RODENT
barb: 5 QUILL SPINE
Pore
Leaf: 5 STOMA
over: 4 READ
Pores
Plant: 7 STOMATA
Porfirio
Mexican dictator: 4 DIAZ
Porgy: 4 FISH
Love of: 4 **BESS**
variety: 4 SCUP
"Porgy and Bess": 5 OPERA
Pork: 4 MEAT
cut: 4 CHOP LOIN
place: 3 STY
Preserve: 4 SALT
Pork-barreler: 3 POL
Porker
in pictures: 4 BABE
Mother: 3 SOW
place: 3 **STY**
plaint: 4 OINK
Porkpie: 3 HAT
feature: 4 BRIM
Porky: 3 PIG 4 TOON
Love of: 7 PETUNIA
Voice of: 3 MEL
Porn: 4 SMUT
Porous: 5 LEAKY
Porridge
Bear with cold: 4 MAMA
Buckwheat: 5 KASHA
ingredient: 3 OAT
Like some ~, to Goldilocks:
6 TOOHOT
Thin: 5 GRUEL
___ porridge: 5 PEASE
"___ Porridge Hot": 5 PEASE
Porsche
Old ~ model: 6 SPYDER

Port
alternative: 7 MADEIRA
Any ~ in a storm: 5 HAVEN
Israel: 5 EILAT
Leave: 4 SAIL 7 SETSAIL
of Algeria: 4 ORAN
of Brazil: 5 BELEM
of Crete: 5 CANEA
of Iraq: 5 BASRA
of Okinawa: 4 NAHA
of Phoenicia: 5 SIDON
of Yemen: 4 ADEN
Old Rome: 5 OSTIA
on the Loire: 6 NANTES
on the Seine: 5 ROUEN
opening: 4 HELI
Out of: 4 **ASEA** 5 TOSEA
prefix: 4 HELI TELE
vessel: 3 VAT 6 CARAFE
Port-___ (cheese): 5 SALUT
Portable
bed: 3 COT
computer: 6 LAPTOP
cutter: 8 SABERSAW
home: 5 TEPEE
platform: 4 SKID
~ PC: 6 LAPTOP
Portal: 4 DOOR GATE
Popular: 5 YAHOO
Port-au-Prince
land: 5 HAITI
Port du ___ (cheese): 5 SALUT
Port ___, Egypt: 4 SAID
Portend: 4 BODE
Portent: 4 OMEN
Porter: 3 ALE 6 BEARER
Baggage: 6 REDCAP
burden: 4 BAGS
or Younger: 4 COLE
Popular: 6 SHERPA
Pullman: 6 REDCAP
Regretful Miss of: 4 OTIS
Porter, Cole
1929 ~ song: 5 PAREE
birthplace: 5 PERU
title city: 5 PAREE
tune: 7 ROSALIE
~, schoolwise: 3 ELI
Porterhouse: 5 STEAK

alternative: 5 TBONE
request: 4 RARE

Porters
Where to find: 3 PUB

Portfolio
component: 5 STOCK
item: 5 ASSET
part: 3 IRA 4 FUND

Porthos
Friend of: 5 ATHOS 6 ARAMIS
~, to Athos: 3 AMI

Portico
Greek: 4 **STOA**

Portion: 4 DOSE METE PART
     5 PIECE SHARE
(abbr.): 3 SEG
Butter: 3 PAT
Corn: 3 EAR
Game: 4 HALF
(out): 4 METE
Sound: 5 AUDIO

Portland
college: 4 REED
st.: 4 OREG

Portly: 5 STOUT 6 ROTUND
plus: 5 OBESE

Portman
Actress: 7 NATALIE

Portnoy
creator: 4 ROTH

"Portnoy's Complaint"
author: 4 ROTH

Pôrto ___, Brazil: 6 ALEGRE

Portoferraio
island: 4 ELBA

Portrait: 5 IMAGE
     8 LIKENESS
medium: 4 OILS
Penny: 3 ABE
place: 4 HALL
Sit for a: 4 POSE
Stand for a: 5 EASEL
subject: 4 SELF

Portraitist
American Revolutionary:
     5 PEALE
Dutch ~ Frans: 4 HALS
Edwardian: 7 SARGENT
medium: 4 OILS

Portray: 4 LIMN 5 ENACT
     6 DEPICT
again: 7 REENACT

Portrayer: 5 ACTOR

Port St. ___, Florida: 5 LUCIE

Portugal
Euro's predecessor in: 6 ESCUDO
Islands off: 6 AZORES
Lady of: 4 DONA
place: 6 IBERIA
Spain and: 6 IBERIA

Portuguese
city: 6 OPORTO
Former ~ colony: 5 MACAO
Former ~ colony in India: 3 GOA
islands: 6 AZORES
king: 3 REI
king, 1861–89: 4 LUIZ
Old ~ money: 6 ESCUDO
speaking land: 6 ANGOLA
title: 4 DONA
wine: 7 MADEIRA

Pos.
Opposite of: 3 NEG

Posada: 3 INN

Pose: 3 SIT
again: 7 REFRAME

Posed: 3 PUT SAT

Poseidon: 6 SEAGOD 7 NEPTUNE
Mother of: 4 RHEA
realm: 3 **SEA**
Son of: 5 ORION 6 TRITON
spear: 7 TRIDENT

Poser: 5 MODEL 6 ENIGMA
     7 TOUGHIE
Present a: 3 ASK

Posh: 5 RITZY 7 ELEGANT
Far from: 5 SEEDY
property: 6 ESTATE

Posit
prefix: 3 OVI

Position: 3 JOB PUT SET 4 RANK
     ROLE SITE 5 STAND
     STEAD TENET 6 STANCE
at sea: 4 ALEE
Central: 5 MIDST
In a tough: 5 TREED
It may put you in a difficult:
     4 YOGA

Kind of: 4 POLE 5 FETAL
  LOTUS
of authority: 5 CHAIR
of control: 4 HELM
Precarious: 7 THINICE
Put in: 3 SET
Put in a: 4 HIRE
Rough: 3 LIE
to fill: 4 ROLE SLOT
Top: 3 ONE
Uncomfortable: 7 HOTSEAT

Positioned
Is: 4 LIES
Properly: 7 INPLACE

Positive: 4 SURE
aspect: 6 UPSIDE
feedback: 5 YESES
It may be: 3 ION
pole: 5 ANODE
principle: 4 YANG
response: 3 YES
thinker: 5 PEALE
vote: 3 AYE YEA
Was: 4 KNEW

Positively
State: 4 AVER 6 ASSERT

Positron
place: 4 ATOM

Posse: 4 GANG
Picture with a: 5 OATER

Possess: 3 OWN 4 HAVE
Does not: 5 HASNT
~, to Burns: 3 HAE

Possessed: 3 HAD

Possesses: 3 **HAS**
~, old-style: 4 HATH

Possession
Keep ~ of: 6 RETAIN

"Possession of fools"
~, to Herodotus: 5 PRIDE

Possessions
Worldly: 6 ESTATE

Possessive
Biblical: 5 THINE
Dogpatch: 4 HISN
French: 3 SES TES 4 AMOI ATOI
Italian: 3 MIO
pronoun: 3 ITS

Possibilities: 3 IFS

Possibility
Word of: 3 MAY

Possible
All: 5 EVERY
Best: 5 IDEAL
Least: 7 MINIMAL
Make: 6 **ENABLE**

Possibly: 5 MAYBE

Possum
Comics: 4 POGO

Post: 4 MAIL SEND 7 AVIATOR
Aviator: 5 WILEY
delivery (abbr.): 3 ENV
ending: 3 URE
Go from pillar to: 4 ROVE
Hitching: 5 **ALTAR**
in a flight: 5 NEWEL
Not pre or: 3 MID
of etiquette: 5 EMILY
Opposite of: 3 PRE
position: 6 EDITOR
production: 4 NEWS 6 CEREAL
Read but not: 4 LURK
Ready to: 7 STAMPED
Skipper's: 4 HELM
Stairway: 5 NEWEL

Post-___: 6 MORTEM

Post, Wilbur
horse: 4 MRED

Post-accident
statement: 4 IMOK

Postage
item: 5 STAMP
meter unit: 5 OUNCE
sheet: 4 PANE

Postal
abbr.: 3 RFD
creed word: 3 **NOR**
delivery: 4 MAIL
Go: 4 SNAP 6 LOSEIT

Post-Baroque: 6 ROCOCO

Post-blizzard
stuff: 5 SLUSH

Postcards
Like early: 7 ONECENT

Posted: 4 SENT
It's: 4 BAIL

Poster
1960s ~ genre: 5 OPART

boy: **6** ADONIS
heading: **6** REWARD WANTED
letters: **3** AKA
person: **4** IDOL
Post-ER
place: **3** ICU
Posterior: 4 HIND
Postgame
summary: **5** RECAP
Postgrad
deg.: **3** MBA
degrees: **3** MAS
Postgraduate
hurdle: **4** ORAL
study: **3** LAW
Post-It: 4 NOTE
"Postman Always Rings Twice, The"
wife: **4** CORA
Postman's Creed
word: **3** NOR
Post-mark
currency: **4** EURO
Postmortem
bio: **4** OBIT
Post office
activity: **4** KISS
gizmo: **5** DATER
machine: **6** SORTER
motto word: **3** NOR
Post-op
time: **5** REHAB
Postpaid
enc.: **4** SASE
Postpone: 5 DEFER TABLE
Postponement: 4 STAY
cause: **4** RAIN
Postprandial
handout: **5** MINTS
libation: **4** PORT
Postscript
Literary: **6** EPILOG
Musical: **4** CODA
PostScript
creator: **5** ADOBE
Postscripts: 7 ADDENDA
Posture
Having poor: **7** UNERECT
problem: **5** STOOP

Yoga: **5** ASANA
Posturepedic
maker: **5** SEALY
Postwar
period: **9** PEACETIME
Post-workout
woe: **4** ACHE
Post-WWII
alliance: **4** NATO
Pot: 6 KETTLE
contents: **4** BETS
Earthen cooking: **4** <u>**OLLA**</u>
grower: **4** ANTE
Hot: **4** STEW
In debt to the: **3** SHY
It might go into a: **4** CHIT
Meal in a: **4** STEW
Pouring: **5** CRUSE
Spanish: **4** OLLA
starter: **4** <u>**ANTE**</u>
Sweeten the: **5** RAISE
top: **3** LID
Potable
Make: **6** DESALT
Potent: **3** ALE RUM RYE
Pub: **3** ALE **5** STOUT
Potala Palace
setting: **5** LHASA TIBET
Potash
Caustic: **3** LYE
Potassium ___ (food preservative): 7 SORBATE
Potassium hydroxide: 3 LYE
Potatlon
Pirate: **4** GROG
Pub: **3** ALE
Potato: 4 SPUD **5** TUBER
alternative: **4** RICE **5** PASTA PILAF
choice: **6** MASHED
covering: **4** SKIN
feature: **3** EYE
holder: **4** SACK
pancake: **5** <u>**LATKE**</u>
Quality: **5** IDAHO
state: **5** IDAHO
Sweet: **3** <u>**YAM**</u>
7 OCARINA
tool: **5** RICER

Potato chip
accompanier: 8 ONIONDIP
brand: 4 LAYS
feature: 5 RIDGE
flavor: 3 BBQ 5 CHIVE
Like a: 5 SALTY
Like a ~, perhaps: 6 RIDGED
Wise ~ symbol: 3 OWL
~, to a Brit: 5 CRISP
Potatoes: 5 CARBS
Meat and: 4 FOOD
Partner of: 4 MEAT
Peeling ~, perhaps: 4 ONKP
Prepare: 4 MASH RICE
Word before: 5 SMALL
Potatoes au ___: 6 GRATIN
Potato sack
material: 6 BURLAP
wt.: 5 TENLB
Potbelly: 5 STOVE
Potemkin
setting: 6 ODESSA
Potent
mixture: 11 WITCHESBREW
potable: 3 ALE RYE
prefix: 4 **OMNI**
Potentate: 6 DYNAST
Mideast: 4 EMIR
Persian: 4 SHAH
Turkish: 4 AGHA
Potential: 6 LATENT
7 PROMISE
Potentially
explosive situation:
9 POWDERKEG
"Potent Potables for 200, ___":
4 ALEX
Pother: 3 ADO 4 STIR
Pothook
shape: 3 **ESS**
Potion: 6 ELIXIR
Potions
Potter's ~ professor: 5 SNAPE
Potluck
choice: 4 DISH
dish: 9 CASSEROLE
15 NOODLECASSEROLE
Potok
Author: 5 CHAIM

Potomac
Army of the ~ leader: 5 MEADE
Potpie
veggie: 3 **PEA**
Potpourri: 4 **OLIO**
bag: 6 SACHET
bit: 5 PETAL
container: 3 JAR
ingredient: 9 ROSEPETAL
Like: 8 AROMATIC
output: 5 SCENT
Pots: 7 TINWARE 8 IRONWARE
Fish caught in: 4 EELS
Potsdam
please: 5 BITTE
Potshots
Take: 5 **SNIPE**
Pot-shy
Plays: 4 OWES
Potsie
portrayer: 5 ANSON
Potsticker
cooker: 3 WOK
Potted: 3 LIT
plant place: 4 SILL 5 LEDGE
Potter: 8 CERAMIST
English ~ Josiah: 5 SPODE
material: 4 CLAY
need: 4 CLAY SOIL
oven: 4 KILN
rank (abbr.): 3 COL
Potter, Harry: 4 TEEN
Hedwig belonging to: 3 OWL
lightning bolt: 4 SCAR
potions professor: 5 SNAPE
prop: 4 WAND
study: 5 MAGIC
Pottery: 4 WARE
Blue and white: 5 DELFT
Dutch: 5 DELFT
finish: 5 GLAZE
fragment: 5 SHARD
oven: 4 KILN
worker: 8 ENAMELER
Potting
need: 4 SOIL
soil: 4 LOAM
POTUS
part (abbr.): 4 PRES

Title akin to: 4 CINC
Potvin
  of hockey: 5 DENIS
Pou ___ (vantage point): 3 STO
Pouch: 3 **SAC**
  Anatomical: 3 **SAC**
  Animal in a: 3 ROO
  Animal with a: 7 OPOSSUM
  Highlander: 7 SPORRAN
Poughkeepsie
  college: 6 MARIST VASSAR
Poultry
  chicken: 7 ROASTER
  choice: 5 CAPON
  giant: 5 TYSON
  product: 3 EGG
Pounce
  (upon): 4 LEAP
Pound: 4 MASH 5 SMITE
      THROB
  and others: 5 POETS
  and Stone: 5 EZRAS
  (down): 4 TAMP
  Foot in a: 3 PAW
  notes: 6 ARFARF
  of flesh, e.g.: 4 DEBT
  One ~ and one shilling, once:
      6 GUINEA
  part: 5 OUNCE **PENCE**
  poem part: 5 CANTO
  Poet: 4 EZRA
  resident: 4 MUTT 5 STRAY
      8 STRAYDOG
  sound: 3 **ARF** GRR YAP YIP
      4 THUD WOOF YELP
  sterling: 4 QUID
  unrelentingly: 4 PELT
Pound, Ezra: 4 POET 7 IDAHOAN
Pounder
  Actress: 3 CCH
  Door ~ demand: 6 OPENUP
  Gavel ~ word: 5 ORDER
Pounding
  tool: 6 PESTLE
Pounds
  2.2 ~: 4 KILO
  14 ~, in Britain: 5 STONE
  100 ~ (abbr.): 3 CWT
  100 ~ of nails: 3 KEG

140 ~, in Britain: 8 TENSTONE
2,000 ~: 3 TON
Put on: 4 GAIN
Pour: 4 RAIN
  down: 4 RAIN
  Here's one ~ vous: 3 UNE
  out: 5 EMPTY 6 DECANT
  Pub: 3 ALE
  Ready to: 5 ONTAP
  ~, as wine: 6 DECANT
Pour ___: 4 ITON
Pourer: 4 EWER
  pot: 5 CRUSE
  request: 7 SAYWHEN
Pout: 4 **MOUE** SULK
Poverty: 4 NEED WANT
  ~, symbolically: 4 RAGS
Poverty-stricken: 5 NEEDY
POW
  Sitcom: 5 HOGAN
"Pow!": 3 BAM 4 WHAM
Powder: 4 SNOW TALC
  Bath: 4 **TALC**
  Chilly: 4 SNOW
  Cleansing: 5 BORAX
  holder: 4 HORN
  Printer: 5 TONER
  room: 7 ARSENAL
  Soothing: 4 TALC
  Take a: 3 LAM 5 SCRAM
  Took a: 4 FLED LEFT
Powdery: 4 FINE
Powell
  area: 15 STATEDEPARTMENT
  Frequent ~ costar: 3 LOY
  General: 5 COLIN
  Like Gen. ~: 3 RET
  of baseball: 4 BOOG
  Secretary: 5 COLIN
  Tap dancer: 7 ELEANOR
Power: 3 GAS 5 JUICE MIGHT
      SINEW 6 ENERGY
  Actor: 6 TYRONE
  Center of: 5 LOCUS
  Centers of: 4 LOCI
  choice: 4 ACDC
  co. product: 4 ELEC
  Exercise: 5 WIELD
  Give ~ to: 4 VEST 6 ENABLE

Government in: **6** REGIME
Has ~ over: **4** OWNS
Have staying: **4** LAST
High: **3** NTH
holders: **3** INS
Increase in: **5** SURGE
jolt: **5** SURGE
Kind of: **3** NTH **5** SOLAR
Lost: **4** DIED
Muscle: **5** SINEW
network: **4** GRID
Not at full: **5** ONLOW
period: **5** REIGN
problem: **5** SURGE **6** OUTAGE
Put in: **8** ENTHRONE
Raise to the third: **4** CUBE
Reflective: **6** ALBEDO
Remove from: **8** DETHRONE
source: **5** MOTOR STEAM
Southern ~ inits.: **3** TVA
stats: **3** RBI
Staying: **4** LEGS **7** INERTIA
    STAMINA
Super: **3** ESP
symbol: **3** ORB
Those in: **3** INS
Topple from: **4** OUST
unit: **4** WATT
"Power"
star: **4** GERE
Power ___: 4 LOOM
"Power and the Glory, The"
author: **6** GREENE
"Power Broker, The"
author Robert: **4** CARO
Powerful
blow: **4** SWAT
person: **5** NABOB
stream: **3** JET
stuff: **3** TNT
Powerless: 5 ATBAY **6** UNABLE
to move: **5** INERT
"Power Lunch"
network: **4** CNBC
"Power of Positive Thinking, The"
author: **5** PEALE
Powers
Actress: **4** MALA
Judicial ~ part: **10** ARTICLEIII

or Smart: **5** AGENT
player: **5** MYERS
that be: **3** INS
Powwow: 4 CHAT TALK
    7 PALAVER
Pox: 5 CURSE
PR
concern: **5** IMAGE
output: **4** HYPE
person: **3** AGT **5** AGENT
Practical: 5 OFUSE UTILE
It may be: **4** JOKE
joke: **3** GAG **4** JAPE **5** PRANK
    7 LEGPULL
literary genre: **5** HOWTO
Not: **8** ACADEMIC
Practice: 3 PLY **4** WONT **5** DRILL
    USAGE
a part: **8** REHEARSE
Ballet: **4** LEAP
Customary: **4** RITE **5** USAGE
elocution: **5** ORATE
for a rodeo: **5** LASSO
in the outfield: **4** SHAG
Marching: **5** DRILL
Out of: **5** **RUSTY**
piece: **5** **ETUDE**
punching: **4** **SPAR**
"Practice, The"
actress Boyle: **4** LARA
event: **5** TRIAL
Practicing
Prevent from: **6** DISBAR
Practitioner
Divination: **4** SEER
Yoga: **5** HINDU
Prado
Some ~ works: **5** GOYAS
works: **4** ARTE
Pragmatic
one: **7** REALIST
Prague
native: **5** CZECH
premiere of 1921: **3** RUR
Prairie
Argentine: **5** PAMPA
building: **4** SILO
home material: **3** SOD
wolf: **6** COYOTE

Prairie State
  hub: 5 OHARE
Praise: 4 **LAUD** 5 EXALT EXTOL
    KUDOS 7 APPLAUD
    COMMEND
  Overdo the: 4 GUSH
  Poem of: 3 **ODE**
  Shout of: 7 HOSANNA
  Song of: 4 HYMN 5 **PAEAN**
    8 CANTICLE
  to the skies: 5 EXALT EXTOL
  Work of: 3 ODE
"Praise of Folly, The"
  author: 7 ERASMUS
Praiser
  Poetic: 5 ODIST
"Praise the Lord!": 8 ALLELUIA
Praiseworthy: 8 LAUDABLE
    11 MERITORIOUS
Praline
  nut: 5 PECAN
Prance
  about: 6 CAVORT
Prancer
  Forest: 4 DEER
Prank: 3 GAG 4 **DIDO** 5 ANTIC
    CAPER TRICK
  Major: 4 HOAX
  Merry: 4 JEST
  Start of a: 4 DARE
  suffix: 4 STER
Prankster: 3 IMP
  projectile: 3 EGG PEA
Prattle: 3 GAB YAK
Pravda
  provider: 4 TASS
Prawn
  Large: 6 SCAMPI
Pray: 7 ENTREAT
  One way to: 5 ALOUD
  Prepare to: 5 KNEEL
  ~, in Latin: 3 ORA
"___ pray": 5 LETUS
Prayer: 6 ORISON
  beads: 6 ROSARY
  book: 6 MISSAL 7 PSALTER
  ending: 4 **AMEN**
  leader: 4 IMAM
  period: 6 NOVENA

  pronoun: 4 THEE
  response: 4 AMEN
  Rosary: 8 AVEMARIA
  She fought school: 5 OHAIR
  Start of a: 4 NOWI 5 OLORD
  Use a ~ rug: 5 KNEEL
  wheel user: 4 LAMA
  ___ prayer: 4 SAYA
"Prayer for ___ Meany, A":
    4 OWEN
Prayers
  Object of many: 5 ALLAH
Praying
  figure: 5 **ORANT**
  insect: 6 MANTIS
Praying ___: 6 MANTIS
Preach: 5 ORATE
Preacher
  post: 5 ALTAR
  subject: 3 SIN
"Preach on, brother!": 4 AMEN
Preakness: 4 RACE
  1942 ~ winner: 5 ALSAB
Preamble: 5 INTRO PROEM
Prebirth
  berth: 4 WOMB
Precalc
  part: 4 TRIG
Precambrian: 3 ERA
Precarious: 5 SHAKY
  perch: 4 LIMB
  position: 7 THINICE
Precaution
  As a: 6 INCASE
  ___ precaution: 3 ASA
Precede: 6 FOREGO 7 FORERUN
    8 ANTEDATE LEADUPTO
Precedent
  setter: 8 TESTCASE
  ___ precedent: 4 SETA
Preceding
  period: 3 **EVE**
Precept: 4 RULE 5 TENET
  Moral: 5 ETHIC
Precinct: 4 AREA WARD ZONE
    6 SECTOR
Precious: 4 CUTE DEAR
    6 CUTESY
  Act: 7 GETCUTE

instrument: 5 STRAD
metal: 4 GOLD
stone: 3 **GEM** 5 JEWEL
Precipice: 4 EDGE
Precipitate: 4 RAIN RASH
    5 HASTY 6 HASTEN
Precipitation: 4 RAIN
  Icy: 4 HAIL 5 SLEET
  Winter: 4 SNOW 5 SLEET
Precipitous: 5 STEEP
  Make more: 7 STEEPEN
Precise: 5 EXACT 6 DEADON
  Aim at the ~ center: 6 ZEROIN
Precisely: 4 TOAT 6 TOATEE
  11 TOTHELETTER
Precision
  group: 9 DRILLTEAM
Preclude: 5 DEBAR
Precollege: 4 ELHI
Preconditions: 3 IFS
Precook: 7 PARBOIL
Predator: 5 SHARK
  Black-and-white: 4 ORCA
  Ocean: 4 ORCA
    10 NURSESHARK
  seabird: 4 ERNE SKUA
  Veldt: 4 LION
  WWII: 5 UBOAT
  Young: 5 OWLET
Predatory
  bird: 6 RAPTOR
  dolphin: 4 ORCA
  group: 4 PACK
Predestine: 6 ORDAIN
Predicament: 3 JAM 4 BIND MESS
  SPOT 6 SCRAPE
  Golfer: 6 BADLIE
  In a: 8 UPACREEK
Predictable
  pattern: 8 SYNDROME
Predicted: 7 FORESAW
Prediction
  Capt.'s: 3 ETA
  maker: 4 SEER
  tool: 5 TAROT
Predilection: 4 BENT 5 TASTE
Predisposed: 5 PRONE
Predisposition: 4 BIAS
Preface: 5 INTRO PROEM

Prefecture
  Honshu: 5 OSAKA
Prefer: 5 FAVOR
  charges: 3 SUE
Preference: 5 TASTE
  In ~ to: 4 OVER
  Pie: 7 ALAMODE
Preferred: 6 BETTER
  invitees: 5 ALIST
  Most: 3 PET
  strategy: 5 PLANA
Pregame
  ritual: 4 TOSS 6 ANTHEM
Pregnancy
  Kind of: 5 TUBAL
Prego
  rival: 4 **RAGU**
Prehistoric: 3 OLD
  threat: 4 TREX
  time: 8 STONEAGE
Prejudice: 4 **BIAS**
Prelate
  honorific (abbr.): 4 MSGR
Prelim: 5 INTRO
Preliminary
  races: 4 HEAT
  text: 5 DRAFT
  Was ~ (to): 5 LEDUP
Prelude: 5 INTRO
  to a deal: 4 ANTE
  to a duel: 4 SLAP
"Prelude to a Kiss"
  actor Baldwin: 4 ALEC
Prematurely: 7 TOOSOON
Premed
  subj.: 4 ANAT
Premiere: 5 DEBUT
  sight: 4 LIMO
Preminger
  1944 ~ suspense classic: 5 LAURA
  Director: 4 **OTTO**
Premises
  Remove from the: 5 EVICT
Premium
  At a: 4 RARE
  channel: 3 HBO
  Exchange: 4 AGIO
  ___ premium (scarce): 3 ATA
Premonition: 5 HUNCH 6 BODING

Have a: 5 SENSE
Prenatal
prefix: 5 UTERO
test, for short: 5 AMNIO
Preoccupy: 6 OBSESS
Preoperative
delivery of old: 5 ETHER
Preordain: 7 DESTINE
Preowned: 4 USED
Prep
for a marathon, with "up":
4 CARB
sch.: 4 ACAD
Prepaid
Not: 3 COD
Preparation: 5 SETUP
Party: 3 DIP
Preparations
Make: 4 PLAN
Make final: 4 CRAM
Prepare: 3 SET 5 GROOM READY
TRAIN 6 GETSET
8 GETREADY
~, as a hook: 4 BAIT
~, as leftovers: 6 REHEAT
~, as mushroom: 5 SAUTE
~, as new students: 6 ORIENT
~, as salad: 4 TOSS
~, as tea: 5 STEEP
Prepared: 3 SET 5 READY
9 MADEREADY
Preparer
Food: 4 CHEF COOK
Salad: 6 TOSSER
Tax: 3 CPA
Preparers
MS. ~: 3 EDS
Preposterous: 5 INANE 6 INSANE
Preppy
brand: 4 IZOD
jacket: 4 ETON
Preprandial
drink: 8 APERITIF
Prep school
British: 4 **ETON**
New Hampshire: 6 EXETER
Prerecorded
Not: 4 LIVE
Prerequisite: 4 NEED

Deal: 4 ANTE
Two-run homer: 5 ONEON
Prerogative
Director: 6 RETAKE
Presidential: 4 VETO
Pres.
33rd ~: 3 HST
appointee: 4 SECY
Four-term: 3 FDR
New Deal: 3 FDR
title: 3 CIC 4 CINC
Presbyter: 5 ELDER
Preschool
attendee: 3 TOT
Preschooler: 3 **TOT**
Preschoolers: 3 ROE
Prescient
one: 4 SEER
Prescribed: 3 SET
amount: 4 DOSE
doctrine: 5 DOGMA
Prescribers
(abbr.): 3 MDS
Prescription
Available without a ~ (abbr.):
3 OTC
Four times a day, in a: 3 QID
info: 4 DOSE
overseer in D.C.: 3 FDA
phrase: 8 ASNEEDED
Three times a day, in a: 3 TID
Three times, in a: 3 TER
Presence: 8 CHARISMA
Having physical:
15 BRICKSANDMORTAR
Stage: 5 ACTOR
Present: 4 GIFT GIVE HERE
5 NONCE TENSE
6 ONHAND ONSITE
9 INTRODUCE
and past: 6 TENSES
a poser: 3 ASK
a problem: 4 POSE
but hidden: 6 LATENT
from birth: 6 INNATE
mo.: 3 DEC
occasion: 5 NONCE
opener: 4 OMNI
prefix: 4 OMNI

Prepare a: 4 WRAP
time: 4 NOEL XMAS
   9 CHRISTMAS
Was: 4 CAME

Presentation
Kind of: 4 ORAL
staple: 5 CHART

Presenter: 5 EMCEE
Presently: 4 ANON SOON

Preservative
Common: 3 BHT

Preserve: 3 CAN 4 SALT SAVE
for burial: 6 EMBALM
~, as hay: 6 ENSILE
~, as meat: 4 CURE

Preserved: 4 KEPT 5 ONICE

Preserver
Fossil: 5 AMBER
Life: 4 OBIT
of a sort: 6 SALTER
Secret identity: 4 MASK
The ~, in Hinduism: 6 VISHNU

Preserves: 3 JAM
preserver: 3 JAR

Preside
at tea: 4 POUR
over: 4 RULE 5 CHAIR

President
2nd: 5 ADAMS
6th: 5 ADAMS
11th ~: 4 POLK
27th ~: 4 TAFT
44th ~: 5 OBAMA
1950s French: 4 COTY
Bolivia: 5 SUCRE
Czech: 5 HAVEL
Disney: 4 IGER
Fair Deal: 6 TRUMAN
First ~ to marry while in office:
   5 TYLER
First AFL-CIO: 5 MEANY
Former Nicaraguan: 6 ORTEGA
Former SAG: 5 ASNER
French ~ residence: 6 ELYSEE
Kenyan: 3 MOI
Last mustachioed: 4 TAFT
Like the U.S. ~ office: 4 OVAL
Mexican War: 4 POLK
Pakistani ~ of the 1980s: 3 ZIA

Philippines: 5 RAMOS
South Korean: 4 RHEE
Syrian: 5 ASSAD
Unlikely class: 4 NERD
Where le ~ presides: 5 SENAT

President ___ (acting head):
   6 PROTEM
___ President: 5 MADAM

Presidential
1992 ~ candidate: 7 TSONGAS
1996 ~ candidate: 5 PEROT
1996 ~ candidate Alexander:
   5 LAMAR
2000 ~ candidate: 4 BUSH
   5 NADER 6 ALGORE
advisory gp.: 3 NSC
Frequent ~ aspirant Harold:
   7 STASSEN
middle name: 4 ALAN 6 DELANO
monogram: 3 DDE HST
nickname: 3 **ABE** CAL IKE
   5 TEDDY
office shape: 4 OVAL
time: 4 TERM
turndown: 4 VETO

President pro ___: 3 **TEM**

Presidents
Birthplace of seven: 4 OHIO
Name of three: 6 GEORGE
Name of two: 5 ADAMS

Presidents' Day
event: 4 SALE
mo.: 3 FEB

Presley, Elvis
1958 hit: 4 DONT
hit: 13 JAILHOUSEROCK
middle name: 4 ARON

Presley, Elvis ___: 4 **ARON**

Presque Isle
locale: 4 ERIE

Press: 4 **IRON** URGE 5 MEDIA
agent: 4 IRON
conference activity: 5 QANDA
coverage: 3 INK
down: 4 TAMP
for: 4 URGE
for payment: 3 **DUN**
Hot off the: 3 NEW
into service: 3 USE

Kind of: 5 CIDER DRILL
need: 3 INK
on: 4 URGE 5 IMPEL
pass: 5 IDTAG
Ready the: 3 INK
release: 4 WINE 5 CIDER
suffix: 3 URE
Word with: 3 KIT
~, slangily: 3 INK

Pressed
for time: 7 INARUSH
It is ~ for cash: 3 ATM

Presser
Bench ~ pride: 4 PECS
Clothes: 4 IRON

Pressing: 5 ACUTE 6 URGENT
need: 4 **IRON**
One with ~ duties: 6 IRONER

Press Secretary
Ford: 6 NESSEN
Former ~ Myers: 6 DEEDEE
George W's: 3 ARI

Pressure: 4 HEAT 6 LEANON
     STRESS
Apply: 5 EXERT
Collapse under: 4 GIVE 5 CHOKE
Give in to: 3 SAG
Grace under: 5 POISE
Its walls withstand a lot of:
     5 AORTA
Kind of: 4 PEER
meas.: 3 PSI
Operated by air: 9 PNEUMATIC
Position of: 7 HOTSEAT
prefix: 3 ACU
source: 4 PEER
Under: 7 ONADARE
     8 STRESSED
unit: 4 TORR 7 KILOBAR
     8 MILLIBAR
unit (abbr.): 3 PSI

Prestige: 6 CACHET

Prestigious
boys' school: 4 ETON
institutions: 5 IVIES
prize: 5 NOBEL
sch.: 3 MIT

Presto: 5 TEMPO

"Presto!": 4 TADA

Preston: 3 SGT

Preston, Robert
1966 ~ musical: 6 IDOIDO

Preston, Sgt.
home: 5 YUKON
org.: 4 RCMP

Presumed
facts: 6 GIVENS

"Presumed Innocent"
actress Scacchi: 5 GRETA
author: 5 TUROW
     10 SCOTTTUROW

Presumptive: 7 APRIORI

Presupposed: 7 APRIORI

Pretend: 5 FEIGN **LETON**
     7 PLAYACT
to be: 3 ACT
to sing: 7 LIPSYNC

Pretended: 4 SHAM

Pretense: 3 **ACT** 4 AIRS POSE
     SHAM VEIL 5 GUISE
     PUTON 6 FACADE
     7 CHARADE

Pretentious: 4 **ARTY** 5 ARTSY
     6 LADIDA
attitude: 4 AIRS
display: 4 RITZ

Preternatural: 5 EERIE

Prettify: 5 ADORN PREEN PRIMP

Pretty: 4 CUTE 5 QUITE
It's not: 7 EYESORE
Make: 5 ADORN
Not a ~ fruit: 4 UGLI

"___ Pretty": 5 IFEEL

"Pretty nice!": 6 NOTBAD

"Pretty please?": 4 CANI

"Pretty Poison"
star: 11 TUESDAYWELD

"Pretty Woman"
actor Richard: 4 GERE
pretty woman: 7 ROBERTS

Pretzel
bag resealer: 4 CLIP
shape: 4 KNOT
topping: 4 SALT

Pretzels
Like most: 5 SALTY

Prevail: 6 WINOUT
Begin to: 5 SETIN

Prevailed: 3 WON
Prevailing
conditions: 7 CLIMATE
tendency: 5 TREND
Préval
of Haiti: 4 RENE
Prevalent: 4 RIFE
Become: 5 SETIN
Prevaricate: 3 **LIE** 8 TELLALIE
Prevaricator: 4 LIAR
Prevent: 3 BAR 5 AVERT DEBAR
DETER
from practicing: 6 DISBAR
legally: 5 **ESTOP**
Preventer
Slip: 3 MAT
Whiplash: 8 HEADREST
Prevention
unit: 5 OUNCE
Preview: 9 SNEAKPEEK
Kind of: 5 SNEAK
TV: 6 TEASER
Previewer
Movie: 5 RATER
Previn
Conductor: 5 **ANDRE**
Previous: 4 PAST
Not based on ~ study: 7 APRIORI
to, old-style: 5 AFORE
Previously: 3 NEE 4 ONCE
5 AFORE 7 ALREADY
9 ATONETIME
As ~ mentioned: 4 IDEM
owned: 4 USED
Prévost
Novelist: 4 ABBE
Prexy
partner: 4 VEEP
Prey: 6 VICTIM
Bird of: 6 RAPTOR
gripper: 5 TALON
on the mind: 5 EATAT
Search for: 5 PROWL
Prez: 4 EXEC
34th ~: 3 IKE
backup: 4 VEEP
on a penny: 3 ABE
Priam
home: 4 TROY

Son of: 5 PARIS 6 HECTOR
7 TROILUS
Wife of: 6 HECUBA
Price: 4 COST
abbr.: 3 CTS
At a reduced: 6 ONSALE
Change the: 5 RETAG
For the stock issue: 5 ATPAR
indicator: 3 TAG
Kind of: 4 LIST UNIT 6 ASKING
RESALE
List: 6 RETAIL
Market: 5 VALUE
of a ride: 4 FARE
of a visit: 3 FEE
offering: 4 ARIA
or Callas: 4 DIVA
paid: 4 COST
performance: 5 OPERA
place: 3 TAG
Put a ~ on freedom:
7 SETBAIL
Resell at an inflated: 5 SCALP
Retail: 4 COST
Set a: 3 **ASK**
Small ~ to pay: 4 CENT
Stock: 5 QUOTE
tag: 4 COST
tag qualifier: 4 ASIS
word: 3 PER
___ price: 3 ATA
Price, T. ___: 4 ROWE
Priced
Be ~ at: 7 SELLFOR
to move: 6 ONSALE
Price/earnings: 5 RATIO
Price-fixing
group: 6 CARTEL
Priceless: 4 FREE
Prices
Compare: 4 SHOP
Cut, as: 5 SLASH
Like some: 3 NET
Pricey: 4 DEAR 5 **STEEP**
cracker spread: 3 ROE
fur: 5 SABLE
gown: 4 DIOR
import: 3 BMW
watch: 5 ROLEX

Pricing
Kind of: 4 UNIT
word: 3 PER 6 APIECE
Prickle: 5 THORN
Prickly
heat: 4 RASH
plant: 5 BRIER 6 CACTUS
    TEASEL
plants: 5 CACTI
seed case: 3 BUR
sensation: 6 TINGLE
Prickly ___: 4 PEAR
Pride: 3 EGO SIN
Burst with: 5 KVELL
Excessive: 6 HUBRIS
member: 4 LION
of Joy: 4 ELSA
Pitcher's: 3 ARM ERA
She has her: 7 LIONESS
sound: 4 ROAR
Sultan: 5 HAREM
Swallowed one's: 7 ATEDIRT
"Pride and Prejudice"
author: 6 AUSTEN
"Pride's Crossing"
playwright Howe: 4 TINA
Prie-___ (prayer bench): 4 DIEU
Prie-dieu
Use a: 5 KNEEL
Priest
Ancient Celtic: 5 DRUID
and minister cohort: 5 RABBI
at a mosque: 4 IMAM
High ~, in Exodus: 5 AARON
of I Samuel: 3 ELI
of the East: 4 LAMA
Old Testament: 3 ELI
Parish: 5 VICAR 6 CURATE
sch.: 3 SEM
Tibetan: 4 **LAMA**
vestment: 3 ALB
Priestess
at Delphi: 6 ORACLE
Bizet opera: 5 LEILA
Priestley
Actor: 5 JASON
Priestly
attire: 5 ORALE
vestment: 3 ALB

Prig: 8 BLUENOSE
Prima
ballerina: 6 **ETOILE**
Prima donna: 4 DIVA
problem: 3 EGO
Prima ___ evidence: 5 FACIE
Primal
impulse: 4 URGE
Visit through ~ therapy:
    6 RELIVE
"Primal Fear"
actor Richard: 4 GERE
Primary: 4 MAIN
color: 3 RED 4 BLUE
color of printing: 4 CYAN
strategy: 5 PLANA
"Primary Colors"
author: 5 KLEIN
Primate: 3 APE
Big-eyed: 5 LORIS
Hypothetical: 6 APEMAN
Nocturnal: 5 LEMUR
Primatologist
study: 4 APES
~ Fossey: 4 DIAN
Primavera
It's sometimes served: 5 PASTA
Prime: 4 AONE
draft status: 4 ONEA
Even ~ number: 3 TWO
Past one's: 4 AGED
purchases: 6 STEAKS
the pot: 4 ANTE
time: 4 NINE
time hour: 6 NINEPM
Primed: 3 SET 5 READY
Prime Minister
1950s British ~: 4 EDEN
    6 ATTLEE
1960s Japanese ~: 4 SATO
British ~ Benjamin: 8 DISRAELI
British ~ William: 4 PITT
First Burmese: 3 UNU
First Indian: 5 NEHRU
Former Israeli ~ Golda: 4 MEIR
Former Israeli ~ Shimon:
    5 PERES
from 1947 to 1964: 5 NEHRU
Postwar: 6 ATTLEE

Primer: 5 PAINT
  pooch: 4 SPOT
  subject: 4 ABCS
Prime rib au ___: 3 JUS
Primero
  mes: 5 ENERO
Primitive: 5 EARLY
  counters: 5 ABACI
  creature: 5 AMEBA
  home: 3 HUT 5 TEPEE
  percussion instrument: 5 GOURD
  time: 8 STONEAGE
  weapon: 5 SPEAR
Primo: 4 AONE
  Italian writer: 4 LEVI
Primogeniture
  beneficiary: 3 SON
Primordial
  stuff: 4 OOZE
Primp: 5 **PREEN**
Primrose
  variety: 5 OXLIP
Prince: 3 SON 4 HEIR
  Arabian: 4 EMIR
  Indian: 4 RAJA 5 RAJAH
  in Ezekiel: 3 GOG
  Mideast: 4 EMIR
  of Broadway: 3 HAL
  of Darkness: 5 SATAN
  of India: 4 RAJA 5 RAJAH
  of opera: 4 IGOR
  school: 4 ETON
  Shakespearean: 3 **HAL**
Prince Charles
  Sister of: 4 ANNE
Prince ___ Coast: 4 OLAV
Princedom
  of Charles: 5 WALES
Prince ___ Khan: 3 ALY
Princely
  monogram: 3 HRH
  ~ Italian surname: 4 ESTE
"Prince of Tides, The"
  actor Nick: 5 NOLTE
Princess
  Emerald City: 4 OZMA
  Gilbert and Sullivan: 3 **IDA**
  Indian: 4 **RANI** 5 RANEE
  Movie: 4 LEIA

Punjab: 4 **RANI** 5 RANEE
  Sci-fi: 4 LEIA
  Spanish: 5 ELENA
  topper: 5 TIARA
  tormentor: 3 PEA
  TV warrior: 4 **XENA**
  vessels: 6 LINERS
"Princess Bride, The"
  actor Cary: 5 ELWES
  director: 6 REINER
Princess Leia ___: 6 ORGANA
Princess of Wales
  Late: 5 DIANA
Princess Royal: 4 ANNE
Princeton
  and others: 5 IVIES
  mascot: 5 TIGER
  team: 6 TIGERS
Prince Valiant
  Son of: 3 **ARN**
  Wife of: 5 **ALETA**
"Prince Valiant"
  cartoonist Foster: 3 HAL
Prince William: 7 ETONIAN
  school: 4 **ETON**
Principal: 4 ARCH HEAD **MAIN**
          STAR 5 CHIEF
  part: 4 BODY
Principality
  British: 5 WALES
Principal McGee
  portrayer: 5 ARDEN
          8 EVEARDEN
Principle: 5 **TENET**
  Accounting: 4 LIFO
  Chinese: 3 TAO
  Female: 3 YIN
  Guiding: 5 CREDO TENET
  Jungian: 5 ANIMA
  Kwanzaa: 5 UNITY
  Man of: 5 PETER
  of economy:
        15 WASTENOTWANTNOT
  Positive: 4 YANG
  Underlying: 5 BASIS
  Universal: 5 AXIOM
Principles
  Basic: 4 ABCS
  Lacking: 6 AMORAL

Set of: 5 ETHIC
Print
  Kind of: 5 LITHO
  Like some: 4 FINE
  made using stone: 5 LITHO
  Malign in: 5 LIBEL
  measures: 3 EMS ENS
  Ready for: 4 EDIT
  See: 3 RUN
  tint: 5 SEPIA
  Words in: 4 TEXT
Printed
  matter: 4 TEXT
  mistake: 4 TYPO
  Was: 3 RAN
Printemps
  follower: 3 **ETE**
  month: 3 MAI 5 AVRIL
Printer
  !, to a: 4 BANG
  ad abbr.: 3 PPM
  company: 5 EPSON
  measure: 4 PICA
  powder: 5 TONER
  primary color: 4 CYAN
  problem: 3 JAM
  proof: 5 REPRO
  spec.: 3 DPI
  supplies: 4 INKS
  type: 5 LASER 6 INKJET
  unit: 4 REAM
  widths: 3 **EMS** ENS
Printing
  Book: 7 EDITION
  flourish: 5 SERIF
  measures: 3 EMS ENS
  method: 6 OFFSET
  mistakes: 6 ERRATA
  Prepare for: 4 EDIT 7 TYPESET
  press part: 5 INKER
  process, for short: 4 ROTO
    5 LITHO
  woe: 4 BLOT
Printout
  Hosp.: 3 ECG
Prints
  and such: 3 ART
  Blue: 7 EROTICA
  Look for: 4 DUST

Prior
  From a ~ era: 3 OLD
  superior: 5 ABBOT
  to: 3 **ERE** 5 UNTIL
  to, old-style: 5 AFORE
Prioritizing
  Medical: 6 TRIAGE
Priscilla
  John who courted: 5 ALDEN
Prison: 3 PEN
  area: 4 WARD YARD
  camp: 6 STALAG
  guard: 5 SCREW
  in a Cash tune: 6 FOLSOM
  Like ~ windows: 6 BARRED
  Notorious London:
    7 NEWGATE
  One way out of: 6 PAROLE
  sentence: 4 TERM
  uprising: 4 RIOT
  weapon: 4 SHIV
  Women's ~ figure: 6 MATRON
Prisoner: 3 CON
  for good: 5 LIFER
  It's entered by a: 4 PLEA
  of Jabba the Hutt: 4 LEIA
  Take: 7 CAPTURE
  term: 7 STRETCH
"Prisoner of ___, The":
  5 ZENDA
Prison-related: 5 PENAL
Pristine: 4 MINT PURE
Private: 5 INNER
    8 ONEONONE
  address: 3 APO
  bed: 3 COT
  chat: 9 TETEATETE
  club: 3 USO
  dinner: 4 MESS
  filmmaker: 5 INDIE
  instructor: 5 TUTOR
  language: 4 CANT
  lines: 5 ASIDE
  response: 5 NOSIR 6 YESSIR
  sch.: 4 ACAD
  student: 5 TUTEE
  ~, at times: 7 SALUTER
"Private Dancer"
  singer Turner: 4 TINA

Private eye: 3 TEC 5 SNOOP
      6 SHAMUS
  Attire popular with a:
      10 TRENCHCOAT
  Do a ~ job: 6 DETECT
  Like Britain's ~ magazine:
      9 SATIRICAL
Privately: 8 INCAMERA
Privileged
  group: 5 ELITE
  The: 5 HAVES
Privy: 3 LOO
  Made ~ to: 7 LETINON
  to: 4 **INON**
Prix ___: 4 FIXE
Prix fixe
  offering: 4 MEAL
Prize: 5 AWARD VALUE
      6 ESTEEM
  Acting: 5 OSCAR
  Boxing: 4 BELT
  Derby: 5 PURSE ROSES
  Drama: 4 OBIE
  Film: 5 OSCAR
  money: 5 PURSE
  name: 5 NOBEL
  Olympic: 5 MEDAL
  since 1949: 4 EMMY
  Taking the booby: 4 LAST
  Top: 7 JACKPOT
  TV: 4 EMMY
___ prize: 5 BOOBY
"Prize, The"
  actress Sommer: 4 ELKE
Prized: 3 PET
  name: 5 NOBEL
  people: 5 DEARS
  person: 3 GEM
  salmon: 4 TYEE
  violin: 5 AMATI
Prizm
  maker: 3 GEO
"Prizzi's Honor"
  heroine: 5 IRENE
PRNDL
  Part of: 4 PARK
  pick: 4 GEAR
Pro: 3 ACE **FOR** 4 WHIZ
      9 INFAVOROF

  Balancing: 3 CPA
  choice: 4 IRON 7 ONEIRON
  CPR: 3 EMT
  follower: 3 TEM 4 RATA
      5 FORMA
  Kitchen: 4 CHEF
  Not: 4 **ANTI**
  Numbers: 3 CPA
  opponent: 4 **ANTI**
  opposite: 3 CON
  or con: 4 SIDE
  shop item: 3 TEE
  Theatrical: 7 ARTISTE
  vote: 3 **AYE**
Pro ___: 3 TEM 4 BONO **RATA**
      5 FORMA
Pro-___ (some tourneys): 3 AMS
Probability: 4 ODDS
  pioneer: 6 PASCAL
Probable: 6 LIKELY
___ probandi (burden of proof):
      4 ONUS
Probate
  subject: 6 ESTATE
Probe: 4 FEEL TEST
  Busybody: 4 NOSE
  Surgical: 6 STYLET
  ~, with "into": 5 DELVE
Problem: 3 ILL 4 SNAG
  conclusion: 4 ATIC
  for Pauline: 5 PERIL
  of the middle ages: 3 SAG
  Present a: 4 POSE
  Tending to the: 4 ONIT
  Thorny: 7 DILEMMA
Problematic: 4 IFFY
Pro bono: 6 UNPAID
  ~ TV spot: 3 PSA
Pro Bowl
  letters: 3 AFC NFC
Procedure: 6 SYSTEM
  (abbr.): 4 SYST
  Backup: 5 PLANB
  part: 4 STEP
Proceed: 4 GOON WEND
  tediously: 4 PLOD
Proceeded: 4 WENT
  confidently: 6 STRODE
Proceedings: 4 ACTA

Like some legal: 5 INREM
Proceeds: 3 SUM 4 GATE GOES TAKE
  ~, biblically: 5 GOETH
Process
  Part of a: 4 STEP
  Repetitive: 4 ROTE
  ~, as ore: 5 SMELT
Procession: 7 CORTEGE
  Public: 6 PARADE
Proclaim: 4 AVOW 6 ASSERT 7 TRUMPET
  noisily: 5 BLARE
  with pomp: 5 ORATE
Proclamation: 5 EDICT
  Wedding: 5 BANNS
Proclivity: 4 BENT
Procol ___: 5 HARUM
Procrastinator
  promise: 4 SOON
  word: 5 LATER 6 MANANA 8 TOMORROW
Procter & Gamble
  detergent: 3 ERA 4 TIDE
  shampoo: 4 PERT 5 PRELL
  soap: 3 DUZ 4 LAVA 5 IVORY
Proctor
  call: 4 TIME 7 TIMESUP
  handout: 4 TEST
Procyon
  constellation: 10 CANISMINOR
Prod: 3 EGG 4 GOAD URGE 5 EGGON
  gently: 4 COAX 5 NUDGE
Prodder: 4 SPUR
Prodigal: 7 SPENDER
Prodigal Son
  Where the ~ saw the light: 3 STY
Prodigy
  alternative: 3 AOL
Produce: 4 SIRE 5 BREED SPAWN STAGE YIELD 8 GENERATE
  hurriedly, with "out": 5 CHURN
Producer: 5 MAKER
  Commercial: 7 SPONSOR
  Oil: 6 ARTIST
  Private film: 5 INDIE
  Wool: 5 LLAMA

"Producers, The"
  award: 4 TONY
  director Mel: 6 BROOKS
  Max's partner in: 3 LEO
Produce-scale
  word: 4 TARE
Product
  End: 6 RESULT
  makers (abbr.): 4 MFRS
  of erosion: 6 RAVINE
  package abbr.: 4 NTWT 5 NETWT
  rollout: 6 LAUNCH
  testing org.: 3 FDA
Production: 6 OUTPUT
  Big: 4 EPIC
  Iron: 5 STEAM
  Met: 5 OPERA
  Post: 4 NEWS 6 CEREAL
Productive
  activity: 4 WORK
  one: 4 DOER
Prof
  degree: 3 PHD
  helpers: 3 TAS
  Kind of: 4 ASST
  Law ~ degree: 3 LLD
  protection: 6 TENURE
  ___ prof.: 4 ASST
Profane
  Least: 7 HOLIEST
Profanity
  Bit of: 4 OATH
Profess: 4 **AVER** AVOW 6 ALLEGE
Profession: 5 TRADE 6 CAREER METIER
  ~, in slang: 3 BIZ
Professional
  org.: 3 AMA 4 ASSN
  payment: 3 FEE
  pitcher: 5 ADMAN
  prefix: 3 NON
  runner: 3 POL
  suffix: 3 IST
Professor: 8 EDUCATOR
  Do a ~ job: 5 TEACH
  Hogwarts: 5 SNAPE
  Retired: 8 EMERITUS
  ~ Brainard: 3 NED
  ~ Corey: 5 IRWIN

~ Higgins, to Eliza: 4 ENRY
~ Hill: 5 ANITA
~ Jones: 4 INDY
~ Plum game: 4 CLUE
"Professor and the Madman, The"
  subj.: 3 OED
Professors
  Some: 7 EMERITI
Proficiency: 4 EASE 5 SKILL
  H.S. ~ test: 3 GED
Proficient: 4 ABLE 5 ADEPT
  in: 6 GOODAT
  Not ~ in: 5 BADAT
Profile
  Distinctive: 4 OGEE
  Short: 3 BIO
Profit: 3 NET 4 GAIN 5 **AVAIL**
      LUCRE 7 NETGAIN
  ending: 3 EER
  For no: 6 ATCOST
  Net ~ or loss: 10 BOTTOMLINE
  Opposite of: 4 LOSS
  prefix: 3 NON
  Resell for a: 5 SCALP
  unfairly: 15 LINEONESPOCKETS
  ___ profit (make money):
      5 TURNA
Profitable
  ~ Internet business: 4 PORN
Profiteer
  Ticket: 7 SCALPER
Profits: 4 TAKE
  Deplete, as: 7 EATINTO
Profligate: 4 ROUE
Profound: 4 **DEEP**
Profundity: 5 DEPTH
  ___ profundo: 5 BASSO
Prog.
  New Deal: 3 CCC NRA REA TVA
      WPA
  Reagan: 3 **SDI**
  Web ~ code: 4 HTML
Progenitor: 4 SIRE
Progeny: 4 SEED 5 ISSUE SCION
  Some: 4 SONS
Prognosis
  Unfavorable: 5 WORSE
Prognosticator: 4 SEER
Program: 4 SHOW

airing: 8 TELECAST
Coll. military: 4 ROTC
Community: 8 OUTREACH
Computer ~ input: 8 DATABASE
Fed. monetary aid: 3 SSI
file extension: 3 EXE
Fix a computer: 5 DEBUG
interruption: 10 NEWSREPORT
interruptions: 3 ADS
listing: 4 CAST
Mail ~ command: 4 SEND
Mil. training: 3 OCS
Moonshot: 6 APOLLO
offerer: 5 USHER
PC: 3 APP
Post-op: 5 REHAB
Reagan R&D: 3 SDI
Small: 6 APPLET
Software: 3 APP
trial: 8 BETATEST
Programmer: 5 CODER
  output: 4 CODE
  solution: 3 APP
Programming
  language: 4 JAVA 5 COBOL
Progress: 5 GAINS 7 HEADWAY
      INROADS STRIDES
  Delay: 6 RETARD
  impeder: 4 SNAG
  In: 5 **AFOOT**
  Initial: 7 TOEHOLD
  Intelligently planned: 7 TELESIS
  Making no: 6 INARUT
  Slight: 4 DENT
  slowly: 4 INCH
Progresso
  product: 4 SOUP
Prohibit: 3 **BAN** BAR NIX
      5 DEBAR 6 ENJOIN
Prohibited: 5 TABOO 7 FORBADE
      ILLEGAL ILLICIT
  act: 4 NONO
Prohibition: 3 BAN 4 NONO
      5 TABOO
  Apartment: 6 NOPETS
  opener: 5 DONOT
  promoter: 3 DRY
  supporters: 4 DRYS
Prohibition ___: 3 ERA

Prohibitionists: 4 **DRYS**
Project: 3 JUT 7 RADIATE
  conclusion: 3 ILE
  Dives into a: 7 HASATIT
  FDR: 3 TVA
  step: 5 PHASE
  TVA: 3 DAM
Projectile
  path: 3 ARC
  Prankster: 3 PEA
  Pub: 4 **DART**
  Quitter: 5 TOWEL
Projecting
  part: 5 PRONG 6 FLANGE
    7 SALIENT
  window: 5 ORIEL
Projection: 4 EAVE 5 LEDGE
  Church: 4 APSE
  Hook: 4 BARB
  Kind of: 6 ASTRAL
  Rocky: 4 CRAG
  Roof: 4 EAVE
  room spool: 4 REEL
  Soft palate: 5 UVULA
  Warship: 3 RAM
  Window: 5 LEDGE
Prokofiev
  character: 5 PETER
  Composer: 6 SERGEI
  ~ Piano Concerto #1 key:
    5 DFLAT
Prolific
  author: 4 ANON
  De. 4 TEEM
Prolix: 5 WORDY 7 VERBOSE
  Hardly: 5 TERSE
Prologue: 5 INTRO
  follower: 4 ACTI 6 ACTONE
Prolonged
  attack: 5 **SIEGE**
Prolonger
  Life ~, supposedly: 6 ELIXIR
Prom: 5 DANCE
  attendee: 4 TEEN 6 SENIOR
  attendees (abbr.): 3 SRS
  At the: 7 ONADATE
  date: 6 ESCORT
  dress fabric: 5 TULLE
  night safety gp.: 4 SADD

  night woe: 4 ACNE
  partner: 4 DATE
  pursuit: 4 DATE
  queen prop: 5 TIARA
  rental: 4 LIMO
  ride: 4 LIMO
  Unlikely ~ king: 4 NERD
  wear: 3 TUX 4 GOWN 6 ORCHID
    TUXEDO
Promenade: 7 SAUNTER
  Greek: 4 STOA
  Public: 5 PASEO
  Tree-lined: 7 ALAMEDA
Prometheus
  Brother of: 5 ATLAS
  Gift from: 4 FIRE
Prominence: 3 TOR 4 CRAG NAME
Prominent: 4 STAR 5 NOTED
  It has a ~ bridge:
    9 ROMANNOSE
  time: 3 ERA
  ~ U.S. mayor: 5 DALEY
Promise: 3 VOW 4 OATH **OLEO**
    WORD 6 ASSURE
  Bud: 5 BLOOM
  Campaign: 6 TAXCUT
  Go back on a: 6 RENEGE
  Oft-broken: 3 IDO
  product: 4 OLEO
  Solemn: 3 VOW 4 OATH
  to pay: 3 IOU
  Words of: 3 IDO
Promised Land: 6 CANAAN
    UTOPIA
  promisee: 7 ABRAHAM
"Promised Land"
  author: 4 EBAN
Promises
  Like some: 5 EMPTY
Promising: 4 ROSY
  letters: 3 IOU
  Not: 5 BLEAK
  person: 5 COMER
  rocks: 3 ORE
  words: 3 IDO 4 IDOS OATH
Promissory
  Govt. ~ note: 5 TBILL
  note: 3 IOU
Promo: 6 TEASER

Movie: 7 TRAILER
pro: 5 ADMAN
tape: 4 DEMO
Promontory: 4 NESS
Promos
Some: 3 ADS
Promote: 4 ABET SELL TOUT
5 BOOST EXALT
6 FOSTER
Heavily: 4 HYPE
Promoted
Is: 7 MOVESUP
Promoter
H.S.: 3 PTA
Product: 5 ADMAN
Promotion
basis: 5 MERIT
recipient: 4 PAWN
Promotional
link: 5 TIEIN
Prompt: 3 CUE 4 GOAD SPUR
URGE 6 ONTIME REMIND
SPEEDY 7 INSPIRE
PrompTer
prefix: 4 TELE
Prompting
Urgent: 6 BEHEST
Promptly: 4 ASAP SOON 5 APACE
Promulgate: 3 SOW
Prone: 3 APT
Get: 3 LIE
to fidgeting: 5 ANTSY
to imitation: 5 APISH
to pry: 4 NOSY
Prong: 4 TINE
Pronghorn: 8 ANTELOPE
"___ pro nobis": 3 ORA
Pronoun
Biblical: 3 THY 4 THEE THOU
5 THINE
Dixie: 4 YALL
French: 3 CES ILS LUI MOI
MON SES TES TOI
German: 3 ICH SIE
Italian: 3 MIA
Latin: 3 MEA 4 ILLE
Nuptial: 4 OURS
Oft-mispunctuated: 3 ITS
Pointer: 4 THAT

Quaker: 3 THY 4 THEE THOU
5 THINE
Seagoing: 3 HER SHE
Spanish: 3 ESA 4 ESAS ESTA
ESTO 5 ELLAS
Pronounce: 3 SAY 5 UTTER
Fail to: 5 ELIDE
indistinctly: 4 SLUR
"___ pronounce ...": 4 INOW
Pronouncement: 5 EDICT
Pronouncements: 5 DICTA
One making: 5 SAYER
Pronto: 4 ASAP 6 ATONCE
Pronunciation
mark: 5 BREVE SCHWA
Omit in: 5 ELIDE
Proof
Burden of: 4 ONUS
Claim without: 6 ALLEGE
finale: 3 QED
Fire: 3 ASH
letters: 3 QED
of ownership: 4 DEED 5 TITLE
of purchase (abbr.): 4 RCPT
Printer's: 5 REPRO
Show ~ of: 6 EVINCE
They have the burden of: 3 TAS
word: 4 ERAT ERGO STET
Proofer
find: 4 TYPO
mark: 4 DELE STET
Proofreader
find: 4 TYPO 5 ERROR
"leave it": 4 STET
mark: 4 DELE STET
oversights: 6 ERRATA
Proofreading
mark: 4 STET
symbol: 5 CARET
Proofs
Go over: 4 EDIT
of age: 3 IDS
Prop
place: 3 SET
prefix: 5 TURBO
suffix: 3 ANE
up: 5 BRACE SHORE
Propagate: 3 SOW
Propel: 5 PEDAL

a boat: **3** OAR ROW
a gondola: **4** POLE
Propeller: 3 OAR **5** SCREW
holder: **6** BEANIE
part: **5** BLADE
Pellet: **8** AIRRIFLE
sound: **4** WHIR
Propensity: 4 BENT
Proper: 5 STAID
As is: **5** APTLY
Deem: **6** SEEFIT
In a ~ manner: **4** DULY
It may be: **4** NOUN
Like ~ children: **4** SEEN
Overly ~ person: **5** PRUDE
Partner of: **4** PRIM
Properly: 6 ARIGHT
Act: **6** BEHAVE
Operate: **4** WORK
pitched: **5** ONKEY
positioned: **7** INPLACE
Property: 5 TRAIT **6** ESTATE
    REALTY
claim: **4** **LIEN**
Govt. ~ overseer: **3** **GSA**
Landed: **6** ESTATE
recipient: **7** ALIENEE
right: **4** LIEN
seller: **7** ALIENOR
title: **4** DEED
Turn over a: **6** RESELL
Prophecies
Book of: **4** AMOS **5** HOSEA
    6 ISAIAH
Prophet: 4 SEER
at Delphi: **6** ORACLE
Minor: **4** AMOS **5** JONAH MICAH
Old Testament: **4** AMOS
    5 HOSEA **6** ISAIAH
Prophetess: 5 SIBYL
of Greek myth: **9** CASSANDRA
Prophetic: 8 ORACULAR
sign: **4** OMEN
Propitiate: 7 APPEASE
Propitiatory
present: **3** SOP
Proportion: 5 RATIO
Proportional: 7 INSCALE
share: **5** QUOTA

Proportionately: 7 TOSCALE
Proportions
Of great: **4** EPIC
Proposal: 4 IDEA **5** OFFER
    6 THESIS
defeated in 1982: **3** ERA
Freelancer: **5** QUERY
Makes a:
    15 POPSTHEQUESTION
Parliamentary: **6** MOTION
Propose: 5 OFFER POSIT
    8 PUTFORTH
at a meeting: **4** MOVE
Prepare to: **5** **KNEEL**
Proposer
prop: **4** **KNEE**
Proposition
Auxiliary: **5** LEMMA
Losing: **4** DIET
Money-losing: **4** SCAM
Provable: **7** THEOREM
Proprietor: 5 OWNER
Proprietresses
Pub: **8** ALEWIVES
Propyl
finish: **3** ENE
prefix: **3** ISO
Pros and ___: 4 CONS
Prosciutto: 3 HAM
Proscribed: 5 TABOO **7** FORBADE
Proscription: 3 BAN **4** NONO
Prose
piece: **5** ESSAY
Polish: **4** EDIT
Prosecute: 3 TRY
They ~ perps: **3** DAS
Prosecutors
Perp: **3** DAS
Subordinate ~ (abbr.): **4** ADAS
___ prosequi: **5** NOLLE
Prosodic
foot: **4** IAMB
Prospect
Derby: **4** COLT
Impractical: **11** PIEINTHESKY
Prospecting
tool: **3** PAN
Prospector
beast: **4** MULE

find: 3 ORE
property: 5 CLAIM
strike: 4 LODE
Prosper: 6 DOWELL THRIVE
French writer: 7 MERIMEE
Prosperity: 4 BOOM EASE
6 WEALTH
Prospero
Daughter of: 7 MIRANDA
servant: 5 ARIEL
Prosperous
Not: 4 LEAN
time: 4 BOOM
times: 3 UPS
Prost
of racing: 5 ALAIN
Prot.: 3 REL
Certain: 4 EPIS METH
Protagonist
Unlikely: 7 NONHERO
8 ANTIHERO
Protect: 5 GUARD 6 DEFEND
from floods: 6 EMBANK
~, as freshness: 6 SEALIN
~, in a way: 6 ENCASE
INSURE PATENT
8 LAMINATE
9 INOCULATE
Protected: 4 SAFE 6 IMMUNE
area: 7 WETLAND
bird: 5 EGRET
from the elements: 6 INDOOR
from the wind: 4 ALEE
Protection: 4 CARE EGIS 5 AEGIS
ARMOR
Protective
charm: 6 AMULET
container: 3 POD
embankment: 6 ESCARP
garment: 5 SMOCK
plastic: 7 ACETATE
Protectively
Hold: 6 CRADLE
Protectorate
Former British: 4 ADEN OMAN
6 UGANDA
Former French: 4 LAOS
Protegé
maker: 5 MAZDA

Protein
acid: 5 AMINO
component: 9 AMINOACID
Muscle: 5 ACTIN
production aid: 3 RNA
source: 3 NUT 4 TOFU
7 SOYBEAN
Protest: 4 BEEF 5 DEMUR SITIN
6 OPPOSE
1960s ~ org.: 3 SDS
French ~ phrase: 4 ABAS
tactic: 5 SITIN
Protestant
Certain: 8 LUTHERAN
denom.: 3 BAP 4 EPIS
French: 8 HUGUENOT
Protester: 4 ANTI
ploy: 5 SITIN
prop: 8 BULLHORN
Proteus
and others: 8 VERONESE
Proto
suffix: 5 PLASM
Protocol: 6 RUBRIC
Proton
holder: 4 ATOM
part: 5 QUARK
prefix: 4 ANTI
Protopopov
Skater: 4 OLEG
Prototype: 5 MODEL
Protozoan: 5 AMEBA 6 AMEBIC
AMOEBA
propellers: 5 CILIA
Protracted: 4 LONG
Protractor
measure: 5 ANGLE
Protrude: 3 JUT 5 BULGE
Protuberance: 4 NODE
Small: 3 NUB
Tree: 4 KNAR
Proudly
Presents ~, with "out":
5 TROTS
Walk: 5 STRUT
Proud ___ peacock: 3 ASA
Proust
protagonist: 5 SWANN
Writer: 6 MARCEL

Prov.
 Book after: 4 ECCL
 Canadian: 3 **ONT** PEI QUE
  4 ALTA
Prove
 false: 5 BELIE
 successful: 6 PANOUT
 to be human: 3 ERR
 useful: 5 AVAIL
"Proved!"
 letters: 3 QED
"Prove it!": 6 SHOWME
Proven: 4 SURE 6 TESTED
Provençal
 pal: 4 AMIE
 ___ provençale: 3 ALA
Provence
 city: 5 ARLES
Proverb: 3 SAW 5 ADAGE MAXIM
 ending: 3 IAL
Proverbial
 amount of bricks: 3 TON
 backbreaker: 5 STRAW
 battlers: 5 SEXES
 heirs: 4 MEEK
 In the ~ cellar: 4 LAST
 More, in a ~ sense: 4 LESS
 sword beater: 3 PEN
Proverbs
 Bk. after: 4 ECCL
Provide: 5 ENDUE 6 RENDER
 an address: 5 ORATE
 an upper surface for: 4 CEIL
 food for: 5 CATER
 (for): 4 FEND
 guidance: 6 MENTOR
 new equipment for: 5 REFIT
 temporarily: 4 LEND
 with funds: 5 ENDOW
 with gear: 5 EQUIP
 with workers: 5 STAFF
Provide ___ (save face): 5 ANOUT
Provided
 that: 8 ASLONGAS
Providence
 sch.: 3 URI
"Providence"
 Lead role in: 3 SYD
Province: 4 AREA 5 REALM

 Austrian: 5 TYROL
 Canadian: 7 ALBERTA ONTARIO
 Chinese: 5 HONAN HUNAN
 Italian: 4 ASTI 5 SIENA UDINE
  7 SALERNO
 South African: 5 NATAL
 Spanish: 4 LEON 5 AVILA
  6 ARAGON
Provinces
 Like some: 8 MARITIME
Provincetown
 catch: 3 COD
Provincial: 4 HICK
 one: 5 YOKEL
Provision
 Contract: 6 CLAUSE
  15 ESCALATORCLAUSE
Proviso
 Auction: 4 ASIS
Provo
 coll.: 3 BYU
 neighbor: 4 LEHI **OREM**
 resident: 5 UTAHN 6 UTAHAN
 state: 5 UTAH
Provocative
 look: 4 LEER
 Most: 7 EDGIEST
Provoke: 3 IRE IRK VEX 4 DARE
  GOAD RILE ROIL SPUR
  STIR 5 ANGER TEASE
  TEMPT 6 AROUSE INCITE
  NETTLE STIRUP
Provoked
 Easily: 5 SHORT
Prowler
 Night: 6 TOMCAT 8 ALLEYCAT
Proximate: 4 NEAR 7 NEAREST
Proximity: 8 NEARNESS
Prude: 8 BLUENOSE
Prudent: 4 SAGE WARY WISE
Prudential
 rival: 5 **AETNA**
Prudhomme
 Cajun cookbook author: 5 ENOLA
Prufrock
 creator: 5 ELIOT 7 TSELIOT
 creator monogram: 3 TSE
Prufrock, J. Alfred
 poet: 3 TSE 7 TSELIOT

Prune: 3 LOP 4 EDIT PARE
    TRIM
  Like a: 5 DRIED
  Prepare a: 4 STEW
  ~, formerly: 4 PLUM
Prurient
  look: 4 LEER
Pruritus: 4 ITCH
Prussian
  Palindromic: 4 OTTO
  pronoun: 3 SIE
Pry: 5 SNOOP
  Apt to: 4 NOSY
  bar: 5 LEVER
Prying: 4 NOSY
Pryor, Richard
  1982 ~ movie: 6 THETOY
Psalm
  word: 5 SELAH
Psalms
  interjection: 5 SELAH
  preceder: 3 JOB
PSAT
  takers: 3 **JRS**
Pseudo: 4 MOCK
Pseudocultural: 4 ARTY
Pseudodocumentary
  1983 ~: 5 ZELIG
Pseudologue: 4 LIAR
Pseudonym: 5 ALIAS
  Anne Brontë: 5 ACTON
  Lamb: 4 **ELIA**
  Munro: 4 SAKI
  Romain de Tirtoff: 4 ERTE
Pseudopod
  former: 5 AMEBA 6 AMOEBA
Pseudosophisticated: 4 ARTY
Psi
  follower: 5 OMEGA
  preceder: 3 CHI
"Psst!": 3 HEY 8 OVERHERE
  follower: 6 INHERE
  relative: 4 AHEM
PST
  Part of: 3 STD
Psych
  suffix: 4 OSIS OTIC
Psych.
  research subject: 3 ESP

Psyche
  Damage, as the: 4 SCAR
  Lover of: 4 EROS
  part: 3 **EGO**
  parts: 3 IDS
Psyched: 5 EAGER
  about: 5 UPFOR
  up: 4 AGOG
Psychedelic
  drug: 3 LSD
Psychiatrist
  response: 4 ISEE
  ~ Alfred: 5 ADLER
  ~ Carl: 4 JUNG
Psychic: 4 SEER
  A ~ may see it: 4 AURA
  power: 3 ESP
  reading material: 4 AURA
  ~ Edgar: 5 CAYCE
  ~ Geller: 3 URI
  ~ "Miss": 4 CLEO
"Psycho"
  actor Bates: 6 NORMAN
  actress Anne: 5 HECHE
  actress Miles: 4 VERA
  motel: 5 BATES
  setting: 5 MOTEL
Psychoanalysis
  subject: 3 EGO
Psychoanalyst
  term: 12 FREUDIANSLIP
  ~ Fromm: 5 **ERICH**
Psychological
  shock: 6 TRAUMA
  ~ Burton-Firth film: 5 EQUUS
Psychologist
  Giant of a: 4 JUNG
  study: 6 AUTISM
  Swiss: 6 PIAGET
  ~ Bettelheim: 5 BRUNO
  ~ Jean: 6 PIAGET
  ~ Jung: 4 CARL
  ~ May: 5 ROLLO
Pt.
  or qt.: 3 AMT
P.T.
  boat officer: 3 ENS
  boats are in it: 3 USN
  program: 5 REHAB

PTA
  concern (abbr.): 4 EDUC
  meeting place (abbr.): 3 SCH
  member: 6 PARENT
  part: 4 ASSN
Pterodactyl
  Screen: 5 RODAN
Pts.
  8 ~: 3 GAL
  parts: 3 OZS
  They're worth 6: 3 TDS
Pub
  fixture: 3 TAP
  game: 5 **DARTS** 7 SNOOKER
  Go from ~ to pub: 6 BARHOP
  order: 3 **ALE** 4 PINT 5 LAGER
      STEIN STOUT 6 PORTER
      7 PALEALE
  projectile: 4 DART
  proprietresses: 8 ALEWIVES
  purchase: 4 PINT
  stock: 4 ALES
Public: 5 OVERT
  announcers: 6 CRIERS
  English ~ school: 4 ETON
  hanging: 3 ART
  hangings: 7 ARTSHOW
  house: 3 INN
  image, for short: 3 REP
  In the ~ eye: 4 SEEN
  Make: 3 **AIR** 4 BARE 7 RELEASE
      8 ANNOUNCE
  opinion: 6 VOXPOP
  outburst: 5 SCENE
  performer: 7 ARTISTE
  persona: 5 IMAGE
  procession: 6 PARADE
  reader: 6 LECTOR
  relations concern: 4 SPIN
      5 IMAGE
  role: 7 PERSONA
  row: 5 SCENE
  sentiment: 5 ETHOS
  Sought ~ office: 3 RAN
  speaker: 6 ORATOR
  speech: 7 ORATION
  square: 5 **PLAZA**
  square of old: 5 AGORA
  to-do: 5 SCENE

  transport: 3 BUS
  ___ public: 6 NOTARY
  ___ publica: 3 RES
Publican
  potable: 3 ALE
Publication
  Fan: 4 ZINE
  Humor: 11 MADMAGAZINE
  Online: 5 EZINE
  Prepare for: 4 EDIT
Public Citizen
  founder: 5 NADER
Publicist
  concern: 5 IMAGE
Publicity: 3 **INK**
  Exaggerated: 4 HYPE
  Major: 6 HOOPLA
  person: 5 AGENT
  piece: 7 RELEASE
  seeker act: 5 STUNT
Publicize: 3 AIR
Publish: 5 ISSUE
Published: 3 RAN 7 INPRINT
Publisher: 6 ISSUER
  Available from the: 7 INPRINT
  Big paperback: 3 TOR 4 AVON
  Famous jour.: 3 AMA
  Playboy: 6 HEFNER
  pursuit: 12 SERIALRIGHTS
  ~ Adolph: 4 OCHS
  ~ Ballantine: 3 IAN
  ~ Chandler: 4 OTIS
  ~ Henry: 4 LUCE
Publishers
  Like some textbook: 4 ELHI
Publishing
  Big inits. in paperback: 3 NAL
  Big name in book: 5 KNOPF
  Big name in newspaper:
      4 OCHS
  employee: 6 EDITOR READER
Pubmates: 4 LADS
Pucci
  Designer: 6 EMILIO
Puccini
  heroine: 5 TOSCA
  opera: 5 EDGAR **TOSCA**
      8 LABOHEME
  piece: 4 ARIA 5 OPERA

work: 5 TOSCA
Puck: 3 IMP
Pass the ~ to: 4 FEED
stopper: 6 GOALIE
The ~ stops here: 3 NET
Pucker: 5 PURSE
producing: 4 TART
Puckered
fabric: 6 PLISSE
Puckish: 5 ELFIN
Pudding: 7 DESSERT
flavor: 7 TAPIOCA
ingredient: 3 EGG FIG 4 SAGO
    SUET
Kind of: 4 RICE 5 HASTY
starch: 4 SAGO
Puddle
Play in a: 5 SLOSH 6 SPLOSH
Puddle-jumper: 7 AIRTAXI
Pudgy
Beyond: 5 OBESE
Pueblo
chamber: 4 KIVA
home: 5 ADOBE
material: 5 **ADOBE**
New Mexico: 4 TAOS
pot: 4 OLLA
Pueblo Indian: 4 **HOPI** ZUNI
Puente
Bandleader: 4 **TITO**
music: 5 SALSA
specialty: 5 MAMBO
Puerto ___ : 4 **RICO** 5 RICAN
Puerto Rican
city: 7 ARECIBO
port: 5 PONCE
___ Puf (softener brand): 3 STA
Puff: 4 GASP TOKE WISP
    6 DRAGON
Cream: 4 WIMP 6 ECLAIR
Huff and: 4 BLOW PANT
Move on a ~ of air: 4 WAFT
of smoke: 4 WISP
up: 4 RISE 5 BLOAT ELATE
Puff ___ : 5 ADDER
Puff Daddy
music: 3 RAP
Puffed: 4 BLEW
up: 4 SMUG VAIN 7 SWOLLEN

Puffin
relative: 3 AUK
Puffy
Ex of: 3 JLO
white hat person: 4 CHEF
Pug: 3 DOG
Practice with a: 4 SPAR
workplace: 5 ARENA
Puget Sound
city: 6 **TACOMA** 7 SEATTLE
Pugilism
Practice: 4 SPAR
Pugilist
gp.: 3 IBF WBA
Poetic: 3 **ALI**
punch: 3 JAB
"Rope-a-dope": 3 ALI
weapon: 4 FIST
~ Laila: 3 ALI
"Puh-leeze!": 7 SPAREME
Pulitzer
1934 ~ writer: 4 AGAR
1953 ~ playwright: 4 INGE
1958 ~ author: 4 AGEE
1975 ~ critic: 5 EBERT
1977 ~ winner: 5 HALEY
    9 ALEXHALEY
1999 ~ play: 3 WIT
category: 5 DRAMA
critic Richard: 4 EDER
novelist Glasgow: 5 ELLEN
paper: 5 WORLD
playwright Akins: 3 ZOE
poet Van Duyn: 4 MONA
Posthumous ~ winner: 4 AGEE
winner James: 4 **AGEE**
winner Pyle: 5 ERNIE
winner Welty: 6 EUDORA
winning biographer Leon: 4 EDEL
winning biographer Nevins:
    5 ALLAN
winning columnist Mike:
    5 ROYKO
winning humorist Barry: 4 DAVE
winning novel of 1925: 5 SOBIG
Pulka
rider: 4 LAPP
Pull: 3 TOW TUG 5 CLOUT
a boner: 3 ERR 4 GOOF

along: 3 TOW 4 HAUL
an all-nighter: **4 CRAM**
apart: 4 REND TEAR
   8 SEPARATE
a plow: 4 TILL
a sulky: 4 TROT
back: 6 REININ
down: **4 EARN**
Gp. with: 3 ADA
in: 6 ARRIVE
(in): 4 REIN
on: 5 TUGAT
out: 6 SECEDE
out all the stops: 6 LETRIP
Quick: 4 JERK
the plug on: 3 END 4 STOP
They have: 4 OXEN
up stakes: 4 MOVE 6 DECAMP
up to a bar: 4 CHIN
with effort: 3 LUG
Pull-down
Word after: 4 MENU
Pulled: 4 DREW
apart: 4 TORE
It's ~ on a farm: 5 UDDER
off: 3 DID
Puller
Nail: 4 CLAW
Plow: 4 TEAM
Pullers
Plow: 4 OXEN TEAM
Pullet
Former: 3 HEN
Pulley: 7 MACHINE
Pulling
One ~ strings: 5 TUNER
Pullman: 3 CAR
place: 5 BERTH
porter: 6 REDCAP
Pull-off: 8 RESTAREA
   RESTSTOP
Pull ___ one: 5 AFAST
Pullover: 4 POLO
African: 7 DASHIKI
Colorful: 7 DASHIKI
Pulls: 3 INS
It ~ a bit: 4 REIN
Pull-up
Do a: 4 CHIN

Pulp
Beat to a: 4 MASH
"Pulp Fiction"
actress Plummer: 6 AMANDA
actress Thurman: 3 **UMA**
costar of John: 3 UMA
She played Mia in: 3 UMA
Uma role in: 3 MIA
Pulpit
Early: 4 AMBO
Pulpits: 6 ROSTRA
Pulsate: 5 **THROB**
Pulse
alternative: 4 TONE
Pulver
rank (abbr.): 3 **ENS**
Pulverize: 4 MASH 5 CRUSH
   SMASH
Puma: 3 CAT
rival: 6 ADIDAS
Pumice
feature: 4 PORE
source: 4 LAVA
Pummel: 4 MAUL 6 BEATON
Pump: 3 ASK 4 SHOE
Bodybuilders ~ it: 4 IRON
Fix a: 6 REHEEL RESOLE
Gas ~ choice (abbr.): 3 REG
levy: 6 GASTAX
number: 6 OCTANE
Old ~ name: 4 ESSO
part: 4 HEEL SOLE 6 INSOLE
Prepare the: 5 PRIME
preserver: 8 SHOETREE
rating: 6 OCTANE
Vital: 5 HEART
Pumped: 4 SHOD
It may be: 4 **IRON**
Pumper
Iron ~ pride: 3 ABS 4 PECS
Pumpernickel
alternative: 3 RYE
"Pumping ___": 4 IRON
Pumpkin
and pecan: 4 PIES
color: 6 ORANGE
kin: 5 GOURD
Noted ~ eater: 5 PETER
seed: 6 PEPITA

Pumps
In: 4 SHOD
Letters on some: 3 EEE
Pun: 7 GROANER
conclusion: 4 STER
React to a bad: 4 MOAN OUCH
    5 GROAN WINCE
response: 4 HAHA 5 GROAN
Punch: 3 JAB 4 SOCK TANG
bowl item: 5 LADLE
card remnant: 4 CHAD
in: 5 ENTER
ingredient: 4 FIST
It may give ~ punch: 3 RUM
Juice with: 9 HARDCIDER
Kind of: 6 ONETWO
Packing a: 6 POTENT
Partner of: 4 JUDY
Pleased as: 4 GLAD 6 ELATED
Poem with a ~ line: 8 LIMERICK
Prepared to: 9 HAULEDOFF
Quick: 3 **JAB**
Reaction to a stomach: 3 OOF
server: 5 LADLE
Small: 3 AWL
sound: 3 POW
Spike the: 4 LACE
with punch: 7 SANGRIA
Puncher
Hole: 3 AWL 8 STILETTO
Punches
Roll with the: 5 ADAPT
Some: 4 AWLS 5 LEFTS
Trade: 4 SPAR
Punching
Practice: 4 SPAR
tool: 3 AWL
Punctual: 6 ONTIME
Punctually: 8 ONTHEDOT
Punctuation
Bit of: 6 EMDASH
mark: 4 DASH 5 COLON COMMA
Telegram: 4 STOP
Puncture: 4 STAB 5 PRICK
prefix: 3 ACU
sound: 3 SSS 4 SISS
Pundit: 4 SAGE 5 SWAMI
    6 SAVANT
TV ~ Rooney: 4 ANDY

~ Gary: 5 BAUER
Pungent: 5 ACRID TANGY
    6 STRONG
bulb: 5 ONION
cheese: 6 ASIAGO
green: 5 CRESS
pepper: 8 JALAPENO
veggie: 5 ONION
Punic Wars
side: 8 CARTHAGE
Punish: 7 CHASTEN
by fine: 6 AMERCE
Serving to: 5 PENAL
~, in a way: 4 CANE FINE
    5 SPANK
Punishment
Civil: 4 FINE
Kid's: 4 NOTV
Light: 4 SLAP
Makeshift ~ tool: 5 RULER
Partner of: 5 CRIME
Subject to: 5 PENAL
symbol: 3 ROD
unit: 4 LASH
Punjab
Capital of ~ province: 6 LAHORE
Early invader of the: 5 ARYAN
princess: 4 RANI
sect member: 4 SIKH
Punjabi
believer: 4 SIKH
princess: 4 RANI
Punk
Feels: 4 AILS
genre: 3 EMO
icon Joey: 6 RAMONE
Pop of: 4 IGGY
rock outgrowth: 7 NEWWAVE
"Punk'd"
network: 3 MTV
Punkie: 4 GNAT
Punster: 3 WIT
Punt: 4 BOAT
path: 3 ARC
Punta ___, Chile: 6 ARENAS
Punta del ___, Uruguay: 4 **ESTE**
Punter: 7 BOATMAN
Punxsutawney
groundhog: 4 PHIL

Puny
pest: 4 GNAT
Pup
Bite like a: 3 NIP
cry: 3 YIP 4 YELP
Primer: 4 SPOT
Smallest: 4 RUNT
Pup ___: 4 TENT
Pupa
graduate: 5 IMAGO
preceder: 5 LARVA
protection: 6 COCOON
Pupil: 5 TUTEE
Act like a: 9 TAKENOTES
Constriction of the: 6 MIOSIS
controller: 4 IRIS
French: 5 ELEVE
of Jane Eyre: 5 ADELE
place: 3 EYE 4 **IRIS**
protector: 3 LID 6 CORNEA
surrounder: 4 IRIS 6 AREOLA
Where a ~ sits: 4 IRIS
Puppet
dragon: 5 OLLIE
Kukla's ~ pal: 5 OLLIE
Shari Lewis: 8 LAMBCHOP
Puppeteer
~ Baird: 3 BIL
~ Bil: 5 BAIRD
~ Lewis: 5 **SHARI**
~ Tony: 4 SARG
Puppies
Have: 5 WHELP
Like: 4 CUTE
Puppy
bite: 3 NIP
Go after, like a: 5 NIPAT
love: 5 CRUSH
sound: 3 YAP YIP 4 YELP
"Puppy Love"
singer: 4 ANKA 6 OSMOND
Pups
Praises for: 4 PATS
Some: 5 SEALS
Pupu platter
party: 4 LUAU
___ pura: 4 AQUA
Purchase: 3 BUY
incentive: 6 REBATE

Prime: 5 STEAK
Proof of ~ (abbr.): 4 RCPT
Risky: 10 PIGINAPOKE
Purchased
How some stocks are: 5 ATPAR
Purchasing
Govt. ~ org.: 3 **GSA**
Purdue Univ.
major: 3 AGR
Pure: 6 CHASTE
and simple: 4 MERE
Make: 6 REFINE
"Pure ___" (1994 jazz album):
4 ELLA
Purebred
Not: 4 MUTT
Purée
Red: 10 TOMATOSOUP
Puréed
peas eater: 4 BABY
Purely
academic: 4 MOOT
"Pure Woman"
Hardy's: 4 TESS
"Purgatorio"
poet: 5 DANTE
Purge: 3 **RID** 7 CLEANSE
Purged: 3 RID
Purify: 6 REFINE 7 CLEANSE
Purim
honoree: 6 ESTHER
month: 4 **ADAR**
Purina
rival: 4 **ALPO**
Puritan: 4 PRIG
Puritanical
one: 5 PRISS 8 BLUENOSE
Purity
Mythical symbol of: 7 UNICORN
symbol: 4 LILY
unit: 5 KARAT
Purlieu: 4 AREA
Purloin: 5 STEAL
Purloined: 5 STOLE
"Purloined Letter, The"
detective: 5 DUPIN
writer: 3 POE
Purple
bloom: 5 LILAC

Bluish: 5 MAUVE
Dark: 4 PUCE
fruit: 4 PLUM SLOE
Pale reddish: 5 LILAC
Shade of: 4 PUCE 5 GRAPE
    LILAC MAUVE
Purple Heart: 5 MEDAL
"Purple People Eater, The"
singer Wooley: 4 SHEB
Purplish
hue: 5 LILAC
red: 7 MAGENTA
shade: 5 MAUVE
Tree with ~ flowers: 5 PAPAW
Purport: 5 CLAIM TENOR
Purpose: 3 AIM END **USE** 4 SAKE
    5 SENSE 6 INTENT
For a specific: 5 **ADHOC**
Lose on: 5 THROW
Sans: 4 IDLY
Serve the: 5 AVAIL
Serving a: 5 UTILE
Ultimate: 6 ENDALL ENDUSE
Walked with: 6 STRODE
Without: 4 IDLY
Purposeful: 7 EARNEST
Purring
animal: 3 CAT
Purse: 3 BAG
alternative: 7 SATCHEL
holder: 5 STRAP
Pursue: 4 HUNT SEEK SHAG
    5 CHASE STALK TRAIL
as a trade: 3 PLY
relentlessly: 3 DOG 5 HOUND
Pursuer
of the Pleiades: 5 ORION
Pusher: 4 NARC
Pursuing: 5 AFTER
Pursuit: 4 HUNT 5 CHASE QUEST
In ~ of: 5 AFTER
Vein: 3 **ORE**
Purviance
Actress: 4 EDNA
Purview: 5 SCOPE 6 SPHERE
Pusan
native: 6 KOREAN
Push: 4 PROD SELL URGE
    5 SHOVE

(around): 4 BOSS
forward: 4 URGE 5 IMPEL
Give a little: 5 NUDGE
out of bed: 5 ROUST
roughly: 5 SHOVE
~, so to speak: 6 PEDDLE
Push-button
Not: 4 DIAL
Pushed
It may get ~ around: 4 CART
the doorbell: 4 RANG
Pusher
customer: 4 USER
Harbor: 3 TUG
Pedal: 4 FOOT
Pencil: 6 WRITER
Petal: 3 BEE
pursuer: 4 NARC
Pushkin
hero: 5 BORIS 6 ONEGIN
Pushover: 5 PATSY 6 SOFTIE
Pushrod
pusher: 3 CAM
Push-up
Kind of: 6 ONEARM
muscle: 3 PEC
Pushy
Get: 5 PRESS
Pusillanimous: 5 TIMID
Puss: 3 MUG
Wear a: 4 POUT
Pussy
foot: 3 PAW
Pussycat
shipmate: 3 OWL
Pussycats
Leader of the: 5 JOSIE
Pussyfoot: 5 SNEAK
Put: 3 LAY 7 SITUATE
a cap on: 5 LIMIT
a match to: 3 LIT 6 IGNITE
an early end to:
    11 NIPINTHEBUD
an edge on: 4 HONE WHET
    5 HONED
an end to: 4 STOP 5 CEASE
another way: 7 REWRITE
aside: 5 ALLOT 6 SHELVE
a strain on: 3 TAX 5 TAXED

at risk: 7 IMPERIL
   8 ENDANGER
a value on: 6 ASSESS
away: 3 ATE EAT ICE 4 ICED
   SAVE **STOW** 5 EATEN
   SAVED STASH STORE
   6 ENTOMB STORED
   STOWED 7 SHEATHE
   8 STOREDUP
back: 4 STET 5 RESET
   7 RESTORE
down: 3 DIS LAY SET 4 LAID
   5 ABASE QUELL WROTE
   6 ABASED BERATE DEMEAN
   DISSED STIFLE 7 ASPERSE
   DERIDED
down in writing: 5 LIBEL
down roots: 6 SETTLE
forth: 3 ASK 5 EXERT POSIT
forward: 5 OFFER POSED POSIT
   6 ASSERT
in: 3 ADD
in a kiln: 3 DRY
in cipher: 6 ENCODE
in office: 5 ELECT
in order: 4 SORT 7 ARRANGE
in place: 5 SITED
in power: 8 ENTHRONE
in rollers: 3 SET
in stitches: 3 **SEW** 4 DARN
   SEWN SLAY 5 SEWED
in the bank: 5 SAVED
in the cup: 5 HOLED
in the hold: 4 LADE STOW
in the mail: 4 SEND SENT
in the pot: 4 ANTE
into action: 3 USE 5 EXERT
into law: 5 ENACT
into motion: 7 ACTUATE
into piles: 4 SORT
into service: 3 USE
into words: 3 SAY 5 UTTER
   7 UTTERED
it to: 3 ASK
next to: 6 APPOSE
Not stay: 4 ROAM
off: 5 **DEFER** DELAY DETER
   REPEL TABLE 8 ALIENATE
   POSTPONE

on: 3 ADD **DON** 4 GAIN WEAR
   5 AIRED APPLY LADED
   STAGE 6 STAGED
on again: 7 RESTAGE
on a happy face: 5 SMILE
on a pedestal: 5 ADORE EXALT
   6 ADORED ESTEEM
   7 ADULATE
on a scale: 4 RATE
on a spare tire: 4 GAIN
on board: 4 LADE STOW
on cargo: 4 LADE
on cloud nine: 5 ELATE
on cuffs: 5 ALTER
one over on: 6 SNOWED
one past: 3 ACE 4 ACED
one's finger on: 7 PINDOWN
one's foot down: 4 **STEP** TROD
   5 STOMP
one's two cents in: 4 ANTE
   5 OPINE
on ice: 5 CHILL TABLE
on notice: 4 WARN
on the books: 5 **ENACT**
on the line: 4 RISK
on the market: 4 SELL
on the payroll: 4 HIRE
   5 HIRED
on the rack: 7 TORTURE
on TV: 3 AIR 5 AIRED
out: 3 IRK TAG 4 EMIT IRED
   SORE 5 DOUSE EVICT
   IRATE ISSUE 6 DOUSED
   ISSUED
out (effort): 5 EXERT
out of commission: 7 DISABLE
out of sight: 4 HIDE
right: 5 AMEND 6 INDENT
spin on: 4 SKEW
Stay: 6 REMAIN
the collar on: 3 NAB
   6 ARREST
the kibosh on: 3 END **NIX**
   4 VETO 5 ENDED NIXED
the pedal to the metal: 4 SPED
the squeeze on: 5 PRESS
the whammy on: 5 HEXED
They're ~ on: 4 AIRS
through a sieve: 5 RICED

together: 4 MADE 5 AMASS
RIGUP UNITE
to rest: 5 ALLAY
to shame: 5 ABASH
to sleep: 4 BORE LULL
to the grindstone: 5 HONED
to the test: 3 USE 5 ASSAY
7 ESSAYED
to use: 5 EXERT
to work: 3 USE 4 USED
6 EMPLOY
two and two together: 3 ADD
under: 6 SEDATE
up: 4 POST 5 BUILD BUILT
ERECT HOUSE STORE
6 HOUSED 7 ERECTED
up a fight: 6 RESIST
up a fuss: 6 BEEFED
up for sale: 5 OFFER
up on the wall: 4 HANG
up with: 5 ABIDE STAND
STOOD 6 ABIDED
Well: 3 APT
your hands together: 4 CLAP
Put ___ (ask a hard question):
4 ITTO
"Put a lid ___!": 4 ONIT
"Put a lid on it!": 3 SHH
Put an ___ (stop): 5 ENDTO
"Put a sock ___!": 4 INIT
"Put a sock in it!": 3 SHH
"Put a tiger in your tank"
company: 4 ESSO
Put-down: 4 SLAP SLUR
Put ___ good word for: 3 INA
"Put ___ Happy Face": 3 ONA
Putin
denial: 4 NYET
Former ~ org.: 3 KGB
Putin, Vladimir
former org.: 3 KGB
Put in ___ for: 4 ABID
"... ___ put it another way ...":
4 ORTO
"Put ___ my bill": 4 ITON
"Put ___ my tab": 4 ITON
Putnam
Revolutionary War patriot:
5 RUFUS

Put-on: 3 ACT 4 HOAX SHAM
Put one's ___ (meddle): 5 OARIN
"Put ___ on it!": 4 ALID
Putt
First to ~, usually: 4 AWAY
Make a: 5 SINK
Sank, as a: 5 HOLED
Short: 5 TAPIN
Sink a: 7 HOLEOUT
Very short ~, say: 5 GIMME
Putter
Shot: 7 SYRINGE
target: 3 CUP 4 HOLE
Putterer: 7 AMATEUR
"Put the gun down!": 6 DROPIT
"Puttin' On the ___": 4 RITZ
Put ___ to: 5 ANEND ASTOP
Put to ___ (outdo): 5 SHAME
"Put ___ writing!": 4 ITIN
"Put Your Head on My Shoulder"
singer: 4 ANKA
Puzo
Author: 5 MARIO
novel: 6 OMERTA
subject: 5 MAFIA
Puzzle: 5 POSER 6 BEMUSE
ENIGMA
pattern: 4 GRID
Pencil: 4 MAZE
Picture: 5 REBUS
Seven-piece: 7 TANGRAM
solver's shout: 3 AHA
suffix: 4 MENT
Tough: 5 POSER
unit: 5 PIECE
Puzzled: 5 ATSEA 7 ATALOSS
comments: 3 EHS
Puzzlement: 6 ENIGMA
Puzzles: 8 ENIGMATA
First word in: 6 ACROSS
Pvt.
Like a ~ washing dishes: 4 ONKP
superior: 3 CPL SGT
PX
patrons: 3 GIS 4 NCOS
Pygmalion
Love of: 7 GALATEA
"Pygmalion"
heroine: 5 ELIZA

monogram: 3 GBS
playwright: 4 **SHAW**
Pygmy
antelope: 5 ORIBI
Pyle
Journalist: 5 ERNIE
of Mayberry: 5 GOMER
player: 6 NABORS
Pyle, Gomer: 6 MARINE
org.: 4 USMC
Pym
Creator of Miss: 3 TEY
Pymt.
Homeowner: 4 MTGE
Pyramid: 4 TOMB
Bill with a: 3 ONE
builders: 5 MAYAS
6 MAYANS

Food ~ org.: 4 USDA
scheme: 4 SCAM
Pyramide du Louvre
designer: 5 IMPEI
Pyramus
Lover of: 6 THISBE
Pyrenees
Info: Spanish cue
realm: 7 ANDORRA
Pysanky
need: 3 EGG
Pythagorean
proposition: 7 THEOREM
~ P: 3 RHO
Pythias
Pal of: 5 DAMON
Python: 5 SNAKE
Kipling: 3 KAA

Qq

Q
Queue after: 3 RST 4 RSTU
Queue before: 3 NOP 4 MNOP

Q45
maker: 8 INFINITI

Qabus bin Said: 5 OMANI
country: 4 OMAN

Qaddafi: 6 LIBYAN
country: 5 LIBYA

Q&A
Part of: 3 ANS

Qantas
symbol: 5 KOALA

Qatar
capital: 4 **DOHA**
leader: 4 EMIR
place: 6 ARABIA
resident: 4 ARAB

Qatari: 4 ARAB
leader: 4 EMIR

QB: 6 PASSER
mistake: 3 INT
stat: 3 TDS YDS

"QB ___": 3 VII

"QB VII"
author: 4 URIS

QED
Part of: 4 **ERAT** QUOD

Qintars
100 ~: 3 LEK

Qom
country: 4 IRAN
money: 4 RIAL
resident: 5 IRANI

"Q ___ queen": 4 ASIN

Qt.: 3 AMT
couple: 3 PTS

Q-Tip: 4 SWAB
target: 3 EAR 6 EARWAX

Qtr.
starter: 3 OCT

Qtrs.
Fifth: 3 OTS

Transient: 3 SRO

Qts.: 4 AMTS
Four: 3 GAL
Parts of: 3 PTS

Qty.: 3 **AMT**
Egg: 3 DOZ

Q-U
connection: 3 **RST**

Quaalude
Give a ~ to: 6 SEDATE

Quad
building: 4 DORM
~ VIP: 4 BMOC

Quadrennial
candidate Harold: 7 STASSEN
games org.: 3 IOC
pol. event: 4 CONV

Quadri-
Cousin of: 3 TRI UNI 4 HEXA
OCTA 5 TETRA
preceder: 3 TRI

Quaff
Green: 7 LIMEADE
Herbal: 3 TEA 7 MINTTEA
Holiday: 3 NOG 6 EGGNOG
Japanese: 4 SAKE
Middle Ages: 4 MEAD
Minty: 5 JULEP
Pub: 3 ALE 4 BEER
Radar's: 4 NEHI
Sailor's: 4 GROG
Summer: 3 ADE

Quagmire: 3 BOG FEN 5 MARSH
SWAMP 6 MORASS

Quahog: 4 CLAM

Quaid, Dennis
film: 3 DOA

Quai d'Orsay
river: 5 SEINE

Quail: 5 COWER
group: 4 BEVY 5 COVEY

Quaint: 3 ODD
contraction: 5 TWERE

establishment: **6** SHOPPE
expletive: **4** EGAD
lodging: **3** INN
road: **4** LANE
sigh: **4** AHME
Quake: 5 SEISM **6** TREMOR
Quaker: 5 ASPEN **6** FRIEND
cereal: **3** OHS
colonist: **4** PENN
in the woods: **5** ASPEN
pronoun: **3** THY **4** THEE THOU
        5 THINE
Quaker ___: 4 OATS
Quakers: 4 SECT
Quaker State
port: **4** ERIE
Quaking: 8 ATREMBLE
in one's boots: **6** SCARED
tree: **5** ASPEN
Qualcomm Stadium
player: **5** PADRE
Qualification
Without: **6** FLATLY
Qualified: 3 APT **4** **ABLE**
        8 ELIGIBLE
Most ~ to serve: **4** ONEA
to work: **7** HIRABLE
Qualifiers: 3 IFS
Qualify: 7 ENTITLE
Qualifying
race: **4** HEAT
Quality: 4 GOOD ODOR TONE
        5 TRAIT
Attractive: **6** APPEAL
Carpet: **4** PILE
Cool: **7** HIPNESS
Gung-ho: **4** ZEAL ZEST
Laid-back: **4** EASE
Muscle: **4** **TONE**
Pervasive: **4** AURA
Sound: **4** TONE **6** TIMBRE
Valuable: **5** ASSET
Winter air: **3** NIP
Qualm: 4 PANG
**___ quam videri (North Carolina
        motto): 4** ESSE
Quandary: 3 FIX **7** DILEMMA
In a: **5** ATSEA
___ quandary: 3 INA

___ qua non: 4 SINE
Quant, Mary
design: **4** MINI **9** MINISKIRT
look: **3** MOD
Quantity: 6 AMOUNT
(abbr.): **3** AMT
Cookie: **5** BATCH
Fixed: **4** UNIT
Large: **3** SEA **4** HEAP MUCH
        RAFT SCAD SLEW **5** OCEAN
        6 OODLES
Medicinal: **4** DOSE
Paper: **4** REAM
Small: **4** IOTA
Unspecified: **3** ANY **4** SOME
Yarn: **5** SKEIN
Quantum: 6 AMOUNT
event: **4** LEAP
physics particle: **5** MESON
Quarantine: 6 ENISLE **7** ISOLATE
"Quare Fellow, The"
author: **5** BEHAN
Quark
A ~ and an antiquark: **5** MESON
place: **4** ATOM
Quarrel: 3 ROW **4** SPAT TIFF
        5 ARGUE RUNIN SCRAP
        SETTO **6** BICKER DUSTUP
settler: **4** DUEL
Quarry: 3 PIT **4** MINE PREY
Cop's: **4** PERP
Hunter's: **3** ELK
MP's: **4** **AWOL**
Sniggler's: **3** EEL
Quart
British: **5** LITRE
fractions (abbr.): **3** PTS
Metric: **5** LITER
quartet: **4** CUPS
Quarter: 4 AREA COIN **6** LOCALE
        7 TWOBITS
Algerian: **6** CASBAH
back: **5** EAGLE
millennium: **3** CCL
of four: **3** ONE
Word on a: **4** UNUM
Quarterback: 6 PASSER
        7 OVERSEE
option: **4** PASS **5** SNEAK

setback: 4 LOSS
target: 3 END
Quarterfinal
group: 5 OCTET
Quarter note
line: 4 STEM
Quarters: 5 ABODE AREAS
Camper's: 4 TENT
Campus: 4 DORM
Clergyman's: 5 MANSE
Conical: 5 TEPEE
Cruise: 5 CABIN
Four: 3 ONE 4 YEAR
Frozen: 5 IGLOO
Skier's: 5 LODGE
Two: 4 HALF
Quartet
Alphabet: 4 ABCD BCDE
     CDEF *etc.*
Country: 7 ALABAMA
Deck: 4 ACES
Half of a pop: 5 MAMAS PAPAS
member: 4 ALTO BASS 5 CELLO
     VIOLA
minus one: 4 TRIO
Swedish: 4 ABBA
"___ Quartet, The": 3 RAJ
Quartz
Golden-brown ~ stone:
     9 TIGERSEYE
material: 6 SILICA
variety: 4 ONYX OPAL 5 AGATE
     TOPAZ 6 JASPER
Quash: 3 END 4 STOP VETO
Quasimodo
creator: 4 HUGO
portrayer: 3 LON
Quaternary
division: 6 ICEAGE
Quatrain: 6 STANZA
rhyme scheme: 4 ABAA ABAB
     ABBA
Quatro
Singer: 4 SUZI
Quattro
maker: 4 **AUDI**
preceder: 3 TRE
Tre plus: 5 SETTE
Quaver: 4 NOTE

Quay: 4 PIER 5 WHARF
Quayle
successor: 4 GORE
Vice president: 3 DAN
Que
follower, in song: 4 SERA
Que.
neighbor: 3 ONT
"Qué ___?": 4 PASA
Queasiness: 6 NAUSEA
Queasy: 3 ILL
Feel: 3 AIL
feeling: 6 NAUSEA
Québec
campus: 5 LAVAL
connections: 3 ETS
friend: 3 AMI
Hot time in: 3 ETE 4 AOUT
Part of many ~ place names:
     3 STE
peninsula: 5 GASPE
school: 5 ECOLE
vote: 3 NON
Quechua
speaker: 4 INCA
Where ~ is spoken: 4 PERU
     7 BOLIVIA
Queeg
creator: 4 WOUK
ship: 5 **CAINE**
Queen: 4 CARD
Babar's: 7 CELESTE
county: 5 SHIRE
Fairy: 3 MAB
Fit for a: 5 REGAL ROYAL
French: 5 REINE
Hindu: 4 RANI 5 RANEE
Jordanian: 4 NOOR
Land of a biblical: 5 SHEBA
Nile: 4 CLEO
Norse underworld: 3 HEL
of Carthage: 4 DIDO
of fiction: 6 ELLERY
of Persia, in the Bible:
     6 ESTHER
of rap: 7 LATIFAH
of Thebes: 5 NIOBE 7 JOCASTA
Olympus: 4 HERA
Scat: 4 ELLA

Spanish: 3 ENA
Spartan: 4 LEDA
subject: 3 ANT
topper: 5 TIARA
Queen ___: 3 MUM
Queendom
  Biblical: 5 SHEBA
  Cleopatra's: 5 EGYPT
"___ Queene, The": 6 FAERIE
Queen Elizabeth II: 5 LINER
  Daughter of: 4 ANNE
  Letters that precede: 3 HRH
Queen ___ lace: 5 ANNES
Queenly
  crown: 5 TIARA
Queen Margarethe
  land: 7 DENMARK
  subjects: 5 DANES
Queen of Country
  singer McEntire: 4 REBA
Queen of Hearts
  dessert: 5 TARTS
  tart thief: 5 KNAVE
"Queen of Mean"
  ~ Helmsley: 5 LEONA
Queen of Soul
  ~ Franklin: 6 ARETHA
Queens
  section: 7 ASTORIA
  stadium: 4 ASHE **SHEA**
  team: 4 METS
Queenside
  castle, in chess notation: 3 OOO
Queen Victoria
  granddaughter: 3 ENA
  house: 7 HANOVER
  prince: 6 ALBERT
Queequeg: 6 WHALER
  captain: 4 AHAB
"Queer Eye for the Straight Guy"
  channel: 5 BRAVO
Quemoy
  neighbor: 5 MATSU
Quench: 5 **SLAKE**
Quencher
  Citrus: 3 ADE 7 LIMEADE
  Pub: 3 ALE 4 BEER
  Summer: 8 LEMONADE
___ Quentin: 3 SAN

Query: 3 ASK
  Biblical: 5 ISITI
  Cabbie's: 7 WHERETO
  Comic's: 5 GETIT
  Reporter's: 3 HOW WHO WHY
    4 WHAT 4 WHERE
  sounds: 3 EHS
  Tot's: 3 WHY
Ques.
  response: 3 **ANS**
Quest
  One on a: 6 SEEKER
___ Quested: 5 ADELA
Question: 3 ASK 5 DOUBT POSIT
  9 CHALLENGE
  A ~ of identity: 3 WHO
  A ~ of motive: 3 WHY
  A ~ of timing: 4 WHEN
  Biblical: 5 ISITI
  Cabbie's: 7 WHERETO
  Call into: 6 OPPUGN
  Comic's: 5 GETIT
  Gift recipient's: 5 FORME
  Kind of: 5 **YESNO**
  Long-answer: 5 ESSAY
  Optimist's: 6 WHYNOT
  Pop the: 7 PROPOSE
  Put forth a: 4 POSE
  Reporter's: HOW WHO WHY
    4 WHAT WHEN 4 WHERE
  Throw in, as a: 9 INTERPOSE
  to Mom or Dad: 4 CANI
  Tough: 5 POSER
  Zen master's: 4 KOAN
Questionable: 4 IFFY 5 FISHY
  7 SUSPECT
Questionnaire
  choice: 3 YES 4 MALE NONE
    5 OTHER
  datum: 3 AGE SEX
  Kind of: 6 MAILIN
Quetzalcoatl
  worshipper: 5 AZTEC MAYAN
    6 TOLTEC
Queue: 4 LINE 5 BRAID
  7 PIGTAIL
  after A: 3 BCD
  after Q: 3 RST 4 RSTU
  after R: 3 STU 4 STUV

before Q: 3 NOP 4 MNOP
    5 LMNOP
before U: 3 RST
call: 4 NEXT
Form a: 6 LINEUP
Queued up: 6 INAROW INLINE
    7 INALINE
Quibble: 4 CARP 5 CAVIL
    7 NITPICK
Quiche: 3 PIE
  ingredient: 3 EGG HAM 4 EGGS
    7 SPINACH
Quiche Lorraine
  ingredient: 5 BACON
Quick: 3 APT 4 SPRY 5 AGILE
    SHARP WITTY 6 ASTUTE
    SPEEDY
  bread: 5 SCONE
  gait: 4 TROT 6 GALLOP
  look: 4 PEEK 6 GLANCE
  Not very: 5 DENSE
  pull: 4 JERK
  to the helm: 3 YAR
  trip: 4 SPIN
Quickly: 4 ASAP FAST SOON
    5 APACE 6 ATONCE
    PRESTO 8 CHOPCHOP
  Very: 8 INAFLASH INATRICE
    INNOTIME
Quick on the ___: 6 UPTAKE
Quick-witted: 3 APT 4 KEEN
    5 AGILE SHARP SMART
    6 ADROIT
Quid: 4 CHAW
Quiddity: 7 ESSENCE
Quid pro ___: 3 QUO
Quid pro quo: 4 SWAP
    9 TITFORTAT
"Quién ___?": 4 SABE
Quiescent: 6 ATREST
    7 DORMANT
Quiet: 3 MUM 4 CALM HUSH
    MUTE 5 MUTED STILL
    6 HUSHED 8 RETICENT
  Be: 4 REST
  Be ~, musically: 5 TACET
  companion: 5 PEACE
  period: 4 LULL
  protest: 5 SITIN

"Quiet!": 3 **SHH** 4 HUSH SHHH
Quietly
  Move: 5 STEAL 6 TIPTOE
"Quiet on the ___!": 3 SET
Quill: 3 NIB 5 SPINE
Quilled
  critter: 9 PORCUPINE
"Quills"
  subject: 4 SADE
Quilt
  Crazy: 4 OLIO
  filler: 5 EIDER
  part: 5 PATCH
  Work on a: 3 SEW
Quilting
  party: 3 BEE
Quince: 4 POME
Quincy
  actor: 3 ITO
  of music: 5 JONES
Quincy, Dr.
  and colleagues: 3 MES
Quindlen
  Writer: 4 ANNA
Quinine
  target: 7 MALARIA
  water: 5 TONIC
Quinn
  Actor: 5 **AIDAN**
  Annie portrayer: 6 AILEEN
Quinn, Anthony
  role: 5 ZORBA
Quint
  family name: 6 DIONNE
Quintessence: 7 EPITOME
Quintet
  Alphabet: 5 AEIOU
  Ark: 5 TORAH
  Corporeal: 6 SENSES
  HOMES: 5 LAKES
  member: 5 ALTO
  Vowel: 5 AEIOU
  Wind ~ member: 4 OBOE
    6 OBOIST
Quintuplet
  1934 ~: 6 DIONNE
Quip: 3 MOT 4 JAPE JEST
  suffix: 4 STER
Quipster: 3 WAG WIT

Quipu
maker: 4 INCA
Quire
member: 5 SHEET
Quirk: 3 TIC 6 FOIBLE ODDITY
Language: 5 IDIOM
Personal: 3 TIC
Quirky: 3 ODD
habit: 3 TIC
Quisling: 7 TRAITOR
City of: 4 OSLO
Quit: 4 EXIT FOLD STOP
5 CEASE 6 RESIGN
"___ quit!": 3 ORI
Quite: 4 VERY
a bit: 4 LOTS MANY TONS
5 OFTEN
a way: 4 AFAR
a while: 3 EON 4 AGES
5 YEARS
Not: 6 ALMOST HARDLY
NEARLY
"Quite contrary"
girl: 4 MARY
Quito
Capital south of: 4 LIMA
coin: 5 SUCRE
country: 7 ECUADOR
country (abbr.): 4 ECUA
quencher: 4 AGUA
Quitter
comment: 5 ICANT
cry: 5 UNCLE
throw-in: 5 TOWEL
word: 4 CANT
"Quit that!": 6 STOPIT
Quitting time: 4 FIVE
Quiver: 5 SHAKE 7 VIBRATE
carrier: 6 ARCHER
item: 5 ARROW
Quivering: 7 TREMBLY
tree: 5 ASPEN

Quiz: 3 ASK 4 EXAM TEST
answer: 4 TRUE 5 FALSE
Quiz show
group: 5 PANEL
host Trebek: 4 ALEX
Old radio: 4 DRIQ
sound: 4 DING
"Quiz Show"
actor: 7 FIENNES
Qum
coin: 4 RIAL
country: 4 IRAN
native: 5 IRANI
Qumran
dweller: 6 ESSENE
"Quo ___?": 5 VADIS
Quod ___ demonstrandum:
4 ERAT
Quod ___ faciendum: 4 ERAT
Quoits
Good shot in: 6 RINGER
target: 3 HOB
Quorum
Company: 3 TWO
Football: 6 ELEVEN
Solitaire: 3 ONE
Tango: 3 TWO
Teetertotter: 3 TWO
Quotable
catcher: 4 YOGI 5 BERRA
Quotation
notation: 3 SIC 4 ANON
Quote: 4 CITE
Probability: 4 ODDS
___ quote ...: 4 ANDI
"___ quote you?": 4 CANI
Quotidian: 5 DAILY
"Quo Vadis"
role: 4 NERO
QWERTY
alternative: 6 DVORAK
QxQ: 4 MOVE

Rr

R
Geometry: **6** RADIUS
Give an ~ to: **4** RATE
Greek: **3** RHO
Queue after: **3** STU **4** STUV
Reason for an ~ rating: **3** SEX
    4 GORE
R ___: 4 ANDR
R2-D2: 5 DROID
Ra: 3 GOD
Rabanne
Fashion designer: **4** PACO
Rabaud
role: **3** ALI
"Rabbi Ben ___": 4 EZRA
Rabbinical
text: **6** TALMUD
Rabbit: 4 CONY **6** ANGORA
Cereal promoted by a: **4** TRIX
chaser: **5** ALICE
ears: **6** DIPOLE **7** ANTENNA
Female: **3** DOE
food: **5** SALAD
foot: **3** PAW
fur: **4** CONY **5** LAPIN **6** ANGORA
home: **5** HUTCH **6** WARREN
hunter Fudd: **5** ELMER
Kind of: **10** COTTONTAIL
relative: **4** HARE
Rock: **4** PIKA
Rodent like a: **6** AGOUTI
Run like a: **7** SCAMPER
season: **6** EASTER
Storied: **5** MOPSY
tail: **4** SCUT
title: **4** BRER
Toon: **5** ROGER
Rabbit ___: 4 EARS
"Rabbit ___": 5 REDUX
___ Rabbit: 4 BRER
"Rabbit, Run"
author: **6** UPDIKE
Rabble-rouse: 7 AGITATE

Rabelaisian
giant: **9** GARGANTUA
Rabi
Nobel physicist: **6** ISIDOR
Rabin: 7 ISRAELI
Mrs.: **4** LEAH
predecessor: **4** **MEIR**
successor: **5** PERES
Raccoon
relative: **5** COATI PANDA
Race: 3 REV **4** TEAR **5** SPEED
Alaskan sled dog: **8** IDITAROD
Annual: **5** DERBY
Baton-passing: **5** RELAY
British ~ site: **5** ASCOT
climax: **7** LASTLAP
distance: **4** MILE TENK
Drag: **6** HOTROD
Early political: **7** PRIMARY
End of a: **8** ELECTION
Enter the: **3** RUN
Fabled ~ loser: **4** HARE
Fabled ~ winner: **8** TORTOISE
finish: **4** TAPE WIRE
French auto: **6** LEMANS
Harness: **4** TROT
Harness ~ horse: **5** PACER
Kind of: **3** RAT **4** ARMS DRAG
    5 ALIEN HUMAN RELAY
Memorial Day: **4** INDY
of Norse gods: **5** AESIR
pace: **4** TROT
place: **4** INDY OVAL **5** ASCOT
    TRACK **7** DAYTONA
Qualifying: **4** HEAT
Sailing: **7** REGATTA
Short: **4** DASH
Ski: **6** SLALOM
starter: **3** EVE **4** ADAM
unit: **3** LAP LEG
Racecar
feature: **7** ROLLBAR
gauge: **4** TACH

Racehorse
classification: 3 AGE
Like a former: 6 ATSTUD

Racer
Downhill: 4 LUGE SLED
5 LUGER SKIER
Edge for a: 9 HEADSTART
Harness: 5 PACER
Iditarod: 4 SLED
Kiddie: 6 GOKART
Miniature: 4 KART
7 SLOTCAR
Tortoise: 4 HARE
Toy: 7 SLOTCAR

"Racer's Edge, The": 3 STP

Racetrack: 4 OVAL
boundary: 4 **RAIL**
figure: 4 TOUT
info: 4 ODDS
NYC: 4 BIGA

Rachel
Brother-in-law of: 4 ESAU
Father of: 5 LABAN
Husband of: 5 JACOB
Sister of: 4 LEAH

Rachmaninoff
Composer: 6 SERGEI
piece: 5 ETUDE

Racine
play part: 4 ACTE
tragedy: 6 ESTHER PHEDRE

Racing
Big name in: 5 UNSER
boat. 5 SCULL
circuit: 3 LAP
form site, briefly: 3 OTB
initials: 3 STP
org.: 6 NASCAR
sled: 4 LUGE
vehicle: 4 AUTO 6 GOCART
GOKART 8 DRAGSTER

Rack: 7 ANTLERS
Discount ~ abbr.: 3 IRR 5 IRREG
item: 3 BAT HAT TIE 4 COAT
5 SPICE
Kind of: 3 HAT
Partner of: 4 RUIN 6 PINION
Put on the: 7 TORTURE
site: 4 OVEN

Racket: 3 ADO **DIN** 4 SCAM
5 NOISE 6 CLAMOR
7 CLATTER
game: 6 SQUASH
It makes a: 6 CATGUT
Suffix with: 3 **EER**

Raconteur
offering: 4 TALE 8 ANECDOTE

Racy
Hardly: 4 TAME

"Rad!": 4 COOL NEAT 5 NEATO
7 AWESOME

Radames
Love of: 4 AIDA

Radar
anomaly: 3 UFO
detector: 10 FUZZBUSTER
Favorite drink of: 4 **NEHI**
Home of: 4 IOWA
Last name of: 7 OREILLY
principle: 4 ECHO
screen: 4 GRID
signal: 4 **BLIP**

Radarange
maker: 5 AMANA

Radar gun
meas.: 3 MPH
pointer: 3 COP 7 TROOPER

Radcliffe
grads: 7 ALUMNAE
Novelist: 3 ANN

Radial: 4 TIRE
British: 4 **TYRE**
pattern: 5 TREAD
Perpendicular to: 5 AXIAL

Radiance: 4 AURA GLOW
5 SHEEN
Social: 5 ECLAT

Radians
Angle measured in: 7 ARCSINE

Radiant: 5 **AGLOW** 6 AGLEAM
glow: 4 AURA
smile: 4 BEAM

Radiate: 4 **EMIT** OOZE 5 EXUDE
SHINE

Radiation
unit: 3 **REM**

Radiator
adjunct: 7 FANBELT

front: 6 GRILLE
output: 4 HEAT
part: 3 FIN 4 COIL
sound: 3 SSS 4 HISS SSSS

Radical
1960s ~ gp.: 3 **SDS**
1970s ~ gp.: 3 SLA
Sixties: 6 YIPPIE
Vinegar: 6 ACETYL

Radii
neighbors: 5 ULNAE

Radio: 4 SEND 5 MEDIA
amateur: 3 HAM
Car ~ button: 6 PRESET
Celestial ~ source: 6 PULSAR
component: 6 PREAMP
feature: 4 DIAL KNOB 5 TUNER
format: 4 ROCK TALK
6 OLDIES
Get a program on the:
6 TUNEIN
good buddy: 4 CBER
host Hansen: 5 LIANE
Kind of: 3 HAM 4 **AMFM**
9 SHORTWAVE
O in old ~ lingo: 4 OBOE
okay: 5 ROGER
Old ~ quiz show: 4 DRIQ
partner of Abner: 3 LUM
partner of Andy: 4 AMOS
personality: 7 DONIMUS
11 HOWARDSTERN
Police ~ alert, briefly: 3 APB
settings: 3 AMS FMS
Sitcom ~ station: 4 WKRP
spots: 3 ADS
talk show participant: 6 CALLER
tube gas: 5 ARGON XENON

Radioactive
gas: 5 RADON
isotope: 6 IONIUM

Radioactivity
unit: 5 CURIE

Radio City
Like: 4 DECO 7 ARTDECO

Radio Flyer
bar: 4 AXLE

Radiola
maker: 3 RCA

Radish: 4 ROOT

Radium
discoverer: 5 CURIE

Radius: 7 ARMBONE
neighbor: 4 **ULNA**

Radner
Comedienne: 5 GILDA
role: 8 BABAWAWA

Radon: 3 GAS
lacks it: 4 ODOR
Like: 5 INERT

___ **Rae:** 5 NORMA

Reasonable: 4 SANE
Sound: 5 ADDUP

RAF
award: 3 DSO
flyer: 4 BRIT
~, to Churchill: 5 SOFEW

___ **Rafael:** 3 SAN

Raffle
ticket: 6 CHANCE

Raft: 3 TON 4 BEVY HEAP SLEW
Move a: 4 POLE
operator: 5 POLER
wood: 5 BALSA

Rafter: 4 BEAM
connector: 7 TIEBEAM

Rag: 3 KID 5 TAUNT TEASE
WIPER 6 TATTER
Chew the: 3 YAK 4 CHAT

Raga
First name in: 4 RAVI
instrument: 5 SITAR
rhythm-maker: 5 TABLA

Ragamuffin: 4 WAIF 6 URCHIN

Rage: 3 FAD **IRE** 4 FURY
5 ANGER FUROR MANIA
STORM STYLE 6 LATEST
All the: 3 HOT MOD 4 CHIC
6 REDHOT TRENDY
7 INSTYLE POPULAR

Ragged: 6 UNEVEN
Make: 4 FRAY

"Ragged Dick"
author: 5 ALGER

Raggedy
doll: 3 **ANN** 4 ANDY

Raggedy Ann: 4 DOLL

Raging: 5 ANGRY 7 ONATEAR

"Raging Bull"
  subject: 7 LAMOTTA
"Rag Mop"
  brothers: 4 AMES
Ragout: 4 STEW
  Game: 5 SALMI
Rags-to-riches
  author: 5 ALGER
Ragtime
  Blake of: 5 EUBIE
  dance: 7 ONESTEP
"Ragtime"
  actress Steenburgen: 4 MARY
  author: 10 ELDOCTOROW
Ragú
  rival: 5 **PREGO**
Rah
  Ring: 3 OLE
Rah-rah: 4 AVID 6 ARDENT
Raid: 6 INROAD SORTIE
  1976 ~ site: 7 ENTEBBE
  Cause of a Boston Harbor:
    6 TEAACT
  Drug: 4 BUST
  Quick: 5 FORAY
  rival: 4 DCON
  target: 4 PEST 5 ROACH
    6 INSECT
  the fridge: 4 NOSH
Raider
  Cornfield: 4 CROW
  Corporate ~ Carl: 5 ICAHN
  of the 10th century:
    8 NORSEMAN
  Pantry: 3 ANT
  Picnic: 3 ANT
Raiders
  gp.: 3 DEA FBI
  Home of the: 7 OAKLAND
  Treasury Dept.: 3 ATF
"Raiders of the Lost ___": 3 ARK
"Raiders of the Lost Ark"
  danger: 4 ASPS
  setting: 5 NEPAL
"Raid on Entebbe"
  airline: 4 ELAL
Rail
  Ballet: 5 BARRE
  Like a: 4 THIN

  rider: 4 **HOBO**
  runner: 4 TRAM 5 TRAIN
  Short-billed: 4 SORA
  support: 3 TIE
  Windy City ~ system (abbr.):
    3 CTA
Raillery: 3 WIT
Railroad
  area: 4 YARD
  bridge: 7 TRESTLE
  car: 5 DINER
  Certain model ~ *(plural)*: 3 HOS
  measure: 5 GAUGE
  siding: 4 SPUR
  station: 5 DEPOT
  stop (abbr.): 3 STA
  support: 3 TIE
  switch: 5 SHUNT
  Trans-Siberian ~ city: 4 OMSK
  unit: 3 CAR
  worker: 6 REDCAP STOKER
Railway
  car problem: 6 HOTBOX
  D.C.: 5 METRO
Railways
  Raised: 3 ELS
Raiment: 4 GARB 6 ATTIRE
  Raipur: 4 SARI
  Roman: 4 TOGA
Rain
  alternative: 5 SHINE
  Bit of: 4 DROP
  check: 4 STUB
  clouds. 5 NIMDI
  delay protection: 4 TARP
  Frozen: 5 SLEET
  gear: 7 OILSKIN SLICKER
  Hard: 4 HAIL
  heavily: 4 POUR TEEM
  It may be called on account of:
    3 CAB
  Kind of: 4 ACID
  The ~ in Spain: 4 AGUA
  ___ rain: 4 ACID
Rainbow: 3 ARC 4 IRIS
  color: 6 INDIGO
  End of a: 6 VIOLET
  goddess: 4 **IRIS**
  Like a: 5 **ARCED**

maker: **5** PRISM
Part of a: **3** HUE
shape: **3** ARC **4** ARCH
Rainbow ___: **5** TROUT
Rainbow Bridge
locale: **4** UTAH
Raincoat
British: **3** MAC
Raindrop
sound: **4** PLOP
**"Raindrops Keep Fallin' ___
Head"**: **4** ONMY
Rainer
Actress: **5** LUISE
Oscar role for: **4** OLAN
Raines
Actress: **4** ELLA
Rainfall
measure: **4** INCH
Rain forest
feature: **4** MIST
Like a: **4** LUSH **5** DENSE
ruminant: **5** OKAPI
vine: **5** LIANA
Raingear
brand: **5** TOTES
Rainier
and others (abbr.): **3** MTS
locale: **6** MONACO
Rainless: **4** ARID SERE
Rains
Actor: **6** CLAUDE
Rainy: **3** WET
Rainy day
fund: **7** NESTEGG
Prepare for a: **4** SAVE
Raipur
wrap: **4** SARI
Raise: **3** BET **4** HIKE LIFT REAR
5 ERECT EXALT HOIST
6 UPREAR **7** ELEVATE
(abbr.): **4** INCR
a glass to: **5** TOAST
an outcry: **6** CLAMOR
a stink: **4** REEK **5** GRIPE
canines: **6** TEETHE
in relief: **6** EMBOSS
It helps ~ dough: **5** YEAST
Kind of: **5** MERIT

Match a: **3** SEE
Refuse to: **4** CALL
Something to: **4** CAIN HELL
spirits: **5** ELATE
the cost of: **5** BIDUP
the hackles of: **4** RILE
the hem: **5** ALTER
your voice: **4** YELL
~ Cain: **4** RAGE
Raise ___: **4** CAIN
Raised: **4** BRED **5** ERECT UPPED
eyebrow remarks: **3** OHS
He ~ Cain: **4** ADAM
It is ~ on a farm: **4** BARN SILO
platform: **4** DAIS **5** ALTAR
platforms: **6** ROSTRA
railways: **3** ELS
ridge: **4** WELT
seam: **4** WELT
She ~ Cain: **3** EVE
Raiser: **6** PARENT
Cain: **3** EVE **4** ADAM
Curtain: **4** ACTI
Dough: **5** YEAST
Hair: **3** GEL
Ham: **4** NOAH
Reindeer: **4** LAPP
Spirit: **6** SEANCE
Tarzan: **3** APE
Raises: **3** UPS
Raisin
California ~ center: **6** FRESNO
Like a: **5** DRIED
rum cake: **4** BABA
Seedless: **7** SULTANA
~, originally: **5** GRAPE
Raising
heck: **5** ROWDY **7** ONATEAR
"Raisin in the Sun, A"
heroine: **4** LENA
Raison ___: **5** DETRE
Rajah
land: **5** INDIA
Wife of: **4** RANI **5** RANEE
Rajiv
Mother of: **6** INDIRA
Wife of: **5** SONIA
Rake: **3** CAD **4** ROUE **6** LECHER
8 LOTHARIO

home: 4 SHED
in: 4 EARN
over the coals: 5 ROAST
part: 4 TINE
Rakehell: 4 ROUE
Raleigh
state (abbr.): 4 NCAR
title: 3 SIR
to Philly heading (abbr.): 3 NNE
Rall
Political cartoonist: 3 TED
Rally: 5 ROUSE 7 RECOVER
cry: 3 RAH 6 GOTEAM
Kind of: 3 PEP
They may: 5 CRIES
Ralph
1950s slugger ~: 5 KINER
Consumerist: 5 NADER
Designer: 6 LAUREN
Ed, to: 3 PAL
Wife of: 5 ALICE
Ram: 4 BUTT MALE
       7 REAREND
Astrological: 5 **ARIES**
mate: 3 EWE
remark: 3 **BAA** MAA 5 BLEAT
RAM
Part of: 6 ACCESS RANDOM
unit: 3 MEG 4 ONEK
Rama
~, to Vishnu: 6 AVATAR
Ramadan: 5 MONTH
observance: 4 FAST
Ramble: 3 GAD 4 ROAM ROVE
       6 WANDER 7 MEANDER
on: 3 YAK
Rambler
maker: 3 AMC 4 NASH
"Rambling Rose"
actress Laura: 4 DERN
"__ ramblin' wreck": 3 IMA
**"Ramblin' Wreck From
       Georgia __":** 4 TECH
Rambo: 5 HEMAN
       10 ONEMANARMY
Like: 5 MACHO
Rambunctious: 5 ROWDY
Ramee
pen name: 5 OUIDA

Ramirez
of tennis: 4 RAUL
Ramis
Actor: 6 HAROLD
Ramone
Late rocker: 6 DEEDEE
Ramones, The: 11 PUNKROCKERS
music: 4 PUNK
Ramp
Off: 4 EXIT
Rampage: 4 TEAR
__ rampage: 3 ONA
Rampager
Ring: 4 TORO
Rampaging: 7 ONATEAR
Rampal
instrument: 5 FLUTE
Rampant: 4 RIFE
Rampart: 4 WALL
part: 7 PARAPET
Rams
home: 3 STL
Like: 5 OVINE
The ~ sch.: 3 URI
Ramses I
Son of: 4 SETI
Ramses II
Father of: 4 SETI
Site of ~ temples: 9 ABUSIMBEL
"__ Ramsey" (1970s TV western):
       3 HEC
Ramshackle
structure: 7 RATTRAP
Ran: 3 LED 4 BLED FLED TORE
       5 LOPED RACED
a tab: 4 OWED
away: 4 FLED
easily: 5 LOPED
first: 3 LED
in: 8 ARRESTED
in neutral: 5 IDLED
in the wash: 4 **BLED**
into: 3 **MET**
like heck: 4 TORE
off: 6 ELOPED
on: 6 PRATED
out: 6 LAPSED
Ranch
alternative: 7 ITALIAN RUSSIAN

brush: 4 SAGE
bunch: 4 HERD
Kind of: 4 DUDE
Large: 8 HACIENDA
Like a ~ house:
   8 ONESTORY
moniker: 3 TEX
Pres. with a: 3 LBJ
rope: 5 RIATA 6 LARIAT
suffix: 3 ERO
unit: 4 ACRE HEAD
visitor: 4 DUDE
wear: 6 DENIMS
worker: 4 HAND 7 COWPOKE
   9 HIREDHAND
Rancher: 9 CATTLEMAN
enemy: 6 COYOTE
mark: 5 BRAND
Rancidity
retardant: 3 BHT
Rancor: 5 SPITE
Rand
Author: 3 **AYN**
Shrugger of: 5 ATLAS
Rand, Ayn
book: 6 ANTHEM
   13 ATLASSHRUGGED
Randall
1964 ~ title role: 5 DRLAO
Actor: 4 TONY
Dr. played by: 3 LAO
~ TV role: 5 UNGER
R&B
1970s ~ member: 4 OJAY
singer Braxton: 4 TONI
singer Bryson: 5 PEABO
singer Hill: 3 DRU
singer James: 4 **ETTA**
singer Redding: 4 OTIS
R&D
Part of: 3 DEV RES
Reagan ~ program: 3 SDI
Rand McNally
book: 5 ATLAS
Random: 5 STRAY
criticism: 7 POTSHOT
number generator: 3 DIE
scrap: 6 TAGEND
Select at: 4 DRAW

Random House
founder: 4 CERF
Randomizer: 3 DIE
R&R
Part of: 4 REST
place: 3 SPA 6 RESORT
Randy
Country singer: 6 TRAVIS
Ranee
wrap: 5 SAREE
Rang: 6 PEALED TOLLED
out: 6 PEALED 7 SOUNDED
"___ rang?": 3 YOU
Range: 4 ROAM ROVE 5 GAMUT
   SCOPE STOVE STRAY
   SWEEP
animal: 4 DEER 8 ANTELOPE
Asian: 5 URALS
Audible: 7 EARSHOT
Chilean: 5 ANDES
Complete: 4 ATOZ 5 GAMUT
Curriculum ~, briefly: 4 ELHI
Driving ~ item: 3 TEE
Entire: 4 ATOZ 5 GAMUT
Gp. on the: 3 NRA
Home on the: 5 **TEPEE**
influence: 6 SPHERE
It is within your: 4 OVEN
Light on the: 5 PILOT
Low: 4 BASS 5 BASSO
maker: 5 **AMANA**
Minnesota: 6 MESABI
Name on the: 3 TEX 5 AMANA
newcomer: 4 CALF
of view: 5 SCOPE
of vision: 3 KEN 7 EYESHOT
orphan: 5 DOGIE
Peruvian: 5 ANDES
Rating: 8 ONETOTEN
rover: 4 HERD 5 STEER
Rugged: 6 SIERRA
Russian: 5 URALS
Sax: 4 ALTO 5 TENOR
stray: 5 DOGIE
units (abbr.): 3 MTS 4 MTNS
Voice: 4 ALTO BASS 5 TENOR
   7 SOPRANO
Wyoming: 6 TETONS
Yodeler: 8 FALSETTO

Ranger: 5 EDSEL
  sidekick: 5 TONTO
  slugger, once: 4 AROD
___ Ranger (trendy Londoner):
      6 SLOANE
"___ Ranger, The": 4 LONE
Rangers
  gp.: 3 NHL
Rani
  wrap: 4 **SARI**
Rank: 4 RATE TIER 5 FETID
      GRADE PLACE 6 ROTTEN
  GI: 3 PFC
  Mil.: 3 COL MAJ PFC SGT
     5 LTCOL
  Nav.: 3 CPO **ENS**
  NCO: 4 MSGT SSGT
  Partner of: 4 NAME
  P.D.: 3 DET 4 INSP
  Reduce in: 5 ABASE 6 DEMOTE
  Scout: 5 EAGLE
  Sign of: 6 STRIPE
  Social: 5 CLASS
  Tournament: 4 SEED
Ranked: 4 AROW
Ranking: 5 CLASS
  player: 5 SEED
Rankle: 3 IRK VEX 5 ANNOY
      6 FESTER 8 EMBITTER
Ransack: 4 LOOT RAID 5 RIFLE
Ransom
  Automaker: 4 OLDS
  Hold for: 6 KIDNAP
  payoff: 4 DROP
"Ransom"
  actress Russo: 4 **RENE**
  actress Taylor: 4 LILI
Rant: 6 TIRADE
  Partner of: 4 RAVE
"___ Ran the Circus": 3 IFI
"___ Ran the Zoo": 3 IFI
Raoul
  Director: 5 WALSH
Rap: 3 GAB 4 CHAT 5 BLAME
      14 CRIMINALCHARGE
  artist: 4 ICET 6 COOLIO
  fans: 5 BBOYS
  Give a: 4 CARE
  session: 6 SEANCE

sheet data: 3 **AKA** 5 ALIAS
     PRIOR 6 THEFTS
     7 ARRESTS
  variety: 7 GANGSTA
  ~ Dr.: 3 **DRE**
Rapa ___ (Easter Island): 3 **NUI**
Rapid: 6 SPEEDY
  transit: 3 SST
Rapid-fire
  weapon: 3 UZI
Rapidly: 4 FAST 5 APACE
Rapids
  transit: 4 RAFT 5 CANOE KAYAK
Rapier
  Fencing: 4 **EPEE**
Rapper
  Cool: 4 ICET
  sound: 7 RATATAT
  ~ Dr.: 3 **DRE**
  ~ Lil': 3 KIM
  ~ Queen: 7 LATIFAH
  ~ Snoop: 4 DOGG
  ~ Tone: 3 LOC
Rapscallion: 3 IMP 5 ROGUE
     SCAMP
Raptor
  claw: 5 TALON
  Coastal: 3 ERN 4 ERNE
  Young: 6 EAGLET
Raptors
  city: 7 TORONTO
Rapture: 3 JOY 5 BLISS
Rapunzel
  feature: 4 HAIR 5 TRESS
  hair color: 6 FLAXEN
  Like: 6 TRESSY
  prison: 5 TOWER
Raquel
  Actress: 5 WELCH
Rara ___: 4 AVIS
Rara avis: 4 ONER
Rare: 4 PINK 6 EXOTIC SCARCE
  bill: 3 TWO
  bird: 4 ONER
  blood: 6 TYPEAB
  golf shot: 3 ACE
  It may be: 5 STEAK
  Like a ~ game: 5 NOHIT
  Not even: 3 RAW

Rarer than: 3 RAW 7 TARTARE
trick taker: 4 TREY
"Rare and radiant maiden"
of Poe: 6 LENORE
Rarefied: 4 THIN
Rarely: 6 SELDOM
       15 ONCEINABLUEMOON
Raring
to go: 4 AVID 5 AFIRE **EAGER**
   6 ALLSET
___ rasa: 6 TABULA
Rascal: 3 CAD IMP 5 KNAVE
     ROGUE **SCAMP** 6 VARLET
     8 SCALAWAG
Rash: 5 HASTY SPATE 6 MADCAP
     SUDDEN
feature: 7 REDNESS
reaction: 4 ITCH
treatment: 4 TALC
Rashad
Sportscaster: 5 AHMAD
Rasp: 4 FILE
Raspberry: 4 JEER
     10 BRONXCHEER
Raspy: 6 HOARSE
Rasta
messiah: 8 SELASSIE
music: 6 REGGAE
Rat: 4 SING TELL 6 TATTLE
     7 STOOLIE TRAITOR
challenge: 4 MAZE
Dirty: 5 LOUSE 7 SOANDSO
Film: 3 BEN
(on): 4 TELL
out: 6 TELLON
Pack: 5 SAVER
Rug: 3 **TOT** 4 TYKE
tail: 4 ATAT
White: 6 ALBINO
Rat-___: 4 **ATAT**
Rat-a-___: 3 TAT
Ratatouille: 4 STEW
ingredient: 8 ZUCCHINI
Ratched, Nurse
creator: 5 KESEY
Ratchet
engager: 4 PAWL
Rate: 4 CLIP PACE 5 MERIT
     7 DESERVE

Data transfer: 4 BAUD
Flat: 4 RENT
of return: 5 YIELD
The going: 4 FARE TOLL
     5 SPEED
Tpk.: 3 MPH
Rate ___ (be perfect): 4 ATEN
Rated
Highly: 3 AAA 4 ACES AONE
Rater
Meat ~ (abbr.): 4 USDA
Motel: 3 AAA
MPG: 3 **EPA**
Ratfink: 7 STOOLIE
Rathbone
Actor: 5 BASIL
role: 6 HOLMES
Rather: 4 ABIT 5 QUITE
     6 SORTOF 7 INSTEAD
     8 PREFERTO
Newsman: 3 **DAN**
report: 4 NEWS
~, informally: 5 KINDA SORTA
Rather, Dan: 7 NEWSMAN
network: 3 CBS
Rathskeller: 8 BEERHALL
item: 5 STEIN
quaff: 3 ALE
Ratify: 4 PASS
Rating
a 10: 5 IDEAL
Bond: 3 AAA BBB CCC
Draft: 4 ONEA
Excellent: 4 AONE
Film ~ gp.: 4 MPAA
Gas: 6 OCTANE
Kind of: 3 EPA 7 NIELSEN
Mileage ~ gp.: 3 EPA
Movie ~ (plural): 3 PGS
Perfect: 3 TEN
Poor: 7 ONESTAR
range: 8 ONETOTEN
unit: 4 **STAR**
Ratio
Betting: 4 ODDS
indicator: 5 COLON
Math: 4 SINE
phrase: 4 **ISTO**
Speed: 4 MACH

Trig: 3 COS TAN 4 **SINE**
     5 COSEC 6 COSINE SECANT
Ration: 4 DOLE METE 5 ALLOT
Rational: 4 SANE
   religion: 5 DEISM
Rationality: 5 SENSE 8 SANENESS
Ratios
   Circle: 3 PIS
Rat Island
   resident: 5 ALEUT
Ratite
   bird: 3 EMU
Ratlike
   rodent: 4 VOLE
   ___ Raton: 4 **BOCA**
Rat Pack
   leader: 7 SINATRA
   name: 4 DINO 5 SAMMY
     10 JOEYBISHOP
"Rats!": 4 DARN 6 DARNIT
     PHOOEY
Ratso
   portrayer: 6 DUSTIN
Ratted: 4 SANG TOLD
Rattle: 3 JAR 4 FAZE 6 MARACA
     7 UNHINGE UNNERVE
   in a whistle: 3 PEA
   on: 3 YAK
   sabers: 6 MENACE
   Something to: 4 CAGE 5 SABER
Rattletrap: 5 CRATE
Rattrap: 3 STY
Ratty
   place: 5 SEWER
Raucous: 4 LOUD 5 NOISY
   diver: 4 LOON
   noise: 5 BLARE
Rave
   music: 6 TECHNO
   Partner of: 4 RANT
   ~ VIPs: 3 DJS
Ravel
   classic: 6 BOLERO
   Composer: 7 MAURICE
Raveled
   fuzz: 4 LINT
Raven
   call: 3 CAW 5 CROAK
   haven: 4 NEST

maven: 3 POE
"Raven, The"
   actor: 5 LORRE
   author: 3 POE 5 EAPOE
     13 EDGARALLANPOE
   maiden: 6 LENORE
   monogram: 3 EAP
   opener: 4 ONCE
Ravens
   God attended by two: 4 ODIN
   gp.: 3 NFL
Ravi
   Sitarist: 7 SHANKAR
Ravioli: 5 PASTA
Raw: 7 TARTARE
   facts: 4 DATA
   fish dish: 5 SUSHI
   In the: 4 BARE NUDE
   It may be: 4 DEAL
   linen color: 4 ECRU
   material: 3 ORE
   Run in the: 6 STREAK
   silk color: 4 ECRU
   ~, as diamonds: 5 UNCUT
Rawboned: 5 LANKY
     7 ANGULAR
Rawhide
   Cure: 3 TAN
"Rawhide"
   Eastwood role in: 5 YATES
   singer: 5 LAINE
Rawlings
   Writer: 8 MARJORIE
Rawls
   Singer: 3 **LOU**
Ray
   Actor: 4 **ALDO** 6 LIOTTA
   Big Band singer: 6 EBERLE
   Kind of: 4 HEAT 5 GAMMA
     MANTA SKATE
   McDonald's founder: 4 KROC
   of light: 4 BEAM 7 SUNBEAM
   of the Kinks: 6 DAVIES
   Shoot a: 4 LASE
   Use a ~ gun: 3 ZAP
Ray, Johnnie
   song: 3 CRY
Ray, Man
   genre: 4 DADA

Rayburn
  Game show host: 4 GENE
  Politico: 3 SAM
Raymond
  Actor: 4 BURR 6 MASSEY
  Mystery writer: 8 CHANDLER
  on TV: 6 ROMANO
  Songwriter: 4 EGAN
Rays
  Catch some: 3 SUN **TAN** 4 BASK
      6 SUNTAN 8 SUNBATHE
  Give off: 4 EMIT
Raze: 5 LEVEL
Razor
  brand: 3 BIC 4 **ATRA** 6 SENSOR
      7 NORELCO
  brand ___ II: 4 TRAC
  feature: 4 EDGE
  He had a: 5 OCCAM
  Sharpen a: 4 HONE
  sharpener: 5 **STROP**
  Use a: 5 SHAVE
Razor-billed
  bird: 3 AUK
Razorfish: 6 WRASSE
"Razor's ___, The": 4 EDGE
Razz: 4 GIBE JEER 5 TAUNT
      TEASE 6 NEEDLE
Razzle-dazzle: 5 ECLAT GLITZ
RB
  gains: 3 YDS
RBI: 4 **STAT**
  Part of: 3 RUN 4 RUNS
  recordholder: 5 AARON
RC: 4 COLA
  rival: 4 COKE 5 PEPSI
RCA: 5 LABEL
  Nipper of: 3 DOG
  products: 3 TVS
  rival: 3 EMI
RCA Dome
  team: 5 COLTS
Rd.
  Major: 3 HWY
  Numbered: 3 **RTE**
  Toll: 3 TPK 4 TPKE
Re: 4 ASTO NOTE 5 ANENT
Reach: 3 GET 5 GETAT GETTO
      6 ATTAIN 7 CONTACT

across: 4 **SPAN**
a peak: 5 CREST
for: 6 GRABAT
in amount: 5 RUNTO
the beach: 4 LAND
Within: 4 **NEAR** 5 HANDY
      6 ATHAND
___ reach: 6 WITHIN
Reachable: 7 INRANGE
Reaches: 8 GETSUPTO
React
  Not quick to: 5 INERT
  to a blow: 4 REEL 8 SEESTARS
  to a pun: 5 WINCE
  to snuff: 6 SNEEZE
Reaction
  Allergic: 4 ITCH RASH 5 ACHOO
      6 ASTHMA SNEEZE
  Angry: 4 RISE
  Bad news: 5 GROAN
  Cold: 3 BRR
  Gut: 3 OOF
  Hostile: 4 FLAK
  Kind of: 3 GUT 8 ALLERGIC
      KNEEJERK
  Mouse: 3 EEK
  Rash: 4 ITCH
  Shocked: 4 GASP
  source: 3 GUT
Reactor: 10 ATOMICPILE
  part: 3 ROD 4 CORE
  unit: 3 RAD
Read: 7 PERUSED
  a bar code: 4 **SCAN**
  Make hard to: 6 ENCODE
  One way to: 5 **ALOUD**
  quickly: 4 SCAN SKIM
  Something to: 4 PALM 5 METER
      7 RIOTACT
Read ___ (study): 4 UPON
"Read 'em and ___!": 4 WEEP
Reader
  Manual: 4 USER
  Meter: 6 GASMAN
  Mind ~ claim: 3 ESP
  Palm: 4 SEER
  Public: 6 LECTOR
  Speed: 5 RADAR
  Tarot: 4 SEER

"___ Reader, The": 4 **UTNE**
"Reader's ___": 6 DIGEST
"Reader's Digest"
  Wallace of: 4 LILA
Readily
  available: 5 ONTAP 6 ONCALL
    ONHAND
Readiness
  In: 5 ONICE
Reading: 4 GAOL
  Bar Mitzvah: 5 TORAH
  Heavy: 4 **TOME**
  light: 4 LAMP
  material: 9 TEALEAVES
  Meter: 4 FARE
  Odometer: 5 MILES
  Restaurant: 4 MENU
  room: 3 DEN 5 STUDY
  Sunday: 6 COMICS 8 MASSBOOK
  Sundial: 3 III VII XII
  Tach: 3 RPM 4 REVS
"Reading Rainbow"
  host Burton: 5 LEVAR
Readout
  Digital ~, for short: 3 **LCD**
  Hosp.: 3 ECG EEG EKG
Read the ___ act: 4 RIOT
Ready: 3 SET 4 PREP RIPE
        5 ALERT ONTAP 6 ALLSET
        PRIMED
  and willing partner: 4 ABLE
  Be ~ for: 5 AWAIT
  follower: 3 AIM
  for: 4 UPTO 6 OPENTO
  for battle: 5 ARMED
      15 ARMEDTOTHETEETH
  for drawing: 5 ONTAP
  Get: 4 **PREP** 5 TEEUP
      6 GEARUP 7 PREPARE
  to fire: 5 ARMED 6 COCKED
      PRIMED
  to go: 3 SET 5 EAGER 6 ALLSET
  to hit: 5 ATBAT
  to pluck: 4 RIPE
  to roll: 6 INGEAR
  to serve: 4 DONE
"Ready ___ ...": 5 ORNOT
Ready for the World
  hit: 8 OHSHEILA

"Ready or not, ___ ...": 5 HEREI
"Ready or not, here ___!":
    5 ICOME
"Ready to Wear"
  actor Stephen: 3 REA
Reagan
  aide Nofziger: 3 LYN
  Attorney General under:
      5 **MEESE** 7 EDMEESE
  costar in 1951: 5 BONZO
  court appointee: 6 SCALIA
  Daughter of: 5 PATTI
  era prog.: 3 **SDI**
  First wife of: 5 WYMAN
  Interior Secretary under:
      4 WATT
  President: 6 RONALD
  Secretary of State under: 4 HAIG
  Son of: 3 RON
  speechwriter: 6 NOONAN
  Surgeon General under: 4 KOOP
Real: 4 TRUE 6 ACTUAL INESSE
      7 SINCERE
  Be: 5 EXIST
  For: 5 LEGIT
  Not: 4 SHAM 5 BOGUS
" ___ real!": 3 GET
Real estate
  abbr.: 3 RMS 4 APTS BDRM
      BSMT
  company: 3 ERA
  document: 4 DEED
  info: 5 RENTS
  map: 4 PLAT
  Move, in ~ lingo: 4 RELO
  parcel: 3 LOT
  sign: 4 SOLD
  unit: 4 ACRE
Realism
  prefix: 3 NEO
Reality: 4 FACT
  In: 7 ATHEART DEFACTO
Realize: 3 GET NET SEE 4 GAIN
      REAP 6 ATTAIN
      7 ACHIEVE
Really: 6 INFACT
"Really!": 3 GEE 5 NOLIE
      6 DOTELL
"Really?": 4 ITIS 8 ISTHATSO

"___ Really Going Out With Him?": 5 ISSHE
"Really lookin' fine"
  car in a '64 song: 3 GTO
Realm: 4 AREA 6 SPHERE
"___ real nowhere man ...": 4 HESA
Realtor
  database (abbr.): 3 MLS
  Move, in ~ lingo: 4 RELO
  sign: 4 SOLD
  tactic: 9 OPENHOUSE
  unit: 3 LOT 4 ACRE
Realty
  unit: 3 LOT 4 ACRE
Ream
  fraction: 5 QUIRE
  unit: 5 SHEET
Reaper
  tool: 6 SCYTHE
Rear: 4 DUFF HIND 5 RAISE
      STERN 6 BREECH PARENT
      7 TAILEND
  Bringing up the: 4 LAST
  Bring up the: 3 LAG 4 MOON
      5 TRAIL 6 BELAST
  end: 3 RAM 4 PRAT RUMP
      TUSH 5 FANNY 6 HEINIE
  To the: 3 AFT 5 ABAFT
      6 ASTERN
Rear-___: 5 ENDER
Reason: 3 WHY 5 CAUSE LOGIC
      6 DEDUCE MOTIVE
      SANITY
  For any: 5 ATALL
  For this: 5 HENCE
  Partner of: 5 RHYME
  Within: 4 SANE
  ___ reason: 6 WITHIN
Reasoning: 5 LOGIC
Reassurance
  Words of: 4 IMOK
Reassuring
  phrase: 4 IMOK 5 ITSOK
Reb
  Foe of: 4 YANK
  outfit: 3 CSA
Rebate
  Kind of: 6 MAILIN

Rebbe
  locale: 4 SHUL
Rebecca
  Author: 4 WEST
  of the WNBA: 4 LOBO
"Rebecca"
  1997 Emmy winner for ~: 4 RIGG
Rebecca ___ (née Pocahontas):
      5 ROLFE
Rebekah
  Husband of: 5 ISAAC
  Son of: 4 ESAU
Rebel
  ~ Turner: 3 NAT
Rebel ___: 4 YELL
"___ Rebel" (Crystals hit): 4 HESA
___ Rebellion
  of 1786: 5 SHAYS
  of 1857–59: 5 SEPOY
Rebellious
  time: 5 TEENS
  ~ Turner: 3 NAT
Rebels: 5 RIOTS 6 ARISES
      7 UPRISES
Rebels, The: 7 OLEMISS
"Rebel Without a Cause"
  actor: 8 SALMINEO
      9 JAMESDEAN
  actor Mineo: 3 SAL
  actor Sal: 5 MINEO
"Rebel Yell"
  rocker Billy: 4 IDOL
Rebound: 5 CAROM
  basket: 5 TAPIN
  Sound: 4 ECHO
Rebounds: 4 STAT
Rebozo
  Nixon pal: 4 BEBE
Rebuff: 4 SLAP SNUB
Rebuffs: 3 NOS
Rebuke
  Ides: 4 ETTU
  Recital: 3 SHH
  Sharp: 4 SLAP
  Verbal: 6 EARFUL
  Word of: 3 TUT
Rebukes
  How some ~ are made:
      7 CROSSLY

sharply: **7** SNAPSAT
Rec
  center: **4** YMCA
  room: **3** DEN
Recall
  1982 ~ subject: **7** TYLENOL
  beginning: **9** IREMEMBER
  "___ recall ...": **3** ASI
Recant: **6** ABJURE
Recap: **5** SUMUP
Recede: **3** __EBB__
Receipt: **9** SALESSLIP
  Abbr. on a: **3** CHG
  stamp: **4** PAID
Receipts: **4** GATE TAKE
Receive: **3** GET **5** GREET
        6 ACCEPT
  enthusiastically: **5** LAPUP
Receiver: **5** RADIO
  Audio: **3** EAR
  Gift: **5** DONEE
  Image: **6** RETINA
  Pass: **3** END
  Property: **7** ALIENEE
  Signal: **4** DISH **7** ANTENNA
        13 SATELLITEDISH
Recent: **3** NEW **4** LATE
  arrival: **6** NEWKID **7** NEONATE
        8 NEWCOMER
  In ~ times: **6** LATELY OFLATE
  prefix: **3** NEO **4** CENO
  ~, in German: **3** NEU
Recently: **5** NEWLY **6** __OFLATE__
  As ~ as: **4** ONLY
  discovered: **8** NEWFOUND
Receptacle
  Barbecue: **6** ASHPIT
  Garbage: **6** ASHCAN
  Holy water: **4** FONT
  Recycling: **3** BIN
Reception
  Afternoon: **3** TEA
  aid: **6** AERIAL **7** ANTENNA
  Bad: **4** HISS **6** STATIC
  Handle a: **5** CATER
  Line before a: **3** IDO
  medium: **5** CABLE
  staple: **5** TOAST
  Wedding ~ centerpiece: **4** CAKE

Receptionist
  cry: **4** NEXT
Receptive: **4** OPEN **7** TUNEDIN
Recess: **4** NOOK REST **5** BREAK
        NICHE **6** ALCOVE
  Carpentry: **7** MORTISE
  Church: **4** __APSE__
  Shoreline: **4** COVE **5** INLET
  Wall: **5** NICHE
Recession: **5** SLUMP **7** DECLINE
Rechargeable
  battery: **5** NICAD
Recharging
  In need of: **4** DEAD
Recherché: **4** RARE **6** ARCANE
Recipe
  amt.: **3** TBS __TSP__ **4** TBSP
  direction: **4** BOIL SEAR __STIR__
        5 SAUTE STEAM **6** FOLDIN
        STIRIN
  guesstimate: **4** DASH **5** ADASH
  info (abbr.): **3** AMT
  phrase: **7** TOTASTE
  title words: **3** ALA
Recipient
  Award: **7** HONOREE
  Bond: **7** OBLIGEE
  Charity: **5** __DONEE__
  Check: **5** PAYEE
  Gift: **5** __DONEE__
  Gold watch: **7** RETIREE
  Legacy: **4** HEIR
  Medal: **4** HERO
  Property: **7** ALIENEE
Reciprocal
  Cosecant: **4** SINE
  Sine: **5** COSEC
Reciprocity
  Law of quadratic ~ formulator:
        5 EULER
Recital
  hall: **5** ODEUM
  piece: **4** SOLO **5** ETUDE
        6 SONATA
  pieces: **4** SOLI
  Rosary: **8** AVEMARIA
Recitation
  Kindergarten: **4** ABCS
  Religious: **6** ROSARY

8 AVEMARIA
Scout: 4 OATH
Recite: 3 SAY 6 INTONE
Easily: 7 REELOFF
Reckless: 4 RASH 6 MADCAP
sort: 9 DAREDEVIL
Recklessly
Dance: 4 MOSH
Drive: 6 CAREEN
Recklessness
Goddess of: 3 ATE
Reckon: 5 GUESS OPINE
6 FIGURE
Recline: 3 LIE 4 LOLL
Reclined: 3 LAY 4 **LAIN**
Recliner: 5 CHAIR
part: 7 ARMREST LEGREST
Room with a: 3 DEN
Recluse: 5 LONER 6 HERMIT
SHUTIN 7 EREMITE
Recognition: 4 FAME 6 CREDIT
response: 3 AHA
Words to elicit: 5 ITSME
Recognize: 3 SEE 4 KNOW
7 DISCERN
Recoil: 3 SHY 4 KICK
Recolor: 3 DYE
Recombinant
stuff: 3 DNA
Recommend: 4 URGE 6 ADVISE
Recompense: 5 WAGES
6 AMENDS
Recon
unit: 6 PATROL
Reconcile: 7 IRONOUT
MEDIATE
Reconditioned: 4 USED
Reconnoiter: 5 SCOUT 6 PATROL
Reconsideration
Mark of: 4 STET
Record: 3 LOG 4 DISC TAPE
5 ALBUM ENTER
6 ANNALS 8 RAPSHEET
Ancestry: 4 TREE
book entry: 4 STAT
Checkbook: 4 STUB
collection: 8 DATABASE
company: 5 LABEL
company receipt: 8 DEMOTAPE

cutter: 6 STYLUS
flaw: 4 SKIP
Half a: 7 SIDEONE
holder: 4 FILE 6 JACKET
SLEEVE 7 DOSSIER
SPINDLE
label: 3 BMI **EMI** MCA 4 ATCO
KTEL 5 ASCAP DECCA
6 ARISTA
material: 5 VINYL
of one year: 5 ANNAL
One with a: 3 CON
output: 5 AUDIO
Phonograph: 4 DISC
player: 4 HIFI 5 PHONO
6 DEEJAY STEREO
problem: 4 SKIP
store purchases: 3 CDS
store section: 3 RAP
World: 5 ATLAS
___ record: 4 SETA
Recorded: 5 TAPED 6 **ONTAPE**
Not: 4 LIVE
proceedings: 4 ACTA
Recorder
Modern: 4 TIVO
Recording
Early: 4 MONO
medium: 3 DAT 4 TAPE
studio effect: 4 ECHO
Trial: 4 DEMO
Records
Computer: 7 DATASET
Court: 4 ACTA
Diamond of: 4 NEIL
Vinyl: 3 LPS
Recount: 4 TELL
Recourse
Lender: 4 LIEN
Recover: 4 HEAL 5 RALLY
from: 7 GETOVER
Recovered
car: 4 REPO
Recovery
clinic: 5 **REHAB**
Recreation: 4 PLAY 5 SPORT
Recreational
four-wheeler: 3 ATV
vehicle: 10 MOBILEHOME

Recruit
Like a new: 3 RAW
response: 5 NOSIR 6 YESSIR
Recruiter
Corporate: 10 HEADHUNTER
Lafayette ~ Silas: 5 DEANE
Univ.: 4 ROTC
Recruitment
Campus: 4 RUSH
Rectangle: 6 OBLONG
(abbr.): 3 OBL
Rectangular
pier: 4 ANTA
Rector
income: 5 TITHE
Recumbent: 5 LYING
Recuperate: 4 HEAL MEND
Place to: 3 SPA
Recur: 5 ACTUP
Recurring
melody: 5 THEMA
period: 5 CYCLE
theme: 5 **MOTIF**
Recyclable: 4 USED
item: 3 CAN 5 EMPTY
7 SODACAN 8 ALUMINUM
11 ALUMINUMCAN
Recycling
receptacle: 3 BIN
Red: 3 SEA 4 NLER 5 ROUGE
algae: 7 SEAMOSS
bearded god: 4 THOR
Be in the: 3 **OWE**
Big: 3 MAO 5 LENIN 6 STALIN
buoy: 3 NUN
cap: 3 FEZ
carpet recipient: 7 HONOREE
Cause to see: 6 ENRAGE
Cheese in: 4 EDAM
coat: 4 RUST
coin: 4 CENT
Comedian: 7 SKELTON
Cool ~ giant: 5 SSTAR
Dark: 4 LAKE PUCE RUBY
WINE 6 CERISE MAROON
dye: 5 EOSIN HENNA
Firefighter: 5 **ADAIR**
fish: 7 SNAPPER
flag: 5 ALERT

Former ~ Rose: 4 PETE
giant: 7 ANTARES
head: 3 MAO 5 LENIN 6 STALIN
herring: 4 PLOY
In the: 4 ASEA 5 OWING
in the middle: 4 RARE
It might be: 4 CENT 5 ALERT
letters: 4 USSR
One in the: 4 OWER
pigment: 4 LAKE
planet: 4 MARS
prefix: 5 INFRA
Purplish: 4 PUCE WINE
5 GRAPE 6 CERISE
7 CARMINE MAGENTA
See: 3 **OWE** 4 FUME RAGE
STOP 5 STEAM 6 GETMAD
SEETHE
Seeing: 3 MAD 4 IRED SORE
5 IRATE RILED
Shade of: 4 BEET 6 CERISE
sky: 4 OMEN
state: 4 DEBT 5 ALERT ANGER
tag event: 4 SALE
team: 3 SOX
Turn: 3 DYE 5 BLUSH FLUSH
RIPEN SHAME
vegetable: 4 BEET
Vivid: 7 PIMENTO
wine: 4 PORT 5 MEDOC PINOT
6 CLARET MERLOT
9 PINOTNOIR
~ Muppet: 4 ELMO
Red ___ : 3 ANT SEA TAI 4 CENT
HOTS 5 ALERT APPLE
BARON 7 SNAPPER
___ red: 4 BEET
___ Red
(apple variety): 3 IDA
"Red, The"
Explorer called: 4 ERIC
Red Army
founder: 7 TROTSKY
leader: 3 MAO
member: 3 ANT
Red as ___: 5 **ABEET**
"Red Badge of Courage, The"
author: 5 CRANE
Red Baron: 3 ACE 7 AVIATOR

foe: **6** SNOOPY
Red-blooded: 5 LUSTY **6** ROBUST
Redbone
Folk singer: **4** LEON
Redbreast: 5 ROBIN
Redcap
burden: **4** BAGS
workplace: **5** DEPOT
Red carpet
recipient: **7** HONOREE
Roll out the: **5** GREET
Red Cloud: 5 SIOUX
Red Cross
course: **3** CPR
Former ~ head: **4** DOLE
founder: **6** BARTON
founder Barton: **5** CLARA
supply: **4** SERA **5** BLOOD
6 PLASMA
Redding
Peak north of: **8** MTSHASTA
Singer: **4** **OTIS**
Reddish: 4 RARE
purple: **5** LILAC
yellow: **5** OCHER
Reddish brown: 4 RUST **5** HENNA
6 RUSSET SIENNA
SORREL TITIAN WALNUT
8 MAHOGANY
gem: **4** SARD
horse: **3** BAY **4** ROAN **6** SORREL
Red-dog: 5 BLITZ
Reddy
Singer: **5** HELEN
Reddy, Helen
hit: **9** DELTADAWN
Redecorate: 6 DOOVER
Redeem: 4 CASH SAVE
6 CASHIN
Red-eye
gravy base: **3** HAM
Red-faced: 7 ABASHED
ASHAMED
Redford: 5 BLOND
1969 ~ role: **11** SUNDANCEKID
1975 ~ role: **11** WALDOPEPPER
1984 ~ film: **10** THENATURAL
1984 ~ role: **5** HOBBS
1992 ~ film: **8** SNEAKERS

1994 ~ film: **8** QUIZSHOW
Redgrave
1968 ~ film: **7** ISADORA
Actress: **4** LYNN **7** VANESSA
title role: **5** JULIA **6** AGATHA
Red Guard
leader: **3** MAO
member: **6** MAOIST
Red-handed
Catch: **3** NAB **4** NAIL
Redhead
dye: **5** HENNA
Mayberry: **4** OPIE
Raggedy: **3** ANN
Riverdale: **6** ARCHIE
~, slangily: **9** CARROTTOP
Red-hot: 6 WIENER
one: **4** MAMA
"Red House Mystery, The"
author: **5** MILNE **7** AAMILNE
Red-hunting
gp.: **4** HUAC
Red ink: 4 DEBT
amount: **4** LOSS
Redness
Symbol of: **4** BEET
Redo: 4 EDIT
Redolence: 4 ODOR **5** AROMA
7 PERFUME
Redress
Seek: **3** SUE
Red Riding Hood
accessory: **6** BASKET
burden: **6** BASKET
Red River
capital: **5** HANOI
"Red River": 5 OATER
actress Joanne: **3** DRU
Reds: 4 TEAM **5** NLERS
7 SOVIETS
Red Sea
gulf: **5** AQABA
nation: **5** SUDAN YEMEN
7 ERITREA
peninsula: **5** SINAI
port: **4** ADEN SUEZ
vessel: **4** DHOW
"Red Shoes, The"
actress Shearer: **5** MOIRA

Red Skelton
  catchphrase: **7** IDOODIT
  character: **4** CLEM
Red Sox
  Garciaparra of the: **5** NOMAR
Red-spotted
  creature: **3** EFT **4** NEWT
Red Square
  figure: **5** LENIN
Reduce: 4 DIET EASE PARE
       5 ABATE LOWER PRUNE
       6 LESSEN
  to mush: **5** PUREE
Reduced: 6 ONSALE
  by: **4** LESS
  fare: **4** DIET
Reduction: 3 CUT **4** DROP
       8 CUTPRICE
Redwood City
  county: **8** SANMATEO
Reebok: 7 SNEAKER
  rival: **4** AVIA FILA NIKE PUMA
       6 ADIDAS
Reed
  Film critic: **3** REX
  home: **5** MARSH
  instrument: **3** SAX **4** OBOE
  Musical: **3** LOU
  of TV: **5** DONNA
  player: **6** OBOIST
  Weaver: **4** SLEY
Reedlike: 7 SLENDER
Reef
  dweller: **3** EEL **5** MORAY
  material: **5** CORAL
  Ring-shaped: **5** ATOLL
Reek: 5 FETOR STINK
Reel: 5 DANCE **7** STAGGER
       8 SEESTARS
  Fishing ~ winder: **5** SPOOL
  in: **4** LAND
  off: **6** RECITE
  Partner of: **3** ROD
  person: **5** ACTOR
Reese
  Actress: **5** DELLA
  of the Dodgers: **6** PEEWEE
  Singer: **5** DELLA
Reese, ___ Wee: 3 PEE

Reeve
  role: **4** KENT **8** SUPERMAN
Reeves
  Actor: **5** KEANU
  Bodybuilder: **5** STEVE
  Country singer: **3** DEL
  film: **5** SPEED **9** THEMATRIX
  role: **3** NEO
Ref
  call: **3** TKO **4** TIME
  counterpart: **3** UMP
Ref.
  book: **4** DICT
  Large ~ work: **3** ENC OED
       5 ENCYC
Refer: 6 ALLUDE
  to: **4** CITE
Referee: 7 MEDIATE
  ~, slangily: **5** ZEBRA
Reference: 8 ALLUSION
  20-vol. ~ work: **3** OED
  Annual ~ book: **7** ALMANAC
  Astronomy: **7** STARMAP
  Chef's: **8** COOKBOOK
  Credit as a: **4** CITE
  Geographical: **5** ATLAS
  Make: **6** ALLUDE
  Many ~ works: **5** TOMES
  Microsoft: **7** ENCARTA
  Paper: **8** FOOTNOTE
  Pianist ~ material:
       10 SHEETMUSIC
  words: **4** INRE
  Writing: **5** ROGET
Referendum
  choice: **3** YES
Refill
  Needing a: **3** LOW
Refinable
  rock: **3** ORE
Refine: 4 HONE **5** SMELT
Refined: 6 POLITE **7** ELEGANT
  iron: **5** STEEL
  Not: **3** RAW **4** BASE **5** CRUDE
       6 COARSE
Refinement: 5 TASTE **6** NICETY
       8 ELEGANCE
  Place of: **7** SMELTER
  They lack: **4** ORES

Refinery
   refuse: 4 SLAG
Reflect: 4 MUSE
   Something to ~ on: 6 MIRROR
Reflection: 5 IMAGE
   ___ reflection: 4 UPON
"Reflections on Ice-Breaking"
   poet Ogden: 4 NASH
Reflex
   Conditioned ~ researcher:
      6 PAVLOV
   Gag: 4 HAHA
   test site: 4 KNEE
Reflux: 3 EBB
Reform
   targets: 4 ILLS
Reformer
   ~ Bloomer: 6 AMELIA
   ~ Dorothea: 3 DIX
   ~ Jacob: 4 **RIIS**
   ~ Julia Ward ___: 4 HOWE
   ~ Wells: 3 IDA
Reformist
   Aggressive: 9 YOUNGTURK
Reform Party
   founder: 5 PEROT
   member: 5 TRUMP
Refractor
   Light: 5 PRISM
Refrain
   Common: 5 TRALA 7 TRALALA
   from taking action: 6 SITPAT
   King of Siam: 8 ETCETERA
   "Old MacDonald": 5 EIEIO
   Part of a Beatles: 4 YEAH
   Part of a pirate: 6 YOHOHO
   syllable: 3 SHA **TRA** 4 LALA
   Tyrolean: 5 YODEL
Refresh: 6 AERATE
Refresher
   Daytime: 3 NAP
   Summer: 3 ADE
Refreshing
   place: 3 SPA 5 OASIS
Refreshment
   Boardwalk: 3 ICE
   site: 5 OASIS
   Summer: 3 ADE
Refrigerant: 5 FREON

   Cryogenic: 4 NEON
Refrigerate: 4 COOL 5 CHILL
Refrigerator
   decoration: 6 MAGNET
   name: 5 AMANA
   part: 7 CRISPER
   precursor: 6 ICEBOX
Refuel: 5 GASUP
Refueling
   area: 3 PIT
   opportunity: 7 PITSTOP
Refuge
   Place of: 3 ARK 4 LAIR NEST
      5 HAVEN
   Take: 6 HOLEUP
Refugee
   Dust Bowl: 4 OKIE
   Political: 6 EMIGRE
Refuges: 5 ASYLA
Refund
   check issuer (abbr.): 3 IRS
   Due a: 12 OVERWITHHELD
   How a ~ may be made:
      7 PRORATA
Refusal
   Emphatic: 5 NEVER NOHOW
      6 NOMAAM 7 NOSIREE
   French: 3 **NON**
   German: 4 **NEIN**
   Polite: 5 NOSIR 6 NOMAAM
   Russian: 4 **NYET**
   Scottish: 3 NAE
   Slangy: 3 **NAH** 4 NOPE
   Terse: 5 IWONT
Refusals: 3 **NOS** 4 NOES
Refuse: 3 ASH 4 DENY LEES
      SCUM 5 CHAFF DROSS
      OFFAL SAYNO TRASH
      WASTE 6 LITTER
      7 GARBAGE
   aid: 8 TRASHCAN
   Kitchen: 4 SLOP
   Metal: 4 SLAG
   to talk: 6 CLAMUP
   to yield: 6 INSIST
   transport: 4 SCOW
   visitor: 3 RAT
Refuses
   to: 4 WONT

Refute: 4 DENY 5 BELIE
    8 DISPROVE
Reg.: 3 STD
  City: 3 ORD
Regal: 7 STATELY
  address: 4 SIRE
  fur: 6 ERMINE
  headwear: 5 TIARA
  letters: 3 HRH
  material: 4 SILK
  residence: 6 PALACE
  symbol: 3 ORB
Regale: 4 FETE
Regalia
  item: 3 ORB
Regan
  Father of: 4 **LEAR**
Regard: 3 EYE SEE 4 CARE DEEM
    VIEW 6 ESTEEM
  highly: 6 ADMIRE **ESTEEM**
  In ~ to: 5 ANENT ASFOR
  with awe: 8 VENERATE
Regarding: 4 **ASTO** INRE
    5 ABOUT ANENT
  this point: 6 HERETO
Regardless: 6 ANYWAY
    7 ANYWAYS
Regatta: 4 RACE 8 BOATRACE
  implement: 3 OAR
  racer: 5 SCULL SLOOP YACHT
  site: 6 HENLEY
  team: 4 CREW
Reggae
  fan: 5 RASTA
  Gregory of: 6 ISAACS
  Kamoze of: 3 INI
  Peter of: 4 TOSH
  relative: 3 **SKA**
  ___ régime: 6 ANCIEN
Regimen: 4 DIET 7 PROGRAM
  Pool: 4 LAPS
  Post-op: 5 REHAB
  vitamin: 7 ONEADAY
Reginald
  Actor: 4 OWEN
"Reginald"
  author: 4 SAKI
Region: 4 **AREA** ZONE
  (abbr.): 4 TERR

Upper ~ of space: 3 SKY
    5 ETHER
Regional: 7 ENDEMIC
  dialect: 5 IDIOM 6 PATOIS
  foliage: 5 FLORA
  life: 5 BIOTA
  wildlife: 5 FAUNA
Regis
  cohost Kelly: 4 RIPA
Register: 5 **ENROL** ENTER
    LOGIN 6 ENLIST ENROLL
    SIGNIN SIGNUP SINKIN
  key: 6 NOSALE
  output: 7 RECEIPT
  signer: 5 GUEST
  transaction: 4 SALE
Registered
  It may be: 9 TRADENAME
Registration
  datum: 5 OWNER
  Mil. ~ group: 3 SSS
Regret: 3 **RUE** 6 LAMENT
    7 REMORSE
  Express: 4 MOAN SIGH
  Word of: 4 **ALAS**
Regretful
  feeling: 4 PANG
  one: 4 RUER
  ~ Miss of song: 4 OTIS
Regrets
  Send ~, maybe: 4 RSVP
Regrettable: 3 SAD
Regular: 5 USUAL 6 PATRON
    7 HABITUE
  (abbr.): 3 STD
  guy: 3 JOE 4 BEAU
  hangout: 5 HAUNT
    7 PURLIEU
  order: 5 USUAL
Regulation: 3 LAW 4 RULE
    7 STATUTE
  Judge's: 10 COURTORDER
Regulator
  Current: 8 RHEOSTAT
  Former RR: 3 ICC
  JFK: 3 FAA
  Light: 4 IRIS
  NYSE: 3 SEC
  TV: 3 FCC

Workplace: 4 OSHA
Regulatory
Fed. ~ gp.: 3 AEC FDA
Rehab
candidate: 4 USER
process: 5 DETOX
Rehan
Actress: 3 ADA
Rehearsal
Kind of: 5 DRESS
request: 4 LINE
Rehearse
in the ring: 4 SPAR
Rehem: 5 ALTER
Reid
Actor: 3 TIM
Actress: 4 TARA
Reign: 4 RULE
Rein
in: 4 CURB
Reindeer
herder: 4 LAPP
kin: 3 ELK 7 CARIBOU
name: 5 COMET CUPID VIXEN
6 DANCER DASHER
DONNER 7 BLITZEN
PRANCER
Santa's: 5 OCTAD OCTET
Reiner
Director: 3 ROB 4 CARL
Reinforcement
Blue jeans: 5 RIVET
Concrete: 5 REBAR
Tire: 3 PLY
Reinking
Dancer: 3 **ANN**
Reins
Take the: 4 LEAD 5 STEER
Reiterate: 4 ECHO
Reitman
Director: 4 IVAN
Reject: 3 NIX 4 DENY JILT VETO
5 SPURN
Rejection: 6 REBUFF
Russian: 4 NYET
Rejections: 3 NOS 4 NOES
Rejoice: 5 EXULT
Relate: 4 TELL 5 TIETO
6 BEARON

Related: 3 KIN 4 **AKIN** TOLD
7 SIMILAR
Maternally: 5 **ENATE**
(to): 4 AKIN TIED
Relation
In ~ to: 7 VISAVIS
Relations: 7 KINFOLK
Break in: 4 RIFT
Good: 5 AMITY
Relationship: 5 RATIO
Kind of: 6 CASUAL
8 ONETOONE
Relationships
Like some: 7 SAMESEX SPATIAL
8 PLATONIC
Relative: 3 SIB 5 FLESH
7 KINSMAN
by marriage: 5 INLAW
of mine: 4 OURS
Relax: 4 EASE LAZE LOLL REST
5 CHILL LETUP 6 COOLIT
EASEUP GOEASY LOOSEN
UNWIND 7 TAKETEN
8 CHILLOUT TAKEFIVE
Place to: 3 DEN SPA 6 RESORT
~, as rules: 4 BEND
~, with "out": 3 VEG
"Relax!": 6 ATEASE
8 LOOSENUP
Relaxation: 4 **EASE**
Relaxed: 4 CALM 5 EASED LOOSE
6 **ATEASE**
Relaxing: 6 ATEASE
place: 3 **SPA**
"Relax, soldier!": 6 **ATEASE**
Relay: 6 PASSON SENDON
part: 3 LEG
stick: 5 BATON
Release: 4 EMIT FREE 5 LETGO
UNTIE 6 SPRING
7 SETFREE 8 LETLOOSE
Conditional: 6 PAROLE
Early: 6 PAROLE
money: 4 BAIL
Press: 4 WINE
Released: 8 ONPAROLE
Be: 6 GOFREE
Relent: 6 EASEUP GIVEIN
Relevance: 7 APTNESS

Relevant: 3 APT 5 ADREM
    7 GERMANE
  Be: 5 TIEIN 7 PERTAIN
  Be ~ to: 6 BEARON
Reliable: 4 SAFE TRUE 5 LOYAL
    SOLID 6 TRUSTY
Reliant
  Plymouth: 4 KCAR
Relief: 3 AID SUB 4 DOLE
    6 SOLACE 7 RESPITE
  Carve in: 6 EMBOSS
  carving: 5 CAMEO
  Cries of: 3 AHS
  Cry of: 3 **AAH** 4 PHEW SIGH
    TGIF WHEW 6 ATLAST
  Disaster ~ org.: 4 FEMA
  It is a: 7 ASPIRIN
  Kind of: 3 BAS 5 COMIC
  Source of: 4 BALM
  spot: 5 OASIS
  ___ relief: 3 BAS
Relief pitcher: 5 SAVER
    7 FIREMAN
  goal: 4 SAVE
Relieve: 3 RID 4 EASE 5 ALLAY
    SALVE SLAKE
Reliever: 5 EASER
  Pain: 6 ICEBAG OPIATE
    7 ANODYNE
  Pain ~ brand: 5 ALEVE BAYER
  stat: 3 ERA 5 SAVES
Religion: 5 FAITH
  Japanese: 6 SHINTO
  Mideast: 5 ISLAM
  Persian: 5 BAHAI
Religious: 5 PIOUS
  artifact: 4 ICON
  belief: 6 THEISM
  Bygone ~ group: 7 SHAKERS
  ceremony: 4 RITE
  council: 5 SYNOD
  dissenter: 7 HERETIC
  Extremist ~ group: 4 CULT
  group: 4 SECT
  Iowa ~ sect: 5 AMANA
  offshoot: 4 SECT
  principle: 5 TENET
  recitation: 6 ROSARY
  recluse: 4 MONK 7 EREMITE

  retreat: 5 ABBEY 6 ASHRAM
  sch.: 3 SEM
  scroll: 5 TORAH
  sculpture: 5 PIETA
  symbol: 4 ICON
  war: 7 CRUSADE
Relinquish: 4 **CEDE** QUIT
    5 DEMIT WAIVE
Relish: 4 TANG ZEST 5 EATUP
    ENJOY GUSTO **SAVOR**
Relocate: 4 MOVE
Reluctant: 3 COY 5 **LOATH**
    6 AVERSE
Rely: 6 DEPEND
  on: 5 TRUST 6 LOOKTO
    7 SWEARBY TRUSTIN
REM
  Part of: 3 EYE 5 RAPID
  venue: 3 MTV
  ~ singer Michael: 5 **STIPE**
Remain: 3 ARE 4 **BIDE** STAY
    6 STAYON
  at home: 5 STAYIN
  How some shall: 8 NAMELESS
  undecided: 4 **PEND**
Remainder: 4 REST
  ~, in French: 5 RESTE
Remained: 3 SAT 6 ABIDED
Remaining: 4 LEFT 5 OTHER
Remains: 4 LEES 5 ASHES DREGS
    6 DEBRIS
  Smoldering: 6 EMBERS
  to be seen: 5 RUINS
Remark
  Barbed: 4 GIBE
  Cutting: 4 **BARB**
  Defiant: 7 SOTHERE
  Parenthetical: 5 ASIDE
  Sheepish: 3 BAA
  Sotto voce: 5 ASIDE
  Witty: 3 MOT 4 JEST QUIP
Remarkable: 6 OFNOTE
    7 AMAZING UNCANNY
    10 NOTEWORTHY
  person: 5 LULU
  thing: 5 DILLY 8 CATSMEOW
Remarks
  Like some: 5 SNIDE 6 SEXIST
    7 POINTED

Opening: 5 INTRO
Remarque
  Author: 5 ERICH
Re/Max
  rival: 3 ERA
Rembrandt
  Artist: 5 PEALE
  Artist ~ van ___ : 3 RYN
  Emulate: 4 ETCH
  medium: 4 OILS
Remedy: 4 CURE HEAL
    7 REDRESS 8 ANTIDOTE
  Burn: 4 ALOE
  Sunburn ~, originally:
    7 NOXZEMA
Remember
  Mission to: 5 ALAMO
  Ship to: 5 MAINE
  Time to: 3 **ERA** 5 EPOCH
  You must ~ this: 5 ALAMO
  "___ Remember": 5 TRYTO
  "Remember the ___!": 5 ALAMO
    MAINE
Remembrance Day
  mo.: 3 NOV
Remind: 5 NUDGE
  too much: 3 NAG
Reminder: 4 NOTE
  Office: 4 MEMO
  product: 6 POSTIT
  Stage: 3 CUE
  Surgery: 4 SCAR
  to Santa: 4 LIST
Remington
  rival: 7 NORELCO
  TV detective: 6 STEELE
  "Remington ___": 6 STEELE
Remini
  Actress: 4 LEAH
Remit: 3 PAY 4 SEND
Remnant: 3 END 4 DREG 5 SCRAP
    SHRED TRACE 6 TAGEND
    7 RESIDUE VESTIGE
  Fire: 3 ASH 5 EMBER
  ___ Remo, Italy: 3 SAN
Remora
  ride: 5 SHARK
Remorse: 7 SADNESS
  Feel ~ for: 3 **RUE** 6 REPENT

Remorseful
  one: 4 RUER
Remote: 3 FAR 7 FARAWAY
    8 ISOLATED
  ancestor: 4 DIAL
  button: 3 REC 4 MENU **MUTE**
    6 VOLUME
  location: 4 SOFA
  room: 3 DEN
  target: 4 VCR 5 TVSET
  targets: 3 TVS
Removable
  car roof: 4 TTOP
Remove: 3 AXE 4 DELE DOFF
    SHED 5 ERASE EVICT
  a splinter: 6 TWEEZE
  branches: 5 PRUNE
  from office: 4 OUST 6 UNSEAT
  rind: 4 PARE
  the fat from: 4 TRIM
Removed
  Commonly ~ tissue: 6 TONSIL
    8 ADENOIDS
Remover
  Hair: 5 RAZOR
  Hair ~ brand: 4 NEET
  Mistake: 6 ERASER
  Polish: 7 ACETONE
  Stubble: 5 RAZOR
  Wrinkle: 4 **IRON**
Remsen
  Chemist: 3 IRA
Remus: 4 TWIN 5 UNCLE
Remus, Uncle: 4 TALE
  address: 4 BRER
Ren: 4 TOON
Renaissance
  family: 4 **ESTE**
  fiddle: 5 REBEC
  instrument: 4 LUTE
  patron: 4 ESTE
Renaissance ___: 5 FAIRE
Renata
  Soprano: 6 SCOTTO
Renault
  Old: 5 LECAR
Rend: 4 TEAR
Render
  harmless: 5 UNARM 6 DEFUSE

DISARM
speechless: **3** AWE GAG **4** STUN
unnecessary: **7** OBVIATE
"Render therefore ___ Caesar ...":
    4 UNTO
Rendezvous: 4 MEET **5 TRYST**
    6 MEETUP
Rene
    Actress: **5** RUSSO
René
    1950s French president ~:
        4 COTY
    of tennis: **7** LACOSTE
Renée
    Actress: **6 ADOREE**
Renege: 6 COPOUT
Renewable
    energy type: **5** SOLAR
Renewal
    Kind of: **5** URBAN
    target: **4** SLUM
Renfrew
    org., in old radio: **4** RCMP
Reno
    formerly in Washington: **5** JANET
    predecessor: **4** BARR
    resident: **7** NEVADAN
    roller: **3** DIE
    state: **6** NEVADA
Renoir
    subject: **4** NUDE
Renounce: 6 DISOWN
Renown: 4 FAME **5** ECLAT GLORY
Rent: 3 LET RIP **4** HIRE TEAR
        TORE TORN **5** LEASE
    again: **5** RELET
    alternative: **3** OWN
    For: **5** TOLET
    payer: **6** LESSEE TENANT
"Rent"
    Basis for: **8** LABOHEME
Rent-___: 4 ACAR ACOP
"Rent-___" (1988 film): 4 ACOP
Renta, Oscar ___ : 4 DELA
Rental
    ad abbr.: **3** RMS
    agent: **6** LEASER
    agreement: **5 LEASE**
    Common: **4** TAPE **5** VIDEO

Lake: **5** CANOE
Links: **4** CART
Moving: **5** UHAUL
Prom: **3** TUX **4** LIMO
Renter: 6 LESSEE TENANT
    paper: **5** LEASE
    Room: **3** INN
Reo: 3 CAR
    maker: **4** OLDS
    Part of: **3** ELI **4** OLDS
        6 RANSOM
    rival: **5** ESSEX
Rep: 5 AGENT
    presentation: **4** DEMO
Rep.: 3 AGT
    City council: **3** ALD
    counterpart: **3** SEN
    Legal: **3** ATT **4** ATTY
    Not ~ or Dem.: **3** IND
    rival: **3** DEM
Repair: 3 FIX **4** MEND
    cost: **5** LABOR PARTS
    shop substitute: **6** LOANER
    Wreck beyond: **5** TOTAL
Repairman: 5 FIXER
    Brand with a lonely: **6** MAYTAG
Reparation: 6 AMENDS
    Make: **5** ATONE
Repartee: 3 WIT
    Bit of: **3** MOT
    Part of a: **3** TAT
Repast: 4 MEAL
Repay: 6 AVENGE
Repeat: 4 ECHO 6 PARROT
        7 ITERATE
    performance: **6** ENCORE
    verbatim: **4** ECHO **5** QUOTE
Repeatedly: 3 OFT **5** OFTEN
    Say: **7** ITERATE
Repeating: 7 ITERANT
        9 ITERATIVE
Repellent
    Evil: **6** AMULET
    Insect: **4** DEET
    Moth: **5** CEDAR
    Mugger: **4** MACE
    Vampire: **5** CROSS **6** GARLIC
Repent: 5 ATONE
    of: **3** RUE

Repentant
one: 4 RUER
Repetition
Musical ~ mark: 5 SEGNO
Unthinking: 4 ROTE
Repetitious: 7 ITERANT
Repetitive
card game: 3 WAR
process: 4 ROTE
Rephrase: 4 EDIT 5 AMEND
Replace: 9 SUPERSEDE
Replay
feature: 5 **SLOMO**
Replayed
shot: 3 LET
Replete
Render: 4 SATE
Replica: 4 COPY 5 MODEL
Replicate: 5 CLONE
Reply: 4 RSVP
(abbr.): 3 ANS
Defiant: 5 NEVER
Off-the-wall: 4 ECHO
Private: 5 NOSIR
Respectful: 4 YESM
Roll call: 4 HERE
Sheepish: 3 BAA
to "Am not!": 4 AMSO 5 ARESO
to "Am too!": 6 ARENOT
to "That so?": 4 ITIS
to the captain: 3 AYE 6 AYEAYE
to "You are not!": 5 IAMSO
Repo
man: 6 SEIZER
Report: 4 BANG 7 WRITEUP
1977 ~ author: 4 HITE
1998 ~ author: 5 STARR
by phone: 6 CALLIN
card stat: 3 GPA
of an insured: 4 LOSS
of a report:
15 HEARSAYEVIDENCE
of a shooting: 4 BANG
Police ~ letters: 3 AKA
Rather: 4 NEWS
Short: 3 POP
Reporter
angle: 5 SLANT
bailiwick: 4 BEAT

CNN: 11 WOLFBLITZER
Comics: 5 STARR
contact: 6 SOURCE
coup: 5 SCOOP
Court: 5 STENO
Daily Planet: 4 KENT LANE
LOIS 5 OLSEN 8 LOISLANE
need: 7 NOTEPAD
place: 4 DESK
query: 3 HOW WHO WHY
4 WHAT WHEN 5 WHERE
source: 4 LEAK
~ Donaldson: 3 SAM
~ Roberts: 5 COKIE
Reporters: 5 PRESS
Like some: 6 ROVING
Reporting
Credit ~ co.: 3 TRW
to: 5 BELOW UNDER
Repose: 4 EASE REST 5 SLEEP
Reposed: 4 LAIN
Repository
Corneal: 7 EYEBANK
Tool: 4 SHED
Wine: 6 CELLAR
Reprehensible: 4 BASE VILE
Morally: 6 SORDID
Represent: 5 ACTAS 6 DENOTE
8 SPEAKFOR
What candles sometimes: 3 AGE
Representation: 5 IMAGE
Representative: 5 **AGENT** ENVOY
TOKEN 6 ICONIC
Repress: 5 QUASH 6 HOLDIN
KEEPIN
Reprieve: 4 STAY
15 STAYOFEXECUTION
Reprimand: 5 CHIDE SCOLD
6 BERATE REBUKE
7 CENSURE
15 CALLONTHECARPET
for Rover: 3 BAD
~, with "out": 4 CHEW REAM
Reprints
Magazine of: 4 UTNE
10 UTNEREADER
Reproach
Famed: 4 ETTU
Sound of: 3 TSK TUT 6 TSKTSK

Word of: **5** SHAME
Reproduce: 4 COPY **5** BREED
    SPAWN
Reproduction
  Exact: **5** CLONE
  needs: **3** OVA
Reproductive
  body: **5** SPORE
  cell: **5** OVULE **6** GAMETE
  cells: **3** **OVA**
  gland: **5** OVARY
Reproof
  Sound of: **3** TUT
Reps
  Company whose ~ have a calling:
    4 AVON
  Several ~, in the gym: **3** SET
Reptile: 5 SNAKE **6** LIZARD
  Company with a ~ logo: **4** IZOD
  Long ~, in short: **4** CROC
  Nile: **3** **ASP**
  prefix: **4** SAUR
Republic
  Asian: **4** IRAN LAOS
  Baltic: **7** ESTONIA
  Black Sea: **7** GEORGIA
    ROMANIA
  Caribbean: **5** HAITI
  Irish: **4** EIRE
  Islamic: **4** IRAN
  Landlocked African: **4** MALI
  South Pacific: **4** FIJI
  West African: **4** MALI TOGO
    5 BENIN GABON
    7 NIGERIA
"Republic, The"
  author: **5** PLATO
Republican: 3 GOP
  elephant creator: **4** NAST
Repudiate: 4 DENY **6** DISOWN
Repugnant: 6 ODIOUS
  Find: **5** ABHOR
Repulsive: 4 ICKY VILE
  Find: **5** ABHOR
Reputation: 4 NAME ODOR
  tarnisher: **4** BLOT
  threat: **5** SMEAR
  Worse than a bad: **6** INFAMY
Repute: 4 FAME ODOR

Req.
  Not: **3** OPT
Request: 3 ASK **4** PLEA SEEK
    6 ASKFOR
  before a shot: **5** SMILE
  sweetener: **6** PLEASE
Requested
  Do as: **6** OBLIGE
Requiem
  word: **4** IRAE
**"Requiem for ___" (Faulkner
    book): 4** ANUN
Require: 4 **NEED** **6** COMPEL
    ENTAIL OBLIGE
Requirement: 4 MUST **NEED**
Requiring
  help: **6** INNEED
Requisite: 4 NEED **6** NEEDED
Requisition: 6 ASKFOR
Requital: 7 PAYMENT
Requite: 6 AVENGE
Rescue: 3 AID **4** HELP SAVE
    7 BAILOUT
  squad VIP: **3** EMT
Rescuer: 4 HERO **6** SAVIOR
Research: 5 DELVE
  facil.: **4** INST
  institute: **9** THINKTANK
  Medical ~ agcy.: **3** NIH
  money: **5** GRANT
  paper: **6** THESIS
  site: **3** LAB
___ Research Center: 4 AMES
Researcher
  quest: **5** GRANT
Resell
  illegally: **5** SCALP
Resemble: 6 BELIKE
  Closely: **5** MIMIC
  ~, with "after": **4** TAKE
Resembling: 3 ALA **4** LIKE
    5 QUASI
Resentful: 4 SORE **6** BITTER
Resentment: 3 IRE **5** PIQUE
    7 UMBRAGE
  Cause: **6** RANKLE
Reservation: 3 BUT **5** QUALM
  Course: **7** TEETIME
  Make a: **4** BOOK

Plane: 4 SEAT
Reserve: 4 HOLD SAVE 5 CACHE
    STORE 7 ICINESS
    8 BOTTLEUP SETASIDE
    9 RETICENCE
In: 5 APART **ASIDE** ONICE
Reserved: 3 SHY 4 KEPT 5 ALOOF
    ONICE STAID TAKEN
    6 DEMURE SEDATE
    8 SETASIDE
Reserves: 7 MILITIA
Reservoir
  filler: 4 RAIN
Reset
  setting: 3 OOO 4 OOOO
Reside: 5 DWELL
Resided: 5 **DWELT** LIVED
Residence
  (abbr.): 3 HSE
  Bird: 4 NEST
  Cockney: 3 OME
  First family: 4 EDEN
  French president: 6 ELYSEE
  Northern: 5 IGLOO
  Regal: 6 PALACE
  Take up: 6 MOVEIN
Resident: 6 INTERN
  suffix: 3 ESE ITE
Residents
  (abbr.): 3 DRS MDS
Residue: 3 **ASH**
  Chimney: 4 SOOT
  Dryer: 4 LINT
  Pipe: 6 DOTTLE
  Smelting: 4 **SLAG**
Resign: 4 QUIT 5 DEMIT
Resignation
  Phrase of: 5 IQUIT
Resignee
  1973 ~: 5 **AGNEW**
  1974 ~: 3 RMN 5 NIXON
Resilient: 7 ELASTIC
  wood: 3 ASH
Resin: 3 **LAC**
  Adhesive: 5 EPOXY
  Fossil: 5 AMBER
  Fragrant: 5 **ELEMI**
  Varnish: 5 COPAL ELEMI
    6 MASTIC

Resist: 4 DEFY 6 OPPOSE
  change: 8 STANDPAT
  Not: 4 OBEY
Resistance
  Air: 4 DRAG
  figure: 6 OHMAGE
  Symbol of: 5 OMEGA
  to change: 7 INERTIA
  unit: 3 **OHM**
Resistant: 6 AVERSE
Resister: 5 REBEL
  Roman invasion: 5 DRUID
Res ___ loquitur: 4 IPSA
Resnais
  Director: 5 ALAIN
Resolution
  Accept a: 5 ADOPT
  Fill with: 5 STEEL
  Printer (abbr.): 3 DPI
  Typical New Year: 4 DIET
Resolve: 3 VOW 6 SETTLE
    7 IRONOUT
  Tough to: 5 MESSY
Resolved: 7 DEADSET
  Not yet: 4 OPEN
Resonance
  Magnetic ~ device: 6 IMAGER
Resonant
  Not: 5 TINNY
Resort
  Belgian: 3 SPA
  Brazilian: 3 RIO
  California: 5 TAHOE
    11 PALMSPRINGS
  Caribbean: 5 ARUBA
  Colorado: 4 VAIL 5 ASPEN
  German: 3 EMS
  Health: 3 **SPA**
  Italian: 4 **LIDO**
  Italian ~ lake: 4 COMO
  Maine: 9 BARHARBOR
  Mediterranean: 7 RIVIERA
  near Venezuela: 5 ARUBA
  Nevada: 5 TAHOE
  New Mexico: 4 TAOS
  Pennsylvanian: 7 POCONOS
  Riviera: 4 NICE 7 SANREMO
  Sicilian: 4 ENNA
  Sierra Madres: 4 OJAI

site: **5** SHORE
Utah: **4 ALTA**
Vermont: **5** STOWE
Resound: 4 ECHO PEAL
Resource: 5 ASSET
Natural: **3** ORE
Resourcefulness: 4 WITS
Resp.: 3 ANS
Respect: 6 ADMIRE ESTEEM
In any: **5** ATALL
Indian title of: **3** SRI **5** SAHIB
Japanese title of: **3** SAN
Show: **3** BOW **4** RISE **5** KNEEL
Term of: **4** MAAM **5** MADAM
Treat with: **5** HONOR
With ~ to: **4** INRE **5** ASFOR
Respected
one: **5** DOYEN ELDER
"Respect for Acting"
author: **8** UTAHAGEN
author Hagen: **3** UTA
Respectful
gesture: **6** SALUTE
Respecting: 4 ASTO
Respiration: 6 BREATH
Respire: 7 BREATHE
Respond: 6 ANSWER
angrily: **15** BITEONESHEADOFF
suffix: **3** ENT
(to): **5** REACT
to a bore: **4** YAWN
to a sneeze: **5** BLESS
to reveille: **4** RISE **5** ARISE
Respondent
911 ~: **3 EMT**
Response
Glib: **9** PATANSWER
Military: **5** NOSIR **6** YESSIR
Polite: **7** YESMAAM
Positive: **3** YES
Prayer: **4** AMEN
to a compliment: **4** ITRY
to a ques.: **3** ANS
Responsibilities
Face: **4** COPE
~, figuratively: **4** HATS
Responsibility: 4 DUTY **ONUS**
5 BLAME
Avoid: **11** PASSTHEBUCK

Falls on, as a: **8** LIESWITH
Responsible: 8 INCHARGE
Be ~ for: **5** SEETO
Hold: **5** BLAME
Legally: **5** OFAGE **6** LIABLE
Rest: 3 LIE NAP SIT **4** EASE
6 REPOSE **7** LIEDOWN
against: **6** LEANON
And the ~ (abbr.): **3** ETC **4** ETAL
area: **3** BED SPA **5** OASIS
area sight: **4** SEMI
At: **4** IDLE
atop: **5** LIEON
Came to: **4** ALIT
Come to: **5** ENDUP
Day of: **7** SABBATH
Lay to: **5 INTER** 6 ENTOMB
of the afternoon: **6** SIESTA
Put to: **5** ALLAY
room sign: **3** MEN **5** GENTS
INUSE **6** LADIES
stop: **3** BED **5** OASIS
Restaurant
Avoid the: **5** EATIN
chain: **4** IHOP
employee: **4** CHEF
fish: **7** SEABASS
freebie: **4** MINT ROLL **5** WATER
8 ICEWATER
Go to a: **5** EATAT **6** EATOUT
Like some ~ orders: **4** TOGO
list: **4** MENU
of "Alice": **4** MELS
offering: **4** MEAL
owner of song: **5** ALICE
review symbol: **4** STAR
Surf, in a: **7** SEAFOOD
Toots in a: **4** SHOR
Word in French ~ names:
4 CHEZ
___ **Restaurant:** 6 ALICES
Restaurateur
New York: **4** SHOR **5** SARDI
Rested: 3 SAT **4** LAIN **5** LEANT
Resting: 4 ABED **6** ATEASE
on: **4 ATOP**
place: **3** BED DEN INN **4** BASE
LAIR MOOR SOFA TOMB
5 OASIS ROOST

Restless: 4 EDGY 5 ANTSY
    6 UNEASY
  desire: 4 ITCH
  Have a ~ night: 4 TOSS
  on a score: 7 AGITATO
Restlessness: 4 ITCH 6 UNEASE
    15 ANTSINONESPANTS
Restorative: 5 SALVE TONIC
Restore
  confidence to: 8 REASSURE
  to health: 4 CURE
Restrain: 4 BATE CURB REIN
    STEM 6 HOLDIN REININ
    TETHER
Restraint: 4 CURB REIN 5 LEASH
    7 LIMITER
  Dungeon: 5 IRONS
  Free from: 5 UNTIE
  Pet: 5 LEASH 6 TETHER
Restrict: 5 CRAMP HEMIN LIMIT
Restricted __: 4 AREA
Restriction: 5 LIMIT
Restroom: 3 LAV
Result: 3 END 5 ENDUP **ENSUE**
    6 UPSHOT
  As a: 4 ERGO THUS
  As a ~ of: 5 DUETO
  End: 6 UPSHOT
  Get as a: 4 REAP
  in: 6 LEADTO
  of a crack: 4 HAHA
  Ring: 3 TKO 4 DRAW
  Unexpected: 5 UPSET
Results
  They get: 5 DOERS
Résumé
  relative: 3 BIO
  ~, for short: 4 VITA
Resurrection
  Egyptian symbol of: 6 SCARAB
"Resurrection"
  composer Gustav: 6 MAHLER
Ret.
  plan: 3 IRA
Retail
  area: 5 STRIP
  center: 4 MALL
  outlet: 4 MART 5 STORE
  outlets: 7 EMPORIA

  price: 4 COST
  revenue: 5 SALES
  store opening: 3 WAL
Retailer: 6 DEALER SELLER
  Swedish: 4 IKEA
Retain: 4 HOLD KEEP
Retainer: 3 FEE 4 DIKE
Retaliate: 7 GETEVEN
Retardant
  Apple growth: 4 ALAR
  Rancidity: 3 BHT
Retina
  cell: 3 ROD
  feature: 4 CONE
  layers: 6 TAPETA
Retin-A
  treats it: 4 ACNE
Retinue: 5 TRAIN
Retire
  Place to: 3 BED
  When to: 7 BEDTIME
Retired: 4 ABED 7 EMERITA
  as a prof.: 4 EMER
  flier: 3 SST
  His #4 was: 3 OTT 6 MELOTT
  His #7 was: 6 MANTLE
  His #12 was: 6 NAMATH
  professors: 7 EMERITI
  quarterback: 7 ESIASON
  U.S. brand ~ in 1972: 4 ESSO
Retiree
  asset: 3 IRA
  of 1979: 3 ALI
  title: 7 EMERITA
Retirees
  Agcy. for: 3 SSA
  Titled: 7 EMERITI
Retirement
  agcy.: 3 SSA
  benefit: 7 PENSION
  home: 3 BED
  mecca: 6 STPETE
  plan: 5 KEOGH
  Put off: 6 STAYUP
  savings: 4 IRAS
Retiring: 3 SHY 5 TIMID
Retort
  Cynic's: 4 IBET
  Unconcerned: 6 SOWHAT

Retract: 5 UNSAY 8 TAKEBACK
Retraction
  Make a: 7 EATCROW
Retreat: 3 DEN SPA 4 EXIT **LAIR**
    5 OASIS 9 BACKPEDAL
  Hindu: 6 ASHRAM
  Luxurious: 5 VILLA
  Mountain: 5 CABIN
  Russian: 5 DACHA
  Shady: 5 ARBOR
Retribution: 9 TITFORTAT
  Agent of: 7 NEMESIS
Retrieve: 3 GET 6 REELIN
Retriever
  Type of: 8 LABRADOR
  ~, for short: 3 LAB
Retro
  car: 6 BEETLE
  hairdo: 4 AFRO
  phone feature: 4 DIAL
  sign word: 4 OLDE
  style: 4 DECO
Retroactive
  Make: 8 BACKDATE
Retrovirus
  material: 3 RNA
Retsyn
  Mint with: 4 CERT
Return: 6 PROFIT
  addressee: 3 IRS
  call: 4 ECHO
  Get in: 4 REAP
  High: 3 LOB
  mail courtesy (abbr.): 4 SASE
  Rate of: 5 YIELD
  requirement: 7 RECEIPT
    9 SALESSLIP
  to base: 5 TAGUP
  to office: 7 REELECT
  ~ ID: 3 SSN
Returnee
  cry: 6 IMHOME
  Lucas: 4 JEDI
Returnees
  Homecoming: 6 ALUMNI
Returner
  Hardy: 6 NATIVE
"Return of the Jedi"
  creature: 4 **EWOK**

Returns
  No: 4 ASIS
  org.: 3 IRS
"Return to ___": 6 SENDER
Reuben
  bread: 3 **RYE**
  Brother of: 4 LEVI
  ingredient: 5 KRAUT SWISS
  Mother of: 4 LEAH
"Reuben, Reuben"
  actor Tom: 5 **CONTI**
Reunifier
  German: 4 KOHL
Reunion
  attendee: 3 SIS 4 **ALUM** AUNT
    GRAD 5 FRERE NIECE
    UNCLE
  attendee (abbr.): 3 REL
  group: 3 KIN 4 CLAN
    5 CLASS
Reuss River
  origin: 3 URI
Reuters
  rival: 3 UPI
Reuther, Walter
  org.: 3 UAW
Rev: 3 GUN
Rev.
  address: 3 SER
  initials: 3 MLK
  ~ Jackson: 5 JESSE
  ~ Roberts: 4 ORAL
Reveal: 4 BARE 5 LETON
    6 IMPART UNVEIL
    7 LAYBARE
  by accident: 7 LETSLIP
  ~, in poetry: 3 **OPE**
Revealed: 3 OUT 4 TOLD
Revealing: 8 TELLTALE
    10 TATTLETALE
  attire: 4 MINI
  cry from above: 6 UPHERE
  pictures: 5 XRAYS
  swimwear: 5 THONG
Reveille
  horn: 5 BUGLE
  Opposite of: 4 TAPS
  Respond to: 4 RISE 5 ARISE
"___ Reveille" (Kyser hit): 3 TIL

Revel
 in: 5 EATUP
 noisily: 7 ROISTER
Revelation: 6 EXPOSE
  9 EYEOPENER
 Divine: 6 ORACLE
 response: 3 AHA
Revelations
 nation: 5 MAGOG
Reveler
 Greek ~ utterance: 4 EVOE
 Mythical: 5 SATYR
Revelry
 Wild: 4 ORGY
Revenge
 Have ~ on: 3 GET
 Take: 7 GETEVEN
Revenue
 sources: 3 ADS
 State ~ generator: 5 LOTTO
 ~, in French: 5 RENTE
Revenuer: 4 TMAN
Reverberate: 4 **ECHO**
Reverberation: 4 ECHO
Revere: 5 ADORE HONOR
  6 ESTEEM
 When ~ rode: 5 APRIL
Revered: 6 SACRED
 leader: 9 STATESMAN
 one: 4 GURU IDOL
Reverence: 3 **AWE** 9 PIOUSNESS
Reverend Jim
 Sitcom with: 4 TAXI
Reverent: 5 PIOUS
Reverie: 5 DREAM
 Lost in: 5 MOONY
Reversal: 3 UEY 5 UTURN
  7 SETBACK
"Reversal of Fortune"
 star Jeremy: 5 IRONS
Reverse: 4 GEAR **UNDO**
  7 COUNTER
 a dele: 4 STET
 Coin: 5 TAILS
 Game with ~ cards: 3 UNO
 side: 4 BACK
 stitch: 4 PURL
Reversible
 fabric: 6 DAMASK

Reversion: 7 ATAVISM
Revert: 5 RESET
Review: 6 ASSESS GOOVER
  7 BRUSHUP RUNOVER
  WRITEUP 8 CRITIQUE
  HASHOVER
 Bad: 3 **PAN**
 Four-star: 4 **RAVE**
 IRS: 3 AUD
 Kind of: 4 RAVE 5 MIXED
Reviewer
 Book: 3 CPA
 ~ Reed: 3 REX
 ~ Roger: 5 EBERT
Revise: 4 EDIT 5 AMEND EMEND
Revision: 4 EDIT
Revival
 shelter: 4 TENT
 shout: 4 AMEN
 technique: 3 CPR
Revivalist: 3 NEO
 chic: 5 RETRO
Revlon
 rival: 4 AVON
Revolt: 5 REBEL 6 APPALL
  RISEUP UPRISE
  8 NAUSEATE
Revolting: 4 VILE 5 LURID
 one: 5 REBEL
Revolution: 5 TWIRL
 period: 4 YEAR
Revolutionary
 French: 5 MARAT
 loyalist: 4 TORY
 mercenary: 7 HESSIAN
 Mexican: 5 VILLA 6 ZAPATA
 Old-style: 6 ANARCH
 Russian: 5 LENIN
 ~ Luxemburg: 4 ROSA
"Revolutionary"
 of Chopin: 5 ETUDE
Revolve: 4 SPIN TURN 5 TWIRL
Revolver: 3 GUN 4 DOOR
 feature: 8 SNUBNOSE
 inventor: 4 **COLT**
 Small: 4 EDDY
 Space: 6 PLANET
Revolving
 firework: 8 PINWHEEL

part: 5 ROTOR
Revue
1978 Broadway ~: 5 EUBIE
1998 Broadway ~: 5 FOSSE
bit: 4 **SKIT**
Weekend: 3 SNL
Reward
Employee: 5 BONUS RAISE
for a dog: 4 BONE 5 TREAT
for a hero: 5 MEDAL
for waiting: 3 TIP
Rework: 4 EDIT 5 ADAPT AMEND
Rewrite: 4 EDIT
Rex
Contemporary of: 4 ERLE
Critic: 4 REED
Sleuth created by: 4 **NERO**
Rey, Lester ___ (sci-fi author):
3 DEL
Reykjavik
nation: 7 ICELAND
Reynolds
Actor: 4 BURT
competitor: 5 ALCOA
Pitcher: 5 ALLIE
Reynolds, Burt
1976 ~ film: 5 GATOR
1978 ~ film: 6 HOOPER
THEEND
1988 ~ film: 8 RENTACOP
Reynolds, Debbie
1973 ~ Broadway revival:
5 IRENE
Reynolds, R.J.
brand: 5 DORAL SALEM
Reza Khan: 4 SHAH
RFD
Part of: 5 RURAL
RFK: 4 ATTY
Rhapsodic
Make: 5 ELATE
rhyme: 3 ODE
Rhea
Daughter of: 4 HERA
relative: 3 EMU
role: 5 CARLA
Roman equivalent of: 3 OPS
Rhein
blocker: 3 EIS

city: 4 KOLN
feeder: 3 AAR
"___ Rheingold": 3 DAS
Rheinland
route: 4 BAHN
Rhetoric: 6 HOTAIR
Recite: 5 ORATE
Rhett
Last word of: 4 DAMN
Last words of: 5 ADAMN
Rhine
Catcher in the: 5 SEINE
City on the: 4 BONN 5 BASEL
feeder: 3 AAR 4 AARE RUHR
Region along the: 6 ALSACE
siren: 7 LORELEI
whine: 3 **ACH**
Rhine, Dr.
Field of: 3 ESP
Rhineland
refusal: 4 NEIN
region: 4 SAAR
Rhino
feature: 4 HORN
relative: 5 TAPIR
Rhinoplasty: 7 NOSEJOB
Rho
follower: 5 SIGMA
Rhoda
Mom of: 3 **IDA**
"Rhoda"
David of: 4 GROH
mom: 3 IDA
production co.: 3 MTM
star Harper: 7 VALERIE
Rhode Island
Former ~ senator: 4 PELL
motto: 4 HOPE
nickname: 10 OCEANSTATE
state tree: 8 REDMAPLE
Rhodes
Actor: 4 HARI
of Rhodesia: 5 CECIL
Rhododendron
kin: 6 **AZALEA**
Rhody: 4 AUNT
Little: 10 OCEANSTATE
Rhone
capital: 4 LYON 5 LYONS

City on the: 4 LYON 5 **ARLES**
feeder: 5 **ISERE** SAONE
Rhubarb: 3 ADO ROW 5 SCRAP
    SETTO 6 FRACAS
Rhyme: 4 POEM
Dieter of: 5 **SPRAT**
Gardener of: 4 MARY
Nightgown wearer of:
    15 WEEWILLIEWINKIE
Old king of: 4 COLE
Rhapsodic: 3 ODE
Runaway of: 5 SPOON
scheme: 4 ABAB ABBA
Seesaw sitter of: 4 ESAU
Shepherdess of: 6 BOPEEP
Simpleton of: 5 SIMON
Start of a counting: 4 EENY
time: 3 EEN
Tumbler of: 4 JILL
Without ~ or reason:
    8 ATRANDOM
writer: 11 MOTHERGOOSE
"Rhyme Pays"
rapper: 4 ICET
Rhymer: 4 POET
Wry Rye: 4 NASH
Rhymes
Busta Rhymes: 8 RAPSONGS
of rap: 5 BUSTA
Rhys, Jean
Sea in a ~ title: 8 SARGASSO
Rhythm: 4 BEAT 5 TEMPO
Dramatic: 6 PACING
instrument: 4 DRUM 6 MARACA
Jaunty: 4 LILT
keeper: 3 TOE
Rio: 5 SAMBA
"___ Rhythm": 4 IGOT
Rhythmic: 6 CADENT 7 METERED
    8 CADENCED
cadence: 4 LILT
dance: 5 SAMBA
feet: 5 IAMBS
speech: 4 LILT
Rial
spender: 5 IRANI OMANI
Rib: 4 BONE JOSH 5 COSTA
    TEASE 6 NEEDLE
connection: 7 STERNUM

Corduroy: 4 WALE
donor: 4 ADAM
order: 4 RACK
Ribald: 4 LEWD RACY
Ribbed
fabric: 5 TWILL 6 FAILLE
Ribbon
Get a blue: 3 WIN
ornament: 7 ROSETTE
Yellow ~ site: 7 OAKTREE
Ribosomal ___: 3 RNA
___ Rica: 5 **COSTA**
Ricardo
landlord: 5 MERTZ
~, to Mertz: 6 TENANT
Riccardo
Conductor: 4 MUTI
Ricci
Designer: 4 NINA
Rice
athlete: 3 OWL
Author: 4 **ANNE**
Brown or: 3 JIM
dish: 5 **PILAF** PILAU 6 PAELLA
    7 RISOTTO
field: 5 PADDY
Lyricist: 3 TIM
pad: 4 DORM
Playwright: 5 **ELMER**
White ~ lack: 4 BRAN
wine: 4 **SAKE**
Rice ___: 5 PADDY PILAF
Rice-___: 5 ARONI
Rice-A-___: 4 RONI
Rice/John
musical: 4 AIDA
Rice-shaped
pasta: 4 ORZO
Rice/Webber
musical: 5 EVITA
Rich: 6 LOADED
Actress: 5 IRENE
deposit: 4 LODE
dessert: 5 **TORTE** 6 ECLAIR
dude: 6 FATCAT
fertilizer: 5 GUANO
Kind of: 6 FILTHY
Like ~ soil: 5 LOAMY
Poet: 8 ADRIENNE

soil: **4 LOAM**
tapestry: **5** ARRAS
voiced: **7** OROTUND
"Rich and Famous"
reporter: **5** LEACH
Richard
1987 Pulitzer critic ~: **4** EDER
Actor: **4** EGAN GERE
Anonymous: **3** ROE
Antarctic explorer: **4** BYRD
Architect: **5** MEIER
Author: **5** ADAMS **6** SCARRY
Comedian: **5** PRYOR
First VP under: **5** SPIRO
Virgin tycoon: **7** BRANSON
who played Jaws: **4** KIEL
Richard ___ : 3 III
Richard ___, Sir
English essayist: **6** STEELE
Richard III
request: **6** AHORSE
Richards
Former Texas governor: **3 ANN**
of tennis: **5** RENEE
Rock musician: **5** KEITH
Richards, Mary
Neighbor of: **5** RHODA
Richardson
Nixon attorney general: **6** ELLIOT
___ riche: **7** NOUVEAU
Richert
Actor: **4** NATE
Richie
Dad of ~, to the Fonz: **3** MRC
Mom of ~, to the Fonz: **4** MRSC
Richie, Lionel
1983 ~ hit: **6** YOUARE
1984 ~ hit: **5** HELLO
Richly
decorated: **6** ORNATE
embellish: **4** GILD
"Rich Man, Poor Man"
actor Nick: **5** NOLTE
actress Kay: **4** LENZ
author: **4** SHAW
novelist Shaw: **5** IRWIN
The rich man in: **4** RUDY
Richmond
Actor: **4** DEON

Richness: 4 LUXE
Richter
concern: **5** SCALE **6** TREMOR
Richthofen: 3 ACE **5** BARON
Rick
Disc jockey: **4** DEES
Indy champ: **5** MEARS
Love of: **4 ILSA**
Where Ilsa met: **5** PARIS
Rickenbacker: 3 ACE **6** AIRACE
Aviator: **5** EDDIE
Rickety: 10 RAMSHACKLE
auto: **10** RATTLETRAP
Rickey
ingredient: **3** GIN **4** LIME
Ricki
rival, once: **5** OPRAH
Talk show host: **4** LAKE
Rickles
Comic: **3** DON
riposte: **6** INSULT
Rickman
Actor: **4** ALAN
Rick's
pianist: **3** SAM
Ricky
Bluegrass musician: **6** SKAGGS
Landlady of: **5** ETHEL
Landlord of: **4** FRED
portrayer: **4** DESI
Rico
Where ~ shot Tony: **4** COPA
___ Rico: **6** PUERTO
Ricochet: 5 CAROM
Sonic: **4** ECHO
"Ricochet"
rapper: **4** ICET
Rid: 6 DIVEST
Get ~ of: **3** AXE **4** LOSE SHED
       5 DITCH ERASE SCRAP
       6 DELETE **7** ABOLISH
       DEEPSIX DISPOSE
of vermin: **5** DERAT
Riddance
Good: **6** NOLOSS
Riddick
Boxer: **5** BOWE
Riddle: 5 POSER **6** ENIGMA
Pose a: **3** ASK

Zen: 4 KOAN
Riddle-me-___: 3 REE
Riddler
  nemesis: 6 BATMAN
Ride: 5 TAUNT TEASE 6 HARASS
  for E.T.: 3 UFO
  Guide the: 5 STEER
  in space: 5 SALLY
  Long: 4 LIMO
  Metered: 3 CAB 4 TAXI
  Prepare for a rough: 7 STRAPIN
  price: 4 FARE
  Short: 4 SPIN
  the banister: 5 SLIDE
  Toddler's: 5 TRIKE
  up the slope: 6 SKITOW
  Winter: 4 SLED
Rider: 5 ADDON
  Broom: 3 HAG
  Champion: 5 AUTRY
  command: 4 WHOA
  Cry of a: 4 WHEE
  grip: 4 REIN
  Like the ~ of Silver: 4 LONE
  Rail: 4 HOBO
  Revolutionary: 6 REVERE
  Rosinante: 7 QUIXOTE
    10 DONQUIXOTE
  Scout: 5 TONTO
  seat: 6 SADDLE
  Sleipnir: 4 ODIN
"Riders of the Purple Sage"
  author Grey: 4 ZANE
"Riders to the Sea"
  playwright: 5 SYNGE
Ridge
  Coin-edge: 5 KNURL
  Coral: 4 REEF
  Corduroy: 4 WALE
  Fingerboard: 4 FRET
  Fingerprint: 5 WHORL
  Glacial: 5 ARETE ESKER SERAC
  in Washington: 3 TOM
  Mountain: 5 **ARETE**
  Rocky: 3 TOR
  ___ Ridge (racehorse): 4 RIVA
Ridicule: 4 JEER MOCK TWIT
    5 TAUNT 6 DERIDE
    7 SNEERAT

Ridiculous: 5 INANE NUTTY
    SILLY 6 INSANE 7 ASININE
"Ridiculous!": 5 PSHAW
Riding: 4 ATOP
  the waves: 4 ASEA 6 AFLOAT
  whip: 4 CROP
Riefenstahl
  Director: 4 **LENI**
Rife: 5 AWASH 7 TEEMING
  Be ~ (with): 4 TEEM
Riffraff: 4 SCUM 5 TRASH
    6 RABBLE
Rifle: 4 LOOT 7 RANSACK
  Air: 5 BBGUN
  Air ~ ammo: 3 **BBS** 6 BBSHOT
  attachment: 5 SCOPE
    7 BAYONET
  M-1 ~ inventor: 6 GARAND
  part: 4 BUTT 6 BREECH
  support: 5 BIPOD
Rift: 3 GAP
Rig
  Big: 4 **SEMI**
  Rod on a: 4 AXLE
Riga
  resident: 4 **LETT** 7 LATVIAN
Rigatoni: 5 PASTA
  kin: 4 ZITI 5 PENNE
Rigby
  of song: 7 ELEANOR
Rigel: 4 STAR
  constellation: 5 ORION
Rigg
  Actress: 5 **DIANA**
Rigg, Diana
  role: 7 MRSPEEL
Rigged: 5 ARMED
  It is: 4 MAST
Rigging
  support: 4 MAST SPAR
Right: 6 PROPER 9 STARBOARD
  Ain't: 4 ISNT 5 ARENT
  angle: 3 **ELL**
  At ~ angles to the keel: 5 ABEAM
  At the ~ time: 5 ONCUE
  away: 3 NOW 4 STAT 6 ATONCE
    PRONTO
  away (abbr.): 4 ASAP
  Exactly: 6 DEADON SPOTON

Game with a ~ bower: **6** EUCHRE
Go: **3** GEE **4** TURN
Indifferent to ~ and wrong:
  6 AMORAL
Is the ~ size: **4** FITS
Just: **4** TOAT **5** IDEAL **6** TOATEE
Leaning to the: **6** ITALIC
Not: **3** ODD OFF **4** LEFT
  5 AMISS
Not ~ now: **4** ANON **5** LATER
of decision: **5** SAYSO
of passage: **8** EASEMENT
on the map: **4** EAST
Point in the ~ direction:
  6 ORIENT
Set: **4** HEAL MEND TRUE
  5 ALIGN AMEND **6** REMEDY
  7 REDRESS **8** FINETUNE
"Right!": **3** YES
"___, right!": **4** YEAH
Right, Mr.
  Hardly: **3** CAD **5** CREEP
"Right away!": **4** ASAP **6** INASEC
Righteous: **4** JUST
Rightful: **3** DUE **4** JUST
  8 DESERVED
Right Guard
  rival: **5** ARRID
Right-hand
  man: **4** AIDE
  man (abbr.): **4** ASST
  page: **5 RECTO**
Rightist
  ~, briefly: **6** NEOCON
"Right on!": **4** AMEN
Rights
  Animal ~ org.: **4** PETA SPCA
  5 ASPCA
  Gun ~ org.: **3** NRA
  Human ~ agcy.: **3** ILO
  org.: **4 ACLU** CORE **5** ASCAP
  Transfer: **6** ASSIGN
  Workers ~ org.: **4** NLRB
"Rights of Man"
  writer: **5** PAINE
"Right Stuff, The"
  role: **5** GLENN **6** YEAGER
Rigid: **3** SET **5** TENSE
  7 ADAMANT

bracelet: **6** BANGLE
"Rigoletto"
  Beloved, in: **4** CARO
  composer: **5** VERDI
  trio: **4** ACTS
Rigor: **8** ASPERITY SEVERITY
Rigorous: **5** STERN **6** SEVERE
  exams: **5** ORALS
___ rigueur (literally): **3** ALA
Riis
  concern: **5** SLUMS
"Rikki-Tikki-___": **4** TAVI
Rile: **4** STIR **5** GRATE
  up: **5** ANGER **6** ENRAGE
Riled
  All ~ up: **5** IRATE **7** INASTIR
  up: **3** HET **4** SORE **6** INAPET
Riley
  Former Knicks coach: **3** PAT
  Life of: **4 EASE** **10** EASYSTREET
  pal Digger: **5** ODELL
Riley, Bridget
  genre: **5** OPART
Rill
  setting: **4** VALE
Rim: **4** EDGE **5** VERGE
  Basketball: **4** HOOP
  Projecting metal: **6** FLANGE
  Watch: **5** BEZEL
Rime: **4** HOAR
Rimes
  Singer: **5 LEANN**
Rind: **4** PEEL
  Cheese with a: **4** BRIE
  Lemon: **4** ZEST
  Remove: **4** PARE
Ring: **4** BAND ECHO HALO **PEAL**
  TOLL **5** ARENA CHIME
  KNELL PHONE
  8 RESONATE
  activity: **4** BOUT
  Anatomical: **6** AREOLA
  Angelic: **4 HALO**
  around the castle: **4** MOAT
  Baby: **7** TEETHER
  bearer: **3** EAR **4** TREE WIFE
  5 FRODO **6** SATURN
  boss: **3** REF
  cheer: **3** OLE

combo: **6** ONETWO
count: **3** TEN
dance: **4** HORA
decision: **3** TKO
Floral: **3** LEI
foe: **4** TORO
Give a: **5** PHONE
great: **3** ALI
Harness: **6** TERRET
Island: **3** LEI
Item thrown in a: **3** HAT
Kind of: **4** MOOD **7** DECODER
leader: **5** CHAMP **6** TORERO
legend: **3** ALI
Light: **4** HALO
master: **7** JEWELER
of color: **6** AREOLA AREOLE
org.: **3** WBA
out: **4** PEAL
Practice in the: **4** SPAR
Reef: **5** ATOLL
Response to a: **5** HELLO
Rubber: **6** GASKET
site: **3** EAR **4** LOBE NOSE TREE
    5 NAVEL PINKY **7** BATHTUB
    EARLOBE
source: **5** ONION
sport: **4** SUMO
Swing in the: **3** BOX
up: **4** CALL DIAL HALO
    5 PHONE
wear: **6** GLOVES
Ringed
planet: **6** SATURN
Ringer: **4** BELL **5** CHIME
Bell: **4** AVON **6** SEXTON
    8 AVONLADY
Near: **6** LEANER
Ringing
site: **3** EAR
sound: **4** PEAL TING
Ringlet: **4** CURL LOCK
Ringling Brothers
One of the: **4** OTTO
Ringmaster: **5** EMCEE
Ringo: **6** BEATLE
Drummer: **5** STARR
John, to: **3** LOO
Part of a ~ kit: **5** SNARE

Rings: **6** ANNULI
Car with four linked: **4** AUDI
Math: **4** TORI
Things on: **4** KEYS
What tree ~ indicate: **3** AGE
Ring-shaped: **5** TORIC
    7 ANNULAR
reef: **5** ATOLL
Ringside
shout: **3** OLE
Ring-tailed
critter: **4** COON **5** COATI
Rink
confrontation: **7** FACEOFF
Enjoy the: **5** SKATE
fakeout: **4** DEKE
jump: **4** AXEL LUTZ
legend: **3** ORR
shape: **4** OVAL
surface: **3** ICE
Rinse
Hair: **5** HENNA
Red: **5** HENNA
with a solvent: **5** ELUTE
Rio
Airline to: **5** VARIG
automaker: **3** KIA
beach: **7** IPANEMA
    10 COPACABANA
contents: **4** AGUA
peak: **9** SUGARLOAF
rhythm: **5** SAMBA
Rio ___: **5** NEGRO **6** GRANDE
"Rio ___" (John Wayne film):
    4 LOBO
Rio de la ___: **5** PLATA
Rio Grande
city: **6** ELPASO LAREDO
Rio Grande do ___ (Brazilian
    state): **5** NORTE
"Rio Lobo"
actor Jack: **4** ELAM
___ Rios, Jamaica: **4** OCHO
Riot: **4** HOOT **5** REBEL **6** SCREAM
1886 ~ site , with "Square":
    9 HAYMARKET
1971 prison ~ site: **6** ATTICA
follower: **3** ACT
participant: **6** LOOTER

Put down a: **5** QUELL
remedy: **7** TEARGAS
spray: **4** MACE
squad item: **7** GASMASK
Rioter: 6 STONER
take: **4** LOOT
___ **Rio, Texas: 3** DEL
Riotous
crowd: **3** MOB
Rio Treaty
implementor (abbr.): **3** OAS
Rip: 4 TEAR 6 SCATHE
apart: **4** REND
into: **5** SETAT **6** TEARAT
off: **3** CON ROB **4** GLOM ROOK
SCAM **5** STEAL SWIPE
6 FLEECE
up: **4** REND **5** SHRED
Ripe
for planting: **6** ARABLE
Way past: **6** ROTTEN
Ripen: 3 AGE 6 MATURE
Ripening
agent: **4 AGER**
Ripken
broke his record: **6** GEHRIG
of baseball: **3 CAL**
was one: **6** ORIOLE
Ripley
End of a claim by: **3** NOT
5 ORNOT
Ready for: **3** ODD
Ripley, Mr.
of film: **5** DAMON
"Ripley's Believe ___ Not": 4 ITOR
Ripoff: 4 SCAM **5** THEFT
Ripped: 4 RENT **TORE** TORN
6 TOREUP
off: **5** STOLE **6** STOLEN
Ripple: 7 WAVELET
maker: **3** OAR
They ~ on bodybuilders: **4** PECS
tippler: **4** WINO
Ripsnorter: 4 LULU
Rise: 4 GOUP HIKE HILL
5 CLIMB GETUP STAND
6 ASCEND
(abbr.): **4** INCR
and shine: **6** AWAKEN

Dow: **4** GAIN
Flat-topped: **4** MESA
Get a ~ out of: **6** LEAVEN
Give ~ to: **4** SIRE **5** BREED
SPAWN **8** ENGENDER
high: **4** SOAR
It will get a: **5** YEAST
quickly: **4** SOAR
up: **4** REAR **5** REBEL
"Rise, Glory, Rise"
composer: **4** ARNE
Riser
Early: **3** SUN
plus tread: **5** STAIR
Rising
locale: **4** OVEN
star: **5** COMER
Rising Sun
Land of the: **5** JAPAN
Risk: 5 PERIL WAGER **6** HAZARD
7 IMPERIL **8** ENDANGER
a fine: **6** LITTER
At: **6** LIABLE **7** INPERIL
8 INDANGER
a ticket: **5** SPEED
Free of: **4** SAFE
Take a: **4** DARE
taker: **5** DARER **9** DAREDEVIL
Transfer the: **8** REINSURE
Worrier: **5** ULCER
"Risk"
adversaries: **6** ARMIES
Risked: 7 ATSTAKE
Risk takers
self-question: **7** DOIDARE
Risky: 6 UNSAFE
business: **4** SPEC
purchase: **10** PIGINAPOKE
undertaking: **7** VENTURE
way to run: **7** ONEMPTY
Risqué: 4 BLUE **RACY 5** SALTY
A bit: **5** SPICY
More than: **4** LEWD
Ristorante
beverage: **4** VINO
course: **5** PASTA
courses: **9** ANTIPASTI
dessert: **6** GELATI GELATO
7 TORTONI

dish: **8** CALAMARI
herb: **7** OREGANO
request: **7** ALDENTE
Rita
  An ex of: **3** <u>**ALY**</u> **5** ORSON
Ritchard
  Actor: **5** CYRIL
Ritchie
  Singer: **6** VALENS
Rite: 8 CEREMONY
  answer: **3** IDO
  Early: **7** BAPTISM
  robe: **3** ALB
  site: **4** PYRE **5** <u>**ALTAR**</u>
Rites
  Waive one's: **5** ELOPE
Ritter
  Actor: **3** TEX
  Singer: **3** <u>**TEX**</u>
Ritter, John
  Father of: **3** TEX
Ritual: 7 LITURGY
  bread: **5** WAFER
  greeting: **6** SALAAM
  Inauguration: **4** OATH
  Nine-day: **6** NOVENA
  Poker: **4** ANTE
  Pregame: **4** TOSS **6** ANTHEM
  Religious: **4** MASS
  Tot: **3** NAP
  Wedding: **5** TOAST
  Yom Kippur: **4** FAST
Ritz
  owner: **8** HOTELIER
  rival: **4** <u>**HIHO**</u>
Ritzy: 4 POSH **5** PLUSH SWANK
    7 OPULENT
  spread: **6** CAVIAR ESTATE
Rival: 3 FOE **4** VIER
River
  African: **4** NILE **5** NIGER
    6 UBANGI
  Alpine: **3** AAR **4** AARE **5** ISERE
  blocker: **3** DAM
  Blue or White: **4** NILE
  crosser: **5** FERRY **6** BRIDGE
  dam: **4** WEIR
  deposit: **4** SILT
  embankment: **5** <u>**LEVEE**</u>

English: **4** AVON TYNE **5** TRENT
  6 THAMES
Eurasian: **4** URAL
European: **4** ELBE ODER
  5 VOLGA
feature: **3** BED **4** BEND FORK
  5 DELTA FALLS MOUTH
feeder: **6** STREAM
French: **4** OISE ORNE **5** ISERE
  LOIRE MARNE RHONE
  SAONE
German: **3** EMS **4** <u>**EDER**</u> ELBE
  ODER RUHR SAAR **5** RHINE
horse: **5** HIPPO
in a 1957 film: **4** KWAI
inlet: **3** <u>**RIA**</u>
island: **3** <u>**AIT**</u>
Longest: **4** NILE
mammal: **5** OTTER
mouth: **5** DELTA
of Hades: **4** STYX **5** LETHE
Sell up the: **6** BETRAY
skipper: **5** STONE
source: **4** HEAD
transport: **4** RAFT **5** BARGE
  CANOE
~, in Spanish: **3** RIO
___ **River: 4** EAST **5** OLMAN
Rivera
  Actress: **5** CHITA
  Artist: **5** DIEGO
  Muralist: **5** DIEGO
Rivera, Diego
  work: **5** MURAL
Riverbank
  romper: **5** OTTER
Riverbed
  Dry: **4** WADI
Riverboat
  hazard: **4** SNAG **5** SHOAL
Riverdale
  redhead: **6** ARCHIE
Rivers
  of comedy: **4** JOAN
Riveter
  of song: **5** ROSIE
Riviera
  resort: **4** <u>**NICE**</u> **7** SANREMO
  season: **3** ETE

view: 3 MER
___ Rivoli (of Paris): 5 RUEDE
Riyadh
  resident: 4 **ARAB** 5 SAUDI
Rizzuto
  contemporary: 5 REESE
  Ex-Yankee: 4 PHIL
  nickname: 7 SCOOTER
R.L.
  "Goosebumps" author: 5 STINE
Rm.
  coolers: 3 ACS
RMN
  Loser to: 3 HHH
R.N.
  forte: 3 **TLC**
  workplaces: 3 ERS ORS 4 ICUS
RNA
  component: 6 URACIL
  sugar: 6 RIBOSE
Roach
  Film producer: 3 HAL
  killing brand: 4 RAID
Road
  Bump in the: 4 SNAG
  caution: 3 SLO 4 BUMP
  closing: 4 STER
  Country: 4 LANE
  cover: 3 TAR
  curve: 3 **ESS** 4 BEND
  Do ~ work: 3 TAR 4 PAVE
  Down the: 5 AHEAD LATER
      6 INTIME
  Fix a: 5 RETAR
  groove: 3 RUT
  guide: 3 MAP
  hazard: 3 ICE 5 SLEET
  Hit the: 4 LEFT MOVE RIDE
      TOUR WENT 5 LEAVE
      SCRAM 6 DEPART
  hugger: 10 RADIALTIRE
  King of the: 4 HOBO
  Mountain ~ sign:
      10 STEEPGRADE
  offense: 3 DWI
  One for the: 3 CAR 4 AUTO
  On the: 4 **AWAY**
  Prepare for a ~ trip: 5 GASUP
  Rig on the: 4 SEMI

  Roman: 4 **ITER**
  runner: 3 CAR 4 AUTO
  Secluded: 5 BYWAY
  shoulder: 4 BERM
  sign word: 4 THRU
  Toll: 4 PIKE 8 TURNPIKE
  Word after: 4 TEST
"Road"
  destination: 3 RIO 4 BALI
"___ Road" (Binchy book): 4 TARA
Roadblock: 4 SNAG 7 IMPASSE
  requests: 3 IDS
Roadhouse: 3 **INN**
  sign: 4 EATS
Roadie
  load: 3 **AMP**
  ride: 7 TOURBUS
Road map
  abbr.: 3 RTE
  feature: 5 INSET
Road Runner
  foe: 6 COYOTE
  sound: 4 BEEP
Roads
  (abbr.): 3 STS
  Like some: 3 ICY 5 RUTTY
      7 ONELANE
Roadside
  distress signal: 5 FLARE
  eatery: 5 DINER
  grazer: 4 DEER
  lodging: 3 INN 5 MOTEL
  sign: 3 GAS
  stop: 3 INN 5 MOTEL
Roadster: 8 RUNABOUT
  feature: 10 RUMBLESEAT
"Road to ___": 4 BALI
Roadwork
  Do: 4 PAVE 5 RETAR
Roald
  Author: 4 **DAHL**
Roam: 5 RANGE
  about: 3 GAD 6 WANDER
Roar: 4 YELL 5 BLARE
  in a ring: 3 OLE
Rorer: 3 LEO 4 LION
Roaring
  Its films have a ~ start: 3 MGM
  start: 3 RIP

Roaring Camp
  creator: 5 HARTE
Roaring Fork River
  City on the: 5 ASPEN
Roaring Twenties: 3 ERA
      6 DECADE
Roast
  Center for a: 7 HONOREE
  French: 4 ROTI
  host: 5 **EMCEE**
  hosts: 3 MCS
  How a ~ may be served: 5 AUJUS
  Moisten a: 5 BASTE
  spot: 4 DAIS
Roast beef
  au ___: 3 JUS
  order: 4 RARE
Roaster: 4 OVEN
  spot: 4 DAIS
Roasting
  rod: 4 **SPIT**
Rob: 5 RIFLE 6 BURGLE
  Actor: 4 **LOWE**
  Director: 6 REINER
Robb
  Pitcher: 3 NEN
Robbe-Grillet
  Author: 5 ALAIN
Robber: 5 THIEF 7 BRIGAND
  chaser: 3 COP
  Grave: 5 GHOUL
Robbery: 5 HEIST THEFT
  Check out before a: 4 CASE
Robbie
  Daredevil dad of: 4 EVEL
Robbins
  Actor: 3 TIM
  Author: 6 HAROLD
  Choreographer: 6 JEROME
Robe
  African: 7 DASHIKI
  fabric: 5 TERRY
  Lounging: 6 CAFTAN
  Priest: 3 ALB
  Roman: 4 **TOGA**
Robert
  Actor: 4 ALDA HAYS RYAN
      5 DONAT URICH 6 DENIRO
  Arctic explorer: 5 PEARY

  Author: 4 CARO 6 LUDLUM
  Baritone: 7 MERRILL
  Comedian: 5 KLEIN
  Director: 6 ALTMAN
  Disney president: 4 IGER
  Irish patriot: 5 EMMET
  Screenwriter: 5 TOWNE
  Synthesizer creator: 4 MOOG
Robert ___
  Gen.: 4 **ELEE**
Roberto
  Boxer: 5 DURAN
  of baseball: 6 ALOMAR
      8 CLEMENTE
Roberts
  Actor: 4 ERIC
  Actress: 5 DORIS JULIA TANYA
  Evangelist: 4 **ORAL**
  Journalist: 5 **COKIE**
  Writer: 4 NORA
Roberts, Julia
  Brother of: 4 ERIC
  Ex of: 4 LYLE
Robertson
  Writer: 6 DAVIES
Robert the ___: 5 BRUCE
Robes
  Roman: 5 TOGAE
Robeson
  role: 7 OTHELLO
Robin
  and Batman: 3 DUO
      10 DYNAMICDUO
  Celeb watcher: 5 LEACH
  mentor: 6 BATMAN
  residence: 4 NEST
  sweetheart: 10 MAIDMARIAN
  Ward who played: 4 BURT
Robin, Christopher
  bear: 4 POOH
Robin Goodfellow: 3 IMP
Robin Hood: 6 ARCHER
  portrayer: 5 ERROL
      8 ALANHALE
"Robin Hood: Men in Tights"
  Roger of: 4 REES
Robinson
  and Thomas:
      14 BALLPARKFRANKS

Brooks: 6 ORIOLE
Game show host: 4 ANNE
of song: 3 MRS
Poet: 5 EDWIN
role: 4 RICO
"___ Robinson": 3 MRS
Robinson, Mrs.
Daughter of: 5 ELAINE
portrayer: 8 BANCROFT
Robot
banker: 3 ATM
coiner: 5 CAPEK
drama: 3 RUR
of Jewish lore: 5 GOLEM
Robotic
rock group: 4 DEVO
Rob Roy: 4 GAEL SCOT
refusal: 3 NAE
"Rob Roy"
actor Neeson: 4 LIAM
star: 6 NEESON
Robt. ___ : 4 **ELEE**
Robust: 3 FIT 4 **HALE** 5 HUSKY
    LUSTY 6 HEARTY
"Robusto!"
Maker of ~ sauces: 4 RAGU
Roc
Like a: 5 AVIAN
Rochester
river: 7 GENESEE
Wife of: 4 EYRE
Rock: 5 GENRE STONE 6 TEETER
1960s ~ musical: 4 HAIR
1986 ~ autobiography: 5 ITINA
Banded: 6 GNEISS
Black: 6 BASALT
blaster: 3 **AMP** TNT
bottom: 5 LEAST NADIR
Comedian: 5 CHRIS
Crystalline: 6 SCHIST
Crystal-lined: 5 GEODE
Easily split: 5 SLATE
First name in: 4 JIMI 5 ELTON
Fissile: 5 SHALE
Flaky: 4 MICA
forerunner: 5 RANDB
garden herb: 5 SEDUM
group: 4 LODE ORES
growth: 4 MOSS 6 LICHEN

Hollow: 5 GEODE
Igneous: 6 BASALT
Kind of: 4 ACID FOLK PUNK
layers: 6 STRATA
ledge: 5 SHELF
Like a: 4 HARD 5 SOLID
Loose ~ debris: 5 SCREE
Made-up ~ group: 4 KISS
Metallic: 3 ORE
Metamorphic: 5 SLATE 6 GNEISS
    SCHIST
Modern ~ genre: 3 EMO
Molten: 4 LAVA 5 **MAGMA**
Monument: 7 GRANITE
music genre: 5 METAL
Oil-bearing: 5 SHALE
Partner of: 4 ROLL
Pop of: 4 IGGY
rabbit: 4 PIKA
Rugged: 4 **CRAG**
salt: 6 HALITE
singer: 5 SIREN 7 LORELEI
Soft: 4 TALC
Stone of: 3 SLY
Third ~ from the sun: 5 EARTH
trailer: 4 ETTE
venue: 5 ARENA
video awards: 4 AVAS
___ Rock: 5 AYERS
"___ Rock": 4 IAMA
"Rock-a-Bye Baby"
setting: 7 TREETOP
Rock and Roll Hall of Fame
architect: 3 PEI 5 IMPEI
singer James: 4 ETTA
View from the: 4 ERIE
"Rock and Roll, Hoochie ___"
('74 song): 3 KOO
Rock-bottom: 5 LEAST
Rock climbing
grip: 4 CRAG
need: 7 TOEHOLD
Rock-clinger
Marine: 7 ABALONE
Rockefeller
asset: 8 OLDMONEY
dish: 7 OYSTERS
Former VP: 6 NELSON
money source: 3 OIL

___ **Rockefeller:** 7 OYSTERS
Rockefeller Center
  muralist: 4 SERT
Rocker
  Country ~ Steve: 5 EARLE
  Folk ~ DiFranco: 3 ANI
  gear: 3 AMP
  Is not off one's: 4 SITS
  Off one's: 3 MAD 4 BATS DAFT
    LOCO
  On one's: 4 SANE
  site: 5 PORCH
  ~ Billy: 4 IDOL 5 OCEAN
  ~ Bob: 5 SEGER
  ~ Bonnie: 5 RAITT
  ~ Brian: 3 **ENO**
  ~ Chris: 3 REA
  ~ Elvis: 8 COSTELLO
  ~ Frank: 5 ZAPPA
  ~ Glenn: 4 FREY
  ~ Joan: 4 JETT
  ~ Julian: 6 LENNON
  ~ Marvin: 4 GAYE
  ~ Patty: 5 SMYTH
Rocket: 4 SOAR
  1950s U.S. ~: 4 THOR
  1960s U.S. ~: 8 REDSTONE
  add-on: 3 EER
  Booster: 5 ATLAS
  European: 6 ARIANE
  French: 6 ARIANE
  fuel: 3 LOX
  fuel component: 5 NITRO
  gasket: 5 ORING
  Inits. on a: 3 USA 4 CCCP
  interceptor: 3 ABM
  launcher: 4 NASA 7 BAZOOKA
  launch site: 3 PAD
  Moon: 6 APOLLO
  path: 3 ARC
  pioneer: 7 GODDARD
  section: 5 STAGE 8 NOSECONE
  stage: 5 AGENA
Rockies: 3 MTS
  Home of the: 8 COLORADO
  Range of the: 5 TETON
  resort: 4 VAIL 5 ASPEN
  summer setting (abbr.): 3 MDT
  wind: 7 CHINOOK

Rockne
  Coach: 5 KNUTE
"Rock 'n' Roll Is King"
  band: 3 ELO
"Rock of ___": 4 AGES
Rocks: 3 ICE
  Hot: 4 LAVA
  Not on the: 4 NEAT
  On the: 4 **ICED**
  Pet: 3 FAD
  Throw ~ at: 4 PELT 5 STONE
Rock Wren
  habitat: 4 MESA
Rocky
  cliff: 4 SCAR
  debris: 5 SCREE
  Foe of: 6 APOLLO
  peak: 3 **TOR**
  projection: 4 CRAG
  ridge: 5 ARETE
  ~, for Stallone: 4 ROLE
"Rocky"
  actress Shire: 5 **TALIA**
  actress Talia: 5 SHIRE
  composer Bill: 5 CONTI
"Rocky II"
  He was dethroned in: 6 APOLLO
"Rocky III"
  actor: 3 MRT
"Rocky IV"
  actor Lundgren: 5 DOLPH
Rocky Mountain
  Indian: 3 UTE
  state: 4 UTAH
  tree: 5 ASPEN
Rococo: 5 STYLE 6 ORNATE
Rod: 3 GAT 6 HEATER PISTOL
    ROSCOE
  Actor: 7 STEIGER
  attachment: 4 REEL
  Barbecue: 4 **SPIT**
  Baseball Hall of Famer: 5 **CAREW**
  Conducting: 5 BATON
  divs.: 3 YDS
  Ex of: 5 ALANA
  of tennis: 5 LAVER
  Partner of: 4 REEL
  Roasting: 4 SPIT
  Schoolmaster: 6 FERULE

squad (abbr.): **3** NRA
Surveyor: **9** RANGEPOLE
Use a divining: **5 DOWSE**
Wheel: **4 AXLE 5** SPOKE
Wooden: **5** DOWEL
___ Rod: **6** AARONS

Roddick
of tennis: **4** ANDY

Rodent
Bushy-tailed: **6** MARMOT
Rabbitlike: **6** AGOUTI
Ratlike: **4** VOLE
Reaction to a: **3** EEK
South American: **4** PACA
    5 COYPU **6** AGOUTI
Tailless: **4** PACA

Rodeo
bucker: **5** BRONC
bull: **6** BRAHMA
Compete in a: **4** ROPE
holler: **5** WAHOO
Immobilize, at a: **6** HOGTIE
performer: **5** ROPER
producer: **5** ISUZU
rope: **5 LASSO** REATA RIATA
    6 LARIAT
sight: **5** CLOWN **6** BARREL

Rodgers
and Hart song: **8** BLUEMOON
Musical partner of: **4** HART

Rodham
Word before: **3** NEE

Rodin
Emulate: **6** SCULPT
sculpture: **4** ADAM

Rodney
Quarterback: **5** PEETE

Rodnina
Figure skater: **5** IRINA

Rodolfo
Love of: **4** MIMI

Rodomontade: 4 RANT

Rodriguez
Catcher: **4** IVAN
Golfer: **6** CHICHI
Shortstop: **4** ALEX

Rods
160 square ~: **4** ACRE
It has: **6** RETINA

Rod-shaped
germ: **5** ECOLI **7** BACILLI

Roe: 4 EGGS
source: **4 SHAD**

Roebuck: 4 DEER
Partner of: **5** SEARS

Roeper
Partner of: **5** EBERT

Rogaine
promise: **4** HAIR

Roger
1960s slugger ~: **5** MARIS
Actor: **5** MOORE
Critic: **5 EBERT**
Fictional: **6** RABBIT
follower: **5** WILCO
Media exec: **5** AILES
Newsman: **4** MUDD **5** ONEIL
Sportswriter: **4** KAHN

"Roger, ___ and out!": 4 OVER

Rogers
Actor: **5** WAYNE
Actress: **4** MIMI
Cowboy: **3** ROY
partner: **7** ASTAIRE
Sci-fi hero: **4** BUCK
Singer: **5** KENNY

Rogers, Buck
ladylove: **5** WILMA

Rogers, Ginger
role: **5** FOYLE **10** KITTYFOYLE
    11 IRENECASTLE

Rogers, Kenny
hit: **4** LADY

Rogers, Mister: 4 FRED

Rogers, Roy
movie type: **5** OATER
Real last name of: **4** SLYE
Wife of: **4** DALE **5** EVANS

Rogers, Will
prop: **5** LASSO

Roget
wd.: **3** SYN

Rogue: 3 CAD **5 SCAMP**
    6 PICARO RASCAL

Roguish: 3 SLY **4** ARCH

Rohmer
Director: **4** ERIC
Writer: **3** SAX

Roker
and others: 3 ALS
show: 5 TODAY
Rolaids
rival: 4 TUMS
Role: 4 PART 7 PERSONA
Has the lead: 5 STARS
It has a supporting: 3 BRA
model: 4 HERO **IDOL** 5 IDEAL
Play a: 3 ACT
player: 5 ACTOR
Play the ~ of: 5 **ACTAS**
Primary: 4 LEAD
Public: 7 PERSONA
Put in an expected:
    8 TYPECAST
Small: 5 CAMEO
Rolex
rival: 5 ELGIN OMEGA
Roll: 3 WAD 4 LIST
back: 5 RESET
Big: 3 WAD 6 ELEVEN
Common: 5 SEVEN
Dice: 5 THROW
Holey: 5 BAGEL
It may be on a: 4 OLEO
Kind of: 3 EGG 5 HONOR PIANO
    6 KAISER 8 CRESCENT
of coins: 7 ROULEAU
of fabric: 4 BOLT
of stamps: 4 COIL
On a: 3 **HOT**
Onion: 5 BIALY
out: 6 UNFURL
partner: 4 ROCK
Place to: 5 AISLE
player: 5 PIANO
up: 4 FURL 5 AMASS
with the punches: 5 ADAPT
___ roll: 3 BED EGG LOG **ONA**
    5 HONOR 6 KAISER
    7 TOOTSIE
Rollaway
kin: 3 COT
Roll-call
no-show: 4 AWOL
response: 3 NAY YEA 4 **HERE**
Rolle
Actress: 6 ESTHER

Rolled
It can be ~ over: 3 IRA
items: 4 DICE EGGS EYES OATS
model: 5 PINUP
Roller: 5 WHEEL 6 CASTER
High: 4 SEMI 7 SPENDER
High ~ roll: 3 WAD
Mine: 4 TRAM
on the road: 4 TIRE
Reno: 3 DIE
Typewriter: 6 PLATEN
Rollerblade: 5 SKATE
protection: 6 HELMET
    7 KNEEPAD
Roller coaster: 4 RIDE
cry: 4 WHEE
feature: 4 DROP LOOP
unit: 3 CAR
Roller derby
item: 3 PAD 5 SKATE
Rollers
High: 3 **ELS**
Put in: 3 SET 6 CURLED
Vegas: 4 DICE
Rolling
Get the ball: 4 OPEN 5 START
Have ~ in the aisles: 4 SLAY
in dough: 4 RICH
lands: 5 HILLS
musician: 5 STONE
rock: 4 LAVA
stone lack: 4 MOSS
veggie: 3 PEA
Rolling ___: 4 INIT 6 STONES
Rolling Stone
founder Jann: 6 WENNER
Rolling Stones
1965 ~ hit:
    15 GETOFFOFMYCLOUD
1966 ~ hit: 12 PAINTITBLACK
1967 ~ hit: 11 RUBYTUESDAY
1968 ~ hit:
    15 JUMPINJACKFLASH
1973 ~ hit: 5 **ANGIE**
1980 ~ hit:
    15 EMOTIONALRESCUE
Former ~ member Bill: 5 WYMAN
label: 3 EMI
One of the: 5 WATTS

Richards of the: 5 KEITH
Wood of the: 3 RON
Roll-on
  brand: 3 BAN 5 ARRID
  target: 4 ODOR
Rollout
  Ballpark: 4 TARP
  Product: 6 LAUNCH
Rollover
  target: 3 IRA
Rolls
  filler: 6 PETROL
  Partner of: 5 ROYCE
  radial: 4 TYRE
Rolls-___: 5 ROYCE
Rolodex
  abbr.: 3 **TEL**
Roly-___ : 4 POLY
Roly-poly: 5 PLUMP PUDGY
ROM
  Part of: 4 ONLY READ
      6 MEMORY
  storage units: 3 CDS
Rom.
  Not: 4 ITAL
Roma
  Bishop of: 4 PAPA
  currency: 4 LIRE
  Love, in: 5 AMORE
  Seaport southeast of: 6 NAPOLI
  Where ~ is: 6 ITALIA
Romain de Tirtoff: 4 ERTE
Romaine
  lettuce: 3 COS
Roman
  censor: 4 CATO
  commoner: 4 PLEB
  date: 4 IDES
  dictator: 5 SULLA
  emperor: 4 NERO OTHO
      6 CAESAR TRAJAN
  fountain: 5 TREVI
  Four Holy ~ emperors: 5 OTTOS
  goddess of agriculture: 5 CERES
  goddess of plenty: 3 OPS
  goddess of the moon: 4 LUNA
      5 DIANA
  god of love: 4 AMOR
  hearth goddess: 5 VESTA

  historian: 4 LIVY
  holiday: 5 FESTA
  Holy ~ emperor: 4 OTTO
      5 OTTOI 7 LOTHAIR
  household god: 3 LAR
  invasion resister: 5 DRUID
  law: 3 LEX
  magistrate: 5 EDILE
  meeting place: 5 FORUM
  naturalist: 5 PLINY
  official: 7 SENATOR
  orator: 4 **CATO** 6 CICERO
  philosopher: 6 SENECA
  poet: 4 **OVID**
  road: 4 **ITER**
  robe: 4 **TOGA** 5 STOLA
  sandal: 5 SOLEA
  suffix: 5 ESQUE
  sun god: 3 SOL
  temple: 8 PANTHEON
  trio: 3 TRE
  well: 4 BENE
  ~ Zeus: 4 JOVE
Roman ___: 4 NOSE 7 NUMERAL
___-Roman
  wrestling: 5 GRECO
  ___ Romana: 3 PAX
Romance: 3 WOO 4 TALE
      5 GENRE GESTE
  Big name in ~ fiction: 4 AVON
      9 HARLEQUIN
  Call off the: 5 ENDIT
  French: 5 AMOUR
  Hero of medieval. 6 ROLAND
  lang.: 4 ITAL
  Melville's: 4 OMOO
  writer award: 4 RITA
"___ Romance" (Kern tune):
      5 AFINE
Roman Empire
  invader: 4 GOTH
Roman-fleuve: 4 SAGA
Romanian
  coin: 3 LEU
  Former ~ president: 7 ILIESCU
  Former ~ president Iliescu: 3 ION
  ~ Wiesel: 4 ELIE
"Romanian Rhapsodies"
  composer: 6 ENESCO

Romano
cheese source: 3 EWE
TV star: 3 RAY
Romanov
ruler: 4 **TSAR**
Romans: 7 EPISTLE
Book before: 4 ACTS
Romantic: 5 LOVER
interlude: 4 IDYL 5 IDYLL
lead-in: 3 NEO
Like ~ evenings: 7 MOONLIT
rendezvous: 5 TRYST
situation:
    15 ETERNALTRIANGLE
song: 6 BALLAD
writing: 10 LOVELETTER
Romantically
Murmur: 3 COO
Rombauer
Cookbook author: 4 **IRMA**
Rome
Ancient invader of: 4 GOTH
Behold, in old: 4 ECCE
Bishop of: 4 POPE
Capital of: 4 LIRE
First bishop of: 7 STPETER
It was in old: 4 ERAT
Land in old: 5 TERRA
neighbor: 5 UTICA
    7 ATLANTA
Nothing in old: 5 NIHIL
Port of old: 5 **OSTIA**
River of: 5 **TIBER**
Road to old: 4 ITER
To be, in old: 4 ESSE
Year in: 4 ANNO
Years in old: 4 ANNI
Romeo
Emulate: 5 ELOPE
Juliet, to: 3 SUN
Last words of: 4 IDIE
Rival of: 5 PARIS
___ **Romeo:** 4 **ALFA**
"Romeo and Juliet"
Churchyard tree in: 3 YEW
Like: 6 TRAGIC
setting: 6 VERONA
"Romeo Is Bleeding"
actress Lena: 4 OLIN

Romero
Actor: 5 **CESAR**
Rommel
Field marshal: 5 ERWIN
milieu: 6 DESERT
nickname: 9 DESERTFOX
Where ~ was routed:
    9 ELALAMEIN
Romp: 4 LARK SAIL 6 FROLIC
Romper
River: 5 OTTER
"Romper Room"
role model: 5 DOBEE
Romulus: 4 TWIN 6 EPONYM
Twin of: 5 REMUS
Ron
Actor: 3 ELY 5 ONEAL
of baseball: 3 CEY
TV Tarzan: 3 ELY
Rona
Author: 5 JAFFE
Ronnie
Football Hall of Famer: 4 LOTT
Singer: 6 MILSAP
Ronny
Role for: 4 OPIE
Ronny & the Daytonas
1964 ~ hit: 3 GTO
Ronstadt
Singer: 5 LINDA
Roo
Mom of: 5 KANGA
Pal of: 6 EEYORE
Roods
Four: 4 ACRE
Roof
Car ~ variety: 4 TTOP
covering: 3 TAR
edge: 4 EAVE
Hit the: 6 SEERED
Like a bad: 5 LEAKY
of the mouth: 6 PALATE
On the ~ of: 4 ATOP
ornament: 3 EPI
overhang: 4 EAVE
piece: 7 SHINGLE
Restaurant with an orange:
    4 HOJO
support: 6 RAFTER

type: **5** SLATE **6** LEANTO
   7 MANSARD
Roofer: 6 NAILER
Roofing
  material: **3** TAR **4** TILE **5** SLATE
   6 THATCH **8** TARPAPER
  specialist: **6** SLATER
Rooftop
  device: **4** VANE
  fixture: **4** DISH
Rook: 3 GYP **4** BILK **6** CASTLE
  call: **3** CAW
  home: **4** NEST
Rookie: 4 TIRO TYRO **6** NOVICE
   9 GREENHORN
  socialite: **3** DEB
Rookie of the Year
  1951 N.L. ~: **4** MAYS
  1964 A.L. ~: **5** OLIVA
  1966 A.L. ~: **4** AGEE
  1967 NHL ~: **3** ORR
  1968 N.L. ~: **5** BENCH
  1975 A.L. ~: **4** LYNN
  1982 N.L. ~: **8** STEVESAX
  1988 N.L. ~: **4** SABO
  1993 AFC ~: **5** MIRER
  1993 NBA ~: **5** ONEAL
  1995 N.L. ~: **4** NOMO
  1996 A.L. ~: **5** JETER
  1997 N.L. ~: **5** ROLEN
Room: 5 SPACE **6** LEEWAY
  at the top: **4** LOFT **5** **ATTIC**
  Baby: **7** NURSERY
  Chat ~ chuckle: **3** **LOL**
  Clue: **5** STUDY
  Cozy: **3** **DEN**
  décor: **9** WALLPAPER
  divider: **4** WALL
  Drawing: **5** SALON
  Family: **3** DEN
  Growing: **4** ACRE
  Hacienda: **4** SALA
  Harem: **3** **ODA**
  Kind of: **3** **REC** **4** MENS
   5 ELBOW **6** ROMPER
  meas.: **4** SQFT
  on board: **5** CABIN
  Powder: **7** ARSENAL
  Provide a ~ for: **6** RENTTO

Reading: **3** DEN
renter: **3** INN
Sitting: **6** LOUNGE PARLOR
Spa: **5** SAUNA
Style of a: **5** DECOR
TV: **3** DEN
Vaulted: **4** APSE
Waiting ~ call: **4** NEXT
Wash: **7** LAUNDRY
Wiggle: **6** LEEWAY
With ~ to spare: **5** AMPLY
~, in French: **5** SALLE
~, in Spanish: **4** SALA
___ room: **3** REC
Roommate
  of Bert: **5** ERNIE
  of Felix: **5** OSCAR
  of Madison: **5** UNGER
"Room of One's Own, A"
  author: **5** WOOLF
Rooms
  Skylit: **5** ATRIA
Room to swing ___: 4 ACAT
"Room With ___, A": 5 AVIEW
Roomy
  bag: **8** CARRYALL
  dress: **4** TENT **5** ALINE
  vehicle: **3** VAN **5** SEDAN
Roone
  TV exec: **7** ARLEDGE
Rooney
  Commentator: **4** ANDY
Roosevelt: 4 SARA **5** TEDDY
   7 ELEANOR
Roosevelt, Teddy
  group: **11** ROUGHRIDERS
  Home of: **12** SAGAMOREHILL
Roost: 5 PERCH
  Lofty: **5** AERIE
Rooster: 4 COCK MALE
  mate: **3** HEN
  Roof: **4** VANE
  topper: **4** COMB
Root: 5 CAUSE **6** ORIGIN
  Agave: **5** AMOLE
  Edible: **3** YAM **4** TARO
  for: **6** URGEON **7** CHEERON
  Fragrant: **5** ORRIS
  Nobelist: **5** **ELIHU**

Plant: 5 RADIX
Poi: 4 TARO
Take: 5 SETIN
Taro: 4 EDDO
vegetable: 7 PARSNIP
word: 3 OLE RAH

Root beer
brand: 4 DADS NEHI 5 AANDW
  BARQS HIRES
root: 9 SASSAFRAS

Rooter: 3 FAN

Rootlessness: 6 ANOMIE

Roots
Put down: 7 SETTLED
Work on: 3 DYE

"Roots": 4 EPIC SAGA
actor Burton: 5 LEVAR
author Alex: 5 HALEY
author Haley: 4 **ALEX**
Captain Davies on: 7 EDASNER
hero ___ Kinte: 5 KUNTA
role: 5 KINTE
~ Emmy winner: 5 ASNER
  7 EDASNER

Rope
Attach with a: 5 TIEON
Bind with: 4 LASH
Cowboy: 5 LASSO REATA
  RIATA
fiber: 4 BAST HEMP JUTE
  5 **SISAL**
Gaucho: 5 **REATA** RIATA
Horse-training: 5 LONGE
in: 5 LASSO 7 ENSNARE
Looped: 5 NOOSE
Mooring: 6 HAWSER
Separate ~ strands: 5 UNLAY
Unravel a: 4 FRAY

"Rope-a-dope"
boxer: 3 ALI

Roper
Pollster: 4 ELMO
report: 4 POLL

Roper, Mrs.
portrayer Lindley: 5 AUDRA

Ropes: 4 GEAR
One learning the: 7 TRAINEE
Show the ~ to: 5 TEACH TRAIN
  6 ORIENT 7 EDUCATE

Roping
venue: 5 RODEO

Roquefort
hue: 4 BLEU

Rorem
Composer: 3 **NED**

Rorschach
image: 4 **BLOT** 7 INKBLOT

Rosa
of civil rights fame: 5 PARKS

Rosalynn
Daughter of: 3 AMY
successor: 5 NANCY

"Rosanna"
band: 4 TOTO

Rosary
prayer: 8 AVEMARIA
Say the: 4 PRAY
unit: 4 BEAD

Roscoe: 3 GAT ROD 6 HEATER

Rose: 4 GREW 5 STOOD
  7 CLIMBED
home: 3 BED
Love of: 4 **ABIE**
oil: 5 **ATTAR**
part: 3 HIP 4 STEM 5 PETAL
protector: 5 THORN
Red: 4 **PETE**
Rock singer: 3 AXL
shrub family: 4 SLOE 6 SPIREA
___ Rose: 5 TOKYO
"___ Rose": 4 LIDA

Roseanne
1989 ~ film: 8 SHEDEVIL
Comic: 4 BARR
TV daughter of: 7 DARLENE

"Roseanne"
actress Gilbert: 4 **SARA**
Darlene player on: 4 SARA
star: 4 BARR

Rose Bowl
20-time ~ winner: 3 USC
city: 8 PASADENA
team: 3 MSU OSU 4 UCLA

Rosebud: 4 SLED
owner: 4 KANE

"Rose is a rose is a rose"
speaker: 5 STEIN

Rosemary: 4 HERB

portrayer: 3 MIA
"Rosemary's Baby"
  author Ira: 5 LEVIN
  author Levin: 3 IRA
Rosencrantz: 4 DANE 8 COURTIER
"___ Rosenkavalier": 3 **DER**
"Rose of ___, The": 6 TRALEE
"Rose ___ rose ...": 3 ISA
Roses
  Goddess with a crown of:
    5 ERATO
  Oil of: 5 ATTAR
"Roses ___ red ...": 3 ARE
Rosetta
  river: 4 NILE
Rosetta Stone
  stuff: 6 BASALT
Rosewall
  of tennis: 3 KEN
Rosie
  Actress: 5 PEREZ
  Fastener for: 5 RIVET
  Muppet friend of: 4 ELMO
  of tennis: 6 CASALS
  Runner: 4 RUIZ
Rosie the ___: 7 RIVETER
Rosinante
  rider: 10 DONQUIXOTE
"Rosmersholm"
  playwright: 5 IBSEN
Ross
  Flagmaker: 5 BETSY
  Singer: 5 DIANA
Ross, Betsy
  Emulate: 3 SEW
Ross, Diana
  1975 ~ film: 8 MAHOGANY
  1980 ~ hit: 9 ITSMYTURN
  musical: 6 THEWIZ
Ross, Katharine
  1969 ~ role: 9 ETTAPLACE
Rossellini
  Director: 7 ROBERTO
Rossi
  of soccer: 5 PAOLO
Rossini
  creation: 5 OPERA
  song: 4 ARIA
  subject: 4 TELL

Ross Sea
  sight: 4 FLOE
Rostand
  hero: 6 CYRANO
Rosten
  Author: 3 LEO
Roster: 4 ROLL ROTA
  abbr.: 4 ETAL
  Playbill: 4 CAST
  Society: 5 ALIST
Rostropovich
  instrument: 5 CELLO
Roswell
  sighting: 3 UFO
  visitor: 5 ALIEN
Rosy
  Hardly: 4 GRIM 5 ASHEN
Rot: 4 TOSH 5 DECAY GOBAD
    HOOEY 7 TWADDLE
Rota
  Composer: 4 NINO
Rotary
  current: 4 EDDY
  Use a ~ phone: 4 DIAL
Rotate: 4 SPIN TURN 5 TWIRL
Rotating
  disc: 3 **CAM**
Rotation
  About the line of: 5 AXIAL
  Center of: 4 AXIS
  Force of: 6 TORQUE
  Star of the: 3 ACE
ROTC
  relative: 3 OCS
Rote
  exercise: 5 DRILL
Roth
  plan: 3 **IRA**
  Writer: 6 PHILIP
Rotini: 5 PASTA
Rotisserie: 4 OVEN
  part: 3 ROD 4 SPIT
Rotten: 3 BAD 5 AWFUL LOUSY
    6 NOGOOD
  Dirty ~ scoundrel: 5 CREEP
    SWINE
Rotter: 3 CAD CUR
Rotterdam
  Revered name in: 7 ERASMUS

Rotunda
 feature: **4 DOME**
Rouen
 refusal: **3 NON**
 river: **5 SEINE**
 room: **5 SALLE**
"Rouen Cathedral"
 painter: **5 MONET**
Rouge
 In need of: **4 PALE**
 It may be: **3 VIN**
Rough: 4 RUDE 6 COARSE
  SEVERE 7 CRAGGED
  8 UNGENTLE
 cliff: **4 CRAG**
 file: **4 RASP**
 guess: **4 STAB**
 house: **6 LEANTO**
 it: **4 CAMP**
 Prepare for a ~ ride:
  7 STRAPIN
 stuff: **3 ORE 5 EMERY GRASS**
 up: **4 MAUL 5 ABUSE**
 waters: **4 CHOP**
Roughage: 5 FIBER
Roughly: 4 ORSO 5 ABOUT
  CIRCA 6 AROUND
  10 MOREORLESS
 Handle: **4 MAUL 5 PAWAT**
 Tear: **8 LACERATE**
Roulette
 bet: **3 ODD RED 4 EVEN NOIR**
  5 ROUGE
 try: **4 SPIN**
Round
 Bar: **4 ALES**
 building: **4 SILO**
 cheese: **4 EDAM**
 dance: **4 HORA**
 Early: **6 PRELIM**
 ender: **4 BELL**
 figure: **5 BOXER**
 Go a: **4 SPAR**
 Kind of: **5 OVATE**
 Not quite: **4 OVAL 5 OVOID**
 number: **4 ZERO 8 ESTIMATE**
 of applause: **4 HAND**
 of four: **5 SEMIS**
 Pub: **4 ALES**

 roof: **4 DOME**
 sandwich: **4 OREO**
 trip: **5 ORBIT**
 window: **5 OXEYE**
Roundabout
 path: **6 DETOUR**
"Roundabout"
 band: **3 YES**
"Round and Round"
 rock group: **4 RATT**
 singer Perry: **4 COMO**
Rounded
 hammer part: **4 PEEN**
 lump: **4 GLOB**
 up: **6 HERDED**
Roundish: 4 OVAL 5 OVATE
  OVOID
Rounds: 4 AMMO
Round Table
 address: **3 SIR**
 knight: **3 KAY 4 BORS 6 GARETH**
  8 LANCELOT
 ruler: **6 ARTHUR**
Roundup
 rope: **5 LASSO RIATA**
 sound: **3 MOO**
Roundworm: 8 NEMATODE
Rouse: 4 WAKE 6 AWAKEN
Rouser: 5 ALARM
Roush
 of baseball: **3 EDD**
Rousseau
 Artist: **5 HENRI**
 novel: **5 EMILE**
Roustabout
 raising: **4 TENT**
Route: 3 WAY 4 LINE PATH
  6 COURSE
 Bus: **4 LINE**
 Cop: **4 BEAT**
 Direct: **7 BEELINE**
 Main: **7 SEALANE**
 Rheinland: **4 BAHN**
 Rural: **4 LANE**
 Shipping: **7 SEALANE**
 Wheelchair: **4 RAMP**
"Route 66"
 actor George: **7 MAHARIS**
 When ~ was on (abbr.): **3 FRI**

Routes
Like some: **6** SCENIC
Routine: 4 ROTE **5** DRILL
HOHUM USUAL **6** OLDHAT
Comedy: **3** BIT **6** SHTICK
Dull: **3** RUT **4** ROTE
Frenzied: **7** RATRACE
Healthful: **7** REGIMEN
Laborious: **5** GRIND
task: **5** CHORE
Routing
word: **3** VIA
Rover: 5 NOMAD
Command to: **3** SIT **4** HEEL STAY
5 FETCH SPEAK
Friend of: **3** REX **4** FIDO
Ordeal for: **4** BATH
Range: **5** STEER
reprimand: **3** BAD
restraint: **5** CHAIN LEASH
reward: **4** BONE
Scrap for: **3** ORT
warning: **3** GRR **5** SNARL
Roving
adventurously: **6** ERRANT
Row: 3 OAR **4** FRAY RANK SPAT
TIER **5** MELEE SCULL
SETTO **6** FRACAS STROKE
Cannery: **4** TINS
Classroom: **5** DESKS
of bushes: **5** HEDGE
One in a: **3** OAR
Play to the back: **5** EMOTE
producer: **3** HOE
Public: **5** SCENE
Stadium: **4** TIER
Tough ~ to hoe: **6** ORDEAL
Rowan
Designer: **4** RENA
Rowboat
blade: **3** OAR
pair: **4** OARS
Small: **5** SKIFF
**Rowdy ___ ("Rawhide" role):
5** YATES
Rower: 3 OAR
Rowing
need: **3** OAR
team: **4** CREW

Rowland
Actress: **4 GENA**
Columnist: **5** EVANS
Rowling, J.K.
creation: **6** POTTER
Honour given to: **3** OBE
**"Row, Row, Row Your Boat":
5** ROUND
Life, in: **5** DREAM
"Roxanne"
Martin of: **5** STEVE
Roxette
style: **7** EUROPOP
Roxy Music
cofounder: **3 ENO**
Roy
Cartoonist: **4** DOTY
Country singer: **5** ACUFF
Former Colorado governor:
5 ROMER
Lawyer: **4** COHN
of CORE: **5** INNIS
Wife of: **4 DALE**
Royal
address: **4** SIRE **6** MYLORD
ball: **3** ORB
British: **4** ANNE
decree: **5** EDICT
domain: **5** REALM
Eastern: **4** RAJA **RANI**
educator: **4** ETON
elephant: **5** BABAR
flush card: **3** ACE TEN
fur: **5** SABLE **6** ERMINE
headgear: **5** CROWN TIARA
6 DIADEM
home: **6** CASTLE PALACE
Indian: **4** RAJA RANI
irritant: **3** PEA
issue: **6** PRINCE
jelly maker: **3** BEE
messenger: **6** HERALD
Mideast ~ name: **4** SAUD
Norwegian ~ name: **4** OLAF
OLAV
pain: **4** PEST
princess: **4** ANNE
rule: **5** REIGN
Russian: **4** TSAR

Saudi ~ name: **4** FAHD **6** FAISAL
seat: **6** THRONE
symbol: **3** ORB
wish: **3** SON
Royal Botanical Gardens
locale: **3** KEW
Royal Crown: 4 COLA
brand: **4** NEHI
Royale
automaker: **3** REO
___ Royale: 4 ISLE
"___ Royale": 6 CASINO
Royalty
Indian: **4** RANI **5** RANIS
receiver: **6** AUTHOR
Spanish: **5** REYES **6** REINAS
"Star Wars": **4** LEIA
ROY G. ___ : 3 BIV
ROY G. BIV
Part of: **3** RED **6** INDIGO
VIOLET
Roz
portrayer on "Frasier": **4** PERI
Role for: **4** MAME
Rozelle
Football exec: **4** **PETE**
RPI
grad: **4** ENGR
grads: **3** EES
Part of: **4** INST
RPM
indicator: **4** TACH
The P in: **3** PER
RR
employee: **4** ENGR
Former ~ regulator: **3** ICC
stop: **3** **STA** STN
RR ___ : 4 XING
R-rated
~, maybe: **4** GORY RACY
5 ADULT **6** EROTIC STEAMY
RSVP
enclosure: **4** SASE
Part of: **3** **SIL** **4** VOUS **5** PLAIT
Rte.: 3 HWY RDS *(plural)* TPK
Backwoods: **3** RFD
City: **3** AVE
East Coast: **5** USONE
recommenders: **3** AAA

Ruark
novel: **5** UHURU
Rub: 4 WIPE **6** ABRADE
and rub: **5** SCOUR
it in: **5** GLOAT
off: **6** ABRADE
on: **6** ANOINT
out: **3** OFF **4** DOIN KILL SLAY
5 **ERASE**
the right way: **3** PET
the wrong way: **3** IRK **4** RILE
5 CHAFE **6** NETTLE
together: **5** GNASH
Violinist's: **5** ROSIN
You might ~ one out: **5** GENIE
Rub-___ : 4 ADUB
"Rubáiyát"
poet: **4** OMAR
Rubber: 5 TIRES **6** ERASER
7 MASSEUR **8** MASSEUSE
Burn: **5** SPEED
center: **5** AKRON
ducky spot: **4** BATH
gasket: **5** ORING
Hard: **7** EBONITE
Kind of: **4** FOAM **5** INDIA
Leave: **5** ERASE
Letters on a ~ check: **3** NSF
Pitcher: **4** SLAB
Prepare to burn: **3** REV
ring: **6** GASKET
source: **5** LATEX
Synthetic ~ componet:
7 STYRENE
Rubber ___ : 6 CEMENT
"Rubber Duckie"
singer: **5** ERNIE
Rubbermaid
Home of: **4** OHIO
Rubberneck: 3 EYE **4** GAPE
GAWK OGLE **5** CRANE
STARE
Rubber-stamp: 4 OKAY
Rubbish: 3 ROT **4** CRUD
5 DROSS OFFAL **TRIPE**
6 DEBRIS
Rubble
maker: **3** TNT
Rocky: **5** SCREE

Rubdown
  target: 4 ACHE
Rube: 4 HICK 5 RURAL YOKEL
    7 HAYSEED
  of Red: 4 CLEM
Rubella
  symptom: 4 RASH
Rubenesque: 6 ZAFTIG
Rubicon
  crosser: 6 CAESAR
Rubicund: 3 RED
Rubik
  creation: 4 CUBE
Rubik's Cube
  inventor Rubik: 4 **ERNO**
Rubinstein
  Pianist: 5 ANTON ARTUR
Ruble
  part: 5 KOPEK 6 KOPECK
Ruby: 3 GEM 7 CARMINE
    DEEPRED
  Actress: 3 **DEE**
Ruby-like
  gem: 6 SPINEL
Ruckus: 3 **ADO** DIN 4 FLAP STIR
    TODO 5 HOOHA MELEE
    NOISE SCENE
Rudder
  control: 6 TILLER
  locale: 5 STERN
  support: 4 SKEG
  Take the: 5 STEER
  Toward the: 3 AFT 6 ASTERN
Ruddy
  Hardly: 3 WAN 4 ASHY PALE
    5 PASTY
Rude: 5 SURLY 8 INSOLENT
  Be ~ in line: 5 SHOVE
  Less: 5 NICER
  look: 4 LEER 5 STARE
  one: 3 CAD 4 BOOR 5 CHURL
Rudely
  Awaken: 5 ROUST
  brief: 4 CURT
  ignore: 4 SNUB
  Nudge: 5 ELBOW
  sarcastic: 5 SNIDE
  Stare: 4 OGLE
  Take: 4 GRAB

  Treat: 5 SHOVE
Rudge
  Fictional: 7 BARNABY
Rudimentary: 5 BASIC CRUDE
  seed: 5 OVULE
Rudiments: 4 **ABCS**
Rudner
  Comic: 4 **RITA**
Rudolf
  Infamous: 4 HESS
  Pianist: 6 SERKIN
Rudolph
  Runner: 5 WILMA
  trademark: 7 REDNOSE
Rue: 6 REGRET
  Costar of: 3 BEA
  the run: 4 ACHE
Rueful: 5 SORRY
"Rue Morgue"
  author: 3 POE
  culprit: 3 APE
Ruff
  stuff: 4 LACE
Ruffian: 4 GOON THUG 5 BRUTE
    6 MAULER
Ruffle: 3 IRK 4 STIR
  feathers: 4 RILE
Rug: 6 TOUPEE
  cleaner, for short: 3 VAC
  Cut a: 5 DANCE
  fiber: 5 SISAL
  Fix a: 7 REWEAVE
  Kind of: 3 RYA 4 AREA 5 SISAL
    6 NAVAJO
  Like a bug in a: 4 SNUG
  rat: 3 **TOT** 4 TYKE 6 MOPPET
  Scandinavian: 3 RYA
  Shag ~ feature: 4 PILE
  Small: 3 MAT
  Sweep under the: 4 HIDE
  Use a prayer: 5 KNEEL
Rugby
  formation: 5 SCRUM
Rugged
  range: 6 SIERRA
  ridge: 5 **ARETE**
  rock: 4 **CRAG**
Rugrat: 3 TOT 4 TYKE
    6 MOPPET

"Rugrats"
dad: 3 STU
Tommy's kid brother on: 3 DIL
Ruhr
city: 5 **ESSEN**
refusal: 4 NEIN
Ruin: 3 MAR 4 BANE DOIN DOOM
HARM UNDO 5 WRACK
WRECK
Bring ~ on: 6 RAVAGE
Cause of: 4 BANE
Partner of: 4 RACK 5 WRACK
Rack and: 5 HAVOC
~, old-style: 5 STROY
Ruination: 4 **BANE** DOOM
Ruined: 4 SHOT 5 KAPUT
6 SPOILT
Rukeyser
Host: 5 LOUIS
Rule: 5 REIGN 6 GOVERN
Actress: 6 JANICE
As a: 9 INGENERAL
Brief: 3 REG
British ~ in India: 3 **RAJ**
Corporate: 5 BYLAW
Golden ~ word: 4 **UNTO**
Kind of: 3 MOB 4 HOME
Last word of the golden: 3 YOU
out: 3 BAN BAR NIX 6 NEGATE
Standard: 5 BYLAW
to live by: 5 TENET
___ rule: 3 ASA
"Rule, Britannia"
composer: 4 **ARNE**
Ruled: 3 RAN 4 LINY
"___ Ruled the World" (1965 hit):
3 IFI
Ruler
at Karnak: 6 RAMSES
Bygone: 3 DEY 4 CZAR SHAH
TSAR
Hereditary: 6 DYNAST
in Borneo: 5 RAJAH
length: 4 FOOT 7 ONEFOOT
Mesopotamian: 6 SARGON
Mideast: 4 EMIR SHAH 5 AMEER
EMEER
Olympian: 4 ZEUS
Petty: 6 SATRAP

Terrible: 4 IVAN
Turkish: 5 PASHA
unit: 4 INCH
Rules
Follow the: 4 OBEY
maven: 5 HOYLE
of conduct: 6 ETHICS
One who ~ the roast: 5 EMCEE
Org. with eligibility: 4 NCAA
Relax, as: 4 BEND
System of: 4 CODE
Ruling
body: 6 REGIME
Court: 3 LET
group: 5 JUNTA
Ref: 3 TKO
"Ruling Class, The"
star: 6 OTOOLE
Rulings: 5 DICTA
Rum
cake: 4 **BABA**
Cuban: 3 RON
drink: 4 GROG 6 COLADA
MAITAI
~, to some: 5 DEMON
Rumba: 5 DANCE
relative: 5 MAMBO
Rum-based
liqueur: 8 TIAMARIA
Rumble: 4 ROAR 5 MELEE
Car with a ~ seat: 8 ROADSTER
"Rumble in the Jungle"
site: 5 ZAIRE
Rumbler
Sicilian: 4 ETNA
Rumblers
Chicago: 3 ELS
Ruminant
chew: 3 CUD
Rain forest: 5 OKAPI
Third stomach of a: 6 OMASUM
Ruminate: 4 CHEW MUSE
Rummikub
piece: 4 TILE
Rummy: 3 SOT 5 SOUSE
game: 3 GIN 4 TONK
variety: 3 GIN 7 CANASTA
Rumor: 4 TALE 6 GOSSIP
REPORT

generator: 4 MILL
Nasty: 6 CANARD
starter: 5 IHEAR
Rumormonger: 5 YENTA
Rumors
Like some: 4 IDLE
Rump
neighbor: 7 SIRLOIN
Rumpelstiltskin
Imitated: 4 SPUN
Rumple: 4 MUSS
Rumpled: 5 MESSY
Rumpus: 3 ADO 4 TODO
6 SHINDY
Rumsfeld
org.: 3 DOD
predecessor: 5 COHEN
Rum ___ Tugger ("Cats"
character): 3 TUM
Run: 3 HIE LAM 4 COST FLEE
LOPE 5 BLEED SCOOT
SPATE 6 DIRECT MANAGE
SERIES 7 **OPERATE**
after: 5 CHASE
Alphabet: 3 ABC BCD CDE *etc.*
amok: 4 RIOT
a tab: 3 OWE
away: 4 FLEE
Bond on the: 5 ELOPE
Bull: 3 LEA
Dry: 4 TEST 5 TRIAL
easily: 4 LOPE TROT
Good: 6 STREAK
in: 3 NAB 6 ARREST
in neutral: 4 **IDLE**
in the raw: 6 STREAK
in the wash: 5 BLEED
into: 3 RAM 4 **MEET**
7 REAREND
like heck: 4 TEAR
off: 4 BOLT FLEE 5 PRINT
REPEL
One on the: 5 FLEER 7 ESCAPEE
One way to: 3 JOG 4 **AMOK**
WILD 6 SCARED
Opening: 4 ABCD
out: 3 END 5 LAPSE 6 ELAPSE
EXPIRE
out of: 5 USEUP

out of gas: 3 DIE 4 TIRE
out of steam: 3 DIE 4 TIRE
out on: 6 DESERT 7 ABANDON
playfully: 4 ROMP
Prepare to: 4 EDIT
Risky way to: 7 ONEMPTY
Short: 4 DASH
Ski: 5 PISTE SLOPE
smoothly: 3 HUM 4 FLOW PURR
the show: 4 RULE 5 EMCEE
REIGN
They ~ errands: 6 GOFERS
They ~ in the kitchen: 4 TAPS
They ~ when broken: 4 EGGS
through: 4 GORE STAB 5 USEUP
6 IMPALE PIERCE SKEWER
8 REHEARSE
Trial: 4 PREP
up: 5 AMASS INCUR
Wrong way to: 7 AGROUND
Run ___ : 4 AMOK ATAB
Run-___ (of hip-hop): 3 DMC
"Runaround Sue"
singer: 4 DION
Runaway: 4 ROMP 7 RAMPANT
of rhyme: 5 SPOON
"Runaway"
singer Shannon: 3 DEL
"Runaway Bride"
Richard of: 4 GERE
Rundgren
Singer: 4 TODD
Rundown: 5 RECAP
Run-down: 5 SEAMY **SEEDY**
6 SORDID
area: 4 SLUM 6 GHETTO
building: 8 TENEMENT
Rung: 4 STEP
Rope ~ on a ship: 7 RATLINE
Run-in: 3 ROW 4 SPAT
Runner: 5 GOFER 7 ATHLETE
Australian: 3 EMU
Distance: 5 MILER
Easy: 5 LOPER
Errand: 5 GOFER
Fast: 4 HARE
Forest: 3 SAP
goal: 4 TAPE
Graceful: 7 ARABIAN

Maze: **3** RAT **6** LABRAT
Nov.: **3** POL
Pamplona: **4** TORO
path: **8** BASELINE
Road: **3** CAR **4** AUTO
Senate: **4** PAGE
Winter: **4** SLED
Runners: 4 LEGS
carry it: **4** SLED
Runner-up: 5 LOSER
Fabled: **4** HARE
to Ike: **5** ADLAI
Running: 8 ONTHELAM
behind: **4** LATE **5** TARDY
game: **3** TAG
mates: **3** VPS **5** VEEPS
Stop: **3** DIE
things: **8** INCHARGE
Those ~ the place (abbr.):
    4 MGMT
total: **5** TALLY
track: **4** OVAL
wild: **4** AMOK **5** ARIOT
    7 ONATEAR
Running mate
1968 ~ of Wallace: **5** LEMAY
Adlai's: **5 ESTES**
Dole's: **4 KEMP**
Mondale's: **7** FERRARO
Nixon's: **5** AGNEW
"Running on Empty"
singer: **13** JACKSONBROWNE
"Runnin' Rebels, The": 4 UNLV
Run ___ of: 5 AFOUL
Runoff
spot: **6** RAVINE
Typographical: **5** WIDOW
Run ___ of the law: 5 AFOUL
Run-of-the-mill: 4 SOSO **5** USUAL
    6 COMMON **7** AVERAGE
(abbr.): **3** ORD
"Run ___ Run" (1998 film):
    4 LOLA
Runs: 4 GOES
It ~ from stem to stern:
    4 KEEL
Runt: 8 LITTLEST
Like a: **7** WEAKEST
Runway: 6 TARMAC

Banks on the: **4** TYRA
Hit the: **4** LAND **6** ALIGHT
model: **5** PLANE
Move down the: **6** SASHAY
Roll on a: **4** TAXI
walker: **5** MODEL
Runyon
Writer: **5** DAMON
Rupees
Where ~ are spent: **5** INDIA
    NEPAL
Rupert
Actor: **7** EVERETT
Rupture: 4 REND TEAR
"R.U.R."
playwright: **5** CAPEK
Rural: 6 RUSTIC
carriage: **4** SHAY
expanse: **3** LEA
fight: **6** RASSLE
get-together: **3** BEE
hotel: **3** INN
Like many ~ roads: **7** ONELANE
Not: **5** URBAN
outing: **7** HAYRIDE
    9 STATEFAIR
route: **4** LANE
storehouse: **4** SILO
structure: **4** BARN
Ruse: 3 CON **4** PLOY WILE
Rush: 3 HIE **4** RACE REED ZOOM
    5 HASTE HURRY RUNAT
    SPURT STORM SURGE
    6 HASTEN SCURRY
    8 STEPONIT
letters: **4 ASAP**
People ~ to get in here: **4** FRAT
site: **5** MARSH
Sudden: **5** SPATE
"Rush!": 4 ASAP
Rush, Geoffrey
Oscar-winning film starring:
    5 SHINE
Rushdie
Author: **6** SALMAN
Like the Verses of: **7** SATANIC
Rushed: 5 HADAT RANAT
Rush hour: 3 SIX
subway rarity: **4** SEAT

traffic facilitator: 7 HOVLANE
"Rush Hour"
    star Jackie: 4 CHAN
Rushing
    place: 4 FRAT
    sound: 6 SWOOSH
Rushlike
    plant: 5 SEDGE
"Rushmore"
    director Anderson: 3 WES
    ___ Rushmore: 5 MOUNT
"Rush, Rush"
    singer Abdul: 5 PAULA
    singer Paula: 5 ABDUL
Russ
    Director: 5 MEYER
Russell
    Actor: 4 KURT
    Actress: 7 THERESA
    "Felicity" star: 4 KERI
    Oscar winner: 5 CROWE
    Rocker: 4 LEON
Russell, Rosalind
    1948 ~ film, with "The":
        11 VELVETTOUCH
    1958 ~ comedy:
        10 AUNTIEMAME
    role: 4 MAME
Russell Cave Natl. Mon.
    locale: 3 ALA
Russert
    Moderator: 3 TIM
Russert, Tim
    venue: 4 CNBC
Russia
    Popular game from: 6 TETRIS
    Trotsky of: 4 LEON
"___ Russia $1200" (Bob Hope
book): 4 IOWE
Russian
    alternative: 5 RANCH
    auto make: 4 LADA
    ballet company: 5 KIROV
    blue: 3 CAT
    capital: 6 MOSCOW
    carriage: 6 TROIKA
    city: 4 OMSK OREL
    coin: 5 RUBLE
    comrade: 8 TOVARICH

cooperative: 5 ARTEL
country home: 5 **DACHA**
czar known as "The Great":
    6 PETERI
dish: 5 BLINI
empress: 7 TSARINA
fighter: 3 **MIG**
Former ~ council: 6 SOVIET
Former ~ space station: 3 **MIR**
grassland: 6 STEPPE
John, in: 4 IVAN
legislature: 4 DUMA
mountains: 5 URALS
name meaning holy: 4 OLGA
news agency: 4 TASS
novelist: 5 GOGOL GORKI
Old ~ ruler: 4 CZAR **TSAR**
pancakes: 5 BLINI
peace: 3 MIR
plain: 6 STEPPE
range: 5 URALS
refusal: 4 NYET
retreat: 5 DACHA
revolutionary: 5 LENIN
river: 3 OKA 4 LENA NEVA
    URAL
urn: 7 SAMOVAR
wolfhound: 6 BORZOI
Russian America
    Capital of: 5 SITKA
Russian-born
    artist: 4 ERTE
Russian Orthodox
    First ~ saint: 4 OLGA
Russians
    Some: 6 ASIANS TATARS
Russo
    Actress: 4 **RENE**
Rust: 5 **OXIDE** 7 OXIDATE
Rustic: 4 HICK RUBE 5 YOKEL
    digs: 5 CABIN
    locale: 3 LEA
    pipe: 4 REED
Rustle: 5 SWISH
Rustler
    chaser: 5 POSSE
    target: 4 HERD
Rustling
    sound: 6 SWOOSH

Rusty
  of baseball: 5 STAUB
Rut
  In a: 5 STUCK
  Words before: 3 INA
Rutabaga: 5 SWEDE 6 TURNIP
Rutger
  Actor: 5 HAUER
Rutgers
  river: 7 RARITAN
  team color: 7 SCARLET
Ruth
  Colleague of: 4 ARTE
  Husband of: 4 BOAZ
  Mother-in-law of: 5 NAOMI
  nickname: 4 BABE 7 BAMBINO
      THEBABE
  Retired number of: 5 THREE
  successor: 5 AARON
  sultanate: 4 SWAT
Ruthless: 9 CUTTHROAT
      DOGEATDOG
  boss: 4 AXER
RV
  connection: 3 STU
  stop: 3 KOA
R-V
  hookup: 3 STU
  link: 3 **STU**
Rwanda
  native: 4 HUTU
RWE
  Part of: 5 WALDO
Rwy.
  stop: 3 STA
Rx
  amount: 4 DOSE

  amt.: 3 TSP
  dispenser (abbr.): 4 PHAR
  Four times a day, in an: 3 QID
  Needing no: 3 OTC
  Three times, in an: 3 TER
  watchdog: 3 FDA
  writers: 3 DRS MDS
Ryan
  (abbr.): 3 PVT
  Actor: 5 ONEAL
  Actress: 3 **MEG** 4 JERI 5 IRENE
  Daughter of: 5 TATUM
  Hall of Fame pitcher: 5 **NOLAN**
  Like seven ~ games: 5 NOHIT
  portrayer: 5 DAMON
Ryan, Meg
  1989 ~ film: 3 DOA
Ryan, Nolan
  ~, once: 5 ASTRO
Ryan, Robert
  1949 ~ film: 8 THESETUP
"Ryan Express, The": 5 NOLAN
"Ryan's Hope"
  actress Kristen: 5 ILENE
Ryder
  Actress: 6 WINONA
  rival: 5 UHAUL
  ___-Ryder Open: 5 DORAL
Rye: 5 BREAD
  alternative: 10 WHITEBREAD
      WHOLEWHEAT
  buy: 4 LOAF
  Deli meat on: 8 PASTRAMI
  fungus: 5 ERGOT
  Wry ~ rhymer: 4 NASH
Ryun, Jim
  distance: 4 MILE

Ss

S: 3 DIR 4 SIZE
    15 SYMBOLFORSULFUR
  Code word for: 6 SIERRA
  in RSVP: 3 SIL
  in WASP: 5 SAXON
  Not quite: 3 SSE
  of CBS: 3 SYS
  shape: 4 OGEE
Saab
  Fashion designer: 4 ELIE
  model: 4 AERO
Saarinen
  Architect: 4 **EERO**
  The elder: 5 ELIEL
Saatchi & Saatchi
  award: 4 CLIO
  employees: 5 ADMEN
Sábado: 3 DIA
Sabbath
  Observe the: 4 REST
  talk (abbr.): 3 SER
  ___ Sabe: 4 KEMO
Saber
  relative: 4 EPEE
Saberhagen
  of baseball: 4 BRET
Saber-rattling: 6 THREAT
Sabin
  Like the ~ vaccine: 4 ORAL
  rival: 4 SALK
Sabina, Poppaea
  Husband of: 4 NERO
Sable: 3 FUR
  kin: 6 MARTEN
  maker, for short: 4 MERC
Sabres
  gp.: 3 NHL
Sac
  Anatomical: 4 CYST
    5 BURSA
  Form into a: 6 ENCYST
  Of the embryo: 8 AMNIOTIC
  prefix: 3 OVI

SAC
  letters: 4 USAF
Sacajawea: 5 GUIDE
  craft: 5 CANOE
  denomination: 3 ONE
Saccharin
  discoverer Remsen: 3 IRA
Saccharine: 5 SWEET 6 SUGARY
Sacco
  of Sacco and Vanzetti:
    6 NICOLA
Sacher
  dessert: 5 TORTE
Sachet
  emanation: 5 AROMA SCENT
  scent: 5 LILAC
Sachs
  Poet: 5 NELLY
Sack: 3 AXE BAG BED CAN ROB
    4 BOOT LOOT 6 RAVAGE
    7 PILLAGE
  Camp: 3 COT
  Give the: 4 FIRE
  In the: 4 ABED
  Leave the: 5 ARISE
  out: 5 SLEEP
  Out of the: 5 ASTIR RISEN
  Ready for the: 4 BEAT
  Simple: 3 COT
  sound: 5 SNORE
  weight: 5 TENLB
Sackcloth
  Don: 6 REPENT
  partner: 5 ASHES
Sacked: 5 INBED
  out: 5 INBED SLEPT
"Sack Look"
  designer Christian: 4 DIOR
Sacramento
  arena: 4 ARCO
  City near: 4 LODI
"Sacre ___!": 4 BLEU
Sacred: 4 HOLY

beetle: 6 SCARAB
bird: 4 **IBIS**
bull: 4 APIS
chest: 3 ARK
cow: 4 IDOL
hymn: 5 PSALM
image: 4 ICON IKON
Make: 6 ANOINT
place: 5 ALTAR
poem: 5 PSALM
prefix: 5 HIERO
river: 4 ALPH
scroll: 5 TORAH
song: 5 MOTET **PSALM**
syllables: 3 OMS
text: 5 KORAN TORAH
"Sacred Wood, The"
writer: 5 ELIOT
Sacrifice
Certain: 4 BUNT
fly stat: 3 RBI
site: 5 ALTAR
Sacro
suffix: 5 ILIAC
Sacs: 6 BURSAE
Spore: 4 ASCI
Sad: 3 LOW 4 BLUE DOWN GLUM
5 TEARY
notice: 4 OBIT
piece: 5 ELEGY
song: 5 **DIRGE**
sound: 3 SOB
to say: 4 ALAS
___ Sad: 4 NOVI
Sadat
of Egypt: 5 **ANWAR**
predecessor: 6 NASSER
Saddam: 5 IRAQI
Sadden: 7 DEPRESS
Saddle
In the: 7 ASTRIDE
part: 4 HORN
Saddler
tool: 3 AWL
Sad-faced
comedian: 7 BENBLUE
"___ Sadie" (Beatles song):
4 SEXY
"Sadly ...": 4 ALAS

Sadness: 3 WOE 5 TEARS
6 SORROW
Sign of: 4 TEAR
Sound of: 4 MOAN
"Sad to say ...": 4 ALAS
Safari: 4 TREK
gateway: 7 NAIROBI
leader: 5 BWANA
lodging: 4 TENT
park: 3 ZOO
sight: 3 GNU 4 LION 5 RHINO
Safe
deposit box item: 4 DEED
harbor: 4 COVE
havens: 5 ASYLA
Make: 6 SECURE
on board: 4 ALEE
On the ~ side: 4 **ALEE**
or out: 4 CALL
Person with a ~ job: 4 YEGG
place: 4 BANK 5 HAVEN VAULT
6 REFUGE
spot: 4 WALL 5 HAVEN
Symbol of ~ passage: 3 ARK
to consume: 6 EDIBLE
Safecracker: 4 YEGG
Safeguard: 4 KEEP 6 ENSURE
INSURE
Safekeeper
Sailor's: 6 STELMO
Safekeeping: 4 CARE
Safer
coworker: 5 STAHL
8 REASONER
network: 3 CBS
Newsman: 6 MORLEY
On the ~ side: 4 ALEE
Safety: 4 BACK
Air ~ gp.: 3 FAA
Auto ~ device: 6 AIRBAG
7 ROLLBAR
device: 3 NET
gp.: 4 MADD SADD
org.: 4 OSHA
signal: 8 ALLCLEAR
Staircase ~ feature: 4 RAIL
Workplace ~ org.: 4 OSHA
Saffron
Dish made with: 6 PAELLA

Safin
 2000 U.S. Open winner ~:
  5 MARAT
Safire
 subject: 5 USAGE
Sag: 5 DROOP
SAG
 Former ~ president: 5 ASNER
 member: 5 ACTOR
Saga: 4 EPIC TALE
 Icelandic: 4 EDDA
Sagacious: 4 WISE
Sagacity: 6 ACUMEN
Sagal
 Actress: 5 KATEY
Sagan
 Astronomer: 4 CARL
 book and series: 6 COSMOS
 subj.: 4 ASTR
Sage: 4 HERB WISE 5 SOLON
  6 SAVANT
 Hindu: 5 RISHI SWAMI
 Sci-fi: 4 YODA
Sagebrush State: 6 NEVADA
 native: 7 NEVADAN
Sage of Concord, The:
  7 EMERSON
Sager, ___ Bayer
 Songwriter: 6 CAROLE
Saginaw Bay
 lake: 5 HURON
Sagittarius: 6 ARCHER
Saguaro
 and others: 5 CACTI
Sahara: 6 DESERT
 beast: 5 CAMEL
 Like the: 4 ARID SERE
 rarity: 4 RAIN
 sight: 4 DUNE
 stop: 5 OASIS
 stops: 5 OASES
Saharan: 4 ARID
 nation: 4 MALI 5 LIBYA
 sight: 4 DUNE
 wind: 7 SIROCCO
Sahib
 in Swahili: 5 BWANA
Sahl
 Humorist: 4 **MORT**

Said: 6 STATED 7 UTTERED
 "#@$%!": 5 SWORE
 with a sneer: 5 SNIDE
 ~, old-style: 5 SPAKE
"___ said ...": 3 ASI
Saigon
 former enemy: 5 HANOI
 site, for short: 3 NAM
 ~ New Year: 3 TET
"Saigon"
 star Alan: 4 LADD
Sail
 extender: 5 SPRIT
 Forward: 3 JIB
 holder: 4 MAST
 Ready, as a: 5 ATRIP
 Set: 3 RIG 6 EMBARK
  8 PUTTOSEA
 spar: 5 SPRIT
 support: 4 MAST 7 YARDARM
 through: 3 ACE
 Triangular: 3 **JIB** 6 LATEEN
  9 GOOSEWING
 Under: 4 ASEA 5 ATSEA
Sailboat
 Arab: 4 DHOW
 feature: 4 MAST
 pole: 5 SPRIT
Sailcloth
 fiber: 4 HEMP
Sailed: 6 BOATED
Sailer
 of 1492: 4 NINA
Sailing: 4 **ASEA** 5 ATSEA
  8 OUTTOSEA
 hailing: 4 AHOY
 hazard: 4 REEF 5 SHOAL
 maneuver: 4 TACK
 race: 7 REGATTA
 Small ~ vessel: 4 YAWL
 Smooth: 4 EASE
Sailor: 3 GOB **TAR** 4 SALT
  6 SEAMAN
  8 SEAFARER
 command: 5 AVAST
 direction: 4 ALEE
 drink: 4 GROG
 expertise: 5 KNOTS
 greeting: 4 AHOY

Indian: 6 LASCAR
jail: 4 BRIG
left: 4 PORT
of myth: 6 SINBAD
or boater: 3 HAT
patron: 4 ELMO 6 STELMO
punishment: 4 LASH
saint: 4 **ELMO**
speed: 5 KNOTS
stop: 5 AVAST
tale: 4 YARN
temptress: 7 LORELEI
Veteran: 6 SEADOG
yes: 3 AYE
Sailors: 4 CREW
"Sailor's Song"
Words repeated in: 5 TOSEA
Sailplane: 4 SOAR
"Sail ___ Ship of State!": 3 ONO
Saint
Actress: 8 EVAMARIE
Canterbury: 6 ANSELM
Fiery: 4 ELMO
Home of a: 6 ASSISI
Norwegian: 4 **OLAF** OLAV
Patron ~ of France: 5 DENIS
picture: 4 ICON
Russian Orthodox: 4 OLGA
Sailor: 4 **ELMO**
"Venerable": 4 BEDE
Saint, ___ Marie
Actress: 3 EVA
Saint-___
(French resort): 6 TROPEZ
(Loire's capital): 7 ETIENNE
Saint-___, Camille
Composer: 5 SAENS
"Saint, The"
actor Kilmer: 3 VAL
actress Elisabeth: 4 SHUE
Saint Catherine
home: 5 SIENA
Saint Clare
home: 6 ASSISI
Sainted
king: 4 OLAV
~ 5th-century pope: 4 LEOI
~ 7th-century pope: 5 LEOII
Sainte-___, Quebec: 3 FOY

Saint-Exupéry
classic: 15 THELITTLEPRINCE
Writer ___ de ~: 7 ANTOINE
Saint Francis
home: 6 ASSISI
Sainthood
Fit for: 4 HOLY
"Saint Joan"
monogram: 3 GBS
playwright: 4 SHAW
star Jean: 6 SEBERG
Saintly: 4 GOOD 7 ANGELIC
glow: 4 AURA HALO
symbol: 4 HALO
Saint Patrick
land: 4 EIRE
Saint Philip ___: 4 NERI
Saints
gp.: 3 NFC NFL
Some: 7 MARTYRS
Saint-___, Switzerland: 6 MORITZ
Saint Teresa
Home of: 5 AVILA
Saint-Tropez
locale: 7 RIVIERA
Saison
Une: 3 ETE
"___ Saison en Enfer": 3 UNE
Sajak: 5 EMCEE
Request to: 3 ANE
show: 5 WHEEL
Sake
Dish seasoned with: 8 TERIYAKI
For safety's: 6 INCASE
Source of: 4 RICE
Sakharov
Nobelist: 6 **ANDREI**
Saki: 7 PENNAME
real name: 5 MUNRO
title: 4 ESME
Sal
Actor: 5 MINEO
canal: 4 **ERIE**
of song: 3 GAL
Salaam: 3 BOW 9 OBEISANCE
Salacious: 4 LEWD
look: 4 LEER
Salad
Bitter ~ item: 6 ENDIVE

9 DANDELION
Cabbage: 4 SLAW
Caesar ~ ingredient: 3 OVA
cheese: 4 **FETA**
choice: 6 CAESAR
Cobb ~ ingredient: 5 BACON
Crunchy ~ bit: 4 BACO
dressing choice: 5 RANCH
dressing ingredient: 3 OIL
fish: 4 TUNA
follower: 6 ENTREE
fruit: 4 KIWI 7 AVOCADO
garnish: 5 CRESS
green: 5 **CRESS** 6 ENDIVE
    8 ESCAROLE
ingredient: 4 CUKE 5 FRUIT
    OLIVE ONION 6 ENDIVE
    TOMATO 7 ARUGULA
    LETTUCE ROMAINE
    8 CHICKPEA
    10 BELLPEPPER
In one's ~ days: 5 YOUNG
Kind of: 4 TACO TUNA 5 CHEFS
    PASTA 6 CAESAR POTATO
leaf: 6 ENDIVE
Like much: 6 TOSSED
Like some ~ dressings:
    6 ONIONY
oil holder: 5 CRUET
Prepare a: 4 TOSS
preparer: 6 TOSSER
servers: 5 TONGS
slice: 6 RADISH
sort: 5 CHEFS
topping: 3 OIL 8 CROUTONS
veggie: 4 CUKE 5 CRESS
    6 ENDIVE
Waldorf ~ ingredient: 6 CELERY
Salad bowl
wood: 4 TEAK
Salad dressing
ingredient: 3 OIL
Salade Niçoise
ingredient: 4 TUNA
Salamander: 3 EFT 4 **NEWT**
Two-legged: 6 MUDEEL
Salami
choice: 5 **GENOA**
hangout: 4 DELI

Salary: 3 PAY 4 WAGE 5 WAGES
increase: 5 RAISE
limit: 3 CAP
Salchow
relative: 4 AXEL
Sale
abbr.: 3 IRR
condition: 4 **ASIS**
Fabrics for: 8 DRYGOODS
item, often: 4 **DEMO**
Kind of: 6 ESTATE REDTAG
Like some ~ items: 4 USED
Put up for: 5 OFFER
Records a: 7 RINGSUP
sign: 4 ASIS
site: 4 YARD
word: 4 ONLY
Salem
City between Boston and: 4 LYNN
state: 6 OREGON
Salerno
Info: Italian cue
send-off: 4 CIAO
She, in: 4 ESSA
Sales
agents: 4 REPS
booth: 5 KIOSK
dept. worker: 3 AGT
force: 4 REPS
goal: 5 QUOTA
incentive: 6 REBATE
meeting aid: 5 GRAPH
online: 5 ETAIL
pitch: 3 PIE 5 SPIEL
rep.: 3 AGT
slip (abbr.): 3 RCT 4 RCPT
Ticket: 4 GATE
Salesman: 3 REP
Fictional: 5 LOMAN
goal: 5 ORDER
Miller: 5 LOMAN
pitch: 5 SPIEL
place: 4 ROAD
stock: 4 LINE
Salesperson: 3 REP 5 CLERK
Salieri
Slow, to: 5 LENTO
Saline
drop: 4 TEAR

Salinger
  character: 4 ESME 6 HOLDEN
  dedicatee: 4 **ESME**
  girl: 4 **ESME**
  hero: 15 HOLDENCAULFIELD
  or Trudeau: 6 PIERRE
  title character: 4 ESME 5 ZOOEY
Salisbury
  Capital once known as:
    6 HARARE
Salisbury Plain
  monument: 10 STONEHENGE
Saliva: 7 SPITTLE
Salivate: 5 DROOL
Salk
  and Pepper (abbr.): 3 DRS
  conquest: 5 POLIO
  contemporary: 5 SABIN
  Dr.: 5 JONAS
Sallie ___: 3 MAE
Sally
  and Ayn: 5 RANDS
  Astronaut: 4 RIDE
  ~, to Charlie Brown: 6 SISTER
Sally Ann
  Actress: 5 HOWES
Sally ___ cake: 4 LUNN
Salma
  Actress: 5 HAYEK
Salmon: 7 SPAWNER
  Brine-cured: 3 LOX
  do it: 5 SPAWN
  Prized: 4 TYEE
  Reproduce like: 5 SPAWN
  Smoked: 3 LOX
  variety: 4 COHO
  Where the ~ flows: 5 IDAHO
  Young: 4 **PARR** 5 SMOLT
"Salome"
  prop: 4 VEIL
  solo: 4 ARIA
Salon
  activity: 7 STYLING
  appliance: 5 DRYER
  application: 3 DYE GEL
  coloring: 5 HENNA
  creation: 4 COIF
  cut: 4 SHAG
  dye: 5 HENNA

  employee: 4 DYER 6 TINTER
    7 STYLIST
  goo: 3 GEL
  job: 3 CUT SET 4 PERM TINT
    5 RINSE
  locks: 4 HAIR
  or Slate: 4 EMAG
  sound: 4 SNIP
  styles: 3 DOS
  supplies: 4 DYES GELS 5 COMBS
    TINTS 7 ROLLERS
  sweepings: 4 HAIR
  Touch up at a: 7 RECOLOR
  treatment: 4 PERM 6 FACIAL
Salonen, ___-Pekka
  Conductor: 3 ESA
Salonga
  Actress: 3 LEA
Salons
  Like some: 6 UNISEX
Saloon: 3 BAR 7 CANTINA
  bill: 6 BARTAB
  Old ~ sight: 5 PIANO
  order: 3 ALE RYE
  request: 7 ANOTHER
  seat: 5 STOOL
  sign: 5 ONTAP
  worker: 5 BGIRL
Salsa
  dipper: 5 NACHO
  Like some: 4 MILD 5 ZESTY
  quality: 4 TANG
  singer Blades: 5 RUBEN
  singer Cruz: 5 CELIA
  topped entrée: 4 TACO
Salt: 3 GOB **TAR** 4 NACL
    6 DEICER SAILOR SEADOG
  Add ~ to: 6 SEASON
  amount: 4 DASH
  assent: 3 AYE
  away: 5 STASH STORE
  Call for the: 4 AHOY
  Chemical: 6 IODIDE
  Chemical ~ in ink: 7 TANNATE
  direction: 4 ALEE
  Element 53: 6 IODATE IODIDE
  Halt, to a: 5 **AVAST**
  holder: 4 BOAT 6 CELLAR
  lick visitor: 4 DEER

Old: 3 **TAR**
Olive with a little: 3 OYL
Organic: 5 ESTER
Rock: 6 HALITE
Sea: 3 TAR
shaker: 7 TSUNAMI
source: 3 SEA
Soviet ~ lake: 4 ARAL
Spilled: 4 OMEN
Table: 4 NACL
Treat as table: 6 IODIZE
~, in French: 3 SEL
~, symbolically: 4 NACL

SALT
Part of: 4 ARMS
signer: 4 USSR
subject: 4 ICBM 5 NTEST

Salt-___: 5 NPEPA

Salten
deer: 5 BAMBI

Saltimbocca
ingredient: 4 VEAL

Saltine
brand: 5 ZESTA

Salting
In need of: 3 ICY

Salt Lake City
athlete: 3 **UTE**
City near: 4 OREM 5 OGDEN
native: 5 UTAHN
state: 4 UTAH

Salt-N-___: 4 PEPA

Salt-N-Pepa
Emulate: 3 RAP

Salton ___: 3 SEA

Saltpeter: 5 NITER
British: 5 NITRE

Saltpetre: 5 NITRE

Salts
Kind of: 5 EPSOM
Need smelling: 5 SWOON
___ salts: 5 **EPSOM**

Saltwater
catch: 7 SEABASS
Like ~ taffy: 5 CHEWY

Salty: 5 BRINY 6 SALINE
assents: 4 AYES
drop: 4 TEAR
lake: 4 ARAL

Man with a ~ wife: 3 LOT
sauce: 3 SOY
shout: 4 AHOY

Salutation
Islamic: 6 SALAAM
Island: 5 ALOHA
Latin: 3 AVE
Sailor's: 4 AHOY
Sideline: 5 HIMOM
Sydney: 4 GDAY

Salute: 4 HAIL
Answer with a: 3 SIR 6 YESSIR
Gun: 5 SALVO
Raised glass: 5 TOAST

Salvador
Artist: 4 DALI
Surrealist: 4 **DALI**
___ Salvador: 3 SAN

Salvage
gear: 5 SONAR

Salvation
Person in need of: 8 LOSTSOUL

Salvation Army
collection: 4 ALMS

Salve
ingredient: 4 ALOE

Salyut 7
cosmonaut Atkov: 4 OLEG
Successor to: 3 MIR

Salzburg
vista: 4 ALPS

Sam: 5 UNCLE
Actor: 5 NEILL
Detective: 5 SPADE
Director: 5 RAIMI
Former senator: 4 NUNN
Golfer: 5 **SNEAD**
of Watergate fame: 5 ERVIN
played for her: 4 ILSA
Singer: 5 COOKE

Sam-___ (Seuss character): 3 IAM

"___ Sam" (Sean Penn film): 3 IAM

Samantha
Actress: 5 **EGGAR**
Sister of: 6 SERENA

Samara
bearer: 3 ELM

Samaritan
Be a good ~ to: 3 AID

Samba
place: 3 RIO
relative: 7 CARIOCA
Sambuca
flavoring: 5 ANISE
Same: 5 ALIKE
Be of the ~ mind: 5 AGREE
Do the ~ as: 3 APE
Feel the: 5 AGREE
In the ~ place: 6 IBIDEM
In the ~ place (abbr.): 4 IBID
More of the: 7 WHATNOT
Much the: 5 ALIKE
Not the: 7 ALTERED
Of the ~ cloth: 4 AKIN
prefix: 3 ISO 4 EQUI
Regard as the: 6 EQUATE
The ~ as: 7 EQUALTO
The ~ as before: 4 IDEM
Treat the: 6 EQUATE
~, in French: 4 EGAL
"Same here!": 5 ASAMI **DITTO**
    METOO SODOI
Same old, same old: 3 RUT
    5 USUAL
    10 DAILYGRIND
"Same Time, Next Year"
actor: 4 ALDA
Sam Goody
purchases: 3 CDS
Sami
speaker: 4 LAPP
Samisen
player: 6 GEISHA
Samms
Actress: 4 EMMA
Sammy
Composer: 4 FAIN
Lyricist: 4 CAHN
of baseball: 4 SOSA
Slammin': 4 SOSA 5 SNEAD
Slugger: 4 **SOSA**
Samoa
Capital of: 4 **APIA**
coin: 4 TALA
staple: 3 POI
studier: 4 MEAD
Samos
Site of ancient: 5 IONIA

Samothrace
figure: 4 NIKE
Samovar: 3 **URN**
Sampan
paddle: 3 OAR
Sample: 3 SIP TRY 4 BITE DEMO
    POLL TEST 5 TASTE
Band: 4 DEMO
check word: 4 VOID
Cloth: 6 SWATCH
tray sign: 6 TRYONE
Sampler: 6 TESTER
Music: 4 DEMO
Sampras
asset: 5 SERVE
feat: 3 ACE
foe: 6 AGASSI
of tennis: 4 PETE
~, at times: 4 ACER
Samson
Like the weakened: 5 SHORN
suffix: 3 ITE
Where ~ defeated the Philistines:
    4 LEHI
Where ~ died: 4 GAZA
"Samson and Delilah"
actress Lamarr: 4 HEDY
Delilah in: 6 LAMARR
Sam the ___ and the Pharaohs:
    4 SHAM
Samuel
Diarist: 5 **PEPYS**
teacher: 3 **ELI**
with a code: 5 MORSE
Samurai
home: 3 EDO
sash: 3 OBI
"Samurai, The"
novelist Shusaku: 4 ENDO
San ___
(Argentina): 6 ISIDRO
(California): 4 JOSE 5 DIEGO
    MATEO RAMON
(Italy): 4 **REMO**
(Puerto Rico): 4 JUAN
(Riviera resort): 4 REMO
(Theological Seminary site):
    7 ANSELMO
(Texas, familiarly): 6 ANTONE

San'a
land: 5 YEMEN
native: 6 YEMENI
San Antonio
arena: 9 ALAMODOME
cagers: 5 SPURS
landmark: 5 **ALAMO**
San Bernardino County
Part of: 6 MOHAVE MOJAVE
Sanctified: 5 BLEST
Sanctify: 5 BLESS 6 HALLOW
Sanction: 3 LET 4 OKAY 5 BLESS
             6 PERMIT
"___ Sanction, The": 5 EIGER
Sanctioned: 3 OKD 5 LEGAL
             LEGIT
Sanctions: 3 OKS
Subject of U.N.: 4 IRAQ
Sanctity
Sign of: 4 HALO
___ Sanctorum: 4 ACTA
Sanctuaries: 5 ASYLA
Sanctuary: 3 ARK 5 HAVEN OASIS
             6 ASYLUM REFUGE
___ sanctum: 5 INNER
"___ Sanctum, The": 5 INNER
Sand: 4 GRIT
bar: 5 **SHOAL**
club: 5 WEDGE
hill: 4 DUNE
holder: 4 PAIL TRAP
lover: 6 CHOPIN
~, to Chopin: 4 AMIE
Sand, George: 5 ALIAS WOMAN
Composer who loved.
             6 CHOPIN
Sandal
feature: 5 STRAP THONG
             7 OPENTOE
Japanese: 4 ZORI
Like a: 7 TOELESS
Mexican: 8 HUARACHE
Roman: 5 SOLEA
Sporting a: 4 SHOD
San ___ Dam, California: 4 LUIS
Sandbank: 5 SHOAL
Sandbar: 5 SHOAL
Sandberg
of baseball: 4 **RYNE**

Sandbox
sharer: 8 PLAYMATE
toy: 4 PAIL
"Sandbox, The"
playwright: 5 ALBEE
Sandburg: 4 POET
Poet: 4 **CARL**
Sandcastle
spot: 5 SHORE
Sanders
of football: 5 DEION
rank: 3 COL 7 COLONEL
Sanders, Colonel
chain: 3 KFC
feature: 6 GOATEE
San Diego
attraction: 3 ZOO
baseballer: 5 PADRE
City near: 6 DELMAR LAMESA
It's south of: 4 BAJA
pro: 5 PADRE
Sanding
In need of: 3 ICY
Sandinista
leader Daniel: 6 ORTEGA
S&L
convenience: 3 ATM
customer: 4 ACCT
offering: 3 IRA
offerings: 3 CDS
payment: 3 INT
Sandler
Comic: 4 **ADAM**
Sandlot
game: 7 ONEOCAT
S&P 500
stock: 3 AOL
Sandpaper
coating: 4 GRIT
Like: 5 ROUGH 6 COARSE
Use: 6 ABRADE
"Sand Pebbles, The"
actress Richard: 6 CRENNA
Sandpiper: 3 REE
Sandra
Actress: 3 **DEE**
and Ruby: 4 DEES
Sands
Singer: 4 EVIE

"Sands of ___ Jima": 3 **IWO**
Sandstone:
    15 SEDIMENTARYROCK
Sandusky
  lake: 4 **ERIE**
Sandwich
  Big: 4 HERO
  Black and white: 4 OREO
  bread: 3 RYE 4 PITA
  Cheesy: 4 MELT
  cookie: 4 **OREO**
  Crunchy: 3 BLT 4 TACO
  Deli: 4 HERO 6 REUBEN
  Diner: 3 BLT
  filler: 4 TUNA 8 TUNAFISH
  fish: 4 TUNA
  Greek: 4 GYRO
  Grilled: 6 PANINI
  Hot: 4 MELT
  initials: 3 BLT
  Kind of: 4 PITA
  Layered: 4 CLUB
  Long: 3 SUB
  man: 4 EARL
  meat: 3 HAM
  Mexican: 4 TACO
  New Orleans: 5 POBOY
  option: 5 WHEAT
    15 WHOLEWHEATBREAD
  order: 5 ONRYE
  Round: 4 OREO
  shop: 4 **DELI**
  spread: 4 MAYO
  Submarine: 4 HERO
    6 HOAGIE
  Sweet: 4 **OREO**
  Trendy: 4 WRAP
  with sauerkraut: 6 REUBEN
Sandy
  color: 4 ECRU 5 BEIGE
  expanse: 6 DESERT
  Golfer: 4 LYLE
  hill: 4 DUNE
  of baseball: 6 ALOMAR
  owner: 5 ANNIE
  particles: 4 GRIT
  sound: 3 ARF 6 ARFARF
  tract, to a Brit: 4 DENE
Sane: 8 ALLTHERE

San Fernando Valley
  city: 6 ENCINO
Sanford
  Actress: 6 ISABEL
  or son: 7 JUNKMAN
Sanford, John
  He was born: 8 REDDFOXX
"Sanford and ___": 3 SON
"Sanford and Son"
  actor Foxx: 4 **REDD**
  son: 6 LAMONT
San Francisco
  and environs: 7 BAYAREA
  County north of: 5 MARIN
  footballer: 5 NINER
  hill: 3 NOB
  Late ~ columnist: 4 CAEN
  neighbor: 7 OAKLAND
  Onetime mayor of: 6 ALIOTO
  paper: 8 EXAMINER
  sight: 9 CABLECARS
  tower: 4 COIT
  transport: 8 CABLECAR
San Francisco Bay
  City on: 7 ALAMEDA
    8 PALOALTO
Sang: 6 RATTED
San Gabriel Valley
  city: 5 AZUSA
Sang-froid: 4 CALM COOL
    5 POISE
San Giacomo
  Actress: 5 LAURA
San Joaquin Valley
  city: 4 LODI 6 DELANO
    FRESNO
Sank
  a putt: 5 HOLED
  into the sofa: 3 SAT
___ San Lucas (Baja resort):
    4 CABO
San Luis ___, California: 6 OBISPO
San Marino
  cash: 4 LIRE
  surrounder: 5 ITALY
San ___ Obispo, California:
    4 LUIS
San Quentin
  room: 4 CELL

San Rafael
  county: 5 MARIN
Sans
  company: 5 ALONE
  ice: 4 NEAT
  Opposite of: 4 AVEC
  purpose: 4 IDLY
  sense: 5 INANE
Sans ___ (carefree): 5 SOUCI
San Simeon
  builder: 6 HEARST
Sanskrit
  word for color: 4 RAGA
Sans-___ type: 5 SERIF
Santa
  California: 3 ANA
  delivery: 3 TOY
  helper: 3 ELF
  helpers: 5 ELVES
  image creator: 4 NAST
  landing spot: 4 ROOF
      7 ROOFTOP
  Letter to: 8 WISHLIST
  Like ~ cheeks: 4 ROSY
  Like ~ helpers: 5 ELFIN
  mail: 5 LISTS
  mo.: 3 DEC
  pole: 5 NORTH
  reindeer: 5 COMET CUPID
      VIXEN 6 DANCER DASHER
      DONNER 7 BLITZEN
      PRANCER
  reindeer team: 5 OCTAD
  reminder: 4 LIST
  sackful: 4 TOYS
  season: 4 YULE
  Sidewalk: 4 TEMP
  soiler: 4 SOOT
  sound: 4 HOHO
  sounds: 3 HOS
  They track: 5 NORAD
  transport: 4 SLED
Santa ___
  (California): 3 **ANA** 4 CRUZ
      ROSA 5 CLARA MARIA
  (hot winds): 4 ANAS
  (racetrack): 5 ANITA
Santa Anita
  doings: 5 RACES

Santa Anita Racetrack
  site: 7 ARCADIA
Santa Anna
  target: 5 ALAMO
"Santa Baby"
  singer: 4 KITT
Santa Barbara
  Resort east of: 4 OJAI
Santa Claus
  artist: 4 NAST
  feature: 5 BEARD
Santa Fe
  and others: 3 RRS
  neighbor: 4 TAOS
Santa Fe Trail
  town: 4 TAOS
Santana
  hit: 8 EVILWAYS 9 OYECOMOVA
"___ santé!": 6 AVOTRE
___ Sant'Gria (wine): 4 YAGO
Santha Rama ___
  Author: 3 RAU
Santiago
  backdrop: 5 ANDES
  charger: 4 TORO
  land: 5 CHILE
Sanyo
  rival: 3 RCA 4 AIWA SONY
São ___: 5 PAULO
São ___ (Cape Verde island):
      5 TIAGO
São Miguel
  islands: 6 AZORES
Saône
  City on the: 4 LYON 5 LYONS
São Paulo
  Part of: 5 TILDE
Sap: 5 CHUMP DRAIN ERODE
      6 WEAKEN 8 ENERVATE
  Play for a: 3 USE
  source: 5 MAPLE
  sucker: 5 APHID
Saperstein
  of basketball: 3 ABE
___ sapiens: 4 HOMO
Sapphire
  Birthstone after: 4 OPAL
  mo.: 4 SEPT
Sappho: 4 POET

home: 6 LESBOS
Muse of: 5 ERATO
poem: 3 ODE
Sapporo
sash: 3 **OBI**
sport: 4 SUMO
Sap-sucking
genus: 5 APHIS
Sara
Actress: 3 MIA
in the market: 3 LEE
Poet: 8 TEASDALE
Saragossa
river: 4 EBRO
Sarah
Son of: 5 ISAAC
Sarajevo
locale: 6 BOSNIA
Saran: 4 WRAP
Sarandon
Actress: 5 SUSAN
Saratoga Springs: 3 SPA
Sarcasm
Subtle: 5 IRONY
Sarcastic: 4 ACID 5 **SNIDE**
    6 IRONIC
response: 4 IBET
syllables: 4 HAHA
Sarcophagus: 4 TOMB
Sardine
holder: 3 TIN
relative: 7 HERRING
Sardonic: 3 WRY
smile: 5 SNEER
Sarducci, Father ___:
    5 GUIDO
Sargasso: 3 SEA
plant: 7 SEAWEED
swimmer: 3 EEL
Sarge: 3 NCO 6 NONCOM
pooch: 4 OTTO
superior: 5 LOOIE
Sargents
Where ~ hang: 4 TATE
Sari
wearer: 4 RANI
___ **Sark:** 5 CUTTY
Sarnoff
org.: 3 RCA

Saroyan
title character: 4 ARAM
___ **Sarto, Andrea**
Artist: 3 DEL
Sartre
Info: French cue
article: 3 LES
being: 4 ETRE
novel: 6 NAUSEA
play: 6 NOEXIT
sea: 3 MER
Soul, to: 3 AME
SAS
listing (abbr.): 3 ETA
SASE: 3 **ENC** 4 ENCL
enclosures (abbr.): 3 MSS
Part of: 3 ENV 4 SELF
Sash
Kimono: 3 OBI
Sasha
Skater: 5 COHEN
Sashimi
fare: 3 EEL
Like: 3 RAW
Sask.
neighbor: 3 ALB 4 ALTA NDAK
Saskatchewan
capital: 6 REGINA
native: 4 CREE
Sasquatch
cousin: 4 YETI
Sass: 3 **LIP** 5 CHEEK
Lots of: 5 ESSES
Sassafras
Struggle with: 4 LISP
Sassoon
Hair maven: 5 VIDAL
Sassy: 4 PERT 5 FRESH
one: 4 SNIP
Sastre
Supermodel: 4 INES
Sat: 5 POSED
around: 5 IDLED
in a cask: 4 AGED
tight: 5 BIDED
SAT: 5 BOARD
company: 3 ETS
relative: 3 GRE
section: 4 MATH 6 VERBAL

taker need: **6** PENCIL
takers: **3** SRS
Satan: 7 EVILONE
  Like: **4** EVIL
  work: **4** EVIL
Satanic: 4 EVIL
  moniker: **7** EVILONE
"Satanic Verses"
  author: **7** RUSHDIE
Satchel
  of baseball: **5** PAIGE
Satchmo
  instrument: **7** TRUMPET
  Sound like: **4** RASP
  style: **4** JAZZ
Satellite: 4 MOON
  Communications: **4** ECHO
    7 TELSTAR
  Data path to a: **6** UPLINK
  First man-made: **7** SPUTNIK
  French ~ launcher: **6** ARIANE
  of Jupiter: **4** LEDA **6** EUROPA
  of Saturn: **4** RHEA **5** DIONE
    TITAN
  path: **5** ORBIT
  transmission: **4** FEED
  Weather: **4** ESSA **5** TIROS
Satellite-tracking
  program: **5** NORAD
Satiate: 4 CLOY FILL
Satie
  Composer: **4 ERIK**
Satinlike: 5 SILKY
Satire
  magazine: **3** MAD
  Voltaire: **7** CANDIDE
Satirical
  cartoonist: **4** ARNO
  essay: **4** SKIT
  newspaper, with "The": **5** ONION
Satirist
  Freberg: **4** STAN
  Mort: **4 SAHL**
  Sahl: **4** MORT
Satirize: 7 LAMPOON
Satisfaction: 7 REDRESS
  Exact ~ for: **6** AVENGE
  Focus on: **11** AIMTOPLEASE
  Show: **5** GLOAT

Sound of: **3** AAH
  Sounds of: **3** AHS **4** AAHS
  Ultimate: **9** LASTLAUGH
Satisfactorily
  Performed: **5** DIDOK
Satisfactory
  Be: **11** FILLTHEBILL
Satisfied: 3 MET
  sigh: **3** AAH
  sighs: **3** AHS
Satisfy: 4 MEET SUIT **5** SLAKE
  6 PLEASE
  a debt: **5 REPAY**
  fully: **4** SATE
  the munchies: **4** NOSH
Satori
  Pursuit of: **3** ZEN
Saturate: 3 SOP **4** SOAK **5** IMBUE
  STEEP
Saturated: 3 WET
  substances: **4** FATS
"Saturday Night Fever"
  group: **7** BEEGEES
  music: **5** DISCO
"Saturday Night Live"
  announcer: **5** PARDO
  piece: **4** SKIT
  producer Michaels: **5** LORNE
  regular Cheri: **5** OTERI
  regular Gasteyer: **3** ANA
Saturn: 3 CAR GOD **4** AUTO
  5 DEITY
  compact: **3** ION
  features: **5** RINGS
  model: **3 ION** VUE
  Moon of: **4** RHEA **5** DIONE
    TITAN
  neighbor: **6** URANUS
  vehicle: **3** UFO
  Wife of: **3 OPS**
Saturnalia: 4 ORGY
Saturnine: 4 DOUR GLUM
Satyr: 4 LECH
  Look like a: **4** LEER
  stare: **4** LEER
  ~, in part: **4** GOAT
Sauce
  Basil: **5 PESTO**
  Béarnaise ~ herb: **8** TARRAGON

brand: **4** RAGU **5** PREGO
Falafel: **6** TAHINI
Floury: **4** ROUX
Garlicky: **5** AIOLI
Green: **5** PESTO
herb: **5** BASIL
Highly seasoned: **8** RAVIGOTE
Hot: **5** SALSA **7** TABASCO
Italian: **5** PESTO
Kind of: **3** SOY
Off the: **5** SOBER
Pasta ~ maker: **4** RAGU
Salty: **3** SOY
source: **3** SOY
Spicy: **5** SALSA
Steak: **4** AONE
style: **5** BARBQ
Tend the: **4** STIR
thickener: **4** ROUX
with fish: **6** TARTAR
Saucer
crew: **3** ETS
Flying: **3** UFO
person: **5** ALIEN
Sauciness: 4 SASS
Saucy: 4 **PERT**
sort: **4** SNIP
Saud
Brother of: **6** FAISAL
___ Saud: **3** IBN
Saudi: 4 **ARAB**
citizen: **4** ARAB
city: **6** MEDINA
king: **4** FAHD **6** FAISAL
neighbor: **5** OMANI
royal name: **4** FAHD
Saudi ___: **6** ARABIA
Saudi Arabia
capital: **6** RIYADH
Gulf between ~ and Egypt:
    5 AQABA
neighbor: **4** IRAQ **OMAN**
    5 QATAR YEMEN
region: **4** ASIR
Sauerkraut
Sandwich with: **6** REUBEN
Sault ___ Marie: 3 **STE**
Sauna
attire: **5** TOWEL

Like a: **6** STEAMY
siding: **5** CEDAR
site: **3** **SPA**
Saunders
Jazzman: **4** MERL
Saunter: 5 AMBLE MOSEY
Sausage: 5 WURST
Deli: **6** SALAMI
Polish: **8** KIELBASA
skin: **6** CASING
Spicy: **6** SALAMI
unit: **4** LINK
Sausalito
county: **5** MARIN
Sauté: 3 FRY
Sautéed
Battered and ~ in butter:
    8 MEUNIERE
dish: **4** HASH
shrimp dish: **6** SCAMPI
Savage: 5 BEAST BRUTE CRUEL
        FERAL **6** FIERCE
on TV: **4** FRED
Savalas
Actor: **5** TELLY
Savalas, Telly
Like: **4** BALD
role: **5** KOJAK
Savannah
summer hrs.: **3** EDT
___ Savant, Marilyn: **3** **VOS**
Save: 3 BUT **6** EXCEPT RESCUE
        8 SALTAWAY
Partner of: **6** SCRIMP
Saved: 9 LAIDASIDE
It may be: **4** FACE
on dinner: **5** ATEIN
up: **9** INRESERVE
"Save Me"
singer Mann: **5** AIMEE
"Save me ___" (movie request):
        5 ASEAT
Saver
Day: **4** HERO
Life: **4** HERO
option: **3** IRA
Shoe: **4** TREE
Saves
on postage: **8** PRESORTS

"Saving Private ___": 4 RYAN
"Saving Private Ryan"
  actor Matt: 5 DAMON
  craft: 3 LST
  event: 4 DDAY
Savings: 7 NESTEGG
  acct. earning: 3 INT
  bond abbr.: 3 SER
  plan: 3 IRA
  Some ~ accts.: 3 CDS 4 IRAS
Savior: 4 HERO
Savoie
  Summer in: 3 ETE
Savoir-faire: 4 **TACT**
Savor: 5 TASTE
Savory
  jelly: 5 **ASPIC**
  smell: 5 AROMA
Savoy ___: 4 ALPS
Savvy: 3 HEP HIP 4 KNOW
     5 SMART 6 SMARTS
  about: 4 ONTO
"Savvy?": 3 SEE 5 GETME
Saw: 4 EYED TOOL 5 **ADAGE**
     DATED MAXIM 6 ESPIED
     7 NOTICED
     10 LAIDEYESON
  eye to eye: 6 AGREED
  logs: 5 SNORE
  red: 4 OWED
  suffix: 3 YER
  the sights: 6 TOURED
  things: 5 TEETH
  through: 6 XRAYED
  with the grain: 3 RIP
  wood: 5 SNORE
Sawbones: 3 DOC 6 MEDICO
  org.: 3 AMA
Sawbuck: 3 **TEN** 6 TENNER
     7 TENSPOT
  fraction: 3 ONE
  Half a: 3 FIN 4 FIVE
Sawbucks
  100 ~: 4 ONEG
  Bill worth 10: 5 CNOTE
"... ___ saw Elba": 4 **EREI**
Sawing
  logs: 6 ASLEEP
Saw-toothed: 7 SERRATE

formation: 6 SIERRA
Sawtooth Mountains
  state: 5 IDAHO
Sawyer
  Journalist: 5 DIANE
  pal Huck: 4 FINN
Sawyer, Tom
  creator: 5 TWAIN
  Half brother of: 3 SID
  Love of: 5 BECKY
  Polly, to: 4 AUNT
Sax
  How a ~ sounds: 5 REEDY
  Kind of: 4 **ALTO** 5 TENOR
  object: 4 REED
  player G: 5 KENNY
  player Getz: 4 STAN
Saxon
  prefix: 5 ANGLO
Saxony
  river: 3 EMS
  seaport: 5 EMDEN
Saxophone: 4 REED
  Kind of: 4 ALTO
  part: 4 REED
Saxophonist
  Popular: 6 KENNYG
  ~ Getz: 4 STAN
  ~ Stan: 4 GETZ
  ~ Zoot: 4 SIMS
Say: 5 STATE UTTER
  "#@$%!": 4 CUSS 5 SWEAR
  again: 4 ECHO 6 REPEAT
     9 REITERATE
  by heart: 6 RECITE
  for sure: 4 AVER
  further: 3 ADD
  "hey" to: 5 GREET
  it isn't so: 4 DENY
  it's so: 4 AVER AVOW
  Just ~ no: 4 DENY
  Never ~ this: 3 DIE
  no to: 4 VETO
  over: 7 ITERATE
  Sad to: 4 ALAS
  so: 4 AVER
  suddenly: 5 BLURT
  yes: 5 AGREE 6 ACCEDE
  You can ~ that again!: 6 MANTRA

"Say ___": 3 AAH 4 WHEN
"Say ___ ?": 4 WHAT
Say ___ (deny): 4 NOTO
"Say cheese!": 5 SMILE
Sayer
  Nae: 4 SCOT
  Nay: 4 **ANTI**
  Neigh: 5 HORSE
Sayers
  detective Lord Peter: 6 WIMSEY
Say Hey Kid, The: 4 MAYS
Saying: 5 ADAGE
  Familiar: 6 OLDSAW
  Old: 3 SAW 5 ADAGE
  One who sees what you're:
    9 LIPREADER
  Say without: 5 IMPLY
  Trite: 7 BROMIDE
  Witty: 3 MOT
Sayings
  Collected: 3 ANA
"Say it isn't so!": 4 OHNO
"Say it ___ so!": 4 AINT ISNT
"___ say more?": 5 NEEDI
"Say no more!": 4 STOP
"Sayonara"
  ~ Oscar-winner Miyoshi:
    5 UMEKI
___ Says (child's game): 5 SIMON
Say-so
  On the ~ of: 5 ASPER
"Say what?": 3 HUH 5 AGAIN
"Say You, Say Me"
  singer Lionel: 6 RICHIE
Scacchi
  Actress: 5 **GRETA**
Scads: 4 ALOT ATON LOTS SLEW
    5 AHEAP
Scaggs
  Singer: 3 BOZ
Scalawag: 5 ROGUE 6 RASCAL
Scale: 4 GOUP 5 CLIMB 6 ASCEND
  amts.: 3 LBS WTS
  button: 4 TARE
  divs.: 3 LBS
  down: 4 PARE
  Fifth on the: 3 SOL
  It uses a higher: 5 INSET
  Kind of: 4 MOHS 6 POSTAL

  model: 6 MOCKUP
  notes: 3 FAS LAS MIS **RES** TIS
  On a grand: 4 EPIC
  pair: 4 DORE REMI MIFA FASO
    SOLA LATI TIDO
  Postal ~ unit: 5 OUNCE
  Put on a: 4 RATE
  start: 4 DORE 6 DOREMI
  Steps on a: 5 TONES
  Temperature: 7 CELSIUS
  Top of a: 3 TEN
___ scale: 4 MOHS
Scaleless
  fish: 3 EEL
Scales
  Celestial: 5 LIBRA
  They have: 4 MAPS
  up: 5 LIBRA
Scalia
  Justice: 7 ANTONIN
Scallion: 4 LEEK
Scallop: 8 SEASHELL
  Kind of: 3 BAY
Scaloppine
  Make: 5 SAUTE
  ~, usually: 4 VEAL
Scalp
  tickets: 6 RESELL
Scaly
  squeezer: 3 BOA
Scam: 3 CON 4 TAKE
  Three-card: 5 MONTE
  victims: 4 SAPS
Scammed: 3 HAD 4 TOOK
Scamp: 5 ROGUE 6 RASCAL
    URCHIN
Scampered: 3 RAN
Scampi
  ingredient: 5 PRAWN 6 GARLIC
    SHRIMP
Scan: 4 READ
  Brain: 3 EEG
  Hosp.: 3 MRI
Scand.
  land: 3 NOR 4 NORW SWED
Scandal
  1920s ~: 10 TEAPOTDOME
  1950s recording: 6 PAYOLA
  1980s ~: 8 IRANGATE

2002 ~: 5 ENRON
fodder: 4 DIRT
sheet: 3 RAG
suffix: 3 OLA 4 GATE
Scandalous
gossip: 4 DIRT
~ 1980s initials: 3 PTL
Scandinavia
From: 6 NORDIC
native: 4 LAPP
Scandinavian: 4 DANE 5 NORSE
capital: 4 OSLO
Certain: 4 LAPP
coin word: 5 NORGE
epic: 4 EDDA
god: 4 ODIN
king: 4 OLAV
native: 4 SAMI
royal name: 4 OLAF
rug: 3 RYA
saint: 4 OLAF
toast: 5 SKOAL
Scanned
Something: 3 UPC 7 BARCODE
Scanner
Cat: 3 VET
Diagnostic: 3 MRI
Kind of: 7 OPTICAL
Text: 3 OCR
Scant: 4 MERE 6 MEAGER
Scanty: 4 SLIM 6 SPARSE
~, to a Brit: 6 MEAGRE
Scar
Car.: 4 DENT
Scarab: 6 BEETLE
Scarce: 4 RARE
Hardly: 4 RIFE
Scarcely: 3 ILL
scruffy: 5 KEMPT
Scarcity: 6 DEARTH
Scare
It may ~ you: 3 BOO
off: 5 DETER SPOOK
word: 3 BOO
Scarecrow
lack: 5 BRAIN
stuffing: 5 STRAW
Scared
Visibly: 5 ASHEN

Scarf: 3 BOA
Broad: 5 ASCOT
down: 3 EAT 6 INHALE
Feathery: 3 **BOA**
Furry: 5 STOLE
Spanish: 8 MANTILLA
Wide: 5 STOLE
Scarface
portrayer: 6 PACINO
~ Al: 6 CAPONE
Scarfed
down: 3 ATE 5 EATEN
Scarlatti
Typical ~ work:
  10 OPERASERIA
Scarlet: 3 RED
bird: 7 TANAGER
It may be: 7 TANAGER
letter: 6 STIGMA
The ~ letter: 4 REDA
"Scarlet Letter, The"
woman: 6 HESTER PRYNNE
Scarlett
admirer: 5 RHETT
Daughter of: 4 ELLA
First love of: 6 ASHLEY
home: 4 TARA
love: 5 RHETT
  11 RHETTBUTLER
of Tara: 5 **OHARA**
Scarpia
killer: 5 TOSCA
Scary: 5 EERIE
snake: 3 ASP
street: 3 ELM
"Scary Movie"
actress Cheri: 5 OTERI
actress Faris: 4 ANNA
Scat
First name in: 4 **ELLA**
"Scat, cat!": 4 SHOO
Scatter: 5 **STREW**
seed: 3 SOW
~ Anita: 4 ODAY
~ Fitzgerald: 4 ELLA
Scatterbrain: 4 DITZ
Scatterbrained: 5 DITSY
Scattered: 6 SPARSE STREWN
~, as seed: 4 SOWN

Scavenger
Beach: 4 GULL
Laughing: 5 HYENA
Serengeti: 5 HYENA
Scene: 4 VIEW 5 VENUE
At the: 6 ONSITE
Chaotic: 3 ZOO
Chase ~ noise: 5 SIREN
Completed: 4 WRAP
Crime ~ find: 5 PRINT
Crowd ~ actor: 5 EXTRA
Made a: 5 ACTED
Made the: 4 CAME
Mob: 4 RIOT
Nativity: 6 CRECHE
One who makes a: 6 ARTIST
On the: 7 PRESENT
Stable: 6 CRECHE
Temptation: 4 EDEN
Scene-ending
cry: 3 CUT
Scenery
chewer: 3 HAM 6 EMOTER
Chew the: 5 **EMOTE**
Part of the: 8 SETPIECE
Stage: 3 SET
Scenes
Behind the: 8 OFFSTAGE
Scenic
view: 5 VISTA
Scent: 4 **ODOR** 5 AROMA
SMELL
Animal: 4 MUSK
Cleanser: 4 PINE
finder: 4 NOSE
Polish: 5 LEMON
Sachet: 5 LILAC
Scented
bag: 6 SACHET
"Scent of a Woman"
~ Oscar winner: 6 PACINO
Scepter: 3 ROD
Crown and: 7 REGALIA
mate: 3 ORB
Sch.
Grade: 4 ELEM
group: 3 **PTA**
High ~ exam: 4 PSAT
Kind of: 4 **ELEM**

Prep: 4 ACAD
subject: 3 ENG SCI
supporter: 3 PTA
Technical: 4 INST
Theological: 3 SEM
Scharnhorst
admiral: 4 SPEE
Sched.
Business: 3 HRS
entry: 3 ETA ETD 4 APPT
Not yet on the: 3 TBA
Schedule: 5 SLATE
abbr.: 3 ARR ETA ETD TBA
again: 7 RESLATE
Behind: 4 LATE
contingency: 8 RAINDATE
Meeting: 6 AGENDA
On the: 6 SLATED 7 SLOTTED
opening: 4 SLOT
Part of a flexible: 8 OPENDATE
Space on the: 4 SLOT
TV ~ abbr.: 3 TBA
Was behind: 7 RANLATE
Schedule A
Use: 7 ITEMIZE
Schedule C
figure: 7 NETLOSS
Scheduled: 3 DUE
Schedules
Org. with many: 3 IRS
They work with: 4 CPAS
Scheherazade
offering: 4 TALE
Scheme: 4 PLAN PLOT 5 CAPER
SETUP
Get-rich-quick: 5 HEIST
Pyramid: 4 SCAM
Rhyme: 4 ABAB ABBA
Sneaky: 4 RUSE
Support a: 4 ABET
Schemer
"Othello": 4 IAGO
Schemers: 5 CABAL
Scheming
bunch: 5 CABAL
Schenectady
river: 6 MOHAWK
Schiaparelli
Designer: 4 **ELSA**

Schiele
Painter: 4 EGON
Schifrin
Composer: 4 **LALO**
Schiller
poem used by Beethoven:
8 ODETOJOY
Schindler
Herr: 5 **OSKAR**
portrayer: 6 NEESON
"Schindler's List"
Oskar portrayer in: 4 LIAM
Schindler of: 5 OSKAR
star: 6 NEESON
Schipa
Tenor: 4 TITO
Schiphol Airport
Carrier to: 3 KLM
Schisgal, Murray
1964 ~ play: 3 LUV
Schism: 4 RIFT SECT
Schlemiel: 3 SAP 4 JERK
5 LOSER
Schlep: 3 LUG 4 DRAG HAUL
TOTE
Schlepper: 5 TOTER
Schlesinger
1995 ~ film:
15 COLDCOMFORTFARM
Schlessinger, Dr.
of radio: 5 LAURA
Schlimazel: 5 LOSER
Schmaltz: 3 GOO
Schmear
The whole: 3 ALL
Schmidt
of Novell: 4 ERIC
successor: 4 KOHL
Schmooze: 3 GAB
Schnabel
Pianist: 5 ARTUR
Schnauzer
of whodunits: 4 ASTA
Schneider
Actress: 4 ROMY
Schnoz: 4 BEAK NOSE 5 SNOUT
7 SMELLER
Schnozz
suffix: 3 **OLA**

Schnozzola: 4 BEAK NOSE
5 SNOOT SNOUT
of vaudeville: 7 DURANTE
Schoenberg
Like ~ music: 6 ATONAL
Scholar: 6 SAVANT
goal: 3 PHD
Jewish: 5 RABBI
Legal: 6 JURIST
Legal ~ deg.: 3 LLD
Old Jewish: 4 ABBA
sphere: 8 ACADEMIA
Venerable: 4 BEDE
volume: 4 TOME
Scholarly
In a ~ fashion: 9 ERUDITELY
Scholarship
criterion: 4 **NEED**
founder: 6 RHODES
Rhodes with a: 5 CECIL
Scholastic
stereotype: 4 NERD
Scholasticism
founder: 6 ANSELM
Scholl, Dr.
product: 6 INSOLE
Schon
Guitarist: 4 NEAL
School: 5 TEACH 7 EDUCATE
007 ~: 4 ETON
adviser: 4 DEAN
assignment: 5 ESSAY 6 REPORT
Avoid summer: 4 PASS
basics: 3 RRR
book: 4 TEXT
break: 6 RECESS
British secondary ~ exam:
6 ALEVEL OLEVEL
cheer: 4 YELL 6 GOTEAM
course part: 4 UNIT
dance: 3 HOP
division: 5 GRADE
Eli: 4 YALE
furniture: 5 DESKS
Future: 3 ROE
gp.: 3 **PTA**
grad: 4 ALUM
Grammar ~ trio: 3 RRR
group: 4 FISH

house: 4 FRAT
Kick out of: 5 EXPEL
Kind of: 3 MED 4 ELEM PREP
Martial arts: 4 **DOJO**
Med. ~ subj.: 4 **ANAT**
Mil.: 4 ACAD
Military: 7 ACADEMY
mo.: 3 OCT 4 SEPT
Night ~ subj.: 3 ESL
of Buddhism: 3 ZEN
of the future: 3 ROE
of thought: 3 **ISM**
of whales: 3 **GAM** POD
Old ~ figure: 4 MARM
org.: 3 NEA **PTA** 4 ROTC
period: 4 TERM
prayer fighter: 5 OHAIR
Preppy: 4 ETON
Reason to cancel: 4 SNOW
session: 4 TERM
setting: 3 SEA
since 1440: 4 ETON
Southern: 4 BAMA
sports org.: 4 NCAA
Start for: 3 PRE
Stick in: 5 RULER
subj.: 3 ENG SCI 4 HIST MATH
tie: 3 PTA
tool: 5 RULER
transport: 3 BUS
website ender: 3 EDU
zone sign: 3 SLO 4 SLOW
~, in French: 5 ECOLE LYCEE
___ School: 6 ASHCAN
Schoolbook: 4 **TEXT**
Schoolboy: 3 LAD
collar: 4 ETON
"Schoolboy"
of baseball: 4 ROWE
Schooling
Get: 5 LEARN
Schoolmarm
do: 3 BUN
Like a: 4 PRIM
rod: 6 FERULE
Schoolmaster
rod: 6 FERULE
Schoolroom
fixture: 4 DESK

Schoolteacher
Old-time: 4 MARM
Schoolwork
Do: 5 TEACH
Some: 4 ROTE
Schoolyard
challenge: 4 DARE 6 MAKEME
game: 3 TAG
retort: 4 AMSO
Schooner
filler: 3 **ALE** 4 BEER
part: 4 MAST
Schott
Former baseball owner: 5 MARGE
Schroeder
Former Rep.: 8 PATRICIA
toy: 5 PIANO
Schubert
chamber work:
    15 THETROUTQUINTET
song: 4 LIED 8 AVEMARIA
Schuss: 3 SKI
Schusser
lift: 4 TBAR
locale: 5 SLOPE
___ **Schwarz (toy store)**: 3 FAO
Schwarzenegger
1988 ~ film: 7 REDHEAT
1996 ~ film: 6 ERASER
Gov.: 6 ARNOLD
middle name: 5 ALOIS
role: 5 CONAN
Schwarzkopf, Gen.
Like: 3 RET 4 RETD
Sci.
Biological: 4 ANAT
course: 4 ANAT
Earth: 4 **ECOL** GEOL
Environmental: 4 **ECOL**
of the body: 4 ANAT
of the stars: 4 ASTR
Social: 4 ECON
Structural: 4 ANAT
___ **sci (coll. course)**: 4 POLI
Science
Bygone ~ magazine: 4 OMNI
class: 3 LAB
Occult: 6 CABALA
of light: 6 OPTICS

PBS ~ series: 4 **NOVA**
prefix: 4 OMNI
show: 4 NOVA
Winemaking: 8 OENOLOGY
~, informally: 5 OLOGY
Science fiction
award: 4 HUGO
magazine: 6 ANALOG
"Science Guy"
~ Bill: 3 **NYE**
Sciences
Partner of: 4 ARTS
Scientific
org.: 4 INST
Scientist
employer: 4 NASA
hangout: 3 LAB
Scientology
founder Hubbard: 4 **LRON**
Sci-fi: 5 GENRE
1956 ~ film:
    15 FORBIDDENPLANET
1958 ~ menace: 4 BLOB
1960s ~ series: 11 LOSTINSPACE
1966 ~ film:
    15 FANTASTICVOYAGE
1979 ~ film: 5 ALIEN
1982 ~ film: 4 TRON
1986 ~ film: 6 ALIENS
Asimov of: 5 ISAAC
author Ellison: 6 HARLAN
author Frederik: 4 POHL
author Isaac: 6 ASIMOV
author Lester ___ Rey: 3 DEL
author ___ Scott Card: 5 ORSON
Change, in ~ films: 5 MORPH
creatures: 3 ETS
Disney ~ film: 4 TRON
Doctor of: 3 WHO
drug: 3 TEK
Earth, in: 5 TERRA
Earthling, in: 6 TERRAN
escape vehicle: 3 POD
figure: 5 DROID ROBOT
film extra: 5 ALIEN
film extras: 3 ETS
Flying monster of: 5 RODAN
Furry ~ critter: 4 EWOK
Herbert ~ opus: 4 DUNE

killer: 3 RAY
mag of old: 4 OMNI
Miniature ~ vehicle: 3 POD
play: 3 RUR
princess: 4 LEIA
sage: 4 YODA
Serling of: 3 ROD
Shatner ~ novel: 6 TEKWAR
sighting: 3 UFO
Solo of: 3 HAN
subjects: 3 ETS
vehicle: 3 UFO
visitor: 5 ALIEN
visitors: 3 ETS
weapon: 3 RAY 5 LASER
    6 PHASER RAYGUN
Scimitar: 5 SABER
Scintilla: 4 ATOM **IOTA** 5 SHRED
    TRACE
Scion: 4 HEIR
Woody: 4 ARLO
Scissor
sound: 4 SNIP
Scissorhands
portrayer: 4 DEPP
Scissors
Cut with: 4 SNIP
Place for: 4 ETUI
sound: 4 SNIP
Scoff: 4 JEER 5 SNEER
at: 4 GIBE 6 DERIDE
Skeptic's: 4 **IBET**
Scoffer
cry: 4 HAH
Scold: 3 NAG 4 LASH RATE
    5 CHIDE 6 BERATE
    SNAPAT YELLAT
    7 BAWLOUT CHEWOUT
    REAMOUT
severely: 4 FLAY
Scolder
sound: 3 TSK
Scolding: 6 EARFUL
    8 HARANGUE
sound: 3 TSK
syllable: 3 TUT
word: 3 BAD
Sconce
spot: 4 WALL

Scooby-___ (cartoon dog):
  3 DOO
Scooby-Doo
  Pal of: 5 VELMA
Scoop: 4 DOPE INFO
  holder: 4 CONE
  Inside: 4 DIRT DOPE
  Soup: 5 LADLE
Scoot: 3 HIE RUN 4 TEAR
Scooter: 5 MOPED
Scope: 3 KEN 4 **AREA** ROOM
  5 AMBIT RANGE
  Grand in: 4 EPIC
  prefix: 4 ENDO PERI TELE
    6 STETHO
  Use a: 3 AIM
Scopes
  advocate: 6 DARROW
  The ~ ___: 5 TRIAL
Scopes Trial
  org.: 4 ACLU
Scorch: 4 BURN CHAR **SEAR**
  5 SCALD SINGE
Score: 6 TWENTY
  after deuce: 4 **ADIN** 5 ADOUT
  Arc on a: 4 SLUR
  before 15: 4 LOVE
  Best golf: 6 FEWEST
  Court: 4 ADIN
  direction: 8 STACCATO
  Early game: 6 ONEONE
  Even: 3 TIE
  Free throw: 3 ONE
  Got a perfect ~ on: 4 ACED
  Great: 3 TEN
  Half: 3 TEN
  Hockey: 4 GOAL
  in horseshoes: 6 LEANER
  Like a 4-4: 4 TIED
  Line ~ letters: 3 RHE
  mark: 3 TIE 4 REST SLUR
  Miner: 3 ORE
  Ore: 4 VEIN
  Part of a: 4 ARIA
  Settle the: 7 GETEVEN
  Slowly, on a: 5 **LENTO**
  Soccer: 4 GOAL
  Standard: 3 PAR
  Tennis: 4 **ADIN** 5 ADOUT

  Together, on a: 4 ADUE
  unit: 4 NOTE
  Worst: 4 ZERO
Scoreboard
  info: 3 PTS 4 DOWN OUTS
    RUNS
  initials: 3 RHE
Scorecard
  bunt: 3 SAC
  line: 3 PAR
Score-producing
  stat: 3 RBI
Scorer
  of 1,281 career goals: 4 PELE
Scores: 4 ALOT LOTS MANY
  5 DEBTS
  Apiece, in: 3 ALL
  Lively, in: 7 ANIMATO
  NFL: 3 **TDS**
  Smooth, in: 6 LEGATO
Scorn: 7 DISDAIN SNEERAT
  Show: 5 SNEER
Scornful
  cry: 3 BAH
  look: 5 SNEER
Scorpio: 4 SIGN
  star: 7 ANTARES
Scorpion: 8 ARACHNID
  attack: 5 STING
  product: 5 VENOM
Scorpius
  Neighbor of: 3 **ARA**
  Star in: 7 ANTARES
Scot: 4 GAEL
  Ancient: 4 PICT
  Certain: 10 ABERDONIAN
  group: 4 CLAN
  Not, to a: 3 NAE
  topper: 3 TAM
Scotch
  and Drambuie drink:
    9 RUSTYNAIL
  concoction: 6 ROBROY
  datum: 3 AGE
  ingredient: 4 MALT
  partner: 4 SODA
  servings: 5 SHOTS
Scotch ___: 4 PINE TAPE
___ Scotia: 4 NOVA

Scotland
Island of: 4 IONA
John of: 3 IAN
Longest river of: 3 TAY
Since, in: 4 SYNE
Tiny, in: 3 SMA
Scotland yard: 5 METRE
Scotland Yard
div.: 3 CID
title (abbr.): 4 INSP
Scots
toss it: 5 CABER
trill: 4 BURR
~ Gaelic: 4 **ERSE**
"Scots Wha ___" (Burns poem):
3 HAE
Scott
Author: 5 ODELL TUROW
Cartoonist: 5 ADAMS
Historic: 4 DRED
in 1857 news: 4 DRED
Newbery-winning: 5 ODELL
novel: 6 ROBROY 7 IVANHOE
of TV: 4 BAIO
role: 6 PATTON
Scott, Dred
~ Chief Justice: 5 TANEY
Scott, Paul
series: 13 THERAJQUARTET
___ Scott Decision: 4 DRED
Scott-Heron
Novelist: 3 GIL
Scottie: 7 TERRIER
White House: 4 FALA
Scottish
bay: 4 LOCH
cap: 3 TAM
cattle breed: 5 ANGUS
child: 5 BAIRN
county: 6 ARGYLL
dagger: 4 DIRK
dish: 6 HAGGIS
explorer John: 3 RAE
family: 4 CLAN
girl: 4 LASS
highlander: 4 GAEL
hillside: 4 BRAE
inlet: 4 LOCH 5 FIRTH
inventor James: 4 WATT

isle: 4 IONA
lake: 4 LOCH NESS
landholder: 5 **LAIRD**
loch: 4 NESS
monster: 6 NESSIE
no: 3 NAE
Old ~ landholder: 5 THANE
philosopher David: 4 HUME
quickbread: 5 SCONE
refusal: 3 NAE
river: 3 TAY
topper: 3 TAM
uncle: 3 EME
~ Gaelic: 4 ERSE
~ "Gee!": 3 OCH
~ John: 3 IAN
Scotto: 4 DIVA
solo: 4 ARIA
Soprano: 6 RENATA
Scoundrel: 3 CAD CUR **RAT**
4 HEEL 5 KNAVE ROGUE
6 RASCAL 8 DIRTYDOG
SCALAWAG
Dirty rotten: 5 CREEP
Stevenson: 4 HYDE
Scour: 4 COMB
Scourge: 4 BANE
African: 5 EBOLA 6 TSETSE
"Scourge of God, The": 6 ATTILA
Scout
creation: 4 KNOT
discovery: 6 TALENT
doing: 4 DEED
group: 3 DEN 5 TROOP
High: 5 EAGLE
job: 5 RECON
Kind of: 6 TALENT
leader: 5 TONTO
master: 5 TONTO
Memorable: 9 KITCARSON
Novice: 10 TENDERFOOT
outing: 4 HIKE 5 RECON
rank: 5 EAGLE
recitation: 4 OATH
skill: 8 EAGLEEYE
Tonto, to: 5 RIDER
Top: 5 EAGLE
unit: 3 DEN 5 TROOP
~, at times: 5 HIKER

Scow: 4 BOAT
Scowcroft
  Bush adviser: 5 BRENT
Scowl: 5 GLARE
Scrabble
  Low-count ~ quintet: 5 AEIOU
  piece: 4 **TILE**
  Valuable ~ tile: 3 ESS
  ~ 3-pointers: 3 EMS
  ~ 10-pointer: 3 ZEE 5 ZTILE
Scram
  suffix: 3 OLA
"Scram!": 3 GIT 4 SHOO 5 LEAVE
        6 BEATIT GETOUT
        7 GETLOST
Scrambled
  It may be: 3 EGG
Scrammed: 3 RAN
Scrap: 3 **ORT** RAG ROW 4 SPAT
        5 SETTO 6 TAGEND
        7 REMNANT
  Food: 3 ORT
  paper: 5 SHRED
  Random: 6 TAGEND
  Stable: 3 OAT
  Table: 3 **ORT**
Scrapbook
  Affix in a: 5 PASTE
  pastings: 3 ANA
Scrape: 3 ROW 4 BIND MESS
        RASP SKIN 6 ABRADE
        8 ABRASION
  aftermath: 4 SCAB
  Bow and: 4 FAWN
  More than: 4 GASH
  (out): 3 EKE
  site: 4 KNEE
  together: 5 RAISE 6 EKEOUT
Scratch: 3 **MAR** 4 CLAW 5 MOOLA
        6 MOOLAH
  a dele: 4 STET
  From: 4 **ANEW** 6 AFRESH
  Needing to: 5 ITCHY
  Old: 5 SATAN 7 EVILONE
  (out): 3 EKE
  Start from: 4 REDO
  target: 4 ITCH
  the surface: 3 MAR
  up: 3 MAR

Scratcher
  Cat: 4 CLAW
Scrawny: 4 BONY THIN 5 GAUNT
        WEEDY
  one: 5 SCRAG
Scream: 4 RIOT 6 SHRIEK
  Comics: 3 EEK
  Type of: 6 PRIMAL
"Scream"
  actress Campbell: 4 **NEVE**
  director Craven: 3 WES
"Scream 2"
  actor Omar: 4 **EPPS**
Screamers:
        15 BANNERHEADLINES
  Some: 4 FANS
Screecher: 3 OWL
Screen: 4 HIDE SIFT VEIL
  award: 5 OSCAR
  Big ~ name: 4 IMAX
  dot: 5 PIXEL
  image: 4 ICON
  Kind of: 4 LINT 5 RADAR
  letters: 5 EMAIL
  Letters on a: 5 EMAIL
  material: 4 MESH
  PC: 3 CRT
  pet: 4 ASTA
  Put on the small: 3 AIR
  Radar: 4 GRID
  Radar ~ image: 4 BLIP
  symbol: 4 ICON
  TV ~ grid: 6 RASTER
Screened: 3 HID
Screening
  device: 5 VCHIP
Screenwriter
  1972 Oscar-winning ~: 4 PUZO
  creation: 8 SCENARIO
  ~ Ephron: 4 **NORA** 5 DELIA
  ~ James: 4 **AGEE**
  ~ Robert: 5 TOWNE
Screw
  Bar with two ~ threads: 5 UBOLT
  up: 3 **ERR**
Screwball: 3 NUT 4 LOON
        5 WACKO WACKY
        7 NUTCASE
Screwdriver: 4 **TOOL**

hue: **6** ORANGE
Part of a: **5** VODKA
  place: **3** BAR
"Screwtape Letters, The"
  writer: **7** CSLEWIS
Scribble: 3 JOT **4** NOTE
     6 DOODLE
Scribe: 6 PENMAN
  Dead Sea Scrolls: **6** ESSENE
Scrimp
  partner: **4** SAVE
Scrimshaw
  medium: **5** IVORY
Script
  Ignore the: **5** ADLIB
  suffix: **3** URE
  When the ~ demands: **5** ONCUE
Scriptural
  interpretation: **8** EXEGESIS
Scripture
  Jewish: **5** TORAH
  Of Hindu: **5** VEDIC
  volume: **5** CODEX
Scroll
  holder: **3** ARK
  Holy: **5** TORAH
  Scriptures: **5** CODEX
  Synagogue: **4** TORA **5 TORAH**
Scrolls
  site: **7** DEADSEA
Scrollwork
  shape: **3** ESS
Scrooge: 5 MISER
  cry. **3** BAH
  look: **5** SNEER
  portrayer: **3** SIM
  ~, for short: **4** EBEN
Scrounge
  (for): **4** GRUB
Scrub: 4 WASH **5** ABORT SCOUR
     6 CANCEL
  NASA: **4** NOGO **5** ABORT
  nurse sites (abbr.): **3** ORS
Scrubbed: 4 NOGO
Scruff: 4 NAPE
Scruffy
  Scarcely: **5** KEMPT
Scruggs
  Banjoist: **4 EARL**

instrument: **5** BANJO
  partner: **5** FLATT
Scrum
  game: **5** RUGBY
Scrumptious: 5 YUMMY
Scruples
  Without: **6** AMORAL
Scrutinize: 3 EYE
  ~, with "over": **4** PORE
Scrutiny: 7 PERUSAL
Scuba
  gear: **4** TANK **7** WETSUIT
Scud
  downer (abbr.): **3** ABM
Scuff: 3 MAR
  up: **3** MAR
Scuffle: 4 FRAY
  More than a: **5** MELEE
Scull: 3 OAR
  propeller: **3** OAR
  Use your: **3** ROW
Sculler
  need: **3** OAR
Scully: 5 AGENT
  abbr.: **3** AGT
  Agent: **4** DANA
  Case for: **5** XFILE
  employer: **3** FBI
  Sportscaster: **3** VIN
Sculpt: 5 SHAPE **6** CHISEL
Sculpted
  form: **5** TORSO
Sculpting
  medium: **3** ICE **4** CLAY
Sculptor
  Dadaist: **3** ARP
  French: **5** RODIN
  medium: **3** ICE
  subject: **4** BUST **5** TORSO
  ~ Henry: **5** MOORE
  ~ Hesse: **3** EVA
  ~ Jean: **3** ARP
  ~ Nadelman: **4** ELIE
Sculptors
  Family of: **7** PISANOS
Sculpture
  alloy: **6** BRONZE
  forms: **5** TORSI
  Religious: **5** PIETA

subject: 5 TORSO
Type of: 7 RELIEVO
with fixed parts: 7 STABILE

Scum
Pond: 4 ALGA 5 ALGAE

Scummy
place: 4 POND

Scurrier
Little: 3 ANT
Slum: 3 RAT

Scurrilous: 6 RIBALD

Scurry: 3 HIE RUN

Scut
Critter with a: 4 HARE

Scuttle: 4 SINK
Coal: 3 HOD
filler: 4 COAL

Scuttlebutt: 4 DIRT INFO POOP
5 RUMOR 7 HEARSAY

Scuttler
Ocean: 8 SANDCRAB

Scythe
handle: 5 SNATH
Use a: 4 REAP

S. Dak.
neighbor: 3 NEB

SDS
antithesis: 4 ROTC
target: 3 SSS

Sea: 5 BRINY OCEAN
Antarctic: 4 ROSS
Arm of the: 5 INLET
Back at: 3 AFT 6 ASTERN
bird: 3 ERN 4 ERNE GULL
cow: 7 MANATEE
creature: 5 OTTER 7 ANEMONE
dog: 3 GOB TAR 4 SALT
duck: 5 EIDER
eagle: 3 ERN 4 **ERNE**
flier: 4 ERNE
god: 7 NEPTUNE
Go out to: 3 EBB
Go to: 4 SAIL
Greek: 6 AEGEAN
growth: 5 ALGAE
Inland: 4 **ARAL**
Killer at: 4 ORCA
Left at: 4 PORT 5 APORT
letters: 3 HMS USS

life: 5 ALGAE
Like a ~ lion: 5 EARED
monster: 3 ORC
nymph: 6 NEREID 7 OCEANID
Pair at: 4 OARS
palm: 4 KELP
phase: 4 TIDE
plea: 3 SOS
predator: 4 ORCA
Room at: 5 CABIN
salt: 3 TAR
She at: 4 SHIP
shell seller: 3 SHE
spots: 5 ISLES 6 ISLETS
suffix: 5 SCAPE
Support at: 4 MAST
swallow: 4 **TERN**
urchin food: 4 KELP
Where river meets: 7 ESTUARY
~, in French: 3 MER
~, in Spanish: 3 MAR

Sea ___: 5 OTTER

___ Sea: 4 **ARAL**

Sea-___ Airport: 3 TAC

Seabees
mil. branch: 6 USNAVY
motto: 5 CANDO

Seabird: 3 ERN 4 ERNE TERN
Diving: 3 AUK 6 PETREL
Predatory: 4 SKUA
Tube-nosed: 6 PETREL

Seaboard: 5 COAST

Sea-ear: 7 ABALONE

Seafarer: 3 TAR 7 OLDSALT

Seafood
choice: 4 CRAB SOLE
7 LOBSTER
delicacy: 3 ROE
dish: 6 SCAMPI
entrée: 4 SOLE 5 SCROD
6 SALMON 8 SCALLOPS
10 REDSNAPPER
11 FILETOFSOLE
lover: 3 ERN

Seagal, Steven
1997 ~ movie:
13 FIREDOWNBELOW

Seagoing
(abbr.): 4 NAUT

letters: 3 USS
pronoun: 3 HER SHE
sort: 3 TAR
Seahawks
home: 7 SEATTLE
Seal: 4 SHUT 6 CACHET
Baby: 3 PUP
Eared: 5 OTARY
hunter: 4 ORCA
in the juices: 4 SEAR
Kind of: 5 EARED 6 EASTER
meal: 3 EEL
Official: 6 SIGNET
ring: 6 SIGNET
Solomon's: 4 STAR
Young: 3 PUP
Sealant: 3 TAR
Sealed: 4 SHUT 6 UNOPEN
They may be: 4 LIPS
Sealer
Carton: 4 TAPE
Street: 3 TAR
wax ingredient: 3 LAC
Windowpane: 5 PUTTY
Seals
Herd of: 3 POD
Like: 7 AQUATIC
Like some: 5 **EARED**
        7 EARLESS
Male ~ have them: 6 HAREMS
singing partner: 6 CROFTS
Sealskin
wearer: 5 ALEUT
Sealy
rival: 5 **SERTA**
Seam
content: 3 ORE
Fix a: 3 SEW
Garment: 4 DART
Raised: 4 WELT
Seaman: 3 TAR 4 SALT
assent: 3 AYE
Seams
Burst at the: 4 TEEM
Come apart at the: 4 FRAY
They come out at the: 4 ORES
Seamstress
fastener: 3 PIN
~ Betsy: 4 ROSS

Seamy
stuff: 3 ORE
Sean
Actor: 4 PENN 5 ASTIN
Séance
board: 5 OUIJA
phenomenon: 6 TRANCE
sound: 3 **RAP**
Sea of ___ (Black Sea arm):
        4 **AZOV**
"Sea of Love"
star: 6 PACINO
Seaplane
part: 5 FLOAT
Seaport
Adriatic: 4 BARI
Alaskan: 4 NOME
Algerian: 4 **ORAN**
Brazilian: 5 BELEM NATAL
Danish: 6 ODENSE
French: 5 BREST
German: 5 EMDEN
Hawaiian: 4 HILO
Indian: 6 MADRAS
Irish: 6 TRALEE
Israeli: 4 ACRE 5 HAIFA
Italia: 6 NAPOLI
Italian: 4 BARI 5 GENOA
        7 SALERNO
Japanese: 4 KOBE
Mediterranean: 4 GAZA
New Jersey: 10 PERTHAMBOY
Polish: 6 GDANSK
Saxony: 5 EMDEN
southeast of Roma: 6 NAPOLI
south of Milan: 5 GENOA
Ukrainian: 6 ODESSA
Vietnamese: 6 DANANG
Yemen: 4 **ADEN**
Seaquake
aftermath: 7 TSUNAMI
Search: 5 QUEST
a perp: 5 FRISK
blindly: 5 GROPE
engine result: 3 HIT
for: 4 SEEK
for food: 6 FORAGE
for gold: 3 PAN
for prey: 5 PROWL

for the unknown: 7 ALGEBRA
for water: 5 DOWSE
high and low: 5 SCOUR
In ~ of: 5 AFTER
(into): 5 DELVE
party: 5 POSSE
thoroughly: 4 COMB 5 SCOUR

Searcher
need: 7 WARRANT

Searle
Artist: 6 RONALD

Sears
rival: 5 KMART

Seascape
color: 4 AQUA

"Seascape"
playwright: 5 ALBEE

Seashell
Colorful: 6 TRITON
seller: 3 **SHE**

Seashore: 5 COAST

Season: 3 AGE
Allergy ~ sound: 5 ACHOO
Christmas: 4 NOEL YULE
French: 3 ETE
Like monsoon: 5 RAINY
opener: 3 MID PRE
Rabbit: 6 EASTER

Seasonal
air: 4 NOEL
drink: 3 NOG
employee: 3 ELF
schedule abbr.: 3 EDT
song: 4 NOEL 5 CAROL
song end: 4 SYNE
visitor: 5 SANTA

Seasoned: 4 AGED
Highly ~ stew: 6 BURGOO
one: 3 VET
pro: 3 ACE
sailor: 4 SALT
stew: 6 RAGOUT
vet: 6 OLDPRO

Seasoning: 5 SPICE
Add: 4 SALT
Chef: 4 HERB
French: 3 SEL
Get some: 3 AGE
Goulash: 7 PAPRIKA

Meat: 4 SAGE
Soup: 5 THYME
Spaghetti: 7 OREGANO
Stuffing: 4 SAGE

Seasons
Four: 4 YEAR
Goddesses of the: 5 HORAE

"Seasons, The": 8 ORATORIO

Seat: 3 USH
Airline ~ feature: 7 ARMREST
a jury: 7 IMPANEL
Baby: 3 LAP
Back ~ driver: 3 NAG
Bar: 5 STOOL
Bridge: 4 **EAST** WEST 5 NORTH
   SOUTH
Catbird: 4 NEST
Child: 3 LAP
choice: 5 AISLE
Church: 3 PEW
Cowboy: 6 SADDLE
Deluxe: 3 BOX
Elephant: 6 HOWDAH
for two or more: 6 SETTEE
Give a ~ to: 5 ELECT
Greet and: 5 SEEIN
holders: 3 INS
Judge: 4 **BANC**
Kind of: 3 BOX 5 AISLE
   6 SENATE
Left one's: 5 AROSE
Occupied, as a: 5 TAKEN
of Allen County: 4 IOLA
of County Kerry: 6 TRALEE
of Garfield County: 4 ENID
of Greene County: 5 XENIA
of Hawaii County: 4 HILO
of Jackson County: 4 EDNA
of Marion County: 5 OCALA
of Silver Bow County: 5 BUTTE
of Ward County: 5 MINOT
of Washoe County: 4 RENO
of White Pine County: 3 ELY
Provide a ~ for: 5 ELECT
Return to one's: 7 REELECT
Saloon: 5 STOOL
seeker: 3 POL
Simple: 5 STOOL
Soft: 4 SOFA 6 SETTEE

Sought a: **3** RAN
Sunday: **3** PEW
Tried to keep one's: **5** RERAN
Seater: 5 USHER
Seating
  Mass: **3** PEW
  request: **5** AISLE
  sect.: **4** ORCH
  section: **4** TIER
  Soft: **4** SOFA
  Stadium: **10** GRANDSTAND
SEATO
  Part of: **4** ASIA EAST
Seattle
  ballplayer: **7** MARINER
  City east of: **8** BELLEVUE
  forecast: **4** RAIN
  Gp. protested in: **3** WTO
  hoopster: **5** SONIC
  sound: **5** PUGET
  team: **6** SONICS
Seawater: 5 BRINE
  Like: **6** SALINE
  part: **4** NACL
  Treat, as: **6** DESALT
Seaweed: 4 ALGA KELP **5 ALGAE**
  extract: **4** AGAR
  product: **4 AGAR**
Seaweed-wrapped
  fare: **5** SUSHI
SeaWorld
  attraction: **4** ORCA **5 SHAMU**
  performer: **4** SEAL
Sebastian
  Explorer: **5** CABOT
  Runner: **3 COE**
Sec: 4 JIFF **5** TRICE
SEC
  eleven: **4** BAMA
Secant: 5 RATIO
Seceder
  of 1967: **6** BIAFRA
Secessionist
  of '67: **7** BIAFRAN
Secessionists
  ~, initially: **3** CSA
Sechs
  Half of: **4** DREI
Seckel: 4 PEAR

kin: **4** BOSC
Secluded
  corner: **4** NOOK
  road: **5** BYWAY
  spot: **4** GLEN
  valley: **4** DELL **GLEN**
Second: 4 ECHO
  (abbr.): **4** ASST
  afterthought: **3** PPS
  Begin a ~ hitch: **4** REUP
  busiest U.S. airport: **5** OHARE
  chance: **15** ANEWLEASEONLIFE
  chance for a student: **6** RETEST
  Come in: **4** LOSE **5** PLACE
  coming: **6** ENCORE
  degree: **3** MBA
  Do a ~ draft: **6** RETYPE
  Dove into: **4** SLID
  Fairy tale ~ word: **4** UPON
  family of the 1990s: **5** GORES
  Finish: **5** PLACE
  First and: **5** GEARS **8** ORDINALS
  Got to ~ base: **5** STOLE
  half of an album: **5** SIDEB
  Have ~ thoughts: **3** RUE
    8 REASSESS
  in a series: **4** BETA
  in command: **4** VEEP
  man on the moon: **6** ALDRIN
  name in inventions: **4** ALVA
  name in rock: **4** ARON
  of Adam: **4** ABEL
  of all: **3** EVE
  of Eric: **4** LEIF
  of Eve: **4** ABEL
  of Frank: **3** AVA
  of Henry VIII: **4** ANNE
  of Jackie: **3 ARI**
  of two: **6** LATTER
  person: **3** EVE YOU
  prefix: **4 NANO**
  president: **5** ADAMS
  section: **5** PARTB
  sequel tag: **3** III
  shot: **6** RETAKE
  showing: **5** RERUN
  sight: **3** ESP
  sinner: **4** ADAM
  son: **4** ABEL

start: 4 NANO
Take: 5 STEAL
Take a ~ look at: 6 REREAD
to none: 4 BEST
Second ___ (tops): 6 TONONE
Second Amendment
org.: 3 NRA
word: 4 ARMS
Secondary: 5 MINOR
British ~ school exam: 6 OLEVEL
Second-century
anatomist: 5 GALEN
"Second Coming, The"
poet: 5 YEATS
Second-generation
Japanese: 5 NISEI
Second-guessing: 9 HINDSIGHT
Secondhand: 4 USED
deal: 6 RESALE
Second-in-command: 6 DEPUTY
Second-rate: 6 LESSER
Seconds: 4 MORE
Factory ~ (abbr.): 4 IRRS
Second-stringer: 3 SUB 5 SCRUB
Second-year
student: 4 SOPH
Secrecy
Breach of: 4 LEAK
Sign of: 4 VEIL
Secret: 5 CODED INNER
6 ARCANE CLOSET
agent: 3 SPY
author: 11 GHOSTWRITER
Blonde's: 3 DYE
Chef's: 4 HERB
Chinese ~ society: 4 TONG
competitor: 3 BAN 5 ARRID
doctrine: 6 CABALA
East German ~ police: 5 STASI
ending: 3 IVE
exit: 8 TRAPDOOR
gp.: 3 NSA
language: 4 CODE
Make: 6 ENCODE
meeting: 5 **TRYST**
Member of a ~ order: 5 MASON
motive: 5 ANGLE
No longer: 4 SEEN
offering: 6 ROLLON

Redhead's: 5 HENNA
rendezvous: 5 TRYST
retreat: 4 LAIR
society: 5 MAFIA
society secret: 6 RITUAL
Soviet ~ police: 3 KGB
Spill a: 4 BLAB
store: 5 CACHE STASH
stuff: 6 ARCANA
supply: 5 CACHE STASH
target: 4 ODOR
Well-kept ~, to some: 3 AGE
writing: 4 CODE
Secretarial
position: 4 DESK
Secretary: 4 DESK 5 FILER
Oscar Madison's: 5 MYRNA
Perry's: 5 **DELLA**
~ Powell: 5 COLIN
Secretary-General
First U.N.: 3 LIE
Secretary of Defense
Nixon's: 5 LAIRD
Secretary of State
1960s ~: 4 RUSK
1980s ~: 4 HAIG
Carter's: 5 VANCE
Clinton's: 5 COHEN
Eisenhower's: 6 DULLES
FDR's: 4 HULL
Kennedy's: 4 RUSK
Lincoln's: 6 SEWARD
Reagan's: 4 HAIG
Truman's: 7 ACHESON
~ Vance: 5 CYRUS
Secretary of the Interior
Kennedy's: 5 UDALL
Secretary of War
First: 4 KNOX
WWII: 7 STIMSON
Secreted: 3 HID
Secreter
Musk: 5 OTTER
Secretion
Resinous: 3 LAC
Squid: 3 INK
Secretly: 7 ONTHEQT
tie the knot: 5 ELOPE
watch: 5 SPYON

"Secret of ___, The": 4 NIMH
Secrets: 6 ARCANA
Secs.
  60 ~: 3 MIN
Sect
  Buddhist: 3 **ZEN**
  Iowa religious: 5 AMANA
  Lancaster-area: 5 AMISH
  leader: 3 TRI
  Meditative: 3 ZEN
  Mennonite: 5 AMISH
  Muslim: 5 SUNNI
  Plain-living: 5 AMISH
  Punjab ~ member: 4 SIKH
  Religious: 4 CULT
  suffix: 5 ARIAN
Sect.
  Bookstore: 4 BIOG
  Seating: 4 ORCH
  Yearbook: 3 SRS
Sectarian
  Jamaican: 5 RASTA
Section: 4 AREA PART UNIT
        ZONE 5 PIECE
  Big ~ in a dictionary: 3 ESS
  Grass: 3 SOD
  of Queens: 7 ASTORIA
  Seating: 4 TIER
  section: 4 ACRE
  Semi: 3 CAB
Sector: 4 AREA ZONE
  boundary: 3 ARC
Secular: 4 **LAIC** 6 LAICAL
Secure: 3 GET ICE TIE 4 MOOR
        SAFE SHUT 5 CLAMP
        6 ANCHOR ATTACH
        ATTAIN FASTEN OBTAIN
  a ship: 4 MOOR
  a victory: 3 ICE
  tightly: 5 TRUSS
  with lines: 4 MOOR
Secured:
        15 UNDERLOCKANDKEY
Securities
  Like some: 3 OTC
  trader, for short: 3 ARB
Security
  agreement: 4 LIEN
  breach: 4 LEAK

Company with famous: 4 ELAL
  concern: 4 LEAK
  Form of: 4 LIEN
  Govt.: 5 TBILL **TNOTE**
  holder: 6 BAILEE
  Loan: 4 LIEN
  pmt.: 3 DEP
  problem: 4 LEAK
  Professor's: 6 TENURE
  system part: 6 SENSOR
  U.S.: 5 TNOTE
Security Council
  Former ~ member: 4 USSR
  member: 3 USA
  vote: 3 NON
Secy.: 4 ASST
Sedaka
  Singer: 4 NEIL
Sedan: 3 CAR 4 AUTO
  Nissan: 6 ALTIMA
  Oldsmobile: 5 ALERO
  sweetie: 4 AMIE
Sedate: 5 STAID
Sedation
  Under: 5 DOPED
Sedative: 6 OPIATE
Seder
  serving: 5 MATZO
Sedgwick
  Actress: 4 **KYRA**
  Warhol pal: 4 EDIE
Sedgy
  stretch: 5 MARSH
Sediment: 4 LEES SILT 5 DREGS
  Wine: 4 **LEES**
Sedimentary
  rock beds: 6 STRATA
Sedona
  automaker: 3 KIA
Seducer
  of Tess: 4 ALEC
"Seduction of Joe Tynan, The"
  star: 4 ALDA 8 ALANALDA
"Seduction of the Minotaur"
  author: 3 NIN
Seductive: 4 SEXY
Seductress: 5 SIREN
See: 4 DATE SPOT
  Able to ~ through: 4 ONTO

A psychic may ~ it: 4 AURA
As much as one cares to:
    6 EYEFUL
Cause to ~ red: 6 ENRAGE
Does more than: 6 RAISES
eye to eye: 4 JIBE 5 **AGREE**
Fail to: 4 MISS
For all to: 5 OVERT 6 OPENLY
It helps you ~ plays: 5 SLOMO
It may make you ~ things: 3 LSD
Just like you ~ it: 4 ASIS
One way to: 8 EYETOEYE
Plain to: 5 OVERT
red: 3 **OWE** 4 FUME RAGE STOP
    5 STEAM 6 GETMAD
socially: 4 DATE
stars: 4 GAZE
the old gang: 5 REUNE
the sights: 4 TOUR
to: 4 TEND
You can ~ right through them:
    6 LENSES
See-___: 4 THRU
"See?": 5 GETIT
"See!": 10 ITOLDYOUSO
"See ___" (news program):
    5 ITNOW
"___ see!": 3 SOI
"___ See Clearly Now": 4 ICAN
Seed: 5 SPORE
Caffeinated: 4 KOLA
case: 4 ARIL
Citrus: 3 PIP
coat: 4 ARIL 5 TESTA
covering: 4 **ARIL**
Feed: 3 OAT
Go to: 3 ROT
Plant more: 5 RESOW
Prickly ~ cover: 3 BUR
Pumpkin: 6 PEPITA
Rudimentary: 5 OVULE
Scatter: 3 **SOW**
shell: 4 HULL
source: 6 SESAME
Spread: 5 SOW
Seed-bearing
organ: 6 PISTIL
Seeded
It may be: 3 RYE

Seedless
plant: 4 FERN
raisin: 7 SULTANA
Seeds: 3 OVA
Apple ~ site: 4 CORE
Seed-to-be: 5 OVULE
Seedy
joint: 4 DIVE
Seeger
Folk singer: 4 **PETE**
"See if ___!": 5 ICARE
Seeing
Not ~ eye to eye: 6 ATODDS
red: 3 MAD 4 SORE 5 IRATE
    6 INDEBT
Respond to ~ red: 4 STOP
things: 4 EYES
"___ seeing you": 5 ILLBE
"___ see it ...": 3 ASI
Seek
answers: 3 ASK
approval from: 6 PLAYTO
change: 3 BEG
damages: 3 SUE
Didn't go: 3 HID
help from: 6 PRAYTO TURNTO
info: 3 ASK
the hand of: 3 **WOO**
What some scouts: 6 TALENT
Seeker
Asylum: 6 EMIGRE
Evaded the: 3 HID
Food: 7 FORAGER
Office: 3 POL
Pleasure: 8 HEDONIST
Pole: 5 PEARY
Solitude: 5 LONER
Vein: 5 MINER
Seeking: 5 AFTER
Seeming: 5 QUASI
Seemingly
boundless: 4 VAST
forever: 3 EON 4 AEON AGES
    EONS
limitless: 4 VAST
"___ seems": 4 SOIT
Seen
enough: 5 HADIT
Hardly: 4 RARE

Remains to be: 5 RUINS
Seldom: 4 **RARE**
"See no ___ ...": 4 EVIL
Seep: 4 OOZE
Seepage
  at sea: 5 BILGE
Seer: 6 ORACLE
  card: 5 TAROT
  deck: 5 TAROT
  reading matter: 9 TEALEAVES
  sign: 4 OMEN
  Spanish: 3 OJO
  suffix: 3 ESS
Sees
  One who ~ what you mean:
    9 LIPREADER
Seesaw: 6 TEETER
  requirement: 3 TWO
  sitter of rhyme: 4 ESAU
"See Spot run"
  book: 6 READER
Seethe: 4 BOIL
Seething: 5 ABOIL
See-through: 5 CLEAR SHEER
  item: 4 LENS PANE
  wrap: 5 SARAN
"See ya!": 3 BYE 4 CIAO TATA
    5 ADIEU ADIOS IMOFF
    LATER
Sega
  rival: 3 NES
  user: 5 GAMER
Segal
  Author: 5 ERICH
Segment: 4 PART 5 PIECE
  ___ segno: 3 DAL
Sego lily
  state: 4 UTAH
Segovia
  Guitarist: 6 ANDRES
Segue: 6 LEADIN
  Communiqué: 4 ASTO
Sei
  halved: 3 TRE
Seiji
  Conductor: 5 OZAWA
Seine
  City on the: 5 PARIS ROUEN
  contents: 3 EAU

feeder: 4 **OISE** 5 MARNE
port: 5 ROUEN
sight: 3 ILE
Summer on the: 3 **ETE**
tributary: 4 **OISE** 5 MARNE
"Seinfeld"
  A Costanza on: 7 ESTELLE
  Any ~ episode, now: 5 RERUN
  character Elaine: 5 BENES
  character Kramer: 5 COSMO
  postal worker: 6 NEWMAN
  role: 6 ELAINE GEORGE
    KRAMER
  uncle: 3 LEO
Seinfeldesque: 3 WRY
Seis
  halved: 4 TRES
Seismic
  event: 5 QUAKE 6 TREMOR
Seize: 3 NAB 4 GRAB TAKE
    5 USURP WREST
    6 SNATCH
  firmly: 4 GRIP
  ~, à la Caesar: 5 CARPE
Seized
  the opportunity: 7 MADEHAY
  vehicle: 4 REPO
Seko, Mobutu ___: 4 **SESE**
Selassie
  of Ethiopia: 5 **HAILE**
Selassie, Haile
  follower: 5 **RASTA**
  ~, originally: 9 RASTAFARI
Seldom: 6 RARELY
  seen: 4 RARE
Select: 3 OPT TAP 4 CULL PICK
    5 ELITE 6 CHOOSE
  at random: 4 DRAW
  for jury duty: 7 EMPANEL
  group: 5 ALIST ELITE
  ~, with "for": 3 OPT
Selected: 5 CHOSE 6 CHOSEN
Selection
  Auto: 5 SEDAN
  Brunch: 5 CREPE 6 OMELET
  Caucus: 8 DELEGATE
  Dairy: 4 OLEO
  Golf: 4 IRON
  Make a: 3 OPT

Pub: 3 ALE
Selective: 6 CHOOSY
Selena
  Music style of: 6 TEJANO
Selene
  realm: 4 MOON
  Sister of: 3 EOS
Selenic: 5 LUNAR
Seles
  of tennis: 6 MONICA
  rival: 4 GRAF
Self: 3 **EGO**
  expression: 3 IAM
  Inner: 5 ANIMA
  prefix: 3 AUT
  starter: 3 ESS HER 4 AUTO
Self-___: 7 RELIANT
Self-assurance
  Spirited: 4 ELAN
Self-assured: 6 POISED
Self-centered
  sort: 6 EGOIST
Self-conceit: 3 EGO
Self-confidence: 5 POIŚE
      6 APLOMB
  Destroy the ~ of: 5 ABASH
Self-congratulatory: 4 SMUG
Self-conscious
  giggle: 6 TITTER
Self-contradictory
  thing: 7 PARADOX
Self-defense: 4 PLEA
  method: 4 JUDO 6 KARATE
Self-employed
  people: 3 EDS
  professional: 9 FREELANCE
Self-esteem: 3 EGO
Self-evident
  It's: 6 TRUISM
  truth: 5 **AXIOM**
Self-government
  Local: 8 HOMERULE
Self-guided
  tour: 7 EGOTRIP
Self-identifying
  response: 5 ITSME
Self-image: 3 **EGO**
Self-importance: 3 EGO
Self-important

pace: 5 STRUT
Self-indulgent
  act: 7 EGOTRIP
Selfish
  Harbor ~ motives:
      15 HAVEANAXTOGRIND
  sort: 5 TAKER
      14 DOGINTHEMANGER
Selfishness: 6 EGOISM
Self-mover
  rental: 5 UHAUL
Self-proclaimed
  "greatest": 3 ALI
Self-produced
  CD: 4 DEMO
Self-question: 7 DOIDARE
Self-regard: 3 EGO
Self-righteous
  sort: 4 PRIG
Self-satisfied: 4 **SMUG**
      15 PROUDASAPEACOCK
Self-server: 6 EGOIST
Self-styled
  superior: 4 SNOB
Self-titled
  1982 ~ album: 6 ARETHA
Sell: 4 VEND 6 MARKET RETAIL
  at an inflated price: 5 SCALP
  Buy and: 5 TRADE 6 DEALIN
  for: 4 COST 5 FETCH
  (for): 3 REP
  off: 6 DIVEST
  out: 5 RATON 6 BETRAY
Sellecca
  Actress: 6 CONNIE
  Spouse of: 4 TESH
Selleck
  Actor: 3 TOM
  film of 1992: 10 MRBASEBALL
  ~ TV role: 6 MAGNUM
Seller
  Birthright: 4 **ESAU**
  caveat: 4 ASIS
  Insurance: 5 AGENT
  Property: 7 ALIENOR
  Seashell: 3 **SHE**
  Ticket: 5 AGENT
Sellers
  Actor: 5 PETER

role: 6 ORIENT
Tip: 5 TOUTS
Selling
  liquor: 3 WET
  point: 5 ASSET KIOSK STORE
  well: 3 HOT
Sellout: 3 HIT 5 SMASH
  sign: 3 **SRO**
"___ sells": 3 SEX
"___ sells seashells ...": 3 SHE
Selma
  ~, to Bart: 4 AUNT
Seltzer
  starter: 4 ALKA
Selves: 4 EGOS
Sem.
  study: 3 REL
Semana
  part: 3 DIA
Semaphore
  equipment: 4 FLAG
Semblance: 5 GHOST
Semester: 4 TERM
  ender: 4 EXAM
Semesters
  Two: 4 YEAR
Semi: 3 **RIG**
  compartment: 3 CAB
  conductor: 4 CBER
  engine: 6 DIESEL
  part: 3 CAB
  support: 4 AXLE
Semiaquatic
  salamander: 3 EFT 4 NEWT
Semicircle: 3 ARC
Semicircular
  molding: 4 TORI
  recess: 4 APSE
Semi-colon: 3 DOT
Semiconductor: 5 DIODE
Semidiurnal
  occurrence: 4 TIDE
Semiformal
  outfit: 3 TUX
Semimonthly
  tide: 4 NEAP
Seminary
  deg.: 3 STB
  subj.: 3 REL

Seminole
  leader: 7 OSCEOLA
Seminoles
  sch.: 3 FSU
Semiprecious
  stone: 5 AGATE
Semiquaver: 4 NOTE
"Semiramide"
  composer: 7 ROSSINI
Semiramis
  realm: 7 ASSYRIA
Semirural: 7 EXURBAN
Semisolid: 3 GEL
Semisweet
  wine: 8 SAUTERNE
Semite
  Ancient: 6 ESSENE
Semitic
  deity: 4 BAAL
  Demon of ~ lore: 6 LILITH
"Semi-Tough"
  actress Lotte: 5 LENYA
"Semper fidelis": 5 MOTTO
"Semper Fidelis"
  composer: 5 SOUSA
"___ semper tyrannis": 3 SIC
Sen
  division: 3 RIN
Senate
  accusation: 4 ETTU
  attire: 4 TOGA
  declaration: 3 YEA
  employee: 4 PAGE
  event: 6 DEBATE
  Former ~ leader: 4 LOTT
  gofer: 4 PAGE
  Hatch in the: 5 ORRIN
  Lott of the: 5 TRENT
  position: 4 SEAT
  shower: 5 CSPAN
  Speak in the: 5 ORATE
  spot: 4 SEAT
  Words heard in the: 4 ETTU
Senator
  California: 12 BARBARABOXER
  Connecticut: 4 DODD
  Delaware: 4 ROTH 5 BIDEN
  Former ~ Sam: 4 NUNN
  Former Georgia: 4 NUNN

Former Indiana: 4 BAYH
Former New York: 6 DAMATO
Former Rhode Island: 4 PELL
Former Tennessee: 5 ESTES
Former Virginia: 4 ROBB
Hawaiian: 6 INOUYE
Indiana: 5 LUGAR
in space: 4 GARN 5 GLENN
Massachusetts: 5 KERRY
Mississippi: 4 LOTT
    9 TRENTLOTT
Nevada: 4 REID
Six years, to a: 4 TERM
Vermont: 5 LEAHY
Watergate: 5 ERVIN
~ Bayh: 4 EVAN
~ Feinstein: 6 DIANNE
~ Hatch: 5 ORRIN
~ Kefauver: 5 ESTES
~ Kennedy: 3 TED
~ Lott: 5 TRENT
~ Sam: 5 ERVIN
~ Specter: 5 ARLEN
~ Thurmond: 5 STROM
~ Trent: 4 LOTT
Senators
home: 6 OTTAWA
org.: 3 NHL
Send: 4 SHIP WIRE 5 ELATE
    RADIO REMIT
again: 6 REPOST RESHIP
another way: 7 REROUTE
a telegram: 4 WIRE 6 TAPOUT
back: 4 ECHO 6 REMAND
by FedEx: 4 RUSH
elsewhere: 5 REFER
forth: 4 EMIT
headlong: 4 TRIP
in: 5 REMIT
off: 4 EMIT SHIP
on: 5 REFER
on an impulse: 5 EMAIL
out: 4 **EMIT**
packing: 3 AXE CAN 4 FIRE
    OUST
payment: 5 REMIT
sprawling: 4 TRIP
(to): 5 REFER
to a mainframe: 6 UPLOAD

via phone: 3 FAX
"Send help!": 3 SOS
"Send in the Clowns"
First word of: 4 ISNT
Seneca
Student of: 4 NERO
Senegal
Capital of: 5 DAKAR
suffix: 3 ESE
Senescence: 6 OLDAGE
Senile
one: 6 DOTARD
Senior: 4 YEAR 5 ELDER
    7 OLDSTER
Coll. ~ test: 3 GRE
event: 4 PROM
Former: 4 ALUM
in French names: 4 PERE
Junior, to: 8 NAMESAKE
Knievel: 4 EVEL
member: 4 DEAN 5 **DOYEN**
moment: 4 PROM
org.: 4 AARP
Organization for ~ travelers:
    11 ELDERHOSTEL
Seniors: 5 CLASS
exam: 3 SAT
gp.: 4 AARP
Sennett
character: 3 KOP
Señor
Answer to a: 4 SISI
feature: 5 TILDE
of old TV: 6 WENCES
suffix: 3 **ITA**
Señora
That: 3 ESA
Señorita: 6 LATINA
need: 5 TILDE
Sensation: 4 VIBE 5 ECLAT
Excited: 6 TINGLE
It's a: 4 ITCH
Lingering: 10 AFTERTASTE
Sudden: 4 STAB
Sensational: 5 LURID
Something: 7 SCANDAL
    SHOCKER
Sense: 4 FEEL 6 DETECT
6th ~: 3 ESP

Common: 5 SIGHT SMELL
    TASTE 6 SMARTS
Kind of: 5 HORSE
Make: 5 **ADDUP**
Making no: 5 INANE
Musical: 3 EAR
of completeness: 7 CLOSURE
of humor: 3 WIT
of manliness: 8 MACHISMO
of self: 3 EGO
of taste: 6 PALATE
Sixth: 3 **ESP**
Uncommon: 3 **ESP**
___ sense: 3 INA
"Sense and Sensibility"
  actress Thompson: 4 EMMA
  heroine: 6 ELINOR
Sensed: 4 FELT
Senseless: 5 INANE
  Knock: 4 STUN
Senses
  The human: 6 PENTAD
Sensible: 4 **SANE**
  More: 5 SANER WISER
Sensitive
  spot: 4 SORE
  subject: 3 AGE
  topic: 8 SORESPOT
  Very: 4 KEEN
Sensitivity: 3 EAR 4 TACT
Sensor
  forerunner: 4 ATRA
  Oral: 8 TASTEBUD
Sensory
  stimulus: 4 ODOR
  ___-sen, Sun: 3 YAT
Sent
  back (abbr.): 4 RETD
  to the mat: 3 KOD
  with a click: 7 EMAILED
Sentence: 4 DOOM
  Analyze a: 5 PARSE
  Complete a: 9 SERVETIME
  ending abbr.: 3 ETC
  Kind of: 5 RUNON
  Long: 4 LIFE
  modifier: 7 REMORSE
  One with a shortened:
    7 PAROLEE

part (abbr.): 4 PRED
Reduce a: 4 EDIT
Serve a: 6 DOTIME
shortener: 6 PAROLE
subject: 4 NOUN
Word preceding a: 6 GUILTY
Sentences
  Life: 4 OBIT
Sentient: 5 AWARE
Sentiment
  Public: 5 ETHOS
  Sampler: 13 HOMESWEETHOME
  Valentine: 4 LOVE
Sentimental: 8 DEWYEYED
  drivel: 3 GOO
  Get: 4 GUSH
  one: 6 MOONER SOFTIE
  Overly: 4 ICKY 5 SAPPY
  song: 6 BALLAD
Sentimentality
  Contrived: 7 TREACLE
  Excessive: 8 SCHMALTZ
Sentinel
  site: 10 WATCHTOWER
Sentry
  cry: 4 HALT
  Dangerous answer to a: 3 FOE
  duty: 5 WATCH
  Obey the: 4 HALT
Seoul
  Citizen of: 6 KOREAN
  soldier: 3 ROK
  Where ~ is: 5 KOREA
SEP: 3 IRA
Separate: 5 ALONE SPLIT
    6 DETACH UNGLUE
    7 SPLITUP
  flour: 4 SIFT
  Go ~ ways: 4 PART
Separated: 5 **APART**
Separately
  Not: 5 ASONE
  When sold: 4 EACH
"Separate Tables"
  star: 5 NIVEN
Separation
  Adjective relating to the ~ of
    church and state:
    9 TAXEXEMPT[*]

Sephia
maker: **3** KIA
Sept.
follower: **3** OCT
September
birthstone: **8** SAPPHIRE
bloom: **5** ASTER
Many a ~ birth: **5** VIRGO
The first of: **3** ESS
Third of: **3** PEE
"September ___" (Neil Diamond hit): 4 MORN
Septembre
It ends in: **3** ETE
Septennial
problem: **4** ITCH
Septet
One of a fairy tale: **3** DOC
Salty: **4** SEAS
Sepulcher: 4 TOMB **6** ENTOMB
Sequel
of 1847: **4** OMOO
Sci-fi: **6** ALIENS
tag: **3** III
Words used in a: **5** SONOF
Sequence: 6 SERIES
Alphabet: **3** ABC BCD CDE *etc.*
Boxer: **6** ONETWO
End of a: **3** ZEE
of amino acids: **11** GENETICCODE
Position in a: **4** SLOT
Scale: **4** DORE REMI MIFA FASO
SOLA LATI TIDO
that may end in "y": **5** AEIOU
Sequential
evidence: **10** PAPERTRAIL
Sequentially: 6 INTURN
Sequester: 7 ISOLATE
Sequins: 8 SPANGLES
Seraglio: 5 HAREM
chamber: **3** ODA
Seraph
circle: **4** HALO
French: **4** ANGE
"___ Sera, Sera": 3 QUE
Serb: 4 SLAV
neighbor: **5** CROAT
Serbian
city: **3** NIS

Sere: 4 ARID
Serenade: 6 SINGTO
the moon: **4** HOWL
Serenaded: 6 SANGTO
Serendip
Land once known as: **8** SRILANKA
"Serendipities"
author: **3** ECO
Serene: 4 CALM
Serengeti
family: **5** PRIDE
grazer: **3** GNU **5** ELAND
6 IMPALA
scavenger: **5** HYENA
sound: **4** ROAR
trek: **6** SAFARI
Serenity: 4 EASE **5** PEACE QUIET
Serf: 4 ESNE **5** HELOT
Sergeant: 3 NCO
command: **6** ATEASE FALLIN
in a 1941 film: **4** YORK
Obey the drill:
15 SNAPTOATTENTION
TV: **5** BILKO
What to call a: **3** SIR
Sergeant Friday
request: **5** FACTS
Sergeant Preston
horse: **3** REX
Sergeant York: 5 ALVIN
"Sergeant York"
star: **6** COOPER
Sergio
Director: **5** LEONE
Se Ri
of the LPGA: **3** PAK
Serial
for lunch: **4** SOAP
Partner of ~ number and rank:
4 NAME
segment: **7** EPISODE
Serials
Spaceman of: **11** FLASHGORDON
Series
1969 ~ winners: **4** METS
2000 ~ losers: **4** METS
CBS hit: **3** CSI
ender: **3** ETC ZEE **4** ETAL
5 OMEGA

End of a: **3** ZED ZEE **5** OMEGA
First in a: **5** ALPHA
Fourth in a: **3** DEE
Last in a: **3** NTH ZEE **5** OMEGA
Like one in a: **3** NTH
of engagements: **4** TOUR
opener: **3** ESS **5** ALPHA
prototype: **5** PILOT
Repeated: **5** CYCLE
Second in a: **4** BETA
separator: **5** COMMA
starter: **6** OPENER
Start of a German: **4** EINS
___ serif: **4** SANS
Serious: 4 DIRE **5** ACUTE GRAVE
       SOBER **6** SOLEMN
       10 NONONSENSE
about: **4** INTO
Get: **5** SOBER
       11 KNUCKLEDOWN
hang-ups: **3** ART
Isn't: **4** KIDS **5** JESTS
Not: **6** JOKING
play: **5** DRAMA
sign: **4** OMEN
trouble: **3** WOE **8** HOTWATER
Seriously
Not: **5** INFUN
Take: **4** HEED
Serkin
Pianist: **6** RUDOLF
Serling
Host: **3** ROD
Like ~ tales: **5** EERIE
Like ~ tales (var.): **4** EERY
series: **15** THETWILIGHTZONE
Sermon
basis: **4** TEXT
Deliver a: **6** PREACH
ender: **4** AMEN ETTE
subject: **3** SIN **4** EVIL
       11 ORIGINALSIN
Sermonize: 6 PREACH
Serpent
African: **3** ASP
Beany's ~ buddy: **5** CECIL
home: **4** EDEN
Nine-headed: **5** HYDRA
sound: **3** SSS **4** HISS

suffix: **3** INE
tail: **3** INE
Serpentine: 5 SNAKY
curve: **3** ESS
shape: **3** **ESS**
swimmer: **3** EEL
"Serpico"
author Peter: **4** **MAAS**
director Sidney: **5** LUMET
producer De Laurentiis: **4** DINO
Serta
rival: **5** SEALY
Serum
holder: **4** VIAL
Serval: 3 CAT
Servant
Eastern: **4** AMAH
Future: **5** ROBOT
Prospero's: **5** ARIEL
Servants: 4 HELP
Serve: 5 AVAIL DOFOR LADLE
       6 DOTIME
a sentence: **6** DOTIME
at parties: **5** CATER
drinks: **4** POUR
Fit to: **4** ONEA
Great: **3** ACE
How to ~ Welsh rabbit:
       7 ONTOAST
in the capacity of: **5** ACTAS
Net-touching: **3** LET
Ready to: **4** DONE ONEA
       5 ONTAP
Score on a: **3** ACE
soup: **5** LADLE
Super: **3** ACE
the purpose: **5** AVAIL
to be replayed: **3** LET
Server: 6 WAITER
Caesar: **9** SALADBOWL
Coffee: **3** **URN**
Drive-in: **6** CARHOP
edge: **4** ADIN
Frank: **4** DELI
item: **4** FILE
reward: **3** TIP
Salad: **5** TONGS
Situation for a: **4** ADIN
Soup: **5** LADLE **6** LADLER

Water: 4 EWER
Wheeled: 7 TEACART
Service
Afternoon: 6 TEASET
Auto: 4 LUBE
Be of ~ to: 5 AVAIL
call: 3 LET
charge: 3 FEE
Church: 4 MASS
club: 7 KIWANIS
expert: 4 ACER
Fit for: 4 ONEA
Great: 3 ACE
group: 6 TEASET
holder: 5 PADRE
Join the: 6 ENLIST
Kind of: 3 CAR LIP TEA 4 ROOM
    TAXI WIRE
Length of: 6 TENURE
Of: 5 **UTILE** 6 USABLE
One in the: 3 HUP
Out of ~ (abbr.): 3 RET
Press into: 3 USE
Put back into: 5 REUSE
Put into: 3 **USE**
Social: 3 TEA
status: 4 ONEA
Sunday: 4 MASS
volunteer: 8 ENLISTEE
Wire: 3 **UPI**
Wonderland: 6 TEASET
Serviceable: 4 ONEA 5 OFUSE
    UTILE
Service station: 6 CHAPEL
    TEMPLE
container: 6 OILCAN
service: 4 LUBE
Servicewoman
British: 4 WREN
Servile
Act: 6 GROVEL
Servilely: 7 ADULATE
Serving: 9 WAITINGON
a purpose: 5 UTILE
bowl: 6 TUREEN
of butter: 3 PAT
perfectly: 5 ACING
Wee: 4 DRAM
Servitude: 7 PEONAGE

Sesame: 7 OILSEED
paste: 6 TAHINI
plant: 3 TIL
treat (var.): 5 HALVA
Word before: 4 OPEN
"Sesame Street"
channel: 3 PBS
character: 4 BERT ELMO
    5 ERNIE 8 THECOUNT
grouch: 5 OSCAR
lesson: 4 ABCS
puppeteer: 7 FRANKOZ
Spanish speaker on: 6 ROSITA
Sess.: 3 MTG
Session
Be in: 3 SIT
Held ~ again: 5 REMET
Kind of: 5 QANDA
Rap: 6 SEANCE
Returned to: 5 RESAT
School: 4 TERM
Training: 7 SEMINAR
Was in: 3 SAT
with an M.D.: 4 APPT
Sessions
org. (1987–93): 3 FBI
successor: 5 FREEH
Set: 3 **GEL** 8 ARRANGED
afire: 3 LIT 6 IGNITE
(against): 3 PIT
All: 5 READY
apart: 5 ALLOT 7 ISOLATE
a price: 3 ASK
aside: 4 SAVE 5 ALLOT
    8 RESERVED
back: 7 SCENERY
do-overs: 7 RETAKES
down: 3 LAY PUT 4 ALIT LAID
    5 WROTE
Empty math: 4 NULL
fire to: 5 TORCH
firmly: 5 EMBED
foot in: 5 ENTER
foot (on): 4 TROD
free: 5 UNTIE 7 UNLOOSE
Gym: 4 REPS
Head: 4 EARS EYES
Kind of: 7 DINETTE ERECTOR
loose: 5 UNTIE

Mind: **5** IDEAS **6** IMAGES
of beliefs: **5** CREDO
off: **3** IRK **5** APART **6** IGNITE
    8 DETONATE
of moral principles: **5** ETHIC
of plates: **5** ARMOR
of sheets: **4** REAM
of supplies: **3** KIT
of values: **5** ETHIC
(on): **3** SIC
One of a matched: **3** HIS **4** HERS
one's sights: **3** AIM **5** AIMED
out: **5** ARRAY **6** EMBARK
piece: **4** PROP
right: **4** MEND **5** AMEND
    7 REDRESS
sail: **3** RIG **6** EMBARK
    8 PUTTOSEA
shout: **3** CUT
Smart: **5** MENSA
Sock: **4** PAIR
straight: **4** TRUE **5** **ALIGN**
    6 ORIENT
Super: **4** KEYS
the pace: **3** LED
to go: **5** READY
to rest: **5** ALLAY
up: **3** RIG **5** ERECT FRAME
    6 RIGGED **7** ARRANGE
    PREPARE
~, in French: **4** FIXE
Set-___: 3 TOS
___ Set: 7 ERECTOR
Setback: 4 LOSS **7** RELAPSE
Minor: **4** SNAG
Set ___ by: 5 STORE
Seth
Brother of: **4** ABEL
Father of: **4** ADAM
Son of: **4** **ENOS**
Seton
Author: **4** **ANYA**
Sets: 3 TVS **5** JELLS
upon: **5** HASAT
Sette
successor: **4** OTTO
Settee: 4 SOFA
Setter
Precedent: **8** TESTCASE

Trap: **6** SNARER
Setting: 5 **ARENA** PLACE
35mm ~: **5** FSTOP
Settle: 3 PAY SAG **4** SINK **5** REPAY
    6 LOCATE **7** RESOLVE
down: **5** ROOST
in: **4** NEST
once and for all: **8** NAILDOWN
One who won't ~ down:
    5 NOMAD
snugly: **8** ENSCONCE
Tough to: **5** MESSY
up: **5** REPAY
Settled: 3 LIT **4** ALIT PAID
down: **4** ALIT
Got: **8** HADASEAT
in: **6** NESTED
Settlement
Frontier: **7** OUTPOST
Settler
Andes: **4** INCA
building material: **3** SOD
Quarrel: **4** DUEL
Transvaal: **4** BOER
Set-to: 3 ROW
Set-top
box: **4** TIVO
Setup
Circus: **4** TENT
Sound: **6** STEREO
___ seul (dance solo): 3 PAS
Seuss
character: **5** LORAX **6** SAMIAM
turtle: **6** YERTLE
Sevareid
Newsman: **4** **ERIC**
Sevastopol
locale: **6** CRIMEA
Seven
Best of: **6** SERIES
City of ~ hills: **4** ROME
Explore the ~ seas: **4** SAIL
Group of: **6** HEPTAD
Largest of: **4** ASIA
One of: **3** SEA **4** ASIA
One of Salome's: **4** VEIL
There are ~ in a semana: **4** DIAS
Three before: **8** AREACODE
Winner of ~ Emmys: **5** ASNER

~, in Spanish: **5** SIETE
"Seven Brides for Seven Brothers"
  actor Howard: **4** KEEL
Seven deadly sins
  One of the: **4** ENVY LUST
     5 ANGER PRIDE SLOTH
Seven Dwarfs
  One of the: **3** DOC **5** DOPEY
     HAPPY **6** GRUMPY SLEEPY
     SNEEZY **7** BASHFUL
Seven Little ___: 4 FOYS
"Seven-Per-Cent Solution, The"
  actor Williamson: **5** NICOL
  author Nicholas: **5** MEYER
Seven-piece
  puzzle: **7** TANGRAM
Sevens
  Card game also called: **6** FANTAN
  It uses ~ through aces: **4** SKAT
Seventh
  grader: **7** PRETEEN
  letter: **3** **ETA**
  planet: **6** URANUS
  sign: **5** LIBRA
Seventh-century
  date: **3** DCI DCL
Seventh heaven: 5 BLISS
     7 ECSTASY **8** EUPHORIA
     9 CLOUDNINE
  In: **6** ELATED
  Put in: **5** ELATE
Seven-time
  batting champ Rod: **5** CAREW
  home run champ: **5** KINER
  ~ Best Actor nominee:
    11 PETEROTOOLE
  ~ Emmy winner: **5** ASNER
    7 EDASNER
  ~ Wimbledon champ: **4** GRAF
    7 SAMPRAS
"Seven Year Itch, The"
  actor Tom: **5** EWELL
"Seven Years in Tibet"
  star: **4** PITT
Sever: 3 CUT HEW LOP **4** REND
Several
  czars: **5** IVANS
  periods: **4** ERAS
  reps: **3** SET

Sondheim's: **5** TONYS
Severe: 5 ACUTE HARSH STERN
  Became less: **8** RELENTED
  blow: **4** GALE
  Less: **5** LAXER
  pang: **5** THROE
  test: **6** ORDEAL
Severinsen
  Bandleader: **3** DOC
Severity: 5 RIGOR
Severn
  feeder: **4** AVON
Seville: 3 CAR **4** AUTO
  Info: Spanish cue
  Lady of: **4** DONA
  sir: **5** SENOR
  six: **4** SEIS
  snack: **4** TAPA
  some: **4** UNOS
Sèvres
  Info: French cue
Sew
  loosely: **5** BASTE
  up: **3** ICE **4** DARN MEND
Seward
  Folly of: **6** ALASKA
Seward Peninsula
  city: **4** **NOME**
Sewell
  Author: **4** ANNA
Sewer
  line: **3** HEM **4** SEAM **6** THREAD
  of note: **4** ROSS
  protector: **7** THIMBLE
  ~ Howe: **5** ELIAS
Sewing
  case: **4** **ETUI**
  connection: **4** SEAM
  kit item: **3** PIN **5** SPOOL
    10 PINCUSHION
  requirement: **6** NEEDLE
  tool: **3** AWL
Sewing machine
  attachments: **7** HEMMERS
  inventor: **4** HOWE **9** ELIASHOWE
  inventor Howe: **5** ELIAS
Sewn
  edge: **3** HEM
  It may be ~ in: **5** IDTAG

Sex
  An end to: **3** ISM
  appeal: **5** OOMPH
  determinant: **11** XCHROMOSOME
  Intro to: **3** UNI
  prefix: **3** UNI
  researcher Hite: **5** SHERE
  suffix: **3** ISM
Sex ___ : 6 APPEAL
"Sex and the City"
  heroine: **6** CARRIE
  network: **3** HBO
Sex-changing
  suffix: **3** INE
Sexennial
  affair: **10** SENATERACE
Sexes
  For both: **7** EPICENE
"sex, lies, and videotape"
  actress MacDowell: **5** ANDIE
Sexologist
  ~ Shere: **4** HITE
Sextet
  halves: **4** TRIO
  Inning: **4** OUTS
Sexton: 4 POET
Sexual
  prefix: **4** AMBI
Sexy: 3 HOT
  skirt: **4** MINI
  skirt feature: **4** SLIT
  ~ Beatles girl: **5** SADIE
"___ sez ...": 3 SOI
S.F
  hours: **3** PST
  summer setting: **3** PDT
S.F. Giant: 4 NLER
SFO
  posting: **3** ARR ETA ETD
Sgt.: 3 <u>NCO</u>
  charges: **4** PFCS
"Sgt. Pepper"
  album song:
    15 WHENIMSIXTYFOUR
Shabbily
  Treat: **3** USE
Shabby: 5 RATTY SEEDY
    6 RAGTAG
    10 DOWNATHEEL

Shack: 3 HUT **5** HOVEL **6** LEANTO
  Caddy: **6** GARAGE
Shackle: 6 FETTER **7** ENSLAVE
    LEGIRON
Shackles: 5 IRONS
Shackleton
  Antarctic explorer: **6** ERNEST
Shad
  delicacy: **3** <u>ROE</u>
  Had: **3** ATE
Shade: 3 <u>HUE</u> **4** TINT TONE
    5 TINGE **6** NUANCE
  Beach: **3** TAN
  Eye: **5** HAZEL
  Fall: **4** RUST
  giver: **3** ELM **4** TREE
  maker: **3** ELM
  Marine: **4** AQUA
  Neutral: **3** ASH **4** ECRU **5** BEIGE
  of black: **3** JET **4** COAL EBON
    5 RAVEN
  of blond: **3** <u>ASH</u>
  of blue: **3** SKY **4** ANIL AQUA
    CYAN NAVY NILE OPAL
    TEAL **5** AZURE ROYAL
    6 COBALT
  of brown: **4** ECRU RUST **5** BEIGE
    COCOA SEPIA UMBER
  of green: **3** PEA **4** JADE LIME
    MOSS NILE **5** BERYL KELLY
    OLIVE **7** AVOCADO
  of meaning: **6** NUANCE
  of purple: **4** PUCE **5** LILAC
    MAUVE
  of red: **4** BEET **6** CERISE
  Pastel: **4** AQUA **5** LILAC
  provider: **3** ELM **4** TREE
    6 AWNING **7** ELMTREE
  Sky: **5** AZURE
  Soft: **4** AQUA **6** PASTEL
  tree: **3** <u>ELM</u> **5** BEECH
Shading: 4 TINT TONE
Shadow: 4 <u>TAIL</u> **5** UMBRA
  Eclipse: **5** UMBRA
  Five o'clock: **7** STUBBLE
  Five o'clock ~ remover: **5** RAZOR
  Get rid of a: **5** SHAVE
"Shadow, The"
  actor Baldwin: **4** ALEC

character Cranston:
6 LAMONT
Shadowbox: 4 SPAR
Shadows
When ~ are shortest: **4** NOON
Shadowy: 6 UMBRAL
Shady
group: **4** ELMS
It may be: **4** PAST
spot: **5** **ARBOR** BOWER
Shaffer
play: **5** EQUUS
Shaft
Auto: **4** AXLE
find: **3** ORE
of light: **3** RAY
They get the: **6** MINERS
Wheel: **4** AXLE
Shag
rug feature: **4** PILE
Shaggy: 7 HIRSUTE
ape: **5** ORANG
bovine: **5** BISON
ox: **3** YAK
Shah
homeland, once: **4** IRAN
subject, once: **5** IRANI
Shah ___ (Taj Mahal builder):
5 JAHAN
Shaheen
Pol. designation for Gov. Jeanne:
3 DNH
Shahn
Painter: **3** BEN
___ Shah Pahlavi: 4 REZA
Shake: 3 JAR **4** LOSE **5** ELUDE
6 WAGGLE
a leg: **3** HIE
alternative: **6** MALTED
hands with: **4** MEET
it or break it: **4** ALEG
off: **4** LOSE **5** ELUDE EVADE
slightly: **3** JOG
Something to: **4** HAND
up: **3** **JAR** MAR **4** FAZE JOLT
ROIL **5** ROUSE SCARE
7 AGITATE STARTLE
"Shake ___!": 4 ALEG
Shake like ___: 5 ALEAF

Shaken
It may be: **4** SALT
Shaker
Abbr. after: **3** HTS
contents: **4** SALT
leader: **6** ANNLEE
Mover and: **4** DOER **5** NABOB
Salt: **7** TSUNAMI
shaker: **6** SALTER
Shaker ___, OH: 3 HTS
Shakers
and others: **5** SECTS
founder Lee: **3** ANN
leader: **6** ANNLEE
partners: **6** MOVERS
Shakes
No great: **4** SOSO
Two: **3** SEC
~, for short: **3** DTS
Shakespeare: 4 BARD
character Andronicus: **5** TITUS
character Katharina: **5** SHREW
foot: **4** IAMB
king: **4** LEAR
Like a ~ sonnet: **6** IAMBIC
Mrs.: **4** ANNE
Performed, per: **5** DIDST
river: **4** AVON
suffix: **3** ANA
teen: **5** ROMEO
theatre: **5** GLOBE
title starter: **4** ALLS
Trouble, per: **3** ADO
villain: **4** IAGO
Witch, to: **3** HAG
Word repeated in a ~ title:
7 MEASURE
work: **4** PLAY
Shakespearean
actor Edmund: **4** KEAN
bad guy: **4** IAGO
contraction: **5** TWERE
ensign: **4** IAGO
exclamation: **3** FIE
forest: **5** ARDEN
king: **4** **LEAR** **6** OBERON
prince: **3** **HAL**
setting: **6** VERONA
sprite: **5** **ARIEL**

suffix: 3 EST ETH
title start: 4 ALLS 5 ASYOU
tragedy: 7 OTHELLO
verb: 4 DOTH HATH
villain: 4 IAGO
~ Moor: 7 OTHELLO
Shakespeare Festival
New York ~ founder: 4 PAPP
"Shakespeare in Love"
prop: 4 EPEE
~ Oscar winner: 5 DENCH
Shaking
spell: 4 AGUE
Shakur
Rapper: 5 TUPAC
Shalala
Former HHS Secretary: 5 DONNA
Shale
extract: 3 OIL
features: 6 STRATA
Shalhoub, Tony
~ TV role: 4 MONK
Shalit
Critic: 4 GENE
"... ___ shall die": 3 ORI
Shallow
Bake in a ~ dish: 5 SHIRR
container: 4 TRAY 5 PLATE
Get into ~ water: 4 WADE
Not: 4 DEEP
"Shallow ___" (Paltrow film):
3 HAL
"Shall we?"
Answer to: 4 LETS
"Shalom!": 5 PEACE
Sham: 4 FAKE HOAX 5 BOGUS
FALSE 6 ERSATZ PSEUDO
7 PRETEND
Shaman: 6 HEALER
Shambles: 4 MESS RUIN
Make a ~ of: 5 TRASH
Shame
Crying: 4 PITY
Put to: 5 ABASH
Show: 6 REDDEN
"Shame ___!": 5 ONYOU
Shamefaced: 7 HANGDOG
Shameless: 6 BRAZEN
joy: 4 GLEE

promotion: 4 PLUG
"Shame on you!": 3 TSK
Shampoo
bottle word: 4 OILY
brand: 5 PRELL
ingredient: 4 **ALOE**
step: 5 RINSE
"Shampoo"
screenwriter Robert: 5 TOWNE
~ Oscar winner: 8 LEEGRANT
Shamrock
land: 4 EIRE ERIN
Shamu: 4 **ORCA**
Shamus: 3 TEC
Shandy
creator: 6 STERNE
ingredient: 3 ALE 8 LEMONADE
"Shane"
actor Jack: 7 PALANCE
star: 4 **LADD** 8 ALANLADD
Shanghai: 6 ABDUCT
"Shanghai Express"
actress Anna May: 4 WONG
"Shanghai Noon"
actor Jackie: 4 CHAN
actor Wilson: 4 OWEN
actress Lucy: 3 LIU
Shangri-La: 4 EDEN
Man of: 4 LAMA
Shankar
instrument: 5 SITAR
Sitarist: 4 **RAVI**
tune: 4 RAGA
Shannon
Singer: 3 **DEL**
Where the ~ flows: 4 EIRE
Shanty: 3 HUT 5 HOVEL
6 LEANTO
Shape: 4 MOLD
Angular: 3 ELL
Bent out of: 5 IRATE 6 WARPED
Get in: 5 TRAIN 6 TONEUP
In fighting: 4 TRIM
In good: 3 FIT 4 HALE TRIM
5 SOUND TONED
In sorry: 5 SEEDY
Out of: 4 BENT SOFT
Take: 4 JELL
Twist out of: 4 WARP 5 GNARL

up: 6 SNAPTO
Shapeless
mass: 4 GLOB
Shapely
leg: 3 GAM
Shaper
Gelatin: 4 MOLD
Shoe: 4 TREE
Shop: 5 LATHE
Tool: 3 DIE
Wood: 3 ADZ
Shaping
tool: 4 RASP 5 LATHE
Shapiro
Jazzman: 5 ARTIE
Shaq
alma mater: 3 LSU
Former teammate of: 4 KOBE
Former team of: 4 HEAT
     5 MAGIC 6 LAKERS
of basketball: 5 ONEAL
org.: 3 NBA
Shar-___ (dog): 3 PEI
Share: 3 CUT 4 DOLE 6 RATION
     7 PARTAKE PORTION
a border with: 4 ABUT
a role: 10 SPLITAPART
Don't: 3 HOG
equally: 5 HALVE SPLIT
Even: 4 HALF
Lion's: 4 MOST
Pay one's ~, with "up": 4 ANTE
Proportional: 5 QUOTA
Shared: 6 MUTUAL
between us: 4 OURS
computer sys.: 3 LAN
with: 6 TOLDTO
Sharer
Apartment: 6 ROOMIE
Bedroom: 3 SIB
Lead: 6 COSTAR
Legacy: 6 COHEIR
word: 3 OUR 4 OURS
Shares
Corp.: 3 STK
Fewer than 100: 6 ODDLOT
How some ~ are bought/sold:
     5 ATPAR
Like some: 7 PRORATA

Shari
Puppeteer: 5 LEWIS
Sharif
Actor: 4 **OMAR**
homeland: 5 EGYPT
title role: 3 CHE
Sharing
word: 6 APIECE
Sharjah: 7 EMIRATE
Shark: 8 MANEATER
clinger: 6 REMORA
hangout: 8 POOLHALL
home: 3 SEA 5 OCEAN
Kind of: 4 LOAN MAKO
Loan: 6 USURER
Loan ~ offense: 5 USURY
movie: 4 JAWS
offer: 4 LOAN
omen: 3 FIN
Small: 7 DOGFISH
Thresher: 6 SEAFOX
Sharkey
~ TV rank: 3 CPO
Sharks
or Jets: 4 GANG
Sharon: 7 ISRAELI
Actress: 5 GLESS
Land of: 6 ISRAEL
of Israel: 5 **ARIEL**
Sharp: 3 SLY 4 ACID **KEEN** TART
     5 ACERB ACRID ACUTE
     ALERT 6 ASTUTE CLEVER
     POINTY
bark: 3 YIP 4 YELP
blow: 4 SLAP
C: 5 DFLAT
change in direction: 3 ZIG
cheese: 6 ROMANO
competitor: 3 RCA 4 SONY
curve: 3 ESS
D: 5 EFLAT
F: 5 GFLAT
feller: 3 AXE
fight: 5 SETTO
flavor: 4 TANG
Having one: 3 ING
Key with one: 6 EMINOR
knock: 3 RAP
left or right: 3 JAB

Like ~ cheese: 4 AGED
Make a ~ turn: 4 VEER
Neither ~ nor flat: 5 ONKEY
part: 4 EDGE
punch: 3 AWL JAB
rebuke: 4 SLAP
ridge: 5 ARETE
taste: 4 **TANG**
turn: 3 ZAG ZIG
Very: 5 ACUTE
weapon: 5 SPEAR
Sharp as ___ : 5 ATACK
"Sharp Dressed Man"
band: 5 ZZTOP
Sharpen: 4 EDGE **HONE** WHET
    5 STROP
again: 6 REHONE
Sharpener: 5 HONER
    8 OILSTONE
Razor: 5 **STROP**
Sharper: 5 CHEAT
Sharp-eyed
hunter: 5 EAGLE
Sharply
dressed: 5 NATTY
stinging: 5 ACRID
Turn: 3 ZIG 4 SLEW VEER
Whack: 4 SWAT
Sharpness: 3 WIT 4 BITE EDGE
    TANG 6 ACUITY ACUMEN
Sharp-pointed
instrument: 6 STYLET
Sharps
Having five: 3 INB
Having four: 3 INE
Key with four: 6 EMAJOR
Key with no ~ or flats:
    6 AMINOR
Key with three ~ (abbr.):
    4 AMAJ
Sharpshooter: 7 DEADEYE
asset: 3 AIM
~ Oakley: 5 ANNIE
Sharp-smelling: 5 ACRID
Sharp-tasting: 4 TART 5 ACRID
    6 ACIDIC
Sharpton
and others: 3 ALS
Sharp-tongued: 5 ACERB

Sharp-toothed
fish: 5 MORAY
Sharp-witted: 6 ASTUTE
Shatner
sci-fi series: 6 TEKWAR
Word in ~ titles: 3 TEK
Shatt-al-Arab
port: 5 BASRA
Shave
Close: 5 SCARE
Prepare to: 6 LATHER
"Shave ___ haircut": 4 ANDA
Shaver
brand: 4 ATRA
Little: 3 LAD TOT 4 TYKE
need: 5 RAZOR
Shavers
Women with: 3 MAS
Shavetails
(abbr.): 3 LTS
Shaving
accessory: 5 STROP
brand: 4 ATRA
mishap: 4 **NICK**
stuff: 4 FOAM
tool: 5 RAZOR
Shaving cream
feature: 4 FOAM
ingredient: 4 ALOE
Shaw
Author: 5 IRWIN
Bandleader: 5 **ARTIE**
Clarinetist: 5 **ARTIE**
Doolittle created by: 5 ELIZA
play: 7 CANDIDA
title starter: 4 ARMS
Shawl: 4 WRAP
Fur: 5 STOLE
Mexican: 6 SERAPE
Shawm
descendant: 4 OBOE
Shawn
Dancer: 3 TED
of the NBA: 4 KEMP
Pitcher: 5 ESTES
Shawnee
Honorary: 5 BOONE
"Shawshank Redemption, The"
extra: 6 INMATE

Shays's Rebellion
Shays of: 6 DANIEL
She
gets what she wants: 4 LOLA
had a little lamb: 3 EWE
has a ball: 3 DEB
He and: 4 THEY
sheep: 3 EWE 4 EWES
~, in French: 4 ELLE
~, in Italian: 4 ESSA
Shea
and others: 6 STADIA
player: 3 MET 5 NYMET
Stadium near: 4 ASHE
Shearer
Actress: 5 MOIRA NORMA
Ballerina: 5 MOIRA
Shearing
candidate: 3 EWE
protest: 3 BAA
Shears
Use: 4 SNIP
Shearson
Ex-partner of: 6 LEHMAN
Sheathe: 6 ENCASE
Sheaves
Bring in the: 4 REAP
Sheba
creator: 4 INGE
today: 5 YEMEN
Shebang
The whole: 3 **ALL** 4 ATOZ
Shebat
follower: 4 ADAR
She-bear
~, in Latin: 4 URSA
~, in Spanish: 3 OSA
"She Believes ___": 4 INME
"___ she blows!": 4 THAR
Shed: 3 HUT 4 CAST EMIT LOSE
MOLT 6 HANGAR
LEANTO
feathers: 4 MOLT
item: 3 HOE 4 RAKE TEAR
tears: 4 WEEP WEPT
Shed ___ : 5 ATEAR
"She Done ___ Wrong": 3 HIM
Sheedy
Actress: 4 ALLY

Sheehan
Pulitzer writer: 4 NEIL
Sheehy
Author: 4 GAIL
Sheen: 6 LUSTER
Sheena
Singer: 6 EASTON
Sheep
Bear young, as: 4 YEAN
Clip: 5 SHEAR
coat: 4 WOOL 6 FLEECE
Dolly the: 5 CLONE
Female: 3 EWE
Like: 5 OVINE
Like clipped: 5 SHORN
Male: 3 RAM
place: 3 LEA
She: 3 EWE 4 EWES
shelter: 4 COTE
sound: 3 BAA 5 BLEAT
Stop counting: 5 SLEEP
type: 6 MERINO
Words to a black: 6 BAABAA
Young: 4 LAMB
Sheepdog: 6 HERDER
British: 7 SHELTIE
Hungarian: 4 PULI
Sheepish: 5 **OVINE**
remark: 3 BAA MAA 6 BAABAA
Sound: 5 BLEAT
Sheep-related: 5 OVINE
Sheepshank: 4 KNOT
Make another: 5 RETIE
Sheepskin
bearer: 4 GRAD
leather: 4 ROAN
Sheer: 5 UTTER
fabric: 5 NINON **TOILE** VOILE
Sheet
Animation: 3 CEL
Balance ~ item: 5 ASSET
Cheat: 4 TROT
Four-page: 5 FOLIO
Kind of: 4 SPEC
material: 5 SATIN 6 MUSLIN
7 PERCALE
of glass: 4 PANE
of ice: 4 FLOE
of stamps: 4 **PANE**

Scandal: **3** RAG
White as a: **4** PALE **5** ASHEN
Sheetful
of cookies: **5** BATCH
Sheet music
abbr.: **3** ARR
symbol: **4** CLEF REST **5** SEGNO
Sheets: 5 LINEN **6** STRATA
24 ~: **5** QUIRE
500 ~: **4** REAM
Material in: **4** MICA
Set of: **4** REAM
Three ~ to the wind: **3** LIT
    6 BLOTTO
Sheffield
Info: British cue
She-goat: 3 DOE
Sheik: 4 ARAB
bevy: **5** HAREM
of Ray Stevens:
    11 AHABTHEARAB
peer: **4** EMIR
Sheikdom
Gulf: **7** BAHRAIN
of song: **5 ARABY**
"Sheik of ___, The": 5 ARABY
Shelby
Historian: **5** FOOTE
Writer: **6** STEELE
Shelf: 5 LEDGE
bracket: **3** ELL
Fireplace: **3** HOB **6** MANTEL
Take off the: **3** USE
Shell
alternative: **4** HESS **5** AMOCO
    EXXON GETTY MOBIL
    6 SUNOCO
Deep-fried: **7** TIMBALE
figure: **6** OCTANE
food: **4** TACO
Food in a: **4** TACO
game: **4** SCAM
game need: **3** PEA
Kind of: **4** TACO
lining: **5** NACRE
mover: **3** OAR
Ornamental: **7** ABALONE
out: **5** SPEND
Propel a: **3** OAR

Racing: **5** SCULL
Seafood in a: **6** OYSTER
Seed: **4** HULL
Spiral: **5** CONCH
Stick a ~ in: **4** LOAD
team: **4** CREW
Shellac: 4 DRUB **5** TROMP
Shellacking: 4 BATH
Sheller
Sea: **6** ARMADA
Shelley: 5 ODIST
Actress: **4** LONG
alma mater: **4** ETON
Keats, to: **7** ADONAIS
Novelist: **4** MARY
poem: **3 ODE**
queen: **3** MAB
role: **5** DIANE
Shortly, to: **4** ANON
Sundown, to: **3** EEN
Shellfish: 7 ABALONE
bane: **7** REDTIDE
Shells: 4 AMMO **5** PASTA
"___ She Lovely": 4 ISNT
"She loves me"
flower: **5** DAISY
Shelter: 3 LEE **5** HAVEN
    6 HARBOR HOSTEL
and food: **5** NEEDS
Animal: **3** ARK **4** LAIR
Beach: **6** CABANA
Camp: **4** TENT
Crude: **3** HUT
Dugout: **4** ABRI
Gave ~ to: **6** HOUSED
gp.: **4** SPCA
Leafy: **5** ARBOR BOWER
Open: **6** RAMADA
Plains: **5** TEPEE
Sheep: **4** COTE
Toward: **4 ALEE**
Sheltered: 4 ALEE
inlet: **4** COVE
side: **3** LEE
spot: **4** COVE **5** HAVEN
Shelters: 5 ASYLA
Some tax: **8** ROTHIRAS
"Shelters of Stone, The"
author: **4** AUEL

Shelve: 5 DEFER TABLE
Shelved
  for now: **6** ONHOLD
Shelves
  Set of display: **7** ETAGERE
Shem
  Father of: **4** NOAH
Shemp: 6 STOOGE
  Brother of: **3** MOE
Shenanigan: 5 ANTIC PRANK
  Assist in a: **4** ABET
Shepard
  Astronaut: **4 ALAN**
  Playwright: **3** SAM
Shepard, Sam
  genre: **5** DRAMA
Shepherd
  boy of opera: **5** AMAHL
  Cry to a: **3** BAA
  Genesis: **4** ABEL
  locale: **3** LEA
Shepherd, Jean
  book:
      15 ACHRISTMASSTORY
Shepherdess
  of rhyme: **6** BOPEEP
Sheraton
  Food critic: **4** MIMI
Sheraton Hotels
  owner: **3** ITT
Sherbet
  choice: **6** ORANGE
  kin: **3** ICE
Shere
  Sexologist: **4** HITE
Sheridan
  Actress: **3** ANN
Sheriff
  aide: **6** DEPUTY
  asst.: **3** DEP
  badge: **4** STAR **7** TINSTAR
  band: **5** POSSE
  Mayberry: **4** ANDY
  star: **5** BADGE
  TV: **4** LOBO
Sheriff Lobo
  portrayer: **5** AKINS
Sheriff Taylor
  boy: **4 OPIE**

Sherilyn
  Actress: **4** FENN
Sherlock
  Going on, to: **5** AFOOT
  lead: **4** CLUE
  portrayer: **5** BASIL
  "The Woman," to: **5** IRENE
Sherman
  Comic: **5** ALLAN
  took it: **7** ATLANTA
  War, to: **4** HELL
  was his veep: **4** TAFT
Sherman ___, California: 4 OAKS
Sherman Oaks
  City near: **6** ENCINO
Sherpa
  land: **5** NEPAL
  sighting: **4** YETI
Sherry
  casks: **6** SOLERA
  Drank: **5** WINED
  Semisweet: **7** OLOROSO
  Spanish: **7** AMOROSO
Sherwood: 6 FOREST
"She's a Lady"
  songwriter: **4** ANKA
"She's ___ Have It": 5 GOTTA
"She's So High"
  singer Bachman: **3** TAL
" ___ She Sweet?": 4 AINT
Shetland: 4 PONY
Shevat
  follower: **4** ADAR
Shield: 5 BADGE
  border: **4** ORLE
  Driver: **5** VISOR
  Heat ~ locale: **8** NOSECONE
  of Athena: **5** AEGIS
  of Zeus: **5** AEGIS
  Sun: **7** PARASOL
"Shield, The"
  actress Pounder: **3** CCH
Shields
  Lyricist: **3** REN
  on stage: **6** BROOKE
Shields, Brooke
  TV role for: **5** SUSAN
Shift: 5 DRESS **7** CHEMISE
  Late: **8** DOGWATCH

neighbor: 5 ENTER
start: 4 NINE
Work: 4 DAYS
Shifted
They may be: 5 GEARS
9 TENSPEEDS
Shiftless: 4 LAZY
Shifty
one: 5 SNEAK
Shih ___: 3 TZU
Shih Tzu: 3 TOY 6 LAPDOG
origin: 5 TIBET
Shiite
deity: 5 ALLAH
leader: 4 IMAM
Shiites: 4 SECT
Shill
Audience: 5 PLANT
for: 4 ABET
Shilling
A pound and a: 6 GUINEA
Fifth of a: 5 PENCE
Shillong
state: 5 ASSAM
Shilly-shally: 5 WAVER
Shiloh
commander: 5 GRANT
general: 5 BUELL
priest: 3 ELI
Shimmering
stone: 4 OPAL
"Shimmy, Shimmy, ___-Bop":
4 KOKO
Shimon
of Israel: 5 **PERES**
Shinbone: 5 **TIBIA**
Shindig: 4 BASH GALA 5 PARTY
Island: 4 LUAU
Shindigs: 3 DOS
Shine: 5 EXCEL GLEAM
7 RADIATE
in ads: 3 **GLO**
Partner of: 4 RISE
Rise and: 6 AWAKEN
Take a ~ to: 3 WAX 4 LIKE
"Shine a Little Love"
rock gp.: 3 ELO
"Shine On, Harvest Moon"
co-composer Bayes: 4 NORA

Shiner: 4 STAR
Big: 3 SUN
Shingle
abbr.: 3 ESQ
letters: 3 DDS
material: 5 CEDAR
words: 5 ATLAW
Shingles
Get new: 6 REROOF
Shining: 5 AGLOW
brightly: 6 AGLARE
example: 3 SUN
faintly: 8 AGLIMMER
"Shining, The"
actor Crothers: 7 SCATMAN
author: 4 KING
Shinny: 5 CLIMB
Shinto
temple gateway: 5 TORII
Shiny
fabric: 4 LAME 6 SATEEN
mineral: 4 MICA
on top: 4 BALD
"Shiny Happy People"
band: 3 REM
Ship: 4 SEND
1492 ~: 4 NINA 5 PINTA
50-oared ~: 4 ARGO
Any: 3 SHE
backbone: 4 KEEL
Behind, on a: 3 AFT
Big: 5 LINER
board: 5 PLANK
class: 8 STEERAGE
Clumsy: 3 TUB
company: 4 CREW
Crosswise, on a: 5 ABEAM
Cruise: 5 LINER
deck: 5 ORLOP
Easily handled, as a: 4 YARE
Fasten a ~ rope: 5 BELAY
frame: 4 HULL
front: 4 PROW
Gulf: 5 OILER
heading: 3 ENE ESE NNE SSE
Historic: 4 NINA
in news of 1898: 5 MAINE
landing: 4 PORT
Legendary: 4 ARGO

load: 5 CARGO
Lowest ~ deck: 5 ORLOP
mast: 4 SPAR
Memorable: 5 MAINE
Merchant: 6 ARGOSY
money-handler: 6 PURSER
Mutinied: 7 AMISTAD
of fuels: 5 OILER
of myth: 4 ARGO
part: 4 KEEL
Part of a ~ bow: 5 HAWSE
pole: 4 MAST
pronoun: 3 SHE
Ready to: 6 CRATED
rear: 5 STERN
rope: 3 TYE
Rope rung on a: 7 RATLINE
Secure a: 4 MOOR
shape: 4 HULL
Sinking ~ signal: 3 SOS
stabilizer: 4 KEEL
staff: 4 CREW
Steer a: 4 CONN
steering wheel: 4 HELM
Swerve, as a: 3 YAW
That: 3 HER SHE
To the back, on a: 6 ASTERN
To the left, on a: 5 APORT
wood: 4 TEAK
Shipboard
direction: 6 ASTERN
Shipbuilder
Biblical: 4 NOAH
Shipbuilding
wood: 4 TEAK
Shipman
prefix: 3 MID
Shipped: 4 <u>SENT</u>
Shipping
container: 5 CRATE
deduction: 4 TARE
dept. stamp: 4 RECD
hazard: 4 BERG FLOE
7 ICEBERG
inquiry: 6 TRACER
line: 6 HAWSER
nickname: 3 ARI
Remove from a ~ box:
7 UNCRATE

route: 7 SEALANE
unit: 3 TON
weight: 4 TARE
Ships
Group of: 5 FLEET 6 ARGOSY
Shipshape: 4 <u>NEAT</u> TIDY TRIM
Ship-to-ship
call: 4 AHOY
Shipworm: 5 BORER
Shipwreck
site: 4 REEF
Shiraz
locale: 4 IRAN
native: 5 IRANI
resident: 7 IRANIAN
Shire
Actress: 5 TALIA
Shirelles
hit: 10 SOLDIERBOY
Shirk: 5 EVADE
15 LIEDOWNONTHEJOB
Shirkers ~ it: 4 DUTY
Shirley
1963 role for ~: 4 IRMA
1994 role for ~: 4 TESS
Roommate of: 7 LAVERNE
Shirt: 3 TOP
brand: 4 <u>IZOD</u>
Casual: 3 TEE
Kind of: 3 TEE 4 POLO
opponent: 4 SKIN
part: 3 ARM 6 SLEEVE
shape: 3 TEE
size: 5 LARGE
size (abbr.): 3 LGE MED
spoiler: 5 STAIN
Striped ~ wearer: 3 REF
Stuffed: 4 PRIG SNOB
5 SNOOT
with a slogan: 3 TEE
with a reptilian logo: 4 IZOD
___ shirt: 5 ALOHA
Shirts
and skins: 5 TEAMS
Like Hawaiian: 4 LOUD
Shish ___: 6 KEBABS
Shish kebab
Like: 8 SKEWERED
pin: 6 SKEWER

Shiva
Wife of: 4 KALI
Shiver
producing: 5 EERIE
Shivering
fit: 4 AGUE
sound: 3 BRR
Shmoo
creator Al: 4 CAPP
SHO
alternative: 3 AMC HBO TMC
    TNT
Shoal: 4 REEF
Long: 4 SPIT
Shoat
place: 3 STY
Shock: 3 JAR ZAP 4 JOLT STUN
    5 AMAZE APPAL 6 APPALL
    TRAUMA
Cry of: 4 EGAD
Emotional: 6 TRAUMA
Express: 4 GASP
In: 6 AGHAST
Partner of: 3 AWE
React to a: 4 REEL
Show: 4 GASP
Shocked: 5 AGASP 6 **AGHAST**
reaction: 4 GASP
Visibly: 5 AGAPE ASHEN
"___ shocked!": 3 IAM
Shocker
Sea: 3 EEL
Sports: 5 UPSET
Shocking: 5 LURID
It can be: 3 EEL 5 TASER
sound: 3 ZAP
swimmer: 3 EEL
Shock jock
Don: 4 IMUS
Howard: 5 STERN
Shoddy: 4 POOR 5 CHEAP
    6 SLEAZY
Shoe
accessory: 6 INSOLE
Big: 3 EEE 4 EEEE
blemish: 5 SCUFF
bottom: 4 **SOLE**
box letters: 3 AAA EEE
Clunky: 5 SABOT

Comfy: 3 MOC
cover: 4 SPAT
Dancing ~ attachment: 3 TAP
Danish ~ brand: 4 ECCO
designation: 3 EEE
Do a ~ repair: 6 RESOLE
feature: 6 EYELET
forms: 5 LASTS
Golf ~ feature: 5 CLEAT
Heelless: 4 FLAT
holder: 4 TREE
hue: 3 TAN
insert: 4 TREE
lift: 7 HEELTAP
Low-heeled: 6 BROGUE
material: 5 SUEDE
name: 4 MCAN
part: 3 TOE 4 ARCH HEEL SOLE
    WELT 5 UPPER 6 INSOLE
    INSTEP
Pointy ~ wearer: 3 ELF
polish brand: 4 KIWI
saver: 4 TREE
seller Thom: 4 MCAN
shaper: 4 TREE
Soft: 3 MOC
style: 7 OPENTOE
Thick-soled: 4 CLOG
tie: 4 LACE
touting dog: 4 TIGE
Wide: 3 **EEE**
Woman's: 6 TSTRAP WEDGIE
Wooden: 4 CLOG 5 SABOT
Shoebox
letters: 3 **EEE**
"___ shoe fits ...": 5 IFTHE
Shoelace: 3 TIE
alternative: 6 VELCRO
hole: 6 EYELET
problem: 4 **KNOT**
tip: 5 **AGLET**
Shoeless
cobbler: 3 PIE
"Shoeless Joe"
portrayer: 6 LIOTTA
Shoemaker
form: 4 LAST
helper: 3 ELF
McAn: 4 THOM

strip: 4 WELT
Thom: 4 MCAN
tool: 3 AWL
Shoes
Big name in: 4 ECCO MCAN
   6 DEXTER
Feature of some: 6 TSTRAP
First name in: 6 IMELDA
Fix: 6 REHEEL RESOLE
Like some: 7 OPENTOE
   TWOTONE
Some: 5 NIKES
Thom of: 4 MCAN
Tied, as: 5 LACED
"Shoes of the Fisherman, The"
author: 4 WEST
Shoestring: 4 LACE
___ shoestring: 3 ONA
Shofar
source: 3 RAM
Shogun
capital: 3 EDO
sash: 3 OBI
Sholem
Author: 4 ASCH
Sholom
Author: 8 ALEICHEM
"Shoo!": 3 GIT 4 AWAY SCAT
Shoo-___: 3 INS
"Shooby-doo"
Sing: 4 SCAT
Shook
hands with: 7 GREETED
up: 6 JARRED 8 STARTLED
"Shoop Shoop Song"
syllables: 6 NANANA
Shoot: 4 DART FILM SPEW TWIG
   5 SPRIG
a ray: 4 LASE
at: 5 PLINK
down: 3 NIX
End of a: 4 WRAP
for: 5 AIMAT 6 ASPIRE
Get set to: 5 AIMAT
Grafting: 5 SCION
off: 4 EMIT
One about to: 5 AIMER
Prepared to: 4 DREW
Prepare to: 3 AIM

Something to ~ for: 3 PAR
   5 IDEAL SKEET
the breeze: 3 FAN **GAB** JAW RAP
   YAK 4 CHAT
up: 4 SOAR 5 SPIKE
"Shoot!": 3 **ASK** 4 DANG DARN
   DRAT 5 ASKME
   6 DARNIT
Shoot-'em-up: 5 OATER
Shooter: 3 TAW 4 GUNN
ammo: 3 PEA
Arrow: 4 EROS
filler: 4 AMMO
Glass: 3 TAW
gp.: 3 NRA
Hood's: 3 GAT
order: 9 SAYCHEESE
pellet: 3 PEA
setting: 5 FSTOP
Shot: 4 HYPO
Showy: 3 TAW
Shootin'
The whole ~ match: 3 ALL
Shooting
End of a: 4 WRAP
game: 5 SKEET
Kind of: 5 SKEET
marble: 5 AGATE IMMIE
org.: 3 NRA
Report of a: 4 BANG
site: 3 SET
sport: 5 SKEET
star: 6 METEOR
Start: 8 OPENFIRE
The whole ~ match: 3 ALL
"Shooting of Dan ___, The":
   6 MCGREW
Shootout
shout: 4 DRAW
site: 8 OKCORRAL
time: 4 NOON
Shop: 4 MART 5 STORE
C's in: 6 CLAMPS
Food: 4 DELI
holder: 4 VISE 5 CLAMP
   6 CCLAMP
item: 4 TOOL
piercer: 3 AWL
Reason to close: 6 SIESTA

shaper: 5 LATHE
Specialty: 5 SALON
Sweat: 3 SPA
talk: 5 LINGO
without buying: 6 BROWSE
Shopaholic
binge: 5 SPREE
delight: 4 SALE
heaven: 4 MALL
___ Shop Boys: 3 PET
Shopkeeper: 6 SELLER
on TV: 3 APU
Shoplift: 5 BOOST STEAL
Shoplifter
giveaway: 5 BULGE
Shoppe
sign word: 4 **OLDE**
Shopper
aid: 4 CART LIST
bag: 4 TOTE
binge: 5 SPREE
burden: 4 BAGS
Car ~ option: 5 LEASE
concern: 5 PRICE
notes: 4 LIST
stopper: 4 SALE
Shopping
aid: 4 CART LIST
binge: 5 SPREE
center: 4 MALL MART 5 PLAZA
channel: 3 QVC
Like some: 7 ONESTOP
London ~ district: 4 SOHO
Popular   spot: 6 THEWEB
Tokyo ~ district: 5 GINZA
Shoptalk: 5 **ARGOT** LINGO
Shopworn: 5 TRITE
"Shop ___ you drop": 3 TIL
Shore
bird: 3 ERN 4 ERNE GULL
TERN 5 HERON
dinner entrée: 4 CLAM CRAB
Far from: 4 ASEA
Off: 4 ASEA
Singer: 5 DINAH
Stay near the: 4 WADE
thing: 4 DUNE SAND
Shore, Pauly
1992 ~ film: 9 ENCINOMAN

Shorebird: 4 GULL TERN
6 AVOCET PLOVER
Shoreline
feature: 4 COVE 5 INLET
problem: 7 EROSION
shelter: 4 COVE
Shorelines
Like some: 6 ERODED
Short: 3 SHY 4 CURT 5 BRIEF
Info: Abbr. cue
and sweet: 5 TERSE
Are: 4 LACK
Be: 3 OWE
Be ~ with: 6 SNAPAT
bio: 4 OBIT VITA
blast: 4 TOOT
branch track: 4 SPUR
breath: 4 GASP
change: 3 CTS
Come up: 3 OWE 4 FAIL FALL
LOSE
coming: 3 ARR
Cut: 3 BOB END 4 CLIP CROP
5 ABORT
cuts: 4 BOBS 5 SNIPS
distance: 4 STEP
11 STONESTHROW
dog: 3 POM 4 PEKE
drama: 7 PLAYLET
drink: 4 DRAM
drive: 4 SPIN
end: 4 STUB
end of the stick: 7 BUMDEAL
RAWDEAL
Fall: 4 FAIL
flight: 3 **HOP**
form: 4 ABBR
Get ~ with: 6 SNAPAT
haircut: 3 BOB
holiday: 4 XMAS
In ~ supply: 5 SCANT
In a ~ time: 4 ANON
Is: 4 OWES
It may be ~ or long: 3 TON
jacket: 4 ETON
joke: 8 ONELINER
letter: 4 NOTE
life: 3 BIO
meeting: 4 SESS

news bit: 5 SQUIB
No ~ story: 4 EPIC SAGA
note: 4 MEMO
of shut: 4 AJAR
opera piece: 7 ARIETTA
order: 3 **BLT**
pan: 3 UGH
pants: 4 TROU
Partner of: 5 SWEET
people might write them: 4 IOUS
period: 3 SEC
poem: 6 RONDEL
punch: 3 JAB
putt: 5 TAPIN
race: 4 DASH 6 SPRINT
relative: 3 SIS
report: 3 POP
ride: 4 SPIN
run: 4 DASH
shot: 3 PIC
skirt: 4 **MINI**
sleep: 3 NAP
smoke: 3 CIG
snooze: 3 **NAP** 6 CATNAP
snort: 3 NIP 4 SHOT
sock: 6 **ANKLET**
solo: 7 ARIETTA
solos: 7 ARIOSOS
stop: 3 STA
stories: 3 LIT
story: 7 NOVELLA
street: 4 LANE
stroke: 4 PUTT
summary: 5 RECAP
swim: 3 DIP
tail: 4 SCUT
Take a ~ cut: 4 SNIP
time: 3 BIT MIN SEC 5 SPELL
    TRICE 6 MOMENT
time out: 4 DOZE
trader: 3 ARB
trip: 3 HOP
wave: 4 PERM
way to go: 3 RTE
Shortage: 4 LACK NEED
        6 DEARTH
Extreme: 6 FAMINE
Short-billed
rail: 4 SORA

Shortcut: 10 SIDESTREET
Chore: 9 TIMESAVER
Computer: 5 **MACRO**
Shorten: 3 MOW 4 EDIT
        7 ABRIDGE
again: 5 RECUT REHEM RESAW
Shortener
Fight: 3 TKO
List: 3 ETC 4 **ETAL**
Sentence: 6 PAROLE
Shortening: 4 LARD
Short-fused: 5 TESTY
Shorthand
inventor: 5 GREGG
pro: 5 **STENO**
Short-legged
dog: 6 BASSET
Short-lived
fashion: 3 FAD
particle: 4 MUON
success: 13 FLASHINTHEPAN
~ Ford: 5 EDSEL
Shortly: 4 **ANON** SOON 6 INABIT
        INASEC
before: 3 ERE
Short-range
plane: 6 AIRBUS
Short-sheeting: 5 PRANK
Shortsighted
one: 5 MYOPE
Shortsightedness: 6 MYOPIA
Short-spoken: 5 TERSE
Shortstop
Famous: 5 REESE
Like a: 5 AGILE
nickname: 4 AROD
~ Aparicio: 4 LUIS
~ Derek: 5 JETER
~ Garciaparra: 5 NOMAR
~ Jeter: 5 DEREK
~ Rodriguez: 4 ALEX
~ Vizquel: 4 OMAR
Short-straw
drawer: 5 LOSER
Short-tailed
wildcat: 4 LYNX
Short-tempered: 5 TESTY
Short-term
hire: 4 TEMP

Short-winded: 5 TERSE
Shoshone
  speaker: 3 UTE
Shostakovich
  Composer: 6 DMITRI
Shot: 3 BBS TRY 4 AMMO STAB
      5 GUESS KAPUT PHOTO
      SNORT
  A: 3 PER
  amount: 4 DOSE
  Arcing: 3 LOB
  Being: 8 ONCAMERA
  Big: 3 **VIP** 4 CZAR 5 CELEB
      MOGUL NABOB 6 FATCAT
      7 CLOSEUP
  Billiards: 5 CAROM MASSE
  Camera: 3 PAN
  contents: 4 SERA
  Drop: 4 DINK
  Easy: 5 TAPIN
  from a tee: 5 DRIVE
  Give it a: 3 TRY
  Good: 4 GOAL
  Had a: 5 DRANK
  Hot: 3 ACE
  Inside: 4 XRAY
  in the arm: 4 HYPO 5 BOOST
  in the dark: 4 STAB 5 GUESS
  Kind of: 3 FLU MUG 4 CHIP
  Last: 4 PUTT
  Long: 8 ONEINTEN
  Movie: 4 TAKE
  Not-so-big: 3 BBS
  of booze: 4 BELT SLUG 5 SNORT
  orderer: 3 DOC
  Overhead: 5 SMASH
  Prepare to be: 4 POSE
  put: 5 EVENT
  putter: 7 SYRINGE
  Replayed: 3 LET
  Second: 6 RETAKE
  shooter: 4 HYPO
  Small: 3 BBS 6 PELLET
  spot: 3 ARM
  Sweeping: 3 PAN
  Take a ~ at: 3 TRY
  Take another: 5 RETRY
  Tennis: 3 LOB
  Took a: 5 TRIED

  Tricky: 5 MASSE
  up: 4 GREW
  Voided: 3 LET
Shotgun
  shot: 6 PELLET
Shots
  Call the: 4 LEAD 6 DIRECT
  Some: 8 VACCINES
Should
  that be the case: 4 IFSO
  ~, with "to": 5 OUGHT
Shoulder
  blade: 7 SCAPULA
  Cold: 4 SNUB
  extension: 6 SLEEVE
  Give the cold: 4 SHUN SNUB
      5 SPURN 6 IGNORE
  muscle: 7 DELTOID ROTATOR
  muscle, briefly: 4 **DELT**
  ornament: 7 EPAULET
  Road: 4 BERM
  Touch on the: 3 TAP
  wrap: 5 SHAWL STOLE
Shouldered: 5 BORNE
Shoulders
  It has: 4 ROAD
Shout: 3 CRY 4 YELL
  from the stands: 3 RAH
  in church: 4 AMEN
  of adoration: 7 HOSANNA
  of disapproval: 3 BOO
  of encouragement: 5 CHEER
  of praise: 7 HOSANNA
  of support: 3 OLE
  of surprise: 3 OHO
  of triumph: 4 TADA
  to an unruly group:
      10 ONEATATIME
Shove: 4 PUSH
  off: 4 SAIL 5 LEAVE 6 DEPART
      7 SETSAIL
  Upward: 5 BOOST
Shovel
  Use a: 3 DIG
Shoving
  match: 4 SUMO
Show: 3 AIR 4 BARE 6 EVINCE
      7 PRESENT
  Afternoon: 7 MATINEE

again: 5 REAIR
appreciation: 4 CLAP 5 THANK
assent: 3 NOD
backer: 5 ANGEL
Big: 4 EXPO
Boffo: 5 SMASH
clearly: 6 EVINCE
concern for: 8 ASKAFTER
contempt: 5 SNEER
curiosity: 3 ASK
Daytime: 4 SOAP
disapproval: 3 BOO
disdain: 5 SCORN SNEER
fear: 4 PALE 5 COWER START
   7 TREMBLE
flexibility: 4 BEND 5 ADAPT
gratitude: 5 THANK
Hit ~ sign: 3 SRO
horse: 4 ARAB 5 THIRD
host: 5 EMCEE
how: 5 TEACH
interest in: 8 ASKABOUT
Kick off the: 4 OPEN
Kind of: 4 STAG TENT 5 RAREE
   6 ONEMAN 7 PREGAME
Light: 6 AURORA
Like ~ horses: 4 SHOD
mercy to: 5 SPARE
need (abbr.): 3 TKT
off: 5 SPORT 6 FLAUNT
off muscles: 4 FLEX
of hands: 4 VOTE
on TV: 3 AIR
opener: 4 ACTI 5 EMCEE
partner: 4 TELL
piece: 3 ACT 7 EPISODE
place: 5 STAGE THIRD
Postgame: 5 RECAP
presenter: 3 USO
proof of: 6 EVINCE
respect: 4 RISE 5 KNEEL
Run the: 4 RULE 5 EMCEE
   6 DIRECT
Science: 4 NOVA
scorn: 5 SNEER
shame: 6 REDDEN
shock: 4 GASP
showers: 3 TVS
signs of life: 4 STIR

souvenir: 4 STUB
starter: 4 ACTI
stoppers: 3 ADS
Street: 5 RAREE
surprise: 4 GASP
Take the ~ on the road: 4 TOUR
team spirit: 4 ROOT
the ropes to: 5 TEACH TRAIN
   6 ORIENT
They'll ~ you the world:
   7 ATLASES
to a seat: 3 USH
to be false: 5 BELIE
to be true: 5 PROVE
Trade: 4 EXPO
uncertainty: 6 SEESAW
up: 4 COME 6 APPEAR ARRIVE
up again: 5 RECUR
up for: 6 ATTEND
Variety: 5 REVUE
When the ~ must go on:
   7 AIRTIME
with skits: 3 SNL
Show ___: 3 BIZ
___ show (carnival): 5 RAREE
Show biz
org.: 5 ASCAP *
parent: 8 STAGEMOM
prize: 5 OSCAR
"Show Boat"
author Ferber: 4 EDNA
cap'n: 4 ANDY
composer Jerome: 4 KERN
song: 10 OLMANRIVER
Showdown: 4 DUEL
Showed
again: 5 RERAN
interest: 5 SATUP
up: 4 **CAME** 6 BLEWIN
Shower: 4 PELT RAIN 5 BATHE
affection: 4 DOTE
alternative: 4 BATH
Bridal: 4 RICE
Cold: 5 SLEET
gel additive: 4 ALOE
Get ready to: 6 UNROBE
House: 5 CSPAN
Kind of: 6 BRIDAL
Like a cold: 6 SLEETY

Local flick: 4 NABE
part: 6 METEOR
powder: 4 TALC
shower: 5 RADAR
sponge: 5 LOOFA
square: 4 TILE
time: 5 APRIL
Showers
Show: 3 TVS
Showery
month: 5 APRIL
"Show Girl"
tune: 4 LIZA
Showing
a fancy for: 4 INTO
awe: 5 AGAPE
distress: 6 PAINED
fatigue: 3 WAN
off: 10 HOTDOGGING
Second: 5 RERUN
wonder: 5 AGAPE
Showman
~ Ziegfeld: 3 FLO
"Show Me the Way"
band: 4 STYX
Show-off: 3 HAM
Educated: 6 PEDANT
Showplaces
Tree: 8 ARBORETA
Showroom
model: 4 DEMO
Shows
It ~ the way: 5 ARROW
Showtime
rival: 3 HBO
"___ show time!": 3 ITS
Showy: 4 ARTY GALA 6 FLORID
        ORNATE
bloom: 4 IRIS 5 ASTER
Culturally: 4 ARTY
display: 5 **ECLAT**
feather: 5 PLUME
Female with a ~ mate:
        6 PEAHEN
flower: 4 GLAD IRIS LILY ROSE
        5 ASTER CALLA PEONY
        6 AZALEA DAHLIA
        8 HIBISCUS
flowers: 5 CROCI 8 GLADIOLI

lily: 4 SEGO
moths: 3 IOS
parrot: 8 COCKATOO
shooter: 3 TAW
shrub: 6 AZALEA
trinket: 4 GAUD
Shred: 3 RIP 4 ATOM IOTA REND
        TEAR WHIT 5 RIPUP
        6 TATTER TEARUP
Shredded: 4 TORE TORN
        9 INTATTERS
Shredder
in the news: 5 ENRON
Shrek: 4 **OGRE**
Like: 6 RATEDG
Shrew: 3 HAG NAG 6 VIRAGO
Shrewd: 3 SLY 4 CAGY CUTE
        5 CAGEY CANNY SHARP
        SMART 6 ASTUTE
Shrewdness: 6 ACUMEN
Shriek
Comics: 3 **EEK** 4 YEOW
Shrill
cry: 4 YELP
insect: 6 CICADA
Shrimp: 4 RUNT 7 SHORTIE
dish: 6 **SCAMPI**
kin: 5 PRAWN
Shrimper
needs: 4 NETS
net: 5 TRAWL
Shrine
Buddhist: 5 STUPA
Cavelike: 6 GROTTO
Delphic: 6 ORACLE
Eastern: 6 PAGODA
Israeli: 6 MASADA
San Antonio: 5 ALAMO
Texas: 5 ALAMO
Shrine Game
side: 4 EAST WEST
Shriner
cap: 3 FEZ
Humorist: 3 WIL
Shrink: 3 SHY 7 ANALYST
        15 PSYCHOTHERAPIST
in fear: 6 CRINGE
org.: 3 APA
reply: 4 ISEE

Shrinking
Like a ~ violet: 3 SHY
sea: 4 **ARAL**
Shrivel: 4 WILT 5 WIZEN
6 WITHER
Shriver
Newswoman: 5 MARIA
of tennis: 3 **PAM**
Philanthropist: 6 EUNICE
Shriver, Maria
Mother of: 6 EUNICE
Shropshire
she: 3 EWE
Shroud
site: 5 TURIN
Shrovetide
serving: 5 BLINI
Shrove Tuesday
follower: 4 LENT
Shrub
Asian: 5 HENNA
Cashew family: 5 SUMAC
Flowering: 6 AZALEA SPIREA
Fragrant: 5 LILAC
Garden: 6 AZALEA
Indigo: 4 ANIL
Medicinal: 5 SENNA 6 CASSIA
Ornamental: 6 SPIREA
8 OLEANDER
Poison: 5 SUMAC
Rose family: 4 SLOE 6 SPIREA
Showy: 6 AZALEA
Shrubby
wasteland: 5 HEATH
Shrug
Eliciting a ~, maybe: 4 SOSO
off: 6 IGNORE
Shtick: 3 ACT BIT
Pick up: 4 LINE
Shucker
unit: 3 EAR
"Shucks!": 4 DANG DARN DRAT
HECK RATS 5 AWGEE
OHGEE 6 DARNIT
Shuffleboard
locale: 4 DECK
___ shui: 4 FENG
Shul
scroll: 5 TORAH

Shula
Coach: 3 DON
Shun: 5 AVOID 6 ESCHEW
Shuriken
thrower: 5 NINJA
"Shush!": 5 QUIET
Shut: 5 CLOSE
in: 4 PENT
loudly: 4 SLAM
Not quite: 4 **AJAR**
up: 4 SEAL 5 CLOSE
(up): 4 CLAM PENT
Shutdown
End a: 6 REOPEN
Shute
Author: 5 NEVIL
Shuteye: 5 SLEEP
Get some extra: 7 SLEEPIN
Got some: 5 SLEPT
Shutout
line score: 4 OOOO
score: 3 NIL
spoilers: 4 RUNS
Shutter
strip: 4 SLAT
Shutterbug
request: 5 SMILE
setting: 5 **FSTOP**
Shuttle
org.: 4 NASA
piece: 4 TILE
plane: 6 AIRBUS
seal: 5 ORING
site: 4 LOOM
Use a: 3 TAT 5 WEAVE
Shuttlecock: 4 BIRD
"Shut up!": 5 CANIT 6 STOWIT
7 SILENCE
Shy: 3 COY 5 SHORT 6 DEMURE
Be: 3 OWE
creature: 4 DEER
Not: 5 VOCAL
person: 15 SHRINKINGVIOLET
Shylock
doing: 5 USURY
offering: 4 LOAN
Play: 4 LEND
Sí: 3 YES
SI: 3 MAG

Siam
King of ~ phrase: **8** ETCETERA
suffix: **3** ESE
Visitor to: **4** **ANNA**
Siamang: 9 LESSERAPE
Siamese: 3 CAT **4** THAI
sound: **4** MEOW PURR
Tutor of ~ royalty: **4** ANNA
twin name: **3** ENG
Sib: 3 BRO **SIS**
Sibelius
Composer: **4** JEAN
Siberia
City in: **4** OMSK
locale: **4** ASIA
People of: **5** YAKUT
Send to: **5** EXILE
Siberian
Like ~ winters: **5** HARSH
plain: **6** STEPPE
relative: **5** ALEUT
river: **4** URAL
Sibilant
letters: **5** ESSES
Suffer with a: **4** LISP
summons: **4** PSST
Sibling
Biblical: **4** ABEL CAIN
Bro: **3** SIS
offspring: **5** NIECE
of Jo, Meg, and Amy: **4** BETH
Sis: **3** BRO
Spouse's: **5** INLAW
Siblings
Having no: **4** ONLY
Kid with no: **9** ONLYCHILD
Sibyl: 4 SEER **7** SEERESS
"Sic 'em!": 6 ATTACK
Sicilia: 5 ISOLA
Sicilian
city: **4** ENNA **7** PALERMO
peak: **4** ETNA
resort: **4** ENNA
volcano: **4** ETNA
wine: **7** MARSALA
Sicily
Capital of: **7** PALERMO
Island near: **5** MALTA
volcano: **4** ETNA **6** MTETNA

Sick: 3 ILL
and tired: **5** FEDUP
Feel: **3** AIL
Partner of: **5** TIRED
~, in French: **6** MALADE
Sick as ___: 4 ADOG
Sickle: 4 **TOOL**
Use a: **4** REAP
Sickly
looking: **6** SALLOW
"Sic semper tyrannis!"
crier: **5** BOOTH
Sid
TV costar of: **7** IMOGENE
"Siddhartha"
author: **5** **HESSE**
Side: 6 ASPECT
Calm: **3** LEE
Chopped: **4** SLAW
Coin: **7** OBVERSE
Cutting: **4** EDGE
Debate: **3** CON **PRO** **4** ANTI
Diamond: **5** FACET
Favor one: **4** LIMP
Flip: **5** HEADS
Go to the other: **6** DEFECT
It has a broad: **4** BARN
Lean to one: **4** LIST
Lee: **3** CSA **4** GRAY
Move to the: **5** SHUNT
One on your: **4** ALLY
On the other: **3** FOE
On the safe: **4** **ALEE**
On the small: **3** WEE
Other: **3** FOE **5** ENEMY
South: **3** ERN
squared: **4** AREA
The bright: **4** YANG
The dark: **3** YIN
Tip to one: **6** CAREEN
To one: **5** APART ASKEW
Toward the sheltered: **4** ALEE
track: **4** SPUR
Window: **4** JAMB
with: **4** ABUT
Word on either ~ of "-à-": **3** VIS
Sidearm
Cavalry: **5** SABER
Sideboard: 8 CREDENZA

Side by side: 4 AREA 7 ABREAST
  Live: 7 COEXIST
  Place: 6 APPOSE
Side dish: 4 **SLAW** 5 BEANS
    FRIES 8 COLESLAW
    9 RICEARONI
    11 IDAHOPOTATO
Sidekick: 3 **PAL** 4 AIDE 5 CRONY
  Batman's: 5 ROBIN
  Boris's: 7 NATASHA
  Captain Hook's: 4 SMEE
  Garfield's: 4 ODIE
  Green Hornet's: 4 KATO
  Lone Ranger's: 5 TONTO
  Ollie's: 4 STAN
  Stimpy's: 3 **REN**
  with a headband: 5 TONTO
Sideless
  cart: 4 DRAY
Sidelines
  brand: 8 GATORADE
  greeting: 5 HIMOM
  shout: 3 RAH
Sidelong
  glance: 4 LEER
Sidepiece: 4 JAMB
Sides
  Attack from all: 5 **BESET**
  Cricket: 3 ONS
  in some wars: 5 GANGS
  It has six: 4 UTAH
  On both ~ of: 7 ASTRIDE
Sideshow
  performer: 4 GEEK
  setting: 4 TENT
  site: 6 MIDWAY
Side-splitter: 4 RIOT
Sidestep: 5 AVERT AVOID DODGE
    ELUDE **EVADE** SKIRT
Sidestroke
  feature: 12 SCISSORSKICK
Side to side
  From: 7 ATHWART
  Move from: 4 SWAY
  Move rapidly from: 6 WAGGLE
Sidewalk
  eatery: 4 CAFE
  edge: 4 CURB
  Install a: 4 PAVE

stand drink: 3 **ADE**
  ~ Santa: 4 TEMP
Sideways
  look: 4 LEER
  Move: 4 CRAB
Sidewinder: 5 SNAKE
  React to a: 8 SEESTARS
  trail: 3 ESS
  warning: 6 RATTLE
Siding
  Railroad: 4 SPUR
  wood: 5 CEDAR
Sidle: 4 EDGE
Sidler
  Beach: 4 CRAB
Sidney
  Charlie Chan portrayer: 5 TOLER
  Director: 5 LUMET
Sieben
  follower: 4 ACHT
Siege
  1836 ~ site: 5 ALAMO
  defense: 4 MOAT
  Under: 5 BESET
Siegfried
  Partner of: 3 ROY
Siegmeister
  Composer: 4 ELIE
Siemens
  Electrical units now called:
    4 MHOS
Sierra ___: 5 **LEONE** MADRE
    6 NEVADA
Sierra Club
  cofounder: 4 MUIR
  concern (abbr.): 4 ECOL
Sierra Madre
  treasure: 3 ORO
Sierra Madres
  resort: 4 OJAI
Sierra Nevada
  City at the foot of the: 4 RENO
  lake: 5 TAHOE
  resort: 5 TAHOE
Siesta: 3 **NAP** 4 REST 5 SLEEP
  covering: 6 SERAPE
  Take a: 4 DOZE REST
  takers: 7 NAPPERS
  time (abbr.): 3 AFT

Siete
follower: **4** OCHO
minus seis: **3** UNO

Sieve
bottom: **4** MESH
Put through a: **4** RICE
Use a: **6** STRAIN

Sift
through: **6** WINNOW

Sigh
of relief: **4** PHEW
Quaint: **4** AHME
Satisfied: **3** AAH

Sighed
aside: **4** AHME
line: **4** AHME

Sigher
word: **4** ALAS

Sighs
of distress: **3** OHS

Sight: 5 SENSE
Catch ~ of: **4 ESPY** SPOT
     6 DESCRY
Out of: **4** GONE **6** HIDDEN
Put out of: **4** HIDE
Second: **3** ESP
Stay out of: **4** HIDE **6** HOLEUP
     LIELOW
"___ sight!": **4** OUTA **5** OUTTA

Sighting: 6 ESPIAL

Sights
See the: **4** TOUR
Set one's: **3** AIM
Set one's ~ on: **5** AIMAT

Sightseeing
trip: **4** TOUR

Sigma
follower: **3 TAU**
preceder: **3** RHO

Sigma ___: 3 CHI

Sigma Chi
Sweatheart of: **4** COED

Sigmoid
shape: **3** ESS

Sigmund: 5 FREUD
Daughter of: **4** ANNA

Sign: 3 INK **4 OMEN**
an agreement: **9** ENTERINTO
a new lease: **5** RELET

Apartment: **5** TOLET
away: **4** CEDE
Be a ~ of: **4** BODE
Broadcast: **5** ONAIR
Business: **4** ESTD **5** ESTAB
B'way: **3 SRO**
Danger: **7** REDFLAG
Diner: **4 EATS 7** EATHERE
Door: **3** MEN **4** EXIT **5** ENTER
Fall: **5** LIBRA **7** SCORPIO
First: **5** ARIES
Flat: **5** TOLET
for another hitch: **4** REUP
Foreboding: **4** OMEN **7** PORTENT
for short: **7** INITIAL
from above: **4** OMEN
gas: **4** NEON
Good: **4** HALO
Healing: **4** SCAB
Hit: **3** SRO
How to: **5** ININK
in the dark: **4** EXIT
Kind of: **4** NEON
Lighted: **4** EXIT
Musical: **4** CLEF
Octagonal: **4** STOP
of a mistake: **7** ERASURE
of approval: **3** NOD
of a winner: **3** VEE
of boredom: **4** YAWN
of disuse: **4** RUST
off: **3** END
off on: **4** OKAY
of life: **5** PULSE
of spring: **4** THAW **5 ARIES**
     6 GEMINI
of success: **3** SRO
of summer: **3 LEO 5** VIRGO
     7 THECRAB
of things to come: **4 OMEN**
on: **4** HIRE **5** ENROL LOGIN
     6 ENLIST
on again: **4** REUP
over: **4** CEDE
Pause: **5** COMMA
Peace: **4** DOVE
Place to: **10** DOTTEDLINE
Retro ~ word: **4** OLDE
Sale: **4** ASIS

Store: 4 OPEN SALE
Studio: 5 **ONAIR**
up: 4 JOIN 5 **ENROL** 6 ENLIST
   ENROLL HIREON
   7 RECRUIT
Signal: 3 CUE 5 NODTO
a cab: 4 HAIL
approval: 3 NOD
for help: 3 SOS
light: 5 FLARE
receivers: 15 SATELLITEDISHES
Sortie: 8 AIRALERT
to enter: 3 CUE
TV ~ carrier: 5 CABLE
Two-palms-down: 4 SAFE
Warning: 5 SIREN
Signature
piece: 3 PEN
Signatures
Simple: 3 XES
Signe
Actress: 5 HASSO
Signed: 3 XED
note: 3 IOU
off on: 3 OKD
Signer
~, at times: 3 XER
Signet: 4 SEAL
Significance: 6 IMPORT
Significant: 3 KEY 5 MAJOR
   6 OFNOTE
event: 9 MILESTONE
Least: 6 MEREST
period: 3 **ERA**
They may be: 6 OTHERS
Significant ___ : 5 OTHER
Signify: 4 BODE MEAN 6 DENOTE
   7 ADDUPTO
Sikorsky
Inventor: 4 **IGOR**
Silas
Diplomat: 5 **DEANE**
"Silas Marner"
author: 5 ELIOT
girl: 5 EPPIE
Sildenafil ___ (Viagra):
   7 CITRATE
Silence: 3 GAG 4 HUSH MUTE
   5 SITON STILL

Code of: 6 OMERTA
Musical: 4 REST
Silenced: 5 SATON
"Silence of the Lambs, The"
director: 5 DEMME
org.: 3 FBI
Silencer: 3 SHH
Commercial: 4 MUTE
Squeak: 3 OIL
Silent: 3 MUM 4 MUTE 5 TACIT
assent: 3 **NOD**
Be ~, in music: 5 TACET
communication syst.: 3 ASL
film star: 5 HARPO
greeting: 4 WAVE
one: 4 CLAM
performer: 4 MIME
president: 3 CAL
"Silent Movie"
costar: 6 PETERS
"Silent Running"
star Bruce: 4 DERN
Silent-screen
siren: 4 VAMP
"Silent Spring"
killer: 3 DDT
Silesia
River of: 4 ODER
Silica
gem: 4 OPAL
Silicate
Soft: 4 TALC
Silicon
gem: 4 OPAL
Silicone
valley: 8 CLEAVAGE
Silicon Valley
city: 8 PALOALTO
giant: 5 INTEL
Silk
fabric: 5 TULLE 6 PONGEE
French ~ center: 4 LYON
   5 LYONS
Indian ~ center: 5 ASSAM
pattern: 5 MOIRE
Raw ~ color: 4 ECRU
tie: 3 OBI
topper: 8 OPERAHAT
wrap: 4 SARI

~, in French: 4 SOIE
"Silk Stockings"
    actress Charisse: 3 CYD
    actress Cyd: 8 CHARISSE
    star: 7 ASTAIRE
"Silkwood"
    character Silkwood: 5 KAREN
    star: 6 STREEP
Silkworm: 3 ERI
Silky
    coated cat/rabbit: 6 ANGORA
    coated dog: 7 SPANIEL
        11 AFGHANHOUND
    synthetic: 5 RAYON
Sill: 5 LEDGE
Silliness
    Symbols of: 5 GEESE
Sillitoe
    Author: 4 ALAN
Sills: 4 DIVA
    solo: 4 **ARIA**
Silly: 4 DAFT 5 **INANE** 7 ASININE
    goose: 3 ASS 5 NINNY
    It might be: 4 GRIN
    Knock: 4 DAZE
    ones: 5 GEESE
    Really: 5 APISH
    stuff: 5 PUTTY
    trick: 5 APERY
Silly Putty
    holder: 3 **EGG**
"___ silly question ...": 4 **ASKA**
Silo
    missile: 5 TITAN
    neighbor: 4 BARN
    occupant: 4 ICBM
Silt
    deposit: 5 LOESS
Silver: 5 METAL 6 ARGENT
    Actor: 3 RON
    eagle wearer: 7 COLONEL
    Fine: 8 STERLING
    lead: 4 REIN
    leaf wearer (abbr.): 5 LTCOL
    rider: 10 LONERANGER
    salmon: 4 COHO
    Shout to: 4 HIYO
    source: 3 ORE 4 LODE MINE
    Take the: 5 PLACE

type (abbr.): 4 STER
    ~, in Spanish: 5 PLATA
Silver ___ (cloud seed):
        6 IODIDE
"___ Silver, away!": 4 HIYO
Silver Bow County
    seat: 5 BUTTE
Silverdome
    team: 5 LIONS
Silverheels, Jay
    role: 5 TONTO
Silvers
    Comedian: 4 PHIL
    role: 5 BILKO
Silversmith
    Colonial: 6 REVERE
Silver Springs
    neighbor: 5 OCALA
Silver State (abbr.): 3 NEV
Silverstein
    Author: 4 **SHEL**
Silverstone
    Actress: 6 ALICIA
Silver-tongued: 4 GLIB
    speaker: 6 ORATOR
Silverwork
    Mexican ~ center: 5 TAXCO
Silvery: 6 ARGENT
    fish: 5 **SMELT**
    gray: 3 ASH
    white: 6 ARGENT
Sim
    Actor: 8 ALASTAIR
Simba: 4 LION
    cry: 4 ROAR
    Mate of: 4 NALA
    Uncle of: 4 SCAR
___ Simbel: 3 ABU
Simferopol
    Its capital is: 6 CRIMEA
Simian: 3 APE 7 APELIKE
    Sumatran: 5 ORANG
Similar: 4 **AKIN** 5 ALIKE
    in sound: 8 ASSONANT
    prefix: 5 HOMEO
    to: 4 LIKE
    version: 8 ANALOGUE
Similarity
    symbol: 5 TILDE

Similarly: 5 ALIKE
Simile
  center: 3 **ASA**
  words: 3 **ASA** 4 ASAN
Simmer: 4 STEW 6 BRAISE
  eggs: 5 POACH
  More than: 4 BOIL
Simmering: 5 ONLOW
Simmons
  of Kiss: 4 GENE
  rival: 5 SEALY SERTA
  rock band: 4 KISS
Simoleon: 4 BUCK CLAM
  Spanish: 6 PESETA
Simoleons: 5 MOOLA
Simon
  Apostle: 5 PETER
  Baritone: 5 ESTES
  Playwright: 4 NEIL
  TV detective: 7 TEMPLAR
  Villainous: 6 LEGREE
Simon ___: 4 SAYS
Simon, Carly
  hit: 11 YOURESOVAIN
Simon, Neil
  play: 10 CHAPTERTWO
      15 CALIFORNIASUITE
Simon, Paul
  musical: 7 CAPEMAN
  song: 7 AMERICA
Simon & Garfunkel: 3 DUO
  1966 ~ hit: 8 IAMAROCK
  hit: 7 CECILIA
Simone
  Info: French cue
  Author: 4 WEIL
  Sea, to: 3 MER
  Singer: 4 **NINA**
Simpatico: 7 LIKABLE
  reply: 8 IHEARYOU
Simple: 4 EASY MERE
  fellow: 5 SIMON
  Pure and: 4 MERE
  Something: 4 SNAP
  stuff: 4 ABCS
Simpler
  Make: 4 EASE
Simpleton: 3 ASS OAF 4 BOOB
      CLOD DODO DOLT DOPE

      LOON 5 GOOSE NINNY
      NODDY
Simplicity: 4 **EASE**
  Epitome of: 3 ABC
Simplify: 4 **EASE**
  10 STREAMLINE
Simpson
  Blue-haired: 5 MARGE
  boy: 4 BART
  Designer: 5 **ADELE**
  Former Senator: 4 ALAN
  Grandpa: 3 **ABE**
  Novelist: 4 MONA
  sister: 4 LISA
  trial judge: 3 **ITO**
Simpson, Homer
  bartender: 3 MOE
  Dad of: 3 ABE
  favorite bar: 4 MOES
  neighbor: 3 NED
  outburst: 3 **DOH**
  Son of: 4 BART
Simpson, Marge
  voice: 6 KAVNER
"Simpsons, The"
  bartender: 3 MOE
  bus driver: 4 OTTO
  character Disco ___: 3 STU
  character Nahasapeemapetilon:
    3 APU
  creator Groening: 4 MATT
  neighbor Flanders: 3 NED
  storekeeper: 3 APU
  tavern: 4 MOES
  teacher Krabappel: 4 EDNA
Sims
  of jazz: 4 ZOOT
Simulate
  ~, in a way: 7 REENACT
Simultaneously: 7 ATATIME
Sin: 3 ERR 5 STRAY 7 MISDEED
  A deadly: 4 ENVY LUST
      5 ANGER GREED SLOTH
  city: 5 SODOM
Sinai
  and others (abbr.): 3 MTS
  climber: 5 MOSES
  Desert near: 5 NEGEV
Sinatra: 4 TINA 8 BARITONE

1961 ~ album:
   13 RINGADINGDING
1993 ~ album: 5 DUETS
circle: 7 RATPACK
employer: 6 DORSEY
Former Mrs.: 3 AVA MIA
hometown: 7 HOBOKEN
standard: 5 MYWAY
   9 HIGHHOPES
Sinbad
bird: 3 ROC
realm: 3 SEA
transport: 3 ROC
Since: 4 **ASOF** 6 INTHAT
~, in Scotland: 4 SYNE
Sincere: 4 REAL TRUE
"Since ___ You Baby": 4 IMET
Sinclair
Author: 5 **UPTON**
rival: 4 **ESSO**
Sine: 5 **RATIO**
language: 4 TRIG
Sine ___ non: 3 **QUA**
Sine qua non: 4 NEED
Sinew: 6 TENDON
Sinewy: 4 WIRY
Sinful: 4 EVIL
Sing: 3 RAT 4 BLAB 5 TROLL
along: 6 JOININ
cheerfully: 4 LILT
in the Alps: 5 YODEL
in the snow: 5 CAROL
like Bing: 5 **CROON**
like Ella: 4 SCAT
like the birds: 5 TRILL TWEET
Not really: 7 LIPSYNC
softly: 5 CROON
Something to: 4 TUNE
the blues: 4 WAIL
the praises of: 4 LAUD
   5 EXTOL
without words: 3 HUM
Word after: 5 ALONG
Sing.
Opposite of: 3 PLU
Sing-along
Bar: 7 KARAOKE
syllable: 3 TRA
"___ Sing America": 4 ITOO

Singapore
Island near: 7 SUMATRA
setting: 4 ASIA
"Singapore"
actress Gardner: 3 AVA
Singaraja
setting: 4 BALI
Singe: 4 CHAR
Singer: 3 RAT 4 FINK 7 STOOLIE
Actress: 4 LORI
at Woodstock: 4 BAEZ
Author: 5 ISAAC
One-named: 4 CHER ENYA SADE
   5 CHARO 6 **ODETTA**
syllable: 3 **TRA**
syllables: 3 LAS 4 LALA
Synagogue: 6 CANTOR
Use a: 3 SEW
~ Amos: 4 **TORI**
~ Anita: 4 **ODAY**
~ Anthony: 4 MARC
~ Arnold: 4 EDDY
~ Billy: 4 JOEL
~ Bonnie: 5 **RAITT**
~ Bryant: 5 ANITA
~ Burl: 4 IVES
~ Celine: 4 DION
~ Cleo: 5 LAINE
~ Della: 5 REESE
~ Diana: 4 ROSS
~ Dinah: 5 SHORE
~ Ed: 4 AMES
~ Edith: 4 PIAF
   Frankie: 5 LAINE
~ Irene: 4 CARA
~ Jackson: 6 BROWNE
~ Jacques: 4 BREL
~ Janis: 3 **IAN**
~ Jennifer: 5 LOPEZ
~ Jerry: 4 VALE
~ Joan: 4 JETT
~ Johnny: 6 MATHIS
~ k.d.: 4 LANG
~ Kiki: 3 DEE
~ K.T.: 5 OSLIN
~ LeAnn: 5 RIMES
~ Lena: 5 HORNE
~ Leon: 7 REDBONE
~ Lou: 5 RAWLS

~ Mariah: 5 CAREY
~ Marvin: 4 GAYE
~ Mel: 5 TORME
~ Nelson: 4 EDDY
~ Patsy: 5 CLINE
~ Patti: 7 LABELLE
~ Paul: 4 **ANKA**
~ Paula: 5 ABDUL
~ Peggy: 3 LEE
~ Perry: 4 COMO
~ Phil: 4 OCHS
~ Sheena: 6 EASTON
~ Tori: 4 **AMOS**
~ Travis: 5 TRITT
~ Vikki: 4 CARR
~ Yma: 5 SUMAC
~ Yoko: 3 ONO

Singers
Church: 5 CHOIR
Some: 5 ALTOS BASSI

"Sing, goddess, the wrath of ..."
It begins: 5 ILIAD

Singing
brothers: 4 **AMES**
cowboy: 5 AUTRY
First name in: 4 ELLA
group: 5 CHOIR
Half a ~ group: 5 MAMAS
      PAPAS
One of a ~ quartet: 6 EDAMES
Refrain from: 3 TRA
      7 TRALALA
soldier: 6 SADLER
style: 4 SCAT
syllable: 3 **TRA**
syllables: 4 LALA 5 TRALA
the blues: 3 SAD
voice: 4 ALTO
Wordless: 4 SCAT

Single: 3 **ONE** 4 LONE ONLY
      SOLE 5 UNWED 7 BASEHIT
A ~ time: 4 **ONCE**
Card with a ~ pip: 3 ACE
entity: 5 MONAD
Not a ~ person: 5 NOONE
On a ~ occasion: 4 ONCE
out: 6 SELECT
piece: 4 UNIT
With a ~ voice: 5 ASONE

Single-celled
organism: 5 AMEBA MONAD
      6 AMOEBA
Single-channel: 4 MONO
Single-handed: 4 SOLO 5 ALONE
Single-handedly: 5 **ALONE**
Single-masted
vessel: 5 SLOOP
Single-named
4 CHER ENYA SADE 5 CHARO
      6 **ODETTA**
supermodel: 4 IMAN
Singles
players: 3 DJS
Some: 4 EXES
Single-sailed
vessel: 7 CATBOAT
Single-strand
molecule: 3 RNA
Singleton: 3 ONE
Singly: 3 PER 4 APOP EACH
      ONCE 5 ALONE
      10 ONEATATIME
Sing Sing: 6 PRISON
inhabitant: 3 CON
room: 4 CELL
Singsong
syllable: 3 TRA
Singular: 3 ODD 4 RARE
person: 4 ONER
Sinister: 4 EVIL
look: 4 LEER
Sink: 3 EBB SAG SET 4 FALL
      5 BASIN 7 SCUTTLE
      TORPEDO
clutter: 6 DISHES
feature: 5 DRAIN
hole: 5 DRAIN
in the middle: 3 SAG
jam: 4 CLOG
Kitchen ~ item: 10 LIQUIDSOAP
opposite: 4 SWIM
or swim: 4 VERB
trap shape: 3 ESS
unclogging brand: 5 DRANO
Sinker
Lusitania: 5 UBOAT
material: 4 LEAD
Sub: 6 ASHCAN

Titanic: 4 BERG 7 ICEBERG
Sinking
It may be: 4 FUND
Not: 6 AFLOAT
signal: 3 SOS
Sinn ___: 4 FEIN
Sinner
Original: 3 EVE
Second: 4 ADAM
What a ~ does: 7 PENANCE
Sinn Fein
land: 4 EIRE
org.: 3 IRA
Sins
Deadly ~ number: 5 SEVEN
Sinuous
curve: 3 ESS
shocker: 3 EEL
squeezer: 3 BOA
swimmer: 3 EEL
Sinus: 4 ITER
specialist, briefly: 3 ENT
suffix: 4 ITIS
Siouan
Largest ~ tribe: 6 DAKOTA
speaker: 3 OTO 4 IOWA **OTOE**
    5 OMAHA OSAGE
Sioux
foe: 6 PAWNEE
speaker: 3 OTO 4 OTOE
trophy: 5 SCALP
Sioux City
site: 4 IOWA
Sip: 5 NURSE TASTE
More than: 4 SWIG
Sipowicz
employer: 4 NYPD
Sipping
aid: 5 STRAW
Sir: 5 TITLE
counterpart: 4 MAAM 5 MADAM
Deer: 4 STAG
in India: 5 SAHIB
~, in Spanish: 5 SENOR
Sire: 5 BEGET
Sired: 5 BEGAT BEGOT
Siren: 4 VAMP 5 ALARM ALERT
    7 ALLURER LORELEI
    9 SEXKITTEN

on the Rhine: 7 LORELEI
Play the: 4 LURE 5 TEMPT
Sound like a: 4 WAIL
"Sirens"
actress Macpherson: 4 ELLE
Sirius: 5 ASTAR
Sirloin: 5 STEAK
part: 3 TIP
Sis: 3 REL **SIB**
sibling: 3 **BRO**
Sisal: 5 AGAVE
Siskel
One-time partner of: 5 EBERT
Sissy
Actress: 6 SPACEK
No: 5 HEMAN
role: 6 CARRIE 7 LORETTA
Sister
and brother: 3 KIN
attire: 5 HABIT
Dad's: 4 AUNT
Daughter of: 5 NIECE
Holy: 3 NUN
Mom's: 4 AUNT
Sorority: 4 COED
Word with: 3 SOB
"Sister Act"
extra: 3 NUN
Sisterhood
member: 3 NUN
Sisterly: 7 SORORAL
"Sisters"
actress Ward: 4 **SELA**
sister: 4 ALEX
Sistine Chapel
figure: 4 ADAM
Sit: 4 POSE REST
around: 4 LOAF
Don't just ~ there: 3 ACT
(down): 4 PLOP
for: 4 POSE
in on: 5 AUDIT 6 ATTEND
in the sun: 4 BASK
in traffic: 4 IDLE
Just ~, like food: 7 GETCOLD
on: 5 QUASH 6 STIFLE
One way to: 4 IDLY
Place to: 5 CHAIR
through again: 5 RESEE

Unable to ~ still: **5** ANTSY
Words after: **4** ONIT
Sitar
  accompaniment: **5** TABLA
  player Shankar: **4** **RAVI**
Sitarist
  Ravi: **7** SHANKAR
  Shankar: **4** **RAVI**
Sitcom
  1950s ~: **9** MRPEEPERS
  1950s ~ family: **6** NELSON
  1950s ~ mom: **4** REED
  1950s ~ name: **4** DESI
  1970s ~: **5** ARNIE RHODA
  1980s ~: **4** AMEN
  1990s ~: **5** ELLEN **7** FRIENDS
  alien: **3** ALF
  aunt: **3** BEE
  British: **5** ABFAB
  diner: **4** MELS
  Former ABC: **5** ELLEN
  Furry: **3** ALF
  Groundbreaking: **5** ELLEN
  Half a ~ duo: **7** LAVERNE
  in a garage: **4** TAXI
  landlord: **5** MERTZ
  newsman Baxter: **3** TED
  Part of a ~ sign-off: **4** NANU
  planet: **3** ORK
  segment: **7** EPISODE
  Self-titled: **4** REBA
  set in Korea: **4** MASH
  Starring in a: **4** ONTV
  station: **4** WKRP
  WB: **4** REBA
  Young: **15** FATHERKNOWSBEST
Site: 6 LOCALE
  of a fall: **4** EDEN
  of many firings: **4** KILN
  of some famous hangings:
      5 PRADO
Sites: 4 LOCI
Sit-in
  Old ~ org.: **3** SDS
  participant: **9** PROTESTER
Sitka
  of Stooge shorts: **4** EMIL
Sitter
  charge: **3** TOT

creation: **3** LAP
handful: **3** IMP
on the farm: **3** HEN
Sitting: 7 SESSION
  around: **4** IDLE
  duck: **5** DECOY
  muscles: **6** GLUTEI
  Not ~ well: **5** ANTSY
  on: **4** ATOP
  on one's hands: **4** IDLE
  room: **6** PARLOR
  spot: **5** STOOP
  Stand for a: **5** EASEL
Sitting Bull: 5 SIOUX **6** DAKOTA
Situate: 6 ORIENT
Situated
  Be ~ above: **7** OVERLIE
  Is: **4** LIES
Situation: 8 BALLGAME
  Embarrassing: **7** HOTSEAT
  Handle the: **4** COPE
  Kind of: **5** NOWIN
  Messy: **5** SNAFU
  No-win: **3** TIE **4** DRAW
  Potentially explosive:
      9 POWDERKEG
  Romantic:
      15 ETERNALTRIANGLE
  Tennis: **4** ADIN
  Tough: **4** SPOT
  Unpleasant: **4** MESS
Situations
  Like some: **5** NOWIN
Sit-up
  targets: **3** ABS
Sitwell
  Poet: **5** EDITH
Siva
  sounds: **3** OMS
Six
  It has ~ sides: **4** CUBE UTAH
  Last ~ lines of a sonnet:
      6 SESTET
  make a fl. oz.: **4** TSPS
  o'clock fare: **4** NEWS
  on a phone: **3** MNO
  years, for a senator: **4** TERM
  ~, in Italian: **3** SEI
  ~, in Spanish: **4** SEIS

"Six ___ ...": 5 OFONE
"Six Characters in Search of an Author"
dramatist: 15 LUIGIPIRANDELLO
"Six Days, Seven Nights"
actress: 5 HECHE
Six-Day War
hero: 5 DAYAN
side: 6 ISRAEL
"Six Feet Under"
network: 3 HBO
son: 4 NATE
Six Flags
attraction: 4 RIDE
Six-foot
~ Australian: 3 EMU
Six-footer: 3 ANT
Six-legged
soldier: 7 ARMYANT
Six-line
poem: 6 SESTET
Six-pack
component: 3 CAN
makeup: 3 ABS
Six-packs
Four: 4 CASE
Six-pointers: 3 TDS
Six-shooter: 3 GUN
Six-sided
state: 4 UTAH
Six-stringed
instrument: 4 VIOL
Sixteen
Kasparov's: 3 MEN
oz.: 5 ONELB
Sixth
Henry VIII's: 4 **PARR**
president: 5 ADAMS
sense: 3 **ESP**
~ Greek letter: 4 ZETA
Sixth-century
date: 3 DII DLI DXI 4 DIII
storyteller: 5 AESOP
Sixth-day
creation: 3 MAN
"Sixth Sense, The"
actress Collette: 4 TONI
Six-time
homer champ: 3 OTT

~ Rose Bowl champs: 3 OSU
~ Super Bowl coach: 5 SHULA
~ U.S. Open champ: 5 EVERT
Sixty
Of ~ minutes: 5 HORAL
Six-winged
angel: 6 SERAPH
Six-yr.
term holder: 3 SEN
Size
abbr.: 3 LGE MED REG
Battery: 3 **AAA**
Bed: 4 TWIN
Big: 3 EEE
Book: 6 OCTAVO
Bottle: 5 LITER
Broad: 3 EEE
Clothing: 6 PETITE
Coffee: 4 TALL 5 VENTI
Egg: 5 LARGE
Is the right: 4 FITS
Paper: 5 LEGAL
Type: 4 PICA 5 AGATE ELITE
up: 4 CASE RATE 6 **ASSESS**
Sizes
Ascending ~ (abbr.): 3 SML
Big: 3 XLS
Sizing
up: 5 EYING
Sizzler
Breakfast: 5 BACON
Sizzling: 3 HOT
Skate: 3 RAY
kin: 5 MANTA
Loosen, as a: 5 UNTIE
Prepare to: 6 LACEUP
Skater: 5 LACER
jump: 4 **AXEL** LUTZ
surface: 3 ICE
~ Apolo Anton: 4 OHNO
~ Brian: 5 ORSER
~ Katarina: 4 WITT
~ Michelle: 4 KWAN
~ Sonja: 5 **HENIE**
Skates
Kind of: 6 INLINE
Skating
event: 5 PAIRS
jump: 4 AXEL 7 SALCHOW

legend: 3 ORR
rink: 4 OVAL
spin: 5 CAMEL
venue: 7 ICERINK
Skavar: 4 IVAN
Sked
guess: 3 ETA
TV ~ abbr.: 3 TBA
Skedaddle: 3 GIT HIE LAM
 4 FLEE SCAT 5 SCOOT
 SCRAM 7 VAMOOSE
"Skedaddle!": 3 **GIT** 4 SHOO
Skedaddled: 3 RAN 4 FLED TORE
Skee-Ball
site: 6 ARCADE
Skeet
device: 4 TRAP
target: 10 CLAYPIGEON
Skeeter
Smack a: 4 SWAT
Skein
formers: 5 GEESE
sound: 4 HONK
Skeleton
Kind of: 5 AXIAL
part: 4 BONE ULNA
place: 6 CLOSET
prefix: 3 EXO 4 ENDO
Skelton
catchphrase: 7 IDOODIT
character: 4 CLEM
Comic: 3 RED
persona: 4 HOBO
Skeptic: 7 DOUBTER
grain: 4 SALT
scoff: 4 **IBET**
Skeptical: 5 LEERY
Be: 5 DOUBT
response: 4 IBET
sort: 5 CYNIC
Skeptically: 7 ASKANCE
Sketch: 4 DRAW LIMN SKIT
again: 6 REDRAW
Brief: 8 VIGNETTE
Funny: 4 SKIT
out: 4 PLAN
TV ~ show: 3 SNL
Sketched: 4 DREW 5 DRAWN
"Sketches by ___": 3 BOZ

Skewed: 4 AWRY 5 ATILT
view: 4 BIAS
Skewer: 4 SPIT STAB
Skewered
meal: 5 KABOB KEBAB
Ski
event: 6 SLALOM
house style: 6 AFRAME
lift: 3 TOW 4 **TBAR**
lodge fare: 5 COCOA
run: 5 SLOPE
trail: 5 PISTE
Ski-___ (snowmobile): 3 DOO
Skidded: 4 SLID
Skid row
denizen: 4 WINO
woe: 3 **DTS**
Skier
aid: 4 JBAR TBAR
quarters: 5 LODGE
run: 5 SLOPE
transport: 4 TBAR
~ Hermann: 5 MAIER
~ Phil: 5 MAHRE
~ Tommy: 3 MOE
Skies
Praise to the: 5 EXALT EXTOL
Skiff: 4 BOAT
mover: 3 OAR
stabilizer: 4 KEEL
That: 3 SHE
Skiing
category: 6 ALPINE
event: 6 SLALOM
Kind of: 6 NORDIC
mecca: 4 ALPS 5 ASPEN
spot: 5 SLOPE
Skill: 3 **ART** 5 CRAFT KNACK
 6 TALENT
EMT: 3 CPR
Having: 4 ABLE
Improve a: 4 HONE
Lacking: 5 INEPT
Mediator's: 4 TACT
Medium's: 3 ESP
R.N.'s: 3 TLC
Special: 5 KNACK
With: 4 **ABLY** 7 ADEPTLY
 8 ADROITLY

Skilled: 4 ABLE DEFT 5 **ADEPT**
  in: 6 GOODAT
  Not ~ in: 6 POORAT
  stalker: 4 LION
Skillet: 3 PAN
  lubricant: 4 OLEO
  material: 4 IRON
Skillful: 4 ABLE **DEFT** 5 ADEPT
    6 ADROIT HABILE
Skills
  Basic: 4 ABCS
  Office ~ meas.: 3 WPM
Skim
  along: 4 FLIT
  ~, as milk: 5 DEFAT
Skimmer: 3 HAT
Skim milk
  lack: 3 FAT
  Like: 6 NONFAT
  Produce: 5 DEFAT
Skimpy
  skirt: 4 MINI
Skin: 4 FLAY HIDE PARE PEEL
    5 FLESH 6 SCRAPE
  Animal: 4 HIDE PELT
  art: 6 TATTOO
  blemish: 4 MOLE WART
  care name: 4 OLAY 5 ESTEE
    NIVEA
  cream ingredient: 4 **ALOE**
  Get under one's: 3 IRK
  layer: 5 DERMA
  Like a lizard's: 5 SCALY
  Of the: 6 DERMAL
  opening: 4 **PORE**
  pigment: 7 MELANIN
  prefix: 4 DERM 5 DERMO
  problem: 4 ACNE 5 TINEA
  Shed one's: 4 MOLT
  Soak to the: 6 DRENCH
  soother: 4 **ALOE** 5 CREAM
    6 LOTION
  Tough: 4 HIDE
"Skin Deep"
  actor John: 6 RITTER
Skinflint: 5 MISER PIKER
Skinflinty: 5 CHEAP
Skinnay
  Bandleader: 5 ENNIS

Skinner
  Actor: 4 OTIS
Skinny: 4 BONY DIRT DOPE INFO
    LEAN POOP SLIM THIN
    6 LATEST
  dipper: 3 EEL
  one: 5 SCRAG
Skinny-dipper
  Like a: 4 BARE NUDE
Skins
  Shirts and: 5 TEAMS
Skin-So-Soft
  maker: 4 AVON
Skip: 4 MISS **OMIT** 5 ELIDE
    6 PASSUP SITOUT
  along the water: 3 DAP
  a turn: 4 PASS
  Game with ~ cards: 3 UNO
  it: 4 ROPE
  off: 5 ELOPE
  over: 4 **OMIT** 5 ELIDE
  the commercials: 3 ZAP
  You can ~ it: 4 ROPE
Skip ___: 5 ABEAT
Skipjack: 4 TUNA
Skipped: 6 SATOUT 8 BYPASSED
Skipper: 10 SEACAPTAIN
  Genesis: 4 NOAH
  Nautilus: 4 NEMO
  Pequod: 4 AHAB
  portrayer: 8 ALANHALE
  post: 4 HELM
  River: 5 STONE
  syllable: 3 TRA
  Yankee: 5 TORRE
"Skip to My ___": 3 LOU
Ski resort
  Alberta: 5 BANFF
  Colorado: 4 VAIL 5 ASPEN
  Utah: 4 **ALTA**
  Vermont: 4 PICO 5 STOWE
Skirmish: 4 FRAY 5 MELEE
    6 TUSSLE
  Marital: 4 SPAT
Skirt: 5 AVOID EVADE
    8 SIDESTEP
  Ankle-length: 4 MAXI
  Ballerina: 4 TUTU
  Calf-length: 4 MIDI

edge: 3 HEM
feature: 4 SLIT 5 PLEAT
fold: 5 PLEAT
Full: 6 DIRNDL
Hula ~ material: 5 GRASS
insert: 4 GORE
Kind of: 4 HULA MAXI MINI
    SLIT 5 ALINE 6 POODLE
Layered: 4 TUTU
length: 4 MAXI MIDI MINI
line: 3 HEM
Long: 4 **MAXI**
panel: 4 GORE
shape: 4 HOOP
Short: 4 **MINI**

Skit
NBC ~ show: 3 SNL

Skits
Show with: 3 SNL 5 REVUE

Skittish: 4 WARY 5 TIMID
Acts: 5 SHIES
move: 5 START

Skittle: 7 NINEPIN

"Skittle Players"
artist: 5 STEEN

___ Ski Valley: 4 TAOS

Skivvies: 4 BVDS

Skosh: 3 TAD

Skulk: 4 LURK 5 SNEAK

Skull: 7 CRANIUM

Skull and Bones
member: 3 ELI

Skullcap: 8 YARMULKE

Skull Island
find: 4 KONG

Skunk: 7 POLECAT
Cartoon: 4 PEPE 5 LEPEW
City on the: 4 **AMES**
defense: 4 **ODOR** 5 SCENT
feature: 6 STRIPE

Sky: 5 LIMIT
Altar in the: 3 ARA
bear: 4 **URSA**
blue: 5 AZURE
box: 4 KITE
Clear: 5 ETHER
color: 5 AZURE
Drops from the: 4 RAIN
High in the: 5 ALOFT

light: 3 UFO 4 STAR
    6 AURORA
Pie in the: 3 UFO
pilot: 5 PADRE
Red ~ at morning: 4 OMEN
shade: 5 AZURE
Take to the: 6 AVIATE
~, in French: 4 CIEL

Skybox
locale: 5 ARENA

Skydiving
need: 5 CHUTE

SkyDome
setting: 7 TORONTO
song: 7 OCANADA

Skye
Actress: 4 **IONE**
cap: 3 **TAM**
guy: 4 SCOT
talk: 4 ERSE

Sky-high
Go: 4 SOAR

"___ Skylark": 3 TOA

Skylighted
courts: 5 ATRIA

Skyline
European ~ sight: 3 ALP
feature: 5 SPIRE 7 STEEPLE
obscurer: 4 HAZE SMOG
Rural ~ sight: 4 SILO

Skylines
Like some: 8 STEEPLED

Skylit
courts: 5 **ATRIA**

SkyMiles
offerer: 5 DELTA

Skyrocket: 4 RISE **SOAR** ZOOM

Skyscraper
Boston ~, with "the": 3 PRU
He made the ~ possible: 4 OTIS
Rural: 4 SILO
support: 5 IBEAM

Skywalker: 4 JEDI
foe: 5 VADER
mentor: 4 YODA

Skywalker, Anakin
Son of: 4 LUKE

Skyward: 5 ALOFT
Directed: 6 UPCAST

SLA
Hearst ~ name: 5 TANIA
Slab
Stone: 5 STELE
Slack: 6 UNTAUT
Give some: 6 LOOSEN
Lacking: 4 **TAUT** 5 TENSE
TIGHT
off: 4 EASE 5 ABATE
Slacken: 4 EASE 5 ABATE
Slacker
bane: 3 JOB
Slack-jawed: 4 AGOG 5 **AGAPE**
feeling: 3 AWE
Leave: 4 STUN
look: 4 GAPE
Slacks
material: 5 CHINO
measure: 6 INSEAM
Slake: 4 SATE 6 QUENCH
Slalom: 3 SKI
contestant: 5 SKIER
curve: 3 **ESS**
obstacle: 4 GATE
Slam: 4 SHUT
preventer: 8 DOORSTOP
Slam-dance: 4 MOSH
Slammed: 7 LITINTO
Slammer: 3 PEN 4 COOP JAIL
STIR 5 CLINK POKEY
6 PRISON 8 HOOSEGOW
Ship: 4 BRIG
"Slammin' Sammy": 4 SOSA
5 SNEAD
Slander: 3 TAR 5 SMEAR
7 ASPERSE TRADUCE
Like: 4 ORAL
Slang
expert Partridge: 4 ERIC
Shop: 5 LINGO
Slangy
assent: 3 YEH **YEP** 4 YEAH
greeting: 4 HIHO
hat: 3 LID
intensifier: 3 OLA
money: 4 KALE
no: 5 IXNAY
refusal: 3 **NAH** NAW 4 NOPE
suffix: 3 OLA 4 **AROO** EROO

Slant: 4 **BIAS** CANT LEAN SKEW
TILT 5 ANGLE BEVEL
Political: 4 SPIN
Slanted: 5 ATILT 6 ITALIC
type: 6 ITALIC
type (abbr.): 4 **ITAL**
Slanting: 6 ASLOPE
Slap
cuffs on: 3 NAB
Deserving a: 4 RUDE 5 FRESH
It may follow a: 4 DUEL
target: 5 WRIST
Slapper
in shorts: 3 MOE
Slapstick
comedy: 5 FARCE
missile: 3 **PIE**
trio member: 3 MOE 6 STOOGE
Slash
Bandmate of: 3 AXL
mark: 4 SCAR
Words separated by a: 5 ANDOR
Slasher
of films: 5 ZORRO
Slat: 4 LATH
Slate: 6 AGENDA ROSTER
Clean: 10 TABULARASA
Clear the: 5 ERASE
name: 7 NOMINEE
Was on a: 3 RAN
~, for one: 4 EMAG
~, for short: 4 SKED
Slaughter: 4 ROUT
of baseball: 4 **ENOS**
Slaughterhouse: 8 ABATTOIR
Slav
Certain: 4 SERB
Slave: 4 PEON SERF 5 HELOT
6 THRALL
11 BONDSERVANT
away: 4 TOIL
girl of opera: 4 AIDA
name: 4 TOBY
response: 5 GROAN
~ Turner: 3 NAT
Slavery
Amendment abolishing: 4 XIII
Slaves
Country founded by: 7 LIBERIA

"Slaves of New York"
  author Janowitz: 4 TAMA
Slaving
  away: 4 ATIT
"Slavonic Dances"
  composer: 6 DVORAK
Slaw: 4 SIDE
  ___ slaw: 4 COLE
Slay: 3 OFF 4 DOIN KILL
Slayer
  Vampire: 5 STAKE
  "___ slayeth the silly one":
      4 ENVY
Slayton
  Astronaut: 4 DEKE
Sleaze: 5 CREEP
Sleazy: 6 SORDID
  paper: 3 RAG
Sled
  Olympic: 4 LUGE
  Travel by: 4 MUSH
Sledding
  spot: 4 HILL
Sleek
  fabric: 5 SATIN
  jet: 3 SST
  looking: 11 STREAMLINED
  swimmer: 5 OTTER
  ~, in lingo: 4 AERO
Sleekly
  designed: 4 AERO
Sleep
  acronym: 3 REM
  Bit of: 3 ZEE
  Deep: 4 **COMA** 5 SOPOR
  disorder: 5 **APNEA**
  Forego: 6 STAYUP
  Get some: 6 RESTUP
  He may put you to: 7 SANDMAN
  inducer: 6 OPIATE
  Like ~, ideally: 7 RESTFUL
  Lose ~ over: 4 STEW
  Put to: 4 BORE LULL
  research tool: 3 EEG
  restlessly: 4 TOSS
  Short: 3 NAP
  sound: 5 SNORE
  soundly: 5 SNORE
  spoiler: 5 ALARM

  stage: 3 REM
  unit: 3 ZEE
  You'll ~ through it: 5 DREAM
Sleep ___: 4 ONIT
Sleeper: 3 CAR
  film of 1978: 4 COMA
  Noisy: 6 SNORER
  Restless: 6 TOSSER
  Sound: 6 SNORER
  Storied: 3 RIP
  Upside-down: 5 SLOTH
  woe: 5 APNEA
Sleepers: 7 PAJAMAS
  "___ Sleep, for Every Favor":
      4 EREI
Sleeping: 3 OUT 4 ABED
      5 NOTUP 6 ATREST
  disorder: 5 APNEA
  Like a ~ bag: 5 LINED
  sickness carrier: 6 TSETSE
  Stopped: 4 WOKE
"Sleepless in Seattle"
  director Ephron: 4 NORA
  director Nora: 6 EPHRON
Sleepover
  wear: 3 PJS
Sleepy: 5 DWARF
  Get: 4 FADE
  pal: 3 DOC
Sleepy Hollow
  character: 4 BROM
"Sleepy Hollow"
  star: 4 DEPP
"Sleepy Time ___": 3 GAL
"Sleepy Time Gal"
  songwriter: 4 EGAN
Sleet
  covered: 3 ICY
  Slide in: 4 SKID
Sleeve
  card: 3 ACE
  filler: 3 ARM
Sleeveless
  cloak: 6 MANTLE
  garment: 4 CAPE VEST
Sleeves
  Discs with: 3 LPS
Sleigh
  Russian: 6 TROIKA

Sleighmate
of Cupid: 5 COMET
Sleipnir
rider: 4 ODIN
Slender: 4 LANK SLIM THIN
       5 REEDY
blade: 4 EPEE
candle: 5 TAPER
cigar: 8 PANATELA
dagger: 6 STYLET 8 STILETTO
girl: 5 SYLPH
Gracefully: 6 SVELTE
gull: 4 TERN
instrument: 4 OBOE
nail: 4 BRAD
reed: 4 OBOE
stinger: 4 WASP
sword: 6 RAPIER
Slender-waisted
insect: 4 WASP
Sleuth: 3 TEC
Bogart's: 5 SPADE
dog: 4 ASTA
Film: 4 CHAN
find: 4 CLUE
Hammett's: 5 SPADE
Marquand's: 4 MOTO
Rex's: 4 **NERO**
~ Charlie: 4 CHAN
~ Lupin: 6 ARSENE
~ Wolfe: 4 NERO
"Sleuth"
star: 5 CAINE
Slew: 3 TON 4 RAFT 5 DIDIN
       OCEAN SMOTE
Whole ~ of: 7 ZILLION
Slezak
Actress: 5 **ERIKA**
Slice: 3 CUT
and dice: 4 HASH
(off): 3 LOP
of history: 3 ERA
Salad: 6 RADISH
Thick: 4 **SLAB**
Thin: 7 SCALLOP
Slicer
site: 4 DELI
Slick: 3 ICY WET 4 OILY WILY
       5 SUAVE

stuff: 3 OIL
Slicker: 3 MAC 5 ICIER 7 OILSKIN
place: 4 CITY
Slid
It may be ~ on: 8 BANISTER
Slide
Lab ~ critter: 5 AMEBA
       6 AMOEBA
Lab ~ subjects: 6 AMEBAE
       7 AMOEBAE
on ice: 4 SKID 5 SKATE
Spot for a: 4 BASE
Water: 5 CHUTE
Word with: 4 RULE
Sliding
machine part: 6 TAPPET
Vehicle with ~ doors: 3 VAN
Slight: 4 MERE SNUB 6 IGNORE
       7 SLENDER
advantage: 4 EDGE
color: 4 TINT 5 TINGE
decrease: 3 DIP
fight: 4 SPAT
odor: 5 WHIFF
progress: 4 DENT
Social: 4 SNUB
variation: 5 SHADE
Slightest: 5 LEAST
In the: 5 ATALL
sound: 4 PEEP
The ~ bit: 4 ATAD
Slightly: 4 ABIT **ATAD** 7 ALITTLE
       ATRIFLE
~, in music: 4 POCO
Slim
and muscular: 4 WIRY
and trim: 6 SVELTE
swimmer: 3 EEL
Very ~ margin: 4 HAIR
Slime: 3 GOO 4 GOOK GOOP
       GUCK GUNK MUCK OOZE
"Slim Shady": 6 EMINEM
Slimy
stuff: 4 OOZE
Sling: 4 HURL
ammo: 5 STONE
mud at: 4 SLUR 5 SMEAR
       7 ASPERSE
What some slingers: 4 HASH

Slingshot
ammo: 5 STONE
Like a: 7 YSHAPED
Slink: 4 LURK
Slinky: 3 TOY
shape: 4 COIL
Slip: 3 **ERR** 5 ERROR LAPSE
7 FAUXPAS
a cog: 3 ERR
away: 5 ELOPE 6 ELAPSE
back: 7 RELAPSE
behind: 3 LAG
by: 5 ELUDE 6 ELAPSE
cover: 5 DRESS
Give a pink ~ to: 3 AXE CAN
Give the ~ to: 4 LOSE 5 **ELUDE**
EVADE
into: 3 DON 7 THROWON
(into): 4 EASE
Let: 4 TELL
of the tongue: 5 ERROR
on: 3 DON
Pink: 13 WALKINGPAPERS
preventer: 3 MAT
Sign of a: 7 ERASURE
Slips on a: 6 ERRATA
through the cracks: 4 SEEP
up: 3 **ERR**
Slip ___ : 4 ACOG
"Slip ___ Away": 6 SLIDIN
Slipknot: 5 NOOSE
Slip-on
shoe: 6 LOAFER
Slipper
Ballet: 7 TOESHOE
Lounging: 4 MULE
Slipperiness
Symbol of: 3 EEL
Slippery: 3 ICY SLY 4 **EELY**
7 ELUSIVE
Get: 5 ICEUP 7 ICEOVER
It may be: 5 SLOPE
one: 3 EEL 6 EVADER
slope: 6 SKIRUN
swimmer: 3 **EEL**
Thin and: 7 EELLIKE
tree: 3 ELM
Wiggly and: 4 EELY
Slippery as ___ : 5 ANEEL

Slippery-eel
link: 4 ASAN
Slips: 6 ERRATA
"Slips my mind": 7 IFORGET
Slip-up: 4 GOOF 5 BONER ERROR
Slit: 8 APERTURE
Garment: 4 VENT
Slither: 5 CREEP
Slitherer: 5 SNAKE
Nile: 3 **ASP**
Slithering
squeezer: 3 BOA
Slithery
swimmer: 3 EEL
"Slithy"
critter: 4 TOVE
"Sliver"
author: 5 LEVIN
Sliwa
topper: 5 BERET
Slob
home: 3 STY
napkin: 6 SLEEVE
of Broadway: 5 OSCAR
Slobber: 5 DROOL
Slog: 4 PLOD
Slogan
Clothes with a: 7 TSHIRTS
ending: 3 EER
Shirt with a: 3 TEE
writer: 5 ADMAN
Sloganeer: 5 ADMAN
Sloop
slip: 5 BERTH
Slop
eaters: 5 SWINE
spot: 3 STY
Slope: 4 CANT RAKE RISE
5 GRADE 8 HILLSIDE
Gentle: 6 GLACIS
Slippery: 6 SKIRUN
Steep: 5 SCARP 6 ESCARP
Stick on a: 7 SKIPOLE
Tackle a: 3 SKI
Way up the: 4 TBAR
Sloping
walk: 4 RAMP
Sloppy
condition: 4 MESS

Evidence of ~ editing: 5 TYPOS
    place: 3 STY
Sloshed
    Slightly: 5 TIPSY
Slot
    Broadcast: 7 AIRTIME
    filler: 3 TAB
    spot: 6 CASINO
Sloth: 3 SIN
    home: 4 **TREE**
    Two-___: 4 TOED
Slothful: 4 LAZY 6 OTIOSE
Slot machine
    feature: 3 ARM
    fruit: 5 LEMON
Slots: 15 ONEARMEDBANDITS
    It's full of: 4 RENO 6 CASINO
Slouched
    over: 7 UNERECT
Slough: 3 BOG 4 MIRE
    off: 4 SHED
    School near: 4 ETON
Slovenia
    Alliance that includes: 4 NATO
    Port near: 7 TRIESTE
Slow: 4 POKY 5 DENSE LARGO
        LENTO
    dance: 8 HABANERA
    Do a ~ burn: 4 STEW 6 **SEETHE**
        7 SMOLDER
    down: 5 BRAKE 6 RETARD
    down, in music: 3 RIT
    flow: 4 OOZE 7 TRICKLE
    Make a ~ transition: 6 EASEIN
    More than ~, in retail: 4 DEAD
    movement: 4 OOZE 5 LARGO
        6 ADAGIO 9 ANDANTE
    mover: 5 **SNAIL**
    one: 4 POKE
    on the uptake: 5 DENSE
    outflow: 7 SEEPAGE
    pace: 3 JOG
    pitch: 3 LOB
    Take it: 4 LAZE LOLL
    tempo: 5 LARGO LENTO
    train: 5 LOCAL
    ~, in music: 5 LARGO LENTO
        TARDO
Slow-cook: 4 STEW

Slowdown: 3 LAG
"Slow down!": 4 WHOA
Slowly: 6 ADAGIO
    destroy: 5 ERODE
    Move: 4 INCH OOZE
    Moved: 5 CREPT
    Run: 4 TROT
    Speak: 5 DRAWL
    ~, in music: 5 LARGO **LENTO**
        6 ADAGIO
Slow-moving
    mammal: 5 SLOTH
    one: 5 SNAIL
Slowness
    Epitome of: 5 SNAIL
        8 MOLASSES
Slow on the ___: 6 UPTAKE
Slowpoke: 5 **SNAIL** 8 TORTOISE
Slow-witted: 3 DIM 4 DULL DUMB
        5 DENSE
SLR
    setting: 5 FSTOP
Sludge: 4 CRUD GOOK OOZE
Slug
    kin: 5 SNAIL
    Like a: 5 BOGUS
    suffix: 4 FEST
    trail: 5 SLIME
Slugfest: 4 FRAY
    souvenir: 6 SHINER
Sluggard: 4 POKE 5 SNAIL
Slugger: 4 FIST
    Cub: 4 SOSA
    Louisville: 3 ALI BAT
    Louisville ~ wood: 3 ASH
    Mudville: 5 CASEY
    opportunity: 5 ATBAT
    stat: 3 HRS RBI
    Yankee: 4 AROD
    ~ Hank: 5 AARON
    ~ Johnny: 4 MIZE
    ~ Mel: 3 OTT
    ~ Moises: 4 ALOU
    ~ Ralph: 5 KINER
    ~ Roger: 5 MARIS
    ~ Sammy: 4 **SOSA**
Sluggish: 4 LAZY LOGY SLOW
        5 INERT 6 LEADEN
        TORPID

In a ~ way: 7 INERTLY
water: 5 BAYOU
Sluggishness: 6 TORPOR
7 INERTIA
Sluglike
mollusk: 7 SEAHARE
Slum
life author: 9 JACOBRIIS
sight: 3 RAT
Slumber
sound: 5 SNORE
Slump: 3 SAG
Slung
dish: 4 HASH
It may be: 3 MUD
Slur
over: 5 **ELIDE**
Slutskaya
Skater: 5 IRINA
Sly: 4 ARCH CAGY WILY 5 CAGEY
6 CRAFTY
character: 5 RAMBO ROCKY
costar: 5 TALIA
look: 4 **LEER**
sort: 3 FOX
stratagem: 4 RUSE
trick: 4 WILE
Slyly
Eye: 4 OGLE
suggest: 9 INSINUATE
Smack: 3 HIT RAM 4 BUSS KISS
SLAP SWAT 5 PASTE
TASTE 6 SMOOCH
dab in the middle:
10 DEADCENTER
in the face: 4 KISS
suffix: 4 EROO
Smacker: 3 LIP 4 CLAM
Smackers: 4 ONES
100 ~: 5 CNOTE
Smacking
sound: 4 WHAP
Small: 3 LIL 4 PUNY SIZE
5 DINKY PETTY 6 PETITE
amount: 3 BIT DAB SOU **TAD**
4 DRAM DRIB IOTA MITE
WHIT 5 TRACE
and mischievous: 5 ELFIN
and weak: 4 PUNY

band: 4 TRIO 5 COMBO
Extremely: 5 MICRO
It carries a ~ charge: 3 ION
Like a ~ garage: 6 ONECAR
suffix: 3 ULE
Very: 3 WEE 4 ITSY TINY
5 TEENY 6 MINUTE
~, in French: 5 PETIT
Small-business
mag: 3 INC
Smaller
amount: 4 LESS
Get: 6 SHRINK
than small: 6 TEENSY
Smallest: 5 LEAST
Small-minded: 5 PETTY
Smallmouth: 4 BASS
Small-plane
maker: 6 CESSNA
Smallpox
vaccine discoverer: 6 JENNER
Small-screen
heartthrob: 6 TVIDOL
Small-time: 5 DINKY 6 TWOBIT
7 TINHORN 9 PENNYANTE
"Smallville"
character Lang: 4 LANA
family: 5 KENTS
friend: 5 CHLOE
"___ small world": 4 ITSA
Smarmy: 4 OILY
Smart: 4 ACHE CHIC HURT NEAT
5 NATTY SASSY STING
dresser: 3 FOP
employer: 7 CONTROL
Get: 4 SASS 5 LEARN 6 WISEUP
group: 5 MENSA
guy: 4 ALEC 5 **ALECK** BRAIN
Not: 3 DIM
or Bond: 5 AGENT
player: 5 ADAMS
set: 5 MENSA
talk: 4 SASS
Unusually: 3 APT
Smart ___: 4 ALEC 5 **ALECK**
Smart, Maxwell: 5 AGENT
Smart-alecky: 4 FLIP PERT WISE
Smarten
up: 7 GETWISE

Smartly
Dress: **5** PREEN
Smart-mouthed: 4 PERT
5 SASSY
Smarts: 4 WITS **5** SENSE
10 HORSESENSE
Having more: **5** SORER
Smart ___ whip: 3 ASA
Smash: 3 HIT
Box office: **4** BOFF
into: **3** RAM
Sign of a: **3** SRO
suffix: **4** EROO
up: **4** RUIN **5** TOTAL
Smashed: 3 LIT **6** BLOTTO
It may get: **4** ATOM
Smasheroo: 3 HIT
Smashing
serve: **3** ACE
Smattering
A ~ of: **4** SOME
Smear: 3 TAR **4** BLUR DAUB
5 LIBEL **6** BEDAUB
STREAK
Ink: **4** BLOT
Smell: 4 **ODOR** REEK **5** SCENT
SENSE STINK WHIFF
Awful: **5** FETOR
bad: **4** REEK
like: **6** REEKOF
Pleasant: **5** AROMA
What the suspicious: **4** ARAT
Smell ___: 4 **ARAT**
Smeller: 4 NOSE
Smelling ___: 5 SALTS
Smells
It: **4** **NOSE**
Smelly
smoke: **6** STOGIE
Smelter
input: **3** ORE
waste: **4** SLAG
Smeltery
fodder: **7** IRONORE
input: **3** **ORE**
waste: **4** SLAG **5** DROSS
Smidge: 3 DAB TAD
Smidgen: 3 BIT DAB JOT TAD
4 ATOM DRIB **IOTA** WHIT

5 PINCH SKOSH SPECK
TRACE
Smile: 4 BEAM GRIN
Bring a ~ to: **5** AMUSE
Scornful: **5** SNEER
shape: **3** ARC
Word that brings a: **6** CHEESE
"Smile!": 9 SAYCHEESE
"___ Smile": 4 SARA
"___ Smile Be Your Umbrella":
4 LETA
Smiles
All: **5** HAPPY
Like some: **6** TOOTHY
Smiley: 5 AGENT
creator: **7** LECARRE
Smiley, Jane
novel: **3** MOO
Smiling: 5 AGRIN RIANT
6 AMUSED
Smirk: 4 LEER
Smirnoff
Comedian: **5** YAKOV
rival: **5** STOLI
Smith: 5 SHOER
and Gore: **3** ALS
and Jones, often: **7** ALIASES
Blues singer: **6** BESSIE
Columnist: **3** LIZ
Did a ~ job: **4** SHOD **5** SHOED
Do a ~ job: **6** RESHOE
Economist: **4** **ADAM**
Gossipy: **3** LIZ
Granny: **5** APPLE
iron: **5** ANVIL
Jockey: **5** ROBYN
NFL rusher: **6** EMMITT
of tennis: **4** STAN
Partner of: **6** WESSON
Rock singer: **5** PATTI
role: **3** ALI
Singer: **4** KATE
___ Smith: 6 GRANNY
Smith, Buffalo Bob
puppet: **10** HOWDYDOODY
Smith, Hannibal
group: **5** ATEAM
Smith, John
~, perhaps: **5** ALIAS

Smith, Jos.
follower: 3 LDS
Smith, Mrs.
product: 3 PIE
Smith, ___ Pinkett
Actress: 4 JADA
Smith, Snuffy: 6 RUSTIC
Inquired, to: 3 AST
Son of: 5 TATER
Smith, Will
1997 ~ film, briefly: 3 MIB
2001 ~ role: 3 **ALI**
Mrs.: 4 JADA
songs: 4 RAPS
Smithereens: 4 BITS 6 PIECES
Break to: 5 SMASH TOTAL
maker: 3 TNT
Smithfield
product: 3 HAM
Smithsonian
(abbr.): 4 INST
stuff: 9 AMERICANA
Smithsonite: 3 ORE
Smithy: 5 FORGE SHOER
Did a ~ job: 5 SHOED
sight: 5 ANVIL
Smits
former show: 5 LALAW
of basketball: 3 RIK
Smitten: 4 GAGA 6 INLOVE
      8 ENAMORED
Smog: 4 HAZE
component: 4 SOOT
watchdog (abbr.): 3 EPA
Smoke: 3 CIG 4 CURE
Bit of: 4 PUFF WISP
Celebratory: 5 CIGAR
Cheap: 6 STOGIE
conduit: 4 FLUE
detector: 4 NOSE
Good: 6 HAVANA
Mild: 5 CLARO
out: 6 EXPOSE
site: 7 ASHTRAY
Small: 9 CIGARILLO
solids: 3 TAR
___ smoke: 4 UPIN
Smoked
delicacy: 3 EEL

meat: 3 HAM
salmon: 3 LOX
Smoke-filled
room folks: 4 POLS
"Smoke Gets In Your Eyes"
composer: 4 KERN
lyricist Harbach: 4 OTTO
Smokehouse
item: 3 HAM
Smokejumper
need: 5 CHUTE
Smoker: 3 CAR 4 STAG
concern: 3 TAR
purchase: 4 PACK
request: 5 LIGHT
Sicilian: 4 **ETNA**
Smokey: 4 BEAR
spotter: 4 CBER
Smoking
alternative: 3 NON
and nonsmoking: 5 AREAS
gun: 5 PROOF
Quit: 12 KICKTHEHABIT
Started: 5 LITUP
"Smoking or ___?": 3 NON
Smoky
stone: 4 OPAL
"Smoky Mountain Rain"
singer Ronnie: 6 MILSAP
Smoldering
remains: 5 EMBER
Smooch: 4 BUSS KISS
Willing to: 5 KISSY
Smooth: 4 EASE EVEN FILE GLIB
      IRON SAND 5 SILKY
      SUAVE 6 FLUENT SATINY
      SHAVEN 7 UNLINED
and lustrous: 5 SLEEK
and soft: 6 SILKEN
Make: 4 EASE SAND
Make a ~ transition: 5 SEGUE
musically: 6 LEGATO
out: 4 EVEN
Overly: 4 GLIB
sailing: 4 EASE
the way: 4 EASE
transition: 5 SEGUE
Smoother: 4 RASP
Make even: 6 RESAND

Smoothing
tool: **6** PLANER
Smoothly
Go: **4** FLOW
Mix: **5** BLEND
Move: **5** GLIDE
Run: **3** HUM **4** PURR
Switch: **5** SEGUE
"Smooth Operator"
singer: **4** <u>SADE</u>
Smooth-talking: 4 <u>GLIB</u>
Smooth-tongued: 4 <u>GLIB</u>
Smothers Brothers: 3 DUO
One of the: **3** TOM
Smudge: 4 BLOT SOIL SPOT
5 SMEAR
Solver's: **7** ERASURE
Smug
Be: **5** GLOAT
smile: **5** SMIRK
Smurf
Bearded: **4** PAPA
Like a: **4** BLUE
Smut: 4 PORN
Smythe
Cartoonist: **3** REG
Sn
Its symbol is: **3** TIN
Snack: 3 EAT **4** BITE **NOSH**
After-school: **4** OREO
bar: **7** GRANOLA
cake: **5** SUZYQ
Cheesy: **5** NACHO
chip. **5** NACHO
chips: **6** FRITOS
Coffee break: **5** DONUT
Creme-filled: **4** OREO
Have a: **3** EAT **4** NOSH
Hiker's: **4** GORP
Hostess: **5** HOHOS
in a shell: **4** TACO
in a stack: **4** OREO
Marshmallow: **5** SMORE
7 MOONPIE
Mexican: **4** TACO
since 1912: **4** OREO
Snail's: **5** ALGAE
Squirrel: **5** ACORN
Stadium: **6** NACHOS

Tex-Mex: **4** TACO **6** TAMALE
~, in Spanish: **4** TAPA
Snafu: 4 MESS **5** MIXUP
6 MESSUP
Snag: 3 NET **5** HITCH LASSO
Snail: 8 SLOWPOKE
Edible: **8** ESCARGOT
Like a: **4** SLOW
mail attachment: **5** STAMP
Marine: **5** WHELK
snack: **5** ALGAE
trail: **5** SLIME
Snaillike: 4 POKY SLOW
___ snail's pace: **3** ATA
Snake: 4 APOD
African: **3** ASP **5** MAMBA
charmee: **3** EVE
Charmer's: **5** COBRA
dancers: **4** HOPI
Deadly: **5** COBRA KRAIT VIPER
eye: **7** ONESPOT
eyes: **3** TWO **4** ONES
Hooded: **3** ASP **5** COBRA
Kind of: **5** ADDER
Longest venomous:
10 BUSHMASTER
Many a: **6** HISSER
Milk: **5** ADDER
Place for a: **5** DRAIN
poison: **5** VENOM
shape: **3** ESS
sound: **3** SSS **4** HISS
Squeezing: **3** BOA
venom: **5** TOXIN
Venomous: **3** ASP **5** ADDER
COBRA KRAIT MAMBA
10 COPPERHEAD
Venomous, as a: **6** ASPISH
Word with: **3** SEA
~, to Medusa: **5** TRESS
Snake-haired
woman of myth: **6** MEDUSA
Snakelike
fish: **3** <u>EEL</u>
Snake River
locale: **5** IDAHO
Snaky
curve: **3** ESS
fish: **3** EEL

shape: 3 ESS 4 COIL
sound: 3 SSS
Snap: 3 PIC 4 ELAN ZING
    5 CINCH CLICK GOAPE
    PHOTO 6 LOSEIT
  course: 5 EASYA
  It's a: 3 PIC 4 HIKE 5 PHOTO
  It's heard at a: 3 HUT
  Liable to: 5 CROSS
  Sit for a: 4 POSE
Snapper: 6 TURTLE
  competitor: 4 TORO
  Swamp: 4 CROC 5 GATOR
  trapper: 3 NET
Snappish: 4 CURT 5 **TESTY**
Snapple
  rival: 6 NESTEA
  specialty: 3 TEA
Snappy
  comeback: 6 RETORT
Snaps: 3 PIX 10 BLOWSAFUSE
    15 LOSESONESTEMPER
Snapshot: 3 PIC 5 PHOTO
Snare: 3 NET 4 DRUM TRAP
    5 NOOSE 6 ENTRAP
  Sniggler: 6 EELPOT
Snarl: 4 GNAR 6 TANGLE
  Traffic: 3 JAM
Snarler
  Traffic: 5 CRASH
Snatch: 4 **GRAB**
Snead
  of golf: 3 SAM
Sneak
  a look: 4 PEEK
  attack: 6 AMBUSH
  peek (var.): 6 PREVUE
Sneak ___: 5 APEEK
Sneaker: 4 SHOE 7 GYMSHOE
  bottoms: 6 TREADS
  brand: 4 KEDS 5 NIKES
  feature: 4 LACE 6 EYELET
  Former ~ brand: 4 AVIA
  problem: 4 ODOR
Sneakily
  Criticize: 5 SNIPE
  Injured: 5 KNEED
Sneaking
  suspicion: 4 IDEA

Sneaky: 3 SLY
  guy: 4 PETE
  laugh: 3 HEH
  scheme: 4 RUSE
Sneaky ___: 4 PETE
Sneer
  Said with a: 5 SNIDE
Sneetches
  creator: 5 SEUSS
Sneeze
  inducer: 7 ALLERGY
  Respond to a: 5 BLESS
  sound: 5 ACHOO
Sneezy
  friend: 3 DOC
  Sound from: 5 ACHOO
Snicker: 5 TEHEE
  Like a: 5 SNIDE
  sound: 3 HEE
Snicker-___: 4 SNEE
Snickers
  maker: 4 MARS
Snick-or-___: 4 **SNEE**
Snidely
  Look from: 5 SNEER
Snider
  teammate: 5 REESE
Sniff: 6 INHALE
  out: 6 DETECT
Sniffer: 4 NOSE
Sniffles
  Get the: 9 CATCHCOLD
  Have the: 3 AIL
Sniggler: 5 EELER
  quarry: 3 **EEL**
  snare: 6 EELPOT
Snip: 3 CUT
Snipes
  Actor: 6 WESLEY
Snippet
  Cinema: 4 CLIP
  Dramatic: 5 SCENE
Snippy: 4 TART
  Get ~ with: 4 SASS
Snit
  fit: 5 ANGER
Snitch: 3 **RAT**
  Act the: 6 TATTLE
  Be a: 4 TELL 5 RATON

Snitched: 4 TOLD
Snitches
  spill them: 5 BEANS
Snivel: 5 WHINE
"SNL"
  bit: 4 SKIT
  Early ~ comic: 7 PISCOPO
  Early ~ name: 5 GILDA
  Kevin on: 6 NEALON
  Part of: 4 LIVE
  player Cheri: 5 OTERI
  player Dunn: 4 NORA
  player Kevin: 6 NEALON
  producer Michaels: 5 LORNE
  segment: 4 SKIT
  When ~ ends: 5 ONEAM
Snob: 7 ELITIST
Snobbery: 7 ELITISM
Snobbish: 6 UPPITY 7 HIGHHAT
  behavior: 4 AIRS
Snobs
  put them on: 4 AIRS
Snockered: 3 LIT
Snood: 7 HAIRNET
Snooker
  shot: 5 MASSE
Snookums: 3 HON 6 DEARIE
        7 PETNAME
Snoop: 3 PRY SPY 5 PRIER
  Act the: 3 PRY
  (around): 4 NOSE
  gp.: 3 CIA
  Like a: 4 NOSY
  Rapper: 4 DOGG
Snooping: 4 NOSY
Snoopy: 4 NOSY 6 BEAGLE
  foe: 8 REDBARON
Snoot: 4 NOSE
Snootiness: 4 AIRS
Snooty
  one: 4 SNOB
Snooze: 3 NAP
  Short: 3 NAP 6 CATNAP
  Sonora: 6 SIESTA
Snore
  letter: 3 ZEE
Snorer
  disorder: 5 APNEA
Snorkel: 5 SARGE

  (abbr.): 3 SGT
  dog: 4 **OTTO**
Snorkeler
  locale: 4 REEF
  sight: 5 CORAL
Snorkeling
  accessory: 3 FIN
  milieu: 5 CORAL
  site: 4 REEF
Snort: 3 NIP 4 BELT
  Cynic's: 4 IBET
  Short: 3 NIP 4 SHOT
Snorter
  Corrida: 4 TORO
  starter: 3 RIP
Snout
  Animal with a: 5 TAPIR
Snow
  boot: 3 PAC
  Clear: 4 PLOW
  coaster: 4 SLED
  cover: 5 IGLOO
  Glide on: 3 SKI
  Lift in the: 4 TBAR
  Like the driven: 4 PURE
  Loose: 6 POWDER
  pea holder: 3 POD
  prowler: 4 YETI
  remover: 6 SHOVEL
  structure: 4 FORT
  toy: 4 SLED
  unit: 5 FLAKE
  vehicle: 4 SLED
Snowball: 8 ESCALATE
Snowballs: 4 AMMO
  Attack with: 4 PELT
Snowbird
  Resort near: 4 ALTA
"Snowbird"
  singer Murray: 4 ANNE
Snowe, Sen.
  state: 5 MAINE
Snowed
  Not ~ by: 4 ONTO
Snowfall
  measure: 4 INCH
Snowman
  Abominable: 4 **YETI**
  carrot: 4 NOSE

of song: 6 FROSTY
prop: 4 PIPE
Snowmass
Enjoy: 3 SKI
Snowmobile
part: 3 SKI
Snow White
and the dwarfs: 5 OCTET
dwarfs: 6 SEPTET
Snowy
bird: 5 EGRET
Enjoy a ~ slope: 3 SKI 4 SLED
Snub: 4 SHUN 6 IGNORE
7 HIGHHAT
12 COLDSHOULDER
Snub-nosed
dog: 3 PUG 4 PEKE
Snuff
Isn't up to: 4 AILS
Not up to: 3 BAD OFF 4 POOR
6 SUBPAR
React to: 6 SNEEZE
Up to: 4 ABLE
___ snuff: 4 UPTO
Snuffleupagus
street: 6 SESAME
Snug: 4 COZY 5 COMFY
bug locale: 3 RUG
retreat: 4 NEST
"Snug as ___ ...": 4 ABUG
Snuggle: 6 NESTLE
up: 6 NESTLE
Snugly
Fit: 4 NEST
Settle: 6 NESTLE 8 ENSCONCE
So: 4 ERGO NOTE THUS TRUE
And ~ on: 3 ETC 8 ETCETERA
and so: 5 NOTES
be it: 4 AMEN
Even: 3 YET 5 STILL
far: 3 YET YTD 5 **ASYET**
6 TODATE 7 UPTONOW
Just: 4 TOAT 6 TOATEE
Like: 4 THUS
Say it ain't: 4 DENY
Say it's: 4 AVER AVOW
to speak: 8 ASITWERE
"So?": 15 WHATSTHEBIGDEAL
"So!": 3 AHA

"So ___": 4 BEIT
Soak: 3 SOP SOT 6 DRENCH
flax: 3 RET
in the tub: 5 BATHE
Place for a: 3 SPA
starter: 3 PRE
tea: 5 STEEP
up: 4 BLOT 6 ABSORB
(up): 3 SOP
up again: 6 RESORB
up some sun: 4 BASK
Soaked: 3 WET 5 AWASH SOGGY
6 SODDEN
Soaking
Make ~ wet: 3 SOP
spot: 3 TUB 4 BATH
Soap: 5 DRAMA 6 SERIAL
acid: 5 OLEIC
Bar of: 4 CAKE
box: 6 TEEVEE
brand: 3 LUX 4 LAVA 5 CAMAY
follower: 5 OPERA
ingredient: 3 LYE 6 OLEATE
POTASH
Like ~ operas: 8 EPISODIC
neighbor: 7 SHAMPOO
opera: 5 DRAMA
plant: 5 AMOLE
Popular: 4 DAYS
segment: 7 EPISODE
substitute: 5 AMOLE
unit: 3 BAR 4 CAKE
Wash off: 5 RINSE
"Soap"
family: 5 TATES
family name: 4 TATE
spin-off: 6 BENSON
Soapbox
person: 6 ORATOR
Use a: 5 **ORATE**
Soap Box Derby
city: 5 AKRON
entrant: 5 RACER
Soap-making
need: 3 LYE
Soapstone: 4 TALC
Soar: 4 RISE
Soaring
hairdo: 7 UPSWEEP

Send spirits: 5 ELATE
Soave: 4 WINE
Sob: 4 BAWL WAIL WEEP
  syllable: 3 HOO
Sobbed: 4 WEPT
Sobbing: 7 INTEARS
"So be it": 4 AMEN
Sober: 5 STAID
Sober-minded: 5 STAID
Sobieski
  Actress: 6 LEELEE
"So Big"
  author Ferber: 4 EDNA
Sobriquet
  Cowboy's: 3 TEX
  Hemingway's: 4 PAPA
  Springsteen's: 4 BOSS
  Stallone's: 3 SLY
Soc.
  Patriotic: 3 DAR
Soccer
  announcer's cry: 4 GOAL
  Common ~ score: 6 ONENIL
    ONEONE
  First name in: 3 MIA
  great: 4 **PELE**
  great Rossi: 5 PAOLO
  Mia of: 4 HAMM
  period: 4 HALF
  score: 4 GOAL
  shot: 6 HEADER
  star: 4 PELE 7 MIAHAMM
Social: 3 BEE TEA 5 DANCE
    MIXER 8 TEAPARTY
  A ~ sci.: 4 ECON
  Afternoon: 3 **TEA**
  asset: 4 TACT 5 POISE
  blunder: 5 GAFFE
  brew: 3 TEA
  butterfly: 8 GADABOUT
  class: 5 CASTE
  climber's goal: 6 STATUS
  connections: 3 INS
  customs: 5 MORES
  division: 5 CASTE
  dud: 4 NERD 6 MISFIT
  ending: 3 ITE
  equal: 4 **PEER**
  finale: 3 ITE

  gathering: 3 BEE
  group: 5 CASTE
  Hindu ~ division: 5 CASTE
  insect: 3 ANT
  instability: 6 ANOMIE
  introduction: 4 ANTI
  Lodge: 8 APRESSKI
  misfit: 4 GEEK **NERD**
  note: 4 ITEM
  outcast: 6 PARIAH
  outing: 4 DATE
  radiance: 5 ECLAT
  rank: 5 CLASS
  rebuff: 4 SNUB
  reformer Bloomer: 6 AMELIA
  reformer Jacob: 4 **RIIS**
  service: 3 TEA
  skill: 4 TACT
  slight: 4 SNUB
  standing: 6 STATUS
  stratum: 5 **CASTE**
  suffix: 3 ITE
  welfare org.: 6 UNICEF
  worker: 3 ANT
  worker load: 5 CASES
"Social Contract, The"
  author: 8 ROUSSEAU
Socialist
  ~ Eugene: 4 DEBS
Socialite
  ~ Maxwell: 4 ELSA
  ~ Mesta: 5 PERLE
  ~ Young: 3 DEB
Socialites
  Certain: 6 JETSET
Socially
  challenged one: 4 DRIP GEEK
    NERD
  chosen: 5 ALIST
  dominant: 5 ALPHA
  inept: 5 NERDY
  See: 4 **DATE**
Social Register
  word: 3 NEE
Societal
  breakdown: 5 ANOMY 6 ANOMIE
  no-no: 5 TABOO
  oddball: 4 GEEK
  woes: 4 ILLS

Society
Born, in the ~ page: 3 NEE
Chinese secret: 4 **TONG**
Cream of: 5 ELITE
girl: 3 DEB
High: 4 JETS SOTS 5 ELITE
Levels of: 6 STRATA
newcomer: 3 **DEB**
page word: 3 **NEE**
roster: 5 ALIST
Secret: 5 MAFIA
stalwart: 6 PILLAR
Society Islands
Largest of the: 6 TAHITI
"Society's Child"
singer Janis: 3 IAN
Sociologist
~ Durkheim: 5 EMILE
~ Max: 5 WEBER
Sock
away: 4 SAVE 5 STASH
clinger: 3 BUR
Fix a: 4 DARN
front: 3 TOE
hard: 5 PASTE
hop: 5 DANCE
hop number: 5 OLDIE
Kind of: 4 TUBE
part: 3 TOE
pattern: 6 ARGYLE
Short: 6 ANKLET
suffix: 4 EROO
Socket
filler: 7 EYEBALL
Golf club: 5 HOSEL
Word with: 3 EYE
Sock-in-the-gut
sound: 3 OOF
"Sock it ___!": 4 TOME
"Sock ___ me!": 4 ITTO
Socks: 4 HOSE 7 HOSIERY
Darn, as: 4 MEND
Kind of: 4 KNEE
Knock the ~ off: 3 AWE WOW
    5 AMAZE 6 DAZZLE
Like matched: 6 PAIRED
Like some: 3 ODD
Pair of: 6 ONETWO
set: 4 PAIR

"Socrate"
composer Erik: 5 SATIE
Socrates
end: 5 OMEGA
Student of: 5 PLATO
Soc. Sec.
On: 3 RET 4 RETD
supplement: 3 IRA
Soda
bottle size: 5 LITER
can feature: 3 TAB
choice: 5 PEPSI
Classic ~ brand: 4 **NEHI**
Club: 7 SELTZER
container: 3 CAN
    11 ALUMINUMCAN
flavor: 4 COLA 5 GRAPE
Fruit ~ brand: 5 FANTA
Kind of: 3 SAL 6 BAKING
Per bottle of: 4 APOP
server: 4 JERK
___ soda: 3 SAL
Soda fountain
choice: 4 COKE MALT
freebie: 5 STRAW
New England: 3 SPA
Sodium
chloride: 4 SALT
hydroxide: 3 LYE 4 NAOH
Sodom
escapee: 3 LOT
"___ So Easy": 3 ITS
Soeur
sibling: 5 FRERE
Sofa: 4 SEAT 5 DIVAN
    6 SETTEE
Backless: 5 DIVAN
Convertible: 3 BED
feature: 3 ARM
How to move a: 7 ENDWISE
Relax on the: 4 LOLL
Sank into the: 3 SAT
Sofer
Soap actress: 4 **RENA**
"So few"
of WWII: 3 RAF
Sofia: 5 REINA
portrayer: 5 OPRAH
"___ So Fine": 3 HES

Soft: 5 DOWNY PIANO
7 LENIENT
and smooth: 6 SILKEN
and wet: 7 SQUISHY
ball: 4 **NERF**
cheese: 4 **BRIE**
diet: 3 PAP
ending: 4 WARE
fabric: 5 TERRY 6 SATEEN
felt hat: 6 FEDORA
food: 3 PAP
Go: 4 MELT
kid: 5 SUEDE
leather: 5 SUEDE
metal: 3 TIN
mineral: 4 **TALC**
Not too: 7 ALDENTE
rock: 4 TALC
seat: 4 SOFA 6 SETTEE
shade: 6 PASTEL
shoe: 3 **MOC**
shot: 3 LOB
spread: 4 OLEO
suffix: 4 WARE
throw: 3 LOB
tissue: 7 KLEENEX
touch: 3 DAB PAT
Soft & ___ : 3 DRI
Softball
team: 3 TEN
Soft drink: 4 **COLA** SODA
7 SODAPOP
brand: 4 NEHI 6 RCCOLA
SHASTA
Classic: 4 NEHI
nut: 4 KOLA
Popular: 4 COKE COLA
size: 5 LITER
Soften: 4 EASE MELT 5 ALLAY
6 EASEUP RELENT
up: 4 THAW
~, with "down": 4 TONE
Softener
Skin: 4 ALOE 5 CREAM
Softest
mineral: 4 TALC
Soft-focus
effect: 4 HAZE
Softhead: 3 SAP

Softly: 5 PIANO
Sing: 5 CROON
Very, very ~, in music: 3 PPP
Walk: 3 PAD 6 TIPTOE
Soft-money
source: 3 PAC
Soft palate: 5 VELUM
Of the: 5 VELAR
projection: 5 UVULA
Soft-shell
clam: 7 STEAMER
Software
All-in-one: 5 SUITE
Big name in: 5 ADOBE LOTUS
box encl.: 5 CDROM
buyer: 4 **USER**
Newer: 7 UPGRADE
Old PC: 5 MSDOS
Prerelease ~ version: 4 BETA
program: 3 APP
security fix: 5 PATCH
selection: 4 MENU
test version: 4 BETA
Soggy: 3 WET
ground: 4 MIRE
Soglow
Cartoonist: 4 OTTO
"So help me!": 6 HONEST
Soho
digs: 4 LOFT
Like some ~ shops: 4 ARTY
social: 3 TEA
So long, in: 4 TATA
Soil: 4 DIRT 5 **EARTH**
Clayey: 4 MARL 5 ADOBE
component: 5 HUMUS
embankment: 4 BERM
Fertile: 4 LOAM 5 LOESS
Like ~ near trees: 5 ROOTY
Like good: 5 LOAMY
Loamy: 5 LOESS
prefix: 4 AGRO
Rich: 4 **LOAM**
sweetener: 4 LIME
Windblown: 5 **LOESS**
Work the: 3 HOE 4 TILL
Soiled: 5 DIRTY
Soissons
summer: 3 ETE

"___ soit qui mal y pense": 4 HONI
"So it's you!": 3 AHA
Sojourn: 4 STAY
Sojourner
  Cell: **3** CON
Sokolova
  Skater: **5** ELENA
Sol: 4 NOTE
  Impresario: **5** HUROK
  prefix: **4** AERO
  Where el ~ rises: **4** ESTE
Sol.: 3 ANS
Solar
  deity: **4** ATEN
  event: **7** ECLIPSE
  phenomenon: **5** FLARE
    6 CORONA **7** SUNSPOT
  product: **3** RAY
  system model: **6** ORRERY
Solar ___: 6 SYSTEM
"Solaris"
  author Stanislaw: **3** LEM
Sold
  Bought and: **5** DEALT
  It's ~ in bags: **3** ICE
  It's ~ in bars: **4** OLEO SOAP
  It's ~ in sticks: **4** OLEO
  out: **4** GONE
  When ~ separately: **4** EACH
Solder
  element: **3** TIN
Soldier
  assignment: **4** DUTY
  Career: **5** LIFER
  Cavalry: **6** LANCER
  Confederate: **3** REB
  cops: **3** MPS
  CSA: **3** REB
  Down Under: **5** ANZAC
  French: **5** POILU
  helmet: **6** TINHAT
  Inept: **7** SADSACK
  in gray: **3** REB **5** REBEL
  knapsack: **6** KITBAG
  Korean: **3** ROK
  material: **3** TIN
  of fortune: **4** MERC
  Small: **3** ANT
  Seoul: **3** ROK

  topper: **6** TINHAT
  Toy: **5** GIJOE
  utensils: **7** MESSKIT
Soldiers: 3 GIS
Sold-out
  sign: **3** SRO
Sole: 3 ONE **4** LONE ONLY
  attachment: **5** CLEAT
  Kind of: **5** CREPE
  pattern: **5** TREAD
  point: **5** CLEAT
Soleil Moon ___: 4 FRYE
Solely: 3 ALL
Solemn: 5 GRAVE
  ceremony: **4** RITE
  promise: **3** VOW **4** OATH
  response: **4** AMEN
  song: **5** DIRGE
  stretch: **4** LENT
  vow: **4** OATH
"___ Solemnis": 5 MISSA
Solemnly
  affirm: **7** SWEARTO
  state: **4** AVOW
Solicit: 3 BEG **6** ASKFOR
  from: **5** ASKOF HITUP
Solicitous
  reply: **4** ISEE
Solid
  alcohol: **6** STEROL
  Become: **3** GEL
  Biochemical: **6** STEROL
  Freeze: **5** ICEUP
  ground: **10** TERRAFIRMA
  Not: **4** IFFY
  On ~ ground: **6** ASHORE
  suffix: **3** ITY
Solidarity
  city: **6** GDANSK
  First name in: **4** LECH
  name: **6** WALESA
Solidify: 3 GEL SET **4** CAKE CLOT
    JELL
Solidity
  Symbol of: **3** OAK
Solids
  Geometric: **4** TORI
Soliloquy
  start: **4** **TOBE**

Solitaire: 3 GEM
  Playing: 5 ALONE
  stone: 4 OPAL
Solitary: 3 ONE 4 **LONE** 5 ALONE
  one: 5 LONER 7 EREMITE
Solitude
  seeker: 5 LONER
Solo: 4 ARIA LONE STAG
     5 **ALONE** 6 ONEMAN
     7 UNAIDED 8 ALLALONE
     9 GOITALONE
  in space: 3 HAN
  org.: 5 UNCLE
  performance: 4 ARIA
  Short vocal: 6 ARIOSO
Solo, Han
  love: 4 LEIA
Soloist: 5 LONER
Solomon: 4 SAGE
  asset: 6 WISDOM
  Like: 4 SAGE WISE
  seal: 4 STAR
"Solomon and Sheba"
  costar: 4 GINA
"So long!": 4 CIAO TATA 5 ADIOS
     SEEYA
"___ So Long": 4 BEEN
Solti
  Conductor: 5 GEORG
  Slowly, to: 5 LENTO
  Smoothly, to: 6 LEGATO
  Softly, to: 5 PIANO
  Speeds, to: 5 TEMPI
Solution
  (abbr.): 3 ANS
  Bleaching: 3 LYE
  Caustic: 3 LYE
  Hospital: 6 SALINE
  Office: 5 TONER
  Pickling: 5 BRINE
  product: 3 ION
  Programmer's: 3 APP
  strength: 5 TITER
  Strong-smelling: 7 AMMONIA
  Temporary: 7 STOPGAP
Solve: 5 CRACK 7 UNRAVEL
  a cryptogram: 6 DECODE
  Confident way to: 5 ININK
    INPEN

Solvent: 6 AFLOAT
  Alcohol-based: 6 ACETAL
  Common: 5 ETHER 7 ACETONE
  Financially: 6 AFLOAT
  Hydrocarbon: 6 HEXANE
  Paint: 6 ACETAL 7 ACETONE
  Rinse, as with: 5 ELUTE
  Volatile: 5 ETHER
Solver
  Confident ~ tool: 3 PEN
  cry: 3 AHA
  need: 6 ERASER
  smudge: 7 ERASURE
Solzhenitsyn
  punishment: 5 EXILE
  topic: 5 GULAG
Somalia
  Gulf near: 4 ADEN
Somalian
  model: 4 **IMAN**
Somber: 4 GRIM 5 GRAVE
  In a ~ way: 5 SADLY
Sombrero: 3 HAT
Some: 3 **ANY** 4 ABIT AFEW ATAD
    6 ABITOF 7 ALITTLE
  ~, in Spanish: 4 UNOS
"So ___ me!": 3 SUE
Somebody: 4 NAME
Somebody ___ (not mine):
    5 ELSES
Somehow: 8 INASENSE
    15 ONEWAYORANOTHER
"Some ___ meat and canna eat":
    Burns: 3 HAE
Somersault: 4 FLIP ROLL
Something
  Certain: 4 AURA
  Come up with: 6 IDEATE
  Do: 3 **ACT**
  Do ~ with: 3 USE
  Have: 3 AIL EAT 4 DINE
  Have ~ at home: 5 EATIN
  It may follow: 4 ELSE
"___ something I said?": 4 ISIT
"Something's ___ Give":
    5 GOTTA
"Something to Talk About"
  singer Bonnie: 5 RAITT
Sometime: 6 ONEDAY

"Sometimes a Great Notion"
  author: 5 KESEY
"Sometimes you feel like ___":
  4 ANUT
Somewhat: 4 ABIT **ATAD**
  5 SORTA 6 KINDOF
  RATHER SORTOF
  8 INASENSE
  suffix: 3 ISH
  ~, in music: 4 POCO
"Somewhere in Time"
  actor: 5 REEVE
Somme
  Info: French cue
  city: 6 AMIENS
  Set, in: 4 FIXE
  state: 4 ETAT
  summer: 3 **ETE**
Sommelier
  Do a ~ job: 6 DECANT
  offering: 3 RED 4 WINE
  prefix: 4 OENO
Sommer
  Actress: 4 **ELKE**
"Sommersby"
  actor: 4 GERE
Sommers, Jaime
  Like: 6 BIONIC
Somnambulist
  Like a: 6 ASLEEP
"So Much in Love"
  singers: 5 TYMES
Son: 8 MANCHILD
  Favorite ~, perhaps:
    6 ELDEST
  of a son: 3 III
  ~, in French: 4 FILS
Sonar
  signal: 4 ECHO
  sound: 4 PING
  spot: 4 BLIP
Sonata: 4 OPUS
  finale: 4 CODA
  movement: 5 **RONDO**
Sondheim
  character: 4 TODD
Song
  Alpine: 5 YODEL
  and dance: 4 ARTS

Battle: 4 ARIA
Biblical: 5 PSALM
Cheerful: 4 LILT
Christmas: 4 NOEL 5 CAROL
Church: 4 HYMN
ending: 4 FEST
For a: 5 CHEAP
  9 DIRTCHEAP
Kind of: 4 SWAN 5 SIREN
Like a: 6 ARIOSE ARIOSO
Minstrel: 3 LAY
Nostalgic: 5 OLDIE
of praise: 3 ODE 4 HYMN
  5 PAEAN 8 CANTICLE
Part: 4 GLEE
Sacred: 5 MOTET **PSALM**
Sad: 5 DIRGE
section: 5 VERSE
Sentimental: 6 BALLAD
Simple: 5 DITTY
syllable: 3 **TRA**
syllables: 3 LAS 4 LALA 5 LALAS
  TRALA
thrush: 5 MAVIS
Words of a: 5 LYRIC 6 LYRICS
___ song (cheaply): 4 FORA
"___ Song" (John Denver hit):
  6 ANNIES
Song-and-dance
  act: 5 REVUE
Songbird
  Small: 3 TIT 4 LARK **WREN**
    5 PIPIT VIREO 6 TOMTIT
    7 SPARROW
"___ Song Go Out of My Heart":
  5 ILETA
Songka River
  capital: 5 HANOI
Songlike: 6 ARIOSE ARIOSO
"Song of the Golden Calf":
  4 ARIA
"Song of the South"
  syllables: 4 ADEE
  title: 4 BRER
Songs
  Art: 6 LIEDER
  for one: 4 SOLI
  for two: 5 DUETS
  German: 6 LIEDER

Top 40: 4 HITS
Songsmith
~ Jacques: 4 BREL
"Son ___ gun!": 3 OFA
Songwriter
org.: 5 **ASCAP**
~ Gus: 4 KAHN
~ Jacques: 4 BREL
~ Leonard: 5 COHEN
~ Sammy: 4 CAHN
Sonia
Actress: 5 BRAGA
Sonic
boom source: 3 SST
bounce: 4 **ECHO**
unit: 4 MACH
Sonic the Hedgehog
maker: 4 SEGA
Son-in-law
of LBJ: 4 ROBB
of Muhammad: 3 ALI
Sonja
Skater: 5 **HENIE**
Sonnet: 4 POEM
component: 7 COUPLET
ending: 3 EER 6 SESTET
Italian ~ closing: 6 SESTET
starter: 5 OCTET
unit: 4 IAMB
Sonneteer: 4 BARD POET
Muse of a: 5 ERATO
Sonnets
Like most: 6 IAMBIC
"Sonnets of Orpheus, The"
poet: 5 RILKE
Sonntag
Never, on: 3 NIE
Sonny
Boxer: 6 LISTON
boy: 3 LAD
Ex of: 4 CHER
or Chastity: 4 BONO
sibling: 3 SIS
"Son of"
in Arabic: 3 IBN
"Son of ___!": 4 AGUN
"Son of a gun!": 5 ILLBE
"Son of Frankenstein"
role: 4 YGOR

Sonoma
neighbor: 4 NAPA
Sonora
Info: Spanish cue
shawl: 6 SERAPE
snack: 4 TACO
snooze: 6 SIESTA
"so long": 5 ADIOS
Sons
Fathers and: 3 HES
of, in Hebrew: 4 BNAI
Some: 3 JRS
Sontag
Writer: 5 SUSAN
Sony
cofounder Morita: 4 AKIO
product: 7 WALKMAN
rival: 3 RCA 4 AIWA 5 SANYO
Soon: 4 **ANON** 7 ERELONG
          SHORTLY 9 INAMINUTE
after: 4 UPON
As ~ as: 4 **ONCE**
None too: 6 ATLAST
Sometime: 6 ONEDAY
Start too: 10 JUMPTHEGUN
Very: 6 INASEC
~, in poems: 4 **ANON**
Sooner
Certain: 6 TULSAN
city: 4 ENID 5 TULSA
migrant: 4 OKIE
state (abbr.): 4 OKLA
Sooner State
native: 4 OTOE
Soot
particle: 4 SMUT
Sooth
Word following: 5 SAYER
Soothe: 4 EASE LULL 5 ALLAY
Soother: 4 BALM
Burn: 4 **ALOE** 8 ALOEVERA
Mineral: 4 TALC
Skin: 4 BALM 6 LOTION
Sprain: 6 ICEBAG 8 LINIMENT
Throat: 7 LOZENGE
Soothing
hue: 4 AQUA
medicine: 7 NERVINE
ointment: 4 BALM 5 SALVE

plant: 4 **ALOE**
powder: 4 TALC
sound: 3 AAH
spot: 3 SPA
Soothsayer: 4 SEER 5 SIBYL
clue: 4 OMEN
Sooty
spot: 4 FLUE
Soph.
and others: 3 YRS
Sophia
Actress: 5 **LOREN**
Carlo, husband of: 5 PONTI
Husband of: 5 CARLO
Sophie
Oscar winner as: 5 MERYL
"Sophie's Choice"
actress: 6 STREEP
author: 6 STYRON
Sophie, in: 5 MERYL
Sophisticated: 5 SUAVE
6 URBANE
Like ~ software:
8 HIGHTECH
Sophisticates
they're not: 5 HICKS RUBES
Sophocles
tragedy: 4 AJAX 7 ELECTRA
8 ANTIGONE
10 OEDIPUSREX
Sophomore: 4 YEAR
Former: 6 JUNIOR
Sophs.
in two years: 3 SRS
Soporific: 6 OPIATE
substance: 6 OPIATE
Soprano
nicknamed "Bubbles": 5 SILLS
Puccini: 5 TOSCA
Range below: 4 ALTO
solo: 4 ARIA
~ Beverly: 5 SILLS
~ Jenny: 4 LIND
~ Lily: 4 PONS
~ Nellie: 5 MELBA
~ Renata: 6 SCOTTO
~ Wagner: 3 EVA
Soprano, A.J.
Robert who plays: 4 ILER

Soprano, Tony
Mother of: 5 LIVIA
"Sopranos, The"
actor Robert: 4 ILER
actress Falco: 4 **EDIE**
actress Turturro: 4 AIDA
award: 4 EMMY
Carmela portrayer on: 4 EDIE
James role on: 4 TONY
network: 3 **HBO**
Sorbet: 3 ICE
Sorbonne: 5 ECOLE
Info: French cue
article: 3 UNE
Head of the: 4 TETE
student: 5 ELEVE
summer: 3 ETE
To be, at the: 4 ETRE
Sorcerer: 4 MAGE
Sorcerers: 4 MAGI
Sorceress
of myth: 5 CIRCE MEDEA
Sorcery: 10 BLACKMAGIC
Goddess of: 6 HECATE
West Indies: 5 OBEAH
Sordid: 5 SEAMY
Sore: 3 MAD 4 **ACHY** 5 IRATE
IRKED ULCER VEXED
6 ACHING TENDER
Be: 4 ACHE
Eye: 4 **STYE**
Feel: 4 **ACHE**
Feeling: 4 ACHY
loser attitude: 10 SOURGRAPES
More: 6 ACHIER
spot: 4 ACHE
throat cause: 5 STREP
Soreness: 4 ACHE
Sorenstam
Golfer: 6 ANNIKA
org.: 4 LPGA
Sorghum
variety: 4 MILO 5 DURRA
Sor Juana ___
Poet: 4 INES
Sorority
letter: 3 CHI ETA PHI PSI RHO
4 ZETA 5 DELTA OMEGA
THETA

member: 4 COED

Sorrel
Cold ~ dish: 5 SCHAV
horse: 4 ROAN
Wood: 3 OCA 6 OXALIS

Sorrow: 3 RUE WOE 5 DOLOR TEARS
Expression of: 4 ALAS 6 LAMENT
Feel ~ for: 3 RUE
Sign of: 4 TEAR 8 TEARDROP
Sound of: 4 SIGH

Sorrowful
poem: 5 ELEGY
sigh: 4 ALAS
sound: 3 SOB 6 PLAINT
words: 4 AHME

Sorry: 3 SAD 4 LAME
Be ~ for: 4 PITY
Being ~ for: 5 RUING
Feel ~ about: 3 RUE 6 LAMENT
Feel ~ for: 4 PITY 6 REPENT
In ~ shape: 5 SEEDY
situations: 5 ILLS
sort: 4 RUER
to say: 4 ALAS

"Sorry!": 4 OOPS 8 PARDONME

"___ sorry!": 4 IMSO

"Sorry about that!": 4 OOPS

"Sorry to say ...": 4 ALAS

Sort: 3 **ILK** 4 KIND TYPE
of: 6 INAWAY RATHER 8 INASENSE

Sortie: 4 RAID

Sorting
device: 5 SIZER

"Sort of"
suffix: 3 ISH OID

Sorts
Out of: 3 **ILL** 5 ALIBI UPSET

Sorvino
Actress: 4 **MIRA**

SOS
alternative: 6 BRILLO
part, supposedly: 3 OUR
responder: 4 USCG

"S.O.S."
band: 4 ABBA

Sosa: 3 CUB
Stat for: 3 HRS RBI

stick: 3 BAT

"So ___ say": 4 THEY

So-so: 4 FAIR
connection: 3 AND
grade: 3 **CEE**

So ___ so forth: 5 ONAND

"So's ___ old man!": 3 YER

Sot: 4 LUSH 5 TOPER 7 TOSSPOT
Certain: 4 WINO
Mayberry: 4 OTIS
problem: 3 DTS
sound: 3 **HIC**
spot: 3 BAR
state: 6 STUPOR
symptoms: 3 DTS
Walk like a: 4 REEL

"So that's it!": 3 **AHA** OHO

"So that's your game!": 3 OHO

Sotheby's
signal: 3 BID NOD
stock: 3 ART

"So there!": 3 HAH SEE 4 TADA

Sothern
Actress: 3 **ANN**

Sothern, Ann
role: 6 MAISIE

Sotto ___ : 4 VOCE

Sotto voce
Not: 5 ALOUD
remark: 5 ASIDE

Souchong: 3 TEA
___ souci: 4 SANS

Soufflé
Like a: 4 EGGY
start: 4 EGGS

Sought: 7 QUESTED
an office: 6 RANFOR
answers: 5 ASKED
a seat: 3 RAN
damages: 4 SUED
office: 3 **RAN**

Soul: 5 ANIMA
mate: 4 BODY
Nary a: 5 **NOONE** 6 NOTONE
Not a: 5 NOONE
Queen of: 6 ARETHA
Solitary: 5 LONER
Sorry: 4 RUER
~, in French: 3 AME

"Soul Food"
actress Long: 3 NIA
Sound: 4 GOOD HALE OKAY
SANE TOLL TONE WELL
5 AUDIO INLET SOLID
6 COGENT
asleep: 5 SNORE
at the door: 3 RAP
bite: 5 QUOTE
booster: 3 AMP
effect: 4 ECHO
investment: 3 AMP 6 STEREO
Make: 4 **HEAL**
Of ~ mind: 4 SANE
Of ~ quality: 5 TONAL
off: 4 RANT 5 OPINE ORATE
Ominous: 5 KNELL
portion: 5 AUDIO
purchase: 6 STEREO
quality: 4 TONE 6 HEALTH
TIMBRE
reasonable: 5 ADDUP
rebound: 4 ECHO
setup: 6 STEREO
sleeper: 6 SNORER
start: 5 ULTRA
the alarm: 4 WARN
track: 5 AUDIO
unit: 4 SONE
upstairs: 4 SANE
~, as a bell: 4 PEAL
Sounded: 4 RANG
"Sounder"
actress Cicely: 5 TYSON
Soundness
of mind: 6 SANITY
"Sound of Music, The"
backdrop: 4 ALPS
extra: 3 NUN
figure: 6 ABBESS
heroine: 5 MARIA
name: 5 TRAPP
song: 5 MARIA
"Sounds good to me!": 4 IMIN
Sound system: 4 HIFI 6 **STEREO**
Old ~ component: 8 TAPEDECK
Soundtrack
Fix the: 5 REDUB
Work on a: 3 DUB

Soup
alternative: 5 SALAD
bean: 4 LIMA 6 LENTIL
Chilled: 5 SCHAV
Clear: 8 CONSOMME
container: 3 CAN
cracker: 7 SALTINE
Duck: 4 EASY
flavoring: 4 DILL
holder: 3 CAN 6 TUREEN
Hot and sour ~ ingredient:
4 TOFU
ingredient: 6 LENTIL OXTAIL
Italian ~ ingredient: 4 ORZO
9 SPLITPEAS
Japanese: 4 **MISO** 5 RAMEN
legume: 3 PEA 6 LENTIL
pasta: 4 ORZO
pod: 4 OKRA
scoop: 5 LADLE
Serve: 5 LADLE
served cold: 5 SCHAV
served with sour cream:
7 BORSCHT
server: 5 LADLE 6 LADLER
TUREEN
Simple: 5 BROTH
source: 3 CAN
spheroid: 3 PEA
Thick: 5 PUREE 6 POTAGE
Thin: 5 BROTH
veggie: 3 **PEA** 4 LEEK OKRA
vessel: 3 POT
with sushi: 4 MISO
Soupçon: 3 TAD 4 DASH HINT
TANG 5 TASTE TINGE
TRACE
Soup du ___: 4 JOUR
Souped-up
car: 6 HOTROD
Soupy
Comic: 5 SALES
Sour: 4 TART 5 ACERB ACIDY
SPOIL 6 ACETIC ACIDIC
CURDLE MOROSE
brew: 6 ALEGAR
fruit: 4 SLOE 5 LEMON
Go: 4 TURN
note: 7 CLINKER

Without a ~ note: **6** INTUNE
Sour ___ : 4 MASH
Sourball
  Like a: **4** TART
Source: 4 FONT LODE ROOT
      5 FOUNT **6** ORIGIN
Sourdough
  find: **3** ORE
Sourpuss: 4 CRAB
Sour-tasting: 4 ACID TART
      5 ACERB
Sousaphone
  kin: **4** TUBA
Souse
  Sitcom: **4** OTIS
Soused: 3 LIT
Souter
  Justice replaced by: **7** BRENNAN
South: 5 DIXIE
  Commodity in the old:
      10 KINGCOTTON
  end: **3** ERN
  Go ~, maybe: **7** MIGRATE
  side: **3** ERN
  suffix: **3** ERN
  The ~, once: **3** CSA
  ~, in Spanish: **3** SUR
South Africa
  area: **5** NATAL
  Country inside: **7** LESOTHO
  Golfer from: **3** ELS
  Mandela of: **6** NELSON
South African
  Certain: **4** BOER
  fox: **4** ASSE
  grassland: **4** VELD **5** VELDT
  money: **4** RAND
  playwright Fugard: **5** ATHOL
  pres.: **7** PWBOTHA
  president: **5** BOTHA
  province: **5** NATAL
  ~ Peace Nobelist: **4** TUTU
South America
  Flightless bird of: **4** RHEA
  It's spotted in: **6** OCELOT
  Landlocked country of:
      7 BOLIVIA
South American
  Ancient: **4** INCA

beast: **5** LLAMA
bird: **4** RHEA
capital: **4** LIMA **5** LAPAZ QUITO
      SUCRE
dance: **5** SAMBA
monkey: **4** TITI
plain: **5** LLANO
range: **5** ANDES
rodent: **4** CAVY PACA **5** COYPU
      6 AGOUTI
tuber: **3** OCA
~ Indian: **4** INCA
South Australia
  Capital of: **8** ADELAIDE
South Beach ___ : 4 DIET
South Bend
  City near: **7** ELKHART
South Carolina
  motto word: **5** SPERO
South Dakota
  athlete: **6** COYOTE
  capital: **6** PIERRE
  city: **5** HURON **7** YANKTON
  feature: **7** BADLAND
  ~, to Pierre: **4** ETAT
South Devon
  river: **3** EXE
Southeast Asian: 3 LAO **4** THAI
Southeastern Conference
  team, informally: **4** BAMA
Southend-on-Sea
  site: **5** ESSEX
Southern
  bread: **4** PONE
  breakfast dish: **5** GRITS
  city: **8** SAOPAULO
  constellation: **3** ARA
  gal: **5** BELLE
  legume: **6** COWPEA
  lights: **15** AURORAAUSTRALIS
  power inits.: **3** TVA
  school: **4** BAMA
  sibling: **4** BRER
  side: **4** OKRA
  vacation spot: **3** RIO
Southernmost
  of the Marianas: **4** GUAM
  ~ Great Lake: **4** ERIE
  ~ U.S. city: **4** HILO

Southfork: 5 RANCH
 matriarch: 5 ELLIE
South ___, Indiana: 4 BEND
South Korea
 capital: 5 SEOUL
 First president of: 4 RHEE
 Roh ___ Woo of: 3 TAE
 Syngman of: 4 RHEE
South Korean
 1950s ~ president: 4 RHEE
 auto: 3 KIA
 port: 5 PUSAN
South-of-the-border
 Info: Spanish cue
 friend: 5 AMIGO
 shout: 3 OLE
 uncle: 3 TIO
South Pacific
 island: 5 SAMOA 6 EASTER
  TAHITI 8 BORABORA
 kingdom: 5 TONGA
 region: 7 OCEANIA
 republic: 4 FIJI
"South Pacific"
 actor Pinza: 4 EZIO
 actress Gaynor: 5 MITZI
 director Josh: 5 LOGAN
 Emile portrayer in: 4 EZIO
 girl: 4 LIAT
 hero: 5 EMILE
 heroine: 6 NELLIE
 song: 7 BALIHAI
"South Park"
 casualty: 5 KENNY
 character Cartman: 4 ERIC
 creator Parker: 4 TREY
 creator Stone: 4 MATT
 kid: 3 IKE 4 KYLE STAN
 voice actor Hayes: 5 ISAAC
Southpaw: 5 LEFTY
 strength: 4 LEFT
 Winningest: 5 SPAHN
South Pole
 explorer Amundsen: 5 ROALD
South Seas
 attire: 6 SARONG
 island: 6 TAHITI
 islander: 6 SAMOAN
 island group: 4 FIJI 5 SAMOA

 kingdom: 5 TONGA
 staple: 4 TARO
 tale: 4 OMOO
South Vietnam
 president Ngo Dinh: 4 DIEM
Southwest
 friend: 5 AMIGO
 poplar: 5 ALAMO
 sight: 4 MESA
 ~ Indian: 4 HOPI PIMA
Southwestern
 art colony: 4 TAOS
 brick: 5 ADOBE
 gulch: 6 ARROYO
 monster: 4 GILA
 native: 3 **UTE**
 plateau: 4 MESA
 poplar: 5 ALAMO
 pot: 4 OLLA
 river: 4 GILA
 saloon: 7 CANTINA
 stewpot: 4 OLLA
 ~ Indian: 3 UTE 4 HOPI
Souvenir: 5 RELIC TOKEN
  7 MEMENTO
 item: 3 TEE 6 TSHIRT
  8 TEESHIRT
Souvlaki
 ingredient: 4 LAMB
" ___ So Vain": 5 YOURE
Sovereign: 5 ROYAL RULER
 stand-in: 6 REGENT
Sovereignty: 6 THRONE
 Symbol of: 3 ORB
Soviet
 co-op: 5 ARTEL
 First ~ premier: 5 LENIN
 Former ~ First Lady: 5 RAISA
 founder: 5 LENIN
 labor camp: 5 GULAG
 military force: 7 REDARMY
 news agency: 4 **TASS**
 Old ~ initials: 4 CCCP
 satellite: 7 SPUTNIK
 space probe: 4 LUNA
 spy agcy.: 3 KGB
Sow: 3 **SHE** 4 SEED 5 PLANT
  6 FEMALE
 chow: 4 SLOP

mate: 4 BOAR
pen: 3 STY
sound: 4 OINK
"___ sow ...": 4 ASYE
"So what?!": 7 BIGDEAL
"So what ___ is new?": 4 **ELSE**
Sowing
  machine: 6 SEEDER
Sox
  city: 3 CHI
  on scoreboards: 3 BOS
Soy
  product: 4 TOFU
  What ~ can mean: 3 IAM
Soybean
  product: 4 TOFU
  soup: 4 MISO
Soyuz
  Inits. on a ~ rocket: 4 CCCP
  launcher: 4 USSR
Spa: 5 BATHS 6 HOTTUB
      RESORT
  Day ~ offering: 4 ROBE
  English: 4 BATH
  feature: 5 SAUNA 6 HOTTUB
  French: 5 EVIAN
  German: 5 BADEN
      10 BADENBADEN
  handout: 5 TOWEL
  Lake Geneva: 5 EVIAN
  offering: 5 SAUNA
      7 MUDBATH
  sounds: 3 AHS 4 AAHS
  treatment: 6 FACIAL
Space: 3 AIR GAP 4 AREA HOLE
      ROOM VOID 5 REALM
  between: 5 AISLE
  between teeth: 8 DIASTEMA
  Buzz in: 6 ALDRIN
  cadet's place: 8 LALALAND
  chimp: 4 ENOS
  cloud: 6 NEBULA
  Empty: 4 VOID
  explorer: 5 PROBE
  Fill: 3 ARE
  First guy in: 4 YURI
  Had ~ for: 6 SEATED
  heater: 3 SOL
  Intro to: 4 AERO

invaders: 3 ETS
Kind of: 5 OUTER
leader: 4 AERO
Like outer: 4 VAST
Link in: 4 DOCK
occupier: 6 MATTER
on a schedule: 4 SLOT
opening: 4 AERO
org.: 4 NASA
prefix: 4 **AERO**
revolver: 6 PLANET
Ride in: 5 SALLY
rock: 6 METEOR
Senator in: 4 GARN 5 GLENN
Shepard in: 4 ALAN
shuttle org.: 4 NASA
Solo in: 3 HAN
Soviet ~ program: 6 VOSTOK
spiral: 6 NEBULA
Tight on: 7 CRAMPED
Upper regions of: 5 ETHER
Vaulted: 4 APSE
walk (abbr.): 3 EVA
~, poetically: 5 ETHER
Space ___: 5 CADET
___ space: 5 OUTER
Spacecraft
  component: 3 POD
  segment: 6 MODULE
Space Invaders
  maker: 5 ATARI
Spacek
  Actress: 5 SISSY
  role: 4 LYNN
Spaceman
  of serials: 11 FLASHGORDON
Space Needle
  city: 7 SEATTLE
Space-saving
  abbr.: 3 ETC 4 ETAL
Spaceship
  Mork's: 3 EGG
Spaceship Earth
  setting: 5 EPCOT
Space station
  1970s ~: 6 SKYLAB
  Former Russian: 3 **MIR**
Spacewalk
  initials: 3 EVA

Spacey
 Actor: 5 KEVIN
Spacious: 4 AIRY 5 AMPLE
  ROOMY
Spackle
 target: 8 NAILHOLE
Spade: 6 SLEUTH
 Doesn't call a ~ a spade: 4 ERRS
 portrayer: 6 BOGART
 the sleuth: 3 SAM
 Use a: 3 DIG
 ~, to Bogart: 4 ROLE
Spades: 4 SUIT
 Game with 13 ~ laid out:
  4 FARO
Spaghetti: 5 PASTA
 specification: 7 ALDENTE
 strainer: 5 SIEVE
 topping: 5 SAUCE
Spaghetti sauce
 brand: 4 RAGU 5 PREGO
 herb: 5 BASIL
Spaghetti western
 director Sergio: 5 LEONE
 topper: 7 STETSON
Spain
 and Portugal: 6 IBERIA
 Capital of: 6 MADRID
 City in: 4 LEON 5 AVILA LORCA
  6 ORENSE OVIEDO TOLEDO
 is in it (abbr.): 3 EEC
 Lady of: 4 **DONA** 6 SENORA
 Money of: 6 PESETA
 Onetime queen of: 3 ENA
 Province in: 4 LEON 5 AVILA
 Region in: 6 ARAGON
 River in: 4 EBRO
 The rain in: 4 AGUA
Spam: 4 MEAT
 container: 3 CAN TIN 5 EMAIL
 maker: 6 HORMEL
 Much: 3 ADS
Span: 5 CROSS
 Animals in a: 4 OXEN
 Calendar: 5 YEAR
 Geological: 3 EON
 Historical: 3 ERA
 Pianist's: 6 OCTAVE
 Singer's: 5 RANGE

Spanakopita
 cheese: 4 FETA
Spandau
 Last inmate at: 4 HESS
Spangle: 6 SEQUIN
Spaniard
 Legendary: 5 ELCID
Spaniel
 breed: 8 SPRINGER
 Kind of: 6 SUSSEX
Spanish
 1930s ~ queen: 3 ENA
 actress Carmen: 5 MAURA
 and pearl: 6 ONIONS
 appetizer: 4 **TAPA**
 article: 3 LAS LOS **UNA** UNO
 aunt: 3 **TIA**
 ayes: 3 SIS 4 **SISI**
 babe: 4 NENE
 beach: 5 PLAYA
 bear: 3 OSO
 bread: 6 PESETA
 cheer: 3 OLE
 Common ~ verb: 4 **ESTA**
 count start: 3 UNO
 cowboy: 7 LLANERO
 crowd: 4 TRES
 custard: 4 FLAN
 day: 3 DIA
 dessert: 4 FLAN
 dessert wine: 6 MALAGA
 diminutive: 3 ITA
 direction: 3 SUR 4 ESTE
 dish: 6 PAELLA
 Dry ~ wine: 5 RIOJA
 explorer: 6 DESOTO
 eye: 3 **OJO**
 girlfriend: 5 AMIGA
 gold: 3 **ORO**
 grocery: 6 BODEGA
 hand: 4 MANO
 hero: 5 ELCID
 house: 4 CASA
 inn: 6 POSADA
 king: 3 REY
 lady: 4 DONA 6 SENORA
 language drama of 1984:
  7 ELNORTE
 liqueur: 4 ANIS

love: 4 AMOR
mark: 5 TILDE
miss (abbr.): 4 SRTA
muralist: 4 SERT
nobleman: 7 GRANDEE
Old ~ coins: 6 REALES
or Denver: 6 OMELET
painter: 4 DALI GOYA MIRO
    SERT
poet: 5 LORCA
port: 5 CADIZ
pot: 4 OLLA
princess: 5 ELENA
pronoun: 3 ESA ESO 4 ELLO
    ESAS ESTA ESTO
    5 ELLAS
queen: 5 REINA
rice: 5 ARROZ
rice dish: 6 PAELLA
river: 3 RIO 4 EBRO
room: 4 SALA
root word: 3 OLE
royalty: 5 REYES 6 REINAS
shawl: 6 SERAPE
sherry: 7 AMOROSO
silver: 5 PLATA
sir: 5 SENOR
snack: 4 TAPA
stew: 4 OLLA
stewpot: 4 OLLA
surrealist: 4 DALI MIRO
tar: 4 BREA
tourist town: 5 AVILA
uncle: 3 TIO
vessel: 4 OLLA
walled city: 5 AVILA
water: 4 AGUA
wave: 3 OLA
~ Mrs.: 3 SRA
~ Muppet: 6 ROSITA
Spanish ___: 6 OMELET
"Spanish Harlem"
singer: 6 ARETHA
Spanish Steps
city: 4 ROME
"Spanish Tragedy, The"
dramatist Thomas: 3 KYD
Spank: 3 TAN 4 LICK SWAT
Spanker: 4 SAIL

Spanking
follower: 3 NEW
spot: 4 KNEE REAR
Spanky
Pal of: 7 ALFALFA
~, for one: 6 RASCAL
Spann
Bluesman: 4 OTIS
Spar: 3 BOX 4 MAST POLE YARD
Sail: 5 SPRIT
Spare: 4 LEAN TIRE 7 AUSTERE
change: 4 TIRE
hair: 3 WIG
holder: 5 TRUNK
part: 3 PIN RIB
Put on a ~ tire: 4 GAIN
Seek ~ change: 3 BEG
target: 6 TENPIN 7 NINEPIN
With room to: 5 AMPLY
Spared
It may be: 6 THEROD
Spare tire: 3 FAT 4 FLAB
site: 5 WAIST
Spark: 4 ELAN GERM 6 EXCITE
    7 ANIMATE 8 CATALYST
Creative: 4 **IDEA**
follower: 4 PLUG
plug feature: 3 GAP
Sparkle: 3 PEP 4 ELAN 5 ECLAT
    GLINT SHINE 6 ESPRIT
    7 GLISTEN
Add some: 6 AERATE
Wine with a: 4 ASTI
Sparkled: 5 SHONE
Sparkler: 3 GEM
Sparkling: 8 AGLITTER
headwear: 5 TIARA
It might be: 4 WINE
wine: 4 ASTI
Sparks
City near: 4 RENO
loc.: 3 NEV
Old film comic: 3 NED
setting: 6 NEVADA
Sparky
Cy Young winner: 4 LYLE
Sparrow: 5 FINCH
Sparrow of Paris, The
Singer known as: 4 PIAF

Sparse: 4 THIN 6 SCANTY
Sparta
  Rival of: 5 ARGOS
  Serf of ancient: 5 HELOT
Spartacus: 5 SLAVE
Spartan: 5 HARSH STARK
    7 AUSTERE
  foe: 8 ATHENIAN
  queen: 4 LEDA
  serf: 5 HELOT
Spasm: 3 **TIC** 4 PANG 5 THROE
  Neck: 5 CRICK
Spasmodic: 5 JERKY
Spat: 3 ROW 4 TIFF TODO
    5 SETTO
  Public: 5 SCENE
  spot: 5 ANKLE
Spate: 4 RASH 7 TORRENT
Spathe
  Flower with a: 5 CALLA
Spatting: 4 ATIT
Spatula
  Toss with a: 4 FLIP
Spawn: 3 OVA ROE
Spawning
  fish: 3 EEL 4 SHAD
Spay: 6 NEUTER
SPCA
  Part of: 3 SOC
Speak: 3 SAY 4 TALK 5 ORATE
    UTTER
  As we: 3 NOW
  at all: 6 SAYBOO
  at length: 5 ORATE RUNON
  derisively: 5 SCOFF
  hesitantly: 3 HAW
  hoarsely: 4 RASP
  in a monotone: 5 DRONE
  irritably to: 6 SNAPAT
  like a tough guy: 4 RASP
  like Sylvester: 4 LISP
  lovingly: 3 COO
  off the cuff: 5 ADLIB
  one's mind: 5 OPINE
  pompously: 5 ORATE
  slowly: 5 DRAWL
  So to: 8 ASITWERE
  unclearly: 4 SLUR
  with a Jersey accent: 3 MOO

  ~, old-style: 5 SAYST
  ___ speak: 4 SOTO
Speakeasy
  event: 4 RAID
Speaker
  aid: 5 NOTES
  Loud: 6 RANTER 7 STENTOR
  of baseball: 4 **TRIS**
  Old ~ name: 4 NEWT
  part: 7 TWEETER
  pauses: 3 ERS
  platform: 4 **DAIS**
  Public: 6 ORATOR
  spot: 4 DAIS 7 LECTERN
  systems, for short: 3 PAS
Speaking
  Generally: 7 ASARULE
  Manner of: 4 TONE 5 IDIOM
  Plain: 5 PROSE
  sites: 6 ROSTRA
Spear
  carrier: 5 EXTRA
  carrier venue: 5 OPERA
  handle: 5 SHAFT
  Poseidon's: 7 TRIDENT
Spearhead: 4 LEAD
Spears, Britney
  fan: 4 TEEN
  hit: 15 OOPSIDIDITAGAIN
  Product hawked by: 5 PEPSI
Spec.
  Not: 3 GEN
  Shoe: 3 EEE
Special: 3 PET 6 ENTREE
  attention, for short: 3 TLC
  case: 4 ETUI
  connections: 3 INS
  edition: 5 EXTRA
  group: 5 ELITE
  Kind of: 5 KMART
  Nothing: 5 SOSO
  skill: 4 GIFT 5 KNACK
  suffix: 3 IST
  They may be: 9 INTERESTS
  time: 3 ERA
  vocabulary: 5 ARGOT
Special Forces
  cap: 5 BERET
  unit: 5 **ATEAM**

weapon: 3 UZI
Special-interest
  gp.: 3 ORG 4 ASSN
Specialist: 3 PRO 5 MAVEN
Specialized
  angler: 5 EELER
  idiom: 5 ARGOT
  sch.: 4 ACAD
  slang: 5 LINGO
Specialty: 4 **AREA** 5 FIELD
    FORTE NICHE 6 METIER
Specific
  For a ~ purpose: 5 ADHOC
  Get: 9 NAMENAMES
Specifically: 5 TOWIT
Specification: 6 DETAIL
Specifics: 7 DETAILS
Specified: 3 SET
Specify: 4 NAME
Specimen
  Assay: 3 ORE
  collector: 4 SWAB
  holder: 4 VIAL
  New: 7 NEOTYPE
Specious
  debater: 7 SOPHIST
Speck: 3 DOT TAD 4 ATOM IOTA
    MOTE
  in the ocean: 4 ISLE 5 ISLET
Speckled
  fish: 5 TROUT
  horse: 4 **ROAN**
Spectacle: 5 SCENE
Spectacles
  Spot for: 4 NOSE
Spectacular: 4 EPIC 7 AWESOME
  star: 4 NOVA
Spectator
  No mere: 4 DOER
  Unhappy: 5 BOOER
Spectator, The
  essayist: 6 STEELE
Specter: 5 BOGIE GHOST
    6 WRAITH
  Senator: 5 **ARLEN**
Spectra
  maker: 3 KIA
Spectrum
  band: 3 HUE

Beyond the visible: 8 ULTRARED
  11 ULTRAVIOLET
component: 3 RED 4 BLUE
  6 INDIGO
One end of the: 3 RED
producer: 5 PRISM
The whole: 4 ATOZ
Speculative: 5 RISKY
  Least: 6 SAFEST
Sped: 3 RAN ZIP 4 FLEW **TORE**
Speech: 7 ADDRESS ORATION
  Acceptance ~ word: 5 THANK
  Body of a: 4 TEXT
  characteristic: 4 ACCENT
  difficulty: 4 LISP
  enlivener: 8 ANECDOTE
  Figure of: 5 IDIOM **TROPE**
    6 ORATOR
  Formal: 7 ORATION
  Free ~ obstacle: 3 GAG
  Give a: 5 **ORATE**
  Imperfect: 4 LISP
  Informal: 5 SLANG
  Long ~, often: 4 BORE
  Make a: 5 **ORATE**
  Omit, in: 5 ELIDE
  Part of: 4 NOUN 8 SENTENCE
  problem: 4 LISP
  Pt. of: 3 ADV 4 PRON
  Public: 7 ORATION
  Some ~ sounds: 6 NASALS
  study: 9 PHONETICS
  stumbles: 3 UHS
  Sun.: 3 SER
Speechify: 5 **ORATE**
Speechless: 3 MUM 4 MUTE
    6 AGHAST SILENT
  Leave: 3 AWE 4 STUN
  one: 5 MIMER
Speechwriter
  ~ Peggy: 6 NOONAN
Speed: 3 HIE 5 HASTE 6 GOFAST
  At full: 5 **AMAIN**
  Built for: 5 SLEEK
  Burst of: 6 SPRINT
  Check: 4 TIME
  contest: 4 RACE
  demon: 5 RACER
  Demonstrate raw: 6 STREAK

Hi-tech ~ rate: **4** BAUD
limit letters: **3** MPH
Musical: **5** TEMPO
prefix: **3** VEL
ratio: **4** MACH
reader: **5** RADAR **8** RADARGUN
Tape ~ (abbr.): **3** IPS
Undue: **5** HASTE
unit: **4** KNOT MACH
up: **3** REV
Up to: **4** ABLE
Walking: **4** PACE
With: **5** APACE
Word with: **4** TRAP
"Speed"
actor: **6** REEVES
actor Reeves: **5** KEANU
actress Bullock: **6** SANDRA
setting: **3** BUS
"Speed ___": **5** RACER
Speeder
A ~ makes it: **5** HASTE
A ~ steps on it: **3** GAS
penalty: **4** FINE
spotter: **5** RADAR
stopper: **3** COP
Speedily: **5** APACE
Speed-of-sound
exceeder: **3** SST
number: **4** MACH
Speedometer
letters: **3** **MPH**
Speeds
Musical: **5** TEMPI
Speedster
Retired: **3** SST
Speed Stick
maker: **6** MENNEN
___ **Speedwagon:** **3** **REO**
Speedway
Florida: **7** DAYTONA
Speedy: **4** FAST **5** FLEET RAPID
flier: **3** SST
one-seater: **6** GOKART
steed: **4** ARAB
Speleologist: **5** CAVER
Spell: **3** HEX **4** BOUT **5** STINT
7 RELIEVE
Bad: **3** HEX

Cold: **6** ICEAGE
For a: **6** AWHILE
of excess: **5** SPREE
Sit a: **4** REST
Under Cupid's: **6** INLOVE
Under the ~ (of): **8** ENAMORED
Voodoo: **4** MOJO
Where one stands for a: **3** BEE
Spellbinding
sort: **6** ORATOR
Spellbound: **4** AGOG AWED RAPT
Spelled
Not ~ out: **5** TACIT
Song title ~ out: **4** YMCA
Speller
phrase: **4** ASIN
Spelling
Actress: **4** **TORI**
Alt.: **3** VAR
and Amos: **5** TORIS
contest: **3** **BEE**
game: **5** GHOST
TV producer: **5** AARON
Spell-off: **3** BEE
Spelunker: **5** CAVER
Spelunking
site: **4** CAVE **6** GROTTO
Spend: **5** USEUP
the night: **4** STAY
Spender
Big: **10** HIGHROLLER
Spending
binge: **5** SPREE
limit: **3** CAP
Spendthrift: **7** WASTREL
Not a: **5** MISER SAVER
Spenser
portrayer: **5** URICH
"Spenser: For Hire"
actor Robert: **5** URICH
Spenserian
work: **6** SONNET
Spent: **4** WORN **5** ALLIN TIRED
WEARY **6** POOPED
USEDUP **7** ALLGONE
Money: **5** OUTGO
Spew: **4** EMIT
fire and brimstone: **4** RANT
forth: **4** GUSH **5** ERUPT SPOUT

SPUME

Volcanic: 3 ASH

Spewer

Sicilian: 4 **ETNA**

Sphagnous: 5 MOSSY

Sphagnum: 4 MOSS

moss: 4 PEAT

Sphere: 3 **ORB** 4 AREA 5 ARENA
GLOBE REALM 6 REGION

prefix: 3 ECO 4 **ATMO** HEMI
IONO 5 TROPO 6 STRATO

Spherical: 5 ORBIC ROUND

veggies: 4 PEAS

Spheroid: 3 ORB

Edible: 3 PEA

hairdo: 4 AFRO

Sphinx

site: 4 GIZA

~, in part: 4 LION

Spice: 4 ZEST

Add ~ to: 6 SEASON

amt.: 3 TSP

Cookie: 6 GINGER

Eggnog: 6 NUTMEG

holder: 4 RACK

Nutmeg: 4 MACE

rack spice: 9 ONIONSALT

Spiced

It may be: 3 TEA

stew: 4 OLLA

tea: 4 CHAI

Spice Girls

genre: 7 EUROPOP

singer Halliwell: 4 GERI

Spick-and-span: 4 NEAT

Spicy: 3 HOT 5 ZESTY 7 PEPPERY

candies: 7 REDHOTS

cuisine: 4 **THAI** 5 CAJUN
HUNAN 6 CREOLE TEXMEX
7 MEXICAN

dip: 5 SALSA

ingredient: 5 CHILI

Not: 4 MILD 5 BLAND

sauce: 5 SALSA

sausage: 6 SALAMI

stew: 4 **OLLA** SAMI 6 RAGOUT

Very: 6 REDHOT

Spider

creation: 3 WEB 6 COBWEB

maker: 4 FIAT

prey: 3 FLY

She was changed into a:
7 ARACHNE

web: 4 TRAP

Spiderlike

bug: 13 DADDYLONGLEGS

Spider-Man

creator: 7 STANLEE

creator Lee: 4 STAN

creator Stan: 3 LEE

"Spider-Man"

actress Kirsten: 5 DUNST

director: 5 RAIMI 8 SAMRAIMI

___ Spiegel: 3 DER

Spiegelman, Art

critter: 4 MAUS

Spiel: 4 LINE 5 ORATE 6 PATTER

Emcee: 5 INTRO

Sales: 5 PITCH

Spielberg

Director: 6 STEVEN

film: 4 JAWS 7 AMISTAD

Spiff

(up): 6 SPRUCE

Spiffy: 4 **NEAT** POSH 6 RAKISH

Make: 4 DOUP

Spigot: 3 **TAP**

Container with a: 3 URN

Spike: 4 LACE

Climbing: 5 PITON

Corn: 3 EAR

Director: 3 **LEE**

Golden ~ state: 4 UTAH

greeting: 3 GRR

Shoe: 5 CLEAT

Volleyball: 8 KILLSHOT

Spiked

club: 4 MACE

Spikes

They might end in: 3 TDS

Spike TV

former name: 3 TNN

Spiky

Doll with ~ hair: 5 TROLL

Spill: 4 TRIP 5 WASTE 6 HEADER
TUMBLE

Clean, as a: 5 MOPUP

(over): 4 SLOP

Snitches ~ them: 5 BEANS
the beans: 3 RAT 4 **BLAB** SING
    TALK TELL 5 BLURT LETON
    6 TATTLE

Spilt
Cry over ~ milk: 5 WHINE

Spin: 4 REEL TURN 5 TWIRL
        6 ROTATE 7 REVOLVE
Apply: 4 SKEW
Go for a: 4 REEL
Put a ~ on: 5 SLANT
Rink: 5 CAMEL
What DJs: 3 LPS
You might go for a ~ in it:
    4 TUTU

Spinach
Like: 5 LEAFY

Spinach-like
plant: 6 ORACH

Spinal
column feature: 4 DISC

Spinal cord
Brain and ~ (abbr.): 3 CNS
Of the: 6 NEURAL

"Spin City"
star: 5 SHEEN

Spindle: 3 MAR 4 AXLE
Grinding wheel: 7 MANDREL

Spin doctor: 5 PRMAN
concern: 5 **IMAGE**

Spine
line: 5 TITLE

Spine-chilling: 5 EERIE

Spiner
Actor: 5 BRENT
role: 4 DATA

Spine-tingling: 5 **EERIE**

Spingarn Medal
awarder: 5 NAACP

Spinks
Boxer: 4 **LEON**
defeater: 3 ALI

Spin like ___: 4 ATOP

Spinnaker: 4 SAIL
site: 5 YACHT

Spinner: 3 TOP 4 GYRO 5 PRMAN
of lore: 15 RUMPELSTILTSKIN
Plane: 4 PROP
Record: 6 DEEJAY

Yarn: 4 LIAR

Spinners: 3 DJS

Spinning: 5 AREEL 6 AWHIRL
part: 5 ROTOR
toy: 3 TOP
wheels, perhaps: 5 MIRED

Spin-off
Religious: 4 SECT

Spiny
anteater: 7 ECHIDNA
cactus: 6 CHOLLA
houseplant: 4 **ALOE**
plant: 6 CACTUS
plants: 5 CACTI

Spiny-rayed
fish: 7 CICHLID

Spiral: 4 LOOP 5 HELIX
        6 GYRATE
shell: 5 CONCH 6 TRITON
Space: 6 NEBULA

Spiral-horned
antelope: 4 KUDU 5 **ELAND**

Spiral-shelled
mollusk: 5 SNAIL WHELK
        6 TRITON

Spirit: 3 PEP VIM 4 AURA BRIO
        ELAN LIFE SOUL 5 ARDOR
        GENIE GHOST HEART
        SPUNK 6 MORALE
        WRAITH
Blithe: 4 ELAN
Bottled: 5 GENIE
Break the ~ of: 5 UNMAN
Community: 5 **ETHOS**
Evil: 5 DEMON
Full of school: 6 RAHRAH
Group: 6 MORALE
Household: 3 LAR
Indomitable: 4 GRIT
Irish: 7 BANSHEE
Islamic: 5 DJINN
Kind of: 4 TEAM
Obliging: 5 GENIE
of a people: 5 ETHOS
of the time: 9 ZEITGEIST
raiser: 6 SEANCE
Shakespearean: 5 ARIEL
Show team: 4 ROOT
Word before: 4 TEAM

Spirited
attack: 5 SALVO
horse: 4 ARAB 5 STEED
self-assurance: 4 ELAN
session: 6 SEANCE
Spiritedness: 4 ELAN
Spirits: 7 ALCOHOL
Bottled: 5 GENII
Evil: 6 INCUBI
Guardian: 5 GENII
High: 3 PEP 4 **GLEE** 5 CHEER
    7 ELATION
home: 3 BAR
In low: 3 SAD
Island: 4 RUMS
Japanese: 5 SAKES SAKIS
Lift the ~ of: 5 ELATE
Roman household: 5 LARES
Spiritual: 4 SONG 5 INNER
adviser: 4 GURU
Endow with ~ awareness:
    6 ENSOUL
guide: 4 GURU
Islamic ~ leader: 6 CALIPH
leader: 5 REBBE
path: 3 TAO ZEN
Spiritualist
session: 6 SEANCE
Spiritually
Uplift: 5 EDIFY
Spiro
predecessor: 6 HUBERT
Vice President: 5 AGNEW
Spit
Frog: 4 ALGA
out: 4 SPEW
Ready to: 5 IRATE
Spitchcock: 3 EEL
Spite: 5 VENOM 6 MALICE
In ~ of: 3 THO 5 ALTHO
Spiteful: 4 MEAN 5 CATTY NASTY
Spitfire
fliers: 3 RAF
Spitter
sound: 4 PTUI
South American: 5 LLAMA
Spitting
sound: 4 PTUI
thing: 5 IMAGE

Splash: 4 ELAN SLOP
Big: 5 ECLAT
Cause of a big: 9 BELLYFLOP
Make a: 4 PLOP
Splasher
Playful: 5 OTTER
Splashy
resort: 3 SPA
Splatter
protector: 3 BIB
Spleen: 3 **IRE** 4 BILE
Splendid: 5 GRAND REGAL
    SUPER
array: 7 PANOPLY
"Splendid Splinter, The"
~ Williams: 3 TED
Splendor: 4 POMP
"Splendor in the Grass"
screenwriter: 4 INGE
Splice: 4 EDIT
Spliced
Get: 3 WED
item: 4 GENE
Splicer
need: 3 DNA
target: 4 GENE
Splint
site: 4 SHIN
Splinter
group: 4 **SECT**
Remove a: 6 TWEEZE
"Splish Splash"
singer Bobby: 5 DARIN
Split: 3 RAN 4 BOLT CHAP GAPE
    GULF PART **REND** RENT
    RIFT RIVE TEAR TORE
    5 CLEFT HALVE INTWO
    LEAVE RIVED RIVEN
    6 BISECT CLEAVE CLOVEN
    DIVIDE
apart: 4 REND
bit: 4 ATOM
country: 5 KOREA
decision: 7 DIVORCE
Easily ~ rock: 4 MICA 5 SLATE
evenly: 6 BISECT
Family: 6 ESTATE
for church: 5 TITHE
hairs: 7 NITPICK

in two: **6** CLEAVE
It might be: **3** PEA **4** ATOM
land: **5** KOREA
open: **3** RIP
personalities: **4** EXES
Some are: **4** ENDS
They've: **4** EXES
to unite: **5** **ELOPE**
up: **7** DIVORCE
Split-off
group: **4** SECT
Split ___ soup: 3 PEA
Splitsville: 4 RENO
parties: **4** EXES
Splitter
Beam: **5** PRISM
Wood: **3** AXE
Splitting
headache: **13** CUSTODYBATTLE
Splotch: 4 BLOB
Spock
(abbr.): **3** CDR
forte: **5** LOGIC
Like: **7** LOGICAL
portrayer: **5** NIMOY
Spode
offering: **6** TEASET
Spoil: 3 MAR ROT **4** RUIN TURN
    5 GOBAD GUMUP TAINT
a picnic: **6** RAINON
Didn't: **4** KEPT
~, with "on": **4** DOTE
Spoiled: 3 BAD **6** BRATTY
    8 INEDIBLE
kid: **4** BRAT
Spoiler: 4 BANE **6** RUINER
~, of a sort: **5** DOTER
Spoils: 4 LOOT SWAG **5** BOOTY
    7 DOTESON
taker: **6** VICTOR
Spoilsport: 9 SORELOSER
Spoke: 4 SAID
(up): **5** PIPED
Spoken: 4 **ORAL** SAID **5** ALOUD
    6 STATED
for: **5** TAKEN
Not: **5** TACIT
Spokes: 5 **RADII**
center: **3** HUB

Umbrella: **4** RIBS
Spokescow: 5 ELSIE
Spokes-elf: 5 ERNIE
Spokeslizard: 5 GECKO
Spokesman
for Moses: **5** AARON
Keebler: **3** ELF
~ Fleischer: **3** **ARI**
Sponge: 3 BUM DAB SOT **4** GRUB
    5 CADGE DIPSO LEECH
    MOOCH **6** CADGER
    7 MOISTEN **8** FREELOAD
Bath: **5** LOOFA **6** LOOFAH
feature: **4** **PORE**
gently: **5** DABAT
target: **4** SLOP
Spongy
cake: **5** BABKA
earth: **4** MIRE
ground: **3** BOG
toy ball: **4** NERF
Sponsor
GI show: **3** USO
Jack Benny: **5** JELLO
Racecar: **3** STP
spots: **3** ADS
Words from the: **3** ADS
Sponsored
One ~ at baptism: **6** GODSON
Sponsorship: 4 EGIS **5** AEGIS
Spontaneous
response: **5** ADLIB
Spoof: 5 PUTON
1966 spy ~: **11** OURMANFLINT
1974 Sutherland/Gould ~:
    4 SPYS
Spook: 3 SPY **5** SCARE
gp.: **3** CIA
Spooky: 4 EERY **5** **EERIE** SCARY
    WEIRD
In a ~ way: **6** EERILY
sight: **3** UFO
Spool
Film: **4** REEL
Spoon: 7 UTENSIL
Greasy: **5** DINER
Greasy ~ sign: **4** EATS
Use a: **4** STIR
___ spoon (diner): 6 GREASY

Spoon-bender
~ Geller: 3 URI
Spoonbill
cousin: 4 IBIS
Spoonful: 4 DOSE 5 TASTE
6 DOLLOP
Spoon-playing
site: 4 KNEE
Spoons
Like some: 7 SLOTTED
Spoony
Make: 6 ENAMOR
Sporadic: 15 ONAGAINOFFAGAIN
Spore
prefix: 4 ENDO
producer: 4 FERN
sacs: 4 ASCI
Spork
part: 4 TINE
Sport: 4 JEST
blade: 4 EPEE
Clay pigeon: 5 SKEET
Court: 7 JAIALAI
Cowboy: 5 RODEO
for heavyweights: 4 SUMO
full of traps: 5 SKEET
Japanese: 4 SUMO
NCAA: 8 LACROSSE
Royal: 4 POLO
Self-defense: 4 JUDO
Shooting: 5 SKEET
Sword: 4 EPEE
Winter: 4 LUGE
with horses: 4 POLO
World Cup: 6 SOCCER
Sport ___: 3 **UTE** 4 TRAC
Sportage
maker: 3 KIA
Sported: 4 **WORE** 5 HADON
Sporting
blade: 4 **EPEE**
sandals: 4 SHOD
Sports: 5 HASON WEARS
2001 ~ biopic: 3 ALI
Amateur ~ org.: 4 NCAA
Annual ~ event: 6 USOPEN
arenas: 6 STADIA
award: 4 ESPY
basket: 5 CESTA

Big name in ~ cards: 5 FLEER
Cable ~ award: 4 ESPY
center: 5 **ARENA**
College ~ org.: 4 NCAA
column: 4 LOSS WINS
complex: 5 ARENA
data: 5 STATS
drink suffix: 3 ADE
elite: 6 ALLPRO
event: 4 MEET
facilities: 6 STADIA
facility: 5 ARENA
figure: 4 STAT
Former ~ org.: 3 AFL
gp.: 3 AAU
HBO ~ agent: 6 ARLISS
Like many ~ telecasts: 4 LIVE
Like no-holds-barred:
7 EXTREME
mag: 4 ESPN
Nonpro ~ org.: 3 AAU
NYC ~ venue: 3 MSG
org.: 4 NCAA
page number: 4 STAT
palace: 5 ARENA
replay tool: 5 SLOMO
shocker: 5 UPSET
show tool: 5 SLOMO
squad: 4 TEAM
stadium: 5 **ARENA**
surprise: 5 UPSET
team: 5 SQUAD
trivia: 5 STATS
Unlv. ~ gp.: 4 NCAA
venue: 5 ARENA
Sports car: 3 JAG 4 ALFA
Classic: 5 TBIRD
engine: 5 TURBO
English: 3 JAG
Italian: 4 ALFA
Sports cars
British: 3 **MGS**
Some: 3 GTS
Sportscast
feature: 5 RECAP SLOMO
insight: 5 COLOR
Sportscaster
device: 5 SLOMO 6 REPLAY
offering: 5 COLOR

~ Dick: 6 ENBERG
~ Howard: 6 COSELL
~ Mel: 5 ALLEN
~ Merlin: 5 OLSEN

"SportsCenter"
network: 4 ESPN

Sportsman
Sports Illustrated's 1974 ~ of the
    Year: 3 ALI
Sports Illustrated's ~ of the
    Century: 3 ALI

Sportster
Chevy: 5 VETTE

Sportswear
brand: 4 IZOD

Sporty
auto: 3 GTO 6 CAMARO
car roof: 4 TTOP
scarf: 5 ASCOT
truck: 3 UTE
~ Chevy: 5 VETTE 6 CAMARO
~ Ford: 5 TBIRD
~ Italian car: 4 ALFA
~ Mazda: 5 **MIATA**
~ Pontiac: 3 GTO
~ Studebaker: 6 AVANTI
~ Volkswagen: 3 GTI

Spot: 3 DAB EYE SEE SPY 4 AREA
    ESPY LOAN SITE TVAD
    5 PLACE STAIN 6 DAPPLE
    LOCALE LOCATE
broadcast: 5 PROMO
checker: 5 ASPCA LEASH
markers: 4 EXES
of land: 4 ISLE
of relief: 5 OASIS
of wine: 4 ASTI
on radar: 4 BLIP

Spotless: 15 CLEANASAWHISTLE

Spots: 3 ADS 4 LOCI
Central: 4 LOCI
Paid: 3 ADS
TV: 3 ADS

Spotted: 3 SAW 4 LENT **SEEN**
    6 CALICO
beetle: 7 LADYBUG
butterfly: 5 SATYR
cat: 6 **OCELOT**
cavy: 4 PACA

predator: 5 HYENA
~, to Tweety: 3 TAW

Spotter
Smokey: 4 CBER
Speeder: 5 RADAR

Spouse: 4 MATE 7 PARTNER
    8 HELPMATE
denial: 6 NODEAR
kin: 5 INLAW
sibling: 5 INLAW
Take a: 3 WED

Spouses
Former: 4 **EXES**
of a sultan: 5 HAREM

Spout: 5 ORATE
off: 5 ORATE

Spouter
Sicilian: 4 **ETNA**

Sprain
soother: 6 ICEBAG 8 LINIMENT
spot: 5 ANKLE
Treat a: 3 ICE

Sprang: 5 AROSE LEAPT
up: 5 AROSE

Sprat: 5 EATER
regimen: 5 NOFAT

Sprat, Jack
bane: 3 FAT
choice: 4 LEAN
diet: 4 LEAN

Sprawl: 3 LIE
Kind of: 5 URBAN

Sprawling
Send: 4 TRIP

Spray: 3 WET 4 MIST 7 AEROSOL
alternative: 6 ROLLON
Anti-attacker: 4 MACE
Asthma: 8 INHALANT
Banned: 4 **ALAR**
can: 7 AEROSOL
Cooking: 3 **PAM**
Fine: 4 MIST
Kind of: 5 NASAL
Nasal: 5 SINEX
target: 4 ODOR

Spread: 3 SOW 4 FARM MEAL
    5 FEAST SPLAY STREW
    WIDEN
apart: 5 SPLAY

around: 5 STREW
BLT: 4 MAYO
Bread: 3 JAM 4 MAYO **OLEO**
Deli: 4 MAYO
Expensive: 3 ROE 6 CAVIAR
Fancy: 4 PATE
Garlicky: 5 AIOLI
Had a: 5 DINED
Hors d'oeuvre: 4 PATE
in a tub: 4 OLEO
joy: 5 ELATE
Nondairy: 4 OLEO
out: 3 FAN 4 SOWN 5 ARRAY
    SPLAY 6 SPARSE
Part of a: 4 ACRE
Party: 4 BRIE PATE
seed: 5 SOWED
Significant: 6 ESTATE
Sweet: 5 ICING
thickly: 7 SLATHER
Thinly: 6 SPARSE
unchecked: 4 RAGE
Vegetable: 4 OLEO

Spreadable
cheese: 4 BRIE
stick: 4 OLEO

Spreading
tree: 3 ELM

Spreadsheet
entry: 5 DATUM
filler: 4 DATA
Like a: 7 TABULAR
line: 3 ROW
pros: 4 CPAS

"Sprechen ___ Deutsch?": 3 SIE

Spree: 3 JAG 4 LARK ORGY TEAR
    TOOT 5 BINGE 6 BENDER
Go on a: 5 SPEND
site: 4 MALL

Spreeing: 7 ONATEAR

Sprightly: 4 PERT 5 AGILE ELFIN

Spring: 3 HOP SPA 4 COIL LEAP
    5 ARISE BOUND LETGO
    6 SEASON 7 EMANATE
ahead, perhaps: 5 RESET
bloom: 4 IRIS 5 LILAC PEONY
    6 AZALEA CROCUS
cleaning event: 7 TAGSALE
collection org.: 3 IRS

Do a ~ chore: 5 CLEAN
event: 4 THAW
    11 APRILSHOWER
feast: 5 SEDER
feature: 4 COIL
festival: 6 EASTER
formal: 4 PROM
harbinger: 5 ROBIN
Like many ~ days: 4 MILD
locale: 3 SPA 5 OASIS
Mineral: 3 SPA
mo.: 3 **APR** MAR
month: 3 MAY
Opposite of: 4 NEAP
Pertaining to: 6 VERNAL
purchase: 4 SEED
Showy ~ flower: 5 PEONY
Sign of: 4 THAW 5 **ARIES**
    ROBIN 6 GEMINI
sound: 5 BOING
summer: 3 CPA
thing: 4 COIL
time: 3 MAY 4 LENT 5 APRIL
    7 EQUINOX
Toy on a: 9 POGOSTICK
up: 5 ARISE

Spring ___ (start dripping):
    5 ALEAK

"Spring ahead"
hrs.: 3 DST

Springlike: 6 VERNAL

Springs
It ~ eternal: 4 HOPE
___ Springs, Florida:
    9 ALTAMONTE

Springsteen
birthplace: 3 USA
nickname: 7 THEBOSS
tune: 8 IMONFIRE

Springtime
dance site: 7 MAYPOLE
hunter's find: 9 EASTEREGG

Springy: 6 VERNAL 7 ELASTIC

Sprinkle
around: 5 STREW
Post-shower: 4 TALC
Scientist's: 4 NACL
with oil: 6 ANOINT
~, as powdered sugar: 4 SIFT

Sprinkler
attachment: 4 HOSE
Sprint: 3 RUN 4 DASH RACE
rival: 3 MCI
Sprinted: 3 RAN
Sprinter
assignment: 4 LANE
goal: 4 TAPE
path: 4 LANE
Sprite: 3 ELF IMP 4 PERI PIXY
5 PIXIE
Mischievous: 5 PIXIE
rival: 6 FRESCA
Shakespearean: 5 **ARIEL**
Water: 5 NIXIE
Spritely: 5 ELFIN 6 ELFISH
Sprocket: 3 COG
Sprout: 3 LAD TOT 4 GROW
Bean: 3 EAR 4 IDEA
up: 4 GROW
Spruce: 4 NEAT TIDY TRIM
5 NATTY 6 DAPPER
relative: 3 FIR
up, in a way: 6 REFACE
Spruced
All ~ up: 4 NEAT
up: 8 NEATENED
Sprung: 6 ARISEN
Spry: 5 AGILE
Spud: 5 **TATER**
bud: 3 EYE
source: 5 IDAHO
Spuds
Prepare: 4 MASH
Spumante
source: 4 ASTI
___ spumante: 4 **ASTI**
Spun: 7 ROTATED
It may be: 4 TALE YARN
tales: 6 YARNED
Yarn that is: 4 TALE
Spunk: 4 GRIT 5 MOXIE
6 METTLE SPIRIT
Full of: 6 FEISTY
Spur: 4 GOAD PROD URGE
5 EGG ON IMPEL ROUSE
6 INCITE
part: 5 ROWEL
Silver: 4 HIYO

Spurt: 5 SPASM
Had a growth: 6 SHOT UP
of activity: 5 SPASM
Sputnik
coverer: 4 TASS
letters: 4 CCCP
Month when ~ was launched:
7 OCTOBER
Sputter
and stall: 3 DIE
Spy: 4 MOLE 5 AGENT PLANT
alias: 8 CODENAME
Biblical: 5 CALEB
disguise: 5 COVER
exchanged for Powers: 4 ABEL
Fictional ~ Helm: 4 MATT
Former ~ org.: 3 KGB
Northern: 5 APPLE
Old ~ org.: 3 OSS
org.: 3 **CIA**
Seductive: 8 MATAHARI
writing: 4 CODE
WWII ~ org.: 3 OSS
~ Aldrich: 4 AMES
Spydom
First name in: 4 MATA
Last name in: 4 HARI
Spyglass
Use a: 4 PEER
"Spy in the House of Love, A"
novelist: 3 NIN 8 ANAISNIN
Spymaster
worry: 4 MOLE
Spyri, Johanna
classic novel: 5 HEIDI
S*P*Y*S
org.: 3 CIA
"Spy vs. Spy"
magazine: 3 **MAD**
**"Spy Who Came In From the
Cold, The"**
spy: 4 ALEC
Squabble: 3 ADO 4 FEUD RIFT
SPAT TIFF 5 ARGUE
RUNIN SCRAP 6 BICKER
HASSLE 7 RHUBARB
Squabbling: 4 ATIT
Squad: 4 TEAM
car: 7 CRUISER

Crack: 5 ATEAM
Firing: 3 NRA
Football: 6 ELEVEN
Military: 4 UNIT
Rescue ~ VIP: 3 EMT
Riot ~ item: 7 GASMASK
"___ Squad, The": 3 MOD
Squads
GI: 3 KPS
Squalid: 5 DIRTY SEAMY SEEDY
     6 SORDID
digs: 4 SLUM
Squander: 4 BLOW BURN LOSE
     5 WASTE
Squandered: 4 BLEW
Square: 4 BOXY EVEN KNOT
     NERD 5 ALIGN NERDY
     UNHIP 6 HONEST
1/640 of a ~ mile: 4 ACRE
100 ~ meters: 3 ARE
160 ~ rods: 4 ACRE
4,840 ~ yards: 4 ACRE
     7 ONEACRE
6,272,640 ~ inches: 4 ACRE
Butter: 3 PAT
Calendar: 3 DAY
Ceramic: 4 TILE
Floor: 4 TILE
footage: 4 **AREA** SIZE
Glass: 4 PANE
Grass: 3 SOD
Greek: 5 AGORA
Half the ~ dancers: 4 GALS
It can be measured in ~ feet:
     4 AREA
It may be: 4 MEAL
matrix, in math: 7 ADJOINT
measure: 4 AREA
mileage: 4 AREA
Monopoly: 4 **JAIL** 6 CHANCE
Not: 3 HEP
one: 5 GETGO START
On the: 7 ETHICAL
peg in a round hole: 6 MISFIT
Public: 5 AGORA **PLAZA**
They may be: 5 DEALS
things: 5 AMEND ATONE
Town: 5 PLAZA
(with): 5 AGREE

Square dance
call: 6 DOSIDO
group: 5 OCTET
neckwear: 4 BOLO
partner: 3 GAL
site: 4 BARN
Square-ended
boat: 4 SCOW
Squarely: 8 SMACKDAB
Met: 5 FACED
Square-mile
fraction: 4 ACRE
Square one
From: 4 ANEW 5 AGAIN
     6 AFRESH
Go back to: 9 STARTANEW
Take from: 4 REDO
Squaretail: 5 TROUT
Squarish: 4 BOXY
Squash: 9 VEGETABLE
Kind of: 5 ACORN
Squashed
circle: 4 OVAL
Squat: 3 NIL
(down): 6 HUNKER
One ~, say: 3 REP
Squawk: 4 YAWP
box: 8 INTERCOM
Squawker
Colorful: 5 MACAW
Squeak
Fix a: 3 OIL
(out): 3 EKE
Peke: 3 YIP
silencer: 3 OIL
Squeakers: 4 MICE
Squeaky: 7 UNOILED
clean: 6 CHASTE
wheel need: 3 OIL
Squeal: 3 **RAT** 4 SING TELL
     6 TATTLE
Cartoon: 3 EEK
Squealed: 4 SANG
Squeegee: 4 WIPE 5 WIPER
Squeeze: 3 HUG 4 BEAU CRAM
     5 PRESS
(from): 5 EXACT
It may put the ~ on you: 3 BOA
     8 ANACONDA

(out): 3 **EKE**
play start: 4 BUNT
Suicide ~ stat: 3 RBI
Squeezer: 3 BOA 4 VISE
Squelch: 5 SITON 6 STIFLE
Squelched: 5 **SATON**
Squib: 4 ITEM 5 BLURB
Squid
 on a plate: 8 CALAMARI
 relatives: 6 OCTOPI
 squirt: 3 INK
 squirter: 6 INKSAC
Squiggle
 Sheet music: 4 CLEF
 Type: 5 TILDE
Squiggles
 Make: 6 DOODLE
Squiggly
 mark: 5 TILDE
Squint: 4 PEER
Squinting
 eye: 4 SLIT
Squirm: 6 WIGGLE WRITHE
Squirrel: 6 RODENT STORER
 away: 4 SAVE 5 HOARD STASH
  STORE
 food: 3 NUT 5 ACORN
 Go like a flying: 5 GLIDE
 hangout: 3 OAK
 home: 4 TREE
Squirt: 3 TOT 4 TYKE 6 SPRITZ
Squirter: 6 INKSAC OILCAN
Sr.
 and jr.: 3 YRS
 test: 3 GRE SAT 4 LSAT
Sra.
 French: 3 MME
Sri ___: 5 **LANKA**
Sri Lanka
 capital: 7 COLOMBO
 export: 3 TEA 5 PEKOE
  8 PEKOETEA
 language: 5 TAMIL
 money: 5 RUPEE
 native: 5 TAMIL
 ~, formerly: 6 CEYLON
SRO
 affair: 7 SELLOUT
 Part of: 4 ONLY

show: 3 HIT
Srta.
 French: 4 MLLE
SSE: 3 DIR
 Opposite of: 3 NNW
S-shaped
 molding: 4 **OGEE**
SSS
 category: 4 ONEA
 Eligible, to the: 4 ONEA
 Pt. of: 3 SYS 4 SYST
SST
 It's crossed by an: 3 ATL
 Part of: 5 SONIC
SSW
 Opposite of: 3 **NNE**
St.
 Broad: 3 AVE
 crosser: 3 **AVE**
St. ___: 5 CROIX LUCIA MARYS
  6 MORITZ
Stab: 3 **TRY** 5 GUESS SPEAR
  7 ATTEMPT BAYONET
 Take a ~ (at): 5 LUNGE
 Take another ~ at: 5 RETRY
Stabber: 4 TINE
Stability
 Symbol of: 8 EVENKEEL
Stabilize: 6 STEADY
Stabilizer
 Cello: 4 KNEE
 Food: 4 AGAR
 Kite: 4 TAIL
 Ship: 4 KEEL 7 BALLAST
Stable
 area: 5 STALL
 babe: 4 FOAL
 bit: 3 OAT
 British: 4 MEWS
 diet: 3 HAY 4 OATS
 employee: 6 OSTLER
 Gave birth in a: 6 FOALED
 locks: 4 MANE
 mate: 4 MARE
 More: 5 SANER
 parent: 4 **SIRE**
 scene: 6 CRECHE
 sound: 4 BRAY CLOP 5 NEIGH
  SNORT

staple: 3 HAY OAT 4 OATS
talker: 4 MRED
Staccato
Not: 6 LEGATO
symbol: 3 DOT
Stack: 4 PILE
Cafeteria: 5 TRAYS
DJ's: 3 CDS
In a: 5 PILED
Monopoly: 5 DEEDS
role: 4 NESS
Snack in a: 4 OREO
Teller's: 4 ONES
Stackable
snack: 4 OREO
Stacked: 7 INAPILE
Stacks
Chain with: 4 IHOP
It's found in: 4 SOOT
Lighted: 5 PYRES
Stadia: 6 ARENAS
Stadium: 4 OVAL PARK 5 **ARENA**
area: 4 TIER
Big Apple: 4 ASHE SHEA
cheer: 3 RAH
cover: 4 DOME
D.C.: 3 RFK
feature: 4 TIER
hoverer: 5 BLIMP
level: 4 LOGE **TIER**
Like a ~ crowd: 5 AROAR
receipts: 4 GATE
shot: 3 RAH
snack: 6 NACHOS
sound: 3 **RAH** 4 ROAR
stat: 3 RBI 5 SEATS
walkway: 4 RAMP
worker: 5 USHER
Stadiumgoer: 3 FAN
Staff: 3 MAN ROD 4 CANE
    5 AIDES
Add: 4 HIRE
anew: 5 REMAN
associate: 3 ROD
Captain's: 4 CREW
Ceremonial: 4 MACE
Cut from the: 3 AXE
Executive's: 5 AIDES
leader: 4 CLEF 5 CCLEF GCLEF

Lines on a: 5 EGBDF
Mag: 3 EDS
member: 4 NOTE REST
Music ~ symbol: 4 CLEF
    5 CCLEF
note: 3 SOL 4 MEMO
of Life: 3 EDS
Part of a univ.: 3 FAC
PC support: 5 TECHS
Sails: 4 MAST
sgt.: 3 NCO
Silence of the: 4 REST
Supply: 3 MAN
Support: 4 CANE
symbol: 4 **CLEF** REST 5 GCLEF
Staffer: 4 AIDE
Hosp.: 3 LPN
Hospital: 4 AIDE
Tabloid: 6 EDITOR
Staffers
Hosp.: 3 DRS MDS RNS
Stafford
Singer ~, et al.: 3 JOS
Staffordshire
river: 5 TRENT
Stag: 4 DEER HART MALE SOLO
    5 **ALONE**
attendees: 3 MEN
partner: 3 DOE
party: 4 DEER
Stage: 3 LEG 4 STEP 5 PHASE
accessory: 4 PROP
All the world is his: 5 ACTOR
area: 5 APRON
assistant: 4 CUER
award: 4 OBIE
Bean on: 5 ORSON
Chase on: 4 ILKA
comment: 5 ASIDE
construction: 3 SET
curtain: 5 SCRIM
direction: 4 EXIT 5 **ENTER**
Do ~ work: 3 ACT
Early: 5 ONSET
Final: 7 ENDGAME
front: 5 APRON
Go on: 5 ENTER
Got ~ fright: 5 FROZE
Has the: 4 ISON

hog: 3 HAM
Insect: 4 PUPA 5 IMAGO
 LARVA
item: 4 PROP
Leave the: 4 EXIT
Moon: 5 PHASE
of a race: 3 LEG
of development: 5 PHASE
opening: 4 ACTI
org.: 4 ANTA
Overdo on the: 5 EMOTE
part: 4 ROLE
Perform on: 3 ACT
piece: 4 PROP
presence: 5 ACTOR
prompt: 3 CUE
remark: 5 ASIDE
Rocket: 5 AGENA
scenery: 3 SET
signal: 3 CUE
Sleep: 3 REM
success sgn: 3 SRO
Terrible age: 4 TWOS
whisper: **ASIDE**
Stagecoach
 controls: 5 REINS
Stagehand: 4 GRIP
Stagg, ___ Alonzo: 4 AMOS
Stagg, Amos ___: 6 ALONZO
Stagger: 4 **REEL** 5 LURCH
 SHOCK 6 CAREEN
Staggering: 5 AREEL
Stagnant
 water problem: 4 ALGA
Stagnation: 3 RUT
St. Agnes's ___: 3 EVE
Stain: 3 DYE MAR 4 BLOT SLUR
 SOIL 5 SULLY TAINT
 6 BLOTCH IMBRUE
 7 SPLOTCH
Biological: 5 EOSIN
Collar: 4 RING
Garage: 3 OIL
Ink: 4 BLOT
Stained-glass
 site: 4 APSE
Stainless: 6 CHASTE
What ~ steel is resistant to:
 4 RUST

Stair
 part: 4 STEP 5 **RISER** TREAD
 post: 5 NEWEL
Staircase
 safety feature: 4 RAIL
 shape: 6 SPIRAL
 support: 5 NEWEL
Stake: 3 BET 5 WAGER
 driver: 4 MAUL 6 SLEDGE
 Initial: 4 ANTE
 Thing to have a ~ in: 4 TENT
Staked
 Something: 5 CLAIM
"Stakeout"
 Richard's costar in: 6 EMILIO
Stakes
 Pull up: 4 MOVE 6 DECAMP
 Put down: 4 ANTE
 race stakes: 5 PURSE
Stalactite
 former: 4 DRIP
 site: 4 CAVE 6 CAVERN
"Stalag 17"
 star: 6 HOLDEN
Stale: 3 OLD 5 DATED TIRED
 TRITE
Stalemate: 3 TIE 7 IMPASSE
Stalin
 challenger: 4 TITO
 domain: 4 USSR
 predecessor: 5 LENIN
 State under: 3 SSR
Stalk: 4 HUNT STEM 6 PREYON
 Marsh: 4 REED
 Salad: 6 CELERY
Stalker
 Skilled: 4 LION
Stall
 bedding: 5 STRAW
 call: 5 SNORT
 Mall: 5 KIOSK
 Sputter and: 3 DIE
Stalling
 Stop: 3 ACT
Stallion
 mate: 4 MARE
 Young: 4 COLT
Stallone
 nickname: 3 SLY

role: 5 DREDD RAMBO ROCKY
Stalls
Place with: 10 FLEAMARKET
Stalwart
Society: 6 PILLAR
Stamen
counterpart: 6 PISTIL
Stamina: 4 WIND
Have: 4 LAST
Lose: 4 FADE
Stammerer
sounds: 3 ERS
words: 5 IMEAN
Stamp: 4 SEAL
Actor: 7 TERENCE
Bill: 3 DUE 4 PAID
Christmas ~ subject:
    7 MADONNA
Food: 4 USDA
Invoice: 4 PAID
mill input: 3 ORE
of approval: 4 USDA
Office: 4 RECD 5 DATER
Passport: 4 VISA
purchase: 4 COIL
sheet: 4 PANE
Stampeders: 4 HERD
Stamper
need: 3 PAD
Stamps: 7 POSTAGE
Letters without: 5 EMAIL
Roll of: 4 COIL
Sheet of: 4 **PANE**
Stan
Funny: 6 LAUREL
Jazzman: 4 GETZ
of hockey: 6 MIKITA
Partner of: 5 **OLLIE**
Spider-Man creator: 3 LEE
Stance: 4 POSE
Stand: 4 BEAR DAIS RISE
    5 ABIDE ARISE EASEL
    GETUP GROVE
    7 STOMACH 8 TOLERATE
against: 6 OPPOSE
Artist's: 5 **EASEL**
at a wake: 4 BIER
at home: 3 BAT
Bric-a-brac: 7 ETAGERE

buy: 3 ADE
by: 5 AWAIT
Can't: 4 HATE 5 ABHOR HATES
    6 DETEST LOATHE
    7 DETESTS
Didn't ~ pat: 4 DREW
Don't just ~ there: 5 REACT
Famous last: 5 **ALAMO**
firm: 6 INSIST
for: 4 MEAN 5 ABIDE 6 DENOTE
Hat: 4 HEAD
in: 3 SUB
in line: 4 WAIT
Kind of: 4 TAXI
Let: 4 STET
Mall: 5 KIOSK
One way to: 3 **PAT** 4 TALL
    5 ALONE INAWE ONEND
    6 UNITED
One way to ~ by: 4 IDLY
out: 5 EXCEL SHINE
Place to ~ a round: 3 BAR
Sidewalk ~ buy: 3 ADE
Something to ~ on: 3 LEG
Take the: 7 TESTIFY
The way things ~ now: 6 ASITIS
up: 4 RISE 5 ARISE
up and speak: 5 ORATE
up for: 6 DEFEND
up to: 4 DEFY FACE 6 RESIST
You ~ to lose it: 3 LAP
"Stand"
band: 3 REM
"___ stand" (Martin Luther):
    5 HEREI
"Stand and Deliver"
star Edward James: 5 OLMOS
Standard: 3 PAR 4 NORM
    5 STOCK 6 NORMAL
axes: 5 XANDY
Clock ~ (abbr.): 3 GMT
deviation symbol: 5 SIGMA
Double: 3 TWO
Gold: 5 KARAT
High: 5 IDEAL
Links: 3 PAR
Moral: 5 ETHIC
Naval: 6 ENSIGN
of excellence: 5 IDEAL

partner: 5 POORS
product: 3 OIL
score: 3 PAR
stuff: 3 OIL 4 GOLD
Standard & ___: 5 POORS
Standard Oil
   acronym: 4 ESSO
Standards: 8 CRITERIA
"Stand by Me"
   actor Wheaton: 3 WIL
   singer King: 4 BENE
Standee
   support: 5 STRAP
Stand-in: 3 SUB
   Rest-of-the-team: 4 ETAL
Standing: 4 RANK 5 ERECT
        ONEND PLACE 6 REPUTE
   by: 5 ONICE
   Of long: 3 OLD
   on: 4 ATOP
   rule: 5 BYLAW
   Run while: 4 IDLE
   Social: 5 CASTE 6 ESTATE
        STATUS
   straight: 5 ERECT
Stand in good ___: 5 STEAD
Standings
   column: 4 WINS 6 LOSSES
Standish
   Pilgrim: 5 MYLES
Standoff: 3 TIE 7 IMPASSE
Standoffish: 3 ICY 5 **ALOOF**
Standout: 4 STAR
Standstill: 4 HALT
   ___ **standstill:** 3 **ATA**
Stand-up
   guy: 5 COMIC
   offering: 3 BIT
   staple: 4 JOKE
Stanford-Binet
   figs.: 3 IQS
Stanford-___ test: 5 BINET
Stanislaw
   Author: 3 LEM
Stanley
   Director: 5 DONEN 6 KRAMER
   Jazzman: 6 CLARKE
   Mystery writer: 5 ELLIN
   offering: 4 TOOL

Stanley Cup
   org.: 3 NHL
   winners of 1999: 5 STARS
Stanley Falls
   river: 8 THECONGO
Stannary
   stock: 3 TIN
Stannous
   element: 3 TIN
Stansfield
   Pop singer: 4 LISA
St. Anthony's cross: 3 TAU
Stanton, Elizabeth ___
   Suffragist: 4 CADY
Stanza
   Final: 5 ENVOI
   Six-line: 6 SESTET
Staple
   Bar: 3 RYE
   Breakfast: 3 EGG 4 EGGS
   Brunch: 6 OMELET
   Cajun: 4 OKRA
   Daytime TV: 5 OPRAH
   Dorm room: 6 STEREO
   Drawing board: 7 TSQUARE
   Frat party: 3 KEG
   Italian: 5 PASTA
   Luau: 3 POI
   Passover: 5 MATZO
   Presentation: 5 CHART
   South Seas: 4 TARO
   Stable: 3 HAY OAT 4 OATS
   Sushi bar: 8 SOYSAUCE
   Table: 4 SALT
   Vegan: 4 TOFU
   Wedding: 4 BAND
Staples
   purchase: 4 REAM
   Sci-fi: 3 ETS
Staples Center: 5 ARENA
   Former ~ center: 4 SHAQ
        5 ONEAL
   player: 5 LAKER
Staple Singers
   #1 hit: 15 ILLTAKEYOUTHERE
Stapleton
   Actress: 4 JEAN
Star: 4 HERO 5 CELEB 6 ETOILE
   bit: 5 CAMEO

Bright: 4 BETA NOVA
Dog: 4 ASTA 5 BENJI 6 LASSIE
Exploding: 4 NOVA
Faded: 7 HASBEEN
Falling: 6 METEOR
followers: 4 MAGI
go-between: 5 AGENT
It can move a: 4 LIMO
Kind of: 5 NATAL
Little: 5 CELEB
material: 3 TIN
Matinee: 4 IDOL
Night: 4 LENO
One-named: 8 ROSEANNE
Our: 3 SOL SUN
Pitching: 3 ACE
Pop: 4 IDOL 8 TEENIDOL
prefix: 4 MEGA
quality: 4 AURA
rep: 5 AGENT
Rising: 5 COMER
Shooting: 6 METEOR
Spectacular: 4 NOVA
vehicle: 4 LIMO
witnesses: 4 MAGI
~, in French: 6 ETOILE
"Star ___": 4 TREK WARS
Starboard
Opposite of: 4 PORT
Starbuck
boss: 4 **AHAB**
Skater: 4 JOJO
Starbucks
asset: 5 AROMA
container: 3 URN
flavor: 5 MOCHA
order: 5 DECAF **LATTE**
    MOCHA 6 GRANDE
    8 ESPRESSO
size: 5 VENTI 6 GRANDE
Starch
Palm: 4 SAGO
source: 4 TARO
~, for short: 4 CARB
Starched
collar: 4 ETON
Starchy
pudding stuff: 4 SAGO
tuber: 3 YAM

Star-crossed
lover: 5 ROMEO
Stare: 4 GAPE GAWK GAZE
at: 4 **OGLE**
Impertinent: 4 OGLE
Like an unfriendly: 3 ICY
open-mouthed: 4 GAPE
Satyr's: 4 LEER
stupidly: 4 GAWK
Stares
Like some: 3 ICY 6 VACANT
Starfire: 4 OLDS
Starfleet Academy
grad.: 3 ENS
Starfire — (see below)
Staring: 5 AGAZE
angrily: 6 AGLARE
Stark
raving sort: 6 MANIAC
Starker
Cellist: 5 JANOS
Starless
Like a ~ night: 4 INKY
Starlet
dream: 4 FAME
persona: 7 INGENUE
Starlike: 6 ASTRAL
Starling
org.: 3 FBI
relative: 4 MYNA
Starliters, The
Joey of: 3 DEE
"Starpeace"
musician: 3 ONO
Slurr
of song: 3 KAY
of the Beatles: 5 RINGO
of the Wild West: 5 BELLE
Quarterback: 4 BART
Starring
in a sitcom: 4 ONTV
role: 4 LEAD
Starry: 6 ASTRAL
bear: 4 URSA
Stars
Give ~ to: 4 RATE
Give more ~ to: 6 RERATE
Give no: 3 PAN
Movie that rates 0: 7 STINKER
Of the: 6 ASTRAL

Wearer of three ~ (abbr.):
   5 LTGEN
~, in Latin: 5 ASTRA
"Stars above!": 6 DEARME
Stars and Bars
   org.: 3 CSA
Stars and Stripes
   land: 3 USA
"Stars and Stripes Forever"
   composer: 5 SOUSA
Star-shaped: 6 ASTRAL
      8 STELLATE
   flower: 5 ASTER
Starship
   1986 ~ hit: 4 SARA
Starsky
   Partner of: 5 HUTCH
"Star-Spangled Banner"
   lyricist: 3 KEY
   word: 3 OER
Start: 5 GETGO **ONSET** SCARE
      WINCE 6 ADVENT
      LAUNCH OPENER
      OUTSET SETOUT
   Info: Prefix cue
   again: 6 REOPEN
   a hand: 4 ANTE DEAL
   a hole: 5 TEEUP
   all over: 4 REDO
   an occupation: 6 MOVEIN
   another hitch: 4 REUP
   a pot: 4 ANTE
   eating: 5 DIGIN
   fishing: 4 CAST
   from scratch: 4 REDO
   From the: 4 ANEW
   Head: 4 EDGE
   of a polite offer: 9 IFYOUWISH
   over: 4 REDO
   up: 4 BOOT 8 INITIATE
Starter
   Info: Prefix cue
   need: 3 GUN
Starters: 5 ATEAM
"Star Time"
   star Michael: 8 STGERARD
Starting: 4 ASOF
   from: 4 ASOF
   gait: 4 TROT

gate: 4 POST
lineup: 4 ABCD
on: 4 ASOF
place: 4 EDEN
point: 4 GERM SEED WOMB
      5 GITGO 6 ORIGIN
points: 7 GENESES
stake: 4 ANTE
to develop: 7 NASCENT
with: 4 ASOF
Startled
   cries: 3 OHS
Star-to-be: 5 COMER
Start-over
   button: 5 RESET
"Star Trek"
   actor Burton: 5 LEVAR
   actor George: 5 TAKEI
   actor Spiner: 5 BRENT
   address: 6 MRSULU
   android: 4 DATA
   bad guy: 7 ROMULAN
   communications officer: 5 UHURA
   counselor Deanna: 4 TROI
   doctor: 5 MCCOY
   engineer: 6 SCOTTY
   extra: 5 ALIEN
   genre: 5 SCIFI
   helmsman: 4 SULU
   lieutenant: 5 UHURA
   navigator: 4 **SULU**
   phaser setting: 4 STUN
   rank (abbr.): 3 ENS
   speed: 4 WARP
   star: 5 NIMOY
   weapon: 6 PHASER
"Star Trek: Deep Space Nine"
   character: 3 ODO
"Star Trek II"
   villain: 4 KHAN
"Star Trek: The Next Generation"
   actor Burton: 5 LEVAR
   counselor Deanna: 4 TROI
   role: 4 TROI
"Star Trek: Voyager"
   actress Kate: 7 MULGREW
   actress Ryan: 4 JERI
Starts
   Partner of: 4 FITS

Star-___ tuna: 4 KIST
Starve: 8 EMACIATE
Star Wars
  inits.: 3 **SDI**
"Star Wars"
  actor Guinness: 4 ALEC
  character: 11 JARJARBINKS
  character Han: 4 SOLO
  creature: 4 EWOK
  director George: 5 LUCAS
  droid: 5 ARTOO
  gangster: 5 JABBA
  knight: 4 JEDI
  mentor: 4 YODA
  name: 3 HAN 5 VADER
  princess: 4 **LEIA**
  prog.: 3 SDI
  role for Ford: 4 SOLO
  sage: 4 YODA
  star: 12 ALECGUINNESS
  villain: 5 VADER
      10 DARTHVADER
  warrior: 4 JEDI
Starwood
  acquisition: 3 ITT
Starwort: 5 ASTER
Stash: 4 HIDE STOW
  away: 4 SAVE STOW 5 HOARD
  finder: 4 NARC
  Secret: 5 CACHE
Stashed: 3 HID
Stat: 3 PDQ 4 ASAP 6 ATONCE
      PRONTO
  prefix: 4 RHEO
"Stat!": 3 NOW 4 ASAP
      6 PRONTO
State: 4 AVER AVOW 5 VOICE
      6 ASSERT 7 DECLARE
  as fact: 4 AVER 5 SAYSO
  confidently: 4 AVER 6 ASSERT
      ASSURE
  firmly: 4 AVER
  further: 3 ADD
  of mind: 4 MOOD
  one's view: 5 **OPINE**
  positively: 4 AVER 6 ASSERT
  since 1948: 6 ISRAEL
  solemnly: 4 AVOW
  treasury: 4 FISC

~, in French: 4 **ETAT**
Stated: 3 PUT 4 SAID
  one's case: 4 PLED
"State Fair"
  setting: 4 IOWA
State Farm
  rival: 5 AETNA
Statehouse
  ~ VIP: 3 GOV
Stately: 5 NOBLE REGAL
  dance: 6 MINUET PAVANE
  home: 5 MANOR MANSE
  shade-giver: 3 ELM 7 ELMTREE
Statement
  Court: 4 PLEA
  Definitive: 8 LASTWORD
  of belief: 5 CREDO CREED
  Sworn: 4 OATH
Staten Island
  boat: 5 FERRY
State-of-the-art: 6 NEWEST
State-run
  game: 5 LOTTO
Statesman
  Israeli: 4 EBAN
  Roman: 4 CATO
Statesmen
  Like some: 5 ELDER
Static: 5 NOISE
Static ___: 5 CLING
Station: 4 DESK STOP 5 DEPOT
  Bus: 5 DEPOT
  High: 3 MIR
  Kind of: 3 GAS WAY 5 RELAY
      6 AMTRAK
  Military: 4 POST
  Old ~ name: 4 ESSO
  sign: 5 ONAIR
  Sub: 4 DELI
  suffix: 3 ARY ERY
  Took to the ~ house: 5 RANIN
  Train: 4 STOP 5 DEPOT
  Union: 5 ALTAR
  wagon abroad: 9 ESTATECAR
  Work: 4 DESK
  ___ Station: 4 PENN
Stationary: 5 STILL 6 ATREST
  Be ~, nautically: 5 LIETO
Stationed: 3 PUT 5 BASED

Stationer
  supply: 4 PADS PENS
Stationery
  brand: 5 EATON
  imprint: 10 LETTERHEAD
  quantity: 4 REAM
  store stock (abbr.): 4 ENVS
Station wagon
  abroad: 9 ESTATECAR
Statistic
  Court: 6 ASSIST
  Econ.: 3 GNP
  Gazetteer: 4 AREA
  Vital: 3 AGE
Statistical
  boundary: 8 QUARTILE
  info: 4 DATA
  measure: 4 MEAN MODE
      5 RANGE
Statistician: 11 BEANCOUNTER
Statistics: 4 DATA
  Like some: 5 VITAL
Stats: 4 DATA INFO RECS
Statuary
  Bit of: 5 TORSO
Statue
  base: 6 PLINTH
  Gold: 5 OSCAR
  inscription: 8 EPIGRAPH
  Made like a: 5 FROZE
  Michelangelo: 5 PIETA
  place: 5 NICHE
Statue of Liberty
  ship: 5 ISERE
  skin: 6 COPPER
Statues
  Giant: 7 COLOSSI
Statuesque: 4 TALL
Statuette
  Cinema: 5 OSCAR
  Winged: 4 EMMY
Status
  Attain: 4 RISE
  Current: 4 ACDC
  Draft: 4 ONEA 5 ONTAP
  follower: 3 QUO
  Have: 4 RATE
  Service: 4 ONEA
Status ___: 3 QUO

Statute: 3 ACT LAW
  Make a: 5 ENACT
Staunch: 4 TRUE 8 TRUEBLUE
Stave
  off: 5 AVERT REPEL
**Stay: 4 BIDE 5 ABIDE VISIT
      6 REMAIN**
  away from: 4 SHUN 5 AVOID
      NOTDO
  behind: 6 REMAIN
  dry: 8 TEETOTAL
  fresh: 4 KEEP
  glued to: 7 STAREAT
  home for dinner: 5 EATIN
  How long one might: 6 AWHILE
  idle: 3 SIT
  in the cooler: 6 DOTIME
  Not ~ put: 4 ROAM
  out of sight: 4 HIDE 6 HOLEUP
      LIELOW
  Place to: 3 INN
  put: 6 REMAIN
  Some ~ at home: 4 DADS
  still, at sea: 5 LIETO
  to the finish: 4 LAST
"Stay!": 6 DONTGO
"Stay (I Missed You)"
  singer Lisa: 4 LOEB
  singer Loeb: 4 LISA
Staying
  Have ~ power: 4 LAST
  power: 4 LEGS 6 TENURE
      7 INERTIA STAMINA
St. Bernard
  bark: 4 WOOF
St. Catherine
  Home of: 5 SIENA
St. Clare
  Home of: 6 ASSISI
Std.
  Not: 3 IRR
Stead: 4 LIEU
**Steadfast: 4 TRUE 5 LOYAL
      6 STABLE**
Steadily
  Keep at: 7 STANDTO
  Pursued: 5 PLIED
Steady: 4 BEAU SURE 5 BRACE
  devotion: 9 ADHERENCE

flow: 6 STREAM
Go ~ with: 4 DATE
Jacques': 4 AMIE
"Steady Eddie"
of baseball: 5 LOPAT
"Steady ___ goes": 5 ASSHE
Steadying
rope: 3 GUY
Steak: 4 MEAT
Blacken, as: 4 CHAR
Char a: 4 SEAR
Club: 9 DELMONICO
Cook, as: 5 BROIL
cut: 5 FLANK TBONE
Hearty: 5 TBONE
Kind of: 4 TUNA 5 STRIP SWISS
Like ~ tartare: 3 RAW
Like a good: 6 TENDER
Loin: 5 TBONE
order: 4 **RARE** WELL 5 TBONE
Pink, as a: 4 RARE
sauce brand: 4 AONE
style: 5 DIANE 7 TARTARE
type: 5 TBONE
Steak ___: 5 DIANE 7 TARTARE
Steakhouse
offering: 5 **TBONE** 6 RIBEYE
order: 4 RARE 5 TBONE
sound: 6 SIZZLE
Steak tartare
ingredient: 6 RAWEGG
Steal: 3 ROB 4 GLOM TAKE
5 POACH SWIPE 6 PILFER
THIEVE
attention from: 7 UPSTAGE
away: 5 ELOPE
cattle: 6 RUSTLE
from: 3 ROB
It's a: 5 THEFT
steers: 6 RUSTLE
Stealth
Move with: 6 TIPTOE
What ~ may avoid: 5 RADAR
Stealthily
Approach: 7 CREEPUP
Enter: 6 EDGEIN
Move: 5 SKULK SLINK SNEAK
Moved: 5 CREPT
Pick up: 4 PALM

"Steal This Book"
author Hoffman: 5 ABBIE
Stealthy: 7 CATLIKE
sort: 5 NINJA SNEAK
Steam: 5 VAPOR
bath: 5 SAUNA
Blow off: 4 HISS RANT VENT
Burn with: 5 SCALD
It blows off: 6 GEYSER
Lose: 4 TIRE
room: 5 SAUNA
Run out of: 3 DIE 4 TIRE
up: 3 IRE 4 RILE 5 ANGER
Steamed: 3 MAD 4 IRED SORE
5 ANGRY **IRATE** LIVID
RILED 6 FUMING INAPET
7 INARAGE INASNIT
dish: 6 TAMALE
Get: 4 BOIL 6 SEERED
Get ~ up: 4 FUME
up: 4 IRED
Steam engine
developer: 4 WATT
Steamer
creator: 7 STANLEY
trunk feature: 4 HASP
Steaming: 5 IRATE
Steamroll: 7 RUNOVER
Steamy: 3 HOT 4 DAMP 6 EROTIC
RRATED TORRID
spot: 5 SAUNA
~ 1998 Broadway revue: 5 FOSSE
Steed: 5 HORSE
Speckled: 4 ROAN
Spirited: 4 ARAB 7 ARABIAN
steerer: 4 REIN
Swift: 4 ARAB
Steel
component: 4 IRON
factory input: 7 IRONORE
German ~ city: 5 ESSEN
girder: 5 IBEAM
industry pioneer: 8 BESSEMER
Man of: 5 ROBOT 8 CARNEGIE
Man of ~ portrayer: 5 REEVE
mill refuse: 4 SLAG
plow maker: 5 DEERE
source: 4 IRON 7 PIGIRON
toughener: 8 TITANIUM

Use ~ wool: 5 SCOUR
Steele
  Partner of: 7 ADDISON
Steeler
  Former ~ coach Chuck: 4 NOLL
Steelhead: 5 TROUT
Steelie
  alternative: 5 AGATE
Steelworkers
  Former ~ head: 4 ABEL
Steely Dan
  album: 3 AJA
Steen
  Painter: 3 JAN
  Stand for: 5 EASEL
Steenburgen
  Actress: 4 MARY
Steep: 4 BREW DEAR SOAK
        5 CLIFF
  cliff: 4 CRAG
  slope: 4 DROP 5 SCARP
        6 ESCARP
Steeple: 5 SPIRE
Steep-roofed
  house: 6 AFRAME
Steep-sided
  valley: 6 RAVINE
Steer: 3 TIP 5 PILOT
  clear of: 4 SHUN 5 **AVOID**
        ELUDE EVADE
Steerer: 6 DROVER
Steering
  adjustment: 5 TOEIN
  aid: 6 RUDDER
  station: 4 CONN HELM
  strap: 4 REIN
  system link: 6 TIEROD
  wheel: 4 HELM
Stefani
  Singer: 4 GWEN
Steffi
  of tennis: 4 GRAF
Stein
  and Stiller: 4 BENS
  filler: 3 ALE 4 BEER 5 LAGER
  Part of a ~ line: 3 ISA 5 AROSE
  relative: 7 TANKARD
Stein, Jean
  bestseller: 4 EDIE

Steinbeck
  birthplace: 7 SALINAS
  character: 4 **OKIE**
  family: 5 JOADS
  migrant: 4 OKIE
  name: 4 JOAD
  novel: 10 CANNERYROW
  title varmints: 4 MICE
Steinful: 3 ALE 5 LAGER
Steinway
  product: 5 PIANO
**Ste. Jeanne ___ : 4 DARC
Stellar: 6 ASTRAL
  altar: 3 ARA
  bear: 4 URSA
  spectacular: 4 NOVA
"St. Elmo's Fire"
  actor: 4 LOWE
Stem: 4 PROW 6 ARREST
  Base of a plant: 4 CORM
  joint: 4 NODE
  Mushroom: 5 STIPE
  Opposite of: 5 STERN
  Plant: 5 STALK 6 STOLON
  to stern runner: 4 KEEL
  Twining: 4 BINE
___ Ste. Marie: 5 SAULT
Stemmed
  It may be: 4 TIDE
Stemware: 7 GLASSES
Sten
  or Magnani: 4 ANNA
Stench: 4 ODOR REEK 5 FETOR
        7 MALODOR
Stengel
  1960s ~ crew: 4 METS
  of baseball: 5 CASEY
Steno
  need: 3 PAD 7 NOTEPAD
Stenographer
  group: 4 POOL
Step: 3 PAS 4 PACE 5 STAIR
        TREAD
  Ballet: 3 **PAS**
  Big: 6 STRIDE
  Bouncy: 4 LILT
  Dance: 3 CHA PAS
  down: 8 ABDICATE
  Gliding dance: 6 CHASSE

in: 5 ENTER
into character: 3 ACT
Ladder: 4 **RUNG**
Laundering: 5 RINSE
Miss a: 6 FALTER
on a scale: 4 TONE
One: 5 STAIR
on it: 3 GAS HIE 4 PATH SOLE
    5 PEDAL SCALE 6 INSOLE
    8 GASPEDAL
on the scale: 3 SOL
part: 5 RISER
Place to: 5 ASIDE
Project: 5 PHASE
"Step ___!" ("Hurry!"): 4 **ONIT**
"Step by Step"
    actress Keanan: 5 STACI
"Stepford Wives, The"
    author: 8 IRALEVIN
    author Levin: 3 IRA
___ step further: 3 GOA
Stephanie
    Father of: 5 EFREM
Stephen
    Actor: 3 **REA** 4 BOYD
    Brother of ~ and Billy:
        4 ALEC
    ~, in French: 7 ETIENNE
Stephen Vincent ___
    Poet: 5 BENET
"Step on it!": 5 HURRY
Stepped: 4 TROD
    down: 4 ALIT
    on: 4 TROD
    on it: 4 SPED
"Steppenwolf"
    author: 5 **HESSE**
Steppes
    settler: 5 TATAR
Steps
    alternative: 4 RAMP
    Castle with many: 5 IRENE
    over a fence: 5 STILE
    Porch: 5 STOOP
    Take: 3 **ACT**
    Take baby: 6 TODDLE
    Took: 6 STRODE
"Steps in Time"
    autobiographer: 7 ASTAIRE

Stepsisters
    Like Cinderella's: 4 UGLY
Stereo
    component: 3 AMP 5 TUNER
    forerunner: 4 MONO
    Not: 4 MONO
    system: 4 HIFI
Stereotype
    Studious: 4 NERD
Sterile
    hybrid: 4 MULE
Sterling
    Pound: 4 QUID
Stern: 4 **REAR**
    Article in: 3 EIN
    Opposite of: 4 STEM
    rival: 4 IMUS
    Toward the: 3 **AFT**
    Violinist: 5 **ISAAC**
    with a bow: 5 ISAAC
___ Stern (German newspaper):
        3 DER
Sternutation: 6 SNEEZE
Sternward: 3 AFT 5 ABAFT
Steroid
    Kind of: 8 ANABOLIC
Stertorous
    Be: 5 SNORE
Stet: 7 LEAVEIN
    Opposite of: 4 DELE
Stethoscope
    sound: 5 THUMP
    user: 3 DOC
St.-Étienne
    capital: 5 LOIRE
Stetson: 3 HAT
    Like a: 7 BRIMMED
Steve
    Host: 5 ALLEN
    Muscleman: 6 REEVES
    Quarterback: 6 MCNAIR
    Runner: 5 OVETT
    Singer: 5 EARLE
    Singing partner of: 5 EYDIE
    Skier: 5 MAHRE
"Steve Allen Show, The"
    regular: 3 NYE
Stevedore: 4 LADE 5 LADER
        6 LOADER

concern: 5 CARGO
org.: 3 ILA

Steven
Actor: 6 SEAGAL

Stevens
Actress: 5 INGER 6 STELLA
Senator: 3 TED

Stevenson
fiend: 4 HYDE
Politician: 5 **ADLAI**
retirement home: 5 SAMOA
scoundrel: 6 MRHYDE

Stevie
Singer: 5 NICKS

Stew: 4 **FRET** OLIO SNIT SULK
    6 RAGOUT SEETHE
    SIMMER
bean: 4 LIMA
cooker: 3 POT
First name in: 5 DINTY
Get into a: 3 EAT
Highly seasoned: 6 BURGOO
ingredient: 3 PEA 4 LEEK OKRA
It may be in a: 5 LADLE
Kind of: 5 IRISH 6 HOTPOT
Okra: 5 GUMBO
Spicy: 4 **OLLA** 5 SALMI
    6 RAGOUT

Steward
offer: 4 WINE

Stewart
film: 6 DESTRY
Golfer: 5 PAYNE
Journalist: 5 ALSOP
Politico: 5 UDALL
role: 4 DOWD
Singer: 3 ROD
Style expert: 6 MARTHA
successor on the bench:
    7 OCONNOR

Stewart, Jimmy
Speak like: 5 DRAWL
syllables: 3 AWS

Stewbum: 3 SOT

Stewed: 3 LIT 5 OILED TIPSY
    6 BLOTTO WASTED
dude: 3 SOT

Stewpot: 4 **OLLA**

"St. ___ Fire": 5 ELMOS

St. Francis
Home of: 6 **ASSISI**

St.-Germain
river: 5 SEINE

St. Helens
and others: 3 MTS

Stick: 4 CANE POKE STAB
    5 CLING PASTE 6 **ADHERE**
    CLEAVE COHERE
around: 4 STAY WAIT
a shell in: 4 LOAD
Beat with a: 4 FLOG
Candy on a: 5 LOLLY
Dangerous: 4 TNT
Fiddle: 3 BOW
Game: 6 CROSSE
Get the short end of the:
    7 LOSEOUT
Grocery: 4 OLEO
in a paint can: 7 STIRRER
in school: 5 RULER
in the fridge: 4 OLEO
in the mud: 4 MIRE 5 EMBED
in the water: 3 OAR
it in your ear: 4 QTIP
it out: 4 STAY
it to: 5 SHAFT
Kind of: 4 JOSS POGO
Knight: 5 LANCE
like glue: 6 ADHERE
Magic: 4 WAND
Night: 5 ROOST
on: 3 ADD 5 AFFIX 6 ATTACH
    GLUETO
on a stick: 6 IMPALE
or split: 6 CLEAVE
out: 3 JUT 4 SHOW 5 BULGE
    6 ENDURE 8 PROTRUDE
(out): 3 JUT
Place to ~ a pick: 4 AFRO
Pool: 3 CUE
Short end of the: 7 BUMDEAL
    RAWDEAL
Swizzle: 7 STIRRER
(to): 6 ADHERE CLEAVE
together: 4 BIND GLUE
    5 CLUMP PASTE 6 **COHERE**
up: 3 ROB
Walking: 4 **CANE**

Where something may: **4** CRAW
with: **6** HOLDTO **8** ADHERETO
with a kick: **3** TNT
with a pin: **5** BURST
Yellow: **4** OLEO
Stick ___ (maltreat): **4** ITTO
___ stick
(clarinet): **8** LICORICE
(toy): **4** POGO
Stickball
venue: **6** STREET
"Stick 'em up!": **5** REACH
Sticker: **3** BUR PIN **4** GLUE HYPO
    TACK **5** DECAL EPOXY
    THORN **6** CACTUS
    NEEDLE **7** IMPALER
    8 PRICETAG
Direct-mail: **3** YES
Food: **4** TINE
Game: **5** SPEAR
Leather: **3** AWL
Price: **3** TAG
response: **4** HONK
stat: **3** MPG
Window: **5** DECAL
Sticking
point: **3** RUT **4** CRAW SNAG
    TINE **5** THORN
Stick in one's ___: **4** CRAW
Stick-in-the-mud: **4** FOGY
Stickler: **6** PURIST
Stick-on: **5** DECAL
Sticks
Gp. that ~ to its guns: **3** NRA
It comes in: **3** GUM
partners: **6** STONES
Stick-to-it-___: **3** IVE
Stick-to-itiveness: **4** GRIT
Stickum: **4** GLUE **5** PASTE
Sticky: **5** GOOEY HUMID **6** VISCID
roll: **4** TAPE
strip: **4** TAPE
stuff: **3** <u>**GOO**</u> TAR **4** GLUE GOOK
    GOOP TAPE **5** EPOXY PASTE
Sticky-tongued
critter: **4** TOAD
Stiff: **4** TAUT **6** FRIGID WOODEN
and sore: **4** ACHY
collar: **4** ETON

drink: **6** BRACER
hair: **4** SETA
hairs: **5** SETAE
Not: **4** LIMP
wind: **4** GALE
Working: **4** PEON **5** PROLE
Stiff ___ board: **3** ASA
Stiffen: **3** SET **5** STEEL TENSE
Stiffener
Collar: **4** STAY
Laundry: **6** STARCH
Salon: **3** GEL
Stiffly
formal: **4** PRIM **7** STILTED
Walk: **5** STALK
Stiffness: **4** KINK
Stiff-upper-lip
sort: **5** STOIC
Still: **3** <u>**YET**</u> **4** CALM EVEN IDLE
    MUTE **5** INERT **6** ATREST
    EVENSO SILENT
    8 STAGNANT
and all: **3** YET
Be ~, at sea: **5** LIETO
for rent: **5** UNLET
fresh: **7** UNJADED
going: **5** ALIVE
not there: **4** LATE
on the plate: **7** UNEATEN
Stood: **5** FROZE
stuff: **7** ALCOHOL
Unable to sit: **5** ANTSY
with us: **5** ALIVE
··, in poetry: **3** EEN
"Still ___" (1999 rap song): **3** DRE
"Still Crazy"
star Stephen: **3** REA
"Stille ___": **5** NACHT
Stiller
Comedian: **3** BEN
Partner of: **5** <u>**MEARA**</u>
Stiller, Ben
~, to Meara: **3** SON
Still-life
item: **4** PEAR
subject: **3** URN **4** EWER VASE
    5 FRUIT
Stills
bandmate: **4** NASH

Crosby, ~, and Nash: 4 TRIO
Stillwater
  City near: 4 ENID
Stilt
  relative: 6 AVOCET
  spot: 4 NEST
Stimpy: 3 CAT 4 TOON
  pal: 3 **REN**
Stimulant: 5 UPPER
  yielder: 4 COCA
Stimulate: 4 FUEL PROD SPUR
      URGE **WHET** 5 PIQUE
      6 AROUSE EXCITE
Stimulating
  drink: 6 BRACER
  nut: 4 KOLA
Stimulus: 4 GOAD PROD SPUR
  Olfactory: 4 ODOR 5 AROMA
      SMELL
  Respond to a: 5 REACT
  Taste: 4 ODOR
Sting: 3 CON 4 BILK SCAM TRAP
      5 SMART
  It has no: 5 DRONE
  operation: 4 TRAP
  Ring king with a: 3 ALI
"Sting, The"
  character Henry: 8 GONDORFF
  Oscar winner: 4 HEAD
Stinger: 3 BEE 4 **WASP**
      6 HORNET 8 SCORPION
  Big: 9 BUMBLEBEE
Stinging: 4 ACID 5 ACRID
  insect: 4 **WASP** 6 HORNET
  remark: 4 BARB
  shot: 3 BBS
Stingless
  bee: 5 DRONE
"... sting like ___": 4 ABEE
"Sting like a bee"
  boxer: 3 ALI
Stingy: 4 MEAN NEAR 5 CHEAP
      CLOSE 11 TIGHTFISTED
  one: 5 MISER PIKER
Stink: 3 ADO 4 ODOR REEK
      5 SMELL
  Make a: 3 ROT 4 REEK
  suffix: 4 AROO EROO
  to high heaven: 4 REEK

Stinker: 3 RAT 5 LOUSE SKUNK
      6 MEANIE
  Real: 7 SOANDSO
  Warner Bros.: 4 PEPE
Stinkeroo
  Cinematic: 4 BOMB
Stinkpot: 6 MEANIE
Stint
  Do another: 4 REUP
Stipe, Michael
  band: 3 REM
Stipend: 3 FEE PAY 4 WAGE
Stipulation: 5 GIVEN
  Added: 3 AND
  Auction: 4 ASIS
Stipulations: 3 IFS
Stir: 3 **ADO** MIX 4 RILE ROIL
      TODO WAKE 5 BUDGE
      HOOHA ROUSE
      6 AROUSE HOOPLA
      INCITE THECAN
  in: 3 ADD
  It can cause a: 5 SPOON
  to action: 4 PROD URGE
      6 AROUSE
  up: 3 FAN 4 RILE **ROIL**
      5 ROUSE STOKE WAKEN
      6 AROUSE EXCITE FOMENT
      INCITE 7 AGITATE
"Stir Crazy"
  actor Richard: 5 PRYOR
Stir-fry
  pan: 3 **WOK**
  tidbit: 7 SNOWPEA
Stirred: 4 WOKE
Stirrer: 5 SPOON
  Cauldron: 3 HAG
Stirrup
  site: 3 EAR
Stitch: 3 SEW
  caretaker: 4 LILO
  Knitting: 4 PURL
  loosely: 5 BASTE
  over: 5 RESEW
  Pal of: 4 LILO
  up: 3 SEW
  Without a: 5 NAKED
Stitched: 4 **SEWN**
  fold: 5 PLEAT

Stitches
In: **4** SEWN
It may need: **4** GASH
Line of: **4** SEAM
Put in: **3** <u>**SEW**</u> **4** DARN KNIT
    SEWN SLAY **5** BASTE
Remove ~ from: **5** UNSEW
Stitching
Towel: **3** HIS **4** HERS
St. Ives
riddle start: **3** ASI
St.-John's-___: 4 WORT
St. Johns, ___ Rogers
Author: **5** <u>**ADELA**</u>
St. Kitts
partner: **5** NEVIS
St. Louis
bridge designer: **4** EADS
footballer: **3** RAM
hrs.: **3** CST
landmark: **4** <u>**ARCH**</u>
summer setting: **3** CDT
St. Louis Browns
successor: **6** ORIOLE
St. Moritz
backdrop: **4** ALPS
Stock: 5 BROTH GOODS HOARD
(abbr.): **4** MDSE
buyer's objective: **6** GROWTH
collection: **4** HERD
European ~ exchange: **6** BOURSE
figure: **3** PAR **5** RATIO
For the ~ issue price: **5** ATPAR
holder: **3** PEN **4** BARN SAFE
    5 LADLE LASSO STORE
In: **6** ONHAND UNSOLD
Kind of: **5** NOPAR
Lock, ~, and barrel: **3** ALL
market abbr.: **3** IPO OTC
Not in ~ yet: **7** ONORDER
option: **3** PUT **5** TRADE
or bond: **5** ASSET
page abbr.: **3** OTC **4** AMEX
phrase: **5** ATPAR NOPAR
response: **3** MOO
Risky ~ tradng: **4** SPEC
S&P 500: **3** AOL
Secret: **5** STASH
suffix: **3** ADE

Take: **5** LASSO **6** RUSTLE
Take ~ of: **6** ASSESS
Tech: **3** IBM
Tech-heavy ~ exchange:
    6 NASDAQ
ticker inventor: **6** EDISON
unit: **3** COW **4** HEAD **5** SHARE
    STEER
unit (abbr.): **3** SHR
Unload: **4** SELL
up: **5** HOARD
up on: **5** AMASS
up on again: **7** REORDER
word: **3** PAR
Stockbroker
freebie: **3** TIP
Stockdale
was his running mate: **5** PEROT
Stock exchange: 3 MOO
area: **3** PIT
membership: **4** SEAT
worker: **6** TRADER
Stockholder
vote: **5** PROXY
Stockholm
Airline to: **3** <u>**SAS**</u>
Capital west of: **4** OSLO
coin: **5** KRONA
native: **5** SWEDE
sedan: **4** SAAB
Stocking
flaws: **4** RUNS
lines: **5** SEAMS
material: **5** LISLE NYLON
merchandise: **4** TOYS
No longer: **5** OUTOF
problem: **4** SNAG
shade: **4** ECRU NUDE **5** BEIGE
stuffer: **3** TOE TOY **5** SANTA
stuffer for a brat: **4** COAL
Stockings: 4 HOSE
Like some: **6** SEAMED
    8 SEAMLESS
Stockpile: 5 <u>**AMASS**</u> CACHE
    HOARD **6** GATHER
    SAVEUP
Stogie: 5 CIGAR
Stoic
Original: **4** ZENO

Stoicism
  Founder of: 4 ZENO
Stoker
  Author: 4 **BRAM**
Stole: 3 FUR 4 WRAP 5 CREPT
    6 LIFTED SWIPED
  Feathered: 3 BOA
  material: 4 MINK
Stolen
  goods: 4 LOOT
  It can be: 4 BASE 5 SCENE
  Like ~ goods: 3 HOT
Stoltz
  Actor: 4 ERIC
Stomach: 3 GUT MAW 5 ABIDE
    BROOK STAND 6 ENDURE
    8 TOLERATE
  Animal: 4 CRAW
  Can't: 4 HATE 5 ABHOR
    6 LOATHE
  muscles: 3 **ABS**
  settler: 5 BROMO 6 BICARB
    7 ANTACID
  Sound of a ~ punch: 3 OOF
  woe: 4 KNOT 5 ULCER
Stomachache
  cause: 5 ECOLI
Stomachs
  Like some: 8 CASTIRON
Stomp: 5 DANCE 7 TRAMPLE
"Stompin' at the ___": 5 SAVOY
Stone
  Actress: 6 SHARON
  and Pound: 5 EZRAS
  and Stallone: 4 SLYS
  Banded: 5 AGATE
  Blue: 5 LAPIS
  Cameo: 4 **ONYX**
  Cherry: 3 PIT
  Crystal-lined: 5 GEODE
  for a Libra: 4 OPAL
  foundation: 6 RIPRAP
  Glittery: 5 GEODE
  Green: 4 JADE
  Hollow: 5 GEODE
  Inscribed: 5 STELA STELE
  Iridescent: 4 OPAL
  Letters carved in: 3 RIP
  Marbled: 5 AGATE

  marker: 5 STELA STELE
  memorial: 5 CAIRN
  Milky: 4 OPAL
  mound: 5 CAIRN
  name: 7 ROSETTA
  of rock: 3 SLY
  Ornamental: 9 TIGERSEYE
  pillar: 5 STELA
  Precious: 3 **GEM** 5 JEWEL
  Print made using: 5 LITHO
  Rolling ~ lack: 4 MOSS
  Smoky: 4 OPAL
  Striped: 5 AGATE
  Unlike a rolling: 5 MOSSY
  Weight of a: 5 CARAT
  Words in: 7 EPITAPH
  ___ Stone: 7 ROSETTA
Stone, Oliver
  film: 3 JFK 5 NIXON
Stone Age
  implement: 7 NEOLITH
  tool: 6 EOLITH
"Stoned Soul Picnic"
  songwriter Laura: 4 NYRO
Stone-faced: 6 STOLID
Stonehenge
  worker: 4 CELT
  worshipper: 5 DRUID
Stones: 4 BAND
  Board game with: 5 PENTE
  Spa rooms with heated:
    6 SAUNAS
Stoneworker: 5 MASON
"Stoney End"
  composer Laura: 4 NYRO
Stood: 4 ROSE 5 AROSE BORNE
    GOTUP
  firm: 4 HELD
  for: 5 MEANT
  on a soapbox: 6 ORATED
  still: 5 FROZE
  up: 5 AROSE
  up to: 5 FACED
Stooge: 3 MOE 5 CURLY LARRY
    SHEMP
  Head: 3 MOE
  with bangs: 3 MOE
Stooges: 4 TRIO
Stool: 4 SEAT 5 PERCH

Stoolie: 3 RAT
  Play the: **4** BLAB
  ~, to a Brit: **4** NARK
Stool pigeon: 3 RAT
  Be a: **4** SING
"___ Stoops to Conquer": 3 SHE
Stop: 3 DIE END **4** CORK HALT
         QUIT **5** CEASE DEPOT
         DETER EMBAR LETUP
         6 DESIST **11** CALLITQUITS
  by: **5** ENDAT POPIN VISIT
       6 DROPIN
  Didn't: **4** WENT **5** RANON
  Don't: **6** KEEPAT
  fasting: **3** EAT
  Kind of: **3** BUS **4** REST
  on a line: **3** STA **5** DEPOT
  One way to: **7** ONADIME
  on the way: **8** RESTAREA
  order: **4** DONT
  Put a ~ to: **3** END **5** CEASE
  running: **3** DIE
  signal: **3** RED
  start: **3** NON
  talking: **6** CLAMUP
  Train ~ (abbr.): **3** STA
  Travel: **3** INN **5** MOTEL
  Truck: **5** DINER
  Truckee: **4** RENO
  up: **3** DAM **4** CLOG CORK PLUG
  Wayside: **3** INN
  working: **6** RETIRE
  ~, in French: **5** ARRET
"Stop!": 4 DON'T HALT WHOA
         5 AVAST **6** ENOUGH
         NOMORE
"Stop already!": 6 ENOUGH
"Stop behaving like a child!":
         10 ACTYOURAGE
Stop ___ dime: 3 ONA
Stoplight
  color: **3** RED
Stop on ___: 5 ADIME
Stopover: 3 INN **5** MOTEL
  Cruise: **4** ISLE
  Desert: **5** OASIS
  in la mar: **3** ILE
Stoppage
  Blood flow: **4** CLOT

Flow: 6 STASIS
WBA: 3 TKO
Stopped
  fasting: **3** ATE
  lying: **5** AROSE
  sleeping: **4** WOKE
Stopper: 4 CORK PLUG **5** BRAKE
  Bottle: **4** CORK
  Debate: **7** GAGRULE
  Fight: **3** TKO
  Flow: **4** CLOG
  Keg: **4** BUNG
  Parade: **4** RAIN
  Shopper: **4** SALE
  Speeder: **3** COP
Stoppers
  Show: **3** ADS
Stopping
  place: **3** INN
  Without: **7** ATACLIP
"Stop right there!": 4 HALT
         WHOA **6** HOLDIT
Stops
  It ~ often: **5** LOCAL
  Pull out all the: **6** LETRIP
  Rest: **5** OASES
  Where the buck: **3** DOE **4** HERE
"Stop that!": 4 DONT
"Stop the clock!": 4 TIME
Stopwatch
  button: **5** RESET
  Use a: **4** TIME
Storage
  area. **5** **ATTIC** **6** GARAGE
  battery type: **5** NICAD
  box: **3** BIN
  building: **4** SHED
  Coal: **3** BIN
  Computer ~ acronym: **5** ASCII
  container: **3** BIN
  cylinder: **4** SILO
  Farm ~ area: **4** SILO
  Food ~ material: **5** SARAN
  Hay ~ space: **4** LOFT
  PC ~ medium: **5** CDROM
  place: **3** BIN **6** CLOSET
  room: **5** ATTIC
  space: **3** BIN **5** ATTIC **6** CLOSET
  unit: **4** BYTE

Store: 4 FILE MART STOW
    5 CACHE
Be in ~ for: 5 AWAIT
event: 4 SALE
goods (abbr.): 4 MDSE
Kind of: 4 DIME
of ore: 4 LODE
on a farm: 6 ENSILE
posting (abbr.): 3 HRS
prefix: 4 MEGA
Retail: 4 MART
Retail ~ opening: 3 WAL
Secret: 5 CACHE STASH
selection: 5 SIZES
sign: 4 OPEN SALE
up: 8 PUTASIDE
wine: 6 CELLAR
~, as fodder: 6 ENSILE
Stored: 6 LAIDUP
in barrels: 4 AGED
on board: 5 LADED
Storefront
cover: 6 AWNING
sign: 4 OPEN
Storehouse
Rural: 4 SILO
Stores: 7 EMPORIA
Mil.: 3 PXS
Stories: 4 LORE
Body of legendary: 6 MYTHOS
Like ghost: 5 EERIE
Stork
kin: 4 IBIS 5 CRANE
Storm: 4 RAGE 6 ASSAIL
        ATTACK
Away from a: 4 ALEE
center: 3 **EYE**
Let up, as a: 5 ABATE
maker: 3 GEO
preceder: 4 CALM
tracker: 5 RADAR
Stormy
bird: 6 PETREL
"Stormy Weather"
composer: 5 ARLEN
singer: 5 HORNE
singer Horne: 4 LENA
Stornoway
It's spoken in: 4 ERSE

Storrs
coll.: 5 UCONN
Storting
Where the ~ meets: 4 OSLO
Story: 4 MYTH **TALE** 7 ACCOUNT
approach: 5 ANGLE
Bear of: 4 PAPA
Bedtime: 5 DREAM
Big: 4 EPIC
connector: 5 STAIR
Continuing: 6 SERIAL
Cover: 5 **ALIBI**
Creative: 3 LIE
dance: 4 HULA
Epic: 4 SAGA
Fairy: 4 TALE
Final: 4 OBIT
Fish: 3 LIE 4 TALE YARN
Fish ~ suffix: 3 EST
Folk: 4 TALE
Heroic: 4 EPIC
It's a long: 4 EPIC **SAGA**
It's an old: 5 FABLE
Kind of: 3 SAD SOB
Legendary: 4 MYTH
Life: 3 BIO
Like a hard-to-believe: 4 TALL
line: 4 **PLOT** 5 ANGLE
Long: 4 **SAGA**
Make a long ~ short: 4 EDIT
    5 RECAP
Never-ending: 4 SOAP
    9 SOAPOPERA
of Jesus: 7 PARABLE
Old war: 5 ILIAD
Ongoing: 6 SERIAL
setting: 5 SCENE
Shorter: 7 NOVELLA
starter: 4 **ONCE**
Suspect's: 5 ALIBI
Sweeping: 4 EPIC
Tall: 4 TALE YARN
Tell a: 7 NARRATE
teller: 4 LIAR
that may hold secrets: 5 ATTIC
Troy: 5 **ILIAD**
Trumped-up: 3 LIE
Unlikely: 4 TALE
War: 5 ILIAD

with a moral: 7 PARABLE
~, in French: 5 ETAGE

Storybook
elephant: 5 BABAR
ending: 5 MORAL
How a ~ is read: 5 ALOUD
monster: 4 OGRE
start: 4 ONCE

"Story of Civilization, The"
author: 6 DURANT

"Story of ___ H., The": 5 ADELE

Storyteller: 4 LIAR 6 FIBBER
7 RELATER
Noted: 5 AESOP

Storytelling
~ Uncle: 5 REMUS

Stout: 3 ALE 5 BEEFY LUSTY
6 PORTLY ROTUND
Half ale, half:
11 BLACKANDTAN
Make: 4 BREW 6 FATTEN
Mystery writer: 3 REX
relative: 3 ALE
sleuth: 4 NERO

Stove
Bubbling on the: 5 ABOIL
light: 5 PILOT
option: 3 GAS
section: 4 OVEN
workspace: 7 COOKTOP

Stovepipe: 3 HAT

Stoves
Like some: 5 SETIN

Stovetop
sights: 4 PANS POTS
whistler: 6 KETTLE

Stow
cargo: 4 LADE

Stowe
1856 ~ novel: 4 DRED
character: 3 EVA 5 TOPSY
Enjoy: 3 SKI
gear: 4 SKIS
tow: 4 TBAR
villain: 6 LEGREE

St. Patrick
Home of: 4 EIRE ERIN

St. Paul: 8 TWINCITY
architect: 4 **WREN**

St. Pete
Home of: 3 FLA

St. Peter
was the first: 4 POPE

St. Petersburg
neighbor: 5 TAMPA
river: 4 **NEVA**
st.: 3 FLA

St. Philip ___: 4 NERI

St. Pierre: 3 ILE
and others: 4 ILES

Strabismus: 8 CROSSEYE

Straddle: 4 SPAN

Straddling: 4 ATOP 6 ACROSS
7 ASTRIDE

Stradivari
Teacher of: 5 **AMATI**

Strads
Some: 5 CELLI

Straggle: 3 LAG

Straight: 3 DUE 4 NEAT TRUE
6 HETERO HONEST
LINEAR UNBENT
and tall: 5 ERECT
Didn't go: 5 ARCED
Don't go: 4 VEER
Get: 5 ALIGN
Get ~ A's: 5 EXCEL
Isn't: 5 LEANS
Isn't ~ with: 6 LIESTO
line through a circle: 6 SECANT
Make: 6 NEATEN
man: 4 FOIL 6 STOOGE
Not: 3 GAY WRY 4 ALOP AWRY
BENT WAVY 5 ATILT CURLY
6 ANGLED
Not walk: 4 REEL
path: 7 BEELINE
prefix: 5 ORTHO
Set: 4 TRUE 5 **ALIGN**
6 ORIENT
Standing: 5 ERECT
up: 4 NEAT 5 ERECT
Wasn't: 4 LIED

Straight ___ arrow: 4 ASAN

Straight as ___: 4 ADIE

Straightaway: 3 NOW

Straight-billed
game bird: 5 SNIPE

Straight-bladed
  dagger: 4 DIRK
Straighten: 5 ALIGN 6 UNBEND
    UNCURL 8 UNTANGLE
  up: 6 NEATEN
Straightened: 4 NEAT
Straightforward
  Less: 5 SLIER
Straight-grained
  wood: 3 ASH
Straightness
  Epitome of: 5 ARROW
"Straight Up"
  singer: 5 ABDUL
Strain: 3 TAX 4 ONUS 5 BREED
    EXERT 6 MELODY STRESS
    9 OVEREXERT
  Dangerous: 5 EBOLA ECOLI
  One with "I": 6 EGOIST
  Put a ~ on: 3 TAX 5 TAXED
Strain at a ___: 4 GNAT
Strained
  Became: 6 TENSED
Strainer: 5 **SIEVE** 8 COLANDER
Strains: 5 TRIES
Strait
  European: 7 OTRANTO
  ___ Strait: 6 BERING
Strait-laced: 4 PRIM 5 STAID
    9 VICTORIAN
  one: 5 PRISS
Strait of ___ (Malaysia):
    7 MALACCA
Strait of Dover
  county: 4 KENT
  French city on the: 6 CALAIS
Strait of Hormuz
  land: 4 IRAN OMAN
Strait of Messina
  monster: 6 SCYLLA
Straits
  In dire: 5 NEEDY
  Like some: 4 **DIRE**
  ___ Straits: 4 DIRE
Strand: 5 BEACH LEAVE SHORE
    6 DESERT ENISLE
    MAROON
  Curly: 7 TENDRIL
  in winter: 5 ICEIN

  Thin: 4 WISP
Stranded
  It's: 3 DNA RNA
  motorist's need: 3 TOW 5 FLARE
Strands
  Separate rope: 5 UNLAY
Strange: 3 ODD 5 ALIEN EERIE
    OUTRE
  Frightfully: 5 EERIE
  In a ~ way: 5 ODDLY 6 EERILY
  sighting: 3 UFO
  sounding city: 4 ERIE
  to say: 5 ODDLY
  Very: 5 WEIRD
Strangelove
  and No: 3 DRS
"Strange Magic"
  band: 3 ELO
"Stranger, The"
  author Albert: 5 CAMUS
"Strangers and Brothers"
  novelist: 6 CPSNOW
Strap
  Bridle: 4 REIN
  Jockey: 4 REIN
  Kind of: 3 BRA
  Sandal: 5 THONG
Straphanger: 7 STANDEE
  buy: 5 TOKEN
  lack: 4 SEAT
Strapped: 5 BROKE NEEDY
  for cash: 5 SHORT
Strapping: 6 ROBUST
Strasbourg
  Info: French cue
  school: 5 ECOLE
  summer: 3 ETE
Strata: 6 LAYERS
  Social: 6 CASTES
Stratagem: 4 PLAN PLOY RUSE
    6 TACTIC
  Sly: 4 RUSE
  Tennis: 3 LOB
Strategically
  Arrange: 6 DEPLOY
Stratego
  piece: 3 SPY 4 FLAG
Strategy: 8 GAMEPLAN
  Backup: 5 PLANB

Desperate: **10** LASTRESORT
Fallback: **5** PLANB
First: **5** PLANA
Poker: **5** RAISE
Wall St.: **3** LBO

Stratford
river: **4** __AVON__

Stratford-___-Avon: 4 UPON

Stratosphere
Head for the: **4** SOAR

Stratum: 5 LAYER
Coal: **4** SEAM
Social: **5** CASTE CLASS ELITE
Thin: **4** SEAM

Strauss
Composer: **6** JOHANN
Jeans maker: **4** __LEVI__
opera: **6** DAPHNE __SALOME__
waltz river: **6** DANUBE

Stravinsky
ballet: **4** AGON
Composer: **4** __IGOR__

Straw
Bundled, as: **5** BALED
Drink with a: **5** FLOAT
hat: **6** BOATER
in the wind: **4** OMEN
It contains: **5** ADOBE
Japanese ~ mat: **6** TATAMI
Last: **5** LIMIT
Like the unlucky: **5** SHORT
Small bundle of: **4** WISP
Use a: **4** SUCK

Strawberry: 5 EXMET
~ was one: **3** MET

Strawberry ___: 4 ROAN

Stray: 3 __ERR__ SIN **4** ROAM WAIF
    6 ERRANT **8** ALLEYCAT
animal: **4** WAIF
calf: **5** DOGIE
Cowboy's: **5** DOGIE
from the script: **5** ADLIB
gp.: **5** ASPCA
Take in a: **5** ADOPT

Straying: 6 ERRANT

Streak
Go on a winning: **6** GETHOT
On a lucky: **3** HOT
Ready to: **5** NAKED

Talk a blue: **3** GAB YAK **4** CUSS
    5 RUNON SWEAR
Winning: **3** RUN

Streaked: 4 LINY SPED TORE
    7 STRIATE

Streaker
Celestial: **5** COMET **6** METEOR
European: **3** SST
Sleek: **3** SST

Stream: 5 CREEK
Block, as a: **5** DAMUP
Burns: **5** AFTON
Cross a: **4** WADE
Electron: **7** BETARAY
Shakespeare: **4** AVON
Small: **4** RILL **5** BROOK
spot: **4** VALE
Swiss: **3** AAR **4** AARE
Word before: **3** AIR

Streambed
African: **4** WADI

"Streamers"
playwright David: **4** RABE

Streamlet: 3 RIA **4** RILL

Streamlined: 5 SLEEK

Streep
Actress: **5** MERYL
film: **8** SHEDEVIL
Title role for: **6** SOPHIE
~ Oscar role: **6** KRAMER

Street: 4 ROAD
34th ~ happening: **7** MIRACLE
Back: **5** ALLEY
border: **4** CURB
boss: **5** MASON
caution: **3** SLO
Central: **4** MAIN
Common ~ name: **3** ELM **4** MAIN
Complete a: **3** TAR
crosser: **6** AVENUE
Dead-end: **8** CULDESAC
fixture: **4** LAMP
fleet: **4** CABS
Freddy's: **3** ELM
Horror film: **3** ELM
Is not on the: **4** AINT
Memphis: **5** BEALE
Narrow: **4** LANE
Nightmare: **3** ELM

of fiction: 5 DELLA
of Olympics fame: 6 PICABO
Parisian: 3 RUE
performer: 4 MIME
Reason for a ~ closing:
    10 BLOCKPARTY
Scary: 3 ELM
shader: 3 ELM
Short: 4 LANE
show: 5 RAREE
sign: 5 YIELD 6 ONEWAY
urchin: 5 GAMIN
    10 RAGAMUFFIN
    11 GUTTERSNIPE
vendor: 7 PEDDLER
Street ___ (believability): 4 CRED
Streetcar: 4 TRAM 7 TROLLEY
"Streetcar Named Desire, A"
role: 6 STELLA
Street corner
box: 6 USMAIL
sign: 4 STOP
Streets
Like some: 4 THRU
Protest in the: 4 RIOT
Street-smart: 5 CANNY
Streisand
Film directed by: 5 YENTL
title role: 5 YENTL
~, familiarly: 4 BABS
Strength: 5 FORTE MIGHT
    POWER SINEW 7 POTENCE
Brute: 8 RAWPOWER
Current: 8 AMPERAGE
Drain: 3 SAP
Gather one's: 6 RESTUP
Kind of: 5 INNER 7 TENSILE
Lose: 3 EBB 4 FADE FLAG TIRE
    WANE
Muscular: 5 SINEW
Solution: 5 TITER
Source of: 5 ASSET UNITY
    6 SINEWS
Symbol of: 3 **OAK** 5 STEEL
With all one's: 5 AMAIN
~, in Latin: 3 VIS
Strengthen: 4 GIRD TONE
    6 ANNEAL BEEFUP
    TONEUP

Strengthener
Ab: 5 SITUP
Stress: 4 AGER 7 ITERATE
Sign of: 6 ACCENT 7 ITALICS
Stressed: 4 BOLD 5 TENSE
type (abbr.): 4 ITAL
Stressful
spot: 7 HOTSEAT
Stress-reducing
discipline: 4 YOGA
Stretch: 4 AREA 5 CRANE STINT
    TRACT 8 ELONGATE
across: 4 SPAN
in a stretch: 8 LIMORIDE
Intervening: 8 MEANTIME
It can be a: 4 LIMO
Long: 3 EON
More than a: 3 LIE
of land: 5 TRACT
out: 3 LIE 8 ELONGATE
(out): 3 EKE
Sedgy: 5 MARSH
Significant: 3 ERA
Solemn: 4 LENT
the truth: 3 LIE
time: 7 SEVENTH
Stretchable: 7 ELASTIC
Stretched
out: 4 LAIN
Tightly: 4 TAUT
Stretcher
Pay: 3 OLA
Shoe: 4 TREE
Stretching
muscle: 6 TENSOR
Stretchy: 7 ELASTIC
Strict
Hardly: 3 LAX
Less: 5 LAXER 6 EASIER
Morally: 7 PURITAN
Not: 7 LENIENT
suffix: 3 URE
Strictly
precise: 5 EXACT
Strictness: 5 RIGOR
Stride: 4 PACE STEP
Easy: 4 LOPE
Steed: 4 GAIT
Strident: 5 HARSH

sound: 5 BLARE
Stridex
  target: 4 ACNE
Strife
  Free from: 7 ATPEACE
  Norse god of: 3 TYR
Strike: 3 HIT NIX 4 DELE XOUT
        5 CLOUT SMITE 6 ATTACK
        DELETE SEEMTO
  back: 5 REACT
  caller: 3 UMP 5 UNION
        6 UMPIRE
  Didst: 5 SMOTE
  down: 5 SMITE
  from a list: 4 XOUT
  lightly: 3 TAP
  Lucky: 3 OIL ORE 5 TROVE
  Not quite a: 5 SPARE
  out: 3 FAN 4 **DELE** FAIL OMIT
        5 ERASE 6 DELETE
  participant: 3 PIN
  Prepare to: 4 COIL
  setting: 4 LANE
  site: 5 ALLEY
  Try to: 5 HITAT
  Wildcat: 3 OIL
  zone: 4 LANE
  zone boundary: 5 KNEES
Strike ___ : 5 ADEAL APOSE
Strike ___ blow: 4 ALOW
Strikebreaker: 4 **SCAB**
Strikeout
  king Nolan: 4 RYAN
  king Ryan: 5 NOLAN
Striker
  anathema: 4 SCAB
  cry: 5 UNITE
Strikers
  demand: 5 RAISE
  org.: 3 PBA
"Strike up the band!": 5 HITIT
Strike while the iron ___ : 5 ISHOT
Striking
  end: 4 PEEN
String
  Drum: 5 SNARE
  group: 5 OCTET
  Item attached to a: 6 TEABAG
  of flowers: 3 LEI

Package: 5 TWINE
  sound: 5 TWANG
  Strong: 5 TWINE
  tie: 4 BOLO
  Toy on a: 4 KITE YOYO
  Word after: 5 ALONG
String bean
  opposite: 5 FATSO
Stringed
  instrument: 4 HARP LYRE VIOL
        5 CELLO 6 ZITHER
  toy: 4 YOYO
String quartet
  member: 5 CELLO VIOLA
Strings
  Hawaiian: 3 UKE 7 UKELELE
        UKULELE
  Heavenly: 4 HARP
  Old: 5 LYRES
  One pulling: 5 TUNER
  Precious: 5 STRAD
  Pull: 5 STRUM
  Some: 5 CELLI
Stringy: 4 ROPY
Strip: 4 PARE PEEL SLAT
        5 SWATH 6 UNROBE
        7 DISROBE
  a ship: 5 UNRIG
  Backing: 4 LATH
  Barrel: 5 STAVE
  Blind: 4 SLAT
  blubber: 6 FLENSE
  Decorative ~ of fabric: 6 RIBAND
  Mideast: 4 GAZA
  Musical based on a: 5 ANNIE
  Narrow: 4 SLAT 7 ISTHMUS
  Shoe: 4 WELT
  Stem-to-stern: 4 KEEL
  Sticky: 4 TAPE
  Wood: 4 LATH SLAT 6 SPLINE
___ Strip: 4 GAZA 6 MOBIUS
Stripe: 3 ILK 4 KIND
  Lowest: 4 NINE
  Tear a ~ off: 6 DEMOTE
Striped
  animal: 5 OKAPI TIGER
  cat: 5 TABBY
  chalcedony: 5 AGATE
  equine: 5 ZEBRA

fish: 4 BASS
shirt wearer: 3 REF
stone: 5 AGATE
Stripling: 3 LAD
Stripped
They're sometimes: 5 GEARS
Stripper
garb: 7 GSTRING
Strips
of land: 6 ISTHMI
Stritch
Tony winner: 6 **ELAINE**
Strive: 3 TRY VIE 5 ASSAY
    6 ASPIRE
Stroheim, Erich ___: 3 VON
Stroke: 3 PET RUB 6 CARESS
Back: 3 PAT
Billiards: 5 MASSE
Finishing: 4 COUP
Gentle: 6 CARESS
gently: 3 PAT PET
Golf: 4 PUTT SHOT
of luck: 5 BREAK FLUKE
of the pen: 5 SERIF
Short: 4 PUTT
Something to: 3 EGO
Swimming: 5 CRAWL
Tennis: 3 LOB 4 CHOP
Violin: 5 UPBOW
Strokes
Like some swimming:
    7 OVERARM
Stroll: 4 ROAM WALK
    5 AMBLE MOSEY
    6 RAMBLE
Easy: 5 PASEO
Leisurely: 5 PASEO
Stroller
London: 4 PRAM
Strolling
area: 4 PIER
Stromboli
output: 4 LAVA
Strong: 5 HARDY 6 POTENT
    7 INTENSE
acid: 3 HCL 6 NITRIC
adhesive: 5 EPOXY
alkali: 3 LYE
and sharp: 5 ACRID

cleaner: 3 LYE
cord: 4 ROPE
cotton: 4 PIMA
craving: 4 LUST
criticism: 4 FLAK
desire: 3 YEN
fiber: 5 RAMIE
glue: 5 EPOXY
Going: 4 ATIT
impulse: 4 URGE
insect: 3 ANT
It may be: 4 SUIT
Lean and: 4 WIRY
point: 5 ASSET FORTE
preference: 4 BIAS
string: 5 TWINE
suit: 5 ARMOR FORTE
wind: 4 **GALE**
Strong-arm: 6 COERCE
Strong as ___: 4 ANOX
Strongbox: 4 SAFE 5 CHEST
    6 COFFER
"Strong Enough to Bend"
singer Tucker: 5 TANYA
Stronghold: 4 FORT 7 BASTION
    CITADEL
Military: 4 FORT
Mormon: 4 UTAH
Strongman
Biblical: 6 SAMSON
Mythical: 5 ATLAS
Onetime African: 4 AMIN
Strong ___ ox: 4 ASAN
"Strong Poison"
author: 6 SAYERS
Strong-scented
herb: 3 RUE
Strong-willed: 4 IRON
Strop: 4 HONE
user: 5 HONER
Stroud, Robert
nickname: 7 BIRDMAN
Strove: 4 VIED
Struck: 7 EXEDOUT
by Cupid: 7 SMITTEN
down: 5 SMOTE
hard: 5 SMOTE
It may be: 3 OIL 4 POSE
out: 4 EXED 5 DELED

prefix: 4 DUMB
~, old-style: 4 SMIT
Structural
beam: 4 IBAR
member: 5 IBEAM
sci.: 4 ANAT
support: 6 PILING
Structure
Baglike: 3 SAC
Circus: 4 TENT
Cylindrical: 4 SILO
Farm: 4 BARN SILO
Multiroofed: 6 PAGODA
Offshore: 3 RIG
prefix: 5 INFRA
Ramshackle: 7 RATTRAP
Snow: 4 FORT
Storage: 4 SHED
Struggle: 3 VIE WAR 6 TUSSLE
Class: 4 TEST
for air: 4 GASP
(through): 4 SLOG
Violent: 5 THROE
with struggle: 4 LISP
Struggling: 7 INAHOLE
Strummed
instrument: 3 UKE
Strung
along: 5 LEDON
tightly: 4 TAUT
Strut: 6 SASHAY 7 SWAGGER
like a peacock: 6 PARADE
Stc.: 3 RDS
St. Teresa
Home of: 5 **AVILA**
St. Thomas: 4 ISLE
who was murdered: 6 BECKET
Stu
Actor: 5 IRWIN
Stuart
CSA general: 3 JEB
Last ~ monarch: 4 **ANNE**
Stuart, J.E.B.
country: 3 CSA
Stuarti
Singer: 4 **ENZO**
"Stuart Little"
actress Davis: 5 GEENA
Stub ___: 4 ATOE

Stubbed
item: 3 TOE
Stubble
remover: 5 RAZOR
Stubborn: 6 MULISH
animal: 4 MULE
dirt: 5 GRIME
one: 3 ASS 4 MULE
things of Twain: 5 FACTS
Stubborn as ___: 5 AMULE
Stubbornness
Symbol of: 4 MULE
Stubbs
of the Four Tops: 4 LEVI
Stubby: 4 KAYE
Stuck: 5 GLUED MIRED TREED
        6 INAFIX INAJAM INARUT
        LODGED 7 ADHERED
        INABIND INASPOT
        UPATREE
around: 6 STAYED
by a thorn: 7 PRICKED
Get: 5 LODGE
on oneself: 4 VAIN
Place to get: 4 MIRE
Stuck in ___: 4 ARUT
Stuck-up
sort: 4 SNOB 7 EGOTIST
Stud: 5 HEMAN POKER
        7 EARRING
Emulate a: 4 SIRE
Farm: 8 STALLION
fee: 4 ANTE
Pay a ~ fee: 6 ANTEUP
poker: 4 SPUR
remark: 5 IMIN
site: 3 EAR 4 LOBE 7 EARLOBE
Studdard
"American Idol" winner:
  5 RUBEN
Studebaker
Sporty: 6 AVANTI
Student: 5 PUPIL TUTEE
        7 LEARNER
Academy: 5 CADET
book: 4 TEXT
concern: 4 EXAM
driver, usually: 4 TEEN
First-year law: 4 ONEL

Flight ~ test: 4 SOLO
focused org.: 3 PTA
jottings: 5 NOTES
Kind of: 3 MED
Mil. ~ body: 4 ROTC
Military: 5 CADET
New Haven: 3 **ELI** 5 YALIE
of Seneca: 4 NERO
of Socrates: 5 PLATO
of Zeno: 5 STOIC
overseer: 4 DEAN
Private: 5 TUTEE
purchase: 4 TEXT
res.: 4 DORM
second chance: 6 RETEST
Second-yr.: 4 SOPH
stat: 3 GPA
surprise: 7 POPQUIZ
West Point: 5 CADET
Yale: 3 **ELI**
Yeshiva: 3 JEW
~, in French: 5 ELEVE
Students
Fourth-yr.: 3 SRS
Group of: 5 CLASS
Like Anna's: 7 SIAMESE
Pertaining to most: 4 ELHI
play it: 5 HOOKY
Prepare new: 6 ORIENT
Some college: 5 COEDS
Studied
~, with "over": 5 PORED
Studio 7 ATELIER
alert: 5 ONAIR
Artist's: 7 ATELIER
Ball's: 6 DESILU
Dance ~ feature: 5 BARRE
Film: 3 LOT
output: 7 RELEASE
sight: 3 SET
sign: 5 **ONAIR**
stand: 5 EASEL 6 TRIPOD
stock: 4 REEL
structure: 3 SET
with a lion: 3 MGM
with a troubled history: 5 ORION
worker: 6 ARTIST
Study: 3 DEN 4 READ ROOM
    6 BONEUP PERUSE

7 EXAMINE LIBRARY
    8 POREOVER
Advanced ~ group: 7 SEMINAR
at the last minute: 4 CRAM
Field of: 4 **AREA**
hard: 4 CRAM
Not based on previous: 7 APRIORI
Stuff: 3 RAM 4 CRAM FILL GEAR
    GLUT **SATE** 5 ITEMS
    7 SATIATE
and nonsense: 3 ROT
in a cell: 3 RNA
in a closet: 5 LINEN
one's face: 6 PIGOUT
to the gills: 4 SATE 5 GORGE
Unimportant: 6 TRIVIA
Unusual: 6 CURIOS
Stuffed: 7 OVERFED REPLETE
animal of the '80s: 8 CAREBEAR
Get: 7 OVEREAT
It might be: 9 BALLOTBOX
shirt: 4 PRIG SNOB 5 SNOOT
~ Italian pockets: 7 RAVIOLI
Stuffer
Bagel: 3 LOX 4 NOVA
Stocking: 3 TOE TOY 4 COAL
    FOOT 5 SANTA
Stuffers
Wallet: 4 ONES
Stuffing
Cotton: 4 BATT
herb: 4 **SAGE**
Pillow: 5 EIDER KAPOK
Scarecrow: 5 STRAW
Stuffy: 4 PRIM
sounding: 5 NASAL
Stumble: 3 ERR 4 TRIP 6 FALTER
Stumblebum: 3 OAF 4 CLOD
    LOUT 5 KLUTZ
Stumbles
Verbal: 3 ERS UHS UMS
Stumbling
block: 4 SNAG
Stump
man: 6 ORATOR
Take the: 5 ORATE
Stumped: 5 ATSEA 7 ATALOSS
    UPATREE
Help for the: 4 HINT

Stumper: 3 POL 6 ENIGMA
    ORATOR
Stun: 3 AWE JAR WOW ZAP
    4 DAZE 5 AMAZE FLOOR
  gun: 5 TASER
Stung
  He ~ like a bee: 3 ALI
Stunned: 5 AGAPE AGASP INAWE
    7 INADAZE
  state: 4 DAZE
Stunning
  It's: 6 PHASER
  success: 4 COUP
  swimmer: 3 EEL
Stunt: 4 FEAT 5 CAPER
  double: 7 STANDIN
  Plane: 4 LOOP
Stunted: 5 RUNTY
Stuntman
  Knievel: 4 EVEL
"Stunt Man, The"
  star: 6 OTOOLE
Stunts
  First name in: 4 **EVEL**
Stupefy: 3 AWE 4 **DAZE** STUN
    5 AMAZE BESOT
    6 BEMUSE BOGGLE
  with drink: 5 BESOT
Stupid: 5 DENSE DOPEY INANE
    7 ASININE
  jerk: 3 ASS 4 BOZO 5 SCHMO
Stupidly
  Stare: 4 GAPE GAWK
"Stupid me!": 3 DOH 4 OOPS
Stupor: 4 DAZE
Sturdiness
  Symbol of: 3 OAK
Sturdy: 5 OAKEN
  cart: 4 **DRAY**
  wood: 3 ASH OAK
Sturgeon
  output: 3 **ROE**
Sturluson
  Icelandic poet: 6 SNORRI
  work: 4 EDDA
Sturm ___ Drang: 3 **UND**
Sturm und ___: 5 DRANG
Stuttered
  Name ~ in a song: 4 KATY

Stuttgart
  title: 4 HERR
Stutz
  auto: 7 BEARCAT
  contemporary: 3 **REO**
Stutz Bearcat
  contemporary: 3 REO
Sty
  cry: 4 **OINK**
  dweller: 3 HOG SOW
  fare: 4 SLOP 5 SWILL
  guy: 4 BOAR
  offspring: 5 STOAT
  resident: 3 PIG
  sound: 4 OINK 5 GRUNT SNORT
Style: 4 ELAN MODE VEIN
    5 DECOR GENRE TASTE
    TREND 6 MANNER
    7 PANACHE
  1920s ~: 7 ARTDECO
  1960s ~: 3 MOD 5 OPART
  In the ~ of: 3 **ALA**
  No longer in: 5 PASSE
  Nostalgic: 5 RETRO
  of a room: 5 DECOR
  of dress: 5 ALINE
  Ornate: 6 ROCOCO
  Out of: 5 DATED PASSE
  Suffix of: 5 ESQUE
  Type: 5 ELITE
  ~, in French: 3 TON
Styling
  goo: 3 GEL
Stylish: 3 MOD 4 **CHIC** TONY
    5 DASHY SHARP 6 CLASSY
  dresser: 3 FOP
  Elegantly: 6 CLASSY
  More: 6 TONIER 7 SMARTER
  Overly: 6 CHICHI
  suit: 6 ARMANI
Stylishly
  old: 5 RETRO
  smooth: 5 SLEEK
Stylist
  spot: 5 SALON
Stylistically
  bold: 5 AVANT
Stylus
  channel: 6 GROOVE

Styne
  Tony winner: 4 JULE
Styptic
  stuff: 4 **ALUM**
Styron
  heroine: 6 SOPHIE
  ~ Turner: 3 NAT
Styx
  ferryman: 6 CHARON
  setting: 5 HADES
Suave: 6 URBANE
  competitor: 5 PRELL
  Overly: 4 OILY
  "___ Suave": 4 RICO
Sub: 4 HERO TEMP 5 UBOAT
    6 HOAGIE 7 STANDIN
  Attack a: 3 EAT
  contractor: 4 DELI
  detector: 5 SONAR
  Downed a: 3 ATE
  German: 5 **UBOAT**
  Ill-fated: 5 KURSK
  in a tub: 4 OLEO
  launching: 7 TORPEDO
  New Orleans: 7 POORBOY
  sinker: 4 MINE 6 ASHCAN
  station: 4 **DELI**
  system: 5 SONAR
  viewer: 5 SCOPE
  WWII: 5 **UBOAT**
Sub ___ (in secret): 4 **ROSA**
Subarctic
  forest: 5 TAIGA
Subatomic
  particle: 4 MUON PION
    5 MESON QUARK 6 PROTON
Subbed: 5 SATIN
Subcompact: 4 MINI
Subcontinental
  prefix: 4 INDO
Subdivision
  Family: 5 GENUS
  Military: 4 UNIT
  of a legion: 7 MANIPLE
  Phylum: 5 CLASS
  subdivision: 3 LOT 4 ACRE
Subdivisions
  Taxonomic: 5 PHYLA
Subdue: 4 TAME

Subdued: 4 TAME
  color: 6 PASTEL
Subject: 4 NOUN 5 THEME TOPIC
    6 MATTER
  preceder: 4 INRE
  word: 4 NOUN
Subjective
  atmosphere: 4 AURA
Subjoin: 3 ADD 6 APPEND
Sublease: 5 RELET
Sublime: 8 ETHEREAL
Submachine gun
  British: 4 **STEN**
  Clip-fed: 4 BREN
  Israeli: 3 **UZI**
Submarine: 4 HERO
    12 HEROSANDWICH
  base: 4 DELI
  class: 4 ALFA
  detector: 5 SONAR
  First atomic: 8 NAUTILUS
  German: 5 UBOAT
  on sonar: 4 BLIP
  sandwich: 4 HERO 6 HOAGIE
  Work on a: 3 EAT
  WWII: 5 UBOAT
Submariner
  Fictional: 4 NEMO
Submerged: 4 SANK SUNK
  Partially ~ part: 4 HULL
Submission
  Aspiring singer's: 4 DEMO
  Contest: 5 ENTRY
  enc.: 4 SASE
Submissions
  to eds.: 3 **MSS**
Submissive: 4 MEEK TAME
    6 DOCILE
  group: 5 SHEEP
Submit: 3 BOW 5 ENTER OFFER
    YIELD 6 ACCEDE HANDIN
    SENDIN TENDER
Submitted: 6 SENTIN
Subordinate
  Brig. Gen.: 3 COL
  Claus's: 3 ELF
  deity: 6 DAEMON
  Looie: 5 SARGE
  ruler: 6 SATRAP

Santa's: 3 ELF
title (abbr.): 4 ASST
Subordinates
Capt.: 3 LTS
Subpoena: 4 WRIT
Subscriber: 4 USER
option: 7 RENEWAL
Subscription
End, as a: 5 LAPSE
Extend a: 5 **RENEW**
period: 4 YEAR
Subsection
Document: 7 ARTICLE
Subsequently: 4 THEN 5 AFTER
        HENCE LATER **SINCE**
Subservience
Show: 5 KNEEL
Subside: 3 **EBB** 4 WANE 5 ABATE
        6 LESSEN
Subsidiary: 4 UNIT
ExxonMobil: 4 ESSO
GE: 3 NBC
Maytag: 5 AMANA
theorem: 5 LEMMA
Subsidy: 3 AID
Subsist: 3 ARE 4 LIVE
Subspecies
Adaptable: 7 ECOTYPE
Substance: 4 GIST MEAT
Lacking: 4 AIRY 5 INANE
Slick: 3 OIL
Soothing: 5 SALVE
Substantial: 5 AMPLE HEFTY
        LARGE MEATY
Substantive: 5 MEATY
Substitute: 5 PROXY SCRUB
        6 FILLIN 8 ALTEREGO
As a: 7 INSTEAD
Butter: 4 **OLEO**
Chocolate: 5 **CAROB**
Fat: 5 OLEAN 7 OLESTRA
for: 5 ACTAS
Gelatin: 4 AGAR
Meat: 4 TOFU
Money: 5 SCRIP
place: 5 STEAD
Repair shop: 6 LOANER
ruler: 6 REGENT
Soap: 5 AMOLE

spread: 4 OLEO
Sugar: 4 DEAR
Substituted: 7 STOODIN
Substitution
word: 4 LIEU
Subterfuge: 4 RUSE TRAP
        5 TRICK
Subterranean
dwarf: 5 GNOME
pest: 4 MOLE
soldier: 3 ANT
Subtle: 4 FINE
atmosphere: 4 AURA
difference: 6 NUANCE
emanation: 4 AURA
tone: 3 HUE
Subtlety: 6 NUANCE
Lacking: 5 CORNY
Subtraction
Account: 5 DEBIT
amt.: 3 DIF
subject: 4 MATH
word: 4 LESS
Suburb: 4 AREA
Suburban
expanse: 4 LAWN
hangout: 4 MALL
plot: 4 ACRE
suffix: 3 ITE
Suburbanite
concern: 4 LAWN
Suburbia
sight: 4 LAWN
Subway: 5 METRO
alternative: 3 BUS CAB 4 TAXI
alternatives: 3 ELS
barrier: 5 STILE
coin: 5 TOKEN
entrance: 5 STILE
fare: 4 HERO
handhold: 5 STRAP
map point: 4 STOP
NYC: 3 BMT IND **IRT** MTA
NYC ~ stop, for short: 3 LEX
of song: 6 ATRAIN
Paris: 5 METRO
S.F. ~ system: 4 BART
stop (abbr.): 3 STA
track: 4 RAIL

wish: 4 SEAT
~, to a Brit: 4 TUBE
"Subway Series"
manager: 5 TORRE
stop: 4 SHEA
team: 4 METS
Succeed: 5 ENSUE GOFAR
6 FOLLOW MAKEIT
PANOUT 7 PROSPER
REPLACE 8 GETAHEAD
GOPLACES
Might: 8 HASASHOT
Success: 3 HIT
Achieve: 6 ARRIVE
Big: 3 HIT 5 ECLAT SMASH
Brilliant: 5 **ECLAT**
Letters of: 3 SRO
Short-lived: 13 FLASHINTHEPAN
Sign of: 3 **SRO**
Successful: 5 ONTOP
Become: 6 GETHOT
Very: 5 BOFFO SOCKO
Where the ~ go: 3 FAR
Succession
Arranged in: 7 SERIATE
Successively: 5 ONEND 6 INTURN
Successor: 4 HEIR
Succinct: 5 BRIEF PITHY TERSE
Succor: 3 AID
Succotash
bean: 4 **LIMA**
morsel: 8 LIMABEAN
Succulent
Soothing: 4 **ALOE**
They're: 5 CACTI
Suck
in: 4 LURE 6 ENTICE
up: 6 ABSORB
Sucker: 3 SAP 5 PATSY
7 ENSNARE LIVEONE
8 LOLLIPOP
British: 5 LOLLY
It's for a: 5 STRAW
Play for a: 3 USE
Sap: 5 APHID
Sucking
fish: 6 REMORA
Suckling
spot: 4 TEAT

Sucks
It: 6 VACUUM
Sucres
Where to spend: 7 ECUADOR
Sucrose
source: 4 BEET
Suction
device: 6 SIPHON 9 ASPIRATOR
prefix: 4 LIPO
Sud
Opposite of: 4 NORD
Sudan
neighbor: 4 CHAD
river: 4 NILE
suffix: 3 ESE
Sudden: 6 ABRUPT
attack: 4 RAID
burst: 4 GUST 5 SPASM SPURT
enlightenment: 6 SATORI
fancy: 4 WHIM
fright: 5 PANIC START
impulse: 4 URGE
move: 4 DART
outpouring: 5 **SPATE**
pain: 6 TWINGE
rush: 5 SPATE SURGE
sensation: 4 STAB
thought: 4 IDEA
transition: 4 LEAP
wind: 4 GUST
Suddenly
Appear: 5 POPUP
Awaken: 5 ROUST
Become ~ aware: 6 SNAPTO
Erupt: 5 FLARE
Intensify: 7 FLAREUP
Move: 4 DART
Open: 3 POP
Pull: 4 JERK
Say: 5 BLURT
Seize: 4 GRAB 6 SNATCH
Turn: 6 SWERVE
Veer: 3 ZAG
"Suddenly"
singer: 10 BILLYOCEAN
Suds: 4 BEER BREW FOAM
Bath: 3 ALE
Get the ~ off: 5 RINSE
holder: 3 KEG

Make: 4 BREW
Pub: 3 ALE
source: 3 PUB TAP

Suez ___ : 5 CANAL

Suez Canal
land: 5 EGYPT
sight: 5 OILER
terminus: 6 REDSEA

Suffer: 3 AIL 7 AGONIZE
a "brain cramp": 3 ERR
defeat, slangily: 5 EATIT
from: 4 HAVE
humiliation: 7 EATCROW
in summer: 7 SWELTER
suffix: 4 ANCE

Sufferer
Allergy: 7 SNEEZER
Cold ~ sound: 7 SNIFFLE

Suffering: 3 ILL WOE
Intense: 5 AGONY
partner: 4 PAIN

"... ___ suffer the slings ...":
4 ORTO

Suffice: 11 FILLTHEBILL
More than: 4 SATE

"Suffice ___ say ...": 4 ITTO

Sufficient: 5 AMPLE 6 ENOUGH
Barely: 5 SCANT 6 SKIMPY
Fully: 5 AMPLE
Marginally: 4 MERE
~, informally: 4 ENUF
~, poetically: 4 ENOW

Suffragist
~ Carrie: 4 **CATT**

Suffuse: 5 BATHE IMBUE

Sugar: 3 HON 4 CARB DOLL
Add ~ to: 7 SWEETEN
amt.: 3 TSP
bowl marchers: 4 ANTS
coat: 5 GLAZE ICING
Corn: 8 DEXTROSE
cube: 4 LUMP
in some fruits: 7 GLUCOSE
Like table: 8 GRANULAR
Milk: 7 LACTOSE
pill: 7 PLACEBO
Potatoes high in: 4 YAMS
source: 4 **BEET** CANE 5 MAPLE
Sprinkle: 4 SIFT

substitute: 4 DEAR
suffix: 3 **OSE**
unit: 4 CUBE LUMP

Sugar ___ : 3 PIE 4 BEET 5 MAPLE

Sugar Bowl
1993 ~ champs: 4 BAMA
Eight-time ~ champs: 4 BAMA

Sugarcoat: 5 GLAZE

Sugarcoated: 5 GLACE

Sugar-free: 5 NOCAL

"Sugar Lips"
trumpeter: 4 HIRT

Sugarloaf
1970 ~ hit:
13 GREENEYEDLADY

Sugarloaf Mountain
city: 3 RIO

Sugary: 5 SWEET
drink: 3 ADE
Sort of: 8 SWEETISH
suffix: 3 **OSE**

Suggest: 4 MEAN 5 GETAT IMPLY
INFER OPINE POSIT
6 HINTAT 7 CONNOTE
PROPOSE
More than: 4 URGE

Suggested
amt.: 3 RDA

Suggestion: 4 HINT IDEA
5 SCENT

Suggestions: 5 INPUT

Suggestive: 4 RACY 6 RISQUE
look: 4 LEER

Suicidal: 8 KAMIKAZE

"Suicide Blonde"
rock group: 4 INXS

Suicide squeeze
stat: 3 RBI

Suit: 4 CASE EXEC 5 BEFIT
accessory: 3 TIE
Big: 3 CEO
Birthday: 4 SKIN
Change to: 5 ADAPT
Dark: 6 SPADES
fabric: 4 WOOL 5 **SERGE**
TWEED TWILL
Fail to follow: 6 RENEGE
in a suit: 6 LAWYER
Kind of: 4 ZOOT 5 CIVIL LIBEL

UNION
Knight: 5 ARMOR
Like a leisure ~, now: 5 RETRO
Long: 5 ASSET FORTE
Man in a: 5 SANTA
One in a: 3 ACE
One in a black: 5 SPADE
part: 4 VEST 5 PANTS
Press a: 3 WOO
Reason for a: 4 TORT
Revealing: 6 BIKINI
spec: 4 LONG
Strong: 5 ARMOR FORTE
Stylish: 6 ARMANI
Tarot: 4 CUPS
Three-piece ~ part: 4 VEST
top: 3 ACE BRA
___ suit: 4 ZOOT
Suitability: 7 APTNESS
Suitable: 3 APT
for all audiences: 6 RATEDG
for evening wear: 6 DRESSY
for farming: 6 ARABLE
for service: 4 ONEA
In a ~ manner: 5 FITLY
Not: 5 INAPT UNFIT
place: 5 NICHE
Suitcase: 3 BAG 4 GRIP 6 VALISE
Suite: 7 RETINUE
amenity: 6 WETBAR
section: 4 ROOM
spot: 5 HOTEL
Suited
Best: 6 APTEST
Not: 5 UNFIT
___ suiter: 4 ZOOT
Suitor: 4 BEAU 5 SWAIN
It's pitched by a: 3 WOO
Suits
It ~ you: 6 ATTIRE
"Suits me!": 7 IMHAPPY
Suit to ___: 4 **ATEE**
Sukiyaki
ingredient: 4 TOFU
Sulawesi
Former name of: 7 CELEBES
Sulf-
suffix: 3 IDE
Sulk: 4 MOPE POUT SNIT

Sulky: 6 INAPET MOROSE
gait: 4 TROT
horse: 7 TROTTER
leader: 5 PACER
Pull a: 4 TROT
state: 3 PET
Sullen: 4 DOUR GLUM 5 POUTY
          6 MOROSE
Look: 4 POUT
Sullivan
and others: 3 **EDS**
had a really big one: 4 SHEW
Sully: 3 MAR TAR 4 SOIL 5 STAIN
          TAINT 6 DEFILE SMIRCH
          7 BESMEAR
Sultan
Spouses of a: 5 HAREM
Sultana
chamber: 3 ODA
**"Sultan after Sultan with his
      Pomp"**
poet: 4 OMAR
Sultanate
Arabian: 4 **OMAN**
Diamond: 4 SWAT
Pacific: 6 BRUNEI
"Sultan of Sulu, The"
writer: 3 ADE
Sultans
One of three Ottoman: 5 AHMED
Sulu
portrayer: 5 TAKEI
shipmate: 5 UHURA
Sum: 5 TOTAL
Considerable: 11 PRETTYPENNY
In: 7 ALLTOLD
part: 6 ADDEND
thing: 6 ADDEND
Tidy: 4 PILE
Tiny: 4 MITE
total: 6 AMOUNT
total (abbr.): 3 AMT
up: 3 ADD 5 RECAP
Sumac
Singer: 3 **YMA**
Sumatra
neighbor: 4 JAVA
simian: 5 ORANG
Three-toed ~ beast: 5 TAPIR

Summa cum ___ : 5 LAUDE
Summa ___ laude: 3 CUM
Summarize: 5 RECAP
Summary: 5 RECAP 6 APERCU
    PRECIS
    holder: 8 NUTSHELL
Summation: 5 RECAP
Summer: 6 SEASON
    A ~ place: 4 CAMP
    attire: 6 SHORTS
    Avoid ~ school: 4 PASS
    clock setting (abbr.): 3 DST EDT
    cooler: 3 **ADE** FAN 4 POOL
        6 ICETEA 7 ICEDTEA
    coolers: 3 ACS 4 ICES
    cottage: 6 RENTAL
    D.C. ~ hrs.: 3 EDT
    Denver ~ hrs.: 3 MDT
    drink: 3 **ADE**
    ermine: 5 **STOAT**
    fare: 7 REPEATS
    footwear: 6 SANDAL 7 SANDALS
    getaway: 4 CAMP
    hire: 4 TEMP
    hrs.: 3 DST EDT MDT
    KS ~ hrs.: 3 CDT
    L.A. ~ hrs.: 3 PDT
    Like ~ drinks: 4 ICED
    Middle of: 3 EMS
    mo.: 3 **AUG** JUL
    music: 5 DISCO
    music festival site: 5 ASPEN
    Part of a ~ forecast: 4 HAZE
    pest: 4 GNAT 7 SKEETER
    quaff: 3 **ADE**
    shade: 3 TAN
    shirt: 3 TEE
    shoe: 6 SANDAL
    Showed during the: 5 RERAN
    Sign of: 3 **LEO** 5 VIRGO
        7 THECRAB
    Singer: 5 DONNA
    Spring: 3 CPA
    Sticky in: 5 HUMID
    Sultry part of: 7 DOGDAYS
    top: 3 TEE 6 HALTER
    wear: 3 TEE
    ~, in French: 3 **ETE**
    ~ TV fare: 5 RERUN

Summer, Donna
    song: 10 ONTHERADIO
"Summer and Smoke"
    heroine: 4 ALMA
Summer Games
    event: 4 EPEE
    org.: 3 IOC
Summerhouse: 6 GAZEBO
Summerlike: 7 ESTIVAL
"Summer Nights"
    Musical with the song: 6 GREASE
"Summer of ___": 3 SAM
"Summer of Sam"
    director Spike: 3 LEE
"Summer Place, A"
    actor Richard: 4 EGAN
    actress Sandra: 3 DEE
Summers
    in the East: 5 ABACI
"Summertime": 4 ARIA
"Summertime, Summertime"
    group: 6 JAMIES
Summery: 7 ESTIVAL
Summing
    up: 5 INALL
Summit: 3 TIP TOP 4 ACME
        APEX 6 VERTEX
    1945 ~ site: 5 YALTA
    At the ~ of: 4 **ATOP** 5 ONTOP
    Gangland ~ figure: 3 DON
    offering: 5 VISTA
Summon: 4 CALL PAGE
        7 SENDFOR
    up: 5 EVOKE 6 MUSTER
    with a beeper: 4 PAGE
    ~, in a way: 4 BEEP
Summoned: 4 BADE RANG
        7 SENTFOR
Summoner: 5 PAGER
    Genie: 7 ALADDIN
Summons: 4 BEEP CALL
    (abbr.): 3 CIT
    Answered a: 4 CAME
    Brief: 5 SEEME
    Court: 8 SUBPOENA
    from the boss: 5 SEEME
    Furtive: 4 PSST
    Gave a ~ to: 5 CITED
    Sibilant: 4 PSST

Teacher's: 5 SEEME
Sumner, Gordon
stage name: 5 STING
Sumo
land: 5 JAPAN
Like ~ wrestlers: 5 OBESE
Sumptuous: 4 POSH RICH
7 OPULENT
meal: 5 FEAST
Sumptuously
Eat: 5 FEAST
Sumptuousness: 4 LUXE
Sumter: 4 FORT
and others (abbr.): 3 FTS
Sun: 3 ORB **SOL**
Bit of: 3 RAY
block: 5 CLOUD 7 ECLIPSE
PARASOL
dancer: 4 HOPI 7 ARAPAHO
Egyptian: 4 ATEN
emanations: 4 RAYS
Enjoy the: 4 BASK
follower: 3 MON 6 MOONIE
Get some: 3 TAN
He flew too near to the: 6 ICARUS
Indian with a ~ dance: 3 UTE
Lie in the: 4 BAKE BASK
Look into the: 6 SQUINT
offering: 4 JAVA
Of the: 5 SOLAR
Once around the: 4 YEAR
orbiter: 6 PLANET
or moon: 3 **ORB**
Our: 3 SOL
prefix: 5 HELIO
Roman ~ god: 3 SOL
Sag in the: 4 WILT
screen: 5 VISOR
Setting of the: 3 SKY
shade: 3 TAN
Shade from the: 3 TAN
shield: 5 VISOR 6 AWNING
7 PARASOL
Soak up some: 4 BASK
The ~ is one: 5 GSTAR
Third rock from the: 5 EARTH
Where the ~ comes up: 4 EAST
~, in French: 6 SOLEIL
~, in Spanish: 3 SOL

Sun.
delivery: 3 SER
follower: 3 MON
speech: 3 SER
talk: 3 **SER**
Sunbather
goal: 3 TAN
Riverside: 4 CROC
Sunbathers
catch them: 4 RAYS
Sunbeam: 3 RAY
Sunblock: 6 LOTION
letters: 3 SPF
Sunbow
producer: 4 MIST
Sun Bowl
city: 6 ELPASO
Sunburn
Get a: 3 FRY
Lose a: 4 PEEL
Product once sold as a ~ remedy:
7 NOXZEMA
soother: 4 **ALOE**
Sunburned: 3 RED
Sun-cracked: 4 SERE
Sundance Kid: 5 ALIAS
girlfriend: 4 **ETTA**
partner: 5 BUTCH
Sunday
address (abbr.): 3 SER
celebration: 4 MASS
clothes: 6 FINERY
delivery: 6 SERMON
dinner: 5 ROAST
8 POTROAST
drive: 4 SPIN
Put on one's ~ best:
7 DRESSUP
reading: 6 COMICS
8 MASSBOOK
seat: 3 PEW
service: 4 MASS
supplement: 6 INSERT
talk topic: 3 SIN
wrap-up: 4 AMEN
Sundays
A month of: 3 EON 4 AGES
Sun Devils
sch.: 3 **ASU**

Sundial
numeral: 3 **III** VII XII 4 IIII VIII
Sundown
~, poetically: 3 EEN
Sun-dried
brick: 5 **ADOBE**
Sundry: 7 DIVERSE
Sunfish: 5 BREAM
Sunflower: 5 OXEYE
or daisy: 5 ASTER
product: 3 OIL
seed: 6 ACHENE
start: 4 SEED
"Sunflowers"
setting: 5 ARLES
Sunflower St.: 3 KAN
Sunflower State: 6 KANSAS
Sung
syllable: 3 TRA
Sunken
cooking site: 7 FIREPIT
Sun King
number: 3 XIV
Sunni: 4 SECT
faith: 5 ISLAM
Sunny: 5 SOLAR
opening: 5 HELIO
"Sunny"
singer Bobby: 4 HEBB
Sunnyside up
It may be served: 3 EGG
The sun in: 4 YOLK
Sunrise: 4 DAWN
direction: 4 EAST
Sonora: 4 ESTE
to sunset to sunrise: 5 CYCLE
"Sun ___ Rises, The": 4 ALSO
Sunrooms: 7 SOLARIA
Suns: 4 TEAM
Exploding: 5 NOVAE
spot: 7 PHOENIX
Sunscreen: 6 AWNING
abbr.: 3 SPF
ingredient: 4 ALOE **PABA**
Sunset
direction: 4 WEST
Like a: 3 RED
On ~ Blvd., perhaps: 4 INLA
shade: 4 ROSE

time, in verse: 3 EEN
"Sunset Boulevard"
actress Nancy: 5 OLSON
heroine Desmond: 5 NORMA
Sunshade: 7 PARASOL
Sunshine
Bit of: 3 **RAY**
cracker: 4 HIHO
~, in French: 6 SOLEIL
Sunshine St.: 3 FLA
Sunshine State
city: 5 MIAMI OCALA
Sun-Times
rival: 4 TRIB
Sunup
direction: 4 EAST
Sun Valley
setting: 5 IDAHO
"Sun Valley Serenade"
star: 5 HENIE
Sup: 3 EAT 4 DINE
Super: 4 AONE PHAT 5 GREAT
ULTRA
apartment: 4 AONE
bargain: 5 STEAL
duper: 5 FRAUD
mark: 5 APLUS
power: 3 ESP
serve: 3 ACE
server: 4 ACER
set: 4 KEYS
star: 4 NOVA
time (abbr.): 3 TUE
"Super!": 5 NEATO
Super ___ : 3 NES
Superabundance: 4 GLUT
Superaggressive
one: 5 RAMBO
Superb: 4 AONE
Superbly
Did: 5 SHONE
Serve: 3 ACE
Super Bowl
1984 ~ champs: 7 RAIDERS
1999 ~ MVP: 5 ELWAY
2000 ~ champs: 4 RAMS
2002 ~ champs: 4 PATS
First ~ MVP: 5 STARR
Five-time ~ champs:

    8 STEELERS
Four-time ~ winning coach:
    4 NOLL
Namath: 3 III
sight: 5 BLIMP
Six-time ~ coach: 5 SHULA
stat: 3 TDS
Three-time ~ MVP:
    10 JOEMONTANA
~ MVP Brett: 5 FAVRE
Super Bowl I
winner: 8 GREENBAY
Super Bowl III
winners: 4 JETS
~ MVP: 6 NAMATH
Super Bowl VII
winner: 5 MIAMI
Super Bowl VIII
~ MVP Larry: 6 CSONKA
Super Bowl X
~ MVP Swann: 4 LYNN
Super Bowl XIV
losers: 4 RAMS
winners: 8 STEELERS
Super Bowl XX
winning coach: 5 DITKA
Super Bowl XXI
~ MVP: 5 SIMMS
Super Bowl XXIX
winners: 6 NINERS
Super Bowl XXXIII
~ MVP: 5 ELWAY
Super Bowl XXXIV
champs: 4 RAMS
Super Bowl XXXV
champs: 6 RAVENS
Superboy
girlfriend Lana: 4 LANG
girlfriend Lang: 4 **LANA**
Supercharger: 5 TURBO
Supercilious
sort: 4 SNOB
Superciliousness: 4 AIRS
Supercomputer
name: 4 CRAY
Superdome
team: 6 SAINTS
Super-duper: 4 ACES AONE TOPS
    5 GREAT NEATO

Superfecta: 3 BET
Superficial: 5 SLICK 7 SHALLOW
Superfluous: 5 EXTRA
Superfund
org.: 3 EPA
Supergarb: 4 CAPE
Supergiant
in Scorpius: 7 ANTARES
Supergirl
alias Linda: 3 LEE
Krypton name of: 4 KARA
Supergroup
Comics: 4 XMEN
Superhero
accessory: 4 CAPE MASK
Diminutive DC Comics: 4 ATOM
garment: 4 CAPE
group: 4 XMEN
Marvel Comics: 4 THOR
    7 IRONMAN
Superimpose: 7 OVERLAY
Superimposed: 4 ATOP
Superior: 4 AONE BEST LAKE
    5 ELECT 6 CHOICE
    8 HIGHERUP
Be: 5 EXCEL
Be ~ to: 8 OUTCLASS
city: 6 DULUTH
group: 5 ELITE
inferior: 4 ERIE
skill: 3 ART
to: 4 ATOP OVER 5 ABOVE
Superlative
ending: 3 **EST**
suffix: 3 **EST** 4 IEST
Superman
accessory: 4 CAPE
alias: 4 KENT
birth name: 5 KALEL
co-creator: 6 SIEGEL
Father of: 5 JOREL
insignia: 3 ESS
Like: 6 HEROIC
Mother of: 4 **LARA**
portrayer: 4 CAIN 5 REEVE
skill: 10 XRAYVISION
symbol: 3 ESS
~, to Reeve or Reeves: 4 ROLE
"Superman"

actor Christopher: 5 REEVE
Margot's ~ role: 4 LOIS
star: 5 REEVE
villainess: 4 URSA
villain Luthor: 3 LEX
"Super, man!": 3 RAD
Supermarket
area: 5 AISLE
chain: 5 AANDP
checkout item: 7 SCANNER
division: 5 AISLE
Do a ~ job: 3 BAG
employee: 6 PRICER
It's bagged at the: 3 TEA
lines: 8 BARCODES
section: **4 DELI** 5 AISLE DAIRY
    MEATS
Supermodel
One-named: 4 EMME **IMAN**
    5 FABIO
~ Carol: 3 ALT
~ Heidi: 4 KLUM
Super Monkey Ball
producer: 4 SEGA
Supernatural: 5 EERIE 6 OCCULT
Superpower
Former: 4 USSR
Supersecret
org.: 3 NSA
Super-secure
carrier: 4 ELAL
Super-sharp
knife: 5 GINSU
Supersized: 5 LARGE
Supersonic
reading: 4 MACH
Superstar
Temporary: 4 NOVA
Superstation
Cable: 3 **TBS**
Supervise: 7 OVERSEE
Supervised: 7 OVERSAW
Supervision: 4 CARE
Supervisor: 4 BOSS 8 OVERSEER
Casino: 7 PITBOSS
Supervisors
Dorm: 3 RAS
Superwide: 3 EEE
Supped: 3 ATE

Supper: 6 DINNER REPAST
Has: 5 DINES
in a sty: 4 SLOP 5 SWILL
It's set for: 5 TABLE
Saved on ~, perhaps: 5 ATEIN
scrap: 3 ORT
Serve ~ to: 4 FEED
Suppertime
~, for some: 3 SIX
Supple: 5 **LITHE** 7 LISSOME
Supplement: 3 ADD 5 ADDIN
    ADDON ADDTO
    7 ADDONTO
Article: 7 SIDEBAR
Pension: 3 IRA
Sunday: 6 INSERT
Vitamin: 4 IRON
Will: 7 CODICIL
~, with "out": 3 **EKE**
Supplements: 7 ADDENDA
Supplicate: 4 PRAY
Supplied: 3 FED
Supply: 4 FUND 5 EQUIP
    6 SELLTO
Hidden: 5 CACHE STASH
In short: 5 SCANT 6 SCARCE
    SPARSE
more weapons to: 5 REARM
of arms: 7 ARSENAL
Partner of: 6 DEMAND
the food: 5 CATER SERVE
with weapons: 3 ARM
Supply-and-demand
subj.: 4 **ECON**
Support: 3 AID 4 ABET BACK
    HELP PROP 5 AEGIS
    BRACE CHEER 6 PROPUP
    UPHOLD 7 BOLSTER
    8 UNDERPIN
a foundation: 6 DONATE
a scheme: 4 ABET
at sea: 4 MAST
beam: 4 IBAR
Give ~ to: 4 BACK
group: 4 BRAS 6 ALANON
In ~ of: 3 FOR
Insincere: 10 LIPSERVICE
Kind of: 4 TECH 7 SPOUSAL
Letter-shaped: 5 IBEAM

Limited: 5 RAILS
person: 5 AIDER
piece: 4 SLAT
provider: 3 BRA
Sound of: 3 RAH
system: 3 BRA 7 SHORING
Use for: 6 LEANON RELYON
Vote of: 3 YEA
Without: 5 ALONE
Words of: 5 ICARE
~, with "up": 4 PROP
~, with "with": 4 SIDE
___ support: 4 TECH
Supporter: 3 LEG PRO 4 ALLY
    CANE 6 PATRON
of arms: 3 NRA
of the arts: 5 DONOR EASEL
Supporting: 3 FOR PRO
Not: 4 ANTI
vote: 3 YEA
Supportive
of: 3 FOR
Suppose: 4 DEEM 5 GUESS
    OPINE
"Suppose ...": 6 WHATIF
Suppositions: 3 IFS
Suppress: 5 QUASH QUELL
    SITON 6 STIFLE
Suppressed: 5 SATON 6 PENTUP
"___ supra" (as above): 3 UBI
Supreme
being: 3 GOD
leader: 4 ROSS
ruler: 7 EMPEROR
~ Diana: 4 ROSS
~ Greek deity: 4 ZEUS
~ Norse deity: 4 ODIN
~ Supreme: 4 ROSS 5 DIANA
~ Theban deity: 6 AMENRA
Supreme Court
1973 ~ case: 3 ROE
count: 4 NINE
David of the: 6 SOUTER
justices, e.g.: 6 ENNEAD
justice since 1975: 7 STEVENS
middle name: 5 BADER
Reagan ~ nominee: 4 BORK
    6 SCALIA
Scott of an 1857 ~ case: 4 DRED

Supremes, The: 4 TRIO
**___ supuesto (of course, in
    Spanish):** 3 POR
Sur
Opposite of: 5 NORTE
Suras
It has 114: 5 KORAN
Sure
Be ~ of: 4 KNOW
competitor: 3 BAN 5 ARRID
Isn't: 6 DOUBTS
Make: 7 SEETOIT
Make ~ of: 3 ICE 5 SEETO
Say for: 4 AVER
shooter: 7 DEADEYE
target: 4 ODOR
thing: 4 FACT 5 CINCH
    6 SHOOIN
to succeed: 5 ONICE
Was ~ of: 4 KNEW
"Sure!": 3 YEP YES 5 NATCH
    6 YOUBET
Surefire: 6 NORISK
winner: 6 SHOOIN
Sure-footed
animal: 3 ASS
goat: 4 IBEX
"Surely you ___!": 4 JEST
"Surely you jest!": 4 UHUH
"Sure thing!": 3 YES 4 OKAY
    6 RIGHTO YOUBET
Sure-to-succeed: 6 NOLOSE
"Sure, why not?": 4 LETS OKAY
Surf
feature: 5 SPRAY
in restaurants: 7 SEAFOOD
Loud, as the: 5 AROAR
Place to: 3 NET
Prepare to: 5 LOGIN LOGON
Slog through the: 4 WADE
sound: 4 **ROAR**
The "turf" in ~ and turf:
    5 STEAK
Wade through the: 4 SLOG
Surface: 4 PAVE 5 ARISE
    6 EMERGE
Condense on the: 6 ADSORB
Downy: 3 NAP
Flat: 5 PLANE

Near the: 4 RISE
On the: 6 INAREA
Surfaced: 5 AROSE
Surfboard •
    coat: 3 WAX
    flaw: 4 DING
Surfeit: 4 CLOY SATE 7 SATIATE
        SATIETY
Surfer: 4 USER
    enabler: 5 MODEM
    entry: 3 URL
    mart: 4 EBAY
    Net: 4 USER
    spot: 3 WEB
    surface: 4 WAVE
    wannabe: 5 **HODAD**
Surfing: 6 ONLINE
    equipment: 5 MODEM
    mecca: 5 OAHU
    site: 3 NET WEB 6 THENET
    the Net: 6 ONLINE
    wannabe: 5 HODAD
Surg.
    locales: 3 ORS
    specialty: 4 ORTH
Surge: 6 ONRUSH
Surgeon: 6 DOCTOR
    Army ~ Walter: 4 REED
    assistant: 5 NURSE
    Immediately, to a: 4 STAT
    insertion: 5 STENT
    Kind of: 4 ORAL
    Noted heart: 7 DEBAKEY
    Oral ~ deg.: 3 DDS
    outfit: 6 SCRUBS
    prefix: 5 NEURO
    tool: 6 LANCET
    Unwelcome word from a: 4 OOPS
Surgeon General
    Former: 4 KOOP 6 ELDERS
    Former ~ C. Everett: 4 KOOP
    under Reagan: 4 KOOP
Surgery
    Before: 5 PREOP
    Do eye: 4 LASE
    Eye ~ procedure: 5 LASIK
    Fat-removing: 4 LIPO
    Get ready for: 4 PREP
    It may require: 4 TREE

Kind of: 4 ORAL 5 LASER
        9 OPENHEART
    reminder: 4 SCAR
    sites: 3 ORS
    souvenir: 4 SCAR
Surgical
    beam: 5 LASER
    dressing: 5 GAUZE
    glove material: 5 LATEX
    instrument: 6 LANCET
    Modern ~ tool: 5 LASER
    opening: 5 NEURO
    probe: 6 STYLET
    tube: 5 STENT
    Use a ~ beam: 4 LASE
Suribachi
    ~, et al.: 3 MTS
Suriname
    neighbor: 6 GUYANA
    region: 6 GUIANA
Surly: 5 GRUFF 6 ORNERY
    sort: 3 CUR 5 CHURL
Surmise: 5 INFER
Surmounting: 4 ATOP
Surname
    Common: 5 SMITH
    Fictional ~ of 1847: 4 EYRE
    French ~ start: 3 DES
    Italian noble: 4 ESTE
    Marionette: 5 DOODY
    Number One Son's: 4 CHAN
    O.K. Corral: 4 EARP
    Singing brothers': 4 AMES
    Steinbeck: 4 JOAD
    Tara: 5 OHARA
Surnames
    Abbr. before multiple: 6 MESSRS
Surpass: 3 TOP 5 EXCEL ONEUP
        OUTDO UPEND 7 ECLIPSE
        OVERTOP
Surplus: 4 GLUT
Surprise
    attack: 4 RAID
    By: 5 ABACK 8 UNAWARES
    Cry of: 3 AHA GEE HEY **OHO**
        4 YIPE 5 WOWIE
    from a lamp: 5 GENIE
    greatly: 4 STUN
    Grunt of: 3 HUH

hit: 7 SLEEPER
Show: 4 GASP 5 REACT
Sounds of: 3 EHS OHS 5 GASPS
Sports: 5 UPSET
Student: 4 QUIZ
Surprised
Cry of ~ disgust: 3 ACK
Obviously: 5 AGAPE
"Surprised by Joy"
autobiographer: 7 CSLEWIS
Surprisingly: 6 NOLESS
Surreal
suffix: 3 ISM
Surrealism
pioneer: 5 ERNST
Surrealist
German: 5 ERNST
Mustachioed: 4 DALI
Some ~ works: 5 DALIS MIROS
Spanish: 4 MIRO
~ Jean: 3 ARP
~ Joan: 4 MIRO
~ Max: 5 **ERNST**
~ Salvador: 4 **DALI**
Surrender: 4 CEDE
Cry of: 5 IQUIT UNCLE
Formally: 4 CEDE
Word of: 5 UNCLE
Surreptitious: 3 SLY
look: 4 PEEK
summons: 4 PSST
Surrey
town: 5 EPSOM
Surrogate
Child in a 1980s ~ case: 5 BABYM
Surround: 4 GIRD 5 BATHE
HEMIN 6 ENFOLD
ENWRAP 7 BESIEGE
ENCLOSE
snugly: 5 EMBED
with an aura: 6 ENHALO
Surrounded: 4 GIRT 5 BESET
by: 4 **AMID** 5 AMONG 6 AMIDST
7 AMONGST
~, poetically: 6 ENGIRT
Surrounder
Lagoon: 5 ATOLL
Pupil: 4 IRIS 6 AREOLA
San Marino: 5 ITALY

Shower: 4 TILE
Surrounding
Completely: 7 AMBIENT
glow: 4 AURA
light: 4 HALO
Surroundings: 6 MILIEU
Surveil: 5 SPYON
Survey: 4 POLL
choice: 3 YES 4 MALE 5 OTHER
6 FEMALE
no.: 3 PCT
Unscientific: 8 SPOTTEST
~, for short: 5 RECON
Surveyor
assistant: 6 RODMAN
calculation: 4 AREA
map: 4 **PLAT**
support: 6 TRIPOD
unit: 4 ACRE
Survive: 4 LAST 5 GETBY
7 OUTLIVE
Surviving
trace: 5 RELIC
Survivor
concern: 11 ESTATETAXES
Flood: 4 NOAH
Lions' den: 6 DANIEL
Sodom: 3 LOT
"Survivor"
group: 5 TRIBE
network: 3 CBS
Susan
Actress: 3 **DEY** 5 ANTON
Author: 6 ISAACS
Emmy role for: 5 ERICA
Essayist: 6 SONTAG
Lazy: 4 TRAY
of soaps: 5 LUCCI
Susceptible
Not: 6 IMMUNE
Sushi
bar staple: 8 SOYSAUCE
condiment: 6 WASABI
Drink with: 4 SAKE
fish: 3 **EEL** TAI 4 TUNA
7 ABALONE
ingredient: 4 KELP RICE
item: 3 UNI
land: 5 JAPAN

Like: 3 RAW
Soup with: 4 MISO
supplier: 5 EELER
Tuna belly: 4 TORO
wrap: 7 SEAWEED
Suspect: 5 SENSE
dishonesty: 9 SMELLARAT
story: 5 ALIBI
Suspected
More than: 4 KNEW
"___ suspected!": 3 ASI
Suspects
Like some: 5 USUAL
Suspend: 4 HALT HANG 5 PAUSE
Suspended
ride: 4 TRAM
Suspender
Curtain: 3 ROD
Suspends
One who ~ an action: 6 ABATOR
Suspenseful
ending: 11 CLIFFHANGER
Suspicion: 5 DOUBT
Sneaking: 4 IDEA
"Suspicion"
studio: 3 RKO
Suspicious: 4 WARY 5 FISHY
        LEERY
Be: 9 SMELLARAT
More than ~ of: 4 ONTO
of: 4 ONTO
What ~ folks smell: 4 ARAT
~, as in Hamlet's Denmark:
        6 ROTTEN
Susquehanna
City on the: 7 ONEONTA
Sussex
Info: British cue
school exam: 6 ALEVEL
stoolie: 4 NARK
streetcar: 4 TRAM
sword: 5 SABRE
Sustain: 4 FEED 5 INCUR
Sustenance: 4 FOOD FUEL
        7 ALIMENT
Sutcliffe
Early Beatle: 3 **STU**
Sutherland: 4 DIVA
1971 ~ title role: 5 KLUTE

1974 ~ film: 4 SPYS
Actor: 6 DONALD KIEFER
song: 4 ARIA
"___ Sutra": 4 **KAMA**
Sutton
Golfer: 3 HAL
SUV: 3 UTE
Chevy: 5 TAHOE 6 BLAZER
Suva
land: 4 **FIJI**
Suvari
Actress: 4 MENA
Suzanne
Actress: 6 SOMERS
Singer: 4 VEGA
"Suzanne"
songwriter Leonard: 5 COHEN
Svelte: 4 SLIM THIN TRIM
Sven
Cousin of: 4 LARS
Svgs.
fund: 3 IRA
Swab: 3 MOP TAR 5 MATEY
        6 WETMOP
again: 5 REMOP
Cotton: 4 QTIP
Swabber: 3 MOP
org.: 3 USN
Swabbie: 3 GOB **TAR**
Swaddle: 4 WRAP
Swag: 4 LOOT 5 BOOTY
Swagger: 4 BRAG 5 STRUT
        SWASH 7 BRAVADO
Swahili: 5 BANTU
for "boss": 5 BWANA
for "freedom": 5 UHURA
Swain: 4 BEAU 5 ROMEO WOOER
        6 SUITOR
SWAK
Part of: 4 KISS 6 SEALED
Swallow: 4 DOWN GULP SWIG
        6 ACCEPT INGEST
flat: 4 NEST
It may be hard to: 4 PILL
Prepare to: 4 CHEW
Sea: 4 **TERN**
up: 6 ENGULF
Swallowed: 3 ATE
one's pride: 7 ATEDIRT

Swallower
Jonah's: 5 WHALE
Swallow-tailed
bird: 4 KITE
Swami: 4 GURU SAGE SEER
5 HINDU
Swamp: 3 BOG FEN 4 MIRE
5 DROWN MARSH
6 ENGULF MORASS
critter: 4 CROC 5 GATOR
goo: 4 OOZE
plant: 4 REED 5 SEDGE
Stalk in the: 4 REED
thing: 4 CROC PEAT REED
5 GATOR
Swampland
swindle: 5 BUNCO
Swamplike: 4 MIRY
"Swamp Thing"
director Craven: 3 WES
Swampy
ground: 3 BOG 4 MIRE
stretch: 5 SWALE
Swan
City on the: 5 PERTH
lady: 4 LEDA
Male: 3 COB
song: 3 END
Star in the ~ constellation:
5 DENEB
Young: 6 CYGNET
Swank: 4 CHIC 5 RITZY 6 CLASSY
7 ELEGANT
Husband of: 4 LOWE
Swanky: 4 POSH
"Swan Lake"
heroine: 6 ODETTE
role: 5 ODILE
skirt: 4 **TUTU**
swan: 5 ODILE
Swann
of football: 4 LYNN
"Swann's Way"
author: 6 PROUST
Swansea
locale: 5 WALES
Swanson
film: 15 SUNSETBOULEVARD
Swap: 5 **TRADE** 6 BARTER

Swarm: 3 MOB 4 HOST **TEEM**
5 HORDE
Swarming: 5 ALIVE
Swarms
Like some: 5 APIAN
Swarthy: 4 DARK
Swashbuckler
Flynn: 5 **ERROL**
weapon: 5 SABER SWORD
Swath
producer: 6 SCYTHE
SWAT team
member: 6 SNIPER
Sway: 4 REEL ROLL TILT
6 CAREEN TOTTER
7 IMPRESS
Hold: 4 **RULE** 5 REIGN
Swayback
woe: 3 SAG
Swayze
1987 ~ film: 12 DIRTYDANCING
1990 ~ film: 5 GHOST
Swe.
neighbor: 3 NOR
Swear: 4 AVER **AVOW** 6 ATTEST
by, with "on": 4 RELY
word: 4 OATH
words: 3 **IDO**
Swearing-in: 4 OATH
words: 3 IDO 4 OATH
Swear ___ stack of Bibles: 3 ONA
Sweat
Bit of: 4 BEAD
bullets: 4 FRET STEW
Don't ~ it: 8 RESTEASY
drop: 4 BEAD
it: 4 FRET
It might make you: 3 SPA
it out: 6 ENDURE
No: 4 EASY
Place to ~ it out: 5 SAUNA
shop: 3 SPA
spot: 4 PORE 5 SAUNA
Sweatband
spot: 5 WRIST
Sweater: 3 TOP 4 KNIT PORE
eater: 4 MOTH
Hole in a: 4 PORE
Kind of: 5 VNECK 6 PULLON

RAGLAN 8 PULLOVER
10 TURTLENECK
letter: 3 ETA RHO VEE 4 ZETA
    5 THETA
Make a: 4 KNIT
material: 6 ANGORA MOHAIR
problem: 4 SNAG
size: 5 LARGE
style: 5 VNECK
synthetic: 5 ORLON
Work up a: 4 KNIT
"Sweater Girl"
~ Turner: 4 LANA
Sweaters
Pair of ~ worn together:
    7 TWINSET
Sweatshirt
part: 4 HOOD
Swed.
neighbor: 3 NOR 4 NORW
Sweden
Airline to: 3 SAS
capital: 3 ESS
Coin of: 5 KRONA
Furniture store from: 4 IKEA
Import from: 4 SAAB
Swedish
auto: 4 **SAAB**
chain: 4 IKEA
city: 7 UPPSALA
diva Jenny: 4 LIND
flier: 3 SAS
Flower named for a ~ botanist:
    6 DAHLIA
Former ~ P.M. Palme: 4 OLOF
import: 4 SAAB 5 VOLVO
money: 5 KRONA
quartet: 4 ABBA
"Swedish Nightingale, The":
    4 LIND
"Sweeney ___": 4 TODD
Sweeney, Julia
film: 6 ITSPAT
"Sweeney Todd"
actor Cariou: 3 LEN
prop: 5 RAZOR
Sweep: 3 OAR 5 CLEAN GAMUT
    7 EXPANSE
Like a chimney: 5 SOOTY

target: 4 SOOT
under the rug: 4 HIDE
Sweeper: 5 BROOM
accessory: 7 DUSTPAN
Sweeping: 3 BIG 4 EPIC VAST
    5 BROAD 7 OVERALL
cut: 5 SLASH
shot: 3 PAN
story: 4 EPIC
Sweepings
Salon: 4 HAIR
Sweepstakes
hopeful: 7 ENTRANT
Mailed, as a ~ entry: 6 SENTIN
Sweet: 4 DEAR KIND
Be ~ on: 5 ADORE
cherry: 4 BING
drink: 4 COLA MEAD 5 JULEP
    6 NECTAR
ending: 3 OSE
flower: 5 AFTON
It may be: 5 TOOTH
Least: 6 DRIEST
liqueur: 5 CREME
    8 ANISETTE
Not: 3 DRY SEC
nothing: 10 ENDEARMENT
potato: 3 **YAM** 7 OCARINA
prefix: 4 SEMI
sandwich: 4 **OREO**
Short and: 5 TERSE
spread: 5 ICING
stuff: 5 SUGAR 6 NECTAR
    7 TREACLE
suffix: 3 OSE
They can be: 4 PEAS
treat: 3 ICE 4 FLAN 5 FUDGE
    7 DESSERT
Whisper ~ nothings: 3 **COO**
Whisper ~ nothings to: 3 WOO
wine: 4 PORT 6 MALAGA
    7 MARSALA 8 MUSCATEL
"Sweet"
girl of song: 7 ADELINE
herb: 5 BASIL
stream of poetry: 5 AFTON
"Sweet!": 3 RAD 5 NEATO
Sweet 16
org.: 4 NCAA

"Sweet and Lowdown"
  actress Thurman: 3 UMA
"Sweet as apple cider"
  girl: 3 IDA
Sweetbrier: 8 WILDROSE
"Sweet Dreams"
  Singer profiled in: 5 CLINE
Sweeten: 5 SUGAR
  the pot: 5 RAISE
Sweetener
  brand: 5 EQUAL
  Request: 6 PLEASE
  Soil: 4 LIME
"Sweetest Taboo, The"
  singer: 4 SADE
Sweetheart: 4 BABY BEAU DEAR
      LASS LOVE 5 DEARY
      FLAME HONEY 6 DEARIE
      8 TRUELOVE
"Sweetheart of Sigma ___, The":
  3 CHI
"Sweet Home ___": 7 ALABAMA
"Sweet Home Alabama"
  actress Witherspoon: 5 REESE
Sweetie: 3 HON 4 DEAR DOLL
      LAMB 5 ANGEL FLAME
      SUGAR TOOTS
      8 SUGARPIE
  pie: 3 HON 4 DEAR DOLL LOVE
      5 CUTEY CUTIE HONEY
      TOOTS
"Sweet Liberty"
  director/star: 4 ALDA
"Sweet Love"
  singer Anita: 5 BAKER
Sweetly
  (Italian): 5 DOLCE
Sweetness: 5 SAPOR
  Overwhelm with: 4 CLOY
Sweet 'N Low
  rival: 5 EQUAL
Sweet-sounding: 6 DULCET
Sweet-talk: 4 COAX
Sweetums: 3 HON 5 TOOTS
Swell: 3 FOP 4 NICE RISE WAVE
      5 BLOAT NEATO SUPER
      7 BREAKER ENLARGE
  Cause to: 5 BLOAT
  place: 3 **SEA** 5 OCEAN

"Swell!": 5 NEATO
Swelled
  head: 3 **EGO**
Swellhead: 7 EGOTIST
  indulgence: 7 EGOTRIP
  problem: 3 EGO
Swelling
  Eyelid: 4 STYE
  Plant: 5 **EDEMA**
  reducer: 3 ICE 6 ICEBAG
  Where ~ occurs: 3 SEA
Swelter: 3 FRY 4 BOIL 5 BROIL
      ROAST
Sweltering: 3 HOT
Swenson
  Actress: 4 **INGA**
Swerve: 4 VEER
  off course: 3 YAW
Swift: 4 FAST 5 RAPID 6 SPEEDY
      8 SATIRIST
  bird: 3 EMU
  boat: 4 PROA
  forte: 5 IRONY
  horse: 4 ARAB 9 HOUYHNHNM
  Not too: 5 DENSE 7 SLOWISH
  piece: 6 SATIRE
  vehicle: 6 SATIRE
  watercraft: 9 HYDROFOIL
  work: 5 ESSAY 6 SATIRE
Swift, Jonathan: 8 SATIRIST
  1729 ~ pamphlet:
      15 AMODESTPROPOSAL
  piece: 6 SATIRE
Swiftly: 5 APACE
  Move: 4 DART DASH TEAR
Swiftness: 5 HASTE
Swifty
  Hollywood agent: 5 LAZAR
Swig
  Big: 4 BELT CHUG
Swill: 4 SLOP
Swim
  alternative: 4 SINK
  competition: 4 MEET
  Quick: 3 **DIP**
  Sink or: 4 VERB
Swimmer
  1920s Olympics ~: 6 EDERLE
  Aquarium: 5 TETRA

assignment: 4 LANE
Channel ~ Gertrude: 6 **EDERLE**
concern: 5 CRAMP
count: 3 LAP
Electric: 3 **EEL**
Furry: 5 OTTER
Lab: 5 AMEBA
Long-jawed: 3 GAR
Long-nosed: 4 PIKE
Park: 4 SWAN
Playful: 5 OTTER
Pond: 4 TEAL
regimen: 4 LAPS
Slippery: 3 **EEL**
~ Janet: 5 EVANS
~ Kristin: 4 OTTO
~ Mark: 5 SPITZ
~ Matt: 6 BIONDI
~ Thorpe: 3 IAN
Swimmers
Leggy: 6 OCTOPI
One-celled: 7 AMOEBAE
Swimming: 6 NATANT
competition: 4 MEET
Like some ~ strokes:
    7 OVERARM
site: 4 HOLE LAKE POND POOL
Swimming pool
shade: 4 AQUA
site: 4 YMCA 5 MOTEL
sound: 6 SPLASH
tester: 3 TOE
Swimsuit
brand: 6 SPEEDO
part: 3 **BRA**
Revealing: 5 THONG
Swimwear
Big name in: 6 SPEEDO
Minimal: 5 THONG
Swindle: 3 CON GYP RIP ROB
    4 BILK BURN CLIP DOIN
    HOSE ROOK **SCAM**
    5 BUNKO CHEAT COZEN
    GOUGE GRIFT MULCT
    6 CHISEL CONJOB
    EUCHRE FLEECE RIPOFF
    7 CONGAME
    9 SHELLGAME
Swindled: 5 STUNG

Swindler: 5 CHEAT CROOK
    SHARP THIEF
    6 CONMAN
~, slangily: 5 GANEF
Swine: 4 BOAR
food: 4 SLOP
She turned men into: 5 CIRCE
spot: 3 STY
Swing: 3 BAT
and others: 4 ERAS
around: 4 **SLUE**
a sickle: 4 REAP
Couples may ~ here: 3 TEE
First name in: 5 ARTIE
in a ring: 3 BOX
Kind of: 4 MOOD
Makeshift: 4 TIRE
music: 4 JIVE
One way to: 3 FRO
One who knows how to:
    7 GOLFPRO
Ready to: 5 ATBAT
site: 3 TEE
wildly: 5 FLAIL
Swinger: 6 HEPCAT
club: 3 BAT
joint: 5 HINGE
Jungle: 3 APE
Sumatra: 5 ORANG
Swingers
org.: 3 PGA
Swinging: 3 HIP
Word after: 4 DOOR
"Swing Time"
star: 7 ASTAIRE
Swipe: 3 COP 4 GLOM 5 STEAL
Swiped: 4 TOOK 5 STOLE TAKEN
    6 STOLEN
Swirl: 4 **EDDY**
Swiss
A ~ army knife has many:
    4 USES
abstractionist Paul: 4 **KLEE**
canton: 3 **URI** 4 BERN
    6 GENEVA
capital: 4 BERN 5 BERNE
    FRANC
chard: 4 BEET
city: 5 BASEL BERNE

cottage: 6 CHALET
hero: 4 TELL
It has ~ banks: 4 **AARE**
mathematician: 5 **EULER**
miss: 5 **HEIDI**
Of ~ peaks: 6 ALPINE
painter Paul: 4 **KLEE**
peak: 3 ALP
river: 3 AAR 4 AARE
skyline: 3 ALP
state: 6 CANTON
stream: 3 AAR
tourist center: 7 LUCERNE
vendor: 4 DELI
watch: 5 OMEGA
Swiss cheese: 7 GRUYERE
feature: 4 HOLE
hole: 3 EYE
Like: 5 HOLEY
"Swiss Family Robinson"
author Johann: 4 WYSS
Swit
Actress: 7 LORETTA
costar: 4 ALDA
Switch: 4 SWAP 9 TRANSPOSE
Bait and: 6 TACTIC
ending: 4 **EROO**
handles: 6 RENAME
Kind of: 5 ONOFF 6 DIMMER
material: 5 BIRCH
partner: 4 BAIT
position: 3 OFF
positions: 3 **ONS** 4 OFFS
Radio: 4 AMFM
Railroad: 5 SHUNT
suffix: 4 **EROO**
words: 5 ONOFF
Switchback
curve: 3 ESS
Switchblade: 4 SHIV
Switz.
neighbor: 3 AUS
Where ~ is: 3 EUR
Switzerland
canton: 3 URI
Capital of: 3 ESS 4 BERN
It has banks in: 4 AARE
loc.: 3 EUR
river: 4 AARE

Swiveling
joint: 3 HIP
Swizzle: 4 **STIR**
stick: 7 STIRRER
Use a ~ stick: 4 **STIR**
Swoboda
of baseball: 3 RON
Swoon: 5 FAINT
cause: 4 IDOL
Swoop: 6 POUNCE
Swoopes
gp.: 4 WNBA
Swoosh
company: 4 NIKE
Nike's: 4 LOGO
Swoosie
Tony winner: 5 KURTZ
Sword
beater: 3 PEN
Blunted: 4 **EPEE**
Cavalry: 5 SABER
Curved: 5 SABER 8 SCIMITAR
Fencing: 4 **EPEE** 5 SABER
6 RAPIER
fight: 4 DUEL
handle: 4 HAFT **HILT**
of Damocles: 5 PERIL
Olympic: 4 EPEE
Put a ~ away: 7 SHEATHE
Slender: 6 RAPIER
with a guarded tip: 4 EPEE
Swordfight
reminder: 4 SCAR
Swordplay
Japanese: 5 KENDO
Swords
Beat ~ into plowshares:
5 UNARM
Crossing: 5 ATWAR
Like: 5 EDGED
Sword-shaped
Plant with ~ leaves: 4 IXIA
5 YUCCA 8 GLADIOLA
Swordsman: 5 BLADE
Dumas': 5 ATHOS
Masked: 5 ZORRO
ploy: 5 LUNGE
Swore: 6 CUSSED
by: 8 RELIEDON

Sworn: 6 AVOWED
  statement: 3 VOW 4 OATH
  They may be: 7 ENEMIES
Sycophant: 5 TOADY 6 LACKEY
      YESMAN
  response: 3 YES
Sydney
  Astrologer: 5 **OMARR**
  band: 4 ACDC
  salutation: 4 GDAY
  st.: 3 NSW
Sylphlike: 6 SVELTE
Sylvan: 5 WOODY
  deity: 5 SATYR
Sylvania
  unit: 4 WATT
Sylvester
  costar: 5 TALIA
  problem letters: 5 ESSES
  Speak like: 4 LISP
  ~, to Tweety: 3 TAT
Sylvia
  Singer: 4 SYMS
Sylvius
  Aqueduct of: 4 ITER
Symbol: 4 ICON 5 TOKEN
      6 EMBLEM
  of Americanism: 8 APPLEPIE
  of authority: 6 MANTLE
  of craziness: 4 LOON
  of easiness: 3 ABC PIE
  of elusiveness: 3 EEL
  of freshness: 5 DAISY
  of goodness: 4 HALO
  of grace: 4 SWAN
  of happiness: 4 CLAM
  of holiness: 4 HALO
  of industry: 3 ANT
  of life: 4 ANKH
  of love: 7 REDROSE
  of meanness: 11 JUNKYARDDOG
  of might: 3 OAK
  of redness: 4 BEET
  of resistance: 5 OMEGA
  of royalty: 3 ORB
  of slowness: 5 SNAIL
  of stability: 8 EVENKEEL
  of strength: 3 **OAK** 5 STEEL
  of stubbornness: 4 MULE

Symmetry
  Kind of: 5 **AXIAL** 6 RADIAL
Sympathetic: 4 KIND 5 HUMAN
      6 CARING
  attention: 3 EAR
  Make: 6 ENDEAR
  sounds: 3 AWS
Sympathy
  Feel ~ (for): 4 ACHE
  partner: 3 TEA
  Words of: 5 ICARE
Symphonic
  poem creator: 5 LISZT
"Symphonie espagnole"
  composer Édouard: 4 LALO
"Symphonie fantastique"
  composer: 7 BERLIOZ
Symphony: 4 OPUS
  member: 4 OBOE
  nickname: 6 EROICA
  performers (abbr.): 4 ORCH
"Symphony ___" (Bizet): 3 INC
"Symphony of a Thousand"
  composer: 6 MAHLER
"Symposium"
  author: 5 PLATO
Symptom: 4 SIGN
  suffix: 4 ATIC
Synagogue: 4 SHUL
  chest: 3 ARK
  leader: 5 RABBI
  scroll: 4 TORA 5 **TORAH**
  singer: 6 CANTOR
Sync
  Get in ~ again: 6 RETUNE
  In: 5 ASONE
Synchronous: 7 INPHASE
Syncopated
  music: 3 RAG
Syndicate: 3 MOB 6 CARTEL
  boss: 4 CAPO
  head: 3 DON
Syndicated
  astrologer: 5 OMARR
  deejay: 4 IMUS
Synfuel
  source: 5 SHALE
Syngman
  of Korea: 4 RHEE

Synonym
 man: 5 ROGET
Synonymist
 ~ Peter: 5 ROGET
Syntax
 Analyze the ~ of: 5 PARSE
Synthesizer
 inventor: 4 MOOG
 Speech: 7 VOCODER
 ___ synthesizer: 4 MOOG
Synthetic: 4 FAUX MADE
  6 ERSATZ 7 MANMADE
  8 TESTTUBE
 fabric: 5 ORLON
 fiber: 5 ARNEL NYLON **ORLON**
  RAYON 7 ACETATE
 rubber component: 7 STYRENE
 Silky: 5 RAYON
Syr.
 and Eg., once: 3 UAR
 neighbor: 3 **ISR** LEB
Syracuse
 athletes: 9 ORANGEMEN
 City near: 5 UTICA
 College in: 7 LEMOYNE
 Lake near: 6 ONEIDA
Syria
 and Egypt, once: 3 UAR

 Bashar of: 5 ASSAD
 Capital of ancient: 7 ANTIOCH
 Great Mosque site of: 6 ALEPPO
Syrian: 4 ARAB
 city: 4 HAMA 6 ALEPPO
 Early: 7 HITTITE
 leader: 5 **ASSAD**
Syringe: 4 HYPO
 amt.: 3 CCS
Syrup
 brand: 4 KARO
 flavor: 5 MAPLE
 Item with: 5 CREPE
 Medicinal: 6 IPECAC
 source: 3 SAP 4 CORN 5 MAPLE
System: 6 METHOD
 Belief: 3 ISM
 Exercise: 4 YOGA 5 TAEBO
 Kind of: 5 CASTE MERIT SOLAR
 Learning: 4 ROTE
 Operating: 4 UNIX 5 MSDOS
 Power: 4 GRID
 prefix: 3 **ECO**
 Sound: 4 HIFI 6 **STEREO**
 Sub: 5 SONAR
 Support: 3 BRA 7 SHORING
 Value: 5 ETHIC
Systematize: 4 SORT 6 CODIFY

Tt

T: 5 SHIRT
Greek: 3 TAU
Morse: 4 DASH
or F: 3 ANS
T. ___: 3 REX
___ T: 3 TOA
Tab: 4 BILL COLA 8 DIETCOLA
    DIETSODA
Accumulate a: 5 RUNUP
competitor: 8 DIETCOKE
Have a: 3 OWE
Opening for a: 4 SLOT
Pick up the: 3 PAY 5 **TREAT**
Run a: 3 OWE
Settle a: 5 PAYUP
Tabasco
Info: Spanish cue
quality: 4 ZEST
Tabby: 3 CAT
cry: 4 MEOW
mate: 3 TOM
tempter: 6 CATNIP
treater: 3 VET
Word to a: 4 SCAT
Table: 5 DEFER
Bar on the: 4 OLEO
Buffet ~ item: 3 URN 6 STERNO
Chip on the: 4 ANTE
Clear the: 3 BUS
Coffee ~ item: 7 ARTBOOK
Dinner: 4 MENU
extender: 4 LEAF
Find another ~ for: 6 RESEAT
Have a ~ for one: 8 EATALONE
insert: 4 LEAF
It's found in a: 7 ELEMENT
It's shaken at the: 4 SALT
Like ~ sugar: 8 GRANULAR
linen: 6 NAPERY
linen fabric: 6 DAMASK
No longer at the: 5 EATEN
Occupy a: 5 SITAT
part: 3 LEG

Point at the: 4 TINE
protector: 6 TRIVET
    8 PLACEMAT
salt: 4 NACL 8 CHLORIDE
scrap: 3 **ORT**
spread: 4 OLEO
staple: 4 SALT
support: 3 LEG
tennis need: 6 PADDLE
Three-legged ornamental:
    6 TEAPOY
Under the: 3 LIT
wine: 4 ROSE
Tablecloth
material: 4 LACE 5 LINEN
Tablecloths
and such: 6 NAPERY
Table d'___: 4 **HOTE**
Table-hop: 3 MIX
Tableland: 4 **MESA** 7 PLATEAU
Tables
Clear: 3 BUS
How times ~ are learned:
    6 BYROTE
Like some: 6 NESTED
Workplaces with: 3 ORS
Tablet: 3 PAD 4 DOSE PILL
holder: 3 ARK
Writing: 3 PAD
Tabletop
farm animals: 4 ANTS
Tablets: 4 MEDS
He took two: 5 MOSES
Holder of two: 3 ARK
Two: 4 DOSE
Tabloid: 3 RAG
abductor: 5 ALIEN
couple: 4 ITEM
fliers: 3 ETS
fodder: 4 DIRT
Like ~ stories: 5 LURID
monster: 6 NESSIE
staffer: 6 EDITOR

subject: 3 UFO
talk: 4 DIRT
target: 5 CELEB
tidbit: 4 ITEM
topic: 3 UFO
twosome: 4 **ITEM**
Taboo: 3 BAN 4 **NONO**
   8 VERBOTEN
Taboos: 5 DONTS
Tabouli
bread: 4 PITA
Tabriz
country: 4 IRAN
resident: 5 **IRANI**
Tabula ___ : 4 **RASA**
"___ Tac Dough": 3 TIC
Tach
reading: 3 **RPM** 4 REVS
Tachometer
abbr.: 3 RPM
Tacit: 6 UNSAID 8 UNSPOKEN
approval: 3 NOD
Taciturn: 11 TIGHTLIPPED
Tack
Like a: 5 SHARP
Sharp as a: 4 KEEN 5 ACUTE
   SMART 6 ASTUTE
Tacked
on: 5 ADDED
Tackle: 3 TRY 4 GEAR 7 ATTEMPT
box item: 4 **LURE** 5 SNELL
   6 SCALER
Get up after a: 6 UNPILE
hard: 4 NAIL
teammate: 3 END
Tacks
Spots for: 4 TIES
Tacky: 5 SHARP
Taco
alternative: 7 TOSTADA
topper: 5 SALSA
Taconite: 7 IRONORE
Tact
suffix: 3 ILE
Tactful
one: 8 DIPLOMAT
Tactfully
Remove: 7 EASEOUT
Tactic: 4 PLOY RUSE

Basketball: 5 PRESS
   9 FASTBREAK
Campaign: 5 SMEAR
Deceptive: 4 RUSE
Economic warfare: 7 EMBARGO
Evasive: 6 ENDRUN
Ring: 3 JAB
Tennis: 3 LOB
Wheedler: 5 GUILE
Tactical
station: 3 OPS
Tactile
Like ~ hair: 7 SENSORY
Tactless: 5 BLUNT
   10 INDELICATE
Tad: 3 KID TOT 4 IOTA MITE
"Ta-da!": 5 THERE VOILA
Tadpole
home: 4 POND
Tadzhik
~, once (abbr.): 3 SSR
TAE
Part of: 4 ALVA
Tae ___ do: 4 KWON
___ Tafari (Haile Selassie):
   3 **RAS**
Taffy
Like: 5 CHEWY
Taft
alma mater: 4 YALE
birth state: 4 OHIO
Tag: 5 LABEL
abbr.: 3 LGE
along: 4 COME
disclaimer: 4 ASIS
Dog ~ datum: 5 OWNER
Gift ~ word: 4 FROM
info: 4 SIZE
line: 4 ASIS 5 NOTIT PRICE
Price: 4 COST
pursuers: 3 ITS
Red ~ event: 4 SALE
Sale: 4 ASIS
Sale ~ (abbr.): 3 IRR
Second sequel: 3 III
___ tag: 5 PHONE
"___ Tag!": 5 GUTEN
Tagalong
cry: 5 METOO

Tagging
 along: **5** INTOW
Tags: 3 IDS
 Switch: **6** RENAME
Tagus
 City on the: **6** LISBON
Tahini
 base: **6** SESAME
Tahiti: 3 ILE
 Island near: **8** BORABORA
Tahitian
 Language akin to: **5** MAORI
 port: **7** PAPEETE
Tahoe: 4 LAKE
 City near: **4** RENO
 topper: **6** SKICAP
___ tai: 3 MAI
Tail: 3 DOG **5** TRAIL
   6 SHADOW
 Info: Suffix cue
 Buck: **4** AROO
 Chick: **4** ADEE
 Dino: **4** SAUR
 Dog with a curled: **3** PUG
  5 AKITA
 end: **4** REAR
 Gator: **3** ADE
 Hippo: **5** DROME
 Human: **3** OID
 Meteor: **3** ITE
 Move one's: **3** WAG
 off: **5** ABATE
 Ox: **3** IDE
 Pig: **3** LET
 prefix: **3** URO
 Rabbit: **4** SCUT
 Rat: **4** ATAT
 Rocket: **3** EER
 Serpent: **3** INE
 Toward the: **3** AFT
 Toy with a: **4** KITE
 Turn: **3** RUN **4** FLEE
Tailbone: 6 COCCYX
Tailless
 amphibian: **4** TOAD
 cat: **4** MANX
 primate: **3** APE
 rodent: **4** PACA
 simian: **3** APE

Taillike: 6 CAUDAL
Tailor: 3 SEW **5** ADAPT
  6 MENDER SEAMER
  7 ALTERER
 concern: **3** FIT HEM
 Do a ~ job: **3** HEM SEW
 line: **4** SEAM
 measurement: **6** INSEAM
 of yore: **6** SARTOR
 tool: **6** SHEARS
  11 TAPEMEASURE
Tails
 It goes with: **6** TOPHAT
Tailward: 3 AFT
Taina
 Dancer: **3 ELG**
Taint: 3 MAR **7** CORRUPT
Tainted
 Least: **6** PUREST
Taipei
 Where ~ is: **6** TAIWAN
Taiwan
 capital: **6** TAIPEI
 is in it: **8** CHINASEA
 ~, formerly: **7** FORMOSA
Taiwanese: 5 ASIAN
Taj ___ : 5 MAHAL
Taj Mahal
 city: **4 AGRA**
 site: **4 AGRA**
Take: 3 NAB **4** GATE GRAB
  5 CHEAT
 after: **7** EMULATE
 apart: **4** UNDO
 as a given: **5** POSIT
 as one's own: **5 ADOPT**
 away: **4** LESS **6** DEDUCT
  REMOVE **7** DETRACT
 back: **4** UNDO **5** UNSAY
  6 RECANT
 by force: **5** SEIZE USURP
  WREST
 Can't: **5** ABHOR
 care of: **4** TEND **5 SEETO**
  6 HANDLE TENDTO
  8 SEEAFTER
 cover: **4** HIDE
 credit: **3** OWE
 Did a double: **6** RESHOT

Didn't ~ part, with "out":
    5 OPTED
Do a double: 5 REACT
effect: 5 INURE SETIN
exception: 5 DEMUR
five: 4 **REST** 5 RELAX
Get ready to ~ off: 4 TAXI
Give and: 4 SWAP 5 TRADE
Give or: 4 ORSO 5 ABOUT
home: 3 **NET**
in: 3 EAT SEE 4 EARN 5 ADOPT
    ALTER
It doesn't ~ much: 4 TREY
it easy: 4 LOLL REST
most of: 3 HOG
Not ~ off: 4 STAY
off: 3 LAM 4 SHED SOAR
    6 DEPART
on: 4 HIRE 5 ADOPT
out: 4 DATE DELE
over: 5 USURP
Put in or ~ out: 4 EDIT
Some people can't ~ them:
    5 HINTS
steps: 3 ACT 4 PACE
turns: 6 ROTATE
~, as advice: 5 ACTON
Take-___: 5 ALONG
"Take ___"
    (host's request): 5 ASEAT
    (Madonna song): 4 ABOW
"Take ___!": 4 THAT
"Take a Chance on Me"
    group: 4 ABBA
Take a crack ___: 4 ATIT
"Take a hike!": 5 SCRAM
"Take a load off!": 3 SIT
"... ___ take arms against ...":
    4 ORTO
Take-away
    game: 3 NIM
Takeback
    Bank: 4 **REPO**
"Take care of that!":
    7 SEETOIT
Take down ___: 4 APEG
Take ___ down memory lane:
    5 ATRIP
Take ___ for the worse: 5 ATURN

"Take ___ from me": 4 **ATIP**
Take-home: 3 NET 6 NETPAY
Takei, George
    role: 4 SULU
"Take it easy!": 5 RELAX
    6 NOWNOW
"Take it or leave it": 4 ASIS
"Take ___ leave it!": 4 ITOR
"Take my wife, please!"
    speaker Youngman: 5 HENNY
Taken: 3 HAD 5 INUSE
    alone: 5 PERSE
    by force, once: 4 REFT
    How some are: 5 ABACK
    in: 3 HAD 4 SEEN
    Not ~ in by: 4 ONTO
    One ~ in: 7 ADOPTEE
Taken ___: 5 ABACK
Takeoff: 5 SPOOF 6 PARODY
    SATIRE
    approx.: 3 ETD
    Clear for: 5 DEICE
    Do a ~ on: 3 APE
    Prepare for: 4 TAXI
"Take one!": 4 HERE
Takeout
    Chinese ~ freebie: 4 RICE
    choice: 7 CHINESE
    For: 4 TOGO
    Get: 5 EATIN
    order: 4 **DELE**
Takeover
    Corp.: 3 LBO
    Sudden: 4 COUP
"___ takers?": 3 **ANY**
Takes
    Having what it: 4 ABLE
    It ~ two: 4 TREY
    off: 4 GOES
    too much: 3 ODS
"Take ___, She's Mine": 3 HER
Take ___ stride: 4 ITIN
"Take that!": 7 SOTHERE
"Take this!": 4 **HERE**
"Take ___ Train": 4 THEA
"Take ___ your leader": 4 METO
"Take your pick": 3 ANY
    8 EITHEROR
"Take your time!": 6 NORUSH

Taking
after: 3 ALA
For the: 4 FREE
liberty: 6 ASHORE
One ~ off: 4 APER
Taking-off
place: 3 SPA
"Takin' ___ the Streets": 4 ITTO
Talbot
Actress: 4 NITA
Talcum
and walcum rhymer: 4 NASH
target: 4 RASH
Tale: 4 YARN 5 STORY
Epic: 4 SAGA
Grand-scale: 4 EPIC
Heroic: 4 EPIC **SAGA**
Moralistic: 5 FABLE
of adventure: 4 GEST 5 GESTE
of woe: 8 SOBSTORY
Old wives': 4 MYTH
starter: 4 ONCE
Tall: 4 **YARN**
teller: 3 POE 4 BARD LIAR
Told, as a: 4 SPUN
Talent: 4 BENT GIFT 5 KNACK
SKILL 8 APTITUDE
Furnish with: 5 ENDOW
Look for: 5 SCOUT
Medium's: 3 ESP
Musical: 3 EAR
Natural: 4 GIFT 5 FLAIR
Special: 5 KNACK
Talented: 3 APT 4 ABLE 5 ADEPT
"Talented Mr. Ripley, The"
actor Jude: 3 LAW
actor Matt: 5 DAMON
"Tale of ___ Saltan, The": 4 TSAR
Tales
Folk ~ and such: 4 LORE
Like some: 4 TALL
Tell: 3 LIE 7 NARRATE
"Tales From the Vienna Woods"
composer: 7 STRAUSS
Tales of ___ : 3 WOE
"... tale told by an ___ ": 5 IDIOT
Talia
Actress: 5 SHIRE
Cousin of: 7 NICOLAS

Taliban
mullah: 4 OMAR
Talisman: 4 MOJO 5 CHARM
6 AMULET FETISH
Egyptian: 6 SCARAB
Talk: 3 GAB 4 CHAT
a blue streak: 4 CUSS 5 RUNON
SWEAR
about: 7 SPEAKOF
amorously: 3 COO
and talk: 3 YAK
Baby: 6 GOOGOO
Back: 3 LIP 4 ECHO GUFF **SASS**
6 STATIC
big: 4 BRAG CROW 5 BOAST
Casual: 4 CHAT
Colorful: 5 SLANG
effusively: 4 GUSH
Empty: 3 GAS 4 WIND
6 HOTAIR
First name in: 4 MERV 5 CONAN
ELLEN LEEZA OPRAH
REGIS RICKI ROSIE
6 MONTEL 7 ARSENIO
Fresh: 4 SASS
incessantly: 3 YAP
Insincere: 4 CANT
It's mostly: 7 AMRADIO
Jazzy: 4 JIVE
Kind of: 3 PEP
King of: 5 LARRY
like crazy: 4 RANT
Like some: 5 SMALL
Loose: 5 SLANG
(over): 4 HASH
Playful: 6 BANTER
Small: 4 CHAT 8 CHITCHAT
Something to ~ about: 5 TOPIC
Sun.: 3 **SER**
too much: 4 BLAB 6 YAMMER
Trade: 5 ARGOT
up: 4 HYPE PRAY TOUT
wildly: 4 RANT
with one's hands: 4 SIGN
Talk ___ : 4 SHOP
"___ talk?": 5 CANWE
Talkathon: 7 GABFEST
Talkative: 4 GLIB 6 CHATTY
bird: 4 MYNA

Talked
  a blue streak: 5 SWORE
  monotonously: 8 DRONEDON
Talker
  Caged: 4 MYNA
  Morning: 4 IMUS
Talking
  bird: 4 MYNA
  bird of poetry: 5 RAVEN
  heads: 5 PANEL
  horse of TV: 4 MRED
  Not: 3 MUM
  point: 3 JAW 5 TOPIC
  She's not: 4 MIME
  Stop: 6 CLAMUP
  trees: 4 ENTS
Talking-___ (lectures): 3 TOS
"Talking in Your Sleep"
  singer: 5 GAYLE
"Talking Straight"
  author: 7 IACOCCA
"Talk Radio"
  actor Baldwin: 4 ALEC
  director Oliver: 5 STONE
Talks
  It: 5 MONEY
Talk show
  group: 5 PANEL
  host Jay: 4 LENO
  host Joe: 4 PYNE
  host Tom: 6 SNYDER
  lineup: 6 GUESTS
  partner: 6 COHOST
  pioneer: 4 PAAR
  Radio ~ participant: 6 CALLER
  Try to reach a: 6 DIALIN
Tall
  and trim: 4 LANK
  bird: 3 EMU
  hat wearer: 4 CHEF
  It may be: 4 TALE
  stalk: 4 REED
  story: 4 TALE YARN
  Straight and: 5 ERECT
  tale: 4 **YARN**
Tallchief, Maria
  tribe: 5 OSAGE
Taller
  Get: 4 GROW

Tallies
  NBA: 3 PTS
Tallinn
  native: 4 ESTH
  resident: 8 ESTONIAN
Tallow
  ingredient: 4 **SUET**
Tally: 3 ADD
  mark: 5 NOTCH
Talmadge
  Actress: 5 NORMA
Talmud
  expert: 5 RABBI
  language: 6 HEBREW
Talmudic
  Noted ~ sage: 6 HILLEL
Talon: 4 **CLAW**
Talus
  area: 5 ANKLE
Tam: 3 CAP
  wearer's tongue: 4 ERSE
Tamale
  topping: 5 SALSA
Tamblyn
  Actor: 4 **RUSS**
"Tamburlaine the Great"
  playwright: 7 MARLOWE
Tamed
  Easily ~ bird: 3 EMU
"Tamerlane"
  dramatist Nicholas: 4 ROWE
"Taming of the Shrew, The"
  setting: 5 PADUA
  shrew: 4 KATE
Tamiroff
  Actor: 4 AKIM
Tammany Hall
  caricaturist: 4 NAST
  leader: 5 TWEED
Tammy
  Actress: 6 GRIMES
  Jim and ~ gp.: 3 PTL
  Singer: 7 WYNETTE
"Tammy"
  singer Debbie: 8 REYNOLDS
Tammy Faye
  former org.: 3 PTL
Tampa
  City south of: 8 SARASOTA

neighbor: 6 STPETE
paper, for short: 4 TRIB
Tampa Bay
player, for short: 3 BUC
Tamper
with: 3 RIG
Tamper-resistant: 6 SEALED
Tan: 3 SUN 4 ECRU
Author: 3 AMY
Black and ~ ingredient: 3 ALE
Light: 4 ECRU
too long: 4 BAKE
Tandem
Go by: 5 PEDAL
Tandoor: 4 OVEN
baked bread: 3 NAN
Tang: 3 NIP 4 ZEST
T'ang dynasty
poet: 4 LIPO
Tangelo
variety: 4 **UGLI**
Tangent: 5 RATIO
Go off on a: 7 DIGRESS
Tangible: 4 REAL 8 CONCRETE
Tangier
Port east of: 4 ORAN
Tangle: 3 MAT WEB 5 MELEE
      RAVEL SKEIN SNARL
      6 ENMESH 7 ENSNARL
Bureaucratic: 7 REDTAPE
Traffic: 5 SNARL
up: 6 ENMESH 7 ENSNARL
Tangled: 5 MESSY
Tanglewood
town: 5 LENOX
Tango: 5 DANCE
move: 3 DIP
number: 3 TWO
Tanguy
Painter: 4 YVES
Tangy
drink: 7 LIMEADE
Most: 7 TARTEST
pie flavor: 5 LEMON
Tank: 3 VAT
Brewery: 3 VAT
filler: 3 **GAS**
Fill the: 5 GASUP
fish: 5 TETRA

Kind of: 6 SEPTIC 7 SHERMAN
Rainwater: 7 CISTERN
suffix: 3 ARD
top: 6 GASCAP TURRET
Tankard
filler: 3 **ALE**
Tanker: 4 SHIP 5 OILER
mishap: 5 SPILL
Tankful: 3 GAS
"Tank Girl"
actress Petty: 4 LORI
rapper: 4 ICET
Tanks: 7 AQUARIA
and such: 5 ARMOR
Tanned
Hardly: 4 PALE
Tanner: 3 SUN
tub: 3 VAT
wares: 5 HIDES
Tanners
catch them: 4 RAYS
Tannery
tool: 3 AWL
Tanning
abbr.: 3 UVA
lotion letters: 3 SPF
Tannish: 4 ECRU
Tantalize: 5 TEMPT
Tantalus
Daughter of: 5 NIOBE
Tantara: 5 BLARE
Tantrum: 3 FIT 4 RAGE
Tanzanian
neighbor: 7 RWANDAN
park: 9 SERENGETI
tongue: 7 SWAHILI
Tao
founder: 6 LAOTSE
~, literally: 6 THEWAY
Taoism
emerging dynasty: 4 CHOU
founder: 6 **LAOTSE**
Taormina
Peak near: 4 ETNA
Taos
material: 5 ADOBE
Tap: 6 DRAWON SPIGOT
Back: 3 PAT
choice: 3 ALE

Green: 4 PUTT
label: 3 HOT
Morse: 3 DIT
output: 3 ALE
problem: 4 DRIP
Type of: 6 SPINAL
"Tap"
Gregory of: 5 HINES
Tape
Audition: 4 **DEMO**
Beat to the: 6 OUTRAN
    7 OUTRACE
Break the: 3 WIN
Clear the: 5 ERASE
deck button: 3 REC 5 EJECT
    ERASE
holder: 8 CASSETTE
Kind of: 4 BETA DEMO DUCT
    5 VIDEO
Linen: 5 INKLE
Not on: 4 LIVE
Obsolete: 10 EIGHTTRACK
over: 5 ERASE
rec. jack: 3 MIC
Ticker: 3 EKG
Trimming: 5 INKLE
Taper: 3 VCR
off: 4 WANE 5 ABATE
Tapered
Cylindrical and: 6 TERETE
end: 5 POINT
feature: 7 STEEPLE
tuck: 4 DART
Tapestry: 5 **ARRAS**
beast: 7 UNICORN
Tapioca
source: 7 CASSAVA
Tapir
feature: 5 SNOUT
Tappan ___ Bridge: 3 ZEE
Tapped
It's: 3 KEG
Taproom
site: 3 INN
"Taps"
instrument: 5 BUGLE
time: 3 TEN
Taqueria
order: 7 TOSTADA

Tar: 3 GOB 4 SALT SWAB
    6 SEADOG SEAMAN
British: 5 LIMEY
tale: 4 YARN
~, in Spanish: 4 BREA
Tara
Butler at: 5 RHETT
family: 6 OHARAS
Scarlett of: 5 **OHARA**
Taradiddle: 3 FIB
Tarantino
Director: 7 QUENTIN
Like most ~ films: 6 RATEDR
Tarantula: 6 SPIDER
"Taras Bulba"
author: 5 GOGOL
extra: 7 COSSACK
Tarbell
Author: 3 **IDA**
Tarboosh
feature: 6 TASSEL
kin: 3 FEZ
Tardiness
excuse: 8 LATEPASS
Tardy: 4 LATE
Somewhat: 6 LATISH
Target: 3 AIM 4 PREY 5 AIMAT
1969 ~: 4 MOON
competitor: 5 KMART SEARS
On: 3 APT
Pick a: 3 AIM
Tell tale: 5 APPLE
Tar Heel State
(abbr.): 4 NCAR
campus: 4 ELON
sch.: 3 UNC
Tariff: 3 FEE
1930 ~ cosponsor: 5 SMOOT
eliminating pact: 5 NAFTA
Tariq
Former Iraqi diplomat: 4 AZIZ
Tarkenton
of football: 4 FRAN
Tarkington
novel: 6 PENROD
Tarmac
Hit the: 4 LAND
Touched the: 4 ALIT
"Tarnation!": 4 EGAD

Tarnish: 3 MAR 4 SOIL 5 STAIN
TAINT
Tarnisher
Reputation: 4 BLOT
Taro
dish: 3 **POI**
root: 4 EDDO
Tarot
reader: 4 SEER
suit: 4 CUPS
Tarpon: 4 FISH
Tarragon: 4 HERB
Tarry: 4 BIDE
Tarsal
prefix: 4 META
Tart: 4 ACID 5 ACERB ACRID
6 ACIDIC
fruit: 4 **SLOE**
taste: 4 TANG
thief: 5 KNAVE
Very: 5 **ACERB**
Tartan
cap: 3 TAM
garb: 4 KILT
pattern: 5 PLAID
sporters: 4 CLAN
"Tartuffe"
author: 7 MOLIERE
Tarzan: 6 APEMAN
actor Ely: 3 RON
actor Ron: 3 ELY
companion: 3 APE
kid: 3 BOY
mate: 4 JANE
transportation: 4 VINE
Task: 3 JOB 5 CHORE STINT
Equal to the: 4 ABLE
Is up to the: 3 CAN
Not up to the: 5 INEPT
Routine: 5 CHORE
Tough: 4 ONUS
Up to the: 4 **ABLE**
Tasman
Explorer: 4 **ABEL**
Tasmania
capital: 6 HOBART
Peak in: 4 OSSA
Tass
country: 4 USSR

Tasseled
topper: 3 **FEZ** TAM
Taste: 3 BIT SIP TRY 5 **SENSE**
6 LIKING SAMPLE
Enjoy the: 5 SAVOR
Personal: 8 CUPOFTEA
Sense of: 6 PALATE
Sharp: 4 TANG
Small: 3 SIP
stimulus: 4 ODOR
test label: 6 BRANDX
Zingy: 4 TANG
Tasteless: 4 BLAH 5 BLAND
CRASS GAUDY TACKY
Tastelessly
affected: 6 TOOTOO
"Taste of Honey, A"
playwright: 7 DELANEY
Taster
Wine ~ concern: 4 YEAR
"Tastes awful!": 3 UGH
Tastiness: 5 SAPOR
Tasting
Bitter: 5 ACERB
like Tokay: 4 WINY
of wood: 4 OAKY
Wine: 3 SIP
Tasty: 4 GOOD 5 SAPID
dish: 5 VIAND
mushroom: 5 MOREL
tuber: 3 YAM
"Tasty!": 3 MMM YUM 4 MMMM
Tat
equivalent: 3 TIT
"Ta-ta!": 4 CIAO 5 ADIEU SEEYA
7 CHEERIO
Tatar
ruler: 4 KHAN
Tate
British poet: 5 NAHUM
collection: 3 ART
Tater: 4 **SPUD**
state: 5 IDAHO
Taters
Some: 7 IDAHOES
Tater Tots
maker: 6 OREIDA
Tati
character: 5 HULOT

"Tatler, The"
founder: 6 STEELE
Tatter: 3 RAG
product: 4 LACE
Tattered: 4 TORN WORN 5 RATTY
6 INRAGS
attire: 4 RAGS
"Tattered Tom"
author: 5 ALGER
Tatting
material: 4 LACE
Tattle: 3 RAT 4 BLAB TELL
6 TELLON
Tattled: 4 TOLD
Tattletale: 3 RAT 6 SNITCH
7 BLABBER
Tattoo
fluid: 3 INK
for kids: 5 DECAL
Popeye: 6 ANCHOR
site: 3 ARM
word: 3 MOM
"Tattooed lady"
of song: 5 LYDIA
Tatum
Father of: 4 RYAN
Jazzman: 3 ART
Oscar winner: 5 ONEAL
Tatyana
Singer: 3 ALI
Taught: 8 SCHOOLED
Taunt: 4 **GIBE** GOAD JEST TWIT
5 RAGON TEASE
Taunting
cry: 3 OHO
remark: 4 GIBE
Tauromachian
cheer: 3 OLE
Taurus: 3 CAR 4 AUTO
Constellation next to: 5 ORION
Sign after: 6 GEMINI
Sign before: 5 ARIES
Star in: 9 ALDEBARAN
Taut: 12 TIGHTASADRUM
Tautness
Lose: 3 SAG 5 DROOP
Tauto-
What ~ means: 4 SAME
Tavern: 3 BAR INN PUB

inventory: 4 KEGS
offering: 4 BEER
order: 3 ALE RYE
sign abbr.: 4 ESTD 5 ESTAB
temptress: 5 BGIRL
Tax: 3 TRY 4 DUTY LEVY
agcy.: 3 IRS
British: 4 CESS
cheat catchers: 4 TMEN
cheat's risk: 5 AUDIT
form ID: 3 SSN
form info (abbr.): 3 IRA
Imposed a: 6 LEVIED
Kind of: 3 SIN USE 6 EXCISE
mo.: 3 APR
pro: 3 CPA 8 ASSESSOR
Protectionist: 6 TARIFF
Some ~ shelters: 8 ROTHIRAS
time: 5 APRIL
Tax-___ : 6 EXEMPT
Tax-deferred
acct.: 3 IRA 7 ROTHIRA
Taxes
Earn after: 3 NET
Impose: 4 LEVY
Take home, after: 5 CLEAR
Taxi: 3 **CAB** 4 HACK
feature: 4 HORN 5 METER
fee: 4 FARE
Like a: 7 METERED
Typical: 5 SEDAN
"Taxi"
Danny on: 5 LOUIE
driver: 4 ALEX
Judd on: 4 ALEX
Marilu on: 6 ELAINE
mechanic: 5 LATKA
Taxidermy
Perform: 5 STUFF
Taxing
Do ~ work: 6 ASSESS
Less: 6 EASIER
mo.: 3 APR
org.: 3 IRS
trip: 4 TREK
Taxonomic
subdivisions: 5 PHYLA
suffix: 3 OTA
Taxpayer: 5 FILER

dread: **5** AUDIT **8** IRSAUDIT
~ ID: **3** SSN
Tay: **4** LOCH
Tiny, on the: **3** SMA
Taylor
1963 ~ role: **4** CLEO
A ~ husband: **4** TODD
Actress: **4** LILI **5** RENEE
Blues singer: **4** KOKO
boy: **4** OPIE
Entertainer: **3** RIP
nickname: **3** LIZ
Pop singer: **5** DAYNE
predecessor: **4** POLK
~, for one: **4** WHIG
Taylor, Claudia ___: 4 ALTA
Tazer
Use a ~ on: **4** STUN
T-bar: 3 TOW
T-Bird
Old ~ features: **4** FINS
T-bone: 5 **STEAK**
Tbsp.: 3 AMT
fractions: **4** TSPS
Tchaikovsky
ballet: **8** SWANLAKE
ballet role: **4** SWAN
middle name: **5** ILICH
Tchotchke: 7 TRINKET
holder: **7** ETAGERE
TDK
rival: **7** MEMOREX
Te-___ (cigar brand): 3 AMO
Tea: SOCIAL
biscuit: **5** SCONE
Black: **5** PEKOE
brand: **6** LIPTON SALADA
    6 TETLEY
Brit's bit of: **4** SPOT
Chinese: **3** **CHA**
Grade of: **5** PEKOE
growing state: **5** ASSAM
holder: **3** BAG TIN
Iced ~ garnish: **5** LEMON
Interpret ~ leaves: **4** READ
leaf reader: **4** SEER
Like some: **4** ICED **6** HERBAL
party member: **5** ALICE
    8 DORMOUSE

Prepare: **4** BREW **5** STEEP
quantity: **4** SPOT
server: **3** URN
Spiced: **4** CHAI
Texas: **3** OIL
time: **4** FOUR
type: **5** PEKOE **6** HERBAL
    OOLONG
Téa
Actress: **5** LEONI
Teach: 5 TRAIN **7** EDUCATE
Teacher: 4 PROF
Bauhaus: **4** KLEE
charges: **5** CLASS
favorite: **3** PET
goal: **6** TENURE
Hindu: **4** GURU **5** SWAMI
Jewish: **5** REBBE
joy: **8** ASTUDENT
Martial arts: **6** SENSEI
of Bart: **4** EDNA
of Heifetz: **4** AUER
of Luke: **4** YODA
of Samuel: **3** **ELI**
of Stradivari: **5** **AMATI**
org.: **3** **NEA**
request: **5** SEEME
TV: **4** GABE
Wise: **6** MENTOR
Word a ~ likes to hear: **3** AHA
~, sometimes: **6** TESTER
Teaching
deg.: **3** EDB EDD MED **4** BSED
Do a ~ job: **5** GRADE
Elders: **4** LORE
"Teach not thy lip such ___":
    5 SCORN
Teacup
handle: **3** EAR
"Tea for Two"
musical: **11** NONONANETTE
Teal
Color similar to: **4** AQUA
hangout: **4** POND
Team: 4 SIDE **5** SQUAD
    6 TANDEM
Competing: **4** SIDE
Crew: **4** OARS
Farm: **4** **OXEN** SPAN

Football: **6** ELEVEN
Greet the opposing: **3** BOO
Hockey: **6** SEXTET
It keeps the ~ together: **4** YOKE
Kind of: **3** TAG **4** AWAY FARM
    SWAT
Lacrosse: **3** TEN
leader: **7** CAPTAIN
lineup: **6** ROSTER
members: **4** OXEN
morale: **6** SPIRIT
Mule: **4** ARMY
Police: **4** SWAT
Show ~ spirit: **4** ROOT
Small: **3** DUO
Sports: **5** SQUAD
The other: **4** THEM
Word to a: **4** MUSH
Teamsters
notable: **5** HOFFA
rig: **4** SEMI
Teamwork
deterrent: **3** EGO
Teapot
cover: **4** COZY
feature: **5** SPOUT
Tempest in a: **3** ADO **4** FUSS
Teapot Dome
figure: **10** ALBERTFALL
Tear: 3 RIP **4** RACE REND RENT
    5 SPREE **8** LACERATE
apart: **3** RIP **4** **REND** RIVE
carrier: **4** DUCT
Doesn't just ~ up: **4** SOBS
down: **4** RAZE
down (British): **4** RASE
Fix a: **4** DARN
in little pieces: **5** SHRED
into: **6** ASSAIL ATTACK
It brings a ~ to the eye: **4** DUCT
jerker: **5** ONION
More than a ~ up: **4** BAWL WEEP
open: **5** UNRIP
Partner of: **4** WEAR
roughly: **8** LACERATE
Shed a: **4** WEPT
to pieces: **4** REND **5** RIPUP
up: **3** CRY RIP **4** MIST REND
    WEEP

Wear and: **3** USE
Words before: **3** ONA
Tearful: 3 SAD **5** WEEPY
Tearjerker: 5 ONION
necessity: **6** TISSUE
React to a: **3** CRY
Tearoom: 4 CAFE
Tears
Blur with: **5** BLEAR
into: **5** HASAT
Like: **5** SALTY **6** SALINE
Shed: **4** WEEP WEPT
Teasdale
Poet: **4** **SARA**
Tease: 3 KID RAG **RIB** **4** BAIT
    JOSH RAZZ RIDE TWIT
    5 RAGON **6** LEADON
    NEEDLE
Teased: 4 RODE
Teaser
Kitty: **6** CATNIP
TV: **5** PROMO
Teasing
result: **7** BIGHAIR
Teaspoon: 4 DOSE
Teatime
treat: **5** SCONE
Teatro alla ___ : 5 SCALA
Teatro Costanzi
debut of 1900: **5** TOSCA
Teatro ___ Scala: 4 ALLA
Tebaldi
Soprano: **6** RENATA
Tech
sch. grad: **4** ENGR
stock: **3** IBM
___ Tech: 3 CAL
Techie
client: **4** USER
Kind of: **14** SYSTEMSANALYST
~, maybe: **4** NERD
"___ Te Ching": 3 TAO
Technical
data: **5** SPECS
sch.: **4** INST
Technicality
Kind of: **4** MERE
Technician
Piano: **5** TUNER

spot: 3 LAB
Technique: 3 ART 4 MODE
  Film editing: 4 WIPE
  Jazz: 4 SCAT
  Memorization: 4 ROTE
  Mosaic: 5 INLAY
  Mountain climbing: 6 RAPPEL
  Replay: 5 SLOMO
Techno
  Popular ~ musician: 4 MOBY
  suffix: 4 CRAT
Technological
  advance of the 50's: 7 COLORTV
  marvel of 1951: 6 UNIVAC
Technologically
  advanced: 13 STATEOFTHEART
Technology
  prefix: 4 NANO
Techs
  It has many: 6 NASDAQ
Tecs: 3 PIS
Tecumseh: 7 SHAWNEE
Ted
  Rocker: 6 NUGENT
Teddies: 8 LINGERIE
Teddy
  Eleanor, to: 5 NIECE
Tedious: 5 PROSY 8 TIRESOME
  situation: 4 DRAG
  task: 4 ONUS 5 CHORE
Tediously
  Proceed: 4 PLOD
Tedium: 5 ENNUI
Tee
  follower: 3 HEE
  Hit from a: 5 DRIVE
  off: 3 IRE IRK 4 RILE 5 ANGER
    DRIVE
  preceder: 3 ESS
  To a: 3 PAT
  user: 6 GOLFER
  ___ tee: 3 TOA
Teed
  off: 4 SORE 5 IRATE
Tee-hee
  More than a: 4 HAHA
Teem: 6 ABOUND
Teeming: 4 RIFE 6 ASWARM
Teen: 7 MALLRAT

affliction: 4 ACNE
fave: 4 IDOL 7 POPSTAR
hangout: 4 MALL
Much ~ talk: 5 SLANG
of comics: 6 ARCHIE
outcast: 4 NERD
party: 9 SLEEPOVER
spots: 4 ACNE
suffix: 4 AGER
wall décor: 6 POSTER
woe: 3 ZIT 4 ACNE
Teen ___: 4 IDOL
Teena
  Singer: 5 MARIE
Teenage
  hooligan, to a Brit: 3 YOB
  Like some ~ turtles: 6 MUTANT
Teenage Mutant ___ Turtles:
    5 NINJA
Teenager
  Many a ~ room: 4 MESS
  woe: 4 ACNE
"___ Teen-age Werewolf":
    5 IWASA
Teens
  Great, to: 3 RAD
  Not for most: 6 RATEDR
  Rock star, to: 4 IDOL
Teensy: 3 WEE
  bit: 4 ATOM IOTA
Teeny: 3 WEE 4 ITSY 5 BITSY
    6 PETITE 9 ITSYBITSY
  parasites: 5 MITES
Teeter-totter: 6 SEESAW
Teeth: 4 COGS
  Deg. with: 3 DDS
  Gear: 4 COGS
  Grind, as: 5 GNASH
  Grinding: 6 MOLARS
  Like hen's: 4 RARE
  One with sharp: 3 SAW
  Sink one's ~ into: 4 BITE
  Space between: 8 DIASTEMA
  Tool with: 3 SAW 4 RAKE
Teetotaler: 3 DRY 7 NONUSER
  order: 4 SODA
Teflon
  maker: 6 DUPONT
"Teflon Don, The": 5 GOTTI

Teheran
City SW of: 3 QOM
coin: 4 RIAL
country: 4 **IRAN**
Former ~ ruler: 4 SHAH
native: 5 **IRANI**
tongue: 5 FARSI
Tehrani
tongue: 5 FARSI
Tejano
singer: 6 SELENA
Te Kanawa
Soprano: 4 KIRI
Tel.
book listings: 3 NOS
line: 3 EXT
Tel ___: 4 AVIV
Tel Aviv
Airline to: 4 **ELAL**
Airport near: 3 LOD
native: 5 SABRA 7 ISRAELI
server: 4 ELAL
Telecast
component: 5 AUDIO
over: 5 RERUN
Telecom
Former ~ giant: 3 GTE ITT
giant: 3 ATT
Telecommunications
Old ~ name: 5 NYNEX
speed unit: 4 BAUD
Telecommuter
Where a ~ works: 6 ATHOME
Telegram: 4 WIRE
period: 4 STOP
Send, as a: 6 TAPOUT
Telegrams
Like some: 4 SUNG
Telegraph
click: 3 DIT
inventor: 5 MORSE
key: 6 TAPPER
Telepathy: 3 ESP PSI
Telephone: 4 CALL
6 on a ~: 3 MNO
abbr.: 4 OPER
button: 4 STAR
button with no letters: 3 ONE
greeting: 5 HELLO

location: 5 BOOTH
part: 4 CORD 6 CRADLE
    7 HANDSET
trio: 3 ABC DEF GHI JKL MNO
    PRS TUV WXY
user: 5 PARTY
~, in slang: 4 HORN
Telephoned: 4 RANG
"Telephone Line"
gp.: 3 **ELO**
TelePrompter
filler: 4 TEXT
input: 6 SCRIPT
Telescope
Hale ~ site: 7 PALOMAR
part: 4 LENS
pioneer: 7 GALILEO
sights: 5 STARS
Small: 8 SPYGLASS
Telescopium
Constellation next to: 3 ARA
Telesthesia: 3 ESP
TeleTax
org.: 3 IRS
Televise: 3 AIR
Television: 5 MEDIA
announcer Don: 5 PARDO
award: 4 EMMY
cabinet: 7 CONSOLE
Show on: 3 AIR
Tell: 6 INFORM RELATE
    7 NARRATE
a good one: 3 LIE
all: 4 BLAB SING
a thing or two: 5 SCOLD
a whopper: 3 LIE
Could: 6 SENSED
Didn't mean to: 7 LETSLIP
forte: 7 ARCHERY
it like it isn't: 3 LIE
It's hard to: 5 SAGA
projectile: 5 ARROW
tales: 3 LIE 7 NARRATE
Tell-___ (some biographies):
    4 ALLS
Tell, William: 6 ARCHER
canton: 3 URI
Teller: 3 RAT
Bygone tale: 4 BARD

call: 4 NEXT
Fortune: 4 SEER 5 TAROT
    6 ORACLE
Partner of: 4 PENN
post: 4 CAGE
stack: 4 ONES TENS
Tale: 3 POE 4 LIAR
Telling: 6 COGENT
trial: 8 ACIDTEST
"Tell It to My Heart"
singer Taylor: 5 DAYNE
"Tell ___ lies": 4 MENO
"Tell Mama"
singer James: 4 ETTA
"Tell ___ story": 3 MEA
Telltale
sign: 4 ODOR OMEN
"Tell-Tale Heart, The"
author: 3 POE
"Tell ___ the judge!": 4 ITTO
"Tell ___ the Marines!": 4 ITTO
Telly
network: 3 BBC
on the telly: 7 SAVALAS
Temp
Year-end: 5 SANTA
Tempe
sch.: 3 **ASU**
Temper: 3 IRE 4 HUFF MOOD
    5 IRISH 6 ANNEAL
Ill: 3 **IRE** 4 BILE
Lose one's: 13 HITTHECEILING
Tempera
painting surface: 5 GESSO
Temperament: 4 MOOD
    6 NATURE
Temperamental: 5 MOODY
star: 4 DIVA
tizzy: 4 SNIT
Temperate: 4 MILD
Temperature: 4 HEAT
Body ~, etc.: 6 VITALS
scale: 7 CELSIUS
taker: 5 NURSE
___ temperature: 4 RANA
Temperatures
Freezing: 5 TEENS
Tempest: 5 STORM
in a teapot: 3 ADO 4 FUSS

"Tempest, The"
fairy: 5 ARIEL
king: 6 ALONSO
magician: 8 PROSPERO
Sci-fi version of:
    15 FORBIDDENPLANET
slave: 7 CALIBAN
Tempest ___ teapot: 3 INA
Temple
athlete: 3 OWL
Chinese: 6 PAGODA
Common ~ name: 7 EMANUEL
Greek: 4 NAOS
image: 4 IDOL
leader: 5 RABBI
Object near a: 3 EAR
player: 3 OWL
Roman: 8 PANTHEON
Shinto ~ gateway: 5 TORII
text: 5 TORAH
Temple, Shirley
role: 5 HEIDI
Temple of ___: 4 ARES ZEUS
Temple of Apollo
site: 6 DELPHI
Temple of Zeus
site: 5 NEMEA
Temples
Site of two: 9 ABUSIMBEL
They're found beside:
    7 GLASSES
Templeton
Pianist: 4 ALEC
Tempo: 4 PACE RATE 5 SPEED
Fast: 6 PRESTO
Slow: 5 LARGO LENTO
Temporarily: 6 FORNOW
    8 FORATIME
be: 5 ACTAS
Give: 4 **LEND** LOAN
Joined: 5 SATIN
put aside: 5 ONICE
Temporary: 5 ADHOC 6 ACTING
    7 INTERIM
fashion: 3 FAD
fix: 7 STOPGAP
gift: 4 LOAN
money: 5 SCRIP
wheels: 6 LOANER

Tempt: 4 BAIT LURE 6 ENTICE
  SEDUCE
  fate: 4 DARE
Temptation
  Dieter's: 5 AROMA
  location: 4 EDEN
"Temptation of St. Anthony, The"
  artist: 5 BOSCH ERNST
Temptations
  1965 ~ hit: 6 MYGIRL
Tempted
  It may be: 4 FATE
Tempter: 5 SATAN SIREN WOOER
  Eve: 7 SERPENT
  Fish: 4 LURE
Temptress: 5 SIREN
  Joe Hardy: 4 LOLA
  Play the: 6 SEDUCE
  Rhine: 7 LORELEI
  Tavern: 5 BGIRL
Ten
  Hang: 4 SURF
  or higher: 5 HONOR
  percenter (abbr.): 3 AGT
  prefix: 4 DECA
  sawbucks: 5 CNOTE
  Take: 4 REST
  Top ~, for one: 4 LIST
  Top ~ item: 3 HIT
  Worth a: 5 IDEAL
Tenacious: 6 DOGGED
Tenant: 6 LESSEE RENTER
  ROOMER
  Feudal: 6 VASSAL
  Find a new ~ for: 5 RELET
  Joint: 3 CON 5 FELON
  Mall: 4 SHOP 5 STORE
  payment: 4 RENT
  protest: 10 RENTSTRIKE
  Tent: 6 CAMPER
  Throw out a: 5 EVICT
Ten Commandments
  mount: 5 SINAI
  word: 5 SHALT
  ~, for the most part: 5 NONOS
"Ten Commandments, The":
  4 EPIC
  actress Debra: 5 PAGET
  director: 7 DEMILLE

  Ramses portrayer, in: 3 YUL
Tend: 5 SEETO
Tended: 5 SAWTO
Tendency: 4 BENT 5 TREND
  Had a: 5 LEANT
  toward chaos: 7 ENTROPY
Tender: 4 SORE
  Bar: 9 BEERMONEY
  ender: 4 LOIN
  Some legal: 6 TNOTES
  spot: 3 BAR 4 SORE
  Tijuana: 4 PESO
  touch: 6 CARESS
"Tender ___": 7 MERCIES
Tenderfoot: 4 TYRO
  org.: 3 BSA
Tender-hearted: 4 SOFT
Tenderized
  cut: 9 CUBESTEAK
Tendon: 5 SINEW
  connector: 5 BURSA
Tendril: 4 WISP
Tenement
  locale: 4 SLUM
  ___ tenens (substitute): 5 LOCUM
Tenerife: 4 ISLA
Tenet: 5 CREDO DOGMA
Tenet, George
  org.: 3 CIA
"Ten-hut!"
  opposite: 6 ATEASE
Tenn.
  athlete: 3 VOL
  hours: 3 CST
  neighbor: 3 ALA 4 NCAR
Tennessee
  aluminum town: 5 ALCOA
  athlete: 3 VOL
  footballer: 3 VOL 5 TITAN
  Former ~ senator Kefauver:
    5 ESTES
  singer Ford: 5 ERNIE
  state flower: 4 IRIS
  Veep from: 6 ALGORE
Tennille
  Singer: 4 TONI
Tennis: 5 SPORT
  1965 NCAA ~ champ: 4 ASHE
  1970s ~ star: 4 ASHE BORG

call: 3 **LET**
Czech ~ player: 5 LENDL
deuce: 3 TIE
divider: 3 NET
do-over: 3 **LET**
drop shot: 4 DINK
First name in 1970s: 4 ILIE
game point: 4 ADIN
Great ~ server: 4 ACER
instructor: 3 PRO
miscue: 5 FAULT
New York ~ stadium: 4 ASHE
Palindromic ~ star: 5 SELES
ploy: 3 LOB
Quick round of: 6 ONESET
ranking: 4 SEED
score: 4 ADIN 5 ADOUT
score after deuce: 4 **ADIN**
shot: 3 LOB
Start a ~ game: 5 SERVE
whiz: 4 ACER
zero: 4 LOVE
"Tennis, ___?": 6 ANYONE
Tennis player
~ Andre: 6 AGASSI
~ Arthur: 4 **ASHE**
~ Becker: 5 BORIS
~ Borg: 5 BJORN
~ Edberg: 6 STEFAN
~ Emerson: 3 ROY
~ Fraser: 5 NEALE
~ Gibson: 6 ALTHEA
~ Hingis: 7 MARTINA
~ Hoad: 3 LEW
~ Huber: 4 ANKE
~ Ilie: 7 NASTASE
~ Kournikova: 4 ANNA
~ Lacoste: 4 **RENE**
~ Lendl: 4 **IVAN**
~ Makarova: 5 ELENA
~ Mandlikova: 4 **HANA**
~ Martina: 6 HINGIS
~ Michael: 5 CHANG
~ Monica: 5 SELES
~ Nastase: 4 **ILIE**
~ René: 7 LACOSTE
~ Richards: 5 RENEE
~ Rod: 5 LAVER
~ Sampras: 4 PETE

~ Shriver: 3 PAM
~ Smith: 4 STAN
~ Steffi: 4 GRAF
~ Tanner: 6 ROSCOE
~ Williams: 5 VENUS
              6 SERENA
"Ten North Frederick"
writer: 5 OHARA
Tennyson
Arden of: 5 ENOCH
lady: 4 ENID
maid: 6 ELAINE
poem: 5 IDYLL
Tenochtitlán
resident: 5 AZTEC
Tenor
top note: 5 HIGHC
tune: 4 ARIA
Voice above: 4 ALTO
warhorse: 8 OSOLEMIO
Tenpenny: 4 NAIL
Ten-percenter: 5 **AGENT**
Tense: 4 EDGY TAUT 6 ONEDGE
Get less: 4 THAW
Kind of: 4 PAST
Make less: 6 DEFUSE
~, with "up": 5 KEYED
Ten-sided
figure: 7 DECAGON
Tension: 6 STRESS
Ten-speed: 4 BIKE
Tent
caterpillar: 5 EGGER
Conical: 5 TEPEE
event: 4 SALE
furnishing: 3 COT
holder: 3 PEG 5 STAKE
Mongol: 4 YURT
Pitch a: 4 CAMP 6 ENCAMP
tenant: 6 CAMPER
Tentacle: 3 ARM
Tentacled
animal: 5 POLYP SQUID
        7 ANEMONE
        10 SEAANEMONE
Tentative
taste: 3 SIP
Tenterhooks
On: 4 EDGY 5 TENSE

Tenth
anniversary gift: 3 TIN
Break the ~ Commandment:
    5 COVET
part: 5 TITHE
prefix: 4 DECI
Tenth-grader: 4 SOPH
    9 SOPHOMORE
Tentmaker
Literary: 4 OMAR
Tenuous: 8 ETHEREAL
Tenure: 5 STINT
Military: 4 TOUR
of office: 4 TERM
Tenzing
Sherpa guide: 6 NORGAY
Teo
of racing: 4 FABI
Tepee
makeup: 4 HIDE
shape: 4 CONE
shaped: 5 CONIC
Tequila
serving: 4 SHOT
source: 5 AGAVE
Teresa, Mother: 3 NUN
~, by birth: 8 ALBANIAN
Teresa, Saint
birthplace: 5 **AVILA**
Terfel
Opera singer: 4 BRYN
Terhune
classic: 7 LADADOG
dog: 3 LAD
Teri
Actress: 4 GARR
Role for: 4 LOIS
Teriyaki
seasoning: 6 GINGER
Terkel
Author: 5 STUDS
Term: 5 STINT 7 SESSION
Academic: 8 SEMESTER
of affection: 5 CUTIE
of endearment: 3 HON PET
    4 BABE 5 HONEY TOOTS
    10 HONEYBUNCH
of respect: 3 SIR 4 MAAM
paper abbr.: 4 IBID

paper citation: 6 IBIDEM
Prison: 7 STRETCH
Termagant: 5 SHREW
    8 SHREWISH
Term-ending
test: 5 FINAL
Terminal: 3 END 5 DEPOT FATAL
abbr.: 3 POS
Battery: 5 **ANODE**
Battery ~ (abbr.): 3 NEG POS
Cell: 7 CATHODE
Chicago: 5 OHARE
info: 3 ETA
JFK: 3 TWA
Like a battery: 6 ANODAL
list (abbr.): 4 ARRS
Network: 4 NODE
posting: 3 ETA
R.R.: 3 STA
"Terminal Bliss"
actress Chandler: 5 ESTEE
Terminate: 3 AXE CAN END
    4 FIRE 5 CEASE
Terminator
Pasta: 3 INI
"Terminator, The"
heroine: 5 SARAH
Termini: 4 ENDS
Modem: 3 EMS
Terminus: 3 END
Chisholm Trail: 7 ABILENE
I-79: 4 ERIE
Iditarod: 4 **NOME**
Race: 4 TAPE
Suez Canal: 6 REDSEA
Termitarium: 4 NEST
Termite: 4 PEST
hunter: 8 ANTEATER
relative: 3 ANT
Terms
Come to: 5 **AGREE**
Tern: 7 SEABIRD
Terpsichore
Sister of: 5 ERATO
Terr.
Former U.S.: 3 DAK
Terra ___: 5 **COTTA** FIRMA
Terra firma: 4 LAND SOIL
    5 EARTH

On: 6 ASHORE
Terrapin: 6 TURTLE
Terrarium
  growth: 4 MOSS
  plant: 4 FERN
  youngster: 3 EFT
Terre
  Opposite of: 3 MER
Terre ___ : 5 HAUTE
Terre Haute
  river: 6 WABASH
  sch.: 3 ISU
Terrestrial
  newt: 3 EFT
Terrible
  He was: 4 IVAN
  More: 5 DIRER
  time: 4 TWOS
  twos: 5 PHASE
  type: 6 ENFANT
"Terrible"
  tsar: 4 **IVAN** 6 IVANIV
___ terrible (brat): 6 ENFANT
"... ___ terrible thing to waste":
    3 ISA
Terribly
  Bother: 5 EATAT
Terrier
  cry: 3 ARF
  Kind of: 4 SKYE 5 CAIRN
    8 AIREDALE WIREHAIR
  Largest: 8 AIREDALE
  Movie: 4 **ASTA** TOTO
  type: 7 SCOTTIE
  Welsh: 8 SEALYHAM
  White: 6 WESTIE
"Terrif!": 3 FAB
Terrific: 5 GREAT SUPER SWELL
  time: 5 BLAST
  ~, in slang: 4 PHAT
Terrified: 5 ASHEN
  Was ~ by: 7 DREADED
Terrify: 5 SCARE
Terrifying: 5 SCARY
Territory: 4 **AREA** LAND ZONE
    6 DOMAIN
  Canadian: 5 YUKON
  east of Manila: 4 GUAM
  Former U.S.: 6 DAKOTA

Fowl: 4 COOP 5 ROOST
Gang: 4 TURF
Give up: 4 CEDE
Gold rush: 5 YUKON
Indian: 5 DELHI
Kind of: 5 ENEMY
Terror
  Cry of: 5 OHGOD
  Prehistoric: 4 TREX
  Squeals of: 4 EEKS
Terrorism
  prefix: 3 ECO
Terrorist
  Kenyan: 6 MAUMAU
  of renown: 5 CARLO
  weapon: 3 UZI
Terrorize: 6 MENACE
Terry
  Clockmaker: 3 **ELI**
  garment: 4 ROBE
  Teammate of Hubbell and: 3 OTT
Terse: 4 CURT 5 PITHY SHORT
  denial: 5 NOTME
  review: 3 UGH
  summons: 5 SEEME
  warning: 4 DONT
Tertiary Period
  epoch: 6 EOCENE
Terza ___ : 4 RIMA
Tesla
  Inventor: 6 NICOLA
Tessie
  Actress: 5 OSHEA
"Tess of the D'Urbervilles"
  seducer: 4 ALEC
Test: 3 TRY 4 EXAM 5 TRIAL
    8 TRIALRUN
  answer: 4 TRUE 5 FALSE
  area: 3 LAB
  Big: 5 FINAL
  Brain: 3 EEG
  Breeze through a: 3 ACE
  choice: 4 TRUE
  Diagnostic: 4 SCAN
  Difficult: 6 ORDEAL
  ER: 3 ECG EKG
  F on a: 5 FALSE
  for a sr.: 3 **GRE**
  for fit: 5 TRYON

Geometry ~ answer: 4 AREA
Hosp.: 3 ECG EKG
H.S. junior: 4 PSAT
H.S. proficiency: 3 GED
IQ ~ name: 5 BINET
Kind of: 3 DNA 4 ACID BETA
 ORAL 5 ESSAY TASTE
M.A. entry: 3 GRE
material: 3 DNA
Nonwritten: 4 ORAL
Prenatal: 5 AMNIO
Preop: 3 ECG EKG
Prepare for a: 5 STUDY
proctor call: 4 TIME
Put to the: 3 TRY USE 5 ASSAY
 ESSAY
site: 3 LAB
Some ~ answers: 5 TRUES
Tough: 4 ORAL
Testarossa
and others: 8 FERRARIS
Test-driven
car: 4 DEMO
Tester
Air ~ (abbr.): 3 EPA
Beta: 4 USER
IQ: 5 BINET
Water: 3 **TOE**
Testify: 4 AVOW 5 SWEAR
 6 DEPONE DEPOSE
Testimonial
dinner: 5 HONOR 7 TRIBUTE
Testimony
Like court: 5 SWORN
Like some: 4 **ORAL**
starter: 4 OATH
Take ~ from: 4 HEAR
Testing
site: 3 LAB
Test-marketing
city: 6 PEORIA
Testy: 5 SHORT
Get ~ with: 6 SNAPAT
state: 4 SNIT
Tet
observer: 5 ASIAN
Tête
thought: 4 IDEE
topper: 5 BERET

Tête-à-tête: 4 CHAT TALK
Have a ~ with: 8 SEEALONE
Tether: 5 LEASH
Tethys
Daughter of: 7 OCEANID
Tetley
alternative: 6 NESTEA SALADA
product: 3 TEA
Tet Offensive
city: 6 SAIGON
Tetra-
~, twice: 4 OCTA OCTO
Tetrazzini
Soprano: 5 LUISA
Teutonic: 8 GERMANIC
cry: 3 ACH
lang.: 3 GER
name part: 3 VON
three: 4 DREI
turndown: 4 NEIN
Tevere
city: 4 ROMA
Tevye
portrayer: 5 TOPOL
Tex
Animator: 5 AVERY
Singer: 6 RITTER
Tex.
neighbor: 4 OKLA
or Mex.: 4 ABBR
Tex-___: 3 MEX
Texaco
symbol: 4 STAR
"Texaco Star Theater"
star: 5 BERLE
Texan
Many a: 5 OILER
tie: 4 BOLO
"Texan, The"
actor Calhoun: 4 RORY
Texas
border city: 6 DELRIO ELPASO
 LAREDO
border river: 6 SABINE
city: 4 WACO 6 DALLAS ELPASO
 LAREDO ODESSA
city on the Brazos: 4 WACO
city on the Rio Grande:
 6 LAREDO

cook-off dish: 5 CHILI
county: 5 LAMAR
flag symbol: 4 STAR
Houston of: 3 SAM
Hutchinson of: 3 KAY
landmark: 5 ALAMO
leaguer: 5 ASTRO
mission: 5 ALAMO
oil city: 6 ODESSA
player: 5 ASTRO
Richards of: 3 ANN
sch.: 3 SMU
shortstop, once: 4 AROD
shrine: 5 **ALAMO**
state flower: 10 BLUEBONNET
state tree: 5 PECAN
tea: 3 OIL
town: 4 WACO 5 ENNIS
    PLANO
university: 5 LAMAR
Texas ___: 3 TEA
Texas A&M
player: 5 AGGIE
Texas Mustangs (abbr.): 3 SMU
Tex-Mex
condiment: 5 SALSA
sauce: 5 SALSA
snack: 4 TACO 6 TAMALE
treat: 6 FAJITA TAMALE
Text
Authoritative: 5 BIBLE
Change: 4 EDIT
Computer: 5 ASCII
Correct. 5 EMEND
ending: 3 URE
Fix: 4 EDIT 5 EMEND
Islamic: 5 KORAN
Rabbinical: 6 TALMUD
Remove from: 4 DELE
Sacred: 5 KORAN TORAH
Tilted ~ (abbr.): 4 ITAL
Textbook
division: 4 UNIT
Like some ~ publishing: 4 ELHI
Textile
colorer: 3 DYE
French ~ city: 5 LILLE
trademark: 5 ARNEL
Trousers: 5 CHINO

worker: 4 DYER
Texts
Orig.: 3 MSS
TGIF
Part of: 3 FRI **ITS**
Thai: 5 ASIAN
currency: 4 BAHT
language: 3 LAO
neighbor: 3 LAO
Some: 3 LAO
Thailand
neighbor: 4 LAOS
~, once: 4 **SIAM**
Thais: 6 ASIANS
Thalia
Sister of: 4 CLIO 5 ERATO
Thames
College on the: 4 **ETON**
Land in the: 3 AIT
town: 4 **ETON**
"Thank God ___ Country Boy":
3 IMA
"Thank goodness!": 4 PHEW
"Thank Heaven for Little Girls"
musical: 4 GIGI
Thankless
one: 7 INGRATE
Thanks
Island: 6 MAHALO
~, in French: 5 MERCI
~, in German: 5 DANKE
"Thanks ___!": 4 ALOT
"Thanks a ___!": 3 MIL
Thanksgiving
Alice's ~ guest: 4 ARLO
celebration: 5 FEAST
day (abbr.): 5 THURS
dish: 4 YAMS
Do the ~ honors: 5 CARVE
Hymn of: 5 PAEAN
mo.: 3 NOV
veggie: 3 YAM
Thanksgiving Day
event: 6 PARADE
"Thanks, I already ___": 3 ATE
"Thank U"
singer Morissette: 6 ALANIS
Thank you
(Japanese): 7 ARIGATO

partner: 6 PLEASE
"Thank You"
  singer: 4 DIDO
Thank-you-___: 4 MAAM
Thank-yous
  Brits': 3 TAS
"Thar ___ blows!": 3 SHE
Tharp
  Choreographer: 5 TWYLA
That
  and that: 5 THOSE
  being the case: 4 IFSO
  guy's: 3 HIS
  is: 5 **IDEST**
  objeto: 3 ESO
  This and: 4 BOTH OLIO
    5 THESE
  ~, in French: 3 CET
  ~, in Spanish: 3 ESA **ESO**
  ~, once: 3 YON
"___ That a Shame": 4 AINT
Thataway: 6 YONDER
Thatch
  Bit of: 4 REED
Thatcher, Margaret: 4 TORY
Thatching
  palm: 4 NIPA
"That ___ excuse!": 4 ISNO
"That feels good!": 3 AAH OOH
"That Girl"
  actress Thomas: 5 MARLO
  girl: 3 ANN
"That hurts!": 3 YOW 4 OUCH
"That is" (to Caesar): 5 IDEST
"That is ___ ...": 5 TOSAY
"That is a riot!": 4 HAHA
    7 GOODONE
"That is my understanding":
    10 IBELIEVESO
"That is right!": 4 TRUE
"That is so funny": 4 HAHA
"That is to say ...": 5 IMEAN
"That'll be the day!": 4 IBET
"That'll show you!": 3 HAH
"That makes me mad!": 3 GRR
"That makes sense!": 4 ISEE
"That means ___!": 3 YOU
"That's ___!": 4 ALIE
"That's ___ ...": 3 ODD

"That's ___" (Dean Martin hit):
    5 AMORE
"That's a go": 3 YES
"That's a laugh!": 3 HAH
"That's a lie!": 5 NOTSO
    6 UNTRUE
"That's all, folks!"
  speaker: 8 PORKYPIG
  voice: 5 BLANC
"That's all there ___ it!": 4 ISTO
"That's all ___ wrote!": 3 SHE
"That's a relief!": 4 WHEW
"That's a riot!": 4 HAHA
"That's ___ ask!": 4 ALLI
"That's awful!": 3 UGH
"That's ___ blow!": 4 ALOW
"That's cheating!": 6 NOFAIR
"That's clear": 4 ISEE
"That's disgusting!": 3 ICK UGH
    4 YECH 5 YECCH**
"That's enough!": 4 STOP
    6 NOMORE STOPIT
    11 PUTALIDONIT
"That's gotta hurt!": 3 OOH
"That's gross!": 3 UGH
"That's ___ haven't heard":
    4 ONEI
"That's it!": 3 AHA 5 BINGO
"That's nice!": 3 AAH
"That's not ___!": 4 ATOY
"That sounds good!": 3 OOH
"___ that special!": 4 ISNT
"That's really something!":
    3 MAN
"That's right!": 4 TRUE
"That's show ___!": 3 BIZ
"That's so-o-o-o nice!": 3 AAH
"That's so true": 6 IAGREE
"That's ___ subject": 5 ASORE
"That's terrible!": 4 OHNO
"That's the way ___": 4 ITIS
"that thing you do!"
  setting: 4 ERIE
"That was close!": 4 PHEW
    WHEW
"That wasn't nice!": 3 TSK
"That Was the Week That Was"
  host: 10 DAVIDFROST
"That ___ you!": 4 ISSO

Thaw: 4 MELT 5 DEICE
    7 DETENTE
The ___ (Netherlands city):
    5 HAGUE
Theater: 4 CINE
  abbr.: 3 SRO
  Ancient Greek: 5 ODEON
  and other things: 4 ARTS
  area: 4 LOGE 6 RIALTO
  award: **4 OBIE** TONY
  backdrop: 5 SCRIM
  Best of: 4 EDNA
  Big-screen: 4 IMAX
  box: 4 LOGE
  Classic ~ name: 4 ROXY
    6 RIALTO
  company, briefly: 3 REP
  district: 6 RIALTO
  divider: 5 AISLE
  employee: 5 USHER
  for some vets: 3 NAM
  guide: 5 USHER
  Harlem: 6 APOLLO
  Holds, as a: 5 SEATS
  level: 4 LOGE TIER
  light: 4 SPOT
  litter: 5 STUBS
  Local ~, in slang: 4 NABE
  London: 6 OLDVIC
  Movie: 4 CINE 6 CINEMA
  section: 4 LOGE
  Shakespeare: 5 GLOBE
  sign: 3 SRO 4 EXIT
  Some: 7 CABARET
  sound: 3 SHH
  souvenir: 4 STUB
  space: 8 ENTRACTE
  ticket word: 3 ROW
  walkway: 5 AISLE
  warning: 3 SHH
  Worth of the: 5 IRENE
Theater of the Absurd
  pioneer: 7 IONESCO
Theaters
  Ancient: 4 ODEA
  Big name in: 5 LOEWS
  Bygone: 4 RKOS
  They are shared in:
    8 ARMRESTS

Théâtre
  division: 4 ACTE
Theatrical: 5 SHOWY
  award: 4 OBIE
  backdrop: 5 SCRIM
  Be: 5 EMOTE
  Extravagantly: 4 CAMP
  Overly: 5 STAGY
  pro: 7 ARTISTE
  Wax: 5 EMOTE
Theban
  deity: 4 AMON
  Supreme ~ deity: 6 AMENRA
Thebes
  Opera set in: 4 AIDA
  Queen of: 5 NIOBE
"The best ___ to come": 5 ISYET
___ the chase: 5 CUTTO
Theda
  Actress: 4 **BARA**
  Vamp: 4 BARA
"The Day the Earth Stood Still"
  robot: 4 GORT
"The doctor ___": 4 ISIN
"The heck with you!": 5 NERTS
"The jig ___!": 4 ISUP
"The joke is ___!": 4 ONME
  5 ONYOU
The ___ knees: 4 BEES
"The lady ___ protest ...":
  4 DOTH
"The law is a ___": Mr. Bumble:
  3 ASS
"The light dawns!": 3 AHA 4 ISEE
Thelma
  Actress: 4 TODD
  Movie partner of: 6 LOUISE
"Thelma & Louise"
  actress Davis: 5 GEENA
  star: 10 GEENADAVIS
  Thelma in: 5 GEENA
"The loneliest number": 3 ONE
Thelonious
  Jazzman: 4 MONK
Them: 5 ENEMY 6 OTHERS
  ~, to us: 4 FOES 5 ENEMY
"Them": 3 FOE 5 ENEMY
  author: 5 OATES
  or "us": 4 SIDE

"Them!"
  creatures: 4 ANTS
"The magic word": 6 PLEASE
Theme: 4 IDEA 5 ESSAY MOTIF
    TOPIC
  Main: 5 MOTIF
  Recurring: 5 MOTIF
"___ Theme": 5 **LARAS**
Theme park
  acronym: 5 EPCOT
  attraction: 4 RIDE
Then
  Now and: 7 ATTIMES
  ~, in French: 5 ALORS
"Then what?": 3 AND
Theobald
  Flute innovator: 5 BOEHM
  ___ the occasion: 6 RISETO
Theocracy
  Mideast: 4 IRAN
Theocritus
  work: 4 IDYL
Theodore
  Eleanor, to: 5 NIECE
  of Broadway: 5 BIKEL
  ~, to Wally: 4 BEAV
Theodore Roosevelt Award
  org.: 4 NCAA
Theologian
  Kierkegaard: 5 SOREN
  sch.: 3 SEM
  subj.: 3 REL
  who opposed Martin Luther:
    3 ECK
Theological
  no-no: 3 SIN
  sch.: 3 SEM
"The one that got away": 4 YARN
Theophilus
  New Haven founder: 5 EATON
Theorem
  Auxiliary: 5 LEMMA
  ender: 3 QED
  name: 6 FERMAT
Theoretically: 7 ONPAPER
Theory: 3 ISM
  In: 7 IDEALLY
  Put forth a: 5 POSIT
  suffix: 3 ISM

"The other white meat": 4 PORK
___ the rainbow: 4 OVER
"___ the ramparts ...": 3 **OER**
Therapeutic
  bath: 4 SITZ
  Employ a ~ technique:
    8 ROLEPLAY
  plant: 4 ALOE
  scent: 5 AROMA
Therapist
  Animated: 4 KATZ
  response: 4 ISEE
  Speech ~ concern: 4 LISP
Therapy
  Kind of: 4 GENE
  Primal ~ sound: 6 SCREAM
  prog.: 5 REHAB
  Visit through primal: 6 RELIVE
There
  All: 4 **SANE** 6 INTACT
  Be: 6 ATTEND
  Get: 6 ARRIVE MAKEIT
  Go here and: 4 ROAM ROVE
  Here and: 5 ABOUT APART
    6 PASSIM
  Here, ~, and everywhere:
    7 ALLOVER
  is, in French: 4 ILYA
  It's up: 3 SKY
  Neither here nor: 7 ENROUTE
    INLIMBO
  Not all: 5 DOTTY
  Out: 4 AFAR 6 YONDER
  Over: 3 **YON** 6 YONDER
  Still not: 4 LATE
  The one over: 4 THAT
  Way out: 4 AFAR
"There!": 4 LOOK TADA 5 VOILA
"___ there?": 4 WHOS
Thereabout: 4 ORSO
"There ___ atheists ...": 5 ARENO
"There but for the grace of
    God ___": 3 GOI
"Thereby hangs ___": 5 ATALE
"___ there, done that": 4 BEEN
Therefore: 4 **ERGO** THUS
    5 ANDSO HENCE
"There Is Nothin' Like ___":
    5 ADAME

"There it is!": 3 AHA
"There'll be ___ time ...": 4 AHOT
"There oughta be ___!": 4 ALAW
Theresa
 St. ~ home: 5 AVILA
"There's a Wocket in My Pocket!"
 writer: 5 SEUSS
Thérèse: 3 STE
___ Thérèse, Quebec: 3 STE
"Thérèse Raquin"
 novelist: 4 ZOLA
"There's ___ every crowd!":
   5 ONEIN
"There's many ___ ...": 5 ASLIP
"There's more ...": 3 AND
"The rest ___ to you": 4 ISUP
"The results ___!": 5 AREIN
"There, there": 5 ITSOK
"There ___ tide ...": 3 ISA
"There was ___ woman ...":
   5 ANOLD
Therewithal: 4 ALSO
"___ there yet?": 5 AREWE
"There you are!": 3 AHA
Therm
 prefix: 3 ISO
Thermal
 prefix: 3 GEO ISO
Thermodynamics
 Second law of: 7 ENTROPY
Thermometer
 Kind of: 4 ORAL
Thermonuclear
 explosive: 5 HBOMB
Thermopylae
 victor: 6 XERXES
Thermos
 inventer James: 5 DEWAR
Thermostat: 6 SENSOR
Thesaurus
 author: 5 ROGET
 entry (abbr.): 3 **SYN**
These
 Not: 5 THOSE 6 OTHERS
 ~, in French: 3 CES
 ~, in Spanish: 5 ESTAS ESTOS
Theseus
 land: 6 ATTICA
 She helped ~ escape: 7 ARIADNE

"The sign of extra service"
 sloganeer: 4 ESSO
Thesis
 defense: 4 ORAL
 prefix: 3 SYN
Thespian: 5 ACTOR
 part: 4 ROLE
Thessaly
 peak: 4 **OSSA**
"The sweetest gift of heaven":
   Virgil: 5 SLEEP
Theta
 Letter after: 4 **IOTA**
 Letter before: 3 ETA
"The ___ Tale" (Chaucer segment):
   6 REEVES
"The ___ the limit!": 4 **SKYS**
"The thief of bad gags": 5 BERLE
"___ the Top" (Porter tune):
   5 YOURE
"The Twilight ___": 4 ZONE
"The very ___!": 4 IDEA
"___ the Walrus" (Beatles tune):
   3 IAM
___ the way: 4 PAVE
"The wolf ___ the door": 4 ISAT
The writing ___ the wall: 4 ISON
They
 ~, in French: 3 ILS 5 ELLES
 ~, in Italian: 4 ESSE
"They Died With Their Boots On":
   5 OATER
"They're ___!": 3 OFF
"They're ___ again!": 4 ATIT
"___ they run": 6 SEEHOW
Thiamine
 deficiency: 8 BERIBERI
Thick: 3 FAT 5 DENSE MIDST
 as a brick: 5 DENSE
 carpet: 4 SHAG
 cornmeal mush: 7 POLENTA
 cut: 4 SLAB
 fog: 7 PEASOUP
 hair: 3 MOP 4 MANE
 In the ~ of: 3 MID 4 **AMID**
   5 AMONG 6 AMIDST
 Lay on: 7 SLATHER
 liqueur: 5 CREME
 piece: 4 **SLAB**

slice: 4 **SLAB**
soup: 5 PUREE 6 POTAGE
    7 CHOWDER
Thick ___ brick: 3 ASA
Thicke
  Actor: 4 **ALAN**
Thicken: 4 CLOT
Thickener
  Food: 4 **AGAR**
  Sauce: 4 ROUX
  Soup: 4 OKRA
Thickening: 4 CLOT
  agent: 4 AGAR
Thicket: 5 **COPSE**
Thickheaded: 5 **DENSE**
        6 OBTUSE
Thickly
  packed: 5 DENSE
  Spread: 7 SLATHER
Thickness: 3 **PLY**
  measure: 3 MIL
  measurer: 7 CALIPER
Thick ___ plank: 3 ASA
Thick-skinned
  creature: 5 RHINO
Thick-soled
  shoe: 4 CLOG
Thick-trunked
  tree: 6 BAOBAB
Thief
  Give relief to a: 4 ABET
  "savings": 5 STASH
  Seagoing: 6 PIRATE
  Tart: 5 KNAVE
"Thief"
  actor James: 4 CAAN
"Thief of Bagdad, The"
  star: 4 SABU
Thieves
  hangout: 3 DEN
  take: 4 HAUL
Thigh
  muscles: 5 QUADS
Thighbone: 5 FEMUR
Thimbleful: 3 SIP
Thimblerig
  item: 3 PEA
"Thimble Theater"
  name: 3 OYL

Thimbleweed: 7 ANEMONE
Thin: 4 LANK LEAN RARE SLIM
        6 SPARSE WATERY
  and nasal: 5 REEDY
  and slippery: 7 EELLIKE
  board: 4 SLAT
  coat: 4 FILM
  coin: 4 DIME
  fastener: 4 BRAD
  fog: 4 MIST
  layer: 6 LAMINA VENEER
  layers: 7 LAMINAE
  mattress: 5 FUTON
  model: 4 WAIF
  nail: 4 BRAD
  opening: 4 SLIT
  out: 9 ATTENUATE
  pancake: 5 CREPE
  paper: 9 ONIONSKIN
  porridge: 5 GRUEL
  puff: 4 WISP
  slice: 7 SCALLOP
  soup: 5 BROTH
  strand: 4 WISP
  stratum: 4 SEAM
  strip: 4 SLAT
  tie: 4 BOLO
  Very: 4 LANK
  wedge: 4 SHIM
Thin ___: 7 ASARAIL
Thin as ___: 5 ARAIL AREED
Thing: 4 ITEM 6 ENTITY
  Directed against a: 5 INREM
  Good: 4 PLUS 5 **ASSET**
  Had a ~ for: 5 LIKED
  In: 5 STYLE
  Latest: 4 RAGE
  Legal: 3 **RES**
  Living: 5 BEING
  Not a: 3 NIL
  of the past: 5 RELIC
  of value: 5 ASSET
  One ~ after another: 6 SERIES
  Play: 4 PROP ROLE
  Tell a ~ or two: 5 SCOLD
  to avoid: 4 NONO
  Wonderful: 12 THEBEESKNEES
"Thing, The"
  He played the Thing in:

6 ARNESS
Thingamabob: 6 DOODAD
Thingamajig: 5 GIZMO 6 DOODAD
    7 WHATSIT
Thingie: 6 DOODAD GADGET
Things: 5 STUFF
  Fine: 4 ARTS
  lacking: 5 NEEDS
  One of those: 4 THAT
  Saw: 5 TEETH
  The way ~ are going: 5 TREND
  The way ~ stand: 6 ASITIS
  to do: 5 TASKS 6 AGENDA
    7 ERRANDS
  to mind: 7 PSANDQS
  What little ~ mean: 4 ALOT
Thingy: 4 ITEM 6 DOODAD
"Thin Ice"
  skater Sonja: 5 HENIE
Think: 5 OPINE 6 IDEATE
  ahead: 4 PLAN
  alike: 5 AGREE
  fit: 5 DEIGN
  hard: 8 COGITATE
  highly of: 6 ADMIRE ESTEEM
  logically: 6 REASON
  of it: 4 IDEA
  One way to: 5 ALOUD
  out loud: 5 OPINE
  (over): 4 MULL
  piece: 4 IDEA 5 ESSAY
  Something to ~ about: 4 IDEA
  the world of: 5 **ADORE**
    6 ADMIRE
  Things to ~ about: 5 IDEAS
  through: 6 REASON
  up: 6 DEVISE IDEATE
Thinker: 4 SAGE
  French: 4 TETE
  Positive: 5 PEALE
"Thinker, The"
  creator: 5 RODIN
Thinking
  Kind of: 9 NONLINEAR
  Positive ~ proponent: 5 PEALE
  Say without: 5 BLURT
  Way of: 7 MINDSET
  Wishful: 5 IHOPE
  Without: 6 RASHLY

"Think nothing ___!": 4 OFIT
ThinkPad
  maker: 3 IBM
Think tank
  member: 7 IDEAMAN
  output: 4 **IDEA**
"... think, therefore ___": 3 IAM
Thinly
  spread: 6 SPARSE
"Thin Man, The"
  actress Loy: 5 MYRNA
  actress Myrna: 3 LOY
  dog: 4 **ASTA**
  wife: 4 NORA
Thinner
  component: 7 ACETONE
Thinness
  Epitome of: 4 RAIL REED
    5 RAZOR
Thinnest
  coin: 4 DIME
"Thin Red Line, The"
  actor Sean: 4 PENN
Thin-waisted
  flier: 4 WASP
Third
  Adam's: 4 SETH
  Beethoven's: 6 **EROICA**
  century date: 3 CCI
  Come in: 4 SHOW
  degree: 3 PHD
  Finish: 4 SHOW
  Frank's: 3 MIA
  from center: 3 END
  Give the ~ degree: 5 GRILL
  Held by a ~ party:
    8 INESCROW
  man: 4 **ABEL**
  man in the ring: 3 REF
  of eight: 5 EARTH
  of September: 3 PEE
  party holding: 6 ESCROW
  place: 4 SHOW
  Raise to the ~ power: 4 CUBE
  rock from the sun: 5 EARTH
  Scarlett's: 5 RHETT
  smallest of eight: 4 MARS
  Taylor's: 4 TODD
  ~ Greek letter: 5 GAMMA

"Third Man, The"
  actress Valli: 5 ALIDA
  setting: 6 VIENNA
  star: 6 WELLES
"Third of May"
  painter: 4 GOYA
Thirds
  Cut in: 7 TRISECT
Third-stringer: 5 SCRUB
Thirst: 3 YEN
  Quench, as: 5 SLAKE
  quencher: 3 ADE
Thirsty: 3 DRY
Thirteen
  popes: 4 LEOS
"Thirty days ___ ...": 4 HATH
"thirtysomething"
  actor Ken: 4 OLIN
  actress Harris: 3 MEL
This
  and that: 4 BOTH OLIO 5 THESE
  Apart from: 4 ELSE
  At ~ point: 4 HERE
  Exactly like: 6 JUSTSO
  Give ~ for that: 5 TRADE
  In ~ manner: 6 LIKESO
  In ~ way: 4 THUS 6 LIKESO
  instant: 3 NOW
  is one: 4 CLUE
  Never say: 3 DIE
  Not: 4 THAT
  one and that: 4 BOTH
  Other than: 4 ELSE
  way, or that: 3 FRO
  What ~ isn't: 4 THAT
  ~, in French: 3 CET
  ~, in Spanish: 4 **ESTA** ESTE
    ESTO
"This ___" (1979 Loggins hit):
  4 ISIT
"This ___" (carton label):
  5 ENDUP
This-and-that
  dish: 4 STEW
"This can't be!": 4 OHNO
"This comes ___ surprise": 4 ASNO
___ this earth: 5 NOTOF
"This Gun for Hire"
  star: 4 LADD

"This guy walks into ___ ...":
  4 ABAR
"This instant!": 6 ATONCE
"This is ___": 5 ATEST
"This is fun!": 4 WHEE
"This is just ___": 5 ATEST
"This is no joke!": 7 IMEANIT
"This is only ___": 5 ATEST
"This is serious!": 7 IMEANIT
"This looks bad": 4 UHOH
"This means ___!": 3 WAR
"This must weigh ___!":
  4 ATON
"This Old House"
  network: 3 PBS
"This one's ___!": 4 ONME
"This ___ outrage!": 4 ISAN
"This ___ recording": 3 ISA
"This round is ___!": 4 ONME
"This ___ stickup!": 3 ISA
"This ___ sudden!": 4 ISSO
"This ___ test": 3 ISA
"This won't hurt ___!": 4 ABIT
Thom
  Shoemaker: 4 MCAN
Thomas
  Actress: 5 MARLO
  Author: 5 WOLFE
  Cartoonist: 4 NAST
  Clockmaker: 4 **SETH**
  Colleague of Kennedy and:
    6 SCALIA
  Columnist: 3 CAL
  Composer: 4 ARNE
  Doubting: 5 CYNIC
  Dramatist: 3 KYD
  of basketball: 5 ISIAH
  Pamphleteer: 5 PAINE
  Poet: 5 DYLAN
  Revolutionary War general:
    4 GAGE
  Skater: 4 DEBI
  Soul singer: 4 IRMA
"Thomas Crown Affair, The"
  actress: 9 RENERUSSO
Thomas Stearns ___: 5 ELIOT
Thompson
  Actress: 3 LEA 4 EMMA **SADA**
  Oscar winner: 4 EMMA

Thompson, Kay
  character: 6 ELOISE
Thong: 5 STRAP
"Thong Song"
  rapper: 5 SISQO
Thor
  and others: 5 AESIR
  Father of: 4 ODIN
  Like: 5 NORSE
Thoracic
  muscle: 3 PEC
Thorn
  relative: 3 EDH
  Stuck by a: 7 PRICKED
"Thorn Birds, The"
  novelist McCullough: 7 COLLEEN
Thornburgh
  predecessor: 5 MEESE
      7 EDMEESE
Thornfield Hall
  governess: 4 EYRE
Thorny: 6 BRIERY
  bloom: 4 ROSE
  subject: 5 BRIAR 8 ROSEBUSH
Thorough: 10 EXHAUSTIVE
Thoroughfare: 4 ROAD 6 AVENUE
    STREET
  German: 7 STRASSE
Thoroughfares
  (abbr.): 3 STS
Thoroughly: 4 ATOZ 5 NOEND
    15 FROMSTEMTOSTERN
  enjoyed: 5 ATEUP
  investigate: 3 VET
Thorpe
  Swimmer: 3 IAN
Those
  against: 5 ANTIS
  for: 4 YEAS
  Not: 5 THESE
  One of: 4 THAT
  over there: 4 THEM
  people: 4 THEY
  ~, in Spanish: 4 ESAS ESOS
"Those ___ the Days": 4 WERE
Thoth
  had the head of one: 4 IBIS
Thou: 3 GEE 4 ONEG 5 GRAND
  A thousand: 3 MIL

squared: 3 MIL
  Verb with: 4 DOST HAST
Though: 6 ALBEIT
  Even: 6 ALBEIT
Thought: 4 IDEA 5 MUSED
      6 OPINED 7 IDEATED
  Lines of: 4 EEGS
  Lost in: 7 PENSIVE
  prefix: 4 IDEO
  School of: 3 **ISM**
  the world of: 6 ADORED
  waves: 3 ESP
  Without: 4 IDLY
Thought-provoking: 4 DEEP
Thoughts
  Have second: 3 RUE
  Have second ~ about:
    8 REASSESS
  Offer: 5 OPINE
"Thou ___ not ...": 5 SHALT
"___ Thou Now O Soul" (Whitman
    poem): 6 DAREST
Thousand
  thou: 3 MIL
  ~, in French: 5 MILLE
Thousand ___, California: 4 OAKS
Thousandth
  of a yen: 3 RIN
  One: 5 MILLI
"... ___ thousand times ...": 3 NOA
Thou-shall-not: 4 NONO
"Thpeak like thith": 4 LISP
Thrash: 3 LAM TAN 4 FLOG
    5 BASTE FLAIL WHALE
    6 LARRUP
Thread
  and other things: 7 NOTIONS
  Cotton: 5 LISLE
  Fine: 5 LISLE
  holder: 5 **SPOOL**
  Twisted: 5 LISLE
  Unit of wound: 5 SKEIN
  Use needle and: 3 SEW
Threadbare: 4 WORN 5 RATTY
    6 SHABBY
Threaded
  fastener: 4 TNUT 5 **SCREW**
Threads: 6 ATTIRE
Threat: 5 PERIL 6 MENACE

ender: 4 ELSE 6 **ORELSE**
Threaten: 4 WARN 6 IMPEND
    MENACE
like a dog: 7 SNARLAT
Threatening
  word: 4 ELSE
  words: 6 ORELSE
Threats
  Like some: 4 IDLE
Three: 4 TREY
  About ~ grains: 5 CARAT
  are a match: 4 SETS
  before seven: 8 AREACODE
  Consisting of: 6 TRIUNE
  dots: 3 ESS
  Group of: 5 TRIAD
  in one: 6 TRIUNE
  (Italian): 3 **TRE**
  months abroad: 3 ETE
  on a clock: 3 III
  One of ~ squares: 4 MEAL
  or four: 4 AFEW
  sheets to the wind: 3 LIT
    6 BLOTTO
  times, in an Rx: 3 **TER**
  wood: 5 SPOON
  ~, at times: 5 CROWD
  ~, in French: 5 TROIS
  ~, in German: 4 DREI
Three Bears
  One of the: 4 MAMA PAPA
Three B's
  One of the: 4 BACH
Three-card
  game: 5 MONTE
  monte: 4 SCAM
"Three Coins in the Fountain"
  fountain: 5 TREVI
  lyricist: 4 CAHN
Three-digit
  number: 8 AREACODE
Three-dimensional: 5 CUBIC
  SOLID 7 SPATIAL
Three-faced
  woman: 3 EVE
"Three Faces ___, The":
  5 OFEVE
Three-handed
  card game: 4 SKAT

Three-horse
  carriage: 6 TROIKA
Three-layer
  snack: 4 OREO
Three-legged
  endeavor: 4 RACE
  table: 6 TEAPOY
Three-letter
  sequence: 7 TRIGRAM
Three-line
  verse: 5 HAIKU
Three Little Kittens
  reward: 3 PIE
" ___ Three Lives": 4 **ILED**
Three-match
  link: 3 ONA
Three ___ match: 3 **ONA**
"Three men in ___": 4 ATUB
Three-mile
  Area beyond the ~ limit:
    7 OPENSEA
Three Musketeers
  One of the: 5 ATHOS 6 ARAMIS
  unit: 3 BAR
Three-note
  chord: 5 TRIAD
Three-panel
  picture: 8 TRIPTYCH
"Threepenny Opera"
  composer: 5 WEILL
Three-piece
  apparel: 4 SUIT
  suit piece: 4 **VEST**
Threepio
  pal: 5 ARTOO
Three-pronged
  weapon: 7 TRIDENT
Three-reeler: 5 MOVIE
"Three's Company"
  actor John: 6 RITTER
  actress Suzanne: 6 SOMERS
Threescore: 5 SIXTY
Three-seater: 4 SOFA
Three-sided
  sword: 4 EPEE
"Three Sisters"
  sister: 4 **OLGA** 5 IRINA MASHA
Threesome: 4 **TRIO**
  Easy: 3 ABC

TV: 4 SONS
Three-spot: 4 TREY
Three-star
off.: 5 LTGEN
Three Stooges
One of the: 3 MOE 5 SHEMP
Three-strikes
result: 3 OUT
Three-striper
(abbr.): 3 NCO SGT
"Three Tall Women"
playwright: 5 ALBEE
Three-time
heavyweight champ: 3 ALI
~ 60-homer man: 4 SOSA
~ A.L. batting champ: 5 BRETT
    OLIVA
~ A.L. MVP: 5 BERRA
~ Best Director: 5 CAPRA
~ Burmese leader: 3 UNU
~ Cy Young Award winner:
    6 SEAVER
~ French Open champ: 5 SELES
~ Hart Trophy winner: 3 ORR
~ Masters champ: 5 FALDO
    SNEAD 8 SAMSNEAD
~ PGA champ: 5 SNEAD
~ Super Bowl MVP:
    10 JOEMONTANA
~ U.S. Open champ: 5 LENDL
    9 IVANLENDL
~ Wimbledon champ: 5 EVERT
    6 TILDEN 7 MCENROE
Three-toed
animal: 5 TAPIR
bird: 4 RHEA
Three-way
joint: 3 TEE
Threnody: 5 ELEGY 6 LAMENT
Thresh: 5 FLAIL
Thresher
shark: 6 SEAFOX
Threshing
tool: 5 FLAIL
Threshold: 3 EVE 4 DOOR EDGE
    SILL 5 BRINK
Cross the: 5 ENTER 6 STEPIN
Thrice
daily, in prescriptions: 3 TID

~, in prescriptions: 3 **TER**
Thrift shop
condition: 4 USED
stipulation: 4 ASIS
What a ~ does: 7 RESELLS
Thrifty
competitor: 4 AVIS
one: 5 SAVER
Too: 6 SKIMPY
Thrill: 3 WOW 4 KICK RUSH
    SEND 5 ELATE
"Thrilla in Manila"
boxer: 3 ALI
Thrilled: 4 GLAD SENT
"Thriller"
singer nickname: 5 JACKO
Thrilling: 5 HEADY 8 ELECTRIC
"Thrill Is Gone, The"
singer: 6 BBKING
Thrill-seeker
cord: 6 BUNGEE
Throat
ailment: 5 STREP
clearer: 4 AHEM
dangler: 5 UVULA
feature: 6 TONSIL
problem: 4 FROG
___ throat: 5 STREP
___ Throat (of Watergate): 4 DEEP
Throat-clearing
sound: 4 **AHEM**
Throat-culture
finding: 5 STREP
Throaty: 6 HOARSE
Throb: 4 ACHE PANG 5 POUND
    PULSE
Throne
eyer: 4 HEIR
Hold the: 5 REIGN
Occupy the: 3 SIT 4 RULE
On the: 7 REGNANT
Place for a: 4 DAIS
Throneberry
of baseball: 4 MARV
~, once: 3 MET
Throng: 3 MOB 4 HOST SLEW
    5 CROWD HORDE
"___ Thro' the Rye": 5 COMIN
Throttle: 3 GAS

At full: 5 AMAIN
Through: 3 PER **VIA** 4 DONE
    OVER 5 ENDED
  Get ~ to: 5 REACH
  Go: 4 SIFT 5 SPEND
  Run: 4 GORE STAB 6 PIERCE
    8 REHEARSE
Throw: 3 PEG 4 CAST FAZE HURL
    TOSS 5 AMAZE HEAVE
  A: 4 EACH
  dice: 4 CAST ROLL
  down the gauntlet: 4 DARE
  Easy: 3 LOB 4 TOSS
  in: 3 ADD 9 INTERPOSE
  in the towel: 4 QUIT
  off: 4 **EMIT** SHED
  out: 3 CAN 4 CAST TOSS
    5 EJECT EVICT EXPEL
    SCRAP
  rocks at: 4 PELT
  Slow: 3 LOB
  water on: 5 DOUSE
  with effort: 5 HEAVE
Throw ___: 4 AFIT
Throwaway
  Apple: 4 CORE
  Cookout: 3 COB
  Fruit: 4 RIND SEED
Throwback: 7 ATAVISM
Thrower
  Party: 4 HOST
Throwing
  in the towel result: 3 TKO
Thrown
  disk: 7 FRISBEE
  Item ~ in a ring: 3 HAT
Thrown for ___: 5 ALOOP ALOSS
Thrush: 5 VEERY
  Song: 5 MAVIS
Thrust: 4 STAB 5 LUNGE
Thrusting
  sword: 6 RAPIER
Thu.
  follower: 3 FRI
Thud
  Loud: 3 BAM
Thug: 3 APE 4 **GOON** HOOD
    5 BRUTE 7 GORILLA
  knife: 4 SHIV

Thumb: 5 HITCH
  owner: 5 EBERT
  (through): 4 LEAF
Thumb-and-forefinger
  sign: 4 OKAY
Thumb-raising
  critic: 5 EBERT
Thumbs
  All: 5 **INEPT** 6 CLUMSY
    7 AWKWARD
  down: 3 NAY
  down reactions: 4 NOES
  Give a ~ down: 3 NIX PAN
  ups: 3 YES
Thumbscrew
  ridge: 5 KNURL
Thumbs-up: 3 YES 4 OKAY
    6 ASSENT
  Gave the ~ to: 3 OKD
  response: 3 AOK
  vote: 3 **YEA** YES
  write-up: 4 RAVE
Thumb-twiddling: 4 IDLE
Thump: 3 RAP
Thumper
  pal: 5 BAMBI
Thunder: 4 ROAR
  God of: 4 THOR
  sound: 4 **CLAP** PEAL
Thunder Bay
  prov.: 3 ONT
Thundering: 5 AROAR
  group: 4 HERD
Thunderstorm
  product: 5 OZONE
Thunderstruck: 4 AWED 5 AGAPE
    INAWE
Thurber
  dreamer: 5 MITTY
Thurible
  Use a: 5 CENSE
Thüringen
  Info: German cue
  trio: 4 DREI
Thurman
  Actress: 3 UMA
  role: 4 PEEL
Thurmond
  of basketball: 4 **NATE**

Senator: 5 STROM
Thurs.
follower: 3 FRI
___ Thursday: 6 MAUNDY
Thus: 3 SIC 4 ERGO
far: 3 YET 5 ASYET TONOW
6 TODATE
Thusly: 6 LIKESO
Thwack: 3 RAP
Thwart: 4 FOIL 5 AVERT CROSS
DETER 6 STYMIE
7 PREVENT
"Thy hair ___ a flock of goats":
4 ISAS
Thyme: 4 HERB 7 POTHERB
"Thy Neighbor's Wife"
author: 6 TALESE
Thyroid: 5 GLAND
treatment: 6 IODINE
Tia
Actress: 7 CARRERE
___ Tiago: 3 SAO
Tiant
of baseball: 4 LUIS
Tiara
inlays: 4 GEMS
wearer: 4 POPE
Tibbets, Colonel
Mother of: 5 ENOLA
Tiber
City on the: 4 ROME
River connected to the:
4 ARNO
Tiberius
Mother of: 5 LIVIA
That is, to: 5 IDEST
To be, to: 4 ESSE
Tibet
capital: 5 **LHASA**
From: 5 ASIAN
neighbor: 5 NEPAL
setting: 5 ASIA
Tibetan
legend: 4 YETI
monk: 4 **LAMA**
ox: 3 YAK
prefix: 4 SINO
Tibia: 4 BONE SHIN
connectors: 5 TARSI

Tic: 5 SPASM
follower: 3 TAC
Tic ___: 3 TAC
"Tic ___ Dough": 3 TAC
Tick
away: 6 ELAPSE
off: 3 IRE IRK 4 GALL LIST
MIFF **RILE** 5 ANGER
ANNOY COUNT PEEVE
6 ENRAGE 7 INCENSE
Ticked: 3 MAD 4 SORE
5 IRATE
Get ~ off: 5 STEAM 6 SEERED
off: 3 MAD 4 **SORE** 5 ANGRY
IRATE 7 INASNIT
(off): 4 TEED
Ticker
locale (abbr.): 4 NYSE
tape (abbr.): 3 ECG EKG
Taxi: 5 METER
Ticket: 4 CITE 5 DUCAT SLATE
buyer alert: 3 SRO
category: 5 ADULT
end: 4 STUB
Free: 4 COMP **PASS**
Give a ~ to: 4 CITE
High-priced ~ area: 4 LOGE
info: 3 ROW 4 GATE SEAT
TIER
issuer: 3 COP
Kind of: 4 MEAL 5 LOTTO SPLIT
6 SEASON
leftover: 4 STUB
Overcharge for a: 5 SCALP
Political: 5 SLATE
profiteer: 7 SCALPER
Risk a: 5 **SPEED**
sales: 4 GATE
seller: 5 AGENT
9 BOXOFFICE
word: 3 ROW 5 **ADMIT**
Tickle: 5 **AMUSE** ELATE
pink: 5 **ELATE** 6 PLEASE
the ivories: 4 PLAY
Tickled: 4 GLAD
He's: 4 ELMO
pink: 4 **GLAD**
Tickled-pink
feeling: 4 GLEE

"Tickle Me"
 doll: 4 **ELMO**
Ticklish
 doll: 4 **ELMO**
Tic-tac-toe
 loser: 3 OOX **OXO** XOO XXO
 plays: 7 XSANDOS
 win: 3 **OOO**
Tic-___-toe: 3 **TAC**
Tidal
 reflux: 3 EBB
 wave: 7 TSUNAMI
Tidbit: 4 ITEM 6 MORSEL
 Try a: 5 TASTE
Tiddlywink: 4 DISC
Tide
 Kind of: 3 EBB 4 **NEAP** YULE
 Receding: 3 EBB
 rival: 3 ALL ERA FAB
 Semimonthly: 4 NEAP
 target: 4 DIRT 5 STAIN
Tidy: 4 **NEAT** TRIM 9 SHIPSHAPE
 sum: 4 PILE
 up: 6 NEATEN
Tie: 4 DRAW KNOT YOKE
   5 NEXUS TRUSS UNITE
   6 CRAVAT 8 DEADHEAT
 Broad: 5 ASCOT
 Eastern: 3 OBI
 fabric: 3 REP
 Fancy: 5 ASCOT
 holder: 3 TAC
 indicator: 3 ALL
 Parts to: 4 ENDS
 School: 3 PTA
 Shoe: 4 LACE
 String: 4 **BOLO**
 the knot: 3 WED
 type: 4 BOLO 5 ASCOT
 up: 4 BIND DOCK LACE LASH
   5 TRUSS 6 TETHER
 up at the dock: 4 MOOR
 up the line: 3 YAK
Tie ___: 3 TAC
Tiebreaker: 7 PLAYOFF
Tiebreakers: 3 **OTS**
Tied: 4 EVEN 10 EVENSTEVEN
 All ~ up: 4 EVEN
 bundle: 4 BALE

 Fit to be: 3 MAD 5 IRATE LOOSE
   RILED 7 INARAGE
   STEAMED
 It's ~ at the back: 3 OBI
 It's fit to be: 7 SNEAKER
 up: 4 EVEN 5 BOUND
   6 MOORED
Tie-dye
 alternative: 5 BATIK
Tier: 5 LAYER
Tierney
 Actress: 5 MAURA
Tierney, Gene
 role: 5 LAURA
Tierra del ___: 5 FUEGO
Tierra del Fuego
 sight: 5 ANDES
Tierra ___ Fuego: 3 DEL
Ties: 8 NECKWEAR
 Like some: 6 CLIPON
Tie-twiddling
 comedian: 5 OLLIE
Tie-up: 5 SNARL
 Traffic: 3 JAM 5 SNARL
   10 BOTTLENECK
Tiff: 3 ROW 4 SNIT **SPAT**
   5 RUNIN
Tiffin
 Take: 3 EAT
Tiger: 3 CAT 8 MANEATER
 Cereal box: 4 TONY
 Comic strip: 6 HOBBES
 cry: 4 FORE
 feet: 4 PAWS
 game: 4 GOLF
 Like a: 6 FIERCE
 org.: 3 PGA
 pocketful: 4 TEES
 position: 3 LIE
 Start of a rhyme about a: 4 EENY
 support: 3 TEE
 target: 4 HOLE
 tooth: 4 FANG
 with a club: 5 WOODS
Tiger Beat
 reader: 4 TEEN
Tiger-in-your-tank
 brand: 4 ESSO
Tigers: 4 TEAM

of South Carolina: **7** CLEMSON
sch.: **3** LSU
"Tiger Walks, A"
  star: **4** SABU
Tigger
  Friend of: **3** ROO **4** POOH
Tiggywinkle: 3 MRS
Tight: 4 SNUG TAUT **5** TENSE
     6 STINGY
  Close: **6** SEALUP
  Got: **6** TENSED
  He may be: **3** END
  hold: **4** GRIP
  Make: **4** SEAL
  Not: **5** LOOSE SOBER
  Not quite: **4** SNUG
  Not shut: **4** AJAR
  Sit: **4** BIDE STAY
  spot: **4** BIND
  ~, budgetwise: **7** AUSTERE
Tight as ___: 5 ADRUM
Tighten: 5 RETIE
  up: **5** TENSE
Tightener
  Tummy: **5** SITUP **6** CORSET
Tight-fisted: 5 CHEAP
Tightfitting: 4 SNUG
Tight-knit
  group: **5** CADRE
Tight-lipped: 3 MUM
Tightly
  packed: **5** DENSE
  stretched: **4** TAUT
Tightwad: 5 MISER PIKER
Tiglon: 6 HYBRID
Tigris
  land: **4** IRAQ
Tijuana
  Info: Spanish cue
  gold: **3** ORO
  region: **4** BAJA
  tender: **4** PESO
  That, in: **3** ESA ESO
  This, in: **4** **ESTO**
  title: **5** SENOR
  toast: **5** SALUD
  Today, in: **3** HOY
  Tomorrow, in: **6** MANANA
  treat: **4** TACO

two: **3** DOS
Tijuana Brass
  leader: **6** ALPERT
Tiki
  carver: **5** MAORI
Tikkanen
  of hockey: **3** **ESA**
Tilde
  PC ~ topper: **3** ESC
  wearers: **3** ENS
Tilden
  topper: **5** HAYES
Tile
  Clean a ~ floor, maybe:
     7 DAMPMOP
  protector: **7** BATHMAT
Tiler
  need: **5** GROUT
Tiles
  Game with: **8** SCRABBLE
Till: 3 HOE **4** PLOW UPTO
     6 DRAWER
  bill: **3** ONE
  compartment: **4** ONES TENS
  fill: **4** CASH ONES
  now: **3** YET
  stack: **4** ONES TENS
Tiller
  locale: **4** HELM
  prefix: **4** ROTO
  Take the: **5** STEER
Tillie
  Novelist: **5** OLSEN
Tilling
  tool: **3** HOE
Tillis
  Singer: **3** MEL PAM
Tilly
  Actress: **3** **MEG**
Tilt: 3 TIP **4** CANT LEAN LIST
     5 TIPUP
  Going full: **4** ATIT
Tilt-a-Whirl: 4 RIDE
Tilted: 5 LEANT **6** ASLANT
     ASLOPE
  type, for short: **4** ITAL
Tilter
  mount: **5** STEED
  weapon: **5** LANCE

Tilting
  tower town: 4 PISA
  weapon: 5 LANCE
Tim
  Actor: 4 REID
  collaborator: 5 ELTON
  of comedy: 5 ALLEN
  of the Yankees: 6 RAINES
Timber
  problem: 6 DRYROT
  Stem-to-stern: 4 KEEL
  tab: 5 TENON
  tool: 3 ADZ 4 ADZE
  tree: 3 ASH
  Western: 6 REDFIR
  wolf: 4 **LOBO**
Timbering
  tool: 3 AXE
Timberlake, Justin
  band: 5 NSYNC
Timberwolves
  org.: 3 NBA
Timbuktu
  land: 4 MALI
Time: 3 ERA 4 AGER HOUR
     5 CLOCK
     15 FOURTHDIMENSION
  after time: 4 OFTEN
  Ahead of: 5 EARLY
  All the: 4 ALOT 5 OFTEN
  and again: 3 OFT 5 OFTEN
  and time again: 4 EONS ERAS
  Another: 5 AGAIN
  Any: 5 ISSUE
  Any ~ now: 4 SOON
  At another: 4 ANON
  At any: 4 **EVER**
  At no: 4 NEER 5 NEVER
  At that: 4 THEN
  At the ~ of: 4 UPON
  At the right: 5 ONCUE
  At what: 4 WHEN
  Back in: 3 AGO
  Bad: 4 IDES
  before: 3 EVE
  Before this: 6 ERENOW
  Behind: 4 LATE
  being: 5 NONCE
  Big: 3 AGE **ERA** 4 ALOT

Cold: 6 ICEAGE
critic: 4 AGEE
Dark: 5 NIGHT
Decisive: 4 DDAY
delay: 3 LAG
div.: 3 MIN
division: 4 ZONE
During the ~ that: 5 WHILE
Fast: 4 LENT 7 RAMADAN
Festive: 4 YULE
follower: 4 SPAN
for a revolution: 4 YEAR
for one doing time: 7 STRETCH
For the ~ being: 6 PROTEM
For the second: 4 ANEW
frame: 3 ERA
Gay: 8 NINETIES
Get to work on: 4 EDIT
Give a hard ~ to: 6 HASSLE
gone by: 4 PAST
Great: 3 ERA GAS 4 BALL
    5 BLAST
High: 4 BOOM NOON
Hit the big: 6 ARRIVE MAKEIT
Holiday: 4 YULE
Important: 3 **ERA**
In a short: 4 ANON
In due: 4 ANON
in history: 3 AGE EON ERA
In no: 4 SOON
Keep: 3 TAP 5 RENEW
keeper: 6 EDITOR
Kill: 4 IDLE
Kind of: 3 NAP TEE 4 REAL
Knight: 4 YORE
Length of: 5 SPELL
Life: 3 AGE
line segment: 3 ERA
Long: 3 AGE CEN **EON** 4 AEON
    AGES 5 EPOCH YEARS
    7 DOGSAGE
long past: 4 YORE
Make-or-break: 4 DDAY
Many a: 3 OFT 5 OFTEN
March: 4 IDES
Mark: 4 IDLE TICK
Memorable: 3 ERA 5 EPOCH
Notable: 3 **ERA**
Not in: 4 LATE 5 TARDY

7 TOOLATE
Of all: 4 EVER
of anticipation: 3 EVE
of decision: 4 DDAY
off: 4 REST 5 LEAVE RANDR
   7 HOLIDAY LEISURE
of note: 3 ERA
of one's life: 3 AGE
of the year: 6 SEASON
One: 5 ISSUE
One more: 4 ANEW 5 AGAIN
on end: 3 EON
on the job: 5 STINT
Opening: 4 NINE
out: 3 NAP 4 COMA REST
   6 RECESS
Palindromic: 4 NOON
Partner of: 5 AGAIN
Pass, as: 5 SPEND 6 ELAPSE
Past: 4 **YORE**
period: 3 **ERA** 4 SPAN 5 SPELL
piece: 3 ERA MIN 6 OCLOCK
pieces: 3 HRS
Play for: 5 **STALL**
Poetic: 3 **EEN** 4 MORN
Present: 4 NOEL XMAS
Pressed for: 7 INARUSH
Primitive: 8 STONEAGE
Quiet: 4 LULL
Short: 3 BIT MIN SEC 5 TRICE
   6 MOMENT
Single: 4 **ONCE**
Some: 6 AWHILE
Some ~ ago: 4 ONCE
Some ~ back: 9 AWHILEAGO
Some other: 5 LATER
Spring: 3 MAY 4 LENT
   7 EQUINOX
Stretch: 7 SEVENTH
Take more: 5 RENEW
Terrible: 4 TWOS
Terrific: 5 BLAST
Tiny ~ div.: 4 MSEC NSEC
to act: 4 DDAY
to beware: 4 IDES
to celebrate: 3 EVE
to crow: 4 DAWN
to dye: 6 EASTER
to give up: 4 **LENT**

to remember: 3 ERA
Trying: 6 ORDEAL
Up to the ~ that: 5 UNTIL
Very long: 3 **EON** 4 AEON
   8 BLUEMOON
Waste: 4 IDLE KILL 6 DAWDLE
when both hands are up: 4 NOON
While away the: 4 LAZE
Whistle: 4 NOON
Wild: 5 SPREE
without end: 4 AEON
~, so to speak: 5 SANDS
"Time ___" (old sci-fi series):
   4 TRAX
___ time: 4 **ATNO** INNO
"___ time": 3 ITS
"___ Time" (1970s musical):
   5 ONEMO
Time and ___: 5 AHALF
"Time ___ a premium": 4 ISAT
Timecard
   (abbr.): 3 HRS
Time-consuming: 4 LONG
"Timecop"
   actress Mia: 4 SARA
Timed
   Perfectly: 5 ONCUE
   ___ time flat: 4 INNO
Time ___ half: 4 ANDA
Time-honored
   practice: 4 RITE
   saying: 5 ADAGE
"Time in a Bottle"
   singer Jim: 5 CROCE
"Time is money": 5 ADAGE
   AXIOM
Timeless: 7 ETERNAL
~, to a poet: 6 ETERNE
Timeline
   division: 3 **ERA**
Timely
   benefit: 4 BOON
   In a ~ way: 5 ONCUE
"Time Machine, The"
   people: 4 **ELOI**
Time Magazine
   ~ Person of the Year of 2005:
   4 BONO
"Time ___ My Side": 4 ISON

Time-out: 3 NAP
Timepiece: 5 WATCH
  Novelty: **11 CUCKOOCLOCK**
  Pricey: 5 ROLEX
Timer
  Lot: 5 METER
  place: 4 OVEN
Times
  At all: 4 EVER
  Change with the: 5 ADAPT
  Good: 3 **UPS**
  High: 3 UPS
  Old: 4 YORE
  P.M.: 3 NTS 4 AFTS
Timesaver
  PC: 5 MACRO
"Time's a-wastin'!": 4 CMON
Time-share: 6 RENTAL
"Times of Your Life"
  singer: 4 ANKA
Timetable: 4 **SKED**
  abbr.: 3 ARR ETD
"Time ___ the essence!":
    4 ISOF
"... ___ time to do't": Lady
    Macbeth: 3 TIS
Time Warner
  buyer: 3 AOL
Timeworn: 3 OLD
Timex
  rival: 5 CASIO SEIKO
Timid: 3 SHY 5 MOUSY
  creature: 4 DEER
  one: 5 MOUSE
Timing
  A question of: 4 WHEN
Timmy
  Dog of: 6 LASSIE
Timothy
  1960s tripper: 5 LEARY
  Actor: 4 DALY
Timothy Q. Mouse
  Friend of: 5 DUMBO
Timpani: 4 DRUM
Tin
  alloy: 6 PEWTER
  Award that is mostly: 5 OSCAR
  Fish in a: 7 SARDINE
  foil: 4 WRAP

Tina
  Ex of: 3 IKE
  "SNL" writer: 3 FEY
Tin ___ Alley: 3 PAN
"Tin Cup"
  actress Rene: 5 RUSSO
  costar of Kevin: 4 RENE
"Tin Drum, The"
  author Gunter: 5 GRASS
Tine: 5 PRONG
Tined
  tool: 4 FORK
Tinged: 4 HUED
Tiniest
  bit: 4 ATOM DROP IOTA
      5 LEAST SHRED
  The ~ bit: 7 ONEIOTA
Tinker: 3 CUB
  target: 5 EVERS
  with: 4 EDIT
Tinkerbell: 5 PIXIE
  prop: 4 WAND
"Tinker to ___ to Chance":
    5 EVERS
Tin Lizzie: 6 MODELT
Tin Man
  Dorothy, to the: 5 OILER
  necessity: 6 OILCAN
  need: 3 OIL
  portrayer: 5 HALEY
Tinny: 7 STANNIC
Tin Pan Alley
  Ardor, in: 4 PASH
  org.: 5 ASCAP
  product: 4 SONG
Tinsel: 7 ADORNER
Tint: 3 DYE **HUE** 5 COLOR
    SHADE
  Photo: 5 **SEPIA**
Tintern: 5 ABBEY
___ Tin Tin: 3 RIN
Tintinnabulation: 4 PEAL
Tintype
  tint: 5 SEPIA
Tinware
  Painted: 4 TOLE
Tiny: 3 **WEE** 4 ITSY 5 ELFIN
    MICRO 6 MINUTE
  amount: 3 SOU TAD 4 ATOM

DRIB **IOTA** MITE WHIT
5 AMITE GRAIN TRACE
buzzer: 4 GNAT
(Scottish): 3 SMA

"Tiny"
guy: 3 TIM

"Tiny ___": 5 ALICE

"Tiny Alice"
playwright: 5 ALBEE

"Tiny Bubbles"
singer: 5 DONHO

Tiny-capped
mushroom: 5 ENOKI

Tiny Tim
Father of: 3 BOB
flower: 5 TULIP
instrument: 3 UKE 7 UKELELE
    UKULELE
~, to Bob Cratchit: 3 SON

Tiomkin
Film composer: 6 DMITRI

Tip: 3 END 4 ACME DOFF HINT
    LEAN STEER UPEND
Info: Suffix cue
a hat: 4 DOFF
Follow a: 5 ACTON
for a dealer: 4 TOKE
Leave no: 5 STIFF
of a wing tip: 3 TOE
off: 4 CLUE TELL WARN
    5 ALERT 6 CLUEIN
    8 FOREWARN
of the House: 6 ONEILL
politely: 4 DOFF
seller: 4 TOUT
suffix: 4 STER
to one side: 6 CAREEN
Tout: 5 HORSE

Tippecanoe
mate: 5 TYLER

Tipped
It may be: 3 HAT

Tipper
Mate of: 6 ALGORE
or Al: 4 GORE

Tipperary
County west of: 5 CLARE

Tippi
Actress: 6 HEDREN

Daughter of: 7 MELANIE

Tippled: 7 HADANIP

Tippler: 3 **SOT**
Big: 4 WINO
Mayberry: 4 OTIS

Tippy
craft: 5 CANOE

Tips: 6 INCOME

Tipsy: 4 HIGH
Beyond: 3 LIT 6 STEWED

Tiptoe: 5 SNEAK STEAL

Tiptop: 4 ACME AONE APEX
    PEAK

Tirade: 4 **RANT**
One on a: 6 RANTER

Tiranë
land: 7 ALBANIA
land (abbr.): 3 ALB

Tire
abbr.: 3 PSI
channel: 3 RUT
filler: 3 AIR
in the trunk: 5 SPARE
Leaky ~ sound: 4 SSSS
meas.: 3 PSI
Ohio ~ city: 5 AKRON
(out): 4 POOP
part: 5 TREAD
pattern: 5 TREAD
Put on a spare: 4 GAIN
reinforcement: 3 PLY
Spare: 3 FAT 4 FLAB
Spare ~ site: 5 WAIST
Type of: 5 RECAP 6 RADIAL
    7 RETREAD
~, in French: 4 PNEU

Tired: 5 ALLIN STALE TRITE
    WEARY
Sick and: 3 ILL 5 FEDUP

Tireless
It's: 4 SLED

Tires
Feature of some: 9 STEELBELT
Like most: 7 TREADED
Like old: 4 BALD
Work on: 5 ALIGN

Tiresias: 4 SEER

Tiresome: 3 OLD
Become: 4 PALL WEAR

grind: 3 RUT
one: 4 BORE
Tirtoff
alias: 4 ERTE
Tishri
Month before: 4 ELUL
Tissue
additive: 4 **ALOE**
Connective: 6 TENDON
Fatty: 4 SUET
Kind of: 4 SCAR
layer: 3 PLY
Mass of: 4 NODE
Plant: 5 XYLEM
Relating to: 5 TELAR
Soft: 7 KLEENEX
suffix: 5 PLASM
Throat: 6 TONSIL
Tit
for tat: 4 TYPO 5 TRADE
Titan
Memorable: 5 ATLAS
place: 4 SILO
Titania: 4 MOON
Husband of: 6 OBERON
Titanic: 5 LINER
casualty: 5 ASTOR
It was left on the: 4 PORT
message: 3 SOS
sinker: 4 BERG 7 ICEBERG
totaler: 4 BERG
"Titanic"
actor Billy: 4 ZANE
actress Winslet: 4 KATE
director: 7 CAMERON
heroine: 4 ROSE
sight: 4 BERG
soundtrack singer: 4 DION
Titan II: 4 ICBM
Titans
Father of the: 6 URANUS
Mother of the: 4 GAEA
One of the: 5 ATLAS
7 OCEANUS
org.: 3 NFL
quarterback Steve: 6 MCNAIR
Tit for ___ : 3 **TAT**
Tithe
amount: 5 TENTH

Tither
amount: 8 ONETENTH
Titian Venus: 4 NUDE
Titicaca: 4 LAGO
Titillating: 4 RACY SEXY
6 EROTIC
Titillation: 5 AROMA
Title: 4 DEED NAME
bandit of opera: 6 ERNANI
British: 4 DAME EARL
car of song: 3 GTO
cloud: 4 LIEN
Common ~ word: 3 THE
document: 4 DEED
Eastern: 3 AGA
Esteemed: 3 SIR
Have ~ to: 3 **OWN**
Hindu: 3 SRI
holder: 5 CHAMP OWNER
Islamic: 4 EMIR
Knight: 3 **SIR**
Lady: 3 MRS 5 MADAM
Muslim: 4 IMAM
of respect: 3 SIR SRI 5 SAHIB
page: 4 DEED
Palindromic: 3 AGA 4 MAAM
5 MADAM
Property: 4 DEED
Retiree: 7 EMERITA
Take the: 3 WIN
Turkish: 3 **AGA** 4 AGHA
5 PASHA
~, in French: 3 MME 4 MLLE
~, in Spanish: 3 SRA 4 SRTA
Titled: 5 NOBLE
lady: 4 DAME
nobleman: 4 LORD
Titleist
holder: 3 TEE
Titmouse
Kind of: 6 TUFTED
Tito
Bandleader: 6 PUENTE
predecessor: 7 PETERII
Real first name of:
5 JOSIP
Real name of: 4 BROZ
Titter: 5 TEHEE
Tittle: 4 IOTA

TiVo
alternative: 3 VCR
Tivoli
family name: 4 ESTE
Three, in: 3 TRE
Tix: 6 DUCATS
Free: 5 COMPS
Tizzy: 5 **SNIT** 5 HOOHA
6 LATHER
In a: 4 AGOG 5 MANIC UPSET
TKO
caller: 3 REF
Tlaloc
~, to the Aztecs: 7 RAINGOD
TLC
dispensers: 3 RNS
Part of: 4 CARE
provider: 5 NURSE
~, for one: 4 TRIO
T-man: 3 FED
T-men: 4 FEDS
TNT
alternative: 3 AMC HBO SHO
USA
ending: 3 ENE
inventor: 5 NOBEL
Part of: 3 **TRI** 5 NITRO
7 TOLUENE
Use: 5 BLAST
To
any extent: 5 **ATALL**
a tee: 3 PAT
be *(plural)*: 3 ARE
be, in French: 4 **ETRE**
be, in Latin: 4 **ESSE**
be, in Spanish: 3 **SER** 5 ESTAR
boot: 3 TOO 4 **ALSO**
6 NOLESS
date: 3 YET 4 AFAR 5 **ASYET**
SOFAR
have, in French: 5 AVOIR
love (Italian): 5 AMARE
me, in French: 4 AMOI
Partner of: 3 **FRO**
pieces: 5 APART
wit: 6 NAMELY
To ___: 4 AMAN **ATEE**
"To a ..."
poem: 3 ODE

Toad
feature: 4 WART
"Toad of Toad Hall"
playwright: 7 AAMILNE
Toadstool
Unlike a: 6 EDIBLE
Toady: 6 YESMAN
13 APPLEPOLISHER
Acted the: 5 YESED
response: 3 YES
To and ___: 3 **FRO**
Toast: 4 CHAR 5 SKOAL 6 SALUTE
7 DRINKTO
choice: 3 RYE 5 WHEAT
Cockney ~ start: 4 ERES
Danish: 5 SKOAL
Dish served on: 7 RAREBIT
French: 5 SALUT
French ~ portion: 5 SANTE
German: 6 PROSIT
Kind of: 5 MELBA
On ~, at a diner: 4 DOWN
opener: 5 HERES 7 HERESTO
Spanish: 5 SALUD
topper: 3 JAM 4 **OLEO** 5 JELLY
Yuletide: 7 WASSAIL
~, to a GI: 7 SHINGLE
___ toast: 5 MELBA
Toasted
brand: 4 EGGO
sandwich, for short: 3 BLT
Toaster
oven setting: 5 BROIL
sound: 5 CLINK
treat: 7 POPTART
type: 5 POPUP
waffle brand: 4 EGGO
word: 5 SKOAL
Toastmaster: 5 EMCEE
"Toastmaster General": 6 JESSEL
"Toast of the Town"
host: 10 EDSULLIVAN
Toasty: 4 WARM
"To Autumn": 3 ODE
Tobacco: 4 ROAD
Coarse: 4 SHAG
holder: 3 TIN
kiln: 4 OAST
Kind of: 9 SMOKELESS

mouthful: 4 CHAW
Pack down: 4 TAMP
pipe part: 4 STEM
Plug of: 4 CHAW
~, et al. (abbr.): 3 RDS

Tobacconist
offering: 5 BLEND

"To be, or not to be"
speaker: 6 HAMLET

Tobias
Author: 5 WOLFF

Toboggan: 4 SLED
site: 4 HILL

Toby ___, Sir: 5 BELCH

Today
~, in Italian: 4 OGGI
~, in Spanish: 3 HOY

"Today"
cohost Lauer: 4 MATT
cohost Matt: 5 LAUER
forecaster Al: 5 ROKER
Former ~ cohost Couric: 5 KATIE
weatherman: 7 ALROKER
___ Today: 3 USA

Todd
of baseball: 5 ZEILE
Oldtime actress: 6 THELMA

Todd, Mary
Hubby of: 3 ABE

Todd, Sweeney
weapon: 5 RAZOR

Toddler: 3 TOT 4 TYKE 6 RUGRAT
break: 3 NAP
glassful: 4 WAWA
perch: 3 LAP 4 KNEE
place: 4 CRIB
query: 3 WHY
taboo: 4 NONO

To-do: 3 ROW 4 FLAP FUSS SPAT
STIR 6 FRACAS HOOPLA
list: 6 AGENDA
list item: 4 **TASK** 5 CHORE
Public: 5 SCENE

Toe: 5 DIGIT PIGGY 6 DACTYL
cover: 4 NAIL
Hurt a: 4 STUB
in the water: 4 TEST
More than dip a: 4 WADE
the line: 4 **OBEY**

woe: 4 CORN GOUT

Toes
On one's: 4 ATIP 5 **ALERT**
AWAKE READY
She's on her: 9 BALLERINA

"... to fetch ___ of water": 5 APAIL

Tofu
base: 3 SOY 7 SOYBEAN
source: 4 SOYA

Tog
up: 6 ENROBE

Toga
party site: 4 FRAT
sporter: 5 ROMAN

Together: 3 ONE WED 4 SANE
5 **ASONE** INALL 6 INSYNC
7 ATATIME ENMASSE
8 INTANDEM
All: 5 ASONE 6 INTOTO
7 **ENMASSE**
Band: 5 UNITE 6 TEAMUP
Bring: 5 **UNITE**
Come: 3 **GEL** 4 JELL KNIT
MASS MESH 5 MASS
MERGE UNITE 8 COALESCE
Do: 5 COACT
Fit: 4 MESH NEST
Gather: 5 **AMASS**
Get: 4 MEET 5 AMASS UNITE
Get ~ again: 5 REUNE
Got: 3 MET
Grind: 5 GNASH
Grow: 7 ACCRETE
Hold: 6 COHERE
Join: 4 YOKE 5 UNITE
Melt: 4 **FUSE**
Mix: 4 STIR 5 BLEND
Most: 6 SANEST
musically: 4 **ADUE**
Not: 5 APART
Pieced: 4 SEWN
Put: 4 MADE 5 AMASS RIGUP
UNITE
Rub: 5 GNASH
Scrape: 5 RAISE 6 EKEOUT
Stick: 4 GLUE JOIN 5 PASTE
6 COHERE
They're no longer: 4 EXES
When both hands are: 4 NOON

(with): 5 ALONG
Working: 6 INSYNC 8 INLEAGUE
Togetherness: 5 UNITY 6 UNISON
Toggery: 5 DRESS
Tognazzi
  Actor: 3 UGO
Togo
  capital: 4 LOME
  neighbor: 5 BENIN GHANA
  ___ Toguri (Tokyo Rose): 3 IVA
"To ___ his own": 4 EACH
"To ___ human ...": 5 ERRIS
Toil: 5 LABOR SLAVE
  and trouble: 3 ADO
  wearily: 4 SLOG
  with a crew: 3 OAR
Toiler: 4 PEON SERF
  Autumn: 5 RAKER
  Tiny: 3 ANT
Toiletries
  case: 4 ETUI
Toiling
  away: 4 ATIT
"To ___ is human ...": 3 ERR
Token: 4 SIGN 7 MEMENTO
            8 KEEPSAKE
  Counterfeit: 4 SLUG
  Engagement: 4 RING
  Monopoly: 3 HAT 4 IRON SHOE
  of welcome: 3 LEI
  Poker: 4 CHIP
  taker: 4 SLOT 5 STILE
"To Kill a Mockingbird"
  actor Gregory: 4 PECK
  author: 9 HARPERLEE
  author Harper: 3 LEE
  author Lee: 6 HARPER
Toklas
  partner: 5 STEIN
Tokyo
  Airline to: 3 ANA
  airport: 6 NARITA
  carrier: 3 JAL
  district: 5 GINZA
  Former name of: 3 **EDO**
  island: 6 HONSHU
  Singer born in: 3 ONO
  tie-on: 3 OBI
  trasher: 5 RODAN

Told
  all: 4 SANG
  a tale: 4 SPUN
  a whopper: 4 **LIED**
  Do as: 4 OBEY
  on: 6 RATTED
"___ Told Every Little Star": 3 IVE
"Told you!": 3 HAH SEE
            7 IKNEWIT SOTHERE
Toledo
  Info: Spanish cue
  lake: 4 **ERIE**
  river: 6 MAUMEE
  title: 5 SENOR
  viewer: 7 ELGRECO
  View from: 8 LAKEERIE
Tolerable: 4 SOSO
Tolerate: 4 BEAR TAKE 5 **ABIDE**
            BROOK STAND 6 ENDURE
            7 STOMACH 8 STANDFOR
"To Live and Die ___": 4 **INLA**
Tolkien
  beast: 3 ORC
  creature: 3 **ENT** 6 HOBBIT
  protagonist: 5 FRODO
  tree creature: 3 **ENT**
  wrote one: 7 TRILOGY
Toll: 3 FEE 5 KNELL 7 USERFEE
  rd.: 3 TPK 4 TPKE
  road: 4 PIKE
  Take a: 3 TAX 4 PEAL
  unit: 4 AXLE
Tollbooth
  area: 5 PLAZA
Tolled: 4 RANG
Toll-free
  Part of a ~ number: 3 ATT
Tolls
  For whom the bell: 4 THEE
Tolstoy
  Author: 3 LEO
  heroine: 4 ANNA 8 KARENINA
  novel: 11 WARANDPEACE
Tom: 3 CAT
  Actor: 5 EWELL WOPAT
  Author: 5 WOLFE
  cry: 4 MEOW
  Father of: 5 PIPER
  Golfer: 4 KITE 6 WATSON

Lyricist: 5 ADAIR
mate: 3 HEN
Oscar role for: 7 FORREST
Peeping: 4 EYER 5 SPIER
Polly, to: 4 AUNT
Talk host: 6 SNYDER
~, Dick, and Harry: 4 TRIO
    5 MALES
~, Dick, or Harry: 4 NAME
    6 ANYONE 8 FORENAME
Tomahawk: 3 AXE
Tomás
  Info: Spanish cue
Tomato: 9 LOVEAPPLE
  blight: 5 EDEMA
  jelly: 5 ASPIC
  Tossed ~ sound: 5 SPLAT
  variety: 4 PLUM ROMA
Tomb
  His ~ was found in 1922: 3 TUT
Tomboy: 6 HOYDEN
"Tomb Raider"
  character Croft: 4 LARA
  character Lara: 5 CROFT
Tombstone
  inscription: 3 RIP
  lawman: 4 EARP
  locale: 7 ARIZONA
  newspaper: 7 EPITAPH
"Tombstone"
  actor Kilmer: 3 VAL
  role: 4 EARP
Tomcat: 3 GIB
Tome: 4 BOOK
  Brit. ref.: 3 OED
  filling tales: 5 SAGAS
  ___ Tomé: 3 **SAO**
Tomei
  Oscar winner: 6 MARISA
Tomlin, Lily
  character: 8 EDITHANN
  character Ernestine:
    8 OPERATOR
Tommie
  of baseball: 4 **AGEE**
Tommy
  gun: 4 STEN
  of Broadway: 4 TUNE
  Rocker: 3 LEE

Singer: 3 ROE
Skier: 3 MOE
"Tommy": 5 OPERA
  band: 6 THEWHO
Tommy Lee ___ : 5 JONES
Tomorrow
  Here today, gone: 9 EPHEMERAL
  School of: 3 ROE
  ~, in Spanish: 6 MANANA
"Tomorrow"
  musical: 5 ANNIE
"___ Tomorrow" (Sammy Kaye
    tune): 5 UNTIL
Tomorrow's
  woman: 4 GIRL
Tomoyuki
  Godzilla creator: 6 TANAKA
"Tom Sawyer"
  author: 5 TWAIN
"Tom's Diner"
  singer Suzanne: 4 VEGA
"Tom Thumb"
  composer: 4 ARNE
  star Tamblyn: 4 RUSS
Tom-tom: 4 DRUM
Ton: 4 LOTS 5 LOADS PILES
    SCADS
  fractions (abbr.): 3 LBS
  portion (abbr.): 3 CWT
  Type of: 6 METRIC
Tone
  arm item: 6 NEEDLE
  Complexion: 5 OLIVE
  down: 4 EASE MUTE 6 SOFTEN
    SUBDUE
  Earth: 4 ECRU 5 OCHER
    OCHRE
  Nasal: 5 TWANG
  Neutral: 4 ECRU
  Photo: 5 SEPIA
  Subtle: 3 HUE
  Triangle: 4 TING
  Word after: 4 DEAF
Toner: 6 DRYINK
Tongue
  Asian: 4 THAI
  Boot ~ (abbr.): 4 ITAL
  Caesar's: 5 LATIN
  Celtic: 4 ERSE

Dog with a blue-black: 4 CHOW
Gaelic: 4 **ERSE**
Indian: 3 UTE 4 ZUNI 5 TAMIL
of Jesus: 7 ARAMAIC
Pakistani: 4 URDU
Siouan: 5 OMAHA OSAGE
Speak with forked: 3 LIE
Tehran: 5 FARSI
tip: 3 ESE
Turkic: 5 TATAR
Tongue-clucking
sound: 3 TSK
Tongue-lash: 5 SCOLD 6 BERATE
Tongue-lashing: 6 TIRADE
Tongues
do it: 3 WAG
Like gossiping: 4 AWAG
Tongue-tied
one: 4 SHOE
Toni
Pop singer: 7 BRAXTON
Tonic
partner: 3 GIN
prefix: 3 ISO
Tonics
and tablets, briefly: 4 MEDS
"Tonight Show, The"
first host: 5 ALLEN
former announcer Hall: 3 EDD
host: 4 LENO
host before Carson: 4 PAAR
Tonkin
delta city: 5 HANOI
To no ___ : 5 AVAIL
"To ___ not to ...": 4 BEOR
Tons: 4 **LOTS** MANY 5 AHEAP
ALOAD HEAPS SCADS
SLEWS 6 OCEANS OODLES
Tonsil
neighbor: 5 UVULA
suffix: 4 ITIS
Tonsillitis
cause: 5 STREP
Tonsorial
offering: 5 SHAVE
touch-up: 4 TRIM
Tony: 4 CHIC 5 AWARD
1964 ~ winner: 4 LAHR
1980 ~ winner: 5 EVITA

1982 ~ winner: 4 NINE
1996 ~ winner: 4 RENT
1998 ~ winner: 3 ART
Actor: 5 DANZA
Batting champ: 5 OLIVA
British P.M.: 5 BLAIR
candidate: 4 PLAY
kin: 4 **OBIE**
Middleweight champ: 4 ZALE
of baseball: 4 PENA 5 OLIVA
      PEREZ
of golf: 4 LEMA
Puppeteer: 4 **SARG**
winner: 10 HELENHAYES
winner Caldwell: 3 ZOE
winner Hagen: 3 UTA
winner Judith: 4 IVEY
winner Neuwirth: 4 BEBE
winner Rivera: 5 CHITA
winner Styne: 4 JULE
winner Swoosie: 5 KURTZ
winner Uta: 5 HAGEN
winner Worth: 5 IRENE
winning role for Morse: 3 **TRU**
Too: 4 **ALSO** 6 ASWELL
      OVERLY
big: 5 OBESE
hasty: 4 RASH
inquisitive: 4 NOSY
much, musically: 6 TROPPO
quickly: 7 INHASTE
snug: 5 TIGHT
"Too bad!": 4 ALAS PITY
      5 TOUGH
"Toodle-oo!": 4 **TATA**
Toulouse: 5 ADIEU
"Toodles!": 3 BYE 4 TATA
      5 IMOFF 6 SOLONG
Took: 5 STOLE 7 FLEECED
care of: 5 SAWTO
charge: 3 LED
cover: 3 HID
first: 3 WON
five: 6 RESTED
from the top: 5 REDID
home: 6 NETTED
in: 3 ATE
measures: 5 ACTED
notice: 5 SATUP

off: 3 RAN 4 FLED FLEW LEFT
   WENT
off on: 4 APED
on: 5 HIRED
out: 5 DELED
place: 3 WAS
steps: 5 ACTED 6 STRODE
the cake: 3 ATE WON
the wrong way: 5 STOLE
too much: 4 ODED
up: 7 GOTINTO
Tool: 4 PAWN 7 CATSPAW
  Abrasive: 7 SCRAPER
  arm: 4 SCYTHE
  Axelike: 4 ADZE
  Boring: 5 AUGER 6 REAMER
  Branding: 4 IRON
  building: 4 SHED
  Carpentry: 3 ADZ SAW 4 RASP
    VISE 5 DRILL LEVEL PLANE
    6 RIPSAW
  Climbing: 5 PITON
  Cutting: 3 ADZ AXE BUR 4 ADZE
  Digging: 5 SPADE 6 SHOVEL
  Duel: 4 EPEE
  Fall: 4 RAKE
  Garden: 3 HOE 4 RAKE 5 EDGER
    SPADE 6 WEEDER
  Grinding: 6 PESTLE
  Kitchen: 6 PEELER
  Metalworker: 8 BALLPEEN
  Piercing: 3 AWL
  shaper: 3 DIE
  Shaping: 4 RASP
  sharpener: 8 OILSTONE
  Surgical: 5 LASER
  Threshing: 5 FLAIL
  Trimming: 3 ADZ 5 EDGER
  Turning: 5 LATHE
  with a belt: 6 SANDER
  with teeth: 3 SAW 4 RAKE
  Woodworking: 3 ADZ 4 ADZE
    5 LATHE 6 CHISEL SHAPER
"Too many cooks ...": 5 ADAGE
Toon
  Blue: 5 SMURF
  chihuahua: 3 REN
  dog: 3 REN
  Early ~ clown: 4 KOKO

fowl: 9 DAFFYDUCK
frame: 3 CEL
Futuristic ~ family: 7 JETSONS
MTV: 3 REN
panda: 4 ANDY
pooch: 3 REN
rabbit: 5 ROGER
skunk: 9 PEPELEPEW
Twister-like: 3 TAZ
unit: 3 CEL
~ Betty: 4 BOOP
___ to one's ears: 4 INUP
"___ Too Proud to Beg": 4 AINT
"Too-Ra-Loo-Ra-Loo-___": 3 RAL
Toot: 3 JAG 4 BEEP BLOW TEAR
    5 BINGE SPREE 6 BENDER
  one's own horn: 4 CROW
    5 BOAST
Tooter
  Popeye's: 4 PIPE
Tooth: 3 COG
  Artificial: 7 DENTURE
  Back: 5 MOLAR
  covering: 6 ENAMEL
  Gear: 3 COG
  Long: 4 FANG
  Long in the: 3 OLD 4 **AGED**
  Machine: 3 COG
  org.: 3 ADA
  part: 4 ROOT 6 ENAMEL
  Partner of: 4 NAIL
  prefix: 5 DENTI 6 ODONTO
  trouble: 4 ACHE 5 DECAY
  Wheel: 3 COG
  Wisdom: 5 MOLAR
Toothbrush
  brand: 5 **ORALB**
Toothed: 7 DENTATE
  tool: 3 SAW 4 RAKE
Toothless: 8 EDENTATE
Toothpaste
  box abbr.: 3 ADA
  brand: 5 CREST
  Classic: 5 IPANA
  holder: 4 TUBE
  type: 3 **GEL**
Toothpick
  item: 5 OLIVE
Toothsome: 5 TASTY

Toothy
fish: 3 GAR
menace: 4 CROC
tool: 3 SAW
Toots: 3 HON 5 HONEY
Restaurateur: 4 **SHOR**
"Tootsie"
actress Garr: 4 **TERI**
actress Jessica: 5 LANGE
~ Oscar nominee: 8 TERIGARR
Tootsies
Tabby: 4 PAWS
Top: 3 BRA CAP LID TOY 4 ACME
      APEX BEST PEAK
      5 OUTDO 6 BLOUSE
athlete: 7 ALLSTAR
banana: 4 STAR
Big: 4 TENT
Bikini: 3 BRA
Blow one's: 5 ERUPT
Box: 3 LID
card: 3 ACE
Casual: 3 TEE 6 TSHIRT
choices: 5 ALIST
Come out on: 3 WIN
contractor: 6 ROOFER
dog: 5 CHAMP MRBIG
    9 NUMEROUNO
draft level: 4 ONEA
floor: 5 ATTIC
From the: 4 **ANEW** 5 AGAIN
From the ~, in music: 6 DACAPO
grade: 5 APLUS
gun: 3 ACE
kick: 6 NONCOM
Kind of: 4 TANK 6 HALTER
of some scales: 3 TEN
of the head: 4 PATE
of the morning: 5 ONEAM
of the world: 4 POLE
On: 5 AHEAD
On ~ of: 4 OVER UPON
    5 ABOVE
position: 3 ONE
prize: 7 JACKPOT
rating: 3 TEN 4 AONE
scout: 5 EAGLE
spot: 4 ACME APEX
Take from the: 4 REDO SKIM

Take off the: 4 SKIM
Tank: 6 GASCAP TURRET
Tatar: 4 KHAN
Tube: 3 CAP
Very: 4 ACME
Wave: 5 CREST
Way to get to the: 6 SKITOW
Top 40
song list: 9 HITPARADE
songs: 4 HITS
Topaz: 3 GEM
"Topaz"
author Leon: 4 **URIS**
Top-drawer: 4 AONE 5 ELITE
Topeka
state (abbr.): 4 KANS
Toper: 3 SOT 4 SOAK
Mayberry: 4 OTIS
Top-flight: 4 AONE
"Top Hat"
star: 7 ASTAIRE
Topiary
Like: 6 SHAPED
Topic: 5 THEME
list: 6 AGENDA
of gossip: 4 ITEM
"Top ___ morning!": 4 OTHE
Top-notch: 3 ACE 4 ACES **AONE**
    5 APLUS
Top-of-the-line: 4 AONE BEST
Topology
shapes: 4 TORI
Topper: 3 CAP HAT LID TAM
Topple: 5 UPEND UPSET
    6 UNSEAT
from power: 4 OUST
(over): 4 KEEL
Topps
rival: 5 FLEER
Top-rated: 4 AONE
Tops: 4 **AONE** BEST 6 ATMOST
    ONEUPS
~, in sports: 11 ALLAMERICAN
Top-shelf: 4 AONE
Topsoil
Added ~ to: 6 LOAMED
Lose: 5 ERODE
Topsy
playmate: 3 EVA

Topsy-turvy: 7 INAMESS
  Turn: 5 UPEND UPSET
Toque: 3 HAT
Torah
  holder: 3 **ARK**
  teacher: 5 RABBI
Torch
  1996 Olympic ~ lighter: 3 ALI
  carrier: 6 SCONCE
  Carry a ~ (for): 4 PINE
  crime: 5 ARSON
  job: 5 ARSON
  Kind of: 4 TIKI
  user: 6 WELDER
Torched: 3 LIT
Torch Red
  Car available in: 5 TBIRD
Tore: 3 RAN 4 SPED
  down: 5 RAZED
Toreador
  Cheer for a: 3 OLE
"To recap ...": 5 INSUM
"To reiterate ...": 7 ASISAID
Torero
  encouragement: 3 OLE
Tori
  Singer: 4 **AMOS**
Torino
  Info: Italian cue
  locale: 6 ITALIA
  Three, in: 3 TRE
Tormé
  forte: 4 SCAT
  nickname, with "The":
    9 VELVETFOG
  Singer: 3 MEL
Torment: 3 VEX 4 BAIT RIDE
    5 AGONY EATAT NAGAT
    TEASE
Tormentor
  of Curly: 3 MOE
  of Margaret: 6 DENNIS
  Princess: 3 PEA
  Tiny: 4 GNAT
Torn: 4 RENT
  Actor: 3 RIP
  and tattered: 5 RATTY
Tornado: 8 ACTOFGOD
  siren: 5 ALERT

"Tornado"
  Pitcher nicknamed: 4 NOMO
Toro
  competitor: 5 DEERE
  opponent: 7 MATADOR
  ___ Toro, Benicio: 3 DEL
Toronto
  media inits.: 3 CBC
  team: 4 JAYS 5 LEAFS
    10 MAPLELEAFS
  ~ Argonauts' org.: 3 CFL
Toronto Maple ___: 5 LEAFS
Torpedo: 3 SUB 4 RUIN SINK
  vessel: 5 EBOAT UBOAT
Torpor: 7 INERTIA
Torquato
  Italian poet: 5 TASSO
Torre
  team member: 6 YANKEE
Torrent: 4 RAIN RASH
    5 SPATE 6 DELUGE
    ONRUSH
Torrijos
  of Panama: 4 OMAR
Torso: 4 BODY 6 MIDDLE
Torte
  Top a: 3 ICE
  topper: 4 ICER
Tortelli, Carla
  portrayer: 11 RHEAPERLMAN
Tortilla
  chip dip: 5 SALSA
  Filled: 4 TACO
  sandwich: 4 WRAP
  snack: 5 NACHO
"Tortilla Soup"
  actress Elizabeth: 4 PENA
Tortoise
  and hare event: 4 RACE
  racer: 4 HARE
"Tortoise and the Hare, The":
    5 FABLE
  writer: 5 AESOP
Tortosa
  river: 4 EBRO
Torts
  prof.'s degree: 3 LLD
Tortuga
  neighbor: 5 HAITI

Torture
device: 4 RACK
Torturer: 6 SADIST
Tory
rival: 4 **WHIG**
"Tosca": 5 OPERA
composer: 7 PUCCINI
tune: 4 ARIA
Toscanini: 7 MAESTRO
Conductor: 6 **ARTURO**
Together, to: 4 ADUE
~, et al.: 7 MAESTRI
Tosh, Peter: 5 RASTA
Toshiba
competitor: 3 NEC RCA 4 SONY
5 SANYO
"To Sir With Love"
singer: 4 LULU
Toss: 3 LOB 4 FLIP HURL
5 THROW
about: 5 STREW
High: 3 LOB
option: 5 TAILS
out: 4 BOOT EMIT 5 EJECT
EVICT SCRAP 6 DEPOSE
Scots ~ it: 5 CABER
Tossed
dish: 5 SALAD
It may be: 5 SALAD
Tosser
Caber: 4 SCOT
Mortarboard: 4 GRAD
Tosspot: 3 SOT
"To summarize ...":
7 INSHORT
Tot: 3 ADD 4 DRAM 5 CHILD
break: 3 NAP
piggies: 4 TOES
Reminder to a: 9 SAYPLEASE
ritual: 3 NAP
Seat for a: 4 KNEE
song start: 4 ABCD
spot: 4 CRIB
tender: 5 NANNY
toter: 4 PRAM
trailer: 5 WAGON
wheels: 5 TRIKE
Words to a: 7 ISEEYOU
Tot.: 3 AMT

Total: 3 ADD SUM 4 FULL RUIN
5 ADDUP INALL RUNTO
UTTER 6 ALLOUT
AMOUNT COMETO
ENTIRE 7 ADDUPTO
8 DEMOLISH
(abbr.): 3 AMT
again: 5 READD
confusion: 5 CHAOS
failure: 6 FIASCO
reversal: 5 UTURN
Running: 5 TALLY
Sum: 6 AMOUNT
"Total ___" (1990 film): 6 RECALL
Totaled: 5 **RANTO**
Totality: 3 ALL
Totally: 3 ALL 5 INALL
"Totally rad": 7 AWESOME
"Total Recall"
setting: 4 MARS
"Total Request Live"
network: 3 MTV
Tote: 3 LUG 5 CARRY 6 SCHLEP
8 CARRYALL
figures: 4 ODDS
Roadie: 3 AMP
Totenberg
of NPR: 4 NINA
Toter
Blanket: 5 LINUS
To the ___: 3 MAX 4 HILT
To the ___ degree: 3 **NTH**
**"To ___ their golden eyes"
("Cymbeline"):** 3 OPE
"To the max"
indicator: 3 EST
"To thine own ___ be true":
4 SELF
Toto
hit song: 7 ROSANNA
Tottenham
Info: British cue
Totter: 4 REEL
Toucan
feature: 4 BEAK
Touch: 3 BIT TAD TAG 4 **ABUT**
HINT 5 SENSE
base: 5 TAGUP
down: 4 LAND

Encouraging: 3 PAT
Gentle: 6 CARESS
Get in: 7 CONTACT
Kind of: 5 MIDAS
Light: 3 PAT
lovingly: 6 FONDLE
Nice: 6 CARESS
of color: 5 TINCT
off: 4 TRIP 5 SPARK START
of frost: 3 NIP
on: 4 **ABUT**
on the shoulder: 3 TAP
Perceive by: 4 FEEL
Special: 3 TLC
up: 4 EDIT 5 AMEND EMEND
    6 REVISE 7 ENHANCE
up, at the salon: 7 RECOLOR
upon: 4 ABUT
Touchdown: 7 ARRIVAL
Chicago: 5 OHARE
datum: 3 ETA
Made a: 4 ALIT
spot: 7 AIRPORT
time (abbr.): 3 ETA
Touched: 5 DOTTY
down: 4 **ALIT**
"Touched by an Angel"
actress Downey: 4 ROMA
actress Reese: 5 DELLA
costar: 5 REESE
role: 4 TESS
Touching: 7 TANGENT
"Touch of Evil"
director Orson: 6 WELLES
"Touch the Wind"
Hit subtitled: 6 ERESTU
Touch-up: 4 TRIM
Touchy: 7 TACTILE
subject: 3 AGE 8 SORESPOT
Touchy-___: 5 FEELY
Tough: 4 GOON HARD HOOD
    THUG 9 HARDNOSED
boss: 10 TASKMASTER
companion: 4 MOLL
curve: 3 ESS
exam: 4 ORAL
exterior: 4 HIDE
guy: 7 IRONMAN 8 HARDNOSE
In a ~ spot: 5 TREED

journey: 4 TREK
look: 5 SNEER
Make: 5 STEEL
Mob: 8 ENFORCER
Not so: 8 TENDERER
nut: 5 POSER
nut to crack: 6 ENIGMA
question: 5 POSER
row to hoe: 6 ORDEAL
situation: 4 SPOT
spot: 3 JAM 4 BIND HOLE
    KNOT MESS 5 PINCH
    6 PLIGHT SCRAPE
    8 KNOTHOLE
task: 4 ONUS
test: 4 ORAL
to climb: 5 STEEP
to grasp: 4 DEEP
to settle: 5 MESSY
trip: 4 **TREK**
watchdog: 5 AKITA
wood: 3 ASH 5 LARCH
Toughen: 5 ENURE INURE
up: 5 INURE STEEL
    6 ANNEAL
Toughener
Steel: 8 TITANIUM
Tough-guy
actor Ray: 4 ALDO
Toughie: 5 POSER
"Tough-Minded Optimist, The"
author: 5 PEALE
Toughness
symbol: 5 NAILS
Toujours ___: 3 GAI
Toulon
Info: French cue
To be, in: 4 ETRE
View from: 3 MER
Toulouse
Info: French cue
Thanks, in: 5 MERCI
time: 3 ETE
To be, in: 4 **ETRE**
"Toodle-oo" in: 5 ADIEU
Toulouse-___: 7 LAUTREC
Toulouse-Lautrec
album of women: 5 ELLES
Artist: 5 HENRI

Toupee: 3 RUG WIG
Tour
  gp.: **3** PGA **4** LPGA
  guide listings: **4** INNS
  helper: **6** ROADIE
  leader: **5** GUIDE
  of duty: **5** STINT
  Take a: **8** SIGHTSEE
Tour de France
  entrant: **6** CYCLER
Touring
  car: **5** SEDAN
  company: **8** ROADSHOW
  Early ~ car: **3** REO
  prefix: **3** ECO
  troupe: **8** ROADSHOW
Tourist
  aid: **3** MAP **5** GUIDE
  draw: **5** MECCA
  tote: **6** CAMERA
  transport: **3** CAB
Tourist spot
  Arizona: **6** SEDONA
  Indian: **4 AGRA**
  Mediterranean: **5** IBIZA
  New Mexico: **4** TAOS
  San Diego: **3** ZOO
  Spanish: **5** AVILA
  Swiss: **7** LUCERNE
Tournament
  Big: **4** OPEN
  Early ~ match: **6** PRELIM
  exemption: **3** BYE
  favorite. **4** SEED
  Hoops: **3** NIT **4** NCAA
  Kind of: **4** OPEN **5** PROAM
  Like many ~ events: **5** TIMED
  match: **4** SEMI
  pass: **3 BYE**
  ranking: **4** SEED
  round: **5** SEMIS
  type: **4** OPEN
Tourney
  Hoops: **3** NIT
  March: **4** NCAA
  pass: **3** BYE
  rank: **4** SEED
  round: **5** SEMIS
  type: **4** OPEN **5** PROAM

Tours
  Info: French cue
  river: **5** LOIRE
  season: **3** ETE
  Ta-ta, in: **5** ADIEU
  thanks: **5** MERCI
  toast: **5** SALUT
  To be, in: **4** ETRE
  turndown: **3** NON
  with: **4** AVEC
  Yours, in: **4 ATOI**
Tousle: 4 MUSS
Tout: 4 LAUD
  figures: **4** ODDS
  hangout (abbr.): **3** OTB
  spot: **4** RAIL
  tidbit: **6** HOTTIP
  tip: **5** HORSE
Toves
  Like Carroll's: **6** SLITHY
Tow: 4 HAUL
  Horse: **4** SHAY
  job: **4** REPO
  Ski: **4** TBAR
  Tug: **5** BARGE
Toward
  Head: **7** MAKEFOR
  Lean: **5** FAVOR **6** PREFER
  Move: **4** NEAR
  Point: **5** AIMAT
  shelter: **4 ALEE**
  sunrise: **4** EAST
  sunset: **4** WEST
  the back: **5** AREAR
  the dawn: **4** EAST
  the mouth: **4** ORAD
  the rear: **3** AFT **6** ASTERN
  the rudder: **3** AFT **6** ASTERN
  the stern: **3 AFT**
  Turn: **4** FACE
Towel
  feature: **3** NAP
  holder: **3** ROD
  inscription: **3** HIS **4** HERS
  material: **5** TERRY
  Needing a: **3** WET
  off: **3** DRY
  Result of throwing in the: **3** TKO
  Throw in the: **4** QUIT

word: 3 HIS 4 **HERS**
Tower: 4 LOOM SOAR
  Bell ~ emanation: 4 PEAL
  Biblical: 5 BABEL
  Bridge: 5 PYLON
  Control ~ image: 4 BLIP
  Farm: 4 SILO
  in the water: 3 TUG
  Leaning ~ home: 4 PISA
  Mosque: 7 MINARET
  over: 5 DWARF
  Rural: 4 SILO
  site: 4 PISA 5 BABEL 6 LONDON
  topper: 5 SPIRE
  town: 4 PISA
___ Tower
  (Chicago): 5 SEARS
  (Honolulu): 5 ALOHA
  (San Francisco): 4 COIT
"Tower, The"
  poet: 5 YEATS
Towering: 4 TALL 5 LOFTY
"Towering Inferno, The"
  ~ Oscar nominee: 7 ASTAIRE
Tower of London
  treasure: 11 CROWNJEWELS
"To what do I ___ ...?": 3 OWE
"To whom ___ concern ...": 5 ITMAY
"To ___ With Love": 3 SIR
Town: 4 BURG
  Bean: 4 **LIMA**
  destroyed during WWI: 5 YPRES
  destroyed in 1944: 4 STLO
  employee: 5 CRIER
  German: 5 STADT
  In: 5 LOCAL
  in a novel: 5 ADANO
  in County Kerry: 6 TRALEE
  Italian: 6 ASSISI
  Italian wine: 4 ASTI
  Like a tiny: 8 ONEHORSE
  Market: 5 BOURG
  meeting: 5 FORUM
  near Bangor: 5 ORONO
  near Caen: 4 STLO
  near Padua: 4 ESTE
  Noted cathedral: 3 ELY
  official: 5 CRIER

  on the Thames: 4 **ETON**
  on the Vire: 4 STLO
  Outlying: 5 EXURB
  Out of: 4 AWAY
  outside Harrisburg: 5 ENOLA
  Paint the ~ red: 7 CAROUSE
  Skip: 4 FLEE 5 ELOPE
  Small: 4 BURG
  Spanish wine: 5 JEREZ
  square: 5 PLAZA
  ~ NNE of Santa Fe: 4 TAOS
Town ___: 5 CRIER
"___ Town" (Wilder play): 3 OUR
Townhouse
  type: 5 CONDO
Townie: 5 LOCAL
Town-line
  sign (abbr.): 4 ESTD
Townshend
  of the Who: 4 **PETE**
  Rocker: 4 PETE
"To Wong ___, Thanks for Everything, Julie Newmar: 3 FOO
"___ to worry!": 3 NOT
Tow truck
  abbr.: 3 AAA
  pickup, at times: 4 REPO
Toxic
  compound (abbr.): 3 PCB
  shrub: 5 SUMAC
Toxin
  fighters: 4 SERA
Toy
  ball: 4 NERF
  Beach: 4 PAIL
  block: 4 LEGO
  boat spot: 4 POND
  Boy: 3 KEN
  Building: 4 LEGO
  Child's: 10 JACKINABOX
  Christmas: 4 SLED
  Crib: 6 RATTLE
  disk: 7 FRISBEE
  dog: 4 PEKE
  for windy days: 4 KITE
  gun ammo: 4 CAPS
  Musical: 5 KAZOO
  on a string: 4 KITE YOYO

Paper: 4 KITE
racer: 7 SLOTCAR
Sandbox: 4 PAIL
since 1902: 9 TEDDYBEAR
Snow: 4 SLED
soldier: 5 GIJOE
Spinning: 3 TOP
Spring: 6 SLINKY
that does tricks: 4 YOYO
Ticklish: 4 ELMO
train maker: 6 LIONEL
truck: 5 TONKA
Wind-up: 4 KITE
Winter: 4 SLED
with a tail: 4 KITE

Toyland
visitors: 5 BABES

Toymaker: 3 ELF

Toyota
model: 5 CAMRY PASEO SUPRA
    6 AVALON CELICA TERCEL
    7 COROLLA

"To your health!": 5 SALUD
    SKOAL 6 PROSIT

Tpk.: 3 RTE
rate: 3 MPH

Tra ___ : 4 **LALA**

Trace: 4 CLUE HINT IOTA WISP
    7 SOUPCON VESTIGE
    9 SCINTILLA
Memory: 6 ENGRAM
of color: 5 TINGE
of dishonor: 5 TAINT
of smoke: 4 WISP

Tracey
Comedienne: 6 ULLMAN

Trac II
alternative: 4 ATRA

Track: 3 DOG 4 OVAL RAIL SONG
action: 3 BET
Animal: 5 SPOOR
athlete: 5 MILER
Auxiliary: 4 SPUR
Back at the: 5 BETON
down: 6 LOCATE
event: 4 DASH HEAT **MEET**
    RACE TROT 5 RELAY
    6 SPRINT
    11 HAMMERTHROW

figure: 4 TOUT
figures: 4 ODDS
Go off the: 6 DERAIL
has-been: 3 NAG
Laugh ~ sound: 4 HAHA
Like some ~ meets: 4 DUAL
Lose: 6 DERAIL
numbers: 4 ODDS
official: 5 TIMER
Off the: 6 ASTRAY
Once around the: 3 LAP
Pass again on the: 5 RELAP
Race: 4 OVAL
Railroad ~ part: 8 CROSSTIE
regular: 6 BETTOR
shape: 4 **OVAL**
Slalom: 3 ESS
specialist: 5 MILER
support: 7 TRESTLE
tipster: 4 TOUT
transaction: 3 BET
trial: 4 HEAT
Trodden: 4 PATH
Wheel: 3 RUT

Track-and-field
org.: 3 AAU

Trackball
alternatives: 4 MICE

Tracker: 3 GEO
Airplane: 5 RADAR
Storm: 5 RADAR
UV index: 3 EPA

Tracking
device: 5 RADAR

Tracks
(down): 5 HUNTS
Made: 3 RAN 4 FLED SPED
    TORE
Make: 3 HIE LAM SKI 4 FLEE
    RACE 6 HASTEN

Tract: 3 LOT 4 AREA PLOT
Low: 4 VALE
Open: 3 LEA 5 LLANO
Overgrown: 5 HEATH
Peaty: 4 MOOR
Uncultivated: 5 HEATH
Wet: 4 MIRE

Traction
aid: 5 CLEAT

Tractor
Lose: 4 SKID
Lost: 4 **SLID**

Tractor
blade: 4 PLOW
handle: 5 DEERE
maker: 5 DEERE
name: 5 DEERE

Tractor-trailer: 3 **RIG** 4 SEMI

Tracy
of the comics: 4 DICK

Tracy, Dick
Mrs.: 4 **TESS**

Tracy, Spencer
film of 1958:
13 THELASTHURRAH

Tracy/Hepburn
1949 ~ film: 8 ADAMSRIB
1957 ~ film: 7 DESKSET

Trade: 3 BIZ 4 LINE **SWAP**
5 SKILL 6 BARTER
CAREER METIER
8 EXCHANGE
Carry on: 3 PLY
center: 4 MART
International ~ spot:
8 OPENPORT
jabs: 4 SPAR
Make a: 4 SWAP
Place to: 4 MART
punches: 4 SPAR
show: 4 EXPO
talk: 5 ARGOT
Where some stks.: 3 OTC
___ trade: 3 RAG

Trade-in
item: 7 USEDCAR
reason: 5 DENTS

Trademark: 4 LOGO 5 BRAND
LABEL
Chevalier: 8 STRAWHAT
Churchill: 5 VSIGN
Elvis: 5 SNEER
Indiana Jones: 6 FEDORA
Tangelo: 4 UGLI
Textile: 5 ARNEL

Trader
Bond ~ phrase: 5 ATPAR
Kind of: 3 DAY FUR
place: 3 PIT

Wall St.: 3 ARB

Trader ___ : 4 VICS

Trading
abbr.: 3 OTC
area: 3 PIT
card name: 5 FLEER
center: 4 MART
Early ~ town: 7 ASTORIA
letters: 4 NYSE
Nonstandard ~ unit: 6 ODDLOT
Risky stock: 4 SPEC
U.S. ~ partner: 3 EEC

"Trading Spaces": 6 TVSHOW
Emulate ~ folk: 4 REDO

Tradition
Kind of: 4 ORAL
Local: 4 LORE

Traditional
knowledge: 4 LORE
saying: 5 ADAGE

Trafalgar Square
honoree: 6 NELSON

Traffic: 5 TRADE
Air ~ control device: 5 RADAR
Air ~ screen sight: 4 BLIP
Blend with: 5 MERGE
caution: 3 SLO
circle: 6 ROTARY
cone: 5 PYLON
controller: 5 LIGHT
cop, at times: 5 CITER
director: 4 CONE 5 ARROW
jam: 5 SNARL TIEUP
Kind of: 4 THRU
light color: 5 AMBER
marker: 4 CONE
problem: 5 SNARL 8 GRIDLOCK
Rush-hour ~ facilitator:
7 HOVLANE
Sit in: 4 IDLE
slower: 9 SPEEDBUMP
snarl: 3 JAM
sound: 5 BLARE
tie-up: 3 JAM 5 SNARL
10 BOTTLENECK

"Traffic"
cop: 4 NARC
org.: 3 DEA

Traffic ___ : 4 CONE

Traffic-stopping
  org.: 3 DEA
Tragedy
  Euripides: 5 MEDEA 7 ORESTES
  King of: 4 LEAR
  Racine: 6 ESTHER PHEDRE
  Shakespearean: 7 OTHELLO
  Sophocles: 4 AJAX 7 ELECTRA
    8 ANTIGONE
    10 OEDIPUSREX
"Tragedy of ___, The": 3 NAN
Tragic
  It may be: 4 FLAW
Trail: 3 LAG 4 PATH 5 SCENT
  Animal: 5 SPOOR
  Blazed a: 3 LED
  Follow a: 4 HIKE
  Hound: 5 SCENT
  Hunter: 5 SPOOR
  On the ~ of: 5 AFTER
  shelter: 6 LEANTO
  Ski: 5 PISTE SLOPE
  Snail: 5 SLIME
  the pack: 3 LAG
  ___ Trail: 7 TAMIAMI
Trailblazer: 7 PIONEER
Trailer: 5 PROMO
  Info: Suffix cue
  Boat: 4 WAKE
  hauler: 7 TRACTOR
  Motor: 4 CADE
  Movie: 4 GOER
  Rock: 4 ETTE
  Tot: 5 WAGON
  unit: 5 SCENE
Trailing: 5 INTOW
Trail mix: 4 GORP
  fruit: 6 RAISIN
Train: 5 COACH TEACH TUTOR
  Amtrak's bullet: 5 **ACELA**
  bridge: 7 TRESTLE
  cos.: 3 RRS
  Drive ~ part: 4 AXLE
  for a match: 4 SPAR
  Freight ~ part: 6 BOXCAR
  Half a: 4 CHOO
  Last ~ car: 7 CABOOSE
  line to NYC: 4 LIRR
  name: 6 LIONEL

On the: 6 ABOARD
part: 3 CAR
Place on a: 5 BERTH
schedule abbr.: 3 ETD
schedule listing: 4 STOP
Slow: 5 LOCAL
Speedy: 5 ACELA
station: 4 STOP 5 DEPOT
stop (abbr.): 3 STA
Took the: 4 RODE
Toy ~ maker: 6 LIONEL
track: 4 RAIL
unit: 3 CAR
Wagon ~ direction: 4 WEST
with gloves: 4 SPAR
Trained
  Better: 5 ABLER
Trainee: 5 CADET 6 INTERN
  education: 5 ROPES
Trainer
  Ali: 6 ANGELO
  Lt.: 3 OTC
  place: 3 GYM
Training
  group: 5 CADRE
  Kind of: 5 BASIC
  Like some: 6 ONSITE
  Mil. ~ acad.: 3 OCS
  Military ~ group: 5 CADRE
  Military ~ site: 8 BOOTCAMP
  Pugilist in: 11 SHADOWBOXER
  session: 7 SEMINAR
Trains
  Big name in: 4 TYCO 6 AMTRAK
    LIONEL
  Chicago: 3 **ELS**
  Overhead: 3 **ELS**
"Trainspotting"
  actor McGregor: 4 EWAN
Trait
  carrier: 4 **GENE**
  Desirable: 5 ASSET
  transmitter: 4 GENE
Traitor: 5 JUDAS REBEL
  Noted: 6 ARNOLD
Traits
  Like some: 7 GENETIC
Trajan
  Year ~ conquered Dacia: 3 CVI

Year ~ was born: 4 LIII
Year in the reign of ~: 3 CII
Trajectory: 3 ARC
Tralee
county: 5 KERRY
Tram
load: 3 **ORE**
Tramp: 4 HOBO 7 TRAIPSE
Love of: 4 LADY
Tramped: 4 TROD
Trample: 6 STEPON 7 TREADON
Trampled: 4 TROD
Tranquil: 4 CALM 6 **SERENE**
7 ATPEACE
discipline: 4 YOGA
Tranquilize: 6 SEDATE
Tranquilizer: 6 OPIATE
transport: 7 DARTGUN
Tranquillity: 4 EASE 6 REPOSE
Transaction: 4 DEAL
Bank: 4 LOAN
Business: 4 DEAL
Flea market: 6 RESALE
Team: 5 TRADE
Track: 3 BET
Used car: 6 RESALE
Video store: 6 RENTAL
Transactional analysis
phrase: 4 IMOK
Transatlantic
flyer: 3 SST
Transcriber
~, for short: 5 STENO
Transcript
fig.: 3 **GPA**
letter: 5 GRADE
Transcriptionist: 5 STENO
Transfer: 5 DECAL
Data ~ speed rate: 4 BAUD
port: 6 DECANT
property: 6 ASSIGN
title: 4 DEED
Transfer ___: 3 RNA
Transferee
concern (abbr.): 4 RELO
Transfix: 5 RIVET 6 IMPALE
Transform: 5 MORPH
Transfusion
fluids: 4 SERA

Transgress: 3 ERR 7 VIOLATE
Transgression: 3 SIN 7 OFFENSE
Transient
qtrs.: 3 SRO
Transistor
electrode: 7 EMITTER
forerunner: 6 TRIODE
Transit
Boston ~ syst.: 3 MTA
Capital: 5 METRO
Like some: 5 RAPID
Mass ~ carrier: 3 BUS
Rapid: 3 SST
Rapids: 5 CANOE KAYAK RAFTS
Some ~ lines: 6 METROS
Transition: 5 SEGUE
Abrupt: 4 LEAP
Astrological ~ point: 4 CUSP
Logician: 4 ERGO
Make a slow: 6 EASEIN
Smooth: 5 SEGUE
Transitional
being: 6 APEMAN
Transitory: 10 FLYBYNIGHT
Translate: 6 DECODE
from plaintext: 6 ENCODE
Translation
Bible ~ (abbr.): 3 VER
Translator: 8 LINGUIST
obstacle: 5 IDIOM
Translucent
computer: 4 IMAC
gem: 4 OPAL
mineral: 4 MICA 5 TOPAZ
paper: 9 ONIONSKIN
Transmission
part: 4 GEAR
Satellite: 4 FEED
Sound: 5 AUDIO
Transmit: 3 FAX 4 **SEND**
Transmitted: 4 SENT
Transmitter: 6 SENDER
Impulse: 4 AXON
Neural: 4 AXON
prefix: 5 NEURO
Trait: 4 GENE
Transmitting: 5 ONAIR
Transmutation
Process of: 7 ALCHEMY

Transparency: 7 ACETATE
Transparent: 5 SHEER
      7 SEETHRU
  It's: 4 PANE
  linen: 5 **TOILE**
  Not: 6 OPAQUE
  plastic: 6 LUCITE
  wrap: 5 SARAN
Transpire: 5 OCCUR 6 HAPPEN
Transplant: 5 REPOT 6 REROOT
  Kind of: 5 ORGAN
  Prepare to: 5 UNPOT
  taker: 5 DONEE
Transplanting
  need: 4 SOIL
Transport
  Bermuda: 5 MOPED
  D-Day: 3 LST
  E.T.: 3 UFO
  Final: 6 HEARSE
  Golfer's: 4 CART
  Huck: 4 RAFT
  Kiddie: 7 SCOOTER
  Off-road: 3 ATV
  on treads: 6 SNOCAT
  School: 3 BUS
  sci-fi style: 6 BEAMUP
  Skier's: 4 TBAR
  Tippy: 5 CANOE
  to Oz: 7 TORNADO
  Tot's: 5 TRIKE
  Tourist: 3 CAB
  Urban: 3 BUS CAB
  Western: 5 STAGE
  Winter: 4 SLED
Transportation
  Urban: 3 ELS
Transported: 5 BORNE
      6 ENRAPT
Trans ___ range: 4 ALAI
Trans-Siberian Railroad
  city: 4 OMSK
Transvaal
  settler: 4 **BOER**
Transversely: 6 ACROSS
Trans World Dome
  player: 3 RAM
Transylvania
  locale: 7 ROMANIA

Trap: 3 NAB YAP 5 ICEIN **SNARE**
      7 ENSNARE
  Booby: 5 SNARE
  Dryer ~ content: 4 LINT
  Fly: 3 WEB
  It's a: 5 SNARE
  Like a dryer: 5 LINTY
  Lint: 5 INNIE
  setter: 6 SNARER
  Simple: 5 SNARE
  trigger: 8 TRIPWIRE
  Type of: 5 STEEL
Trapeze
  expert: 9 AERIALIST
Trapped: 5 ATBAY 6 INAJAM
      7 INABIND INASPOT
      UPATREE 8 ENSNARED
Trapped like ___: 4 ARAT
Trapper
  Bug: 5 RESIN
  device: 5 SNARE
  prize: 4 PELT
  Snapper: 3 NET
Trapper John
  Last name of: 8 MCINTYRE
Trappist
  Head: 5 ABBOT
Trapshooting: 5 **SKEET**
Trash: 3 DIS 4 JUNK 5 WASTE
      6 GRUNGE REFUSE
  bag accessory: 3 TIE
  collector: 3 BIN 8 WASTEBIN
  Desktop ~ can: 4 ICON
  place: 4 DUMP
  prefix: 4 EURO
  Talk ~ to: 4 SASS
Trask
  One of the ~ brothers: 4 ARON
Trattoria
  bottle: 4 VINO
  course: 5 PASTA
  dessert: 7 TORTONI
  order: 7 LASAGNA RISOTTO
  quaff: 4 VINO
  sauce: 5 PESTO
  topping: 5 PESTO
  treat: 6 GELATO
  treats: 6 GELATI
  tubes: 4 ZITI

Trauma
ctrs.: **3** ERS
evidence: **4** SCAR
Teen: **4** ACNE
Travel
agent suggestion: **7** AIRLINE
aimlessly: **3** GAD
Air ~ expediter: **7** ETICKET
around: **4** TOUR
before takeoff: **4** TAXI
by air: **4** WAFT
Fast way to: **5** BYAIR
method: **3** AIR
need: **4** VISA
on snow: **3** SKI
option: **4** RAIL
org.: **3** AAA
papers: **5** VISAS
Ready to: **6** ABOARD
stop: **3** INN
When ~ is restricted: **7** WARTIME
Traveler: 4 GOER **5** FARER
aid: **3** MAP **5** ATLAS
bag: **6** VALISE
digs: **5** HOTEL
info: **3** ETA
need: **4** VISA
reference: **5** ATLAS
stop: **3** INN **5** MOTEL
Time ~ stop: **4** PAST
Travelers
Horse-and-buggy: **5** AMISH
to Bethlehem: **4** MAGI
Travel guide: 3 MAP
list: **4** INNS
name: **5** FODOR
Traveling: 4 AWAY **6** AFIELD
9 ONTHEROAD
carriage: **4** SHAY
trio: **4** MAGI
Traveling Wilburys
Bob of the: **5** DYLAN
"Travelin' Man"
Opening words of: **3** IMA
Travels
Fabric that ~ well: **5** ORLON
Travesty: 5 FARCE
Travis
Country singer: **5** MERLE

RANDY **TRITT**
Fictional sleuth: **5** MCGEE
Last stand for: **5** ALAMO
Travolta
1980 ~ film: **11** URBANCOWBOY
musical: **6** GREASE
Trawl
Use a: **4** DRAG
Trawled: 6 SEINED
Trawler
gear: **3** NET
Tray
cheese: **4** EDAM
deposit: **3** ASH
Sign on a ~ of samples:
6 TRYONE
Tre
~ + quattro: **5** SETTE
~ + tre: **3** SEI
Treacherous: 5 FALSE
one: **5** VIPER
sort: **15** SNAKEINTHEGRASS
type: **7** SERPENT
Tread: 4 STEP
mate: **5** RISER
plus riser: **5** STAIR
tediously: **4** PLOD
the boards: **3** ACT
Tread-bare: 4 BALD
Treading
the boards: **7** ONSTAGE
Treadless: 4 BALD
Treadmill
ordeal: **10** STRESSTEST
unit: **4** MILE
Treasure: 3 GEM **5** ADORE TROVE
6 ESTEEM **7** CHERISH
Buried: **3** ORE
cache: **5** TROVE
guardian: **5** GNOME
Hidden: **5** TROVE
holder: **5** CHEST
hunter aid: **3** MAP
Legendary ~ city: **8** ELDORADO
map measure: **4** PACE
Spanish: **3** ORO
Treasure-___ : 5 TROVE
Treasured
violin: **5** AMATI

"Treasure Island"
  character: 4 GUNN
  monogram: 3 **RLS**
Treasurer
  Corp.: 3 CPA
Treasure State
  capital: 6 HELENA
Treasure-trove: 4 LODE
Treasury
  bill: 3 TEN
  State: 4 FISC
Treasury Dept.
  branch: 3 **ATF** IRS
Treasury secretary
  Former: 5 RUBIN
  of Bush: 6 ONEILL
Treat: 3 PAY 6 PAYFOR
          11 FOOTTHEBILL
  as a celebrity: 7 LIONIZE
  badly: 5 ABUSE
  Black-and-white: 4 **OREO**
  Breakfast: 5 CREPE
          12 CINNAMONROLL
  Campfire: 5 SMORE
  Carnival: 7 SNOCONE
  Cool: 7 SHERBET SNOCONE
  Custard: 4 FLAN
  Dog: 4 BONE
  Dutch: 4 **EDAM** 5 GOUDA
  Fountain: 4 MALT 6 MALTED
          11 BANANASPLIT
  harshly: 5 ABUSE
  like a dog: 3 PET
  like dirt: 5 ABUSE
  Luau: 3 POI 4 HULA
  Lunchbox: 4 OREO
  maliciously: 5 SPITE
  meat: 4 CORN CURE
  Meat-filled: 4 TACO
  poorly: 5 ABUSE
  Rich: 5 TORTE
  salt: 6 IODIZE
  Sesame ~ (var.): 5 HALVA
  shabbily: 3 USE
  Teatime: 5 SCONE
  Tex-Mex: 4 TACO 6 FAJITA
          TAMALE
  Toaster: 7 POPTART
  Tubular: 7 CANNOLI

  Twisted: 7 PRETZEL
  with contempt: 5 SPURN
          6 DERIDE
  with gas: 6 AERATE
  with milk: 4 OREO
  with tea: 5 SCONE
Treater
  phrase: 4 **ONME** 7 ITSONME
  pickup: 3 TAB
"Treatise of Human Nature, A"
  author: 4 HUME
Treatment
  Bad: 5 ABUSE
  Emergency: 8 FIRSTAID
  Harsh: 4 GAFF
  Ill: 5 ABUSE
  Kind of: 3 VIP 5 ROYAL
  Rash: 4 TALC
  R.N.: 3 TLC
  Salon: 4 PERM 6 FACIAL
  Window: 5 DRAPE 7 DRAPERY
Treaty: 4 **PACT**
  1814 ~ city: 5 GHENT
  1993 ~: 5 NAFTA
  Defunct ~ org.: 5 SEATO
  gp. since 1948: 3 OAS
  Joined by: 6 ALLIED
  signer: 4 ALLY
  subject: 4 ARMS 7 TESTBAN
  Western ~ gp.: 3 **OAS**
Trebek
  Emcee: 4 **ALEX**
Trebek, Alex: 5 EMCEE
          8 CANADIAN
Treble: 4 CLEF
  clef lines: 5 EGBDF
  clef reader: 4 ALTO
Tree
  African: 4 KOLA 5 MAMBA
  Bark up the wrong: 3 ERR
  branch: 4 LIMB
  Chinese: 6 LITCHI
  chopper: 3 AXE
  Christmas: 3 FIR
  Cone-bearing: 3 FIR 7 CYPRESS
  Cottonwood: 5 ALAMO
  creature: 3 **ENT**
  Cut down a: 4 FELL
  Dwarf: 6 BONSAI

European: **4** SORB
Evergreen: **3** YEW
exudate: **3** SAP
Fam. ~ member: **4** DESC
Fam. ~ word: **3** NEE
feller: **3** AXE
fluid: **3** SAP
Fluttering: **5** ASPEN
Fruit: **4** PEAR
Hardwood: **3** ASH **5** MAPLE
Hawaiian: **3** KOA
house: **4** __NEST__
in Miami: **4** PALM
juice: **3** SAP
knot: **4** BURL KNAR **5** GNARL
Liberty: **3** ELM
Like soil around a: **5** ROOTY
Like some ~ trunks: **5** MOSSY
Mighty: **3** OAK
Mountain: **3** ASH
Nut: **5** BEECH
of life locale: **4** __EDEN__
Quaking: **5** ASPEN
ring: **7** ANNULUS
rings indication: **3** AGE
Shade: **3** __ELM__
Slippery: **3** ELM
Small: **6** ACACIA
Spreading: **3** ELM
Sturdy: **3** OAK
surgeon: **6** PRUNER
that spreads: **6** BANYAN
Thick-trunked: **6** BAOBAB
Trembling: **5** ASPEN
Trim a: **3** LOP
Tropical: **4** PALM **5** CACAO
trunk: **4** __BOLE__
type: **3** ASH
with catkins: **5** __ALDER__
with cones: **4** PINE
with triangular nuts: **5** BEECH
with yellow ribbons: **3** OAK
___ tree: **3** UPA **5** TULIP
Treebeard: 3 ENT
Tree-dwelling: 8 ARBOREAL
primate: **5** LEMUR
"___ tree falls ...": **3** IFA
"Tree Grows in Brooklyn, A"
family: **5** NOLAN

Treeless
expanse: **5** PAMPA
plain: **5** LLANO **6** STEPPE
Tree-lined
Like a ~ area: **5** SHADY
promenade: **7** ALAMEDA
walk: **5** ALLEE
Tree-man: 3 ENT
Tree of Knowledge
site: **4** EDEN
Tree-planting
org.: **3** CCC
"Trees"
poet Kilmer: **5** JOYCE
Treetop
ornament: **5** ANGEL
Trek
Great ~ participant: **4** BOER
to Mecca: **4** HADJ
Trekker
Transvaal: **4** BOER
Trekkers
Star: **4** MAGI
Trellis: 8 ESPALIER
climber: **3** IVY
Tremble: 5 QUAKE **6** DODDER
QUAVER QUIVER
Trembled: 5 SHOOK
Trembling: 6 ASHAKE
tree: **5** ASPEN
Tremendous: 4 EPIC HUGE
Tremendously: 4 ALOT
Tremor: 5 QUAKE SEISM
Trench
Lunar: **4** RILL **5** RILLE
suffix: **4** COAT
Watery: **4** MOAT
Trencherman: 5 EATER
Trend
determiner: **4** POLL
Hot: **3** FAD
Trendy: 3 HIP HOT NOW **4** CHIC
6 LATEST WITHIT
cuisine: **4** THAI
protein source: **4** TOFU
sandwich: **4** WRAP
Trent
Senator: **4** __LOTT__
Trepidation: 5 DREAD

Tres
  menos dos: **3** UNO
  y cinco: **4** OCHO
  y tres: **4** SEIS
"Très ___!": 4 BIEN
Trespass: 3 SIN
Tresses: 4 HAIR **5** LOCKS
  Long: **5** MANES
Trevanian
  novel peak: **5** EIGER
Trevi Fountain
  coin: **4** LIRA
  coins: **4** LIRE
  locale: **4** ROME
Trevino
  Golfer: **3** LEE
Trevor
  Director: **4** NUNN
Trey: 4 CARD
  Loser to a: **5** DEUCE
  topper: **4** FOUR
Tri
  plus two: **5** PENTA
Triage
  ctrs.: **3** __ERS__
  team member: **5** MEDIC
Trial: 3 WOE **4** TEST **6** ORDEAL
    7 TESTRUN
  Avoid a: **6** SETTLE
  balloon: **4** TEST **6** FEELER
  Bikini: **5** ATEST
  Conclusive: **8** ACIDTEST
  evidence: **3** DNA
  Explosive: **5** NTEST
  figure: **5** STENO
  Military: **5** NTEST
  partner: **5** ERROR
  Program: **8** BETATEST
  run: **4** PREP TEST
  setting: **5** VENUE
  Telling: **8** ACIDTEST
  town: **5** SALEM
  Track: **4** HEAT
"Trial, The"
  author: **5** KAFKA
Triangle
  Kind of: **7** SCALENE
  part: **3** LEG
  part (abbr.): **3** HYP

Pool: **4** RACK
  ratio: **4** SINE
  River: **5** DELTA
  tone: **4** TING
Triangular
  deposit: **5** DELTA
  formation: **5** DELTA
  house: **6** AFRAME
  road sign: **5** YIELD
  sail: **3** __JIB__ **6** LATEEN
    9 GOOSEWING
Triangular-bladed
  weapon: **4** EPEE
Triathlete: 7 IRONMAN
  quality: **7** STAMINA
Triathlon
  leg: **3** RUN **4** SWIM
  need: **4** BIKE
Tribal
  chief: **4** KHAN **6** SACHEM
  doctor: **6** SHAMAN
  figure: **5** TOTEM
  history: **4** LORE
  leader: **5** ELDER
  magician: **6** SHAMAN
  symbol: **5** TOTEM
  tales: **4** LORE
  warrior: **5** BRAVE
Tribe
  called the Cat Nation: **4** ERIE
  defeated by the Iroquois: **4** ERIE
  Eastern: **4** ERIE
  for whom a sea is named:
    5 CARIB
  Indian: **6** NATION
  Lake: **4** ERIE
  Largest U.S.: **6** NAVAJO
  Midwest: **4** OTOE
  Plains: **4** OTOE **5** KIOWA
    6 PAWNEE
  Respected ~ member: **5** ELDER
  Western: **3** UTE **4** UTES
TriBeCa
  neighbor: **4** __SOHO__
Tribes
  One of the 12: **3** DAN **4** LEVI
    5 ASHER
Tribesman
  North African: **6** BERBER

Plains: 3 OTO
Western: 3 UTE
Tribulation: 3 **WOE** 6 ORDEAL
Tribunal
Vatican: 4 ROTA
Tributary: 6 FEEDER
Tribute: 4 KUDO 6 HOMAGE
Comic: 5 ROAST
Flowery: 3 ODE
Pay ~ to: 5 HONOR 6 SALUTE
Poetic: 3 ODE
Spoken: 6 EULOGY
Triceratops
feature: 4 HORN
Trick: 3 CON FOX 4 DUPE RUSE
SCAM WILE 5 CATCH
6 DELUDE ENTRAP
LEADON TAKEIN
7 MISLEAD SLEIGHT
Beguiling: 4 WILE
Does a dog: 4 BEGS
Do the: 5 AVAIL
joint: 4 KNEE
Part of a hat: 4 GOAL
Playful: 5 ANTIC
Rare ~ taker: 4 TREY
Silly: 5 APERY
Sly: 4 WILE
suffix: 3 ERY 4 STER
taker: 3 ACE
Tricked
Not ~ by: 4 **ONTO** 6 WISETO
Trickery: 3 ART 5 WILES
6 DECEIT
Trickle: 4 DRIP OOZE **SEEP**
"Trick or ___": 5 TREAT
Trick-or-treater: 5 GHOST
Tricks
Play: 4 JAPE
Trickster: 3 IMP
of myth: 4 LOKI
"Tricksy spirit": 5 ARIEL
Trick-taking
game: 5 WHIST 6 ECARTE
EUCHRE
Tricky: 3 SLY 4 WILY
curve: 3 **ESS**
maneuver: 4 PLOY
shot: 5 MASSE

Trident
feature: 4 TINE
Like a: 5 TINED
shaped letter: 3 **PSI**
Tried: 6 TESTED
and true: 5 SOLID 6 TESTED
Fit to be: 4 SANE
hard: 6 STROVE
Partner of: 4 TRUE
~, with "at": 6 HADAGO
Trieste
Info: Italian cue
They, in: 4 ESSE
Trifecta: 3 BET
Trifle: 3 SOU TOY
Trifling: 4 MERE 5 PETTY
7 NOMINAL
amount: 3 FIG SOU 4 IOTA MITE
fruit: 3 FIG
Most: 5 LEAST
Trig: 4 MATH
abbr.: 3 COS TAN
function: 4 **SINE** 5 COSEC
COTAN 6 COSINE SECANT
7 ARCSINE
ratio: 4 **SINE** 5 COSEC
Trigger: 8 PALOMINO
puller: 4 REIN
rider: 3 ROY
tidbit: 3 OAT
Trap: 8 TRIPWIRE
Triglyceride: 5 ESTER
Trigonometric
function: 4 SINE
Trigonometry
abbr.: 3 COS
ratio: 4 SINE 6 SECANT
Trigram
Cinema: 3 MGM
Phone: 3 ABC DEF GHI JKL
MNO PRS TUV WXY
Trike
power: 5 PEDAL
Trilby: 3 HAT
Trill
Insect: 5 CHIRR
Sheep: 3 BAA
Trillion
About 5.88 ~ mi.: 4 LTYR

prefix: 4 **TERA**
Trillions
  No. in ~ of dollars: 3 GNP
Trilogy
  Aeschylus: 8 ORESTEIA
  Dos Passos: 3 USA
Trim: 3 LOP MOW 4 CROP LEAN
      NEAT PARE SNIP 5 ADORN
      PRUNE SHAVE 6 EDGING
  and graceful: 5 SLEEK
  Auto: 6 CHROME
  Decorative: 4 LACE
  Not just: 5 SLASH
  Robe: 6 ERMINE
  Slim and: 6 SVELTE
  to fit: 4 EDIT
Trimmer
  Lawn: 5 EDGER
  Wood: 4 ADZE
Trimming
  Ready for ~, as a sail: 5 ATRIP
  tape: 5 INKLE
  tool: 3 ADZ 5 EDGER
Trinidad
  partner: 6 TOBAGO
Trinity
  Hindu ~ member: 4 SIVA
    5 SHIVA
  member: 3 SON
"Trinity"
  author: 4 URIS
Trinity College Library
  architect: 4 WREN
Trinket: 5 CHARM 6 BAUBLE
      10 KNICKKNACK
  Exquisite: 5 BIJOU
  Showy: 4 GAUD
Trio
  Alphabetic: 3 ABC BCD CDE *etc.*
  Basic ed: 3 RRR
  Biblical: 4 MAGI
  Female rap: 3 TLC
  German: 4 DREI
  Italian: 3 TRE
  Mythological: 5 FATES HORAE
  One of a 1492: 4 NINA 5 PINTA
  One of a daily: 4 MEAL
  One of a Latin: 3 AMO 4 AMAS
    AMAT VENI

One of a slapstick: 3 MOE
Phone: 3 ABC DEF GHI JKL
    MNO PRS TUV WXY
Pop: 3 AHA
Rock: 5 ZZTOP
times two: 6 SESTET
Traveling: 4 MAGI
trebled: 5 NONET
Trident: 5 TINES
Triple: 5 NONET
Upscale: 6 DOREMI
Yule: 4 MAGI
___ **Triomphe:** 5 ARCDE
Trip: 3 ERR 5 JAUNT 6 VOYAGE
  choice (abbr.): 3 RTE
  Guided: 4 TOUR
  Hard: 4 TREK
  inducer: 3 LSD
  Kind of: 3 EGO LSD
  Newlywed: 9 HONEYMOON
  odometer button: 5 RESET
  Oversea: 6 SAFARI
  part: 3 LEG
  Prepare for a: 5 GASUP
  Quick: 4 SPIN
  Round: 5 ORBIT
  segment: 3 LEG
  Sightseeing: 4 TOUR
  starter: 3 LSD
  taker: 3 EGO
  Took a: 4 FELL
  to the plate: 5 ATBAT
  Tough: 4 **TREK**
  up: 6 ASCENT
  Wee-hours: 6 REDEYE
Triple
  in a triple play: 4 OUTS
  trio: 5 NONET
Triple ___: 3 SEC
Triple Crown
  1930 ~ jockey: 5 SANDE
  1930 ~ winner: 10 GALLANTFOX
  1935 ~ winner: 5 OMAHA
  1937 ~ winner: 10 WARADMIRAL
  1978 ~ winner: 8 AFFIRMED
  stat: 3 RBI
  Two-time ~ jockey: 6 ARCARO
Triple-decker
  lunch: 12 CLUBSANDWICH

treat: 4 OREO
Triple sec
  flavoring: 6 ORANGE
Triplets: 6 THREES
Tripmeter
  button: 5 RESET
Tripod
  feature: 3 LEG
Tripoli
  land: 5 LIBYA
  resident: 6 LIBYAN
Tripper
  turn-on: 3 LSD
Tripping
  air: 4 LILT
Triptik
  abbr.: 3 RTE
  org.: 3 AAA
Trireme
  gear: 4 OARS
Tristan
  Love of: 6 **ISOLDE**
  "___ Triste": 5 VALSE
"Tristia"
  poet: 4 OVID
Tristram
  Beloved of: 6 ISEULT ISOLDE
"Tristram ___": 6 SHANDY
"Tristram Shandy"
  author: 6 STERNE
Trite: 3 PAT 5 BANAL CORNY
      DATED STALE
  saying: 3 SAW 7 BROMIDE
  writer: 4 HACK
Tritt
  Country singer: 6 TRAVIS
Triumph: 3 WIN 7 PREVAIL
      SUCCESS
  Cry of: 3 AHA HAH
  Reliever: 4 SAVE
  Shout of: 4 TADA
  Song of: 5 PAEAN
Triumphant
  cry: 3 AHA 4 IWON TADA
  shout: 3 YES
Triumphed: 3 WON
"Triumph of the Will"
  director Riefenstahl: 4 LENI
Triumvirate: 6 TROIKA

Trivia
  Bit of: 4 FACT 7 FACTOID
  category: 6 SPORTS
  collection: 3 ANA
  Sports: 5 STATS
Trivial: 5 MINOR 6 PALTRY
      13 NICKELANDDIME
  detail: 3 NIT
  objection: 5 CAVIL
Trivial Pursuit
  edition: 5 GENUS
  piece: 3 PIE
Trixie
  Pal of: 5 ALICE
Trodden
  track: 4 PATH
Troglodyte
  home: 4 CAVE
Troilus
  Lover of: 8 CRESSIDA
Trois
  less deux: 3 UNE
Trojan
  hero: 6 AENEAS
  horse: 4 RUSE
  rival: 5 BRUIN UCLAN
Trojans, The: 3 USC 5 SOCAL
Trojan War
  adviser: 6 NESTOR
  beauty: 5 HELEN
  epic: 5 ILIAD
  hero: 4 **AJAX** 6 AENEAS
      HECTOR
  king: 5 PRIAM
Troll: 5 GNOME
Trolley: 4 TRAM
  Off one's: 4 DAFT 5 NUTSY
      NUTTY
  shelter: 7 CARBARN
  sound: 5 CLANG
Trollhättan
  Car from: 4 SAAB
Trollop: 6 HARLOT
Trombone: 5 BRASS
  attachment: 4 MUTE
  feature: 5 SLIDE
Trombonist
  ~ "Kid": 3 ORY
  ~ Winding: 3 KAI

Trompe l'___ : 4 **OEIL**
Trône
  occupant: 3 ROI
Troon
  Info: Scottish cue
  Tiny, in: 3 SMA
Troop
  carrier (abbr.): 3 LST
  encampment: 5 ETAPE
  entertainment spon.: 3 USO
  gp.: 3 BSA 4 REGT
  group: 4 ARMY **UNIT**
    7 BRIGADE
  movement: 6 SORTIE
  truant: 4 AWOL
Trooper
  maker: 5 ISUZU
  Tempt a: 5 SPEED
Troops
  Have more ~ than: 6 OUTMAN
  Move: 6 DEPLOY
  WWI: 3 AEF
Trophy: 3 CUP 5 AWARD PRIZE
  Branch in a ~ room: 6 ANTLER
  Frontier: 5 SCALP
  locale: 3 DEN
  NHL: 4 HART
  shelf: 6 MANTEL
  Took the: 3 WON
  Trapper: 4 PELT
  TV: 4 EMMY
Tropical
  animal: 5 TAPIR
  bird: 3 ANI 5 MACAW 6 TOUCAN
  climber: 5 LIANA
  cocktail: 6 MAITAI
  cooler: 9 TRADEWIND
  cuckoo: 3 ANI
  evergreen: 5 CACAO
  fish: 4 SCAD 5 TETRA
  fruit: 4 DATE 5 DATES GUAVA
    MANGO 6 BANANA PAPAYA
  jelly source: 5 GUAVA
  lizard: 6 IGUANA
  nut: 4 KOLA 5 BETEL
    6 CASHEW
  palm: 5 ARECA
  parrot: 5 MACAW
  plain: 7 SAVANNA

  ray: 5 MANTA
  root: 4 TARO
  spot: 4 ISLE
  tree: 4 PALM 5 CACAO
    6 BAOBAB
  tuber: 4 **TARO**
  vine: 5 **LIANA** LIANE
  wader: 4 IBIS
Tropicana
  rival: 10 MINUTEMAID
Tropicana Field
  locale: 6 STPETE
Trot: 4 **GAIT**
  Hot to: 4 AGOG AVID KEEN
    5 EAGER
  More than a: 4 LOPE
Trotsky
  Revolutionary: 4 **LEON**
Trotter
  rhythm: 4 PACE
Troubadour
  instrument: 4 LUTE
  song: 3 LAI
Trouble: 3 ADO AIL ILL IRK VEX
    WOE 4 CARE FLAP
    5 BESET EATAT 6 HARASS
    7 DISTURB 8 HOTWATER
  Athlete ~ spot: 4 KNEE
  Big: 8 HOTWATER
  Cause: 15 CREATEANUISANCE
  Eye: 4 STYE
  Get out of: 6 RESCUE
  Have ~ deciding: 6 SEESAW
  Having: 7 INASPOT
  Hose: 4 SNAG
  "I": 6 EGOISM
  In: 8 UPACREEK
  Partner of: 4 TOIL
  Ready for: 7 ONALERT
  Serious: 8 HOTWATER
  Sleep: 5 APNEA
  spots: 4 ACNE
  Tap: 4 DRIP LEAK
  Teen: 4 ACNE
  Throat: 4 FROG 5 STREP
  Timber: 6 DRYROT
  Tooth: 5 DECAY
  Tummy: 4 ACHE 5 ULCER
  with esses: 4 LISP

"T-R-O-U-B-L-E"
   singer Travis: 5 TRITT
Troubled: 5 ATEAT
   Not: 6 ATEASE
   state: 6 UNREST
Troublemaker: 3 IMP 4 BRAT
      6 BADLOT 7 GREMLIN
      HELLION
Troubleshooter
   PC: 4 TECH
Trough
   filler: 4 SLOP
   Mason: 3 HOD
   site: 3 STY 4 EAVE
Trounce: 4 ROUT 5 WHOMP
Troupe
   gp.: 3 USO
   group: 6 ACTORS
   Touring: 8 ROADSHOW
Trouser
   cuffs: 7 TURNUPS
   fold: 6 CREASE
   part: 3 LEG
Trousers: 5 PANTS 6 SLACKS
   Old-fashioned: 9 KNEEPANTS
   textile: 5 CHINO
Trout
   fisherman's wear: 6 WADERS
   tempter: 4 LURE
   Way to prepare: 8 AMANDINE
Troutlike
   fish: 5 SMELT
Troy
   Ancient: 5 ILIUM
   coll.: 3 RPI
   Counselor at: 6 NESTOR
   It's headquartered in: 5 KMART
   King of: 5 PRIAM
   lady: 5 HELEN
   Mount near: 3 IDA
   sch.: 3 RPI
   story: 5 **ILIAD**
   Tactics at: 5 SIEGE
   Tale of: 5 ILIAD
   Warrior at: 4 AJAX
Troyanos
   Opera singer: 7 TATIANA
TRS-80
   computer maker: 5 TANDY

Truant
   Mil.: 4 AWOL
Truce
   talk: 6 PARLEY
Trucial
   potentate: 4 EMIR
Truck
   All-purpose: 3 UTE
   British: 5 LORRY
   Chevy: 5 TAHOE
   compartment: 3 CAB
   Dump ~ filler: 6 LOADER
   Fire ~ item: 3 AXE
   garage: 4 BARN
   GMC: 6 SIERRA
   Large: 4 SEMI
   Like a money: 7 ARMORED
   name: 4 MACK
   part: 3 CAB
   Rental ~ company: 5 RYDER
   Shallow: 7 FLATBED
   Sporty: 3 UTE
   Versatile: 3 UTE
   weight: 4 TARE 6 ONETON
Truckee
   Source of the ~ River:
      5 TAHOE
   stop: 4 **RENO**
Trucker
   competition: 6 ROADEO
   expense: 5 TOLLS
   in a union: 8 TEAMSTER
   rig: 4 SEMI
   watchdog (abbr.): 3 ICC
   with a handle: 4 **CBER**
Trucking
   rig: 4 SEMI
Truckload: 3 TON 4 ALOT
Trucks
   Big name in: 5 TONKA
   Co. with brown: 3 UPS
   Gas company known for toy:
      4 HESS
   initials: 3 GMC
   Some toy: 6 TONKAS
Truck stop: 5 DINER
   fare: 4 HASH
   sight: 3 RIG 4 SEMI
   sign: 4 EATS

Trudeau
  Canadian P.M.: **6** PIERRE
  Cartoonist: **5** GARRY
Trudge: 4 PLOD SLOG TREK
True: 4 REAL **5** ALIGN LEVEL
        LOYAL
  blue: **5** LOYAL
  It's: **4** FACT
  It's not: **4** MYTH
  Make: **5** ALIGN
  partner: **5** TRIED
  Regard as: **6** ACCEPT
  Show to be: **5** PROVE
  Tried and: **6** TESTED
  up: **5** ALIGN ALINE
"True ___" (Wayne film): 4 GRIT
"___ true!": 3 ITS
"True Colors"
  singer Lauper: **5** CYNDI
"True Grit"
  ~ Oscar winner: **5** WAYNE
Trueheart
  beau: **5** TRACY
  of the comics: **4 TESS**
True-to-life: 4 REAL
Truffaut
  character: **5** ADELE
Truffle
  and others: **5** FUNGI
  coating: **5** COCOA
Truism: 4 FACT **5** ADAGE AXIOM
Truly: 3 YEA **5** QUITE **6** INDEED
        7 FORREAL
Truman
  adviser: **7** ACHESON
  birthplace: **5** LAMAR
  Mrs.: **4 BESS**
  nuclear agcy.: **3** AEC
  program: **8** FAIRDEAL
  veep Barkley: **5** ALBEN
"Truman"
  portrayer: **6** SINISE
Trump: 4 BEST
  Former Mrs.: **5 IVANA** MARLA
  Game with ~ cards: **4** SKAT
  ~, at times: **5** CLUBS **6** HEARTS
        SPADES **8** DIAMONDS
Trumped-up
  story: **3** LIE

Trumpet: 4 HORN
  accessory: **4** MUTE
  blast: **7** TANTARA
  feature: **5** VALVE
  Half a ~ sound: **3** WAH
  muffler: **4** MUTE
  sound: **4** WAWA **5** BLARE
        7 CLARION
Trumpeter: 4 SWAN
  accessory: **4** MUTE
  Jazz: **6** ALHIRT
Trumpeting: 6 ABLARE
Trumpets: 5 BRASS
Truncation
  abbreviation: **3** ETC
Trunk: 4 BOLE **5** AORTA **TORSO**
  fastener: **4** HASP
  growth: **4** MOSS
  Human: **5** TORSO
  item: **4** JACK TIRE **5** FLARE
        SPARE **8** TIREIRON
        9 SPARETIRE
  It has a: **4** TREE
  line: **5** AORTA
  Main: **5** AORTA
  One year in a: **4** RING
  site: **4** TREE
  Tree: **4 BOLE**
  with a chest: **5** TORSO
Trunkmate
  of McCarthy: **5** SNERD
Trunks: 5 TORSI **6** TORSOS
Trust: 6 BANKON RELYON
        8 RELIANCE
  Have: **4** RELY
  Hold in: **6** ESCROW
  Kind of: **5** BLIND
  prefix: **4** ANTI
  ~, with "on": **4** BANK RELY
Trusted
  friend: **8** ALTEREGO
Trustful: 7 RELIANT
Trusting
  act: **11** LEAPOFFAITH
  Less: **6** WARIER
Trustworthy: 4 SURE **8** RELIABLE
  sort: **7** GOODEGG
Trusty
  mount: **5** STEED

Truth
Absolute: **6** GOSPEL
Assumed: **5** AXIOM
Central: **3** TAO
It's the: **4** FACT
Kind of: **5** NAKED
Not facing the: **8** INDENIAL
Old-style: **5** SOOTH
Self-evident: **5** **AXIOM**
Stretch the: **3** FIB LIE
twister: **4** LIAR
Truth ___ : **5** SERUM
Truthful: 6 HONEST
Try: 3 TAX VIE **4** SHOT STAB
TEST **5** TASTE **6** SAMPLE
7 HAVEAGO
again: **6** REHEAR
Eager to: **6** KEENON
Give a: **5** ESSAY
hard: **6** STRIVE
Hardly: **5** COAST
out: **4** **TEST**
They ~ harder: **4** AVIS
Willing to: **6** OPENTO
~, as a case: **4** **HEAR**
Trying
experience: **6** ORDEAL
one: **7** ESSAYER
"Try ___ might ...": 3 ASI
Tryon, Thomas
novel, with "The": **5** OTHER
Tryout: 4 TEST **7** TESTRUN
Bikini: **5** ATEST
of a sort: **10** SCREENTEST
Trypanosome
transmitter: **6** TSETSE
Trypsin: 6 ENZYME
Tryptophan: 9 AMINOACID
"Try ___ see": 5 ITAND
Tryst
spot: **5** MOTEL
"Try this!": 4 HERE **5** TASTE
T.S. ___ (poet): 5 ELIOT
Tsar
"Terrible": **4** **IVAN** **6** IVANIV
Tse-___, Mao: 4 TUNG
Tse-tung, ___ : 3 MAO
T-shirt
Old ~, perhaps: **3** RAG

size: **5** LARGE
size (abbr.): **3** **LGE**
"Tsk!": 3 TUT **4** PITY
Tsp.: 3 AMT
Tswana
pest: **6** TSETSE
T ___ Tom: 4 ASIN
"___ Tu" (1974 hit): 4 **ERES**
"___ tu" (Verdi aria): 3 **ERI**
Tu-144: 3 SST
Tub: 4 BATH SCOW
contents: **4** OLEO **9** MARGARINE
Hot: **3** **SPA**
Industrial: **3** VAT
Linger in the: **4** SOAK
Soak in the: **5** **BATHE**
Spread in a: **4** OLEO
Sub in a: **4** OLEO
Tuba: 8 BASSHORN
role: **8** BASSPART
sound: **3** PAH **6** OOMPAH
Tubb
Country singer: **6** ERNEST
Tubby: 3 FAT
More than: **5** OBESE
Tube: 5 TVSET **6** TEEVEE
Air on the: **8** TELECAST
Boob: **5** TVSET
Electron: **5** DIODE **6** TRIODE
Exhaust: **8** TAILPIPE
Kind of: **4** BOOB **5** INNER
Lab: **5** PIPET **7** PIPETTE
Old: **6** TRIODE
Radio ~ gas: **5** ARGON XENON
Surgical: **5** STENT
Toothpaste ~ abbr.: **3** **ADA**
top: **3** **CAP**
traveler: **4** OVUM
travelers: **3** OVA
___ tube: 5 INNER
Tube-nosed
seabird: **6** PETREL
Tuber
Edible: **3** OCA YAM **4** **TARO**
Tubes
Boob: **3** TVS
Inner ~, e.g.: **4** TORI
Pasta: **4** ZITI **5** PENNE
8 RIGATONI **9** MANICOTTI

Tubing
Insulating: **9** SPAGHETTI
Tubman: 7 HARRIET
Tub-thump: 4 RANT
Tubular
fare: **4** ZITI **5** PENNE
8 RIGATONI
treat: **7** CANNOLI
Tuck
away: **3** EAT **4** STOW
partner: **3 NIP**
Tapered: **4** DART
title: **5** FRIAR
Tucked
away: **3** ATE
in: **4** ABED SNUG
Tucker
Country singer: **5 TANYA**
Entertainer: **6** SOPHIE
out: **4** TIRE
partner: **3** BIB
Tuckered
out: **4** BEAT **5** ALLIN SPENT
Tucson
plants: **5** CACTI
Tudor
queen: **4** MARY
Tues.
preceder: **3** MON
Tuesday
at the movies: **4** WELD
~, in French: **5** MARDI
___ Tuesday: **5** SUPER **6** SHROVE
(Mardi Gras): **3** FAT
___ Tuesday (1980s pop group):
3 TIL
Tuffet
Use a: **3** SIT
Tuft
Ornamental: **6** POMPOM
Thin: **4** WISP
Tufts
Cat with ear: **4** LYNX
Tug: 4 YANK
task: **3** TOW
tow: **4** SCOW **5** BARGE
Tugboat
line: **7** TOWROPE
sound: **4** TOOT

Tuition
Kind of: **7** INSTATE
Tulip
Future: **4** BULB
Tulips
Traverse the: **6** TIPTOE
"Tulips and Chimneys"
poet: **10** EECUMMINGS
Tully
Philanthropist: **5** ALICE
Tulsa
City south of: **3** ADA
City west of: **4 ENID**
sch.: **3** ORU
state (abbr.): **4** OKLA
Tumble: 4 FALL
Tumbler: 5 GLASS **7** ACROBAT
of rhyme: **4** JILL
"Tumbleweeds"
cartoonist: **6** TKRYAN
cartoonist Tom: **4** RYAN
Tumbling
need: **3** MAT
Tummy
muscles: **3 ABS**
tightener: **6** CORSET
trouble: **4 ACHE 5** ULCER
upsetter: **4** ACID
Tums
alternative: **7** ROLAIDS
Tumult: 3 ADO **4** ROAR STIR
6 CLAMOR
Tumultuous: 6 STORMY
Tuna: 4 FISH
at a sushi bar: **4** TORO
container: **3** TIN
Hawaiian: **3** AHI
How some ~ is ordered:
7 ONTOAST
How some ~ is packed: **5** INOIL
type: **8** ALBACORE
Tuna ___: 4 MELT
"Tuna Fishing"
artist: **4** DALI
___ Tunas: **3** LAS
Tundra
Like the: **8** TREELESS
wanderer: **3** ELK
Tune: 3 AIR **4** SONG **6** MELODY

1950s ~: 5 OLDIE
Cheery: 4 LILT
for two: 4 DUET
Holiday: 4 NOEL 5 CAROL
Light: 4 LILT
Nostalgic: 5 OLDIE
Operatic: 4 ARIA
out: 6 IGNORE

Tuned
in: 5 AWARE

Tuneful: 7 MELODIC
transition: 5 SEGUE

Tuner: 4 DIAL
choices: 4 AMFM

___ Tunes (cartoon series):
6 LOONEY

Tunesmith
org.: 5 ASCAP

Tune-up
item: 9 SPARKPLUG

Tunic
Knight's: 6 TABARD
Roman: 5 STOLA

Tuning fork
Orchestral: 4 OBOE

Tunis
gp.: 3 PLO

Tunisian
Old ~ title: 3 BEY CEY
port: 4 SFAX

Tunnel
maker: 3 ANT 4 MOLE
___ tunnel syndrome: 6 CARPAL

Tunney
Boxer: 4 GENE

Tupolev
creation: 3 SST

Tupperware
Mr. Tupper of: 4 EARL
sound: 4 BURP

"Turandot"
slave girl: 3 LIU

Turban
wearer: 4 SIKH 5 SWAMI

Turbid
Make: 3 MUD

Turbine
part: 5 ROTOR
pivot: 6 STATOR

Turbo
maker: 4 SAAB

Turbulent
water: 3 RIP

Turcotte
Jockey: 3 RON

Tureen
spoon: 5 LADLE

Turf: 3 SOD 4 AREA 5 SWARD
Cover with: 3 **SOD**
grabber: 5 CLEAT
group: 4 GANG
Homeboy: 4 HOOD
in "surf and turf": 5 STEAK

Turgenev
Author: 4 **IVAN**
birthplace: 4 OREL
heroine: 5 ELENA

Turin
Info: Italian cue
City near: 4 ASTI
Cloth of: 6 SHROUD
goodbye: 4 CIAO
Three, in: 3 TRE
Today, in: 4 OGGI

Turing
Mathematician: 4 **ALAN**

Turk
neighbor: 3 SYR 5 IRANI IRAQI
title: 3 AGA

Turkey: 3 DUD 4 FLOP NERD
5 LEMON
Capital of: 6 ANKARA
follower: 4 TROT
Fruit from: 6 CASABA
Go cold: 4 QUIT
helping: 3 LEG
herb: 4 SAGE
Highest point in: 6 ARARAT
Male: 3 TOM
Moisten a: 5 BASTE
neighbor: 4 IRAN IRAQ
5 SYRIA
part: 3 LEG 9 ASIAMINOR
Peak in: 5 MTIDA
roaster: 4 OVEN
Tend to a: 5 BASTE
topper: 5 GRAVY
Young: 5 POULT

Turkic
speaker: 5 TATAR
Turkish
bigwig: 3 **AGA** 4 AGHA 5 PASHA
city: 5 ADANA
coin: 4 LIRA
fruit: 3 FIG
honorific: 3 AGA 4 AGHA
inn: 5 SERAI 6 IMARET
money: 4 LIRA
mount: 6 ARARAT
native: 4 KURD
title: 3 **AGA** 4 AGHA 5 PASHA
Turkish Empire
founder: 5 OSMAN
Turkmenistan
neighbor: 4 IRAN
Turks
Home to most: 4 ASIA
Like most: 5 ASIAN
Turmoil: 4 STIR 5 MELEE
6 UNREST
Inner: 5 ANGST
Turn: 4 MOVE SOUR VEER
5 SPOIL
180-degree ~: 3 UEY
about: 4 SLUE 6 ROTATE
abruptly: 6 SWERVE
aside: 4 SNUB 5 **AVERT** PARRY
SHUNT 6 DIVERT
away: 5 **AVERT** REPEL SPURN
back: 5 REPEL 6 REVERT
blue: 3 DYE 6 SADDEN
color: 5 RIPEN
down: 3 DIM 4 DENY VETO
5 LOWER SPURN 6 PASSUP
REFUSE REJECT
in: 6 RETIRE
Indicate a: 6 SIGNAL
informer: 3 RAT
inside out: 5 EVERT
Kind of: 7 HAIRPIN
left: 3 HAW
loose: 7 RELEASE
Make a sharp: 4 VEER
off: 8 ALIENATE
off course: 4 VEER
on: 5 START 6 AROUSE
on an axis: 4 SLUE 6 ROTATE

out: 5 ENDUP
out to be: 5 ENDUP
outward: 5 EVERT SPLAY
over: 4 **CEDE** GIVE 5 UPEND
6 HANDIN INVERT
pale: 6 BLANCH
Partner of: 4 TOSS
Player's: 4 MOVE ROLL
Ready to ~ in: 6 SLEEPY
red: 3 DYE 5 BLUSH RIPEN
right: 3 GEE
Sharp: 3 **ZAG** ZIG
sharply: 3 ZIG 4 VEER 5 ANGLE
Skip a: 4 PASS
suddenly: 6 SWERVE
tail: 3 RUN WAG 4 FLEE
Takes a: 4 GOES
Took a: 4 WENT
toward: 4 FACE
Tricky: 3 ESS
up one's nose at: 4 SNUB
___-turn: 3 NOU
Turnaround: 3 UIE
Turncoat: 8 DESERTER
RENEGADE
Turndown
Emphatic: 5 NOSIR
Polite: 5 NOSIR 6 NOMAAM
Presidential: 4 VETO
Slangy: 3 NAH NAW 4 NOPE
Teutonic: 4 NEIN
Tours: 3 NON
Vocal: 3 NAY
words: 3 NOS
Turndowns: 3 **NOS** 4 NOES
Turned: 5 SWUNG
into: 6 BECAME
on: 3 LIT
on by: 4 INTO
Turner
Actress: 4 **LANA**
autobiography: 5 ITINA
Cable kingpin: 3 TED
creation: 3 CNN
Head: 4 HUNK
Insurrectionist: 3 NAT
of records: 3 IKE
Rebellious: 3 **NAT**
Singer: 4 **TINA**

Tycoon: **3** TED
Wheel: **4** AXLE
Turner Field
site: **7** ATLANTA
team, on scoreboards: **3** ATL
Turning
meas.: **3** RPM RPS
part: **5** ROTOR
point: **3** ELL HUB **4** AXIS AXLE
DDAY EDDY **5** HINGE PIVOT
6 CRISIS
tool: **5** LATHE
WWII ~ point: **4 DDAY**
Turnip: 4 ROOT
variety: **8** RUTABAGA
Turnoff: 4 EXIT
Turnpike: **4** RAMP
8 RESTAREA
Turn-on
Certain: **3** LSD
"Turn on, tune in, drop out"
adviser: **5** LEARY
Turnover: 5 KNISH
Small: **6** SAMOSA
Turnovers
Small Russian: **8** PIROSHKI
Turnpike: 4 ROAD
charge: **4** TOLL
no-no: **5** UTURN
turnoff: **4** EXIT RAMP
8 RESTSTOP
Turn ___ profit: 4 ANET
Turns
It ~ in its work: **5** LATHE
Some: **5** LEFTS
Take: **6 ROTATE**
Turnstile
coin: **5** TOKEN
Turntable
speed (abbr.): **3** RPM
topper: **5** ALBUM
turners: **3** LPS
"Turn to Stone"
gp.: **3** ELO
"Turn! Turn! Turn!"
group: **5** BYRDS
songwriter: **6** SEEGER
Turow, Scott
book: **4 ONEL**

Turpentine
source: **4** PINE
Turpitude: 4 EVIL
Turquoise: 4 AQUA
8 GEMSTONE
relative: **4** AQUA **8** NILEBLUE
Turret
site: **4** TANK
Turtle
shell: **8** CARAPACE
"Turtle, The"
poet: **4** NASH
Turtledove: 4 DEAR
Turtles
Like some teenage: **5** NINJA
6 MUTANT
Turtles, The
1968 hit song by ~:
7 ELENORE
Turturro
Actress: **4** AIDA
Tuscaloosa
univ.: **4** BAMA
Tuscan
city: **5** SIENA
island: **4** ELBA
marble city: **5** MASSA
river: **4** ARNO
Tuscany
city: **4** PISA **5** SIENA
island: **4** ELBA
Old name for: **7** ETRURIA
river: **4** ARNO
Talk of ~ (abbr.): **4** ITAL
wine: **7** CHIANTI
Tush: 4 REAR
"Tush!": 4 POOH
Tushingham
Actress: **4** RITA
Tusk
material: **5** IVORY
Tusked
animal: **4** BOAR **6** WALRUS
Tussaud
establishment: **9** WAXMUSEUM
first name: **5** MARIE
medium: **3** WAX
Title for: **3** MME **6** MADAME
Tussle: 5 SCRAP

Brief: 5 SETTO
Tut
  country: 5 EGYPT
  relative: 3 TSK
Tutee
  Henry's: 5 ELIZA
Tutor
  Fictional: 4 ANNA
  session: 6 LESSON
Tutu: 5 SKIRT
  material: 5 TULLE
Tutuila
  harbor: 8 PAGOPAGO
Tuxedo
  button: 4 STUD
  Like many a: 6 RENTED
  Put on a: 7 DRESSUP
TV
  adjunct: 3 VCR
  adjustment: 3 HOR
  alien: 3 ALF 4 MORK
  angel portrayer: 5 REESE
  antenna: 6 AERIAL
      10 RABBITEARS
  appearance: 6 AIRING
  award: 4 EMMY
  band: 3 UHF VHF
  cabinet: 7 CONSOLE
  cartoon dog: 3 REN 5 ASTRO
  chef: 4 KERR
  choice: 3 RCA
  clown: 4 BOZO
  collie: 6 LASSIE
  commercial: 4 SPOT
  component: 3 CRT
  control: 3 VOL 4 DIAL TINT
  diner: 4 MELS
  doctor: 4 PHIL 5 ULENE
  dog: 3 REN 6 LASSIE
  et al.: 5 MEDIA
  from D.C.: 5 CSPAN
  genie: 4 EDEN
  guide: 6 RATING
  handyman: 4 VILA
  hookup: 3 VCR
  horse: 4 MRED
  host: 5 EMCEE
  hosts: 3 MCS
  inits.: 3 RCA

inits. since 1975: 3 SNL
interference: 4 SNOW
interruptions: 3 ADS
judge: 3 AMY
knob: 4 TINT
lawyer: 4 ALLY
listing: 4 SKED 7 AIRTIME
maker: 3 RCA 4 SONY
monitor: 3 FCC 5 **VCHIP**
music vendor: 4 KTEL
news source: 3 CNN
palomino: 4 MRED
part: 3 CRT 4 TELE
planet: 3 ORK
preview: 6 TEASER
receiver: 4 DISH
remote button: 3 SEL
room: 3 **DEN**
screen grid: 6 RASTER
series precursor: 5 PILOT
sheriff: 4 LOBO
sked letters: 3 TBA
spots: 3 ADS
studio sign: 5 ONAIR
teaser: 5 PROMO
trophy: 4 EMMY
Unpaid ~ ad: 3 PSA
warrior: 4 XENA
Was on: 5 AIRED
watchdog: 3 FCC
Weekend ~ show: 3 SNL
Words mouthed to a ~ camera:
      5 HIMOM
workers' union: 5 AFTRA
~ E.T.: 3 ALF
~ Marine: 4 PYLE
TVA
  output: 4 ELEC
  project: 3 DAM
  proponent: 3 FDR
TV Guide
  abbr.: 3 TBS
  notation: 3 TBA
  span: 4 WEEK
TWA
  exec Carl: 5 ICAHN
  Former ~ rival: 5 PANAM
Twaddle: 3 PAP ROT 4 BOSH
      5 PRATE 6 DRIVEL

Twain
  character: **4** FINN HUCK
    6 SAWYER
  contemporary: **5** HARTE
  Country singer: **6** SHANIA
  frog: **4** DANL
  Onetime ~ home: **6** ELMIRA
  resting place: **6** ELMIRA
Twain, Mark: 7 PENNAME
Twain/Harte
  play: **5** AHSIN
Twangy: 5 NASAL
TWA Terminal
  designer Saarinen: **4** EERO
Tweak: 3 NIP **8** FINETUNE
Tweed
  Boss ~ caricaturist: **4** NAST
  ___ Tweed (fabric): **6** HARRIS
Tweeter
  output: **6** TREBLE
Tweety
  home: **4** CAGE
  Sylvester, to: **3** TAT
"Twelfth Night"
  Belch of: **4** TOBY
  countess: **6** OLIVIA
  duke: **6** ORSINO
  role: **5** VIOLA
  Sir Toby of: **5** BELCH
Twelve: 4 NOON
  A cube has: **5** EDGES
  doz.: **3** GRO
Twelve ___: 4 OAKS
"Twelve Days of Christmas, The"
  musician: **5** PIPER
Twelve Oaks
  neighbor: **4** TARA
Twelve-year-old: 7 PRETEEN
  Last year's: **4** TEEN
Twenties
  dispenser: **3** ATM
  Roaring: **3** ERA
Twenty
  Change for a: **4** TENS
  fins: **5** CNOTE
"Twenty-One"
  host: **5** BARRY
Twenty Questions
  answer: **3** YES

  category: **6** ANIMAL
Twice: 3 BIS **5** AGAIN
  chewed food: **3** CUD
  Pass: **5** RELAP
  Price: **5** RETAG
  tetra: **4** OCTA OCTO
  tre: **4** SEIS
Twiddled
  one's thumbs: **5** IDLED
Twiddling
  one's thumbs: **4** IDLE
Twig
  Basketry: **5** OSIER
  broom: **5** BESOM
  Willow: **5** OSIER
Twiggy
  abode: **4** NEST
Twigs
  Digs of: **4** NEST **5** NESTS
Twilight
  times: **4** EVES
  ~, old-style: **5** GLOAM
  ~, to a poet: **3** EEN
"Twilight Zone, The"
  host: **10** RODSERLING
  host Serling: **3** ROD
  Like: **5** EERIE
Twill
  Khaki: **5** CHINO
Twilled
  fabric: **5** SERGE
Twin: 4 DUAL
  Biblical: **4** ESAU
  in chemistry: **6** ISOMER
  Minnesota: **6** STPAUL
  of Abby: **3** ANN
  of Apollo: **7** ARTEMIS
  of Artemis: **6** APOLLO
  of Bert: **3** NAN
  of Chang: **3** ENG
  of Esau: **5** JACOB
  of Jacob: **4** ESAU
  of myth: **5** REMUS
  of Pollux: **6** CASTOR
  of Romulus: **5** REMUS
Twin Cities
  suburb: **5** EDINA
Twine: 4 CORD **6** ENLACE
  fiber: **5** SISAL

Twin Falls
Capital NW of: 5 BOISE
Twinge: 4 ACHE PANG
Twining
stem: 4 BINE
Twinings
product: 3 TEA
Twinkie
alternatives: 5 HOHOS
filler: 5 CREME
maker: 7 HOSTESS
Twinkler: 4 STAR
Twinkle-toed: 4 SPRY 5 AGILE
Twinkling: 5 TRICE
"Twin Peaks"
actress Piper: 6 LAURIE
Twins
Father of: 5 ISAAC
Minnesota: 3 ENS
"Twins"
twin: 6 DEVITO
Twirl: 4 SPIN
Twirler
stick: 5 BATON
Twist: 4 SKEW WARP 5 DANCE
    GNARL SCREW
    7 CONTORT
about: 7 ENTWINE
creator: 7 DICKENS
derivative: 4 FRUG
Double: 3 ESS
Fruit for a: 4 LIME
Humor with a: 5 IRONY
It might have a: 4 PLOT
Novel: 6 OLIVER
of phrase: 7 ANAGRAM
out of shape: 4 WARP 5 GNARL
together: 6 ENLACE
Wry: 5 IRONY
Twistable
cookie: 4 OREO
Twisted: 3 WRY 4 AWRY BENT
    SICK 5 WOUND
Antelope with ~ horns: 5 ELAND
Mentally: 4 SICK
person: 5 SICKO
They can be: 6 ANKLES
thread: 5 LISLE
treat: 7 PRETZEL

Twister
Truth: 4 LIAR
Wrist: 4 ULNA
~ Joey: 3 DEE
Twister-like
toon: 3 TAZ
Twisting: 5 SNAKY
Act of: 7 TORSION
the truth: 5 LYING
turns: 5 ESSES
Twit: 5 TAUNT
Twitch: 3 **TIC** 5 SPASM
Twitter: 4 PEEP
"Twittering Machine"
artist: 4 **KLEE**
Twix
maker: 4 MARS
Two: 4 BOTH PAIR
Any one of: 6 EITHER
bells: 3 ONE 5 ONEPM
Bicycle for: 6 TANDEM
bits: 7 QUARTER
Break in: 5 HALVE
Brew for: 3 TEA
caplets: 4 DOSE
cents worth: 3 SAY 7 OPINION
Contest for: 4 DUEL
cups: 3 BRA
Dance for: 5 TANGO
Divisible by: 4 EVEN
fins: 3 TEN 7 TENSPOT
Game with ~ bases: 7 ONEACAT
Give ~ thumbs down to: 3 PAN
Group of: 4 DYAD
hearts: 3 BID
He put ~ and two together:
    4 NOAH
He took ~ tablets: 5 MOSES
How ~ hearts may beat:
    5 ASONE
In ~ parts: 4 DUAL
It has ~ doors: 5 COUPE
It takes: 4 TREY
Music for: 4 DUET
Number: 4 VEEP VICE
of a kind: 4 PAIR
of fifty: 4 EFFS
of nine: 3 ENS
One of: 6 EITHER

or three: 4 AFEW
out of two: 4 BOTH
points: 5 COLON
Put ~ and two together: 3 ADD
  6 TOTEUP
Put in ~ cents' worth: 4 ANTE
  5 OPINE
quarters: 4 HALF
Seat for ~ or more: 6 SETTEE
Second of: 6 LATTER
shakes: 3 SEC
Song for: 4 **DUET**
Split in: 6 CLEAVE
together: 4 BOTH
trios: 6 SEXTET
under par: 5 EAGLE
~, in Spanish: 3 DOS
Two-___: 6 SEATER
Two-bagger
  (abbr.): 3 DBL
Two-band
  radio: 4 AMFM
Two-by-four: 5 BOARD
  Trim a: 3 SAW
Two-by-two
  vessel: 3 ARK
"Two by Two"
  focus: 8 NOAHSARK
  role: 4 NOAH
Two-dimensional: 5 PLANE
    6 PLANAR
  measure: 4 AREA
Two-door: 5 COUPE
Two-faced: 5 FALSE
  deity: 5 JANUS
Two-finger
  sign: 3 VEE
Two fives for ___: 4 ATEN
Twofold: 4 **DUAL**
Two-footed
  animal: 5 BIPED
"Two Laundresses"
  painter: 5 DEGAS
Two-legged
  salamander: 6 MUDEEL
Two-masted
  vessel: 4 BRIG YAWL 5 KETCH
"Two Mules for Sister ___":
    4 SARA

Two-palms-down
  signal: 4 SAFE
Two-part: 4 DUAL
Two-piece: 6 BIKINI
  piece: 3 **BRA**
Two-player
  hoops game: 8 ONEONONE
Two-pointer: 6 SAFETY
  Easy: 4 DUNK 5 TIPIN
Two-run
  homer prerequisite: 5 ONEON
Two-seaters
  Classic: 3 MGS
Two-___ sloth: 4 TOED
Twosome: 3 **DUO** 4 DYAD ITEM
    PAIR
  Tabloid: 4 **ITEM**
Two-stage
  missile: 5 TITAN
Two-star: 4 SOSO
Two-syllable
  foot: 4 IAMB
Two-tiered
  galley: 6 BIREME
Two-ton
  beast: 5 RHINO
Two-tone
  treat: 4 **OREO**
"Two Treatises of Government"
  author: 5 LOCKE
"Two Virgins"
  musician: 3 ONO
Two-way
  preposition: 3 ERE
Two-wheeled
  carriage: 4 SHAY
Two-wheeler: 4 BIKE 5 MOPED
    7 SCOOTER
  Old: 7 CHARIOT
"Two Women"
  ~ Oscar winner: 5 **LOREN**
Two-year-old: 3 TOT
  stride: 6 TODDLE
"Two Years Before the ___":
    4 MAST
"Two Years Before the Mast"
  author: 4 DANA
Twyla
  Choreographer: 5 THARP

Ty
of baseball: 4 COBB
Tycho
Astronomer: 5 BRAHE
Tycoon: 5 BARON
Fur: 5 ASTOR
nickname: 3 ARI
Virgin: 7 BRANSON
"Tyger! Tyger!"
poet: 5 BLAKE
Tyke: 3 TAD TOT
"Blondie": 4 ELMO
Mayberry: 4 OPIE
Unruly: 4 BRAT
Tylenol
alternative: 5 ADVIL ALEVE
  6 ANACIN
target: 4 **ACHE** PAIN
Tyler
Actress: 3 LIV
Author: 4 ANNE
successor: 4 POLK
~, politically: 4 WHIG
Tympanic
membrane: 7 EARDRUM
Tynan, Joe
portrayer: 4 ALDA
Tyne
Actress: 4 **DALY**
Type: 3 **ILK** 4 KIND SORT
choice: 4 FONT
detail: 5 SERIF
in again: 5 REKEY 7 REENTER
measures: 3 EMS ENS
redundantly: 7 ENTERIN
Slanted ~ (abbr.): 4 **ITAL**
Stressed ~ (abbr.): 4 ITAL
Type A
ailment: 5 ULCER
"Typee"
sequel: 4 OMOO
Typeface: 4 FONT
detail: 5 SERIF
extension: 4 KERN
PC: 5 ARIAL
Typesetter
option: 4 FONT

unit: 4 PICA
Typesetting
unit: 4 PICA
units: 3 ENS
Typewriter
feature: 6 TABSET
key: 3 TAB 5 SHIFT 6 RETURN
  SPACER
part: 6 PLATEN
settings: 4 TABS
type: 4 PICA
Typical: 5 USUAL
Least: 6 ODDEST
prefix: 5 PROTO
Typically: 9 ONAVERAGE
Typing
Blood ~ system: 3 ABO
Typist
purchase: 4 REAM
stat: 3 WPM
Typo: 5 ERROR
Typographic
unit: 4 PICA
Typographical
runover: 5 WIDOW
Typos: 6 ERRATA
Check for: 4 EDIT
Tyrannical: 8 DESPOTIC
sort: 4 OGRE
Tyrannosaurus ___: 3 REX
Tyranny
First name in: 3 IDI
Tyrant: 4 OGRE 6 DESPOT
Petty: 6 SATRAP
Tyre
King of: 5 HIRAM
Tyro: 6 NEWBIE ROOKIE
Tyrolean
garb: 6 DIRNDL
refrain: 5 YODEL
Tyrrhenian Sea
island: 4 ELBA
Tyson
Actress: 6 CICELY
moniker: 8 IRONMIKE
___ Tzu: 4 SHIH

Uu

U
- Drainpipe: 4 TRAP
- follower: 4 HAUL
- of the United Nations: 5 THANT
- Queue before: 3 RST 4 QRST
- senior test: 3 GRE

U2
- lead singer: 4 BONO

UAE
- Part of: 4 ARAB

UAR
- Half the ~, once: 3 SYR 5 SYRIA
- Part of: 4 ARAB

Ubangi
- River to the: 4 **UELE**

Ucayali
- Where the ~ flows: 4 PERU

UCLA
- Part of: 3 CAL **LOS** 4 UNIV
    5 CALIF
- rival: 3 USC
- team: 6 BRUINS

Udder
- part: 4 TEAT

Udon
- Order with: 5 SUSHI

Uffizi
- display: 3 ART 4 ARTE

UFO
- crew: 3 **ETS** 6 ALIENS
- shape: 4 DISK

Uganda
- Amin of: 3 **IDI**
- city: 7 ENTEBBE
- Deposed ~ leader: 5 OBOTE
- despot: 4 **AMIN** 7 IDIAMIN
- neighbor: 5 KENYA SUDAN
    6 RWANDA

"Ugh!": 3 ICK 4 YECH
    8 ITSAMESS

Ugly
- Make: 3 MAR
- weather: 5 SLEET

Ugly Duckling
- ~, eventually: 4 SWAN

U-Haul
- rival: 5 RYDER
- unit: 3 VAN
- Use: 4 RENT

UHF
- Part of: 5 **ULTRA**

"Uh-huh": 3 YEP 4 ISEE YEAH

"Uh-oh!": 4 OOPS

"Uh-uh!": 3 NAH 4 **NOPE**
    5 NOWAY 6 NODICE
    NOSOAP

Uintah Reservation
- ~ Indian: 3 UTE

U.K.
- award: 3 MBE OBE
- Fast way to the: 3 SST
- fliers: 3 RAF
- honour: 3 MBE OBE
- Inc., in the: 3 LTD
- lexicon: 3 OED
- locale: 3 EUR
- native: 4 BRIT
- network: 3 BBC
- Part of the: 3 ENG IRE
- record label: 3 EMI

Ukr.
- neighbor: 3 RUS
- ~, once: 3 **SSR**

Ukraine
- capital: 4 KIEV
- citizen: 7 ODESSAN
- city: 4 LVOV 5 YALTA 6 **ODESSA**
- port: 6 ODESSA
- ~, once (abbr.): 3 **SSR**

Ukulele
- Play a: 5 STRUM

"Ulalume"
- poet: 3 POE

Ulan ___ : 5 **BATOR**

Ullman
- Comedienne: 6 TRACEY

Ullmann
Actress: 3 **LIV**
Ulna: 4 BONE
neighbor: 6 RADIUS
Ulrich
Metallica drummer: 4 LARS
Ulster: 4 COAT
Ultimate: 3 END NTH 4 LAST
5 FINAL 6 ENDALL
8 EVENTUAL
purpose: 6 ENDALL ENDUSE
Ultimatum: 6 THREAT
ender: 4 **ELSE** 6 ORELSE
Ultrasecret
org.: 3 NSA
Ultraviolet
blocker: 5 OZONE
Ulvaeus
group: 4 ABBA
"Ulysses"
author: 5 JOYCE
Last word of: 3 YES
Uma
1998 ~ role: 4 EMMA
role: 3 MIA
Umberto
Author: 3 **ECO**
Umbrage: 3 IRE
Take ~ at: 4 MIND 6 RESENT
Umbrella: 5 AEGIS
Lightweight: 7 PARASOL
part: 3 RIB
Umbrian
city: 6 ASSISI
Umlaut
Half an: 3 DOT
Rotated: 5 COLON
Ump
call: 3 **OUT** 4 SAFE TIME
6 STRIKE
Kin of: 3 REF
"Um, pardon me": 4 AHEM
Umpire
call: 3 **LET** OUT 4 SAFE TIME
Umpteen: 4 MANY 5 SCADS
U.N.
ambassador under JFK: 3 AES
15 ADLAIESTEVENSON
Annan of the: 4 KOFI

delegate (abbr.): 3 AMB
First ~ head: 3 LIE
First Israeli ~ ambassador:
4 EBAN 8 ABBAEBAN
Former ~ member: 4 USSR
6 TAIWAN
Hammarskjöld of the: 3 DAG
head of the 1960s: 6 UTHANT
headquarters site: 3 NYC
intervention site: 7 SOMALIA
Kofi of the: 5 ANNAN
member since 1949: 3 ISR
6 ISRAEL
member since 1960: 4 TOGO
observer group: 3 PLO
worker agency: 3 **ILO**
~ Security Council member:
3 USA
Unable
Is ~ to: 4 CANT
to decide: 4 **TORN**
to escape: 5 TREED
to flee: 5 ATBAY
to play: 4 HURT
to sit still: 5 ANTSY
Unabridged: 6 ENTIRE
dictionary: 4 TOME
Unacceptable: 6 NOGOOD
Is: 6 WONTDO
Unaccompanied: 4 LONE SOLE
SOLO STAG 5 **ALONE**
part song: 4 GLEE
"Unaccustomed   am ..."; 3 ASI
Unacquainted
Be ~ with:
15 NOTKNOWFROMADAM
Unadorned: 4 BARE 5 NAKED
PLAIN
Unadulterated: 4 **PURE**
Unaffected: 4 REAL 5 NAIVE
manner: 4 EASE
Unaffiliated
(abbr.): 3 IND
~, slangily: 5 INDIE
Unagi: 3 EEL
Unaided: 5 ALONE
sight: 8 NAKEDEYE
Unalaska
resident: 5 ALEUT

Unanimously: 5 ASONE
6 TOAMAN
"Unanswered Question, The"
composer: 4 IVES
Unappealing: 4 BLAH UGLY
15 NOTONESCUPOFTEA
Unappetizing: 7 INSIPID
food: 4 GLOP MUSH SLOP
5 GRUEL
Unarmed: 5 CLEAN
Unassuming: 3 SHY 4 MEEK
6 MODEST
Unattached: 6 SINGLE
Unattended: 4 LONE 8 SOLITARY
Unattractive
feature: 4 WART
fruit: 4 UGLI
Unbalanced: 4 ALOP
"Un Ballo in Maschera"
aria: 5 ERITU
Unbar
~, to Byron: 3 OPE
"Unbearable Bassington, The"
author: 4 SAKI 5 MUNRO
**"Unbearable Lightness of Being,
The"**
author Kundera: 5 MILAN
Unbegotten: 7 ETERNAL
Unbelievable: 4 TALL
"Unbelievable"
rock band: 3 EMF
Unbending: 4 TAUT 5 RIGID
6 STEELY
Unbleached
hue: 4 ECRU
Unbound: 5 LOOSE
Unbreakable: 8 IRONCLAD
Unbroken: 3 ONE 4 WILD
5 SOLID 6 ENTIRE
Unburden: 3 RID
Uncalled
for: 8 NEEDLESS
Uncanny: 5 **EERIE** WEIRD
ability: 3 ESP
Uncap: 4 OPEN
Unceasingly: 4 EVER
Uncertain: 4 IFFY 5 ATSEA
ROCKY 7 NOTSURE
things: 3 IFS 6 DOUBTS

___ **uncertain terms:** 4 INNO
Uncertainty
Schedule ~ (abbr.): 3 TBA
Show: 6 SEESAW
Unchanged: 4 ASIS SAME
Unchanging: 6 STABLE STATIC
Unchecked: 7 RAMPANT
Spread: 4 RAGE
Unchic: 5 PASSE
Uncivil: 4 RUDE
Uncle: 3 MAN
(abbr.): 3 REL
American: 3 **SAM**
Chekov: 5 VANYA
Fictional: 5 REMUS
of a donkey: 3 ASS
of a monkey: 3 APE
of Antigone: 5 CREON
of Simba: 4 SCAR
Scottish: 3 EME
Seinfeld: 3 LEO
She may cry: 5 NIECE
~, in Spanish: 3 TIO
"Uncle!": 5 IGIVE
Uncle ___ : 3 SAM 4 BENS
"Uncle ___" (Chekov): 5 VANYA
Unclear: 4 HAZY 6 OPAQUE
Unclearly
Speak: 4 SLUR
Uncle Ben
speciality: 4 RICE
"Uncle Miltie": 5 BERLE
Uncle Remus
character: 7 BRERFOX
8 BRERBEAR
offering: 4 TALE
title: 4 BRER
"Uncle Tom's Cabin"
author: 5 STOWE
Friend of Topsy in: 3 EVA
girl: 3 **EVA**
"Uncle Vanya"
role: 5 ELENA
Unclose: 3 OPE
Uncluttered: 4 NEAT
Uncomfortable: 9 ILLATEASE
position: 7 HOTSEAT
weather measure (abbr.): 3 THI
Uncommon: 4 RARE

bill: **3** TWO
major: **5** CFLAT
sense: **3** ESP
~, in Latin: **4** RARA
Uncomplaining: 5 STOIC
Uncomplicate: 4 EASE
Uncompromising: 5 RIGID STERN
offer: **9** ALLORNONE
Unconcealed: 5 OVERT
Unconcerned: 5 ALOOF
retort: **6** SOWHAT
with right and wrong: **6** AMORAL
Unconfined: 5 LOOSE
Unconscious: 3 OUT
state: **4** COMA
Uncontaminated: 4 PURE
Uncontrolled: 4 AMOK
cry: **3** SOB
Unconventional: 5 **OUTRE**
7 OFFBEAT
Unconvincing: 4 LAME
Uncooked: 3 **RAW** **7** TARTARE
Uncool
sort: **4** **NERD** **5** DWEEB
Uncountable
years: **3** EON
Uncouth: 4 RUDE **5** CRASS
CRUDE
one: **3** APE
Uncover: 4 OPEN **5** DIGUP
6 DETECT REVEAL
Uncovered: 4 BARE
Uncrashable
party: **9** OPENHOUSE
Uncreative
response: **4** ROTE
Uncredited
actor: **5** EXTRA
Unctuous: 4 OILY **6** SMARMY
flattery: **5** SMARM
Uncultivated: 6 FALLOW
tract: **5** HEATH
Uncut: 6 ENTIRE
U.N. Day
month: **3** OCT
___ und Drang: **5** STURM
Undecided: 4 OPEN TORN
10 ONTHEFENCE
Be: **4** HANG **5** WAVER

Remain: **4** PEND
seat: **5** FENCE
Undecorated: 4 BARE
Undeliverable
letter: **5** NIXIE
Undemanding: 4 EASY **5** CUSHY
Undeniable: 4 TRUE
Under: 5 BELOW **6** NETHER
7 SEDATED
any circumstances: **5** ATALL
control: **4** TAME **6** INHAND
INLINE
debate: **7** ATISSUE
Go: **4** SINK
Not: **7** ATLEAST
pressure: **8** STRESSED
Put: **6** SEDATE
sail: **4** ASEA **5** ATSEA
siege: **5** BESET
the covers: **4** ABED **5** INBED
the deck: **5** BELOW
the spell (of): **8** ENAMORED
the table: **3** LIT
the weather: **3** **ILL** **4** SICK
way: **5** AFOOT BEGUN
7 STARTED
wraps: **6** SECRET
~, in verse: **5** NEATH
Underage
temptation: **8** JAILBAIT
"Under a Glass Bell"
author: **3** NIN
Underbodice: 8 CAMISOLE
Undercoat: 6 PRIMER SEALER
Undercover
agent: **3** SPY **4** NARC
Like some ~ cops: **5** WIRED
operation: **5** STING
Went: **5** SPIED
Undercut: 6 ERODED
Underdog
win: **5** UPSET
Underestimate: 9 SELLSHORT
Underfoot
It may be: **3** RUG **6** INSOLE
Undergarment: 3 BRA **4** SLIP
5 PANTY TEDDY **6** PANTIE
One-piece: **9** UNIONSUIT
Undergoes: 3 HAS

Undergrad: 4 SOPH
  degs.: 3 BAS
  Some ~ studies: 6 PRELAW
Underground
  chamber: 4 CAVE 5 CRYPT
    8 CATACOMB
  conduit: 5 SEWER
  deposit: 3 ORE
  figure: 4 MOLE
  Go: 4 HIDE
  org.: 3 UMW
  Paris: 5 METRO
Underground Railroad
  leader: 6 TUBMAN
Underhanded: 3 **SLY** 5 CHEAP
  one: 5 SNEAK 6 WEASEL
Underline: 6 STRESS
Underling: 4 AIDE 6 MENIAL
    MINION STOOGE
  (abbr.): 4 ASST
  Hook: 4 SMEE
Underlining
  equiv.: 4 ITAL
Underlying: 5 BASIC
  cause: 4 ROOT
  principle: 5 BASIS
Undermine: 3 SAP 5 ERODE
    6 WEAKEN
Underscore: 6 STRESS
Underside: 4 SOLE
"Under Siege"
  star Steven: 6 SEAGAL
Understand: 3 DIG **GET** SEE
    4 READ 5 GRASP
  Hard to: 6 OPAQUE
  ~, à la Heinlein: 4 GROK
"Understand?": 5 GETME
Understanding: 3 **KEN** 4 GRIP
    ONTO 5 GRASP
    7 ENTENTE
  Phrase of: 4 AHSO ISEE
    6 IGETIT
  Political: 7 ENTENTE
  Sounds of: 3 AHS
Understated: 6 LOWKEY SUBTLE
Understood: 3 DUG GOT 4 KNEW
    5 CLEAR KNOWN TACIT
"Understood!": 4 ISEE
  Slangy: 4 IDIG 5 IMHIP

Undertake: 4 GOAT WAGE
    5 START
Undertaking: 3 ACT 4 TASK
Under-the-table
  activity: 8 KNEESIES
Underwater
  asteroid: 7 SEASTAR
  device: 5 SONAR
  habitat: 6 SEALAB
  missile: 7 POLARIS
  obstacle: 4 REEF
  shelf: 5 LEDGE
  shocker: 3 EEL
Underway: 5 AFOOT BEGUN
  Get: 5 START
Underwear: 6 BRIEFS 8 SKIVVIES
  brand: 4 BVDS 5 HANES
  Kind of: 7 THERMAL
Underwood
  Pound on an: 4 TYPE
Underworld
  boss: 4 CAPO
  Egyptian ~ god: 6 OSIRIS
  Egyptian ~ queen: 4 ISIS
  Greek: 5 HADES
  Norse ~ queen: 3 HEL
  river: 4 STYX 5 LETHE
Underwrite: 4 FUND 6 ASSURE
    7 SPONSOR
Undeserved
  charge: 6 BADRAP BUMRAP
Undesirable
  condition: 6 MALADY
Undiluted: 4 NEAT PURE
    6 STRONG
Undissembling: 7 SINCERE
Undisturbed: 6 INSITU
Undivided: 3 ONE 4 RAPT SOLE
    5 WHOLE 6 ENTIRE
Undo: 4 RUIN 5 ANNUL
    6 NEGATE REPEAL
    7 REVERSE
  a dele: 4 STET
  PC ~ key: 3 ESC
Undocumented
  one: 5 ALIEN
Undoing: 4 BANE RUIN
Undone
  Wish: 3 **RUE** 6 REGRET

"Undoubtedly": 3 YES
Undress: 4 PEEL
Undulate: 4 ROLL WAVE
Unduly: 3 TOO
  interested: 4 NOSY
Undying: 7 AGELESS ETERNAL
Unearned
  run cause: 5 ERROR
Unearth: 5 DIGUP
Unearthly: 5 ALIEN EERIE
    WEIRD
Uneasy
  feeling: 5 ANGST DREAD
    QUALM
Unedited: 3 RAW 5 ROUGH
  version: 5 DRAFT
Unemotional: 3 DRY 5 STOIC
    STONY 6 STOLID
Unemployed: 4 IDLE
Unending: 7 ETERNAL
Unenthusiastic: 5 TEPID
Unequal: 5 ALONE
  on all three sides: 7 SCALENE
Unescorted: 4 SOLO 5 ALONE
Uneven: 3 ODD 4 ALOP 5 EROSE
    JERKY 7 STREAKY
  hairdo: 4 SHAG
Unexciting: 4 BLAH DRAB FLAT
    SOSO TAME
  grade: 3 CEE
  poker hand: 4 PAIR
Unexpected: 6 ABRUPT
  blow: 4 GUST
  development: 5 TWIST
    11 TWISTOFFATE
  pleasure: 5 TREAT
  result: 5 UPSET
Unexploded: 4 LIVE
Unfair: 6 BIASED 8 ONESIDED
  shake: 6 BUMRAP
Unfairly
  Depict: 4 **SKEW**
  Treat: 5 SHAFT WRONG
"Unfaithful"
  costar: 4 GERE
Unfamiliar: 3 NEW 5 ALIEN
    7 STRANGE
  with: 5 NEWAT
Unfavorable: 7 ADVERSE

  prognosis: 5 WORSE
Unfavorably: 3 ILL
  Review: 3 PAN
Unfeeling: 4 COLD NUMB
    5 STONY 8 RUTHLESS
Unfettered: 4 FREE 5 LOOSE
Unflappable: 4 CALM 6 SERENE
    STOLID
Unfold: 4 OPEN 6 EVOLVE
    OPENUP
  ~, in verse: 3 OPE
"Unforgettable"
  singer: 4 COLE
  ~ Cole: 3 NAT
Unforseen
  problem: 4 SNAG
Unfortunate: 3 SAD 7 HAPLESS
"Unfortunately ...": 4 ALAS
Unfounded
  ~, as gossip: 4 IDLE
Unfriendly: 3 ICY 4 COLD
  quality: 7 ICINESS
  welcome:
    15 CHILLYRECEPTION
Unger, Felix: 9 NEATFREAK
  Daughter of: 4 EDNA
  Like: 4 NEAT TIDY
Ungulate
  Odd-toed: 5 TAPIR
"Unhand me!": 5 LETGO
Unhastily: 9 ATLEISURE
Unhealthy
  atmosphere: 6 MIASMA
Unhearing: 4 DEAF
Unheeding: 4 DEAF
Unhinged: 3 MAD 4 BATS
  Become: 4 SNAP
Unhip
  type: 4 NERD
Unholster: 4 DRAW
Unholy: 4 EVIL
"Unholy Loves"
  author: 5 OATES
"Un Homme et une Femme"
  actress: 10 ANOUKAIMEE
Unhurried: 4 EASY SLOW
    8 LEISURED
Unicellular
  critter: 5 AMEBA

Unidentified
man: 7 JOHNDOE MISTERX
plane: 5 BOGIE
woman: 7 JANEDOE
Unification Church
head: 4 MOON
member: 6 MOONIE
Unified: 3 **ONE** 5 ASONE ATONE
Uniform: 4 **EVEN** 5 DRESS
color: 5 KHAKI OLIVE
9 OLIVEDRAB
fabric: 5 CHINO KHAKI
frill: 7 EPAULET
GI ~ *(plural):* 3 ODS
Lady in: 3 WAC 4 WAAC
part: 3 CAP
Uniform Crime Report
org.: 3 FBI
Unifying
idea: 5 THEME
Unimaginative: 4 ARID
Unimportant: 4 MERE 5 MINOR
Unimpressed: 5 BLASE
Uninteresting: 3 DRY 4 ARID
BLAH DRAB DULL
5 BLAND HOHUM
Uninvited
Enter: 5 CRASH
guest: 11 GATECRASHER
Uninvolved: 5 ALOOF 7 NEUTRAL
Union: 4 BLOC 7 WEDDING
(abbr.): 3 STA
Actors': 3 SAG
agreement: 3 IDO
branch: 5 LOCAL
concern: 4 JOBS 5 LABOR
dealing agcy.: 4 NLRB
demand: 5 RAISE
Detroit: 3 UAW
foe: 3 REB 4 SCAB
Former ~ member (abbr.): 3 SSR
Largest U.S.: 3 NEA
Leave the: 6 SECEDE
letters: 3 AFL SSR
Media: 5 AFTRA
member: 5 BRIDE STATE
6 YANKEE
of D.C.: 3 STA
site: 5 ALTAR 10 CLOSEDSHOP

Teachers': 3 NEA
TV: 5 AFTRA
Waterfront: 3 ILA
Unique: 4 ONLY SOLE 5 ALONE
person: 4 ONER
~, in Latin: 4 RARA
Uniquely: 4 ONCE
___ **Unis:** 5 ETATS
Unison
In: 5 **ASONE** 8 ASONEMAN
In ~, musically: 4 ADUE
Unit
A/C: 3 BTU
Animation: 3 CEL
Astronomical: 6 PARSEC
Auction: 3 LOT
Bridge toll: 4 AXLE
Burpee: 4 SEED
Butter: 3 PAT
Capacitance: 5 FARAD
Cargo: 3 TON
Cloth: 4 BOLT
Conductance: 3 MHO
Corn: 3 COB **EAR**
Cotton: 4 BALE
Dance: 4 STEP
Dorm: 4 ROOM
Dosage: 3 RAD 4 PILL
Ecological: 5 BIOME
Electrical: 3 AMP OHM REL
4 **VOLT** WATT 5 FARAD
TESLA 6 AMPERE
Energy: 3 ERG 4 DYNE 5 JOULE
Exercise: 3 REP 5 SITUP
Farm: 4 **ACRE**
Film: 4 REEL
Flight: 5 STAIR
Force: 4 **DYNE**
Frequency: 5 HERTZ
Fuse: 3 AMP 6 AMPERE
Glazier: 4 PANE
Grass: 5 BLADE
Hay: 4 BALE
Heat: 5 THERM
Heredity: 4 GENE
Hospital: 3 BED 4 WARD
Information: 3 BIT 4 BYTE
Jeweler: 5 **CARAT** KARAT
Kind of: 4 ARMY 6 METRIC

Land: 4 ACRE
Leaf: 4 PAGE
Lettuce: 4 HEAD
Light: 5 LUMEN
Loudness: 3 BEL 4 SONE
  7 DECIBEL
Magnetic: 5 GAUSS TESLA
  WEBER
Mall: 5 STORE
Marathon: 4 MILE
Metric: 4 GRAM IAMB KILO
  5 STERE TONNE
Mil.: 4 REGT
Monogram ~ (abbr.): 4 INIT
NYSE: 3 SHR
Per: 4 APOP 6 APIECE
Petrol: 5 LITRE
Play: 5 SCENE
Power: 4 WATT
Pressure: 4 TORR
Printing: 4 PICA REAM
Punishment: 4 LASH
Race: 3 LAP LEG
Radiation: 3 REM
Rating: 4 STAR
Recon: 6 PATROL
Resistance: 3 OHM
Rosary: 4 BEAD
Soap: 4 CAKE
Sound: 3 BEL 4 PHON SONE
  7 DECIBEL
Special forces: 5 ATEAM
Speed: 4 KNOT
Stock: 5 SHARE STEER
Sugar: 4 LUMP
Train: 3 CAR
UPS: 3 CTN
USAF: 3 SAC
Work: 3 **ERG** 4 CREW WEEK
  5 JOULE
Zoning: 4 ACRE
Unitas
  team: 5 COLTS
Unite: 3 WED 4 JOIN KNIT WELD
  5 MERGE 6 SPLICE
  Split to: 5 ELOPE
United: 3 **ONE** WED 5 ASONE
  7 AIRLINE
  Be: 6 COHERE

  group: 4 BLOC
  rival: 3 TWA 8 AMERICAN
United Arab Emirates
  capital: 8 ABUDHABI
  neighbor: 4 OMAN
United ___ Emirates: 4 ARAB
United Nations
  display: 5 FLAGS
United Nations Day
  mo.: 3 OCT
"___: United States Marshal"
  (Wayne film): 6 CAHILL
Unity: 7 ONENESS
"Unity of India, The"
  writer: 5 NEHRU
Univ.: 3 SCH
  aides: 3 TAS
  conference: 3 ACC
  dorm supervisors: 3 RAS
  hotshot: 4 BMOC
  military program: 4 ROTC
  sports gp.: 4 NCAA
  teacher: 4 PROF
  test: 3 GRE
Universal: 6 COSMIC
  blood recipient: 6 TYPEAB
  donor: 5 TYPEO
  ideal: 3 TAO
  principle: 5 AXIOM
Universal Studios
  company: 3 MCA
Universe: 6 COSMOS
  Egyptian god of the: 6 AMENRA
  Protomatter of the: 4 YLEM
University
  Atlanta: 5 **EMORY**
  Chicago: 6 LOYOLA
  Denver: 5 REGIS
  English ~ city: 5 LEEDS
  founder Cornell: 4 EZRA
  head: 5 PREXY
  Houston: 4 RICE
  life: 8 ACADEMIA
  Long Island: 7 ADELPHI
  Maine ~ town: 5 ORONO
  New Orleans: 6 TULANE
  New York: 7 CORNELL
  North Carolina: 4 ELON
  Oxford: 7 OLEMISS

Philadelphia: 7 LASALLE
Swedish: 7 UPPSALA
~ URL ending: 3 EDU
~ VIP: 4 DEAN 6 REGENT
University of California
site: 5 DAVIS
University of Cincinnati
player: 7 BEARCAT
University of Wyoming
site: 7 LARAMIE
Unjust
charge: 6 BUMRAP
Unkempt: 5 MESSY SEEDY
6 RAGGED
one: 4 SLOB
place: 3 STY
Unkept
Like ~ yards: 5 WEEDY
Unkeyed: 6 ATONAL
Unkind: 4 MEAN 5 CATTY
nickname: 5 FATSO
Unknown
author (abbr.): 4 ANON
influence: 7 XFACTOR
sched.: 3 TBA
Search for the: 7 ALGEBRA
~ John: 3 DOE
Unlatch
~, in poetry: 3 OPE
Unlawful
firing: 5 ARSON
removal: 5 THEFT
Unleaded
alternative (abbr.): 3 REG
Unleash: 3 SIC 4 FREE 5 WREAK
Unless
~, in law: 4 NISI
Unlikely: 4 SLIM 6 REMOTE
class president: 4 NERD
donor: 5 MISER
protagonist: 7 NONHERO
8 ANTIHERO
story: 4 TALE
to bite: 4 TAME
Unlit: 4 DARK 5 SOBER
Unload: 3 RID 4 DUMP SELL
Unlock: 4 OPEN
~, in verse: 3 OPE
Unlucky: 7 HAPLESS

UNLV
Part of: 3 LAS
Unmannered: 5 CRASS
sort: 3 CAD 4 BOOR
Unmask: 6 REVEAL
Unmatched: 3 **ODD** 4 AONE SOLE
Unmitigated: 5 UTTER 6 ARRANT
Unmixed: 4 NEAT PURE
Unmoved: 5 STOIC 6 INSITU
Unmoving: 5 INERT
Unnamed
alternative: 4 ELSE
litigant: 3 ROE
ones: 4 THEM THEY
Unnatural: 5 EERIE 6 FORCED
blonde: 4 DYER
Unnecessary
Render: 7 OBVIATE
Unnerve: 3 COW 4 FAZE 5 DAUNT
6 DISMAY
Uno: 6 NUMERO
and dos: 4 TRES
and due: 3 TRE
and uno: 3 DOS
minus uno: 4 CERO
___ uno: 6 NUMERO
Unobtainable
Nearly: 4 RARE
Unoccupied: 4 IDLE
Unoriginal: 5 APISH STALE
TRITE
reply: 4 ECHO
Unpaid
debt: 6 ARREAR
Have ~ bills: 3 OWE
servant: 5 ROBOT
~ TV ad (abbr.): 3 PSA
Unpleasant: 4 GRIM SOUR
5 MESSY
fuss: 5 STINK
look: 4 LEER
situation: 4 MESS
Very: 4 VILE 5 NASTY
"___ Unplugged": 6 ALANIS
Unpolished: 4 RUDE 5 CRASS
leather: 6 RUSSET
Unpopular
More than: 5 HATED
one: 4 NERD

spots: 4 ACNE
worker: 4 SCAB
Unpredictable: 7 ERRATIC
Unpretentious: 5 LOWLY
          6 MODEST
          11 DOWNTOEARTH
Unprincipled: 6 **AMORAL**
person: 6 RASCAL
Unprocessed: 3 RAW 5 CRUDE
Unproductive: 6 INARUT
          7 STERILE
Unprotected: 5 NAKED
Unproven
ability: 3 ESP
Unqualified: 5 UTTER
Unravel: 4 FRAY 5 SOLVE
Unreactive: 5 INERT
Unrealistic
hope: 9 PIPEDREAM
Unrealized
gain: 11 PAPERPROFIT
Unrefined: 3 RAW 4 BASE
          5 CRASS CRUDE 6 COARSE
          EARTHY
metal: 3 ORE
Unrehearsed: 5 ADLIB
Unreliable
witness: 4 LIAR
Unrepaired: 4 ASIS
Unresolved
detail: 8 LOOSEEND
Leave things:
          15 AGREETODISAGREE
Unrest
1965 ~ site: 5 WATTS
Urban: 4 RIOT
Unrestricted: 4 OPEN 5 LOOSE
Unreturnable
serve: 3 ACE
Unruffled: 4 CALM COOL
          6 PLACID SEDATE
          SERENE
Unruly: 4 WILD 5 ROWDY
bunch: 3 MOB 4 HERD 5 HORDE
          6 RABBLE
locks: 3 MOP
"Unsafe at Any Speed"
author: 5 NADER
Unsaid: 5 TACIT

Leave: 4 OMIT
Unsatisfactory: 4 POOR
grade: 3 DEE
Most: 5 WORST
outcome: 3 TIE
Unsavory: 5 SHADY
one: 5 CREEP 6 SLEAZE
Unscheduled
(abbr.): 3 TBA
Unscrupulous: 6 AMORAL
sort: 6 RASCAL
Unseal: 4 OPEN
Unseat: 4 **OUST** 6 DEPOSE
Unseen
Hang around: 4 LURK
Present but: 6 LATENT
Unseld
of basketball: 3 WES
Unselfish
sort: 5 GIVER
Unsers
of racing: 3 **ALS**
Unsettle: 3 JAR
Unsettled: 4 OPEN 6 QUEASY
          10 INQUESTION
Remain: 4 PEND
Unshackle: 4 FREE
Unskilled: 4 POOR
worker: 4 **PEON**
writer: 4 HACK
Unsmiling: 5 STERN 6 SOLEMN
Unsociable
sort: 5 LONER
Unsophisticated: 5 NAIVE
          6 RUSTIC
sort: 4 RUBE
Unsound: 6 FAULTY
Unspecified
amount: 3 ANY 4 SOME
degree: 3 NTH
person: 3 ONE
Unspoiled: 4 PURE
spot: 4 EDEN
Unspoken: 5 **TACIT**
Unstable
Be: 6 TEETER
particle: 4 MUON
Unstamped
letters: 5 EMAIL

Unstated: 5 TACIT
Unsteady: 5 SHAKY TIPSY
  Be: 4 REEL
Unstressed
  vowel: 5 SCHWA
Unstrict: 3 LAX
Unstructured: 5 LOOSE
Unsubstantial: 4 AERY AIRY
Unsuccessful
  one: 7 ALSORAN
Unsuitable: 5 INAPT
Unsullied: 4 PURE 6 CHASTE
Unsurpassed: 4 BEST 7 ALLTIME
Untagged: 5 NOTIT
Untainted: 4 PURE 5 CLEAN
Untamed: 4 WILD 5 FERAL
      6 SAVAGE
Unter
  Opposite of: 4 UBER
Unthought-out: 4 RASH
Untidy: 5 MESSY
  one: 4 SLOB 6 SLOVEN
Until: 4 UPTO
  now: 3 YET 5 ASYET SOFAR
      6 TODATE
  ~, in Spanish: 5 HASTA
"___ unto Caesar ...": 6 RENDER
___ unto himself: 4 ALAW
"Unto the Sons"
  author Gay: 6 TALESE
Untouchable: 4 SAFE 6 SACRED
  ~ Eliot: 4 NESS
  ~ Ness: 5 ELIOT
Untouchables: 4 TMEN 5 CASTE
"Untouchables, The": 4 FEDS
      TMEN
  composer Morricone: 5 ENNIO
  leader: 4 NESS 9 ELIOTNESS
  role for Costner: 4 NESS
  villain: 5 NITTI
  ~ Oscar winner: 7 CONNERY
"Unto us ___ is given ...": 4 ASON
Untrained: 3 RAW
Untroubled: 7 ATPEACE PACIFIC
Untrue: 5 **NOTSO**
  Declare: 4 **DENY**
Untrustworthy
  one: 3 CAD 5 SNEAK
Untruth: 3 LIE

Untruthful
  Be ~ with: 5 LIETO
Untruths
  Many: 10 PACKOFLIES
Unused: 3 NEW 4 IDLE
  Remain: 3 SIT
Unusual: 3 ODD 4 RARE
  item: 5 CURIO
  partner: 5 CRUEL
Unveiling
  cry: 4 TADA
Unwakable
  state: 4 COMA
Unwanted
  buildup: 4 LINT 6 TARTAR
  e-mail: 4 **SPAM**
  flora: 4 WEED
  look: 4 LEER
Unwarm
  welcome: 4 HISS
Unwashed
  Like ~ hair: 4 OILY
  The great: 5 PLEBS
Unwavering: 5 SOLID 6 STEADY
Unwelcome
  guest: 4 PEST
  look: 5 SNEER
  mail: 4 BILL
  one: 6 PARIAH
Unwell: 3 ILL
  Be: 3 AIL
Unwilling: 5 LOATH 6 AVERSE
  to listen: 4 DEAF
Unwind: 4 REST 5 RELAX
  Place to: 3 SPA TUB
Unwise
  undertaking: 5 FOLLY
Unwitting
  one: 4 DUPE PAWN
Unworldly: 5 NAIVE
Unwrap: 4 OPEN
  in a hurry: 8 TEAROPEN
Unwritten: 4 ORAL
Unyielding: 4 GRIM IRON 5 RIGID
      STERN STIFF STOIC
      6 STEELY 7 ADAMANT
      8 HARDLINE OBDURATE
Up: 5 AHEAD ALOFT ASTIR
      ATBAT AWAKE BOOST

RAISE RISEN 6 ARISEN
    7 ELEVATE 8 INCREASE
above: 4 ATOP
and about: 5 **ASTIR** AWAKE
    RISEN 6 ACTIVE ARISEN
for grabs: 4 FREE 7 ANYONES
for it: 4 GAME
in arms: 5 IRATE
in the air: 4 IFFY 5 **ALOFT**
Is ~ to the task: 3 CAN
Not: 3 SAD 4 ABED 5 INBED
Not ~ (to): 6 UNABLE
Not ~ to much: 4 IDLE
One who is: 6 BATTER
Partner of: 5 ABOUT
the ante: 5 RAISE
the creek: 7 INASPOT
    9 INTROUBLE
to: 3 TIL 5 **UNTIL** 6 ATMOST
to it: 4 **ABLE**
to now: 3 YET 5 ASYET SOFAR
to the task: 4 **ABLE**
Up ___ : 5 **ATREE**
___ up
(admit): 4 FESS
(angry): 3 HET
(clinch): 3 SEW
(dress): 3 TOG
(get ready): 4 GEAR
(hide): 4 HOLE
(invigorate): 3 PEP
(prepare to drive): 3 TEE
"Up and ___!": 4 **ATEM**
Up-and-comer: 7 STARLET
Up-and-up
On the: 5 LEGAL LEGIT LICIT
    6 KOSHER RISING
Upbraid: 5 SCOLD
UPC
Part of: 4 CODE
Update: 4 REDO 7 REFRESH
a chart: 5 REMAP
a factory: 6 RETOOL
"___ up, doc?": 5 WHATS
Up-front
money: 4 ANTE
Up ___ good: 4 TONO
Upgrade: 4 REDO
Upheaval: 5 THROE

Upholstered
piece: 4 SOFA
Thickly ~ seat: 9 CLUBCHAIR
Upholstery
fabric: 5 FRISE TOILE
flaw: 3 RIP
Uplift: 4 BUOY 5 EDIFY RAISE
Uplifting
attire: 3 BRA
talk (abbr.): 3 SER
Upon: 4 ATOP
"___ upon a time": 4 ONCE
Upper
body: 5 TORSO
crust: 5 **ELITE**
hand: 4 EDGE
house: 6 SENATE
left key: 3 ESC
limit: 3 CAP MAX
regions: 5 ETHER SKIES
story: 4 LOFT
Upper ___ (Burkina Faso):
    5 VOLTA
Upperclassmen
(abbr.): 3 SRS
Uppity
one: 4 SNOB 5 SNOOT
Up ___ point: 3 TOA
Upright: 4 POST 5 ERECT MORAL
    ONEND PIANO PROUD
    6 HONEST SPINET
    7 ETHICAL 8 GOALPOST
Door frame: 4 JAMB
Not: 5 ALIST ATILT
Uprising: 4 RIOT 6 REVOLT
1976 ~ site: 6 SOWETO
Uproar: 3 ADO DIN 4 RIOT TODO
    5 FUROR HAVOC HOOHA
    6 OUTCRY TUMULT
___ uproar: 4 **INAN**
Ups: 5 HIKES
It has its ~ and downs: 4 YOYO
    6 SEESAW 8 ELEVATOR
Switch: 3 ONS
UPS
delivery: 3 CTN PKG
rival: 5 FEDEX
Use: 4 SHIP
Upscale: 4 TONY 5 ELITE

More: 5 NICER
trio: 6 DOREMI
wheels: 3 BMW
Upset: 3 ADO 4 IRED RILE SORE
      5 EVERT IRKED RILED
      6 RATTLE 7 AGITATE
  with: 5 MADAT
Upshot: 3 END 6 RESULT
Upside-down
  "e": 5 SCHWA
  sleeper: 5 SLOTH
Upsilon
  follower: 3 PHI
  preceder: 3 TAU
Upstairs: 5 ABOVE
  Sound: 4 SANE
  ___ upswing: 4 ONAN
Uptake
  Quick on the: 3 APT 5 ALERT
      SMART 6 ASTUTE
  Slow on the: 5 DENSE
Uptight: 4 EDGY 5 **TENSE**
      6 ONEDGE
Up-to-date: 3 MOD
  Most: 6 LATEST
  Not be: 3 LAG
Upton
  Writer: 8 SINCLAIR
Uptown
  in NYC: 3 NNE
"___ up to you": 3 ITS
Upturn
  Brief: 4 BLIP
  Sudden: 5 SPIKE
Upturned: 5 ONEND
  slope: 4 RISE 6 ASCENT
"Up, up and away"
  co.: 3 TWA
"Up Where We Belong": 4 DUET
Ur
  Locale of ancient: 5 SUMER
Uracil
  It contains: 3 RNA
Uraeus
  figure: 3 ASP
Ural
  City on the: 4 ORSK
Urals
  East of the: 4 ASIA

  West of the: 6 EUROPE
Urania: 4 MUSE
  Sister of: 5 ERATO
Uranium
  ~ 235 or 238: 7 ISOTOPE
Uranus
  Moon of: 5 ARIEL 6 OBERON
      7 MIRANDA TITANIA
  Wife of: 4 GAEA
Urban: 5 CIVIC
  air problem: 4 SMOG 5 SMAZE
  blight: 4 SLUM
  play area: 7 SANDLOT
  polluter: 5 NOISE
  problem: 6 SPRAWL
  suffix: 3 ITE
  unrest: 4 RIOT
  vehicle: 3 BUS CAB 4 TAXI
  vermin: 3 RAT
Urbane: 5 SUAVE
Urchin
  Street: 4 WAIF 5 GAMIN SCAMP
      11 GUTTERSNIPE
Urge: 3 YEN 4 GOAD ITCH PROD
      5 IMPEL PRESS 6 EXHORT
  (on): 4 SPUR
  to attack: 3 SIC
Urgency: 5 HASTE
Urgent: 4 DIRE STAT 5 ACUTE
  call: 3 SOS
  letters: 4 ASAP
  need: 6 DEMAND
  request: 6 BEHEST
Uriah ___ (Dickens character):
      4 HEEP
Urich, Robert
  ~ TV series: 5 VEGAS
Uris
  Author: 4 **LEON**
  hero: 3 **ARI**
  novel: 5 QBVII TOPAZ 6 THEHAJ
  novel, with "The": 3 HAJ
URL
  ending: 3 COM EDU GOV NET
      ORG
  part: 3 DOT
  start: 4 HTTP
Urn: 4 VASE
  Decorative: 7 SAMOVAR

Russian: 7 SAMOVAR
tribute: 3 ODE
Ursula
Author: 6 LEGUIN
Uru.
neighbor: 3 ARG
Uruguay: 3 RIO
Us
Not: 4 THEM
Still with: 5 ALIVE
Them, to: 4 FOES
U.S.
First ~ capital: 3 NYC
Former ~ territory: 6 DAKOTA
From the: 4 AMER
Southernmost ~ city: 4 HILO
The ~, to Mexicans:
    7 ELNORTE
trading partner: 3 EEC
USA
50 of the ~: 3 STS
alternative: 3 TBS TNT
Part of: 4 AMER
~ ID: 3 SSN
"U.S.A.": 7 TRILOGY
Usable
Make: 5 ADAPT
USAF
bigwig: 3 GEN
unit: 3 SAC
~ NCO: 4 TSGT
U.S. Airways
rival: 3 TWA
U.S. Army
medal: 3 DSC
"___ us a son ...": 4 UNTO
USC
athlete: 6 TROJAN
rival: 4 UCLA
U.S./Canadian
security acronym: 5 NORAD
USCG
call: 3 SOS
rank: 3 CPO ENS
U.S. Constitution
article: 3 THE
USDA
Part of: 3 AGR 4 DEPT
rating: 6 CHOICE

Use: 3 PLY 4 WEAR 5 AVAIL
    6 EMPLOY
Allow to: 4 LEND
Already in: 5 TAKEN
Be of: 5 **AVAIL** SERVE
Do not: 4 OMIT 5 WASTE
Have no ~ for: 4 HATE 5 ABHOR
    6 DETEST
In widespread: 4 RIFE
Make good ~ of: 3 TAP
    6 DRAWON
Not in: 4 FREE IDLE
Of no: 6 OTIOSE
Put to: 5 APPLY EXERT
Ready to: 5 ONTAP
Used: 3 OLD 4 WORN
Get ~ (to): 5 ADAPT ENURE
    INURE
Hardly: 7 LIKENEW
Not: 3 NEW 4 LEFT
to be: 3 **WAS** 4 WERE
to own: 3 HAD
up: 4 GONE 5 SPENT
Useful: 5 HANDY UTILE
article: 3 THE
Prove: 5 AVAIL
thing: 5 ASSET
Useless: 6 NOGOOD NOHELP
    7 INUTILE
User: 6 ADDICT
Kind of: 3 END
U.S./Eur.
link: 3 ATL
U-shaped
river bend: 5 OXBOW
Usher: 6 ESCORT LEADIN
    SEATER
beat: 5 **AISLE**
creator: 3 POE
in: 4 SEAT 5 ADMIT 6 HERALD
offering: 3 ARM 4 SEAT
Using: 3 VIA
USMA
freshman: 4 PLEB
grads: 3 LTS
Part of: 4 ACAD
USMC
Highest ~ rank: 3 GEN
one-striper: 3 PFC

Part of: 5 CORPS
USN
  rank: 3 ADM CDR CPO ENS
      4 CAPT CMDR
USNA
  freshman: 5 PLEBE
  grad: 3 **ENS**
  Part of: 3 NAV 4 ACAD
USO
  attendees: 3 GIS
U.S. Open
  1955 ~ winner: 7 TRABERT
  1966 ~ winner: 6 STOLLE
  1968 ~ winner: 4 ASHE
  1972 ~ runner-up: 4 ASHE
  1972 ~ winner: 7 NASTASE
  1977 ~ winner: 5 VILAS
  1991–92 ~ winner: 5 SELES
  1992 ~ winner: 4 KITE
      7 TOMKITE
  1994 ~ winner: 3 ELS
  1997 ~ winner: 3 ELS
  1999 ~ winner: 6 AGASSI
  2000 ~ winner: 5 SAFIN
  2000 ~ winner Safin: 5 MARAT
  Former ~ site:
      11 FORESTHILLS
  Four-time ~ winner: 5 HOGAN
  Six-time ~ winner: 5 EVERT
  stadium: 4 ASHE
  Three-time ~ winner: 5 IRWIN
      LENDL 9 IVANLENDL
  Two-time ~ winner: 3 **ELS**
      5 PAYNE SELES 6 AGASSI
      8 ERNIEELS
  Two-time ~ winner Fraser:
      5 NEALE
  unit: 3 SET
  ___ U.S. Pat. Off.: 3 REG
U.S. president
  10th ~: 5 TYLER
  11th ~: 4 POLK
  27th ~: 4 TAFT
  First name of six ~: 5 JAMES
USPS
  alternative: 3 FAX 5 EMAIL
  delivery: 3 LTR
  limbo: 3 DLO
  option: 3 COD

USSR
  Part of: 3 SOV
  state (abbr.): 3 RUS
  successor: 3 CIS
U.S. Steel
  founder: 8 JPMORGAN
Ustinov
  Actor: 5 PETER
Usual: 3 PAR 6 NORMAL
      7 ROUTINE
  (abbr.): 3 STD
  routine (abbr.): 3 SOP
Usually: 7 ASARULE
Usurer: 9 LOANSHARK
  offering: 4 LOAN
U.S. vice president
  First: 5 ADAMS
Uta
  Tony winner: 5 HAGEN
Utah
  canyon: 4 SEGO 5 BRYCE
  city: 4 **OREM** 5 OGDEN PROVO
  Hatch of: 5 ORRIN
  landmark: 13 GREATSALTLAKE
  lily: 4 SEGO
  mountain range: 5 UINTA
  national park: 4 ZION
  ski resort: 4 **ALTA**
  Young in ~ history: 7 BRIGHAM
Utensil: 4 TOOL
  Cooking: 3 PAN WOK
  Holey: 5 SIEVE
  Kitchen: 5 CORER PARER
Utensils: 8 FLATWARE
  Military ~ set: 7 MESSKIT
UTEP
  Part of: 4 PASO
Utica
  county: 6 ONEIDA
Utility
  (abbr.): 3 TEL 4 ELEC
  bill enc.: 3 SAE
  customer: 4 USER
  pipe: 4 MAIN
Utilize: 6 DRAWON
Utmost: 3 **NTH** 7 EXTREME
      9 NTHDEGREE
Utopia: 4 **EDEN** 9 SHANGRILA
  Onetime New York: 6 ONEIDA

Utopian: 5 **IDEAL** 8 IDEALIST
  novel: 7 EREWHON
Utrecht
  From: 5 DUTCH
Utrillo
  Stand for: 5 EASEL
Uttar Pradesh
  city: 4 **AGRA**
Utter: 3 SAY 4 EMIT PURE TELL
      5 SHEER STATE TOTAL
      6 ENTIRE
  suffix: 4 ANCE
Uttered: 4 ORAL SAID 6 SPOKEN
  with contempt: 4 SPAT
U-turn
  from ENE: 3 WSW

from ESE: 3 WNW
from NNE: 3 SSW
from NNW: 3 SSE
from SSE: 3 NNW
from SSW: 3 NNE
from WNW: 3 ESE
from WSW: 3 **ENE**
UV
  index tracker: 3 EPA
Uzbek
  body of water: 7 ARALSEA
Uzbekistan
  sea: 4 **ARAL**
  ~, once (abbr.): 3 SSR
Uzi: 3 GUN
  relative: 4 STEN

Vv

V: 4 FIVE
  formers: 5 GEESE
  preceders: 3 STU 4 RSTU
  sign: 5 PEACE
V8
  ingredient: 6 CELERY TOMATO
    7 SPINACH
V-8: 6 ENGINE
  unit (abbr.): 3 CYL
Vacances
  Time for les: 3 ETE
Vacancy: 4 VOID
  sign: 5 TOLET
Vacant: 5 EMPTY INANE
    UNLET
  look: 5 STARE
Vacation: 4 TRIP 7 GETAWAY
    HOLIDAY
  aid: 3 MAP
  home: 5 VILLA 7 COTTAGE
  On: 3 OFF 4 AWAY
  plan: 4 REST TRIP 5 RANDR
  Popular ~ spot: 3 RIO 4 KEYS
    5 ARUBA CRETE
    7 BAHAMAS POCONOS
    RIVIERA
  rental: 3 CAR
  souvenir: 3 LEI TEE 6 TSHIRT
  spot: 3 SPA 4 CAPE ISLE LAKE
    5 SHORE 6 RESORT
    7 SEASIDE 8 SEASHORE
  stop: 3 INN
  time in France: 3 ETE
  Wild: 6 SAFARI
Vacationing: 3 OFF 4 AWAY
    7 ONATRIP
Vaccination: 4 SHOT
  fluids: 4 SERA
Vaccine
  developer Salk: 5 JONAS
  Smallpox ~ developer: 6 JENNER
  Type of: 4 ORAL SALK
Vaccines: 4 **SERA**

Vacillate: 4 SWAY YOYO 5 HEDGE
    WAVER 6 SEESAW TEETER
Vaclav
  Czech leader: 5 HAVEL
Vacuous: 5 INANE
Vacuum: 4 VOID 5 CLEAN
  part: 3 BAG 4 HOSE
  target: 4 DIRT 5 CRUMB
Vacuum tube
  gas: 5 ARGON
  Type of: 5 DIODE 6 TRIODE
___ Vader: 5 DARTH
Vader, Darth
  Like: 4 EVIL
Vaderesque: 4 EVIL
"___ Vadis?": 3 QUO
Vagabond: 4 HOBO 5 NOMAD
    ROGUE ROVER TRAMP
    6 PICARO ROAMER
Vagrant: 3 BUM 4 HOBO
    5 TRAMP
Vague: 4 HAZY
  quality: 4 AURA
Vail
  alternative: 5 ASPEN
  Enjoy: 3 SKI
  surface: 4 SNOW
  trail: 6 SKIRUN
  visitor: 5 SKIER
Vain
  claim: 5 BOAST
  voyage: 7 EGOTRIP
  walk: 5 STRUT
"Valachi Papers, The"
  author Peter: 4 MAAS
Valais
  capital: 4 SION
Val d'___: 4 ARNO
Valdai Hills
  river: 5 VOLGA
Valdez
  vessel: 5 OILER
Vale: 4 DELL GLEN

Valedictorian
pride (abbr.): **3** GPA
Valedictory
Give a: **5** ORATE
Valencia
Info: Spanish cue
conqueror: **5** ELCID
Very, in: **3** MUY
Valens, Ritchie
hit song: **5** DONNA
Valentine: 5 HEART SAINT
Actress: **5** KAREN
figure: **4** EROS **5** CUPID
flowers: **5** ROSES
month (abbr.): **3** FEB
team: **4** METS
word: **4** LOVE
words: **5** ILOVE
Valentine's Day
gift: **4** CARD **5** ROSES
letters: **3** FTD
Valentino
Lover of: **5** NEGRI
role: **5** SHEIK
Valhalla
~ VIP: **4 ODIN**
Valiant: 5 BRAVE GUTSY
6 HEROIC
Valid: 5 LEGIT SOUND
Established as: **8** PROBATED
No longer: **4** NULL VOID
Valium
manufacturer: **5** ROCHE
Valkyries: 5 NORSE
God attended by the: **4** ODIN
Mother of the: **4** ERDA
___ **Vallarta: 6** PUERTO
Valle del Bove
site: **4** ETNA
Valle del Cauca
capital: **4** CALI
Vallee
Singer: **4** RUDY
Vallejo
City near: **4** NAPA
Valletta
island: **5** MALTA
Valley: 4 DALE DELL **GLEN**
California: **4 NAPA** SIMI

French wine: **5** LOIRE
German: **4 RUHR** SAAR
5 MOSEL RHINE
Moon: **5 RILLE**
Wine: **4 NAPA**
Valley ___: **5** FORGE
___ Valley: **4 SIMI**
"Valley Girl"
singer: **5** ZAPPA
"Valley of the Dolls"
actress: **4** TATE
author: **6** SUSANN
character: **5** NEELY
Valli
Actress: **5** ALIDA
Valor: 6 METTLE
Valorous: 5 BRAVE
Valova
Skater: **5** ELENA
"Valse ___": 6 TRISTE
Valuable: 4 DEAR **5** OFUSE
UTILE **6** NEEDED
collection: **5** TROVE
deposit: **3** ORE **4** LODE
item: **5** ASSET
Least ~ part: **5** DREGS
quality: **5** ASSET
Value: 5 PRIZE WORTH **6** ASSESS
ESTEEM **8** APPRAISE
Add ~ to: **6** ENRICH
Base: **3** PAR
Of: **5** UTILE **7** AINTHAY
system: **5** ETHIC ETHOS
Thing of: **5** ASSET
Without: **4** NULL
Without face: **5** NOPAR
Valued: 4 DEAR
Valve
Place for a: **5** AORTA
prefix: **3** UNI
Type of: **6** AORTIC INTAKE
MITRAL
"Vamoose!": 3 GIT **4** SCAT SHOO
5 SCRAM **6** GETOUT
Vamp: 5 FLIRT SIREN TEASE
6 SEDUCE **7** SEDUCER
accessory: **3** BOA
Vampire
Anne Rice: **6** LESTAT

Famous: 7 DRACULA
feature: 5 FANGS
Female: 5 LAMIA
hideaway: 4 TOMB
killer: 5 STAKE
repellent: 5 CROSS 6 GARLIC
Van: 7 VEHICLE
starter: 4 MINI
Took the: 3 LED
Van ___, Anthony
Artist: 4 DYCK
Van ___, Charles
Quiz show contestant: 5 DOREN
Van ___, Eddie
Guitarist: 5 HALEN
Van ___, Gus
Director: 4 SANT
Van ___, Jan
Artist: 4 EYCK
Van ___, Jean-Claude
Actor: 5 DAMME
Van ___, Mark
Poet: 5 DOREN
Van ___, Martin
President: 5 BUREN
Van ___, Rembrandt
Artist: 3 RYN
Van ___, Vincent
Artist: 4 GOGH
Van ___, William
Architect: 4 ALEN
Van ___, California: 4 NUYS
Vance
(abbr.): 3 AFB
Detective: 5 PHILO
Vance AFB
locale: 4 ENID
Vance Air Force Base
City near: 4 ENID
Van Cleef
Actor: 3 LEE
Vandal: 3 HUN 7 RAVAGER
Vandalize: 3 MAR 5 TRASH
6 DAMAGE DEFACE
Vandenberg: 3 AFB
Van der ___, Jan
Artist: 4 MEER
Van Der Beek, James
role: 6 DAWSON

Vanderbilt: 3 AMY 6 GLORIA
9 CORNELIUS
___ van der Rohe, Ludwig
Architect: 4 MIES
van der Rohe, Mies
motto: 10 LESSISMORE
Van Devere
Actress: 5 TRISH
Van Doren
Actress: 5 MAMIE
of quiz show fame: 7 CHARLES
Van Duyn
Poet: 4 MONA
Vandyke: 5 BEARD
Van Dyke
Actor: 4 DICK
role: 6 PETRIE
Vane
dir.: 3 ENE ESE NNE NNW SSE
SSW WNW WSW
direction: 4 EAST WEST
5 NORTH SOUTH
turner: 4 WIND
Vanessa
Role for: 7 ISADORA
Van Gogh, Vincent: 6 ARTIST
7 PAINTER
Brother of: 4 THEO
home: 5 ARLES
offering: 3 EAR
painting: 6 IRISES
Vanguard
Took the: 3 LED
Vanilla: 5 PLAIN
Rapper: 3 ICE
___ Vanilli: 5 MILLI
Vanish: 4 FADE 9 DISAPPEAR
EVAPORATE
Cause to: 6 DISPEL
Vanished: 4 **GONE**
Vanishing
sound: 4 POOF
Vanity: 3 EGO 5 PRIDE
affair: 7 EGOTRIP
Sign of: 4 AIRS
Voyage of: 7 EGOTRIP
Vanna
Boss of: 4 MERV
Partner of: 3 PAT

Request to: **3** ANA ANO
~, to Pat: **6** COHOST
Vannelli
Singer: **4** GINO
Vanquish: 4 BEAT BEST ROUT
6 DEFEAT **8** OVERCOME
Van Sant
Director: **3** GUS
van Susteren
Analyst: **5** GRETA
Vantage
point: **4** VIEW **5** ANGLE COIGN
PERCH
Vanuatu
neighbor: **4** FIJI
Part of: **7** OCEANIA
Vanzetti
partner: **5** SACCO
___ vapeur: **3** ALA
Vapor: 4 MIST **5** STEAM
Vaporize: 8 EVANESCE
Vaquero
rope: **5** LASSO REATA RIATA
Vardalos
Actress: **3** NIA
Vargas ___, Mario
Author: **5** LLOSA
Variable
star: **4** NOVA
Varicolored: 4 PIED
horse: **5** PINTO
Most: **8** MOTLIEST
Varied: 8 ECLECTIC
mixture: **4** OLIO
Variegated: 4 PIED
Variety: 3 **ILK** **4** KIND SORT
TYPE **5** GENRE
Lacking in: **7** ONENOTE
show: **5** **REVUE**
Various: 6 SUNDRY
Varner
Faulkner character: **4** EULA
Varney, Jim
character: **6** ERNEST
Varnish: 5 STAIN
ingredient: **3** **LAC** **5** RESIN
7 TUNGOIL
resin: **5** ELEMI **6** MASTIC
thinner: **7** ACETONE

Varsity: 5 ATEAM
award: **6** LETTER
Vasarely
genre: **5** OPART
Vasco ___
Explorer: **6** DAGAMA
Vasco da ___
Explorer: **4** **GAMA**
Vase: 3 **URN** **4** EWER
handle: **4** ANSA
handles: **5** ANSAE
Valuable: **4** MING
Verse on a: **3** ODE
Vassal: 4 SERF **5** LIEGE
Vassar
Like: **4** COED
Vast: 5 BROAD LARGE
7 IMMENSE OCEANIC
amount: **5** OCEAN
chasm: **5** ABYSS
expanse: **3** SEA **5** OCEAN
extents: **5** DEEPS
~, old-style: **5** ENORM
Vat: 3 TUN **4** CASK
Wine ~ waste: **4** LEES
worker: **4** DYER
Vatican
court: **4** ROTA
emissary: **6** NUNCIO
figure: **4** POPE
government: **7** HOLYSEE
locale: **4** ROME
period: **6** PAPACY
Related to the: **5** PAPAL
sculpture: **5** PIETA
vestment: **3** ALB
Vaudeville
bit: **3** ACT **4** SKIT
brothers: **4** RITZ
family: **4** FOYS
prop: **3** BOA **4** CANE
Sad-faced ~ comedian:
7 BENBLUE
show: **5** REVUE
star: **9** TOPBANANA
Vaughan
Jazz singer: **5** SARAH
nickname: **5** SASSY
of baseball: **4** ARKY

Vaughan, ___ Ray
  Guitarist: 6 STEVIE
Vaughn
  Actor: 5 VINCE
Vault: 4 ARCH **LEAP** SAFE
  Burial: 5 CRYPT
  cracker: 4 YEGG
  locale: 4 **APSE** BANK
  part: 3 RIB
Vaulted
  area: 4 **APSE**
Vaulter
  aid: 4 POLE
Vaunt: 4 BRAG 5 BOAST
    9 BRAGABOUT
"Vaya Con ___": 4 DIOS
Vb.
  form: 3 INF
  target: 3 OBJ
  Type of: 3 AUX **IRR** 4 INTR
V-chip
  target: 4 GORE PORN
VCR
  alternative: 4 TIVO
  button: 3 **REC** REW 4 PLAY
    5 EJECT PAUSE RESET
    6 REWIND
  connections: 3 TVS
  feature: 5 TIMER
  format: 3 VHS 4 BETA
  insert: 4 TAPE
  location: 3 DEN
  maker: 3 RCA 4 SONY 5 SANYO
  The "V" of: 5 VIDEO
Veal: 4 MEAT
  cut: 4 CHOP
  serving: 6 CUTLET
  ___ Vecchio: 5 PONTE
Veda
  devotee: 5 HINDU
  language: 8 SANSKRIT
V-E Day
  celebrants: 6 ALLIES
  initials: 3 HST
Vedder
  Illustrator: 5 ELIHU
Vedic
  deity: 5 INDRA
  god of fire: 4 AGNI

Vee, Bobby
  hit song: 8 RUNTOHIM
Veejay
  employer: 3 MTV
Veep
  before Al: 3 DAN
  before Ford: 5 AGNEW
  of Coolidge: 5 DAWES
  of LBJ: 3 HHH
  of Nixon: 5 AGNEW SPIRO
Veer: 3 ZAG 4 SKEW 6 CAREEN
    SWERVE
Vega
  constellation: 4 LYRA
Vegan
  no-no: 4 MEAT 5 STEAK
  staple: 4 TOFU
Vegas
  area: 5 STRIP 8 THESTRIP
  attraction: 4 SLOT 6 CASINO
  calculation: 4 ODDS
  casino of old: 5 SANDS
  cubes: 4 DICE
  game: 4 FARO KENO
  Hot, in: 7 ONAROLL
  machine: 4 SLOT
  natural: 5 SEVEN 6 ELEVEN
  opening: 3 LAS
  Run off to: 5 ELOPE
  sign: 4 NEON
  TV show set in: 3 CSI
"Vega$"
  actor: 5 URICH
  ___ Vegas: 3 **LAS**
Vegetable
  Borscht: 4 BEET
  Cabbagelike: 4 KALE
  container: 3 POD 6 PEAPOD
  Creole: 4 OKRA
  fat: 4 OLEO
  fuel: 4 PEAT
  Gumbo: 4 OKRA
  Japanese: 3 UDO
  Leafy: 4 KALE 5 CRESS
  Pungent: 5 ONION
  Red: 4 BEET
  Root: 7 PARSNIP
  Salad: 4 CUKE 5 CRESS
    6 ENDIVE

Soup: 3 PEA 4 LEEK OKRA
sponge: 5 LOOFA
spread: 4 OLEO
Vegetable oil: 5 ESTER
part: 5 OLEIN
Vegetarian
no-no: 4 MEAT
staple: 4 TOFU
Vegetation: 4 ALGA 5 FLORA
Like desert: 6 SPARSE
Lush with: 7 VERDANT
Veg out: 4 LAZE LOAF LOLL
Vehemence: 4 HEAT 5 ARDOR
Vehicle: 3 CAR 4 AUTO
All-purpose: 3 UTE
Apollo: 3 LEM
Army: 4 JEEP TANK
Auctioned: 4 REPO
Autobahn: 4 AUDI
Celebrity: 4 LIMO
E.T.: 3 UFO
Family: 5 SEDAN
Farm: 7 TRACTOR
Grocery: 4 CART
Iditarod: 4 SLED
Metered: 3 CAB 4 TAXI
Mine: 4 TRAM
Moving: 3 VAN
Musher: 4 SLED
NASA: 3 LEM 7 SHUTTLE
Off-road: 8 DIRTBIKE
Olympics: 5 KAYAK 7 BOBSLED
Racing: 4 AUTO 6 GOKART
      7 RACECAR 8 DRAGSTER
      STOCKCAR
Roomy: 5 SEDAN
Sci-fi: 3 UFO 8 STARSHIP
Seized: 4 REPO
Swift: 6 SATIRE
Urban: 3 BUS CAB 4 TAXI
Winter: 4 SLED 6 SNOCAT
Veil
material: 5 TULLE
Veiled
oath: 3 IDO
Vein: 4 LODE SEAM 7 DEPOSIT
contents: 3 **ORE**
Leaf: 3 RIB 6 MIDRIB
Leaf ~ space: 6 AREOLA

seeker: 5 MINER
site: 4 MINE
Velcro
alternative: 4 SNAP 5 LACES
      6 ZIPPER
Veldt
grazer: 5 ELAND HIPPO
predator: 4 LION
vacation: 6 SAFARI
Velez
Actress: 4 LUPE
Velocity: 5 SPEED
Meas. of: 3 FPS IPS
Velodrome
vehicle: 7 BICYCLE
___ Velva: 4 AQUA
Velveeta
maker: 5 KRAFT
Velvet
finish: 3 **EEN**
Lustrous: 5 PANNE
Velvet Fog, The: 5 TORME
Velvety
growth: 4 MOSS
Vena ___ : 4 CAVA
Vena cava
neighbor: 5 AORTA
Venae ___ : 5 CAVAE
Vend: 4 SELL 6 PEDDLE
Vendetta: 4 FEUD
Vending machine
input: 4 ONES
purchase: 4 COLA SODA
Vendor
stand: 4 CART
Street: 7 PEDDLER
Veneer: 4 COAT FACE FILM
      5 LAYER 6 FACADE
Veneman, Ann
dept.: 3 AGR
Venerable: 3 OLD
one: 5 ELDER
ref. set: 3 OED
saint: 4 **BEDE**
Venerate: 5 ADORE HONOR
      6 ADMIRE HALLOW
Venerated
symbol: 5 TOTEM
tribe member: 5 ELDER

Veneration: 3 AWE
Venetian
  blind part: 4 **SLAT**
  explorer: 4 POLO
  magistrate: 4 **DOGE**
  painter: 6 TITIAN
  resort: 4 LIDO
  taxi: 7 GONDOLA
  villain: 4 IAGO
  ___ Veneto: 3 VIA
Venezuela
  capital: 7 CARACAS
  export: 3 OIL
  Group that includes ~ (abbr.):
    4 OPEC
  Island near: 5 **ARUBA**
  neighbor: 6 GUYANA TOBAGO
  river: 7 ORINOCO
Vengeful
  feeling: 5 SPITE
Veni: 5 ICAME
Venice
  City near: 5 UDINE
  Coin of old: 5 DUCAT
  marketplace: 6 RIALTO
  Resort near: 4 LIDO
Venice-to-Naples
  dir.: 3 SSE
Venison: 4 MEAT
  Like: 4 GAMY
  source: 4 DEER
"Veni, ___, vici": 4 VIDI
"Veni, vidi, ___": 4 VICI
Venner
  of fiction: 5 ELSIE
Venom: 4 BILE HATE 5 TOXIN
    6 MALICE
  Snake: 5 TOXIN
  source: 3 ASP 5 SNAKE
Venomous
  snake: 3 ASP 5 **ADDER** COBRA
    KRAIT MAMBA
    10 COPPERHEAD
Venous
  prefix: 5 INTRA
Vent: 4 EMIT SLIT 6 AIRWAY
    OUTLET
Ventilate: 3 AIR 6 AERATE
    AIROUT

Ventilated: 4 AIRY 5 AIRED
Ventilation: 3 AIR
  channel: 4 DUCT
  source: 7 AIRHOLE
Ventral
  Fish without ~ fins: 3 EEL
Ventricle
  Left ~ attachment: 5 AORTA
Ventriloquist
  Head-in-a-box: 6 WENCES
  ~ Bergen: 5 EDGAR
  ~ Lewis: 5 SHARI
Ventura
  Former governor: 5 JESSE
Ventura County
  city: 6 OXNARD
  valley: 4 SIMI
Venture: 3 BET TRY 4 DARE RISK
Venue: 4 SITE 6 LOCALE
  Hockey: 4 RINK
  Mead: 5 SAMOA
  NYC opera: 6 THEMET
  NYC sports: 3 MSG
  Olympics: 4 OSLO
  Roping: 5 RODEO
  Skiing: 5 SLOPE
  Sports: 5 **ARENA**
  Workout: 3 SPA
Venus: 3 ORB 5 DEITY 6 PLANET
  home: 4 MILO
  neighbor: 5 EARTH
  Sister of: 6 SERENA
  Son of: 4 AMOR
"Venus"
  pop group: 10 BANANARAMA
  singer: 6 AVALON
"Venus and ___": 6 ADONIS
"Venus and Adonis"
  painter: 6 RUBENS
Venus de ___: 4 MILO
Venus de Milo
  lack: 4 ARMS
Venus Flytrap
  radio station: 4 WKRP
Venusian: 5 ALIEN
  (plural): 3 ETS
"___ Vep" (1996 film): 4 IRMA
Vera
  Actress: 5 MILES

Fashion designer: 4 WANG
Vera ___: 4 CRUZ
___ vera: 4 **ALOE**
Veracious: 4 TRUE
Veranda: 5 PORCH
Hawaiian: 5 **LANAI**
Verb
Archaic ~ ending: 3 ETH
Biblical: 4 DOST DOTH HAST
  HATH 5 HADST SHALT
Biblical ~ ending: 3 EST **ETH**
British ~ ending: 3 **ISE**
ending: 3 OSE
French 101: 4 ETRE
Latin 101: 3 AMO 4 AMAS AMAT
  ESSE
preceder: 4 NOUN
Spanish 101: 4 ESTA
suffix: 3 ING
type (abbr.): 3 INT IRR
  4 INTR
~, for one: 4 NOUN
Verbal
assault: 4 SLAM
gem: 3 MOT
hesitations: 3 ERS UMS
nudge: 4 PSST
white flag: 5 UNCLE
Verbatim: 7 LITERAL
Quoted: 3 SIC
Repeat: 4 ECHO 5 QUOTE
Verbena: 7 LANTANA
tree: 4 TEAK
Verbose: 5 GASSY WORDY
opposite: 5 TERSE
Verboten: 5 TABOO 6 BANNED
act: 4 NONO
(var.): 4 TABU
Verdant: 4 LUSH 5 GREEN
___ Verde: 4 MESA
Verde Sao ___: 5 TIAGO
Verdi
aria: 5 ERITU
genre: 5 OPERA
heroine: 4 **AIDA**
opera: 4 **AIDA** 6 ERNANI
  OTELLO 8 FALSTAFF
solo: 4 ARIA
Very, to: 5 ASSAI MOLTO

villain: 4 IAGO
Verdict
Hand down, as a: 6 RENDER
Unjust: 6 BUMRAP
"Verdict, The"
actor Milo: 5 OSHEA
Verdigris: 6 PATINA
Verdon
Dancer: 4 GWEN
Verdon, Gwen
role: 4 LOLA
Verdugo
Actress: 5 **ELENA**
Verdun
Done, in: 4 FINI
river: 5 MEUSE
Vereen
Tony winner: 3 BEN
Vereen, Ben
musical: 6 PIPPIN
Verge: 4 EDGE 5 BRINK
Is on the ~ of: 5 NEARS
on: 4 ABUT
Vergil: 4 POET
epic: 6 AENEID
hero: 6 AENEAS
Verifier
Balance sheet ~ (abbr.): 3 AUD
Verily: 3 YEA 4 AMEN 5 TRULY
  6 INDEED
"___, verily!": 3 YEA
Verizon
predecessor: 3 GTE
Vermeer
contemporary: 4 HALS 5 STEEN
Painter: 3 JAN
Vermin: 4 LICE RATS 5 PESTS
Clear of: 5 DERAT
Vermont
city: 5 BARRE 7 RUTLAND
harvest: 3 SAP
patriot Allen: 5 ETHAN
product: 5 SYRUP
senator: 5 LEAHY
ski area: 4 PICO
ski resort: 5 STOWE
stop: 3 INN
Vermouth: 8 APERITIF
name: 5 ROSSI

Vern
Neighbor of: 6 ERNEST
Vernacular: 5 ARGOT LINGO
SLANG
Verne
Author: 5 JULES
captain: 4 NEMO
genre: 5 SCIFI
traveler: 4 FOGG
Vernon
Dancing partner of: 5 IRENE
Verona
A gentleman of: 5 ROMEO
family name: 7 CAPULET
wine: 5 SOAVE
Veronese
painter: 5 PAOLO
Veronica
Actress: 4 LAKE 5 HAMEL
Supermodel: 4 WEBB
"Veronica's Closet"
actress: 5 ALLEY
12 KIRSTIEALLEY
Véronique: 3 STE
___ versa: 4 VICE
Versace
Designer: 6 GIANNI
Versailles
agreement: 6 TREATY
Eye, in: 4 OEIL
ruler: 3 ROI
verb: 4 ETRE
Very, in: 4 TRES
Versatile
bean: 4 SOYA
Electrically: 4 ACDC
opener: 11 SKELETONKEY
transport: 3 ATV
vehicle: 3 UTE 4 JEEP
Verse: 4 POEM 6 POETRY
STANZA
adverb: 3 EEN EER
Analyze: 4 SCAN
Japanese: 5 HAIKU
Narrative: 4 EPOS
on a vase: 3 ODE
prefix: 3 UNI
reciter: 4 BARD
tribute: 3 ODE

writer: 4 POET
Versed: 5 ADEPT
in: 4 UPON
Versifier: 4 BARD POET
Version
Basic ~ (abbr.): 3 STD
Easier ~, in music: 5 OSSIA
New: 6 REMAKE 7 REWRITE
Pop song: 5 REMIX
Similar: 8 ANALOGUE
Small: 4 MINI
Software: 4 BETA
Verso: 4 PAGE
counterpart: 5 RECTO
Vert.
opposite: 3 HOR
Vertebra
locale: 5 SPINE
Type of: 6 LUMBAR
Vertical: 5 APEAK
graph line: 5 YAXIS
Not exactly: 5 ATILT
Perfectly: 5 PLUMB
pipe: 5 RISER
stabilizer: 3 FIN 4 KEEL
~, at sea: 5 APEAK
"Vertigo"
actress Kim: 5 NOVAK
actress Novak: 3 KIM
Verve: 3 PEP 4 BRIO **ELAN** ZEST
6 ESPRIT SPIRIT
7 PANACHE
Very: 4 MOST OHSO SAME SUCH
5 QUITE
~, in French: 4 TRES
~, in German: 4 SEHR
~, in music: 5 ASSAI MOLTO
"Very funny!": 4 HAHA
Very much: 4 **ALOT** 5 NOEND
6 SORELY
"Very well!": 6 SOBEIT
Vespasian
Son of: 5 TITUS
Vespers
preceder: 5 NONES
time: 7 EVENING
Vespucci
Explorer: 7 AMERIGO
Vessel: 4 BOAT SHIP 5 CRAFT

15th-century ~: 4 NINA 5 PINTA
Ablutionary: 4 EWER
Beer: 5 STEIN
Biblical: 3 ARK
Blood: 5 AORTA 6 ARTERY
Coffee: 3 URN
D-Day: 3 LST
Harbor: 3 TUG 7 TOWBOAT
Indian Ocean: 4 DHOW
Jason's: 4 ARGO
Kitchen: 3 POT
Lake: 5 CANOE
Large: 3 VAT
Ocean: 4 SHIP 5 LINER
Port: 3 VAT
Queeg's: 5 CAINE
Red Sea: 4 DHOW
Sailing: 4 YAWL 5 SLOOP
Spanish: 4 OLLA
That: 3 SHE
Torpedo: 5 EBOAT
Vintner's: 3 TUN VAT
Wine: 3 VAT 6 CARAFE
WWII: 3 **LST** 5 UBOAT
    6 PTBOAT
Vest
  lack: 7 SLEEVES
Vesta: 8 ASTEROID
Vestibule: 5 ENTRY FOYER
    7 HALLWAY
Vestige: 4 DREG SIGN 5 RELIC
    SHRED **TRACE**
Vestment: 3 **ALB** 5 AMICE
  Papal: 5 ORALE
Vesture: 4 ROBE
Vesuvio
  City near: 6 NAPOLI
Vesuvius
  City near: 6 NAPLES
  output: 3 ASH 4 LAVA
  Vent, like: 5 ERUPT
Vet: 3 DOC 4 EXGI 6 OLDPRO
    7 OLDHAND 8 OLDTIMER
  task: 4 SPAY 6 DEFLEA
  text: 4 EDIT
  theater, maybe: 3 NAM
Veteran: 3 PRO 6 OLDPRO
    7 OLDHAND 8 OLDTIMER
    SEASONED

  sailor: 3 TAR 4 SALT 6 SEADOG
    7 OLDSALT
Veto: 3 **NIX** 4 KILL 6 REJECT
    8 OVERRULE
  Opposite of: 6 ASSENT
Vex: 3 IRK 4 GALL **RILE** ROIL
    5 EATAT 6 PESTER
Vexation: 3 IRE
___ vez (again, in Spanish):
    4 OTRA
Vezina Trophy
  org.: 3 NHL
V-formation
  group: 5 GEESE 8 SQUADRON
VFW
  Part of: 4 WARS
VH1
  rival: 3 MTV
VHS
  alternative: 4 BETA
Via: 3 PER 5 USING
Via ___ (Rome): 6 VENETO
Viacom
  cable channel: 3 TNN
Via del Corso
  locale: 4 ROMA
Viagra
  alternative: 6 CIALIS
  maker: 6 PFIZER
Vial: 6 AMPULE
Viands: 7 EDIBLES
Via Veneto
  car: 4 FIAT
Vibes: 4 AURA
  Pick up: 5 SENSE
Vibrant: 5 ALIVE
  Not: 4 DRAB
Vibrating
  effect: 7 TREMOLO
Vibration: 6 TREMOR
Vibrato: 7 TREMOLO
Vic
  Radio wife of: 4 SADE
  Singer: 6 DAMONE
"Vic and ___" (old radio show):
    4 SADE
Vicar of Christ: 4 POPE
Vice ___: 5 **VERSA**
"___ Vice": 5 MIAMI

Vice president
First: 5 ADAMS
under Clinton: 4 GORE
   6 ALGORE
under Coolidge: 5 DAWES
under Lincoln: 6 HAMLIN
under Madison: 5 GERRY
~ Agnew: 5 SPIRO
Vichy: 3 SPA
verb: 4 ETRE
Very, in: 4 **TRES**
Void, in: 3 NUL
water: 3 **EAU**
Vichyssoise
ingredient: 4 **LEEK** 6 POTATO
Vicinity: 4 **AREA** 6 LOCALE
   REGION
In the: 4 NEAR 5 ABOUT
   6 AROUND
Vicious: 4 EVIL 5 CRUEL
Punk rocker: 3 SID
Vicksburg
fighter: 3 REB
victor: 5 GRANT
Victim: 4 GOAT PREY
April 1st: 4 FOOL
Blight: 3 ELM
Corday: 5 **MARAT**
Genesis: 4 **ABEL**
of Brutus: 6 CAESAR
of deflation: 3 EGO
Pizarro: 4 INCA
Raid: 4 PEST 5 ROACH
Victimize: 6 PREYON
Victor: 5 CHAMP
Actor: 5 BUONO
Author: 4 HUGO
by one electoral vote: 5 HAYES
Comedic musician: 5 BORGE
Cry of a: 4 IWIN IWON
Gettysburg: 5 MEADE
initials: 3 RCA
___ Victor: 3 RCA
Victoria: 4 LAKE
Novelist: 4 HOLT
Victoria Island
explorer: 3 RAE
Victorian: 4 PRIM
expletive: 4 EGAD

time period: 3 ERA
type: 5 PRUDE
Victorian ___ : 3 ERA
Victoria's Secret
item: 3 **BRA**
Victories
Ring: 3 KOS
Victorious: 5 ONTOP
Victory: 3 WIN
Clinch, as a: 3 ICE 5 SEWUP
Easy: 4 ROMP ROUT
   7 RUNAWAY
emblem: 6 LAUREL
goddess: 4 NIKE
Narrow margin of: 4 NOSE
One-sided: 9 LANDSLIDE
sign: 3 VEE
Unexpected: 5 UPSET
~, in German: 4 SIEG
"Victory ___ !": 5 ATSEA
"___ victory!": 4 ONTO
Victrola
company: 3 RCA
Victuals: 4 EATS
Vicuna
home: 5 ANDES
kin: 5 LLAMA
Like the: 6 ANDEAN
Vidal
Author: 4 GORE
book: 4 BURR
character Breckenridge: 4 MYRA
Vidalia: 5 **ONION**
Video
dot: 5 PIXEL
Make a: 4 TAPE
meaning: 4 ISEE
network: 3 MTV
Old ~ format: 4 BETA
partner: 5 AUDIO
recorder, for short: 3 CAM
Video game: 6 PACMAN TETRIS
adventurer: 5 MARIO
company: 4 SEGA 5 **ATARI**
Early: 4 PONG
hangout: 6 ARCADE
letters: 3 NES
Video store
offering: 3 DVD 6 RENTAL

section: 5 DRAMA SCIFI
   6 HORROR
Vidi
  meaning: 4 ISAW
Vie: 7 COMPETE CONTEND
"___ Vie" (novel): 3 UNE
Vienna
  group (abbr.): 4 OPEC
  home (abbr.): 3 AUS
Vientiane
  land: 4 **LAOS**
  native: 3 LAO 7 LAOTIAN
Vier
  Half of: 4 ZWEI
  preceder: 4 DREI
Viet ___: 4 CONG
Vietnam
  capital: 5 **HANOI**
  coin: 3 HAO
  dictator: 4 DIEM
  general: 6 ABRAMS
  holiday: 3 **TET**
  neighbor: 4 **LAOS**
  patrol boat: 8 RIVERRAT
  port: 6 DANANG
  suffix: 3 ESE
Vietnam Veterans Memorial
  designer: 3 LIN 7 MAYALIN
View: 3 EYE SEE 5 SCENE
   7 EYESHOT OPINION
  Come into: 4 LOOM 6 EMERGE
  Express a: 5 OPINE
  Extensive: 5 VISTA
  finder: 3 EYE
  Have in: 6 INTEND
  In: 4 SEEN
  Inside: 4 XRAY
  Nice: 3 MER
  Open to: 5 OVERT
  Panoramic: 5 VISTA
  Point of: 5 ANGLE SLANT
  quickly: 6 PEEKAT
  Scenic: 8 PANORAMA
  Skewed: 4 BIAS
"View, The"
  cohost: 5 BEHAR
Viewable: 7 INSIGHT
Viewer: 4 EYER
  MTV: 4 TEEN

Viewpoint: 5 ANGLE SLANT
   6 ASPECT
  page: 4 OPED
Vigilant: 5 ALERT AWARE
   7 ONALERT
  Wasn't: 5 SLEPT
Vigilius
  Year of ~ papacy: 3 DLI
Vigoda
  Actor: 3 **ABE**
Vigor: 3 PEP ZIP 4 BRIO ELAN
  Lack of: 6 ANEMIA
  Lose: 3 SAG
  partner: 3 VIM
Vigorous: 4 HALE 5 PEPPY
   6 HEARTY ROBUST
  dance: 8 FLAMENCO
  effort: 11 ELBOWGREASE
  spirit: 4 ELAN
Viking
  destination: 4 MARS
  of the comics: 5 **HAGAR**
Vikki
  Singer: 4 **CARR**
Vile: 4 BASE EVIL 5 NASTY
   SLIMY 6 SORDID
  smile: 5 SNEER
Vilify: 5 SMEAR 6 DEFAME
Villa
  Russian: 5 DACHA
Villa ___: 5 DESTE
Villa d'___: 4 **ESTE**
Villa d'Este
  city: 6 TIVOLI
Village: 4 DORP
  African: 4 STAD
  Tiny: 6 HAMLET
Village People
  hit song: 4 YMCA
Village Voice
  award: 4 **OBIE**
Villain: 6 BADDIE BADMAN
  Biblical: 5 HEROD
  expletive: 6 CURSES
  Fairytale: 4 OGRE
  Greet the: 3 BOO 4 HISS
  Opera ~, often: 5 BASSO
  ~, at times: 7 SNEERER
Villainous: 4 EVIL MEAN

look: 4 LEER 5 SNEER
Villechaize
  Actor: 5 HERVE
Villon
  offering: 5 POEME
    7 RONDEAU
Vim: 3 **PEP** 4 ELAN ZEST
    5 GUSTO
Vin
  choice: 5 BLANC
Viña ___ Mar: 3 DEL
Vince
  Country singer: 4 GILL
Vincent
  Actor: 5 SPANO
  Brother of: 4 THEO
Vincente
  Daughter of: 4 LIZA
___ vincit amor: 5 **OMNIA**
Vindictive
  goddess: 4 HERA
Vine
  Climbing: 3 IVY
  Tropical: 5 **LIANA**
Vine-covered
  area: 5 ARBOR
  passageway: 7 PERGOLA
Vinegar
  bottle: 5 CRUET
  Full of: 6 ACETIC
  partner: 3 OIL
  prefix: 5 ACETO
  radical: 6 ACETYL
  type: 8 BALSAMIC
Vinegary: 6 **ACETIC**
  Prefix meaning: 5 ACETO
Vineyard
  container: 4 CASK
  French: 3 CRU
  valley: 4 NAPA
Vingt-___ (blackjack): 4 ETUN
Vinland
  discoverer: 8 ERICSSON
Vino
  region: 4 ASTI
Vintage: 3 OLD 4 YEAR
  auto: 3 **REO** 5 ESSEX
  ~ Ford: 6 MODELA
  ~ Jag: 3 XKE

Vintner
  cache: 7 RESERVE
  dregs: 4 LEES
  Prefix used by a: 3 OEN 4 OENO
  valley: 4 NAPA
  vessel: 3 TUN VAT
Vinton
  Singer: 5 BOBBY
Vinton, Bobby
  hit song: 11 ROSESARERED
    14 RAINRAINGOAWAY
Vinyl
  records: 3 LPS
Viol
  precursor: 5 REBEC
Viola
  kin: 5 CELLO
  range: 5 TENOR
  Valuable: 5 AMATI
Viola da ___: 5 GAMBA
Violation: 7 OFFENSE
  Commandment: 3 SIN
Violent: 4 GORY 5 ROUGH
    6 STORMY
  Like a ~ film: 6 RATEDR
  struggles: 6 THROES
  weather: 5 STORM
Violet: 5 PANSY
  Kind of: 7 AFRICAN
  Like a shrinking: 3 SHY
  prefix: 5 ULTRA
Violin
  holder: 4 CHIN
  Like a ~ bow: 6 ROSINY
  maker Amati: 6 NICOLO
  part: 4 NECK
  precursor: 5 REBEC
  string holder: 3 PEG
  stroke: 5 UPBOW
  Valuable: 5 **AMATI** STRAD
Violinist
  accessory: 5 ROSIN
Violist
  clef: 4 **ALTO**
VIP: 4 EXEC 5 MOVER 6 CHEESE
    7 SOMEONE
  Ambulance: 3 EMT
  Business: 3 CEO
  Campus: 4 BMOC DEAN PROF

Capitol: 3 SEN
Church: 5 ELDER
Computer: 5 SYSOP
Cotillion: 3 DEB
Court ~, in 1995: 3 ITO
Mideast: 4 AMIR **EMIR** 5 EMEER
  6 SULTAN
Mosque: 4 IMAM
Political: 4 BOSS
Valhalla: 4 ODIN
vehicle: 4 LIMO
Viper: 3 **ASP** 5 **ADDER** SNAKE
feature: 4 FANG
home: 4 NEST
sound: 3 SSS
VIPs
Baseball: 3 GMS
Courtroom: 3 DAS
Hospital: 3 DRS MDS RNS
Magazine: 3 EDS
Radio: 3 DJS
Vire
Town on the: 4 STLO
Virgil: 4 POET
epic: 6 AENEID
hero: 6 AENEAS
Virgin: 6 UNTROD
Like a: 6 CHASTE VESTAL
  9 UNTRODDEN
tycoon: 7 BRANSON
Virginia
Author: 5 WOOLF
city: 7 ROANOKE
dance: 4 REEL
family: 4 LEES
North of: 5 OLLIE
player: 3 CAV
resource: 8 COALMINE
senator: 4 ROBB
settler: 5 ROLFE
willow: 4 ITEA
Virginia ___ : 4 REEL
"Virginian, The"
actor Doug: 7 MCCLURE
actor Gulager: 3 CLU
actor McClure: 4 DOUG
author Wister: 4 OWEN
Virgin Islands
Smallest of the: 6 STJOHN

Westernmost of the:
  8 STTHOMAS
~, for one (abbr.): 4 TERR
Virgo
Sign after: 5 LIBRA
Sign before: 3 LEO
star: 5 SPICA
Virgule: 5 SLASH
Virile: 5 MACHO MANLY
person: 5 HEMAN
Virna
Actress: 4 **LISI**
Virtue
Paragon of: 5 SAINT
Symbol of: 4 HALO
Virtuoso: 3 ACE 4 WHIZ
Virtuous: 4 PURE 5 MORAL
  6 CHASTE
Virus
African: 5 EBOLA
carrier, sometimes: 5 EMAIL
type: 3 RNA
Visa
rival: 4 AMEX
statement abbr.: 3 APR
Visage
Villainous: 4 LEER 5 SNEER
Viscosity
symbol: 3 ETA
Viscount
superior: 4 **EARL**
Viscous: 5 SLIMY
substance: 4 GOOP
Vise
part: 5 CLAMP
Portable: 6 CCLAMP
Vishnu: 3 GOD
avatar: 4 RAMA 7 KRISHNA
Rama, to: 6 AVATAR
Sounds of: 3 OMS
worshiper: 5 HINDU
Visibility
problem: 3 FOG 4 HAZE MIST
  SMOG 5 SMAZE
Visible: 4 SEEN
Barely: 5 FAINT
Become: 6 EMERGE
Visine
units: 5 DROPS

Vision: 4 IDEA 5 DREAM SIGHT
  Dull: 5 BLEAR
  Having keen: 9 EAGLEEYED
  Inner: 4 XRAY
  Night: 5 DREAM
  Person of: 4 SEER 6 ORACLE
  prefix: 4 TELE
  Range of: 7 EYESHOT
Visionary: 4 **SEER** 6 DREAMY
      7 DREAMER UTOPIAN
      8 IDEALIST
  drama: 3 RUR
  words: 4 ISEE
Visit: 3 SEE 5 GOSEE POPIN
      6 CALLON DROPIN
      STOPBY STOPIN
      8 CALLUPON
Visited: 3 SAW 6 CAMEBY
"Visit From St. Nicholas, A"
  opener: 4 TWAS
  poet: 5 MOORE
Visitor: 5 GUEST 6 DROPIN
  China: 4 POLO
  Christmas: 5 SANTA
  Holiday: 5 INLAW
  Sci-fi: 3 UFO 5 ALIEN
  Siam: 4 ANNA
Visored
  cap: 4 KEPI
  helmet: 5 ARMET
"Vissi d'arte": 4 ARIA
  opera: 5 TOSCA
Vista: 5 SCAPE SCENE
  Desert: 5 CACTI
  ___ **Vista**
  (battle site): 5 BUENA
  (San Diego suburb): 5 CHULA
Vistula River
  city: 6 WARSAW
Visual: 5 OPTIC 6 OCULAR
  aid: 5 SPECS
  assent: 3 NOD
  illusions: 5 OPART
  prefix: 5 AUDIO
Visualize: 3 SEE
Vital: 3 KEY 5 ALIVE BASIC
      6 NEEDED
  fluid: 3 SAP
  sign: 5 PULSE

  Some are: 6 ORGANS
  statistic: 3 AGE
  vessel: 5 AORTA
Vitality: 3 PEP 4 ELAN LIFE
      ZING 5 OOMPH PULSE
      VERVE
  Lacking: 6 ANEMIC
  Lack of: 6 ANEMIA
  Lose: 3 SAG
Vitamin
  acid: 5 FOLIC
  bottle abbr.: 3 **RDA**
  prefix: 5 MULTI
  regimen: 7 ONEADAY
  supplement: 4 IRON
Vitamin A: 7 RETINOL
  source: 8 CAROTENE
      12 BETACAROTENE
Vitamin B: 6 NIACIN
Vitamin C: 4 ACID
  source: 3 ADE 4 LIME
Vit. info: 3 RDA
Vitro
  In ~ items: 3 OVA
Vittles: 4 CHOW·**EATS** GRUB
Vittorio
  Director: 6 DESICA
Vituperate: 5 ABUSE 7 CURSEAT
Viva ___: 4 VOCE
Vivacious
  wit: 6 ESPRIT
Vivacity: 4 BRIO DASH ELAN
      LIFE 6 ESPRIT
  ___ **vivant:** 3 BON
Vivarin
  rival: 5 NODOZ
"Viva ___ Vegas": 3 LAS
Viva voce: 4 ORAL 5 ALOUD
"Viva Zapata!"
  star: 6 BRANDO
"Vive ___!": 5 LEROI
"Vive le ___!": 3 ROI
Vivid: 5 LURID 7 GRAPHIC
  display: 4 RIOT
  red: 7 PIMENTO
Vizquel
  of baseball: 4 **OMAR**
VJ
  employer: 3 MTV

V-J Day
It ended with: 4 WWII
pres.: 3 HST
Vladivostok
villa: 5 DACHA
Vlad the Impaler: 6 DESPOT
V-mail
address: 3 APO
VMI
program: 4 ROTC
student: 5 CADET
V-neck: 7 SWEATER
Vocabulary
Specialized: 5 **ARGOT**
Vocal: 4 ORAL
cords: 5 PIPES
effect: 7 TREMOLO
group: 5 OCTET
part: 6 ARIOSO
quality: 4 TONE
range: 4 ALTO
solo: 4 ARIA
Vocalize: 5 SPEAK UTTER
6 INTONE
Vocalized: 4 SUNG
Vocally: 5 ALOUD
expressed: 4 ORAL
Vocation: 6 CAREER
Voce
Not sotto: 5 ALOUD
Viva: 4 ORAL 5 ALOUD
___ voce: 4 VIVA 5 **SOTTO**
" ___ voce poco va": 3 UNA
Vociferate: 4 YELL 5 SHOUT
Vodka
(abbr.): 3 ALC
brand, familiarly: 5 STOLI
cocktail: 6 GIMLET
Vogue: 4 RAGE 5 STYLE
TREND
competitor: 4 ELLE
In: 4 CHIC 6 TRENDY
No longer in: 3 OUT 5 PASSE
photographer: 6 AVEDON
Voice
above tenor: 4 ALTO
a view: 5 OPINE
below soprano: 4 ALTO
Choir: 4 **ALTO**

Give ~ to: 5 UTTER
Like a whiny: 5 NASAL
Low: 4 BASS 5 BASSO
of Bugs: 3 MEL
of Elmer: 3 MEL
of Porky: 3 MEL
quality: 4 TONE
range: 4 ALTO BASS 5 TENOR
7 SOPRANO
vote: 3 NAY YEA
With a single: 5 ASONE
Voiced: 4 ORAL SAID TOLD
6 SONANT
Voice of America
gp.: 4 USIA
"Voice of Israel"
author: 4 EBAN
Voices: 4 ALTI 5 BASSI
"Voices Carry"
pop group: 10 TILTUESDAY
Void: 3 GAP 5 ANNUL 6 CANCEL
NEGATE 7 INVALID
Make: 5 ANNUL
partner: 4 **NULL**
~, in Vichy: 3 NUL
Voided: 5 UNDID
tennis play: 3 LET
Voight
Actor: 3 JON
role: 6 COSELL
"Voilà!": 4 **TADA** 5 THERE
6 PRESTO
Voir ___ : 4 DIRE
Vojvodina
resident: 4 SERB
Volatile
liquid: 5 NITRO
solvent: 5 ETHER 7 ACETONE
**"___ volat propriis" (Oregon
motto):** 4 ALIS
Volcanic
crater: 7 CALDERA
output: 3 ASH 4 LAVA
5 MAGMA
peak: 6 MTHOOD SHASTA
rock: 6 BASALT
Volcano: 6 SPEWER
Alaskan: 6 KATMAI
Japanese: 4 FUJI

Martinique: 5 PELEE
output: 3 ASH 4 LAVA SLAG
part: 4 CONE
Sicilian: 4 **ETNA** 6 MTETNA
"Volcano Lover, The"
author: 6 SONTAG
___ volente (God willing): 3 DEO
Volga
dweller: 5 TATAR
outlet: 7 CASPIAN
River to the: 3 OKA
Volkswagen
model: 3 GTI 4 GOLF 5 JETTA
6 PASSAT
rival: 4 OPEL
Volley: 5 BURST SALVO
7 BARRAGE
Volleyball
birthplace: 7 HOLYOKE
divider: 3 NET
player: 6 SETTER
smash: 4 KILL 5 SPIKE
Volt: 4 UNIT
Voltage
letters: 3 EMF
Voltaire
satire: 7 CANDIDE
~, religiously: 5 DEIST
Volume: 4 BOOK **TOME** 5 ATLAS
Metric: 5 STERE
supporter: 7 BOOKEND
Two-dimensional: 4 AREA
unit: 4 SONE
Volunteer: 5 ENROL OFFER
6 ENLIST 8 ENLISTEE
phrase: 4 ICAN 5 IWILL
Volunteer State
(abbr.): 4 TENN
Voluptuous: 4 SEXY
Volvo: 4 AUTO
competitor: 4 SAAB
von ___, Carl Maria
Composer: 5 WEBER
von Bismarck
Chancellor: 4 OTTO
von Bulow: 5 CLAUS
portrayer: 5 IRONS
von Dohnányi
Composer: 4 ERNO

von Furstenberg
Designer: 4 EGON 5 DIANE
Vonnegut
Author: 4 KURT
von Richtofen
title: 5 BARON
von Sternberg
Director: 5 JOSEF
von Stroheim
Director: 5 ERICH
von Sydow
Actor: 3 MAX
von Trapp
family member: 4 KURT
5 GEORG MARIA MARTA
title: 5 BARON
von Trier
Director: 4 LARS
Voodoo
charm: 4 MOJO
cousin: 5 OBEAH
Voom
preceder: 4 VAVA
Vortex: 4 EDDY
"___ Vos Prec" (T.S. Eliot work):
3 ARA
Vote
Affirmative: 3 AYE YEA
Decline to: 7 ABSTAIN
French: 3 NON OUI
German: 4 NEIN
in: 5 ELECT
Negative: 3 NAY
out: 6 UNSEAT
Russian: 4 NYET
to accept: 5 ADOPT
Type of: 4 ORAL
Voters: 10 ELECTORATE
Like-minded: 4 BLOC
problem: 6 APATHY
Some: 4 INDS
Voting
district: 4 WARD
group: 4 **BLOC**
no: 4 ANTI
place: 4 POLL
Voucher: 4 CHIT
Vous
Verb with: 4 ETES

"___ vous plait": 3 SIL
Vow: 4 **OATH** 5 SWEAR
    7 PROMISE
Altar: 3 **IDO**
taker: 3 NUN 4 MONK
Vowel
Greek: 3 **ETA** 4 IOTA
group: 5 AEIOU
slur: 5 ELIDE
sound: 5 SCHWA
Unstressed: 5 SCHWA
Vows
Exchange: 3 WED
Like some: 6 SACRED
    7 NUPTIAL
Wedding: 4 IDOS
Voyage: 4 TREK TRIP
end: 8 LANDFALL
for the vain: 7 EGOTRIP
preceder: 3 BON
type: 6 MAIDEN
"___ voyage!": 3 **BON**
Voyager: 7 MINIVAN
Voyageurs Natl. Park
locale (abbr.): 4 MINN
Voyeur: 6 PEEPER

VP: 4 EXEC
of LBJ: 3 HHH
"VR.5"
actress Singer: 4 LORI
V-shaped
cut: 5 NOTCH
fortification: 5 REDAN
Vt.
neighbor: 3 QUE
___ vu: 4 **DEJA**
Vulcan: 5 ALIEN
home: 4 ETNA
Vulcanologist
study: 4 LAVA
Vulgar: 3 RAW 5 CRASS
person: 6 SLEAZE
Vulgarian: 4 BORE LOUT
    SLOB 5 YAHOO
    6 SLEAZE
Vulnerable
area: 10 UNDERBELLY
hero: 8 ACHILLES
to shooting: 7 INRANGE
Vulpine: 3 SLY
VW: 4 AUTO 6 BEETLE
predecessors: 3 STU 4 RSTU

Ww

W: 8 TUNGSTEN
  Affiliation of: 3 GOP
  Brother of: 3 JEB
W-2
  info: 3 SSN 5 WAGES
Wabbit
  chaser: 5 ELMER
Wacko: 3 MAD NUT 4 DAFT
    LOON NUTS 5 LOONY
Wacky: 4 DAFT LOCO NUTS
    ZANY 5 AMISS 6 INSANE
Wad
  Tobacco: 4 CHAW
  Wallet: 4 ONES
Wade
  across: 4 FORD
  of baseball: 5 BOGGS
  opponent: 3 **ROE**
  through: 4 SLOG 5 SLOSH
Wader
  Everglades: 5 EGRET
  Marsh: 4 IBIS 5 EGRET HERON
  Pinkish: 8 FLAMINGO
  White: 4 IBIS 5 **EGRET**
Wading
  bird: 4 **IBIS** RAIL 5 CRANE
    EGRET HERON SNIPE
    STILT STORK 8 FLAMINGO
Wadkins
  Golfer: 5 LANNY
Wafer
  Like a: 4 THIN
  Nabisco: 5 NILLA
Wafer-and-creme
  cookie: 4 OREO
Waffle: 5 HEDGE 6 SEESAW
  brand: 4 **EGGO**
  topping: 5 SYRUP
Waffling
  Stop: 3 OPT
Wag: 4 CARD 5 JOKER
    8 JOKESTER
  words: 4 QUIP

Wage: 6 SALARY
  Hourly: 4 RATE
  Minimum: 5 SCALE
Wage ___: 6 EARNER
Wager: 3 **BET** PUT 5 PUTUP
    STAKE
  Extra: 7 SIDEBET
  handler (abbr.): 3 OTB
  Place a ~ towards: 5 BETON
  Risked a: 6 STAKED
  type: 6 EXACTA PARLAY
Wagered: 4 LAID
  Amount: 5 STAKE
Wagering
  locale (abbr.): 3 OTB
Wages: 3 PAY 6 INCOME
  Like some: 6 HOURLY
Wagga Wagga
  resident: 6 AUSSIE
Waggish: 5 DROLL 7 JOCULAR
Waggle
  dancer: 3 BEE
Waggoner
  Actor: 4 LYLE
Wagnalls
  collaborator: 4 FUNK
Wagner
  Father-in-law of: 5 LISZT
  hero: 7 TRISTAN
  heroine: 6 ISOLDE
  of baseball: 5 HONUS
  opera: 6 RIENZI 8 PARSIFAL
  soprano: 3 EVA 4 ELSA
  Very, to: 4 SEHR
  work: 5 OPERA
Wagon: 4 CART DRAY
    9 CONESTOGA
  On the: 5 SOBER
  part: 4 AXLE
  track: 3 RUT
Wagons-___ : 3 LIT
Wagon train
  direction: 4 WEST

"Wag the Dog"
actress Anne: 5 HECHE
Wahine
dance: 4 HULA
feast: 4 LUAU
gift: 3 **LEI**
wear: 4 **LEI**
welcome: 5 ALOHA
Wahlberg
Singer: 6 DONNIE
Waif: 5 GAMIN STRAY 6 URCHIN
Waiflike: 4 THIN
Waikiki
locale: 4 OAHU
wannabe: 5 HODAD
wear: 3 LEI
welcome: 3 LEI 5 ALOHA
wiggle: 4 HULA
wingding: 4 LUAU
woman: 6 WAHINE
wreath: 3 **LEI**
Wail: 3 CRY SOB 4 BAWL KEEN
YOWL
Dramatic: 4 ALAS
Warning: 5 SIREN
Wailer
Irish: 7 BANSHEE
Warning: 5 SIREN
Waist
circler: 3 OBI 4 BELT
type: 4 WASP
Waistband: 4 SASH
Waist-length
jacket. 4 ETON
Waistline: 6 MIDDLE
It lacks a: 9 TENTDRESS
Wait: 3 SIT 4 BIDE 8 SITTIGHT
After a long: 6 ATLAST
at the light: 4 IDLE
impatiently: 4 PACE
Lie in: 4 LURK 5 SKULK
Long: 3 EON
on: 3 SIT 4 TEND 5 SERVE
6 ATTEND 7 CATERTO
Some ~ for this: 3 CUE TIP
"Wait ___!": 4 **ASEC**
___ wait: 5 LIEIN
Waite
Hall of Fame pitcher: 4 HOYT

Waiter: 6 SERVER
Airport: 3 CAB 4 TAXI
boss: 7 MAITRED
burden: 4 TRAY
French: 6 GARCON
handout: 4 MENU
helper: 6 BUSBOY
on wheels: 6 CARHOP
parting word: 5 ENJOY
Place for a: 4 LINE
request: 5 ORDER
reward: 3 TIP
type: 4 DUMB
"Waiter, there's a fly ___ soup!":
4 INMY
Waiting: 4 IDLE 6 INLINE
ONDECK ONHOLD
7 INSTORE
area: 6 LOUNGE
8 ANTEROOM
9 GREENROOM
period: 3 EON
Reward for: 3 TIP
room call: 4 NEXT
"Waiting for ___": 5 GODOT
"Waiting for Lefty"
playwright: 5 **ODETS**
"Waiting for the Robert ___":
4 **ELEE**
"Waiting to ___ " (McMillan novel):
6 EXHALE
"Wait just a minute!": 4 WHOA
Waitress
at Mel's Diner: 3 FLO 4 VERA
5 ALICE
Waits, Tom
Sing like: 4 RASP
"Wait ___ the Sun Shines, Nellie":
3 TIL
"Wait Until Dark"
actor: 5 ARKIN
Waitz
Marathoner: 5 GRETE
Waitz, Grete
birthplace: 4 OSLO
Waive
your rites: 5 ELOPE
Wakayama
woofer: 5 AKITA

Wake
Begin to: 4 STIR
site: 3 AFT 6 ASTERN
up: 5 ARISE ROUSE 6 COMETO
Wakefield
cleric: 5 VICAR
Wake Island: 5 ATOLL
Waken: 5 ROUSE 6 AROUSE
rudely: 5 ROUST
Waker-upper: 5 ALARM BUGLE
6 ROUSER
Wake-up
call: 5 ALARM 7 AROUSAL
"Wake Up Little ___": 5 SUSIE
Waking: 5 ASTIR
"Waking ___ Devine" (1998 film):
3 NED
Walden: 4 POND
Waldheim
predecessor: 5 THANT
6 UTHANT
Secretary General: 4 KURT
Waldorf
salad ingredient: 4 MAYO
6 CELERY 7 WALNUTS
serving: 5 SALAD
Wales
capital: 7 CARDIFF
dog: 5 CORGI
Former Princess of: 5 DIANA
Motto of the Prince of:
7 ICHDIEN
symbol: 4 LEEK
~ John: 4 EVAN
Walesa
homeland: 6 POLAND
Polish leader: 4 **LECH**
Walk: 4 GAIT 5 AMBLE LEGIT
TREAD 6 HOOFIT
14 CONSTITUTIONAL
a beat: 6 PATROL
all over: 3 USE
back and forth: 4 PACE
Faster than a: 4 TROT
heavily: 4 PLOD SLOG
5 CLOMP STOMP TRAMP
TROMP
in the woods: 4 HIKE
It is used to ~ the dog: 4 YOYO

leisurely: 5 AMBLE 6 SASHAY
STROLL
like a cat: 5 PROWL
like a child: 6 TODDLE
like a duck: 6 WADDLE
Long: 4 HIKE
One learning to: 3 TOT
out: 4 EXIT QUIT
over: 6 STEPON
proudly: 5 STRUT
Shady: 5 ALLEE 7 ALAMEDA
Sloping: 4 RAMP
slowly: 5 MOSEY
softly: 3 PAD 6 TIPTOE
Space ~ (abbr.): 3 EVA
through water: 4 WADE 5 SLOSH
unsteadily: 4 REEL
Waterfront: 4 PIER
Where the elated: 5 ONAIR
Where to ~ very carefully:
6 ONEGGS
with effort: 4 PLOD SLOG
6 TRUDGE
Walk-___: 3 ONS
"Walk ___" (Warwick hit): 4 ONBY
"Walkabout"
director Nicolas: 4 ROEG
"Walk Away ___" (1966 hit):
5 RENEE
"Walk, Don't Run"
costar: 5 EGGAR
Walked: 4 TROD 6 STRODE
"___ Walked Into My Life": 4 IFHE
Walker
Author: 5 ALICE
Beat: 3 COP
Cartoonist: 4 MORT
Distiller: 5 **HIRAM**
New: 3 TOT
of football: 4 DOAK
Runway: 5 MODEL
~, for short: 3 PED
Walker, Mort
pooch: 4 OTTO
Walkie-talkie
word: 4 **OVER** 5 ROGER
Walking: 5 AFOOT 6 ONFOOT
difficulty: 4 GIMP LIMP
on air: 6 ELATED

papers: 5 THEAX 7 RELEASE
speed: 4 PACE
stick: 4 CANE
Way of: 4 GAIT
Walking ___: 5 ONAIR
"Walking Man"
of baseball: 4 YOST
"Walking on Thin Ice"
singer: 3 ONO
"Walk Like ___" (Four Seasons hit): 4 AMAN
Walkman
batteries: 3 AAS
maker: 4 SONY
Walk of Fame
sight: 4 STAR
Walk-on
role: 5 CAMEO
"Walk on the Wild Side"
singer: 4 REED
Walkover: 4 ROMP
"___ walks in beauty ...": Byron: 3 SHE
Walk-up
resident: 6 TENANT
Walkway: 4 PATH 5 AISLE
Covered: 4 STOA
material: 5 SLATE
Stadium: 4 RAMP
Tree-lined: 7 ALAMEDA
Wall: 6 STREET
Bounce off the: 4 ECHO
bracket: 6 SCONCE
British ~ builder: 7 HADRIAN
climber: 3 IVY
covering: 5 PAINT PAPER
décor: 5 MURAL
Defensive: 7 PARAPET
Drive up the: 3 IRK 6 MADDEN
hanging: 3 ART OIL 5 ARRAS 6 POSTER
hanging for an M.D.: 3 DEG
Hole in the: 4 SAFE VENT 6 SOCKET
layer: 4 COAT
Off the: 4 LOCO 5 DAFFY NUTTY WACKO
Pass through a: 4 GATE
plaster: 5 GROUT 6 STUCCO

Put up on the: 4 HANG
recess: 5 NICHE
tapestry: 5 **ARRAS**
Word on a: 4 MENE
work: 3 ART OIL 6 POSTER
Writing on the: 4 OMEN SIGN
Wallace
Actor: 5 BEERY
Actress: 3 DEE
Author: 3 **LEW**
cohort: 5 SAFER
of Reader's Digest: 4 LILA
Running mate of: 5 LEMAY
Wallace, George
Home of: 7 ALABAMA
Wallach
Actor: 3 **ELI**
Wallboard: 5 PANEL
Walled
~ Spanish city: 5 **AVILA**
Wallenda
patriarch: 4 KARL
Waller
Jazzman: 4 FATS
Wallet
items: 3 IDS 7 IDCARDS
material: 3 EEL 7 EELSKIN
stuffers: 4 CASH **ONES**
wad: 4 **ONES**
Walletful: 3 WAD
Walleye: 8 PICKEREL
Wallflower
Like a: 3 SHY 4 MEEK 5 TIMID
Wallop: 3 TAG 4 BANG BELT DECK SLUG SOCK 5 PASTE SMITE
Added a ~ to: 5 LACED
Packing a: 6 POTENT
Wallow
Place to: 3 STY 4 MIRE
Walls
Bouncing off the: 5 HYPER
Its ~ can withstand a lot of pressure: 5 AORTA
Like some college: 5 **IVIED**
Wall Street
Boesky of: 4 IVAN
deal (abbr.): 3 LBO
debut (abbr.): 3 **IPO**

deg.: 3 MBA
Good news on: 3 UPS 4 RISE
   5 RALLY
gp.: 4 AMEX NASD NYSE
index: 3 DOW
index (abbr.): 5 SANDP
letters: 4 AMEX NASD NYSE
optimist: 4 BULL
org.: 3 ASE
pessimist: 4 BEAR
purchase: 5 STOCK 6 OPTION
regulator (abbr.): 3 SEC
site: 13 STOCKEXCHANGE
transaction: 3 BUY PUT 4 SELL
   5 TRADE
whiz, for short: 3 ARB
worker: 6 BROKER TRADER
   7 ANALYST
worry: 5 PANIC
Wally
Bother of: 4 BEAV
Cookie maker: 4 AMOS
Wal-Mart: 5 CHAIN
competitor: 5 SEARS 6 TARGET
founder: 9 SAMWALTON
founder Walton: 3 SAM
Walnut: 4 TREE
Walpole
title: 4 EARL
Walrus
feature: 4 TUSK
Walsh
Director: 5 RAOUL
Walsh, M. ___
Actor: 5 EMMET
Walston
Actor: 3 RAY
Walter
Army surgeon: 4 REED
Cartoonist: 5 LANTZ
Conductor: 5 BRUNO
Golfer: 5 HAGEN
Labor leader: 7 REUTHER
Singer: 4 EGAN
Thurber character: 5 MITTY
Walter ___, Sir: 5 SCOTT
Walton
Author: 5 IZAAK
daughter: 4 ERIN

Grandpa ~ portrayer: 4 GEER
   8 WILLGEER
of Wal-Mart: 3 SAM
Walton, Izaak
Pastime of: 7 FISHING
___ Walton League: 5 IZAAK
"Waltons, The"
actor Ralph: 5 WAITE
actor Will: 4 **GEER**
actress Corby: 5 ELLEN
character: 4 ERIN 6 OLIVIA
   7 GRANDPA
Waltz
King of: 7 STRAUSS
Waltzing
woman: 7 MATILDA
"Waltzing Matilda"
First words of: 5 ONCEA
Waltz King, The: 7 STRAUSS
Wampum: 5 BEADS
Wan: 4 ASHY PALE 5 ASHEN
   6 PALLID
Rather: 6 PALISH
Wanamaker
Actress: 3 ZOE
Wand
Conductor: 5 BATON
Majorette: 5 BATON
Wander: 3 ERR GAD 4 ROAM
   ROVE
about: 5 MOSEY
aimlessly: 4 MILL 5 DRIFT
   6 STROLL 7 MEANDER
   TRAIPSE
off: 5 STRAY
Wanderer: 4 HOBO 5 GYPSY
   NOMAD ROVER STRAY
   8 WAYFARER
Alley: 8 STRAYDOG
Web: 6 SURFER
Wandering: 6 ADRIFT ASTRAY
   ERRANT 7 NOMADIC
Wane: 3 EBB LAG SAG 5 ABATE
Wang
Designer: 4 VERA
Wangle: 7 FINAGLE
Wankle: 6 ENGINE
engine part: 5 ROTOR
"Wanna ___?": 3 BET

"___ Wanna Do": 4 **ALLI**
"Wanna make ___?": 4 ABET
Want: 4 NEED 5 CRAVE
      6 DEARTH DESIRE
  badly: 5 COVET
  to avoid: 5 DREAD
  to know: 3 ASK
Want ad
  abbr.: 3 EEO EOE
  listing (abbr.): 4 APTS
Wanted
  Help ~ notice: 3 SOS
Wanted poster
  letters: 3 **AKA**
  word: 5 ALIAS ARMED
"___ want for Christmas": 4 **ALLI**
Wanting: 5 NEEDY 6 INNEED
  company: 8 LONESOME
"___ want a room
    somewhere ...": 4 ALLI
Wanton
  look: 4 LEER
Wants
  He ~ you: 8 UNCLESAM
Wapiti: 3 **ELK**
  kin: 5 MOOSE
War
  1899–1902 ~ participant: 4 BOER
  1950s ~ site: 5 KOREA
  1960s ~ zone: 3 NAM
  1967 ~ site: 5 SINAI
  1991 ~ zone: 4 IRAQ
  2003 invasion locale: 4 IRAQ
  Act of: 3 TUG
  correspondent Pyle: 5 ERNIE
  Drawn-out ~ tactic: 5 SIEGE
  ender: 4 PACT 6 TREATY
  film, when tripled: 4 TORA
  First Secretary of: 4 KNOX
  Friend in: 4 ALLY
  game: 8 STRATEGO
  god: 4 **ARES** MARS
  goddess: 6 ATHENA
  Holy: 5 JIHAD 7 CRUSADE
  horse: 5 **STEED**
  party: 4 ARMY
  Prepare for: 3 ARM
  Pro: 4 HAWK
  Religious: 7 CRUSADE

  room item: 3 MAP
  Side in a 1980s: 4 IRAN
  stat: 3 MIA
  story: 5 ILIAD
  ~, to Sherman: 4 HELL
  ___ War: 4 MANO
"War and Peace"
  actor Herbert: 3 LOM
  author: 7 TOLSTOY
  heroine: 7 NATASHA
Warble: 5 CROON TRILL
Warbled: 4 SANG SUNG
Warbucks
  Annie, to: 4 WARD
  henchman: 3 ASP 6 THEASP
  ward: 5 ANNIE
Ward: 5 STAVE
  Actress: 4 **SELA**
  healers (abbr.): 3 MDS RNS
  heeler: 3 POL
  Hosp.: 3 ICU
  off: 4 FEND 5 **AVERT** DETER
    REPEL
  Satirist: 3 NED
Ward-___ (politico): 6 HEELER
Ward ___, Julia
  Reformer: 4 HOWE
Ward County
  seat: 5 MINOT
Warden
  Kind of: 4 GAME
Wardrobe: 7 ARMOIRE
  ___ ware: 5 IMARI
Warehouse: 4 STOW 5 DEPOT
  STORE
  supply (abbr.): 4 CTNS
Warfare
  Kind of: 4 GANG GERM 5 CLASS
  tactic: 5 SIEGE 7 EMBARGO
"WarGames"
  org.: 5 NORAD
Warhead
  toter: 4 ICBM
Warhol: 9 POPARTIST
  Artist: 4 ANDY
  genre: 6 POPART
  protégé Sedgwick: 4 EDIE
  subject: 3 MAO 7 SOUPCAN
"War is ___": 4 HELL

Warm: 4 NEAR **6** TOASTY
TROPIC **7** AFFABLE
and comfy: **4** COZY SNUG
5 HOMEY **6** TOASTY
drink: **5** COCOA TODDY
Getting: **4** NEAR **5** CLOSE
Nice ~ time: **3** ETE
Set to keep: **5** ONLOW
the bench: **3** SIT
up: **4** THAW
up again: **6** REHEAT
welcome: **3** HUG **5** ALOHA
When it's ~ in Chile: **5** ENERO
Warmer
Egg: **3** HEN
Hand: **5** GLOVE **6** MITTEN
Winter: **4** WOOL **5** COCOA
SCARF STOLE
~, perhaps: **4** HINT
Warm-hearted: 4 KIND NICE
Warmth: 5 ARDOR
Without: **5** ICILY
Warm-up: 4 PREP **7** PRELUDE
Warn: 5 ALERT **6** TIPOFF
7 CAUTION
Warner
Chan portrayer: **5** OLAND
Revolutionary War hero: **4** SETH
Warner ___: 4 BROS
Warner Bros.
collectible: **3** CEL
creation: **4** TOON
toon: **4** FUDD
Work for: **7** ANIMATE
Warning: 5 ALERT **6** CAVEAT
TIPOFF
Advance: **5** ALERT
Fairway: **4** FORE
Fencer: **7** ENGARDE
Highway: **3** SLO **5** FLARE
Jungle: **4** ROAR
Library: **3** SHH
sign: **4** OMEN
10 DONOTENTER
sound: **3** GRR **4** HISS **5** GROWL
SIREN SNARL
Studio ~ sign: **5** ONAIR
Theater: **3** SHH
Word of: **4** DONT

Words of: **5** DONOT **6** ORELSE
7 LOOKOUT
War of 1812
battle site: **4** ERIE
treaty site: **5** GHENT
"War of the ___": 5 ROSES
"War of the ___, The": 6 WORLDS
"War of the Worlds, The"
author: **5** WELLS
enemy: **4** MARS **7** MARTIAN
invader: **4** MARS **7** MARTIAN
War on Poverty
org.: **3** OEO
Warp: 4 SKEW
Warp-knit
fabric: **6** TRICOT
Warplane: 6 BOMBER
10 DIVEBOMBER
fleet: **6** ARMADA
Warrant: 3 LET
officer (abbr.): **4** BOSN
Warranty
purchaser: **4** USER
Without: **4** ASIS
Warren
Football player: **4** SAPP
Hall of Fame pitcher: **5** SPAHN
Jurist: **4** EARL
resident: **4** HARE **6** RABBIT
Wife of: **7** ANNETTE
Warren, Robert ___
Author: **4** PENN
Warrior
Female: **6** AMAZON
Fifth-century: **3** HUN
Japanese: **5** NINJA **7** SAMURAI
Olympian: **4** ARES
princess: **5** XENA
Trojan War: **4** AJAX **6** AENEAS
"Warrior Princess"
of TV: **4** XENA
Warriors
org.: **3** NBA
"___ Wars": 4 STAR
Warsaw
coin: **5** ZLOTY
native: **4** POLE
resident: **4** POLE
river: **7** VISTULA

Warsaw ___: 4 PACT
Warsaw Pact
Former ~ member: 4 USSR
"War Scenes"
composer: 8 NEDROREM
Warship: 7 FRIGATE
9 DESTROYER
danger: 4 MINE
group: 5 FLEET 6 ARMADA
Old: 7 TRIREME
projection: 3 RAM
Wars of the Roses
house: 4 YORK
Wartime
Detain during: 6 INTERN
sub: 5 UBOAT
Warts
and all: 4 **ASIS**
Warty
hopper: 4 **TOAD**
Warwick
hit: 5 ALFIE
Singer: 6 DIONNE
Warwickshire
forest: 5 ARDEN
Wary: 5 LEERY
Was
What: 4 PAST
~, in Latin: 4 ERAT
"Was ___ blame?": 3 ITO
Wash: 4 **LAVE** 5 BATHE
7 CLEANSE
against: 5 LAPAT
away: 5 ERODE
Bleed in the: 3 RUN
cycle: 4 SPIN 5 RINSE
Dry: 4 WADI
English river to the: 4 OUSE
out: 4 FADE 5 ERODE RINSE
room: 7 LAUNDRY
Run in the: 5 **BLEED**
thoroughly: 5 SCRUB
Wash.
bigwig: 3 SEN
hours: 3 PST
neighbor: 3 IDA ORE 4 OREG
Washboard
muscles: 3 ABS
Washbowl: 5 BASIN

Washday
brand: 3 ALL DUZ 4 TIDE
unit: 4 LOAD
Washed-out: 3 WAN 4 PALE
5 ASHEN FADED
Washer
Beach: 4 TIDE
companion: 5 DRYER
cycle: 4 SPIN 5 **RINSE**
Shore: 4 TIDE
Washerful: 4 LOAD
Washing: 6 LAVAGE
Washington: 4 CITY 5 MOUNT
STATE
(abbr.): 3 GEN
Actor: 6 DENZEL
airport: 6 SEATAC
and others (abbr.): 3 MTS
bill: 3 ONE
Bill in: 5 GATES
biographer: 5 WEEMS
Blues singer: 5 DINAH
city: 6 TACOMA 7 SPOKANE
10 WALLAWALLA
city, when doubled: 5 WALLA
gallery: 5 FREER
insider: 3 POL 8 POLITICO
Lyricist: 3 NED
Mrs.: 6 MARTHA
neighbor: 6 OREGON
paper: 4 POST
Part of a ~ address:
15 ICANNOTTELLALIE
post: 10 SENATESEAT
Pres.: 3 GEO
product: 5 APPLE
river: 7 POTOMAC
Send to: 5 ELECT
sound: 5 PUGET
stadium: 3 RFK
successor: 5 ADAMS
summit: 7 RAINIER
What ~ could not tell: 4 ALIE
wheeler-dealer: 3 POL
8 POLITICO
Washington, Denzel
movie: 5 GLORY
role: 8 MALCOLMX
15 HURRICANECARTER

Washington Sq.
School at: 3 NYU
"Washington Week"
airer: 3 PBS
Wash n ___: 3 DRI
Washoe
~ County seat: 4 RENO
Washout: 3 DUD 4 FLOP
Washroom: 3 **LAV**
Washstand
pitcher: 4 **EWER**
"___ was in the beginning":
4 ASIT
Wasp
home: 4 NEST
nest site: 4 EAVE
type: 3 MUD
12 YELLOWJACKET
woe: 5 STING
WASP
part: 5 ANGLO SAXON
Wassailing
Go: 5 CAROL
quaff: 6 EGGNOG
song: 4 NOEL
"___ was saying": 3 **ASI**
Wasser
Frozen: 3 **EIS**
Wasserstein, Wendy
heroine: 5 HEIDI
Waste: 4 LOSE SLAG 5 DROSS
6 DEBRIS SEWAGE
allowance: 4 TRET
away: 3 ROT 5 ERODE
effort: 14 SPINONESWHEELS
Go to: 3 ROT
Lay ~ to: 4 RUIN
maker: 5 **HASTE**
not: 3 USE
pipe: 5 SEWER
receptacle: 3 BIN 6 ASHCAN
Smeltery: 4 SLAG 5 DROSS
time: 4 LOAF 6 DAWDLE
DIDDLE
watchers (abbr.): 3 EPA
Wine: 4 LEES
~, as time: 4 KILL
Wasted: 4 ICED 6 STINKO
Wasteland: 4 MOOR 5 HEATH

"Waste Land, The"
monogram: 3 **TSE**
poet: 5 **ELIOT** 7 TSELIOT
"Waste not, want not": 5 ADAGE
Waster
Time: 5 IDLER 7 DAWDLER
"Was to be"
~, in Latin: 4 ERAT
Watch: 3 EYE 4 TEND 5 GUARD
VIGIL
Adjust a: 3 SET
again: 5 RESEE
brand: 5 CASIO OMEGA SEIKO
6 BULOVA
chain: 3 **FOB**
closely: 3 EYE
15 KEEPASHARPEYEON
display, briefly: 3 LCD LED
face: 4 DIAL
for: 5 AWAIT
innards: 5 WORKS
Limp ~ painter: 4 DALI
One to ~ in a pinch: 6 KLEPTO
over: 4 TEND
part: 4 FACE STEM 5 BEZEL
STRAP
Place for a: 5 WRIST
pocket: 3 FOB
secretly: 5 SPYON
Something to: 4 STEP
sound: 4 TICK
the figures: 4 OGLE
the kids: 3 SIT 7 BABYSIT
type: 6 ANALOG
wide-eyed: 6 GAPEAT
winder: 4 STEM
Watchband: 5 STRAP
Watchdog
Airline ~ gp.: 3 FAA
breed: 5 AKITA
Ecol.: 3 **EPA**
Govt. narcotics: 3 DEA
org.: 4 SPCA 5 ASPCA
Rx: 3 FDA
Trucking: 3 ICC
TV: 3 FCC
Wall St.: 3 SEC
warning: 3 GRR
Workplace ~ org.: 4 OSHA

Watched: 3 SAW
  Just: 5 SATBY
Watcher: 4 EYER
  Bambino: 5 MAMMA
  Junior: 6 SITTER
  Kid: 6 SITTER
Watchful: 5 ALERT 8 OPENEYED
  one: 4 EYER
Watching: 7 ONALERT
  Tanks for: 7 AQUARIA
"Watching ___" (Julia Louis-
    Dreyfus sitcom): 5 ELLIE
"Watch it, buster!": 3 HEY
"Watch out!": 4 FORE
Water: 4 AQUA 8 IRRIGATE
  Add ~ to: 6 DILUTE
  balloon sound: 5 SPLAT
  barrier: 4 DIKE MOAT 5 LEVEE
  Bath: 4 AVON
  Bath ~ unit: 5 LITRE
  bird: 4 COOT SWAN
  Body of: 3 SEA 4 POND 5 OCEAN
    6 LAGOON
  Burn with: 5 SCALD
  cannon target: 6 RIOTER
  carrier: 4 MAIN PAIL VASE
  channel: 6 SLUICE
  Clean ~ org.: 3 EPA
  color: 4 **AQUA**
  cooler: 3 ICE
  edge: 5 SHORE
  French ~ source: 5 EVIAN
  gate: 3 DAM
  Hard: 3 ICE 4 HAIL 5 SLEET
  hazard: 4 REEF
  High ~ alternative: 4 HELL
  holder: 3 DAM JUG 4 PAIL VASE
    WELL 5 BASIN GLASS
  Holy ~ receptacle: 4 FONT
  Italian body of: 4 LAGO
  It gets into hot: 5 PASTA
    6 TEABAG
  It will not hold: 3 NET 5 SIEVE
  Lake name meaning big:
    5 TAHOE
  Land in the: 4 ISLE 5 ISLET
  Leaves in hot: 3 TEA
  Like running: 7 EROSIVE
  Muddy the: 4 ROIL

Narrow body of ~ (abbr.): 3 STR
Narrow passage of: 5 INLET
nymph: 5 NAIAD
park feature: 5 CHUTE SLIDE
pipe: 4 BONG MAIN
pitcher: 4 **EWER**
plant: 4 ALGA
platform: 4 PIER 5 WHARF
Playful ~ animal: 5 OTTER
prefix: 5 HYDRO
Put in boiling: 5 STEEP
Salt: 5 BRINE
Scottish body of: 4 LOCH
Search for: 5 DOWSE
skiing apparatus: 4 RAMP
Skip on: 3 DAP
slide: 5 CHUTE
source: 3 TAP 4 MAIN WELL
sprite: 5 NIXIE
tester: 3 **TOE**
Test the: 3 SIP
Throw ~ on: 5 DOUSE
Toe in the: 4 TEST
Tower in the: 3 TUG
Turbulent: 3 RIP
under the bridge: 4 PAST
under the drawbridge: 4 MOAT
vapor: 5 STEAM
Vichy: 3 **EAU**
Walk through: 4 WADE 5 SLOSH
Wanting: 4 ARID
Weaken with: 6 DILUTE
Whirling: 4 **EDDY**
White: 6 RAPIDS
~, in French: 3 EAU
~, in German: 6 WASSER
~, in Spanish: 4 AGUA
Water ___: 3 PIK 4 LILY
___ water: 5 INHOT 6 TOILET
Watercolors
  alternative: 4 OILS
  Do: 5 PAINT
Watercraft
  Birchbark: 5 CANOE
  Brand of: 6 JETSKI
  Swift: 9 HYDROFOIL
Watered
  down: 3 WET 4 THIN WEAK
    5 HOSED

silk: 5 MOIRE
Waterfall: 7 CASCADE
    8 CATARACT
effect: 4 MIST 5 SPRAY
Waterfront
org.: 3 ILA
walk: 4 PIER
" ___ Waterfront": 5 ONTHE
Watergate: 7 SCANDAL
Chuck of: 6 COLSON
co-conspirator: 5 LIDDY
evidence: 4 TAPE
informant John: 4 DEAN
Jaworski of: 4 LEON
Magruder of: 3 JEB
reporter Bernstein: 4 CARL
senator Sam: 5 ERVIN
Watering hole: 3 BAR INN PUB
    SPA 4 POND WELL 5 OASIS
    6 TAVERN
Waterless: 4 ARID SERE
"Water Lilies"
painter Claude: 5 MONET
Waterlogged: 5 SOGGY
    6 SODDEN
land: 3 FEN 5 MARSH
Waterloo: 6 DEFEAT
loser: 8 NAPOLEON
Marshall at: 3 NEY
victor: 10 WELLINGTON
"Waterloo"
group: 4 ABBA
Waterman: 3 PEN
"Watermark"
singer: 4 ENYA
Watermelon
part: 4 RIND SEED
Waterproof
coat: 7 SLICKER
cover: 4 TARP 8 OILCLOTH
material: 3 TAR 7 LANOLIN
    8 OILPAPER PARAFFIN
    TARPAPER
Waters: 5 AQUAE AQUAS
Antarctic: 7 ROSSSEA
Blues singer: 5 ETHEL
International: 7 OPENSEA
Jazz singer: 5 ETHEL
Muddy the: 4 ROIL

~, in French: 4 EAUX
~, in Latin: 5 AQUAE
Waters, Muddy
Music of: 5 BLUES
"Watership Down"
author Richard: 5 ADAMS
Waterside
inn: 6 BOATEL
Waterspout
scaler: 15 ITSYBITSYSPIDER
Waterston
Actor: 3 SAM
Watertight
Make: 5 CAULK 6 SEALUP
Not: 5 LEAKY
Water-to-wine
town: 4 CANA
Waterway
Artificial: 5 CANAL
Cajun: 5 BAYOU
Narrow: 6 STRAIT
Waterwheel: 5 NORIA
Waterworks
Turn on the: 3 SOB 4 WEEP
Watery: 4 THIN WEAK
expanse: 3 SEA 5 OCEAN
porridge: 5 GRUEL
Watkins ___, New York: 4 GLEN
Watley
Singer: 4 JODY
WATS
Part of: 4 AREA
Watson
code letters: 3 DNA
creator: 5 DOYLE
Partner of: 6 HOLMES
Watson, Dr.
portrayer Bruce: 5 NIGEL
Watt: 4 UNIT
Inspiration for: 5 STEAM
Watteau
Painter: 7 ANTOINE
Watterson
tiger: 6 HOBBES
Watts
Actress: 5 NAOMI
Pianist: 5 **ANDRE**
Waugh
Novelist: 4 **ALEC** 6 EVELYN

Wave

Brain: 4 IDEA

Brain ~ (abbr.): 3 EEG

carrier: 3 SEA

catcher: 6 AERIAL 7 ANTENNA

Electromagnetic ~ amplifier:
  5 MASER

Hair: 4 PERM

It is said with a: 4 SHOO

Kind of: 4 HEAT SINE 5 ALPHA
  CRIME TIDAL

Long: 6 ROLLER

Short: 4 PERM

The ~ performers: 4 FANS

Tidal: 7 TSUNAMI

top: 5 CREST

~, in French: 4 ONDE

~, in Spanish: 3 OLA

___ wave: 5 TIDAL

Wavelength

Put on the right: 6 ATTUNE

symbol: 6 LAMBDA

Waveless: 4 CALM

Waves: 4 SURF

Make: 4 PERM 5 SLOSH
  6 SPLASH

Riding the: 4 ASEA

Thought: 4 ESP

Wavy: 7 SINUATE

lines, in comics: 4 ODOR

pattern: 5 MOIRE

___ Wawa: 4 BABA

Wax: 4 GROW 5 LIPID 6 SEALER

Big name in: 7 TUSSAUD

coated cheese: 4 **EDAM**

eloquent: 5 ORATE

Hand-dye with: 5 BATIK

producer: 3 BEE EAR
  8 HONEYBEE

remover: 4 QTIP

Sealing ~ ingredient: 3 LAC

stamper: 4 SEAL

theatrical: 5 EMOTE

Way: 3 TAO 4 LANE PATH ROAD
  5 ROUTE 6 AVENUE
  STREET

back when: 3 AGO 4 ONCE
  7 AGESAGO LONGAGO

By ~ of: 3 ALA PER **VIA** 4 THRU

By the: 3 SAY

cool: 3 RAD

Feel one's: 5 GROPE

Get in the ~ of: 5 DETER
  6 IMPEDE

Give: 5 YIELD

in: 4 DOOR GATE 5 ENTRY
  6 ENTREE PORTAL
  8 ENTRANCE

In a: 5 SORTA 6 KINDOF
  SORTOF

In a bad: 4 ILLY 6 EVILLY

In any: 4 EVER 5 **ATALL**

In a weird: 5 ODDLY 6 EERILY

In no: 7 NOTABIT

In this: 4 THUS 6 LIKESO

In what: 3 HOW 5 HOWSO

It shows the: 5 ARROW

No: 3 NAH 4 ASIF IBET **UHUH**
  5 ICANT NEVER 6 CANTBE
  10 NOTACHANCE

Not in any: 5 NOHOW 6 NOWISE

off: 3 FAR 4 **AFAR** RAMP
  6 REMOTE

of walking: 4 GAIT

On the: 3 DUE 4 SENT 5 ALONG
  7 ENROUTE

out: 4 AFAR DOOR **EXIT** 5 ALIBI
  6 EGRESS ESCAPE PORTAL

out there: 4 **AFAR**

Show the: 5 POINT 6 LEADIN

Smooth the: 4 EASE PAVE

The ~ things stand: 6 ASITIS

This ~ or that: 3 FRO

to go: 4 EXIT PATH ROAD
  5 ROUTE 6 AVENUE

to go (abbr.): 3 **RTE**

to stand: 3 PAT

to the altar: 5 AISLE

to walk: 5 ONAIR

Under: 5 AFOOT BEGUN
  7 STARTED

up: 4 RAMP STEP 5 STAIR
  6 ASCENT

up the slope: 4 TBAR
  9 CHAIRLIFT

Wild ~ to go: 3 APE

Wild ~ to run: 4 AMOK

with words: 4 TACT

Wrong ~ to run: 7 AGROUND
___ way: 3 INA
___ Way (Rome): 6 APPIAN
Wayans
brother: 5 DAMON 6 KEENEN
"Way cool!": 3 RAD
Wayfarer
stop: 3 INN
Waylay: 6 ACCOST
Wayne
Author: 4 DYER
Buddy of: 5 GARTH
Wayne, Bruce
butler: 6 ALFRED
cavemate: 3 BAT
home: 5 MANOR
~, to Batman: 8 ALTEREGO
Wayne, John
birthplace: 4 IOWA
film: 3 MCQ 5 HONDO
 6 DAKOTA HATARI
 7 BIGJAKE RIOLOBO
 8 ELDORADO RIOBRAVO
 THEALAMO TRUEGRIT
 10 FORTAPACHE
 14 SANDSOFIWOJIMA
 15 LEGENDOFTHELOST
 REUNIONINFRANCE
 TALLINTHESADDLE
film, with "The": 5 ALAMO
genre: 5 OATER
 9 SHOOTEMUP
nickname: 4 DUKE
role: 14 ROOSTERCOGBURN
title word: 3 RIO
"Wayne's World"
actor Carvey: 4 DANA
actor Mike: 5 MYERS
actress Carrere: 3 TIA
Where ~ began (abbr.): 3 SNL
word: 3 NOT
"Way of All ___, The": 5 FLESH
"Way of the gods": 6 SHINTO
Ways
partner: 5 MEANS
Wayside
stop: 3 **INN**
"Way to go!": 7 NICEONE
 8 ATTAGIRL

Wayward
Like a ~ GI: 4 AWOL
"Wayward Wind, The"
singer Grant: 4 GOGI
"Way We ___, The": 4 WERE
WB
competitor: 3 UPN
network mascot: 4 FROG
sitcom: 4 REBA
WBA
official: 3 REF
outcome: 3 TKO
stats: 3 KOS 4 TKOS
W.C.
in the U.K.: 3 LOO
Wd.
part: 3 LTR SYL
We
As ~ speak: 3 NOW
Weak: 4 PUNY SOFT THIN
 6 ANEMIC FEEBLE
 7 FLACCID
brew: 8 NEARBEER
~, as an excuse: 4 LAME
"___ Weak" (Belinda Carlisle hit):
 4 IGET
Weaken: 3 EBB SAG SAP 4 FADE
 5 ABATE ERODE 6 DILUTE
 8 ENERVATE
"Weakest Link, The"
host Robinson: 4 ANNE
Weakness: 6 ANEMIA
 9 BLINDSPOT
"___ we all?": 5 ARENT
Wealth: 3 FAT 5 MEANS 6 ASSETS
 RICHES
A lot of: 6 ESTATE
Inherited: 8 OLDMONEY
Source of sudden: 7 JACKPOT
Wealthy: 10 RAKINGITIN
 WELLHEELED
contributor: 6 FATCAT
one: 4 HAVE 5 NABOB
~, in Spanish: 4 RICO
Weapon
Animal: 4 CLAW 5 TALON
Antitank: 7 BAZOOKA
Cavalry: 5 LANCE SABER
Caveman: 4 CLUB

David's: 5 SLING
Defense system without a:
   4 JUDO
Fencing: 4 EPEE FOIL 5 SABER
   SWORD
Gangster: 3 GAT 4 SHIV
   6 ROSCOE
Gaucho: 4 **BOLA**
Guided ~, for short: 4 ICBM
handle: 4 HAFT HILT
in Clue: 4 ROPE 8 LEADPIPE
   REVOLVER
Jousting: 5 **LANCE**
Medieval: 4 MACE PIKE
   6 POLEAX 7 POLEAXE
   8 CROSSBOW
Mob ~: 7 GAROTTE GARROTE
Nuclear: 5 ABOMB HBOMB
Olympic: 4 EPEE
Sci-fi: 3 RAY 5 LASER 6 PHASER
   RAYGUN
Sharp: 5 LANCE SABER SPEAR
Slapstick: 3 PIE
Special Forces: 3 **UZI**
Sport: 4 EPEE
Take away a: 5 UNARM
Terrorist: 3 UZI
Tilting: 5 LANCE
WWII: 4 **STEN**
~, in French: 4 ARME
"___ Weapon": 6 LETHAL
Weaponry: 4 ARMS
Weapons: 4 ARMS
  Big: 9 ARTILLERY
  experiment, for short: 5 NTEST
  Search for: 5 FRISK
  supply: 6 ARMORY 7 ARSENAL
  Supply more ~ to: 5 REARM
Wear: 5 ERODE SPORT 6 ATTIRE
       HAVEON 7 APPAREL
  After-bath: 4 ROBE
  a long face: 4 MOPE POUT
  and tear: 3 USE
  at the edges: 4 FRAY
  away: 4 FRET 5 **ERODE**
    6 ABRADE
  Casual: 3 TEE
  down: 4 TIRE 5 **ERODE**
    6 ABRADE 7 TIREOUT

Formal: 3 TUX 5 TAILS
   6 TUXEDO
Hard: 5 ARMOR
out: 4 TIRE
out your welcome: 8 OVERSTAY
Partner of: 4 WASH
Summer: 3 TEE
well: 4 LAST
___ wear: 4 MENS
"___ we are!": 4 HERE
Wearily
  Walk: 4 PLOD SLOG
Weariness: 5 ENNUI
Wearing: 7 EROSIVE
  Is: 5 HASON
Wearisome
  Become: 4 PALL
Wears: 5 HASON
Weary: 4 BEAT FLAG LIMP TIRE
  Sound: 4 SIGH
Weasel: 3 RAT 5 SNEAK
    6 FISHER 10 EQUIVOCATE
  kin: 4 MINK 5 OTTER SABLE
    6 MARTEN 7 POLECAT
  out: 6 RENEGE
  out of: 5 EVADE
  type: 5 STOAT 6 ERMINE
  word: 3 POP 5 MAYBE
Weather: 5 ERODE 6 ENDURE
    8 ELEMENTS
  Be under the: 3 AIL
  forecasting aid: 5 RADAR
  indicator: 4 VANE
  Like some winter: 5 SNOWY
    6 SLEETY
  London: 3 FOG
  map area: 3 LOW 4 HIGH
    5 FRONT
  map line: 6 ISOBAR
  Mild, as: 5 BALMY
  phenomenon: 6 ELNINO
    LANINA
  Prevailing: 5 CLIME
  satellite: 4 ESSA 5 TIROS
  stat: 3 LOW 4 HIGH
  system: 3 LOW 4 HIGH
  Under the: 3 **ILL** 4 SICK
  Wet: 4 RAIN
Weathercock: 4 VANE

Weatherman
  TV: 7 ALROKER
Weatherspoon
  of the WNBA: 6 TERESA
Weave: 4 MESH
  Partner of: 3 BOB
Weaver
  apparatus: 4 LOOM
  Basket ~ material: 5 OSIER
  Fictional: 6 MARNER
  Former manager: 4 EARL
  of myth: 7 ARACHNE
  reed: 4 SLEY
Weaver, Charley
  hometown: Mount ___: 3 IDY
Weaver, Sigourney
  film: 5 ALIEN
  role: 10 DIANFOSSEY
  sequel: 6 ALIENS
Weavers, The
  One of: 6 SEEGER
Web
  Access the: 5 LOGON
  Bit of ~ programming:
    10 JAVAAPPLET
  conversation: 4 CHAT
  letters: 5 EMAIL
  Make a: 4 SPIN
  master: 6 SPIDER
  place: 4 SITE
  pop-ups: 3 ADS
  surfer: 4 USER 7 NETIZEN
  user: 6 SURFER
  user's need: 5 MODEM
Web address
  (abbr.): 3 URL
  ending: 3 COM EDU GOV NET
    ORG
  part: 3 DOT
  start: 4 HTTP
Webb, Karrie
  org.: 4 LPGA
Webber, Andrew Lloyd: 6 KNIGHT
  musical: 4 CATS 5 EVITA
  title: 3 SIR
Weber
  One ~ per square meter: 5 TESLA
Web-footed
  mammal: 5 OTTER

  swallow: 4 TERN
Web page
  feature: 4 LINK
  Main: 4 HOME
Web site: 4 FOOT 5 **ATTIC**
  Auction: 4 EBAY
  help: 3 FAQ
  language: 4 JAVA
  unit: 4 PAGE
  visit: 3 HIT
  worker: 5 SYSOP
Webster
  Emulate: 5 ORATE
  Wordsmith: 4 **NOAH**
  ~, for short: 4 DANL
Webster, Daniel: 6 ORATOR
Webster, Norma ___: 3 RAE
Webzine: 4 EMAG
Wed: 3 TIE 5 UNITE
  on the run: 5 **ELOPE**
Wed.
  follower: 3 THU
  preceder: 3 TUE
"___ We Dance?": 5 SHALL
Wedded: 3 ONE
Wedding: 4 RITE 5 UNION
  announcement: 5 BANNS
  band: 4 RING 5 OCTET
  cake feature: 4 **TIER**
  dance: 4 HORA
  day sight: 4 LIMO
  dessert: 4 CAKE
  helper: 5 USHER
  keepsake: 5 ALBUM
  Like a ~ cake: 6 TIERED
  Make ~ plans: 8 SETADATE
  Many ~ guests: 3 KIN
  page word: 3 **NEE**
  ritual: 5 TOAST
  seater: 5 USHER
  shower: 4 RICE
  site: 5 ALTAR 6 CHAPEL
  symbol: 4 BAND
  vow: 3 IDO
  wear: 3 TUX 4 VEIL
    6 TUXEDO
  ~ VIP: 5 BRIDE 7 BESTMAN
    10 RINGBEARER
"___ Wedding": 6 BETSYS

Wedel: 3 SKI
"___ we devils?": 5 ARENT
Wedge: 4 **SHIM**
  driver: 4 MAUL
  Wheel: 5 CHOCK
Wedges
  It has: 3 PIE
Wednesday
  was named for him: 4 ODIN
  ___ Wednesday: 3 **ASH**
Wednesday's child
  Fate of: 3 WOE
"**We Do Our Part**"
  org.: 3 NRA
Wee: 3 LIL SMA 4 PUNY TINY
     5 SMALL TEENY
     6 MINUTE TEENSY
  bit: 3 **TAD** 4 ATOM IOTA MITE
  hour: 3 ONE TWO 5 ONEAM
     THREE TWOAM 6 FOURAM
  hour flight: 6 REDEYE
  hours: 4 LATE
  one: 3 ELF TAD TOT 4 RUNT
     TYKE 6 INFANT
  worker: 3 ANT
  ~, in Scotland: 3 SMA
Wee ___: 3 UNS
Weed: 3 CIG
  Biblical: 4 TARE
  killer: 3 HOE 4 HOER
  whacker: 3 **HOE** 4 HOER
Week
  before Easter: 10 PALMSUNDAY
  Big in TV. 6 SWEEPS
  Day of the ~ (abbr.): 3 FRI MON
     SAT SUN THU TUE WED
  ending abbr.: 4 TGIF
  ~, in Spanish: 6 SEMANA
Weekend
  getaway site: 3 INN
  inits.: 4 TGIF
  ~ TV show: 3 SNL
Weena: 4 ELOI
Weenie: 4 NERD 5 TWERP
Weep: 3 CRY SOB
Weeper: 5 LOSER
  of myth: 5 **NIOBE**
Weevil
  home: 4 BOLL

___ weevil: 4 BOLL
"**We ___ Family**": 3 ARE
"___ we forget ...": 4 **LEST**
"... we have seen his ___ the
     east": 6 STARIN
"___ we having fun yet?": 3 ARE
Weigh: 6 ASSESS 8 EVALUATE
Weighed
  down: 5 **LADEN**
Weighing
  device: 5 SCALE
Weight: 4 **HEFT** ONUS
  abbr.: 3 LBS
  Apothecary: 4 DRAM
  Asian: 4 TAEL
  Big name in~ loss:
     10 JENNYCRAIG
  British: 5 STONE
  Container: 4 **TARE**
  Gem: 5 CARAT
  Heavy: 3 **TON**
  Kind of: 4 TROY
  Light: 4 GRAM 5 OUNCE
  loss plan: 4 DIET
  Metric: 4 GRAM KILO 5 TONNE
  Middle: 9 SPARETIRE
  room reps: 3 SET
  room unit: 3 REP
  Test the ~ of: 4 HEFT
Weightlifter
  count: 3 REP
  lift: 4 CURL
  muscles: 3 ABS 4 LATS 6 BICEPS
  unit: 3 REP
Weighty
  book: 4 TOME
  Way too: 5 OBESE
Weill
  Composer: 4 KURT
  Mrs.: 5 LENYA LOTTE
Weinberger
  Ex-Secretary: 6 CASPAR
Weinmeister
  of football: 5 ARNIE
Weird: 3 ODD 5 **EERIE** OUTRE
     6 FREAKY SPOOKY
     7 BIZARRE ODDBALL
"**Weird Al**"
  movie: 3 UHF

Weirdo: 3 NUT 4 GEEK KOOK
    5 CREEP FLAKE
    7 DEVIANT ODDBALL
Weiss, Erich: 7 HOUDINI
Weisshorn: 3 ALP
Weizman
  Israeli statesman: 4 EZER
Wek
  Fashion model: 4 ALEK
Welcome: 5 ASKIN GREET SEEIN
    6 ACCEPT
  forecast: 5 CLEAR
  Hawaiian: 3 LEI 5 **ALOHA**
  item: 3 MAT
  Openly: 5 ASKIN
  Roman: 3 AVE
  sight: 5 OASIS
  site: 3 MAT
  Symbol of: 8 OPENARMS
    OPENDOOR
  Wear out your: 8 OVERSTAY
  Word of: 5 ALOHA HELLO
  words to a hitchhiker: 5 HOPIN
Welcome ___: 3 MAT
"Welcome Back, Kotter"
  actor Kaplan: 4 GABE
  actor Palillo: 3 RON
Welcomer: 4 HOST
"Welcome to Waikiki!":
  5 ALOHA
Weld: 4 BOND FUSE
Welder
  Kind of: 3 ARC
Weldon
  Writer: 3 FAY
Welfare
  Animal ~ org.: 4 SPCA
  Child ~ gp.: 3 PTA
  factor: 4 NEED
  grant: 4 DOLE
  state: 4 NEED
  Worker ~ org.: 4 OSHA
Welk
  intro part: 4 AONE ATWO
  speciality: 5 POLKA
Well: 4 ABLY HALE SUMP
    7 CISTERN
  As: 3 **TOO** 4 ALSO 6 TOBOOT
  As ~ as: 3 AND

Do: 5 EXCEL 6 THRIVE
    7 PROSPER
Is not: 4 AILS
Make: 4 CURE HEAL
Not: 3 DIM ILL 4 RARE SICK
    6 POORLY
put: 3 APT
Run: 3 HUM
Serve: 3 ACE
Type of: 8 ARTESIAN
Very: 6 SOBEIT
~, in French: 4 BIEN
~, in Spanish: 4 BIEN
"Well!": 6 INEVER 8 IDECLARE
Well-___: 6 HEELED
"Well, ___!": 6 INEVER LADIDA
"___ well": 4 ALLS 5 ALLIS
"Wellaway!": 5 ALACK
"Well, ___ be!": 3 ILL
Well-behaved: 4 GOOD 6 POLITE
  Hardly: 3 BAD
  kid: 4 DOLL
Well-built: 5 SOLID 6 STURDY
WellCare: 3 HMO
Well-chosen: 3 APT
Well-coordinated: 5 AGILE
"Well, ___-di-dah!": 3 LAH
"Well, Did You ___?" (Cole Porter
    song): 4 EVAH
"Well done!": 4 **NICE**
  ~, in Italian: 4 BENE
Welles
  Actor: 5 **ORSON**
  Director: 5 ORSON
  Old studio of: 3 RKO
  role: 4 **KANE**
Wellesley
  grad: 6 ALUMNA
Well-founded: 5 VALID
Well-groomed: 4 NEAT TRIM
    5 KEMPT SLEEK
    7 SOIGNEE
  Not: 5 MESSY
Well-heeled: 4 RICH
"Well, I ___!": 5 NEVER
Well-informed: 5 AWARE
  about: 4 UPON
Wellington
  Napoleon, to: 3 FOE

NFL Hall of Famer: 4 MARA
"Well, lah-di-___!": 3 DAH
"Wellll ...?": 3 SOO
"Well, lookee here!": 3 OHO
Well-mannered: 5 CIVIL
    6 POLITE
Wellness
  org.: 3 NIH
Well-ordered: 4 NEAT
Well-pitched: 5 ONKEY
  Like some ~ games: 5 NOHIT
Well-read
  types: 8 LITERATI
Wells
  race: 4 ELOI
  Reformer: 3 IDA
Wells, H.G.
  doctor: 6 MOREAU
  novel: 15 THEINVISIBLEMAN
  race: 4 ELOI
"Well said!": 6 TOUCHE
Wells Fargo
  vehicle: 5 STAGE
Well-spoken: 6 FLUENT
Wellspring: 5 FOUNT 6 ORIGIN
"We'll tak ___ o' kindness yet ...":
    4 ACUP
"___ Well That Ends Well": 4 ALLS
"Well, ___ that special!": 4 ISNT
Well-to-do
  suffix: 4 AIRE
Well-ventilated: 4 AIRY
"Well, well!": 3 AHA OHO 4 ISAY
Well-worn: 3 OLD 5 BANAL
    FADED
Welsh
  dog: 5 CORGI
  symbol: 4 LEEK
Welsh ___: 5 CORGI 7 RAREBIT
Welshman: 4 CELT
Welty
  Author: 6 EUDORA
Wembley Stadium
  borough: 5 BRENT
"___ we meet again": 5 UNTIL
Wences
  title: 5 SENOR
Wenders
  Director: 3 WIM

Wendy
  Dog of: 4 NANA
  Kidnapper of: 4 HOOK
Wendy's
  Went to: 6 ATEOUT
"We ___ Not Alone": 3 ARE
Went
  after: 4 SUED 5 SETAT WOOED
    6 CHASED 8 ASSAILED
  ahead: 3 LED
  alone: 6 SOLOED
  around: 7 AVOIDED
  astray: 5 ERRED
  bad: 6 ROTTED SOURED
  ballistic: 5 RAGED 6 LOSTIT
  down: 4 FELL SANK SLID
  fast: 3 RAN 4 FLEW HIED SPED
    TORE 5 RACED RANBY
    7 SCOOTED
  for: 5 CHOSE LIKED
    7 AIMEDAT
    9 HOMEDINON
  gaga over: 5 LOVED 6 ADORED
  off: 4 BLEW 5 ERRED
  off course: 5 YAWED
  out: 5 EBBED 6 EXITED
  out of business: 8 FOLDEDUP
  out with: 5 DATED
  over: 7 RANLATE
  too far: 9 OVERDIDIT
  too fast: 4 SPED
  under: 4 DOVE SANK
  undercover: 5 SPIED
  underground: 3 HID
  wild: 5 RAVED 7 RANRIOT
  with: 5 DATED
  wrong: 5 ERRED
"___ Went Mad": Riley: 4 EREI
"___ went thataway!": 4 THEY
"We ___ Overcome": 5 SHALL
"We ___ please": 5 AIMTO
Wept: 5 CRIED
___ were: 4 ASIT
"___ Were a Rich Man": 3 IFI
"We're in big trouble!": 4 OHOH
"We're number ___!": 3 ONE
"We're Off ___ the Wizard":
    5 TOSEE
"___ Were the Days": 5 THOSE

"Werewolves of London"
singer: 5 ZEVON
"___ were you ...": 3 IFI
"Were you born in ___?":
5 ABARN
Werner
Actor: 5 OSKAR
Wertmuller
Director: 4 **LINA**
Wesley, John
denom.: 4 METH
West
Actress: 3 **MAE**
Contest in the: 5 RODEO
end: 3 ERN
Land ~ of Nod: 4 EDEN
of Batman: 4 ADAM
West ___: 6 INDIES
___ West: 3 MAE
West, Mae
Final film of: 8 SEXTETTE
Move like: 5 SLINK
play: 10 DIAMONDLIL
song: 10 MYOLDFLAME
wraparound: 3 BOA
West African
desert: 5 NAMIB
republic: 4 MALI 5 BENIN
GABON 7 NIGERIA
10 IVORYCOAST
West Bank
gp.: 3 PLO
West Coast
sch.: 4 UCLA
time: 3 PDT
Western: 5 OATER
airline: 5 ALOHA
alliance: 3 OAS 4 NATO
capital: 5 BOISE SALEM
6 HELENA
classic of 1953: 5 SHANE
elevation: 4 MESA
film: 5 OATER
friend: 4 PARD
hat: 7 STETSON
law group: 5 POSSE
lily: 4 SEGO
locale: 4 FORT
moniker: 3 TEX

Old ~ fort: 3 ORD
omelet ingredient: 3 HAM
plateau: 4 MESA
resort lake: 5 TAHOE
show: 5 RODEO
star Lash: 5 LARUE
tie: 4 BOLO
timber: 6 REDFIR
topper: 7 STETSON
treaty org.: 3 OAS
tribe: 3 UTE 4 OTOE UTES
TV: 6 LAREDO
wine valley: 4 NAPA
wolf: 4 LOBO
writer: 4 GREY 5 HARTE
writer Grey: 4 ZANE
writer Wister: 4 OWEN
Western Athletic Conference
sch.: 3 SMU TCU 4 UTEP
Western Australia
capital: 5 PERTH
Westernmost
African capital: 5 DAKAR
Aleutian: 4 **ATTU**
Western Samoa
capital: 4 APIA
Western Union
founder Cornell: 4 EZRA
West Indies: 5 ISLES
island: 5 ARUBA 7 ANTIGUA
language: 5 CARIB
music: 7 CALYPSO
native: 5 CARIB
sorcery: 5 OBEAH
Westminster: 5 ABBEY
"Westminster Alice, The"
author: 4 SAKI
West Point
alt.: 4 ROTC
athletes: 4 ARMY
frosh: 5 PLEBE
sch.: 4 ACAD USMA
student: 5 CADET
"West Side Story"
actor Tamblyn: 4 RUSS
actress Moreno: 4 RITA
gang: 4 JETS 6 SHARKS
girl: 5 ANITA MARIA
Maria's friend in: 5 ANITA

role: 4 TONY 5 ANITA
song: 5 MARIA 7 AMERICA
  TONIGHT
~ Oscar winner: 6 MORENO
  10 RITAMORENO
West Virginia
resource: 8 COALMINE
"West Wing, The"
actor Rob: 4 **LOWE**
award: 4 EMMY
network: 3 NBC
star: 5 SHEEN
worker: 4 AIDE
"Westworld"
actor Brynner: 3 YUL
Wet: 4 DAMP DEWY SOAK
  5 RAINY 7 MOISTEN
bar: 4 SOAP
behind the ears: 3 RAW
  5 NAIVE
blanket: 7 KILLJOY
  11 PARTYPOOPER
course: 4 SOUP
Get one's feet: 4 WADE
Like ~ ink: 6 SMEARY
Like a ~ noodle: 4 LIMP
nurse: 4 AMAH
septet: 4 SEAS
Sound of ~ impact: 5 SPLAT
weather: 4 RAIN
wiggler: 3 EEL
zapper: 3 EEL
"We ___ the Champions" (Queen
  hit): 3 ARE
"We, the Living"
author: 4 RAND 7 AYNRAND
"___ we there yet?": 3 **ARE**
"We ___ the World": 3 ARE
Wetland: 3 BOG FEN 5 MARSH
"We try harder"
company: 4 AVIS
"We've got trouble!": 4 UHOH
"We want ___!" (ballpark chant):
  4 AHIT
Whack: 3 BAT BOP HIT OFF RAP
  4 BELT STAB SWAT
  5 SMITE
Out of: 4 AWRY 5 AMISS ASKEW
  8 COCKEYED

Whacker
Weed: 3 **HOE** 4 HOER
Whale
Baby: 4 CALF
Female: 3 COW
finder: 5 SONAR
First name of a: 4 MOBY
group: 3 GAM POD
Killer: 4 **ORCA**
Kind of: 5 SPERM
movie: 4 ORCA
One in a: 5 JONAH
SeaWorld: 5 SHAMU
White ~ pursuer: 4 AHAB
Whaler: 6 SEAMAN
direction: 4 THAR
Melville: 4 AHAB
"Wham!": 3 POW 5 KAPOW
Whammy: 3 HEX
Wham-O
fad item: 8 HULAHOOP
Wharf: 4 PIER **QUAY**
locale: 4 PORT
pest: 3 RAT
worker org.: 3 ILA
Wharton
deg.: 3 **MBA**
grad: 3 **MBA**
subj.: 4 ECON
title character: 5 ETHAN FROME
Writer: 5 EDITH
What
a mess: 3 STY
Give ~ for: 5 SCOLD 7 TELLOFF
Having ~ it takes: 4 ABLE
In ~ way?: 3 HOW 5 HOWSO
No matter:
  15 COMERAINORSHINE
Then: 3 AND
this is not: 4 THAT
to do: 4 TASK 6 AGENDA
we have: 4 OURS
you eat: 4 DIET
you will: 6 ESTATE
~, in French: 4 QUOI
~, in Spanish: 3 QUE
"What?": 3 HUH
syllables: 3 EHS
Words after: 5 ISAID

"What ___!": 4 AGAS 5 ADEAL AMESS

"What ___ ...": 3 THE

"What ___?": 4 ELSE

"What, again?!": 4 OHNO

"What a Girl Wants"
singer Christina: 8 AGUILERA

"What a good boy ___!": 3 AMI

"What am ___?" (auction query):
4 IBID

"What am I supposed to ___?":
5 DONOW

"What a pity!": 4 ALAS

"What a rare mood ___": 4 IMIN

"What a relief!": 3 AAH 4 PHEW

"What are the ___?": 4 ODDS

"What a ride!": 4 WHEE

"What a shame!": 4 ALAS
6 TOOBAD

"What a surprise!": 3 OHO

"What a week!": 4 TGIF

"What ___ can I say?": 4 ELSE

"Whatcha ___?": 4 DOIN

"What ___, chopped liver?":
3 AMI

"What'd ___" (Ray Charles hit):
4 ISAY

"What did I tell you?": 3 SEE

"What'd I tell ya?": 3 SEE

"What'd you say?": 3 HUH

"What else?": 3 AND

Whatever: 3 ANY

"Whatever": 9 IDONTCARE

"Whatever ___ Wants" (1955
song): 4 LOLA

"What fools these mortals be"
writer: 6 SENECA

"What ___ for Love": 4 IDID

"What ___ God wrought?":
4 HATH

"What happened next?": 3 AND

"What have we here?!": 3 OHO

"What I Am"
singer Brickell: 4 EDIE

"What ___ is new?": 4 ELSE

"What Kind of Fool ___?": 3 AMI

"What Kind of Fool Am I?"
singer Anthony: 6 NEWLEY

"What'll ___?": 4 ITBE

"What, me ___?": 5 WORRY

"What ___ mind reader?": 4 AMIA

"What ___ now?": 4 ISIT

What's
expected: 4 NORM
happening: 4 NEWS 5 EVENT
TREND
here: 5 THESE
left: 4 REST 6 ESTATE
more: 3 AND 4 ALSO
up: 3 SKY

"What's ___?": 3 NEW

"What ___ say?": 4 CANI

"What's ___ for me?": 4 INIT

"What's Going On?"
singer: 4 GAYE

"What's gotten ___ you?": 4 INTO

"What's in ___?": Shakespeare:
5 ANAME

"What's more ...": 3 AND

"What's My Line?"
crew: 5 PANEL
panelist Bennett: 4 CERF
panelist Francis: 6 ARLENE

Whatsoever: 5 ATALL

"What's the ___?": 3 DIF USE

"What's the big ___?": 4 IDEA

"What's this?": 5 HELLO

"What's up, ___?": 3 DOC

"What's ___ you?": 4 ITTO
6 EATING

"What ___ that?": 3 WAS

"What the Butler Saw"
playwright: 5 ORTON

"What ___ the odds?": 3 ARE

"What time ___?": 4 ISIT

"What've you been ___?":
4 UPTO

"What was ___ do?": 3 ITO

"What was that?": 3 HUH

"What was ___ think?": 3 ITO

"What Women Want"
actor Alan: 4 ALDA
actress Marisa: 5 TOMEI

"Whazzat?": 3 HUH

Wheat: 4 CROP 5 GRAIN
Beat the: 6 THRESH
bundle: 5 SHEAF
covering: 3 AWN

holder: 4 SILO
husk: 4 BRAN
Pasta: 5 DURUM
Type of: 5 SPELT

Wheaties
box figure: 7 ATHLETE

Wheaton
Actor: 3 WIL

Wheedle: 4 COAX 6 CAJOLE

Wheedler
tactic: 5 GUILE

Wheel
alignment: 5 TOEIN
Be at the: 5 STEER
Big: 5 CHIEF NABOB
Color ~ display: 5 TONES
connector: 4 **AXLE**
cover: 6 HUBCAP
Engine: 3 CAM
hub: 4 NAVE
Kind of: 3 MAG
man: 5 SAJAK 6 FERRIS
part: 3 HUB RIM 5 SPOKE
Pet on a: 7 HAMSTER
shaft: 4 AXLE
Ship: 4 HELM
spokes: 5 RADII
Spur: 5 ROWEL
Take the: 5 STEER
Tend the squeaky: 3 OIL
tooth: 3 COG
track: 3 RUT
turner: 4 AXLE

Wheelchair
access: 4 RAMP

Wheeler-dealer: 8 OPERATOR
D.C.: 3 POL
Wall St.: 3 ARB

Wheelhouse
direction: 4 ALEE

Wheeling
River of: 4 OHIO

Wheelless
vehicle: 6 SLEDGE

"Wheel of Fortune"
buy: 3 ANA ANE ANI ANO
5 VOWEL
category: 5 EVENT THING
6 PHRASE

choice: 4 SPIN
creator Griffin: 4 MERV
host: 5 SAJAK
quintet: 5 AEIOU
singer: 5 STARR

Wheels: 3 CAR 4 AUTO
10 AUTOMOBILE
Early: 5 TRIKE
Eccentric: 4 CAMS
Fast: 7 PORSCHE
Furniture: 7 CASTERS
Homes on: 3 RVS
Off-road ~, for short: 3 ATV
Teamster: 4 SEMI
Temporary: 6 LOANER
Upscale: 3 BMW
Vintage: 3 REO
VIP: 4 LIMO

Whelk: 5 SNAIL

W. Hemisphere
gp.: 3 OAS

When: 8 ASSOONAS
Back: 3 AGO

"___ when?": 5 SINCE
"When ___ door ...?": 3 ISA
"When ___ eat?": 4 DOWE

Whenever
you like: 6 ATWILL

"Whenever": 7 ANYTIME

"When Harry Met Sally"
actress Ryan: 3 MEG
director Rob: 6 REINER

"When hell freezes over!":
5 NEVER

"When in ___ ...": 4 ROME

"When in Rome, ___ the ...":
4 DOAS

"When I put out ___": Tennyson:
5 TOSEA

"When it's ___" (old riddle
answer): 4 AJAR

"When I was ___ ...": 4 **ALAD**

"When pigs fly!": 5 NEVER

"When ___ said and done ...":
4 ALLS

"When the frost ___ the
punkin ...": 4 ISON

"When the moon hits your eye"
emotion: 5 AMORE

"When We Were Kings"
subject: 3 ALI
"When Will ___ Loved": 3 IBE
"When You Wish Upon ___":
5 ASTAR
Where
From: 6 WHENCE
to get down: 5 EIDER
to get off: 4 EXIT STOP
you live: 5 ABODE
~, in Latin: 3 UBI
Where ___: 5 ITSAT
"Where ___?": 3 AMI 4 WASI
Whereabouts: 4 AREA SITE
"Where America's Day Begins":
4 GUAM
"Where Angels Fear to Tread"
author: 7 FORSTER
"Where Eagles Dare"
actress Mary: 3 URE
gun: 4 STEN
Wherefores
Partner of: 4 WHYS
"Wherefore ___ thou ...": 3 ART
"Where pines and maples grow"
Words before: 7 OCANADA
"Where's ___?" (1970 film):
5 POPPA
"Where's Daddy?"
dramatist: 4 INGE
"Where's Poppa?"
actor George: 5 SEGAL
"Where the Boys ___": 3 ARE
"Where the heart is": 4 HOME
"Where there's ___ ...": 5 AWILL
"Where the Wild Things ___":
3 ARE
Wherewithal: 5 MEANS
Lacks the: 6 CANNOT
Provide the: 5 EQUIP
"Where ___ you?": 4 WERE
Wherry: 4 BOAT
Whet: 4 HONE 6 AROUSE
Whether ___: 4 ORNO
"Whether ___ nobler ...": Hamlet:
3 TIS
Whetstone
Use a: 4 HONE
"Whew!": 3 BOY MAN 6 IMBEAT

Reason to say: 8 NEARMISS
Whey
companion: 5 CURDS
Wheyfaced: 3 WAN 5 ASHEN
Which
By ~, in Latin: 3 QUA
person: 3 WHO
Whichever: 3 **ANY**
"___ which will live in infamy":
FDR: 5 ADATE
Whiff: 3 FAN 4 HINT ODOR
5 SMELL
Get a ~ of: 5 SCENT SMELL
SNIFF
king Ryan: 5 NOLAN
Whiffenpoof: 3 ELI
Whig
leader: 4 CLAY
orator William: 4 PITT
rival: 4 TORY
While: 8 SOLONGAS
A ~ back: 4 ONCE
After a: 4 ANON
away: 4 IDLE LAZE
Give for a: 4 LEND
In a: 4 **ANON** SOON 5 LATER
lead-in: 4 ERST
Once in a: 7 ATTIMES
Quite a: 3 EON 4 AGES
5 YEARS
"While ___ it ...": 4 IMAT
"While you're ___ ...": 4 ATIT
Whillikers
lead-in: 3 GEE
___ whim: 3 ONA
Whimper: 3 SOB 4 **MEWL** PULE
WEEP
Whimsical: 3 FEY 5 DROLL
Whine: 4 MEWL PULE 6 SNIVEL
YAMMER
Rhine: 3 ACH
Whinny: 5 NEIGH
Whip: 3 **TAN** 4 BEST LASH
Like a: 5 SMART
mark: 4 WALE WELT
One with a: 5 TAMER
9 LIONTAMER
Riding: 4 CROP
up: 5 CHURN 7 PREPARE

"Whip It"
  band: 4 **DEVO**

Whiplash
  of cartoons: 7 SNIDELY
  preventer: 8 HEADREST

Whiplash, Snidely
  Emulate: 5 SNEER

Whipped: 6 BEATEN
  cream serving: 4 GLOP
      6 DOLLOP
  dessert: 6 MOUSSE
  up: 4 MADE

Whippersnapper: 5 WHELP

Whipping
  boy: 4 GOAT

Whirl: 3 TRY 4 EDDY REEL SPIN
  Give it a: 3 TRY

Whirling: 5 AREEL ASPIN
  water: 4 **EDDY** 6 VORTEX

Whirlpool: 4 **EDDY** 6 VORTEX
  competitor: 5 AMANA 6 MAYTAG
  feature: 3 JET
  site: 3 SPA

Whirlybird
  relative: 4 GIRO
  whirler: 5 ROTOR

Whirring
  sound: 4 BIRR

Whisker
  Beat by a: 4 EDGE

Whiskers
  Animal with: 3 CAT 4 SEAL

Whiskey
  drink: 4 SOUR 6 ROBROY
      9 MANHATTAN
  follower: 4 SOUR 5 AGOGO
  grain: 3 RYE
  Kind of: 3 RYE 5 IRISH
  Language that gives us: 4 ERSE
  Noted name in: 5 DEWAR
  Walker of: 5 HIRAM

Whisper
  Furtive: 4 PSST
  Stage: 5 ASIDE
  sweet nothings: 3 **COO**

Whispering
  No: 3 SHH

Whistle: 5 ALERT
  blower: 3 COP REF 6 TOOTER

  Blow the: 3 RAT 4 TELL TOOT
  cord: 7 LANYARD
  hour: 4 NOON
  Kitchen ~ cause: 5 STEAM
  Old ~ tune: 5 DIXIE
  part: 3 PEA
  sound: 4 TOOT 5 TWEET

Whistler: 3 REF 4 WOLF 6 ARTIST
      KETTLE TEAPOT
      7 REFEREE 9 TEAKETTLE

Whistles
  partners: 5 BELLS

Whit: 3 FIG 4 ATOM IOTA

Whitcomb
  Poet: 5 RILEY

White: 3 SEA WAN 4 ASHY
      PALE 5 ANGLO ASHEN
      SNOWY
  animal: 6 ALBINO
  Celtics great: 4 JOJO
  cheese: 4 BRIE
  chip, often: 4 ANTE
  Choreographer: 4 ONNA
  cliffs locale: 5 DOVER
  Complement of: 4 YOLK
  Creamy: 5 IVORY
  dwarf: 3 DOC
  flag message: 5 TRUCE
  fur: 6 ERMINE
  Great ~ ___ : 5 HERON
  hat wearer: 4 CHEF HERO
      5 NURSE
  heron: 5 EGRET
  house: 5 IGLOO
  lie: 3 FIB
  Little ~ thing: 3 LIE
  Lustrous: 6 PEARLY
  Milky ~ gem: 4 OPAL
  oak: 5 ROBLE
  of the eye: 6 SCLERA
  poplar: 5 **ABELE**
  sale item: 5 LINEN SHEET
      TOWEL
  Silvery: 6 ARGENT
  The other ~ meat: 4 PORK
  Verbal ~ flag: 5 UNCLE
  vestment: 3 ALB 5 AMICE
  wader: 4 IBIS 5 EGRET
  water: 6 RAPIDS

whale pursuer: 4 AHAB
wine: 5 PINOT RHINE SOAVE
    8 SAUTERNE
wine aperitif: 3 KIR
White ___: 3 ANT SOX 5 NOISE
White, Perry: 5 CHIEF 6 EDITOR
employee: 8 LOISLANE
White, Snow
and the dwarfs: 5 OCTET
Whiteboard
wiper: 6 ERASER
"White Christmas"
Danny of: 4 KAYE
The "white" of: 4 SNOW
Whiteclaw
Journalist: 4 REID
White Cloud
People of: 4 IOWA
White-collar
crook: 5 KITER
worker: 6 CLERIC PRIEST
"White Fang"
author: 6 LONDON
Whitefish: 4 CHUB 5 CISCO
White-haired
fellow: 7 GRANDPA
Whitehall
whitewall: 4 TYRE
Whitehorse
Chief: 4 OTOE
White House
dog: 3 HER HIM 4 FALA
monogram: 3 DDE FDR HST
    RMN
nickname: 3 ABE CAL IKE RON
spokesman Fleischer: 3 **ARI**
staffer: 4 **AIDE**
~ Office: 4 OVAL
~ Room: 4 EAST 5 GREEN
~ Scottie: 4 FALA
White Rabbit: 6 ALBINO
cry: 6 IMLATE
Like the: 4 LATE
Whites
Flash the pearly: 5 SMILE
Pearly: 5 TEETH
Whitetail: 4 DEER
White-tailed
bird: 3 ERN 4 **ERNE**

Whitewash: 4 HIDE LIME
    7 COVERUP
Whitewater
craft: 4 RAFT 5 CANOE KAYAK
~ VIP: 5 STARR
Whitey
teammate: 4 YOGI
Whitman
bloomer: 5 LILAC
Poet: 4 WALT
Whitman, C. Todd
org.: 3 EPA
Whitney
and others (abbr.): 3 MTS
Author: 4 OTTO
invention: 9 COTTONGIN
Inventor: 3 **ELI**
Partner of ~ in planes: 5 PRATT
Whittle: 4 PARE
away: 5 ERODE
Whitty, May
title: 4 DAME
Whiz: 3 **ACE** PRO ZIP 4 GURU
    5 MAVEN SPEED 6 EXPERT
Computer: 6 TECHIE
Electronics: 6 TECHIE
Gee: 4 GOSH
opener: 3 GEE
Shorthand: 5 STENO
Tennis: 4 ACER
Wall St.: 3 ARB
Who
follower: 3 AMI
"Who ___?": 3 DAT 4 ISIT
    6 DOESNT
"___ who?": 3 SEZ
Who, The
Like ~, in the 1960s: 3 MOD
Townshend of: 4 PETE
"Whoa, ___!": 6 NELLIE
"Who am ___ judge?": 3 ITO
"Who am ___ say?": 3 ITO
"Who cares?": 6 SOWHAT
"Who Do You Love?"
singer: 9 BODIDDLEY
Whodunit
plot element: 6 MOTIVE
suspect: 4 HEIR
terrier: 4 ASTA

"Who goes there?"
Word before: 4 HALT
"Who is there?"
reply: 5 ITSME
"Who knew?!": 10 IHADNOIDEA
Whole: 3 ONE 6 ENTIRE INTACT
7 UNITARY
As a: 5 INALL 6 ENBLOC
bunch: 3 TON 4 ALOT LOTS
RAFT SCAD **SLEW**
6 OCEANS 9 AGGREGATE
Double ~ note: 5 BREVE
lot: 3 TON 4 RAFT SCAD **SLEW**
6 OCEANS 9 AGGREGATE
Make: 4 HEAL MEND
number: 7 INTEGER
Opposite of: 6 NONFAT
Part of a: 4 UNIT
slew of: 8 ZILLIONS
The ~ shebang: 3 **ALL** 4 ATOZ
"Whole ___ Love" (1970 hit):
5 LOTTA
"Whole ___ Shakin' Goin' On":
5 LOTTA
"Who Let the Dogs Out"
band: 7 BAHAMEN
Wholly: 3 ALL 6 INTOTO
absorbed: 4 RAPT
"Who, me?": 3 MOI
Whoop: 4 YELL 5 SHOUT YAHOO
it up: 5 PARTY REVEL
Whoop-de-do: 4 STIR 5 HOOHA
Whooped: 5 SMOTE
"Whoopee!": 3 **YAY** 6 HURRAY
Whooping
bird: 5 CRANE
"Whoops!": 4 OHOH UHOH
Whopper: 3 **LIE** 4 LULU TALE
YARN
rival: 6 BIGMAC
teller: 4 LIAR
topper: 5 ONION 7 KETCHUP
"Who's Afraid of Virginia Woolf?"
playwright: 5 ALBEE
"Whose Life ___ Anyway?" (1981
movie): 4 ISIT
"Who's on ___?": 5 FIRST
"Who's on First?"
comic: 6 ABBOTT

"Who's That Girl?"
rapper: 3 EVE
"Who's the Boss?"
costar: 5 DANZA
role: 4 MONA
"Who's there?"
response: 5 ITISI ITSME
"Who's Who"
entry: 3 BIO
"Who Wants to Be a Millionaire"
network: 3 ABC
option: 8 LIFELINE
"Who ___ we kidding?": 3 ARE
"Who ___ you?": 3 ARE
Whup: 3 TAN 4 BEAT FLOG LICK
Why: 6 REASON
"Why don't we ?": 4 LETS
"Why not?": 4 OKAY SURE
"Why should ___?": 5 ICARE
"Why should ___ you?": 4 ILET
"Why would ___?": 4 ILIE
Wiccan: 8 PAGANIST
Wichita
winter hrs.: 3 CST
Wicked: 4 **EVIL** VILE 6 UNHOLY
"Wicked Game"
singer Chris: 5 ISAAK
Wicker
material: 6 RATTAN
palm: 6 RATTAN
source: 5 OSIER
willow: 5 OSIER
Wicket
Cricket: 3 END
Wickiup: 3 HUT
Wide
belt: 4 SASH
body: 3 SEA
Give a ~ berth: 5 AVOID
key: 5 ENTER
of the mark: 3 OFF 6 ERRANT
Open: 4 GAPE YAWN
opening: 5 **AGAPE** 6 GAPING
Partner of: 3 FAR
shoe size: 3 **EEE**
tie: 5 ASCOT
Wide-area
alert: 3 APB
Widebody: 3 JET

Wide-eyed: 4 **AGOG** GAGA
  5 ALERT
Widen: 4 REAM 5 FLARE
  6 DILATE
"Wide Sargasso Sea"
  author Jean: 4 RHYS
"___ Wide Shut": 4 EYES
Widespread: 4 RIFE VAST
  5 BROAD 7 GENERAL
  RAMPANT 8 EPIDEMIC
  damage: 5 HAVOC
"Wide World of Sports"
  creator Arledge: 5 ROONE
Width
  Lacking ~ and depth: 4 ONED
  Length ×: 4 AREA
  Shoe: 3 **EEE**
___ Wiedersehen: 3 **AUF**
Wield: 3 PLY USE 5 EXERT
  6 EMPLOY
Wiener
  holder: 4 ROLL
Wiener schnitzel
  meat: 4 VEAL
Wiesbaden
  state: 5 HESSE
Wiesel
  birthplace: 7 ROMANIA
  Nobelist: 4 **ELIE**
Wiest
  Oscar winner: 6 DIANNE
Wife: 3 MRS 4 MATE 5 WOMAN
  6 MISSUS 7 OLDLADY
  Run for your: 5 ELOPE
  ~, in legalese: 4 UXOR
Wiggle
  room: 4 PLAY 6 LEEWAY
  Wahine: 4 HULA
  Waikiki: 4 HULA
Wiggy
  Get all: 9 GOBANANAS
Wight: 4 **ISLE**
Wigwam: 4 TENT 5 TEPEE
Wilcox, ___ Wheeler
  Poet: 4 ELLA
Wild: 4 AMOK ZANY 5 FERAL
  OUTRE 6 MADCAP SAVAGE
  UNTAME 7 LAWLESS
  UNTAMED

about: 4 INTO
animal home: 4 LAIR
animal trail: 5 SPOOR
blue yonder: 3 **SKY** 5 ETHER
bugler: 3 ELK
bunch: 3 MOB 4 PACK
Call of the: 4 ROAR
cat: 4 LION PUMA
dog: 5 DINGO 6 JACKAL
fancy: 5 DREAM
Go: 4 RIOT 7 RUNAMOK
goat: 4 **IBEX**
Going: 7 ONATEAR
guess: 4 SHOT **STAB**
Not: 4 SANE TAME 5 STAID
party: 4 BASH ORGY RAVE
  5 BLAST
pig: 4 BOAR
plum: 4 SLOE
Running: 4 AMOK 5 ARIOT
They may be: 4 OATS
  6 DEUCES
thing: 6 SAVAGE
throw: 5 ERROR
time: 5 SPREE
way to go: 3 APE
way to run: 4 AMOK
Wildcat
  Short-tailed: 4 LYNX
  Spotted: 6 OCELOT
  strike: 3 OIL
Wildcats
  of the Big 12 Conf.: 3 KSU
  org.: 4 NCAA
Wildcatter
  dream: 6 GUSHER
  find: 3 OIL
"Wild Duck, The"
  playwright: 5 IBSEN
Wilde
  forte: 5 FARCE
  genre: 5 FARCE
  play: 6 SALOME
  quality: 3 WIT
  Writer: 5 OSCAR
Wildebeest: 3 **GNU**
Wilder
  Actor: 4 GENE
  Author: 5 LAURA

Wilderness Road
  blazer: 5 BOONE
Wildflower
  Yellow: 9 BUTTERCUP
Wildlife
  marker: 6 EARTAG
  refuge: 4 LAIR
"Wild Swans at Coole, The"
  poet: 5 YEATS
"Wild Thing"
  rapper: 7 TONELOC
Wild West: 3 MAE
  justice: 5 NOOSE
  knot: 5 NOOSE
  showman: 4 CODY
  vehicle: 5 STAGE
  watering hole: 6 SALOON
Wile E. Coyote
  Supply company to: 4 **ACME**
Wilhelm
  Hall of Fame pitcher: 4 HOYT
Wilkes-___, Pennsylvania:
    5 BARRE
Will
  be, in song: 4 SERA
  beneficiary: 4 HEIR
  Having a: 7 TESTATE
  Ill: 3 IRE 4 HATE 5 SPITE
    6 ANIMUS ENMITY MALICE
    RANCOR
  matter: 6 ESTATE
  subject: 6 ESTATE
  supplement: 7 CODICIL
  What you: 6 ESTATE
Willa
  Novelist: 6 CATHER
Willamette
  Capital on the: 5 SALEM
"Will & Grace"
  actor McCormack: 4 ERIC
  actress Messing: 5 DEBRA
  actress Mullally: 5 MEGAN
  Grace on: 5 ADLER
  Maid on: 7 ROSARIO
Willard
  Boxing champ: 4 JESS
"Will be"
  What ~ will be: 3 ARE
  Word before and after: 4 BOYS

"___ will be done ...": 3 THY
Willem
  Actor: 5 **DEFOE**
Willful: 10 HEADSTRONG
Willfully
  Behave: 5 ACTUP
William: 6 PRINCE
  Actor: 6 DEVANE
  Archer: 4 TELL
  Bathysphere designer: 5 BEEBE
  Ex-Defense Secretary: 5 COHEN
  Mother of: 5 DIANA
  of westerns: 4 BOYD
  Playwright: 4 INGE
  Quaker: 4 PENN
William ___, Sir: 5 OSLER
William of ___: 5 OCCAM
William Randolph
  Publisher: 6 HEARST
Williams
  Actress: 6 JOBETH
  Adventure hero: 4 REMO
  of baseball: 3 TED
  of tennis: 5 VENUS 6 SERENA
  Singer: 4 ANDY
  Talk host: 6 MONTEL
  title start: 5 CATON 6 CATONA
Williams, Andy
  hit tune: 9 DEARHEART
    10 LIPSOFWINE
Williams, Billy ___
  Actor: 3 DEE
Williams, Robin
  film: 4 TOYS 7 ALADDIN
    JUMANJI 10 PATCHADAMS
  film role: 4 GARP 5 GENIE
  ~ TV role: 4 MORK
Williams, Ted
  number: 4 NINE
Williamson
  Actor: 5 NICOL
William the Conqueror
  Daughter of: 5 ADELA
  Son of: 6 HENRYI
Willie
  Hall of Famer: 4 MAYS
  Pool champ: 7 MOSCONI
Willing: 4 GAME GLAD
  Is ~ to: 5 WOULD

More: **5** GAMER
partner: **4** ABLE
to try: **6** OPENTO
Willingly: 4 FAIN LIEF
Willis, Bruce
Ex of: **4** DEMI **5** MOORE
film: **7** DIEHARD
Willow: 4 TREE **5 OSIER**
relative: **6** POPLAR
Will-___-wisp: 4 OTHE
Willy
Fictional salesman: **5** LOMAN
follower: **5** NILLY
"Willy Wonka and the Chocolate Factory"
song part: **5** OOMPA
Wilmington
state (abbr.): **3** DEL
Wilson
Cartoonist: **5** GAHAN
Former Philly mayor: **5** GOODE
Jazz pianist: **5** TEDDY
Pianist-actor: **6** DOOLEY
President before: **4** TAFT
Wilson, Marie
role: **4** IRMA
Wilson, Woodrow
school: **9** PRINCETON
Wilt: 3 SAG
Built like: **4** TALL
Wily: 3 SLY
Wimbledon
1955 ~ champ: **7** TRABERT
1956–57 ~ champ Lew: **4** HOAD
1960 ~ champ Fraser: **5** NEALE
1972 ~ champ Smith: **4** STAN
1975 ~ champ: **4 ASHE**
1976–80 ~ champ: **4** BORG
1977 ~ champ: **4** WADE
1986 ~ champ: **5** EVERT
1987 ~ champ: **4** CASH
1988 ~ champ: **4** GRAF
   6 EDBERG
1991 ~ champ: **5** STICH
1992 ~ champ: **6** AGASSI
1998 ~ champ Novotna: **4** JANA
call: **3** LET
Five-time ~ champ: **4** BORG
   9 BJORNBORG

Four-time ~ champ: **5** LAVER
Seven-time ~ champ: **4** GRAF
   7 SAMPRAS
Three-time ~ champ: **5** EVERT
   6 TILDEN **7** MCENROE
unit: **3** SET
Wimp: 4 WUSS **5** SISSY
   7 MILKSOP NEBBISH
Wimple
wearer: **3** NUN
Wimpy: 4 MEEK
Hardly: **5** MACHO
They are hardly: **5** HEMEN
Wimsey
creator: **6** SAYERS
title: **4** LORD
Win: 4 REAP **6** GARNER OBTAIN
   7 TRIUMPH
back: **6** RECOUP
Boxing: **3** TKO **4** KAYO
Easy: **4** ROMP
every game: **5** SWEEP
Lopsided: **4** ROUT
of an underdog: **5** UPSET
over: **6** ENDEAR SEDUCE
the heart of: **6** ENAMOR
Try to: **3** WOO
Wrestling: **3** PIN
Winans
Singer: **4** BEBE CECE
Win by ___: 5 ANECK **ANOSE**
Wince: 5 REACT
Winchester: 5 RIFLE
Rank of: **3** MAJ
Wind
word form: **5** ANEMO
Windbag
output: **6** HOTAIR
Windblown: 6 EOLIAN
soil: **5 LOESS**
Winder
Fishing reel: **5** SPOOL
Watch: **4** STEM
Windex
target: **4** PANE
Windfall: 4 BOON **7** BONANZA
Windflower: 7 ANEMONE
Winding
path: **3 ESS**

Trombonist: 3 KAI
way: 3 ESS
"Wind in the Willows, The"
  author: 7 GRAHAME
  character: 4 TOAD 5 OTTER
Windless: 4 CALM 5 STILL
Windmill
  part: 4 **VANE** 5 BLADE
Window
  alternative: 5 AISLE
  Bay: 5 **ORIEL**
  blind piece: 4 SLAT
  Choose the ~ instead of the aisle:
    5 ELOPE
  dressing: 5 DRAPE 6 FACADE
    7 DRAPERY
  frame: 4 SASH
  inset: 6 SCREEN
  It may have a ~ (abbr.): 3 ENV
  ledge: 4 SILL
  Look through a: 6 PEERIN
  Oval: 5 OXEYE
  Oxeye ~ shape: 4 OVAL
  part: 5 PANE SASH SILL
  Projecting: 5 ORIEL
  Round: 5 OXEYE
  Ship: 8 PORTHOLE
  side: 4 JAMB
  sign: 4 OPEN SALE 5 TOLET
  sticker: 5 DECAL
  treatment: 5 DRAPE 6 FACADE
    7 DRAPERY
  Upstairs: 6 DORMER
"___ Window": 4 REAR
Windows
  boxes: 3 PCS
  Like: 5 PANED
  picture: 4 ICON
  predecessor: 3 DOS 5 MSDOS
  typeface: 5 ARIAL
Windpipe: 6 AIRWAY 7 TRACHEA
Winds
  California: 8 SANTAANA
Windshield
  cleaner: 5 WIPER
  Clear a: 5 DEFOG DEICE
  option: 4 **TINT**
  sticker: 5 DECAL
"Winds of ___, The": 3 WAR

Windsor: 4 KNOT 6 CASTLE
  prov.: 3 ONT
  river: 6 THAMES
  School near: 4 ETON
Windswept
  spot: 3 TOR
Windup: 3 END 6 FINALE
Wind-up
  toy: 4 KITE
Windward
  Not: 4 ALEE
Windy
  Not: 5 TERSE
Windy City
  airport: 5 OHARE
  train initials: 3 CTA
  trains: 3 ELS
  ~, briefly: 3 CHI
Wine
  Amber: 7 MADEIRA
  and dine: 3 WOO 4 FETE
    6 REGALE
  Big name in: 5 GALLO
  Bordeaux: 5 MEDOC 6 CLARET
  bottle datum: 4 YEAR
  bottle word: 3 CRU SEC
  bouquet: 4 NOSE 5 AROMA
  California ~ region: 4 NAPA
    6 SONOMA
  cask: 3 TUN
  choice: 4 ROSE
  container: 3 JUG VAT 4 CASK
    6 BARREL CELLAR FLAGON
  Dessert: 4 PORT 8 SAUTERNE
  Dry, as: 3 **SEC**
  expert: 6 TASTER
  French ~ region: 6 ALSACE
  German: 5 RHINE 7 MOSELLE
  grape: 5 PINOT 8 RIESLING
  Hungarian: 5 **TOKAY**
  Italian: 4 VINO 5 SOAVE
    7 MARSALA
  Italian ~ area: 4 **ASTI**
  Like fine: 4 **AGED**
  order: 6 CARAFE
  Partner of: 4 DINE
  Piedmont ~ center: 4 ASTI
  Portuguese: 7 MADEIRA
  Pour, as: 6 DECANT

prefix: 3 OEN 4 **OENO**
Red: 5 MEDOC PINOT
    6 CLARET 7 CHIANTI
    9 PINOTNOIR
Rice: 4 **SAKE**
Seal the ~ bottle again:
    6 RECORK
sediment: 4 **LEES**
Sicilian: 7 MARSALA
source: 5 GRAPE
Sparkling: 4 ASTI
Sweet: 4 PORT 6 MALAGA
    7 MARSALA 8 MUSCATEL
    SAUTERNE
valley: 4 NAPA 5 LOIRE MOSEL
    RHINE
Very dry, as: 4 BRUT
waste: 4 LEES
White: 5 BLANC SOAVE
    7 CHABLIS
White ~ aperitif: 3 KIR
word form: 4 OENO
Wineglass
part: 4 **STEM**
Winemaker
~ Carlo: 5 ROSSI
~ Ernest or Julio: 5 GALLO
Winemaking
partner of Martini: 5 ROSSI
science: 8 OENOLOGY
Winery
fixture: 3 VAT
process: 5 AGING
Wineshop: 6 BODEGA
Winfield
General: 5 SCOTT
Winfrey
Former ~ rival: 7 DONAHUE
of TV: 5 OPRAH
Wing: 3 **ELL** 4 SIDE 5 ANNEX
    FLANK
Building: 3 **ELL**
Dumbo: 3 EAR
it: 3 JAM 5 ADLIB
measurement: 4 SPAN
New: 5 ANNEX
prefix: 4 PTER 5 PTERO
Take: 3 FLY 4 SOAR 6 AVIATE
Take under one's: 5 ADOPT

tip: 4 SHOE
Wright: 3 ELL
Wingding: 4 BASH FETE GALA
    5 ROAST
Waikiki: 4 LUAU
Winged: 4 **ALAR** 5 ALATE
god: 4 **EROS**
youth: 4 **EROS**
Winger
Actress: 5 **DEBRA**
Wingless
parasites: 4 LICE
Winglike: 4 **ALAR** 5 ALATE
Wings
~, in Latin: 4 **ALAE**
"Wings"
actress: 8 CLARABOW
Wink
Done with a: 3 SLY
Winks
count: 5 FORTY
Winless
horse: 6 MAIDEN
Winnebago
nation member: 4 OTOE
~ County seat: 7 OSHKOSH
Winnebagos: 3 RVS
Winner: 5 CHAMP 6 VICTOR
Be a bad: 4 CROW 5 GLOAT
Cry of a game: 3 GIN
Headpiece of a: 5 TIARA
Not a: 7 ALSORAN
November: 7 ELECTEE
Olympic: 8 MEDALIST
Sign of a: 3 VEE
Take of a: 3 ALL POT
Tic-tac-toe: 3 OOO
Winners
Bred: 5 SIRED
Clio: 3 ADS
Election: 3 INS
Winnie ___: 3 MAE
"Winnie ___ Pu": 4 ILLE
"Winnie-the-___": 4 POOH
"Winnie-the-Pooh"
baby: 3 ROO
creator: 5 MILNE 7 AAMILNE
friend: 3 OWL 6 EEYORE
Winning: 5 AHEAD ONTOP

Barely: **5** UPONE
Go on a ~ streak: **6** GETHOT
margin: **4** EDGE NOSE
roll at Caesar's: **3** VII
streak: **3** RUN
"Winning ___ everything!":
    4 ISNT
Winnings: 3 POT **5** PURSE
Winnow: 4 CULL SIFT SORT
Winona
  Actress: **5** RYDER
Winslet
  Actress: **4** KATE
Winslow
  Painter: **5** HOMER
Winsome: 7 LIKABLE
Winsor
  Cartoonist: **5** MCCAY
Winston Cup
  org.: **6** NASCAR
Winter
  ailment: **3** FLU **4** COLD
    6 GRIPPE
  air: **4** NOEL **5** CAROL
  air quality: **3** NIP
  apple: **6** RUSSET
  arrival: **6** PISCES
  blanket: **4** SNOW
  break: **4** THAW **7** SNOWDAY
  budget item: **4** HEAT
  bug: **3** FLU **4** COLD
  coat: **4** HOAR RIME **5** FROST
    6 ANORAK ULSTER
  comment: **4** BRRR
  drink: **3** NOG **5** COCOA TODDY
  fall: **4** SNOW **5** SLEET
  fish: **4** SHAD
  forecast: **4** SNOW **5** SLEET
  forecast word: **5** TEENS
  fruit: **9** SNOWAPPLE
  hat part: **6** EARLAP **7** EARFLAP
  hazard: **3** ICE **5** SLEET
  hrs. in Wichita: **3** CST
  Like ~ roads: **3** ICY
  melon: **6** CASABA
  mo.: **3** DEC FEB JAN
  pear: **4** BOSC **5** ANJOU
  toy: **4** SLED
  vehicle: **4** SLED **6** SNOCAT

wear: **4** WOOL **5** PARKA SCARF
  7 WOOLENS **8** OVERCOAT
Wintergreen
  fruit: **8** TEABERRY
Winter Olympian: 5 LUGER
  SKIER
Winter Olympics
  1952 ~ site: **4** OSLO
  1984 ~ site: **8** SARAJEVO
  2002 ~ host: **3** USA
  2002 ~ site: **4** UTAH
  event: **4** LUGE **6** SLALOM
    7 SKIJUMP **10** SKIJUMPING
Winter Palace
  resident: **4** CZAR **TSAR**
Wintry: 3 ICY **4** COLD
Winwood
  Actress: **7** ESTELLE
Wipe
  out: **3** END **5** **ERASE** PURGE
    6 DELETE EFFACE NEGATE
    8 MASSACRE **9** ERADICATE
Wiped
  out: **5** SPENT TIRED
Wipe out: 5 ERASE
Wire: 5 CABLE TELEX
    7 MESSAGE **8** TELEGRAM
  Live: **4** DOER **6** DYNAMO
  measure: **3** **MIL**
  nail: **4** BRAD
  point: **4** BARB
  service inits.: **3** UPI
Wired: 4 EDGY **5** HYPER TENSE
    6 ONLINE
Wirehair: 7 TERRIER
  Fictional: **4** ASTA
Wiry
  dog: **8** AIREDALE
Wisc.
  neighbor: **4** MICH MINN
Wisconsin
  city: **6** BELOIT
  college: **5** RIPON **6** BELOIT
  senator Herb: **4** KOHL
Wisdom
  Folk: **4** LORE
  Goddess of: **6** ATHENA
  tooth: **5** MOLAR
  Unit of: **5** PEARL

Words of: **5** ADAGE **6** ADAGES
Wise: 3 HEP **4** SAGE
about: **4** ONTO
competitor: **4** LAYS
guy: **3** OWL **4** GURU SAGE
    5 SWAMI **6** SMARTY
    11 SMARTYPANTS
men: **4** MAGI
one: **3** OWL **4** GURU **SAGE**
    SEER YOGI **5** ELDER SOLON
    SWAMI **6** ORACLE PUNDIT
    SAVANT SMARTY
saying: **5** ADAGE
teacher: **6** MENTOR
to: **4** INON
trio: **4** MAGI
Word to the: **3** TIP **6** TIPOFF
Wisecrack: 4 GIBE QUIP
"Wiseguy"
writer Nicholas: **7** PILEGGI
Wiseman, Joseph
role: **4** DRNO
Wisenheimer: 6 SMARTY
    9 KNOWITALL
    10 SMARTALECK
Wise ___ owl: 4 ASAN
Wiser: 5 SAGER
partner: **5** OLDER
Wish
(for): **4** HOPE LONG PINE
    5 YEARN
granter: **5** **GENIE**
Royal: **3** SON
undone: **3** **RUE** **6** REGRET
~, with "to": **6** ASPIRE
___ wish!: 3 YOU
Wishful
words: **5** IHOPE **7** IHOPESO
"Wish I could help": 7 NOCANDO
"Wishing won't make ___":
    4 ITSO
"Wish ___, wish ...": 4 IMAY
Wishy-___: 5 WASHY
Wishy-washy
Be: **6** WAFFLE
Wisk
rival: **3** ALL ERA
Wister
Author: **4** **OWEN**

Wistful
wishing: **3** YEN
word: **4** ALAS
Wistfully
thoughtful: **7** PENSIVE
Wit: 3 WAG **4** CARD SALT
Biting: **4** ACID
Bit of: **3** PUN
Lively: **6** ESPRIT
To: **6** NAMELY
Witch: 3 HAG **5** CRONE
Biblical ~ place: **5** ENDOR
blemish: **4** WART
Comic strip: **10** BROOMHILDA
concoction: **4** BREW
craft: **5** BROOM
trials town: **5** SALEM
work: **3** HEX **5** CURSE SPELL
Witchcraft
Goddess of: **6** HECATE
West Indies: **5** OBEAH
Witches
brew ingredient: **4** NEWT
Group of: **5** COVEN
"Witches, The"
director: **4** ROEG
Witching
hour: **3** XII
"Witching Hour, The"
author: **8** ANNERICE
With
it: **3** HEP **HIP** NOW **4** CHIC
    5 ALERT AWARE SHARP
    SMART **7** TUNEDIN
~, in French: **4** AVEC
~, in Spanish: **3** CON
"___ With a View": 5 AROOM
"With a wink and ___": 4 ANOD
"___ With a Z": 4 LIZA
Withdraw: 4 QUIT WEAN
    6 BOWOUT RECEDE
    RETIRE SECEDE
Withdrawal
site: **3** ATM
Withdrawn: 3 SHY **7** ASOCIAL
Wither: 5 DRYUP **7** SHRIVEL
Withered: 4 **SERE**
Withers, Bill
tune: **5** USEME **8** LEANONME

Witherspoon
  Actress: 4 CORA 5 **REESE**
Withhold: 4 DENY KEEP
Within: 4 AMID
  Fit: 4 NEST
  It is ~ range: 4 OVEN
  prefix: 4 ENDO **ENTO** 5 INTRA
  reach: 4 NEAR 5 HANDY
    6 ATHAND
"With ___ in My Heart": 5 ASONG
Within ___ of: 5 ANACE
"___, With Love": 5 TOSIR
"___ With Music": 5 SAYIT
"With ___ of thousands!":
    5 ACAST
"With or Without You"
  singer: 4 BONO
Without: 4 LESS **SANS** 5 MINUS
  a bal.: 3 PPD
  Cannot do: 4 **NEED**
  ~, in French: 4 SANS
  ~, in Latin: 4 SINE
Without ___: 4 ANET 5 ACARE
    ACENT
"Without further ___ ...": 3 ADO
"With Reagan"
  author: 7 EDMEESE
Withstand: 4 BEAR 5 ABIDE
    6 RESIST
"With the jawbone of ___":
    5 ANASS
Witness: 3 SEE 6 LOOKON
  Bear: 6 **ATTEST**
  Unreliable: 4 LIAR
  vow: 4 OATH
  words: 3 IDO
"Witness"
  actor Lukas: 4 **HAAS**
  director Peter: 4 WEIR
  sect: 5 AMISH
Witnesses
  Like some: 7 HOSTILE
  Star: 4 MAGI
"Witness for the Prosecution"
  Tyrone's wife in: 7 MARLENE
Wits
  Battle of: 5 CHESS
Witt
  Actress: 6 ALICIA

  jump: 4 AXEL
Witticism: 3 MOT 4 JEST JOKE
    QUIP
  Critical: 4 BARB
"Wiz, The"
  Glinda in: 4 LENA 5 HORNE
    9 LENAHORNE
  star: 4 ROSS
  Wiz in: 5 PRYOR
Wizard: 4 GURU SAGE
    8 SORCERER
"Wizard ___, The": 4 OFID OFOZ
"Wizard of Menlo Park, The":
    6 EDISON
"Wizard of Oz, The"
  actor: 4 LAHR 5 HALEY
  actor Bert: 4 LAHR
  author: 4 BAUM
  composer: 5 ARLEN
  dog: 4 TOTO
  farmhand: 4 ZEKE
  producer: 5 LEROY
  prop: 6 OILCAN
  revealer: 4 TOTO
  studio: 3 MGM
Wizardry: 5 MAGIC
Wizards: 5 MAGES
  org.: 3 NBA
Wizened: 7 DRIEDUP
WJM
  anchorman: 3 TED
Wk.
  Day of the: 3 FRI MON SAT SUN
    THU TUE WED
"WKRP"
  actress Anderson: 4 LONI
  Nessman of: 3 LES
  news director Les: 7 NESSMAN
  She was Jennifer on: 4 LONI
  Tim of: 4 REID
WNBA
  Lisa of the: 6 LESLIE
  Rebecca of the: 4 LOBO
WNW
  opposite: 3 **ESE**
Woe: 3 **ILL** 6 SORROW
  Word of: 4 **ALAS** 5 ALACK
  Words of: 4 **AHME** OHME OHNO
    5 OYVEY

"Woe ___" (grammar bestseller):
3 ISI
"Woe ___!": 4 ISME
Woebegone: 3 SAD
"Woe is me!": 4 **ALAS** 5 ALACK
Wok: 3 PAN
 Use a: 3 FRY 5 SAUTE
  7 STIRFRY
Wolf: 5 SCARF 6 CANINE
  8 PREDATOR
 down: 3 EAT 6 DEVOUR INHALE
 Feminist author: 5 NAOMI
 Gray: 4 **LOBO**
 in a Kipling tale: 5 AKELA
 Kind of: 4 LONE
 Look like a: 4 LEER OGLE
 pack member: 5 UBOAT
 pack rank: 5 ALPHA
 Prairie: 6 COYOTE
 preceder: 3 SHE 4 WERE
 Timber: 4 LOBO
Wolfe
 Detective: 4 **NERO**
Wolfgang
 Physicist: 5 PAULI
Wolfhound
 Russian: 6 BORZOI
Wolflike: 6 LUPINE
Woman
 Fr. holy: 3 **STE**
 in distress: 6 DAMSEL
 Loos: 7 LORELEI
 Low-voiced: 4 ALTO
 name suffix: 4 ETTE
 of distinction: 4 DAME
 of letters: 5 VANNA
 of the haus: 4 FRAU
 of tomorrow: 4 GIRL
 Old: 5 CRONE
 Sp.: 3 SRA
 That: 3 HER SHE
 Waikiki: 6 WAHINE
 Witchy: 5 CRONE
 Young: 4 LASS
"Woman"
 The woman in: 3 ONO
"___ Woman"
 (Beatles tune): 5 SHESA
 (Maria Muldaur tune): 3 IMA

 (Reddy tune): 3 IAM
"Woman ___, The"
 (1984 Wilder film): 5 INRED
Womanizer: 4 RAKE ROUE
"Woman With a ___" (Vermeer):
  4 LUTE
Wombs: 5 UTERI
Women: 4 GALS
 Figure in a prison for: 6 MATRON
 (French abbr.): 4 MMES
 Group of: 5 HAREM
 Magazine for: 4 ELLE SELF
  5 COSMO
 Org. of: 3 DAR 4 LPGA
 Without: 4 STAG
 ~, to poets: 7 FAIRSEX
"Women, The"
 playwright: 4 LUCE
 writer: 4 LOOS
"Women and Love"
 author: 4 HITE
"Women Ironing"
 artist: 5 DEGAS
"Women, Race and Class"
 author Davis: 6 ANGELA
Women's ___: 3 **LIB**
**"Women Who Run With the
  Wolves"**
 author: 5 ESTES
Won
 every game: 5 SWEPT
Won ___: 3 **TON**
Wonder: 3 AWE
 Full of: 5 INAWE
 Kind of: 6 ONEHIT
 of music: 6 STEVIE
 Word of: 3 GEE
Wonder, Stevie
 tune: 5 IWISH
Wonderful: 5 NEATO SUPER
 thing, once: 12 THEBEESKNEES
 ~, in slang: 3 RAD
"Wonderful!": 3 AAH
"___ Wonderful Life": 4 ITSA
Wonderland
 bird: 4 DODO
 cake phrase: 5 **EATME**
 character: 4 HARE
 girl: 5 ALICE

Like the ~ Hatter: 3 MAD
Wonderment: 3 **AWE**
  Show: 3 AAH OOH
Wonder Woman: 6 AMAZON
  alias: 5 DIANA
Wonder-worker
  Hindu: 5 FAKIR
Wong, ___ May: 4 ANNA
Wonka
  creator: 4 **DAHL**
"___ won't!": 3 NOI
"___ won't be afraid" ("Stand by
    Me" lyric): 3 NOI
Woo: 7 ROMANCE
Woo, Roh ___ (of South Korea):
  3 TAE
Wood
  Actress: 4 LANA 7 NATALIE
  alternative: 4 IRON
  Archery: 3 YEW
  basecoat: 6 SEALER
  Bat: 3 **ASH**
  Bowling pin: 5 MAPLE
  Cabinet: 5 ALDER
  Chest: 5 CEDAR
  cutter: 3 ADZ AXE SAW 4 ADZE
    6 RIPSAW
  Durable: 3 ASH ELM OAK
    4 TEAK
  file: 4 RASP
  finish: 5 STAIN
  Fragrant: 5 CEDAR 8 REDCEDAR
  Guitarist: 3 RON
  Hard: 3 ASH ELM OAK 4 TEAK
    5 EBONY LARCH
  Knotty: 4 PINE
  Light: 5 BALSA
  Model: 5 **BALSA**
  nymph: 5 DRYAD
  pattern: 5 GRAIN
  problem: 6 DRYROT
  Saw: 5 SNORE
  Shipbuilding: 4 TEAK
  Smooth: 4 SAND
  sorrel: 3 OCA 6 OXALIS
  strip: 4 LATH SLAT 6 SPLINE
  Three: 5 SPOON
  trimmer: 3 ADZ AXE SAW
    4 ADZE

  Two: 7 BRASSIE
  Wickerwork: 5 OSIER
  Work on: 7 WHITTLE
Woodard
  Actress: 5 **ALFRE**
"... ___ woodchuck": 3 IFA
Woodcutter
  of fiction: 7 ALIBABA
Wooded: 6 SYLVAN
  shelter: 5 ARBOR
  valley: 4 DELL
Wooden
  container: 6 BARREL
  duck: 5 DECOY
  pin: 3 PEG 5 DOWEL
  shoe: 5 **SABOT**
Wooden, John
  team: 4 UCLA
Woodhouse
  of fiction: 4 EMMA
Woodland
  creature: 4 DEER
  deity: 4 FAUN 5 **SATYR**
Woods
  Actor: 5 JAMES
  Babe in the: 4 FAWN **NAIF**
  Golfer: 5 TIGER
  Neck of the: 4 **AREA**
  org.: 3 PGA
  prop: 3 TEE
  Quaker in the: 5 ASPEN
  Walk in the: 4 HIKE
  Way into the: 4 PATH
Woodskin: 5 CANOE
Woodstock
  do: 4 AFRO
  First name at: 4 ARLO JIMI
  gear: 4 AMPS
  setting: 4 FARM
  Singer at: 4 BAEZ
Woodward
  Actress: 6 JOANNE
  Husband of: 6 NEWMAN
Woodward, Joanne
  role: 3 EVE
Woodwind: 4 **OBOE** REED
Woodworking
  groove: 4 DADO
  tool: 3 ADZ AWL 4 ADZE RASP

5 LATHE PLANE 6 RIPSAW
SHAPER

Woody
Arlo, to: 3 SON
Colleague of Ted and: 4 RHEA
Ex of: 3 MIA
Filmmaker: 5 ALLEN
Son of: **4 ARLO**
vine: 5 LIANA
Wife of: 6 SOONYI

Woody Woodpecker
creator: 5 LANTZ

Wooer: 4 BEAU 6 SUITOR
of Cleo: 4 MARC

"Woof!": 3 ARF

Woofer
output: 3 ARF 4 BASS
Wakayama: 5 AKITA

Wool: 7 TEXTILE
Coarse ~ cloth: 5 TWEED
fat: 7 LANOLIN
Fine: 6 ANGORA MERINO
Harvest: 5 SHEAR
Kind of: 5 LAMBS STEEL
Low-grade: 5 MUNGO
source: 3 EWE 5 **LLAMA**
6 ALPACA ANGORA

Woolen
cap: 3 TAM

Wooley
Actor and singer: 4 SHEB

Woolly: 5 OVINE 6 LANATE
LANOSE
mama: 3 EWE
yarn: 4 TALE
~ Andean: 5 LLAMA

Woolworth's
First ~ store city: 5 UTICA

Woosnam
Golfer: 3 IAN

Word: 3 VOW 4 NEWS 5 SAYSO
Encouraging: 3 OLE RAH TRY
YES 4 AMEN CMON
7 ATTABOY 8 ATTAGIRL
Final: 3 END 4 AMEN OBIT
5 ADIEU SAYSO
for the wise: 4 SAGE
game: 5 GHOST
Get the: 4 HEAR

Give one's: 5 SWEAR 6 ASSURE
on either side of -à-: 3 VIS 4 TETE
on the wall: 4 MENE
origin: 6 ETYMON
part (abbr.): 3 SYL
The magic: 6 PLEASE
to the wise: 3 TIP
You can take his ~ for it:
5 ROGET

Word for word: 3 MOT 7 LITERAL
8 VERBATIM

Wordless
agreement: 3 NOD
singing: 4 SCAT

Wordplay
Some: 4 PUNS

Word processor
command: 4 REDO SAVE SORT
UNDO 5 PASTE
function: 6 TABSET
menu: 4 EDIT

Words
Have ~ with: 4 SPAR 5 ARGUE
6 TALKTO
In other: 5 IDEST 6 THATIS
Man of many: 5 ROGET
7 WEBSTER
to live by: 5 ADAGE AXIOM
CREDO CREED DOGMA
MORAL MOTTO TENET

Wordsmith
~ Webster: 4 NOAH

Wordsworth: 5 ODIST
8 LAKEPOET
muse: 5 ERATO
work: 3 ODE 4 POEM

Wordy: 4 LONG
Not: 5 TERSE

Wore: 5 HADON
away: 3 ATE 6 ERODED
He ~ a 4: 3 ORR OTT
6 MELOTT

Workhorse
Harbor: 3 TUG

Working: 4 **ATIT** 6 ONDUTY
class: 5 PROLE
Get by: 4 EARN
In ~ order: 6 USABLE
8 OPERABLE

No longer ~ (abbr.): 3 RET
  4 RETD
Not: 3 OFF 4 DEAD **IDLE**
  6 BROKEN 7 ONLEAVE
  RETIRED 8 ONSTRIKE
on a chair: 6 CANING
stiff: 4 PEON 5 PROLE
Stop: 6 RETIRE
together: 6 TEAMED
  8 INLEAGUE
"Working Girl"
  actress Griffith: 7 MELANIE
  girl: 4 TESS
Working without ___ : 4 ANET
Workout
  Achy after a: 4 SORE
  aftereffect: 4 ACHE
  center: 3 GYM SPA 4 YMCA
  exercise: 5 SITUP
  result: 5 SWEAT
  spot: 3 GYM SPA 4 YMCA
  system: 5 TAEBO
  target: 4 DELT FLAB LATS PECS
  type: 7 AEROBIC
  unit: 3 REP SET
  wear: 6 SWEATS
  woe: 4 SORE
Workplace
  safety org.: 4 **OSHA**
Workshop: 7 ATELIER
  of Hephaestus: 4 ETNA
  tool: 4 RASP VISE 5 CLAMP
  PLANE
Work ___ sweat: 3 UPA
Workweek
  Cry at the end of a: 4 TGIF
World
  book: 5 **ATLAS**
  College: 7 ACADEME
  8 ACADEMIA
  Dead to the: 5 INERT 6 ASLEEP
  7 OUTCOLD
  End of the: 4 POLE
  financial gp.: 3 IMF
  Game of ~ conquest: 4 RISK
  Go around the: 5 ORBIT
  In the: 7 ONEARTH
  It goes around the: 7 ORBITER
  It might go around the: 4 YOYO

Lat.: 5 MUNDI
leader: 6 NETHER
leader, 1959–2008: 6 CASTRO
leader, 1961–71: 6 UTHANT
Man of the: 5 ATLAS
Out of this: 5 ALIEN EERIE
record: 5 ATLAS
religion: 5 ISLAM
(Russian): 3 MIR
They'll show you the: 7 ATLASES
Think the ~ of: 5 ADORE
  6 ADMIRE ESTEEM
~, in French: 5 MONDE
~, in Spanish: 5 MONDO
World ___ : 6 SERIES
"___ World": 6 WAYNES
"___ World, The" (MTV): 4 REAL
"World According to ___ , The":
  4 GARP
World Bank
  offering: 3 AID
World Court
  site: 5 HAGUE
World Cup
  1958 ~ sensation: 4 PELE
  1974 ~ site: 11 WESTGERMANY
  1982 ~ site: 5 SPAIN
  1994 ~ host: 3 USA
  1998 ~ winner: 6 FRANCE
  2002 ~ cohost: 5 KOREA
  cry: 3 OLE
  power (abbr.): 3 ARG 4 ITAL
  powerhouse: 5 ITALY
  sport: 6 SOCCER
World Heritage
  gp.: 6 UNESCO
Worldly: 5 SUAVE 7 SECULAR
  Least: 7 NAIVEST
"World of Suzie ___ , The":
  4 WONG
World Series
  1956 ~ perfect game pitcher:
    6 LARSEN
  1960 ~ hero, familiarly: 3 MAZ
  1969 ~ champs: 4 METS
  1972–74 ~ champs: 5 THEAS
  1973 ~ site: 4 SHEA
  1975–76 ~ champs: 4 REDS
  1979 ~ champs: 7 PIRATES

1983 ~ champs: 7 ORIOLES
1984 ~ champs: 6 TIGERS
1986 ~ champs: 4 METS
1986 ~ site: 4 SHEA
1990 ~ champs: 4 REDS
1990 ~ MVP: 4 RIJO
1991 ~ champs: 5 TWINS
1992–93 ~ champs: 8 BLUEJAYS
1992–93 ~ site: 7 TORONTO
1995 ~ champs (abbr.): 3 ATL
1999 ~ losers: 7 ATLANTA ·
2000 ~ MVP: 5 JETER
   10 DEREKJETER
2000 ~ site: 4 SHEA
2000 ~ team: 4 METS
2002 ~ champs: 6 ANGELS
College ~ site: 5 OMAHA
Four-game: 5 SWEEP
mo.: 3 **OCT**
winning manager in '98, '99, and
  '00: 5 TORRE

World Series of Golf
site: 5 AKRON

World's Fair
1962 ~ city: 7 SEATTLE
1964 ~ symbol: 9 UNISPHERE
1970 ~ site: 5 OSAKA
~, for short: 4 EXPO

"___ World Turns": 5 ASTHE

World War I
battle site: 6 VERDUN
  7 ARGONNE

World War II
gun: 4 STEN

World-weariness: 5 ENNUI

World-weary: 5 BLASE JADED

Worldwide
(abbr.): 4 INTL
law enforcement group:
  8 INTERPOL
workers gp.: 3 ILO

Worm: 4 BAIT
container: 3 CAN
follower: 5 EATEN
Like the bird that catches the:
  5 EARLY
product: 4 SILK

Worms
conclave: 4 DIET

Like: 7 LEGLESS
One in: 3 EIN
Worn: 3 OLD 4 USED 7 ABRADED
away: 5 EATEN 6 ERODED
down: 6 ERODED 7 ABRADED
out: 3 OLD 4 SHOT 5 JADED
  SPENT 6 DONEIN
to a frazzle: 4 SHOT 5 TIRED
Unevenly: 5 EROSE
Worrier
risk: 5 ULCER
Worry: 3 NAG 4 CARE **FRET**
  STEW 5 ANGST BROOD
  EATAT SWEAT 7 SWEATIT
Bank: 3 RUN
excessively: 4 FUSS 6 OBSESS
Freedom from: 4 EASE
Grower's: 6 FREEZE
Illegal parker's: 5 TOWER
Not: 8 RESTEASY
Not to: 4 IMOK 5 ITSOK
Old car: 4 RUST
Things to ~ over: 5 BEADS
Winter: 3 ICE
"___ worry!": 5 NOTTO
Worry-free
locale: 4 EDEN
Worrywart
Act the: 4 FRET STEW
woe: 5 ULCER
Worse
Could be: 4 SOSO 8 NOTSOBAD
None the: 6 UNHURT
  9 UNSCARRED
"___ worse than death": 5 AFATE
Worship: 5 **ADORE** 6 REVERE
  9 ADORATION
House of: 4 SHUL 5 ABBEY
  6 CHURCH TEMPLE
Nature: 5 WICCA
Object of: 3 GOD 4 HERO
  5 DEITY **IDOLS**
Place of: 5 ALTAR 6 CHAPEL
Seat of: 3 PEW
Where some ~ from: 4 AFAR
Worthy of: 4 HOLY 6 SACRED
Worshiper: 5 DEIST 6 ADORER
Haile Selassie: 5 RASTA
Hero: 7 LEANDER

Idol: 3 FAN
Islamic: 6 MUSLIM
Machu Picchu: 4 INCA
Quetzalcoatl: 5 AZTEC MAYAN
   6 TOLTEC
Shiva: 5 HINDU
Stonehenge: 5 DRUID
Tree: 5 DRUID
Vishnu: 5 HINDU
Worst: 6 DEFEAT
Absolute: 4 PITS
In the ~ way: 5 BADLY
   6 SORELY
score: 4 ZERO

Worsted
cloth: 5 SERGE 6 TRICOT
Worth: 5 MERIT VALUE
   8 VALUEDAT
a C: 4 FAIR SOSO
Actress: 5 **IRENE**
a D: 4 POOR
having: 5 OFUSE UTILE
Is ~ it: 4 PAYS
mentioning: 6 OFNOTE
Not ~ debating: 4 MOOT
Two cents': 3 SAY 5 INPUT
   7 OPINION
Worthless: 3 BUM TIN 4 NULL
   7 INUTILE
amount: 3 FIG
coin: 3 SOU
talk: 5 BILGE 6 DRIVEL
Worthwhile: 5 UTILE
Is: 4 PAYS
Worthy: 3 FIT
Be ~ of: 4 EARN RATE 5 MERIT
   7 DESERVE
of worship: 4 HOLY 6 SACRED
Wouk
ship: 5 CAINE
work: 5 NOVEL
"Would I lie?": 6 HONEST
"Would ___ to you?": 4 ILIE
"Would you look at that?!":
   5 ILLBE
Wound: 4 GASH HURT SORE
   6 COILED INJURE LESION
cover: 4 SCAB
Item that is: 5 SKEIN

Old: 4 SCAR
Piercing: 4 STAB
Seriously: 4 MAIM
Shaving: 4 NICK
Small: 5 PRICK
up: 5 ENDED TENSE WIRED
   6 ONEDGE
Wounded Knee
locale (abbr.): 4 SDAK
Woven: 7 BRAIDED
fabric: 4 MESH 6 DAMASK
   7 TEXTILE
rattan: 4 CANE
Wow: 3 AWE 4 SLAY STUN
   5 AMAZE
"Wow!": 3 GEE MAN OOH
   12 HOLYMACKEREL
Wozniak
Computer pioneer: 5 STEVE
"Wozzeck": 5 OPERA
composer: 4 BERG
WPM
part: 3 MIN PER WDS
Wraith: 5 SPOOK 7 SPECTER
Wrangle: 4 SPAR 6 HAGGLE
Wrangler: 4 JEEP
alternative: 3 LEE 5 LEVIS
rope: 6 LARIAT
Wrap: 3 BOA FUR OBI 4 COAT
   FOIL PITA SARI 5 SARAN
   SAREE SHAWL STOLE
   6 ENFOLD ENROBE
   MANTLE SARONG SERAPE
   7 SWADDLE TINFOIL
   8 ENVELOPE
around: 4 FURL 5 TWINE
   7 ENTWINE
artist: 7 CHRISTO
Delhi: 4 **SARI**
Feathery: 3 **BOA**
Fur: 5 STOLE
Indian: 4 SARI
like a baby: 7 SWADDLE
Mexican: 6 SERAPE
Neck: 5 SCARF
Plastic: 5 SARAN
Ranee: 5 SAREE
Roman: 4 TOGA 5 STOLA
tightly: 4 BIND 6 SWATHE

up: 3 **END** ICE 6 ENCASE
   ENFOLD 7 ENVELOP
(up): 3 SEW
"___ wrap!": 4 ITSA
Wraparound
dress: 4 SARI
Japanese: 3 OBI
Polynesian: 5 PAREU 6 SARONG
Tartan: 4 KILT
Wrapped
up: 4 CLAD DONE OVER
Wrapper
Body: 4 SKIN
Flapper: 3 BOA
weight: 4 TARE
Wrapping
material: 5 SARAN
Wraps
Keep under: 4 HIDE 5 SITON
Under: 6 SECRET 7 CLOAKED
Wrap-up
Musical: 4 CODA
Play: 6 EPILOG
Sports: 5 RECAP
Wrath: 3 **IRE** 4 FURY 5 ANGER
Fit of: 4 RAGE
Roman: 4 IRAE
Wray
Actress: 3 FAY
Wreak
Bad thing to: 5 HAVOC
Wreath
Hawaiian floral: 3 LEI
Head: 6 ANADEM
Wreck: 3 MAR 4 BUST RAZE
   RUIN 5 **TOTAL** TRASH
   6 DERAIL
Wreckage: 4 RUIN 6 DEBRIS
Wrecked: 4 SHOT
Wrecker
Home: 6 VANDAL 7 TERMITE
Job for a: 3 TOW
Wrecking ball
alternative: 3 TNT
Use a: 4 RAZE
"Wreck of the Mary ___, The":
   5 DEARE
"Wreck of the Mary Deare, The"
author: 5 INNES

Wren: 4 BIRD 6 TOMTIT
Wing of: 3 ELL
Wrench: 4 TOOL TURN 6 SPRAIN
   7 SPANNER
Monkey: 4 SNAG
type: 5 ALLEN 6 SOCKET
   7 SPANNER
Wrestle: 6 TUSSLE
(with): 7 GRAPPLE
Wrestler: 6 PINNER
goal: 3 **PIN**
Japanese: 4 SUMO
knowledge: 5 HOLDS
surface: 3 MAT
~ Hogan: 4 HULK
Wrestling
contest: 4 MEET
event: 4 MEET
Giant of: 5 ANDRE
hold: 4 LOCK 6 NELSON
   9 WRISTLOCK
Hulk of: 5 HOGAN
Japanese: 4 **SUMO**
Kind of: 3 ARM 4 SUMO
   6 INDIAN
move: 12 SCISSORSHOLD
official: 3 REF
pair: 7 TAGTEAM
round: 4 FALL
surface: 3 **MAT** 6 CANVAS
venue: 3 MUD 5 ARENA
win: 3 PIN
Wretched: 5 LOUSY RATTY
   SEEDY 6 ROTTEN
   SORDID
Wretchedness: 3 WOE
Wriggler: 3 EEL 4 WORM
Wriggling: 4 EELY
Wriggly
fish: 3 **EEL**
swimmer: 3 EEL
Wright: 4 ISLE 5 MAKER
Actress: 6 TERESA
angle: 3 ELL
Comic: 6 STEVEN
Do the ~ thing: 6 AVIATE
wing: 3 ELL
Wright, Steven
quip: 8 ONELINER

Wright brothers: 7 OHIOANS
    8 AVIATORS
  home: 4 OHIO
  hometown: 6 DAYTON
Wrigley
  field: 3 GUM
Wrigley Field
  flora: 3 IVY
  Like ~ walls: 5 IVIED
  slugger: 4 SOSA
  team: 4 CUBS
Wrinkle: 4 SEAM 6 CREASE
    RUMPLE
  a brow: 4 KNIT
  cause: 3 AGE
  remover: 4 **IRON**
Wrinkled: 4 LINY 7 CREASED
    9 DEPRESSED
Wrinkler
  Nose: 4 ODOR
Wrinkle-resistant
  fabric: 5 ORLON 6 DACRON
Wrinkly
  canine: 3 PUG 7 SHARPEI
  fruit: 4 UGLI 5 PRUNE
Wrist
  action: 5 FLICK
  attachment: 4 ULNA
  bones: 5 CARPI
  Of the: 6 CARPAL
Writ
  of a debtor: 6 ELEGIT
Write: 3 JOT PEN 6 NOTATE
    9 DROPALINE
  anew: 5 REPEN
  down: 3 LOG
  for another: 5 GHOST
  illegibly: 6 SCRAWL
  Nothing to ~ home about:
    4 SOSO
  on metal: 4 ETCH 7 ENGRAVE
  quickly: 3 JOT 9 DROPALINE
  software: 4 CODE
  up: 4 CITE
  with a point: 4 ETCH
Write-off: 4 LOSS 7 BADDEBT
Writer: 3 PEN 6 AUTHOR
    PENMAN SCRIBE
  A ~ may work on it: 4 SPEC

  Bakery: 4 ICER
  Check: 5 PAYER
  deg.: 3 MFA
  Jingle: 5 ADMAN
  Mediocre: 4 HACK
  Praiseful: 5 ODIST
  problem: 5 CRAMP
  reference: 5 ROGET
  rep: 5 AGENT
  Slogan: 5 ADMAN
  submissions (abbr.): 3 MSS
  Unknown ~ (abbr.): 4 ANON
  Verse: 4 POET
  woe: 5 CRAMP
Writers
  Rx: 3 DRS MDS
Write-up
  Doctor: 9 CASESTUDY
  Preliminary: 5 DRAFT
  Research: 9 LABREPORT
Writing: 5 PROSE
  Dull, as: 5 PROSY
  Icelandic: 4 EDDA
  on the wall: 4 OMEN SIGN
  pad: 6 TABLET
  point: 3 NIB
  Portable ~ surface:
    9 CLIPBOARD
  Put down in: 3 PAN 5 LIBEL
  Secret: 4 CODE
  style: 8 LONGHAND
  table: 4 DESK
  tablet: 3 PAD
Writings
  Some ancient: 6 PAPYRI
Writ of ___ corpus: 6 HABEAS
Written
  As: 3 SIC
  assurance: 9 GUARANTEE
  It is: 4 TEXT
  Not: 4 ORAL
  record: 4 MEMO 5 ANNAL
    ENTRY
Wrong: 3 SIN 4 AWRY TORT
    5 ABUSE AMISS
    7 INERROR
  Civil: 4 **TORT**
  Completely: 6 ALLWET
  end: 4 DOER

Go: 3 **ERR**
Gone: 4 AWOL
Isn't: 4 AINT
Legal: 4 TORT
move: 5 ERROR
prefix: 3 MIS
Prove: 6 NEGATE
Right, as a: 6 AVENGE
Rub the ~ way: 3 IRK 4 RILE
    5 CHAFE 6 ABRADE NETTLE
Sense of right and: 6 MORALS
start: 3 MIS
Take the ~ way: 3 ROB 5 STEAL
way to run: 7 AGROUND
Went: 5 ERRED
"Wrong!": 5 NOTSO
Wrongdoing: 3 SIN 4 EVIL
    5 ERROR
Assist in: 4 **ABET**
Wrongful
  act: 4 **TORT**
Wrote: 6 PENNED 7 EMAILED
for: 7 GHOSTED
Wrought
  It may be:.4 IRON
  Richly: 6 ORNATE
Wry: 5 DROLL
  Catcher in the: 5 BERRA
  twist: 5 IRONY
W's
  One of the five: 3 WHO WHY
    4 WHAT WHEN 5 WHERE
WSW
  Opposite of: 3 **ENE**
Wt.
  Sack: 5 TENLB
  system: 5 AVOIR
  units: 3 LBS
Wts.
  Heavy: 3 TNS
Wurst: 7 SAUSAGE
Wuss: 5 PANSY SISSY WEENY
"Wuthering Heights"
  actress Oberon: 5 MERLE
  author: 6 BRONTE
  setting: 4 MOOR
WWI
  battle site: 5 MARNE SOMME
    YPRES

line: 6 TRENCH
plane: 4 SPAD
river: 4 YSER 5 MARNE
spy: 8 MATAHARI
troops: 3 AEF
victor: 3 AEF
~ French soldier: 5 POILU
~ German admiral: 4 SPEE
~ U.S. soldier: 4 YANK
    8 DOUGHBOY
WWII
⅓ of a ~ film title: 4 TORA
admiral: 6 HALSEY
ally: 4 USSR
anti-subversive gp.: 4 HUAC
arena: 3 ETO
battle site: 4 STLO 6 BATAAN
battle site, for short: 3 IWO
beach: 5 OMAHA
beachhead: 5 ANZIO
buy: 5 EBOND
captive: 3 POW
center of French resistance:
    4 LYON
code machine: 6 ENIGMA
command: 3 **ETO**
conference site: 5 CAIRO YALTA
correspondent: 4 PYLE
    9 ERNIEPYLE
correspondent Pyle: 5 ERNIE
covert gp.: 3 OSS
craft: 3 **LST** 5 EBOAT UBOAT
    6 PTBOAT
enlistee: 5 GIJOE 7 DOGFACE
enlistees: 3 GIS
entertainers: 3 USO
female enlistee: 3 WAC 4 SPAR
    WAAC
general: 11 OMARBRADLEY
gun: 4 **STEN**
hero Murphy: 5 AUDIE
island: 4 TRUK 5 LEYTE
journalist: 4 PYLE 9 ERNIEPYLE
losers: 4 AXIS
menace: 5 UBOAT
neutral country (abbr.): 3 ARG
nickname: 3 IKE 4 DUCE
    5 MONTY
pinup: 6 GRABLE

plane: **4** ZERO **5** STUKA
  8 ENOLAGAY
power: **4** USSR
pres.: **3** FDR
prison camp: **6** STALAG
rationing agcy.: **3** OPA
rifle: **6** GARAND
riveter: **5** ROSIE
side: **4** AXIS
spy gp.: **3** OSS
sub: **5** **UBOAT**
tank: **6** PANZER **7** SHERMAN
town: **4** STLO **6** BATAAN
turning point: **4** DDAY
vessel: **3** **LST** **5** EBOAT UBOAT
  6 PTBOAT
weapon: **4** **STEN** **6** GARAND
  7 ENFIELD
winners: **6** ALLIES
~ Brit. flyers: **3** RAF
~ GI: **5** AMVET
~ Japanese general: **4** TOJO
~ Russian leader: **6** STALIN
WWW
address: **3** **URL**
address starter: **4** HTTP
moniker: **6** USERID
One way to the: **3** AOL
Part of: **3** WEB

Wyatt
Marshal: **4** **EARP**
Wye
follower: **3** ZED ZEE
Wyeth
Artist: **5** JAMIE **6** ANDREW
Wyeth, Andrew
subject/model: **5** HELGA
Wyeth, ___ Convers: 6 NEWELL
Wylie
Poet: **6** ELINOR
Wynken
Partner of: **3** NOD
Wynn
Actor: **6** KEENAN
and others: **3** EDS
of baseball: **5** EARLY
Wynn, Ed
Son of: **6** KEENAN
Wynonna
Mother of: **5** **NAOMI**
Wyo.
neighbor: **3** **IDA** NEB **4** NEBR
  SDAK
Wyoming
city: **6** CASPER **7** LARAMIE
neighbor: **4** UTAH
range: **5** TETON **6** TETONS
river: **7** LARAMIE

Xx

X: 3 CHI TEN 4 KISS 5 TIMES
  (abbr.): 3 LTR
  Center: 3 TAC
  First: 3 TIC
  Greek: 3 **CHI**
  on a map: 4 HERE
  out: 6 DELETE
  rating: 3 TEN
  Third: 3 TOE
  ~, Y, or Z: 4 **AXIS**
Xanadu
  resident: 4 KANE
"Xanadu"
  rock gp.: 3 ELO
Xanthippe: 3 NAG
  Where ~ shopped: 5 AGORA
Xavier
  Bandleader: 5 CUGAT
  ex: 5 CHARO
  Singer with: 4 ABBE
Xavier, Professor
  Team of: 4 XMEN
Xbox
  fan: 5 GAMER
Xena
  foe: 4 ARES
  portrayer Lucy: 7 LAWLESS
"Xena: Warrior Princess"
  actress O'Connor: 5 RENEE
  god: 4 ARES
Xenia
  locale: 4 OHIO
Xenon: 3 GAS 7 RAREGAS
     8 INERTGAS
  Like: 5 INERT
Xenophobe
  dread: 5 ALIEN
  ___ Xer: 3 GEN
Xerox
  competitor: 5 RICOH
  insert (abbr.): 4 ORIG
Xerxes
  land: 6 PERSIA

"X-Files, The"
  actor Nicholas: 3 LEA
  agent: 6 SCULLY
  agent Scully: 4 DANA
  extras: 3 ETS 4 GMEN
  Like: 5 EERIE
  network: 3 FOX
  org.: 3 FBI 4 SETI
  role for Gillian: 4 DANA
  sight: 3 UFO
  subject: 3 ETS
  worker: 5 AGENT
X-Games
  network: 4 ESPN
Xhosa: 5 BANTU
Xi
  preceders: 3 NUS
Xiamen: 4 AMOY
Xiaoping
  Chinese leader: 4 DENG
  ___ Xing: 3 **PED** 4 DEER
Xings
  They have: 3 RRS
XL: 4 SIZE
Xmas
  mo.: 3 DEC
  poem opener: 4 TWAS
"X-Men"
  actor McKellen: 3 IAN
X-rated: 5 ADULT DIRTY
  stuff: 4 SMUT
X-ray
  alternative: 3 MRI
  blocker: 4 LEAD
  dose: 3 RAD
  unit: 3 RAD
  vision blocker: 4 LEAD
XXX: 4 CHIS
  counterpart: 3 OOO
X ___ xylophone: 4 ASIN
Xylophone
  need: 6 MALLET
  relative: 7 MARIMBA

Yy

Y: 4 AXIS
(abbr.): 3 LTR
chromosome carrier: 4 MALE
Like: 10 NEXTTOLAST
of YSL: 4 YVES
room: 3 GYM
Series that may end in: 5 AEIOU
sporter: 3 ELI
wearer: 3 ELI
X, ~, or Z: 4 **AXIS**

Y2K
Language linked to ~ problem:
5 COBOL

Y.A.
Giants QB: 6 TITTLE

Yacht
maneuver: 4 TACK
Maneuverable, as a: 4 YARE
spot: 4 PIER 5 BASIN 6 MARINA
yes: 3 AYE
Yonder: 3 SHE

Yachting: 4 ASEA 5 ATSEA
event: 7 REGATTA SEARACE
Go: 4 SAIL
hazard: 4 REEF
woe: 4 CALM

"Yadda yadda yadda": 3 **ETC**
6 ETCETC 7 ANDSOON
8 ETCETERA

Yagudin
Skater: 6 ALEXEI

Yahoo: 4 BOOR HICK LOUT

Yahoo!: 3 ISP 6 PORTAL
competitor: 3 AOL
feature: 5 EMAIL

Yahoo.com: 4 SITE

Yahtzee
cube: 3 DIE
equipment: 4 DICE

Yak: 3 GAB JAW 4 BLAB 5 RUNON
6 NATTER
home: 5 TIBET
pack: 4 OXEN

Yakutsk
river: 4 LENA

Yale: 3 IVY
alumni: 4 **ELIS**
and others: 5 IVIES
Either Clinton, to: 4 ALUM
founder: 5 ELIHU
Half a ~ cheer: 5 BOOLA
NFL Hall of Famer: 4 LARY
student: 3 **ELI**
students since 1969: 5 COEDS

Yalie: 3 **ELI**

"Y'all"
Say: 5 ELIDE

Yalow
Nobelist: 7 ROSALYN

Yalta
attendee: 6 STALIN
monogram: 3 FDR

Yam
sayer: 6 POPEYE

Yamaguchi
Figure skater: 6 KRISTI
rival: 3 ITO

Yamaha
product: 5 PIANO
user: 5 BIKER

Yamuna
City on the ~ river: 4 AGRA

Yang
Concept with yin and: 3 TAO
opposite: 3 **YIN**

Yangtze
feeder: 3 HAN

Yank: 3 TUG 4 ALER PULL
ally: 4 BRIT
foe: 3 **REB**
out of bed: 5 ROUST

Yankee: 4 ALER 6 GRINGO
admonition: 6 GOHOME
announcer: 8 MELALLEN
div.: 6 ALEAST
epithet: 4 DAMN

home: 5 BRONX
manager Joe: 5 **TORRE**
manager Stengel: 5 CASEY
nickname: 4 AROD YOGI
    5 DIMAG
number 3: 4 RUTH
pitcher Eddie: 5 LOPAT
Quotable: 5 BERRA
Yankee Clipper
airline: 5 PANAM
Yankee Conference
town: 5 ORONO
Yankee Doodle
feather: 8 MACARONI
"Yankee Doodle Dandy"
beginning: 3 **IMA**
songwriter: 5 COHAN
"Yank in the ___, A": 3 RAF
Yankovic, "___ Al": 5 WEIRD
Yankovic, "Weird Al"
hit: 5 **EATIT**
"Yanks"
star: 4 GERE
Yao
of basketball: 4 MING
Yap: 4 TRAP 5 MOUTH 6 KISSER
Yaphet
Actor: 5 KOTTO
role: 3 IDI
Yapper: 7 SCOTTIE
Little: 4 PEKE
Yarborough
Racer: 4 CALE
Yard: 4 LAWN
Big ~, perhaps: 4 ACRE
contents: 3 ALE
Do ~ work: 3 MOW SOD 4 RAKE
enclosure: 5 FENCE HEDGE
follower: 4 SALE
holder: 4 MAST
It's served by the: 3 ALE
part: 4 FOOT
pest: 4 MOLE
tool: 4 RAKE 5 EDGER
Yardage
pickup: 4 GAIN
Yardarm: 4 SPAR
Yardbirds
tune: 6 IMAMAN

Yards
5.5 ~: 3 ROD
1,760 ~: 4 MILE
4,840 square ~: 4 ACRE
    7 ONEACRE
About 1.3 cubic: 5 STERE
About 120 square: 3 ARE
The whole nine: 3 ALL 4 ATOZ
Yard sale
buys: 3 LPS
caveat: 4 ASIS
label: 3 TAG
tag: 4 ASIS
Yardstick: 5 GAUGE
(abbr.): 3 STD
Econ.: 3 GNP
Yarn: 4 **TALE**
Ball of: 4 CLEW
Bit of: 4 HANK
Embroidery: 6 CREWEL
Fishy: 4 TALE
quantity: 5 **SKEIN**
spinner: 4 LIAR
Work with: 4 KNIT
Yashin
of hockey: 6 ALEXEI
Yashmak: 4 VEIL
Yasir
Former Palestinian leader:
    6 ARAFAT
Yasmine
Actress: 6 BLEETH
Yastrzemski
of baseball: 4 CARL
Yat-___, Sun: 3 SEN
Yaw: 4 VEER
Yawl: 4 BOAT 5 YACHT
call: 4 AHOY
relative: 5 KETCH
Yawn: 4 GAPE
Cause to: 4 BORE
inducer: 4 BORE
sound: 5 HOHUM
Yawner: 4 BORE
Yawn-inducing: 4 BLAH DULL
    5 BANAL HOHUM
Yawning: 4 DEEP 5 AGAPE
fissure: 5 CHASM
gulf: 5 ABYSS

"Yay!": 3 OLE RAH 6 HOORAH

"Yay, team!": 3 RAH

Ye
follower: 4 **OLDE**

Yea
opposite: 3 NAY

"Yeah, ___!": 3 YOU

"Yeah, man!": 4 IDIG

"Yeah, right!": 3 HAH 4 **ASIF**
　　IBET 6 ILLBET IMSURE
　　OHSURE

"Yeah, sure!": 4 ASIF IBET

Yeanling
producer: 3 EWE

Year
Add another: 5 RENEW
divs.: 3 MOS
Lunar new: 3 TET
Once a: 6 ANNUAL
One ~ in a trunk: 4 RING
record: 5 ANNAL
~, in French: 5 ANNEE
~, in Italian: 4 ANNO
~, in Spanish: 3 ANO
___ year: 4 LEAP

Yearbook: 6 ANNUAL
sect.: 3 SRS

Year-end
reward: 5 BONUS
temp: 5 SANTA

"Yearling, The"
animal: 4 DEER

Yearly: 6 ANNUAL
record: 5 ANNAL

Yearn: 4 **ACHE** LONG PINE
　　6 ASPIRE HUNGER
for: 4 MISS NEED 5 COVET
　　CRAVE 6 DESIRE

Yearning: 3 YEN 4 ACHE ITCH
　　LUST

Years
A billion: 3 EON 4 AEON
Add ~ to: 3 AGE
ago: 4 ONCE
Early: 5 YOUTH
Getting on in: 6 OLDISH
Golden: 6 OLDAGE
of note: 3 ERA
Ten: 6 DECADE

Uncountable: 3 EON
Up in: 4 AGED 5 OLDER
~, in Italian: 4 ANNI

Years ___: 3 AGO

"Years Alone, The"
Biography subtitled: 7 ELEANOR

Years and years: 3 EON 4 AGES
　　EONS 7 DECADES

Yearwood
Singer: 6 TRISHA

Yeast
Add ~ to: 6 LEAVEN
React to: 4 RISE

Yeasty
brew: 3 ALE

Yeats: 4 POET
heroine: 7 DEIRDRE
Home for: 4 EIRE ERIN
　　7 IRELAND

"Yea, verily": 6 ITISSO

"Yecch!": 3 UGH

Yegg: 11 SAFECRACKER
haul: 3 ICE
target: 4 SAFE

Yell: 3 CRY 5 SHOUT 6 HOLLER
Bowl: 3 RAH
Outfielder: 6 IGOTIT
Sporting: 3 RAH

Yeller
Old: 5 CRIER
___ Yello (soda brand): 5 MELLO

Yellow: 3 SEA 5 AMBER MAIZE
　　OCHER RIPEN 6 AFRAID
　　CRAVEN FLAXEN
blazer: 3 SUN
brown: 5 TAWNY
cheese: 4 EDAM
flower: 5 TANSY 9 BUTTERCUP
fruit: 5 GUAVA PAPAW
　　6 BANANA CASABA PAPAYA
Grayish: 4 ECRU
jacket: 4 WASP
Pale: 5 MAIZE
paper: 6 MANILA
part: 4 YOLK
Pinkish: 5 CORAL 7 APRICOT
Reddish: 5 OCHER
spread: 4 OLEO
Tree with ~ ribbons: 3 OAK

wildflower: 9 BUTTERCUP
Yellowbelly: 6 COWARD
Yellow fever
  fighter: 4 REED
  mosquito: 5 AEDES
Yellowfin: 4 TUNA
  tuna: 3 AHI
Yellowish: 5 OCHER 6 SALLOW
  brown: 5 AMBER CAMEL
     OCHER TAWNY 6 SIENNA
     7 CARAMEL
  pigment: 5 OCHER
  pink: 6 SALMON 7 TEAROSE
  red: 5 CORAL SANDY
  white: 8 EGGSHELL
Yellow Pages
  entries: 3 ADS
"___ yellow ribbon ...": 4 TIEA
Yellowstone: 4 PARK
  animal: 3 ELK 4 BEAR 5 BISON
     6 WAPITI
  City near: 4 CODY
  figure: 6 RANGER
     10 PARKRANGER
  spewer: 6 GEYSER
"Yellow Submarine"
  villain: 6 MEANIE
Yelp
  Mouse-induced: 3 EEK
Yeltsin
  Mr.: 5 BORIS
  Mrs.: 5 NAINA
  successor: 5 PUTIN
  villa: 5 DACHA
Yemana
  portrayer: 3 SOO
Yemen
  capital: 4 ADEN **SANA** 5 SANAA
  city: 4 ADEN TAIZ
  gulf: 4 ADEN
  native: 4 ADENI
  neighbor: 4 **OMAN**
  peninsula: 6 ARABIA
  port: 4 **ADEN**
  ~, long ago: 5 SHEBA
Yemeni: 4 **ARAB**
  money: 4 RIAL 5 RIYAL
  neighbor: 5 OMANI
  port: 4 **ADEN**

Yen: 4 ACHE ITCH URGE
    6 DESIRE
  Have a: 4 ACHE
  Have a ~ for: 4 WANT 5 CRAVE
    6 HANKER
  part: 3 SEN
  thousandth: 3 RIN
Yenta
  Like a: 4 NOSY
Yeoman
  yes: 3 **AYE**
"Yep"
  on a yacht: 3 AYE
  opposite: 4 NOPE
"Yer darn ___!": 6 TOOTIN
"___ yer old man!": 3 SOS
"Yertle the Turtle"
  author: 5 SEUSS
Yes
  at sea: 3 AYE
  Emphatic: 6 IDOIDO
  Emphatic ~, in Spanish: 4 SISI
  follower: 5 SIREE
  (Japanese): 3 HAI
  Say: 5 AGREE 6 ASSENT
  Say ~ to: 6 ACCEDE ACCEPT
  vote: 3 AYE
  ~, in French: 3 OUI
"Yes!": 4 AMEN 10 ABSOLUTELY
    BYALLMEANS
    11 BUTOFCOURSE
"Yes ___?": 4 ORNO
"Yes, ___!": 4 MAAM 6 SIRREE
"Yes ___" (Sammy Davis Jr. bio):
    4 ICAN
"Yes ___, Bob!": 6 SIRREE
Yeshiva
  graduate: 5 RABBI
  teacher: 5 REBBE
Ye ___ Shoppe: 4 OLDE
Yes-man: 5 TOADY 6 NODDER
    8 ASSENTER
Yesterday
  ~, in French: 4 HIER
  ~, in Italian: 4 IERI
"Yesterday!": 4 ASAP
Yesteryear: 4 YORE
"Yes, there is ___!": 4 AGOD
"Yes! Yes!": 6 IDOIDO

Yet: 5 BYNOW SOFAR 6 TODATE
  again: 4 ANEW
  As: 5 SOFAR 6 ERENOW
  Not in: 7 ONORDER
  to come: 5 AHEAD
  ~, poetically: 3 **EEN**
Yiddish
  gossip: 5 YENTE
  plaints: 3 OYS
  writer Aleichem: 6 SHOLOM
Yield: 3 BOW PAY 4 BEAR BEND
      CAVE **CEDE** EMIT GIVE
      5 DEFER 6 ASSENT
      GIVEIN RELENT RETURN
      7 SUCCUMB
  Field: 4 CROP
  Maple: 3 SAP
  Mine: 3 ORE
  Refuse to: 6 INSIST
Yielding: 6 PLIANT
"Yikes!": 3 EEK 4 **EGAD** OHNO
     5 EGADS 7 OMIGOSH
Yin
  opposite: 4 YANG
"Yipe!": 4 EGAD
"Yippee!": 5 OHBOY WAHOO
Yitzhak
  predecessor: 5 GOLDA
YM: 3 MAG
Yma
  Singer: 5 SUMAC
YMCA
  class: 3 CPR
  part: 4 ASSN MENS
"Yo!": 3 HEY 6 HEYYOU
  Subtle: 4 PSST
Yodel
  recall: 4 ECHO
Yodeler
  perch: 3 ALP
  range: 8 FALSETTO
  reply: 4 ECHO
Yoga
  accessory: 3 MAT
  position: 5 ASANA LOTUS
  practitioner: 5 HINDU
  type: 5 HATHA
  ___ yoga: 5 HATHA
Yogi: 4 BEAR

  Baseball catcher: 5 BERRA
  Buddy of: 10 BOOBOOBEAR
Yogi Bear: 4 TOON
  co-creator: 5 HANNA
  Voice of: 4 DAWS
Yogurt
  Like some: 5 NOFAT
     6 NONFAT
Yoke: 5 UNITE
  mates: 4 **OXEN**
  The ~ is on them: 4 OXEN
Yokel: 4 BOOR CLOD RUBE
Yoko
  Singer: 3 **ONO**
  Son of: 4 SEAN
Yokohama
  drama: 3 NOH
  yes: 3 HAI
Yokozuna
  Its champion is called: 4 SUMO
Yokum
  boy: 5 ABNER
  creator: 4 CAPP 6 ALCAPP
  dad: 5 PAPPY
  mom: 5 MAMMY
Yokum, Daisy ___: 3 MAE
Yokum, Mammy
  First name of: 5 PANSY
Yolk
  encloser: 3 SAC
Yom ___: 3 TOV
Yom Kippur
  Observe: 5 ATONE
  observer: 6 **ATONER**
  ritual: 4 FAST
Yon: 4 AFAR
  companion: 6 HITHER
  damsel: 3 HER SHE
"Yond Cassius has ___ and hungry
    look": 5 ALEAN
Yonder: 4 AFAR THAT 5 THERE
  Off: 4 **AFAR**
  Over: 4 THAR 5 THERE
  woman: 3 SHE
  yacht: 3 SHE
Yoo
  follower: 3 HOO
"Yoo-___!": 3 HOO
"Yoo-hoo!": 8 OVERHERE

Yoplait
  competitor: 6 DANNON
Yorba ___: 5 LINDA
Yore
  Car of: 3 GTO
  Days of: 4 ELD 4 PAST
  News source of: 5 CRIER
  Oath of: 4 EGAD
  Of: 3 AGO 4 PAST 5 OLDEN
  Ruler of: 4 TSAR 6 SHOGUN
  Your of: 3 THY 5 THINE
Yorick
  Like: 4 POOR
  Word for: 4 ALAS
York: 3 NCO **SGT**
  Actress: 8 SUSANNAH
  John of: 3 LOO
  river: 4 OUSE
  Sergeant: 5 ALVIN
Yorkshire
  city: 5 **LEEDS**
  literary name: 6 BRONTE
  river: 3 URE 4 AIRE OUSE
Yosemite: 4 PARK
  photographer: 5 ADAMS
      10 ANSELADAMS
Yossarian
  bunkmate: 3 ORR
"Yo te ___": 3 AMO
Yothers
  Actress: 4 TINA
You
  are here: 5 EARTH
  ~, formerly: 4 THEE THOU
  ~, in French: 3 TOI
  ~, in German: 3 SIE
  ~, in Spanish: 5 USTED
  ~, right now: 6 SOLVER
You ___!": 6 BETCHA
"You ___?": 4 RANG
"You ___" (Lionel Richie hit):
      3 ARE
"You are ___": 4 HERE
"You are here"
  place: 3 MAP
"You Are My Destiny"
  singer Paul: 4 ANKA
"You are not!"
  reply: 5 IAMSO 6 IAMTOO

"You are, too!"
  preceder: 6 IAMNOT
"___ you asked ...": 5 SINCE
"___ You Babe": 4 IGOT
"You ___ Beautiful" (Joe Cocker
      hit): 5 ARESO
"You Belong to Me"
  singer Glenn: 4 FREY
"You bet!": 3 YEP **YES** 4 SURE
      YEAH 6 ANDHOW
"You betcha!": 3 YEP YES YUP
      4 SURE 8 YESSIREE
"You Bet Your Life"
  prop: 5 CIGAR
  sponsor: 6 DESOTO
"You ___ bother!": 6 NEEDNT
"You Can Call Me Al"
  singer Paul: 5 SIMON
"You can count on me!":
      7 ILLDOIT
"You can ___ horse ...":
      5 LEADA
"You can observe a lot by
      watching"
  speaker: 5 BERRA
"You can say that again!":
      4 **AMEN**
"You can't play at my house!":
      6 GOHOME
"You Can't Take It With You"
  director: 5 CAPRA
  playwright: 8 MOSSHART
  star: 10 JEANARTHUR
"You can't teach ___ dog ...":
      5 ANOLD
"You da ___!": 3 MAN
"___ you don't!": 4 OHNO
"You Don't Bring Me Flowers":
      4 DUET
"You don't mean me?!": 3 MOI
"You don't say!": 3 GEE
      6 INDEED
"You don't think I'd do it, do
      you?": 6 DAREME
"You ___ for it!": 5 ASKED
"___ you for real?": 3 ARE
"___ you glad ...": 5 ARENT
"___ You Glad You're You?":
      5 ARENT

"You go not till ___ you up a
    glass": 4 ISET
"You gotta be kidding!": 4 OHNO
"You got that right!": 6 ILLSAY
"You haven't started yet, have
    you?": 7 AMILATE
"You have to see this!":
    6 OHLOOK
"You ___ here": 3 ARE
"You ___ kidding!": 5 ARENT
"___ you kidding?": 3 ARE
"You know how ___": 4 ITIS
"You Light Up My Life"
  singer Boone: 5 DEBBY
"You'll regret it otherwise!":
    6 ORELSE
"You look like you ___ ghost!":
    4 SAWA
"___ you loud and clear!":
    5 IREAD
Youmans
  heroine: 7 NANETTE
  musical: 11 NONONANETTE
"You missed it": 7 TOOLATE
"You ___ mouthful!": 5 SAIDA
"You Must Remember This"
  author: 5 OATES
"You ___ My Sunshine": 3 ARE
Young
  Actor: 4 ALAN
  Actress: 4 SEAN 7 LORETTA
  bear: 3 CUB
  Bear ~, as sheep: 4 YEAN
  "Blondie" creator: 4 CHIC
  boy: 3 LAD TAD
  codfish: 5 SCROD
  deer: 4 FAWN
  eel: 5 ELVER
  follower: 3 UNS
  Forever: 7 AGELESS
  fowl: 5 POULT
  fox: 3 KIT
  goat: 3 KID
  haddock: 5 SCROD
  hare: 7 LEVERET
  hooter: 5 OWLET
  horse: 4 COLT FOAL
  hotshot: 6 PHENOM
  lady: 4 GIRL LASS MISS

lady of Sp.: 4 SRTA
lion: 5 WHELP
man: 3 BOY LAD
newt: 3 **EFT**
Not: 4 AGED
of Utah history: 7 BRIGHAM
Org. for ~ men: 3 BSA
Partner of ~ in accounting:
    5 ERNST
pig: 5 SHOAT
pigeon: 5 SQUAB
predator: 5 OWLET
raptor: 6 EAGLET
salmon: 4 PARR 5 SMOLT
seal: 3 PUP
sheep: 4 LAMB
Singer: 4 NEIL
socialite: 3 DEB
suffix: 4 STER
swan: 6 CYGNET
turkey: 5 POULT
wolf: 5 WHELP
woman: 4 LASS
Young ___: 3 **UNS**
Young, Brigham
  place: 4 UTAH
Young, Robert
  sitcom: 15 FATHERKNOWSBEST
"Young and the Restless, The":
    4 SOAP 9 SOAPOPERA
Youngest
  Greek god: 4 EROS
"Young Frankenstein"
  Actress Garr: 4 **TERI**
  assistant: 4 IGOR
  role for Marty: 4 IGOR
  woman: 4 INGA
Youngman
  Funnyman: 5 HENNY
  specialty: 8 ONELINER
Youngster: 3 KID LAD TAD TOT
    4 TYKE 5 CHILD 6 SHAVER
Young 'un: 3 LAD TAD TOT
    4 TYKE
"___ you nuts?": 3 ARE
"___ you one!": 4 IOWE
Your
  and my: 3 OUR
  highness: 4 SIRE

of yore: 3 THY
~, in French: 3 TES
"You rang?": 3 YES
"___ your disposal": 4 IMAT
"You're it!"
Word before: 3 TAG
"You're joshing!": 5 PSHAW
"You're ___ mistaken!": 5 SADLY
"You're ___ Need to Get By":
    4 ALLI
"You're on!": 8 ITSADEAL
"Your Erroneous Zones"
author Wayne: 4 DYER
"You're So ___" (Carly Simon hit):
    4 VAIN
"You're ___ talk!": 5 ONETO
"You're the ___ Care For":
    4 ONEI
"You're ___, ya know that?":
    Archie Bunker: 4 APIP
"You ___ right!": 5 ARESO
"___ your life!": 5 NOTON
"Your majesty": 4 SIRE
"___ your pardon!": 4 IBEG
"Your point being ...?": 3 AND
Yours
and mine: 4 OURS
Not: 4 MINE
of yore: 5 THINE
~, in French: 4 ATOI
Yours ___: 5 TRULY
"___ yourself": 5 BRACE
"Your Show of Shows"
regular: 4 COCA
"Yours truly": 5 CLOSE
"Your turn": 4 OVER
"You said it!": 3 YES 4 AMEN
    6 ANDHOW 7 RIGHTON
"___ you serious?": 3 ARE
"You sly one, you!": 3 OHO
"You stink!": 3 BOO
Youth: 3 LAD 5 MINOR TEENS
    9 SALADDAYS
Goddess of: 4 HEBE
Impudent: 5 WHELP
org.: 3 BSA 4 YMCA YMHA
Winged: 4 EROS
"You there!": 3 HEY
"You there?": 5 HELLO

"You ___ There": 3 ARE
Youthful
times: 9 SALADDAYS
"You've got ___": 5 ADEAL
"You've Got ___": 4 MAIL
"You've got mail"
co.: 3 AOL
One who hears: 5 AOLER
"You've Got Mail"
director Ephron: 4 NORA
Ryan of: 3 MEG
"You've Made ___ Very Happy":
    4 MESO
"You ___ what you eat": 3 ARE
"You will regret it otherwise!":
    6 ORELSE
"You win": 5 ILOSE
"You wish!": 4 ASIF
    7 DREAMON
"You Won't ___" (Beatles tune):
    5 SEEME
"You ___ worry": 6 NEEDNT
"You wouldn't dare!"
response: 5 TRYME
"Yowl!": 4 OUCH
Yowler
Alley: 3 TOM
Yo-yo: 3 TOY
maker: 6 DUNCAN
trick: 13 WALKINGTHEDOG
"___ y Plata" (Montana's motto):
    3 ORO
Yr.
end adviser: 3 CPA
ender: 3 DEC
fourth: 3 QTR
parts: 3 MOS
School ~ part: 3 SEM
Yrs.
100 ~: 3 CEN
Golden ~ cache: 3 IRA
YSL
part: 4 YVES
Yttrium: 9 RAREEARTH
Yucatán
Early ~ dweller: 4 MAYA
yay!: 3 OLE
year: 3 ANO
you: 5 USTED

~ Indian: 5 MAYAN
Yucca
  family: 5 AGAVE
  fiber: 5 ISTLE
  relative: 4 ALOE
"Yuck!": 3 UGH
Yugo.
  neighbor: 3 ALB
Yugoslav
  Former ~ leader: 4 **TITO**
Yugoslavs
  Many: 5 SERBS
Yukon: 4 TERR
  country: 6 CANADA
  letters: 3 GMC
"Yuk yuk": 4 HAHA
Yule: 4 NOEL
  drink: 3 NOG
  garland: 6 WREATH
  song: 4 NOEL
  trio: 4 MAGI
  ~, informally: 4 XMAS
Yuletide: 4 NOEL
  décor: 5 HOLLY

door décor: 6 WREATH
drink: 3 NOG 6 EGGNOG
song: 4 NOEL 5 CAROL
sweet: 4 CANE
trio: 4 MAGI
visitor: 5 SANTA
"Yum!": 5 TASTY
Yuma
  river: 4 GILA
Yummy: 4 GOOD
"Yummy": 3 MMM
Yup
  opposite: 4 NOPE
Yuppie
  auto: 3 BMW
Yuri
  Love of: 4 LARA
  player: 4 OMAR
Yutang
  Author: 3 **LIN**
Yvonne
  Actress: 7 DECARLO
YWCA
  part: 4 ASSN

Zz

Z
A to: 5 GAMUT
British: 3 ZED
Greek: 4 ZETA
X, Y, or: 4 **AXIS**

"Z"
actor Montand: 4 YVES
actress Papas: 5 IRENE
___ Z: 3 ATO
From: 3 **ATO**
Z3: 3 BMW

Zadora
Actress/singer: 3 PIA

Zag: 3 YAW 4 VEER

Zagreb
location: 7 CROATIA
resident: 5 **CROAT** 8 CROATIAN

Zahn
Newswoman: 5 PAULA

Zaire
dictator Mobuto ___ Seko:
4 **SESE**
dictator Mobuto Sese ___: 4 SEKO

Zaius, Dr.: 3 APE

Zambia
neighbor: 6 ANGOLA

Zamboni
site: 4 RINK
surface: 3 ICE

Zane
Author: 4 GREY

Zany: 6 MADCAP

Zap: 4 LASE NUKE STUN

Zapata
Info: Spanish cue
Zilch, to: 4 **NADA**
" ___ Zapata": 4 VIVA

Zapped
They might be: 3 ADS

Zapper: 3 EEL
target: 3 ADS BUG

Zaragoza
river: 4 EBRO

Zasu
Comic: 5 PITTS

Zátopek
Olympic runner: 4 **EMIL**

Zayak
Skater: 6 ELAINE

Zeal: 5 ARDOR

Zealot: 3 NUT 5 ULTRA
6 MANIAC 7 FANATIC

Zealous: 4 AVID 5 EAGER
6 ABLAZE ARDENT

Zebra: 3 REF 6 EQUINE
feature: 4 MANE
relative: 3 ASS

Zebulon
Explorer: 4 PIKE

Zedong, ___: 3 MAO

Zee
preceder: 3 WYE

Zeke
portrayer: 4 LAHR

"Zelig"
director: 5 ALLEN

Zelle
familiar name: 4 HARI

Zellweger
Actress: 5 **RENEE**

Zelnicek, ___: 5 IVANA

Zen: 4 SECT
Do: 8 MEDITATE
enlightenment: 6 **SATORI**

Zenith: 3 TOP 4 **ACME** APEX
6 APOGEE
opposite: 5 NADIR
product: 3 VCR
rival: 3 RCA

Zeno
birthplace: 4 **ELEA**
follower: 5 **STOIC**

platform: 4 STOA
Zephyr: 6 BREEZE
Zephyrous: 4 AIRY
___ **Zeppelin:** 3 LED
Zeppo: 4 MARX
  Brother of: 5 CHICO HARPO
Zero: 3 **NIL** 4 LOVE NADA NONE
      NULL 5 AUGHT 6 NAUGHT
      NOTANY NOTONE
      7 NOTABIT 8 GOOSEEGG
  Actor: 6 MOSTEL
  Less than ~ (abbr.): 3 NEG
  Letters above: 4 OPER
  Put back to: 5 RESET
  With ~ chance: 5 NOHOW
Zero-star
  fare: 4 SLOP
  movie: 4 BOMB
  review: 3 PAN
Zero-wheeled
  vehicle: 4 SLED
Zest: 4 BRIO ELAN RIND
      5 GUSTO SAVOR
  Fruit: 4 PEEL RIND
Zesty
  dip: 5 SALSA
Zeta
  follower: 3 **ETA**
Zetterling
  Actress: 3 MAI
Zeus
  abductee: 6 EUROPA
  Consort of: 4 HERA
  Daughter of: 4 HEBE 5 HELEN
      6 ATHENA
  Mother of: 4 RHEA
  Queen wooed by: 4 LEDA
  Roman: 4 JOVE
  Shield of: 5 AEGIS
  Son of: 4 **ARES** 6 APOLLO
  temple site: 5 NEMEA
  Wife of: 4 **HERA**
Zhivago
  Love of: 4 **LARA**
  portrayer: 6 SHARIF
Zhou
  Communist leader: 5 **ENLAI**
Ziegfeld
  designer: 4 ERTE

  Producer: 3 **FLO**
  production: 5 REVUE
"Ziegfeld Follies"
  designer: 4 ERTE
  star Naldi: 4 NITA
  Ziegfeld of: 3 FLO
Ziering
  Actor: 3 IAN
Zig: 3 YAW 4 TURN VEER
Ziggy
  Jazz trumpeter: 5 ELMAN
Zigzag: 3 SEW 5 WEAVE
      6 SLALOM
Zilch: 3 **NIL** 4 NADA NONE ZERO
      6 NAUGHT NOTANY
Zillion: 3 TON 4 MANY
Zillions: 4 ALOT
  of years: 3 EON
Zimbabwe
  capital: 3 ZEE 6 HARARE
  Lang. of: 3 ENG
  ~, formerly: 8 RHODESIA
Zimbalist
  Actor: 5 EFREM
  Violinist: 5 EFREM
Zinc
  sulfide: 6 BLENDE
Zinc ___: 5 OXIDE
Zine
  Online: 4 EMAG
Zinfandel
  Like: 3 DRY
Zing: 3 PEP 4 ELAN 5 NOISE
      OOMPII
Zinger: 3 MOT 4 BARB
      6 RETORT 7 RIPOSTE
      8 ONELINER
  producer: 3 WIT
Zingy
  taste: 4 TANG
Zinnemann
  Director: 4 FRED
Zion National Park
  home: 4 UTAH
Zip: 3 **NIL** PEP 4 DART ELAN
      NADA NONE NULL TEAR
      ZERO 5 SPEED ZILCH
      6 ENERGY 7 NOTAONE
      8 GOOSEEGG

Bike that can: 5 MOPED
Full of: 4 PERT
"Zip-A-Dee-___-Dah": 3 DOO
"Zip-A-Dee-Doo-___": 3 DAH
"Zip-A-___-Doo-Dah": 3 DEE
Zip code
  10001 ~: 4 NYNY
"Zip-___-Doo-Dah": 4 **ADEE**
Zipped: 4 FLEW SPED TORE
  through: 4 ACED
Zipper
  alternative: 4 SNAP 6 VELCRO
  cover: 3 FLY
  Name on a: 4 IZOD
Zippo: 3 NIL 4 **NADA** NONE
  part: 4 WICK
Zippy
  dip: 5 SALSA
  flavor: 4 TANG
  watercraft: 6 JETSKI
Zither
  Japanese: 4 KOTO
Ziti: 5 **PASTA**
  relative: 5 PENNE
Zodiac
  animal: 3 **RAM** 4 BULL CRAB
    GOAT LION 8 SCORPION
  border: 4 CUSP
  sign: 3 **LEO** 5 ARIES LIBRA
    VIRGO 6 GEMINI PISCES
  symbol: 6 ARCHER SCALES
Zoe
  Friend of: 4 ELMO
  Playwright: 5 AKINS
Zog I
  domain: 7 ALBANIA
Zola
  Author: 5 **EMILE**
  heroine: 4 NANA
  letter: 7 JACCUSE
  novel: 4 **NANA**
  portrayer: 4 MUNI
Zoltan
  Director: 5 KORDA
Zone: 4 **AREA** 6 REGION
    SECTOR
  Canal: 3 EAR
  Flying: 8 AIRSPACE
  Narrow: 4 BELT

School ~ sign: 3 SLO 4 SLOW
Strike ~ boundary: 5 KNEES
Time: 3 CST EST PST
War: 3 NAM 4 IRAQ 5 ARENA
  6 SECTOR
WWII: 3 **ETO**
Zoning
  unit: 4 **ACRE**
Zoo
  barrier: 4 MOAT
  beast: 3 **APE** 5 HIPPO KOALA
    LLAMA ORANG OTTER
    PANDA RHINO TIGER
  enclosure: 4 CAGE
  Floating: 3 ARK
  section: 6 AVIARY
  sound: 4 ROAR
  trench: 4 MOAT
Zoo de Madrid
  animal: 3 OSO 5 TIGRE
Zooey
  Father of: 3 LES
Zool.: 3 SCI
Zoologist
  study: 5 FAUNA
  ~ Fossey: 4 DIAN
Zoology: 7 SCIENCE
  bones: 4 OSSA
  classification: 6 FAMILY
  foot: 3 PES
  mouths: 3 ORA
Zoom: 4 LENS SOAR TEAR
    5 NOISE SPEED
  photo: 7 CLOSEUP
Zoophyte: 7 ANEMONE
"Zoo Story, The":
    8 ONEACTER
  playwright: 5 ALBEE
Zoot
  Jazzman: 4 SIMS
"Zorba the Greek"
  actress Irene: 5 PAPAS
  actress Papas: 5 IRENE
Zoroastrian: 5 PARSI
  scriptures: 4 ZEND 6 AVESTA
Zorro
  Daughter of: 5 ELENA
  garb: 4 CAPE
  mark: 3 ZEE 4 SCAR

"Zounds!": 4 **EGAD** 5 **EGADS**
Zoysia: 5 GRASS
Z's
  Catch some: 3 NAP 4 DOZE
    5 SLEEP 6 SNOOZE
  Catch some extra: 7 SLEEPIN
  ~, in Zaragoza: 6 SIESTA
Zsa Zsa: 5 GABOR
  Sister of: 3 **EVA** 5 MAGDA
    8 EVAGABOR
Zubin
  Conductor: 5 **MEHTA**
"Zuckerman Unbound"
  author: 4 ROTH
Zugspitze: 3 ALP
Zuider ___: 3 ZEE
Zukor
  Producer: 6 ADOLPH

Zulu: 5 **BANTU**
Zumwalt
  Admiral: 4 ELMO
Zurich
  peak: 3 ALP
Zurich-to-Munich
  dir.: 3 ENE
Zuyder ___: 3 ZEE
Zwei
  cubed: 4 ACHT
  doubled: 4 VIER
  follower: 4 **DREI**
  Half of: 4 EINS
Zygomatic
  Flex one's ~ muscles: 5 SMILE
Z ___ zebra: 4 ASIN
ZZ Top: 4 TRIO
Zzz: 5 SNORE

About the Authors

KEVIN MCCANN is an IT specialist residing in Ottawa, Canada, with his wife, Paula, and their Chihuahuas, Archie and Mindy. He has contributed crossword puzzles to *The New York Times*, and is also the creator of cruciverb.com, a website for crossword constructors. In his spare time McCann enjoys guitar, billiards, golf, and the music of Leon Redbone.

MARK DIEHL is a full-time dentist, for 30 years and counting, with the Veterans Affairs Hospital in Palo Alto, California. He lives in San Jose with his wife, Lee Ann, and two of three daughters. When time allows, Diehl constructs crosswords for *The New York Times*, the *Los Angeles Times*, and other puzzle venues.